Completely updated to 1982, the new Fourth Edition reaffirms the position of *The Negro Almanac* as *the* definitive reference on the history, culture and contributions of black Americans. In previous editions, this monumental, one-volume work received acclaim from a wide spectrum of educators, scholars, statesmen, librarians and students. The Fourth Edition, while retaining the same successful, fast-access format, represents a major review, revision and expansion of material that spans nearly 500 years and now surpasses 1,400 pages. Among the numerous changes and additions in the new edition are:

- New material in the Chronology section, covering the 6-year period from 1976 through 1981

- A major shift in emphasis, from issues of litigation and social equality and toward issues of greater economic rights—including the attempted coalition between poor blacks and whites, and the controversies over black involvement in Mid-East politics and energy issues

- Greater analysis of black voter trends in light of the Democratic Party's new conservatism; the Congressional Black Caucus

- Revised material on the black family, including new analysis on the effects of unemployment, budget cuts, and the decline of the family farm

- Expanded treatment of the progress of black women's rights and of the movement's leaders

- Plus . . . updated material on blacks and religion, blacks in film, blacks and the media, prominent black Americans, as well as an analysis of social, political and economic trends in black Africa and the Western Hemisphere

This commitment to distinguished scholarship, reflected by these many vital additions and revisions, has already earned *The Negro Almanac* a special citation from the Library Journal (in conjunction with the American Library Association) for overall excellence as a reference tool in libraries and institutions throughout the country.

THE NEGRO ALMANAC

A Reference Work on

THE AFRO-AMERICAN

Black mariners were with Columbus when he discovered America.

THE NEGRO ALMANAC

A Reference Work on

THE AFRO-AMERICAN

Fourth Edition

compiled and edited by

HARRY A. PLOSKI
New York University

and

JAMES WILLIAMS
Director of Communications
National Urban League

A Wiley-Interscience Publication

JOHN WILEY & SONS

New York ■ Chichester ■ Brisbane ■ Toronto ■ Singapore

Copyright © 1983 by John Wiley & Sons, Inc.

All rights reserved. Published simultaneously in Canada.

Reproduction or translation of any part of this work
beyond that permitted by Section 107 or 108 of the
1976 United States Copyright Act without the permission
of the copyright owner is unlawful. Requests for
permission or further information should be addressed to
the Permissions Department, John Wiley & Sons, Inc.

Library of Congress Cataloging in Publication Data:

Main entry under title:

The Negro almanac.

"A Wiley-Interscience publication."
Includes index.
1. Afro-Americans—Dictionaries and encyclopedias.
I. Ploski, Harry A.   II. Williams, James D. (James
De Bois), 1926–

E185.N385   1982   973'.0496073'00321   82–17469
ISBN 0–471–87710–7

Printed in the United States of America

10 9 8 7 6 5 4 3 2 1

MANAGING EDITOR: RICHARD ROSENTHAL

SPECIAL PROJECTS EDITOR: ERNIE JOHNSTON

Contributing Editors

John E. Brown
Rutgers University

Ernest Kaiser
New York Public Library Schomberg Collection
Freedomways

Joseph Carbone
Board of Education
Harrison, New York

Linda Lambert
Educational Consultant

Gylbert Coker
Art Consultant

Aaron Lipton
Associate Professor of English
State University of New York at Stony Brook

Conrad Eberstein
Law Consultant

Larry Long
Bureau of the Census

William Gale

Bill Mackey
Instructor of Afro-American Studies
City College of New York

Robert B. Hill
Bureau of Social Science Research

Lola Meisel

Faustine Jones
Howard University

Jim Murray
NBC

Research Assistants

Paula Braverman
Carol Cox
Joan Deutsch

Tereas Lewis
Sherry Turkletaub

Special Photographic Work

Ed Druck

Bill Mackey

EDITOR'S NOTE

When *The Negro Almanac* was first published in 1967, it was immediately hailed as the most comprehensive reference work of its kind on the history and culture of black Americans and their significant contributions to our society. It was subsequently cited by *Library Journal,* in conjunction with the American Library Association, as one of the outstanding reference works of the decade. The 1971 second edition met with even greater praise. Our objectives in undertaking the third edition, which was a major revision, were both to update the scholarship of the first two editions and to substantially broaden their scope and coverage.

Appearing on the 200th anniversary of American independence, the third edition of The Negro Almanac had a special bicentennial emphasis. A principal consideration in that volume was the lack of generally available information on black participation in the American Revolution and in subsequent United States history. To remedy this information gap, the edition paid particular attention to the black role in colonial and revolutionary America and to the black contribution to the growth and development of the American nation since its inception. This book was chosen by the National Urban League to be an integral part of its own Bicentennial Project.

This fourth edition reflects our awareness of the expanding dimensions of the black cultural and social experience in the United States. After examining the role of blacks in the settlement and growth of this country, we proceeded to consider the contemporary situation within the framework of American society.

Special attention is given to the black woman, and the section detailing her achievements and aspirations has been expanded. We continue to supply biographical data on an imposing roster of historical and contemporary personalities—men and women of achievement from all walks of life. Our volume is generously stocked with valuable statistical material—including tables, charts, and graphs—all of which provide technical insights into the scope and importance of the black experience in the United States. This edition also expands our exploration of the significance of a wide spectrum of groups within the contemporary black community, seeking not only to discover their historical roots but also to assess their ongoing importance, without bias or partisanship. The strength of this volume, we believe, lies both in the breadth of its investigations and in the analytical potential of its organization and material.

Information on the wide variety and extensive range of topics which are covered here can be obtained only from multiple sources in a few specialized library collections and, as such, has been relatively inaccessible to all but highly trained and well-placed researchers. By laying the groundwork for a far broader dissemination of such information in an enlarged format, we hope to provide the widest possible audience with an accurate, comprehensive, and well-documented study of black culture in the United States, and around the world as well.

HARRY A. PLOSKI

PUBLISHER'S NOTE

John Wiley acquired the rights to *The Negro Almanac* in 1981 and retained the original publisher and editor, Harry A. Ploski, as the editor-in-chief. We feel that his experience with the previous editions and his commitment to bringing the country's attention to black culture and its importance to our national life make him the best possible person to supervise the preparation of the fourth edition.

A great deal of effort and time has gone into the revision. We endeavored to retain all the powerful and useful features of the Bicentennial Edition of 1976. At the same time we have tried to modernize the book.

All the statistical information has been updated with the latest information available to June 1982. Wherever possible and necessary, new facts have been added to all the sections. Biographies as well as socioeconomic, cultural, and historical material reflect current data and research.

We extend our appreciation and gratitude to everyone, those outside John Wiley & Sons as well as those inside, who have contributed to this new edition.

JOHN WILEY & SONS, INC.
January 1983

CONTENTS

CHRONOLOGY: A HISTORICAL REVIEW

Major Events in Black History (1492–1953) ■ The Civil Rights Revolution (1954–1964) ■ The March of News (1965–1970) ■ Consolidation and Reverses (1971–1982)

Black history in the Western Hemisphere can probably be traced back to the *Santa Maria,* with Columbus's crewman Pedro Alonzo Niño identified as a black sailor. Without any doubt, black seamen and explorers figured importantly in many of the subsequent Spanish expeditions as well as in the successful English colonization that birthed the United States of America. Nevertheless, standard references have largely ignored the historical role of the black American. For the most part blacks have been viewed as outside the mainstream of American history rather than as active participants in its creation and greatness. The following chronology attempts to redress this error by specifically reviewing the important events of Afro-American history. In addition to providing a developmental outline of the black American presence, the chronology stands as a record of the contributions of blacks to the nation's growth, achievements, and vitality that should not be overlooked. Subsequent sections of this volume will flesh out the record with respect to specific eras and fields, but the chronology by itself documents the great range and depth of the black contribution to the social, cultural, and economic strength of this nation.

MAJOR EVENTS IN BLACK HISTORY (1492–1953)

1492 The New World Blacks are among the first explorers to the New World. Pedro Alonzo Niño, identified by some scholars as a black, arrives with Columbus; other blacks accompany Balboa, Ponce de Leon, Cortes, Pizarro, and Menendez on their travels and explorations.

1501 Spain The Spanish throne officially approves the use of black slaves in the New World.

1502 Latin America Portugal lands its first slave cargo in the Western Hemisphere.

1513 Latin America Spain authorizes use of black slaves in Cuba. Thirty blacks accompany Balboa when he discovers the Pacific Ocean.

1526 South Carolina The first group of blacks to set foot on what is now the United States are brought by a Spanish explorer to South Carolina to erect a settlement. However, they soon flee to the interior and settle with the native Americans.

1538 Arizona; New Mexico Estevanico, a black explorer, leads an expedition from Mexico into the territory of the American Southwest and is credited with the discovery of what is now Arizona and New Mexico.

1562 Hispaniola Britain enters the slave trade when John Hawkins sells a large cargo of blacks to Spanish planters. Though Queen Elizabeth allows Hawkins to include the figure of a bound black in his coat of arms, she denies that he transports slaves.

1600 Latin America Historical records indicate that by 1600, 900,000 slaves have been brought to Latin America. In the next century, 2,750,000 are added to that total. Slave revolts in the sixteenth century were reported in Hispaniolo, Puerto Rico, Panama, Cuba, and Mexico.

1618 England The government grants monopolies to

A SLAVE-SHED.

A slave shed in Africa.

a group of companies, established for the purpose of slave trading.

1619 Jamestown, Virginia   The forerunner of slavery in the English colonies begins with the arrival of 20 black indentured servants aboard a Dutch vessel. Most indentured servants are released after serving a term, usually seven years, and are allowed to own property and participate in political affairs.

1624 New Amsterdam   The Dutch, who had entered the slave trade in 1621 with the formation of the Dutch West Indies Co., import blacks to serve on Hudson Valley farms. According to Dutch law, the children of manumitted (freed) slaves are bound to slavery.

1629–1637 The English Colonies   Black slaves are imported into Connecticut (1629), Maryland and Massachusetts (1634), and New York City (1637).

1630 Massachusetts   A law protecting slaves who flee owners because of ill treatment is enacted.

1639 Salem, Massachusetts   New England seamen enter slave trade as Captain William Pierce sails to West Indies and exchanges Indian slaves for blacks.

1640–1650 The "Western Hemisphere"   Spurred by the increasing use of sugar as a money crop, the slave population of the West Indies multiplies rapidly, but growth in mainland English colonies is slow. The black slave population in Barbados, for example, grows from a few hundred in 1640 to 6,000 in 1645. But by 1649, there are only 300 black slaves in Virginia, and by 1671 only 2,000.

1640–1699 The English Colonies   Punitive fugitive laws applying to both indentured servants and slaves are enacted in Connecticut, Maryland, New Jersey, South Carolina, and Virginia. The Virginia law, passed in 1642, penalizes people sheltering runaways 20 pounds worth of tobacco for each night of refuge granted. Slaves are branded after a second escape attempt.

1641 Massachusetts   Massachusetts becomes the first colony to legalize slavery, adding a modification that forbids capture by "unjust violence." This provision was subsequently adopted by all of the New England colonies.

1643 New England   The groundwork is laid for eighteenth and nineteenth century fugitive slave laws in the United States when an intercolonial agreement of the New England Confederation declares that mere certification by a magistrate is sufficient evidence to convict a runaway slave.

1651 North Hampton County, Virginia   Anthony Johnson, himself a black, imports five servants and thus qualifies to receive a 200 acre land grant along the Puwgoteague River in Virginia. Other blacks soon join Johnson and attempt to launch an independent black community. At its height, the settlement has 12 black homesteads with sizable holdings.

1662 Virginia   The colony passes a law which provides that the status of children—bound or free— will be determined by the condition of the mother.

1663 Gloucester, Virginia   A planned uprising, involving many black slaves and white indentured servants, is betrayed by a house servant.

1663 Maryland Settlers pass a law stipulating that all imported blacks are to be given the status of slaves. Free white women who marry black slaves are to be slaves during the lives of their spouses; children of the union are also classified as slaves. Ironically, children born of white servant women and blacks are regarded as free by a later law (1681).

1670 Virginia Voting rights are removed from recently freed slaves and indentured servants. All non-Christians imported to the territory, "by shipping," are to be slaves for life, whereas those who enter by land are to serve until the age of 30 if they are adult men and women when their period of servitude commences.

1672 Virginia A law is enacted providing for a bounty on the heads of "Maroons"—black fugitives who form communities in the mountains, swamps, and forests of southern colonies. Many Maroon communities attack towns and plantations.

1685 French West Indies The French Code Noir is enacted. It requires religious instruction for slaves, permits intermarriage, outlaws working of slaves on Sundays and holidays, but forbids liberation of mulatto children reaching 21 if their mothers are still enslaved. However, the Code is largely ignored by the French settlers.

1688 Germantown, Pennsylvania Mennonite Quakers sign an anti-slavery resolution, the first formal protest against slavery in the Western Hemisphere.

In 1696 Quakers importing slaves are threatened with expulsion from the Society.

1700 English North American Colonies Slave population is placed at 28,000, with 23,000 in the South.

1704 New York City Elias Neau, a French immigrant, opens the "Catechism School" for black slaves.

1705 Virginia The Assembly declares that "no Negro, mulatto, or Indian shall presume to take upon him, act in or exercise any office, ecclesiastic, civil or military." Blacks are forbidden to serve as witnesses in court cases and are condemned to life-long servitude, unless they have either been Christians in their native land or free men in a Christian country.

1711 Pennsylvania Spurred by the Mennonites and Quakers, the colonial legislature outlaws slavery but is overruled by the British Crown.

1712 New York City An early slave revolt claims the lives of nine whites and results in the execution of 21 blacks. Six others commit suicide.

1723 Virginia The colony enacts laws to limit the increase of free blacks to those who are born into this class or manumitted by special acts of the legislature. Free blacks are denied the right to vote and forbidden to carry weapons of any sort.

1727 Philadelphia The Junto, a benevolent association founded by Benjamin Franklin, opposes slavery.

1735 New York Dutch Burgher John Van Zandt

The first black immigrants to the British colonies entered Jamestown as indentured servants in 1619, but later arrivals were condemned to slavery.

whips his slave to death for being picked up outside of his quarters. Van Zandt is tried by a coroner's jury which asserts that the slave was killed "by the visitation of God."

1739 South Carolina Three black revolts occur, resulting in known deaths to 51 whites and many more slaves. One of the insurrections led by the slave, Cato, results in death of 30 whites.

1740 South Carolina The colony passes a slave code which forbids slaves from raising livestock, provides that any animals owned by slaves be forfeited and fixes severe penalties for slaves who make "false appeals" to the governor on the grounds that they have been placed in bondage illegally.

1741 New York A series of arsonist acts throughout the city prompts a massive white backlash which results in the burning of 11 blacks and the hanging of 18 others. Public suspicion of slaves stems solely from their presence, rather than from any circumstantial or direct proof of their connection with the crimes.

1744 Virginia The colony amends its 1705 law declaring that blacks cannot serve as witnesses in court cases; it decides, instead, to admit "any free negro, mulatto, or Indian being a Christian," as a witness in a criminal or civil suit *involving another Negro*, mulatto, or Indian.

1746 Deerfield, Massachusetts Slave poet Lucy Terry pens "Bars Fight," a commemorative poem recreating the Deerfield Massacre. Terry, generally considered the first black poet in America, later tried unsuccessfully to convince the Board of Trustees at Williams College to admit her son to the school.

1747 South Carolina The Assembly commends black slaves for demonstrating "great faithfulness and courage in repelling attacks of His Majesty's enemies." It then makes cautious provisions for utilizing black recruits in the event of danger or emergency. No more than half of all able-bodied slaves aged 16–20 is authorized to enlist. Once mustered in, slaves are to be integrated among the companies so that they never constitute more than one-third of the white men in the company.

1749 Georgia Prohibitions on the importation of slaves are repealed in a law which also attempts

The earliest English settlement in America was on Roanoke Island in Pamlico Sound, shown here in a sixteenth-century navigator's map. The sinking ships warn captains of the banks.

to protect slaves from cruel treatment and from being hired out.

1750 Framingham, Massachusetts Crispus Attucks, later to become one of the first heroes of the American Revolution, escapes from his master.

1750 The English Colonies Slave population reaches 236,400, with over 206,000 of the total living south of Pennsylvania. Slaves comprise about 20% of colonies' population, over 40% of Virginia's.

1752 Mount Vernon There are 18 slaves at Mount Vernon at the time George Washington acquires the estate there. Under Washington, the number grows to 200. Washington's record shows a concern for their physical welfare, but vacillation about their right to freedom and his willingness to dispense with their services.

1754 Philadelphia Quaker John Woolman publishes *Some Considerations On the Keeping Of Negroes,* an exhortation to fellow members of the Society of Friends to consider manumitting their slaves on grounds of morality. Three years later, some Quakers take formal action against members who ignore this plea and continue to own slaves.

1754 Baltimore Benjamin Banneker, a 22-year-old free black, becomes the first person in the North American colonies to build a clock, though he has never before seen one. The clock chimes the hour accurately for more than 20 years.

1760 New York City Jupiter Hammon, a black poet, publishes *Salvation By Christ With Penitential Cries.*

1760 Rhode Island Despite the exhortation of some Friends and official statements from other Quaker communities, Quaker policy is not uniform on the slavery issue. One group in Rhode Island continues to be active in the slave trade. A few Quakers in the Carolinas and Virginia refuse to relinquish slaves.

1764 Massachusetts Slave ship captains and merchants oppose efforts to raise the price of sugar and molasses, declaring them essential to the slave trade, which they deem the "vital commerce" of New England. But, representing another viewpoint, Samuel Adams refuses the offer of a slave for his sick wife. Though penniless, Adams insists the woman be freed before she enters his house.

1766 Virginia George Washington orders that one of his slaves, "Negro Tom," who had run away, be sold in the West Indies for molasses, rum, limes, tamarinds, sweet meats, and good old spirits.

1767 Boston Phillis Wheatley, a 14-year-old slave to the wife of a prosperous Boston tailor, publishes a poem, *The University of Cambridge in New England.* She is soon hailed as a prodigy and feted in New England and London.

1769 Virginia In the Virginia House of Burgesses, Thomas Jefferson unsuccessfully presses for a bill to emancipate slaves.

1770 Boston, Massachusetts Crispus Attucks is shot and killed during the Boston Massacre.

1770 Philadelphia, Pennsylvania Led by Anthony Benezet, the Quakers open a school for blacks.

1773 Savannah, Georgia George Lisle and Andrew Bryan organize the first Negro Baptist church in the state.

1774 The Continental Colonies The Continental Congress demands elimination of the slave trade and economic embargoes on all countries participating in it. Rhode Island enacts a law freeing slaves henceforth brought into the colony, but not those presently there.

1775 Germany Johann Friedrich Blumenbach publishes the first telling attack on theories declaring blacks to be racially inferior. In *On the Natural Variety of Mankind,* Blumenbach proves that the skulls and brains of blacks are the same as those of Europeans. Blumenbach's paper serves as a counter to the views of Voltaire, Hume, and Linne that blacks are akin to apes.

1775 Philadelphia Organization of the first abolitionist society in the United States.

1775 Fort Ticonderoga Black patriots join Ethan Allen and the Green Mountain Boys in the capture of Fort Ticonderoga.

1775 Bunker Hill Peter Salem, Salem Poor, and others are among blacks to fight heroically at Bunker Hill.

1775 Philadelphia The Continental Congress bars blacks from the American Revolutionary army.

1775 Virginia Lord Dunmore, British governor of Virginia, offers freedom to all male slaves who join the loyalist forces. General George Washington, originally opposed to the enlistment of blacks, is alarmed by the response to the Dunmore proclamation and orders recruiting officers to accept free blacks for service.

1776 Philadelphia Adoption of the amended form of the Declaration of Independence, which eliminates the Jefferson proposal denouncing slavery.

1776 The Continental Colonies Lafayette praises black soldiers for successfully covering Washington's retreat to Long Island. Blacks also help cover Washington's retreat at Trenton and Princeton, but many rebel leaders oppose integrated forces and two all-black companies are formed.

1776 Delaware River Two blacks—Prince Whipple and Oliver Cromwell—cross the Delaware with

Much of the work on colonial docks was done by slaves.

Washington enroute to an attack on the British and their Hessian mercenaries in Trenton, New Jersey.

1778 Rhode Island A black battalion consisting of 300 former slaves is formed. They are compensated on a par with their white comrades-in-arms and promised freedom after the war. In August, the battalion kills 1,000 Hessians and later sees action under Colonel Green at Ponts Bridge in New York.

1779 New York Alexander Hamilton endorses the plan of South Carolina's Henry Laurens to use slaves as soldiers in the south. "I have not the least doubt that the Negroes will make very excellent soldiers," says Hamilton, ". . . for their natural faculties are as good as ours." Hamilton reminds the Continental Congress that the British will make use of Negroes if the Americans do not. In Hamilton's words: "The best way to counteract the temptations they will hold out, will be to offer them ourselves."

1781 Virginia Black soldiers participate in defeat of Cornwallis at Yorktown. Maroon attacks on plantations and an uprising in Williamsburg are reported.

1782 Virginia Thomas Jefferson's *Notes on Virginia* exhibits a curious mixture of perception and naivete with regard to blacks. On the one hand, Jefferson believes that "the whole commerce between master and slave is a perpetual exercise of the most boisterous passions," on the other, he invents the fantasy that blacks' "griefs are transient."

1782 Massachusetts Deborah Gannet, a female black disguised as a man, serves in the 4th Massachusetts Regiment and is later cited for bravery.

1783 The United States The war ends. Some 10,000 blacks had served in the continental armies, 5,000 as regular soldiers. The famed "Black Regiment" is deactivated.

1783 Massachusetts Slavery in The Commonwealth is abolished by the Massachusetts Supreme Court. Blacks in taxable categories are granted suffrage.

1785 Wilmington, North Carolina Birth of black abolitionist David Walker, who in 1827 establishes a second-hand clothing business in Boston and, two years later, writes *Walker's Appeal,* a call to revolt in the South. The document creates such a furor among slaveowners that at least one southern legislature makes circulation of it a capital offense.

1787 Philadelphia Black preachers Richard Allen and Absalom Jones organize the Free African Society. Prince Hall organizes the first black Masonic Lodge in America—African Lodge No. 459.

1787 Northwest Territory Congressional passage of the "Northwest Ordinance" forbids the extension of slavery into this area.

1787 New York City Opening of the African Free School by the New York Manumission Society.

1787 The United States The Constitution is adopted. In it, importation of slaves cannot be prohibited before 1808 and five slaves are considered the equivalent of three freemen in Congressional apportionment.

1788 Newport, Rhode Island The Negro Union advocates emigration of free blacks to Africa. Its stand is opposed by the Philadelphia Free African Society.

1790 The United States According to the first census, there are 757,000 blacks in the United States, comprising 19% of the total population. Nine percent of blacks are free.

1790 West Indies Blacks comprise seven-eighths of the islands' 529,000 inhabitants. Less than 3% are free. Mulattoes in French Santo Domingo own 10% of the slaves and land.

1790 The Western Territories Jean Baptiste Pointe du Sable, the son of a French mariner and African slave mother, establishes the first permanent settlement at what is to become Chicago.

1791 Haiti Toussaint L'Ouverture, a self-educated slave, leads unsuccessful uprising, but the French grant suffrage to mulattoes born of free parents.

1791 Louisiana Twenty-three slaves are hanged and three white sympathizers deported, following suppression of a black revolt.

1791 District of Columbia On the recommendation of Thomas Jefferson, Benjamin Banneker—astronomer, inventor, mathematician and gazetteer—is appointed to serve as a member of the commission charged with laying out plans for the city of Washington.

Jean Baptiste Pointe Du Sable, a black fur trapper, established the first permanent settlement at what was to become Chicago.

Private Edward Hector, Artillery.

1791 Philadelphia Congress excludes blacks and Indians from peacetime militia. Kentucky is admitted as a slave state.

1793 Philadelphia Passage of the Fugitive Slave Act, which makes it criminal to harbor a slave or prevent his arrest.

1793 Mulberry Grove, Georgia Eli Whitney patents the cotton gin, which strengthens slavery by vastly increasing profits in cotton growing.

1793 Virginia Passage of a state law which forbids free blacks from entering the state.

1794 Philadelphia Dedication of the First African Church of St. Thomas, the first black Episcopal Congregation in the United States. In the same year, Richard Allen organizes the Bethel Church, a Negro Methodist Episcopal Church. Allen and Absalom Jones are well known to the citizens of Philadelphia, having been commended by the Mayor for organizing blacks to minister to the sick and bury the dead during an outbreak of yellow fever.

1795 Louisiana More slave uprisings are suppressed with some 50 blacks killed and executed.

1795 Virginia George Washington advertises for the return of one of his slaves, stipulating that the notice for his retrieval not be run north of Virginia. This same year, John Adams writes: "I have never owned a Negro or any other slave [even] when it has cost me thousands of dollars for the labor and sustenance of free men, which I might have saved by the purchase of Negroes at times when they were very cheap."

The British prison ship Jersey, *aboard which many white and black Revolutionary soldiers died.*

1796 Tennessee Admission of Tennessee to the Union as a slave state. The state's constitution, however, does not deny suffrage to free blacks.

1796 New York City Organization of the Zion Methodist Church.

1797 North Carolina Congress refuses to accept the first recorded anti-slavery petition seeking redress against a North Carolina law which requires that slaves, although freed by their Quaker masters, be returned to the state and to their former condition.

1797 Hurley, New York and Chapel Hill, North Carolina Births of Sojourner Truth and George Moses Horton. Miss Truth, freed in 1827, feels herself singled out for a divinely inspired crusade involving emancipation and women's liberation. During the Civil War, she is a nurse; later, she is a touring lecturer. A janitor, George Moses Horton writes love poems for students and later publishes a book of verse. Horton is freed after the Civil War and finishes a second volume, *Naked Genius.*

1798 Washington, D.C. Secretary of the Navy Stoddert forbids the deployment of black sailors on men-of-war, thus disrupting a nonracial enlistment policy which had been operative in the Navy for many years. Nevertheless, a few blacks slip past the ban,

including William Brown, a "powder monkey" on the *Constellation* and George Diggs, quartermaster of the schooner *Experiment.* Enlistments in the Marine Corps are also forbidden.

1799 Mount Vernon, Virginia George Washington's will declares: "It is my will and desire that all the slaves which I hold in my right, shall receive their freedom."

1799 Boston First minstrel performance is given by Gottlieb Graupner, a young German who had studied songs sung by blacks in Charleston. Graupner later forms the Boston Philharmonic Society.

1800 Richmond Betrayal of Gabriel Prosser's plan to lead thousands of slaves in an attack on Richmond. Prosser and 15 of his followers are later hanged.

1800 Washington, D.C. By a vote of 85 to 1, Congress rejects petition by free blacks of Philadelphia to gradually end slavery in the United States.

1803 South Carolina The Legislature, which had been trying to limit importation of slaves, reopens slave trade with Latin America and the West Indies.

1803 New York City Blacks of New York burn parts of the city and destroy several homes.

1804 Ohio The legislature enacts the first of the

"Black Laws" restricting the rights and movements of blacks. Other Western states soon follow suit. Illinois, Indiana, and Oregon later have anti-immigration clauses in their state constitutions.

1804 New Jersey New Jersey passes an emancipation law. All states north of the Mason-Dixon Line now have laws forbidding slavery or providing for its gradual elimination. However, there are to be some slaves in New Jersey right up to the Civil War.

1807 New Jersey The state alters its 1776 Constitution by limiting the vote to free white males.

1807 Washington, D.C. Congress bars the importation of any new slaves into the territory of the United States (effective January 1, 1808). Law is widely ignored.

1808 United States Ban on the importation of slaves is scheduled to take effect. There are one million slaves in the country.

1810 Louisiana Courts declare, in *Adelle* v. *Beauregard,* that a black is free unless it is otherwise proven.

1811 Westport, Connecticut Paul Cuffee (1759–1818), son of black and Indian parents and later a wealthy shipbuilder, sails with small group of blacks to Sierra Leone to underscore his advocacy of a black return to Africa.

1811 Delaware The state forbids the immigration of free blacks and declares that any native-born free black who has been out of Delaware for more than six months will be deemed a nonresident.

1811 Louisiana U.S. troops suppress a slave uprising in two parishes some 35 miles from New Orleans. The revolt is led by Charles Deslands. Some 100 slaves are killed or executed.

1812 Louisiana Admission of Louisiana to the Union as a slave state. State law enables freedmen to serve in the state militia.

1813 Lake Erie Of Admiral Perry's victorious force in naval battle with British, 10 to 25% are blacks. Many are cited for bravery.

1814 The United States Blacks participate in victories at Plattsburg and on Lake Champlain. Andrew Jackson praises blacks for bravery in battle.

1815 New Orleans Six hundred blacks, many led by black officers, fight with Andrew Jackson in successful defense of New Orleans.

1815 Fort Blount, Florida Blacks and Creek Indians capture the fort from Seminoles and use it as haven for escaped slaves and base for attacks on slave owners. But an American army detachment eventually recaptures the fort.

1816 Louisiana State law prohibits slaves from testifying against whites and free blacks, except in cases involving slave uprisings.

1816 Philadelphia Organization of the African Methodist Episcopal Church.

1816 Washington, D.C. Organization of the American Colonization Society, which seeks to transport free blacks to Africa. (Protest meetings are subsequently held by many such blacks in opposition

Chained for the voyage, Africans were at the mercy of brutal crewmen.

to the Society's efforts "to exile us from the land of our nativity.")

1816 Virginia Failure of slave rebellion led by George Boxley, a white man.

1816 Baltimore Founding of Bethel Charity School for Negroes by Daniel Coker, a black.

1816 New Orleans James P. Beckwourth, who was to become one of the great explorers of the nineteenth century, signs on as a scout for General Henry Ashley's Rocky Mountain expedition.

1817 The United States Mississippi enters the union as a slave state. New York passes a gradual abolition act.

1818 Connecticut Blacks are disenfranchised.

1818 Philadelphia Free blacks form the Pennsylvania Augustine Society "for the education of people of colour." Schools for blacks receive public aid.

1819 Washington, D.C. James Madison, who wishes slavery to cease but believes in separatism, argues that slavery should end gradually and that slaves be allotted land in the West because the barriers to "incorporation of the people are insuperable."

1819 Alabama Alabama enters the Union as a slave state, although its constitution provides the Legislature with the power to abolish slavery and compensate slaveowners. Other measures include jury trials for slaves figuring in crimes above petty larceny and penalties for malicious killing of slaves.

1820 Washington, D.C. The Missouri Compromise provides for Missouri's entry into the Union as a slave state and Maine's entry as a free state. There are thus 12 slave and 12 free states in the United States. All territory north of 36° 30' is declared free; all territory south of that line open to slavery. The Army is forbidden from accepting blacks and mulattoes.

1820 New York City The *Mayflower of Liberia* sails for the west coast of Africa (Sierra Leone) with 86 blacks aboard.

1821 New York The State Constitutional Convention alters the voting requirements of the 1777 N.Y. Convention by establishing higher property and longer residence requirements for blacks.

1821 New York City Founding of the African Methodist Episcopal Zion Church, with James Varick as its first bishop.

1821 New York The African Company performs Shakespeare in a theater on Mercer Street.

1822 Charleston, South Carolina Betrayal of the Denmark Vesey conspiracy, one of the most elaborate on record. Vesey, a sailor and carpenter, and 36 collaborators are hanged, an additional 130 blacks and four whites are arrested, and stricter controls are imposed on free blacks and slaves. Following this insurrection, South Carolina and other slave states adopt laws and policies that further restrict the mobility and education of blacks.

1822 Western Africa Liberia is founded by blacks of the American Colonization Society.

1822 Rhode Island Free blacks are disenfranchised.

1823 Washington, D.C. and Philadelphia U.S. Circuit Court declares that removal of a slave to a

Arab slaves entering a West African village—as the slave trade intensified, European guns made tribal resistance futile.

free state bestows freedom and that malicious, cruel, or inhuman treatment of a slave is an indictable offense of a common law.

1823 Mississippi   Law prohibiting teaching of reading and writing to blacks and meetings of more than five slaves or free blacks is enacted.

1824 The United States   As the country moves toward universal male suffrage, more states in the North and West as well as the South move to deny the vote to blacks. Illinois, Indiana, Iowa, and Michigan require blacks to post bond in guarantee of good behavior.

1825 Maryland   Josiah Henson, prototype for the original "Uncle Tom," leads a group of slaves to freedom in Kentucky. Henson later crosses the border into Ontario and becomes leader of a community of ex-slaves.

1826 London   Frederick Ira Aldridge, a black actor born in New York City and educated in The African Free School, makes his London debut playing Othello at the Royal Theater. Aldridge is later acclaimed in Europe as one of the great actors of the nineteenth century.

1826 Virginia   Thomas Jefferson's will frees only five of his many slaves, the remainder being bequeathed to heirs.

1827 New York City   *Freedom's Journal,* the first black newspaper, begins publication on March 16. States the publication: "In the spirit of candor and humility we intend . . . to lay our case before the public with a view to arrest the progress of prejudice, and to shield ourselves against its consequent evils."

1827 New York   Slavery is abolished in New York State on July 4; 10,000 are freed.

1828 Bennington, Vermont   William Lloyd Garrison begins attacks on slavery in the *National Philanthropist.*

1829 Cincinnati   After riot in which whites attack black residents and loot and burn their homes, 1,200 blacks flee to Canada.

1829 Boston   Publication by David Walker, a free black, of a militant antislavery pamphlet *An Appeal to the Colored People of the World* which is distributed throughout the country and arouses a furor among slaveholders.

1830 North Carolina   Masters fearing violation of state law manumit more than 400 slaves to Quaker residents of North Carolina, who retain theoretical ownership, but allow slaves virtual freedom until they can afford to transport them to free states.

1830 Washington, D.C.   The U.S. Census Bureau reports that 3,777 Negro heads of families own slaves, mostly in Louisiana, Maryland, Virginia, North Carolina, and South Carolina.

1830 Philadelphia   Chaired by Richard Allen, the first National Negro Convention meets from September 20 to 24 at Philadelphia's Bethel Church. It launches a church-affiliated program to improve the social status of the American Negro.

1830 The United States   As a counter to the increasing strength of the abolitionist movement a number of states pass laws restricting the education, legal safeguards, and citizenship rights of slaves and free blacks. Many states require the deportation of free blacks; slave codes are enforced more strictly and the number of manumissions decline.

1831 Boston   The *Liberator,* an abolitionist organ, is founded by William Garrison. Proclaims Garrison: "I am in earnest—I will not equivocate—I will not excuse—I will not retreat a single inch—AND I WILL BE HEARD."

1831 Southampton County, Virginia   Nat Turner, a brilliant and moody slave, leads the greatest slave rebellion in history. Some 60 whites are killed and the entire South is thrown into panic. Turner is captured on October 30 and hanged in Jerusalem (Virginia) 12 days later.

1831 Philadelphia   Convocation of the first Annual Convention of the People of Color at Wesleyan Church, where delegates from five states resolve to study black conditions, explore settlement possibilities in Canada, and raise money for an industrial college in New Haven. Delegates oppose the American Colonization Society and recommend annual meetings.

1831 Virginia   Thomas Dew, a legislator, proudly refers to Virginia as a "Negro-raising state" for other states. Between 1830 and 1860, Virginia exports some 300,000 slaves, South Carolina 179,000. The price of slaves increases sharply due to expanding territory in which slaves are permitted and a booming economy in products harvested and processed by slave labor.

1832 Boston   The New England Anti-Slavery Society is established by 12 whites at the African Baptist Church on Boston's Beacon Hill.

1833 Philadelphia   Black, and white, abolitionists organize the American Anti-Slavery Society.

1833 Canterbury, Connecticut   Miss Prudence Crandall, a white liberal, is arrested for conducting an academy for black girls.

1833 Ohio   Founding of Oberlin College, integrated from the outset and a leader in the abolitionist cause. At the start of the Civil War, blacks constitute one-third of Oberlin's students.

Slaves were stowed "spoon-fashion" after the trade became illegal in 1808.

1834 British Empire Parliament abolishes slavery in the British Empire; 700,000 are liberated at cost of 20 million British pounds sterling.

1834 South Carolina State enacts a law prohibiting the teaching of black children, free or slave.

1835 Washington, D.C. President Jackson seeks to restrict the mailing of abolitionist literature to the South.

1835 North Carolina The last southern state to deny suffrage to blacks, North Carolina repeals a voting rights provision of the state constitution. The state also makes it illegal for whites to teach free blacks.

1836 The United States The Methodist Church softens its opposition to slavery and declares its intention to avoid interference in civil and political relationships between masters and slaves.

1836 Washington, D.C. The House of Representatives adopts the "gag rule" which prevents Congressional action on antislavery resolutions or legislation.

1837 Alton, Illinois Elijah P. Lovejoy is murdered by a mob in Alton after refusing to stop publishing antislavery material.

1837 Florida John Horse, a black, is a commander of Seminole Indians in their victory over American troops at Battle of Okeechobee.

1837 New York City James McCune Smith establishes medical practice after studying medicine in Scotland.

1837 Boston Series of abolitionist works are published, including Reverend Hosea Eaton's *A Treatise on the Intellectual Character and Political Condition of the Colored People of the United States.*

1837 Virginia The price for a slave, "prime field hand," that is, a black male between 18 and 25 years of age, in good physical condition reaches $1,300, then declines in wake of a recession.

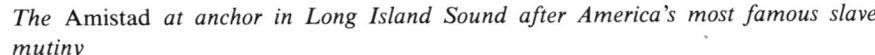

The Amistad *at anchor in Long Island Sound after America's most famous slave mutiny*

1837 Canada Blacks are given right to vote.

1838 Southern States Black preachers are increasingly forbidden to conduct services, as slaves are required to worship under the supervision of their masters.

1838 Montauk, Long Island The slave ship *Amistad* is brought into Montauk by a group of Africans who have revolted against their captors. The young African leader Cinqué and his followers are defended before the Supreme Court by former President John Quincy Adams, and awarded their freedom.

1839 Washington, D.C. The State Department rejects a black's application for a passport on the grounds that blacks are not citizens.

1839 Warsaw, New York Founding of the first anti-slavery political organization, the Liberty Party, with black abolitionists Samuel Ringgold Ward and Henry Highland Garnet among its leading supporters. Party urges boycotts and exclusion of southern crops and products.

1840 The Vatican Pope Gregory XVI declares opposition to slavery and the slave trade.

1840 New York and Vermont Jury trial for fugitive slaves is instituted. Vermont law is overturned in 1843, reinstated in 1850.

1840 Massachusetts Running counter to a nation-wide trend, Massachusetts repeals law forbidding intermarriage between whites and blacks, mulattoes, or Indians.

1841 Virginia Slaves revolt on the vessel *Creole* en route from Hampton, Virginia to New Orleans. Overpowering the crew and sailing the ship to the Bahamas, the slaves are granted asylum and freedom.

1841 Massachusetts Frederick Douglass begins his career as a lecturer with the Massachusetts Anti-Slavery Society.

1841 The United States Increasingly restrictive segregation statutes are enacted. The New York State Legislature grants school districts the right to segregate their educational facilities. South Carolina forbids white and black mill hands from looking out the same window. Whites and blacks in Atlanta are required to swear on different bibles in court.

1842 Boston The capture of George Latimer, an escaped slave, precipitates the first of several famous fugitive slave cases straining North–South relations. Latimer is later purchased from his master by Boston abolitionists. Agitation for Latimer is marked by Frederick Douglass's first appearance in print.

1842 Rhode Island Suffrage is granted to blacks.

1842 Pennsylvania An early challenge to the Fugitive Slave Act (of 1793) occurs when a state court convicts Edward Prigg of kidnapping for his recapture of an escaped slave, Margaret Morgan. The Pennsylvania Court denies that the Fugitive Slave Law applies in Prigg's behalf, on grounds that it must be enforced by federal officials. An early dispute between immigrant and black laborers erupts in coal mining areas, where black and Irish miners clash.

The execution of Captain Ferrer under mutiny-leader Joseph Cinque's watchful eyes, from a Harper's etching. Defended in court by John Quincy Adams, the mutineers were set free and returned to Africa.

1843 Buffalo, New York Henry Highland Garnet calls for a slave revolt and general strike while addressing the National Convention of Colored Men. Garnet, Samuel R. Ward, and Charles B. Ray participate in the Liberty Party convention, becoming the first blacks to take part in a national political gathering.

1843 Massachusetts and Vermont Legislatures defy the Fugitive Slave Act and forbid state officials from imprisoning or assisting federal authorities in recapture of escaped slaves.

1843 Washington, D.C. Approval of Webster–Ashburton Treaty in which Britain and the United States agree to keep ships off African Coast to suppress the slave trade there. No agreement is reached, however, to restrict slave trade within the Western Hemisphere.

1844 Philadelphia Birth of Richard Greener, the first black to receive a degree from Harvard (1870). Active as a teacher and editor, Greener is admitted to the South Carolina bar in 1876 and becomes dean of Howard's Law School in 1879.

1844 California Jim Beckwourth discovers a pass through the Sierra Nevada Mountains to California and the Pacific Ocean.

1845 Worcester, Massachusetts Macon B. Allen becomes the first black formally admitted to the bar in the United States.

1845 Washington, D.C. Congress overturns the gag rule of 1836. Texas is admitted to the Union as a slave state.

1846 Louisiana Norbert Rillieux, son of a white engineer and free mulatto mother, patents the multiple-effect vacuum evaporation process which becomes the basic method for processing sugar.

1847 New York Abolitionist Gerritt Smith's plans to parcel up thousands of acres of his land in New York fails to attract prospective black farmers. Lack of capital among blacks and the infertility of the land doom the project. New York voters reject a constitutional amendment to grant equal suffrage to blacks.

1847 St. Louis Dred Scott files suit for his freedom in the Circuit Court of St. Louis.

1847 Rochester, New York Frederick Douglass publishes the first issue of his abolitionist newspaper, *The North Star.*

1848 Buffalo The convention of the Free Soil Party is attended by a number of black abolitionists.

1848 Virginia Postmasters are forced to inform police of arrival of pro-abolition literature and turn it over to authorities for burning.

1849 Maryland Harriet Tubman, soon to be a conductor on the "Underground Railroad," escapes from slavery. Tubman later returns to the South no less than 19 times to help transport more than 300 slaves to freedom. In the same year, the Maryland legislature enacts laws to override restrictions on the importation of slaves.

1849 Maryland The state's Supreme Court establishes the "separate but equal" doctrine in response to suit brought by Benjamin Roberts to have his daughter admitted to a white school.

1850 Washington, D.C. The Clay Compromise is enacted, strengthening the 1793 Fugitive Slave Act. Federal officers are now offered a fee for the slaves they apprehend. California is admitted to union as a free state.

1850 New York Samuel R. Ward becomes president of the American League of Colored Laborers, a union of skilled black workers who develop black craftsmen and encourage black-owned business.

1851 Virginia New laws require freed slaves to leave the state within a year or be enslaved again.

1852 Akron, Ohio Sojourner Truth addresses the National Women's Suffrage Convention.

1852 Rochester Frederick Douglass delivers his scathing "What to the Slave is the Fourth of July?" oration—" . . . your celebration a sham; your boasted liberty an unholy license, your national greatness, swelling vanity. . . ."

1852 Boston Publication of the first edition of Harriet Beecher Stowe's controversial *Uncle Tom's Cabin.*

1852 Cincinnati Some 200 of the 3,500 Cincinnati blacks are prosperous property owners whose aggregate worth is $500,000 and who pay real estate taxes on their accumulated wealth. However, violent incidents between white and black communities are frequent.

1853 London William Wells Brown publishes *Clotel,* the first novel written by an American black.

1853 The United States Moves to deport free blacks to Africa gain support. Virginia imposes poll tax on free blacks to obtain funds for deportation and the *New York Herald Tribune* declares that black "racial inferiority" renders their emigration desirable.

1853 Oxford, Pennsylvania Lincoln University, the first black college, is founded as Ashmum Institute.

1854 Boston Anthony Burns, a fugitive slave, is arrested and escorted through streets lined with abolitionist sympathizers, by U.S. troops prior to being returned to his master, who refuses an offer of $1,200 from Boston citizens attempting to purchase his freedom.

1854 Washington, D.C. The Kansas–Nebraska Act,

The Fugitive Slave Law, part of the Compromise of 1850, was more ruthlessly enforced than its predecessor, the Fugitive Slave Act of 1793.

authored by Stephen Douglas, admits the territories of Kansas and Nebraska to the Union without slavery restrictions, in direct contradiction to the provisions of the Missouri Compromise of 1820.

1854 Paris, France James Augustine Healy, later the first American black Roman Catholic bishop, is ordained a priest in Notre Dame Cathedral.

1854 Ohio John Mercer Langston, who was born a slave in Virginia, is admitted to the Ohio bar. Langston is to become dean of Howard University and the first black to win elective office in the history of the United States.

1854 New England The New England Emigration Society organizes to settle ex-slaves in Kansas.

1854 Peoria, Illinois In his first statement on slavery, Abraham Lincoln opposes its extension to Western Territories.

1855 New York The Liberty Party nominates Frederick Douglass for Secretary of State, the first black nominated for statewide office.

1855 Maine, Massachusetts, and Michigan The slavery issue is further polarized by enactment, in these states, of laws forbidding state officials from aiding the federal government in enforcement of the Fugitive Slave Laws. The Massachusetts Legislature abolishes school segregation and integration proceeds without incident.

1856 Ohio Wilberforce University is founded by the Methodist Episcopal Church. Blacks in Ohio are given control of their own schools.

1856 Missouri and Kansas Pro-slavery forces sack the town of Lawrence, noted for its abolitionist, free-soil sentiment.

1856 The United States George Vashon publishes an anthology of his poetry, including *Victor Oge*, an antislavery work about a Haitian mulatto.

1856 Washington, D.C. Senator Sumner of Massachusetts is severely beaten on the Senate floor by Representative Brooks of South Carolina; Sumner is in the midst of attacking slaveowners and those who favor pro-slavery legislation.

1857 Washington, D.C. In the Dred Scott decision, the U.S. Supreme Court, by a 6 to 3 vote, opens federal territory to slavery, denies citizenship rights to blacks, and decrees that slaves do not become free when taken into free territory. (Scott himself is freed by his owner.) The Dred Scott decision is followed by a ruling that blacks are not entitled to land grants.

1857 Maine and New Hampshire Continuing to defy Fugitive Slave Laws, these states grant freedom and citizenship to people of African descent.

1858 Illinois In debates with Douglas, Lincoln states opposition to slavery, but declares that equality between the races is impossible.

1858 Washington, D.C. U.S. Attorney rules slaves cannot patent inventions because they are not citizens. Jefferson Davis is unable to patent a boat propellor invented by a slave of his, Benjamin Montgomery, because slaves cannot assign inventions to owners.

1859 Harpers Ferry John Brown and his band (13 whites, 5 blacks) attack Harpers Ferry. Two blacks are killed, two are captured, one escapes. (Brown is later hanged at Charles Town, West Virginia.)

1859 Baltimore Businessmen complain at slaveholders convention that free black laborers and entrepreneurs monopolize some service industries. How-

This famous painting of John Brown being led to the gallows presents him as the kindly, gentle leader the North imagined.

ever, a resolution to expel free blacks from the state fails.

1858 Vicksburg, Mississippi The Southern Commercial Convention calls for reestablishment of the slave trade, despite opposition from Tennessee and Florida delegations.

1860 The United States Policies of pro- and anti-slave forces continue to polarize, as the country edges toward Civil War. In Virginia, a law provides that free blacks can be sold into slavery for committing imprisonable offenses. Maryland forbids manumission. President Buchanan advocates a constitutional amendment confirming the Fugitive Slave Acts. The Democratic Party platform supports the Dred Scott decision. The Republican platform opposes the expansion of slavery into the western territories and Lincoln, still a moderate on the subject of abolition, is elected President. On December 17, South Carolina secedes from the Union.

1861 The Confederacy The Confederates attack Fort Sumter, South Carolina, marking the beginning of Civil War. Jefferson Davis is elected President of Confederate States of America and defends slavery as necessary to "self-preservation." The Confederates conscript slaves for military supporting jobs. Some Confederate states use free blacks in armed forces.

1861 Washington, D.C. The Secretary of the Navy solicits enlistment of blacks, but most black offers to help militarily are rejected. Federal policy toward liberated slaves is erratic, depending mostly on the viewpoint of individual commanders. Lincoln moves warily, countermanding General Freemont's order that slaves of masters who fight against the Union are to be "declared free men."

1861 Boston William C. Nell is appointed a post office clerk, becoming the first black person to hold a federal civilian job.

1862 Washington, D.C. President Lincoln proposes plan for gradual, compensated emancipation of slaves. Included is a provision to subsidize emigration to Haiti or Liberia. Lincoln's cautious policies are clarified in a letter to Horace Greeley in which he states his paramount objective as saving the Union "not either to save or destroy slavery." However, Lincoln does sign bills abolishing slavery in the territories and freeing slaves of masters disloyal to the United States. Military commanders are forbidden from returning fugitive slaves to owners and, in September, Lincoln issues an ultimatum giving hostile areas until January 1 to cease fighting or lose their slaves.

1862 New York Formation of the National Freedmen's Relief Association, one of many groups dedicated to assist the black slave in making the transition to freedom. Groups in Philadelphia, Cincinnati, and Chicago are eventually consolidated as the American Freedmen's Aid Commission.

1862 Charleston, South Carolina Black pilot Robert Smalls, later a congressman, sails the *Planter*, a

With Bible in one hand and rifle in the other, militant abolitionist John Brown is depicted as a giant battling to make Kansas a free state. Mural by John Steuart Curry adorns Kansas State Capitol.

Confederate steamer, out of Charleston harbor and turns the ship over to Union forces as war booty.

1862 Washington, D.C. Congress authorizes the enlistment of blacks for military service.

1862 The Confederacy Captured black union troops are hanged or pressed into forced labor. Union generals using black troops are declared subject to execution.

1863 Washington, D.C. Lincoln issues Emancipation Proclamation, declaring all slaves in rebellious areas to be free. The War Department forms the USCT (United States Colored Troops) group to federalize black regiments. Between 75 and 100 blacks become officers, most of them serving in Louisiana, many with distinction.

1863 New York In anti-draft riots, 1,200 people, mostly blacks, are killed. Riot is spurred in part by provision that exemption from military service can be bought for $300, a provision bitterly resented by poor white immigrants, who vent their frustrations on blacks.

1863 Cow Island, Haiti Lincoln sends ship to bring back 500 black settlers as colonization attempt fails.

1864 The Louisiana Territory Legislature, elected under auspices of occupying Union forces, votes to abolish slavery, but denies suffrage to blacks.

1864 The Union Reports of ill-treatment and withheld wages of black troops and officers continue despite efforts of the Department of War to improve matters.

1864 Virginia Fourteen of 37 Congressional Medal of Honor winners at Battle of Chaffin's Farm are black.

1865 Washington, D.C. John Rock becomes the first black admitted to practice before the Supreme Court. Congress approves the Thirteenth Amendment and establishes the Freedmen's Bureau.

1865 Montgomery, Alabama Jefferson Davis authorizes the Confederacy to fill its military quota by enlisting blacks in number not to exceed 25% of the able-bodied slave population. The measure comes one month before Appomatox and is too late to have an impact on the war.

1865 Appomatox, Virginia The Confederacy surrenders: 179,000 blacks served in the Union army, 3,000 were killed in battle, 26,000 died from disease, 14,700 deserted. Blacks represented 9 to 10% of the armed forces and 7% of the desertions.

1865 Washington, D.C. Death of Abraham Lincoln. The new President, Andrew Johnson, calls for ratification of the Thirteenth Amendment, which forbids slavery, but opposes black suffrage.

1865 Southern States All-white legislatures in many states enact black codes, which seek to maintain many features of prewar restrictions on blacks. Laws impose heavy penalties for "vagrancy," "insulting gestures," "curfew violations," and "seditious speeches." South Carolina requires blacks entering state to pose $1,000 bond in guarantee of good behavior and entitles employers to whip black employees.

1865 Davis Bend, Mississippi Blacks are settled on confiscated land, but President Johnson pardons owners and returns land to them. Johnson is also to return confiscated land in Georgia and South Carolina.

1865 The Union Wisconsin, Connecticut, and Minnesota deny suffrage to blacks.

1865 Tennessee The Ku Klux Klan is formed with the purpose of reasserting white supremacy and minimizing the influence of the Union in the South.

1866 Massachusetts Edward G. Walker and Charles L. Mitchell are elected to the Massachusetts House of Representatives, becoming the first blacks to serve in a legislative assembly in the United States.

1866 Nashville, Tennessee Opening of Fisk University.

1866 Washington, D.C. Passage of the Civil Rights Bill of 1866 despite President Johnson's veto. Its intention is to nullify the black codes. A bill is introduced in the District of Columbia to provide for black suffrage. White voters are asked to indicate their sentiments in a referendum. Over 6,500 vote against extension of the franchise to blacks; only 35 favor it. The Fourteenth Amendment passes the House and Senate despite opposition from Johnson. After considerable wrangling, a compromise bill, modestly extending the authority of the Freedman's Bureau, is passed over a Johnson veto. The bill pro-vides for military protection of blacks, distribution of food to members of both races, expansion of educational facilities, and return of expropriated land to original owners.

1866 Tennessee and Louisiana In a race riot in Memphis 48 blacks and two white sympathizers are killed; 35 blacks are killed in a riot in New Orleans.

1866 Washington Two black cavalry units are formed to serve in the west.

1866 London The *London Art Journal* selects Robert Duncanson, a black painter born in Cincinnati, as one of the day's outstanding landscape artists.

1867 Atlanta and Washington, D.C. Openings of Morehouse College and Howard University.

1867 Washington, D.C. Congress passes, over another veto by President Johnson, the first Reconstruction Act, which provides for military rule pending organization of state governments loyal to the Union. The Act requires occupied states to ratify the Fourteenth Amendment and guarantee the vote to blacks. Secretary of War Sumner fails in efforts to have Act order Freedman's Bureau to provide homes and schools for blacks.

1867 Southern and Border States Enforcement of the Reconstruction Act provides blacks with majority of vote in most southern states and alliances of blacks and white Republicans control in border states.

1867 The West Iowa and Dakota grant suffrage to blacks, Ohio rejects it.

1868 Hampton, Virginia Opening of Hampton Institute by an ex-Union officer, Samuel Chapman Armstrong.

Trent River settlement, a black village opposite Newbern, North Carolina

1868 Southern States Oscar Dunn, an ex-slave and captain in the Union army, is elected Lieutenant Governor of Louisiana. Blacks outnumber whites 87 to 40 in South Carolina Legislature, but whites have majority in state Senate.

1868 Washington, D.C. The Fourteenth Amendment is ratified, establishing the concept of "equal protection" for all citizens under the U.S. Constitution. President Johnson's veto of the bill granting vote to blacks in District of Columbia is overridden by Congress. Congress passes the Fifteenth Amendment, guaranteeing vote to blacks, and bill denying Supreme Court right to rule on cases involving constitutionality of the Reconstruction Act. The Senate declines by one vote short of needed two thirds (35 to 19) to find Johnson guilty of offenses for which he was indicted by the House of Representatives.

1868 Louisiana Louisiana's senators and representatives are readmitted to the U.S. Congress. The move follows the systematic terror initiated by the Ku Klux Klan against members of the Republican Party and emancipated blacks. Killings, lynchings, and beatings are recorded in several Louisiana parishes.

1868 The South Many states are readmitted to Union. Alabama legislature votes to segregate races in schools.

1868 North and West Nine states grant suffrage to blacks; two deny it. Republican platform omits demand for black suffrage in northern states.

1868 Great Barrington, Massachusetts Birth of William DuBois, the great activist and writer, an early advocate of racial pride.

1869 Washington, D.C. Organization of The Colored National Labor Union advocates purchase and distribution of land. Ebenezer Don Carlos Bassett, believed to be the first black to receive an appointment in the diplomatic service, becomes U.S. Minister to Haiti.

1870 Washington, D.C. The Fifteenth Amendment, guaranteeing all citizens right to vote, is ratified. In "Ku Klux Klan Acts," the Army is empowered to maintain order in federal elections. The Supreme Court refuses to review the Reconstruction Act. Hiram Revels of Mississippi, America's first black senator, delivers his maiden speech on March 16 and says: "I maintain that the past record of my race is a true index of the feelings which today animate them . . . They aim not to elevate themselves by sacrificing one single interest of their white fellow citizens." Between 1870 and 1900, 22 blacks, 13 of them ex-slaves are to serve in Congress. The

Census of 1870 finds only 19% of blacks literate. The figure reaches 43% in 1890.

1870 Washington, D.C. Recruitment of blacks for cavalry intensifies. By 1890, 14 were to receive Congressional Medals of Honor for bravery in Indian Wars.

1870 The South Democrats regain control of many states from Republicans. Some attribute this to intimidation by the Ku Klux Klan. A Congressional investigation reports that in nine South Carolina counties, the Klan murdered 35 men and whipped 262 men and women. The Florida Secretary of State reports 153 Klan murders in Jackson County.

1871 Nashville The renowned Fisk Jubilee Singers go on an international tour to raise money for the college and to present black spirituals to wider and ever-growing audiences.

1872 Washington, D.C. Charlotte E. Ray becomes the first black woman to graduate from a university law school (Howard) in the United States.

1872 Louisiana P. B. S. Pinchback becomes acting governor of the state upon impeachment of the incumbent.

1872 Washington, D.C. Congress passes Amnesty Act, enabling officials of the Confederacy to hold office. Ku Klux Klan Act expires and is not renewed.

1874 Washington, D.C. Reverend Patrick F. Healy, S.J., is named President of Georgetown, the oldest Catholic University in the United States.

1874 Virginia State rearranges election districts and local government system thereby reducing political power of blacks.

1875 Washington, D.C. Congress passes the Civil Rights Bill of 1875, prohibiting discrimination in such public accommodations as hotels, theaters, and amusement parks. A key piece of legislation in the post-Civil War era, it seeks to "mete out equal and exact justice to all, of whatever nativity, race, color, or persuasions, religious or political. . . ."

1875 Mayesville, South Carolina Birth of Mary McLeod Bethune, who was to become advisor on youth affairs to President Franklin Roosevelt.

1875 Washington, D.C. Blanche K. Bruce of Mississippi becomes only black man to serve full term in Senate until the middle of the twentieth century. Bruce soon becomes a respected and articulate advocate for blacks, whose rights and influence he feels are insufficiently protected by Congress or President Grant.

1875 Kentucky Oliver Lewis, a black jockey, rides Aristides to victory in the first Kentucky Derby.

1876 Washington, D.C. The Senate, after three years

of controversy, refuses to seat H. R. Pinchback, a black who had been elected from Louisiana in 1873. In two decisions, the Supreme Court decides that the Fourteenth and Fifteenth Amendments do not guarantee suffrage. In *U.S.* v. *Cruikshank,* the Court declares that the Fourteenth Amendment provides blacks with equal protection under the law but does not add anything "to the rights which one citizen has under the Constitution against another." The Court rules that "the right of suffrage is not a necessary attribute of national citizenship."

1876 South Carolina Federal troops are sent by President Grant to restore order after five blacks are killed in Hamburg.

1876 Philadelphia Black landscape painter Robert Bannister and sculptress Edmonia Lewis, born of black and Indian parents, win critical praise at Centennial Exhibition.

1877 The United States Many historians regard 1877 as the start of a prolonged, adverse period, in which the legal and economic status of blacks declines. Major factors involved are the re-establishment of white political control in the South and the widespread use of blacks as cheap labor and strike breakers in nation's rapid economic expansion.

1877 Washington, D.C. In the aftermath of the inconclusive presidential election of 1876, Rutherford Hayes, a Republican, promises southern delegates he will withdraw federal troops from the South. This contributes to his selection for the presidency over Samuel J. Tilden by the House of Representatives. Democrats control Congress, deny funds to Army, and in 1878 remove presidential authority to use troops to guarantee fair elections.

1878 Washington, D.C. The U.S. Attorney General reveals widespread intimidation of blacks attempting to vote and stuffing of ballot boxes in several southern states.

1879 The South Frustrated by poverty and discrimination, large numbers of blacks start to emigrate north and west. A leader of the emigration movement is Benjamin Singleton, a mulatto ex-slave who had earlier escaped to Canada and favors separate black communities. Emigration is vigorously opposed by many whites, some of whom prevent ships from transporting blacks on the Mississippi River. Between 1870 and 1880, 21% of black males between 15 and 34 in Alabama leave.

1880 The United States Garfield is elected President, promising protection to southern blacks. Only two blacks are elected to Congress. Bruce is defeated for reelection to the Senate as whites regain control of state's Legislature.

1881 Washington, D.C. Chester Arthur succeeds Garfield, who is assassinated, and implies belief that blacks are not sufficiently educated to vote. Ex-Senator Bruce is appointed Registrar of the Treasury after refusing two other minor federal appointments, one a ministerial post in Brazil.

1881 Tennessee Tennessee passes a "Jim Crow" railroad law which sets a trend soon taken up by Florida (1887), Mississippi (1888), Texas (1889), Louisiana (1890), and a host of other southern and border states.

1881 Tuskegee, Alabama Booker T. Washington opens Tuskegee Institute with a $2,000 appropriation from the Alabama Legislature.

1881 Washington, D.C. Patent for first incandescent electric lamp with carbon filament is granted Lewis Latimer, a black inventor. Latimer also makes drawings for Alexander Graham Bell's telephone and eventually becomes chief draftsman for General Electric and Westinghouse.

1883 Washington, D.C. The Supreme Court declares the Civil Rights Act of 1875 unconstitutional.

1883 Lynn, Massachusetts The shoe-lasting machine of Jan Matzeliger, a black from Dutch Guiana, so revolutionizes the industry that Lynn becomes the "shoe-capital of the world."

1884 New York First issue of the New York Age, a successful black newspaper by T. Thomas Fortune, a mulatto born in Florida.

Ex-slaves formed a pool of cheap manual labor.

Frederick Douglass accepts congratulations on his appointment as minister to Haiti.

1884 Washington, D.C. Former black Reconstruction Congressman John Roy Lynch is elected temporary chairman of the Republican convention—the first black to preside over a national political gathering.

1887 Chicago Formation of first black baseball team, the Union Giants.

1888 Richmond and Washington, D.C. Founding of two black banks—The Savings Bank of the Grand Fountain United Order of True Reformers in Virginia and the Capital Savings Bank in Washington.

1889 Washington, D.C. Frederick Douglass is appointed U.S. Minister to Haiti. Three blacks, one each from North Carolina, South Carolina, and Virginia, take seats in Congress.

1890 Mississippi The Mississippi Constitutional Convention begins the systematic exclusion of blacks from the political arena by adopting literacy and other complex "understanding" texts as prerequisites to voting. Seven other southern states follow suit by 1910.

1890 Washington, D.C. In the *In Re Green* decision, the Supreme Court sanctions control of elections by state officials, thus weakening federal protection for southern black voters. Court also permits states to segregate public transportation facilities.

1891 Baffin Bay, Greenland Matthew Henson, a Maryland-born black, accompanies Admiral Perry in exploration of the Arctic. Henson, a skilled navigator with fluent command of the Eskimo language, is indispensible to expedition's success.

1891 Chicago, Illinois Dr. Daniel Hale Williams founds Provident Hospital, with the first training school for black nurses in the United States.

1891 Washington, D.C. The number of lynchings in the United States is reported to be 112. The great majority of victims are blacks residing in the South.

1892 St. Louis Georgia Populists, at the Populist Convention, strive to unite poor black and white farmers in the South, who, according to gubernatorial candidate Tom Watson, are kept at loggerheads by landed interests. Watson argues that wealthy Southerners perpetuate racial antagonisms so that poor whites and their black counterparts will resent each other, rather than cooperate for mutually advantageous ends.

1893 Washington, D.C. George Murray of South Carolina is the only black to take a seat in the 53rd Congress. National lynch count is 117.

1893 Cambridge, Massachusetts William Henry Lewis, black football player at Harvard, makes Walter Camp's All-American team.

1894 Cambridge, Massachusetts William DuBois becomes first black to be awarded Ph.D. by Harvard.

1894 Washington, D.C. Section of Emancipation Act dealing with right of blacks to vote is repealed.

1894 Detroit Publication of *Appointed*, a militant, politically conscious novel by William Anderson and Walter Stowers.

1895 Washington, D.C. George Murray is, again, the only black to take seat in Congress.

1895 Atlanta, Georgia Booker T. Washington delivers his famous "Atlanta Compromise" address at the Cotton Exposition—"To those of my race who depend on bettering their condition in a foreign land, or who underestimate the importance of cultivating friendly relations with the Southern white

The black 10th Cavalry distinguished itself charging Spanish cannon at the Battle of San Juan Hill, Santiago, Cuba, July 1, 1898.

man . . . I would say: 'Cast down your bucket where you are. . . .' "

1896 Washington, D.C. The Supreme Court in the *Plessy* v. *Ferguson* decision upholds the doctrine of "separate but equal," paving the way for segregation of blacks in all walks of life. Justice Harlan, dissenting, calls the ruling as "pernicious as the Dred Scott case."

1896 Cambridge, Massachusetts DuBois, who is emerging as a militant counterforce to Booker T. Washington, publishes *Suppression of the African Slave Trade,* the first of some 20 annual sociological studies of blacks in the United States.

1896 The Southern States Riots erupt in bitter elections, as diverse factions seek to control or eliminate the black vote. Racism increases within Populist ranks. G. H. White of North Carolina is only black elected to Congress.

1896 Washington, D.C. Formation of The National Association of Colored Women, a politically active self-help group.

1897 United States Andrew J. Beard is awarded $50,000 for invention of railroad coupler.

1898 Santiago, Cuba Four black regiments in the regular army compile an outstanding combat record in and around Santiago during the Spanish-American War. Five blacks receive Congressional Medals of Honor. At the close of the war, over 100 blacks are officers.

1898 Louisiana Addition of a "grandfather clause" to the Constitution enables poor whites to qualify for the franchise while curtailing black registration. In 1896 there were over 130,000 black voters on the Louisiana rolls. Four years later, the number is about 5,000.

1900 London, England W. E. B. DuBois attends the conference of the African and New World Intellectuals, where he delivers an address incorporating his famous dictum: "The problem of the twentieth century is the problem of the color line." DuBois also attends the first Pan-African Congress, an international body of concerned African nations protesting Western imperialism and promoting the concept of self-government among colonized peoples.

1900 Boston Formation by Booker T. Washington of the National Negro Business League.

1900 The United States Two contrasting works by blacks receive wide attention. Booker T. Washington's *Up from Slavery* describes success through acceptance of white domination. Charles W. Chestnutt's *The House Behind the Cedars* portrays desperate plight of the mulatto, whom he perceives as an outcast from both black and white worlds.

1901 Washington, D.C. Congressman George White delivers his farewell address in the House of Representatives "in behalf of an outraged, heart-broken, bruised and bleeding, but God-fearing people, faithful, industrious, loyal people—rising people, full of force." No black was to serve in Congress again until 1928.

1901 The United States Joe Walcott becomes welterweight champion, Joe Gans the lightweight champion.

1902 Richmond, Virginia Virginia joins other southern states in adopting the "grandfather clause."

1902 Paris, France *Off Bloomingdale Avenue,* a satirical comedy, is the first film to use blacks.

1903 The United States John D. Rockefeller starts large donations to the General Education Board, which stresses training of black teachers for southern schools. Within six years, Rockefeller donates over $50 million to the Board.

1903 New York City A black real estate man starts promoting Harlem as a community for blacks. Countee Cullen, poet, is born.

1903 Georgia and Ohio Whites attack blacks in riots, which are spurred by charges blacks have murdered whites.

1904 Atlanta Financier Andrew Carnegie brings together a parcel of prominent black leaders, including Booker T. Washington and W. E. B. DuBois, who discuss "the interests of the Negro Race." The personal and ideological clash between the two men is evident at the meeting, though there is agreement that the group should press for "absolute civil, political, and public equality." The group shows little fire in advancing familiar proposals for black self-help.

1905 Fort Erie, New York Twenty-nine militant black intellectuals from 14 states organize the Niagara Movement (a forerunner of the NAACP) in opposition to the conciliatory policies of Booker T. Washington. Delegates to the convention demand the abolition of all distinctions based on race.

1906 Atlanta An extended riot in which respected black citizens are killed brings the city to a standstill for several days. After the riot interracial groups are formed to better conditions for blacks, but many blacks emigrate and moderates lose influence.

1906 Brownsville, Texas Several black soldiers of the 25th Infantry Division are involved in a riot with Brownsville police and merchants. Following the incident, President Roosevelt dishonorably discharges three companies without a trial. These dishonorable discharges are finally reversed by the Army in 1972. The lone survivor is awarded $25,000 by the Army in 1973.

1907 Washington, D.C. The Supreme Court upholds the right of railroads to segregate passengers traveling between states, even when this runs counter to the laws of states in which the train is traveling.

1908 Washington, D.C. The first black sorority, Alpha Kappa Alpha, is founded at Howard University.

1909 New York City Partly in reaction to continuing riots, the National Association for the Advancement of Colored People (NAACP) is founded in New York, on the 100th anniversary of Lincoln's birth. The signers of the original charter of incorporation include Jane Addams, John Dewey, Dr. W. E. B. DuBois, William Dean Howells, and Lincoln Steffens. Booker T. Washington is opposed to the group. NAACP concentrates on legal abuses of blacks. In 1910 it succeeds in having Baltimore residential segregation statute declared unconstitutional, but the city succeeds later, with more carefully drafted laws. In New Jersey the NAACP secures the release of two blacks being held without evidence on murder charges.

1909 North Pole Matthew Henson places the flag of the United States at the North Pole.

1909 Memphis, Tennessee William Handy composes campaign music for Edward Crump, the "Mayor Crump Blues."

1909 The United States Sambo and Rastus comedy shorts, in which blacks are depicted as childlike and incompetent, become popular.

1910 New York The first edition of *Crisis Magazine,* edited by W. E. B. DuBois, appears. Only 1,000 copies are in print, but before the end of the decade, circulation of the magazine has increased one hundred fold. Among the articles in the first edition, is one by DuBois in which he maintains that individuals should be free to marry whomever they choose. He concedes, however, that such an enlightened policy would cause a social calamity in the United States.

1910 Reno, Nevada Jack Johnson wins heavyweight championship from James Jeffries in fifteenth round knockout.

1910 England On separate lecture tours of Great Britain, DuBois and Washington paint contrasting versions of the black condition in the United States. Washington tells the British that blacks are making strides; DuBois underscores injustices and claims Washington kowtows to powerful white interests. In 1911 DuBois joins the Socialist Party and publishes a novel, *The Quest of the Silver Fleece,* which relates racism to economic causes.

1911 New York City The National Urban League is founded with support from wealthy whites and Booker T. Washington. The League stresses employment and industrial opportunities for blacks. Eugene Kinckle Jones is the first executive secretary.

1911 Jamaica Marcus Garvey forms the Universal Negro Improvement Association.

1912 The United States Despite his southern back-

Lieutenant Colonel Charles Young on the trail of Pancho Villa

ground and apparent indifference to black rights, Woodrow Wilson is supported for President by Du-Bois and NAACP, who feel Wilson is a decent and principled man.

1912 New York James Weldon Johnson's *The Autobiography of an Ex-Colored Man* is published, spurring white recognition of black culture and advent of the "Harlem Renaissance." Theaters in New York City are desegregated.

1913 Washington, D.C. President Wilson refuses to appoint a National Race Commission to study the social and economic status of blacks, rejecting a proposal sponsored by Oswald Garrison Villard. The President also appoints white foreign service officers to Haiti and Santo Domingo, among the few consular posts open to blacks by custom and practice.

1914 The United States Blacks make first noteworthy appearance in films. Bert Williams stars in *The Darktown Jubilee* and Sam Lucas plays Uncle Tom. Heretofore, blacks had been portrayed by whites in blackface.

1915 Southern States Spurred by boll weevil devastation of cotton crops, the great migration of blacks to the north begins. In a year and a half the total is 350,000. Dr. Carter G. Woodson establishes the Association for the Study of Negro Life and History and launches the *Journal of Negro History,* with himself as its editor.

1915 Washington, D.C. U.S. Supreme Court in *Guinn* v. *United States* declares the "grandfather clause" in the Oklahoma constitution unconstitutional.

1916 New York City Oswald Villard resigns from NAACP Board in protest against DuBois's militancy. Black leaders meet at the home of Joel Spingarn and agree that suffrage, equal education, and cessation of violence against blacks are priorities. The NAACP expands to the South, naming James Weldon Johnson to organize local chapters there.

1916 Mexico Colonel Charles Young, highest ranking black in the U.S. Army, commands a squadron in an expedition against Pancho Villa.

1917 Washington, D.C. U.S. Supreme Court declares Louisville "block" segregation ordinance unconstitutional.

1917 New York City Some 10,000 blacks parade down Fifth Avenue in protest against lynchings and the East St. Louis riot. Marchers include DuBois and James Weldon Johnson.

1917 Washington, D.C. The United States enters World War I. Joel Spingarn presses the War Department to establish an officers' training camp for blacks, thus alienating many of his NAACP colleagues who feel that such a camp only perpetuates segregation and in effect gives substance to the notion of black inferiority. Others concede that the move is prudent, since it is the only way for black officers to be trained. The organization ultimately puts itself on record in favor of separate camps. In October, over 600 blacks are commissioned officers; 700,000 blacks register in the draft.

This "Silent Protest Parade" was held in New York City in 1917 by blacks protesting lynchings in the South.

1918 The United States Most blacks and black papers support the War, as 365,000 blacks are drafted for military service. Blacks comprise 11% of troops sent overseas.

1918 France Two black infantry battalions are awarded the Croix de Guerre and two black officers win the French Legion of Honor as blacks are in the forefront of fighting from 1917 until the defeat of Germany.

1919 Atlantic City Samuel Gompers of the American Federation of Labor delivers an address to the Federation's annual conference in which he vows to remove "every class and race distinction" from the movement and pledges himself to the total abolition of all discrimination in union membership. Gompers professes to see a new era in the struggle for black rights "as well as an advance in the history of political and economic liberty in America." However, Gompers does not support antidiscrimination resolutions at AFL conventions of 1921 and 1924.

1919 The United States Membership of NAACP approaches 100,000 despite attempts in some areas, such as Texas, to make it illegal. During second half of the year, there are 75 lynchings and 27 race riots, the severest in Chicago and Washington, D.C. Charles Evans Hughes, leading jurist and defeated Presidential candidate, supports NAACP efforts to have lynching outlawed.

1919 West Virginia The State Supreme Court rules blacks should be admitted to juries.

1919 Paris W. E. B. DuBois organizes the first Pan-African Congress at the Grand Hotel; says DuBois: "The Natives of Africa must have the right to participate in the government as fast as their development permits." Jazz and ragtime sweep the French capital. A representative of the Casino de Paris comes to New York to assemble orchestra of 50 blacks.

1920 New York James Weldon Johnson becomes first black secretary of NAACP and campaigns for withdrawal of U.S. troops occupying Haiti.

1921 St. Louis. At the age of 15, Josephine Baker runs away from home, becomes Bessie Smith's maid, and soon proves her own singing ability.

1921 Tulsa, Oklahoma Twenty one blacks and ten whites are killed in a riot.

1922 Washington, D.C. After it is approved by the House, Republican Senators vote to abandon the Dyer Anti-Lynching Bill, which provides severe penalties and fines for "any state or municipal officer" convicted of negligence in affording protection to individuals in custody who are attacked by a mob bent on lynching, torture, or physical intimidation. The Bill had also provided for compensation to the families of victims.

1922 New York Publication of *Harlem Shadows* by Claude McKay.

1923 New York Marcus Garvey, sentenced to five-year term for mail fraud, charges that most of his troubles stem "from my opponents of the colored race . . . light colored Negroes who think that the

Negro can always develop in this country (and) . . . resent . . . that I, a black Negro, am their leader."

1924 Washington, D.C. New York Representative Emanuel Cellar introduces legislation to provide for the formation of a blue-ribbon panel to study the racial question. The idea is met with disdain from the black press, particularly the *Chicago Defender,* which editorializes: "We have been commissioned to death . . . We have too many studies and reports already." The *Defender* asserts that blacks need only to look after their own interests through the creation of a strong party vehicle and potent political leadership in the halls of Congress.

1924 Washington, D.C. Immigration Act excludes blacks of African descent from entering the country.

1925 New York Publication of *Color,* poetry by Countee Cullen and *The New Negro,* an anthology of poetry edited by Alain Locke.

1925 New York Black physicians are admitted to practice in Harlem Hospital.

1926 The United States Founding of the Brotherhood of Sleeping Car Porters by A. Philip Randolph.

1926 Washington, D.C. President Coolidge tells Congress that the country must provide "for the amelioration of race prejudice and the extension to all elements of equal opportunity and equal protection under the laws, which are guaranteed by the Constitution." Twenty-three blacks are reported lynched during the year.

1926 New York Controversy rages among the black intelligentsia after publication of *Nigger Heaven* by white writer Carl van Vechten. The book glamorizes the freewheeling style of Harlem life amid the general contention that blacks are less ashamed of sex and more morally honest than whites. DuBois finds the assumptions deplorable; James Weldone Johnson, on the other hand, believes the treatment is neither scandalous nor insulting.

1926 Washington, D.C. Negro History Week is introduced by Dr. Carter G. Woodson and the Association for the Study of Negro Life and History.

1926 New York City Langston Hughes, writing in *The Nation* magazine, urges black artists to write from their experience and to stop imitating white writers.

1927 The United States In assorted legislation and judicial verdicts, Colorado, Illinois, and New Jersey lessen segregation in schools, but segregation statutes are firmed in southern states.

1927 Chicago Urban League organizes boycott of stores that don't hire blacks. In 1929 boycotts are started in several other Midwest cities.

1927 Atlanta Marcus Garvey is released from prison and deported to the British West Indies.

1927 New York City Formation of the Harlem Globetrotters basketball team. Bill "Bojangles" Robinson and Ethel Waters star on Broadway in *Blackbirds.*

1927 Pennsylvania and West Virginia Nonunion black labor is brought from the South to the coal fields, weakening the position of the United Mine Workers. Racial strife ensues as hysterical rumors of rape and miscegenation spread through white mining communities.

1927 Washington, D.C. The U.S. Supreme Court strikes down the Texas law which bars blacks from voting in party primaries. Texas then enacts a law allowing local committees to determine voter qualifications.

1928 Illinois The election of Oscar De Priest, a Republican, as the first black Congressman from a northern state.

1929 New York Oscar De Priest tells an audience of 2500 gathered at a rally at Harlem's Abyssinian Baptist Church that blacks will never make substan-

Langston Hughes at Tuskegee Institute in 1926 with Jessie Fauset and Zora Neale Hurston. Hughes urged black writers to draw on their own experiences and stop imitating white writers.

tial progress until they elect political leaders whose fortunes are dependent on their ability to fight for black interests in Congress. De Priest concludes: "No one can really lead you but one who has been Jim Crowed as you have."

1930 Washington, D.C. An NAACP campaign helps prevent confirmation of U.S. Supreme Court nominee John H. Parker, one-time self-admitted opponent of the franchise for blacks. The NAACP also helps unseat three of the senators who voted for him in later Congressional elections.

1930 Detroit Founding, by Fard Mohammed, of the Temple of Islam, later to become the "Black Muslims."

1931 Alabama First trial of the Scottsboro Nine results in battle between NAACP and the International Labor Defense, a Communist-controlled group, for right to represent the young defendants who are charged with rape. The case, which becomes a worldwide *cause celebre* and important propaganda weapon for Communists, drags on for 20 years despite recanting of charge by one of the two plaintiffs and medical testimony that rape was not committed.

1932 The United States Franklin Roosevelt is elected President, but with little support from blacks who observe omission of their objectives from the Democratic Platform. However, in coming years Roosevelt's popularity rises as he appoints blacks to responsible posts and his wife, Eleanor, shows sensitivity to black problems.

1933 The United States More than one-fourth of urban blacks are on relief. New Deal programs aid housing and education of blacks, but traditional segregation policies are generally followed. One exception is the Civilian Conservation Corps camps in New England and the Pacific states, which are integrated.

1934 The United States In northern and border states 52% of blacks, compared with about 12% of whites, are on relief. The American Federation of Labor's organization committee rejects a resolution introduced by A. Philip Randolph to end discrimination, stating that no discrimination exists in the labor organization.

1934 Chicago Arthur Mitchell becomes the first black Democrat of the twentieth century to be elected to Congress, succeeding De Priest.

1934 Washington, D.C. Antilynch bill fails, as Roosevelt does not support it. American troops are withdrawn from Haiti.

1934 Chicago Black Muslim Headquarters are established. Elijah Muhammed is leader.

1935 New York City Founding by Mary McLeod Bethune of the National Council for Negro Women.

1935 Washington, D.C. U.S. Supreme Court Justice Roberts upholds the Texas law that prevents blacks from voting in the Texas Democratic primary. The decision is a setback to the NAACP, which has waged several effective legal battles to equalize the ballot potential of the black voter.

1935 St. Louis NAACP bitterly criticizes Roosevelt for failure to present or support civil rights legislation.

1935 The United States Percy Julian, a black chemist, develops physostigmine, a drug for treatment of glaucoma.

1936 The United States Roosevelt wins overwhelming reelection victory, gains increasing support from blacks who feel he would like to achieve more for them than Congress allows.

1936 Berlin, Germany Jesse Owens wins four gold medals in the 1936 Olympics, but is snubbed by the Chancellor of Germany, Adolf Hitler.

1936 Washington, D.C. U.S. Supreme Court requires Maryland University to admit a black student, Donald Murray, to its graduate law school.

1936 Philadelphia Birth of Wilt Chamberlain.

1937 Virgin Island William H. Hastie is confirmed Judge of the Federal District Court in the Virgin Islands, thereby becoming the first black to serve as a federal judge in the history of the United States.

1937 The United States Blacks continue to benefit from New Deal programs but not to same degree as whites. In South, black tenants leave farms as government policies encourage use of wage labor. U.S. Supreme Court rules that picketing is a legal means for blacks to seek redress of grievances.

1937 Pennsylvania New law denies many state services to unions discriminating against blacks.

1937 New York Richard Wright becomes editor of *Challenge Magazine,* changes title to *New Challenge,* and urges blacks to write with greater "social realism."

1937 Spain Between 60 to 80 of the 3200 Americans who fight for Republican side in the Civil War are black. Oliver Law, a black from Chicago, commands the Lincoln Battalion.

1938 New York Adam Clayton Powell, Jr. and other black leaders convince white merchants in Harlem to hire at least one third blacks and to promise equal promotion opportunities.

1938 New York Billie Holiday appears with Artie Shaw's band. Boogie woogie is popularized at a Carnegie Hall concert given by three blacks. Boxer Henry Armstrong defeats Barney Ross for welterweight championship and Lou Ambers for lightweight championship. Armstrong is also featherweight champion and thus holds three championships concurrently.

1938 Pennsylvania Crystal Bird Fauset of Philadelphia, the first black woman state legislator, is elected to the Pennsylvania House of Representatives.

1939 Washington, D.C. Marian Anderson, denied the use of Constitution Hall by the Daughters of the American Revolution, sings on Easter Sunday before 75,000 people assembled at the Lincoln Memorial.

1939 New York City Jane Bolin is appointed Judge of the Court of Domestic Relations in New York City, becoming the first female black judge in the United States.

1939 Miami, Florida Intimidation and cross-burnings by the Ku Klux Klan in the black ghetto of Miami fail to discourage over 1,000 of the city's registered blacks from appearing at the polls. The Klan parades with effigies of blacks who will allegedly be slain for daring to vote.

1940 Washington, D.C. Census places black life expectancy at 51 years, white at 62. Nearly one fourth of blacks live in North and West. U.S. Supreme Court rules that black teachers cannot be denied wage parity with white teachers.

1940 Virginia The Virginia Legislature chooses "Carry Me Back to Ole Virginny," written by black composer James A. Bland, as the official state song.

1940 Washington, D.C. Appointment of Benjamin O. Davis, Sr. as the first black general in the history of the U.S. Armed Forces. Responding to NAACP pressure, Franklin Delano Roosevelt announces that black strength in the Armed Forces will be proportionate to black population totals. Several branches of the military service and several occupational specialties are to be opened to blacks. But Roosevelt rules out troop integration because it will be "destructive to morale and detrimental to . . . preparation for national defense." At start of Selective Service, less than 5000 of 230,000 men in the Army are black and there are only two black combat officers. Approximately 888,000 black men and 4,000 black women are to serve in the Armed Forces during World War II. Blacks are mostly confined to service units.

1940 New York Mass meeting of West Indians here oppose transfer of West Indian islands to United States.

1940 Southern States Eighty thousand blacks vote in eight southern states. Five percent of voting age blacks are registered.

Messman Dorie Miller wears Navy Cross he won at Pearl Harbor. When Japanese bombers attacked U.S. ships, Miller voluntarily manned a deck machine gun and downed four enemy planes.

1941 Washington, D.C. Dr. Robert Weaver is appointed director of the government office charged with integrating blacks into the National Defense program.

1941 Washington, D.C. The U.S. Supreme Court, in a case brought by Congressman Arthur Mitchell, rules that separate facilities in railroad travel must be *substantially* equal.

1941 Washington, D.C. Blacks' threat to stage massive protest march on nation's capital results in the issuance of Executive Order 8802, prohibiting discrimination in the defense establishment. The order states: "There shall be no discrimination in the employment of workers in defense industries or Government because of race, creed, color or national origin."

1941 Pearl Harbor Dorie Miller, messman aboard the *USS Arizona,* mans a machine gun during the

Pearl Harbor attack, downs four enemy planes, and wins the Navy Cross.

1941 Washington, D.C. Dr. Charles R. Drew, a black physician, sets up the blood bank.

1942 Washington, D.C. The Justice Department threatens to file suit against a number of black newspapers which it believes are guilty of sedition in their strong criticism of the government's racial policies in the Armed Services. The NAACP steps in to suggest guidelines which will satisfy the Justice Department. The clear alternative is suppression of the black press, should it remain unruly.

1942 Chicago Founding of the Congress of Racial Equality (CORE), a civil rights group dedicated to a direct-action, nonviolent program. In 1943 CORE stages its first sit-in in a Chicago restaurant.

1944 The European Theater of War The black 99th Pursuit Squadron flies its 500th mission in the Mediterranean Theater. The 92nd Division enters combat in Italy. On D-Day, 500 blacks land on Omaha Beach, France, among them the 761st tank battalion which spends 183 days in action and is cited for conspicuous courage. Also cited in January 1945, is the 969th Field Artillery Battalion, for support in the defense of Bastogne.

1944 Washington, D.C. Restrictions of black seamen to shore duty are ended, as is exclusion of blacks from the Coast Guard and Marine Corps. War Department officially ends segregation in all Army posts, but order is widely ignored. U.S. Supreme Court rules that "white primaries" violate the Fifteenth Amendment.

1944 New York City Election to House of Representatives of Adam Clayton Powell, Jr., the first black congressman from the Northeast.

1944 Guam, San Francisco, and New York NAACP secures release of servicemen detained for protests of discrimination in Armed Forces.

1944 New York City Frank Yerby wins O. Henry short story award.

1945 Kentucky Benjamin O. Davis, Jr., is named Commander of Godman Field.

1945 New York The first state Fair Employment Practices Commission (FEPC) is established in New York as a result of the Ives-Quinn Bill.

1945 Washington, D.C. Congress denies funds to federal FEPC established during the war to enforce fair employment policies. Ralph Bunche becomes a division head in the State Department.

1945 European Theater Black troops in forefront of victorious assaults in Germany and Northern Italy. However, the use of black troops in World War II was more confined and beset by prejudice than in World War I or the Spanish-American War. Despite efforts by some enlightened Naval officers, over 90% of blacks in the Navy are still messmen when the war ends.

1946 Washington, D.C. U.S. Supreme Court rules that segregation on interstate buses is unconstitutional.

President Truman presents scroll to Brigadier General Davis upon his retirement after 50 years of Army service. At right, during World War II, Davis talks with Staff Sergeant Joe Louis, then heavyweight champion of the world.

U.N. Undersecretary Ralph Bunche (left) *is shown conferring with Roy Wilkins of the NAACP.*

1947 Atlanta The Southern Regional Council releases figures which demonstrate that only 12% (c. 600,000) of the blacks in the Deep South meet voting qualifications. In the states of Louisiana, Alabama, and Mississippi, the figure is approximately 3%. In Tennessee more than one in four adult blacks meets state voting requirements.

1947 Washington, D.C. The Truman Committee on civil rights formally condemns racial injustice in America in the widely quoted report, "To Secure These Rights."

1947 Tuskegee, Alabama Tuskegee statistics indicate the 3,426 blacks have been lynched in the United States in the period 1882–1947. Of these, 1,217 were lynched in the decade 1890–1900. From 1947 to 1962, 12 blacks are lynched.

1947 Winston Salem, North Carolina A black is elected to the City Council.

1947 Southern States CORE's first "freedom ride" travels through southern states to integrate transportation facilities.

1947 New York City Jackie Robinson breaks the color bar in major league baseball, playing second base for the Brooklyn Dodgers.

1948 Washington, D.C. U.S. Supreme Court in *Shelley* v. *Kraemer* rules that federal and state courts may not enforce restrictive covenants. But the Court does not declare the covenants illegal.

1948 Washington, D.C. President Truman issues Executive Order 9981 directing "equality of treatment and opportunity" in the Armed Forces and creates the Fair Practices Board of the Civil Service Commission to deal with complaints of discrimination in government employment.

1948 New York Ralph Bunche is confirmed by the U.N. Security Council as Acting U.N. mediator in Palestine.

1948 California The California Supreme Court declares the state statute banning racial intermarriage unconstitutional.

1948 The United States Truman is elected President in surprise victory. The States Rights (Dixiecrat) Party takes four states.

1949 Connecticut The state becomes the first in the Union to extend the jurisdiction of the Civil Rights Commission into the domain of public housing.

1949 Washington, D.C. Congressman William L. Dawson becomes the first black to head a Congressional committee, when he is named Chairman of the House Committee on Government Operations.

1949 New York City Jackie Robinson is voted most valuable player in the National League. Joe Louis retires from boxing after holding heavyweight championship for 11 years.

1950 Chicago Gwendolyn Brooks is awarded a Pulitzer Prize for poetry—the first black so honored.

1950 New York City Edith Sampson is appointed an alternate delegate to the United Nations.

1950 Oslo, Norway Ralph Bunche wins the Nobel Peace Prize.

1950 Washington, D.C. Census puts net 10-year black emigration from South at 1.6 million. Various U.S. Supreme Court decisions open university facilities to blacks. A special committee reports to President Truman that black servicemen are still barred from many military specialties and training programs, but that the Armed Forces has largely been desegregated.

1950 Korea The black 24th Infantry Regiment recaptures city of Yech'on, the first American victory in the Korean War.

1951 Korea Private-First-Class William Thompson is awarded the Congressional Medal of Honor during the Korean War, becoming the first black since the Spanish-American War to win the nation's highest military citation.

1952 The United States In a series of legal maneuvers, the NAACP and other black groups succeed in desegregating a number of colleges and high schools in southern and border areas. In addition, public housing projects are opened to blacks in some northern and western cities and desegregation is achieved in several businesses and unions. A public swimming pool is integrated in Kansas City, a golf course in Louisville, and Ford's Theater in Baltimore.

1952 The United States Eisenhower is elected President, though he gets only 21% of the black vote. In the South over one fourth of voting-age blacks register to vote.

1952 Tuskegee A Tuskegee report indicates that, for the first time in its 71 years of tabulation, no lynchings have occurred in the United States.

1953 Washington, D.C. U.S. Supreme Court asks to re-hear five school segregation cases first argued in 1942. Sensing a major opportunity, the NAACP puts 100 lawyers, scholars and researchers to work in preparation. NAACP also files complaint with the Interstate Commerce Commission to execute earlier Supreme Court desegregation orders in transportation facilities.

1953 New York City Hulan Jack is sworn in as Borough President of Manhattan.

1953 District of Columbia D.C. Commissioners order the abolition of segregation in several district agencies. The Fire Department is among those which escape the mandate. The Defense Department orders an end to segregation in schools on military bases and in Veterans Hospitals.

THE CIVIL RIGHTS REVOLUTION (1954–1964)

1954 Washington, D.C. On May 17, by a unanimous 9 to 0 vote, the Supreme Court declares that "separate but equal" educational facilities are "inherently unequal" and that segregation is therefore unconstitutional. The decision is reached in the case of *Brown* v. *Board of Education* (of Topeka) and overturns the "separate but equal" doctrine that since 1896 has legitimized segregation. In another case, the court rules that the University of Florida must admit blacks regardless of any "public mischief" it might cause.

1954 The United States In the autumn following the *Brown* decision, 150 formerly segregated school districts in eight states and the District of Columbia integrate. But a number of groups opposing segregation emerge in the South. Most prominent among these are White Citizens Councils, which soon claim 80,000 members and propose constitutional amendments reinstating segregation.

1954 Washington, D.C. President Eisenhower appoints a black, J. Ernest Wilkins, to be Undersecretary of Labor, but pointedly does not endorse Civil Rights Legislation. The Department of Defense reports that "all-Negro" units in the Army no longer exist. However, some bases still evade integration. The Veteran's Administration announces their hospitals have been desegregated, but the Department of Health, Education and Welfare declares it will continue to give funds to segregated hospitals. Charles H. Mahoney becomes the first black American appointed as a permanent delegate to the United Nations.

1955 Montgomery, Alabama Mrs. Rosa Parks takes a seat in the front of a Cleveland Avenue bus, refuses to surrender it to a white man, and is arrested. Four days later, on December 5, the Reverend Martin Luther King, Jr. urges the city's black community to boycott the buses. Thus begins the Montgomery Bus Boycott which was to end with desegregation the following year and start the era of passive resistance that culminated in the Civil Rights Acts of the 1960s.

1955 Washington, D.C. U.S. Supreme Court orders school boards to draw up desegregation procedures "with all deliberate speed." In accordance with Supreme Court edicts, the Interstate Commerce Commission outlaws segregated buses and waiting rooms for interstate passengers, but many communities ignore order.

1955 The Southern States While such states as Kansas, Oklahoma, Missouri, and parts of Texas desegregate schools with minimal fuss, states in the Deep South dig in to fight. Georgia's Board of Education adopts a resolution revoking the license of any teacher who teaches integrated classes. Mississippi repeals its compulsory school attendance law and establishes a branch of government for the sole purpose of maintaining segregation. White Citizens

Councils in Mississippi initiate economic pressures against blacks who try to register to vote, while more extreme groups resort to direct terror.

1955 Washington, D.C. The Eisenhower administration continues to discourage civil rights legislation. The House of Representatives defeats attempts by Adam Clayton Powell, Jr. to deny funds to segregated schools.

1955 New York State The Metcalf-Baker Law is passed, forbidding discrimination in housing assisted by FHA or Veterans Administration funds. Robert Weaver is appointed State Rent Commissioner.

1955 New York City Walter White, head of NAACP since 1931, dies and is succeeded by Roy Wilkins. Marian Anderson becomes the first black to sing on the stage of the Metropolitan Opera House, appearing in Verdi's *The Masked Ball.*

1956 Southern States By the fall term, some 800 school districts containing 320,000 black children had desegregated since the 1954 Supreme Court decision. However, nearly 2.5 million black children remain in segregated schools and there are still no desegregated districts in Virginia, North and South Carolina, Georgia, Florida, Mississippi, Alabama, and Louisiana. Autherine Lucy is admitted to the University of Alabama by court order, but riots ensue and she is expelled on a technicality.

1956 Washington, D.C. Southern senators, led by Harry Byrd of Virginia, fight integration. Byrd obtains signatures of 100 congressmen on a "Southern Manifesto," which attacks the Supreme Court. Southern nonsigners include Senators Kefauver and Gore of Tennessee and Lyndon B. Johnson of Texas.

1956 Washington, D.C. U.S. Supreme Court rules bus segregation unconstitutional. Montgomery boycott ends in victory for boycotters on December 21.

1957 Southern States President Eisenhower orders paratroopers to Little Rock to enforce an integration order for 18 black pupils in Central High School. Token school desegregation starts in some North Carolina cities. Tennessee announces desegregation of state universities to start in 1958. The Southern Christian Leadership Conference is formed by Martin Luther King, Jr., Bayard Rustin, and Stanley Levinson to coordinate activities of nonviolent groups devoted to integration and citizenship for blacks.

1957 Washington, D.C. A civil rights bill, affirming the right to vote, is enacted after provisions strengthening school integration are withdrawn.

1957 Milwaukee Henry Aaron is voted the most valuable player in National League and wins his first home run title, with 44.

1958 Southern States Black voter registration rises slowly, as states institute complicated delaying tactics. Black registration reaches 72% in Tennessee, 39% in Florida, and 36% in North Carolina and Texas, but is only 3% in Mississippi.

1959 Southern States Blacks are elected to local offices in North Carolina. In other areas, however, blacks are disenfranchised and in Tennessee, black landowners registering to vote are denied their usual preharvest loans. In Virginia, Prince Edward

Elderly black woman boards bus on day that Montgomery City Lines acceded to five-month boycott by blacks and abandoned segregation.

Among the first to ride were activist ministers Ralph David Abernathy (front) and Martin Luther King, Jr. (rear).

County abolishes its public school system rather than comply with an integration order.

1959 Western States California abolishes antimiscegenation act and passes a law forbidding discrimination in public housing.

1960 Washington, D.C. President Eisenhower signs bill authorizing judges to appoint referees to aid blacks to register and vote in federal elections. Bill also outlaws bombing and mob action to restrict voting.

1960 The United States John F. Kennedy, the Democratic candidate for President, telephones Coretta King to express concern about her husband's arrest during an Atlanta sit-in. Kennedy then sends his brother, Robert, to speak to the judge handling the case. The Republican candidate, Richard Nixon, remains aloof. Kennedy's actions are credited with tipping the states of Michigan and Illinois into his column and enabling him to win in a very close election. In all, Kennedy receives over two thirds of the black vote.

1960 Southern States The "sit-in" era starts at a Woolworth lunch counter in Greensboro, North

Announcing plans for the "March on Washington" are (left to right) Reverend Martin Luther King, Jr., A. Philip Randolph, and Roy Wilkins. The civil rights leaders called all Americans to take part in a "prayer pilgrimage" to end discrimination in education, housing, employment, and the courts.

Carolina, when four blacks from a local college sit down and refuse to move. Soon blacks and white supporters are being trained in passive resistance techniques by the Congress of Racial Equality. Sit-ins spread to Nashville, Montgomery, and other cities. Before the year is over, lunch counters in Greensboro, San Antonio, and other places are desegregated. In Atlanta, the Student Non-Violent Coordinating Committee is formed to organize activities. Church kneel-ins and beach wade-ins soon join lunch counter and bus station sit-ins. Houston desegregates schools, but delay tactics stall progress in other parts of the South.

1960 New York The Negro American Labor Council is founded by A. Philip Randolph, who believes the AFL-CIO is paying little more than lip service to desegregation in unions.

1960 New Rochelle, New York First integration suit in North occurs as black parents sue to end *de facto* segregation of New Rochelle schools. Case is won in 1961.

1961 Washington, D.C. Several busloads of Freedom Riders organized by CORE set out on a ride through the South to test compliance of bus stations with Interstate Commerce Commission desegregation order. They are arrested and attacked in many places. Attorney General Robert Kennedy orders 600 federal marshalls to Montgomery, Alabama to maintain order. Adam Clayton Powell, Jr. becomes

New York college youths sit-in at a Woolworth's lunch counter.

Chairman of House Education and Labor Committee. Robert Weaver is appointed Administrator of Federal Housing and Home Finance Administration. James P. Parsons is appointed to Federal District Court, becoming first black District Judge. Fred Moore becomes first black sentry to guard the tomb of the unknown soldier.

1961 The United States Six more states pass laws forbidding desegregation in housing, raising total to 10.

1962 Washington, D.C. The Kennedy Administration issues orders banning segregation in southern paper mills and federally financed housing. Military commanders are ordered to actively oppose discriminatory practices in the Armed Forces.

1962 Jackson, Mississippi Twelve thousand federal troops are ordered to the University of Mississippi campus to maintain order as riots erupt in protest over the admission of James Meredith, a 29-year-old black veteran, to the university.

1962 Washington, D.C. Army reports 3% of its officers and 12% of its enlisted men are black. Figures for the Navy are much lower—only 3% officers and 5% enlisted men. The Navy appoints its first black to a ship command, Lt. Commander Samuel L. Gravely to destroyer escort, *U.S.S. Falgout.* Gravely later becomes the first black Admiral.

1963 Jackson, Mississippi Medgar Evers, a prominent civil rights leader, is assassinated in the doorway of his home.

1963 Washington, D.C. President Kennedy becomes first President to declare that segregation is "morally wrong." More than 200,000 Americans of all races and colors gather at the Lincoln Memorial in the "March on Washington," the largest protest in the nation's history. Marchers demand legislation to end discrimination in education, housing, and employment, and courts. On the day of Evers' funeral, President Kennedy asks Congress to vote equal rights in public accommodations and to outlaw discrimination in employment, housing, and labor unions.

1963 Birmingham, Alabama Four black children are killed in bombing of the 16th Street Baptist Church.

1963 Southern States Less than 10% of black public school students attend integrated classes in the fall term. Governor George Wallace of Alabama declares: "I draw the line in the dust and toss the gauntlet before the feet of tyranny and I say 'segregation now, segregation tomorrow, segregation forever.'" Martin Luther King, Jr. targets Birmingham for a drive against discrimination. This soon results in famous, televised confrontations between demonstrators and the policemen and police dogs of Birmingham Police Chief Eugene "Bull" Connor.

1963 Dallas,Texas and Washington, D.C. President Kennedy is assassinated. His successor, Lyndon B. Johnson, promises to support strong civil rights legislation.

1964 Washington, D.C. A major Civil Rights Bill, forbidding discrimination in public accommodations and employment, is enacted with strong support from President Johnson, as the Senate finally votes cloture to shut off filibuster by southern opponents.

1964 Oslo, Norway Martin Luther King, Jr. wins the Nobel Peace Prize.

1964 Philadelphia, Mississippi Three young civil rights volunteers, James Chaney, Michael Schwerner, and Andrew Goodman, the latter two whites, are murdered. A number of arrests on federal charges, less severe than murder, follow. Among the 19 suspects are the sheriff and a deputy sheriff of Neshoba County. But no convictions are obtained and charges are dismissed in December.

More than 200,000 Americans of all races advanced toward the Lincoln Memorial in the "March on Washington," the largest protest in the nation's history.

1964 Tuskegee, Alabama Two blacks are elected to the City Council.

1964 Northern Cities Blacks in New York and Cleveland stage brief school boycotts to protest inadequate facilities.

1964 New York City One person is killed, 140 injured, and 500 arrested in riot in Harlem. This is generally considered to be the first of the wave of large riots that were to strike urban black neighborhoods during the sixties. Shortly after the Harlem disturbances, riots erupt in Brooklyn and Rochester, New York, and Jersey City and Paterson, New Jersey. The riots produce split in civil rights movement, with Roy Wilkins condemning the "criminal elements" which instigate them, while other blacks are more reserved in their criticism.

1964 New York City Malcolm X resigns from the Black Muslim Movement and forms the Organization for Afro-American Unity.

1964 The United States George Wallace receives large number of votes in Democratic Party primaries, including 30% in Indiana and 43% in Maryland. However, Lyndon B. Johnson is renominated easily and reelected in a landslide over Senator Barry Goldwater. Johnson receives about 95% of the black vote.

1964 Forest Hills, New York Arthur Ashe becomes the first black man to win the American singles tennis championship and to play on the U.S. Davis Cup Team.

1964 Miami Beach, Florida Cassius Clay, to become known as Muhammad Ali, knocks out Sonny Liston in the seventh round of a scheduled 15-round fight and wins the heavyweight championship of the world.

THE MARCH OF NEWS (1965–1970)

An epochal point in the march of Afro-American history was reached when the Supreme Court in *Brown v. Board of Education* (May 17, 1954) ruled that racial segregation in the nation's public schools was unconstitutional. This major legal victory was viewed by blacks as a breakthrough in the painstaking process of achieving total integration into the cultural fabric of the United States. From hopes raised by the *Brown* decision came the militancy and activism now known as the Civil Rights Revolution (see Civil Rights section). The Voting Rights Act of 1965 was enacted and, under Martin Luther King's urging, the question "What is America for?" was brought up for national reappraisal. Questions regarding civil rights, human rights, activism, militancy, and "black power" dominated media

Leaders of the mid-1960s were Malcolm X, black nationalist spokesman and dissident; Bayard Rustin, organizing genius of the March on Washington; and Martin Luther King, Jr., here congratulated by King Olav V of Norway after receiving the 1964 Nobel Peace Prize.

attention. What followed was a turbulent period of progress, backlash, action, and reaction. Major events from 1965 to 1970 are chronologized here to help recapture the prevailing mood of those years.

1965, January 2–23 On January 2, Reverend Martin Luther King, Jr. announces his intention to call for demonstrations if Alabama blacks are not permitted to register and vote in appropriate numbers. Twelve blacks, including Dr. King himself, book rooms on January 18 at Selma's Hotel Albert, becoming the first blacks accepted for this formerly all-white hotel. While signing the register, Dr. King is accosted by a white segregationist who is later fined $100 and given a 60-day jail sentence. On January 19, Sheriff James G. Clark arrests 62 blacks in Selma after they refuse to enter the Dallas County court-house through an alley door. Clark and his deputies arrest 150 other black voter-registration applicants the very next day. A federal district court order issued on January 23 bars law enforcement officials from interfering with voter registration and warns against violence.

1965, January 4 The U.S. House of Representatives votes to seat five white Congressmen elected from Mississippi. Some 600 blacks assemble in protest outside the House chamber.

1965, January 15 A Jackson, Mississippi federal grand jury hands down indictments for the June 1964 slaying of three civil rights workers—James E. Chaney, Andrew Goodman, and Michael Schwerner. The following day, 18 men (including two law enforcement officers from the state of Mississippi) are arrested.

1965, February 1–4 Reverend Martin Luther King, Jr. and some 770 blacks are arrested in Selma, Alabama during protest demonstrations against discrimination in black voter registration (February 1). Dr. King remains in jail for four days before posting bond. During this time, more than 3,000 persons are arrested. On February 4, a federal district court orders the county board of registrars to refrain from using an unduly difficult literacy test on voter applicants or from rejecting their application on petty technicalities.

The Selma Story

Martin Luther King and thousands of civil rights supporters made a five-day, 54-mile march from Selma to the Alabama state capital of Montgomery from March 21 to 25, 1965, in an effort to dramatize the denial of voting rights to blacks who had attempted to register in Selma.

When the march ended in front of the state capitol building, the number of participants had swelled to 25,000. Dr. King addressed the throng, and later sought to present an equal rights petition to Governor George C. Wallace, who twice turned away a delegation before finally meeting with it on March 30.

The march, which captured national headlines, was first attempted on March 7, 1965, at which time some 200 Alabama state troopers and possemen of the Dallas County Sheriff's office halted the 525 black marchers by charging into their ranks, using tear gas, nightsticks, and whips in a reputed effort to enforce Governor Wallace's order banning the demonstration. Seventeen blacks were hospitalized and 67 others treated for injuries of varying severity, including exposure to tear gas.

On March 8, Governor Wallace denied that the police had made an intemperate display of force, and maintained further that police action in dispersing marchers had undoubtedly saved many black lives. Dr. King then returned to Selma to lead another March on Montgomery.

On March 9, President Lyndon B. Johnson stated that he was certain that all Americans "joined in deploring the brutality with which a number of black citizens of Alabama were treated when they sought to dramatize their deep and sincere interest in attaining the precious right to vote."

On the same day, 1500 blacks and whites, among them hundreds of northern clergymen and civil rights workers, began a second march to Montgomery, with Martin Luther King in the front rank. By that time, however, Federal Judge Frank M. Johnson, Jr. had already issued a restraining order against the march. The demonstrators again turned back, although they were allowed to pass a few minutes in prayer before doing so.

On March 17, Judge Johnson upheld the right of black demonstrators to stage the march as originally planned and enjoined Governor Wallace and other Alabama officials from intimidating the participants in any way. Furthermore, the judge ordered the governor to provide police protection for the march.

After the march had begun, some 2,900 of the original 3,200 participants returned to Selma on the evening of March 21. Thereafter, in accordance with a court order, the number of marchers was limited to 300 each day.

1965, February 16 Three blacks and a white woman from Canada (described by police as pro-Castro left-wingers) are arrested in New York City on charges

Troopers charge into freedom marchers in Selma.

Martin Luther King, Jr., fellow Nobelist Ralph Bunche, and Coretta King lead last lap of Selma march.

of plotting to blow up the Statue of Liberty, the Liberty Bell, and the Washington Monument.

1965, February 18 Some 300 school-boycotting black students sweep through the streets of downtown Brooklyn, New York, hurling bricks at policemen and breaking store windows. The following day, an estimated 5,500 students are absent from 27 schools.

1965, February 21 Malcolm X, 39-year-old black nationalist leader and former member of the Black Muslim sect, is shot to death in the Audubon Ballroom, New York City, as he is about to deliver an address before a rally of several hundred followers.

After the murder, Black Muslim headquarters in New York City and San Francisco are burned, and most Muslim leaders are placed under heavy police guard. Three blacks—Talmadge Hayer, Norman 3X Butler, and Thomas 15X Johnson—are later taken into custody, and charged with first-degree murder. The trio is convicted and sentenced to life imprisonment on March 10, 1966.

Suspended from the Black Muslims by Elijah Muhammad after he had referred to President John F. Kennedy's assassination as a case of "chickens coming home to roost," Malcolm X had retired for a time to the Middle East, where he had engaged

in a serious study of the Moslem faith before returning to the United States and founding his own nationalist group, the Organization of Afro-American Unity.

1965, February 25 U.S. District Court Judge W. Harold Cox dismisses a federal indictment against 17 of the men accused of conspiracy in the June 1964 murder of three civil rights workers in Philadelphia, Mississippi. (See January 15 entry.)

1965, February 26 Jimmie Lee Jackson, a 26-year-old black, dies in Selma, eight days after having been clubbed and shot during a night march in Marion, Alabama.

1965, March 9–15 Three white Unitarian ministers are beaten on March 9 in Selma, Alabama while assisting in the civil rights drive being directed by Martin Luther King, Jr. Reverend James J. Reeb, a 38-year-old white Boston minister, is critically injured and dies in a Birmingham hospital on March 11. A federal judge arranges with law-enforcement officials in Selma to allow more than 2,000 white and black sympathizers to hold memorial services there on March 15.

1965, March 13 Colonel Al Lingo, head of the Alabama Highway Patrol, admits that Jimmie Lee Jackson (see February 26 entry) was shot in Marion by a state trooper.

Peaceful moment on the 54-mile Selma-to-Montgomery road after Alabama Governor Wallace and his state troopers were muzzled by a federal court order enjoining them from "harassing or threatening" the freedom marchers in any way. Although more than 3,000 civil rights people volunteered to march, the court limited the number of marchers to 300 each day.

1965, March 26–30 President Johnson announces the arrest of four Ku Klux Klan members in connection with the murder of Mrs. Viola Gregg Liuzzo, a 39-year-old white civil rights worker from Detroit slain on a Lowndes County highway during the Selma-to-Montgomery Freedom March. The President goes on to declare war on the Klan, calling it a "hooded society of bigots." Robert M. Shelton, Jr. Imperial Wizard of the United Klans of America, Inc., answers the President's charges by branding him "a damn liar." On March 30, the House Un-American Activities Committee votes to open a full investigation of the activities of the Klan. The Committee chairman, a Louisiana Democrat, asserts that the Klan is perpetrating "shocking crimes."

1965, April 1–2 Martin Luther King, Jr. announces plans for an economic boycott of Alabama during a meeting of the executive board of the Southern Christian Leadership Conference (SCLC) in Baltimore. The three-stage program outlined by King calls for: (1) suspension by the business community of all plant location and expansion in Alabama, (2) withdrawal of federal tax funds from Alabama banks coupled with an appeal to private institutions, churches, and labor unions to make certain their investments are not used to support racism in the state, and (3) a boycott of Alabama-produced goods.

President Johnson warns against full execution of such a program, maintaining that it would endanger the security of innocent people.

1965, April 13 A grand jury in Selma, Alabama indicts three white men for the murder of Reverend James J. Reeb. (See March 9–15 entry.) They are William S. Hoggle, Namon O. Hoggle (his brother), and Elmer L. Cook.

1965, April 23 Martin Luther King, Jr. leads a three-mile civil rights demonstration in Boston, parading from the predominantly black section of Roxbury to the Boston Common. There he tells a crowd of 20,000 that America cannot afford to become a nation of "onlookers" in the struggle against segregation.

1965, April 29 The autumn of 1967 is set by the federal government as a deadline for integration at all grade levels of public schools seeking to qualify for federal funds. In addition, Commissioner of Education Francis Keppel states that school districts must also show a "good faith substantial start" toward desegregation by September of 1965. (This is defined as desegregation of at least four of the first 12 grades.)

1965, May 3–7 A mistrial is declared in the trial of Collie Leroy Wilkins, a Ku Klux Klansman charged with the murder of Mrs. Viola Gregg Liuzzo. (See entry dated March 26.) The all-male, all-white jury is hopelessly deadlocked after two days of deliberation, the vote being split 10–2 in favor of conviction. At the opening of the trial (May

Mississippi: Freedom marchers (above) *approach Jackson, a center of Klan power; marcher* (below) *escapes tear gas and clubs of night-riding state highway patrolmen.*

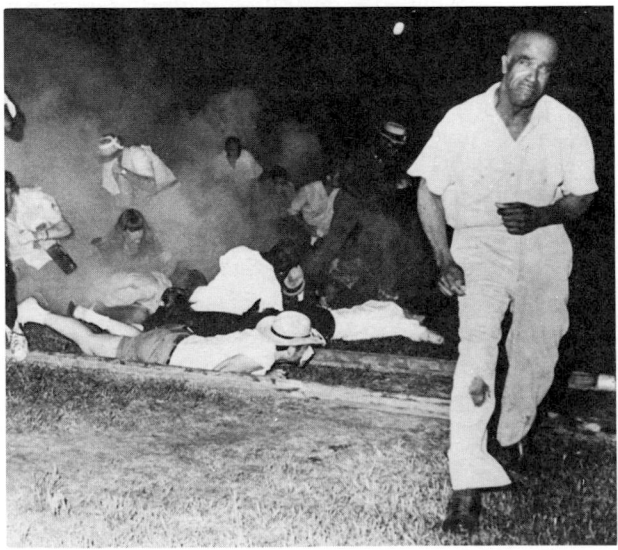

3), FBI informer and undercover agent Gary Thomas Rowe, Jr., who was allegedly in the car at the time of the murder, testifies that Wilkins and a fellow passenger fired shots at Mrs. Liuzzo after driving their own car alongside hers. The FBI presents the weapons as evidence, indicating that tests prove the bullets which killed Mrs. Liuzzo were fired from them. The defense attorney, however, attempts to discredit Rowe as a witness by maintaining that he has broken the oath of secrecy associated with membership in the Ku Klux Klan (Rowe had joined the organization as part of his assignment) and, therefore, cannot be believed. Moreover, witnesses are produced who testify that they have seen Wilkins elsewhere at the approximate time of the shooting. In closing the defense attorney maintains that what happened to Mrs. Liuzzo was her own fault since she was riding in a vehicle with a black passenger. The jury is instructed that it can convict Wilkins on a lesser charge than first-degree murder and quickly settles on a charge of first-degree manslaughter.

1965, May 26 The Senate passes the Voting Rights Bill, 77–19.

1965, May 30 Vivian Malone becomes the first black to graduate from the University of Alabama.

1965, June 6 Louisiana law-enforcement officials express growing concern over the activities of the Deacons for Defense and Justice, an armed black group with the professed aim of protecting blacks from terrorism by whites. Members of this group are reported to have twice fired on whites who were caught harasing blacks.

1965, June 10–16 Mass demonstrations, marches to City Hall, and other gestures of protest begin in Chicago on June 10, drawing attention to the slow pace of desegregation in the city's public school system. On June 11, 225 persons are arrested, including comedian Dick Gregory and CORE director James Farmer. Within four days, the arrest total reaches 530. On June 16, a final march culminates in a meeting between Chicago Mayor Richard Daley and a delegation led by the Reverend John Porter, leader of the Chicago branch of the NAACP.

1965, June 17 Pope Paul VI names John Patrick Cody of New Orleans, a staunch advocate of civil rights, to the post of Archbishop of Chicago, the nation's largest Roman Catholic see.

1965, June 18 More than 850 persons are arrested in Jackson, Mississippi after five days of protest demonstrations there.

1965, July 1–19 Between July 1 and July 5, the Congress of Racial Equality (CORE) lays the groundwork for a "major assault" in Bogalusa, Louisiana, scene of alleged police brutality against blacks. On July 7, a march is made on the Bogalusa City Hall to present desegregation demands. The following day, during a second march, a white man attacks two blacks, one of whom shoots and seriously wounds the man. On July 10, a federal district court judge enjoins Bogalusa authorities from blocking civil rights demonstrations, and orders protection for blacks who are being harassed by whites. Marches resume on July 11 with James Farmer of CORE in the vanguard. On July 12, Louisiana Governor John J. McKeithen flies to Bogalusa and appeals for a 30-day cooling-off period. On July 19, as the marches still continue, the Justice Department files criminal and civil contempt actions against Bogalusa officials. On July 22, the governor announces the formation of a 40-member biracial committee.

1965, July 2 Title VII of the 1964 Civil Rights Act prohibiting job discrimination in private business goes into effect.

1965, July 13 Thurgood Marshall is nominated as Solicitor General of the United States, the first black to hold this office.

1965, July 24–26 Martin Luther King, Jr. and the Southern Christian Leadership Conference (SCLC) conduct a civil rights campaign in Chicago, leading 18 rallies and church services in black neighborhoods, as well as in the primarily white suburb of Winnetka. On July 26, King and some 10,000 to 20,000 marchers assemble at the city hall, where King assails the city's *de facto* segregation patterns.

1965, August 6 President Johnson signs the 1965 Voting Rights Act, providing for the registration by federal examiners of those black voters turned away by state officials.

1965, August 8 Some 700 members of the Ku Klux Klan stage a silent march and memorial service in Americus, Georgia for a white youth slain in a racial conflict.

1965, August 11–21 A six-day orgy of looting, burning, and rioting plunges the predominantly black section of Watts, Los Angeles into a state of virtual anarchy. Thousands of National Guardsmen and state police are rushed in to quell the rioting which is traced to the arrest and alleged mistreatment of a black youth by white policemen on charges of drunken driving. The death toll is 35; 883 are injured, 3598 arrested. Fire damage: 175 million dollars. Property damage: 46 million dollars.

1965, August 20 President Johnson denounces the Los Angeles rioters, comparing them in one sense to Ku Klux Klan extremists. He declares that the existence of legitimate grievances in such communities as Watts is no justification for lawlessness. "We cannot . . . in one breath demand laws to protect the rights of all our citizens, and then turn our back . . . and . . . allow laws to be broken that protect the safety of our citizens."

1965, September 27–30 An all-white Alabama jury acquits part-time deputy sheriff Thomas L. Coleman of manslaughter charges in connection with the slaying of Jonathan M. Daniels, 26, a white Episcopal seminarian and civil rights worker from Keene, New Hampshire (September 30). State Attorney General Richmond Flowers calls the verdict "appalling" and a "license to kill."

1965, October 2 Pope Paul appoints the first black bishop in the United States in the twentieth century, the Very Reverend Harold R. Perry (Auxiliary Bishop of New Orleans).

1965, October 19 The House Un-American Activities Committee opens public hearings in the nation's capitol on the activities of the Ku Klux Klan. Robert M. Shelton, Jr., Imperial Wizard of the largest Klan group, invokes his constitutional rights and refuses to answer any of the committee's questions. Federal investigators charge Klan leaders with misappropriation of funds and the frequent use of violence against individuals and groups they consider to be enemies.

1965, October 22 An all-white Alabama jury acquits

Six days of burning and looting reduce Watts, California, to a disaster area.

Ku Klux Klansman Collie Leroy Wilkins in the slaying of Mrs. Viola Gregg Liuzzo. (See entries dated March 26–30; May 3–7.) The verdict is greeted with a storm of applause in the courthouse. The first Wilkins trial (see entry dated May 3–7) ended in a hung jury. At the second trial, the prosecution was handled by State Attorney General Richmond Flowers, who said of Wilkins: "The blood of this man's sins, if you do not find him guilty, will stain the very soul of our country for an eternity." Flowers attempted to disqualify the jury after several members admitted they felt civil rights workers were inferior beings. The Alabama Supreme Court, however, ruled against him, with the result that six self-styled white supremacists and eight present or former members of the White Citizens Council were selected to pass judgment on the case.

1965, November 23 A federal court in Montgomery, Alabama nullifies state court injunctions against the enrollment of federally registered voters in six Alabama counties.

1965, December 2 Segregationist Hubert D. Strange, 23, is convicted by a state court in Anniston, Alabama of second-degree murder in the slaying of Willie Brester, a 38-year-old black. Strange is sentenced to 10 years in prison by an all-white jury.

1965, December 3 An all-white jury convicts Collie Leroy Wilkins, 22, Eugene Thomas, 42, and William Orville Eaton, 42, on charges of conspiracy in the murder of Mrs. Viola Gregg Liuzzo. (See entries dated March 26; May 3; October 22.) Convictions are based on an 1870 federal civil rights law.

1965, December 10 A Selma, Alabama jury acquits three white businessmen charged with the murder of Reverend James J. Reeb, a Boston clergyman slain in Selma civil rights demonstrations.

1966, January 13 Robert Weaver is named head of the Department of Housing and Urban Development (HUD), the first black appointed to serve in a Presidential cabinet in U.S. history.

1966, January 15 President Johnson names Lisle Carter, a black, as an assistant secretary in the Department of Health, Education and Welfare (HEW).

1966, January 25 Constance Baker Motley, former NAACP lawyer and Borough President of Manhattan, becomes the first black woman to be named to a federal judgeship in the history of the United States.

1966, February 7 A federal court finds Lowndes County, Alabama guilty of "gross, systematic exclusion of members of the black race from jury duty." County officials are ordered to prepare a new jury list, one taking into account the added fact that an Alabama law barring women from juries has been declared unconstitutional. Lowndes County is also ordered to desegregate its school system within two years, to close 24 black-schools staffed with only one teacher each, and to introduce remedial programs designed to close the educational gap between white and black pupils.

1966, March 7 The Office of Education, Department of Health, Education and Welfare (HEW), issues tighter guidelines to end discrimination in schools and hospitals, threatening to cut off federal funds in both areas.

1966, March 15 A renewed outbreak of violence in Watts results in two deaths, injury to 26 people, 34 arrests, and damage to 15 buildings. Government studies indicate little change in the economic prospects of the average Watts citizen, with unemployment still running around 35%.

1966, March 25 U.S. Supreme Court outlaws the poll tax for all elections, a ruling which complements the Twenty-Fourth Amendment to the U.S. Constitution, barring such a tax in federal elections.

1966, April 12 Emmett Ashford becomes the first black major league umpire when he opens the season umpiring an American League game between Washington and Cleveland.

1966, April 1–24 The first World Festival of Black Arts is held in Dakar, Senegal. Black art the world over is brought for exhibit, with several American black artists being awarded prizes for their work.

1966, April 29 President Johnson sends his third civil rights bill to Congress. This one makes the racial murder of a civil rights worker, a student seeking education, or a citizen attempting to vote a federal crime punishable by life imprisonment. The Johnson bill is also designed to force the desegregation of schools and other public facilities, and to outlaw discrimination on racial and religious grounds in the sale, rental, or occupancy of *all* housing.

1966, May 4 Over 80% of Alabama's more than 235,000 registered blacks turn out for the Democratic primary election in which Lurleen Wallace is nominated by the party to succeed her husband as governor of the state. Sheriffs James Clark (Selma) and Al Lingo (Birmingham) fail in their bid for renomination.

1966, May 16 Stokely Carmichael is named as the new head of the Student Nonviolent Coordinating Committee (SNCC), replacing John Lewis, while Ruby Smith Robinson is appointed to fill the post of James Forman as SNCC executive secretary. The shakeup is interpreted to mean that the organization is charting a more militant course.

1966, June 6 James Meredith is shot from ambush shortly after beginning a 220-mile voting rights pilgrimage from Memphis, Tennessee to Jackson, Mississippi. Aubrey James Norvell, 40, is arrested at the scene and taken to jail where, according to authorities, he admits to the shooting. Meredith suffers multiple injuries, but recovers.

1966, June 22 A federal grand jury in Biloxi, Mississippi returns indictments against 15 alleged members of the Ku Klux Klan in connection with the January 10 slaying of Vernon F. Dahmer, a black active in promoting voter registration.

1966, June 26 The Mississippi march begun by James Meredith ends with a rally in front of the state capitol in Jackson. Addresses are delivered by Meredith himself, Martin Luther King, Jr., and Stokely Carmichael, who urges the 15,000 blacks in attendance to "built a power base . . . so strong that we will bring them (whites) to their knees every time they mess with us." (The "Meredith March Against Fear," taken up on June 7 by an assortment of civil rights groups, covers 260 miles, and results in the registration of about 4,000 blacks.)

1966, July 1–4 The national convention of the Congress of Racial Equality (CORE) votes to adopt a resolution endorsing the concept of "black power" as enunciated by Stokely Carmichael during the "Meredith March." CORE National Director Floyd McKissick says: "As long as the white man has all the power and money, nothing will happen, because we have nothing. The only way to achieve meaningful change is to take power."

1966, July 4–9 The National Association for the Advancement of Colored People (NAACP) disassociates itself from the "black power" doctrine.

1966, July 10 Martin Luther King, Jr. launches a drive to make Chicago an "open city," addressing a predominantly black crowd of 30,000 to 45,000 at Soldier Field. The rally is sponsored by the Coordinating Council of Committee Organizations (CCCO), a coalition consisting of some 45 local civil rights groups.

1966, July 12–15 Three nights of rioting sweep Chicago's West Side black district in the wake of a police decision to shut off a fire hydrant which had been open illegally to give black children relief from the stifling heat. Two blacks are killed, scores of police and civilians wounded, and 372 persons are arrested.

1966, July 18–23 Shooting, fire-bombing, and looting sweeps through the black area of Hough on Cleveland's East Side. Four are killed and 50 are injured amid widespread property damage. Most of the 164 persons arrested are charged with looting.

1966, July 22 John Lewis resigns from the Student Nonviolent Coordinating Committee, vowing to remain active in the civil rights movement.

1966, July 29–31 Martin Luther King launches demonstrations in a Southwest Side Chicago neighborhood as part of the "open city" campaign begun by his Southern Christian Leadership Conference (SCLC). Jeering whites pelt marchers with rocks and bottles before being driven off by police. In the Gage Park section, some 300 white hecklers overturn five cars belonging to black demonstrators.

1966, August 5 Martin Luther King is stoned in Chicago as he leads a march of 600 demonstrators through crowds of angry white residents in the Gage Park section of Chicago's Southwest Side. Near rioting ensues between 4,000 whites and 960 policemen, including 160 members of a riot-control force. King leaves Chicago on August 6, but pledges to "keep coming back until we are safe from harassment."

1966, August 9 By a vote of 259–157, the House of Representatives passes and sends to the Senate an amended version of the Administration's proposed Civil Rights Bill of 1966. Most of the long debate centers around the bill's controversial "openhousing" section embodied in Title IV. The Mathias Amendment, added to the bill, exempts some 60% of the nation's housing from its anti-discrimination provisions. Other sections of the bill concern jury selection, interference with the civil rights of individuals, and initiation of court action to desegregate schools and public accommodations.

1966, October Huey Newton and Bobby Seale found the Black Panther Party in Oakland, California. They propose a 10-point program, which includes reparations for past abuses of blacks, release of all black prisoners, and trial of blacks by all-black juries.

1966, October Bill Russell becomes the first black to coach a major professional athletic team, as a player-coach with the Boston Celtics of the National Basketball Association.

1966, November 8 Edward Brooke, a Massachusetts Republican, becomes the first black elected to the U.S. Senate since Reconstruction. Floyd McCree, a black, is elected Mayor of Flint, Michigan.

1967, January-March Representative Adam Clayton Powell, Jr. of New York is stripped of his chairmanship of the House Committee on Education and Labor, and then barred from assuming his seat in the 90th Congress. A Congressional committee investigating the case later proposes public censure, loss of seniority, and a $40,000 fine, stipulating, however, that he be returned to his seat. Congress, on the other hand, votes for exclusion, whereupon

Powell and his lawyers indicate their intention to challenge the constitutionality of this decision in federal court.

1967, February 15 President Johnson requests that Congress consider and pass new civil rights legislation in the area pertaining to the sale and rental of housing. In his special message, Johnson outlines the scope of the proposed bill, specifying that it be designed to end discrimination in jury selection, to permit the Equal Opportunity Commission (EEOC) to issue cease-and-desist orders, to extend the life of the U.S. Commission on Civil Rights, and to authorize 2.7 million dollars in appropriations for the Community Relations Service. Violators are to be subject to court orders and fines issued by the Secretary of Housing and Urban Development. The law is also to address itself to the matter of the civil rights to individuals, particularly insofar as it will enable them to file damage suits in cases where they are being victimized by discrimination. Civil rights workers, too, would be in a position to seek injunctions to combat discriminatory practices.

1967, February 27 A federal grand jury returns federal conspiracy indictments against 19 men in connection with the 1964 slayings of civil rights workers Michael Schwerner, Andrew Goodman, and James Earl Chaney. Another 12 men are indicted in connection with the 1966 firebombing of black leader Vernon Dahmer.

1967, March 1–8 Representative Powell is barred from the 90th Congress by a vote of 307–116, and immediately files suit in U.S. District Court to combat his ouster. Powell argues that he has met all Constitutional requirements for House membership: citizenship, age, and residency. The Congressman also charges that his constituency is left without representation, and hence subject to discrimination.

1967, March 7–13 James Meredith announces he will run against Adam Powell, calling the impending special election "one of the most important in the history of this country." Though he declares himself an independent Democrat, Meredith plans to run on the Democratic ticket. Meredith withdraws on March 13 after meeting with CORE leader Floyd McKissick and Charles Evers, NAACP field secretary from Mississippi.

1967, March 22 A three-judge federal court in Montgomery, Alabama orders the state board of education and the governor to begin desegregation of public schools in the fall term. This is the first instance in which an entire state is under a single injunction to end discrimination.

1967, March 29 The 5th Circuit Court of Appeals

Ejected Congressman Adam Clayton Powell relaxes during his two-year exile in Bimini.

upholds the legality of revised federal school desegregation guidelines in an 8–4 ruling which calls for the desegregation of all students, teachers, school transportation facilities, and school-related activities in six Deep South states. The guidelines establish rough percentage goals to be used in determining compliance with the Civil Rights Act of 1964.

1967, April 7–11 Adam Clayton Powell appeals a U.S. District Court dismissal of his suit seeking reinstatement in the House. The Court declares it has no jurisdiction in the matter and is unable to tell Congress how to govern itself. Powell next seeks and receives a popular mandate, being returned to office by more than 74% of the Harlem electorate in a special election. The Congressman conducts his campaign from his Bimini retreat partly because he would risk possible arrest on contempt charges if he were to return to New York, but also as a means of demonstrating his enormous popularity. He is a landslide winner in the special runoff election for the 18th Congressional District, which has been left unrepresented since Powell's exclusion from the House. Powell wins 27,900 votes to 4,091 for Republican candidate Lucille Pickett Williams and only 427 for Reverend Erwin Yearling, Conservative Party standard bearer.

1967, April 11–24 Demonstrations escalate in Louisville, Kentucky following rejection of a proposed open-housing ordinance by the city's Board of Aldermen. In the vanguard of the march are Reverend A. D. Williams King and comedian/activist Dick Gregory. White youth harassing the marchers chant "We Want Wallace," and carry banners saying "We Don't Want Any Niggers." On April 13, a band of some 75 whites burn a cross on the lawn of the Southern Junior High School. A circuit court judge issues a restraining order seeking to curb the marches, but attorneys for the demonstrators petition to dissolve the injunction. Police use tear gas and smoke bombs to disperse whites who interfere with the march, and arrest black demonstrators for violating the injunction. Demonstrations are extended into affluent white suburbs and exclusive east side sections of Louisville; arrests, trials, and convictions follow in their wake. On April 24, county and city leaders agree to hold "hard bargaining sessions" to resolve the problems.

1967, April 15–24 Ignoring the criticisms of some of his black colleagues, Martin Luther King, Jr. signals his full-fledged entry into the peace movement by leading thousands of demonstrators through New York's Central Park to the U.N. building, where he and other prominent leaders deliver a series of forceful addresses attacking U.S. policy in Vietnam. More than 100,000 attend the rally, only one of several staged at campuses and in cities across the country. King later announces the formation of Negotiation Now, a pressure group dedicated to the accumulation of one million signatures on a peace petition to be submitted to the President.

1967, May 3 A federal district court in Montgomery overturns the Alabama statute countering guidelines for school desegregation. The court rules that no state may nullify the action of "a federal department or agency without initiating Court action" reviewable by the U.S. Supreme Court.

1967, May 10–13 A black delivery man, Benjamin Brown, on his way to a restaurant, is shot and killed during riots on the campus of Jackson State College. Within full view of police, Brown is left at the scene unattended until he is taken to the University Hospital by black bystanders. Rioters are apparently "not rioting over any specific grievance," according to Kenneth Dean, director of the Mississippi Council of Human Relations. Police, unable to contain the demonstrators whose ranks are swelled by participants from nearby Tougaloo College, are reinforced by more than 1,000 National Guardsmen.

1967, May 12–16 H. Rap Brown replaces Stokely Carmichael as chairman of the Student Non-Violent Coordinating Committee. Brown calls a news conference to announce that SNCC's Black Power policy will remain intact, and pledges to build a strong anti-draft program and movement among black youth. Carmichael vows to stay on at SNCC as field secretary in Washington, D.C.

1967, June 2–5 Scores of persons are injured; 75–100 are arrested in an outbreak of rioting in Boston's predominantly black section of Roxbury. The disturbance occurs in the wake of an attempt by welfare mothers to barricade themselves inside a building as a protest against departmental policies and police rudeness. Police who try to enter the building are struck by stones and bottles; others inside the building form a flying wedge and charge out the center, only to be bombarded by various missiles.

1967, June 6 Legal Defense Fund director/counsel Jack Greenberg announces the creation of a new educational project to inform blacks of their rights in housing, health, and employment. The program, known as the Division of Legal Information and Community Service and funded by a matching $300,000 Rockefeller grant, is headed by Jean Fairfax.

1967, June 12–15 More than 300 persons are arrested

National Guardsman returns snipers' fire from behind concrete stanchion in Milwaukee's north side during 1967 civil disorders that swept several major cities.

Striking worker is removed from premises during the Charleston hospital strike.

in Cincinnati racial disturbances which include incidents of looting and arson. H. Rap Brown arrives in the city on June 15, advising city fathers to remove National Guard patrols and "honkie cops" and urging that 12 imprisoned blacks be released. The cause of the rioting, originally identified as a protest aired against a death sentence imposed on a black convict, turns out to be the familiar litany of grievances associated with urban unrest, primarily police brutality, and lack of job opportunity.

1967, June 13 Thurgood Marshall is appointed an Associate Justice of the Supreme Court, the first black so designated. President Johnson calls Marshall "the right man," the Court "the right place," and the appointment "the right thing to do."

1967, June 14 Nine prominent civil rights leaders, meeting secretly in Suffern, New York, announce plans to ease racial tensions in Cleveland, a city they regard as one in which "underlying causes of unrest and despair" have reached crisis proportions. One of the leaders, Martin Luther King, Jr., confirms SCLS's previously announced plans for initiating organized civil rights action during the summer, and singles out the bread industry for a selective buying campaign. The NAACP's Roy Wilkins expresses reservations about King's plans to "stir up trouble," although he hastens to add that slums, poor schools, and lack of jobs are the real causes of trouble. The FBI's J. Edgar Hoover faults King

for issuing an "open invitation" to summer violence by naming cities where it is likely to occur.

1967, June 12–17 The "long hot summer" begins in earnest in Newark, New Jersey, scene of the most devastating riot to sweep an urban center since the 1965 Watts uprising.

1967, June 18–22 Stokely Carmichael is arrested as he joins a crowd of 200–500 persons gathered in the Dixie Hill section of Atlanta to protest the arrest of a citizen accused of "malicious mischief." Carmichael tells the crowd that the police have "everybody marked, ready to shoot" and exhorts them to take to the streets. State Senator Leroy Johnson tries to organize a youth patrol to cool tempers, but the move does not prevent a confrontation between police and crowds gathered in a shopping center. One black is killed; three others are injured. Carmichael is convicted on June 22 of fomenting a riot and sentenced to 50 days in jail.

1967, June 19 U.S. District Judge J. Skelly Wright rules that *de facto* segregation of blacks in the District of Columbia is unconstitutional, and orders the public school system to abolish the "track system," the assignment of some children to special courses for gifted students. Wright orders the complete desegregation of D.C. schools by the fall.

1967, June 24 James Meredith and four others resume the "March Against Fear" in Mississippi mainly, as Meredith says, to complete unfinished business, to demonstrate that local police can protect blacks if they choose to, and because "the black has a whole history of failure and incompletions," based on the fear which he seeks to expose and extinguish.

1967, June 27–30 Three days of rioting in Buffalo, New York, result in more than 85 injuries, 205 arrests, and property damage estimated at $100,000.

1967, July 10–15 The fifty-eighth NAACP convention is a tense and at times bitter affair in which Executive Director Roy Wilkins defends black militants for shaking up the establishment, but warns against the endorsement of the kind of radicalization that will force whites out of the movement altogether.

1967, July 19 The House of Representatives passes legislation which declares it a federal crime to cross state lines or to use interstate facilities for the purpose of inciting a riot. The bill is aimed at alleged professional agitators who travel from city to city to inflame the people. New York's Emanuel Celler finds the bill "neither preventive nor curative," and fears it will only arouse black hostility even further.

1967, July 20–23 Despite objections by New Jersey Governor Hughes, a four-day conclave of black leaders, many of them Black Power advocates, convenes in Newark. Militancy and a call for separate nationhood dominates the meeting, as most delegates concur with the estimate offered by one participant. Alfred Black of the Newark Human Relations Commission: "The black today is either a radical or an Uncle Tom. There is no middle ground." On July 22, riots erupt in Detroit.

1967, July 25–28 "You'd better get yourselves some guns. The only thing honkies respect is guns." These words, attributed to SNCC leader H. Rap Brown, are cited as the cause of the rioting and arson that inflict wholesale damage on the black business section of Cambridge, Maryland. Governor Spiro Agnew later tours the district and tells the press that Brown is responsible for the trouble. The Governor orders 700 National Guardsmen to take up positions in Cambridge. On July 28, the Governor calls the city "sick" and obviously segregated.

1967, July 27 President Johnson appoints a blue-ribbon panel to "investigate the origins of the recent disorders in our cities." The President instructs the commission to leave aside political considerations and concern itself solely with the health and safety of American society and its citizens. The President imposes only three guidelines on the panel, three basic questions which he deems it indispensable to answer: (1) what happened (2) why did it happen,

Thurgood Marshall was the first black justice appointed to the U.S. Supreme Court.

and (3) how can it be prevented from happening again.

1967, August 10 The National Advisory Commission on Civil Disorders urges President Johnson to increase the number of blacks in the Army and Air National Guard. The panel also recommends increased riot-control training for the Guard, as well as a review of promotion procedures. The recommendations, delivered in a letter to LBJ, are forwarded to Defense Secretary Robert McNamara.

1967, August 14–22 H. Rap Brown is indicted *in absentia* by a Dorchester County grand jury on charges of inciting to riot, arson, and other related actions inimical to the public peace. Brown is arrested in New York on August 19 and charged with carrying a gun across state lines while under indictment. After strenuous objections are voiced by his white lawyer, William Kunstler, Brown's bail is reduced to $15,000 on August 22, and he is released in time to address a crowd of 100 blacks on the steps of the Foley Square courthouse. Pointing to whites nearby, Brown says: "That's your enemy out there. And you better not forget, because I ain't going to."

1967, August 14–21 The Student Nonviolent Coordinating Committee (SNCC) publishes an article in its newsletter denouncing Zionism and charging Israelis with inflicting atrocities against the Arabs. The article accuses Israel of practicing segregation against Arabs still in their country, and of assigning second-class status to dark-skinned Jews. Author Harry Golden and folksinger Theodore Bikel resign from SNCC following the charges posted in the article. The article is later defended by SNCC as being anti-Zionist, not anti-Semitic.

1967, August 16 The House passes an amended Administration bill to defend persons exercising federally protected civil rights. The vote is 326–93.

1967, August 19–23 Nearly 450 persons are arrested during five days of looting, arson, and vandalism in New Haven, Connecticut. No serious injuries are reported, and no shots are fired by police despite frequent curfew violations. New Haven Mayor Richard C. Lee declares: "We've done a lot, but for everything we've done, there are five that we haven't."

1967, September 6 President Johnson discloses he will nominate Walter E. Washington to head the newly reorganized municipal government of Washington, D.C. Washington is the first black to govern a major American city.

1967, September 19 An open-housing ordinance is introduced in the Milwaukee Common Council following weeks of open-housing demonstrations led by the militant Catholic priest, Reverend James E. Groppi. Committeemen fail to agree on specific provisions of the ordinance.

1967, October 3–5 Black Power at the polls is evidenced by the Democratic primary victory of Representative Carl Stokes, who unseats incumbent Ralph Locher in the race for Cleveland mayor. Wealthy black lawyer and businessman A. W. Willis, Jr. is less successful, however, running a poor fourth in a nonpartisan election for mayor of Memphis on October 5.

1967, October 6 The Equal Employment Opportunity Commission (EEOC) declares that there is widespread discrimination against blacks in the nation's drug industry. EEOC Chairman Clifford Alexander meets with Food and Drugs Commissioner James L. Goddard and some 24 representatives of the industry whose companies account for 70% of the drug business. Alexander threatens to institute the "complaint process" unless hiring and upgrading of blacks commences immediately.

1967, October 20 An all-white Mississippi federal jury of five men and seven women returns a verdict of guilty in the 1964 murder trial of three civil rights workers near Philadelphia. Seven men are convicted of conspiracy; eight, however, are acquitted, and three are declared to be victims of mistrial. Among the guilty are Chief Deputy Sheriff Cecil Price and Sam Bowers, Imperial Wizard of the Ku Klux Klan.

1967, November 7 Richard Hatcher is elected Mayor of Gary, Indiana, Carl Stokes of Cleveland, Ohio.

1967, November 28 Martin Luther King, Jr. announces significant victories for SCLC's Operation Breadbasket, a program of skillful buying and selective pressure designed to convince white chain stores operating in ghetto neighborhoods to hire and upgrade more blacks.

1967, December 4 Martin Luther King, Jr. announces plans for a massive civil disobedience campaign scheduled for Washington, D.C. in the spring of 1968 and designed to apply pressure on Congress and the Johnson Administration to end poverty by providing jobs and income for all of America's citizens.

1967, December 27 Roy Innis is named to succeed Lincoln Lynch as Associate National Director of CORE. Innis, a militant black nationalist, was formerly chairman of CORE's New York (Harlem) chapter.

1968, January 4 Black poet-playwright Imamu Amiri Baraka (Leroi Jones) is sentenced to 2½–3 years in prison and fined $1,000 for illegal possession of firearms during the July 1967 riots in Newark. Two others are sentenced with Baraka, but their terms are far less severe.

1968, January 8 NAACP Executive Director Roy Wilkins concedes that his organization's membership decreased by 3% in 1967, with a consequent loss in operating revenue as well. Wilkins attributes the decline to the problems of central cities, and the violence which invariably produces a loss of sympathy for all black organizations. He ignores reference to the appeal of other militant black groups at odds with NAACP strategy.

1968, January 8–13 Adam Clayton Powell, rejected by the House in 1967 after having been excluded from that body due to irregularities in the use of Congressional funds, goes on a speaking tour of California campuses, exhorting his white listeners "to join the Black Revolution" and classifying Black Power as "the saving grace of the United States."

1968, January 16 Lucius Amerson is elected Sheriff of Macon County, Alabama, the first black sheriff in the South since Reconstruction.

1968, January 24 President Johnson appeals to Congress to enact his pending 1967 civil rights proposals in the areas of housing, jobs, jury selection, and federal protection of persons exercising their civil rights. The President recognizes that minorities in America are subject to social, educational, and economic disparities, not merely the equities or inequities of law. He places heavy stress on the denial of equal justice and opportunity as the primary factors behind the tragedy of urban riots, but he insists that such lawlessness must be curbed, if only because its prime victims are ghetto residents themselves.

1968, February 5–26 Three black youths are shot to death and more than 30 people are wounded in a racial outburst involving police and students at Orangeburg's South Carolina State College. The violence is the culmination of student protest against the segregation of a local bowling alley. Students begin the protests on February 5 and continue them the next evening when 15 are arrested on trespassing charges. One policeman and seven students are injured and hospitalized. On February 7, the campus is sealed off and classes are suspended in the wake of rock and bottle-throwing incidents. The three students shot on February 8 are fired on by police who mistakenly believe one of their troopers has been shot when, in reality, he has been knocked down by a piece of lumber heaved by a demonstrator. On February 9, Governor McNair orders a curfew, and attributes the violence to "Black Power" advocates, including Cleveland Sellers, state coordinator for SNCC. Sellers, under arrest, is held on $50,000 bond. On February 11, local blacks call for the removal of the National Guard, and announce plans for a boycott of white business. The city fathers counter by establishing a Human Relations Commission which resolves to prevent further outbreaks by determining the causes of the present one. On February 13, the NAACP criticizes the commission for failing to consult with it before appointing the black members. On February 24, the Southern Regional Council issues a report analyzing the Orangeburg upheaval and tracing it to such things as the emotional appeal of black power to young blacks, white overreaction against this euphoria, the tendency of blacks to see violence as being more and more necessary in the face of continued failure to enforce federal laws (in this case, the 1964 Civil Rights Act), and the expectation by whites that police power and military force must be utilized to cope with all forms of public demonstrations. The analysis does not prevent later violence after the resumption of classes at the College on February 26.

1968, February 15–17 McGeorge Bundy of the Ford Foundation says his organization will work to eliminate racial prejudice even if it is forced to lend its support to black separatists. The Foundation announces grants to three experimental projects in school decentralization in New York City—the IS 201 complex, Ocean Hill–Brownsville in Brooklyn, and Two Bridges in lower New York.

1968, February 29 The President's National Advisory Commission on Civil Disorders issues an exhaustive report on the causes of the civil disorder that disrupted the nation in 1967. The commission identifies the major cause of the rioting as the existence of two separate bodies in America—"one black, one white, separate and unequal." It charges that white racism, more than anything else, was the chief catalyst in the already explosive mixture of discrimination, poverty, and frustration that ignited so many urban ghettos in the tragic summer of 1967. It reminds white America how deeply it is implicated in the existence of the ghetto. "White institutions created it, white institutions maintain it, and white society condones it." To overcome this terrible and crushing legacy, the Commission implores the nation to initiate a massive and sustained commitment to action and reform, and appeals for unprecedented levels of "funding and performance" in housing, education, employment, welfare, law enforcement, and the mass media.

1968, March 11 The Senate passes the Civil Rights Bill of 1968, prompting President Johnson to hail the "nation's commitment to human rights under law." Among its major provisions are sweeping housing and anti-riot measures which go far beyond the federal protections offered to civil rights workers in the 1967 House version of the bill.

1968, March 12 Though he was victorious in the primary, Charles Evers is defeated by a 2–1 margin in the special runoff election for the Congressional seat in Mississippi's Third District. His rival, Charles Griffin, outpolls him 87,761 to 43,083. Evers carries two of the district's 12 counties, Jefferson and Claiborne.

1968, March 18 The Department of Health, Education and Welfare (HEW) extends its school desegregation guidelines to northern schools. It calls for the elimination of such concrete examples of unequal treatment as overcrowded classes, lower per-pupil expenditures, less-qualified teachers, and inadequate textbooks.

1968, March 22–24 Adam Clayton Powell returns to New York City and surrenders on criminal contempt-of-court charges. On March 24, Powell tells his congregation at Abyssinian Baptist Church that nonviolence is no longer the most effective strategy in the civil rights struggle. Powell says black leadership is in the hands of a "new breed," dedicated to retaliatory violence. His words: "Think big, think black, and think like a child of God."

1968, March 29–29 A teen-aged black youth is slain in Memphis after a protest march led by Martin Luther King, Jr. deteriorates into violence and looting. The march culminates six weeks of labor strike activity involving the sanitation workers of the city,

President Johnson signs Voting Rights bill into law; Roy Wilkins is among those looking on.

90% of whom are black. The workers seek a pay raise, a dues checkoff system, seniority rights, health and hospitalization insurance, and recognition of the American Federation of State, County and Municipal Employees as bargaining agents. City officials, including the mayor, contend the strike is illegal under the terms of a State Supreme Court decision banning strikes by public employees. Civil rights leaders and black ministers call for a boycott of downtown business and urge massive civil disobedience to express support for the strikers. Such action broadens the thrust of the strike and transforms it into a general civil rights action. On the day of the march, disturbances begin almost immediately. Some black students who have been refused the right to leave school and participate in the march begin pelting police with bricks; others smash department store windows along Beale Street and steal merchandise. Still, most of the marchers (estimates vary from 6,000 to 20,000) are peaceful until city and county police join the National Guard in quelling the disturbances. After Dr. King is spirited away to safety at a nearby hotel, tear gas is fired at the crowds, and more than 150 persons are arrested, 40 of them on looting charges.

1968, April 4–11 The world is shocked by the assassination of Martin Luther King, by a sniper's bullet in Memphis. The killing triggers a wave of violence in over 100 cities, including such urban centers as Baltimore, Chicago, Kansas City, Missouri, and Washington, D.C., where looting, burning, and shooting are most pronounced. Some 70,000 federal troops and guardsmen are dispatched to restore order. Official figures report 46 dead: 41 blacks, five whites. Thousands are injured and arrested.

Felled by a single bullet fired from a distance of only 50–100 yards from the point of impact, Dr. King was pronounced dead at St. Joseph's Hospital at 7:05 P.M. CST, barely an hour after he had been hit. Attorney General Ramsey Clark, on hand to conduct the preliminary investigation in person, de-

Assassin's view of Martin Luther King, Jr.'s balcony is recaptured down a rifle barrel.

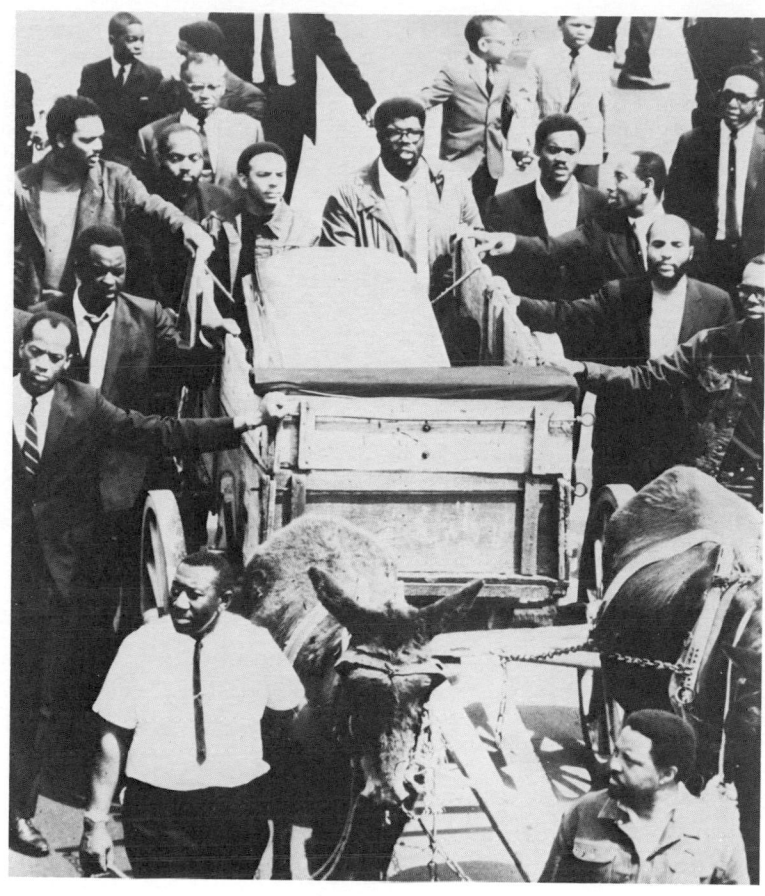

Slain leader is carried to his grave in a farm wagon pulled by two Georgia mules.

clares that the early evidence points to the crime as being the work of a single assassin. Witnesses report seeing a white man running from the doorway of a rooming house at 420 South Main Street minutes after the shooting. On April 5, Reverend Ralph Abernathy is named to succeed King and discloses that SCLC's first public gesture will be to lead the march King himself was planning. Three days later, Coretta Scott King takes her place in the front ranks of the marchers, locking arms with two of the 42,000 people on hand for the demonstration. King's body is put on public view at Ebenezer Baptist Church on April 6. He is buried at South View Cemetery on April 9 after funeral services are held at the church and a general memorial service is conducted at Morehouse College, his alma mater. There is an eerie magnificence and a sublime dignity to the last gesture in the proceedings before interment when the coffin is carried through the streets on a faded green farm wagon pulled by two Georgia mules. In accordance with a request of Mrs. King, the tape-recorded voice of King echoes through the crowd at the funeral service as a last reminder of the man and a vivid testimony to his courage: "Say . . . that I tried to love and serve

humanity . . . say that I was a drum major for peace . . . for righteousness . . ." Following King's death, riots break out in several cities.

1968, April 10–11 The assassination moves the House to submit to the President a Senate-passed civil rights bill prohibiting racial discrimination in the sale or rental of 80% of the nation's housing. The President signs the measure on April 11, and counsels the nation to stay on the road to progress by recognizing "the process of law."

1968, April 16 An accord is reached in the Memphis sanitation men's strike, the issue which brought Martin Luther King, Jr. to the beleaguered southern city. Most of the workers' demands are met, including dues checkoff, recognition of a bargaining agent, and an immediate pay raise.

1968, April 23 Roman Catholic bishops call on the faithful to "declare war" on racism in housing, education, and employment. The National Conference of Catholic Bishops appropriates $25,000 to "Operation Connection," an interfaith group raising money to finance black-sponsored programs in five cities.

1968, May 11-June 10 Nine caravans of poor people

begin arriving in Washington, D.C., the vanguard of the Poor People's Campaign. The Defense Department alerts "selected troop units" to help D.C. police in the event of violence. On Mother's Day, May 12, Coretta Scott King leads a march of welfare mothers from 20 cities and declares at a subsequent rally that she will try to enlist the support of all the nation's women "in a campaign of conscience." The next day, Ralph Abernathy, clad in blue denims and using carpenter's tools, presides at the christening of Resurrection City, the plywood shantytown erected within walking distance of the White House and the Capitol. Demonstrations follow almost immediately as the SCLC staff leadership begins to put pressure on Congress and the Administration to declare its dedication to the goal of eliminating poverty in the United States. Meanwhile, bad weather contributes to the mounting internal crises being faced by residents of the city. Inadequate cooking, bathing, and sanitation facilities create health hazards for some, and induce others to leave the campsite. Bayard Rustin, called in to lead a special Solidarity Day March on June 19, resigns on June 7 following a dispute among staff hierarchy as to the exact nature of Rustin's role. The controversy stems from Rustin's association with reformist sentiments and pressure on Abernathy from other quarters to adopt a more revolutionary stance. Abernathy explains that Rustin does not intend to press for jobs, a minimum guaranteed income, major housing and welfare reform, and an end to the war in Vietnam. Rustin's replacement, Sterling Tucker of the Washington Urban League, drafts a revised list of demands which include the establishment of strong federal gun control laws and a commitment to deescalate the Vietnam war. On the positive side, Abernathy is able to report, as the campaign draws to a close, that certain gains have been recorded. The Department of Agriculture, for instance, agrees to "provide food to the neediest counties in this country"; the Senate approves an amendment removing restrictions on the Agriculture Department's use of contingency funds for this purpose; the Senate approves a bill to increase low-income housing construction; and the OEO allocates 25 million dollars for expanded programs, including one encouraging participation of the poor.

1968, June 5–8 Senator Robert Kennedy is shot and killed in Los Angeles moments after leaving a rally in celebration of his victory over Eugene McCarthy in the California Democratic primary. Seized almost immediately after the shooting is Sirhan Sirhan, a young Jordanian resident of the Los Angeles area who is disarmed by Roosevelt Grier, one of the black bodyguards and aides who had been accompa-

Poor People's Crusade: escorted by supporters, Reverend Ralph D. Abernathy and other leaders march toward Labor Department.

"Resurrection City," the architect-designed shantytown where 2,500 camped to bring poverty home to the nation's legislators.

Robert Kennedy, moments before he was assassinated. Behind his left shoulder stands bodyguard Roosevelt Grier, who disarmed murderer.

nying Kennedy throughout his California campaign to protect him from excitable crowds. (The other two are Rafer Johnson, former Olympic decathlon champion, and Deacon Jones, Los Angeles footballer.) Kennedy is flown by presidential jet to New York on June 6. Among the passengers consoling his grieving widow Ethel are Mrs. Martin Luther King, Jr. and Mrs. Medgar Evers, both of whom have seen their own husbands fall victim to the assassin's bullet.

1968, June 8   James Earl Ray, alleged assassin of Dr. Martin Luther King, Jr. is arrested at a London airport on June 8, the same day on which Senator Kennedy is buried at Arlington. Four days later, the United States applies for extradition, ending what is said to have been the most extensive manhunt in U.S. history. Ray had been under indictment as Eric Starvo Galt since April 23, and was first indicted under his real name on May 7. After Ray's capture, rumors of conspiracy again multiply, but Attorney General Ramsey Clark continues to make numerous public statements discounting them.

1968, June 25–27   Ralph Abernathy is sentenced to 20 days in jail for leading an unlawful assembly at the foot of Capitol Hill. From his cell, he issues a letter encouraging the clergy to join in a demon-

stration the next day. The letter, reminiscent of Dr. King's Letter from a Birmingham Jail, is distributed nationally, but less than 25 clergymen respond. Abernathy announces his intention to fast for spiritual strength.

1968, July 8   CORE National Director Floyd McKissick takes a leave of absence from the organization, whereupon Roy Innis assumes the directorship. Innis pledges to tighten up the organization and give it direction.

1968, July 16   Black comedian Dick Gregory is released from an Olympia, Washington jail after being held for six weeks following his conviction on charges of illegal net fishing during a 1966 Indian fishing-rights demonstration. While in custody, Gregory fasted for six weeks in order to call attention to the civil rights struggle of the Indian minority.

1968, July 23–27   A racial outburst in Cleveland's Glenville district results in the death of 11 persons, eight of them black (including three labeled as nationalists) and three white policemen. Black Mayor Carl Stokes helps restore order with relative rapidity after a night of burnings and lootings which result in over a million dollars worth of property damage. Over 3,000 National Guardsmen are on the scene, but they are not widely utilized. Blame for the attack is laid to Ahmed (Fred) Evans, 37-year-old anti-poverty worker and head of the Black Nationalists of New Libya. At the height of the shoot-out, followers of Evans occupy several Glenville buildings, exchanging gunfire with black community leaders who agree to help organize citizen's patrols and assist regular police to maintain order. The distressed areas are cordoned off, but the renewed outbreak of looting and violence forces Stokes to send in guard units once more, albeit sparingly. Within a day, calm is restored, and the Stokes 9 P.M.-6 A.M. curfew is lifted. On June 26, Ahmed Evans is arraigned on three charges of first degree murder; a day later, Stokes offers an analysis of the incident in which he claims it is "uniquely different" from those experienced elsewhere in the country. In this case, Stokes feels that the episode was part of a deliberate, premeditated attempt to attack police in a revolutionary manner. SNCC program director Phil Hutchings confirms this estimate in a New York press conference.

1968, July 27 The Kerner Commission releases preliminary findings that indicate a sharp rise in the number of blacks who accept urban riots as a justifiable or inevitable response to conditions prevailing in the nation's ghettos. One study totally rejects the so-called riff-raff theory, the assumption that the riots were caused by a small dissatisfied portion of the black community subjected to outside agitation.

1968, August 1 President Johnson signs into law the Housing and Urban Development Act of 1968, authorizing more than 5 billion dollars worth of funds for a three-year program aimed at providing 1.7 million units of new or rehabilitated housing for families with low-income status. The bill sets up a homeownership assistance program that will provide eligible low-income purchasers with an interest-rate subsidy. Other subsidies cover construction or rehabilitation of rental and cooperative housing.

1968, August 6 Representatives of the Poor People's Campaign put in various appearances at the convention headquarters of various Republican Presidential hopefuls, receiving an enthusiastic welcome from New York's Governor Rockefeller, a lukewarm reception from the Nixon entourage, and a flat rejection from California's Governor Reagan, who bars them from his news conference. Claiming to represent the "51st state—that of poverty," Abernathy calls for a platform "to end poverty and injustice in America," and declares that Rockefeller is the last hope of the party to capture "the black vote."

1968, August 7–8 Two days of looting, fire bombing, and shooting in the black section of Miami culminate in Florida Governor Claude Kirk's decision to summon the National Guard to quell disorders. Despite Ralph Abernathy's plea for "an end to this violence," crowds of blacks battle police in the eight-block area which the latter have cordoned off. On August 8, three blacks are killed in gun battles with law enforcement officials. Although Dade County Mayor Chuck Hall accuses outsiders of instigating the trouble, particularly to gain exposure before a nationwide audience, the 10% rate of unemployment, particularly among blacks in the 16–22 age bracket, is certainly a factor producing the explosive situation.

1968, August 29 Ralph Abernathy, appearing with his Poor People's entourage, addresses an August 29 rally in Chicago and accuses Democratic officials of rebuffing his requests to address the convention and offering little encouragement or support for Poor People campaigners. Abernathy demands a personal apology from Democratic nominee Hubert Humphrey. Elsewhere on the streets, comedian Dick Gregory and 300 other demonstrators marching toward the convention site are halted by police, who arrest 150 persons and disperse the others by using tear gas.

1968, August 29 Dr. Nathan Wright announces that white newsmen will be barred from the Third National Conference on Black Power due to the allegedly false stories they filed at the previous conference. During the four-day meeting, some 4,000 delegates approve more than 100 formal proposals in such areas as politics, education, and economics. One of them calls for a national black party.

1968, September 4 More than 150 whites, many said to be off-duty policemen, allegedly attack a handful of Black Panthers and white sympathizers standing in a hallway of Brooklyn's Criminal Court building. The policemen, said to be members of a right-wing group within the department, are reported to have proclaimed themselves "the white tigers" and to have swung blackjacks while stomping the outnumbered group. Mayor Lindsay orders an investigation, but no arrests are made, nor is disciplinary action taken.

1968, September 8–27 Black Panther Huey P. Newton is tried and convicted of manslaughter in the October 28, 1967 fatal shooting of a white patrolman. Nearly three weeks later, Newton is sentenced to 2–15 years imprisonment. The trial and the conviction introduce the nation at large to a new and formidable organization of black militants: the Black Panthers. Who they are and what they represent is the subject of occasionally hysterical inquiry.

1968, September 9 Opening day of the New York teacher's strike immobilizes the public school system in the city and keeps a million pupils out of the schools for several weeks. The dispute carries strong racial overtones, centering as it does on the Ocean Hill–Brownsville School Demonstration District, a predominantly black and Puerto Rican district in Brooklyn, most of whose 500 teachers are white. Teachers, fearing student and community harassment, and administrators, seeking to implement the notion of community control or involvement in the operation of the schools, clash head-on over jurisdiction, procedures, tenure, seniority, the right to teach, etc. The union vows to remain out on strike until its members are assured they cannot be arbitrarily dismissed. The community, on the other hand, feels the teachers show callous disregard for the needs of the children, plus a disturbing unwillingness to submit to some form of periodic evaluation or quality control. Battle lines in the dispute crystallize around three basic positions: complete retention of the status quo, creation of a decentralized system recognizing neighborhood or local residential patterns, the establishment of full-fledged community control based on local self-determination in matters pertaining to funding, hiring and firing, and direction of curriculum.

1968, September 10 The Gallup poll reports that 50% of union members interviewed in the South favor Governor Wallace over both major party nominees, Humphrey (29%) and Nixon (16%). The poll shows that labor's traditional support of the Democratic nominee is being overridden by increasing blue-collar disenchantment with the pace of black progress in the labor market and with the social strength of the black movement.

1968, September 17–24 News that Eldridge Cleaver has been asked to deliver a series of 10 lectures at the Berkeley campus of the University of California touches off a furious battle between radical student supporters of the idea and conservatives who denounce the Black Panther leader as an "advocate of racism and violence." Governor Reagan is among those who oppose Cleaver; the Board of Regents takes the stand that he should be allowed to appear as a one-time guest lecturer; students demand that all conditions restricting his appearance be rescinded. Cleaver eventually delivers a single lecture entitled "The Roots of Racism." The lecture is well received and regarded as scholarly and moderate.

1968, October 1–20 More than half the professional basketball players opening the season are black. Nearly one third of major league football and baseball players are also black.

1968, October 8 Some 250 Washington, D.C. blacks protest the fatal shooting of a black pedestrian by a motorcycle policeman who reportedly tried to stop the victim on a jaywalking charge. Demonstrators set fires and block traffic until police reinforcements disperse them with tear gas. The patrolman is eventually charged by a federal grand jury and exonerated of guilt.

1968, October 4 Gary Mayor Richard Hatcher and Detroit Congressman John Conyers, members of an all-black National Committee of Inquiry, propose that black voters withhold their support of Democratic nominee Hubert Humphrey unless he takes an unequivocal stand on the war in Vietnam and agrees in advance to support programs designed to cope meaningfully with problems indigenous to all-black communities across the nation.

1968, November 5 Richard Nixon defeats Hubert Humphrey for President in a very close election. Some 90% of the black vote goes to Humphrey despite his weaker advocacy of the black cause than in his previous campaigns. However, blacks are unresponsive to Nixon's "law and order" campaign and promises of aid to blacks wishing to go into business for themselves. In local and state elections, seven blacks become mayors, 97 are elected to state legislatures, Shirley Chisholm becomes the first black woman elected to the House of Representatives. Four hundred blacks are elected to various local offices in the eleven states of the old Confederacy, compared to 70 in 1965.

1968, November 13–19 Two gunbattles involving Panthers in California keep the feud between the party and the police in the national spotlight. On November 13, in Berkeley, one Panther and one patrolman are injured in a shooting fracas after police stop a car whose driver is accused of a traffic violation. Six days later, three police are wounded in a gunfight with eight blacks wanted for questioning in a service station holdup. The eight blacks are in possession of a panel truck identified as a vehicle of "The Black Panther Black Community News Service."

1968, November 27–29 Eldridge Cleaver, Black Panther Minister of Information and Presidential candidate of the Peace and Freedom Party, is sought by police as a parole violator on a fugitive warrant issued in San Francisco. Cleaver is believed to have left the United States for Montreal to attend an international conference of antiwar militants. Local officials ask the FBI to join in the manhunt.

1968, December 1–5 Three members of the Panthers are arrested on charges of carrying out a machine gun attack on a Jersey City police station on November 29. A Panther spokesman claims that a December 1 bombing of party headquarters in Newark is in response to the Jersey City attack. A police sergeant cites the arrest of seven Newark Panthers on November 28 as the cause of the precinct attack. Amid such frequent speculation and wholesale accusations on both sides, little explanation can be offered save the conscientious reporting of the kaleidoscopic incidents and the conflicting versions of what happened.

1969, January 3 After long and entangled debate concerning his qualifications and conduct, the House of Representatives votes to seat Adam Clayton Powell. However, it fines him $25,000 for alleged misuse of payroll funds and travel allowances, and demotes him to freshman status by stripping him of his seniority rank.

1969, January 29 Barely a week after his inauguration, President Nixon stirs the apprehensions of the liberal alliance by postpoining for 60 days a deadline that would have cut off federal funds for five southern school districts which have failed to abolish segregated schooling. HEW secretary Robert Finch asks for more time to study the cases, but others interpret the moves as a calculated and familiar stall.

1969, February 6 President Nixon admits he is not regarded as "a friend by many of our black citizens," professing instead a desire to be a "friend to all the people." At his press conference, he reaffirms his reluctance to cut off federal funds to school districts refusing to foster integration. Nixon appoints only three blacks to important cabinet positions, James Farmer as an Assistant Secretary of Health, Education and Welfare, Arthur Fletcher as an As-

sistant Secretary of Labor, and William Brown III, as Chairman of the Equal Employment Opportunities Commission.

1969, March 10 Confessed murderer James Earl Ray is sentenced to 99 years for the slaying of Dr. Martin Luther King, Jr. The Department of Justice brings no evidence to bear that Ray was part of a larger conspiracy, although it leaves open that possibility by continuing its investigation.

1969, April 8 The Justice Department moves against Cannon Mills, a Southern textile company, accusing it of bias in employment and housing. The move marks the first time the government has exerted legal pressure in the question of company-owned housing facilities which are segregated by design.

1969, April 9 Harvard-trained Clifford Alexander, Jr., resigns as Chairman of the Equal Employment Opportunity Commission (EEOC), citing "a crippling lack of administration support" as the main grounds of his departure. Mr. Alexander alludes specifically to a threat made by Republican Senator Dirksen to have him ousted for harassing businessmen on the issue of job discrimination.

April 19–20 Student members of the campus Afro-American Society seize a student center at Cornell University, protesting, among other things, the alleged harassment of black coeds and the burning of a cross on campus. Whites try unsuccessfully to remove them, and four are injured in the brief skirmish. After the administration yields to their demands, students relinquish control of the building and leave peacefully, though with weapons poised for action. Campus radicals cheer; most students and faculty are appalled.

1969, April 22–26 More than 700 striking Charleston

Armed black students occupied Cornell University building as protest.

Charles Evers (right) *is sworn in as Mayor of Fayette, Mississippi.*

hospital workers are led by Reverend Ralph Abernathy of the Southern Christian Leadership Conference (SCLC) in a march designed to dramatize their deplorable working conditions and draw national support for their unionizing efforts. Coretta Scott King lends her presence to support the strikers. On April 26, 100 black students are thrown in jail when they try to march down the city's main street in support of the workers. National Guardsmen and state troopers on duty in the city arrest over 200 people.

1969, May 2   The Department of Health, Education and Welfare (HEW) authorizes Antioch College to operate an all-black black studies program on the condition that nonblacks are excluded only on the ground that their background is not "relevant" to the courses, not because of arbitrary distinctions based on race, color, or national origin.

1969, May 6   Howard Lee is elected Mayor of Chapel Hill, North Carolina, the first black man to hold such an office in a predominantly white North Carolinian city.

1969, May 13   Charles Evers joins a host of successful black candidates who win assorted political posts in the state of Mississippi. Evers defeats a white incumbent in an election free from violence and harassment and becomes Mayor of Fayette.

1969, May 28   Los Angeles City Councilman Thomas Bradley, a heavy favorite, is upset by incumbent Mayor Sam Yorty in a mayoralty election that is riddled with unsavory campaign tactics and blatant appeals to prejudice. Yorty resorts to unsubstanti-

ated smears and guilt-by-association moves that polarize the voting community and heighten racial tension.

1969, June 6–20   Testimony released in a federal court in Houston, Texas indicates that the telephones of Martin Luther King, Jr. and Elijah Muhammad were tapped by the FBI, despite the fact that President Johnson had ordered a halt to all wiretaps in 1965. The loophole in the order stems from the Attorney General's discretion in reported cases of "national security." Former Attorney General Ramsey Clark labels as misleading the statement FBI Director J. Edgar Hoover made that Robert Kennedy ordered wiretaps on Dr. King.

1969, June 16   The Supreme Court slaps down the House of Representatives' suspension of Harlem Congressman Adam Clayton Powell and terms that action a violation of the U.S. Constitution.

1969, July 3   The Nixon Administration affirms its intention to hold Southern school districts to the September deadline for school desegregation, but its exemption of some districts from the mandate on grounds that they have "bona fide . . . problems causes the NAACP's Roy Wilkins to accuse the government of breaking the law."

1969, July 6   James Forman of the National Black Economic Development Conference receives a check for $15,000 from the Washington Square United Methodist Church in New York City. The church is the first predominantly white organization to come up with some money in the aftermath of Forman's earlier demand made on American churches that they owe 500 million dollars in reparations for helping to perpetuate slavery.

1969, July 9   The Justice Department accuses the Chicago Board of Education and the State Board in Georgia of practicing segregation. The latter group is said to be maintaining a dual system that is unconstitutional, while the former is singled out for segregating faculty.

1969, July 18   The 113-day-old Charleston hospital strike comes to a close. Its most notable achievement is the cooperation achieved between labor and civil rights groups seeking union representation and racial justice.

1969, July 29   Black candidates win four of five seats on the County Commission of Alabama's Green County and also capture two of the five school board seats in a special election victory which Ralph Abernathy calls "the most significant achievement by black men since the Emancipation."

1969, August 1   The Justice Department files suit against the state of Georgia to end segregation in its schools in the first desegregation suit against an entire state. Governor Lester G. Maddox condemns the action as criminal and declares the state will "win the war against these tyrants."

1969, August 18–23 President Nixon nominates Southern judicial conservative Clement Haynsworth, Jr. to occupy the seat vacated by departing Justice Abe Fortas. Investigation of Haynsworth's holdings reveals that the judge tried a 1963 case involving a textile concern depending for supplies on a vending-machine company in which he owned stock.

1969, August 20 Bobby Seale's defense attorney accuses the Justice Department of initiating a national campaign to intimidate and harass the Black Panther Party. Seale, being held on $25,000 bail, is under indictment for the May 1969 slaying of an alleged Panther informer in Connecticut.

1969, August 21–25 The 600 delegates at the National Welfare Rights Organization convention in Detroit assail President Nixon's $1600 annual minimum family assistance figure as inadequate, and call for a figure of $3,200.

1969, August 25–29 Five construction sites in Pittsburgh are closed by several hundred black construction workers and members of the Black Construction Coalition to protest "discriminatory hiring practices." Four hundred angry white workers stage counterdemonstrations on August 28 and 29 to protest the work stoppage agreed to by the construction project owner while negotiations for a black job training project were in progress.

1969, August 26–27 Civil rights lawyers in the Nixon Administration make known their dissatisfaction with the government's request in the application of desegregation guidelines. The lawyers say that the Nixon braintrust is instituting a slowdown in virtually all areas of civil rights enforcement. When news reaches them that the government has called for a delay in Mississippi school integration, more than half of the Justice Department's Civil Rights Division joins in protest against the decision.

1969, September 2 After a comparatively quiet summer, the nation is stunned at the news that Hartford, Connecticut is the scene of widespread ghetto disorders including firebombings and snipings. Scores of people are placed under arrest, and a dusk-to-dawn curfew is imposed.

1969, September 2 Governor Nelson Rockefeller of New York urges a federal takeover of all welfare costs at the meeting of the National Governors Conference in Colorado Springs.

1969, September 3 The Episcopal Church's House of Deputies votes James Forman's Black Economic Development Conference $200,000, part of the 500 million dollars the organization has demanded for injustices to the black man.

1969, September 3 General Leonard F. Chapman, Jr., Marine Corps Commander, orders an end to discrimination against blacks in promotions, assignments, and social activities on marine posts.

1969, September 12 A 105-page report by the U.S. Commission on Civil Rights, chaired by Father Theodore Hesburgh, President of Notre Dame University, charges the Nixon administration with choosing the wrong school desegregation policy and covering its actions with overly optimistic statistics.

1969, September 12 Black militant Robert F. Williams lands in Detroit and is arrested in connection with a kidnapping charge. The kidnapping was supposed to have occurred in North Carolina eight years previously. Since that time Williams had been in self-imposed exile in Cuba, China, and Africa.

1969, September 23 Labor Secretary George P. Shultz orders federally assisted construction projects in Philadelphia to follow the guidelines for minority hiring suggested in the so-called "Philadelphia Plan."

1969, October 17 Dr. Clifton Reginald Wharton, Jr., a black economist from New York City, is elected President of Michigan State University. Dr. Wharton becomes the first black to head a major public and predominantly white university.

1969, October 29 The Supreme Court orders an end to all school desegregation "at once." The decision replaces the Warren court's doctrine of "all deliberate speed," and is regarded as a setback for the Nixon administration.

1969, October 29 Judge Julius J. Hoffman orders Bobby Seale, on trial for conspiracy to incite to riot in Chicago, gagged and chained after Seale disrupts court proceeding by jumping up and shouting insults at the judge.

1969, November 4 Carl B. Stokes is reelected Mayor of Cleveland. He is the first black mayor of a major American city.

1969, November 5 Black Panther leader Bobby Seale is sentenced to four years in prison for contempt of court by Chicago 7 Judge Julius Hoffman.

1969, November 21 The Senate rejects the nomination of Clement F. Haynsworth, Jr. of South Carolina to the Supreme Court by a vote of 55 to 45.

1969, December 4 Two Black Panther leaders, Fred Hampton and Mark Clark, are killed by police in Chicago, four others are wounded. Panthers charge police with premeditated murder and a Grand Jury later calls police action "excessive."

Supreme Court post for Clement F. Haynsworth was rejected by Senate.

1970, January 2 J. Edgar Hoover, Director of the Federal Bureau of Investigation, states that in 1969, there were over 100 attacks on police by "hate-type" black groups, among which he includes the Black Panthers.

1970, January 3 Mississippi Governor John Bell Williams announces his intention to submit to the state legislature a proposal to authorize income tax credits of up to $500 a year for contributors to "private" educational institutions. The plan is designed to create a "workable alternative" to school desegregation. That same day, HEW reports that a comprehensive survey indicates that 61% of the nation's black students and 65.6% of its white students were attending segregated schools as of 1968.

1970, January 5–6 Black children are enrolled in three formerly all-white Mississippi districts under the watchful eyes of federal marshals and Justice Department officials. Scores of white parents picket the schools, while others keep their children home, relying on the new private schools which have been chartered to circumvent desegregation. HEW Secretary Robert Finch supports a countermove to cut off tax exemptions for the 300–400 "private schools" which have opened in the South since the 1964 Civil Rights Act was enacted.

1970, January 10–23 Four southern governors—Maddox of Georgia, Brewer of Alabama, McKeithen of Louisiana, and Kirk of Florida—promise to reject all busing plans designed for their states by the federal government or the courts. Each moves independently to block the busing order. Maddox asks the legislature to abolish compulsory attendance; McKeithen reveals no plan, but describes himself as one "drawing the line in the dust"; Brewer denies the courts have the constitutional authority to order busing as a device to achieve racial balance and promises to use his full executive powers to prevent it; Kirk vows to issue an executive order to block further desegregation of Florida schools.

1970, January 12 The Supreme Court refuses to review the ruling of an Ohio State Court which upholds an equal employment plan comparable to the Nixon Administration's "Philadelphia Plan." The plan requires state contractors to give assurances that they will employ a specified number of black workers in projects constructed with federal funds or sponsored *in toto* by the federal government. The Ohio contractor who brought suit in the case had refused to provide such assurances.

1970, January 13 A three-judge federal court orders the Internal Revenue Service to refuse tax-exemption status for more segregated private academies in Mississippi. Those already in existence are immune from the ruling.

1970, January 14 The Supreme Court overturns a December 1, 1969 Circuit Court of Appeals ruling which sets September 1, 1970 as a pupil desegregation deadline date for six Southern states. The Court sets February 1, 1970 as the new deadline, rejecting a Justice Department bid for postponement. Four Justices concur without reservation in reaffirming the conclusion of the Court's October 29, 1969 ruling in *Alexander* v. *Holmes Board of Education* (see that entry). The words "at once" are requoted from the Alexander decision.

1970, January 15 Though the day is not yet a national holiday, the anniversary of the birth of Martin Luther King, Jr. is celebrated with impressive ceremonies, eulogies, and church services in many parts of the country. Public schools are closed in many cities; in others, they are kept open for formal study of Dr. King's work and utterances. In Atlanta, Coretta King dedicates the Martin Luther King, Jr. Memorial Center, which includes his home, the Ebenezer Baptist Church, and the crypt where his remains are housed.

1970, January 16 Black Panther Warren Kimbro, head of the party's New Haven chapter, pleads guilty to second-degree murder in the killing of alleged Panther informer Alex Rackley. Kimbro faces a possible life term.

1970, January 19 Florida Governor Claude Kirk petitions the U.S. Supreme Court for a rehearing of its January 14 ruling ordering immediate school desegregation. Kirk claims the state is "financially and physically unable" to meet the Court's deadline, and says he will instruct school districts not to change their calendar in mid-year. Two attorneys representing school districts in Louisiana inform the Court that they are encountering insurmountable difficulties in complying with the Court order.

1970, January 19–20 The nomination to the U.S. Supreme Court of G. Harrold Carswell draws the immediate fire of civil rights advocates.

1970, January 20 A Los Angeles District Court judge orders the Pasadena school district to submit a desegregation plan for its public schools no later than February 16, 1970. Pasadena is the first northern school district pressed by the federal government to produce an educational plan in which no single school has a majority of nonwhite students. The plan is slated to take effect in September 1970.

1970, January 21–27 Civil rights organizations and labor groups begin a salvo of criticism against the Carswell Supreme Court nomination. On January 21, the NAACP leads off by condemning his "pro-segregation record." Two days later, the SCLC's Ralph Abernathy sends a telegram to Senate leaders pleading for "reassurance to the black community that there is . . . understanding and support . . . for our needs." AFL-CIO President George Meany calls the appointment "a slap in the face to the nation's black citizens." Testifying before the Senate Judiciary Committee on January 27, Carswell states: "I am not a racist. I have no notions, secretive or otherwise, of racial superiority." This statement contrasts sharply with a 1948 remark that Carswell would yield to no man "in the firm, vigorous belief in the principles of white supremacy." Carswell is also accused of helping form a private golf club in 1956 in an effort to prevent desegregation.

1970, February 1 Three districts in Louisiana, two in Mississippi, and one in Florida comply with the Supreme Court order setting February 1 as the date for establishing integration. About 15 others are granted delays by district court judges, whereas 20 districts choose to disobey the order either by closing schools or supporting parent-organized boycotts. Vice President Agnew announces a Presidential plan to appoint a cabinet-level committee to advise the districts on how best to implement the court's order without causing wholesale disruption.

Elsewhere, South Carolina (January 27) announces that it will comply with the desegregation mandate.

1970, February 5–9 Senators John Stennis and Strom Thurmond demand that northern school districts be obliged to observe federal desegregation guidelines in the same way as their southern counterparts. On February 9, Connecticut Senator Abraham Ribicoff endorses the Stennis Amendment, a rider to the House-passed education bill then before the Senate. The Stennis bill is a virtual duplication of the text of the 1969 New York State bill prohibiting the assignment of students to schools according to race. Ribicoff condemns northern liberals who blame the South for resistance to integration while, at the same time, failing to recognize and assail similar policies in the North. He chides northern communities for their "systematic and consistent" denial of educational opportunity to black children.

1970, February 6 Some one third of Denver buses slated to put into effect the city's plan to achieve racial balance by busing the city's school children are destroyed by dynamite bombs believed to have been set by fanatic opponents of busing.

1970, February 7 The NAACP asks the U.S. government to examine and ban a fourth-grade Alabama history textbook that "glorifies the Ku Klux Klan" by claiming that the vigilante organization appeared only sporadically, and then only to prevent carpetbaggers from taking refuge behind unjust laws.

1970, February 11–16 Black neurosurgeon Dr. Thomas W. Matthew, head of the National Economic Growth and Reconstruction Organization (NEGRO), criticizes the NAACP for its continued harassment of Supreme Court nominee G. Harrold Carswell. Matthew endorses Carswell, citing his "public renunciation of racist views." The Senate Judiciary Committee clears the Carswell nomination on February 16.

1970, February 16 President Nixon establishes a cabinet-level task force to assist and counsel local school districts which have been ordered to desegregate their school immediately. The objective is to spare the public school system undue disruption while, at the same time, insuring compliance with the law.

1970, February 16 Joe Frazier knocks out Jimmy Ellis to assume undisputed possession of the heavyweight championship of the world. After the match, Frazier indicates he will retire unless a match can be arranged with Muhammad Ali, the former title holder.

1970, February 17 Leon E. Panetta, Director of the Office for Civil Rights in the Department of Health, Education and Welfare (HEW), resigns in protest against the Nixon Administration's lax enforcement of the nation's civil rights laws. Panetta states that, though Nixon himself may be sincere in wishing for greater unity among Americans, he is surrounded by others who are perfectly willing to subvert that goal if it is necessary to win the next election.

1970, February 18 The Senate passes, by a 56–36 margin, an amendment to deny federal funds to *all school districts* whose racial imbalance stems from residential segregation. Mississippi Senator Stennis hails the move as an endorsement of his proposal to force northern districts to grapple with the same guidelines and policies which are being imposed on the South. The text of the Stennis amendment reads as follows:

It is the policy of the U.S. that guidelines and criteria pursuant to Title VI of the Civil Rights Act of 1964 and Section 182 of the Elementary and Secondary Amendments of 1966 shall be applied uniformly in all regions of the U.S. in dealing with conditions of segregation by race, whether *de jure* or *de facto,* in the schools of the local education agencies of any state without regard to the origin or cause of such segregation.

1970, February 18 Hearings on the extension of the 1965 Voting Rights Act open in Congress with the NAACP's Clarence Mitchell seeking to reinstate the government's power to veto allegedly discriminatory voting laws in the South. The House amendments to the law seek to curb the government's veto power, a policy which would reduce the pressure on these states to conform to federally approved voting guidelines. The use of federal registrars and the reliance on the enforcement power of the Attorney General's office have added almost 900,000 blacks to the voting rolls in the South.

1970, February 19 Southerners in the House and Senate incorporate into two appropriations bills riders designed to restore "freedom-of-choice" school plans and to prevent the federal government from resorting to busing as a vehicle to promote racial balance.

1970, February 21–23 Texas Governor Preston Smith recommends a statewide referendum to give voters the opportunity to declare approval or rejection of public school busing. Governors Maddox and McKeithen sign bills prohibiting busing and student/teacher transfers to achieve racial balance. Governor Brewer calls a special session of the legislature to sponsor a similar bill for Alabama.

1970, February 21–25 Three gasoline bombs explode in front of the New York home of State Supreme Court Justice John Murtaugh, presiding judge at the Panther hearings. Though no one is injured, there is some property damage and a warning

scrawled on the pavement: "Free the Panther 21." On February 25, Murtaugh halts the hearings, demanding from the defendants a written pledge to observe American courtroom procedures.

1970, February 28 The Senate approves the Education Appropriations Bill after first voting down three southern riders aimed at diluting the government's power to enforce school desegregation laws. The Senate succeeds entirely in blocking southern efforts to reinstate "freedom of choice" plans. The Mathias Amendment weakens the restrictive language of the House's antibusing amendment by making it conform to the requirements of the Constitution, which already required integration.

1970, February 28 The "benign neglect" memorandum from Daniel Patrick Moynihan to President Nixon is revealed. In this memo, Moynihan, domestic advisor to the President, counseled him that "the time may have come when the issue of race could benefit from a period of 'benign neglect.'" Moynihan explains that the memo was intended to suggest ways that the "extraordinary black progress" in the last decade could be "consolidated." However, black leaders such as Bayard Rustin and Representative John Conyers, charge that the memo is "symptomatic of a calculated, aggressive, systematic effort of the Nixon Administration to wipe out civil rights progress of the past 20 years."

1970, March 3 State troopers intervene with riot guns and tear gas to dispense an angry mob, armed with ax handles and baseball bats, that smashes windows and menaces a bus transporting 39 black students to an all-white school in Lamar, South Carolina. Two empty buses are overturned; both troopers and mob members are injured, none severely.

1970, March 4–7 White House Aide John D. Ehrlichman says he is opposed to school integration if its real purpose is to foster social integration without an accompanying improvement in the caliber of education. Sociologist James S. Coleman, however, suggests that integration is the most effective instrument yet discovered to upgrade the education of poor black children.

1970, March 6 The Mississippi State Senate clears a tax relief bill designed to grant financial support to white parents who intend to enroll their children in private academies.

1970, March 9 The U.S. Supreme Court orders the Memphis school system, consisting of 74,000 black students and 60,000 whites, to end racial segregation, and remands the case to a lower court where it issues instructions to develop an effective desegregation plan.

1970, March 21 Federal Reserve Board member Andrew Brimmer, a leading black economist, declares that there is "a deepening schism" in the black community, despite the economic gains that are being recorded. Upon studying the figures further, Brimmer concludes that the gap is widening between the able and the less able, between the more prepared and those with few skills. In Brimmer's view, this accounts, in part for the growing militancy at the bottom end of the scale, where the disparity is most keenly felt.

1970, March 24 President Nixon's long-awaited statement on school desegregation expected with hope by some blacks, affirms his "personal belief" that the 1954 Supreme Court decision (*Brown* v. *Board of Education*) is right "in both constitutional and human terms." The President vows to bring the full force of his office and authority to bear toward eliminating *de jure* segregation, but balks at applying the same standard to the question of *de facto* segregation, stating that the courts have not yet provided clear-cut mandates in this domain. Nixon, however, rejects the concept of school busing and offers instead financial aid to upgrade ghetto schools. Most civil rights groups regard the statement as bland, evasive, and retrogressive.

1970, March 25 Self-imposed exile Stokely Carmichael testifies before a closed session of the Senate Internal Security Subcommittee in Washington, D.C. Carmichael discusses his travels and associations in Cuba, Africa, China, and Puerto Rico, and explains that his return is linked to his desire to curb drug abuse in the black community. Some observers brand the sessions "an inquisition," others are vexed that they were uninformed about schedules for the proceedings.

1970, April 7 HEW Secretary Finch predicts the number of black children in schools with whites will double by the fall of 1970. Finch maintains that busing will be one of the practices used to enforce desegregation, claiming that 90% of the South's schools already utilize buses for comparable functions. The Secretary admits, however, that the decision as to whether discrimination is *de facto* or *de jure* will have to be rendered on an individual basis.

1970, April 7 The recessed pretrial hearings of 13 Black Panthers are resumed in a courtroom atmosphere of calm and restraint on both sides. Justice Murtaugh, unable to obtain a signed pledge from the defendants to uphold the decorum of the court, proceeds nonetheless with the legal issue at hand.

1970, April 7 The Detroit school board approves a busing plan for some 3,000 high school students and announces the initiation of a decentralization

G. Harrold Carswell, Nixon's second unsuccessful nominee, had avowed white supremacy.

plan aimed at dispersing white minority students among the city's secondary schools. In Detroit, 63% of the system's 294,000 students are nonwhite, as are 42% of the teachers.

1970, April 8 In what is regarded as a major Administration defeat, Supreme Court nominee G. Harrold Carswell is rejected by the Senate in a 51–45 vote. Among the key swing senators who influence the outcome are Winston Prouty of Vermont and Margaret Chase Smith of Maine. Instrumental in the defeat of Carswell are the quiet and diplomatic moves of Senator Edward A. Brooke. Brooke's gentle prodding of Republican colleagues and his constant reminders that Carswell's record not only stamps him as racially biased but as judicially intemperate are held as vital factors influencing some of the last-minute shifts which upended Carswell.

1970, April 11 The Commission on Civil Rights criticizes President Nixon's March 24 policy statement as inadequate, overcautious, and indicative of a possible retreat in the area of school integration. The panel maintains that *de jure* segregation is not confined to the South, and indicates that the President could apply great pressure to eliminate it in this area of the country as well.

1970, April 20   Sociologist Kenneth Clark, Director of the Metropolitan Applied Research Center, testifies that segregation is even more damaging to white school children than to those from minority groups. Clark maintains that the President's March 24 statement constitutes an important withdrawal from the situation, a failure to assess its moral, ethical, and educational implications, and a slackening of the momentum generated by the courts and by some segments of society.

1970, April 22–23   A student strike is called at Yale in support of the eight Black Panthers awaiting trial in New Haven. Yale President Kingman Brewster asserts he is "skeptical" that such black revolutionaries can have a fair trial in the United States.

1970, May 4   A warrant is issued for the arrest of H. Rap Brown who again fails to appear in court to resume his trial. Brown's bond is forfeited, and the FBI is asked to join Maryland authorities in the search. Days later, Brown's name is added to the list of the nation's 10 most-wanted fugitives.

1970, May 8   All charges against seven Panthers indicted on January 30 on charges of instigating a shootout with Chicago police are dropped. The State Attorney admits that the evidence gathered may not satisfy "judicial standards of proof."

1970, May 12   Six blacks are shot and 20 other people are wounded in Augusta, Georgia, during a night of violence punctuated by looting, burning, and sniper activity. The immediate cause of the violence is said to be the killing of a black youth in a county jail a few days earlier. Autopsies of the slain blacks establish that they were shot in the back. The *New York Times* later reports that at least three of the dead were unarmed bystanders.

1970, May 14–17   Two black students are shot and killed after a night of violence outside a women's dormitory at Jackson State College in Mississippi. Witnesses charge that police simply moved in and indiscriminately blasted the residence hall with shotguns. President Nixon dispatches Justice Department officials to ferret out the facts, but contradictory explanations make it impossible to assemble a wholly coherent story. On May 17, the Mississippi United Front vows to provide students and other groups with independent protection.

1970, May 23   A five-day, 100-mile march against repression ends in downtown Atlanta with a rally by the SCLC and the NAACP. Speakers include Ralph Abernathy, Coretta King, and Senator George McGovern. Jointly, they condemn racism, the Vietnam war, student killings at Kent State and Jackson State, and alleged police brutality in Augusta.

1970, May 29   A California Court of Appeals over-

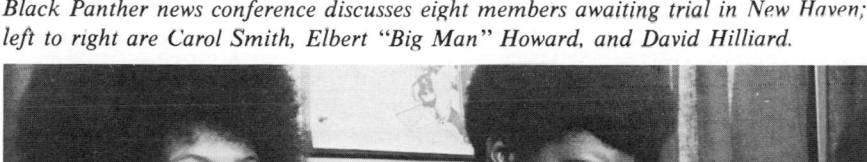

Black Panther news conference discusses eight members awaiting trial in New Haven; left to right are Carol Smith, Elbert "Big Man" Howard, and David Hilliard.

U.S. Attorney General John Mitchell (left) *and Dr. John Peoples, president of Jackson State College, examine campus dormitory where two black youths were killed by police bullets. Bullet-riddled windows bear out eyewitness charges that police simply moved in and blasted the residence hall with shotguns.*

turns the manslaughter conviction of Huey Newton, finding that procedural errors had deprived the Black Panther leader of a fair trial.

1970, June 13 The NAACP announces a $50,000 grant to a panel of independent citizens created in December 1969 to study clashes between the Black Panthers and the police in various cities across the United States. The commission, hoping for funds from the Ford Foundation, is disappointed at the lack of interest shown by this group, and confesses it will be unable to function until it can raise its budget to $150,000.

1970, June 29 Spottswood Robinson and a host of other black leaders who address the sixty-first annual NAACP convention brand the Nixon Administration antiblack and catalog a list of grievances to support their contention. These include the signing of defense contracts with firms practicing discrimination, the retreat on enforcement of school desegregation, the nominations of Supreme Court Justices whose record and outlook brand them as insensitive to black aspirations, and the systematic attempt to emasculate the Voting Rights Act.

1970, July 1 Kenneth Gibson becomes Mayor of Newark, New Jersey, defeating Hugh Addonizio, whose administration had been racked by charges of kickbacks from contractors doing business with the city.

1970, July 10 The Internal Revenue Service an-

nounces its intention to tax private academies practicing racial discrimination in their admissions policies. The greatest impact of the policy is expected to be felt in the South, although schools there will presumably receive ample time to adjust their policies should they be branded racist. Thus, the new policy promises these schools sufficient flexibility to avoid immediate revocation of their tax-exempt status.

1970, July 19 Whitney Young refuses to follow the hard line taken by the NAACP in denouncing Administration policy toward the black. Instead, Young characterizes that policy as "pro-political," designed exclusively to win political votes from a beguiled majority. To offset this "white magic" policy, Young encourages the total spectrum of black groups—from the Panthers to the Baptists—to enter the arena of decision-making by forging a coalition of agreement on vital issues affecting the total black community.

1970, August 1 Figures released by the Pentagon reveal a decline in the proportion of black fatalities in the Indo-China War. In 1969 blacks accounted for 13.5% of battle deaths and represented only 9.5% of troops there. In the first three months of 1970, however, blacks represented about 10% of the total force and 8.5% of battle fatalities.

1970, August 7 A dramatic shootout outside the San Rafael courthouse results in the death of Superior

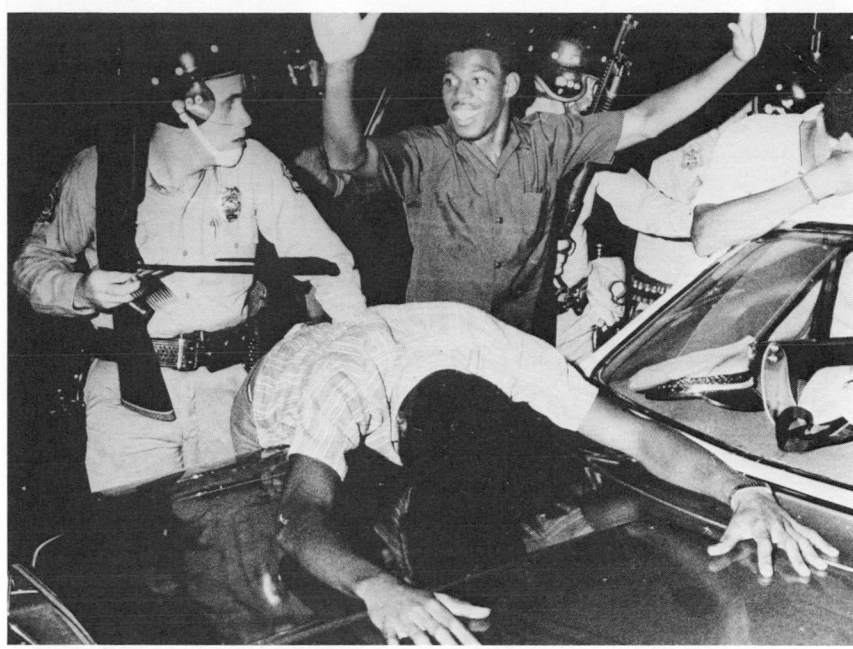

Police search three suspects in Melbourne, Florida, where over 600 youths took to streets with rocks and firebombs during several hours of racial violence. Thirty-five people were arrested.

Court Judge Harold Haley and three other men—all black prisoners on trial. The shootout follows a daring escape plan in which weapons are smuggled into the courtroom, while the court is in session, by a 17-year-old youth. The prisoners take control of the court, seize the judge and members of the jury at gunpoint, and try to effect their escape. Police reinforcements open fire on the escape van, killing its driver and the other fugitives. The judge, too, is slain by a shotgun blast from the weapon of one of the fugitives. Later investigation traces the sale of the weapons used in the shootout to Angela Davis, controversial UCLA professor and longtime defender of the so-called Soledad Brothers. Davis, a self-admitted Communist, has been the center of considerable dispute over her right to teach at UCLA. Though dismissed by the Board of Regents, she has strong faculty and student backing, and benefits from a court decision invalidating dismissal for political beliefs. After the shootout, Davis disappears. In accordance with California law, she is charged with murder and kidnapping. The FBI places her on its list of the 10 most-wanted fugitives in the nation.

1970, August 29 Some whites in Fort Pierce, Florida threaten to remove bodies of relatives from a local all-white cemetery, after a federal judge orders it to accept the remains of Poindexter E. Williams, a black soldier killed in action in Vietnam. The burial plot had been given to William's family by a white women.

1970, September 1–10 Some 300,000 black children are integrated in over 200 southern school districts,

but parental boycotts and delaying tactics by states and cities slow desegregation pace. Whites opposed to desegregation are encouraged by the Nixon Administration's "southern policy" which delays enforcement of integration orders and seeks exemptions for private "academies." However, the

Whitney Young urged the total spectrum of black groups—from the Panthers to the Baptists—to forge a coalition on vital issues affecting the total black community.

Rifle-bearing policeman guards downtown Asbury Park, New Jersey, after resort town was rocked by several days of disturbances.

Internal Revenue Service revokes a large number of these exemptions.

1970, September 12 California's Governor Reagan signs a bill forbidding busing of school children without the written consent of their parents or guardians.

1970, September 13 Eldridge Cleaver, in exile in Algiers, presides at an "international section" meeting of the Black Panther Party. The Algerian government had granted the party status of a "liberation movement."

1970, October 1 A three-judge federal court convening in Buffalo declares void New York States antibusing law which made it illegal for appointed school boards to reshuffle pupil assignment plans for the purpose of achieving racial balance. The law had been copied by several southern school districts to forestall desegregation. Earlier, Governor Reagan had signed into California law a bill prohibiting the busing of students "for any . . . reason without the written permission of the parent or guardian."

1970, October 1–30 Two northern cities, Pontiac, Michigan and Trenton, New Jersey, are the scenes of violent clashes connected with integration efforts. Four whites and one black are shot in Pontiac. Trenton schools are shut for two days following fight between 100 white and black students.

1970, October 12 Father Theodore M. Hesburgh, Chairman of the U.S. Commission on Civil Rights, announces in a 1,115-page report that there has been a "major breakdown" in the enforcement of national mandates outlawing racial discrimination. The Commission maintains that the absence of pressures from the White House contributes to the general breakdown in the enforcement of pertinent laws.

1970, October 13 On October 19, the NAACP files suit against HEW, charging it with general and calculated default in enforcement of desegregation guidelines.

1970, October 13 Angela Davis is arrested in New York and arraigned in federal court on charges of unlawful flight to avoid prosecution for her alleged role in a California kidnap-escape plot. Seized with Davis is David R. Poindexter, a 36-year-old Chicago black accused of knowingly aiding a fugitive.

1970, October 19   The government dismisses conspiracy charges against Bobby Seale in connection with the Chicago riot of 1968, but Seale must still contend with a four-year prison term for contempt of court plus kidnapping and murder charges in connection with the slaying in New Haven of Alex Rackley.

1970, October 24-November 24   Violent confrontations erupt in a number of northern cities between police and extremist black groups. In Cicero, Illinois, a group of blacks fire at the police station. There are no injuries. In Detroit, 15 blacks, reputedly connected with the National Committee to Combat Fascism, are arrested after the slaying of a black policeman. In Arkansas, a riot erupts on the Cumming Prison Farm following agitation for racially segregated living quarters.

1970, November 5   Shooting and fires break out in Henderson, North Carolina, where blacks had been protesting a decision to reopen an all-black school. The National Guard was called out to restore order and the Board of Education agreed to close the school. Over 100 arrests are made.

1970, November 30   Senator Abraham Ribicoff of Connecticut introduces legislation to bring about total integration of the nation's schools, both urban and suburban. The target date: 1982.

1970, December 7   James Farmer resigns as Assistant Secretary for Administration of the Department of Health, Education and Welfare. Farmer declines to criticize Nixon Administration policies.

1970, December 17   A Pentagon task force reports "frustration and anger" among black troops stationed in Germany. At stake is the morale of black troops subjected to racial indignities by the civilian population.

1970, December 30   A U.S. Court of Appeals in Philadelphia rules that the Department of Housing and Urban Development must promote fair housing when it considers applications for mortgage insurance and rent supplements.

CONSOLIDATION AND REVERSES (1971–1975)

The period between 1971 and 1975 was full of contrasts. Political leaders increasingly cooled to the political and economic demands of the black electorate, yet there were more black officeholders than at any time in American history, many elected in areas where whites comprise a majority. Opposition to school integration spread from the South to the North, and within the black community, but more blacks than ever were attending integrated schools and colleges. Discontent among blacks in the Armed Forces was manifest, particularly in the Navy, but there were more black servicemen and officers than ever. Many blacks, popularly classified as radicals, were apparently singled out for surveillance, harassment, and prosecution by federal and local officials, but black defendants were successful in a number of landmark courtroom battles. The federal government and much of the business sector clearly failed to follow up on the promise of the civil rights legislation and job training programs of the 1960s, yet more blacks than ever held skilled and responsible positions.

Much of the period was ugly. An increasing number of politicians appealed to, even stimulated, the fears and prejudices of white "ethnics." Instances of extralegal action by the police seemed to increase. But blacks increasingly united, at a series of caucuses and conventions, to present their demands and proclaim pride in their race and culture. This closing of the ranks was symbolized at the Gary Convention in 1972 where Coretta King, widow of the Reverend Martin Luther King, Jr., and Bobby Seale, a leader of the Black Panthers, sat side by side on the same podium.

1971, January 1   James A. Floyd, a black, is appointed Mayor of Princeton, New Jersey, an affluent university town. His Chief of Police is also black.

1971, January 4   Reverend Leon Howard Sullivan is elected to the Board of Directors of General Motors, the first black man to participate in the direction of a U.S. auto company.

1971, January 5   Bethlehem Steel is charged with job bias through the use of a seniority system which effectively discriminates against blacks. Bethlehem denies the charge, but agrees to establish new hiring, training, and promotion quotas for black employees.

1971, January 6   J. Edgar Hoover reports that attacks on police by black extremists are increasing, but that racial incidents in schools are declining. He concludes that America is "far from the realization of racial harmony."

1971, January 16   Preliminary reports on 1970 census indicate that since 1960 black population in cities increased 3 million and white urban population decreased about 2.5 million. Reports also indicate that 1.4 million blacks emigrated from the South in the 1960s and nearly half of these settled in New York or California. Since 1940, the percentage of blacks living in the South declined from 77 to 53%.

1971, February 4   Eight black federal employees file suit in federal court claiming that the principal test qualifying college graduates for civil service posts is "culturally and racially discriminatory." Defendants in the suit include HUD Secretary Romney.

1971, March 8 FBI files stolen from a Pennsylvania office and released to the press reveal that in November 1970 J. Edgar Hoover ordered an investigation of all groups "organized to project the demands of black (college) students, because they posed a threat to the nation's stability and security."

1971, March 29 President Nixon grants audience to the Congressional black caucus that had been trying to see him for months. The black Congressmen request stronger welfare services, desegregation, housing, and social justice programs. President Nixon reportedly promises stronger enforcement of civil rights laws. In May, he promises "jobs, income and tangible benefits." Caucus leaders express disappointment.

1971, April 8 Heavyweight champion Joe Frazier becomes the first black man to address the South Carolina Legislature since Reconstruction. He chides the Legislature for not having invited a black sooner.

1971, April 23 The African Heritage Studies Association meeting in Baton Rouge, Louisiana, urges black scholars to study their African heritage and use it to unify their "fragmented race."

1971, April 30 The Joint Center for Political Studies in Washington, D.C. reports that 1,860 blacks now hold elective office in the United States; almost four times the 475 who held office in 1967. However, only three of every 1,000 officeholders in the United States are black, while blacks now represent 12% of the population.

1971, May 4 Georgia's Governor Carter says that it is fortunate the North forced the South to deal with its racial problems and that the South now has a healthier racial climate than the North. Governor Carter's remarks come a week after Tom Wicker, Southern-born columnist for the *New York Times,* noted that Carter and Governor West of South Carolina believe that white southerners are tired of old racial patterns and think the battle to maintain them has been lost.

1971, May 5 A riot erupts in the Brownsville section of Brooklyn, New York after thousands of residents take to streets to protest cuts in state welfare, Medicaid, food stamps, and educational programs. One policeman is shot; 12 are injured. Residents blame police for firing first shots. Police say it was in self-defense. The government is forced by a District Judge to release David Hilliard, Chief of Staff of the Black Panther Party, when it refuses to reveal wiretaps of Hilliard conversations. Hilliard had been arrested on charges of threatening the life of President Nixon during a speech in San Francisco.

1971, May 13 Thirteen Black Panthers are acquitted on all of 156 counts of conspiracy to bomb police stations and department stores in New York. The trial lasts nine months, the longest in the history of New York City.

1971, May 17 Senator McGovern of South Dakota urges the government to divert $31 billion of current federal spending in an effort to end racial discrimination by the end of the century. Dr. Milton Eisenhower, former Chairman of President Johnson's Commission on Causes and Preventions of Violence, warns that the United States faces a racial war if it does not remedy the social injustice, inequitable law enforcement, and easy availability of firearms that pervade the nation.

1971, June 1 By a vote of 5 to 4 the Supreme Court declares unconstitutional a Cincinnati city ordinance making it unlawful for small groups of people to loiter in an annoying manner in public places. Blacks claimed the ordinance had been used by police to harass them. Other cities passed similar laws in recent years.

1971, June 2 President Nixon invites a group of 36 black Republicans from various parts of the country to the White House for a briefing on his replies to the Congressional black caucus. The meeting occurs just before representatives of the Congressional caucus are to appear on a television program to criticize the President's response to their demands. The White House denies that it is considering a countercaucus.

1971, June 4 The Department of Labor announces it is removing support from the voluntary "Chicago Plan," which was to hire 4,000 blacks and Spanish-speaking Americans for construction jobs on federal projects. After 18 months, less than 900 had been accepted in training programs and only a few had been admitted to Chicago construction unions. Plans are to replace the Chicago Plan with a compulsory program similar to the Philadelphia Plan which requires a quota on federal construction projects costing more than $500,000.

1971, June 7 The Supreme Court rules unanimously that people can sue in Civil Court against individuals who conspire to deprive them of their civil rights. The decision orders a hearing in the Federal District Court of Mississippi on a suit by four blacks who were beaten by two whites who mistook them for civil rights workers. The decision reverses a 1951 decision that such suits could only be filed against public officials.

1971, June 15 By a vote of 5 to 4 the Supreme Court rules that a community can close publicly owned recreational facilities rather than desegregate them.

The ruling upholds the closing of the Jackson, Mississippi swimming pools in 1963 after federal courts ordered them integrated. Justice Hugo Black, known as a stalwart of integration, wrote the majority decision, a factor widely interpreted as indicating growing resistance of the court to expanding integration. Jackson contended it closed pools to both races from economic need and desire to avert violence.

1971, June 15 Governor King of New Mexico summons the National Guard to quell a disturbance attributed to marauding bands of blacks, Chicanos, and white "hippies." Thirty-three people including four policemen are injured and some 200 are arrested. Violence started after a public rock concert was canceled and five youths were arrested for drinking. The Black Berets, a coalition of Chicanos and blacks, is allowed to hold a meeting in a public park at which the state Attorney General promises to investigate charges of police brutality.

1971, June 24 Secretary of Defense Laird states that civilian authorities in the Johnson Administration, not the military, ordered the Army to spy on black leaders after the riots following the assassination of Martin Luther King, Jr. in 1968. The Administration's directive was implemented after Clark Clifford, then Secretary of Defense, ordered the establishment of a riot command center at the Pentagon. In a related statement, J. Edgar Hoover, Director of the Federal Bureau of Investigation declares that terrorism by black extremists is rising and necessitates more federal investigation. A spokesman for the New York City Police Department states that the slaying of a white and a black policeman in Harlem may signal the beginning of guerrilla warfare by radical blacks against the police, but feels the shootings were directed more against the "establishment" than against whites.

1971, June 27 James Meredith announces that he is returning to Mississippi from New York because the South now has a better racial climate than the North. Meredith says he will try to get blacks to concentrate more on attaining economic power.

1971, June 28 By an 8 to 0 vote, with Justice Marshall abstaining, the Supreme Court overturns draft evasion charges against Muhammad Ali. In its decision, the Court agreed that Ali, a Black Muslim, was objecting to military service sincerely and on religious grounds, rather than on a political basis, as the Department of Justice had charged.

1971, July 5 Addressing the annual convention of the NAACP, Roy Wilkins, Executive Director, states that young black activists differ most markedly from their predecessors in their distrust of white men. Black youth, he adds, may have repudiated, NAACP's "slow and careful methods," but not its basic philosophy. Indeed, he states, most contemporary black groups have adopted policies that are essentially variations of NAACP themes.

1971, July 17 Vice President Agnew, while traveling from Africa to Spain, criticizes American blacks who have "arrogated unto themselves the positions of black leaders and spend their time in querulous complaint and constant recrimination against the rest of society instead of undertaking constructive action." Agnew adds that American black leaders, who he would not identify, could learn much from African leaders, who more truly represent the wishes of their constituents. American blacks, says Agnew, refuse to recognize efforts made on their behalf. Black leaders criticizing Agnew's remarks include R. L. Grant, Special Assistant to HUD, Assistant Secretary Hyde, and Representative William Clay of Missouri, who reportedly charges that the Vice President is "seriously ill" and then refuses a demand of Republican House Leader Gerald Ford that he apologize to the Vice President. Grant is dismissed from his post on July 30 by HUD Secretary Romney.

1971, July 24–27 Fifteen blacks are arrested and several hospitalized during racial disturbances in Columbus, Georgia following the dismissal of eight black policemen. Firebombings and snipings are reported. Seventy-five state troopers are summoned to maintain order as both black and white communities become apprehensive of bloodshed.

1971, August 4 The U.S. Civil Rights Commission writes detailed recommendations to Representative Wilbur Mills, Chairman of the House Ways and Means Committee, warning that without strong antidiscrimination provisions the Administration's $5 billion revenue-sharing plan will be used to continue racial discrimination. Representative Mills notes that these recommendations confirm his opposition to revenue sharing because they threaten state and local governments with extensive federal controls.

1971, August 7–14 Julian Bond, a member of the Georgia House of Representatives, tours his state to spark the political interests of blacks who remain unregistered six years after passage of Voting Rights Act. Bond notes that due to a blend of apathy and activism many blacks do not perceive the ballot as an effective political weapon that can be used to bring a change in their lives. Bond cites as an example the failure of blacks in 1970 to elect black officials in an area where they were a majority of registered voters. However, leaders of the Southern Leadership Conference announce that their goal of electing a Southern black to Congress is feasible in view of the redistricting in a number of southern states.

1971, August 21 Roy Innis, Executive Director of CORE, upon his return from a four-week African trip, urges massive American support for black African interests, including a Washington lobby, economic assistance, and a response to military threats from foreign attacks. Innis includes Caribbean and South American countries in his definition of Africa.

1971, August 18–23 Eleven members of the Republic of New Africa, including I. Obadele, leader of the organization, are charged with murder and assault of federal officers after the death of Lieutenant I. Skinner, a Mississippi policeman. Skinner was shot when police and FBI agents raided the Jackson headquarters of the Republic of New Africa, a black separatist organization, in order to serve fugitive warrants on three members. The FBI claims that the separatists were tipped off about the coming raid by informers hired and paid by the FBI. Mississippi Attorney General Summer says the incident would not have occurred if U.S. Attorney General John Mitchell had complied with a request made by the state for action to be taken against the group. Following the death of Lieutenant Skinner, the District Attorney of Hinds County asks a special grand jury to charge the 11 separatists with treason and requests the Justice Department to allow these charges to take precedence over any federal prosecution.

1971, August 28 Blacks differ on events leading to the death of George Jackson, author of *Soledad Brothers,* and a folk hero to many black and white radicals. Jackson was shot and killed while trying to escape from San Quentin Prison in California. Some supporters of Jackson claim he was "set-up" for assassination. Others feel the official version is essentially correct and that Jackson was shot during a serious, premeditated escape attempt.

1971, August 30 Roy Wilkins, at ceremonies honoring his seventieth birthday, reports that the term "colored" must remain part of his organization's title because the initials NAACP are too well known to drop.

1971, August 31 The indictment is revealed of 14 Chicago lawmen for conspiring to obstruct justice in the investigation of the December 1969 deaths of Mark Clark and Fred Hampton, leaders of the Illinois Black Panther Party. Among those indicted is the Chief Prosecutor of Cook County, Edward V. Hanrahan, widely regarded as the heir apparent to Richard Daley as Mayor of Chicago. The Grand Jury cited 20 examples of police and official misconduct.

1971, September 4 Trade reports box office boom in black movies. The gross of *Sweet Sweetback's Baadaass Song* reportedly reaches $10 million, the more recently released *Shaft,* directed by Gordon Parks, $6 million.

1971, September 4 A massive return of blacks to the South is urged by Dr. J. Cashin, Chairman of the National Democratic Party of Alabama, an interracial group that is challenging control of the state's regular party. Dr. Cashin believes blacks are becoming disillusioned with the North and that an additional 200,000 to 400,000 blacks in each southern state would effect dramatic and positive changes in them.

1971, September 5 A survey conducted by Michigan University's Social Research Institute indicates Americans think police should shoot, but not shoot to kill, blacks in order to control riots.

1971, September 9–13 During riot by 1,200 inmates at the Attica Correctional Facility, Attica, New York, 32 inmates and 11 correctional employees die. Of the 43, 39 are killed and some 80 others wounded during a 15-minute attack by New York State police to retake the prison. Of 11 slain prison employees, 10 were hostages killed by police gunfire during the assault. The Attica riot was spawned and compounded by a number of elements: black and Puerto Rican militancy, a growing "law and order" political climate, poor prison conditions, and rehabilitation programs and, after the riot started, false and exaggerated reports of castration and other brutality to the 39 white hostages by black inmates. The demands of the prisoners ranged from popularly accepted but perpetually rejected areas of penal reform, such as better food, library facilities, and legal assistance, to proposals for complete amnesty for rioters and an option for them to relocate to "nonimperialist" nations. A number of prominent citizens, including Bobby Seale of the Black Panthers and Jose Paris of the Young Lords, a Puerto Rican group, attempted to mediate the dispute and persuade Governor Rockefeller to show his concern for better conditions by visiting Attica personally. But the Governor refuses, negotiations collapse, and the assault is ordered.

1971, September 20 The National Urban Coalition's Committee on Cities reports that if present trends continue, the majority of American cities will be predominantly black, brown, and bankrupt by 1980. The Committee, headed by Senator Harris of Oklahoma and Mayor Lindsay of New York, is encouraged by the growth of black self-help organizations,

Insurrectionary Attica inmates dispute surrender terms conveyed by State Correction Commissioner Russell G. Oswald (lower left). Refusing to visit the scene personally, Governor Rockefeller ordered heavily armed police to retake the prison; 35 persons were killed and some 80 others wounded in the ensuing attack.

but contends that conditions in slums have become more polarized and that the commitment of the federal government to correct urban problems has eased.

1971, October "Black Expo," a cultural and business exposition attracts some 800,000 people during its four day run in Chicago. The exposition is run by Jesse Jackson, of "Operation Breadbasket," and a number of black businessmen.

1971, October Dick Gregory, black comedian and presidential candidate in 1968, urges blacks to have large families as a counter to "genocide" attempts by whites to reduce the black population. Gregory adds that whites want to dictate the bedroom habits of blacks.

1971, November The Newark, New Jersey Board of Education votes to hang the Black Liberation flag in all schools were blacks comprise a majority, but implementation of the decision is prevented by a New Jersey state court.

1971, November Decline of confidence by blacks in the government is indicated by attitude survey conducted by the University of Michigan which reports that only 34% of blacks believe that the government is run for the benefit of all people. In 1958 some 78% of blacks held this view.

1971, November For the third time in 1971, the U.S. Commission on Civil Rights accuses the government of inadequate enforcement of civil rights laws. The Commission grants that in many cases enforcement machinery has been set up, but objects that little progress has stemmed from this.

1971, December The National Opinion Research Center reports that whites seem more ready to accept racial integration than in 1942. It concedes that many whites who claim to favor integration may be hiding their true feelings, but adds that whites will respond affirmatively if the government's presentation of the case for integration is positive.

1972, January A federal judge in Richmond, Virginia orders consolidation of Richmond's predominantly black school system with the nearly all-white system of two suburbs. Judge Robert Mehirge bases his decision on the failure of state officials to take *positive action* to reverse *de facto* segregation. The decision goes beyond recent verdicts of courts in Detroit and Pontiac, Michigan, which required busing because officials *condoned* segregation. Richmond announces it will appeal the decision.

1972, January Hunter Nicolas, an 18-year-old researcher from Boston, becomes the first precollege student in the United States to present a paper to the American Federation for Clinical Research.

1972, January In the worst violence in the South for two years, two white policemen and two young blacks, identifying themselves as Black Muslims, are killed in a shootout in Baton Rouge, Louisiana. After 31 bystanders are wounded, 700 National Guardsmen are sent by the Governor to establish order. Black Muslim headquarters in Chicago disavows the blacks.

1972, March President Nixon proposes a moratorium until July 1973 on all court-ordered busing and diversion of $1.5 billion for "impoverished" schools. Blacks in Congress claim the President is suggesting a return to separate but equal schools and that the moratorium would be unconstitutional. Roy Wilkins warns that the plan will precipitate a constitutional crisis.

1972, March Some 8,000 blacks, representing a wide spectrum of political views, attend the first National Black Political Convention in Gary, Indiana. The convention is chaired by Imamu Amiri Baraka of Newark. Mayor Richard Hatcher of Gary is the keynote speaker. The group approves a political platform, the "Black Agenda," which demands reparations, proportional Congressional representation for blacks, an increase in federal spending to combat crime and the drug traffic, reduction of the military budget, and a guaranteed annual income of $6,500 for a family of four. The Caucus also approves, after heated debate, a resolution opposing

integration of schools, demanding as an alternative control of schools by local school boards. The Congressional Black Caucus, however, repeats its support of busing and school integration. The Convention does not take a position in support of the many candidates for the Democratic Party's presidential nomination. A resolution to support Congresswoman Shirley Chisholm does not come to a vote.

1972, May Mrs. Esther Hunt Moore, the first black woman to register in Hickory, North Carolina, becomes the second black "mother of the year" in the award's 37-year history.

1972, May Stanford University rejects a proposal by Dr. William Shockley, Nobel Prize winning physicist, to teach a graduate course in which he would present his views that blacks are genetically inferior to whites. The University's rejection is based on grounds that Shockley's suggested reading material for the course is biased and that he is insufficiently familiar with the field of genetics. Shockley continues with the University as a teacher of electrical engineering.

1972, June Hank Aaron hits home run number 648 to tie Willie Mays, now with the New York Mets, for second place on the all-time home run list. Following the game, Aaron expresses belief he has a chance to surpass Babe Ruth's record of 714.

1972, June A U.S. Appeals Court, by a 5 to 1 vote, overturns the "Richmond" decision that would have required busing of school children between the city and two nearly "all-white" suburbs.

Gary mayor Richard Hatcher (center) *urges National Black Convention to build political and economic power; also on dais are Imamu Baraka* (left) *and Jesse Jackson.*

Frank Wills, who captured the Watergate burglars in the act, is honored with Ralph Abernathy at a 1974 ceremony. If not for Wills, Nixon's "secret police" operations and other subversions of democracy might never have been revealed to the American public.

1972, June   In San Jose, California, after 13 hours of deliberation, a jury of 11 whites and one Mexican-American acquits Angela Davis of murder and other charges in connection with the 1970 "court house shootout" in San Rafael, California.

1972, June   Frank Wills, a black security guard in Washington, D.C.'s Watergate office complex, detects and detains a group of men installing surveillance equipment in the Democratic Party National Headquarters. The men are arrested by the city police whom Wills summons and within a year the highest reaches of the Nixon Administration is racked by the Watergate scandal. Congressman Andrew Young of Georgia later asserts that Wills refused to accept bribes from the intruders in return for letting them escape.

1972, June   Jerome H. Holland, former Ambassador to Sweden, becomes the first black to be nominated a director of the New York Stock Exchange.

1972, July   At the sixty-third annual NAACP convention, Herbert Hill charges that minority membership in building trades unions is actually declining despite federally-prodded programs in Chicago, Philadelphia, Pittsburgh, and New York City.

1972, July   Senator George McGovern of South Dakota obtains the Democratic nomination for the presidency at a convention in which 400 blacks (15% of the total) are delegates. The vote of black delegates is largely divided between McGovern and Shirley Chisholm. Chisholm's showing is lessened by the fact that the black vote in the primaries was divided. Her total never exceeded 6%. After his nomination, McGovern names State Senator Basil Patterson of New York, Deputy Chairman of the Democratic Party.

1972, August   Attorney General Richard Kleindienst files suit against Los Angeles and Montgomery, Alabama for discrimination in hiring for public service jobs. Montgomery is accused of assigning whites to better jobs than blacks and with paying less to blacks in the same jobs as whites. Los Angeles is accused of discriminating against blacks in hiring and promotion of minorities in the Fire Department, which has only 48 blacks, 94 Mexican-Americans, and no Americans of Asian descent.

1972, August   James Baker, a 37-year-old diplomat, is appointed by the U.S. State Department to a post in the intensely segregated Union of South Africa, which coolly announces he will be able to live in the same area as whites because he is a "distinguished foreigner." Baker's appointment follows a controversy in March in which Roy Wilkins denied defending the role of American businesses operating in South Africa. Wilkins had noted he was unsure South African blacks were better off working for South African than American employers.

1972, August   The "Coalition Against Blax-ploitation," a combination of major civil rights groups in Los Angeles, announces its intention to rate black films, notes that "the transformation from the stereotype Stepin Fetchit to Super Nigger on the screen is just another form of cultural genocide."

1972, August   American black athletes become embroiled in a number of issues at the Munich Olympic Games. Some support African blacks in an attempt to deny acceptance of the team from Rhodesia. Two American runners are severely criticized for appearing lackadaisical on the victory stand during the playing of the Star Spangled Banner.

1972, August   Richard Nixon, renominated for President at Miami Beach, restates opposition to busing and "statistical targets" for use of blacks and other minorities in jobs and education. Says Nixon: "The way to end discrimination against some is not to begin discrimination against others." Many observers interpret Nixon's comments as a step in the rejection of special programs and quotas for blacks in construction and other skilled trades.

1972, September A special New York State Commission, reporting on the 1971 uprising at Attica prison, criticizes inmates for taking hostages and New York State authorities for "clearly indiscriminate firing by men who did not value inmates' lives." The report confirms that hostages were killed by gunfire from state forces retaking the prison.

1972, October Algernon Cooper, the great-great grandson of a black slave and a Confederate general, is inaugurated Mayor of Prichard, Alabama, a town of 41,000. A moderate who seeks to attract business to his community, Cooper pays a call on Governor George Wallace, who is recovering from an assassination attempt.

1972, October Demonstrations by white parents in Canarsie and other sections of Brooklyn and Queens, New York successfully halt busing of black children to three schools. Parents groups say they do not favor segregation but feel the schools are "tilting" too strongly to a black student body.

1972, November Richard Nixon is reelected President in landslide victory over Senator George McGovern, despite the fact that some 86% of the black vote went to McGovern. However, blacks achieve a number of electoral successes. Among them are: An increase of black Congressmen from 12 to 15; election of the first black Congress members from the South, Andrew Young from Atlanta and Yvonne Jordan from Houston, since the days of Reconstruction; a landslide victory for Republican Senator Edward Brooke in Massachusetts, even though Massachusetts was the only state to be carried by George McGovern; an increase in black representation in state legislatures, from 206 in 31 states before the election to 229 in 39 states after the election; election of blacks to the Arkansas state legislature for the first time in the history of that state; election of blacks to the Minnesota and Oregon legislatures, where they were not represented in the previous session. Blacks also suffered some setbacks. Black candidates for statewide offices lost in Indiana, Washington, and Pennsylvania. Blacks were unseated from state legislatures in the same states. The percentage of blacks of voting age who cast a ballot was 44 compared with 54 in 1968, but whites also voted in lesser numbers, 55 compared with 69 in 1968.

1972, November The Association for the Study of Black Life History, meeting in Cincinnati for its fifty-seventh annual convention, changes its name to the Association for the Study of African American History. The change is based on a mail ballot of the Association's membership, some two thirds of whom opted to substitute "African-American"

for "black" in the title. Prominent speakers at the convention include Andrew F. Brimmer, a governor of the Federal Reserve Board, Congressman Louis Stokes of Cleveland, Dr. John Hope Franklin, Professor of History at the University of Chicago, and Dr. Rayford W. Logan, Distinguished Professor of History at Howard University.

1972, November Admiral Elmo R. Zumwalt, Jr., Chief of Naval Operations, and Secretary of the Navy John W. Warner summon some 90 admirals and Marine Corps generals to a "stern lecture" on the "failure" of the commanders to achieve racial harmony on their ships and stations. Admiral Zumwalt orders the commanders to punish any act of bias or violation of its equal opportunity program. The issue was brought to a head by disturbances, strikes, and sabotage aboard a number of warships in Asia and domestic waters and the ensuing arrest pattern in which black sailors were questioned and confined in much greater numbers than whites. Zumwalt notes the incidents "were clearly due to the failure of commands to implement new racial programs with a whole heart." Blacks only were arrested in October after disturbances aboard the aircraft carrier *Kitty Hawk* and the Navy oiler *Hassayampa*. A multimillion dollar fire on the carrier *Forrestal* on July 10 and sabotage on the carrier *Ranger* were linked to racial tensions and antiwar feeling despite the fact that sailors arrested for these actions were white. A number of Admirals and Congressmen reply that the Navy has been too "permissive" with blacks.

1972, November Secretary of Defense Laird releases and praises a report by a bi-racial panel of military officers and civilians which declares that systematic and intentional discrimination exists against blacks in the military services.

1972, November Father Theodore M. Hesburgh, President of Notre Dame University, resigns as Chairman of the U.S. Commission on Civil Rights. The White House concedes it had sought the resignation of Father Hesburgh, an outspoken critic of President Nixon's antibusing policy, and the Commission's five other members. Father Hesburgh had served on the Commission since its formation in 1957.

1972, November Two young black men, Denver A. Smith and Leonard Douglas Brown, are killed on the Baton Rouge, Louisiana campus of Southern University during a confrontation between students, state police and sheriff deputies of East Baton Rouge Parish. The students had been pressing for the resignation of University President Dr. G. Leon Netterville, whom they charged had arbitrarily dismissed teachers he regarded as militant and was unreceptive to student demands for better living and academic facilities.

Following the shootings, Louisiana Governor Edwin W. Edwards closes the school and sends the National Guard to the Baton Rouge campus. After declaring that law enforcement officers had not used firearms in the Baton Rouge confrontation, the Governor concedes that a deputy might have mistaken a shot gun shell for a tear gas shell which resembled it. Students declare that they had not attacked police except to hurl back a tear gas shell that had been fired into their ranks.

Earlier in November, students had occupied the administration building of the New Orleans campus until the campus administrator, Dr. Emmet W. Bashful, resigned. However, the state Board of Education did not accept the resignation and the issue was cloudy at the time of the violence in Baton Rouge.

1972, November A Newark, New Jersey Superior Court judge lifts a temporary restraining order that had halted construction of the Kawaida Towers apartment building in a white middle-class neighborhood. The 16-story, 210-apartment project is sponsored by Temple Kawaida, whose spiritual leader is Imamu Baraka. Court action to halt construction was brought by a group of four whites, led by Assemblyman Anthony Imperiale. Numer-

Imamu Baraka and Anthony Imperiale head the opposing factions in Newark's Kawaida Towers housing controversy.

ous battles in court and the City Council ensue before construction proceeds.

1972, November The NAACP announces opposition to the nomination of Peter J. Brennan as Secretary of Labor. Roy Wilkins charges that the appointment of Brennan, President of the New York Building Trades Council, is "appalling in the nature of a disaster" and that Brennan did nothing to aid the acceptance of blacks and other minority members into craft union membership programs." President Nixon replies that Brennan has been "instrumental" in helping minorities gain access to such programs.

1972, December In a guarded statement in the Black Panther newspaper, Huey P. Newton, Chief of the Panthers, offers assistance to Eldridge Cleaver, former head of the Panthers, in the event that Cleaver should return from exile in Algeria to face trial in the United States. Cleaver, who once headed the Panthers, and Newton had split over policy, with Cleaver generally believed to hold the more revolutionary philosophy. Cleaver, who authored the best-selling autobiography *Soul On Ice,* fled the country

Father Theodore Hesburgh, President of Notre Dame College and an outspoken critic of ex-President Nixon's civil rights policies

in 1968 when he was scheduled to go to prison for parole violation. Cleaver had recently announced an intention to return to the United States and demand a trial. Newton states that the Panthers cannot forget Cleaver's attacks, but adds that Cleaver is "not an oppressor, but is himself oppressed."

1972, December The Supreme Court rules unanimously that residents of racially segregated housing projects can sue to integrate them. The decision states that white residents suffer social and economic injury as do people denied entry to them, and can thus be stigmatized as residents of a "white ghetto."

1972, December The Reverend W. Sterling Cary, 45-year-old Administrator of the United Church of Christ's Greater New York District, becomes the first black President of the National Council of Churches when he is elected unanimously in Dallas by the Council's General Assembly at its triennial meeting. After his election, Reverend Cary advocates that the 33 Protestant and Orthodox denominations belonging to the Council finance nonprofit housing programs can "help to pull the country together again." Cary adds that white liberals are suffering from "battle fatigue." The meeting is calmer than the session in 1969 at which James Forman pressed for reparations to blacks and a black candidate challenged Dr. Cynthia C. Wedel, the woman president whom Reverend Cary is succeeding. In an address to the Council, Imamu Baraka notes that organized religion must espouse representative government and "equitable distribution of wealth or be destroyed."

1972, December Leaders of the East Harlem Parents Council in New York announce the end of a school boycott which had kept over 10,000 of the area's 13,000 pupils out of 13 elementary schools for nearly two weeks. The boycott fails in its attempt to force the New York City Board of Education to restore funds and personnel cuts from local schools, but does focus widespread attention on the neighborhood's educational problems. It also indicates a high level of cooperation between blacks and Puerto Ricans.

1972, December Johnnie Rodgers, controversial black halfback for the University of Nebraska, is awarded the Heisman Trophy as the "country's outstanding college football player." Rodgers, once convicted for a holdup, was opposed by some people who felt this selection would set a bad example for American youth, who presumably wish to emulate athletic heroes. But Nebraska coach Bob Devaney supports Rodgers, as does O. J. Simpson, the 1968 winner, who observes: "I just missed getting

into some scrapes when I was growing up and so did everybody else from the ghettoes."

1973, January The American Telephone and Telegraph Company settles a suit by the Federal Equal Employment Opportunities Commission when it promises to pay $15 million in back wages to 15,000 women and minority group men. A T & T also agrees to give $23 million in raises to 36,000 employees who had been advanced to more responsible positions, but allegedly had not been granted sufficient wage increases. EEOC officials promise more suits would follow if business did not act on its own.

1973, January At the start of its second term in office, spokesmen for the Nixon Administration note the following policies and claims with respect to blacks: Hiring preference for blacks to make up for past injustices and oversights is to be replaced by a merit system, ostensibly without regard to race. Civil rights laws are to be enforced less stringently. Discrimination clearly in violation of the law must be established for the government to act. The government will no longer attempt to force integration in schools or suburban housing. Busing is to be opposed, if necessary by a constitutional amendment. Welfare legislation will be pursued but with less emphasis on cost cutting, work requirements and establishment of eligibility than in the 1969 Bill which was not enacted. The Administration claims that between 1969 and 1973 it increased appropriations to enforce civil rights legislation, helped minority business enterprises, and raised the number of children in legally depressed schools in the South from 32 to 91%.

1973, April Paul Robeson is honored on his seventy-fifth birthday by Rutgers University, which he attended, and many other institutions and groups. The homage to Robeson, who is ill at the time, marks attempts at reconciliation between American institutions and the great singer, actor, and long-time Communist sympathizer.

1973, April Bobby Seale, running as a Democrat, finishes second in the mayoral race in Oakland, California, earns the right to a runoff against the incumbent, John Reading, who just fails to attain the needed 50% necessary for election without a runoff.

1973, May The Supreme Court, in a 4 to 4 tie, fails to overturn a circuit court rejection of the Mehirge decision which would have required Richmond, Virginia to integrate its school system with that of two suburbs. Thus, for the time being at least, the Court rejects the concept that racial imbalance in a few schools justifies revision of school boundaries.

1973, June Thomas Bradley, a former policeman,

who is the son of a sharecropper, is elected Mayor of Los Angeles, defeating the incumbent Sam Yorty by 100,000 votes. Yorty had defeated Bradley in 1969 in a vote in which Bradley's race had been a major issue.

1973, June Howard University's Joint Center for Political Studies reports that as of April 1973, 2,621 blacks hold 2,627 elective offices in the United States at every level from school boards to the Congress. When the first list was compiled, in 1969, the total was 1,185. In 1972 the figure was 2,264. Michigan leads the states with 179, followed in order by New York, Mississippi, Alabama, and Arkansas.

1973, July Alonzo Crim, Atlanta's new, black Superintendent of Schools, launches a "school compromise plan" which would leave some 80 of the city's 140 schools all-black, limit busing to 3% of the school population, and increase the number of desegregated schools by only eight. A number of blacks, among them Roy Wilkins, condemn the plan, as setting a dangerous precedent. Defenders feel the plan is the best route to effective education and racial harmony.

1973, September Willie Mays, now of the New York Mets, announces his retirement as an active player, though he is to appear in the World Series. Mays's lifetime batting average is .302, his homer total 660. Hank Aaron ends the season with 713 home runs, one short of Babe Ruth's record.

1973, November The number of black elected officials in the United States rises from 370 to 2,991, in an election held mostly for municipal and county offices. The number of black mayors rose from 81 to 108 with notable victories in Detroit and Atlanta.

1973, November Governor George Wallace of Alabama is warmly applauded as he addresses meeting of the National Conference of Black Mayors in Tuskegee. The black mayor of Tuskegee, Johnny Ford, stresses need for black mayors to forget old racial hostilities and get along with Wallace, but many blacks attack the spread of "creeping respectability" for the Alabama Governor. In May 1974 Wallace and the Reverend Ralph Abernathy, head of The Southern Christian Leadership Conference, meet and shake hands.

1974, January A group of prominent black leaders, including Roy Wilkins, Reverend Jesse Jackson, Floyd McKissick, and Mayors Bradley, Young, and Jackson, visit Vice President Ford and report that the meeting was courteous and say they hope blacks now have a friendly ear in the Nixon Administration.

1974, January Rabbi Balfour Brickner of the New York Federation of Reform Synagogues urges both blacks and Jews, in the spirit of the late Martin Luther King, Jr., to reestablish the cooperation that prevailed in the 1960s and says that negative atmosphere in New York City is partly attributable to separatism within both communities.

1974, March The Department of Justice releases memos revealing that in the 1960s and early 1970s the Federal Bureau of Investigation had waged a campaign designed to disrupt, discredit, and neutralize black nationalist groups, including the Black Panther Party. A major objective of the effort, according to the memo, was to prevent the emergence of a black leader capable of uniting disparate factions and inspiring violence. Reverend Jesse Jackson asserts the documents give credence to charges that the FBI figured in the deaths of Malcolm X, Reverend King, and Fred Hampton.

1974, March The Second Black National Political Convention meets in Little Rock; Mayors Hatcher of Gary and Jackson of Atlanta and Imamu Baraka are among speakers. However, many prominent black leaders are absent, among them Representative Charles Diggs, who resigned as co-chairman.

1974, April Henry Aaron of the Atlanta Braves ties Babe Ruth's home run record of 714 in his team's opening game in Cincinnati, breaking it with number 715 a few days later in Atlanta against Al Downing of the Los Angeles Dodgers.

1974, May Alvin F. Poussaint, a black Harvard professor, charges that the women's liberation movement is regarded as a threat by many blacks who feel it is being used as an excuse to perpetuate discriminatory practices in employment. While praising the contributions of the women's movement to human rights, Poussaint asks women to be aware of efforts by racists to use them as pawns.

1974, June A draft report of the Senate "Watergate" investigating staff indicates that reelection efforts on behalf of President Nixon in 1972 sought to gain the support or neutrality of prominent blacks by means of an expeditious proferring and withholding of federal aid. Two black targets were the Reverend Jesse Jackson, head of Operation PUSH, and James Farmer, an official during Nixon's first term.

1974, July By a vote of 5 to 4 the Supreme Court nullifies an attempt to effect "metropolitan integration" of predominantly black schools in Detroit with those of nearby white suburbs. Chief Justice Burger in his majority decision declares that segregation in a city's schools does not justify its combination with schools in its suburbs. Justice Thurgood Marshall, dissenting, calls the decision an emasculation of the constitutional guarantee of equal opportunity.

1974, August Richard Nixon resigns as President as

likelihood of his conviction and removal from office on three counts of impeachment becomes apparent. Three blacks, Conyers, Jordan, and Rangel, serve on the Committee. Nixon is succeeded by Vice President Gerald Ford who, a few days after the inauguration, holds a meeting with the Congressional Black Caucus. Though Ford promises little in the way of civil rights activity, the meeting is cordial, a marked change from encounters between the Caucus and the Nixon Administration.

1974, November The number of black elected officials rises at federal, state, and local levels. All blacks in Congress are reelected and one new member, Harold Ford of Memphis, Tennessee is added. Blacks are elected lieutenant governor in California and Colorado.

1974, December Riots against integration of public schools in Boston peak as police struggle to restrain violence which wrenches much of the city. President Ford deplores the violence, but is criticized by black leaders as actually encouraging it by his comment that he opposes busing to integrate schools.

1975, February A wide range of black leaders attack President Ford's budget which proposes to reduce and eliminate humanitarian programs and to raise the cost of food stamps. Democrats declare opposition to much of the plan.

1975, March William T. Coleman is appointed Secretary of Transportation by President Ford, becoming the second black in the nation's history to hold a cabinet post.

1975, May Department of Labor figures report the national unemployment rate at 9%, the black rate at 15%. Vernon L. Jordan, Jr. of the National Urban League reports that the black rate is actually 26% when undercounts and "discouraged" workers are considered.

1975, June *Focus,* the publication of the Joint Center for Political Studies, charges that the proportion of blacks being recruited for the Armed Forces is being deliberately reduced.

1975, June President Ford addresses the NAACP's annual convention in Washington, D.C. He asks blacks, in the interest of economic stability, to accept his reduced spending policies, which mean lower aid to minorities and poor people. Black leaders differ strongly with the President's programs.

1975, July 1 Wallace Muhammed, supreme minister of the Nation of Islam, delivers a historic speech, opening the Muslim Nation to members of all races.

1975, July The NAACP's sixty-sixth annual convention in Washington, D.C. focuses on the country's bitter economic situation with over 12% of adult black workers and as much as 40% of black youth unemployed. Discussion centers on programs for creating new jobs and on organized labor's seniority system, which unintentionally, but automatically, discriminates against blacks. President Ford addresses the convention but refuses to create special programs for unemployed or underemployed blacks.

1975, August 18 District of Columbia Appellate Court Judge Julia Cooper is confirmed by the Senate, becoming the highest ranking black woman in the federal courts.

1975, August 20 Senator Edward Brooke calls for a $10 billion federal employment program to end the economic "depression" in black America by creating 1 million public service jobs.

1975, August 22 In a celebrated North Carolina trial, 21-year-old Joan Little is freed of the charge of murdering a white jailer while she was a prisoner in a county jail; the defense contended she slew the jailer while being raped.

1975, August 29 General Daniel "Chappie" James, Jr., becomes commander-in-chief of the North American Air Defense Command (NORAD). On the same day he is promoted to become the first black four-star general in U.S. history.

1975, September The U.S. Civil Rights Commission rebukes President Ford for voicing public opposition to a federal court's busing plan for Boston, saying that the President's stand has contributed to the entrenched and sometimes violent resistance to busing.

1975, September 27–28 The Congressional Black Caucus, now 17 members strong, holds its fifth annual dinner, an event that has grown into a two-day, 2,800-person civil rights convention. The major theme of the affair is "From Changing Structures to Using Structures—1879–1976." Panelists recommend federal takeover of the welfare system and poverty assistance, that the states assume more fiscal responsibility for education, and that Caucus-directed programs develop a national black position on matters of policy.

1975, September 29 WGPR-TV, the first black-owned, black-operated television station in the United States, goes on the air in Detroit.

1975, September 30 The case of Rubin "Hurricane" Carter and John Artis, who have been serving life sentences for murder since 1967, despite the fact that the two chief prosecution witnesses recanted in September 1974 (asserting they were coerced into perjury by the Passaic County Prosecutor's office) was sent by New Jersey Governor Byrne to the Assembly Judiciary Committee for review and to determine whether pardons should be granted. Carter has long claimed that he was framed because of his outspoken views about racism and police brutality in Paterson.

1975, December U.S. Attorney General Edward Levy opens an official review of the Martin Luther King assassination. Although self-confessed James Ray was convicted of the crime, many facts point to a conspiracy and suggest that those really responsible for the murder are still at large. These facts move the Justice Department to open a secret investigation as early as 1970, but the FBI refuses to turn over necessary records. The major questions are: Could Ray, a stranger to Memphis, find the perfect assassination spot in just 2½ hours if he were acting alone? What are the New Orleans connections the assassin was afraid to discuss even while on trial for his life? Where did his escape money come from?

1975, December 4 Pointing to recently discovered graves and statues, archeologists announce that Africans, rather than Columbus or the Vikings, were the first overseas explorers to set foot in the New World. Probably the first to come, perhaps as early as 4000 B.C., were fishermen from the Liberian area. Mali King Zabu Bakiri II is believed to have headed one of the last expeditions from Africa to the New World in the early 1300s, using compasses and navigational instruments developed for crossing the Sahara desert. The great Olmec civilization of ancient Mexico is now thought to have been a largely black culture.

1976, March 24 The Supreme Court decides that blacks who have been denied jobs in violation of the 1964 Civil Rights Act must receive retroactive seniority once they have been hired in those jobs.

1976, April 20 The Supreme Court rules that federal courts may order minority low-cost public housing in white suburbs of a city even when those suburbs have not been guilty of racially discriminatory housing practices. The Department of Housing and Urban Development can be ordered to provide such housing.

1976, April 26 The Metropolitan Applied Research Center, a major black research organization founded to serve as advocate for the urban poor, announces that it must close due to declining funds.

1976, June 1 A study by The Joint Center for Political Studies shows that blacks hold almost 4,000 elected posts in government, more than any other time in history. Still blacks comprise only 0.05% of the total elected officials in the country.

1976, June 14 The Supreme Court refuses without comment to review court-ordered busing for desegregation of Boston public schools. In January, the U.S. Court of Appeals for the First Circuit upheld a May 1975 ruling by U.S. District Court Judge Arthur Garrity ordering busing to achieve racial integration in the Boston school system. In April of that same year, a period of prolonged violence erupts in Boston after the topic of busing becomes the object of a bitter and simmering dispute.

1976, July Mayor Kenneth A. Gibson of Newark, New Jersey is elected the first black president of the 43-year old U.S. Conference of Mayors.

1976, August 31 A Chancellery Court in Mississippi awards $1,250,058 to 12 white Port Gibson merchants in damages from the NAACP due to the organization's successful boycott in 1966.

1976, October 2 U.S. Agriculture Secretary Earl Butz is reprimanded by President Gerald Ford for making "highly offensive" remarks about blacks. Butz issues an apology for his remarks.

1976, November 2 Blacks play a vital role as Jimmy Carter narrowly defeats President Gerald Ford in the presidential election. Carter received about 94% of some 6.6 million black votes.

1976, November 14 The congregation of President-Elect Jimmy Carter's Baptist church in Plains, Georgia votes to drop its 11-year ban on attendance by blacks.

1976, December 16–21 President-Elect Jimmy Carter appoints Andrew Young as Chief Delegate to the United Nations and Patricia Roberts Harris as Secretary of the Department of Housing and Urban Development.

1977, February 6 Griffin Bell is confirmed as Attorney General despite opposition from leading blacks. Bell soon appoints two blacks—Wade H. McCree as Solicitor General and Drew Days as Assistant Attorney General for Civil Rights. However, Coretta King declares that Bell has an image that is almost segregationist and Congressman Parren Mitchell reveals Bell's membership in three social clubs that exclude blacks. During the Senate confirmation hearings, Bell saw himself as a voice of moderation, and despite the efforts of the NAACP to keep the hearings open, they were closed and after a bitter Senate battle.

1977, January 20 Clifford Alexander, Jr. is sworn in as the first black Secretary of the Army. Appointees by President Carter include 19 blacks in the White House and 37 in other executive positions.

1977, March 23 Representative Charles C. Diggs of Michigan is indicted on charges of taking kickbacks from three Congressional employees and keeping on his payroll three other employees who did not work in Congress.

1977, March 9 Joseph Lawson Hawze is installed as Bishop of the Roman Catholic Diocese of Biloxi, Mississippi. He becomes the first black bishop of an American diocese since James Healy of Portland, Maine in 1875. The diocese has over 42 parishes with 48,000 Catholics, including about 9,000 blacks.

1977, April 19 Author Alex Haley receives a special Pulitzer Prize for his book *Roots*. The book becomes a best seller among blacks and its popularity is further boosted through the television movie *Roots*.

1977, July 24–25 National Urban League Executive Director Vernon Jordan, thought to be one of the black leaders closest to President Carter, criticizes the Administration's policies in a speech to his organization. Carter replies that he has no apologies for his record on blacks and the poor.

1977, July 2 Colston A. Lewis, a member of the EEOC, charges President Carter with racism and failure to keep his promise to bring more blacks into the Administration. He then defies a White House order to vacate his office immediately.

1977, July 18 The once radical Black Panther Party becomes integrated into the political system of Oakland, California, as it works to elect Lionel Wilson

In 1978 Benjamin Hooks became executive director of the NAACP after the retirement of Roy Wilkins.

as the city's first black mayor and John George as the first black Alameda County supervisor.

1977, July 29 Roy Wilkins, a 42-year veteran of the NAACP serving the last 22 as Executive Director, announces his intention to retire during the organization's sixty-eighth annual convention in St. Louis, his hometown. Wilkins was 75 when he announced his retirement.

1977, September 4 A meeting of 15 black leaders at the National Urban League produces two general agreements: A loose coalition of members will work against perceived antiblack sentiment in the nation and top priority would be given to increasing job opportunities for minorities.

1977, October 27 Dr. Clifton R. Wharton, President of Michigan State University, is appointed President of the State University of New York, the nation's largest state university.

1977, November 19 Robert E. Chambliss, a 73-year-old former member of the Ku Klux Klan, is convicted of first-degree murder in the 1963 bombing of the 16th Street Baptist Church where four black girls were killed. He is sentenced to life in prison. Chambliss protests his innocence.

1977, December 28 Karen Farmer becomes the first black member of the Daughters of American Revolution, when she proves her worthiness by tracing her ancestry to William Hood, a soldier in the patriot army during the American Revolution.

1978, January 8 Benjamin Hooks, the new Executive Director of the NAACP, announces plans to revitalize the civil rights organization with new chapters and a greater stress on fundraising.

1977, May 14 Reverend Jesse Jackson accuses President Carter of assuming a conservative stance on blacks and the poor and moves to organize a coalition of all groups of blacks and whites to secure economic and social justice. In June NAACP Chairwoman Margaret Bush Wilson attacks Carter, stating that his means of attempting a balanced budget will be harmful to the interests of blacks. EEOC member Colston A. Lewis charges Carter with racism and defies an order that strips him of his position.

1978, January 17 Major Guion S. Bluford, Jr., Major Frederick D. Gregory, and Dr. Ronald E. McNair join the space program and begin training as astronauts for future space missions.

1978, May 2 Ernest Morial, a former judge, is inaugurated as the first black mayor of New Orleans.

1978, May 23 Wallace D. Muhammad, leader of the World Community of Islam in the West, says that his organization will abandon its separatist philosophy and become a patriotic group in the belief that minorities may have asked too much and not done enough for themselves.

1978, May 29 FBI files made public reveal that an unidentified black leader worked with the agency during the 1960s in an effort to remove Dr. Martin Luther King from national prominence in the civil rights movement. The information released is from files of J. Edgar Hoover.

1978, July 22 NAACP leader Benjamin Hooks asserts that if the Republican Party's efforts to gain more black political support were to be effective, the party would have to demonstrate more concern for the needs of disadvantaged Americans and that programs such as lower taxes for those in lower income brackets and full employment legislation would be basic considerations. The Republican Party had announced a $640,000 public relations campaign to garner more black votes.

1978, June 28 The Supreme Court in a 5–4 decision orders that white student Allan P. Bakke be admitted to The University of California, Davis's Medical College, indicating that the refusal to admit Bakke was tantamount to reverse discrimination and that use of racial or ethnic quotas was an improper means of achieving racial balance. The Court held that the college affirmative action program was invalid since it had the effect of discriminating against qualified white applicants although the Court perceived the goal of attaining a diverse student body constitutional and permissible. The decision, however, creates a need to reevaluate affirmative action programs in general and how best to achieve greater minority equality in education and the economy. Justice Thurgood Marshall writes a separate opinion (see Legal section).

1978, June 9 The Church of the Latter Day Saints (Mormons) revokes its 148-year-old policy of excluding black men from the priesthood.

1978, June 30 Assistant Attorney General Drew Days states that federal agencies will be able to continue vigorous enforcement of antidiscrimination laws in wake of the Bakke decision, but must be more careful in doing so.

1978, August 14–18 The House of Representatives holds public hearings on the assassinations of Dr. Martin Luther King and President John F. Kennedy. James Earl Ray, convicted of killing Dr. King, denies his guilt and charges that he was framed.

1978, December 3 The Census Bureau reports that during the period of 1960 to 1977, the number of blacks living in suburbs increased from 2.4 million to 4.6 million and that 55% of the 24.5 million

In 1980 Representative Charles C. Diggs (shown here in better days) abruptly resigned his house seat after conviction on mail fraud and payroll kickbacks.

blacks in the United States live in central cities, indicating a decline from the 1970 figure of 59%.

1978, September 9 President Carter acts to heal a rift with the Congressional Black Caucus following an angry meeting during which Representative John Conyers walks out after a heated verbal exchange with Carter and Vice President Mondale. Conyers was demanding a "Camp David summit" to discuss employment.

1978, October 10 Representative Charles Diggs (D., Mich.), considered the "dean" of blacks in the House of Representatives, is convicted on 11 counts of mail fraud and 18 counts of falsified Congressional payroll vouchers. He announces his intention to appeal and is later reelected despite the conviction.

1978, October 27 President Carter signs the Humphrey-Hawkins Full Employment Bill, which states the government's desire to reduce unemployment to 4% and continue the CETA program for four more years. However, it does not provide for funds to pursue its goals.

1978, November 8 U.S. Senator Edward Brooke of Massachusetts, the only black in the upper house of Congress, loses to Paul Tsongas following a period of bad publicity about his divorce and personal finances.

1978, July Debate rages within the civil rights movement over charges that many groups and leaders serve two masters by accepting large donations and board of directors positions with large corporations. The greatest argument centers on the NAACP's generally favorable position on deregulation of energy prices. Some black opponents of deregulation contend that the NAACP had difficulty achieving objectivity on the issue because of members of its energy committee were employed by energy interests.

1979, October 3 Councilman Richard Arrington of Birmingham, Alabama is elected as that city's first black mayor. Arrington garnered 52% of the vote.

1979, December 22 The Joint Center for Political Studies reveals that between 1978 and 1979 the number of blacks elected to public office increased by 104. This 2% increase is considered meager and that such officials were elected in states with substantial black populations.

1979, October 18 Benjamin Hooks, M. Carl Holman, James Farmer, Dr. Kenneth Clark, and Vernon Jordan express concern that meetings between black leaders and the Palestine Liberation Organization could damage the black movement.

1979, November 19 Ayatollah Khomeini releases eight blacks and five white women while continuing to hold other hostages at the U.S. Embassy in Teheran.

1979, July 20 Patricia Roberts Harris moves within the Carter Administration from Secretary of Housing and Urban Development to Secretary of Health, Education and Welfare.

1979, August 16 Andrew Young resigns as Chief U.S. Delegate to the United Nations after being publicly criticized for unauthorized talks with the Palestine Liberation Organization in New York. The resignation sets off a storm of controversy and animosity between segments of the Jewish and black communities.

1979, September 10 The NAACP announces plans to establish ties with representatives of African and Caribbean nations in a move to increase the influence of blacks on world affairs.

1979, September 15 The FBI admits it planted a rumor in 1970 that actress Jean Seberg, who later committed suicide, was pregnant by a member of the Black Panther Party. The rumor was circulated in an effort to discredit her support for the black nationalist movement.

1979, September 20 A delegation of 10 black Americans representing the Southern Christian Leadership Conference meets in Lebanon with guerrillas of the Palestine Liberation Organization. The visit stems from the resignation of Andrew Young from his post as U.S. Ambassador to the United Nations.

1979, September 24 Donald McHenry replaces Andrew Young as U.S. Ambassador to the United Nations.

1979, October 17 Sir Arthur Lewis, a professor at Princeton, is named winner of the Nobel Prize in Economic Science for his work in the subject of problems of developing nations. He shares the award with Theodore W. Schultz of the University of Chicago.

1979, June 11 Statistics gathered by the tribunal of the U.S. Supreme Court demonstrates that the majority of individuals employed by the courts are white and male and that black employees are concentrated at the lowest levels. There have been only two black law clerks in the Court's history.

1979, June 25 Amalya L. Kearse receives an appointment to the U.S. Court of Appeals for the Second Circuit and becomes the first woman to sit on that bench and the second black ever in such a position. The first black was Thurgood Marshall, who is now a justice of the Supreme Court.

1979, September 20 A survey conducted by the Southern Regional Council of 11 southern states and four cities in other areas of the country discloses that three of five southern judges belong to all-white social organizations and the probability exists that such is the case throughout the country.

1979, September 25 One of every five firms receiving federal aid for minority businessmen and the disadvantaged has been demonstrated to be a front for white contractors, an audit by the Small Business Administration concludes. In effect, of the 1,505 firms granted assistance, 256 should not have been funded.

1979, March 28 In a bid to become the first black mayor of Kansas City, Missouri, Bruce R. Watkins fails as the city divides along racial rather than political lines and elects Republican Richard L. Berkley by a 20,000 plurality.

1979, February 18 It is reported that the most rapidly growing minority group in America, the Hispanics, at the present growth rate, will displace blacks as the nation's largest minority by 1985.

1979, April 15 Imperial Wizard Bill Wilkinson leads 100 members of the KKK through Selma, Alabama shouting "white power." They are confronted by stone-throwing blacks who attempt to disrupt the procession.

1979, May 27 A march led by Reverend Joseph Lowery of SCLC erupts into a fight with some 100 KKK members as the Klan attempts to block the march. Two klansmen are shot during the disturbance.

1979, January 24 President Carter sends his budget to Congress and the response of most blacks in government and in leadership positions across the nation is negative. Ronald H. Brown of the Washington-based operations committee of the National Urban League states, "we're concerned and disturbed about any budget that doesn't meet the needs of the poor and this one doesn't."

1979, January 30 Franklin A. Thomas, former president of Bedford-Stuyvesant Restoration Corporation and a director of New York Life Insurance Company, becomes the first black president of the Ford Foundation.

1979, February 24 President Carter honors Jesse Owens, Reverend Martin Luther King, Sr., and 15 other elderly blacks selected for their contributions by the National Caucus on Black Aged.

1979, April 20 The National Association of Black Social Workers calls for a national black political convention in 1980 to develop strategies to counteract racism in health, housing, employment, and social programs.

1979, May 16 News of a series of private meetings between middle-level black officials in the Carter Administration becomes known. The group meets over a period of several months to discuss its concerns over the Administration's record on minority issues.

1979, May 28 The Congressional Black Caucus and delegates from 11 southern states set up an "action alert communications network" to help them exert pressure on at least 100 white Congressional representatives from heavily black districts to vote with the caucus on important issues.

1979, June 19 The Bureau of the Census announces a study indicating that despite the fact that black Americans have made enormous advances in employment, income, health, housing, political power, and other measures of social well-being in recent decades, they remain far behind white Americans.

1979, February 27 The Department of Housing and Urban Development announces it will foreclose the financially troubled Soul City, a new town in rural North Carolina that was to have been controlled by blacks but open to all. Since 1969, when Floyd B. McKissick announced the idea for the city, $27 million had been spent by federal, state, and local sources. McKissick vows to continue efforts to keep the project alive.

1979, May 1 New York State Senator Vander Beatty announces he has collected 63,000 signatures calling for the City Council in New York City to schedule a referendum in the fall on whether a recall procedure should be included in the City Charter. Beatty started his campaign accusing Mayor Edward Koch of racism. However, Beatty's efforts failed.

1979, June 29 The U.S. Supreme court rules 5–2, in *U.S. Steel* v. *Brian Weber,* that private employers can legally give special preference to black workers to eliminate "manifest racial imbalance" in traditionally white jobs.

1979, July 26 The U.S. Justice Department announces that it will sponsor a seminar for police officials on the use of deadly force as a result of policemen killing nonwhites in controversial circumstances in several cities during previous months.

1979, August 1 The House of Representatives votes 408–1 to place a bust of Martin Luther King, Jr. in the Capitol. The work will be the first to honor any black American in Congress.

1980, January 18 A survey conducted by Data Black, a major black commercial polling organization, indicates widespread dissatisfaction with President Carter's efforts among blacks.

1980, February 6 The Congressional Black Caucus attacks President Carter's fiscal 1981 budget proposals, criticizing increases in military spending that lead to cuts for social programs. Caucus members promise to initiate legislation to reduce military spending increases and pronounce the budget "an unmitigated disaster for the poor, the unemployed and minorities."

1980, February 6 Georgia State Senator Julian Bond suffers a political setback in a bid for a largely ceremonial post of majority whip. He is defeated in a Democratic caucus by Senator Loyce Turner of Valdosta by a vote of 27 to 21.

1980, February 6 The American Bar Association votes to defer action on a measure requiring law schools to adopt affirmative action plans for the admission of minority students. The measure would amend the Standards for the Approval of Law Schools and would require schools seeking to obtain or maintain accreditation to demonstrate "concrete action" in expanding opportunities for racial minorities and women in the study and entry into the law profession.

1980, March 3 The "National Conference for a Black Agenda" meets with limited success. A special "presidential forum" in which the presidential candidates were to discuss issues of importance to black Americans, is canceled when Senator Edward Kennedy, Representative John Anderson, and Governor

Jerry Brown decide not to attend. However, 1,000 national black leaders conduct in-depth discussions on strategies and goals pertaining to maximizing black political clout, employment, housing, and affirmative action. The conference is sponsored by organizations such as the NAACP, the National Urban League, PUSH—groups that had already endorsed President Carter—so that candidates saw no purpose in speaking.

1980, March 17 A study released by the Radio and Television News Directors Association indicates that women are making greater employment advances than minorities in the broadcasting industry. Only 71% of all television stations employed minorities, while 94% of those stations employed women, according to the survey conducted in 1979. In radio, only 20% of the country's stations employ minorities, a figure unchanged in 9 years.

1980, April 22 The U.S. Supreme Court, in a 6–3 decision, overturns a lower court ruling that an at-large city electoral system in Mobile, Alabama is unconstitutional because it dilutes the voting strength of blacks.

1980, April 23 In an unprecedented decision, the Supreme Court votes 6 to 3 that intentional discrimination must be proven to declare a local election system unconstitutional. Mobile, Alabama's, at-large voting system was found constitutional, overturning the rulings of two lower courts. Not one black had been elected city commissioner or to the county school board in the city's history, although blacks comprise 35.4% of its population. Justices William Brennan, Byron White, and Thurgood Marshall wrote dissenting opinions.

1980, April 30 Amoco Oil Co., a division of Standard Oil of Indiana, agrees to pay a record civil penalty of $200,000 to settle charges of discrimination against blacks, Hispanics, and women, in the issuance of credit cards. The company's use of zip codes to determine which applicants obtained credit fostered the discrimination charges, and Amoco agreed to reconsider, upon request, applicants rejected over the past three years. The action could result in 30,000 to 50,000 new card holders. The civil penalty is the largest ever levied under the Equal Credit Opportunity Act.

1980, May 11 Early primary results reveal that the black community is supporting President Carter's second-term bid despite criticism of his record by naional black leaders, according to reports. The "resounding" victories won by Carter in the southern primaries are interpreted as blacks lacking faith in their ability to enact a "Great Society-style social renewal" agenda as proposed by Senator Edward M. Kennedy.

1980, May 14 J. B. Stoner, a white supremacist, is convicted for the 1958 bombing of a black church in Birmingham, Alabama.

1980, May 18 The black Liberty City area and predominantly black Coconut Grove section of Miami erupt into riotous violence, ending with 9 dead and 163 injured, following the acquittal of four white Dade County police officers in the beating death of a black man. In the night-long unrest, stores are looted, property burned, and whites fatally beaten. During the violence, blacks are heard screaming the name "McDuffie" (Arthur), the black insurance executive beaten to death following a high-speed chase with Dade County police officers for a traffic violation. Dade County officials impose an 8 P.M. to 6 A.M. curfew; 350 National Guard troops set up headquarters in an armory, with 450 more en route from Orlando.

1980, May 29 Vernon E. Jordan, Jr., President of the National Urban League, is shot and seriously wounded by an unknown assailant in Fort Wayne, Indiana. Stating that the shooting evidenced "an element of premeditation," William H. Webster, Director of the Federal Bureau of Investigation, says "the shooting was not accidental, and was in furtherance of an apparent conspiracy to deprive Vernon Jordan of his civil rights." The shooting occurred just outside Jordan's motel room.

1980, June 4 Representative Charles C. Diggs, Jr. (D. Mich.) abruptly resigns his House seat after the Supreme Court refuses to review his case presented to the U.S. Court of Appeals, which was denied. Diggs, a senior black Congressman, ends a 26-year career marred by formal House censure, resignation of committee and subcommittee chairmanships, and conviction on charges of mail fraud and the diversion of $60,000 in payroll kickbacks. He agrees to pay $40,000 and will leave Congress with a "clear conscience."

1980, July 3 In a consent decree with the Justice Department, the City of Cincinnati agrees to hire and promote more blacks and women within the police department. The decree permanently enjoins the city from engaging in any employment discrimination. Over a 5-year, 34% of new police officer vacancies will be filled by blacks and 23% by women. The Fire Department of the City of Chicago, in a similar action (April 2, 1980), was permanently prohibited from discriminating against any candidate for promotion on the basis of race or national origin. The settlement of this discrimination action was filed in federal district court and resulted from a suit charging violations of the Civil Rights Act of 1964 and the Federal Sharing Act of 1972. In New York City, the U.S. Court of Appeals (August 1, 1980) overturned a lower court ruling that 50% of all new police officer hirings be black and Hispanic. The Appeals Court, however, ruled that the written test used for hiring had "significant disparate racial impact" in violation of the Civil Rights Act of 1964. It concluded that until a new test was implemented one third of all newly hired police must be black or Hispanic.

1980, June 14 Based on a recent ruling by the U.S. Supreme Court, the Justice Department drops a voting rights discrimination suit against Hattiesburg, Mississippi. The high court rules in Mobile, Alabama that it must be proven that "at large" voting systems were intentionally established and excluded black voters. The Justice Department contends that "at large" elections for three members of the Hattiesburg City Commission diluted black voting strength in violation of the Voting Rights Act of 1965 and the Fourteenth and Fifteenth Amendments.

1980, June 25 The nomination of Alabama State Senator U. W. Clemon is unanimously approved by the Senate Judiciary Committee. Ranking Republican committee member Senator Strom Thurmond endorses Clemon and says although he does not condone his (Clemon's) late filing of tax returns, there was "no indication whatsoever of fraud." If confirmed by the Senate, Clemon would be the thirty-second black appointed to a federal judgship by President Carter. At the start of his administration, only 19 blacks sat on the bench.

1980, July 1 Presidential candidate Ronald Reagan declines an invitation to address the NAACP national convention. Executive Director Benjamin Hooks then criticizes the candidate for "writing off" black votes. Reagan soon responds by accepting an invitation to speak at the National Urban League convention.

1980, July 2 The U.S. Supreme Court decides that Congress' award of federal funds on the basis of race was to redress racial discrimination.

1980, July 3 A ruling authorizing Congress to impose racial quotas to remedy past discrimination against minority contractors in federal jobs programs is upheld by the Supreme Court in a 6-3 vote. It validates the 10% minority set-aside of federal public works contracts, challenged by white contractors in *Fullilove* v. *Klutznick*.

1980, July 18 A federal district court in Montgomery rules that the State of Alabama cannot prosecute Gary Thomas Rowe, Jr., a chief informant of the

FBI during the 1960s, even though the Justice Department issued a report indicating that the FBI knew about and apparently covered up illegal acts by Rowe, including attacks on blacks, civil rights activists, and newsmen.

1980, September 3 St. Louis schools are desegregated peacefully after eight years of struggle. Over 16,000 students are bused on the first day of classes under court-ordered power. No violence is reported.

1980, September 26 Federal District Judge Horace W. Gilmore invalidates the 1980 census on the ground that it undercounts blacks and Hispanics, thus violating the one-person, one-vote principle. The action was precipitated by a suit initiated by the city of Detroit with support from dozens of other cities. The census was later upheld in higher courts.

1980, September 26 The Congressional Black Caucus marks its tenth anniversary with its annual legislative weekend. The group of bipartisan representatives cite as their major achievements the Humphrey-Hawkins Full Employment Bill and the 10% "minority-set-aside," law established to ensure minority firms a nearly representative share of federal contracts. The caucus identifies its current concern as the potential reapportionment of congressional districts affected by the outcome of the 1980 census.

1980, September 29 Blacks are warned to mobilize against growing evangelical Christian political organizations to protect their social progress by the Congressional Black Caucus. During its legislative weekend, the caucus announces plans to spearhead the mobilization effort, which will include other national leaders.

1980, September 29 The Schomburg Center for Research in Black Culture opens a new $3.8 million building in New York City's Harlem.

1980, September 30 The first annual Black College Day in Washington, D.C. is attended by 18,000 black students. Speeches on the preservation of black colleges and universities are given by black officials and student leaders. The march is organized by black journalist Tony Brown in an effort to draw public attention to the impact of integration and merging of black private and public colleges and universities. Brown contends seven out of 10 blacks attending predominantly white colleges do not graduate.

1980, October 17 The candidacy of Republican nominee Ronald Reagan for President is endorsed by two long-time civil rights leaders, the Reverend Ralph David Abernathy and Hosea Williams. Reverend Abernathy cited President Carter's broken 1976 campaign promises as spurring the endorse-

Because of President Carter's "broken promises" to blacks, the Reverend Ralph Abernathy endorsed 1980 presidential candidate Ronald Reagan.

ment, which came after a private meeting with Reagan.

1980, October 24 Discrimination against blacks and women by the South's largest bank, Republic National, is found in a 272-page ruling by U.S. District Judge Patrick Higginbotham. Discrimination in salaries, promotions, and hiring occurred over a 10-year period, according to Higginbotham. Out of the bank's 570 officers, only 15 were black and none had reached the rank of vice president.

1980, November By an electoral landslide of 483 to 49, Ronald Reagan sweeps Jimmy Carter out of the presidency. The wake of his victory sweeps some of the best senatorial liberal friends of blacks away as well. Heroic liberals such as George McGovern, Frank Church, Birch Bayh, Warren Magnusson, and John Culver lose their senate seats to Republicans and for the first time in almost 30 years, conservatives control the U.S. Senate. Very few voters are enthralled by either Carter or Reagan and had it not been for Carter's maneuvering of the Iranian hostage crisis for his advantage, he might well have lost the nomination to Senator Edward Kennedy. Kennedy's campaign got off to a slow start, but as the months wore on and the disillusion with Car-

ter grew, Kennedy's primary victories increased. It was generally believed that the contest between Carter, a virtually discredited president, and Reagan, the most conservative Republican nominee since Herbert Hoover, would be much closer than the final result. The vast majority of blacks, though disillusioned with Carter, do not vote for him. Many chose to stay home along with whites as only 52% of registered voters vote. Ronald Reagan is elected by only 26% of the eligible voters. With the election of Ronald Reagan and the loss of a Democratic Senate, blacks have little to cheer about and voice concern about the future of the hard-won gains of the past 50 years. There is small minority of blacks, an emerging group with conservative thoughts, such as Gloria Toote, a black senior advisor in Reagan's successful campaign, who says, "Governor Reagan's approach, our approach, is the economic approach. We talk in terms of entrepreneurship and reducing welfare roles simultaneously with increasing work opportunities and full employment." Says Urban League President Vernon Jordan, "We survived Nixon and we can survive Reagan. . . . If you take Mr. Reagan at his word that he is going to put America back to work again, he can't put just white people back to work."

1980, November 23 About 1,000 people from 25 states attend a convention in Philadelphia and form the National Black Independent Party. The idea grows out of a National Black Political Assembly in Gary, Indiana in 1972.

1980, November 30 A special report says that violence and rioting erupted in Miami on May 17 because of the black community's perception of racist conditions and of a local political system stacked against them. Issued by an eight-member private citizens's committee appointed by Governor Bob Graham, it also criticizes the State Attorney's office handling of the Arthur McDuffie case (the black insurance executive beaten to death while in police custody). The report also pointed to the underlying problems of poverty, slum housing, functional illiteracy, and others as causing the rioting.

1980, December 4 Congress sends a $9.1 billion appropriations bill, with controversial legislation preventing the Justice Department from ordering busing to achieve school desegregation, to President Carter. The constitutionality of the anti-busing rider, which prohibits the use of funds "to bring any sort of action to require" busing, is publicly questioned by Attorney General Benjamin Civiletti. In addition, black leaders meet with President Carter to urge him to veto the measure, and on December 14, 1980 President Carter vetoes the funding bill which includes an anti-busing rider that prohib-

Samuel Pierce, President Reagan's Secretary of Housing and Urban Development.

its the Justice Department from initiating court cases to require busing to achieve school desegregation. A spokesman for House Speaker Thomas (Tip) O'Neill, Jr. says no attempt will be made to override the veto. Anti-busing proponents vow to resume their efforts in the next session of Congress.

1980, December 12 Testifying for the government in the civil rights trial of a former Dade County police officer, Dr. Roland Wright says that Arthur McDuffie "died of blunt impact injuries on the head [caused] by a beating." Dr. Wright's testimony challenges police claims that the black insurance executive died from injuries resulting from a motorcycle accident. The officer, Charles Veverka, 30, is charged with assisting in the falsification of reports to make the beating appear an accident. The trial is conducted in San Antonio after being switched from three other cities because of racial tension.

1980, December 12 Black leaders of the nation's major civil rights organizations meet with President-Elect Ronald Reagan, who says he will defend the civil rights of minorities. The leaders urge him to appoint a black to a Cabinet position in his Administration, and include Vernon E. Jordan, Jr., President of the National Urban League, Benjamin Hooks, Executive Director, NAACP, and Dorothy I. Height, President of the National Council of Negro Women.

1980, December 18 A federal grand jury acquits

Charles Veverka, 30, of four counts of violating the civil rights of Arthur McDuffie, a black who was beaten to death while in police custody. The jury deliberated for 16 hours, finally breaking an 11-1 deadlock that threatened a mistrial. Veverka was indicted following violent riots in Miami resulting from the acquittal of four white police officers accused of executing the fatal beating.

1980, December 23 Samuel R. Pierce, Jr., 58, is named by President-Elect Reagan to the Cabinet post of Secretary of the Department of Housing and Urban Development. As such, Pierce is the highest ranking black appointee of the new Administration. According to reports, Pierce is a life-long Republican, widely respected in legal, financial, and civil rights circles.

1981, January 14 Ruth B. Love, 48, is voted the first black general superintendent of Chicago's schools, following the rejection of a black deputy superintendent who has been with the school system for 26 years. The school board, comprised of five blacks, three Hispanics, and three whites, voted 8 to 2 to hire Love. The initial vote rejecting Manford Byrd, Jr., by the white and Hispanic board members was reportedly a reaffirmation of their efforts to bring in an outsider for the job. Love, who had been superintendent of Oakland Public Schools, is also a member of the board of trustees of the National Urban League.

1981, January 17 President Carter disavows the urban policy findings of the President's Commission for a National Agenda for the Eighties, stating that he disagrees with the Commission's recommendation that the federal government should play a role in facilitating the population trend from the Frost Belt to the Sun Belt, and that "we cannot abandon our older urban areas." After receiving a copy of the 44-member Commission's final report, Carter says he agrees with many of its recommendations, but that he opposes many others. He says the older urban areas of the Northeast and Midwest have "unique values and resources" and that their present and future contributions to the national economy must be recognized. The Commission was appointed by Carter in 1979.

1981, January 23 Samuel Pierce, Jr. receives Senate confirmation as Secretary of Housing and Urban Development. He is the only black member of the Reagan Cabinet.

1981, February 7 Three Miami youths are convicted of murder, in connection with the beating deaths of three whites during the Liberty City riots in May 1980. A fourth youth, who was tried with the others, is acquitted. Attorneys for the defendants announce plans to appeal the verdicts.

1981, April 7 The Southern Regional Council issues a report entitled "A Decade of Frustration," finding that public schools in the "black belt" of the Deep South remain inferior to other southern schools despite desegregation efforts. An 18-month examination of these schools in 34 rural counties in Georgia and Alabama, where blacks constitute a majority of the population, found that inferior public schools are often a result of local government decision making. According to the report, exceptions result from two factors—mandatory state and federal standards and school boards with a black majority.

1981, April 16 Incumbent Mayor Tom Bradley of Los Angeles wins his third term with 63.6% of the vote, beating 18 opponents. According to the report, part of Bradley's success is attributed to a successful campaign strategy in which he stayed away from the city's volatile busing issues and was projected as thoughtful and articulate on the issues of fiscal restraint and crime.

1981, May 7 Representative Robert S. Walker (R. Penn.) introduces a bill which prohibits the use of numerical quotas devised to increase the hiring or school enrollment of minorities and women. Entitled the "Equal Employment Opportunity Act," it seeks to amend the Civil Rights Act of 1964 and prevents the federal government from imposing rules on employers or schools to hire workers or to admit students on the basis of race, sex, or national origin. In effect, the proposal no longer requires companies and educational institutions to make up for past discrimination by taking on a set number of minorities and women within a specified time frame.

1981, May 13 The Labor Department proposes revisions of Executive Order 11246 (prohibiting employment discrimination by federal contractors based on race, sex, color, national origin, or religion) in its continuing effort to ease job-discrimination rules for federal contractors. The contents of an internal memorandum reveal the effort seems targeted toward reducing the record keeping and affirmative action requirements for small contractors and eliminating "unnecessary confrontations" with all contractors. Timothy Ryan, Labor Department Solicitor, says that the revisions make the program more manageable and cuts the number of companies covered by two thirds for certain requirements. Secretary Raymond Donovan maintains that a final decision on revisions within the Office of Federal Contracts Compliance Programs has not been made. Administration officials plan to alter the proposal before its effective date of June 29.

1981, May 17 A special study conducted for the Ford Foundation concludes that the Miami riots of 1980 were dramatically different from those of the 1960s, noting that such spontaneous uprisings by blacks to beat or kill whites have not occurred since the slave uprisings before the Civil War. According to the report, unlike the rioters of the 1960s, the Liberty City rioters were from a more law-abiding and representative group.

1981, May 23 Calling them "ineffective" and unfair remedies to discrimination, Attorney General William French Smith announces that the Justice Department will no longer continue its vigorous pursuit of mandatory busing and the use of racial quotas in employment discrimination cases. In effect, the Department will no longer intervene in school desegregation cases dealing with mandatory busing and will abandon its advocacy of affirmative action plans, including quotas in the Supreme Court and elsewhere. It also considers amendments which would make "reverse discrimination" illegal under the Civil Rights Act of 1964.

1981, June 10 The House once again approves an anti-busing provision by a vote of 265 to 122, forbidding the Justice Department from taking any direct or indirect action to require the busing of students to schools other than those closest to where they live, with the exception of cases involving special education needs. The provision is known as an "anti-busing rider" because of its attachment to the Department's $2.3 billion authorized bill.

1981, June 16 The Reagan Administration, in a letter to Attorney General William French Smith, requests the Justice Department to determine whether the political rights of minority Americans are best served by the Voting Rights Act of 1965. Stating that the act marks the nation's commitment to full equality for all Americans, the Administration says that what must be answered is whether the act continues to be the most appropriate means of guaranteeing their rights. The completed report is due October 1.

1981, June 21 Wayne B. Williams, a 23-year-old talent scout and freelance photographer, is charged with the slaying of two of 28 young blacks murdered in Atlanta. He is indicted within a month and the reports of missing persons drop in the city. Williams pleads not guilty.

1981, June 30 Speaking to the NAACP national convention in Denver, President Reagan states that government programs have created a "new kind of bondage for blacks" and calls on the delegates to join him in an effort to allow business and industry to bring about "economic emancipation" for the poor. Generally, the President receives a cold reception from the audience.

1981, July 1 A bipartisan group of 12 Senators takes exception to efforts by "conservative" legislators to limit the role of federal courts in school busing desegregation cases in a "Dear Colleague" letter. The Senators contend that such efforts will "radically alter our basic constitutional framework," and they specifically criticize the business measure sponsored by Senators Jesse Helms (R. N.C.) and J. Bennett Johnston (D. La.). The letter reflects growing concern among "liberals," constitutional scholars, and rights groups, on 25 bills before Congress which seek to restrict the authority of federal courts in school desegregation cases and other controversial issues. Among the senators signing the letter were Edward M. Kennedy (D. Mass.) and Lowell P. Weicker, Jr. (R. Conn.).

1981, July 16 The Reagan Administration sends mixed signals to blacks on its affirmative action and civil rights policy by cutting back the enforcement powers of the Justice Department and by weakening regulations against racial discrimination in employment. A July deadline date for the publication of affirmative action guidelines by the Office of Federal Contract Compliance Practices is delayed until August 26. In addition, the Justice Department's civil rights division only initiates five civil lawsuits on discrimination issues as compared to 17 filed by the Carter Administration in its first six months in office. According to William Bradford Reynolds, Assistant Attorney General-Designate for Civil Rights in the Department, the Administration's actions are not indicative of its unwillingness to litigate civil rights violations but instead constitute its intention to "look at more remedies than those tried in the past that failed."

1981, July 30 According to this report, the House reaches a tentative agreement on a compromise for the extension of the Voting Rights Act of 1965. In what would be a major change in the existing law, some counties would no longer be required to undergo federal review of their local election practices, once they have met stringent requirements dealing with their voting records. Counties in the states covered by the provision would have to prove their compliance with "the letter and spirit of the act," for 10 years. If the proposal is approved, nine states including seven in the South, and portions of 13 other states, may win exemption from seeking Justice Department approval when making changes in local election laws or voting procedures.

1981, August 13 Reagan Administration undertakes its review of 30 federal regulations, including rules on civil rights guidelines, to determine whether they are "burdensome, unnecessary or counterproductive." The review is the third in a series conducted by the Presidential Task Force on Regulatory Relief, which will examine, among other such rules, Title IX regulations requiring companies to maintain hiring guidelines and records to prevent job discrimination against blacks and other minorities. According to Vice President Bush, who announced the start of the study, the regulations are to receive a fair review, which is intended to help stimulate the economy by reducing the rules and record-keeping load on business.

1981, September 9 Roy Wilkins, former head of the NAACP and one of the key players in the Civil Rights movement of the 1960s, dies at New York University Medical Center of uremia at the age of 80.

1981, September 10 Vernon Jordan announces his plans to resign as Executive Director of the National Urban League and join the Dallas-based law firm of Akin, Grump, Hauer and Field. Jordan's office will be in Washington, D.C.

1981, September 11 In a brief to the Supreme Court, the Justice Department indicates that a Washington state law barring a voluntary busing plan in Seattle is no longer considered unconstitutional. Filed by the solicitor general, Rex E. Lee, and William Bardford Reynolds, head of the civil rights division, it

Roy Wilkins, one of the major players in the Civil Rights movement of the sixties, died at the age of 80 in September 1981.

may affect some 10,000 students being bused under the voluntary plan. The Department's reversal is characterized as "unethical and a breech of legal canons" by a school board attorney. A previous ruling by the Ninth U.S. Circuit Court of Appeals found that the law violated the equal protection clause of the constitution's Fourteenth Amendment.

1981, September 13 William Bradford Reynolds, in a reversal of his earlier action, disapproves a staff recommendation that the Justice Department file a legal brief supporting allegations that the voting rights of blacks in Edgefield County, South Carolina have been violated. Black residents contend the county violated the Voting Rights Act by changing its local government from an appointed to an elected form, without submitting the plan to either the Justice Department or the federal district court, as law requires.

1981, October 7 A House vote, 389-24, in favor of extending the Voting Rights Act of 1965, seems to ensure the likelihood of an equally strong measure in the Senate, according to Capitol Hill analysts. The House version makes the preclearance provisions of the act permanent (requiring six southern states and Alaska to submit proposed changes in election laws to the Justice Department before implementation), but also features the so-called bailout

provision that exempts jurisdiction from the requirement if they can prove a clean 10-year, voting rights record and efforts to encourage minority voting.

1981, October 29 Andrew Young defeats Sidney Marcus to succeed Maynard Jackson as Mayor of Atlanta, Georgia.

1981, November 28 The nomination of Clarence M. Pendleton, President of the Urban League of San Diego, to head the U.S. Commission on Civil Rights, results in divided opinion over his suitability for the post. Pendleton's selection is controversial because of his promotion of private industry as a cure-all for black economic problems and because of his opposition to other positions taken traditionally by the civil rights movement on issues such as busing and affirmative action.

1981, December 8 William Bradford Reynolds, Assistant Attorney General of the Justice Department's civil rights division, announces plans to seek a ruling by the Supreme Court which would find it unconstitutional to give minorities and women preference in hiring and promotion. Reynolds wants a reversal of the high court's decision in *Weber* v. *Kaiser Aluminum and Chemical Corp.*, which upheld the legality of affirmative action hiring and promotion practices negotiated by the company and the United Steelworkers of America. Reynolds contends the *Weber* decision was "wrongly decided" and that different sets of rules for the public sector and the private sector should not exist. Under his direction, the Justice Department has ceased such hiring preferences; the action sought by Reynolds would prohibit individuals, the Labor Department, or the Equal Employment Opportunity Commission from seeking such preferences.

1981, December 8 The selection of John E. Jacob, 46, to succeed Vernon E. Jordan, Jr., as President of the National Urban League is announced at a news conference at the agency's headquarters in New York City. Jacob, the NUL's Executive Vice President, is unanimously selected by a special search committee as the best choice among the final contenders. The League's Board of Trustees approves the recommendation. In accepting the appointment, effective January 1, 1982, Jacob says his task is to "make a difference—to help guide the Urban League movement to new heights of effectiveness, to help educate the nation to its unfinished responsibilities, and to help bring fresh opportunities to the black and poor people who are the constituency of the Urban League."

1981, December 11 A filibuster against an anti-busing amendment in the Senate is halted by a vote of

64 to 35. The amendment by Senator J. Bennett Johnston (D. La.) would ban judges deciding school desegregation cases from requiring busing of students for more than five miles or 15 minutes away from their homes. Senator Lowell Weicker, Jr. (R. Conn.), who conducted the filibuster, succeeds in delaying a vote on the measure by proposing a series of procedural motions. Weicker views the entire bill as an unconstitutional attempt by Congress to usurp the authority of the judicial and executive branches.

1982, January 4 Former U.S. Ambassador to the United Nations Andrew Young is inaugurated as Mayor of Atlanta. Young becomes mayor following a runoff election with white State Representative Sidney Marcus.

1982, January Stating that rent in its current New York office headquarters would quadruple, the NAACP asks for help from the offices of Mayor Edward Koch as it sought a new location for its national headquarters. A search committee announced that the civil rights organization was surveying other cities and the group did receive some criticism for allegedly failing to seek out a location in a black neighborhood such as New York City's Harlem.

1982, January 20 Two black civil rights workers, Julia Wilder and Maggie Bozeman, are imprisoned in Alabama after multiple appeals and pleas for leniency, charged with vote fraud.

1982, January 25 Sandra Antoinette Wilson is ordained as the first black female priest in New York City's Episcopal Diocese. She is the fourth in the nation to be ordained.

1982, January 27 Mayor Tom Bradley of Los Angeles opens his campaign to become the first black governor of California. The 64-year-old former policeman has been elected to the mayoralty three times.

1982, January 27 Before a Senate Judiciary subcommittee, the Reagan Administration throws its support behind extension of key provisions of the Voting Rights Act. The Administration, in doing so, states that there is a continuing need to protect the rights of voters who are minorities.

1982, February 5 Mayor Ernest N. "Dutch" Morial, the first black to be elected mayor in New Orleans, wins a second term of office.

1982, February 6 A small band of southern civil rights workers, followed by 300 sympathizers, start a 140-mile march in support of the Federal voting Rights Act and in protest against the vote fraud conviction of two black political activists. The marchers travel from Carrollton, Alabama through Selma to the state capitol, Montgomery, a route made famous in early civil rights marches.

1982, February 7 A key person in the Mississippi voter registration drive in the 1960s, Amzie Moore, dies at the age of 69. Mr. Moore was responsible for bringing students into the state to register voters and also recruited local students to work.

1982, February 8 Wesleyan University ends an admission policy that does not consider the student's ability to pay, which in effect will bar some poor students because of proposed cuts in federal student aid.

1982, February 9 John E. Jacob, new President of the Urban League, announces that the organization will concentrate on four priority issues: pregnancy among black teen-agers, the plight of poor households headed by women, crime in black neighborhoods, and voting registration and education.

1982, February 10 Representative Shirley Chisholm, a Democrat of New York and the first black woman to win a seat in Congress, announces that she will not seek another term. She has served the Brooklyn communities of Bedford-Stuyvesant and Bushwick since 1968.

1982, February 10 The Black and Puerto Rican Caucus of the State Legislature of New York sues to

Representative Shirley Chisholm announced in February 1982 that she would not seek reelection.

force the body's leaders to adopt new Senate, Assembly, and Congressional district lines by March 1.

1982, February 11 The Justice Department proposes that the City of Chicago be allowed to try to desegregate its schools following a plan that would rely mainly on vountary student transfers rather than mandatory busing.

1982, February 12 Bowing to opposition from civil rights groups and several Democratic senators, President Reagan withdraws the nomination of William M. Bell as chairman of the Equal Employment Opportunity Commission and announces that he will instead nominate Clarence Thomas, an Assistant Secretary for Civil Rights in the Department of Education.

1982, February 13 The American Civil Liberties Union accuses southern states of continuous discrimination against black voters in light of the federal enforcement under the Voting Rights Act of 1965.

1982, February 14 Hundreds of voting rights marchers going from Carrollton to Montgomery march peacefully across the four-lane Edmund Pettus Bridge, where as police wielding clubs attacked participants in the Selma-to-Montgomery march.

1982, February 14 The New York State Black and Puerto Rican Legislative Caucus met for its eleventh Legislative Weekend with 700 participants present and hear chairman Assemblyman Albert Vann call for more effort to increase the political power of minority groups in the state.

1982, February 17 Sixty rank-and-file lawyers of the Justice Department's Civil Rights Division question their boss William Bradford Reynolds about his policies, especially tax exemptions for private segregationist schools. Earlier, both the White House and the Justice Department stated that those who had objected to the Administration's policies were free to resign.

1982, February 25 President Reagan announces his decision to request the Supreme Court for a decision about whether racially discriminatory schools should receive tax-exempt status. The move is the latest in a series of moves to resolve a politically explosive issue precipitated by the Administration's support for tax-exempt status for such schools.

1982, February 27 A jury in Atlanta finds Wayne Williams guilty in the sensational murder case involving two slain young men. He is sentenced to consecutive life terms but indicates he will seek a new trial. Within days after the conviction, Atlanta authorities dismantle the task force which had worked for months to solve the murders of 28 young black people in Atlanta.

Representative Parren J. Mitchell attacked Reagan's Urban Enterprise Zone program.

1982, March Reverend Sam B. Hart, nominated by President Reagan for a position on the U.S. Civil Rights Commission, resigns after pressure against his nomination due to outrage by a number of groups over positions he had taken regarding individual rights and some concern about his past financial status.

1982, March 2 Representative Parren J. Mitchell makes public a 63-page report, "Urban Policy Issues," and states that the national policy is in disarray and that the cities will not be aided by President Reagan's proposed Urban Enterprise Zone program designed to encourage business development of inner cities through tax incentives.

1982, March 3 After the Senate passes a sweeping anti-busing bill by a vote of 57–37 (following a filibuster of eight months), House Speaker Thomas P. O'Neill, Jr. says he will take no action on the legislation unless asked to do so by two key committee chairmen.

1982, March 4 The Federal Bureau of Investigation is asked by the White House to reopen an investigation into the background of Clarence M. Pendleton, who had been nominated for the chairmanship of the U.S. Commission on Civil Rights.

1982, March 13 The Reagan Administration is defended by Assistant Attorney General William Bradford on its rejection of preferential hiring and promotion of minority groups. Reynolds states that "this administration is firmly committed to the view that the Constitution and laws of the United States protect the rights of every person, whether black or white, male or female, to pursue his or her goals in an environment of racial and sexual neutrality."

1982, April 4 The Bureau of Census reports that the 1980 census missed counting 1.3 million blacks and that the undercount represented 4.8% of the nation's 28 million blacks. The Bureau says that in 1970 the census missed 1.9 million out of 24.4 million blacks.

1982, April 14 Eight surviving black members of "the Golden 13" hold a reunion at sea aboard the U.S.S. Kidd off Virginia. The Golden 13 were the first blacks to wear the gold stripes of commissioned officers.

1982, April 18 A study of national test results shows that black children closed the gap on whites in educational achievement tests during the 1970s. Dr. Lyle V. Jones, author of the study, says that blacks probably had an increased motivation to succeed.

1982, April 27 Private Joseph C. Christopher, a 26-year-old white Army private is found guilty of murdering four blacks in Buffalo and a Hispanic man in New York City.

1982, June 8 Mayor Tom Bradley of Los Angeles wins the Democratic nomination for Governor of California. Bradley will face Attorney General George Deukmejian in the general election. If elected, Bradley would become the first black governor in the United States.

1982, June 15 Kenneth A. Gibson is elected to a fourth term as Mayor of Newark, New Jersey, defeating City Council President Earl Harris in a runoff election. Gibson is the Mayor of New Jersey's largest city for a record fourth time.

1982, June 18 and 23 The Senate approves the landmark Voting Rights Act of 1965 by a vote of 85–8, as a quarter-century renewal of the enforcement provisions designed to guarantee free access to the polls for blacks and other minorities. Senator Jesse Helms of North Carolina delayed the voting for 10 days after he vowed to block the extension of the bill. The House approved the extension on June 23.

SIGNIFICANT DOCUMENTS IN AFRO–AMERICAN HISTORY (1688–1975)

Resolutions ■ Declarations ■ Constitutional Provisions and Amendments ■ Editorials ■ Laws ■ Proclamations ■ Speeches ■ Executive Orders ■ Manifestos

The documents included in this section—whether they be resolutions, legislative enactments, amendments to the Constitution, executive proclamations, or presidential speeches—have all been chosen because they bear a special relevance to black history in the United States. Some—like the Declaration of Independence, the Constitution, the Emancipation Proclamation—are household words which are an explicit part of every American's heritage; others, though less known, deserve comparable status. In themselves, they offer eloquent testimony to the impact of the black on American history—as slave, as freedman, and, ultimately, as full-fledged American citizen.

THE GERMANTOWN MENNONITE RESOLUTION AGAINST SLAVERY (1688)

The Germantown Mennonite Resolution Against Slavery represents the earliest such protest formally voiced in Colonial America. It was passed 69 years after the introduction of the first black slaves in America—at a time when the number of slaves in the Colonies was comparatively small. It was not until 1775, however, that the Quakers, a religious group similarly opposed to the institution, formed the first antislavery society in the Colonies.

This is to the monthly meeting held at Richard Worrell's:

These are the reasons why we are against the traffic of men-body, as followeth: Is there any that would be done or handled at this manner? viz., to be sold or made a slave for all the time of his life? How fearful and faint-hearted are many at sea, when they see a strange vessel, being afraid it should be a Turk, and they should be taken, and sold for slaves into Turkey. Now, what is *this* better done, than Turks do? Yea, rather it is worse for them, which say they are Christians; for we hear that the most part of such negers are brought hither against their will and consent, and that many of them are stolen. Now, though they are black, we cannot conceive there is more liberty to have them slaves, as it is to have other white ones. There is a saying, that we should do to all men like as we will be done ourselves; making no difference of what generation, descent, or colour they are. And

95

These half-starved and physically weak slaves have just disembarked in America.

those who steal or rob men, and those who buy or purchase them, are they not all alike? Here is liberty of conscience, which is right and reasonable; here ought to be likewise liberty of the body, except of evil-doers, which is another case. But to bring men hither, or to rob and sell them against their will, we stand against. In Europe there are many oppressed for conscience-sake; and here there are those oppressed which are of a black colour. And we who know that men must not commit adultery—some do commit adultery *in* others, separating wives from their husbands, and giving them to others: and some sell the children of these poor creatures to other men. Ah! do consider well this thing, you who do it, if

you would be done at this manner—and if it is done according to Christianity! You surpass Holland and Germany in this thing. This makes an ill report in all those countries of Europe, where they hear of [it], that the Quakers do here handel men as they handel there the cattle. And for that reason some have no mind or inclination to come hither. And who shall maintain this your cause, or plead for it? Truly, we cannot do so, except you shall inform us better hereof, viz.: that Christians have liberty to practice these things. Pray, what thing in the world can be done worse towards us, than if men should rob or steal us away, and sell us for slaves to strange countries; separating husbands from their wives and children. Being now this is not done in the manner we would be done at; therefore, we contradict, and are against his traffic of men-body. And we who profess that it is not lawful to steal, must, likewise, avoid to purchase such things as are stolen, but rather help to stop this robbing and stealing, if possible. And such men ought to be delivered out of the hands of the robbers, and set free as in Europe. Then is Pennsylvania to have a good report, instead, it hath now a bad one, for this sake, in other countries; especially whereas the Europeans are desirous to know in what manner *the Quakers* do rule in *their* province; and most of them do look upon us with an envious eye. But if this is done well, what shall we say is done evil?

If once these slaves (which they say are so wicked and stubborn men) should join themselves—fight for their freedom, and handel their masters and mistresses, as they did handel them before; will these masters and mistresses take the sword at hand and war against these poor slaves, like, as we are able to believe, some will not refuse to do? Or, have these poor negers not as much right to fight for their freedom, as you have to keep them slaves?

Now consider well this thing, if it is good or bad. And in case you find it to be good to handel these black in that manner, we desire and require you hereby lovingly, that you may inform us herein, which at this time never was done, viz., that Christians have such a liberty to do so. To the end we shall be satisfied on this point, and satisfy likewise our good friends and acquaintances in our native country, to whom it is a terror, or fearful thing, that men should be handelled so in Pennsylvania.

This is from our meeting at Germantown, held ye 18th of the 2d month, 1688, to be delivered to the monthly meeting at Richard Worrell's.

Garret Henderich,
Derick op de Graeff,
Francis Daniel Pastorius,
Abram op de Graeff.

THE DECLARATION OF INDEPENDENCE (1776)

The final version of the Declaration of Independence, as accepted by Congress, did not contain the following paragraph written by Thomas Jefferson as part of an initial draft of the document:

"He has waged cruel war against human nature itself, violating its most sacred rights of life and liberty in the persons of a distant people who never offended him, captivating and carrying them into slavery in another hemisphere, or to incur miserable death in their transportation thither. This piratical warfare, the opprobrium of infidel *powers, is the warfare of the Christian king of Great Britain. Determined to keep open a market where MEN should be bought and sold, he has prostituted his negative for suppressing every legislative attempt to prohibit or to restrain this execrable commerce; and that this assemblage of horrors might want no fact of distinguished die, he is now exciting these very people to rise in arms among us, and to purchase that liberty of which* he *deprived them by murdering the people upon whom he also obtruded them; thus paying off former crimes committed against the liberties of one people, with crimes which he urges them to commit against the lives of another."*

The omission of this passage reflected the awareness on the part of some Congressmen that a number of New England merchants were profitably engaged in the slave trade. Other legislators were simply in favor of slavery as an institution, and felt that the inclusion of such sentiments would prejudice the case for its continuation.

Many historians and critics have understandably concluded that the elimination of this passage offers adequate proof that the American black, unlike his white counterpart, was never meant to share in the fruits of independence and equality in his adopted homeland.

When in the Course of human events, it becomes necessary for one people to dissolve the political bands which have connected them with another, and to assume among the Powers of the earth, the separate and equal station to which the Laws of Nature and of Nature's God entitle them, a decent respect to the opinions of mankind requires that they should declare the causes which impel them to the separation.

We hold these truths to be self-evident, that all men are created equal, that they are endowed by their Creator with certain unalienable Rights, that among these are Life, Liberty and the pursuit of Happi

When his attacks on the Crown shocked other Virginia legislators, Patrick Henry shouted: "Give me liberty or give me death!"

ness. That to secure these rights, Governments are instituted among Men, deriving their just powers from the consent of the governed, That whenever any Form of Government becomes destructive of these ends, it is the Right of the People to alter or to abolish it, and to institute new Government, laying its foundation on such principles and organizing its powers in such form, as to them shall seem most likely to effect their Safety and Happiness. Prudence, indeed, will dictate that Governments long established should not be changed for light and transient causes; and accordingly all experience hath shown, that mankind are more disposed to suffer, while evils are sufferable, than to right themselves by abolishing the forms to which they are accustomed. But when a long train of abuses and usurpations, pursuing invariably the same Object evinces a design to reduce them under absolute Despotism, it is their right, it is their duty, to throw off such Government, and to provide new Guards for their future security.—Such has been the patient sufferance of these Colonies; and such is now the necessity which constrains them to alter their former Systems of Government. The history of the present King of Great Britain is a history of repeated injuries and usurpations, all having in direct object the establishment of an absolute Tyranny over these States. To prove this, let Facts be submitted to a candid world.

He has refused his Assent to Laws, the most wholesome and necessary for the public good.

He has forbidden his Governors to pass Laws of immediate and pressing importance, unless suspended in their operation till his Assent should be obtained; and when so suspended, he has utterly neglected to attend to them.

He has refused to pass other Laws for the accommodation of large districts of people, unless those people would relinquish the right of Representation in the Legislature, a right inestimable to them and formidable to tyrants only.

He has called together legislative bodies at places unusual, uncomfortable, and distant from the depository of their Public Records, for the sole purpose of Fatiguing them into compliance with his measures.

He has dissolved Representative Houses repeatedly, for opposing with manly firmness his invasions on the rights of the people.

He has refused for a long time, after such dissolutions, to cause others to be elected; whereby the Legislative Powers, incapable of Annihilation, have returned to the People at large for their exercise; the State remaining in the mean time exposed to all the dangers of invasion from without, and convulsions within.

He has endeavoured to prevent the population of these States; for that purpose obstructing the Laws of Naturalization of Foreigners; refusing to pass others to encourage their migration hither, and raising the conditions of new Appropriations of Lands.

He has obstructed the Administration of Justice, by refusing his Assent to Laws for establishing Judiciary Powers.

He has made Judges dependent on his Will alone, for the tenure of their offices, and the amount and payment of their salaries.

He has erected a multitude of New Offices, and sent hither swarms of Officers to harass our People, and eat out their substance.

He has kept among us, in times of peace, Standing Armies without the Consent of our legislature.

He has affected to render the Military independent of and superior to the Civil Power.

He has combined with others to subject us to a jurisdiction foreign to our constitution, and unacknowledged by our laws; giving his Assent to their acts of pretended legislation:

For quartering large bodies of armed troops among us:

For protecting them, by a mock Trial, from Punishment for any Murders which they should commit on the Inhabitants of these States:

For cutting off our Trade with all parts of the world:

For imposing taxes on us without our Consent:

For depriving us in many cases, of the benefits of Trial by Jury:

For transporting us beyond Seas to be tried for pretended offences:

For abolishing the free System of English Laws in a neighbouring Province, establishing therein an Arbitrary government, and enlarging its Boundaries so as to render it at once an example and fit instrument for introducing the same absolute rule into these Colonies:

For taking away our Charters, abolishing our most valuable Laws, and altering fundamentally the Forms of our Governments:

For suspending our own Legislature, and declaring themselves invested with Power to legislate for us in all cases whatsoever.

He has abdicated Government here, by declaring us out of his Protection and waging War against us.

He has plundered our seas, ravaged our Coasts, burnt our towns, and destroyed the lives of our people.

He is at this time transporting large armies of foreign mercenaries to compleat the works of death, desolation and tyranny, already begun with circumstances of Cruelty & perfidy scarcely paralleled in the most barbarous ages, and totally unworthy the Head of a civilized nation.

He has constrained our fellow Citizens taken Captive on the high Seas to bear Arms against their Country, to become the executioners of their friends and Brethren, or to fall themselves by their Hands.

He has excited domestic insurrections amongst us, and has endeavoured to bring on the inhabitants of our frontiers, the merciless Indian Savages, whose known rule of warfare, is an undistinguished destruction of all ages, sexes and conditions.

In every stage of these Oppressions We have Petitioned for Redress in the most humble terms: Our repeated Petitions have been answered only by repeated injury. A Prince, whose character is thus marked by every act which may define a Tyrant, is unfit to be the ruler of a free People.

Nor have We been wanting in attention to our British brethren. We have warned them from time to time of attempts by their legislature to extend an unwarrantable jurisdiction over us. We have reminded them of the circumstances of our emigration and settlement here. We have appealed to their native justice and magnanimity, and we have conjured them by the ties of our common kindred to disavow these usurpations, which would inevitably interrupt our connections and correspondence. They too have been deaf to the voice of justice and of consanguinity. We must, therefore, acquiesce in the necessity, which denounces our Separation, and hold them, as we hold the rest of mankind, Enemies in War, in Peace Friends.

We, therefore, the Representatives of the United States of America, in General Congress, Assembled, appealing to the Supreme Judge of the world for the rectitude of our intentions, do, in the Name, and by Authority of the good People of these Colonies, solemnly publish and declare, That these United Colonies are, and of Right ought to be Free and Independent States; that they are Absolved from all Allegiance to the British Crown, and that all political connection between them and the State of Great Britain, is and ought to be totally dissolved; and that as Free and Independent States, they have full Power to levy War, conclude Peace, contract Alliances, establish Commerce, and to do all other Acts and Things which Independent States may of right do. And for the support of this Declaration, with a firm reliance on the Protection of Divine Providence, we mutually pledge to each other our Lives, our Fortunes and our sacred Honor.

JOHN HANCOCK.

Massachusetts-Bay
SAML. ADAMS,
JOHN ADAMS,
ROBT. TREAT PAINE,
ELBRIDGE GERRY.

New Hampshire
JOSIAH BARTLETT,
WM. WHIPPLE,
MATTHEW THORNTON.

Rhode Island
STEP. HOPKINS,
WILLIAM ELLERY.

Pennsylvania
ROBT. MORRIS,
BENJAMIN RUSH,
BENJA. FRANKLIN,
JOHN MORTON,
GEO. CLYMER,
JAS. SMITH,
GEO. TAYLOR,
JAMES WILSON,
GEO. ROSS.

Connecticut
ROGER SHERMAN,

SAM'EL HUNTINGTON,
WM. WILLIAMS,
OLIVER WOLCOTT,
GEO. READ,
THO. M'KEAN.

Georgia
BUTTON GWINNETT,
LYMAN HALL,
GEO. WALTON.

Delaware
CAESAR RODNEY.

North Carolina
WM. HOOPER,
JOSEPH HEWES,
JOHN PENN.

Maryland
SAMUEL CHASE,
WM. PACA,
THOS. STONE,
CHARLES CARROLL
of Carrollton.

New York
WM. FLOYD,

PHIL. LIVINGSTON,
FRANS. LEWIS,
LEWIS MORRIS.

South Carolina
EDWARD RUTLEDGE,
THOS. HEYWARD, JUNR.,
THOMAS LYNCH, JUNR.,
ARTHUR MIDDLETON.

New Jersey
RICHD. STOCKTON,
JNO. WITHERSPOON,
FRAS. HOPKINSON,
JOHN HART,
ABRA. CLARK.

Virginia
GEORGE WYTHE,
RICHARD HENRY LEE,
TH. JEFFERSON,
BENJA. HARRISON,
THS. NELSON, JR.,
FRANCIS LIGHTFOOT LEE,
CARTER BRAXTON.

THE OMITTED ANTI-SLAVERY CLAUSE (1776)

Thomas Jefferson's attitudes to blacks varied during his lifetime. In his early years, Jefferson thought blacks were biologically inferior, then decided that slavery had a destructive conditioning effect which stamped blacks with "odious peculiarities." With this view, and spurred by his conviction that "natural rights" accrued to all men, Jefferson penned a short, passionate attack on King George III's indulgence of the slave traffic, for inclusion in the Declaration of Independence. But, at the behest of delegates from South Carolina and Georgia, and with the indulgence of northern delegates whose ports sheltered and profited from slave ships, the clause was omitted from the final version.

He [King George III] has waged cruel war against human nature itself, violating its most sacred rights of life and liberty in the persons of a distant people who never offended him, captivating and carrying them into slavery in another hemisphere, or to incur miserable death in their transportation thither. This piratical warfare, the opprobrium of *infidel* powers, is the warfare of the *Christian* king of Great Britain. Determined to keep open a market where MEN should be bought and sold, he has prostituted his negative for suppressing every legislative attempt to prohibit or restrain this execrable commerce.

THE CONSTITUTION OF THE UNITED STATES (1787)

Although we have chosen to print the Constitution and the Bill of Rights in their entirety, we are more concerned—within the framework of this volume—with two passages in particular: Sections 2 and 9 of Article I. Section 2, containing the so-called three-fifths compromise (see paragraph 3, section 2, first sentence set in italic), in effect defines the black ("other Persons") as three-fifths of the white man ("free Persons"). Section 9 (the first two paragraphs of which are also in italic) provides both for the extension of the slave trade for a 20-year period, and for the return of runaway slaves. Such passages attest to the strong element of conservatism that existed in the United States in the critical period following the Revolutionary War.

WE THE PEOPLE of the United States, in Order to form a more perfect Union, establish Justice, insure domestic Tranquility, provide for the common defence, promote the general Welfare, and secure the Blessings of Liberty to ourselves and our Posterity, do ordain and establish this Constitution for the United States of America.

ART. I

SEC. 1. All legislative Powers herein granted shall be vested in a Congress of the United States, which shall consist of a Senate and House of Representatives.

SEC. 2. The House of Representatives shall be composed of Members chosen every second Year by the People of the several States, and the Electors in each State shall have the Qualifications requisite for Electors of the most numerous Branch of the State Legislature.

No person shall be a Representative who shall not have attained to the Age of twenty-five Years, and been seven Years a Citizen of the United States, and who shall not, when elected, be an Inhabitant of that State in which he shall be chosen.

Representatives and direct Taxes shall be apportioned among the several States which may be included within this Union, according to their respective Numbers, which shall be determined by adding to the whole Number of free Persons, including those bound to Service for a Term of Years, and excluding Indians not taxed, three-fifths of all other Persons. The actual Enumeration shall be made within three Years after the first Meeting of the Congress of the United States, and within every subsequent Term of ten Years, in such Manner as they shall by Law direct. The Number of Representatives shall not exceed one for every thirty Thousand, but each State shall have at Least one Representative; and until such enumeration shall be made, the State of New Hampshire shall be entitled to chuse three, Massachusetts eight, Rhode-Island and Providence Plantations one, Connecticut five, New York six, New Jersey four, Pennsylvania eight, Delaware one, Maryland six, Virginia ten, North Carolina five, South Carolina five, and Georgia three.

When vacancies happen in the Representation from any State, the Executive Authority thereof shall issue Writs of Election to fill such Vacancies.

The House of Representatives shall chuse their Speaker and other Officers; and shall have the sole Power of Impeachment.

SEC. 3. The Senate of the United States shall be composed of two Senators from each State, chosen by the Legislature thereof, for six Years; and each Senator shall have one Vote.

Immediately after they shall be assembled in Consequence of the first Election, they shall be divided as equally as may be into three Classes. The Seats of the Senators of the first Class shall be vacated at

Jefferson's denunciation of the slave trade was voted out of the Declaration of Independence.

the Expiration of the second Year, of the second Class at the Expiration of the fourth Year, and of the third Class at the Expiration of the sixth Year, so that one third may be chosen every second Year; and if Vacancies happen by Resignation, or otherwise, during the Recess of the Legislature of any State, the Executive thereof may make temporary Appointments until the next Meeting of the Legislature, which shall then fill such Vacancies.

No Person shall be a Senator who shall not have attained to the Age of thirty Years, and been nine Years a Citizen of the United States, and who shall not, when elected, be an Inhabitant of that State for which he shall be chosen.

The Vice President of the United States shall be President of the Senate, but shall have no Vote, unless they be equally divided.

The Senate shall chuse their other Officers, and also a President protempore, in the Absence of the Vice President, or when he shall exercise the Office of President of the United States.

The Senate shall have the sole Power to try all Impeachments. When sitting for that Purpose, they shall be on Oath or Affirmation. When the President of the United States is tried, the Chief Justice shall preside: And no Person shall be convicted without the Concurrence of two thirds of the Members present.

Judgment in Cases of Impeachment shall not extend further than to removal from Office, and disqualification to hold and enjoy any Office of honor, Trust or Profit under the United States: but the Party convicted shall nevertheless be liable and subject to Indictment, Trial, Judgment and Punishment, according to Law.

SEC. 4. The Times, Places and Manner of holding Elections for Senators and Representatives, shall be prescribed in each State by the Legislature thereof; but the Congress may at any time by Law make or alter such Regulations, except as to the Places of chusing Senators.

The Congress shall assemble at least once in every Year, and such Meeting shall be on the first Monday in December, unless they shall by Law appoint a different Day.

SEC. 5. Each House shall be the Judge of the Elections, Returns and Qualifications of its own Members, and a Majority of each shall constitute a Quorum to do Business; but a smaller Number may adjourn from day to day, and may be authorized to compel the Attendance of absent Members, in such Manner, and under such Penalties as each House may provide.

Each House may determine the Rules of its Proceedings, Punish its Members for disorderly Behaviour, and, with the Concurrence of two thirds, expel a Member.

Each House shall keep a Journal of its Proceedings, and from time to time publish the same, excepting such Parts as may in their Judgment require Secrecy; and the Yeas and Nays of the Members of either House on any question shall, at the Desire of one fifth of those Present, be entered on the Journal.

Neither House, during the Session of Congress, shall, without the Consent of the other, adjourn for more than three days, nor to any other Place than that in which the two Houses shall be sitting.

SEC. 6. The Senators and Representatives shall receive a Compensation for their Services, to be ascertained by Law, and paid out of the Treasury of the United States. They shall in all Cases, except Treason, felony and Breach of the Peace, be privileged from Arrest during their Attendance at the Session of their respective Houses, and in going to and returning from the same; and for any speech or Debate in either House, they shall not be questioned in any other Place.

No Senator or Representative shall, during the Time for which he was elected, be appointed to any civil Office under the Authority of the United States which shall have been created, or the Emoluments whereof shall have been encreased during such time; and no Person holding any Office under the United States, shall be a Member of either House during his Continuance in Office.

SEC. 7. All Bills for raising Revenue shall originate in the House of Representatives; but the Senate may propose or concur with Amendments as on other Bills.

Every Bill which shall have passed the House of Representatives and the Senate, shall, before it becomes a Law, be presented to the President of the United States; If he approves he shall sign it, but if not he shall return it, with his Objections to that House in which it shall have originated, who shall enter the Objections at large on their Journal, and proceed to reconsider it. If after such Reconsideration two thirds of that House shall agree to pass the Bill, it shall be sent, together with the Objections, to the other House, by which it shall likewise be reconsidered, and if approved by two thirds of that House, it shall become a Law. But in all such Cases the Votes of both Houses shall be determined by Yeas and Nays, and the Names of the Persons voting for and against the Bill shall be entered on the Journal of each House respectively. If any Bill shall not be returned by the President within ten Days (Sundays excepted) after it shall have been presented to him, the Same shall be a Law, in like Manner as if he had signed it, unless the Congress by their Adjournment prevent its Return, in which Case it shall not be a Law.

Every Order, Resolution, or Vote to which the Concurrence of the Senate and House of Representatives may be necessary (except on a question of Adjournment) shall be presented to the President of the United States; and before the Same shall take Effect, shall be approved by him, or being disapproved by him, shall be repassed by two thirds of the Senate and House of Representatives, according to the Rules and Limitations prescribed in the Case of a Bill.

SEC. 8. The Congress shall have Power To lay and collect Taxes, Duties, Imposts and Excises, to pay the Debts and provide for the common Defence and general Welfare of the United States; but all Duties, Imposts and Excises shall be uniform throughout the United States;

To borrow Money on the credit of the United States;

To regulate Commerce with foreign Nations, and among the several States, and with the Indian Tribes;

To establish a uniform Rule of Naturalization, and uniform Laws on the subject of Bankruptcies throughout the United States;

To coin Money, regulate the Value thereof, and of foreign Coin, and fix the Standard of Weights and Measures;

To provide for the Punishment of counterfeiting and Securities and current Coin of the United States;

To establish Post Offices and post Roads;

To promote the Progress of Science and useful Arts, by securing for limited Times to Authors and Inventors the exclusive Right to their respective Writings and Discoveries;

To constitute Tribunals inferior to the supreme Court;

To define and punish Piracies and Felonies committed on the high Seas, and Offences against the Law of Nations;

To declare War, grant Letters of Marque and Reprisal, and make Rules concerning Captures on Land and Water;

To raise and support Armies, but no Appropriation of Money to that Use shall be for a longer Term than two Years;

To provide and maintain a Navy;

To make Rules for the Government and Regulation of the land and naval Forces;

To provide for calling forth the Militia to execute the Laws of the Union, suppress Insurrections and repel Invasions;

To provide for organizing, arming, and disciplining, the Militia, and for governing such Part of them as may be employed in the Service of the United States, reserving to the States respectively, the Appointment of the Officers, and the Authority of training the Militia according to the discipline prescribed by Congress;

To exercise exclusive Legislation in all Cases whatsoever, over such District (not exceeding ten Miles square) as may, by Cession of particular States, and the Acceptance of Congress, become the Seat of the Government of the United States, and to exercise like Authority over all Places purchased by the Consent of the Legislature of the State in which the Same shall be, for the Erection of Forts, Magazines, Arsenals, dock-Yards, and other needful Buildings;—And

To make all Laws which shall be necessary and proper for carrying into Execution the foregoing Powers, and all other Powers vested by this Constitution in the Government of the United States, or in any Department or Officer thereof.

SEC. 9. *The Migration or Importation of such Persons as any of the States now existing shall think proper to admit, shall not be prohibited by the Congress prior to the Year one thousand eight hundred and eight, but a Tax or duty may be imposed on such*

Importation, not exceeding ten dollars for each Person.

The Privilege of the Writ of Habeas Corpus shall not be suspended, unless when in Cases of Rebellion or Invasion the public Safety may require it.

No Bill of Attainder or ex post facto Law shall be passed.

No Capitation, or other direct, Tax shall be laid, unless in Proportion to the Census or Enumeration before directed to be taken.

No Tax or Duty shall be laid on Articles exported from any State.

No Preference shall be given by any Regulation of Commerce or Revenue to the Ports of one State over those of another: nor shall Vessels bound to, or from, one State, be obliged to enter, clear, or pay Duties in another.

No Money shall be drawn from the Treasury, but in Consequence of Appropriations made by Law; and a regular Statement and Account of the Receipts and Expenditures of all public Money shall be published from time to time.

No Title of Nobility shall be granted by the United States: And no Person holding any Office of Profit or Trust under them, shall, without the Consent of the Congress, accept of any present, Emolument, Office, or Title, of any kind whatever, from any King, Prince or foreign State.

SEC. 10. No State shall enter into any Treaty, Alliance, or Confederation; grant Letters of Marque and Reprisal; coin Money; emit Bills of Credit; make any Thing but gold and silver Coin a Tender in Payment of Debts; pass any Bill of Attainder, ex post facto Law, or Law impairing the Obligation of Contracts, or grant any Title of Nobility.

No State shall, without the Consent of the Congress, lay any Imposts or Duties on Imports or Exports, except what may be absolutely necessary for executing its inspection Laws: and the net Produce of all duties and Imposts, laid by any State on Imports or Exports, shall be for the Use of the Treasury of the United States; and all such Laws shall be subject to the Revision and Control of the Congress.

No State shall, without the Consent of Congress, lay any Duty of Tonnage, keep Troops, or Ships of War in time of Peace, enter into any Agreement or Compact with another State, or with a foreign Power, or engage in War, unless actually invaded, or in such imminent Danger as will not admit of delay.

ART. II

SEC. 1. The executive Power shall be vested in a President of the United States of America. He shall hold his Office during the Term of four Years, and, together with the Vice President, chosen for the same Term, be elected, as follows

Each State shall appoint, in such Manner as the Legislature thereof may direct, a Number of Electors,

Colonial slave markets such as this one were given a twenty-year lease by the Constitution.

equal to the whole Number of Senators and Representatives to which the State may be entitled in the Congress: but no Senator or Representative, or Person holding an Office of Trust or Profit under the United States, shall be appointed an Elector.

The electors shall meet in their respective States, and vote by Ballot for two Persons, of whom one at least shall not be an inhabitant of the same State with themselves. And they shall make a List of all the Persons voted for, and of the Number of Votes for each; which List they shall sign and certify, and transmit sealed to the Seat of the Government of the United States, directed to the President of the Senate. The President of the Senate shall, in the Presence of the Senate and House of Representatives, open all the Certificates, and the Votes shall then be counted. The Person having the greatest Number of Votes shall be the President, if such Number be a Majority of the whole Number of Electors appointed; and if there be more than one who have such Majority, and have an equal Number of Votes, then the House of Representatives shall immediately chuse by Ballot one of them for President; and if no person have a Majority, then from the five highest on the List the said House shall in like Manner chuse the President. But in chusing the President, the Votes shall be taken by States, the Representation from each State having one Vote; A quorum for this Purpose shall consist of a Member or Members from two thirds of the States, and a Majority of all the states shall be necessary to a choice. In every case, after the choice of the president, the person having the greatest number of Votes of the Electors shall be the Vice President. If there should remain two or more who have equal Votes, the Senate shall chuse from them by Ballot the Vice President.

The Congress may determine the Time of chusing the Electors, and the Day on which they shall give their Votes; which Day shall be the same throughout the United States.

No Person except a natural born Citizen, or a Citizen of the United States, at the time of the Adoption of this Constitution, shall be eligible to the Office of President; neither shall any Person be eligible to that Office who shall not have attained to the Age of thirty-five Years, and been fourteen Years a Resident within the United States.

In Case of the Removal of the President from Office, or of his Death, resignation, or Inability to discharge the Powers and Duties of the said Office, the Same shall devolve on the Vice President, and the Congress may by Law provide for the Case of Removal, Death, Resignation or Inability, both of the President and Vice President, declaring what Officer shall then act as President, and such Officer shall act accordingly, until the Disability be removed, or a President shall be elected.

The President shall, at stated Times, receive for his Services, a Compensation, which shall neither be encreased nor diminished during the Period for which he shall have been elected, and he shall not receive within that Period any other Emolument from the United States, or any of them.

Before he enter on the execution of his Office, he shall take the following Oath or Affirmation:—"I do solemnly swear (or affirm) that I will faithfully execute the Office of President of the United States, and will to the best of my Ability, preserve, protect and defend the Constitution of the United States."

SEC. 2. The President shall be Commander in Chief of the Army and Navy of the United States, and of the Militia of the several States, when called into the actual Service of the United States; he may require the Opinion, in writing, of the principal Officer in each of the executive Departments, upon any Subject relating to the Duties of their respective Offices, and he shall have Power to grant Reprieves and Pardons for Offences against the United States, except in cases of Impeachment.

He shall have Power, by and with the Advice and Consent of the Senate, to make Treaties, provided two thirds of the Senators present concur; and he shall nominate, and by and with the Advice and Consent of the Senate, shall appoint Ambassadors, other public Ministers and Consuls, Judges of the Supreme Court, and all other Offices of the United States, whose Appointments are not herein otherwise provided for, and which shall be established by Law; but the Congress may by Law vest the Appointment of such inferior Officers, as they think proper, in the President alone, in the Courts of Law, or in the Heads of Departments.

The President shall have Power to fill up all Vacancies that may happen during the Recess of the Senate, by granting Commissions which shall expire at the end of their next Session.

SEC. 3. He shall from time to time give to the Congress Information of the State of the Union, and recommend to their Consideration such Measures as he shall judge necessary and expedient; he may, on extraordinary Occasions, convene both Houses, or either of them, and in Case of Disagreement between them, with Respect to the Time of Adjournment, he may adjourn them to such Time as he shall think proper; he shall receive Ambassadors and other public Ministers; he shall take care that the Laws be faithfully executed, and shall Commission all the Officers of the United States.

SEC. 4. The President, Vice President and all civil Officers of the United States, shall be removed from Office on Impeachment for, and Conviction of, Treason, Bribery, or other high Crimes and Misdemeanors.

Many of the revolutionaries who declared independence from Britain reconvened to draw up the Constitution.

ART. III

SEC. 1. The judicial Power of the United States, shall be vested in one supreme Court. And in such inferior Courts as the Congress may from time to time ordain and establish. The Judges, both of the supreme and inferior Courts, shall hold their Offices during good Behaviour, and shall, at stated Times, receive for their Services, a Compensation which shall not be diminished during their Continuance in Office.

SEC. 2. The judicial Power shall extend to all Cases, in Law and Equity, arising under this Constitution, the Laws of the United States, and Treaties made, or which shall be made, under their Authority;—to all Cases affecting Ambassadors, other public Ministers and Consuls;—to all Cases of admiralty and maritime Jurisdiction;—to Controversies to which the United States shall be a Party;—to Controversies between two or more States;—between a State and Citizens of another State;—between Citizens of different states,—between Citizens of the same State claiming Lands under Grants of different States, and between a State, or the Citizens thereof, and foreign States, Citizens or Subjects.

In all Cases affecting Ambassadors, other public Ministers and Consuls, and those in which a State shall be Party, the supreme Court shall have original Jurisdiction. In all the other Cases before mentioned, the supreme Court shall have appellate Jurisdiction, both as to Law and Fact, with such Exceptions, and under such Regulations as the Congress shall make.

The Trial of all Crimes, except in Cases of Impeachment, shall be by Jury; and such Trial shall be held in the State where the said Crimes shall have been committed; but when not committed within any State, the Trial shall be at such Place or Places as the Congress may by Law have directed.

SEC. 3. Treason against the United States, shall consist only in levying War against them, or in adhering to their Enemies, giving them Aid and Comfort. No Person shall be convicted of Treason unless on the Testimony of two Witnesses to the same overt Act, or on Confession in open Court.

The Congress shall have Power to declare the Punishment of Treason, but no Attainder of Treason shall work Corruption of Blood, or Forfeiture except during the Life of the Person attainted.

ART. IV

SEC. 1. Full Faith and Credit shall be given in each state to the Public Acts, Records, and judicial Proceedings of every other State. And the Congress may by general Laws prescribe the Manner in which such Act, Records and Proceedings shall be proved, and the Effect thereof.

SEC. 2. The Citizens of each State shall be entitled to all Privileges and Immunities of Citizens in the several States.

A Person charged in any State with Treason, Felony, or other Crime, who shall flee from Justice, and be found in another State, shall on Demand of the executive authority of the State from which he fled, be delivered up, to be removed to the State having Jurisdiction of the Crime.

No Person held to Service or Labour in one State, under the Laws thereof, escaping into another, shall, in Consequence of any Law or Regulation therein, be discharged from such Service or Labour, but shall be delivered up on Claim of the Party to whom such Service or Labour may be due.

SEC. 3. New States may be admitted by the Congress into this Union; but no new States shall be formed or erected within the Jurisdiction of any other State; nor any State be formed by the Junction of two or more States, or Parts of States, without the Consent of the Legislatures of the States concerned as well as of the Congress.

The Congress shall have Power to dispose of and make all needful Rules and Regulations respecting the Territory or other Property belonging to the United States; and nothing in this Constitution shall be so construed as to Prejudice any Claims of the United States, or of any particular State.

SEC. 4. The United States shall guarantee to every State in this Union a Republican Form of Government, and shall protect each of them against Invasion; and on Application of the Legislature, or of the Executive (when the Legislature cannot be convened) against domestic Violence.

Art. V

The Congress, whenever two thirds of both Houses shall deem it necessary, shall propose Amendments to this Constitution, or, on the Application of the Legislatures of two thirds of the several States, shall call a Convention for proposing Amendments, which, in either Case, shall be valid to all Intents and Purposes, as Part of this Constitution, when ratified by the Legislatures of three-fourths of the several States, or by Conventions in three-fourths thereof, as the one or the other Mode of Ratification may be proposed by the Congress; Provided that no Amendment which may be made prior to the Year One thousand eight hundred and eight shall in any Manner affect the first and fourth Clauses in the Ninth Section of the first Article; and that no State, without its Consent, shall be deprived of its equal Suffrage in the Senate.

Art. VI

All Debts contracted and Engagements entered into, before the Adoption of this Constitution, shall be as valid against the United States under this Constitution, as under the Confederation.

This Constitution, and the Laws of the United States which shall be made in Pursuance thereof; and all Treaties made, or which shall be made, under the authority of the United States, shall be the supreme Law of the Land; and the Judges in every State shall be bound thereby, any Thing in the Constitution or Laws of any state to the Contrary notwithstanding.

The Senators and Representatives before mentioned, and the Members of the several State Legislatures, and all executive and judicial Officers, both of the United States and of the several States, shall be bound by Oath or Affirmation, to support this Constitution; but no religious Test shall ever be required as a Qualification to any Office or public Trust under the United States.

Art. VII

The Ratification of the Conventions of Nine States, shall be sufficient for the Establishment of this Constitution between the States so ratifying the Same.

Done in Convention by the Unanimous Consent of the States present the Seventeenth Day of September in the Year of our Lord one thousand seven hundred and Eighty seven and of the Independence of the United States of America the Twelfth. In witness whereof We have hereunto subscribed our Names,

G° WASHINGTON—Presid^t
and deputy from Virginia

New Hampshire	JOHN LANGDON NICHOLAS GILMAN
Massachusetts	NATHANIEL GORHAM RUFUS KING
Connecticut	W^M SAM^L JOHNSON ROGER SHERMAN
New York	ALEXANDER HAMILTON
New Jersey	WIL: LIVINGSTON DAVID BREARLEY W^M PATERSON JONA: DAYTON
Pennsylvania	B FRANKLIN THOMAS MIFFLIN ROB^T MORRIS GEO. CLYMER THO^S FITZSIMONS JARED INGERSOLL JAMES WILSON GOUV MORRIS GEO: READ
Delaware	GUNNING BEDFORD jun JOHN DICKINSON RICHARD BASSETT JACO: BROOM
Maryland	JAMES M^{C}HENRY DAN OF S^T THO^S JENIFER DAN^L CARROLL
Virginia	JOHN BLAIR— JAMES MADISON JR
North Carolina	W^M BLOUNT RICH^D DOBBS SPAIGHT HU WILLIAMSON
South Carolina	J. RUTLEDGE CHARLES COTESWORTH PINCKNEY CHARLES PINCKNEY PIERCE BUTLER
Georgia	WILLIAM FEW ABR BALDWIN

THE BILL OF RIGHTS (1791)

Art. I

Congress shall make no law respecting an establishment of religion, or prohibiting the free exercise thereof; or abridging the freedom of speech, or of the press; or the right of the people peaceably to assemble, and to petition the government for a redress of grievances.

Art. II

A well regulated Militia, being necessary to the security of a free State, the right of the people to keep and bear Arms, shall not be infringed.

Art. III

No Soldier, shall, in time of peace be quartered in any house, without the consent of the Owner, nor in time of war, but in a manner to be prescribed by law.

Art. IV

The right of the people to be secure in their persons, houses, papers, and effects, against unreasonable searches and seizures, shall not be violated, and no Warrants shall issue, but upon probable cause, supported by Oath or affirmation, and particularly describing the place to be searched, and the persons or things to be seized.

Art. V

No person shall be held to answer for a capital, or otherwise infamous crime, unless on a presentment or indictment of a Grand Jury, except in cases arising in the land or naval forces, or in the Militia, when in actual service in time of War or public danger; nor shall any person be subject for the same offence to be twice put in jeopardy of life or limb; nor shall be compelled in any criminal case to be a witness against himself, nor be deprived of life, liberty, or propety, without due process of law; nor shall private property be taken for public use, without just compensation.

Art. VI

In all criminal prosecutions, the accused shall enjoy the right to a speedy and public trial, by an impartial jury of the State and district wherein the crime shall have been committed, which district shall have been previously ascertained by law, and to be informed of the nature and cause of the accusation; to be confronted with the witnesses against him; to have compulsory process for obtaining witnesses in his favor, and to have the Assistance of Counsel for his defence.

Art. VII

In Suits at common law, where the value in controversy shall exceed twenty dollars, the right of trial by jury shall be perserved, and no fact tried by a jury, shall be otherwise re-examined in any Court of the United States, than according to the rules of the common law.

Art. VIII

Excessive bail shall not be required, nor excessive fines imposed, nor cruel and unusual punishments inflicted.

Art. IX

The enumeration in the Constitution, of certain rights, shall not be construed to deny or disparage others retained by the people.

Art. X

The powers not delegated to the United States by the Constitution, nor prohibited by it to the States, are reserved to the States respectively, or to the people.

THE FUGITIVE SLAVE ACT OF 1793

The Fugitive Slave Act of 1793 was designed to secure enforcement of Article IV, Section 2 of the Constitution and incur penalties against those who aided or abetted attempts of slaves to escape bondage.

Sec. 1. *Be it enacted by the Senate and House of Representatives of the United States of America in Congress assembled,* That whenever the executive authority of any state in the Union, or of either of the territories northwest or south of the river Ohio, shall demand any person as a fugitive from justice, of the executive authority of any such state or territory to which such person shall have fled, and shall moreover produce the copy of an indictment found, or an affidavit made before a magistrate of any state of territory as aforesaid, charging the person so demanded, with having committed treason, felony or other crime, certified as authentic by the governor or chief magistrate of the state or territory from whence the person so changed fled, it shall be the duty of the executive authority of the state or territory to which such person shall have fled, to cause him or her to be arrested and secured, and notice of the arrest to be given to the executive authority making such demand, or to the agent of such authority appointed to receive the fugitive, and to cause the fugitive to be delivered to such agent when he shall appear: But if no such agent shall appear within six months from the time of the arrest, the prisoner may be discharged. And all costs or expenses incurred to the state or territory making such demand, shall be paid by such state or territory.

SEC. 2. *And be it further enacted,* That any agent, appointed as aforesaid, who shall receive the fugitive into his custody, shall be empowered to transport him or her to the state or territory from which he or she shall have fled. And if any person or persons shall by force set at liberty, or rescue the fugitive from such agent while transporting, as aforesaid, the person or persons so offending shall, on conviction, be fined not exceeding five hundred dollars, and be imprisoned not exceeding one year.

SEC. 3. *And be it also enacted,* That when a person held to labour in any of the United States, or in either of the territories on the northwest or south of the river Ohio, under the laws thereof, shall escape into any other of the said states or territory, the person to whom such labour or service may be due, his agent or attorney, is hereby empowered to seize or arrest such fugitive from labour, and to take him or her before any judge of the circuit or district courts of the United States, residing or being within the state, or before any magistrate of a county, city or town corporate, wherein such seizure or arrest shall be made, and upon proof to the satisfaction of such judge or magistrate, either by oral testimony or affidavit taken before and certified by a magistrate of any such state or territory, that the person so seized or arrested, doth, under the laws of the state or territory from which he or she fled, owe service or labour to the person claiming him or her, it shall be the duty of such judge or magistrate to give a certificate thereof to such claimant, his agent or attorney, which shall be sufficient warrant for removing the said fugitive from labour, to the state or territory from which he or she fled.

SEC. 4. *And be it further enacted,* That any person who shall knowingly and willing obstruct or hinder such claimant, his agent or attorney in so seizing or arresting such fugitive from labour, or shall rescue such fugitive from such claimant, his agent or attorney when so arrested pursuant to the authority herein given or declared; or shall harbor or conceal such person after notice that he or she was a fugitive from labour, as aforesaid shall, for either of the said offences, forfeit and pay the sum of five hundred dollars.

Which penalty may be recovered by and for the benefit of such claimant, by action of debt, in any court proper to try the same; saving moreover to the person claiming such labour or service, his right of action for or on account of the said injuries or either of them.

AN ADDRESS TO THE PUBLIC BY BENJAMIN FRANKLIN (1798)

The failure of the Constitutional Convention to include Thomas Jefferson's antislavery proposal did not diminish the debate between the proslavery states of the South and many antislavery Congreemen of the North. Influential antislavery groups attempted to exert pressure on the Congress to enact an antislavery amendment to the Constitution. Among such groups was the Pennsylvania Society for Promoting the Abolition of Slavery and the Relief of Free Negroes unlawfully held in Bondage. Over the signature of the President of the Society, Benjamin Franklin, the following "Address to the Public," urging abolition, was sent to the Congress of the United States.

Benjamin Franklin termed slavery "an atrocious debasement of human nature."

It is with peculiar satisfaction we assure the friends of humanity, that, in prosecuting the design of our association, our endeavors have proved successful, far beyond our most sanguine expectations.

Encouraged by this success, and by the daily progress of that luminous and benign spirit of liberty which is diffusing itself throughout the world, and humbly hoping for the continuance of the divine blessing on our labors, we have ventured to make an important addition to our original plan; and do therefore earnestly solicit the support and assistance of all who can feel the tender emotions of sympathy and compassion, or relish the exalted pleasure of beneficence.

Slavery is such an atrocious debasement of human nature, that its very extirpation, if not performed with solicitous care, may sometimes open a source of serious evils.

The unhappy man, who has long been treated as a brute animal, too frequently sinks beneath the common standard of the human species. The galling chains that bind his body do also fetter his intellectual faculties, and impair the social affections of his heart. Accustomed to move like a mere machine, by the will of a master, reflection is suspended; he has not the power of choice; and reason and conscience have but little influence over his conduct, because he is chiefly governed by the passion of fear. He is poor and friendless; perhaps worn out by extreme labor, age, and disease.

Under such circumstances, freedom may often prove a misfortune to himself, and prejudicial to society.

Attention to emancipated black people, it is therefore to be hoped, will become a branch of our national police; but, as far as we contribute to promote this emancipation, so far that attention is evidently a serious duty incumbent on us, and which we mean to discharge to the best of our judgment and abilities.

To instruct, to advise, to qualify those who have been restored to freedom, for the exercise and enjoyment of civil liberty; to promote in them habits of industry; to furnish them with employments suited to their age, sex, talents, and other circumstances; and to procure their children an education calculated for their future situation if life,—these are the great outlines of the annexed plan, which we have adopted, and which we conceive will essentially promote the public good, and the happiness of these our hitherto too much neglected fellow-creatures.

A plan so extensive cannot be carried into execution without considerable pecuniary resources, beyond the present ordinary funds of the Society. We hope much from the generosity of enlightened and benevolent freemen, and will gratefully receive any donations or subscriptions for this purpose which may

be made to our Treasurer, James Starr, or to James Pemberton, Chairman of our Committee of Correspondence.

Signed by order of the Society,
B. FRANKLIN, *President*

PHILADELPHIA, 9th of November, 1789

GEORGE WASHINGTON'S LAST WILL AND TESTAMENT: THE FIRST PRESIDENT FREES HIS SLAVES (1799)

During the eighteenth century, Negro slavery was a firmly entrenched institution of American life, particularly in the South where it was justified mainly as an economic necessity. This argument notwithstanding, it was Washington's decision, at the writing of his last will and testament in 1799, to free all those slaves which he held in his "own right." Washington's will also reflected his concern for the financial welfare and educational support of his former charges.

In the Name of God Amen

I George Washington of Mount Vernon—a citizen of the United States,—and lately President of the same, do make, ordain and declare this Instrument; which is written with my own hand and every page thereof

Accompanying George Washington on this land survey is a black miner.

Arab slavers marching their captives to the coast. Any attempt at resistance meant death.

subscribed with my name, to be my last Will & Testament, revoking all others. ... . Upon the decease of my wife, it is my Will & desire that all the Slaves which I hold in *my own right,* shall receive their freedom. . . . And whereas among those who will receive freedom according to this devise, there may be some, who from old age or bodily infirmities, and others who on account of their infancy, that will be unable to support themselves; it is my Will and desire that all who come under the first & second description shall be comfortably cloathed & fed by my heirs while they live;—and that such of the latter description as have no parents living, or if living are unable, or unwilling to provide for them, shall be bound by the Court until they shall arrive at the age of twenty five years;—and in cases where no record can be produced, whereby their ages can be ascertained, the judgment of the Court upon its own view of the subject, shall be adequate and final.—The Negros thus bound, are (by their Masters or Mistresses) to be taught to read & write; and to be brought up to some useful occupation, agreeably to the Laws of the Commonwealth of Virginia, providing for the support of Orphan and other poor Children.—And I do hereby expressly forbid the Sale, or transportation out of the said Commonwealth of any Slave I may die possessed of, under

any pretence whatsoever.—And I do moreover most pointedly, and most solemnly enjoin it upon my Executors hereafter named, or the Survivors of them, to see that *this* clause respecting Slaves, and every part thereof be religiously fulfilled at the Epoch at which it is directed to take place; without evasion, neglect or delay, after the Crops which may then be on the ground are harvested, particularly as it respects the aged and infirm;—Seeing that a regular and permanent fund be established for their Support so long as there are subjects requiring it; not trusting to the uncertain provision to be made by individuals.—And to my Mulatto man William (calling himself William Lee) I give immediate freedom; or if he should prefer it (on account of the accidents which have befallen him, and which have rendered him incapable of walking or of any active employment) to remain in the situation he now is, it shall be optional in him to do so: In either case however, I allow him an annuity of thirty dollars during his natural life, which shall be independent of the victuals and cloaths he has been accustomed to receive, if he chuses the last alternative; but in full, with his freedom, if he prefers the first;—& this I give him as a testimony of my sense of his attachment to me, and for his faithful services during the Revolutionary War.

THE ACT TO PROHIBIT THE IMPORTATION OF SLAVES (1807)

The Act of 1807 (which, although dated March 2, 1897, actually went into effect on January 1, 1808, and thereby did not interfere with the provisions of Article I, Section 9 of the U.S. Constitution) sought to end the slave trade by prohibiting the importation of "men-body" onto the North American mainland. The act, however, was not rigidly enforced, despite the appeals of Presidents Martin Van Buren and John Tyler. Evidence of this can be found in the fact that, between 1808 and 1860, some 250,000 slaves were illegally imported into the United States.

An Act to prohibit the importation of Slaves into any port or place within the jurisdiction of the United States, from and after the first day of January, in the year of our Lord one thousand eight hundred and eight.

Be it enacted, That from and after the first day of January, one thousand eight hundred and eight, it shall not be lawful to import or bring into the United States or the territories thereof from any foreign kingdom, place, or country, any negro, mulatto, or person or colour, as a slave, or to be held to service or labour.

SEC. 2. That no citizen of the United States, or any other person, shall, from and after the first day of January, in the year of our Lord one thousand eight

A slave being branded as punishment for a minor offense.

hundred and eight, for himself, or themselves, or any other person whatsoever, either as master, factor, or owner, build, fit, equip, load or to otherwise prepare any ship or vessel, in any port or place within the jurisdiction of the United States, nor shall cause any ship or vessel to sail from any port or place within the same, for the purpose of procuring any negro, mulatto, or person of colour, from any foreign kingdom, place, or country, to be transported to any port or place whatsoever within the jurisdiction of the United States, to be held, sold, or disposed of as slaves, or to be held to service or labour: and if any ship or vessel shall be so fitted out for the purpose aforesaid, or shall be caused to sail so as aforesaid, every such ship or vessel, her tackle, apparel, and furniture, shall be forfeited to the United States, and shall be liable to be seized, prosecuted, and condemned in any of the circuit courts or district courts, for the district where the said ship or vessel may be found or seized. . . .

SEC. 4. If any citizen or citizens of the United States, or any person resident within the jurisdiction of the same, shall, from and after the first day of January, one thousand eight hundred and eight, take on board, receive or transport from any of the coasts or kingdoms of Africa, or from any other foreign kingdom, place, or country, any negro, mulatto, or person of

TO BE SOLD on board the Ship *Bance-Island*, on tuesday the 6th of *May* next, at *Ashley-Ferry*; a choice cargo of about 250 fine healthy

NEGROES, just arrived from the Windward & Rice Coast. —The utmost care has already been taken, and shall be continued, to keep them free from the least danger of being infected with the SMALL-POX, no boat having been on board, and all other communication with people from *Charles-Town* prevented.

Austin, Laurens, & Appleby.

N. B. Full one Half of the above Negroes have had the SMALL-POX in their own Country.

This handbill circulated in Charleston, South Carolina, during a smallpox epidemic.

colour in any ship or vessel, for the purpose of selling them in any port or place within the jurisdiction of the United States as slaves, or be to held to service or labour, or shall be in any ways aiding or abetting therein, such citizen or citizens, or person, shall severally forfeit and pay five thousand dollars, one moiety thereof to the use of any person or persons who shall sue for and prosecute the same to effect. . . .

SEC. 6. That if any person or persons whatsoever, shall, from and after the first day of January, one thousand eight hundred and eight, purchase or sell any negro, mulatto, or person, of colour, for a slave, or to be held to service or labour, who shall have been imported, or brought from any foreign kingdom, place, or country, or from the dominions of any foreign state, immediately adjoining to the United States, after the last day of December, one thousand eight hundred and seven, knowing at the time of such purchase or sale, such negro, mulatto, or person of colour, was so brought within the jurisdiction of the United States, as aforesaid, such purchaser and seller shall severally forfeit and pay for every negro, mulatto, or person of colour, so purchased or sold as aforesaid, eight hundred dollars. . . .

SEC. 7. That if any ship or vessel shall be found, from and after the first day of January, one thousand eight hundred and eight, in any river, port, bay, or harbor, or on the high seas, within the jurisdictional limits of the United States, or hovering on the coast thereof, having on board any negro, mulatto, or person of colour, for the purpose of selling them as slaves, or with intent to land the same, in any port or place within the jurisdiction of the United States, contrary to the prohibition of the act, every such ship or vessel, together with her tackle, apparel, and furniture, and the goods or effects which shall be found on board the same, shall be forfeited to the use of the United States, and may be seized, prosecuted, and condemned, in any court of the United States, having jurisdiction thereof. And it shall be lawful for the President of the United States, and he is hereby authorized, should he deem it expedient, to cause any of the armed vessels of the United States to be manned and employed to cruise on any part of the coast of the United States, or territories thereof, where he may judge attempts will be made to violate the provisions of this act, and to instruct and direct the commanders of armed vessels of the United States, to seize, take, and bring into any port of the United States all such ships or vessels, and moreover to seize, take, or bring into any port of the U.S. all ships or vessel of the U.S. wheresoever found on the high seas, contravening the provisions of this act, to be proceeded against according to law. . . .

James Monroe, fifth President of the United States. His administration designed the Missouri Compromise to appease both slavery and antislavery factions.

THE MISSOURI COMPROMISE (1819–1821)

Under the terms of the Missouri Compromise (1819–1821), Missouri was admitted to the Union as a slave state. (It was followed in short order by Maine, a free state.) However, slavery was prohibited from that time onward in all Louisiana Territory lying north of latitude 36° 30'. For a certain period, the Compromise appeased both pro and antislavery spokesmen. However, the question of slavery once again vaulted into the national spotlight with the outbreak of the Mexican War, which gave promise of greatly increasing the potential territory open to slavery. (See Compromise of 1850 entry.)

1. The Tallmadge Amendment
February 13, 1819

And provided also, That the further introduction of slavery or involuntary servitude be prohibited, except for the punishment of crimes, whereof the party shall be duly convicted; and that all children of slaves, born within the said state, after the admission thereof into the Union, shall be free but may be held to service until the age of twenty-five years.

2. The Taylor Amendment
January 26, 1820

The reading of the bill proceeded as far as the fourth section; when

MR. TAYLOR, of New York, proposed to amend the bill by incorporating in that section the following provision:

Section 4, line 25, insert the following after the word "States"; "And shall ordain and establish, that there shall be neither slavery nor involuntary servitude in the said State, otherwise than in the punishment of crimes, whereof the party shall have been duly convicted: *Provided, always,* That any person escaping into the same, from whom labor or service is lawfully claimed in any other State, such fugitive may be lawfully reclaimed, and conveyed to the person claiming his or her labor or service as aforesaid: *And provided, also,* That the said provision shall not be construed to alter the condition or civil rights of any person now held to service or labor in the said Territory."

3. The Thomas Amendment
February 17, 1820

And be it further enacted, That, in all that territory ceded by France to the United States, under the name of Louisiana, which lies north of thirty-six degrees and thirty minutes north latitude, excepting only such part thereof as is included within the limits of the State contemplated by this act, slavery and involuntary servitude, otherwise than in the punishment of crimes whereof the party shall have been duly convicted, shall be and is hereby forever prohibited: *Provided always,* That any person escaping into the same, from whom labor or service is lawfully claimed in any State or Territory of the United States, such fugitive may be lawfully reclaimed, and conveyed to the person claiming his or her labor or service, as aforesaid.

4. Missouri Enabling Act
March 6, 1820

An Act to authorize the people of the Missouri territory to form a constitution and state government, and for the admission of such state into the Union on an equal footing with the original states, and to prohibit slavery in certain territories.

Be it enacted That the inhabitants of that portion of the Missouri territory included within the boundaries hereinafter designated, be, and they are hereby, authorized to form for themselves a constitution and state government, and to assume such name as they shall deem proper; and the said state, when formed, shall be admitted into the Union, upon an equal footing with the original states, in all respects whatsoever.

SEC. 2. That the said state shall consist of all the territory included within the following boundaries, to wit: Beginning in the middle of the Mississippi river, on the parallel of thirty-six degrees of north latitude; thence west, along that parallel of latitude, to the St. Francois river; thence up, and following the course of that river, in the middle of the main channel thereof, to the parallel of latitude of thirty-six degrees and thirty minutes; thence west, along the same, to a point where the said parallel is intersected by meridian line passing through the middle of the mouth of the Kansas river, where the same empties into the Missouri river, thence, from the point aforesaid north, along the said meridian line, to the intersection of the parallel of latitude which passes through the rapids of the river Des Moines, making the said line to correspond with the Indian boundary line; thence east, from the point of intersection last aforesaid, along the said parallel of latitude, to the middle of the channel of the main fork of the said river Des Moines; thence down and along the middle of the main channel of the said river Des Moines, to the mouth of the same, where it empties into the Mississippi river; thence, due east, to the middle of the main channel of the Mississippi river; thence down, and following the course of the Mississippi river, in the middle of the main channel thereof, to the place of beginning: . . .

SEC. 3. That all free white male citizens of the United States, who shall have arrived at the age of twenty-one years, and have resided in said territory three months previous to the day of election, and all other persons qualified to vote for representatives to the general assembly of the said territory, shall be qualified to be elected, and they are hereby qualified and authorized to vote, and choose representatives to form a convention. . . .

SEC. 8 That in all that territory ceded by France to the United States, under the name of Louisiana, which lies north of thirty-six degrees and thirty minutes north latitude, not included within the limits of the state, contemplated by this act, slavery and involuntary servitude, otherwise than in the punishment of crimes, whereof the parties shall have been duly convicted, shall be, and is hereby, forever prohibited: *Provided always,* That any person escaping into the same, from whom labour or service is lawfully claimed, in any state or territory of the United States, such fugitive may be lawfully reclaimed and conveyed to the person claiming his or her labour or service as aforesaid.

5. The Constitution of Missouri
July 19, 1820

SEC. 26. The general assembly shall not have power to pass laws—

1. For the emancipation of slaves without the consent of their owners; or without paying them, before such emancipation, a full equivalent for such slaves so emancipated; and,

2. To prevent *bona-fide* immigrants to this State, or actual settlers therein, from bringing from any of the United States, or from any of their Territories, such persons as may there be deemed to be slaves, so long as any persons of the same description are allowed to be held as slaves by the laws of this State.

They shall have power to pass laws—

1. To prevent *bona-fide* immigrants to this State of any slaves who may have committed any high crime in any other State or Territory;

2. To prohibit the introduction of any slave for the purpose of speculation, or as an article of trade or merchandise;

3. To prohibit the introduction of any slave, or the offspring of any slave, who heretofore may have been, or who hereafter may be, imported from any foreign country into the United States, or any Territory thereof, in contravention of any existing statute of the United States; and,

4. To permit the owners of slaves to emancipate them, saving the right of creditors, where the person so emancipating will give security that the slave so emancipated shall not become a public charge.

It shall be their duty, as soon as may be, to pass such laws as may be necessary

1. To prevent free negroes end [and] mulattoes from coming to and settling in this State, under any pretext whatsoever; and,

2. To oblige the owners of slaves to treat them with humanity, and to abstain from all injuries to them extending to life or limb.

6. Resolution for the Admission of Missouri
March 2, 1821

Resolution *providing for the admission of the State of Missouri into the Union, on a certain condition. Resolved,* That Missouri shall be admitted into this union on an equal footing with the original states, in all respects whatever, upon the fundamental condition, that the fourth clause of the twenty-sixth section of the third article of the constitution submitted on the part of said state to Congress, shall never be construed to authorize the passage of any law, and that no law shall be passed in conformity thereto, by which any citizen, of either of the states in this Union, shall be excluded from the enjoyment of any of the privileges and immunities to which such citizen is entitled under the constitution of the United States: *Provided,* That the legislature of the said-state, by a solemn public act, shall declare the assent of the said state to the said fundamental condition, and shall transmit to the President of the United States, on or before the fourth Monday in November next, an authentic copy of the said act; upon the receipt whereof, the President, by proclamation, shall announce the fact; whereupon, and without any further proceeding on the part of Congress, the admission of the said state into this Union shall be considered as complete.

THE INAUGURAL EDITION ON *FREEDOM'S JOURNAL:* THE FIRST NEGRO NEWSPAPER IN THE UNITED STATES (1827)

Freedom's Journal, owned and edited by Samuel Cornish and John B. Russwurm, put its first issue on the streets of New York City in 1827. This editorial, printed here in its entirety, devoted itself to slavery and discrimination.

To Our Patrons
In presenting our first number to our Patrons, we feel all the diffidence of persons entering upon a new and untried line of business. But a moment's reflection upon the noble objects, which we have in view by the publication of this Journal; the expediency of its appearance at this time, when so many schemes are in action concerning our people—encourage us to come boldly before an enlightened publick. For we believe, that a paper devoted to the dissemination of useful knowledge among our brethren, and to their moral and religious improvement, must meet with the cordial approbation of every friend to humanity.

The peculiarities of this Journal, renders it important that we should advertise to the world our motives by which we are actuated, and the objects which we contemplate.

We wish to plead our own cause. Too long have others spoken for us. Too long has the publick been deceived by misrepresentations, in things which concern us dearly, though in the estimation of some mere trifles; for though there are many in society who exercise towards us benevolent feelings; still (with sorrow we confess it) there are others who make it their business to enlarge upon the least trifle, which tends to the discredit of any person of colour; and pronounce anathemas and denounce our whole body for the misconduct of this guilty one. We are aware that there are many instances of vice among us, but we avow that it is because no one has taught its subjects to be virtuous; many instances of poverty, because no sufficient efforts accommodated to minds contracted by slavery, and deprived of early education have been made, to teach them how to husband their hard earnings, and to secure to themselves comfort.

Education being an object of the highest importance to the welfare of society, we shall endeavour to present just and adequate views of it, and to urge upon our brethren the necessity and expediency of training their children, while young, to habits of industry, and thus forming them for becoming useful members of society. It is surely time that we should awake from this lethargy of years, and make a concentrated effort for the education of our youth. We form a spoke in the human wheel, and it is necessary that we should understand our pendence on the different parts, and theirs on us, in order to perform our part with propriety.

Though not desiring of dictating, we shall feel it our incumbent duty to dwell occasionally upon the general principles and rules of economy. The world has grown too enlightened, to estimate any man's character by his personal appearance. Though all men acknowledge the excellency of Franklin's maxims, yet comparatively few practise upon them. We may deplore when it is too late, the neglect of these self-evident truths, but it avails little to mourn. Ours will be the task of admonishing our brethren on these points.

The civil rights of a people being of the greatest value, it shall ever be our duty to vindicate our brethren, when oppressed; and to lay the case before the publick. We shall also urge upon our brethren, (who are qualified by the laws of the different states) the expediency of using their elective franchise; and of making an independent use of the same. We wish them not to become the tools of party.

And as much time is frequently lost, and wrong principles instilled, by the perusal of works of trivial importance, we shall consider it a part of our duty to recommend to our young readers, such authors as will not only enlarge their stock of useful knowledge, but such as will also serve to stimulate them to higher attainments in science.

We trust also, that through the columns of the FREEDOM'S JOURNAL, many practical pieces, having for their bases, the improvement of our brethren, will be presented to them, from the pens of many of our respected friends, who have kindly promised their assistance.

It is our earnest wish to make our Journal a medium of intercourse between our brethren in the different states of this great confederacy: that through its columns an expression of our sentiments, on many interesting subjects which concern us, may be offered to the publick: that plans which apparently are beneficial may be candidly discussed and properly weighed; if worth, receive our cordial approbation; if not, our marked disapprobation.

Useful knowledge of every kind, and everything that relates to Africa, shall find a ready admission into our columns; and as that vast continent becomes daily more known, we trust that many things will come to light, proving that the natives of it are neither so ignorant nor stupid as they have generally been supposed to be.

And while these important subjects shall occupy the columns of the FREEDOM'S JOURNAL, we would not be unmindful of our brethren who are still in the iron fetters of bondage. They are our kindred by all the ties of nature; and though but little can be effected by us, still let our sympathies be poured forth and our prayers in their behalf, ascend to Him who is able to succour them.

From the press and the pulpit we have suffered much by being incorrectly represented. Men whom we equally love and admire have not hesitated to represent us disadvantageously, without becoming personally acquainted with the true state of things, nor discerning between virtue and vice among us. The virtuous part of our people feel themselves sorely aggrieved under the existing state of things—they are not appreciated.

Our vices and our degradation are ever arrayed against us, but our virtues are passed by unnoticed. And what is still more lamentable, our friends, to whom we concede all the principles of humanity and religion, from these very causes seem to have fallen into the current of popular feeling and are imperceptibly floating on the stream-actually living in the practice of prejudice, while they abjure it in theory, and feel it not in their hearts. Is it not very desirable that such should know more of our actual condition; and of our efforts and feelings, that in forming or advocating plans for our amelioration, they may do it more understandingly? In the spirit of candor and humility we intend by a simple representation of facts to lay our case before the public, with a view to arrest the progress of prejudice, and to shield ourselves against the consequent evils. We wish to conciliate all and to irritate none, yet we must be firm and unwavering in our principles, and persevering in our efforts.

If ignorance, poverty and degradation have hitherto

been our unhappy lot; has the Eternal decree gone forth, that our race alone are to remain in this state, while knowledge and civilization are shedding their enlivening rays over the rest of the human family? The recent travels of Denham and Clapperton in the interior of Africa, and the interesting narrative which they have published; the establishment of the republic of Haiti after years of sanguinary warfare; its subsequent progress in all the arts of civilization; and the advancement of liberal ideas in South America, where despotism has given place to free governments, and where many of our brethren now fill important civil and military stations, prove the contrary.

The interesting fact that there are FIVE HUNDRED THOUSAND free persons of colour, one half of whom might peruse, and the whole be benefitted by the publication of the Journal; that no publication, as yet, has been devoted exclusively to their improvement—that many selections from approved standard authors, which are within the reach of few, may occasionally be made—and more important still, that this large body of our citizens have no public channel—all serve to prove the real necessity, at present, for the appearance of the FREEDOM'S JOURNAL.

It shall ever be our desire so to conduct the editorial department of our paper as to give offence to none of our patrons; as nothing is farther from us than to make it the advocate of any partial views, either in politics or religion. What few days we can number, have been devoted to the improvement of our brethren; and it is our earnest wish that the remainder may be spent in the same delightful service.

In conclusion, whatever concerns us as a people, will ever find a ready admission into the FREEDOM'S JOURNAL, interwoven with all the principal news of the day.

And while every thing in our power shall be performed to support the character of our Journal, we would respectfully invite our numerous friends to assist by their communications, and our coloured brethren to strengthen our hands by their subscriptions, as our labour is one of common cause, and worthy of their consideration and support. And we most earnestly solicit the latter, that if at any time we should seem to be zealous, or too pointed in the inculcation of any important lesson, they will remember, that they are equally interested in the cause in which we are engaged, and attribute our zeal to the peculiarities of our situation; and our earnest engagedness in their well-being.

Foes cartooned William Lloyd Garrison as helping southern secessionists to destroy the Union.

THE LIBERATOR: THE MOST FAMOUS ABOLITIONIST NEWSPAPER IN THE UNITED STATES (1831)

The Liberator *was published weekly in Boston, Massachusetts from 1831 to 1865. Most of its subscribers were blacks, although its founder, William Lloyd Garrison ("I have a system to destroy, and I have no time to waste") was himself white.*

A key organ of abolitionist propaganda, The Liberator *succeeded in shifting the sentiment of much of the nation away from the notion of gradual emancipation, and more toward that of total abolition.*

. . . During my recent tour for the purpose of exciting the minds of the people by a series of discourses on the subject of slavery, every place that I visited gave fresh evidence of the fact, that a greater revolution in public sentiment was to be effected in the free states—and particularly in New England—than at the south. I found contempt more bitter, opposition more active, detraction more relentless, prejudice more stubborn, and apathy more frozen, than among slave owners themselves. Of course, there were individual exceptions to the contrary. This state of things afflicted, but did not dishearten me. I determined, at every hazard, to lift up the standard of emancipation in the eyes of the nation, within sight of Bunker Hill and in the birth place of liberty. That standard is now unfurled; and long may if float, unhurt by the spoliations of time or the missiles of a desperate foe—yea, till every chain be broken, and every bondman set free! Let Southern oppressors tremble—let their secret abettors tremble—let their Northern apologists tremble—let all the enemies of the persecuted blacks tremble. . . .

I am aware, that many object to the severity of my language; but is there not cause for severity? I will be as harsh as truth, and as uncompromising as justice. On this subject, I do not wish to think, or speak, or write, with moderation. No! No! Tell a man whose house is on fire, to give a moderate alarm; tell him to moderately rescue his wife from the hands of the ravisher; tell the mother to gradually extricate her babe from the fire into which it has fallen;—but urge me not to use moderation in a cause like the present. I am in earnest—I will not equivocate—I will not excuse—I will not retreat a single inch—AND I WILL BE HEARD. . . .

WILLIAM LLOYD GARRISON

AN INDICTMENT OF SLAVERY (1839)

In 1839, The American Anti-Slavery Society compiled a massive portfolio of testimony which sought to document the inhumanities and illegalities of slavery. The introduction was written much as a prosecutor would address a court. The following introduction, by Theodore D. Weld of New York, stirred abolitionist sentiments in the North while being attacked as demagogic in the South.

READER, YOU ARE empanelled as a juror to try a plain case and bring in an honest verdict. The question at issue is not one of law, but of fact—"What is the actual condition of slaves in the United States?"

A plainer case never went to a jury. Look at it.

An international antislavery society was planned by Garrison, George Thompson, and Wendell Phillips.

TWENTYSEVEN HUNDRED THOUSAND PERSONS in this country, men, women, and children, are in SLAVERY. Is slavery, as a condition for human beings, good, bad, or indifferent?

We submit the question without argument. You have common sense, and conscience, and a human heart—pronounce upon it. You have a wife, or a husband, a child, a father, a mother, a brother or a sister—make the case your own, make it theirs, and bring in your verdict.

The case of Human Rights against Slavery has been adjudicated in the court of conscience times innumerable. The same verdict has always been rendered—''Guilty;'' the same sentence has always been pronounced ''Let it be accursed;'' and human nature, with her million echoes, has rung it round the world in every language under heaven. ''Let it be accursed. . . .''

As slaveholders and their apologists are volunteer witnesses in their own cause, and are flooding the world with testimony that their slaves are kindly treated; that they are well fed, well clothed, well housed, well lodged, moderately worked, and bountifully provided with all things needful for their comfort, we propose,—first, to disprove their assertions by the testimony of a multitude of impartial witnesses, and then to put slaveholders themselves through a course of cross-questioning which will draw their condemnation out of their own mouths.

We will prove that the slaves in the United States are treated with barbarous inhumanity; that they are overworked, underfed, wretchedly clad and lodged, and have insufficient sleep; that they are often made to wear round their necks iron collars armed with prongs, to drag heavy chains and weights at their feet while working in the field, and to wear yokes and bells, and iron horns; that they are often kept confined in the stocks day and night for weeks together, made to wear gags in their mouths for hours or days, have some of their front teeth torn out or broken off, that they may be easily detected when they run away; that they are frequently flogged with terrible severity, have red pepper rubbed into their lacerated flesh, and hot brine, spirits of turpentine, &c., poured over the gashes to increase the torture; that they are often stripped naked, their backs and limbs cut with knives, bruised and mangled by scores and hundreds of blows with the paddle, and terribly torn by the claws of cats, drawn over them by their tormentors; that they are often hunted with bloodhounds and shot down like beasts, or torn in pieces by dogs; that they are often suspended by the arms and whipped and beaten till they faint, and when revived by restoratives, beaten again till they faint, and sometimes till they die; that their ears are often cut off, their eyes knocked out, their bones broken, their flesh branded with red hot irons; that they are maimed, mutilated and burned to death, over slow fires. All these things, and more, and worse, we shall *prove*. . . .

We shall show, not merely that such deeds are

Pro-slavery hoodlums destroy an abolitionist printing press.

This drawing headlined newspaper advertisements for runaway slaves.

committed, but that they are frequent; not done in corners, but before the sun; not in one of the slave states, but in all of them; not perpetrated by brutal overseers and drivers merely, but by magistrates, by legislators, by professors of religion, by preachers of the gospel, by governors of states, by "gentlemen of property and standing," and by delicate females moving in the "highest circles of society."

We know, full well, the outcry that will be made by multitudes, at these declarations; the multiform cavils, the flat denials, the charges of "exaggeration" and "falsehood" so often bandied, the sneers of affected contempt at the credulity that can believe such things, and the rage and imprecations against those who give them currency. We know, too, the threadbare sophistries by which slaveholders and their apologists seek to evade such testimony. If they admit that such deeds are committed, they tell us that they are exceedingly rare, and therefore furnish no grounds for judging of the general treatment of slaves; that occasionally a brutal wretch in the *free* states barbarously butchers his wife, but that no one thinks of inferring from that, the general treatment of wives at the North and West.

They tell us, also, that the slaveholders of the South are proverbially hospitable, kind, and generous, and it is incredible that they can perpetrate such enormities

upon human beings; further, that it is absurd to suppose that they would thus injure their own property, that self-interest would prompt them to treat their slaves with kindness, as none but fools and madmen wantonly destroy their own property; further, that Northern visitors at the South come back testifying to the kind treatment of the slaves, and that the slaves themselves corroborate such representations. All these pleas, and scores of others, are bruited in every corner of the free States; and who that hath eyes to see, has not sickened at the blindness that saw not, at the palsy of heart that felt not, or at the cowardice and sycophancy that dared not expose such shallow fallacies. We are not to be turned from our purpose by such vapid babblings. In their appropriate places, we propose to consider these objections and various others, and to show their emptiness and folly.

THE NORTH STAR: THE ABOLITIONIST ORGAN OF FREDERICK DOUGLASS (1847)

Frederick Douglass, a leading Negro spokesman in the abolitionist movement, founded his newspaper on December 3, 1847 in Rochester, New York. Douglass conceded in his first editorial that he would plead the cause of the Negro before all else, but did not exclude the possibility that several other major topics might also occupy the editorial spotlight from time to time.

To Our Oppressed Countrymen

We solemnly dedicate the *North Star* to the cause of our long oppressed and plundered fellow countrymen. May God bless the offering to your good! It shall fearlessly asset your rights, faithfully proclaim your wrongs, and earnestly demand for you instant and even-handed justice. Giving no quarter to slavery at the South, it will hold no truce with oppressors at the North. While it shall boldly advocate emancipation for our enslaved brethren, it will omit no opportunity to gain for the nominally free, complete enfranchisement. Every effort to injure or degrade you or your cause—originating wheresoever, or with whomsoever—shall find in it a constant, unswerving and inflexible foe.

We shall energetically assail the ramparts of Slavery and Prejudice, be they composed of church or state, and seek the destruction of every refuge of lies, under which tyranny may aim to conceal and protect itself. . . .

While our paper shall be mainly Anti-Slavery, its columns shall be freely opened to the candid and decorous discussions of all measures and topics of a moral and humane character, which may serve to

THE FUGITIVE'S SONG.

As a fugitive slave, Frederick Douglass held uncommon views about Independence Day.

enlighten, improve, and elevate mankind. Temperance, Peace, Capital Punishment, Education,—all subjects claiming the attention of the public mind may be freely and fully discussed here.

While advocating your rights, the *North Star* will strive to throw light on your duties: while it will not fail to make known your virtues, it will not shun to discover your faults. To be faithful to our foes it must be faithful to ourselves, in all things.

Remember that we are one, that our cause is one, and that we must help each other, if we would succeed. We have drunk to the dregs the bitter cup of slavery; we have worn the heavy yoke; we have sighed beneath our bonds, and writhed beneath the bloody lash;—cruel mementoes of our oneness are indelibly marked in our living flesh. We are one with you under the ban of prejudice and proscription— one with you under the slander of inferiority—one with you in social and political disfranchisement. What you suffer, we suffer; what you endure, we endure. We are indissolubly united, and must fall or flourish together. . . .

We shall be the advocates of learning, from the very want of it, and shall most readily yield the defer-

ence due to men of education among us; but shall always bear in mind to accord most merit to those who have labored hardest, and overcome most, in the praiseworthy pursuit of knowledge, remembering "that the whole need not a physician, but they that are sick," and that "the strong ought to bear the infirmities of the weak."

Brethren, the first number of the paper is before you. It is dedicated to your cause. Through the kindness of our friends in England, we are in possession of an excellent printing press, types, and all other materials necessary for printing a paper. Shall this gift be blest to our good, or shall it result in our injury? It is for you to say. With your aid, cooperation and assistance, our enterprise will be entirely successful. We pledge ourselves that no effort on our part shall be wanting, and that no subscriber shall lose his subscription—"The *North Star* Shall Live."

THE COMPROMISE OF 1850

The Compromise of 1850 was occasioned by a revival of the slavery question pursuant to the Mexican War. Henry Clay, chief architect of the compromise, made five key points upon which the document is based:

1. *That California be admitted to the Union as a free state.*
2. *That territorial governments be established in New Mexico and Utah without any immediate decision as to whether they would be slave or free.*
3. *That a stricter fugitive slave law be passed.*
4. *That the slave trade be abolished in the District of Columbia.*
5. *That the Texas-New Mexico boundary be settled, and that the federal government liquidate any debts incurred by Texas.*

Clay's Resolutions
January 29, 1850

1. *Resolved,* That California, with suitable boundaries, ought, upon her application to be admitted as one of the States of this Union, without the imposition by Congress of any restriction in respect to the exclusion or introduction of slavery within those boundaries.

2. *Resolved,* That as slavery does not exist by law, and is not likely to be introduced into any of the territory acquired by the United States from the republic of Mexico, it is inexpedient for Congress to provide

by law either for its introduction into, or exclusion from, any part of the said territory; and that appropriate territorial governments ought to be established by Congress in all of the said territory, not assigned as the boundaries of the proposed State of California, without the adoption of any restriction or condition on the subject of slavery.

3. *Resolved,* That the western boundary of the State of Texas ought to be fixed on the Rio del Norte, commencing one marine league from its mouth, and running up that river to the southern line of New Mexico; thence with that line eastwardly, and so continuing in the same direction to the line as established between the United States and Spain, excluding any portion of New Mexico, whether lying on the east or west of that river.

4. *Resolved,* That it be proposed to the State of Texas, that the United States will provide for the payment of all that portion of the legitimate and bona fide public debt of that State contracted prior to its annexation to the United States, and for which the duties on foreign imports were pledged by the said State to its creditors, not exceeding the sum of_____dollars, in consideration of the said duties so pledged having been no longer applicable to that object after the said annexation, but having thenceforward become payable to the United States; and upon the condition, also, that the said State of Texas shall, by some solemn and authentic act of her legislature or of a convention, relinquish to the United States any claim which it has to any part of New Mexico.

5. *Resolved,* That it is inexpedient to abolish slavery in the District of Columbia whilst that institution continues to exist in the State of Maryland, without the consent of that State, without the consent of the people of the District, and without just compensation to the owners of slaves within the District.

6. *But, resolved,* That it is expedient to prohibit, within the District, the slave trade in slaves brought into it from States or places beyond the limits of the District, either to be sold therein as merchandise, or to be transported to other markets without the District of Columbia.

7. *Resolved,* That more effectual provision ought to be made by law, according to the requirement of the constitution, for the restitution and delivery of persons bound to service or labor in any State, who may escape into any other State or Territory in the Union. And,

8. *Resolved,* That Congress has no power to promote or obstruct the trade in slaves between the slaveholding States; but that the admission or exclusion of slaves brought from one into another of them, depends exclusively upon their own particular laws.

The Texas and New Mexico Act
September 9, 1850

An Act proposing to the State of Texas the Establishment of her Northern and Western Boundaries, the Relinquishment by the said State of all Territory claimed by her exterior to said Boundaries, and of all her claims upon the United States, and to establish a territorial Government for New Mexico.

First. The State of Texas will agree that her boundary on the north shall commence at the point at which the meridian of one hundred degrees west from Greenwich is intersected by the parallel of thirty-six degrees thirty minutes north latitude, and shall run from said point due west to the meridian of one hundred and three degrees west from Greenwich; thence her boundary shall run due south to the thirty-second degree of north latitude; thence on the said parallel of thirty-two degrees of north latitude to the Rio Bravo del Norte, and thence with the channel of said river to the Gulf of Mexico.

Second. The State of Texas cedes to the United States all her claim to territory exterior to the limits and boundaries which she agrees to establish by the first article of this agreement.

Third. The State of Texas relinquishes all claim upon the United States for liability of the debts of Texas, and for compensation or indemnity for the surrender to the United States of her ships, forts, arsenals, custom-houses, custom-house revenue, arms and munitions of war, and public buildings with their sites, which became the property of the United States at the time of the annexation.

Fourth. The United States, in consideration of said establishment of boundaries, cession of claim to territory, and relinquishment of claims, will pay to the State of Texas the sum of ten millions of dollars in a stock bearing five per cent interest, and redeemable at the end of fourteen years, the interest payable half-yearly at the treasury of the United States. . . .

Fugitive Slave Act
[September 18, 1850]

An Act to amend, and supplementary to, the Act entitled "An Act respecting Fugitives from Justice, and Persons escaping from the Service of their Masters," approved—[February 12, 1793].

Sec. 5. That it shall be the duty of all marshals and deputy marshals to obey and execute all warrants and precepts issued under the provisions of this act, when to them directed; and should any marshal or deputy marshal refuse to receive such warrant, or other process, when tendered, or to use all proper means diligently to execute the same, he shall, on conviction thereof, be fined in the sum of one thousand dollars, to the use of such claimant, . . . and after arrest of such fugitive, by such marshal or his deputy, or whilst at any time in his custody under the provisions of this act, should such fugitive escape, whether with or without the assent of such marshal or his deputy, such marshal shall be liable, on his official bond, to be prosecuted for the benefit of such claimant, for the full value of the service or labor of said fugitive in the State, Territory, or District whence he escaped: and the better to enable the said commissioners, when thus appointed, to execute their duties faithfully and efficiently, in conformity with the requirements of the Constitution of the United States and of this act, they are hereby authorized and empowered, within their counties respectively, to appoint, . . . any one or more suitable persons, from time to time, to execute all such warrants and other process as may be issued by them in the lawful performance of their respective duties;

Sec. 6. That when a person held to service or labor in any State or Territory of the United States, has heretofore or shall hereafter escape into another State or Territory of the United States, the person or persons to whom such service or labor may be due, . . . may pursue and reclaim such fugitive person, either by procuring a warrant from some one of the courts, judges, or commissioners aforesaid, of the proper circuit, district, or county, for the apprehension of such fugitive from service or labor, or by seizing and arresting such fugitive, where the same can be done without process, and by taking, or causing such person to be taken, forthwith before such court, judge, or commissioner, whose duty it shall be to hear and determine the case of such claimant in a summary manner; and upon satisfactory proof being made, by deposition or affidavit, in writing, to be taken and certified by such court, judge, or commissioner, or by other satisfactory testimony, duly taken and certified by some court, . . . and with proof, also by affidavit, of the identity of the person whose service or labor is claimed to be due as aforesaid, that the person so arrested does in fact owe service or labor to the person or persons claiming him or her, in the State or Territory from which such fugitive may have escaped as aforesaid, and that said person escaped, to make out and deliver to such claimant, his or her agent or attorney, a certificate setting forth the substantial facts as to the service or labor due from such fugitive to the claimant, and of his or her escape from the State or Territory in which he or she was arrested, with authority to such claimant, . . . to use such reasonable force and restraint as may be necessary, under the circum-

stances of the case, to take and remove such fugitive person back to the State or Territory whence he or she may have escaped as aforesaid.

Sec. 7. That any persons who shall knowingly and willingly obstruct, hinder, or prevent such claimant, his agent or attorney, or any person or persons lawfully assisting him, her, or them, from arresting such a fugitive from service or labor, either with or without process as aforesaid, or shall rescue, or attempt to rescue, such fugitive from service or labor, from the custody of such claimant, . . . or other person or persons lawfully assisting as aforesaid, when so arrested, . . . or shall aid, abet, or assist such person so owing service or labor as aforesaid, directly or indirectly, to escape from such claimant, . . . or shall harbor or conceal such fugitive, so as to prevent the discovery and arrest of such person, after notice or knowledge of the fact that such person was a fugitive from service or labor . . . shall, for either of said offences, be subject to a fine not exceeding one thousand dollars, and imprisonment not exceeding six months . . . ; and shall moreover forfeit and pay, by way of civil damages to the party injured by such illegal conduct, the sum of one thousand dollars, for each fugitive so lost as aforesaid. . . .

Sec. 9. That, upon affidavit made by the claimant of such fugitive, . . . that he has reason to apprehend that such fugitive will be rescued by force from his or their possession before he can be taken beyond the limits of the State in which the arrest is made, it shall be the duty of the officer making the arrest to retain such fugitive in his custody, and to remove him to the State whence he fled, and there to deliver him to said claimant, his agent, or attorney. And to this end, the officer aforesaid is hereby authorized and required to employ so many persons as he may deem necessary to overcome such force, and to retain them in his service so long as circumstances may require.

Act Abolishing the Slave Trade in the District of Columbia
September 20, 1850

An Act to suppress the Slave Trade in the District of Columbia.

Be it enacted . . . , That from and after January 1, 1851, it shall not be lawful to bring into the District of Columbia any slave whatever, for the purpose of being sold, or for the purpose of being placed in depot, to be subsequently transferred to any other State or place to be sold as merchandize. And if any slave shall be brought into the said District by its owner, or by the authority or consent of its owner, contrary to the provisions of this act, such slave shall thereupon become liberated and free.

WHAT TO THE SLAVES IS THE FOURTH OF JULY?: FREDERICK DOUGLASS' INDEPENDENCE DAY ADDRESS (1852)

Perceiving full well the irony implicit in his delivering an address which commemorated the coming of independence to the United States, Frederick Douglass lost little time in laying bare the contradiction inherent in allowing slavery to exist within a society professedly dedicated to individual freedom.

Fellow Citizens

Pardon me, and allow me to ask, why am I called upon to speak here today? What have I or those I represent to do with your national independence? Are the great principles of political freedom and of natural justice, embodied in that Declaration of Independence, extended to us? And am I, therefore, called upon to bring our humble offering to the national altar, and to confess the benefits, and express devout gratitude for the blessings resulting from your independence to us?

Would to God, both for your sakes and ours, that an affirmative answer could be truthfully returned to these questions. Then would my task be light, and my burden easy and delightful. For who is there so cold that a nation's sympathy could not warm him? Who so obdurate and dead to the claims of gratitude, that would not thankfully acknowledge such priceless benefits? Who so stolid and selfish that would not give his voice to swell the halleluiahs of a nation's jubilee, when the chains of servitude had been torn from his limbs? I am not that man. . . .

I am not included within the pale of this glorious anniversary! Your high independence only reveals the immeasurable distance between us. The blessings in which you this day rejoice are not enjoyed in common. The rich inheritance of justice, liberty, prosperity, and independence bequeathed by your fathers is shared by you, not by me. The sunlight that brought life and healing to you has brought stripes and death to me. This Fourth of July is *yours,* not *mine. You* may rejoice, *I* must mourn. To drag a man in fetters into the grand illuminated temple of liberty, and call upon him to join you in joyous anthems, were inhuman mockery and sacrilegious irony. Do you mean, citizens, to mock me, by asking me to speak today? . . .

Fellow citizens, above your national, tumultuous joy, I hear the mournful wail of millions, whose chains, heavy and grievous yesterday, are today rendered more intolerable by the jubilant shouts that reach them. If I do forget, if I do not remember those bleeding children of sorrow this day, "may my right hand forget her cunning, and may my tongue cleave to the roof of my mouth!" To forget them, to pass lightly over their wrongs, and to chime in with the popular theme, would be treason most scandalous and shocking, and would make me a reproach before God and the world. My subject, then, fellow citizens, is "American Slavery." I shall see this day and its popular characteristics from the slave's point of view. Standing here, identified with the American bondman, making his wrongs mine, I do not hesitate to declare, with all my soul, that the character and conduct of this nation never looked blacker to me than on this Fourth of July. Whether we turn to the declarations of the past, or to the professions of the present, the conduct of the nation seems equally hideous and revolting. America is false to the past, false to the present, and solemnly binds herself to be false to the future. Standing with God and the crushed and bleeding slave on this occasion, I will, in the name of humanity, which is outraged, in the name of liberty, which is fettered, in the name of the Constitution and the Bible, which are disregarded and trampled upon, dare to call in question and to denounce, with all the emphasis I can command, everything that serves to perpetuate slavery—the great sin and shame of America! "I will not equivocate; I will not excuse"; I will use the severest language I can command, and yet not one word shall escape me that any man, whose judgment is not blinded by prejudice, or who is not at heart a slave-holder, shall not confess to be right and just.

But I fancy I hear some of my audience say it is just in this circumstance that you and your brother Abolitionists fail to make a favorable impression on the public mind. Would you argue more and denounce less, would you persuade more and rebuke less, your cause would be much more likely to succeed. But, I submit, where all is plain there is nothing to be argued. What point in the anti-slavery creed would you have me argue? On what branch of the subject do the people of this country need light? Must I undertake to prove that the slave is a man? That point is conceded already. Nobody doubts it. The slave-holders themselves acknowledge it in the enactment of laws for their government. They acknowledge it when they punish disobedience on the part of the slave. There are seventy-two crimes in the State of Virginia, which, if committed by a black man (no matter how ignorant he be), subject him to the punishment of death; while only two of these same crimes will subject a white man to like punishment. What is this but the acknowledgment that the slave is a moral, intellectual, and responsible being? The manhood of the slave is conceded. It is admitted in the fact that Southern statute-books are covered with enactments, forbidding, under severe fines and penalties, the teaching of the slave to read and write. When you can point to any such laws in reference to the beasts of the field, then I may consent to argue the manhood of the slave. When the dogs in your streets, when the fowls of the air, when the cattle on your hills, when the fish of the sea, and the reptiles that crawl, shall be unable to distinguish the slave from a brute, then I will argue with you that the slave is a man!

For the present it is enough to affirm the equal manhood of the Negro race. Is it not astonishing that, while we are plowing, planting, and reaping, using all kinds of mechanical tools, erecting houses, constructing bridges, building ships, working in metals of brass, iron, copper, silver, and gold; that while we are reading, writing, and cyphering, acting as clerks, merchants, and secretaries, having among us lawyers, doctors, ministers, poets, authors, editors, orators, and teachers; that while we are engaged in all the enterprises common to other men—digging gold in California, capturing the whale in the Pacific, feeding sheep and cattle on the hillside, living, moving, acting, thinking, planning, living in families as husbands, wives, and children, and above all, confessing and worshipping the Christian God, and looking hopefully for life and immortality beyond the grave—we are called upon to prove that we are men?

Would you have me argue that man is entitled to liberty? That he is the rightful owner of his own body? You have already declared it. Must I argue the wrongfulness of slavery? Is that a question for republicans? Is it to be settled by the rules of logic and argumentation, as a matter beset with great difficulty, involving a doubtful application of the principle of justice, hard to understand? How should I look today in the presence of Americans, dividing and subdividing a discourse, to show that men have a natural right to freedom, speaking of it relatively and positively, negatively and affirmatively? To do so would be to make myself ridiculous, and to offer an insult to your understanding. There is not a man beneath the canopy of heaven who does not know that slavery is wrong *for him*.

What! Am I to argue that it is wrong to make men brutes, to rob them of their liberty, to work them without wages, to keep them ignorant of their relations to their fellow men, to beat them with sticks, to flay their flesh with the last, to load their limbs with irons, to hunt them with dogs, to sell them at auction, to sunder their families, to knock out their teeth, to burn their flesh, to starve them into obedience and submission to their masters? Must I argue that a system thus marked with blood and stained with pollution is

wrong? No; I will not. I have better employment for my time and strength than such arguments would imply.

What, then, remains to be argued? Is it that slavery is not divine; that God did not establish it; that our doctors of divinity are mistaken? There is blasphemy in the thought. That which is inhuman cannot be divine. Who can reason on such a proposition? They that can, may; I cannot. The time for such argument is past.

At a time like this, scorching irony, not convincing argument, is needed. Oh! had I the ability, and could I reach the nation's ear, I would today pour out a fiery stream of biting ridicule, blasting reproach, withering sarcasm, and stern rebuke. For it is not light that is needed, but fire; it is not the gentle shower, but thunder. We need the storm, the whirlwind, and the earthquake. The feeling of the nation must be quickened; the conscience of the nation must be roused; the propriety of the nation must be startled; the hypocrisy of the nation must be exposed; and its crimes against God and man must be denounced.

What to the American slave is your Fourth of July? I answer, a day that reveals to him more than all other days of the year, the gross injustice and cruelty to which he is the constant victim. To him your celebration is a sham; your boasted liberty an unholy license; your national greatness, swelling vanity; your sounds of rejoicing are empty and heartless; your denunciation of tyrants, brass-fronted impudence; your shouts of liberty and equality, hollow mockery; your prayers and hymns, your sermons and thanksgivings, with all your religious parade and solemnity, are to him mere bombast, fraud, deception, impiety, and hypocrisy—a thin veil to cover up crimes which would disgrace a nation of savages. There is not a nation of the earth guilty of practices more shocking and bloody than are the people of these United States at this very hour.

Go where you may, search where you will, roam through all the monarchies and despotisms of the Old World, travel through South America, search out every abuse and when you have found the last, lay your facts by the side of the every-day practices of this nation, and you will say with me that, for revolting barbarity and shameless hypocrisy, America reigns without a rival.

THE KANSAS–NEBRASKA ACT (1854)

The Kansas–Nebraska Act repealed the Missouri Compromise, placing in the hands of the territories themselves the ultimate decision as to whether they would be slave or free.

Kansas ballot boxes were stuffed with fraudulent votes.

An Act to Organize the Territories of Nebraska and Kansas

Be it enacted . . . , That all that part of the territory of the United States included within the following limits, except such portions thereof as are hereinafter expressly exempted from the operations of this act, to wit: beginning at a point in the Missouri River where the fortieth parallel of north latitude crosses the same; thence west on said parallel to the east boundary of the Territory of Utah, on the summit of the Rocky Mountains; thence on said summit northward to the forty-ninth parallel of north latitude; thence east on said parallel to the western boundary of the territory of Minnesota; thence southward on said boundary

Stephen Douglas is shown as a squatter prepared to defend slavery in Kansas.

to the Missouri River; thence down the main channel of said river to the place of beginning, be, and the same is hereby, created into a temporary government by the name of the Territory of Nebraska; and when admitted as a State or States, the said Territory, or any portion of the same, shall be received into the Union with or without slavery, as their constitution may prescribe at the time of their admission: . . .

SEC. 14. *And be it further enacted, . . .* That the Constitution, and all laws of the United States which are not locally inapplicable, shall have the same force and effect within the said Territory of Nebraska as elsewhere within the United States, except the eighth section of the act preparatory to the admission of Missouri into the Union, approved March 6, 1820, which, being inconsistent with the principle of nonintervention by Congress with slavery in the States and Territories, as recognized by the legislation of eighteen hundred and fifty, commonly called the Compromise Measures, is hereby declared inoperative and void; it being the true intent and meaning of this act not to legislate slavery into any Territory or State, nor to exclude it therefrom, but to leave the people thereof perfectly free to form and regulate their domestic institutions in their own way, subject only to the Constitution of the United States: *Provided,* That nothing herein contained shall be construed to revive or put in force any law or regulation which may have existed prior to the act of March 6, 1820, either protecting, establishing, prohibiting, or abolishing slavery. . . .

SEC. 19. *And be it further enacted,* That all that part of the Territory of the United States included within the following limits, except such portions thereof as are hereinafter expressly exempted from the operations of this act, to wit, beginning at a point on the western boundary of the State of Missouri, where the thirty-seventh parallel of north latitude crosses the same; thence west on said parallel to the eastern boundary of New Mexico; thence north on said boundary to latitude thirty-eight; thence following said boundary westward to the east boundary of the Territory of Utah, on the summit of the Rocky Mountains; thence northward on said summit to the fortieth parallel of latitude; thence east on said parallel to the western boundary of the State of Missouri; thence south with the western boundary of said state to the place of beginning, be, and the same is hereby, created into a temporary government by the name of the Territory of Kansas; and when admitted as a State or States, the said Territory, or any portion of the same, shall be received into the Union with or without slavery, as their constitution may prescribe at the time of their admission: . . .

THE EMANCIPATION PROCLAMATION (1863)

The Emancipation Proclamation, drafted in 1862 and put into effect on January 1, 1863, freed the slaves in those states that had seceded from the Union. All other slaves—and there were some 800,000 unaffected by the provisions of this act—were not yet free.

By the President of the United States of America: A Proclamation

Whereas on the 22d day of September, A.D. 1862, a proclamation was issued by the President of the United States, containing, among other things, the following, to wit:

"That on the 1st day of January, A.D. 1863, all persons held as slaves within any State or designated part of a State the people whereof shall then be in rebellion against the United States shall be then, thenceforward, and forever free; and the executive government of the United States, including the military and naval authority thereof, will recognize and maintain the freedom of such persons and will do no act or acts to repress such persons, or any of them, in any efforts they may make for their actual freedom.

"That the executive will on the 1st day of January aforesaid, by proclamation, designate the States and parts of States, if any, in which the people thereof, respectively, shall then be in rebellion against the United States; and the fact that any State or the people thereof shall on that day be in good faith represented in the Congress of the United States by members chosen thereto at elections wherein a majority of the qualified voters of such States shall have participated shall, in the absence of strong countervailing testimony, be deemed conclusive evidence that such State and the people thereof are not then in rebellion against the United States."

Now, therefore, I, Abraham Lincoln, President of the United States, by virtue of the power in me vested as Commander-in-Chief of the Army and Navy of the United States in time of actual armed rebellion against the authority and government of the United States, and as a fit and necessary war measure for suppressing said rebellion, do, on this 1st day of January, A.D. 1863, and in accordance with my purpose so to do, publicly proclaimed for the full period of one hundred days from the first day above mentioned, order and designate as the States and parts of States wherein the people thereof, respectively, are this day in rebellion against the United States the following, to wit:

Arkansas, Texas, Louisiana (except the parishes of St. Bernard, Plaquemines, Jefferson, St. John, St. Charles, St. James, Ascension, Assumption, Terrebonne, Lafourche, St. Mary, St. Martin, and Orleans,

Northern soldiers read the Proclamation's message of freedom to astonished slaves throughout the South.

including the city of New Orleans), Mississippi, Alabama, Florida, Georgia, South Carolina, North Carolina, and Virginia (except the forty-eight counties designated as West Virginia, and also the counties of Berkeley, Accomac, Northhampton, Elizabeth City, York, Princess Anne, and Norfolk, including the cities of Norfolk and Portsmouth), and which excepted parts are for the present left precisely as if this proclamation were not issued.

And by virtue of the power and for the purpose aforesaid, I do order and declare that all persons held as slaves within said designated States and parts of States are, and henceforward shall be, free; and that the Executive Government of the United States, including the military and naval authorities thereof, will recognize and maintain the freedom of said persons.

And I hereby enjoin upon the people so declared to be free to abstain from all violence, unless in necessary self-defense; and I recommend to them that, in all cases when allowed, they labor faithfully for reasonable wages.

And I further declare and make known that such persons of suitable condition will be received into the armed service of the United States to garrison forts, positions, stations, and other places, and to man vessels of all sorts in said service.

And upon this act, sincerely believed to be an act of justice, warranted by the Constitution upon military necessity, I invoke the considerate judgment of mankind and the gracious favor of Almighty God.

The Emancipation Proclamation freed all slaves in the southern states that had seceded from the Union.

ABRAHAM LINCOLN

AND HIS

Emancipation Proclamation

Whereas On the Twenty-second day of September, in the year of our Lord one thousand eight hundred and sixty-two, a Proclamation was issued by the President of the United States, containing among other things the following, to-wit:

"That on the first day of January, in the year of our Lord one thousand eight hundred and sixty-three, all persons held as slaves within any State, or designated part of a State, the people whereof shall then be in rebellion against the United States, shall be then, thenceforward and forever free, and the executive government of the United States, including the military and naval authority thereof, will recognize and maintain the freedom of such persons, and will do no act or acts to repress such persons, or any of them, in any efforts they may make for their actual freedom.

"That the executive will, on the first day of January aforesaid, by proclamation, designate the States and parts of States, if any, in which the people thereof respectively shall then be in rebellion against the United States, and the fact that any State, or the people thereof, shall on that day be in good faith represented in the Congress of the United States by members chosen thereto at elections wherein a majority of the qualified voters of such State shall have participated, shall, in the absence of strong countervailing testimony, be deemed conclusive evidence that such State and the people thereof are not then in rebellion against the United States."

Now, therefore, I, ABRAHAM LINCOLN, President of the United States, by virtue of the power in me vested as Commander-in-Chief of the Army and Navy of the United States in time of actual armed rebellion against the authority and government of the United States, and as a fit and necessary war measure for suppressing said rebellion, do, on this first day of January, in the year of our Lord one thousand eight hundred and sixty-three, and in accordance with my purpose so to do, publicly proclaim for the full period of one hundred days from the day the first above mentioned order, and designate as the States and parts of States wherein the people thereof respectively are this day in rebellion against the United States, the following, to-wit: ARKANSAS, TEXAS, LOUISIANA (except the parishes of St. Bernard, Plaquemines, Jefferson, St. John, St. Charles, St. James, Ascension, Assumption, Terre Bonne, Lafourche, St. Mary, St. Martin, and Orleans, including the city of New Orleans), MISSISSIPPI, ALABAMA, FLORIDA, GEORGIA, SOUTH CAROLINA, NORTH CAROLINA and VIRGINIA (except the forty-eight counties designated as West Virginia, and also the counties of Berkley, Accomac, Northampton, Elizabeth City, York, Princess Ann and Norfolk, including the cities of Norfolk and Portsmouth), and which excepted parts are, for the present, left precisely as if this Proclamation were not issued.

And by virtue of the power and for the purpose aforesaid, I do order and declare that all persons held as slaves within said designated States and parts of States are and henceforward shall be free; and that the executive government of the United States, including the military and naval authorities thereof, will recognize and maintain the freedom of said persons.

And I hereby enjoin upon the people so declared to be free, to abstain from all violence, unless in necessary self-defence, and I recommend to them that in all cases, when allowed, they labor faithfully for reasonable wages.

And I further declare and make known that such persons of suitable condition, will be received into the armed service of the United States to garrison forts, positions, stations and other places, and to man vessels of all sorts in said service.

And upon this act, sincerely believed to be an act of justice, warranted by the Constitution, upon military necessity, I invoke the considerate judgment of mankind, and the gracious favor of Almighty God.

In testimony whereof, I have hereunto set my name, and caused the seal of the United States to be affixed.

Done at the City of Washington, this first day of January, in the year of our Lord one thousand eight hundred and sixty-three, and of the Independence of the United States the eighty-Seventh.

By the President: ABRAHAM LINCOLN.

WILLIAM H. SEWARD, Secretary of State.

NOTE.---The rest of the slaves were afterwards freed by Legislation and Constitutional Amendments.

The Freedmen's Bureau sought to keep peace between bands of white southerners and former slaves.

THE FREEDMEN'S BUREAU (1865)

The Freedmen's Bureau, brought into being in 1865, was designed to provide basic health and educational services for freedmen and to administer all land abandoned in the South. The life of the bureau was extended after the war, despite the veto of President Andrew Johnson.

An Act to Establish a Bureau for the Relief of Freedmen and Refugees

Be it enacted, That there is hereby established in the War Department, to continue during the present war of rebellion, and for one year thereafter, a bureau of refugees, freedmen, and abandoned lands, to which shall be committed, as hereinafter provided, the supervision and management of all abandoned lands, and the control of all subjects relating to refugees and freedmen from rebel states, or from any district of country within the territory embraced in the operations of the army, under such rules and regulations as may be prescribed by the head of the bureau and approved by the President. The said bureau shall be under the management and control of a commissioner to be appointed by the President, by and with the advice and consent of the Senate.

SEC. 2. That the Secretary of War may direct such issues of provisions, clothing, and fuel, as he may deem needful for the immediate and temporary shelter and supply of destitute and suffering refugees and freedmen and their wives and children, under such rules and regulations as he may direct.

SEC. 3. That the President may, by and with the advice and consent of the Senate, appoint an assistant commissioner for each of the states declared to be in insurrection, not exceeding ten in number, who shall, under the direction of the commissioner, aid in the execution of the provisions of this act; . . . And any military officer may be detailed and assigned to duty under this act without increase of pay of allowances. . . .

SEC 4. That the commissioner, under the direction of the President, shall have authority to set apart, for the use of loyal refugees and freedmen, such tracts of land within the insurrectionary states as shall have been abandoned, or to which the United States shall have acquired title by confiscation or sale, or otherwise, and to every male citizen, whether refugee or freedman, as aforesaid, there shall be assigned not more than forty acres of such land, and the person to whom it was so assigned shall be protected in the use and enjoyment of the land for the term of three years at an annual rent not exceeding six per centum upon the value of such land, as it was appraised by the state authorities in the year eighteen hundred and sixty, for the purpose of taxation, and in case no such appraisal can be found, then the rental shall be based upon the estimated value of the land in said year, to be ascertained in such manner as the commissioner may by regulation prescribe. At the end of said term, or at any time during said term, the occupants of any parcels so assigned may purchase the land and receive such title thereto as the United States can convey, upon paying therefor the value of the land, as ascertained and fixed for the purpose of determining the annual rent aforesaid. . . .

THE THIRTEENTH AMENDMENT (1865)

Brief and to the point, the Thirteenth Amendment to the U.S. Constitution, ratified December 18, 1865, abolishes slavery "within the United States," thus completing the job begun by the Emancipation Proclamation.

SEC. 1. Neither slavery nor involuntary servitude, except as a punishment for crime whereof the party shall have been duly convicted, shall exist within the United States, or any place subject to their jurisdiction.

SEC. 2. Congress shall have power to enforce this article by appropriate legislation.

THE CIVIL RIGHTS ACT (1866)

The Civil Rights Act of 1866 was designed to protect the freedman from the Black Codes and other repressive legislation. This measure conferred citizenship on Negroes and set the stage for the more inclusive Fourteenth Amendment.

An Act to Protect All Persons in the United States in Their Civil Rights, and Furnish the Means of Their Vindication

Be it enacted, That all persons born in the United States and not subject to any foreign power, excluding Indians not taxed, are hereby declared to be citizens of the United States; and such citizens, of every race and color, without regard to any previous condition of slavery or involuntary servitude, except as a punishment for crime whereof the party shall have been duly convicted, shall have the same right, in every State and Territory in the United States, to make and enforce contracts, to sue, be parties, and give evidence, to inherit, purchase, lease, sell, hold, and convey real and personal property and to full and equal benefit of all laws and proceedings for the security of person and property, as is enjoyed by white citizens, and shall be subject to like punishment, pains, and penalties, and to none other, any law, statute,

ordinance, regulation, or custom, to the contrary notwithstanding.

SEC. 2. *And be it further enacted,* That any person who, under color of any law, statute, ordinance, regulation, or custom, shall subject, or cause to be subjected, any inhabitant of any State or Territory to the deprivation of any right secured or protected by this act, or to different punishment, pains, or penalties on account of such person having at any time been held in a condition of slavery or involuntary servitude, except as a punishment for crime whereof the party shall have been duly convicted, or by reason of his color or race, than is prescribed for the punishment of white persons, shall be deemed guilty of a misdemeanor, and, on conviction, shall be punished by fine not exceeding one thousand dollars, or imprisonment not exceeding one year, or both, in the discretion of the court.

SEC. 3. *And be it further enacted,* That the district courts of the United States, . . . shall have, exclusively of the courts of the several States, cognizance of all crimes and offences committed against the provisions of this act, and also, concurrently with the circuit court of the United States, of all causes, civil and criminal, affecting persons who are denied or cannot enforce in the courts or judicial tribunals of the State or locality where they may be any of the rights secured to them by the first section of this act. . . .

SEC. 4. *And be it further enacted,* That the district attorneys, marshals, and deputy marshals of the United States, the commissioners appointed by the Circuit and territorial courts of the United States, with powers of arresting, imprisoning, or bailing offenders against the laws of the United States, the officers and agents of the Freedmen's Bureau, and every other officer who may be specially empowered by the President of the United States, shall be, and they are hereby, specially authorized and required, at the expense of the United States, to institute proceedings against all and every person who shall violate the provisions of this act, and cause him or them to be arrested and imprisoned, or bailed, as the case may be, for trial before such court of the United States or territorial court as by this act has cognizance of the offence. . . .

SEC. 8. *And be it further enacted,* That whenever the President of the United States shall have reason to believe that offences have been or are likely to be committed against the provisions of this act within any judicial district, it shall be lawful for him, in his discretion, to direct the judge, marshal, and district attorney of such district to attend at such place within the district, and for such time as he may designate, for the purpose of the more speedy arrest and trial of persons charged with a violation of this act; and it shall be the duty of every judge or other officer, when any such requisition shall be received by him, to attend at the place and for the time therein designated.

SEC. 9. *And be it further enacted,* That it shall be lawful for the President of the United States, or such person as he may empower for that purpose, to employ such part of the land or naval forces of the United States, or of the militia, as shall be necessary to prevent the violation and enforce the due execution of this act.

SEC. 10. *And be it further enacted,* That upon all questions of law arising in any cause under the provisions of this act a final appeal may be taken to the Supreme Court of the United States.

THE FIRST RECONSTRUCTION ACT (1867)

The First Reconstruction Act of 1867 contained the general principles which governed Congressional Reconstruction. President Andrew Johnson vetoed the bill in vain, inasmuch as the Radical Republicans were able to muster the two-thirds majority necessary to override his veto.

An Act to Provide for the More Efficient Government of the Rebel States

Whereas no legal State governments or adequate protection for life or property now exists in the rebel States of Virginia, North Carolina, South Carolina, Georgia, Mississippi, Alabama, Louisiana, Florida, Texas, and Arkansas; and whereas it is necessary that peace and good order should be enforced in said States until loyal and republican State governments can be legally established: Therefore,

Be it enacted, That said rebel States shall be divided into military districts and made subject to the military authority of the United States as hereinafter prescribed, and for that purpose Virginia shall constitute the first district; North Carolina and South Carolina the second district; Georgia, Alabama, and Florida the third district; Mississippi and Arkansas the fourth district; and Louisiana and Texas the fifth district.

SEC. 2. That it shall be the duty of the President to assign to the command of each of said districts an officer of the army, not below the rank of brigadier-general, and to detail a sufficient military force to enable such officer to perform his duties and enforce his authority within the district to which he is assigned.

SEC. 3. That it shall be the duty of each officer assigned as aforesaid, to protect all persons in their rights of persons and property, to suppress insurrection, disorder, and violence, and to punish, or cause to be punished, all disturbers of the public peace and criminals; and to this end he may allow local civil tribunals to take jurisdiction of and to try offenders, or, when in his judgment it may be necessary for the trial of offenders, he shall have power to organize military commissions or tribunals for that purpose, and all interference under color of State authority with the exercise of military authority under this act, shall be null and void.

SEC. 4. That all persons put under military arrest by virtue of this act shall be tried without unnecessary delay, and no cruel or unusual punishment shall be inflicted, and no sentence of any military commission or tribunal hereby authorized, affecting the life or liberty of any person, shall be executed until it is approved by the officer in command of the district, and the laws and regulations for the government of the army shall not be affected by this act, except in so far as they conflict with its provisions: *Provided,* That no sentence of death under the provisions of this act shall be carried into effect without the approval of the President.

SEC. 5. That when the people of any one of said rebel States shall have formed a constitution of government in conformity with the Constitution of the United States in all respects, framed by a convention of delegates elected by the male citizens of said State, twenty-one years old and upward, of whatever race, color, or previous condition, who have been resident in said State for one year previous to the day of such election, except such as may be disfranchised for participation in the rebellion or for felony at common law, and when such constitution shall provide that the elective franchise shall be enjoyed by all such persons as have the qualifications herein stated for electors of delegates, and when such constitution shall be ratified by a majority of the persons voting on the question of ratification who are qualified as electors for delegates, and when such constitution shall have been submitted to Congress for examination and approval, and Congress shall have approved the same, and when said State, by a vote of its legislature elected said constitution, shall have adopted the amendment to the Constitution of the United States, proposed by the Thirty-ninth Congress, and known as article fourteen, and when said article shall have become a part of the Constitution of the United States said State shall be declared entitled to representation in Congress, and senators and representatives shall be admitted therefrom on their taking the oath prescribed by law, and then and thereafter the preceding sections of this act shall be inoperative in said State: *Provided,* That no person excluded from the privilege of holding office by said proposed amendment to the Constitution of the United States, shall be eligible to election as a member of the convention to frame a constitution for any of said rebel States, nor shall any such person vote for members of such convention.

Sec. 6. That, until the people of said rebel States shall be by law admitted to representation in the Congress of the United States, any civil governments which may exist therein shall be deemed provisional only, and in all respects subject to the paramount authority of the United States at any time to abolish, modify, control, or supersede the same; and in all elections to any office under such provisional governments all persons shall be entitled to vote, and none others, who are entitled to vote, under the provisions of the fifth section of this act; and no persons shall be eligible to any office under any such provisional governments who would be disqualified from holding office under the provisions of the third *article* of said constitutional amendment.

THE FOURTEENTH AMENDMENT (1868)

The Fourteenth Amendment, ratified July 23, 1868, defined U.S. citizenship and reversed the traditional federal-state relationship by providing for the intervention of the federal government in cases where state governments were accused of violating the Constitutional rights of the individual.

Sec. 1. All persons born or naturalized in the United States, and subject to the jurisdiction thereof, are citizens of the United States and of the State wherein they reside. No state shall make or enforce any law which shall abridge the privileges or immunities of citizens of the United States; nor shall any State deprive any person of life, liberty, or property, without due process of law; nor deny to any person within its jurisdiction the equal protection of the laws.

Sec. 2. Representatives shall be apportioned among the several States according to their respective numbers, counting the whole number of persons in each State, excluding Indians not taxed. But when the right to vote at any election for the choice of electors for President and Vice President of the United States, Representatives in Congress, the Executive and Judicial officers of a State, or the members of the Legislature thereof, is denied to any of the male inhabitants of such State, being twenty-one years of age, and citizens of the United States, or in any way abridged, except for participation in rebellion, or other crime, the basis of representation therein shall be reduced in the proportion which the number of such male

citizens shall bear to the whole number of male citizens twenty-one years of age in such State.

Sec. 3. No person shall be a Senator or Representative in Congress, or elector of President and Vice President, or hold any office, civil or military, under the United States, or under any State, who, having previously taken an oath, as a member of Congress, or as an officer of the United States, or as a member of any State legislature, or as an executive or judicial officer of any State, to support the Constitution of the United States, shall have engaged in insurrection or rebellion against the same, or given aid or comfort to the enemies thereof. But Congress may by a vote of two-thirds of each House, remove such disability.

Sec. 4. The validity of the public debt of the United States, authorized by law, including debts incurred for payment of pensions and bounties for services in suppressing insurrection or rebellion shall not be questioned. But neither the United States nor any State shall assume or pay any debt or obligation incurred in aid of insurrection or rebellion against the United States, or any claim for the loss or emancipation of any slave; but all such debts, obligations and claims shall be held illegal and void.

Sec. 5. The Congress shall have power to enforce, by appropriate legislation, the provisions of this article.

THE FIFTEENTH AMENDMENT (1870)

Ratified March 30, 1870, the Fifteenth Amendment, like the Thirteenth a model of brevity, established the right to vote for all citizens.

Sec. 1. The right of citizens of the United States to vote shall not be denied or abridged by the United States or by any State on account of race, color, or previous conditions of servitude.

Sec. 2. The Congress shall have power to enforce this article by appropriate legislation.

THE CIVIL RIGHTS ACT (1875)

The Civil Rights Act of 1875 concerned itself primarily with the prohibition of racial discrimination in places of public accommodation. Eight years later, however, the Supreme Court ruled that the law was unconstitutional, stating that Congress did not have the authority to regulate the prevalent social mores of any state. This decision virtually removed the federal government from the civil rights arena, particularly as regarded enforcement of the Fourteenth Amendment.

Cartoons of the 1876 elections show each political party accusing the other of intimidating black voters. Loyal to Lincoln's memory, most blacks voted Republican.

An Act to Protect All Citizens in Their Civil and Legal Rights

Whereas it is essential to just government we recognize the equality of all men before the law, and hold that it is the duty of government in its dealings with the people to mete out equal and exact justice to all, of whatever nativity, race, color, or persuasion, religious or political; and it being the appropriate object of legislation to enact great fundamental principles into law: Therefore,

Be it enacted, That all persons within the jurisdiction of the United States shall be entitled to the full and equal enjoyment of the accommodations, advantages, facilities, and privileges of inns, public conveyances on land or water, theaters, and other places of public amusement; subject only to the conditions and limitations established by law, and applicable alike to citizens of every race and color, regardless of any previous condition of servitude.

SEC. 2. That any person who shall violate the foregoing section by denying to any citizen, except for reasons by law applicable to citizens of every race and color, and regardless of any previous condition of servitude, the full enjoyment of any of the accommodations, advantages, facilities, or privileges in said section enumerated, or by aiding or inciting such denial, shall, for every such offense, forfeit and pay the sum of

five hundred dollars to the person aggrieved thereby, . . . and shall also, for every such offense, be deemed guilty of a misdemeanor, and upon conviction thereof, shall be fined not less than five hundred nor more than one thousand dollars, or shall be imprisoned not less than thirty days nor more than one year . . .

SEC. 3. That the district and circuit courts of the United States shall have, exclusively of the courts of the several States, cognizance of all crimes and offenses against, and violations of, the provisions of this act . . .

SEC. 4. That no citizen possessing all other qualifications which are or may be prescribed by law shall be disqualified for service as grand or petit juror in any court of the United States, or of any State, on account of race, color, or previous condition of servitude; and any officer or other person charged with any duty in the selection or summoning of jurors who shall exclude or fail to summon any citizen for the cause aforesaid shall, on conviction thereof, be deemed guilty of a misdemeanor, and be fined not more than five thousand dollars.

SEC. 5. That all cases arising under the provisions of this act . . . shall be renewable by the Supreme Court of the United States, without regard to the sum in controversy. . . .

BOOKER T. WASHINGTON'S "ATLANTA COMPROMISE" SPEECH (1895)

Booker T. Washington, at one time the sole voice in the movement for Negro advancement, is often criticized today for having encouraged the Negro to cultivate a spirit of peaceful coexistence with the white Southerner. Washington advocated technical and industrial self-help programs for the Negro, even if they tended to discount the importance of his cultivating intellectual and aesthetic values as well.

Mr. President and Gentlemen of the Board of Directors and Citizens:

One third of the population of the South is of the Negro race. No enterprise seeking the material, civil, or moral welfare of this section can disregard this element of our population and reach the highest success. I but convey to you, Mr. President and Directors, the sentiment of the masses of my race when I say that in no way have the value and manhood of the American Negro been more fittingly and generously recognized than by the managers of this magnificent Exposition at every stage of its progress. It is a recognition that will do more to cement the friendship of the two races than any occurrence since the dawn of our freedom.

Not only this, but the opportunity here afforded will awaken among us a new era of industrial progress. Ignorant and inexperienced, it is not strange that in the first years of our new life we began at the top instead of at the bottom; that a seat in Congress or the State Legislature was more sought than real estate or industrial skill; that the political convention or stump speaking had more attractions than starting a dairy farm or truck garden.

A ship lost at sea for many days suddenly sighted a friendly vessel. From the mast of the unfortunate vessel was seen a signal: "Water, water; we die of thirst!" The answer from the friendly vessel at once came back: "Cast down your bucket where you are." A second time the signal, "Water, water; send us water!" ran up from the distressed vessel, and was answered: "Cast down your bucket where you are." And a third and fourth signal for water was answered: "Cast down your bucket where you are." The captain of the distressed vessel, at last heeding the injunction, cast down his bucket, and it came up full of fresh, sparkling water from the mouth of the Amazon River. To those of my race who depend on bettering their condition in a foreign land, or who underestimate the importance of cultivating friendly relations with the Southern white man, who is their next door neighbor, I would say: "Cast down your bucket where you are"—cast it down in making friends in every manly way of the people of all races by whom we are surrounded.

Cast it down in agriculture, mechanics, in commerce, in domestic service, and in the professions. And in this connection it is well to bear in mind that whatever other sins the South may be called to bear, when it comes to business, pure and simple, it is in the South that the Negro is given a man's chance in the commercial world, and in nothing is this Exposition more eloquent than in emphasizing this chance. Our greatest danger is, that in the great leap from slavery to freedom we may overlook the fact that the masses of us are to live by the productions of our hands, and fail to keep in mind that we shall prosper in proportion as we learn to dignify and glorify common labor, and put brains and skill into the common occupations of life; shall prosper in proportion as we learn to draw the line between the superficial and the substantial, the ornamental gewgaws of life and the useful. No race can prosper till it learns that there is as much dignity in tilling a field as in writing a poem. It is at the bottom of life we must begin, and not at the top. Nor should we permit our grievances to overshadow our opportunities.

To those of the white race who look to the incom-

Accepting Booker T. Washington's (center) *invitation, Theodore Roosevelt addresses the National Negro Business League.*

ing of those of foreign birth and strange tongue and habits for the prosperity of the South, were I permitted, I would repeat what I say to my own race, "Cast down your bucket where you are." Cast it down among the 8,000,000 Negroes whose habits you know, whose fidelity and love you have tested in days when to have proved treacherous meant the ruin of your firesides. Cast down your bucket among these people who have, without strikes and labor wars, tilled your fields, cleared your forests, builded your railroads and cities, and brought forth treasures from the bowels of the earth, and helped make possible this magnificent representation of the progress of the South. Casting down your bucket among my people, helping and encouraging them as you are doing on these grounds, and, with education of head, hand and heart, you will find that they will buy your surplus land, make blossom the waste place in your fields, and run your factories. While doing this, you can be sure in the future, as in the past, that you and your families will be surrounded by the most patient, faithful, law-abiding, and unresentful people that the world has seen. As we have proved our loyalty to you in the past, in nursing your children, watching by the sick bed of your mothers and fathers, and often following them with tear-dimmed eyes to their graves, so in the future, in our humble way, we shall stand by you with a devotion that no foreigner can approach, ready to lay down our lives, if need be, in defense of yours, interlacing our industrial, commercial, civil, and religious life with yours in a way that shall make the interests of both races one. In all things that are purely social we can be as separate as the fingers, yet one as the hand in all things essential to mutual progress.

There is no defense or security for any of us except in the highest intelligence and development of all. If anywhere there are efforts tending to curtail the fullest growth of the Negro, let these efforts be turned into stimulating, encouraging, and making him the most useful and intelligent citizen. Effort or means so invested will pay a thousand percent interest. These efforts will be twice blessed—"blessing him that gives and him that takes."

There is no escape through law of man or God from the inevitable:

> The laws of changeless justice bind
> Oppressor with oppressed;
> And close as sin and suffering joined
> We march to fate abreast.

Nearly sixteen millions of hands will aid you in pulling the load upwards, or they will pull against you the load downwards. We shall constitute one-third and more of the ignorance and crime of the South, or one-third its intelligence and progress; we shall contribute one-third to the business and industrial prosperity of the South, or we shall prove a veritable body of death, stagnating, depressing, retarding every effort to advance the body politic.

Gentlemen of the Exposition, as we present to you our humble effort at an exhibition of our progress, you must not expect overmuch. Starting thirty years ago with ownership here and there in a few quilts and pumpkins and chickens (gathered from miscellaneous sources), remember the path that has led from these to the invention and production of agricultural implements, buggies, steam engines, newspapers, books, statuary, carving, paintings, the management of drug stores and banks, has not been trodden without contact with thorns and thistles. While we take pride in what we exhibit as a result of our independent efforts, we do not for a moment forget that our part in this exhibition would fall far short of your expectations but for the constant help that has come to our educational life, not only from the Southern States, but especially from Northern philanthropists, who have made their gifts a constant stream of blessing and encouragement.

The wisest among my race understand that the agitation of questions of social equality is the extremist folly, and that progress in the enjoyment of all the privileges that will come to us must be the result of severe and constant struggle rather than of artificial forcing. No race that has anything to contribute to the markets of the world is long in any degree ostracized. It is important and right that all privileges of the law be ours, but it is vastly more important that we be prepared for the exercise of those privileges. The opportunity to earn a dollar in a factory just now is worth infinitely more than the opportunity to spend a dollar in an opera house.

In conclusion, may I repeat that nothing in thirty years has given us more hope and encouragement, and drawn us so near to you of the white race, as this opportunity offered by the Exposition; and here bending, as it were, over the altar that represents the results of the struggles of your race and mine, both starting practically empty-handed three decades ago, I pledge that, in your effort to work out the great and intricate problem which God has laid at the doors of the South, you shall have at all time the patient, sympathetic help of my race; only let this be constantly in mind that, while from representations in these buildings of the product of field, of forest, of mine, of factory, letters, and art, much good will come, yet far above and beyond material benefits will be that higher good, that let us pray God will come, in a blotting out of sectional differences and racial animosities and suspicions, in a determination to administer absolute justice, in a willing obedience among all classes to the mandates of law. This, coupled with our material prosperity, will bring into our beloved South a new heaven and a new earth.

THE UNIVERSAL NEGRO IMPROVEMENT ASSOCIATION: SPEECH AT LIBERTY HALL, NEW YORK CITY (1922)

The Universal Negro Improvement Association (UNIA) was founded by Marcus Garvey—a West Indian Negro who, in the decade following World War I, won a large following in the United States. Garveyism was the precursor of present-day black nationalist movements. It represented a sharp repudiation of Washington's ideas, as did the work of Negro scholar W. E. B. DuBois, one of the founding fathers of the NAACP.

Over five years ago the Universal Negro Improvement

Marcus Garvey was one of the pioneer advocates of Black Nationalism.

Association placed itself before the world as the movement through which the new and rising Negro would give expression of his feelings. This Association adopts an attitude not of hostility to other races and peoples of the world, but an attitude of self-respect. . . .

. . . Wheresoever human rights are denied to any group, wheresoever justice is denied to any group, there the U.N.I.A. finds a cause. And at this time among all the peoples of the world, the group that suffers most from injustice, the group that is denied most of those rights that belong to all humanity, is the black group . . . even so under the leadership of the U.N.I.A., we are marshaling the 400,000,000 Negroes of the world to fight for the emancipation of the race and of the redemption of the country of our fathers.

We represent a new line of thought among Negroes. Whether you call it advanced thought or reactionary thought, I do not care. If it is reactionary for people to seek independence in government, then we are reactionary. If it is advanced thought for people to seek liberty and freedom, then we represent the advanced school of thought among the Negroes of this country. We of the U.N.I.A. believe that what is good for the other folks is good for us. If Government is something that is worth while; if government is something that is appreciable and helpful and protective to others, then we also want to experiment in government. We do not mean a government that will make us citizens without rights or subjects without consideration. We mean a kind of government that will place our race in control, even as other races are in control of their own government.

. . . The U.N.I.A. is not advocating the cause of church building, because we have a sufficiently large number of churches among us to minister to the spiritual needs of the people, and we are not going to compete with those who are engaged in so splendid a work; we are not engaged in building any new social institutions, . . . because there are enough social workers engaged in those praiseworthy efforts. We are not engaged in politics because we have enough local politicians, . . . and the political situation is well taken care of. We are not engaged in domestic politics, in church building or in social uplift work, but we are engaged in nation building.

In advocating the principles of this Association we find we have been very much misunderstood and very much misrepresented by men from within our own race, as well as others from without. Any reform movement that seeks to bring about changes for the benefit of humanity is bound to be misrepresented by those who have always taken it upon themselves to administer to, and lead the unfortunate. . . .

. . . The Universal Negro Improvement Association stands for the Bigger Brotherhood; the Universal Negro Improvement Association stands for human rights, not only for Negroes, but for all races. The Universal Negro Improvement Association believes in the rights of not only the black race, but the white race, the yellow race and the brown race. The Universal Negro Improvement Association believes that the white man has as much right to be considered, the yellow man has as much right to be considered, the brown man has as much right to be considered as the black man of Africa. In view of the fact that the black man of Africa has contributed as much to the world as the white man of Europe, and the brown man and yellow man of Asia, we of the Universal Negro Improvement Association demand that the white, yellow and brown races give to the black man his place in the civilization of the world. We ask for nothing more than the rights of 400,000,000 Negroes. We are not seeking, as I said before, to destroy or disrupt the society of the government of other races, but we are determined that 400,000,000 of us shall unite ourselves to free our motherland from the grasp of the invader. . . .

The Universal Negro Improvement Association is not seeking to build up another government within the bounds or borders of the United States of America. The Universal Negro Improvement Association is not seeking to disrupt any organized system of government, but the Association is determined to bring Negroes together for the building up of a nation of their own. And why? Because we have been forced to it. We have been forced to it throughout the world; not only in America, not only in Europe, not only in the British Empire, but wheresoever the black man happens to find himself, he has been forced to do for himself.

To talk about Government is a little more than some of our people can appreciate. . . . The average man . . . seems to say, "Why should there be need for any other government?" We are French, English or American. But we of the U.N.I.A. have studied seriously this question of nationality among Negroes— this American nationality, this British nationality, this French, Italian or Spanish nationality, and have discovered that it counts for nought when that nationality comes in conflict with the racial idealism of the group that rules. When our interests clash with those of the ruling faction, then we find that we have absolutely no rights. In times of peace, when everything is all right, Negroes have a hard time, wherever we go, wheresoever we find ourselves, getting those rights that belong to us in common with others whom we claim as fellow citizens; getting that consideration that should be ours by right of the constitution, by right of the law; but in the time of trouble they make us all partners in the cause, as happened in the last war. . . .

We have saved many nations in this manner, and we have lost our lives doing that before. Hundreds of thousands—nay, millions of black men, lie buried under the ground due to that old-time camouflage of saving the nation. We saved the British Empire; we saved the French Empire; we saved this glorious country more than once; and all that we have received for our sacrifices, all that we have received for what we have done, even in giving up our lives, is just what you are receiving now, just what I am receiving now.

You and I fare no better in America, in the British Empire, or any other part of the white world; we fare no better than any black man wheresoever he shows his head. . . .

The U.N.I.A. is reversing the old-time order of things. We refuse to be followers anymore. We are leading ourselves. That means, if any saving is to be done, . . . we are going to seek a method of saving Africa first. Why? And why Africa? Because Africa has become the grand prize of the nations. Africa has become the big game of the nation hunters. Today

Africa looms as the greatest commercial, industrial and political prize in the world.

The difference between the Universal Negro Improvement Association and the other movements of this country, and probably the world, is that the Universal Negro Improvement Association seeks independence of government, while the other organizations seek to make the Negro a secondary part of existing governments. We differ from the organizations in America because they seek to subordinate the Negro as a secondary consideration in a great civilization, knowing that in America the Negro will never reach his highest ambition, knowing that the Negro in America will never get his constitutional rights. All other organizations which are fostering the improvement of Negroes in the British Empire know that the Negro in the British Empire will never reach the height of his constitutional rights. What do I mean by constitutional rights in America? If the black man is to reach the height of his ambition in this country—if the black man is to get all of his constitutional rights in America—then the black man should have the same chance in the nation as any other man to become president of the nation, or a street cleaner in New York. If the black man in the British Empire is to have all his constitutional rights it means that the Negro in the British Empire should have at least the same right to become premier of Great Britain as he has to become street cleaner in the city of London. Are they prepared to give us such political equality? You and I can live in the United States of America for 100 more years, and our generations may live for 200 years or for 5000 more years, and so long as there is a black and white population, when the majority is on the side of the white race, you and I will never get political justice or get political equality in this country. Then why should a black man with rising ambition, after preparing himself in every possible way to give expression to that highest ambition, allow himself to be kept down by racial prejudice within a country? If I am as educated as the next man, if I am as prepared as the next man, if I have passed through the best schools and colleges and universities as the other fellow, why should I not have a fair chance to compete with the other fellow for the biggest position in the nation? . . .

We are not preaching a propaganda of hate against anybody. We love the white man; we love all humanity. . . . The white man is as necessary to the existence of the Negro as the Negro is necessary to his existence. There is a common relationship that we cannot escape. Africa has certain things that Europe wants, and Europe has certain things that Africa wants, . . . it is impossible for us to escape it. Africa has oil, diamonds, copper, gold and rubber and all the minerals that Europe wants, and there must be some kind of relationship between Africa and Europe for a fair exchange, so we cannot afford to hate anybody.

The question often asked is what does it require to redeem a race and free a country? If it takes man power, if it takes scientific intelligence, if it takes education of any kind, or if it takes blood, then the 400,000,000 Negroes of the world have it.

It took the combined power of the Allies to put down the mad determination of the Kaiser to impose German will upon the world and upon humanity. Among those who suppressed his mad ambition were two million Negroes who have not yet forgotten how to drive men across the firing line. . . . when so many white men refused to answer to the call and dodged behind all kinds of excuses, 400,000 black men were ready without a question. It was because we were told it was a war of democracy; it was a war for the liberation of the weaker peoples of the world. We heard the cry of Woodrow Wilson, not because we liked him so, but because the things he said were of such a nature that they appealed to us as men. Wheresoever the cause of humanity stands in need of assistance, there you will find the Negro ever ready to serve.

He has done it from the time of Christ up to now. When the whole world turned its back upon the Christ, the man who was said to be the Son of God, when the world cried out "Crucify Him," when the world spurned Him and spat upon Him, it was a black man, Simon, the Cyrenian, who took up the cross. Why? Because the cause of humanity appealed to him. When the black man saw the suffering Jew, struggling under the heavy cross, he was willing to go to His assistance, and he bore that cross up to the heights of Calvary. In the spirit of Simon, the Cyrenian, 1900 years ago, we answered the call of Woodrow Wilson, the call to a larger humanity, and it was for that that we willingly rushed into the war. . . .

We shall march out, yes, as black American citizens, as black British subjects, as black French citizens, as black Italians or as black Spaniards, but we shall march out with a greater loyalty, the loyalty of race. We shall march out in answer to the cry of our fathers, who cry out to us for the redemption of our own country, our motherland, Africa.

We shall march out, not forgetting the blessings of America. We shall march out, not forgetting the blessings of civilization. We shall march out with a history of peace before and behind us, and surely

that history shall be our breast-plate, for how can man fight better than knowing that the cause for which he fights is righteous? . . . Glorious shall be the battle when the time comes to fight for our people and our race.

We should say to the millions who are in Africa to hold the fort, for we are coming 400,000,000 strong.

EXECUTIVE ORDER 8802 (1941)

Executive Order 8802, signed by President Franklin D. Roosevelt, eliminated discriminatory practices in the defense industry during World War II. Since then, such orders have often been supplemented by comprehensive legislation designed to cope with the very grievances outlined by men like Garvey.

. . . I do hereby reaffirm the policy of the United States that there shall be no discrimination in the employment of workers in defense industries or Government because of race, creed, color, or national origin, and I do hereby declare that it is the duty of employers and of labor organizations, in furtherance of said policy and of this order, to provide for the full and equitable participation of all workers in defense industries, without discrimination because of race, creed, color, or national origin. . . .

President Franklin D. Roosevelt cracked down on discriminatory hiring in the defense industry.

EXECUTIVE ORDER 9981 (1948)

Executive Order 9981, signed by President Harry S. Truman, ended segregation in the Armed Forces of the United States.

Whereas it is essential that there be maintained in the armed services of the United States the highest standards of democracy, with equality of treatment and opportunity for all those who serve in our country's defense:

Now, therefore, by virtue of the authority vested in me as President of the United States, by the Constitution and the statutes of the United States, and as Commander-in-Chief of the armed services, it is hereby ordered as follows:

1. It is hereby declared to be the policy of the President that there shall be equality of treatment and opportunity for all persons in the armed services without regard to race, color, religion or national origin. This policy shall be put into effect as rapidly as possible, having due regard to the time required to effectuate any necessary changes without impairing efficiency or morals.

2. There shall be created in the National Military Establishment an advisory committee to be known as the President's Committee on Equality of Treatment and Opportunity in the Armed Services, which shall be composed of seven members to be designated by the President.

3. The Committee is authorized on behalf of the President to examine into the rules, procedures and practices of the armed services in order to determine in what respect such rules, procedures and practices may be altered or improved with a view to carrying out the policy of this order. The Committee shall confer and advise with the Secretary of Defense, the Secretary of the Army, the Secretary of the Air Force, and shall make such recommendations to the President and to said Secretaries as in the judgment of the Committee will effectuate the policy hereof.

4. All executive departments and agencies of the Federal Government are authorized and directed to cooperate with the Committee in its work, and to furnish the Committee such information or the services of such persons as the Committee may require in the performance of its duties.

5. When requested by the Committee to do so, persons in the armed services or in any of the executive departments and agencies of the Federal Government shall testify before the Committee and shall make available for the use of the Committee such documents and other information as the Committee may require.

6. The Committee shall continue to exist until such time as the President shall terminate its existence by Executive order.

THE CIVIL RIGHTS ACTS OF 1957 AND 1960

The Civil Rights Acts of 1957 and 1960, both passed during the Eisenhower Administration, represented the first comprehensive federal legislation in this area in the twentieth century. (Both these documents are presented in summary form.)

Provisions of the Act of 1957

TITLE I

Created an executive Commission on Civil Rights composed of six members, not more than three from the same political party, to be appointed by the President with the advice and consent of the Senate.

Established rules of procedure for the Commission.

Authorized the Commission to receive in executive session any testimony that might defame or incriminate anyone.

Provided that penalties for unauthorized persons who released information from executive hearings of the Commission would apply only to persons whose services were paid for by the Government.

Barred the Commission for issuing subpenas for witnesses who were found, resided or transacted business outside the state in which the hearing would be held.

Placed the pay for Commissioners at $50 per day—plus $12 per day for expenses away from home.

Empowered the Commission to investigate allegations that U.S. citizens were being deprived of their right to vote and have that vote counted by reason of color, race, religion, or national origin; to study and collect information concerning legal developments constituting a denial of equal protection of the laws under the Constitution; to appraise the laws and policies of the Federal Government with respect to equal protection of the laws.

Directed the Commission to submit interim reports to the President and Congress and a final report of its activities, findings and recommendations not later than two years following enactment of the bill.

Authorized the President, with the advice and con-

Black leaders meet with President Eisenhower at the White House in 1958. Left to right: *Martin Luther King, Jr., E. Frederick Morrow, President Eisenhower, A. Philip Randolph, Attorney General William Rogers, Presidential Assistant Rocco Siciliano, and Roy Wilkins.*

sent of the Senate, to appoint a full-time staff director of the Commission whose pay would not exceed $22,500 a year.

Barred the Commission from accepting or utilizing the services of voluntary or uncompensated personnel.

TITLE II

Authorized the President to appoint, with the advice and consent of the Senate, one additional Assistant Attorney General in the Department of Justice.

TITLE III

Extended the jurisdiction of the district courts to include any civil action begun to recover damages or secure equitable relief under any act of Congress providing for the protection of civil rights, including the right to vote.

Repealed a statute of 1866 giving the President power to employ troops to enforce or to prevent violation of civil rights legislation.

TITLE IV

Prohibited attempts to intimidate or prevent persons from voting in general or primary elections for federal offices.

Empowered the Attorney General to seek an in-junction when an individual was deprived or about to be deprived of his right to vote.

Gave the district courts jurisdiction over such proceedings, without requiring that administrative remedies be exhausted.

Provided that any person cited for contempt should be defended by counsel and allowed to compel witnesses to appear.

TITLE V

Provided that in all criminal contempt cases arising from the provisions of the Civil Rights Act of 1957, the accused, upon conviction, would be punished by fine or imprisonment or both.

Placed the maximum fine for an individual under those provisions at $1,000 or six months in jail.

Allowed the judge to decide whether a defendant in a criminal contempt case involving voting rights would be tried with or without a jury.

Provided that in the event a criminal contempt case was tried before a judge without a jury and the sentence upon conviction was more than $300 or more than 45 days in jail, the defendant could demand and receive a jury trial.

Stated that the section would not apply to contempts committed in the presence of the court or so near as to interfere directly with the administration of justice, nor to the behavior or misconduct of any officer of the court in respect to the process of the court.

Provided that any U.S. citizen over 21, who had resided for one year within a judicial district would be competent to serve as a grand or petit juror unless: (1) he had been convicted of a crime punishable by imprisonment for more than one year and his civil rights not restored; (2) he was unable to read, write, speak and understand the English language; (3) he was incapable, either physically or mentally, to give efficient jury service.

Provisions of the Act of 1960

TITLE I

Provided that persons who obstructed or interfered with any order issued by a federal court, or attempted to do so, by threats or force, could be punished by a fine of up to $1,000, imprisonment of up to one year, or both. Such acts could also be prevented by private suits seeking court injunctions against them.

TITLE II

Made it a federal crime to cross state lines to avoid prosecution or punishment for, or giving evidence on, the bombing or burning of any building, facility or vehicle, or an attempt to do so. Penalties could be a fine of up to $5,000, or imprisonment of up to five years, or both.

Made it a federal crime to transport or possess explosives with the knowledge or intent that they would be used to blow up any vehicle or building. Allowed the presumption, after any bombing occurred, that the explosives used were transported across state lines (therefore allowing the FBI to investigate any bombing case), but stipulated that this would have to be proved before the person could be convicted. Penalties could be imprisonment of up to one year and/or $10,000 fine; if personal injury resulted, 10 years and/or $10,000 fine; if death resulted, life imprisonment or a death penalty if recommended by a jury.

Made it a federal crime to use interstate facilities, such as telephones, to threaten a bombing or give a false bombscare, punishable by imprisonment of up to one year or a fine of up to $1,000, or both.

TITLE III

Required that voting records and registration papers for all federal elections, including primaries, must be preserved for 22 months. Penalties for failing to comply or for stealing, destroying or mutilating the records could be a fine of up to $1,000, and/or imprisonment for one year.

Directed that the records, upon written application, be turned over to the Attorney General "or his representative" at the office of the records' custodian.

Unless directed otherwise by a court, the Justice Department representative must not disclose the content of the records except to Congress, a government agency, or in a court proceeding.

TITLE IV

Empowered the Civil Rights Commission, which was extended for two years in 1959, to administer oaths and take sworn statements.

TITLE V

Stated that arrangements might be made to provide for the education of children of members of the armed forces when the schools those children regularly attended had been closed to avoid integration and the U.S. Commissioner of Education had decided that no other educational agency would provide for their schooling. Amended the laws on aid to impacted school districts (PL 81–815, PL 81–874) to this effect.

TITLE VI

Provided that after the Attorney General won a civil suit brought under the 1957 Civil Rights Act to protect Negroes' right to vote, he could then ask the court to hold another adversary proceeding and make a separate finding that there was a "pattern or practice" of depriving Negroes of the right to vote in the area involved in the suit.

If a court found such a "pattern or practice," any Negro living in that area could apply to the court to issue an order declaring him qualified to vote if he proved (1) he was qualified to vote under state law; (2) he had tried to register after the "pattern or practice" finding; and (3) he had not been allowed to register or had been found unqualified by someone acting under color of law. The court would have to hear the Negro's application within 10 days and its order would be effective for as long a period as that for which he would have been qualified to vote if registered under state law.

State officials would be notified of the order, and they would then be bound to permit the person to vote. Disobedience would be subject to contempt proceedings.

To carry out these provisions, the court may appoint one or more voting referees, who must be qualified voters in the judicial district. The referees would receive the applications, take evidence, and report their findings to the court. The referee must take the Negro's application and proof in an *ex parte* proceeding (without cross-examination by opponents) and the court may set the time and place for the referee's hearing.

The court may fix a time limit of up to 10 days, in which state officials may challenge the referee's report. Challenges on points of law must be accompanied by a memorandum and on points of fact by a verified copy of a public record or an affidavit by those with personal knowledge of the controverting evidence. Either the court or the referee may decide the challenges in accordance with court-directed procedures. Hearings on issues of fact could be held only when the affidavits show there is a real issue of fact.

If a Negro has applied for a court certificate 20 or more days before the election, his application is challenged, and the case is not decided by election day, the court must allow him to vote provisionally, provided he is "entitled to vote under state law," and impound his ballot pending a decision on his application. If he applies within 20 days before the election, the court has the option of whether or not to let him vote.

The court would not be limited in its powers to enforce its decree that these Negroes be allowed to vote and their votes be counted and may authorize the referee to take action to enforce it.

The referees would have the powers conferred on court masters by rule 53 (c) of the Federal Rules of Civil Procedure. (Rule 53 (c) gives masters the right to subpena records, administer oaths and cross-examine witnesses.)

In any suit instituted under these provisions, the state would be held responsible for the actions of its officials and, in the event state officials resign and are not replaced, the state itself could be sued.

EXECUTIVE ORDER 10730 (1957)

Executive Order 10730, signed by President Dwight D. Eisenhower, ended segregation in Little Rock's Central High School.

Whereas on September 23, 1957, I issued Proclamation No. 3204 reading in part as follows:

Whereas certain persons in the State of Arkansas, individually and in unlawful assemblages, combinations, and conspiracies, have wilfully obstructed the enforcement of orders of the United States District Court for the Eastern District of Arkansas with respect to matters relating to enrollment and attendance at public schools, particularly at Central High School,

located in Little Rock School District, Little Rock, Arkansas; and

Whereas such wilful obstruction of justice hinders the execution of the laws of that State and of the United States, and makes it impracticable to enforce such laws by the ordinary course of judicial proceedings; and

Whereas such obstructions of justice constitutes a denial of the equal protection of the laws secured by the Constitution of the United States and impedes the course of justice under those laws;

Now, therefore, I, Dwight D. Eisenhower, President of the United States, under and by virtue of the authority vested in me by the Constitution and Statutes of the United States, including Chapter 15 of Title 10 of the United States Code, particularly sections 332, 333 and 334 thereof, do command all persons engaged in such obstruction of justice to cease and desist therefrom, and to disperse forthwith, and

Whereas the command contained in that Proclamation has not been obeyed and wilful obstruction of enforcement of said court orders still exists and threatens to continue:

Now, therefore, by virtue of the authority vested in me by the Constitution and Statutes of the United States, including Chapter 15 of Title 10, particularly sections 332, 333 and 334 thereof, and section 301 of Title 3 of the United States Code, it is hereby ordered as follows:

SEC. 1. I hereby authorize and direct the Secretary of Defense to order into the active military service of the United States as he may deem appropriate to carry out the purposes of this Order, any or all of the units of the National Guard of the United States

President Eisenhower initiated use of Army troops to override southern obstructions to school desegregation.

and of the Air National Guard of the United States within the State of Arkansas to serve in the active military service of the United States for an indefinite period and until relieved by appropriate orders.

SEC. 2. The Secretary of Defense is authorized and directed to take all appropriate steps to enforce any orders of the United States District Court for the Eastern District of Arkansas for the removal of obstruction of justice in the State of Arkansas with respect to matters relating to enrollment and attendance at public schools in the Little Rock School District, Little Rock, Arkansas. In carrying out the provisions of this section, the Secretary of Defense is authorized to use the units, and members thereof, ordered into the active military service of the United States pursuant to Section 1 of this Order.

SEC. 3. In furtherance of the enforcement of the aforementioned orders of the United States District Court for the Eastern District of Arkansas, the Secretary of Defense is authorized to use such of the armed forces of the United States as he may deem necessary.

SEC. 4. The Secretary of Defense is authorized to delegate to the Secretary of the Army or the Secretary of the Air Force, or both, any of the authority conferred upon him by this Order.

EXECUTIVE ORDER 11053 (1962)

Executive Order 11053, signed by President John F. Kennedy, authorized the use of federal troops in integrating the University of Mississippi.

Whereas on September 30, 1962, I issued Proclamation No. 3497 reading in part as follows:

Whereas the Governor of the State of Mississippi and certain law enforcement officers and other officials of that State, and other persons, individually and in unlawful opposing and obstructing the enforcement of orders entered by the United States District Court for the Southern District of Mississippi and the United States Court of Appeals for the Fifth Circuit; and

Whereas such unlawful assemblies, combinations, and conspiracies oppose and obstruct the execution of the laws of the United States, impede the course of justice under those laws and make it impracticable to enforce those laws in the State of Mississippi by the ordinary course of judicial proceedings; and

Whereas I have expressly called the attention of the Governor of Mississippi to the perilous situation that exists and to his duties in the premises, and have requested but have not received from him adequate assurances that the orders of the courts of the United States will be obeyed and that law and order will be maintained:

Now, therefore, I, John F. Kennedy, President of the United States, under and by virtue of the authority vested in me by the Constitution and laws of the United States, including Chapter 15 of Title 10 of the United States Code, particularly sections 332, 333 and 334 thereof, do command all persons engaged in such obstructions of justice to cease and desist therefrom and to disperse and retire peaceably forthwith; and

Whereas the commands contained in that proclamation have not been obeyed and obstruction of enforcement of those court orders still exists and threatens to continue:

Now, therefore, by virtue of the authority vested in me by the Constitution and laws of the United States, including Chapter 15 of Title 10, particularly Sections 332, 333 and 334 thereof, and Section 301 of Title 3 of the United States Code, it is hereby ordered as follows:

SEC. 1. The Secretary of Defense is authorized and directed to take all appropriate steps to enforce all orders of the United States District Court for the Southern District of Mississippi and the United States Court of Appeals for the Fifth Circuit and to remove all obstructions of justice in the State of Mississippi.

SEC. 2. In furtherance of the enforcement of the aforementioned orders of the United States District Court for the Southern District of Mississippi and the United States Court of Appeals for the Fifth Circuit, the Secretary of Defense is authorized to use such of the armed forces of the United States as he may deem necessary.

SEC. 3. I hereby authorize the Secretary of Defense to call into the active military service of the United States, as he may deem appropriate to carry out the purposes of this order, any or all of the units of the Army National Guard and of the Air National Guard of the State of Mississippi to serve in the active military service of the United States for an indefinite period and until relieved by appropriate orders. In carrying out the provisions of Section 1, the Secretary of Defense is authorized to use the units, and members thereof, ordered into the active military service of the United States pursuant to this section.

SEC. 4. The Secretary of Defense is authorized to delegate to the Secretary of the Army or the Secretary of the Air Force, or both, any of the authority conferred upon him by this order.

THE BIRMINGHAM MANIFESTO (1963)

In 1963, a series of events in Birmingham, Alabama dramatized the Negro's plight to the nation at large.

Black citizens were arrested en masse during peaceful demonstrations which were subsequently quelled by local police using dogs and by firemen using hoses. The Manifesto, dated April 3, 1963, embodied the hope of the Negro community in Birmingham that law, order, and peace would somehow prevail.

The patience of an oppressed people cannot endure forever. The Negro citizens of Birmingham for the last several years have hoped in vain for some evidence . . . [of the] . . . resolution of our just grievances.

Birmingham is part of the United States and we are bona fide citizens. Yet the history of Birmingham reveals that very little of the democratic process touches the life of the Negro in Birmingham. We have been segregated racially, exploited economically, and dominated politically. Under the leadership of the Alabama Christian Movement for Human Rights, we sought relief by petition for the repeal of city ordinances requiring segregation and the institution of a merit hiring policy in city employment. We were rebuffed. We then turned to the system of the courts. We weathered set-back after set-back, with all of its costliness, finally winning the terminal, bus, parks and airport cases. The bus decision has been implemented begrudgingly and the parks decision prompted the closing of all municipally-owned recreational facilities with the exception of the zoo and Legion Field. . . .

We have always been a peaceful people, bearing our oppression with superhuman effort. Yet we have been the victims of repeated violence, not only that inflicted by the hoodlum element but also that inflicted by the blatant misuse of police power. . . . For years, while our homes and churches were being bombed, we heard nothing but the rantings and ravings of racist city officials.

The Negro protest for equality and justice has been a voice crying in the wilderness. Most of Birmingham has remained silent, probably out of fear. In the meanwhile, our city has acquired the dubious reputation of being the worst big city in race relations in the United States. Last fall, for a flickering moment, it appeared that sincere community leaders from religion, business and industry discerned the inevitable confrontation in race relations approaching. Their concern for the city's image and commonweal of all its citizens did not run deep enough. Solemn promises were made, pending a postponement of direct action, that we would be joined in a suit seeking the relief of segregation ordinances. Some merchants agreed to desegregate their rest-rooms as a good faith start, some actually complying, only to retreat shortly thereafter. We hold in our hands now, broken faith and broken promises. We believe in the American Dream of democracy, in the Jeffersonian doctrine that "all men are created equal and are endowed by their Creator with certain inalienable rights, among these being life, liberty and the pursuit of happiness."

Twice since September we have deferred our direct action thrust in order that a change in city government would not be made in the hysteria of a community crisis. We act today in full concert with our Hebraic-Christian traditions, the law of morality and the Constitution of our nation. The absence of justice and progress in Birmingham demands that we make a moral witness to give our community a chance to survive. We demonstrate our faith that we believe that the beloved community can come to Birmingham. We appeal to the citizenry of Birmingham, Negro and white, to join us in this witness for decency, morality, self-respect and human dignity. Your individual and corporate support can hasten the day of "liberty and justice for all." This is Birmingham's moment of truth in which every citizen can play his part in her larger destiny. . . .

LETTER FROM A BIRMINGHAM JAIL (1963)

In the spring of 1963, Martin Luther King, Jr. was hauled off to jail in the aftermath of the Birmingham confrontation with Public Safety Commissioner "Bull" Connor and municipal authorities. Beatings, hosings, and the unleashing of vicious dogs could not deter thousands of demonstrating Negroes from risking serious injury, even death, in peaceful parades into the heart of downtown Birmingham. When King was criticized by a group of white clergymen who blamed him for precipitating the violence, he penned a subdued, but passionate letter of reply to his colleagues, smuggling it out on toilet tissue, the margins of newspapers, indeed any scrap of paper available to him. Excerpts of the letter indicate more than just extreme despair and anxiety; they offer eloquent testimony to the flaming moral concern for oppressed humanity which was King's legacy to his fellow Americans.

We have waited for more than 340 years for our constitutional and God-given rights. The nations of Asia and Africa are moving with jetlike speed toward the goal of political independence, and we still creep at horse-and-buggy pace toward the gaining of a cup of coffee at a lunch counter. I guess it is easy for those who have never felt the stinging darts of segregation to say "wait."

But when you have seen vicious mobs lynch your

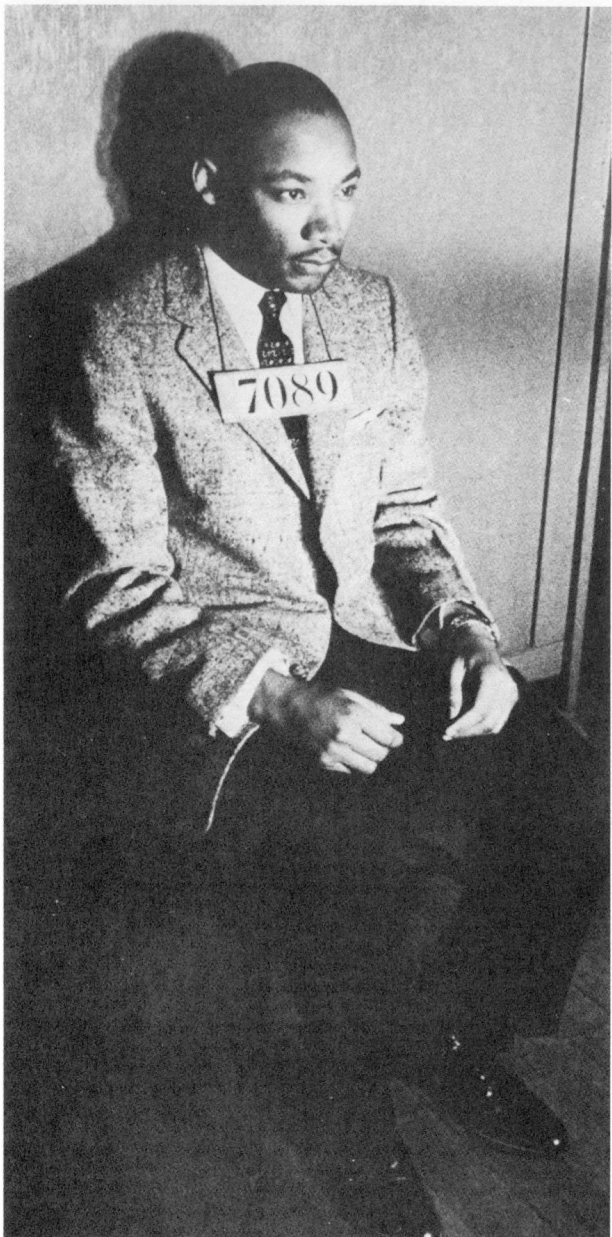

Martin Luther King, Jr., calmly faces his arraignment in Birmingham Jail after being arrested by "Bull" Connor.

mothers and fathers at will and drown your sisters and brothers at whim; when you have seen hate-filled policemen curse, kick, brutalize and even kill your black brothers and sisters; when you suddenly find your tongue twisted and your speech stammering as you seek to explain to your six-year-old daughter why she can't go to the public amusement park that has just been advertised on television, and see tears welling up in her little eyes when she is told that "Funtown" is closed to colored children, and see the de-

pressing clouds of inferiority begin to form in her little mental sky, and see her begin to distort her little personality by unconsciously developing a bitterness toward white people; when you are humiliated day in and day out by nagging signs reading "white" and "colored," when your first name becomes "nigger" and your middle name becomes "boy" (however old you are) and your last name becomes "John," and when your wife and mother are never given the respected title "Mrs."; when you are harried by day and haunted by night by the fact that you are a Negro, living constantly at tiptoe stance, never quite knowing what to expect next, and plagued with inner fears and outer resentments; when you are forever fighting a degenerating sense of "nobodyness"—then you will understand why we find it difficult to wait.

In your statement you asserted that our actions, even though peaceful, must be condemned because they precipitate violence. Isn't this like condemning the robbed man because his possession of money precipitated the evil act of robbery? Isn't this like condemning Socrates because his unswerving commitment to truth and his philosophical delvings precipitated the misguided popular mind to make him drink the hemlock? Isn't this like condemning Jesus because his unique God-consciousness and never-ceasing devotion to God's will precipitated the evil act of the Crucifixion?

The question is not whether we will be extremist but what kind of extremist will we be. Will we be extremists for hate or will we be extremists for love? Will we be extremists for the preservation of injustice—or will we be extremists for the cause of justice? In that dramatic scene on Calvary's hill, three men were crucified for the same crime—the crime of extremism. Two were extremists for immorality, and thus fell below their environment. The other, Jesus Christ, was an extremist for love, truth, and goodness, and thereby rose above his environment. So, after all, maybe the South, the nation and the world are in dire need of creative extremists.

Before the Pilgrims landed at Plymouth, we were here. Before the pen of Jefferson etched across the pages of history the majestic words of the Declaration of Independence, we were here. For more than two centuries, our foreparents labored in this country without wages; they made cotton "king," and they built the homes of their masters in the midst of brutal injustice and shameful humiliation—and yet out of a bottomless vitality, they continued to thrive and develop. If the inexpressible cruelties of slavery could not stop us, the opposition we now face will surely fail. We will win our freedom because the sacred heritage of our nation and the eternal will of God are embodied in our echoing demands.

A DIGEST OF THE CIVIL RIGHTS ACT OF 1964

The Civil Rights Act of 1964 is subdivided into 11 titles, as follows:

Title I   Voting
Title II   Public accommodations
Title III   Public facilities
Title IV   Public schools
Title V   Civil Rights Commission
Title VI   Federal aid
Title VII   Employment
Title VIII   Statistics
Title IX   Courts
Title X   Conciliatory services
Title XI   Miscellaneous

Title I (voting) prohibits registrars to apply different standards for Negro and white voting applicants, and prevents registrars from disqualifying applicants due to trivial mistakes made on their forms. It also establishes written literacy tests (except for the blind), and provides that an applicant be given a copy of the questions and his answers, should he desire to have it. A sixth-grade education is considered to be a sufficient basis for the presumption of literacy.

Title II (public accommodations) prohibits discrimination in the use of public accommodations—i.e., hotels, motels, restaurants, gasoline stations, and places of amusement whose operations involve interstate commerce. The constitutionality of this title has already been upheld by the Supreme Court of the United States in two test cases, both of which were decided on December 14, 1964. These are: *Heart of Atlanta* v. *United States,* and *Katzenbach* v. *McClung* (379 U.S. 802, 803). Title II also enables the Attorney General to bring suit in a federal court against all persons or groups found to be resisting enforcement of its provisions.

Title III (public facilities) is designed to guarantee that Negroes be accorded equal access to, and treatment in, all public-owned and-operated facilities, including parks, stadiums, and swimming pools. As in the case of Title II, this section makes it possible for the Attorney General to bring suit for its enforcement if private individuals are unable to do so.

Title IV (public schools) authorizes the federal government to provide technical and financial aid to all school districts engaged in the process of desegregation. Once again, the Attorney General is empowered to sue for school desegregation, provided private citizens are not in a position to do so.

Title V (Civil Rights Commission) extends the tenure of the Civil Rights Commission until January 31, 1968.

Title VI (federal aid) guarantees that no person shall be subject to any form of racial discrimination in any program which is receiving federal financial aid. It also empowers federal agencies to take appropriate steps to counteract any such discrimination, particularly by denying federal funds to any state or local agencies which practice discrimination.

Title VII (employment) prohibits discrimination on the part of employers or unions with more than 100 employees or members during the first year from the date the Act takes effect. Four years from that date, the number of employees for both unions and employers is to be reduced to 25. This title also establishes a commission to investigate charges of discrimination in employment or employee organizations and, where necessary, to take appropriate steps in mediating such charges. Where a "pattern or practice" of resistance to the provisions of this title becomes definitely identifiable, the Attorney General is empowered to bring suit before a three-judge federal court.

Title VIII (statistics) directs the Census Bureau to compile voting statistics by race in areas of the country designated by the Civil Rights Commission.

Title IX (courts) allows higher federal courts to prevent lower federal courts from sending a civil rights case back to a state or local court—particularly when such a step by the lower court might compromise the case of an appellant. This reverses a former trend whereby the decision of such a federal court to return a case to a state or local court could not be voided.

Title X (conciliatory services) establishes a Community Relations Service (CRS) in the Department of Commerce for the purpose of mediating racial disputes at the local level. The CRS generally intervenes only after it has received a request to do so from appropriate local officials.

Title XI (miscellaneous) assures the right of jury trial in criminal contempt cases which grow out of any part of the act, save Title I. This title in no way supercedes state laws which already afford protection similar to that which is offered in the provisions of the Civil Rights Act. Furthermore, it provides that the Civil Rights Act as a whole will not be affected by the possible invalidation of any single portion of it. . .

PRESIDENT JOHNSON'S VOTING RIGHTS ADDRESS: WE SHALL OVERCOME

In an address delivered before a joint session of Congress on March 15, 1965, President Lyndon B. Johnson placed the full weight of his office behind the passage of legislation needed to enforce the Fifteenth Amendment, which guarantees all Americans the right to vote. The speech takes its name from the following lines:

". . . it's not just Negroes, but really it's all of us who must overcome the crippling legacy of bigotry and injustice. And we shall overcome." (*Emphasis added.*)

Mr. Speaker, Mr. President, members of the Congress, I speak tonight for the dignity of man and the destiny of democracy.

I urge every member of both parties, Americans of all religions and of all colors, from every section of this country, to join me in that cause.

At times, history and fate meet at a single time in a single place to shape a turning point in man's unending search for freedom.

So it was at Lexington and Concord. So it was a century ago at Appomattox. So it was last week in Selma, Ala.

There, long suffering men and women peacefully protested the denial of their rights as Americans. Many were brutally assaulted. One good man—a man of God—was killed. . . .

There is no Negro problem. There is no Southern problem. There is no Northern problem. There is only an American problem.

Our fathers believed that if this noble view of the rights of man was to flourish it must be rooted in democracy. The most basic right of all was the right to choose your own leaders.

The history of this country in large measure is the history of expansion of that right to all of our people. Many of the issues of civil rights are very complex and most difficult. But about this there can and should be no argument: every American citizen must have an equal right to vote. . . .

Wednesday, I will send to Congress a law designed to eliminate illegal barriers to the right to vote. . . .

This bill will strike down restrictions to voting in all elections, Federal, state and local, which have been used to deny Negroes the right to vote.

This bill will establish a simple, uniform standard which cannot be used, however ingenious the effort, to flout our Constitution. It will provide for citizens to be registered by officials of the United States Government, if the state officials refuse to register them.

It will eliminate tedious, unnecessary lawsuits which delay the right to vote.

Finally, this legislation will insure that properly registered individuals are not prohibited from voting.

I will welcome the suggestions from all the members of Congress—I have no doubt that I will get some—on ways and means to strengthen this law and to make it effective.

But experience has plainly shown that this is the only path to carry out the command of the Constitu-

tion. To those who seek to avoid action by their national Government in their home communities, who want to and who seek to maintain purely local control over elections, the answer is simple: Open your polling places to all your people.

Allow men and women to register and vote whatever the color of their skin. . . .

There is no constitutional issue here. The command of the Constitution is plain. There is no moral issue. It is wrong—deadly wrong—to deny any of your fellow Americans the right to vote in this country.

There is no issue of states rights, or national rights. There is only the struggle for human rights. . . .

So I ask you to join me in working long hours and nights and weekends, if necessary, to pass this bill.

And I don't make that request lightly, for from the window where I sit with the problems of our country I recognize that from outside this chamber is the outraged conscience of a nation, the grave concern of many nations and the harsh judgment of history on our acts.

But even if we pass this bill the battle will not be over.

What happened in Selma is part of a far larger movement which reaches into every section and state of America. It is the effort of American Negroes to secure for themselves the full blessings of American life.

Their cause must be our cause too. Because it's not just Negroes, but really it's all of us who must overcome the crippling legacy of bigotry and injustice. And we shall overcome. . . .

A century has passed—more than 100 years—since equality was promised, and yet the Negro is not equal.

A century has passed since the day of promise, and the promise is unkept. The time of justice has now come, and I tell you that I believe sincerely that no force can hold it back. It is right in the eyes of man and God that it should come, and when it does, I think that day will brighten the lives of every American.

For Negroes are not the only victims. How many white children have gone uneducated? How many white families have lived in stark poverty?

How many white lives have been scarred by fear? . . .

There is really no part of America where the promise of equality has been fully kept. In Buffalo as well as in Birmingham, in Philadelphia as well as Selma, Americans are struggling for the fruits of freedom. This is one nation. What happens in Selma and Cincinnati is a matter of legitimate concern to every American. . . .

And I have not the slightest doubt that good men

from everywhere in this country, from the Great Lakes to the Gulf of Mexico, from the Golden Gate to the harbors along the Atlantic, will rally now together in this cause to vindicate the freedom of all Americans.

For all of us owe this duty and I believe that all of us will respond to it. Your President makes that request of every American.

The real hero of this struggle is the American Negro. His actions and protests, his courage to risk safety, and even to risk his life, have awakened the conscience of this nation. His demonstrations have been designed to call attention to injustice, designed to provoke change; designed to stir reform.

He has called upon us to make good the promise of America. And who among us can say that we would have made the same progress were it not for his persistent bravery and his faith in American democracy?

For at the real heart of the battle for equality is a deep-seated belief in the democratic process. Equality depends, not on the force of arms or tear gas, but depends upon the force of moral right—not on recourse to violence, but on respect for law and order.

There have been many pressures upon your President and there will be others as the days come and go. But I pledge you tonight that we intend to fight this battle where it should be fought—in the courts, and in the Congress, and in the hearts of men.

We must preserve the right of free speech and the right of free assembly.

But the right of free speech does not carry with it—as has been said—the right to holler fire in a crowded theatre.

We must preserve the right to free assembly. But free assembly does not carry with it the right to block public thoroughfares to traffic.

We do have a right to protest. And a right to march under conditions that do not infringe the constitutional rights of our neighbors. And I intend to protect all those rights as long as I am permitted to serve in this office.

We will guard against violence, knowing it strikes from our hands the very weapons which we seek—progress, obedience to law, and belief in American values. . . .

The bill I am presenting to you will be known as a civil rights bill.

But in a larger sense, most of the program I am recommending is a civil rights program. Its object is to open the city of hope to all people of all races, because all Americans just must have the right to vote, and we are going to give them that right.

All Americans must have the privileges of citizenship, regardless of race, and they are going to have those privileges of citizenship regardless of race.

But I would like to caution you and remind you that to exercise these privileges takes much more than just legal right. It requires a trained mind and a healthy body. It requires a decent home and the chance to find a job and the opportunity to escape from the clutches of poverty.

Of course people cannot contribute to the nation if they are never taught to read or write; if their bodies are stunted from hunger; if their sickness goes untended; if their life is spent in hopeless poverty, just drawing a welfare check.

So we want to open the gates to opportunity. But we're also going to give all our people, black and white, the help that they need to walk through those gates. . . .

I want to be the President who helped to feed the hungry and to prepare them to be taxpayers instead of tax eaters.

Above the pyramid on the great seal of the United States it says in Latin, "God has favored our undertaking." God will not favor everything that we do. It is rather our duty to divine His will. But I cannot help believe that He truly understands and that He really favors the undertaking that we begin here tonight.

THE VOTING RIGHTS ACT OF 1965

The 1965 Voting Rights Act was an outgrowth of the protest demonstrations organized by blacks to draw attention to discriminatory voter-registration practices in several Southern states. These were particularly prevalent in Alabama, Arkansas, Mississippi, Texas, and Virginia, which, until passage of the Twenty-Fourth Amendment to the U.S. Constitution, still required payment of a poll tax as a prerequisite for voting in national elections.

The 1965 law abolished literacy, knowledge, and character tests as qualifications for voting in those states where less than one-half of the eligible population had voted, or been entitled to vote, in November 1964. It empowered federal registrars to register potential voters in any county where such tests had been suspended, and where, in the judgment of the Attorney General of the United States, registrars were indeed necessary to enforce the Fifteenth Amendment. The Attorney General also was given the right to take whatever legal action he deemed necessary to eliminate any equivalent of the poll tax. The text of the act follows.

Be it enacted by the Senate and House of Representatives of the United States of America in Congress assembled, That this Act shall be known as the "Voting Rights Act of 1965."

Sec. 2. No voting qualification or prerequisite to voting, or standard, practice, or procedure shall be imposed or applied by any State or political subdivision to deny or abridge the right of any citizen of the United States to vote on account of race or color.

Sec. 3. (a) Whenever the Attorney General institutes a proceeding under any statute to enforce the guarantees of the fifteenth amendment in any State or political subdivision the court shall authorize the appointment of Federal examiners by the United States Civil Service Commission in accordance with section 6 to serve for such period of time and for such political subdivisions as the court shall determine is appropriate to enforce the guarantees of the fifteenth amendment (1) as part of any interlocutory order if the court determines that the appointment of such examiners is necessary to enforce such guarantees or (2) as part of any final judgment if the court finds that violations of the fifteenth amendment justifying equitable relief have occurred in such State or subdivision: *Provided,* That the court need not authorize the appointment of examiners if any incidents of denial or abridgement of the right to vote on account of race or color (1) have been few in number and have been promptly and effectively corrected by State or local action, (2) the continuing effect of such incidents has been eliminated, and (3) there is no reasonable probability of their recurrence in the future.

Sec. 4. (a) To assure that the right of citizens of the United States to vote is not denied or abridged on account of race or color, no citizen shall be denied the right to vote in any Federal, State, or local election because of his failure to comply with any test or device in any State with respect to which the determinations have been made under subsection (b) or in any political subdivision with respect to which such determinations have been made as a separate unit, unless the United States District Court for the District of Columbia in an action for a declaratory judgment brought by such State or subdivision against the United States has determined that no such test or device has been used during the five years preceding the filing of the action for the purpose or with the effect of denying or abridging the right to vote on account of race or color: *Provided,* That no such declaratory judgment shall issue with respect to any plaintiff for a period of five years after the entry of a final judgment of any court of the United States, other than the denial of a declaratory judgment under this section, whether entered prior to or after the enactment of this Act, determining that denials or abridgments of the right to vote on account of race or color through the use of such tests or devices have occurred anywhere in the territory of such plaintiff.

(2) No person who demonstrates that he has suc-

cessfully completed the sixth primary grade in a public school in, or a private school accredited by, any State or territory, the District of Columbia, or the Commonwealth of Puerto Rico in which the predominant classroom language was other than English, shall be denied the right to vote in any Federal, State, or local election because of his inability to read, write, understand, or interpret any matter in the English language, except that in States in which State law provides that a different level of education is presumptive of literacy, he shall demonstrate that he has successfully completed an equivalent level of education in a public school in, or a private school accredited by, any State or territory, the District of Columbia, or the Commonwealth of Puerto Rico in which the predominant classroom language was other than English.

Sec. 5. Whenever a State or political subdivision with respect to which the prohibitions set forth in section 4(a) are in effect shall enact or seek to administer any voting qualification or prerequisite to voting, or standard, practice, or procedure with respect to voting different from that in force or effect on November 1, 1964, such State or subdivision may institute an action in the United States District Court for the District of Columbia for a declaratory judgment that such qualification, prerequisite, standard, practice, or procedure does not have the purpose and will not have the effect of denying or abridging the right to vote on account of race or color, and unless and until the court enters such judgment no person shall be denied the right to vote for failure to comply with such qualification, prerequisite, standard, practice, or procedure.

Sec. 9. (a) Any challenge to a listing on an eligibility list prepared by an examiner shall be heard and determined by a hearing officer appointed by and responsible to the Civil Service Commission and under such rules as the Commission shall by regulation prescribe.

Sec. 10. (a) The Congress finds that the requirement of the payment of a poll tax as a precondition to voting (i) precludes persons of limited means from voting or imposes unreasonable financial hardship upon such persons as a precondition to their exercise of the franchise, (ii) does not bear a reasonable relationship to any legitimate State interest in the conduct of elections, and (iii) in some areas has the purpose or effect of denying persons the right to vote because of race or color. Upon the basis of these findings, Congress declares that the constitutional right of citizens to vote is denied or abridged in some areas by the requirement of the payment of a poll tax as a precondition to voting.

Sec. 11. (a) No person acting under color of law shall fail or refuse to permit any person to vote who is entitled to vote under any provision of this Act or is otherwise qualified to vote, or willfully fail or refuse to tabulate, count, and report such person's vote.

(b) No person, whether acting under color of law or otherwise, shall intimidate, threaten, or coerce, or atempt to intimidate, threaten or coerce any person for voting or attempting to vote, or intimidate, threaten, or coerce, or attempt to intimidate, threaten, or coerce any person for urging or aiding any person to vote or attempt to vote, or intimidate, threaten, or coerce any person for exercising any powers or duties under section 3 (a), 6, 8, 9, 10, or 12(e). . . .

Sec. 14. (a) All cases of criminal contempt arising under the provisions of this Act shall be governed by section 151 of the Civil Rights Act of 1957 (42 U.S.C. 1995).

(b) No court other than the District Court for the District of Columbia or a court of appeals in any proceeding under section 9 shall have jurisdiction to issue any declaratory judgment pursuant to section 4 or section 5 or any restraining order or temporary or permanent injunction against the execution or enforcement of any provision of this Act or any action of any Federal officer or employee pursuant hereto.

(c) (1) The terms "vote" or "voting" shall include all action necessary to make a vote effective in any primary, special, or general election, including, but not limited to, registration, listing pursuant to this Act, or other action required by law prerequisite to voting, casting a ballot, and having such ballot counted properly and included in the appropriate totals of votes cast with respect to candidates for public or party office and propositions for which votes are received in an election.

Sec. 16. The Attorney General and the Secretary of Defense, jointly, shall make a full and complete study to determine whether, under the laws or practices of any State or States, there are preconditions to voting, which might tend to result in discrimination against citizens serving in the Armed Forces of the United States seeking to vote. Such officials shall, jointly, make a report to the Congress not later than June 30, 1966, containing the results of such study, together with a list of any States in which such preconditions exist, and shall include in such report such recommendations for legislation as they deem advisable to prevent discrimination in voting against citizens serving in the Armed Forces of the United States.

BLACK PANTHER MANIFESTO (1966)

The tightly knit, close-fisted Black Panther Party relies on a strict and uncompromising regimen to mold its members into a unified and cohesive revolutionary force. Like the Muslims, the party denounces all intoxicants, drugs, and artificial stimulants "while doing party work." The intellectual fare of every party member is the 10-point program (supplemented by daily reading of political developments), which every member is obliged to know and understand, presumably even to commit to memory. Military training and political education courses are mandatory; strict adherence to central directives is also prescribed. Grants, poverty funds, and other "outside money" may not be accepted by chapters, branches, or members of the party unless National Headquarters first lends its approval. Apart from policy, there is the matter of consistent ideology. This is embodied in the 10-point program drafted in 1966 and enumerated below.

1. **We want freedom. We want power to determine the destiny of our Black Community.**

We believe that black people will not be free until we are able to determine our destiny.

2. **We want full employment for our people.**
We believe that the federal government is responsible and obligated to give every man employment or a guaranteed income. We believe that if the white American businessman will not give full employment, then the means of production should be taken from the businessmen and placed in the community so that the people of the community can organize and employ all of its people and give a high standard of living.

3. **We want an end to the robbery by the CAPITALIST of our Black Community.**
We believe that this racist government has robbed us and now we are demanding the overdue debt of forty acres and two mules. Forty acres and two mules was promised 100 years ago as restitution for slave labor and mass murder of black people. We will accept the payment in currency which will be distributed to our many communities. The Germans are now aiding the Jews in Israel for the genocide of the Jewish people. The Germans murdered six million Jews. The American racist has taken part in the slaughter of over fifty million black people, therefore, we feel that this is a modest demand that we make.

4. **We want decent housing, fit for shelter of human beings.**
We believe that if the white landlords will not give decent housing to our black community, then the housing and the land should be made into cooperatives so that our community, with government aid, can build and make decent housing for its people.

5. **We want education for our people that ex-**

poses the true nature of this decadent American society. **We want education that teaches us our true history and our role in the present-day society.**

We believe in an educational system that will give to our people a knowledge of self. If a man does not have knowledge of himself and his position in society and the world, then he has little chance to relate to anything else.

6. We want all black men to be exempt from military service.

We believe that Black people should not be forced to fight in the military service to defend a racist government that does not protect us. We will not fight and kill other people of color in the world who, like black people, are being victimized by the white racist government of America. We will protect ourselves from the force and violence of the racist police and the racist military, by whatever means necessary.

7. We want an immediate end to POLICE BRUTALITY and MURDER of black people.

We believe we can end police brutality in our black community by organizing black self-defense groups that are dedicated to defending our black community from racist police oppression and brutality. The Second Amendment to the Constitution of the United States gives a right to bear arms. We therefore believe that all black people should arm themselves for self-defense.

8. We want freedom for all black men held in federal, state, county and city prisons and jails.

We believe that all black people should be released from the many jails and prisons because they have not received a fair and impartial trial.

9. We want all black people when brought to trial to be tried in court by a jury of their peer group or people from their black communities, as defined by the constitution of the United States.

We believe that the courts should follow the United States Constitution so that black people will receive fair trials. The 14th Amendment of the U.S. Constitution gives a man a right to be tried by his peer group. A peer is a person from a similar economic, social, religious, geographical, environmental, historical and racial background. To do this the court will be forced to select a jury from the black community from which the black defendant came. We have been, and are being tried by all-white juries that have no understanding of the "average reasoning man" of the black community.

10. We want land, bread, housing, education, clothing, justice and peace. And as our major political objective, a United Nations-supervised plebiscite to be held throughout the black colony in which only black colonial subjects will be allowed to participate, for the purpose of determining the will of black people as to their national destiny.

When, in the course of human events, it becomes necessary for one people to dissolve the political bands which have connected them with another, and to assume, among the powers of the earth, the separate and equal station to which the laws of nature and nature's God entitle them, a decent respect to the opinions of mankind requires that they should declare the causes which impel them to the separation.

We hold these truths to be self-evident, that all men are created equal; that they are endowed by their Creator with certain unalienable rights; that among these are life, liberty, and the pursuit of happiness. **That, to secure these rights, governments are instituted among men, deriving their just powers from the consent of the governed; that, whenever any form of government becomes destructive of these ends, it is the right of the people to alter or to abolish it, and to institute a new government, laying its foundation on such principles, and organizing its powers in such form, as to them shall seem most likely to effect their safety and happiness.** Prudence, indeed, will dictate that governments long established should not be changed for light and transient causes; and, accordingly, all experience hath shown, that mankind are more disposed to suffer, while evils are sufferable, than to right themselves by abolishing the forms to which they are accustomed. **But, when a long train of abuses and usurpations, pursuing invariably the same object, evinces a design to reduce them under absolute despotism, it is their right, it is their duty, to throw off such government, and to provide new guards for their future security.**

THE CIVIL RIGHTS ACT OF 1968: PROVISION FOR OPEN HOUSING

Just as the 1964 Civil Rights Bill reflected the nation's belatedly noble attempt to pay tribute to the memory of an assassinated President, John F. Kennedy, so too did the 1968 Civil Rights Act represent a memorial gesture in honor of an assassinated national figure, Martin Luther King, Jr. In both cases it was Lyndon B. Johnson who presided over the

Flanked by lawmakers, President Johnson signs the Civil Rights Act of 1968 into law. Among the witnesses are Senator Edward Brooke and Justice Thurgood Marshall. Johnson's administration produced more civil rights legislation than any predecessor.

formal passage of the legislation. As originally drafted in the House, the bill was impotent and uninspiring; in the Senate, however, liberal Democrats and Republicans shaped an open-housing provision with some teeth in it and created an expanded package covering the Constitutional rights of Indians and containing two antiriot clauses. Had it not been for King's death, however, chances are that the conservative mood of the 1968 House would have prevailed, and the bill would have been shelved. With the death of Dr. King, however, the issue became, in the words of House Speaker John McCormack, one of "human dignity" rather than political partisanship. Within a week of King's death, the bill passed the House by a 249–171 margin. NAACP lobbyists for the bill were delighted; black militants, on the other hand, branded the legislation a colossal hoax. To the moderates, the opening of 80% of the nation's housing to Negroes represented the key to unlocking the prison of the ghetto; to the mili-

tants, however, 80% of the nation's housing was out of the economic reach of most ghetto residents and so nothing more than an unattainable luxury.

Discrimination in the Sale or Rental of Housing

SEC. 804. As made applicable by section 803 and except as exempted by sections 803(b) and 807, it shall be unlawful—

(a) To refuse to sell or rent after the making of a bona fide offer, or to refuse to negotiate for the sale or rental of, or otherwise made unavailable or deny, a dwelling to any person because of race, color, religion, or national origin.

(b) To discriminate against any person in the terms, conditions, or privileges of sale or rental of a dwelling, or in the provision of services or facilities in connection therewith, because of race, color, religion, or national origin.

(c) To make, print, or publish or cause to be made,

printed, or published any notice, statement, or advertisement, with respect to the sale or rental of a dwelling that indicates any preference, limitation, or discrimination based on race, color, religion, or national origin, or an intention to make any such preference, limitation, or discrimination.

(d) To represent to any person because of race, color, religion, or national origin that any dwelling is not available for inspection, sale, or rental when such dwelling is in fact so available.

(e) For profit, to induce or attempt to induce any person to sell or rent any dwelling by representations regarding the entry or prospective entry into the neighborhood of a person or persons of a particular race, color, religion, or national origin.

Title IX—Prevention of Intimidation in Fair Housing Cases

SEC. 901. Whoever, whether or not acting under color of law, by force or threat of force willfully injures, intimidates or interferes with, or attempts to injure, intimidate or interfere with—

(a) any person because of his race, color, religion or national origin and because he is or has been selling, purchasing, renting, financing, occupying, or contracting or negotiating for the sale . . . of any dwelling . . . shall be fined not more than $1,000, or imprisoned not more than one year, or both; and if bodily

injury results shall be fined not more than $10,000, or imprisoned not more than ten years, or both; and if death results shall be subject to imprisonment for any term of years or for life.

Title I—Interference with Federally Protected Activities

(b) Whoever, whether or not acting under color of law, by force or threat of force willfully injures, intimidates or interferes with, or attempts to injure, intimidate or interfere with—

(1) any person because he is or has been, or in order to intimidate such person or any other person or any class of persons from—

(A) voting or qualifying to vote, qualifying or campaigning as a candidate for elective office, or qualifying or acting as a poll watcher, or any legally authorized election official, in any primary, special, or general election; . . .

(2) any person because of his race, color, religion or national origin . . .

(3) during or incident to a riot or civil disorder, any person engaged in a business in commerce or affecting commerce . . . shall be fined not more than $1,000, or imprisoned not more than one year, or both; and if bodily injury results shall be fined not more than $10,000, or imprisoned not more than ten years, or both; and if death results shall be subject to imprisonment for any term of years or for life.

President Johnson is congratulated at Howard University after delivering an extremely effective civil rights speech.

THE NIXON DOCTRINE ON SCHOOLS, THE COURTS, SOCIETY, AND RACE: "THE COMPROMISE OF 1970"

On March 24, 1970, the Nixon Administration issued a carefully drafted comprehensive 8,000-word statement on the status of school desegregation in the United States. The President attempted to establish two philosophical and administrative priorities: one, to provide compensatory educational help to minority group children in de facto segregated classrooms; two, to relieve the pressure on local districts to conform to de jure federal desegregation guidelines. The President also summarized the findings of various court rulings which have sought to untangle the complexities stemming from support for neighborhood school patterns in the North and freedom of choice plans in the South. His conclusion: de facto segregation does not violate the Constitution; de jure desegregation as practiced in the South does "in both Constitutional and human terms." The statement was attacked by most members of the black middle-class establishment as a retreat on school desegregation ("desegregation yes, integration no"), and a tacit endorsement of tax-exempt status for separate white "private" schools in the South. At the NAACP convention in July 1970, critics of Nixon ticked off other grievances: Nixon's retreat on the use of federal registrars to enforce the Voting Rights Act of 1965, his emasculation of the cease-and-desist powers of the Equal Employment Opportunity Commission (EEOC), his willingness to sign defense contracts with textile companies not complying with desegregation guidelines, and his Supreme Court nominations. Although this statement does not explicitly contend with all these accusations, it does summarize Nixon's views on the principles for human advancement and the policies he was prepared to back in order to guarantee black progress within the framework of American society. The document is printed in its virtual entirety as a statement of the President's intention to press for "a free and open society" in hiring, housing practices, and higher education.

My purpose in this statement is to set forth in detail this Administration's policies on the subject of desegregation of America's elementary and secondary schools.

My specific objectives in this statement are:

To reaffirm my personal belief that the 1954 decision of the Supreme Court in Brown v. Board of Education was right in both constitutional and human terms.

To assess our progress in the 16 years since Brown and to point the way to continuing progress.

To clarify the present state of the law, as developed by the courts and the Congress, and the Administration policies guided by it.

To discuss some of the difficulties encountered by courts and communities as desegregation has accelerated in recent years, and to suggest approaches that can mitigate such problems as we complete the process of compliance with Brown.

To place the question of school desegregation in its larger context, as part of America's historic commitment to the achievement of a free and open society.

The Context

Progress toward school desegregation is part of two larger processes, each equally essential:

The improvement of educational opportunities for all of America's children.

The lowering of artificial racial barriers in all aspects of American life.

Only if we keep each of these considerations clearly in mind—and only if we recognize their sepa-

rate natures—can we approach the question of school desegregation realistically.

It may be helpful to step back for a moment and to consider the problem of school desegregation in its larger context.

The school stands in a unique relationship to the community, to the family and to the individual students. It is a focal point of community life. It has a powerful impact on the future of all who attend.

It is a place not only of learning, but also of living—where a child's friendships center, where he learns to measure himself against others, to share, to compete, to cooperate—and it is the one institution above all others with which the parent shares the child. . . .

Overburdening the Schools

One of the mistakes of past policy has been to demand too much of our schools: They have been expected not only to educate, but also to accomplish a social transformation. Children in many instances have not been served, but used—in what all too often has proved a tragically futile effort to achieve in the schools the kind of a multiracial society which the adult community has failed to achieve for itself.

If we are to be realists, we must recognize that in a free society there are limits to the amount of government coercion that can reasonably be used; that in achieving desegregation we must proceed with the least possible disruption of the education of the nation's children; and that our children are highly sensitive to conflict, and highly vulnerable to lasting psychic injury.

Failing to recognize these factors, past policies have placed on the schools and the children too great a share of the burden of eliminating racial disparities throughout our society. A major part of this task falls to the schools. But they cannot do it all or even most of it by themselves.

Other institutions can share the burden of breaking down racial barriers, but only the schools can perform the task of education itself. If our schools fail to educate, then whatever they may achieve in integrating the races will turn out to be only a Pyrrhic victory. . . .

Policies and Enforcement: The Nixon Approach

It will be the purpose of this Administration to carry out the law fully and fairly. And where problems exist that are beyond the mandate of legal requirements, it will be our purpose to seek solutions that are both realistic and appropriate.

I have instructed the Attorney General, the Secretary of Health, Education and Welfare and other appropriate officials of the Government to be guided by these basic principles and policies:

Deliberate racial segregation of pupils by official action is unlawful, wherever it exists. In the words of the Supreme Court, it must be eliminated "root and branch"—and it must be eliminated at once.

Segregation of teachers must be eliminated. To this end, each school system in this nation, North and South, East and West, must move immediately, as the Supreme Court has ruled, toward a goal under which "in each school the ratio of white to Negro faculty members is substantially the same as it is throughout the system."

With respect to school facilities, school administrators throughout the nation, North and South, East and West, must move immediately, also in conformance with the Court's ruling, to assure that schools within individual school districts do not discriminate with respect to the quality of facilities or the quality of education delivered to the children within the district.

In devising local compliance plans primary weight should be given to the considered judgment of local school boards—provided they act in good faith and within constitutional limits.

The neighborhood school will be deemed the most appropriate base for such a system.

Transportation of pupils beyond normal geographic school zones for the purpose of achieving racial balance will not be required.

Federal advice and assistance will be made available on request, but Federal officials should not go beyond the requirements of law in attempting to impose their own judgment on the local school district.

Job Incentives

We have inaugurated new minority business enterprise programs—not only to help minority members get started in business themselves, but also, by developing more black and brown entrepreneurs, to demonstrate to young blacks, Mexican-Americans and others that they, too, can aspire to this same sort of upward economic mobility.

In our education programs, we have stressed the need for far greater diversity in offerings to match the diversity of individual needs—including more and better vocational and technical training, and a greater development of two-year community colleges.

Such approaches have been based essentially on faith in the individual—knowing that he sometimes needs help, but believing that in the long run he usually knows what is best for himself. . . .

We have overcome many problems in our 190 years as a nation. We can overcome this problem.

We have managed to extend opportunity in other areas. We can extend it in this area. Just as other rights have been secured, so too can these rights be secured—and once again the nation will be better for having done so.

I am confident that we can preserve and improve our schools, carry out the mandate of our Constitution, and be true to our national conscience.

CONGRESSIONAL BLACK CAUCUS: LEGISLATIVE AGENDA, 94TH CONGRESS (1975)

On February 27, 1975, Representative Charles Rangel of New York announced the legislative program and objectives of the Congressional Black Caucus to the House of Representatives. It was the first formal statement of legislative goals and activities by the Caucus for an upcoming session of Congress.

Though it received little attention in the general press, the document was remarkable for its thorough and concise discussion of the problems and solutions of paramount importance to blacks and other minorities, and for the perception with which it drew on the legislative achievements of the 1960s to further the cause of the minorities and low-income groups in the 1970s.

Following is an abridged version of the Agenda.

Representative Charles Rangel, chairman of the Congressional Black Caucus.

The 1971 House Black Caucus accuses the Nixon administration of trying to justify the status quo.

Areas of Major Legislative Focus

FULL EMPLOYMENT

The Congressional Black Caucus sees as one of its highest priorities, the passage of comprehensive legislation which establishes both the policy and the mechanism for guaranteeing the right to useful and meaningful employment for all adult Americans able and willing to work. It is most important that the full employment concept be understood as reaching far beyond the public service program to create both the right and the opportunity to meaningful jobs.

As unemployment skyrockets, with some predicting that January's 8.2 percent national unemployment rate will pass 10 percent this year, the need for relief is unquestioned. Black unemployment in January was over 13 percent and black teenage unemployment in the same month was at 41 percent. However, even many of those who recognize the need to not fully understand that Bureau of Labor Statistics figures show that the real national unemployment rate—which included the under-employed, those employed part-time who seek full-time work, and those who need work but are discouraged from looking—is over 15 percent. For blacks, that means a real unemployment rate in the neighborhood of 30 percent nationally, and even higher in depressed areas.

The major thrust of the effort to attain full employment legislation centers around a bill introduced by Caucus member Augustus Hawkins. That measure would create a Job Guarantee Office and a Standby Job Corps, as well as requiring the President to develop a national full employment and production program. Full employment would be achieved through both private and public employers. Central to the proposal is the concept that there is no tolerable level of official unemployment for a narrowly-defined labor force in contrast to present practice.

As the legislative process proceeds, the specifics of a full employment program will, of course, be refined and sharpened. Complementary proposals, such as that of Congressman John Conyers to require the federal government to become the employer of last resort, will also help shape the final legislation. There should also be legislation passed providing for flexible working hours, as in Congresswoman Burke's Career Opportunity Act. Any legislation supported by the Caucus must have an adequate mechanism at the local level for ensuring jobs and eliminating red tape.

Congressman Hawkins has also introduced a bill providing for an additional one million public service jobs, which the Caucus supports. Further, a youth unemployment program aimed at getting young people from school into the labor force, including provisions for summer jobs must be established immediately.

TAX REFORM

If we are to solve our nation's basic problems of unemployment, inadequate housing, health care, public education and other social ills, it will take lots of money. When the question is raised 'how shall we fund these programs,' the inevitable answer given is that the average American taxpayer is already overburdened with the cost of government and simply is not willing to have taxes raised to fund desperately needed human needs programs.

The Congressional Black Caucus agrees with that assessment. We also agree that if the money to attack these basic domestic problems—which just happen to be reflected most acutely in the black experience—is ever to be raised, it must come through extensive tax reform that will close up gaping loopholes in the tax law by which rich individuals and multi-national corporations get away with over $50 billion a year in revenues which would come to the federal Treasury were they taxed today. That amounts to an enormous "welfare payment," "a free ride" for the rich in our nation today.

The noted Brookings Institution economist and Director of the Congressional Budget Office, Alice Rivlin, believes that with the annual yield from tax reform applied to our national budget we could house all of our low and moderate income families, and fund health manpower, health research, and a health care system that would meet the needs of all our citizens. Over several years, we could also create jobs for all our unemployed and train less-skilled people to fill socially useful jobs on a permanent basis and substantially increase our spending on public education at every level from pre-school through college. The Congressional Black Caucus agrees.

For too long, we have seen no fundamental change in our national policies and priorities in response to domestic needs. In the 1930's, the Great Depression led to a system of Social Security. Following the War, the Employment Act of 1946 was passed. In the 1960's major civil rights laws were passed. And in the mid-'60's, a belated and only partial response to the problems of poverty was begun.

Today, we face a period of economic turmoil following closely an era of tragic international and American political turmoil. Yet, as in the '30's, these great events have served to create a common understanding among most Americans as to our common dilemma. It is not the rich against the poor, black against white. Instead, there is a mutual recognition that any of us may be the next victim of unemployment, and that all of us will most certainly be the next victim of inflation.

The Congressional Black Caucus has as its motto that "we have no permanent friends and no permanent enemies, only permanent interests." At this time of economic distress, we feel we have many more friends than enemies, as our interests are even more clearly those of the nation. While our foremost concerns are those of blacks, those concerns and their remedies are inextricably intertwined with those of all Americans.

This legislative agenda begins to address both economic and political problems common to the nation and the black community.

There are several legislative issues to be decided this year which the Caucus considers of primary importance. These are bills of broad scope with major implications for blacks and others, on which major national attention will be focused. They fall into three broad categories: (1) economic issues, (2) access and political participation issues, and (3) issues involving federal domestic assistance programs.

1. Economic issues

Our economic program will focus on full employment, tax reform, and a careful review of congressional appropriations in the framework of national priorities. . . . The Caucus does not agree that every time Congress asks for more money it adds to the deficit, for the reordering of priorities will permit the use of old funds for new purposes.

2. Political participation issues

The second major goal of the Caucus' program this year, will be to increase voter participation by removing barriers to voting.

3. Federal domestic assistance programs

Our third major priority will involve federal domestic assistance programs. Four broad and timely issues here are revenue sharing, health care, social insurance, and education.

At the same time as we press the legislative agenda, the Caucus will expand its oversight of federal activities, continuously evaluating the impact of federal programs on our constituents, to review civil rights enforcement, affirmative action, and substantive program effectiveness and equity. We have a particular concern this year with surveillance activities of the CIA and FBI, much of which appears to have been directed at black organizations and individuals. A more aggressive Congress will, we hope, further this oversight function. Further, we will be carefully scrutinizing nominees for federal appointive posts for their suitability with respect to the black community.

The Congressional Black Caucus will be pressing in the 94th Congress, therefore, to effect such reforms of the tax law as:

Repeal of the oil depletion allowance.

Enactment of a minimum tax to ensure that those who earn incomes are taxed on it.

Restructuring of capital gains provisions to fully tax income from whatever source.

Elimination of hobby-farm tax deductions.

Repeal of tax credit provisions which enable multinational corporations to fully deduct foreign taxes from their U.S. tax obligations and thereby avoid U.S. taxes.

Elimination of tax incentives for foreign investments that move industry and jobs from the U.S., thereby eroding the domestic tax base.

Tightening of provisions for business activity to present taxpayer subsidies of a high standard of living not legitimately related to business activity.

THE BUDGET AND APPROPRIATIONS PROCESS

While we can agree that there must be limits on federal spending, for us the key issue is where cuts and limits should be made. We have already worked to defeat the Administration's proposed cuts in the Food Stamp program and we will continue to work to keep the burden of antirecessionary measures from the backs of the poor.

The time is ripe for a more realistic view of the military and foreign aid budgets and a hard questioning of the premises on which they are built.

There are numerous budget areas which deserve paring. These include:

The B-1 Bomber

The Trident Submarine.

Overseas troop level, by 100,000 troops.

AWACS Air Warning System.

MARV Counterforce.

Additional military aid to Southeast Asia.

$2.3 billion for inflationary costs for shipbuilding.

$1.6 billion for 20 percent increase in research and development.

VOTING RIGHTS ACT OF 1965

The Voting Rights Act of 1965 has been perhaps the most effective piece of civil rights legislation ever passed. Focusing on areas where the exclusion of black voters was greatest, largely in the South, the Voting Rights Act has resulted in the registration of over 1 million persons since 1965. Black registration rates in covered areas in the South have risen from about 30 percent of those of voting age in 1965 to 57 percent of those eligible in those same areas in 1972. Black elected officials have increased from fewer than 100 in these same areas in considerable evidence such as in the recent U.S. Civil Rights Commission Study, that the problems persist, and that without the Act, there would be serious regression in black voting rights.

The Congressional Black Caucus strongly supports extension of the Voting Rights Act for an additional 10 years. We feel that it is particularly crucial that the extension be for 10 years so as to cover reappor-

Vice President Rockefeller confers with Representatives Charles Rangel of New York and Walter Fauntroy of Washington, D.C.

tionment which will follow the 1980 census. Experience under the Act has shown it to be especially effective in overcoming racial gerrymandering. The Caucus also supports a permanent ban on literacy tests. Section 5 of the Act, which requires submission of any 'change with respect to voting' in covered areas to the Justice Department or C.D. Federal District Court, has proved to be the heart of the legislation. It must be retained in the extension. Congresswoman Barbara Jordan has introduced a bill to extend the protections of the Act.

Further, the Caucus supports efforts to extend the Act's coverage to Spanish-speaking and other minorities who face severe problems of disenfranchisement.

UNIVERSAL VOTER REGISTRATION

The continuing decline in voter participation since 1960 challenges the nation's democratic principles. While voter registration and participation among blacks has increased greatly since the Voting Rights Act of 1965, it still lags significantly behind that for whites. The nationwide voter participation rate has declined from 64% of those eligible in 1960 to 55% of those eligible in 1975. In 1974 only 39% of those eligible voted in the congressional elections. Black voter participation in 1974 is estimated at under 30% of those eligible.

Over the past several years, proposals have been made to institute a system of universal voter registration. Largely, they have been bills which would simplify registration through the use of postcards for registering for federal elections. Provisions to protect against fraud and to give financial incentives for states and localities to utilize the federal postcard registrations have been included in the major bills.

Last year, H.R. 8053, the Voter Registration Act, failed to gain a rule in the House by a vote of 197 to 204. The members of the Congressional Black Caucus supported that bill, and continue to strongly support similar legislation this year.

The states of Maryland, Minnesota, Texas and New Jersey have systems of registration by mail and have found them to be tremendously successful.

GENERAL REVENUE SHARING

Revenue sharing was initially proposed during the mid-1960's as a means of distributing a budget surplus to states and localities as a flexible additional sum of money to supplement categorical programs. Under the Nixon Administration, general revenue sharing became a political weapon to shift the locus of decision-making to units of government less responsive to social needs of poor and minorities. Categorical program cutbacks, despite promises to contrary, heightened

the withdrawal from commitments to national priorities supported by the Congressional Black Caucus and its constituents. Reports and studies which have appeared to date, such as those by the National Clearinghouse on Revenue Sharing, civil rights organizations, the General Accounting Office, and the Brookings Institution, generally indicate the general revenue sharing funds have gone to purposes other than to meet most basic social needs. Few benefits of revenue sharing expenditures have reached blacks and the poor.

We understand the need for continuing funds for general city services at a time of financial crisis. Yet we see the review and debate concerning general revenue sharing as a focal point for discussion of our national priorities.

Any extension of the general revenue sharing program should contain . . . Stronger civil rights provisions, which put a greater responsibility for effective enforcement on the federal government.

There must be a specific requirement for citizen participation in the decision-making process for fund use. Citizen participation should include at least public hearings, better notification of minority groups, and public reports on planned and actual uses which indicate the nature and type of projects as well as the real impact in terms of a locality's overall budget.

The formula and permissible use categories must result in greater benefits to lower-income communities and individuals.

Data used in the formula [must] be responsive to the known census undercount.

HEALTH CARE

The United States is the only industrialized nation in the world that does not have a comprehensive health care system. Medicaid and Medicare reach only a minimal number of people and with a relatively low level of benefits. A large number of persons have no medical plan at all, and even those with medical plans frequently do not have regular preventive care.

Unfortunately, the medical industry and the country have forced us to choose between the high costs of comprehensive coverage and a gamble with our own health.

Caucus members Congressman Andrew Young and Congressman Ronald Dellums will introduce major health care legislation. There are a number of principles which must be incorporated in any bill finally passed.

1. It must include preventive services, health maintenance and community education for personal and community health.

2. Health care must be recognized as a right, not merely as a privilege.

3. Health coverage must include the full range of health care, preventive, diagnosis, treatment and rehabilitation regardless of one's ability to pay.

4. There must be progressive trust fund financing so that health care is insured of continuation as a permanent program.

5. Consumers must be permitted and encouraged to participate in health care program operations.

6. Finally, the health care program must be reinforced with adequate financing for research, planning and administration.

SOCIAL INSURANCE

Welfare or income security must be addressed this year both in terms of the amount of money and resources consumed by the program.

In particular, we will take a close look at the concept of a negative income tax.

However, any measure which receives final Caucus approval cannot be laden down with punitive, counter-productive amendments, such as has happened in the past. As one simple example, it is ludicrous to talk about forced work requirements at a time of spiraling unemployment. Moreover, it is necessary to remove procedures and activities which result in invasions of privacy. It is also crucial to recognize that the majority of welfare recipients are heads of single-parent households, frequently with young children.

Any welfare replacement or income supplement program is doomed to failure unless it is tied to job development, job training, a vastly expanded child care program, and a thorough and far-reaching program to eradicate sex and racial discrimination in education, job training and unemployment.

We also support expansion and increased funding of programs authorized by the Older Americans Act of 1965.

EDUCATION

During the past several years, important education policy questions have taken second place to a misleading, and emotional debate over the question of busing. As misdirected discussion continues to take place, education for black children, as well as for many others, continues to suffer. While elementary and secondary education are of primary importance for our constituents, legislative activity in education this year will mostly concern higher education and vocational education.

Two major pieces of legislation, the Higher Educa-

tion Act and Vocational Education Act expire this year and are likely to be renewed. We support their renewal, but we are concerned that they be strengthened, and not weakened.

In extending the Higher Education Act, there are three important issues which must be addressed: 1. Eligibility criteria must concentrate on aiding those students with the greatest needs; 2. the Strengthening Developing Institutions program must be continued at at least the same funding level: 3. There must be no provisions which restrict the affirmative action obligations of institutions to hire and promote minorities.

A renewed Vocational Education Act must contain provisions to ensure that handicapped and disadvantaged students receive substantial benefits from the program. Moreover, legislative provisions must be added to see that administrative costs at the state level are substantially diminished.

Individual Legislative Initiatives

In addition to the preceding areas of major focus, following are some forty pieces of legislation in ten major categories which are being introduced by members of the Congressional Black Caucus.

1. Child care (Chisholm)

Would establish federally aided child development programs to provide comprehensive services to children under the age of six. Building on the Headstart experience, there would be multi-service programs for young children and their families. While the program would serve a broad population definite priorities are established for poor children and those with special needs including migrants, handicapped and bilingual children. This would also include children of working mothers and single-parent families. The bill would allow public and private organizations and institutions to operate programs.

2. Civil and political rights and liberties

Voting Representation for the District of Columbia (Fauntroy, Diggs). A bill to be introduced later this year will provide for full voting members of the Senate and House from Washington, D.C.

To ameliorate the severe and inequitable social and economic consequences of dishonorable discharges, legislation is being introduced to require that there be only a single category of discharge from the armed forces and that reasons for separation be kept confidential.

Amnesty (Dellums). Provides automatic general amnesty for failing to comply with any requirement of, or relating to service in the Armed Forces during our Indochina involvement.

Discrimination in Bar Examination (Hawkins). Would provide for federal bar examiners for temporary periods in those states in which there is substantial and long standing evidence of discrimination in the administration of bar examinations.

Psychosurgery Prohibition (Stokes). Under proposed legislation psychosurgery, including lobotomy, psychiatric surgery, behavioral surgery to modify thoughts, action and behavior would be prohibited in any federally connected health care facility.

Mexican-American Land Rights (Hawkins). Two bills have been introduced to guarantee, protect and, when necessary, to restore the community land grants belonging to descendants of former Mexican Citizens. Further, the civil, religious, political and property rights of these persons are protected, as is their right to self determination.

3. Criminal justice

Gun Control (Dellums, Fauntroy, Metcalfe, Nix). The use of handguns and other firearms has become an overwhelming threat to the life and safety to Americans of all races. Black on black crime is an especially prevalent problem. Several bills offered by Caucus members and by others would ban the importation, manufacture, sale, purchase, transfer, transportation, receipt, possession and ownership of handguns, except in certain circumstances. These special circumstances would involve gun clubs, collectors, security guards and similar persons. An effective registration and reporting system would be established. A tax credit system for turning in handguns is proposed in some bills. The Caucus supports the strongest bill using these elements which can be passed.

Grand Jury Reform (Conyers, Rangel). The Grand Jury Reform Act of 1975 provides rules and safeguards assuring the appearance of witnesses, protecting their constitutional rights and apprising grand jury members of their inquiry powers. A witness could be given immunity and a corresponding order to testify only if he or she agrees to this exchange. A favorable vote by a grand jury majority would be necessary to subpoena a witness and to request a contempt citation. Use immunity would be eliminated.

Commodity Price Marketing (Ford). To protect consumer's right and ability to accurately determine prices, particularly in food stores, price marking on individual commodity items must be made mandatory. A bill to this end has been introduced in response to the growing use of computer checkout pricing in the supermarkets. In addition, the Caucus strongly supports the establishment of an independent consumer protection agency with the power to investigate anticonsumer activities and go to court with its own attorneys.

4. Consumer protection

F.U.E.L. Subsidy Program for Energy Costs (Stokes). To relieve the burden of rising energy costs on lower-income families, the F.U.E.L. program would make subsidies available for electricity, heating fuel and gas, allowing voluntary participation by needy families.

Antitrust (Jordan). To increase the effectiveness of antitrust laws by such means as permitting state Attorneys General the authority to file class action antitrust suits in federal courts, repealing state fair trade laws, and by preventing leading conglomerates from controlling alternative sources of energy. Also the antitrust exemption for agricultural cooperatives should be re-evaluated.

5. Foreign affairs

Rhodesian Chrome (Diggs). The Byrd Amendment passed in 1971, authorizes the President, in disregard of the United Nations sanctions, to import Rhodesian Chrome. The world community recognizes the illegitimacy of the Rhodesian regime.

Fair Employment Practices for U.S. Firms in South Africa (Diggs). Contracts between the U.S. Government and any person or firm doing business in South Africa should be prohibited unless such person or firm is doing business in accordance with fair employment practices.

African Development Funding Act (Young). Would provide for multilateral trade and technical assistance commitments based on the development priorities of African nations.

6. Governmental structure and responsibility

Bureaucratic Accountability (Dellums). In response to hearings on governmental lawlessness held by the Congressional Black Caucus in 1972, the Bureaucratic Accountability Act has been introduced to insure that citizens may obtain information and redress concerning federal activities. The bill would extend due process requirements under the Administrative Procedures Act to social programs and other aspects of positive governments.

Census Undercount (Rangel). Would require federal agencies administering domestic assistance programs utilizing population based formulas to adjust data in determining allocations to be responsive to census undercount rates determined by the U.S. Bureau of the Census.

Cabinet Level Minority Enterprises Agency (Mitchell). The minority business components of the Small Business Administration, the office of Minority Business Enterprise and those within the Department of Health, Education, and Welfare would be combined into a single cabinet level agency.

Independent Office of Civil Rights Enforcement (Hawkins). The Civil Rights Enforcement Act of 1975 would create the Civil Rights Enforcement Agency as an independent agency of the federal government with a director as chief executive officer who would be appointed by the Supreme Court of the United States and confirmed by the Senate.

Veterans' Pensions (Ford). Legislation should be enacted to ensure that recipients of Veterans' pension and compensation will not have the amount reduced because of increase in monthly social security benefits.

Hatch Act Reform (Clay). Federal government employees, who are presently prohibited from participating in partisan politics should be permitted to participate in election campaigns and other aspects of the political process.

Social Security Disability Benefits (Stokes). To provide that an individual may qualify for disability insurance benefits and the disability freeze if he has enough quarters of coverage to be fully insured for old-age benefit purposes, regardless of when such quarters were earned.

Criminal Justice Reform (Conyers, Jordan, Rangel). (1) Citizens should be enlisted in the war against crime by such programs as citizens patrols and block security programs. (2) Criminal offenses, especially non-violent victimless crimes should be redefined. (3) Programs of deferred prosecution in federal criminal cases should be created. (4) A federal grand jury investigating executive branch officials should have the opportunity to appoint a special prosecutor if it is felt that the investigation is being compromised.

Dum-Dum Bullets (Burke, Metcalfe). The Hollow Bullet Control Act would bar the importation, manufacture, possession or use of the so-called dum-dum bullet or any similar hollow point bullet.

Office of Federal Correctional Ombudsman (Metcalfe). An independent third party system for investigating and arbitrating complaints of both inmates and the staffs of the federal prison system and those who are under the direction of the federal parole board should be established.

To Permit Suits Against States and Localities (Metcalfe). Inability under the law to sue states and localities frequently leave many persons without a remedy for injuries.

Drugstore Robbery (Nix). Provides fines up to $5,000 and/or imprisonment for up to 2 years for robbing a pharmacy of any narcotic as defined under the Controlled Substances Act.

7. Health

Narcotics (Rangel). Legislative and appropriations efforts to (1) increase the Drug Enforcement Agency's budget, (2) provide funding for supportive services such as education and employment counseling.

Mobile Health Units (Burke). Under the Mobile Health Units Act, health care delivery assistance to medically underserved urban and rural areas would be provided through special project grants for the purchase of mobile health units.

Amniocentesis Research (Burke). To further research into the early detection of birth defects, funds should be provided for research to extend the availability of amniocentesis to those who cannot now afford such tests.

8. Housing

Low-Income Housing (Mitchell). A 3-year emergency housing program based on legislation now on the books, should be put into effect. Three million units in three years are required: one million public housing; one million 236 or 515 with rent supplements; one million 235 or 502 with interest credits. Sixty percent of the units should be in metropolitan areas, forty percent outside.

Limited Moratorium on Repayment of FHA and Va-Guaranteed Loans (Burke). Persons faced with loss of employment, temporary layoffs, etc. would be permitted to defer loan repayment under FHA and VA guarantee program for six months without penalty.

Condominium Conversion Protection (Collins). Would provide national condominium standards for condominium projects utilizing federal funds, and would create the post of Assistant Secretary of HUD for Condominiums to administer the protections for condominiums.

Low Interest Loans for Rehabilitation (Metcalfe). Housing rehabilitation loans should be provided for low and middle income individuals. The legislation introduced also calls for a General Accounting Office evaluation of all ongoing housing programs on a regular basis to determine whether congressional intent is being met.

9. Martin Luther King Birthday National Holiday (Conyers)

January 15th of each year, the date of Dr. Martin Luther King's birth, should be designated as a legal public holiday. Making Dr. King's birthdate a national holiday would provide at least one day during the year when all Americans would have an opportunity to reflect on the ideals for which Dr. King lived and died.

10. Women's Rights

Rape Prevention and Control (Burke). To provide financial assistance for a research and demonstration program into the causes, consequences, prevention, treatment and control of rape.

Pap Smear Test (Collins). To provide for coverage under the Medicare program for routine Papanicolaou (Pap) tests for the diagnosis of uterine cancer.

Social Security Coverage for Homemakers (Jordan). A bill has been introduced which recognizes household employees as self-employed workers and provides them with all the social security benefits available to other workers.

KEYNOTE ADDRESS OF VERNON JORDAN AT THE ANNUAL CONFERENCE OF THE NATIONAL URBAN LEAGUE (1981)

The keynote speech that Vernon E. Jordan delivered on Sunday, July 18, 1981, at the Sheraton Washington Hotel in Washington, D.C., to open the Annual Conference of the National Urban League was his last as president of the agency. Several months later he announced that after ten years as the head of the League, he was stepping down. While no one in the audience knew that they were witnessing a historic event, Jordan's eloquent and passionate speech, describing the hardships imposed on blacks and the poor by the Reagan Administration and calling for a "return to basics," was regarded as one of his finest moments.

My first Urban League Conference address was in 1971. Then too, it dealt with a conservative Administration in Washington. But that Administration, while hostile to black people, was pragmatic. It had to be. There was still a strong national consensus that operated to preserve black gains. The Congress was a bulwark against attempts to dismantle important social programs. We had a two-party system then.

Today, there is another conservative Administration in Washington. But this time, much has changed.

This Administration is wedded to an ideology of radical conservatism. This Administration has introduced a new political vocabulary—"budget reconciliation," "truly needy," "supply side economics," and other phrases. But it has dropped from the political vocabulary the one word that makes government relevant to the governed, the one word that grants legitimacy to its laws—"compassion."

This is not mere semantics. The Administration's refusal to temper ideology with compassion makes it a clear and present danger to black people and to poor people. . . .

Yes, outmoded. The President claims to be bringing us new ideas and new policies. But they are actually a recycled version of ideas and policies that were buried in the Great Depression. And with good reason.

What are the new ideas the Administration is ramming down the throats of the nation? Get government off our backs. Give power and programs to the states.

Federal programs have failed. Rely on the free enterprise system. Build more missiles.

Black people don't need to be told that government is on our backs because we know it has been by our side, helping to counterbalance the vicious racism that deprived us of our lives, our liberty, and our rights.

Black people don't need to be told that power and programs should go to the states, because we know the few, feeble programs that have helped us were those mandated by Washington. It was the state and local governments that excluded us from everything from voting to paved streets. And it is they who will trample on our interests again if this Administration dumps the programs we need into block grants.

Black people don't need to be told federal programs have failed because we know many have succeeded. The Pentagon may not be able to land helicopters in Iran, but the Food Stamp program has fed the hungry; social security has wiped out poverty for most older citizens; CETA has put the jobless to work, compensatory education programs have improved reading scores of disadvantaged youth, and Legal Services has given poor people access to the justice system.

Black people don't need to be told to rely on the free enterprise system. We believe in the free enterprise system. We want to be part of it. We want our fair share of it.

And we know that will not happen without a federal government that pushes the private sector into affirmative action programs. It will not happen without a federal government that has setasides for minority enterprises and job and training programs for the disadvantaged.

America, we will not get our fair share unless there is more for everyone. But we also know that we will not get our fair share just because there is more. America has managed to push us from the table of prosperity in good times as in bad.

So it is not enough just to have growth. What we want to know is "economic growth for whom?" "A rising tide lifts all boats" is no answer. A rising tide lifts only those boats in the water; our boats are in the drydock of America's economy. And we know we will be stranded on dry land, far from the rising tide, unless government steps in with the programs and protection that help launch us into the mainstream.

That will not happen with an economic program that gives to the wealthy in the vague hopes that some of it will trickle down to the poor. What little trickles down is soaked up long before it reaches us.

Let us cut through the rhetoric of a supply-side economics that supplies misery to the poor: this Administration's economic program amounts to a massive transfer of resources from the poor to the rich.

It takes money, programs, and opportunities from poor people and promises them in return an end to inflation and prosperity for all. It says to poor people: give up the little you have today and we promise you a lot more in the bye and bye. Well, black people aren't buying pie-in-the-sky economics. . . .

A brief look at what happened to some of the major domestic programs will demonstrate that black people are the major victims of a budget that tears huge, gaping holes in our safety net:

Social security. The minimum benefit—a measly $122 a month is eliminated. Who gets hurt? Poor black people who spent their working lives on their knees cleaning floors. Disability benefits are tightened. Who gets hurt? Workers who are injured or fall sick and can't work anymore—a disproportionate number of them black.

Food Stamps—A million people will lose their food stamps, millions more will have their benefits reduced. Who gets hurt? The working poor. Over a third of all food stamp recipients are black.

Public service jobs ended; CETA training cut back—Who gets hurt? Over a third of all CETA workers are black.

Medicaid is capped; poor people will suffer reductions in access to health care—Who gets hurt? Over a third of Medicaid recipients are black.

Legal Services—The Administration wanted to kill it, but our compassionate Congress just cut its budget by two-thirds. Who gets hurt? People who can't afford a lawyer. Poor people. A third are black.

Welfare is cut and a forced work program authorized in the hope that unpleasant make-work jobs will drive people off the rolls—Who gets hurt? Almost half the recipients are black children and black mothers. Who gets hurt most? Working mothers who get small welfare checks to supplement their low earnings.

Education aid cut heavily—Who gets hurt? Disadvantaged children, over a third of them black.

Defenders of that budget will tell us black people are not being singled out. That's true. It's only poor people who are being victimized. And we are twelve percent of the population but a third of the poor—so we are the main victims.

We are told the nation can no longer afford to help the poor. But it can afford to throw one-and-a-half trillion dollars at the Pentagon over the next five years.

We are told social programs don't help poor people: they help the people in social service professions. Tell that to the families deprived of their food stamps, their welfare checks, their public service jobs.

We are told social programs breed dependency. Tell that to the working mothers who will have to quit their jobs or lose benefits. Tell it to young people in training programs who will lose their chance to learn and to earn their way out of poverty. Tell it to sick people whose public health clinics are shut down.

We are told that it's bad to look to government for special help—everyone should be treated the same. Tell that to the affluent who will get huge tax cuts on top of their loopholes. Tell it to the corporations on welfare. Tell it to the special interests who still get their subsidies while poor people lose their life-lines.

Last month, with no real debate, the programs that help the poor were cut to ribbons. With no real debate, years of slow, patient progress were swept out to sea by the rising tide of radical conservatism.

Never have so few taken so much from so many in so little time!

Where was the outcry against that outrage? Where were the Democrats? Where were the liberals? Where were the Congressmen who once fought for the programs that give poor people opportunities?

With some honorable exceptions, they were in a last-ditch fight to save benefits for the middle class and farm interests. Roosevelt led a party concerned with the "ill-housed, ill-clad, ill-nourished." Today his successors are concerned with the upper-middle class.

Democrats and Republicans alike need some arithmetic lessons. They need to learn that poll results still show significant public support for social programs that work.

They need to learn that when they cut social programs whose beneficiaries are one-third to one-half black, the remainder are white. Whites make up half to two-thirds of the victims of the cuts.

When the poor have no more programs left to cut, the cuts will start reaching into the middle-class constituency the Democrats are now courting.

One last word for the Democrats who take the black vote for granted—an opposition that does not oppose is not worthy of governing.

But the silence extends well beyond a passive Congress. When aid to the arts is cut, there are full-page newspaper ads of protest. There are petitions, and loud protest. When an aggressive foreign policy is implemented, there is the same. But where are the voices raised in behalf of poor people? Where are the churches, the universities, the other sectors of our society that once marched with us and supported us?

And where is the enlightened business community? Will they keep their silence as the price for their tax cuts? Will they choose short-term profits over the long-term social stability that ultimately is the surest guarantee of the free enterprise system? Will they silently pocket billions in tax cuts without speaking out on behalf of poor working people who lose their food stamps?

The silence is frightening because the real issue extends beyond the specific budget cuts. The real issue is the grand design of substituting charity for entitlements, local tyranny for federal protection, and unbridled, law-of-the-jungle capitalism for a balanced cooperation between the public and private sectors. . . .

Thus, the real issue is the nature of our society. . . . The black community today feels itself under siege. It is victimized by the budget cuts. It is harassed by attacks on affirmative action. It is alarmed that state legislatures will redistrict our representatives out of the Congress and out of local offices. It is outraged by the Administration's tilt toward racist South Africa. It is threatened by block grants.

And it is burdened by events beyond the political arena: by growing racial insensitivity and rising anti-black attitudes; by the murders of black children in Atlanta and violence against blacks elsewhere; by the continued deterioration of black neighborhoods; by the flow of drugs and the increase of crime; and by the rise of the fanatics of the far right like the Klan and the Nazis.

. . . The fight for voting rights symbolizes the erosion of black gains. We are now fighting the fight we fought sixteen years ago. And in some ways, we are dealing with basic issues like better race relations that were issues of the 1950s. We moved far beyond that stage, and now we are thrust back to square one.

. . . The complexities of today's racial, economic, and political issues are such that there is no one grand strategy or leader to deliver us. We will have to draw on our immense resources of survival skills to get us through these hard times. And we will have to cultivate our bonds of unity to once again overcome.

In many ways, it is back to basics for black people. That means a recommitment to the slow, agonizing work of building community strengths and community institutions. Throughout history, it has been our churches, our press, our colleges, our community organizations that have fought on our behalf.

Back to basics also means a recommitment to group progress. We reject completely the notion that individual progress is meaningful while half of our black brothers and sisters are mired in ghetto poverty.

Back to basics also means a recommitment to excellence. There is no margin granted to black Americans—we've got to be better than others in order to get what other Americans take for granted.

Back to basics also means political action. It's hard to break through the cynicism that grips people who have seen subjected to brutalizing poverty and hopelessness.

Back to basics also means building coalitions. We've got to reach across class and ethnic lines to win victories for all people. America's tragedy is the racism that drives a wedge between whites and blacks who have so much to gain by working together.

Back to basics also means devising new strategies, alternatives for a nation that thinks old ideas that led to the Great Depression are new ideas for an uncertain future; alternatives like the Urban League's income maintenance plan.

Back to basics also means challenging America's institutions. It means challenging the Administration and the Congress to discover compassion, to make their conservatism humane. It means challenging the private sector to live up to its job creation and affirmative action obligations. It means challenging the churches to practice the morality they preach. It means challenging weak-kneed liberals and hard-hearted conservatives wherever they may be found. It means reminding America's institutions that black people are Americans too, that our blood, sweat, and tears helped make this country what it is, and all we want is our fair share.

And back to basics means back to protesting our condition. Protest has been the basic response of black Americans, from the protest of the slave revolts to the protest of the March on Washington.

Now, when all about us is dark with despair, now is the time to raise high a fresh banner of protest. Now is the time to speak out loud and clear. Now is the time to tell the Administration that poor people can't live on a diet of jellybeans, to tell local officials they can't close our hospitals, to tell corporations they can't hire us last and fire us first, to tell the school boards they are failing their duty to our children, to tell all of America's institutions that they must root out the racism at the core of our national life.

That is our duty, to our nation, to ourselves, to our children, and to our children's children. Let us then get back to the basic job of building new foundations for a new thrust for equality. Let us get back to the basic job of making America America again—this time for everyone!

LIFT EVERY VOICE AND SING (1900)

Lift Every Voice and Sing *was written by the noted black poet and civil rights leader James Weldon Johnson. It was originally intended for use in a program given by a group of Jacksonville, Florida schoolchildren to celebrate Lincoln's birthday. Inasmuch as its words tend to convey a sense of birthright and* heritage, it is often referred to as the "Negro National Anthem" and sung at the opening of various public gatherings.

Lift every voice and sing
Till earth and heaven ring,
Ring with the harmonies of Liberty;
Let our rejoicing rise
High as the listening skies,
Let it resound loud as the rolling sea.
Sing a song full of the faith that the dark past has
    taught us,
Sing a song full of the hope that the present has
    brought us,
Facing the rising sun of our new day begun
Let us march on till victory is won.

Stony the road we trod,
Bitter the chastening rod,
Felt in the days when hope unborn had died;
Yet with a steady beat,
Have not our weary feet
Come to the place for which our fathers sighed?
We have come over a way that with tears have been
    watered,
We have come, treading our path through the blood
    of the slaughtered,
Out from the gloomy past,
Till now we stand at last
Where the white gleam of our bright star is cast.

God of our weary years,
God of our silent tears,
Thou who has brought us thus far on the way;
Thou who has by Thy might
Led us into the light,
Keep us forever in the path, we pray.
Lest our feet stray from the places, Our God, where
    we met Thee,
Lest, our hearts drunk with the wine of the world,
    we forget Thee;
Shadowed beneath Thy hand,
May we forever stand.
True to our GOD,
True to our native land.

UNITED NATIONS PROCLAMATIONS: UNIVERSAL DECLARATION OF HUMAN RIGHTS (1947–1948)

The Universal Declaration of Human Rights was drawn up in 1947 and 1948 by the Commission on Human Rights, headed by Eleanor Roosevelt, widow of President Franklin D. Roosevelt. It was

adopted at the Paris session of the UN General Assembly on December 10, 1948 without a dissenting vote, although there were eight abstentions. At the time of its adoption, it was widely regarded as a definitive statement of the basic rights and fundamental freedoms to which all men *are entitled.*

While the first two and the last three of the Declaration's 30 articles are general in character, the main body of the document covers personal, civil and political rights (Articles 3–21) as well as economic, social, and cultural rights (Articles 22–27).

Preamble

Whereas recognition of the inherent dignity and of the equal and inalienable rights of all members of the human family is the foundation of freedom, justice and peace in the world.

Whereas disregard and contempt for human rights have resulted in barbarous acts which have outraged the conscience of mankind, and the advent of a world in which human beings shall enjoy freedom of speech and belief and freedom from fear and want has been proclaimed as the highest aspiration of the common people,

Whereas it is essential, if man is not to be compelled to have recourse, as a last resort, to rebellion against tyranny and oppression, that human rights should be protected by the rule of law,

Whereas it is essential to promote the development of friendly relations between nations,

Whereas the peoples of the United Nations have in the Charter reaffirmed their faith in fundamental human rights, in the dignity and worth of the human person and in the equal rights of men and women and have determined to promote social progress and better standards of life in larger freedom,

Whereas Member States have pledged themselves to achieve, in co-operation with the United Nations, the promotion of universal respect for and observance of human rights and fundamental freedoms,

Whereas a common understanding of these rights and freedoms is of the greatest importance for the full realisation of this pledge,

Now therefore

The General Assembly

Proclaims This Universal Declaration of Human Rights as a common standard of achievement for all peoples and all nations, to the end that every individual and every organ of society, keeping this Declaration constantly in mind, shall strive by teaching and education to promote respect for these rights and freedoms and by progressive measures, national and international, to secure their universal and effective recognition and observance, both among the peoples of Member States themselves and among the peoples of territories under their jurisdiction.

ART. 1. All human beings are born free and equal in dignity rights. They are endowed with reason and conscience and should act towards one another in a spirit of brotherhood.

ART. 2. Everyone is entitled to all the rights and freedoms set forth in this Declaration, without distinction of any kind, such as race, colour, sex, language, religion, political or other opinion, national or social origin, property, birth or other status. Furthermore, no distinction shall be made on the basis of the political, jurisdictional or international status of the country or territory to which a person belongs, whether it be independent, trust, nonself-governing or under any other limitation of sovereignty.

ART. 3. Everyone has the right to life, liberty and security of person.

ART. 4. No one shall be held in slavery or servitude; slavery and the slave trade shall be prohibited in all their forms.

ART. 5. No one shall be subjected to torture or to cruel, inhuman or degrading treatment or punishment.

ART. 6. Everyone has the right to recognition everywhere as a person before the law.

ART. 7. All are equal before the law and are entitled without any discrimination to equal protection of the law. All are entitled to equal protection against any discrimination in violation of this Declaration and against any incitement to such discrimination.

ART. 8. Everyone has the right to an effective remedy by the competent national tribunals for acts violating the fundamental rights granted him by the constitution or by law.

ART. 9. No one shall be subjected to arbitrary arrest, detention or exile.

ART. 10. Everyone is entitled in full equality to a fair and public hearing by an independent and impartial tribunal, in the determination of his rights and obligations and of any criminal charge against him.

ART. 11. (1) Everyone charged with a penal offence has the right to be presumed innocent until proved guilty according to law in a public trial at which he has had all the guarantees necessary for his defence.

(2) No one shall be held guilty of any penal offence on account of any act or omission which did not constitute a penal offence, under national or international law, at the time when it was committed. Nor shall a heavier penalty be imposed than the one that was applicable at the time the penal offence was committed.

ART. 12. No one shall be subjected to arbitrary inter-ference with his privacy, family, home or correspondence, nor to attacks upon his honour and reputation. Everyone has the right to the protection of the law against such interference or attacks.

ART. 13. (1) Everyone has the right to freedom of movement and residence within the borders of each state.

(2) Everyone has the right to leave any country, including his own, and to return to his country.

ART. 14. (1) Everyone has the right to seek and to enjoy in other countries asylum from persecution.

(2) This right may not be invoked in the case of prosecutions genuinely arising from non-political crimes or from acts contrary to the purposes and principles of the United Nations.

ART. 15. (1) Everyone has the right to a nationality. (2) No one shall be arbitrarily deprived of his nationality nor denied the right to change his nationality.

ART. 16. (1) Men and women of full age, without any limitation due to race, nationality or religion, have the right to marry and to found a family. They are entitled to equal rights as to marriage, during marriage and at its dissolution.

(2) Marriage shall be entered into only with the free and full consent of the intending spouses.

(3) The family is the natural and fundamental group unit of society and is entitled to protection by society and the State.

ART. 17. (1) Everyone has the right to own property alone as well as in association with others.

(2) No one shall be arbitrarily deprived of his property.

ART. 18. Everyone has the right to freedom of thought, conscience and religion; this right includes freedom to change his religion or belief, and freedom, either alone or in community with others and in public or private, to manifest his religion or belief in teaching, practice, worship and observance.

ART. 19. Everyone has the right to freedom of opinion and expression; this right includes freedom to hold opinions without interference and to seek, receive and impart information and ideas through any media and regardless of frontiers.

ART. 20. (1) Everyone has the right to freedom of peaceful assembly and association.

(2) No one may be compelled to belong to an association.

ART. 21. (1) Everyone has the right to take part in the government of his country, directly or through freely chosen representatives.

(2) Everyone has the right of equal access to public service in his country.

(3) The will of the people shall be the basis of the

authority of government; this will shall be expressed in periodic and genuine elections which shall be by universal and equal suffrage and shall be held by secret vote or by equivalent free voting procedures.

ART. 22. Everyone, as a member of society, has the right to social security and is entitled to realisation, through national effort and international cooperation and in accordance with the organisation and resources of each State, of the economic, social and cultural rights indispensable for his dignity and the free development of his personality.

ART. 23. (1) Everyone has the right to work, to free choice of employment, to just and favourable conditions of work and to protection against unemployment.

(2) Everyone, without any discrimination, has the right to equal pay for equal work.

(3) Everyone who works has the right to just and favourable remuneration insuring for himself and his family an existence worthy of human dignity, and supplemented, if necessary, by other means of social protection.

(4) Everyone has the right to form and to join trade unions for the protection of his interests.

ART. 24. Everyone has the right to rest and leisure, including reasonable limitation of working hours and periodic holidays with pay.

ART. 25. (1) Everyone has the right to a standard of living adequate for the health and well-being of himself and of his family, including food, clothing, housing and medical care and necessary social services, and the right to security in the event of unemployment, sickness, disability, widowhood, old age or other lack of livelihood in circumstances beyond his control.

(2) Motherhood and childhood are entitled to special care and assistance. All children, whether born in or out of wedlock, shall enjoy the same social protection.

ART. 26. (1) Everyone has the right to education. Education shall be free, at least in the elementary and fundamental stages. Elementary education shall be compulsory. Technical and professional education shall be made generally available and higher education shall be equally accessible to all on the basis of merit.

(2) Education shall be directed to the full development of the human personality and to the strengthening of respect for human rights and fundamental freedoms. It shall promote understanding, tolerance and friendship among all nations, racial or religious groups, and shall further the activities of the United Nations for the maintenance of peace.

(3) Parents have a prior right to choose the kind of education that shall be given to their children.

ART. 27. (1) Everyone has the right freely to participate in the cultural life of the community, to enjoy the arts and to share in scientific advancement and its benefits.

(2) Everyone has the right to the protection of the moral and material interests resulting from any scientific, literary or artistic production of which he is the author.

ART. 28. Everyone is entitled to a social and international order in which the rights and freedoms set forth in this Declaration can be fully realised.

ART. 29. (1) Everyone has duties to the community in which alone the free and full development of his personality is possible.

(2) In the exercise of his rights and freedoms, everyone shall be subject only to such limitations as are determined by law solely for the purpose of securing due recognition and respect for the rights and freedoms of others and of meeting the just requirements of morality, public order and the general welfare in a democratic society.

(3) These rights and freedoms may in no case be exercised contrary to the purposes and principles of the United Nations.

ART. 30. Noting in this Declaration may be interpreted as implying for any State, group or person any right to engage in any activity or to perform any act aimed at the destruction of any of the rights and freedoms set forth herein.

DECLARATION OF THE RIGHTS OF THE CHILD (1959)

The Declaration of the Rights of the Child was adopted on November 20, 1959 as an extension of the Universal Declaration of Human Rights. Its general objective is to create a climate in which the children of the world can enjoy a safe, happy, and wholesome life.

The document, consisting of a preamble and 10 "principles," addresses itself not only to governments, but also to parents, voluntary organizations, and local authorities—encouraging them to recognize the rights of children and to adopt appropriate legal and social measures for the safeguarding of these rights. Great care was taken by various UN agencies to formulate the principles in a way that would not conflict with the political, religious, and ideological beliefs of any member nations.

Preamble

Whereas the peoples of the United Nations have, in the Charter, reaffirmed their faith in fundamental

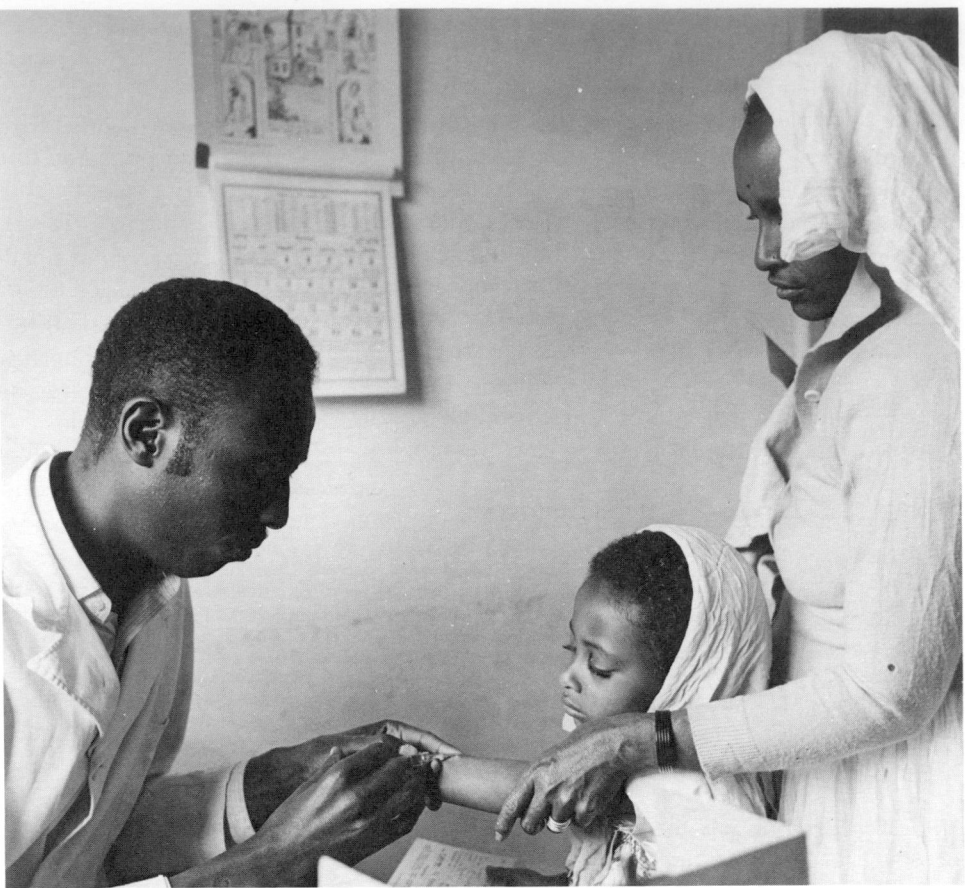

A medical technician gives an Ethiopian youngster an injection against tuberculosis.

human rights, and in the dignity and worth of the human person, and have determined to promote social progress and better standards of life in larger freedom,

Whereas the United Nations has, in the Universal Declaration of Human Rights, proclaimed that everyone is entitled to all the rights and freedoms set forth therein, without distinction of any kind, such as race, color, sex, language, religion, political or other opinion, national or social origin, property, birth or other status,

Whereas the child, by reason of his physical and mental immaturity, needs special safeguards and care, including appropriate legal protection, before as well as after birth,

Whereas the need for such special safeguards has been stated in the Geneva Declaration of the Rights of the Child of 1924, and recognized in the Universal Declaration of Human Rights and in the statutes of specialized agencies and international organizations concerned with the welfare of children.

Whereas mankind owes to the child the best it has to give,

Now therefore,

The General Assembly

Proclaims this *Declaration of the Rights of the Child* to the end that he may have a happy childhood and enjoy for his own good and for the good of society the rights and freedoms herein set forth, and calls upon parents, upon men and women as individuals and upon voluntary organizations, local authorities and national Governments to recognize these rights and strive for their observance by legislative and other measures progressively taken in accordance with the following principles:

Principle 1

The child shall enjoy all the rights set forth in this Declaration. All children, without any exception whatsoever, shall be entitled to these rights, without distinction or discrimination on account of race, color, sex, language, religion, political or other opinion, national or social origin, property, birth or other status, whether of himself or of his family.

Principle 2

The child shall enjoy special protection, and shall be given opportunities and facilities, by law and by other means, to enable him to develop physically, mentally, morally, spiritually and socially in a healthy and normal manner and in conditions of freedom and dignity. In the enactment of laws for this purpose the best interests of the child shall be the paramount consideration.

Principle 3

The child shall be entitled from his birth to a name and a nationality.

Principle 4

The child shall enjoy the benefits of social security. He shall be entitled to grow and develop in health; to this end special care and protection shall be provided both to him and to his mother, including adequate pre-natal and post-natal care. The child shall have the right to adequate nutrition, housing, recreation and medical services.

Principle 5

The child who is physically, mentally or socially handicapped shall be given the special treatment, education and care required by his particular condition.

Principle 6

The child, for the full and harmonious development of his personality, needs love and understanding. He shall, wherever possible, grow up in the care and under the responsibility of his parents, and in any case in an atmosphere of affection and of moral and material security; a child of tender years shall not, save in exceptional circumstances, be separated from his mother. Society and the public authorities shall have the duty to extend particular care to children without a family and to those without adequate means of support. Payment of State and other assistance to-

wards the maintenance of children of large families is desirable.

Principle 7

The child is entitled to receive education, which shall be free and compulsory, at least in the elementary stages. He shall be given an education which will promote his general culture, and enable him on a basis of equal opportunity to develop his abilities, his individual judgment, and his sense of moral and social responsibility, and to become a useful member of society.

The best interest of the child shall be the guiding principle of those responsible for his education and guidance; that responsibility lies in the first place with his parents.

The child shall have full opportunity for play and recreation, which should be directed to the same purposes as education; society and the public authorities shall endeavor to promote the enjoyment of this right.

Principle 8

The child shall in all circumstances be among the first to receive protection and relief.

Principle 9

The child shall be protected against all forms of neglect, cruelty and exploitation. He shall not be the subject of traffic in any form.

The child shall not be admitted to employment before an appropriate minimum age; he shall in no case be caused or permitted to engage in any occupation or employment which would prejudice his health or education, or interfere with his physical, mental or moral development.

Principle 10

The child shall be protected from practices which may foster racial, religious and any other form of discrimination. He shall be brought up in a spirit of understanding, tolerance, friendship among peoples, peace and universal brotherhood and in the consciousness that his energy and talents should be devoted to the service of his fellow men.

HISTORIC LANDMARKS OF BLACK AMERICA

A Survey of Afro-American Historic Sites, Buildings, Monuments, and Shrines Across the United States

No more substantial testimony to the black role in the growth and development of this nation can be found than the numerous historical landmarks in various regions of the country which are associated with black Americans. Many of these—like the Alamo and Bunker Hill—are not conventionally known as sites involving chapters of black history.

Alabama

Florence
Handy Heights Housing Development and Museum

The Development and Museum is named for composer W. C. Handy, who was born in Florence in 1873. It includes a restored cabin in which are housed his piano, trumpet, and other mementoes.

Mobile
Fort Gaines (on Dauphin Island)

Site of the Battle of Mobile Bay (August 1864) during the Civil War. One of the key battles of the day was the engagement between Admiral David Farragut's flagship, the *Hartford,* and the Confederate ironclad, *Tennessee.* During the battle, black naval hero John Lawson manned his duty station despite serious injury;

his role in keeping Union guns operative may well have saved the ship from destruction. For his valor, the Pennsylvania black was awarded the Medal of Honor. Black infantry units also participated in the capture of Fort Gaines and, later, the capture of Mobile itself. When nearby Fort Blakely fell, nine black regiments were included in the 1st Division of the federal force commanded by General John Hawkins.

Montgomery
Dexter Avenue Baptist Church
454 Dexter Avenue

The Dexter Avenue Baptist Church was the church where Dr. Martin Luther King, Jr. organized the black boycott of segregated city buses in Montgomery in 1955. The church, which has been in existence since 1878, was declared a National Historic Landmark by the Department of Interior on March 30, 1974. Dr. King pastored the church from 1954 to 1959 and in the church is a mural depicting scenes and related data of the civil rights movement as well as a Martin Luther King Library containing personal mementoes of Dr. King and his family as well as resource data on him. It was the boycott of buses in Montgomery, which he led, that brought Dr. King into national prominence as a civil rights leader.

The Battle of Mobile Bay, where John Lawson, a Pennsylvania black, was awarded the Medal of Honor.

Talladega
Talladega College and Swayne Hall

Home of the first college for blacks in Alabama, Talladega was founded by the American Missionary Association as a primary school in 1867. Its Slavery Library houses three fresco panels by Hale Woodruff (the celebrated Amistad Murals). Professor Woodruff studied abroad in France under the renowned Henry Ossawa Tanner, and also at the Herron Institute in Indianapolis.

Swayne Hall, built in 1857, is the oldest building on the campus of Talladega College. The building was declared a National Historic Landmark by the Department of Interior on December 2, 1974. The building was built by slave labor before the school was established. Talladega pursued a liberal arts program at a time when vocationalism dominated Negro education.

Tuskegee
Tuskegee Institute

The Institute is a world-famous center for agricultural research and extension work. First opened on July 4, 1881 with a $2,000 appropriation from the Alabama State Legislature, it consisted of a single shanty, a student body of 30, and one teacher—Booker T. Washington. Tuskegee functioned originally as a normal school for the training of black teachers, the first of its kind established in the United States. Eventually it came to specialize in agricultural and manual training, areas which were to make both the school and Booker T. Washington famous.

In 1882, Washington moved the school to a 100-acre plantation and began a self-help program which enabled students to finance their education. Most of the early buildings were built with the aid of student labor.

Next to Washington, the most famous person to be associated with the Institute was George Washington Carver, who became its director of agricultural research in 1896. Carver persuaded many Southern farmers to plant peanuts, sweet potatoes, and other crops instead of cotton, which was rapidly depleting the soil. Ultimately, Carver's research programs helped

Under construction at Tuskegee Institute are a $2 million cultural center (left) *and a new wing for the John A. Andrew Memorial Hospital.*

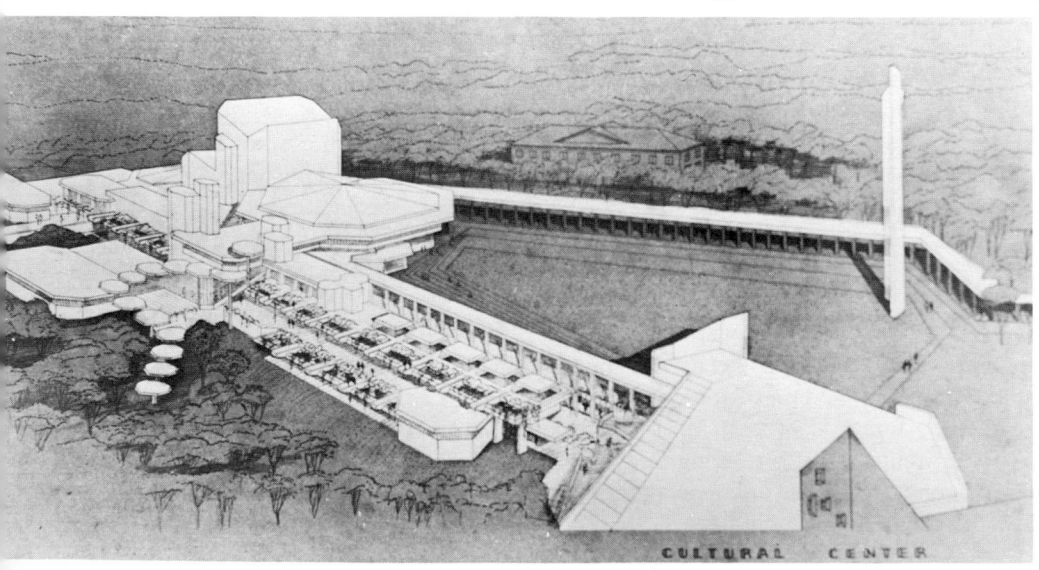

Sent out with no recompense for past labors, emancipated slaves built for themselves.

develop 300 derivative products from peanuts and 118 from sweet potatoes. At one point, he even succeeded in making synthetic marble from wood pulp.

Today, Tuskegee covers nearly 5,000 acres and has more than 150 buildings. Notable places to visit there include the Founder's Marker (the site of Washington's original shanty), the Oaks (Washington's home), the Booker T. Washington Monument, and the George Washington Carver Museum.

The Carver Museum houses the scientist's plant, mineral, and bird collections, and includes exhibits of various products he developed, as well as a number of his paintings and research papers.

Tuskegee is also the home of the George Washington Carver Foundation, a research center founded by Carver in 1940.

Alaska

Fairbanks
Pioneers Home

One of the few surviving black pioneers of Alaska is Mattie Crosby, who first came to the wilderness in 1900 with a Maine family that adopted her. Miss Crosby later opened a bathhouse and became famous as one of Alaska's best cooks. Some blacks came into the territory during the era of the Gold Rush, and others were occasionally seen on board ships which brought in supplies. Still, for nearly 17 years, Mattie Crosby lived in Fairbanks without meeting another black. In her advancing years, she wrote a book about

her experiences, but it has unfortunately since been lost.

Arizona

Apache
Geronimo Monument

Geronimo was one of the last Apache chieftains to resist the oncoming hordes of white settlers and immigrants moving into the Southwest. Black cavalrymen finally escorted Geronimo and his renegades into exile at Fort Dickens, Florida and later returned with him to Fort Sill, where he died.

Bonita
Old Fort Grant

Site of a fort at which black soldiers were housed during the Indian Wars. Two soldiers of the fort, Isaiah Mays and Benjamin Brown, received Congressional Medals of Honor while on duty at this station.

Fort Apache
Old Fort Apache

Another fort at which black units served during the Indian Wars. The punitive expedition led by John

On steep mountainside trails, cavalrymen became foot soldiers.

Cavalry troopers drawn by Frederic Remington during the time he spent with this unit for Harpers Weekly *in 1888.*

Pershing in search of Pancho Villa originated at this point, the 10th Cavalry in the vanguard. This unit was stationed at the fort beginning in 1913, after having seen service in Cuba and the Philippines.

Fort Thomas
Camp Thomas

This camp was a base of operations from which both black cavalry units operated in their mission to keep peace among the Apache tribes. One black, Sergeant William McBryar, won the Congressional Medal of Honor for demonstrating "coolness" and "bravery" under combat stress during the pursuit of a renegade Apache.

Phoenix
State House

Among the eight murals at the State Capitol Building in Phoenix depicting vital episodes from Arizona's history is one portraying Estevanico, the black guide of Fray Marcos de Niza, the Franciscan missionary whose search for the Seven Cities of Gold brought him into Arizona in 1539. Estevanico was killed at one of the seven Zuni pueblos after trying to escape.

San Carlos
San Carlos Indian Reservation

The 9th and 10th Cavalry, black regiments formed after the Civil War, were often sent out to combat the Cheyenne and Apache Indians in the American Southwest. The Indians called them *Buffalo Soldiers;* their own white officers referred to them as *The Brunettes*. Whatever their designation, however, they were considered to be among the best troops in the area. The first black officer assigned to the 10th Cavalry was Lieutenant Henry O. Flipper, who was the first black to graduate from West Point.

Blacks were among the troops under General Crook's command at the time of the surrender of the famed Apache chief Geronimo in 1876.

Today, the tribal council of the San Carlos Apaches meets regularly on the site where the reservation of the Warm Springs Apaches was once found.

Sierra Vista
Fort Huachuca

Fort Huachuca quartered troops of the 9th and 10th Cavalry during the Indian Wars. Elements of the 10th were stationed here in the first decade of the twentieth century. During World War II, the men of the all-black 92nd Division trained here before being sent overseas to Africa and Europe.

Springerville
Apache National Forest

Site, in the White Mountains, where troopers of the 10th Cavalry captured Mangas Coloradas on September 18, 1886. Coloradas was one of those fierce Apache chiefs who fought desperately for choice grazing lands for his people. Today the reservation at Springerville contains millions of acres of fertile land, the legacy of the tenacious resistance of the Apaches.

Tombstone
John Swain (Slaughter) Grave in Boot Hill

Born a slave in 1845, John Swain went to Tombstone in 1879 as a cowhand in the employ of John Slaughter, who was later to become sheriff of this town. Swain was an expert rider, and only one of several blacks to work for Slaughter.

In 1884 Swain fought and lost a one-round boxing match with John L. Sullivan, then heavyweight champion of the world. He died just three months short of his hundredth birthday, and was buried with honors by the citizens of Tombstone. A special tablet stands on the gravesite, commemorating the close ties between the two men.

Tortilla Flat
Battle of the Caves

Site, during 1872–1873, of General Crook's campaign to wipe out Apache bands holed up in distant, and virtually inaccessible, mountain retreats. Black units approached the Indian hideout under cover of darkness, pinned down the enemy in their cave, and scored a notable victory. Few of the marauders escaped; several were killed by ricocheting bullets.

Arkansas

Camden
Poison Spring State Park

Site of an 1864 Civil War battle in which the 1st Kansas Colored Regiment suffered heavy casualties, some of which were apparently inflicted by Confederates on captured or wounded black soldiers. Black troops, as they did at Fort Pillow, vowed to take no more rebel prisoners.

Helena
The Battle of Helena

Among the defenders of this Mississippi River port were members of the 2nd Infantry Regiment of African Descent. Black soldiers fought shoulder to shoulder with whites in repulsing a Confederate siege of the city in July 1863. The experience of one black unit stationed there—the 56th U.S. Colored Troops—is typical of many which confronted blacks during the war. Disease was an even more potent enemy than combat. Only a handful of men lost their lives as a result of armed conflict, whereas literally hundreds fell victim to disease and poor medical treatment.

Little Rock
Philander Smith College

Opened in 1877 under the sponsorship of the Methodist Episcopal Church, Philander Smith (then known as Walder College) was renamed five years later after receiving a large donation which enabled the school to construct a permanent brick edifice.

Sheridan
Jenkins Ferry State Park

Two weeks after the Poison Spring engagement—on April 30, 1864, to be exact—the 1st and 2nd Kansas Colored Regiments saw action along the Sabine River, where they overran a Confederate battery, shouting, "Remember Poison Spring" and inflicting 150 casualties on the enemy.

California

Allensworth
Allensworth Colony

The town of Allensworth, an all black community, was founded by Allen Allensworth in 1910 and is still in existence. Now a historic monument, this landmark is being developed by a black historical group as a memorial to the founder. The town is named after Allen Allensworth, who as a slave, just prior to the Civil War, was a well-known racing jockey in Louisville, Kentucky. With the beginning of the Civil War, Allensworth was allowed to enter the Navy where he advanced to rank of Chief Petty Officer. After the War, Allensworth studied for the ministry and returned to the military service as Chaplain of the famed 24th U.S. Infantry. Around 1900 he migrated to California where he dedicated himself to improving the lot of his black brothers. The founding of Allensworth was a result.

Arcadia
Santa Anita Race Track

Santa Anita Race Track is located on the former site of the E. J. "Lucky" Baldwin ranch, a spread at which John Fisher, a black man and former slave, was a prominent breeder and trainer. Fisher, a native of St. Louis, was at first reluctant to follow Baldwin to California out of fear of Indians, but was eventually persuaded to join him. He later became a foreman on the ranch.

Beckwourth
Beckwourth Pass (U.S. Alt. 40, east of the junction with U.S. Rte. 395)

Beckwourth Pass, which runs through the Sierra Nevada mountains, was discovered by James P. Beckwourth, one of a number of black traders and trappers dubbed *The Mountain Men* by many writers of American history.

Fond of telling a good yarn, Beckwourth not surprisingly added spice to his own life with a number of romantic legends, in which it is often difficult to separate fact from fantasy.

One such story has it that, toward the end of his life, he killed a man in an argument in Denver, and was held in custody for a time before being acquitted on a plea of self-defense. Beckwourth, who claimed to be a Crow chief, was subsequently welcomed by the tribe, which believed him to be a symbol of good fortune. When he talked of leaving, the Crow decided to keep their "talisman" with them forever by planning a sumptuous feast in his honor and then poisoning the stew.

A less embellished account of his end has it that he died on the trail two days after leaving Denver for a rendezvous with the Crow.

Jim Beckwourth, the black frontiersman for whom Beckwourth Pass in the Sierras is named.

Beverly Hills
Beverly-Wilshire Hotel

Black architect Paul R. Williams designed this plush hotel, one of the most elegant in the area. Many stunning private residences of famous Hollywood stars have been designed by Williams, the Spingarn medalist for 1953.

Downieville
The Pioneer Museum

Site of an 1849 gold strike involving a Scotch immigrant, William Downie, and 10 blacks. One of the black adventurers was Waller Jackson, an Easterner who journeyed " 'round the Horn" in 1849 and found his fortune with the rest of the prospecting party.

Allensworth, California, was founded by a famous nineteenth-century jockey.

Folsom Lake
"Negro Bar" Marker

Folsom Lake now covers the site of an old mining camp anonymously associated with black gold miners. Remains of these intrepid pioneers have been reburied at nearby Mormon Island Pioneer Cemetery.

Fremont Park
Fremont Peak State Park

John C. Fremont—soldier of fortune, explorer, writer, politician—was a key figure in the development of California and in the war which was fought against Mexico to make this vast territory a part of the Union.

Fremont led four exploratory and mapping missions into California and took along blacks on two of them. John Dodson, a free black who was a servant of Fremont's father-in-law, Senator Thomas Hart Benton, accompanied the second of these expeditions, while Saunders Jackson, likewise a servant of Benton, volunteered for the fourth in order to raise the $1,700 needed to buy his family's freedom.

After considerable hardship, the ill-fated fourth expedition ended with Fremont and his party finally arriving in California via a southern route. Once there, Fremont discovered that, in his absence, gold had been discovered on land he owned. Jackson was given permission to prospect for gold and within a few days had dug out nuggets valued at $1,700. He then returned to Missouri, emancipated his family as planned, and disappeared from history.

Having become a millionaire, Fremont, whose political ideology was abolitionist, was to experience several ups and downs, both in military and in political affairs, during his later career. Ultimately, however, he became territorial governor of Arizona before his death in 1890.

Hollywood
Grauman's Chinese Theater

In 1967 Sidney Poitier became the first black actor to record his footprints in the concrete of Grauman's Chinese Theater, a ritual which has become synonymous with stardom and success in Hollywood film circles.

Hornitos
Gold Mining Camp

Home of Moses Rodgers, a successful and affluent black mine owner who was one of the finest engineers and metallurgists in the state. Rodgers was only one of several black miners who struck it rich in gold and

Black and white prospectors washing gold at Spanish Flats, California, in 1852.

quartz. One black, known to history only as Dick, reputedly amassed a fortune of more than $100,000 but lost it all on the Sacramento gaming tables and, in despair, blew his brains out.

Mokelumme Hill
Gold Discovery Marker

Site of a legendary strike involving a black miner allegedly the butt of a white prank. According to the story, a befuddled black prospector asked his white colleagues where to dig and was told, with great fanfare, that a barren hillside in town was the most likely place to strike it rich. What took shape as an elaborate joke turned out, however, to be a startling prophecy, fulfilled inside of two days by a happy black prospector carrying a sack of gold. The butt of the joke had returned to thank his "friends" for their generous and abundant advice.

Oakland
Oakland Art Museum

The museum has several pieces done by prominent black artists, including Sargent Johnson's *Forever Free* and lithographs by Grafton T. Brown, believed to be the first black artist active in the state.

Leidesdorff's San Francisco hotel.

Red Bluff
Oak Hill Cemetery

Burial place of Aaron Coffey, only black man in the Society of California Pioneers. Coffey, descendant of an officer who fought under Jackson at New Orleans, came to California a slave in 1849. By day, he worked at his master's claim; by night, as a cobbler, accumulating money toward his $1,000 emancipation fee. Betrayed by his owner, he was forced to return to Missouri, where he was again sold. Coffey pleaded with his new master to allow him to return to California and earn the necessary money to free himself and his family, which he left behind as collateral. That mission accomplished, Coffey returned to Red Bluff, took up farming, and settled down to a contented family life.

Sacramento
St. Andrew's African Methodist Church

The first AME church in California, organized in a private residence in 1850. Within four years, the congregation organized a school for black, Oriental, and Indian children in the church basement.

San Francisco
Leidesdorff Street

Named after William Alexander Leidesdorff, a wealthy and influential California pioneer of black and Danish ancestry and a native of the Danish West Indies. A merchant, Leidesdorff operated the first steamer to pass through the Golden Gate, was later appointed U.S. vice-consul, and ultimately became a civic and educational leader in San Francisco.

Colorado

Breckenridge
Barney Ford Hill (just southeast of city limits)

A fugitive slave who went to Colorado in 1860 in search of gold, Barney Ford had once operated a station in Chicago's Underground Railroad and been involved with the famed revolutionary John Brown.

Ford found gold but was cheated out of his claim by outlaws. He managed to get back to Denver, where rumors began to spread that he had buried a fortune in the hill which now bears his name.

Fugitive slave Barney L. Ford discovered gold in California.

Ford actually became a wealthy hotel owner and restauranteur (repeating the success he had originally had in Nicaragua) but, in spite of this, people persisted in believing his wealth was really derived from the hillside treasure-trove. The result was that, over the years, the hill became pockmarked with the diggings of those who refused to believe Ford's protestations and denials. Later in life, Ford was beleaguered by hoodlums and other riffraff who insisted on spying upon his every move in the hope that he would one day betray a vital clue to the whereabouts of the alleged treasure.

Central City
"Aunt Clara" Brown Chair (Central City Opera House)

This chair is a tribute to "Aunt Clara" Brown, believed to have been the first black resident of Colorado. Aunt Clara died in 1877, in her eighties.

Born a slave in Virginia, Aunt Clara moved to Missouri where her husband and children were sold before she herself gained freedom through her master's last will and testament. From Missouri she headed for Kansas and then for the gold fields of Colorado, where she opened the territory's first laundry. From her earnings she soon began putting aside money for the purchase of her family.

Even though the Emancipation intervened and her immediate family was set free, she nonetheless returned to Missouri and brought back with her to Central City a group of 38 relatives. She remained in the mining community for the rest of her life, nursing the sick and performing other charitable works.

She was buried with honors by the Colorado Pio-

Charity working Clara Brown became the leading citizen of Central City, Colorado.

neers Association, of which she was a member. Her chair was dedicated in 1932.

Denver
Inter-Ocean Hotel
16th and Market Streets

The Inter-Ocean Hotel, once a showplace for millionaires and presidents, was built by Barney Ford, a black entrepreneur active during the gold rush days. (See first Colorado entry.)

Ford and his cohorts joined the fight over the organization of the Colorado territory and the question of statehood. Originally allowed to vote, they had seen this privilege abrogated by the territorial constitution and, as a result, sought to delay statehood for the territory until black voting rights were reinstated. Enlisting the aid of the famed Massachusetts abolitionist Senator Charles Sumner, Ford urged President Andrew Johnson to veto the bill for statehood.

Ultimately, Johnson adopted this course of action and, as an ironic consequence, Colorado was unable to vote on the question of Johnson's impeachment. Had the territory become a state then, it is believed likely that the two provisional senators would have voted for impeachment, inasmuch as they were known to be vehemently anti-Johnson.

In Colorado, Ford was blamed for attempting to block statehood and for keeping Johnson in office. Once the fifteenth Amendment had been passed, however, Ford began to work vigorously on behalf of statehood. He supported the Republican state legislature and its representatives on the electoral commission which voted in the Hayes-Tilden election. Some claimed Ford was responsible for the deciding commission vote. In any event, the advent of Hayes to the presidency signaled the end of Reconstruction and paved the way for a series of laws which soon deprived the black throughout the South of his precious and newly won voting right.

Ford retired and spent the remainder of his life in Denver where he died in December 1902. He is buried alongside his wife Julia in Denver's Riverside Cemetery.

Pueblo
El Pueblo Museum
905 S. Prairie Avenue

The El Pueblo Museum houses a replica of the Gantt-Blackwell Fort which Jim Beckwourth, black explorer, scout, and trader, claimed to have founded in 1842. The validity of the claim has not been established, inasmuch as Beckwourth is known to have had something of a reputation as a teller of tall tales.

Connecticut

Canterbury
Home of Prince Goodin

A parcel of land in Canterbury, once the home of Prince Goodin, a free black who fought with the British against the French in the French and Indian War. Goodin enlisted in 1757 after hearing a fiery speech of Canterbury's Reverend James Cogswell which stressed the danger of encroachment against "properties, liberties, religion and our lives." He served at Fort William Henry and was captured during a French attack upon the fort and taken to Montreal where he was sold into slavery. After three years of captivity he was freed when the British took the city in 1760. Goodin later petitioned the colony of Connecticut for compensation.

Farmington
First Church of Christ (Hartford County)

As the center of the community life of the Amistad captives after their famous 1840–1841 trial, the First Church of Christ commemorates the importance of this famous trial in the history of the abolition movement. The church was designated a National Historic Landmark on December 8, 1976.

Groton Heights
Fort Griswold State Park

Freeman was the black orderly of the American commander Colonel William Ledyard, who was forced to surrender the fort to superior British forces. The British officer who accepted the surrender behaved ignobly, however. Ledyard was first induced to give up the sword and then run through with his own weapon, presumably in revenge for the death of a British officer at the hands of Freeman. Another black, Lambert Latham, avenged Ledyard's death by killing the treacherous British officer.

Washington
Jeff Liberty Grave

In the Judea Cemetery in Washington, Connecticut lies the grave of Jeff Liberty, a soldier in the Continental Army during the Revolution. His grave marker, erected by the Sons of the American Revolution, states simply "in remembrance of Jeff Liberty and his colored patriots." Liberty, a slave at the time of the rebellion, asked his owner to be allowed to serve in the struggle for independence. His request granted, he fought throughout the revolution with a black Connecticut

Jeff Liberty's grave marker placed by the Sons of the American Revolution.

regiment and was granted freedman status at the end of the war.

New Haven
James Weldon Johnson Collection, Temple Street Church

Temple Street Church was one of the foremost stopping-off points for fugitive slaves en route to Canada. It was founded by two Underground Railroad agents, Reverends Simeon S. Jocelyn and Amos G. Beman, the latter of whom was the church's first black pastor. The town of New Haven lived up to its name both prior to and during the Civil War, providing shelter to many slaves bound for freedom. Many New Haven citizens were involved in the work.

Delaware

Wilmington
Asbury Methodist Episcopal Church

This church, located at Third and Walnut Streets, was dedicated in 1789 by the distinguished orator Bishop Francis Asbury. Tradition has it that, on one occasion, a number of the town's leading citizens, many of whom were eager to hear Asbury preach but considered Methodism beneath them socially, refused to enter the church but stayed outside within hearing distance of the sermon. The listeners were impressed by the eloquence of the man they heard—not, as it turned out, the bishop, but his black servant Harry whose compelling testimony reached their ears and inspired their admiration. By 1805, however, blacks had left this church, driven out by the decision of white worshippers to confine black members to the gallery. The blacks who left formed their own church.

District of Columbia

Association for the Study of Negro Life and History
1538 Ninth Street, N.W.

The Association was long the sole professional agency concerned with preserving the historical record of the black in American life. The organizing pioneer behind the Association was Carter Woodson, a scholar and lecturer who began publication of the *Journal of Negro History* in 1916. Ten years later, Woodson inaugurated observance of "Negro History Week," during which leaders of the black freedom struggle were appropriately honored, primarily in schools. Negro History Week is always celebrated in February, as close as possible to the birthdays of both Frederick Douglass and Abraham Lincoln. Woodson and his later colleague, Dr. Charles Wesley of Central State, collaborated on many historical studies.

Mary McLeod Bethune Memorial

The Mary McLeod Bethune Memorial, unveiled in 1974, is the first monument to a black person, or a woman, erected on public land in the nation's capitol. The $100,000 monument is located in Lincoln Park. It is inscribed with the words:

I leave you love, I leave you hope. I leave you the challenge of developing confidence in one another. I leave you a thirst for education. I leave you respect for the use of power. I leave you faith. I leave you racial dignity.

Mrs. Bethune was a black educator who was concerned about the children of the laborers who worked on the Florida East Coast Railroad.

In 1904 she established the Daytona Normal and Industrial Institute for black girls. In 1926 she merged with Cookman Institute of Jacksonville to form the Bethune and Cookman College.

Mrs. Bethune helped President Roosevelt organize the National Youth Administration, and in 1936 she became Director of the Division of Black Affairs. She received the Spingarn Award in 1935.

Blanche K. Bruce House
909 M Street, N.W.

A Senator from Mississippi, Blanche K. Bruce was the first black American to serve a full term in the U.S. Senate from 1875 to 1881. Bruce was born in

Farmville, Virginia and learned the printer's trade in Missouri. In 1861, prior to the Civil War, he escaped to Hannibal, Missouri and set up a school for blacks. He studied at Oberlin College in Oberlin, Ohio and after moving to Mississippi he became a wealthy planter. His positions in Mississippi included that of sheriff, tax collector, a member of the levee board in Mississippi, and superintendent of schools for the county. A Republican, Bruce was elected by the Mississippi state legislature to the U.S. Senate in 1874. The Blanche K. Bruce House was designated a National Historic Landmark on May 15, 1975.

Mary Ann Shadd Cary House
1421 W Street, N.W.

Mary Ann Shadd Cary was the first black newspaperwoman in America and lived in the house between 1881 and 1886. She was also a writer, educator, lawyer, and antislavery abolitionist. A forceful lecturer, she appeared before audiences throughout the country, usually speaking on topics of slavery and women's suffrage. During the Civil War she held the position of recruiting officer for the Union Army. The house was designated a National Historic Landmark on December 8, 1976.

Frederick Douglass Home
1411 W Street, S.E.

Cedar Hill, the 20-room colonial mansion in which Frederick Douglass lived for the last 13 years of his life, has been preserved as a monument to the great nineteenth-century abolitionist. In 1964 Secretary of the Interior Stewart Udall declared it a national shrine.

Credit for the restoration and preservation of the home belongs largely to the National Association of Colored Women's Clubs, which worked hand in hand with the Douglass Association.

Birthplace of Edward Kennedy "Duke" Ellington
1212 T Street, N.W.

On 1212 T Street N.W., Washington, D.C. stands the building in which "Duke" Ellington was born on April 29, 1899. Ellington, one of the world's great exponents of jazz, was enormously versatile. In addition to being a great bandleader, Ellington was a talented pianist, and a composer in his idiom without peer. He died in May 1974.

Emancipation Statue: Lincoln Park

Former black slaves were responsible for financing and

Freed slaves contributed the money for this statue of Lincoln the Emancipator.

erecting the oldest memorial to Abraham Lincoln in the Washington, D.C. area.

After Lincoln's assassination in 1865, the first five dollars for the statue was donated by a Mrs. Charlotte Scott of Marietta, Ohio. Contributions were soon pouring in, whereupon Congress finally set aside appropriate grounds for Thomas Bell's statue of Lincoln breaking slavery's chains. The memorial was dedicated on April 14, 1876—the eleventh anniversary of the assassination of the Great Emancipator.

Charlotte Forten Grimké House
1608 R Street, N.W.

Charlotte Forten Grimké, born of wealthy free black parents in Philadelphia, was among the first wave of northerners engaged in educating slaves in the occupied Union territories of the South. Her activities as a female black activist, writer, poet, and educator forged a path for the participation of other females in education, social welfare, and humanitarian endeavors. The house was designated a National Historic Landmark on May 11, 1976.

Howard University

Howard University, founded in 1867, is the largest institution of higher learning established for the black in the immediate post-Civil War period.

Covering more than 50 acres on one of the highest elevations in the District of Columbia, the campus grounds and the physical plant are valued at more than 40 million dollars. Of particular interest is the famed Founders Library, which contains more than 300,000 volumes and includes the Moorland Collection, one of the finest collections on black life and history in the United States.

Lincoln Memorial

The Lincoln Memorial has been the site of several important events underscoring the black's quest for dignity and struggle for opportunity. One involves refusal of permission for Marian Anderson to sing at Constitution Hall, an auditorium owned by the Daughters of the American Revolution. The DAR offered no explanation beyond the fact that it was conforming to local custom in excluding her. The District of Columbia public school system followed suit by refusing to allow Miss Anderson to appear, prompting an aroused and indignant public to question local policy toward blacks in every area of public accommodations. Rejection of such arbitrary exclusion of blacks led to the eventual integration of amusement parks and places of entertainment in the city. For Miss Anderson, the episode was a prelude to one of her greatest triumphs— an Easter Sunday concert on the steps of the Lincoln Memorial. Her rendition of "Nobody Knows the Trouble I've Seen" prompted NAACP Executive Secretary Walter White to foresee the advent of "a new affirmation of democracy." In 1968, the mall before the Memorial was the site of Resurrection City, the encampment erected for participants in the "Poor People's March."

National Gallery of Art
6th Street and Constitution Avenue, N.W.

The Gallery houses many of the world's greatest paintings, and has, in recent years at least, sought to find representative samples of early Americana by black painters. Among its paintings is one by the first black American portraitist, Joshua Johnston. Known as *The Westwood Children,* it was probably done during Johnston's most active period, roughly 1796–1824. Many of the families who owned Johnston's work thought he was a slave, but he is listed as a "free householder of color" in the Baltimore directory of 1817.

Phillips Gallery
1612 21st Street, N.W.

Thirty of Jacob Lawrence's famous 60-panel study on black migration in America is housed in the Phillips Gallery. (Others are in the permanent collection of the New York Museum of Modern Art.) Lawrence, a native of Atlantic City, New Jersey paints in a stark and vivid style that brings to life the human despair implicit in many of the historical situations he uses as subject matter. Lawrence's work has been exhibited in most of the nation's top museums. In 1970 he was the recipient on the NAACP's coveted Spingarn Medal, emblematic of special preeminence in his field.

St. Luke's Episcopal Church
15th and Church Streets, N.W.

From 1879 until 1934, the pulpit of St. Luke's Episcopal Church was filled by Alexander Crummell, a talented and articulate black scholar who became a leading spokesman for black liberation both at home and in Africa. He was the founder of the American Negro Academy, established with the intention of forming a cadre of black intellectuals and scholars. The church was designated a National Historic Landmark on May 11, 1976.

Carter G. Woodson House
1538 Ninth Street, N.W.

This was the home of Carter G. Woodson from 1915 until his death in 1950. Recognizing the need for recording black contributions in the development of the nation and for correcting distortions, Woodson established the Association for the Study of Negro Life and History, the Associated Publishers, and the official organ of the Association, the *Journal of Negro History*. Each of them helped bring to the consciousness of the nation the roles and contributions of Afro-Americans in the development and progress of America. On May 11, 1976, the Carter G. Woodson house was designated a National Historic Landmark.

Tidal Basin Bridge

It is often said that the Tidal Basin Bridge commands the most impressive view of the annual cherry blossom extravaganza in Washington, D.C. each spring. Few are aware that the bridge was engineered and built by a black designer, Archie A. Alexander, once governor of the Virgin Islands. The "outstanding graduate" of the class of 1912 at the State University of Iowa, Alexander was known as a fairminded and witty man who enjoyed his work and expected to be judged for his ability, not his color. He once removed the "White" and "Colored" signs adorning segregated bathrooms, and replaced them with the words "Skilled" and "Unskilled."

Florida

Daytona Beach
Bethune-Cookman College

One of the leading institutions in the South for the training of Negro teachers, Bethune-Cookman College was founded in 1904 by Mary McLeod Bethune on "faith and a dollar-and-a-half."

In her day, Mrs. Bethune, advisor to Presidents Franklin D. Roosevelt and Harry S Truman, was one of the most powerful and influential blacks in the United States.

Mary McLeod Bethune Home
Campus of Bethune-Cookman College

The two-story frame house belonging to the black activist Mary McLeod Bethune was built in 1920 on the campus of the school she established in 1904. Following the tradition of Mary McLeod Bethune, the college has made important and significant contributions to black education in the South. The house was proclaimed a National Historic Landmark on December 2, 1974.

Fort George Island
Kingsley Plantation

Kingsley traded extensively in slaves, and the headquarters for his operation was on his plantation on Fort George Island. It is the oldest known plantation house in Florida and was established in 1763. Kingsley was known for training slaves to be exceptionally skilled craftsmen and productive farmers. The plantation, which has been restored as a house museum, displays exhibits and furnishings that reflect the plantations and island life during the period 1763–1783.

Franklin County
British Fort Gadsen (six miles southwest of Sumatra)

This British fort was a place where runaway slaves lived alongside Seminole Indians. Its destruction in 1816 precipitated the First Seminole War. In 1814 the British built the fort as a base for recruiting Indians and blacks during the War of 1812. The British abandoned it to their allies in 1815 along with its artillery and military supplies. It became known as the Negro Fort and served as a beacon for rebellious slaves and a threat to supply vessels on the river. On May 15, 1975, British Fort was named a National Historic Landmark.

Battle of Olustee, fought by the 8th and 54th Colored Troops.

Olustee
Olustee Battlefield Historic Memorial

Olustee was the site of a bloody Civil War battle during which the unseasoned soldiers of the 8th U.S. Colored Troops lost more than 300 men, many of them untutored in the operation of their weapons and equipment. The veteran 54th Massachusetts, one of the two other black regiments serving among Union forces there, fared better in the battle, checked the enemy, and held its position while it covered the retreat of the corps it had been sent in to rescue. Cited for valor in combat, Stephen A. Swails became the first black to be commissioned in the 54th. Federal troops retired to Jacksonville after the engagement at Olustee, remaining there until the end of the war.

Georgia

Andersonville
Andersonville Prison

Andersonville, the infamous Confederate prison where thousands of Union soldiers perished as a result of the inhuman manner in which they were contained, is now a national monument. Andersonville was the shame of the Confederacy. Here on July 19, 1864, Corporal Henry Gooding of the black 54th Massachusetts regiment was imprisoned and died. It was Corporal Gooding who had started a protest with the military

regarding the pay of black soldiers and went over the heads of brass to write President Lincoln. At that time the pay of blacks was a flat $7 per month. For whites, it ranged from $9 to $30. Encouraged by Colonel Robert Shaw, the black soldiers of the 54th refused to accept any remuneration unless it was equal to that of white comrades. This financial inequity was subsequently rectified. But, with tragic irony, Corporal Gooding died at Andersonville without ever having drawn a day's pay.

Atlanta
Martin Luther King, Jr. Historic District

The district, within several blocks of Atlanta's Auburn Avenue and Boulevard, includes Dr. Martin Luther King, Jr.'s birthplace home, gravesite, and the church where King served as assistant pastor. The environs of his childhood are largely intact. Private efforts to create a living monument to Dr. King and his beliefs are carried on primarily through the Martin Luther King Jr. Center for Non-Violent Social Change, Inc., which is building a Freedom Hall complex adjacent to the present memorial. Surrounding the prime historic area are two National Register Historic Districts: The Martin Luther King Jr. National Register Historic District and the Sweet Auburn National Landmark Historic District. The MLK Historic District was designated a National Historic Landmark on May 5, 1977.

Martin Luther King and his place of birth (below).

Atlanta University System

The campus of the Atlanta University System (consisting of Atlanta University and Morris Brown, Clark, Morehouse, and Spelman Colleges) is one of the most beautiful to be found anywhere in the South.

Ebenezer Baptist Church

Ebenezer Baptist Church had as its associate pastor the Reverend Martin Luther King, Jr., the most celebrated spokesman for nonviolent protest produced in America in the twentieth century. It was from this church that Dr. King radiated outward through the rest of the South, organizing chapters of the Southern Christian Leadership Conference (SCLC), the civil rights coalition which he served as president. Funeral services for Dr. King were held in this church, attended by a host of notables from all over the world. As millions watched on television, mourners lined up for miles behind the muledrawn wagon that carried Dr. King from Ebenezer to Morehouse College, his alma mater. There, the eulogies were delivered, and more than 150,000 paid their last respects to a great and fearless American martyr.

South View Cemetery

Dr. King was laid to rest in South View Cemetery, where a marble crypt was inscribed with the words he had used to conclude his famous speech delivered on the occasion of the 1963 March on Washington. The words, taken from an old slave song, are: "Free at last, free at last, thank God Almighty I'm free at last." South View was founded in 1886 by blacks who balked at a prevailing policy which required that they be buried in the rear of the municipal cemetery.

Stone Hall

Built in 1882, Stone Hall is most closely associated with the history of the Atlanta University. The institution was founded in 1866 by the American Missionary Association to provide education for freed Negroes. Noted writer W. E. B. DuBois taught at the university. The building was named a National Historic Landmark on December 2, 1974.

Sweet Auburn Historic District
Auburn Avenue

Although only a remnant of its original sprawling expanse of one mile, Sweet Auburn Historic District typifies the rapid growth of black enterprise in the post-Civil War period, forced to adjust to segregated resi-

Atlanta University held its first classes in abandoned railway cars.

dential and commercial patterns. Auburn Avenue was once called the "richest negro street in the world." The district was designated a National Historic Landmark December 8, 1976.

Columbus
"Blind Tom" Marker (U.S. Rte. 27A)

The "Blind Tom" Marker refers visitors and pedestrians to the gravesite of the famous black pianist "Blind Tom" Bethune, son of a slave, but a remarkably gifted prodigy whose astonishing talent brought him into the salons of Europe, where royalty marveled at his virtu-

oso performances. "Blind Tom" also toured his own country and excited the wonder and admiration of appreciative audiences everywhere.

Bragg Smith Marker

The Bragg Smith Marker, located in the Columbus Colored Cemetery, marks the gravesite and marble memorial built by the city in memory of Bragg Smith, who was killed while attempting to rescue the city engineer from a cave-in.

Savannah
Reverend George Lisle Monument
(First Bryan Baptist Church, 559 West Bryan Street)

The Reverend George Lisle Monument is dedicated to the first American black Baptist missionary.

Illinois

Chicago
Robert S. Abbott House
4742 Martin Luther King Drive

The house was occupied by Robert Stengstacke Abbott from 1926 to 1940, the year of his death. Under Abbott, the *Chicago Defender,* a newspaper appealing to black readers, encouraged southern blacks to migrate northward, particularly to Chicago. Probably more than any other publication, the *Defender* was responsible for the large northward migration of blacks during the first half of the twentieth century. The house was named a National Historic Landmark on December 8, 1976.

Blind Tom's piano music delighted concert audiences throughout Europe and America.

Robert S. Abbott, who founded the influential and militant black newspaper the Chicago Defender.

The Art Institute

Among the Nation's great art galleries, the Art Institute has works by black artists and sculptors, including Tanner's *The Two Disciples at the Tomb,* Richard Hunt's *Hero Construction,* and Marion Perkins' *Man of Sorrows.*

Oscar Stanton DePriest House
4536–4538 Dr. Martin Luther King, Jr. Drive

The house is the residence of the first black American elected to the House of Representatives from a northern state. DePriest was born in Florence, Alabama but moved with his family to Kansas and later to Chicago. He was a real estate broker in Chicago. In 1928 Oscar DePriest was elected to the U.S. House of Representatives as a Republican. He was a congressman for three terms and following his tenure, he returned to the real estate business but was still involved politically in Chicago. DePriest was also vice chairman of the Cook County Republican Committee. The DePriest home was designated a National Historic Landmark on May 15, 1975.

Du Sable Marker

The Du Sable Marker on the Michigan Avenue Bridge marks the site of the first building in the area that is now part of the city of Chicago. It was also the home of Jean Baptiste Pointe Du Sable, a black fur trapper and trader from Santo Domingo.

According to records in Cahokia, Illinois, Du Sable was married to a Potawatamie Indian in the year 1788. The earliest known reference to him appears in an army report by a British colonel in 1779, but there are several other descriptions of him and his home after that date. For instance, he is known to have owned a farm in Peoria, Illinois, as well as other property in St. Charles, Missouri, where his son eventually settled.

In 1796, Du Sable sold his Chicago home, and went to live with his son in St. Charles, where he died in 1814.

The site of Du Sable's home is marked by a plaque on the northeast approach to the Michigan Avenue Bridge. Two other plaques exist—one in the Chicago Historical Society, the other in the lobby of Du Sable High School, at 49th and State Streets.

The Historical Society

Among the treasures and exhibits of the Chicago Historical Society are many which relate to blacks, including a replica of the cabin built by Jean Du Sable (see entry above) and numerous other artifacts relative to the days of slavery. John Jones (1811–1879), a successful businessman who settled in Chicago in 1845 and was Cook County Commissioner from 1871 to 1875, and his wife Mary are preserved for posterity by two Aaron Darling portraits. Other material explores the role played by black units from Illinois during campaigns of the Civil War.

Museum of African American History and Art

The Museum of African-American History and Art was founded recently by Mrs. Margaret Burroughs in an effort to "inspire Afro-American people by acquainting them with contributions other members of their race have made to society in the past." Of the many artifacts, including books and periodicals, relating to the black, perhaps the most distinctive is the powderhorn carried during the Revolutionary War by the black fifer Barzillai Lew.

Milton L. Olive Park

Milton L. Olive Park was dedicated by Chicago Mayor Richard Daley in honor of the first black soldier to be awarded a Congressional Medal of Honor during the Vietnam conflict. Olive died in action after exhibiting extraordinary heroism which saved the lives of several other soldiers exposed to a live grenade.

Jean Baptiste Point Du Sable Homesite
401 North Michigan Avenue

Jean Baptiste Point Du Sable, a black man born in Haiti to a French mariner father and a black mother,

PFC Milton Olive III saved five comrades from death by leaping on an enemy grenade thrown into their midst and smothering the explosion with his body.

Jean Baptiste Point DuSable and the fur trading settlement which became the city of Chicago.

immigrated to French Louisiana and became a fur trapper. He established trading posts on the sites of the present cities of Michigan City, Indiana, Peoria, Illinois, and Port Huron, Michigan but the most important post was on the site of Chicago, Illinois. This site, where he constructed a log home for his wife and family, is recognized as the first settlement of Chicago. The homesite was designated a National Historic Landmark on May 11, 1976.

Provident Hospital and Training School
51st Street and Vincennes Avenue

Provident Hospital and Training School is the first training school for black nurses in the United States. It was founded by Dr. Daniel Hale Williams, the renowned surgeon who performed the first successful operation on the human heart in 1893.

Underground Railway Marker

An Underground Railway Marker, which represents an in-transit point for slaves escaping into Canada, is located at 9955 South Beverly Avenue.

Victory Monument
35th Street and South Park Way

Victory Monument is a memorial statue by Leonard Crunelle honoring the black soldiers of Illinois who

served in World War I. Just opposite this statue is the Lake Meadows Shopping Center and Housing Development. The monument and tomb of Stephen A. Douglas, once the owner of much of the land in the area, is likewise located near 35th Street.

Ida B. Wells-Barnett House
3624 S. Dr. Martin Luther King, Jr. Drive

The home of the 1890s civil rights advocate and crusader for the rights of black women, Ida Wells-Barnett, who carried on her crusades in the pages of her newspaper, the *Memphis Free Speech*. The Wells house was designated a National Historic Landmark on May 30, 1974.

Daniel Hale Williams House
445 East 42nd Street

This is the home of one of America's first black surgeons, whose accomplishments include one of the first successful heart operations in 1893 and the establishment of quality medical facilities for blacks. Daniel Hale Williams was born in Hollidaysburg, Pennsylvania. He had operated a barber shop prior to apprenticing under Dr. Henry Palmer, who was surgeon-general of Wisconsin. In 1883, Williams received his M.D. degree from Chicago Medical College and later opened an office in Chicago. He was the first black to win a fellowship of the American College of Surgeons. The Williams home was designated a National Historic Landmark on May 15, 1975.

Indiana

Bloomingdale
Underground Railroad Marker (U.S. Rte. 41)

This marker is only one of several once used to assist fugitive slaves brave enough to risk death by fleeing from the South and seeking freedom and safety in Canada. One of these, William Trail, liked Indiana so much he decided instead to stay on and go into farming. His efforts were met with success, and he became one of many prosperous farmers active in Union County, Indiana.

Fountain City
Levi Coffin Home, North Main Street

Levi Coffin, a Quaker abolitionist referred to as "The President of the Underground Railroad," used his own home as a way station in which, from 1827 to 1847, he hid more than 300 slaves heading for Illinois, Michigan, or Canada.

Levi Coffin, referred to as "President of the Underground Railway."

Born in North Carolina in 1798, Coffin moved to Fountain City (then known as Newport) at the age of 28. From there he went to Ohio where he continued his activities, eventually helping over 3,000 slaves escape from the South. One of the founders of the Freedmen's Bureau (1865), he was still engaged in the resettlement of former slaves long after the Civil War had ended. Coffin died in Avondale, Ohio in 1877.

Iowa

Clinton
Underground Railroad Station

Before the Lafayette Hotel was built, the small house that once stood at Sixth Street South and South Second Street is known to have been a point of shelter and sustenance for black fugitives escaping from Missouri. Iowa was a free territory by virtue of both the Northwest Ordinance (1787) and the Missouri Compromise of 1820. Many Quakers who had come to the state before the Civil War took great pains to organize an efficient and effective Underground Railroad network.

Des Moines
Fort Des Moines Provisional Army Officer Training School

Camp Des Moines was an all black "West Point" established during World War I, on June 15, 1917, for the purpose of training talented black soldiers to hold officer's rank. On October 14, 1917, 639 black soldiers were commissioned as Second Lieutenants and assigned to the American Expeditionary Forces being sent to France. Black units led by men trained at the school were assembled in France as the 92nd Division.

The camp was abandoned at the end of the war. The site was designated a National Historic Landmark on May 30, 1974.

Slaves like these sought escape from the South via the Underground Railroad.

Sioux City
Pearl Street

Once the city's main thoroughfare, Pearl Street is named for a black pioneer who arrived in the town by boat more than a century ago and achieved widespread popularity as a cook. Another black cook, Aunty Wooden by name, impressed many leading citizens with her specialty, an opossum dinner. Civil War veteran Henry Riding was another black pioneer who staked a claim to Iowa land and had a successful career as a homesteader. He once prevented a railroad crew at gunpoint from laying track across his land, and forced the company to settle for $21,000 before granting them the right of access. Sioux City was a refuge for many slaves escaping from Missouri.

Kansas

Beeler
George Washington Carver Marker

Along Route K-96 in Ness County lies the plot of land once homesteaded by George Washington Carver, famed black agricultural scientist. He spent two years there before going to college in Iowa.

Fort Scott

Fort Scott was the home of the First Kansas Colored Volunteers, a black unit organized by the Union Army in August 1862. The first such unit to go into combat during the Civil War, it beat back a superior Confederate force at the battle of Island Mount, Missouri on October 28, 1862.

Dodge City
Fort Dodge

Established in 1865, Fort Dodge was often used as a base of operations by the all-black 10th U.S. Cavalry, a unit which saw much action on the plains protecting settlers, pioneers, and cattlemen from Indian uprisings, but which was equally active in Dodge City itself, a haven for gamblers, rustlers, and even desperate killers. When a black named Taylor was murdered, the Fort Dodge commandant decided to take action against the town's criminal element. County government and a string of fearless sheriffs eventually quieted the town, reducing the major crime to less serious proportions. Many of the black cowboys active on the trail stopped at Dodge and many of them matched their white counterparts in letting off steam and raising cain. Ben

Hodges was not among these transients, partly because his game called for a smoother operation. Hodges was fond of bilking ranchers by posing as a wealthy man and getting financial backing for supposedly reputable projects. Though he was eventually unmasked as an imposter, he was spared the rope or the bullet and lived to a ripe old age, regaling youngsters with pioneer tales and eventually coming to be regarded as a revered and respectable old-timer.

Leavenworth
Fort Leavenworth

Fort Leavenworth was the first home of the 10th Cavalry, the all-black unit which not only participated in many important battles during the Indian wars, but also served with valor and distinction during the Spanish-American War. It was at Leavenworth that the Independent Kansas Colored Battery, a unit with several black officers, was recruited in 1864. Among its members was Captain H. Ford Douglass, son of the noted abolitionist Frederick Douglass. The younger Douglass joined the Illinois Volunteers as far back as 1862.

Nicodemus
Nicodemus Colony

Located along U.S. Rte. 24 two miles west of the Rooks-Graham county line, Nicodemus Colony is the last of three now-virtually-deserted colonies which were founded by the Exodusters—a group of black homesteaders active in Kansas during the 1870s. The name "Nicodemus" was derived from a slave who, according to legend, foretold the coming of the Civil War.

Arriving in 1877, the first settlers lived in dugouts and burrows during the cold weather. From the outset, they were plagued by crop failures. Although never more than 500 in number, they managed nonetheless to create a real community—with teachers, ministers, civil servants, etc. The state of Kansas has commemorated this site with a historical marker located in a roadside park in Nicodemus.

Osawatomie
John Brown Memorial State Park

This state park, named in honor of the fiery insurrectionist, contains the cabin in which he lived during his brief sojourn in Kansas.

Wallace
Fort Wallace

Only a roadside marker and a cemetery are left as identifying marks of Fort Wallace, another of the military outposts used by the 10th Cavalry. One white officer who came to Fort Wallace as commandant of the 5th Cavalry after having refused a regiment of black troopers changed his attitude in the field when black soldiers whom he fought alongside proved their

Sod houses were built by the first settlers of Nicodemus.

mettle in battle against the Cheyenne. The black cavalrymen marched 230 miles in nine days and killed 10 Cheyenne who had surrounded the escort party which was taking the major to his new regiment.

Kentucky

Berea (Madison County)
Lincoln Hall, Berea College

Lincoln Hall was built in 1887 at Berea College. Berea is significant in the history of black education in that it was the first college established in the United States for the specific purpose of educating blacks and whites together. Lincoln Hall, closely associated with Berea's history, was designated by the Department of Interior as a National Historic Landmark on December 2, 1974.

Louisiana

Baton Rouge
Southern University

Located in Baton Rouge since 1914, Southern University is the successor to an institute founded in New Orleans after the Civil War. The modern and well-financed plant now serves some 12,000 students on a breathtakingly landscaped site that includes a huge lake. The two university satellites now in existence are located in Shreveport and New Orleans.

New Orleans
Chalmette National Historical Park—Louisiana State Museum

Chalmette National Historical Park is the more precise site of what is usually recorded in history as the Battle of New Orleans, fought during the War of 1812. The battle pitted the motley forces of General Andrew Jackson against 5,400 seasoned English veterans of the Napoleonic campaigns fighting under Sir Edward Pakenham. About 200 of Jackson's soldiers were free blacks commanded by Colonel Joseph Savary. These men, according to Jackson, manifested great bravery, "although they were poorly armed and sometimes forced to fight with empty guns used as clubs." After the first attack on December 23, 1814, Jackson withdrew his men to Chalmette, where he built a defensive breastwork which shielded his 4,000-man force. On Christmas Day, Pakenham arrived with his men, and sought immediately to engage Jackson's Creoles, Indians, Negroes, Kentuckians, and pirates. The Americans repulsed two attacks before girding for the decisive engagement on January 8. Pakenham was felled in this last desperate charge, struck, according to Jackson, "from the bullet of a free man of color, who was a famous rifle shot and came from the Attakapas region of Louisiana." Among the hundreds of Negroes who had contributed to the victory was Jordan Noble, a 14-year-old drummer boy whose drum has been preserved at the Louisiana State Museum.

About 200 of General Andrew Jackson's soldiers at New Orleans were free black riflemen who volunteered for the battle.

James H. Dillard Home
571 Audubon Street

The home was built during the nineteenth century and James Dillard lived there from 1894 to 1913. Dillard played an important role in black education in the nineteenth century, strengthening vocational and teacher-training programs. Dillard's home was designated a National Historic Landmark on December 2, 1975 by the Department of Interior. Dillard University was named for the educator.

The Louisiana State Museum
751 Charles Street

The Louisiana State Museum contains a tablet inscribed to the memory of Norbert Rillieux, the New Orleans "quadroon libre" whose invention of the sugar evaporating pan revolutionized the sugar refining industry by reducing labor and costs to a bare minimum. Rillieux's father was a wealthy engineer and plantation owner; his mother was a slave.

Melrose
Yucca Plantation

The plantation was established by a former slave who became a wealthy businesswoman. It is located on Louisiana Rte. 119, just east of the intersection with Louisiana Rte. 493, Natchitoches Parish. The plantation was established during the eighteenth and nineteenth centuries. The African House on the plantation, which is a unique structure with an umbrellalike roof, may be of direct African derivation. The site was declared a National Historic Landmark by the Department of Interior on May 30, 1974.

Port Hudson
Port Hudson Siege Marker

The besieged city of Port Hudson was the scene of numerous acts of gallantry involving black troops from the 1st and 3rd Louisiana Native Guards—freedmen who were recruited in New Orleans by Union general Ben Butler. The city fell in July, but the bombardment began as far back as March of 1863. The New York *Times* wrote:

Official testimony settles the question that the Negro race can fight with great prowess. Those black soldiers had never before been in any severe engagement. They were comparatively raw troops, and were yet subjected to . . . the charging upon fortifications through the crash of belching batteries. The men, white or black, who will not flinch from that, will flinch from nothing. It is no longer possible to doubt the bravery and steadiness of the colored race.

The great majority of the Negro units in the battle were led by Negro officers, including Captain Andre Cailloux, who was given a state funeral after he fell on the battlefield. The funeral pageant was "the like of which" had never before been seen "in honor of a dead Negro." The site was declared a National Historic Landmark by the Department of Interior on July 1, 1974.

Yucca plantation established by a former slave who became a wealthy businesswoman.

The first man to walk on the North Pole was Matthew Henson.

Maryland

Annapolis
Matthew Henson Plaque

The Matthew Henson Plaque honors the memory of
the only man to accompany Admiral Robert E. Peary
on all of his polar expeditions. Henson was also the
first man actually to reach the North Pole (April 6,
1909). Peary himself, barely able to walk, arrived there
after Henson had taken a reading of his position and
proudly planted the flag of the United States.

Baltimore
Morgan State College Frederick Douglass Monument

Morgan State College has an interesting collection of
artifacts on Benjamin Banneker, noted astronomer,
compiler of almanacs, and—together with L'Enfant—
surveyor of the District of Columbia. It also houses
a number of artifacts on Fredrick Douglass and Matthew Henson. On the campus of Morgan State College,
in Baltimore, is the Fredrick Douglass Memorial statue
created by the noted black sculptor James Lewis. The
work, completed in 1956, stands 12 feet tall with pedes-
tal. Its simple inscription reads, "Fredrick Douglass
1817–1895 Humanitarian, Statesman."

Baltimore County
Banneker Marker
Westchester Avenue at Westchester School

This marker is a tribute to Benjamin Banneker, the
black mathematician, astronomer, and inventor who,
in 1792, produced an almanac regarded as one of the
most reliable of his day. His scientific knowledge, as
well as the international renown that accrued to him,
led to his assignment as a member of the surveying

and planning team which helped lay out the nation's
capital.

Banneker's correspondence with President Thomas
Jefferson can be seen at the Library of Congress.

Rockville
Uncle Tom's Cabin

Site of the log cabin believed to be the birthplace of
Josiah Henson, the escaped slave immortalized as Uncle Tom in Harriet Beecher Stowe's famous abolitionist

*"Uncle Tom" as he appeared in theater posters. Between 1852
and 1931 Uncle Tom was playing continually somewhere in
the United States.*

A scene from an early dramatization of the novel.

study. Born in 1789, Henson was sold at auction at an early age and transferred to many masters until he managed to escape in 1830. After setting up a community for fugitive slaves in Dawn, Canada, Henson frequently returned to the South to liberate others. Later a minister and mill owner, Henson journeyed to London in 1851, meeting the Archbishop of Canterbury, who asked him from which university he had graduated. Henson replied cryptically: "The University of Adversity." Two years earlier, he had met Mrs. Stowe and given her the outline of his slave experiences which formed the bases for her celebrated story. In the introduction to Henson's *Autobiography*, published some years later, she acknowledged his story as the source of her own tale.

Massachusetts

Boston
Crispus Attucks Monument

The Crispus Attucks Monument, located in the Boston Common, was dedicated in 1888 to honor the five victims of the Boston Massacre—Crispus Attucks, Samuel Maverick, James Caldwell, Samuel Gray, and Patrick Carr. The site of the Massacre is marked by a plaque on State Street, near the Old State House.

Attucks is believed by many historians to have been the same man who in 1750 was advertised as a runaway black slave from Framingham, Massachusetts. A stranger to Boston, he led a group which converged on a British garrison quartered in King Street to help enforce the Townshend Acts. One of the soldiers of the garrison panicked and fired, and Attucks was the first to fall. (Gray and Caldwell were also killed on the same spot. Maverick and Carr died later of wounds

The Crispus Attucks Monument.

sustained during the clash. The British soldiers were later tried for murder and acquitted.)

The five men are buried in Granary Burying Ground, together with such famous Revolutionary War figures as John Adams and John Hancock, as well as Governor William Bradford of Plymouth Colony.

Bunker Hill Monument

Standing in the Charlestown district of Boston, the Bunker Hill Monument commemorates the famous Revolutionary War battle, which—contrary to popular belief—was actually fought on Breed's Hill on June 17, 1775.

A number of blacks fought alongside the colonists during the battle, including Peter Salem, Salem Poor, Titus Coburn, Cato Howe, Alexander Ames, Seymour Burr, Pomp Fiske, and Prince Hall, founder of the Negro Masonic order.

The cornerstone for the monument was laid by the Marquis de Lafayette in 1825. A ceremony at which Daniel Webster was a featured speaker marked the completion of the monument in 1843.

William C. Nell Residence
3 Smith Court

From the 1830s to the end of the Civil War, William C. Nell was a leading black abolitionist and spokesman for his race. He was born in Boston and studied law in the office of William I. Bowditch. Nell refused to take an oath to be admitted to the bar because he did not want to support the Constitution of the United States, which he felt compromised the powers of slaves. He then began organizing meetings and lecturing in support of the antislavery movement. Nell's residence was designated a National Historic Landmark by the Department of Interior on May 11, 1976.

Shaw Monument

Executed by the famed sculptor Augustus Saint-Gaudens, the Shaw Monument, on Beacon Street facing the State House, is a group statue of Colonel Robert Gould Shaw and the 54th Massachusetts Volunteers, a black regiment which served in the Union Army. The regiment particularly distinguished itself in the battle for Fort Wagner during which Colonel Shaw was killed. Sergeant William H. Carney's valiant exploits during this battle later won him the Congressional Medal of Honor.

Paul Cuffe used his merchant fortune to fight for black civil rights.

Cambridge
Maria Baldwin House
196 Prospect H Street

This house was the permanent address of Maria Baldwin from 1892 until her death in 1922. As principal and later as "master" of the Agassiz School in Cambridge, as a leader in community organizations such as the League for Community Service, as a gifted and popular speaker on the lecture circuit, and as a sponsor of charitable activities like the first kindergarten in Atlanta, Georgia, Maria Baldwin exemplified the achievements that were attainable by a black person in a predominantly white society. The house was designated by the Department of Interior as a National Historic Landmark on May 11, 1976.

Phillis Wheatley Folio

During her celebrated trip to England in 1773, Phillis Wheatley, the first American black woman to write a book, was presented with a folio edition of John Milton's *Paradise Lost*. It now resides in the library of Harvard University.

Miss Wheatley, who came to America in 1761 as a child of seven or eight, made rapid strides in mastering the English language and, by the time she was 14, had already completed her first poem. Always in

delicate health, she died in Boston on December 5, 1784.

Central Village
Memorial to Paul Cuffe

Cuffe, son of a freedman, was born in 1759, became a prosperous merchant seaman, and resolved to use his wealth and position to campaign for the extension of civil rights for blacks. On one occasion, Cuffe refused to pay his personal property tax on the grounds that he was being denied full citizenship rights. A court of law eventually upheld his action, whereupon he was granted the same privileges and immunities enjoyed by white citizens of the state. In 1815, Cuffe transported 38 blacks to Sierra Leone in what was intended to become a systematic attempt at repatriating the black inhabitants of the United States. With the growth of abolitionist sentiment in the colonies, repatriation lost favor among both blacks and whites as a means of solving the black question.

William E. B. DuBois Boyhood Homesite
Route 23

This is the boyhood homesite of William E. B. DuBois, the prominent black sociologist and writer who was a major figure in the Negro civil rights movement during the first half of the twentieth century. DuBois advocated the elimination of discrimination and inequality against blacks through his writing, as a college professor, and as a lecturer. He received his B.A. degree in 1888 from Fisk University and another B.A. degree from Harvard University in 1890. The DuBois homesite was designated May 11, 1976 as a National Historic Landmark by the Department of Interior.

Great Barrington
DuBois Memorial Marker

William Edward Burghardt DuBois was born here in Great Barrington on February 23, 1868. He is considered one of the most influencial black intellectuals of the twentieth century. A founder of the NAACP and author of many books, DuBois died in 1963 at the age of 95. At his homesite, the people of Great Barrington have erected a memorial to one of the city's great citizens.

Lynn
Jan Ernst Matzeliger Statue

The Matzeliger Statue is one of the few extant honors accorded the black inventor whose shoc-last machine revolutionized the industry and made mass-produced shoes a reality in the United States. A native of Dutch Guiana, Matzeliger came to the United States in 1876, learned the cobbler's trade, and set out to design a machine which would simplify shoe manufacture. Sickly, he died at an early age, unable to capitalize on his successful patent, which was purchased by the United Shoe Machinery Company of Boston. After his death, Matzeliger was awarded a gold medal at the 1901 Pan-American Exposition.

Nantucket
Nantucket Whaling Museum

In the whaling museum on beautiful Nantucket Island is stored a treasury of whaling lore among which are recorded the names and histories of blacks who participated in the whaling industry such as Peter Green, a black sailor and second mate of the whaling ship *John*

The most important man in a whaleboat was the harpooner, who was often black.

Adams. In August 1823, after a violent storm in which the captain and first mate were lost at sea, Green brought his ship and crew out of the maelstrom to safety.

Suffolk County
William Monroe Trotter House
97 Sawyer Avenue

This is the home of William Monroe Trotter, noted black journalist and militant civil rights activist during the first decades of the twentieth century. Trotter was the first black member of Phi Beta Kappa. He was an insurance and mortgage broker in Boston from 1897 to 1906. In 1901 he became publisher and editor of *The Guardian,* which was a crusading newspaper, and he edited the publication until his death in 1934. The Sawyer Avenue house was designated a National Historical Landmark by the Department of Interior on May 11, 1976.

Westport
Paul Cuffe Farm
1504 Drift Road

Paul Cuffe was a self-educated black man who became a prosperous merchant. He also pioneered in the strug-

gle for minority rights in the eighteenth and early nineteenth centuries. Cuffe was also active in the movement for black settlement in Africa. The Paul Cuffe Farm was designated by the Department of Interior as a National Historic Landmark on May 30, 1974.

Michigan

Battle Creek
Sojourner Truth Grave

The Sojourner Truth Grave in Oak Hill Cemetery marks the resting place of one of the most powerful abolitionist lecturers of the nineteenth century.

Sojourner settled in Battle Creek after the Civil War but continued to travel on lecture tours until a few years before her death in 1883, at the approximate age of 85.

Cassopolis
Underground Railroad Marker

There is an Underground Railroad Marker located 2½ miles east of Cassopolis on Route M-60.

Dred Scott sued for his freedom in 1847 on the grounds that his master had taken him to live in Minnesota, which did not allow slavery. The southern-dominated Supreme Court denied Scott's suit, ruling that slaves were not American citizens.

Sojourner Truth believed God had assigned her the mission of traveling across the country to spread the truth about slavery. Huge crowds gathered to hear her speak, for she had a very sharp mind and great powers of oratory.

Detroit
Detroit Public Library
5201 Woodward Avenue

The Azalia Hackley Memorial Collection is one of the major treasures available for public perusal at the Detroit Public Library. Madame Hackley did pioneering work in the field of music, promoting black concert talent and seeking recognition for works by black composers. Talented black musicians like Clarence Cameron White and Nathaniel Dett were among those who benefited from scholarship aid provided by this tireless crusader. Included in her collection of artifacts, clippings, and memorabilia are more than 600 books, sheet music for many popular songs, assorted photographs, and printed programs.

Douglass-Brown Marker

The Douglass-Brown Marker, on East Congress Street and St. Antoine, marks the site of the William Webb House, where fellow abolitionists John Brown and Frederick Douglass met in March of 1859 to map out the strategy which ultimately led to the abortive Harpers Ferry revolt. Douglass was strongly opposed to this course of action.

Marshall
Crosswhite Boulder

In Triangle Park, on Michigan Avenue and Mansion Street, stands *Crosswhite Boulder*—the site of the pitched battle fought in 1846 in defense of Adam Crosswhite, a fugitive slave who had fled from Kentucky. The Crosswhite case is said to have been instrumental in the enactment of the Fugitive Slave Law of 1850.

Minnesota

St. Paul
Fort Snelling State Park

Fort Snelling was that outpost in the Wisconsin Territory to which the slave later to become known as Dred Scott was transported from Illinois in 1836.

Scott met and married his wife Harriet at the fort, and also saw his first child born there. After having been taken to Missouri by his master, he filed suit for his freedom and became a national figure as his case was tried, from 1847 to 1857, before numerous tribunals en route to the U.S. Supreme Court. Scott argued that he should be considered free by virtue of his having previously resided in Illinois and at Fort Snelling.

(See St. Louis, Missouri entry for discussion of the Dred Scott decision.)

Mississippi

Alcorn
Oakland Memorial Chapel, Alcorn University

The chapel on the Alcorn campus was built in 1838. It is the oldest and the most venerable building on the Alcorn University campus. Oakland Chapel symbolizes the importance of Alcorn as the first black land grant college in the United States. The chapel was designated a National Historic Landmark by the Department of Interior on May 11, 1976.

Mound Bayou
I. T. Montgomery House
West Main Street

This is the home of Isiah Thornton Montgomery, who in 1887 founded in the town of Mound Bayou a place where black Americans could obtain social, political, and economic rights in a white supremacy South. The house was declared a National Historic Landmark by the Department of Interior on May 11, 1976.

Natchez
Natchez National Cemetery
61 Cemetery Road

This cemetery is the final resting place of many black war dead, including landsman Wilson Brown, a Medal of Honor recipient during the Civil War. Brown and fellow seaman John Lawson received their medals for courage in action while serving aboard the U.S.S. *Hartford* in its Mobile Bay engagement of August 5, 1864. Another prominent black from Natchez, Hiram R. Revels, was the first black elected to the U.S. Senate. A Methodist minister, Revels recruited blacks for the Union side during the war, and served as Chaplain of a Union regiment from Mississippi. He later became president of Alcorn A & M, and is buried in Holly Springs.

Missouri

Diamond
Carver National Monument

Located in a park, Carver National Monument commemorates the place where the great black scientist George Washington Carver was born and spent his early childhood.

Kidnapped when he was just six weeks old, Carver was eventually ransomed for a horse valued at $300. Raised in Missouri by the family of Moses Carver, his owner, he made his way through Minnesota, Kansas, and Iowa before being "discovered" by Booker

T. Washington in 1896. That same year, Carver joined the faculty of Tuskegee Institute where he conducted most of the research for which he is famous.

The monument is the first created in honor of a black. It contains a statue of Carver as a boy, and encloses several trails leading to places of which he was particularly fond. The park also houses a visitors' center and a museum displaying many of his discoveries and personal belongings, as well as other artifacts of his day. It can be reached on U.S. Alt. 71, just west of Diamond.

Jefferson City
Lincoln University

More than $6,000 raised by the black fighting men of the 62nd and 65th U.S. Colored Infantry constituted the initial endowment for a 22-foot-square room in which classes first began in 1866 at what is now Lincoln University in Jefferson City. Known then as Lincoln Institute, the school began receiving state aid to expand its teacher-training program in 1870. It became a state institution nine years later, and instituted college-level courses in 1887. It has been known as Lincoln University since 1921, and has had graduate school status since 1940. The more than 2,000 students now attending the school are often reminded that Lincoln was launched through the generous philanthropy of former slaves, many of them illiterate, who fought for their freedom and the freedom of succeeding generations.

St. Joseph
Pony Express Station

The famed pony express was a privately owned postal service which carried mail from St. Joseph, Missouri to Sacramento, California in 1860. The riders, a most select group, had to make the run in 10 days, riding in relays, regardless of the weather, terrain, food, or hostile Indians. At its height, the service employed 125 riders, 400 station men and assistants, and 420 horses. Two of the most famous, well known for their other exploits, were Buffalo Bill Cody and Wild Bill Hickok. Two black men, for the most part forgotten, who rode the pony express were George Monroe and William Robinson; little else is known of them except that they made their contribution to this epic saga in western history.

St. Louis
Old Courthouse (Jefferson National Expansion Memorial)

It was in the Old Courthouse in 1847 that Dred Scott, the most famous fugitive slave of his day, first filed suit to gain his freedom. For the next 10 years, the Dred Scott case was a burning political and social issue across the country. In 1857 it reached the Supreme Court. There, Chief Justice Roger Taney handed down the decision that slaves could not become free by escaping—or by being taken—into free territory, nor could they be considered American citizens.

Ironically, a few weeks after the decision was rendered, Scott was set free by his new owner. He died a year later.

Scott Joplin Residence
2685-A Morgan Street

The Scott Joplin residence was built in the 1890s and was the last surviving residence of Joplin. Joplin was called the "king of ragtime" and was one of the most creative black musicians of the late nineteenth and early twentieth centuries. Joplin was born in Texarkana, Texas but he left home to earn a living when he was 14 years of age. Joplin played piano in the St. Louis and Sedalia, Missouri area in such places as saloons, gambling parlors, and vaudeville houses. His residence was declared a National Historic Landmark by the Department of Interior on December 8, 1976.

Montana

Big Horn Station
Fort Manuel Marker

Captain William Clark and his party, including the lively and valuable slave York, camped at this site on July 26, 1806, a year before Manuel Lisa established Montana's first trading post. This site, too, was chosen by Major Andrew Henry as the Rocky Mountain Fur Company's first trading post. Leader of that expedition was Edward Rose, another of the famed black mountainmen and explorers active in the territory.

Crow Agency
Custer Battlefield National Monument—Reno-Benteen Battlefield National Monument

These two monuments commemorate the famed Battle of the Little Big Horn, in which three batteries commanded by General George Armstrong Custer were slaughtered on June 25, 1876 by a group of Indian tribes led by Chief Sitting Bull.

The first skirmish that day involved an advance party under the command of Major Marcus Reno. One of the first to fall was Isaiah Dorman, a black who had lived among the Sioux and was serving as an army interpreter. Dorman was known to the Indians as "Teat," or sometimes referred to as the "black white man."

Among those killed at the Battle of Little Big Horn was Isaiah Dorman, a black army interpreter who had lived among the Sioux. According to one account, Sitting Bull himself ordered that the body of the dying black man not be mutilated in token of their past friendship.

According to one account, the dying black was found by Sitting Bull himself, who ordered that his body not be mutilated in any way.

Fort Shaw
Site of Fort Shaw

This military outpost was founded in 1867 and named after Colonel Robert Gould Shaw, commandant of the heroic 54th Massachusetts who fell during his unit's spirited, valiant, and unsuccessful charge against the breastworks of Fort Wagner during the Civil War. Fort Shaw was the home base of the 25th Infantry, one of the units sent into the wilderness to protect the territory's few pioneering settlers and indefatigable miners from Indian attacks.

Pompey's Pillar

This pillar, named for the Indian Pomp, was discovered by Captain William Clark of the famed Lewis and Clark expedition. One of the members of Clark's group was a slave named York, a giant of a man who proved to be an invaluable asset to Clark—not only because of his prodigious strength and endurance, but also because he got along so well with the Indians, who were impressed with his dancing ability.

Nevada

Reno
The Jim Beckwourth Trail

In the early days of pioneer settlement, the barren stretch of trail between Reno and the California line was the last obstacle to be overcome before passing through the gateway to the Golden West. The original trail was laid out by the loquacious and cantankerous Jim Beckwourth, one of the legendary mountain men whose exploits lend spice and sparkle to the Western saga. Beckwourth Pass helped put the city of Reno on the map, particularly after the railroad decided to put a station there and began selling acreage in the neighborhood. Reno was later the site of the famous Jim Jeffries-Jack Johnson heavyweight fight, won by the famed black champion who had bested Tommy Burns in Australia, in 1908. Johnson held the crown for seven years, losing it to Jess Willard on a 26-round knockout.

New Hampshire

Jaffrey
Amos Fortune Grave

The Amos Fortune Grave is the resting place of an eighteenth-century black slave who purchased his free-

Indians did not believe Lewis and Clark's slave York was black. They tried to rub off his color.

dom in 1770 at the age of 60 and went on to become one of the leading citizens of Jaffrey, his adopted hometown.

Nine years later, Fortune was able to buy freedom for his wife, Violet Baldwin, and his adopted daughter, Celyndia. In 1781, he moved to Jaffrey and set himself up as a tanner, employing both black and white apprentices. In 1795, six years before his death, Fortune founded the Jaffrey Social Library and, in his will, directed that money be left to the church and to the local school district.

The school fund begun by Fortune is still in existence, having grown from $233 to the present total of $1,600. Proceeds from the fund are used to provide annual prizes for high-school debating and oratorical contests.

Each year during July and August, the Amos Fortune Forum is held as a memorial to the Old Meeting House where the ex-slave attended church services. Both Fortune and his wife lie in the meetinghouse burial ground.

Fortune's freedom papers and several receipt slips for the sale of his leather are on file at the Jaffrey Public Library. Similarly, the Fortune house and barn still stand intact.

New Jersey

Red Bank
T. Thomas Fortune House
94 West Bergen Place

From 1901 to 1915 the West Bergen Place address was the home of T. Thomas Fortune, the crusading black journalist who in his newspapers articulated the cause of Negro rights at the turn of the twentieth century. Fortune was born a slave in Marianna, Florida. He was freed by proclamation in 1865. He received training as a printer as a youngster and founded the *New York Age* newspaper. Fortune was a close friend and advisor to Booker T. Washington. The Fortune house was designated a National Historic Landmark on December 8, 1976.

Newark
The Newark Museum

This museum, located at 43–49 Washington Street, owns the paintings of such famous black artists as Henry Ossawa Tanner (*The Good Shepherd*), Charles W. White (*Sojourner Truth and Booker T. Washing-*

ton), and Hale Woodruff (*Poor Man's Cotton*). Tanner was a student under Thomas Eakins and spent most of his life abroad. He excelled in religious subjects and sacred themes. White and Woodruff are among the most prominent black painters at work today.

New Mexico

Columbus
Fort Stanton

It was from Fort Stanton that black troopers of the 9th Cavalry fanned out in pursuit of the Apache chief Victorio and his warriors in 1879. Two black troopers—Sergeants Thomas Boyne and John Denny—were awarded Medals of Honor for heroism displayed during this engagement with the Apaches. At least one other frontier military post in New Mexico was the scene of a fierce battle involving Victorio: Fort Tularosa. There, in May 1880, Sergeant George Jordan and a detachment of 25 cavalrymen held off the Apache chieftain and 100 braves. Jordan, too, was awarded the Medal of Honor for gallantry under fire.

The Pancho Villa Expedition

After one of his patented border raids had resulted in the burning of half of Columbus and the loss of many lives, Pancho Villa and his bandit army so aroused the ire of the U.S. government that it dispatched a punitive expedition into Mexico to track down Villa and eliminate him. "Black Jack" Pershing was in command of the 10th U.S. Cavalry during the strenuous journey. With only two days' rations in their knapsacks, the black troopers were forced to live off the land while in pursuit of the canny and fearless Mexican outlaw. The 10th engaged the Villistas at Carrizal, Mexico, and lost 10 men in a bloody skirmish. The expedition then returned to Fort Huachuca, its permanent base.

Folsom
Archaeological Folsom Man Discovery

In the spring of 1925 George Majunkin, a black cowhand, while riding the range and arroyos in the northeast corner of New Mexico near the town of Folsom, chanced to see a glittering object in the back of a tree. In examining the oddity, he took out his knife and began to pry out a number of bone fragments and a spear tip. With acute curiosity, he sent his find to J. D. Figgers, director of the Colorado Museum of Natural History, who determined that they were the bones of a bison that became extinct some 10,000 years ago. Figgers directed excavations at the site of Majunkins find and established proof that the weapon

Troopers of the 10th Cavalry photographed during their expedition to capture Pancho Villa's rebel band. Since speed and flexibility were essential the cavalrymen were forced to live off the land in Mexico's desolate mountains for several months.

and the animal belonged together and that man had been in that area over 10,000 years ago.

Lincoln
Old Court House

During the Lincoln County Cattle War of 1877–1878, Billy the Kid, the notorious outlaw, was held in custody at the Old Court House, now a frontier museum. Black cowhands were involved on both sides of this struggle and, on one occasion, a group of black cavalrymen surrounded Billy the Kid during a particularly bloody battle. The outlaw, however, managed to escape the ambush. (Incidentally, it was a black trooper who delivered Governor Lew Wallace's proclamation declaring a cessation to hostilities and the granting of amnesty to all those involved.)

Zuni
Zuni Pueblo

Zuni Pueblo was discovered in 1539 by Estevanico, a Moorish slave who was one of the original party of Spanish explorers to land in Tampa Bay in 1528. After a succession of disasters, the party was ultimately reduced to four (including Estevanico) who, marooned on the Texas shore near what is now Galveston, were soon captured and enslaved by Indians. After seven years in captivity, Estevanico and the others escaped to New Spain.

Having heard of the legend of the Seven Cities of Gold, reputed to be located in the Southwest, Estevanico signed on as an advance scout for an expedition led by a Father Marco. Often traveling ahead of the main party, Estevanico sent most of his messages back via friendly Indians. His last message—a giant cross emblematic of a major discovery—led the expedition to the Zuni Pueblo, which Estevanico apparently thought was part of the legendary Seven Cities. By the time the expedition arrived, however, the suspicious Zuni had already put Estevanico to death.

Today, Estevanico is credited with the discovery of a territory which comprises the states of Arizona and New Mexico.

New York

Albany
Emancipation Proclamation

The New York State Library houses President Abraham Lincoln's original draft of the preliminary Emancipation Proclamation issued in September 1862. It was purchased by Gerrit Smith, a wealthy abolitionist and patron of the famed revolutionary John Brown.

The January 1, 1863 version of the proclamation resides in the National Archives of Washington, D.C. The draft of this document was destroyed in the Chicago fire of 1871.

Auburn
Harriet Tubman Home

The Harriet Tubman Home stands as a monument to the woman who is believed to have led some 300 slaves to freedom via the Underground Railroad.

Miss Tubman settled in this home at the close of the Civil War—years after it had outlived its original function as a major way station on the northbound freedom route of fugitive slaves. In 1953 the house was restored at a cost of $21,000. Born a slave in Maryland, Miss Tubman fled at the age of 25, only to return South at least 19 times to lead others to freedom. Rewards of up to $40,000 were offered for her capture, but she was never arrested, nor did she

After escaping from slavery herself, Harriet Tubman led at least 19 missions into the South to conduct hundreds of others to freedom on the Underground Railroad.

ever lose one of her passengers in transit. During the Civil War, she served as a spy for Union forces.

Harriet Tubman Home for the Aged
180–182 South Street

The Home for the Aged was established in 1908 for aged and indigent Negroes by the most famous "conductor" on the Underground Railroad. Harriet Tubman had led more than 300 slaves to freedom. The home was declared a National Historic Landmark by the Department of Interior on May 30, 1974.

Greenburgh (Westchester County)
Villa Lewaro

Designed by the noted black architect Vertner Woodson Tandy for Madame C. J. Walker, the successful cosmetics manufacturer, Villa Lewaro illustrates the achievements of Negroes in both architecture and business. The Villa Lewaro was declared a National Historic Landmark on May 11, 1976.

New York City
African Methodist Episcopal Zion Church
151 West 136th Street

The African Methodist Episcopal Zion (AMEZ) Church was dedicated in 1801 on a plot of land located at Church and Leonard Streets in New York City. A year later, the trustees of the church signed an agreement with the General Conference of the Methodist Episcopal Church, thereby consenting to place themselves under the jurisdiction of the bishops from this latter church. The conference was also given the right to appoint a preacher for the black church. By 1820, however, the AMEZ Church had found this arrangement so unsatisfactory that it bolted from the General Conference. At this juncture, the leader of the black congregation was a former slave named Peter Williams. The first three ordained black ministers of the new church were Abraham Thompson, James Scott, and Thomas Miller, while the first exhorter (an unordained person authorized to preach) was William Miller. James Varick was the first bishop.

Amsterdam News
2340 Frederick Douglass Boulevard

The Amsterdam News, now New York City's largest Negro-owned newspaper as well as the largest weekly community paper in the United States, was founded on December 4, 1909 in the home of James H. Anderson (132 West 65th Street). At that time one of only 50 black "news sheets" in the country, the *Amsterdam*

News had a staff of 10, consisted of six printed pages, and sold for 2¢ a copy. Since then, the paper has been printed at several Harlem addresses.

Altogether, the *Amsterdam News* must be considered one of the most vital organs of information in any campaign to reach blacks in New York City. Its pages have historically reflected the interests and concerns of black Americans. It is currently the largest circulating black weekly in the country and publishes on Thursday of each week. The New York Amsterdam News Building, at 2293 Seventh Avenue, was designated a landmark on May 11, 1976 by the Department of Interior.

Apollo Theater
125th Street, between 7th and 8th Avenues

The Apollo Theater in Harlem, an entertainment mecca for all races, is one of the last great vaudeville houses in the United States. For 50 weeks of every year, the Apollo presents live entertainment—featuring rising young stars as well as established black professionals who play there not so much for the financial reward as for the importance of exposure to a popular audience.

Louis Armstrong House
3456 107th Street, Corona, Queens

For years this was the home of Louis Armstrong, the famous jazz musician whose talents entertained millions throughout the world. Whenever Louie was at his Corona home on a break from his concert dates, he was a favorite with neighborhood youngsters. He would often entertain them in his home and on the street. His wife, Lucille, still lives at the address. The house was designated a historical landmark on May 11, 1976 by the Department of Interior.

Bethel A.M.E. Church
60 West 132nd Street

In the autumn of 1819 Bishop Richard Allen of Philadelphia dispatched William Lambert to New York City for the purpose of organizing an African Methodist Episcopal church there. Mother Bethel Church, the oldest and largest AME church in Manhattan, came into being both as a religious body and as a kind of protest organization.

Booker T. Washington Plaque

Booker T. Washington, educator and founder of Tuskegee Institute, is the only black honored by a plaque in the Hall of Fame, New York University.

Ralph Bunche House
115–125 Grosvenor Road, Kew Gardens, Queens

The home of Ralph Bunche, the distinguished Afro-American diplomat and scholar who served as Undersecretary of the United Nations and who received the Nobel Peace Prize for his 1949 contribution to peace in the Middle East. The house was designated a National Historic Landmark on May 11, 1976 by the Department of Interior.

Calvary Baptist Church
111–10 New York Boulevard, Jamaica, Queens

Reverend Walter S. Pinn has been pastor of Calvary Baptist Church since 1946, at which time it was still housed in a tiny, one-story building with a seating capacity of only 100. Today it is the largest black congregation on Long Island, meeting in a beautiful, spacious structure which can seat some 2,000 persons. The new building contains several classrooms and meeting halls, a wedding chapel, and a modern kitchen. There are two Sunday services, supplemented by a 150-voice chorale under the direction of Mr. Samuel Daniels.

Cornerstone Baptist Church
Lewis and Madison Streets, Brooklyn

The Cornerstone Baptist Church, a congregation now boasting over 5,000 members, was founded on September 10, 1917 by eight faithful churchgoers assembled for communal worship in a single room of a private residence at 933 DeKalb Avenue, Brooklyn, New York. The church began to expand rapidly under the pastorship of Reverend T. W. Fentress, who linked it in 1932 with the Unity Baptist Church.

Will Marion Cook House
221 West 138th Street

This was the home of the early-twentieth-century black composer Will Marion Cook, whom Duke Ellington called "the master of all masters of our people." Cook was born in Washington, D.C. He began studying violin at 13 years of age, and at 15 he won a scholarship to study with Joseph Joachim at the Berlin Conservatory. Syncopated ragtime music was introduced to theatergoers in New York City for the first time with Cook's operetta *Clorinda*. The house was designated a National Historic Landmark by the Department of Interior on May 11, 1976.

Edward Kennedy "Duke" Ellington Residence
935 St. Nicholas Avenue, Apt. 4A

When Duke Ellington recorded "Take the A Train" to Harlem, he meant just that because the A train express stops on St. Nicholas Avenue and it was the quickest and fastest way for Ellington to get home. The St. Nicholas Avenue address was the long-term residence of Ellington, who has been regarded by critics as the most creative Afro-American composer of the twentieth century. The residence was designated a National Historic Landmark by the Department of Interior on May 11, 1976.

Franks Restaurant
312 West 125th Street

The largest black-owned restaurant in Harlem is Franks, run by the eminent East Coast restauranteur Lloyd Von Blaine and the equally well-known caterer Selwyn Joseph. Franks has been *the* place for quality dining along Harlem's "main stem" for over 50 years.

Fraunces Tavern
Broad and Pearl Streets

One of the most famous landmarks in New York City, Fraunces Tavern was bought in 1762 from a wealthy Huguenot by Samuel Fraunces, a West Indian of black and French extraction. In those days, Fraunces called his establishment the Queen's Head Tavern. Before the Revolutionary War began it served as a kind of meetingplace for numerous patriots already chafing under the tyranny of King George III.

On April 24, 1774, the Sons of Liberty and the Vigilance Committee met at the tavern to map out much of the strategy later used during the war. George Washington himself was a frequenter of the tavern, as were many of his senior officers. Washington's association with Fraunces continued for a number of years, with Fraunces eventually coming to be known as "Steward of the Household" in New York City. It was at Fraunces Tavern, in fact, that Washington took leave of his trusted officers in 1783 before retiring to Mount Vernon.

Much of the tavern's original furnishings and decor are still intact. The third floor—now a museum—contains several Revolutionary War artifacts, while on the fourth floor one can find a historical library featuring paintings by John Ward Dunsmore. A restaurant, patronized by leading New York citizens as well as by tourists from all over the country, is maintained on the ground floor.

Restored to its Revolutionary elegance, Fraunces Tavern is a popular New York restaurant.

Freedom National Bank
275 West 125th Street

Freedom National Bank is Harlem's first black-chartered, black-run commercial bank. Founded in 1965, it already has 10,000 customers and assets of over 10 million dollars—a figure which, by comparison with other banks maintaining branches in Harlem (Chase Manhattan, Citibank, Manufacturers Hanover, Chemical), is small.

The most significant thing about this bank, however, is the fact that the Harlemite has come to refer to it as *his* bank, a symbolic phrase for residents of an area in which most fixed property and real estate continue to be controlled by white people. A former chairman of the board of Freedom National is Jackie Robinson, the baseball great. The president is William R. Hudgins, who has lived and worked in Harlem for the past 37 years.

(The first bank in Harlem—the Dunbar Bank—was founded by John D. Rockefeller in 1928 but folded 10 years later. In 1949 the Carver Federal Savings and Loan Association was established, with Hudgins serving as a member of the board. Today, Carver has two branches—one in Manhattan, the other in Brooklyn—and assets totaling some 30 million dollars.)

Matthew Henson Residence
Dunbar Apartments, 246 West 150th Street

This was a late home of Matthew Henson, a black explorer who served as an assistant to Robert E. Peary and whose best known achievement came in 1909 when he became the first man to reach the North Pole. The residence was designated a National Historic Landmark by the Department of Interior on May 15, 1975.

Hotel Theresa
2090 7th Avenue (corner of 125th Street)

Built in 1913, the Hotel Theresa was once a luxury hotel serving white clientele from lower Manhattan and accommodating "white only" dinner patrons in its luxurious Skyline Room. In 1936, a corporation headed by Love B. Woods tried to take over the hotel and transform it into a black business establishment. This move failed when Seidenberg Estates, the realtors, set a price on it beyond the reach of the group. Woods did eventually manage to purchase the hotel. (Its most publicized guest in recent years has been Cuban premier Fidel Castro.) Nowadays, the hotel has lost some of its original lustre.

James Weldon Johnson Residence
187 West 135th Street

From 1925 to 1938, this was the home of James Weldon Johnson, the versatile black composer of popular songs, as well as being a poet, writer, general secretary of the NAACP and a civil rights activist. Johnson is best known for composing such songs as "Congo Love Song," "Since You Went Away," and "Lift Every Voice and Sing." "Lift Every Voice and Sing" has been called the national anthem for black people. Johnson was born in Jacksonville, Florida and did graduate study at Columbia University. The residence was named a National Historic Landmark by the Department of Interior on May 11, 1976.

Maiden Lane—First Slave Revolt in New York

In 1712 on Maiden Lane and William Street the first organized slave revolt in New York City occurred.

Approximately 30 slaves organized and attempted to fight their way to freedom. Many people were injured in the melee which ensued as the slaves took to the woods with the militia close behind. Surrounded in the woods, several slaves committed suicide. The rest were captured and subsequently executed.

Claude McKay Residence
180 West 135th Street

From 1941 to 1946 this was the residence of the black poet and writer Claude McKay, who has often been called the father of the Harlem Renaissance. McKay was born in Jamaica, British West Indies and was in Kingston's constabulary prior to coming to the United States. His residence was named a National Historic Landmark by the Department of Interior on December 8, 1976.

Messiah Baptist Church
866 Sutter Avenue, Brooklyn

Messiah Baptist Church has been in existence since March 1965, having been founded by its current pastor, Reverend Elijah Pope. Starting with a group of 15, the congregation has already grown to over 200. The dedicatory sermon was preached by Reverend Sandy F. Ray, pastor of Brooklyn's famous Cornerstone Baptist Church.

Reverend Pope has already organized several auxiliaries, as well as a Boy Scout troop and a street block association.

Florence Mills House
220 West 135th Street

This was the home of the popular black singer who in the 1920s achieved stardom on Broadway and in Europe. Following that, she became a symbol of success for black Americans. The Mills residence was designated a National Historic Landmark by the Department of Interior on December 8, 1976.

Paul Robeson Residence
555 Edgecomb Avenue

This was the residence of the famous black actor and singer Paul Robeson. In the 1940s and the 1950s, Robeson suffered public condemnation for his political sympathies while he was widely acclaimed for his artistic talents. The residence was named a National Historic Landmark on December 8, 1976 by the Department of Interior.

John Roosevelt "Jackie" Robinson Residence
5224 Tilden Street, Brooklyn

This was the home of Jackie Robinson, the baseball player who in 1947 became the first black to play in the major leagues. His signing to a baseball contract broke the color barrier to full black participation in professional sports. While a Brooklyn Dodger, Robinson lived for many years in the same borough of New York City where he played baseball. The residence was designated a National Historic Landmark on May 11, 1976.

St. George's Episcopal Church
Third Avenue and First Street

This was the home church of Harry Thacker Burleigh, the black composer, arranger, and singer who helped establish the Negro spiritual as an integral part of American culture. The church was designated a National Historical Landmark by the Department of Interior on December 8, 1976.

Schomburg Collection of Negro Literature and History
103 West 135th Street

The Schomburg Collection of Negro Literature and History is a library and archive of materials devoted to black life around the world.

This collection is built around the private library of Arthur A. Schomburg, a Puerto Rican of African descent. It contains books, pamphlets, manuscripts, photographs, art objects, and recordings which cover virtually every aspect of black life—from ancient Africa to present-day black America.

Among the treasured items in the collection are:

1. The work of America's first black poet—Jupiter Hammon's Address to the blacks in the State of New York (1787).

2. Manuscript poems and early editions of the works of Phillis Wheatley.

3. Copies of the 1792 and 1793 Almanacs of Benjamin Banneker.

4. The scrapbook of Ira Aldridge, the black Shakespearean actor who achieved fame in Europe in the nineteenth century.

5. *Clotel,* the first novel by an American black (William Wells Brown).

Material in the Schomburg is not circulated but can be used or viewed in the library. G. K. Hall and Co., 97 Oliver Street, Boston, Massachusetts has published a nine-volume edition of the *Dictionary Catalog of the Schomburg Collection of Black Literature and History,* priced at $605.00.

Sugar Hill, Harlem

Sugar Hill is a handsome residential section in uptown Harlem. It is bordered on the west by Amsterdam Avenue, on the north by 160th Street, on the east by Colonial Park, and on the South by 145th Street. An area of tall apartment buildings and private homes, it is peopled largely by middle-class blacks, sometimes referred to as the *black bourgeoisie.* Its only counterparts in the area of central Harlem are Riverton and Lenox Terrace.

North Elba
John Brown's Grave

Just six miles south of Lake Placid on Rte. 86A, John Brown's Grave is located on a farm he purchased after he had left Ohio. Brown lived there until he joined the free-soil fight in Kansas.

The farm was part of 100,000 acres set aside for both freedmen and slaves by Gerritt Smith, a wealthy abolitionist. Smith hoped to build an independent community peopled by former slaves who had learned farming and other trades. Brown joined Smith in the venture, but the idea failed to take hold and was eventually abandoned.

Ogdensburg
Remington Art Memorial

Artist/journalist Frederic Remington is easily the greatest visual chronicler of the saga and splendor of the Old West. Remington fashioned several durable portraits and sketches of black cavalrymen in action in the field, on bivouac, and even during ceremonial exercises. Remington was also a correspondent during the Spanish-American War, and did a painting entitled *The Charge of the Rough Riders at San Juan Hill.* The painting shows only one of the many blacks who accompanied Teddy Roosevelt's men on their celebrated charge. The Ogdensburg Museum houses the Remington portrait in its permanent collection.

Rochester
Frederick Douglass Monument

New York Governor Theodore Roosevelt dedicated the Frederick Douglass Monument in 1899. The noted black abolitionist had helped organize all-black volunteer regiments during the Civil War and saw two of his sons volunteer for duty.

Frederick Douglass.

South Granville
Lemuel Haynes House
Route 149

The house, located in Washington County, was built in 1793. It was the later-day home of Lemuel Haynes, the first black ordained minister in the United States. Haynes was also the first black minister to a white congregation. The South Granville homesite was declared a National Historic Landmark by the Department of Interior on May 15, 1975.

Ticonderoga
Fort Ticonderoga

Leading the Revolutionary War assault on the fort at Ticonderoga were Ethan Allen and his famed Green Mountain Boys, many of whom were blacks, including Lemuel Haynes, Primus Black, and Epheram Blackman. After the American victory, some of the cannons were transported to Boston, where they were instrumental in providing heavy weapons support for General George Washington's thrust into, and capture of, the city.

North Carolina

Durham
North Carolina Mutual Life Insurance Company
114–116 West Parish Street

The Parish Street address is the home office of North Carolina Mutual Life Insurance Company, which is a black-managed enterprise founded in 1898. The company achieved financial success in an age of Jim Crow.

The British storming Fort Ticonderoga after it was taken by American patriots, many of whom were black.

The site was declared a National Historical Landmark by the Department of Interior on May 15, 1975.

Milton
The Yellow Tavern
Also Known as Union Tavern

For more than 30 years, the Yellow Tavern was the workshop of Tom Day, one of the great black artisans and furniture makers of the Deep South prior to the Civil War. Day began making hand-wrought mahogany furniture in 1818 and within five years accumulated enough money to convert the old Yellow Tavern into a miniature factory. Both white apprentices and black slaves were taught this skilled trade under his coveted tutelage. Day's artistry was so revered by the citizens of Milton that they went to great pains to secure a special dispensation from a North Carolina law which made it illegal for any free black or mulatto to migrate into the state. The dispensation was needed because Day had married Acquilla Wilson in 1829, two years after the law took effect. The legislature actually went so far as to pass a law which exempted Day and his wife from the "fines and penalties of the Act of 1827."

Day also found an ingenious way to integrate the Presbyterian church in Milton by offering to replace the worn-down mahogany pews on the main floor of the church—in return for the "privilege" of sitting in them, rather than in the gallery, during services.

Day built the pews, but he confounded the parishioners by using maple instead of mahogany. The church, the pews, the Yellow Tavern, and Tom Day's home and grave have all survived and are accessible to this day. The Yellow Tavern was declared a National Historic Landmark by the Department of Interior on May 15, 1975.

Raleigh
John Chavis Memorial Park
E. Lenoir at Worth Street

This park is named after John Chavis, a black educator and preacher who founded an interracial school in Raleigh which later numbered among its graduates several important public figures, including senators, congressmen, and governors. As a result of the abortive Nat Turner slave rebellion in 1831, however, blacks were barred from preaching in North Carolina, obliging Chavis to retire from the pulpit. He died in 1838.

Ohio

Akron
John Brown Monument

The John Brown Monument was built in honor of the fiery abolitionist whose ill-fated Harpers Ferry revolt led to his conviction for treason and execution by hanging in 1859.

Harriet Beecher Stowe.

Cincinnati
Harriet Beecher Stowe Home

The Harriet Beecher Stowe Home has been preserved as a memorial to the internationally known author of *Uncle Tom's Cabin.*

Taft Museum

An exceptionally fine black American artist, Robert S. Duncanson, took up residence in Cincinnati sometime during the 1840s. A friend and patron of Duncanson was the philanthropist Nicholas Longworth, who commissioned him to do the decorative work on the walls of the main entrance of the mansion. Duncanson completed a series of eight murals and several pieces for over doors. The building was sold to the Tafts of Cincinnati and later became the Taft Museum of Art.

Dayton
Paul Laurence Dunbar Home
219 Summit Street

The Paul Laurence Dunbar Home has been preserved much as the poet left it at the time of his death in 1906, just prior to his thirty-fourth birthday. Along with his personal effects, several original manuscripts can be seen.

Dunbar, the first black poet after Phillis Wheatley to gain anything approaching a national reputation

in the United States, was also the first to concentrate on dialect poetry and exclusively black themes. His first collection of poetry, *Oak and Ivory,* was published before he was 20. By 1896 his book *Majors and Minors* had won critical favor in a *Harper's Weekly* review. Dunbar contracted tuberculosis in 1899 and was in failing health until his death on February 9, 1906.

John Mercer Langston House
207 East College Street

This was the home of John Mercer Langston, the first black American to be elected to public office in 1855. Langston later served the Freedman's Bureau and was the first dean of the Howard University Law School. He was also a minister to Haiti. The house was designated a National Historical Landmark by the Department of Interior on May 15, 1975.

Oberlin
Oberlin College

Before the Civil War, Oberlin was one of the centers of underground abolitionist planning and a haven for activists of every stamp and hue. On one occasion, 20 Oberlin villagers actually snatched away a black fugitive who was being returned to his Kentucky owner by Federal agents. Later, three of John Brown's raiding party at Harper's Ferry were identified as blacks from Oberlin.

After the war, Oberlin was able to devote more time to its stated mission: providing quality education to all regardless of race. Among the distinguished alumni of Oberlin was Blanche Kelso Bruce, who served a full term in the U.S. Senate (1875–1881). Another Oberlin graduate was Moses "Fleet" Walker, who once played baseball with Toledo of the American Association, then recognized as a major league. Jackie Robinson was the first black player to play major league baseball in the accepted modern sense of that term.

Put-in-Bay
Battle of Lake Erie Memorial National Monument

The memorial draws attention to the Battle of Lake Erie, fought during the War of 1812, and to the impatient and impetuous American sea captain who became immortal by virtue of his defeat of the British: Oliver Hazard Perry. Perry had at first criticized his superior, Commodore Isaac Chauncey, for sending him a motley lot of replacements, including blacks. After the actual battle, however, these same men prompted him to revise his original estimate and praise the black seamen for being "absolutely insensible to danger."

Ripley
John Rankin House Museum

An Underground Railroad station prior to the Civil War, the John Rankin House Museum is believed to have been the haven of the fugitive slave on whose story the novelist Harriet Beecher Stowe based the flight incident in *Uncle Tom's Cabin.*

Upper Sanduskey
Wyandotte Indian Mission Church

John Stewart, self-appointed missionary to the Wyandotte Indians, was of French, black, and Indian stock. His missionary labors among this tribe began in 1816. He was assisted in this work by Jonathan Poynter, a black who had been raised by the Wyandottes and acted as Stewart's interpreter.

Stewart converted the Indians to Christianity with the help of a fine tenor voice which he used to good advantage in singing them the spirituals and hymns he had learned in Virginia. He died in 1823, one year before the construction of his church was completed.

When the Wyandottes signed the treaty which resulted in their move to Kansas, one of its conditions was that the church remain within the Methodist Episcopal Conference. In 1960, the latter listed the Stewart grave and the missionary church among the 10 official shrines of American Methodism.

Wilberforce
Colonel Charles Young House
Columbus Pike between Clifton and
Stevenson Roads

The Columbus Pike address was the residence of the highest ranking black officer in World War I and the first black military attaché. Colonel Charles Young was the son of former slaves and was born in Mays Lick, Kentucky. The Army had declared Young unfit physically because of high blood pressure, so to prove that he was physically fit, he rode horseback 500 miles from Wilberforce to Washington, D.C. in 16 days. The Army, however, still stuck by its ruling. The house was declared a National Historical Landmark by the Department of Interior on May 30, 1974.

Oklahoma

Boley
Boley Historic District

This is the largest of the Negro towns established in Oklahoma to provide black Americans with the oppor-

Battle of Lake Erie.

tunity for self-government in an era of white supremacy and segregation. The Boley Historic District was designated a National Historic Landmark by the Department of Interior on May 15, 1975.

Lawton
Fort Sill

Units of the 10th Cavalry and the 24th Infantry were among those which served at Fort Sill in the aftermath of the Civil War. Like most black troopers in the territories, they did escort and patrol duty, but they were often called upon to round up cattle thieves and whiskey runners. It was to Fort Sill that the black cavalrymen of the 10th escorted the famed Apache chieftain Geronimo. Geronimo spent his last days at the fort and is buried in the Apache cemetery.

Marland (*Kay County*)
101 Ranch Historic District

This is a large cattle ranch and home base of the 101 Wild West Show, which featured Bill Pickett, the well-known black cowboy who invented steer wrestling and who was elected to the Cowboy Hall of Fame. The ranch was established in 1879. On May 15, 1975, the ranch was declared a National Historic Landmark.

Bill Pickett of the 101 Ranch.

Ponca City
101 Ranch (five miles south of Ponca City on U.S. Rte. 77)

During the latter part of the nineteenth century, the 101 Ranch was one of the largest and most famous in the West. In its prime, it employed several black cowhands, the most celebrated of whom was Bill Pickett.

The originator of the art of bulldogging or steer wrestling, Pickett also perfected a unique style unlike any used by current rodeo participants. He would leap from his horse, grab the steer around the neck or by the horns, and then sink his teeth into the animal's upper lip. In Mexico City, he once wrestled a fighting bull for a full six minutes to win a bet. In March 1932, though then in his seventies, Pickett was still active—the last of the original 101 hands. He died a month later, on April 21, 1932, after being kicked by a horse, and was buried on a knoll near the White Eagle Monument.

Pennsylvania

Erie
Harry T. Burleigh Birthplace Marker

A friend of famed Czech composer Dvorak, and a composer/arranger in his own right, Harry T. Burleigh was born in 1866. Burleigh set to music many of the stirring poems of Walt Whitman and arranged such unforgettable spirituals as "Deep River." He died in 1949.

Lancaster
Thaddeus Stevens Grave

When Thaddeus Stevens was dying, he was attended

Thaddeus Stevens, a dedicated antislavery spokesman.

by Lydia Smith and two nuns from a charity hospital for blacks that Stevens had helped with a grant of $30,000 from Congress.

Upon his death five black and three white pallbearers escorted the body to Washington, D.C., where it lay in state on the same catafalque that had borne the body of Lincoln and was guarded by black soldiers of a Massachusetts Regiment. Two days later the body was returned to Lancaster, where over 10,000 blacks attended the funeral, and was buried in Schreiner's Cemetery, a cemetery for blacks. Stevens, a white abolitionist and civil rights activist, in his will, rejected burial in a white cemetery because of the segregation policy.

Lower Merion Township (Montgomery County)
James A. Bland Grave

In Montgomery County lies the grave of black composer James A. Bland, who wrote "Carry Me Back to Old Virginny," now the state song of Virginia.

Philadelphia
Frances Ellen Watkins Harper House
1006 Bainbridge Street

This was the home of the black writer and social activist Frances Ellen Watkins Harper, who participated in the nineteenth-century abolitionist, Negro rights, woman's suffrage, and temperance movements. The house was named a National Historical Landmark on December 8, 1976.

Mother Bethel African Methodist Episcopal Church
419 S. Sixth Street

The Mother Bethel African Methodist Episcopal (AME) Church was the fourth church to be erected on the site where Richard Allen and Absalom Jones founded the Free African Society in 1787. This later grew into the AME, one of the largest black religious denominations in the United States.

Allen, the first black bishop, was born a slave and became a minister and circuit rider after winning his freedom. In 1814 he and James Forten organized a force of 2,500 free blacks to defend Philadelphia against the British. Sixteen years later, Allen organized the first black convention in Philadelphia and was instrumental in getting the group to adopt a strong platform denouncing slavery and encouraging abolitionist activities. Allen died in 1831 and was buried in a basement vault at Mother Bethel's.

As for Forten, he had been born free in 1766 and, despite his youth, served aboard a Philadelphia privateer during the Revolutionary War. In 1800 he was

Mother Bethel Chapel stands on the site where the A.M.E. Church was founded.

one of the signers of a petition requesting Congress to alter the Fugitive Slave Act of 1793. Opposed to the idea of resettling slaves in Africa, Forten chaired an 1817 meeting held at Bethel to protest existing colonization schemes. In 1833, he put up the funds which William Lloyd Garrison needed to found *The Liberator*.

After his death, Forten's work was continued by his offspring, who remained active in the abolitionist cause throughout the Civil War, and on behalf of the freedmen during Reconstruction. The Forten home was a meeting place for many of the leading figures in the movement.

The church was named a National Historic Landmark by the Department of Interior on May 30, 1974.

Negro Soldiers Monument
Lansdowne Drive, West Fairmount Park

The Negro Soldiers Monument was erected by the state of Pennsylvania in 1934 to pay tribute to her fallen black soldiers.

Henry O. Tanner Homesite
2903 West Diamond Street

This was the boyhood home of the late nineteenth- and early twentieth-century black expatriate painter Henry O. Tanner, whose work earned recognition in Europe and the United States. Tanner was born in Pittsburgh, Pennsylvania. He was the first black to be elected to the National Academy of Design. The homesite was designated a historical landmark by the Department of Interior on May 11, 1976.

Valley Forge
Valley Forge State Park

Blacks were among those who endured the winter hardships of Valley Forge with the bedraggled Continental Army of George Washington in 1777. One of the blacks who died was Phillip Field, a New Yorker; among those who survived was Salem Poor, the very same black who had fought at Bunker Hill as a member of Colonel Frye's Massachusetts Regiment and been officially cited for having "behaved like an experienced officer, as well as an excellent soldier." The citation concluded as follows: ". . . in the person of this said black centers a brave and gallant soldier."

Rhode Island

Portsmouth
Site of the Battle of Rhode Island

This was the site of the only Revolutionary War battle in which an all-black unit, the 1st Rhode Island Regi-

ment, participated. The unit joined John Sullivan's army in attacking British garrison troops in Newport. The site was named a National Historic Landmark on May 30, 1974.

South Carolina

Beaufort
Robert Smalls House
511 Prince Street

Robert Smalls was a former slave who served in the state legislature and in Congress. He had lived in Beaufort both as a slave and as a free man. Smalls fought for black rights while in office. His house was designated a National Historic Landmark on May 30, 1973.

Charleston
Denmark Vesey House
56 Bull Street

This was the residence of Denmark Vesey, a free black Charleston carpenter whose 1822 plans for a slave insurrection illustrated Negro resistance to slavery. The Denmark Vesey House was declared a National Historic Landmark on May 11, 1976.

Fort Sumter National Monument

Site of the first shelling of the Civil War on April 12, 1861, Fort Sumter is an important site in black history due to the daring exploits of a black coastal pilot, Robert Smalls. On May 13, 1862, Smalls took

Robert Smalls and the captured gunboat Planter.

control of the Confederate steamboat *Planter,* loading into it his family and a few other brave crewmen who endorsed his resourceful and cunning escape plan. Smalls sailed the ship past the Confederate checkpoints, imitating the captain at each vital juncture during which he was being observed from a distance. Once beyond the reach of Confederate shore batteries, Smalls hoisted the white flag of surrender, and delivered the ship into Union hands. Smalls was later elected to several terms as U.S. Congressman from South Carolina.

Charleston County
Stono River Slave Rebellion Site
Rantowles Vicinity

This was the site of the serious slave insurrection in the Colonial period. It was during that time when some 100 escaped slaves burned plantations and murdered whites before being stopped by the militia. The site was named a National Historic Landmark on July 4, 1974.

Columbia
Chapelle Administration Building
1530 Harden Street

This building was one of the finest works of John Anderson Lankfor, a pioneer black architect who helped gain recognition for Afro-American architects among the architectural community. The building was named a historical landmark by the Department of Interior on December 8, 1976.

Frogmore
Penn School Historic District

The northern missionaries organized one of the first southern schools for Negroes in Frogmore. The Penn School Historic District pioneered in health services and self-help programs. It is the oldest existing structure in Brick Church. On December 2, 1974, the district was named a National Historic Landmark.

South Dakota

Deadwood
Adams Memorial Museum

Only one of the legendary claimants to the title of "Deadwood Dick" is a black, but he can back his assertion with a colorful and richly tapestried autobiography which takes the reader through his childhood in slavery, his early bronc-busting efforts, and his fabled life as a range rider and Indian fighter in the old West. Nat Love claimed he won the title during a public competition held in Deadwood on the Fourth of July in 1876. The presence of other black cowboys, gambling house operators, and escort soldiers in the area during these years, as well as the convincing style of Love's narrative, lend a high degree of credibility to his adventurous tales although, like Jim Beckwourth, he was probably given to moments of wanton exaggeration.

Tennessee

Henning
Fort Pillow Marker

Taken originally by Union Forces in 1862, Fort Pillow was recaptured by Confederate troops under the command of the wily Nathan B. Forrest on April 12, 1864.

Indianfighter Nat Love claimed the title "Deadwood Dick" after a public competition on July 4, 1876. Born a slave, he grew up to live the fabled life of a cowboy and range rider in the Old West.

the song about Casey Jones' legendary train ride. The song, which became popularized in vaudeville and music halls, was written by Wallace Saunders, a black fireman aboard Jones' locomotive. The Railroad Museum is a symbolic inclusion that represents the enormous unsung contributions of blacks to the railroad industry in the United States.

Memphis
W. C. Handy Park—Tom Lee Memorial (foot of Beale Street on the river bank) Lorraine Hotel

The city of Memphis pays tribute to famed blues composer W. C. Handy in the form of a park and a heroic bronze statue overlooking the very same Beale Street which he immortalized. The statue shows Handy standing with horn poised, about to play. Executed by Leone Tomassi of Italy, it was dedicated in 1960 at the close of a memorial campaign instituted by the city shortly after Handy's death in 1958. (Though born in Florence, Alabama, Handy lived most of his life in the Tennessee city.)

Tom Lee

The 30-foot-high Tom Lee granite memorial was erected in 1954 to honor a black who, on May 8, 1925, saved the lives of 32 passengers aboard the *M. E. Norman,* an excursion boat which had capsized some 20 miles below Memphis near Cow Island. Alerted to the disaster, Lee pulled 32 people from the water onto his skiff. He was honored for his feat by the Memphis

Gunfighter Isom Dart. Although no landmark is listed in this section for Dart, he was part of the lore of the old frontier.

The few black survivors of the engagement testified before the Federal Committee on the Conduct of the War, and documented several instances of massacre after their surrender. Southerners claimed the defenders had simply refused to surrender. The fort was declared a National Historic Landmark by the Department of Interior on May 30, 1974.

Jackson
Casey Jones Railroad Museum

On Chester Street in Jackson, Tennessee one will find the Casey Jones Railroad Museum filled with memorabilia of a bygone era. Jones was immortalized through

Massacre at Fort Pillow.

Black firemen stoked the first locomotive (left) built in the United States. At right is a horse-propelled bus which could travel 12 miles per hour. Blacks deserve much credit for the growth of the U.S. railroad industry from its earliest days. Memorabilia of those times are preserved in the Casey Jones Railroad Museum in Tennessee. The famous song about Casey was written by Wallace Saunders, the black fireman aboard his locomotive.

Engineers Club, which provided him with money for the duration of his life. A fund was also raised to purchase him a home. After his death in 1952, a committee raised the money needed to erect the memorial.

Lorraine Hotel

It was on the balcony of the Lorraine Hotel that Martin Luther King, Jr. was assassinated while emerging from a second-floor room, in the presence of a pair of his trusted advisers, Ralph Abernathy and Jesse Jackson. King died in the emergency room of St. Joseph's Hospital on April 4, 1968.

Nashville
Fisk University, Meharry Medical School and Jubilee Hall

Founded in 1866, Fisk University is today one of the most prestigious institutions of higher learning originally for blacks in the United States. Much the same can be said of Meharry Medical School, one of the leading training centers for black doctors in the U.S.A.

Jubilee Hall is of Victorian Gothic structure and is the oldest building on the Fisk University campus. Fisk was founded by the American Missionary Association to provide a liberal arts education for blacks

W. C. Handy, "Father of the Blues."

following the Civil War. When Fisk first began operation, it was called Fisk Free School. The hall was named a National Historic Landmark on December 2, 1974.

Texas

Amarillo
First Black School

Matthew Bones Hooks was born in central Texas in 1867. The story goes that he rode wild horses at 8, had his first paid job as a cowhand at the age of 10, and later herded cattle for Colonel Charles Goodnight, taking them from Texas to Dodge City, Kansas. Hooks homesteaded in New Mexico, rode broncos in Romfa, Texas in 1910, and then moved to Amarillo, where he established the first school for blacks in that city. The school was in the north heights section, an all-black community. He also founded the Dogie Club, an organization for underprivileged boys in cooperation with the Boy Scouts. He was the only black member of the old Settlers Association of Amarillo and the first black of Amarillo to serve on a grand jury.

San Antonio
The Alamo

Mystery shrouds the identity of all who fought at The Alamo in 1836, but evidence exists that there were some blacks serving with the Texas troops defending this post. The most famous of them is known only as "Joe," the slave of Colonel W. B. Travis (a senior officer at the Alamo). After his release by the Mexican general Santa Anna, Joe reported the results of the battle to another contingent of Texas troops in what is believed to be the first known description of the Mexican assault.

It is also believed that Joe was later reenslaved. According to a newspaper ad dated in 1837, a slave named Joe who had survived The Alamo had stolen a horse and run away from his master. No records exist to verify whether Joe or the horse was ever found.

Utah

Fort Douglas
The Old Fort

Home of the 24th Infantry Regiment, a black unit which served in the trenches of San Juan Hill and

Several blacks were among the 179 Texans who died rather than surrender the Alamo to a Mexican Army.

later was utilized to combat the yellow fever epidemic at Siboney. Weakened and reduced in number because of the sickness, the men returned to a huge welcome in New York but were barely able to get through the parade after their strenuous ordeal. More men died of yellow fever in Cuba than of combat wounds sustained in battle.

Virginia

Arlington

Arlington National Cemetery

Being interred at the Arlington National Cemetery is reserved to those men and women who served in the military. It is the resting place of the Unknown Soldier and also President John Kennedy and Senator Robert Kennedy. Many black soldiers are buried here and their gravesites may be visited. Among them are Lieutenant Colonel A. T. Augusta of the Medical Corps during the Civil War, known as a strong civil rights activist. Also buried at Arlington is Colonel Charles Young, the third black cadet to graduate from West Point.

Benjamin Banneker: SW-9 Intermediate Boundary Stone
18th and Van Buren Streets

The boundary stone commemorates the accomplishment of Benjamin Banneker, who helped survey the city of Washington, D.C. and who was perhaps the most famous black man in Colonial America. Banneker, a mathematician and scientist, was born in Ellicott Mills, Maryland and received his early schooling with the aid of a Quaker family. Banneker was known as a national hero for black people and many schools have been named for him. The boundary stone was declared a National Historic Landmark on May 11, 1976.

Charles Richard Drew House
2505 First Street South

This was the home address of Charles Richard Drew from 1920 to 1939. Drew was the noted black physician and teacher best remembered for his pioneer work in discovering means to preserve blood plasma. The house was named a National Historic Landmark by the Department of Interior on May 11, 1976.

Fort Monroe

This was one of the few military posts not seized by the Confederacy at the outbreak of the Civil War and hence became a haven for fugitive blacks escaping into Union lines. Known as "contraband" (the term was extended by Union General Ben Butler to cover runaways), these able-bodied blacks were put to work building roads, erecting fortifications, and as teamsters and foragers. Many eventually saw combat duty in the Army of the James after restrictions on enlistments were lifted.

Glen Allen

Virginia Randolph Cottage
2200 Mountain Road

Under the Jeanes Fund set up by a wealthy Philadelphia Quaker to aid black education, Virginia Randolph became the first Jeanes supervisor, working to upgrade black vocational training. The cottage was named a National Historic Landmark on December 2, 1974.

Hampton

Hampton Institute

One of the earliest institutions of higher learning for blacks in the United States, Hampton Institute was attended by the great Booker T. Washington before he went to Tuskegee. Washington also taught for a time at Hampton.

Richmond

Jackson Ward Historic District
Bounded by 4th, Marshall, and Smith Streets and the Richmond-Petersburg Turnpike

This is the foremost Afro-American community of the nineteenth and early twentieth centuries and an early center for ethnic social organizations and protective banking institutions. The district was named a National Historic Landmark on June 2, 1978.

Richmond National Battlefield Park

The area around Richmond was the scene of several combat engagements involving black troops active in the Civil War. Among these engagements were Chaffin's Farm, New Market Heights, and Deep Bottom. General Butler found that the gallantry of these men merited special consideration, and so authorized the issuance of 200 medals which he presented personally to those outstanding soldiers who were recommended to his attention.

Maggie Lena Walker House
110A East Leigh Street

In 1903 Maggie Lena Walker, a black woman, founded the successful Saint Luke Penny Savings Bank and

The campus of Hampton Institute—one of the most beautiful in the entire South.

became the first woman to establish and head a bank. The life and career of Maggie Walker have inspired many. In addition to being the first woman president of a bank, she was editor of a newspaper which was considered to be one of the best journals of its class in America. She was also a concerned community leader. The house is located in the Jackson Ward Historic District of Richmond and is an impressive two-story red brick structure. It was declared a National Historic Landmark May 15, 1975.

Rocky Mount
Booker T. Washington National Monument

The Burroughs plantation, on which Booker T. Washington was born a slave in 1856, can be found in a 200-acre park located in Rocky Mount.

Washington

Centralia
George Washington Park

The park is named after a liberated slave who escaped from slavery in Virginia when he was adopted by a white couple and taken to Missouri. He then left Missouri with a wagon train heading for the Pacific Northwest, settling on a homestead along the Chehalis River which was ultimately reached by the Northern Pacific Railroad. Washington subsequently laid out a town, setting aside acreage for parks, a cemetery, and churches. Soon over 2,000 lots were in the hands of a thriving population which formed the nucleus of Centerville.

West Virginia

Harpers Ferry
Harpers Ferry National Monument

Harpers Ferry derives its historical fame from the much-publicized antislavery raid conducted by John Brown and a party of 18 men (including five blacks) from October 16 to 18, 1859. Brown hoped to set up a fortress and refuge for fugitive slaves which he could transform into an important way station for escapees en route to Pennsylvania.

Brown lost two of his sons in the battle and was himself seriously wounded. Later tried and convicted of treason, he was hanged at Charles Town on December 2, 1859.

Malden
Booker T. Washington Monument

This monument, erected in 1963, marks the site where the great black educator labored for several years in the salt works. At the time, Washington credited his employer, Mrs. Violla Ruffner, with having encouraged him to pursue a higher education at Hampton Institute.

Wisconsin

Madison
State Historical Society of Wisconsin

The Wisconsin Historical Society has taken the impressive initiative of building up an archival collection of documents and other written materials relating to the modern-day civil rights struggle. Although it goes back only to 1960, archivists have already amassed the papers of more than 300 civil rights workers and agencies. The purpose of the collection is to create a repository of information for later historians and scholars who will seek to interpret the movement and extract its vital essence. Also included in the collection are broadsides of the black in the Civil War, and items pertaining to slavery.

John Brown's fort at Harpers Ferry.

Milton
Milton House Museum

The Milton House Museum (the oldest cement building in the United States) was once used as a hideaway for fugitive slaves escaping by means of the Underground Railroad.

Portage
Silver Lake Cemetery

Ansel Clark, "born a slave, died a respected citizen," settled in Wisconsin after the Civil War, during which he served as an impressed laborer in the Confederate cause for a time, then escaped. He became a nurse in a Union hospital. There he tended a Wisconsin resident who brought him home after the war to settle in Portage, where he became town constable and deputy sheriff. For 30 years he worked in law enforcement, standing up to the town's rough characters and keeping them in line with "firmness and dignity." It was said, however, that he was such a gentle man with animals that his undertaker feared to crack the whip on the horses driving his hearse lest "Old Anse be out of that box and on my neck."

Wyoming
Fort Washakie Blockhouse

The blockhouse served as headquarters for both the 9th and 10th Cavalry regiments during their assorted campaigns on the Indian frontier. On one occasion, the 9th rescued a unit of infantry from Fort Steele, which was being attacked by a Ute war party. The dug-in infantrymen, exhausted and low on provisions, were relieved to be reinforced by the black troopers who drove off the Indians and stayed at the site to start construction on what was to become Fort Duchesne.

CIVIL RIGHTS ORGANIZATIONS AND BLACK POWER ADVOCATES—PAST AND PRESENT

A Brief History of Civil Rights in the United States ■ Civil Rights Organizations ■ Past Civil Rights and Black Militant Groups ■ Civil Rights and Black Power Leaders ■ Former Contemporary Civil Rights Leaders ■ Past Civil Rights Leaders ■ National Private Organizations with Civil Rights Programs ■ State and Federal Agencies with Civil Rights Responsibilities

The history of the struggle of blacks to gain equality and freedom in America can be divided into three broad phases. Two of them are over, the third is still in progress, and it is not inconceivable that there may still be more phases to come. Simply stated, the first phase involved bringing down the house of slavery. The second was concerned with achieving equality under the law. The third is the current effort to secure economic equity with the supposition that this carries social equity with it.

The pursuit of these goals has, at the very least, been consistent in Black America. There have been peaks and valleys—a spurt of effort and then a leveling off. Nevertheless, when viewed from a broad historical perspective, the struggle has never really stopped nor,

given the realities that still separate black and white, does it seem likely to stop in the near future.

Consistency, however, has not meant uniformity. There have been different approaches to the black struggle from its beginning, just as there are today. Arrayed on one side have been those blacks who have seen the redemption of their dreams of freedom coming within the framework of an integrated pluralistic society. Their values, to a large measure, reflect those of the mainstream of American society—race excepted—and they form the backbone of the traditional Civil Rights Movement. An opposite view has been taken by those who favor an independent black society built outside of white-controlled and dominated institutions. Those who take this view see integration as a sham, a device to keep blacks in some form of bondage. It has been called black nationalism and, more recently, black power.

What must be pointed out, however, is that the line between the two views is not always sharply drawn and they are not totally at war with each other. One can favor the civil rights approach and still work to build independent black institutions. And those who hold black power views can still, on a pragmatic basis, recognize the need to maintain some degree of contact with white groups and institutions.

Both civil rights and black power advocacy go back to the early days of colonial America. Concepts of liberty and equality, common to the civil rights movement, were stated in the Mennonite Quaker Resolution of 1688, which defended the right of "negers" to the liberty of their bodies. Black power may have an even older history on these shores. As far back as 1671 Maroons (escaped slaves) had established separate communities in Rappahannock and Middlesex counties, Virginia, surviving for years before being hunted down by white settlers and troops.

In the not too distant past, historians assumed that blacks had acquiesced almost completely to their status as slaves. The notion was put forth that blacks are fundamentally childlike and docile and that slavery was therefore necessary for their protection and contentment. This "southern view" was widely disseminated in American education until the 1930s, at which time a more thoughtful approach gained acceptance. This view stated that blacks are not docile or incompetent but had to accept their inferior status because of oppression and social conditioning. Blacks were far from content with their lot. But the sheer strength of white police and military power plus the fragmentation of black families and social organization by slavery rendered protest or resistance physical and emotional impossibilities.

Proponents of this view wanted to be fair and unprejudiced, but they underestimated the efforts of blacks to improve their position. Historical records, recently examined, reveal that during colonial and early days of the Republic, many blacks struggled bravely, and occasionally successfully, for their freedom and rights.

Early Movements

Foremost among black protest and self-help efforts was the Free African Society organized in 1787 in Philadelphia by the Reverend Richard Allen and Absalom Jones. As with many black movements to follow, the Free African Society was somewhat religious in its principles and program. Indeed, Jones was to become Rector of a Protestant Episcopal Church for blacks and Allen to form the Bethel African Methodist Church.

The Free African Society was an important source of political consciousness and welfare for blacks throughout the country. It combined economic and medical aid for poor blacks with support of abolition and sub-rosa communication with blacks in the South.

As was to be the case with civil rights leaders of the nineteenth and twentieth centuries, Allen, who eventually became sole leader of the Society, had a strong appeal to whites. The Free African Society was formed in response to insistence by whites that Allen not preach to integrated congregations.

Blacks were also leaders in plans to resettle them in Africa, plans which led to the founding of Liberia in 1820. Paul Cuffee, a black merchant and shipbuilder who lived in Connecticut, was a leader of recolonization efforts but withdrew in disillusionment at the growing association between recolonization and the pro-slavery forces of Senator John Calhoun.

The Abolitionist Movement, customarily dated from the first publication of *The Liberator* in 1831, reflected both civil rights and black power strains. Such black abolitionist leaders as Harriet Tubman, Frederick Douglass, and Henry Highland Garnet were concerned not only with erasing slavery but with the growing discrimination and cruelty against free blacks in both the South and North.

The first obvious influence of blacks on a presidential election occurred in 1844 when the Liberty Party, which counted Douglass and Garnet among its leaders, deprived Henry Clay of enough votes in New York to swing the state and the White House to James Polk.

On the whole, black abolitionists opposed separatist doctrines and favored working with whites to change the system. They foresaw a society in which blacks and whites would cooperate peacefully. However, some very potent black abolitionists, such as Garnet and David Walker, stressed the uniqueness of blacks and from the early days of the abolitionist movement urged that slavery be abolished, if necessary, by violence. The differences between Garnet, who advocated the overthrow of slavery by armed revolt and a general strike, and Douglass, who proposed more moderate methods, were in many respects forerunners of disputes which were to split the civil rights movement more than a century later, in the 1960s.

Both moderates and militants had a profound effect on events leading up to the Civil War and on the thinking of an articulate young politician from the West, Abraham Lincoln.

Slave Insurrections

While the Abolitionist movement was forming and flowering in the North, many slaves in the South es-

[1839] *Anti-Slavery Almanac.* 19

Free blacks were frequently kidnapped and sold into slavery.

caped to found their own communities, in defiance of their overlords and military authorities.

Historians sympathetic to the black cause have concentrated their research and writing on the underground slave "escape trains" and more recently on the slave uprisings of Nat Turner and Denmark Vesey. Still unexplored and relatively unknown are the numerous Maroon communities which thrived in the South nearly two centuries before the Civil War.

Maroon societies have, until recently, been regarded as a phenomenon almost exclusive to Latin American and Caribbean countries. Maroon groups in Brazil, Jamaica, Surinam, and other areas survived for centuries, came to number thousands and attained official recognition of their freedom from colonial authorities. In Surinam, the Saranaka Maroon society remains viable today, over 300 years after its founding by escaped slaves, a tribute to the economic and military prowess of its seventeenth-century forebears.

Maroon achievements in the United States were less

dramatic but nonetheless real and of great concern to Southern slaveholders and military commanders.

Southern newspapers and military proclamations of the seventeenth, eighteenth, and nineteenth centuries attest to numerous battles and occasional trade between whites and communities of escaped slaves and free blacks. Some 50 such communities are known to have existed during the 200 years preceding the Civil War. Many lasted for years. And today, communities reflecting intermarriage between Maroons and Indians can be found in the hills and swamps from New Jersey to Florida, westward from Florida to Texas and across the border into Mexico.

The following example of a battle between whites and Maroons appears in *Maroon Societies,* edited by Richard Price, associate professor of anthropology at Yale:

A letter of August 25, 1856 to Governor Thomas Bragg of North Carolina, signed by Richard A. Lewis and twenty-one

Abolitionists William Lloyd Garrison and George Thompson mobbed in Boston in 1838.

The branding of Captain Jonathan Walker for ferrying escaped slaves to the Bahamas.

Many escaped slaves joined maroon bands deep in the wilderness.

other citizens, informed him of a "very secure retreat for runaway blacks" in a large swamp between Bladen and Robison Counties (Governor's Letter Book, No. 43, pp. 514–515, Historical Commission, Raleigh). There "for many years past, and at this time, there are several runaways of bad and daring character—destructive to all kinds of stock and dangerous to all persons living by or near said swamp." Slaveholders attacked these blacks on August 1, 1856 but accomplished nothing and saw one of their own number killed. "The blacks ran off cursing and swearing and telling them to come on, they were ready for them again." The Wilmington Journal *of August 14 mentioned that these runaways "had cleared a place for a garden, had cows in the swamp."*

Such reports abounded throughout the antebellum South. In several South Carolina counties in 1830, slaveholders complained that the example of Maroons induced slaves to become almost uncontrollable. Maroons comprised much of the leadership and strength of Seminole forces in their six-year war (1837 to 1843) against the United States. In 1851, some 1500 ex-slaves were reported fighting as allies of the Comanche Indians against Texas slaveholders. During the Civil War, Maroons together with the white deserters from the Confederate Army evoked requests for martial law in parts of Florida, Alabama, and Virginia.

Acknowledgment of the Maroons and the teachings of such blacks as Garnet and David Walker provide an essential balance to the understanding of black history in the United States. For it then becomes clear that blacks have sought to assert their identity as well as to attain acceptance and justice within white-dominated institutions.

Civil Rights after the Civil War

Perhaps the era in which blacks were least assertive in their own cause extends from the end of Reconstruction in the 1870s to the formation of the Niagara Movement in 1905. During the period, some blacks sought unsuccessfully to forge alliances with whites in labor unions and political parties. Others, through such leaders as Booker T. Washington, tried to assuage fears of whites that blacks sought "social equality." In the 1890s, however, William Edward Burghardt DuBois—a young black historian who had recently been awarded a Ph.D. at Harvard for his thesis on the slave trade—emerged as an aggressive civil rights advocate. A brilliant debater, DuBois was soon to capture the interest and respect of blacks, who were being oppressed by Klan-style violence in the South and urban riots in the West and North.

Hidden behind their bedsheet masks KKK terrorists tried to keep southern blacks in virtual slavery.

police patrols who fired volley after volley into the night air in a futile attempt to disperse the crowds. In comparison with what was to come, the Harlem casualty figures were paltry. One man died, and 144 were injured. Prophetically, though, things had exploded in Harlem, the prototype black ghetto in the consciousness of white America. Few cared then that virtually every major American city was structured in the same way New York was, with an invisible wall encircling the black ghetto and buttressing white city dwellers from exposure to, and contact with, their black counterparts.

The Watts Riot (1965)

The Watts section of southwest Los Angeles, a 20-square-mile black ghetto with an estimated population of 90,000, was the scene of one of the worst riots in the history of the United States, August 11–16, 1965. Thirty-five people were killed, and property damage due to looting and arson reached the staggering total of 200 million dollars. Black deaths numbered 28.

Stores were looted; entire city blocks burned to the ground; buses and ambulances were stoned; and firemen, policemen, and airplanes were shot at in a 150-block area which, after six days, lay under a virtual state of siege.

The incident that sparked the outburst occurred on August 11 when state highway patrolmen chased an automobile around a six-block area and arrested its driver on a charge of drunken driving.

A crowd gathered as word of the arrest spread, and rumors of brutality were passed on by eyewitnesses. Rocks were thrown, and police summoned to disperse the rioters, who soon began stoning cars and smashing windows. A semblance of order was restored by 3 the next morning, but rioting again broke out on the evening of August 12.

The March on Washington was the peak of civil rights mass action.

Washington newsboy vends special edition.

Los Angeles Mayor Samuel Yorty and Chief of Police William Parker summoned the National Guard to assist beleaguered police and deputies. Between August 13 and August 16, 12,634 guardsmen, 1,430 city police, 1,017 county sheriff's deputies, and 68 state highway patrolmen served on riot duty.

Causes of the Riots

A number of causes were advanced to explain the riots. Among them were:

1. Poverty and lack of job opportunities.
2. "Racial humiliation," the failure of whites to accept the dignity of blacks.
3. Lack of black leadership.
4. Agitation of the civil rights movement.
5. Police brutality.
6. Hot weather.
7. The criminal element.

Whatever the relative weight of these factors, the riots demonstrated the axiom that violence is an inevitable result of failure to cope with the root causes underlying discontent.

Statistics told much of the story. At the time, two-thirds of Watts residents had less than a high school education; one-eighth were illiterate. Only one in eight homes in the area was less than 25 years old, the remainder being in various stages of decay and disrepair. Three of every ten school children came from broken

Large sections of the black Watts community were burned down in the 1965 riots.

Troopers attempt to break up march to Montgomery in 1965.

homes. The school dropout rate in Watts was 2.2 times above the Los Angeles average. And children grew up among an assortment of social outcasts—prison parolees, prostitutes, narcotics addicts, and the like.

Many black and white observers believed that the riots boosted the pride of blacks. Noted black psychiatrist J. Alfred Cannon:

They have developed a feeling of potency. They feel the whole world is watching now. And out of the violence, no matter how wrong the acts were, they have developed a sense of pride.

The rallying cry of the mob ("Get Whitey") revealed another aspect of the problem. Aggressive "Get Whitey" cries were counterbalanced by the protective signs of "Brother" or "Blood" which appeared in the windows of black shopkeepers. In the view of some observers, however, "Whitey"—the white policeman, the white merchant, the white social worker—was attacked mainly because they were symbols of the black's oppression.

"Black Power" Surfaces

A further indication that nonviolence was becoming less relevant occurred in June 1966, when Stokely Carmichael of the Student Non-Violence Coordinating Committee used the phrase "black power" in Greenville, Mississippi. Carmichael, along with other civil rights leaders, had come to the state after James Meredith, the first black to be admitted to the University of Mississippi, had been shot as he attempted a protest march across the state.

In the days following the Mississippi march, many civil rights leaders analyzed and condemned the concept of "black power." Martin Luther King, Jr., for example, whose philosophy of nonviolence appeared to be antithetical to the position taken by the advocates of black power, said:

I happen to believe that a doctrine of Black Supremacy is as evil as White Supremacy. I don't think that anything can be more tragic than the attitude that the Black Man can solve his problems by himself.

On July 5, the NAACP heard its executive secretary, Roy Wilkins, denounce black power at its annual convention in Los Angeles:

No matter how endlessly they try to explain it, the term "black power" means anti-white power. In a racially pluralistic society, the concept, the formation and the exercise of an ethnically tagged power means opposition to other ethnic powers.

In the black-white relationship, it means that every other ethnic power is the rival and the antagonist of "black power." It has to mean "going it alone." It has to mean separatism.

The National Urban League, the last of the civil rights groups to comment on the controversy, issued a press

Mississippi freedom marchers enter a small farm town. CORE chairman Floyd McKissick (left front) hails onlookers to join march. CORE's leadership role in confronting racial injustice through the United States was built by activist members dedicated to principles of what James Farmer called "nonviolent self-sacrifice."

release on July 11, disassociating itself from black power both semantically and philosophically:

The National Urban League does not intend to invent slogans, however appealing they may be to the press. What we will continue to do through our unique structure is expand and develop positive programs of action which bring jobs to the unemployed, housing to the dispossessed, education to the deprived, and necessary voter education to the disenfranchised. The Urban League is dedicated to an interracial approach to solving the problems faced by the nation. We are equally dedicated to the expansion of the services and programs which have helped hundreds of thousands of people find jobs and get the training, education, and counseling they need. Our interracial staff is at work in 76 cities with programs, not slogans.

The Congress of Racial Equality (CORE), on the other hand, adopted a resolution at one of its conventions endorsing the concept of black power in these terms:

Black Power is not hatred. It is a means to bring the Black Americans into the covenant of Brotherhood. Black Power is not Black Supremacy; it is a unified Black Voice reflecting racial pride in the tradition of our heterogeneous nation.

Stokely Carmichael elaborated further on the subject:

Black power seems to me a number of things. Number one, that black people in this country are oppressed for one reason— and that's because of their color, and that's what this country has to face . . . their rally cry must be the issue around which they are oppressed, as it was for unions. The workers came together, they were oppressed because they were workers. And we must come together around the issue that oppressed us—which is our blackness. Unions—they needed power to stop their oppression. We need power to stop ours. So it's black power. And black power just means black people coming together and getting people to represent their needs and to stop that oppression.

Some observers explained black power in terms of the collective frame of mind inevitable in a people emerging from a long period of inferior status. Others found that black power reflected a new ethnic integrity among blacks. Still others interpreted it as a phenomenon embracing many deep-seated antiwhite emotions, and saw in it further a rejection of existing political and social institutions, a voluntary form of separatism nurtured by personal pride, and a desire to meet violence with counterviolence.

The Newark Riot (1967)

Further evidence that nonviolence had perhaps reached the point of diminishing returns was provided later in the summer of 1966 when Martin Luther King attempted to take his philosophy to Chicago in an assault on segregated housing and was greeted with mobs of hostile and violent whites. So entrenched was the opposition that the effort had to be abandoned.

Rioting broke out again in the summer of 1967 first in Newark, New Jersey, and then in other cities, with such ferocity that the "long hot summer" became a catch phrase.

The spark of Newark's ghastly and tragic uprising in the summer of 1967 was a single arrest and the false rumors it generated. On the evening of July 12, black cabdriver John Smith tried to hurry past a prowl car patrolling in a black neighborhood. Carrying a passenger, Smith darted by the slow-moving vehicle, was cut off by police, and was hauled down to the station following a heated argument. (It developed that he was an illegal driver since his license had been revoked for numerous violations and accidents.) Central Ward witnesses who saw police dragging a limp and stiff body into the station concluded hastily that a hackie had been beaten up and killed. (Smith's injuries were serious enough to require a doctor's treatment.) He seems to have been roughed up to such an extent that he could not have cooperated peacefully with arresting officers even if he were so disposed.

Reports of death on the ghetto grapevine, however, escalated the tension and pushed residents and police toward open confrontation. By midnight, rocks and bottles were clattering against the walls of the station-house. Inside, the police girded for action; outside, the grapevine telegraphed a message calling for more manpower and other reinforcements.

Meanwhile, civil rights leaders, black militants, community officials, and police authorities met to sort out the facts and quiet the hostility and hysteria of the gathering throng. As black participants at the meeting were attempting to persuade police to initiate an investigation to determine just how Smith had been injured, the unruly people outside became a matter of pressing concern. Soon Molotov cocktails were hurled against the wall of the stationhouse, starting minor fires. These were quickly extinguished, but they were ominous enough to persuade the police to set up a line of defense in front of the station.

Once the moderating black leaders sensed they could not disperse the crowd, they decided shrewdly to try to organize an instantaneous march on City Hall to protest Smith's arrest and demand a thorough investigation. Some of the crowd positioned itself for such a march; others, however, milled around, disgruntled and unappeased. People in the line of march were struck by rocks; windows continued to be shattered; a car was set afire. Seeing the situation deteriorating still further, police rushed the crowd and sent it fleeing in all directions. Late-night reports of the episode carried references to a few isolated lootings, but otherwise indicated that the disturbances had run their course.

Police Chief Dominick Spina, however, sensed the seriousness of the situation, and realized that tensions had been aroused beyond a simple outburst. The next evening, a "Police Brutality Protest Rally" was organized by assorted black power advocates, including the Black Muslims, the United Afro-American Association, and other black nationalists. Together, they planned to picket the Fourth Precinct Station.

Despite the announcement that the Smith incident would be investigated, the blacks remained unsatisfied. In short order, the police station was again under a virtual state of siege, whereupon police once again charged into the crowds, hurrying them off into the night. They did not, however, return to their homes or quiet their anger.

In the early morning hours of Friday, July 14, Mayor Hugh Addonizio finally conceded the situation was beyond his control, and sent in an urgent request to New Jersey Governor Richard J. Hughes for state police and National Guard units.

After daybreak, more than 2,600 National Guard reinforcements were deployed throughout the area. Arrests were made systematically, and roadblocks effectively deterred entrance into, or flight from, the area. Command of the anti-riot operations was assumed by the governor, who declared Newark a city in open rebellion and defined the restoration of order as his first priority. Hughes ordered all guns and ammunition confiscated from stores that were selling them, imposed three separate curfews, and toured the area accompanied by a protective task force which arrested looters on sight.

However, neither the armored personnel carriers, the .50 caliber rifles, nor the other war equipment could diminish the defiance of looters and the persistent barrage of small arms sniper fire.

A three-year-old girl lost the sight of an eye and the hearing of an ear when she was hit by a police bullet fired at fleeing snipers; a 73-year-old man was felled by another police bullet fired as part of a sortie aimed at a group of looters who had attracted a crowd of milling spectators. The imprudent spectators, too, were quickly dispersed by the barrage of bullets, and innocent people were exposed to danger and injury simply by being on the scene. A garage mechanic was shot in the side while jacking up a car; a man standing on a porch was hit in the eye by a bullet; a 10-year-old boy riding in the family car was shot through the head.

Later testimony before the House of Representatives uncovered a hideous skein of events in which it became apparent that the amount of sniper fire was being grossly exaggerated and that, in many cases, it was more likely that frightened Guardsmen and fidgety police were exchanging gunfire.

Other incidents of brutality, anonymous killing, and savage behavior were too numerous to report; official reports after state police and Guardsmen were recalled on July 17 read as follows: 23 dead (21 of them black and two of them—a policeman and a fireman—white). Of these, six were black women, and two black children. Damage was over 10 million dollars, about 20% of it to buildings and fixtures, and the overwhelming majority due to stock loss at supermarkets, liquor stores, clothing shops, and other stores. More than 1,000 people were injured, and another 1,600 under arrest. Among them was black poet/activist Imamu Baraka, who was snatched from a Volkswagen, beaten, and hauled off to jail after being relieved of two .32 caliber pistols.

And Newark was only the first city to burn in 1967.

The Detroit Riot (1967)

The Detroit riot also stemmed, on the surface at least, from an arrest that attracted widespread attention on the ghetto streets. It began at 3:45 A.M. Sunday morning, July 22 when the police raided a so-called blind pig, an after-hours drinking and gambling spot crowded with patrons attending a party thrown in honor of a group of black servicemen, two of whom had recently returned from Vietnam. All 82 patrons were arrested. As they were being carted off, however, a crowd of 200 gathered, and a mood of ugly resentment soon prevailed.

Shortly after 5 A.M., an empty bottle smashed into a police car, and a litter basket was hurled through a store window. Police reinforcements were summoned as riot tensions mounted, but few police were on duty in the immediate riot area. By 6 A.M., hundreds of irate blacks were already massed on the street. Assorted window-smashing and looting had begun along 12th Street, a high-density area of substandard and deteriorating housing.

A curfew ordered by the mayor had little effect on the situation. Looters continued to raid supermarkets recklessly, and street fights, beatings, knifings, and gun battles were common. A 23-year-old white woman was hit at close range after she and her husband had dropped off two black friends; less than two hours later, she was dead. A 45-year-old white man collaborating with black companions was shot from a car by the owner of the supermarket he was looting. A 68-year-old white shoe repairman was beaten to death by a black youth for interfering with looters cleaning out a nearby store. Fallen power lines killed a white fireman and a black homeowner.

By 2 A.M. Monday, 8,000 National Guardsmen were on their way to bolster the 800 state police officers and 1,200 National Guardsmen already on duty. By this time, Governor Romney and Mayor Cavanaugh had both decided to request federal assistance. The Attorney General's office replied that if state and local police could not control the situation, the governor would have to declare a "state of insurrection." Romney declined to follow this course once he realized that insurance companies would be relieved of financial responsibility for the damages pursuant to such a declaration.

President Johnson then authorized the sending of a paratrooper task force which arrived at Selfridge Air Force Base near the city at about 4 P.M. Monday.

By 11:30 P.M., federal observers (primarily Cyrus Vance and General John L. Throckmorton) advised President Johnson to authorize the use of paratroopers. The President signed the executive order federalizing the Guard, and thus committed the jittery young guardsmen to what amounted to a complex battle situation.

The casualties in the Detroit riot outstripped those of Newark. Altogether, 43 persons were killed, 33 of them black and 10 white. Two of the 17 looters who died were white; the rest, black. Fifteen citizens (four whites), one white National Guardsman, one white fireman, and one black private guard fell victim to gunshot wounds. Property damage soared to 22 million dollars, not counting business stock, private furnishings, churches, and charitable institutions, many of which were covered by insurance.

In all, over 7,000 persons were arrested—3,000 on the second day of the riot and over 4,000 by midnight Monday. Some were kept in such makeshift jails as buses and underground garages.

When the curfew was lifted and the National Guard removed from the city on Saturday, July 29, most of Detroit's black area was a charred mess of tangled rubble and waterlogged ashes. For some, dreams were broken; for others, hopes were seemingly shattered. Some blacks who had lost the work of a lifetime sobbed in dismay and gave up hope; conversely, others who had never accumulated many possessions seemed relieved of rage and inclined to build.

For the white establishment—another day of reckoning had passed, with many still too timid or too angry to press for real change. Walter Reuther found the words to describe the needs dramatized by Detroit:

Those Americans [who] do not feel a part of society . . .
don't behave like responsible people. Only when they get their

fair share of America will they respond in terms of responsibility.

The Kerner Report (1968)

While the riots in Newark and Detroit were the most serious during the summer of 1967, a number of other disturbances also broke out and President Lyndon B. Johnson appointed a Commission on Civil Disorders to study what happened, why it happened, and what could be done. The Commission, which was given a year to make its report, subsequently came to be known as the Kerner Commission, after its chairman, Governor Otto Kerner of Illinois.

It did not require a full year for the 11-member Kerner Commission to issue its provocative report on the mangled status of black society in the United States in the aftermath of the urban riots of 1967. One reason for the early appearance of the report may have been the fear that procrastination might only serve as fuel for a possible repetition of the holocaust. Another was assuredly the elementary recognition that the causes of the rioting were implicit in the situations and conditions of ghetto life, and these were not, after all, mysteriously unknown factors.

In gathering the facts, the Commission discovered that mass hysteria and exaggeration had reached as far as the nation's media, which had rendered estimates of damage and destruction far out of proportion to true figures. There were, in truth, 164 disorders—eight of them "major," 33 of them "serious," and the rest hardly worthy of attention under normal circumstances. No evidence existed to substantiate the notion that the uprisings were caused by a deliberate conspiracy, Communist or otherwise. Each riot had its own unique and complex character, and was a product of both general grievances and particular circumstances. Most rioters were young men, aged 15–24, high school dropouts, lifelong ghetto residents with a growing measure of racial pride, hostility to the middle class (black or white), and a basic distrust of the political system and the role of police enforcers.

Among the facts cited and exhaustively documented were a distressing crime rate (sometimes 35 times higher than in white neighborhoods), the lack of health facilities and municipal services (infant mortality among blacks was reported to be 58% higher than among whites; poor garbage collection and sanitation provisions helped account for 14,000 cases of rat bite in 1965 alone), and the increasing compression of poor black citizens within the urban ghetto itself. These problems were compounded by poor educational opportunity, inadequate recreational facilities, biased administration of justice, discriminatory credit and consumer practices, feeble welfare programs, and in-

credibly high unemployment. In other words, it was not possible to contemplate wholesale escape, nor was it likely that internal change could be undertaken effectively without wholesale assistance.

The recommendations outlined by the Commission called for a program "equal to the dimension of the problems." Such proposals did not take into account matters of obvious caste or political opposition; instead, they concentrated strictly on the issues and the policies which exacerbated tensions and produced an atmosphere of popular readiness to riot.

The proposals constituted an irrefutable admission that the nation was in fact racially polarized, and that blacks were now so aroused that, whenever it suited their strategy or their mood, they would not shy away from open racial warfare. Nevertheless, a fundamental gulf remained between the Kerner Commission's analysis of the situation (with which black militants generally concurred) and the mood of the nation. To the militants, it was clear that, though the message was couched in urgent, indeed "shocking" terms, it was still being directed to a sluggish and unresponsive source: the U.S. government, Congress, the Establishment in general.

President Johnson accepted the report but never endorsed it and very little was done to implement its recommendations.

The Assassination Riots (April 4–11, 1968)

The Kerner Commission issued its report in March 1968. A month later, on April 4, Martin Luther King, the man who had played the leading role in the Civil Rights Movement, was shot and killed by an assassin in Memphis, Tennessee. Gunfire, looting, and burning erupted in some 125 cities following his death.

The government's prompt, strong reaction to these riots marked a turning point in black history and American politics. Unlike the response to earlier riots in Watts, Newark, and Detroit, troops were summoned immediately. In some cities, seasoned troops were dispatched, rather than the relatively green National Guardsmen. Undoubtedly, the existence of rioting in many cities at once, and the fact that one of the cities was the nation's capital, was a factor in the reaction. Fear of the growing anti-Vietnam War movement and occasional violence on college campuses may also have played a part, even though black participation in antiwar disturbances was minimal. But whatever provoked such a large scale use of troops (the total reached 70,000) from this point on, the incidence and intensity of urban riots subsided and many militant black leaders became blunt in their counsel to "cool it."

The riots had another effect. The fear they engendered among whites contributed to a "law and order" reaction that was to exert a strong influence on the American political scene for years to come.

The Fading of Militancy (1964–1974)

Following the riots of 1968, violence and influence of black leaders who seemed to advocate it declined. The summer of 1969, and those that followed, were "cool," outbreaks increasingly becoming limited in duration and scope.

It could be argued, from a fatalistic point of view at least, that black discontent and frustration had simply reached a pitch of frenzy which had to subside, just as a convulsive attack of epilepsy runs its course for no precisely discernible reason. Far more encouraging and constructive explanations for the cessation of violence could be advanced, however. For one thing, both ghetto residents and black middle-class leaders recognized the excruciating reality that the riots only destroyed their own turf and left many homeless, totally unprotected, and utterly devoid of marketable resources.

Militant groups, such as the Black Panthers, while able to attract the interest of the media were unable to sell their messages on a broad scale in the black community. Eventually they faded into impotence.

The Black Power Conferences (1966–1970)

In the waning days of the nonviolent Civil Rights Movement, the shape of organized "black power" be-

gan to emerge. The First National Conference on Black Power was convened in Washington, D.C. on September 3, 1966, by Congressman Adam Clayton Powell. It was attended by 169 delegates from 37 cities, 18 states, and 64 organizations. Out of this grew the Second National Conference on Black Power held in Newark July 20–23, 1967.

The largest and most broadly representative gathering of black Americans ever to attend such a meeting poured into Newark—more than 1,000 strong from 36 states and 42 cities. Its atmosphere and style were distinctly different from any previously scheduled meeting of national consequence involving black leaders. For one thing, white authorities—the Administration and the press—were not given ringside seats at the event, nor were their opinions and analyses solicited. The meeting was a closed-circuit black affair, a four-day private parley that took place at the conference headquarters of Cathedral House in the heart of Newark's Episcopal Diocese.

The serious nature of the issues produced a shroud of secrecy which enveloped the participants in the 14 workshops organized to grapple with the theme and establish key points of programmatic accord. The black representatives clearly wished to keep their divergent opinions private until they could hammer out some form of unified approach to a particular aspect of the problem.

The spectrum of black organizations represented at the meeting ranged from so-called conservative groups like the NAACP, the SCLC, and the Urban

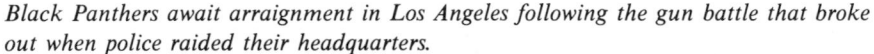
Black Panthers await arraignment in Los Angeles following the gun battle that broke out when police raided their headquarters.

League to the so-called orthodox radicals (CORE and SNCC) to the more abrasive and occasionally strident paramilitary groups (Ron Karenga's US of Los Angeles and Charles 37X Kenyatta's Mau Mau of New York).

The sporadic reports of violence bubbling up in several American cities lent added vigor to the proclamations of the paramilitary groups who advocated organized military training for black youth and self-defense courses for all black families, castigation of Christianity as a selfish and corrupt religion preaching love and practicing hate and materialism, and rejection of the word "Negro" for the word "black." Other resolutions called for the formal partitioning of the United States into two separate nations, the refusal of blacks to accept induction into the Armed Forces, the censure of all Congressmen who voted to unseat Congressman Adam Clayton Powell, and the support of a black boycott of the 1968 Olympics in the event Muhammad Ali's title remained unrestored.

At the Third National Conference on Black Power, held in Philadelphia in the last week of August 1968, more than 3,000 delegates were in attendance. Not all resolutions of the Conference were made public. Among those released to the press were:

Neutrality in the Nigeria-Biafra war and a statement that both sides move for a settlement

Immediate withdrawal of U.S. forces from Vietnam

Boycott of the draft by all eligible black youths

Implementation of the goal of creating a black urban army in the city's ghettos for the protection of black citizens

Denunciation of the term "ghetto"

In 1969, delegates to the black power confab took a different approach, scheduling the meeting for Hamilton, Bermuda, and viewing it as an attempt to create an international black power organization. Delegates who attended came from the United States, Africa, Canada, and the Caribbean.

As in the previous year, the resolutions offered by the Black Power Conference dwindled in number. They included:

An end to media distortion of the black population

A return of all documents, art, and artifacts relating to black people from the world's museums

A protest against the trial of black Canadian students

A call for immediate withdrawal from Vietnam and a boycott of draft induction by black youths

The 1970 conference was held in Atlanta amid the continuing rhetoric that its aim was to develop institutions that would promote the liberation of black people. Significantly, the term black power was removed from the title of the conference, and the scope of the group was broadened to further upgrade the identity of other-than-American black people. Hence the name: The Congress of African People.

The Second National Conference on Black Power pressed beyond traditional civil rights goals toward black control of all black affairs.

H. Rap Brown, president of SNCC, called for violence.

The meeting was attended by delegates from North America, Latin America, the Caribbean, and Africa. The internationalist outlook of the participants was apparent in the tendency to identify people by religion rather than by nation.

What was clear from five years of conferences, meetings, encounters, confrontations, violent upheavals, and position papers was that black power was a new driving force in the black community, not just a clever slogan that achieved momentary fashion and then faded into oblivion. Every black leader has had more than just an incidental curiosity about its real meaning; each has somehow been subject to its demands even as he has sought to harness and comprehend its implications.

Inflation, Recession, and Populism (1974–1975)

In the early 1970s the very successes of the black power concept began to lessen its strengths. The black leaders who met in Gary, Indiana, in 1972 for another black power conference, were conspicuous by the fact that they had succeeded within the system. The host, Richard Hatcher, was mayor of Gary; the chairman, Imamu Amiri Baraka, was accepted, though often resentfully, as a leading writer and political advocate. In 1972, enough blacks were elected to Congress (16) to make the Congressional Black Caucus an important political force. And blacks were being elected mayors of major cities.

These successes contributed to a blurring of the sharp divisions between advocates of black power and the civil rights leaders who, though moving toward greater militance, had persisted in pursuing traditional paths of reconciliation and integration.

But perhaps of greater long-term importance in the early 1970s was the reemergence, after a lapse of some 70 years, of a populist feeling among blacks, a belief that low- and low-middle income whites and blacks had vital interests in common and should work together toward guarantees of these interests.

The most conspicuous early supporter of this position was Dr. George Wiley, founder of the National Welfare Rights Organization. Wiley's untimely death greatly weakened the NWRO, but with the advent of "double digit" inflation in 1973 and the economic decline of 1974, both moderate and militant black leaders increasingly advocated reconciliation between the races and pursuit of such goals as minimum welfare standards, rent controls, increased taxes on corporations, National Health Insurance subsidies, and im-

Playwright Imamu Baraka leads the fight for Kawaida Towers housing in Newark, New Jersey.

provement of mass transit and other measures that would balance income and provide every citizen with guarantees of a decent living standard.

Included in this shift to interracial cooperation by low- and middle-income whites and blacks were such diverse leaders as black power advocate Imamu Baraka, who tended to a Marxist position, and Vernon Jordan of the Urban League. More moderate policies were also discernible among such groups as the Black Panthers and Black Muslims.

The Civil Rights Movement had produced new leaders, and others emerged from the ranks of black power advocates, to be joined by those who had been provided with leadership opportunities because of the War on Poverty and its funding of community groups.

The Period of Retrenchment (1976–1981)

By the mid-1970s it was evident that the Civil Rights Movement had entered a new era, completely different from that of the 1950s and 1960s when it had achieved notable substantive victories and a respected status throughout the land. Basically, what the Movement accomplished during the 1950s and 1960s was to force the removal of the legal base that supported racial discrimination and segregation, forge a broad-based consensus that overt acts of racism were not morally

Bobby Seale, co-founder of the Black Panther Party.

Malcolm X addressing a Black Muslim convocation.

tolerable in American society, enlist the support of the national government in the pursuit of racial equality, and establish a powerful coalition that brought together the church, labor, intellectuals, idealists, other ethnic groups, and the young. It also created the public image of a highly moral and vibrant crusade led by strong and committed black leaders (most notably Martin Luther King) who spoke in a united voice and accurately reflected the hopes and aspirations of their followers.

At its zenith, the Civil Rights Movement was the most important event taking place in America. It aroused the national conscience as it pitted the forces of good (as represented by the Movement) against the forces of evil (as represented by racist police). Through demonstrations, sit-ins, marches, and soaring rhetoric, the Movement aroused widespread public indignation, primarily through television, which was its passport into millions of living rooms, at the injustices being inflicted on a suffering people in the name of the law, thus creating a political atmosphere in which it was possible to make changes.

Once the oppressive laws had been rendered null and void, however, the Movement began to lose momentum. It had won major victories through the Civil Rights Act of 1964, the Voting Rights Act of 1965, court decisions and Presidential directives, but these were behind it and the challenges that it faced in the 1970s and beyond had more to do with the results of discrimination and segregation than with the law.

The accomplishments of the Civil Rights Movement were indeed remarkable and accounted for more progress in less time than blacks had made since they first arrived in America in 1619. The legal structure that kept blacks in the back of the bus in the South, out of hotels and restaurants and other places of public accommodation was outlawed. The segregation of public schools was effectively ended. The Voting Rights Act enfranchised millions of black voters and helped elect hundreds of southern blacks to public office. The Movement brought a fresh sense of pride to many blacks who, while they may not have been a part of it, drew inspiration from its achievements. And, the Movement helped to develop a whole new generation of black leaders.

Despite Success, Many Untouched

As momentous as these achievements were, however, they failed to materially alter the lives of the mass of black people who remained disproportionately poor, badly educated, and unable to avail themselves of the opportunities that went to better prepared blacks. The Movement hardly touched them at all. Unemployment for blacks remained at double the rate for whites, the ghettos continued to deteriorate, crime still plagued black neighborhoods, and the various government programs that sought to address these problems were never funded at the proper level or maintained long enough to make any real difference.

Bluntly stated, the successes of the Civil Rights Movement did not improve the economic and social conditions of the masses of blacks, nor did they reach to the depth and complexity of the subtle racism that permeates almost every aspect of American life. One astute commentator, Carey McWilliams, noted:

The struggle for civil rights was not a social revolution. It has limited objectives, though objectives of critical importance. Legal barriers and discrimination had to be removed before more significant progress could be made.

Unfortunately, the same type of national consensus that helped bring about the victories of the Civil Rights Movement could not be developed to deal with the endemic economic and social problems of the black community, or with ingrained racism that said in effect that blacks could come so far, and then no further. The mass of people that could be mobilized to demonstrate and march so that the walls of segregation would come tumbling down could not be mobilized over such issues as unemployment, welfare reform, better housing, improved health care. The glamour had gone out of the Movement.

Progress Slows—Coalitions Break Down

Additionally, as long as the Movement concentrated its energies on attacking the most odious manifestations of racial injustice in the South, it benefited from general public support. But when the emphasis shifted to securing economic equality for blacks and dismantling institutional racism, the support dwindled primarily because many whites saw such actions as jeopardizing their own status. This "me first" attitude became more pronounced as the national economic picture worsened.

The roots for the disintegration of the consensus can be traced back to the urban riots of the 1960s, which did, in fact, whether rightly or wrongly, frighten a number of white people and lessen their ardor for black-oriented causes. At about this same time, the role of national leadership in supporting the Movement began to diminish as President Lyndon B. Johnson turned his attention away from what he had called The Great Society and to the waging of the war in Vietnam. The Nixon-Ford Administration, with its attitude of benign neglect toward blacks and coolness toward many of the goals of the Movement, helped further dilute the consensus. For its part, the Carter Administration squandered what political capital it had in such an untidy fashion and was faced with some other critical issues (e.g., Iran and a souring economy) that it could do little in rebuilding consensus.

The Movement was further weakened when old allies began to break ranks because they had either grown weary, felt that they were no longer needed or wanted, turned to other causes such as Vietnam and the antiwar mood, the environment, or equal rights for women, or encountered philosophical differences with civil rights leadership. This latter was most pronounced in the deterioration of relationships between blacks and Jews over two matters—affirmative action and Andrew Young. The former involved primarily black and Jewish leadership while the latter was so emotionally charged that it went far beyond the ranks of the leaders to touch a sizable part of the black community.

At the center of the falling out over affirmative action—a process for assuring that blacks were treated equitably in hiring and in promotions—was the use of numbers or quotas as a method of insuring that affirmative action was actually working. Blacks took the position that quotas were essential. Jews, on the other hand, recalling that quotas had traditionally been used to limit their entry into certain professions and occupations, were opposed to them.

The Bakke Case

This clash of views simmered for several years and finally came to a critical point in 1978 over the *Bakke*

Case. The plaintiff, Alan Bakke, a white man, sued the medical school at the University of California at Davis because it had reserved 16 places for minorities out of the 100 available spaces for first-year students. Bakke's contention was that the establishment of a quota for minority students denied Bakke admittance even though on the basis of his test scores he was more qualified than some of the minority group members who were admitted.

Bakke's position was supported by a number of the most powerful Jewish groups in the country and unanimously opposed by black civil rights leadership. By a vote of 5–4, the U.S. Supreme Court sustained Bakke and ruled that the special program at Davis, and presumably others molded along the same lines, violated the 14th Amendment because Bakke had been rejected on the basis of his race. Black leaders were especially bitter over the decision since it came at a time when the concept of affirmative action was coming under increased assault by some whites as a form of "reverse discrimination." Blacks felt they had been deserted by their former Jewish allies, and they feared that an adverse decision in Bakke would have a "chilling effect" on other schools with affirmative action programs. Whether Bakke was to blame or not, black enrollments in professional schools did in fact decline after Bakke.

This feeling of an alliance gone wrong was reinforced in 1979 when the two groups once again found themselves on opposite sides of the affirmative action question. The case was *Weber* vs. *Kaiser Aluminum* and it involved a claim by Brian Weber, a white man, that a voluntary training program set up by Kaiser to train blacks for positions that had previously been closed to them was unconstitutional since he had been denied admittance to the program. In this instance, the Supreme Court ruled 5–2 that such voluntary plans were constitutional, but once again blacks and Jews were at odds.

Andrew Young and Black-Jewish Relations

Black-Jewish relations were further damaged that same year over the Andrew Young incident. Young, once a close and trusted associate of the late Martin Luther King, a civil rights leader in his own right, a former congressman from Atlanta, and one of the most admired blacks in America, was at that time serving as the U.S. Ambassador to the United Nations.

Already under heavy criticism by some whites because of his candor and outspokenness, Young violated official U.S. policy by meeting with a representative of the Palestine Liberation Organization to discuss pending business at the United Nations. The policy prohibited any U.S. official from meeting with any PLO

Black and Jewish relations were severely damaged by Ambassador Andrew Young's violation of U.S. policy by secretly meeting with the Palestine Liberation Organization.

representative as long as that organization refused to recognize the right of Israel to exist as a state. The restriction was a matter of great concern not only to Israelis but to American Jews as well because of the violent enmity of the PLO toward Israel.

Young's meeting was secret but news of it leaked out, producing a formal protest from Israel and cries of outrage from American Jews. Initially, Young told the State Department that the meeting had been a chance encounter, but he later conceded that it had been planned and received an official reprimand. Several days later, under mounting pressure, Young submitted his resignation to President Carter, and it was accepted.

The reaction from individual blacks was swift and angry and much of it was directed toward the Jewish community, which was held responsible for forcing Young's resignation. The first organized black response came from the Black Leadership Forum, which had been initiated in 1977 by Vernon Jordan, president of the National Urban League, in an effort to more effectively coordinate the activities of a number of black groups and ease some of the strain existing between them. In addition to the League, other groups comprising the Forum, which is still active, were the National

Business League, Legal Defense and Education Fund, National Council of Negro Women, National Urban Coalition, NAACP, Operation PUSH, Martin Luther King Jr. Center for Social Change, Southern Christian Leadership Conference, Congressional Black Caucus, National Black Caucus of Local Elected Officials, A. Philip Randolph Institute, Opportunities Industrialization Centers, and the Joint Center for Political Studies.

The Forum stopped short of directly blaming Jews for Young's troubles but it did issue a sharp statement that took issue with the manner in which Young was treated and condemned President Carter's action in accepting the Ambassador's resignation.

Then, on August 22, over 200 blacks representing the great range of opinion within the black community including many civil rights, fraternal, professional, religious, and grassroots groups, as well as those organizations at the earlier Forum meeting, gathered in an unprecedented meeting at the New York City headquarters of the NAACP to take up the Young matter. Even at the height of the Civil Rights Movement such a diverse group had not been brought together, so that the meeting indicated the seriousness with which the black community viewed the situation.

Several sharply worded statements came out of the meeting, accusing the Carter Administration of applying a double standard in dealing with Young, reaffirming the right of blacks to become involved in all foreign

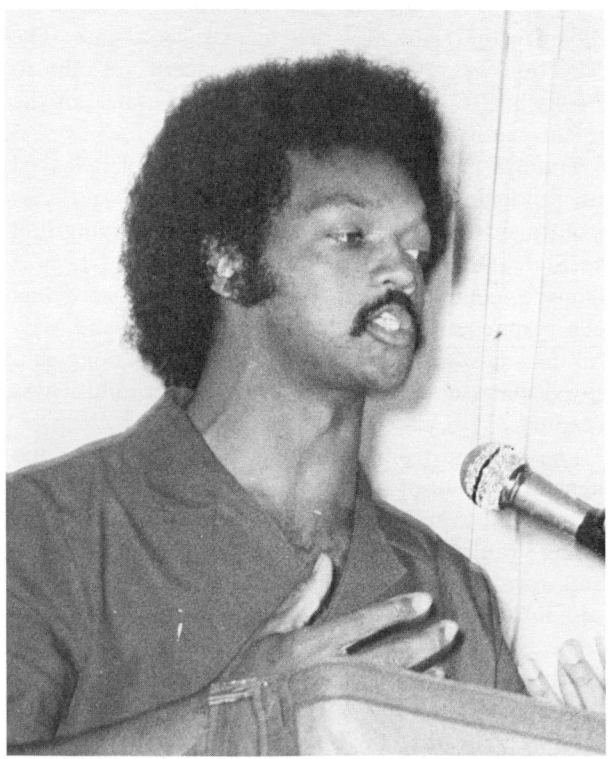

Jesse Jackson attempted to quell the Miami riots.

policy issues, and attributing a major share of the responsibility for Young's departure to Jewish influence. A day later, the National Jewish Community Relations Advisory Board, representing all major national Jewish organizations, responded by denying any involvement in Young's resignation—which was commonly conceded to have been forced. This was the sharpest dispute that had ever occurred between blacks and Jews, and while leaders on both sides sought to repair the rift, the scars were slow in healing.

The dispute also produced division within the ranks of black leadership itself when Jordan, one of the most prominent of the black leaders in the 1970s, criticized Jesse Jackson of Operation PUSH, a powerful leader, and others, for meeting with Yasir Arafat, head of the PLO, in the Middle East, a short time after the Young incident and the exchange of statements.

Jordan warned that "black-Jewish relations should not be endangered by ill-considered flirtations with terrorist groups devoted to the extermination of Israel." Jordan in turn was the object of a barrage of criticism for publicly attacking another black leader and for what some saw as taking the Jewish side.

The Miami Riots of 1980

If white Americans believed, as some of them did, that the absence of major urban riots since the late 1960s indicated that the potential for violence in the inner cities had disappeared, the belief proved to be a fallacy in May 1980 when the city of Miami exploded in an outbreak of rage that left 16 people dead, 371 injured, another 450 under arrest, and property damage in the millions. The spark that touched off the conflagration was the acquittal of four white Dade County police officers in the death of a black insurance man, Arthur McDuffie. There was convincing evidence introduced at the trial that the officers had inflicted a brutal beating on a helpless McDuffie after he was in their custody on a traffic charge. But an all-white jury freed the policemen and black anger spilled over into a full-scale riot.

Several national civil rights leaders, including Benjamin Hooks of the NAACP and Jesse Jackson of Operation PUSH, went to Miami in an effort to calm down the situation, but, as in the past, the peacemaking attempts of "establishment" black leaders were not effective and the rioting went on until it finally sputtered out. The failure of black leaders to exert any influence over the rioters was indicative of the sheer intensity of the problems in the black community that the Civil Rights Movement, the black power advocates, and the most militant of the militant black groups had not been able to solve. Writer Francis Ward several months later in *First World* summed up this state of affairs in the following words:

Miami was a dramatic but timely demonstration that they [younger, low-income blacks] have little if any confidence in black leadership, local or national. Black leadership has no message for the black dispossessed, no offer of jobs, education or new opportunities it can offer to lure the new generation of surly, angry blacks away from potential violence.

And, as in other riots, a report—this one from a special governor's committee—was made and it pointed to all too familiar causes: the black community's perception of racist conditions and a local political system stacked against it, and the always present and underlying problems of poverty, slum housing, functional illiteracy and joblessness. And, once again, it was filed and forgotten.

Vernon Jordan Ambushed

It was also in May that the National Urban League's president, Vernon E. Jordan, was ambushed and seriously wounded by an unknown gunman as he was about to enter his motel after delivering a speech to the Fort Wayne, Indiana Urban League. The bullet from a 30.06 rifle struck Jordan in the back, leaving a hole that physicians described as "almost large enough to put a fist in." Through a strange twist of fate, Jordan's life was saved by another black man, Dr. Jeffrey H. Towles, a gifted surgeon, who performed the initial operation on the civil rights leader.

The FBI mounted a far-ranging investigation but as late as the end of 1981, no arrest had been made in the case. The FBI did identify the prime suspect as a white man possessed of a virulent hatred for blacks who had been convicted of the murders of two black joggers in Salt Lake City, but they admitted they did not have enough evidence to bring him to trial in the Jordan shooting.

After a 90-day stay in the hospital, Jordan returned to his Urban League offices on November 5 and continued as president of that organization until December 31, 1981, when he resigned to become a partner in a major white law firm in Washington, D.C.

Return of the KKK

The mid-1970s and early 1980s also witnessed a rising tide of violence directed against blacks by such hate groups as the Ku Klux Klan and the Nazis. In 1980 alone, at least 24 blacks were killed in unprovoked and obviously racially inspired murders in places as far apart as Cincinnati, Indianapolis, Oklahoma City, Johnstown (Pa.), and Salt Lake City. Aided by extensive media coverage, the Klan and its sister groups, though still relatively small, were able to attract additional converts to their ranks, creating the potential for violence. Assessing the possible impact of this, the

National Urban League said in its "State of Black America—1981" report:

It should be remembered that the old Klan went into decline when the so-called "good people," who had never burned crosses or terrorized the frightened and helpless, became embarrassed at their own racism and withdrew their support. But now racism is becoming legitimized again and there is a direct line between the sophisticates who feel free to make derogatory remarks about blacks and all other racial groups and by the primitives who kill and terrorize. They are only separated by the degree of their activity.

Blacks and President Reagan—New Threats to Hard-Won Gains

The fear that racism was in fact on the rise again was a very real factor to black leadership during this period. The leaders recognized that the country's growing economic problems stiffened white resistance to further black progress, and that there was a corresponding rising tide of conservatism. The latter was reflected most strikingly in the 1980 election, which saw Ronald Reagan win the White House in a landslide and conservatives achieve control of the Senate and make major inroads into the House of Representatives.

With blacks casting only a little over 5% of their votes for Reagan, there was little reason to believe that black leadership would have any influence in his Administration. That fact was underscored when Reagan began to move immediately to either terminate or drastically reduce various social service programs which disproportionately affected black people: job training, CETA, welfare, food stamps, and a host of other programs. These were programs that black leadership had labored to bring about and now they were feeling the axe.

For the first time since the pre-Franklin D. Roosevelt days, black leadership found itself without any allies within the White House. Even the Nixon Administration, despite its public rhetoric, had desegregated southern schools at a faster rate than the Democrats, stepped up funding for job training programs, expanded government hiring of blacks, and greatly increased Federal aid to minority business, banks and colleges and Federal spending on civil rights enforcement.

Reagan, however, was a different story. Not only did he slash many of the programs that civil rights leaders saw as necessary if the economic and social gap between whites and blacks was to be closed, he also moved to roll back some of the gains that had been made in the name of civil rights, gains that prior to Reagan had not appeared to be in any real danger. Several examples are cited below:

In retrospect, President Nixon's administration was effective in enforcing civil rights laws and increasing aid for many sectors of minority concern.

March 1981—The Labor Department announced plans to withdraw a regulation that would bar employers from paying membership fees in private clubs that have discriminatory policies.

June 1981—The Education Department announced acceptance of a North Carolina higher education desegregation plan that included several provisions which had repeatedly been rejected by the Carter Administration.

August 1981—The Labor Department moved to relax antidiscriminatory rules for contractors doing business with the Federal government.

September 1981—The Justice Department said it would no longer go to court to seek the use of goals and timetables by employers found guilty of racial and sexual discrimination.

November 1981—The Office of Management and Budget told the Federal Communications Commission it could abandon a questionnaire used to determine if broadcasters are treating minorities and women fairly in employment.

December 1981—The Justice Department said it is looking for an opportunity to get the Supreme Court to reverse the *Weber* decision, which established the legality of voluntary affirmative action plans.

But this was not all. The Administration allowed the Equal Employment Opportunity Commission to drift for over a year without a chairman. In the interim, President Reagan nominated a black man who was so blatantly unqualified that black leaders, who are traditionally reluctant to criticize another black,

mounted such an outcry that the nomination had to be pulled back. With certain key sections of the Voting Rights Act, universally regarded as the most effective civil rights law ever passed, up for renewal in 1982, President Reagan finally, late in 1981, gave a lukewarm endorsement to the bill, but also expressed support for several changes that civil rights leaders unanimously agreed would seriously weaken it. Then, early in 1982, the Administration touched off a firestorm when it announced that it was reversing a policy, in existence for more than a decade and supported by several Federal court decisions, and would no longer deny tax-exempt status to private schools that practiced racial discrimination.

Despite Reagan's protestations that he was personally free of any racial bias, the actions of his Administration produced a high level of alarm among civil rights leaders, who felt that not only was the clock being turned back on racial progress, but that, given the mood of the country, they had little leverage with which to alter the course of the Administration.

Economic Setback

The mood of the country had in fact undergone a change. Polls taken in the last half of the 1970s and the early 80s showed that while an increasing number of whites were committed to the concept and idea of integration, many of them believed that true equality of opportunity had been achieved as the result of the passage of the civil rights laws and thus there was no longer a need to help blacks through government programs and spending. On the other hand, an increasing number of blacks from all points on the economic spectrum felt that racial discrimination still existed at all levels of employment, job opportunities, and housing. They also felt that things were getting worse for them.

The statistics tended to support this view. At the end of 1981, for example, official black unemployment stood at 15.5%. When workers who had become discouraged and stopped looking for work and those who held part-time jobs only because they could not find full-time employment were added, the unemployment rate skyrocketed to well over 25%. Youth unemployment in the summer of 1981 reached 45.7%. There was also an alarming rise in the number of black households headed by women and in other indices used to measure economic and social well-being.

Unable to deal with the magnitude of these problems, civil rights leaders found themselves under attack by white critics, most notably those from the political right, as being out of touch with the mass of black people. The critics pointed to what they described as a growing social gap between the black middle class, many of whom had left the ghetto, and the black poor who remained behind, and questioned whether black civil rights leadership, being mainly from the middle class, could really speak and act on behalf of the masses. They also lambasted Federal social programs as wasteful and said, in effect, that blacks had to pull themselves up by their own bootstraps and the government's role in the process should be minimal.

The Black Neoconservatives

Attacks also came from black neoconservatives led by Dr. Thomas Sowell, an economist and senior fellow at the Hoover Institute in California. Sowell castigated traditional black leaders for what he saw as their failure to serve the needs of the black masses and their endorsement of federally funded programs, many of which he described as counterproductive and inducing a sense of dependency.

The most visible moment for the black conservatives as a group came in December 1980, one month after the Reagan victory, when they held a conference in San Francisco that attracted several hundred persons and received major media attention. However, the meeting failed to produce a conservative black agenda and a planned follow-up meeting was never held. The conservatives also announced that they would form their own national organization to challenge traditional black leadership, but this never materialized.

Actually, conservatism has little influence in Black America. A number of surveys have revealed that in the main, blacks are economic liberals and differ markedly from conservatives on the role of government in socioeconomic programs. Blacks favor more. Conservatives favor less. Noted political scientist Dr. Charles V. Hamilton has this to say:

To the extent that the black leadership articulates policies aimed at continued and increased government participation in such areas as education, welfare, housing, and health, that leadership speaks in the same way as the mass of blacks.

And while blacks find themselves agreeing with some positions of the conservatives on such issues as law enforcement and sexual morality, they veer off in an entirely different direction on questions of civil rights.

However, if black neoconservatives failed to establish any meaningful role for themselves in the mid-1970s and early 1980s, there were other black leadership groups that did come to prominence and caused a diversification of black leadership that has traditionally been concentrated in civil rights, the church, the professions, and academia.

The first of these is black elected officials, a group which has grown from a handful in the early 1960s to more than 4,000 in the late 1970s. The next is blacks who are managing large public and private (predominantly white) institutions, such as Franklin Thomas at the Ford Foundation and Dr. Clifton Wharton at the State University of New York. The third group comprises blacks who are executives in corporate America. The fourth is the cadre of leaders basically developed through the War on Poverty programs. Many of these are originally grassroots people who, once placed in a position of leadership, had the opportunity to develop their potential. The fifth and final group is the new black businessmen, who have made successes in nontraditional fields.

The Formidability of Civil Rights Organizations Declines

At the same time that these groups were emerging, the influence of the black militants and the Black Power advocates, which had once appeared formidable, was on the wane. Locally, some of the groups continued to function or served as the parents of other self-help and community organizations, but by the beginning of the 1980s, on the national level, the militants and the Black Power advocates were virtually invisible. It was as if after a brief moment in the sky, they had faded like dying rockets. Certainly their leaders from the 1960s were all gone and no others had emerged to take their places.

Eldridge Cleaver of the Black Panthers was a born-again Christian who frequently lectured on the subject of his conversion. H. Rap Brown, the successor to Stokely Carmichael as the head of the Student Non-Violent Coordinating Committee (SNCC), after serving time for armed robbery, was a storekeeper in Atlanta. Carmichael himself was dividing his time between Africa and America without any real base of power. Huey Newton of the Panthers, after losing in an effort to become mayor of Oakland, California, dropped from sight.

As for the five major organizations that were most active during the Civil Rights Movement of the sixties—the NAACP, the National Urban League, CORE, SNCC, and the Southern Christian Leadership Conference—only the first two continued to thrive.

CORE was still on the scene but it had long since ceased to be a truly national organization and its membership was concentrated in New York City under the long-term and stormy leadership of Roy Innis, who was named its national director in 1968. The organization was also buffeted by charges of fraud in connection with its fundraising activities and expenditures of funds, and allegations of intimidation of dissident members, so that its credibility was badly damaged.

Without the dynamic leadership of Martin Luther King, the Southern Christian Leadership Conference was a shadow of its former self, confining its sporadic activities primarily to the South. SNCC had simply gone out of business.

Even within the oldest and most stable of the groups, the NAACP and the Urban League, there were changes. Roy Wilkins, after 22 years as Executive Director of the NAACP, retired in 1977 to be replaced by Benjamin L. Hooks, a Baptist minister, attorney, and a former commissioner on the Federal Communications Commission. (Mr. Wilkins died in 1981.) Vernon Jordan, after ten years at the helm of the Urban League as the successor to the late Whitney M. Young, stepped down at the end of 1981. His post was taken over by John E. Jacob, who had served for several years as the League's executive vice president.

The NAACP during this period experienced a decline in its membership and resulting financial problems. The former was most critical since the strength of the organization has always resided in its broad base of dues-paying members who not only gave it a degree of independence from white philanthropy, but who could be mobilized quickly in more than 1,000 communities whenever the need arose. Its membership is in fact the strength of the NAACP and, fully aware of this, the organization has moved to increase these ranks aided by the fact that it is usually the NAACP black people turn to in times of trouble.

In recent years the NAACP has shifted its emphasis from lobbying for legislation—at which it was very successful—to seeing that the laws it helped put on the books are properly carried out. Therefore, it has increased the number of court cases it argues on behalf of blacks including legal fights for fair housing, school desegregation, and social justice.

Unlike the NAACP, the Urban League does not maintain a national membership, depending for its strength instead on a network of over 100 affiliates staffed by paid personnel. But it also faced financial problems when much of the funding it had been receiving to conduct job training and other programs was cut off in the Reagan economy drive. This reduction in resources forced the League to cut back on staff and terminate several of its largest programs, just as the nation was entering a recession and black unem-

H. Rap Brown, fiery orator of the Black Power Movement, is now a storekeeper in Atlanta.

ployment was on the rise. Facing this dilemma, Vernon Jordan, in what was to be his last keynote speech as head of the League, told its 1981 conference:

The complexities of today's racial, economic and political issues are such that there is no one grand strategy or leader to deliver us. We will have to draw on our immense resources of survival skills to get us through these hard times, and to cultivate our bonds of unity to once again overcome.

He suggested that the future agenda for the League lay in a return to "basics" such as building community strengths and institutions, developing more political muscle, and establishing coalitions. If the League is to do this, the chances are that it will have to continue its traditional focus on funds from the private sector, and this means corporate America.

Under the guidance of the Reverend Jesse Jackson, Operation PUSH (People United to Save Humanity) was the other important national civil rights organization on the scene during this period. In contrast to the NAACP and the League, which had relatively large permanent staffs at their national headquarters and eight chapters or affiliates across the country, PUSH lacked a national structure of any size, engaged in no legal cases on behalf of constituents, and operated only a single program, on an experimental basis, to improve educational achievement.

Most of PUSH's influence was derived through the charismatic personality of Reverend Jackson, which made him one of the most respected and admired figures in the black community, and one of the most effective of all civil rights spokesmen on the airways and in newspapers and magazines.

The Future

As to the future, civil rights groups, whether national or local, face a new set of challenges that will test their sophistication, their endurance, and their ability to devise new strategies to meet these challenges. The national swing to the right, a faltering economy that promotes a meanness of spirit, and increasing indifference to legitimate black needs signal that the position of blacks in this society is still precarious. Most vulnerable are young blacks who enter a world where opportunities are growing scarcer, requiring more skills and training, and where racism is still a factor in who gets what.

To many of these young people the Civil Rights Movement means very little. They were not around when it was at its apex and they can see nothing, or very little, that it has done, or is doing, to make their lives any better. It was one thing to win the right to check into a hotel, but the struggle for jobs and eco-

nomic stability that will enable people to check out of that hotel has still not been won.

Helping to create jobs, improving education, protecting the rights of the disadvantaged, maintaining vigilance to see that the gains of the past are not wiped out, and enriching the quality of life for black people is unglamorous and sometimes harsh. But this is the task that faces the Civil Rights Movement in the eighties and beyond.

CIVIL RIGHTS ORGANIZATIONS

The National Association for the Advancement of Colored People

"I bring you greetings from the oldest, largest, most effective, most consulted, most militant, most feared and to us the most loved of all the civil rights organizations in the world."

From 1961 until his death in 1974, Bishop Stephen Gill Spottswood (African Methodist Episcopal Zion Church) as chairman of the board of the National Association for the Advancement of Colored People, traditionally used those words to open the organization's annual conference. His description was accurate in almost every respect, for the NAACP has more than earned its niche as America's preeminent civil rights organization.

The NAACP came into being on February 12, 1909—the hundredth anniversary of the birth of Abraham Lincoln. It was largely the brainchild of three people: William English Walling, a white Southerner who feared that racists would soon carry "the race war to the North"; Mary White Ovington, a wealthy young white woman who had attended the 1906 meeting of the Niagara group as a reporter for the *New York Evening Post* and had experience with conditions in the black ghettos of New York City; and Dr. Henry Moskowitz, a New York social worker. This trio proposed that a conference be called "for the discussion of present evils, the voicing of protests, and the renewal of the struggle for civil and political liberty."

The three-day conference (May 30–June 1) was followed by four meetings, the results of which were an increase in membership and the choice of an official name: The National Negro Committee. In 1910 the organization adopted its present name and was incorporated in New York state. A year earlier the Niagara movement and the NAACP had merged. By 1914 the association had already established some 50 branches throughout the country.

With the founding of the NAACP, *Crisis* magazine, edited by W. E. B. DuBois, became its chief organ for propoganda and a major vehicle for the dissemina-

Dr. W. E. B. DuBois works at his desk in the old Crisis *office.*

tion of educational and social programs. (*Crisis* is still being published on a monthly basis.)

Over the years, the NAACP attempted to better the black's lot through "litigation, legislation, and education." Perhaps its most significant judicial victory was won in 1954 when the historic *Brown* v. *Board of Education* case threw out the "separate but equal" doctrine established in *Plessy* v. *Ferguson,* thus opening the door for the elimination of segregation in public education.

While other black organizations have tended in recent years to gravitate toward racial separatism, the NAACP has clung tenaciously to its goal of promoting racial integration. It has sought to improve the status of blacks in many fields, including jobs and schools, and has pushed doggedly and perseveringly for civil rights legislation.

Following the failure of legal decisions and legislation championed by the NAACP to evoke fundamental changes in America's racial climate, the NAACP was attacked by many militants and black power advocates as "irrelevant" to the needs of most blacks. These charges reached a climax in 1972 when members of the now defunct National Economic Growth and Reconstruction Organization (NEGRO) occupied part of

NAACP's New York office for a few hours in protest against NAACP's alleged "unresponsiveness" to the needs of the black masses.

Such criticism was short-lived, however, as the NAACP launched a new series of programs that included providing assistance to coalitions of minority contractors to qualify for major construction jobs, the establishment of daycare centers in several communities, the setting-up of "Project Rebound" to aid the reorientation of former prison inmates, and the investigation of military justice in Alaska and West Germany and on some Navy ships.

The leadership of the NAACP changed in 1977 when Roy Wilkins, who had served as executive director for over 25 years, retired and was succeeded by Benjamin L. Hooks, a lawyer, minister, civil rights activist, and at the time of his selection, a commissioner at the Federal Communications Commission—the first black to hold such a post.

With its efforts to secure civil rights legislation crowned by success, the NAACP has in recent years devoted more of its attention to seeing that the laws are carried out. It argues many court cases on behalf of blacks, including legal fights for fair housing, school desegregation, and political equality. The NAACP Legal Department has been active in 38 states and the District of Columbia, filing motions, arguing cases, meeting with local branch people, interviewing clients, or conferring with cooperating retained counsel.

J. W. Johnson, former secretary of the NAACP.

Roy Wilkins outlines a needed federal program to President Johnson.

The rise of violence against blacks, beginning in the early eighties is another matter to which the NAACP has given high priority, successfully seeking the intervention of the Justice Department on a number of occasions.

On the programmatic side, the NAACP is active in housing, education, labor, voter education/registration, and prisons. It also has a very effective program to reach young people that operates through its Youth and College Division.

The NAACP maintains a powerful Washington bureau which, for many years (until his retirement in 1978) was headed by Clarence Mitchell, Jr., whose efforts as a lobbyist on behalf of black people earned him the title "the 101st Senator." This bureau was a key factor in the passage of all of the civil rights legislation of the 1960s and has continually maintained its posture as an effective national defender of the rights of blacks. At the local level, the individual chapters of the NAACP are often the most influential civil rights organizations.

The NAACP's chief regional offices are located in San Francisco, Dallas, and Atlanta. It is headquartered in New York City. The latter office was reorganized in 1973, when national headquarters differed with its support of a plan which seemed to minimize the prospects for integrating Atlanta's schools.

The National Urban League

The National Urban League, in existence since 1919, began as an organization to help black migrants to New York City find suitable employment and make as smooth a transition as possible from rural southern to urban northern life.

Black migrants to the cities stemmed largely from an agricultural environment, and had often lived in virtual peonage in the Black Belt. Unschooled and unguided, they faced the competition of the northern labor markets, including the craft unions, with virtually no preparation, and without the protection of any governmental guidelines for their prospective employers.

In 1906, at the urging of William H. Baldwin, president of the Long Island Railroad, a group of blacks and whites met for the purpose of studying the work needs of the black. This group, known as the Committee for Improving the Industrial Conditions among Negroes in New York, studied the racial aspects of the labor market (particularly the attitudes and policies of employers and unions), and sought to find openings for qualified blacks.

At the same time, the League for the Protection of Colored Women was established to provide similar services for black women who were coming into New

Original Seal of the National Urban League.

York and Philadelphia from various parts of the South. These women often had no friends or relatives to meet and welcome them, and so fell prey to unscrupulous employment agencies which led them into jobs at wages far less than they had expected to receive.

A third organization, the Committee on Urban Conditions Among Negroes, appeared on the New York scene in 1910. It was organized by Mrs. Ruth Standish Baldwin, widow of the former Long Island Railroad president, and Dr. George Edmond Haynes, one of only three trained black social workers in the country and the first black person to receive a doctorate from Columbia University. Haynes was named as the first executive secretary of the new agency and a year later it merged with the Committee for the Improvement of Industrial Conditions Among Negroes in New York and the National League for the Protection of Colored Women to form the National League on Urban Conditions Among Negroes. That name was later shortened to the now-familiar National Urban League.

From the outset, the Committee focused more on dealing with the social and economic needs of blacks than it did with the civil rights aspect of their existence. The latter area was one in which the NAACP was active and the League sought instead to involve itself in the training of black social workers, and in housing, health, sanitation, recreation, self-improvement, and job assistance.

The organizational model that the League had established in New York City attracted attention and soon affiliates began to be formed in various cities across the country. Traditionally, the affiliates, like the prototype, were full-time operations, staffed by professionals, and dependent on private philanthropy for funding. A major goal of the League and its affiliates was to broaden economic opportunities for blacks by using the techniques of persuasion and conciliation to open up doors that had been closed before.

The NUL was one of the first black organizations to become involved in research. This occurred in 1920 when Dr. Charles S. Johnson, a classic figure in black scholarship, organized the NUL's Research Department. Dr. Johnson produced numerous landmark studies on the black condition and also edited the magazine *Opportunity: Journal of Negro Life,* which became a mainstay of what was known as "the Harlem Renaissance" of the 1930s, publishing almost every leading black poet and writer of the day.

It was not, however, until the 1960s when Whitney M. Young, Jr. became its new leader that the League began to emerge as a force in the civil rights struggle. The League's strategy was to deal with fundamental social problems through influencing decision makers and becoming part of the process by which basic decisions affecting black people are made. Thus a typical technique of the sixties was for the League to work with more obviously militant organizations whose marches the League backed up in boardroom and public policy confrontations.

In the late sixties the League embarked on a program called "New Thrust," which was designed to assist inner-city residents to increase their own economic and political power through programs and community organization. This grassroots involvement has continued.

Young had achieved status as a major spokesman for black people when his career was cut short in a drowning accident off the coast of Africa in 1971. He was succeeded by Vernon E. Jordan, Jr., a lawyer and the first non-social worker to head the League. Jordan continued the forceful advocacy of Young, enhancing the civil rights posture of the League. In his ten years at the helm (Jordan resigned December 31, 1981) he took the League into new programmatic fields such as energy and the environment, challenged national leadership over its failure to deal with the problems of the poor, and increased the number of League affiliates from 99 to 118 with over 4,200 employees and 30,000 volunteers.

The growth of the League was due primarily to expansion of its direct services, which annually provided over one million people with programs like job training, education, health, housing, criminal justice. The League, over a period of years, had demonstrated an ability to operate such programs effectively and as a result, under both Democrats and Republicans, it received a large number of government grants. However, with the decision of the Reagan Administration when it took office in 1981 to cut back on domestic spending, the League lost a sizable portion of its Fed-

President Ford meets with Vernon E. Jordan, Jr., executive director of the Urban League.

eral funding, which in the fiscal year ending June 30, 1981 totaled some $19 million. But still intact was the basic general budget of the League of some $5 million raised in the main from the corporate community and foundations.

The League has been brought under attack by some critics who charge that it is middle class in orientation and therefore cannot be responsive to the needs of the mass of black people. The League responds by pointing out that while it relies for staff on trained professionals, who are middle class, the overwhelming majority of its activities are geared toward improving the economic and social status of the black poor.

Headquartered in New York City, the National Urban League also has four regional offices, in Atlanta, Chicago, Los Angeles, and New York City. In addition, it has a Washington Bureau and Research Department in Washington, D.C.

The Urban League has been interracial since its founding. It has a board of some 60 members drawn from all sectors of the community. The League is headed by a chairman of the board and a president and chief executive officer who is responsible for the day-to-day operation of the agency. The former has traditionally been white and the latter black. The League now describes itself as "an interracial, non-profit community service organization that uses the tools and methods of social work, economics, law and other disciplines, to secure equal opportunity in all sectors of our society for black Americans and other minorities."

The current president of the League is John E. Jacob, a social worker, who succeeded Vernon Jordan on January 1, 1982. Mr. Jacob had served in the number two position at the League as Executive Vice President since February 1, 1979. At the time of his election by the board, he had served in the Urban League Movement for over 15 years.

The Southern Christian Leadership Conference

Born out of the Montgomery bus boycott of the 1950s, the Southern Christian Leadership Conference came into being just as the civil rights movement in the American south was about to explode. Even as young as it was, SCLC was destined to play a leading role in that explosion.

And the time was right for an organization such as SCLC. In some areas of the South, the NAACP was prohibited from operating and the Urban League, with its traditional emphasis on social work as opposed to direct action, was in no position to provide direction for the growing movement. However, led by a gifted young black minister, Martin Luther King, Jr., the Montgomery Improvement Association, after a non-violent struggle that lasted over a year, achieved its

Reverend Martin Luther King, Jr., leads Chicago march for housing.

goal of desegregating the bus system in a city that was known for its harsh racial attitudes.

Encouraged by this demonstration of the power that could be employed through a mass movement, representatives from ten southern states, consisting mainly of black ministers at the grassroots level, met at Atlanta's Ebenezer Baptist Church in January 1957, shortly after the victory in Montgomery, and organized SCLC. They elected Dr. King as president.

SCLC appealed to blacks "to assert their human dignity by refusing further cooperation with evil." Specifically, SCLC contended that blacks should feel a moral obligation to reinforce traditional legal action in the courts with nonviolent direct action to desegregate public transportation, public places, and public schools. Beyond these accomplishments, the ballot and civil rights laws stood as goals to be achieved.

For the rest of the decade of the 1950s and until the assassination of Dr. King in 1968, SCLC, as one of the most influential and effective of all the civil rights groups, espoused, most often through the eloquence of Dr. King, a doctrine of nonviolent protest and passive resistance in its assault on segregation and discrimination.

The basic strength of SCLC was rooted in the black church, the single most important and influential institution within Black America. By emphasizing the morality of the civil rights crusade, by sharply drawing in religious terms the contrast between racial justice and racial injustice, and by the predominance of ministers in leadership positions, SCLC secured the support of a sizable part of the black church community which gave freely of its resources, even in the face of threatened or actual violence directed against it. The church

also encouraged its members to support SCLC. Further, the appeal of SCLC, under King's leadership, to basic principles of humanity, was so great that it drew support from the white community as well.

SCLC was a driving force under King. Its confrontations with the forces of bigotry in such places as Birmingham and Selma, Alabama helped not only arouse the conscience of what had until then been a complacent America, but also spurred the passage of the various civil rights laws of the 1960s. The murder of Dr. King dealt SCLC a severe blow. More than any other person, he had come to symbolize SCLC and there was real concern that without his charismatic leadership the organization would fall apart.

The Reverend Ralph David Abernathy, one of Dr. King's closest associates, was elected by the SCLC board to succeed the slain leader. Prior to his death, Dr. King had planned a massive "Poor People's Campaign" that was to bring thousands of people of all races from all across the country to Washington, D.C. in the spring of 1968 to demand help from the government for the poor. The campaign was continued under Dr. Abernathy, but it was plagued from the very start by a series of almost insurmountable difficulties, including inadequate logistics, internal disputes, general public indifference and seemingly unending rainstorms that turned "Resurrection City," the site where tents had been erected for the demonstrators, into a sea of mud and misery that sapped the spirit and morale of the demonstrators. This was the last major public demonstration that SCLC was to mount outside the South, but in that area of the country, where it had its greatest strength, it continued as a viable organization, albeit with a lower profile.

Many of SCLC's recent activities have been centered on its efforts to strengthen the black family, and since 1980 it has held an annual Martin Luther King Jr. Memorial Weekend at which it brings together experts and concerned citizens to examine various aspects of the black family. SCLC has also taken an interest in foreign affairs, particularly those related to the Mideast and Africa. It maintains its ongoing commitment to protecting and increasing the political power of blacks, and in 1982, as a renewal of the Voting Rights Act of 1965 was being debated in Congress, it duplicated the historic march of Dr. King from Selma to Montgomery, which has been credited with having a major influence in the passage of the original legislation.

SCLC is interracial in character and has supporters among people of all faiths, religions, and creeds. Its headquarters is in Atlanta and it maintains affiliates in six Southern and boarder states. Its board of some 50 members is composed of both ministers and lay people. Board chairman is Representative Walter Fauntroy (a Democrat from Washington, D.C.), who was one of the earliest members of SCLC. The president is Reverend Joseph Lowery, who was elected in 1977.

"Stride Toward Freedom" speech.

Individuals hold membership in SCLC through such affiliated organizations as churches, fraternal orders, and civic bodies. Bona fide affiliates are restricted to the 17 southern states and the District of Columbia, but supporting affiliates are not under this geographical restriction.

Funds for SCLC are raised through the fees and pledges of affiliated organizations, mass rallies, and direct mail appeals. SCLC does not make available the size of its staff or its annual budget.

One of the major interests of SCLC is its Operation Breadbasket, which it formed in 1962 to deal with the problems blacks faced as workers, consumers, professionals, and businessmen.

Operation PUSH (People United to Save Humanity)

Through the leadership of its founder and president, the Reverend Jessee Jackson, Operation PUSH has developed, within a short time, into a nationally known and respected civil rights organization. One of the most sought after speakers in the country, gifted with the ability to communicate with virtually every sector of society, Jackson through his organization has been especially effective in motivating young people through the PUSH-EXCEL Program.

Basically, the program instills a sense of pride in young high school students, builds up their confidence that they can succeed, and encourages disciplined study. PUSH-EXCEL operates in seven cities—Buffalo, N.Y.; Chattanooga, Tenn.; Kansas City, Mo.; Chicago; Denver; Takoma Park, Md.; and Rochester, N.Y. PUSH also awards a $10,000 annual scholarship through the program.

In the early 1980s PUSH scored major breakthroughs on the economic front when it negotiated national agreements with Coca Cola and Hueblein, Inc. to expand the number of black distributors and wholesalers handling their products, increase employment opportunities, use black media more for advertising, place money in black banks, and generally put more financial resources in the black community. This approach is continuing with other major firms.

This type of activity is not new to PUSH, for in 1972 it signed a similar agreement with the Joseph Schlitz Brewing Co. for blacks to comprise 15% of its work force and black business to receive 15% of its advertising, insurance, and construction expenditures. A similar agreement with the General Food Corp. increased that company's employment of blacks and use of black business.

Operation PUSH's viewpoint is stated in the following preamble and 15-point platform, signed by leading members of its board of directors.

Operation PUSH dinner in 1972: Manhattan Borough President Percy Sutton, Reverend Jesse Jackson, presidential candidate George McGovern (left to right).

Operation PUSH Platform

We, the People United to Save Humanity, believe that humanity will be saved and served only when justice is done for all people. We believe that we must challenge the economic, political, and social forces that make us subservient to others; and that we must assume the power (of being) given us by the Power of God. We believe that our worth as humane people is expressed in our united efforts to secure justice for all persons. We, therefore, state our declaration of goals.

1. PUSH for a comprehensive economic plan for the development of Black and poor people. This plan will include status as underdeveloped enclaves entitled to consideration by the World Bank and the International Monetary Fund.
2. PUSH for human alternatives to the welfare system.
3. PUSH for the revival of the labor movement to protect organized workers and to organize unorganized workers.
4. PUSH for a survival Bill of Rights for all children up to the age of 18 guaranteeing their food, clothing, shelter, medical care and education.
5. PUSH for a survival Bill of Rights for the aging, guaranteeing adequate food, clothing, shelter, medical care and meaningful programs.
6. PUSH for full political participation including an automatic voter registration as a right of citizenship.
7. PUSH to elect to local, state and federal offices persons committed to humane economic and social programs.
8. PUSH for humane conditions in prisons and sound rehabilitative programs.
9. PUSH for a Bill of Rights for veterans whose needs are ignored.
10. PUSH for adequate health care for all people based upon need.
11. PUSH for quality education regardless of race, religion or creed.
12. PUSH for economic and social relationships with the nations of Africa in order to build African/Afro-American unity.

13. PUSH for national unity among all organizations working for the humane economic, political and social development of people.
14. PUSH for a relevant theology geared to regenerating depressed and oppressed peoples.
15. PUSH for black excellence.

We are dedicated to reaching our goals through the research, education, development and execution of direct action programs that provide for economic, political and cultural independence.

Congress of Racial Equality

The Congress of Racial Equality (CORE) was founded in 1942 by James Farmer as the result of a campaign protesting discrimination at a Chicago restaurant which developed the "sit-in" technique that was to prove so successful during the civil rights movement of the 1960s. CORE began life as an interracial passive-resistance organization committed to confronting racism and discrimination with direct action.

From Chicago, it moved on to other cities and other causes: drug and department stores in St. Louis, a legitimate theater in Baltimore, registration drives in South Carolina, movie theaters in Columbia, Missouri—all the while growing slowly. Then came Greensboro, North Carolina, where in 1960 four young black male students from A&T College staged a sit-in at a Woolworth lunch counter which refused to serve them. Under the auspices of CORE, the sit-ins began to spread rapidly throughout the South, and in many instances they achieved the desegregation of public places. CORE thus began to establish national visibility for itself.

Its status was further enhanced in 1961 when it sponsored a series of Freedom Rides across the South to test compliance with an order of the Interstate Commerce Commission to desegregate bus travel and stations. The riders, both black and white, were brutally assaulted in several cities but the demonstration set the stage for eventual enforcement of the ruling.

In assessing the importance of CORE during those days, the Reverend Jesse Jackson said: "It was the very soul of the civil rights movement. In 1963, it had more people marching for desegregation in Greensboro than Dr. King had in Birmingham." Another evaluation called it more activist than the NAACP, more intergrated than the Southern Christian Leadership Conference, and more established and respected than the Student Non-Violent Coordinating Committee (SNCC).

CORE began to change directions in 1966 as the Black Power philosophy was coming to the fore. Farmer, the founder, turned the national leadership over to Floyd McKissick, a North Carolina lawyer. The new leader began to move CORE closer to being all-black in membership and staff and in 1967 it moved, at its convention, to eliminate the word "multiracial" from its constitution.

When McKissick left in 1968 he was replaced by the present national director, Roy Innis, former chairman of the Harlem chapter of CORE.

In recent years CORE has been beset by a number of difficulties. Its membership and affiliates have dwindled sharply from some 70,000 members and almost 100 affiliates in 33 states and the District of Columbia that it reported in the late 1960s. And CORE itself no longer gives out these figures.

The Black Leadership Forum

The Black Leadership Forum is an informal group of the heads of 14 national predominantly black organizations who meet on a periodic basis to exchange information, discuss mutual concerns, and plan joint strategies where appropriate. The meetings are private and media coverage is discouraged to ensure the confidentiality of the discussions.

However, the Forum does from time to time issue joint statements on matters of specific interest to blacks. It was created in 1977 following a suggestion by Vernon E. Jordan, Jr., then president of the National Urban League, that such a group was needed to better coordinate the various efforts being made on behalf of black people.

One of the first issues to face the Forum was the *Bakke* case involving a white man's claim of reverse discrimination in his failure to be accepted by a medical

Floyd McKissick is an advocate of black economic power.

school. The Forum appealed to the Carter Administration to file a brief in opposition to Bakke's claim.

The Forum can be viewed as a descendant of the Council for United Civil Rights Leadership that was active in the 1950s and 1960s as a coordinating mechanism for the Civil Rights Movement and included the NAACP, the National Urban League, the National Council of Negro Women, the NAACP Legal Defense and Educational Fund, CORE, the Southern Christian Leadership Conference, and the Student Non-Violent Coordinating Committee.

Groups now holding membership in the Forum—and membership is confined to only the leader of each group—are the NAACP, National Urban League, National Business League, NAACP Legal Defense and Education Fund, National Council of Negro Women, National Urban Coalition, Operation PUSH, Martin Luther King, Jr. Center for Social Change, Congressional Black Caucus, National Black Caucus of Local Elected Officials, A. Philip Randolph Institute, Opportunities Industrialization Centers, and Joint Center for Political Studies.

The leadership of the Forum alternates on an annual basis. The current chairman is Reverend Joseph Lowery, president of SCLC.

The Leadership Conference on Civil Rights

The Leadership Conference on Civil Rights was established in 1950 by A. Philip Randolph, Roy Wilkins, and Arnold Aronson to implement the historic report of President Truman's Committee on Civil Rights, "To Secure These Rights."

Beginning with 30 organizations, the Conference has grown in numbers, scope, and effectiveness. It currently consists of approximately 157 national organizations representing blacks, Hispanics, Asian Americans, labor, the major religious groups, women, the handicapped, the aged, and minority businesses and professions.

These organizations speak for a substantial portion of the population and together comprise the most broadly based coalition in the nation. The member groups differ in size, structure, and broad objectives, but are united in seeking an integrated, democratic, plural society, in which each individual is accorded equal rights, equal opportunities, and equal justice without regard to race, sex, religion, ethnic origin, handicap, or age.

Starting with the Civil Rights Act of 1957, the Leadership Conference coordinated the campaigns that resulted in the passage of all the civil rights legislation of this century, including the Civil Rights Acts of 1960 and 1964, the Voting Rights Act of 1965, and the Fair Housing Act of 1968.

The Leadership Conference is committed to establishing, as a matter of right, a useful job at a decent wage for all who are employable or who can be made so by training or retraining, an income sufficient to provide all others with the essentials for living in dignity and self-respect, decent housing in a decent environment for all, medical care for all in health, sickness, and disability, and education to the limit of each person's capacity to benefit from it.

Among the member groups of the Leadership Conference are the African Methodist Episcopal Church,

Flanked by co-workers, Floyd McKissick speaks at a CORE rally in Soul City, North Carolina.

AFL-CIO, Anti-Defamation League of B'nai B'rith, Kappa Alpha Psi Fraternity, Mexican American Legal Defense and Education Fund, the NAACP, the National Urban League, and the Organization of Chinese Americans.

LEADERSHIP CONFERENCE ON CIVIL RIGHTS
2027 Massachusetts Avenue NW
Washington, D.C.   20036
(202) 667-1780

The Black United Front

The newest of the national civil rights organizations, the Black United Front, was organized in July 1980, when 1,000 delegates from 34 states gathered at a Brooklyn church in response to a call from Reverend Herbert Daughtry, a Brooklyn Pentecostal minister. Included among the delegates were many long-time activists who saw the need to build a strong grassroots black movement in light of unemployment and other problems affecting blacks.

Daughtry contended that the situation has reached "genocidal dimensions for blacks" and that there was a vacuum in national black leadership, and "our people are searching for new leaders and new vehicles."

The BUF announced that it would seek to enroll black youth, the elderly, churches, the middle class, and professionals. The only groups that it said it would not recruit was "black leaders created by whites who have sold out to whites and who function to keep community leaders from developing."

Among those present for the organizing session were Imamu Amiri Baraka, the poet and playwright; Amiri Obodeli, President of the New Republic of Africa; Skip Robinson, President of the United League of Mississippi; and Prince Ashiel Ben Israel, Ambassador from the Hebrew Israelites of Dimona, Israel.

The NAACP Legal Defense and Educational Fund, Inc.

Established in 1939 by the NAACP, the NAACP Legal Defense and Educational Fund has had its own board, program, staff, office, and budget for some 20 years. Through the years, it has been in the forefront of legal assaults against discrimination and segregation and has an outstanding record of victories, a tribute to the meticulous care with which it traditionally prepares its cases.

Throughout the years, the LDF has won extremely important legal victories for minorities. In 1972 it succeeded in getting the Supreme Court to nullify the death penalty and to rule that towns with heavy concentrations of white students could not secede from largely black school systems.

Recently, it has been deeply involved in employment, education, the administration of criminal justice, affirmative action, housing, and health care. The greatest concentration has been on employment, where, in the space of just under two years, the LDF secured $10.1 million in back pay awards for minority workers who had been discriminated against. The LDF was also instrumental in reaching agreement with the Federal government to phase out its Professional and Administrative Career Examination (PACE) because of its severe adverse impact on blacks and other minorities.

As it looked to the 1980s, the LDF predicted that its role as the premiere legal defender of the rights of black Americans would not diminish and that the civil rights of blacks would be affected in the following ways:

Across-the-board attacks on affirmative action through executive then legislative and budgetary means.

Appointment of judges unsympathetic to civil rights claims.

Structural changes in the civil rights enforcement authority of agencies such as the Office of Federal Contract Compliance, the Equal Employment Opportunity Commission, and the Departments of Education and Housing and Urban Development.

Support of congressional efforts aimed at crippling effective school desegregation remedies.

Redistricting with the intent to reduce minority representation.

In its 1980 annual report, the LDF said "agencies like LDF will have a more important role in the defense of basic civil rights in the next few years than at any time in the recent past."

In addition to its litigation, the LDF provides scholarships and training for young lawyers, advises lawyers on legal trends and decisions, and monitors federal programs which often fail to deliver their intended services.

The Director-Counsel of LDF is Jack Greenberg, who in 1961 succeeded Thurgood Marshall upon the latter's appointment to the Supreme Court.

THE NAACP LEGAL DEFENSE AND EDUCATION FUND, INC.
10 Columbus Circle
New York, New York   10019
(212) 586-8397

CIVIL RIGHTS AND MILITANT GROUPS OF THE PAST

The cause of blacks in the United States has been represented by a great diversity of organizations. Some, such as the Free African Societies, emerged from organized religious groups; others, such as the Niagara Movement and the Student Non-Violent Coordinating Committee, from intellectuals and students. Following are short descriptions of organizations, no longer active, that have rendered important contributions to the black struggle for equality and respect.

The Free African Society

The Free African Society was formed in Philadelphia in 1787 by Richard Allen and Absalom Jones, two ministers, to help blacks of "orderly and sober life . . . support one another in sickness and for the benefit of their widows and children." Though it adhered to its moral tenets intently, and expelled members who violated them, the Free African Society soon began to help blacks who ran afoul of the law because of opposition to slavery. However, it avoided, wherever possible, all appearances of racial militancy, promising to exclude from membership any person who violated "the laws of their country."

Despite such caution, The Free African Society cooperated with the Pennsylvania Abolition Society and counseled other, more militant, "Free African" groups to form in other northern cities. Similar groups in the South were forbidden by law.

The American Anti-Slavery Society

A number of antislavery societies developed in the eighteenth century, particularly among the Quakers of Pennsylvania, but they lost strength to recolonization movements and the increased demand for slaves to labor on cotton plantations.

Antislavery groups that did exist were generally weak and conservative. Total membership in 1825 did not exceed 8,000 and many advocated recolonization of freed blacks. Several of these groups communicated with one another loosely through the American Anti-Slavery Society.

However, in the early 1830s William Lloyd Garrison formed the New England Anti-Slavery Society and through it succeeded in directing the American Anti-Slavery Society to a stronger position, though many chapters remained moderate. Membership boomed, exceeding 300,000 by 1840.

The influence of the Society in the overall abolitionist movement increased. Blacks, pleased with the Society's stand for racial equality, joined, formed their

Abolitionist newspaperman William Lloyd Garrison raised public outcry for immediate and total abolition of slavery.

own chapters, and sent delegates to national meetings. Some, however, such as Henry Highland Garnet, were to find the Society's position too reserved and called for revolution to end slavery. And in 1851 Frederick Douglass broke with Garrison when Douglass demanded that the Society attack the Constitution as a document which favors slavery. The split weakened the Society, but its contribution as a catalyst and focal point of antislavery sentiment had been fulfilled.

The Niagara Movement

The Niagara Movement was founded by a group of 29 black intellectuals—headed by W. E. B. DuBois, a professor at Atlanta University—who met July 11–13, 1905 in Buffalo, New York.

The Niagara Movement represented a formal renunciation of the policy of accommodation which had been the keynote of Booker T. Washington's program for the black since his famed "Atlanta Compromise" address of 1895. Washington advocated manual and industrial training for the black as a means of gaining economic security, and preferred conciliation rather than agitation as a means of gaining social equality. "It is important and right," he said, "that all privileges of the law be ours, but it is vastly more important that we be prepared for the exercise of those privileges."

The Niagara Movement, on the other hand, maintained that it was even more important for blacks to press for the immediate implementation of their civil rights. In the words of DuBois:

Militant Stokely Carmichael headed the Student Nonviolent Coordinating Committee.

We want full manhood suffrage and we want it now. . . .

We want the Constitution of the country enforced. . . .

We want our children educated . . . We are men! We will be treated as men. And we shall win!

The organization held national conferences in 1906 and 1907 at Harper's Ferry and Boston, respectively, and initiated protest rallies in several American cities in 1908. Every aspect of the black's case was laid before the nation: voting rights, educational and economic opportunity, justice in the courts (the "separate but equal" doctrine of *Plessy* v. *Ferguson* was a particular bone of contention), recognition in labor unions and in the military establishment, acceptance in the Christian church. Moreover, the leaders of the Niagara Movement appended certain duties to its list of basic grievances:

The duty to vote.

The duty to respect the rights of others.

The duty to work.

The duty to obey the laws.

The duty to be clean and orderly.

The duty to send our children to school.

The duty to respect ourselves, even as we respect others.

In 1909, the Niagara Movement was absorbed into the framework of the National Association for the Advancement of Colored People (NAACP), an organization founded on many of the same principles.

The Student Non-Violent Coordinating Committee

Often referred to as "Snick" (SNCC), the Student Non-Violent Coordinating Committee was formed in 1960 to coordinate the activities of students engaged in direct action protest such as sit-ins and jail-ins in the South. SNCC achieved enormous results in the desegregation of public facilities and earned respect from the country for its determination to act peacefully, no matter how violent or demeaning the provocation.

After the 1964 Democratic Convention, however, Stokely Carmichael, a leader of SNCC, tended increasingly to feel that the American system could not be turned around without being threatened by wholesale violence and disruption. Failure to seat the delegation of the SNCC-founded Mississippi Freedom Democratic Party (also known as the Lowndes County Freedom Organization or Black Panther Party) at the convention apparently sealed Carmichael's fate as an advocate of black power and supporter of urban-based guerrilla violence.

The Panthers to whom Carmichael moved represented what was believed to be the new thrust of the liberation movement. SNCC, however, depended heavily on the influx of middle-class black and white youths into what was essentially a civil rights movement. Once aggressive northern ghetto youths roared into the picture, SNCC was left without a constituency.

By leaving the South, SNCC surrendered an essential base of support and a concrete program around which to organize. Never a large membership organization, it lost many of its remaining supporters to graduate study, antipoverty work, teaching, law, etc.

SNCC did not recover its sense of direction or central focus once Carmichael departed. H. Rap Brown, formerly minister of justice in the old organization, renamed the new organization the Student National Coordinating Committee in the summer of 1969, at which time he indicated SNCC would retaliate violently if the situation so demanded.

Brown outlined plans for a new SNCC dimension, the creation of a Peoples Medical Center and a Peoples Sewing Center in Brooklyn. However, Brown's legal troubles made it virtually impossible for him to support these programs with any consistent leadership. As a result, SNCC became virtually defunct.

The Black Panthers

By the 1980s, the Black Panthers, once a powerful force in Black America, especially among inner city youth, had virtually faded from the scene. Under seige by the police, who often brutally trampled on their rights, beset by internal difficulties, with the membership growing older and no new recruits to take their place, the force of the Black Panthers had been spent.

It was not always like this. From its founding by Huey P. Newton and Bobby Seale in October 1966, the Black Panther Party departed from the platform and tactics of all established civil rights organizations.

It condemned institutional structure which, in its view, made American society corrupt; it disavowed established channels of authority and operation which either oppressed or overlooked significant portions of the black community; it rejected middle-class values because they contributed to callous indifference toward, or contempt for, the disinherited youth of the black ghetto. It was, therefore, a revolutionary organization that drew its support almost exclusively from rootless young blacks trapped in large urban slums.

It was to unemployed, undisciplined ghetto youth that the Panthers held out the promise of a bright future, or at least a safer one. The Panthers imposed party discipline on many young males who were responsive to their militaristic regimen, their aggressive rhetoric, and their glorification of machismo. By insisting on the fundmental right of self-defense, the Panthers sought to establish themselves as champions of the black poor against the police.

The National Welfare Rights Organization

Created in 1966, at a time when the nation's attention was focused on the poor through the War on Poverty, the National Welfare Rights Organization at one time had some 800 local groups of welfare recipients and low-income people located in all 50 states. Its founder and moving force was George Wiley, a chemistry professor from Syracuse. Most of its membership was black, although most welfare recipients are white.

At the time of its greatest influence, NWRO spoke in a militant voice for the rights of people on welfare, advocating a minimum annual income of $7,500 for a family of four and adequate health and legal services for the poor. NWRO's stated purpose was to "provide

Black Panthers demonstrate outside Manhattan Criminal Court during murder trial of the "Harlem Six." Beginning as an organization basically dedicated to the defense of the black poor against the police, the Panthers, especially in California, have since expanded their power and range of operations by working within the political system.

for bread, justice, dignity, and democracy for welfare recipients." In 1973 NWRO won a suit against the Department of Health, Education and Welfare denying federal funds for sterilization of human beings.

NWRO provided a forum, for the first time, for welfare recipients to speak out on their own behalf and it helped develop a number of powerful spokesmen. As the welfare recipients themselves became more skilled at organizing, a rift developed with Wiley, the professional, and he resigned early in 1973. Wiley died that same year in a drowning accident.

In 1975 NWRO closed its national office in Washington. Since then there has been no national structure, although a number of local chapters are still active.

CURRENT CIVIL RIGHTS LEADERS

Following are biographical sketches of civil rights leaders who are now active on the national scene. In the main, they head national organizations that work in the field of civil rights on a day-to-day basis. Since the last edition of the *Negro Almanac* in 1976, several of the individuals who were included have gone on to other endeavors so that they can no longer be properly included in this category (they appear in other sections). Some of the names that follow will be new to the reader; their inclusion indicates the changing nature of civil rights leadership. The listing of a fairly limited number of individuals in this section should

not be construed as indicating that there are not other persons in leadership roles in civil rights. There are in fact many individuals who work on behalf of civil rights in their own communities and on a state and regional basis. It would be impossible to list them all. Finally, the reader will note that none of the leaders connected with the Black Power Movement that flourished during the 1960s and the early 1970s appear. The passing years have seen a marked decline in the Movement on the national level, so that it presently lacks national spokesmen, though it is still a force within some communities.

IMAMU AMIRI BARAKA
Community Organizer

Imamu Amiri Baraka, formerly Leroi Jones, is another militant who is successfully using the system to help blacks. Baraka was born in Newark in 1934, the son of a postal superintendent father and social worker mother. He was a scholarship student at Rutgers University and then attended Howard.

After serving in the Air Force, Baraka became a teacher and writer, publishing his first book, *Preface to a Twenty Volume Suicide Note* in 1961. His poetry and fiction won him a John Hay Whitney Fellowship in 1961. Within a few years he had taken powerful steps into the white literary establishment, but he abruptly rejected the values of that world and began to create a radical black literature of highly charged poetry.

Imamu Amiri Baraka (sunglasses) *organized this African Liberation Day rally in Newark.*

In 1964 his play *Dutchman* was acclaimed by New York audiences and critics, receiving the Obie award for the best Off-Broadway play of the season. The shocking honesty of Baraka's treatment of racial conflict in this and later plays became the hallmark of his work. In 1966 Baraka's play *The Slave* won second prize in the drama category at the First World Festival of Dramatic Arts in Dakar, Senegal.

Later, the prolific Baraka published *Four Black Revolutionary Plays* (1969), *Baptism and The Toilet* (1967), and many other plays in black drama anthologies, in magazines, or as booklets. He edited with Larry Neal *Black Fire: An Anthology of Afro-American Writing* (1968), *Afrikan Congress: A Documentary of the First Modern Pan-African Congress* (1972), and other books. In fiction he published *The System of Dante's Hell* (novel, 1965) and *Tales* (short stories, 1967).

In nonfiction, Baraka has published *Black Music* (1967), *Blues People: Negro Music in White America* (1963), *Home: Social Essays* (1966), *In Our Terribleness: Some Elements and Meanings in Black Style* (with Billy Abernathy, 1969), *Raise Race Rays Raze: Essays Since 1965* (1971), *It's Nationtime, Kawaida Studies: The New Nationalism, A Black Value System and Strategy and Tactics of a Pan Afrikan Nationalist Party.* In poetry, in addition to *Preface,* he has published *The Dead Lecturer: Poems* (1964) and *Black Magic: Sabotage, Target Study, Black Art: Collected Poetry 1961–1967* (1969). In the 1970s, Baraka, who had earlier gone from avant garde to black nationalism, changed again to his own version of Marxism-Leninism. Since this ideological metamorphosis, he has published *The Motion of History, Six Other Plays* (1978), which also has the play *Slave Ship; Selected Plays and Prose of Amiri Baraka/LeRoi Jones* (1979), which also has a chapter from his autobiographical unpublished novel *Six Persons;* and *Selected Poetry of Amiri Baraka/LeRoi Jones* (1979), containing some new poems and many poems long out of print. There are five books about Baraka and his writings and three bibliographies of his works.

In the late sixties, though he continued to write, Baraka became a leading black power spokesman in Newark. He was sentenced to prison on a gun-carrying charge and later became head of the Temple of Kawaida, which Baraka describes as an "African religious institution—to increase black consciousness." The Temple and Baraka soon became a focal point of black political activism in the racially polarized city. In 1971 Baraka successfully, and quietly, steered a tax abatement application through the white-dominated Newark City Council and obtained approval of a $6.4 million mortgage through the New Jersey State Finance Agency, for the construction of Kawaida Towers. The site of this 16-story low- and middle-income housing project is in Newark's north ward, an area of the city that is 70% white and presumed to be the turf of Assemblyman Anthony Imperiale, head of the militant white North Ward Citizens Committee.

The ensuing attempts of Imperiale groups to halt construction of Kawaida Towers marked an important point in black history, for Baraka had so successfully used the system to pave the way for his project, it was Baraka's white opponents, rather than Newark's blacks, who found themselves cast in the role of the disgruntled minority. In a series of political, court, and street protest actions, Imperiale tried to stall construction of the Towers, while Baraka urged his supporters to act with restraint and fought off Imperiale's efforts in the courts.

In 1972 Baraka achieved prominence as a black leader as chairman of the often stormy National Black Political Convention in Gary, where he tried adroitly, though not always successfully, to resolve conflicting positions among the 8,000 nationalist and moderate blacks who attended.

MARIAN WRIGHT EDELMAN
President, Children's Defense Fund

The civil rights of children has been one of the principal concerns of Marian Wright Edelman throughout her career. Founder and president of the Children's Defense Fund, based in Washington, D.C., since its incep-

Marian Wright Edelman is president of the Childrens Defense Fund.

tion in 1973 she has been an outspoken advocate of the rights of children, with special emphasis on minority children.

A native of Bennettsville, South Carolina, Edelman received her undergraduate degree from Spelman College and her law degree from Yale. Her civil rights involvement began in 1963 when she joined the NAACP Legal Defense and Education Fund as staff attorney. A year later she founded the NAACP Legal Defense and Education Fund in Jackson, Mississippi, serving as its director until 1968 when she founded the Washington Research Project of the Southern Center for Public Policy that later developed into the Children's Defense Fund.

Edelman was a member of the Yale University Corporation and the Carnegie Council on Children. She served on the Board of Directors of the NAACP Legal Defense and Education Fund and the Aetna Life and Casualty Foundation. She is the author of many articles and several books on children, including "Children Out of School in America," School Suspensions: Are They Helping Children?, and "Portrait of Inequality: Black and White Children in America." Special honors include nine honorary degrees.

DICK GREGORY
Comedian, Civil Rights Activist

Dick Gregory is one of America's best known comedians and, more than anyone else, is responsible for creating the precedent which has since enabled other top-flight black humorists to present personal racial humor to the general public.

Born in St. Louis in 1932, Gregory struggled through the depths of the Depression, determined originally to escape from the ghetto on the strength of his athletic ability. As a high school miler, he won the Missouri State mile championship in 1951 and repeated his victory a year later.

He later attended Southern Illinois University on a track scholarship. While there, he was named the school's outstanding athlete in 1953, but he left after two years to join the army. Once in the service, he began working as a comedian in Special Service shows.

After leaving Southern Illinois for the last time in 1956, he worked at various jobs while trying to establish himself in his chosen field. In 1960 part of his Chicago nightclub routine was seen on a television documentary, and he began to receive a few sporadic offers.

Brilliant satirist Dick Gregory has been jailed several times for his tireless, nonviolent acts of protest.

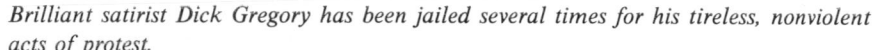

Executive director of the NAACP Benjamin Hooks (third from left) *with friends.*

On January 13, 1961, he filled in at Chicago's Playboy Club for an ailing comedian and was such an astonishing success that he was held over, given special coverage in *Time* magazine, and booked into the country's top night spots.

Gregory has been an avid campaigner in the civil rights movement, often at great personal expense. While attempting to quiet the Watts rioters in 1965, he was shot in the leg, but was not seriously injured.

Perhaps no entertainer entered the civil rights movement with the commitment and courage of Gregory. Within a year of his Playboy Club success, he was going broke from fines, legal fees, and travel expenses incurred while appearing on protest picket lines. He was jailed several times. When told by friends he could achieve more as a comedian than activist, Gregory replied tartly, "They didn't laugh Hitler out of existence, did they?"

In 1966 he ran for Mayor of Chicago against Richard Daley, and in 1968 he ran for President, to highlight his "militant but humble" philosophy of confrontation and nonviolence.

Now a wealthy man—from records, writing, and lecture tours, Gregory continues to propound the truth as he sees it to largely white audiences.

Though he amuses audiences with his entertainer's flair, Gregory takes his position very seriously. He has declared that the CIA plans to wipe out black and nonconforming Americans. He frequently fasts for lengthy periods to clean out his system and protest policies such as the Vietnam War, which he opposed. Typical of Gregory's commitment to causes in which he believes was his 46-day fast in 1981 for hunger research.

M. CARL HOLMAN
President, National Urban Coalition

Often moving behind the scenes, M. Carl Holman has been one of the leading strategists in the Civil Rights Movement for several decades. Since 1971 he has headed the National Urban Coalition, which has come to be recognized as the only broad-based national organization in the country that focuses on the survival and success of the American city, its people, its institutions, its business and industry, and its economic and fiscal well-being.

Holman was born in Minter City, Mississippi, and grew up in St. Louis. He graduated magna cum laude from Lincoln and received masters degrees from Yale University (as a recipient of a Whitney Fellowship) and the University of Chicago. He began his professional career in 1949 as an English professor at Clark College in Atlanta, and also taught at Atlanta University and Hampton Institute.

When the Civil Rights Movement began to develop in the South in the 1950s, Holman emerged as one of its truly important, if unsung heroes, by serving as a wise and compassionate strategist for the student demonstrators who turned to him for guidance, and as a respected and trusted advisor to many civil rights leaders.

In 1962 he joined the U.S. Commission on Civil Rights as its deputy staff director and along with several other highly placed blacks was a member of what was considered the unofficial black cabinet of the Kennedy and Johnson administrations.

BENJAMIN L. HOOKS
Executive Director, National Association for the Advancement of Colored People

Benjamin L. Hooks was unanimously elected Executive Director of the National Association for the Advancement of Colored People by the NAACP National Board of Directors on January 10, 1977, and formally assumed office on August 1, 1977. He succeeded the legendary Roy Wilkins, who retired.

Hooks' highly successful career spans a number of fields. He first gained nationwide recognition upon his nomination in 1972 to serve on the Federal Communications Commission as its first black member. Once on the FCC he became a driving force to improve the portrayal and employment and ownership opportunities for blacks in the electronic media.

As a lawyer in Memphis, he was an assistant public defender and later was the first black judge to serve in the Shelby County (Memphis) Criminal Court. As an ordained minister, he is on leave from both the Middle Baptist Church in Memphis and the Greater New Mt. Moriah Baptist Church in Detroit. As a prominent local businessman, he was the co-founder and vice president of the Mutual Federal Savings and Loan Association in Memphis for 15 years (1955–1969).

Under his progressive leadership, the NAACP took a more aggressive posture on U.S. policies toward African nations through a successful demonstration in Nashville to protest South Africa's participation in the Davis Cup tennis matches, and through testimony before the House Subcommittee on Africa opposing the lifting of sanctions against Rhodesia.

Among his many battles on Capitol Hill, Hooks, led the historical Prayer Vigil in Washington, D.C. in 1979 against the Mott anti-busing amendment, which was eventually defeated in Congress; led in the fight for passage of the D.C. Home Rule bill; and was instrumental in gathering important Senate and House votes on the Humphrey-Hawkins Full Employment Bill.

Through such new programs as the Emergency Relief Program to assist victims of natural disasters and the urban assistance program in Miami following the riots of 1980, he also continues the NAACP's tradition of providing technical and financial assistance to the black community. In 1980 Hooks scored another first by becoming the first national figure to address both national political conventions in the same year.

Known for his highly effective and persuasive oratory, Hooks was born in Memphis and attended Le-

Roy Innes labels busing "obsolete and dangerous."

Moyne College there and Howard University in Washington, D.C. He received his J.D. degree from DePaul University College of Law in 1948. He is a World War II veteran and served in the 92nd Infantry Division's campaign in Italy.

ROY INNIS
National Director, Congress of Racial Equality

Born June 6, 1934 in St. Croix, Virgin Islands, Innis has lived in the United States since he was 12. He attended Stuyvesant High School in New York City and went on to serve two years in the service, disguising his age as 18 though he was only 16. Back in civilian life, he majored in chemistry at City College of New York and did not originally plan to pursue a career in the racial movement.

By 1963, however, he was active in CORE circles, promoting the theme of economic competition and male assertiveness while downgrading the value of integration to blacks. Allies were few at this time, since the organization was multiracial in character and seemed to be irrevocably committed to integration. Patient and persuasive, however, Innis was elected chairman of Harlem CORE in 1965 and went on to become associate national director some three years later. By this time, he was effectively preaching the abandonment of the nonviolent philosophy in favor of a policy of self-defense.

On the economic front, Innis founded the Harlem

Commonwealth Council, an agency designed to create black-owned businesses and black-directed economic institutions in Harlem. To promote his ideas, he also took a plunge into journalism, serving with William Haddad as co-editor of the *Manhattan Tribune,* a weekly New York tabloid stressing the affairs of Harlem and the upper West Side. In print and in action, Innis has continued to stress black strength and black advancement over all other themes.

Innis' leadership of CORE, however, has been marked with controversy. Numerous members have dropped out, charging that Innis has run the organization as a one-man show. CORE was also the subject of a three-year investigation by the New York State Attorney General's Office into allegations that it had misused charitable contributions. An agreement was reached in 1981 that did not require CORE to admit to any wrongdoing in its handling of funds, but stipulated that Innis would have to contribute $35,000 to the organization over the next three years.

Innis also faced a challenge in the early 1980s when a group of former CORE members, headed by James Farmer, the founder and former chairman of CORE,

attempted to oust him. The effort failed and Innis continues to head the organization.

JESSE JACKSON
President, People United to Save Humanity

Jesse Jackson is possibly the most exciting and dynamic young black leader who has decided to work within the system while, at the same time, retaining the appearance, the ardor, and the fervor of a black nationalist or revolutionary. Reared in the black ministry, Jackson has relied on the techniques of pulpit oratory to capture a huge and diverse following, but he has resisted efforts to be cast in the role of a "successor"—particularly to Martin Luther King. "You can be an orator or an organizer," he says. "I am an organizer."

Had Jackson been born white, he could possibly have become another Joe Namath or Tom Seaver. Capable of throwing a football 70 yards and averaging 17 strikeouts per game as a high school pitcher, Jackson won an athletic scholarship to the University of Illinois in 1959 where he was expected to burn up the gridirons and diamonds of the "big Ten."

But Jackson, the son of an Alabama sharecropper, was born black and could not abide the humiliation many white colleges had often inflicted on black athletes. Because he was black, Jackson was not allowed to play at the quarterback position of the football team and was as well subtly excluded from concerts and social events—even those at which black artists, such as Lionel Hampton, performed. Jackson left Illinois for a black college in Greensboro, North Carolina—North Carolina A & T.

While there, Jackson became the "point man" at Greensboro sit-ins. Jackson would enter "whites-only" restaurants alone and when refused service, blacks would start to picket. Such efforts speeded up integration in Greensboro. Upon graduation, Jackson enrolled in the Chicago Theological Seminary. While there he worked briefly, at the precinct level, for a future rival, Mayor Richard Daley, but quit when he concluded that working for the city's Democratic party machine was an affront to his self-respect.

In 1963 Jackson joined the SCLC. He quickly earned a reputation for organizing ability by rallying Chicago's black clergymen behind King. In 1966 Jackson helped unite the SCLC and the Chicago Coordinating Council of Community Organizations into the Chicago Freedom Movement, a group which pressed for integrated schools and open housing. The campaign was one of the first of the postwar years to challenge northern racism, particularly in the Chicago suburb of Cicero, and success in this effort was minor. Shortly

Reverend Jesse Jackson galvanizes Operation PUSH.

thereafter, Operation Breadbasket was launched and Jackson led the campaigns for enlightened hiring and trade policies by the Country Delight Dairy and the A & P. Other businesses in Chicago gradually altered their employment policies, many from fear of the Breadbasket campaign. Recalls Jackson: "You can't calculate the number of jobs made available because they heard those footsteps coming."

While engaged in these battles, Jackson became increasingly concerned about the tendency for money earned and spent by blacks to leave the black community. In part, Breadbasket's effort sought to counter this, but Jackson felt the matter required greater organization and thought. So he formed a group of black leaders and held informal strategy sessions every Saturday morning at the Chicago Theological Seminary. Soon Jackson's Saturday sessions became a platform for Jackson to discuss his views on black pride and a magnet for blacks from all over the country. They are now held in a theater before audiences of several thousand.

Jackson was beside King on the Memphis balcony when the man he so greatly admired was killed. Two weeks later, in Chicago, after sitting through a eulogy to King by Richard Daley, who had opposed King, Jackson rose and in tears said to Daley, "This blood is on the chest and hands of those who would not have welcomed him here yesterday . . . (The best tribute) would not be to sit here looking sad and pious . . . but to behave differently." That Saturday, attendance at Jackson's "strategy session" increased tenfold and to many blacks and whites, Jackson, not Ralph Abernathy, was the inheritor of King's crown.

Through the disappointing years that followed, the failure of the Poor People's March, and the ascendancy of white backlash, Jackson emerged increasingly as the black leader with the organizing ability and charisma necessary to keep the problems and aspirations of blacks before the public eye.

In 1971 Jackson led a march on Springfield, (the capitol of Illinois) which prevented a reduction in state welfare payments. In 1972 he was keynote speaker at the Gary black power convention, where he urged formation of a separate black political party to endorse candidates of both major parties and occasionally run its own.

Jackson has tried to maintain amicable relations with the SCLC and Reverend Abernathy since he left them in 1971. However, the break was not friendly and Jackson's Operation PUSH clearly intrudes on turf SCLC regarded as Breadbasket's. The split occurred in 1971, when Abernathy suspended Jackson for 60 days after learning that Jackson had organized the black fair called "Black Expo" under a separate corporation rather than the aegis of SCLC. Jackson,

who had long wanted to go his own way, set up Operation PUSH.

From that point on, Jackson was on his way to becoming the most visible and sought-after civil rights leader in the country. His magnetic personality came across as appealing on television, and while he described himself as "a country preacher," his command of issues and his ability to reach the heart of matters marked him as an individual of intellectual depth.

Of all the civil rights leaders, Jackson was the one who could relate best to the young. He was possessed with a gift of being able to summon out the best in them, in a phrase that became his trademark, "I am somebody."

Out of this came Jackson's program, PUSH–EXCEL, which sought to motivate young schoolchildren to do better academically. In 1981 *Newsweek* magazine credited Jackson with building a struggling community improvement organization into a nationwide campaign to revive pride, discipline, and the work ethic in inner-city schools. It also characterized him as the charismatic spokesman for Black America. And when *Black Enterprise* magazine conducted a poll in 1980 to determine who was viewed as the premiere spokesman for blacks, Jackson's name led all the rest.

With funding from the federal government under President Carter, the PUSH–EXCEL Program was placed in Chicago and five other cities as a demonstration project. The initial evaluations were mixed as to the success of the programs, and the Reagan Administration revealed that it would reduce funding. Some observers attributed this not only to the evaluation report but to the fact that Jackson had been a supporter of President Carter, whom Reagan defeated.

JOHN E. JACOB
President, National Urban League

Trained as a social worker and a veteran of the Urban League Movement, John E. Jacob had a large pair of shoes to fill when he replaced Vernon E. Jordan, Jr. as president of the NUL on January 1, 1982. In the space of 10 years at the League, Jordan had established a national reputation as an effective and forceful civil rights leader who exerted tremendous influence. He resigned from the League to enter private law practice December 31, 1981, and the board selected Jacob as his successor.

The new president had served since 1979 as executive vice president, the number two staff position at the League, so he was not new to the job. In accepting the new post, Jacob described it as a "signal honor" and added:

This is my goal as I assume this important post: to make a difference; to help guide the Urban League Movement to new

President of the National Urban League John E. Jacob.

heights of effectiveness; to help educate the nation to its unfinished responsibilities; and to help bring fresh opportunities to the black and poor people who are the constituency of the Urban League.

Early in his tenure, Jacob clearly indicated that he would put his own mark on the NUL Presidency by speaking out against the budget cuts of the Reagan Administration, by calling on the black community to resist any efforts to turn back the clock on racial gains, and by setting forth several new areas of interest for the League—the plight of single-female-headed households, teenage pregnancy, voter education and registration, and crime in the black community.

His career with the National Urban League began in 1965 when he was named Director of Education and Youth Incentives at the Washington, D.C. Urban League. He held a number of increasingly important positions with the NUL affiliate, serving as director of its Northern Virginia Branch (1966), associate director for administration of the affiliate (1967), and as its acting executive director from 1968 until 1970. He also spent several months as director of community organization training in the Eastern Regional Office of the NUL.

He left the Washington Urban League to serve as executive director for the San Diego Urban League, a post he held 4½ years (1970–1975) until his return to the Washington Urban League as its president. He

remained there until 1979 when he joined the national office.

Prior to joining the Urban League Movement he worked for the Department of Public Welfare in Baltimore as a Case Supervisor in the areas of services to families, childrens' services, protective and medical services.

Jacob is vice chairman of the Howard University Board of Trustees. He serves as a member of the Board of the Local Initiatives Support Corporation, a national nonprofit enterprise that helps selected local organizations draw new private and public resources into their efforts to revitalize communities and neighborhoods. He is a member of the Board of "A Better Chance, Inc.," a national nonprofit organization whose goal is to increase substantially the number of well-educated minority people who can assume responsibility and leadership in American society. He is also a member of the Community Advisory Board of New York Hospital and the National Advertising Review Board.

He has served as a member of the D.C. Manpower Services Planning Advisory Council and as a member of the Board of Trustees, D.C. Legal Aid Society. Jacob also served as a member of the Judicial Nominating Commission—U.S. District Court and the U.S. Circuit Court for the District of Columbia.

Born in Trout, Louisiana on December 16, 1934, Jacob grew up in Houston. He received his undergraduate and masters degrees from Howard University.

Vernon E. Jordan, Jr., has cut channels into the power centers of government.

VERNON E. JORDAN, JR.
Executive Director, National Urban League

Vernon E. Jordan, Jr. was born in Atlanta in 1935 and grew up there. After graduating from De Pauw University in 1957 and from Howard Law School in 1960, he returned to Georgia, becoming a civil rights lawyer and, in 1962, field secretary for the Georgia branch of the NAACP. Between 1964 and 1968 Jordan was director of the Voter Education Project of the Southern Regional Council and led its successful drives that registered nearly 2 million blacks in the south, leading to an eightfold increase of elected black officials there, from 72 to 564.

In 1970 Jordan moved north to become executive director of the United Negro College Fund, helping to raise record sums for its member colleges until he was tapped by the Urban League as the successor to the late Whitney Young.

Taking over as NUL executive director in January 1972, the energetic Jordan moved the League into new areas, such as voter registration in northern and western cities, while continuing and strengthening the League's traditional social service programs and its role as advocates for the cause of black people and as a bridge to the white community.

While forcefully denouncing the Nixon Administration's racial policies, opposing just about every domestic program offered by it, he was successful in establishing personal links with the White House that softened some federal policies and helped bring federal program contracts to the Urban League and other black institutions.

An outspoken advocate of the cause of the black and the poor, Jordan has taken strong stands in favor of busing, an income maintenance system that ends poverty, scatter-site housing, and a federally financed and administered, consumer-oriented national health system, among others.

As the economy faltered in the early 1970s, Jordan became a leader in the fight for a national full employment policy that "guarantees a decent job at a decent wage for all." Maintaining that the "issues have changed," since the 1960s, Jordan has called for "equal access and employment up to and including top policy-making jobs."

As president of the National Urban League, Jordan's schedule saw him traveling over 100,000 miles a year and often working 70 to 80 hours a week. Much in demand as a speaker, Jordan became one of the most visible and influential leaders of the Civil Rights Movement. In 1977 he was one of the first national spokesmen to criticize the Carter Administration for its emphasis on fiscal conservatism at the expense of human service programs. Still, Jordan maintained his close ties with the President, a fellow Georgian, and with the Administration.

The nation was stunned on May 29, 1980 when Jordan, who had just delivered an address to the Fort Wayne Urban League, was shot in the back by a sniper as he returned to his motel in that city. The bullet was fired from a high-powered rifle and an investigation disclosed that the assailant had lain in wait for some time on a small grassy knoll across from Jordan's room. Jordan narrowly escaped death in the attack and was confined to the hospital, first in Fort Wayne and later in New York City, for some 90 days. He returned to his office in early September 1980. Despite an intensive and widespread investigation by the FBI, as late as May 1982 no suspect had been charged in the shooting.

Jordan made a complete recovery and resumed his demanding schedule within a matter of months. On September 9, 1981, he announced that after 10 years as head of the League, he was stepping down effective December 31, 1981, to enter the private practice of law as partner in the Washington office of a major law firm, Akin, Gump, Strauss, Hauer and Feld. At the time of his resignation, Vernon Jordan said:

My resignation is based on the belief that it is time for a change, personally and institutionally. . . . The goals of the

Urban League and the cause of racial equality will always be dearest to my heart and soul.

During Jordan's tenure, the League increased its affiliates from 99 to 118; employees from 2,100 to 4,200; and its overall budget, involving the affiliates and the national office, from $40 million annually to $150 million.

CORETTA SCOTT KING
Civil Rights Activist

After her husband's assassination, Coretta Scott King made a swift transition from a dedicated wife and parent living in comparative seclusion to a dynamic civil rights and peace crusader in her own right. During

Coretta Scott King works to make her late husband's dream a reality.

her husband's life, she accommodated herself to the mother/wife role; with him gone, it seemed imperative that she carry on his life's work and perpetuate his ideals actively and publicly.

Born one of three children on April 27, 1927, Mrs. King is a native of Heiberger, Alabama. During the Depression she was forced to contribute to the family income by hoeing and picking cotton, but she resolved early to overcome adversity, seek treatment as an equal, and struggle to achieve a sound education.

In 1945 she entered Antioch College in Yellow Springs, Ohio on a scholarship, majoring in education and music. A teaching career appealed to her, but she became badly disillusioned when she was not allowed to do her practice teaching in the public schools of the town. No black had ever taught there, and she was not destined to be the first to break the tradition.

Musical training in voice and on piano absorbed much of her time, with the result that, upon graduation, she decided to continue her studies at the New England Conservatory of Music in Boston, attending on a modest fellowship which covered tuition but made part-time work a necessity. Paradoxically, her financial situation improved when she began receiving state aid from Alabama. (Such aid was available to blacks studying outside the state, but not for black applicants seeking to attend schools within the state itself.)

Her meeting with Martin Luther King thrust her into a whirlwind romance, and also presented her with the opportunity to marry an exceptional young minister whose intense convictions and concern for humanity brought her a measure of rare self-realization early in life. Sensing his incredible dynamism, she suffered no regrets at the prospect of relinquishing her own possible career.

Completing her studies in 1954, Mrs. King moved back South with her husband, who became pastor of Drexel Avenue Baptist Church in Montgomery, Alabama. Within a year, King had led the Montgomery bus boycott, and given birth to a new era of civil rights agitation. Two years later, he was the head of the Southern Christian Leadership Conference (SCLC).

By 1964 Mrs. King was the mother of four children: Yolanda (born 1955); Martin Luther, III (born 1957); Dexter Scott (born 1961); and Bernice Albertine (born 1963).

Over the years, Mrs. King did some teaching and fund-raising work for SCLC, becoming more accustomed to the limelight, particularly after her trip to Oslo in 1964. In was more than such exposure, however, that gave her the strength, the courage, and the determination to deal with the assassination, and, later, to deliver the speeches he had drafted in rough form.

Her speech on Solidarity Day, June 19, 1968, is often identified as a prime example of her emergence from the shadow of her husband's memory. In it, she called upon American women to "unite and form a solid block of women power" to fight the three great evils of racism, poverty, and war.

Much of her subsequent activity revolved around building plans for the creation of a Martin Luther King Jr. Memorial in Atlanta. Mrs. King later published a book of reminiscences, *My Life With Martin Luther King Jr.*

In 1982, 14 years after her husband's death, Mrs. King remains an eloquent and respected spokesperson on behalf of black causes and nonviolent philosophy. Her children are grown and carving their own careers, and she devotes most of her time to the Martin Luther King Jr. Center for Social Change in Atlanta, which has grown into a well-respected institution visited by persons from across the world.

JOSEPH E. LOWERY
President, Southern Christian Leadership Conference

Reverend Joseph E. Lowery continues a tradition begun with the late Dr. Martin Luther King of having the Southern Christian Leadership Conference headed by a clergyman. In 1977 he succeeded Reverend Ralph David Abernathy, who had been picked by Dr. King as his successor. From his first official statement to SCLC, Reverend Lowery made clear what his course would be:

It is with both humility and honor that I accepted the presidency of the Southern Christian Leadership Conference. The mantle was handed from Martin Luther King Jr. to Ralph Abernathy, and now to me. Yet, I have accepted the challenge with prayer and determination, for the "dream" remains unfulfilled. . . .

Yes, we are still engaged in the struggle to replace violence and poverty with a system that will assure the dignity of every person. Much of our struggle, in communities across the nation, is unheralded by the media—struggles against racism expressed in denial of the ballot, unjust wages, high unemployment, inadequate housing and medical care, lack of economic opportunities and oppression in the criminal justice system.

Soft-spoken and unassuming, Reverend Lowery received his first broad-scale national and international exposure when he led a delegation of 10 persons from SCLC on a fact-finding mission to the Mideast in 1979, in the wake of the furor that erupted over a meeting held by U.S. Ambassador Andrew Young with a representative of the Palestine Liberation Organization. Such meetings were contrary to U.S. policy and Young was forced to resign, touching off a squabble between black and Jewish leaders.

On his overseas trip, Lowery met with PLO leaders, and as a consequence, Israeli leaders refused to meet with the SCLC president, touching off massive news coverage.

Reverend Lowery was born in Huntsville, Alabama, and holds several degrees. He has been minister of the Centennial Unity Methodist Church since 1968. His ministry began in 1952 at the Warren Street Church in Birmingham, where he served until 1961 when he became administrative assistant to Bishop Golden. From there he moved on to become pastor of St. Paul Church from 1964 to 1968. He was one of the founders of the Southern Christian Leadership Conference and held several positions with the organization before becoming its president.

Under his leadership, SCLC has broadened its activities to include the reinstitution of its Operation Breadbasket to encourage businesses that earn substantial profits in the black community to reinvest equitably and employ blacks in equitable numbers; involvement in the plight of Haitians who were jailed by the American government after they sought asylum here; and a march from Selma to Washington, D.C. in connection with the renewal of the Voting Rights Act of 1982.

BAYARD RUSTIN
Executive Director, A. Philip Randolph Institute

Bayard Rustin could easily be identified with any number of civil rights organizations, pacifist groups, massive popular demonstrations, etc., but it is through

Bayard Rustin designs radical socioeconomic programs enlisting government support.

his 30-year association with A. Philip Randolph, and his present directorship of the A. Philip Randolph Institute that he is able to give shape to his most abiding and progressive ideas on civil rights, labor management and economic planning.

As executive director of the Institute since its inception in 1964, Rustin has worked unstintingly to develop and promote sound radical programs designed to cure the economic and social ills of the country. Though he does not totally discount the value of federally sponsored poverty programs and other schemes for ensuring every American family a guaranteed annual income, he feels, nonetheless, that real progress can occur only in the wake of a government decision to mobilize all employable persons and assign to them the basic task of improving their environment: rebuilding ghetto neighborhoods, ghetto schools, and ghetto hospitals at public expense.

Tax money allocated for this objective would not only provide decent income for the unemployed but would generate real growth in a sector of the nation which traditionally cannot produce the taxes needed to finance its progress, and so becomes dependent on regular public assistance. In Rustin's view, it is the nation's incredible distortion of public priorities that has led to the bloodbaths of the inner city, the wholesale carnage, destruction, and looting, the ascendancy of the riot mentality, and the burning tempers of disillusioned and explosive youth. Poverty money can only relieve such conditions for a time; it cannot, by definition, assuage the anger because it does not reach the heart of the problem.

Rustin defines the problem as the onslaught of a technology that fails to take into account basic human needs, that displaces unskilled and semiskilled laborers without concern for their welfare or economic adaptability, thus indirectly causing social fragmentation, urban decay, family disintegration, and loss of hope. The solution he advocates calls for the orderly seizure of political power by responsible groups able to agree on the defects and to map strategy for their elimination. The groups which, in his view, engineered such impressive movements as the March on Washington, the passage of the 1964 Civil Rights Act, and the Johnson landslide, must increase their power base, stimulate greater support for their ideology of social reconstruction, and force government to respond to the needs of predominantly urban constituencies. The four identifiable groups present in Rustin's sturdy coalition are: the black community, white liberals, religious parties, and labor unions.

Rustin, in other words, advocates the growth and strengthening of those organizations and agencies identified with the non-Communist political left. He feels black separatism and guerrilla warfare rhetoric are not only suicidal but also criminally destructive and self-defeating. Inevitably, he argues, they play into the hands of reactionary groups able to capitalize on internecine squabbling and disruptive fragmentation.

Rustin's philosophy has not been conceived in Olympian aloofness. More than just a theoretician, he has been arrested 23 times in the cause of peace and civil rights, and has demonstrated time and again his willingness to take to the streets in defense of his beliefs and in promotion of his ideology.

Born in West Chester, Pennsylvania in March 1910, Rustin was raised by his grandparents, though he was particularly influenced by his grandmother, a devout Quaker. At school, he was an honor student and star athlete, experiencing his first real anger at discrimination when he was refused restaurant service in Pennsylvania while on tour with the football team.

After graduation, he studied literature and history at Cheyney State and Wilberforce Colleges, but his most serious interests already lay in politics. In 1936 Rustin joined the Young Communist League, becoming an organizer two years later. Rustin earned an irregular livelihood in New York singing at the old Cafe Society with such notables as Josh White and Leadbelly.

Rustin left the Party in 1941, joining the Fellowship of Reconciliation, a nonviolent antiwar group. That same year, he became a youth organizer for A. Philip Randolph's projected March on Washington to demand better job opportunities for blacks in the defense industry. During World War II, Rustin was imprisoned as a conscientious objector, serving some 2½ years behind bars. Released in 1945, he immediately joined the Indian independence movement and was again jailed for demonstrating before the British Embassy.

In 1947 Rustin participated in a historic "journey of reconciliation," an event now popularly known as a Freedom Ride. The experience brought with it another jail term, but enabled Rustin to expose chain gang abuses in North Carolina which were subsequently abolished. By this time Rustin was not only identified with the Congress of Racial Equality (CORE), the organization which had pioneered in the Freedom Ride movement, but also with A. Philip Randolph's Committee Against Discrimination in the Armed Forces.

Until 1955 Rustin was preoccupied with various peace conventions, efforts to restrict nuclear armaments, and movements toward African independence. That year, he joined Martin Luther King's Southern Christian Leadership Conference (SCLC), again in an organizational capacity as King's Special Assistant. In 1963 he was named chief logistics expert and organizational coordinator of the March on Washington.

In the late 1960s Rustin was increasingly hard pressed to maintain support for the nonviolent philosophy to which he had dedicated his life. His charismatic appeal, relentless logic, and debating effectiveness carried him through crisis after crisis, however. Nonviolence, he argued, was not outdated; it was a necessary and inexorable plan called for by the black's condition in the United States. Guerrilla warfare and armed insurrection, Rustin explained, required friendly border sanctuaries, a steady source of arms and equipment, and the support of the majority of a country's inhabitants.

Still, Rustin was equally appalled by the ignorance and shallowness of government groups who failed to respond to the legitimate appeals of young blacks for better education, increased job opportunity, improved housing, and general medical care. When blacks went on a rampage in Watts in 1965, Rustin, as he had previously in Harlem in 1964, braved jeers and insults in a desperate attempt to explain the hopelessness of violence and to restore order, but he was hooted down by angry militants and the uncontrollable mob.

In response to the difficulty, Rustin set his sights on the enunciation of a broad platform of economic proposals geared primarily to advance the poor and the underprivileged of all races. The general solution involved the acquisition of political power by such groups and a rapid refashioning of the nation's economic priorities.

By taking over the Randolph Institute, Rustin came to occupy a post where his considerable intellectual abilities and rare organizational talents could be combined to create a clearinghouse of information on the viable alternatives to senseless violence and Communist demagoguery.

In 1972 Rustin, writing in *Newsweek* magazine, reasserted his belief in coalition rather than racial solutions to the problems faced by blacks.

"Black power," he wrote, *was born in bitterness and frustration—has left us with a legacy of polarization, division and political nonsense.—Black power was (always)—likely to produce basically conservative answers—The challenge we face is to rebuild a broad-based coalition which embraces intellectuals, organized labor, young people, minorities and liberals.*

Years later, in 1981, when he was 70 and still heading the A. Philip Randolph Institute, Rustin clung to his beliefs.

I do not think it is practical to separate the problems of black poverty from poverty as such. It makes it look as if we're asking for special privileges unless we do it within the context of asking for the elimination of poverty for all.

And he added:

The economic impact of the Reagan Administration is not directed toward blacks. We mustn't fear that. It is directed toward a class of people—the have nots. Today, what you must ask for is education, jobs, hospital care for an entire class of people. So new leadership that will emerge cannot just be a replacement for King, Jordan, Whitney Young and the others.

Rustin continues to be active in the Civil Rights Movement as its leading and most respected theoretician and maintains a heavy speaking schedule.

EDDIE N. WILLIAMS
President, Joint Center for Political Studies

Regarded as the most knowledgeable person in America about the operation of blacks within the political structure, Eddie N. Williams has headed the Joint Center for Political Studies since 1972. While he maintains a low profile, it is generally conceded that through the Center, Williams has been instrumental in strengthening the black presence in politics. Specifically, the

Eddie N. Williams heads the very important Joint Center for Political Studies.

Joining hands to sing "We Shall Overcome" in Selma, 1965 were (from left) *James Foreman, Reverend Fred Shuttlesworth, unidentified man, Reverend Martin Luther King, Reverend Ralph Abernathy, and Reverend James Bevel.*

Center keeps its eyes on the changing tides of politics, shares this information on a wide basis, and provides supportive services to black elected officials.

Before joining the Center, Williams was Vice President of Public Affairs and Director of the Center for Policy Study, both at the University of Chicago.

Trained as a journalist, Williams received his undergraduate degree from the University of Illinois and pursued graduate studies in political science at Atlanta University. He was a reporter for the Atlanta *Daily World*. Williams also served in the State Department for seven years as director of the Department's Office of Equal Employment Opportunity, as staff assistant to the assistant secretary for Near Eastern and South Asian Affairs, and as protocol officer. From 1958 to 1960 he was staff aide to Senator Hubert H. Humphrey. He is also the author of numerous magazine and newspaper articles.

FORMER CONTEMPORARY CIVIL RIGHTS LEADERS

RALPH D. ABERNATHY
Former President, Southern Christian Leadership Conference

Reverend Ralph David Abernathy headed the Southern Christian Leadership Conference from the time of Martin Luther King's death in 1968 until 1977, when he resigned to run for the Congressional seat being vacated by his fellow Atlantan, Andrew Young, who had accepted an appointment from President

Jimmy Carter as the Ambassador to the United Nations.

The race went badly for Abernathy, who came in fourth in the 13-man Democratic primary election with less than 5% of the vote. Abernathy laid the blame at the doorstep of the Atlanta voters and said that they obviously thought that he should remain in civil rights and not go to Congress. However, in the succeeding years, Abernathy became less and less involved with the Movement and turned more of his attention to pastorship at Atlanta's West Hunter Street Baptist Church and to the lecture circuit.

When Martin Luther King lost his life to an assassin's bullet, he had already made it clear that if he fell, his successor was to be his trusted confidante, Reverend Abernathy. The mantle of leadership thus passed smoothly and Abernathy rallied the SCLC staff and thousands of supporters to the side of the garbage workers, who won a settlement of their grievances in short order.

Abernathy continued as a leading figure in the Movement until his resignation in 1977, although SCLC never recovered the influence it had had under King.

H. RAP BROWN
Former Chairman, Student Nonviolent Coordinating Committee

As chairman of the Student Nonviolent Coordinating Committee, H. Rap Brown emerged with Stokely Carmichael in 1966 as a stormy advocate of black power. In 1968 he was charged with inciting a riot in Cambridge, Maryland and was convicted in New Orleans on a federal charge of carrying a gun between states. Brown disappeared in 1970, after being slated for trial in Maryland, and in 1972 he was shot, arrested, and eventually convicted for a saloon holdup in New York City.

In 1974, while still in prison, Brown remained a controversial figure among blacks. Some claimed he had succumbed indulgently to violence, others that he had been framed and harassed by law enforcement officials who feared him.

While in prison, Brown converted to the Islamic faith and took the name of Jamil Abdullah Al-Amin. On his release, he went to Atlanta where he opened a grocery store.

STOKELY CARMICHAEL
Former Chairman, Student Nonviolent Coordinating Committee

If there was one individual during the sixties who stood at the forefront of the Black Power Movement it was Stokely Carmichael. Gifted, handsome, and articulate, he soared to fame as popularizer of the dynamic phrase "black power" and as leader, until 1977, of the Student Nonviolent Coordinating Committee. In the short life of SNCC, he was its most powerful and influential leader.

The son of a carpenter, Carmichael was born in Trinidad in 1941 and came to the United States when he was 11. As a teenager, Carmichael was jolted by ghetto life in which "black" and "impotent" seemed to be synonymous terms. He was not reassured later when he was admitted to the Bronx High School of Science, encountered white liberals, and felt he had been adopted by them as a "mascot."

In 1960 Carmichael joined CORE in its efforts to integrate public accommodations in the South. Though offered scholarships to white universities, he entered Howard, graduating in 1964. He then joined SNCC, was elected its leader, and was instrumental in altering its orientation from peaceful integration to "black liberation."

Carmichael not only drove a wedge into the civil rights movement but emerged as the foremost spokesman for the black power concept and became a symbol of violence to whites fearful at the time of uprisings in America's cities.

Carmichael subsequently resigned from SNCC and joined the Black Panthers.

However, he differed with Eldridge Cleaver's view that coalitions could be formed with white radicals, and he soon resigned from the Panthers, declaring himself a Pan-Africanist whose duty it was to wage unrelenting war against the white Western Empire. He moved to Guinea.

Expatriate Eldridge Cleaver has returned to the United States.

In 1968 Carmichael married Mariam Makeba, the South African singer. In 1972 he returned to the United States and espoused his Pan-African ideology, which he depicted as an increased awareness and acceptance by American blacks of the culture, heritage, and ideals of Africans. He stresses that this is not a new course but the ultimate extension of black power.

His activities as a civil rights figure have virtually ceased, and rarely is he heard from.

ELDRIDGE CLEAVER
Former Minister of Information, Black Panther Party

It was in the late 1970s that the life of Eldridge Cleaver underwent a dramatic change from that of a black militant to that of a "born-again Christian" who shunned all forms of violence. Cleaver first came to prominence as a revolutionary social critic and as the chief theoretician and spokesman for the Black Panther Party. He was also the author of *Soul on Ice*, a collection of impassioned love letters and brilliant essays probing the depth and conundrums of the modern black psyche.

Born in 1935 in Wabbeseka, Arkansas (near Little Rock), Cleaver was convicted of possessing marijuana at age 18 and, in 1954, began a 12-year cycle of assorted prison terms at Soledad, Folsom, and San Quentin. While in prison, he obtained a diploma from Bay View High School, was converted to the Black Muslim faith (he was an ardent follower of Malcolm X), and began writing for the first time in earnest.

After his release from prison, he became a staff writer for *Ramparts* magazine and much-publicized lecturer on college campuses, where he sought to inspire and motivate black students, particularly those with ghetto backgrounds. He was once invited to address a group of Berkeley students as a black studies lecturer, a move roundly opposed by California governor Ronald Reagan. The course Social Analysis 139X was never conducted regularly.

In 1969 Cleaver left the United States secretly, fleeing a prison sentence which had been imposed on him for violating parole and for alleged involvement in a shoot-out with Oakland police. He was found by a Reuters correspondent in Havana, ostensibly working on a sequel to *Soul on Ice*. Later that year, however, he emerged in Moscow, where he granted an interview which confirmed his connection with the "international proletarian movement." Critical of both the Soviet Union and Red China for pursuing "narrow interests," Cleaver contended that "big communist countries" should invest in the future by pooling their arsenals, supplying more generous arms supplies to fledgling liberation movements, and facing up to the imperialism of the United States.

At this juncture, it developed that Cleaver, his wife, and young son were residing in Algeria.

For a time, Cleaver lived amicably in Algeria, praising its "third world" position between the two giant power blocs of East and West. However, in 1972 a rift between Cleaver and his host government was reported on the issue of skyjacking ransom money. The Algerians, contrary to Cleaver's desire, wished it returned to the airlines which had paid it. In 1973 Cleaver was reported to be under house arrest in Algiers. Meanwhile, reports circulated in California that Cleaver's former associates in the Black Panther Party, with whom he had broken, wanted to reconcile their differences with him.

Cleaver returned to the United States in 1979 and in return for his pleading guilty to assaulting an Oakland policeman more than 10 years earlier, the old murder charge against him was dismissed. He was placed on probation and ordered to do 2,000 hours of community service.

A changed man after his stay out of the country, Cleaver announced that he was a "born-again Christian" and began to make a number of appearances at fundamentalist churches in various sections of the country to speak of his conversion and to urge others to follow suit. Once a critic of the United States,

Cleaver told a group of students at Yale University in 1982 that America was the "freest and most democratic country in the world."

JAMES FARMER
Founder and Former National Director, Congress of Racial Equality

Much of the life of James Farmer has been involved with the Congress of Racial Equality in one way or another. He was one of its founders in 1942 and served as its national director until 1966. CORE was established on the basis of interracial cooperation and during its early years it clung to this philosophy.

During the mid-1960s, CORE moved toward racial separatism and it was at this point that Farmer left, though it was obvious that he did so with regret.

Born in Marshall, Texas on January 12, 1920, Farmer attended public schools throughout the South, and later earned his B.S. in chemistry from Wiley College. At first interested in medicine, he later enrolled in the School of Religion at Howard University with the intention of preparing for the Methodist ministry. Active in the Christian Youth Movement, and once vice-chairman of the National Council of Methodist Youth and the Christian Youth Council of America, Farmer received his Bachelor of Divinity degree in 1941 but refused ordination when confronted with a realization that he would have to practice in a segregated ministry.

In 1941 Farmer accepted a post as race relations secretary of the Fellowship of Reconciliation, a pacifist group. The following year he and a group of University of Chicago students organized CORE, the first American black protest organization which utilized the techniques of nonviolence and passive resistance advocated by the Indian revolutionary Mohandas K. Gandhi. In June 1943 CORE staged the first successful sit-in demonstration at a restaurant in the Chicago Loop. The organization soon supplemented this maneuver with what came to be known as the standing-line, which involved the persistent waiting in line by CORE groups at places of public accommodation where blacks were being denied admission.

Throughout the 1950s Farmer was active on a number of different fronts in the civil rights struggle. In 1958 he was one of a five-man delegation sent to 15 African countries by the International Confederation of Free Trade Unions. He also served as a radio and television commentator on programs sponsored by the United Auto Workers in Detroit, and functioned as program director for the NAACP while contributing several articles to *Crisis* magazine.

In 1961 CORE introduced the Freedom Ride into the vocabulary and methodology of civil rights protest, dispatching a group of bus riders into the South for

James Farmer, former director of CORE.

the purpose of testing whether terminal facilities there had been desegregated. Attacked in Alabama and later arrested in Mississippi, the Freedom Riders eventually succeeded in securing compliance with the Supreme Court decision of 1960 which had outlawed segregated bus terminals.

Farmer left CORE in 1966, phasing out his association with the organization as soon as he discerned what he deemed an irreversible trend toward separatism, and also to restrict the activities of whites who had made a significant commitment to the goals of the organization. Originally, he was slated to head a nationwide literacy program sponsored by the Johnson Administration and funded with a $900,000 grant from the Office of Economic Opportunity (OEO). The project was canceled, however, ostensibly because some urban politicians feared it would produce a black voter registration drive that would disrupt the voting patterns which kept them in power. Farmer later ran for Congress against Shirley Chisholm but was defeated despite the fact that his name appeared on both the Liberal and the Republican line.

President Nixon appointed Farmer as Assistant Secretary of Health, Education and Welfare in 1969, creating a furor in some black circles where it was felt that it was inappropriate for a former civil rights leader to serve in such an Administration. However, the appointment was praised by many who thought it necessary for blacks to be represented in all political parties. Farmer, himself, found that there was little of substance that he could do in the post and he resigned in a short period of time.

He began to give lectures and for a while headed a "think tank" at Howard University. In 1976 he broke all ties with CORE, criticizing its leader, Roy Innis, for such things as attempting to recruit black Vietnam veterans as mercenaries in Angola's civil war. In 1977 Farmer became executive director of the Coalition of

American Public Employees in Washington, D.C., a post that he still retains.

Disturbed over the course that CORE had taken, Farmer and a score of former CORE members attempted to create a new racially mixed civil rights organization in 1980. Farmer and Floyd McKissick later met with Innis at McKissick's Soul City, in an effort to reach an agreement about the future of the organization, but nothing developed and Innis remained in command. Farmer's civil rights activities ceased at this point.

JOHN LEWIS
Former Chairman, Student Nonviolent Coordinating Committee

John Lewis was always the quiet but totally dedicated young man of the Civil Rights Movement. A graduate of Fisk and a Baptist minister, Lewis headed the Student Nonviolent Coordinating Committee from 1963 to 1966, when he was defeated by forces less devoted than he to the nonviolent approach.

Lewis joined the sit-in Movement when he was a seminarian in Nashville, and soon, in addition to Bible training, he had a jail record, much to the grief of his mother, who tried to get him to serve the Movement in some way other than going to jail. However, Lewis told her he felt compelled to act "according to my

John Lewis heads the Voter Registration Project, which is changing southern politics.

convictions and according to my Christian conscience."

His most traumatic experience probably occurred at the March on Washington in 1963 when he, as the youngest, was to join such speakers as Martin Luther King, Walter Reuther of the United Auto Workers, Whitney Young of the National Urban League, Roy Wilkins of the NAACP, and Catholic Archbishop Patrick O'Boyle of Washington, D.C., before several hundred thousand people.

Lewis had prepared a strong speech in which he lashed out at the Kennedy Administration and urged basic changes in the social order to correct brutalities and injustices suffered by blacks and civil rights workers in the Deep South. Objections were raised by some of his elders and Archbishop O'Boyle threatened to withdraw if the program was to be too radical.

Under this pressure, Lewis dropped certain parts of the speech. After leaving SNCC, Lewis remained active in the Movement, later heading the Voter Education Project, an Atlanta-based organization that coordinates voter registration drives and provides assistance to elected black officials in the South.

After the election of Jimmy Carter as President in 1976, Lewis went to Washington as an official with ACTION, the government agency that was responsible for volunteer activities such as VISTA. When Carter left office, Lewis returned to Atlanta, where he was elected a city councilman in 1981.

FLOYD B. McKISSICK
Former National Director, Congress of Racial Equality

When Floyd Bixler McKissick replaced James Farmer as head of CORE on January 3, 1966, the organization completed a 180-degree turn that saw it change from an interracial, integrationist civil rights agency pledged to uphold nonviolence into a militant and uncompromising advocate of the ideology of black power.

McKissick refused to support Martin Luther King's call for massive nonviolent civil disobedience in northern cities, concentrating instead on programs aimed at increasing the political power and improving the economic position of the ghetto dweller.

It was also under McKissick's leadership that CORE moved in 1967 to eliminate the word "multiracial" from its constitution. McKissick and Roy Innis, who at that time was the head of the Harlem chapter of CORE, were close allies, and when McKissick left CORE in 1968, Innis took over.

After leaving CORE, McKissick launched a plan to build a new community, Soul City, on Warren County, North Carolina farmland.

Born in Asheville, North Carolina on March 9, 1922, McKissick did his undergraduate work at More-house and North Carolina colleges, and later graduated from the University of North Carolina Law School.

During World War II McKissick served in the European theater as a sergeant. After the war, he began legal practice in Durham, North Carolina, where he once represented his own daughter in her successful bid to gain admission to a previously all-white public school.

Despite the victory, McKissick later decided that "integration" itself only magnified the perils faced by many black children, McKissick bitterly recalled that his children had been taunted and harassed: "Patches cut out of their hair, pages torn out of books, water thrown on them in the dead of winter, ink down the front of their dresses"—a demoralizing array of constant and relentless pressures designed to crack their composure and destroy their will to learn. The adversity no doubt deepened McKissick's nascent radicalism and militant zeal.

As a lawyer, McKissick's most publicized efforts involved a segregated black local in the Tobacco Workers International, an AFL-CIO member. McKissick pressed to have black workers admitted to the skilled scale without loss of their seniority rating. McKissick also successfully defended "sit-in" protestors in the south.

It was at this time that the rupture widened between the older, established civil rights groups, dependent for their programming on a coalition of educated blacks and affluent white liberals, and the younger, more rancorous black militants who turned their backs on most institutional white support. The militants argued that the civil rights groups did not appreciate the urgency of many problems affecting black urban majorities, particularly in the job area where technology often reduced people to useless ciphers.

McKissick saw Soul City as an integrated community with sufficient industry to support a population of 55,000. For his venture, he received a $14 million bond issue guarantee from the Department of Housing and Urban Development and a loan of $500,000 from the First Pennsylvania Bank.

Soul City, however, ran into difficulties and despite the best efforts of McKissick, the project never developed as he had anticipated. Finally, in June 1980, the Soul City Corporation and the federal government reached an agreement that would allow the government to assume control the following January. Under the agreement, the company retained 88 acres of the project, including the site of a mobile home park and a 60,000 square foot building that had served as the project's headquarters.

The Department of Housing and Urban Development paid off $10 million in loans and agreed to pay an additional $175,000 of the project's outstanding debts. In exchange, McKissick agreed to drop a lawsuit brought to block HUD from shutting down the project.

HUEY P. NEWTON
Supreme Commander, Black Panther Party

The youngest of seven children, Newton was born in Monroe, Louisiana on February 17, 1942. He attended Oakland City College, where he founded the Afro-American Society, and later studied at San Francisco Law School.

In 1966 Newton and Bobby Seale joined forces to establish the Black Panther Party for Self-Defense. The pair systematically set out to survey police practices in the ghetto, scouting through the area with cameras and loaded shotguns.

Newton and his partner almost immediately became the targets of sharp police resentment and uneasiness. The hostility came to a climax in the 1967 fracas during which Newton allegedly killed an Oakland officer. His eight-week trial was a *cause celebre* in which more than 2,500 demonstrators surrounded the courthouse chanting Panther slogans and demanding his release. It was also one of the first public appearances of large numbers of the incipient Black Panther Party. Some 250 strong, they wore the berets and leather jackets which have since become a trademark in the public consciousness.

After his September 1968 conviction on a voluntary manslaughter charge, Newton was sent to the California Men's Colony and placed in solitary confinement for his refusal to work in the mess hall. He agreed, however, to take a job in the institution's industrial training program.

His conviction was overturned by the California Court of Appeals on the grounds that the jury had not received proper instruction from the presiding judge. The Appeals court ruled that the judge should have instructed the jury to recognize Newton's defense as a complete one if it accepted his contention that he was unconscious at the time of the killing. Besides the "omitted instructions," the court cited several other prejudicial errors as grounds for overturning the conviction.

Newton, out on $50,000 bail, was slated for retrial on a manslaughter charge stemming from the shooting of the patrolman.

As early as 1972, Newton gave signals that he was beginning to moderate his position. "The gun itself is not revolutionary," he said, adding that the Panthers had "defected from black people" by becoming too militant.

Newton fled to Cuba in 1974 and voluntarily returned to the United States in 1977. He was convicted again in 1978 of the shooting of the policeman, but that conviction was reversed. He went on trial again on a murder charge stemming from the shooting of a woman in 1974, but after two juries could not reach a verdict, the charge was dropped.

In 1980 Newton received his Ph.D. degree from the University of California. His doctoral thesis was "War Against the Panthers—Study of Repression in America." Newton is no longer active in the Black Power Movement.

Huey P. Newton leaves Alameda County Jail on $50,000 bail.

BOBBY SEALE
Co-Founder, Black Panther Party

In 1966 there were but three Black Panthers: Huey P. Newton, Bobby Seale, and Bobby Hutton. Newton and Seale were summer youth workers for the Richmond, California poverty program; Hutton was only 15 and a high school dropout.

At 29, Seale, then foreman in a car wash, was in a position to carve out a satisfactory career in the poverty program, concentrating on "trades and technical skills, . . . a little black history . . . , and then cleaning lawns, repairing houses, chopping weeds."

When Seale took up residence at the North Oakland Service Center, his patience with such a program was wearing thin; it disintegrated completely one night when he led a group of black youths on a tour of Oakland's police headquarters and heard a white police lieutenant advise members of the party to turn in "people who burn down houses. Why don't you give us their names?"

Sensing then that he was involved in what he regarded as an insidious attempt to propagandize these youths and to distort their loyalties and sense of justice,

Seale and Newton withdrew from such work, deciding instead to patrol the ghetto in their own fashion, "unified around the gun." Their objective: to monitor the movement of cops on the beat. The effort was designed to establish a mutual tolerance, Seale said, not to challenge the right of police to do their duty. It was also designed to show young blacks that they had every right to demand respect and due process from police who patrolled their area.

Still, such a policy invariably involved more racial confrontation than programmatic performance. Seale and his cohorts succeeded in luring many youngsters away from the rootlessness and spiritual starvation of ghetto streets but were unable to attract the kind of support from black intellectuals and professionals that might have complemented their emotionally resuscitating ideology.

By 1969 the cream of the Panther hierarchy—men like Huey Newton, Eldridge Cleaver, Fred Hampton, and Bobby Hutton—were either dead or in exile. Seale himself was in jail on charges stemming from the 1968 Chicago convention riots, and was one of the 13 Panthers being held in custody for the alleged execution of suspected Panther informer Alex Rackley.

Awaiting trial for the murder of a fellow Black Panther member, Bobby Seale (left) *describes his experiences in San Francisco City Jail to television producer Francisco Newman.*

Some encouragement stemmed from the party's attempts to enlist radical support in 1969 from such lawyers as Charles R. Garry of New York and William M. Kunstler of New York. That same year, the Panthers convoked a three-day conference of 3,500 young radicals from more than 300 organizations.

Significant among the changes evident in the Panther positions was the group's emphasis on "people's" problems, rather than just those of the black ghetto. Seale spoke at the 1969 meeting, stressing "unity of the people" and pledging that Panthers would "not fight racism with more racism."

Seale was shifting the emphasis away from the issue of race and committing the Panthers to the idea that class struggle was the deciding factor in American life:

We will not fight capitalism with more capitalism—black capitalism. We will fight it with basic socialistic programs. We will not fight fire with fire. The best way to put out fire is with water.

Seale thus acknowledged the need to resort to propaganda, organization, and political activity as alternate tactics beyond arming people and tutoring them in guerilla warfare. In 1973, Seale ran unsuccessfully for Mayor of Oakland, California, finishing second in a field of eight and thus forcing the incumbent to engage in a runoff election.

In 1974 Seale resigned as chairman of the Black Panther Party and later wrote his autobiography, *A Lonely Rage*. In recent years Seale has lectured widely and is reported to be writing another book. He is no longer active in the Black Power Movement.

CIVIL RIGHTS AND BLACK POWER LEADERS OF THE PAST

Following are brief biographies of blacks, no longer living, who made profound contributions to the civil rights and political awareness of blacks in the United States. The *Negro Almanac* has selected this group on the basis of the contributions and fame of each individual. All shades of the political spectrum are represented, from carefully moderate Booker T. Washington to William DuBois, who supported the Communist Party in his late years.

RICHARD ALLEN
1760–1831

Richard Allen was among the first black preachers to become prominent as a political activist. When still in his teens, Allen converted his master to Christianity and was permitted to buy his freedom.

Allen thought of people first as children of God

Reverend Richard Allen founded the Free African Society.

and only then as members of a racial group. He believed that he could preach to both whites and blacks, and in this view Allen was supported by the Bishop of the Methodist Church. However, in 1787 Allen encountered intense bigotry at a church in Philadelphia and as a result, together with Absalam Jones, established the first black church in the United States, the African Methodist Episcopal. In 1816 Allen organized black Methodist congregations from several states into one group and was elected bishop.

Allen was aware that the prejudice which denied him the means to address integrated congregations also denied blacks the means to live in dignity. In 1787 he founded the Free African Society, which sought to further the social welfare and racial and religious awareness of blacks.

Allen remained a patriot throughout his life, strongly supporting the United States in the war of 1812 against Great Britain. In 1830 he formed a movement for settling blacks in Canada but opposed with intensity and vigor all efforts to resettle blacks in Africa.

FREDERICK DOUGLASS
1817–1895

One of a handful of names which immediately leaps to mind at the mention of the American black is that of Frederick Douglass, probably the foremost voice in the abolitionist movement of the nineteenth century.

Born in February 1817 in Talbot County, Maryland, Douglass was sent to Baltimore as a house servant at the age of eight. He learned to read and write under the instruction of his mistress. At the death of her husband, Douglass was sent to the country as a field

Frederick Douglass was foremost speaker of the Abolitionist movement.

hand. In his early teens, he began to teach in a Sunday school which was foricbly shut down by hostile southerners. Douglass himself was severely flogged for his resistance to slavery.

After one unsuccessful attempt to escape, Douglass managed to make his way to New York disguised as a sailor. Once in the North, he found his true calling—leader in the antislavery crusade. Taken on as an agent by the Massachusetts Anti-Slavery Society, he began his great lifework.

Douglass soon became an increasingly familiar figure to abolitionists throughout the country. In 1845, after having published his *Narrative* at great personal risk (that of reenslavement as a fugitive), he went to England, where he raised enough money, through lectures on slavery and women's rights, to buy his freedom. Upon his return to his native shores, he founded the famous newspaper *The North Star.* Later he was forced to flee to Canada when the governor of Virginia swore out a warrant for his arrest on charges that he had conspired with John Brown, leader of the Harpers Ferry revolt.

With the outbreak of the Civil War, Douglass—once again back in the United States—met with President Lincoln and assisted him in recruiting the celebrated 54th and 55th Massachusetts Negro regiments.

In 1871, during the Reconstruction period, he was appointed to the territorial legislature of the District of Columbia; in 1872 he served as one of the presidential electors-at-large for New York and, shortly thereafter, became secretary of the Santo Domingo Commission.

In 1877, after a short term as a police commissioner of the District of Columbia, Douglass was appointed marshal—a post he held until he was named recorder of deeds in 1881.

Eight years later, in return for his support of the presidential campaign of Benjamin Harrison, Douglass was appointed to the most important federal posts he was to hold—minister resident and counsul general to the Republic of Haiti and, later, chargé d'affaires for Santo Domingo. However, when he saw his efforts being undermined by unscrupulous American businessmen interested solely in exploiting Haiti, he resigned his post in 1891.

Four years later, Frederick Douglass died at his home in Washington, D.C.

W. E. B. DUBOIS
1868–1963

An outstanding critic, editor, scholar, author, and civil rights leader, William Edward Burghardt DuBois is certainly among the most influential blacks of the twentieth century.

Born in Great Barrington, Massachusetts on February 23, 1868, DuBois received a bachelors degree from Fisk University and went on to win a second bachelors, as well as a Ph.D., from Harvard. He was for a time professor of Latin and Greek at Wilberforce and the University of Pennsylvania, and also served as a professor of economics and history at Atlanta University.

One of the founders of the National Association for the Advancement of Colored People (NAACP) in 1909, DuBois served as that organization's director of publications and editor of *Crisis* magazine until 1934. In 1944 he returned from Atlanta University to become head of the NAACP's special research department, a post he held until 1948. Dr. DuBois emigrated to Africa in 1961 and became editor-in-chief of the *Encyclopedia Africana,* an enormous publishing venture which had been planned by Kwame Nkrumah, since then deposed as president of Ghana. DuBois died in Ghana in 1963 at the age of 95.

His numerous books include *The Suppression of the Slave Trade* (1896), *The Philadelphia Negro* (1899), *The Souls of Black Folk* (1903), *John Brown* (1909), *Quest of the Silver Fleece* (1911), *The Negro* (1915), *Darkwater* (1920), *The Gift of Black Folk* (1924), *Dark Princess* (1928), *Black Folk: Then and Now* (1939), *Dusk of Dawn* (1940), *Color and Democracy* (1945), *The World and Africa* (1947), *In Battle for Peace* (1952), and a trilogy, *Black Flame* (1957–1961).

It is this enormous literary output on such a wide variety of themes which offers the most convincing testimony to DuBois' lifetime position that it was vital for blacks to cultivate their own aesthetic and cultural values even as they made valuable strides toward social emancipation. In this he was opposed by Booker T. Washington, who felt that the black should concentrate on developing technical and mechanical skills before all else.

In 1961 at age 93, DuBois joined the Communist Party. He died two years later.

It was DuBois' affiliation with the Communist Party that prompted a spirited protest against the plan to erect a memorial in his hometown in 1969. Though DuBois was a lifelong radical, he functioned within the pale of society as an American during his most productive years.

T. THOMAS FORTUNE
1856–1928

T. Thomas Fortune was one of the most prominent black journalists involved in the flourishing black press of the post-Civil War era.

Born in Florida, the son of a Reconstruction politician, Fortune was particularly productive before his thirtieth year, completing such important literature as *Black and White: Land, Labor and Politics in the South* and *The Negro in Politics* while in his twenties.

Fortune attended Howard University for two years, leaving to marry Miss Carrie Smiley of Jacksonville, Florida. The couple went to New York in 1878, with Fortune taking a job as a printer for the New York *Sun.* In time, Fortune caught the attention of *Sun* editor Charles A. Dana, who eventually promoted him to the editorial staff of the paper.

Fortune also edited *The Globe,* a black daily, and was later chief editorial writer and polemicist on the staff of *The Negro World.* In 1900 Fortune joined Booker T. Washington in helping to organize the successful National Negro Business League. His later activity with Washington gained him more notoriety than his earlier writing, although the latter is clearly more vital in affording him an important niche in the history of black protest.

In 1883 Fortune founded the New York *Age,* the paper with which he sought to "champion the cause" of his race. In time, the *Age* became the leading black journal of opinion in the United States. One of Fortune's early crusades was against the practice of separate schools for the races in the New York educational system.

Fortune was later responsible for coining the term "Afro-American" as a substitute for Negro in New York newspapers. He also set up the Afro-American Council, an organization which he regarded as the precursor of the Niagara Movement. In 1907 Fortune sold the *Age,* although he remained active in journalism as an editorial writer for several black newspapers.

At the time of his death in 1928, Fortune was writing for the *Negro World.*

HENRY HIGHLAND GARNET
1815–1882

Like Frederick Douglass, Henry Highland Garnet achieved fame as an antislavery crusader and in his later years served his country in appointed office.

Garnet was born a slave in Maryland, escaped with his parents to Pennsylvania when he was nine, and graduated from Oneida Institute in 1840. His eloquent antislavery oratory soon gained him a following. In 1843 he made his famous speech at the Free Colored People Convention in Buffalo, in which he called for a general strike and armed rebellion. The speech was too rousing, even for Douglass, who recessed the meeting to let the assemblage cool down. But Garnet, a pastor as well as a political activist, continued to advocate violence to end slavery, if peaceful methods failed.

After the Civil War, Garnet was a pastor in Washington and New York, president of Avery College in Pittsburgh, and U.S. Minister to Liberia.

MARCUS GARVEY
1887–1940

Marcus Garvey was a West Indian by birth and a revolutionary by disposition. Garvey dedicated his life to what he called the "uplifting" of the black people of the world through the creation of the Universal Negro Improvement Association (UNIA) and the African Communities League. Like Malcolm X a generation later, he believed that blacks could never achieve equality unless they became independent—founding their own nations, governments, businesses, industrial enterprises, and military establishments—in short, those same institutions by which other peoples of the world had risen to power.

The youngest of 11 children, Garvey moved to Kingston at age 14, found work in a print shop, and became acquainted with the abysmal living conditions of the laboring class. He quickly involved himself in social reform, participating in the first Printers' Union strike on Jamaica and setting up a newspaper called *The Watchman.* Leaving the island to earn money to finance his projects, he visited Central and South America, amassing evidence that black people everywhere were victims of discrimination.

Back in Jamaica in 1911, he laid the groundwork of the Universal Negro Improvement Association, to which he was to devote his life. Undaunted by lack of enthusiasm for his plans, Garvey left for England in 1912 in search of additional financial backing. While there, he worked for an Egyptian scholar and learned much of the history of Africa—particularly with reference to the exploitation of black peoples by colonial powers.

In 1916, acquainted with the work of Booker T. Washington, he came to the United States, where he

Marcus Garvey held that black people would never enjoy equality until they became independent, founding their own nations, businesses, and industrial enterprises.

formulated what he called the "Back to Africa" program for the resettlement of the black in his ancestral homeland. In New York City particularly his ideas attracted popular support, and thousands enrolled in the UNIA. He began publishing the newspaper *The Negro World* and toured the United States preaching black nationalism to popular audiences. In a matter of months, he had founded over 30 UNIA branches and launched some ambitious business ventures, notably the Black Star Line, a black steamship company. On the negative side, he ran into trouble with the New York District Attorney's Office, which he had publicly criticized, and other enemies began to appear.

In 1920 the UNIA convened a 31-day international conclave in Madison Square Garden, where they presented a policy statement on the Back to Africa program and proclaimed a formal Declaration of Rights for blacks all over the world. Following this, Garvey set himself the task of negotiating for the repatriation of blacks to Liberia. Rumors that Garvey's real intention was to seize power in Liberia and build a personal empire there caused Liberia to withdraw all support from the venture, leaving Garvey stunned from the realization that he had actually been rebuffed by a black African nation.

With the Black Star Line in serious financial difficulties, Garvey promoted two new business organizations—the African Communities League and the Negro Factories Corporation. He also tried to salvage his colonization scheme by sending a delegation to appeal to the League of Nations for transfer to the UNIA of the African colonies taken from Germany during World War I.

Financial betrayal by trusted aides and a host of legal entanglements (based on charges that he had used the U.S. mails to defraud prospective investors) eventually led to Garvey's imprisonment in Atlanta Federal Penitentiary for a five-year term. In 1927 his half-served sentence was commuted, and he was deported to Jamaica by order of President Calvin Coolidge.

Garvey then turned his energies to Jamaican politics, campaigning on a platform of self-government, minimum wage laws, and land and judicial reform. He was soundly defeated at the polls, however, because most of his followers did not have the necessary voting qualifications.

In 1935 Garvey left for England where, in near obscurity, he died five years later in a cottage in West Kensington.

Critics have labeled Garvey a pretentious mountebank, whereas his supporters call him a genius. From a historical viewpoint he must be regarded as a fanatic visionary, a man literally driven by the notion that the blacks' sole means for surviving in the twentieth century was through the foundation of a unified, separatist empire in Africa. Although his ideas were rejected by most people of his day, it is clear that, since then, these very ideas have strongly influenced the policies of black leaders all over the world.

LESTER B. GRANGER
1896–1976

Lester Granger served as executive director of the National Urban League from 1941 to 1961. His vigorous leadership transformed the League into an effective instrument for integrating blacks into the war effort and was responsible for greatly increasing the size and strength of the organization.

Born in Newport News, Virginia, Granger graduated from Dartmouth College in 1917 and served in the 92nd Infantry Division in France during World War I. A social worker by professional training and disposition, he joined the New Jersey Urban League in 1919 and rose to the national directorship in 1941. During the ensuing world war, he worked tirelessly as a special assistant to the Secretary of the Navy, traveling more than 60,000 miles to talk with servicemen, defense contractors, and workers. Presenting him with the Medal of Merit for his work, President Truman said that Granger had contributed "more than any other person to the effective utilization of Negro personnel in the service."

Granger was responsible for a number of major innovations within the League, including the development of a Pilot Placement Project in which blacks were placed in significant jobs previously barred to them, and the establishment of a Commerce and Industry Council and Trade Union Advisory Council. During his tenure in office, the number of League affiliates grew from 41 to 65, and the budget increased from $600,000 to $4.5 million.

When he retired in 1961, Granger was praised by President Eisenhower as a "man of the highest character and integrity." From a historical vantage, it is clear that Granger's contributions both to the League and to the course of American life were profound.

GEORGE EDMUND HAYNES
1875–1960

Dr. George E. Haynes, co-founder and first executive secretary of the Department of Race Relations of the Federal Council of Churches of Christ in America, was born in Pine Bluff, Arkansas. He received an A.B. from Fisk University and later became the first black

to receive a doctorate from New York's Columbia University. While studying economics and social science in New York, Haynes developed a keen sensitivity to the urban problems of recently migrated southern blacks and in 1910, along with Ruth Baldwin and Frances Kellor, he launched the National Urban League. He served as executive director until resigning in 1918 to become a special assistant to the Secretary of Labor for three years. Beginning in 1921, he took on the executive secretaryship with the Federal Council of Churches, a post to which he devoted 26 years of service. Following World War II, he organized the Interracial Clinic, an agency dedicated to easing racial tensions.

JAMES WELDON JOHNSON
1871–1938

Like DuBois, black intellectual James Weldon Johnson played a vital role in the civil rights movement of the twentieth century—as poet, teacher, critic, diplomat, and NAACP official. Johnson is perhaps most often popularly remembered as the lyricist for *Lift Every Voice and Sing,* the poem which is often referred to as the black national anthem.

Born in 1871 in Jacksonville, Florida, Johnson was educated at Atlanta and Columbia universities. His career included service as a school principal, a lawyer, and a diplomat (U.S. Consul at Puerto Cabello, Venezuela and, later, in Nicaragua). From 1916 to 1930 he was a key policy maker of the NAACP, eventually serving as the organization's executive secretary.

In his early days, Johnson's fame rested largely on his lyrics for popular songs, but in 1917 he completed his first book of poetry, *Fifty Years and Other Poems.* Five years later, he followed this with *The Book of American Negro Poetry,* and in 1927 he established his literary reputation with *God's Trombones,* a collection of seven folk sermons in verse. Over the years, this work has been performed countless times, on stage and television.

In 1930 Johnson finished *St. Peter Relates an Incident of the Resurrection* and, three years later, his lengthy autobiography, *Along This Way.*

Johnson died in 1938 following an automobile accident in Maine.

EUGENE KINCKLE JONES
1884–1951

Eugene K. Jones had a long career with the National Urban League, serving as its second executive director from 1918 to 1941, and held many important government posts. Born in Richmond, Virginia, he was educated at Virginia Union and Cornell University. In addition to helping structure the Urban League, he served as Negro Affairs advisor to the U.S. Department of Commerce from 1933 to 1943, chaired the Negro Advisory committees for the Texas Centennial Exposition of 1936 and the New York World's Fair of 1939, and joined the Fair Employment Board of the U.S. Civil Service Commission in 1948.

MARTIN LUTHER KING, JR.
1929–1968

Any number of historic moments in the civil rights struggle have been used to identify Martin Luther King, Jr.—prime mover of the Montgomery bus boycott (1956), keynote speaker at the March on Washington (1963), youngest Nobel Peace Prize laureate (1964). But in retrospect, single events are less important than the fact that King, and his policy of nonviolent protest, was the dominant force in the civil rights movement during its decade of greatest achievement, from 1957 to 1968.

King was born Michael Luther King in Atlanta on January 15, 1929—one of the three children of Martin Luther King, Sr., pastor of Ebenezer Baptist Church, and Alberta (Williams) King, a former schoolteacher. (He did not receive the name of "Martin" until he was about six years of age.)

After attending grammar and high school locally, King enrolled in Morehouse College (also in Atlanta) in 1944. At this time he was not inclined to enter the ministry, but while there he came under the influence of Dr. Benjamin Mays, a scholar whose manner and bearing convinced him that a religious career could have its intellectual satisfactions as well. After receiving his B.A. in 1948, King attended Crozer Theological Seminary in Chester, Pennsylvania, winning the Plafker Award as the outstanding student of the graduating class, and the J. Lewis Crozer Fellowship as well. King completed the course work for his doctorate in 1953, and was granted the degree two years later upon completion of his dissertation.

Married by then, King returned South, accepting the pastorate of the Dexter Avenue Baptist Church in Montgomery, Alabama. It was here that he made his first mark on the civil rights movement, by mobiliz-

Martin Luther King in a pensive moment.

ing the black community during a 382-day boycott of the city's bus lines. Working through the Montgomery Improvement Association, King overcame arrest and other violent harassment, including the bombing of his home. Ultimately, the U.S. Supreme Court declared the Alabama laws requiring bus segregation unconstitutional, with the result that blacks were allowed to ride Montgomery buses on equal footing with whites.

A national hero and a civil rights figure of growing importance, King summoned together a number of black leaders in 1957 and laid the groundwork for the organization now known as the Southern Christian Leadership Conference (SCLC). Elected its president, he soon sought to assist other communities in the organization of protest campaigns against discrimination, and in voter-registration activities as well.

After completing his first book and making a trip to India, King returned to the United States in 1960 to become co-pastor, with his father, of Ebenezer Baptist Church.

Three years later, King's nonviolent tactics were put to their most severe test in Birmingham, Alabama during a mass protest for fair hiring practices, the establishment of a biracial committee, and the desegregation of department-store facilities. Police brutality used against the marchers dramatized the plight of blacks to the nation at large with enormous impact. King was arrested, but his voice was not silenced as he issued his classic "Letter from a Birmingham Jail" to refute his critics.

Later that year King was a principal speaker at the historic March on Washington (1963), where he delivered one of the most passionate addresses of his career. At the beginning of the next year *Time* magazine designated him as its Man of the Year for 1963. A few months later he was named recipient of the 1964 Nobel Peace Prize.

Upon his return from Oslo, where he had gone to accept the award, King entered a new battle, in Selma, Alabama, where he led a voter-registration campaign which culminated in the Selma-to-Montgomery Freedom March.

King next brought his crusade to Chicago where he launched a slum-rehabilitation and open-housing program.

In the North, however, King soon discovered that young and angry blacks (such as the ones in Watts who once replied "Martin Luther Who?" to a question about whether the civil rights leader would approve of their behavior) cared little for his pulpit oratory and even less for his solemn pleas for peaceful protest.

Their disenchantment was clearly one of the factors influencing his decision to rally behind a new cause and stake out a fresh battleground: the war in Vietnam.

King himself antagonized many civil rights leaders by declaring the United States to be "the greatest purveyor of violence in the world." His clear aim was to fuse a new coalition of dissent based on equal support for the peace crusade and the civil rights movement.

The rift was immediate. The NAACP saw King's shift of emphasis as "a serious tactical mistake"; the Urban League warned that the "limited resources" of the civil rights movement would be spread too thin; Bayard Rustin claimed black support of the peace movement would be negligible; Ralph Bunche felt King was undertaking an impossible mission in trying to bring the campaign for peace in step with the goals of the civil rights movement.

From the vantage point of history, King's timing could only be regarded as superb. In announcing his opposition to the war, and in characterizing it as a "tragic adventure" which was playing "havoc with the destiny of the entire world," King again forced the white middle class to concede that no movement could dramatically affect the course of government in the United States unless it involved deliberate and restrained aggressiveness, persistent dissent, and even militant confrontation. These were precisely the ingredients of the civil rights struggle in the South in the early 1960s.

Speaking at the U.N., King again found words to prod the conscience of white America:

Let us save our national honor—stop the bombing.

Let us save American lives and Vietnamese lives—stop the bombing.

Let us take a single instantaneous step to the peace table— stop the bombing.

Let our voices ring out across the land to say the American people are not vainglorious conquerors—stop the bombing.

As students, professors, intellectuals, clergymen and reformers of every stripe rushed into the movement (in a sense forcing fiery black militants like Stokely Carmichael and Floyd McKissick to surrender their control over antiwar polemics), King turned his attention to the domestic issue which, in his view, was directly related to the Vietnam struggle: the War on Poverty.

At one point, he called for a guaranteed family income, he threatened national boycotts, and spoke of disrupting entire cities by nonviolent "camp-ins." With this in mind, he began to draw up plans for a massive march of the poor on Washington, D.C. itself, envisioning a popular demonstration of unsurpassed intensity and magnitude designed to force Congress and the political parties to recognize and deal with the unseen and ignored masses of desperate and downtrodden Americans.

King's decision to interrupt these plans to lend his support to the Memphis sanitationmen's strike was based in part on his desire to discourage violence, as well as to focus national attention on the plight of the poor, unorganized workers of the city. The men were bargaining for little else beyond basic union representation and long-overdue salary considerations.

Though he was unable to eliminate the violence which had resulted in the summoning and subsequent departure of the National Guard, King stayed on in Memphis and was in the process of planning for a march which he vowed to carry out in defiance of a federal court injunction if necessary.

On the night of April 3, 1968, he told a church congregation: "Well I don't know what will happen now . . . But it really doesn't matter . . ." (At other times, musing over the possibility he might be killed, King had assured his colleagues that he had "the advantage over most people" because he had "conquered the fear of death.")

Death came for King on the balcony of the black-owned Lorraine Motel just off Beale Street on the evening of April 4. While standing outside with Jesse Jackson and Ralph Abernathy, a shot rang out. King fell over, struck in the neck by a rifle bullet which left him moribund. At 7:05 P.M. he was pronounced dead at St. Joseph's Hospital.

King's death caused a wave of violence in such major cities as Washington, D.C. (11 dead; 24 million dollars property damage, over 8,000 arrests, over 1,000 injuries); Chicago (nine dead, 11 million dollars property damage, nearly 3,000 arrests, 500 injured), and Baltimore (6 dead, 14 million dollars property damage, 5800 arrests, and 900 injured). Without restraint against looters, death tolls would have been even higher. Both grief and anger suffused the black community. The anger was assuredly all the more fanatic precisely because King had been so irretrievably dedicated to nonviolence.

King's birthday, January 15, is now recognized as a national holiday.

MALCOLM X
1925–1965

Malcolm X was one of the most fiery and controversial blacks of the twentieth century.

Born Malcolm Little in Omaha on May 19, 1925, Malcolm was the son of a Baptist preacher who was an avid supporter of Marcus Garvey's United Negro Improvement Association. At an early age, Malcolm moved to Lansing, Michigan with his parents, both of whom were tragically lost to him in childhood. (His father was run over by a streetcar, and his mother was committed to a mental institution.)

Leaving school after the eighth grade, Malcolm

Fiery Malcolm X rose from the underworld to become an outspoken Black Muslim apostle; he was assassinated after starting his own movement.

made his way to New York, working for a time as a waiter at Smalls Paradise in Harlem. Soon part of the seamy underworld life of the ghetto, Malcolm began selling and using drugs, turned to burglary, and was sentenced to a 10-year prison term in 1946.

While in prison, he became acquainted with the Black Muslim sect headed by Elijah Muhammad and was quickly converted to its utopian and racist point of view. Paroled from prison in 1952, he soon became an outspoken defender of Muslim doctrines, accepting the basic argument that evil was an inherent characteristic of the "white man's Christian world."

Unlike Muhammad, Malcolm sought publicity, making several provocative and inflammatory statements to predominantly white civic groups and college campus audiences. Branding white people "devils," he spoke bitterly of a philosophy of vengeance and "an eye for an eye." When, in 1963, he characterized the Kennedy assassination as a case of "chickens coming home to roost," he was suspended from the Black Muslim movement by Elijah Muhammad, and soon formed his own protest group, the Organization of Afro-American Unity.

The group had built only a small following at the time of Malcolm X's murder in 1965. He was buried as Al Hajj Mali al-Shabazz, the name he had taken in 1964 after making his holy pilgrimage to Mecca.

Malcolm X had a profound influence on both blacks and whites. Many blacks responded to a feeling that he was a man of the people, experienced in the ways of the street rather than the pulpit or the college campus, which traditionally have provided the preponderance of black leaders. And many young whites responded to Malcolm's blunt, colorful language and unwillingness to retreat in the face of hostility. By the 1970s, it had become apparent that Malcolm X would be lionized, or even beatified, by those who sought as much to revere his memory as to promote their own distorted view of the true meaning of his ideology and striving. In practical terms, he was an advocate of self-help, self-defense, and education; as a philosopher and pedagogue, he succeeded in integrating history, religion, and mythology to establish a framework for his ultimate belief in world brotherhood and in human justice. Faith, in his view, was a prelude to action; ideas were feckless without policy. At least three books published since his death effectively present his most enduring thoughts. They are his own classic *Autobiography,* a collection of *Speeches* given at Harvard, and *Malcolm X: The Man and His Times.*

KELLY MILLER
1863–1939

A voice of reason and scholarship, Kelly Miller was one of the major black spokesmen and teachers of the early twentieth century. His thoughtful essays analyzed racial problems in terms of their global development, the potency and promise of the black race, and viable solutions. For Miller, who devoted his life to teaching, the surest release from the house of bondage was by the road of education.

Born in Winnsboro, South Carolina, during the Civil War, he worked his way through school, graduating from Howard University in 1886, studying postgraduate mathematics and physics at Johns Hopkins (1887–1889), and eventually earning from Howard his A.M. (1901) and LL.D. (1903) degrees. After a short stint teaching in the public schools of Washington, D.C., he joined Howard's faculty, where he was to remain for most of his academic career, serving variously as professor of mathematics, chairman of the department of sociology, dean of the junior college, and dean of the College of Arts and Sciences. In addi-

tion to his collegial responsibilities, he published many important essays, became the first black academician to write a regular column for the black press, and helped W. E. B. DuBois edit the journal *Crisis.*

In the face of prevailing pessimism about race relations, Miller emphasized the great capacity for progress the black race had shown in the 50 years since emancipation. Literacy had increased enormously, a managerial and professional class was crystallizing, property ownership had swelled, and the masses' need for self-expression and self-government had given birth to the unique socioreligious institution of the black church. Armed with the belief that no people in world history had made such great advances in so brief a span, and convinced of the inherently democratizing effect of American institutions, Miller proclaimed certainty that the black race would eventually assume its rightful position of equality in the United States. Unlike DuBois, who felt that color would always single blacks out for prejudicial treatment, Miller held that the evolution of similar behavior patterns would obviate the import of physical differences.

Miller's major publications were *Race Adjustment* (1903), *Out of the House of Bondage* (1917), *History of the World War and the Important Part Taken by the Negroes* (1919), and *The Everlasting Stain* (1924).

WILLIAM MONROE TROTTER
1872–1934

Many Civil Rights leaders of the past 100 years, men such as DuBois, Johnson, Wilkins, and Fortune, have been writers. William Monroe Trotter was perhaps the most militant of them. An honor student and Phi Beta Kappa at Harvard, Trotter founded the *Guardian,* a militant newspaper, in 1901, for the purpose of "propaganda against discrimination."

In 1905 Trotter joined DuBois in founding the Niagara Movement but refused to move with him into the NAACP because he felt it would be too moderate. Instead, Trotter formed the National Equal Rights League. In 1919 Trotter appeared at the Paris Peace Conference in an unsuccessful effort to have it outlaw racial discrimination. The State Department had denied him a passport to attend, but he had reached Paris nonetheless, by having himself hired as a cook on a ship.

Because of his strident unwillingness to work with established groups, the Civil Rights Movement has been slow to recognize Trotter. But many of his methods were to be adopted in the 1950s, notably his use of nonviolent protest. In 1903 Trotter deliberately disrupted a meeting in Boston at which Booker T. Washington was preaching support of segregation; Trotter's purpose was to be arrested to gain publicity for his militant position. Trotter also led demonstrations against plays and films which glorified the Ku Klux Klan.

SOJOURNER TRUTH
1797–1883

Isabella Baumfree—popularly known as Sojourner Truth—became famous in her lifetime as a preacher, abolitionist, and lecturer. Born, it is believed, in 1797 in Ulster County, New York, she is known to have been freed from slavery by the New York State Emancipation Act of 1827, and to have lived for a time in New York City.

Soon disillusioned with life there, she adopted the name Sojourner Truth (a name she felt God had given her) and assumed as her "mission" in life the task of traveling across the country and spreading "the truth." It was not long before this self-styled prophetess had become famous as an itinerant preacher. Wherever she appeared, huge crowds would gather to hear her, for she was reputed to have not only "mystical gifts" but great powers of oratory as well.

Since black women were early and active participants in the antislavery movement, it was not surprising that, before long, Sojourner Truth was addressing countless meetings in the abolitionist cause. She soon became friendly with such leading white abolitionists as James and Lucretia Mott and Harriet Beecher Stowe.

Sojourner Truth, born Isabella Baumfree, a gifted orator who traveled across the nation to speak against the evils of her time.

With the outbreak of hostilities, she raised money to buy gifts for the soldiers, and went into the army camps to distribute them herself. She also aided blacks who had managed to escape North, helping them to find work and places to live.

After the war, Sojourner Truth continued traveling on behalf of her people, campaigning in particular for better educational opportunities. Her *Narrative,* published in 1875, recounts her war experiences, as well as a meeting with Abraham Lincoln.

Age and ill health finally forced her to give up traveling and then even the less demanding schedule of lectures at her Battle Creek sanatorium.

She died in Michigan on November 26, 1883.

HARRIET ROSS TUBMAN
1820–1913

The greatest "conductor" on the Underground Railroad—an organized network of way stations which helped black slaves escape from the South to the free states and as far north as Canada—was a former slave and a woman, Harriet Ross Tubman.

Believed to have been born about 1820 in Dorchester County, Maryland, Tubman had a childhood similar to that of most slave children—no schooling, little play, much hard work, and often severe punishment. In 1848 she succeeded in escaping from this life, leaving her husband John Tubman, who threatened to report her to their master.

Once free, she began to devise practical ways to help other slaves escape. Over the next 10 years, she made some 20 trips from the North to the South, rescuing more than 300 slaves. A price of $40,000 was set on her head.

Harriet Tubman's reputation spread rapidly. She won the admiration of leading white abolitionists, some of whom sheltered her "passengers".

One of her major disappointments was the ultimate failure of John Brown's raid on Harpers Ferry. She had met and aided Brown in recruiting soldiers for his cause (in fact, he called her "General Tubman"), and she was always to regard him, rather than Lincoln, as the true emancipator of her people.

In 1860 Harriet Tubman began to canvass the nation, appearing at antislavery meetings and speaking on behalf of women's rights. Shortly before the outbreak of the Civil War, she was forced for a time to leave for Canada, but she soon returned to the United States, serving the Union cause openly and actively as nurse, soldier, spy, and scout. She was particularly valuable in this latter capacity, since her work on the Railroad had made her thoroughly familiar with much of the terrain.

Two years after the end of the war, John Tubman died, and in 1869 Harriet Tubman married Nelson

Harriet Tubman (left with pan) *was the Underground Railroad's best known conductor.*

Davis, a war veteran. A year earlier, her biography had been written by Sarah Bradford, and the proceeds from the sales of the book were given to her to help ease her financial burden.

Despite her many honors and tributes (including a medal from Queen Victoria of England), Harriet Tubman spent her last years in poverty. She did not receive a pension until more than 30 years after the close of the Civil War. Awarded $20 a month for the remainder of her life, she used most of this money to help found a place for the aged and needy—later to be called The Harriet Tubman Home.

She died in Auburn in March 1913.

DAVID WALKER
1785–1830

David Walker is something of a mystery, both as a literary figure and as a man. His fame rests exclusively on a small but explosive pamphlet which circulated clandestinely through the antebellum South and "rumored" slave uprisings as the only possible solution to the black problem. The full title of Walker's work is *Walker's Appeal in Four Articles Together With A Preamble to the Colored Citizens of the World, But in Particular and Very Expressly to Those of the United States (1829).*

Born of a free mother and a slave father, Walker left his native North Carolina while in his teens, and settled in Boston, where he earned a living as a dealer in old clothes. After his *Appeal* was published, his life was threatened, but he refused to flee to Canada and seek anonymity. Instead, he vowed to fight on. He died shortly thereafter, in circumstances which led many abolitionists to believe that he had been murdered. The blacks of Boston believed him a true martyr to their cause.

BOOKER TALIAFERRO WASHINGTON
1856–1915

Educator and statesman Booker T. Washington was Frederick Douglass' successor as the black leader of his day. Unlike Douglass, Washington was never to hold federal office, but he managed, nonetheless, to exert considerable influence on several areas of public affairs.

Washington was born a slave in Hale's Ford, Virginia, reportedly in April 1856. He entered Hampton Institute in 1872 and graduated four years later. After teaching a while, he continued his studies at Wayland Seminary in Washington, D.C. Washington founded Tuskegee Institute in 1881, at the same time becoming its first president. Later, in addition to instituting a variety of programs for rural extension work, he helped establish the National Negro Business League.

In sharp contrast to Douglass, Washington was intent on setting forth a conciliatory policy with respect to civil rights. Already in 1884 he emphasized that the best cause to pursue in regard to civil rights in the South is to let it alone . . . and it will settle itself.

Some 11 years later, in his famous speech at the opening of the Cotton States Exposition, he expounded moderate views that were to turn black intellectuals against him. It was feared that his stand would encourage the foes of equal rights.

Washington's theme was that blacks would best protect their constitutional rights through their own economic and moral advancement; hence his major task was to win over diverse elements among southern whites, without whose support the program he envisaged would have been impossible.

At the time of his death in 1915, Washington's philosophy had been largely discredited by more militant black groups working toward the achievement of their aims through activist agencies. In the South, however, Washington still managed to play a major role in motivating blacks to improve their lot through self-help programs and the development of skilled labor.

In 1896, shortly after the election of President William McKinley, a movement was set in motion urging that Washington be named to a cabinet post, but Washington withdrew himself from consideration, preferring to work outside the political arena.

WALTER WHITE
1893–1955

Walter White, who could have passed for white, chose instead to identify with his black ancestry, and ultimately came to be the most ardent protagonist in the fight to stamp out lynching in America, particularly after World War I. His most famous work was *Rope and Faggot: A Biography of Judge Lynch* (1929).

Born in Atlanta and educated in that Georgia city as well as in New York, White worked as secretary of the National Association for the Advancement of Colored People (NAACP). He completed his important study after two years as a Guggenheim Fellow. This work stood alongside two earlier novels, *Fire in the Flint* (1924) and *Flight* (1926). White's other work appeared in the leading periodicals of the day, including *Harper's, The Nation,* and *New Republic.* White was awarded a Spingarn Medal in 1937 in recognition of his tireless efforts on behalf of all black Americans.

ROY WILKINS
1910–1981

On September 8, 1981, Roy Wilkins, who had served as Executive Secretary of the NAACP for 22 years, died quietly in New York City at the age of 80. He had retired from the NAACP in 1977 and since then had been in declining health. His death removed from the scene the last of the towering leaders who had played major roles in the Civil Rights Movement of the fifties and sixties—Martin Luther King, Whitney Young, Malcolm X, A. Philip Randolph.

Of his passing, *Newsweek* magazine said:

He was among the last of a generation of civil rights leaders who pulled and tugged and cajoled the nation through decades of change so profound that many Americans cannot imagine, still less remember, what segregation was like.

Once asked to describe what he did for a living, Wilkins said, "I work for Negroes." He could never bring himself to use the word "black," and this, along with his thoughtful, deliberate pace, made him seem out of date to younger blacks. In fact, there were rumblings within the NAACP, even before he retired, that he should step down, but he remained in his position until it became physically impossible for him to continue.

A courtly and gracious man, he was sustained by a determined optimism and a steady faith that "there are more people who want to do good than do evil."

When asked to describe his greatest satisfaction in life, he pointed to the *Brown* decision of 1954 that ended segregation in the public schools and heralded the end of legalized segregation in the country.

Born in St. Louis on August 30, 1901, Wilkins was reared in the home of an aunt and uncle living in St. Paul, Minnesota. Though poor, he was able to attend integrated schools in the city, and he grew up in what might be termed a racially mixed community.

Wilkins majored in sociology and minored in journalism while attending the University of Minnesota, supporting himself by doing a variety of odd jobs. He also served as night editor of the Minnesota *Daily* (the school paper) and edited a black weekly, the St. Paul *Appeal.* After receiving his B.A. in 1923, he joined the staff of the Kansas City *Call,* a leading black weekly. While in Missouri, Wilkins gained his first insight into segregation as an entrenched system, and resolved to broaden his activities in the NAACP, an organization which he had first joined while in college.

In 1931 Wilkins left the *Call* to serve under Walter White as assistant executive secretary of the NAACP. A year later, he substantiated charges of discrimination on a federally financed flood control project in Mississippi and played an instrumental role in getting Congress to take action to curb its practice there.

One of the great leaders of the Civil Rights Movement, the quiet, gentle, but most effective Roy Wilkins.

In 1934 he joined a picket march in Washington, D.C., protesting the failure of the Attorney General to include lynching on the agenda of a national conference on crime. For his pains, he suffered the first arrest of his career. Beginning in this same year, Wilkins put his editorial talent to work for the NAACP, succeeding W. E. B. DuBois as editor of *Crisis* magazine. (He held this post for some 15 years.) In 1945, after having served as an advisor in the War Department, he acted as a consultant to the American delegation at the United Nations conference in San Francisco.

Wilkins was named acting executive secretary of the NAACP in 1949, the year Walter White took a year's leave of absence from the organization. At the same time, he functioned as chairman of the National Emergency Civil Rights Mobilization, a pressure group which sent numerous lobbyists to Washington, D.C. to campaign for civil rights and fair employment legislation.

Wilkins assumed his position as executive secretary of the NAACP in 1955, upon the death of Walter White. He quickly established himself as one of the most articulate spokesmen in the civil rights movement. He testified before innumerable Congressional hearings, conferred with all the Presidents, and wrote extensively for all manner of publications. His training as a journalist stood him in good stead, for he never used a ghost writer.

Although Wilkins and the NAACP became more militant in the 1970s, both he and his organization were, nevertheless, subjected to attack by more radical groups, such as the Black Muslims. However, he never wavered in his determination to use all constitutional means at his disposal to help blacks achieve the rights of full citizenship within the democratic framework of American society.

For a number of years, Wilkins was the chairman of the Leadership Conference on Civil Rights, a group composed of over 100 national civic, labor, fraternal, and religious organizations. He was a trustee of the Eleanor Roosevelt Foundation, the Kennedy Memorial Library Foundation, and the Estes Kefauver Memorial Foundation. He was also a member of the Board of Directors of the Riverdale Children's Association, the John LaFarge Institute, and the Stockbridge School, as well as Peace with Freedom, an international organization working toward the goals described in its name.

Among the numerous awards conferred on Wilkins were the Anti-Defamation League's American Democratic Legacy Award, the Alpha Phi Alpha Fraternity's Medal of Honor, the Omega Phi Psi fraternity's Outstanding Citizen Award, the American Jewish Congress' Civil Rights Award, and the Boy Scout's Scout of the Year Award. He received the Outstanding Alumni Achievement Award of the University of Minnesota, and awards from the Japanese-American Citizens' League, the Unitarian Fellowship for Social Justice, B'nai B'rith Lodges, the Jewish War Veterans, the Postal Alliance, the National Medical Association, and the Eastern Star Lodge. He also holds the Russwurm Award of the National Newspaper Publishers Association. In 1964 the NAACP honored him with its own Spingarn Medal.

In 1972, Jesse Jackson, director of Operation PUSH, joined other militants who are increasingly praising Wilkins. Jackson told the NAACP convention that blacks need both the vitality of the Panthers and the wisdom of Wilkins.

Toward the end of his life there was a reevaluation of Wilkins by younger blacks. Recognition was given to the many positive things the NAACP had accomplished for blacks under his leadership and there was a growing understanding of how important he had been to Black America.

In a final tribute, President Reagan ordered American flags flown at half staff on all government buildings and at all installations.

WHITNEY M. YOUNG, JR.
1922–1971

Whitney M. Young, Jr., executive director of the Urban League from 1961 to 1971, was born in Lincoln Ridge, Kentucky, and received his B.S. degree at Kentucky State College in 1941. He later did graduate work at Massachusetts Institute of Technology and earned an M.A. in social work from the University of Minnesota in 1947.

From 1954 to 1961 Young served as dean of the Atlanta University School of Social Work. During the academic year 1960–1961 he was a visiting scholar at Harvard University under a Rockefeller Foundation grant.

A prominent lecturer and author of several articles which appeared in professional journals, Young completed his first full-length book, *To Be Equal,* in 1964. A second, *Beyond Racism,* was published in 1969.

Young was president of the National Association of Social Workers and the National Conference on Social Welfare. He served on the boards and advisory committees of the Rockefeller Foundation, Urban Coalition, and Urban Institute, and on seven Presidential Commissions of the Kennedy and Johnson administrations.

In 1969 Young was one of the 20 Americans selected by President Johnson to receive the Medal of Freedom, the nation's highest civilian award.

Young's many friendships with business and political leaders of the United States stirred much controversy within the black community. Though these relationships were important to the achievement of the Urban League's objectives of jobs for blacks, the epithet "Uncle Tom" was frequently hurled at him. Young, however, was far from an Uncle Tom. He spoke out forcefully, right up to his untimely death, against the slow pace with which businesses and government agencies were fulfilling their promises to blacks. But to Young, the important point was to maintain communication with America's centers of financial and political power, no matter how tense race relations might become in the nation's streets and schools. Young died while visiting Africa in 1971.

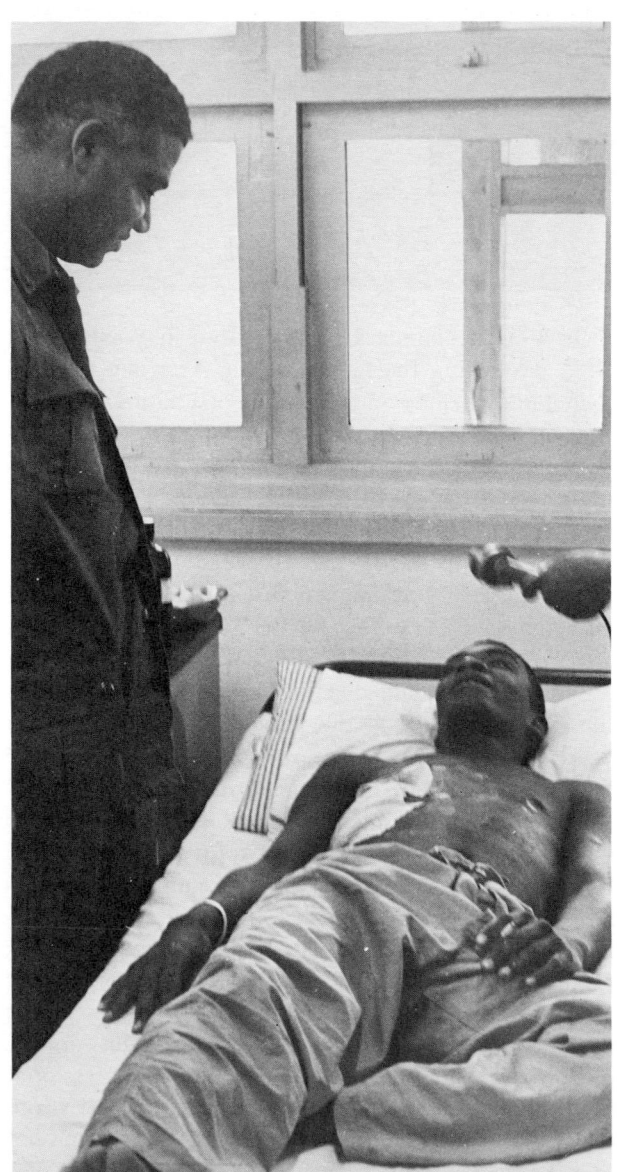

Whitney Young chats with a wounded soldier in Vietnam.

NATIONAL PRIVATE ORGANIZATIONS WITH CIVIL RIGHTS PROGRAMS

Alpha Kappa Alpha

5211 South Greenwood Avenue
Chicago, IL 60615
(312) MU 4-1282

National black sorority. Voter education program and voter registration campaigns, providing transportation and baby sitting services.

Alpha Phi Alpha

4432 South King Drive
Chicago, IL 60653
(312) DR 3-1819

National Negro fraternity. Program includes political action and education and sponsorship of an annual citizenship week to encourage voter registration.

American Civil Liberties Union

156 Fifth Avenue
New York, NY 10010
(212) 675-5990 or
(212) 989-7702 —Press Relations
Southern Regional Office:

5 Forsyth Street, N.W.
Atlanta, GA 30303
(404) 523-2721
Washington Office:

1424 16th Street, N.W.
Suite 501
Washington, DC 20036
(202) 483-9832

National legal assistance group. Concerned with abuses of civil liberties, administration of justice, and local and national problems.

AFL-CIO

Department of Civil Rights
815 16th Street, N.W.
Washington, DC 20006
(212) 293-5270

Department of Civil Rights is staff arm to AFL-CIO Committee of Civil Rights. It helps to implement AFL-CIO policies on equal opportunity, handles complaints involving any form of union discrimination, prepares materials concerning civil rights issues and programs, aids affiliates in the development of affirmative programs and policies, and serves as official liaison with civil rights organizations and government agencies working in the field of equal opportunity.

American Federation of Teachers, AFL-CIO

1012 14th Street, N.W.
6th Floor
Washington, DC 20005
(202) 737-6141

Organization to improve status of teachers and public education in United States. Civil rights programs include Freedom Schools in Mississippi and various conferences on Negro history, especially pertaining to textbooks in elementary and secondary schools.

American Veterans Committee (AVC) Inc.

1333 Connecticut Avenue, N.W.
Washington, DC 20036
(202) 293-4890

National veterans organization with strong civil rights program. Has served as watchdog on integration of Regular Armed Forces, Reserves, and National Guard. Veterans claims activities focus on discriminatory situations. Has been member of Leadership Conference on Civil Rights, assisted in planning 1963 March on Washington, and lobbied for civil rights and voting legislation.

Americans for Democratic Action

1424 16th Street, N.W.
Washington, DC 20036
(202) 265-5771

National political action organization concerned with local and national civil rights legislation, education, and poverty programs.

Anti-Defamation League of B'nai B'rith

315 Lexington Avenue
New York, NY 10016
(212) MU 9-7400

National human relations organization. Develops extensive resource materials for community education programs (including audiovisual), and research on intergroup relations. Educational and human relations arm of B'nai B'rith.

Board of Christian Social Concerns of the United Methodist Church

Division of Human Relations
100 Maryland Avenue, N.E.
Washington, DC 20002
(202) 546-1000

Conducts programs of research, education, and action centering around the following Christian social concerns: race relations, civil liberties, public policy on education, church and state relations, civic responsibility, labor-management relations.

Board of Social Ministry Lutheran Church in America

Justice and Social Change—
Urban Crisis
231 Madison Avenue
New York, NY 10016
(212) LE 2-3410

Designed to help people understand the nature of prejudice, see their own share in bringing about and perpetuating conditions of deprivation and injustice for minority groups, and take effective action.

Brotherhood-in-Action, Inc.

560 Seventh Avenue
New York, NY 10018
(212) LW 4-0350

To foster intergroup progress and understanding, offering programs, services, and facilities to qualified intergroup relations agencies for conferences and training programs.

California Rural Legal Assistance

1212 Market Street
San Francisco, CA 94102
(415) 863-4911

Established in 1966, California Rural Legal Assistance gives legal aid to the poor without fee in civil cases in rural California. It is a nonprofit organization funded by the Office of Economic Opportunity.

Chamber of Commerce of the U.S.

Human Resources Development Group
1615 H Street, N.W.
Washington, DC 20006
(202) 659-6100

Serves as educational arm to U.S. Chamber of Commerce. Concerned with civil rights policies affecting employment and other aspects of management-employee relations.

Church Women United

475 Riverside Drive
New York, NY 10027
(212) 870-2353

Civil Rights program called "Assignment Race." Councils sponsor direct action programs to end discrimination in housing, education, and employment.

Citizens' Advocate Center

1211 Connecticut Avenue, N.W.
Suite 304
Washington, DC 20036
(202) 293-1515

The Citizens' Advocate Center functions as a privately funded ombudsman to receive complaints and to monitor the administration of Federal programs.

Congress of Racial Equality (CORE)

200 West 135th Street
New York, NY 10030
(212) 281-9650
New Orleans Office:
2209 Dryad Street
New Orleans, LA 70113
(504) 523-7625

National human relations, direct action group. Initiates nonviolent direct action to end discrimination in education, housing, employment, and public accommodations. Program being extended into social, economic, and political fields.

National Newspaper Publishers Association

2400 S. Michigan Avenue
Chicago, IL 60616

National professional society. Membership comprised of publishers of Negro newspapers. Initiates action programs, disseminates information, supports other phases of civil rights movement.

National Office for the Rights of the Indigent (NORI)

10 Columbus Circle
Suite 2030
New York, NY 10019
(212) JU 6-8397

Established in 1966 by Ford Foundation grant under sponsorship

of NAACP Legal Defense and Educational Fund, Inc., to plan and coordinate significant legal actions affecting rights of the poor. Principal task is making precedents in courts dealing with poverty law.

National Afro-American Labor Council

13 Astor Place
New York, NY 10003
(212) 673-5120

National association of Negro trade union members working to eliminate discrimination in employment and in unions. Committed to militant trade union movement. Works in cooperation with official labor bodies.

Omega Psi Phi Fraternity

2714 Georgia Avenue, N.W.
Washington, DC 20001
(202) 667-7158

National Negro fraternity. Social action committee develops civil rights programs involving employment, housing, public accommodations, and political action.

National Sharecroppers Fund, Inc.

112 East 19th Street
New York, NY 10003
(212) GR 3-0284

Fay Bennett, Executive Director
Alan Swenson Administrative Director
Leonard Smith, Field Director
Michael Bruland, Research Director

Created to aid in the solution of the problems of the needy southern United States agricultural population by financing and otherwise fostering constructive efforts to improve their conditions of life.

National Urban League

500 East 62nd Street
New York, NY 10021
(212) 644-6500
Washington Bureau:
425—13th Street, N.W.
Suite 515
Washington, DC 20004
(202) 393-4332
Region I:
Eastern Regional Office
420 Madison Avenue
New York, NY 10017
(212) 751-0300

Region II:
Mideastern Regional Office
1316 First National Tower
106 South Main Street
Akron, OH 44308
(216) 726-6233
Region III:
Midwestern Regional Office
7212 Olive Street
Suite 1012
St. Louis, MO 63101
(314) 421-6393
Region IV:
Southern Regional Office
136 Marietta Street, N.W.
Atlanta, GA 30303
(404) MU 8-8778
Region V:
Western Regional Office
955 South Western Avenue
Los Angeles, CA 90006
(213) 731-8261
Field Services Department
1424-16th Street, N.W.
Washington, DC 20036
Sterling Tucker
Director

A professional community service organization committed to securing equal opportunities for Negroes and other minorities in all areas of American life. It is nonpartisan and interracial in its leadership and staff. Not largely a membership organization. Community Chest funds support many local affiliates.

Opportunities Industrialization Center Institute, Inc.

100 West Coulter Street
Philadelphia, PA 19144
(215) 849-3010

The national and three regional directors operate out of the Philadelphia headquarters. Western Region office is at 100 McAllister Street, San Francisco, CA.

The local OIC programs are designed to motivate, train, develop, and utilize the technical skills of members of our communities, regardless of race, creed, color, or sex, in manufacturing and industrialization.

A. Philip Randolph Institute

260 Park Avenue South
New York, NY 10010
(212) 533-8000

Group formed to raise economic issues that underlie the civil rights movement. Services all existing civil rights groups by preparing educational materials—pamphlets, testimony, conference programs.

Scholarship, Education and Defense Fund for Racial Equality, Inc.

164 Madison Avenue
New York, NY 10016
(212) 532-8216

Formed to develop leadership programs and community organization techniques, handle legal problems, engage in voter registration, and provide scholarship assistance to students who have demonstrated leadership in civil rights activities.

Southern Christian Leadership Conference (SCLC)

334 Auburn Avenue, N.E.
Atlanta, GA 30303
(404) 522-1420

National civil rights group organized around affiliate organizations that operate out of Negro churches. Program includes nonviolent direct action, voter registration, citizenship schools, and selective buying campaign. Founded by the late Dr. Martin Luther King, Jr.

Southern Conference Educational Fund, Inc.

3210 West Broadway
Louisville, KY 40211
(502) 778-3348

Group works with community groups and other civil rights organizations. Gives staff and financial assistance on education, social welfare, voter registration, and community organizing.

Southern Regional Council

5 Forsyth Street, N.W.
Atlanta, GA 30303
(404) 522-8764

Regional development program with emphasis on race relations. One hundred persons from throughout the South are the members. No general membership. Cooperates closely with Councils on Human Relations in the 11 southeastern states.

United Automobile Workers Fair Practices Department

8000 East Jefferson Street
Detroit, MI 48214
(313) 926-5000
William H. Oliver, Co-Director

Acting as the civil rights department of the UAW, it serves its membership in all civil rights matters. It is the contact agent between UAW, other international unions, and private organizations.

United Church Board for Homeland Ministries

Amistad Research Center and
Race Relations Department
Fisk University
Nashville, TN 37203

To promote better human relations through research and education. Collecting source materials for study of Negro life and history.

United Farm Workers Organizing Committee, AFL-CIO

P.O. Box 130
Delano, CA 93215
(805) 725-1314
Washington:

United Farm Workers Organizing Committee Boycott, Washington, DC
7332 Piney Branch Road
Takoma Park, MD 20012
(202) 587-0510

Organization to represent farm laborers for collective bargaining purposes. Civil rights, poverty, and clearinghouse programs handled through Delano office.

United States Catholic Conference

Department of Social Development
1312 Massachusetts Avenue, N.W.
Washington, DC 20005
(202) 659-6600

Action and public affairs agency of Catholic Church in United States. Divisions of Urban Life, Rural Life, Family Life. Task force on urban problems is information and coordinating agency for race- and poverty-related programs conducted in 156 dioceses in United States.

United States Jaycees

Program for Human Resource Development
Box 7
Tulsa, OK 74102
(918) 584-2481

Programs are aimed at helping the disadvantaged of all races and creeds help themselves. The program concentrates on employment, education, recreation, government awareness, personal development, environmental improvement, and housing.

The Urban Coalition

2100 M Street, N.W.
Washington, DC 20037
(202) 293-1530

Seeks to alleviate the crisis in the nation's urban centers through all-out attack on the unemployment problem. The Coalition works with businessmen to promote programs for the recruitment, training, and employment of the hard-core unemployed. Assists local communities in organizing coalitions to solve local problems.

Western Center on Law and Poverty

1709 West 8th Street
Los Angeles, CA 90017
(213) 483-1491

Legal services resource for the war on poverty in Southern California. It engages in test cases and appellate litigation and seeks to aid neighborhood law offices for the poor and to help improve their effectiveness.

Women's International League for Peace and Freedom

1738 Pine Street
Philadelphia, PA 19103
(215) 546-6082

Has human rights division with active committees on civil rights and civil liberties. Members of local branches carry on variety of civil rights community projects.

Young Men's Christian Association

National Board
291 Broadway
New York, NY 10007
(212) DI 9-0700

Advisory group formed to advance racial integration in YMCA and to work in area of special racial problems.

Additional programs also include developing plans for action, studies, and intercultural programs.

Young Women's Christian Association

Office of Racial Justice
National Board
600 Lexington Avenue
New York, NY 10022
(212) 753-4700

Seeks to be an agent of social change, keeping abreast of developments in civil and human rights, pressing toward full integration in all aspects of its own life and in local community.

Zeta Phi Beta Sorority, Inc.

1734 New Hampshire Avenue, N.W.
Washington, DC 20009
(202) 387-3103

National Negro sorority. Program includes leadership development, human and civil rights, youth and adult leadership programs, and social and welfare projects.

STATE AND FEDERAL AGENCIES WITH CIVIL RIGHTS RESPONSIBILITIES

Alaska

Alaska State Commission for Human Rights
520 MacKay Building
338 Denali Street
Anchorage, 99501
(907) 272-9504

Arizona

Arizona Civil Rights Division, Arizona State Department of Law
1502 West Jefferson Street
Phoenix, 85007
(602) 271-5263

California

California Fair Employment Practices Commission
455 Golden Gate Avenue
San Francisco, 94102
(415) 557-2000

Colorado

Colorado Civil Rights Commission
312 State Services Building
1525 Sherman Street
Denver, 80203
(303) 892-2621

Connecticut

Connecticut Commission on Human Rights and Opportunities
90 Washington Street
Hartford, 06106
(203) 566-3350

Delaware

Department of Labor and Industrial Relations Division Against Discrimination
618 North Union
Wilmington, 19801
(302) 658-9251 Ext. 276, 277

District of Columbia

District of Columbia Human Relations Commission
Room 5
District Building
14th and E Street, N.W.
(202) 629-4723

Florida

Florida Commission on Human Relations
Department of Community Affairs
2711 Apalachee Parkway
Tallahassee, 32301
(904) 878-1489

Georgia

Governor's Council on Human Relations
Room 104
State Capital
Atlanta, 30334
(404) 656-1735

Hawaii

Department of Labor and Industrial Relations
825 Mililani Street
Honolulu, 96813
(808) 548-3150

Idaho

Idaho Commission on Human Rights
State House
Boise, 83702
(208) 384-3550

Illinois

Illinois Commission on Human Relations
160 North LaSalle Street
Chicago, 60601
(312) 793-2893

Indiana

Indiana Civil Rights Commission
319 State Office Building
100 North Senate Avenue
Indianapolis, 46204
(317) 633-4855

Iowa

Iowa Civil Rights Commission
State Capitol Building
Des Moines, 50319
(515) 281-5129

Kansas

Kansas Commission on Civil Rights
Room 1155 W
State Office Building
Topeka, 66612
(913) 296-3206

Kentucky

Kentucky Commission on Human Rights
Mammoth Life Building
600 West Walnut Street
Louisville, 40203
(502) 585-3363

Louisiana

Louisiana Commission on Human Relations, Rights, and Responsibilities
State Office Building
150 Riverside Mall
Suite 402
Baton Rouge, 70801
(504) 389-6601

Maine

Maine Human Rights Commission
State House
Augusta, 04330
(207) 289-2326

Maryland

Maryland Commission on Human
Rights
The Mount Vernon Building
701 St. Paul Street
Baltimore, 21202
(301) 383-3680

Massachusetts

Massachusetts Commission Against
Discrimination
120 Tremont Street
Boston, 02108
(617) 727-3990

Michigan

Michigan Civil Rights Commission
1000 Cadillac Square Building
Detroit, 48226
(313) 222-1810

Minnesota

Department of Human Rights
60 State Office Building
St. Paul, 55155
(612) 296-2931

Missouri

Missouri Commission on Human
Rights
P.O. Box 1129
314 East High Street
Jefferson City, 65101
(314) 751-3325

Montana

Montana Department of Labor and
Industry
1336 Helena Avenue
Helena, 59601
(406) 449-3472

Nebraska

Nebraska Equal Opportunity
Commission
233 South 14th
Lincoln, 68508
(402) 471-2024

Nevada

Nevada Commission on Equal Rights
of Citizens
State Office Building
Room 100-B
215 East Bonanza
Las Vegas, 89101
(702) 385-0104

New Hampshire

New Hampshire Commission on
Human Rights
66 South Street
Concord, 03301
(603) 271-2767

New Jersey

New Jersey Division on Civil Rights
1100 Raymond Boulevard
Newark, 07102
(201) 648-2700

New Mexico

Human Rights Commission of New
Mexico
120 Villagra Building
Santa Fe, 87501
(505) 827-2713

New York

New York State Division of Human
Rights
270 Broadway
New York, 10007
(212) 488-7610

North Carolina

North Carolina Human Relations
Commission
P.O. Box 12525
Raleigh, 27605
(919) 829-7996

Ohio

Ohio Civil Rights Commission
240 Parsons Avenue
Columbus, 43215
(614) 469-2785

Oklahoma

Oklahoma Human Rights
Commission
P.O. Box 52945
Oklahoma City, 73105
(405) 521-2360

Oregon

Civil Rights Division
466 State Office Building
Portland, 97201
(503) 229-5741

Pennsylvania

Pennsylvania Human Relations
Commission
4th Floor
100 North Cameron Street
Harrisburg, 17001
(717) 787-4410

Rhode Island

Rhode Island Commission for Human
Rights
244 Broad Street
Providence, 02903
(401) 277-2661

South Dakota

South Dakota Human Relations
Commission
State Capitol Building
Pierre, 57501
(605) 224-3692

Tennessee

Tennessee Commission for Human
Development
Cordell Hull Building
Nashville, 37219
(615) 741-2424

Texas

Good Neighbor Commission of Texas
P.O. Box 12007
Austin, 78711
(512) 475-3581

Utah

Anti-Discrimination Division
Industrial Commission of Utah
State Office Building
Salt Lake City, 84114
(801) 328-5552

Vermont

Vermont State Human Rights
Commission
c/o Attorney General's Office
Montpelier, 05602
(802) 828-2717

Washington

Washington State Human Rights
Commission
W.E.A. Building
319 Seventh Avenue East
Olympia, 98501
(206) 753-6770

West Virginia

West Virginia Human Rights
Commission
1591 East Washington Street
Charleston, 25305
(304) 348-2616

Wisconsin

Equal Rights Division
Department of Industry
310 Price Place
Madison, 53702
(608) 266-3145

Wyoming

Department of Labor and Statistics
304 State Capitol Building
Cheyenne, 82001
(307) 777-7261

FEDERAL AGENCIES WITH CIVIL RIGHTS OFFICES

Department of Health, Education, and
Welfare
Office for Civil Rights
North Building
300 Independence Avenue, S.W.
Washington, DC 20201

Department of Housing and Urban
Development
Equal Opportunity Office
415 Seventh Street, S.W.
Washington, DC 20410

Department of Justice
Civil Rights Division
Constitution Avenue and Tenth
Street, S.W.
Washington, DC 20530

Department of Transportation
Departmental Office of Civil Rights
400 Seventh Street, S.W.
Washington, DC 20590

Department of Transportation
National Highway Traffic Safety
Administration
Office of Civil Rights
400 Seventh Street, S.W.
Washington, DC 20590

Department of Transportation
Urban Mass Transportation
Administration
Office of Civil Rights and Service
Development
400 Seventh Street, S.W.
Washington, DC 20590

Environmental Protection Agency
Office of Civil Rights and Urban
Affairs
Waterside Mall West Tower
401 M Street, S.W.
Washington, DC 20460

Equal Employment Opportunity
Commission
Room 1246
1800 G Street, N.W.
Washington, DC 20506

Small Business Administration
Office of Minority Enterprise
1441 L Street, N.W.
Washington, DC 20416

Small Business Administration
Office of Equal Employment
Opportunity and Compliance
1441 L Street, N.W.
Washington, DC 20416

THE LEGAL STATUS OF BLACK AMERICANS

Current Problems ■ Blacks and the Supreme Court ■ Due Process ■ Education ■ Forced Confessions ■ Housing ■ Jury Service ■ Public Accommodations ■ Recreation ■ Transportation ■ Voting (Registration and Primaries) ■ Requirements for Legislative Membership ■ Employment ■ Racial Intermarriage ■ Notable Adverse U.S. Supreme Court Decisions ■ State Antidiscrimination Laws ■ Lynching ■ Blacks in the Judiciary ■

At the start of the 1980s, blacks were on the defensive, struggling to maintain the progress toward desegregation and equal opportunity that had received such impetus from the great Court and Congressional victories of the fifties and sixties.

In a very important sense, blacks had won. Racist doctrine was no longer embodied in law. Legal segregation had all but disappeared from public life. But for all this, the march toward equal opportunity was being turned back by a series of events and policies that were thwarting the translation of legal equality into daily reality.

The roadblocks stemmed from all branches of government. The Supreme Court was proving receptive to claims that affirmative action for minorities produced "reverse discrimination" against whites. Congress was legislating limits and exemptions to measures vital to the actual achievement of equality, such as limits on busing. And, most threatening of all, the Reagan Administration was rapidly detaching itself from enforcement of civil rights laws. As a result, the legal status of equality blacks had fought long to achieve was losing strong enforcement. To many

blacks, such gains were coming to resemble a trophy for past victories rather than a body of rules by which the nation would live.

BLACKS AND THE SUPREME COURT

For most of the twentieth century the Supreme Court exercised a profound beneficial effect on the progress of blacks. In case after case, the Court invalidated legal and regulatory barriers which had legitimized the withholding of first-class citizenship from minorities. Decisions favorable to minorities occurred most frequently during the 16-year tenure of Chief Justice Earl Warren, from 1953 to 1969. During that period, the Court declared separate school facilities unconstitutional, sought to guarantee the rights of people under arrest and in scores of other decisions to erase discrimination in education, due process, housing, employment, recreation, jury service, transportation, and other areas.

Starting in 1969, however, the Court's decisions reflected a more conservative view. Under Warren

In 1956 white and black bus passengers board a public transit bus as an order by the Supreme Court went into effect.

Burger, who replaced Chief Justice Warren, and with three new justices appointed by President Nixon, decisions tended to allow state and local governments more discretion in law enforcement and integration procedures, with a resultant relaxation of efforts to end discriminatory practices. A factor in the change was the reduction of government representations to the Court on behalf of minorities and liberal views of due process. During the Eisenhower, Kennedy, and Johnson administrations, the Solicitor General and federal agencies frequently urged the Court to reach "liberal" decisions. But after 1969, the government frequently counseled enforcement delays or reversals of earlier liberal verdicts.

By early 1975 "court-watchers" differed in their forecasts of the Court's path. Some feared the Court might retreat to a course of decisions that would again make discrimination respectable. Most observers, however, felt that progress was still possible and that despite its retreats, the Court had no wish to return to the era of "legal racism."

Retreat and Dismantlement

An important group to suffer extensively from the Reagan Administration's policies was the Legal Services Corporation, which over the years has provided services to millions of poor people through 320 local programs. Though it survived attempts to eliminate it completely in fiscal year 1982, LSC's funding and powers were sharply curtailed in the spring of 1982.

President Reagan was still advocating its eradication in fiscal year 1983.

LSC's 1982 funds were reduced one third. Its lawyers were prohibited from filing class action suits against federal, state, or local governments and from providing legal help related to segregation. The government's opposition to class action suits extended to other areas, such as affirmative action in employment, where it proposed that discrimination suits could be filed only by individuals. Such a rule would place a heavy financial burden on disadvantaged individuals seeking to use the courts to achieve equality and, additionally, to restrict the impact of the legal victories they might win.

The administration also proposed enactment of a Federal Assistance Reform Act, which would reduce the Congress's ability to examine and amend block grant proposals. The probable result: evasion of enforcement procedures that have been made part of civil rights programs.

Other proposals affecting civil rights included:

Limiting the jurisdiction of courts to correct discrimination.

Attempts through legislation to weaken the Voting Rights Act, so intent to discriminate rather than a *de facto* result of discrimination had to be proven to obtain redress.

Constitutional amendments to prohibit affirmative action and busing.

Many of the steps taken by the administration involved administrative dismantlement of existing laws through nonenforcement, underfunding, and rule changes. Among these were:

Relaxing requirements for enforcement agencies, such as the Department of Justice, to conduct legally required investigations.

Rules requiring victims to bear the burden of proof in discrimination cases and exempting employers from maintaining records to prove they are not discriminating.

Elimination of efforts by the Justice Department to use busing to integrate schools, even where discrimination has been proved.

Granting tax-exempt status to private schools that discriminate against blacks.

In the latter case, public outcry produced challenges that were unresolved as this book was going to press. But for the most part, the government's withdrawal from civil rights enforcement was not seriously challenged.

As a result, blacks faced a future with reduced access to courts, reduced enforcement of civil rights laws, and a government that no longer regarded itself as a forum for redress of grievances.

Blacks and Police

Tensions between blacks and local judicial and law enforcement officials persisted in many areas throughout the 1970s and into the 1980s. One problem was excessive time required to bring defendants to trial. As a result, many persons spent long periods of time in jail when they were in fact innocent of the charges against them.

The most explosive issue, however, was the frequent failure of law enforcement agencies to forestall use of excessive force against minorities during arrest and incarceration procedures. An extreme example occurred in Miami, when Arthur McDuffie, a black insurance executive, died shortly after his arrest by white police officers. The Miami Liberty City riots of May and July 1980, in which 16 people were killed, erupted when officers charged with murdering McDuffie were acquitted.

Serious confrontations between blacks and police also occurred in Brooklyn, New York following the death by strangulation of a black businessman in a police car after his arrest.

The degree of polarization found in some cities was underscored in 1981 by a poll of attitudes toward police in Milwaukee where a young black, Ernest Lacy, died while in custody for a rape he did not commit. Two thirds of whites felt the Milwaukee police were doing a good job while two thirds of blacks felt they were not.

An issue in Milwaukee was the absence of high-ranking blacks on the police force. A consent decree in 1975 between the city and EEOC induced the city to hire some 200 black police but by December 1981 no black held higher rank than sergeant.

There were, however, positive signs from the white community. A jury in Wisconsin awarded $1.8 million to the family of Daniel Bell, a black man killed by Milwaukee police in 1958, and a Boston jury awarded $150,000 to the wife of James Bowden, shot to death by police in 1975. In 1981 Milwaukee's District Attorney took a firm public position against police excesses. And during the 1970s, EEOC achieved gains toward recruitment of minorities for the police forces in several cities (See employment section.)

Federal Legislation Affecting Blacks

A compilation of significant federal legislation enacted by the Congress since the Civil Rights Act of 1957 indicates that the fight for equality has shifted from civil rights to economic rights. A summary of the salient features of such legislation is included here (a more detailed presentation is made in the second chapter).

Civil Rights Act of 1957
Created the Commission on Civil Rights and empowered it to investigate allegations of deprivation of a U.S. citizen's right to vote and to appraise laws and policies of the federal government with respect to equal protection of the law and to submit a report to the President and to the Congress within two years.

Civil Rights Act of 1960
Provided for criminal penalties in the event a person crossed state lines to avoid legal process for the actual or attempted bombing or burning of any vehicle or building and provided penalties for persons who obstructed or interfered with any order of a federal court.

Civil Rights Act of 1964
Prohibited discrimination in the use of public accommodations whose operations involve interstate commerce and provided enforcement remedies to ensure equal access to public facilities. Also prohibited racial discrimination in any program receiving federal aid and prohibited discrimination in most areas of employment.

Voting Rights Act of 1965
Struck down restrictions such as literacy and knowledge tests and poll tax payments which had been used

to restrict black participation in voting, and provided for federal registrars to register voters should state registrars refuse to do so. It further provided that registered voters not be prohibited from voting.

Civil Rights Act of 1968

Provided for open housing by prohibiting discrimination based on race, color, religion, or national origin.

Housing and Urban Development Act of 1968

Provided for equal employment oppportunities for lower income persons by requiring that minimum numbers of minorities be hired to work on housing projects funded by the federal government and provided for housing for lower income families.

Equal Employment Opportunity Act of 1972

Provided the Equal Employment Opportunity Commission (which was established by the Civil Rights Act of 1964) with authority to issue judicially enforceably cease and desist orders in cases involving discriminatory employment practices.

Comprehensive Employment and Training Act of 1973 (CETA)

Provided federal funding to employ and train unskilled minority workers in various federally assisted programs.

Public Works Employment Act of 1977

Provided that 10% of funds expended as a result of federal grants be earmarked for and paid to minority business enterprises (so-called set-asides).

Full Employment and Balanced Growth Act of 1978 (Humphrey-Hawkins Bill)

Asserted the responsibility of the federal government to promote full employment, production, and real income; and required the President to set forth explicit short- and medium-term economic goals each year.

During the 1970s and early 1980s, signals from the Supreme Court were mixed. Many busing and affirmative employment action plans were upheld, especially those reached voluntarily between institutions and minorities, as in the *Weber* and *AT&T* cases. On the other hand, as noted, the Court acceded to charges of reverse discrimination against whites, as in *Bakke*. Also, in the Mobile, Alabama voting rights case, the Court stated that intent to discriminate, rather than mere result, had to be established to prove that the Voting Rights Act had been violated.

In 1981, in a sharp departure from its predecessors, the Reagan Administration stated an intention to use the Court to reverse steps taken toward integration

and affirmative action. Notable among these was its announced intention to seek reversal of the voluntary affirmative action plan approved in *Weber* and a voluntary integration plan reached between minorities and the Seattle School Board. With conservative appointees now a majority of the Court and liberals the eldest justices, there was concern among blacks that the Court would become receptive to such petitions.

Congressional conservatives also indicated interest in reversing civil rights gains through constitutional amendements. An amendment prohibiting busing was receiving the most attention.

IMPORTANT CASES

The following important cases are presented in digest form and arranged in general categories.

Due Process

Moore v. *Dempsey*
261 US 86 (1923)
Justice Holmes delivered the opinion.

In 1919, during an Arkansas race riot, one white man was killed and several people of both races were injured. At the trial, 12 blacks were sentenced to death and 67 to lengthy prison terms.

Black witnesses appearing at the trial were whipped until they consented to testify against the accused. The all-white jury heard the case in the presence of a mob threatening violence if there were no convictions. The court-appointed counsel did not ask for a change of venue and called no witnesses—not even the defendants themselves. The trial lasted 45 minutes, and the jury brought in a verdict of guilty after five minutes.

NAACP attorneys then applied for a writ of habeas corpus on the grounds that the trial was a trial in form only and no due process was accorded in view of the mob pressure. The petition was at first dismissed. The U.S. Supreme Court ultimately ruled that the petition should be heard, and reversed the decision of the Arkansas District Court, with Justice Holmes stating in his opinion that "counsel, jury and judge were swept to the fatal end by an irresistible wave of public passion."

United States v. *Adams, Bordenave and Mitchell*
319 US 312 (1943)

The three defendants in this case were convicted in a local U.S. court of the rape of a civilian while within the confines of Camp Claiborne, Louisiana. They were represented by a court-appointed lawyer, and sentenced to death. The men then appealed for assistance to the NAACP, which applied for a writ of habeas corpus on the ground that the local court was without jurisdiction. The U.S. Court of Appeals for the Fifth Circuit, unable to decide the issue, forwarded the case to the U.S. Supreme Court.

This Court ruled that the lower court was without juridiction in the case, with the result that the men were subsequently released from the custody of civilian authorities and returned to the Army for court-martial proceedings.

Sniadach v. *Family Finance Corp.*
395 US 337 (1969)

The Supreme Court ruled that a debtor's wages cannot be garnisheed without court determination in a fair proceeding with notice to the debtor that a debt does exist and an opportunity extended to defend. In this case, the plaintiff's wages had, under Wisconsin law, been withheld without proving the existence of a debt. In all, 17 states had permitted courts to tie up half an employee's wages without establishing proof of debt.

Williams v. *Illinois*
399 US 235 (1970)

An indigent defendant was convicted of a misdemeanor, sentenced to one year in jail, and fined $500, as permitted by state law. He was required to remain in jail and work off, at a rate of $5 per day, the amount to which he might be in default of the fee at the expiration of his imprisonment.

The defendant's appeal of the work-off provision of the sentence was denied by the trial judge. The Supreme Court, however, ruled for the defendant, declaring the work-off portion to be in violation of the Fourteenth Amendment because the aggregate imprisonment of an indigent would exceed the maximum period fixed by the statute and noted that a person with sufficient funds would not have been subjected to such a penalty.

Furman v. *Georgia*
408 US 238 (1972)

The Supreme Court declared the death penalty to be cruel and unusual punishment in violation of the Eighth Amendment, since it is generally applied arbitrarily by judges and juries. However, the Court left room for state legislators to enact laws in which capital punishment would be applied less capriciously.

Lloyd Gaines disappeared after winning 1938 case for admission to University of Missouri Law School.

Education

State of Missouri, ex rel. Lloyd Gaines v. *University of Missouri*
305 US 337 (1938)
Chief Justice Hughes delivered the opinion.

After Lloyd Gaines, a black, had been refused admission to the law school of the State University of Missouri, he applied to state courts for an order to compel admission on the grounds that refusal constituted a denial of his rights under the Fourteenth Amendment of the U.S. Constitution.

The University of Missouri defended its action by maintaining that Lincoln University (a predominantly black institution of higher learning) would eventually establish its own law school, which Gaines could then attend, and that, in the meantime, he could exercise the option of pursuing his studies outside the state on a scholarship. The Supreme Court of Missouri dismissed Gaines' petition for mandamus, and upheld the university's decision to reject his application.

The U.S. Supreme Court, however, reversed this decision, maintaining that the state of Missouri was obliged to provide equal facilities for Negroes or, in the absence of such facilities, to admit them to the existing facility.

Sipuel v. *University of Oklahoma*
332 US 631 (1948)

Ada Lois Sipuel, a black, was denied admission to the law school of the University of Oklahoma and thereupon promptly requested legal assistance from the NAACP, which filed a petition in the Oklahoma courts requesting an order directing her admission. The petition was denied on the grounds that the *Gaines*

decision (see above) did not require a state with segregation laws to admit a black to its white schools. Further, the Oklahoma court maintained that the state itself was not obligated to set up a separate school unless first requested to do so by blacks desiring a legal education. The decision was affirmed by the Supreme Court of Oklahoma. The U.S. Supreme Court, however, reversed this decision, and held that the state was required to provide Negroes with equal educational opportunities as soon as it did so for whites.

Sweatt v. *Painter*
339 US 629 (1950)
Chief Justice Vinson delivered the opinion.

The black petitioner in this case was refused admission to the law school of the University of Texas on the grounds that substantially equivalent facilities were already available in another Texas school open to blacks only.

The US Supreme Court ruled that the petitioner be admitted to the University of Texas law school, since "in terms of number of the faculty, variety of courses and opportunity for specialization, size of the student body, scope of the library, availability of law review and similar activities, the University of Texas Law School is superior."

McLaurin v. *Oklahoma State Regents for Higher Education*
339 US 637 (1950)
Chief Justice Vinson delivered the opinion.

After having been admitted to the state university, G. W. McLaurin, a black, was required to occupy a special seat in the classroom and a designated table in both the library and the cafeteria—all because of his race.

The U.S. Supreme Court declared unanimously that the black student must receive the same treatment at the hands of the state as other students, and could not be segregated.

Gray v. *University of Tennessee*
342 US 517 (1952)

This case resulted from the refusal of a three-judge U.S. District Court to accept jurisdiction in the matter of enjoining the exclusion of blacks from a state university. The lone judge to whom the matter was then referred ruled that plaintiffs were entitled to admission but did not order the university to do so.

The Supreme Court was asked to refer the case back to the three-judge District Court for further proceedings. Pending this appeal, however, one of the stu-

G. W. McLaurin won a court order to end segregation at the University of Oklahoma.

dents seeking admission was in fact admitted. Since the court found no suggestion that persons "similarly situated would not be afforded similar treatment," the case was dismissed as moot.

Brown v. *Board of Education*
347 US 483 (1954)
Chief Justice Warren delivered the opinion.

This case involved the practice of denying black children equal access to state public schools due to state laws requiring or permitting racial segregation. The U.S. Supreme Court unanimously held that segregation deprived the children of equal protection under the Fourteenth Amendment to the U.S. Constitution. The "separate but equal" doctrine of *Plessy* v. *Ferguson* was overruled. After reargument a year later, the case was remanded (along with its four companion cases) to the District Court, which was instructed to enter such orders as were necessary to ensure the admission of all parties to public schools on a racially nondiscriminatory basis.

Hawkins v. *Board of Control*
347 US 971 (1954)

This case resulted from a ruling of the Florida Supreme Court which denied a black the right to enter the University of Florida on the grounds that he had failed to show that a separate law school for blacks was not substantively equal to the one for whites. The U.S. Supreme Court vacated the judgment and remanded the case to the Florida Supreme Court for a decision in light of the ruling in *Brown* which overruled the separate but equal doctrine.

After two years, the Florida Supreme Court was still denying the petitioner the right to enter the University of Florida. By that time, however, it had appointed a commissioner to determine when in the future he could be admitted "without causing public mischief." This time, the U.S. Supreme Court ruled that the petitioner should be admitted to the school promptly, since there was no palpable reason for any delay.

Turead v. Board of Supervisors
347 US 971 (1954)

This case stemmed from a provisional injunction requiring the admittance of blacks to Louisiana State University. The State Court of Appeals reversed this action, declaring that it required the decision of a District Court of three judges. The U.S. Supreme Court vacated this judgment and remanded the case for consideration, again in light of *Brown*.

Frazier v. University of North Carolina
350 US 979 (1956)

The U.S. Supreme Court affirmed a district court judgment that blacks may not be excluded from institutions of higher learning because of their race or color.

Cooper v. Aaron
358 US 1 (1958)

The Supreme Court voted unanimously to set aside a 2½-year delay in the integration of Central High School, Little Rock.

Lucy v. Adams
224 F. Supp. 79 (1963)

The University of Alabama was ordered by a Federal District Court to admit two black students, Vivian Malone and James Hood. Governor Wallace of Alabama tried to thwart their admission by "standing in

The NAACP generated nationwide pressure for 1954 Brown *decision making segregated public schools illegal.*

the school house door," but he backed down when President Kennedy mobilized the National Guard.

Lee v. *Macon County Board of Education*
389 US 25 (1967)

The Supreme Court affirmed a lower court decision ordering the desegregation of Alabama's school districts and declared state school grants to whites attending segregated private schools unconstitutional.

Alexander v. *Holmes County Board of Education.*
396 US 19 (1969)

The Supreme Court ended the "all deliberate speed" doctrine when, by a vote of 8 to 0, it ordered 33 districts in Mississippi to desegregate. The Department of Health, Education and Welfare had asked that the districts be granted more time to desegregate, the first time HEW had sought a delay in integration. But the Court ordered that integration proceed "at once."

The twenty-first anniversary of the Supreme Court's Brown *v.* Board of Education *decision is celebrated at a meeting of the NAACP.*

Swann v. *Charlotte Mecklenburg Board of Education*
402 US 1 (1971)

The Supreme Court affirmed the use of busing and faculty transfers to overcome the effects of dual school systems. Writing the decision, Chief Justice Burger noted that "bus transportation has long been a part of all public educational systems and it is unlikely that a truly effective remedy could be devised without continued reliance upon it." However, the decision left local district judges the authority to decide whether a desegregation plan was constitutionally adequate.

Wright v. *City of Emporia*
407 US 451 (1972)

Cotton v. *Scotland Neck Board of Education*
407 US 485 (1972)

The Supreme Court held that two towns with heavy concentrations of white students could not secede from a largely black county school system and form its own school district in an attempt to frustrate integration.

Richmond, Virginia School Board v. *State Board of Education*
412 US 92 (1973)

By a 4 to 4 vote the Supreme Court declined to order the integration of the predominantly black schools in Richmond with those of two white suburbs. Though the Court wrote no decision, integrationists express concern that permitting *de facto* segregation to stand in this manner will hinder corrective action in other metropolitan areas, perpetuate "neighborhood" one-race schools, and lessen the extent of integration in unitary school systems.

Keyes v. *School District 1*
413 US 189 (1973)

The Supreme Court, for the first time, ordered integration in a northern school system. By a 7 to 1 vote, it ruled that a substantial part of the schools of Denver were administratively segregated, that the system must therefore be considered "dual" and thus be desegregated. The suit had been brought by 11 black, Hispanic, and white parents, marking a trend for black and Hispanic minorities to cooperate.

University of California Regents v. *Bakke*
438 US 265 (1978)

Allen Bakke, a white, was denied admission to the University of California at Davis Medical School and claimed that he was unlawfully discriminated against.

Although not able to agree on an opinion concerning the major issues raised about the school's admission policies, the result of the Court's decision was that the school's special admissions program violated law by totally excluding nonminority applicants from consideration for 16 (out of 100) places irrespective of qualifications.

Third-party presidential candidate George Wallace resisted Supreme Court orders to desegregate Alabama schools.

Forced Confessions

Brown, Ellington and Shields v. *State of Mississippi*
297 US 278 (1936)
Chief Justice Hughes delivered the opinion.

On April 4, 1934, a few days after the murder of one Raymond Stewart, three blacks were indicted for the crime. They were arraigned, tried, found guilty and sentenced to death.

The only evidence presented against them during the trial was that they had confessed—admittedly after both force and physical torture had been applied. One had been hanged by a rope to a tree, severely beaten, and then permitted to return home after still refusing to "confess." A day or two later, he was again seized and whipped until he agreed to confess. At the time of the trial, the marks of violence were still visible on this victim's neck.

The conviction in this case was affirmed by the Supreme Court of Mississippi, but it was reversed by the U.S. Supreme Court, which held that the rack and the torture chamber could not be used in place of, or as a prelude to, the witness stand.

Chambers v. *Florida*
309 US 227 (1940)
Justice Black delivered the opinion.

This case involved four blacks convicted of murder in Pompano, Florida. The U.S. Supreme Court reversed the conviction on the grounds that the confessions used to convict the men had been extorted by force and violence and, thus denied the defendants due process as guaranteed by the Fourteenth Amendment.

Canty v. *Alabama*
309 US 629 (March 11, 1940)

The U.S. Supreme Court—in a memorandum opinion—reversed without argument the decision of the Supreme Court of Alabama, which had upheld the conviction and sentence of Dave Canty for murder, in view of the *Chambers* case.

White v. *Texas*
309 US 631 (1940)

On the authority of the *Chambers* and *Canty* cases, the U.S. Supreme Court reversed the conviction and sentencing of Bob White, which had been upheld by the Texas Court of Criminal Appeals.

Political cartoons of the nineteenth century spotlighted abuses and pushed for reforms. Resistance to Jim Crow on Nashville streetcars (above) led blacks to pool finances and buy their own buses. Thomas Nast's "Justice" (right) points out racist inequity of numbers of death penalties.

Ward v. *State of Texas*
316 US 547 (1942)

This case involved William Ward, a black, who, in 1939, was indicted in Texas for the murder of a white man. At his first trial, the jury was unable to agree on a verdict. At the second one, he was found guilty of murder (without malice) and sentenced to three years in the state penitentiary. The Texas Court of Criminal Appeals affirmed the lower court decision but was reversed by the U.S. Supreme Court on the grounds that Ward had originally been convicted as the result of a forced confession.

Lee v. *Mississippi*
332 US 742 (1948)
Justice Murphy delivered the opinion.

Albert Lee, a 17-year-old black, was indicted and convicted of assault with the intent to rape, his conviction having been based on a confession which had allegedly been coerced. The Mississippi Supreme Court affirmed the conviction, but the U.S. Supreme Court reversed it on the grounds that the confession had been coerced.

to rape, the defendant attacked the conviction on the grounds that it was based on a coerced confession and because blacks had been systematically excluded from service on the jury. The U.S. Supreme Court reversed the conviction on a number of grounds, including the fact that the prisoner was mentally retarded and had not had the assistance of counsel while being held incommunicado.

Housing (Right of Sale and Restrictive Covenants)

Buchanan v. *Warley*
245 US 60 (1917)
Justice Day delivered the opinion.

The plaintiff Buchanan brought an action in this case for the performance of a sale of certain real estate in Louisville, Kentucky. The purchaser, Warley (a black), maintained that he would be unable to occupy the land since it was located within what was defined by a Louisville ordinance as a white block. (The ordinance prohibited whites from living in black districts, and vice versa.) Buchanan alleged that the ordinance was in conflict with the Fourteenth Amendment to the U.S. Constitution.

The U.S. Supreme Court maintained that the ordinance was unconstitutional.

Harmon v. *Tyler*
273 US 668 (1927)

On the authority of *Buchanan* v. *Warley,* a similar New Orleans residential ordinance which was upheld by the lower court was declared unconstitutional by the U.S. Supreme Court.

City of Richmond v. *Deans*
281 US 704 (1930)

The U.S. Supreme Court, again on the basis of *Buchanan* v. *Warley,* struck down the ruling of a lower court and declared a Richmond residential segregation ordinance unconstitutional.

Shelley v. *Kraemer*
334 US 1 (1948)

Hurd v. *Hodge*
334 US 26 (1948)
Chief Justice Vinson delivered both opinions.

On August 11, 1945, a black family, the Shelleys, received a warranty deed to a parcel of land whch, unknown to them, was subject to a restrictive covenant barring its sale to blacks. Suit was subsequently brought in the Circuit Court of St. Louis seeking to

Watts v. *Indiana*
338 US 49 (1949)

The U.S. Supreme Court reversed the conviction and death sentence of a black in a rape and murder case on the grounds that the confession had been coerced.

Reeves v. *Alabama*
348 US 891 (1954)

The defendant, sentenced to death for rape, attached the conviction on the ground that it was based on a coerced confession and that blacks had been improperly excluded from service on the jury. The U.S. Supreme Court reversed the conviction holding that a conviction based on a coerced confession denied the due process guarantees of the Fourteenth Amendment to the U.S. Constitution.

Fikes v. *Alabama*
352 US 191 (1957)
Chief Justice Warren delivered the opinion

Sentenced to death for the crime of burglary with intent

After the Civil War white terrorist societies sprang up in the South with the intention of keeping black people in a slavelike condition. KKK members murdered children, lynched, and burned to frighten blacks from using their new rights as citizens.

divest the Shelleys of title to the land. The Supreme Court of Missouri directed the trial court to strip the petitioners of said title.

The U.S. Supreme Court reversed this decision, maintaining that restrictive covenants, though valid contracts, could not be enforced by state courts. In the *Hurd* v. *Hodge* case, involving a similar set of circumstances, federal courts were similarly prohibited from enforcing such restrictive covenants.

Barrows v. *Jackson*
346 US 249 (1953)

The U.S. Supreme Court in this case held it to be a violation of the equal protection and due process clauses of the Fourteenth Amendment for a state court to award damages for the violation of a restrictive covenant.

Reitman v. *Mulkey*
387 US 369 (1967)

In 1964 the California electorate voted in favor of a referendum granting "absolute discretion" to real estate owners in the sale and rental of real property, in effect voiding the state's fair housing laws. Lincoln Mulkey filed suit against property owners in Orange County to challenge the validity of the referendum. Mulkey's position failed in the lower courts but was sustained 5 to 2 by the California Supreme Court on the grounds that the California referendum violated the Fourteenth Amendment of the U.S. Constitution. The U.S. Supreme Court upheld the decision.

Thorpe v. *Housing Authority*
393 US 268 (1969)
Chief Justice Warren delivered the opinion.

The Supreme Court declared that tenants of federally assisted housing projects cannot be evicted without being first informed of the reason and given an opportunity to reply or explain.

Kennedy Park Homes Assn. v. *City of Lackawanna*
401 US 1010 (1971)

The Supreme Court refused to review a lower court decision granting blacks the right to build a low-income housing project in a section of the city largely inhabited by whites.

Trafficante v. *Metropolitan Life Insurance*
409 US 205 (1972)
Justice Douglas delivered the opinion.

The Supreme Court ruled that a complaint of racial discrimination in housing may be brought by parties who have not themselves been refused accommodation but who, as members of the same housing unit, allege injury by discriminatory housing practices. The suit had been filed by a black and a white resident of a housing development in San Francisco, who contended that the owner of the development, in maintaining a "white ghetto," was depriving plaintiffs of the right to live in a racially integrated community.

James v. *Valtierra*
402 US 137 (1971)

The Supreme Court upheld a ruling that local voters could veto projected plans for low-rent housing projects. The ruling affirmed a decision which held that no low-income projects could be developed without the majority vote of a city, town, or county in a referendum where such process was duly provided for in law.

Jury Service

Hollins v. *Oklahoma*
295 US 394 (1935)

Charged with rape, the defendant in this case was convicted on December 29, 1931 at a trial held in the basement of the jail in Sapula, Oklahoma. Three days before the scheduled execution, the NAACP secured

A mixed jury in 1867. The Fourteenth Amendment protects black people from conviction by juries which exclude black jurors.

a stay and, later, a reversal of his conviction by the Supreme Court of Oklahoma.

The U.S. Supreme Court—in a memorandum opinion—affirmed the principle that the conviction of a black by a jury from which all blacks had been excluded was a denial of the equal protection clause of the Fourteenth Amendment to the U.S. Constitution.

Hale v. *Commonwealth of Kentucky*
303 US 613 (1938)

Charged with murder in McCracken County, Kentucky in 1936, Joe Hale moved to set aside the indictment on the grounds that the jury commissioners had systematically excluded blacks from jury lists.

Hale established that one out of every six residents of the county was black, and that there were at least 70 blacks out of a total of 6,700 persons qualified for jury duty. Still, there had not been a black on jury duty between 1906 and 1936.

Hale's conviction and death sentence were upheld by the Court of Appeals of Kentucky, but both were struck down by the U.S. Supreme Court on the grounds that he had been denied equal protection of the laws.

Patton v. *Mississippi*
332 US 463 (1947)
Justice Black delivered the opinion.

This case involved Eddie Patton, a black who was indicted, tried, and convicted of the murder of a white man in Mississippi. At his trial and as part of his appeal, Patton alleged that all qualified blacks had been systematically excluded from jury service in Lauderdale County (the place of the trial) solely because of race. The state maintained that, since jury service was limited by statute to qualified voters, and since few blacks were qualified to vote, such a procedure was valid in the eyes of the law.

The U.S. Supreme Court, however, reversed Patton's conviction on the grounds that such a jury plan, resulting in the almost automatic elimination of blacks from jury service, constituted an infringement of his rights under the Fourteenth Amendment.

Shepherd v. *Florida*
341 US 50 (1951)

The U.S. Supreme Court reversed the conviction of a state court involving black defendants solely on the grounds that the method of selecting the grand jury discriminated against blacks.

Rosa Parks, the "Little Lady Who Started It All" in Montgomery, is honored by black leaders.

Turner v. *Fouche*
396 US 346 (1970)

The Supreme Court affirmed the right to bring an action in Federal Court to end discrimination in jury selection.

Public Accommodations

Katzenbach v. *McClung*
379 US 802

Heart of Atlanta v. *United States*
379 US 803
Both cases were decided on the same day in 1964; both opinions were delivered by Justice Clark.

In the *Katzenbach* case, the Attorney General of the United States sued Ollie's Barbecue Restaurant in Birmingham, Alabama for its refusal to serve blacks in its dining accommodations—in direct violation of the antidiscriminatory public accommodations clause of the 1964 Civil Rights Act. The U.S. District Court, Northern District of Alabama, held that the Civil Rights Act could not be applied under the Fourteenth Amendment to the U.S. Constitution, inasmuch as there was no "demonstrable connection" between food purchased in interstate commerce and sold in a restaurant that would affect commerce. The U.S. Supreme Court, however, held that "the Civil Rights Act of 1964, as here applied, [is] plainly appropriate in the resolution of what . . . [Congress has] . . . found to be a national commercial problem of the first magnitude."

Heart of Atlanta dealt with a Georgia motel which solicited patronage in national advertising and had several out-of-state residents as guests from time to time. The motel had already instituted the practice of refusing to rent rooms to blacks prior to the passage of the 1964 Civil Rights Act, and stated thereafter that it intended to continue this practice. The motel owner filed suit, maintaining that the 1964 Civil Rights Act violated both the Fifth and the Thirteenth Amendments. The United States countered with the argument that the refusal to accept Negroes interfered with interstate travel, and that the Congress in voting to apply nondiscriminatory standards to interstate commerce was not violating either amendment. The U.S. Supreme Court upheld the right of Congressional regulation, stating that the power of Congress was not confined to the regulation of commerce among the states. "It extends to those activities intra-state which so affect interstate commerce or the exercise of the power of Congress over it as to make regulation of them appropriate means to the attainment of a legitimate end."

Bell v. *Maryland*
378 US 226 (1964)

The Supreme Court ordered a Maryland district court to reconsider its affirmation of a state court conviction of 12 blacks for trespass when they refused to leave a restaurant that refused to serve them, entirely on the basis of their color.

Shuttlesworth v. *Birmingham*
394 US 147 (1969)

The Supreme Court invalidated Birmingham's Parade-Permit law which had been used in 1963 to harass Martin Luther King, Jr.'s Easter March.

Recreation

Rice v. *Arnold*
340 US 848 (October 16, 1950)

This case involved the successful attempt to abolish segregation on a Miami (Florida) golf course owned and operated by the city. The U.S. Supreme Court granted a writ of certiorari and vacated the judgment of the Florida Supreme Court which authorized the segregated use of the course—in light of the *McLaurin* and *Sweatt* decisions. (See education section above.)

Muir v. *Louisville Park Theatrical Association*
347 US 971 (1954)

Blacks were refused admission to an amphitheater located in a Louisville city park leased and operated by a privately owned group not affiliated in any way with the city. The Kentucky Court of Appeals found no evidence of unlawful discrimination, but the U.S. Supreme Court vacated this judgment and remanded the case for consideration in the light of the prevailing legal climate as articulated in *Brown* v. *Board of Education*.

Mayor and City Council of Baltimore v. *Dawson*
350 US 377 (1955)

The U.S. Supreme Court affirmed a judgment that the enforcement of racial segregation in public beaches and bathhouses maintained by public authorities is unconstitutional.

Holmes v. *Atlanta*
350 US 859 (1955)

This case involved a suit brought by blacks to integrate a city-owned and city-operated golf course in Atlanta. The segregated arrangements were ordered sustained by the lower court, but that order was vacated by the U.S. Supreme Court and the case remanded to the District Court with directions to enter a decree for plaintiffs in conformity with the *Baltimore* case above.

Evans v. *Newton*
382 US 296 (1966)

The Supreme Court ruled that transfer of a city park from municipal ownership to a board of private trustees does not remove its obligations under the Fourteenth Amendment.

Transportation

Morgan v. *Commonwealth of Virginia*
328 US 373 (1946)
Justice Reed delivered the opinion.

Irene Morgan, a black, refused to move to the rear seat of a Greyhound bus which was traveling from Virginia to Washington, D.C., and was subsequently convicted in the lower Virginia courts for violating a state statute requiring segregation of the races on all public vehicles.

NAACP attorneys then carried the case through the Virginia courts and on to the U.S. Supreme Court, where it was decided that the Virginia statute could not apply to interstate passengers or motor vehicles engaged in such traffic. (The ruling was of such a nature that it lent itself to application on railroads, in airplanes, etc.)

Bob-Lo v. *Michigan*
333 US 28 (1948)
Justice Rutledge delivered the opinion.

In this case, the operator of a line of vessels used to transport patrons from Detroit to an amusement park owned by the city on an island in Canadian waters was convicted of violating the Michigan Civil Rights Act for refusing passage to a black.

The U.S. Supreme Court upheld the application of the Michigan statute.

Flemming v. *South Carolina Electric and Gas Company*
351 US 901 (1956)

This case involved a suit brought by a black passenger against a bus company for damages due to the bus driver's having required her to change seats in accordance with South Carolina's segregation law. The trial judge dismissed the case on the grounds that the statute in question was valid, but the Court of Appeals reversed this decision, holding that the "separate but equal" doctrine was no longer valid. The U.S. Supreme Court upheld the Court of Appeals.

Gayle v. *Browder*
352 US 114 (1956)

This action challenged the constitutionality of state statutes and ordinances in effect in the city of Montgomery, Alabama, which required the segregation of whites and blacks on public buses.

These statutes were first declared unconstitutional by the decision of a three-judge federal district court. The U.S. Supreme Court then affirmed this judgment.

Voting (Registration and Primaries)

Guinn v. *United States*
238 US 347 (1915)
Chief Justice White delivered the opinion.

By an amendment passed in 1910, the Constitution of Oklahoma restricted the franchise according to a "grandfather clause" which provided that no illiterate person could be registered to vote. The clause, however, granted an exemption for such a person provided he had lived in a foreign country prior to January 1, 1866; had been eligible to register prior to that date, or if his lineal ancestor was eligible to vote at that time. Since no blacks were eligible to vote in Oklahoma prior to 1866, the law disenfranchised all blacks.

The U.S. Supreme Court held the grandfather clause invalid in Oklahoma, as well as in any other state where one was in effect.

Nixon v. *Herndon*
273 US 536 (1927)
Justice Holmes delivered the opinion.

By reason of a state statute providing that no black shall be "eligible to participate in a Democratic Party election held in the State of Texas," Dr. L. A. Nixon, a black, was refused the right to vote in a Texas primary election. Nixon filed suit against the election officials, and his case ultimately reached the U.S. Supreme Court. In his opinion, Justice Holmes said: "It is too clear for extended argument that color cannot be made the basis of a statutory classification affecting the right set up in this case," and, as such, declared the Texas statute unconstitutional.

Nixon v. *Condon*
286 US 73 (1932)
Justice Cardozo delivered the opinion.

Pursuant to the decision in the above case, the Texas legislature passed a new statute, empowering the state Democratic executive committee to set up its own rules regarding the primary. The party promptly adopted a resolution stipulating that only white Democrats be allowed to participate in the primary. Dr. Nixon again filed suit, and his right to vote was again upheld by the U.S. Supreme Court.

Lane v. *Wilson*
307 US 268 (1939)
Justice Frankfurter delivered the opinion.

In an attempt to restrict voter registration, the Oklahoma legislature provided that all those who were already registered would remain qualified voters, but that all others would have to register within 12 days (from April 30 to May 11, 1916), or be forever barred from the polls. In 1934 I. W. Lane, a black, was refused registration on the basis of this statute. The U.S. Supreme Court declared that the statute was in conflict with the Fifteenth Amendment to the U.S. Constitution, and, as such, was unconstitutional.

Smith v. *Allwright*
321 US 649 (1944)

The Texas State Democratic party, in convention, limited the right of membership to white electors, thereby denying nonwhites the right to participate in a Democratic party primary. In *Grovey* v. *Townsend* (295 US 45), the Supreme Court had upheld this limitation as not being unconstitutional because the determination was made by the party in convention, not by a party executive committee as in *Condon.* Here the Supreme Court overruled *Grovey,* stating, "The United States is a constitutional democracy. Its organic law grants to all citizens a right to participate in the choice of elected officials without restriction by any state because of race." The Court noted that the political party makes its selection of candidates as an agency of the state and, as such, could not exclude participation based on race and remain consistent with the Fifteenth Amendment.

Baker v. *Carr*
369 US 186 (1962)

This case was brought by electors in several counties of the state of Tennessee who asserted that the 1901 legislative reapportionment statute was unconstitutional because the numbers of voters in the various districts had changed substantially since then. The plaintiffs requested that the court either direct a reapportionment by mathematical application of the Tennessee constitutional formula to the 1960 census or instruct the state to hold direct at-large elections. The district court dismissed the case on the grounds that it was a political question and, as such, did not fall within the protection of the Fourteenth Amendment. The U.S. Supreme Court ruled that the case involved a basic constitutional right and thereby was within court jurisdiction and remanded the case to the district court.

Requirements for Legislative Membership

Bond v. *Floyd*
251 F Supp 333 (1966)

This was the first of two crucial admissions cases involving issues other than the legal qualifications of an elected official to serve in a state legislature. Julian Bond, duly elected to the Georgia House of Representatives, was prevented from taking the oath of office constitutionally required of such representatives and thus excluded from membership in two successive sessions of the Georgia House. Grounds for his exclusion involved alleged statements he had either made or supported, in which U.S. policy in Vietnam, as well as the operation of the Selective Service laws, were attacked. Bond then brought an action in U.S. District Court, Northern District of Georgia, on the grounds that the House action depriving him of his seat was unauthorized and a clear violation of his rights under the First Amendment. The District Court, Griffin Bell, Circuit Judge, declared that it had jurisdiction to decide the Constitutionality of the case, that the Georgia

House was autorized by state law to take such exclusionary action, and that the plaintiff's right to free speech was not violated. The Supreme Court, however, ruled that Bond's statements did not constitute any incitement to violation of law and reversed the lower court on the question of his right to freedom of expression as guaranteed by the First Amendment.

Powell v. *McCormack*
395 US 486 (1969)

According to the Constitution, only three basic factors govern eligibility to serve as a legislator in the U.S. House of Representatives: the proper age, the possession of U.S. citizenship, and the fulfillment of the state's residency requirement. When Congressman Adam Clayton Powell, Jr., was excluded from the 90th Congress on the grounds that he had misused public funds and defied the courts of his home state, the duly elected Congressman from New York's 18th Congressional District filed suit in Federal Court in an attempt to force the House to review only the necessary credentials for membership. The district court dismissed the first petition on the grounds that it lacked jurisdiction.

Julian Bond won his court battle to be seated in the Georgia legislature.

By the time the case was finally heard before the U.S. Supreme Court, the 90th Congress had adjourned. Powell, however, was reelected and finally seated in the 91st Congress, a gesture which, in the view of the court, did not moot the case. The legal point on which the case hinged involved the distinction between "expulsion" and "exclusion." Despite the more than two-thirds majority required for expulsion, the Court ruled that the intent of the House was to "exclude," not to "expel." Many House members entertained severe doubts about their ability to expel a member for misconduct occurring during a prior session. The Court summation stated flatly that "the House was without power to exclude him from its membership."

Employment

Quarles v. Philip Morris
279 F Supp 505 (1968)

A Federal Court required equal pay for equal work and maintenance of seniority when an employee is promoted from one department to another. The effect of this decision was to be felt in a number of subsequent administrative decisions including the Labor Department's 1973 order to Bethlehem Steel to make sweeping changes in its seniority system at its Sparrows Point, Md. plant, and an agreement in 1973 signed between the government and The American Telephone and Telegraph Co. in which the latter agreed to promote and grant retroactive pay increases to thousands of minority employees.

The House of Representatives could not exclude Adam Clayton Powell.

Ali v. State Athletic Commission
316 F Supp 1246 (1970)

A federal district court ruled that Muhammad Ali was discriminated against when the New York State Athletic Commission denied him the right to box because of a Selective Service violation and ordered the commission to renew his boxing license. Ali's claim to be a conscientious objector had been denied by Selective Service officials, but was under appeal. The Court noted that boxers convicted of more serious crimes than Ali's had not been deprived of their licenses. (In 1971, the Supreme Court declared Ali to be a sincere conscientious objector and reversed his five-year jail term; 403 US 698.)

Griggs v. Duke Power
401 US 424 (1971)

The Supreme Court ruled that under Title VII of the 1964 Civil Rights Act tests for hiring and promotion must be related to job performance and cannot be used to exclude minorities, even though the tests, such as high school IQ tests, seem to be neutral on their face. In writing the decision, approved by an 8 to 0 vote, Chief Justice Burger stated that "any tests used must measure the person for the job and not the person in the abstract." The case was initiated by 13 black employees of the Duke Power Co., in Draper, N.D., who had been denied promotion.

Teamsters v. United States
431 US 324 (1977)

In enforcing the Civil Rights Act of 1964, the Supreme Court held that because of proven union and employer discrimination, post-1964 Act discrimination victims were entitled to full relief available to make them whole, including retroactive seniority. The court required proof of "intent to discriminate," however, to establish that a given seniority system is illegal. (Subsequent late 1970s cases in lower Federal Courts have resulted in relief being granted which, in addition to retroactive seniority, included retroactive back pay.)

Kaiser Aluminum v. Weber
443 US 193 (1979)

The Supreme Court held that Kaiser Aluminum's voluntary affirmative action plan, created as a result of collective bargaining between Kaiser and the United Steel Workers of America, which granted preference to black employees over more senior white employees in advancement, did not violate the antidiscrimination sections of the 1964 Civil Rights Act. In 1981 the

U.S. Department of Justice indicated it would seek to have this decision reversed.

Fullilove v. *Klutznick*
448 US 448 (1980)

The U.S. Supreme Court upheld a provision of the Public Works Employment Act of 1977 that required a 10% set-aside of Federal funds for minority business enterprises on local public work projects. The provision had been challenged as violative of the equal protection clause of the Fifth Amendment.

Gulf Oil Company v. *Bernard*
68L Ed 2d693 (1981)

In an employee class action suit, an order limiting communications to class members was held to be an abuse of the discretion provided under the Federal Civil Procedure Rules. Here, Gulf proposed to provide back pay to alleged victims of discrimination in exchange for waivers releasing the company from all discrimination claims. However, some employees felt that proposal, fostered by the Equal Employment Opportunity Commission, was inadequate and sought to initiate proceedings to secure what they thought would be adequate relief.

A district court imposed a "gag order" which restricted the dissidents from communicating their point of view to other Gulf employees. The Supreme Court invalidated the gag order as an unconstitutional prior restraint on the First Amendment right of expression because there was no showing of a need to justify such a restraint.

Racial Intermarriage

Loving v. *Virginia*
388 US 1 (1967)

This case virtually nullified the antimiscegenation laws, many of which remain in southern state constitutions and legal codes. It concerned a white man and black woman, residents of Virginia, who married in Washington, D.C. Virginia indicted and convicted them of violating its laws against racial intermarriage when the couple returned to Virginia and attempted to reside there, but released them when the couple agreed not to reside in the state for 25 years. The Lovings, however, decided to challenge the agreement and the law. Their appeal was rejected by the Virginia courts but upheld by the U.S. Supreme Court, which ruled the Virginia law unconstitutional. Soon thereafter, federal district courts in other states which forbade intermarriage were ordering local officials to issue marriage

Court decisions guarantee equal pay for equal work and require that tests for hiring and promotion must be related to job performance and cannot be used to exclude minorities.

licenses to interracial couples applying for them. (Text of antimiscegenation statutes and state constitutional restrictions can be found in the second edition of the *Negro Almanac,* pages 254-263).

NOTABLE ADVERSE U.S. SUPREME COURT DECISIONS

In two cases, *Scott* v. *Sandford* and *Plessy* v. *Ferguson,* the U.S. Supreme Court issued monumental decisions which adversely affected the legal progress of the Negro in the United States. The Dred Scott case denied the black all rights of citizenship in accordance with the U.S. Constitution while the Plessy dictum not only institutionalized the concept of "separate but equal" facilities in public carriers but also paved the way for the development of the "Jim Crow" system throughout the South.

Scott v. Sandford (1856)
Chief Justice Taney delivered the opinion.

In 1835 Dred Scott, born a slave in Virginia, became the property of John Emerson, an Army doctor, in the slave state of Missouri. From there, he was taken into the free state of Illinois and later to the free territory of Minnesota.

In 1847 Scott instituted suit in the Circuit Court of the County of St. Louis, Missouri, arguing that he should be given his freedom by virtue of his having resided on free soil. After nine years, his case was certified to the U.S. Supreme Court, where five of the nine justices, including Chief Justice Taney, were Southerners.

The Court considered three basic questions:

1. Was Scott a citizen of Missouri, and hence within the jurisdiction of the Federal Court there?
2. Did residence in a free area of the United States automatically entitle Scott to his freedom?
3. Was the Missouri Compromise constitutional?

Mr. and Mrs. Richard P. Loving vanquished Virginia's miscegenation law.

In delivering his opinion, Chief Justice Taney declared that, by virtue of both the Declaration of Independence and the Constitution, blacks could not be regarded as citizens of the United States. Moreover, the Court could not deprive slaveholders of their right to take slaves into any part of the Union, North or South. In effect, therefore, the Missouri Compromise, as well as other antislavery legislation, was declared to be unconstitutuional.

. . . if the Constitution recognizes the right of property of the master in a slave, and makes no distinction between that description of property and other property owned by a citizen, no tribunal, acting under the authority of the United States, whether it be legislative, executive, or judicial, has a right to draw such a distinction, or deny to it the benefit of the provisions and guarantees which have been provided for the protection of private property against the encroachments of the government. . . .

Upon the whole, therefore, it is the judgment of this court, that it appears by the record before us that the plaintiff in error is not a citizen of Missouri, in the sense in which that word is used in the Constitution; and that the Circuit Court of the United States, for that reason, had no jurisdiction in the case, and could give no judgment in it.

Plessy v. Ferguson (1896)
Justice Brown delivered the opinion.

The Plessy case was a test of the constitutionality of an 1890 Louisiana law providing for separate railway carriages for whites and blacks.

The information filed in the criminal District Court charged

A PUBLIC MEETING

WILL BE HELD ON

THURSDAY EVENING, 2D INSTANT,

at 7½ o'clock, in ISRAEL CHURCH, to consider the atrocious decision of the Supreme Court in the

DRED SCOTT CASE,

and other outrages to which the colored people are subject under the Constitution of the United States.

C. L. REMOND,
ROBERT PURVIS,

and others will be speakers on the occasion. Mrs. MOTT, Mr. M'KIM and B. S. JONES of Ohio, have also accepted invitations to be present.

All persons are invited to attend. Admittance free.

Key figures in the historic Dred Scott case, which denied blacks the rights of citizenship, were President James Buchanan (caricatured below right), Chief Justice Roger B. Taney (below left), and Dred Scott. Black protest meetings, like the one handbilled for Philadelphia (above), rallied against the racist ruling.

321

in substance that (Homer) Plessy, being a passenger between two stations within the state of Louisiana, was assigned by officers of the company to the coach used by the race to which he did not belong.

In the majority opinion of the Court, "separate but equal" accommodations for blacks constituted a "reasonable" use of state police power. Furthermore, it was said that the Fourteenth Amendment "could not have been intended to abolish distinctions based on color, or to enforce social . . . equality, or a co-mingling of the two races upon terms unsatisfactory to either."

Justice John Marshall Harlan delivered a dissenting opinion in this case which proved to be a prophetic one: "The judgment this day rendered will, in time, prove to be quite as pernicious as the decision made by this tribunal in the Dred Scott case. The thin disguise of equal accommodations for passengers in railroad coaches will not mislead anyone nor atone for the wrong this day done."

Civil Rights Cases (1883)

This group of civil rights cases was heard before the Supreme Court in an effort to determine the constitutionality of the 1875 Civil Rights Act, the first piece of national legislation which attempted to guarantee people of all races "full and equal enjoyment" of all public accommodations, including inns, public conveyances, theaters, and other places of amusement. The Court ruled, however, that the Act was unconstitutional inasmuch as it did not spring directly from the Thirteenth and Fourteenth amendments to the Constitution. In the view of the Court, the Thirteenth Amendment was concerned exclusively with the narrow confines of slavery and involuntary servitude. The Fourteenth Amendment, by a comparable yardstick of interpretation, did not empower Congress to enact direct legislation to counteract the effect of state laws or policies. The effect of this ruling was to deprive the black of the very protections which the three postwar Freedom Amendments were designed to provide.

American Tobacco Company v. John Patterson, et al.
No. 80–1199 (1982)
Justice White delivered the opinion.

The petitioner, American Tobacco Company, operates two plants in Richmond, Virginia, one of which manufactures cigarettes and the other, pipe tobacco. Each plant is divided into a prefabrication department, which blends and prepares tobacco for further processing, and a fabrication department, which manufactures the final product. It is uncontested that prior to 1963 the company and the union, The Bakery, Confectionary and Tobacco Workers Union, and its affiliate Local 182 had engaged in overt racial discrimination. The union maintained two segregated locals, and black employees were assigned to jobs in the lower-paying prefabrication departments. Higher-paying jobs in the fabrication departments were largely reserved for white employees. An employee could transfer from one of the predominantly black prefabrication departments to one of the predominantly white fabrication departments by forfeiting his seniority.

On January 3, 1969, respondent John Patterson and two other black employees filed charges with the Equal Employment Opportunity Commission alleging that the petitioners had discriminated against them on the basis of race. After conciliation failed, the employees filed a class action suit in District Court in 1973 charging the American Tobacco Company with racial discrimination.

In November 1968 the company proposed the establishment of nine lines of progression, six of which were at issue in the case. Four of the six lines of progression at issue consisted mainly of all-white top jobs from the fabrication departments linked with nearly all-white bottom jobs from the fabrication departments. The other two consisted of all-black top jobs from the prefabrication departments linked with all-black bottom jobs from the prefabrication departments. The top jobs in the white lines of progression were among the best paying jobs in the plant. The actions were consolidated for trial and injunctive relief was initially granted, but ultimately the Court of Appeals, without deciding whether the lines of progression were part of a seniority system, held that even if they were, Section 703(h) does not apply to seniority systems adopted after the effective date of the Civil Rights Acts.

City of Mobile, Alabama v. Wiley L. Bolden et al.
446 US 55 (1980)

A class action was brought in the U.S. District Court for the Southern District of Alabama on behalf of a class of all-black citizens of Mobile, alleging among other things that the defendant city's practice of electing commissioners at large by a majority vote unfairly diluted the voting strength of blacks in violation of the Fourteenth and Fifteenth amendments. The District Court, although finding that blacks in the city registered and voted without hindrance, nonetheless held that the plaintiff's Constitutional rights had been violated, and entered a judgment in their favor, ordering that Mobile's city commissioners be disestablished and replaced by a municipal government consisting of a mayor and a city council composed of members selected from single member districts (423F Supp 384).

Pullman Standard v. *Louis Swint and Willie Johnson*
United Steelworkers of America v.
Louis Swint and Willie Johnson
72L Ed 2d66 (1982)
Justice White delivered the opinion.

Black employees of Pullman Standard brought a suit in Federal District Court against Pullman Standard and against the union, alleging that Title VII of the Civil Rights Act of 1964 was violated by a seniority system. The District Court found "that the difference in terms, conditions or privileges of employment resulting from the seniority system are not the result of an intention to discriminate because of race or color" and held therefore that the system satisfied the requirements of Section 703(h) of the Civil Rights Act. In reversing the decision, the Court of Appeals for the Fifth Circuit said, "because we find the differences in the terms, conditions and standards of employment for black workers and white workers at Pullman Standard resulted from an intent to discriminate because of race, we hold that the system is not legally valid under section 703(h) of Title VII US. C. 2000e-2(h)."

Regents of the University of California v.
Allan Bakke
438 US 265 (1978)

A white male, Alan Bakke, who had been denied admission to the University of California Medical School at Davis for two consecutive years, instituted an action for declaratory and injunctive relief against the Regents of the University in the Superior Court of Yolo County, citing the equal protection clause of the Fourteenth Amendment, a provision of the California constitution, and the proscription in Title VI of the Civil Rights Act of 1964 against racial discrimination in any program receiving Federal financial assistance in alleging the invalidity of the medical school's special admission program under which only disadvantaged members of certain minority races were considered for 16% of the 100 places in each year's class. Whereas members of any race could qualify under the school's general admission program for the other 84 places in the class, the plaintiff had been denied admission to the school under the general admission program even though applicants with substantially lower entrance examination scores had been admitted under the special admissions program. Finding that the special admissions program operated as a racial quota because minority applicants in the special program were rated only against one another and 16 places in the class of 100 were reserved for them, the trial court (1) declared that the school could not take race into account in making the admissions decision, and (2) held that

the challenged admissions program violated the federal and state constitutions and Title VI, but (3) refused to order the plantiff's admission because he had failed to prove that he would have been admitted but for the existence of the special program. On direct appeal, the Supreme Court of California affirmed the trial court's judgment insofar as it determined that the special admissions program was invalid under the equal protection clause, but reversed it insofar as it denied an injunction ordering that the plaintiff be admitted to the medical school, having ruled that the university had the burden of demonstration that the plaintiff would not have been admitted even in the absence of the special admissions program, and the university conceded its inability to carry that burden.

STATE ANTIDISCRIMINATION LAWS

In 1974, 33 states encompassing three fourths of the nation's population had laws on the books which were specifically designed to protect minorities from discrimination in one or more of the following categories: housing, employment, recreation and education. Most of these laws were enacted prior to the federal civil rights acts of the 1960s and sought to have an educative rather than coercive effect. Enforcement was usually in response to a complaint of discrimination filed by one or a few people and was rarely applied as a whole to industries, large employers, or real estate developers.

With the passage of the federal Civil Rights Acts in 1964, 1965, and 1968, activity on the state level receded still more in expectation that Washington

Clarence Mitchell, director of the NAACP's Washington Bureau.

would assume the role of fighting discrimination. However, such enforcement has not been vigorous and state laws and commissions remain important, especially in two respects. They are:

As a course of redress for victims of discrimination who find the federal machinery cumbersome or indifferent.

As a legal weapon for civil rights advocates who feel agreements between the federal government and specific industries are insufficiently protective of minorities. An example of such use of state laws occurred in April 1974 when the Legal Defense Fund sued in federal court to reverse a consent agreement between the government and steel company employers and unions. The Legal Defense Fund charged that the consent decree violated the Fair Employment laws of some 17 states.

LYNCHING

For the first half of the twentieth century, lynching, far more than desegregation or voting rights, was regarded as the major issue facing blacks. Lynching has not been an easy term to define. The following is a paraphrase of the definition which has been offered in most proposed federal antilynching legislation:

Lynching is an act of mob violence which results in the death or maiming of a person or persons in the custody of a peace officer, or suspected of, charged with, or convicted of, a serious crime, often one punishable by death.

Other criteria for lynching were established in a conference arranged by F. D. Patterson at Tuskegee Institute in 1940. These include:

1. Legal evidence of a person's illegal death.
2. Group participation in a killing under the pretext of service to justice, race, or tradition.

Since 1882 the trend in lynchings in the United States has gone downward, as an examination of the following tables provided through the courtesy of Tuskegee Institute will clearly show. In 1963 Tuskegee Institute ceased issuing data on lynchings. Though blacks are still victims of mob violence performed under the guise of justice, death from lynch mobs has become very rare.

BLACKS IN THE JUDICIARY

Inasmuch as blacks have not always been able to regard the law as an impartial, justice-seeking force, it is not surprising that they do not have a long and extensive history in the legal profession. In some states in particular, the law tended to become an instrument of oppression, rather than a vehicle of redress. Before the Civil War, for example, the law constituted one of the forces that prevented the black's escape from slavery. Again, toward the end of Reconstruction, the laws of the South were clearly intended in part to institutionalize the practices of white supremacy.

Despite these obstacles, blacks gradually began to enter the legal profession, albeit predominantly in the North, where they were given some degree of status and the right to represent their clients on equal footing with their white counterparts. The formation of the National Association for the Advancement of Colored People (NAACP) played a vital role in broadening the legal horizons of both the black citizen and the prospective practitioner of law in the twentieth century. By 1939, the year the NAACP Legal Defense and Educational Fund was incorporated, the black had ample reason to believe that the legal institutions of the nation were undergoing a profound metamorphosis—judging particularly from the large number of cases regularly being won by black petitioners before the U.S. Supreme Court. Most legal landmarks in the black's fight for constitutional privileges have been won with the assistance of the NAACP, many by a host of lawyers now active as federal judges in the courts of the United States.

Supreme Court Justice Thurgood Marshall.

Almost all black judges currently on the bench have received their appointments only since the mid-1960s. Only one black has served as a member of the U.S. Supreme Court: Thurgood Marshall. Marshall's appointment to the Court in 1967 was among the most momentous decisions rendered during the Johnson Administration. Even before his confirmation, the former NAACP counsel and Solicitor General was subject to the irksome goading of Southern critics like South Carolina's Strom Thurmond, who denounced Marshall's "activist" legal outlook as a judicial liability. Most U.S. Senators rallied to support the nomination, however, with the result that only 11 men voted against confirmation, while 69 favored it. Marshall spoke himself and for the black in general when he pledged "that I shall be ever mindful of my obligation to the Constitution and to the goal of equal justice under law." On October 2, 1967, in the presence of President Lyndon Johnson, Marshall took the oath before the court's oldest member, Hugo Black. Reference to race was not part of the impressive words Marshall repeated in the five-minute ceremony: "I Thurgood Marshall, do solemnly swear that I will administer justice without respect to persons, and do equal right to the poor and to the rich, and that I will faithfully and impartially discharge and perform all the duties incumbent on me as Associate Justice of the United States according to the best of my abilities and understanding, agreeable to the Constitution and laws of the United States. So help me God."

Number and Distribution of Black Judges

The number of black judges in the United States continues to rise, particularly at the state level. However, black judges still represent a disproportionately small percentage of the total number of judges.

Between 1971 and 1974, the number of black judges sitting in Federal Supreme, Appellate, and District level courts increased from 18 to 20. Blacks still comprise only about 5% of the judges sitting on the Appellate and Supreme courts (five of 104) and only about 3% of the judges sitting on Federal District level courts (15 of 437). Also, significantly, black federal judges sit in only eight states and territories, none of them in the South.

From 1971 to 1974 the number of black state-level judges increased from 184 to 314. However, they too comprise a small percentage of the total. And 15 states have no black judges whatever. Some of these states, such as Mississippi and Arkansas, have large black populations.

During the period of 1974 to 1980, the number of black state judges totaled 291, a decrease from the previous six years. There were still no black state judges in Arkansas and Mississippi, and during that time, West Virginia was also without a black judge either in the federal or state court.

Table 4 and the list of black judges have been provided by the National Bar Association.

BIOGRAPHIES OF BLACK FEDERAL JUDGES

WILLIAM BENSON BRYANT
U.S. District Judge
District of Columbia

Born in Wetumpka, Alabama on September 18, 1911, Bryant received both his A.B. and LL.B. degrees from Howard University.

Before going on active military duty during World War II (he was honorably discharged with the rank of lieutenant-colonel), Bryant had served briefly with the Works Project Administration (WPA) and then with the Bureau of Intelligence in the Office of War Information.

In 1948 he opened a law office in Washington, D.C., practicing there until 1951 when he entered federal service as an assistant in the office of the U.S. Attorney for the District of Columbia. After three years, Bryant resigned from this post in order to become a member of a private law firm. He had already become a partner in this firm when in 1965 President Lyndon B. Johnson announced his appointment to the federal bench.

ROBERT LEE CARTER
U.S. District Judge
Southern District of New York

Judge Carter was appointed U.S. District Judge for the Southern District of New York in 1972, capping a distinguished career for this veteran of scores of civil rights campaigns.

Carter was born in Florida in 1917, received his A.B. degree from Lincoln University in 1937 and law degrees from Howard and Columbia universities in 1940 and 1942. During World War II Carter served in the Air Force.

After the war, Carter was appointed to a number of challenging posts. He has been Vice Chairman of the New York City Community Action for Legal Services, member of the New York State Special Commission on Attica; member of the Temporary Commission on the State Court System; member of the Mayor's Committee on the Judiciary; member of the Mayor's Special Task Force on Minority Employment in the Construction Trades; member of the Mayor's Advisory Panel to the Board of Higher Education; Special Assistant U.S. Attorney for the Southern District of New York; and Member of the Departmental Committee

Judge Robert L. Carter served on the Special Commission on Attica.

on Court Administration of the First and Second Judicial Department, Supreme Court of New York.

ALMERIC CHRISTIAN
Judge of the District Court
Territory of the Virgin Islands

Judge Christian was born in Christiansted on the Virgin Island of St. Croix in 1919, only two years after the United States acquired the islands from Denmark. He attended the University of Puerto Rico, then came to the mainland where he graduated with an A.B. degree from Columbia University in 1942. In 1947 he received his Bachelor of Laws (LL.B.) degree from the Columbia Law School.

Christian was appointed Judge for the Virgin Islands District Court by President Nixon in 1969. In 1970 he became Chief Judge.

ROBERT F. COLLINS
U.S. District Judge
Eastern District of Louisiana

Judge Robert Frederick Collins was born January 27, 1931 in New Orleans. He received his undergraduate degree in 1951 from Dillard University and his law degree from Louisiana State University in 1954. Judge Collins is a former city attorney with the New Orleans police department, and from 1967 to 1969 he was judge ad hoc of the traffic court of the city of New Orleans. Prior to his appointment to the U.S. District Court,

Judge Collins was Judge Magistrate to the Criminal District Court in Orleans Parish, Louisiana.

JULIAN ABELE COOK, JR.
U.S. District Judge
Eastern District of Michigan

Julian Abele Cook, Jr. was appointed U.S. District Judge for the Eastern District of Michigan September 23, 1978 by President Jimmy Carter. Judge Cook was born June 22, 1930 in Washington, D.C. He is the co-author of "Some Current Problems of Human Relations Administration" (*Journal of Urban Law,* Volume 49, 1971). He has received a number of honors and awards, among them the Distinguished Citizen of the Year, NAACP of Oakland County, Michigan in 1970; a Citation of Merit in 1971 by the Pontiac, Michigan Area Urban League; and the Pathfinders Award from Oakland University in 1977. Judge Cook is a member of a number of community organizations and a participant in numerous activities benefiting his local Michigan area.

RICHARD C. ERWIN
U.S. District Judge
Middle District of North Carolina

Judge Erwin was born August 23, 1923 in McDowell County, North Carolina. He was appointed U.S. District Judge October 31, 1980. From January 1978 to October 1980, he was judge, North Carolina Court of Appeals and the first black person in the history of that state to win a statewide race for any elective office.

Judge Erwin received his undergraduate degree from Johnson C. Smith University in Charlotte, North Carolina and his law degree from Howard University. He is a member of the North Carolina Penal Study Commission, a life member of the North Carolina P.T.A. Association, a member of the Board of Visitors of Johnson C. Smith University, and a trustee of the Western North Carolina Conference of the Methodist Church.

CLIFFORD SCOTT GREEN
U.S. District Judge
Eastern District of Pennsylvania

Born in Philadelphia in 1923, Green received his undergraduate and graduate degrees from Temple University, obtaining a Doctor of Laws (J.D.) in 1951.

Judge Green was formerly an Assistant Deputy Attorney General of Pennsylvania, 1964; Judge of the Court of Common Pleas of Pennsylvania, 1964–1972; a member of the Juvenile Court Judges' Commission, 1965–1972; Co-Chairman of the Philadelphia City White House Conference on Children and Youth,

1970; a member of the Philadelphia Regional Selection Panel of the President's Commission on White House Fellows; and a member of the President's Advisory Council on Intergovernmental Personnel Policy. During World War II he served in the United States Air Force.

He was appointed to his current position in December 1971.

JOSEPH W. HATCHETT
U.S. Circuit Judge
Fifth Circuit, Tallahassee, Florida

Judge Joseph W. Hatchett was appointed a U.S. Circuit Judge of the United States Court of Appeals October 1, 1981. He received his undergraduate degree in political science from Florida A&M University in 1954 and his law degree from Howard University in 1959.

Judge Hatchett has written a number of articles for law journals and received numerous awards. He is listed in *Who's Who in the South and Southwest, Who's Who in American Law, Who's Who Among Black Americans, The American Bench, Notable Americans, Who's Who in America,* and he is also listed as a Notable Black American. Judge Hatchett was the first black to be appointed to the highest court of a state since Reconstruction and the first black to serve on a federal appellate court in the South.

A. LEON HIGGINBOTHAM, JR.
U.S. Circuit Judge
Third Circuit

Leon Higginbotham, Jr. was appointed October 13, 1977 by President Jimmy Carter as U.S. Circuit Judge. Just prior to this appointment, he had served on the Federal Trade Commission—the first black and the youngest person ever to hold the post of commissioner.

Higginbotham was born in Trenton, New Jersey in 1927. Originally an engineering student at Purdue University, he later enrolled at Antioch College as a liberal arts student, and received his LL.B. in 1952 from Yale.

He was soon appointed assistant district attorney in Philadelphia; then joined a private law firm; and later was chosen by Pennsylvania's Governor David Lawrence to serve as a member of the Pennsylvania Human Rights Commission.

Judge Richard C. Erwin.

In 1959 he was elected president of the Philadelphia chapter of the NAACP and, four years later, was cited as "one of the 10 outstanding young men in America" by the U.S. Junior Chamber of Commerce.

Judge Higginbotham has published more than 40 articles in major scholarly journals and his recent book, *In the Matter of Color: Race and the American Legal Process; The Colonial Period,* has received several national awards.

ODELL HORTON
U.S. District Judge
Western District of Tennessee

Judge Odell Horton received his law degree from Howard University in 1956 and his undergraduate degree from Moorhouse College in Atlanta in 1951. He is a native of Bolivar, Tennessee. Judge Horton was one of three Memphis attorneys selected by the Memphis City Council to investigate citizen complaints against the Memphis Police Department. In 1962 Horton was appointed Assistant U.S. Attorney for the Western District of Tennessee by Attorney General Robert F. Kennedy on the recommendation of Senators Estes Kefauver and Albert Gore and the Shelby County Democratic Club. As an Assistant U.S. Attorney, Horton represented the United States in the prosecution of persons charged with violating criminal laws of the United States as well as civil and criminal legal matters arising in the Western District of Tennessee. Judge Horton also served as president of LeMoyne-Owen College in Memphis from 1970 to 1974.

He has received numerous awards and citations and has held directorships in a number of educational, private, and community organizations.

Judge Odell Horton placing a memorial wreath for Martin Luther King.

NATHANIEL R. JONES
U.S. Court of Appeals, Sixth Circuit
Ohio, Michigan, Kentucky, Tennessee

Judge Nathaniel R. Jones is a former NAACP general counsel and during his tenure, he coordinated the attack against northern school segregation and twice argued in the U.S. Supreme Court the Detroit school case, *Bradley* v. *Milliken.* In addition, in 1979, he successfully organized the presentation to the Supreme Court of the issues in the Dayton and Columbus, Ohio school desegregation cases. Judge Jones also directed the NAACP's response to the attacks against affirmative action and led an inquiry into discrimination against black servicemen. President Jimmy Carter appointed Jones to the Sixth Circuit Court of Appeals in Cincinnati, Ohio on October 15, 1979. Judge Jones is a graduate of Youngstown University, where he received his Bachelor of Arts degree in 1951 and his law degree in 1956. He also received honorary doctor of laws degrees from Youngstown University in 1970 and from Syracuse University in 1972.

DAMON JEROME KEITH
U.S. District Judge
Eastern District of Michigan

Keith, a judicial appointee of President Lyndon Johnson, was born in Detroit in 1922. He received his A.B. degree from West Virginia State College in 1943 and then served three years in the Army. Upon his return to civilian life, he entered Howard Law School, receiving a Bachelor of Laws degree in 1949.

From 1951 to 1955 Keith was with the Office of the Friend of the Court in Detroit. He then returned to college, obtaining his Master of Law Degree from Wayne State University in 1956. From 1958 to 1967 he was President of the Detroit Housing Commission. From 1964 to 1967 he was also Chairman and Co-Chairman of the Michigan Civil Rights Commission.

THURGOOD MARSHALL
Associate Justice
Supreme Court of the United States

In July 1965 Thurgood Marshall was appointed to one of the most prestigious positions ever held by a black in the federal government—that of Solicitor General of the United States. Marshall assumed the task of acting as the government's chief legal spokesman in cases brought before the Supreme Court.

Marshall was born in Baltimore, Maryland on July 2, 1908. After receiving a B.A. degree from Lincoln University as a pre-dental student, he decided instead to become a lawyer and was admitted to Howard University's Law School, graduating in 1933 at the top of his class.

Judge Nathaniel R. Jones.

After five years of private practice in Baltimore, Marshall began what was to become a long and distinguished career with the NAACP—interrupted only briefly by an assignment as President John F. Kennedy's personal representative to the independence ceremonies of Sierra Leone.

In 1938, as national special counsel, he handled all cases involving questions of Negro constitutional rights. Then, in 1950, he was named director-counsel of the organization's 11-year-old Legal Defense and

Judge Keith was chairman of the Michigan Civil Rights Commission.

Educational Fund. In 1954, as part of an imposing team of lawyers, he played a key role in the now-historic Supreme Court decision on school desegregation. He also figured prominently in such important cases as *Sweatt* v. *Painter* (requiring the admission of a qualified black student to the law school of Texas University), and *Smith* v. *Allwright* (establishing the right of Texas Negroes to vote in Democratic primaries).

In 1961 Marshall sat on a federal bench as circuit judge for the Second Circuit. His outstanding achievements in the field of law led in 1946 to his winning the coveted Spingarn Medal, only one of the numerous citations he holds.

The climax of Marshall's legal and judicial career came in 1967 when he was nominated for a seat on the U.S. Supreme Court. At 59, the son of a sleeping-car porter and great grandson of a slave became the ninety-sixth man—and the first black—to sit among the nine Supreme Court justices.

GABRIELLE K. McDONALD
U.S. District Judge
Southern District of Texas

Judge Gabrielle K. McDonald was born April 12, 1942 in St. Paul, Minnesota and received her law degree from Howard University in 1966. While at Howard, Judge McDonald was presented with the Kappa Beta Pi Legal Sorority award for academic excellence as well as the Book Award, The Petitioners, for best oral argument and brief in Appellate Practice. She graduated first in her class at Howard.

Judge McDonald was employed as a staff attorney from 1966 to 1969 with the NAACP Legal Defense and Educational Fund in New York City. She has received awards from the National Bar Association, the Houston Citizens Chamber of Commerce, and Howard University.

CONSTANCE BAKER MOTLEY
U.S. District Judge
Southern District of New York

Born in Connecticut of West Indian parents, Constance Baker Motley was appointed by President Johnson to the U.S. District Court for Southern New York in 1966, thus becoming the nation's first black woman federal judge. The appointment marked the high point of her long career in politics and civic affairs.

While still a law student at Columbia University, Mrs. Motley began working with the NAACP Legal Defense and Educational Fund, Inc., beginning an association that was to make her famous as a defender of civil rights. After receiving her law degree, she began to work full-time with this organization, eventually becoming one of its associate counsels.

President Johnson announcing he will nominate Constance Baker Motley to be a federal judge for the southern district of New York.

Before leaving the organization in 1964 to run for the New York State Senate, Mrs. Motley had argued nine successful NAACP cases before the U.S. Supreme Court, having participated in almost every important civil rights case that had passed through the courts since 1954—from Autherine Lucy in Alabama to James Meredith in Mississippi. By winning election to the state senate in February of 1964, Mrs. Motley became the first Negro woman in New York state history to sit in the upper chamber.

Then, one year later, the state senator ran for the position of Manhattan Borough President, emerging the victor by the unanimous final vote of the City Council. She thus became the first woman to serve as a city borough president, and therefore also the first woman on the Board of Estimate.

A resident of Manhattan's Upper West Side, Judge Motley hopes that her career "will be an inspiration to other Negro women," and feels that "it is important for women, and especially black women, to become involved and to hold public office."

In June 1982, Judge Constance Baker Motley was named chief judge of the Federal District Court that covers Manhattan, the Bronx, and six counties north of New York City. Judge Motley succeeded Judge Lloyd F. MacMahon, who relinquished his administrative duties.

BARRINGTON DANIELS PARKER
U.S. District Judge
District of Columbia

Judge Parker was born in Rosslyn, Virginia in 1915 and attended Lincoln University where he received an A.B. degree in 1936. He was awarded an M.A. degree from the University of Pennsylvania in 1938 and his law degree from University of Chicago in 1947.

Following his graduation, Judge Parker was active in private law practice in Washington, D.C.. He was a partner in the firm of Parker & Parker when President Nixon appointed him to the District Court in 1969.

JAMES BENTON PARSONS
U.S. District Judge
Northern District of Illinois

James Benton Parsons, chosen by President John F. Kennedy in 1961 and installed on the bench the following year, became the first black appointed a lifetime federal district judge within the continental United States (U.S. District Court for the Northern District of Illinois). Prior to this, he had been elected judge of the Superior Court of Cook County, Illinois, and had also held the office of Assistant U.S. Attorney.

A native of Kansas City, Missouri, Parsons was born on August 13, 1911. At first a student of music at the James Milliken University and Conservatory of Music, and, from 1938 to 1940, acting head of the Department of Music at Lincoln University, he attended summer sessions at Wisconsin University with an eye toward changing his major to political science. This plan was temporarily interrupted by four years of military service but, with the end of World War II, he pursued his graduate studies—this time at the University of Chicago. He ultimately received an M.A. in political science in 1946 and a Doctor of Laws Degree three years later.

After a brief stint as a teacher at the John Marshall School of Law, Parsons worked for two years as assistant corporation counsel for the City of Chicago, appearing often before the Illinois Appellate Court as well as the State Supreme Court. He was then appointed to the U.S. Attorney's Office, serving there with distinction for nine years. During this period, he was particularly active with cases relating to juvenile delinquency and rehabilitation, as well as with those involving both civil rights and the selective service. For his success in prosecuting some 60 selective service violators, Parsons was presented with the first Selective Service System Certificate of Appreciation.

WARREN LAWRENCE PIERCE
U.S. District Judge
Southern District of New York

Judge Pierce had been Deputy Commissioner of New York City Police Department.

Judge Pierce was born in 1924 in Philadelphia. He received his B.S. from St. Joseph's College there in 1948 and his law degree from Fordham in 1951.

From 1954 to 1961 Pierce was an Assistant District Attorney in Brooklyn, New York. In 1961 he was named Deputy Commissioner of the New York City Police Department. In 1963 he became Director of the New York State Division for Youth and in 1966, Chairman of the New York State Narcotic Addiction Control Commission. Thus Judge Pierce had a solid foundation in law enforcement procedures and problems when he was appointed to the federal bench in 1970.

SCOVEL RICHARDSON
U.S. Customs Court Judge

In 1957 Scovel Richardson was named judge to the U.S. Customs Court for New York State, having previously acquired considerable legal experience both as a practicing lawyer and a professor of law.

Born in Nashville, Tennessee on February 4, 1912, Richardson obtained his B.A. and M.A. degrees from the University of Illinois and, in 1937, his LL.B. from Howard University.

Thurgood Marshall speaks with Senator Robert Kennedy after being confirmed as U.S. Solicitor General in 1965. Two years later, Marshall became the nation's first black Supreme Court justice.

With the exception of one year (1938) when he served as a private attorney in Chicago, and another year (1943) when he was a senior attorney for the Office of Price Administration (OPA), Richardson was associated with Lincoln University as a professor of law and dean of the law school. He left Lincoln in 1953 to accept an appointment from President Dwight D. Eisenhower to the U.S. Board of Parole, becoming its chairman the following year.

AUBREY EUGENE ROBINSON JR.
U.S. District Judge
District of Columbia

Judge Robinson was appointed to the United States District Court for the District of Columbia on November 3, 1966, and entered on duty November 16, 1966.

He received an A.B. degree from Cornell University in 1943 and an LL.B. degree from Cornell Law School in 1947. He served as a First Sergeant in the United States Army, 1943–1946.

Prior to his appointment to the federal bench Judge Robinson was an Associate Judge of the Juvenile Court for the District of Columbia, 1965–1966. He is a member of the Judicial Conference Ad Hoc Committee on Court Facilities and Design and the District of Columbia Commission on Judicial Disabilities and Tenure.

From 1948 to 1965 Robinson practiced law in Washington, D.C. and acted on behalf of several black petitioners in civil rights cases.

In addition to serving on the federal bench, Robinson is a member of the Special Police Trial Board of the Washington, D.C. Police Department and of the Advisory Committee to the Special Project of the National Council on the Aging.

SPOTTSWOOD W. ROBINSON III
U.S. Circuit Judge
District of Columbia Circuit

Judge Robinson was named Circuit Judge in 1966 by President Johnson, a promotion from his previous position of District Judge, a post to which he had been appointed in 1963.

Prior to becoming a judge, Robinson had served in the legal field for many years—first as a private attorney, then as faculty member, and ultimately as Dean of the Howard University Law School.

Robinson was born in Richmond, Virginia on July 26, 1916. He received his B.A. at Virginia Union University and his LL.B. from the Howard University Law School in 1939.

Judge Robinson was the Virginia representative of the NAACP Legal Defense and Educational Fund from 1948 to 1950 and later served for nine years as its southeast regional counsel. He was a member of the U.S. Commission on Civil Rights from 1961 to 1963.

PAUL A. SIMMONS
U.S. District Judge
Western District of Pennsylvania

Judge Simmons was appointed in 1978 to the Western District of Pennsylvania and was the first merit-selected federal judge in the history of that state. He was born on August 31, 1921 in Monongahela, Pennsylvania where he still resides.

Judge Simmons graduated with high honors from the University of Pittsburgh in 1946 and from Harvard Law School in 1949. While attending school, Judge Simmons worked in the construction industry and on the Pennsylvania Railroad. Following graduation from law school, he was a professor of law at South Carolina College Law School from 1949 to 1952, and at the North Carolina College of Law from 1952 to 1956. From 1956 to 1973 he practiced law in Washington County and the surrounding counties.

In 1973 he was appointed Judge of the Court of Common Pleas of Washington County, and in 1975 he was nominated by both the Democratic and Republican parties and elected to a full 10-year term to that court.

Over the years, Judge Simmons has been a member of various commissions and authorities, including the Pennsylvania Human Relations Commission, the Pennsylvania Minor Judiciary Education Board, and the Washington County Redevelopment Authority. He was also on the Founding Board of Directors of the Monongahela Valley United Health Services. Judge Simmons is a member of the Pennsylvania Bar Association, the American Judicature Society, and many other bar associations.

JACK EDWARD TANNER
U.S. District Judge
Western District of Washington

Judge Tanner was appointed U.S. District Judge for the Western District of Washington on May 19, 1978. He is a member of the Washington State Bar Association, the Loren Miller Law Club, the National Bar Association, and the Board of Visitors of the University of Puget Sound Law School, the NAACP, and was a member of its National Board of Directors from 1962 to 1968.

JOSEPH C. WADDY
U.S. District Judge
District of Columbia

Joseph Waddy was appointed to the District Court bench in 1967, after lending his expertise in government operations to a number of advisory commissions.

Born in Virginia in 1911, Waddy received an A.B. degree from Lincoln University in 1935 and an LL.B. from Howard University Law School in 1938. He served as Associate Judge of the Domestic Relations Branch of the Municipal Court of the District of Columbia from 1962 to 1967. Prior to that time, he was a member of the Citizens Advisory Council to the District of Columbia Commissioners.

Since 1971 Judge Waddy has also served as a Commissioner of the National Conference of Commissioners on Uniform State Laws.

Judge Jack Edward Tanner.

JAMES L. WATSON
U.S. Customs Court Judge

Judge Watson was born in New York City in 1922,

the son of James S. Watson, the first black jurist elected in New York State.

Judge Watson was decorated for bravery in Italy in World War II, where he served with the 92nd Infantry Division. He was graduated from Brooklyn Law School in 1951, served on the Board of Immigration Appeals, and in 1954 was elected to the New York State Senate. In 1963 he resigned from the Senate and was elected Judge of the Civil Court of New York City. In 1966 President Johnson named him to serve on the Customs Court.

DAVID W. WILLIAMS
U.S. District Judge
Central District of California

Judge Williams was appointed United States District Judge for the Central District of California on June 20, 1969. He is a graduate of Los Angeles Junior College, the University of California at Los Angeles, receiving an A.B. degree in 1934, and the University of Southern California Law School, receiving an LL.B. degree in 1937.

Prior to his appointment to the federal bench, Williams served as a Judge of the Los Angeles County Superior Court, 1963–1969; and Judge of the Los Angeles Municipal Court, 1956–1962. He was born in Atlanta in 1910.

ROSTER OF BLACK JUDICIAL OFFICERS[a]

Supreme Court of U.S.

Hon. Thurgood Marshall
Associate Justice
Supreme Court of the United States
Washington, DC

U.S. Court of Appeals

Hon. Harry Edwards
District of Columbia Circuit
U.S. Courthouse
Third and Constitution Avenue, N. W.
Washington, DC 20001

[a] Courtesy of the American Judicature Society and the Judicial Council of the National Bar Association.

Hon. J. Jerome Farris
Ninth Circuit
910 U.S. Courthouse
1010 Fifth Avenue
Seattle, WA 98104

Hon. Joseph Hatchett
Fifth Circuit
P.O. Box 10429
Tallahassee, FL 32302

Hon. A. Leon Higginbotham, Jr.
Third Circuit
15613 U.S. Courthouse
601 Market Street
Philadelphia, PA 19106

Hon. Andrew L. Jefferson, Jr.
Fifth Circuit
(confirmation pending)

Hon. Nathaniel Jones
Sixth Circuit
Room 541
U.S. Post Office and Courthouse
Cincinnati, OH 45202

Hon. Amalya Kearse
Second Circuit
U.S. Courthouse
Room 1006
Foley Square
New York, NY 10007

Hon. Damon Keith, Jr.
Sixth Circuit
730 Federal Building
231 West Lafayette Street
Detroit, MI 48226

Hon. Theodore McMillian
Eighth Circuit
1114 Market Street
St. Louis, MO 63101

Hon. Cecil F. Poole
Ninth Circuit
Federal Building
450 Golden Gate Avenue
San Francisco, CA 94101

Hon. Spottswood W. Robinson, I
District of Columbia Circuit

U.S. Courthouse
Third & Constitution Ave. N.W.
Washington, DC 20001

U.S. District Court

Hon. Henry Bramwell
New York Eastern District
U.S. Courthouse
225 Cadman Plaza East
Brooklyn, NY 11201

Hon. William B. Bryant
Chief Judge
U.S. District Court for the District of
Columbia
U.S. Courthouse
Third and Constitution Avenue, N.W.
Washington, DC 20001

Hon. Clyde S. Cahill, Jr.
Missouri Eastern District
Room 541
1114 Market Street
St. Louis, MO 63101

Hon. Robert L. Carter
New York Southern District
U.S. Courthouse
Foley Square
New York, NY 10007

Hon. U. W. Clemon
Alabama Northern District
Federal Courthouse
Birmingham, AL 35203

Hon. Robert F. Collins
Louisiana Eastern District
C-465 U.S. District Courthouse
500 Camp Street
New Orleans, LA 70130

Hon. Julian A. Cook
Michigan Eastern District
Federal Building, Room 272
Detroit, MI 48226

Hon. Anna Diggs-Taylor
Michigan Eastern District
Federal Building, Room 235
Detroit, MI 48226

Hon. Robert M. Duncan
Ohio Southern District
85 Marconi Boulevard
Columbus, OH 43215

Hon. Benjamin Gibson
Michigan Western District
438 Federal Building
110 Michigan Street, N.W.
Grand Rapids, MI 49503

Hon. James Giles
Pennsylvania Eastern District
U.S. Courthouse, Room 8613
601 Market Street
Philadelphia, PA 19106

Hon. Earl Gilliam
California Southern District
(confirmation pending)

Fred D. Gray
Alabama Middle District
(confirmation pending)

Hon. Clifford Scott Green
Pennsylvania Eastern District
15613 U.S. Courthouse
Independence Mall West
Philadelphia, PA 19106

Hon. Alcee Hastings
Florida Southern District
P.O. Box 013200
Miami, FL 33101

Hon. Terry J. Hatter, Jr.
California Central District
U.S. Courthouse
312 North Spring Street
Los Angeles, CA 90012

Thelton Henderson
California Northern District
(confirmation pending)

Hon. Odell Horton
Tennessee Western District
Federal Building
167 North Main
Memphis, TN 38103

Hon. Joseph C. Howard
U.S. District Court for Maryland
U.S. Courthouse, Room 120
101 West Lombard Street
Baltimore, MD 21201

Hon. Norma H. Johnson
U.S. District Court for the District of
Columbia
U.S. Courthouse
Third and Constitution Avenue, N.W.
Washington, DC 20001

Hon. George N. Leighton
Illinois Northern District
219 South Dearborn Street
Room 2156
Chicago, IL 60604

Hon. Mary Johnson Lowe
New York Southern District
40 Foley Square
New York, NY 10007

Hon. Gabrielle McDonald
Texas Southern District
U.S. Courthouse
515 Rusk Avenue
Houston, TX 77208

Hon. Constance B. Motley
New York Southern District
U.S. Courthouse
Foley Square
New York, NY 10007

Hon. David S. Nelson
U.S. District Court for Massachusetts
McCormack Post Office and
Courthouse Building
Room 1525
Boston, MA 02109

Hon. Barrington Parker
U.S. District Court for the District of
Columbia
U.S. Courthouse
Third and Constitution Avenue, N.W.
Washington, DC 20001

Hon. James B. Parsons
Chief Judge
Illinois Northern District
219 South Dearborn Street
Chicago, IL 60604

Hon John G. Penn
U.S. District Court for the District of
Columbia
613 G Street, N.W.
Washington, DC 20001

Hon. Matthew Perry
U.S. District Court for South Carolina
P.O. Box 10024
Greenville, SC 29603

Hon. Lawrence W. Pierce
New York Southern District
40 Centre Street
New York, NY 10007

Hon. Aubrey E. Robinson, Jr.
U.S. District Court for the District of
Columbia
U.S. Courthouse
Third and Constitution Avenue, N.W.
Washington, DC 20001

Hon. James Sheffield
Virginia Eastern District
(confirmation pending)

Hon. Paul A. Simmons
Pennsylvania Western District
U.S. Post Office and Courthouse
Building
6th Floor
Pittsburg, PA 15219

Hon. Jack E. Tanner
Washington Eastern and Western
Districts
304 Post Office Building
P.O. Box 2015
Tacoma, WA 98401

Hon. Anne E. Thompson
U.S. District Court for New Jersey
U.S. Courthouse
Trenton, NJ 08605

Hon. Horace B. Ward
Georgia Northern District
75 Spring Street, S.W.

Suite 2388
Atlanta, GA 30303

Hon. George White
Ohio Northern District
U.S. Courthouse
Cleveland, OH 44114

Hon. David W. Williams
California Central District
312 North Spring Street
Los Angeles, CA 90012

U.S. District Court (Term)

Hon. Almerie Christian
Chief Judge
Charlotte Amalie, Virgin Islands

U.S. Customs Court

Hon. Scovel Richardson
U.S. Customs Court
One Federal Plaza
New York, NY 10007

Hon. James L. Watson
U.S. Customs Court
One Federal Plaza
New York, NY 10007

U.S. Referees in Bankruptcy

Hon. Charles N. Clevert
U.S. District Court for
Wisconsin Eastern District
517 East Wisconsin Avenue
Milwaukee, WI 53202

Hon. James Dooley
U.S. District Court
California Central District
312 North Spring Street
Los Angeles, CA 90012

Hon. Benjamin E. Franklin
U.S. District Court
for Kansas
Federal Building
812 North Seventh Street
P.O. Box 1339
Kansas City, KN 66117

Hon. Harry G. Hackett
U.S. District Court for
Michigan Eastern District
Federal Building
Detroit, MI 48226

Hon. Grady L. Pettigrew
U.S. District Court for Ohio
Southern District
U.S. Courthouse
85 Marconi Boulevard
Columbus, OH 43215

Hon. Edward B. Toles
U.S. District Court for
Illinois Northern District
219 South Dearborn Street
Chicago, IL 60604

U.S. Magistrates

Hon. Joyce L. Alexander
U.S. District Court for
Massachusetts
932 Post Office—Courthouse
Boston, MA 02109

Hon. Calvin Botley
U.S. District Court
Texas Southern District
U.S. Courthouse
515 Rusk Avenue
Houston, TX 77208

Hon. Arthur Burnett
U.S. District Court
District of Columbia
U.S. Courthouse
Third and Constitution Avenue, N.W.
Washington, DC 20001

Hon. William F. Hall, Jr.
U.S. District Court
Pennsylvania Eastern District
U.S. Courthouse, Room 5918
601 Market Street
Philadelphia, PA 19106

Hon. Henry L. Jones
U.S. District Court
Arkansas Eastern District
U.S. Courthouse
Little Rock, AR 72203

Hon. Chris E. Stith
U.S. District Court
Michigan Eastern District
U.S. Courthouse
Detroit, MI 48226

Hon. Ruth Washington
U.S. District Court
New York Southern District
U.S. Courthouse
Foley Square
New York, NY 10007

U.S. Trustee

David Coar
Department of Justice
U.S. Trustee's Office
175 West Jackson Boulevard
Room A1303
Chicago, IL 60604

U.S. Administrative Judge

Hon. Paul L. Brady

Occupational Safety and
Health Review Commission
Atlanta, GA 30303

Hon. Ralph Brown
Social Security Administration
Columbia, SC

Hon. Jesse H. Butler
Social Security
Office of Hearings and Appeals
477 Michigan Avenue
Detroit, MI 48226

Hon. Charles Cook
Hearing Officer, E.E.O.C.
1365 Ontario Street
Cleveland, OH 44114

Hon. Oliver T. Denning
Social Security Administration
Greensboro, NC

Hon. William Fowler
National Transportation Safety Board
Washington, DC

Hon. Elbert D. Gadsden
National Labor Relations Board
Washington, DC

Hon. William H. Harris
U.S. Maritime Commission

Hon. Julius A. Johnson
Department of Labor
Washington, DC

Hon. Harvey L. McCormick
Social Security Administration
Kansas City, MO

Gordon J. Myatt
National Labor Relations Board
450 Golden Gate Avenue
San Francisco, CA 94102

District of Columbia

District of Columbia Court of Appeals

500 Indiana Avenue, N.W.
Washington, DC 20001

Hon. Theodore R. Newman, Jr.
Chief Judge

Hon. Julia Cooper Mack

Hon. Hubert B. Pair
(Retired; sitting as visiting judge)

Hon. William C. Pryor

Superior Court of the District of Columbia

500 Indiana Avenue, N.W.
Washington, DC 20001

Hon. H. Carl Moultrie, I
Chief Judge

Hon. Shellie F. Bowers

Hon. John D. Fauntleroy

Hon. Eugene N. Hamilton
Hon. Margaret A. Haywood
Hon. Henry H. Kennedy, Jr.
Hon. Luke C. Moore
Hon. Carlisle E. Pratt
Hon. William S. Thompson
Hon. Annice M. Wagner
Hon. James A. Washington, Jr.
Hon. Paul R. Webber, III

Alabama

Circuit Court

Hon. Cain Kennedy
Mobile County Court House
Mobile, AL 36602

District Court

Hon. Aubrey Ford
Macon County District Court
Tuskegee, AL 36083

Hon. Nathaniel Owens
Calhoun County District Court
Anniston, AL 36202

Probate Court

Hon. William McKinley Branch
(nonlawyer)
Probate Court
Green County
Eutaw, AL 35462

Hon. Rufus C. Huffman
Probate Court
Bullock County
P.O. Box 71
Union Springs, AL 36089

Municipal Court

Hon. Frankie Fields
Associate Judge
Municipal Court
Mobile, AL

Hon. Charles Price
Assistant Judge
Municipal Court
Montgomery, AL

Recorder's Court

Hon. Orzell Billingsley, Jr.
Recorder's Court
Masonic Temple Building
Roosevelt City, AL

Hon. Peter A. Hall
Recorder's Court
City Hall
Birmingham, AL 35203

Hon. David H. Hood
Brighton, AL

Alaska

None

Arizona

City Court

Hon. Jean F. Williams
City Magistrate
12 North Fourth Avenue
Phoenix, AZ

Arkansas

Supreme Court

Hon. Richard L. Mays
Supreme Court
Justice Building
Little Rock, AR 72201

Court of Appeals

Hon. George Howard, Jr.
Court of Appeals
Justice Building
Little Rock, AR 72201

California

Supreme Court

Hon. Wiley W. Manuel
350 McAllister Street
San Francisco, CA 94102

Courts of Appeal

First Appellate District
4154 State Building
Civic Center
San Francisco, CA 94104
Hon. John J. Miller
Associate Justice, Division Two
Hon. Clinton W. White
Presiding Justice, Division Three

Second Appellate District
3580 Wilshire Boulevard
Room 301
Los Angeles, CA 90010
Hon. Bernard S. Jefferson
Presiding Justice, Division One
Hon. Arleigh Woods
Associate Justice, Division Four

Los Angeles County

CENTRAL DISTRICT

111 North Hill Street
Los Angeles, CA 90012
Hon. Gilbert Alston
Hon. David F. Cunningham
Hon. Stanley R. Malone, Jr.

Hon. Consuelo Marshall
Hon. Albert D. Matthews
Hon. Billy G. Mills
Hon. Henry Nelson

SOUTH CENTRAL DISTRICT

200 West Compton Boulevard
Compton, CA 90220
Hon. William Clay
Hon. Dion G. Morrow
Hon. William A. Ross

EASTERN DISTRICT

400 Civic Center Plaza
Pomona, CA 91766
Hon. Charles E. Jones
Hon. Loren Miller, Jr.
Hon. Florence Pickard
Hon. James Reese
Hon. Everett E. Ricks
Hon. Robert Roberson, Jr.
Hon. Charles Scarlett
Hon. Huey Shepard
Hon. Vaino Spencer
Hon. Leon Thompson

San Diego County
200 West Broadway
San Diego, CA 92101
Hon. Alpha Montgomery

Alameda County
1225 Fallon Street
Oakland, CA 94112
Hon. Richard Bancroft
Hon. Allen E. Broussard

Sacramento County
720 Ninth Street
Sacramento, CA 95814
Hon. William K. Morgan

San Francisco County
480 City Hall
San Francisco, CA 94102
Hon. John Dearman
Hon. Donald P. McCullum
Hon. Wilmont Sweeney

Berkeley-Albany Judicial District
2120 Grove Street
Berkeley, CA 94704
Hon. Dawn B. Girard

Oakland-Piedmont Judicial District
600 Washington Street
Oakland, CA 94607
Hon. Benjamin Travis
Hon. James S. White

Bay Judicial District

An antisegregation sit-in during the 1960s.

100–37th Street, Room 202
Richmond, CA 94805

Hon. George D. Carroll

Beverly Hills Judicial District
9355 Burton Way
Beverly Hills, CA

Hon. Charles Boags

Compton Municipal Court
200 West Compton Boulevard
Compton, CA 90220

Hon. Dean Farrar

Hon. Homer L. Garrot

Hon. Hugo E. Hill

Hon. G. Tom Thompson

Inglewood Municipal Court
1 Regent Street
Inglewood, CA 90301

Hon. Roosevelt F. Dorn

Hon. Roosevelt Robinson, Jr.

Long Beach Municipal Court
415 West Ocean Boulevard
Long Beach, CA 90802

Hon. William Dunn

Hon. Marcus O. Tucker

Los Angeles Judicial District
110 North Grand Avenue
Los Angeles, CA 90012

Hon. Ernest L. Aubry

Hon. Glenette Blackwell

Hon. Candace Cooper

Hon. Giles B. Jackson

Hon. Xenophon F. Lang

Hon. H. Randolph Moore

Hon. L. C. Nunley

Hon. Marion L. Obera

Hon. Everett M. Porter

Hon. Harold J. Sinclair

Hon. Sherman W. Smith, Jr.

Hon. Maxine Thomas

Central Judicial District
Hall of Justice
Room C-10
San Rafael, CA 94903

Hon. William H. Stephens

West Orange Judicial District
8141–13th Street
Westminster, CA 92638

Hon. Marvin G. Weeks

Sacramento County
720 Ninth Street, Room 102
Sacramento, CA 94814

Hon. Thomas G. Daugherty

Chino Division
13260 Central Avenue
Chino, CA 91710

Hon. Holly Graham

Victorville Division
14455 Civic Drive
Victorville, CA 92392

Hon. H. Trevor Hamilton

El Cajon Judicial District
110 East Lexington Avenue
El Cajon, CA 92020

Hon. Elizabeth Riggs

San Diego Judicial District
220 West Broadway
San Diego, CA 92101

Hon. Napoleon A. Jones, Jr.

Stockton Judicial District

222 East Weber Avenue
Room 200
Stockton, CA 95202

Hon. John F. Cruikshank, Jr.

Southern Judicial District
800 North Humbolt Street
San Mateo, CA 94401

Hon. Phrasel L. Shelton

Central District
111 North Hill Street
Los Angeles, CA 90012

Hon. Hugh E. MacBeth, Jr.
Family Law

Hon. Donald F. Pitts
Juvenile-Justice

South Central District
Juvenile Court
200 West Compton Boulevard
Compton, CA 90220

Hon. James A. Braggs

Hon. Ivy G. Roberts

South Gate Branch
8640 California Avenue
South Gate, CA 90280

Hon. Charles A. Pope

Inglewood Branch
1 Regent Street
Inglewood, CA 90301

Hon. Wardell G. Moss

Hon. Vince M. Townsend, Jr.

Colorado

District Court

City-County Building
Denver, CO 80202

Hon. Gilbert A. Alexander
Hon. James C. Flanigan
Hon. Raymond D. Jones

Juvenile Court

Hon. Morris E. Cole
Denver Juvenile Court
City-County Building
Denver, CO 80202

Quasi-Judicial Officers

Daniel E. Muse
Member Public Utility Commission
1525 Sherman St., 3rd Floor
Denver, CO 80203

Connecticut

Superior Court

Hon. Robert D. Glass
365 Buckingham Street
Oakville, CT

Hon. William D. Graham
95 Tower Avenue
Hartford, CT 06120

Hon. Robert L. Levister
874 Schofield Town Road
Stamford, CT

Hon. L. Scott Melville
100 Chatham Terrace
Bridgeport, CT 06606

Hon. Fleming L. Norcutt, Jr.
15 Birch Drive
New Haven, CT 06515

Hon. William B. Ramsey
c/o Clerk, Superior Court
355 Main Street
West Haven, CT 06516

Delaware

Municipal Court

Hon. Leonard L. Williams
Associate Judge
Wilmington Municipal Court
1020 King Street
Wilmington, DE 19801

Justices of the Peace

Kent County
Hon. Courtney P. Houston, Jr.
Senior Justice
Dover, DE

New Castle County
Hon. Robert F. Jackson
Wilmington, DE

Hon. Rosilyn L. Toulson
Wilmington, DE

Sussex County
Hon. Robert F. Handy
Seaford, DE

Florida

District Courts of Appeal

Hon. Leander Shaw
First District Court of Appeals
Supreme Court Building
Tallahassee, FL 32304

Circuit Courts

Hon. Henry L. Adams, Jr.
Duval County Courthouse
Jacksonville, FL

Hon. Wilkie Ferguson
Dade County Courthouse
Miami, FL

Hon. Henry Latimer
Broward County Courthouse
Fort Lauderdale, FL

Hon. Thomas J. Reddick
Broward County Courthouse
Fort Lauderdale, FL

Hon. Edward Rogers
Palm Beach County Courthouse
West Palm Beach, FL

Hon. James B. Sanderlin
Pinellas County Courthouse
Clearwater, FL

Hon. Emerson R. Thompson, Jr.
Orange County Courthouse
Orlando, FL

County Courts

Hon. Perry A. Little
Hillsborough County Courthouse
Tampa, FL

Hon. Calvin R. Mapp
Dade County
1125 N.W. 88th Street
Miami, FL

Hon. Stephen Mickle
204 University Drive
Gainesville, FL 32601

Hon. Frank H. White
Pinellas County Building
St. Petersburg, FL 33701

Quasi-Judicial Officers

Hon. William Johnson
Deputy Commissioner
Bureau of Workmen's Compensation
Miami, FL

Georgia

Superior Courts

Hon. E. H. Gasden

Eastern Judicial Circuit
Chatham County Courthouse
Savannah, GA 31402

Hon. Issac Jenrette
Atlanta Judicial Circuit
136 Pryor Street, S.W.
Atlanta, GA 30303

State Court

Hon. William H. Alexander
State Court of Fulton County
Room 68, State Court Building
Atlanta, GA 30303

Probate Court

Hon. Edith Jacqueline Ingram
Probate Court of Hancock County
718 New Street
Sparta, GA 31087

Juvenile Court

Hon. Romae Turner Powell
Juvenile Court of Fulton County
445 Capitol Avenue, S.W.
Atlanta, GA 30312

Municipal Courts

Atlanta
Hon. Edward Baety
(Traffic Court)
104 Trinity Avenue, S.W.
Atlanta, GA 30303

Hon. Thelma Cummings
(Traffic Court)
104 Trinity Avenue, S.W.
Atlanta, GA 30303

Hon. Clarence Cooper
175 Decatur Street, S.E.
Atlanta, GA 30303

Hon. Louise Hornsby
(Traffic Court)
104 Trinity Avenue, S.W.
Atlanta, GA 30303

Hon. J. L. Jordan
(Part-time)
244 Ashby Street, N.W.
Atlanta, GA 30314

Hon. W. M. Matthews, Jr.
(Part-time)
197½ Auburn Avenue, N.E.
Atlanta, GA 30303

Macon
Hon. Thomas Jackson
(Part-time)
P. O. Box 247
Macon, GA 31201

Hon. Earlene Montgomery
Referee, Juvenile Court

of Fulton County
445 Capitol Avenue, S.W.
Atlanta, GA 30312

Hawaii

None

Idaho

None

Illinois

Illinois Appellate Court

Daley Civic Center
Chicago, IL 60602

Hon. Calvin C. Campbell
Hon. Glenn T. Johnson
Hon. Kenneth E. Wilson

Circuit Court

Cook County
Daley Civic Center
Chicago, IL 60602

Hon. Archibald J. Carey
Hon. James D. Crosson
Hon. William Cousins, Jr.
Hon. Russell R. DeBow
Hon. Charles J. Durham
Hon. Charles Freeman
Hon. Marion W. Garnett
Hon. Arthur Hamilton
Hon. E. C. Johnson
Hon. Mark E. Jones
Hon. Sidney A. Jones, Jr.
Hon. Howard M. Miller
Hon. William E. Peterson
Hon. R. Eugene Pincham
Hon. Maurice Pompey
Hon. Albert S. Porter
Hon. Earl Strayhorn
Hon. Lucia T. Thomas
Hon. William S. White
Presiding Judge
Juvenile Division
Hon. Willie Whiting
Hon. James M. Walton

Circuit Court Associate Judges

Cook County
Daley Civic Center
Chicago, Illinois 60602

Hon. Clarence Bryant
Hon. Lawrence Chambers

Hon. Chauncey Eskridge
Hon. Marvin E. Gavin
Hon. Joseph W. Handy

Downstate Illinois
Hon. Louis K. Fontenot
12th Judicial Circuit
P.O. Box 417
Joliet, IL 60431
Hon. Billy Jones
20th Judicial Circuit
City Hall
East St. Louis, IL 62203
Hon. James L. Harris
Hon. Blanche M. Manning
Hon. John W. Rogers
Hon. Alvin H. Turner
Hon. Claude E. Wittaker
Hon. Milton Wharton
20th Judicial Circuit
East St. Louis, IL 62203
Hon. Clayton R. Williams
3rd Judicial Circuit
Alton, IL

Quasi-Judicial Officers

Hon. Ted Black
Commissioner
Illinois Industrial Commission
160 North LaSalle Street
Room 1201
Chicago, IL

Indiana

Superior Court

Hon. J. Chester Allen, Jr.
St. Joseph County
City-County Building
South Bend, IN 46601
Hon. Webster L. Brewer
Marion County City-County Building
Indianapolis, IN 46204
Hon. James C. Kimbrough
Lake County
2293 North Main Street
Crown Point, IN 46307

Municipal Court

Hon. Taylor Baker, Jr.
City-County Building
Indianapolis, IN 46204
Hon. Clarence D. Bolden
City-County Building
Indianapolis, IN 46204
Hon. John T. Grimes
City Court
Kokomo, IN

Hon. Frederick T. Work
1300 Broadway
Gary, IN

Justice of the Peace

Hon. Hoyt Brown
35 West Fifth Street
Gary, IN

Iowa

District Court

Hon. Luther T. Glanton, Jr.
Fifth Judicial District
Polk County Courthouse
Fifth and Mulberry Street
Des Moines, IA 50309

District Court Magistrates

Hon. George L. Stigler
Judicial Magistrate
First Judicial District
Black Hawk County Courthouse
Waterloo, IA
Hon. Emmit J. George
Judicial Magistrate (part-time)
Sixth Judicial District
Johnson County Courthouse
Iowa City, IA 52240

Kansas

Court of Appeals

Hon. Sherman A. Parks
Statehouse
Topeka, KS 66612

District Court

Hon. Cordell D. Meeks, Sr.
29th Judicial District
Wyandotte County Courthouse
Kansas City, KS 66101

Municipal Courts

Hon. Cordell D. Meeks, Jr.
Kansas City, KS
Hon. John E. Pyles
Wichita, KS

Kentucky

Circuit Court

Jefferson County
Hall of Justice
600 West Jefferson Street
Louisville, KY 40202

Hon. Charles H. Anderson
Hon. Benjamin F. Shobe

District Courts

Hon. J. Daniel S. Massie
Christian County District Court
Hopkinsville, KY

Hon. William E. McAnulty, Jr.
Jefferson County District Court
Louisville, KY 40402

Hon. Prather Walker
Fayette County District Court
Lexington, KY

Quasi-Judicial Officers

Hon. Darryl T. Owens
Commissioner
Kentucky Workmen's Compensation
Board
1300 West Broadway Street
Louisville, KY 40203

Louisiana

District Courts

Hon. Israel M. Augustine, Jr.
Criminal District Court
Parish of Orleans, Section I
2700 Tulane Avenue
New Orleans, LA 70119

Hon. Lionel Collins
24th Judicial District Court
Jefferson Parish, Division L
New Gretna Court House
Gretna, LA 70053

Hon. Paul Lynch
First Judicial District Court
Caddo Parish Court House
Suite 300C
Shreveport, LA 71101

Hon. Revius O. Ortique
Civil District Court
Orleans Parish, Division H
421 Loyola Avenue
New Orleans, LA 70112

Limited Trial Court Judges

District Court Magistrate
Hon. Nils R. Douglas
Criminal District Court Parish of
Orleans
2700 Tulane Avenue
New Orleans, LA 70112

Juvenile Court
Hon. Joan Bernard Armstrong
Juvenile Court for the Parish of
Orleans
421 Loyola Avenue
New Orleans, LA 70112

Commissioner

Hon. Norbert C. Rayford

19th Judicial Circuit
Baton Rouge, LA

Maine

None

Maryland

Court of Appeals

Hon. Harry A. Cole
Court of Appeals Building
Annapolis, MD 21401

Court of Special Appeals

Hon. David T. Mason
Court of Appeals Building
Annapolis, MD 21401

Circuit Court

Eighth Judicial Circuit
Supreme Bench of Baltimore City
Courthouse
Baltimore, MD 21202
Hon. Milton B. Allen
Hon. Solomon Baylor

Seventh Judicial Circuit
Hon. James H. Taylor
Prince George's County
Court House
Upper Marlboro, MD 20870
Hon. John R. Hargrove
Hon. Robert B. Watts

District Court

District One
211 E. Madison Street
Baltimore, MD 21202
Hon. Robert M. Bell
Hon. James L. Bundy
Hon. William H. Murphy

District Five
Hon. Sylvania W. Woods
Prince George's County
Upper Marlboro, MD 20870

Orphans Court of Baltimore City

Court House
Baltimore, MD 20202
Hon. Benjamin Foreman
Hon. Archie D. Williams

Orphans Court, Juvenile Division

Calvert and Fayette Streets
Baltimore, MD 21202
Hon. Leonard A. Briscoe, Master
Hon. Paul A. Smith, Jr., Master

Massachusetts

Appeals Court

Hon. Frederick L. Brown
New Courthouse
Pemberton Square
Boston, MA 02108

Superior Court

New Courthouse
Pemberton Square
Boston, MA 02108
Hon. Joseph S. Mitchell
Hon. Rudolph F. Pierce

District Courts

*Third District Court of Eastern
Middlesex*
40 Thorndike Street
Cambridge, MA 02141
Hon. James W. Bailey
Hon. Marie Jackson
Hon. Baron H. Martin
Wareham District Court
West Wareham, MA 02576
Hon. George A. Sheehy
Springfield District Court
50 State Street
Springfield, MA 01103
Hon. Herbert E. Tucker
Dorchester District Court
510 Washington Street
Dorchester, MA 02124

Roxbury District Court
85 Warren Street
Roxbury, MA 02119
Hon. Richard L. Banks
Hon. Julian T. Houston
Hon. Elwood S. McKenney

Boston Municipal Court

380 Old Court House
Boston, MA 02108
Hon. Harry J. Elam
Chief Justice
Hon. Margaret Burnham

Massachusetts Juvenile Courts

Bristol County Juvenile Courts
Hon. Ronald D. Harper
26 North Sixth Street
New Bedford, MA 02740

Boston Juvenile Court
Hon. Roderick Ireland
Suffolk County Courthouse
Boston, MA 02108

Michigan

Circuit Courts

Wayne County
City-County Building
Detroit, MI 48226

Hon. Charles S. Farmer

Hon. Harold Hood

Hon. Myron H. Wahls

Genesee County
Hon. Ollie B. Bivins, Jr.
120 E. Fifth Street
Flint, MI 48502

Kent County
Hon. John T. Letts
333 Monroe Avenue, N.W.
Grand Rapids, MI 49503

Recorder's Court of Detroit

Frank Murphy Hall of Justice
Detroit, MI 48226

Criminal Division
Hon. Evelyn K. Cooper

Hon. George W. Crockett, III

Hon. Robert L. Evans

Hon. Geraldine Bledsoe Ford

Hon. Samuel C. Gardner, Chief Judge

Hon. Henry L. Heading, Recorder

Hon. Donald L. Hobson

Hon. Vera Massey Jones

Hon. Clarence Laster, Jr.

Hon. Warfield Moore, Jr.

Hon. Dalton A. Roberson

Hon. James E. Roberts

Hon. Craig S. Strong

Hon. Edward M. Thomas

Hon. Leonard Townsend

Traffic and Ordinance Division
Hon. William C. Hague
600 Randolph Street
Detroit, MI 48226

Probate Court
Hon. Willis F. Ward
City-County Building
Detroit, MI 48226

Common Pleas Court of Detroit
Room 1107
2 Woodward
Detroit, MI 48226

Hon. Frederick E. Byrd
Chief Judge

Hon. Arthur Bowman

Hon. John Cozart, Jr.

Hon. Theresa Doss

Hon. John A. Murphy

Hon. Lucille Watts

District Courts

Hon. Christopher Brown
50th District Court
Pontiac, MI

Hon. Shelton C. Penn
10th District Court
Marshall, MI

Hon. Charles A. Pratt
8th District Court
277 West Michigan Avenue
Kalamazoo, MI 49006

Hon. William S. Price, III
68th District Court
1010 Beach Street
Flint, MI 48502

Quasi-Judicial Officers

Recorder's Court
Hon. William A. Haley, Jr., Referee
Traffic and Ordinance Division
Detroit, MI 48226

Probate Court

JUVENILE DIVISION

Detroit, MI 48226

Hon. Clinton Carter, Referee

Hon. Prentis Edwards
Probate Register

Hon. Carl E. Hall, Referee

Hon. Frances Pitts, Referee

*Michigan Workmen's Compensation
Commission*
Detroit, MI 48226

Hon. Andrew Foster
Administrative Judge

Hon. Claudia Morcom
Administrative Judge

*Michigan Employment Security
Commission*
Hon. A. Glenn Epps, Referee
Lansing, MI

Hon. Jeanne C. Harbour
Board of Review
Detroit, MI

Hon. Robert Powell, Referee
Kalamazoo, MI

Hon. Elisha Scott, Jr., Referee
Flint, MI

Hon. Raymond K. Sewell, Jr.,
Referee
Detroit, MI

Minnesota

District Courts

Hon. Stephen L. Maxwell
District Court, Ramsey County
St. Paul, MN 55102

Hon. William S. Posten
District Court, Hennepin County
Minneapolis, MN 55416

Quasi-Judicial Officers

Milton G. Dunham, Referee
Family Court, Hennepin County
Minneapolis, MN 55416

Mississippi

County Court

Hon. Reuban Anderson
Hinds County Courthouse
Jackson, MS 39201

Justice of the Peace Courts

Hon. Irma L. Inge
District 3, P. O. Box 48
Mound Bayou, MS 38762

Missouri

Circuit Courts

Circuit 16
415 East 12th Street
Kansas City, MO 64106

Hon. Lewis Clymer

Circuit 22
Civil Courts Building
12th and Market Street
St. Louis, MO 63101

Hon. Daniel T. Tillman

Circuit Court—Associate Judges
Hon. Michael Calvin
St. Louis, MO

Hon. Harold Fullwood
St. Louis, MO

Municipal Courts

Hon. Leonard S. Hughes, Jr.
Kansas City, Missouri

Hon. Rita Montgomery
St. Louis, Missouri

Hon. Leonard S. Hughes, III
Kansas City, Missouri

Hon. Virgil H. Lucas
St. Louis, Missouri

Montana

None

Nebraska

Municipal Court

Hon. Elizabeth D. Pittman
Omaha, NE

Nevada

District Court

Hon. Addleliar D. Guy
Department 11
200 East Carson
Las Vegas, NV 89101

New Hampshire

District Court

Hon. Ivorey Cobb
Colebrook District Court
Colebrook, NH 03576

New Jersey

Superior Court

Newark
Hon. Van Y. Clinton
Hon. Robert B. Johnson

County Court

Union County
Elizabeth, NJ
Hon. James H. Coleman, Jr.
Hon. Wm. Fillmore Wood

Essex County
Newark, NJ
Hon. Harry Hazelwood, Jr.

District Court

Hon. Herbert S. Jacobs
Atlantic County Court
1201 Bacharach Boulevard
Atlantic City, NJ 08401

Juvenile and Domestic Relations Court

Hon. Donald King
Essex County
Newark, NJ

Hon. Samuel C. Scott
Hudson County
Jersey City, NJ 07306

Municipal Courts

Newark
Hon. Irving B. Booker
Hon. Milton A. Buck

Camden
Hon. Theodore Davis

East Orange
Hon. Hamlet E. Goore
Hon. John J. Teare
Hon. Kenneth Williams

Jersey City
Hon. Shirley Tollentino
Hon. Betty Lester
Hon. Chester A. Morrison

Quasi-Judicial Officers

Department of State, Office of Administrative Law
Hon. Gerald I. Jarrett
185 Washington Street
Newark, NJ 07102

Hon. Geneva Stanford
185 Washington Street
Newark, NJ 07102

Hon. Augustus Thomas
88 East State Street
Trenton, NJ 08625

New Mexico

None

New York

Supreme Court

Hon. Herbert B. Evans
Chief Administrative Judge of
the Courts of the State of New York
270 Broadway
New York, NY 10007

First District, New York County

100 Centre Street
New York, NY 10013
Hon. Fritz W. Alexander, II
Hon. Amos E. Bowman
Hon. Thomas Dickens
Hon. Edward R. Dudley
Also assigned to Appellate Term,
1st Department
Hon. David H. Edwards, Jr.

First District, Bronx County

851 Grand Concourse
Bronx, NY 10451
Hon. Howard E. Bell
Hon. Andrew R. Tyler
Hon. Jawn A. Sandifer
Also assigned Dept. Administrative
Judge of the Criminal Court of the
City of New York
Hon. Clifford A. Scott
Hon. George Bundy Smith

Hon. Oliver C. Sutton
Hon. Albert P. Williams

Second District, Kings County

360 Adams Street
Brooklyn, NY 11201
Hon. Thomas R. Jones
Hon. William C. Thompson
Also designated Administrative
Judge, 2nd District

Second District, Kings County

Civic Center, Montague Street
Brooklyn, NY 11201
Hon. Charles B. Lawrence
Hon. Franklin W. Morton, Jr.
Hon. James H. Shaw

Eighth District, Erie County

Hon. Samuel L. Green
Buffalo, NY

Ninth District, Westchester County

Hon. Harold L. Wood
111 Grove Street
White Plains, NY 10601

Tenth District, Nassau County

Hon. Alfred S. Robbins
County Courthouse
Mineola, NY 11501

Eleventh District, Queens County

125–01 Queens Boulevard
Kew Gardens
Queens, NY 11415
Hon. Kenneth N. Browne
Hon. W. Eugene Sharpe

Court of Claims

Hon. Dorothy A. Cropper
111 Centre Street
New York, NY 10013

Civil Court of the City of New York

New York County
111 Centre Street
New York, NY 11201
Hon. Kenneth L. Shorter
Also Acting Supreme Court Justice
Hon. Thomas V. Sinclair, Jr.
Hon. Bruce McM. Wright

Kings County
141 Livingston Street
Brooklyn, NY 11201
Hon. George M. Fleary
Hon. Thaddeus Owens
Also Acting Supreme Court Justice
Hon. John L. Phillips

Queens County
Hon. Joscelyn E. Smith
120–55 Queens Boulevard
Kew Gardens
Queens, NY 11415

Criminal Court of the City of New York

New York County
100 Centre Street
New York, NY 10013

Hon. George D. Covington
Hon. Dennis Edwards, Jr.
Also Acting Supreme Court Justice
Hon. Leroy Kellam
Hon. William H. Loguen
Also Acting Supreme Court Justice
Hon. Albert R. Murray
Hon. Milton L. Williams
Also Acting Supreme Court Justice
Hon. Livingston L. Wingate

Kings County
120 Schermerhorn Street
Brooklyn, NY 11201

Hon. William H. Booth
Also Acting Supreme Court Justice
Hon. Lewis Douglas
Hon. Claudius S. Matthews

Bronx County
851 Grand Concourse
Bronx, NY 10451

Hon. Maurice Grey
Also Acting Supreme Court Justice

District Court

Hon. Marquette L. Floyd
Suffolk District Court
1000 Veterans Memorial Highway
Hauppauge, NY 11787

City Courts

Hon. Richard L. Baltimore, Jr.
City Court of New Rochelle
900 Beaufort Place
New Rochelle, NY 10801

Hon. Reuben K. Davis
City Court of Rochester
Rochester, NY

Hon. Barbara M. Sims
City Court of Buffalo
Buffalo, NY

Family Courts

New York City
60 Lafayette Street
New York, NY 10013

Hon. Peggy Davis
Hon. Elrich A. Eastman

Hon. Edith Miller
Hon. John F. Pollard
Hon. Phillip D. Roach
Hon. Joseph B. Williams
Also designated Administrative
Judge, Family Court,
New York County

New York County
283 Adams Street
Brooklyn, NY 11201

Hon. Cesar H. Quinones

Queens County
89–14 Parsons Boulevard
Jamaica, NY 11432

Hon. Reginald S. Matthews

North Carolina

Court of Appeals

Hon. Richard C. Erwin
P. O. Box 888
Raleigh, NC 27602

Superior Court

Hon. Clifton E. Johnson
6024 Croftbury Drive
Charlotte, NC 28215

Hon. Arthur Lane
Special Superior Court Judge
Cumberland County Courthouse
Fayetteville, NC 28305

District Courts

Hon. Elreta Alexander
18th Judicial District
Guilford County Courthouse
Greensboro, NC 27402

Hon. Stafford G. Bullock
10th Judicial District
5440 Dixon Drive
Raleigh, NC 27609

Hon. Karen Galloway
14th Judicial District
Durham County Courthouse
Durham, NC 27701

Hon. George R. Greene
10th Judicial District
2101 Lyndhurst Drive
Raleigh, NC 27610

Hon. William G. Pearson
14th Judicial District
126 Masondale Avenue
Durham, NC 27707

Hon. Donald Ramseur
27th Judicial District
1229 North Highland Street
Gastonia, NC 28052

Hon. Herbert L. Richardson
16th Judicial District
Robeson County Courthouse
Lumberton, NC 28358

Hon. T. Michael Todd
26th Judicial District
Mecklenburg County Courthouse
Charlotte, NC 28202

Hon. Joseph Williams
18th Judicial District
County Building
High Point, NC 27261

North Dakota

None

Ohio

Court of Appeals

Hon. Leo A. Jackson
Cuyahoga County Court House
Cleveland, OH 44113

Court of Common Pleas

Cuyahoga County
Justice Center
1200 Ontario Street
Cleveland, OH 44113

Hon. Lloyd O. Brown
Hon. Frederick M. Coleman

Lucas County
Hon. Robert V. Franklin
Adams and Erie Streets
Toledo, OH 43623

Stark County
Hon. Ira Turpin
Courthouse
Canton, OH 44702

Montgomery County
Hon. Arthur O. Fisher
Courthouse
Dayton, OH 45402

Juvenile Court

Hon. Leodis Harris
2163 E. 22nd Street
Cleveland, OH 44115

Municipal Courts

Cleveland Municipal Court
Justice Center
1200 Ontario Street
Cleveland, OH 44113

Hon. Lillian W. Burke
Hon. Jean M. Capers
Hon. C. Ellen Connally
Hon. Charles J. Doneghy

Municipal Court
Toledo, OH

Hon. H. Alfred Glascor
Municipal Court
Columbus, OH

Hon. Lloyd Haynes
Municipal Court
Youngstown, OH

Hon. Alice O. McCullum
Municipal Court
Dayton, OH 45402

Hon. Charles W. Fleming

Hon. Clarence Gaines

Hon. Sara J. Harper

Hon. Bush P. Mitchell
Municipal Court
335 West Third Street
Dayton, OH 45402

Hon. James A. Pearson
Municipal Court
90 West Broad Street
Columbus, OH 43215

Hon. Joseph Rhoulac
Municipal Court
City-County Safety Building
Akron, OH 44308

Quasi-Judicial Officers

Common Pleas Courts
Ramon Basie, Referee
Domestic Relations Court
Cuyahoga County Court House
Cleveland, OH 44113

Carol Buggs, Referee
Juvenile Court
2163 East 22nd Street
Cleveland, OH 44115

Lillian Greene, Referee
Probate Court
Cuyahoga County Court House
Cleveland, OH 44113

David Taylor, Referee
Domestic Relations Court
Toledo, OH

George Trumbo, Referee
1200 Ontario Street
Cleveland, OH 44113

Municipal Court
Justice Center
1200 Ontario Street
Cleveland, OH

Oklahoma

District Court

Hon. Charles L. Owens
District Seven, Oklahoma County

County Courthouse
Oklahoma City, OK 73102

Municipal Court

Hon. Albert V. Alexander
Associate Municipal Judge
Oklahoma City, OK 73102

Oregon

Circuit Court

Hon. Mercedes F. Deiz
Multonomah County
308 County Court House
Portland, OR 97204

District Court

Hon. Aaron Brown, Jr.
County Court House
Portland, OR 97204

Quasi-Judicial Officers

Hon. H. J. Belton Hamilton
Hearings Examiner
Social Security Department
1904 N. E. 45th Street
Portland, OR 97204

Pennsylvania

Supreme Court

Hon. Robert N. C. Nix, Jr.
362 City Hall
Philadelphia, PA 19107

Commonwealth Court of Pennsylvania

Hon. Robert W. Williams
392 City Hall
Philadelphia, PA 19107

Common Pleas

Philadelphia County
Philadelphia, PA 19107
Hon. Matthew W. Bullock, Jr.
Hon. Herbert R. Cain
Hon. Curtis C. Carson
Hon. Eugene H. Clarke
Hon. Paul A. Dandridge
Hon. Charles L. Durham
Hon. Levan Gordon
Hon. Doris M. Harris
Hon. Norman A. Jenkins
Hon. Julian F. King
Hon. Lawrence W. Prattis
Hon. Harvey Schmidt
Hon. Juanita Kidd Stout
Hon. Calvin T. Wilson
Hon. Charles Wright

Allegheny County
Pittsburgh, PA 15219
Hon. Thomas A. Harper
Hon. Livingston M. Johnson
Hon. Henry R. Smith, Jr.
Hon. J. Warren Watson

Montgomery County
Morristown, PA 19494
Hon. Horace A. Davenport

Delaware County
Media, PA 19063
Hon. Robert A. Wright

Municipal Court

One East Penn Square Building
Philadelphia, PA 19107
Hon. Lynwood F. Blount
Hon. Kenneth S. Harris
Hon. Ricardo C. Jackson

District Magistrate

Hon. Jacob Williams
2220 Wylie Avenue
Pittsburgh, PA 15219

Quasi-Judicial Officers

Duane Darkins
Referee, Workmen's Compensation
1510 State Office Building
Pittsburgh, PA 15222

Rhode Island

None

South Carolina

Circuit Court

Hon. Ernest A. Finney, Jr.
Third Judicial Circuit
P. O. Box 1355
Sumter, SC 29150

Family Court

Hon. Harold R. Boulware
5th Judicial Circuit
Route 1, Box 42
Irmo, SC 29603

Hon. Richard E. Fields
9th Judicial Circuit
P. O. Box 934
Charleston, SC 29402

Hon. Willie T. Smith, Jr.
13th Judicial Circuit
601 Jacob Road
Greenville, SC 29605

Magistrate Courts

Hon. Nathan H. Brown
Georgetown County
Route 2, Box 63
Pawleys Island, SC 29585

Hon. Thelma Cook
Fairfield County
Winnsboro, SC

Hon. John O. Johnston, Sr.
Charleston County
Route 1, Box 11
Adams Run, SC 29426

Hon. Eddie Kline
Beaufort County
Route 1
Seabrook, SC 29940

Hon. Verbena DeLee
Dorchester County
Ridgeville, SC 29477

Hon. Aaron Harvey
Charleston County
138 Spring Street
Charleston, SC 29403

Hon. LeRoy Linen
Charleston County
Route 1, Box 34
Wadmalaw Island, SC 29847

Hon. Hattie Sims
Richland County
Route 1, Box 166-B
Hopkins, SC 29061

Hon. Ernest Yarborough
Jasper County
Pineland, SC 29934

Tennessee

Supreme Court

Hon. George H. Brown, Jr.
Supreme Court Building, 3rd Floor
Seventh and Charlotte Streets
Nashville, TN 37219

Circuit Court

Shelby County
157 Poplar
Memphis, TN 38103

Hon. Arthur T. Bennett

Hon. H. T. Lockard

Hon. S. A. Wilbun

Davidson County
609 Metropolitan Courthouse
Nashville, TN 37201

Hon. A. A. Birch, Jr.

Hon. Robert E. Lillard

C. Anthony Johnson
City Court

128 Adams Street
Memphis, TN 38103

Texas

Court of Civil Appeals

Hon. Henry Doyle
Associate Justice
First Court of Civil Appeals
Civil Courts Building
Houston, TX 77002

District Court

Hon. Alice Bonner
80th District Court
Houston, TX

Hon. John W. Peavy, Jr.
246th District Court
Houston, TX

Hon. Thomas H. Routt
208th District Court
Houston, TX

Hon. Joan T. Winn
191st District Court
Dallas, TX

County Courts

Hon. Berland L. Brashear, Jr.
Criminal Court
Dallas County Courthouse
Dallas, TX

Hon. James L. Muldrow
Criminal Court at Law #6
Harris County
401 Caroline Street
Houston, TX 77002

Municipal Courts

Hon. Robert Anderson
Municipal Court
1400 Lubbock Street
Houston, TX 77002

Hon. Howard O. Banks
2014 Main, Room 210
Dallas, TX 75201

Hon. Charlye Farris
Municipal Court
921 Seventh Street
Wichita Falls, TX 76301

Hon. Maryellen Hicks
Municipal Court
Municipal Courts Building
Ft. Worth, TX 76116

Hon. Clarence McGowan
Municipal Court
City Hall
San Antonio, TX

Hon. Cleve Moten
Municipal Court

700 East Seventh Street
Austin, TX

Hon. Harriet Moore Murphy
Municipal Court
City Hall
Austin, TX

Hon. William J. Rice, Jr.
Municipal Court
1400 Lubbock Street
Houston, TX 77002

Hon. Roy Smith
Municipal Court
608 Fannin, Suite 2007
Houston, TX

Hon. Fred L. Tinsley
Municipal Court
7929 Brookriver Drive
Dallas, TX 75247

Hon. Fad Wilson
Municipal Court #5
1400 Lubbock Street
Houston, TX 77002

Justices of the Peace

Hon. George Allen
Sub-Courthouse, South Beckley
Dallas, TX

Hon. Cecil Bush
4900 Fannin Street
Houston, TX 77004

Hon. Alexander Green
Precinct 7, Position 2
5737 Cullen Boulevard
Houston, TX 77021

Hon. Richard E. Scott
Travis County
2113 E. M. L. King, Jr. Boulevard
Suite 104
Austin, TX 78702

Hon. Cleophus R. Steele
810 Main, Suite 623
Dallas, TX 75202

Quasi-Judicial Officers

Hon. Aldrinette Chapital
Master, Family District Court
Houston, TX 77002

Hon. Bonnie Fitch
Referee, Family District Court
Harris County Court
Houston, TX 77002

Hon. Gladys R. Goffney
Master, Family District Court
201 Main Street
Houston, TX 77002

Hon. Carolyn D. Hobson
Referee, Criminal District Court
Houston, TX 77002

Hon. Veronica Morgan
Referee, Juvenile Court of
Harris County
Family Law Center
Houston, TX 77002

Hon. Craig Washington
Master, Civil District Courts
Houston, TX 77002

Hon. Francis Williams
Master, Family District Court
Houston, TX 77002

Utah

None

Vermont

None

Virgin Islands
Territorial Court of the Virgin Islands

St. Thomas
Virgin Islands 00801

Hon. Alphonso Christian

Hon. Verne Hodge
Presiding Judge

St. Croix
Virgin Islands 00803

Hon. Raymond Finch

Hon. Antoine Joseph

Hon. Eileen R. Peterson

Virginia

Circuit Court

Hon. James Edward Sheffield
City of Richmond, Division I
Courts Building
Richmond, VA 23219

District Courts

Hon. Archie Elliot
General District Court

Portsmouth, VA 23704

Hon. Joseph A. Jordan, Jr.
General District Court
811 East City Hall Avenue
Norfolk, VA 23510

Hon. Thomas Monroe
General District Court
Courthouse
Arlington, VA 22201

Hon. James A. Overton
Substitute Judge
General District Court
623 Effingham Street
Portsmouth, VA 23704

Hon. William Stone
Substitute Judge
General District Court
P. O. Box HB
Williamsburg, VA 23185

Hon. I. Douglas Suggs
Substitute Judge
General District Court
South Boston, VA

Hon. Phillip Walker
Substitute Judge
General District Court
1715 25th Street
Hampton, VA

**Juvenile and Domestic Relations
District Courts**

Hon. Willard H. Douglas, Jr.
2000 Mecklenburg Street
Richmond, VA 23223

Hon. Roland D. Ealy
Substitute Judge
420 North First Street
Richmond, VA 23222

Hon. Leonard W. Lambert
Substitute Judge
2307 East Broad Street
Richmond, VA 23223

Hon. Lester V. Moore, Jr.
800 East City Hall Avenue

P. O. Box 3608
Norfolk, VA 23514

Washington

Superior Court

Hon. Herbert M. Stephens
King County Court House
Seattle, WA 98104

Municipal Court

Hon. Charles V. Johnson
Seattle Municipal Court
610 Third Avenue
Seattle, WA 98104

West Virginia

Magistrate Court Kanawha County

Hon. John Miller
City Building
South Charleston, WV

Hon. Nancy Starks
718 Morris Street
Charleston, WV 25301

Quasi-Judicial Officers

Hon. William L. Lonesome
Commissioner of Accounts
Kanawha County Probate Court
P. O. Box 241
Institute, WV 25112

Wisconsin

Circuit Court

Hon. Harold B. Jackson, Jr.
Civil Division
Milwaukee County Court House
3489 North Hackett
Milwaukee, WI 53211

Hon. Clarence R. Parrish
3322 North 105th Street
Milwaukee County Court House
Milwaukee, WI

President Lyndon B. Johnson signs the Voting Rights Act of 1965.

Table 1. Lynchings by State and Race: 1882–1962

State	Whites	Blacks	Total
Alabama	48	299	347
Arizona	31	0	31
Arkansas	58	226	284
California	41	2	43
Colorado	66	2	68
Delaware	0	1	1
Florida	25	257	282
Georgia	39	491	530
Idaho	20	0	20
Illinois	15	19	34
Indiana	33	14	47
Iowa	17	2	19
Kansas	35	19	54
Kentucky	63	142	205
Louisiana	56	335	391
Maryland	2	27	29
Michigan	7	1	8
Minnesota	5	4	9
Mississippi	40	538	578
Missouri	53	69	122
Montana	82	2	84
Nebraska	52	5	57
Nevada	6	0	6

Table 1 (*continued*)

State	Whites	Blacks	Total
New Jersey	0	1	1
New Mexico	33	3	36
New York	1	1	2
North Carolina	15	85	100
North Dakota	13	3	16
Ohio	10	16	26
Oklahoma	82	40	122
Oregon	20	1	21
Pennsylvania	2	6	8
South Carolina	4	156	160
South Dakota	27	0	27
Tennessee	47	204	251
Texas	141	352	493
Utah	6	2	8
Vermont	1	0	1
Virginia	17	83	100
Washington	25	1	26
West Virginia	20	28	48
Wisconsin	6	0	6
Wyoming	30	5	35
Total	1,294	3,442	4,736

No lynchings recorded as of July 19, 1963.

Table 2. Lynchings by Race and Year: 1882–1962

Year	Whites	Blacks	Total	Year	Whites	Blacks	Total
1882	64	49	113	1923	4	29	33
1883	77	53	130	1924	0	16	16
1884	160	51	211	1925	0	17	17
1885	110	74	184	1926	7	23	30
1886	64	74	138	1927	0	16	16
1887	50	70	120	1928	1	10	11
1888	68	69	137	1929	3	7	10
1889	76	94	170	1930	1	20	21
1890	11	85	96	1931	1	12	13
1891	71	113	184	1932	2	6	8
1892	69	161	230	1933	4	24	28
1893	34	118	152	1934	0	15	15
1894	58	134	192	1935	2	18	20
1895	66	113	179	1936	0	8	8
1896	45	78	123	1937	0	8	8
1897	35	123	158	1938	0	6	6
1898	19	101	120	1939	1	2	3
1899	21	85	106	1940	1	4	5
1900	9	106	115	1941	0	4	4
1901	25	105	130	1942	0	6	6
1902	7	85	92	1943	0	3	3
1903	15	84	99	1944	0	2	2
1904	7	76	83	1945	0	1	1
1905	5	57	62	1946	0	6	6
1906	3	62	65	1947	0	1	1
1907	2	58	60	1948	1	1	2
1908	8	89	97	1949	0	3	3
1909	13	69	82	1950	1	1	2
1910	9	67	76	1951	0	1	1
1911	7	60	67	1952	0	0	0
1912	2	61	63	1953	0	0	0
1913	1	51	52	1954	0	0	0
1914	4	51	55	1955	0	3	3
1915	13	56	69	1956	0	0	0
1916	4	50	54	1957	1	0	1
1917	2	36	38	1958	0	0	0
1918	4	60	64	1959	0	1	1
1919	7	76	83	1960	0	0	0
1920	8	53	61	1961	0	1	1
1921	5	59	64	1962	0	0	0
1922	6	51	57	Total	1,294	3,442	4,736

Table 3. Causes of Lynchings Classified: 1882–1962

Year	Homicides	Felonious Assault	Rape	Attempted Rape	Robbery and Theft	Insult to White Persons	All Other Causes
1882	54	0	33	0	16	0	10
1883	71	0	24	3	4	0	28
1884	62	0	36	0	10	0	103
1885	91	2	28	0	1	0	62
1886	70	1	32	0	8	0	27
1887	54	0	41	0	6	0	19
1888	62	0	31	0	3	4	37
1889	73	1	34	6	10	1	45
1890	35	0	31	2	5	0	23
1891	58	14	39	2	12	0	58
1892	93	3	49	12	15	1	57
1893	60	2	34	4	8	2	42
1894	75	1	37	12	5	1	61
1895	68	0	34	13	7	0	57
1896	39	6	35	6	6	0	31
1897	67	2	26	9	14	2	38
1898	68	7	15	6	8	2	14
1899	43	2	17	9	7	1	27
1900	43	5	21	16	7	1	22
1901	51	7	17	8	10	0	37
1902	37	6	18	12	2	0	17
1903	50	7	15	8	0	1	18
1904	37	1	15	7	0	2	21
1905	32	3	11	7	2	0	7
1906	25	7	16	10	2	1	4
1907	16	7	12	12	14	1	8
1908	35	8	15	14	3	1	21
1909	46	5	14	5	3	4	5
1910	41	3	18	5	4	2	3
1911	36	3	6	7	3	4	8
1912	34	2	11	3	4	3	6
1913	25	4	7	3	1	1	11
1914	31	9	6	1	2	1	5
1915	27	9	11	6	9	3	4
1916	21	7	3	9	8	2	4
1917	7	3	7	6	1	6	8
1918	27	3	10	6	5	2	11
1919	29	8	9	10	1	7	19
1920	23	9	15	3	0	3	8
1921	19	8	16	3	0	3	15
1922	15	5	14	5	4	2	12
1923	5	5	6	1	1	2	13
1924	4	2	5	2	0	3	0
1925	8	1	4	2	0	1	1
1926	13	3	2	3	1	1	7
1927	7	2	2	3	0	0	2
1928	5	2	3	0	0	0	1
1929	1	3	3	0	0	2	1
1930	5	0	8	2	3	0	3
1931	5	3	0	5	0	0	0
1932	1	2	1	1	0	1	2
1933	8	4	3	3	1	1	8
1934	2	2	2	4	1	3	1
1935	8	1	3	3	0	1	4

Table 3 (*continued*)

Year	Homicides	Felonious Assault	Rape	Attempted Rape	Robbery and Theft	Insult to White Persons	All Other Causes
1936	1	0	3	3	0	1	0
1937	4	2	1	0	1	0	0
1938	3	0	1	0	0	1	1
1939	2	0	0	0	0	0	1
1940	0	0	0	1	0	1	3
1941	0	0	0	1	1	0	2
1942	1	1	0	3	0	0	1
1943	1	0	0	0	0	1	1
1944	2	0	0	0	0	0	0
1945	0	0	0	1	0	0	0
1946	0	1	0	0	2	0	3
1947	1	0	0	0	0	0	0
1948	0	0	0	0	1	0	1
1949	0	0	0	0	0	0	3
1950	0	0	0	0	0	0	2
1951	0	0	0	0	0	0	1
1952	0	0	0	0	0	0	0
1953	0	0	0	0	0	0	0
1954	0	0	0	0	0	0	0
1955	0	0	0	0	0	1	2
1956	0	0	0	0	0	0	0
1957	0	1	0	0	0	0	0
1958	0	0	0	0	0	0	0
1959	0	0	1	0	0	0	0
1960	0	0	0	0	0	0	0
1961	0	0	0	0	0	0	1
1962	0	0	0	0	0	0	0
Total	1,937	205	911	288	232	85	1,078

Compiled by the Department of Records and Research, Tuskegee Institute, Alabama.

Lynch mobs killed more than 3,300 people between 1882 and 1903, and lynching of blacks continued to be savagely common as late as 1935. Even between 1935 and 1962, 60 blacks were lynched, but no more of these atrocities have been reported since then.

Table 4. Number and Distribution of Black Judges: 1982

State	Federal Courts		State Courts				Total Black State Judges	Total Black Judges
	Appellate Court	Trial Court	Appellate Court	General Jurisdiction	Limited Jurisdiction	Special Courts		
Alabama		1			4		4	5
Arizona					1		1	1
Arkansas	2							2
California	5	1	1	28	34		61	67
Colorado				3	1		4	4
Connecticut				6	2		8	8
Delaware								
District of Columbia	3	4	2	12			14	23
Florida	1			7	4		11	12
Georgia				2	3		5	5
Illinois	3			35			35	38
Indiana				3			3	3
Iowa				1	2		3	3
Kansas	1			1			1	2
Kentucky				2	3		5	5
Louisiana				4	3		7	7
Maryland	2			5	6		11	13
Massachusetts	1			2	8		10	11
Michigan		1		20	10		30	31
Minnesota				2			2	2
Missouri				2	4		6	6
Nebraska								
Nevada				1			1	1
New Hampshire							1	1
New Jersey				2	1		3	3
New York		23						23
North Carolina	1			2	9		11	12
Ohio	1			5			6	7
Oklahoma				1			1	1
Oregon				1	1		2	2
Pennsylvania	2			21	4		25	27
South Carolina				1			1	1
Tennessee	1			5	1		6	7
Texas	1			4			5	5
Virginia				1	7		8	8
Washington				1	2		3	3
Virgin Islands								
West Virginia				5			5	5
Wisconsin				2			2	2
Totals	24	30	3	183	218		291	346

THE BLACK VOTER AND ELECTED OFFICEHOLDERS

The Current Picture ■ Evolution of the Black Vote ■ Coverage of the Voting Rights Act ■ The Black Lobby ■ The Joint Center for Political Studies ■ The Voter Education Project ■ The Congressional Black Caucus ■ Biographies of Current Black Congressmen ■ Black Congressmen of the Past ■ Black Elected Officeholders at the State Level ■ Biographies of Elected State Executives ■ List of State Legislators ■ Black Mayors ■ Biographies ■ Past and Present Appointed Officials and Diplomats ■ Other Prominent Political Personages

The high point of black political power in the 1970s was reached in 1976 when black voters cast some 90% of their vote for the Democratic candidate for president, Jimmy Carter, providing his margin of victory in such key states as Missouri, Pennsylvania, Ohio, Louisiana, Texas, Mississippi, and Maryland. It was true, as Vernon E. Jordan, president of the National Urban League, commented, that hands that had once picked cotton, picked a President. But as the 1980s began, black political power, at least on the national level, sustained what appeared to be a sharp decline when blacks emerged from the 1980 election as the only group to vote overwhelmingly for the soundly beaten incumbent, Jimmy Carter.

As one political analyst drew the analogy, blacks were about the only crew members still aboard when the *Titanic* went down. In fact, while the rest of the electorate was voting overwhelmingly for Ronald Reagan, blacks were casting 90% of their votes for

Carter, only 7% for Reagan, and 2% for independent candidate Congressman John Anderson.

That blacks voted so decisively for Carter, though they had ample reasons to be dissatisfied with the zeal with which he pursued programs and policies that were of importance to them during his term of office, was not surprising. The Reagan campaign, with its markedly conservative philosophy, its call for a return to states' rights, its coolness toward minorities, and the subtle hints that if Reagan was successful, his administration would be tilted toward the rich and the well-to-do, disturbed a large number of black voters who feared that their recent gains would be wiped out if Reagan moved into the White House.

So it was that when the Reagan Administration took office in January 1981 it was almost totally alienated from black political leadership and the black voter. This was something unique in American politics. Through all national administrations, dating back to

President Franklin D. Roosevelt, and including both Republican and Democratic Presidents, there had been black involvement of varying degrees, but never had there been such alienation.

For example, though President Nixon could never capture over 10% of the black vote, and despite his conservative rhetoric and such symbolic acts as dismantling the Office of Economic Opportunity, his record, in retrospect, was not all that bad. He created CETA, a massive public jobs program; made funds available for a number of minority-oriented job training programs; approved the Philadelphia Plan, which set affirmative action standards for government contractors; did not tamper with the enforcement of civil rights laws; and generally made first-class black appointments. True, his Administration could be accused of "benign neglect" toward blacks, but there was not a feeling of overt hostility. And when Nixon was forced from office in the wake of Watergate, his successor, President Ford, did not alter the basic racial policies of his predecessor.

The Reagan Administration, however, was a different matter. It took office owing no allegiance to the black voter and unwilling to listen to the voices of old-line black Republicans who were not cast in the conservative image. While it has been traditional for candidates, once they are elected to the Presidency, to reach out to those constituencies that did not vote for them in an effort to heal the partisan wounds, the Reagan Administration chose not to do this, refusing to even name an individual who would serve as liaison with the black community and embarking on a series of actions, such as its attacks on affirmative action and busing, that further alienated the black voters, whose approval of the Administration continued to decline, reaching a record low level of 7% at the end of 1981.

The inability of the black voter to exert any influence on the Reagan Administration, however, should not be interpreted as meaning that black political power as a force in America had become impotent. Several notable achievements were scored in the late 1970s and early 1980s and these will be discussed later.

To some degree, the loss of influence sustained at the national level during this period was offset by the continued increase of black elected officials at the state, county, and local levels. The number of black elected officials across the country increased by 2.6% between July 1980 and July 1981. From 1969, when the number of black elected officials was 1,160, the number had grown to 5,038 by July 1981.

Despite this, blacks still hold only 1.03% of all elective offices in the United States. While political progress has been steady, it has been painfully slow and has been concentrated primarily in the southern states, which contain 53% of the black population of the country as well as 61% of all its black elected officials.

The 1981 increases were concentrated in a few states. Mississippi had the largest net increase, 52. Georgia gained 43; Illinois and Kentucky each gained

Surprisingly, Richard Nixon's record in regard to programs affecting blacks was far better than that of Jimmy Carter.

17; Ohio gained 13; and Tennessee, 11. Other than these substantial gains, the overall picture remained fairly stable.

According to the Joint Center for Political Studies, as of July 1981, 340 blacks held state-level elected positions; 36 held regional offices; and 542 held judicial and law enforcement positions. By far the largest category of these officials is municipal officials. In 1981 they numbered 2,382, up from the previous year's total of 2,356. The second largest category of elected officials comprises education officials, who represent 25% of the total.

Black women make up about 20% of the total of black elected officials, and their rate of growth has exceeded that of men over the past decade—3.4% as compared to 2.4%. The women officeholders are concentrated in educational offices and hold relatively few judicial and law enforcement positions.

In Congress, black representation remained almost static between 1975 and 1982. The major loss during the period was that of Senator Edward Brooke (D. Mass.), the only black member of the Senate. He had been elected first in 1966 and again in 1972 from a state in which blacks constituted only 3% of the population. He was defeated in the Democratic primary in 1980.

Also lost from the ranks of national black political leadership during this period were such prominent members of Congress as Rep. Barbara Jordan (D. Tex.), who retired in 1978 because of ill health; Rep. Yvonne B. Burke (D. Cal.), who also retired in 1978; Rep. Charles Diggs (D. Mich.), who was forced to resign in 1980 after his conviction on charges of misappropriating federal funds; Rep. Andrew Young (D. Ga.), who gave up his seat in 1977 to serve as the U.S. Ambassador to the United Nations; Rep. Ralph Metcalfe (D. Ill.), who died in 1978; Rep. Robert Nix, (D. Pa.), who was defeated in the same year; and Rep. Shirley Chisholm (D. N.Y.), who retired in 1982.

The ranks of black mayors, however, showed an increase from 108 in 1974 to 109 at the end of 1982. The most symbolically important of the mayoral elections took place in Birmingham in 1979 when Richard Arrington was elected mayor of a city once regarded as the most violently racist in the nation. In another southern state, Louisiana, Ernest N. Dutch Morial became mayor of the largest city, New Orleans, in 1977, and was reelected in 1981. Atlanta elected its second successive black mayor in 1981 when Andrew Young was chosen to take over the office of Maynard Jackson, who could not succeed himself.

And also in 1981, Thirman L. Milner became the first black chief executive office of a major city in New England when he was elected mayor of Hartford, Connecticut.

There is no question but that blacks have made headway in the political arena. But the fact remains that by any standard of measurement, black political power, as the eighties began, had not reached its full potential. It had succeeded in many instances in making itself felt, but too many blacks were still unregistered and too many who were registered did not vote for blacks to exercise the political clout that they were capable of.

Still, blacks have made substantial progress in politics and this becomes evident by reviewing the history of black suffrage.

Evolution of Black Suffrage

The evolution of black American suffrage has had a long and varied history—not only at the national level, but within the individual states as well. These problems have not been confined to the South but have been an issue in every corner of the country.

At the close of the Revolutionary War, more than 1 million of the 3,250,000 people (excluding Indians) living in the United States were not yet free. These included 600,000 black slaves; 300,000 indentured servants, and 50,000 convicts. Of the more than 2 million free Americans, only 120,000 could meet the voting requirements established by individual states at that time. Generally, these requirements took into consideration the following factors: sex, age, residence, morality (character), property, religion, status of freedom, and race.

In the two decades following the end of the Revolutionary War, various criteria were established for voting participation and many previously franchised individuals lost their privilege. Among those denied the vote were non-U.S. citizens, members of the military, paupers, and the mentally impaired, as well as blacks.

The wave of disenfranchisements stemmed in large measure from the failure of the Founding Fathers to agree as to who would be allowed to take part in the critical function of self-government.

The prevailing opinions generally fell into two categories: one embracing those who were in favor of the creation of a strong central government by individual citizens entitled from the very outset to take part through the responsible exercise of the franchise; the other advocating the maintenance of a stable government brought to power by a select group of men whose rank and education made them suitable arbiters of the new nation's initial political course. The latter group feared "mob rule," and sought to make the extension of the franchise subject to a program of massive popular education. This outlook tended to prevail, and it was decided to extend to the states themselves the right to choose their own electorate.

By 1800 eight states had revised their constitutions and three new states had been admitted to the Union. New constitutions had been put into effect in Georgia and New Hampshire, both of which abandoned their property qualifications in favor of taxpaying requirements and also inserted specific provisions limiting the franchise to white males.

As appreciable numbers of blacks gained their freedom the situation deteriorated. Between 1792 and 1838, no less than nine states (generally those confined to the South and border areas) altered their constitutions to exclude blacks. Moreover, blacks were denied the ballot in every new state (except Maine) entering the Union between 1800 and 1861.

At the beginning of the Civil War, free black men were permitted to vote on a par with their white counterparts in only five states: Maine, Massachusetts, New Hampshire, Rhode Island, and Vermont.

The Civil War shattered the pattern of disenfranchising blacks. Some 4 million slaves were suddenly transformed into citizens possessing the right to vote. The radical wing of the Republican party, led by Senator Charles Sumner of Massachusetts and Representative Thaddeus Stevens of Georgia, was committed to Negro enfranchisement, and to a strict and punitive program for the South as well.

The Reconstruction Act, which divided the former Confederate states into military districts, also called for new constitutional conventions elected by permanently enfranchised male delegates, regardless of race. Within three years, the right to vote had been legalized by the Fifteenth Amendment to the U.S. Constitution, a measure which had its particular impact on the South but was not without application in the North.

Reconstruction and Backlash

Following the Civil War, blacks in the South voted in large numbers and elected many blacks to office. The degree of intelligence of black voters and the extent of integrity and competence of blacks elected during Reconstruction has been questioned by many historians in the past. However, present-day reassessments indicate that the performance of Reconstruction blacks has been evaluated with a southern bias. Actually many Reconstruction blacks performed competently and with integrity.

The attempt to discredit black voters and officeholders, according to the late Dr. William DuBois, reflected fear among many whites that blacks would earn a reputation for effective leadership. As DuBois once put it, "If there was one thing South Carolina feared more than bad Negro government it was good Negro government."

Such white self-interest and prejudice, plus the ex-

cesses of Reconstruction, eventually produced the backlash in the South which succeeded in undermining the Fifteenth Amendment and depriving blacks of the vote.

Perhaps the greatest force motivating the disenfranchisement of blacks was the threat posed to the Southern Democratic party by the possibility of a political alliance between the Populist Party and the Republicans. In such an alliance, it was believed that the black would hold the balance of power—a fact which induced most southern states to close ranks behind the concept of racial exclusion at the polls.

Rise in Consciousness

There was a sharp rise in black political consciousness during the 1960s, due in part to the enthusiasm generated by the Civil Rights Movement in the South and the community organization that was going on in the cities as part of the War on Poverty. The first major victories came in 1967 when Carl Stokes was elected mayor of Cleveland, Ohio, and Richard Hatcher took over City Hall in Gary, Indiana, as the nation's first black elected mayors of major cities. In both instances, it was organized black political strength that made victory possible.

In the early 1970s, black political participation became more sophisticated. The Voter Education Project was formed in Atlanta with the express purposes of getting more blacks registered and assisting black candidates elected to political office in the South. The Joint Center for Political Studies in Washington, D.C., sponsored by Howard University and subsidized by the Ford Foundation, provided information of importance to black voters and to officeholders and methods of distributing such information. The Lawyers Com-

Freedmen learning of their political rights.

"THE FIRST VOTE."—Drawn by A. R. Waud.—[See next page.]   (Harper's Weekly)

Following the Civil War, blacks voted in large numbers in the South.

mittee for Civil Rights Under Law, a national organization, offered assistance to lawyers involved in the litigating of matters related to various aspects of the political rights of groups and candidates. The Congressional Black Caucus was formed to lobby the view of blacks elected to the House of Representatives.

Other victories were also achieved, most notably as Kenneth Gibson was elected Mayor of Newark in 1970, and Coleman Young and Maynard Jackson were elected mayors of Detroit and Atlanta, respectively, in 1973.

Blacks climbed aboard the Jimmy Carter bandwagon early in 1976 and their 90% vote for him nailed down the Presidency for the Georgian. Blacks, quite reasonably, expected that their support would earn them some consideration from the Carter Administra-

tion, and it did. During his Administration, Carter appointed more black federal judges than all other Presidents combined, placed hundreds of blacks in key positions throughout his Administration, and backed domestic programs of special concern to blacks.

Personally responsive to black interests, Carter was also a pragmatist, and faced with the worsening economic picture, the growth of conservatism in the country, and his own declining popularity among the voters, his positions grew increasingly conservative, thus alienating some of his black support, which became critical of him.

A further sign of the growing black political maturity was evident in February 1980, during an election year, when the Black Leadership Forum took the initiative in calling together in Richmond, a National Con-

This old illustration of a black orator addressing voters before a Reconstruction election shows the white southern bias, which tried to discredit the electoral performance of newly enfranchised blacks; nevertheless, many blacks performed competently and with integrity both as voters and as members of Congress.

ference on a Black Agenda for the Eighties. Other convenors were the National Council of Negro Women, the National Conference of Black Mayors, the National Black Caucus of State Legislators, and the Congressional Black Caucus. More than 1,000 blacks, representing over 300 organizations, gathered to formulate an agenda on domestic and international issues of special concern to blacks. With so many diverse groups taking part, there were fears that it would be impossible to hammer out such an agenda, but the Conference succeeded in achieving an unprecedented consensus on the broad issues with which blacks should be concerned in the 1980s.

The agenda went far beyond the traditional civil rights concerns and advocated (1) domestic and foreign economic policies aimed at providing full employment opportunities and opportunities for development of black entrepreneurship; (2) reassessment of federal programs to improve the quality of education available to minorities, and provision of adequate financial assistance and health care for the needy; (3) curtailment

of U.S. interaction with South Africa, and extension of a more equitable program of economic assistance to Caribbean countries; (4) steps by the government and political parties to mobilize the electorate and increase opportunities for full minority participation in the political process.

The nominating conventions of the two major parties had not been held yet but the major Democratic and Republican candidates were invited to address the Conference—Ronald Reagan, George Bush, President Carter, and Senator Edward Kennedy. Congressman John Anderson, the independent, was also invited. While each of the candidates sent observers, none attended, presumably because they might have been placed in the position of responding to the Conference agenda, which would not have been a politically feasible thing to do at that point in the campaign.

And even at that early point in the campaign, it was generally agreed that Carter was the front-runner, trailed by Kennedy, who was a popular favorite but lacked organized black support. Carter won 90% of the black vote in the general election that November, but went down to defeat in the Reagan landslide, bringing new problems for black political power. The Reagan Administration virtually ignored blacks. Only a handful of blacks, selected primarily because of their conservative leanings, were appointed to visible positions within the Administration. In addition, the Administration took several actions, including an ill-advised attempt to grant tax-exempt status to schools that discriminate because of race, which demonstrated its lack of concern for blacks.

The Administration seemed perfectly willing to write off black political power as a force to be reckoned with until it was jolted by the gubernatorial election in 1981 in Virginia. The governor's office had been controlled by Republicans for nearly two decades, but the Republican candidate made the mistake of not endorsing the Voting Rights Act and of making subtle racial statements that angered the black electorate. As a result, it turned out in record number to hand the victory to the Democratic candidate, Charles Robb, a son-in-law of the late President Johnson.

This evidence of disenchantment with the Republican Party disturbed Republican leadership on two levels. First, while blacks generally vote Democratic, this is not always the case. Moderate Republicans have in fact done very well with black voters. Governor Dick Thornburg of Pennsylvania and Senators Charles Percy of Illinois, Charles Mathias of Maryland, and Jacob Javits of New York (before he was defeated in a primary election in 1980) have always done very well with black voters. Therefore, it was not that blacks would not vote Republican, it was more a matter of who they were voting for. This was clearly a sign that under the right circumstances, blacks could be attracted to the GOP. It made sense, therefore, for the Republicans to capitalize on this rather than writing off the black vote as a lost cause.

Second, the alienation of blacks from the Republican ranks worried its moderate faction, which did not want the party to become all white or to project a racist image. From a purely pragmatic position, the moderates argued that the party could not afford to write off the black vote, not if it ever intended to establish itself as the predominant party.

This line of thinking led to high-level meetings in the White House early in 1982 for the express purpose of mending fences with the black community. One of the first moves was to make several key black appointments of individuals who would relate to the black community—appointments the Reagan Administration had once vowed it would never make.

What lies ahead for blacks in the 1980s in the political arena depends on how skillfully they can utilize their political strength, and to what degree. The single most important lesson the 1980 election taught was that in a landslide, the black vote cannot do much to alter things. But the 1980 election was unusual. Most elections are not won in a landslide, and when they are not, the black vote can be crucial. Black voters have the ability to reward their friends and punish their enemies, and in many elections, they can make the difference.

Another encouraging sign is the emergence of new faces on the political horizon. Politics is beginning to attract young, talented blacks who have been encour-

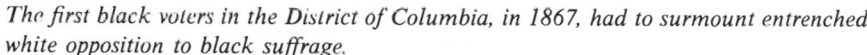

The first black voters in the District of Columbia, in 1867, had to surmount entrenched white opposition to black suffrage.

aged to take the plunge because of other blacks and the example they have set. This bodes well for the future. Blacks are also making more discerning political choices, voting for candidates rather than blindly following party label.

The two most apparent black voting weaknesses are in voter registration and voter participation. As of November 1980, some 33% of the 17,000,000 eligible black voters were not registered. Actual black voter participation tends to lag behind white participation. As an example, in the 1980 election, 40% of the total black voting age population voted, and of registered black voters, only 61.3% exercised the franchise.

At the bottom line, it is the political system that determines how America runs, and blacks, though they are coming somewhat late to the field, have the numbers to make the system work for them, as it has for others.

What is needed is to mobilize that strength, and there were signs during the eighties that this was occurring. One sign was the "Operation Big Vote" campaign that black groups mustered without outside help in 1980. Other voter registration drives in the black community had depended in the past on financing by foundations, labor groups, and the like, but in this instance blacks demonstrated that they could operate on their own. This is an encouraging sign for the future.

BLACKS FAVOR DEMOCRATS

For the most part, beginning in the 1930s with the election of Franklin D. Roosevelt as President, blacks aligned themselves with the Democratic Party. Prior to FDR, blacks had been firmly committed to the Republicans, more because of the revered memory of the Great Emancipator, Abraham Lincoln, than of any meaningful rewards they received for their party loyalty. Roosevelt came along with his promise to "the common man" and was able to weld together an unlikely amalgam of segregationist southerners, big-city political bosses, blue-collar workers, ethnics, labor leaders, intellectuals, poor people, and blacks into a coalition in which blacks felt welcome.

Blacks, over the years, have continued to remain primarily within the ranks of the Democratic Party, which in itself has tended to weaken their political muscle. On the one hand, the Democrats have tended to take the black vote for granted. On the other, the Republicans have generally given the black voter short shrift because of the belief that they were so firmly wedded to the Democrats that overtures to them would be fruitless.

While the political process was opened to blacks in the North, it was virtually closed to them in the

President Harry S. Truman shaking hands with representative William Dawson

South. They were effectively excluded from the process by a variety of methods that included intimidation, unfair registration procedures, and often physical violence.

One of the major goals of the Civil Rights Movement of the 1950s and on into the 1960s was to establish the legal rights of blacks to register and vote in the South. The struggle was not easy, but finally, in 1965, Congress, urged on by President Lyndon B. Johnson, passed the Voting Rights Act, which provided for federal intervention in the registration and voting procedures in areas where blacks and other minorities had been denied the vote.

The impact of the law was electric. In 1961 black voter registration in the states of the Old Confederacy was 1,360,784. Ten years later it was 3,448,565. In 1981 it was 4,254,000. Beyond any question, the Voting Rights Law has been the single most effective piece of civil rights legislation ever passed. Not only did it secure the right to vote for black people, but it also removed race as the major factor in southern politics. Southern legislators who had once used the whipping boy of race to turn out the white voters had to moderate their rhetoric and actions in deference to the newly registered black voters. This downplaying of race encouraged more progressive whites and blacks to enter politics since they did not have to appeal to racist instincts.

The law was extended in 1970 and again in 1975 when it was expanded to protect the voting rights of Mexican Americans and other language minority citizens against discriminatory practices, particularly in the Southwest and West.

Blacks and other minorities also benefited from the one man, one vote ruling of the Supreme Court, which required state legislatures to make certain that Congressional districts fairly represent the population.

COVERAGE OF THE VOTING RIGHTS ACT

As of the spring of 1982 the following areas were covered by the Voting Rights Act:

All of Alabama, Georgia, Louisiana, Mississippi, South Carolina, Virginia.

39 counties in North Carolina: Anson, Beaufort, Bladen, Camden, Caswell, Chowan, Cleveland, Craven, Cumberland, Edgecomb, Franklin, Gaston, Gates, Granville, Greene, Guilford, Halifax, Harnett, Hertford, Hoke, Lee, Lenoir, Martin, Nash, Northampton, Onslow, Pasquotank, Perquimans, Person, Pitt, Robeson, Rockingham, Scotland, Union, Vance, Wake, Washington, Wayne, and Wilson.

9 counties in Arizona: Apache, Cochise, Coconino, Mohave, Navajo, Pima, Pinal, Santa Cruz, and Yuma.

2 counties in California: Monterey and Yuba.

1 county in Idaho: Elmore.

3 counties in New York: Bronx, Kings, New York.

1 county in Wyoming: Campbell.

THE BLACK LOBBY

Since the strengthening of black voting rights in the 1960s, a number of organizations have sought to aid and unite black voters, candidates, and officeholders.

Following are brief descriptions of some groups that have contributed significantly to the growing power of blacks in the American political process.

The Congressional Black Caucus

Officially organized in 1971 when there were 12 black members of the House of Representatives, the Congressional Black Caucus is recognized as the single most important politically oriented black group operating at the national level. Its membership embraces all 18 black members of Congress, when it speaks its voice is listened to, and it has earned high marks both for its commitment to black people and its progressive views.

Blacks have served in Congress since 1870, but it was not until 1969, when Congressman Charles Diggs (D. Mich.) called a meeting of the nine black members then serving in the House and proposed that they join together in a group that there was an effort to establish a unified black presence on the Hill.

Out of this came the Democratic Select Committee, which sought to improve communication among black House members and between those members and the leadership of the House. The structure was kept very informal, which limited its effectiveness. In 1970 Representative William Clay (D. Mo.) suggested that a

President Kennedy greets an NAACP delegation in the White House in 1962. He was the first U.S. president to declare that segregation is "morally wrong."

different type of structure be created, and the idea fell on fertile soil. After some discussion on format and whether the continuing use of "Democratic" in the name might limit membership, the Congressional Black Caucus was created in 1971.

One of its first actions was to appoint a paid staff, something the Democratic Select Committee never had. A method of financing the CBC through an annual dinner was established, and an internal structure was set up consisting of a chairman, executive committee, and policy-oriented subcommittees.

Much of the visibility of the Caucus during the first year came from a series of hearings held around the country on health, education, black enterprise, the mass media, Africa, and racism. Searching for its proper role, the Caucus found itself involved in a number of activities including provision of casework services, gathering and dissemination of information, administrative oversight, articulation of the interests of specialized groups within the black community, and development of legislative proposals. Perhaps it was too broad an agenda for such a young group, for it could not devote enough attention to all these activities.

What also became evident was that while the members of the Caucus were tied together by mutual interests, each of its members was a personality within his or her own right, and as such, individual differences were bound to emerge. This was made evident when Caucus member Shirley Chisholm (D. N.Y.) sought the 1972 Democratic Presidential nomination and discovered that the Caucus was not totally in her corner. This destroyed the myth that the Caucus would always act as one, but at the same time it demonstrated that the Caucus was strong enough to withstand individual differences.

During the Nixon years, the Caucus spent much of its energies in attempting to preserve what remained of the War on Poverty programs and in fighting against the efforts of the President to impound funds for domestic programs. With such a limited agenda, questions were raised whether an elaborate mechanism like the Caucus was needed, and whether the activities in which it was involved might not be handled better by the individual members of Congress.

Through a series of retreats and evaluations, the Caucus stepped back and took a look at itself. This enabled it to focus on three strategies.

The first involved strengthening efforts to get more favorable committee assignments for Caucus members. Such assignments are key elements in determining how influential a Representative can be, and the Caucus was successful in placing its members on all 22 of the standing committees in the House and on the three major ones, Rules, Ways and Means, and Appropriations in the 94th Congress.

The second strategy involved targeting of Representatives from constituencies with high black representation for special lobbying efforts within Congress on such issues as the Home Rule Bill for the District of Columbia. This strategy met with mixed results because of the reluctance of some Caucus members and their staffs to violate existing Congressional mores, which frown on such a strategy.

The third strategy was an expansion of the network of professional and academic advisors outside of Congress. These advisors are divided into groups, according to interests, and meet regularly with a Caucus member to discuss public policy issues and Congressional legislation. This has become an important CBC technique for gaining support and assistance for selected legislative priorities.

Over the years, the CBC has not hesitated to speak out on a variety of issues, regardless of which political party was in office. The present membership of the Caucus is all Democratic, but during his one term (1978–1980) Representative Melvin Evans, the nonvoting Republican delegate from the Virgin Islands, was a member. Former Republican Senator Edward Brooke, the lone black in the Senate during much of the Caucus' history, never chose to join.

When the Reagan Administration took office in 1981, the Caucus, like other black groups, found that its access to the White House was limited and its influence virtually nil. Nevertheless, the Caucus was one of the few organized voices raised in Congress against the sharp cutbacks in social service programs. The Caucus went even further and developed an alternative budget that earned from the Democratic Study Group the accolade of taking "the boldest step of any proposal being offered to the House to deal with the federal deficit and [offering] the largest and fairest tax cut of any of the proposals before the House."

While the Caucus has continued to enhance its role as an effective legislative mechanism, it faces problems with its funding because of actions taken by the House in 1981 that imposed severe restrictions on Congressional caucuses which receive support and funding from non-Congressional sources. In essence, the new restrictions said that if a Congressional caucus received any support from the House in the form of office space, furniture, telephone services, and the like, it could not receive outside funds.

This is crucial to the Caucus since, as an example, in 1980 it received $29,000 in donated Congressional services. In the same year, it raised 95% of its budget, or $550,000, from non-Congressional sources. While it is important that the Caucus keep its offices on Capitol Hill, it obviously cannot operate in the manner that it has without outside funding.

The Caucus maintains a 501(c) tax-exempt organi-

Wendell Gunn, special assistant to President Ronald Reagan. As of July 1982 very few blacks had been appointed by President Reagan.

zation called the Congressional Black Caucus Foundation, which conducts legislative research and public policy analysis. Money can be raised through this entity but because of its tax-exempt status it cannot be involved in advocacy or lobbying, creating a problem for the Caucus, which has to find an acceptable alternative.

The major fund-raising activity of the Caucus, its annual dinner, has become the single most important annual black political gathering. It has been enlarged so that it encompasses an entire weekend filled with workshops, brainstorming sessions, and speeches.

In assessing the accomplishments of the Caucus, Dr. Marguerite Ross Barnett, a political scientist at Columbia University, said:

Ten years of CBC activity has produced an institutionalized organization with a number of experienced, senior legislators with good committee assignments and knowledge of the House and its membership. Translation of CBC potential into positive political realities will depend on a variety of factors, only some of which are in the direct control of the black members of Congress.

The present chairman of the Caucus is Rep. Walter E. Fauntroy (nonvoting delegate, D.C.).

Address

H2–344
House of Representatives Annex
Washington, D.C. 20515
Phone: (202) 255-1691

Edward M. Kennedy, a favorite Democrat of blacks because of his consistent record of support of programs favored by minorities, speaking before the Black Caucus.

The Joint Center for Political Studies

The Joint Center for Political Studies is the most important and authoritative source of information on black political participation in the country. It has been invaluable in enhancing the involvement of blacks in the political process by securing and analyzing data on blacks in the political arena.

The Center was established in 1970 with initial funding from the Ford Foundation. It was originally sponsored by Howard University and the Metropolitan Applied Research Center in New York City. The Center is now independent and is governed by a 10-member board headed by Wendell Freeland, an attorney from Pittsburgh.

The Center describes itself as a national nonprofit institution that conducts research on public policy issues of special concern to black Americans and promotes informed and effective involvement of blacks in the governmental process. The Center provides independent and nonpartisan analysis, publications, and outreach programs. One of its most valuable publications is its annual roster of elected black officials.

Though its basic emphasis remains on the political process, the Center has expanded its interests to include such areas as energy, community development, revenue sharing, crime, and regionalism, and has issued a number of valuable reports.

The Center has been headed since 1972 by Eddie N. Williams, President. Prior to joining the Center he served as the vice president for public affairs at the University of Chicago and director of the Center for Policy Study.

Funding for the Center is obtained through the Ford Foundation as well as other foundations and sources.

Address

Suite 400
1301 Pennsylvania Ave., NW
Washington, D.C. 20004
Phone: (202) 626-3500

Voter Education Project

The Voter Education Project came along at a time when there were the first faint glimmerings of hope that black political strength, which had been penned up so long in the South, might be unshackled. The Civil Rights Movement was on the march and one of its primary goals was to make it possible for black people to vote freely in the South. Already existing was the Southern Regional Conference, a biracial organization based in Atlanta that for many years had been involved in race relations.

The Council was the logical umbrella under which to place a concerted voter registration drive, and in 1961 the Council established the Voter Education Project, which was supported by all the major civil rights groups and endorsed by both the Republican and Democratic National Committees.

VEP's first director was Wiley A. Branton, who was later to become dean of the Howard University Law School. Its activities were limited to the 11 southern states. The programs conducted by the participating national and local agencies were designed to secure voter registration primarily, but in such a way as to gather reports which were submitted to VEP for analysis of methods and techniques used, the problems encountered, solutions developed, and results of the programs.

VEP contributed mightily to the effort which led to the passage of the 1965 Voting Rights Act. Through a combination of supporting locally initiated voter registration efforts and initiating its own voter registration drives, VEP assumed the major responsibility for fulfilling the promise of the 1965 Voting Rights Act. Overall in the South, more than a million black citizens became registered to vote between 1965 and 1969.

As more blacks were elected, VEP started to fulfill the vital function of informing black officeholders on the intricacies of vital issues and on techniques to obtain appropriations important to black voters. A result of this has been more new schools, paved streets, and police protection for many neglected black neighborhoods.

Branton was succeeded in 1965 by Vernon E. Jordan, Jr., who left in 1970 to become head of the United Negro College Fund, and was replaced by John Lewis, the former executive director of the Student Non-Violent Coordinating Committee and a hero of the Selma to Montgomery March in 1965. Lewis resigned in 1977 and was succeeded by Vivian Malone Jones.

THE BLACK CONGRESS

In 1981–1982 there were 17 black members of Congress and a black nonvoting delegate from the District of Columbia serving in the 97th Congress—the largest number of blacks to serve in the House of Representatives at one time since Reconstruction. Four new black members were elected in 1980: George Crockett, Jr. (D. Mich.), Mervyn M. Dymally (D. Calif.), Gus Savage (D. Ill.), and Harold Washington (D. Ill.). Two former members, Bennett Stewart (D. Ill.) and the nonvoting delegate from the Virgin Islands, Melvin Evans (R. V.I.), were not returned to Congress. Representative Shirley Chisholm (D. N.Y.), who was reelected in 1980, announced that she would retire at the end of her term in 1982, but her replacement is certain to be another black.

A. Philip Randolph Institute volunteers preparing posters and literature for distribution during a voter registration drive

Black members now constitute 3.9% of the total House membership of 435. They are all Democrats representing urban areas with only four coming from the South, although 53% of the nation's black population resides there. Most of the black members of Congress have been elected from districts with a majority, or nearly a majority of black voters, although Representatives Ronald V. Dellums and Mervyn M. Dymally (both D. Calif.), are exceptions to the rule with black populations in their districts of 24 and 36%.

As the result of reapportionment following the 1980 Census—each Congressional district must be adjusted so that each House member represents at least 510,000 people—some realignment of district boundaries will take place. Several of the black congressional members will therefore see their districts change since those districts have lost population and are below the mandated population. However, because of political considerations plus the desire not to come into conflict with the Voting Rights Act by reducing black congressional representation, it is generally felt that when boundaries are shifted they will be shifted in a manner to protect the incumbents.

The area of the greatest possible expansion of House membership for blacks is in the South, but the legislatures in these states have shown a reluctance to create districts in which blacks could win.

BIOGRAPHIES OF CURRENT BLACK REPRESENTATIVES

WILLIAM CLAY
First District Missouri
Elected 1969

William Clay, the first black man to represent the state of Missouri in the U.S. Congress, was born in 1931 in the lower end of what is now St. Louis' First District. Clay was educated locally and later took a degree in political science at St. Louis University, where he was one of four blacks in a class of 1,100. After serving in the Army until 1955, Clay became active in a host of civil rights organizations, including the NAACP Youth Council and CORE. During this time he worked as a cardiographic aide, bus driver, and insurance agent, but his heart had already surrendered to politics, at least judging from the number of demonstrations and picket lines he had joined.

In 1959, and again in 1963, Clay was elected alderman of the predominantly black 26th Ward. During his first term, he served nearly four months of a nine-month jail sentence for demonstrations at a local bank. Meanwhile, on the outside, the number of white-collar jobs held by blacks in St. Louis banks began a steady ascent from a low of 16 to a high of 700. In 1964

Clay stepped down from his alderman's post to run for Ward Committeeman, winning handily and being reelected in 1968.

Clay's election platform in 1969 included a number of progressive, even radical, planks. He advocated that all penal institutions make provisions for the creation of facilities in which married prisoners could set up house with their spouses for the duration of their sentences. He branded most testing procedures and diploma requirements, as well as references to arrest records and periods of unemployment, unnecessary obstacles complicating the path of a prospective employee. In his view, a demonstrated willingness to work and an acceptance of responsibility should be the criteria determining one's selection for a job.

Clay's last job before election to Congress was as race relations coordinator for Steamfitters Union Local 562. Subjected to considerable criticism from other St. Louis blacks who labeled the union racist, Clay pointed out that dramatic changes in the hiring practices of the union since he had joined it in 1966 were responsible for the employment of 30 black steamfitters in St. Louis—30 more than the union had previously put to work. Still, Clay conceded that the high-paying job had led him to reduce his active involvement with the civil rights struggle to some degree.

Clay's secure position in the First District, where blacks comprise 55% of the voters, allows him to express his militancy with little compromise, a factor which may have contributed to the fact that in 1972, he ran about 5% behind Senator McGovern in his district. However, Clay still received 64% of the vote and has obtained a seat on the House Education and Labor Committee, which was once chaired by a man Clay greatly admired, the late Adam Clayton Powell.

He serves as the second ranking member of the Committee of Post Office and Civil Service, where he is Chairman of the Subcommittee on Postal Operations and Civil Service; he is fifth ranking member of the House Education and Labor Committee.

Since 1969, when he was seated, Representative Clay has sponsored 592 pieces of legislation including the Hatch Act Reform Bill, the City Earnings Tax Bill, and the IRS Reform Bill.

CARDISS COLLINS
Seventh District Illinois
Elected 1973

Like many wives, Mrs. Cardiss Collins was immensely involved in her late husband's career as a U.S. Congressman. When a tragic accident in December 1972 took his life, she immediately qualified as a viable candidate to succeed him, and in 1973 won a special election to fill the unexpired term of her late husband, George, in the Seventh District in Illinois.

Cardiss Collins succeeded her husband after his tragic death in 1972 and has proved to be an effective voice in Congress.

As a committeewoman in Chicago's 24th Ward Regular Democratic Organization, Congresswoman Collins was no stranger to politics. She had been involved in the successful campaigns waged by her husband for the positions of committeeman and alderman of the 24th Ward and had worked on his campaigns for Congress, first in the Sixth and then in the Seventh District.

Mrs. Collins' District, located on the West Side of Chicago, remains largely loyal to the Democratic machine of Mayor Richard Daley, and still, in some areas, elects white aldermen who are supported by City Hall. In this sense, the District is unlike the South Side, which in 1973 supported Senator Charles Percy over the Democratic candidate.

With Daley's support behind her, Mrs. Collins received over 90% of the vote in the special election of 1973, in which she was chosen to fill her late husband's seat.

Some 55% of Congresswoman Collins' District is black, 22% is foreign born, and 17% Hispanic.

Representative Collins is the first woman and the first black to chair the House Government Operations Subcommittee on Manpower and Housing, which has major oversight responsibility for the Department of Labor, the Department of Housing and Urban Development, ACTION, and the Community Services Administration.

Recognizing her dedication and excellence, her colleagues in the Congressional Black Caucus elected her Chairwoman for the 96th Congress. She had previously served the Caucus as Secretary during the 94th Congress and as Treasurer during the 95th.

JOHN CONYERS, JR.
First District Michigan
Elected 1965

Congressman John Conyers is a native of Detroit, where he was born on May 16, 1929. He received his B.A. and LL.B. degrees from Wayne State University, and served his political apprenticeship for three years as legislative assistant to Congressman John Dingell.

Before election to Congress, Conyers was a referee for the Michigan Workmen's Compensation Department and senior partner in the firm of Conyers, Bell and Townsend. He was general counsel for the Trade Union Leadership Council; a member of Local 900 of the United Auto Workers (UAW) and of Local 42 of the AFL-CIO. He also belonged to the Committee on Political Education in Michigan's 15th Congressional District.

In 1963 President Kennedy appointed Conyers to the National Lawyers Committee for Civil Rights Under Law, an organization designed to foster greater racial tolerance in the legal field. Conyers later served as a member of the Committee to Assist Southern Lawyers (CASL), and represented a number of clients who had been arrested in connection with alleged voter-registration irregularities throughout the South.

Conyers encountered far greater difficulty in gaining the Democratic nomination in Michigan's First Congressional District than in defeating his eventual Republican opponent, Robert Blackwell. Conyers won the primary election by a mere 45 votes, but, aided by his father, a trade unionist, and a group of dedicated volunteers, he then proceeded to trounce Blackwell, emerging with 84% of the total votes cast.

Conyers was co-sponsor of the Johnson Administration's Medicare program and a strong supporter of the 1965 Voting Rights Bill.

The Representative's District in Detroit reflects the rapid change that has transpired in so many cities. Between 1950 and 1970 the black population leaped from 5 to 70% of the total. However, the district is more affluent than most black districts in the United States and some observers have forecast that it will take a Republican turn.

However, neither President Nixon nor Conyers' Republican opponents were able to harvest more than 15% of the vote in the 1968, 1970, and 1972 elections

House Judiciary Committee member John Conyers took part in the impeachment inquiry that led to President Nixon's early retirement.

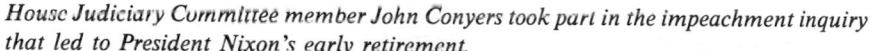

and Conyers was so critical of Nixon that he appeared on the White House's "enemies list," which was revealed in 1973.

The first black man to serve on the House Judiciary Committee, Conyers participated in the impeachment hearings in 1974, at times taking the position that Democrats and Republicans alike were too cautious about confronting the White House's refusal to submit subpeonaed evidence.

In 1980 John Conyers was reelected by 95% of the vote to his ninth term in the U.S. House of Representatives. The fifth ranking member of the Judiciary Committee, he chairs the Subcommittee on Criminal Justice and is a member on the Subcommittee on Crime. He also serves on the Subcommittee on Commerce, Consumer and Monetary Affairs, and Manpower and Housing of the Government Operations Committee.

Representative Conyers is a leader in the full employment movement and was a principal architect of the Humphrey-Hawkins Full Employment and Balanced Growth Act, which became law in 1978. He is a leading critic of federal budget priorities, particularly where this concerns the growth of military spending at the expense of domestic human resources programs and the subsidies awarded to business corporations.

GEORGE W. CROCKETT, JR.
Thirteenth District Michigan
Elected 1980

George W. Crockett, Jr. was elected to Congress in 1980 from the 13th Congressional District of Michigan to fill the vacancy created by the resignation of Charles C. Diggs, Jr. He is the fourteenth ranking member of the Committee on Foreign Affairs, seventeenth ranking member of the Small Business Committee, and serves on the Subcommittees on General Oversight, Export Opportunities, and Special Problems of Small Business, as well as the Select Committee on Aging. He is also a member of the Congressional Arts Caucus, the Congressional Auto Caucus, and the Executive Board of the Democratic Group.

After graduating from the University of Michigan Law School in 1934, Crockett began his legal practice in Jacksonville, Florida. He was admitted to the West Virginia Bar in 1935, the U.S. Supreme Court Bar in 1940, and the Michigan Bar in 1944.

In 1939 he was appointed as the first black lawyer with the U.S. Department of Labor and later became the senior attorney on employee lawsuits under the Fair Labor Standards Act. In 1943 President Roosevelt appointed him one of the first Fair Employment Practices Commission Hearing examiners.

George Crockett founded the International United Auto Workers Fair Employment Practices Department in 1944 and served both as its Director and as General Counsel to the UAW until 1946. From 1946 until 1966 Crockett was in private practice as a senior partner in the law firm Goodman, Crockett, Eden, and Robb. Crockett was elected judge of the Recorders Court in Detroit in 1966 and was reelected to a second term in 1972. In 1974 he became presiding judge of that same court. Following his retirement, he served as visiting judge for the Michigan Court of Appeals, and in 1980 he was acting corporation counsel for the city of Detroit.

RONALD V. DELLUMS
Seventh District California
Elected 1971

An avowed "radical," Ronald Dellums represents one of America's more turbulent Congressional districts, one which combines the black population of Oakland's ghetto with the students and upper-income liberals of Berkeley. It was in this district that both the student movement of the 1960s and the Black Panther Party originated.

A product of the West Oakland ghetto and recipient of a master's degree in social work from the University of California at Berkeley, Dellums was employed prior to his election as a senior consultant to Social Dynamics, Inc., a Berkeley-based enterprise which develops manpower and community organization programs on a national basis.

He was formerly director of an employment program of the San Francisco Economic Opportunity Council, a director at a Bay Area youth center and a community center, lecturer at San Francisco State College and the Graduate School of Social Work at the University of California at Berkeley, and sat on the Berkeley City Council. He served two years in the Marine Corps prior to entering his professional career.

In the Democratic primary of 1970, with only 22% of his district's population black, Dellums challenged the incumbent, Jeffrey Cohelan, a white man who, with strong backing from labor unions, had served 12 consecutive years in Congress. Dellums openly defended some Panther viewpoints and student demonstration tactics, positions that soon attracted considerable conservative opposition and money to defeat him. However, Dellums received 55% of the vote to defeat Cohelan in the primary and 57% in the November contest against the Republican nominee. He was reelected in November 1972, with 56% of the vote, 9% less than the percentage received in his district by Senator McGovern. But in 1974 the coalition which elected Dellums seemed firmly in control of the district.

As a member of the Armed Services Committee,

Ron Dellums represents the district where the Black Panther Party originated.

Dellums has aroused the ire of Republicans and Democrats alike with his charges that the military budget is bloated and that racism remains strong in the armed forces, despite claims by the Department of Defense that it has been eliminated. Dellums remains very much in the minority on the Committee, but his very presence there represents an important departure for black Congressmen, who formerly gravitated to such friendlier environments as the Education and Labor Committee.

He is the Chairperson of both the House Committee on the District of Columbia and the D.C. Subcommittee on Fiscal Affairs and Health.

Dellums is also the tenth ranking member of the House Armed Services Committee, where he serves on the Research and Development Subcommittee. He also chairs the Armed Services Committee Panel dealing with problems on the Island of Vieques.

Representative Dellums is a former vice-chair of the Congressional Black Caucus, a member of its Executive Committee, and he now heads the Caucus Task Force on National Security and Foreign Policy issues. A former member of the Democratic National Committee, he is currently a national co-chair of the New Democratic Coalition.

Dellums is a firm believer in the twin concepts of participatory democracy and "Coalition Politics." In his judgment, when people begin to realize how and why they are being victimized and manipulated by those who control the real levers of power in this society, they will then be able to join together to form a new political majority—one which crosses racial, sexual, and economic barriers.

In his view, Congress is an institution that must be made aware of the forces at work for progressive social and economic change. In his efforts to jolt the House out of its institutional indifference to controversial issues, he has been willing to conduct extraofficial hearings to force "official" Washington to recognize the gravity of a particular situation. For example, he conducted personal investigations into U.S. war crimes in Indochina and the impact of Agent Orange and other toxic agents on the men and women who served in the Indochina theater of operations. In conjunction with the Congressional Black Caucus, he has conducted examinations on the extent of racism in the military and on various aspects of governmental lawlessness and bureaucratic indifference.

JULIAN C. DIXON
Twenty-Eighth District California
Elected 1978

Elected to the House of Representatives from the 28th Congressional District of California in 1978, Julian C. Dixon serves on the powerful House Appropriations Committee as the 25th ranking member. In March 1980 he was selected Chairman of the Subcommittee on the District of Columbia, thus becoming the first freshman legislator in the history of Congress to chair a House Appropriations Subcommittee. Dixon also serves on the Appropriations Subcommittee on Foreign Operations and is formerly a member of the Subcommittee on Energy and Water Development. He is the current treasurer of the Congressional Black Caucus and serves as chair of the Fundraising Committee.

Congressman Dixon's legislative priorities have focused on a wide array of issues ranging from domestic social concerns to African Caribbean affairs. Bills sponsored by Dixon have included the Civil Rights Amendments of 1979, which would prohibit discrimination on the basis of sexual orientation in housing, education, employment, and public accommodations; legislation to establish a Cabinet-level Department of Education; and a bill to provide federal assistance to victims of domestic violence.

His work on the Foreign Operations Subcommittee has succeeded in strengthening U.S. participation in the Sahel Development Program in West Africa and in the African Development Bank. Congressman Dixon has worked for the advancement of alternative forms of energy such as solar, biomass, and wind energy systems.

Dixon's efforts have also centered on issues affecting his own urban district. He was successful in obtaining a federal study of the Baldwin Hills area of Los Angeles—an area nationally recognized for its disastrous mudslides. As a member of the Congressional Olympic Task Force for the 1984 Olympics in Los Angeles, Representative Dixon has been a leading supporter of federal assistance for the games.

From 1973 until his election to Congress, Dixon represented the 49th Assembly District in the California State Assembly. In 1973 he was chairman of the Assembly Democratic Caucus, the first freshman ever elected to that post. He also chaired the Assembly Public Employees and Retirement Committee and was a member of the Committees on Criminal Justice, Ways and Means, and Education. His special assignments included chairman of the Select Committee on Juvenile Violence. In 1979 he received the "Outstanding Legislative Program" award from the National Council of Juvenile and Family Court Judges.

MERVYN M. DYMALLY
Thirty-First District California
Elected 1980

Mervyn Dymally was elected in 1980 to serve as representative of the 31st Congressional District of California. He is presently a member of the Committee on Foreign Affairs where he is the seventeenth ranking member, and the Committee on Science and Technology where he ranks twenty-second. He chairs the Subcommittee on Judiciary and Education of the District of Columbia Committee. Dymally is also a member of the Democratic Study Group and serves as secretary/treasurer of the California Congressional Democratic Delegation.

Representative Dymally brings many years of experience and a deep concern for a broad range of people-oriented problems to the U.S. Congress. Prior to his election in 1980 he served four years as a California Assemblyman (1962–1966) and was elected to the California State Senate in 1966. During his eight years as State Senator, Dymally served as chair of the Senate Democratic Caucus and the committees on Social Welfare; Military and Veterans Affairs; Elections and Reapportionment; and the Subcommittee on Medical Education and Health Needs. He also headed the Senate Select Committee on Children and Youth; the Joint

Committees on Legal Equality, and the Revision of the Election Code.

Dymally served as Lieutenant Governor of California from 1975 to 1979. In this capacity he headed the State Commission for Economic Development and the Commission of the Californias. He was a member of the Board of Regents of the University of California and the Board of Trustees of the State College and University system. Lieutenant Governor Dymally was responsible for organizing the Council on Intergroup Relations, the California Advisory Commission on Youth, and on Food and Nutrition.

Originally from Trinidad, West Indies, Dymally came to this country to attend Lincoln University in Jefferson City, Missouri.

WALTER E. FAUNTROY
Congressman-Delegate District of Columbia
Elected 1971

Congressman Walter E. Fauntroy, also pastor of Washington D.C.'s New Bethel Baptist Church, represents the District of Columbia. A Yale Divinity School alumnus, he was chairman of the Caucus task force for the 1972 Democratic National Committee and of the platform committee of the National Black Political Convention. Fauntroy was Washington, D.C. coordinator for the March on Washington for Jobs and Freedom in 1963, coordinator for the Selma to Montgomery march in 1965, and national coordinator for the Poor People's Campaign in 1969. He is also a Director of the Southern Christian Leadership Conference.

The Reverend Walter E. Fauntroy represents the District of Columbia in Congress.

As of June 1982 the District of Columbia lacked home rule and Fauntroy a vote in Congress. However, he does have a vote on committees. Should the District be awarded statehood, or a corresponding status, Fauntroy would stand an excellent chance of being elected Governor. He has strong support from the city's overwhelmingly black population, especially the large population of black civil servants.

Since his election to Congress, he has continued to build a record of achievement by playing key roles in the mobilization of black political power. In the 95th Congress Fauntroy was a member of the House Select Committee on Assassinations and Chairman of its Subcommittee on the Assassination of Martin Luther King, Jr. He is now the sixth ranking member of the House Banking, Finance, and Urban Affairs Committee and chairman of its Subcommittee on Domestic Monetary Policy. He is also the first ranking member of the House District Committee.

HAROLD FORD
Eighth District Tennessee
Elected 1974

In November 1974 Harold Ford, a 29-year-old Democratic member of the Tennessee House of Representatives, narrowly defeated the Republican incumbent, Dan Kuykendall, to win election to the U.S. House of Representatives. Ford won by 571 votes, 57,715 to 57,141 in a district which takes in most of the city of Memphis.

Elected in 1970 to the State House, Ford was selected majority whip by his fellow Democrats, the first freshman of that body, and probably the youngest to attain that post. While in the State House, Ford sponsored successful bills to regulate Tennessee's utility billing procedures to rehabilitate private housing.

Harold Ford's election to the U.S. Congress was bitter and racially polarized. Kuykendall had been a close ally of former President Nixon, a fact which along with inflation was a major issue in the campaign.

Kuykendall, in addition, had sided with positions of the Congressional Black Caucus in only 10% of Congressional votes in 1973.

Blacks comprise 47% of the district's population. Ford received some 12% of the white vote.

In 1972 Kuykendall had defeated J. D. Patterson, Jr., a black, by nearly 19,000 votes.

The holder of a masters degree in Business Administration from Vanderbilt University, Ford managed a funeral home owned by his father prior to his election to the State House. Two brothers also won office in 1974, his brother John to the State Senate and Emmitt to the State House.

He is currently serving his fourth term and is the eighth ranking member on the House Ways and Means

Harold Ford, now serving in his fourth term.

Committee, where he serves on its Subcommittees of Health, and Oversight; and is also the eighth ranking member of the House Select Committee on Aging.

WILLIAM H. GRAY III
Second District Pennsylvania
Elected 1978

William H. Gray III's election to Congress in 1978 is an extension of his long record of community service as pastor for eight years of Union Baptist Church in Montclair, New Jersey and, since 1972, of the 3,000-member Bright Hope Baptist Church in North Philadelphia.

As a representative in the 97th Congress, Gray remains active through assignments as the thirty-first ranking member of the Appropriations Committee, where he serves on the Transportation and Foreign Operations Subcommittees; and sixth ranking member of the District of Columbia Committee, for which he chairs the Subcommittee on Government Operations and Metropolitan Affairs. In addition, Congressman Gray is vice-chair of the Congressional Black Caucus.

Gray's efforts in the civil rights field included the precedent-setting New Jersey Supreme Court case *Gray v. Serruto,* which ordered that financial damages be paid by those who discriminate on the basis of race in renting multi-family housing. The case later made civil rights history when it became part of a ruling by the U.S. Supreme Court.

During the 96th Congress, Representative Gray served on the House committees on Foreign Affairs, the Budget and the District of Columbia. He was elected secretary of the Congressional Black Caucus and was chosen by his freshman colleagues to represent them on the Leadership's Democratic Steering and Policy Committee.

As a member of the Foreign Affairs Committee in the 96th Congress, Bill Gray moved to increase U.S. visibility in Africa and to make our foreign aid more effective on that continent. He wrote the only new legislation by a freshman to be adopted by the 96th Congress. This legislation established the African Development Foundation, a new mechanism to deliver U.S. aid in a visible manner to the grassroots, village-level people of Africa. Gray also introduced legislation to increase the number of minorities and women in the U.S. Foreign Service and to assure equality in recruitment, promotion, and retention. His amendments to the Foreign Service Personnel Reform Act were adopted by the 96th Congress and signed into law by President Carter.

His work on the Foreign Affairs Committee and active advocacy of majority rule in Rhodesia led to his appointment as a U.S. representative at the inauguration of the government of Zimbabwe. President Carter appointed him to chair the United States/Liberia Presidential Commission, and more recently he headed a special mission to Liberia to begin talks with the government which took office after the 1980 coup. Gray also participated in Vice President Mondale's trade mission to Nigeria.

As a member of the House Budget Committee in the 96th Congress, Bill Gray was deeply involved in the fight to preserve the human needs programs key to the survival of the poor, the elderly, and the minorities of this nation. He continues to be in the forefront of the fight to reorder Federal spending priorities.

AUGUSTUS F. HAWKINS
Twenty-First District California
Elected 1963

Augustus Hawkins was born in Shreveport, Louisiana in 1907 and moved to California at the age of 12. He attended the universities of California and Southern California.

In 1934, when only 27, Hawkins was elected to the California State Assembly. He remained in the state legislature for 28 years, and on a few occasions came close to being elected speaker of the Assembly. During his 28-year tenure, he authored over 100 laws including minimum wage for women; a slum clearance and low-cost housing program; workmen's compensation for domestics; disability insurance; The Fair Housing Act; old age pension; child care centers; The Fair Employment Practices Act of 1959; and the 1961 Metropolitan Transit Authority Act. Eventually as-

Representative Augustus Hawkins is congratulated by his wife on election night.

suming the chairmanship of the Rules Committee, he also served as chairman of the Senate and Assembly Joint Legislative Organization Committee.

Under legislation he sponsored, racial designation was removed from all state documents such as driver's licenses and job orders. He was also instrumental in bringing about the appointment of the first California blacks as judges and as members of the highway patrol and of several state commissions.

Though less militant than younger members of the Black Caucus, Hawkins can be very forceful. In 1970 he was one of the Congressmen who discovered the "tiger cages" in the prisons of South Vietnam, a feat which increased his stature as an opponent of the war.

Hawkins holds an important post in Congress as Chairman of the Education and Labor Committee's Equal Employment Opportunities Subcommittee. His seat situated mainly in the Watts area of Los Angeles is considered safe. Some 54% of the residents are black, 21% Hispanic. In 1972 Hawkins received 84% of the vote.

For the 97th Congress, Representative Hawkins has been appointed chairman of the House Administration Committee. He also serves as chairman of the Joint Committee on the Library and as vice-chairman of the Joint Committee on Printing. Hawkins is first ranking member on the Committee on Education and Labor and is chairman of its Subcommittee on Employment Opportunities.

Representative Hawkins introduced three landmark pieces of legislation during the 93rd Congress: the Juvenile Justice and Delinquency Prevention Act; the Community Services Act; and the Civil Rights Act, Title VII Section amendment to the Equal Employment Opportunities Act.

In the 95th Congress, three other pieces of legislation sponsored by Hawkins became law: the CETA Amendments of 1978; the Youth Employment and Demonstration Projects Act; and the Pregnancy Disability Act. Hawkins witnessed the signing into law of the Humphrey/Hawkins Full Employment Act of 1978 which he began developing in 1974 with Senator Hubert H. Humphrey.

In the 96th Congress, Representative Hawkins introduced the Youth Act of 1980 to combat the disastrously high rate of unemployment among America's youth.

In recognition of Congressman Hawkins' outstanding contribution to education and labor issues, Lincoln University conferred an honorary degree of Doctor of Laws on him during its commencement exercises in May 1978.

MICKEY LELAND
Eighteenth District Texas
Elected 1978

Mickey Leland was elected to the House of Representatives in 1978 and was the freshman whip of the 96th Congress. Reelected in 1980, he is the sixth ranking member of the Committee on Post Office and Civil Service, the eighteenth ranking member of the Committee on Energy and Commerce, and the fourth ranking member of the Committee on the District of Columbia.

Congressman Leland was elected chairman of the Subcommittee on Postal Personnel and Modernization in 1980. He also serves on the Subcommittee on Census and Population, Subcommittee on Energy Conservation and Power, Subcommittee on Fossil and Synthetic Fuels, Subcommittee on Health and the Environment, and the Subcommittee on Manpower, Education, and the Judiciary.

Leland was a member of the Texas House of Representatives from 1972 to 1978. In 1976 he was selected to serve on the Democratic National Committee and was reelected in 1980. While attending the Memphis Midterm Conference of the National Democratic Party in 1978, he helped organize the National Black/Hispanic Democratic Coalition, on which he now serves as co-chair.

He is a member of the Congressional Black Caucus

Fundraising Committee and serves as chair of the Caucus' Energy Braintrust.

PARREN J. MITCHELL
Seventh District Maryland
Elected 1971

Parren J. Mitchell was born in Baltimore in 1922. He received degrees from Morgan State (B.A.) and the University of Maryland (M.S.), and then became a professor of sociology at Morgan State.

Between 1965 and 1968 Mitchell worked as executive director of the Community Action Agency in Baltimore and as executive secretary with the Maryland Commission on Interracial Problems and Relations.

Mitchell is a member of the influential Democratic Policy and Steering Committee, a group which recommends legislative policy and strategy for the Democratic Caucus in the House.

Though Mitchell's district, which is entirely within the city of Baltimore, is 74% black and overwhelmingly Democratic, his seat is far from safe. In 1972 he was challenged in the primary by black supporters of the regular Baltimore Democratic Party and nearly defeated.

Representative Parren Mitchell urges Federal Price Commission to get tough with inner city landlords.

Representative Mitchell's family has long been prominent in politics and civil rights causes. His brother, Clarence, is head Washington lobbyist for the NAACP and his nephew, Clarence, ran for mayor of Baltimore in 1971.

In 1976 he attached to President Carter's $4 billion Public Works Bill an amendment that compelled state, county, and municipal governments seeking federal assistance to set aside 10% of each grant to retain minority firms as contractors, subcontractors, or suppliers. This amendment has led to more than $625 million (15%) going to legitimate minority firms.

Congressman Mitchell also introduced legislation which became Public Law 95–507 in 1978 which requires proposals from federal contractors to spell out goals for awarding contracts to minority subcontractors. This law potentially provides access to billions of dollars for minority businesses.

In the 97th Congress, Parren Mitchell served as chairman of the House Small Business Committee and as whip-at-large. He is a senior member of the House Banking, Finance, and Urban Affairs Committee and a member of the Joint Economic Committee. He is also chairman of the Subcommittee on Housing, Minority Enterprise and Economic Development of the Congressional Black Caucus.

CHARLES RANGEL
Eighteenth District New York
Elected 1970

Harlem-born Charles Rangel vaulted into the national spotlight in 1970 when he defeated Adam Clayton Powell for Democratic nomination in New York's 18th Congressional District. Rangel's upset victory stirred hopes among black leaders that a grassroots political movement generated from within Harlem, rather than stemming from beyond the community, might result in the grooming of an energetic, capable, and untainted successor to the volatile and unpredictable Powell.

Born June 11, 1930, Rangel attended Harlem elementary and secondary schools before volunteering to serve in the U.S. Army during the Korean war. While stationed in Korea with the 2nd Infantry, he saw heavy combat and received the Purple Heart and the Bronze Star Medal for Valor, as well as U.S. and Korean Presidential citations. Discharged honorably as a Staff Sergeant, Rangel returned to finish high school (DeWitt Clinton in 1953) and to study at New York University's School of Commerce, from which he graduated in 1957. The recipient of a scholarship, Rangel then attended St. John's Law School, graduating in 1960.

After being admitted to the bar, Rangel earned a key appointment as Assistant U.S. Attorney in the Southern District of New York in 1961. For the next

Representative Charles Rangel (left) *and State Senator Basil Patterson on the campaign trail.*

five years, he acquired legal experience as legal counsel to the New York City Housing and Redevelopment Board, as legal assistant to Judge James L. Watson, as associate counsel to the speaker of the N.Y. State Assembly, and as general counsel to the National Advisory Commission on Selective Service.

In 1966 Rangel was chosen to represent the 72nd District, Central Harlem, in the State Assembly. Since then, he has served as a member of, and secretary to, the New York State Commission on Revision of the Penal Law and Criminal Code.

In 1972 Rangel easily defeated Livingston Wingate in the Democratic primary and went on to an overwhelming victory in November as the candidate of the Democratic, Republican, and Liberal parties. In 1974 he was elected chairman of the Congressional Black Caucus.

In his first term, he was appointed to the Select Committee on Crime and was influential in passing the 1971 amendment to the drug laws that authorized the President to cut off all military and economic aid to any country that refused to cooperate with the United States in stopping the international traffic in drugs. In 1976 he was appointed to the Select Committee on Narcotics Abuse and Control. Rangel is regarded as one of the leading Congressional experts on the subject.

Representative Rangel served as chairman of the Congressional Black Caucus in 1974–1975 and was a member of the Judiciary Committee when it voted to impeach President Nixon. In 1975 he moved to the Ways and Means Committee, becoming the first black to serve on this committee. Two years later his colleagues in the New York Congressional delegation voted him the majority whip for New York State.

Now serving his sixth term in Congress, Rangel is the third ranking member of the Ways and Means Committee, second ranking member of the Select Committee on Narcotics and has been appointed to the Democratic Steering and Policy Committee.

Blacks comprise 59% of the population in Rangel's district, Spanish-speaking Americans some 17%. His constituency also includes a long stretch of Central Park West and other white middle-class streets of New York's West Side.

AUGUSTUS F. SAVAGE
Second District Illinois
Elected 1980

Augustus F. "Gus" Savage was elected in 1980 to the 97th Congress as Representative of Illinois' Second Congressional District. His election was a continuation of his many years of involvement in the civic and political life of Chicago and the Chicago publishing industry.

Savage is the twenty-third ranking member on the Public Works and Transportation Committee and twenty-second ranking member of the Small Business Committee. He also is a member of the Post Office and Civil Service Committee. For the Congressional Black Caucus he is chairing the Economic Development/Transportation Braintrust Workshop during the CBC Eleventh Annual Legislative Weekend.

Savage has been outspoken in the Chicago community as a political activist, beginning in 1946 with his leading to victory the demonstrations for veterans' housing. He organized demonstrations to win the rights of blacks to be hired as department store clerks, to serve in downtown Chicago restaurants, to live in a middle-income housing development called Lake Meadows, to select school principals in their local areas, to have representation for the 2nd Ward on the City Council and to have a black candidate on the ballot for Mayor of Chicago against former Mayor Michael Bilandic.

In 1950 Savage served as a full-time organizer for the Progressive Party. Thereafter he continued forward despite being subpoenaed into court in 1968 for supporting the Chicago Transit Workers strike, and jailed in 1970 for defending contracts of black home buyers. In 1979 he organized a community conference which enabled Mayor Byrne's transition team to hear the concerns and priorities of the citizens.

Awards that have been bestowed on Savage include the 1965 Independent Journalist of the Year; the City of Chicago Medal of Merit in 1976, by vote of the City Council; the Operation PUSH Award of Merit in 1976, for heroism in risking life to help save women being held as hostages during a robbery; the Businessman of the Year from *Dollars and Sense* magazine in 1978; in 1981 both the Freshman of the Year from the Evanston, Illinois NAACP, and the Presidential Award from the Cook County Bar Association.

Savage wrote the pamphlets "How to Increase the Power of the Negro Vote" in 1959 and "Political Power," in 1969.

LOUIS STOKES
Twenty-First District Ohio
Elected 1969

The older brother of Cleveland's former mayor Carl Stokes, Congressman Louis Stokes skillfully engineered his 1968 victory by welding a successful coalition of ghetto poor and affluent suburbanites in the redrawn 21st Ohio Congressional District (Cleveland's East Side, Garfield Heights, and Newburgh Heights). Stokes garnered some 86,000 votes compared with only 31,000 for his black Republican opponent, Charles Lucas.

Stokes and Lucas had been allies after 1965, the year the Ohio legislature divided the 21st District in such a way that black voting strength was largely emasculated. Under such an arrangement, it would have been virtually impossible for a black Congressional candidate to capture a House seat. Lucas then brought suit before the U.S. Supreme Court protesting the gerrymander, and was joined by Stokes in arguing the case. The merits of their argument were so convincing that the Court instructed the legislature to shelve its original plan, whereupon the Ohioans hatched a new redistricting setup in which the black electorate formed 65% of the voting total. The victory severed the temporary alliance between Stokes and Lucas inasmuch as both were anxious to campaign for the opening.

A native of Cleveland, Stokes shined shoes and sold papers to earn money to help his widowed mother, Mrs. Louise Stokes, and his younger brother, Carl.

Stokes enlisted in the Army after finishing high school and used the GI Bill to finance higher education at Western Reserve University and the Cleveland-Marshall Law School. He later joined the NAACP as a crusading lawyer whose prominence in antidiscrimination lawsuits won him popular favor among the ghetto poor.

Congenial and experienced, Stokes has always impressed people with his ability to circulate comfortably among straitlaced businessmen as well as casual, streetwise billiard parlor habitues.

In 1970 and 1972 Stokes was reelected with some

Congressman Louis Stokes talks with constituents in a Cleveland slum.

80% of the district's vote and his seat is regarded as safe.

From 1972 to 1974 Stokes served as chairman of the Congressional Black Caucus.

Stokes was a member of the Select Committee to Conduct an Investigation and Study of the Circumstances Surrounding the death of President Kennedy and death of Dr. Martin Luther King, Jr., and in 1977 Speaker Thomas P. "Tip" O'Neill appointed him chairman of this committee. On December 31, 1978 Stokes completed these historic investigations and filed with the House of Representatives 27 volumes of hearings, a Final Report, and Recommendations for Administrative and Legislative Reform.

Stokes was appointed to the House Committee on

Standards of Official Conduct (Ethics Committee) in 1980 and early was elected its chairman.

Congressman Stokes has served two terms as chairman of the Congressional Black Caucus and is currently co-chairman of the Caucus Health Braintrust. He has been named by *Ebony* magazine as one of the 100 most influential black Americans each year since 1971, and at the 1980 Congressional Black Caucus Legislative Weekend Awards Program he was presented the William L. Dawson Award by his colleagues in the Caucus in recognition of his "unique leadership in the development of legislation."

HAROLD WASHINGTON
First District Illinois
Elected 1980

Harold Washington, a Democrat, was elected to Congress in 1980. As a freshman he became a member of the Committee on Education and Labor where he is the eighteenth ranking member; the Judiciary Committee where he ranks fourteenth; and the Committee on Government Operations where he ranks twenty-first. He also serves on the Judiciary Subcommittee on Civic and Constitutional Rights, which has jurisdiction over the important Voting Rights Act that expires in August 1982, and the Subcommittee on Manpower and Housing. Congressman Washington currently serves as secretary of the Congressional Black Caucus.

In addition to his committee assignments, Washington is a member of the Northeast-Midwest Congressional Coalition's Auto Task Force and the Congressional Steel Caucus. He also serves on the Executive Board of the Federal Government Service Task Force.

After graduating from Northwestern University School of Law in 1952, Harold Washington was a practicing attorney until his appointment in 1954 as assistant city prosecutor for Chicago. He served for five years as arbitrator for the Illinois Industrial Commission, and in 1965 was elected to the Illinois House of Representatives where he served Chicago's 26th District until his election to the Illinois senate in 1977.

Washington is the founder and president of the Black Taxpayers Federation. He is also a member of the Boards of Directors of the Suburban Southern Christian Leadership Conference and the Mid-South Mental Health Association.

Representative Washington is a member of the Cook County, Illinois and National Bar Associations.

RECENT BLACK CONGRESSMEN

The history of black Congressmen can be divided into three phases.

Reconstruction

Between 1870 and 1901, 22 blacks, two Senators and 20 Representatives, served. All were from the South. Both Senators were from Mississippi. Of the Representatives, eight were from South Carolina, four were from North Carolina, three from Alabama, and one each from Florida, Georgia, Louisiana, Mississippi, and Virginia.

It is not surprising that these black legislators were expected to become a special breed of miracle worker seeking, wherever possible, to establish free public schooling, to abolish debtors' punishments, to extend voting rights—in short, to deliver to the black a host of privileges and rights long taken for granted by the white majority.

Some black legislators were party hacks; some were misguided idealists; some were unprincipled scoundrels. Yet, on the whole, black Congressmen were eager and willing public servants. The majority were not motivated solely by self-interest and political opportunism, nor did they approach government with an overweening desire for revenge against their southern oppressors.

The impact of these men on American history has not been enormous, yet they cannot be regarded merely as historical peculiarities. They were products of their age, but they also made their imprint on that age. With the triumph of white supremacist laws and evasions, the last of these men, George H. White of North Carolina, left Congress in 1901. By 1902 there was not a single black legislator on a national or state level.

The Period of Urbanization: 1902–1965

The rapid emigration of blacks to the North eventually resulted in congressional districts with sufficient black voters to elect a few black legislators. The first was Oscar De Priest of Chicago, a Republican elected to the House in 1928. De Priest was defeated in 1934, during the Roosevelt landslide, by a black Democrat, Arthur Mitchell. During World War II William Dawson and Adam Clayton Powell, Jr. were elected, followed in the 1950s by Charles C. Diggs, who retired in 1980, and Robert N. C. Nix, who was defeated in 1978.

These men fought the long lonely battles for legislation to eliminate the poll tax and make lynching a federal crime. They were extremely important in Congress as a voice for the causes of blacks and as a bridge between blacks and white liberals, the alliance which was to win the civil rights victories of the 1960s.

Legislation and Redistricting: 1965 to the Present

The present period, as noted, finds 16 blacks in the House of Representatives. Much of this achievement is attributable to the Voting Rights Act of 1965, which made possible the election of two black Representatives from the South, Barbara Jordan and Andrew Young, and the Supreme Court's requirements that the one man one vote dictum be applied by state legislatures so that cities be fairly represented.

Following is a list of former black Congressmen. All served in the House of Representatives unless otherwise indicated.

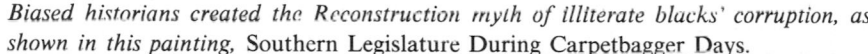

Biased historians created the Reconstruction myth of illiterate blacks' corruption, as shown in this painting, Southern Legislature During Carpetbagger Days.

EDWARD W. BROOKE
Senator from Massachusetts
Elected 1966

During his two terms in the U.S. Senate, Edward W. Brooke, the first black to be elected to that body since 1876, defied conventional political wisdom. In a state that was overwhelmingly Democratic and in which blacks constituted only 3% of the population, he was one of its most popular political figures and a Republican.

He first achieved statewide office in 1962 when he defeated Elliot Richardson to become Attorney General. He established an outstanding record in that post and in 1966 was elected to the Senate over former Massachusetts governor Endicott Peabody.

Born into a middle-class Washington, D.C. environment, Brooke attended public schools locally and went on to graduate from Howard. Inducted into an all-black infantry unit during World War II, Brooke rose to the rank of captain and was ultimately given a Bronze Star for his work in intelligence.

Returning to Massachusetts, Brooke attended the Boston University Law School, compiling an outstanding academic record and editing the *Law Review* in the process. After law school, he established himself as an attorney and also served as chairman of the Boston Finance Commission.

Brooke was later nominated for the attorney general's office, encountering stiff opposition within his own party, but eventually winning both the Republican primary and the general election against his Democratic opponent.

Upon entering the national political scene, Brooke espoused the notion that the Great Society could not become a reality until it was preceded by the "Responsible Society." He called this a society in which "it's more profitable to work than not to work. You don't help a man by constantly giving him more handouts."

Brooke has also hastened to note that he is not merely "the first Negro this or the highest Negro that," but can likewise be described as "a Protestant in a Catholic state and a Republican in a Democratic state."

When first elected, Brooke strongly supported United States participation in the Vietnam War, though most black leaders were increasingly opposing it. However, in 1971 Brooke supported the McGovern-Hatfield Amendment which called for withdrawal of the United States from Vietnam.

As might be expected, matters of race rather than foreign affairs were to become Brooke's area of expertise. Reluctant and subdued, Brooke proceeded carefully at first, waiting to be consulted by President Nixon and loyally accepting the latter's apparent indifference to his views. However, as pressure mounted from the established civil rights groups and impatient black militants he decided to attack the Nixon policies. Brooke was roused into a more active role by the Administration's vacillating school desegregation guidelines, its "firing" of HEW official Leon Panetta, and the nominations to the Supreme Court of judicial conservatives Clement Haynsworth and G. Harrold Carswell.

In 1972 Brooke was reelected to the Senate over-

Senator Edward Brooke went into the streets to get first-hand knowledge of his constituents' grievances.

whelmingly, even though Massachusetts was the only state not carried by his party in the Presidential election. While Brooke seconded the nomination of President Nixon at the 1972 Republican Convention, he became increasingly critical of the Nixon Administration. He also began to appear publicly at meetings of the Congressional Black Caucus, a group he had tended to avoid in the past. Brooke was considered a member of the moderate-to-liberal wing of the Republican Party.

He was defeated for his third term in the Senate in 1978 and returned to the private practice of law.

YVONNE BRAITHWAITE BURKE
Thirty-Seventh District California
Elected 1973

Attorney and former California State Assemblywoman Yvonne Braithwaite Burke became the first black woman from California ever to be elected to the House of Representatives in November 1972.

Congresswoman Burke served in the state Assembly for six years prior to her election to Congress. During her final two years there, she was chairman of the Committee on Urban Development and Housing and a member of the Health, Finance and Insurance committees.

As a state legislator, Burke was responsible for enactment of bills providing for needy children, relocation of tenants and owners of homes taken by governmental action, and one which required major medical insurance programs to grant immediate coverage to newborn infants of the insured.

Burke was recently selected a fellow in the Harvard University Institute of Politics, which is part of the John F. Kennedy School of Government.

Prior to her governmental career, Burke was a practicing attorney, during which time she served as a Deputy Corporation Commissioner, a hearing officer for the Los Angeles Police Commissioner, and an attorney for the McCone Commission, which investigated the Watts riots.

Burke's district, created in 1971 by the California legislature, contains low-and middle-income black and integrated neighborhoods plus some white suburban tracts and beach communities, including Venice, which is noted for its "counterculture" scene.

About 50% of the district's population is black, another 10% of Hispanic and Asian origin. In 1972 the district gave 64% of its vote to Burke, who was, at the time, Miss Braithwaite. She was married in 1972 and in 1973 became the first Congresswoman to give birth while in office, to a daughter, Autumn Roxanne Burke.

In 1978 Representative Burke resigned to run for Attorney General in California. She lost that race and

Representative Yvonne Burke was elected to the U.S. House in 1972.

has since been in the private practice of law although she remains prominent in California politics. She has also taken on a number of civic responsibilities including serving as a member of the University of California Board of Regents.

SHIRLEY CHISHOLM
Twelfth District New York
Elected 1969

Representative Shirley Chisholm stunned a number of people early in 1982 when she announced that after almost 15 years in Congress she would not seek another term because of her desire to return to "a more private life." Her retirement brought an end to a political career that found her as well known nationally as she was in her home district, which encompasses the Bedford-Stuyvesant and Bushwick sections of Brooklyn.

Her decision was not a sudden one. She had been considering such a move for over a year and conceded that the defeat of many liberal lawmakers in the 1980 election and what she considered a growing conservatism in the country had played a part in her decision. At her leaving, she was a member of the all-important House Rules Committee and secretary of the House Democratic Caucus. Hers was one of the loudest voices raised in protest against the Reagan Administration's cutbacks in domestic programs.

Chisholm became the first black woman to sit in the House of Representatives in 1969. Her opponent for the seat was James Farmer, once the leader of CORE and an important figure in the Civil Rights Movement. Farmer allegedly sought to create a whisper campaign around the theme that black women had already exercised far too much influence on the fate of black communities and on the development of black self-assertiveness, but the issue, if it had any relevance at all, did not sway much opinion. Members of the newly created predominantly black and Puerto Rican 12th Congressional District chose the dynamic Chisholm over Farmer by a more than 3–1 margin.

Chisholm originally entered public life in response to local pleas for an honest, conscientious public servant in the New York State Assembly. While there, she sponsored the SEEK program, which offers students from minority groups the opportunity to obtain college-level training even if they do not yet have high school diplomas. She also introduced legislation to establish publicly supported daycare centers and to extend unemployment insurance to domestic workers.

Chisholm's decision to run for higher office was based in part on the continued appeals of people of her district, whose problems she knew because she had chosen to remain in Bedford-Stuyvesant rather than move on to more affluent surroundings.

Born Shirley St. Hill in 1926, Representative Chisholm is descended from West Indian immigrant laborers (her mother was a seamstress from Barbados and her father, a native of British Guiana, worked in a burlap factory). One of three sisters, she was sent to Barbados at the age of three to live with other immediate family members while her parents struggled to save money for the girls' education. At age 11, Shirley returned to Brooklyn, attending grade school and high school before earning a scholarship to pursue higher education. A graduate of both Brooklyn College and Columbia University, holder of a masters in elementary education, Chisholm worked as a nursery school teacher, director of a daycare center, and consultant for the New York Department of Social Services before entering public life as a state representative in Albany.

After her election, Chisholm indicated her early preference for committee assignments which would reflect her interests and areas of expertise (education, labor management, and inner-city conditions in general) and take advantage of her experience in the social services. When saddled with a committee assignment in the area of agriculture, she openly balked at the idea, complaining outspokenly of the gross misuse of her talents.

Chisholm is a tough, tenacious crusader, whose belief in organization is almost as strong as her faith in the good will and basic decency of black people.

Her efforts on their behalf dictate a practical and result-oriented philosophy which focuses on self-determination through the meaningful participation in the economic life of the nation. In her view, this means that black people need sound vocational education, access to higher learning, and sensible business counseling.

Though sympathetic with the goals of militants, she feels that they are often undisciplined and incapable of executing real change in a structured environment serving large numbers of people. She is, however, equally critical of the shallow thinking that produces appeals to law and order without placing equal emphasis on the theme of justice in American society.

In 1972, Representative Chisholm leaped to national prominence when she announced her candidacy for the Democratic Presidential nomination. She entered a large number of primaries and, though her share of the vote never exceeded 7%, she was regarded with the same respect as the white male candidates and

Many were disappointed when Shirley Chisholm announced in 1982 that she would not seek reelection.

was invited to join attempts to prevent the nomination of Senator McGovern.

However, Chisholm received only some 150 of 1,600 delegate votes at the Miami Convention, as a great many blacks supported McGovern or Senator Hubert Humphrey rather than Chisholm.

Chisholm has been the target of considerable criticism from black leaders and her constituents for her avid support of women's liberation. Of particular concern was a remark, attributed to her, to the effect that discrimination against women exceeds discrimination against blacks. Many blacks who agreed with the objectives of "women's lib" feel such views divert attention from the needs of blacks, men and women alike.

However, Chisholm was such a popular figure among her constituents that she continued to win her seat in each election by substantial margins.

CHARLES C. DIGGS
Thirteenth District Michigan
Elected 1954

Following his conviction for using funds from his federal payroll to pay personal bills and his sentencing to three years in prison, Congressman Charles C. Diggs, the senior black representative in the House, resigned in 1980. By resigning, Representative Diggs avoided what was certain to be a vote by his colleagues to expel him.

The resignation removed from Congress one of its most skilled and experienced members, who was particularly effective in his chairmanship of the House Foreign Affairs African Subcommittee.

Diggs was born in Detroit in 1922 and was educated there. In high school he compiled an outstanding academic record and excelled as a debater. Later, at the University of Michigan, Diggs won the university's oratorical championship. In 1942 he transferred to Fisk University in Nashville before being drafted into the Army Air Force where he was ultimately commissioned as a second lieutenant. He was honorably discharged in 1945.

Back in Detroit, Diggs enrolled at the Wayne State University School of Mortuary Science. At the same time, he was radio commentator on a program cosponsored by the House of Diggs, the family business which has come to be the largest funeral home in Michigan.

Diggs entered politics in 1951 when he was elected to the State Senate. Compiling a robust legislative record in civil rights, business, and labor relations, Diggs won the admiration of key figures in the Democratic party and by 1953 was in a position to run, though unsuccessfully for a seat on the Detroit Common Council.

In 1954, at the age of 28, Diggs upset the Democratic incumbent in a landslide primary victory and went on to win election to the House of Representatives. In Washington, he soon acquired a reputation as a diligent and shrewd watchdog of *de facto* discrimination in the armed forces and in federally sponsored programs in the South. Many positive acts by numerous Secretaries of Defense to reduce discrimination can be traced to Diggs.

In 1970, with the death of Congressman William L. Dawson and the defeat of Adam Clayton Powell, Diggs, at 48, became the senior black member of the House. In 1973 he was chosen chairman of the District of Columbia Committee, a position he occupied in addition to his chairmanship of the Foreign Affairs African Subcommittee.

Diggs' district existed entirely within the city of Detroit. It was about 67% black and contained some pockets of Polish and German ethnics. In each of his elections, Diggs faced only token opposition.

MELVIN H. EVANS
Virgin Islands
Elected 1978

As the first elected governor of the U.S. Virgin Islands, and later as its nonvoting congressman in the House of Representatives, Dr. Melvin H. Evans has had two highly successful careers—one in the field of medicine and the other in the political arena. A native of the Virgin Islands, Dr. Evans graduated with honors from Howard University's College of Medicine and later took an advanced degree at the University of California at Berkeley.

He served in a number of medical posts both in the United States and in the Virgin Islands, where he was Commissioner of Health (1959–1967). He was a teaching fellow in Medicine at Howard (1948–1950), a senior assistant surgeon, U.S. Public Health Service (1948–1950), and a fellow in cardiology, Johns Hopkins Hospital (1956–1957). In 1969 he was appointed governor of the Virgin Islands and served until 1971 when he was elected to that post for four years.

In 1975 he was a representative of the State Department on a lecture tour that covered Sierre Leone, Liberia, Zambia, Tanzania, and Kenya. He engaged in the private practice of medicine from 1976 to 1978 when he was elected, as a Republican, to the 96th Congress where he served on the Committee of Armed Services, the Committee on Interior and Insular Affairs, the Committee on Merchant Marine and Fisheries, and the Congressional Tourism Caucus. During his one term in Congress Evans had the distinction of being the first, and as of 1981, the only Republican member of the Congressional Black Caucus.

ROBERT N. C. NIX
Second District Pennsylvania
Elected 1958

Born in Orangeburg, South Carolina in 1905, Robert Nix moved to New York and attended Townsend Harris Hall High School, a prep school with exceptionally high academic requirements. He went on to the Lincoln University and the University of Pennsylvania Law School.

Having passed his bar examination, Nix became a special deputy attorney general for Pennsylvania (Escheats Division of the State Department of Revenue) from 1934 to 1936 and later was active in local Philadelphia politics.

Nix was elected in 1958 to fill the unexpired term of Congressman Earl Chudoff, and thus became the twenty-sixth black Congressman in United States history.

A long-time liberal, Nix was one of the first Congressmen to speak out in support of the Montgomery bus boycott. He was regarded by Speaker of the House Sam Rayburn, Jr. as one of the most brilliant men he had ever known.

However, in the early 1970s, militant blacks charged Nix with indifference to U.S. involvement in Vietnam and to the problems of blacks in his district. He received only 47% of the vote in the 1972 Democratic primary, winning with a plurality over three other candidates. It was obvious then that Nix was likely to encounter ever-increasing challenges from other black Congressional aspirants in the coming years.

In 1978 Congressman Nix was defeated in the Democratic primary election by William Gray, who went on to win the general election.

BARBARA JORDAN
Eighteenth District Texas
Elected 1973

See biography in section on Black Women.

ANDREW YOUNG
Fifth District Georgia
Elected 1973

See biography in section on black mayors.

BLACK CONGRESSMEN OF THE PAST

BLANCHE K. BRUCE
Senator from Mississippi
1875–1881

Blanche K. Bruce was born a slave in Farmville, Prince Edward County, Virginia on March 1, 1841. He received his early formal education in Missouri, where his parents had moved while he was still quite young, and later studied at Oberlin College in Ohio.

In 1868 Bruce settled in Floreyville, Mississippi. He worked as a planter and eventually built up a considerable fortune in property.

Congressman Nix's district was in Pennsylvania.

Blanche K. Bruce was a spokesman for minority rights in the Senate.

Black members of the U.S. Congress during Reconstruction were (left to right) *Senator Hiram Revels and Representatives Benjamin Turner, Robert DeLarge, Josiah T. Walker, Jefferson Long, Joseph M. Rainy, and R. Brown Elliott.*

In 1870 Bruce entered politics and was elected sergeant-at-arms of the Mississippi Senate. A year later he was named assessor of taxes in Bolivar County. In 1872 he served as sheriff of that county and as a member of the Board of Levee Commissioners of Mississippi.

Bruce was nominated for the U.S. Senate from Mississippi in February 1874. Once elected he became an outspoken defender of the rights of minority groups, including the Chinese and Indians. He also investigated alleged election frauds and worked for the improvement of navigation on the Mississippi in the hope of increasing interstate and foreign commerce. Like Hiram Revels, Bruce also supported legislation aimed at eliminating reprisals against those who had opposed Negro emancipation.

After Bruce completed his term in the Senate, he was named Register of the U.S. Treasury Department by President James A. Garfield. Bruce held this position until 1885. In 1889 President Benjamin Harrison appointed him recorder of deeds in Washington, D.C. Seven years later, President William McKinley reappointed him to his former Treasury Department post as register.

Bruce died on March 17, 1898.

RICHARD H. CAIN

South Carolina
1873–1875; 1877–1879

Richard Harvey Cain was born in 1825 in Greenbriar County, Virginia of free parents. While still young, he moved north to Ohio and, like many blacks of his day, found work on steamboats servicing the nation's major waterways.

At the age of 19 Cain became a preacher in Missouri for the Methodist Episcopal Church. Soon disillusioned, he returned to Ohio where he joined the African Methodist Episcopal (AME) Church, and was given a congregation in Iowa.

In the Civil War, Cain served as a minister and also helped publish a newspaper, *The Missionary Record*. In 1868 he was elected a state senator in South Carolina. Subsequently, he served South Carolina in the U.S. Congress, where he established a reputation for clean politics.

On his retirement from public life in 1880, Cain was named AME bishop of the Louisiana and Texas conference, and became president of Paul Quinn College in Waco, Texas. He died in 1887.

HENRY P. CHEATHAM
North Carolina
1889–1893

Henry Plummer Cheatham was born in Henderson, North Carolina in 1857. He won his B.A. and M.A. degrees from Shaw University, and later studied law, although he did not enter practice.

Cheatham first entered public life as register of deeds for Vance County, North Carolina, serving in this post from 1884 to 1888. Thereafter, he was principal of the State Normal School at Plymouth, which was later incorporated into Elizabeth City State Teachers College.

In 1888 Cheatham ran successfully as a Republican candidate for the Second Congressional District of North Carolina. He won reelection in 1890, but was defeated in his try for a third term.

In 1901 Cheatham returned to North Carolina, settling in Oxford where he became superintendent of a black orphan asylum. He helped raise money for this institution, and served its interests unstintingly until his death in 1935.

GEORGE W. COLLINS
Illinois
1970–1972

George W. Collins had a brief, tragic career in Congress. Elected from the Seventh (Chicago West Side) District in 1970 and reelected in 1972, he died in an airplane crash in December, the same crash which killed Dorothy Hunt, wife of E. Howard Hunt, convicted Watergate conspirator.

Collins obtained his seat in 1970 as a result of redistricting in Illinois and the fear of the city's Democratic machine that it was losing support of Chicago's blacks. Mayor Richard Daley encouraged Representative Frank Annunzio, who had represented most of the district to seek election elsewhere, and handed the seat to Collins. Annunzio also won, in a new, white, blue-collar district, after reversing his opposition to antibusing legislation.

Following his death, Collins was succeeded by his wife, Cardiss, who won a special election in 1973.

WILLIAM L. DAWSON
Illinois
1943–1971

William L. Dawson represented the First Congressional District of Illinois for 28 years, from 1943 to 1971.

Born in Albany, Georgia in 1886, Dawson received his early education locally and later graduated *magna cum laude* from Fisk University in Nashville. Interested at first in law, Dawson studied at Kent College

Henry P. Cheatham served two terms in the House of Representatives.

before joining the U.S. Expeditionary Forces in 1917 as an officer. He saw combat with the 365th Infantry in the Argonne offensive, and was wounded and gassed while on the front lines.

At the end of the war, Dawson went back to law, completing his studies at Northwestern University and opening a practice in Illinois. After nine years as an attorney, he ran unsuccessfully as a Republican candidate for Congress in 1928. A year later, while serving as Republican State Committeeman in the First Congressional District, he was called upon to manage Judge John H. Lyle's mayoralty campaign.

Dawson's first political success came in 1935, when he was elected alderman. While serving on the City Council, he crossed party lines and became an avid supporter of President Franklin D. Roosevelt. In 1940 Dawson was elected Democratic committeeman from the Second Ward. Two years later he won a seat in the House of Representatives.

In 1944 Dawson was appointed assistant chairman of the Democratic National Committee, and he soon became the first black to be elected its vice chairman. He campaigned for President Harry S Truman, whose surprise victory over Thomas E. Dewey was later attributed, at least in part, to the black electorate. He was thus able to see to it that, for the first time, blacks were invited in more than token numbers to the Inaugural Ball, a practice which has since been taken for granted.

Dawson occupied a number of key Congressional posts. During the 81st Congress, he was chairman of the House Committee on Expenditures in the Executive Department, and later became chairman of the Committee on Government Operations—considered to be among the most important on Capitol Hill.

Dawson retired in 1971, turning his seat over to Ralph Metcalfe. He died in 1972 at the age of 86.

ROBERT C. DeLARGE
South Carolina
1871–1873

Robert C. DeLarge was born a slave in 1842 in Aiken, South Carolina. He received what was for his day and race an above-average education and, during Reconstruction, became a successful farmer. Turning to politics, he served two years in the state legislature before being elected to Congress. The election, however, was marred by serious voting irregularities, and a Congressional Commission on Elections declared the seat vacant.

In 1873, his health failing, DeLarge was appointed a magistrate in the city of Charleston, a position he held until his death one year later.

OSCAR De PRIEST
Illinois
1929–1935

Oscar De Priest was the first black to win a seat in the U.S. House of Representatives in the twentieth century, and the first to be elected from a northern state.

Born in Florence, Alabama, De Priest moved to Kansas with his family at the age of six. His formal education there consisted of business and bookkeeping classes which he completed before running away to Dayton, Ohio with two white friends. By the year 1889 he had reached Chicago and become a painter and master decorator.

In Chicago De Priest amassed a fortune in real estate and the stock market and in 1904 entered politics successfully when he was elected Cook County commissioner. In 1908 he was appointed an alternate delegate to the Republican National Convention and in 1915 became Chicago's first black alderman.

In 1928 he was a candidate for the post of Republican committeeman for the Third Ward, and a prospective delegate to the Republican National Convention. However, Martin B. Maddew, the Republican Congressman, died suddenly and De Priest waged a successful campaign for the vacant seat.

The unofficial spokesman for the 11 million blacks in the United States during this period, De Priest faced

Robert C. DeLarge, a successful planter.

Oscar De Priest was the first black elected to the House in the twentieth century.

a formidable challenge, particularly since the country was undergoing a profound political and economic transformation during the Depression years. Though sincerely desirous of improving the Negro's lot, he found himself in a difficult partisan position and obliged to shift his support from Republican to Democratic candidates on the local level. On the national level, he usually voted with his party. In 1934 he was defeated by Arthur Mitchell, the first black Democrat elected to serve in Congress.

De Priest remained active in public life, serving from 1943 to 1947 as alderman of the Third Ward in Chicago. His final withdrawal from politics came about after a sharp dispute with his own party. De Priest returned to his real estate business, and he died in 1951.

ROBERT B. ELLIOTT
South Carolina
1871–1875

Robert. B. Elliott was born in Boston, to West Indian parents, in 1842. Much of his education was received abroad—first in the grammar schools of Jamaica, later in High Holborn Academy (London), and finally at Eton, from which he graduated with honors. While in England, he also studied for the law.

Upon his return to the United States, Elliott became an editor with the *Charleston Leader,* was elected to the South Carolina Constitutional Convention, and in 1868 won a seat in the lower house of the state legislature.

Subsequently, he was elected to the 42nd U.S. Congress. After serving two terms, he retired to New Orleans where he practiced law until his death on August 9, 1884.

JEREMIAH HARALSON
Alabama
1875–1877

At one time considered the most influential black in Alabama, Jeremiah Haralson was born a slave in Muscogee County, Georgia in 1846. Haralson was basically self-educated. After Emancipation, he moved to Alabama where, in 1868, he was defeated in his first attempt to win a Congressional seat.

After his election in 1874 Haralson introduced several bills, but none was passed. Accused of fraud, he was forced to submit to a runoff election. He won with a safe majority.

An ardent defender of the principle of amnesty, Haralson encountered widespread opposition from Alabama party regulars, who accused him of trying to maintain too close a relationship with Jefferson Davis, the former president of the Confederate States of America. Among his chief opponents was James T. Rapier, the black Congressman whom he succeeded.

Defeated in the 1878 and 1884 elections, Haralson spent his last days in Colorado where he was killed in a hunting mishap.

JOHN A. HYMAN
North Carolina
1875–1877

Born a slave in 1840 near Warrenton, North Carolina, John A. Hyman was sold and sent to Alabama where he was forced to remain until the end of the Civil War.

In 1868 Hyman, who was self-educated, participated in the Constitutional Convention of North Carolina. Soon thereafter he was selected to the state legislature and served there for six years. In 1875 he won a seat in Congress, but he was not reelected. He remained in Washington, D.C. in a minor post with the Revenue Service until his death in 1891.

JOHN MERCER LANGSTON
Virginia
1889–1891

John Mercer Langston, U.S. Congressman from Virginia, was born in Virginia in 1829 of black, Indian, and English ancestry.

John Langston, politician and diplomat.

Upon the death of his father, Ralph Quarles, an estate owner, young Langston was emancipated and sent to Ohio, where he was given over to the care of a friend of his father. Langston spent his childhood there, attending private school in Cincinnati before graduating from Oberlin College in 1849. Four years later, after getting his degree from the theological department of Oberlin, he studied law and was admitted to the Ohio bar in 1854.

Langston began his practice in Brownhelm, Ohio. He was chosen in 1855 to serve as clerk of this township by the Liberty Party. During the Civil War, he was a recruiting agent for Negro servicemen, helping to raise such famed regiments as the 54th and 55th Massachusetts, and the 5th Ohio.

After the war, Langston served as inspector-general of the Freedmen's Bureau and as dean and vice president of Howard University. In 1877 he was named minister resident to Haiti and charge d'affaires to Santo Domingo, remaining in diplomatic service until 1885.

Soon after his return to the United States and to his law practice, he was named president of the Virginia Normal and Collegiate Institute. In 1888 he was elected to Congress from Virginia, but was not seated for two years until vote-counting irregularities had been investigated. He was defeated in his bid for a second term. In 1894 Langston wrote an autobiography, *From the Virginia Plantation to the National Capital.* (Eleven years earlier, he had published a volume of his speeches, *Freedom and Citizenship.*)

Langston died in 1897.

JEFFERSON F. LONG
Georgia
1869–1871

Jefferson Franklin Long was born a slave in 1836 near Knoxville, Georgia. Primarily self-educated, he moved to Macon at an early age. There, he found work with a merchant tailor and eventually saved enough money to open a shop of his own.

At the close of the Civil War, Long rapidly rose to a position of influence within the local Republican party structure. Elected to the 41st Congress, he campaigned vigorously against the spread of lynch law in Georgia, for enforcement of the Fifteenth Amendment, and for universal suffrage in the District of Columbia.

Long retired in March 1871, returning to his prosperous tailoring business. He attended the Southern Republican Convention in Chattanooga in 1874, and also served as a delegate to the Republican National Convention of 1880.

He died in Macon in 1900.

JOHN R. LYNCH
Mississippi
1873–1877; 1881–1883

The first black to preside over a national convention of the Republican party, Mississippi Congressman John R. Lynch was elected to the House of Representatives in 1873, 1875, and 1881.

Born a slave in Louisiana in 1847, Lynch attended evening classes in Natchez, Mississippi. In 1869 he was named a justice of the peace for Adams County, and elected to the Mississippi State Legislature where he ultimately served as speaker of the House.

From 1871 to 1889—a period which encompassed his Congressional service—Lynch was chairman of the Executive Committee of the Republican party. On three occasions he was a delegate to that party's na-

John Lynch chaired the Republican Party's national convention in 1884.

tional convention, and he presided over it in 1884.

In 1889 Lynch served under Benjamin Harrison as fourth auditor of the United States Treasury, but declined this same appointment when it was offered him four years later by Grover Cleveland. In 1896 he campaigned vigorously on behalf of Presidential candidate William McKinley, who showed his gratitude by naming him U.S. paymaster during the Spanish-American War.

Lynch retired to private law practice in 1911.

During his later years, he wrote two books: *The Facts of the Reconstruction* and *Some Historical Errors of James Ford Rhodes*. He died in Chicago in 1939.

RALPH METCALFE
Illinois
1971–1978

Ralph Metcalfe was born in Atlanta in 1910 and during the 1930s was famed as an Olympic track star who broke or equaled every sprint record between 40 and 220 yards. Metcalfe served in the Army in World War II and entered politics in 1949 when he was named Athletic Commissioner of Illinois.

Between 1954 and 1970, Metcalfe served on the Chicago City Council and was generally considered a loyal supporter of Mayor Richard Daley, a factor which played a role in his nomination and election to the seat held by the late William Dawson.

However, Metcalfe's positions had started to depart from those of the city's Democratic machine. His refusal, in 1972, to support the reelection of state's attorney Edward Hanrahan forced Daley to withhold his endorsement, a factor which led to the defeat of the man widely accused of leading a "cover-up" in the 1969 death of Fred Hampton, leader of the Illinois Black Panthers. Daley and Metcalfe also collided on the issue of police behavior, an ever-present problem that exploded in 1972 when some policemen allegedly beat up two black dentists who were friends of Metcalfe.

The Illinois First is the most solidly black (89%) and solidly Democratic district in the United States. By 1974, Metcalfe was widely acknowledged as the strongest political leader in the South Side, which is the largest black ghetto in the United States. He was reelected in 1976. His career ended with his death in 1978.

THOMAS E. MILLER
South Carolina
1889–1891

Born in Ferebeeville, South Carolina on June 17, 1849, Thomas Ezekiel Miller attended public schools in Charleston and Hudson, New York, before graduating

from Lincoln University. He studied law, passed the bar in 1875, and set up private practice in Beaufort.

Miller held a number of local offices before being elected state senator in 1880. After an unsuccessful campaign for the lieutenant-governorship, Miller was elected for one term to the U.S. House of Representatives. In 1895, after having been chosen a member of the South Carolina Constitutional Convention, he became president of the State Colored College of Orangeburg, South Carolina, the first such institution for the higher education of blacks in the state.

He died in Charleston just before his eighty-ninth birthday, in 1938.

ARTHUR W. MITCHELL
Illinois
1934–1942

The 1934 victory of Arthur W. Mitchell, the first black Democrat ever elected to serve in Congress, was the first major shift in black voting sentiment in the United States since the days of Reconstruction. Conversely, Oscar De Priest, the man he defeated, was the last black Republican to serve in the House.

Born to slave parents in 1883 in Chambers County, Alabama, Mitchell was educated at Tuskegee Institute and at Columbia and Harvard universities. By 1929 he had founded Armstrong Agricultural School in West Butler, Alabama, and become a wealthy landowner and a lawyer with a thriving practice in Washington, D.C. When he left the nation's capital that

Representative Arthur W. Mitchell was the first black Democrat elected to the Congress.

year, it was with the avowed purpose of entering politics and becoming a representative from Illinois.

Mitchell won Democratic approval only after Harry Baker (who had defeated him in the primary) died suddenly, leaving the nomination vacant. Aided by the overwhelming national sentiment for the Democratic party during this period, he unseated Oscar De Priest by the slender margin of 3,000 votes.

Mitchell's most significant victory on behalf of civil rights came, not in the legislative chamber, but in the courts. In 1937 Mitchell brought suit against the Chicago and Rock Island Railroad after having been forced to leave his first-class accommodations en route to Hot Springs, Arkansas, and sit in a "Jim Crow" car. He argued his own case before the Supreme Court in 1941, and won a decision which declared "Jim Crow" practices illegal.

A year later Mitchell retired from Congress and settled on his estate near Petersburg, Virginia, where he died in 1968 at the age of 85.

GEORGE WASHINGTON MURRAY
South Carolina
1893–1897

Long an advocate of free silver and a supporter of stronger federal election laws, George Washington Murray was born a slave in Rembert, South Carolina in 1853. He was left an orphan at Emancipation. Nonetheless, he acquired a substantial education, highlighted by his completion of two years of study at South Carolina University.

A teacher for some 14 years, Murray was chosen Republican party chairman for Sumter County in 1888. President Benjamin Harrison subsequently appointed him Customs Inspector for the port of Charleston. In 1893 he narrowly won a seat in Congress in a disputed election.

An exponent of industrial education, Murray sought to use his office in the promotion of better schooling opportunities for blacks in the South. He also induced Congress to print a list of those inventions which had been patented by blacks, neglecting to mention the fact that eight of these were for his own agricultural implements.

In 1895 Murray was given a leave of absence from his congressional duties for business and health reasons. A year later he was returned to the 54th Congress, this time by a margin of 2,000 votes.

Murray's political aspirations were dashed when he led a faction of dissident blacks in what proved to be an unsuccessful breakaway from the Republican ranks. Returning to Sumter County in 1897, he began a new career in real estate. He died in Chicago in 1926.

CHARLES E. NASH
Louisiana
1875–1877

Born in 1844 in Louisiana, Charles Edmund Nash earned his living as a bricklayer until his enlistment in the Union Army in 1863. A member of the famed *Chasseurs d'Afrique,* Nash lost a leg during the storming of Fort Blakely. After his discharge as a sergeant-major, he was named U.S. Inspector of Customs for his native state.

Elected to the 44th Congress, Nash failed in his bid for reelection. He thereupon became postmaster of a small Louisiana town. Soon after his retirement from this post he moved to New Orleans, where he died in 1913.

JAMES E. O'HARA
North Carolina
1883–1887

Born in New York City in 1844, James E. O'Hara first came to public office as an engrossing clerk for the North Carolina constitutional convention, then served a single term in the state legislature before going on to study law at Howard University. Admitted to the bar in 1873, he became one of six black delegates to the state constitutional convention two years later.

O'Hara first ran for Congress in 1878, but the seat was awarded to his adversary, William Hodges Kitchin. In 1882, however, he was successful—winning by a substantial majority.

Like most other black Reconstruction Congressmen, O'Hara placed the civil rights issue in the forefront of his legislative program. He managed to attach a rider to an interstate commerce bill, thereby sponsoring an amendment which guaranteed to all citizens equal accommodations. He also appended an antidiscrimination clause to the Pension Appropriation Bill. In 1884 O'Hara was renominated for his congressional post and won by a margin of 6,700 votes. However, O'Hara lost his bid for a third term, largely due to party dissension and the resurgence of the Democratic vote. Withdrawing from politics, he practiced law in New Bern, North Carolina, where he died in 1905.

ADAM CLAYTON POWELL, JR.
New York
1945–1971

Adam Clayton Powell, Jr. was a legend in his lifetime and one of the most controversial figures ever to grace American politics.

Born in 1908 to Mattie Fletcher and Adam Clayton Powell, Sr., Adam, Jr. was bred in New York City, attended high school there, and then went to Colgate University.

Powell gives an angry press conference on Bimini island during his exclusion from Congress.

The young Powell launched his career as a crusader for reform during the depth of the Depression. He forced several large corporations to drop their unofficial bans on employing blacks and directed a kitchen and relief operation which fed, clothed, and provided fuel for thousands of Harlem's needy and destitute. He was instrumental in persuading officials of Harlem Hospital to integrate their medical and nursing staffs, helped many blacks find employment along Harlem's "main stem," 125th Street, and campaigned against the city's bus lines, which were discriminating against Negro drivers and mechanics.

When Powell, Sr. retired from Abyssinian Baptist Church in 1937, his son, who had already served as manager and assistant pastor there, was named his successor.

In 1939 Powell served as chairman of the Coordinating Committee on Employment, which organized a picket line before the executive offices of the World's Fair in the Empire State Building and eventually succeeded in getting employment at the fair for hundreds of blacks.

Powell also sought better hospital, housing, and educational facilities for blacks.

Powell won a seat on the New York City Council in 1941 with the third highest number of votes ever cast for a candidate in municipal elections. In 1942 he turned to journalism for a second time (he had already been on the staff of the New York *Evening Post* in 1934), and published and edited the weekly *People's Voice,* which he called "the largest Negro tabloid in the world."

In 1945 Powell went to Washington, D.C. as the sole congressional representative of a community of 300,000, 89% of whom were black. Identified at once as "Mr. Civil Rights," he encountered a host of discriminatory procedures. He could not rent a room in downtown Washington, nor could he attend a movie in which his famed wife Hazel Scott had been starred. Within Congress itself, he was not authorized to use such communal facilities as dining rooms, steam baths, showers, and barber shops. Powell met these rebuffs head on by making use of all such facilities and insisting that his entire staff follow his lead.

As a freshman legislator, Powell engaged in fiery debates with arch-segregationists, fought for the abolition of discriminatory practices at U.S. military installations, and sought—through the controversial Powell amendment—to deny federal funds to any project where discrimination existed. (This amendment eventually became part of the Flanagan School Lunch Bill, making Powell the first black Congressman since Reconstruction to have legislation passed by both houses.)

Powell also sponsored legislation advocating federal aid to education, a minimum-wage scale, and greater benefits for the hard-core unemployed. He also drew attention to certain long-overlooked discriminatory practices on Capitol Hill itself, and in effecting their immediate elimination. It was Powell who first demanded that a Negro journalist be allowed to sit in the Senate and House press galleries, who introduced the first Jim Crow transportation legislation, and the first bill to prohibit segregation in the Armed Forces. At one point in his career, the *Congressional Record* reported that the House Committee on Education and Labor had processed more important legislation than any other major committee.

In 1960 Powell, as senior member of this committee, became its chairman. He had a hand in the development and passage of such significant legislation as the Minimum Wage Bill of 1961, the Manpower Development and Training Act, the Anti-Poverty Bill, the Juvenile Delinquency Act, the Vocational Educational Act, and the National Defense Education Act. (In all, the Powell committee helped pass 48 laws involving a total outlay of 14 billion dollars.)

Powell also displayed considerable foresight in the cause of civil rights when he became the first northerner of any race to endorse Lyndon Johnson for the presidency.

The flamboyant congressman, however, was accused of putting an excessive number of friends on the congressional payroll, of a high rate of absenteeism from congressional votes, and of excessive zeal for the "playboy's" life.

In 1967 the controversies and irregularities surrounding him led to censure in the House and a vote to exclude him from his seat in the 90th Congress. The House based its decision on the allegation that he had misused public funds and was in contempt of the New York courts due to a lengthy and involved defamation case which had resulted in a trial for civil and criminal contempt. Despite his exclusion, Powell was readmitted to the 91st Congress in 1968. In mid-1969, the Supreme Court ruled that the House had violated the Constitution by excluding him from membership, but left open the questions of his loss of 22 years seniority and the chairmanship of the Education and Labor Committee. Also unresolved were the $25,000 fine levied against him and the matter of back pay.

However, rather than return to Congress, Powell spent most of his time on the West Indian island of Bimini, where process servers could not reach him. But photographers did and the ensuing photos of Powell taking the sun on his boat while crucial votes were taken in Congress began to affect Powell in his home district. In 1970 he lost the Democratic primary and his seat to Charles Rangel by 150 votes. Powell's support had dwindled substantially, but it was a tribute to his popularity and achievement that Rangel required a majority of some 1,500 white voters in the district to defeat him. Powell then retired officially to Bimini, and on April 4, 1972, he died in Miami.

The controversy over Powell continues to rage after his death, and tends to follow racial lines. White supporters of the black cause praise his early achievements but feel that he was too difficult to work with. However, many blacks of all shades of the political spectrum defend him and many exult in the memory of his facility for defying the proprieties of the white establishment.

JOSEPH H. RAINEY
South Carolina
1869–1879

Joseph H. Rainey, the first black member of the House of Representatives, was born in 1832 in Georgetown, South Carolina. Drafted to work on Confederate fortifications in Charleston harbor during the Civil War, Rainey escaped to the West Indies and did not return until the close of the war in 1865.

In 1868 Rainey was elected as a delegate to the state constitutional convention and came to occupy a seat in the State Senate. A year later, he was elected to the House of Representatives, remaining in office until 1879.

In Congress, Rainey presented some 10 petitions for a civil rights bill which would have guaranteed blacks full constitutional rights and equal access to public accommodations. On one occasion, Rainey dramatized the latter issue by refusing to leave the dining room of a hotel in Suffolk, Virginia and by allowing himself to be forcibly ejected from the premises.

Rainey advocated passage of a bill to establish an American steamship line between the United States and Haiti, supported the rights of the Chinese minority in California, and became the first black to preside over the House of Representatives during a public debate—in this case, on a proposed bill to improve conditions on Indian reservations.

Upon his retirement from politics, Rainey was appointed a special agent for the U.S. Treasury Department in Washington, D.C. He served until 1881, after which he pursued banking and brokerage interests there.

In 1886 he returned to Georgetown, where he died in 1887.

ALONZO J. RANSIER
South Carolina
1873–1875

Born free in Charleston, South Carolina in 1834, Alonzo J. Ransier received a rudimentary education and, during his youth, worked as a shipping clerk. After serving as registrar of elections in 1865, Ransier attended South Carolina's first Republican convention the following year, and was commissioned to dispatch a memorandum to the U.S. Congress seeking federal protection for blacks.

In 1868 Ransier participated again in the South Carolina convention as a presidential elector and as chairman of the State Executive Committee. Two years later he was elected lieutenant governor of South Carolina, by a 33,000-vote plurality.

In Congress, Ransier became a key figure in the controversy over a "full and complete" civil rights bill. In addition, he advocated the extension of the presidential term to a period of six years, voted for the national tariff and against a salary increase for federal officials, and sought funds for the improvement of Charleston harbor.

Ransier failed to gain his party's nomination for a second term, returned to Charleston, and eventually became a day laborer for the city government. He died in 1882.

JAMES T. RAPIER
Alabama
1873–1875

Active in both the fields of politics and of labor, James T. Rapier was born in Florence, Alabama in 1837. Rapier's father, a successful planter, engaged a private tutor to educate his son, who later studied at Montreal College in Canada, the University of Glasgow in Scotland, and Franklin College in Nashville, Tennessee.

Although reputedly trained as a lawyer, he never practiced.

In 1870 Rapier (by then a successful cotton planter) ran unsuccessfully as a candidate for secretary of state in Alabama.

Rapier later went to Montgomery as one of an enterprising group of reformers who sought to rewrite the state constitution so as to include provisions for universal suffrage and free public schooling. He then helped to form Alabama's first Republican party, and served as its vice-president before turning his attention to the field of labor. Urging urban workers and rural sharecroppers to organize, Rapier was a key force in setting up Alabama's first black labor convention.

In 1872 Rapier won election to Congress by some 3,000 votes, and went to Washington where he worked for the passage of the 1875 Civil Rights Act.

Rapier's congressional career ended with the rapid rise of the Ku Klux Klan and the ascension to power of a Democratic bloc which came to control Alabama's politics. He died in Montgomery in 1882.

HIRAM RHOADES REVELS
Senator from Mississippi
1870–1871

Hiram Rhoades Revels, a native of North Carolina, was the first black to serve in the U.S. Senate. Revels was elected from his adopted state of Mississippi, and served for approximately one year, from February 1870 to March 1871.

A cartoon showing Senator Revels occupying Jefferson Davis's former seat.

Hiram Revels is sworn in as the nation's first black senator.

Born in 1822, Revels was educated in Indiana and attended Knox College in Illinois. Ordained a minister in the African Methodist Church, he worked among black settlers in the Northwest Territory, and in the border states of Kentucky and Missouri before settling in Baltimore. There he served as a church pastor and school principal.

During the Civil War, Revels helped organize a pair of Negro regiments in Maryland, and in 1863 he went to St. Louis to establish a freedmen school and to carry on his work as a recruiter. For a year he served as chaplain of a Mississippi regiment before becoming provost marshall of Vicksburg.

Revels settled in Natchez at the end of the war, and was appointed alderman by the Union military governor of the state. He won the respect of his constituents for his alert grasp of important state issues and for his courageous support of legislation which would have restored voting and office-holding privileges to disenfranchised southerners.

After leaving the senate, Revels was named president of Alcorn University near Lorman, Mississippi. In 1876 he became editor of the *South-western Christian Advocate,* a religious journal.

Revels lived in Holly Springs during his last years, remaining active in religious work until his death on January 16, 1901.

ROBERT SMALLS
South Carolina
1875–1879; 1881–1887

Robert Smalls of South Carolina served a longer period in Congress than any other black Reconstruction congressman.

Born a slave in Beaufort, South Carolina in 1839, Smalls received a limited education before moving to Charleston with the family of his owner.

At the outbreak of the Civil War, Smalls became a Confederate member of the crew of the *Planter,* a transport steamer.

On the morning of May 13, 1862, Smalls smuggled his wife and three children on board, assumed command of the vessel, and sailed it into the hands of the Union squadron blockading Charleston harbor. Singlehanded, he was thus responsible for the freedom of his own family and for that of the 12 black crewmen.

His daring exploit led President Lincoln to name him a pilot in the Union Navy. He was also awarded a large sum of money for what constituted the delivery of war booty.

In December 1863, during the siege of Charleston, Smalls took command of the *Planter* and sailed it to safety—a feat for which he was promoted to captain, the only black to hold such a rank during the Civil War.

After the war, Smalls was elected to the South Carolina State Senate, serving there from 1868 to 1870. In 1875 he began a period of congressional service which was interrupted only by his defeat in the 1878 election. Smalls attributed his defeat to vote-counting irregularities at the polls; however, it is possible that an accusation made a year earlier to the effect that he had accepted a $5,000 bribe while a state senator had diminished his popularity. (Convicted at first, Smalls was eventually exonerated by Governor William Dunlap Simpson of South Carolina.)

An outstanding congressman, Smalls consistently supported a wide variety of progressive legislation, including a bill to provide equal accommodations for blacks in interstate travel and an amendment designed to safeguard the rights of children born of interracial marriages.

Representative Robert Smalls (rear) *was a crewman on the Confederate gunboat* Planter.

Beyond politics, Smalls showed an active interest in military affairs, serving from 1865 to 1877 as an officer in the South Carolina State Militia, where he rose to the rank of major-general.

Smalls died in 1916.

BENJAMIN S. TURNER
Alabama
1871–1873

Born a slave in 1825 in Halifax, North Carolina, Benjamin S. Turner was taken at an early age to Alabama where he was emancipated and then given the rudiments of a private education. As a young man, he served as tax collector of Dallas County and councilman in Salem before becoming a prosperous livery stable owner.

In September of 1870, having manifested a growing interest in politics, he was unanimously nominated by the Republican party for the Congressional seat from the 1st District of Selma, Alabama.

Although renominated in 1872, Turner was the victim of a split within his own party, which led to his defeat and eventual abandonment of politics.

He returned to his home in Alabama and resumed his former business activities. He died in 1894.

JOSIAH T. WALLS
Florida
1871–1877

The only black congressman from Florida, Josiah T. Walls was born free in Winchester, Virginia in 1842, received his early education in Florida, and was a successful farmer when the Civil War broke out.

Drafted into the Confederate Army, he served in an artillery battery until he was taken prisoner by Union forces. He joined the Northern army and, by the end of hostilities, had risen to the rank of sergeant-major.

Walls then returned to Florida and served a term as a member of the Florida legislature.

Elected to the U.S. Congress in 1871, he represented the state during the next five years, although his tenure was interrupted because of a contested election and the opposition of the governor.

As a congressman, Walls favored granting military support to insurgent Cubans in their revolt against Spain, which had introduced African slaves on the island's sugar and tobacco plantations, and had treated the original Indian inhabitants with great brutality.

His congressional career ended, Walls returned to life as a planter, although he remained in politics through his staunch advocacy of Rutherford B. Hayes for the presidency. When a severe frost one year almost ruined him financially, he accepted the post of superintendent of a farm on the campus of Tallahassee State College, remaining there until his death in 1905.

GEORGE H. WHITE
North Carolina
1897–1901

The last black congressman in the aftermath of Reconstruction, George H. White was born in Rosedale, North Carolina in 1852. After graduating from Howard in 1877, he taught school in his native state and studied law. Licensed in 1879 to practice in all state courts, he proved to be a brilliant lawyer, winning several cases against the best of his white colleagues.

In 1880 White entered politics—first as a member of the North Carolina House of Representatives and, four years later, as state senator. At the end of his two-year term, he was chosen state solicitor for the Second Judicial District.

While in Congress, White championed the cause of constitutional liberties and was particularly outspoken in denouncing lynching and mob law.

Once out of politics, White turned his energies to the establishment of an all-black residential community—eventually known as Whitesboro after its founder—near Cape May in New Jersey. He later retired to law practice in Philadelphia where he died on December 28, 1918.

BLACK ELECTED OFFICEHOLDERS AT THE STATE LEVEL

As of May 1981, 341 blacks occupied elected office at the state level. Of the 341, 257 were state representatives, 76 were state senators, and 8 held statewide office.

The 333 state legislators held office in 40 states and the Virgin Islands. They comprise 4.2% of the 8,062 state legislators in the United States, a low figure when compared to the proportion of blacks who are eligible to vote, but more impressive than the total of blacks who occupy statewide elected office.

In 1981 Illinois and Maryland had the most black state senators with six each. Georgia had the most black representatives, 21, nearly 12% of all representatives in its lower house. In Alabama, Maryland, and Michigan more than 10% of the legislators were black.

As of June 1982 there were seven blacks in administrative statewide office: Roland Burris, comptroller of Illinois; Vel Phillips, secretary of state of Wisconsin; Wilson Riles, superintendent of public instruction of California; Richard Austin, secretary of state, and Loren Monroe, treasurer of Michigan; Henry Millin, lieutenant governor of the Virgin Islands; and Henry E. Parker, treasurer of Connecticut.

In 1980 the first black was elected to the Minnesota legislature, Randy Staten, and the first black woman to the Connecticut legislature, Carrie Perry.

Following are brief biographies of black statewide executives and a listing of blacks holding state administrative office as of June 1982.

RICHARD H. AUSTIN
Secretary of State, Michigan
Elected 1970

Richard Austin began his four-year term as head of the Department of State in 1971, after winning statewide election by more than 300,000 votes. He succeeded James M. Hare, who had been secretary of state for 16 years. A Democrat, Austin had served as Wayne County auditor since his election to that post by more than 200,000 in 1966. He had also served as a delegate to Michigan's Constitutional Convention.

Austin was born in Alabama in 1913. His family moved to Pennsylvania in 1917. His father died in 1924 and his mother moved the family to Detroit the following year.

Austin worked while attending school to help his mother support the family, which included two brothers. His scholastic achievements and status as a track star won him a scholarship to Wayne University. However, family circumstances forced Austin to abandon the scholarship. Instead he sold and shined shoes and kept books in a shoe store while studying accounting at the Detroit Institute of Technology at night.

In 1941 Austin became Michigan's first black certified public accountant. He started his own accounting firm and over the years helped organize a number of other businesses, philanthropic foundations, and civic organizations, and has published articles on taxation and legislative apportionment.

Austin ran for mayor of Detroit in 1969. He led the field in the primary but lost the runoff by 6,000 votes, in a racially polarized election, to Roman Gribbs, Wayne County sheriff.

As secretary of state, Austin heads a department of 2,400 employees and over 250 branch offices who serve Michigan residents through the issuance of driver licenses and overseeing elections. In addition, Austin is keeper of the Great Seal and official records and archives of state government.

The secretary of state is the second in line of succession as governor of Michigan.

ROLAND W. BURRIS
Comptroller, State of Illinois

A native of Centralia, Illinois, Roland W. Burris was born August 3, 1937. He received his B.A. degree in sociology from Illinois University and did postgraduate work at the University of Hamburg in Germany. Burris earned his law degree from Howard University in 1963. He has held various positions ranging from tax accountant to second vice president of Continental Illinois National Bank and Trust Company. In 1974 he was named one of ten outstanding business people and in 1979 was one of the 100 most influential blacks in America compiled by Ebony magazine. In 1980 Burris received the Outstanding Alumnus Award from Howard University Law School alumni association.

WILLIAM ALLEN MILLIN
Lieutenant Governor, Virgin Islands

William Allen Millin was born in St. Thomas, Virgin Islands and attended the Inter-American University and Ohio State University. He is the former executive director of the Virgin Islands Housing Authority as well as a former chief clerk in the tax assessor's office. Millin is a member of the Rotary Club and senior warden of All Saints Church Office.

LOREN EUGENE MONROE
Treasurer, State of Michigan

Loren Eugene Monroe was born in Thomasville, Geor-

gia on April 5, 1932 and received his B.S. from Wayne State University in Detroit in 1958. He received his law degree from the same institution in 1970. Monroe is a member of the National Association of Black Accountants and the American Institute of C.P.A.s.

ROBERT N. C. NIX, JR.
Justice, Supreme Court of Pennsylvania
Elected 1972

The son of Robert Nix, the black congressman from Philadelphia, Robert Nix, Jr. is the only black man in the United States who in 1974 was serving in an elected statewide judicial position.

Nix attended Central High School in Philadelphia, received an A.B. from Villanova University and then a Doctorate of Jurisprudence from the University of Pennsylvania. He was admitted to the Pennsylvania Bar in 1956 and appointed a deputy attorney general of the state in the same year. In 1958 he joined the law firm of Nix, Rhodes and Nix with whom he practiced for 10 years. During most of this period, Nix was also a member of the Democratic Party State Committee. In 1968 he became judge of the Common Pleas Court of Philadelphia County and in 1972 assumed his present position.

HENRY E. PARKER
Treasurer, State of Connecticut

Henry E. Parker was born February 14, 1928 in Baltimore and received his B.S. from Hampton Institute

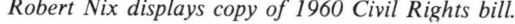

Robert Nix displays copy of 1960 Civil Rights bill.

and his masters degree from Southern Connecticut State College. Parker has done additional college work at Wesleyan University and the University of Connecticut's School of Social Work. Elected treasurer for the State of Connecticut in 1974, Parker was reelected to the post in 1978. Prior to becoming treasurer, he ran a daycare center in New Haven. Parker has also taught in New Haven and was an editorial commentator for radio station WELI there. He was named one of the 100 most influential black men by *Ebony* magazine for four consecutive years and won the Connecticut NAACP Civil Rights Award as well as the Citizenship Award from Hampton Institute. Parker is a member of the NAACP, the Elks, the National Urban League, Prince Hall Masons, and Kappa Alpha Psi Fraternity and is president of the Kappa Alpha Psi Foundation. He is also a member of the Black Americans in Support of Israel.

VEL R. PHILLIPS
Secretary of State of Wisconsin

Vel R. Phillips was born in Milwaukee on February 18, 1924. She received her B.S. from Howard University and her law degree from Wisconsin Law School. She was the first black in the United States ever elected to serve on the National Democratic Convention Committee on Rules and Order of Business. In 1968 she was named Woman of the Year by the Milwaukee University chapter of Theta Sigma Phi Sorority.

WILSON RILES
Superintendent of Public Instruction, California
Elected 1970

Wilson Riles began his career as a teacher in a one-room school on an Indian reservation near Pistol Creek, Arizona. He is now the chief executive of the nation's largest school system, responsible for administration of a program serving 4.5 million students in the public schools.

Riles was first elected state superintendent of public instruction in California in 1970, narrowly defeating the incumbent, Max Rafferty, an ultraconservative who had tried to drastically trim state support of public education. Riles campaigned on the theme "For The Children."

During his first term, Riles so impressed the voters of California that in 1974 he was reelected with an unprecedented 70% of the vote in a field of seven.

Since January 1971, when he took office, Riles has restored the confidence of the Legislature in his department, unified the education profession into a single lobby, and pushed through the largest school aid measure in the state's history.

Riles is also recognized nationally. He was chairman

Wilson Riles, superintendent of the nation's largest school system

of the U.S. Office of Education Task Force on Urban Educational Opportunities. He was selected by President Nixon to serve on the National Council on Educational Research—a presidential appointment which required U.S. Senate confirmation.

A major priority of Riles' is early childhood education. He appointed an Early Childhood Education Task Force soon after he became superintendent, translated its recommendations into legislation, and succeeded in winning the Legislature's and the governor's approval. The goals of the Early Childhood Education program—backed by $50 million for the second year of operation—are to individualize instruction for each child, to lower the adult–pupil ratio in the classroom, and assure that the child has attained competence in the basic skills of reading, arithmetic, and language by the completion of the third grade.

Riles was born in rural Louisiana, near Alexandria, in 1917. He was orphaned as a boy, worked his way through junior and senior high schools delivering milk and laboring in sawmills, and moved to Arizona to enroll at Arizona State College. He received his B.A. degree there in 1940 and—after service in the Army Air Corps during World War II—his M.A. degree in 1947.

After progressing as a teacher and administrator in Arizona schools, he joined the California Department of Education in 1958. In 1965 he was appointed associate superintendent in the Department to organize and administer a $100 million compensatory education program which became a model throughout the nation.

In 1969 he was appointed deputy state superintendent for programs.

In 1973 he was awarded the Spingarn Medal, the highest award of the National Association for the Advancement of Colored People.

ROSTER OF STATE LEGISLATORS

Alabama

Senators

FIGURES, Michael A.
District 33
1407 Davis Ave.
Mobile 36617

HILLIARD, Earl F.
District 15
P.O. Box 11385
Birmingham 35202

PEARSON, J. Richmond
District 13
Exec. Ste. Citizens
Fed. Bldg.
809 Bolin St. S.W.
Birmingham 35211

Representatives

BUSKEY, James E.
District 99
2207 Barretts Lane
Mobile 36617

CLARK, William
District 98
711 S. Atmore Ave.
Prichard 36611

ESCOTT, Sundra
45th District
P.O. Box 8172
Birmingham 35218

HARRISON, Antonio L.
District 44
1630 4th Ave. N.
Birmingham 35203

HOLMES, Alvin A.
District 80
P.O. Box 6064
Montgomery 36106

HORN, William
District 39
333 16th Ave. S.W.
Birmingham 35211

HOWARD, Asbury
District 49
1930 Exeter Ave.
Bessemer 35020

JACKSON, Ronald E.

District 38
1919 Morris Ave. #1170
Birmingham 35203

KENNEDY, Yvonne
District 103
1205 Glennon Ave.
Mobile 36603

LANGFORD, Charles
District 77
918 E. Grove St.
Montgomery 36104

NEVETT, C. Howard
District 41
5028 Parkway Ave.
Fairfield 35064

REED, Thomas
District 67
Drawer E E T
Tuskegee Institute 36088

TUCKER, Jerome
District 43
2121 8th Ave. N. Ste. 1722
Birmingham 35203

Alaska

Borough Assembly Member

MARSHALL, Joseph D.
North Star Borough
P.O. Box 1267
Fairbanks 99701

Arizona

Representatives

HAMILTON, Arthur M.
District 22
State Capitol Bldg.
1700 W. Washington
Phoenix 85007

THOMPSON, Elishia
Leon, Sr.
District 23
2141 S. 6th Ave.
Phoenix 85003

Arkansas

Senator

JEWELL, Jerry
District 3
721 E. 21 St.
Little Rock 72206

Representatives

BROWN, Erma H.
District 3 Pos. 3
1920 S. Summit St.
Little Rock 72206

RICHARDSON,
Grover C., Jr.
District 3
Riffel St. Box 225
College Station 72053

TOWNSEND, William H.
District 3
1304 Wright Ave.
Little Rock 72206

WILKINS, Henry III
District 54
303 N. Maple St.
Pine Bluff 71601

California

Senators

GREENE, Bill
District 29
State Capitol #4031
Sacramento 95814

WATSON, Diane E.
District 30
4401 Crenshaw Blvd.
Los Angeles 90043

Assembly Members

BROWN, Willie L., Jr.
District 17
State Capitol Rm. 2013
Sacramento 95814

HARRIS, Elihu M.
District 13

State Capitol #4015
Sacramento 95814

HUGHES, Teresa P.
District 47
State Capitol
Sacramento 95814

MOORE, Gwen
District 49
3731 Stocker St. Ste. 109
Los Angeles 90008

TUCKER, Curtis R.
District 50
P.O. Box 6500
Inglewood 90306

WATERS, Maxine
District 48
7900 S. Central Ave.
Los Angeles 90001

Colorado

Senators

GROFF, Regis F.
District 3
2841 Colorado Blvd.
Denver 80207

Representatives

TAYLOR, Arie P.
District 7
3328 Magnolia St.
Denver 80207

WEBB, Wilma
District 8
2329 Gaylord St.
Denver 80205

Connecticut

Senators

DANIELS, John C., Jr.
District 10
432 Norton Pkwy.
New Haven 06511

MORTON, Margaret E.

District 23
25 Currier St.
Bridgeport 06607

PERRY, Carrie S.
District 8
203 Ridgefield St.
Hartford 06112

SMITH, Wilbur G.
District 2
196 Palm St.
Hartford 06112

Representatives

BROOKS, Walter S.
District 95
23 Baldwin St.
New Haven 06519

COBLE, Thomas
District 29
188 Deacon St.
Bridgeport 06607

DYSON, William R.
District 94
P.O. Box 2064
New Haven 06521

GILES, Abraham
District 4
188 Cleveland Ave.
Hartford 06120

MILNER, Thirman L.
District 7
41 Kent St.
Hartford 06112

MOSLEY, Maurice B.
District 72
45 Savings St.
Waterbury 06702

Delaware

Senator

HOLLOWAY,
    Herman M., Sr.
District 2
2008 Washington St.
Wilmington 19802

Representatives

HOLLOWAY,
    Herman, Jr.
District 3
609 S. Heald St.
Wilmington 19801

PLANT, Al O., Sr.
District 2
523 Eastlawn Ave.
Wilmington 19802

Florida

Representatives

GIRARDEAU, Arnett E.
District 16
26 E. 6th St.
Jacksonville 32206

KERSHAW, Joe L.
District 105
2539 N.W. 46th St.
Miami 33142

MEEK, Carrie
District 106
6830 N.W. 28th St.
Miami 33147

THOMAS, John
District 17
P.O. Box 40931
Jacksonville 32203

Georgia

Senators

BOND, Julian
District 39
361 West View Dr. S.W.
Atlanta 30310

TATE, Horace E., Sr.
District 38
621 Lilla Dr. S.W.
Atlanta 30310

Representatives

BEAL, Alveda King
District 28
385 Pine St. N.E.
Atlanta 30308

BENN, Lorenzo
District 38
579 Fielding Lane S.W.
Atlanta 30311

BISHOP, Sanford
District 94
4129 Roman Dr.
Columbus 31907

BROOKS, Tyrone
District 34
Station A
P.O. Box 11025
Atlanta 30310

CLARK, Betty J.
District 55
2139 Flat Shoals
    Rd. S.E. #3
Atlanta 30316

DAUGHERTY,
    Julius C., Sr.

District 33
15 Chestnut St. S.W.
Atlanta 30314

DEAN, Douglass C.
District 29
356 Arthur St. S.W.
Atlanta 30310

DENT, Richard A.
District 85
1120 Pine St.
Augusta 30901

GLOVER, Mildred W.
District 32
735 Lawton St.
Atlanta 30310

HAMILTON, Grace T.
District 31
582 Univ. Pl. N.W.
Atlanta 30314

HILL, Bobby L.
District 127
208 E. 34th St.
Savannah 31402

HOLMES, Robert A.
District 39
2073 Cascade Rd. S.W.
Atlanta 30311

LUCAS, David E.
District 102
448 Woolfolk St.
Macon 31201

McKINNEY, James E.
District 35
765 Shorter Terrace N.W.
Atlanta 30318

RANDALL, William C.
District 101
P.O. Box 121
Macon 31202

SCOTT, Albert I., Jr.
District 123
P.O. Box 1704
Savannah 31402

SCOTT, David
District 37
190 Wendell Dr. S.E.
Atlanta 30315

SMYRE, Calvin
District 92
P.O. Box 181
Columbus 31902

THOMPSON,
    Albert W., Sr.
District 93
P.O. Box 587
Columbus 31902

WHITE, John
District 132
P.O. Box 3506
Albany 31706

WILLIAMS, Hosea L.
District 54
551 Houston St. N.E.
Atlanta 30312

Hawaii

Senator

CAMPBELL, Charles M.
District 5
3215 Ala Ilima St.
    #312-A
Honolulu 96818

Illinois

Senators

CHEW, Charles, Jr.
District 29
37 W. 78th St.
Chicago 60620

COLLINS-GRANT,
    Earlean
District 21
5943 W. Madison St.
Chicago 60644

HALL, Kenneth
District 57
1725 Kansas Ave.
East St. Louis 62205

McLENDON, James A.
District 22
1 N. La Salle St.
Chicago 60602

NEWHOUSE, Richard H.
District 24
1900 E. 71st St.
Chicago 60637

TAYLOR, James C.
District 26
6752 S. Morgan St.
Chicago 60621

Representatives

ALEXANDER, Ethel
District 26
610 E. 61st St.
Chicago 60637

BRAUN, Carol Mosley
District 24
5434 S. Hyde Park Blvd.
Chicago 60615

BULLOCK, Larry S.

District 22
400 E. 33rd St. #2112
Chicago 60616

EWELL, Raymond W.
District 29
7902 S. Perry Ave.
Chicago 60620

HENRY, William
District 21
3851 W. Roosevelt
Chicago 60624

HUFF, Douglas
District 20
3037 W. Warren Blvd.
Chicago 60612

JACKSON, Jesse
District 29
9659 S. Halsted St.
Chicago 60628

JONES, Emil, Jr.
District 28
11357 S. Lowe Ave.
Chicago 60628

POUNCEY, Taylor
District 26
1171 W. 71st. St.
Chicago 60621

RHEM, Sylvester O.
District 26
6330 S. Rhodes Ave.
Chicago 60637

SMITH, Margaret
District 22
4949 S. Martin Luther
    King Dr.
Chicago 60615

STEWART, Monica Faith
District 29
640 E. 79th St.
Chicago 60619

TURNER, Arthur
District 21
215 S. Cicero Ave.
Chicago 60644

WHITE, Jesse C., Jr.
District 13
1455 N. Park Ave. B
Chicago 60610

YOUNGE, Wyvetter H.
District 57
1617 N. 46th St.
East St. Louis 62205

Indiana

Senators

CARSON, Julia M.
District 34
2534 N. Park Ave.
Indianapolis 46205

HALL, Katie B.
District 3
1937 Madison St.
Gary 46407

Representatives

CRAWFORD, William A.
District 45
3048 E. Fall Crk. Pkwy.
    N. Dr.
Indianapolis 46205

FISHER, Rayfield
District 5
1982 Hanley St.
Gary 46406

GOODALL, Hurley C.
District 38
1905 Carver Dr.
Muncie 47303

MOSBY, Carolyn
District 5
328 Garfield St.
Gary 46404

SUMMERS, Joseph W.
District 45
3040 N. Capitol Ave.
P.O. Box 88060
Indianapolis 46208

Kansas

Senator

McCRAY, Billy Q.
District 29
1532 N. Ash St.
Wichita 67214

Representatives

CRIBBS, Theo
District 89
1551 N. Minnesota
Wichita 67214

JUSTICE, Norman E.
District 34
506 Washington Blvd.
Kansas City 66101

LITTLEJOHN, J. B.
District 52
2500 Arrowhead Rd.
Topeka 66614

LOVE, Clarence C.
District 35
2853 Parkview
Kansas City 66104

Kentucky

Senator

POWERS, Georgia M.
District 33
733 Cecil Ave.
Louisville 40211

Representatives

HINES, Carl R.
District 43
635 Southwestern Pkwy.
Louisville 40211

STREET-KIDD, Mae
District 41
2308 W. Chestnut St.
Louisville 40211

WILLIAMS, Aubrey
District 42
440 S. 7th St.
Louisville 40203

Louisiana

Senators

BRADEN, Henry E. IV
District 4
612 Gravier St.
New Orleans 70130

JEFFERSON, William J.
District 6
1001 Howard Ave.
New Orleans 70113

Representatives

ALEXANDER, Avery C.
District 93
2803 Martin L.
    King, Jr. Blvd.
New Orleans 70113

BAJOIE, Diana E.
District 91
P.O. Box 15168
New Orleans 70175

CHARBONNET,
    Louis J. III
District 96
1615 St. Phillips St.
New Orleans 70116

CONNOR, George C., Jr.
District 97
2647 Havana St.
New Orleans 70119

DELPIT, Joseph A.
District 67
725 Lettsworth St.
Baton Rouge 70802

JACKSON, Alphonse, Jr.
District 2
3815 Lakeshore Dr.
Shreveport 71109

JACKSON, Johnny, Jr.
District 101
3772 Louisa
New Orleans 70126

JOHNSON, Jon D.
District 102
2223 Deslonde St.
New Orleans 70117

JONES, Charles D.
District 17
1803 Medra Dr.
Monroe 71202

TURNLEY, Richard Jr.
District 63
2757 78th Ave.
Baton Rouge 70807

Maryland

Senators

ALLEN, Aris T.
District 30
James Senate Ofc.
    Bldg. #404
Annapolis 21401

BLOUNT, Clarence W.
District 41
4811 Liberty Hgts. Ave.
Baltimore 21207

BROADWATER,
    Thomas, Jr.
District 25
5611 Landover Rd.
Hyattsville 20784

DOUGLASS, Robert L.
District 45
2503 E. Preston St.
Baltimore 21213

MITCHELL,
    Clarence M. III
District 38
1239 Druid Hill Ave.
Baltimore 21217

WELCOME, Verda F.
District 40
2101 Liberty Hgts. Ave.
Baltimore 21217

Delegates

BRAILEY, Troy F.
District 40
2405 Baker St.
Baltimore 21216

CHESTER, Joseph A., Sr.
District 45
3027 E. Federal St.
Baltimore 21213

CONAWAY, Frank
District 40
3758 W. Belvedere Ave.
Baltimore 21215

DEAN, Walter R., Jr.
District 41
P.O. Box 11937
Baltimore 21207

DIXON, Isaiah, Jr.
District 38
1607 W. North Ave.
Baltimore 21217

DOUGLASS, John W.
District 45
2503 E. Preston St.
Baltimore 21213

EXUM, Nathaniel
District 25
5611 Landover Rd.
Hyattsville 20784

HARRISON, Hattie N.
District 45
2503 E. Preston
Baltimore 21213

LEE, Lena K.
District 38
1816 Madison Ave.
Baltimore 21217

MURPHY, Margaret
District 41
2914 Edmondson Ave.
Baltimore 21223

PHILLIPS, Wendell
District 41
3826 Liberty Hgts. Ave.
Baltimore 21215

RAWLINGS, Howard
District 40
3502 Sequoia Ave.
Baltimore 21215

WOODS, Sylvania W., Jr.
District 25
7816 Fiske Ave.
Glenarden 20706

YOUNG, Larry
District 38
1716 McCulloh St. #2
Baltimore 21217

Massachusetts

Senator

OWENS, William
2nd Suffolk District
115 Hazelton
Boston 02126

Representatives

BOLLING, Royal, Jr.
6th Suffolk District
722 Morton St.
Boston 02126

BUNTE, Doris
7th Suffolk District
State House #127A
Boston 02133

GRAHAM, Saundra M.
28th Middlesex District
State House #38
Boston 02133

JORDAN, Raymond A., Jr.
12th Hampden District
51 Goldenrod Rd.
Springfield 01109

KING, Melvin H.
9th Suffolk District
4 Yarmouth St.
Boston 02116

Michigan

Senators

BROWN, Basil W.
District 3
43 Connecticut
Highland Park 48203

HOLMES, David S., Jr.
District 4
517 E. Kirby
Detroit 48212

VAUGHN, Jackie III
District 5
State Capitol
Lansing 48909

Representatives

COLLINS, Barbara Rose
District 21
State Capitol #114½
Lansing 48909

CUSHINGBERRY,
   George, Jr.
District 4
State Capitol
Detroit 48909

ELLIOTT, Daisy E.

District 8
8701 LaSalle Blvd.
Detroit 48206

HOOD, Morris W., Jr.
District 6
8872 Cloverlawn
Detroit 48204

HOOD, Raymond W.
District 7
State Capitol
Lansing 48901

HUNTER, Teola P.
District 5
14834 Mark Twain
Detroit 48227

KILPATRICK,
   Carolyn C.
District 18
State Capitol #114½
Lansing 48909

McNEELY, Matthew
District 16
P.O. Box 30014
Lansing 48909

SMITH, Virgil C., Jr.
District 10
19637 Ryan Rd.
Detroit 48234

TERRELL, Ethel
District 9
12209 Woodward Ave.
Highland Park 48203

Minnesota

Representative

STATEN, Randolph
270 State Ofc. Bldg.
St. Paul 55155

Mississippi

Senators

ANDERSON, Douglas
District 27
1340 Rockdale Dr.
Jackson 39213

KIRKSEY, Henry
District 28
930 Arbor Vista Blvd.
Jackson 39209

Representatives

BANKS, Fred L., Jr.
District 69
P.O. Drawer 290
Jackson 39201

BUCKLEY, Horace L.
District 70
735 Campbell St.
Jackson 39203

CALHOUN, Credell
District 68
2341 Ludlow Ave.
Jackson 39213

CLARK, Robert G.
District 49
Box 179
Lexington 39095

ELLIS, Tyrone
District 40
Rt. 5, Box 221A
Starksville 39759

FRAZIER, Hillman
District 67
113 California Pl.
Jackson 39213

FREDERICKS, Isiah
District 119
3500 Meadowlark Dr.
Gulfport 39501

GREEN, David
District 98
Rt. 1, Box 152-A
Gloster 39638

HENDERSON, Clayton
District 9
P.O. Box 469
Tunica 38676

HENRY, Aaron
District 26
213 4th St.
Clarksdale 38614

KING, Leslie
District 5
240 N. 6th St.
Greenville 38701

SCHOBY, Barney
District 95
115 Florida Dr.
Natchez 39120

SHEPPARD, Charles
District 87
P.O. Box 254
Lorman 39096

WATSON, Percy
District 104
P.O. Box 1767
Hattiesburg 39401

YOUNG, Charles L.
District 84
500 25th Ave.
Meridian 39301

Missouri

Senators

BANKS, J. B.
District 5
1442-A N. Grand
St. Louis 63106

SWINTON, Lee B.
District 9
Jackson County
6446 Indiana
Kansas City 64132

Representatives

AIKENS, Johnnie S.
District 66
4847 Wabada Ave.
St. Louis 63113

BOYKINS, Billie Anthony
District 82
1509 Lovejoy Lane
St. Louis 63106

CALLOWAY,
De Verne L.
District 81
4309 Enright Ave.
St. Louis 63108

CURTIS, Phillip B. II
District 28
3832 Myrtle
Kansas City 64128

GOWARD, Russell
District 65
4015 Fair Ave.
St. Louis 63115

GROVES BLAND, Mary
District 30
6135 Indiana
Kansas City 64130

JORDAN, Orchid I.
District 25
2745 Garfield Ave.
Kansas City 64109

McKAMEY, Leo
District 36
5260 Elmwood Ave.
Kansas City 64130

PITTS, Earl, Jr.
District 32
7524 Wabash
Kansas City 64132

RIVERS, Nathaniel
District 79
5475 Cabanne Ave.
St. Louis 63112

TINDALL, James

District 23
1231 Garfield
Kansas City 64127

TROUPE, Charles
District 63
5338 Claxton
St. Louis 63120

WALTON, Elbert A., Jr.
District 80
2735 Coleman
St. Louis 63101

WHEAT, Alan D.
District 26
3200½ Brighton #7
Kansas City 64128

WHITEMORE, Jame
District 67
2619 Hodimont
St. Louis 63112

WILLIAMS, Fred
District 78
5852 Julian Ave.
St. Louis 63112

Nebraska

Senator

CHAMBERS, Ernest W.
District 11
1911 Lothrop St.
Omaha 68110

Nevada

Senator

NEAL, Joe
District 4
304 Lance St.
North Las Vegas 89030

Assembly Members

BENNETT, Marion D.
District 6
1911 Goldhill Ave.
Las Vegas 89106

CHANEY, Lonie B.
District 7
504 Kasper Ave.
Las Vegas 89106

New Jersey

Senator

LIPMAN, Wynona M.
District 29
50 Park Pl. #938
Newark 07101

Assembly Members

BARRY-GARVIN,
Mildred
District 27
406 Central Ave.
East Orange 07018

BROWN, Willie B.
District 29
375 Wainwright St.
Newark 07112

MAYS, Charles
District 31
340 Martin Luther
King Dr.
Jersey City 07305

THOMPSON, Eugene
District 29
91 Somerset St.
Newark 07108

New York

Senators

BEATTY, Vander I.
District 23
671 St. Johns Pl.
Brooklyn 11216

BOGUES, Leon
District 28
W. Side Legislative
Serv. Ctr.
720 Columbus Ave.
New York 10025

GALIBER, Joseph L.
District 32
Legislative Ofc. Bldg.
Rm. 51
Albany 12224

OWENS, Major R.
District 17
335 Wyona St.
Brooklyn 11207

Assembly Members

BOYLAND, Thomas S.
District 54
1636 Pitkin Ave.
Brooklyn 11212

BROTHERS, Edith
State Comm. Woman,
Dist. Leader
District 40
265 Livonia Ave.
Brooklyn 11212

EVE, Arthur O.
District 143
184 Jewett Pkwy.

Buffalo 14214

FARRELL,
Herman D., Jr.
District 74
159-00 Riverside Dr. W.
New York 10032

FORTUNE, Thomas R.
District 55
190 Ralph Ave.
Brooklyn 11233

GREEN, Roger
District 57
235 DeKalb Ave.
Brooklyn 11205

GRIFFITH, Edward
District 40
710 Warwick St.
Albany 11207

JENKINS, Andrew
District 29
10 Adelaide Rd.
St. Albans 11433

JOHNSON, Charles
District 76
1188 Grand Concourse
Bronx 10451

LEWIS, Woodrow
District 53
752 Nostrand
Brooklyn 11216

VANN, Albert
District 56
362 McDonough St.
Brooklyn 11233

North Carolina

Senator

FRYE, Henry E.
District 19
1401 S. Benbow Rd.
Greensboro 27406

Representatives

CREECY, C. Meldin
District 5
P.O. Box 526
Rich Square 27869

SPAULDING, Kenneth
District 16
P.O. Box 1346
Durham 27702

Ohio

Senators

BOWEN, William F.
District 9
Statehouse
Columbus 43215

JACKSON, M. Morris
District 21
1723 E. 70th St.
Cleveland 44103

Representatives

BEATTY, Otto, Jr.
330 S. 5th St. #402
Columbus 43215

BELL, Thomas M.
District 10
Statehouse
Columbus 43215

JAMES, Troy Lee
District 9
4216 Cedar Ave.
Cleveland 44103

JONES, Casey C.
District 45
355 Pinewood Ave.
Toledo 43602

MALLORY, William L.
District 23
907 Dayton St.
Cincinnati 45214

McLIN, C. J., Jr.
District 36
1130 Germantown St.
Dayton 45408

MILLER, Ray
District 29
Statehouse
Columbus 43215

RANKIN, L. Helen
District 25
3461 Evanston Ave.
Cincinnati 45207

THOMPSON, Ike
District 13
State House
Columbus 43215

THOMPSON, John D., Jr.
District 15
15611 Stockbridge Ave.
Cleveland 44128

Oklahoma

Senators

PORTER, E. Melvin
District 48
2116 N.E. 23rd St.
Oklahoma City 73111

Representatives

COX, Kevin
District 97
5909 N. Terry
Oklahoma City 73111

McINTYRE, Bernard J.
District 73
P.O. Box 6068
Tulsa 74106

WILLIAMS, Freddye
1145 N. Page Ave.
Oklahoma City 73111

Oregon

Senator

McCOY, William
District 8
6650 N. Amherst St.
Portland 97203

Pennsylvania

Senators

HANKINS, Freeman
District 7
4075 Haverford Ave.
Philadelphia 19104

McKINNEY, Paul
District 8
5741 Chestnut St.
Philadelphia 19143

Representatives

BARBER, James D.
District 190
802 N. 40th St.
Philadelphia 19104

DEAL, Alphonso
District 181
1220 N. Broad St.
Philadelphia 19121

EMERSON, Junius
District 197
2624 W. Lehigh Ave.
Philadelphia 19132

EVANS, Dwight
District 203

7174 Ogontz Ave.
Philadelphia 19138

HARPER, Ruth
District 196
1427 W. Erie Ave.
Philadelphia 19140

IRVIS, K. Leroy
District 19
205 Tennyson Ave.
Pittsburgh 15213

OLIVER, Frank L.
District 195
1309 N. Hollywood St.
Philadelphia 19121

PENDLETON,
William, Sr.
District 24
121 S. Highland Ave.
Pittsburgh 15206

RICHARDSON, David P.,
Jr.
District 201
Main Capitol Bldg. #600
Harrisburg 17120

STREET, Milton
District 181
Box 132
Harrisburg 17120

WHITE, John F., Jr.
District 200
3226 W. Cheltenham Ave.
Philadelphia 19150

WIGGINS, Edward
District 186
2600 Federal St.
Philadelphia 19146

WILLIAMS, Hardy
District 191
5939 Cobbs Creek Pkwy.
Philadelphia 19143

WILLIAMS, James
District 188
801 S. 47th St.
Philadelphia 19143

Rhode Island

Representatives

CASTRO, George A.
57 Carolina Ave.
Providence 02905

WALKER, Leonard
District 19
280 Potters Ave.
Providence 02905

South Carolina

Representatives

BARKSDALE, Hudson L.,
Sr.
District 31
331 N. Dean St.
Spartanburg 29302

BLANDING, Larry
District 70
P.O. Box 1446
Sumter 29150

BROADWATER, Thomas
D., Jr.
District 74
1900 Taylor St.
Columbia 29201

FOSTER, Samuel R.
District 49
P.O. Drawer 10072
Rockhill 29730

GADSON, Tobias, Jr.
District 111
162 Spring St.
Charlestown 29403

GORDON, Benjamin
District 101
P.O. Box 751
Kingstree 29556

JOE, Issac C.
District 51
221 Woodwood St.
Bishopville 29010

MATTHEWS, John W., Jr.
District 94
P.O. Box 460
Bowman 29018

MIDDLETON, Earl M.
District 95
P.O. Drawer 1305
Orangeburg 29115

MITCHELL, Theo W.
District 23
522 Woodland Way
Greenville 29607

MURRAY, Julius
District 81
P.O. Box 11867
Columbia 29211

PATTERSON, Kay
District 73
6815 Gavilan Ave.
Columbia 29203

WASHINGTON,
McKinley, Jr.
District 116

P.O. Box 7
Edisto Island 29438

WHITE, Juanita
District 122
Rt. 1, Box 184
Hardeeville 29927

WOODS, Robert R.
District 109
P.O. Box 2217
Charleston 29403

Tennessee

Senators

DAVIS, Edward
District 33
4924 Sagewood Dr.
Memphis 38116

FORD, John N.
District 29
3655 Summershade Cove
Memphis 38116

WILLIAMS, Avon N., Jr.
District 19
203 2nd Ave. N.
Nashville 37201

WITHERS, Andrew
District 33
480 Brooks St.
Memphis 38109

Representatives

BREWER, Harper, Jr.
District 98
990 N. Idlewild
Memphis 38107

DEBERRY, Lois M.
District 91
680 Alida
Memphis 38106

JONES, Rufus
District 86
War Memorial Bldg.
#113
Nashville 37219

KING, Alvin M.
District 92
1215 Tanglewood
Memphis 38114

LOVE, Harold M.
District 54
4207 Drakes Hill Dr.
Nashville 37218

MURPHY, Ira H.
District 87
Legislative Plaza
Suite 32

Nashville 38126

PRUITT, Charles W.
District 58
1813 Hillside Ave.
Nashville 37203

ROBINSON, Clarence B.
District 28
1909 E. 5th St.
Chattanooga 37404

WITHERS, Dedrick
District 85
480 W. Brooks Rd.
Memphis 38109

Texas

Mayors

MACK, Mary
P.O. Box 75
Clay 77839

REDMOND, John M., Jr.
Ames
P.O. Box 1904
Liberty 77575

SAMS, Eristus
P.O. Box 2809
Prairie View 77445

WALLACE, Matthew
Moore's Station, Rt. 1
Larue 75700

WASHINGTON, Willie
Goodlow
P.O. Box 248
Kerens 75144

Utah

Representative

WILLIAMS, Terry Lee
621 E. 900 S.
Salt Lake City 84105

Virginia

Senator

WILDER, Lawrence D.
District 9
2307 E. Broad St.
Richmond 23223

Delegates

CHRISTIAN, James S., Jr.
District 33
2407 North Ave.
Richmond 23222

LAMBERT,
Benjamin J. III

District 33
801 W. Graham Rd.
Richmond 23222

ROBINSON,
William P., Jr.
District 39
1st VA Bank Twr.,
#1612
Norfolk 23510

SCOTT, Robert C.
District 49
1356 25th St.
Newport News 23607

Washington

Senator

FLEMING, George
District 37
1100 Lake Wash. Blvd. S.
Seattle 98144

Representative

MAXIE, Peggie J.
District 37
1441 Madrona Dr.
Seattle 98122

West Virginia

Delegates

MOORE, Ernest C.
District 14
P.O. Box 67
Thorpe 24888

STEPHENS, Booker
District 14
Drawer E
Keystone 24852

Wisconsin

Administrator

PHILLIPS, Vel
Secretary of State
244 W. Washington A.
Madison 53702

Senator

GEORGE, Gary R.
District 6
319 S. State Capitol
Madison 53702

Representatives

COGGS, Marcia
District 18

325 W. State Capitol
Madison 53702

WILLIAMS, Annette
48 N. State Capitol
Madison 53702

Virgin Islands

Administrator

MILLIN, Henry A.
Lieutenant Governor
P.O. Box 450
Charlotte Amalie
St. Thomas 00801

Senators

BELAIDO, Lilliano
Box D
Christiansted
St. Croix 00820

BELL, John A.
St. Croix District
P.O. Box 3737
Christiansted
St. Croix 00820

DENNIS, Hugo, Jr.
Box 477
St. Thomas 00801

FRETT, Milton A.
Box 477
St. Thomas 00801

HARVEY, William S.
Box D
Christiansted
St. Croix 00820

ILES, Edgar M.
Box D Christiansted
St. Croix 00820

LAWAETZ, Brent
Box D
Christiansted
St. Croix 00820

LEE, Sidney
Box D
Christiansted
St. Croix 00820

PAIEWONSKI, Michael A.
Box 477
St. Thomas 00801

ROEBUCK, Elmo D.
St. Thomas District
P.O. Box 3411
Charlotte Amalie
St. Thomas 00801

ROUSS, Ruby M.
St. Croix District

P.O. Box 865
Christiansted
St. Croix 00820

SIMMONS, Ruby
Box 477
St. Thomas 00801

SPRAUVE, Gilbert A.
Senator-at-Large
P.O. Box 196
Cruz-Bay

St. John 00830

STRIDIRON, Iver A.
Box 477
St. Thomas 00801

WILLIAMS, Lloyd
St. Thomas District
P.O. Box 924
Charlotte Amalie
St. Thomas 00801

BLACK MAYORS

As of April 1982 there were 206 black mayors in the United States, compared to 108 at the same time in 1974 and 80 in 1973. Once a rare breed, they have now become fixtures on the political landscape, though their total number is still very small. The entities they serve range from small all-black towns such as Fairmount Heights, Maryland and Mound Bayou, Mississippi, to several of the nation's largest cities including Los Angeles, New Orleans, Washington, D.C., Atlanta, Detroit, Newark, and Gary.

Along with their white counterparts they face the common problems afflicting many cities, particularly those in the older, more industrialized sections of the country, including changing population patterns, a decreasing industrial base, dwindling tax revenues, and increasing demands for social services. These problems were further exacerbated in the early 1980s by the Reagan Administration's New Federalism, which found the government reducing its flow of dollars to the cities.

While the realities of life put some constraints on what a mayor can do, regardless of whether he or she is black or white, the role of the black mayor continues to be important both symbolically and from a practical viewpoint. Political scientist Dr. Pearl Robinson of Tufts University has made this observation:

Given the frequent setbacks that black elected officials face in federal and state legislative bodies where they are a distinct minority, local level executive offices hold far greater possibilities for forthright leadership. Under present conditions black political power in the United States is generally more viable as a grass roots phenomenon. Getting elected mayor is therefore a significant political milestone.

One of the more interesting developments over recent years is that once blacks win office, competency more than race becomes the test for reelection.

Following are the biographies of a number of black mayors of major U.S. cities.

RICHARD ARRINGTON, JR.
Birmingham, Alabama
1980 Population: 284,413
Percentage Black: 55.6
Elected 1979

One way of measuring how far the South has come from the tumultuous days of the 1960s when the Civil Rights Movement was in full flower is to take a look at Birmingham. If ever a city deserved the description "mean," it was Birmingham. If ever a city was so rigid that blacks and whites never mixed in public, not even in the state-owned liquor stores, where there was a door for the "Coloreds" and a door for the "Whites." The stock came from the same shelves and the money went into the same cash register, but a railing down the center separated the customers.

"Bull" Connor, the director of public safety, ruled Birmingham, or "Bombingham," as it was known among black people, with an iron fist. It was almost inconceivable that the city would ever change, but change it did in 1979 when Richard Arrington, a zoologist and a college professor, was elected mayor.

Arrington had not planned to run for mayor. After eight years as a member of the Birmingham City Council, and a member of two of its most important committees, he was looking to an appointment as president of one of two state colleges where the incumbents had announced plans to retire—Alabama A&M in Huntsville or Alabama State University in Montgomery.

Then came the shooting of 20-year-old Bonita Carter. She was shot three times in the back by a white policeman responding to a robbery call. The policeman claimed that he thought the unarmed woman was the shotgun-wielding bandit. A night of rioting that broke out was followed by a series of demonstrations. At the center was the white mayor who refused to fire the policeman, assigning him instead to a desk job.

Arrington says this incident "was important in my decision to run." He received the support of most blacks, but not the old-line black political leaders who warned that the time was not yet ripe. With limited financial backing—the figure has been put at $19,000—Arrington won 45% of the vote in the October primary, forcing a runoff in November. At this time a record 76% of the registered black voters turned out, giving him 98% of their vote, and white voters gave him 12% of theirs.

Arrington's inauguration was a symphony of irony. With him on the stand were former Alabama Governor George Wallace, once a leading apostle of segregation, as well as Robert Kennedy, Jr., Ethel Kennedy, presidential aide Jack Watson, two other delegates from the Carter White House, both of Alabama's senators, Birmingham Congressman John Buchanan, and Arrington's two predecessors as mayor.

For the son of sharecroppers, Richard Arrington had made it in a big way. But success was nothing new to him.

Arrington started out to be a college professor. He earned his Ph.D. in invertebrate zoology from the University of Oklahoma. He began his teaching career as an assistant professor of biology at Miles College (Birmingham) in 1957. He was named a full professor at the college in 1966 and served as dean from 1967 to 1970. He then served as the fund raising executive director of the Alabama Center for Higher Education, a consortium of eight senior colleges in the state.

He did not neglect the civic side of life, serving as President, Board of Directors, Birmingham Urban League, and President, Board of Directors, Goodwill Industries, among other posts.

Arrington's political involvement began with his election to the Birmingham City Council where he served two terms. His philosophy during that time is summed up in a statement he made to a black magazine.

I was told by the old-line black political leadership that I was going too far out on the limb, that you don't talk about things like police brutality. It didn't work out that way for me, because I was elected by an even bigger margin for my second four-year term. I was able to be independent because I wasn't depending on politics for a livelihood. If I wasn't reelected—well so what?

Arrington's efforts to improve the lot of blacks and the poor in Birmingham have not met with universal approval—he has collided with entrenched interests—but his philosophy remains the same.

MARION S. BARRY
Washington, D.C.
1980 Population: 637,651
Percentage Black: 70.3

Marion S. Barry learned his politics the hard way—in the front ranks of the Civil Rights Movement and as an activist community organizer in the deepest part of the Washington, D.C., ghetto. When he announced in 1978 that he was running for mayor, there were few who gave him an outside chance to end up wearing the victor's crown. He wasn't part of the tightly knit black leadership group in the city—he was more of a freewheeling maverick who never hesitated to tilt against windmills. There seemed to be too many things going against him.

First, he was arrayed against two strong opponents, both black, who between them had most of the backing from the white and black establishment of the city. One of his opponents was the incumbent mayor, Walter E. Washington, a longtime fixture on the Washington

Marion Barry, dynamic mayor of Washington, D.C.

scene who had been named in 1967 by President Lyndon B. Johnson as the District Commissioner, under a reorganization plan for the District which called for replacement of the three-man governing board with a single official. This was the beginning of home rule for the District, which for many years had been under the thumb of Congress. Washington was the first person to hold the post, and he was reappointed by President Nixon in 1969 and 1973. When Washingtonians were able to vote for mayor in 1974, they elected Washington.

The second opponent, also a longtime fixture in Washington, was Sterling Tucker, who had for many years served as executive director of the Washington Urban League and in 1978 was serving as president of the City Council.

In the election, Washington and Tucker virtually canceled each other out since they were competing for the same universe of voters, and Barry won with 35% of the vote in the Democratic primary, which in heavily Democratic Washington ensured his win in the general election.

Mayor Barry was born in Itta Bena, Mississippi, in 1936. He received his undergraduate degree from LaMoyne College and an M.S.W. from Fisk University. He also took graduate work at the University of Kansas and the University of Tennessee. Barry was named the first national chairman of the Student Non-Violent Coordinating Committee in 1960, and moved to Washington in 1965 to take over as Washington director of SNCC. He soon became a familiar figure in the city as one of the principal movers in the civil rights movement.

Barry always had the ability to deal with the young and in 1967 he was a co-founder and chairman of an antipoverty agency, Pride Economic Enterprises. Many of Pride's clients were "street dudes" to whom Pride provided an opportunity to work in jobs that paid them a wage and gave them self-respect. The program was highly successful. Barry severed his connection with Pride in 1970, and in 1972 he was elected president of the D.C. Board of Education. In 1975 he was elected to the City Council as a member-at-large. Barry is a Democrat.

THOMAS BRADLEY
Los Angeles
1980 Population: 2,966,763
Percentage Black: 17.0
Elected 1973

The highly respected California Poll in 1981 reported that Los Angeles Mayor Thomas Bradley was the most popular politician in the state. This was quite an achievement for the son of a Texas sharecropper, but for Bradley, who has always been a superachiever, it was part of a pattern.

Elected as Los Angeles' first black mayor in 1973 with 56% of the vote, reelected in 1977 with 59.1% of the vote, returned for the third time in 1981 with 63.6% of the vote—Bradley has done extremely well in a city where the black population is only 17%. To the people of Los Angeles he is seen as a decent, conciliatory man who works behind the scenes while avoiding public confrontations, even-handedly considering the interests of business, minority groups, and others.

Bradley, age seven, arrived in Los Angeles from Calvert, Texas with his family. He grew up in poverty, was a track star at high school, attended the University of California at Los Angeles on an athletic scholarship, and after graduation became a policeman. After 21 years on the force he retired as a lieutenant in 1960, having earned a law degree at night school. With the encouragement of friends, he ran for the City Council in 1963 and won.

In 1969 he ran for the post of mayor in a race that saw Sam Yorty, the incumbent—a talkative, combative, conservative Democrat—resort to blatant racism. Bradley, also a Democrat, was defeated but in 1973 he was back again and this time he won.

Bradley is regarded as one of the nation's most successful black political leaders. He has been credited with building confidence in Los Angeles, keeping racial conflicts in his city to a minimum in a time of rapid change in ethnic composition. He was a principal force

Mayor Thomas Bradley of Los Angeles won the Democratic nomination for governor of the state of California in 1982.

in securing the 1984 Summer Olympic Games for Los Angeles while helping rebuild the downtown section without subsidies from local taxpayers.

In describing him, Warren M. Christopher, Deputy Secretary of State in the Carter Administration and a longtime California Democratic activist, said, "He has a sense of size and poise and dignity—maybe sturdiness is the best word."

Subsequent to his election to a third term, Bradley announced that he would run for governor of California in 1982.

CHARLES BUSSEY
Little Rock, Arkansas
1980 Population: 158,461
Percentage Black: 32.2

Charles Bussey was born in Stamps, Arkansas in 1920 and was appointed Mayor of Little Rock, Arkansas in November 1981 to fill an unexpired term of Mayor Webb Hubbell, who had resigned. Mayor Bussey became the first black mayor of Little Rock, the city that became nationally known in 1957 following a federal court order that desegregated Central High School. Governor Orval Faubus had called out the

Arkansas National Guard to prevent nine black students from entering the school, prompting President Eisenhower to send U.S. troops to Little Rock to enforce the court order. Mayor Bussey is a member of various civic organizations in Little Rock and is active in the Boy Scout movement. He is a former investigator for the Pulaski County prosecutor's office. Mayor Bussey is a former vice mayor of Little Rock and has served on the Board of Directors of the city. He is on the executive board of the National League of Cities, a member of the Rotary Club, on the executive board of the Boy Scouts of America, and a 32nd degree Mason.

JAMES E. CHASE
Spokane, Washington
1980 Population: 171,300
Percentage Black: 1.3
Elected 1982

A longtime businessman in Spokane, James E. "Jim" Chase won the race for mayor of that city with approximately 62% of the vote. Born in Ballinger, Texas in 1914, Chase moved to Spokane in 1934 and took a job as a porter in a barbershop. That lasted until 1940 when he entered into a partnership in a body and fender repair shop.

During the World War II years he worked at the Gieger Field Air Force Base, and when the war was over he opened his own body and fender repair shop and continued its operation until 1981 when he retired. Active in the civic affairs of his community, he served three terms as president of the Spokane NAACP. He has also been a member of the Municipal League, the Mayor's Committee for Minority Employment, the Chamber of Commerce, and other groups.

He was elected to the Spokane City Council in 1975 and 1979, and served as mayor pro-tem in 1978 and 1979. His term runs until 1985.

PAUL L. GAINES
Newport, Rhode Island
1980 Population: 29,259
Percentage Black: 9.4
Elected 1981

When people think of Newport, they often think of the annual jazz festival that was held there for many years before it moved to New York City, and as a vacation mecca for the very rich. Newport is also a city where one of its favorite sons, Paul L. Gaines, serves as mayor—the first black mayor in the history of Rhode Island and the second in all of New England.

The mayor was educated in the public schools of Newport, earning both academic and athletic honors, the latter in baseball and basketball. He graduated in 1955 from Xavier University in Louisiana, where he captained the baseball and basketball teams and also made the honor roll.

For two years, from 1955 to 1957, he served in the Army in Germany and then joined the Newport School System in 1958 as teacher and basketball coach. He received his M.Ed. in counseling in 1968 from Bridgewater State College in Massachusetts and joined the staff of that college in the same year.

His first entry into the political arena came in 1968 when he was appointed to fill a vacancy on the Newport School Committee. He was elected to a full term the next year, becoming the first black elected to the Newport School Committee in the 1900s. His horizons widened, and in 1977 he ran and won an at-large seat in the City Council, thus becoming its first black member.

There was sentiment then for Gaines to become mayor, under the city's Council/Manager form of government, but he felt that he did not have the necessary experience and declined. He was reelected in 1979 as the Council's top vote getter, but this time, the role of mayor was denied him. The third time around, in 1981, he won his Council seat and the Council members elected him mayor and chairman of the Council.

KENNETH GIBSON
Newark, New Jersey
1980 Population: 329,288
Percentage Black: 58.2
Elected 1970

We must begin to reconcile the community . . . come together to show America that determined people can reverse the trend of decay in our city and other cities across the country.

These words were spoken in triumph June 16, 1970, on a historic night in Newark, when a 38-year-old engineer, Kenneth Gibson, became the first black mayor of a major eastern city.

Acceptance of challenge and a cool temperament were perhaps the major ingredients in the Gibson victory. Born in Enterprise, Alabama in 1932, Gibson migrated to Newark with his parents at the age of eight. Gibson's father took a job as a butcher, his mother as a seamstress.

Gibson and his brother Harold grew up on the streets of Newark's heavily black South Ward. The streets were safe in those days, Gibson remembers, and black youths released their energies in such outdoor activities as track meets and other athletic contests.

Gibson graduated from Central High School and then attended the Newark College of Engineering while he worked in a factory and for the New Jersey Highway Department to support his family. Upon graduation, he was placed on the municipal payroll by Mayor Hugh

Newark mayor Kenneth Gibson waves to supporters after winning reelection.

Addonizio, who was trying to consolidate his standing in the city's growing black community. However, Gibson's ties were closer, Addonizio's regime was racked by scandal, and in 1970 Gibson challenged and defeated the incumbent, obtaining some 54% of the vote.

As mayor, Gibson has been subject to intense pressure from two powerful and colorful political figures. On the right, Assemblyman Anthony Imperiale led a faction of whites aroused by appeals to their backlash fears. On the left, Imamu Baraka charged Gibson with moving too slowly. However, Gibson strengthened his position and in May 1974 was reelected easily, obtaining 54% of the vote in a field of five.

In June 1974 Gibson was elected chairman of the Advisory Board of the U.S. Conference of Mayors, the third highest post in that group.

During his first 12 years as mayor of the largest city in New Jersey, Gibson has enjoyed an illustrious political career. He became a national as well as an international figure. However, during his reelection bid for a fourth term in office in 1982, an indictment was handed down charging the mayor in a no-show job scandal. Dispite the indictment, Gibson drew a sizable number of votes but not enough to win on the first ballot. In the resulting runoff Gibson defeated the City Council President, Earl Harris, who had also been indicted in the no-show scandal.

RICHARD HATCHER
Gary, Indiana
1980 Population: 151,953
Percentage Black: 70.8
Elected 1967

One of the highest tributes an elected official can receive is the approval of his or her peers. Thus the high regard in which the four-time mayor of Gary, Richard Hatcher, is held was demonstrated by his selection in 1980 as the president of the U.S. Conference of Mayors. Another tribute that was paid him was his elections to two terms, 1979–1982, as the president of the National Conference of Black Mayors.

As the first black mayor of a major American city, Hatcher holds a unique place in American politics. He is not only a symbol but a powerful factor in helping to set the black political agenda. As an example, he conceived a now historic meeting in Richmond, Virginia, in 1980, the three-day National Conference on a Black Agenda for the 80s.

Hatcher first won election in 1967 in a startling reversal of the Democratic party policies which had governed the life of Gary for more than a generation.

Gary's Richard Hatcher, first black mayor of a major American city

Gary's black and white population were split along strict racial lines, with the Latin population regarded as the potential holders of the key votes that might ensure a Republican victory.

Richard Hatcher had defeated two white candidates, including the incumbent, in the party's May primary. In normal times, this would have been tantamount to victory. As it was, Hatcher nosed out Joseph B. Radigan in the hotly contested election by an official count of 39,330 to 37,941.

The election was conducted in an atmosphere heavy with the threat of violence, voter intimidation, alleged fraud, charges of militancy, and claims of Communist involvement. County Democratic head John Krupa claimed that Hatcher had "left-wingers in his camp." Hatcher countered by asserting that the so-called left-wing support had been present in the Democratic camp in previous elections without generating comparable charges.

Hatcher's election victory as a reformer placed him in the awkward position of fencing the complaints stemming from white diehards who refused to support any job, housing, or neighborhood programs that would promote any measure of integration and from black citizens equally appalled by his failure to create instant jobs for all.

Hatcher was reelected by a large majority in 1971 and went on to attain a prominent role as a spokesman for black officeholders. He was president of the National Black Caucus of Local Elected Officials in 1972 and was also prominent in the Gary black political convention that year. He was elected to his fourth term in 1980.

JAMES HOWELL McGEE
Dayton, Ohio
1970 Population: 244,000
Percentage Black: 30.9
Elected 1970

One of seven children, James Howell McGee was born in 1918 in Berryburg, Virginia. Raised in Steubenville, Ohio, McGee worked as a floor sweeper in the downtown business district of the city at age 12. He later attended Wilberforce College and, after serving in the Army, Ohio State University's Law School.

After struggling for several years in his profession, McGee began to file legal actions in cases then regarded as revolutionary, particularly one pursuant to the 1954 Supreme Court decision declaring separate public schools unconstitutional. McGee filed one of the first test cases in the North involving *de facto* segregation.

Over the years, McGee built up a considerable following in Dayton's predominantly black West Side wards. This strategy ultimately paid off in November 1969 when he was elected one of the four city-wide

commissioners who govern the Ohio city of 250,000 (including 70,000 blacks).

When McGee's predecessor resigned for health reasons in May 1970, a deadlock developed over his successor. Two commissioners dropped out of the running, however, whereupon McGee was chosen to head the government.

EDWARD M. McINTYRE, SR.
Augusta, Georgia
1980 Population: 47,532
Percentage Black: 53.4

Mayor Edward M. McIntyre, Sr. has had a diverse career, serving as a television host, working as a real estate agent, and holding down the presidency of his own consulting firm. A native of Augusta, he was born in 1931, attended local schools, and earned his B.A. from Morehouse College. He also attended Paine College and Fort Valley State College and took graduate study at Atlanta University and Columbia University.

He was elected mayor of Augusta in 1981 and took office on January 4, 1982. He is a Democrat. He is a member of a number of organizations including the Augusta Mental Health Association, the Augusta Chamber of Commerce, the National Alliance of Businessmen, and the Frontiersmen International Club.

THIRMAN L. MILNER
Hartford, Connecticut
1980 Population: 136,400
Percentage Black: 33.9
Elected 1981

The political pundits called it an "upset victory" when Thirman L. Milner, a two-term state representative, sent a five-term incumbent mayor down to defeat in the Democratic primary election in October 1981. Milner was not supposed to win, and had it not been for his own stubbornness, there probably would not have even been an election in October.

A month before, Milner had lost the first primary election to the incumbent by 94 votes. In heavily Democratic Hartford, winning the Democratic primary virtually assures a win in the general election. Milner wasn't satisfied with the way he lost and he took his case to court, complaining of fraud. The court decided that he was right, threw out the first election, and ordered the second, which Milner won, 9,167 to 6,258 votes.

Milner's romp to victory was aided by an exceptionally large black voter turnout. In black precincts he outpolled the incumbent 11 to 1. Milner also got a hand from such prominent blacks as Reverend Jesse Jackson, Representative Parren Mitchell of Maryland, and H. Carl McCall, former alternate representative to the United Nations. Milner rolled to an easy victory in the general election in November. He thus became the first popularly black elected mayor in New England.

When Milner won the mayor's office, he was no novice in politics. He was first elected to the Connecticut House of Representatives in 1978. He was head of the Black Caucus in the House and demonstrated a flair for leadership, particularly when he held his minority colleagues in line for the Democratic leadership during a crucial budget debate in 1980, and in exchange winning support for a welfare increase that had been in jeopardy.

A third generation native of Hartford, Mayor Milner is a former member of the Southern Christian Leadership Conference and the Student Non-Violent Coordinating Committee, and worked on voter registration and in civil rights demonstrations throughout the South with Dr. Martin Luther King, Andrew Young, and others.

Mayor Milner is known as a low-key legislator. Typically, after he won the election his first instinct was to relax and think about the next hurdle. "Everybody knows me," he said. "I'm trying to get away for a few days."

ERNEST N. MORIAL
New Orleans, Louisiana
1980 Population: 557,500
Percentage Black: 55
Elected 1978

If some master planner had set out to create the ideal profile for the first black mayor of New Orleans, that planner might well have come up with Ernest N. "Dutch" Morial. Born in that city on October 9, 1929, into a family of three brothers and two sisters, Mayor Morial is totally a product of New Orleans. He attended the city's public and parochial schools and was graduated in business administration from Xavier University. In 1954 he became the first black graduate of the Louisiana State University Law School.

The law degree was not an end but a beginning of a number of other firsts. In 1965 he became the first black U.S. attorney in Louisiana; in 1967 he became the state's first black state legislator since Reconstruction and the first black Democrat to ever win a seat; in 1970 he was the first black to be elected to the Juvenile Court; and in 1972 he became the first black to be appointed to the prestigious U.S. Fourth Circuit Court of Appeal.

Morial also served in the U.S. Army Intelligence Corps, 1954–1956, but even more important, early in his law career he made a commitment to the pursuit of civil rights. His early law practice was conducted in association with a legendary southern lawyer, A. P.

Tureaud—a mentor to Morial and other young black lawyers in Louisiana and a pioneer in the movement for equality.

Together with Tureaud, Morial brought and won a number of suits to eliminate segregation in the state and in the city. He was particularly active in suits against discrimination in many of the city's and state's educational institutions. He also filed suits to end discrimination in New Orleans' taxicabs and in its Municipal Auditorium and International Airport. His distinguished record earned him a call from President John Kennedy to be a founding member of the Lawyers' Committee for Civil Rights Under Law. In 1968 he became one of the first black delegates from Louisiana to a Democratic National Convention.

His political career began in 1959 when he ran and lost in a runoff election for a seat on the State Democratic Central Committee. He returned to the fray in 1967 when he won his seat in the State House of Representatives. He tried for the post of councilman-at-large in 1969 and lost in a close runoff election by less than 4% of the total votes cast. However, he continued in the Legislature until 1970, sponsoring such legislation as welfare reform, civil service, employment, consumer credit protection, housing reform, and voter registration. He successfully advocated lowering the voting age to 18.

His judicial career began in 1970, but the urge for the political arena never left him. The opportunity came in 1978 when he won the mayor's office with support of both black and white voters. In his inaugural address on May 1, he promised: "We will reach for the stars and bring the morality of our city government to the highest plane it has ever known."

The problems that plagued New Orleans when Morial took office did not suddenly end. He faced a critical shortage of local tax money, high unemployment, a Police Department seriously short of manpower and low on morale and community respect, and a high crime rate. Morial had his critics in the black community who charged that he was doing more to serve the business interests than the common man.

In the election of 1981, Morial faced a major challenge from a black opponent, State Senator William J. Jefferson, a former supporter. He was also challenged by a white candidate. A political analyist commenting on the election said:

Morial has a quick wit but it comes across to whites as arrogant. Blacks see Morial's personality as tough, he speaks his mind, doesn't take anything off anyone. Whites see that same behavior and call it arrogance. That's the biggest issue in the election. There is no race issue.

The nonpartisan mayoral primary was close enough

to force a runoff, which Morial won to assure his second term as mayor.

CARL E. OFFICER
East St. Louis, Illinois
1980 Population: 55,200
Percentage Black: 95.6
Elected 1979

The Honorable Carl Edward Officer is the mayor of the City of East St. Louis, Illinois, the second most populous city in the southern Illinois region.

Elected by a 95% plurality in May 1979, Officer was confirmed by the U.S. Conference of Mayors as the youngest mayor of a major metropolitan city at that time.

Prior to entering the office of mayor, Officer was the deputy director of Drivers Services for the State of Illinois. He also served as the deputy coroner for St. Clair County.

Shortly after his inauguration, Mayor Officer, realizing that there is strength in unity, founded the Metro-East Conference of Black Mayors, Inc., an organization bringing together the mayors of the four other predominantly black municipalities that surround East St. Louis. He currently serves as president and chief spokesperson for that group.

Mayor Officer was recently selected as one of the future outstanding black leaders for the eighties by *Black Enterprise* magazine.

The youthful mayor holds membership in many professional and fraternal organizations. Included among them are the NAACP, Urban League, Jaycees, U.S. Conference of Mayors, and National Conference of Black Mayors.

Carl Officer is mayor of East St. Louis, Illinois.

LIONEL J. WILSON
Oakland, California
1980 Population: 339,288
Percentage Black: 47.0
Elected 1977

Oakland, which stood for a long time in the shadow of its larger, more famous sister city across the bay, San Francisco, has developed into a city with its own personality and style. With championship professional sports teams, a first-rate symphony orchestra, redevelopment, and a responsive daily newspaper, the *Oakland Tribune,* which has been revitalized under the editorship of a black journalist, Robert Maynard, Oakland is growing. Serving his second term as mayor is Lionel J. Wilson, who came to the city with his family from New Orleans when he was four years old, carved out a career for himself as a lawyer and then a judge, and capped it all by being elected mayor of Oakland in 1977 and being reelected in 1981.

Mayor Wilson is the first black man to govern the city, but he also has a number of other firsts to his credit. In 1960 Governor Edmund G. Brown, Sr., appointed him to the Oakland Piedmont Municipal Court, making him the first black judge in Alameda County. He was serving as presiding judge of that court when Governor Brown elevated him to the Superior Court in 1964. He became presiding judge of the Alameda County Superior Court in 1973.

Wilson grew up in Oakland, the oldest of eight children, and attended public school there. He received his B.A. in Economics from the University of California at Berkeley in 1939, and then served overseas in World War II. After his honorable discharge, he earned his law degree in 1949 from the Hastings College of Law and began his law practice in Oakland.

His career on the bench was distinguished by his service as the chairman of Presiding Judges of California Superior Courts, four terms as the presiding judge of the Criminal Division of the Alameda County Superior Courts, and one year as the presiding judge of the Apellate Department of the Alameda County Superior Court. He was at that time the only black judge to serve as the presiding judge of a Superior Court in California, or of the Appellate Department of a Superior Court, and as chairman of Presiding Judges of California Superior Courts.

Mayor Wilson has also been active in community service, notably with the NAACP in both Berkeley and Oakland. Since his election he has served on the Board of Directors of the League of California Cities, various committees of the U.S. Conference of Mayors, and the National League of Cities. He was appointed by President Jimmy Carter to the U.S. Court of Patents and Appeals. Mayor Wilson is married and the father of three sons, two of whom are graduates of the University of California at Davis School of Law.

ANDREW YOUNG
Atlanta, Georgia
1980 Population: 425,000
Percentage Black: 61.0
Elected 1981

A leading civil rights activist, a congressman from Georgia, the U.S. ambassador to the United Nations, and mayor of the principal city in the South, Atlanta— This has been the career of Andrew Young, who came into national prominence nearly two decades ago and is probably as well known internationally as any living black American, save Muhammad Ali. Soft-spoken while eloquent, Young is widely admired for his incisive thinking and his willingness to speak his mind.

He was born in New Orleans in 1932, and received a B.S. degree from Howard University at 19 and a Bachelor of Divinity degree from Hartford Theological Seminary in 1955. He was ordained a minister in the United Church of Christ and then served in churches in Alabama and Georgia before joining the National Council of Churches in 1957. The turning point of his life came in 1961 when he joined Reverend Martin Luther King and became a trusted aide and close confidante. He did much of the negotiating for the Southern Christian Leadership Conference and was respected for his coolness and rationality. He became executive vice president of SCLC in 1967 and remained with King until the latter's murder in 1968. During those years with SCLC Young also developed several programs including voter registration projects and other major civil rights drives.

In 1970 Young lost a bid for Congress when Fletcher Thompson, a white ultraconservative Republican, beat him by 20,000 votes in a campaign in which Thompson contended that Young sought the demise of Western Civilization. In 1972, however, the Fifth District in Atlanta was redistricted under court order and Thompson, who conceded that he had never met with one black group as a congressman, resigned to run unsuccessfully for the Senate.

Though large segments of the conservative white population had been removed from the Fifth, the race for Congress was not easy for Young. Blacks still comprised only 44% of the registered voters and Young's Republican opponent, Rodney Cook, was a more appealing candidate than Thompson. However, Young captured 23% of the white vote and 54% of the total vote to win by a margin of 8,000, even though Richard Nixon carried the district for president. Young was the first black representative to be elected from Georgia since Jefferson Long in 1870.

Thereafter, Young was elected with ease every two

Andrew Young's audience includes Julius Le Vann Chambers and William T. Coleman, Sr.

years. He was one of the most vocal supporters of his fellow Georgian Jimmy Carter's campaign for the Presidency in 1976. When Carter won, Young left his safe seat in Congress in 1977 to become America's ambassador to the United Nations.

His tenure there was marked by controversy as well as solid achievement. The controversy came because of his outspoken manner, which sometimes ruffled diplomatic feathers. His solid achievements were represented primarily in the tremendous improvement he fostered in relations between America and the Third World.

His career as a diplomat came to an end in 1979 when he met secretly with a representative of the Palestine Liberation Organization to discuss an upcoming vote in the United Nations. America had a policy that none of its representatives would meet with the PLO as long as it refused to recognize the right of Israel to exist as a state. When the news of Young's meeting leaked out, there was an uproar. Young had originally told the State Department that the meeting was by chance, but later he admitted that it had been planned.

Though the meeting had secured a vote in the United Nations that the United States wanted, the pressure mounted and Young tendered his resignation, which President Carter accepted. The incident badly strained black–Jewish relations because of the feeling within the black community that Jewish leaders were instrumental in Young's removal, a charge that they denied.

Young became a private citizen, but not for long. When Maynard Jackson was prevented by law from running for his third term of office as mayor of Atlanta in 1981, Young entered the race. Once again, it was not to be easy. He faced a black candidate and a strong white candidate and was forced into a runoff. Race entered the campaign when the outgoing mayor, himself a black, charged blacks who supported the white candidate, State Legislator Sidney Marcus, with "selling out" the civil rights movement.

Jackson's remarks were widely criticized, and it was feared that they would create a backlash against Young. However, he ended up winning 55% of the total vote. He won 10.6% of the white vote, compared to the 12% he had won in the primary, and 88.4% of the black vote, up from 61% earlier.

Young took office at a time that Atlanta was going through several economic and social problems. Its population was shrinking, the tax base stagnating, almost a quarter of the city's residents were below the poverty line, and the city was still shaken by the murders of 28 black youths and the disappearance of another— even though a man had been convicted of several of the murders.

The new mayor said on inauguration day: "We've gone through the strain and there have been no broken relationships and there will be none in the future."

COLEMAN YOUNG
Detroit, Michigan
1980 Population: 1,203,339
Percentage Black: 63.1
Elected 1973

In 1981 Coleman Young won his third term as mayor of Detroit, which surprised no one. By all odds one of the most popular mayors the Motor City has ever had, if not the most popular, Young won 65.8% of the votes cast. The vote was remarkable because even with the heavy unemployment in Detroit, caused by the difficulties of the automakers, a shortage of cash, and the drying up of funds that the city had received when Jimmy Carter was President, the voters returned Young to office.

What Young had going for him was a sense of revitalization that he breathed into Detroit and the confidence of the voters that though things were rough, the mayor would persevere. A Democrat, and one of the earliest big-city mayors to come out for Jimmy Carter in 1976, Young had a very close relationship with the Carter Administration that proved helpful in securing funds for Detroit. Carter himself said, "There is no other mayor any closer to me than is Coleman Young."

The road that led to the front door of the White House was a long and often tortured one for Young. It started in Tuscaloosa, Alabama, where he was born in 1921. Young's family moved to Detroit's east side

in 1926 after the Ku Klux Klan ransacked a neighborhood in Huntsville where his father was learning to be a tailor. In Detroit, he attended Catholic Central and then Eastern High School, graduating from the latter with honors. He had to reject a scholarship to the University of Michigan when the Eastern High School Alumni Association, in contrast to policies followed with poor white students, declined to assist him with costs other than tuition.

Young entered an electrician's apprentice school at the Ford Motor Company, lost the only available electrician's job to a white man who scored much lower than he in tests, went to work on the assembly line, and soon engaged in underground union activities. One day a man Young describes as a company goon tried to attack him. Young hit him on the head with a steel bar and was fired.

Young then worked to integrate housing in Detroit's Sojourner Truth Housing Project until World War II. During the war he became a navigator in the Army Air Force and was commissioned a second lieutenant. Stationed at Freeman Field, Indiana, he demonstrated against exclusion of blacks from officers' clubs and was arrested along with 100 other black airmen, among them Thurgood Marshall, now an Associate Justice of the Supreme Court, and Percy Sutton, former president of New York's Borough of Manhattan. Young spent three days in jail. Shortly thereafter, the clubs were opened to black officers.

After the war, the future mayor of Detroit returned to his union organizing activities and in 1947 was named director of organization for the Wayne County AFL-CIO. However, the Union fired him in 1948 when he supported Henry Wallace, candidate of the Progressive Party, in the Presidential election. The Union regarded Wallace as a dupe of the Communist Party and supported Harry Truman.

Young managed a dry cleaning plant for a few years and then, in 1951, founded and directed the National Negro Labor Council. According to Young, the Council was way ahead of its time and successfully prevailed on Sears Roebuck & Co. and the San Francisco Transit System to hire blacks. However, the Council also aroused the interest of the House Un-American Activities Committee, which was then holding hearings around the country at which alleged Communists were required to produce names of people allegedly associated with the Party. Young, who denies he was ever a Communist, refused to name anyone. He emerged from the battle with his self-respect intact, but his Labor Council was placed on the Attorney General's subversive list, and in 1956 it disbanded. Says Young of the 1950s: "Anybody who was mentioned by any stool pigeon as being a Communist, lost their jobs. People were really scared." Charges that Young was a Communist were to be used against him, unsuccessfully, 21 years later in his mayoral campaign.

After working at a variety of jobs until 1961, Young won a seat on the Michigan Constitutional Convention. In 1962 he lost a race for state representative but became director of campaign organization for the Democratic gubernatorial candidate in Wayne County (Detroit). He sold life insurance until 1964 when, with Union support, he was elected to the State Senate. In the Senate, he was a leader of the civil rights forces, fighting among other things for low-income housing for people dislocated by urban renewal and for bars to discrimination in the hiring practices of the Detroit Police Force.

In 1969 Young sought to run for mayor but declined when a court ruled he would first have to resign his Senate seat. The black candidate in that race, Richard Austin, lost by 6,000 votes. However, in 1973 the Michigan Supreme Court declared that Young could run, and he won narrowly in a contest in which votes polarized according to race.

ROSTER OF BLACK MAYORS

Alabama

ARRINGTON,
    Richard, Jr.
1245 Mims St. S.W.
Birmingham 35211

BELL, Joe E.
Mosses
Rt. 1, Box 66
Hayneville 36040

CARSON, Rufus
Franklin Co.
Rt. 3, Box 870
Tuskegee 36083

COLVIN, James
Union Co.
Rt. 3, Box 66
Eutaw 35462

FORD, Johnny L., Sr.
City Hall
214 N. Main St.
Tuskegee 36083

FOSTER, Clyde
Town Hall
640 6th St.
Triana 35758

HAYDEN, Andrew M.
P.O. Box 201
Uniontown 36786

HOWARD, Robert B.
P.O. Box 157
Lisman 36912

ISAAC, Jim, Jr.
P.O. Box 36
Forkland 36740

JACKSON, John
Whitehall
Rt. 1 Box 199
Hayneville 36040

KNOX, Eliga G.
P.O. Box 58

Akron 35441

LEWIS, Richard L.
3700 Main St.
Brighton 35020

MARBURY, Howard W.
Rt. 1 Box 413
Ridgeville 35954

ROGERS, Freddie C.
317 Woodward Ave.
Roosevelt City 35020

SAWYER, Geraldine
McMullen Co.
Rt. 1 Box 16B
Aliceville 35442

SMITH, John H.
Prichard
P.O. Box 10427
Prichard 36610

WILLIAMS, Jimmie T.
Old Memphis
Rt. 1 Box 213
Aliceville 35442

Arkansas

BARNES, George
P.O. Box 62
Reed 71670

BORDERS, Doris
509 Vine St.
Newport 72112

BOWENS, Emily
Mitchellville
Rt. 1 Box 308 Vine St.
Dumas 71639

BUSSEY, Charles
Little Rock City Hall
Markham & Broadway
    #203
Little Rock 72201

CONLEY, Emmitt J.

P.O. Box 443
Cotton Plant 72036

DOLTHIN, Silas
Lakeview
Rt. 1
Helena 72342

ENGLISH, Clarence R.
1 Talley Dr.
Menifee 72107

FEIMSTER, Curtis
P.O. Box 93
Huntington 72940

HERPELL, Clyde S.
P.O. Box 95
Humnoke 72072

MINNIS, Clifton, Sr.
General Delivery
Edmondson 72332

STEWART, James A.
Tollette
Rt. 1 Box 299-B
Mineral Springs 71851

WATKINS, Lenice J.
Sunset
Hwy. 77 at Grant St.
Marion 72364

WHITAKER, Willard
P.O. Box 236
Madison 72359

California

BRADLEY, Thomas
City Hall Room 305
200 N. Spring St.
Los Angeles 90012

NEWPORT, Eugene 'Gus'
2180 Milvia St.
Berkeley 94704

TUCKER, Walter R.
Compton City Hall

205 S. Willowbrook St
Compton 90220

WILSON, Lionel J.
City Hall
1421 Washington St.
Oakland 94612

Colorado

BARRY, Odell C.
P.O. Box 33817
Northglenn 80233

Connecticut

MILNER, Thirman
Hartford

Delaware

WRIGHT, George C., Jr.
31 Locust St.
Smyrna 19977

District of Columbia

BARRY, Marion S., Jr.
3607 Suitland Rd. S.E.
Washington 20020

Florida

BARKLEY, Earnest O., Jr.
P.O. Drawer A
Gretna 32332

BROOKS, Bobbie E.
1325 W. 28th St.
Riviera Beach 33404

BYRD, Chester A.
Vice Mayor
100 W. Dania Beach
Dania Beach 33004

DUNMORE, Chester
P.O. Box 73
Micanopy 32667

GORDON, Abraham
P.O. Box 2163
Eatonville 32751

LOGAN, Willie F.
P.O. Box 1163
Opa Locka 33054

Georgia

YOUNG, Andrew
Atlanta

BIVENS, Isaac L., Sr.
P.O. Box 131
Harrison 31035

FAIRCLOTH, Tom
P.O. Box 619
Thomasville 31792

HILL, Richmond D.
P.O. Box 37
Greenville 30222

ISREAL, George
P.O. Box 247
Macon 31202

JACKSON, Maynard H.
City Hall
Atlanta 30303

JOHNSON, B. A.
P.O. Box 572
Wadley 30477

KENT, Carrie
P.O. Box 58
Walthourville 31333

McINTYRE, Edward
Augusta

McIVER, John
P.O. Box 246
Riceboro 31323

Illinois

BALLENTINE, Richard
3327 W. 137th St.
Robbins 60472

BECK, Saul L.
1501 E. 13th Pl.
East Chicago Heights
  60411

DAVIS, James R.
3733 12th St.
Rock Island 61201

ECHOLS, Tyrone
321 Weaver
Madison 62060

FREELON, Joe
115 S. 5th Ave.
Maywood 60153

HARRIS, James C.
725 E. 155th Court
Phoenix 60426

HAYES, Robert E.
Supervisor
Pembroke Twp.
P.O. Box 16
Hopkins Park 60944

JONES, Alex, Sr.
Village of Pembroke
P.O. Box AK
Hopkins Park 60944

JORDAN, Clyde C.
Supervisor
E. St. Louis Twp.
1501 State St.
E. St. Louis 62205

MOBLEY, Callie
4821 Bonds
Alorton 62207

OFFICER, Carl
City Hall
7 Collinsville Ave.
East St. Louis 62201

OWENS, Riley L., III
City Hall
5800 Bond Ave.
Centreville 62203

WEST, Marcellus
312 S. 5th St.
Brooklyn 62059

Indiana

HATCHER, Richard G.
Municipal Bldg.
401 Broadway
Gary 46402

Kansas

BAILEY, Elvin J.
700 N. Vine
Abilene 67410

BLAND, Hy
Fort Dodge Rd.
Dodge City 67801

Kentucky

IRVINE, Bobby Lee
P.O. Box 243
Taylorsville 40071

TWYMAN, Luska J.

City Hall
1208 S. Lewis St.
Glasgow 42141

WASHINGTON, Daniel
Church Street
Drakesboro 42337

Louisiana

MORIAL, Ernest
New Orleans

Maryland

BLACKWELL, Frank
814 Carrington Ave.
Seat Pleasant 20027

GRAY, Robert R.
717 60th Pl.
Fairmount Hghts. 20743

HALL, Raymond A.
3907 Windom Rd.
North Brentwood 20722

Michigan

BLACKWELL, Robert B.
30 Gerald Ave.
Highland Park 48203

CLARK, Leon
Supervisor
Buena Vista Twp.
1160 S. Outer Dr.
Saginaw 48601

COOPER, John B.
P.O. Box 57
17999 State St.
Vandalia 49095

DANIELS, William M.
26754 Kitch
Inkster 48141

GOODMAN, George D.
1610 Gregory
Ypsilanti 48197

HUNT, James
Supervisor
Royal Oak Twp.
21075 Wyoming St.
Ferndale 48220

JONES, Charles W.
905 Carson
Albion 49224

LEWIS, Eugene
Supervisor
Webber Twp.
P.O. Box 626
Baldwin 49304

LITTLE, William
Trustee
Royal Oak Twp.
21075 Wyoming
Ferndale 48220

PATTERSON, Joel
693 Pipestone
Benton Harbor 49022

ROBINSON, William J.
Supervisor
Calvin Twp.
18536 Chain Lake
Cassopolis 49031

SCOTT, Harry Lee
Supervisor
58511 Main St.
New Haven 48048

WINBURN, B. J.
Supervisor
Yales Twp.
P.O. Box 115
Idlewild 49642

YOUNG, Coleman A.
1126 City-Co. Bldg.
Detroit 48226

Mississippi

BARTLEY, Charles
P.O. Box 525
Shaw 38773

BLACKWELL, Unita
P.O. Box 188
Mayersville 39113

BUTLER, Lawrence
P.O. Box 292
Bolton 39041

GRAY, Robert D.
P.O. Drawer J
Shelby 38774

JONES, Franklin
Rt. 1, Box 200
Oakland 38948

JONES, W. J.
P.O. Box 23
Coahoma 38617

LEFLORE, Robert
P.O. Box 216
Pace 38764

LEGGETTE, Violet O.
P.O. Box 191
Gunnison 38746

LINDSEY, S. L.
General Delivery
Metcalfe 38701

LUCAS, Earl

P.O. Drawer H
Mound Bayou 38762

LUCAS, Maurice Fulton
Rt. 1 Box R-6
Revona 38732

MIDDLETON, Kennie
P.O. Box 10
Fayette 39069

PRITCHARD, Daron
Rt. 2 Box 11-C
Edwards 39066

REESE, Henry L.
P.O. Box 38
Glendora 38928

SMITH, Fannie Pearl
General Delivery
Falcon 38728

THOMAS, Richard
P.O. Box 56
Beulah 38726

TODD, Johnny
General Delivery
Rosedale 38769

TUTWILER, Milton D.
Drawer 428
Winstonville 38781

WASHINGTON, James
Box 552
Friars Point 38631

WILKINS, Jim
P.O. Box 337
Jonestown 38639

Missouri

BROWN, Zeke
Penermon
Rt. 1
Essex 63846

CLARK, Theodore L., Sr.
Village of N. Lilbourn
P.O. Box 139
Lilbourn 63862

HARRIS, Betty
Wilson City
P.O. Box 366
Wyatt 63882

HENDERSON, Johnnie L.
6205 Martin Luther
    King Dr.
Wellston 63133

HOWARD, Travis B.
P.O. Box 152
Howardville 63869

HUMES, David R.
Hayti Heights

P.O. Box 426
Hayti 63851

O'KAIN, Roosevelt
6032 Margaretta
Pine Lawn 63121

SHAVERS, James W., Sr.
Homestown
P.O. Box 142
Wardell 63879

WELLS, Joseph L.
5825 Roman Court
Kinloch 63140

WILLIAMS, Lottie
2803 Maywood
Velda Village 63121

New Jersey

ALWAN, Mansour
Chesilhurst Borough Hall
Second & Grant Ave.
Chesilhurst 08089

BRYANT, James W.
Lawnside Borough Hall
4 E. Douglas Ave.
Lawnside 08045

CHERRY, Theodore
Committeemember
S. Brunswick Twsp.
36 New Rd.
Kendall Park 08824

COOKE, Thomas H., Jr.
44 City Hall Plaza
East Orange 07019

GIBSON, Kenneth A.
72 Tuxedo Pwky.
Newark 07106

PRIMAS, Melvin R., Jr.
400 Chambers Ave.
Camden 08102

New York

HOLMES, Everett
Bridgewater 13331

North Carolina

BROWN, Alex
Greenevers
Rt. 2 Box 291
Rose Hill 28458

BROWN, Louis S.
General Delivery
Navassa 28404

CREDLE, Edward Earl

Mesic
Rt. 1 Box 1115B
Bayboro 28515

DIXON, Willie A.
E. Arcadia
Rt. 1 Box 54
Riegelwood 28456

DRAKEFORD, Robert
102 Walters Rd.
Carrboro 27510

GRAY-MELTON, Nellie
P.O. Box 71
Cofield 27922

GREEN, Edith L.
P.O. Box 129
Bolton 28423

JEFFERS, Thebaud
204 W. Walnut Ave.
Gastonia 28052

MASSEY, Reginald
P.O. Box 338
East Spencer 28039

MORGAN, Leander R.
P.O. Box 309
New Bern 28560

PERRY, Wendell
Box 312
Garysburg 27831

PITT, James H.
P.O. Box 126
Parmele 27861

WILKINS, Elmer V.
P.O. Box 357
Roper 27970

Ohio

HUNTER, Richard F., Sr.
3917 N. Fordham Pl.
Silverton 45213

LAWSON, Lawyer
332 Brookhaven St.
Woodlawn 45215

McGEE, James H.
Municipal Bldg. Box 22
101 W. 3rd St.
Dayton 45401

SHARP, Louis D.
2600 Main St.
Urbancrest 43123

SMITH, Rayner J.
3808 Roselawn Rd.
Woodmere Village 44122

WHITE, Albert Andrew
917 13th St.
Portsmouth 45662

Oklahoma

DAVIS, Lelia Foley
Mayor-Councilmember
P.O. Box 157
Taft 74463

GREEN, Theodis G.
P.O. Box 847
Langston 73053

JONES, Cecil, Sr.
P.O. Box 150
Tatums 73087

McCLENDON, Reuben E.
Mayor-Councilmember
P.O. Box 16
Rentiesville 74459

MOORE, Sidney
P.O. Box 1234
Tullahassee 74466

MOSLEY, G.
General Delivery
Red Bird 74558

OLIVER, Lee E.
Brooksville
Rt. 3 Box 137
Tecumseh 74873

PETTIS, John Albert
Mayor-Councilmember
617 W. Clark Box 325
El Reno 73036

RUTLEDGE, Alfred
P.O. Box 127
McLoud 74851

THOMAS, Erma
Mayor-Trustee
Summitt
Rt. 4 Box 436C
Muskogee 74401

WILCOTS, Sam
P.O. Box 975
Boley 74829

Pennsylvania

REID, Robert G.
314 Grant St.
Middletown 17057

Rhode Island

GAINES, Paul
Newport

South Carolina

GOREE, Janie Glymph
P.O. Box 305

Carlisle 29031

GROOMS, Robert
P.O. Box 68
Lamar 29069

HOLMES, William
P.O. Box 551
Allendale 29810

JEFFERSON, Clifton
P.O. Box 146
Lynchburg 29080

PARSON, Hazel S.
Rt. 2 Box 7
Ridgeville 29472

RISHER, James
P.O. Box 172
Gifford 29923

ROBINSON, Henry
1904 Ribaut
Port Royal 29935

ROSS, Charles H.
P.O. Box 536
Lincolnville 29483

SCOTT, Lewis N.
P.O. Box 281
Eastover 29044

SEABROOK, Silas N., Jr.
P.O. Box 424-A
Santee 29142

STEVENS, Cleveland
Atlantic City
P.O. Box 1425
Atlantic Beach 29582

WILSON, Charlie B.
Town Hall
P.O. Box 116
Sellers 29592

Tennessee

BERRY, Hoyt
P.O. Box 142
Charleston 37310

Texas

BELL, Everett
P.O. Box 7391
Easton 75641

BIRMINGHAM, Sam A.
Mayor-Commissioner
2107 Spring St.
Marshall 75670

HUMPHERY,
    Ennis B., Sr.
13714 Willie Melton Blvd.
Kendleton 77451

JENKINS, Ernest Lee
Trinidad
P.O. Box 91
Trinidad 75163

Virginia

BAZEMORE, Willa S.
Vice Mayor
1600 Great Bridge Blvd.
Chesapeake 23320

BEAMER, Ben A., Sr.
Vice Mayor
4308 Templar Dr.
Portsmouth 23703

BUTLER, Wendell H.
Vice Mayor
2118 Andrews Rd. N.W.
Roanoke 24017

DAVIES, Lawrence A.
801 Sophia St.
Fredericksburg 22401

GARLAND, Charles M.
617 Colonial Ave.
Colonial Beach 22443

GOODE, George R., Sr.
700 Pine St.
Clifton Forge 24422

KENT, William A.
Vice Mayor
P.O. Box 251
South Boston 24592

LEWIS, J. B., Jr.
Vice Mayor
420 Wills Rd.
Lexington 24450

MARSH, Henry
Richmond

TAYLOR, Noel C.
2302 Florida Ave. N.W.
Roanoke 24017

Washington

CHASE, James E.
Spokane

West Virginia

HODGE, Charles
P.O. Box 23
Gary 24836

PAST AND PRESENT APPOINTED GOVERNMENT OFFICIALS AND REPRESENTATIVES

Black statesmen are now regularly considered for federal appointments to top-level diplomatic and administrative posts. This positive development is one of the fruits of the capable and skillful service rendered to the nation by the earlier black appointees who blazed a trail to the higher echelons of government. The biographies of several of these eminent men and women, both those still serving at high posts and retirees, are given here.

CLIFFORD ALEXANDER, JR.
Former Associate Counsel to the President
Former Secretary of the Army

A native New Yorker, Clifford Alexander, Jr. was appointed President Lyndon B. Johnson's associate special counsel on August 25, 1965. He had previously served as the President's deputy special assistant. In 1977 Alexander became the first black to lead the Army as its secretary. He was appointed to that post by President Jimmy Carter.

Born in 1933, Alexander graduated from Harvard University and then attended Yale Law School, where he was awarded an LL.B. At the age of 26, he became assistant district attorney of New York County and, two years later, executive director of the Hamilton Grange Neighborhood Conservation District in Manhattanville. After four years at this job, Alexander

Clifford Alexander (left) *and Representative John Conyers at a conference.*

moved to HARYOU in 1963 as an executive program director.

After leaving his post with the EEOC, where he was under constant pressure from Republican Senators like Everett Dirksen who accused him of bullying reluctant employers into complying with federal guidelines for minority employment, Alexander entered private law practice and became a Harvard overseer. His function at Harvard was comparable to the one he was empowered to exercise while in the federal government but, in this case, he was actually involved in working out details with craft unions which were obliged to offer and implement concrete proposals for improving minority group employment opportunities. At Harvard, the pact worked out by Alexander related to "two live buildings" and involved 300 workers, some one-fifth of whom were black and Puerto Rican.

Alexander is currently in the private practice of law.

MARY FRANCES BERRY
Attorney, Government Official

Mary Frances Berry was born in 1938 and received her B.A. degree from Howard University in 1961 and her masters degree in 1962. In 1966 she received the Ph.D. from the University of Michigan and her J.D. from its law school in 1970. Berry was appointed Assistant Secretary of Education, U.S. Department of Health, Education and Welfare by President Jimmy Carter in 1977 and later became commissioner and vice chairman of the U.S. Commission on Civil Rights. She currently is a professor of law and history at Howard University.

MELVIN L. P. BRADLEY
Government Official

Melvin L. P. Bradley was born in Texarkana, Texas and received his B.S. degree from Pepperdine University. He is a former assistant to the vice president of United Airlines and director of public relations. From 1973 to 1975, he was assistant to Governor Ronald Reagan of California as well as a member of Reagan's senior staff participating in cabinet meetings. Bradley currently serves as senior advisor in President Reagan's office of OPD.

Melvin Bradley and President Reagan. Bradley is a special assistant to the President for policy development.

ANDREW FELTON BRIMMER
Former Member Federal Reserve Board

Andrew Brimmer, an eminent black economist and teacher, was named to the Federal Reserve Board in 1966 by President Lyndon B. Johnson.

Born in Newellton, Louisiana on September 13, 1926, Brimmer was awarded a Ph.D. in economics by Harvard University in 1957, having already done some of his graduate studies in India—both at the Delhi School of Economics and at the University of Bombay (1951–1952).

In 1955, after having spent a year at Harvard as a teaching fellow in economics, Brimmer joined the Federal Reserve Bank of New York as an economist—a post he surrendered in 1958 in order to become Assistant Professor of Economics at Michigan State University. In 1961 he joined the faculty of the Wharton School of Finance and Commerce, remaining there until his appointment to the position of Deputy Assistant Secretary of Commerce in May 1963.

His duties involved decisions relevant to the development of the American economy—duties which, under his later title as Assistant Secretary of Commerce, became broad enough to make him one of the key government spokesmen on such varied topics as balance of payments, tourist travel, and U.S. capital investment abroad. He was also in charge of the Bureau of Census and the Office of Business Economics, both of which provide valuable statistical data to the general public.

Aside from having taught at the University of California at Berkeley and at the City College of New York, Brimmer has published a number of books and monographs on his special field of interest, as well as several articles and reviews in some of the nation's leading economic journals. Perhaps his single most important project of 1964 was the research he contributed to the U.S. Supreme Court ruling on the constitutionality of the public accommodations sections of the Civil Rights Act.

Over the years, Brimmer has established himself as the most prominent black economist in the nation. It was natural, then, that he take an active stand pursuant to the Nixon Administration's stated policy of fostering black businesses and lending support to black entrepreneurs. Whereas many critics faulted Nixon for failing to provide a coordinated program of loans to black would-be entrepreneurs, Brimmer attacked the scheme on theoretical grounds, rather than for its organizational shortcomings. How, Brimmer asked, could most black businesses expect to be successful in the ghetto, where so much of the nation's black poor was concentrated? "Self-employment," Brimmer argued, "offers a low and rather risky payoff." In his view, blacks need more jobs as salaried managers and skilled craftsmen with major American companies, companies with the capital resources to command the attention of the national community.

Brimmer now heads his own consulting firm and teaches at Harvard's Graduate Business School.

ROBERT L. BROKENBURR
Former Alternate Delegate to the United Nations

For many years a lawyer, twice state senator from Indiana, and several times at different levels within the Indiana court system, Robert L. Brokenburr served as an alternate delegate to the U.N. General Assembly from 1955 to 1956.

A native of Phoebus, Virginia, Brokenburr was born on November 16, 1886. Educated initially in his hometown, he later attended Hampton Institute in Hampton, Virginia, receiving his B.A. in 1906. He completed his law studies at Howard in 1909.

RALPH J. BUNCHE
Former U.N. Undersecretary for Special Political Affairs

The first American black to win the Nobel Peace Prize, Ralph Bunche was an internationally acclaimed statesman whose record of achievement places him among the most significant American diplomats of the twentieth century. Bunche received the coveted award in 1950 for his role in effecting a cease fire in the Arab–Israeli dispute which threatened to engulf the entire Middle East in armed conflict.

Born in Detroit on August 7, 1904, Bunche graduated from UCLA in 1927 *summa cum laude* and with Phi Beta Kappa honors. A year later he received his M.A. in government from Harvard. Soon thereafter he was named head of the Department of Political Science at Howard University, remaining there until 1932 at which time he was able to resume work toward his doctorate from Harvard. (He later studied at Northwestern University, the London School of Economics, and Capetown University.)

Before World War II broke out, Bunche did field work with the Swedish sociologist Gunnar Myrdal, author of the widely acclaimed *An American Dilemma.* During the war, he served initially as Senior Social Analyst for the Office of the Coordinator of Information in African and Far Eastern Affairs, and was then reassigned to the African section of the Office of Strategic Services. In 1942 he helped draw up the territories and trusteeship sections ultimately earmarked for inclusion in the United Nations charter.

But the single event which brought the name of Ralph Bunche into the international limelight occurred soon after his appointment in 1948 as chief assistant to Count Folke Bernadotte, U.N. mediator in the Palestine crisis. With the latter's assassination, Bunche was faced with the great challenge of somehow continuing cease fire talks between Egypt and Israel. After six weeks of intensive negotiations, Bunche worked out the now-famous "Four Armistice Agreements," which effected an immediate cessation of the hostilities between the two combatants. Once the actual cease fire was signed, Bunche received numerous letters and telegrams from many of the leading heads of state the world over, and was later accorded a hero's welcome upon his return to the United States.

Bunche died on December 9, 1971 after having served as the distinguished Undersecretary-General of the United Nations from 1955 to his retirement in October 1971.

ARCHIBALD J. CAREY
Former Alternate Delegate to the United Nations

Archibald Carey served as an alternate delegate to the United Nations from 1953 to 1956.

A native of Chicago and a graduate of John Marshall Law School, Carey presided for 19 years (1930–1949) as pastor of the Woodlawn A.M.E. Church in that city. Twice elected alderman from Chicago's Third Ward, Carey was on the Chicago city council for eight years, and later became an avid presidential supporter of Dwight D. Eisenhower, from whom he received his U.N. appointment. During the Eisenhower Administration, he was vice chairman of the President's Committee on Government Employment Policy.

Carey currently is a judge on the Supreme Court of Illinois.

LISLE C. CARTER, JR.
Former Assistant Secretary, Department of Health, Education and Welfare (HEW)

Lisle Carter was appointed Assistant Secretary of Health, Education and Welfare (HEW) by President Lyndon B. Johnson in 1966.

Born in New York City on November 18, 1925, Carter moved with his family to Barbados (British West Indies) and began his formal education there. On his return to New York in 1940, he enrolled at Cazenovia Seminary (Syracuse, New York) for one year of junior college before moving on to Dartmouth. In 1944 he received his B.A. in chemistry there and, after an interruption in his schooling caused by his induction into the Armed Forces, finally received an LL.B. from St. John's University School of Law in 1950.

From then until 1961, Carter combined his own

law practice with the job of legal counsel for the National Urban League. Named Deputy Assistant Secretary in the Department of Health, Education and Welfare, he led a departmental team in 1962 through an inspection of health and educational conditions in 11 African countries. Later, he helped conduct a comprehensive survey aimed at ending discrimination in federally assisted programs. Before accepting his present post, Carter was a top aide to Sargent Shriver, Director of the Office of Economic Opportunity (OEO).

Currently he is president of the University of the District of Columbia in Washington, D.C.

ARTHUR A. CHAPIN
Former Director of Equal Employment Opportunity Department of Labor

Arthur Chapin's association with the Department of Labor dates back to 1961. Before accepting his federal assignment, Chapin had worked for many years at the state level as assistant to the president of the New Jersey CIO Council. He was concerned with civil rights legislation and minimum wage and unemployment compensation. He also served as a member of the New Jersey Committee on Housing, and of the State Wage Panel for restaurant employees.

While with the Labor Department, Chapin helped compile an annual *Directory of Negro College Graduates,* which aided business and industry in finding competent and qualified personnel. The directory enabled the Department to maintain close liaison with thousands of college graduates as well as numerous employment agencies.

MERCER COOK
Former Ambassador to Niger, Senegal, and Gambia

Dr. Mercer Cook, the first U.S. Ambassador to the Republic of Niger, also served as Ambassador to the West African nations of Senegal and Gambia.

Born in Washington, D.C. in 1903, Dr. Cook lived across the street from Duke Ellington during his childhood, and attended the famed Dunbar High School in the nation's capital, numbering among his classmates William H. Hastie (now a federal judge), Sterling Brown (noted literary critic and author), and Charles Drew (a pioneer in the development of blood plasma).

After receiving his B.A. from Amherst in 1925, Cook did graduate work at the University of Paris, and later acquired both his M.A. and Ph.D. degrees from Brown University. After a short stint in Haiti on an educational assignment, he returned to the United States to become professor of romance languages at Howard University, a post he held for the next 14 years.

Upon leaving Howard, Dr. Cook traveled widely,

Arthur A. Chapin was director of the Office of Equal Employment Opportunity.

particularly in Africa. In 1963 he served briefly as an alternate delegate to the General Assembly of the United Nations.

Cook completed his diplomatic tour as ambassador to Senegal and Gambia in 1966. He returned to Howard University, where he became head of the Department of Romance Languages.

PRESTON A. DAVIS
Director of Small Business Affairs, U.S. Department of Agriculture

Preston A. Davis, director of Small Business Affairs of the U.S. Department of Agriculture, was born in Norfolk, Virginia. He received his B.S. degree in business administration from West Virginia State College in 1949 and his M.S.W. from George Washington University in 1974. Davis was appointed to his present position in 1979; prior to that he worked in the Department of Agriculture for most of his career life. He was the first black to become a member of Kiwanis International Club and is the winner of the Purple Heart, the Bronze Star, and Army commendation medals as well as the Army Meritorious Service Award. Davis is author of *Firepower Chinese Communist Army* and *Signatures of Soviet Nuclear Missile Systems.*

WILLIAM H. DEAN
Former Chief of the African Unit, Division of Economic Stability and Development

William H. Dean was appointed chief of the African unit in the Division of Economic Stability and Development in 1949, and served in this capacity until his death in 1952.

Born in Lynchburg, Virginia on July 6, 1910, Dean graduated from Bowdoin College in Maine in 1930, and later attended Harvard on a fellowship. He received both his M.A. and Ph.D. degrees from this university in 1932 and 1938, respectively.

During the 1940s, Dean devoted his energies to a number of important posts in government, notably as a consultant to the National Resources Planning Board (1940–1942) and as a member of several technical missions to such places as Haiti, Libya, and the Virgin Islands (1944–1949). He also taught for a time at Atlanta University and City College of New York.

Dean committed suicide on January 9, 1952.

EDWARD RICHARD DUDLEY
Former Ambassador to Liberia

Judge Edward R. Dudley is a justice of the Supreme Court of the State of New York. Born in South Boston, Virginia, he graduated from Johnson C. Smith University (B.S., 1932) and St. John's University Law School (1941). Admitted to the bar in 1941, he became U.S. Ambassador to Liberia (1948–1953) and started the first Point 4 program in Africa. After a term as Borough President of Manhattan (1961–1965), he was appointed an administrative judge of Criminal Court of New York City (1967) and an administrative judge

Thelma Duggin, appointed special assistant to President Reagan as this book went to press.

of the New York Supreme Court (1971). Dudley is a life member of the NAACP and a trustee of the Fund for the City of New York.

ALFRED LEROY EDWARDS
Former Deputy Assistant Secretary of Agriculture

In 1963 President John F. Kennedy appointed Alfred Edwards Deputy Assistant Secretary of Agriculture. Edwards became one of the key coordinators in the department's "Rural Renaissance" movement—a program aimed at reinvigorating those areas affected by a lack of real job opportunities, and the increasing migration of young people to the large cities.

In 1974 he was named Director of the Division of Research and Professional Business Administration, School of Business at the University of Michigan.

Born on August 9, 1920 in Key West, Florida, Edwards received a B.A. from Livingstone College in 1948, an M.A. in economics from the University of Michigan, and a Ph.D. from the University of Iowa in 1958.

Prior to becoming engaged in government service, Dr. Edwards was a faculty member of a number of leading universities. He also helped establish the University of Nigeria at Nsukka—arriving there with the first contingent of American teachers and administrators who were charged with the tremendous task of helping Nigeria organize and oversee the entire venture.

Essentially a social scientist, Dr. Edwards has tried to persuade qualified students to avail themselves of the many opportunities opening up in agriculture—a field which, he feels, has undeservedly been denied the status and importance currently due it.

JAMES FARMER
Former Assistant Secretary of Health, Education and Welfare

For biography see Civil Rights section.

CLARENCE CLYDE FERGUSON, JR.
Former Representative to the Economic and Social Council of the U.N.

Clarence Ferguson was the U.S. Representative to the Economic and Social Council of the United Nations. He was also Deputy Assistant Secretary of State for African Affairs and prior to that U.S. Ambassador to Uganda.

Ferguson joined the Department of State as Special Coordinator for Relief to the Civilian Victims of the Nigerian Civil War with the personal rank of Ambassador in February 1969. Before coming into the Department of State, Ferguson was the Distinguished Professor of Law at Rutgers University Law School. He had

UNESCO Representative Clarence Ferguson helped draft the U.N. Statement on Race.

previously served as the dean of Howard University Law School (1963–1969). During the Kennedy Administration Ferguson was general counsel to the U.S. Commission on Civil Rights.

Ferguson was born November 4, 1924 in Wilmington, North Carolina. He served more than four years in the U.S. Army (1942–1946) in Europe and the Southwest Pacific Theaters. He earned a Battle Star for service with the Third Army in the Central European Campaign (1945).

Educated at Ohio State University, he graduated with High Distinction in Constitutional History in 1948 and was awarded his J.D. *cum laude,* from Harvard Law School in 1951.

Ferguson is a member of the Massachusetts and New York Bars and has practiced in both Massachusetts and New York. In 1954 and 1955 he was an assistant U.S. attorney for the Southern District of New York, having served previously as assistant general counsel to the Moreland-Act Commission to Investigate Harness Racing (1953–1954). From 1951 through 1955, Ferguson was associated as counsel to the firm of Baltimore, Paulson and Canudo, New York City, specializing in corporate and bankruptcy matters.

Ferguson was secretary and research director of the New Jersey State Commission to Study and Report on the Uniform Commercial Code, and author of New Jersey annotations on "Secured Transactions."

In 1952 he was appointed one of the U.S. representatives to the Western Hemisphere UNESCO Conference in Havana, Cuba. In 1963 and 1964 he served as U.S.

alternate in the United Nations Sub-Commission on Prevention of Discrimination Against Minorities, and also as special legal advisor to the U.S. Mission to the United Nations. In April 1965 Ferguson was elected as U.S. expert to the United Nations Sub-Commission on Discrimination. He has also served as consultant to UNESCO on Human Rights (1965). Ferguson is one of the drafters of the UNESCO Statement on Race, 1967. He has headed many U.S. delegations to international conferences and meetings. He was also chairman of the Panel on Humanitarian Problems of International Law of the American Society of International Law.

Ferguson is a member of Phi Beta Kappa and several other honorary societies. In 1956 he was named Outstanding Young Man of New Jersey 1956 by the New Jersey Junior Chamber of Commerce. He has also served as chairman of the New Jersey Committee on Housing for the Aged and as civil rights consultant to Governor Nelson Rockefeller of New York from 1958 to 1964.

Ferguson was a member and treasurer of the East Orange Housing Authority; President of the Newark Rutgers Chapter of the American Association of University Professors, and was a member of the Committee on Racial Discrimination of the American Association of Law Schools. For two years he served on the Executive Committee of the American Association of Law Schools. At the present time, Ferguson is a member of numerous boards and advisory committees as well as consultant to many federal and international agencies. He currently is a member of the Executive Committee of the American Association of International Law as well as professor of law at Harvard Law School.

Ferguson is the author of six legal texts and more than 20 articles on constitutional and international law.

ZELMA GEORGE
Former Alternate Delegate to the United Nations

Zelma George was appointed an alternate delegate to the Fifteenth General Assembly of the United Nations in 1960.

Born in Hearne, Texas, Dr. George moved to Kansas with her family at an early age and later studied voice at the American Conservatory of Music in Chicago. She received an undergraduate degree from the University of Chicago and earned her doctorate in sociology from New York University.

George worked for a time as a probation officer for a juvenile court and then as dean of women at Tennessee State College. In 1955 she was appointed to the Defense Advisory Committee on Women in the Services and, four years later, under the auspices of the State Department, completed a three-month assignment in Southeast Asia, culminating in her attendance at the Pan Pacific and Southeast Asia Women's Assembly which took place in Singapore.

George is currently lecturing, writing, and performing consulting assignments for private business and government. She also serves as a committee member on Ethnic Heritage Studies Development Program Executive Committee.

ERNEST GREEN
Former Assistant Secretary for Employment and Training, U.S. Department of Labor

Ernest Green was appointed Assistant Secretary for Employment and Training of the U.S. Department of Labor by President Carter in 1977. Green was born in 1941 and received his B.A. from Michigan State University in 1962 and his masters degree two years later. Prior to being appointed to the post by President Carter, Green was executive director of Recruitment Training Program and director of the Twentieth Century Fund on employment of black youth and apprenticeship.

PATRICIA ROBERTS HARRIS
Former Ambassador to Luxembourg
Former Secretary, Department of Health and Human Services

As ambassador to Luxembourg, Patricia Harris was the first black woman to hold this diplomatic rank in U.S. history. Until President Ronald Reagan took office in 1980, Harris served as Secretary of the Department of Health and Human Services and also Secretary of Housing and Urban Development under President Jimmy Carter. She served in these positions from 1977 to 1981. Currently Harris is running for the office of mayor in the District of Columbia.

Born in Mattoon, Illinois, Harris attended elementary school in Chicago, and received her undergraduate degree from Howard University in 1945. After completing postgraduate work at the University of Chicago and at American University, she earned her doctorate in jurisprudence from George Washington University Law School in 1960.

Prior to her appointment, Harris had worked for the YWCA in Chicago (1946–1949), and also served as executive director for Delta Sigma Theta in Washington, D.C. An attorney and professor before she entered politics, Harris served under President John F. Kennedy as co-chairman of the National Women's Committee on Civil Rights and was later named to the Commission on the Status of Puerto Rico.

Harris was elected Permanent Chairman of the Democratic National Convention on June 27, 1972.

ANDREW J. HATCHER
Former Associate Press Secretary

In 1960 President John F. Kennedy named Andrew Hatcher as his associate press secretary—thus making him the first major black appointee of the New Frontier. Hatcher was the individual though whom many of the President's important news releases were made.

Born in Princeton, New Jersey in 1925, Hatcher attended Springfield College, graduating with a B.A. degree. During World War II he served for three years in the Army as a second lieutenant and, after his discharge, took a job with the San Francisco *Sun-Reporter*.

In 1960 Hatcher campaigned ardently for Kennedy's election to the presidency. Hatcher resigned after the assassination of the President, and held an executive position with a brewery company in New Jersey.

Hatcher is a business executive in New York City.

CHESTER A. HIGGINS
Former Assistant Chief of Public Affairs to the Secretary of the Army

Chester A. Higgins was born in 1917 and attended Kentucky State College for a year and Louisville Municipal College for two years. Higgins was general assistant to the first black commissioner of the Federal Communications Agency, Benjamin Hooks. Higgins has been a reporter and feature writer for the *Louisville*

Patricia Harris served President Carter as Secretary of Health and Human Services.

Defender, Jet magazine, *Ebony,* and *Tan.* Higgins served as assistant chief of public affairs to the office of Secretary of the Army in the Carter Administration. He is currently editor-in-chief of *Crisis* magazine, the official publication of the NAACP.

JEROME HOLLAND
Former U.S. Ambassador to Sweden

Easily one of President Nixon's shrewdest political appointments, Jerome Holland is an experienced educator whose diplomatic skills often came into play mediating between insistent student radicals and adamant campus authorities. Convivial, articulate, and persuasive, Holland was appropriately discreet and notably confident in his ability to add to the "backlog of cooperation and friendship" which he felt characterized U.S.–Swedish relations. The estimate was perhaps a trifle optimistic in view of the Swedes' policy of granting asylum to U.S. deserters and aid to North Vietnam.

Holland resigned as Ambassador to Sweden in 1972 to become a member of the Board of Directors of the New York Stock Exchange, the first black ever elected to that body.

He currently serves on the boards of several large companies: AT&T, Chrysler Corporation, Continental Corporation, General Foods, Union Carbide, Federated Department Stores, Manufacturers Hanover Trust Company, New York Stock Exchange, Inc., and Zurn Industries, Inc.

MELVIN HUMPHREY
Director of the office of Small Business Development Unit, Department of Transportation

Melvin Humphrey was born in 1921 in St. Louis, Missouri. He received all of his degrees from the University of Illinois, acquiring a Ph.D. in 1955. Before his appointment by President Reagan to the Department of Transportation, Humphrey served as director of research for the Equal Employment Opportunity Commission and co-authored three textbooks: *Principles of Accounting, Principles of Economics,* and *Public Finance.* He also wrote *Black Experience Vs. Black Expectations EEOC 1977.* He has also performed consulting services for private businesses and government and also serves as a committee member on Ethnic Heritage Studies Development Program, executive committee.

SAMUEL C. JACKSON
Former Assistant Secretary, Department of Housing and Urban Development

Samuel C. Jackson was appointed Assistant Secretary of Housing and Urban Development in 1969. At the time of his appointment he was the highest ranking black in federal government.

Born May 8, 1929 at Kansas City, Kansas, Jackson graduated from Washburn University with a B.A. and received an LL.B. from the same school in 1954.

Jackson was a member of the U.S. Equal Employment Opportunity Commission from 1965 to 1968 and headed the U.S. Housing Mission to Africa in 1971.

He is a member of the national board of directors and the legal committee of NAACP and is a past president of the Kansas chapter of the NAACP. Previously, Jackson served as deputy general counsel of the Kansas State Department of Welfare.

HOWARD JENKINS, JR.
Member, National Labor Relations Board

Howard Jenkins, Jr. was appointed by President John F. Kennedy in 1963 to a five-year term as a member of the National Labor Relations Board (NRLB)—the first black ever to serve with this federal government agency. Jenkins has been reappointed to serve as a member of the National Labor Relations Board by four presidents, Democrats and Republicans alike.

Born on June 16, 1915 in Denver, Colorado, Jenkins received his B.A. from the University of Denver in 1936 and soon thereafter became the first black to earn an LL.B. from the same institution. He was likewise the first black to be admitted to the Colorado bar.

After World War II (during which he had worked for the Office of Price Administration, the Denver War Labor Board, and the National Wage Stabilization Board), Jenkins taught labor and administrative law at Howard University for 10 years. In 1956, having completed a graduate program in law at New York University, he became an attorney for the Department of Labor. Over the years, he slowly climbed the rungs of this department's ladder, reaching the post of assistant commissioner in the Bureau of Labor Management Reports in 1962.

BARBARA JORDAN
Attorney, Educator, Former Congresswoman

Barbara Jordan's appointment to President Carter's Advisory Board on Ambassadorial Appointments marked her return to government service after she had resigned as U.S. Representative to the 95th Congress from Texas in 1976.

See section on former members of Congress for more biographical information.

ROBERT WILSON KITCHEN, JR.
Former Deputy Representative to the Economic and Social Council of the U.N.

Previously, Robert Kitchen was stationed in Washington, D.C., as Director of the Office of International

Barbara Jordan, an eloquent and effective voice in Congress.

Training in the Agency for International Development (AID) of the Department of State. He had been with AID and its predecessor organizations since 1952. Beginning as an administrative assistant in the Economic Development Mission to Liberia, Kitchen became acting director of that Mission, then economic advisor to the director of the International Cooperation Administration Mission to Pakistan, Pakistan Desk Officer, and in 1957 Chief of the Special Mission to the Sudan. Kitchen administered the first major AID program in Africa, the U.S. Mission to the Sudan, from 1958 to 1960. Following this assignment he became Special Assistant for Program and Policy in AID's Office of Development Finance and Private Enterprise.

Kitchen graduated from Morehouse College in 1943. He received his M.S. in business administration from Columbia University in 1946, did postgraduate work at American University, and received his LL.D. in industrial management and engineering from Chapman College in 1965. The following year Kitchen participated in the Department of State's Senior Seminar on Foreign Policy, the most advanced training program in international affairs for principal officers of the department. Kitchen also holds the Department of State's Meritorious Service Award.

CLINTON EVERETT KNOX
Former Ambassador to Dahomey

Clinton Knox, a career foreign service officer with more than 20 years experience, was appointed U.S. Ambassador to Dahomey in 1964.

A native of New Bedford, Massachusetts, Knox acquired his Ph.D. from Harvard in 1940. Having taught at Morgan State College for eight years, Knox joined the State Department at the close of World War II, doing research on Northern and Western Europe. In 1957 he was assigned to the NATO Defense College in Paris and subsequently became first secretary in the U.S. mission to NATO. Knox was later counselor and deputy chief of mission in the U.S. Embassy in Tegucigalpa, Honduras.

Knox has retired and is a member of the Diplomatic Consular Officers Association.

JEWEL LAFONTANT
Attorney

Jewel Lafontant is a practicing attorney and civil rights leader in Chicago, where she is a senior partner in the law firm of Stradford, Lafontant, Gibson, Fisher and Cousins.

Robert W. Kitchen, former minister-counselor for economic affairs, U.S. Mission to the United Nations.

Jewel Lafontant was formerly deputy solicitor general of the United States.

Born in Chicago, she took her B.A. at Oberlin College and her LL.D. at the University of Chicago (1946). Admitted to the Illinois Bar in 1947, she became a trial attorney for the Legal Aid Bureau (1947–1954), a member of the law firm of Rogers, Rogers and Strayhorn (1952–1954), and assistant U.S. attorney in Chicago (1955–1958), before taking a part-time position with her present firm in 1958. Her government service has included being a member of the Illinois Advisory Committee to the Commission on Civil Rights (1958–present), a legal advisor for the Inheritance Tax Division of Illinois (1962–1969), and a member of the U.S. Advisory Commission on International, Educational and Cultural Affairs (1969–present). She serves on several corporate boards, one of which is Foote, Cone and Belding Communications, Inc., in Chicago.

CHARLES H. MAHONEY
Former Delegate to the United Nations

Charles H. Mahoney is the first black to become a permanent member of a U.S. delegation to the United Nations.

Born in Decatur, Michigan on March 29, 1886, Mahoney received his B.A. from Fisk University and his LL.B. from the University of Michigan. An attorney for some 30 years, Mahoney was active in a number of civic and business enterprises in Michigan.

During his five-year U.N. tour (1954–1959), Mahoney was an important member of several committees,

and also served on the Panel for Inquiry and Conciliation.

Mahoney died in Detroit on January 29, 1966.

CARMEL CARRINGTON MARR
Former Legal Advisor to the U.S. Mission to the United Nations

An experienced lawyer—particularly in matters pertaining to international law—Carmel Carrington Marr was appointed to the post of legal advisor to the U.S. Mission to the United Nations in 1953.

Apart from her specific duties, she was in close and constant contact with missions from other parts of the world, and served on a number of key committees of the U.N. General Assembly.

A native New Yorker, Marr is a graduate of Hunter College and holds an LL.B. degree from Columbia University.

In 1971 Marr was appointed to the Public Service Commission. She currently serves as a commissioner on the New York State Human Rights Appeal Board.

WADE HAMPTON McCREE
Lawyer, Judge

Wade Hampton McCree was born in Des Moines, Iowa and following his graduation from Fisk University in 1941, he received his LL.B. Degree from Harvard Law School in 1944. He was admitted to the Michigan bar in 1948 at which time he practiced law in Detroit. In 1954 McCree became judge of the Michigan Circuit Court in Wayne County and in 1961 was named judge of the U.S. District Court for the Eastern Michigan District. In 1977 he was appointed solicitor general in the administration of President Jimmy Carter. McCree currently serves as solicitor general of the United States.

DONALD F. McHENRY
Former U.S. Permanent Representative to the United Nations

Donald F. McHenry was appointed U.S. Permanent Representative to the United Nations by President Jimmy Carter in 1979 following the resignation of Andrew Young. McHenry has studied, taught, and worked primarily in the fields of American foreign policy and international law and organizations. He joined the U.S. Department of State in 1963 and served for eight years in various positions related to U.S. policy in international organizations. In 1971, while on leave from the Department, he was a visiting scholar at the Brookings Institution, Washington, D.C. and an international affairs fellow of the Council on Foreign Relations, New York. In 1973, after leaving the State Department, he joined the Carnegie Endowment for International Peace in Washington as director of Humanitarian Policy Studies. In 1976 he served as a member of President Carter's transition staff at the State Department prior to joining the U.S. Mission to the U.N.

During his career, Ambassador McHenry represented the United States in a number of international forums, and as the U.S. Representative on the U.N. Western Five Contact Group he was the chief U.S. negotiator on the question of Namibia.

McHenry was born in St. Louis, Missouri in 1936 and graduated from Illinois State University in 1957, receiving his masters degree two years later from Southern Illinois University. The former ambassador is on the Board of Trustees of the Ford Foundation, a governor of the American Stock Exchange, a director of the First National Boston Corporation, the Coca Cola Company, the International Paper Company, and a member of the Council on Foreign Relations. McHenry is currently university research professor of diplomacy and international affairs at Georgetown University.

FRANK MONTERO
Former Advisor to the U.S. Mission to the United Nations

Frank Montero received his appointment as advisor to the U.S. Mission to the U.N. in 1962 after having

Donald McHenry served as U.N. Ambassador after the resignation of Andrew Young.

served for almost 15 years as the assistant executive director of the National Urban League.

In addition to acting for a time as a special assistant to the late Adlai Stevenson, he represented the United States at the independence celebrations of Niger, Kenya, and Zanzibar, and as senior advisor on economic and social affairs for many of the specialized committees in the U.N. proper.

Born in New York City in 1912, Montero is a graduate of Howard University (1934) and holds graduate degrees from Columbia University (social administration) and New York University (public administration).

E. FREDERIC MORROW
Former Administrative Assistant to President Eisenhower

When President Eisenhower named E. Frederic Morrow as his administrative assistant in 1955, this represented the first time in U.S. history that a black held an executive position on a presidential staff.

Born in Hackensack, New Jersey in April 1909, Morrow graduated from Bowdoin College and later received an LL.B. from the Law School at Rutgers University. In the interim period, he had been business manager of *Opportunity,* the official house organ of the National Urban League, Coordinator of Branches for the NAACP, and a major in the Armed Forces during World War II.

In 1952, after three years in the public affairs division of the Columbia Broadcasting System, he became part of Eisenhower's presidential campaign staff and

President Eisenhower conferring with his administrative assistant E. Frederick Morrow

traveled some 100,000 miles all over the country on behalf of the Republican nominee. The following year, he became Advisor on Business Affairs to the Secretary of Commerce and was in close liaison with Congress on all legislation affecting his department.

After six years of service with President Eisenhower (1955–1961), Morrow left Washington to become vice president of the African-American Institute—the largest privately endowed foundation in the United States. Its main function is to improve American economic and cultural relations with the nations of Africa.

Morrow is currently a vice president of the Bank of America's Department of Communications and Public Affairs in the New York City division.

JOHN HOWARD MORROW
Former Ambassador to Guinea

John Howard Morrow was appointed Ambassador to Guinea by President Dwight D. Eisenhower in 1959, and served in this post for the next two years.

A native of Hackensack, New Jersey, where he was born on February 10, 1910, Morrow received his B.A. from Rutgers and his M.A. and Ph.D. from the University of Pennsylvania. After some 25 years as a teacher, both on the high school and collegiate levels, Morrow was given his first political appointment in 1957 when President Eisenhower made him a member of the Commission on Government Security.

Since completing his assignment in Guinea, Morrow has served in several capacities: first as a member of the U.S. delegation to the U.N. General Assembly; then a vice chairman of a delegation on educational achievement which was posted off to Ethiopia; and, finally, as minister and permanent U.S. representative to UNESCO.

In 1963 he accepted a post with the Foreign Service Institute (Department of State, Washington, D.C.), which helps prepare promising candidates for careers overseas.

Morrow's brother, E. Frederic, once served as an administrative aide to President Eisenhower in the White House.

JAMES M. NABRIT, JR.
Former Ambassador to the United Nations

With his appointment on August 25, 1965 as an ambassador to the U.N., James M. Nabrit, Jr. became the highest ranking black American to serve in any U.S. delegation to the world body.

Born in Atlanta on September 4, 1900, Nabrit received his early education in his home state, and later earned his B.A. from Morehouse. Drawn to the law at an early age, Nabrit set up his own practice in Houston, Texas in 1930, three years after having received his LL.B. from Northwestern University.

At once a specialist in civil rights, Nabrit participated in a number of historic cases tried before the Supreme Court, including one of the five cases connected with the monumental *Brown* v. *Board of Education* decision which outlawed segregation in U.S. public schooling.

During World War II, Nabrit was on both the Selective Service and Price Control boards. In 1954 he served as legal advisor to the Governor of the Virgin Islands and, later, was twice a delegate to the annual International Labor Conference held in Geneva, Switzerland.

Nabrit is president emeritus of Howard University and is an active attorney.

SAMUEL NABRIT
Former Member, Atomic Energy Commission

Dr. Samuel Nabrit is the first black to serve on the Atomic Energy Commission, having been appointed to this post in 1966 by President Lyndon B. Johnson.

Born on February 21, 1905 in Macon, Georgia, Nabrit moved with his family to Augusta, where he attended Walker Baptist Institute. Active in sports, he edited the school newspaper and graduated as class valedictorian. He continued his education at Morehouse, earning his B.A. in 1925. That same year, he began his teaching career at Atlanta University as a biology instructor. (He later became dean of the graduate school of arts and sciences.) In 1932 he won the distinction of being the first black to earn a Ph.D. from Brown University.

Dr. Nabrit taught at Columbia University in 1945, and then spent a year in Brussels doing research. In 1956 he was appointed to a post on the National Science Board by President Dwight D. Eisenhower and during the Kennedy Administration, was made a special ambassador to Nigeria in West Africa.

He has been a marine biologist on the faculty of Texas Southern University. Dr. Nabrit is currently Executive Director of the Southern and National Fellowship Funds of the Council of Southern Universities (one of four black foundation heads in the nation). He served as president of Texas Southern University from 1955 to 1966. Dr. Nabrit is the brother of James M. Nabrit, Jr., formerly the president of Howard University, who was named an Ambassador to the United States delegation to the United Nations in 1965.

SAMUEL RILEY PIERCE
Secretary of Housing and Urban Development

A man who was later to have a broad background in education and government, as well as in private industry, Samuel Pierce served as assistant to the Undersecretary of Labor from 1955 to 1956. Pierce was appointed in 1981 by President Ronald Reagan as Secretary of Housing and Urban Development.

Born in Glen Cove, New York on September 8, 1922, Pierce attended Cornell University where he received his B.A. in 1947 and his LL.B. in 1949. Three

Samuel Pierce has the horrendous task of being President Reagan's Secretary of Housing and Urban Development.

years later, he was awarded an LL.M. (in taxation) from New York University's School of Law.

From 1949 through 1955, he was first assistant district attorney for New York County and then assistant U.S. attorney for the Southern District of New York. Since 1958 Pierce has been a faculty member of the N.Y.U. Law School, served as a judge in the New York Court of General Sessions (1959–1961), and has become a partner in a prominent New York law firm.

THOMAS E. POSEY
Former Chief of the Labor and Industry Division, Agency for International Development

Dr. Thomas Posey is a former chief of the Labor and Industry Division of the Office of International Training within the Agency for International Development (AID).

A native of Washington, D.C., Posey received his B.A. in economics, monetary theory, and labor in 1923 from Syracuse University and, in 1926, his M.A. from the same school.

For the next 25 years he taught economics at West Virginia State College, taking time out, with the aid of a Rosenwald fellowship, to acquire his Ph.D. in 1948 from the University of Wisconsin. During these many years, he was active in the political life of his state, serving as a member of the West Virginia State Planning Board and as advisor to the West Virginia State Federation of Labor.

He also served as a consultant to the Fair Employment Practices Commission (1943), as Supervisory Industrial Economist with the Wage Stabilization Board (1951), and as an economic advisor for the Mutual Security Agency in Burma (1952).

From 1954 to 1960, Dr. Posey served on foreign missions to the Philippines and to Turkey, where his duties involved him primarily with questions of labor productivity and industrial relations. Upon completion of a three-year term as a U.S. delegate to the U.N. Conference in Geneva on the Application of Science and Technology for the Benefit of the Less-Developed Areas of the World, Dr. Posey returned to the United States where he assumed his post with AID.

CARL ROWAN
Former Ambassador to Finland

Carl Rowan has held two major diplomatic and administrative posts in his lifetime: one as Ambassador to Finland (1963), the other as Director of the United States Information Agency (USIA).

Born in Ravenscroft, Tennessee on August 11, 1925, Rowan studied for a year at Tennessee A&I in Nashville and, at the age of 19, became one of the first 15 blacks commissioned by the U.S. Navy during

Journalist Carl Rowan served as director of the United States Information Agency.

U.N. Representative Edith Sampson presents a Booker T. Washington memorial to Ambassador Entezam of Iran.

World War II. After the war, he received his B.A. from Oberlin College in Ohio, and later acquired an M.A. in journalism from the University of Minnesota.

Having established himself as a journalist and much-sought-after feature writer, Rowan soon turned his energies to the writing of full-length books. His first, *South of Freedom,* was based on many of his personal experiences, and was followed by *The Pitiful and the Proud* (1956) and *Go South in Sorrow* (1957). Three years later, he wrote *Wait Till Next Year,* a biography of the famous black baseball player Jackie Robinson.

Rowan returned to journalism after resigning from the USIA in July 1965. At present he writes a thrice-weekly column syndicated in a number of newspapers around the country. His commentaries are also heard on radio stations across the country. As he did in his Minneapolis *Tribune* days, Rowan covers more than just distinctly black stories. Only one in six columns is devoted to racial or civil rights topics.

EDITH SAMPSON
Former Alternate Delegate to the United Nations

The first black woman to be named to the United Nations, Edith Sampson served in this body from 1950 until 1953, first as an appointee of President Harry

S. Truman and later during a portion of the Eisenhower Administration.

A native of Pittsburgh, Sampson acquired a Bachelor of Laws degree from the John Marshall Law School in Chicago in 1925 and, two years later, became the first woman to receive a Master of Laws from Loyola University.

A member of the Illinois bar since 1927, she was admitted to practice before the Supreme Court in 1934. During the 1930s, she maintained her own private practice, specializing particularly in domestic relations and in criminal law.

After her U.N. appointment, Sampson traveled around the world, often as a lecturer under State Department auspices. She was elected Associate Judge of the Municipal Court of Chicago in 1962. In 1978 she retired from Cook County Circuit Court.

Sampson died on October 7, 1979 at Northwestern Hospital in Chicago, Illinois.

ELLIOTT PERCIVAL SKINNER
Former Ambassador to Upper Volta

Dr. Elliott Percival Skinner was appointed by President Lyndon B. Johnson to succeed Thomas S. Estes as Ambassador to Upper Volta, thus becoming the seventh black to hold such a major appointment within the Johnson Administration (the others being Mercer Cook, Patricia Harris, Clinton Knox, Dr. James Nabrit, Hugh Smythe, and Franklin Williams).

An assistant professor of anthropology at New York University, Dr. Skinner was born in 1924 in Port-of-Spain, Trinidad (West Indies), and received his early education in that city. He later acquired his B.A. from N.Y.U. and both his M.A. and Ph.D. degrees from Columbia. He teaches at Columbia University in New York City.

Skinner studied under a Whitney Fellowship in French West Africa from 1953 to 1955, and later continued his academic pursuits in French Guiana under a Ford Foundation Fellowship. A member of several professional associations, and an active participant in the work of the NAACP and the American Society of African Culture (AMSAC), Dr. Skinner has also written or co-authored a number of books, including *An Analysis of the Political Organization of the African People* (1957), *Christianity and Islam Among the Mossi* (1958), *The Mossi of the Upper Volta* (1964), and *A Glorious Age in Africa* (1965).

HUGH H. SMYTHE
Former Ambassador to Syria

Hugh H. Smythe was a former Ambassador to Syria and also was a special advisor to the Senate Foreign Relations Committee, a member of the U.S. delegation to the Sixteenth U.N. General Assembly, and a State Department Research consultant. Smythe who lived in New York City, died in 1977 at the age of 63. He had been appointed Ambassador to Syria in 1965 by President Lyndon B. Johnson, a position he served in until 1967. That was the year that Symthe defied an order by the Syrian government to close the embassy in Damascus within 48 hours during a six-day war in that country.

Born in Pittsburgh in 1914, Smythe was educated locally and later received his B.A. and M.A. degrees from Virginia State College and Atlanta University, respectively. He also studied at Fisk and Chicago universities and, after World War II, won his Ph.D. in anthropology from Northwestern.

As a consequence of his ambassadorial appointment, Dr. Smythe was obliged to take a special leave of absence from Brooklyn College, where he was serving as a deputy chairman in the graduate division of the sociology department. His other governmental posts include lecturer at the Foreign Service Institute of the State Department (1961–1963), trainer of Peace Corps volunteers (1962–1963), and U.S. advisor to the National Research Council of Thailand.

Late in 1964, Symthe became chief consultant to Youth in Action, an organization falling under the Anti-Poverty Program. A year later, he participated in an orientation program designed to train Fulbright grantees bound for Southeast Asia.

HOBART TAYLOR, JR.
Attorney

Hobart Taylor, Jr. was named director to the Export-Import Bank in 1965. In his government career, Taylor had previously served President Lyndon B. Johnson as an associate special counsel and had also been executive vice chairman of the President's Committee on Equal Employment Opportunity. He currently serves as general counsel in the law firm of Jones, Day, Reavis and Pogue in Washington, D.C.

Born in Texarkana, Texas, Taylor graduated from Prairie View College with a B.A., receiving his M.A. from Howard and his LL.B. from the University of Michigan. After a short period as a research assistant for the Chief Justice of Michigan's Supreme Court, he entered a Detroit law firm as a junior and, later, a full partner.

He sits on the board of directors of Aetna Life and Casualty Co., Great Atlantic and Pacific Tea Co., Standard Oil Co., Westinghouse Electric Corporation, and Eastern Airlines.

GLORIA TOOTE
Chairman, Merit System Procurement Board

Gloria Toote received her J.D. degree from Howard Law School and also attended Columbia University Graduate Law School. She is a former member of the editorial staff of national affairs at *Time* magazine. Toote has practiced law in New York City since 1954. In 1971 she joined the Department of Housing and Urban Development as assistant secretary. She is currently chairperson of the Merit System Procurement Board in the Reagan Administration.

EVERETT C. WALLACE
Deputy Assistant Secretary, Fair Housing, HUD

Everett C. Wallace was born in 1951 in Chicago. He received a B.A. degree from Northwestern University in 1973 and a J.D. from the same institution in 1976. He graduated with honors. Prior to his appointment to HUD, Wallace was legal assistant to the office of Senator Howard Baker and senior analyst and energy counsel to the U.S. Senate Budget Committee.

GEORGE LEON-PAUL WEAVER
Former Assistant Secretary of Labor
for International Affairs

George Leon-Paul Weaver, a native of Pittsburgh, was named to the post of Assistant Secretary of Labor for International Affairs by President John F. Kennedy in 1961.

Born on May 18, 1912, Weaver attended Roosevelt

University (at that time the YMCA School in Chicago) and the law school of Howard University.

Weaver has long been active in the labor movement, particularly in the areas of civil rights and international affairs. In 1941, for example, he joined the CIO as a member of the War Relief Committee and, within a year's time, was named assistant to the director of this organization's Civil Rights Committee. For the next 13 years, he continued to serve in both these capacities. In 1955 (the year of the AFL-CIO merger) he was appointed executive secretary of the new body's Civil Rights Committee.

Weaver was obliged to take occasional leaves of absence to handle a number of special government assignments with the International Confederation of Free Trade Unions, and with the National Security Resources Board. Traveling widely, he also was a member (during the mid-1950s) of various missions to the Far East and Southeast Asia. In 1957 he attended the conference of the International Labor Organization (ILO) and, after participating the following year for a second time, was chosen assistant to the president of the International Union of Electrical, Radio and Machine Workers. At present, Weaver serves as a permanent representative to the ILO and as chairman of the U.S. delegation to its annual conference.

Weaver has received, among many other honors, the Eleanor Roosevelt Key for outstanding service to the world community.

In 1969 Weaver became a special assistant to the Director General of the United Nations International Labor Organization in Geneva, Switzerland.

ROBERT WEAVER
Former Secretary of Housing

Robert Weaver became the first black appointed to a presidential cabinet when Lyndon B. Johnson named him to head the newly created Department of Housing and Urban Development (HUD) on January 13, 1966. Previously, Weaver had served as head of the Housing and Home Finance Agency (HHFA).

Robert Weaver was born on December 29, 1907 in Washington, D.C. where he attended Dunbar High School and worked during his teens as an electrician. Encountering discrimination when he attempted to join a union, he decided instead to concentrate on economics, and eventually received his Ph.D. in that field from Harvard University. (Weaver's grandfather, Dr. Robert Tanner Freeman, was the first black American to earn a doctorate in dentistry at Harvard.)

During the 1940s and 1950s, Weaver concentrated his energies on the field of education. (He had already been a professor of economics at the Agricultural and Technical College of North Carolina in Greensboro from 1931 to 1932.) In 1947 he became a lecturer at Northwestern University and, following this, a visiting professor at Teachers College, Columbia University and at the New York University School of Education. During this period, he was also a professor of economics at the New School for Social Research.

From 1949 to 1955 he was director of the Opportunity Fellowships Program of the John Hay Whitney Foundation; served as a member of the National Selection Committee for Fulbright Fellowships; was chairman of the Fellowship Committee of the Julius Rosenwald Fund, and a consultant to the Ford Foundation.

In 1955 Weaver was named Deputy State Rent Commissioner by New York's Governor Averell Harriman. By the end of the year, he had become State Rent Commissioner and the first black to hold state cabinet rank in New York. Still later, he served as vice chairman of the New York City Housing and Redevelopment Board, a three-man body which supervised New York's urban renewal and middle-income housing programs.

Weaver currently teaches in the Department of Urban Affairs at Hunter College in New York City.

SAMUEL Z. WESTERFIELD
Former Deputy Assistant Secretary for Economic Affairs, Bureau of African Affairs, Department of State

Samuel Westerfield was named by President Lyndon B. Johnson in 1964 to the reactivated position of Deputy Assistant Secretary for Economic Affairs within the Bureau of African Affairs of the U.S. Department of State.

Born in Chicago in 1919, Westerfield received an A.B. in economics and political science from Howard University (1939), and later acquired both his M.A. and Ph.D. degrees in economics from Harvard. From 1940 to 1961, apart from a year spent as an economist with the War Labor Board and the United Auto Workers Union, he was actively engaged either in research projects or as a faculty member of such universities as Howard, West Virginia State, Lincoln, and Atlanta.

It was while holding the posts of professor of economics and dean of the school of business administration at the last of these institutions that Westerfield was appointed associate director of the debt analysis staff of the U.S. Treasury. He then became senior advisor to this department's Director of the Office of International Affairs, where he specialized in the economic problems facing the emerging nations of Africa and Latin America. While in this post, he served as a member of the U.S. delegation to the Inter-American Economic and Social Conference held in Mexico City in 1962.

CLIFTON R. WHARTON
Former Ambassador to Norway

Clifton Wharton's appointment as Ambassador to Norway in 1961 was the highlight of more than three decades as a foreign service officer of the U.S. government.

Born in Baltimore on May 11, 1899, Wharton received his LL.B. from Boston University in 1920, the same year he was admitted to the Massachusetts bar. Three years later, he won his LL.M. from Boston University and, the following year, accepted a post as a law clerk in the Department of State.

Wharton entered the U.S. foreign service in 1925, functioning as third secretary to Monrovia, Liberia. Over the next three decades, he held such posts as consul at Tananarive (Malagasy Republic), consul and first secretary to Lisbon (Portugal), and Minister to Rumania (1958). In this last post, he became the first black diplomat to head a U.S. delegation to a European country.

Wharton resigned from his Norway post in 1964.

Wharton is a chancellor of the State University of New York in Albany. In 1977 Wharton was appointed by President Jimmy Carter to the President's Commission on World Hunger. He serves on the board of directors of more than a dozen major American corporations.

FRANKLIN H. WILLIAMS
Former Ambassador to the United Nations;
Ambassador to Ghana

Franklin H. Williams occupied two top-echelon diplomatic posts during the Johnson Administration, one as U.S. Representative to the Economic and Social Council of the United Nations (1964–1965) and, more recently, as U.S. Ambassador to Ghana.

Born in 1917 in Flushing, New York, Williams was educated in the city's public school system and later graduated from Lincoln University in Pennsylvania and from Fordham University Law School. After serving briefly as an assistant to Thurgood Marshall, then special counsel for the NAACP, Williams was sent to the West Coast, where he helped restructure the organization's branch offices in nine states.

A member of the bar in New York and California, Williams has often appeared before the U.S. Supreme Court, particularly in a number of cases involving fundamental constitutional rights. He was once assistant to Sargent Shriver, director of the Peace Corps.

Williams is now president of the Phelps-Stokes Fund and is a director of Consolidated Edison Company.

HOWARD B. WOODS
Associate Director of the United States Information Agency (USIA)

Howard B. Woods was named Associate Director of the USIA in 1965, serving under Carl Rowan, who has since resigned from his post as head of this agency. Woods entered government service after a successful career in journalism, which included 16 years' experience as city editor and then executive editor of the

Franklin Williams addresses the Special Fund Governing Council of the United Nations.

Argus, one of the leading black newspapers in St. Louis, Missouri.

Born in Perry, Oklahoma on January 9, 1917, Woods began his journalistic apprenticeship at the age of 18 and worked for the next seven years with the St. Louis *Call.* In 1942 he acquired his first important journalistic post as St. Louis bureau chief of the Chicago *Defender,* a position he held through 1949.

His current position gives Woods considerable responsibility for USIA programs in the newly emerging countries of Africa, Asia, Latin America, and the Middle East.

BLACKS APPOINTED TO KEY POSITIONS IN THE ADMINISTRATION OF PRESIDENT JIMMY CARTER

The Honorable Hank Aaron
Member, President's Council on Physical Fitness and Sports

The Honorable Sam Frank Abram
Member, Commission on Presidential Scholars

The Honorable O. Rudolph Aggrey
Ambassador to Romania

The Honorable Clifford L. Alexander, Jr.
Secretary of the Army

The Honorable Marcus Alexis
Member, Interstate Commerce Commission

The Honorable Ethel Allen
Member, National Commission on Neighborhoods

The Honorable William Allison
Deputy Director, Community Services Organization

The Honorable Bernard A. Anderson
Member, National Commission for Employment and Unemployment Statistics

Ms. Betty Anderson
Special Assistant to the Executive Director
Equal Employment Opportunity Commission

The Honorable Claud Anderson
Federal Co-Chairman
Coastal Plains Regional Commission

The Honorable Frank Anderson
U.S. Marshall, Southern Indiana

Mr. Joseph Anderson
Special Assistant to the Secretary
U.S. Department of Commerce

Mr. Robert Anderson
Administrator, Office of Comprehensive Employment Development
U.S. Department of Labor

The Honorable Leon B. Applewhaite
Member, Federal Labor Relations Authority

Ms. Milele Archibald
Special Assistant to the President
Overseas Private Investment Corporation

Mr. Ronald Arrington
Special Assistant to the Commissioner
Equal Employment Opportunity Commission

Ms. Ruth Banks
Special Assistant to the Director
Office of Hearings and Appeals
U.S. Department of Interior

Mr. Terry Banks
Associate General Counsel
Federal Communications Commission

Mr. Maurice Barboza
Special Assistant to the Deputy Assistant Secretary for Legislation
U.S. Department of Health, Education and Welfare

The Honorable Maurice Bean
Ambassador to Burma

The Honorable Mary Berry
Assistant Secretary for Education
U.S. Department of Health, Education and Welfare

The Honorable Shallie Bey, Jr.
Superintendent, U.S. Mint, Philadelphia

The Honorable Unita Blackwell
Member, National Commission for the International Year of the Child

Mr. William Blakey
Deputy Assistant Secretary for Legislation
U.S. Department of Health, Education and Welfare

The Honorable David Bolen
Ambassador to the German Democratic Republic

The Honorable Shellie Bowers
Superior Court Judge, District of Columbia

The Honorable Tom Bradley
Member, National Commission on Air Quality

The Honorable Eddie Lee Brandon
Member, National Commission for the International Year of the Child

Mr. William Briggs
Executive Assistant to the Chairman
Commodities Futures Trading Commission

Mr. William Broadwater
Chief, Air Space and Traffic Rules Division
U.S. Department of Transportation

Mr. Benoit Brookens
Special Assistant to the Deputy Assistant Secretary of State for Oceans and Fisheries Affairs

The Honorable Homer Broome, Jr.
Deputy Administrator
Law Enforcement Assistance Administration

The Honorable Tyrone Brown
Member, Federal Communications Commission

The Honorable Hubert Bryant
U.S. Attorney, Northern Oklahoma

The Honorable J. Jerome Bullock
U.S. Marshall, District of Columbia

The Honorable James R. Burgess, Jr.
U.S. Attorney, Eastern Illinois

Mr. John A. Burroughs
Deputy Assistant Secretary of State for Equal Employment Opportunity

The Honorable Goler Butcher
Assistant Administrator for the Bureau for Africa
Agency for International Development

The Honorable James Byrd
U.S. Marshall, Wyoming

The Honorable W. Beverly Carter
Ambassador-at-Large, Office for Liaison with State and Local Governments

The Honorable Lisle Carter
Member, President's Commission on Pension Policy

Mr. William Cheatham
Deputy Director of Program Review,
Office of Civil Rights
U.S. Department of Health, Education
and Welfare

The Honorable Andrew Chisholm
U.S. Marshall, South Carolina

The Honorable Almeric Christian
Judge, District Court of the Virgin
Islands

Mr. William Clement, Jr.
Associate Administrator for Minority
Small Business
Small Business Administration

The Honorable Maurice Clifford
Member, Advisory Commission to the
JFK Center

Ms. Gayletha B. Cobb
Special Assistant to the Assistant
Administrator for Africa
Agency for International
Development

The Honorable Jewel Plummer Cobb
Member, Board of Foreign
Scholarships

Ms. Lovida Coleman
Special Assistant to the Deputy
Attorney General
U.S. Department of Justice

The Honorable Robert Collins
U.S. District Judge, Eastern District
of Louisiana

The Honorable T. R. Coney
U.S. Marshall, Southern District of
Texas

The Honorable Julian Cook
U.S. District Judge, Eastern District
of Michigan

Mr. Stoney Cooks
Executive Assistant to the U.S.
Ambassador to the United Nations

The Honorable William A. Cosby, Jr.
Member, National Commission for the
International Year of the Child

Mr. Jim Crawford
Special Assistant to the Secretary
U.S. Department of Housing and
Urban Development

The Honorable Alonzo Crim
Member, National Council on
Educational Research

Mr. George Dalley
Deputy Assistant Secretary, Office of
International and Organizational
Affairs
U.S. Department of State

**The Honorable William Boone
Darden**
Member, National Highway Safety
Advisory Committee

The Honorable Ann Davis
Member, Small Business Conference
Committee

Mr. Preston Davis
Special Assistant to the Assistant
Secretary for Administration
U.S. Department of Agriculture

The Honorable Drew Days
Assistant Attorney General, Civil
Rights Division
U.S. Department of Justice

The Honorable Anita Defrantz
Member, President's Council on
Physical Fitness and Sports

Ms. Willi Delaney
Special Assistant to the Director,
Women's Bureau
U.S. Department of Labor

Dr. Bernadine Denning
Director, Office of Revenue Sharing
U.S. Department of the Treasury

Mr. Dennis Derryck
Deputy Assistant Director, Office of
Policy and Planning
ACTION

The Honorable Ruth Diggs
Member, President's Committee on
Mental Retardation

The Honorable Anna Diggs-Taylor
U.S. District Judge, Eastern District
of Michigan

Mr. Edwin Dorn
Special Assistant to the Commissioner
of Education
U.S. Department of Health, Education
and Welfare

The Honorable Fannie Dorsey
Member, Federal Council on Aging

The Honorable L. C. Dorsey
Member, National Advisory Council
on Economic Opportunity

The Honorable Elwood Driver
Member, National Transportation
Safety Board

The Honorable Hazel M. Dukes
Member, National Advisory Council
on Economic Opportunity

The Honorable Willie Dean Durham
U.S. Marshall, Western District of
Tennessee

**The Honorable Marion Wright
Edelman**

Member, National Committee on the
International Year of the Child

Mr. Aubrey Edwards
Special Assistant to the Deputy
Assistant Secretary for Regulatory
Functions and Interstate Land Sales
Administration
U.S. Department of Housing and
Urban Development

The Honorable Harry Edwards
Chairman of the Board
National Railroad Passenger
Corporation, AMTRAK

Ms. Judy Ellis
Special Assistant to the Vice
Chairman
Equal Employment Opportunity
Commission

Mr. Darryl Fagin
Special Assistant to the U.S. Treasurer

Ms. Francesta Farmer
Director, Office of Interagency
Coordination
Equal Employment Opportunity
Commission

Ms. Marty Fleetwood
Special Assistant to the Solicitor
General

Ms. Patsy Fleming
Director, Inter-Governmental Affairs,
Office of Civil Rights
U.S. Department of Health, Education
and Welfare

The Honorable Richard Fox
Ambassador to Trinidad and Tobago

The Honorable Alfred W. Francis
U.S. Marshall, Virgin Islands

The Honorable John Hope Franklin
Member, Commission for
International Education and Cultural
Affairs

Ms. Tina Garnett
Special Assistant to the Assistant
Administrator for Africa
Agency for International
Development

Mr. Lucian Gatewood
Special Assistant to the Assistant
Secretary
U.S. Department of Labor

Mr. Gary D. Gayton
Acting Administrator
Urban Mass Transportation
Administration

Mr. Bryant George
Director, Office of Pakistan and Nepal

Agency for International
Development

The Honorable Kenneth Allen Gibson
Member, President's Export Council

Ms. Arleen Gilliam
Executive Assistant to the Assistant
Secretary
U.S. Department of Labor

Mr. Lamond Godwin
Administrator, Office of National
Programs
U.S. Department of Labor

Mr. Quinton Gordan
Director, Office of Policy
Development and Evaluation
U.S. Department of Housing and
Urban Development

Mr. Michael Grace
Special Assistant to the Deputy
Assistant Attorney General
(Antitrust)
U.S. Department of Justice

The Honorable George Grant
U.S. Marshall, Southern District of
New York

Mr. Donald S. Gray
Director, Equal Opportunity
(Military)
U.S. Department of Defense

Ms. Sandra Gray
Assistant Commissioner, Office of
Education
U.S. Department of Health, Education
and Welfare

The Honorable Ernest Green
Assistant Secretary for Employment
and Training
U.S. Department of Labor

The Honorable Frederick Green
Member, National Commission for the
International Year of the Child

The Honorable Robert Lee Green
Member, National Commission for the
International Year of the Child

Mr. Wallace Green
Deputy Under Secretary
U.S. Department of Interior

The Honorable Karl Gregory
Member, Administrative Committee
for Trade Negotiations

Ms. Judy Griffin
Executive Assistant to the Deputy
Commissioner
Bureau of Elementary and Secondary
Education

Mr. Evelio Grillo

Executive Assistant to the Assistant
Secretary for Human Development
U.S. Department of Health, Education
and Welfare

Ms. Lani Guinier
Special Assistant to the Assistant
Attorney General for Civil Rights
U.S. Department of Justice

The Honorable Gladys Gunn
Member, Advisory Council on
Women's Educational Programs

The Honorable Charles V. Hamilton
Member, National Council on the
Humanities

The Honorable Patricia Harris
Secretary
U.S. Department of Housing and
Urban Development

The Honorable Hermene Hartman
Member, Advisory Commission to the
JFK Center

**The Honorable Ulric St. Clair
Haynes, Jr.**
Ambassador to Algeria

The Honorable Alexis Herman
Director, Women's Bureau
U.S. Department of Labor

The Honorable Leon Higginbotham
U.S. Circuit Judge, Third Circuit

Mr. Chester Higgins
Assistant Chief of Public Affairs
Office of the Secretary of the Army

Ms. Janet Hill
Special Assistant to the Secretary of
the Army

The Honorable Jesse Hill
Member, Communications Satellite
Corporation

The Honorable Matthew Holden, Jr.
Commissioner
Federal Energy Regulatory
Commission

Mr. Meldon Hollis
Special Assistant to the Assistant
Secretary of Education
U.S. Department of Health, Education
and Welfare

Ms. Anne Holloway
Director, Washington Office of the
Ambassador to the United Nations

The Honorable Carl Holman
Member, National Council on the
Humanities

Mr. Carl Horton
Special Assistant to the Associate
Administrator

Small Business Administration

The Honorable Joseph Howard
U.S. District Judge, District of
Maryland

Ms. Gloria Hughes
Special Assistant to the Assistant
Secretary for Administration
U.S. Department of the Treasury

The Honorable Teresa Hughes
Member, National Student Loan
Marketing Association

The Honorable G. William Hunter
U.S. Attorney, Northern District of
California

Mr. Ira Hutchinson
Deputy Director, National Park
Service

Ms. Alexis Jackson
Associate Solicitor for General Law
U.S. Department of the Interior

Mr. C. Anthony Jackson
Director, Program Development and
the Office of Community Action
Community Services Administration

The Honorable Maynard Jackson
Member, National Commission on
Neighborhoods

Ms. Gilda Jacobs
Special Assistant to the Director
U.S. Office of Personnel Management

The Honorable Clarence James
Member, Copyright Royalty Tribunal

Ms. Carolyn Jefferson
Congressional Liaison Officer, Office
of Congressional Affairs
U.S. Department of Commerce

The Honorable Howard Jenkins
Member, National Labor Relations
Board

Ms. Elmima Johnson
Special Assistant to the
Commissioner, Office of Education
U.S. Department of Health, Education
and Welfare

Mr. Vernon Johnson
Assistant Secretary, Bureau of African
Affairs
U.S. Department of State

The Honorable Clara Stanton Jones
Member, National Commission on
Libraries and Information Science

The Honorable Franklin Jones
General Counsel, Community Services
Administration

The Honorable James Jones

Member, Federal Service Impasses Panel

Mr. Roosevelt Jones
Executive Assistant to the Assistant Secretary for Community Planning and Development
U.S. Department of Housing and Urban Development

The Honorable Thomas R. Jones
Member, Interagency Commission on Emergency Medical Services

The Honorable William B. Jones
Ambassador to Haiti

The Honorable Barbara Jordan
Member, President's Advisory Board on Ambassadorial Appointments

The Honorable Vernon Jordan
Member, Strategy Council

The Honorable James Joseph
Under Secretary
U.S. Department of the Interior

The Honorable Amalya Kearse
U.S. Circuit Judge, Second Circuit

The Honorable Damon Keith
U.S. Circuit Judge, Sixth Circuit

Mr. Robert Kemp
Executive Director, Interagency Council for Minority Business Enterprise

Ms. Beverly King
Special Assistant to the Director, Office of Civil Rights
Environmental Protection Agency

Mr. Colbert King
Deputy Assistant Secretary for Legislative Affairs
U.S. Department of the Treasury

Mr. Howard King
Deputy Director for Civil Rights
U.S. Department of Transportation

The Honorable Crystal Kuykendall
Member, National Advisory Council on Extension and Continuing Education

Mr. Weldon Latham
Deputy Assistant Secretary, Office of Fair Housing and Equal Opportunity
U.S. Department of Housing and Urban Development

The Honorable Marjorie M. Lawson
Member of the Board, JFK Center for the Performing Arts

The Honorable Lasalle D. Leffall
Member, Advisory Commission to the JFK Center

The Honorable Ronald Le Flore
Member, National Advisory Committee for Juvenile Justice and Delinquency Prevention

The Honorable Wilbert Le Melle
Ambassador to Kenya

The Honorable Walter Leonard
Member, Board of Visitors
U.S. Naval Academy

The Honorable John Lewis
Associate Director of Domestic and Anti-Poverty Operations, ACTION

The Honorable Rufus Lewis
U.S. Marshall, Middle District of Alabama

The Honorable Lee A. Limbs, Jr.
U.S. Marshall, Arizona

The Honorable Bruce Llewellyn
Director, Overseas Private Investment Corporation

The Honorable Mary Johnson Lowe
U.S. District Judge, Southern District of New York

Mr. Richard Lowe
Special Assistant to the Vice Chairman
Equal Employment Opportunity Commission

The Honorable Richard B. Lowe
Deputy Inspector General
U.S. Department of Health, Education and Welfare

Mr. Gerald Lucas
Special Assistant to the Assistant Secretary, Office of Administration
U.S. Department of Commerce

Mr. Myles Lynk
Special Assistant to the Secretary
U.S. Department of Health, Education and Welfare

The Honorable Benjamin Malcolm
Vice Chairman and Commissioner
U.S. Parole Commission

Ms. Dorothy Mann
Executive Assistant to the Deputy Director
ACTION

Mr. Richard Mapp
Special Assistant to the Assistant Secretary for Housing
U.S. Department of Housing and Urban Development

The Honorable Cora B. Marrett
Member, President's Commission on the Accident at Three Mile Island

The Honorable Harry Marshall

U.S. Marshall, Southern District of Illinois

The Honorable Walter Massey
Member, National Science Board

Mr. James W. Mayo
Scientific Advisor to the Assistant Secretary for Energy Technology
U.S. Department of Energy

The Honorable Benjamin Mays
Member, President's Advisory Board on Ambassadorial Appointments

The Honorable William Mays
Member, National Highway Safety Commission

The Honorable Andrew Metcalf
U.S. Marshall, Western District of Michigan

The Honorable Ishmael Meyers
U.S. Attorney, Virgin Islands

The Honorable Henry Michaux, Jr.
U.S. Attorney, Middle District of North Carolina

Ms. Harriet Michel
Director, Office of Community Youth Employment Program
U.S. Department of Labor

Mr. Michael Middleton
Director, Office of Systemic Programs
Equal Employment Opportunity Commission

Mr. Albert Miller
Deputy Under Secretary for Field Coordination
U.S. Department of Housing and Urban Development

Mr. George Miller
Executive Assistant to the Assistant Secretary for Economic Policy
U.S. Department of the Treasury

Ms. Sheila D. Minor
Special Assistant to the Assistant Secretary for Fish, Wildlife and Parks
U.S. Department of the Interior

The Honorable Steven Minter
Member, National Commission for the International Year of the Child

Mr. Tom Minter
Deputy Commissioner of Elementary and Secondary Education
U.S. Department of Health, Education and Welfare

Ms. Beverly Mitchell
Special Assistant to the Director of Congressional Liaison
U.S. Department of Health, Education and Welfare

The Honorable Don Mitchell
Member, Commission on Presidential
Scholars

Mr. George Mitchell
Special Assistant to the Secretary
U.S. Department of State

Ms. Martha Mitchell
Special Assistant to the Deputy
Administrator
Small Business Administration

Mr. Alvin Moore
Special Assistant to the
Administrator, Office of
Comprehensive Employment
Development
U.S. Department of Labor

The Honorable Azie Taylor Morton
Treasurer of the United States
National Director of the U.S. Savings
Bond Division

The Honorable Samuel L. Myers
Member, Commission on Foreign
Language and International Studies

The Honorable Noel Myricks
Member, National Advisory Council
on Extended and Continuing
Education

Mr. Carl McCarden
Executive Assistant to the Assistant
Secretary
U.S. Department of Housing and
Urban Development

Mr. Curtis McClinton
Director, Office of Special Services
Economic Development
Administration

The Honorable Wade McCree
Solicitor General

The Honorable Gabrielle McDonald
U.S. District Judge, Southern District
of Texas

The Honorable Donald F. McHenry
Ambassador to the United Nations

The Honorable W. Philip McLaurin
Member, National Advisory
Commission on Economic
Opportunity

The Honorable Theodore McMillian
U.S. Circuit Judge, Eighth Circuit

The Honorable David Nelson
U.S. District Judge, Massachusetts

Mr. Edward Norton
Acting General Counsel
U.S. Department of Housing and
Urban Development

The Honorable Eleanor Holmes

Norton
Chair
Equal Employment Opportunity
Commission

The Honorable Revius Ortique
Member, Legal Services Corporation

Mr. Ernie Osborne
Commissioner for Public Services and
Human Development
U.S. Department of Health, Education
and Welfare

Ms. Marian Palmer
Executive Assistant to the General
Manager of the New Community
Corporation
U.S. Department of Housing and
Urban Development

Ms. Amelia Parker
Special Assistant, Office of
Telecommunications Policy
U.S. Department of State

The Honorable Paul Parks
Member, Advisory Council on
Women's Educational Programs

The Honorable Franklin Payne
U.S. Marshall, Eastern Missouri

The Honorable John Penn
U.S. District Judge, District of
Columbia

Ms. June Carter Perry
Special Assistant to the Director for
Public Affairs
Community Services Administration

Ms. Yvonne S. Perry
Deputy Assistant Secretary
U.S. Department of Housing and
Urban Development

Ms. Marcella Peterson
Assistant to Director
Office of Revenue Sharing

The Honorable Percy A. Pierre
Assistant Secretary of the Army for
Research, Development and
Acquisition

The Honorable Anderson Pollard
Member, President's Commission on
Mental Retardation

The Honorable Ersa Poston
Vice Chairman, Merit Systems
Protection Board

The Honorable Carlisle Pratt
Judge, District of Columbia Superior
Court

The Honorable Johnnie Prothro
Member, International Food and
Agricultural Development

Commission

The Honorable William C. Pryor
Judge, District of Columbia Court of
Appeals

Mr. Albert Raby
Intergovernmental Relations Officer
ACTION

The Honorable M. Athalie Range
Member, Board of Directors
National Railroad Passenger
Corporation

The Honorable Calvin Raullerson
Assistant Administrator, Private
Development Corporation
Agency for International
Development
U.S. Department of State

Ms. Inez Reid
Deputy General Counsel for
Regulations Review
U.S. Department of Health, Education
and Welfare

The Honorable John Reinhardt
Director, International
Communication Agency

The Honorable Emmett John Rice
Member, Board of Governors
Federal Reserve System

The Honorable Lois D. Rice
Member, Student Loan Marketing
Association

The Honorable Archie Richardson
Member, National Highway Safety
Commission

The Honorable Tyree Richburg
U.S. Marshall, Southern District of
Alabama

The Honorable Wilson Riles
Member, National Council on
Educational Research

The Honorable Glen Robinson
U.S. Marshall, Northern District of
California

Mr. Weldon Rougeau
Director, Office of Federal Contract
Compliance
U.S. Department of Labor

The Honorable Herman J. Russell
Member, National Corporation for
Housing Partnerships

The Honorable Bayard Rustin
Member, President's Commission on
the Holocaust

Mr. Frederick A. Schenck
Deputy Under Secretary
U.S. Department of Commerce

The Honorable Basil Scott
Member, National Highway Safety
Commission

The Honorable Macler Shephard
Member, National Commission on
Neighborhoods

The Honorable Jake J. Simmons III
Member, President's Commission on
Personnel Interchange

The Honorable Paul A. Simmons
U.S. District Judge, Western District
of Pennsylvania

Ms. Genevive C. Sims
Special Assistant to the Vice
Chairman
Merit Systems Protection Board

The Honorable John B. Slaughter
Assistant Director, National Science
Foundation

**The Honorable Constance Slaughter-
Harvey**
Member, Commission on Presidential
Scholars

The Honorable Edith Barksdale Sloan
Member, Consumer Product Safety
Commission

The Honorable J. Clay Smith
Member, Equal Employment
Opportunity Commission

The Honorable Otis Smith
Administrative Conference of the
United States

The Honorable Mabel M. Smythe
Ambassador to Cameroon

Ms. Renee Sprow
Assistant to the Under Secretary of
Defense for Acquisition Policy
U.S. Department of Defense

Mr. Vernon Stansbury
Deputy Director, Bureau of Export
Development
U.S. Department of Commerce

Mr. Allan A. Stephenson
Acting Director, Office of Minority
Business Enterprise
U.S. Department of Commerce

Mr. H. Patrick Swygert
Special Counsel, U.S. Merit Systems
Protection Board

The Honorable Jack Tanner
U.S. District Judge, District of
Washington

The Honorable Horace Tate
Member, National Commission on
Libraries and Information Sciences

The Honorable Quentin Taylor
Deputy Administrator, Federal
Aviation Administration
U.S. Department of Transportation

Ms. Ethel Terry
Special Assistant to the Federal
Co-Chairman
Coastal Plains Regional Commission

Ms. Doris Thompson
Director of Civil Rights
Environmental Protection Agency

The Honorable John D. Thompson
Member, Board of Directors
Federal National Mortgage
Association

Ms. Elizabeth Thorton
Special Assistant to the Commissioner
Equal Employment Opportunity
Commission

The Honorable Terrance Todman
Ambassador to Spain

Ms. Margaret Triplett
Special Assistant, Institute of Law
Enforcement and Criminal Justice
U.S. Department of Justice

The Honorable Benjamin M. Tucker
Member, Advisory Committee to the
JFK Center

The Honorable Sterling Tucker
Assistant Secretary for Fair Housing
and Equal Opportunity
U.S. Department of Housing and
Urban Development

The Honorable Howard J. Turner, Jr.
U.S. Marshall, Western District of
Pennsylvania

Mr. Art Varnado
Special Assistant for Flight Standard
Services
Federal Aviation Administration
U.S. Department of Transportation

The Honorable Shirley Verrett
Member, Commission for the
Preservation of the White House

**The Honorable Annice McBryde
Wagner**
Judge, District of Columbia Superior
Court

The Honorable A. Maceo Walker
Member, Small Business Conference
Committee

The Honorable LeRoy Walker
Member, President's Council on
Physical Fitness and Sports

Dr. Joan S. Wallace
Assistant Secretary for

Administration
U.S. Department of Agriculture

Mr. John Waller
Special Assistant to the Assistant
Secretary for Employment and
Training
U.S. Department of Labor

Mr. William Ware
Director, Congressional Affairs
Equal Employment Opportunity
Commission

Mr. Frank Washington
Acting Chief of Policy and Rules
Divison, Broadcast Bureau
Federal Communications Commission

**The Honorable Warren Morton
Washington**
Member, National Advisory
Committee on Oceans and
Atmosphere

The Honorable Barbara Watson
Assistant Secretary for Consular
Affairs
U.S. Department of State

The Honorable Paul Webber III
Judge, District of Columbia Superior
Court

Mr. Togo West
Special Assistant to the Secretary
U.S. Department of Defense

The Honorable Clifton Wharton
Member, President's Commission on
World Hunger

The Honorable Howard White
Member, Corporation for Public
Broadcasting

Mr. DeWayne Wickham
Special Assistant to the Assistant
Secretary for Education
U.S. Department of Health, Education
and Welfare

Ms. Eve Wilkins
Special Assistant to the Chairman
Equal Employment Opportunity
Commission

The Honorable Bathrus Williams
Member, Commission on
Neighborhoods

Dr. Dorothy Williams
Special Assistant to the Deputy
Assistant Secretary for Urban Affairs
and Development
U.S. Department of Housing and
Urban Development

The Honorable James F. Williams II
Member of the Board of Regents

National Library of Medicine

The Honorable James R. Williams
U.S. Attorney, Northern District of Ohio

The Honorable Thomas Williamson, Jr.
Deputy Inspector General
U.S. Department of Energy

The Honorable Genevieve Wilson
Member, Advisory Council on Juvenile Justice and Delinquency Prevention

The Honorable Margaret Bush Wilson
Member, General Advisory

Commission on Arms Control and Disarmament

Ms. Judith Winston
Executive Assistant to the Chairman
Equal Employment Opportunity Commission

The Honorable Jessie A. Woods
Member, National Council on the Arts

The Honorable Josephine Worthy
Member, Legal Services Corporation

Ms. Patricia Worthy
Deputy Assistant Secretary for Regulatory Functions, Interstate Land Sales

U.S. Department of Housing and Urban Development

Ms. Cheryl Wright
Special Assistant to the Secretary
U.S. Department of Housing and Urban Development

The Honorable Andrew Young
U.S. Ambassador to the United Nations

The Honorable Jean C. Young
Chairman, National Commission for the International Year of the Child

The Honorable Margaret Young
Member, Board of Visitors, U.S. Military Academy

BLACK AND MINORITY KEY WHITE HOUSE STAFF

Dr. Elizabeth Abramowitz
Assisant Director
Domestic Policy Staff

Ms. Raymone Bain
Public Affairs Assistant
Office of Management and Budget

Ms. Julia Dobbs
Legal Deputy to Louis Martin

Ms. Edna Draper
Confidential Assistant to Hamilton Jordan

Mr. James Dyke
Special Assistant to the Vice President

Mr. Christopher Edley
Assistant Director
Domestic Policy Staff

Mr. Nathaniel Fields
Senior Policy Analyst
Office of Science and Technology

Ms. Dianne Hampton

Administrative Assistant to Louis Martin

Ms. Gwendolyn Hemphill
Secretary to Tim Kraft

Mr. Marc Henderson
Associate Press Secretary

Ms. Cecelia Jakovich
Special Assistant to the Deputy Appointments Secretary

Ms. Elizabeth Lumpkin
Press Aide

Mr. Edward Maddox
Staff Assistant
Advance Office

Mr. Robert Malson
Assistant Director
Domestic Policy Staff

Mr. Louis Martin
Special Assistant to the President

Mr. Frederick McKinney

Junior Staff Economist
Council of Economic Advisors

Ms. Valerie Pinson
Special Assistant for Congressional Liaison

Mr. Franklin Raines
Associate Director
Office of Management and Budget

Mr. James Scott
White House Fellow

Ms. Pauline Schneider
Staff Assistant
Office of Intergovernmental Affairs

Mr. Gerald Wallette
Staff Assistant
Presidential Personnel

Mr. Franklin White
Associate Director
Domestic Policy Staff

Ms. Karen Zuniga
Deputy to Louis Martin

BLACKS APPOINTED TO EXECUTIVE LEVEL POSITIONS BY PRESIDENT RONALD REAGAN

William Bell
Chairman
Equal Employment Opportunity Council

Benjamin Bobo
Deputy Assistant Secretary R&D
Department of Housing and Urban Development

Melvin Bradley
Senior Advisor
OPD

Ted Britten

Director, Office of International Affairs
Department of Housing and Urban Development

Carlos Campbell
Assistant Secretary for Economic Development
Department of Commerce

Samuel Cornelius
Deputy Director
CSA

Lawrence Davenport

Assistant Director, Domestic Operations
ACTION

Thelma Duggin
Deputy Special Assistant
OPLiaison

W. Antoinette Ford
Assistant Administrator, Near East
AID

Claire Freeman
Deputy Assistant Secretary, Planning and Evaluation

Department of Housing and Urban
Development

Thaddeus Garrett
Special Assistant to the Vice President

Rosslee Green-Douglass
Director, Economic Impact
Department of Energy

Clarence Hodges
Assistant Director, Community
Action
CSA

Melvin Humphrey
Director, Office SBDU
DOT

Toye Lewis-Byrd
Special Assistant
OPD

Stephanie Lee Miller
Special Assistant
Department of Commerce

Samuel Pierce
Secretary
Department of Housing and Urban
Development

Wes Plummer
Director, Civil Rights

DOT

Vincent Reed
Assistant Secretary
Elementary and Secondary Education

Stephen Rhodes
Deputy Special Assistant,
Intergovernmental Affairs

Harry Singleton
Deputy Assistant Secretary,
Congressional Relations
Department of Commerce

Daniel Smith
Policy Analyst
OPD

Arthur Teele
Administrator, Urban Mass Transit
DOT

John Tiller
Special Assistant
Department of State

Clarence Thomas
Assistant Secretary, Civil Rights
Department of Education

Lennie Marie Tolliver
Commissioner on Aging
Department of Health and Human

Services

Gloria Toote
Chair
Merit System Procurement Board

Everett Wallace
Deputy Assistant Secretary, Fair
Housing
Department of Housing and Urban
Development

Armstrong Williams
Congressional Liaison
Department of Agriculture

Bernice Williams
Office SDBU
Department of Housing and Urban
Development

Lance Wilson
Special Assistant
Department of Housing and Urban
Development

Angela Wright
Public Information, Africa
AID

Robert Wright
Associate Administrator, MBE
SBA

OTHER PROMINENT POLITICAL PERSONAGES

Although elected only to state and local offices, certain black politicians have attained national reputations and influence as a result of their forceful and forward-looking legislative performances. Prominent among this promising group are the six leaders sketched below. The biographies of many other local officeholders can be found in the section on Prominent Black Americans.

JULIAN BOND
State Legislator, Civil Rights Leader
1940

Georgia State Senator Julian Bond, a bellwether of the new politics, continues to be a major force in the advance of civil rights. Articulate and dedicated to his principles, this young leader galvanized the desegregation of Atlanta lunch counters, led a successful insurgent delegation to the 1968 Democratic convention in Chicago, and became the first black American to be nominated for Vice President of the United States.

Born in Nashville to parents who are college educators and administrators, he attended a Quaker prep school and Morehouse College, where he took a philosophy course under Martin Luther King, Jr. While at school he co-founded COHAR, the organization which

began the desegregation of Atlanta lunch counters and eventually merged into SNCC in 1960. In his senior year, he quit college to work full time for the black weekly Atlanta *Inquirer* (ultimately as managing editor) and to become communications director of SNCC until 1965, when he won election to the Georgia House from Atlanta's 111th district.

Julian Bond at the 1968 Democratic convention.

Objecting to Bond's outspoken opposition to the U.S. military adventure in Viet Nam, Georgia's other legislators refused to seat him for over a year, until the U.S. Supreme Court declared such exclusion unconstitutional. Because the state's regular Democratic organization systematically denied significant posts to blacks, Bond and fellow representative Ben Brown then led the insurgent Georgia Loyal National Democratic delegation to Chicago and won half of the state's 42 allotted seats. Bond was reelected as a representative in 1968 and as a state senator in 1974. He currently serves as a state senator of Georgia and is co-chairman of the Georgia Loyal National Democratic Delegation.

He has served as co-chairman of the National Conference for New Politics and is on the boards of the Delta Ministry Project of the National Council of Churches, the Robert F. Kennedy Memorial Fund, and the Martin Luther King Memorial Center.

Known as a hardworking legislator and a responsive ombudsman, Bond is presently concentrating on voter organization. He is chairman of the Southern Elections Fund, an Atlanta-based group that supplies money and technical assistance to black candidates for public office in the South. Focusing on small towns, the fund has helped elect 407 blacks to office since 1969. Its goal, like Bond's, is to change politics in the South.

K. LEROY IRVIS
State Legislator
1919

Speaker of the Pennsylvania House of Representatives and minority leader, K. Leroy Irvis has been instrumental in the passage of much key legislation, including the state's controversial income tax law.

Born in Saugerties, New York, he is an alumnus of New York State Teachers College, New York University, and the University of Pennnsylvania Law School. After serving as a civilian attache of the War Department's Aviation Training Division, he became Pennsylvania's assistant district attorney from 1957 to 1963 and a member of the NAACP's legal redress committee. Elected to the Pennsylvania House in 1958, he has coordinated Democratic legislative proposals as majority leader (1969–1970, 1970–1971) and minority whip (1967–1968, 1973—). Early in his career, Irvis had been a school teacher in Baltimore, a steel chipper in Pittsburgh, and a news correspondent for the *Pittsburgh Courier.*

Irvis is a member of the General State Authority Executive Board and a director of TRIAD, a member of Pennsylvania's Bicentennial Commission and a delegate to the Democratic national conventions of 1968 and 1972. As an attorney, he is a member of Federal, District, and all Pennsylvania courts. He is public rela-

tions secretary and a director of the Urban League of Pittsburgh, and a board member of Pittsburgh's Port Authority, United Black Frontiers, and the University of Pittsburgh.

RICHARD H. NEWHOUSE
State Legislator
1924

Sent to the Illinois State Senate in 1966 as a Democrat from Chicago's 24th election district, Richard Newhouse has proved himself an energetic and responsive legislator.

Born in Louisville, Kentucky, he served in the World War II Air Force from 1943 to 1945, winning 12 battle stars as a staff sergeant in the 448th Signal Construction Unit. After the war he attended Boston University (B.S., 1950; M.S., 1952) and the University of Chicago (J.D., 1960). In the state senate, he sits on the Appropriations, Education, Judiciary, and Welfare committees. He is founder and director of the Black Legislative Clearing House, a fellow of the Adlai Stevenson Institute, and serves on the Intergovernmental Relations Commission and the Council on the Diagnosis and Evaluation of Criminal Defendants. A practicing lawyer in Chicago, he is a member of the American, Cook County, and Chicago bar associations.

A member of many civic groups, such as the National Urban Coalition, he has been singled out by his constituents to receive the "Best Legislator" award from both the Independent Voters of Illinois and the American Legion, and has been named "Outstanding Public Servant" by the Cook County Bar Association, and "Senator of the Year" by the Baptist Ministers Conference of Chicago.

CECIL A. PARTEE
State Legislator
1921

Cecil A. Partee is treasurer for the City of Chicago and is a commissioner for the Department of Human Services and a member of the Democratic National Committee. He has been a member of the Illinois legislature since 1956, when he was first elected to the state's House of Representatives.

Born in Blytheville, Arkansas, he received a B.S. in business administration from Tennssee State University (1944) and a J.D. degree from Northwestern University (1946). After serving as an assistant state's attorney for Cook county from 1948 to 1956, he was elected to the state House in 1956, serving five consecutive terms there before being sent to the upper chamber in 1966. He was president pro tem of the senate from

1971 to 1973. He was a delegate to the Democratic National Convention in 1972.

In the nongovernmental sector, he is a senior partner in the Chicago law firm of Partee & Green and a member of the Cook County, State, American, and National bar associations. Active in many community drives, he belongs to the Chicago City Club, the Jane Dent Home, the NAACP, and the National Urban League. In 1969 he was named "Outstanding State Senator."

BASIL A. PATERSON
State Legislator
1928

Progressive legislator Basil A. Paterson is a former New York State senator from New York City's 26th Senatorial District, and was the Democratic nominee for lieutenant governor in 1970. In addition to authoring many successful bills to improve educational quality, he was a leader in Senate battles for forward-looking social legislation and an opponent of the war in Southeast Asia. Paterson is currently Secretary of State of New York.

Born in New York City, Paterson is a graduate of St. John's College and Law School. He entered the general practice of law in 1952, and is currently a member of the law firm of Paterson, Michael & Murray. In 1964 he was elected president of the New York City branch of the NAACP, and the following year he was elected to the State Senate, where he has served on the Judiciary, Banking, Labor and Industry, Affairs of the City of New York, and Housing and Urban Development committees. He is ranking Democrat on the Joint Legislative Committee on Education Law, and a member of the joint committees on Mental Retardation and Physical Handicaps, and Conservation. He exercises an unusual amount of personal influence on the heavily Republican New York legislature.

Paterson has won many honors, including selection by the Eagleton Institute of Politics in 1967 as one of the two outstanding legislators in New York State. He has also won awards from Kappa Alpha Psi, Omega Psi Phi, and the Distinguished Service Award from the New York City Police Department. Paterson is currently New York State Secretary of State.

PERCY SUTTON
Former City Official, Political Leader
1920

Percy Sutton is the former President of the Borough of Manhattan in New York City. While borough president, Sutton earned a national reputation for his skillful handling of urban problems. Now out of politics, Sutton is chairman of Inner City Broadcasting Company, which owns radio stations in New York City, Detroit,

Basil Paterson (left) *and Charles Rangel attend a Harlem community protest.*

and California. Sutton's group is currently making plans to get into the cable television business with a franchise in Queens, New York. The group is also refurbishing the famed Apollo Theater in Harlem to present entertainment through cable television.

Born in San Antonio, Texas, he relocated to New York as a young man when southern recruiting officers rejected his World War II enlistment, and went on to win combat stars as a captain in Air Force intelligence. Studying on the GI Bill, he graduated from Brooklyn Law School in 1950 and was admitted to the New York bar in 1951. When the Korean conflict erupted, he rejoined the Air Force as a trial advocate judge.

Back in civilian life, Sutton opened his Harlem law firm in 1953 and served in a series of NAACP posts, becoming president on the New York Branch in 1961–1962, but he could make little headway with political leaders. In 1963 he and Charles Rangel formed the insurgent Harlem Democratic Club (now called the Martin Luther King, Jr., Club) which has grown to over 1,000 volunteer workers. Elected to the New York State Assembly in 1964, Sutton united black represen-

Former New York borough president Percy Sutton and Roy Wilkins of the NAACP reviewing veterans' parade.

tatives there into a power bloc that finally won major committee membership and was instrumental in the passage of such significant reform bills as the Wilson-Sutton Divorce Law and the legalization of abortion in New York State. Chosen to finish a vacated term as Manhattan's chief executive in September 1966, he twice won reelection by large majorities. As borough president, he increased citizen participation in government, cut costs though decentralization, and focused municipal attention on the roots of urban problems.

Convinced that "black people must control elements in news media in order to liberate themselves," Sutton formed the groups which purchased the *Amsterdam News,* the nation's second largest black newspaper, and radio station WLIB-AM. He is a national director of the Urban League and Operation Push, an advisor to Harlem Hospital, and a member of the boards of the American Museum of Natural History and the Museum of the City of New York.

GROWTH AND DISTRIBUTION OF THE BLACK POPULATION

Black Population in Colonial America ■ First United States Census (1790) ■ Migration to the Cities ■ Growth of the Black Population ■ The Southern Exodus ■ Urbanization ■ Decline of Black Farmers ■ Beginnings of Deconcentration ■ The Suburbs and Large Cities ■ Population Charts ■ Selected Population Facts ■ Population Tables

Between 1970 and 1980 at least two milestones were recorded in the changing geographical distribution of the nation's black population. One was the reversal of a 100-year migration from the South. The other involved the first signs of significant deconcentration of the black population, primarily the result of greater movement from cities to suburbs.

These two trends mean that by 1980 the long exodus of blacks from the South was over and a new exodus from cities had begun. These changes do not mean that every southern locality is suddenly receiving a large stream of black returnees from the urban North, nor should one conclude that every large city is suddenly losing its black population to suburbs. Viewed nationally, however, the geography of the black population is showing a greater heterogeneity of patterns. No longer is redistribution of blacks simply a movement from the rural South to the urban North. In some ways, migration patterns of blacks are coming to resemble the migration of whites, as more blacks are choosing to stay in or move to the South and as more blacks, like whites, are electing suburban over central city residence. These changes in the last decade or so need to be viewed in their historical context

and are discussed in the subsection on Growth of the Black Population.

Black Population in Colonial America

The beginning of America's black population is usually dated from the year 1619, when 14 or 20 blacks—historians are uncertain—landed in Jamestown, Virginia, from a Dutch man-of-war. These early black immigrants entered Virginia as indentured servants, as did many of their white counterparts, but within a short time the practice of enslaving newly arrived blacks spread its roots. By 1630 there were some 60 slaves in the American colonies, and when Virginia finally legalized slavery in 1662, the number of those condemned to lifetime servitude had reached 3,000.

In the 1680s, the colonies were beginning to flourish. The agrarian society demanded greater manpower to increase productivity, and this manpower was supplied by additional slave labor. By 1690, 70 years after the first importation of black slaves, there were 16,729 people at forced labor in the American colonies. Slavery had taken a firm hold on the economic life of the Southern colonies, and the importation of slaves increased rapidly. In 1700 there were 27,817 slaves in the colonies and, 10 years later, in the year 1710, this population had virtually doubled, to about 50,000. By 1740, the slave population reached 150,000. It was 326,000 in 1760; 462,000 in 1770, and 575,000 in 1780. From 1730 to 1800, the free black population grew at a slower rate than the slave population and by 1780 there was only one free black for every nine slaves.

First United States Census (1790)

The first official census of the new government of the United States was taken in 1790, and 757,181 black people were counted. Not all were slaves. Nine percent, or some 59,557 blacks, had managed to acquire freedom. This group was beginning to become an important factor in the society in general. By 1790, most middle and eastern states—including Pennsylvania, Massachusetts, Connecticut, Rhode Island, New York, New Jersey, and the new Northwest Territory—had enacted legislation providing for gradual emancipation. Table 4 presents the results of the 1790 census.

The slave trade continued almost to the time of the Civil War. By 1860 there were almost 4 million black slaves in the United States, 90% of them in the South. The freedmen population, most of whom were in the North, numbered just short of half a million.

The first exodus from the South occurred in the period 1879–1881 when some 60,000 blacks moved into Kansas. This spontaneous movement was made under difficult circumstances, by riverboat, railroad, deteriorated wagons, and on foot. The in-migration to Kansas created situations that strained the state, and several cities became refugee camps. The motivation behind this initial thrust to new lands was the need for social and economic freedom and the avoidance of political abuse. One of the towns created by this exodus was Nicodemus, which still exists as a small all-black community on the plains of Kansas.

Migration to the Cities

From 1790 to 1900, about 90% of all blacks resided in the South. Even after the Civil War, the rural character of the black population remained virtually intact, although there was some movement into new agricultural areas in Louisiana and Texas. The first large northward migration of blacks occurred between 1910 and 1920, resulting in a drop of the southern black population from 89 to 85%. By 1940 this figure had been reduced to 77%. Since then almost 4 million blacks have migrated northward, most of them to the Northeast and North Central regions of the country.

A newspaper cartoon of the 1880s shows blacks heading west and Chinese heading east to escape racial persecution.

As of 1974 the percentage of blacks in the South dropped to 53.

Statistics for the black population have become more detailed since the Civil War. Earlier census reports reflected greater detail for whites than for blacks. In 1790 the number of slaves was ascertained without distinction of sex or age.

From 1790 to 1850 the black population more than doubled. Earlier increase was in part attributable to importation of slaves during 1790–1808. In 1790 the black population of the United States was 757,181, with 239 Negroes per thousand of the white population. During the period of 90 years from 1790 to 1880, the center of the black population moved from a point in Dinwiddie County, Virginia, to a point 443 miles southwest, located in Walker County, northwestern Georgia.

In 1860, 46.5% of the slave population was located in the South Atlantic states. Of the free black population, 46.2% was in the North and 44.6% in the South. The proportion in the East and West—4.4 and 3.9%, respectively—was much smaller than the proportion of slaves in these regions.

The Vicksburg Wharf from which many blacks departed for the West in the Exodus of 1879–1881.

The census of 1910 provides varied information on the black population. In 1910, the black population of the South numbered 9,827,763, and amounted to 89%, or approximately nine-tenths of the total black population in the country. The southern white population was 20,547,420, or one-fourth of the total white population. The South contained the mass of the black population while the majority of the white population was in the North and West. In the North, for instance, the black population numbered 1,027,674, and in the West 50,662, the white populations for these two sections being respectively 54,640,209 and 6,544,328.

Growth of the Black Population

When the first national census was taken in 1790 blacks were nearly 19% of the nation's population. This figure means that as the Constitution was being ratified nearly one American in five was black. The proportion declined in subsequent decades but remained relatively high. Not until after the importation of slaves was stopped in the early 1800s did the proportion black in the nation's population fall below 18% and begin to show steady and pronounced decline.

European immigration caused the white population to grow faster than the black population during the nineteenth and early twentieth centuries. Blacks declined as a proportion of the nation's population to a low point in 1930, when blacks made up just 9.7% of the U.S. population. Since 1930, however, the black population has grown faster than the national average, and by 1980 blacks made up 11.7% of the U.S. population. The rise in the percentage black since 1930 is the result of higher fertility among blacks than whites.

Blacks are likely to continue to increase faster than the national average, and therefore the proportion black in the total population is likely to continue to rise. One reason is that a momentum to future growth of the black population has been established as a result of higher-than-average fertility levels in the past. As a result of higher fertility in the past, the black population is somewhat younger than the white population and contains a slightly larger proportion of persons in the prime reproductive ages. A second reason is that for at least the next decade or two blacks are likely to continue to have higher age-adjusted fertility rates than whites (i.e., higher fertility even when differences in age composition are taken into account).

By 1980 the U.S. black population had grown to nearly 26.5 million, a figure higher than for many nations. The U.S. black population, for example, is slightly greater than the entire population of Canada. The only African nations with a black population that clearly exceeds the U.S. total of 26.5 million are Nigeria (with an estimated 1980 population of 77 million), Ethiopia (32 million), and Zaire (28 million).

Chart 1. Regional Black Populations and Six Cities with Largest Black Populations: 1981

In 1970 there were six cities in the United States with black populations of over one half million; in 1980 there were only five. Washington, D.C., dropped below one half million with a 16.6% loss since 1970, and from fifth to sixth position of cities having the largest black populations

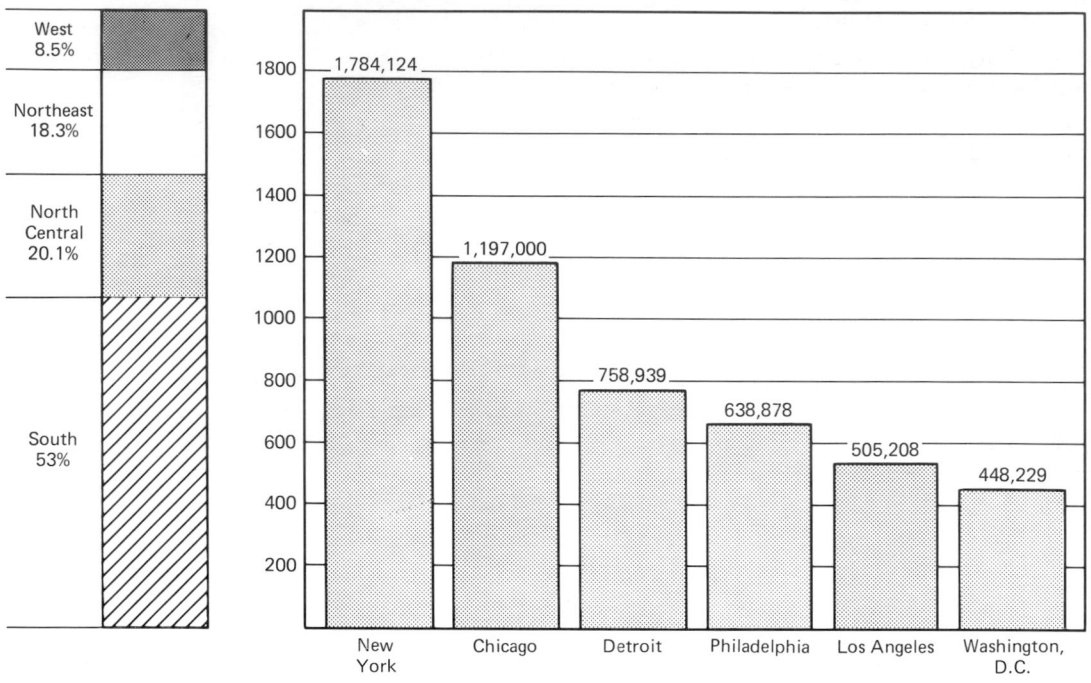

Chart 2. Black Migration between Regions: 1970–1980

After decades of mass exodus from the South by the black population, the 1975–1980 period demonstrates that there is a statistical trend of blacks returning to the South. Most outmigration is occurring from the Northeast

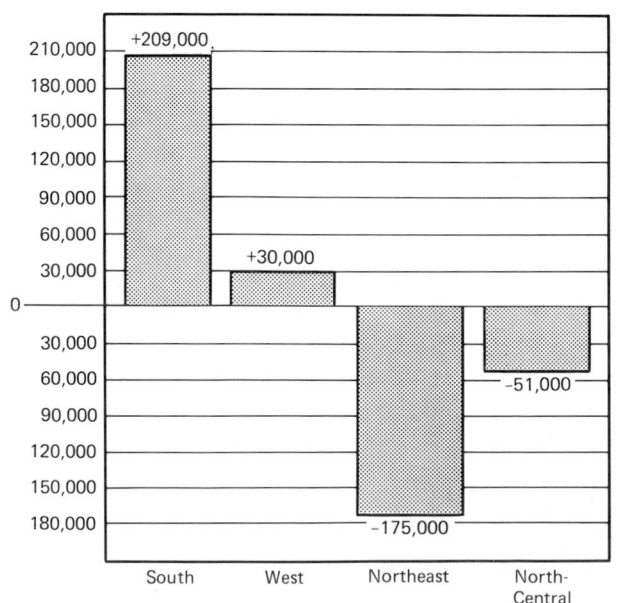

The Southern Exodus

When the Emancipation Proclamation was signed, nine out of every ten blacks lived in the South. With freedom came an apparent inducement to leave the South, but in fact relatively few blacks did so. In 1910, 89% of all blacks still lived in the southern states, and estimates of net migration prepared by demographers show only a small outmigration of blacks from the South to the North in the decades from 1870 to 1910.

Historians and social scientists have long debated why blacks did not leave the South in larger numbers between the end of the Civil War and World War I. Virtually every migration stream is the product of both push and pull factors. Prejudice, discrimination, and a dearth of economic opportunities in the South would seem to have been the strong "push" factors needed to generate outmigration, and a somewhat more open society and the presence of jobs in the industrializing North should have provided the "pull" to establish a strong South-to-North migration steam. Some blacks were leaving the South during this period, typically following transportation routes directly northward from their state of birth, but the number moving north has always seemed smaller than what have been indicated by the combined push and pull forces.

Immigration may be one explanation for the relatively slow start of the southern exodus of blacks. As the North industrialized in the late nineteenth and early twentieth centuries, it generated a huge demand for labor, which was met in large part by massive immigration of Europeans. A great many of the urban factories were filled first by the Irish and German laborers in the nineteenth century and later by immigrants from Italy and southern and eastern Europe. Had northern industries not been able to meet their labor needs through immigration, they might have relied more on domestic sources, including southern blacks. There is substantial evidence that foreign migration can substitute for domestic migration, and this appears to have been the case in the United States in the late nineteenth and very early twentieth centuries.

As immigration to the United States was curtailed by World War I and restrictive legislation passed in the 1920s, blacks began to leave the South in larger numbers. As a consequence, the proportion of the nation's black population living in the South fell more rapidly during the 1910–1920 decade than during the entire period since emancipation.

Black outmigration from the South was reduced somewhat during the depression of the 1930s, but still the proportion of blacks living in the South fell. The greatest volume of outmigration of southern blacks occurred in the 1940–1950 decade and was instituted partly by mobilization during World War II. Therefore, the two world wars of the twentieth century provided a powerful impetus for blacks to leave the South.

A high level of outmigration continued during the 1950s and 1960s, and by 1970 only 53% of the nation's black population resided in the South. By 1980 the exodus was over, and more blacks were moving to the South than from the South (see later section). The proportion of blacks living in the South stopped falling and held steady at 53% between 1970 and 1980. The proportion living in the North (Northeast and North Central regions) fell slightly, and the proportion living in the West rose from 1970 to 1980.

Urbanization

The urbanization of blacks over the last century has been rapid—much more rapid than the urbanization of whites. In 1880 both blacks and whites were predominantly rural populations—12.9% of blacks and 28.3% of whites were "urban" according to the Census Bureau's classification (an incorporated place of at least 2,500 population). By 1920 whites had become predominantly an urban population, but blacks were still predominantly rural; in that year a majority of whites (53.4%) but only 34% of blacks were urban.

After 1920, however, blacks urbanized more rapidly than did whites—partly as a consequence of the growing exodus from the largely rural southern region. The economic depression of the 1930s slowed the pace of urbanization for blacks and actually reversed it for whites. Whites were slightly more urban in 1940 than in 1930; the percentage of whites living in urban areas fell from 57.6 in 1930 to 57.5 in 1940. The ruralization of whites in the 1930s was the result of a back to the-land movement as factories closed and workers lost their jobs. Relatively larger numbers of whites

Chart 3. Population Inside and Outside SMSAs by Race: 1970–1981

From 1960 to 1974 there was a significant exodus of whites from the central cities while the black population grew steadily; however, both white and black populations indicate a trend out of central cities into the suburbs between 1975 and 1981

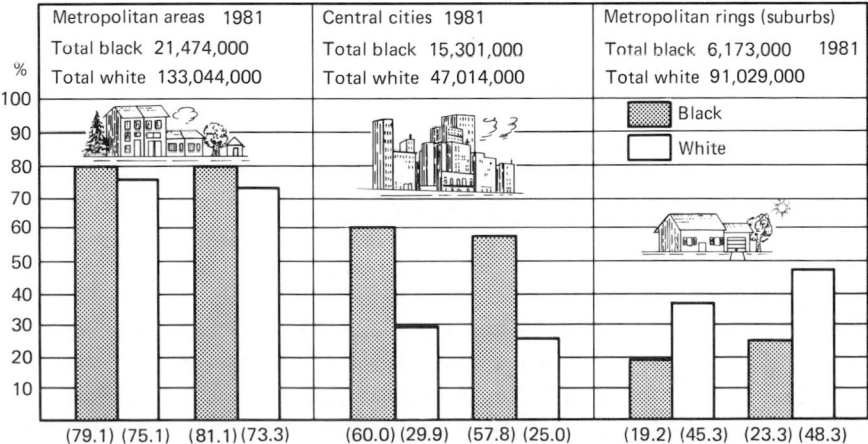

Data: U.S. Department of Commerce, Social and Economic Statistics Administration, Bureau of the Census.

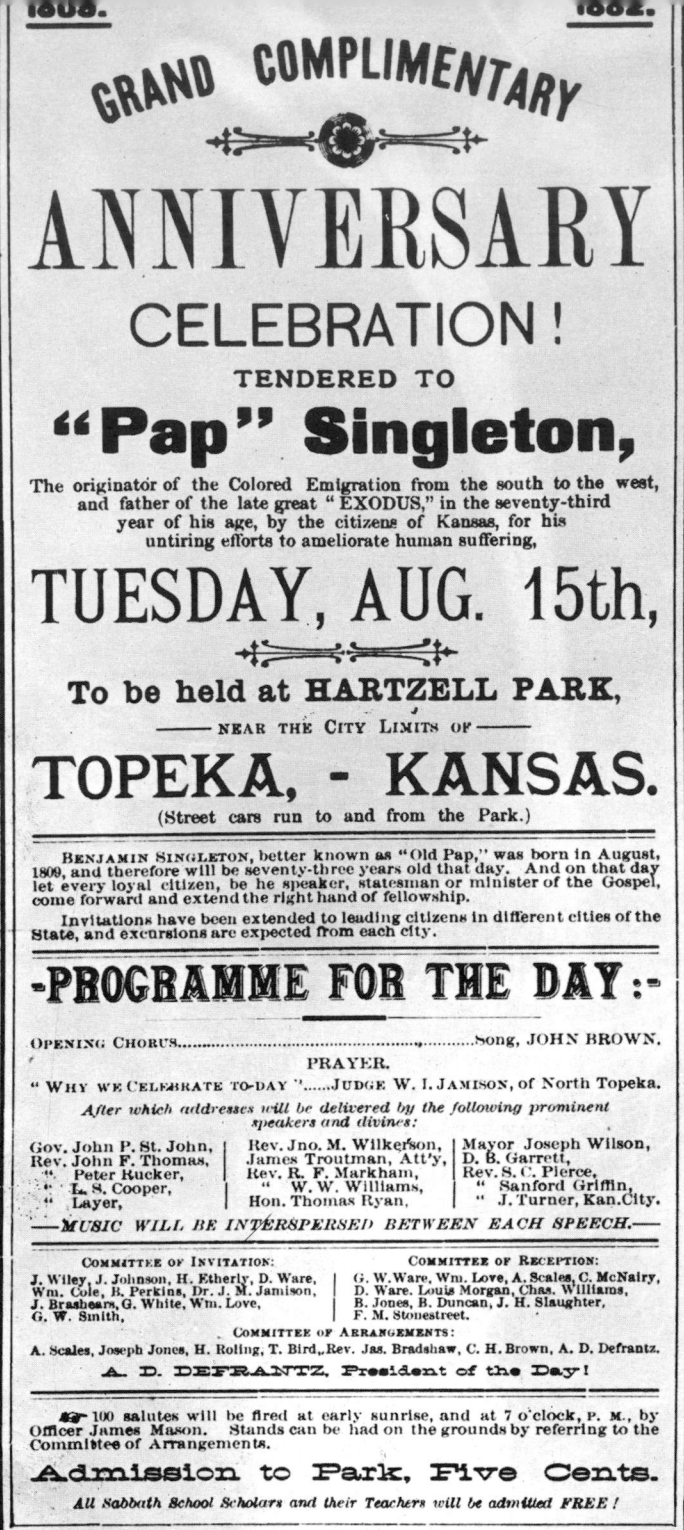

Benjamin "Pop" Singleton was the Moses of black westward migration.

had farms to which they could return or parents or other relatives living in rural areas and with whom the urban expatriates could share residences.

There seems to have been no comparable back-to-the-land movement among blacks during the 1930s. For blacks, the pace of urbanization slowed during this period but blacks, unlike whites, were more highly urban in 1940 than in 1930. Not until 1950, however,

did a majority of blacks become urban, and by 1960 blacks were more highly urbanized than whites. By 1970, 81.3% of blacks lived in urban areas, compared with 72.4% of whites. Final figures from the 1980 census are likely to show a continued increase in the proportion of blacks living in urban areas but little change for whites.

The Decline of Black Farmers

Continued rapid urbanization of the black population has been associated with spectacular decreases in the number of blacks living on farms. In 1920 about 49% of the black population lived on farms. Fifty years later only about 2% of the nation's black population resided on farms. In 1981 only about 222,000 blacks in the entire nation lived on farms.

The decline in the farm population has been more precipitous for blacks than for whites. From 1920 to 1981 the black farm population fell by 96%, whereas the white farm population fell by 79%. Until the early 1960s blacks were much more dependent than whites on agriculture as a way of making a living, but in the last 20 years whites have become more likely than blacks to live on a farm. By 1981 3% of whites and only 1% of blacks were farm residents.

Why has the black farm population fallen so rapidly? There are basically two types of force at work. One is that the demand for farm labor has been falling as a long-term consequence of mechanization and changed farming techniques. At one time many blacks were employed as field hands in the harvesting of cotton, tobacco, and many other crops, but mechanization and shifts toward other agricultural products displaced workers and their families.

Another factor in the decline in the black farm population is the reduction in the number of black farm operators. In the 1930s many black farm operators were tenants, and the consolidation of land holdings displaced many tenant farmers and all but forced their migration to cities. Few black farmers today are tenants, but of the small number of remaining black farmers, many operate under precarious economic conditions. According to the 1978 Census of Agriculture, black farmers, compared with white farmers, have a greater concentration of the elderly, farm smaller acreages, and have a lower dollar value of sales. In 1978 about 52% of black farmers were 55 years old or over (compared with 39% of white farmers). Only 11% of black farmers operated farms of 220 acres or more (compared with 35% of white farm operators), and only 3.5% of black farmers had agricultural sales of $100,000 or more (compared with 9% of whites).

These characteristics mean low incomes for black farm families. In 1978 the median income of black

Chart 4. Percent Distribution of Poor Blacks by Family Status and Region of Residence: 1979

More poor blacks reside in the South than in all other areas combined

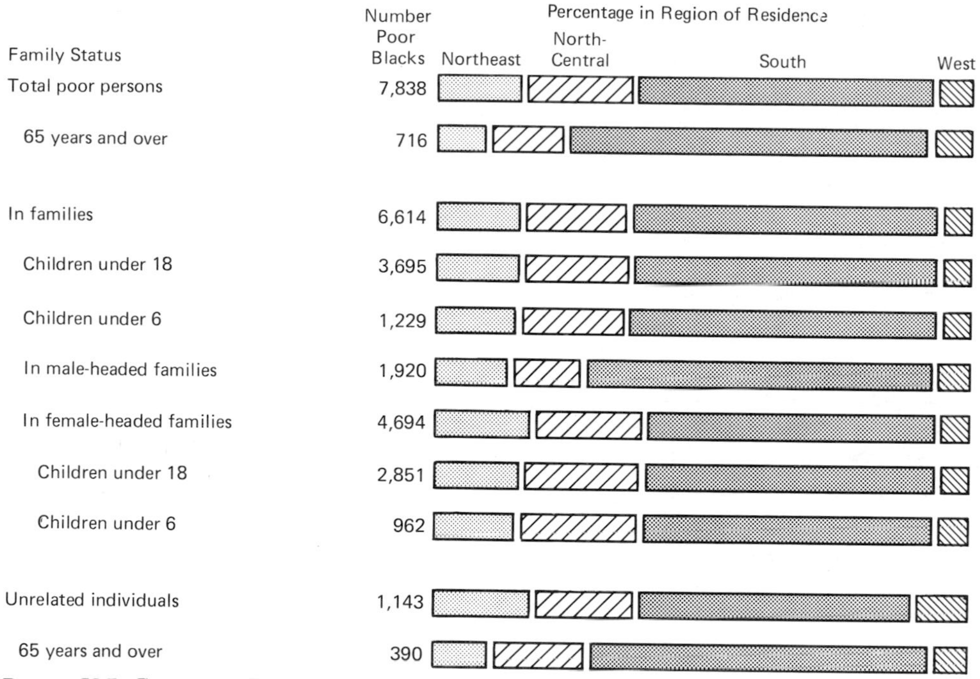

Family Status
Number Poor Blacks
Percentage in Region of Residence
Northeast
North-Central
South
West
Total poor persons 7,838
65 years and over 716
In families 6,614
Children under 18 3,695
Children under 6 1,229
In male-headed families 1,920
In female-headed families 4,694
Children under 18 2,851
Children under 6 962
Unrelated individuals 1,143
65 years and over 390

Data: U.S. Commerce Department, Bureau of the Census.

farm families was only about two-fifths that of white farm families. For the nation as a whole, black families tend to have incomes close to (but slightly below) three-fifths the median income of white families. Hence black–white income differences are greater on farms than off.

At one time, income differences between blacks and whites were strongly influenced by agricultural conditions. This was true when blacks were highly dependent on the agricultural sector of the economy. But today, since only 1% of blacks live on farms, the major influences on inequality between blacks and whites reflect conditions in the various nonagricultural sectors of the economy.

The black farm population has been almost exclusively a southern population. In 1920 nearly 99% of all black farm residents lived in the South, and in 1981 an estimated 99.5% of the few remaining black farm residents lived in the South. Among white farm residents, only 31% lived in the South in 1981.

The Beginnings of Deconcentration

The urbanization of blacks from 1920 to 1970 represented population deconcentration, for not only were blacks leaving farms to go to cities but they were also especially attracted to relatively large cities that constituted the central portions of metropolitan areas. Along with urbanization, there developed a growing proportion of blacks living in central cities of metropolitan areas. The proportion of whites living in central cities has been falling for several decades, as large numbers of whites leave cities to move to the suburbs. But the

Chart 5. Distribution of Poor Blacks Residing Inside and Outside Metropolitan Areas, 1979

71% of poor blacks live in metropolitan areas

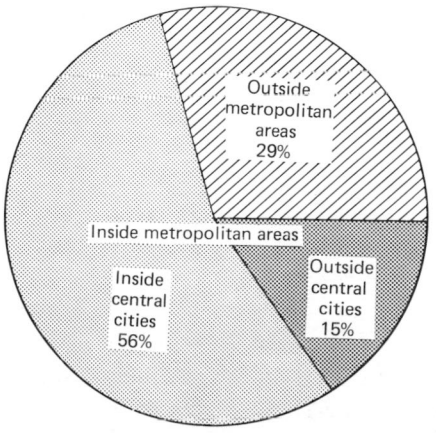

Outside metropolitan areas 29%
Inside metropolitan areas
Inside central cities 56%
Outside central cities 15%

Data: U.S. Commerce Department, Bureau of the Census

Chart 6. Percentage of Population Living on Farms by Race: 1920–1981

In 1920 almost half of the entire black population lived on farms but by 1981 only 1% of the black population was to be found living on farms. In 1920 99% of all black farm residents resided in the South as do 99.5% of the 1% who still reside on farms

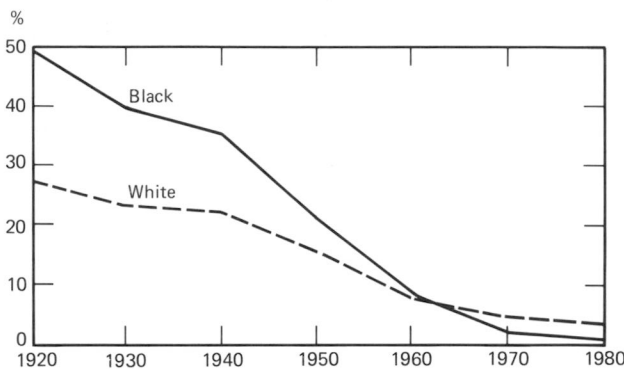

Source: U.S. Bureau of the Census, *Current Population Reports,* Series P-27, No. 55, "Farm Population of the United States: 1981."

proportion of blacks living in central cities has tended to increase.

In the 1970s, however, a turning point was recorded as the proportion of blacks living in central cities began to fall. This is an important development because it signifies that for the first time the number of blacks moving to the suburbs became large enough to significantly affect the overall distribution of the black population. The access of blacks to suburban residences is important for many reasons. One is simply that black suburbanization can further such ideals as open housing, freedom of movement, and the ability to choose a neighborhood that balances a family's income and its preferences and needs, such as aspirations for children's education.

Black suburbanization may be beneficial in other ways as well. Since so many jobs have been moving from cities to suburbs, a greater share of blacks living in suburbs might have long-term consequences for improving employment opportunities and occupational mobility. Finally, for many Americans a move to the suburbs has meant owning a home, a major form of wealth accumulation for middle-class families. Black households have been less likely than white households to own their own home, even when income and other socioeconomic characteristics are taken into account. A trend toward suburbanization might offer more blacks the opportunity to build equity in a home and thus might help to secure middle-class status and the transmission of that status across generations.

For many decades the proportion of blacks living in central cities of metropolitan areas went up, but from 1970 to 1980 it went down (Table 4). By 1970, 58.2% of all blacks were living in central cities, but by 1980 the percentage had fallen to 55.7. This decline is small, but it signifies a break in a trend. For the first time, the black population in the suburbs grew more rapidly than the black population living in central cities. The black city population is continuing to grow—but not growing as rapidly as it did in the past and not as rapidly as the suburban black population.

Chart 7. Population Growth Rates by Decade: 1900–1980

Since 1950 the population growth rates of both blacks and whites have been declining, but the white rate is declining more sharply and is now about three-fifths that of blacks

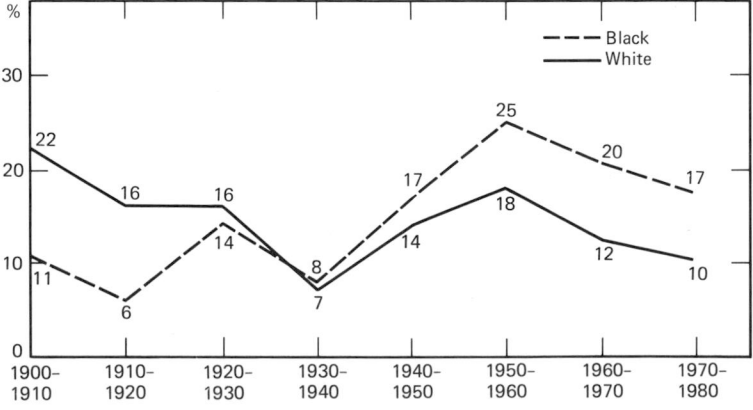

Data: Bureau of the Census.

Chart 8. Population Growth Rates: 1980–1990

During the 1980s it is estimated that the growth rate of the Hispanic population will more than double that of blacks and will be virtually fourfold that of whites

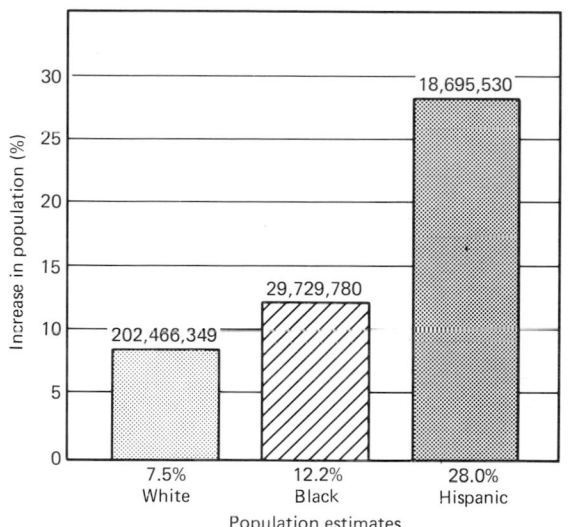

Source: Bureau of the Census and Task Force.

Racial Composition of Suburbs

The black population living in suburbs is growing faster than the white suburban population. Between 1970 and 1980 the total suburban population grew by 17.3% whereas the black population increased by 49.4% (Table 4). In this way, a growing proportion of suburbanites was black. In 1970 blacks constituted 4.8% of all suburbanites, but by 1980 blacks were 6.1% of suburbanites. This change may seem small, but in the 1960s the proportion of blacks in the suburbs hardly changed at all.

As in previous decades, blacks constituted a growing proportion of central city residents. In 1960 blacks were 16.5% of all central city residents; by 1970 blacks were 20.6%, and by 1980 they constituted 23.4% of all central city residents. The growing proportion of blacks in central cities in the 1970s is the product of an absolute decline in the white population and continued growth of the black population (but at a lower rate than in earlier decades).

As central cities and suburban territory were becoming somewhat "blacker" in the 1970s, the territory beyond the suburbs was becoming "whiter." In the outermost suburban fringes (i.e., counties added to the fringes of metropolitan areas between 1970 and 1980), the proportion black fell between 1970 and 1980. In these "exurban" counties blacks made up 9.2% of the population in 1970 and 6.5% in 1980. Beyond these counties, in the residual nonmetropolitan territory, blacks also made up a declining share of the total population.

The overall picture is one of increased movement of blacks from central cities to suburban areas but not to rural areas or small towns that lie beyond the suburban fringe. Whites continue to leave cities for suburbs, but more whites are also moving to locations that lie well beyond the outermost limits of suburban expansion. Whites are not necessarily moving "back to the land," for there is no evidence of growth in the white farm population. But clearly more whites are choosing to live in rural locations even though many commute into cities or towns or otherwise depend on nonagricultural sources of employment.

The reasons for increased movement of blacks to suburbs are doubtlessly heterogeneous. On the one hand, open housing legislation and changing attitudes have contributed to opening up the suburbs. On the otherhand, there is simply an increase in the number of black families possessing middle-income status (even though both husband and wife may have to work), and families of middle-income status seek safety, good schools, large backyards, and the other considerations often cited by city-to-suburb movers in the past.

Individual Large Cities

In some large cities the black population began to decline in the 1970s. Of 14 cities with a black population of at least 200,000 in 1970, four experienced a decrease in the number of black residents between 1970 and 1980 (Table 6). After experiencing growing black populations for many decades, Philadelphia, Washington, D.C., Cleveland, and St. Louis registered losses of blacks between 1970 and 1980.

The transition of some of these cities from growth to decline in the number of blacks was dramatic. In Washington, D.C., the black population grew 30.6% in the 1960s but declined 16.6% in the 1970s. The black population of St. Louis grew 18.6% in the 1960s and then declined 18.8% in the 1970s. In Cleveland the black population grew 14.8% in the 1960s but declined 12.7% in the 1970s. These sudden reversals from growth to decline to some extent reflect the arrival of fewer blacks from rural areas, but most probably they are primarily the product of increases in rates of city-to-suburb moving. Data are not now available on the relative importance of fewer arrivals and more departures in bringing about population declines among blacks in these cities.

Migration data from the 1980 census are expected to show net outmigration of blacks from several cities in addition to the four that had decreases in black population during the 1970s. A black exodus, in addition to the white exodus of longer duration, helps explain why America's older cities generally lost population more rapidly in the 1970s than in the 1960s.

Chart 9. Population Distribution by Age, 1980

In 1980 the median age for U.S. blacks was 24.9 compared with 31.3 for whites

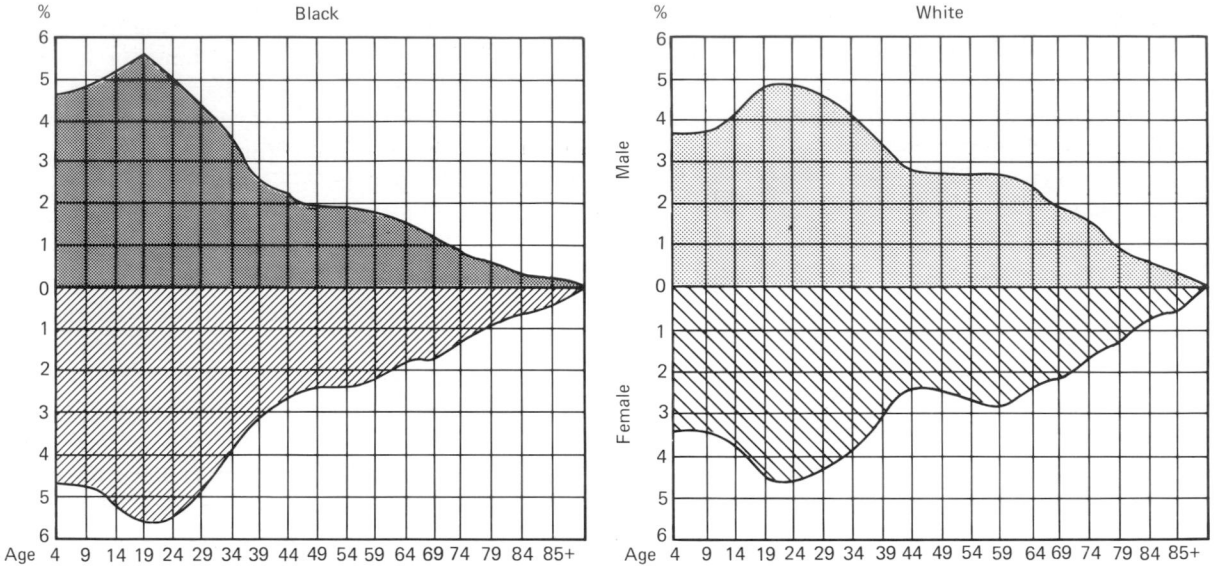

Data: U.S. Department of Commerce, Social and Economic Statistics Administration, Bureau of the Census.

In all but two of the 14 cities the proportion black continued to increase, as it had in previous decades. The two exceptions were Washington, D.C. and Los Angeles. Washington, D.C. went from 71.1% black in 1970 to 70.3% black in 1980 (Table 6). The reason for the declining proportion black in Washington is simply that the non-black population declined somewhat less rapidly than the black population between 1970 and 1980, encouraging speculation that the non-black (mostly white) population of the nation's capital, after declining to less than 30% of the total, may finally be approaching a "hard core" of persons who have a reason for living in the city rather than the suburbs and will stay in the city.

The proportion black in Los Angeles went down for a different reason. The black population of Los Angeles grew in the 1970s, but the non-black population grew even faster, probably because of a rapid influx of Hispanics. In 1970 Los Angeles was 17.9% black, in 1980 blacks made up 17.0% of its population.

Of these 14 cities with the largest black concentrations, two—Washington, D.C. and Atlanta—had black majorities by 1970. By 1980 three more—Detroit, Baltimore, and New Orleans—were majority black. A number of smaller cities also had black majorities, but by 1980 five of the 11 largest cities in the nation were more than 50% black. Demographically speaking, a growing proportion black in the population of large cities has tended to be more the product of a white exodus rather than black inmigration. That is, a grow-

ing proportion black in large cities since World War II has come about more as a result of the "abandonment" of cities by whites rather than a black "invasion." Blacks have not taken over cities so much as whites have deserted them.

Chart 10. Percentage of Population under Age 18: 1980

In 1980 nearly half of the country's black and Hispanic population was 18 years of age or under, while only one-third of the white population was under 18

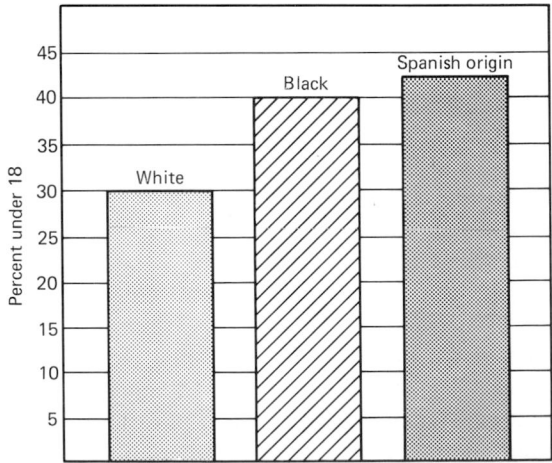

Data: U.S. Department of Commerce, Social and Economic Statistics Administration, Bureau of the Census.

Where is Black Suburbanization Occurring?

The growing black suburban population is concentrated in, but is not limited to, a few large metropolitan areas (Table 6). For the nation as a whole, the black population of the suburbs increased by about 800,000 in the 1960s and 1.8 million in the 1970s. The suburbs of the 14 cities with largest black populations accounted for 64% of the national growth of black suburban population in the 1960s but only 54% in the 1970s.

In the 1960s Los Angeles was the major contributor to black suburbanization. It alone accounted for 15% for the nation's growth of black population in suburbs during that decade.

In the 1970s Washington, D.C., emerged as the major contributor to black suburbanization. Its suburbs accounted for 12.5% of the national increase in the black suburban population between 1970 and 1980. Los Angeles dropped to second place; its suburbs in the 1970s accounted for 8.8% of the national increase in black suburban population.

Atlanta was the third major contributor to black suburbanization in the 1970s. The number of blacks in suburban Atlanta grew only 11,000 in the 1960s, but 124,000 in the 1970s.

A puzzling phenomenon is the smaller black population increase in New York City's suburbs in the 1970s than in the 1960s. The black population in the New York City suburbs grew 77,000 in the 1960s but only 68,000 in the 1970s. With a far larger black population than any other city in the country, New York City is the only one whose suburban black population grew less in the 1970s than the 1960s.

What is clear is that the growth of black population in the suburbs in the 1970s cannot be entirely accounted for by those cities that have the largest black populations. The fact that these cities accounted for a declining share of total black suburban population growth indicates that black suburbanization was more extensive in the 1970s than in the 1960s.

THE UNDERCOUNT

The provisional 1980 Census total of 26,488,218 blacks indicates significant coverage improvement for this group over 1970, according to Census Bureau officials. Comparisons with demographic estimates suggest that the 1980 undercount rate for blacks may be in the range of 4.5–5.5% compared to the estimated miss rate of 7.7% in 1970. In short, the Bureau feels that it may have achieved a 30–40% improvement in the undercount rate for blacks between 1970 and 1980. Similar analyses for other groups have not been completed, but there has been an increase for American Indians, Eskimos, and Aleuts, believed to have resulted from improved census taking and the greater likelihood in 1980 that the people would identify themselves in these categories.

The new figures are the first 1980 data describing characteristics of the nation's population; other data will be released by the Census Bureau as soon as tabulations can be completed. The process of compiling census results continued throughout 1981 and most of 1982. Racial and Spanish-origin count for states, counties, places within states, census tracts, city blocks, and precincts (where these data are needed) will be provided to state governors and legislative officials responsible for redistricting political boundaries. These data help local officials meet requirements of the Federal Voting Rights Act.

Several local jurisdictions, however, challenged the Census Bureau's figures and brought litigation seeking to force the Bureau to acknowledge far greater undercounts. A great deal, of course, is at stake in population figures in that financial aid from federal and state governments for many public services depends on a locality's population. Representation in the House of Representatives and state legislatures is also involved. Blacks are likely to lose representation when the areas they live in are undercounted. Some cities felt they had strong cases. In New York, for example, discrepancies between Census and city figures in city housing projects, which pointed to substantial undercounting, were presented. The courts, however, refused to reverse the Census Bureau.

If the Bureau's own estimate of 5% is accepted, the black population rises from 26.5 million to approximately 27.8 million. *The Afro-American Almanac* estimates the undercount to have been higher, in the neighborhood of 7.2% for blacks, or a total black population of 28.4 million. We also estimate an undercount of 2.2% for the nation's overall population. Under the *Almanac*'s estimate, the proportion of blacks living in the United States in 1980 rises from 11.7 to 12.2%.

SELECTED FACTS

Fact 1

According to the 1980 census the black population of the United States increased by 17½% between 1970 and 1980. Overall the population of the country rose by only 11%.

Fact 2

The median age of blacks was much younger than that of whites, 24.9 compared with 31.3. Persons of Spanish origin were still younger, with a median age of 23.2.

Fact 3
Forty percent of America's black population was under 20 in 1980 compared with only 30% of the white population.

Fact 4
Blacks comprised more than one fourth of the population in five states only: Mississippi (35.3%), South Carolina (30.4%), Louisiana (29.4%), Georgia (26.8%), and Alabama (25.6%).

Fact 5
Seventy-two percent of Illinois' black population lives in Chicago, 74% of blacks in New York state live in New York City, and 64% of Michigan's blacks reside in Detroit.

Fact 6
States with the smallest proportions of blacks in their population were Montana and Vermont, each with about 0.2% blacks. Other states in which blacks comprised less than 1% of residents were Maine, Idaho, Wyoming, Utah, North Dakota, and South Dakota.

Fact 7
Blacks made up 30% of the population of the six cities in the United States that reported populations exceeding 1 million.

Fact 8
Five cities with populations exceeding 500,000 had fewer than 10% blacks. Five in the Far West are San Jose, 4.6%, Pheonix, 4.9%, San Diego, 8.9%, Seattle, 9.5%, and San Antonio, 7.3%. Fifty-four percent of San Antonio's population is Hispanic.

Fact 9
Four cities with populations exceeding 500,000 had more than 50% blacks: Washington D.C., 70.3%, Detroit, 63.1%, New Orleans, 55.3%, and Baltimore, 54.8%.

Fact 10
One of every 12 blacks in the United States lives in the West. In 1930 only one of every hundred lived in that part of the country.

Fact 11
In 1980, three of every five blacks compared with only one of four whites lived inside one of America's cities.

Fact 12
One in every ninety-four whites living in the United States in 1980 was over 85 years of age compared with only one of every 165 blacks.

Fact 13
Metropolitan areas in which over 10% of the black population lived in the suburbs were all located in southern or border states. They were Memphis, where 21% of blacks lived in the suburbs, followed by Washington, D.C., Atlanta, New Orleans, and St. Louis.

Fact 14
According to the 1980 census, 31% of black women lived below the poverty level compared with only 9% of white women. The rate was 20% for black men and 6% for white men.

Fact 15
Median income for a black family, according to the 1980 census, was $11,644. For white families it was $20,502.

Fact 16
Annual income below $10,000 was reported by 43% of black families compared with only 18% of white families; 37% of white families and 17% of black families indicated an annual income in excess of $25,000; 39% of black families and 64% of white families reported annual incomes above $15,000.

Fact 17
Fifty-five percent of black families reported they were a married couple living together, compared with 86% of white families.

Fact 18
Unemployment figures for blacks in the census were 14.1% compared with 6.3% reported by whites.

Fact 19
Black women over 15 years of age accounted for only 6% of the nations' adult population, but 18% of all adults classified as living in poverty.

Fact 20
The percentage of blacks who stated they voted in presidential elections declined from 59 to 49 between 1964 and 1976, but increased to 50.5 in 1980. The percentage of whites voting also declined from 71 to 61 between 1964 and 1976 and remained 61 in 1980.

Fact 21
To a lesser degree, black interest in midterm congressional elections also dropped, from 42% in 1966 to 34% in 1974. It rose to 37% in 1978. Whites reported 57% participation in 1966, 46% in 1975, and 47% in 1978.

Fact 22
Every Pacific and Mountain state except Alaska reported a larger Hispanic than black population. All in all, 18 states had more Hispanic than black residents. In New Mexico, Hispanics outnumber blacks by a ratio of 20 to 1.

Fact 23
The proportion of blacks living in the District of Columbia declined between 1970 and 1980, but blacks made up some 90% of the population growth in the District's metropolitan area.

Fact 24
Rapid population shifts still occur. The town of Pagedale, Missouri, population 4,542, changed from 90% white to 84% black in 10 years.

Table 1.   Growth of Slavery in the Colonies: 1630–1780

	1630	1640	1650	1660	1670	1680	1690	1700
North	10	427	880	1,162	1,125	1,895	3,340	5,206
South	50	170	720	1,758	3,410	5,076	13,389	22,611
Total	60	597	1,600	2,920	4,535	6,971	16,729	27,817

	1710	1720	1730	1740	1750	1760	1770	1780
North	8,303	14,091	17,323	23,958	30,222	40,033	48,460	56,796
South	36,563	54,748	73,698	126,066	206,198	285,773	411,362	518,624
Total	44,866	68,839	91,021	150,024	236,420	325,806	459,822	575,420

Table 2.   Growth of Slave and Freedman Population: 1790–1860

	1790	1800	1810	1820
Slave	697,624	893,602	1,191,362	1,538,022
Free	59,557	108,435	186,446	233,634
Total	757,181	1,002,037	1,377,808	1,771,656

	1830	1840	1850	1860
Slave	2,009,043	2,487,355	3,204,313	3,953,760
Free	319,599	386,293	434,495	488,070
Total	2,328,642	2,873,648	3,638,808	4,441,830

Table 3. Black Population Growth and Percentage of U.S. Total: 1790–1980

Year	Total Population	Black Population	Percentage
1790	3,929,214	757,181	19.3
1800	5,308,483	1,002,037	18.9
1810	7,239,881	1,377,808	19.0
1820	9,638,453	1,771,656	18.4
1830	12,866,020	2,328,642	18.1
1840	17,169,453	2,873,648	16.1
1850	23,191,876	3,638,808	15.7
1860	31,443,790	4,441,830	14.1
1870	39,818,449	4,880,009	12.7
1880	50,155,783	6,580,793	13.0
1890	62,947,714	7,488,676	11.0
1900	75,994,775	8,833,994	11.6
1910	93,402,151	9,827,763	10.7
1920	105,710,620	10,463,131	9.9
1930	122,775,046	11,891,143	9.7
1940	131,669,275	12,865,518	9.8
1950	150,697,361	15,042,286	10.0
1960	179,323,175	18,871,831	10.5
1970	203,302,031	22,580,289	11.1
1980	226,504,825	26,488,218	11.7

Table 4. Black Population by State, Census of 1790

State	Slaves	Free	Black Percentage of State's Population
Connecticut	2,759	2,801	2.3
Delaware	8,887	3,899	21.6
Georgia	29,264	398	35.9
Kentucky	11,830	114	16.3
Maryland	103,036	8,043	34.7
New Hampshire	158	630	.6
New Jersey	11,423	2,762	7.7
New York	21,324	4,654	7.7
North Carolina	100,572	4,975	26.8
Pennsylvania	3,737	6,537	2.4
Rhode Island	952	3,469	6.4
South Carolina	107,094	1,801	43.7
Vermont	17	255	.2
Virginia	293,427	12,766	41.0
Ohio Territory	3,417	5,463	18.8
Maine	None	538	.6

Table 5. Changing Racial Composition and Distribution of Population in Cities, Suburbs, and Nonmetropolitan Areas: 1960–1980

	United States	Central Cities of SMSAs[a]	Balance of SMSAs	Fringe Counties[b]	Residual
Population					
All races					
1960	179,323	59,947	59,648	3,214	56,514
1970	203,212	63,797	75,622	3,953	59,840
1980	226,505	63,111	88,737	5,342	69,314
Black					
1960	18,872	9,914	2,825	323	5,809
1970	22,580	13,140	3,630	326	5,484
1980	26,488	14,751	5,424	347	5,967
Percentage Distribution					
All races					
1960	100.0	33.4	33.3	1.8	31.5
1970	100.0	31.4	37.2	1.9	29.4
1980	100.0	27.9	39.2	2.4	30.6
Black					
1960	100.0	52.5	15.0	1.7	30.8
1970	100.0	58.2	16.1	1.4	24.3
1980	100.0	55.7	20.5	1.3	22.5
Rates of Population Change (in percent)					
All races					
1960–1970	13.3	6.4	26.8	23.0	5.9
1970–1980	11.5	−1.1	17.3	35.1	15.8
Black					
1960–1970	19.7	32.5	28.5	0.7	−5.6
1970–1980	17.3	12.3	49.4	6.6	8.8
Percent Black					
1960	10.5	16.5	4.7	10.1	10.3
1970	11.1	20.6	4.8	8.2	9.2
1980	11.7	23.4	6.1	6.5	8.6

[a] Boundaries of Standard Metropolitan Statistical Areas (SMSAs) as of 1970 are used for all three dates.
[b] Counties added between 1970 and 1980 to the fringes of SMSAs as defined in 1970.

Table 6. Black Population Change in 14 Central Cities and Their Suburbs: 1960–1980

	Black Population	Percentage Change in Black Population		Percentage Black		
	1980	1960–1970	1970–1980	1960	1970	1980
Central Cities						
New York City	1,784,000	53.3	7.0	14.0	21.1	25.2
Chicago	1,197,000	35.7	8.6	22.9	32.7	39.8
Detroit	759,000	37.0	14.9	28.9	43.7	63.1
Philadelphia	639,000	23.5	− 2.3	26.4	33.6	37.8
Los Angeles	505,000	50.4	0.3	13.5	17.9	17.0
Washington, D.C.	448,000	30.6	−16.6	53.9	71.1	70.3
Houston	440,000	47.2	39.1	22.9	25.7	27.6
Baltimore	431,000	29.1	2.6	34.7	46.4	54.8
New Orleans	308,000	14.5	15.3	37.2	45.0	55.3
Memphis	308,000	31.6	26.9	37.0	38.9	47.6
Atlanta	283,000	36.8	12.1	38.3	51.3	66.6
Dallas	266,000	62.7	26.3	19.0	24.9	29.4
Cleveland	251,000	14.8	−12.7	28.6	38.3	43.8
St. Louis	206,000	18.6	−18.8	28.6	40.9	47.4
Suburbs (1970 definition)						
New York City	285,000	55.5	31.4	4.8	5.9	7.6
Chicago	231,000	65.5	79.9	2.9	3.6	5.6
Detroit	128,000	26.1	32.5	3.7	3.6	4.5
Philadelphia	245,000	34.1	28.9	6.1	6.6	8.1
Los Angeles	398,000	105.0	65.7	3.6	6.2	9.6
Washington, D.C.	390,000	98.3	134.9	6.4	7.9	16.6
Houston	80,000	5.2	21.4	12.9	8.8	6.2
Baltimore	126,000	25.6	54.9	7.0	7.0	9.1
New Orleans	79,000	26.3	10.4	15.9	12.5	12.6
Memphis	37,000	−34.8	−18.4	40.2	31.7	21.0
Atlanta	179,000	23.5	222.4	8.5	6.2	14.2
Dallas	50,000	1.1	35.4	8.3	5.2	4.7
Cleveland	94,000	452.8	110.6	0.8	3.4	7.1
St. Louis	201,000	65.0	50.4	6.0	7.7	10.9

Source: Bureau of Census.

Table 7. 1980 Census Population Totals for Racial and Spanish-Origin Groups in the United States

United States	1980	1970	Percentage Distribution 1980	Percentage Distribution 1970
Total	226,504,825	203,211,926	100.0	100.0
White	188,340,790	177,748,975	83.2	87.5
Black	26,488,218	22,580,289	11.7	11.1
American Indian, Eskimo, and Aleut	1,418,195	827,268	0.6	0.4
Asian and Pacific Islander	3,500,636	1,538,721	1.5	0.8
Other	6,756,986	516,673	3.0	0.3
Persons of Spanish origin	14,605,883	9,072,602	6.4	4.5
Persons not of Spanish origin	211,898,942	194,139,324	93.6	95.5

Table 8. Population by Race: 1980

United States, Regions, Divisions, and States	Total	White	Black	American Indian, Eskimo, and Aleut Total	American Indian, Eskimo, and Aleut American Indian	American Indian, Eskimo, and Aleut Eskimo	American Indian, Eskimo, and Aleut Aleut
United States	226,504,825	188,340,790	26,488,218	1,418,195	1,361,869	42,149	14,177
Regions and Divisions							
Northeast	49,136,667	42,328,154	4,848,786	78,182	76,574	890	718
New England	12,348,493	11,585,633	474,549	21,597	21,108	277	212
Middle Atlantic	36,788,174	30,742,521	4,374,237	56,585	55,466	613	506
North Central	58,853,804	52,183,794	5,336,542	248,505	246,456	1,286	763
East North Central	41,669,738	36,138,962	4,547,998	105,881	104,520	834	527
West North Central	17,184,066	16,044,832	788,544	142,624	141,936	452	236
South	75,349,155	58,944,057	14,041,374	372,123	369,497	1,580	1,046
South Atlantic	36,943,139	28,647,762	7,647,743	118,656	117,386	772	498
East South Central	14,662,882	11,699,604	2,868,268	22,454	22,144	199	111
West South Central	23,743,134	18,596,691	3,525,363	231,013	229,967	609	437
West	43,165,199	34,884,785	2,261,516	719,385	669,342	38,393	11,650
Mountain	11,368,330	9,958,545	268,660	363,169	361,988	798	383
Pacific	31,796,869	24,926,240	1,992,856	356,216	307,354	37,595	11,267
States							
New England							
Maine	1,124,660	1,109,850	3,128	4,087	4,057	17	13
New Hampshire	920,610	910,099	3,990	1,352	1,297	41	14
Vermont	511,456	506,736	1,135	984	968	8	8
Massachusetts	5,737,037	5,362,836	221,279	7,743	7,483	129	131
Rhode Island	947,154	896,692	27,584	2,898	2,872	14	12
Connecticut	3,107,576	2,799,420	217,433	4,533	4,431	68	34
Middle Atlantic							
New York	17,557,288	13,961,106	2,401,842	38,732	38,117	330	285
New Jersey	7,364,158	6,127,090	924,786	8,394	8,176	130	88
Pennsylvania	11,866,728	10,654,325	1,047,609	9,459	9,173	153	133

Table 8 (*continued*)

United States, Regions, Divisions, and States	Total	White	Black	American Indian, Eskimo, and Aleut			
				Total	American Indian	Eskimo	Aleut
East North Central							
Ohio	10,797,419	9,597,266	1,076,734	12,240	11,986	167	87
Indiana	5,490,179	5,004,567	414,732	7,835	7,681	107	47
Illinois	11,418,461	9,225,575	1,675,229	16,271	15,833	242	196
Michigan	9,258,344	7,868,956	1,198,710	40,038	39,702	208	128
Wisconsin	4,705,335	4,442,598	182,593	29,497	29,318	110	69
West North Central							
Minnesota	4,077,148	3,936,948	53,342	35,026	34,841	118	67
Iowa	2,913,387	2,838,805	41,700	5,453	5,367	59	27
Missouri	4,917,444	4,346,267	514,274	12,319	12,127	119	73
North Dakota	652,695	625,536	2,568	20,157	20,119	32	6
South Dakota	690,178	638,955	2,144	45,101	45,081	17	3
Nebraska	1,570,006	1,490,569	48,389	9,197	9,147	26	24
Kansas	2,363,208	2,167,752	126,127	15,371	15,254	81	36
South Atlantic							
Delaware	595,225	488,543	95,971	1,330	1,309	13	8
Maryland	4,216,446	3,158,412	958,050	8,021	7,823	113	85
District of Columbia	637,651	171,796	448,229	1,031	996	19	16
Virginia	5,346,279	4,229,734	1,008,311	9,336	9,093	156	87
West Virginia	1,949,644	1,874,751	65,051	1,610	1,555	37	18
North Carolina	5,874,429	4,453,010	1,316,050	64,635	64,519	57	59
South Carolina	3,119,208	2,145,122	948,146	5,758	5,666	70	22
Georgia	5,464,265	3,948,007	1,465,457	7,619	7,444	108	67
Florida	9,739,992	8,178,387	1,342,478	19,316	18,981	199	136
East South Central							
Kentucky	3,661,433	3,379,648	259,490	3,610	3,518	59	33
Tennessee	4,590,750	3,835,078	725,949	5,103	5,012	62	29
Alabama	3,890,061	2,869,688	995,623	7,561	7,483	50	28
Mississippi	2,520,638	1,615,190	887,206	6,180	6,131	28	21
West South Central							
Arkansas	2,285,513	1,890,002	373,192	9,411	9,346	48	17
Louisiana	4,203,972	2,911,243	1,237,263	12,064	11,950	59	55
Oklahoma	3,025,266	2,597,783	204,658	169,464	169,297	107	60
Texas	14,228,383	11,197,663	1,710,250	40,074	39,374	395	305
Mountain							
Montana	786,690	740,148	1,786	37,270	37,153	79	38
Idaho	943,935	901,641	2,716	10,521	10,418	76	27
Wyoming	470,816	447,716	3,364	7,125	7,088	27	10
Colorado	2,888,834	2,570,615	101,702	18,059	17,726	235	98
New Mexico	1,299,968	976,465	24,042	104,777	104,634	88	55
Arizona	2,717,866	2,240,033	75,034	152,857	152,610	138	109
Utah	1,461,037	1,382,550	9,225	19,256	19,158	81	17
Nevada	799,184	699,377	50,791	13,304	13,201	74	29
Pacific							
Washington	4,130,163	3,777,296	105,544	60,771	58,159	1,251	1,361
Oregon	2,632,663	2,490,192	37,059	27,309	26,587	407	315
California	23,668,562	18,031,689	1,819,282	201,311	198,095	1,734	1,482
Alaska	400,481	308,455	13,619	64,047	21,849	34,135	8,063
Hawaii	965,000	318,608	17,352	2,778	2,664	68	46

Table 9. Black Population by Region and State: 1970 and 1980

United States, Regions, Divisions, and States	1980	1970	1980 (%)	1970 (%)
United States	26,488,218	22,580,289	11.7	11.1
Regions and Divisions				
Northeast	4,848,786	4,344,153	9.9	8.9
New England	474,349	388,398	3.8	3.3
Middle Atlantic	4,374,237	3,955,755	11.9	10.6
North Central	5,336,542	4,571,550	9.1	8.1
East North Central	4,547,998	3,872,905	10.9	9.6
West North Central	788,544	698,645	4.6	4.3
South	14,041,374	11,969,961	18.6	19.1
South Atlantic	7,647,743	6,388,496	20.7	20.8
East South Central	2,868,268	2,571,291	19.6	20.1
West South Central	3,525,363	3,010,174	14.8	15.6
West	2,261,516	1,694,625	5.2	4.9
Mountain	268,660	180,382	2.4	2.2
Pacific	1,992,856	1,514,243	6.3	5.7
States				
New England				
Maine	3,128	2,800	0.3	0.3
New Hampshire	3,990	2,505	0.4	0.3
Vermont	1,135	761	0.2	0.2
Massachusetts	221,279	175,817	3.9	3.1
Rhode Island	27,584	25,338	2.9	2.7
Connecticut	217,433	181,177	7.0	6.0
Middle Atlantic				
New York	2,401,842	2,168,949	13.7	11.9
New Jersey	924,786	770,292	12.6	10.7
Pennsylvania	1,047,609	1,016,514	8.8	8.6
East North Central				
Ohio	1,076,734	970,477	10.0	9.1
Indiana	414,732	357,464	7.6	6.9
Illinois	1,675,229	1,425,674	14.7	12.8
Michigan	1,198,710	991,066	12.9	11.2
Wisconsin	182,593	128,224	3.9	2.9
West North Central				
Minnesota	53,342	34,868	1.3	0.9
Iowa	41,700	32,596	1.4	1.2
Missouri	514,274	480,172	10.5	10.3
North Dakota	2,568	2,494	0.4	0.4
South Dakota	2,144	1,627	0.3	0.2
Nebraska	48,389	39,911	3.1	2.7
Kansas	126,127	106,977	5.3	4.8
South Atlantic				
Delaware	95,971	78,276	16.1	14.3
Maryland	958,050	699,479	22.7	17.8
District of Columbia	448,229	537,712	70.3	71.1
Virginia	1,008,311	861,368	18.9	18.5
West·Virginia	65,051	67,342	3.3	3.9
North Carolina	1,316,050	1,126,478	22.4	22.2
South Carolina	948,146	789,041	30.4	30.5
Georgia	1,465,457	1,187,149	26.8	25.9
Florida	1,342,478	1,041,651	13.8	15.3

Table 9 (*continued*)

United States, Regions, Divisions, and States	1980	1970	1980 (%)	1970 (%)
East South Central				
Kentucky	259,490	230,793	7.1	7.2
Tennessee	725,949	621,261	15.8	15.8
Alabama	995,623	903,467	25.6	26.2
Mississippi	887,206	815,770	35.2	36.8
West South Central				
Arkansas	373,192	352,445	16.3	18.3
Louisiana	1,237,263	1,086,832	29.4	29.8
Oklahoma	204,658	171,892	6.8	6.7
Texas	1,710,250	1,399,005	12.0	12.5
Mountain				
Montana	1,786	1,995	0.2	0.3
Idaho	2,716	2,130	0.3	0.3
Wyoming	3,364	2,568	0.7	0.8
Colorado	101,702	66,411	3.5	3.0
New Mexico	24,042	19,555	1.8	1.9
Arizona	75,034	53,344	2.8	3.0
Utah	9,225	6,617	0.6	0.6
Nevada	50,791	27,762	6.4	5.7
Pacific				
Washington	105,544	71,308	2.6	2.1
Oregon	37,059	26,308	1.4	1.3
California	1,819,282	1,400,143	7.7	7.0
Alaska	13,619	8,911	3.4	3.0
Hawaii	17,352	7,573	1.8	1.0

Table 10. Resident Population, by Race and Spanish Origin: April 1, 1980, and April 1, 1970

United States	1980	1970	Percent Distribution 1980	Percent Distribution 1970
Total	226,504,825	203,211,926	100.0	100.0
White	188,340,790	177,748,975	83.2	87.5
Black	26,488,218	22,580,289	11.7	11.1
American Indian, Eskimo, and Aleut	1,418,195	827,268	0.6	0.4
Asian and Pacific Islander[a]	3,500,636	1,538,721	1.5	0.8
Other	6,756,986	516,673	3.0	0.3
Persons of Spanish origin	14,605,883	9,072,602	6.4	4.5
Persons not of Spanish origin	211,898,942	194,139,324	93.6	95.5

Source: U.S. Bureau of the Census, 1980 Census of Population, Supplementary Report, PC80–S1–1; and 1970 Census of Population, Supplementary Report, PC(S1)–104.

[a] Asian and Pacific Islander groups such as Cambodian, Laotian, and Thai are included in the "other" race category. In sample tabulations, these groups will be included in the Asian and Pacific Islander category.

Table 11. Age and Sex Structure of the Resident Population of the United States: April 1, 1980, and April 1, 1970

Age and Sex	Population		Percent Distribution		Population Change, 1970–1980	
	April 1, 1980	April 1, 1970	April 1, 1980	April 1, 1970	Number	Percent
Both Sexes						
All ages	226,504,825	203,235,298	100.0	100.0	23,269,527	11.4
Under 5 years	16,344,407	17,162,836	7.2	8.4	−818,429	−4.8
5 to 9 years	16,697,134	19,969,056	7.4	9.8	−3,271,922	−16.4
10 to 14 years	18,240,919	20,804,063	8.1	10.2	−2,563,144	−12.3
15 to 19 years	21,161,667	19,083,971	9.3	9.4	2,077,696	10.9
20 to 24 years	21,312,557	16,382,893	9.4	8.1	4,929,664	30.1
25 to 34 years	37,075,629	24,922,511	16.4	12.3	12,153,118	48.8
35 to 44 years	25,631,247	23,101,173	11.3	11.4	2,530,074	11.0
45 to 54 years	22,797,367	23,234,790	10.1	11.4	−437,423	−1.9
55 to 64 years	21,699,765	18,601,669	9.6	9.2	3,098,096	16.7
65 to 74 years	15,577,586	12,442,573	6.9	6.1	3,135,013	25.2
75 to 84 years	7,726,826	6,121,627	3.4	3.0	1,605,199	26.2
85 years and over	2,239,721	1,408,136	1.0	0.7	831,585	59.1
Median age (years)	30.0	28.0				
Male						
All ages	110,032,295	98,926,204	100.0	100.0	11,106,091	11.2
Under 5 years	8,360,135	8,750,106	7.6	8.8	−389,971	−4.5
5 to 9 years	8,537,903	10,175,283	7.8	10.3	−1,637,380	−16.1
10 to 14 years	9,315,055	10,598,463	8.5	10.7	−1,283,408	−12.1
15 to 19 years	10,751,544	9,641,372	9.8	9.7	1,110,172	11.5
20 to 24 years	10,660,063	7,924,866	9.7	8.0	2,735,197	34.5
25 to 34 years	18,378,764	12,225,584	16.7	12.4	6,153,180	50.3
35 to 44 years	12,567,786	11,238,084	11.4	11.4	1,329,702	11.8
45 to 54 years	11,007,985	11,206,753	10.0	11.3	−198,768	−1.8
55 to 64 ycars	10,150,459	8,798,748	9.2	8.9	1,351,711	15.4
65 to 74 years	6,755,199	5,440,350	6.1	5.5	1,314,849	24.2
75 to 84 years	2,865,974	2,437,244	2.6	2.5	428,730	17.6
85 years and over	681,428	489,351	0.6	0.5	192,077	39.3
Median age (years)	28.8	26.8				
Female						
All ages	116,472,530	104,309,094	100.0	100.0	12,163,436	11.7
Under 5 years	7,984,272	8,412,730	6.9	8.1	−428,458	−5.1
5 to 9 years	8,159,231	9,793,773	7.0	9.4	−1,634,542	−16.7
10 to 14 years	8,925,864	10,205,600	7.7	9.8	−1,279,736	−12.5
15 to 19 years	10,410,123	9,442,599	8.9	9.1	967,524	10.2
20 to 24 years	10,652,494	8,458,027	9.1	8.1	2,194,467	25.9
25 to 34 years	18,696,865	12,696,927	16.1	12.2	5,999,938	47.3
35 to 44 years	13,063,461	11,863,089	11.2	11.4	1,200,372	10.1
45 to 54 years	11,789,382	12,028,037	10.1	11.5	−238,655	−2.0
55 to 64 years	11,549,306	9,802,921	9.9	9.4	1,746,385	17.8
65 to 74 years	8,822,387	7,002,223	7.6	6.7	1,820,164	26.0
75 to 84 years	4,860,852	3,684,383	4.2	3.5	1,176,469	31.9
85 years and over	1,558,293	918,785	1.3	0.9	639,508	69.6
Median age (years)	31.3	29.3				

Source: 1980 and 1970 censuses.

Table 12. Age of the Resident Population, by Race and Spanish Origin: April 1, 1980

Age	Total	Race					Persons of Spanish Origin
		White	Black	American Indian, Eskimo, and Aleut	Asian and Pacific Islander[a]	Other	
All ages	226,504,825	188,340,790	26,488,218	1,418,195	3,500,636	6,756,986	14,605,883
Under 5 years	16,344,407	12,631,197	2,435,915	149,003	293,470	834,822	1,662,792
5 to 9 years	16,697,134	13,031,017	2,489,947	146,364	302,296	727,510	1,536,895
10 to 14 years	18,240,919	14,460,283	2,672,908	155,731	279,849	672,148	1,474,837
15 to 19 years	21,161,667	16,957,541	2,983,440	170,061	288,550	762,075	1,605,827
20 to 24 years	21,312,557	17,283,385	2,724,355	148,985	320,129	835,703	1,585,651
25 to 34 years	37,075,629	30,625,328	4,208,892	231,775	740,415	1,269,219	2,503,876
35 to 44 years	25,631,247	21,584,367	2,708,418	153,226	497,583	687,653	1,566,200
45 to 54 years	22,797,367	19,612,854	2,271,182	109,589	338,702	465,040	1,185,746
55 to 64 years	21,699,765	19,210,785	1,907,335	78,673	227,808	275,164	775,274
65 to 74 years	15,577,586	13,905,249	1,339,974	48,142	137,765	146,456	457,114
75 to 84 years	7,726,826	6,994,079	586,991	20,794	60,215	64,747	202,841
85 years and over	2,239,721	2,044,705	158,861	5,852	13,854	16,449	48,830
Median age (years)	30.0	31.3	24.9	23.0	28.6	22.8	23.2
Percent Distribution							
All ages	100.0	100.0	100.0	100.0	100.0	100.0	100.0
Under 5 years	7.2	6.7	9.2	10.5	8.4	12.4	11.4
5 to 9 years	7.4	6.9	9.4	10.3	8.6	10.8	10.5
10 to 14 years	8.1	7.7	10.1	11.0	8.0	9.9	10.1
15 to 19 years	9.3	9.0	11.3	12.0	8.2	11.3	11.0
20 to 24 years	9.4	9.2	10.3	10.5	9.1	12.4	10.9
25 to 34 years	16.4	16.3	15.9	16.3	21.2	18.8	17.1
35 to 44 years	11.3	11.5	10.2	10.8	14.2	10.2	10.7
45 to 54 years	10.1	10.4	8.6	7.7	9.7	6.9	8.1
55 to 64 years	9.6	10.2	7.2	5.5	6.5	4.1	5.3
65 to 74 years	6.9	7.4	5.1	3.4	3.9	2.2	3.1
75 to 84 years	3.4	3.7	2.2	1.5	1.7	1.0	1.4
85 years and over	1.0	1.1	0.6	0.4	0.4	0.2	0.3

Source: U.S. Bureau of the Census, 1980 Census of Population, Supplementary Report, PC80–S1–1.

[a] Asian and Pacific Islander groups such as Cambodian, Laotian, and Thai are included in the "other" race category. In sample tabulations, these Asian and Pacific Islander groups will be included in the Asian and Pacific Islander category.

Table 13.   Black Population Change in 14 Central Cities and Their Suburbs, 1960–1980

Area	Black Population 1980	Percent Change in Black Population		Percent Black		
		1960–70	1970–80	1960	1970	1980
Central Cities						
New York City	1,784,000	53.3%	7.0	14.0	12.1	25.2
Chicago	1,197,000	35.7	8.6	22.9	32.7	39.8
Detroit	759,000	37.0	14.9	28.9	43.7	63.1
Philadelphia	639,000	23.5	−2.3	26.4	33.6	37.8
Los Angeles	505,000	50.4	0.3	13.5	17.9	17.0
Washington, D.C.	448,000	30.6	−16.6	53.9	71.1	70.3
Houston	440,000	47.2	39.1	22.9	25.7	27.6
Baltimore	431,000	29.1	2.6	34.7	46.4	54.8
New Orleans	308,000	14.5	15.3	37.2	45.0	55.3
Memphis	308,000	31.6	26.9	37.0	38.9	47.6
Atlanta	283,000	36.8	12.1	38.3	51.3	66.6
Dallas	266,000	62.7	26.3	19.0	24.9	29.4
Cleveland	251,000	14.8	−12.7	28.6	38.3	43.8
St. Louis	206,000	18.6	−18.8	28.6	40.9	47.4
Suburbs (1970 definition)						
New York City	285,000	55.5%	31.4	4.8	5.9	7.6
Chicago	231,000	65.5	79.9	2.9	3.6	5.6
Detroit	128,000	26.1	32.5	3.7	3.6	4.5
Philadelphia	245,000	34.1	28.9	6.1	6.6	8.1
Los Angeles	398,000	105.0	65.7	3.6	6.2	9.6
Washington, D.C.	390,000	98.3	134.9	6.4	7.9	16.6
Houston	36,000	6.2	21.4	12.9	8.8	6.2
Baltimore	126,000	25.6	54.9	7.0	7.0	9.1
New Orleans	79,000	26.9	40.4	15.9	12.5	12.6
Memphis	37,000	−34.8	−18.4	40.2	31.7	21.0
Atlanta	179,000	23.5	222.4	8.5	6.2	14.2
Dallas	50,000	1.1	35.4	8.3	5.2	4.7
Cleveland	94,000	452.8	110.6	0.8	3.4	7.1
St. Louis	201,000	65.0	50.4	6.0	7.7	10.9

Table 14.   Population Inside and Outside SMSAs by Race: 1970 to 1980

Metropolitan Status	All Races	White	Black	Other Races
1980 Census				
Numbers				
United States	226,505	188,341	26,488	11,676
Inside SMSAs	169,405	138,044	21,474	9,887
Inside central cities	67,930	47,014	15,301	5,615
Outside central cities	101,475	91,029	6,173	4,272
Outside SMSAs	57,100	50,297	5,014	1,789
Percent distribution				
United States	100.0	100.0	100.0	100.0
Inside SMSAs	74.8	73.3	81.1	84.7
Inside central cities	30.0	25.0	57.8	48.1
Outside central cities	44.8	48.3	23.3	36.6
Outside SMSAs	25.2	26.7	18.9	15.3

Table 14 (*continued*)

Metropolitan Status	All Races	White	Black	Other Races
Percent of total				
United States	100.0	83.2	11.7	5.2
Inside SMSAs	100.0	81.5	12.7	5.8
Inside central cities	100.0	69.2	22.5	8.3
Outside central cities	100.0	89.7	6.1	4.2
Outside SMSAs	100.0	88.1	8.8	3.1
1970 Census				
Numbers				
United States	203,302	177,749	22,580	2,973
Inside SMSAs	153,694	133,574	17,872	2,247
Inside central cities	67,850	53,100	13,546	1,204
Outside central cities	85,843	80,474	4,326	1,043
Outside SMSAs	49,608	44,175	4,708	725
Percent distribution				
United States	100.0	100.0	100.0	100.0
Inside SMSAs	75.6	75.1	79.1	75.6
Inside central cities	33.4	29.9	60.0	40.5
Outside central cities	42.2	45.3	19.2	35.1
Outside SMSAs	24.4	24.9	20.9	24.4
Percent of total				
United States	100.0	87.4	11.1	1.5
Inside SMSAs	100.0	86.9	11.6	1.5
Inside central cities	100.0	78.3	20.0	1.8
Outside central cities	100.0	93.7	5.0	1.2
Outside·SMSAs	100.0	89.0	9.5	1.5
Change, 1970 to 1980				
Number				
United States	23,203	10,592	3,908	8,703
Inside SMSAs	15,711	4,469	3,602	7,640
Inside central cities	80	−6,086	1,755	4,410
Outside central cities	15,631	10,555	1,847	3,229
Outside SMSAs	7,492	6,122	306	1,063
Percent				
United States	11.4	6.0	17.3	292.8
Inside SMSAs	10.2	3.3	20.2	339.9
Inside central cities	0.1	−11.5	13.0	366.3
Outside central cities	18.2	13.1	42.7	309.6
Outside SMSAs	15.1	13.9	6.5	146.6

Source: U.S. Department of Commerce, Bureau of the Census.

Numbers in thousands. SMSAs defined by Office of Management and Budget as of June 30, 1981.

Table 15. Interregional Migration (numbers in thousands)

Years	Northeast	North Central	South	West
General Population				
1965–1970				
Inmigrants	1,273	2,024	3,142	2,309
Outmigrants	1,988	2,661	2,486	1,613
Net migration	−715	−637	+656	+696
1970–1975				
Inmigrants	1,057	1,731	4,082	2,347
Outmigrants	2,399	2,926	2,253	1,639
Net migration	−1,342	−1,195	+1,829	+708
1975–1980				
Inmigrants	1,106	1,993	4,204	2,838
Outmigrants	2,592	3,166	2,440	1,945
Net migration	−1,486	−1,173	+1,764	+893
Blacks				
1965–1970				
Inmigrants	146	203	162	150
Outmigrants	110	111	378	61
Net migration	+36	+92	−216	+89
1970–1975				
Inmigrants	118	150	302	153
Outmigrants	182	202	288	51
Net migration	−64[a]	−52[a]	+14[a]	+102
1975–1980				
Inmigrants	99	170	415	193
Outmigrants	274	221	220	163
Net migration	−175	−51[a]	+195	+30[a]

[a] Difference from zero not statistically significant at the .05 level.

Table 16. Metropolitan and Nonmetropolitan Migration (numbers in thousands)

	1965–1970	1970–1975	1975–1980
General Population			
Metropolitan			
Inmigrants	5,457	5,127	5,993
Outmigrants	5,809	6,721	7,337
Net migration	−352	−1,594	−1,344
Nonmetropolitan			
Inmigrants	5,809	6,721	7,337
Outmigrants	5,457	5,127	5,993
Net migration	+352	+1,594	+1,344
Blacks			
Metropolitan			
Inmigrants	452	463	469
Outmigrants	234	325	353
Net migration	+218	+138[a]	+116[a]
Nonmetropolitan			
Inmigrants	234	325	353
Outmigrants	452	463	469
Net migration	−218	−138[a]	−116[a]

[a] Difference from zero not statistically significant at the .05 level.

Table 17. Central-City and Suburban Migration (numbers in thousands)

	1970–1975	1975–1980
General Population		
Central Cities		
Inmigrants	5,987	6,891
Outmigrants	13,005	13,237
Net migration	−7,018	−6,346
Suburbs		
Inmigrants	12,732	13,628
Outmigrants	7,309	8,627
Net migration	+5,423	+5,001
Blacks		
Central cities		
Inmigrants	737	724
Outmigrants	980	1,163
Net migration	−243	−439
Suburbs		
Inmigrants	827	1,123
Outmigrants	446	567
Net migration	+381	+556

Table 18. Regional Distribution of the Black Population: 1850–1980

	Percentage of Blacks Living in:			
Year	Northeast	North Central	South	West
1850	4.1	3.7	92.1	<0.1
1860	3.5	4.1	92.2	0.1
1870	3.7	5.6	90.6	0.1
1880	3.5	5.9	90.5	0.2
1890	3.6	5.8	90.3	0.4
1900	4.4	5.6	89.7	0.3
1910	4.9	5.5	89.0	0.5
1920	6.5	7.6	85.2	0.8
1930	9.6	10.6	78.7	1.0
1940	10.6	11.0	77.0	1.3
1950	13.4	14.8	68.0	3.8
1960	16.0	18.3	59.9	5.8
1970	19.2	20.2	53.0	7.5
1980	18.3	20.1	53.0	8.5

Note: The Northeast consists of New England and the Middle Atlantic states of New York, Pennsylvania, and New Jersey. The North Central region consists of the Great Lakes states along with Missouri, Kansas, Iowa, Nebraska, and the Dakotas. The South is made up of all states south of the Mason-Dixon line (including the border states of Delaware, West Virginia, and Kentucky) and extends as far west as Texas and Oklahoma. The remaining states are in the West.

Table 19. Percentage of Population Living in Urban Territory: 1880–1980

Year	Total Population	Blacks	Whites
1880	26.3	12.9	28.3
1890	32.8	17.6	35.1
1900	37.3	20.5	39.7
1910	46.3	27.4	48.7
1920	51.4	34.0	53.4
1930	56.2	43.7	57.6
1940	56.5	48.6	57.5
1950	64.0	62.4	64.3
1960	69.9	73.2	69.5
1970	73.5	81.3	72.4
1980	73.7	Not available	Not available

a Before 1950 "urban" meant everyone living in an incorporated place of 2,500 or greater population. After 1950 the urban total was expanded to include persons living in fairly dense suburban territory surrounding cities of 50,000 or greater population.

Table 20. Increase in Black Population in Suburban Territory, 1960–1980, for the United States and Each of 14 Cities with a 1980 Black Population of 200,000 or more

	Total Increase		Percent Distribution	
	1960–1970	1970–1980	1960–1970	1970–1980
United States	804,953	1,793,313	100.0	100.0
Suburban territory of:				
New York City	77,494	68,127	9.6	3.8
Chicago	50,782	102,528	6.3	5.7
Detroit	20,008	31,378	2.5	1.7
Philadelphia	48,445	55,018	6.0	3.1
Los Angeles	123,148	157,822	15.3	8.8
Washington, D.C.	82,287	224,045	10.2	12.5
Houston	3,819	14,100	0.5	0.8
Baltimore	20,747	44,568	2.6	2.5
New Orleans	11,972	22,789	1.5	1.3
Memphis	−24,744	−8,552	—	—
Atlanta	10,571	123,639	1.3	6.9
Dallas	385	13,066	—[a]	0.7
Cleveland	36,674	49,512	4.6	2.8
St. Louis	52,642	67,339	6.5	3.8
Total of above	514,230	965,379	63.9	53.8
All other suburban territory	290,723	827,934	36.1	46.2

[a] Under 0.05%.

Note: "Suburban territory" refers to the entire balance of SMSAs (as defined in 1970) outside the central cities.

Table 21. 100 Cities With the Largest Black Population, by Rank: 1980

| Rank | City | Black Population | | Total Population |
		Number	Percentage of Total Population	
1	New York, NY	1,784,124	25.2	7,071,030
2	Chicago, IL	1,197,000	39.8	3,005,072
3	Detroit, MI	758,939	63.1	1,203,339
4	Philadelphia, PA	638,878	37.8	1,688,210
5	Los Angeles, CA	505,208	17.0	2,966,763
6	Washington, D.C.	448,229	70.3	637,651
7	Houston, TX	440,257	27.6	1,594,086
8	Baltimore, MD	431,151	54.8	786,775
9	New Orleans, LA	308,136	55.3	557,482
10	Memphis, TN	307,702	47.6	646,356
11	Atlanta, GA	282,912	66.6	425,022
12	Dallas, TX	265,594	29.4	904,078
13	Cleveland, OH	251,347	43.8	573,822
14	St. Louis, MO	206,386	45.6	453,085
15	Newark, NJ	191,743	58.2	329,248
16	Oakland, CA	159,234	46.9	339,288
17	Birmingham, AL	158,223	55.6	284,413
18	Indianapolis, IN	152,626	21.8	700,807
19	Milwaukee, WI	146,940	23.1	636,212
20	Jacksonville, FL	137,324	25.4	540,898
21	Cincinnati, OH	130,467	33.8	385,457
22	Boston, MA	126,229	22.4	562,994
23	Columbus, OH	124,880	22.1	564,871
24	Kansas City, MO	122,699	27.4	448,159
25	Richmond, VA	112,357	51.3	219,214
26	Gary, IN	107,644	70.8	151,953
27	Nashville–Davidson, TN	105,942	23.3	455,651
28	Pittsburgh, PA	101,813	24.0	423,938
29	Charlotte, NC	97,627	31.0	314,447
30	Jackson, MS	95,357	47.0	202,895
31	Buffalo, NY	95,116	26.6	357,870
32	Norfolk, VA	93,987	35.2	266,979
33	Fort Worth, TX	87,723	22.8	385,141
34	Miami, FL	87,110	25.1	346,931
35	San Francisco, CA	86,414	12.7	678,974
36	Shreveport, LA	84,627	41.1	205,815
37	Louisville, KY	84,080	28.2	298,451
38	Baton Rouge, LA	80,119	36.5	219,486
39	San Diego, CA	77,700	8.9	875,504
40	Dayton, OH	75,031	36.9	203,588
41	Mobile, AL	72,568	36.2	200,452
42	Montgomery, AL	69,765	39.2	178,157
43	Savannah, GA	69,441	49.0	141,634
44	Flint, MI	66,124	41.4	159,611
45	East Orange, NJ	64,354	83.5	77,025
46	Tampa, FL	63,835	23.5	271,523
47	Rochester, NY	62,332	25.8	241,741
48	Jersey City, NJ	61,954	27.7	223,532
49	Toledo, OH	61,750	17.4	354,635
50	Compton, CA	60,812	74.8	81,286
51	Denver, CO	59,252	12.1	491,396

Table 21 (*continued*)

Rank	City	Black Population Number	Percentage of Total Population	Total Population
52	Oklahoma City, OK	58,702	14.6	403,213
53	Columbus, GA	57,884	34.2	169,441
54	San Antonio, TX	57,654	7.3	785,410
55	Inglewood, CA	54,010	57.3	94,245
56	Chattanooga, TN	53,716	31.7	169,565
57	Winston-Salem, NC	52,968	40.2	131,885
58	East St. Louis, IL	52,751	95.6	55,200
59	Akron, OH	52,719	22.2	237,177
60	Macon, GA	52,056	44.5	116,860
61	Greensboro, NC	51,373	33.0	155,642
62	Little Rock, AR	51,091	32.2	158,461
63	Durham, NC	47,474	47.1	100,831
64	Portsmouth, VA	47,185	45.1	104,577
65	Paterson, NJ	47,091	34.1	137,970
66	Seattle, WA	46,755	9.5	493,846
67	Hartford, CT	46,186	33.9	136,392
68	Newport News, VA	45,584	31.5	144,903
69	Camden, NJ	45,008	53.0	84,910
70	Beaumont, TX	43,270	36.6	118,102
71	Tulsa, OK	42,594	11.8	360,919
72	Austin, TX	42,118	12.2	345,496
73	Hampton, VA	42,072	34.3	122,617
74	Trenton, NJ	41,860	45.4	92,124
75	Raleigh, NC	41,186	27.5	149,771
76	St. Petersburg, FL	41,000	17.3	236,893
77	Kansas City, KS	40,826	25.3	161,087
78	Long Beach, CA	40,732	11.3	361,334
79	Columbia, SC	40,391	40.7	99,296
80	New Haven, CT	40,235	31.9	125,109
81	Youngstown, OH	38,481	33.3	115,436
82	Orlando, FL	38,390	29.9	128,394
83	Omaha, NE	37,852	12.1	311,681
84	Phoenix, AZ	37,682	4.9	764,911
85	Sacramento, CA	36,866	13.4	275,741
86	Wilmington, DE	35,858	51.1	70,195
87	Richmond, CA	35,799	47.9	74,676
88	Albany, GA	35,173	47.6	73,934
89	Mount Vernon, NY	32,469	48.7	66,713
90	Charleston, SC	32,318	46.5	69,510
91	Fort Lauderdale, FL	32,225	21.0	153,256
92	East Cleveland, OH	31,980	86.5	36,957
93	Chesapeake, VA	31,510	27.6	114,226
94	Wichita, KS	30,200	10.8	279,272
95	Bridgeport, CT	29,898	21.0	142,546
96	Huntsville, AL	29,535	20.7	142,513
97	San Jose, CA	29,157	4.6	636,550
98	Prichard, AL	29,129	73.7	39,541
99	Grand Rapids, MI	28,602	15.7	181,843
100	Pontiac, MI	28,532	37.2	76,715

Table 22. 100 Cities with the Largest Black Population Ranked According to the Highest Proportion of Blacks: 1980

Rank	City	Percentage of Total	Rank	City	Percentage of Total
1	East St. Louis, IL	95.6	51	Greensboro, NC	33.0
2	East Cleveland, OH	86.5	52	Little Rock, AR	32.2
3	East Orange, NJ	83.5	53	New Haven, CT	31.9
4	Compton, CA	74.8	54	Chattanooga, TN	31.7
5	Prichard, AL	73.7	55	Newport News, VA	31.5
6	Gary, IN	70.8	56	Charlotte, NC	31.0
7	Washington, D.C.	70.3	57	Orlando, FL	29.9
8	Atlanta, GA	66.6	58	Dallas, TX	29.4
9	Detroit, MI	63.1	59	Louisville, KY	28.2
10	Newark, NJ	58.2	60	Jersey City, NJ	27.7
11	Inglewood, CA	57.3	61	Houston, TX	27.6
12	Birmingham, AL	55.6	62	Chesapeake, VA	27.6
13	New Orleans, LA	55.3	63	Raleigh, NC	27.5
14	Baltimore, MD	54.8	64	Kansas City, MO	27.4
15	Camden, NJ	53.0	65	Buffalo, NY	26.6
16	Richmond, VA	51.3	66	Rochester, NY	25.3
17	Wilmington, DE	51.1	67	Jacksonville, FL	25.4
18	Savannah, GA	49.0	68	Kansas City, KS	25.3
19	Mount Vernon, NY	48.7	69	New York, NY	25.2
20	Richmond, CA	47.9	70	Miami, FL	25.1
21	Memphis, TN	47.6	71	Pittsburgh, PA	24.0
22	Albany, GA	47.6	72	Tampa, FL	23.5
23	Durham, NC	47.1	73	Nashville–Davidson, TN	23.3
24	Jackson, MS	47.0	74	Milwaukee, WI	23.1
25	Oakland, CA	46.9	75	Fort Worth, TX	22.8
26	Charleston, SC	46.5	76	Boston, MA	22.4
27	St. Louis, MO	45.6	77	Akron, OH	22.2
28	Trenton, NJ	45.4	78	Columbus, OH	22.1
29	Portsmouth, VA	45.1	79	Indianapolis, IN	21.8
30	Macon, GA	44.5	80	Fort Lauderdale, FL	21.0
31	Cleveland, OH	43.8	81	Bridgeport, CT	21.0
32	Flint, MI	41.4	82	Huntsville, AL	20.7
33	Shreveport, LA	41.1	83	Toledo, OH	17.4
34	Columbia, SC	40.7	84	St. Petersburgh, FL	17.3
35	Winston-Salem, NC	40.2	85	Los Angeles, CA	17.0
36	Chicago, IL	39.8	86	Grand Rapids, MI	15.7
37	Montgomery, AL	39.2	87	Oklahoma City, OK	14.6
38	Philadelphia, PA	37.8	88	Sacramento, CA	13.4
39	Pontiac, MI	37.2	89	San Francisco, CA	12.7
40	Dayton, OH	36.9	90	Austin, TX	12.2
41	Beaumont, TX	36.6	91	Omaha, NE	12.1
42	Baton Rouge, LA	36.5	92	Denver, CO	12.1
43	Mobile, AL	36.2	93	Tulsa, OK	11.8
44	Norfolk, VA	35.2	94	Long Beach, CA	11.3
45	Hampton, VA	34.3	95	Wichita, KS	10.8
46	Columbus, GA	34.2	96	Seattle, WA	9.5
47	Paterson, NJ	34.1	97	San Diego, CA	8.9
48	Hartford, CT	33.9	98	San Antonio, TX	7.3
49	Cincinnati, OH	33.8	99	Phoenix, AZ	4.9
50	Youngstown, OH	33.3	100	San Jose, CA	4.6

THE BLACK FAMILY

Current Status ■ Number and Size ■ Shortage of Eligible Males ■ Intermarriage ■ Living Arrangements of Children ■ Income ■ Public Assistance ■ Effects of Unemployment and Poverty ■ Decline of Family Farms ■ Housing ■ Suburban Living ■ Health Care ■ Sickle-Cell Disease ■ Victims of Crime ■ Budget Cuts and the Family ■ Family Charts ■ Selected Family Facts ■ Family Tables

The black family is pressured by two forces: it is black and subject to stresses rooted in race and class differences, and it is a family and thus subject to the divisiveness and disintegration that affect families throughout the United States.

The 1960s were a time of growth and progress for most American families, including those that are black. By comparison, the 1970s were a time of retrogression for most black families, primarily because of economic downturns in the society, but also due to a fretful mood in the nation and the negative political leadership patterns of Presidents Nixon and Ford. The rapidity of social change, coupled with new patterns of permissiveness and personal freedom-seeking, affected most American families.

In 1975 Paul C. Glick, Senior Demographer in the Population Division, Bureau of the Census, issued an analytical report, "Some Recent Changes in American Families." It provides evidence that by the late 1960s and early 1970s marriage typically occurred at a later age, and there was more divorce among upper socioeconomic groups, more single-parent families, and more variety in living arrangements in American families than had been the case in the 1940s and 1950s. The divorce rate was one in three and growing, especially among upper socioeconomic groups, theoretically the most stable of families. By February 1979, the divorce rate approached 40% (p. 22). Also by 1975 there was a sharp rise in unwed motherhood among young females, white and black, some as young as 10 and 11 years old, many under 17.

These evidences of family instability and change were counterbalanced by forces making for stability amidst change. About four of every five persons who divorce do remarry, usually within three years. Single-parent families headed by women or men may be stable family units despite the absence of two adult mates in the home. Many families had fewer children for whom to care since the birth rate declined to an average of 1.9 per woman. These departures in structure and condition on the part of the larger American family from the traditional ideal of lifetime monogamous marriage within which two to four children were produced and reared pervaded at all levels and in all sectors of American society in the late 1960s and throughout the 1970s. This is the context in which the black family operated for those two decades.

Number and Size of Families

The number of black families increased steadily from 4.3 million in 1960 to 5.3 million in 1970, up to 6.7 million in 1978, demonstrating that blacks do believe in the institution of family and maintain families of some type. In 1980, 55.5% of black families were maintained by a married couple, 28.9% by a mother alone, 1.7% by a father alone, 11.3% by a female householder other than the mother, and 2.6% by a male householder other than the father. The proportion of families headed by women alone is growing.

About 40% of all black families were headed by women in 1980. In 1978, 59.3% of black families were

Chart 1. Percentage of Families Headed by Women: 1950, 1960, 1970, 1980

The percentage of families headed by women has increased dramatically since 1950. In 1980, 40% of black families were headed by women

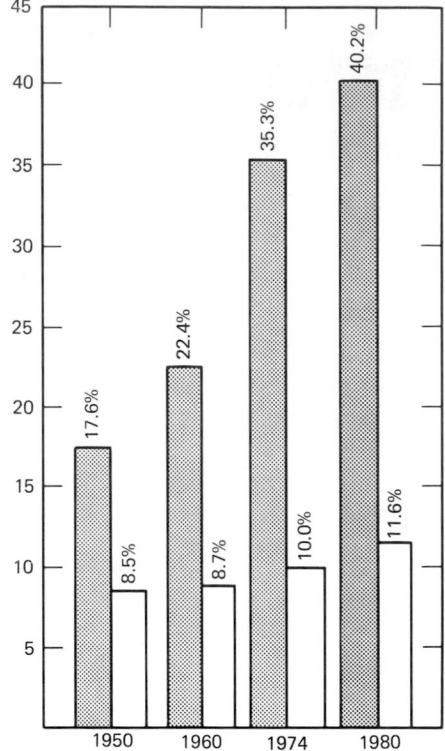

Source: U.S. Department of Commerce, Bureau of the Census.

maintained by a married couple, 36% by a woman with no husband present. The proportion of black families headed by women has increased from about 20% in 1960 to about 36% in 1978 to about 40% in 1980, from 1.0 million families in 1960 to some 2.4 million families in 1978. Much of this change can be attributed to marital separation or divorce. However, although these families may be "broken," they may be very stable in terms of the woman's love for the children under her care and her dependability in maintaining the family unit.

Black family size was smaller in 1978 than it was in 1970. Class differences are visible, with educated middle-income black women producing fewer children than in the past, while less well-educated low-income black women produce more children. In 1978, 73% of black families included four persons or less, and about 27% included five persons or more. This is a change from 1970 when families were larger—35.4% of them included five persons or more, and 64.5% included four persons or fewer. In 1978 black wives aged 18 to 34 years old, in the main reproductive years of life, expressed reduced expectations in terms of life-

time births: 54% of them indicated that they expected two or fewer children in their reproductive period, as compared with 46% who expect to produce three or more children.

Shortage of Eligible Black Males

Some of the single-parent status of black women can be explained by the shortage of eligible black men. This shortage has existed for more than 100 years. Thus some black women never find a husband; others who divorce are not able to remarry because of the shortage of men. The 1970 census revealed that there were over 1 million fewer males than females in the black population. According to data from the *Socioeconomic Status of the Black Population 1974*, there were at that time 91 black males to every 100 black females. But when comparisons of male/female populations 15 years of age and older are made, the proportion drops to 86 males for every 100 females. Thus it is not possible to match every black female of marriageable age with a black male of marriageable age.

Census figures for 1970 indicate that the number of black men in the age group 20–26 years old was only 82% of the number of women 18–24 years old, as contrasted with 93% in the white community. By 1980 these percentages rose to about 89% for blacks

Chart 2. Living Arrangements of Children under 18 by Race: 1980

Almost 58% of all black children come from broken homes. Only 42% of all black children live with both parents

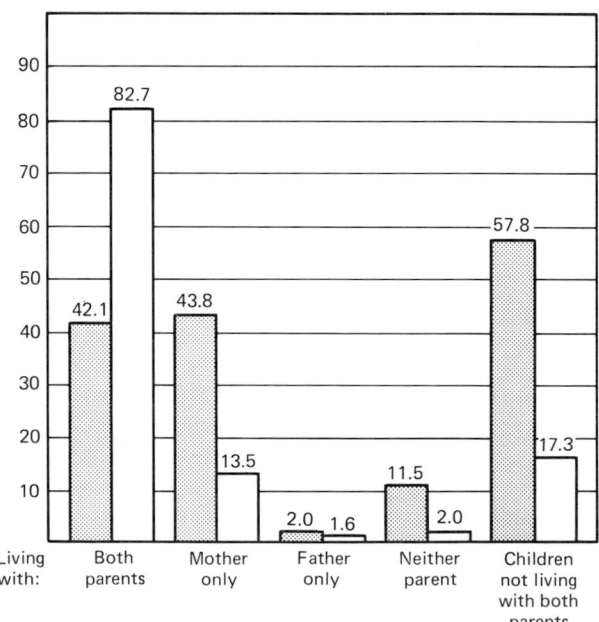

Source: U.S. Department of Commerce, Bureau of the Census.

and 98% for all races. Projections suggest that by 1995 the corresponding figures will rise to 96% and 108%, respectively. Thus marriage prospects will improve for young black women by the end of this century, but they will remain lower than those of white females, assuming interracial marriages remain statistically negligible.

The number of black men eligible for marriage to black women is reduced further by intermarriage. There were 125,000 black-white couples in 1977, almost twice as many as the 65,000 that existed in 1970. Seventy-four percent of those couples (almost ¾) were composed of a black husband and white wife. While this is a small percentage of all black couples, some 3.6%, still numerically it means that about 92,500 black men are not available to black women as marriage partners.

Living Arrangements of Children

In 1979, 43.4% of all black children lived with both of their parents, 41.9% lived with their mothers only, 2.1% lived with their fathers only, and 11.3% lived with neither parent. This last group of children usually resided with grandparent(s) or other relatives.

Thus fewer than half of black children lived with both parents in 1979. Since the grandparent or other relative caring for black children is likely to be female, it seems safe to assume that in 1979, 53.2% of all black children were being cared for by women alone.

When the marital status of mothers rearing their children alone is examined, using 1979 data, 16.2% of these females were married but their spouses were absent (separated). Divorced mothers constituted 9.5% of the group, and widowed mothers comprised 4.3%. Never-married mothers made up 11.9% of the total of mothers rearing children alone. It can be seen that much of the female-headed family situation among blacks can be attributed to marital disruption—separation, divorce, widowhood.

This disruption was part of the American environment in the 1970s, and black families did not escape it at any level. With respect to divorce, for example, Carter and Glick pointed out:

Surprisingly, upper-*level black men included an even higher proportion known to have been divorced than* lower-*level black men* (22 percent versus 19 percent). *Among white men, the situation was the reverse, with nearly twice as large a proportion of lower-level men known to have been divorced (19 percent versus 10 percent). The reasons for the atypical pattern for black men are not apparent, but the pattern is nonetheless noteworthy.* (Hugh Carter and Paul C. Glick, Marriage and Divorce: A Social and Economic Study, *rev. ed. Cambridge, Mass: Harvard University Press, 1976, pp. 405–406*)

Chart 3. Distribution of Public Assistance

Although the public perception is that blacks are by far the major recipients of government social programs, the facts indicate that whites receive 66% of social program aid

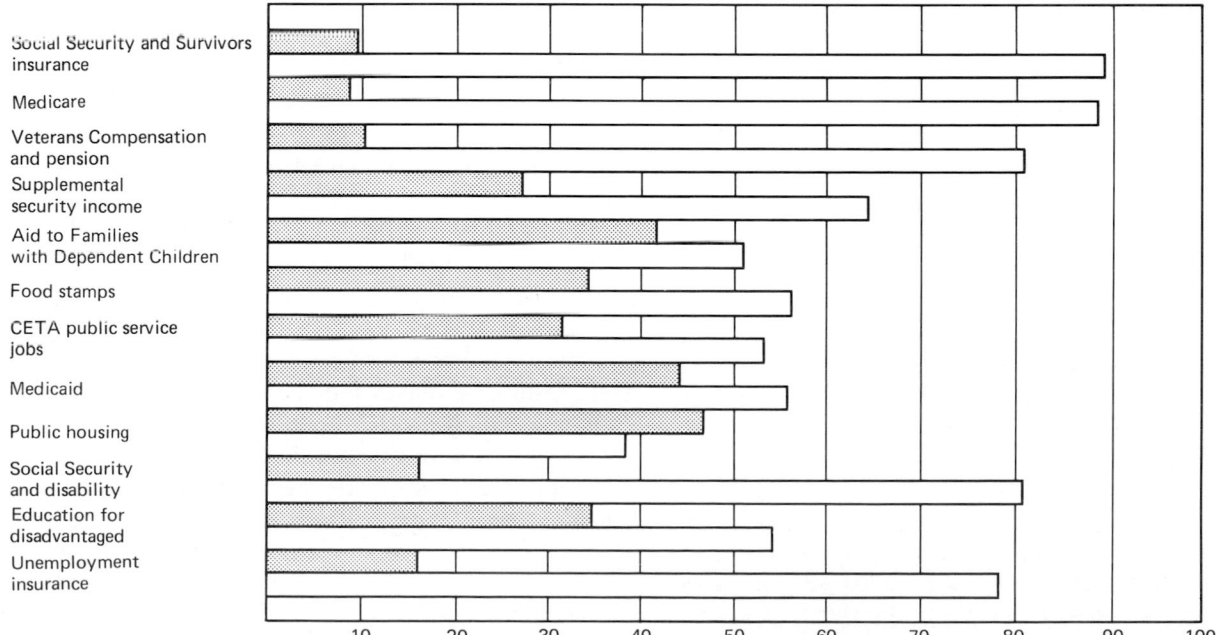

Source: Alex Poinsett, "Who Gets Welfare?" *Ebony Magazine,* Vol. 37, No. 3, January 1982, p. 28.

The effect of marital disruption and the shortage of eligible black male mates certainly had its effect on children. Dr. Robert B. Hill said:

Thus 44 percent of all black children in 1978 lived in families headed by women. Or to put it in numbers instead of percentages, in 1978 five *million black children lived in husband-* *wife families, but* four *million lived in black families headed by women. Since families headed by women are more likely to be poor, many of these four million children are poor— 42 percent of them—or 1,680,000. (Robert B. Hill, "The Economic Status of Black Families," in* The State of Black America 1979. *New York: National Urban League, 1979, p. 35)*

It is very clear that the life chances of these poor children will be restricted because of the economic condition of their families.

Families headed by black women are poor primarily because they do not have jobs, not because they fail to have husbands in the home. Although 75% of unemployed black women heading families were poor in 1977, just 27% of *employed* black women heading families were poor. Thus what black female family heads need are jobs that pay a living wage, so that these adults can provide for themselves and their minor children.

Income

The income that results from employment determines to a very great extent whether one will marry and have children, what housing options are attainable, what one will be able to save or invest, what health care will be available, what educational options will exist for family members, and how family members will prepare for retirement. Blacks have always been far below whites in total income and income expectations.

In 1979, some 36% of black families were able to live moderately or better. Ten percent of all black families were able to maintain themselves at what the Bureau of Labor Statistics defines as the "higher" standard of living, $30,317 for a family of four. This was up 1% from the 9% of such families in 1970, with the income still being produced usually by two or more earners. Also in 1979, some 26% of black families were able to maintain themselves at the "intermediate" standard, $20,517 for a family of four, usually with multiple earners in the labor force, up 2% from the 24% figure in 1970. However, 46% of black families were at the "lower" end of the income spectrum, with incomes of $12,585, up 1% from the 1970 proportion of 45%, and down 2% from the high of 48% in 1978. Middle-income blacks found their salaries eroded by inflation, and were hard-put to retain the standard of living they were able to gain by the late 1960s when the opportunity structure began to open wider for them.

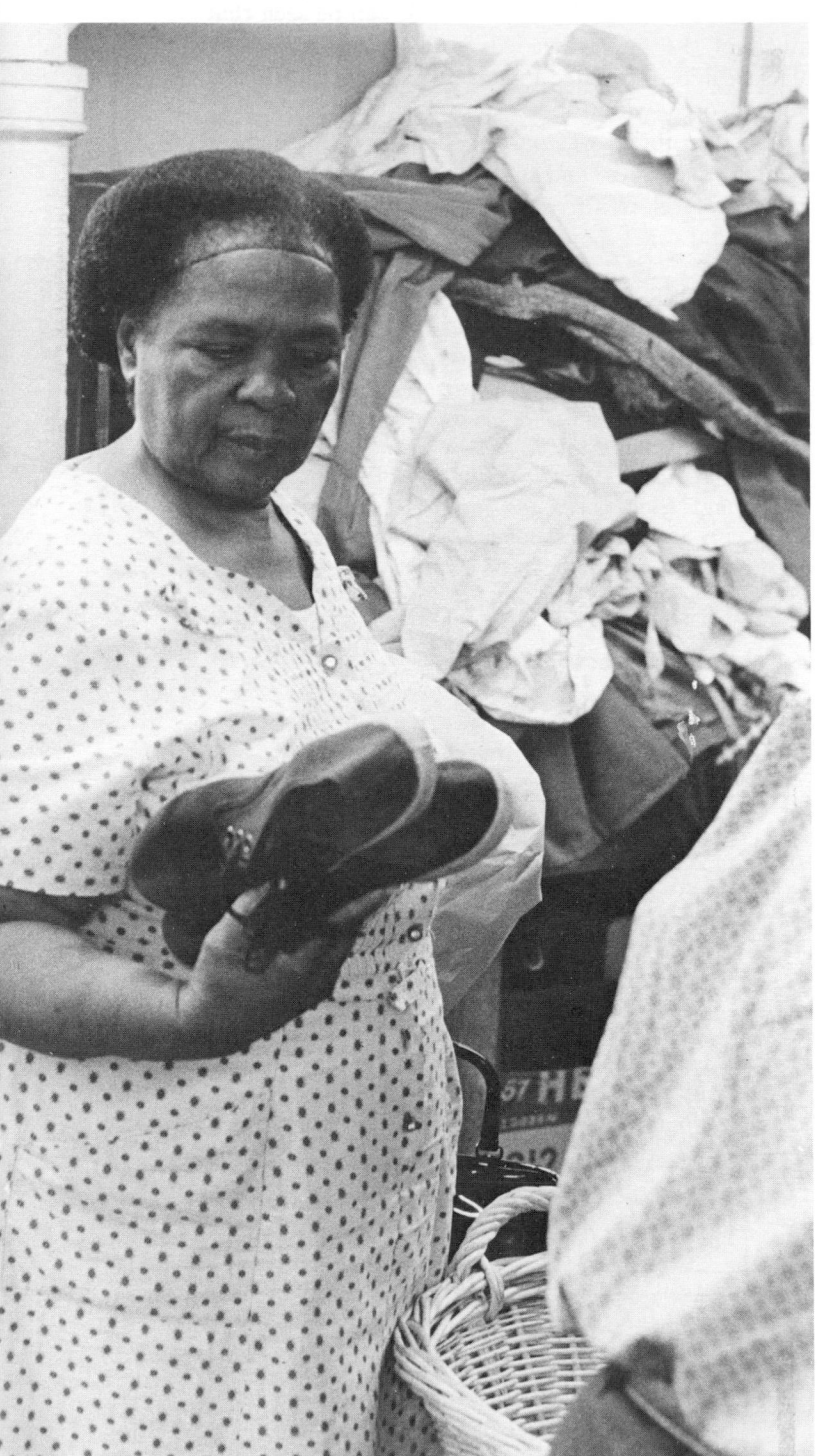

Unemployment, inflation, and federal budget cuts have reduced the standard of living of the poor to marginal subsistence levels.

The income/employment options clearly control what parents or other relatives can provide for children in a family. In 1980, the cost for rearing one child to adulthood ranged from $60,000 to $110,000. Any black family seeking to provide the best in terms of opportunities for its children is likely to spend at the higher end of this range for each child. Black children unfortunate enough to be born in poor families can rarely experience the richness of opportunities provided for their more fortunate peers, black or otherwise.

Families Receiving Public Assistance

In 1980, some 700,000—more than half of poor black families—received no welfare at all, and 70% of all unemployed blacks never received jobless benefits. About 34% of participants in the food-stamp program were black but 40% of poor black families received no food stamps at all.

Because the stereotype is so pervasive that black women and their children dominate the "welfare" rolls (AFDC recipients) a more detailed look at Aid to Families with Dependent Children program figures is in order. In 1977, 3,523,000 recipient families received AFDC monies. Of that number, 43% were black, some 1,514,890 families. Almost all AFDC families (78.8%) had only one adult recipient, usually the mother, and 51% of all these mothers were under 30 years old. This suggests that of some 6 million black families, 1,515,000 received AFDC funds, and of that number approximately 720,000 black AFDC families were headed by mothers under 30 years old.

In 1977 slightly less than 25% of AFDC mothers were known to have graduated from high school. Since a high school diploma was required for most employment in 1977, this suggests that at least 75% of AFDC mothers were unemployable because they were undereducated.

In 1977 one-third of the AFDC children were under age 6, preschoolers. In that year 3,550,354 of 7,835,803 recipient children were black, 45% of the total. Studies have shown that if society spends $6,000 per child in preschool education, the resulting benefits will amount to some $15,000 per child.

There is strong evidence that the vicious cycle of poor education, unemployment, and welfare assistance can be broken by educating all black female heads of AFDC households not known to be high school graduates in order to make them employable. It would also be valuable to such households and to society as a whole to provide preschool education to the children of these mothers.

Studies of low-income children who participated in experimental infant and preschool programs begun in

Chart 4. Aid to Dependent Children: 1960, 1969, 1970, 1973, 1975

Most public assistance goes to aid children. The average monthly stipend for a child is $115

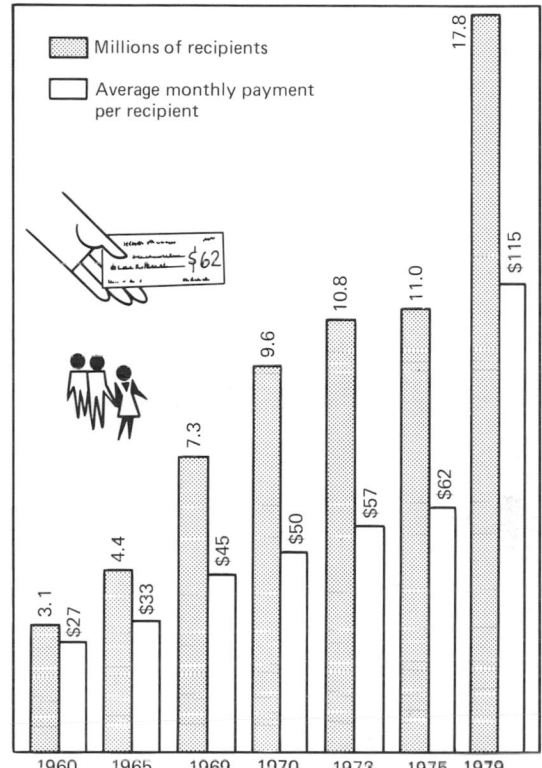

Data: U.S. Department of Commerce, Social and Economic Statistics Administration. Bureau of the Census.

the 1960s show that there are the following lasting effects:

1. Early education programs significantly reduced the number of children assigned to special education classes.

2. The programs significantly reduced the number of children retained in grade.

3. Early education significantly increased children's scores on fourth-grade mathematics achievement tests.

4. Low-income children who attended preschools surpassed their controls on the Stanford-Binet IQ test for up to three years after the programs ended.

5. Children who attended preschool were more likely than control children to give achievement-type reasons for their pride in themselves.

6. Mothers of children who attended preschool had higher vocational aspirations for their children than the children had for themselves.

Chart 5. Median Income of Families by Sex of Head and Labor Force Status of Wife: 1974, 1980

In every type of family status the income of black families has fallen far behind their white counterparts. For all black families the median income in 1980 was $11,644 while for all white families it was $21,824

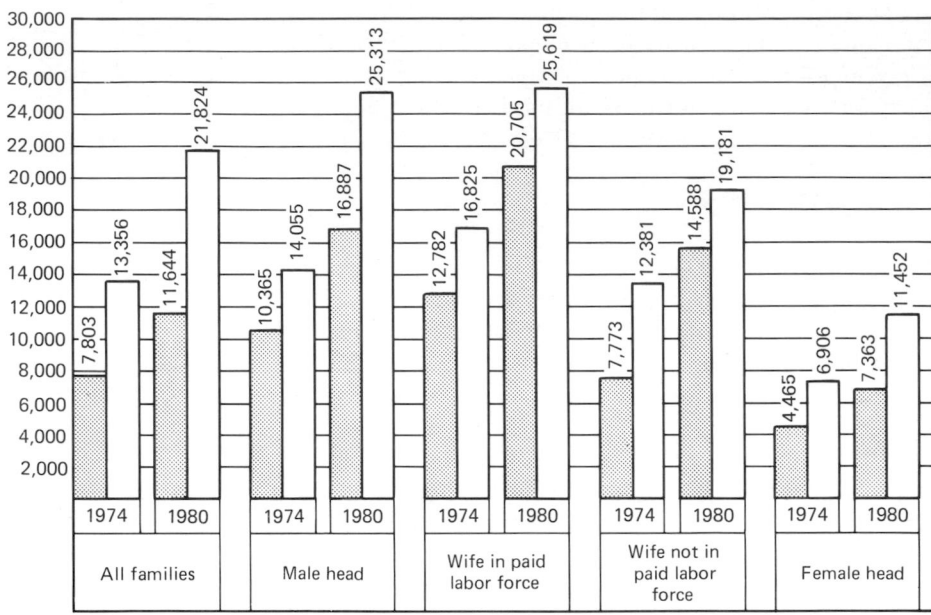

Source: U.S. Department of Commerce.

Women who work usually have fewer children than those who remain at home. Thus to make these AFDC mothers employable would probably reduce the number of children they produce, and the lower birth rate would save public funds in many areas, such as publicly supported day-care centers.

Further, as these mothers are enabled to enter and remain in the labor force, their earnings would increase and they would become taxpayers themselves. They would not need food stamps or medicaid assistance. These are some of the possible benefits to society from an education investment in black women and their children, so many of whom are young.

Life expectancy data support these projections. Years of potential production lie ahead for black female AFDC household heads and their children if they are given the opportunity and skills with which to work.

1978 LIFE EXPECTANCY DATA

	Nonwhite	White
Males	65.0 years of age	70.2 years of age
Females	73.6 years of age	77.8 years of age

Unemployment

The specter and reality of unemployment haunt black families. Black unemployment rates are consistently double those of whites and have been so since 1948

at least. Black unemployment rates have not fallen significantly even in the best of economic times, as during the 1960s. The economic gains of the late sixties eroded under pressures of recession, inflation, and large-scale unemployment. Obviously, families cannot remain intact, grow, and develop without sound economic footing. Black men, particularly, have not been able to count on earning a living wage for themselves and their families. All too often, wages are neither sufficient to enable a man to maintain his self-respect as a provider nor stable enough to make it worthwhile to change the nature of his adaptation to his world. A major reason why low-income men separate from their families is their inability to secure and retain employment that pays respectable wages.

The state of the economy spelled turbulence for black families throughout the 1970s. In 1978 black teenage unemployment rates stood at 52.5%; in some central city areas the unemployment of the young approached 90%. Almost half of those who were officially unemployed were between ages 16 to 24, who needed not only the income from employment, but an opportunity to begin assuming adult responsibilities. Single-parent families headed by black women were hit especially hard by the high unemployment rates; the small earnings of many of these heads-of-households exacerbated the problem. In the rural South, "where many blacks remain on the fringes of the economy, AFDC

Many black families of the rural South still live in conditions similar to these.

has often been the only means of survival." Unemployment rates rose in 1980 and again sharply at the end of 1981. In December 1981, Andrew F. Brimmer stated that an erosion in the relative economic position of blacks could be expected to show up in 1982 in rising unemployment, slower growth of jobs, and only moderate improvement in money income.

Decline of Black Family Farmers

The U.S. Civil Rights Commission announced in February 1982 that America's black family farmers are a rapidly diminishing group. The Commission, in a 196-page report, "The Decline of Black Farming in America," said there were 926,000 farms operated by blacks in 1920. That number had declined to about 57,000 by the end of the 1970s. If such trends continued, there would be only 10,000 by the end of the century. Most of these black farms were in the South, whereas nearly half of the nation's total farm population lived in the North Central region of the United States in 1980.

The Civil Rights Commission noted that the loss of black-owned land is occurring when land values are rising in the South and when there is industrial growth. The Commission held that black family farmers faced special problems of racism, and that their most pressing need was credit.

The Commission was critical of the federal Farmers Home Administration, which loaned only about 2.5% of its total dollars to black farmers in the fiscal year ending September 1981—in spite of the fact that needs of black farmers were greater than those of white farmers. The Commission's report suggests that the FHA may be discriminating against black farmers and contributing to racial inequality. (For more detailed analysis see the section on agriculture.)

Housing

The Fair Housing legislation of 1968 has been weakly and unevenly enforced in the country; it has provided few remedies for those who have experienced discrimination. Realtors have maintained their traditional steering practices; lending institutions and insurance agencies have continued their "red-lining" policies. These practices and others have determined to a very large extent where blacks live and why the Fair Housing Act has not provided the relief anticipated. Housing choices continue to be closely related to skin color. High interest rates, inflated costs for dwellings, and economic adversity compounded the problem. For blacks who have below-average incomes, purchase of a home was almost impossible in 1982. Meanwhile, rental options declined in major cities like Washington, D.C., where apartments, rapidly converted to condominiums, sold at prices far beyond the means of any but the most affluent. The process called "gentrification," the return of whites to central cities, was under way in most major cities in 1982 and blacks were being pushed into the close-in deteriorating suburbs as a result.

Proportions of home ownership did increase among blacks from 1960 to 1975, though not markedly. In 1975 the black home ownership rate was 44%, compared with 42% in 1970 and 38% in 1960. These statistics tell only part of the tale; housing units occupied by blacks, whether as owners or tenants, were generally more overcrowded than those occupied by whites, this being especially true in the South. Further, more housing units occupied by blacks lack some or all plumbing facilities. This was as true in 1970 as in 1960, particularly in the South.

The Suburbs

Census data show that between 1970 and 1977 the number of blacks living in the suburbs increased approximately 34%. This city-to-suburb move included middle-income blacks who actively sought suburban residence as well as low-income blacks being displaced by "gentrification" in cities. The suburbs are, of course, predominantly white. Consequently, blacks who moved to the suburbs from 1974 to 1977 went into predominantly white neighborhoods, gradually integrating them.

A strong relationship was discernible between socioeconomic status of the mover and the suburb chosen. The higher-educated, higher-income blacks were more likely to move into predominantly white neighborhoods. Also, home ownership rates for recent black movers were greatest in white neighborhoods.

Blacks were more likely than whites to be located at the lower end of the neighborhood's socioeconomic scale. In like manner, fewer blacks were to be found in very high-income tracts or tracts of high occupational status.

In 1982, blacks were not a significant force in the suburbs, since the actual number of blacks moving from central cities to suburbs is very small.

White flight in the suburbs has had the effect of creating and reinforcing de facto segregation in housing and schools in some suburban areas. Whites are moving

A large proportion of black families in central cities live in tenements like these.

Chart 6. Number of Recipients of Cash and In-Kind Benefits by Race: 1980

White recipients of public assistance and other cash and noncash benefits outnumber black recipients in every category

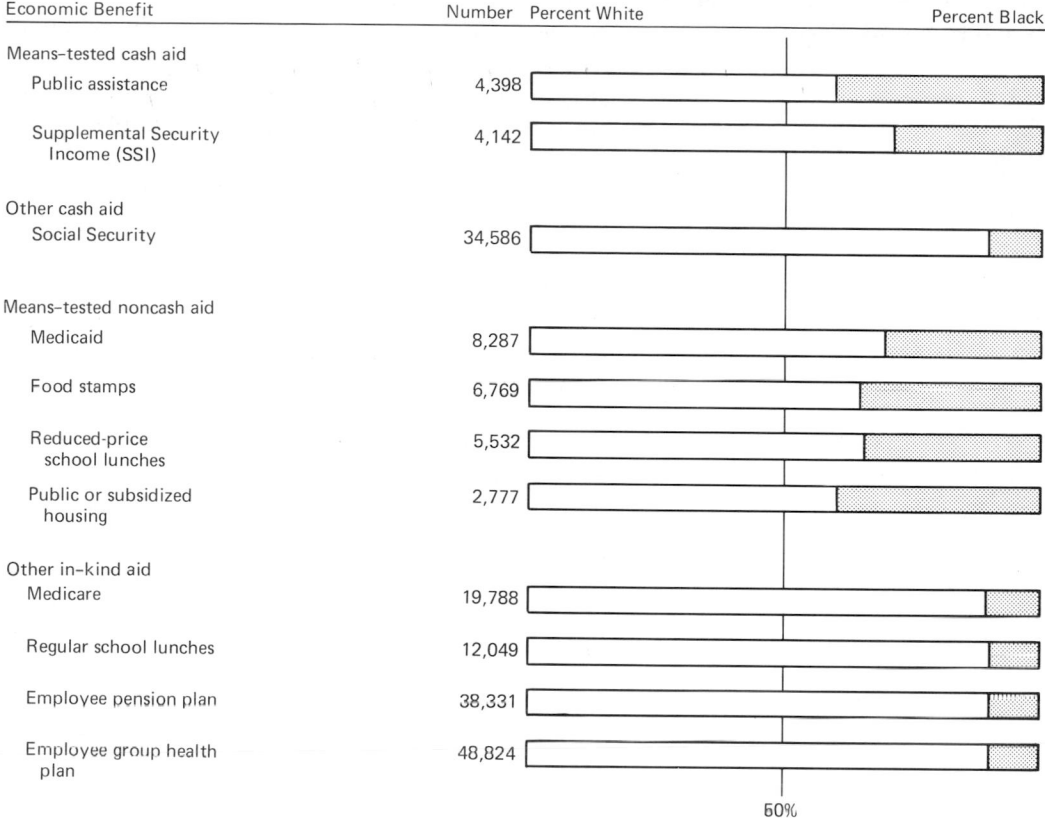

Data: U.S. Department of Commerce, Bureau of the Census.

from one suburban area to more affluent areas farther from the city, or at least from one suburban area to another. Prince Georges and Montgomery counties, in Maryland, are examples of suburban areas that have increasing pockets of de facto segregation in housing and public schools.

Health Care

Low-income Americans have a disproportionate share of health problems and are more likely than more affluent members of the population to perceive their health status as "fair" or "poor." Since blacks are disproportionately represented among the poor, they have a disproportionate share of health problems despite Medicaid and Medicare programs. Access to physician and hospital care has been improved, although in 1982 President Reagan's cutbacks threatened the return of health care to a more primitive level. Dental care has been a special problem for poor people. In 1977, for example, only 34% of persons with family incomes of less than $5,000 visited a dentist once during the

year as contrasted with 62% of persons with family incomes of $15,000 or more.

Infant mortality rates declined from 44.5 infant deaths per 1,000 live births in 1950 to 21.7 deaths per 1,000 live births in 1977. However, the infant mortality rate of blacks and other races was 1.8 times higher than that of white babies in 1977.

Suicide rates were not as high for blacks as whites, but the rates have been increasing in both groups. Among black males, suicide rates increased from 6.8 in 1950 to 11.4 per 100,000 resident population in 1977. For black females the rate increased from 1.6 per 100,000 resident population in 1950 to 3.5 in 1977. In 1978 the rates were highest among 25- to 34-year-olds of both sexes.

Hypertension is prevalent among older blacks. More than half of all black females over 45 years of age and black males 65 or older reported that they had suffered from hypertension. Hypertension can lead to stroke and congestive heart failure.

In spite of warnings that cigarette smoking can be hazardous to health, in 1976, 50.5% of black males

Chart 7. Percentage of Black Elderly and White Elderly Receiving Social Security Benefits: 1978

15% of elderly black heads of families receive at least some Social Security benefits as compared to elderly white family heads

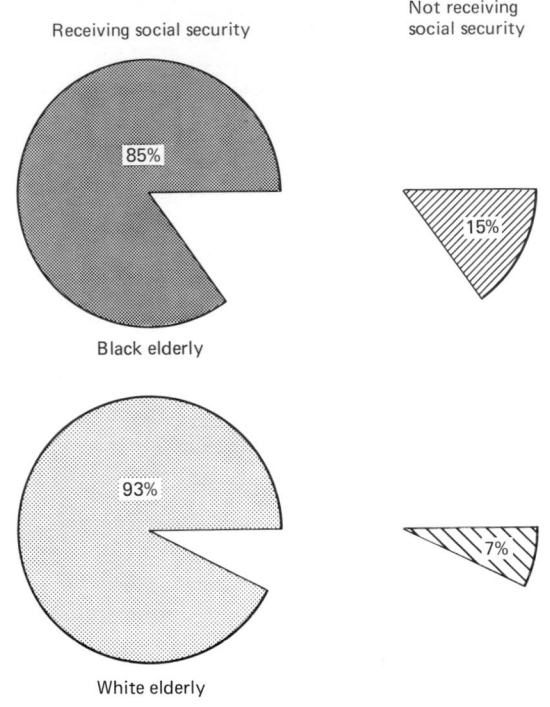

Black elderly

White elderly

Data: U.S. Department of Health and Human Services, Social Security Administration.

and 35.1% of black women reported that they smoked. Blacks consume less alcohol than whites.

Skinfold measurements for 1971–1974 showed that nearly half of black females aged 45–64 in families below the poverty level are obese. Black females are more obese than white females in every age group as well as above and below poverty level. On the other hand, black males usually are less obese than are white males in all groups except age 20–44 years below the poverty level.

Sickle Cell Anemia

Sickle Cell Disease is an inherited affliction in which there is a defect in the hemoglobin. The presence of this defective or abnormal hemoglobin can cause distortion (sickling) of the red blood cells and a decrease in the number of these corpuscles.

Sickled red blood cells have been found in one of every 12 American blacks, but the active disease, SCA, occurs about once in 600 American blacks and once in every 1,200 American whites. It is estimated that about 50,000 persons in the United States suffer from the disease.

Other races are affected by sickle cell anemia. The trait and the anemia affect people from Southern India, Greece, Italy, Syria, Caribbean Islands, South and Central America, Turkey, and other countries.

The disease occurs as a result of the mating of two people, each of whom carries the gene for the sickling trait. The first symptoms usually appear in their child at about 6 months of age. Sickle cell anemia is diagnosed through a study of the blood of the patient microscopically and electrophoretically. This is a chronic disease and medical management is directed both toward the quiescent and active periods (crises) of the malady. "Crisis" occurs when the disease is active, and symptoms usually are fever, pain, loss of appetite, paleness of the skin, generalized weakness, and sometimes a striking decrease in the number of red blood corpuscles.

There is no known cure for sickle cell anemia. Good medical and home care may make it possible for children with the disease to lead reasonably normal lives. Complications and infections have been controlled with antibiotic drugs.

The source of sickle cell disease seems to be malarious countries. People with sickle cell disease are almost always immune to malaria, so it seems that the sickle cell is a defense mechanism against malaria.

Black people who intend to have children are advised to undergo blood tests to determine whether they are carriers of the sickle cell gene. Two such carriers should agree not to produce children, since half of the children will have the trait and one in four the anemia. There is only one chance in four that the child will be free of the disease.

Victims of Crime

From 1960 to 1978 the number of violent crimes in the United States grew threefold, and the number of property crimes increased by about 2.8%. Violent offenses include murder and non-negligent manslaughter, forcible rape, robbery, and aggravated assault. Property crimes include burglary, larceny theft, and motor vehicle theft.

Death rates from homicide have been much higher for black males than for any other race-sex group. In 1977 black males recorded a rate of 60 per 100,000, as compared with 9 for white males. Also in 1977 the homicide rate stood at 13 per 100,000 for black females as compared with 3 for white females.

Blacks have higher victimization rates for crimes of violence than have whites. In 1978 these were 41 per 1,000 population for blacks, and 33 per 1,000 population for whites. The rates for crimes of theft are somewhat higher for whites, 98 versus 90.

Black males were more victimized by crimes of violence than any other group—54 per 1,000 in 1978. They were followed by white males—45 per 1,000; black females—30 per 1,000; and white females—22 per 1,000. On the other hand, with respect to theft white males were most victimized—106 per 1,000 population. They were followed by black males—102 per 1,000; white females—90 per 1,000; and black females—80 per 1,000 people.

Black households were more likely to be burglarized than white households—115 compared with 83 per 1,000. Black households reported a higher incidence of motor vehicle theft, but whites seemed more vulnerable to household larceny. The greatest vulnerability to burglary was for low-income or very high-income families. Middle-income families seemed to experience fewer household burglaries.

Incarcerated Men

Data from the U.S. Department of Justice, the American Correctional Association, and the Criminal Justice Institute, Inc., provide evidence that a disproportionately large segment of the inmate population in the United States is black. Blacks comprised 47% of the inmate population in 1974, but only 11% of the U.S. population at that time. They were overrepresented in the prisoner population by a factor of about 4. This means that these men were not available to be married and at work to provide for their families.

Blacks receive longer sentences than do whites. In part this is because they are more likely to have been convicted of violent crimes, especially robbery, and such crimes carry longer sentences. In 1979 the average sentence for white federal prisoners was 100.5 months (8.3 years) and for other races the average sentence was 132.3 months (11 years).

Black prisoners tend to be younger than their white counterparts. About 66% of all black inmates in 1974 were less than 30 years old, compared with 58% of whites. About 30% of the blacks had no more than an eighth-grade education when they were imprisoned. Some 78% had completed less than high school.

The black prisoners were much more likely than white prisoners to have dependents on welfare. About 43% of the white prisoners and 55% of the black prisoners had dependents on welfare. Thus not only do families pay for the absence of their male members—but society pays three ways in social costs: (1) for the incarceration, (2) for family maintenance and support of dependents of many of the incarcerated, (3) in lost taxes and consumer spending, which would stimulate the economy.

Strengths of Black Families

Most black families have retained the traditional ambitions for themselves and their children. In many of these families the five strengths described by Robert Hill remain supportive elements: strong kinship bonds, strong work orientation, flexibility of family roles,

Chart 8. Families, by Type and Race: 1960, 1970, and 1978

A comparison of white and black married couples indicates that both groups have decreasing numbers; however, the decline for blacks is much steeper and hence a resultant large increase in female heads of families

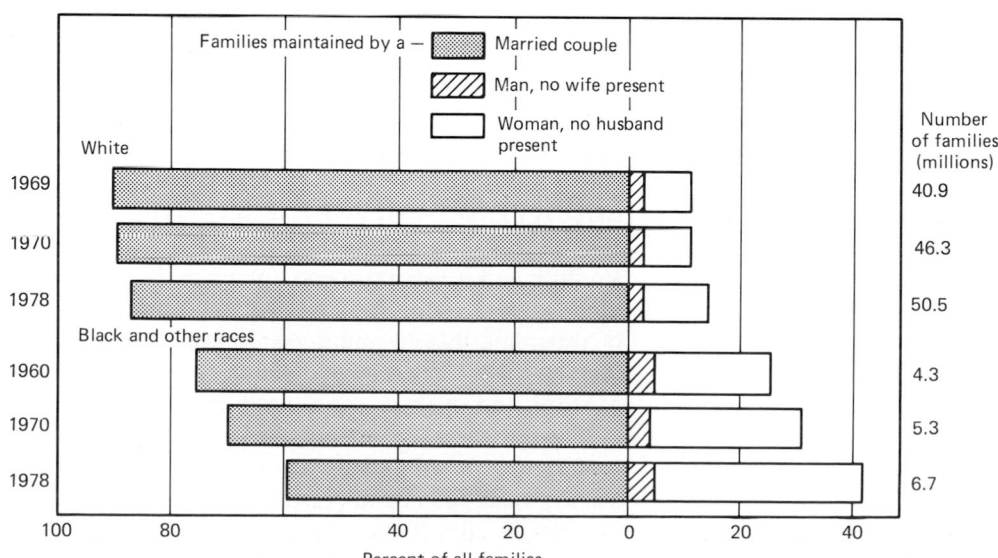

Source: U.S. Bureau of the Census, Social Indicators.

Chart 9. Living Arrangements of the Noninstitutional Population by Race: United States, 1980

In 1980 for both black and white married couples most had one child or none, indicating a steep decline in the number of children for married couples

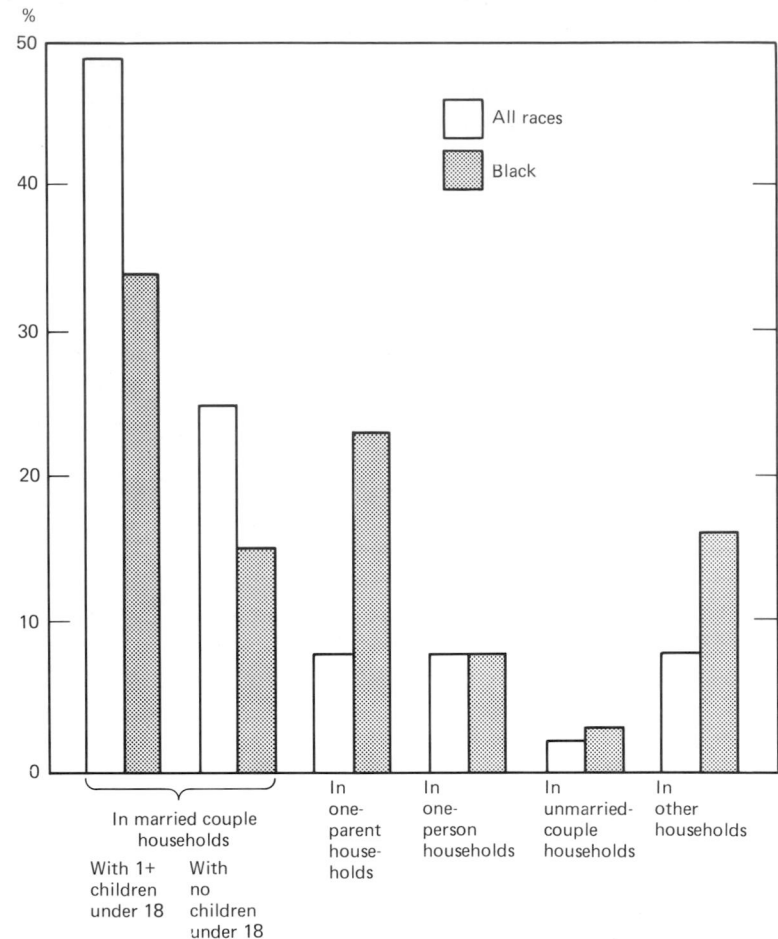

Source: Paul C. Glick, "A Demographic Picture of Black Families," in *Black Families* (Beverly Hills, Calif.: Sage Publications, 1981), p. 114.

strong achievement orientation, and strong religious orientation.

In spite of the forces of change, the extended family/kinship network remains a strong institutional support system for many blacks. Family members may not occupy the same household or live in the same community, but extended families in many cases still give financial assistance, emotional support, child care, assistance with home repairs and chores, clothing and furniture as well as automobiles to their members. This help through the kinship network makes it possible for some families to maintain stability through all the changes that affect them, and to provide opportunity for the young, as well as care for the old. Increasing numbers of black families are having annual or biennial reunions to enable linkages to remain strong. The kinship support pattern is essential for many families, es-

pecially as governmental policies that have harmful effects on the lives of black families persist.

BUDGET CUTS AND THE FAMILY—THE EIGHTIES

In 1981 and 1982, prospects for black families were dimmed by a series of budget cuts and proposed cuts of programs that over the years have provided poor families the wherewithal to obtain food, housing, medical care, and other essential products and services.

Though the administration promised to provide a "safety net" for the "truly needy" and that it would attack "weak claims rather than weak clients," millions of poor families have suffered. A substantial portion of these families have been black.

The services were affected two ways: through direct

Chart 10. Aid to dependent Families and Unemployment Rate: 1948–1979

Aid to dependent children has increased steadily since 1960 even when the unemployment rate drops, though the rise is greater during periods of recession. However, between 1975 and 1979 the AFDC rate rose a dramatic 62%. This figure appears to be related to the enormous increase in female heads of families; during that period of time there were some 5,000,000 divorces involving close to 2,300,000 children. This figure does not include separations or desertions

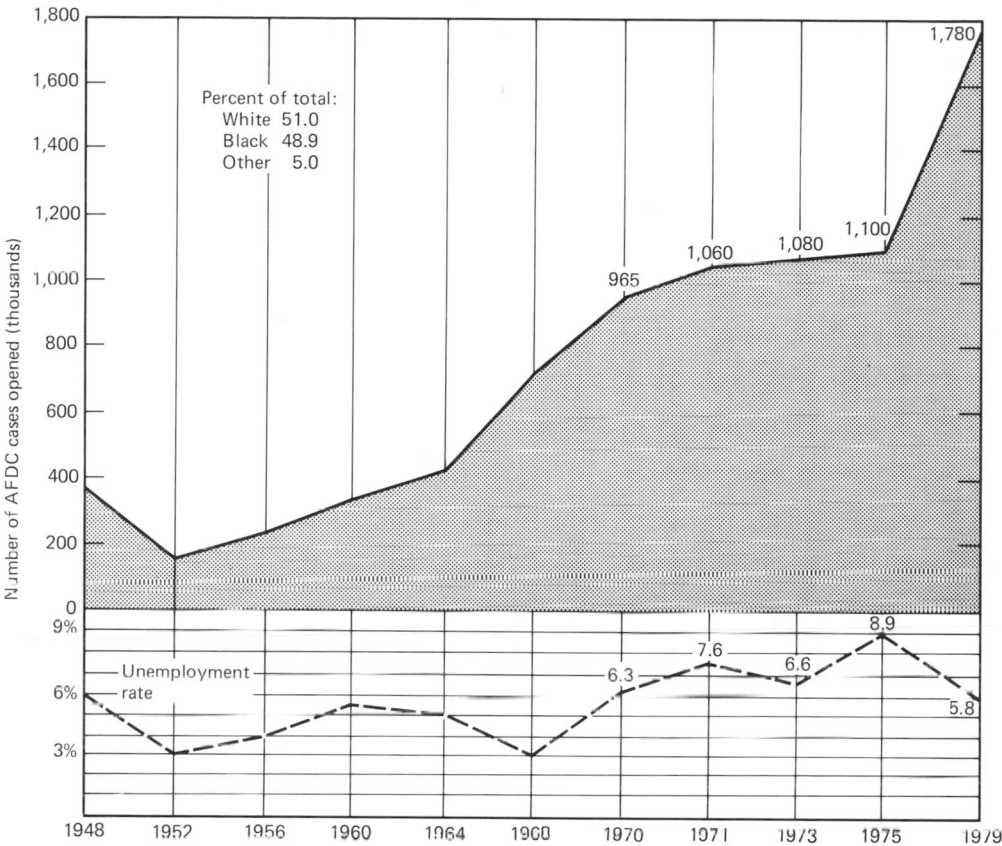

Source: Department of Labor, Bureau of Vital Statistics, Health and Human Services.

budget cuts and through allocation of much of the remaining funds via "block grants," which have weak provisions for the targeting, priorities, and accountability of appropriations.

Following are some of the cuts:

Medicaid
$1 billion cut from fiscal 1982, $2.1 billion proposed cut for fiscal 1983. Procedural cuts increase reductions about $900 billion further. Total reduction: $4 billion, or nearly 20%.

Aid to Families with Dependent Children
For 1982, budget cut $1 billion from $7 billion fiscal 1981 budget. Further cuts of $1.2 billion proposed for 1983. Proposals aim to eliminate many programs within AFDC, such as emergency assistance.

Food Stamps
$2.35 billion cut from 1982, $7 billion projected in cuts for the years 1982–1984. The Children's Defense Fund estimates 1 million people would become completely ineligible for stamps and that 80% of the savings from cuts would come from funds of people below the poverty line. Placing food stamps on block grants is likely to result in further reductions. In the past, many local governmental jurisdictions with the authority to reject fully paid food stamp programs have done so. (The government program calls for a swap, the federal government to take over Medicaid, the states AFDC and food stamps.)

Health Services
The 1982 budgets for a series of successful health programs were cut more than 25%. Among these were:

Community Health Centers, Migrant Health Centers, Family Planning, and several food, nutritional, and counseling programs for families and children. Forty community health centers had to close in 1981. The Reagan Administration proposed to abolish all these programs and replace them with block grants. In some cases, Congress rejected the government's requests, as with the Women's, Infants', and Children's supplemental food plan, but funds for 1982 were cut 10% and the government plans a 35% reduction for 1983, with monies to be distributed through block grants.

Among other health services cut:

School breakfast program, cut 20%, eliminating 400,000 children, 70% poor or near poor

School lunch, cut 30%, amounting to $1 billion

Child Care Food Program, also cut 30%, $130 million

Summer Food Program, cut 50%, with churches and religious organizations prohibited from participating

Special Milk Program, cut 80%

For 1983, further cuts were proposed for all but the school lunch program.

The Head Start Program survived relatively well but also was cut. The Reagan Administration at first accepted an increase proposed by Carter, from $820 million to $950 million, then cut back to $836 million. Current proposals call for $780 million appropriation, under block grants in 1983.

Title XX Day Care Services
(See employment section.)

Housing

Substantial rent increases and reductions in rent subsidies in government-subsidized housing for 1982, reduction of new subsidized units from 260,000 to 140,000 for 1982. Another 100,000-unit cut was proposed for 1983. All in all, public housing was to be cut 40%, Section 8 housing 31% for 1982. Budget authority for public housing was to be cut drastically, in 1982 from $17 billion to $6 billion. Some $9.9 billion in obligations for construction was to be cut in 1982.

Low-Income Energy Assistance

Appropriations were keyed at levels substantially below the Conference Report for the Windfall Profits Tax. As a result, appropriations in 1982 were off 40%, to $1.85 billion, and off 57% in 1982, to $1.75 billion.

DEATH AND ILLNESS CAUSED BY UNEMPLOYMENT

The high correlation between unemployment and indicators of stress has a more meaningful impact when translated to human terms. For example, Table 36 indicates that a 1% rise in unemployment will increase stroke, heart, and kidney disease deaths. How many people will actually be affected? This and similar calculations for the other six evaluated stress indicators are presented in Table 37.

In 1970 unemployment rose 1.4% to 4.9%. This 1.4% increase has been sustained since that time. A 1% sustained rise in unemployment increases CVR disease deaths by a total comparable to 1.9% of all such deaths in the fifth year thereafter. The 1.4% rise

Chart 11. Additional Deaths and Mental Hospitalizations Related to 1.4% Rise in Unemployment

A study by the Joint Economic Committee of Congress indicates that stress related to unemployment increases death and illness rates. The study indicates that some 51,570 deaths and mental hospitalizations were caused by a 1.4% increase in the unemployed population

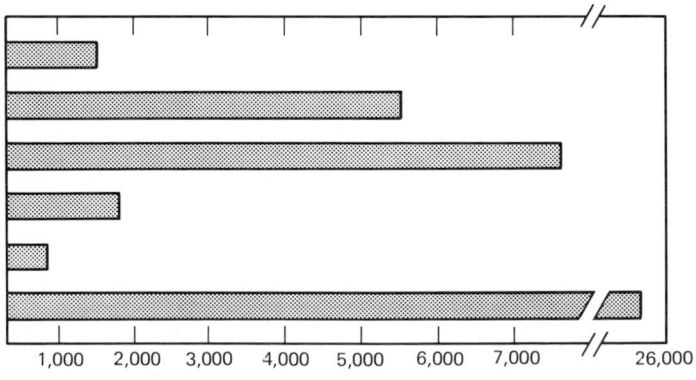

Source: Congress of the United States.

**Chart 12.   Life Expectancy at Ages 20 and 65, by Race and Sex:
1900–1977**

**The life expectancy of black males is approximately 11 years less
than white males; both groups' average life span has increased
proportionately since the 1930s. Life expectancy for black females
has risen very dramatically and has surpassed the expectancy rates
for white males by approximately 5 years**

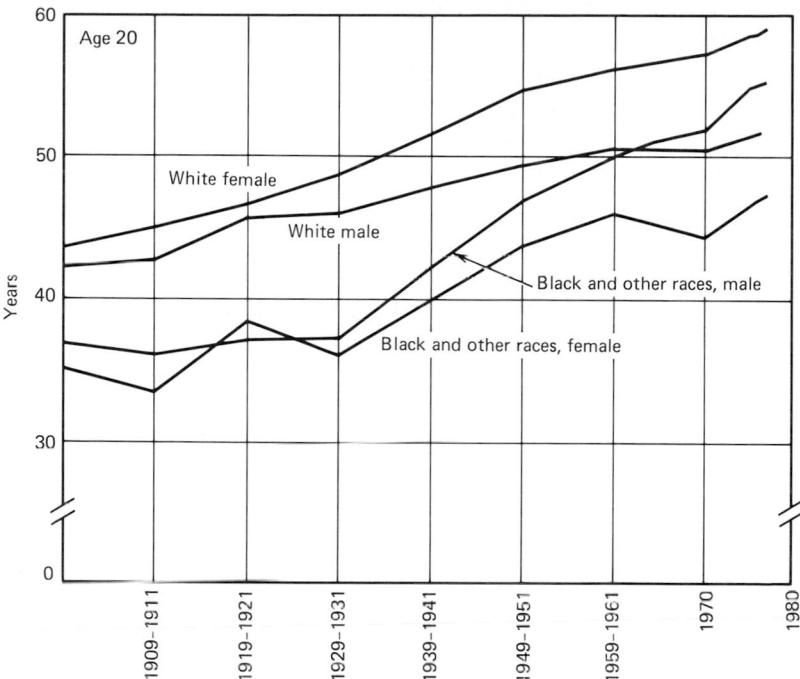

Source: U.S. Bureau of the Census, Social Indicators.

in unemployment during 1970 increased total CVR disease deaths through 1975 by 2.7% (1.9% times 1.4). There were 979,180 CVR disease deaths in 1975. Therefore, 2.7%, or 26,440 CVR deaths, are directly attributal to the rise in unemployment during 1970.

Table 37 shows, in fact, that the 1.4% rise in unemployment during 1970 is directly responsible for some 51,570 total deaths, including 1,740 additional homicides, for 1,540 additional suicides, and for 5,520 additional mental hospitalizations. These are not major portions of the total number of deaths, homicides, suicides, and mental hospitalizations which occurred during 1970 through 1975. But, unlike most other factors which contributed to these statistics, rising unemployment can be readily avoided.

It should be noted that the further increases in unemployment since 1970 are now having an additional impact on individuals and society—an impact which is not in any fashion included in statistics on Table 37. And this more recent rise in unemployment has been striking. From 1970 to 1976, almost 4 million additional men and women have been added to jobless rolls. By 1980 unemployment results in deaths and

institutional admissions were almost three times larger than presented in Table 37.

The low relative size of changes in these stress indicators due to unemployment fluctuations in Table 36 is not surprising. A bewildering variety of factors influence the mental and physical state of contemporary society—many of which are far more influential than jobless status alone. At the same time, this study reveals that unemployment has a strikingly potent impact on society. Even a 1% increase in unemployment, for example, creates a legacy of stress, aggression, and illness affecting society long into the future. This study reveals that it has a multiplier effect far exceeding the relative size of the unemployment rise.

The human tragedy alone of unemployment revealed by this study is shocking—shocking enough to demand a persistent, priority effort by Washington policy planners to reduce unemployment and to keep it low, as well. At the same time, we can go further and attach specific monetary values to the human toll portrayed in Table 37.

In instances of CVR disease, cirrhosis, suicide, homicide, and total mortality, appropriate dollar values include foregone incomes, adjusted for age and sex characteristics. In effect, illness and deaths attributed to unemployment reduce our Nation's resources—our ability to produce goods and services. And one good measure of this loss is the foregone income of deceased or ill workers. Direct medical costs for unemployment-related care should be included as well.

SELECTED FACTS ON THE BLACK FAMILY

Fact 1

The number of black families increased from 5.3 million in 1970 to 6.7 million in 1978, demonstrating that blacks do believe in the institution of family and maintain families of some type.

Fact 2

In 1980, 55.5% of all black families were maintained by a husband-wife couple. Forty percent of all black families in 1980 were headed by women alone, and 4.3% were headed by men alone. Of the 40% of black families headed by women, 28.9% were headed by the mother alone and 11.3% by a female householder other than the mother, usually a grandmother.

Fact 3

The gap between black families and white families with respect to intact marriages has persisted over time. In 1980, 82.5% of all non-black races maintained husband-wife families. Some 11.6% of white families were headed by women alone and 3% were headed by men alone.

Fact 4

Blacks have, since 1960, maintained a consistent pattern of postponing marriage longer than whites in the same age group. In the 20- to 24-year-old group the percentage of never-married black men was 56% in 1960, 57% in 1970, and 79% in 1980, as contrasted with 53% of white males in 1960, 56% in 1970, and 69% in 1980. In like manner, 36% of young black females had never married in 1960, 43% in 1970, and 69% in 1980, as contrasted with 29% of white females in 1960, 36% in 1970, and 50% in 1980.

Fact 5

In the age group 25 to 34 years old, blacks are more likely to be separated or divorced than are whites. In 1980, 13% of black men were separated or divorced, compared with 9% of white men. In this same age group, 28% of black women were separated or divorced, compared with 14% of their white female counterparts.

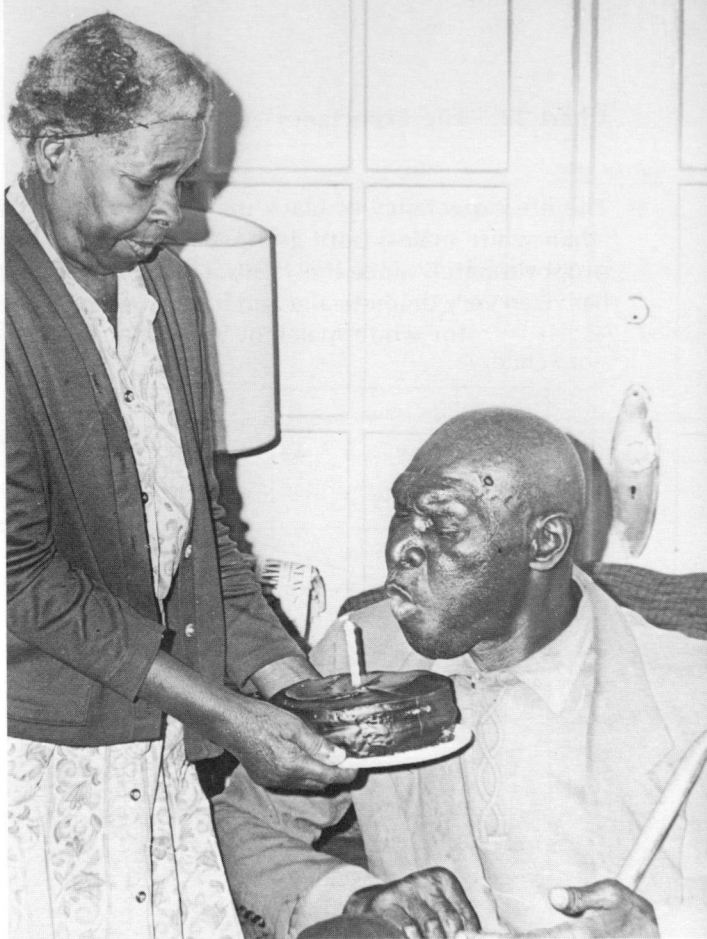

Many poor elderly people are not eligible for Social Security benefits.

Fact 6

In the age group 35–44 years old, 61% of black men were in intact marriages in 1980 as compared with 81% of white men. Only 49% of black women in this age group were in intact marriages, as compared with 84% of white women.

Fact 7

In the age group 55 years old and over, 14% of black men were widowed in 1980, as contrasted with 9% of whites in the same age bracket. Forty-five percent of black women in this age group were widowed, as compared with 37% of women of other races.

Fact 8

In 1980, black families were more likely than other families to include young children. Sixty-two percent of black families had children under 18 at home, whereas 52% of other families were similarly situated.

Fact 9

In 1978, 73% of black families included four persons or fewer, and about 27% included five persons or more. This is a reduction in family size from 1970, when families were larger; at that time 35.4% of them included five persons or more, and 64.5% included four or fewer persons.

Fact 10

In 1978, black wives aged 18–34 years expressed reduced expectations for lifetime births. Fifty-four percent expected to produce two or fewer children, as compared with 46% who expect to produce three or more children.

Fact 11

In 1979, 9% of black women aged 30–34 said they expected to have no children at all.

Fact 12

Highly educated black women tend to have fewer children. In 1979, black women aged 35–44 with less than eight years of schooling averaged 4.6 children, as compared with women with more than eight years schooling, who averaged 3.8 children.

Fact 13

In the 35–44 age group, black women with some college education had 2.4 children, whereas other college-educated women had 2.3 children. Lowest fertility rates of all were displayed by black women 30–39 years old with graduate school education. These black women had 1.9 children, compared with 2.2 children for other similarly educated women.

Fact 14

In 1979, 43.4% of all black children lived with both of their parents, 41.9% lived with their mothers only, 2.1% lived with their fathers only, and 11.3% lived with neither parent. This last group of children usually lived with grandparent(s) or other relative(s). Thus fewer than half of black children lived with both of their parents in 1979, and it seems safe to assume that 53.2% of all black children were being cared for by women alone.

Fact 15

In 1979, only 29% of all black women who had been awarded sole custody of their children were awarded child support payments, as compared with 59% of their counterparts in other races. Only 62.5% of these black women actually received the payments as compared with 75% of all other such women.

Fact 16

In 1979, 14% of women of all races were awarded alimony in connection with divorce proceedings, but only 7% of black women were awarded alimony. Regardless of race, about 7 of every 10 women who were awarded alimony actually received it.

Fact 17

Infant mortality rates have declined from 44.5 deaths per 1,000 live births in 1950 to 21.7 deaths per 1,000 live births in 1977. However, in spite of this decline, the infant mortality rate of black and other races was 1.8 times higher than that of white babies in 1977.

Fact 18

Chances for a long and healthy life are not shared equally by males and females or by blacks and whites. Despite improved life expectancy figures, women generally outlive men and white women can be expected to live longest of all.

Fact 19

Census data show that 19.7 million people below the poverty level in 1980 were white, and 8.6 million were black. The poverty level was $8,414 for a non-farm family of four in 1980.

Fact 20

In 1980, about 8% of white families had incomes below the poverty level, compared with about 19% of all black families and 23% for Spanish-origin families.

Fact 21

In 1980, almost 9.1 million families were maintained by women with no husband present. Thirty-three percent, or 3 million of these families, were below the poverty level, and about half of black and Spanish-origin families maintained by women were below the poverty level.

Fact 22

Central cities had a higher poverty rate in 1980 than did metropolitan areas. The rate was 17.2% for central cities and 11.9% for metropolitan areas. Of all whites in central cities, 12.1%, or 5.4 million, were below the poverty level, but 32.3% of all blacks in central cities were below the poverty level.

Fact 23

In 1980, median income for all black families was only 58% of the median for white families, while Spanish-origin families received 67% of the median for white families.

Fact 24

Median family income was $21,900 for whites in 1980, while that for black families was $12,670, and for Spanish-origin families it was $14,720.

Fact 25

In 1979, 10% of all black families were able to provide for themselves a "higher" standard of living, $30,317

The Restoration Corporation has attempted to create a new inner city urban living environment with their "superblock" in New York City, an award-winning playscaped street. However, such projects are rare.

for a family of four. Some 26% of black families were at the "intermediate" standard, $20,517 for a family of four, usually with multiple earners. Forty-six percent of black families were at the "lower" living standard, with incomes of $12,585.

Fact 26
It costs from $60,000 to $110,000 per child to rear to adulthood in the United States. Any black family seeking to provide the best opportunities for its children will spend at the upper end of this range for each child.

Fact 27
According to the Census Bureau, between 40 and 50% of all black and Spanish-origin households with school-age children received free or reduced-price school lunches in 1980. The school lunch program was, therefore, one of four major non-cash federal programs to assist low-income households. Current public policies are reducing free school lunches to children and will therefore be harmful to low-income households.

Fact 28
Food stamp recipients increased in 1980 among white households, from 3.8 million to 4.2 million, or 12%. Among black households the corresponding figures were 2.4 million in 1980, compared with 2.1 million in 1979, an increase of 11%.

Fact 29
About 8% of all U.S. households received food stamps in 1980, some 6.8 million. Sixty-five percent of these had incomes below the poverty level.

Fact 30
In 1980, 28% of all black households were covered by Medicaid, and 58% of those were below the poverty level.

Fact 31
Black households living in public or other subsidized housing rose from 1.0 million in 1979 to 1.1 million in 1980. White households rose from 1.5 to 1.6 million in 1980. About 25% of black households that were renters lived in publicly owned or subsidized housing.

Fact 32

Many middle-income blacks are priced out of home-buying options because of high interest rates and inflated housing prices. Discrimination remains a problem in some areas where blacks seek to purchase homes.

Fact 33

In 1975, the black home ownership rate was 44%, compared with 42% in 1970 and 38% in 1960.

Fact 34

Older blacks suffer disproportionately from hypertension, heart disease, and arthritis. Obesity is a continuing problem, especially among black females.

Fact 35

In 1980, 50% of black households had one or more members covered by a work-related group health insurance plan, whereas 60% of white households were so covered.

Fact 36

Sickled red blood cells have been found in 1 of every 12 American blacks, but the active disease, sickle cell anemia, occurs about once in 600 American blacks and once in every 1,200 American whites.

Fact 37

In separate reports the Census Bureau joined with the U.S. Department of Agriculture, and the U.S. Civil Rights Commission agreed that black family farmers are a declining group. The Census Bureau/Department of Agriculture report explained that the number of black farm residents declined 550,000, or 65%, between 1970 and 1980, while in the same period white farm residents declined only 22%.

Fact 38

The U.S. Civil Rights Commission fears that black family farmers could disappear almost entirely by the year 2000. Since most of the black family farms are in the South, it seems possible that Southern patterns of discrimination continue into 1982.

Table 1. Selected Characteristics of Families: 1960, 1970, and 1978

Selected Characteristics	1960			1970			1978		
	Total	White	Black and Other Races	Total	White	Black and Other Races	Total	White	Black and Other Races
All families (thousands)	45,149	40,887	4,262	51,586	46,261	5,325	57,215	50,530	6,685
Percent	100.0	100.0	100.0	100.0	100.0	100.0	100.0	100.0	100.0
Families maintained by a:									
Married couple	87.8	89.2	74.9	86.8	88.7	69.6	82.8	85.9	59.3
Man, no wife present	2.9	2.7	4.2	2.4	2.3	3.6	2.8	2.5	4.7
Woman, no husband present	9.3	8.1	20.9	10.8	9.0	26.8	14.4	11.5	36.0
Single, never married	1.1	1.0	2.3	1.2	.8	4.3	2.2	1.2	9.9
Widowed	4.6	4.2	8.4	4.6	4.2	8.2	4.2	3.7	7.7
Divorced	1.6	1.5	2.4	2.4	2.3	3.8	4.9	4.5	8.0
Married, husband absent	2.0	1.4	7.8	2.6	1.7	10.5	3.1	2.2	10.4
Own Children under 18 Years Old									
None under 18	43.1	43.0	43.8	44.1	44.8	38.6	46.9	48.2	37.2
1 child	18.4	18.7	15.6	18.2	18.2	18.1	20.3	19.9	23.3
2 children	18.0	18.5	12.8	17.4	17.7	14.9	19.0	18.9	19.1
3 or more children	20.5	19.7	27.9	20.2	19.3	28.4	13.8	12.9	20.3
Mean number per family	1.33	1.29	1.66	1.27	1.23	1.66	1.04	1.00	1.34
Size of Family									
2 persons	32.7	33.1	28.5	34.6	35.3	28.4	38.5	39.6	29.9
3 persons	21.6	21.9	19.1	20.8	20.9	20.0	22.1	21.9	23.2
4 persons	19.9	20.4	15.0	19.3	19.6	16.1	20.6	20.7	19.9
5 persons	12.8	12.9	11.6	12.5	12.6	11.9	11.0	10.7	12.5
6 or more persons	13.0	11.7	25.7	12.8	11.6	23.5	7.9	7.0	14.4

Source: U.S. Department of Commerce, Bureau of the Census, *1960 Census of Population,* PC(2)-4A, and unpublished 1970 and 1978 data.

Note: Detail may not add to totals shown because of rounding.

Table 2. Distribution of Families, by Type: 1975 (revised), and 1976 to 1978

Type of Family	1975 (revised)	1976	1977	1978
Black				
All families (thousands)	5,491	5,586	5,804	5,806
Percent	100.0	100.0	100.0	100.0
Husband-wife	61.1	60.0	58.7	56.1
Male head, no wife present	3.6	4.1	4.2	4.6
Female head, no husband present	35.2	35.9	37.1	39.2
White				
All families (thousands)	49,440	49,873	50,083	50,530
Percent	100.0	100.0	100.0	100.0
Husband-wife	87.1	86.8	86.7	85.9
Male head, no wife present	2.9	2.4	2.4	2.5
Female head, no husband present	10.5	10.8	10.9	11.5

Source: U.S. Department of Commerce, Bureau of the Census, *The Social and Economic Status of the Black Population in the United States: An Historical View,* Series P-23, No. 80, June 1979, p. 175.

Table 3. Marital Status of Families Maintained by Women: 1975 (revised), 1976, and 1977 (numbers in thousands)

Marital Status	1975 (revised)	1976	1977	Percent Distribution 1975 (revised)	1976	1977
Black						
Total, female head, no husband present	1,934	2,004	2,151	100	100	100
With disrupted marriage	979	989	1,097	51	49	51
Separated	607	602	638	31	30	30
Divorced	372	387	459	19	19	21
Other	955	1,015	1,055	49	51	49
Single (never married)	419	461	486	22	23	23
Widowed	466	480	502	24	24	23
Husband temporarily absent	70	74	67	4	4	3
Armed Forces	18	10	18	1	—	1
Other reasons	52	64	49	3	3	2
White						
Total, female head, no husband present	5,208	5,380	5,467	100	100	100
With disrupted marriage	2,490	2,766	2,870	48	51	52
Separated	777	820	792	15	15	14
Divorced	1,713	1,946	2,078	33	36	38
Other	2,718	2,614	2,595	52	49	47
Single (never married)	486	492	530	9	9	10
Widowed	2,019	1,876	1,850	39	35	34
Husband temporarily absent	213	246	215	4	5	4
Armed Forces	49	28	25	1	1	—
Other reasons	164	218	190	3	4	3

Source: U.S. Department of Commerce, Bureau of the Census, *The Social and Economic Status of the Black Population in the United States: An Historical View,* Series P-23, No. 80, June 1979, p. 176.

Table 4. Selected Characteristics of Families Maintained by Women: 1975 (revised), 1976, and 1977

Selected Characteristic	Black			White		
	1975 (revised)	1976	1977	1975 (revised)	1976	1977
Age						
Total, female head, no husband present (thousands)	1,934	2,004	2,151	5,208	5,380	5,467
Percent	100	100	100	100	100	100
14 to 34 years	42	43	42	29	30	29
35 to 64 years	48	47	48	54	53	54
65 years and over	10	10	10	17	17	17
Presence of Own Children under 18 years						
Total, female head, no husband present (thousands)	1,934	2,004	2,151	5,208	5,380	5,467
Percent	100	100	100	100	100	100
With own children	71	72	72	57	58	58
With no own children	29	28	28	43	42	42
With own children (thousands)	1,378	1,435	1,539	2,972	3,135	3,181
Percent with 2 or more children	67	64	66	56	56	55
Number of Own Children under 18 Years						
Total, in families with female head, no husband present (thousands)	3,336	3,426	3,419	5,735	5,871	5,862
Percent of all children in families	41	42	43	11	11	11

Source: U.S. Department of Commerce, Bureau of the Census, *The Social and Economic Status of the Black Population in the United States: An Historical View,* Series P-23, No. 80, June 1979, p. 177.

Table 5. Marital Status of the Black Population: 1960–1979[a]

Sex and Year	Number of Persons (thousands)					Percent Distribution				
	Total	Single	Married	Widowed	Divorced	Total	Single	Married	Widowed	Divorced
Total										
1960	12,088	3,078	7,461	1,174	376	100.0	25.5	61.7	9.7	3.1
1965	13,273	3,601	7,996	1,194	482	100.0	27.1	60.2	9.0	3.6
1970	12,972	2,668	8,310	1,427	567	100.0	20.6	64.1	11.0	4.4
1975	14,262	3,449	8,373	1,521	920	100.0	24.2	58.7	10.7	6.5
1976	14,668	3,743	8,458	1,452	1,017	100.0	25.5	57.7	9.9	6.9
1977	15,076	4,002	8,476	1,497	1,101	100.0	26.5	56.2	9.9	7.3
1978	15,414	4,434	8,255	1,451	1,273	100.0	28.8	53.6	9.4	8.3
1979	15,728	4,673	8,175	1,597	1,283	100.0	29.7	52.0	10.2	8.2
Male										
1960	5,713	1,692	3,619	264	139	100.0	29.6	63.3	4.6	2.4
1965	6,211	1,980	3,795	245	191	100.0	31.9	61.1	3.9	3.1
1970	5,898	1,435	3,944	307	212	100.0	24.3	66.9	5.2	3.6
1975	6,368	1,733	3,990	319	327	100.0	27.2	62.7	5.0	5.1
1976	6,560	1,861	4,042	271	386	100.0	28.4	61.6	4.1	5.9
1977	6,756	2,039	4,024	327	367	100.0	30.2	59.6	4.8	5.4
1978	6,894	2,160	3,970	285	478	100.0	31.3	57.6	4.1	6.9
1979	6,987	2,283	3,893	310	501	100.0	32.7	55.7	4.4	7.2
Female										
1960	6,375	1,386	3,842	910	237	100.0	21.7	60.3	14.3	3.7
1965	7,062	1,621	4,201	949	291	100.0	23.0	59.5	13.4	4.1
1970	7,074	1,233	4,366	1,120	355	100.0	17.4	61.7	15.8	5.0
1975	7,894	1,716	4,383	1,202	593	100.0	21.7	55.5	15.2	7.5
1976	8,108	1,882	4,416	1,181	631	100.0	23.2	54.5	14.6	7.8
1977	8,320	1,963	4,452	1,170	734	100.0	23.6	53.5	14.1	8.8
1978	8,520	2,274	4,285	1,166	795	100.0	26.7	50.3	13.7	9.3
1979	8,741	2,390	4,282	1,287	782	100.0	27.3	49.0	14.7	8.9

Source: U.S. Bureau of the Census, *Statistical Abstract of the United States: 1980,* 101st ed. (Washington, D.C.: U.S. Government Printing Office, December 1980), p. 42.

[a] 1960 and 1965, persons 14 years old and over; thereafter, 18 and over. 1960 as of April, based on 25% sample; other years, as of March, and based on Current Population Survey.

Table 6. Marital History—Percent Distribution, by Sex, Race, and Year of Birth: 1975 (as of June)

Item	Persons Born, 1900–1959 Total	White	Black	Year of Birth 1945–1954	1935–1944	1925–1934	1915–1924	1900–1914
Men, total	100.0	100.0	100.0	100.0	100.0	100.0	100.0	100.0
Single in 1975	26.1	25.2	33.3	38.0	8.3	5.1	5.3	4.9
Ever married in 1975	73.8	74.8	66.7	62.0	91.7	94.9	94.7	95.1
Once	62.5	63.7	53.2	57.8	78.3	79.6	77.5	73.9
Twice or more	11.3	11.1	13.5	4.2	13.4	15.3	17.2	21.2
Ever divorced, total	12.0	11.8	14.3	7.0	16.9	17.4	17.2	14.9
Ever widowed	3.4	3.3	5.1	.2	.7	2.0	5.2	15.3
Women, total	100.0	100.0	100.0	100.0	100.0	100.0	100.0	100.0
Single in 1975	20.6	19.5	29.0	25.8	5.8	4.2	4.5	6.3
Ever married in 1975	79.4	80.5	71.0	74.2	94.2	95.9	95.5	93.6
Once	67.0	68.1	57.7	67.8	79.8	78.8	77.6	73.9
Twice or more	12.4	12.4	13.3	6.4	14.4	17.1	17.9	19.7
Ever divorced, total	13.9	13.6	16.1	10.8	19.5	20.2	17.0	14.3
Ever widowed	11.1	10.9	31.1	.7	2.7	7.7	17.6	41.2

Source: U.S. Bureau of the Census, *Statistical Abstract of the United States: 1980,* 101st ed. (Washington, D.C.: U.S. Government Printing Office, December 1980), p. 84.

Table 7. Marital Status of the Population 14 Years Old and Over, by Sex, Selected Years: 1950–1978

Marital Status	Male 1950	1960	1970	1978	Female 1950	1960	1970	1978
Total population, 14 years old and over (thousands)	54,762	60,582	70,559	79,863	56,970	64,875	77,766	87,399
Percent	100.0	100.0	100.0	100.0	100.0	100.0	100.0	100.0
Unstandardized								
Single	26.2	25.3	28.1	30.6	19.6	19.0	22.1	23.9
Married	68.0	69.1	66.7	62.8	66.1	65.6	61.9	58.5
Widowed	4.2	3.7	2.9	2.3	12.2	12.8	12.5	11.6
Divorced	1.7	1.9	2.2	4.2	2.2	2.6	3.5	6.0
Standardized[a]								
Single	26.2	25.3	23.9	26.0	20.0	19.0	19.3	20.8
Married	67.4	69.1	70.8	67.0	63.9	65.6	64.9	61.5
Widowed	4.7	3.7	3.0	2.5	14.0	12.8	12.0	11.1
Divorced	1.7	1.9	2.4	4.5	2.1	2.6	3.8	6.5

Source: U.S. Bureau of the Census, *Social Indicators,* Vol. III, p. 50.

Note: Detail may not add to totals shown because of rounding.

[a] Standardized on the basis of the age distribution in 1960.

Table 8. Divorced Persons, by Race, Sex, and Age, Selected Years: 1950–1978 [a]

Race and Year	Male Total, All Ages	Male Under 30 Years Old	Male 30 to 44 Years Old	Male 45 to 64 Years Old	Male 65 Years Old and Over	Female Total, All Ages	Female Under 30 Years Old	Female 30 to 44 Years Old	Female 45 to 64 Years Old	Female 65 Years Old and Over
All Races										
1950	31	25	29	35	30	39	29	42	44	34
1960	28	16	24	38	23	42	29	41	53	43
1970	35	29	34	39	35	60	45	62	66	68
1978	71	82	81	68	39	110	98	136	100	87
White										
1950	30	25	28	33	30	37	28	40	43	33
1960	27	15	23	36	23	38	25	36	49	42
1970	32	27	29	37	35	56	43	57	63	65
1978	65	79	76	63	33	100	93	123	89	81
Black and Other Races										
1950	34	27	37	38	26	53	42	62	56	42
1960	37	17	28	63	19	89	64	97	103	60
1970	60	37	79	62	29	96	59	108	112	113
1978	127	117	130	134	115	213	150	252	230	174

Source: U.S. Department of Commerce, Bureau of the Census, *1950 Census of Population,* Vol. II; *Current Population Reports,* series P-20, nos. 105, 212, and 287; and unpublished 1978 data.

[a] Rate per 1,000 married persons with spouse present.

Table 9. Divorce Decrees Involving Children, by Number of Children Involved: 1960–1976

Year	Number of Divorce Decrees	Number of Children Involved (%) Total	None	1	2	3	4 or More	Not Stated
1960	94,074	100.0	34.5	22.3	16.3	8.0	5.3	13.5
1961	125,128	100.0	35.7	22.6	16.7	8.4	6.7	9.9
1962	147,106	100.0	36.8	21.6	17.5	9.4	7.3	7.4
1963	152,594	100.0	35.1	21.8	17.0	9.7	7.6	8.7
1964	160,987	100.0	33.8	21.8	16.8	10.1	8.0	9.7
1965	164,942	100.0	37.9	21.9	17.0	9.6	7.9	5.7
1966	173,562	100.0	37.9	21.8	17.4	9.9	8.4	4.4
1967	186,628	100.0	37.2	22.2	17.6	9.9	8.5	4.7
1968	315,957	100.0	36.1	21.4	17.3	9.6	8.2	7.4
1969	378,095	100.0	37.3	22.3	17.6	9.6	8.0	5.3
1970	429,498	100.0	38.3	23.5	17.8	9.1	6.7	4.5
1971	466,019	100.0	38.4	23.8	17.9	9.0	6.6	4.4
1972	496,437	100.0	38.3	24.5	18.1	8.7	6.3	4.1
1973	537,943	100.0	38.7	24.4	18.1	8.6	5.7	4.6
1974	571,794	100.0	40.2	24.5	18.0	8.0	5.2	4.1
1975	625,676	100.0	41.1	24.5	18.1	7.7	4.5	4.1
1976	656,535	100.0	42.9	24.5	18.3	7.2	3.9	3.2

Source: U.S. Bureau of the Census, *Social Indicators,* Vol. III, p. 52.

Note: Detail may not add to totals shown because of rounding.

Table 10. Children Under 18 Years Old in Families, by Presence of Parents and Race of Children: 1960, 1970, and 1978

Presence of parents	1960 Total	1960 White	1960 Black [a]	1970 Total	1970 White	1970 Black	1978 Total	1978 White	1978 Black
All children under 18 years old in families (thousands)	62,873	54,492	8,381	68,681	58,506	9,267	62,767	52,261	9,236
Percent	100.0	100.0	100.0	100.0	100.0	100.0	100.0	100.0	100.0
Living with both parents	88.9	91.9	69.2	84.1	88.1	58.7	78.3	84.2	44.3
Living with mother only	8.1	6.2	20.6	11.6	8.6	30.8	17.1	12.6	43.1
Living with father only	1.2	1.0	2.1	1.9	1.8	3.0	1.6	1.5	2.1
All other [b]	1.8	.8	8.2	2.4	1.5	7.5	3.1	1.7	10.5

Source: U.S. Bureau of the Census, *Social Indicators,* Vol. III, p. 50.

Note: Detail may not add to totals shown because of rounding.

[a] Data for 1960 are for blacks and other races. This slightly inflates the proportion of children living with both parents and deflates the share living with the mother only relative to what the distribution would have been if only blacks had been considered.

[b] Children under 18 living with friends, neighbors, or relatives other than parents, or as adopted or foster children.

Table 11. Households and Families, by Type of Householder: 1960–1979 [a]

Type of Householder	Number (thousands) 1960	1965	1970	1975	1979	Percent 1960	1965	1970	1975	1979
Households, total	52,799	57,251	62,874	71,120	77,330					
White	47,665	51,441	56,248	62,945	68,028	100.0	100.0	100.0	100.0	100.0
Married couple	36,175	38,132	40,781	42,951	43,613	76.2	74.1	72.5	68.2	64.1
Male householder [b]	3,365	3,839	4,367	6,295	8,252	6.8	7.5	7.8	10.0	12.1
Female householder [b]	8,125	9,470	11,099	13,700	16,163	17.0	18.4	19.7	21.8	23.8
Black and other	5,134	5,808	6,626	8,175	9,302	100.0	100.0	100.0	100.0	100.0
Married couple	3,079	3,455	3,627	4,000	4,049	60.3	59.5	54.7	48.9	43.5
Male householder [b]	579	599	813	1,103	1,428	11.0	10.3	12.3	13.5	15.4
Female householder [b]	1,476	1,754	2,187	3,073	3,824	28.7	30.2	33.0	37.6	41.1
Families, total	45,111	47,836	51,237	55,712	57,804					
White	40,869	43,081	46,022	49,451	50,910	100.0	100.0	100.0	100.0	100.0
Married couple	36,212	38,171	40,802	42,969	43,636	88.7	88.6	88.7	86.9	85.7
Male householder [b]	1,100	1,028	1,036	1,270	1,355	2.6	2.4	2.3	2.6	2.7
Female householder [b]	3,557	3,882	4,185	5,212	5,918	8.7	9.0	9.1	10.5	11.6
Black and other	4,242	4,752	5,215	6,262	6,894	100.0	100.0	100.0	100.0	100.0
Married couple	3,117	3,474	3,634	4,002	4,056	73.6	73.1	69.7	63.9	58.8
Male householder [b]	175	153	185	230	300	4.0	3.2	3.5	3.7	4.4
Female householder [b]	950	1,125	1,395	2,030	2,540	22.4	23.7	26.7	32.4	36.6

Source: U.S. Bureau of the Census, *Statistical Abstract of the United States: 1980 (101st ed.)*

[a] As of March. Based on Current Population Survey; see also *Historical Statistics, Colonial Times to 1970,* series A 292–295 and A 320–334.

[b] No spouse present.

Table 12. Percent Distribution of Families, by Number of Own Children Under 18 Years Old: 1950–1979[a]

Number of Children	1950	1955	1960	1965	1970	1975	1976	1977	1978	1979
All families (thousands)	38,453	41,951	45,147	47,956	51,586	55,712	56,245	56,710	57,215	57,804
Percent distribution	100.0	100.0	100.0	100.0	100.0	100.0	100.0	100.0	100.0	100.0
No children	48.4	44.7	43.1	43.4	44.1	46.0	46.3	46.8	46.9	47.5
1 child	21.0	19.1	18.4	17.7	18.2	19.7	19.7	19.6	20.3	20.6
2 children	16.5	18.7	18.0	16.8	17.4	18.0	18.3	18.9	19.0	19.0
3 children	}4.2	{9.9	}20.5	{11.0	10.6	9.3	9.3	9.0	8.8	8.5
4 or more children		}7.6		{11.1	9.8	6.9	6.3	5.7	5.0	4.5
Black families (thousands)	3,432[b]	(NA)[c]	4,262[b]	(NA)	4,887	5,498	5,586	5,804	5,806	5,906
Percent distribution	100.0	(NA)	100.0	(NA)	100.0	100.0	100.0	100.0	100.0	100.0
No children	51.7	(NA)	43.8	(NA)	38.9	36.8	37.8	38.2	37.3	37.5
1 child	16.6	(NA)	15.6	(NA)	17.6	22.0	22.3	21.5	23.3	23.5
2 children	11.4	(NA)	12.8	(NA)	14.8	17.0	16.5	17.6	18.6	19.5
3 children	}20.3	{(NA)	}27.9	{(NA)	10.1	10.6	10.9	11.2	10.9	10.8
4 or more children		{(NA)		{(NA)	18.5	13.6	12.4	11.5	9.9	8.8

Source: U.S. Bureau of the Census, *Statistical Abstract of the United States: 1980 (101st ed.)*

[a] As of March, except 1955 as of April. Prior to 1960, excludes Alaska and Hawaii. Based on Current Population Survey; see also *Historical statistics, Colonial Times to 1970,* series A 353–358.

[b] Black and other races.

[c] NA = not available.

Table 13. Mothers with Children under 18 Years Old, by Work Experience, Poverty Status, and Race: 1978[a]

Work Experience	All Races[b]			White			Black		
	Total (thousands)	Below Poverty Level Number (thousands)	Percent	Total (thousands)	Below Poverty Level Number (thousands)	Percent	Total (thousands)	Below Poverty Level Number (thousands)	Percent
All women with own children	30,493	3,827	12.6	26,112	2,411	9.2	3,740	1,307	35.0
Worked in 1978	18,964	1,592	8.4	16,135	1,011	6.3	2,431	538	22.1
50–52 weeks	9,459	353	3.7	7,850	204	2.6	1,386	137	9.9
27–49 weeks	4,341	340	7.8	3,784	215	5.7	489	123	25.2
1–26 weeks	5,163	899	17.4	4,501	593	13.2	556	277	49.8
Did not work in 1978	11,529	2,235	19.4	9,976	1,400	14.0	1,309	769	58.8
Main reason: Keeping house	10,246	1,699	16.6	9,154	1,165	12.7	887	485	54.6
Families and subfamilies headed by women with own children	5,719	2,372	41.5	3,792	1,249	32.9	1,822	1,078	59.2
Worked in 1978	3,924	1,024	26.1	2,769	556	20.1	1,085	448	41.3
50–52 weeks	2,254	209	9.3	1,617	87	5.4	597	117	19.6
27–49 weeks	808	239	29.6	581	130	22.4	216	108	50.0
1–26 weeks	863	576	66.7	571	338	59.2	273	223	81.7
Did not work in 1978	1,795	1,348	75.1	1,023	694	67.8	737	630	85.5
Main reason: Keeping house	1,225	928	75.8	770	533	69.2	430	377	87.6

Source: U.S. Bureau of the Census, *Statistical Abstract of the United States, 1980.*

[a] As of March of the following year.

[b] Includes races not shown separately.

Table 14. Selected Measures of Family Income, by Type of Family and Labor Force Status of Wife: 1977

Type of Family	Median Income			Index of Income Overlap[a]
	Black	White	Ratio: Black to White	
All families	$ 9,563	$16,740	0.57	0.71
Male head[b]	13,443	17,848	0.75	0.82
Married, wife present	13,716	17,916	0.77	0.83
Wife in paid labor force	17,008	20,518	0.83	0.85
Wife not in paid labor force	9,697	15,389	0.63	0.73
Female head, no husband present	5,598	8,799	0.64	0.75

Source: U.S. Department of Commerce, Bureau of the Census, *The Social and Economic Status of the Black Population in the United States: An Historical View,* Series P-23, No. 80, June 1979.

[a] The Index of Income Overlap of White and Black is a statistical measure which summarizes the degree of overlap between the distributions and is equal to 1.00 when the two distributions are identical. Specifically, the index, which was computed on the basis of detailed income intervals, measures the sum of the commonalities expressed in terms of percents shared between whites and blacks for each income class interval. For a more detailed explanation of Index of Income Overlap, see Bureau of the Census, Technical Paper No. 22, "Measures of Overlap of Income Distribution of White and Black Families in the United States."

[b] Includes heads with wife present or without wife present.

Table 15.   Income of Families and Persons, by Selected Characteristics: 1976 and 1977[a]

Selected Characteristics	Black 1976	Black 1977	White 1976	White 1977
Income of Families				
Distribution by Income Level				
All families (thousands)	5,804	5,806	50,083	50,530
Percent	100	100	100	100
Under $3,000	9	10	3	3
$3,000 to $4,999	15	14	5	5
$5,000 to $6,999	12	13	7	7
$7,000 to $9,999	15	15	11	10
$10,000 to $11,999	8	8	7	7
$12,000 to $14,999	11	10	11	11
$15,000 to $24,999	22	21	34	33
$25,000 and over	8	9	22	24
Median income	$ 9,838	$ 9,563	$16,539	$16,740
Median Income by Region				
United States	$ 9,838	$ 9,563	$16,539	$16,740
South	9,076	8,962	15,343	15,721
North and West	10,846	10,403	17,019	17,200
Northeast	10,355	10,285	16,846	17,302
North Central	11,585	10,690	17,389	17,231
West	10,489	9,917	16,757	16,985
Persons with Income				
Total men, 14 years old and over (thousands)	6,651	6,777	64,946	65,974
Median income	$ 6,369	$ 6,292	$10,578	$10,603
Year-round full-time workers (thousands)	2,953	3,082	34,681	35,591
Median income	$10,881	$10,602	$15,193	$15,378
Total women, 14 years old and over (thousands)	7,188	7,562	55,026	56,813
Median income	$ 3,617	$ 3,455	$ 3,839	$ 4,001
Year-round full-time workers (thousands)	2,138	2,296	15,669	16,610
Median income	$ 8,336	$ 8,290	$ 8,916	$ 8,870

Source: U.S. Department of Commerce, Bureau of the Census, *The Social and Economic Status of the Black Population in the United States: An Historical View.*

[a] Adjusted for price changes in 1977 dollars. Families and persons as of the following year.

Table 16. Earners per Family, by Race: 1967–1978[a]

Race and Number of Earners	1967	1968	1969	1970	1971	1972	1973	1974	1974[b]	1975	1976	1977	1978
White													
Number (thousands)	44,814	45,437	46,022	46,535	47,641	48,477	48,919	49,451	48,595	49,161	49,378	49,898	50,312
Percent	100.0	100.0	100.0	100.0	100.0	100.0	100.0	100.0	100.0	100.0	100.0	100.0	100.0
No earners	8.2	8.0	8.3	8.7	9.1	9.3	10.0	10.5	10.7	11.7	11.8	11.9	11.8
1 earner	39.5	38.8	38.2	37.4	38.1	37.5	35.6	35.1	34.6	35.1	33.6	32.8	31.7
2 earners or more	52.3	53.1	53.5	53.8	52.9	53.2	54.4	54.3	54.7	53.1	54.7	55.3	56.5
2 earners	38.4	39.0	39.0	39.3	38.8	39.4	40.2	39.8	39.9	38.9	39.9	40.3	41.6
3 earners	10.0	10.0	10.1	10.1	9.9	9.6	9.5	9.6	9.8	9.8	9.5	10.0	9.7
4 earners or more	3.9	4.1	4.4	4.4	4.2	.2	4.7	4.9	5.0	4.4	5.3	5.0	5.2
Persons per family	3.59	3.56	3.54	3.52	3.47	3.42	3.38	3.36	3.36	3.32	3.31	3.28	3.25
Earners per family	1.67	1.68	1.68	1.68	1.67	1.67	1.68	1.68	1.68	1.63	1.66	1.67	1.69
Ratio of persons to earners per family	2.15	2.12	2.11	2.10	2.08	2.05	2.01	2.00	2.00	2.04	1.99	1.96	1.92
Black													
Number (thousands)	4,589	4,646	4,774	4,928	5,157	5,265	5,440	5,403	5,498	5,512	5,692	5,699	5,824
Percent	100.0	100.0	100.0	100.0	100.0	100.0	100.0	100.0	100.0	100.0	100.0	100.0	100.0
No earners	10.2	10.0	10.5	11.9	14.4	15.1	15.3	17.0	16.6	17.7	18.1	18.5	17.2
1 earner	31.6	32.9	32.3	33.5	34.4	35.4	35.3	34.1	35.2	35.5	34.7	35.6	36.2
2 earners or more	58.2	57.1	57.3	54.5	51.2	49.5	49.5	48.9	48.2	46.8	47.3	45.9	46.6
2 earners	41.8	41.2	41.7	40.4	37.4	38.0	36.3	36.5	35.8	34.8	35.6	34.2	34.6
3 earners	11.1	10.1	10.2	9.3	9.8	7.9	9.2	8.2	8.3	7.9	8.2	7.8	8.1
4 earners or more	5.3	5.8	5.4	4.8	4.0	3.6	4.0	4.2	4.1	4.1	3.5	4.0	3.8
Persons per family	4.35	4.36	4.31	4.26	4.05	4.01	3.92	3.90	3.90	3.90	3.78	3.77	3.74
Earners per family	1.76	1.72	1.73	1.67	1.58	1.53	1.55	1.52	1.52	1.52	1.50	1.51	1.54
Ration of persons to earners per family	2.47	2.53	2.49	2.55	2.56	2.62	2.53	2.57	2.57	2.57	2.52	2.50	2.43

Source: U.S. Department of Commerce, Bureau of the Census, *Current Population Survey.*

[a] Data as of March of the year following the income year.

[b] From 1974 excludes families with members in the Armed Forces.

Table 17. Actual and Standardized Family Income, by Race: 1967–1978

Year	White			Black			Black-to-White Ratio	
	Actual	Standardized[a]	Drag or Stimulus[b]	Actual	Standardized[a]	Drag or Stimulus[b]	Actual	Standardized[a]
Median Family Income								
1967[c]	8,234	8,234		4,875	4,875		0.59	0.59
1968	8,937	8,905	0.004	5,360	5,395	−0.006	0.60	0.51
1969	9,794	9,744	0.005	5,999	6,069	−0.012	0.61	0.52
1970	10,236	10,156	0.008	6,279	6,543	−0.040	0.61	0.54
1971	10,672	10,600	0.007	6,440	6,965	−0.075	0.60	0.66
1972	11,549	11,514	0.003	6,864	7,610	−0.098	0.59	0.66
1973	12,595	12,480	0.009	7,269	8,017	−0.093	0.58	0.64
1974	13,356	13,198	0.012	7,808	8,853	−0.118	0.58	0.67
1974 (revised)	13,456	13,468	−0.001	7,943	9,007	−0.118	0.59	0.67
1975	14,320	14,503	−0.013	8,723	10,180	−0.143	0.61	0.70
1976	15,571	15,632	−0.004	9,264	10,899	−0.150	0.59	0.70
1977	16,782	16,823	−0.002	9,485	11,287	−0.160	0.57	0.67
1978	18,432	18,368	0.003	10,820	12,877	−0.160	0.59	0.70
Mean Family Income								
1967	9,334	9,334		5,916	5,916		0.63	0.63
1968	10,002	9,972	0.003	6,392	6,423	−0.005	0.64	0.64
1969	10,953	10,905	0.004	6,971	7,032	−0.009	0.64	0.64
1970	11,495	11,461	0.003	7,442	7,687	−0.032	0.65	0.67
1971	11,997	12,031	−0.003	7,695	8,157	−0.057	0.64	0.68
1972	13,106	13,156	−0.004	8,346	9,068	−0.080	0.64	0.69
1973	14,163	14,189	−0.002	8,807	9,522	−0.075	0.62	0.67
1974	15,047	15,075	−0.002	9,515	10,399	−0.085	0.63	0.69
1974 (revised)	15,288	15,302	−0.001	9,612	10,475	−0.082	0.63	0.68
1975	16,150	16,342	−0.012	10,367	11,140	−0.069	0.64	0.68
1976	17,561	17,627	−0.004	11,266	12,518	−0.100	0.64	0.71
1977	19,042	19,083	−0.002	11,944	13,445	−0.112	0.63	0.70
1978	20,916	20,863	0.003	13,387	14,975	−0.106	0.64	0.72

Source: U.S. Department of Commerce, Bureau of the Census, Current Population Survey.

[a] Based on revised methodology.

[b] Actual income estimates divided by standardized income estimates minus 1. Positive estimates represent a stimulus and negative estimates a drag to family income.

[c] Based on the 1967 distribution of families by number of earners.

Table 18. Median Income of All Families and Husband-Wife Families, by Race: 1967–1978[a]

| | All Families | | Husband-Wife Families | | | | Percent of; | | |
| | | | Total | | Wife in Paid Labor Force | | | | |
Year	Number (thousands)	Median Income (dollars)	Number (thousands)	Median Income (dollars)	Number (thousands)	Median Income (dollars)	All Husband-Wife Families to All Families	Husband-Wife Families with Wife in Paid Labor Force to All Families	Husband-Wife Families with Wife in Paid Labor Force to All Husband-Wife Families
White									
1967	44,814	14,945	39,821	15,587	14,134	18,506	88.9	31.5	35.5
1968	45,437	15,567	40,354	16,267	14,862	19,103	88.8	32.7	36.8
1969	46,022	16,190	40,802	16,928	15,562	19,648	88.7	33.8	38.1
1970	46,535	15,974	41,092	16,735	15,651	19,575	88.3	33.6	38.1
1971	47,641	15,968	42,039	16,745	16,367	19,598	88.2	34.4	38.9
1972	48,477	16,729	42,585	17,581	16,899	20,494	87.8	34.9	39.7
1973	48,919	17,175	42,894	18,132	17,470	21,346	87.7	35.7	40.7
1974[b]	49,440	16,476	43,049	17,429	18,283	20,261	87.1	37.0	42.5
1975	49,873	16,065	43,311	17,030	18,609	19,760	86.8	37.3	43.0
1976	50,083	16,539	43,397	17,566	19,272	20,276	86.7	38.5	44.4
1977	50,530	16,740	43,423	17,916	19,662	20,518	85.9	38.9	45.3
1978	50,910	17,070	43,636	18,250	20,624	20,791	85.7	40.5	47.3
Black									
1967	4,589	8,848	3,118	10,542	1,565	13,199	67.9	34.1	50.2
1968	4,646	9,336	3,141	11,641	1,611	13,985	67.6	34.7	51.3

Year									
1969	4,774	9,916	3,249	12,115	1,731	15,099	68.1	36.3	53.3
1970	4,928	9,799	3,235	12,198	1,747	15,171	65.6	35.5	54.0
1971	5,157	9,636	3,289	12,237	1,726	15,373	63.8	33.5	52.5
1972	5,265	9,943	3,233	13,277	1,757	16,420	61.4	33.4	54.3
1973[b]	5,440	9,912	3,360	13,267	1,729	16,726	61.8	31.8	51.5
1974	5,491	9,838	3,357	13,145	1,809	16,195	61.1	32.9	53.9
1975	5,586	9,885	3,352	12,977	1,903	16,163	60.0	34.1	56.8
1976	5,804	9,838	3,406	13,985	1,935	16,716	58.7	33.3	56.8
1977	5,806	9,563	3,260	13,716	1,892	17,008	56.1	32.6	58.0
1978	5,906	10,110	3,244	14,789	1,934	17,725	54.9	32.7	59.6

Ratio of Black
to White

Year						
1967	0.10	0.59	0.08	0.68	0.11	0.71
1968	0.10	0.60	0.08	0.72	0.11	0.73
1969	0.10	0.61	0.08	0.72	0.11	0.77
1970	0.11	0.61	0.08	0.73	0.11	0.78
1971	0.11	0.60	0.08	0.73	0.11	0.78
1972	0.11	0.59	0.08	0.76	0.10	0.80
1973	0.11	0.58	0.08	0.73	0.10	0.78
1974[b]	0.11	0.60	0.08	0.75	0.10	0.80
1975	0.11	0.62	0.08	0.76	0.10	0.82
1976	0.12	0.59	0.08	0.80	0.10	0.82
1977	0.11	0.57	0.08	0.77	0.10	0.83
1978	0.12	0.59	0.07	0.81	0.09	0.85

Source: U.S. Department of Commerce, Bureau of the Census, *Current Population Survey.*

[a] Data as of March of the year following the income year.

[b] Based on revised methodology.

Table 19. Persons below the Poverty Level, by Selected Family Characteristics: 1959–1978[a]

Race, Sex of Head, and Year	Number Below Poverty Level (thousands)							Poverty Rate (percent)						
	Total		In Families				Unrelated Individuals	Total		In Families				Unrelated Individuals
	All Persons	65 Years and Over	Total	Head	Related Children under 18	Other Family Members		All Persons	65 Years and Over	Total	Head	Related Children under 18	Other Family Members	
White														
1959	28,484	4,744	24,443	6,185	11,386	6,872	4,041	18.1	33.1	16.5	15.2	20.6	13.3	44.1
1960	28,309	(NA)	24,262	6,115	11,229	6,918	4,047	17.8	(NA)	16.2	14.9	20.0	13.3	43.0
1961	27,890	(NA)	23,747	6,205	10,614	6,928	4,143	17.4	(NA)	15.8	14.8	18.7	13.3	43.2
1962	26,672	(NA)	22,613	5,887	10,382	6,344	4,059	16.4	(NA)	14.7	13.9	17.9	12.0	42.7
1963	25,238	(NA)	21,149	5,466	9,749	5,934	4,089	15.3	(NA)	13.6	12.8	16.5	11.0	42.0
1964	24,957	(NA)	20,716	5,258	9,573	5,885	4,241	14.9	(NA)	13.2	12.2	16.1	10.8	40.7
1965	22,496	(NA)	18,508	4,824	8,595	5,089	3,988	13.3	(NA)	11.7	11.1	14.4	9.2	38.1
1966	20,751	(NA)	16,732	4,481	7,649	4,602	4,019	12.2	(NA)	10.5	10.2	12.8	8.2	37.3
1966 (revised)	19,290	4,357	15,430	4,106	7,204	4,120	3,860	11.3	26.4	9.7	9.3	12.1	7.4	36.1
1967	18,983	4,646	14,851	4,056	6,729	4,066	4,132	11.0	27.7	9.2	9.0	11.3	7.2	36.5
1968	17,395	3,939	13,546	3,616	6,373	3,557	3,849	10.0	23.1	8.4	8.0	10.7	6.3	32.2
1969	16,659	4,052	12,623	3,575	5,667	3,381	4,036	9.5	23.3	7.8	7.7	9.7	5.8	32.1
1970	17,484	3,984	13,323	3,708	6,138	3,477	4,161	9.9	22.5	8.1	8.0	10.5	5.9	30.8
1971	17,780	3,605	13,566	3,751	6,341	3,474	4,214	9.9	19.9	8.2	7.9	10.9	5.8	29.6
1972	16,203	3,072	12,268	3,441	5,784	3,043	3,935	9.0	16.8	7.4	7.1	10.1	5.1	27.1

Year														
1973	15,142	2,698	11,412	3,219	5,462	2,731	3,730	8.4	14.4	6.9	6.6	9.7	4.5	23.7
1974	16,290	2,642	12,517	3,482	6,180	2,855	3,773	8.9	13.8	7.5	7.0	11.2	4.7	23.2
1974 (revised)	15,736	2,460	12,181	3,352	6,079	2,750	3,555	8.6	12.8	7.3	6.8	11.0	4.5	21.8
1975	17,770	2,634	13,799	3,838	6,748	3,213	3,972	9.7	13.4	8.3	7.7	12.5	5.2	22.7
1976	16,713	2,633	12,500	3,560	6,034	2,906	4,213	9.1	13.2	7.5	7.1	11.3	4.7	22.7
1977	16,416	2,426	12,364	3,540	5,943	2,882	4,051	8.9	11.9	7.5	7.0	11.4	4.6	20.4
1978	16,259	2,530	12,050	3,523	5,674	2,852	4,209	8.7	12.1	7.3	6.9	11.0	4.5	19.8
Black														
1959	9,927	711	9,112	1,860	5,022	2,230	815	55.1	62.5	54.9	48.1	65.5	44.1	57.0
1966	8,867	722	8,090	1,620	4,774	1,696	777	41.8	55.1	40.9	35.5	50.6	29.4	54.4
1967	8,486	715	7,677	1,555	4,558	1,564	809	39.3	53.3	38.4	33.9	47.4	27.1	49.3
1968	7,616	655	6,839	1,366	4,188	1,285	777	34.7	47.7	33.7	29.4	43.1	21.7	46.3
1969	7,095	689	6,245	1,366	3,677	1,202	850	32.2	50.2	30.9	27.9	39.6	20.0	46.7
1970	7,548	683	6,683	1,481	3,922	1,279	865	33.5	48.0	32.2	29.5	41.5	20.5	48.3
1971	7,396	623	6,530	1,484	3,836	1,210	866	32.5	39.3	31.2	28.8	40.7	19.1	46.0
1972	7,710	640	6,841	1,529	4,025	1,287	870	33.3	39.9	32.4	29.0	42.7	20.0	42.9
1973	7,388	620	6,560	1,527	3,822	1,211	828	31.4	37.1	30.8	28.1	40.6	18.7	37.9
1974	7,467	626	6,506	1,530	3,819	1,157	961	31.4	36.4	30.3	27.8	40.7	17.6	41.0
1974 (revised)	7,182	591	6,255	1,479	3,713	1,063	927	30.3	34.3	29.3	26.9	39.6	16.4	39.3
1975	7,545	652	6,533	1,513	3,884	1,136	1,011	31.3	36.3	30.1	27.1	41.4	16.9	42.1
1976	7,595	644	6,576	1,617	3,758	1,201	1,019	31.1	34.8	30.1	27.9	40.4	17.8	39.8
1977	7,726	701	6,667	1,637	3,850	1,181	1,059	31.3	36.3	30.5	28.2	41.6	17.4	37.0
1978	7,625	662	6,493	1,622	3,781	1,094	1,132	30.6	33.9	29.5	27.5	41.2	15.7	38.6

[a] Data as of March of the following year.

Table 20. Who Gets Welfare?

Program	Recipient Total	Percent Black	Percent White
Social Security retirement and survivor's insurance	30.3 million	9.1	89.4
Medicare	30.0 million	8.6	88.7
Veterans' compensation and pension	2.2 million	10.0	81.0
Supplemental security income	4.1 million	27.5	64.2
Aid to families with dependent children	11.0 million	42.0	51.0
Food stamps	22.3 million	34.2	57.0
CETA public service jobs	1.5 million	32.0	53.0
Medicaid	23.0 million	44.1	55.9
Public housing	3.1 million	47.1	38.4
Social Security disability	4.7 million	16.5	81.5
Education for disadvantaged	5.3 million	34.5	54.0
Unemployment insurance	2.8 million	16.7	78.5

Source: Alex Poinsett, "Who Gets Welfare?," *Ebony Magazine,* **37,** No. 3, January 1982, p. 28.

Table 21. Aid to Families with Dependent Children (AFDC)—Percent Distribution of Recipient Families and Children, by Characteristics: 1973–1977[a]

Characteristic	1973	1975	1977	Characteristic	1973	1975	1977
Recipient families (thousands)	2,990	3,420	3,623	Recipient children (thousands)	7,725	8,121	7,836
Percent distribution							
Metropolitan areas[b]	77.9	78.5	77.1	Basis for eligibility			
Nonmetropolitan areas[c]	22.1	21.5	22.9	Father is—			
White	46.9	50.3	52.6	Deceased	4.0	3.7	2.6
Black	45.8	44.3	43.0	Incapacitated	10.2	7.7	5.9
American Indian	1.1	1.1	1.3	Unemployed	4.1	3.7	5.1
Other[c]	6.2	4.3	1.5	Absent from home:			
Number of children				Divorced	17.7	19.4	21.4
1	33.8	37.9	40.3	Separated[f]	28.8	28.6	25.5
2	25.5	26.0	27.3	Not married to mother	31.5	31.0	38.8
3	16.3	16.1	16.1	Other	2.4	4.3	4.1
4 or 5	17.2	15.0	12.7	Mother is absent, not father	1.2	1.6	1.6
6 or more	7.2	5.0	3.6				
Years as recipient[d,e]				Age			
Under 1 year	30.2	27.7	32.7	Under 6, including unborn	34.8	34.6	34.8
1–3 years	34.5	27.3	28.0	6–11	34.7	33.7	38.8
4–5 years	10.9	18.8	15.0	12–17	28.1	28.5	27.5
6–10 years	12.8	19.3	18.1	18–20	2.4	2.4	2.6
11–15 years	3.5	4.3	3.8	Unknown	—	.8	1.2
Over 15 years	1.5	2.0	1.5				

Source: U.S. Department of Commerce, Bureau of the Census, *Statistical Abstract of the U.S.,* 100th ed.

[a] Refers to federally aided state programs providing aid to needy children deprived of parental care or support. Based on a sample and subject to sampling variability; for details, see source.

[b] Refers to 243 standard metropolitan statistical areas as designated in 1970 census publications.

[c] Includes unknown or not reported.

[d] Excludes unknown or not reported.

[e] Since recent opening of case.

[f] Includes legally and non-legally separated.

Table 22. Selected Characteristics of Occupants of All Housing Units and Units Built Since 1970 in SMSA Central Cities, by Region and Tenure: 1977

Characteristic	United States — All Units	United States — Units Built Since 1970	Northeast — All Units	Northeast — Units Built Since 1970	North Central — All Units	North Central — Units Built Since 1970	South — All Units	South — Units Built Since 1970	West — All Units	West — Units Built Since 1970
					Number (thousands)					
Occupied units	23,151	2,731	5,818	294	5,719	483	6,710	1,148	4,904	807
Owner occupied	11,346	1,200	2,153	76	3,101	207	3,527	457	2,565	461
White	9,419	1,052	1,843	64	2,570	181	2,796	385	2,211	422
Black	1,713	115	277	3	521	26	715	70	200	15
Female head, under 65 years old	1,454	142	273	6	400	29	463	48	318	58
1 person, under 65 years old	856	93	143	2	228	18	252	30	233	43
Head 65 years old and over	2,704	81	571	5	786	17	825	33	522	28
Median income in 1976 ($)	15,900	21,200	14,900	18,700	15,700	21,100	15,200	22,700	17,700	20,200
Renter occupied	11,805	1,531	3,665	218	2,618	276	3,183	691	2,339	346
White	8,324	1,233	2,694	176	1,790	209	2,015	546	1,826	301
Black	3,009	263	834	39	769	62	1,121	137	284	25
Female head, under 65 years old	3,800	493	1,142	54	879	82	1,056	251	723	106
1 person, under 65 years old	3,248	472	819	40	793	74	877	241	758	117
Head 65 years old and over	2,066	235	783	67	458	55	455	57	369	55
Median income in 1976 ($)	8,100	10,600	8,200	10,000	7,800	9,700	8,100	10,800	8,400	11,100
					Percent					
Occupied units	100.0	100.0	100.0	100.0	100.0	100.0	100.0	100.0	100.0	100.0
Owner occupied	49.0	43.9	37.0	25.9	54.2	42.9	52.6	39.8	52.3	57.1
White	83.0	87.7	85.6	84.2	82.9	87.4	79.3	84.2	86.2	91.5
Black	15.1	9.6	12.9	3.9	16.8	12.6	20.3	15.3	7.8	3.3
Female head, under 65 years old	12.8	11.8	12.7	7.9	12.9	14.0	13.2	10.5	12.4	12.6
1 person, under 65 years old	7.5	7.8	6.6	2.6	7.4	8.7	7.1	6.6	9.1	9.3
Head 65 years old and over	23.8	6.8	26.5	6.6	25.3	8.2	23.4	7.2	20.4	6.1
Renter occupied	51.0	56.1	63.0	74.1	45.8	57.1	47.4	60.2	47.7	42.9
White	70.5	80.5	73.5	80.7	68.4	75.7	63.3	79.0	78.1	87.0
Black	25.5	17.2	22.8	17.9	29.4	22.5	35.2	19.8	12.1	7.2
Female head, under 65 years old	32.2	32.2	31.2	24.8	33.6	29.7	33.2	36.3	30.9	30.6
1 person, under 65 years old	27.5	30.8	22.3	18.3	30.3	26.8	27.6	34.9	32.4	33.8
Head 65 years old and over	17.5	15.3	21.4	30.7	17.5	19.9	14.3	8.2	15.8	15.9

Source: U.S. Bureau of the Census, *Social Indicators*, Vol. III.

Note: Detail may not add to totals shown because of rounding.

Table 23. Lifetime Births Expected by Wives 18 to 34 Years Old, by Race, Selected Years: 1967–1978

Race and Year	Number of Wives (thousands)	Lifetime Births Expected					
		Total (percent)	None	1	2	3	4 or More
All wives aged 18 to 34 years							
1967	11,676	100.0	2.4	5.8	30.7	29.7	31.4
1972	14,228	100.0	3.9	8.4	47.0	24.0	16.7
1974	14,721	100.0	4.9	10.2	48.3	22.6	14.0
1976	14,880	100.0	5.6	11.2	49.7	22.0	11.5
1978	14,940	100.0	5.6	11.8	49.2	22.5	10.9
Black wives aged 18 to 34 years							
1967	940	100.0	3.0	8.5	25.0	25.1	38.3
1972	1,101	100.0	3.1	12.0	34.0	20.7	30.2
1974	1,113	100.0	4.2	14.5	35.8	21.8	23.7
1976	1,086	100.0	3.0	13.7	39.3	26.1	17.9
1978	1,048	100.0	4.5	13.1	36.2	25.5	20.7
Hispanic[a] wives aged 18 to 34 years							
1974	763	100.0	3.4	11.0	42.2	22.2	21.2
1976	812	100.0	4.2	10.3	37.8	28.1	19.6
1978	970	100.0	3.1	12.2	40.4	23.5	20.8

Source: U.S. Bureau of the Census, *Social Indicators,* Vol. III: *Selected Data on Social Conditions and Trends in the United States.*

Note: Detail may not add to totals shown because of rounding.

[a] Hispanic persons may be of any race.

Table 24. Live Births and Infant Mortality Rates, by Race: 1960–1977

Year	Live Births (thousands)			Deaths of Infants under 1 Year Old per 1,000 Live Births		
	Total	White	Black and Other Races	Total	White	Black and Other Races
1960	4,258	3,601	657	26.0	22.9	43.2
1961	4,268	3,601	667	25.3	22.4	40.7
1962	4,036	3,394	642	25.3	[1]22.3	[1]41.4
1963	3,965	3,326	639	25.2	[1]22.2	[1]41.5
1964	4,027	3,369	658	24.8	21.6	41.1
1965	3,760	3,124	636	24.7	21.5	40.3
1966	3,606	2,993	613	23.7	20.6	38.8
1967	3,521	2,923	598	22.4	19.7	35.9
1968	3,501	2,912	589	21.8	19.2	34.5
1969	3,601	2,994	607	20.9	18.4	32.9
1970	3,731	3,091	640	20.0	17.8	30.9
1971	3,556	2,920	636	19.1	17.1	28.5
1972	3,259	2,656	603	18.5	16.4	27.7
1973	3,137	2,551	586	17.7	15.8	26.2
1974	3,160	2,576	584	16.7	14.8	24.9
1975	3,144	2,552	592	16.1	14.2	24.2
1976	3,168	2,568	600	15.2	13.3	23.5
1977	3,327	2,691	636	14.1	12.3	21.7

Source: U.S. Department of Health, Education, and Welfare, Public Health Services, National Center for Health Statistics, *Vital Statistics of the United States,* Vol. 1, various years.

Note: Beginning in 1970, data exclude births and infant deaths to nonresidents of the United States; 1967 data are based on a 20 to 50% sample of births; data for 1960–1966 and 1968 1971 are based on a 50% sample of births; 1972 data are based on a 50% sample of deaths, and on 100% of births in selected states and a 50% sample in all other states; 1973–1977 data are based on 100% of births in selected states and on a 50% sample in all other states.

Table 25. Life Expectancy at Ages 20 and 65, by Race and Sex: 1900–1977

Years	20 Years Old				65 Years Old			
	White		Black and Other Races		White		Black and Other Races	
	Male	Female	Male	Female	Male	Female	Male	Female
1900–1902	42.2	43.8	35.1	36.9	11.5	12.2	10.4	11.4
1909–1911	42.7	44.9	33.5	36.1	11.3	12.0	9.7	10.8
1919–1921	45.6	46.5	38.4	37.2	12.2	12.8	12.1	12.4
1929–1931	46.0	48.5	36.0	37.2	11.8	12.8	10.9	12.2
1939–1941	47.8	51.4	39.7	42.1	12.1	13.6	12.2	14.0
1949–1951	49.5	54.6	43.7	46.8	12.8	15.0	12.8	14.5
1959–1961	50.3	56.3	45.8	50.1	13.0	15.9	12.8	15.1
1969–1971[a]	50.2	57.2	44.3	51.8	13.0	16.9	12.8	15.9
1975[a]	51.4	58.6	46.3	54.7	13.7	18.1	13.7	17.5
1976[a]	51.6	58.7	46.8	54.9	13.7	18.1	13.8	17.6
1977[a]	51.9	59.1	47.2	55.2	13.9	18.4	14.0	17.8

Source: U.S. Bureau of the Census, *Social Indicators,* Vol. III.

[a] Excludes deaths of nonresidents of the United States.

Table 26. Death Rates, by Race, Sex, and Age, 1970 and 1978[a]

Age (years)	1970			1978								
			Black	All Races			White			Black and Other		
	All Races	White	and Other	Both Sexes	Male	Female	Both Sexes	Male	Female	Both Sexes	Male	Female
All ages	945	946	938	883	994	778	896	1,000	797	805	960	665
Under 1	2,142	1,870	3,597	1,434	1,592	1,270	1,218	1,360	1,070	2,457	2,709	2,207
1–4	85	75	134	69	78	60	63	72	53	99	108	90
5–9	42	40	54	33	39	28	31	36	26	43	52	34
10–14	41	38	53	34	44	25	33	42	24	41	53	29
15–19	110	103	154	101	145	55	102	147	55	96	136	56
20–24	148	131	268	135	203	67	126	191	61	184	278	97
25–29	144	121	311	132	192	73	116	168	63	234	357	129
30–34	173	141	392	140	193	88	121	165	76	271	402	160
35–39	247	205	544	189	254	128	162	215	110	382	549	245
40–44	377	324	785	296	383	214	257	329	188	563	785	381
45–49	584	524	1,093	472	609	341	429	554	308	780	1,021	570
50–54	889	820	1,519	742	981	521	684	907	475	1,217	1,610	877
55–59	1,361	1,283	2,093	1,116	1,490	774	1,046	1,405	717	1,734	2,267	1,272
60–64	2,004	1,917	2,834	1,774	2,412	1,213	1,695	2,318	1,143	2,538	3,339	1,867
65–69	2,969	2,870	3,669	2,463	3,439	1,685	2,413	3,395	1,628	2,878	3,815	2,150
70–74	4,371	4,274	5,418	3,787	5,242	2,725	3,685	5,167	2,613	4,878	5,985	3,980
75–79	6,722	6,703	6,960	6,024	8,066	4,713	5,894	7,996	4,564	7,548	8,724	6,621
80–84	10,158	10,290	8,458	8,954	11,597	7,509	9,081	11,822	7,607	7,573	9,420	6,373
85 and over	16,345	16,890	10,750	14,701	17,259	13,541	15,316	18,100	14,079	9,229	10,678	8,449

Source: U.S. Bureau of the Census, *Statistical Abstract of the United States, 1980, 101st ed.*

[a] Number of deaths per 100,000 population. Excludes deaths of nonresidents of the United States.

514

Table 27. Infant, Maternal, and Neonatal Death Rates, and Fetal Death Ratios, by Race: 1940–1978[a]

Item	1940	1950	1955	1960	1970	1972[b]	1973	1974	1975	1976	1977	1978
Infant deaths[c]	47.0	29.2	24.7	26.0	20.0	18.5	17.7	16.7	16.1	15.2	14.1	13.8
White	43.2	26.8	21.5	22.9	17.8	16.4	15.8	14.8	14.2	13.3	12.3	12.0
Black and other	73.8	44.5	40.3	43.2	30.9	27.7	26.2	24.9	24.2	23.5	21.7	21.1
Maternal deaths[d]	376.0	83.3	31.6	37.1	21.5	18.8	15.2	14.6	12.8	12.3	11.2	9.6
White	319.8	61.1	21.0	26.0	14.4	14.3	10.7	10.0	9.1	9.0	7.7	6.4
Black and other	773.5	221.6	83.7	97.9	55.9	38.5	34.6	35.1	29.0	26.5	26.0	23.0
Fetal deaths[e]		19.2	16.2	16.1	14.2	12.7	12.2	11.5	10.7	10.5	9.8	
White		17.1	13.9	14.1	12.4	11.2	10.8	10.2	9.5	9.3	8.7	
Black and other		32.5	27.2	26.8	22.6	19.5	18.6	17.0	16.0	15.2	14.6	
Neonatal deaths[f]	28.8	20.5	17.7	18.7	15.1	13.6	13.0	12.3	11.6	10.9	9.9	9.5
White	27.2	19.4	16.1	17.2	13.8	12.4	11.8	11.1	10.4	9.7	8.7	8.4
Black and other	39.7	27.5	25.4	26.9	21.4	19.2	17.9	17.2	16.8	16.3	14.7	14.0

Source: U.S. Bureau of the Census, *Statistical Abstract of the United States 1980, 101st ed.*

[a] Deaths per 1,000 live births, except as noted. Prior to 1960, excludes Alaska and Hawaii. Beginning 1970, excludes death of nonresidents of United States.

[b] Based on a 50% sample of deaths.

[c] Represents deaths of infants under 1 year old, exclusive of fetal deaths.

[d] Per 100,000 live births from deliveries and complications of pregnancy, childbirth, and the puerperium. For 1970–1978, deaths are classified according to eighth revision of *International Classification of Diseases, Adapted for Use in the United States;* in prior years classified according to the revision of the International Classification of Diseases in use at the time.

[e] Beginning 1970, includes only those deaths with stated or presumed period of gestation of 20 weeks or more; for prior years, includes gestational age not stated.

[f] Represents deaths of infants under 28 days old, exclusive of fetal deaths.

Table 28. Births and Birth Rates: 1950–1978 [a]

Item	1950	1955	1960	1965	1970	1972	1973	1974	1975	1976	1977	1978
Live births	3,632	4,097	4,258	3,760	3,731	3,258	3,137	3,160	3,144	3,168	3,327	3,333
Average annual percent change [b]	3.6	2.4	.8	−2.5	−.2	−6.6	−3.7	.7	−.5	.8	5.0	.2
White	3,108	3,485	3,601	3,124	3,091	2,656	2,551	2,576	2,552	2,568	2,691	2,681
Black and other	524	613	657	636	640	603	586	584	592	600	636	652
Percent of total	14.4	14.0	15.4	16.9	17.2	18.5	18.7	18.5	18.8	18.9	19.1	19.6
Male	1,863	2,099	2,180	1,927	1,915	1,670	1,608	1,622	1,613	1,624	1,706	1,709
Female	1,768	1,998	2,078	1,833	1,816	1,588	1,529	1,538	1,531	1,543	1,621	1,624
Males per 100 females	105.4	105.1	104.9	105.1	105.5	105.1	105.2	105.5	105.4	105.3	105.3	105.3
Age of mother:												
Under 20 years	425	490	594	599	656	628	617	608	595	571	571	556
20–24 years	1,131	1,274	1,427	1,337	1,419	1,174	1,101	1,108	1,094	1,092	1,146	1,140
25–29 years	1,022	1,119	1,093	926	995	900	888	923	937	972	1,016	1,015
30–34 years	598	722	688	529	428	375	370	373	376	392	447	474
35–39 years	293	345	360	283	180	141	127	118	115	116	121	126
40 years or more	80	93	97	86	53	39	34	30	28	26	25	24
Birth rate per 1,000 population	24.1	25.0	23.7	19.4	18.4	15.6	14.9	14.9	14.8	14.8	15.4	15.3
White	23.0	23.8	22.7	18.3	17.4	14.6	13.9	14.0	13.8	13.8	14.4	14.2
Black and other	33.3	34.5	32.1	27.6	25.1	22.9	21.9	21.4	21.2	21.1	21.9	22.1
Male	24.9	25.8	24.7	20.3	19.4	16.5	15.7	15.8	15.6	15.5	16.2	16.1
Female	23.3	23.9	22.8	18.6	17.4	14.9	14.2	14.2	14.0	14.0	14.6	14.5
Plural birth ratio [c]	20.9	21.2	20.4	20.1		18.4	18.4	18.6	19.2	19.5	19.2	19.6
Birth rate per 1,000 women [d]	106.2	118.3	118.0	96.6	87.9	73.4	69.2	68.4	66.7	65.8	67.8	66.6[e]
White	102.3	113.7	113.2	91.4	84.1	69.2	65.3	64.7	63.0	62.2	64.0	62.7
Black and other [d]	137.3	155.3	153.6	131.9	113.0	100.3	94.3	91.0	89.3	87.6	89.9	89.3
Age of mother:												
10–14 years	1.0	0.9	0.8	0.8	1.2	1.2	1.3	1.2	1.3	1.2	1.2	1.2
15–19 years	81.6	90.5	89.1	70.5	68.3	62.0	59.7	58.1	56.3	53.5	53.7	52.4
20–24 years	196.6	242.0	258.1	195.3	167.8	131.0	120.7	119.0	114.7	112.1	115.2	112.3
25–29 years	166.1	190.5	197.4	161.6	145.1	118.7	113.6	113.3	110.3	108.8	114.2	112.0
30–34 years	103.7	116.2	112.7	94.4	73.3	60.2	56.1	54.4	53.1	54.5	57.5	59.1
35–39 years	52.9	58.7	56.2	46.2	31.7	24.8	22.0	20.2	19.4	19.0	19.2	18.9
40–44 years	15.1	16.1	15.5	12.8	8.1	6.2	5.4	4.8	4.6	4.3	4.2	3.9
45–49 years	1.2[f]	1.0[f]	0.9[f]	0.8	0.5	0.4	0.3	0.3	0.3	0.2	0.2	0.2

Source: U.S. Bureau of the Census, *Statistical Abstract of the United States: 1980 (101st ed.)*

[a] Births in thousands, except as indicated. Prior to 1960, excludes Alaska and Hawaii. For 1950 and 1955, births adjusted for underregistration, except by age of mother; thereafter registered births. Beginning 1970, excludes births to nonresidents of U.S. Minus sign (−) denotes decrease.

[b] For 1950, change from 1940.

[c] Per 1,000 live births.

[d] Per 1,000 women, 15–44 years old.

[e] Provisional live birth rate for 1974 was 68.0; data by race and age not available.

[f] Rate computed by relating births to mothers aged 45 years and over to women aged 45 to 49 years.

Table 29. Unwanted Births of All Mothers, 15–44 Years Old: 1973 and 1976[a]

Characteristic	1973 Number of Mothers (thousands)	1973 Total Live Births[b] (thousands)	1973 Unwanted Births[c] Number (thousands)	1973 Unwanted Births[c] Percent	1976 Number of Mothers (thousands)	1976 Total Live Births[b] (thousands)	1976 Unwanted Births[c] Number (thousands)	1976 Unwanted Births[c] Percent	1976 All Births per Mother	1976 Unwanted Births[c] per Mother
Total mothers[d]	25,803	68,184	8,910	13.1	27,055[e]	67,849[e]	8,125	12.0	2.51	.30
Race										
White	22,182	57,551	6,068	10.5	22,837	56,238	5,350	9.5	2.46	.23
Black	3,359	9,984	2,783	27.9	3,726	10,525	2,716	25.8	2.82	.73
Education										
Less than high school	2,622	9,123	1,501	16.5	2,187	7,274	1,264	17.4	3.33	.58
High school										
1–3 years	5,697	16,884	3,024	17.9	5,478	15,543	2,405	15.5	2.84	.44
4 years	12,161	29,917	3,307	11.1	12,651	30,405	3,391	11.2	2.40	.27
College										
1–3 years	3,182	7,585	734	9.7	3,763	8,391	776	9.3	2.23	.21
4 years or more	2,140	4,675	344	7.4	2,925	6,114	286	4.7	2.09	.10
Currently married mothers[d]	21,816	57,524	6,418	11.2	22,253[e]	55,900[e]	5,516	9.9	2.51	.25
Race										
White	19,764	51,391	5,055	9.8	19,921	49,453	4,299	8.7	2.48	.22
Black	1,822	5,561	1,331	23.9	1,927	5,533	1,177	21.3	2.87	.61
Education										
Less than high school	1,948	6,846	838	12.2	1,663	5,584	832	14.9	3.36	.50
High school										
1–3 years	4,482	13,274	2,114	15.9	3,951	11,226	1,320	11.8	2.84	.33
4 years	10,646	26,494	2,586	9.8	10,741	26,120	2,547	9.8	2.43	.24
College										
1–3 years	2,816	6,722	602	9.0	3,244	7,381	597	8.1	2.28	.18
4 years or more	1,924	4,187	279	6.7	2,613	5,503	219	4.0	2.11	.08

Source: U.S. Bureau of the Census, *Statistical Abstract of the United States. 1980 (101st ed.)*

[a] Data represent the birth experience to date of all mothers 15–44 years old who have been married or are single with children of their own in the household. From the 1973 and 1976 National Survey of Family Growth; based on a multistage area probability sample. Data are subject to sampling variability.

[b] Multiple births counted only once.

[c] All births which mothers report as "not wanted" or "probably not wanted" at time of becoming pregnant.

[d] Includes races not shown separately.

[e] Includes education not reported.

Table 30. Births to Unmarried Women, by Race and Age of Mother: 1950–1978[a]

Race and Age	1950	1955	1960	1965	1970	1973	1974	1975	1976	1977	1978
Total live births (1,000)	141.6	183.3	224.3	291.2	398.7	407.3	418.1	447.9	468.1	515.7	543.9
Percent of all births	4.0	4.5	5.3	7.7	10.7	13.0	13.2	14.2	14.8	15.5	16.3
White (1,000)	53.5	64.2	82.5	123.7	175.1	163.0	168.5	186.4	197.1	220.1	233.6
Black and other (1,000)	88.1	119.2	141.8	167.5	223.6	244.3	249.6	261.6	271.0	295.5	310.2
Percent of total	62.2	65.0	63.2	57.5	56.1	60.0	59.7	58.4	57.9	57.3	57.0
Percent white of all white births	1.7	1.8	2.3	4.0	5.7	6.4	6.5	7.3	7.7	8.2	8.7
Percent black and other of all black and other births	16.8	19.4	21.6	26.3	34.9	41.7	42.7	44.2	45.2	46.5	47.5
Births, by age of mother											
Under 15 years (1,000)	3.2	3.9	4.6	6.1	9.5	10.9	10.6	11.0	10.3	10.1	9.4
15–19 years (1,000)	56.0	68.9	87.1	123.1	190.4	204.9	210.8	222.5	225.0	239.7	239.7
20–24 years (1,000)	43.1	55.7	68.0	90.7	126.7	119.1	122.7	134.0	145.4	168.6	186.5
25–29 years (1,000)	20.9	28.0	32.1	36.8	40.6	43.1	44.9	50.2	55.4	62.4	70.0
30–34 years (1,000)	10.8	16.1	18.9	19.6	19.1	18.5	18.6	19.8	21.0	23.7	26.5
35 years and over (1,000)	7.7	10.7	13.6	15.1	12.4	10.8	10.5	10.4	10.9	11.1	11.7
Percent of births to mothers											
19 years and under	41.8	39.7	40.9	44.4	50.1	53.0	53.0	52.1	50.3	48.4	45.8
20–29 years	45.2	45.7	44.6	43.8	42.0	39.8	40.1	41.1	42.9	44.8	47.2
Birth rate[b]	14.1	19.3	21.6	23.5	26.4	24.5	24.1	24.8	24.7	26.0	26.2
White[b]	6.1	7.9	9.2	11.6	13.8	11.9	11.8	12.6	12.7	13.7	13.9
Black and other[b]	71.2	87.2	98.3	97.6	89.9	84.2	81.5	80.4	78.1	79.4	78.7
15–19 years	12.6	15.1	15.3	16.7	22.4	22.9	23.2	24.2	24.0	25.5	25.4
20–24 years	21.3	33.5	39.7	39.9	38.4	31.8	30.9	31.6	32.2	34.7	36.1
25–29 years	19.9	33.5	45.1	49.3	37.0	30.0	28.4	28.0	27.5	28.5	29.4
30–34 years	13.3	22.0	27.8	37.5	27.1	20.5	18.6	18.1	17.8	17.2	17.3

Source: U.S. Bureau of the Census, *Statistical Abstract of the United States: 1980,* 101st ed.

[a] Prior to 1960, excludes Alaska and Hawaii. Beginning 1970, excludes births to nonresidents of United States. Includes estimates for states in which marital status data were not reported. No estimates included for misstatements on birth records or failures to register births.

[b] Rate per 1,000 unmarried (never-married, widowed, and divorced) women aged 15–44 years enumerated as of April 1 for 1950, 1960, and 1970, and estimated as of July for all other years.

Table 31. Visits to Physicians, by Race, Family Income, and Type of Visit: 1978[a]

| | Visits (million) | | | Percent Distribution by Type of Visit | | | | | | | | |
| | | | | All families | White families | | | | Families of other races | | | |
Type of Visit	Total	White	Other races		Total	Under $5,000	$5,000–$9,999	$10,000 or more	Total	Under $5,000	$5,000–$9,999	$10,000 or more
Total visits[b]	1,017	882	135	100.0	100.0	100.0	100.0	100.0	100.0	100.0	100.0	100.0
Physicians' offices	683	605	78	67.2	68.6	64.2	66.9	69.9	57.8	50.5	55.2	62.6
Phone consultation[c]	128	120	8	12.6	13.7	13.2	12.0	14.3	5.7	3.5	6.3	7.9
Emergency room[d]	138	106	33	13.6	12.0	12.5	15.1	11.0	24.1	31.6	24.4	18.8
Other[f]	61	46	15	6.0	5.2	9.4	5.6	4.4	11.4	13.8	13.9	8.9

Source: U.S. Bureau of the Census, *Statistical Abstract of the United States, 1980 (101st ed.)*

[a] Refers to civilian noninstitutional population. Based on Health Interview Survey.

[b] Includes unknown, not shown separately.

[c] Includes visits to patients' homes.

[d] Includes visits to hospital outpatient department.

[e] Represents schools, insurance offices, health department clinics, and other.

519

Table 32.   Persons with Elevated Blood Pressure, by Race, Sex, and Age: 1960–1962 and 1971–1974[a]

Age Group	Number (thousands)					Rate per 100 Persons				
	Total[b]	White	Black	Female	Male	Total[b]	White	Black	Female	Male
1960–1962, total	19,661	16,131	3,380	10,299	9,363	18.2	17.0	30.2	18.1	18.2
1971–1974, total	23,171	19,359	3,672	11,515	11,656	18.1	17.0	28.2	17.1	19.2
18–24 years old	738	632	106	194	544	3.1	3.1	3.7	1.6	4.8
25–34 years old	1,777	1,373	401	618	1,159	6.6	5.8	13.7	4.4	9.1
35–44 years old	3,492	2,738	696	1,449	2,043	15.5	13.6	32.0	12.3	18.9
45–54 years old	5,702	4,710	975	2,680	3,022	24.2	22.2	44.0	21.9	26.8
55–64 years old	6,257	5,354	865	3,382	2,875	33.2	31.4	52.6	34.0	32.3
65–74 years old	5,205	4,551	628	3,191	2,014	40.7	39.3	55.1	43.9	36.6

Source: U.S. Bureau of the Census, *Statistical Abstract of the United States, 1980 (101st ed.)*

[a] Covers civilian noninstitutional population, 18–74 years old. Based on sample and subject to sampling variability, see source. Data represent number of persons with blood pressure readings of either systolic pressure of 160 mmHg or more or diastolic pressure of 95 mmHg or more.

[b] Includes other races not shown separately.

Table 33. Children 1 to 4 Years Old Immunized Against Measles, Rubella, DPT,[a] and Polio, by Race: 1965–1977

Race	1970	1971	1972	1973	1974	1975	1976	1977
Measles								
Total	62.3	66.6	65.0	64.1	66.6	67.7	67.8	64.7
White	64.9	67.7	67.1	66.1	68.6	70.0	72.3	67.1
Black and other races	50.0	61.3	62.5	54.2	56.3	57.2	56.8	53.9
Rubella								
Total	37.2	51.2	56.9	55.6	59.8	61.9	61.7	59.4
White	38.3	51.8	57.8	57.0	61.0	63.9	68.9	66.1
Black and other races	31.8	48.2	52.6	48.5	53.6	52.0	55.1	54.3
DPT								
Total	76.1	78.7	75.6	72.6	73.9	75.2	71.4	69.5
White	79.7	81.6	78.8	75.8	76.8	78.5	75.3	73.0
Black and other races	58.8	65.1	58.7	56.7	59.6	59.4	53.2	53.2

Polio[b]	1965	1966	1967	1968	1969	1970	1971	1972	1973	1974	1975	1976	1977
Total (thousands)	16,054	15,652	15,113	14,547	13,963	13,645	13,598	13,720	13,613	13,281	12,805	12,319	12,072
Percent immunized	73.9	70.2	70.9	68.3	67.7	65.9	67.3	62.9	60.4	63.1	64.8	61.6	60.1
White (thousands)	13,638	13,262	12,762	12,256	11,736	11,484	11,439	11,508	11,370	11,038	10,578	10,140	9,913
Percent immunized	76.6	72.9	73.2	71.0	70.7	69.2	70.5	66.3	64.4	66.7	68.8	66.2	64.2
Black and other races (thousands)	2,416	2,390	2,351	2,291	2,227	2,161	2,159	2,212	2,243	2,243	2,227	2,179	2,159
Percent immunized	59.6	56.6	60.2	54.5	53.6	50.1	51.9	45.2	39.8	45.0	46.1	39.9	41.0

Source: U.S. Bureau of the Census, *Social Indicators*, Vol. III.

[a] Diphtheria, pertussis, tetanus.

[b] Three or more doses.

Table 34. Persons 20 to 74 Years Old Who Were Determined by Skinfold Measurement to Be Obese, by Sex, Race, and Poverty Status: 1971–1974[a]

| | Male | | | | Female | | | |
| | White | | Black | | White | | Black | |
Age	Below Poverty Level	Above Poverty Level	Below Poverty Level	Above Poverty Level	Below Poverty Level	Above Poverty Level	Below Poverty Level	Above Poverty Level
20 to 44 years	9(1,998)	15(25,204)	11(752)	15(2,250)	21(2,703)	18(26,603)	28(1,450)	24(2,471)
45 to 64 years	5(1,319)	13(16,180)	4(541)	12(1,089)	26(1,375)	29(17,544)	49(700)	40(1,296)
65 to 74 years	10(595)	11(4,127)	5(186)	7(276)	26(1,160)	19(5,118)	23(302)	36(298)

Source: U.S. Department of Health, Education, and Welfare, Public Health Service, National Center for Health, *Health, United States, 1976–1977.*

[a] Numbers in parentheses are estimates of the population age group, in thousands.

Table 35.   Adults Ever Having Hypertension and Interval Since Last Blood Pressure Test, by Sex, Race, and Age: 1974

Race, age, and sex	Both Sexes		Male		Female	
	Number (thousands)	Percent	Number thousands	Percent	Number thousands	Percent
	Have had Hypertension					
All races, 17 years and over [a]	29,789	22.1	11,562	18.8	18,228	24.8
White						
17 years and over	25,598	21.4	10,063	18.4	15,535	24.0
17–24 years	1,789	7.7	761	6.9	1,029	8.3
25–54 years	6,037	14.4	2,617	13.3	3,421	15.3
45–64 years	10,194	28.4	4,252	25.6	5,941	30.8
65 years and over	7,578	41.6	2,433	32.6	5,145	47.8
Black						
17 years and over	3,943	28.8	1,377	23.7	2,566	32.6
17–24 years	270	8.1	76	5.4	194	10.0
25–44 years	1,114	22.5	327	16.2	787	26.7
45–64 years	1,668	45.3	650	39.3	1,018	50.1
65 years and over	890	53.3	324	45.3	567	59.4

Cumulative Percent Distribution

	Now Have Hypertension and Interval since Last Blood Pressure Test			Never Had Hypertension and Interval since Last Blood Pressure Test		
	Less than 6 Months	Less than 1 Year	Less than 2 Years	Less than 6 Months	Less than 1 Year	Less than 2 Years
All persons, 17 years and over [b]	74.1	86.2	92.7	44.5	64.3	78.1
Age						
17–44 years	66.9	81.2	90.2	44.2	65.1	79.3
45–64 years	74.9	87.2	93.4	43.7	63.4	77.2
65 years and over	78.6	88.6	93.5	48.4	62.4	73.9
Sex						
Male	70.4	83.4	91.3	38.8	57.8	72.6
Female	76.3	87.8	93.5	49.7	70.2	83.1
Race						
White	74.3	86.6	93.1	44.0	64.0	78.0
Black	72.8	83.4	90.1	49.6	67.9	80.6

Source: U.S. Bureau of the Census, *Social Indicators,* Vol. III.

[a] Includes white, black and other races.

[b] Includes persons with other and unknown intervals and those having a blood pressure test.

Table 36. Impact of a Sustained 1% Change in Unemployment

Social Stress Indicator	Data Period	Change in the Stress Indicator (%)[a]
Suicide	1940–1973	4.1
State mental hospital admissions	1940–1971	3.4
Males		4.3
Females		2.3
State prison admissions	1935–1973	4.0
Homicide	1940–1973	5.7
Cirrhosis of the liver mortality	1940–1973	1.9
Cardiovascular-renal disease mortality	1940–1973	1.9
Total mortality	1940–1974	1.9

Source: 94th Congress, Joint Economic Committee, Congress of the U.S., Paper No. 5, *Estimating the Social Costs of National Economic Policy: Implications for Mental and Physical Health, and Clinical Aggression* (Washington, D.C.: U.S. Government Printing Office), p. V, Table 1.

[a] Measured as a proportion of the total indicator incidence occurring in the fifth year following the 1% change in unemployment.

Table 37. Cumulative Impact of the 1.4% Rise in Unemployment during 1970

Social Stress Indicator	Stress Incidence 1975	Change in Stress Indicator for a 1.4% Rise in Unemployment	Increase in Stress Incidence Due to the Rise in Unemployment
Suicide	26,960	5.7%	1,540
State mental hospital admission	117,480	4.7	5,520
State prison admission	136,875[a]	5.6	7,660
Homicide	21,730[b]	8.0	1,740
Cirrhosis of the liver mortality	32,080	2.7	870
Cardiovascular-renal disease mortality	979,180	2.7	26,440
Total mortality	1,910,000	2.7	51,570

Source: 94th Congress, Joint Economic Committee, Congress of the U.S. Paper No. 5, *Estimating the Social Costs of National Economic Policy: Implications for Mental and Physical Health, and Clinical Aggression,* (Washington, D.C.: U.S. Government Printing Office), p. VII, Table 11.

[a] 1972 data, age 65 and under.

[b] 1974 data.

REFERENCES

Recent information on the black family comes from the following sources.

AFDC Chartbook, 1977 Recipient Characteristics Study. Part 1: Demographic and Program Statistics (Washington, D.C.: Office of Research and Statistics, Office of Policy, Social Security Administration. U.S. Department of Health and Human Services, 1980), pp. 16–17. (SSA 13–11729)

Aid to Families with Dependent Children: A Chartbook (Washington, D.C.: Office of Research and Statistics, Office of Policy, Social Security Administration, U.S. Department of Health and Human Services, 1979), (SSA 79–11721)

John M. Berry, "Joblessness Rose Again Last Month," *The Washington Post,* March 6, 1982, A-1, A-27.

Norman Bowers, "Young and Marginal: An Overview of Youth Employment," *Young Workers and Families: A Special Section* (Washington, D.C.: Bureau of Labor Statistics, U.S. Department of Labor, Special Labor Force Report 233, 1980.)

Andrew F. Brimmer, "Economic Outlook: Reaganomics and the Black Community," *Black Enterprise,* Vol. 12, No. 5, December 1981, p. 43.

Bureau of the Census, "Black Movers to the Suburbs: Are They Moving to Predominantly White Neighborhoods?" (Washington, D.C.: U.S. Government Printing Office, December 1981), p. 1.

Hugh Carter and Paul C. Glick, *Marriage and Divorce: A Social and Economic Study,* rev. ed. (Cambridge, Mass.: Harvard University Press, 1976), pp. 405–406.

St. Clair Drake, "The Social and Economic Status of the Negro," *Daedalus,* Vol. 94, No. 4, Fall 1965, p. 773.

Paul C. Glick, "A Demographic Picture of Black Families," in Harriette Pipes McAdoo, ed., *Black Families* (Beverly Hills: Sage Publications, 1981), p. 108.

S. David Hicks, *The Corrections Yearbook: Instant Answers to Key Questions in Corrections, 1981 Pocket Guide* (New York: Criminal Justice Institute, 1981).

Robert B. Hill, "Black Families in the 1970s," in *The State of Black America 1980* (New York: National Urban League, 1980), pp. 29–58.

Robert B. Hill, *Black Families in the 1974–75 Depression* (Washington, D.C.: National Urban League Research Department, July 1975).

Robert B. Hill, "The Economic Status of Black America," in *The State of Black America 1981* (New York: National Urban League, 1981), pp. 7, 59.

Robert B. Hill, "The Economic Status of Black Families," in *The State of Black America 1979* (New York: National Urban League, 1979), p. 35.

Robert B. Hill, *The Illusion of Black Progress* (Washington, D.C.: National Urban League Research Department, 1978).

Robert B. Hill, *The Strengths of Black Families* (New York: Emerson Hall, 1971).

Robert B. Hill, *The Widening Economic Gap* (Washington, D.C.: National Urban League Research Department, 1979), p. 10.

Instant Answers to Key Questions in Corrections: 1980 Pocket Guide (New York: Criminal Justice Institute, 1980).

Barbara A. P. Jones, "Utilization of Black Human Resources in the U.S.," *Review of Black Political Economy,* Vol. 10, Fall 1979, pp. 79–96.

Faustine Jones-Wilson, "External Crosscurrents and Internal Diversity: An Assessment of Black Progress, 1960–1980," in *Daedalus,* Vol. 110, No. 2, Spring 1981, p. 82.

Juvenile and Adult Correctional Departments, Institutions, Agencies, and Paroling Authorities, U.S. and Canada, 1981 edition, prepared by Diana Travisono (College Park, Md.: American Correctional Association, 1981).

Lasting Effects after Preschool, A report of the Consortium for Longitudinal Studies, under the supervision of Irving Lazar and Richard B. Darlington. (Ithaca, N.Y.: Cornell University, October 1978). (abstract, findings)

Marc Levinson, "Aid to Families with Dependent Children in Georgia," *The Crisis,* January 1980, pp. 31–33.

Harriette Pipes McAdoo, "Patterns of Upward Mobility in Black Families," in Harriette Pipes McAdoo, ed., *Black Families* (Beverly Hills: Sage Publications, 1981), pp. 155–169.

Dorothy K. Newman et al., *Protest, Politics, and Prosperity: Black Americans and White Institutions, 1940–75* (New York: Pantheon Books, 1978), pp. 5–7.

Alex Poinsett, "Who Gets Welfare?," *Ebony,* Vol. 37, No. 3, January 1982, pp. 28–29.

Population Profile of the United States: 1980. Current Population Reports, Series P-20, No. 363, June 1981.

Profile of State Prison Inmates: Sociodemographic Findings from the 1974 Survey of Inmates of State Correctional Facilities (Washington, D.C.: A National Prisoner Statistics Special Report, National Criminal Justice Information and Statistics Service, Law Enforcement Assistance Administration, U.S. Department of Justice, August 1979).

Lee Rainwater, "Crucible of Identity: The Negro Lower-Class Family," *Daedalus,* Vol. 95, Winter 1966, p. 209.

L. J. Schweinhart and D. P. Weikart, *Young Children Grow Up: The Effects of the Perry Preschool Program on Youths Through Age 15* (Ypsilanti, Mich.: The High/Scope Press, 1980), pp. 69–72.

"The Sickle Cell Story," Published by the Howard University Center for Sickle Cell Disease, Washington, D.C. 20059. Pamphlet revised Spring 1980.

Sourcebook of Criminal Justice Statistics—1977 (Washington, D.C.: National Criminal Justice Information and Statistics Service, Law Enforcement Assistance Administration, U.S. Department of Justice, February 1978).

Statistical Abstract of the U.S., 100th ed. (Washington, D.C.: U.S. Government Printing Office, 1979), p. 181.

Statistical Abstract of the U.S., 101st ed. (Washington, D.C.: U.S. Government Printing Office, 1980), pp. 52, 188, 201.

Lester Thurow, *Poverty and Discrimination* (Washington, D.C.: The Brookings Institution, 1969), pp. 158–159.

Lester C. Thurow, *The Zero-Sum Society: Distribution and the Possibilities for Economic Change* (New York: Basic Books, 1980), p. 63.

U.S. Bureau of the Census, *The Social and Economic Status of the Black Population in the United States: An Historical View, 1790–1978,* Current Population Reports, Series P-23, No. 80 (Washington, D.C.: U.S. Government Printing Office, 1979), pp. 7, 16, 31, 69, 136, 186, 189–191, 209.

U.S. Bureau of the Census, *The Social and Economic Status of the Black Population in the United States 1974* (Washington, D.C.: U.S. Government Printing Office, 1975).

U.S. Bureau of the Census, *Social Indicators III: Selected Data on Social Conditions and Trends in the United States.* (Washington, D.C.: U.S. Government Printing Office, December 1980), pp. 21, 47.

Vital Statistics of the U.S., Mortality Rates, Vol. 2, Part A, Section 5, Table 5–1, pp. 5–9 to 5–11.

THE BLACK WORKER IN THE LABOR MOVEMENT

Overview—The Early Eighties ■ A Brief History of Blacks and Organized Labor ■ The Civil Rights Alliance ■ The 1960s—From Cooperation to Conflict ■ Black Power Focuses on Unions (1968–1970) ■ The Construction Workers ■ Nixon and the Building Trades (1970–1974) ■ Blacks Challenge the Steel Union ■ The Landmark Weber Case ■ The Reagan Administration after Weber ■ Trends for the 1980s ■ Selected Labor Facts ■ Labor Tables

In 1980 blacks comprised nearly 15% of the union membership in the United States—approximately 3 million of the nation's 20 million union members. Black men and women found it to their advantage to belong to unions and joined in larger proportions than their white counterparts: out of a union labor force of 20.1 million, 33.8% were black men and 24% were black women, as compared to 27.8% white men and 14.6% white women.

About one third of organzied black workers were concentrated in the automobile, steel, and teamster unions; a substantial number of blacks also held white-collar occupations, especially clerical jobs, where black workers were more likely than whites to be union members.

The National Union of Hospital and Health Care Employees maintained the highest proportion of black union members—out of 119,000 members in 1981, 70,000 were black.

From 1977 to 1980, the total number of employed wage and salary workers increased 6.2 million, from 81.3 to 87.5 million. More than 90% of these new jobs were white-collar occupations, and industry groups such as transportation, communications, and public utilities saw the greatest growth. Although both blue-collar and service occupations gained workers during this period, the percentage of workers employed in blue-collar occupations declined overall to 32.5% of the 87.5 million-person work force.

Union membership remained a clear financial benefit to blacks. In 1980 the median annual earnings for nonunion white males was $273 a week, and it was $192 a week for nonunion black males. In comparison, white males in the unions received $288 a week and black males in the unions received $249. Nonunion white females earned $160 a week and nonunion black females earned $150, while their union counterparts earned $207 and $201 a week, respectively.

However, much of the American labor movement continued to obstruct blacks, especially in the highly paid skilled jobs such as those in the building trades. Government, union, and employer programs, which

Turpentine was produced by slave labor in this old South Carolina camp.

encouraged minority hiring, made some inroads for blacks through affirmative action, but by the early 1980s the efforts had practically ceased. The end result was that "tokenism" existed in employer programs and blacks remained severely underrepresented.

In addition, blacks in many important unions continued to be locked into separate and unequal seniority systems that retarded their progress. Numerous consent decrees and court orders to employers and unions to alter discriminatory hiring and promotion practices and compensate blacks for past inequalities seemed to be reaping satisfactory results by the late 1970s, but the Reagan administration initiated an about-face in 1981 by relaxing laws governing affirmative action requirements for lucrative government contracts and by declaring that preferential treatment could no longer be given to minorities and women.

A BRIEF HISTORY OF BLACKS AND ORGANIZED LABOR

The Early Years

The labor movement in the United States, as elsewhere, was born and nurtured on a mixture of fear and idealism. As a result, from its very inception, organized labor has been ambiguous toward minorities. On one hand, it has maintained the right of all working men and women to just wages, dignified working conditions, and job security. As such, "labor" has sought to help blacks attain a share of the nation's expanding wealth.

On the other hand, the predominantly white membership and leadership of unions have feared the readiness of poor blacks to work for low wages and the ability of skilled blacks to compete with whites for jobs in better paying trades. As a result, the labor movement also became a vehicle to prevent blacks from fulfilling their talents and ambition.

Ironically, from their earliest days on these shores, many of the skills and trades in which blacks are now employed only tokenly were performed regularly, ably, and often brilliantly by free and slave blacks. This was especially so in the better paying construction trades, whose unions now train and admit blacks to only a minuscule degree. Throughout the seventeenth, eighteenth, and nineteenth centuries, blacks were prevalent, and often predominant, in the ranks of the carpenters, masons, ironworkers, and stonecutters who built the great mansions and government buildings that are now the pride of the South. Blacks also were conspicuous in the ranks of printers, coopers, tailors, and mechanics. In the 1830s blacks comprised a majority of the carpenters in Charleston and a substantial portion of other skilled workmen in Atlanta, Philadelphia, New Orleans, and other cities.

But the organized efforts of whites to exclude blacks also dates back to early American history. In 1686 the legislature of the Carolinas was prevailed upon to enact a law excluding free blacks from trades. Laws enacted in many colonies and states in the eighteenth and nineteenth centuries forbade master workmen to teach black apprentices to read and write. Violence to exclude blacks from skilled and unskilled employment increased along with the arrival of white immigrants from Europe. In 1834 alone, there were riots in Trenton, Philadelphia, and Rochester.

The mad scramble for jobs created by the growth of the industrial revolution produced intense rivalry and competition between native-born whites and for-

Old drawings of a skilled black carpenter and a waiter.

from the bad publicity it received, nor live down the ominous nickname with which it was tagged—the "Black International."

Attempts to End Discrimination

For the first three decades of the twentieth century, organized labor as a whole reflected the hostility of American society toward the black population. In so doing, the trade union movement seemed impotent to deal with the divide-and-conquer attitudes of employers.

However, at various intervals throughout the history of the labor movement attempts have been made to end discrimination and segregation. The tradition begun by the Knights of Labor was continued by the militant members of the International Workers of the World (I.W.W., or the "wobblies" as they were known) who went so far as to organize the underpaid and unskilled lumber workers in the South regardless of race. "Big Bill" Haywood, a leader of the I.W.W., refused to countenance segregated meetings of white

eign-born whites for available jobs. In the early years of the craft or trade union movement, both these groups joined forces in propagating policies of racial exclusion—already part of the prevailing social climate of the United States. By the eve of the Civil War, many labor unions had formed nationally federated associations which incorporated these basic social attitudes as a matter of course.

After the war, black workers were encouraged by organizations like the National Labor Union (the first national federation of trade unions) to form their own counterpart unions within the framework of white-dominated federations. (In this way, the Colored National Labor Union came into being as an arm of the Republican party, falling into decline, however, with the panic of 1873 and the end of Reconstruction in 1877.)

For a brief period, the Noble Order of the Knights of Labor did attempt to maintain a labor organization which would include male and female, skilled and unskilled, and white and Negro workers. Organized in 1869, the Order grew rapidly until 1886, at which time it was in a position to boast of some 60,000 blacks among its more than 700,000 members. That year, however, May Day demonstrations in Chicago* and the Haymarket bombing caused both press and public alike to equate it with destructive anarchism and to brand it a social menace. Though it too had denounced the bombings, the Order itself was never able to recover

* Labor's major quest at the time was the eight-hour working day.

Pioneer black union organizer Willard S. Townsend, president of the United Transport Service Employees.

and black workers in Louisiana even when joint meetings were prohibited by state law.

At its inception, the American Federation of Labor included as part of its credo the statement that "working people must unite and organize, irrespective of creed, color, sex, nationality or politics." But the AFL lacked the power and will to implement policies which counteracted the racist attitudes prevalent within its ranks. Thus it organized Negroes into separate locals, or affiliated them with central unions whenever they were refused admission on the basis of color.

During the whole dark chapter covering the period from the turn of the twentieth century to the 1930s, enlightened blacks, despite the rebuffs they had suffered, continued to recognize the potential usefulness of the labor movement to all American workers and its potential usefulness to blacks.

"I carry on the title page of this magazine the union label," wrote W.E.B. DuBois in the *Crisis* magazine (1918), "and yet I know, and everyone of my Negro readers knows, that the very fact that this label is there is an advertisement that no Negro's hand is engaged in the printing of this magazine." DuBois added:

Collective bargaining has undoubtedly raised modern labor from something like chattel slavery to the threshold of industrial freedom and in this advance of labor white and black have shared.

Progressivism in the CIO

With the Roosevelt era of the 1930s and the passage of the Wagner Act, some leaders within the ranks of

Machinist Frank J. Farrell, a Knights of Labor delegate.

the AFL began to reject the discriminatory policies of the majority of the international union leaders. It became obvious to others that if the international unions continued to exclude blacks, employers would have little trouble in recruiting strikebreakers from the excluded class. Under the rising pressure of Negro protest, a number of AFL leaders launched a series of organizing campaigns in the mass-production industries, and ultimately formed the Congress of Industrial Organizations (CIO).

The resulting AFL-CIO rivalry caused a schism in the ranks of labor—one which led the CIO to concern itself primarily with the organization of the steel, auto, mining, packinghouse, and rubber industries, all of which employed large numbers of blacks. It has been said that no other CIO leader better understood "the importance of equalitarian racial policies for successful unionism that John L. Lewis of the United Mine Workers." In this union, the common economic and occupational hardships endured by all minimized—although they did not totally eliminate—racial differences among members, even those in the South. Lewis' policies in this area were soon followed by Philip Murray, president of the steel workers, and Walter Reuther, head of the auto workers. CIO policies ultimately prompted Thurgood Marshall to declare that "the program (of this organization) has become a Bill of Rights for Negro labor in America."

These new unions broke sharply with traditional racial practices. Segregationist constitutions and by-laws were erased. Locals admitted blacks and, in a few cases, integrated seniority lines. Negroes were elected to executive positions within locals. Some new unions gave priority to lifting wage scales for low-paying jobs, most of which were filled by Negroes, and to training and upgrading "underemployed" black workers. One such union was the Transport Workers Union in New York, which negotiated substantial wage increases for change clerks and saw to the promotion of black workers to skilled, well-paying white-collar positions.

Unfortunately, such achievements were exceptions that proved the rule of discrimination throughout America's labor movement, especially in craft locals (e.g., cooks and electricians) and hall-oriented locals (e.g., seafarers and lumber and sawmill workers). In the South, the black's position in unions was actually weakened when, in reaction to the 1954 Supreme Court desegregation decision, segregationist groups formed alliances with union locals.

Far from being conducted in an aura of secrecy, the cooperation of Southern segregationists and union leaders was widely publicized. In many localities, notices appeared in local papers stating that the White Citizens Council or the Ku Klux Klan would be holding a meeting in a union hall.

Charleston dock workers organized a union of their own after the Civil War.

In 1960, six years after the desegregation decision, the NAACP charged that the "Ku Klux Klan and White Citizen Council Forces, especially in Alabama, have moved into many local unions and made them, in effect, virtual extensions of segregationist organizations." Such union-segregationist alliances were apparent to Southern blacks who were understandably more concerned with the situation in their locality than with pro-civil rights declarations from national union headquarters. As a result, Southern blacks often voted in a bloc, in NLRB elections, against union certification. In some cases, black votes defeated major organizational campaigns. One such election, still discussed in union circles, was held at the South Wire Company, Carrollton, Georgia, where 45 Negro workers out of several hundred are believed to have voted en masse against certification of the International Brotherhood of Electrical Workers. The union lost by 8 votes. At the Savannah River Atomic Energy Project in Aiken, South Carolina, 600 black workers out of 3,100 tipped an election against certification of 17 metal trades unions.

The Merger

It is against this background of erratic progress and racist reaction that the AFL and CIO merged in late 1955. The elimination of racism within unions was announced as a major goal of the new giant union. Its constitution pledged that the AFL-CIO would encourage all workingmen "without regard to race, creed, color or national origin or ancestry to share equally in the benefits of union organization." A Civil Rights Committee was established to achieve these goals.

This pledge was, of course, applauded by civil rights and liberal organizations. But five years later, in a report on racism within organized labor, the NAACP charged that "the national labor organization has failed to eliminate the broad pattern of racial discrimination and segregation," and that "efforts to eliminate discriminatory practices within trade unions have been piecemeal and inadequate and usually the result of protest."

There was considerable evidence to support these charges. Despite the exemplary declarations accompanying the merger, the AFL-CIO shortly thereafter admitted two unions, the Brotherhood of Locomotive Firemen and the Brotherhood of Railroad Trainmen, at a time when they had racist clauses in their constitutions.

The AFL-CIO also ignored defiance of state anti-discrimination orders by segregated locals. In April 1957, the New York State Commission against Discrimination ordered the merger of the all-white George N. Harrison Lodge and the all-black Friendship Lodges of the Brotherhood of Railway and Steamship Clerks. The white union disobeyed the order and the lodges remained segregated for several years.

The AFL-CIO also refrained from pressure or comment when member unions went to court to defend exclusion of blacks. In 1958, after elimination of a "caucasian only" clause from its constitution, the Brotherhood of Locomotive Firemen and Enginemen successfully defended continued exclusion of blacks in a suit brought by Negro firemen in a Cincinnati Federal Court.

Leading black trade unionists observed that the AFL-CIO could expel unions for corruption or Communist ties, but not for violating civil right laws and policies.

Infighting between black and union leaders intensified in the late 1950s. The NAACP brought a number of suits under state fair employment practice laws to force admission of blacks to unions. Activists attacked labor's historic gods. In a scathing article in *Commentary* magazine, Herbert Hill, labor director of the NAACP, charged, with some telling evidence to support him, that Samuel Gompers, after struggling with some early idealism, became a racist who despised blacks and hated Asians. Hill also charged that the East St. Louis and Chicago black pogroms of 1917 and 1919 were incited and executed by white unionists who feared the use of Negro strike breakers, and that Gompers defended the rioters in a debate with Theodore Roosevelt.

The AFL-CIO promised it would try to eliminate discrimination from "within the house of labor." George Meany, president of the AFL-CIO, stated that discrimination only survived in the labor movement as "bootleg product, sneaked in by subterfuge."

Meany added that those "that practice discrimination know that its days are numbered." But other leaders of the federation argued that it could not compel locals to adhere to the national union's egalitarian policies.

The Civil Rights Alliance

Paradoxically, while black and union leaders were fighting one another over union racial practices, they were cooperating in support of state and federal civil rights legislation.

Black and union leaders were in part forced into an alliance because the only strong and consistent political support for each group stemmed from liberal Democrats.

Liberal Democrats favored civil rights legislation and such traditional union objectives as increases in the minimum wage and unemployment compensation, while Republicans and Southern Democrats generally opposed pro-labor and civil rights measures.

Republicans and Southern Democrats had achieved enactment of the Taft-Hartley Act, which increased the government's authority to prevent and end strikes. This same political alliance also combined to prevent cloture of filibusters against civil rights legislation.

Tensions between black and labor leaders were also diminished by the fact that black progress within labor unions was not really a major aim of civil rights leaders. The civil rights movement of the 1950s and early 1960s was far more intense about integration in schools, housing, transportation, and restaurants than in unions.

The reasons for this are complex. Civil rights leadership tended to rest in the hands of black and white professional men—lawyers, ministers, journalists, teachers. There was a tendency among them—perhaps a snobbish tendency—to despise blue-collar work both as a career and as a political issue. Perhaps this attitude was related to an association of blue-collar labor with slavery. At any rate, civil rights leaders of that time obviously felt it far more important for blacks to get degrees from colleges, houses in suburbs, and jobs in corporate suites than to soil their hands on railway engines or scaffolds, no matter how well such work paid.

Also, the immediate objectives of black leaders tended to be legalistic rather than economic. The thrust was for new legislation and constitutional interpretations that would provide legal sanction for equality and integration and would eventually, it was assumed, lead to good economic progress.

It was not until Malcolm X, a criminal who embraced Muslimism while in prison and went on to become a charismatic modern-day black leader, achieved notoriety that a "working man" was to obtain status among the postwar black generation.

Thus, though blacks were bitter about union exclusion, black leaders tended to take it easy on unions—in order to sustain their political alliance with unions and because civil rights advocates were really not all that interested in manual labor, skilled or unskilled.

The AFL-CIO leadership, however, was interested in blacks. The union leadership was not happy about its many surrenders and silences to segregationist affiliates. Many important unions were losing strength in the 1950s, both in terms of real numbers and comparative bargaining strength with employers.

Automation in the coal mines and the weak competitive position of coal vis-à-vis other forms of power forced the United Mine Workers to accept massive layoffs and the closing of marginal pits. Organization in service industries was disappointingly slow, partly because of union racist policies. Corporations were acquiring bargaining strength via mergers and internal expansion. And the prospect of blacks again appearing in large numbers as scabs haunted labor leaders who had come up through the ranks to union leadership and who had long and clear memories of the days when Negro strike breakers received police protection in the mines of the Rocky Mountains and on the rails in Pennsylvania.

Also, a tinge of working-class socialist idealism survived, and still survives, amidst the guild exclusiveness and suburban conservatism of the labor movement. Some labor leaders find it easier to think of solidarity in terms of economic class than race, and of progress in terms of social legislation rather than political reaction.

This idealism was tempered by the McCarthyite red scare of the early 1950s and concern about Communist infiltration of unions. Walter Reuther had been a particular target of "witch hunters."

Thus it was that the 1950s ended on an eccentric note. Individual unions and locals were coolly excluding qualified blacks from good jobs and apprenticeships while union and black leaders were cooperating in attempts to achieve legislation that would guarantee blacks the right to live, learn, vote, and work with whites, and on the same terms as whites.

The 1960s—From Cooperation to Conflict

The 1960s saw profound changes within both the black and labor movements, with the two groups tending to pull in opposite directions. Blacks became more radical and assertive, labor more sluggish and cautious, with the end result that by 1970 the AFL-CIO and selected discriminatory unions were prime targets of both militant and moderate Negro groups.

Negro activity during the 1960s can be traced in terms of its changing targets and ways of exerting pressure.

From 1960 to 1964, the major objective remained civil rights legislation. The main target was Congress and the Kennedy and Johnson administrations. Pressure, however, was exerted more aggressively than during the 1950s, as blacks increasingly resorted to sit-ins, marches, and other forms of direct nonviolent confrontation.

From 1964 until spring 1968, the period of ghetto riots, the objective was immediate improvement of living conditions. The main target was the "business establishment," which black leaders of varying militancy felt had the financial and political muscle to effect rapid change.

From spring 1968 to the end of the decade, the period of conservatism and "law and order," major objectives were economic progress, recognition of black ability and uniqueness, and protection of legislation and constitutional gains made since World War II. Major targets were unions which segregated or otherwise demeaned blacks.

While blacks were becoming more radical in the 1960s, the labor movement, as a whole, was becoming more conservative. As workers prospered, they moved to the suburbs or better urban residential areas where they lost interest in social reform, and saw blacks as a threat to their newfound middle-class status. Resistance to integration in unions, and other changes, became so firm by 1970 that A. H. Raskin, assistant

President Kennedy greets black officials at the Centennial of the Emancipation Proclamation.

editor and labor specialist of the *New York Times,* was to describe labor as "a static force in a chaotic society."

"A movement born as a voice of dissent," continued Raskin, "has become a mainstay of the status quo in a period when even the staidest institutions—educational, corporate, governmental—have felt obliged to take a look at all their most cherished precepts and scrap those made obsolete by changing technology and mores."

Blacks and Labor Elect Kennedy

However, both groups supported civil rights and pro-labor legislation and John F. Kennedy for president. Without an overwhelming black and labor vote, Kennedy would have been soundly defeated by Richard Nixon, who lost narrowly and only after some questionable vote counts in Chicago.

Cooperation at the policy-making level reached its high-water mark during the "1,000 days" of Kennedy and the first year or so of the Johnson administration.

Kennedy had promised strong civil rights legislation during his campaign, but by 1963 was clearly pessimistic of his chances of steering a strong bill through Congress. He was especially cynical about Congress's

AFL-CIO President George Meany.

interest in enacting an equal employment opportunities requirement.

Labor historians credit George Meany with the eventual passage of equal opportunities provisions. Notes Raskin:

The AFL-CIO itself was chiefly responsible for the inclusion of the equal employment opportunities requirement in the Civil Rights Act of 1964. When the original omnibus bill was drawn up in 1963, President Kennedy and Attorney General Robert F. Kennedy were both convinced that it would have trouble enough getting through Congress without a provision forbidding job discrimination by employers or unions. Their view would have prevailed if George Meany had not insisted that such a clause was essential. . . . Through every phase of the long fight that followed on Capitol Hill, the AFL-CIO was a mainstay of the coalition that lobbied for a strong anti-bias law.

Walter Reuther, then an AFL-CIO vice-president, was conspicuous in the 1963 March on Washington, as were the heads and memberships of other unions with large quantities of black members. Black labor leaders A. Philip Randolph and Cleveland Robinson were key organizers of the March.

During this period, blacks were progressing in such service-trades unions as the State, County and Municipal Employees and District 65 of the Retail, Wholesalers, Department Store Union. But in most unions, they were progressing slowly or not at all. Blacks were still excluded from the lucrative referral construction unions. And in large industrial unions, such as the steelworkers, blacks were usually consigned to menial jobs and deprivable seniority lines.

Little was achieved with state Fair Employment Practice Commissions. Although many states have FEP laws, their minuscule staffs and budgets confined the Commissions to slow case-by-case conciliation, where investigation of bias and enforcement of the laws were necessary to effect any real change in the job status of minorities.

The unions generally resisted integrationist pressures. AFL-CIO officials continued to protest that the national union lacked authority to interfere with locals. Negro leaders such as A. Philip Randolph chastised the national union and its Civil Rights Division for their indifferent progress in effecting integration.

The Alliance Collapses

The union-civil rights alliance, strained at the best of times, disintegrated with the passage of civil rights legislation and the urban ghetto riots of 1964–1968.

However, black attention was focused elsewhere. Though blacks continued to challenge discrimination in unions, the main targets of their fury were the police and white ghetto merchants. Their main sources of hope were the government and large corporations, whom blacks hoped would invest money and wield influence to erase employment, health, and housing problems. Thus black leaders made relatively little effort to challenge or work with unions.

White leaders who were seeking progress also displayed little interest in unions. For example, the National Advisory Commission on Civil Disorders (The Kerner Commission) was critical of unions and recommended steps to assure Negroes access to skilled jobs, but obviously regarded exclusion from unions as a lesser matter on the blacks' imposing list of grievances.

The government's response to the riots was to emphasize employment and training of poor blacks. The main responsibility for this was assigned to business. The Johnson administration set up the JOBS Program to subsidize recruiting and training of "hard core" ghetto residents and major corporations formed the National Alliance of Business to guide business in these activities. Unions were merely asked to cooperate and in many instances were granted the right to veto training programs which they felt threatened to glut a labor market. This veto power was, in effect, a continuation of a privilege unions had acquired over Department of Labor training programs earlier in the 1960s.

The reaction of unions to JOBS and NAB was erratic. The AFL-CIO pledged support to recruitment and training efforts. Support was forthcoming from many unions, particularly service industry unions with large numbers of minority-group members. Others were quick to exercise their vetoes.

The New York Teachers Strike

One of the more significant labor disputes of the 1960s occurred in 1968, when a local of the United Federation of Teachers in New York City went out on strike. This strike fought for more than increases in wages and fringe benefits for teachers; it also achieved union control of important segments of public educational policy.

The UFT strike was directed at the city's intention to decentralize its public schools and hand control to community school boards. Such a program was underway in three experimental school districts, notably the black Bedford-Stuyvesant section of Brooklyn. The local school board there exhibited a strong distaste for some white teachers who allegedly had little interest in, or aptitude for, motivating black students. It proceeded to dismiss a number of them and to react sluggishly on behalf of other white teachers who were being harassed in classrooms. Union leader Albert Shanker called a strike which kept over 1,000,000 children out of school for two months. The central issue was the school board's power to hire and fire teachers. Underlying issues were black anti-Semitism and the questionable conscientiousness of many whites who teach in black neighborhoods. The strike was not resolved until the local school board's authority was diminished.

1968–1970: Black Power Focuses on Unions

A number of ideological and practical factors served to divide blacks and unions during the final years of the sixties.

In the face of white backlash, unions tended to increase their resistance to integration. They maintained that this was necessary to prevent a massive defection by union voters from the Democratic Party to George Wallace. After the 1968 Presidential election union leaders claimed, though not for publication, that Wallace's vote in Northern cities, which generally ranged from 5 to 10%, would have been much larger if the unions had not stressed the low wages earned by workers in Wallace's home state of Alabama.

Whatever the case, there can be no doubt that Wallace won substantial support from Northern blue-collar whites.

Blacks and the AFL-CIO were also divided by varying positions on the Vietnam war. The AFL-CIO strongly supported the war while blacks, though fighting there in large numbers, tended to regard it as a racist conflict which was absorbing money needed to improve conditions in American cities.

The civil rights movement had also shifted strongly from its legal-legislative orientation to one of economic improvement. To be sure, court cases were abundant

The Newark Teachers' Union threatens to strike.

and many of them referred to the older issues of school and housing integration. But an increasing number were directed toward economic improvement, toward erasing bias by employers and unions.

The Construction Workers

Unions, contractors, politicians, workers, and the thousands of desperately unemployed all have a stake in the lucrative construction industry, which was worth about $140 billion in 1981. Jobs here are among the highest paying in the country. The average wage-fringe benefit package in the unions is $20 an hour and carries excellent fringe benefits; training requires a minimum of educational background.

During the nineteenth century, many of the skilled craftsmen were black, but since the unions gained tight control of the construction labor market in the early 1900s, blacks had been shut out. Today, despite 20 years of antidiscrimination legislation, ranging from executive orders to federal, state, and city laws, blacks still remain underrepresented in construction fields including asbestos workers, bricklayers, carpenters, cement masons, electrical workers, glaziers, ironworkers, lathers, operating engineers, painters, plasterers, plumbers, roofers, and sheetmetal workers. Blacks had good reason to expect opposition in any reasoned attack they made on exclusive-skill unions, like construction locals.

Artificial scarcity had been created in the 1960s through restrictive apprentice programs and journeyman certifications, and construction unions enjoyed astronomical pay scales. Union plumbers in Philadelphia, for example, negotiated an annual minimum wage of $19,400. Such wages contributed to inflationary pay raises throughout the economy. The addition of black construction workers would reduce the scarcity and give blacks a piece of some well-paid action.

Also, construction unions found themselves in great demand: it was estimated in 1965 that 1,000,000 skilled construction men would have to be added to the labor force by 1975. Unfortunately, the Depression-conscious construction unions worked effectively to minimize entrants into the field.

A number of provisions in federal and local law were instituted to require acceptance of blacks on government-supported construction projects. As Herbert Hill, then-Labor Director for the NAACP, remarked to the Senate Judiciary Committee in October 1969, the public share of the current dollar value of construction rose from 17% in 1947 to 34% in 1967. The government is very much in the construction business. And the construction industry is very dependent on government funds, he said.

The new emphasis on black history, reminding blacks that they were able craftsmen during slavery, may also have contributed to their decision to assault the skilled trades.

It should be said for the unions that economic gain has been a greater factor than racial bias in their exclusionist policies. By limiting the supply of officially qualified workers, they strengthened their position against any recession.

The AFL-CIO replied to black charges by repeating their assertion that national headquarters lacked the power to interfere with local unions, that blacks often failed to pass journeyman and apprenticeship qualification tests, and that under an AFL-CIO "Apprenticeship Outreach" program, the unions had trained 3,862 non-whites in construction trades in two years.

But essentially, 15 years after the highly touted Apprenticeship Outreach and other "hometown" plans were announced, it was found that nothing had been changed and the programs themselves hardly existed any longer. By 1981, for example, the only participants in Apprentice Outreach were members who had started the program several years earlier and were finishing their training. No new trainees were accepted and the program was being phased out.

Discriminatory problems with black construction union members seemed to be perpetuated in two ways: the insistence of employers on hiring white union members, and reluctance of hiring hall bosses to dispatch black workers over whites.

Discriminatory practices are still maintained in the hiring halls of referral unions. Here, an employer puts in a request for a number of workers for a period of time, and the union dispatches the workers from their pool. Ideally, each union worker is rotated up a list until his or her name is called for a job. However, it has proven easy to get around rotation rules and blacks have been discriminated against in the white-dominated hiring halls.

It was a situation with hiring halls that triggered a violent melee in midtown Manhattan in July 1981. Construction opportunities had declined throughout the country in the late 1970s, but in New York City there was a booming hardhat business. Since the 1960s, disgruntled blacks had been picketing construction sites where they had been excluded, but by the 1980s, demonstrations had become more violent. Groups such as Black Economic Survival were formed, and they bused dozens and sometimes hundreds of black and Hispanic workers from construction site to construction site to harass the workers and demand equal employment and the appointment of a "community coordinator" to ensure equal representation.

It was a confrontation like this that generated the July 20, 1981 riot in Manhattan where 325 riot police were needed to quell a violent demonstration during

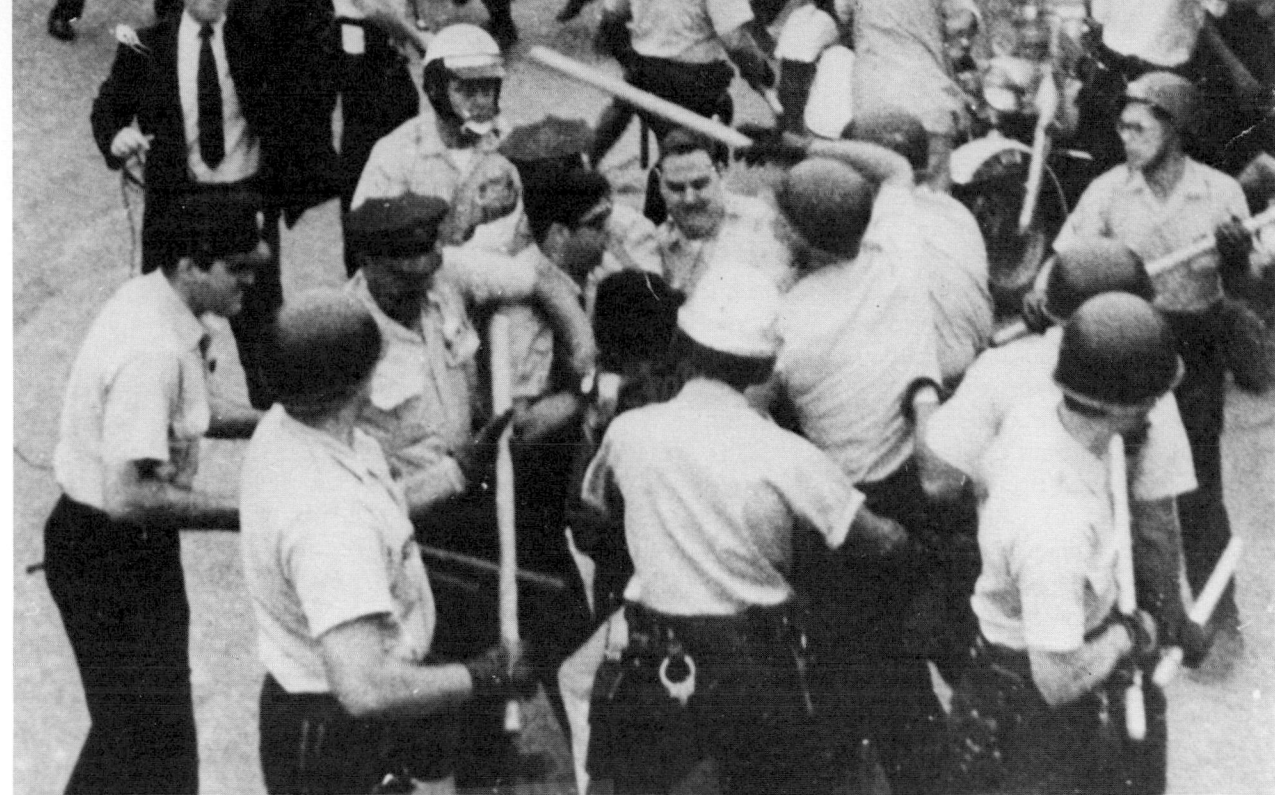

Pittsburgh police scuffle with demonstrators from the Black Construction Coalition at the building site of Three Rivers Stadium.

which some 800 unemployed blacks and Hispanics pitched battle with construction workers at two sites. The fighting raged briefly, with few serious injuries, although 25 workers and 12 police officers required hospitalization. Mayor Edward I. Koch denounced the violence but promised to investigate the allegations of violations of hiring laws. Several protestors were arraigned for assault, but no major action was taken.

A significant case for construction unions is pending in the Supreme Court. On October 19, 1981 the high court accepted a case on appeal from several groups of building contractors in Pennsylvania in order to decide who would be liable for damages in discrimination cases: the union or the contractor. A federal appeals court ruled that 1,488 contractors were jointly responsible with the International Union of Operating Engineers for the virtual absence of blacks in the state's construction business.

The case was first brought by a group of black construction workers, supported by the Pennsylvania state government, who sued both Local 542 of the Operating Engineers, which covers eastern Pennsylvania and all of Delaware, and the employers who patronized the hiring hall. At the time of the 1976 trial, 70% of the employers had never hired a black worker.

In their Supreme Court appeal, the employers and General Buildings Contractors argued that they should not be held liable for the union's discriminatory acts because under the terms of various collective bargaining agreements, they were prohibited from going beyond the hiring hall to employ workers directly. The contractors also argued that the Civil Rights Act of 1966 requires proof that discriminatory intent was present in order to establish a violation.

Following the Supreme Court ruling, a separate trial will be held to determine monetary damage and liability of the contractor and union for past discrimination.

Pittsburgh, Chicago, and the "Philadelphia Plan"

In the early 1960s blacks had demonstrated against hiring bias at construction sites in New York, Philadelphia and elsewhere. These earlier demonstrations were to pale before those which groups undertook in 1969 in Chicago, Pittsburgh, and other cities.

In the summer of 1969, the Pittsburgh Black Construction Coalition, an amalgam of skilled laborers and civil rights groups, blocked entrances to major construction projects for three days. The workers counter-demonstrated, some of them carrying "Wallace in '72" placards. The police were called upon to prevent violence.

In Chicago, also in the summer of 1969, the Chicago Coalition for United Community Action, a group of about 60 minority-group organizations ranging from the Southern Christian Leadership Conference to street gangs, halted work for several days on construction jobs valued at $100 million. The Coalition demanded

10,000 jobs for minorities and the easing of qualification requirements for minorities.

The Chicago & Cook County Building & Construction Trades Council, in a plan endorsed by George Meany, promised in January 1970 to "endeavor to obtain employment for 1,000 qualified journeymen" to be supplied by the Coalition, to accept workers of uncertain skills for 30-day probationary periods, and to expand information, recruiting, and training programs. In February the "agreement" awaited ratification by the unions and Coalition.

In response to rising pressure on construction unions, Secretary of Labor George Schultz in 1969 advanced the Philadelphia Plan, a program which would require builders to display a "good faith effort" toward hiring representative quotas of blacks to skilled jobs on all federally supported construction. The quotas would approximate the percentage of blacks resident in each city included in the plan.

George Meany, a number of Southern senators, and the U.S. Comptroller General opposed the Philadelphia Plan, some of them on the grounds that quotas are illegal under the Civil Rights Act of 1964. But Attorney General John Mitchell, who wielded considerable power in the government, declared the plan to be legal and Schultz stood by it. Black groups tended to support it, though they criticized the enforcement provisions as being too weak. At the start of 1970, the government was proceeding with the Philadelphia Plan and leaking word to the press that it would soon be expanded to 20 other cities.

However, the Philadelphia Plan, which one expert noted "came in with Nixon and left before him," did

Walter Reuther, president of the United Auto Workers, takes part in the massive Mother's Day 1969 march in support of the striking Hospital Workers Union.

not reach more than a few cities—certainly not 20— and dissipated within a few years.

The Charleston Hospital Strike

A large majority of American workers are not highly skilled or even industrial, but are employed in service jobs, many of which are menial, low-paying, and not unionized. Blacks are overrepresented in low-end service trades.

Thus the Charleston College Hospital Strike of 1969 assumes special significance. The strike, conducted by Local 1199 of the RDSWU, was cited by *Business Week* magazine as "a successful union-Negro alliance in which a fight for economic betterment is fused with a fight for racial dignity." The strike was provoked by the hospital's dismissal of 12 black workers. The union won recognition and reinstatement of the workers.

The strike also betrayed some of the conflict common between unions that have varying orientations to blacks. The AFL-CIO supported the strike, but some black union leaders charged that support from the national union was reluctant, tardy, and motivated solely by fear that Local 1199 would withdraw from the RDSWU, as Cleveland Robinson's distributive workers had done a few years earlier.

Nevertheless, the fact remains that the AFL-CIO did support the Charleston strikers and that, for all its internal bickering, organized labor was united on behalf of a group of low-paid service workers, most of them black.

Encouraged by success in Charleston, 1199 branched out to organize hospital and nursing homes in the East and Midwest. In the fall of 1969 it organized the Johns Hopkins in Baltimore and achieved more modest successes in Pennsylvania.

Coretta Scott King was a vocal supporter of the Charleston strike and in 1969 was named honorary chairman of the National Union of Hospital and Nursing Home Employees, the title under which Local 1199 expanded its efforts. The group enlisted the aid of local black and student leaders wherever it could and staged dramatic demonstrations that harvested publicity and thwarted public services. In Charleston, the state police were called out to maintain order as pro-union demonstrations impeded hospital service, reduced the city's tourist and retail revenue, and produced 1,000 arrests. In Pittsburgh, 1199 staged a sit-in at the headquarters of the Mellon National Bank because a hospital trustee had an office there and the bank was a symbol of the "establishment."

In its readiness to frustrate public services on behalf of its aims, Local 1199 was something of a black power counterpart to the United Federation of Teachers in

Coretta King speaks at hospital worker's rally in Charleston, South Carolina.

struction unions occupy a unique and powerful place in both organized labor and the American economy. In most construction work, unions, not employers, determine who is to be hired and who is to be trained in specific skills. This unusual authority has enabled individual locals to exclude almost anyone they chose from employment. It has also enabled them to maintain an artificial shortage of the labor supply, a shortage that strengthens their claims for high wages, wages that frequently exceed $20,000 a year. Inevitably, in such a situation, blacks are the last to be hired.

In 1970 and 1971, construction workers strengthened their position further when they supported President Nixon's Vietnam policies, going to the extent of attacking peace demonstrators in New York City. Nixon rewarded their support by donning, symbolically, a hard hat, appointing Peter Brennan of the New York Building & Construction Trades Council as his Secretary of Labor, and continuing with the coded rhetoric that promised a flaccid approach to enforcement of policies and procedures with which the government had pledged to increase the blacks' share of the lucrative construction union pie.

The administration had, broadly speaking, displayed two plans to increase black building-trades employment: the "hometown solution" and "Operation Outreach." The essence of the hometown approach was voluntary compliance with hiring and training goals approved by the Department of Labor. The Labor Department had two means of persuading unions to comply. They could offer the carrot of federal subsidies for training programs; and through the Office of Federal Contract Compliance, they could threaten to

New York. In 1974 about three fourths of the Districts members were minorities, about 65% were black.

In 1972 District 1199 led a highly controversial strike against over 50 New York hospitals. The dispute was settled with a contract that brought the average weekly wage of orderlies, housekeepers, aides, and dietary employees to $210 with a minimum starting wage of $181. By 1974, District 1199 had organized workers in 15 states with notable success in Philadelphia and Baltimore as well as New York.

Nixon and the Building Trades: 1970–1974

By the early 1970s exclusion of blacks from the better building trades jobs became the major economic and symbolic issue in the efforts of blacks to attain a fair "piece of the action" from organized labor.

The electrical, plumbers, pipefitters, and other con-

Labor Secretary Peter J. Brennan rose from the ranks.

withdraw funds allocated to contractors for specific federal projects.

The results were dismal. Unions in some 90 cities undertook the hometown solution and none reached their goal. In 1974, the Department of Labor singled out 21 cities in which the voluntary goals were declared "mandatory." The report noted that in Boston only 28 craft and local placements had been achieved out of a goal of 121, in New Haven it was 2 out of 121, in Buffalo 4 out of 108, and in Dayton and Evansville, Indiana, none out of seven. Other cities such as Kansas City, Missouri, did better, but still fell far short of their originally unambitious goals.

In New York City in 1972, only 357 minorities were trained out of a goal of 1,000 and about 100 of these were previously involved in a Model Cities Training Program and thus served as "double statistics." In Chicago, fewer than 100 black workers had been hired, and many of them on a temporary basis. In Pittsburgh, few blacks were hired and the Internal Revenue Service found that hundreds of thousands of dollars in government subsidies for job training had been misappropriated.

Local governments wishing to substitute their own goals were threatened with removal of federal funds. This indeed happened in New York City in 1973 when Mayor John Lindsay attempted to substitute a plan he felt would be more productive of jobs.

Another type of hometown solution was attempted in the Philadelphia Plan, in which the government sought to induce builders receiving over $500,000 in government funds to hire specific quotas of blacks in six critical buildings trades. But federal back-up of the Philadelphia Plan was not forthcoming, despite earlier indications of support for it by John Mitchell, then the U.S. Attorney General, and George Schultz, the Secretary of Labor.

Government funds to train minorities in the building trades were also provided an assortment of groups through "Operation Outreach." By 1973, after an expenditure of some $45 million, no reliable figures on the number of blacks trained had been released, but they were few and, again, provided no guarantees of actual employment.

A highly questionable aspect of the Outreach and other programs was their emphasis on apprentice programs. A labor expert at the Columbia University School of Social Work, Russell A. Nixon, estimates that about three fourths of people hired for skilled construction jobs receive training on the job rather than in apprentice programs. Thus the entire procedure

Black membership in all building trades unions increased from 106,263 in 1967 to 133,576 in 1972.

of expensive apprentice programs, in which large sums of money for training are provided unions, are suspect of corruption and political pork-barreling as well as unproductivity of jobs for minorities. In July 1974 the Equal Employment Opportunity Commission released figures detailing the results of building trades' hiring of minorities between 1969 and 1972 in some 2,615 locals (see Table 1). The results showed an overall increase of blacks in building trades from about 1,000,000 to 1,300,000 members during that three-year period. But black membership in the higher wage scale Boilermakers, Electrical Workers, Elevator Constructors, Ironworkers, Plumbers and Pipefitters increased very little, while it rose more rapidly in the lower paying trowel and miscellaneous trades and still more in the lowest paying laborer trades, where blacks comprise one fourth of the total. About three fourths of all blacks in construction trades work in the laborer jobs.

A heavy concentration of black workers fall under the general term "common laborer."

Black Countermoves

Some black groups have attempted, with the limited funds at their disposal, to offer alternative sources of skilled building trades jobs. One such program is the National Association for the Advancement of Colored People's Afro-American Builders Association. This group organized black-owned construction companies in over 500 cities to employ over 3,000 black journeymen at an average annual wage of $10,000. Such efforts, productive for many blacks, cannot make up for the massive tokenism and unemployment of blacks resulting from the policies of construction unions and indulgence of these unions by the government.

Blacks Challenge the Steel Union

The United Steelworkers, a union with 200,000 black members, has long helped legitimize bigoted hiring and promotion policies by incorporating, in labor management pacts, seniority, promotion, and job assignment policies that largely confine blacks to the most menial, uncomfortable, and poorest paying jobs. The NAACP studied and then challenged the steel union policies in the 1950s, but corrective action was inhibited by the union-black civil rights alliance of that era and the absence of laws providing for redress. But the Civil Rights Act of 1964 in its Title VII employ-

ment section, and President Johnson's 1965 Executive Order 11246 forbidding discrimination in companies holding government contracts, provided the government and courts with the legal means necessary to eliminate discriminatory practices. In 1971 a federal judge ruled that 80% of the blacks in the Bethlehem Steel plant in Lackawanna, New York were assigned to 11 departments which contained the hottest and dirtiest jobs in the place. In a rebuke to the union, the Court wrote that "seniority advantages are not indefeasibly vested rights, but mere expectation derived from a bargaining agreement subject to modification." The court also observed that "the Lackawanna Plant was a microcosm of classic job discrimination in the North" and that discriminatory contract provisions were embodied in nationwide master agreements negotiated by the United Steelworkers of America. The court ordered back pay to 1,600 workers.

Shortly thereafter another suit, filed by the Legal Defense Fund against the United Steel Company in an Alabama Federal Court, resulted in a decision permitting LDF to sue for back pay for all black workers in the plant.

Confronted with the possibility of 200,000 black, Hispanic, and woman steelworkers suing for back pay and integrated seniority lines, the companies and union sought a settlement. Fortunately for them, the Nixon administration was in the process of damping the enthusiasm of the Equal Employment Opportunity Commission. In April 1974 the EEOC, Departments of Labor and Justice, the employers and union agreed on a "consent decree" in which each black worker was to be awarded sums ranging from $250 to $775 in return for giving up their right to sue.

The settlement was a dramatic and significant acknowledgment of discrimination by both a giant industry and giant union. On August 18, 1975 nine steel companies agreed to sign consent orders to end racial discrimination against minorities and women by promising to comply with federal antidiscrimination laws and created a $31 million back pay fund.

According to the Justice Department, which had filed an initial discrimination suit in April 1974, the companies produced 73% of the nation's raw steel and employed 347,679 workers, 52,545 of whom were black, 7,646 Spanish-surnamed, and 10,175 women.

The consent orders covered 245 steel plants in 25 states and affected 61,000 minority workers. But the agreement and the way it was negotiated have induced the NAACP and the Legal Defense Fund to challenge it in court. Herbert Hill of the NAACP Labor Department charges that the sums awarded to individuals are "anemic" and not a fraction of what workers would have earned if they had not been discriminated against, that punitive damages were not awarded, and that attorneys for the black workers were excluded from the negotiations. Especially shocking to Hill and others is a provision that the Justice Department will ally itself with the company and union in court against any worker who refuses back pay and sues, establishing a precedent in which future plaintiffs against the USW and steel companies will also have to take on the government.

Other unions have been quick to pick up the cue and try to buy off victims of discrimination with small settlements. One example: in May 1974 blacks and Chicanos who were suing the Pacific Intermountain Express Co. and the Teamsters Union were offered $500 if they signed a waiver of right to sue.

During the 1970s the federal government and Justice Department used "givebacks" to provide recompense to discriminated minority workers. A landmark civil rights case was decided on January 18, 1973 when the American Telephone and Telegraph Company agreed to give $15 million in back pay to 15,000 minority men and women who had suffered employment discrimination. AT&T also agreed to make a $23 million a year pay increase to 36,000 women and minorities who had been moved to higher-paying jobs without being credited with seniority gained in lower category jobs. In return for these actions, the Equal Employment Opportunity Commission agreed to drop its op-

position to proposed AT&T rate increases, provided AT&T complied by January 1979.

Substantive action was taken after July 3, 1979, when the Supreme Court declined to review the case—thus allowing the lower court decisions to stand, and on January 17, 1979, the federal government reported to the federal district court that AT&T had given "substantial compliance" with the orders to end job discrimination. Of an estimated 980,000 national employees, the number of blacks employed rose from 10.6% in 1973 to 12% in 1979, and the percentage of blacks in management rose from 2.2% in 1973 to 5.5% in 1979.

Although the AT&T case was hailed as the largest job bias compensation at the time, union leaders noted that the award was still less than what employees would have earned if promoted earlier. The award also paled in comparison when the nine major steel companies were ordered to give $31 million in back pay in 1979.

The trucking industry was also challenged for its anti-black hiring and job discrimination tactics. On March 20, 1974 the Justice Department obtained a consent decree forcing seven national trucking companies to adopt a percentage hiring plan for blacks and Spanish-surnamed persons. The legal basis for the agreement was a discrimination suit filed the same day against the seven companies, 342 smaller truckers, the International Brotherhood of Teamsters, the International Association of Machinists, and the industry's collective bargaining organization, Trucking Employer's Inc. The decree directed that minorities be hired in 50% of vacancies that appeared in areas where less than 25% of the staff was black or Spanish-surnamed.

The seven companies included Arkansas Best Freight System, Inc., Ft. Smith, Arkansas; Branch Motor Express Co., New York City; Consolidated Freightways Inc., Menlo Park, California; I.M.L. Freight Inc., of Salt Lake City, Utah; Mason & Dixon Lines, Inc., Kingsport, Tennessee; Pacific Intermountain Express Co., Oakland, California; and Smith's Transport Corp., Staunton, Virginia.

Another recent discrimination case involved the Oklahoma City-based Lee Way Motor Freight Inc., which at one time employed only five blacks, eight Hispanics, and no women out of a long-distance trucking labor force of 820.

The company, a subsidiary of Pepsico, Inc., on January 10, 1980 reached a settlement in a job discrimination suit and agreed to pay $2.7 million to 82 black job applicants who were allegedly denied jobs because of race. The company also agreed to employ minorities in the sales and management fields, where no minorities had yet been hired.

Benjamin Hooks praised the Weber ruling as "the most important civil rights decision in recent history."

Another giveback was authorized on April 13, 1981 when the BEOC reached agreement with the Alabama Power Co. requiring the utility to pay $2.2 million to blacks and women to settle discrimination complaints. Final approval was pending from the Federal District Court in Birmingham.

The case was initiated by the commission in 1974 as part of a program to pinpoint patterns of discrimination in industries and companies rather than individual complaints. Awards for the 1,350 maligned workers ranged from $50 to $11,350.

The company also agreed to step up recruitment, hiring, and promotion of blacks and women with affirmative action goals for five years.

The settlement of $1.7 million went for blacks in union or janitorial jobs.

The Landmark Weber Case

The landmark 1977 Supreme Court ruling in the *Bakke* case, which held that educational institutions could take race into account when screening new employees or applicants—especially in order to remedy discrimination—was put to the test when Brian Weber, a white man from Gramercy, Louisiana, brought a suit against both his employer and his union to reclaim his job.

In 1974 the Kaiser Aluminum & Chemical Corpora-

tion and United Steelworkers of America agreed to establish a voluntary program to train minority workers for skilled positions at the Kaiser plants. Half the training positions were to go to blacks and half to whites.

At the Gramercy facility, where Weber, 38, worked, there were 13 positions open for which Weber was a candidate. Seven positions went to blacks and six to whites, and Weber was rejected, although two of the black men accepted had less seniority than he did.

Weber filed a civil suit against the company, claiming that his rights, according to the 1964 Civil Rights Act, which forbids employment discrimination on racial grounds, had been violated.

Weber's position was initially upheld by the Federal District Court and the U.S. Fifth Circuit Court of Appeals, based on Weber's argument that Kaiser Aluminum had maintained a nondiscriminatory policy since 1958. However, the Justice Department filed briefs declaring that there had been a racial bias at the Kaiser plants, and on December 11, 1978, the Supreme Court agreed to review the combined cases of *Kaiser Aluminum & Chemical Corporation* v. *Weber; U.S.* v. *Weber;* and *United Steelworkers of America* v. *Weber.*

"Reverse discrimination," the buzzword given to the landmark *Bakke* case, was also used with *Weber* when the case went to court on March 28, 1979. The largest crowd of spectators since the 1977 *Bakke* case was in attendance.

Weber's lawyer argued long and hard, declaring, "You can't avoid discrimination by discriminating," but on June 27, 1979 the Supreme Court ruled that employers and unions could legally establish voluntary programs, including the use of quotas, to aid minorities and women in employment, turning back Weber's challenge.

NAACP Executive Director Benjamin Hooks praised the ruling as "the most important civil rights decision in recent history. . . . Had we lost this case, the cause of affirmative action would have been set back ten years." AFL-CIO President George Meany called it a "victory for all who believe in racial justice and who are committed to private voluntary action to end discrimination."

The Reagan Administration after Weber

The 1980s under the Reagan Administration saw the relaxing of affirmative action controls that had been built up so carefully during the 1960s and 1970s.

The ball started rolling in May 1981, when Republican Congressman Robert Walker of Pennsylvania introduced legislation that would bar the use of numerical quotas to increase the hiring or school enrollment of women or minorities. The bill, called the Equal Employment Opportunity Act, would amend the Civil Rights Act of 1964 and reflected the views of the Reagan Administration on quotas.

Specifically, the bill called for no timetables for integration and less affirmative action requirements on government contracts. Walker said his bill would cut away the paperwork. He noted that the previous requirements had been imposed by President Johnson's executive order, not constitutional amendment.

The same year, Vice President George Bush was asked to head a special task force to investigate, among other things, affirmative action rules to be reviewed, including those to protect women, blacks, and other minorities from discrimination in hiring.

By August 25 the federal government had taken steps to relax antidiscrimination rules for federal contractors and ease requirements for remedial action. According to Secretary of Labor Raymond Donovan, this move would free three fourths of companies doing business with the federal government of the "burden" of paperwork. In past years, in order to be eligible for a federal contract, an employer would have to file extensive reports about its hiring practices. Under the federal proposal, which went into effect September 25, 1981 (it was filed in the Federal Register August 25, 1981) only businesses with more than 250 employees and a contract worth more than $1 million would have to file formal affirmative action documents. Previously, businesses with more than 50 employees and contracts worth at least $50,000 were subject to the requirements. The proposal was expected to affect 30 million workers and 200,000 contractors.

The action was further supplemented in September when the Justice Department said it would no longer try to remedy discrimination in employment by seeking preferential hiring. Justice Department Head William Brady Reynolds said that the Reagan Administration would enforce civil rights laws but would not tolerate strict preferences for minorities and women in hiring. Reynolds, who could have been quoting Brian Weber's defense attorney, described current practices as "meeting discrimination with discrimination."

Black leaders greeted these changes with concern. In the spring of 1981, the NAACP board of directors advocated requiring private employers to train members of minorities for jobs and to provide daycare centers for the children of employees before a business could qualify for the Reagan Administration's tax cuts and tax benefits on investment and capital equipment.

TRENDS FOR THE 1980s

While economic conditions for many blacks have been improved since the 1960s civil rights struggles, many more black laborers remain locked in a state of economic distress and dependency, and the 1980s have brought conditions which have widened the gap between the more advanced black professionals and blacks who hold unskilled, low-wage jobs.

During the 1970s, both blacks and whites moved into more technical white-collar and professional jobs, with the proportion of black men growing slightly faster than the proportion of white men during the decade. However, the majority of blacks took jobs that were concentrated in occupations at the lower end of the earnings scale, with heavy representation in health technology and counseling. Moreover, in the 1980s, only 8% of all black men were employed as professional, management-level workers, compared to 16% of employed white men.

The largest economic advances were made by black women, who gained more jobs and, more significantly, attained virtual parity in earning power with white women. But the earnings of *all* women remained only slightly more than half that of men and thus remained an obstacle to hurdle.

A pattern of employment from 1960 to 1976 showed that more than half of the growth of nonagricultural employment for blacks was in the public sector, especially in social welfare work.

Today, this pattern of employment appears certain to cause difficulties for the black middle class as federal budget cuts for domestic social programs take their toll. For example, in Washington, D.C., the Department of Health and Human Services, which is a major agency for black employees, will sustain about half the 6,000 layoffs scheduled for 1982. In addition, the Community Service administration, which had a staff of 900 workers—60% of which was black—was abolished in October 1981.

In other unionized, blue-collar jobs, blacks seemed to be making some progress in that they enjoyed steady pay increases, job security, and good fringe benefits through collective bargaining in the nation's automobile, steel, rubber, and manufacturing industries. Black workers continued to remain in mostly nonmanagement positions, but wages were very high in comparison to the economy as a whole and many black families achieved a comfortable standard of living.

By 1982, however, many of these gains were threatened by economic upheavals in those same industries. More than 1 million auto workers lost their jobs, a disproportionate number of them blacks. Additional black workers were unemployed when steel plants closed in Western Pennsylvania and Ohio.

The Reagan Administration's new economic policy, introduced in 1981, was expected to allow both the increase of black unemployment and decline of black income levels as the recession continues, although the

Reagan Administration projected that 13 million new jobs would be created through the economic revitalization program.

According to the Bureau of Labor Statistics, employment in the services sectors are expected to rise from 17.3% of all jobs in 1973 to 22.9% in 1990—a total of 27 million service workers. On the other hand, the prospect for significant growth in the basic manufacturing industries, where large numbers of blacks held well-paying jobs, is quite small.

Trends indicate that the American economy will become increasingly international, and semiskilled manufacturing operations will face competition from Third World countries. Therefore, if black workers are to gain a stronger foothold in the American economy, they must seek higher-level training and jobs in areas such as defense, where federal monies will be flowing.

SELECTED LABOR FACTS

Fact 1

Blacks comprise less than half of the minority membership in the construction referral unions, 11.1% compared with 12.5% for other minorities.

Fact 2

In 1978 blacks comprised only 3% of the workers in such well-paying skills as elevator construction, plumbers, and iron and sheet metal workers; Hispanics make up 4% of this work force.

Fact 3

There were three times as many Hispanics as blacks in the International Ladies Garment Workers Union, but Hispanics accounted for more than seven times as many blacks in the longshoreman's union.

Fact 4

By 1978 women had made only minimal inroads in skilled building trade unions. In 1979 three black women qualified as elevator constructors, three as lathers, three as bricklayers, 18 as iron workers, and 194 as plumbers.

Fact 5

Black women were represented to a slightly greater degree than white women in skilled building trade unions in porportion to their population. Black women comprised 17% of all female lathers, 20% of elevator constructors, 11% of bricklayers, and 22% of all women who were plumbers.

The jobs of assembly line workers in the nation's automobile plants are threatened by both automation and poor sales.

Fact 6

In 1970 blacks were underrepresented in the musicians union—comprising 3.7% of the total membership.

Fact 7

The referral union with the largest proportion of blacks was the Laundry and Dry Cleaning Union, in which blacks made up 55% of membership. Forty-two percent of longshoremen and warehousemen were black.

Fact 8

A black worker is more likely than a white worker to be represented by a union. In 1980 blacks comprised 11.8% of the nation's work force but 14.7% of workers represented by unions. Hispanics were also represented in greater proportion, comprising 5.4% of the labor force and 6.1% of union membership.

Fact 9

In most industries, contract coverage for blacks exceeded that for whites. In durable goods manufacturing, for example, more than half of black workers, but less than two fifths of white workers, were covered by union contracts.

Fact 10

Black women in the labor force are more likely than black men to be represented by unions. Nearly one fifth of the nation's female union members are black, compared with only one eighth of male workers.

Fact 11

Black union members tend to be slightly younger than white union members. The median age for white male union members is 38, compared with 37 for blacks. Median ages for women are 34 for whites, 37 for blacks.

Table 1. Membership in Building Trades Union Locals by Race and Sex

International	Number of Locals	Sex	Total		Black	
			Number	Percent of Total	Number	Percent of Total
Lathers	10	Total	3,343	100	231	6.9
		Male	3,328	99.6	228	6.8
		Female	15	0.4	3	0.1
Marble Polishers	4	Total	823	100	28	3.4
		Male	818	99.4	28	3.4
		Female	5	0.6	0	0.0
Operating Engineers	56	Total	165,517	100	9,455	5.7
		Male	163,449	98.8	8,987	5.4
		Female	2,068	1.2	468	0.3
Plaster and Cement Workers	62	Total	21,366	100	3,344	16.2
		Male	21,272	99.6	3,455	16.0
		Female	94	0.4	26	0.1
Laborers, Painters and Roofers	525	Total	312,541	100	62,728	20.1
		Male	304,011	97.4	60,355	19.3
		Female	8,030	2.6	2,373	0.8
Laborers	348	Total	247,563	100	57,760	23.3
		Male	240,830	97.3	55,704	22.5
		Female	6,733	2.7	2,051	0.8
Plumbers and Pipefitters	301	Total	192,075	100	5,317	2.8
		Male	191,369	99.6	5,123	2.7
		Female	706	0.4	194	0.1
Sheetmetal Workers	83	Total	41,814	100	946	2.3
		Male	41,425	99.1	865	2.1
		Female	389	0.9	81	0.2
Trowel and Miscellaneous Trades	764	Total	509,043	100	27,839	5.5
		Male	504,271	99.1	26,839	5.3
		Female	4,772	0.9	905	0.2

Table 1. (*Continued*)

International	Number of Locals	Sex	Total Number	Total Percent of Total	Black Number	Black Percent of Total
Asbestos Workers	32	Total	6,493	100	248	3.8
		Male	6,455	99.4	241	3.7
		Female	38	0.6	7	0.1
Bricklayers	99	Total	27,232	100	2,441	9.0
		Male	27,208	99.9	2,438	9.0
		Female	24	0.1	3	0.0*
Carpenters	501	Total	284,269	100	11,981	4.2
		Male	281,741	99.1	11,583	4.1
		Female	2,528	0.9	398	0.1
Painters and Allied Trades (laborers)	486	Total	301,160	100	61,068	29.5
		Male	293,228	97.4	58,763	28.2
		Female	7,932	2.6	2,305	1.3
Roofers	39	Total	11,381	100	1,660	14.6
		Male	11,283	99.1	1,592	14.0
		Female	98	0.9	68	0.6

Source: 1978 EEO-3 Report.

Table 2. Black Workers as a Percentage of Employed Wage and Salary Workers by Occupation and Labor Organization Representation, May 1980 (numbers in thousands)

Job Category	All Employed Wage and Salary Workers Total	All Employed Wage and Salary Workers Percent Black	Represented by Labor Organization Total	Represented by Labor Organization Percent Black	Not Represented by Labor Organization Total	Not Represented by Labor Organization Percent Black
Occupation of current job						
All occupations[a]	87,480	11.8	22,493	14.7	64,986	10.8
White-collar occupations	45,955	8.8	8,483	14.2	37,472	7.6
Professional, technical, and kindred workers	14,436	9.6	3,997	12.4	10,439	8.5
Managers and administrators, except farm	8,953	4.9	868	9.9	8,086	4.4
Clerical and kindred workers	17,507	11.3	3,365	17.5	14,142	9.8
Sales workers	5,059	5.4	253	11.7	4,805	5.0
Blue-collar workers	28,414	12.9	11,763	13.3	16,651	12.7
Craft and kindred workers	11,083	8.6	4,571	8.2	6,512	8.9
Carpenters	836	7.4	284	5.2	552	8.6
Construction craft workers, except carpenters	2,212	10.8	1,116	8.5	1,096	13.1
Mechanics and repairers	4,234	7.9	1,815	8.2	2,419	7.8
Other	3,802	8.3	1,357	8.5	2,445	8.2
Operatives and kindred workers	13,208	15.8	5,743	16.3	7,465	15.4
Operatives, except transport	9,982	15.8	4,229	16.6	5,753	15.3
Drivers and delivery workers	2,719	15.0	1,168	15.8	1,551	14.4
Other transport equipment operatives	507	19.4	346	15.4	161	28.1
Nonfarm laborers	4,123	15.5	1,448	17.8	2,674	14.3
Construction	771	15.9	265	18.6	506	14.5
Manufacturing	836	18.0	436	17.0	400	19.1
All other nonfarm laborers	2,516	14.6	747	18.0	1,768	13.1

Table 2. (*Continued*)

Job Category	All Employed Wage and Salary Workers		Represented by Labor Organization		Not Represented by Labor Organization	
	Total	Percent Black	Total	Percent Black	Total	Percent Black
Service workers, including private household	12,074	20.1	2,221	24.3	9,853	19.2
Industry of current job						
All industries	87,480	11.8	22,493	14.7	64,986	10.8
Agriculture	1,455	13.4	55	15.5	1,400	13.3
Mining	892	6.4	314	5.6	578	6.8
Construction	4,982	9.0	1,651	9.4	3,331	8.8
Manufacturing, total	20,976	11.3	7,309	13.9	13,667	10.0
Durable goods, total	12,546	10.7	4,720	13.4	7,826	9.0
Ordnance	235	6.3	86	10.2	148	4.1
Lumber	539	17.9	113	11.4	426	19.6
Furniture	461	10.2	132	7.9	329	11.1
Stone, clay, and glass	618	13.1	305	20.4	313	5.9
Primary metals	1,176	12.9	712	15.1	464	9.5
Fabricated metals	1,359	9.9	530	11.9	828	8.5
Machinery, except electrical	2,779	6.2	851	7.9	1,928	5.4
Electrical equipment	2,230	12.2	672	14.2	1,559	11.3
Transportation equipment	2,031	13.0	1,135	16.1	896	9.0
Automobiles	951	12.3	600	15.7	351	6.3
Aircraft	676	13.0	341	16.4	335	9.4
Other transportation equipment	404	14.7	194	16.5	210	13.0
Instruments	622	7.6	90	3.4	532	8.3
Miscellaneous	497	11.4	93	20.3	403	9.4
Nondurable goods	8,430	12.3	2,589	14.7	5,841	11.3
Food	1,674	12.0	670	15.5	1,004	9.6
Tobacco	60	17.6	21	39.4	39	5.9
Textiles	786	16.9	140	15.5	646	17.2
Apparel	1,298	18.0	353	20.2	945	17.2
Paper	751	9.8	380	12.6	371	6.9
Printing	1,433	8.8	308	11.1	1,125	8.1
Chemicals	1,240	10.8	352	11.7	888	10.5
Petroleum	220	11.9	79	16.9	141	9.0
Rubber and plastics	692	11.4	223	12.2	469	11.1
Leather and not specified manufacturing	275	7.8	64	17.9	212	4.7
Transportation, communication, and public utilities	6,048	11.7	3,113	13.8	2,935	9.5
Railroads	579	9.9	479	10.5	100	7.4
Other transportation	2,662	12.4	1,201	15.0	1,461	10.3
Communication	1,447	12.2	776	15.0	672	8.9
Other public utilities	1,359	10.7	657	12.7	703	8.8
Trade	17,401	8.8	1,896	13.8	15,504	8.2
Wholesale	3,419	8.4	432	18.1	2,988	6.9
Retail	13,981	9.0	1,465	12.6	12,517	8.5
Eating and drinking places	4,031	11.1	212	15.2	3,818	10.8
Other retail	9,950	8.1	1,252	12.1	8,698	7.5

Table 2. (*Continued*)

Job Category	All Employed Wage and Salary Workers		Represented by Labor Organization		Not Represented by Labor Organization	
	Total	Percent Black	Total	Percent Black	Total	Percent Black
Finance, insurance, and real estate	5,152	9.1	250	20.5	4,902	8.5
Banking and other finance	2,356	9.7	67	24.2	2,289	9.2
Insurance and real estate	2,796	8.6	183	19.2	2,613	7.9
Services	25,123	14.8	5,719	17.8	19,404	14.0
Private household service	1,214	32.9	9	24.2	1,205	32.9
Miscellaneous services	23,909	13.9	5,710	17.8	18,199	12.7
Business and repair	2,902	10.6	332	17.0	2,570	9.8
Personal services, except private household	1,653	18.9	238	27.9	1,415	17.4
Entertainment and recreation	902	8.3	140	7.4	762	8.5
Professional services	18,451	14.3	5,000	17.6	13,452	13.0
Medical, except hospitals	2,834	13.2	336	26.0	2,498	11.5
Hospitals	3,901	20.1	841	34.9	3,059	16.0
Welfare and religious	1,541	18.2	246	30.4	1,295	15.8
Educational	8,062	13.3	3,421	12.0	4,641	14.2
Other professional services	2,114	5.9	156	9.8	1,958	5.6
Forestry and fisheries	87	7.5	14	8.9	73	7.2
Public administration	5,364	15.1	2,172	16.6	3,192	14.0
Federal, except postal	1,795	18.9	488	24.0	1,307	17.1
Postal	691	21.0	570	21.5	122	18.5
State	972	10.0	309	9.8	662	10.1
Local	1,906	11.9	805	11.4	1,100	12.3

Note: Due to rounding, sums of individual items may not equal totals.

Source: U.S. Department of Labor, Bureau of Labor Statistics, September 1981.

[a] Includes farm workers not shown separately.

BLACK CAPITALISM

Recent Trends ■ A Brief History ■ Nixon and "A Piece of the Action" ■ Carter's Changes ■ Failure Rates ■ The Largest Black Companies ■ Has Black Capitalism Worked? ■ Blacks in Agriculture

The number of black-owned businesses and their total receipts increased during the 1970s, but failed to keep pace with the growth rate of the nation's economy, or with that of other minority groups. In 1977, the latest year for which figures were available, the number of black-owned enterprises in the United States approximated 231,200, about 3% of the nation's total. Gross receipts were estimated at $8.6 billion, or a scant 0.2% of the total. In 1972 there were 187,600 black-owned firms with a total volume of $5.6 billion.

The 1977 data represent a 12% increase in the number of black firms and a 47% increase in their gross receipts. Inflation for this period was 48%. Thus black business growth declined slightly in terms of constant dollars. Over the same period, the number of firms owned by people of Spanish origin (predicated on Spanish-seeming surnames) rose 53% and their receipts 75%. The category of "other minorities" (Asians and American Indians, for example) also recorded greater gains than blacks.

Figures also indicated black businesses lost support from the black public. Between 1969 and 1977 the proportion of receipts from black businesses to the total income of the black population declined substantially, from 13.5 to 9.9%.

In 1982, though specific figures were not available, there were strong indications black businesses were suffering further declines relative to the overall economy. The reasons: a disproportionate impact of the recession and high interest rates on blacks and on small businesses in general and the misfortune of many black entrepreneurs to own businesses in depressed areas and

industries. There was, for example, a high concentration of blacks as auto dealers and service station proprietors. In 1977 this category accounted for one eighth of gross receipts for all black firms.

Other trends among black-owned businesses included:

An increasing tendency for black entrepreneurs to concentrate in selected services, running the gamut from janitor contracting to hair cutting and styling. Between 1972 and 1977, the proportion of black firms in selected services rose from 35 to 44%, while the proportion of black businesses in retailing, construction, and transportation and public utilities declined.

A sharp increase in the number of firms with paid employees, 46% compared with 6% for firms with no employees. The strongest growth in this category was among smaller companies, with 9 or fewer employees.

A small increase in the total number of employees, only 6% from 1972 to 1977. In 1977 black firms employed 164,000 people, compared with 206,000 for firms owned by Hispanics.

Contrary to the national trend, black firms displayed signs of increasing productivity. Gross receipts per employee between 1972 and 1977 rose 11% in terms of "constant dollars." Manufacturing and wholesaling showed the strongest increases in total volume. Receipts for manufacturers rose 69%, for wholesalers 104%. Auto dealers and service stations led in total

The Hubbard Co. of Emeryville, California, was funded by Urban National Corp. of Boston.

receipts with $1.1 billion. Food stores followed with $786 million.

A BRIEF HISTORY

American blacks have owned businesses since their earliest days on these shores. In the seventeenth and eighteenth centuries, free blacks owned inns, construction, tailoring, farming, catering, and many other small businesses. In the nineteenth century, before the Civil War, some black firms grew sufficiently to hire several employees, black and white. One such was Henry Boyd, a furniture manufacturer in Cincinnati, who eventually had to give up his business because of numerous fires started by whites who resented his success. Another prewar black entrepreneur, William Wormley, had to abandon his riding stable in Washington, D.C., when it too was destroyed by fire.

Blacks have also succeeded as financial speculators—in real estate and other ventures. In the late eighteenth century a black barber in North Carolina, John Stanley, invested in plantations, accumulated wealth valued as high as $35,000, and used much of it to buy freedom for other blacks.

After the Civil War, blacks owned several banks and insurance companies and other enterprises, a factor that led to the formation in Boston in 1900 of the National Black Business League by Booker T. Washington. Some 400 blacks from over 30 states attended. By 1929, about 65,000 blacks were estimated by the League to own businesses in the United States.

However, the climate in the United States has never been conducive to an abundance of black-owned businesses. A major factor in this was the massive immigration to American cities of whites from Europe. Often experienced in business and with sufficient capital and credit standing to start new businesses, these whites rather than blacks were able to start the ventures that grew with the cities. Indeed, whites more than blacks came to be the proprietors of the small retail businesses in neighborhoods where blacks settled, a factor that was to contribute to the racial tensions and violence of the 1960s.

The number and growth of black businesses were also affected, as most businesses in the United States have been, by the trend to concentration of fewer and bigger businesses in virtually every industry. The 1950 census reported that there were some 42,000 self-employed black men in businesses. By the 1960 census the number was down to 32,000.

The 1969 survey of minority-owned business enterprises reported 163,000 businesses, five times the number counted in 1960. However, a preponderance of the increase was attributable to a more thorough census rather than a pronounced increase in black capitalism.

Nixon and "A Piece of the Action"

Following the riots of 1967, increasing attention was devoted to blacks who wished to own businesses. A number of interracial advisory groups were established and various federally assisted programs were promulgated, most conspicuously through the Small Business Administration and the Department of Commerce's Office of Minority Business Enterprise, and to a lesser extent through the Office of Economic Opportunity. Support of such efforts had been stressed in the 1968 Presidential campaign by Richard Nixon, when he noted repeatedly that the government should spend less on providing special aid to blacks, but that in the American tradition, blacks should have a chance to get "a piece of the action."

Some blacks did receive a piece of the action, but

Bruce J. Llewelyn, owner of Fedco Foods, is a prime example of the emerging black entrepreneurial and managerial class.

the preponderance of manufacturing and service businesses in black communities remained white-owned.

Government support of minorities' businesses has also been hindered by red tape and confusion over jurisdiction between various agencies, such as the Small Business Administration and the Office of Minority Business Enterprise, the two major sources of aid to black businesses.

In addition, government offices expressed concern over a reportedly high failure rate among minority businesses that received loans or other subsidies. In 1972 the government announced that it would henceforth place greater emphasis on "success." However, at other times, without citing specific figures, OMBE declared the failure rate of minority businesses it supported to be at or below the national average.

Carter's Changes

The Carter Administration generally supported efforts to strengthen black businesses. In 1978 the President signed PL 95-507, which required companies bidding for prime contracts with the government to submit a plan to subcontract to minority firms.

The law also required each federal agency to set up an Office of Small and Disadvantaged Business Utilization, to seek the fullest possible use of minority businesses in the agency's purchase of goods and services. Enforcement of this provision, however, was difficult and in 1980 such agencies as the Veteran's Ad-

ministration and the Department of Defense had not established their OSDBU divisions.

In 1979 Carter replaced the troubled OMBE with the Minority Business Development Administration and tried to clarify the objectives and purview of the remaining agencies. MBDA was assigned the task of coordinating efforts to break new ground for minority businesses, especially for larger ventures and for businesses in fields where minorities have been underrepresented. Help for smaller businesses was left with the minority division of the Small Business Administration.

In 1982 these and other programs for minority business were still in place, but were weakened by the Reagan Administration's budget cuts and by opposition to affirmative steps to aid minorities. The President declared his support for the development and encouragement of minority business but put limitations on loan, development, and procurement programs and stated that government policy was to rely on the private sector.

Failure Rates

A study by the Georgia Institute of Technology in 1979 indicated that minority firms receiving aid from OMBE/MBDA had only half as good a chance of surviving as nonminority firms not receiving government help. Separate figures for black and other minorities were not reported.

According to the survey, OMBE/MBDA clients showed an annual failure rate of 0.9% and a discontinuance rate of 3.6%, compared with 0.3% and 2.4% for nonclients.

The highest nonsurvival ratio of client to nonclient firms occurred in Washington, D.C., the lowest in Atlanta, Dallas, and San Francisco. In terms of industry clients, firms in wholesale trade had the greatest difficulty surviving; finance, insurance, and real estate, the least.

Minority firms also seemed to have particular trouble after the first two years, surviving almost as well as nonminority companies for the first two.

The Largest Black Companies

In 1980 the largest black business in the United States, according to figures compiled by *Black Enterprise Magazine,* was Motown Industries, the entertainment company based in Los Angeles. Motown, started in 1959, had sales of $91.5 billion. Wallace & Wallace Enterprises of St. Albans, New York, a petroleum sales organization, was second with sales of $82 million.

The 100 largest list highlights both traditions and changes in black entrepreneurship. The oldest company on the list, C. H. James & Co., a wholesale food supplier, was founded in 1883, and The Parker House Sausage Co. dates back to 1921.

The list also contains several new companies in such areas as petroleum sales, broadcasting, electronic and computer systems, and computer software. Some of these have grown rapidly. Wallace & Wallace's sales, for example, more than tripled from 1979 to 1980 and several others in construction, hair care, and computer software more than doubled. Black entrepreneurs were also found in such fledgling areas as solar energy and computer security. In 1982 EDP Audit Controls Inc. of Los Angeles was the largest independent data processing and computer security firm in the country.

Younger companies have also become prominent in banking and insurance. The largest black bank, Independence Bank of Chicago, with assets of $101.9 million, was founded in 1964, and 26 of the 48 largest banks were founded in the 1970s. Three banks on the list were formed prior to 1910 and two savings and loan companies in the 1880s. The largest black insurance company, North Carolina Mutual Life of Durham, with $190 million in assets and 1,400 employees, was formed in 1898.

J. Saunders Thompson (left) *president of Thompson-Piggee Construction Co. in Los Angeles, describing his $2 million housing project to Laurence B. Wilson* (right) *of the United California Bank and Benjamin C. Moore of the Minority Contractors Assistance Project.*

Black-owned Citizens Savings Bank raises new home office in Nashville, Tennessee.

HAS BLACK CAPITALISM WORKED?

By 1982 many blacks had been stunningly successful, and some blacks had made inroads into booming new areas of high technology. But far from achieving a niche in the mainstream of American business life, black entrepreneurs were, on the whole, struggling to stay even. Why was this so, 14 years after black capitalism had received the official blessing of the national government?

Some of the problems resided in black history. Teaching and government service, rather than business, has been the traditional path for college-educated blacks, and few blacks had come to regard business as a way out of poverty. On top of this, racial prejudice continued to deny blacks access to sources of financing and trade information that are essential to the success of any business. And concern about prejudice inhibited blacks from starting retail businesses in white neighborhoods.

These forces were compounded by adverse national

trends. Foremost among these was the decline of the inner cities where blacks logically sought to establish businesses. As a result, many businesses were started, or already existed, in areas that were decaying, both economically and in terms of such vital services as fire and police protection and insurance coverage.

The economic pinch of inflation and frequent recessions reduced the purchasing power of black residents and induced them to buy from larger downtown white merchants who, with lower relative overhead, could undersell black competitors. Add to this the increasing amount of capital needed to start and finance a business and the reluctance of banks to finance inner city ventures and the enormity of the obstacles becomes apparent.

BLACKS IN AGRICULTURE

In 1900 there were about 926,000 black-operated farms in the United States. By 1979 the number had dropped to about 57,000. Though the total number of white-operated farms has also been declining, the drop has been proportionately higher for blacks. Between 1920 and 1978 the proportion of American farms operated by blacks fell from 13 to 6%. The rate of land loss for blacks in 1978 was 2½ times the rate of loss for whites.

The reasons for this decline are manifold and so deeply rooted that in 1982 the U.S. Civil Rights Commission expressed concern that the black farmer might be extinct by the end of the century.

Major obstacles faced by black farmers include:

Government tax and support policies which tend to favor large farms run by corporations.

A stubborn survival of racial bias in federal agricultural support services such as loans and technical assistance.

Financing burdens imposed by high interest rates and inflation.

History

The growth of the cotton industry and the westward expansion of the United States are the two historical factors which have largely determined the black's role in U.S. agriculture for more than three centuries. The Louisiana Purchase (1803) and the doctrine of Manifest Destiny (i.e., the inevitable expansion of the United States) instilled in most Southerners the belief that cotton would remain king as long as fertile land could be acquired by moving westward. By 1850 some 2.8 million slaves lived within the confines of the Cotton Kingdom, working on farms and plantations. Of these, some 1.8 million were engaged in the cultivation of cotton, with the remainder being used to raise tobacco, rice, and sugar cane.

Emancipation did not radically alter the black's role in agriculture, particularly since it did not afford him the opportunity to participate in the great postwar homesteading movement which accompanied the continued westward settlement of the country.

Promises to distribute land to blacks weren't kept, and, though prices were low, blacks lacked the capital to buy it.

The next significant development in the history of the black farmer was the introduction of the tenant system in the South. Under this system, blacks were assigned to work a particular piece of land with the stipulation that they receive a portion of the crop as wages (sharecropping). Tenants were furnished with living supplies over a period of one year under a simple credit system. In return for supplies and equipment, they mortgaged their share of the crops and repaid their debts at harvest time. However, exorbitant interest rates and high-priced goods usually left blacks with very little. In addition, most rural Negroes were disadvantaged by a host of accounting malpractices.

By 1880 blacks owned less than 8% of all farms, had fewer acres of cropland than did white farmers, and were largely restricted to growing cotton by local

The black farmer is rapidly disappearing from American agriculture.

merchants who financed them, and who regarded cotton as a safe crop that could be sold in the event of foreclosure. The fall in the price of cotton, from 29¢ a pound in 1868 to 5¢ in 1889, was especially hard on blacks.

It is important to remember that agricultural education experienced its first real flowering after the Civil War. Hampton Normal and Agricultural Institute was opened at Hampton, Virginia in 1868 and within a decade had graduated Booker T. Washington, who, in turn, founded Tuskegee in 1881. Within the next two decades, the work of Tuskegee's George Washington Carver had revolutionized the growth of soybeans and peanuts throughout the South and helped diversify the economy of the entire region.

The creation of small black-owned banks, plus a strong recovery of cotton prices, greatly aided blacks around the turn of the century. Between 1880 and 1911, 50 black lending institutions were created, and they played a great part in the growth of black farming. By 1910, 240,000 blacks owned their farms and comprised one sixth of all southern landowners. Another 670,000 were tenant farms, which was 40% of that total.

The boom was reversed in the early days of World War I, when cotton again plummeted, this time to 3¢ a pound, and help from private and government sources was largely confined to white farmers. Most black lending institutions collapsed as a result of the depression in cotton. A few years later the boll weevil took a heavy toll of black farmers, few of whom could afford effective insecticides. Many black farmowners returned to tenancy.

A consequence of this depression was the first great urban migration of blacks. Between 1880 and 1910 only 79,000 southern blacks had moved north. Between 1910 and 1920 the number was 227,000, and between 1920 and 1930 it reached 440,000. The great majority of these migrants were sharecroppers or farm laborers.

Racial injustice and violence in rural areas accompanied and spurred the migration. Between 1900 and 1931, 345 of the South's 551 cotton-growing counties had at least one lynching, and 170 (31%) had 10 or more.

Within the tenant system, blacks were generally retarded by being denied renter or share tenant status, an improved position from which tenants could accumulate capital and emerge as landowners. In 1925, 71% of white tenants, but only 46% of blacks, were renters or share tenants.

The Depression of the 1930s brought extreme hardship to both white and black farmers. In 1934 the federal government began to take a hand in reorganizing the nation's agricultural system by providing cheap credit for farmers and helping them become landowners. This was done by purchasing heavily indebted plantations, which were subdivided into smaller farms suitable for one family. Many such plots were sold to former black tenants. In addition, the government put into effect certain crop acreage controls and a system of price supports designed to stabilize the market value of a variety of produce. However, there was little provision in aid programs to assure that monetary benefits would reach black farmers, and much of it was siphoned off by unscrupulous farmowners and local politicians.

Also, outreach programs of financial and technical aid were segregated and did little to help blacks. Black agents were often prevented from reaching black farmers who were tenants on white-owned land.

Dramatic shifts in black agriculture occurred after World War II. Tobacco became more important and by 1959, one sixth of all cigarette tobacco grown in the South was grown on black-operated farms. However, the decline of black agriculture after 1959 swept away both tobacco and cotton farmers. Between 1969 and 1979, the number of black cotton farms in the South declined an extraordinary 96%, the number of tobacco farms 77%, according to the agricultural census. Between 1970 and 1980 black farm population in the South fell at three times the rate of the white farm population (65 to 22%), and in 1980 blacks who remained as farm residents tended to be wage and salary workers rather than self-employed. The median income of black farm families in 1978 was $7,584 compared with $17,323 for their white counterparts. The unemployment rate of black farm workers was four times that of whites.

In the late 1970s and early 1980s, government policies seemed only to exacerbate the situation for black farmers. In 1982 the Civil Rights Commission reported that the number of black Farm Home Administration committee members in southern states had dropped enormously between 1979 and 1980 (see Table 14). Blacks also received a disproportionately small share of farm ownership, farm operating emergency, and soil and water loans.

The Commission concluded that the decline of black farms was especially unfortunate in that they had over the years been a force for stability and economic health for the communities near them.

Hope for rejuvenation rested largely with the Farm Home Administration, which was created to help the small farmer and lends some $6 billion per year. However, in 1982 the FMHA persisted in interpreting its mandate narrowly, much like that of a banking institution that must collect on its loans and that lacks jurisdiction to make loans for social purposes.

Table 1. The 100 Largest Black-Owned Businesses in the United States

Company	Location	Chief Executive	Business	Year Started	Employees	1980 Sales (Billions of Dollars)
Motown Industries	Los Angeles, California	Berry Gordy, Jr.	Entertainment	1959	215	91.700
Wallace & Wallace Enterprises, Inc.	St. Albans, New York	Charles Wallace	Petroleum sales	1969	36	81.935
Johnson Publishing Co., Inc.	Chicago, Illinois	John H. Johnson	Publishing, cosmetics, broadcasting	1942	610	72.974
Fedco Foods Corporation	New York, New York	Samual Berger	Supermarkets	1969	475	51.654
H. J. Russell Construction Co., Inc.	Atlanta, Georgia	Herman J. Russell	Construction	1958	275	51.000
Vanguard Oil & Service Co.	Brooklyn, New York	Kenneth Butler	Petroleum sales	1970	40	51.500
Smith Pipe & Supply, Inc.	Houston, Texas	George Smith, Sr.	Oilfield pipe and supply sales	1976	135	48.000
Johnson Products Co., Inc.	Chicago, Illinois	George E. Johnson	Hair care products and cosmetics	1954	575	41.016
Grimes Oil Company	Dorchester, Massachusetts	Calvin M. Grimes, Jr.	Petroleum sales	1969	65	40.000
Chioke International Corporation	New York, New York	Christopher E. Chioke	Defense equipment and crude oil marketing	1970	14	35.000
Philadelphia International Records	Philadelphia, Pennsylvania	Kenneth Gamble	Phonograph records	1971	150	30.000
Thacker Construction Co.	Alton, Illinois	Floyd O. Thacker	Construction	1970	482	29.400
M & M Products Co., Inc.	Atlanta, Georgia	Cornell McBride	Manufacturer and distributor of hair care products	1973	400	27.000
Pro-Line Corporation	Dallas, Texas	Comer J. Cottrell	Manufacturer and distributor of hair care products	1970	312	22.600
Housing Innovations, Inc.	Boston, Massachusetts	Denis A. Blackett	Real estate, construction	1966	15	22.218
L. H. Smith Oil Corporation	Indianapolis, Indiana	Lannie H. Smith, Jr.	Petroleum sales	1962	49	18.579

Company	Location	Chief Executive	Business	Year Founded	Employees	Sales ($ millions)
Inner City Broadcasting Corp.	New York, New York	Pierre M. Sutton	Radio broadcasting	1971	200	18.300
The Jackson Oil Company	Baltimore, Maryland	Will D. Jackson	Petroleum sales	1965	40	18.213
Community Foods, Inc.	Baltimore, Maryland	Charles T. Burns	Supermarkets	1965	225	18.000
Ebony Oil Corporation	Jamaica, New York	Lawrence J. Cormier	Petroleum sales	1955	45	16.800
Technology Development of California, Inc.	Santa Clara, California	Frank S. Greene, Jr.	Electronic and computer systems	1971	360	16.400
S.T.R. Corporation	Cleveland, Ohio	Steve T. Rogers	Supermarkets	1965	250	15.700
True Transport, Inc.	Newark, New Jersey	Leamon McCoy	Containerized trucking and truck stop	1969	310	15.545
Misso Services Corp. & Assoc.	Falls Church, Virginia	Shelby Coates	Computer sales	1976	5	15.100
International & Domestic Development Corp.	Fayetteville, North Carolina	Marion Harris	Coal sales	1976	12	15.044
Counties Contracting & Construction Co.	Philadelphia, Pennsylvania	William Andrews	Utility contractor	1980	410	14.789
Commonwealth Holding Co., Inc.	New York, New York	James H. Dowdy	Manufacturing, real estate, and building materials	1967	425	14.731
Gourmet Services, Inc.	Atlanta, Georgia	Nathaniel R. Goldston III	Food services management	1975	1300	14.500
Dick Harris Cadillac	Detroit, Michigan	Richard B. Harris	Auto sales and service	1978	57	14.119
American Development Corp.	Charleston, South Carolina	W. Melvin Brown, Jr.	Diversified manufacturing	1972	250	14.000
Essence Communications, Inc.	New York, New York	Edward Lewis	Magazine publishing	1969	65	13.600
Dick Gidron Cadillac, Inc.	Bronx, New York	Richard D. Gidron	Auto sales and service	1972	80	13.600
Porterfield Wilson Pontiac-GMC Truck, Inc.	Detroit, Michigan	Porterfield Wilson	Auto/truck sales and service	1970	55	13.500
Systems & Applied Sciences Corp.	Riverdale, Maryland	Porter L. Bankhead	Information processing/computer software	1973	509	13.235
Bob Ross Buick Inc.	Centerville, Ohio	Robert P. Ross	Auto sales and service	1974	72	12.900
Broadcast Enterprises National, Inc.	Philadelphia, Pennsylvania	Ragar A. Henry	Radio and TV broadcasting	1974	275	12.900

Table 1. The 100 Largest Black-Owned Businesses in the United States (*continued*)

Company	Location	Chief Executive	Business	Year Started	Employees	1980 Sales (Billions of Dollars)
Sam Johnson Lincoln & Mercury Inc.	Charlotte, North Carolina	Sam Johnson	Auto sales and service	1977	40	12.500
Sterling Systems, Inc.	McLean, Virginia	Robert L. Quinichett	Information management/computer systems	1977	300	12.500
Woodruff Oldsmobile, Inc.	Detroit, Michigan	James W. Woodruff	Auto sales and service	1978	55	12.000
Cocoline Chocolate Company, Inc.	Brooklyn, New York	Leonard S. Halpert	Chocolate manufacturers	1974	70	12.000
McAnary Ford, Inc.	Gary, Indiana	Tom P. Gillespie, Sr.	Auto sales and service	1980	75	11.846
Blunt Enterprises, Inc.	Washington, D.C.	Roger R. Blunt, Sr.	Construction/management consulting	1979	150	11.700
Thomas Distributors, Inc.	Chicago, Illinois	Norman M. Thomas	Beer distributors	1975	50	11.115
Fuller Oil Company, Inc.	Fayetteville, North Carolina	Charles C. Fuller	Petroleum sales	1962	19	11.000
Willie Davis Distributing Company	Los Angeles, California	Willie D. Davis	Beer distributors	1970	57	10.500
Micon Construction & Development Corp.	Lynbrook, New York	Charles Peay	Construction	1972	20	10.500
Ran-Der Industries, Inc.	Morgan City, Louisiana	Allison B. Randolph, Jr.	Oilfield chemical sales and engineering services	1972	56	10.034
Delta Enterprises, Inc.	Greenville, Mississippi	Charles D. Bannerman	Diversified manufacturing	1969	550	10.000
Inner City Foods, Inc.	Chicago, Illinois	Garland C. Guice	Fast food restaurants	1976	750	9.600
Prepac, Inc.	Bronx, New York	Howard H. Mackey III	Vinyl and fabric packaging and stationery manufacturing	1978	100	9.500
L. Bennett Ford, Inc.	Flint, Michigan	L. Bennett	Auto sales and service	1972	64	9.400
Gordon Buick, Inc.	Philadelphia, Pennsylvania	Darrell R. Gordon	Auto sales and service	1972	27	9.200

Company	Location	Chief executive	Business	Year	Employees	Sales
Century Chevrolet, Inc.	Upper Darby, Pennsylvania	Robert L. Myers, Jr.	Auto sales and service	1971	40	9.200
Bill Nelson Chevrolet, Inc.	Richmond, California	William W. Nelson	Auto sales and service	1969	50	9.000
Mel Farr Ford, Inc.	Oak Park, Michigan	Mel Farr	Auto sales and service	1976	41	8.600
Systems Management American Corp.	Virginia Beach, Virginia	Herman E. Valentine	Applied information technology	1970	480	8.600
Walton Buick-Opel, Inc.	Medford, Massachusetts	Roland J. Walton	Auto sales and service	1977	40	8.489
Sentry Buick, Inc.	Omaha, Nebraska	Gregory M. Williams	Auto sales and service	1979	41	8.142
Alan Young Buick, Inc.	Lincoln, Nebraska	Alan Young	Auto sales and service	1979	36	8.063
Trans-Bay Engineers & Builders, Inc.	Oakland, California	Ray Dones	General contracting and engineering	1966	25	8.014
Parker House Sausage Company	Chicago, Illinois	Daryl F. Grisham	Sausage manufacturers	1921	84	7.960
D & H Tire Service Co.	Kansas City, Kansas	Luther D. White	Tire sales and service	1965	75	7.900
McLaughlin Oldsmobile, Inc.	Capitol Heights, Maryland	Joseph C. McLaughlin	Auto sales and service, leasing and rental	1975	20	7.700
William Huff Ford, Inc.	Manchester, Georgia	William Huff III	Auto sales and service	1975	20	7.700
Batteast Construction Company, Inc.	South Bend, Indiana	Robert V. Batteast	Construction	1967	60	7.700
The Barfield Companies	Ypsilanti, Michigan	John W. Barfield	Auto parts, manufacturers contract engineers	1955	340	7.600
Conyers Ford, Inc.	Detroit, Michigan	Nathan G. Conyers	Auto sales and service	1970	50	7.600
R. L. Dukes Oldsmobile	Chicago, Illinois	Rufus L. Dukes	Auto sales	1970	60	7.596
Raven Systems and Research, Inc.	Washington, D.C.	Raymond A. Mott	Information processing	1971	400	7.577
Landmark Ford Sales, Inc.	Fairfield, Ohio	Kenneth C. Younger	Auto truck sales and service	1977	53	7.563
The Emanuel Company	Detroit, Michigan	Donald F. Emanual	Construction	1973	34	7.561
Bush Construction Company, Inc.	Chicago, Illinois	Ernest Bush, Sr.	Construction	1971	24	7.556
Teleport Oil Company, Inc.	San Francisco, California	Carl E. Washington	Petroleum sales	1978	12	7.540
Baranco Pontiac, Inc.	Decatur, Georgia	Gregory T. Baranco	Auto sales and service	1978	52	7.517

Table 1. The 100 Largest Black-Owned Businesses in the United States (*continued*)

Company	Location	Chief Executive	Business	Year Started	Employees	1980 Sales (Billions of Dollars)
D.P.S. Protective Systems, Inc.	New York, New York	Dale R. Michael	Security service	1976	1500	7.500
Royal Ridge Management Co., Inc.	Cleveland, Ohio	Narlie Roberts	Fast food restaurants	1970	550	7.435
Earl G. Graves, Ltd.	New York, New York	Earl G. Graves	Magazine publisher/ radio broadcasting	1970	85	7.319
All-Stainless, Inc.	Hingham, Massachusetts	Eugene V. Roundtree	Stainless steel distributor	1952	70	7.250
Keys Group Co.	Detroit, Michigan	Brady Keys, Jr.	Fast food restaurants, coal brokers	1967	250	7.220
Golden Bird, Inc.	Culver City, California	Willie J. Stennis	Fast food restaurants	1955	212	7.200
Tynes Chevrolet-Cadillac, Inc.	Delaware, Ohio	Richard H. Tynes	Auto sales and service	1976	40	7.200
H. F. Henderson Industries	West Caldwell, New Jersey	Henry F. Henderson, Jr.	Automatic weighing and process control systems	1954	55	7.100
The Famous Amos Chocolate Chip Cookie Corporation	Van Nuys, California	Wally Amos	Cookie manufacturer	1975	170	7.000
Ozanne Construction Company, Inc.	Cleveland, Ohio	Leroy Ozanne	Construction	1956	20	7.000
Porterfield Wilson Mazda-Honda	Detroit, Michigan	Barbra J. Wilson	Auto sales and service	1979	15	6.899
Ascension Chemical of America Corp.	Tonawanda, New York	Jesse H. Jackson	Aluminum chloride manufacturer	1972	18	6.800
Yucca Valley Ford	Yucca Valley, California	William E. Shack, Jr.	Auto sales and services	1977	45	6.780
Al Johnson Cadillac, Inc.	Tinley Park, Illinois	Albert W. Johnson, Sr.	Auto sales and service	1971	45	6.770
Payton Wells Ford, Inc.	Indianapolis, Indiana	Payton R. Wells	Auto/truck sales and service	1978	52	6.671

Company	Location	Chief Executive	Business	Year		
Beauchamp Distributing Co.	Los Angeles, California	Patrick L. Beauchamp	Beer distributor	1971	43	6.450
Lismark Distributing Co.	St. Louis, Missouri	C. W. Gates	Beer distributor	1975	33	6.334
Tombs & Sons, Inc.	Bonner Springs, Kansas	Leroy C. Tombs, Sr.	Food, janitorial, and security services		925	5.824
George Hughes Chevrolet, Inc.	Freehold, New Jersey	George Hughes	Auto/truck sales and service	1978	30	5.736
White Buick, Inc.	Manchester, New Hampshire	Luther J. White	Auto sales and service	1974	28	5.549
Bob Neal Pontiac-Toyota, Inc.	Chicago, Illinois	Robert P. Neal	Auto sales and service	1966	37	5.431
Ault, Incorporated	Minneapolis, Minnesota	Luther T. Prince	Electronics manufacturer	1968	140	5.360
Central News-Wave Publications	Los Angeles, California	Chester L. Washington	Newspaper publishing	1971	137	5.300
Seidel Chevrolet, Inc.	Landover, Maryland	John C. Seidel	Auto sales and service	1974	30	5.244
T.W.O./Hillman's Corporation	Chicago, Illinois	Lawrence W. Carroll	Supermarkets	1970	60	5.221
C. H. James & Co.	Charleston, West Virginia	Charles H. James II	Wholesale food supplier	1883	28	5.168

Table 2. Major Black Savings and Loan Associations

Company	Location	Chief Executive	Year Started	Employees	Total Assets (Millions of Dollars)
Family Savings & Loan Association	Los Angeles, California	Robert E. Bowdoin	1948	76	117.200
Illinois/Service Federal Savings & Loan Association of Chicago	Chicago, Illinois	Louise G. Lawson	1935	45	89.600
Carver Federal Savings & Loan Association	New York, New York	Richard T. Greene	1949	54	86.599
Founders Savings & Loan Association	Los Angeles, California	Peter W. Dauterive	1974	66	80.947
Broadway Federal Savings & Loan Association	Los Angeles, California	Elbert T. Hodson	1946	50	65.609
Independent Federal Savings & Loan Association	Washington, D.C.	William B. Fitzgerald	1968	50	56.072
United Federal Savings & Loan Association	New Orleans, Louisiana	Beverly N. Staes	1964	11	28.619
Citizens Federal Savings & Loan Association	Baton Rouge, Louisiana	Louis L. Eames	1956	9	28.438
Citizens Federal Savings & Loan Association	Birmingham, Alabama	A. G. Gaston	1957	18	28.012
Advance Federal Savings & Loan Association	Baltimore, Maryland	W. O. Bryson, Jr.	1957	25	25.574
Mutual Federal Savings & Loan Association of Atlanta	Atlanta, Georgia	Fletcher Coombs	1925	14	24.248
Community Federal Savings & Loan Association	Washington, D.C.	Orlando W. Darden	1974	14	23.102
Home Federal Savings & Loan Association	Detroit, Michigan	Wilburn R. Phillips	1947	15	22.759

Association	Location	President	Year		Assets
Allied Federal Savings & Loan Association	Jamaica, New York	Howard R. Dabney	1959	17	18.331
Mutual Savings & Loan Association	Durham, North Carolina	F. V. Allison, Jr.	1921	10	16.946
Berean Savings Association	Philadelphia, Pennsylvania	I. Maxmilian Martin	1888	10	15.085
Enterprise Savings & Loan Association	Long Beach, California	Cornell R. Kirkland	1963	15	14.484
American Federal Savings & Loan Association of Greensboro	Greensboro, North Carolina	A. S. Webb	1959	7	14.430
Cleveland Community Savings Co.	Cleveland, Ohio	Ray C. Bobo	1952	13	14.184
Tuskegee Federal Savings & Loan Association	Tuskegee Institute, Alabama	Richard R. Harvey	1894	4	14.076
People's Savings & Loan Association	Hampton, Virginia	John E. Coles	1889	9	12.705
Standard Savings Association	Houston, Texas	Mach H. Hannah, Jr.	1959	11	12.464
Berkley Citizens Mutual Savings & Loan Association, Inc.	Norfolk, Virginia	Elbert Stewart	1913	10	11.998
Major Federal Savings & Loan Association	Cincinnati, Ohio	Pauline Allen Strayhorne	1921	10	11.765
New Age Federal Savings & Loan Association	St. Louis, Missouri	A. C. Phillips	1915	8	11.707
Connecticut Savings & Loan Association	Hartford, Connecticut	John A. Hogan	1968	7	10.528
State Mutual Federal Savings & Loan Association	Jackson, Mississippi	James E. Davis	1955	8	9.217
Union Mutual Savings & Loan Association	Richmond, Virginia	Garfield F. Childs	1961	7	8.805
Washington Shores Federal Savings & Loan Association	Orlando, Florida	Charles J. Hawkins	1963	5	8.532

Table 2. Major Black Savings and Loan Associations (*continued*)

Company	Location	Chief Executive	Year Started	Employees	Total Assets (Millions of Dollars)
Community Savings & Loan Association	Newport News, Virginia	George N. Miller, Jr.	1957	5	7.980
Community Federal Savings & Loan Association of Nashville	Nashville, Tennessee	Alfred C. Galloway	1962	5	7.757
Columbia Savings & Loan Association	Milwaukee, Wisconsin	Thalia B. Winfield	1924	7	7.243
Gulf Federal Savings & Loan Association of Mobile	Mobile, Alabama	H. Leroy Davis	1964	5	6.972
Dwelling House Savings & Loan Association	Pittsburgh, Pennsylvania	Robert R. Lavelle	1890	7	6.852
Community Federal Savings & Loan Association of Tampa	Tampa, Florida	James T. Hargrett, Jr.	1967	7	6.841
Inglewood Federal Savings & Loan Association	Inglewood, California	Onie Granville	1980	14	5.200
Magnolia Federal Savings & Loan Association	Knoxville, Tennessee	John Walter Harshaw	1973	5	5.197
Ideal Savings & Loan Association	Baltimore, Maryland	E. Gaines Lansey	1920	4	3.497
Imperial Savings & Loan Association	Martinsville, Virginia	W. B. Muse, Jr.	1929	5	3.406
Equity Savings & Loan Association	Denver, Colorado	Earl M. West	1955	3	3.160
Morgan Park Savings & Loan Association	Chicago, Illinois	Adele White	1921	4	3.107
United Savings & Loan Association of Gary	Gary, Indiana	J. Cameron Wade	1975	1	0.025

Source: Black Enterprise Magazine.

Table 3. Major Black Banks in the United States

Company	Location	Chief Executive	Year Started	Employees	Total Assets (Millions of Dollars)
Independence Bank of Chicago	Chicago, Illinois	Alvin J. Boutte	1964	124	101.891
Seaway National Bank of Chicago	Chicago, Illincis	F. T. Collins	1965	125	72.500
Freedom National Bank of New York	New York, New York	Sharnia Buford	1964	72	63.830
United National Bank of Washington	Washington, D C.	Samuel L. Foggie	1964	90	62.733
Industrial Bank of Washington	Washington, D.C.	B. Doyle Mitchell	1934	80	58.971
First National Bank Association	Cleveland, Ohio	John H. Bustamante	1974	61	58.210
Citizens Trust Bank	Atlanta, Georgia	I. Owen Funderburg	1921	75	52.550
Mechanics and Farmers Bank	Durham, North Carolina	J. J. Sansom, Jr.	1908	85	47.741
First Enterprise Bank	Oakland, Califorria	Lloyd A. Edwards	1972	75	42.518
First Independence National Bank of Detroit	Detroit, Michigan	Donald Davis	1970	65	39.759
Highland Community Bank	Chicago, Illinois	George R. Brokemond	1970	35	38.298
Liberty Bank & Trust Bank	New Orleans, Louisiana	Alden J. McDonald, Jr.	1972	62	36.013
Consolidated Bank & Trust Company	Richmond, Virginia	Vernard W. Henley	1903	60	33.341
First Texas Bank	Dallas, Texas	Lynn D. Turner	1975	44	33.072
Tri-State Bank of Memphis	Memphis, Tennessee	Jesse H. Turner, Sr.	1946	56	30.788
Union National Bank of Chicago	Chicago, Illinois	Charles G. Wells	1950	66	29.161
City National Bank of New Jersey	Newark, New Jersey	Charles L. Whigham	1973	28	28.326

Table 3.   Major Black Banks in the United States (*continued*)

Company	Location	Chief Executive	Year Started	Employees	Total Assets (Millions of Dollars)
Midwest National Bank	Indianapolis, Indiana	John P. Kelly, Jr.	1972	50	28.218
The Douglass State Bank	Kansas City, Kansas	Gerald W. Hall	1947	34	27.516
South Side Bank	Chicago, Illinois	Thomas P. Lewis	1972	45	27.300
Citizens Savings Bank & Trust Co.	Nashville, Tennessee	Richard A. Lewis	1904	47	26.588
Bank of Finance	Los Angeles, California	Herman A. Hendricks	1964	62	23.534
Gateway National Bank of St. Louis	St. Louis, Missouri	David B. Harper	1965	34	23.400
Tri-State Bank	Markham, Illinois	Mitchell M. Nelson	1962	34	21.484
Century National Bank	Jacksonville, Florida	W. Mitchell Hines	1976	26	18.596
Unity Bank & Trust Company	Roxbury, Massachusetts	Theodore S. Wilkins	1968	31	17.222
Carver State Bank	Savannah, Georgia	Robert E. James	1927	43	17.132
Riverside National Bank	Houston, Texas	Carl M. Carroll, Jr.	1963	25	15.044
Community Bank of Lawndale	Chicago, Illinois	Cecil C. Butler	1977	30	13.698
Liberty Bank of Seattle	Seattle, Washington	James C. Purnell	1968	15	13.379
First State Bank	Danville, Virginia	L. Wilson York	1919	16	12.644
Continental National Bank of Kentucky	Louisville, Kentucky	V. Joseph Shipman	1976	15	11.952
American State Bank	Portland, Oregon	Venerable F. Booker	1969	17	11.749
North Milwaukee State Bank	Milwaukee, Wisconsin	Gerard S. Hankins	1971	16	11.672
Atlantic National Bank	Norfolk, Virginia	Charles M. Reynolds, Jr.	1971	24	11.035
American State Bank	Tulsa, Oklahoma	Leroy Thomas, Sr.	1970	19	10.328
Commonwealth National Bank	Mobile, Alabama	E. M. Collins III	1976	21	9.816
Medical Center State Bank	Oklahoma City, Oklahoma	Wilbert Johnson	1973	25	9.756

Bank	Location	Chief Executive	Year		
Greensboro National Bank	Greensboro, North Carolina	Robert S. Chiles, Sr.	1971	23	9.561
National Security Bank	Tyler, Texas	Marie L. Harlin	1975	18	8.881
Unity State Bank	Dayton, Ohio	Ralph C. Jones	1970	18	8.802
Community Bank of Nebraska	Omaha, Nebraska	Leon E. Evans, Jr.	1973	19	7.169
Victory Savings Bank	Columbia, South Carolina	Thomas E. Felder	1921	11	7.000
New World National Bank	Pittsburgh, Pennsylvania	Daniel Smith	1975	15	6.986
United National Bank	Fayetteville, North Carolina	Floyd L. Shorter	1976	16	5.900
Prince George's State Bank	Glenarden, Maryland	Joseph Agyemen-Gyau	1978	11	5.682
Palm Beach Lakes Bank	West Palm Beach, Florida	Dale Kelley	1974	16	5.564
Pacific Coast Bank	San Diego, California	Oscar Knight	1973	16	4.300

Source: Black Enterprise Magazine.

Table 4.   Major Black Life Insurance Companies

Company	Location	Chief Executive	Year Started	Employees	Insurance in Force (Millions of Dollars)
North Carolina Mutual Life Insurance Company	Durham, North Carolina	W. J. Kennedy III	1898	1,390	5,580.249
Atlanta Life Insurance Company	Atlanta, Georgia	Jesse Hill, Jr.	1903	1,000	1,143.362
Golden State Mutual Life Insurance Company	Los Angeles, California	Ivan J. Houston	1925	700	2,904.733
Universal Life Insurance Company	Memphis, Tennessee	A. Maceo Walker, Sr.	1923	885	518.383
Supreme Life Insurance Company of America	Chicago, Illinois	John H. Johnson	1919	400	1,506.933
Chicago Metropolitan Mutual Assurance Company	Chicago, Illinois	Anderson M. Schweich	1927	233	1,341.670
Mammoth Life & Accident Insurance Company	Louisville, Kentucky	J. E. Price, Sr.	1915	275	185.000
Booker T. Washington Insurance Company	Birmingham, Alabama	A. G. Gaston	1932	240	465.000
The Pilgrim Health & Life Insurance Company	Augusta, Georgia	S. W. Walker, II	1897	268	148.090
United Mutual Life Insurance Company	New York, New York	James L. Howard	1933	30	53.429
American Woodmen's Life Insurance Company	Denver, Colorado	Lillie Anne Owens	1966	35	0.160
Afro-American Life Insurance Company	Jacksonville, Florida	J. L. Miller	1901	200	63.528
Central Life Insurance Company of Florida	Tampa, Florida	Joseph A. Henry	1922	126	42.591
Protective Industrial Insurance Company of Alabama	Birmingham, Alabama	Virgil L. Harris	1923	120	40.621

Company	Location	President	Employees	Founded	Assets
Winston Mutual Life Insurance Company	Winston-Salem, North Carolina	George E. Hill	100	1907	218.000
Winnfield Life Insurance Company	Nachitoches, Louisiana	Ben D. Johnson	100	1933	64.648
Golden Circle Life Insurance Company	Brownsville, Tennessee	C. A. Rawis	74	1958	19.028
Virginia Mutual Benefit Life Insurance Company	Richmond, Virginia	D. J. Mack	100	1933	20.000
Southern Aide Life Insurance Company	Richmond, Virginia	E. L. Simon	60	1893	0.041
Wright Mutual Insurance Company	Detroit, Michigan	Wardell C. Croft	50	1942	19.006
Gertrude Geddes Willis Life Insurance Company	New Orleans, Louisiana	Joseph O. Misshore, Jr.	61	1941	23.681
Williams-Progressive Life & Accident Insurance Co.	Opelousas, Louisiana	Borel C. Dauphin	65	1947	29.009
Purple Shield Life Insurance Company	Baton Rouge, Louisiana	Homer J. Sheeler, Sr.	115	1949	58.148
Christian Benevolent Insurance Company	Mobile, Alabama	J. Gary Cooper	74	1926	24.000
Unity Life Insurance Company	Mobile, Alabama	Vance E. Gray	120	1927	24.300
Bradford's Industrial Insurance Company	Birmingham, Alabama	Daniel Kennon, Jr.	19	1932	7.394
Reliable Life Insurance Company	Monroe, Louisiana	Joseph H. Miller, Jr.	70	1940	19.337
Benevolent Life Insurance Company	Shreveport, Louisiana	Granville L. Smith	100	1934	15.711
The Security Life Insurance Company of the South	Jackson, Mississippi	W. H. Williams	89	1940	2.172
Majestic Life Insurance	New Orleans, Louisiana	Adam R. Haydel, Sr.	21	1947	7.498
Southern Life Insurance Company	Baltimore, Maryland	Ida Moore	25	1906	4.000
Valley Life Insurance Group	Phoenix, Arizona	Lincoln J. Ragsdale	8	1958	9.010

Table 4. Major Black Life Insurance Companies (*continued*)

Company	Location	Chief Executive	Year Started	Employees	Insurance in Force (Millions of Dollars)
Superior Life Insurance Company	Baton Rouge, Louisiana	J. K. Haynes	1954	80	10.124
National Service Industrial Life Insurance Company	New Orleans, Louisiana	Duplain Rhodes, Jr.	1948	23	4.807
Lighthouse Life Insurance Company	Shreveport, Louisiana	Bunyan S. Jacobs, Sr.	1949	60	8.261
Lovett's Life & Burial Insurance Company	Mobile, Alabama	L. M. Lovett	1949	20	5.572
People's Progressive Insurance Company	Rayville, Louisiana	Marion Gundy Hill	1936	27	3.772
Progressive Industrial Life Insurance Company	New Orleans, Louisiana	C. L. Dennis	1948	16	0.621

Source: Black Enterprise Magazine

Table 5. Comparative Change in Status of Black-Owned Business between 1972 and 1977

Industry	All U.S. Firms, 1977	1977 Business Firms Owned By—					Percent Change from 1972		
		All Minorities	Percent Minorities of All Firms	Black	Spanish Origins	Other	All Minorities	Black	Spanish Origin
Number of firms, total[a]	9,833[b]	560[b]	5.7	231	219	111	31	12	53
With paid employees	(X)	103	(X)	40	41	24	44	46	35
With no paid employees	(X)	456	(X)	191	178	87	28	6	57
Construction	1,107	52	4.7	21	27	4	31	10	52

Manufacturing	287	12	42	4	6	3	40	16	48
Transportation and public utilities[c]	419	36	8.6	23	11	3	21	8	57
Wholesale trade	⎱ 2,600	⎱ 157	⎱ 6.0	2	4	3	43	30	32
Retail trade	⎰	⎰	⎰	55	58	34	23	3	31
Finance, insurance, real estate	1,404	28	2.0	10	12	6	52	28	85
Selected services	3,623	234	6.5	102	87	46	42	20	85
Business receipts, total[a]	633.1	22.2	3.5	8.6	10.4	7.4	69	47	75
Firms with paid employees	(X)	14.9	(X)	6.4	7.1	5.5	83	75	79
With no paid employees	(X)	7.4	(X)	2.2	3.3	1.9	41	1	66
Construction	72.6	2.1	2.9	.8	1.2	.4	55	21	74
Manufacturing	38.5	.9	2.3	.6	.9	.5	50	69	90
Transportation and public utilities[a]	22.8	.9	3.9	.5	.4	.2	69	42	131
Wholesale trade	⎱ 291.4	⎱ 10.8	⎱ 3.7	.7	.8	.6	78	104	69
Retail trade	⎰	⎰	⎰	3.4	3.8	3.5	59	39	52
Finance, insurance, real estate	66.6	.7	1.1	.6	.4	.3	84	63	129
Selected services	120.1	5.9	4.9	1.9	2.6	1.7	91	57	121
Employment, total[a]	(NA)	(NA)	(NA)	164	206	130	21	6	29
Construction	(NA)	(NA)	(NA)	17	23	5	-2	-22	12
Manufacturing	(NA)	(NA)	(NA)	16	28	16	40	12	45
Transportation and public utilities[c]	(NA)	(NA)	(NA)	8	4	3	—	-3	(Z)
Wholesale trade	(NA)	(NA)	(NA)	5	6	4	17	22	14
Retail trade	(NA)	(NA)	(NA)	46	75	62	25	4	32
Finance, insurance, real estate	(NA)	(NA)	(NA)	15	5	4	—	1	26
Selected services	(NA)	(NA)	(NA)	55	61	34	31	23	35

Source: U.S. Bureau of the Census, *Minority-Owned Businesses: 1977.*

Key: — Represents zero. NA Not available. X Not applicable. Z Less than 0.5%.

[a] Includes industries not shown separately.

[b] Excludes large corporations for comparison to all U.S. firms; breakdown by race includes large corporations.

[c] Excludes railroads.

Table 6. Leading Categories of Black Business, 1977

Type of Business	Gross Receipts of All Firms	Number	Percent of Total Firms	Average Gross Receipts	Average Number of Employees	Number	Percent of Total Firms	Average Gross Receipts
Auto dealers, service stations	$1,107,650,000	2,528	51	$ 390,019	4.3	2,474	49	$49,185
Food stores	$ 785,776,000	2,217	21	$ 224,760	3.3	8,462	79	$33,973
Miscellaneous retailers	$ 589,727,000	2,064	10	$ 192,399	3.0	18,816	90	$10,237
Eating and drinking establishments	$ 572,331,000	4,128	32	$ 103,024	4.2	8,880	68	$16,559
Special trade contractors	$ 496,693,000	4,230	25	$ 82,020	3.1	12,896	75	$11,612
Health services	$ 432,534,000	3,288	23	$ 98,631	3.3	11,272	77	$ 9,602
Personal services	$ 399,274,000	3,785	11	$ 52,420	2.5	31,250	89	$ 6,428
Business services	$ 358,286,000	2,440	16	$ 108,541	7.6	13,021	84	$ 7,177
Trucking, warehousing	$ 353,216,000	1,890	16	$ 83,666	2.6	9,662	84	$20,191
Insurance carriers	$ 249,201,000	53	91	$4,697,736	134.4	5	9	$44,200
General building contractors	$ 214,616,000	1,021	30	$ 155,855	3.4	2,394	70	$23,178
Auto repair and service, garages	$ 184,555,000	1,459	21	$ 75,519	2.6	5,431	79	$13,694
Banking	$ 140,497,000	70	46	$1,986,743	53.8	82	54	$ 9,695

Source: *Black Enterprise*, June 1980.

Table 7. Leading Growth Categories of Black Business, 1972–1977

	All Firms				Firms with Paid Employees			
	Number		Gross Receipts		Number		Gross Receipts	
	1977	Change '72–'77	1977	Change '72–'77	1977	Change '72–'77	1977	Change '72–'77
Banking	152	+54%	$140,497,000	+248%	70	+ 67%	$139,702,000	+254%
Printing and publishing	788	+14%	$122,193,000	+105%	215	+ 27%	$116,318,000	+120%
Wholesale trade	2,212	+30%	$664,052,000	+104%	705	+ 30%	$628,343,000	+113%
Business services	15,461	+48%	$358,286,000	+103%	2,440	+ 87%	$264,839,000	+133%
Fishing, hunting, trapping	885	+66%	$ 11,952,000	+101%	31	+ 35%	$ 2,632,000	+ 65%
Credit agencies	91	– 8%	$ 43,859,000	+ 99%	63	– 1%	$ 43,459,000	+107%
Amusement and recreational services	5,535	+24%	$109,664,000	+ 87%	393	+ 36%	$ 70,035,000	+152%
Lumber and wood products manufacturing	1,935	+29%	$ 83,992,000	+ 87%	923	+ 70%	$ 70,972,000	+132%
Auto repair and service, garages	6,890	+29%	$184,555,000	+ 76%	1,459	+ 65%	$110,183,000	+104%
Real estate	6,606	–30%	$141,267,000	+ 66%	660	+ 68%	$ 85,213,000	+104%
Electric and electronic equipment manufacturing	81	+ 4%	$ 56,412,000	+ 61%	54	none	$ 56,091,000	+ 63%
Food products manufacturing	89	–19%	$ 95,025,000	+ 59%	61	+ 15%	$ 94,405,000	+ 61%
Agricultural services	3,532	+35%	$ 67,269,000	+ 55%	627	+158%	$ 37,184,000	+106%

Source: Black Enterprise.

Note: Covers all categories whose 1977 gross receipts accounted for at least 5% of the total for the pertinent industry group ("Manufacturing," "General Services," etc.) and were at least 50% higher than in 1972. Some additional categories of "General Services" conceivably should be included for which the 1972 and 1977 surveys did not yield directly comparable data. "Credit agencies" obviously excludes banks, which are covered under "banking"; "business services" includes advertising, data processing services, building services, etc. From Census Bureau data.

Table 8. Comparison of Minority Business Enterprises and Black-Owned Firms by Industry Type, 1972–1977

Industry	Percent Owned by All Minorities		Percent Black-Owned	
	1972	1977	1972	1977
Construction	10.4	9.3	10.2	9.1
Manufacturing	2.3	2.2	2.0	1.8
Transportation, public utilities	8.1	6.5	11.4	10.0
Wholesale	1.7	1.7	.9	1.0
Retail	31.5	26.1	28.7	24.0
FIRE	4.8	5.1	4.1	4.2
Selected services	31.6	41.7	35.5	44.0
Total	100	100	100	100

Table 9. Ten Largest SMSAs in Number of Black-Owned Firms, 1977

Rank in 1977	SMSA	Rank in 1972	Number of Firms	Percent of Total	Gross Receipts (Thousands of Dollars)	Percent of Total
1	Los Angeles	2	14,699	6.4	549,514	6.4
2	New York	1	13,966	6.0	480,957	5.6
3	Washington	3	11,645	5.0	331,193	3.8
4	Chicago	4	10,394	4.5	802,095	9.3
5	Houston	7	6,758	2.9	182,144	2.1
6	Philadelphia	5	6,710	2.9	257,058	3.0
7	Detroit	6	6,332	2.7	383,386	4.4
8	San Francisco	8	5,759	2.5	259,499	3.0
9	Baltimore	9	4,526	2.0	154,752	1.8
10	Dallas	NA	4,194	1.8	133,083	1.5

Table 10. Black-Owned Firms by Employee Size

	Number of Firms	Number of Employees	Gross Receipts (Thousands of Dollars)
No employees	191,235	0	2,248,350
1–4	32,581	47,225	2,242,573
5–9	4,556	28,985	958,158
10–19	1,771	23,231	728,161
20–49	717	21,229	914,010
50–99	230	15,540	542,319
100 or more	113	27,967	1,011,629
Total with employees	39,968	164,177	6,396,850
Total firms	231,203	164,177	8,645,200

Table 11. Black Farm Operators in the United States, 1978

	Farms with Sales of $1,000 or More		Farms with Sales of $2,500 or More	
	Farms	Acres in Farms	Farms	Acres in Farms
United States (total)	57,271	4,743,619	23,687	3,282,512
Alabama	4,791	413,354	1,284	218,348
Arizona	92	54,561	51	54,237
Arkansas	2,067	194,969	1,040	153,429
California	388	31,368	196	28,504
Colorado	56	14,035	27	13,262
Connecticut	10	323	4	(D)
Delaware	60	4,378	39	4,007
Florida	2,307	149,780	772	117,300
Georgia	4,485	383,419	1,674	276,644
Idaho	16	9,615	12	9,501
Illinois	169	23,070	126	21,333
Indiana	107	17,838	79	16,884
Iowa	95	23,845	89	23,748
Kansas	139	50,085	103	48,143
Kentucky	1,092	83,155	743	71,442
Louisiana	3,296	225,860	1,080	154,390
Maine	6	3,340	4	(D)
Maryland	953	48,675	610	36,950
Massachusetts	19	836	15	534
Michigan	247	20,377	119	15,755
Minnesota	69	19,913	64	19,539
Mississippi	8,817	677,193	2,204	322,143
Missouri	279	44,998	188	38,796
Montana	8	7,661	7	(D)
Nebraska	74	50,708	63	47,671
Nevada	6	365	1	(D)
New Jersey	104	4,752	54	4,007
New Mexico	12	21,779	3	579
New York	75	10,171	44	7,355
North Carolina	7,680	423,272	4,663	357,348
North Dakota	19	16,696	18	(D)
Ohio	433	31,086	190	25,143
Oklahoma	851	134,144	347	91,500
Oregon	21	2,526	10	1,554
Pennsylvania	70	6,926	45	5,634
South Carolina	6,451	324,665	2,112	219,765
South Dakota	30	35,356	28	(D)
Tennessee	2,405	177,765	1,173	136,674
Texas	5,420	640,411	1,876	392,753
Utah	3	385	2	(D)
Vermont	3	(D)	3	(D)
Virginia	3,895	331,935	2,420	267,445
Washington	42	9,296	30	8,905
West Virginia	46	6,927	23	4,944
Wisconsin	59	10,806	48	10,013
Wyoming	3	231	3	231
All other states	1	(D)	1	(D)

Source: U.S. Department of Commerce, Bureau of the Census, *1978 Census of Agriculture,* Vol. 1, pt. 51, Table 42, p. 209.

Table 12. Farms Operated by Blacks and Whites, 1900–1978

Year	Blacks	Percent Change	Whites	Percent Change
1978	57,271	−57.3	2,398,726	−22.4
1969	133,973	−50.8	3,089,885	− 9.6
1959	272,541	−51.3	3,419,672	−28.8
1950	559,980	−17.9	4,802,520	−10.7
1940	681,790	−22.8	5,378,913	+ .09
1930	882,852	− 4.6	5,373,703	− 2.3
1920	925,710	+ 3.6	5,499,707	+ 1.1
1910	893,377	+19.6	5,440,619	+ 9.5
1900	746,717		4,970,129	
Overall percentage loss between 1920 and 1978		−93.8%		−56.4%

Source: U.S. Department of Commerce, Bureau of the Census, *1974 Census of Agriculture,* Vol. 2, pt. 3, pp. 1-82, 1-10; *1978 Census of Agriculture,* Vol. 1, pt. 51, pp. 2, 209.

Table 13. Black-Operated Commercial Farms in the South[a]

Crop	1959[b]		1969[c]		1974[c]	
	Number	Percent	Number	Percent	Number	Percent
Cotton	87,074	56.4	3,195	13.0	1,569	8.1
Tobacco	40,670	26.4	9,093	37.0	6,963	36.0
Cash grain	2,285	1.5	1,965	8.0	4,332	22.4
Other	24,268	15.7	10,296	41.9	6,485	33.5
Total	154,298	(100%)	24,549	(99.9%)	19,349	(100%)

Sources: *1969 Census of Agriculture,* Vol. 2, chap. 3, p. 107; *1974 Census of Agriculture,* Vol. 2, pt. 3, pp. 1-95; Calvin Beale, "The Negro in American Agriculture," reprinted by USDA from *The American Negro Reference Book,* ed. John P. Davis (1966), p. 177.

[a] Farms with sales of $2,500 or more in a year.

[b] Data for 1959 include all non-white commercial farmers in the South, of whom approximately 98% were black. In addition to farms with sales of $2,500 or more, these data include farms with sales under $2,500 whose operators are not elderly and have little off-farm work. Beale, "The Negro in American Agriculture," pp. 171, 173, 179.

[c] Because of a significant undercount of small and black farmers in the 1969 and 1974 agricultural censuses (resulting from a change in census methodology) these data may be undercounted by as much as one third the true number of farmers.

Table 14. Number of Black Farm Home Administration Committee Members, 1979 and 1980

State	1979	1980	Percent Change
Alabama	37	19	−48.6
Florida	14	10	−28.6
Georgia	61	24	−60.7
Mississippi	48	21	−56.3
North Carolina	47	31	−34.0
South Carolina	27	19	−29.6
Tennessee	33	2	−93.3
Texas	33	18	−45.5
Virginia	49	29	−40.8

Source: U.S. Department of Agriculture, Office of Equal Opportunity, *Equal Opportunity Report: USDA Programs—1980,* pp. 53, 73–76.

Table 15. Farm Operating Loans to Minorities, Fiscal Years 1971–1981

Year	Number of Loans	Percent of Total
1981	3,024	10.3
1980	3,772	11.7
1979	3,344	9.8
1978	4,154	8.8
1977	4,289	10.8
1976	5,294	12.3
1975	6,490	13.8
1974	6,824	13.3
1973	6,403	12.5
1972	5,347	12.3
1971	5,287	12.5

Source: U.S. Department of Agriculture, Farmers Home Administration, Computer data entitled "Racial Program Participation by Fiscal Years" (Fiscal Years 1980 and 1981), Report Code 631. Graph prepared by USDA, Office of Equal Opportunity, entitled "Percent and Number of Operating Loans to Minorities by Fiscal Year" (Fiscal Years 1969–78).

Table 16. Farm Ownership Loans, Fiscal Year 1981

	Number	Percent	Total Amount (Thousands of Dollars)	Percent	Average Loan
Whites	10,991	94.0	756,004	95.1	$68,784
Blacks	226	1.9	10,216	1.3	45,204
Others[a]	476	4.1	29,134	3.7	29,835
Total	11,693	100.0	795,353	100.1	$68,020

Source: U.S. Department of Agriculture, Farmers Home Administration, Computer Data entitled "Distribution of Loans Made by Six Specified Types by Race and Ethnic Group," Report Code 691 (Fiscal Year 1981).

[a] Includes Hispanics, Native Americans, and Asians.

EMPLOYMENT, UNEMPLOYMENT, AND THE LABOR FORCE

A Grim Note ■ Major Trends of the 1970s ■ Unemployment as an Issue ■ Employment and World War II ■ Discrimination After World War II ■ Title VII and EEOC ■ Equal Opportunity and the Carter Years ■ Reagan and Affirmative Action ■ Discrimination in Public Employment ■ Black Immigrants ■ Undocumented Aliens ■ Vietnam Veterans ■ Youth and Structural Unemployment ■ Jobs Programs ■ Nixon and the New Federalism ■ Carter and CETA ■ The Reagan Approach ■ Working Women ■ Occupations ■ Trade-Sensitive Employment ■ The Future

A grim outlook faced the nation's black workers at the start of 1982. In February, by official count nearly one of every six black adults and more than two of five teenagers were unemployed. When the long-term unemployed and part-time workers unable to find full-time work were considered, the predicament of blacks was even bleaker, with unemployment exceeding 25% for adults and 55% for teenagers.

Compounding the situation, long-term prospects were ominous. The recession of 1981–1982, the second within two years, was harsher than expected and exacted an especially heavy toll on blacks, who were concentrated in areas, industries, and skills most affected. Unskilled jobs, traditionally the province of blacks, were increasingly being filled by aliens illegally in the country and willing to work for wages far below the legal minimum. Jobs in the public sector, the em-

ployer of more than half of the nation's black college graduates, were being cut back.

Blacks were also employed at a disproportionately high rate in jobs adversely affected by foreign trade. And skilled craft jobs, in which blacks had attained notable strides during the 1970s, were being erased by employer relocation and automation as the job market relentlessly shifted its orientation to high-technology skills few blacks were in a position to obtain.

As of early 1982, the black labor force had few assets with which to meet the changes and challenges of the 1980s. The private sector, preoccupied with surviving "stagflation" and high interest rates, had little to offer in the way of jobs, training, or upgrading. And the national government, having condemned government as the fount of all economic ills, was withdrawing from the job creation, job training, and affirmative action programs that had done so much to lift

Chart 1. Unemployment Rates in May 1982

As of May 1982 the black unemployment rate was a staggering 18.7% and about 50% of all black youths could not find jobs. This figure does not take into account discouraged people who gave up looking for employment

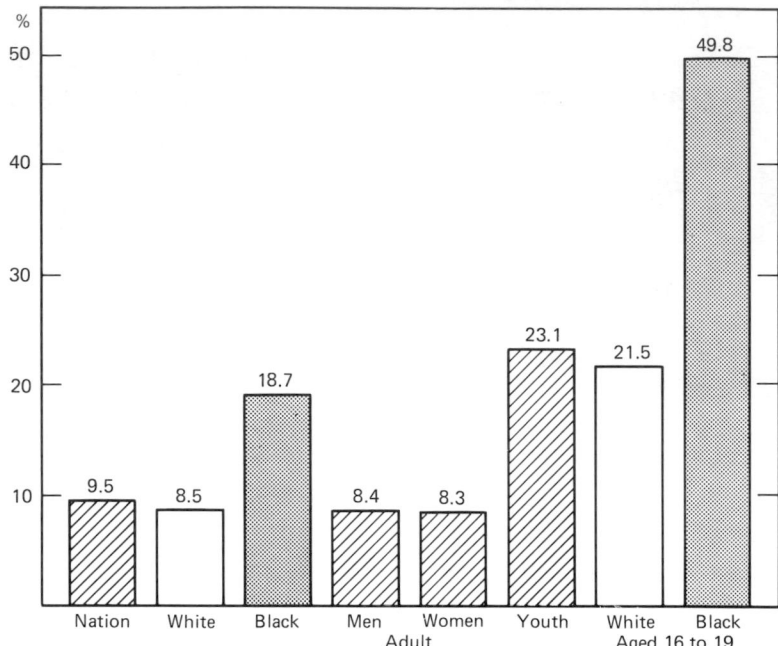

MAJOR TRENDS OF THE 1970S AND EARLY 1980S

Notable among developments of the 1970s were:

The ratio of black to white unemployment rates remained above 2 to 1 for most of the 1970s and in February 1982 was 2.25 to 1.

Teenage unemployment for blacks was above the 30% level throughout most of the decade and averaged over 40% in 1981. Unemployment of black youths rose sharply, nearly doubling for black men between the ages of 20 and 24.

The labor force participation rate of white women increased substantially, from 42% to 52%, while the rate of black women increased only slightly from 50% to 53% and did not change after 1978.

The racial gap in school years completed narrowed. In 1979, median years completed by members of the labor force was 12.7 for whites and 12.3 for blacks.

Reversing a trend, unemployment of black Vietnam veterans declined to a point in 1981 where it was lower than the rate for black nonveterans. Unemployment of white Vietnam era veterans remained higher than for white nonveterans.

The proportion of blacks employed in professional, technical, managerial, and administrative jobs increased at a faster rate than it increased for whites, but blacks remained underrepresented in these positions.

Employment of blacks in upper-level jobs by firms with more than 100 employees increased. Between 1966 and 1978, the proportion of blacks in professional positions more than tripled and the proportion of black managers almost doubled.

Unemployment as an Issue

Long before unemployment rates became part of America's economic literature, blacks comprised a disproportionate share of people who could not find work. Throughout their history in the colonies and the United States, blacks were consistently displaced from trades in which they specialized by white immigrants and relegated by employers, unions, and laws to unskilled and strikebreaking "scab" jobs.

This unemployment and underemployment of blacks thwarted the rise of a skilled black artisan and entrepreneurial class after the Civil War and hindered the spirits, status, and self-sufficiency of blacks during the previous 20 years.

With black unemployment at record levels, the number one priority is jobs.

the integration of blacks and the acceptance of black leaders in important positions in American life.

The relationship of unemployment to discrimination, and also to family instability, was of great concern to W. E. B. DuBois, who spurred and sponsored studies of the problem in the late nineteenth and early twentieth centuries. However, unemployment was only one of many matters which preoccupied the eminent scholar and the NAACP, which he helped found in 1910. The NAACP was more concerned with furthering the legal and political position of blacks than boosting their economic status. Leadership in efforts to help blacks contend with unemployment fell largely to the Urban League, which sought to find work for blacks who had moved to cities.

Progress was slow and retarded by the depression of the thirties, during which unemployment rates commonly exceeded one third of the black and one fourth of the white working force.

Employment and World War II

With the outbreak of World War II, the economic scene changed drastically from competition for employment among workers to a need for full utilization of the nation's workforce in rapidly expanding industries. However, resistance to employing blacks remained entrenched, especially in skilled trades. In 1941, with the nation gearing for war, Asa Philip Randolph, founder of the Brotherhood of Sleeping Car Porters, developed plans for a march on Washington by some 100,000 blacks. The objective was to increase employment opportunities in defense plants, which

were largely confining blacks to menial service jobs, such as janitors. The NAACP declared its support of Randolph's march. An intense behind-the-scenes struggle ensued in Washington—between those who urged action for blacks on the basis of manpower needs and fairness and those who advocated minimal action so as not to divide the country in a time of crisis.

Historians still debate whether Randolph could have made the march come off, but Roosevelt respected the articulate labor leader enough to fear it. On June 25, 1941, a week before the march's scheduled date, FDR signed Executive Order 8802, which forbade discrimination in government and defense job hiring and established a Fair Employment Practices Commission to enforce the order. This was the first of antidiscrimination orders that were to be issued periodically into the 1960s and the first significant step by the government to reduce discrimination in the hiring of minorities.

Roosevelt's order of course did not eliminate discrimination but did reduce it, and it set a precedent for ensuing governmental action against employment barriers.

Discrimination after World War II

Improving the job situation for blacks aroused increasing attention during the 1950s and 1960s and by 1970 was the principal aim of public officials and businessmen interested in reducing racial tensions.

The growing concern about black unemployment and underemployment reflected a significant change in America's approach to racial problems. In the early

1960s, efforts to ease the burdens of blacks were based on the ideal of integration and directed toward a variety of issues—housing, education, welfare, and constitutional justice as much as employment. Response to the integration ideal peaked with the passage of the Civil Rights Act in 1964 and thereafter subsided before the shock waves from ghetto riots and the sudden intensity of black nationalism. Following the violent urban disturbances in the summer of 1967, the nation's "establishment" decided that it was urgent to get blacks "off the streets and into jobs." Integration was downgraded as an unworkable liberal theory that benefited only a minute proportion of blacks. Racial peace and racial justice, it was decided, depended on obtaining jobs for the "hard core," the black who was abandoned, despised, and unemployed in squalid neighborhoods in large cities. Actually, as the National

Advisory Commission on Racial Disorders was to reveal, employed blacks were as prone to riot as the unemployed. Nevertheless, the emphasis turned to jobs.

As a result, scores of federally assisted manpower programs and thousands of diverse, publicly supported training and placement ventures on the state and local levels were set up. Urban-based service industries such as banks and public utilities intensified efforts to recruit and train black and Spanish-speaking employees.

The government programs provided businesses with incentives to employ people whose abilities and job motivation were unproven. The incentives took the form of subsidies to businesses for on-the-job training and referrals of prospective employees who were located and trained at public expense.

These programs reflected a change of approach to

Chart 2.   Unemployment Rates (annual averages): 1948–1982 (above) and Ratio of Black to White Unemployment: 1948–1982 (below)

The unemployment ratios between blacks and whites have been at least 2 to 1 since 1948. This ratio increases substantially during periods of recession and is currently at its highest level since 1948

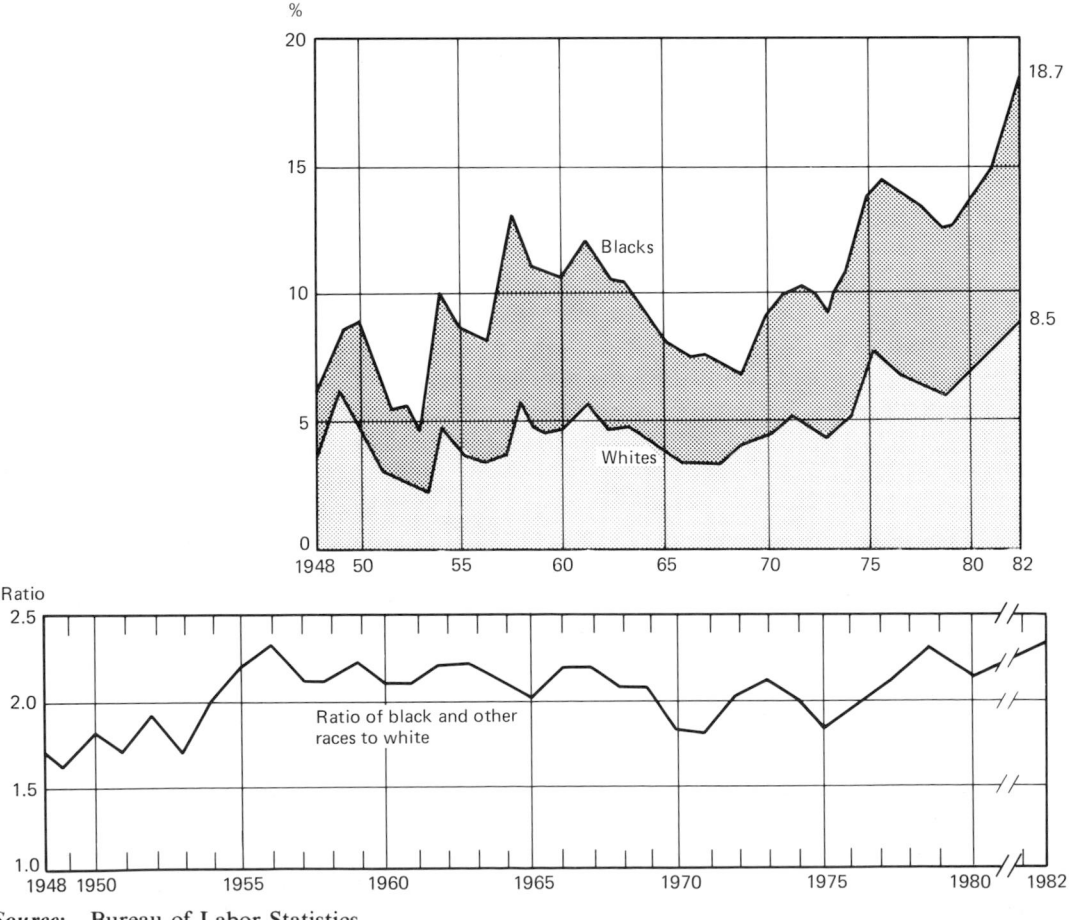

Source: Bureau of Labor Statistics.

employers—a change from pressure to blandishment by public officials charged with the responsibility of bettering the black employment situation. Earlier efforts to rectify the employment status of blacks relied largely on legal and monetary pressure. Employers who discriminated against blacks were threatened with court action or denial of government contracts. In the late 1960s, the emphasis shifted to aiding employers who agreed to hire "underqualified" minorities.

Title VII and the EEOC

There was little significant fair employment legislation on the federal level until the Civil Rights Act of 1964. Title VII of this Act prohibited discrimination on the part of employers and unions who have more than 25 employees or members and who are involved in interstate commerce. Title VII also established the Equal Employment Opportunities Commission to mediate disputes and identify patterns of deliberate and systematic discrimination. As set up, EEOC could refer discrimination cases to the Attorney General, who, in turn, could bring them before a three-judge federal court. The EEOC was also empowered to refer cases of discrimination to the Office of Federal Contract Compliance, which could press businesses dealing with the government to adhere to fair employment practices.

Title VII of the Civil Rights Act of 1964 not only outlawed discrimination in employment but contained an extremely important provision that was scarcely noticed at the time. The law granted courts the power to award fees to attorneys for plaintiffs who successfully sued employers and unions that discriminated. This encouraged lawyers to undertake the arduous and highly detailed leg and legal work essential to proving discrimination.

Until 1972, this provision attracted little attention from the legal profession. EEOC lacked the power to sue. President Nixon was pursuing a "southern strategy" and wooing the "silent majority" with thinly veiled hints that civil rights laws and court decisions would not be enforced. There was little expectation that the Justice and Labor Department divisions empowered to act against unfair employers would do so.

However, the EEOC was strengthened during the 1967–1972 years of Nixon's first term. EEOC's annual budget was raised from $12 million to $42 million and its staff from 250 to 2,500. Critics of Nixon contend that his increasing EEOC's staff and budget were meaningless in the face of its power to do little more than argue and attempt out-of-court conciliation agreements, enforced by voluntary compliance. However, in 1972, with EEOC weak and saddled by a backlog of 60,000 cases, Congress granted EEOC the power to take cases to court, though it refused the agency power to issue cease and desist orders. Nixon signed the bill.

The 1972 Law also granted EEOC power to bring "Pattern and Practice" suits, starting in March 1974. Pattern and Practice suits usually consist of large class actions against large employers and unions whose hiring, promotion, and seniority policies have been systematic in nature.

These suits could involve hundreds of millions, perhaps even billions of dollars in compensation to employees for past "patterns and practices" of discrimination.

The cause of equal rights in employment was also strengthened by the growing expertise and public support of the women's movement for equal rights. This brought more money, legal talent, and political muscle to equal employment ranks.

However, few felt the EEOC would act forcefully. Skeptics pointed out that other government agencies, such as the Interstate Commerce Commission and the Federal Power Commission, had strong regulatory powers but somehow had become allies of the very businesses they were supposed to regulate. It was assumed this would occur with the EEOC.

At the time the 1972 Law passed, EEOC's chairman was William Brown III, a black man with life-long Republican ties and a staunch advocate of the conciliatory approach. It was thus a surprise when Brown, in 1972, developed a "tracking system" which in effect committed EEOC, in cooperation with private "public interest" lawyers, to taking on major corporate violators of equal employment laws. As a part of this approach, EEOC issued some $400,000 in legal contracts among such groups as the Lawyers' Committee For Civil Rights Under Law, and subsidized equal employment legal clinics in major law schools.

Previously filed suits were pursued and new suits were filed. Most actions were undertaken by civil rights groups, such as the Legal Defense Fund, NAACP, The Lawyers' Committee for Civil Rights Under Law, and the National Organization of Women.

The response of most businesses and unions was to sue for peace. It would have been possible for these defendants to drag out cases for several years, but few wanted the publicity and many felt that favorable agreements would become harder to attain under future national administrations.

Reparations and the Telephone Case

The first major company to sign an agreement was the American Telephone & Telegraph Company, the largest employer in the United States. In a 1973 consent decree between EEOC, the Labor Department, and AT&T, the telephone company agreed to pay $15 million in reparations and to allocate $23 million each year to raise the pay of blacks, other minorities, and women to that of the company's white male employees. AT&T also agreed to institute an affirmative action program to increase and improve opportunities for minorities and women. In return, EEOC dropped all pending charges against AT&T.

The settlement was controversial. Critics felt that the company, whose annual profits are some $2.5 billion, owed and could have afforded more. They noted that no employee, under the agreement, would receive back pay of more than $400. EEOC had estimated the actual loss in wages to AT&T minorities at $500 million per year for the eight years preceding the settlement, or a total of $4 billion, not $23 million.

Supporters of the pact emphasized the symbolic and precedent-setting importance of having America's largest business admit, if only implicitly, to charges of bias and to its responsibility to compensate employees for it, however inadequately.

Supporters of the agreement also pointed out that barely two weeks before the agreement was signed, a weaker deal, involving no back pay or substantial affirmative action policy, was very nearly executed between AT&T and the General Services Administration, under President Johnson's Executive Order 11246. This arrangement, which had the support of the Nixon Administration, would have derailed the stronger EEOC settlement, granted no reparations at all, and introduced only a modest affirmative action program. But Chairman Brown personally intervened and, under threat of massive publicity about a sellout of blacks and women, the administration capitulated to the extent of the accord that was reached.

Other Suits

Following the AT&T agreement, precedent-setting decisions were won in suits against the Detroit Edison and New York Telephone companies, with the judge in the Detroit Edison case granting back pay, retroactive from 1973 to 1965 plus punitive damages and forward pay. In 1974, expectations in legal circles were that the court would award several hundred thousand dollars, perhaps a million dollars, in attorney's fees to the lawyers who sued Detroit Edison. Unlike AT&T, Detroit Edison had adopted a hard-line defense.

Within months of the AT&T agreement, EEOC filed over 80 suits, almost all against such powerful and prestigious companies as General Electric and General Motors. These suits, plus the victories against AT&T, Detroit Edison, and steel makers and unions (see the section on unions) frightened the business community, much of which considered itself vulnerable to the bad publicity and high costs of class action litigation.

Brown's presence as head of EEOC was considered a further threat, for despite his solid Republican credentials, he was doing little to restrain the enthusiasm of his staff in their quest to correct current and historic wrongs inflicted on minority workers. And his support of Nixon in the 1972 Presidential election had been tepid.

In the 1973, with the nation's attention on Watergate, the Administration quietly announced that in January 1974, Brown would be replaced by John Powell, Jr. Brown did not learn of his dismissal until he read it in the *Washington Post*.

The agreement that was reached between the government and the steel companies in 1974 was considered weaker because of Brown's pending absence and the presence in the negotiations of the Justice and Labor departments whose involvement followed their exclusion from such cases in the 1972 EEOC Act. A key point in the steel agreement was a provision precluding future suits by requiring workers to execute releases.

Equal Opportunity and the Carter Years

Affirmative action in employment progressed during the Presidential term of Jimmy Carter (1977–1981), though the government never became the activist Carter's earlier stance for equal opportunity had promised.

One serious problem was the immense backlog of cases that besieged EEOC. In April 1976, during the final year of the Ford Administration, EEOC's backlog passed 130,000. By 1978, despite increases in the staff, it reached 340,000, with cases generally requiring two to seven years to resolve. To reduce this burden, Commissioner Eleanor Holmes Norton cut back efforts to consolidate complaints into class action suits and pressed the parties involved to resolve the issues among themselves. The net result of this was that the Commission increasingly confined its best efforts to a few selected cases in the hope that favorable resolution of these would have a ripple effect for blacks among the nation's employers.

This approach had it successes. The very potential of activity by EEOC and the presence of a national administration at least partially committed to affirmative action had a positive effect on employers. Black employment in firms reporting to EEOC during the seventies rose at a significantly greater rate than did the total growth of jobs in these firms, especially in craft and service jobs. The proportion of blacks hired also rose faster in professional and technical fields.

Also encouraging were Supreme Court decisions rejecting "reverse discrimination" challenges brought by whites. Two of the most important suits sought to have the Court reverse voluntary agreements between

Chart 3. Unemployment Rates by Sex, Age, and Race (annual averages): 1981

In every age group or sex group the unemployment rate for blacks is at least twice that of whites. The most disproportionate rates are found among teenage females and those in their early twenties, here the unemployment rate is close to three times that of similar white groups

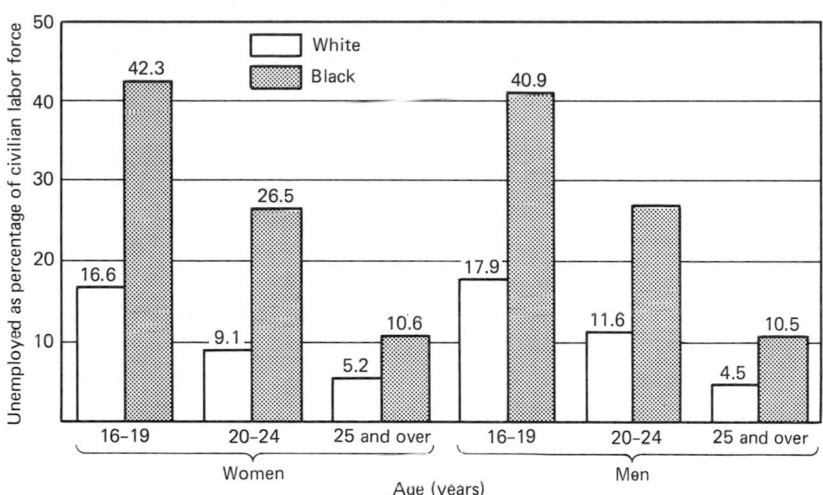

employers and groups championing the cause of minorities.

In July 1978, the Court rejected a challenge brought by the Communications Workers of America to the EEOC-AT&T agreement. And in June 1979, the Court upheld a voluntary affirmative action plan in the Weber Decision, when by a vote of 5 to 2 it declared that an employer can legally give preference to blacks to eliminate racial imbalance in skilled crafts traditionally filled almost exclusively by whites. The Kreps Case (see legal section) was another victory for supporters of affirmative action.

Other Court decisions, however, weakened EEOC by limiting some of its enforcement authority and the award of attorneys' fees and back pay.

Reagan and Affirmative Action

Opposition to affirmative action intensified during the 1970s. Some opponents, many of them erstwhile liberals who had supported the civil rights movement, maintained that affirmative action was bad for the morale and the morality of its recipients. A few blacks such as Thomas Sowell endorsed this stance. Others asserted that government activity to effect equality was a wrongful imposition on individuals and only served to exacerbate discrimination and tension between the races.

Proponents of these views formed behind Ronald Reagan in the Presidential campaign of 1980, and by the fall of 1981, the Reagan Administration had issued a series of sweeping proposals that threatened to erase most of the gains of the last two decades.

In its first year, the Administration announced that it would:

End use of quotas and numerical goals in hiring and promotion.

End timetables and other detailed plans for hiring and promotion of minorities by companies that had yet to comply fully with previous affirmative action commitments.

Eliminate government class action lawsuits and require that cases be brought by individuals.

Seek a reversal of the Weber Decision, which the government contended discriminated unfairly against whites, and thus discourage or terminate voluntary agreements among employers, unions, and minorities.

Recommend a standard of "intent" rather than "effect" in determining the merits of discrimination cases. Intent is, of course, more difficult to prove.

Despite their weakened position within the government, civil rights proponents marshalled a response. In a report titled *Civil Rights in the 1980s: Dismantling the Process of Discrimination,* the Civil Rights Commission endorsed quotas that "select qualified minorities and women according to designated ratios or percentages for limited periods of time."

However, there was little hope that the Civil Rights Commission, never a strong factor in government, could do much to stem the tide, especially since the President had announced prior to issuance of the Report that he was dismissing CRC Chairman Arthur Fleming. And with two vacancies pending at EEOC, it was clear the Administration would soon control that agency.

Of great concern to blacks was the apparent disparity between the President's avowed position and steps initiated by appointees charged with executing his policies. A prime example of this conflict was the President's avowed support for voluntary agreements, as typified in the Kaiser Agreement upheld by the Supreme Court in the Weber Case. Shortly before the government announced its intention to seek a reversal of Weber, the President had declared his personal support for that decision, a position he was soon to retract.

At the start of 1982, blacks hoped the activities of the government reflected only a short-lived swing of the pendulum and not a revival of policies of fear and bigotry that blacks and the civil rights movement had done so much to defeat during the sixties and seventies.

Discrimination in Public Employment

In 1972, amendments to Title VII empowered the EEOC to investigate and try to conciliate complaints of discrimination against state and local governments. Additionally, the Justice Department was empowered to sue on behalf of individuals or groups of public service employees or to remedy "pattern and practice" discrimination in specific locations.

In response to suits brought under these amendments, courts have ruled that public service employment tests which have a racially discriminatory impact are unlawful unless they can be shown to have a demonstrable relationship to job performance. In addition, suits against police and fire departments have brought forth specific numerical goals for hiring minority personnel. Among successful cases were suits against the Boston and Akron fire departments, the San Francisco and Bridgeport, Connecticut police departments, the entire city of Montgomery, Alabama, and the Alabama State Highway Patrol.

This pattern of success continued throughout the 1970s and into 1980 with victories involving police and fire departments in Chicago, Cincinnati, New York, and Los Angeles. In the New York case, the Supreme Court refused to overturn a lower court decision requiring that one-third of police to be hired be black or Hispanic. Los Angeles was required to pay $2 million in back wages to victims of discrimination by its police department and to hire blacks, women, and Hispanics in proportion to their participation in the city's labor force.

Black Immigrants

The elimination of ethnocentric quotas in 1965 encouraged immigration from the West Indies. Not counting Cubans, the number of West Indians entering the United States as permanent residents rose from 44,500 in the 1950s to 263,000 in the 1960s and 304,000 between 1971 and 1977. These numbers were swelled by what is estimated to be a still larger group of illegal aliens from the Caribbean, their number exceeding 500,000.

Black immigrants settled mostly in the northeast, particularly New York City, where in 1977 they comprised about 20% of the city's black population.

In the mid-seventies, nearly 10% of legal black immigrants in New York City held professional and technical jobs compared with 8% for indigenous blacks. By 19 to 15%, a greater proportion of immigrants were employed craftsmen. By 58 to 33%, indigenous blacks were more likely to hold jobs below the level of craftsmen.

There was, however, considerable downward mobility among black immigrants, especially for those who occupied managerial jobs in their countries of origin. White immigrants experienced similar difficulties but were more likely than blacks to regain lost occupational status.

Undocumented Aliens

Only a small portion of the immigrants during the 1970s were black. A much larger group, numbering from 3 million to 5 million, and the vast majority of them in the country illegally, entered the United States from all parts of the world. The largest numbers came from Latin America, mostly from Mexico, and from China, Korea, Eastern and Southeastern Europe.

By the mid-seventies, millions of the "undocumented aliens" were employed in low-paying, sweatshop-type jobs, most frequently in restaurants and garment manufacturing shops and on farms.

In the Los Angeles area, 65% of the restaurants inspected by the state between 1978 and 1980 were breaking wage laws. A Labor Department survey of Chicago restaurants found 91% underpaying workers. In garment shops wages of $1 an hour and less were commonplace.

As Congressman Harold Washington of Illinois noted: "The mere presence of a large number of aliens depresses wages generally and forces unskilled blacks to take dirtier, lower-paying jobs."

Undocumented black immigrants were found work-

Chart 4. Teenage Unemployment Rates by Race and Hispanic Origin (ages 16–19)

The employment to population ratios between black and white youths have become increasingly disproportionate over the past 20 years and have reached historic levels not seen since the 1930s

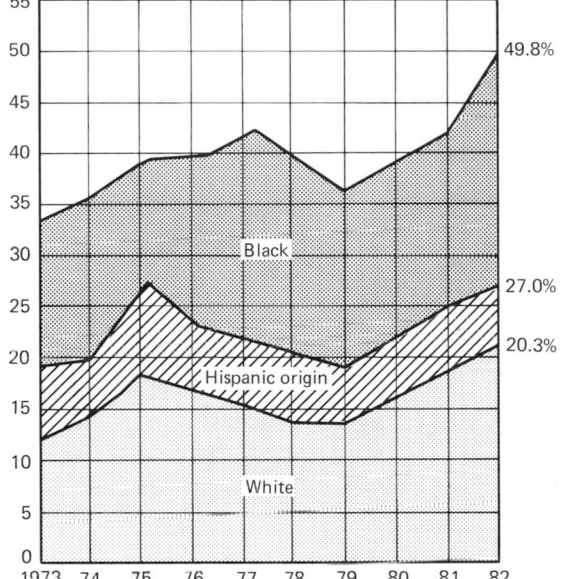

ing in demeaning conditions as migrant farm labor. In 1980 it was revealed that black migrant farm workers, both American and West Indian, were victims of peonage and enslavement on farms in East Coast states between Connecticut and Florida. The Department of Justice appointed an Involuntary Servitude Coordinator and by the end of 1981 had won ten convictions for involuntary servitude and peonage in six cases it prosecuted. The Department conceded that these cases only scratched the surface.

In 1981, President Reagan proposed granting legal status to all aliens who had entered the country prior to 1980, and instituting heavy fines for employers who knowingly hire illegal aliens. The hope was that legal status would reassure exploited aliens to assert their rights. Meanwhile, their prevalence was having a profound adverse effect on the nation's blacks.

Vietnam Veterans

During the 1970s, black Vietnam veterans improved their position within the work force. In 1981, black veterans of the Vietnam era between the ages of 25 and 39 had a lower unemployment rate than nonveterans, 10.5% compared with 12%. Their rate, however, was considerably higher than the rate for white veterans (5.8%) and white nonveterans (5.6%).

An alarming by-product of these figures was a sharp rise in unemployment rates between 1979 and 1981

for veterans of both races, 46% for blacks, 66% for whites. Increases for nonveterans were higher for both races.

Youth—An Endangered Species

The employment situation of young blacks between the ages of 16 and 24 deteriorated in the 1970s. For teenagers between 16 and 19 this continued a long-term trend that first appeared in the recession of 1958. For older youths, however, the decline was startling. Unemployment of non-white men between 20 and 24 rose from 12.6% in 1973 to 24.3% in 1981. The 1981 rate for black males was 26.5%.

The difficulties young blacks encountered were underscored by a tendency for their unemployment rates to remain high after the rest of the labor force has recovered from a recession. The jobless rate for blacks between 16 and 24, for example, was higher in 1978 than in the prerecession year of 1974. The white rate had dropped.

Another notable trend of the 16–24 groups was the declining labor force participation rate of young black men after the mid-seventies and of young black women after 1978.

Several explanations have been advanced for the stubborn severity of youth unemployment. An obvious problem is the rapid population growth of blacks between 16 and 24.

Of greater significance, however, are changes in the structure of the economy that markedly reduce the need for unskilled and semiskilled workers and intensify the demand for people with advanced technological skills. Such skills require degrees of schooling and training that have been available to few blacks.

These and other so-called structural trends have been international in scope. Unemployment rates of

Chart 5. Duration of Teenage Unemployment: 1979

During 1979 slightly over 50% of the black teen-age population managed to work the entire year

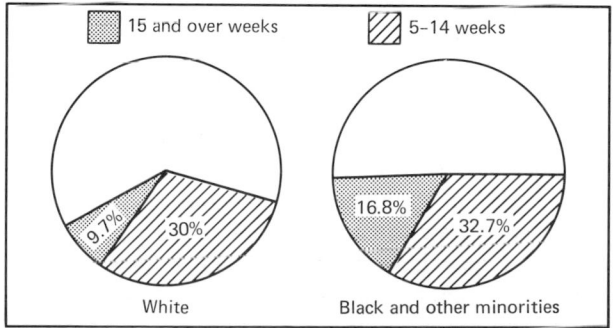

Source: Bureau of Labor Statistics.

Chart 6. The Job Gap for Poor Youth: 1978

Job opportunity for white youth in poverty areas is twice that of their black counterparts

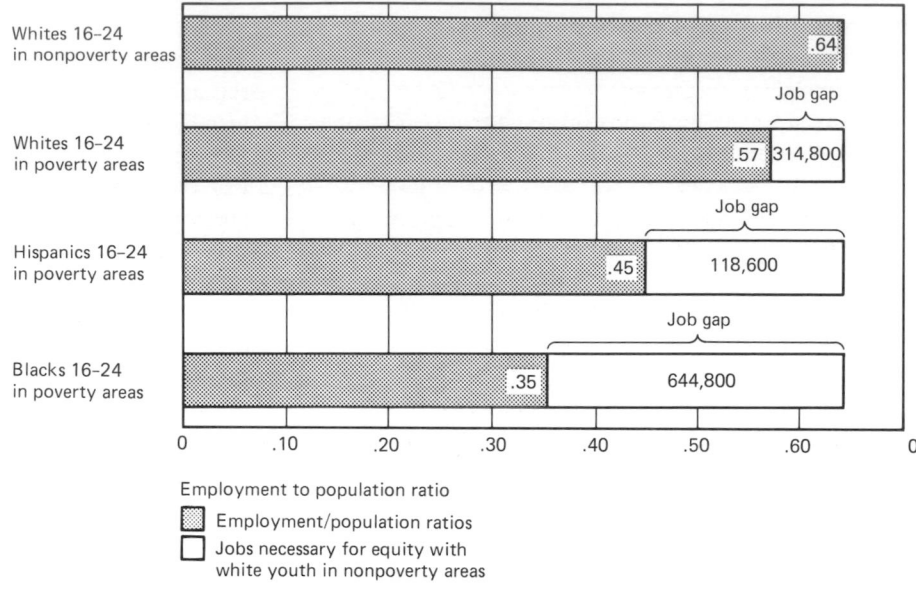

Employment to population ratio

▨ Employment/population ratios
☐ Jobs necessary for equity with white youth in nonpoverty areas

Source: Bureau of Labor Statistics and census data.

teenagers and youths have risen sharply in most industrialized nations.

In the United States, such structural changes combined with rising youth unemployment have sparked concern that a major long-term problem has been brewing and that disadvantaged youths, unable to obtain the necessary training and work experience, will come to form a chronically unemployed underclass far more widespread and resistant to economic upturns than the underclass that grew during the sixties and seventies.

Blacks can be expected to suffer disproportionately under such conditions, and in fact, as the youth unemployment figures testify, already are. (In such countries as Sweden and the United Kingdom, minorities also have suffered disproportionately, though not to the same degree as blacks in the United States; see FACTS.)

In the United States, rising minimum wages were also blamed for higher teenage and youth joblessness. The Urban League challenged this view, noting that the average wage paid teenagers was below the legal minimum anyway, an indication that the minimum is substantially ignored where young people are concerned and not an important hindrance to hiring them.

Another view attributed increases in youth unemployment to a higher rate of black school dropouts between 16 and 24. However, in 1977, 54% of this age group had graduated from high school and another 17% had gone on to college. Also, significantly, in

1977 white high school dropouts between 16 and 24 had a lower unemployment rate than 16 to 24-year-old blacks with some college education (16.7 versus 21.4%).

Jobs Programs

During the depression of the 1930s, and again in the 1960s, the Federal government led efforts to reduce unemployment through an assortment of training and employment activities, identified until the 1970s as "manpower programs."

The Manpower Development and Training Act of 1962 was the first of many legislative measures intended to serve as a base for federal support and activity in job training and placement. Originally designed to retrain workers displaced by technological advances, the MDTA's focus was changed to serve inner-city youth during the 1960s. Among programs operating under MDTA's banner were the Job Corps, Apprenticeship Outreach Program, and the Neighborhood Youth Corps. Blacks comprised a substantial portion of participants in these programs, for example, between 40 and 50% in New York City during the late 1960s. Some blacks, however, were concerned that minorities were more frequently assigned to classrooms than to actual work-experience instruction.

Advocates of federal activity programs cited substantial reduction in unemployment rates of young blacks and proclaimed MDTA's programs a success.

But some conservatives branded them inefficient, indulgent, and corrupt and aided by racial backlash and the nation's disillusion with the Vietnam War were able in 1968 to elect Richard Nixon.

Nixon and "New Federalism"

After 1969, the proportion of blacks enrolled in Department of Labor programs dropped from more than 50% to 40% in 1973. Also in 1973, blacks comprised only 26% of enrollees in the JOBS Program.

These trends stemmed from Nixon's emphasis on a "new federalism" under which programs were shifted from federal to local control, with the federal government financing activities through block grants. The vehicle for this was the Comprehensive Employment and Training Act (CETA) of 1973. By 1975, with Gerald Ford President, the Department of Labor handled only $460 million of CETA's $2.05 billion budget.

Under CETA, the political claims of individual communities frequently replaced the needs of the disadvantaged, thus reducing services for locations with the greatest need. In addition, local communities occasionally overlooked the needy in their allocations. Also, continuing a pattern noticeable during the sixties, blacks tended to be assigned to classroom rather than on-the-job programs.

Carter and CETA

In 1976, Jimmy Carter campaigned on a pledge to increase help for minorities and in 1977 restored much of CETA's emphasis to the disadvantaged and increased its overall budget. In 1978, CETA's peak year, outlays were $5.8 billion, with over 3.5 million people served, a substantial number of them black. Blacks, however, were not always well represented in apprentice activities focusing on development of higher skills. During the first six months of 1979, only 17% of apprentices in training programs were minorities.

During Carter's years, the public came to regard inflation as a more serious problem than unemployment and to accept higher levels of unemployment as normal. Provisions of the Humphrey-Hawkins full employment bill were diluted. The mid-seventies objective of a 3% unemployment maximum was quietly abandoned as a 6% rate came to be regarded as reasonable and proper.

The Reagan Approach

CETA was a major issue in the 1980 Presidential campaign, with champions of governmental jobs activity clearly on the defensive. The public, fatigued and frightened by high living costs and exaggerated anecdotes of coddled welfare cheats, increasingly blamed government activity as the source of economic instability.

Elected on promises to cut taxes, eliminate waste in government, and balance the budget, President Ronald Reagan and his advisors soon unleashed an awesome attack on CETA that caught its defenders in despair and disarray. By 1982, CETA's funds had been cut to $2 billion.

In some areas, cuts were especially devastating. In East St. Louis, Illinois, an impoverished area, with some two-thirds of its black labor force unemployed, CETA funds for 1982 were cut from $2.3 million to $65,000.

Reagan's proposed alternative to these cuts was to induce a spirit of volunteerism among businesses and individuals, in which training and placement of the disadvantaged would reside in the hands of the private sector. Private generosity, claimed the President, would in the long run achieve more for minorities than the government programs of the past twenty years.

Actually, the private sector had often been involved in employment programs, notably in the JOBS (Job Opportunities in the Business Sector) program launched in 1967, and the Opportunities Industrialization Centers of America, founded in 1964 by the Reverend Leon Sullivan. By 1970, 80,000 disadvantaged persons had been hired under JOBS, and OIC soon became a national institution operating in some 100 cities. However, government was deeply involved in these programs. JOBS was a joint venture between the Department of Labor and the National Alliance of Businessmen, and OIC received some 85% of its budget from national, state, and local governments.

In 1978, President Carter signed into law the Private Sector Initiative Program, which claimed to have served some 60,000 individuals in fiscal 1980, 25,000 of them minorities. PSIP was intended to coordinate CETA with the private sector through councils of representatives from business, industry, labor, community organization, and educational institutions.

THE REAGAN CUTS

For fiscal year 1982, the Reagan Administration eliminated:

80% of the funding for the Youth Employment Demonstration Projects Act

20% from the Summer Youth Program

All funding for the Youth Conservation Corps (CETA Title VIII)

All funding for the Public Service Employment Program, which in 1981 helped over 500,000 people

64% of the funding for Title III of CETA, which helped displaced homemakers, the elderly, migrants, and welfare recipients

27% of the funding for Title XX of the Social Security Act, which subsidized daycare centers for low- and moderate-income working parents.

The continuing legislation under which most of these cuts were passed permitted further cuts of 6% and more.

As of March 1982, the Administration proposed for fiscal 1983 to eliminate:

The Summer Youth Employment Program, the only source of jobs for poor youths during the summer (fiscal 1982 funding was $674 million)

Many of the tax exemptions on unemployment insurance

The Work Incentive Program (WIN), which provided jobs for welfare recipients

The total employment and training budget proposed for 1983 was to be $2.4 billion (compared with $8.9 billion for CETA in 1980) of which $1.8 billion was to be earmarked for a private sector program to replace CETA.

By the spring of 1982 the outlines of two plans to reduce unemployment appeared. One would grant tax credits to companies establishing or expanding businesses in impoverished areas which would be labeled "enterprise zones." This approach received a sympathetic hearing from blacks, but by the spring of 1982, little was expected of it. Representative Charles Rangel of New York was dubious of its prospects on the grounds that corporate taxes under the Reagan Administration would be so low or nonexistent that further tax credits would be redundant. Others pointed out that businesses did little to avail themselves of earlier tax credit programs, notably the WIN Program of 1972 and New Jobs Tax Credit Program of 1977.

The second Reagan weapon requested businesses voluntarily to devote a portion of their profits to training and placement of disadvantaged people. In early 1982, a Presidential Task Force on Private Sector Initiative was seeking ways to persuade businesses to cooperate but skeptics pointed out that even massive cooperation would cover only a small portion of the loss sustained by the CETA cuts. Total corporate philanthropic contributions in 1979 were $2.3 billion, mostly to higher education. More than this was cut from CETA alone in 1981, more than $10 billion from other programs serving the disadvantaged.

Private industry already had been unable to fill the gap in jobs erased by budget cuts. Only 180,000 of the 535,000 people in eliminated CETA PSE Projects found employment within a month of their release. Most of these jobs were in state and local government. A year later, one-third of the 535,000 remained out of work.

In March 1982, the Administration proposed a program under which $1.8 billion in block grant money would be granted, via states, to private industry councils to set up job training programs. Local business leaders, through the councils, would have decision-making authority. Training would focus on young members of welfare families between the ages of 16 and 25. Businesses would be compensated for their training costs. Ten percent of the funds could be used to train displaced workers in new skills.

The plan also called for $387 million to continue

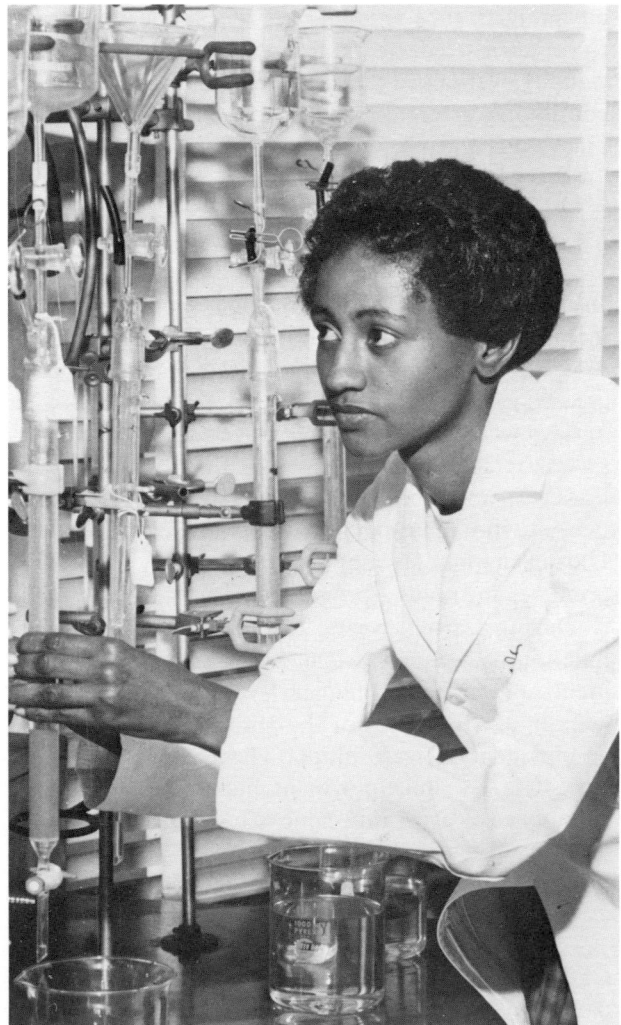

Black women have been making strides in gaining employment in technical fields.

the Jobs Corps at a reduced level. And $200 million would be provided to train special target groups, such as Indians and migratory workers.

Secretary of Labor Raymond Donovan conceded the venture would do little to affect the nation's unemployment rate, but emphasized that despite the $53 billion CETA had spent during its existence, unemployment of minority youths had risen from 28 to 40%. Critics of the proposal charged it was inadequate and that no stipends had been suggested to cover living costs of the welfare youths during training periods. In 1980, CETA programs reached some 3 million people, 40% of whom received stipends.

Working Women

The seventies was a decade of progress and problems for working black women. On one hand, black women moved in large numbers from menial service employment into white-collar professional and clerical work. The declining proportion of black domestic servants was especially dramatic, from 1 in 12 of the female black working population in 1970 to 1 in 38 in 1979.

On the other hand, black women continued in large numbers to be segregated into low-paying dead-end jobs.

The number of working black women increased steadily from about 3.7 million in 1970 to 5.3 million in 1981. The percentage of black women in the labor force, however, remained unchanged from 1978 to 1981. One reason was a large rise in the working age population of black women; another was increasing competition from white women. From 1965 to 1980, labor force participation of white women over age 16 increased by nearly 1 million per year, to approximately 39 million, and their participation rate grew from 38 to 52%. During the same period the participation rate of black women grew from 49 to 53%.

Participation of black women was markedly higher in two-parent familes (64 versus 53% for whites); white participation was higher in one-parent families headed by a woman (66 versus 56%). (Participation by Hispanic women was considerably lower than that of white or black women.) In 1977, unemployment of single black women heading families was 22%, three times the white rate of 7%.

During the 1970s, single mothers were underrepresented in training and placement programs. Single women of both races comprised 56% of the population eligible for CETA in 1977, but only 44% of its enrollees. Their highest CETA participation rate was 46% in 1978 and they were excluded in large numbers from on-the-job training.

An obstacle to progress by disadvantaged women was the paucity of childcare facilities, plus frequent failure of local program administrators to provide information on available daycare centers to program applicants. The number of centers was limited by the block grant approach, which usually meant that the cost of childcare facilities had to be subtracted from training and placement allocations. Statistics in the early seventies indicated that 16% of welfare mothers interested in obtaining jobs were rejected by the WIN Program or not referred to it because childcare facilities weren't available for them. Further, guarantees of childcare for WIN graduates were limited to 30 to 90 days after a parent ended training or obtained employment. As a result, many welfare mothers who successfully completed the program had to leave their jobs to care for their children.

The Administration's budget of 1982 cut childcare funds below previous levels. In January 1982, it was estimated that 150,000 familes would lose federally funded childcare services previously provided under Title XX of the Social Security Act. In 1980, 750,000 persons received subsidized childcare services under this provision.

Occupations

Blacks attained considerable job upgrading in the 1970s. The proportion of black men employed in craft jobs increased from 15 to 18%, while it remained at 21% for white men. The proportion of black women employed in white-collar work rose from 23 to 29%, while remaining stable at 36% for white women. Also, though they remain severely underrepresented, the proportion of black men and women engaged in professional, technical, managerial, and administrative jobs increased so that one black worker in seven now occupies such a position. In 1981, approximately 9% of the nation's teachers, stenographers, and construction craft workers were black. And in 1978, in companies with 100 or more employees, the proportions of blacks employed in white-collar jobs had more than doubled the 1966 rate, though progress had diminished since 1973.

Such gains, however, left blacks far short of an equity position and access to upper-level executive and professional standing. A symptom of the limited access of blacks to such areas appears in the large proportion of black college graduates employed in government—in 1980, 74% for black women college graduates and 58% for men.

Trade-Sensitive Employment

In 1975, non-whites comprised 11.5% of the work force in industries most adversely affected by interna-

Chart 7. Comparison of Extent of Unemployment for Selected Occupational Categories

Occupations having higher ratios of black workers were the hardest hit in the recession of 1981–1982, except for government workers

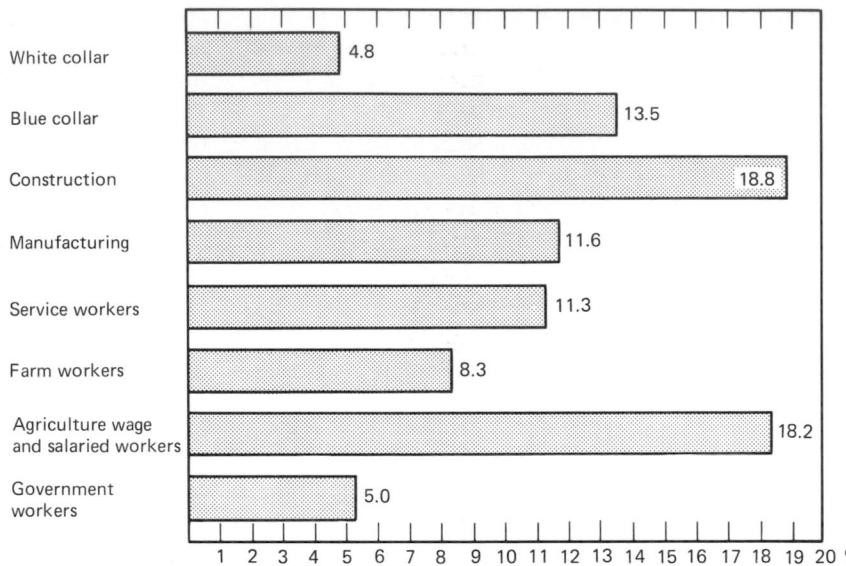

Occupation	%
White collar	4.8
Blue collar	13.5
Construction	18.8
Manufacturing	11.6
Service workers	11.3
Farm workers	8.3
Agriculture wage and salaried workers	18.2
Government workers	5.0

tional trade, and only 7.4% of persons in the 20 most favorably affected industries.

The problems of minorities in such industries relate closely to structural problems reviewed earlier. Industries competing favorably include computers, oil field machinery, aircraft equipment, engines and parts, electronic components, and others that employ a high proportion of scientists and engineers. Only three of the 20 trade-enhanced industries employed more than 7% minorities in 1975. These were logging, plywood, and sawmills. However, in 11 of the 20 adversely affected industries, 10% or more of the work force was nonwhite. The greatest proportion of minorities was employed in steel and motor vehicles, 14% of each in 1975. In 1981, according to the Department of Labor, blacks alone comprised 13.4% of employees in the troubled automobile industry. In March 1982, unemployment in that industry was 21%, and there was also a high rate of discouraged workers.

At the start of 1982, long-range prospects were not propitious. The recession and government retreats from affirmative action reduced incentives for industry and universities to take positive steps. Black enrollment in medical and law schools had leveled off in the late seventies after earlier increases. And, as noted, few blacks had been trained for the increasingly complex technological skills that industry was demanding. Indeed, there was a shortage of skilled whites for many of these areas.

THE FUTURE

Between 1980 and 1985, the black labor force was expected to increase at double the rate of the white labor force. Between 1985 and 1995, the black growth rate is expected to triple the white rate.

Confronted by profound changes in the nation's economic and political climate, the coming generation of black workers will require a full measure of the perseverance and courage that distinguished the efforts of their predecessors.

SELECTED FACTS

Fact 1
The number of unemployed whites declined by over 500,000 between 1975 and 1980. But the number of unemployed blacks increased by more than 200,000.

Fact 2
Between 1975 and 1981, the proportion of unemployed whites decreased by 15%, while the percentage of unemployed black men rose by 5%.

Fact 3
Unemployment of minorities is also more severe for blacks than whites in England. In 1977–1978, Asians and West Indians born in Britain suffered an 11%

rate, compared to 7% for people of white ethnic origin. Approximate unemployment figures in the United States for those years were 6% for whites, 13% for non-whites.

Fact 4

In 1980, 70% of unemployed blacks had never received unemployment insurance.

Fact 5

Blacks have a higher ratio of teenage to adult unemployment than either whites or Hispanics. The ratios in 1980: blacks 3.2, whites 2.9, Hispanics 2.6.

Fact 6

In recent years whites have tended more than blacks to hold extra jobs. In 1973, 5% of each group held two or more jobs, but by 1978 only 3% of blacks were multiple jobholders, compared with 5% of whites.

Fact 7

In March 1978, according to Labor Department figures, there were 626,000 never-married white women heading families, compared with 642,000 black women. Of these, 7.1% of the whites and 22.6% of the black women were unemployed.

Fact 8

Black women tend to hold jobs longer than white women, by 3.6 to 2.6 median years. The median tenure of white men exceeds that of black men by 4.6 to 3.7 years. Tenure rates are about the same for men under 45 regardless of race.

Chart 8. Percentage Change in Various Occupations: 1969–1981

Over the years there was a slow but steady increase in the percentage of blacks employed at occupations which were once largely inaccessible. This growth, however, has leveled off over the past 12 years

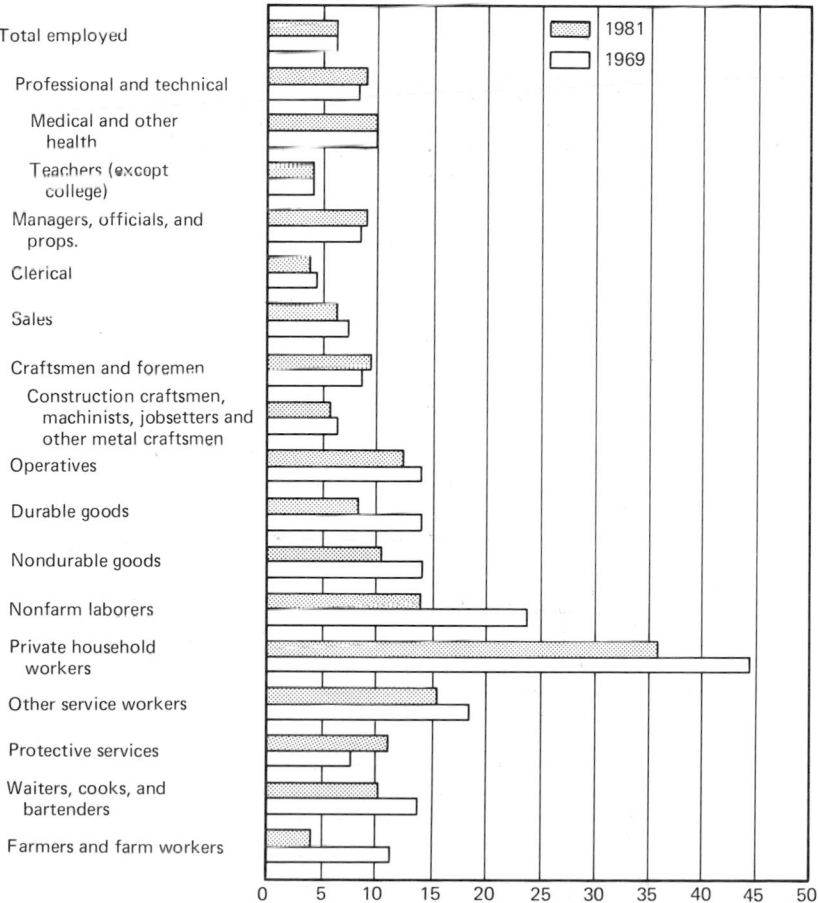

Fact 9

Members of the black labor force are more likely than white workers to return to school after age 35. In 1978, 2.1% of blacks over 35, compared with 1.8% of whites, were attending high school, college, or trade school.

Fact 10

Between 1959 and 1981, the percentage of employed blacks with white-collar jobs rose from 14 to 40%, and the number of blacks in this area rose from 0.95 to 4.5 million. Conversely, the number of blacks estimated to be working on farms dropped from 2.8 to 1.4 million.

Fact 11

In 1979, the unemployment rate of black high school graduates no longer enrolled in school was 24%, compared with only 9.6% for whites and 9.7% for Hispanics of the same status. The rates for students enrolled in college: 23% for blacks, 13% for Hispanics, 8% for whites.

Fact 12

56% of black male college graduates and 72% of female college graduates are employed in public service.

Fact 13

Between 1975 and 1980 whites accounted for 64% of the increase in working-age population and received 75% of the new jobs. Blacks comprised 15% of the population and received 10% of the new jobs.

Chart 9. Ratio of Mean Earnings of Other Workers to All White Male Workers by Occupation, Sex and Race: 1979 (white men = 100)

While black men earn more than women (black or white), they average only 66% of the earnings of white men

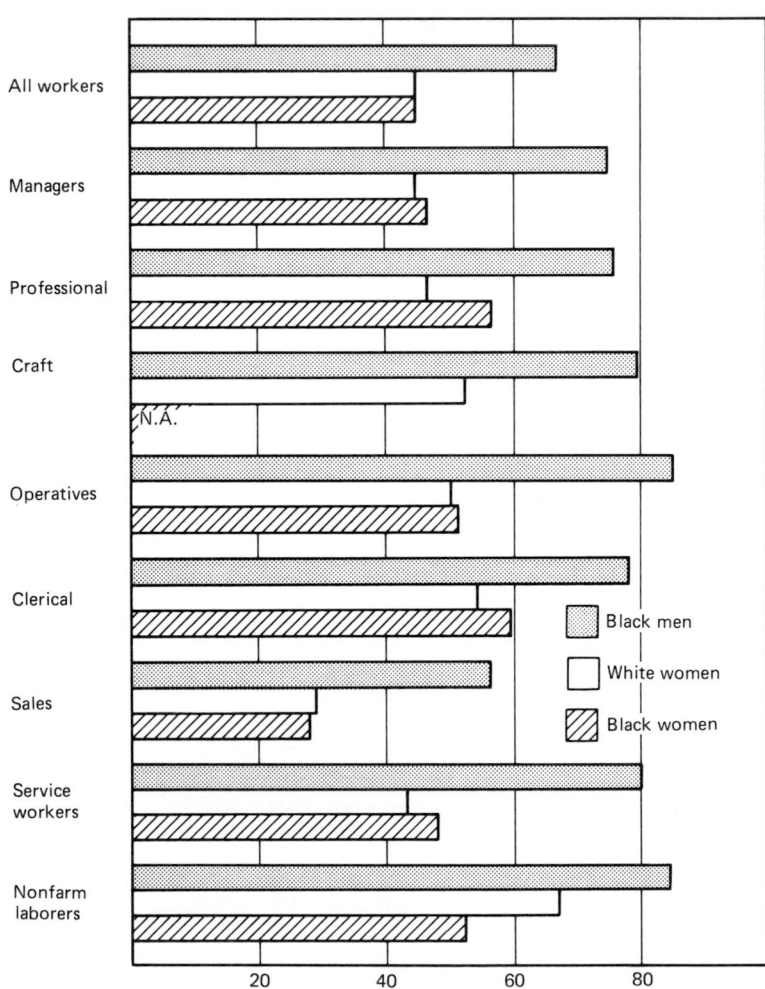

N.A. = not available.

Data: U.S. Department of Commerce, Bureau of the Census.

Fact 14

In 1978 blacks displayed slightly greater job stability than whites. Black median years on the job were 3.7 to 3.6 for whites and 2.6 for Hispanics. 74% of blacks employed had been on the job a year or more, compared with 72% for whites and 66% for Hispanics.

Fact 15

Unemployment of black youth tends to be of longer duration than for whites or Hispanics. In 1979, 50% of all unemployed black teenagers had been out of work over five weeks compared with 40% for whites and 37% for Hispanics.

Fact 16

At the end of 1981, the ratio of black to white unemployment was more than 2 to 1 in every major category. The ratio for adult black men to white men was 2.06, for adult women, 2.13, and for teenagers of both sexes, 2.35 to 1. In the summer of 1981 the unemployment ratio of blacks to whites in the 16–19 age group was nearly 3 to 1.

Fact 17

The labor force participation rate of black women is higher than that of white women, 53 to 52 in December 1981. The reverse is true with men where the rate of

Chart 10. Ratio of Median Earnings of Black Women to White Women Among all Workers: 1969–1978

Black women have achieved earnings levels above those of white women in many job categories, and the gap overall is narrowing

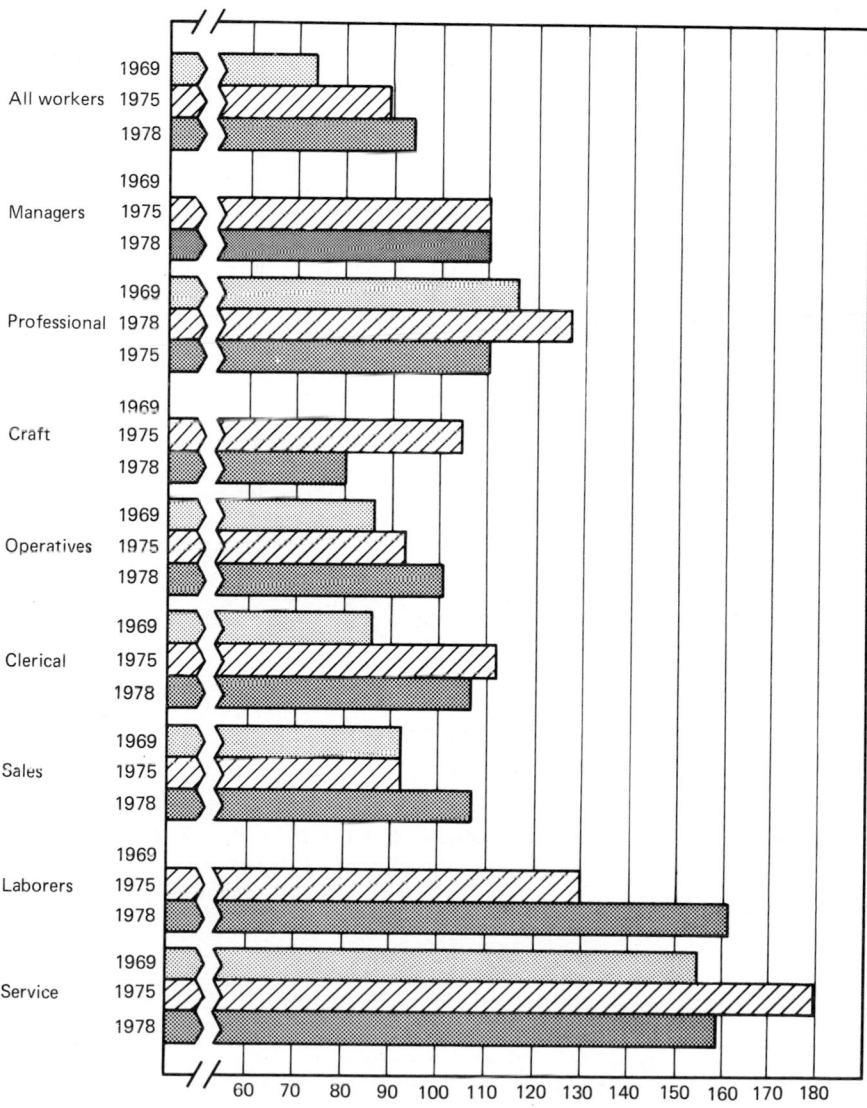

N.A. = not available.

Data: U.S. Department of Commerce, Bureau of the Census.

whites exceeds blacks, 79 to 74%, and among teenagers of both sexes where 57% of whites but only 37% of blacks belong to the labor force.

Fact 18

In the fourth quarter of 1981, 30.5% of the black unemployed had been out of work 15 or more weeks, compared with 23% of the white unemployed and 19% of jobless Hispanics.

Fact 19

In 1979, at the senior high school level, about one-third of blacks, one-fifth of Hispanics, and one-seventh of whites were unemployed.

Fact 20

The percentage of black grammar school dropouts in the labor force has declined drastically since 1959, when 53% of black civilian workers had completed less than eight years of school. In 1979, grammar-school dropouts comprised only 15% of the labor force.

Fact 21

In 1959 the median number of school years attained by whites in the labor force exceeded that of blacks by 12.2 years to 8.6. By 1979, the lead of whites was much smaller, 12.7 to 12.3. However, the proportion of college graduates remains heavily on the side of whites. In 1959, it was 10 to 4% in favor of whites; in 1979, 18 to 9%.

Fact 22

Black women who are college graduates have a substantially higher labor force participation rate than their white counterparts, 81 to 68%. The rates for both black and white men are about 89%.

Fact 23

Black unemployment generally runs higher than for any of the nation's three most populous Hispanic groups. For example, in the third quarter of 1981, the unemployment figure for blacks was 15.9, compared with 13.7 for residents of Puerto Rican origin, 9.4 for Mexicans, and 9.2 for Cubans.

Fact 24

Between the third quarter of 1980 and the third quarter of 1981, unemployment of blacks increased 1% while it declined more than 1% each for the three largest Hispanic groups.

Fact 25

Blacks comprise only about one-ninth of the labor force, but nearly one-third of discouraged workers.

Chart 11. Employment Status of Husbands of Domestic Workers and Other Employed Wives; March 1979

There are virtually no black males in white-collar jobs with wives who are employed as domestic workers

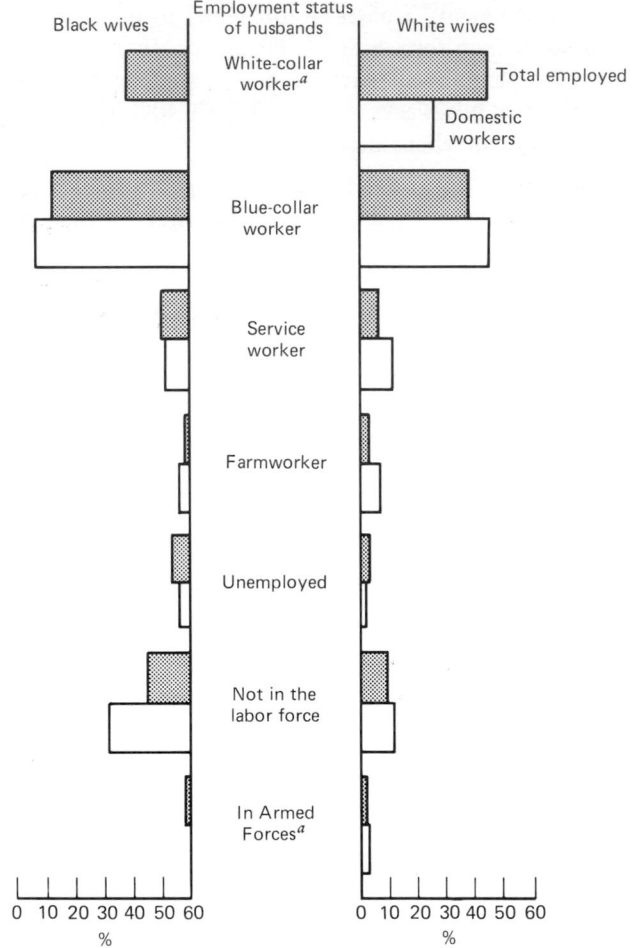

[a] No black domestic workers with husbands in this category.

Fact 26

Blacks experience periodic unemployment at a greater rate than whites. In 1979, only 59% of black men compared with 67% of white men worked the full year at full-time jobs. About one-fourth of all black workers, compared with only one-seventh of white workers, were unemployed during that year.

Fact 27

In one-parent families maintained by women, black children are less likely than white children to have mothers in the labor force by 66 to 57%.

Fact 28

In 1981, black children, by 59 to 53%, were more likely than white children to have mothers working

Blacks have made fair inroads into semi-skilled occupations.

or seeking work. The difference was especially pronounced in two-parent families, where 64% of black children compared with 52% of white children have mothers in the labor force. Hispanic children were less likely than white or black children to have working mothers.

Fact 29

In 1979, 36% of black high school graduates under age 24 were unemployed, compared with 17% Hispanics and 13% whites.

Fact 30

In every area of residence—central cities, suburbs, and nonmetropolitan—the participation rate, in the labor force, of men of Hispanic origin was higher than either white or black men. But in each area the participation rate for Hispanic women was lower than for white or black women.

Fact 31

In central cities in 1980, the labor force participation rate of black women (52.5) was higher than it was for white women (51.6). However, by 69 to 77%, the rate for black men was lower than the rate for white men.

Fact 32

A black worker is more likely to be represented by a union than a white worker. In 1980, blacks comprised 11.8% of the nation's work force but 14.7% of workers represented by unions. Hispanics were also represented in greater proportion, comprising 5.4% of the labor force and 6.1% of union membership.

Fact 33

In most industries, contract coverage for blacks exceeded that for whites. In durable goods manufacturing, for example, more than half of black workers, but less than two-fifths of white workers, were covered by union contracts.

Fact 34

Black women in the labor force are more likely than black men to be represented by unions. Nearly one fifth of the nation's female union members are black, compared with only one-eighth of male workers.

Fact 35

Black union members tend to be younger than white union members. The median age for white male union members is 38 years, compared with 37 for blacks. The median age for women is 37.5 for whites, 37 for blacks.

Fact 36

Ratios of black to white unemployment rose sharply above their 25-year averages in 1981 for all age groups under 35. The sharpest increase was for women between 20 and 24, where the average black-white ratio since 1954 was 2.3 to 1. In 1981, it was 2.9 to 1.

Fact 37

In 1981, the average of duration of unemployment for whites was 13 weeks, for blacks 16 weeks. Median duration was 8.1 weeks for blacks, 6.7 for whites. Black men had the greatest average length of joblessness, 18.3 weeks on average, compared with 14.7 for white males.

Table 1. Employment Status of the Population by Race, Sex, Age, and Hispanic Origin: May 1982 (numbers in thousands)

Employment Status	Not Seasonally Adjusted			Seasonally Adjusted					
	May 1981	April 1982	May 1982	May 1981	January 1982	February 1982	March 1982	April 1982	May 1982
White									
Civilian noninstitutional population[a]	147,670	149,249	149,250	147,670	148,842	148,855	149,132	149,249	149,250
Civilian labor force	95,117	95,252	96,014	95,666	95,120	95,333	95,508	96,015	96,641
Participation rate	64.4	63.8	64.3	64.8	63.9	64.0	64.0	64.3	64.8
Employed	89,134	87,509	88,348	89,237	87,955	87,990	87,956	87,988	88,450
Unemployed	5,983	7,743	7,666	6,429	7,165	7,344	7,552	8,026	8,191
Unemployment rate	6.3	8.1	8.0	6.7	7.5	7.7	7.9	8.4	8.5
Men, 20 years and over									
Civilian labor force	50,799	50,933	51,221	50,920	50,757	50,812	50,903	51,124	51,394
Participation rate	79.9	78.9	79.4	80.1	78.9	79.0	79.0	79.2	79.6
Employed	48,141	47,109	47,583	48,092	47,410	47,430	47,351	47,393	47,535
Unemployed	2,657	3,824	3,639	2,828	3,347	3,382	3,552	3,731	3,859
Unemployment rate	5.2	7.5	7.1	5.6	6.6	6.7	7.0	7.3	7.5
Women, 20 years and over									
Civilian labor force	36,536	37,164	37,337	36,597	36,698	36,860	37,038	37,179	37,428
Participation rate	51.8	51.9	52.2	51.9	51.5	51.7	51.8	52.0	52.3
Employed	34,518	34,696	34,786	34,422	34,380	34,427	34,475	34,489	34,682
Unemployed	2,018	2,469	2,551	2,175	2,319	2,433	2,564	2,690	2,746
Unemployment rate	5.5	6.6	6.8	5.9	6.3	6.6	6.9	7.2	7.3
Both sexes, 16–19 years									
Civilian labor force	7,782	7,155	7,455	8,149	7,665	7,662	7,567	7,712	7,819
Participation rate	57.3	54.3	56.8	60.0	57.8	58.0	57.2	58.6	59.6
Employed	6,475	5,704	5,979	6,723	6,166	6,133	6,130	6,106	6,233
Unemployed	1,308	1,450	1,476	1,426	1,499	1,529	1,437	1,606	1,586
Unemployment rate	16.8	20.3	19.8	17.5	19.6	20.0	19.0	20.8	20.3
Men	16.5	21.6	20.0	17.9	20.8	20.4	20.2	22.3	21.2
Women	17.1	18.8	19.5	17.0	18.2	19.4	17.6	19.2	19.2

Black

Civilian noninstitutional population[a]	18,542	18,511	18,480	18,450	18,423	18,170	18,542	18,511	18,170
Civilian labor force	11,335	11,170	11,217	11,205	11,188	11,126	11,174	10,936	10,974
Participation rate	61.1	60.3	60.7	60.7	60.7	61.2	60.3	59.4	60.4
Employed	9,216	9,111	9,197	9,265	9,314	9,460	9,167	9,031	9,407
Unemployed	2,120	2,058	2,020	1,939	1,874	1,666	2,007	1,955	1,567
Unemployment rate	18.7	18.4	18.0	17.3	16.8	15.0	18.0	17.8	14.3
Men, 20 years and over									
Civilian labor force	5,349	5,350	5,284	5,299	5,284	5,271	5,328	5,310	5,253
Participation rate	74.6	74.8	74.1	74.4	74.3	75.5	74.4	74.3	75.2
Employed	4,439	4,445	4,437	4,450	4,424	4,587	4,448	4,418	4,594
Unemployed	910	906	848	849	860	684	881	894	660
Unemployment rate	17.0	16.9	16.0	16.0	16.3	13.0	16.5	16.8	12.6
Women, 20 years and over									
Civilian labor force	5,140	5,058	5,093	5,063	5,081	4,957	5,074	5,020	4,897
Participation rate	56.4	55.6	56.1	55.8	56.2	55.7	55.6	55.2	55.1
Employed	4,351	4,272	4,307	4,330	4,406	4,306	4,321	4,263	4,275
Unemployed	788	787	786	733	675	651	753	756	622
Unemployment rate	15.3	15.6	15.4	14.5	13.3	13.1	14.8	15.1	12.7
Both sexes, 16–19 years									
Civilian labor force	846	761	839	843	823	898	772	556	824
Participation rate	37.5	33.7	37.1	37.3	36.3	39.2	34.2	29.0	36.0
Employed	425	395	453	486	484	567	398	351	538
Unemployed	421	366	386	357	339	331	373	305	285
Unemployment rate	49.8	48.1	46.0	42.3	41.2	36.9	48.4	45.5	34.6
Men	50.6	48.3	48.5	40.7	36.3	37.6	47.3	43.5	33.9
Women	48.9	47.8	43.1	44.2	46.7	36.0	49.5	44.0	35.4
Hispanic Origin									
Civilian noninstitutional population[a]	9,297	9,235	9,297	9,341	9,400	9,222	9,297	9,235	9,222
Civilian labor force	6,001	5,933	6,024	6,065	6,054	5,960	5,993	5,897	5,957
Participation rate	64.5	64.2	64.8	64.9	64.4	64.6	64.5	63.9	64.6
Employed	5,166	5,191	5,260	5,298	5,330	5,356	5,192	5,170	5,380
Unemployed	834	743	764	767	724	604	801	727	578
Unemployment rate	13.9	12.5	12.7	12.6	12.0	10.1	13.4	12.3	9.7

Note: Detail for the above race and Hispanic-origin groups will not sum to totals because data for the "other races" group are not presented and Hispanics are included in both the white and black population groups.

[a] The population figures are not adjusted for seasonal variations; therefore, identical numbers appear in the unadjusted and seasonally adjusted columns.

Table 2. Employed Persons by Occupation, Race, and Sex

Occupation and Race	Total January 1981	Total January 1982	Males January 1981	Males January 1982	Females January 1981	Females January 1982
Total						
Total, 16 years and over (thousands)	98,139	97,831	55,993	55,300	42,146	42,531
Percent	100.0	100.0	100.0	100.0	100.0	100.0
White-collar workers	53.7	54.0	43.7	44.3	66.9	66.7
Professional and technical	16.8	17.4	16.2	16.9	17.6	18.1
Managers and administrators, except farm	11.8	11.3	14.8	14.6	7.8	7.1
Sales workers	6.4	6.6	6.2	6.4	6.7	6.9
Clerical workers	18.7	18.7	6.5	6.4	34.9	34.7
Blue-collar workers	30.7	29.8	43.6	42.8	13.5	12.9
Craft and kindred workers	12.5	12.3	20.5	20.2	1.8	2.0
Operatives, except transport	10.6	10.0	11.2	10.6	9.8	9.2
Transport equipment operatives	3.4	3.4	5.5	5.5	.7	.7
Nonfarm laborers	4.1	4.1	6.3	6.5	1.2	1.0
Service workers	13.2	13.7	9.1	9.3	18.7	19.4
Private household workers	1.0	1.1	.1	.1	2.3	2.4
Other service workers	12.2	12.6	9.0	9.2	16.5	17.0
Farm workers	2.4	2.4	3.6	3.6	.9	.9
Farmers and farm managers	1.4	1.4	2.2	2.2	.3	.4
Farm laborers and supervisors	1.0	1.0	1.4	1.4	.5	.5
White						
Total, 16 years and over (thousands)	86,535	86,378	49,972	49,454	36,563	36,924
Percent	100.0	100.0	100.0	100.0	100.0	100.0
White-collar workers	55.4	55.5	45.4	45.7	69.0	68.8
Professional and technical	17.2	17.8	16.8	17.3	17.8	18.4
Managers and administrators, except farm	12.5	12.1	15.7	15.4	8.2	7.6
Sales workers	6.9	7.1	6.6	6.8	7.2	7.5
Clerical workers	18.7	18.6	6.3	6.2	35.7	35.3
Blue-collar workers	30.1	29.4	42.7	42.1	12.9	12.4
Craft and kindred workers	12.9	12.7	21.0	20.7	1.8	2.0
Operatives, except transport	10.1	9.5	10.8	10.1	9.2	8.6
Transport equipment operatives	3.2	3.3	5.1	5.2	.7	.8
Nonfarm laborers	3.8	3.9	5.8	6.0	1.2	1.0

Table 2 (*continued*)

Occupation and Race	Total		Males		Females	
	January 1981	January 1982	January 1981	January 1982	January 1981	January 1982
Service workers	12.0	12.5	8.2	8.5	17.1	17.9
Private household workers	.8	.8	.1	(1)	1.8	1.9
Other service workers	11.2	11.7	8.2	8.5	15.4	16.0
Farm workers	2.5	2.6	3.7	3.7	.9	1.0
Farmers and farm managers	1.5	1.6	2.4	2.4	.4	.4
Farm laborers and supervisors	1.0	1.0	1.3	1.3	.6	.6
Black and Other						
Total, 16 years and over (thousands)	11,604	11,453	6,021	5,846	5,583	5,607
Percent	100.0	100.0	100.0	100.0	100.0	100.0
White-collar workers	41.3	42.8	30.2	32.7	53.3	53.3
Professional and technical	13.7	14.5	11.5	13.3	15.9	15.7
Managers and administrators, except farm	6.1	5.9	7.3	7.9	4.8	3.8
Sales workers	2.9	2.9	2.8	2.6	3.1	3.3
Clerical workers	18.6	19.5	8.5	8.9	29.5	30.5
Blue-collar workers	34.6	33.0	51.0	48.6	16.8	16.7
Craft and kindred workers	9.2	8.8	16.5	15.8	1.3	1.5
Operatives, except transport	14.1	14.0	14.7	14.6	13.6	13.4
Transport equipment operatives	5.0	4.4	8.9	7.9	.7	.7
Nonfarm laborers	6.3	5.8	11.0	10.4	1.3	1.1
Service workers	22.5	22.7	16.0	16.0	29.5	29.6
Private household workers	2.9	3.0	.3	.3	5.8	5.8
Other service workers	19.6	19.6	15.8	15.7	23.7	23.8
Farm workers	1.6	1.6	2.8	2.8	.4	.4
Farmers and farm managers	.4	.2	.7	.4	(1)	.1
Farm laborers and supervisors	1.3	1.4	2.1	2.4	.3	.3

Note: 1982 data in this table reflect the introduction of 1980 census population controls into the estimation process, and 1981 data have been revised. See article in this issue for additional information.

Table 3. Unemployment Rates of Persons 16 Years and Over, by Age, Sex, and Race: Annual Averages, 1950–1981

Year	Total, 16 Years and Over	16 and 17 Years	18 and 19 Years	20 to 24 Years	25 to 34 Years	35 to 44 Years	45 to 54 Years	55 to 64 Years	65 Years and Over	14 and 15 Years[a]
White Male										
1950	4.7	13.4	11.7	7.7	3.9	3.2	3.7	4.7	4.6	5.8
1951	2.6	9.5	6.7	3.6	2.0	1.8	2.2	2.7	3.4	4.7
1952	2.5	10.9	7.0	4.3	1.9	1.7	2.0	2.3	2.9	5.5
1953	2.5	8.9	7.1	4.5	2.0	1.8	2.0	2.7	2.3	4.6
1954	4.8	14.0	13.0	9.8	4.2	3.6	3.8	4.3	4.2	4.9
1955	3.7	12.2	10.4	7.0	2.7	2.6	2.9	3.9	3.8	5.1
1956	3.4	11.2	9.7	6.1	2.8	2.2	2.8	3.1	3.4	6.1
1957	3.6	11.9	11.2	7.1	2.7	2.5	3.0	3.4	3.2	6.8
1958	6.1	14.9	16.5	11.7	5.6	4.4	4.8	5.2	5.0	7.9
1959	4.6	15.0	13.0	7.5	3.8	3.2	3.7	4.2	4.5	7.2
1960	4.8	14.6	13.5	8.3	4.1	3.3	3.6	4.1	4.0	8.1
1961	5.7	16.5	15.1	10.0	4.9	4.0	4.4	5.3	5.2	8.0
1962	4.6	15.1	12.7	8.0	3.8	3.1	3.5	4.1	4.1	7.6
1963	4.7	17.8	14.2	7.8	3.9	2.9	3.3	4.0	4.1	7.9
1964	4.1	16.1	13.4	7.4	3.0	2.5	2.9	3.5	3.6	7.7
1965	3.6	14.7	11.4	5.9	2.6	2.3	2.3	3.1	3.4	7.1
1966	2.8	12.5	8.9	4.1	2.1	1.7	1.7	2.5	3.0	7.6
1967	2.7	12.7	9.0	4.2	1.9	1.6	1.8	2.2	2.7	8.9
1968	2.6	12.3	8.2	4.6	1.7	1.4	1.5	1.7	2.8	8.3
1969	2.5	12.5	7.9	4.6	1.7	1.4	1.4	1.7	2.1	8.5
1970	4.0	15.7	12.0	7.8	3.1	2.3	2.3	2.7	3.2	10.1
1971	4.9	17.1	13.5	9.4	4.0	2.9	2.8	3.2	3.4	10.8
1972	4.5	16.4	12.4	8.5	3.4	2.5	2.5	3.0	3.3	10.7
1973	3.7	15.1	10.0	6.5	3.0	1.8	2.0	2.4	2.9	10.7
1974	4.3	16.2	11.5	7.8	3.5	2.4	2.2	2.5	3.0	11.9
1975	7.2	19.7	17.2	13.2	6.3	4.5	4.4	4.1	5.0	13.0
1976	6.4	19.7	15.5	10.9	5.6	3.7	3.7	4.0	4.8	13.7
1977	5.5	17.6	13.0	9.3	5.0	3.1	3.0	3.3	4.9	14.4
1978	4.5	16.9	10.8	7.6	3.7	2.5	2.5	2.6	3.9	14.4
1979	4.4	16.1	12.3	7.4	3.6	2.5	2.5	2.5	3.1	14.2
1980	6.1	18.5	14.6	11.1	6.0	3.6	3.3	3.4	2.5	14.1
1981	6.5	20.0	16.5	11.6	6.2	4.1	3.6	3.4	2.4	
White Female										
1950	5.3	13.8	9.4	6.1	5.2	4.0	4.3	4.3	3.1	8.0
1951	4.2	9.6	6.5	3.9	4.1	3.5	3.6	4.0	3.3	7.1
1952	3.3	9.3	6.2	3.8	3.2	2.8	2.4	2.5	2.3	7.6

Year									
1953	3.1	8.3	6.0	4.1	3.1	2.3	2.3	2.5	1.4	4.0
1954	5.6	12.0	9.4	6.4	5.7	4.9	4.4	4.5	2.8	6.8
1955	4.3	11.6	7.7	5.1	4.3	3.8	3.4	3.6	2.2	7.1
1956	4.2	12.1	8.3	5.1	4.0	3.5	3.3	3.5	2.3	7.8
1957	4.3	11.9	7.9	5.1	4.7	3.7	3.0	3.0	3.5	6.8
1958	6.2	15.6	11.0	7.4	6.6	5.6	4.9	4.3	3.5	5.8
1959	5.3	13.3	11.1	6.7	5.0	4.7	4.0	4.0	3.4	5.2
1960	5.3	14.5	11.5	7.2	5.7	4.2	4.0	3.3	2.8	6.3
1961	6.5	17.0	13.6	8.4	6.6	5.6	4.8	4.3	3.7	6.6
1962	5.5	15.6	11.3	7.7	5.4	4.5	3.7	3.4	4.0	5.6
1963	5.8	18.1	13.2	7.4'	5.8	4.6	3.9	3.5	3.0	5.9
1964	5.5	17.1	13.2	7.1	5.2	4.5	3.6	3.5	3.4	4.1
1965	5.0	15.0	13.4	6.3	4.8	4.1	3.0	2.7	2.7	4.4
1966	4.3	14.5	10.7	5.3	3.7	3.3	2.7	2.2	2.7	4.4
1967	4.6	12.9	10.5	6.0	4.7	3.7	2.9	2.3	2.6	5.2
1968	4.3	13.9	11.0	5.9	3.9	3.1	2.3	2.1	2.7	5.4
1969	4.2	13.8	10.0	5.5	4.2	3.2	2.4	2.1	2.4	6.4
1970	5.4	15.3	11.9	6.9	5.3	4.3	3.4	2.6	3.3	7.4
1971	6.3	16.7	14.1	8.5	6.3	4.9	3.9	3.3	3.6	8.3
1972	5.9	17.0	12.3	8.2	5.5	4.5	3.5	3.3	3.7	8.1
1973	5.3	15.7	10.9	7.0	5.1	3.7	3.1	2.8	2.8	7.8
1974	6.1	16.4	13.0	8.2	5.7	4.3	3.6	3.3	3.9	9.9
1975	8.6	19.2	16.1	11.2	8.5	6.6	5.8	5.1	5.3	10.7
1976	7.9	18.2	15.1	10.4	7.6	5.8	5.0	4.8	5.3	10.3
1977	7.3	18.2	14.2	9.3	6.7	5.3	5.0	4.4	4.9	10.4
1978	6.2	17.1	12.4	8.3	5.8	4.5	3.8	3.0	3.7	10.9
1979	5.9	15.9	12.5	7.8	5.6	4.2	3.7	3.0	3.1	11.0
1980	6.5	17.3	13.0	8.5	6.3	4.9	4.3	3.1	2.9	12.2
1981	6.3	18.4	15.3	9.1	6.6	5.1	4.2	3.8	3.4	

Black and
Other Male

Year									
1950	9.4	12.1	17.7	12.6	10.0	7.9	7.4	8.0	7.0	10.0
1951	4.9	8.7	9.6	6.7	5.5	3.4	3.6	4.1	4.7	4.9
1952	5.2	8.0	10.0	7.9	5.5	4.4	4.2	3.7	4.7	5.5
1953	4.8	8.3	8.1	8.1	4.3	3.6	5.1	3.6	3.1	5.1
1954	10.3	13.4	14.7	16.9	10.1	9.0	9.3	7.5	7.5	5.7
1955	8.8	14.8	12.9	12.4	8.6	8.2	6.4	9.0	7.1	12.1
1956	7.9	15.7	14.9	12.0	7.6	6.6	5.4	8.1	4.9	13.0
1957	8.3	16.3	20.0	12.7	8.5	6.4	6.2	5.5	5.9	14.1
1958	13.8	27.1	26.7	19.5	14.7	11.4	10.3	10.1	9.0	13.0
1959	11.5	22.3	27.2	16.3	12.3	8.9	7.9	8.7	8.4	12.7
1960	10.7	22.7	25.1	13.1	10.7	8.2	8.5	9.5	6.3	13.3

Table 3 (*continued*)

Year	Total, 16 Years and Over	16 and 17 Years	18 and 19 Years	20 to 24 Years	25 to 34 Years	35 to 44 Years	45 to 54 Years	55 to 64 Years	65 Years and Over	14 and 15 Years[a]
1961	12.8	31.0	23.9	15.3	12.9	10.7	10.2	10.5	9.4	14.3
1962	10.9	21.9	21.8	14.6	10.5	8.6	8.3	9.6	11.9	15.2
1963	10.5	27.0	27.4	15.5	9.5	8.0	7.1	7.4	10.1	16.9
1964	8.9	25.9	23.1	12.6	7.7	6.2	5.9	8.1	8.3	19.1
1965	7.4	27.1	20.2	9.3	6.2	5.1	5.1	5.4	5.2	20.3
1966	6.3	22.5	20.5	7.9	4.9	4.2	4.1	4.4	4.9	20.0
1967	6.0	28.9	20.1	8.0	4.4	3.1	3.4	4.1	5.1	24.1
1968	5.6	26.6	19.0	8.3	3.8	2.9	2.5	3.6	4.0	26.0
1969	5.3	24.7	19.0	8.4	3.4	2.4	2.4	3.2	3.2	22.1
1970	7.3	27.8	23.1	12.6	6.1	3.9	3.3	3.4	3.8	29.0
1971	9.1	33.4	26.0	16.2	7.4	4.9	4.5	4.7	3.4	32.2
1972	8.9	35.1	26.2	14.7	6.8	4.8	3.8	4.6	6.9	31.8
1973	7.6	34.4	22.1	12.6	5.8	4.0	3.2	3.1	3.6	34.1
1974	9.1	39.0	26.6	15.4	7.2	4.1	4.0	3.6	5.6	37.9
1975	13.7	39.4	32.9	22.9	11.9	8.3	9.0	6.1	9.5	38.6
1976	12.7	37.7	34.0	20.7	11.0	7.3	7.2	6.2	9.3	41.3
1977	12.4	38.7	36.1	21.7	10.6	6.1	5.2	6.4	8.3	37.4
1978	10.9	40.0	30.8	20.0	8.8	4.9	5.0	4.4	7.1	37.5
1979	10.3	34.4	29.6	17.0	8.6	5.8	5.2	4.8	6.3	37.8
1980	13.3	37.7	33.0	22.3	12.5	7.8	6.6	6.0	8.4	43.2
1981	14.3	40.9	36.7	24.9	13.0	8.7	7.2	6.1	8.1	
Black and Other Female										
1950	8.4	17.6	14.1	13.0	9.1	6.6	5.9	4.8	5.7	
1951	6.1	13.0	15.1	8.8	7.1	5.6	2.8	3.4	1.6	
1952	5.7	6.3	16.8	10.7	6.2	4.0	3.5	2.4	1.5	
1953	4.1	10.3	9.9	5.5	4.9	3.5	2.1	2.1	1.6	
1954	9.3	19.1	21.6	13.2	10.9	7.3	5.9	4.9	5.1	
1955	8.4	15.4	21.4	13.0	10.2	5.5	5.2	5.5	3.3	
1956	8.9	22.0	23.4	14.8	9.1	6.8	5.6	5.3	2.8	
1957	7.3	18.3	21.3	12.2	8.1	4.7	4.2	4.0	4.3	
1958	10.8	25.4	30.0	18.9	11.1	9.2	4.9	6.2	5.6	
1959	9.4	25.8	29.9	14.9	9.7	7.6	6.1	5.0	2.3	
1960	9.4	25.7	24.5	15.3	9.1	8.6	5.7	4.3	4.1	
1961	11.8	31.1	28.2	19.5	11.1	10.7	7.4	6.3	6.5	
1962	11.0	27.8	31.2	18.2	11.5	8.9	7.1	3.6	3.7	

1963	11.2	40.1	31.9	18.7	11.7	8.2	6.1	4.8	3.6	
1964	10.6	36.5	29.2	18.3	11.2	7.8	6.1	3.8	2.2	
1965	9.2	37.8	27.8	13.7	8.4	7.6	4.4	3.9	3.1	
1966	8.6	34.8	29.2	12.6	8.1	5.0	5.0	3.3	4.0	27.1
1967	9.1	32.0	28.3	13.8	8.7	6.2	4.4	3.4	3.4	28.9
1968	8.3	33.7	26.2	12.3	8.4	5.0	3.2	2.8	2.4	23.1
1969	7.8	31.2	25.7	12.0	6.6	4.5	3.7	2.9	1.1	30.9
1970	9.3	36.9	32.9	15.0	7.9	4.8	4.0	3.2	1.9	33.3
1971	10.8	38.5	33.7	17.3	10.7	6.9	4.2	3.5	3.9	39.3
1972	11.3	38.3	38.7	17.4	10.2	7.2	4.7	4.0	2.0	35.6
1973	10.5	36.5	33.3	17.6	9.7	5.3	3.7	3.2	3.9	37.9
1974	10.7	36.2	33.7	18.0	8.6	6.7	4.3	3.3	1.5	41.8
1975	14.0	38.9	38.3	22.5	12.9	8.6	6.7	5.3	3.1	45.5
1976	13.6	46.0	35.0	21.7	13.0	8.1	6.1	5.5	2.6	48.3
1977	14.0	44.7	37.4	23.5	12.9	8.5	5.6	4.9	3.6	47.7
1978	13.1	41.7	36.5	21.3	11.2	7.6	5.6	5.1	4.8	48.8
1979	12.3	38.4	33.4	20.8	11.0	2.0	4.0	4.0	4.0	42.9
1980	13.1	40.4	34.9	21.8	12.3	7.8	6.3	4.7	4.7	
1981	14.4	41.9	36.9	24.5	14.0	8.1	6.7	4.5	5.8	

[a] Rate not shown where base is fewer than 50,000.

Table 4. Employment Status of the Noninstitutional Population in Metropolitan and Nonmetropolitan Areas by Sex, Age, and Race (numbers in thousands)

Employment Status	Metropolitan Areas						Nonmetropolitan Areas					
	Total		Central Cities		Suburbs		Total		Farm		Nonfarm	
	1980	1981	1980	1981	1980	1981	1980	1981	1980	1981	1980	1981
Total												
Civilian noninstitutional population	111,438	112,987	46,224	46,334	65,214	66,653	52,706	53,449	4,532	4,345	48,174	49,104
Civilian labor force	72,207	73,301	28,990	28,978	43,217	44,323	32,512	33,092	2,892	2,796	29,630	30,296
Percent of population	64.8	64.9	62.7	62.5	66.3	66.5	61.7	61.9	63.8	64.4	61.5	61.7
Employed	67,120	67,825	26,560	26,400	40,560	41,425	30,150	30,488	2,801	2,700	27,349	27,788
Unemployed	5,087	5,476	2,429	2,578	2,658	2,898	2,362	2,603	92	96	2,270	2,507
Unemployment rate	7.0	7.5	8.4	8.9	6.2	6.5	7.3	7.9	3.2	3.4	7.7	8.3
Not in labor force	39,230	39,686	17,235	17,355	21,997	22,331	20,194	20,357	1,640	1,548	18,554	18,809
White												
Civilian noninstitutional population	95,516	96,654	35,076	34,959	60,440	61,695	48,141	48,725	4,264	4,098	43,877	44,627
Civilian labor force	62,291	63,229	22,276	22,238	40,015	40,991	29,880	30,357	2,751	2,667	27,129	27,690
Percent of population	65.2	65.4	63.5	63.6	66.2	66.4	62.1	62.3	64.5	65.1	61.8	62.0
Employed	58,503	59,187	20,809	20,711	37,694	38,476	27,877	28,153	2,673	2,585	25,204	25,568
Unemployed	3,788	4,042	1,468	1,527	2,320	2,515	2,003	2,204	78	82	1,925	2,122
Unemployment rate	6.1	6.4	6.6	6.9	5.8	6.1	6.7	7.3	2.8	3.1	7.1	7.6
Not in labor force	33,225	33,425	12,799	12,722	20,426	20,703	18,261	18,368	1,513	1,431	16,748	16,937
Black and Other												
Civilian noninstitutional population	15,922	16,333	11,149	11,374	4,773	4,959	4,565	4,724	268	247	4,297	4,477
Civilian labor force	9,916	10,072	6,713	6,741	3,203	3,331	2,632	2,735	142	129	2,490	2,606
Percent of population	62.3	61.7	60.2	59.3	67.1	67.2	57.7	57.9	52.9	52.4	57.9	58.2
Employed	8,617	8,638	5,752	5,690	2,865	2,948	2,273	2,335	128	116	2,145	2,219
Unemployed	1,299	1,434	962	1,051	337	383	359	399	14	14	345	385
Unemployment rate	13.1	14.2	14.3	15.6	10.5	11.5	13.6	14.6	9.8	10.5	13.9	14.8
Not in labor force	6,006	6,261	4,435	4,633	1,571	1,629	1,933	1,990	126	118	1,807	1,872

Table 5. Percent Distribution of Employed by Occupation, Race, and Sex, 1972 and 1980 Annual Averages (numbers in thousands)

	Men				Women			
	Black		White		Black		White	
Occupation	1972	1980	1972	1980	1972	1980	1972	1980
Total employed	4,347	4,704	47,769	50,337	3,406	4,394	27,305	36,043
Percent distribution	100.0	100.0	100.0	100.0	100.0	100.0	100.0	100.0
Professional and technical	6.4	8.2	14.3	16.1	10.6	13.8	14.9	17.0
Managers and administrators	4.0	5.6	14.0	15.3	2.1	3.4	4.8	7.4
Sales	1.7	2.5	6.6	6.4	2.5	2.8	7.8	7.3
Clerical	7.6	8.4	6.8	6.2	22.7	29.3	36.2	36.0
Craft and kindred workers	14.8	17.6	21.2	21.5	.9	1.4	1.3	1.9
Operatives, except transport	17.4	15.5	12.1	10.7	14.8	13.8	12.5	9.4
Transport equipment operatives	10.3	9.9	5.7	5.4	0.4	0.7	0.4	0.7
Nonfarm laborers	17.4	13.0	6.8	6.5	0.9	1.4	0.9	1.2
Farmers and farm managers	1.0	0.4	3.4	2.6	0.1	—	0.4	0.4
Farm laborers and foremen	3.5	2.4	1.7	1.5	1.1	0.5	1.5	0.8
Private household workers	0.3	0.1	—	—	16.4	7.4	3.0	1.9
All other service workers	15.8	16.4	7.3	7.9	27.6	25.4	16.2	16.0

Table 6. Employment Status of the Female Noninstitutional Population by Sex, Age, and Race: 1981 (numbers in thousands)

			Civilian Labor Force				
	Total Labor Force				Unemployed		Not in Labor Force
Sex and Age	Number	Percent of Population	Total	Employed	Number	Percent of Labor Force	
White							
16 years and over	39,687	52.1	39,559	36,836	2,723	6.9	36,509
16–21 years	6,217	60.7	6,169	5,306	863	14.0	4,034
16–19 years	3,728	55.7	3,707	3,094	614	16.6	2,964
16–17 years	1,486	46.2	1,486	1,212	274	18.4	1,729
18–19 years	2,241	64.5	2,222	1,882	340	15.3	1,235
20 to 64 years	34,928	61.8	34,820	32,746	2,074	6.0	21,592
20–24 years	6,307	71.7	6,245	5,680	565	9.1	2,492
25–54 years	24,508	65.0	24,461	23,107	1,354	5.5	13,205
25–34 years	10,631	66.5	10,589	9,892	697	6.6	5,360
35–44 years	7,734	66.4	7,730	7,333	397	5.1	3,914
45–54 years	6,144	61.0	6,143	5,882	261	4.2	3,931
55–64 years	4,114	41.1	4,114	3,959	154	3.8	5,897
55–59 years	2,594	49.2	2,594	2,492	102	3.9	2,679
60–64 years	1,520	32.1	1,520	1,467	53	3.5	3,217
65 years and over	1,031	7.9	1,031	996	35	3.4	11,953
Black and Other							
16 years and over	6,250	53.7	6,201	5,309	892	14.4	5,398
16–21 years	838	42.1	818	532	286	35.0	1,155
16–19 years	461	34.9	453	278	175	38.6	861
16–17 years	162	24.7	161	94	67	41.8	492
18–19 years	299	44.8	291	184	107	36.9	368

Table 6 (*continued*)

| | Total Labor Force | | Civilian Labor Force | | | | |
| | | | | | Unemployed | | |
Sex and Age	Number	Percent of Population	Total	Employed	Number	Percent of Labor Force	Not in Labor Force
20–64 years	5,662	63.2	5,621	4,911	710	12.6	3,294
20–24 years	1,003	60.7	978	739	239	24.5	649
25–54 years	4,129	67.4	4,112	3,667	446	10.8	1,996
25–34 years	1,913	68.7	1,898	1,632	266	14.0	871
35–44 years	1,290	69.7	1,289	1,171	118	9.1	561
45–54 years	926	62.1	926	864	62	6.7	564
55–64 years	530	44.9	530	506	24	4.5	651
55–59 years	325	50.8	325	309	15	4.7	314
60–64 years	205	37.9	205	197	9	4.2	336
65 years and over	127	9.3	127	120	7	5.8	1,243

Table 7. Employment Status of the Male Noninstitutional Population by Sex, Age, and Race: 1981
(numbers in thousands)

| | Total Labor Force | | Civilian Labor Force | | | | |
| | | | | | Unemployed | | |
Sex and Age	Number	Percent of Population	Total	Employed	Number	Percent of Labor Force	Not in Labor Force
White							
16 years and over	55,542	78.4	54,027	50,504	3,523	6.5	15,284
16–21 years	7,455	70.6	6,963	5,857	1,106	15.9	3,106
16–19 years	4,390	63.7	4,174	3,426	747	17.9	2,502
16–17 years	1,724	51.7	1,710	1,369	341	20.0	1,614
18–19 years	2,665	75.0	2,463	2,057	406	16.5	888
20–64 years	49,472	90.1	48,174	45,439	2,735	5.7	5,447
20–24 years	7,856	87.8	7,304	6,457	847	11.6	1,096
25–54 years	35,152	95.1	34,406	32,738	1,669	4.9	1,793
25–34 years	15,370	96.0	14,881	13,963	918	6.2	643
35–44 years	10,885	96.2	10,661	10,228	433	4.1	428
45–54 years	8,896	92.5	8,865	8,546	318	3.6	723
55–64 years	6,465	71.6	6,463	6,244	219	3.4	2,558
55–59 years	3,976	82.4	3,975	3,840	135	3.4	852
60–64 years	2,489	59.3	2,489	2,404	84	3.4	1,707
65 years and over	1,680	18.6	1,680	1,639	41	2.4	7,335
Black and Other							
16 years and over	7,056	71.2	6,606	5,664	942	14.3	2,852
16–21 years	1,065	54.6	908	598	310	34.2	886
16–19 years	577	44.2	515	318	197	38.3	730
16–17 years	197	30.0	195	115	80	40.9	461
18–19 years	380	58.5	320	202	117	36.7	269

Table 7 (*continued*)

Sex and Age	Total Labor Force		Civilian Labor Force				Not in Labor Force
	Number	Percent of Population	Total	Employed	Unemployed		
					Number	Percent of Labor Force	
20–64 years	6,308	83.1	5,921	5,190	731	12.3	1,280
20–24 years	1,211	80.0	1,016	763	253	24.9	302
25–54 years	4,471	87.9	4,279	3,840	440	10.3	613
25–34 years	2,080	89.1	1,938	1,687	251	13.0	255
35–44 years	1,334	89.9	1,289	1,177	112	8.7	150
45–54 years	1,056	83.5	1,052	976	76	7.2	209
55–64 years	627	63.2	626	588	38	6.1	365
55–59 years	390	72.0	390	365	24	6.2	152
60–64 years	237	52.6	237	223	14	6.0	213
65 years and over	170	16.8	170	156	14	8.1	842

Table 8. Unemployment Trends by Race, Sex, and Age: Selected Years, 1955–1981 (%)

Race, Sex, and Age	1955	1965	1973	1978	1981	% Increase 1955–1981
Total, 16 years and over	4.4	4.5	4.9	6.0	7.3	62
Both sexes, 16–19 years	11.0	14.8	14.5	16.3	19.6	32
Both sexes, 20–24 years	7.0	6.7	7.8	9.5	11.0	73
Both sexes, 25 years and over	3.6	3.2	3.1	4.0	5.4	69
White men						
16–19 years	11.3	12.9	12.3	13.5	17.9	37
16–17 years	12.2	14.7	15.1	16.9	20.0	36
18–19 years	10.4	11.4	10.0	10.8	16.5	45
20–24 years	7.0	5.9	6.5	7.6	11.6	97
25 years and over	3.0	2.5	2.4	3.0	4.6	84
White women						
16–19 years	9.1	14.0	13.0	14.4	16.6	19
16–17 years	11.6	15.0	15.7	17.1	18.4	23
18–19 years	7.7	13.4	10.9	12.4	15.3	14
20–24 years	5.1	6.3	7.0	8.3	9.1	44
25 years and over	3.7	3.6	3.7	4.5	5.0	28
Black and other men						
16–19 years	13.4	23.3	26.9	34.4	38.3	64
16–17 years	14.8	27.1	34.4	40.0	41.7	51
18–19 years	12.9	20.2	22.1	30.8	36.7	82
20–24 years	12.4	9.3	12.6	20.0	24.4	168
25 years and over	8.0	5.5	4.2	6.3	9.3	69
Black and other women						
16–19 years	19.2	31.7	34.5	38.4	38.6	22
16–17 years	15.4	37.8	36.5	41.7	41.8	11
18–19 years	21.4	27.8	33.3	36.5	36.9	33
20–24 years	13.0	13.7	17.6	21.3	24.5	19
25 years and over	6.9	6.4	6.1	8.2	10.1	58

Table 9. Unemployment Rates for Male Vietnam-Era Veterans and Nonveterans, by Age and Race, Fiscal Years 1979–1981

Age, Race, and Veteran Status	Fiscal 1979 Average	Fiscal 1980 Average	Fiscal 1981 Average
Total			
Total, 25 to 39 years			
Veterans	3.9	5.4	—
Nonveterans	3.8	5.6	—
25 to 29 years			
Veterans	5.9	8.9	—
Nonveterans	4.5	6.8	—
30 to 34 years			
Veterans	3.3	4.5	—
Nonveterans	3.3	5.1	—
35 to 39 years			
Veterans	2.7	4.1	—
Nonveterans	2.9	4.0	—
White			
Total, 25 to 39 years			
Veterans	3.5	4.8	5.8
Nonveterans	3.2	4.9	5.6
25 to 29 years			
Veterans	5.2	7.8	9.0
Nonveterans	3.9	6.1	6.7
30 to 34 years			
Veterans	3.1	4.1	5.4
Nonveterans	2.7	4.4	5.1
35 to 39 years			
Veterans	2.5	3.8	4.5
Nonveterans	2.6	3.4	4.0
Black and Other			
Total, 25 to 39 years			
Veterans	7.9	10.9	10.5
Nonveterans	7.6	10.5	12.0
25 to 29 years			
Veterans	12.0	16.2	16.0
Nonveterans	9.3	12.2	14.4
30 to 34 years			
Veterans	6.4	8.9	9.5
Nonveterans	7.5	10.0	16.5
35 to 39 years			
Veterans	5.2	8.1	7.5
Nonveterans	5.0	8.5	8.7

Source: U.S. Department of Labor, Bureau of Labor Statistics, unpublished data.

Table 10. Employment Indicators for Teenagers (ages 16 to 19), by Race, Selected Years: 1970–1981 (in percent)

Measure	1970	1973	1975	1977	1978	1979	1981
Unemployment rate							
Black	29.1	30.2	36.9	38.3	36.3	33.5	41.5
White	13.5	12.6	17.9	15.4	13.9	13.9	17.3
Employment-population ratio[a]							
Black	28.9	28.0	24.6	23.7	26.5	27.1	21.9
White	44.5	49.0	46.6	50.2	52.5	52.7	48.8
Labor force participation rate[b]							
Black	40.5	40.2	39.0	38.3	41.6	40.8	37.4
White	51.5	56.0	56.7	59.4	61.0	61.2	59.0

[a] Civilian employment as a percentage of the civilian noninstitutional population.

[b] Civilian labor force as a percentage of the civilian noninstitutional population.

Table 11. Employment Indicators for Black Youths, Ages 20 to 24, Selected Years: 1970–1981 (in percent)

Measure	1970	1973	1975	1977	1978	1979	1980	1981
Unemployment rate								
Men	12.6	12.6	22.9	21.7	20.0	17.0	23.7	28.3
Women	15.0	17.6	22.5	23.6	21.3	20.8	23.4	28.5
Employment-population ratio[a]								
Men	73.0	71.5	60.4	61.2	62.4	66.5	63.4	58.2
Women	49.0	47.4	43.6	45.4	49.4	48.0	46.3	44.8
Labor force participation rate[b]								
Men	83.5	81.8	78.4	78.2	78.0	80.1	78.9	79.2
Women	57.7	57.5	56.2	59.4	62.8	61.5	60.0	61.1

[a] Civilian employment as a percentage of the civilian noninstitutional population.

[b] Civilian labor force as a percentage of the civilian noninstitutional population.

Table 12. Unemployed Persons by Family Relationship, Race, Hispanic Origin, and Presence of Employed Family Members: 1981

Family Relationship, Race, and Hispanic Origin	Total (thousands)	Percentage of Unemployed [b]		
		With No Employed Persons in Family	With at Least One Employed Person in Family	With at Least One Person in Family Employed Full Time
Total				
Total unemployed	8,080	40.1	59.9	52.6
In families	6,908	29.9	70.1	61.5
Husbands	1,634	44.6	55.4	41.8
With children under 18 years of age	1,057	47.8	55.2	37.5
Wives	1,413	17.2	82.8	77.4
With children under 18 years of age	897	15.1	84.9	79.2
Relatives in married-couple families	1,957	8.6	91.4	86.0
Females who maintain families	566	81.6	18.4	10.7
With children under 18 years of age	469	87.5	12.5	6.0
Relatives in families maintained by females	995	32.9	67.1	55.6
Males who maintain families	130	65.6	34.4	26.1
With children under 18 years of age	54	84.5	15.5	9.4
Relatives in families maintained by males	214	25.5	74.5	67.1
Not in families [a]	1,172	—	—	—
White				
Total unemployed	6,246	38.1	61.9	54.6
In families	5,320	27.4	72.6	64.1
Husbands	1,376	44.7	55.3	40.9
With children under 18 years of age	875	48.3	51.7	35.9
Wives	1,195	16.5	83.5	78.2
With children under 18 years of age	742	14.2	85.8	80.2
Relatives in married-couple families	1,633	8.0	92.0	87.2
Females who maintain families	314	77.2	22.8	13.0
With children under 18 years of age	251	85.0	15.0	6.8
Relatives in families maintained by females	548	30.8	69.2	57.9
Males who maintain families	95	64.8	35.2	27.2
With children under 18 years of age	41	81.6	18.4	11.2
Relatives in families maintained by males	158	25.8	74.2	67.6
Not in families [a]	926	—	—	—
Black				
Total unemployed	1,676	47.1	52.9	45.4
In families	1,454	39.0	61.0	52.3
Husbands	228	43.2	56.8	48.4
With children under 18 years of age	160	44.5	55.5	47.6
Wives	185	21.5	78.5	71.9
With children under 18 years of age	134	19.3	80.7	74.0
Relatives in married-couple families	286	11.3	88.7	80.3
Females who maintain families	240	87.2	12.8	7.7
With children under 18 years of age	208	90.5	9.5	5.0
Relatives in families maintained by females	435	35.3	64.7	53.0
Males who maintain families	30	—	—	—
With children under 18 years of age	12	—	—	—
Relatives in families maintained by males	51	24.4	75.6	65.8
Not in families [a]	222	—	—	—

Table 12 (*continued*)

Family Relationship, Race, and Hispanic Origin	Total (thousands)	Percentage of Unemployed[b]		
		With No Employed Persons in Family	With at Least One Employed Person in Family	With at Least One Person in Family Employed Full Time
Hispanic Origin				
Total unemployed	602	41.2	58.8	51.2
In families	526	32.7	67.3	58.6
Husbands	139	51.2	48.8	37.9
With children under 18 years of age	110	53.1	46.9	36.1
Wives	96	16.9	83.1	77.0
With children under 18 years of age	70	15.7	84.3	79.3
Relatives in married-couple families	138	9.2	90.8	84.2
Females who maintain families	41	75.3	24.7	14.1
With children under 18 years of age	34	—	—	—
Relatives in families maintained by females	76	34.1	65.9	53.1
Males who maintain families	17	—	—	—
With children under 18 years of age	6	—	—	—
Relatives in families maintained by males	20	—	—	—
Not in families[a]	76	—	—	—

[a] The majority of these persons are living alone or with nonrelatives. Also included are persons in married-couple families where the husband is in the Armed Forces, persons in secondary families, and some whose status is unknown.

[b] Percentage not shown where base is less than 35,000.

Table 13.   Unemployment in Families by Type of Family, Race, Hispanic Origin, and Presence of Employed Family Members: 1981 (numbers in thousands)

| | | | With Unemployment | | |
| | | | Percent of Families[a] | | |
Type of Family, Race, and Hispanic Origin	Total Families	Total	With No Employed Person in Family	With at Least One Employed Person in Family	With at Least One Person in Family Employed Full Time
Total					
Total families	59,883	6,267	27.8	72.2	63.7
With children under 18 years of age	30,520	3,905	29.2	70.8	62.3
Married-couple families	48,416	4,572	20.3	79.7	71.6
With children under 18 years of age	24,129	2,897	19.7	80.3	72.0
Families maintained by females	9,109	1,383	50.2	49.8	39.5
With children under 18 years of age	5,579	900	57.7	42.3	32.5
Families maintained by males	2,358	312	38.3	61.7	54.0
With children under 18 years of age	813	109	45.9	54.1	47.7
White					
Total families	52,378	4,897	25.1	74.9	66.4
With children under 18 years of age	25,993	3,006	25.8	74.2	65.5
Married-couple families	44,144	3,873	20.0	80.0	71.9
With children under 18 years of age	21,662	2,426	19.6	80.4	71.9
Families maintained by females	6,310	796	46.5	53.5	42.5
With children under 18 years of age	3,664	495	53.4	46.6	36.0
Families maintained by males	1,923	229	37.4	62.6	55.7
With children under 18 years of age	666	85	41.9	58.1	51.2
Black					
Total families	6,500	1,256	37.7	62.3	53.4
With children under 18 years of age	3,915	825	41.3	58.7	51.0
Married-couple families	3,491	617	21.4	78.6	70.5
With children under 18 years of age	1,977	415	20.2	79.8	72.8
Families maintained by females	2,636	564	55.0	45.0	35.6
With children under 18 years of age	1,812	388	63.0	37.0	28.7
Families maintained by males	373	75	42.1	57.9	47.4
With children under 18 years of age	126	22	—	—	—
Hispanic Origin					
Total families	3,278	469	31.1	68.9	60.6
With children under 18 years of age	2,244	335	33.4	66.6	59.4
Married-couple families	2,395	333	24.9	75.1	67.7
With children under 18 years of age	1,661	253	25.0	75.0	67.9
Families maintained by females	698	105	50.0	50.0	37.7
With children under 18 years of age	517	74	60.8	39.2	31.1
Families maintained by males	185	31	—	—	—
With children under 18 years of age	65	9	—	—	—

[a] Percentage not shown where base is less than 35,000.

Table 14. Unemployed Persons by Duration of Unemployment, Race, and Hispanic Origin
(in thousands)

Weeks of Unemployment	Total 1980	Total 1981	White 1980	White 1981	Black and Other 1980	Black and Other 1981	Hispanic Origin 1980	Hispanic Origin 1981
Duration								
Total, 16 years and over	7,448	8,080	5,790	6,246	1,658	1,833	554	602
Less than 5 weeks	3,208	3,359	2,532	2,653	676	706	255	277
5 to 14 weeks	2,411	2,479	1,879	1,937	532	542	179	192
15 weeks and over	1,829	2,241	1,380	1,656	450	585	120	134
15 to 26 weeks	1,028	1,098	794	837	234	260	73	77
27 weeks and over	802	1,143	586	819	216	325	47	57
Average (mean) duration, in weeks	11.9	13.8	11.5	13.1	13.4	16.1	11.1	11.3
Median duration, in weeks	6.5	7.0	6.3	6.7	7.3	8.1	6.0	6.0
Percent Distribution								
Total unemployed	100.0	100.0	100.0	100.0	100.0	100.0	100.0	100.0
Less than 5 weeks	43.1	41.6	43.7	42.5	40.8	38.5	46.0	45.9
5 to 14 weeks	32.4	30.7	32.5	31.0	32.1	29.6	32.3	31.8
15 weeks and over	24.6	27.7	23.8	26.5	27.1	31.9	21.7	22.2
15 to 26 weeks	13.8	13.6	13.7	13.4	14.1	14.2	13.2	12.8
27 weeks and over	10.8	14.1	10.1	13.1	13.0	17.7	8.5	9.5

Table 15. Unemployed Persons by Reason for Unemployment, Race, and Hispanic Origin
(numbers in thousands)

Reason for Unemployment	Total		White		Black and Other		Hispanic Origin	
	1980	1981	1980	1981	1980	1981	1980	1981
Number of Unemployed								
Total, 16 years and over	7,448	8,080	5,790	6,246	1,658	1,833	554	602
Job losers	3,860	4,178	3,056	3,290	804	888	294	342
On layoff	1,471	1,412	1,235	1,196	237	216	74	101
Other job losers	2,389	2,766	1,821	2,094	567	672	220	240
Job leavers	863	894	717	741	146	153	69	62
Reentrants	1,875	2,048	1,421	1,539	453	510	115	126
New entrants	851	959	595	676	256	283	76	73
Percent Distribution								
Total unemployed	100.0	100.0	100.0	100.0	100.0	100.0	100.0	100.0
Job losers	51.9	51.7	52.8	52.7	48.5	48.5	53.1	56.7
On layoff	19.8	17.5	21.3	19.2	14.3	11.8	13.4	16.7
Other job losers	32.1	34.2	31.5	33.5	34.2	36.7	39.7	39.8
Job leavers	11.6	11.1	12.4	11.9	8.8	8.3	12.5	10.3
Reentrants	25.2	25.4	24.5	24.6	27.3	27.8	20.8	20.9
New entrants	11.4	11.9	10.3	10.8	15.4	15.4	13.7	12.1
Unemployed as a Percentage of the Civilian Labor Force								
Job losers	3.7	3.9	3.3	3.5	6.4	6.9	5.4	5.9
Job leavers	0.8	0.8	0.8	0.8	1.2	1.2	1.3	1.1
Reentrants	1.8	1.9	1.5	1.6	3.6	4.0	2.1	2.2
New entrants	0.8	0.9	0.6	0.7	2.0	2.2	1.4	1.3

Table 16. Unemployment Rates in Poverty and Nonpoverty Areas by Race, Sex, and Age: 1981

Race, Sex, and Age	Total United States		Metropolitan Areas		Nonmetropolitan Areas	
	Poverty Areas	Nonpoverty Areas	Poverty Areas	Nonpoverty Areas	Poverty Areas	Nonpoverty Areas
Total						
Both sexes, 16 years and over	10.7	7.0	14.4	6.9	8.5	7.6
Males, 20 years and over	8.9	5.8	12.8	5.7	6.8	6.2
Females, 20 years and over	9.8	6.3	12.3	6.1	8.2	6.9
Both sexes, 16–19 years	25.9	18.4	34.4	18.5	21.2	18.1
White						
Both sexes, 16 years and over	8.0	6.5	10.1	6.2	7.2	7.3
Males, 20 years and over	6.8	5.4	9.4	5.1	5.9	6.0
Females, 20 years and over	7.0	5.7	7.9	5.4	6.6	6.6
Both sexes, 16–19 years	20.1	16.9	24.7	16.7	18.6	17.4
Black and Other						
Both sexes, 16 years and over	17.8	12.4	19.3	12.3	15.3	13.5
Males, 20 years and over	15.4	10.5	17.4	10.4	12.2	11.0
Females, 20 years and over	15.8	10.7	16.4	10.5	14.8	12.1
Both sexes, 16–19 years	40.5	37.0	43.9	37.6	34.7	33.9

Table 17. Major Unemployment Indicators, Seasonally Adjusted

Category	1981 January	February	March	April	May	June	July	August	September	October	November	December	1982 January
Characteristic													
Total (all civilian workers)	7.4	7.4	7.3	7.3	7.5	7.4	7.2	7.3	7.6	8.0	8.3	8.8	8.5
Males, 20 years and over	6.1	6.0	6.0	5.8	6.3	6.1	5.8	6.0	6.2	6.7	7.1	7.9	7.5
Females, 20 years and over	6.7	6.6	6.6	6.6	6.7	6.6	6.7	6.6	6.9	7.0	7.2	7.4	7.2
Both sexes, 16–19 years	18.9	19.1	19.2	19.0	19.4	19.2	18.7	19.0	19.7	20.4	21.4	21.5	21.7
White	6.6	6.5	6.4	6.4	6.7	6.4	6.3	6.2	6.6	7.0	7.4	7.7	7.5
Black and other	12.8	13.2	13.6	13.2	13.7	14.2	13.8	14.7	14.8	15.2	15.2	15.7	15.1
Married men, spouse present	4.2	4.1	4.1	3.8	4.0	4.2	3.9	4.0	4.4	4.8	5.2	5.7	5.3
Married women, spouse present	6.0	5.8	5.9	5.9	5.8	5.7	5.7	5.5	6.0	6.1	6.5	6.6	6.2
Women who maintain families	10.3	9.8	9.6	9.9	10.4	10.7	11.2	10.1	10.7	10.6	10.8	10.5	10.4
Full-time workers	7.2	7.1	7.1	6.9	7.1	7.1	6.8	6.9	7.3	7.7	8.1	8.7	8.4
Part-time workers	9.1	9.1	9.1	9.2	9.6	9.2	9.3	9.6	9.6	9.5	10.2	9.2	9.6
Unemployed 15 weeks and over[a]	2.2	2.1	2.1	2.0	2.0	2.2	2.0	2.0	2.1	2.1	2.2	2.2	2.2
Labor force time lost[b]	8.3	8.2	8.2	8.2	8.6	7.9	7.9	7.9	8.5	9.1	9.5	10.1	10.0
Occupation													
White-collar workers	3.9	3.8	3.9	4.0	4.0	3.9	4.0	3.9	4.1	4.1	4.2	4.5	4.2
Professional and technical	2.8	2.6	2.7	3.1	2.8	2.8	2.8	2.5	2.8	2.6	2.7	3.4	2.9
Managers and administrators, except farm	2.5	2.5	2.5	2.4	2.6	2.7	2.6	2.7	2.7	2.8	3.0	3.1	2.7

Sales workers	4.3	4.1	4.1	4.2	4.6	4.3	4.9	4.7	5.0	4.9	5.0	4.9	4.5
Clerical workers	5.6	5.4	5.7	5.6	5.6	5.4	5.7	5.7	5.8	6.0	6.0	6.2	6.3
Blue-collar workers	10.2	10.2	10.0	9.7	9.9	9.8	9.5	9.5	10.2	10.9	11.8	12.7	12.5
Craft and kindred workers	6.9	7.1	7.1	6.8	7.2	7.1	6.9	7.0	7.7	8.3	8.5	9.3	9.0
Operatives, except transport	12.2	12.1	11.7	11.6	11.8	11.1	11.1	11.1	11.6	12.8	14.1	15.5	15.4
Transport equipment operatives	9.1	8.6	9.1	8.1	8.2	8.1	7.3	8.0	8.7	8.0	10.4	10.5	10.2
Nonfarm laborers	14.8	14.9	14.2	14.0	13.5	14.7	14.4	13.2	14.6	15.6	16.0	16.9	16.9
Service workers	8.2	8.7	8.3	8.5	9.4	8.9	8.0	8.9	9.0	9.3	9.7	9.6	9.2
Farm workers	5.0	4.9	5.2	3.9	5.2	6.2	4.8	5.4	4.0	6.2	6.2	6.4	6.9
Industry													
Nonagricultural private wage and salary workers[c]	7.6	7.6	7.5	7.3	7.7	7.4	7.2	7.3	7.7	8.1	8.4	9.1	8.8
Construction	13.7	13.7	14.7	14.5	15.7	16.1	15.2	16.2	16.3	17.6	17.8	18.1	18.7
Manufacturing	8.5	8.5	8.1	7.6	7.8	7.4	7.3	7.0	7.9	8.6	9.4	11.0	10.4
Durable goods	8.4	8.7	8.0	7.5	7.4	7.1	7.1	6.5	7.7	8.6	9.5	11.8	11.0
Nondurable goods	8.5	8.3	8.3	7.8	8.6	7.9	7.6	7.9	8.3	8.6	9.3	9.6	9.5
Transportation	5.5	5.4	6.1	5.5	5.7	4.9	4.1	4.8	4.2	4.8	5.5	6.0	6.4
Wholesale and retail trade	7.7	7.7	7.6	7.5	8.3	7.7	7.9	7.9	8.5	8.4	8.6	8.9	8.7
Finance and service industries	5.8	5.9	5.6	5.8	5.8	5.8	5.7	5.7	6.0	6.2	6.1	6.4	5.9
Government workers	4.4	4.3	4.6	4.7	4.7	4.6	4.6	4.5	4.7	4.7	5.2	5.0	4.8
Agricultural wage and salary workers	11.5	11.9	12.1	9.4	11.0	13.3	10.7	12.0	11.0	13.4	14.1	14.8	16.2

[a] Unemployment as a percentage of the civilian labor force.

[b] Aggregate hours lost by the unemployed and persons on part-time for economic reasons as a percentage of potentially available labor force hours.

[c] Includes mining, not shown separately.

Table 18. Employment Status by Race, Sex, and Age, Seasonally Adjusted (numbers in thousands)

Race, Sex, and Age	1981[a]												1982
	January	February	March	April	May	June	July	August	September	October	November	December	January
White													
Total, 16 years and over													
Civilian labor force	94,332	94,552	94,756	95,199	95,666	94,887	95,126	95,163	94,884	95,365	95,535	95,329	95,120
Employed	88,101	88,388	88,653	89,080	89,237	88,799	89,170	89,221	88,628	88,734	88,498	88,010	87,955
Unemployed	6,231	6,164	6,103	6,119	6,429	6,088	5,956	5,942	6,256	6,631	7,037	7,319	7,165
Unemployment rate	6.6	6.5	6.4	6.4	6.7	6.4	6.3	6.2	6.6	7.0	7.4	7.7	7.5
Males, 20 years and over													
Civilian labor force	50,300	50,344	50,505	50,718	50,920	50,633	50,698	50,701	50,712	50,811	50,881	50,948	50,757
Employed	47,547	47,633	47,814	48,070	48,092	47,939	48,157	48,050	47,948	47,790	47,649	47,449	47,410
Unemployed	2,753	2,711	2,691	2,648	2,828	2,694	2,541	2,651	2,764	3,021	3,232	3,499	3,347
Unemployment rate	5.5	5.4	5.3	5.2	5.6	5.3	5.0	5.2	5.5	5.9	6.4	6.9	6.6
Females, 20 years and over													
Civilian labor force	35,852	35,978	36,106	36,274	36,597	36,490	36,612	36,554	36,294	36,742	36,832	36,733	36,698
Employed	33,731	33,939	34,061	34,197	34,422	34,404	34,481	34,534	34,155	34,517	34,513	34,368	34,380
Unemployed	2,121	2,039	2,045	2,077	2,175	2,086	2,131	2,020	2,139	2,225	2,119	2,365	2,119
Unemployment rate	5.9	5.7	5.7	5.7	5.9	5.7	5.8	5.5	5.9	6.1	6.3	6.4	6.3
Both sexes, 16–19 years													
Civilian labor force	8,180	8,230	8,145	8,207	8,149	7,764	7,816	7,908	7,878	7,812	7,822	7,648	7,665
Employed	6,823	6,816	6,778	6,813	6,723	6,456	6,532	6,637	6,525	6,427	6,336	6,193	6,166

Unemployed	1,357	1,414	1,367	1,394	1,426	1,308	1,284	1,271	1,353	1,385	1,486	1,455	1,499
Unemployment rate	16.6	17.2	16.8	17.0	17.5	16.8	16.4	16.1	17.2	17.7	19.0	19.0	19.6
Black and Other													
Total, 16 years and over													
Civilian labor force	13,528	13,476	13,586	13,633	13,649	13,565	13,539	13,632	13,617	13,697	13,757	13,773	13,704
Employed	11,792	11,697	11,742	11,827	11,781	11,643	11,672	11,624	11,607	11,611	11,661	11,610	11,632
Unemployed	1,736	1,779	1,844	1,806	1,868	1,922	1,867	2,008	2,010	2,086	2,096	2,163	2,072
Unemployment rate	12.8	13.2	13.6	13.2	13.7	14.2	13.8	14.7	14.8	15.2	15.2	15.7	15.1
Males, 20 years and over													
Civilian labor force	6,457	6,477	6,517	6,498	6,547	6,479	6,484	6,556	6,551	6,573	6,595	6,614	6,563
Employed	5,786	5,766	5,800	5,796	5,779	5,682	5,722	5,745	5,715	5,711	5,694	5,647	5,630
Unemployed	671	711	717	702	768	797	762	811	836	862	901	967	933
Unemployment rate	10.4	11.0	11.0	10.8	11.7	12.3	11.8	12.4	12.8	13.1	13.7	14.6	14.2
Females, 20 years and over													
Civilian labor force	5,963	5,981	6,032	6,057	6,041	6,081	6,062	6,087	6,085	6,096	6,147	6,163	6,152
Employed	5,300	5,274	5,285	5,337	5,305	5,340	5,321	5,313	5,281	5,301	5,359	5,355	5,388
Unemployed	663	707	747	720	736	741	741	774	804	795	788	808	764
Unemployment rate	11.1	11.8	12.4	11.9	12.2	12.2	12.2	12.7	13.2	13.0	12.8	13.1	12.4
Both sexes, 16–19 years													
Civilian labor force	1,108	1,018	1,037	1,078	1,061	1,005	993	989	981	1,028	1,015	996	989
Employed	706	657	657	694	697	621	629	566	611	599	608	608	614
Unemployed	402	361	380	384	364	384	364	423	370	429	407	388	375
Unemployment rate	36.3	35.5	36.6	35.6	34.3	38.2	36.7	42.8	37.7	41.7	40.1	39.0	37.9

Source: U.S. Department of Labor.

[a] Pre-1982 data in this table have been revised. See article in this issue for additional information.

Table 19. Labor Force Participation and Unemployment Rates by Area of Residence, Sex, Race, and Hispanic Origin, 1980 Annual Averages (%)

Area of Residence	Black			Hispanic Origin			White		
	Total	Men	Women	Total	Men	Women	Total	Men	Women
Central cities									
Participation rate	59.8	69.0	52.5	62.3	80.9	46.2	63.5	77.2	51.6
Unemployment rate	15.3	16.1	14.5	10.4	10.5	10.3	6.6	6.8	6.3
Suburbs									
Participation rate	67.2	76.2	59.6	67.3	83.1	51.9	66.2	80.6	52.9
Unemployment rate	11.8	11.8	11.8	9.6	9.0	10.6	5.8	5.6	6.1
Nonmetropolitan areas									
Participation rate	57.6	68.2	48.8	62.7	81.3	44.6	62.1	76.3	49.0
Unemployment rate	13.7	12.6	15.0	10.1	8.8	12.4	6.7	6.4	7.2

Source: U.S. Department of Commerce.

Table 20. Major Unemployment Indicators: Annual Averages for 1960 and 1970–1980 (civilian noninstitutional population)

Selected Categories	1960	1970	1971	1972	1973	1974	1975	1976	1977	1978	1979	1980
Total	5.5	4.9	5.9	5.6	4.9	5.6	8.5	7.7	7.0	6.0	5.8	7.1
Males, 20 years and over	4.7	3.5	4.4	4.0	3.2	3.8	6.7	5.9	5.2	4.2	4.1	5.9
Females, 20 years and over	5.1	4.8	5.7	5.4	4.8	5.5	8.0	7.4	7.0	6.0	5.7	6.3
Both sexes, 16–19 years	14.7	15.2	16.9	16.2	14.5	16.0	19.9	19.0	17.7	16.3	16.1	17.7
White	4.9	4.5	5.4	5.0	4.3	5.0	7.8	7.0	6.2	5.2	5.1	6.3
Black and other races	10.2	8.2	9.9	10.0	8.9	9.9	13.9	13.1	13.1	11.9	11.3	13.2
Householders		2.9	3.7	3.3	2.9	3.3	5.8	5.1	4.5	3.7	3.6	4.9
Married men, wife present	3.7	2.6	3.2	2.8	2.3	2.7	5.1	4.2	3.6	2.8	2.7	4.2
Married women, husband present		4.9	5.7	5.4	4.6	5.3	7.9	7.1	6.5	5.5	5.1	5.8
Female family householder, No husband present		5.4	7.3	7.2	7.0	7.0	10.0	10.0	9.3	8.5	8.3	9.1

Source: U.S. Department of Commerce, Bureau of the Census.

Table 21. Major Unemployment Indicators, Seasonally Adjusted

Category	Number of Unemployed Persons (in thousands)		Unemployment Rates					
	May 1981	May 1982	May 1981	January 1982	February 1982	March 1982	April 1982	May 1982
Characteristic								
Total, 16 years and over	8,248	10,549	7.5	8.5	8.8	9.0	9.4	9.5
Men, 20 years and over	3,595	4,904	6.3	7.5	7.6	7.9	8.2	8.4
Women, 20 years and over	2,871	3,608	6.7	7.2	7.6	7.9	8.3	8.3
Both sexes, 16–19 years	1,782	2,037	19.4	21.7	22.3	21.9	23.0	23.1
Married men, spouse present	1,632	2,467	4.0	5.3	5.3	5.5	6.0	6.1
Married women, spouse present	1,491	1,947	5.8	6.2	7.0	7.1	7.8	7.4
Women who maintain families	578	669	10.4	10.4	10.2	10.6	11.5	11.8
Full-time workers	6,631	8,717	7.1	8.4	8.5	8.9	9.2	9.2
Part-time workers	1,518	1,674	9.6	9.6	10.8	10.0	10.9	10.5
Labor force time lost[a]	—	—	8.6	10.0	9.8	10.4	10.4	11.1
Occupation[b]								
White-collar workers	2,219	2,722	4.0	4.2	4.6	4.8	4.9	4.8
Professional and technical	463	582	2.8	2.9	3.1	3.2	3.2	3.3
Managers and administrators, except farm	309	417	2.6	2.7	3.1	3.0	3.3	3.5
Sales workers	319	360	4.6	4.5	4.8	5.8	5.6	5.2
Clerical workers	1,128	1,363	5.6	6.3	6.7	6.9	7.2	6.8
Blue-collar workers	3,484	4,663	9.9	12.5	12.5	12.9	13.7	13.5
Craft and kindred workers	1,008	1,273	7.2	9.0	8.4	9.1	9.6	9.4
Operatives, except transport	1,434	1,899	11.8	15.4	15.4	15.9	16.9	16.5
Transport equipment operatives	308	456	8.2	10.2	10.3	10.4	10.7	11.8
Nonfarm laborers	734	1,035	13.5	16.9	17.9	17.9	19.2	18.3
Service workers	1,402	1,755	9.4	9.2	9.8	10.2	11.1	11.3
Farm workers	152	246	5.2	6.9	4.9	5.4	5.8	8.3
Industry[b]								
Nonagricultural private wage and salary workers[c]	6,198	8,135	7.7	8.8	9.0	9.5	9.9	9.9
Construction	823	990	15.7	18.7	18.1	17.9	19.4	18.8
Manufacturing	1,856	2,631	7.8	10.4	10.6	10.8	11.3	11.6
Durable goods	1,047	1,651	7.4	11.0	11.3	10.8	11.9	12.2
Nondurable goods	809	980	8.6	9.5	9.5	10.8	10.5	10.7
Transportation and public utilities	332	381	5.7	6.4	5.9	5.6	7.0	6.5
Wholesale and retail trade	1,669	2,206	8.3	8.7	9.0	10.3	10.1	10.6
Finance and service industries	1,445	1,782	5.8	5.9	6.5	6.9	7.0	6.9
Government workers	780	807	4.7	4.8	5.2	4.9	5.3	5.0
Agricultural wage and salary workers	185	343	11.0	16.2	12.8	14.0	14.6	18.2

[a] Aggregate hours lost by the unemployed and persons on part time for economic reasons as a percentage of potentially available labor force hours.

[b] Unemployment by occupation includes all experienced unemployed persons, whereas that by industry covers only unemployed wage and salary workers.

[c] Includes mining, not shown separately.

Table 22. Minority Race Unemployment, Selected States: 1977–1979[a]

State	Unemployed (thousands) 1977	1978	1979	Rate[b] 1977	1978	1979
U.S.	1,482	1,427	1,386	13.1	11.9	11.3
Alabama	49	43	48	14.5	12.4	13.0
Alaska	5	6	4	15.3	17.8	13.7
Arizona	4	8	5	8.1	13.2	8.2
Arkansas	21	19	23	14.3	12.3	17.3
California	160	152	125	13.2	11.6	9.4
Colorado	6	5	7	12.6	11.5	10.5
Connecticut	11	11	15	10.8	11.2	14.3
D.C.	30	25	20	12.2	10.3	9.3
Delaware	7	5	5	16.5	14.4	14.9
Florida	83	80	74	13.0	11.4	10.9
Georgia	61	47	49	12.2	10.2	11.1
Hawaii	21	22	15	6.7	7.2	5.3
Illinois	92	100	80	14.8	14.8	11.4
Indiana	30	28	31	16.9	14.8	15.2
Kansas	7	7	4	12.3	10.4	7.0
Kentucky	10	10	10	10.0	10.7	9.6
Louisiana	46	53	55	12.6	13.4	12.8
Maryland	41	52	55	11.1	12.3	12.3
Massachusetts	9	10	10	13.1	9.8	7.0
Michigan	70	72	88	15.9	14.4	16.3
Mississippi	45	46	32	13.8	14.0	10.5
Missouri	29	38	32	13.5	13.2	13.4
Montana	1	2	2	8.9	12.9	14.7
New Jersey	60	49	52	16.3	12.4	12.2
New Mexico	5	4	6	11.8	8.4	13.4
New York	122	117	134	12.2	11.0	11.6
North Carolina	57	50	50	10.7	9.0	8.9
Ohio	57	66	66	13.6	14.8	13.6
Oklahoma	15	15	8	14.2	12.8	8.6
Pennsylvania	72	69	71	19.4	17.5	16.2
South Carolina	34	27	23	11.3	8.5	6.9
Tennessee	36	33	38	12.7	11.5	12.8
Texas	68	69	59	9.8	9.5	8.5
Virginia	45	45	47	11.2	10.3	11.1
Washington	13	12	10	18.6	13.5	10.0
Wisconsin	14	12	7	22.2	16.4	9.4

Source: U.S. Bureau of the Census, *Statistical Abstract of the United States, 1980*, 101st ed.

[a] Persons 16 years old and over. United States totals derived by independent population controls; therefore state data may not add to U.S. totals. Minority refers to all races other than White. Data are annual averages based on information collected as part of the Current Population Survey.
[b] Unemployed as percent of civilian labor force.

Table 23. Labor Force Status of the Noninstitutional Population by Age, Sex, Race, and Hispanic Origin Using 1970 and 1980 Census Population Estimates, 1981 Annual Averages (numbers in thousands)

| | Black and Other | | | | | | | | |
| | Total | | | Males | | | Females | | |
Labor Force Status and Age	1970 Base	1980 Base	Net Differ-ence	1970 Base	1980 Base	Net Differ-ence	1970 Base	1980 Base	Net Differ-ence
Civilian Noninstitutional Population									
Total, 16 years and over	21,057	22,222	1,165	9,458	10,032	574	11,599	12,190	591
16–19 years	2,558	2,697	139	1,245	1,328	83	1,313	1,369	56
20–24 years	2,945	3,211	266	1,318	1,471	153	1,627	1,740	113
25–34 years	4,961	5,410	449	2,192	2,422	230	2,768	2,988	220
35–44 years	3,289	3,513	224	1,439	1,587	148	1,850	1,926	76
45–54 years	2,751	2,756	5	1,261	1,237	−24	1,490	1,519	29
55–64 years	2,172	2,271	99	991	1,012	21	1,181	1,259	78
65 years and over	2,382	2,363	−19	1,012	974	−38	1,370	1,388	18
Civilian Labor Force									
Total, 16 years and over	12,807	13,618	811	6,606	7,079	473	6,201	6,539	338
16–19 years	967	1,025	58	515	553	38	453	472	19
20–24 years	1,994	2,173	179	1,016	1,127	111	978	1,045	67
25–34 years	3,835	4,183	348	1,938	2,139	201	1,898	2,045	147
35–44 years	2,579	2,766	187	1,289	1,425	136	1,289	1,341	52
45–54 years	1,978	1,977	−1	1,052	1,032	−20	926	944	18
55–64 years	1,157	1,205	48	626	640	14	530	565	35
65 years and over	297	289	−8	170	162	−8	127	127	0
Employed									
Total, 16 years and over	10,973	11,688	715	5,664	6,083	419	5,309	5,606	297
16–19 years	595	637	42	318	346	28	278	291	13
20–24 years	1,502	1,645	143	763	853	90	739	793	54
25–34 years	3,318	3,630	312	1,687	1,868	181	1,632	1,761	129
35–44 years	2,348	2,528	180	1,177	1,307	130	1,171	1,221	50
45–54 years	1,839	1,840	1	976	959	−17	864	881	17
55–64 years	1,094	1,139	45	588	600	12	506	539	33
65 years and over	276	269	−7	156	149	−7	120	120	0
Agriculture									
Total, 16 years and over	239	259	20	203	219	16	36	40	4
16–19 years	19	21	2	16	18	2	3	3	0
20–24 years	24	27	3	20	23	3	4	4	0

Table 23 (*continued*)

Labor Force Status and Age	Black and Other								
	Total			Males			Females		
	1970 Base	1980 Base	Net Differ-ence	1970 Base	1980 Base	Net Differ-ence	1970 Base	1980 Base	Net Differ-ence
25–34 years	43	50	7	36	42	6	7	8	1
35–44 years	43	47	4	35	39	4	8	8	0
45–54 years	43	44	1	35	35	0	8	8	0
55–64 years	39	43	4	35	38	3	4	5	1
65 years and over	28	27	−1	25	24	−1	3	3	0
Nonagricultural Industries									
Total, 16 years and over	10,735	11,429	694	5,461	5,864	403	5,273	5,566	293
16–19 years	576	616	40	302	328	26	275	288	13
20–24 years	1,478	1,619	141	742	830	88	735	789	54
25–34 years	3,276	3,580	304	1,651	1,827	176	1,625	1,753	128
35–44 years	2,306	2,481	175	1,142	1,267	125	1,164	1,213	49
45–54 years	1,796	1,796	0	941	924	−17	856	872	16
55–64 years	1,055	1,096	41	553	562	9	502	534	32
65 years and over	248	242	−6	131	125	−6	117	117	0
Unemployed									
Total, 16 years and over	1,833	1,930	97	942	997	55	892	933	41
16–19 years	372	388	16	197	208	11	175	181	6
20–24 years	493	527	34	253	274	21	239	253	14
25–34 years	517	554	37	251	270	19	266	284	18
35–44 years	230	238	8	112	119	7	118	119	1
45–54 years	138	137	−1	76	73	−3	62	64	2
55–64 years	63	66	3	38	40	2	24	26	2
65 years and over	21	20	−1	14	13	−1	7	7	0
Unemployment Rate									
Total, 16 years and over	14.3	14.2	−0.1	14.3	14.1	−0.2	14.4	14.3	−0.1
16–19 years	38.4	37.8	−0.6	38.3	37.5	−0.8	38.6	38.3	−0.3
20–24 years	24.7	24.3	−0.4	24.9	24.4	−0.5	24.5	24.2	−0.3
25–34 years	13.5	13.2	−0.3	13.0	12.6	−0.4	14.0	13.9	−0.1
35–44 years	8.9	8.6	−0.3	8.7	8.3	−0.4	9.1	8.9	−0.2
45–54 years	7.0	6.9	−0.1	7.2	7.1	−0.1	6.7	6.7	0
55–64 years	5.4	5.5	0.1	6.1	6.2	0.1	4.5	4.6	0.1
65 years and over	7.1	7.0	−0.1	8.1	8.0	−0.1	5.8	5.7	−0.1

Table 24. Labor Force Status of the Noninstitutional Population by Age, Sex, Race, and Hispanic Origin Using 1970 and 1980 Census Population Estimates, 1981 Annual Averages (numbers in thousands)

Labor Force Status and Age	Black								
	Total			Males			Females		
	1970 Base	1980 Base	Net Difference	1970 Base	1980 Base	Net Difference	1970 Base	1980 Base	Net Difference
Civilian Noninstitutional Population									
Total, 16 years and over	17,808	18,219	411	7,977	8,117	140	9,831	10,102	271
16–19 years	2,227	2,288	61	1,078	1,110	32	1,149	1,178	29
20–24 years	2,499	2,642	143	1,108	1,189	81	1,391	1,453	62
25–34 years	4,073	4,290	217	1,800	1,914	114	2,272	2,376	104
35–44 years	2,755	2,758	3	1,213	1,223	10	1,542	1,534	−8
45–54 years	2,308	2,260	−48	1,068	1,003	−65	1,240	1,257	17
55–64 years	1,887	1,913	26	860	844	−16	1,028	1,069	41
65 years and over	2,060	2,069	9	851	834	−17	1,209	1,234	25
Civilian Labor Force									
Total, 16 years and over	10,810	11,086	276	5,559	5,684	125	5,251	5,401	150
16–19 years	834	862	28	444	462	18	389	400	11
20–24 years	1,724	1,828	104	876	941	65	847	888	41
25–34 years	3,189	3,365	176	1,601	1,702	101	1,588	1,663	75
35–44 years	2,158	2,164	6	1,083	1,093	10	1,075	1,071	−4
45–54 years	1,651	1,608	−43	882	829	−53	769	779	10
55–64 years	1,000	1,009	9	535	524	−11	465	485	20
65 years and over	254	249	−5	138	134	−4	117	115	−2
Employed									
Total, 16 years and over	9,134	9,355	221	4,697	4,794	97	4,437	4,561	124
16–19 years	487	505	18	263	274	11	225	232	7
20–24 years	1,266	1,346	80	643	693	50	623	653	30
25–34 years	2,720	2,872	152	1,368	1,457	89	1,351	1,415	64
35–44 years	1,951	1,957	6	982	991	9	969	966	−3
45–54 years	1,528	1,489	−39	812	764	−48	716	725	9
55–64 years	945	954	9	502	492	−10	444	462	18
65 years and over	237	231	−6	127	123	−4	110	108	−2
Agriculture									
Total, 16 years and over	177	184	7	156	162	6	21	22	1
16–19 years	16	17	1	13	14	1	3	3	0
20–24 years	18	20	2	16	17	1	2	3	1

Table 24 (*continued*)

Labor Force Status and Age	Black								
	Total			Males			Females		
	1970 Base	1980 Base	Net Difference	1970 Base	1980 Base	Net Difference	1970 Base	1980 Base	Net Difference
25–34 years	29	32	3	25	28	3	3	4	1
35–44 years	36	38	2	31	32	1	6	6	0
45–54 years	34	33	−1	30	30	0	3	3	0
55–64 years	25	26	1	23	24	1	2	2	0
65 years and over	19	19	0	18	17	−1	2	2	0
Nonagricultural Industries									
Total, 16 years and over	8,957	9,171	214	4,541	4,632	91	4,416	4,539	123
16–19 years	472	489	17	250	260	10	222	229	7
20–24 years	1,248	1,326	78	628	675	47	621	650	29
25–34 years	2,691	2,840	149	1,343	1,429	86	1,348	1,411	63
35–44 years	1,914	1,919	5	951	959	8	963	960	−3
45–54 years	1,494	1,456	−38	782	735	−47	712	722	10
55–64 years	920	928	8	478	468	−10	442	460	18
65 years and over	217	212	−5	109	106	−3	108	106	−2
Unemployed									
Total, 16 years and over	1,676	1,731	55	861	891	30	814	840	26
16–19 years	346	357	11	182	188	6	165	169	4
20–24 years	457	483	26	233	248	15	225	235	10
25–34 years	469	493	24	232	245	13	237	248	11
35–44 years	208	207	−1	101	101	0	106	105	−1
45–54 years	123	119	−4	70	65	−5	54	54	0
55–64 years	55	55	0	33	33	0	22	23	1
65 years and over	18	17	−1	11	11	0	7	7	0
Unemployment Rate									
Total, 16 years and over	15.5	15.6	0.1	15.5	15.7	−0.2	15.5	15.6	0.1
16–19 years	41.5	41.4	−.1	40.9	40.7	−.2	42.3	42.2	−.1
20–24 years	26.5	26.4	−.1	26.6	26.4	−.2	26.5	26.4	−.1
25–34 years	14.7	14.7	0	14.5	14.4	−.1	14.9	14.9	0
35–44 years	9.6	9.5	−.1	9.4	9.3	−.1	9.9	9.8	−.1
45–54 years	7.5	7.4	−.1	7.9	7.8	−.1	7.0	6.9	−.1
55–64 years	5.5	5.5	0	6.2	6.2	0	4.7	4.7	0
65 years and over	7.0	7.0	0	7.9	7.9	0	6.0	6.0	0

Table 25. Characteristics of Workers and Industries Most Affected by Trade-Related Employment Changes between 1964 and 1975

Item	Average of the 20 Most Favorably Affected Industries	Overall Manufacturing Average	Average of the 20 Most Adversely Affected Industries
Demographic Characteristics of the Labor Force (%)[a]			
Women	21.5	29.4	41.1
Minorities	7.4	10.1	11.5
Under age 25	15.4	16.4	15.8
Over age 50	24.4	26.5	28.0
Family income below poverty level	5.8	7.0	9.8
Annual earnings under $10,000	72.1	77.4	81.7
Annual earnings under $12,000	83.5	87.2	89.7
High school education (4 years)	39.1	36.6	34.0
College education (4 years)	6.9	5.1	3.1
Occupational Measures			
Unionized workers as a percentage of the labor force[b]	40.0	49.0	51.3
Skill measured as a percentage of the average wage in manufacturing (1973)	104.0	100.0	97.8
Skilled workers as a percentage of the labor force[c]	55.8	50.0	38.8
White-collar workers as a percentage of the labor force[c]	36.3	30.3	21.1
Industry Characteristics			
Technical intensity (scientists and engineers as a percentage of the labor force[a]	6.87	3.20	2.29
Technical intensity (research and development as a percentage of sales)[e]	5.90	2.36	1.39
Foreign direct investment proxy (foreign dividends plus tax credits as a percentage of firm's assets)[d]	.53	.34 (median)	.52

[a] From *Census of Population, 1970, Subject Reports: Industrial Characteristics* (Department of Commerce, 1972).

[b] From Richard Freeman and James Medoff, "New Estimates of Private Sector Unionism in the United States," *Industrial and Labor Relations Review,* January 1979, pp. 143–174.

[c] From *Census of Population, 1970, Subject Reports: Occupations by Industry* (Department of Commerce, 1973).

[d] From C. Fred Bergsten, Tom Horst and Ted Moran, *American Multinationals and American Interests* (Washington, Brookings Institution, 1978), Table 3–2.

[e] From Regina Kelly, "The Impact of Technological Innovation on International Trade Patterns," Staff Economist Report, ER-24 (Department of Commerce, December 1977).

Table 26. Persons Holding Two Jobs or More and Multiple Jobholding Rates, by Sex and Race: 1962–1978
(numbers in thousands)

| Year | All Multiple Job-holders | At Least One Job in Agriculture | Two Jobs in Nonagricultural Industries | | | Multiple Jobholding Rate[a] | | | | |
			Total	Two Wage and Salary Jobs	Wage and Salary Job and Self-Employment	Both Sexes	Men	Women	White	Black and Other Races[b]
1962	3,342	868	2,474	1,749	725	4.9	6.4	2.0	4.9	4.6
1963	3,921	1,071	2,850	2,073	777	5.7	7.4	2.4	5.7	5.2
1964	3,726	1,069	2,657	1,928	729	5.2	6.9	2.1	5.3	4.7
1965	3,756	1,065	2,691	1,914	777	5.2	6.7	2.3	5.3	4.0
1966	3,636	936	2,700	1,934	766	4.9	6.4	2.2	5.0	4.3
1969	4,008	939	3,069	2,326	743	5.2	6.9	2.3	5.3	4.5
1970	4,048	943	3,105	2,356	749	5.2	7.0	2.2	5.3	4.4
1971	4,035	851	3,184	2,288	896	5.1	6.7	2.6	5.3	3.8
1972	3,770	831	2,939	2,066	873	4.6	6.0	2.4	4.8	3.7
1973	4,262	987	3,275	2,410	865	5.1	6.6	2.7	5.1	4.7
1974	3,889	848	3,041	2,169	872	4.5	5.8	2.6	4.6	3.8
1975	3,918	890	3,028	2,131	897	4.7	5.8	2.9	4.8	3.7
1976	3,948	819	3,129	2,191	938	4.5	5.8	2.6	4.7	2.8
1977	4,558	922	3,637	2,515	1,122	5.0	6.2	3.4	5.3	2.6
1978	4,493	905	3,587	2,513	1,074	4.8	5.8	3.3	5.0	3.1

[a] Multiple jobholders as a percent of all employed persons.

[b] Starting with 1977, data are for black workers only. Data for prior years are for persons of black and other races except white, about 90 percent of whom are black. The multiple jobholding rate in May 1977 for persons of black and other races was 2.7 percent, not significantly different from the rate for blacks.

Note: Surveys were not conducted in 1967 or 1968.

Table 27. Employed Persons by Detailed Occupation, Sex, and Race: 1981 (numbers in thousands)

Occupation	Total Employed	Percentage of Total Females	Black and Other	Blacks
Total, 16 years and over	98,313	42.9	11.2	
White-collar workers	51,848	53.6	8.6	6.7
Professional and technical	16,055	44.7	9.2	6.6
Accountants	1,096	38.5	9.0	8.3
Architects	91	4.4	8.8	3.3
Computer specialists	613	26.9	8.6	5.7
Computer programmers	357	29.4	9.2	6.7
Computer systems analysts	209	25.8	7.2	5.3
Engineers	1,497	4.3	6.0	2.6
Aeronautical and astronautical engineers	82	1.2	4.9	1.2
Civil engineers	183	1.6	6.0	1.6
Electrical and electronic engineers	370	3.8	6.5	2.7
Industrial engineers	231	11.3	6.5	3.7
Mechanical engineers	247	2.8	4.9	1.6
Foresters and conservationists	57	12.3	3.5	1.8
Lawyers and judges	570	14.0	4.4	3.7
Lawyers	548	14.1	4.4	3.6
Librarians, archivists, and curators	190	83.2	5.3	3.2
Librarians	176	85.8	5.7	3.4
Life and physical scientists	303	21.8	9.6	5.3
Biological scientists	57	40.4	12.3	7.0
Chemists	134	21.6	14.2	7.5
Operations and systems researchers and analysts	196	26.0	6.6	4.6
Personnel and labor relations workers	432	49.8	10.6	4.5
Physicians, dentists, and related practitioners	801	14.2	9.2	2.4
Dentists	127	4.7	5.5	2.4
Pharmacists	147	25.2	7.5	2.0
Physicians, medical and osteopathic	436	13.8	12.2	2.5
Nurses, dietitians, and therapists	1,620	92.7	12.1	9.1
Registered nurses	1,313	96.8	11.7	8.5
Therapists	244	70.5	11.5	9.4
Health technologists and technicians	626	72.5	13.9	10.2
Clinical laboratory technologists and technicians	268	77.2	17.5	10.8
Radiologic technologists and technicians	102	67.6	10.0	10.7
Religious workers	331	11.8	7.6	5.7
Clergy	277	5.1	7.6	6.5
Social scientists	307	33.9	7.2	2.3
Economists	157	24.8	5.7	6.4
Psychologists	115	48.7	8.7	8.7
Social and recreation workers	501	62.7	19.6	18.7
Social workers	383	64.0	20.4	19.6
Recreation workers	119	58.0	16.8	16.0
Teachers, college and university	573	35.3	8.4	5.4
Teachers, except college and university	3,144	70.6	9.8	0.9
Adult education teachers	75	42.7	8.0	8.0
Elementary school teachers	1,389	83.6	11.2	10.3
Prekindergarten and kindergarten teachers	239	98.3	15.5	14.6
Secondary school teachers	1,213	51.3	7.8	7.0
Teachers except college and university, n.e.c.	229	73.8	7.0	5.2
Engineering and science technicians	1,108	18.8	9.0	6.5
Chemical technicians	101	25.7	15.8	14.9
Drafters	332	19.3	7.5	4.2
Electrical and electronic engineering technicians	267	11.2	8.2	5.2
Surveyors	88	1.1	4.5	3.4

634

Table 27 (*continued*)

Occupation	Total Employed	Percentage of Total		
		Females	Black and Other	Blacks
Technicians, except health, engineering, and science	214	22.0	4.7	3.7
Airplane pilots	80	1.3	1.3	.1
Radio operators	61	57.4	4.9	4.9
Vocational and educational counselors	186	53.2	17.2	16.1
Writers, artists, and entertainers	1,358	40.1	5.9	9.1
Athletes and kindred workers	131	44.3	6.9	6.1
Designers	213	29.6	5.6	2.3
Editors and reporters	202	50.5	5.0	4.4
Musicians and composers	142	23.4	5.6	4.9
Painters and sculptors	207	51.2	5.3	2.4
Photographers	99	23.2	7.1	5.0
Public relations specialists and publicity writers	121	45.5	5.0	3.3
Research workers, not specified	188	39.4	10.1	5.3
Managers and administrators, except farm	11,315	27.4	5.4	4.0
Bank officials and financial managers	680	37.4	5.0	3.7
Buyers and purchasing agents				
Buyers, wholesale and retail trade	191	43.5	6.3	4.7
Credit and collection managers				
Health administrators	216	49.5	6.5	5.6
Inspectors, except construction and public administration	108	10.2	8.3	6.5
Managers and superintendents, building	158	50.6	9.5	8.2
Office managers, n.e.c.	494	70.4	3.6	2.6
Officials and administrators; public administration n.e.c.	469	29.0	9.8	8.3
Officials of lodges, societies, and unions	116	28.4	5.2	4.3
Restaurant, cafeteria, and bar managers	707	40.5	9.1	6.1
Sales managers and department heads, retail trade	337	40.4	5.9	4.7
Sales managers, except retail trade	367	13.6	2.5	1.6
School administrators, college	137	35.0	8.0	7.3
School administrators, elementary and secondary	289	36.7	10.0	9.3
All other managers and administrators	6,703	19.6	4.6	3.1
Sales workers	6,291	45.4	5.1	3.8
Advertising agents and sales workers	126	47.6	3.2	3.1
Demonstrators	105	95.2	3.8	2.9
Hucksters and peddlers	167	79.0	7.2	6.0
Insurance agents, brokers, and underwriters	584	23.6	6.0	5.0
Newspaper carriers and vendors	111	29.7	4.5	4.4
Real estate agents and brokers	546	50.0	2.7	1.6
Stock and bond sales agents	156	16.7	2.6	1.3
Sales workers and sales clerks, n.e.c.	4,491	46.6	5.4	3.3
Sales representatives, manufacturing industries	410	20.0	3.7	2.9
Sales representatives, wholesale trade	951	11.9	2.6	1.8
Sales clerks, retail trade	2,380	71.3	7.3	5.8
Sales workers, except clerks, retail trade	514	19.6	3.3	2.3
Sales workers, services and construction	237	43.0	5.1	4.2
Clerical workers	18,187	80.5	11.2	9.3
Bank tellers	558	93.7	7.2	6.1
Billing clerks	151	88.1	9.9	8.6
Bookkeepers	1,922	91.2	5.9	4.2
Cashiers	1,621	86.4	11.3	9.6
Clerical supervisors, n.e.c.	246	70.3	10.6	8.9
Collectors, bill and account	90	64.4	10.0	8.9
Counter clerks, except food	352	76.4	9.9	8.2
Dispatchers and starters, vehicle	113	38.1	8.8	8.0
Enumerators and interviewers	57	75.4	15.8	14.0

Table 27 (*continued*)

Occupation	Total Employed	Percentage of Total		
		Females	Black and Other	Blacks
Estimators and investigators, n.e.c.	529	54.4	10.2	9.1
Expediters and production controllers	249	41.0	8.0	6.9
File clerks	307	83.7	21.8	19.5
Insurance adjusters, examiners, and investigators	186	58.1	9.1	8.1
Library attendants and assistants	149	82.6	13.4	10.7
Mail carriers, post office	239	15.5	13.4	12.1
Mail handlers, except post office	172	47.1	19.8	18.6
Messengers and office helpers	94	26.6	19.1	16.0
Office machine operators	945	73.7	17.0	14.6
Bookkeeping and billing machine operators	47	89.4	12.8	12.7
Computer and peripheral equipment operators	551	63.9	15.2	13.2
Keypunch operators	243	93.8	18.9	16.5
Payroll and timekeeping clerks	226	81.0	8.8	7.1
Postal clerks	263	38.0	25.9	23.6
Receptionists	660	97.4	8.3	6.8
Secretaries	3,847	99.1	6.9	5.7
Secretaries, legal	179	98.9	5.6	3.9
Secretaries, medical	81	100.0	6.2	4.9
Secretaries, n.e.c.	3,587	99.1	7.0	5.8
Shipping and receiving clerks	515	22.5	14.4	13.0
Statistical clerks	361	80.3	14.7	12.2
Stenographers	72	86.1	12.5	8.3
Stock clerks and storekeepers	517	35.0	12.8	10.8
Teachers' aides, except school monitors	373	93.0	18.5	16.4
Telephone operators	301	93.0	16.9	16.3
Ticket, station, and express agents	144	47.2	9.0	6.2
Typists	1,011	96.3	17.2	14.8
Blue-collar workers	30,593	18.6	12.6	10.9
Craft and kindred workers	12,397	6.3	8.1	6.8
Carpenters	1,091	1.8	5.4	4.0
Brickmasons and stonemasons	150	—	11.3	11.2
Cement and concrete finishers	63	—	—	31.7
Electricians	667	1.6	7.5	6.0
Excavating, grading, and road machinery operators	413	.5	11.9	7.6
Painters, construction and maintenance	461	5.6	9.5	8.9
Plumbers and pipefitters	462	.4	7.6	6.5
Structural metal craft workers	80	—	3.8	3.7
Roofers and slaters	135	—	13.3	12.6
Machinists and job setters	657	4.1	7.9	6.1
Job and die setters, metal	93	5.4	8.6	6.5
Machinists	564	3.9	7.8	6.0
Metal craft workers, excluding mechanics, machinists, and job setters	620	4.4	6.8	2.6
Millwrights	102	—	2.9	2.9
Molders, metal	52	17.3	19.2	17.3
Sheet-metal workers and tinsmiths	153	3.3	5.2	3.3
Tool and die makers	176	2.3	2.8	2.3
Mechanics, automobiles	1,217	.7	8.3	7.1
Automobile body repairers	199	1.0	7.5	5.5
Automobile mechanics	1,017	.6	8.5	7.4
Mechanics, except automobiles	2,110	2.6	7.7	6.5
Air-conditioning, heating, and refrigeration mechanics	207	.5	7.2	6.8
Aircraft mechanics	119	3.4	12.6	8.4

Table 27 (*continued*)

Occupation	Total Employed	Percentage of Total		
		Females	Black and Other	Blacks
Data processing machine repairers	97	7.2	7.2	5.2
Farm implement mechanics	46	—	8.7	6.5
Heavy equipment mechanics, including diesel	986	1.8	7.0	6.0
Household appliance and accessory installers and mechanics	130	4.6	8.5	7.7
Office machine repairers	73	4.1	8.2	6.8
Radio and television repairers	107	3.7	5.6	4.5
Railroad and car shop mechanics	59	1.7	10.2	10.2
Printing craft workers	396	25.0	7.8	6.6
Compositors and typesetters	171	35.1	7.6	5.8
Printing press operators	164	11.6	7.9	7.3
Bakers	132	41.7	12.9	11.4
Cabinetmakers	73	2.7	4.1	2.1
Carpet installers	83	—	4.8	3.6
Crane, derrick, and hoist operators	141	.7	15.6	14.9
Decorators and window dressers	123	72.4	7.3	4.9
Electric power line and cable installers and repairers	115	.9	7.8	7.8
Inspectors, n.e.c.	141	8.5	8.5	7.8
Locomotive engineers	46	2.2	2.2	2.2
Stationary engineers	178	1.7	8.4	7.3
Tailors	21	42.9	19.0	4.7
Telephone installers and repairers	318	9.7	8.5	7.5
Telephone line installers and repairers	77	5.2	5.2	3.9
Upholsterers	70	21.4	11.4	10.0
Operatives, except transport	10,316	39.8	15.5	13.2
Assemblers	1,145	52.3	16.4	13.6
Bottling and canning operatives	52	42.3	19.2	17.3
Checkers, examiners, and inspectors; manufacturing	786	53.7	13.0	10.9
Clothing ironers and pressers	115	80.9	38.3	34.8
Cutting operatives, n.e.c.	271	31.4	15.5	14.4
Dressmakers, except factory	114	97.4	14.0	9.6
Drillers, earth	59	—	3.4	1.6
Dry wall installers and lathers	79	—	5.1	2.5
Filers, polishers, sanders, and buffers	113	31.9	16.8	15.9
Furnace tenders, smelters, and pourers; metal	62	3.2	16.1	16.1
Garage workers and gas station attendants	340	5.6	10.3	9.1
Laundry and dry cleaning operatives, n.e.c.	189	66.1	27.5	19.6
Meat cutters and butchers, except manufacturing	173	8.1	9.8	7.5
Meat cutters and butchers, manufacturing	96	29.2	17.7	7.1
Mine operatives, n.e.c.	260	2.3	5.0	4.6
Mixing operatives	77	3.9	15.6	15.6
Packers and wrappers, excluding meat and produce	579	63.4	20.4	18.3
Painters, manufactured articles	162	16.7	13.0	11.7
Photographic process workers	85	50.6	9.4	7.1
Precision machine operatives	348	12.9	9.2	8.3
Drill press operatives	56	25.0	14.3	12.5
Grinding machine operatives	134	10.4	7.9	9.0
Lathe and milling machine operatives	101	5.9	1.9	2.9
Punch and stamping press operatives	106	32.1	10.4	9.4
Sawyers	121	9.9	15.7	14.9
Sewers and stitchers	780	96.0	20.4	14.9

Note: N.E.C. is an abbreviation for "not elsewhere classified" and designates broad categories of occupations which cannot be more specifically identified.

Table 28.   Civilian Labor Force Participation Rates[a] for Persons 16 Years and Over, by Sex, Race, and Age: Annual Averages, 1950–1981

Item	Total, 16 Years and Over	16 and 17 Years	18 and 19 Years	20 to 24 Years	25 to 34 Years	35 to 44 Years	45 to 54 Years	55 to 64 Years	65 Years and Over	14 and 15 Years
Black and Other										
Male										
1954	85.2	46.7	78.4	91.1	96.2	96.6	93.2	83.0	41.2	27.2
1955	85.0	48.2	75.7	89.7	95.8	96.2	94.2	83.1	40.0	27.1
1956	85.1	49.6	76.4	88.9	96.2	96.2	94.4	83.9	39.8	25.5
1957	84.3	47.5	72.0	89.6	96.1	96.5	93.5	82.4	35.9	24.7
1958	84.0	45.1	71.7	88.7	96.3	96.4	93.9	83.3	34.5	21.3
1959	83.4	41.7	72.0	90.8	96.3	95.8	92.8	82.5	33.5	23.9
1960	83.0	45.6	71.2	90.4	96.2	95.5	92.3	82.5	31.2	23.3
1961	82.2	42.5	70.5	89.7	95.9	94.8	92.3	81.6	29.4	19.2
1962	80.8	40.2	68.8	89.3	95.3	94.5	92.2	81.5	27.2	16.5
1963	80.2	37.2	69.1	88.6	94.9	94.9	91.1	82.5	27.6	17.2
1964	80.0	37.3	67.2	89.4	95.9	94.4	91.6	80.6	29.6	18.7
1965	79.6	39.3	66.7	89.8	95.7	94.2	92.0	78.8	27.9	18.9
1966	79.0	41.1	63.7	89.9	95.5	91.1	90.7	81.1	25.6	17.3
1967	78.5	41.2	62.7	87.2	95.5	93.6	91.3	79.3	27.2	18.3
1968	77.6	37.9	63.3	85.0	95.0	93.4	90.1	79.6	26.6	18.1
1969	76.9	37.7	63.2	84.4	94.4	92.7	89.5	77.9	26.1	15.8
1970	76.5	34.8	61.8	83.5	93.7	92.2	88.2	79.2	27.4	16.6
1971	74.9	32.4	58.9	81.5	92.9	92.0	86.9	77.8	24.5	15.2
1972	73.7	34.1	60.1	81.5	92.7	91.4	86.1	73.6	23.6	14.7
1973	73.8	33.4	61.4	81.8	91.7	91.3	88.0	70.7	22.6	13.5
1974	73.3	34.6	62.4	82.1	92.3	90.9	84.7	70.2	21.7	14.8
1975	71.5	30.1	57.5	78.4	91.4	90.0	84.6	68.7	20.9	12.8
1976	70.7	30.2	55.6	78.4	90.6	90.6	83.4	65.7	19.7	12.1
1977	71.0	30.8	57.8	78.2	90.4	91.4	82.7	67.0	19.3	12.6
1978	72.1	33.2	59.5	78.0	90.9	91.0	84.5	69.1	21.3	14.5
1979	71.9	31.7	57.8	80.1	90.6	90.9	85.5	66.9	19.6	12.6
1980	70.8	31.9	56.3	78.9	90.4	89.7	83.9	63.5	17.5	
1981	69.8	29.7	54.3	77.1	88.4	89.6	83.4	63.2	16.8	9.3
Black and Other										
Female										
1954	46.1	24.5	37.7	49.6	49.7	57.5	53.4	41.2	12.2	16.2
1955	46.1	22.7	43.2	46.7	51.3	56.0	54.8	40.7	12.1	11.4
1956	47.3	28.3	44.6	44.9	52.1	57.0	55.3	44.5	14.5	14.4
1957	47.2	24.1	42.8	46.6	50.4	58.7	56.8	44.3	13.6	12.6

1958	48.0	23.2	41.2	48.3	50.8	60.8	59.8	42.8	13.3	11.6
1959	47.7	20.7	36.1	48.8	50.0	60.0	60.0	46.4	12.6	12.6
1960	48.2	22.1	44.3	48.8	49.7	59.8	60.5	47.3	12.8	13.2
1961	48.3	21.6	44.6	47.7	51.2	60.5	61.1	45.2	13.1	11.0
1962	48.0	21.0	45.5	48.6	52.0	59.7	60.5	46.1	12.2	9.7
1963	48.1	21.5	44.9	49.2	53.3	59.4	60.6	47.3	11.8	8.7
1964	48.5	19.5	46.5	53.6	52.8	58.4	62.3	48.4	12.7	8.0
1965	48.6	20.5	40.0	55.2	54.0	59.9	60.2	48.9	12.9	8.1
1966	49.3	23.6	44.0	54.5	54.9	60.9	61.0	49.1	13.0	7.5
1967	49.5	22.8	48.7	54.9	57.5	60.8	59.6	47.1	13.0	9.4
1968	49.3	23.3	46.9	58.4	56.6	59.3	59.8	47.0	11.9	7.2
1969	49.8	24.4	45.4	58.6	57.8	59.5	60.8	47.5	11.9	7.1
1970	49.5	24.3	44.7	57.7	57.6	59.9	60.2	47.1	12.2	9.7
1971	49.2	21.9	41.4	56.0	59.2	61.0	59.4	47.1	11.5	8.3
1972	48.7	21.4	43.9	56.7	60.1	60.7	57.3	43.9	12.8	9.3
1973	49.1	24.3	45.1	57.5	61.0	60.7	56.4	44.7	11.1	7.4
1974	49.1	24.2	44.6	58.2	60.8	61.5	56.9	43.5	10.0	9.1
1975	49.2	26.5	45.1	56.2	61.4	61.7	56.8	43.8	10.5	8.5
1976	50.2	23.9	43.3	57.9	65.3	62.2	57.3	43.4	11.2	8.4
1977	50.9	22.6	44.8	59.4	66.5	63.7	58.7	42.7	9.9	8.7
1978	53.3	27.7	48.6	62.8	68.7	67.1	59.8	43.6	10.7	9.9
1979	53.5	28.7	47.3	61.6	69.0	67.5	60.3	44.3	10.6	8.9
1980	53.4	26.0	45.8	60.0	69.3	68.1	61.7	45.0	9.8	
1981	53.5	24.7	44.1	60.1	68.6	69.7	62.1	44.9	9.3	8.2
Male										
1954	85.6	47.1	70.4	86.4	97.5	98.2	96.8	89.2	40.4	24.5
1955	85.4	48.0	71.7	85.6	97.8	98.3	96.7	88.4	39.5	23.5
1956	85.6	51.3	71.9	87.6	97.4	98.1	96.8	88.9	40.0	26.7
1957	84.8	49.6	71.6	86.7	97.2	98.0	96.6	88.0	37.7	25.1
1958	84.3	46.8	69.4	86.7	97.2	98.0	96.6	88.2	35.7	24.1
1959	83.8	45.4	70.3	87.3	97.5	98.0	96.3	87.9	34.3	24.2
1960	83.4	46.0	69.0	87.8	97.7	97.9	96.1	87.2	33.3	22.2
1961	83.0	44.3	66.2	37.6	97.7	97.9	95.9	87.8	31.9	22.2
1962	82.1	42.9	66.4	86.5	97.4	97.9	96.0	86.7	30.6	22.3
1963	81.5	42.4	67.8	85.8	97.4	97.8	96.2	86.6	28.4	21.4
1964	81.1	43.5	66.6	85.7	97.5	97.6	96.1	86.1	27.9	21.2
1965	80.8	44.6	65.8	85.3	97.4	97.7	95.9	85.2	27.9	21.7
1966	80.6	47.1	65.4	34.4	97.5	97.6	95.8	84.9	27.2	22.3
1967	80.7	47.9	66.1	84.0	97.5	97.7	95.6	84.9	27.1	22.6
1968	80.4	47.7	65.7	82.4	97.2	97.6	95.4	84.7	27.3	22.7
1969	80.2	48.8	66.3	82.6	97.0	97.4	95.1	83.9	27.3	23.0
1970	80.0	48.9	67.4	83.3	96.7	97.3	94.9	83.3	26.7	23.0
1971	79.6	49.2	67.8	83.2	96.3	97.0	94.7	82.6	25.6	23.7
1972	79.6	50.2	71.1	84.3	96.0	97.0	94.0	81.2	24.4	23.5

Table 28 (continued)

Item	Total, 16 Years and Over	16 and 17 Years	18 and 19 Years	20 to 24 Years	25 to 34 Years	35 to 44 Years	45 to 54 Years	55 to 64 Years	65 Years and Over	14 and 15 Years
1973	79.5	52.7	72.3	85.8	96.3	96.8	93.5	79.0	22.8	24.4
1974	79.4	53.3	73.6	86.5	96.3	96.7	93.0	78.1	22.5	24.4
1975	78.7	51.8	72.8	85.5	95.8	96.4	92.9	76.5	21.8	23.1
1976	78.4	51.8	73.5	86.2	95.9	96.0	92.5	75.4	20.3	22.6
1977	78.5	53.8	74.9	86.8	96.0	96.2	92.2	74.7	20.2	25.0
1978	78.6	55.3	75.3	87.2	96.0	96.3	92.1	73.9	20.4	24.8
1979	78.6	55.3	74.5	87.6	96.1	96.4	92.2	73.6	20.1	24.0
1980	78.3	53.6	74.1	87.1	95.9	96.2	92.2	73.3	19.3	
1981	77.9	51.4	73.5	87.0	95.9	96.1	92.5	71.6	18.6	21.0
Female										
1954	33.3	29.3	52.1	44.4	32.5	39.4	39.8	29.1	9.1	10.5
1955	34.5	29.9	52.0	45.8	32.8	39.9	42.7	31.8	10.5	11.2
1956	35.7	33.5	53.0	46.5	33.2	41.5	44.4	34.0	10.6	12.7
1957	35.7	32.1	52.6	45.8	33.6	41.5	45.4	33.7	10.2	12.5
1958	35.8	28.8	52.3	46.1	33.6	41.4	46.5	34.5	10.1	12.2
1959	36.0	29.9	50.8	44.5	33.4	41.4	47.8	35.7	10.2	13.0
1960	36.5	30.0	51.9	45.7	34.1	41.5	48.6	36.2	10.6	12.5
1961	36.9	29.4	51.9	46.9	34.3	41.8	48.9	37.2	10.5	13.5
1962	36.7	27.9	51.6	47.1	34.1	42.2	48.9	38.0	9.8	13.7
1963	37.2	27.9	51.3	47.3	34.8	43.1	49.5	38.9	9.4	12.2
1964	37.5	28.5	49.6	48.8	35.0	43.3	50.2	39.4	9.9	12.7
1965	38.1	28.7	50.6	49.2	36.3	44.3	49.9	40.3	9.7	12.9
1966	39.2	31.8	53.1	51.0	37.7	45.0	50.6	41.1	9.4	14.5
1967	40.1	32.3	52.7	53.1	39.7	46.4	50.9	41.9	9.3	15.4
1968	40.7	33.0	53.3	54.0	40.6	47.5	51.5	42.0	9.4	16.0
1969	41.8	35.2	54.6	56.4	41.7	48.6	53.0	42.6	9.7	16.1
1970	42.6	36.6	55.0	57.7	43.2	49.9	53.7	42.6	9.5	17.3
1971	42.6	36.4	55.0	57.9	43.6	50.2	53.7	42.5	9.3	17.2
1972	43.2	39.3	57.4	59.4	45.8	50.7	53.4	42.0	9.0	17.7
1973	44.1	41.7	58.9	61.6	48.5	52.2	53.4	40.8	8.7	18.9
1974	45.2	43.3	60.4	63.8	51.1	53.7	54.3	40.4	8.0	18.9
1975	45.9	42.7	60.4	65.4	53.5	54.9	54.3	40.7	8.0	18.4
1976	46.9	43.8	61.8	66.2	55.8	57.1	54.7	40.8	8.0	18.4
1977	48.1	45.8	63.3	67.7	58.3	58.9	55.4	40.8	8.0	20.6
1978	49.5	48.9	64.6	69.3	61.0	60.7	56.7	41.2	8.1	21.9
1979	50.6	49.1	65.8	70.5	62.9	63.0	58.1	41.6	8.1	20.7
1980	51.3	47.3	65.1	70.6	64.7	65.5	65.0	41.1	8.0	
1981	52.0	46.2	64.3	71.5	66.4	66.8	66.4	41.0	7.9	17.6

a Percentage of civilian noninstitutional population in the civilian labor force.

Table 29. Occupational Status of Men by Race and Educational Attainment, 1960[a] and 1979[b]

Occupation	College Graduate		High School Graduate		Elementary School Graduate	
	1960	1979	1960	1979	1960	1979
Employed White Men						
Total Employed[c]	4,071	10,630	10,082	18,379	5,736	2,533
Percent	100	100	100	100	100	100
Higher-Level	81	81	46	48	37	36
Professional, managers	77	77	21	18	9	8
Craftsmen	4	4	25	30	28	28
Employed Black Men						
Total Employed[c]	145	409	609	1,656	488	264
Percent	100	100	100	100	100	100
Higher-Level	76	78	22	29	16	27
Professional, managers	72	72	7	7	3	11
Craftsmen	4	6	15	22	13	16

Source: Prepared by NUL Research Department from data in U.S. Census Bureau, *Census of Population: 1960,* Occupation by Earnings and Education," and U.S. Bureau of Labor Statistics "Educational Attainment of Workers, March 1979," *Special Labor Force* Report No. 240, Table K.

[a] Data for 1960 apply to men 18–64 years old.

[b] Data for 1979 apply to men 16 years and over.

[c] Numbers in thousands.

Table 30. Years of School Completed by the Civilian Labor Force, by Sex and Race: 1959–1980[a]

Race and Year	Total (thousands)	Total	Elementary		High School		College		Median School Years Completed
			Less Than 5 Years	5 to 8 Years	1 to 3 Years	4 Years	1 to 3 Years	4 Years or More	
Total									
1959	65,842	100.0	5.3	25.2	19.8	30.7	9.3	9.6	12.0
1962	67,988	100.0	4.6	22.4	19.3	32.1	10.7	11.0	12.1
1964	69,926	100.0	3.7	20.9	19.2	34.5	10.6	11.2	12.2
1965	71,129	100.0	3.7	19.6	19.2	35.5	10.5	11.6	12.2
1966	71,958	100.0	3.3	18.9	19.0	36.3	10.8	11.8	12.2
1967	73,218	100.0	3.1	17.9	18.7	36.6	11.8	12.0	12.3
1968	75,101	100.0	2.9	16.8	18.2	37.5	12.2	12.4	12.3
1969	76,753	100.0	2.7	15.9	17.8	38.4	12.6	12.6	12.4
1970	78,955	100.0	2.4	15.1	17.3	39.0	13.3	12.9	12.4
1971	79,917	100.0	2.2	14.1	16.7	39.4	13.9	13.6	12.4
1972	85,410	100.0	2.1	12.9	19.2	38.7	13.6	13.6	12.4
1973	87,325	100.0	2.0	11.6	18.6	39.4	14.2	14.1	12.5
1974	89,633	100.0	1.8	10.9	18.1	39.2	15.1	15.0	12.5
1975	91,273	100.0	1.7	10.0	17.5	39.7	15.4	15.7	12.5
1976	93,063	100.0	1.5	9.1	17.1	39.8	16.0	16.5	12.6
1977	95,766	100.0	1.5	8.6	17.1	39.5	16.3	16.9	12.6
1978	98,437	100.0	1.4	8.2	16.7	39.6	17.0	16.9	12.6
1979	101,579	100.0	1.4	7.5	15.9	40.0	17.5	17.6	12.6
1980	103,339	100.0	1.2	7.1	15.4	40.2	17.8	18.2	12.7

Table 30 (*continued*)

Race and Year	Total (thousands)	Percent Distribution							Median School Years Completed
		Total	Elementary		High School		College		
			Less Than 5 Years	5 to 8 Years	1 to 3 Years	4 Years	1 to 3 Years	4 Years or More	
White									
1959	58,726	100.0	3.8	23.9	19.6	32.5	9.8	10.3	12.1
1962	60,451	100.0	3.3	21.4	18.8	33.5	11.3	11.8	12.2
1964	62,213	100.0	2.7	19.8	18.5	36.0	11.1	11.9	12.2
1965	63,261	100.0	2.7	18.9	18.4	36.8	11.0	12.2	12.3
1966	63,958	100.0	2.3	17.8	18.3	37.7	11.2	12.5	12.3
1967	65,076	100.0	2.2	16.9	18.1	37.7	12.4	12.8	12.3
1968	66,721	100.0	1.9	16.1	17.4	38.6	12.8	13.2	12.4
1969	68,300	100.0	2.0	15.1	16.9	39.7	13.0	13.4	12.4
1970	70,186	100.0	1.8	14.4	16.4	40.0	13.9	13.6	12.4
1971	71,032	100.0	1.7	13.5	15.8	40.2	14.5	14.4	12.5
1972	76,002	100.0	1.6	12.2	18.4	39.5	14.1	14.3	12.5
1973	77,453	100.0	1.6	11.0	17.8	40.2	14.6	14.8	12.5
1974	79,483	100.0	1.4	10.3	17.4	39.8	15.4	15.7	12.5
1975	81,038	100.0	1.3	9.5	16.8	40.3	15.8	16.3	12.6
1976	82,450	100.0	1.2	8.6	16.4	40.3	16.4	17.2	12.6
1977	84,769	100.0	1.2	8.0	16.3	40.1	16.7	17.6	12.6
1978	86,746	100.0	1.1	7.7	15.9	40.2	17.3	17.7	12.6
1979	89,507	100.0	1.1	7.1	15.2	40.5	17.7	18.4	12.7
1980	91,192	100.0	1.0	6.8	14.7	40.5	17.9	19.1	12.7
Black and Other									
1959	7,116	100.0	17.8	35.5	21.1	16.5	4.9	4.1	8.6
1962	7,537	100.0	15.4	29.8	23.2	21.0	5.7	4.8	9.6
1964	7,713	100.0	11.6	29.2	24.7	22.2	6.6	5.7	10.1
1965	7,868	100.0	11.8	25.7	24.9	24.4	6.1	7.0	10.5
1966	8,000	100.0	11.1	26.7	23.3	24.8	7.1	5.8	10.5
1967	8,142	100.0	10.4	25.5	23.7	27.5	7.2	5.8	10.8
1968	8,380	100.0	9.5	23.5	24.3	28.3	7.7	6.7	11.1
1969	8,453	100.0	8.6	22.6	24.7	28.4	9.0	6.7	11.3
1970	8,769	100.0	7.4	20.6	24.7	31.0	9.0	7.4	11.7
1971	8,885	100.0	6.5	19.5	24.4	32.7	9.5	7.4	11.9
1972	9,408	100.0	6.0	18.6	25.6	32.4	9.4	8.0	12.0
1973	9,872	100.0	5.0	16.5	24.8	33.6	11.0	9.0	12.1
1974	10,150	100.0	5.2	15.7	23.6	34.1	12.1	9.3	12.2
1975	10,234	100.0	5.0	14.1	23.0	34.7	12.4	10.8	12.2
1976	10,612	100.0	4.2	13.2	22.5	36.0	12.8	11.3	12.3
1977	9,408	100.0	3.8	14.0	24.4	35.5	13.4	8.9	12.2
1978	9,909	100.0	3.8	12.0	24.7	35.8	14.9	8.9	12.3
1979	10,144	100.0	3.4	11.6	23.0	37.5	15.5	9.0	12.3
1980	10,203	100.0	2.8	9.9	22.9	39.2	16.1	9.1	12.4

Source: Bureau of Labor Statistics.

[a] Persons 18 years and over for 1957–71, 16 years and over for 1972 forward.

Table 31. Employment of Sophomore and Senior High School Students, by Type of Community and Racial/Ethnic Group: Spring 1980

Type of Community and Racial/Ethnic Group	Sophomores		Seniors	
	Labor Force Participation Rate[a]	Unemployment Rate[b]	Labor Force Participation Rate[a]	Unemployment Rate[b]
Urban	57.9	35.5	76.5	20.3
Black	57.9	51.6	73.2	33.7
Hispanic	54.8	44.3	74.2	22.6
White	58.7	25.2	78.1	15.0
Suburban	60.0	27.7	78.1	15.8
Black	54.7	46.6	70.9	27.9
Hispanic	58.4	33.6	73.8	21.5
White	60.8	25.5	79.0	14.5
Rural	55.9	24.8	72.4	16.8
Black	47.0	37.4	65.1	28.0
Hispanic	57.7	27.5	77.3	14.6
White	56.7	23.5	72.8	16.0

Source: U.S. Department of Education, National Center for Education Statistics, High School and Beyond Survey, *Youth Employment During High School.*

[a] Labor force participation rate is the total number of students, employed and unemployed, participating in the labor force as a percentage of the total population of students.

[b] Unemployment rate is the number of students in the labor force who are unemployed as a percentage of all students in the labor force.

Table 32. Employment Status of Sophomore and Senior High School Students, by Racial/Ethnic Group and Sex: 1980

	Sophomores			Seniors		
	Total Population	Labor Force Participation Rate[a]	Unemployment Rate[b]	Total Population	Labor Force Participation Rate[a]	Unemployment Rate[b]
All students	3,512,055	58.6	28.1	2,924,034	76.2	17.1
Males	1,677,206	62.0	28.6	1,404,098	78.3	16.3
Females	1,819,599	55.3	27.5	1,519,936	74.3	17.8
Blacks	359,887	53.8	47.1	269,068	70.3	30.7
Males	160,428	58.6	43.5	117,185	74.0	27.4
Females	196,111	49.4	50.4	151,883	67.4	33.5
Hispanics	253,714	56.6	37.3	174,362	75.1	20.4
Males	123,001	64.9	33.1	88,471	78.7	19.3
Females	127,342	48.3	42.4	85,891	71.5	21.5
Whites	2,345,642	59.0	24.8	2,093,410	76.7	15.0
Males	1,117,216	61.4	26.6	1,000,735	78.4	14.6
Females	1,222,516	56.7	23.0	1,092,676	75.3	15.4

Source: U.S. Department of Education, National Center for Education Statistics, High School and Beyond Survey, *Youth Employment During High School.*

[a] Labor force participation rate is the total number of students, employed and unemployed, participating in the labor force as a percentage of the total population of students.

[b] Unemployment rate is the number of students in the labor force who are unemployed as a percentage of all students in the labor force.

Table 33. Minimum Wage Workers Among Young People, 16–19 Years Old, by Race and Ethnic Group: 1979

	All Youth	White	Black	Hispanics
Total, 16–19	100	100	100	100
Above minimum[a]	55	55	49	55
Minimum wage	45	45	51	45
At minimum[b]	14	13	19	15
Below minimum[c]	31	31	32	30

Source: Prepared by NUL Research Department from U.S. Labor Department's National Longitudinal Survey of 1979.

[a] Hourly pay rates of $2.91 and over.

[b] At the federal minimum wage of $2.90 as of January 1, 1979.

[c] Hourly pay rates of $2.89 and under.

INCOME, EARNINGS, AND INCIDENCE OF POVERTY

Overview ■ Decade of Recessions and Inflation ■ Ford Administration ■ Carter Administration ■ Reagan Administration ■ Declining Commitments under Nixon-Ford-Carter-Reagan ■ Income and Poverty Patterns

The years between 1971 and 1981 stand out as a period in which many of the economic gains won by blacks over the previous decade appeared to be slipping away. The nation was going through a period of increasing economic difficulties, but for blacks, as always, the difficulties were multiplied. As one observer remarked, when the economy catches a cold, blacks catch pneumonia.

Between 1963 and 1969 the jobless rate for blacks plummeted from 10.8 to 6.4%, reducing the number of unemployed blacks by one third to 570,000, one of the lowest levels in recent times. But by 1981 the jobless rate for blacks had more than doubled to 15.5%, raising the number of unemployed blacks to the largest (1,700,000) ever recorded by the U.S. Bureau of Labor Statistics. Similarly, between 1969 and 1979 the number of black families in poverty jumped from 1,366,000, the lowest level in two decades, to 1,660,000, the highest level ever. And by 1979 the income gap between black and white families had widened from 61% in 1970 to 67% in 1979.

What accounts for the slowing of black economic progress during the 1970s? Two major factors were the lagging national economic growth due to periodic recessions and record level inflation and the development of government policies that reflected a declining commitment to the needs of minorities and the poor. These two factors are examined here in detail along with the status and prospects for both middle-income and low-income blacks.

A DECADE OF RECESSIONS AND INFLATION

Accepted economic theory has traditionally held that unemployment and inflation cannot exist at the same time. This has been a tenet of economists, but in the 1970s a new term, "stagflation," had to be coined to describe the combination of lagging productivity and record level inflation. From 1969 through 1980, this nation had three recessions (1969–1971, 1974–1975, and 1980). Each of these recessions saw black unemployment rise, and at the end of each recession, blacks never regained the ground they had lost. For example, while the number of unemployed white workers declined by 562,000 between 1975 and 1980, there were 200,000 more blacks unemployed in 1980 (1.7 million) than there were at the peak of the 1974–1975 recession (1.5 million).

At the same time this was going on, inflation was rising from an annual rate of 2.3 in the 1960s to an annual rate of 7.1 in the 1970s. How this escalation

Chart 1. Gross Median Income and Ratio of Income of Black to White Families by Family Structure: 1969–1979

Despite some catching up in the early 1970s, the average black family takes home only $57 for each $100 of the average white family

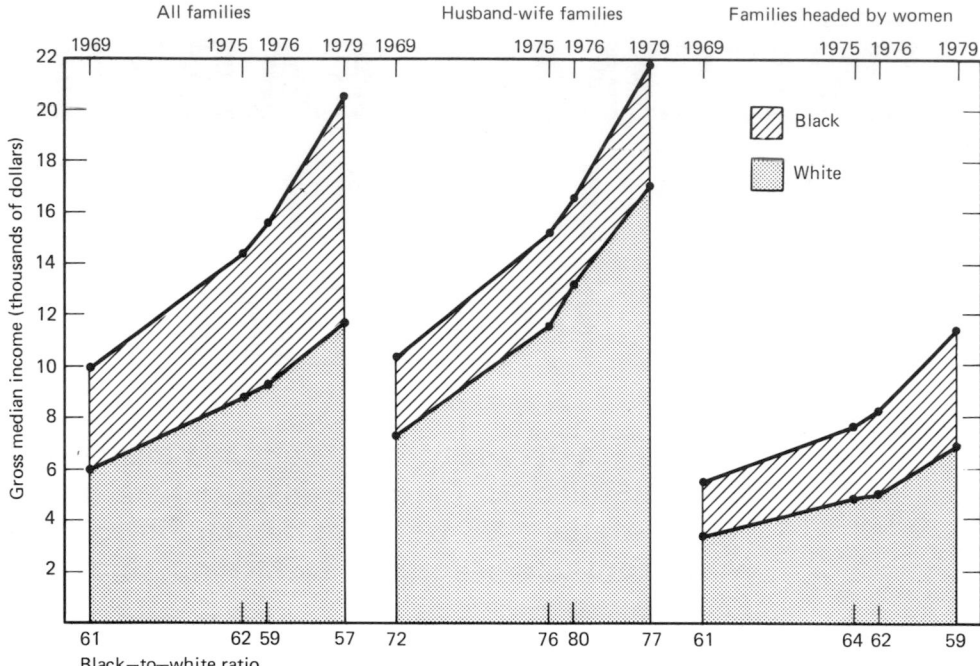

Data: U.S. Department of Commerce, Bureau of the Census.

in inflation affected blacks is illustrated in the statistics that show that between 1970 and 1979, the median income among black families rose $5,330 (from $6,279 to $11,609) while the median income of white families rose $10,209 (from $10,236 to $20,438). But after adjusting for inflation, white family real income showed a gain of $1,304, while black real income fell behind inflation by $128.

Over the past three administrations (Nixon, Ford, Carter) and continuing into the Reagan Administration, the government's efforts to fight inflation have involved inducing unemployment, which has had a disproportionate impact on black workers since in many instances they are most vulnerable by being clustered in industries that are among the first casualties in any downturn of the economy—automobiles, steel, construction, and the like. In a number of cases they are also vulnerable by their lack of seniority, which translates into last hired—first fired.

During the Ford Administration

For more than a decade, the economy has dominated the national consciousness. Americans have seen other nations move into markets where once they were dominant, they have seen the OPEC nations raise the price

of oil almost at will as the nation's energy costs reach staggering levels, and they have experienced the horror of double-digit inflation. In all of this, however, there has been little opportunity for blacks and other minorities—who suffer more as economic problems have a peculiar impact on them—to have any real voice in the formulation of national economic policy. Black leadership was aware of this in August 1974, when Gerald Ford, who had just assumed the Presidency after Richard Nixon's resignation, announced that he would hold an Economic Summit Meeting on Inflation in order to develop strategies for effectively controlling soaring prices.

Disturbed that this meeting would be held without adequate input from the black community, a Black Economic Summit Conference was convened in Washington, D.C., September 21–22, 1974 to develop a unified black economic agenda. Approximately 60 individuals from a broad cross section of black organizations were represented at this historic gathering. At its conclusion, "A Call to Action" was issued and forwarded to the President, on the eve of his own economic meeting. The principal points made in the Call were that (a) the goal of full employment should have equal priority with that of reducing inflation, (b) firm price controls should be quickly instituted, (c) reductions in federal spending should come disproportionately from defense and not social programs, and (d) more targeted monetary and fiscal policies should be utilized.

The proposals were well thought out, received excellent media coverage, and were carried in full in several major newspapers as full-page paid ads. Nevertheless, they were ignored as President Ford announced a "Whip Inflation Now" public relations campaign whose principal contribution was "WIN" buttons, which in a matter of weeks became a national joke as economic data revealed that a severe recession was already under way and that inflation was declining.

During the Carter Administration

When Jimmy Carter took office in 1977 the recession had ended—leaving blacks, as has been noted earlier, less well off—and inflation appeared to be the major problem. Carter had stressed, during the campaign, a pledge to reduce inflation by balancing the budget, and this caused consternation among black leaders who had been urging him to assign equal priority to the goal of full employment. They saw in full employment, which by definition would involve federal expenditures for public sector employment, the only answer to mounting black unemployment.

Specifically, they sought the President's active support of the Humphrey-Hawkins Full Employment Bill in Congress. But the President indicated that he could not support the legislation unless it incorporated more features for controlling inflation.

Consequently, Congress watered down many of the strong employment features of the original bill and installed inflation control provisions. In 1978 Congress passed the Full Employment and Balanced Growth Act, which established a national goal of 3% unem-

Chart 2. Ratio of Gross Median Income of Black to White Families by Region of Residence: 1969–1979

The gap between black and white family income levels is widening, except in the South where it continues to be the greatest

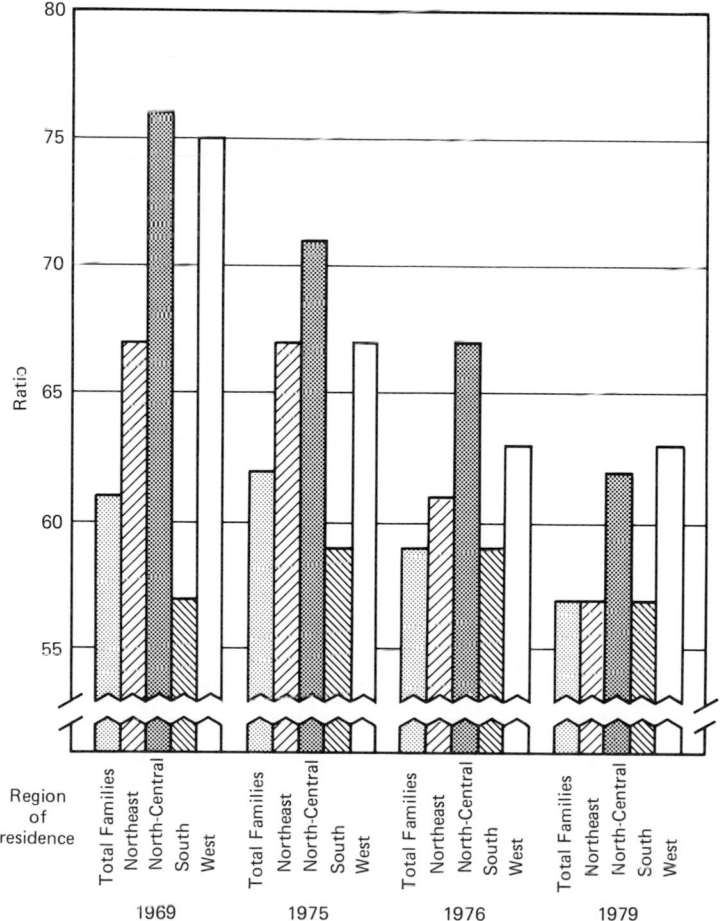

Data: U.S. Department of Commerce, Bureau of the Census.

ployment for adults and 4% for all workers by 1983; a rate of inflation of 3%, declining eventually to zero; an improvement in the balance of trade; a balanced federal budget; and a limit on the growth of the federal government relative to the gross national product. However, with inflation rebounding to double digit levels in 1979, the full employment provisions of the act quickly receded from public concern.

The 1980 recession, in the last year of Carter's Presidency, lasted only seven months and was one of the shortest on record. Despite its brevity, an analysis by the *Wall Street Journal* revealed that in several respects it was more severe than the average of the six post-World War II recessions that preceded it. Based on comparative unemployment rates, the 1980 recession was more devastating for blacks than the 1974–1975 decline. The prime reason was that blacks had not yet recovered from the 1974–1975 recession when they were hit with another. As reported earlier, there were 200,000 more blacks out of work in 1980 than there were at the bottom of the 1974–1975 recession. At the same time, the number of unemployed whites had dropped by half a million.

Yet whites did not escape unscathed, since they experienced an increase in poverty between 1979 and 1980, as did blacks. Furthermore, an unprecedented number of small businesses folded in 1980. An analysis by Dun and Bradstreet revealed that the failure rate of small businesses during the 1980 recession was 14% higher than during the 1974–1975 recession. Black businesses were disproportionately affected, since they, especially, found it difficult to pay off commercial loans at markedly higher interest rates than when they originally obtained those loans. The interest rate problems were further compounded by the credit control policies of the Carter Administration.

During the Reagan Administration

This was the picture in January 1981 when Ronald Reagan was inaugurated as the fortieth President of the United States. The nation appeared to be rebounding from the 1980 slump. Real GNP grew at an impressive 8.4% annual rate during the first quarter of 1981. The prime interest rate was steadily falling from its record 21.5% in December 1980. Inflation, which had eased from 13.3% in 1979 to 12.4% in 1980, dropped even further to an 8.4% annual rate by January 1981.

These were favorable omens, but President Reagan was convinced that a bold new approach was needed to achieve sustained noninflationary economic growth throughout the eighties. Therefore, on February 18, 1981, he unveiled his Economic Recovery Plan, which would cut personal taxes by 30% over the next three years, increase significantly tax incentives for businesses, raise defense spending 17% annually between 1980 and 1984, hold nondefense spending to annual increases of only 1% after 1981, shift the major responsibility for administering and funding major social programs for the poor to state and local governments, eliminate burdensome federal regulations on businesses, sharply reduce inflation, spur job growth, and achieve a balanced budget by 1984.

Reagan's economic strategies are described as "supply-side" economics, since major reliance for spurring economic growth is placed on the "supply-side" (i.e., private business) through tax and other fiscal incentives. "Supply-siders" theorized that the benefits from enhanced business investment would accrue to all groups in the society in the form of more jobs, higher income, and an overall improved quality of life. This approach is in contrast to the "liberal" approach, which is depicted as believing that the most effective way to stimulate productivity is through incentives to the "demand side" (i.e., the consumers) in the form of personal tax cuts, expanding income maintenance programs, and accelerating public works programs during economic downturns.

There were immediate outcries that the Economic Recovery Plan would hurt the poor the most. Many black leaders saw in supply-side economics signs of the old and badly bruised "trickle down" theory that held, in effect, that if there is enough money being gathered at the top, then some of it will trickle down to the bottom. The Administration denied this, but in a moment of candor in an article in the *Atlantic Monthly,* its principal economic spokesman, David Stockman, Director of the Office of Management and Budget, conceded that the "trickle down" theory was really at the heart of the recovery plan.

Several black leaders, most notably Vernon E. Jordan, President of the National Urban League, raised the question of what was to happen to the people who would be thrown out of jobs when federally funded programs ended under Reagan's edict, and to those who were already unemployed, while they waited for the private sector to produce the jobs Reagan had promised that it would. The Administration counseled patience.

What happened, however, is that the continued restrictive monetary policies carried out by the Federal Reserve Board, resulting in high interest rates, cut short the recovery from the 1980 recession and resulted in another recession that began in the second half of 1981 and continued into 1982. Instead of having a balanced budget, many economic analysts predicted that in fiscal year 1983, as a result of the massive tax cuts and sluggish business conditions, the deficit would be over $160 billion, an all-time record. This frightened Wall Street, where the financial power in this country resides, which felt that no significant business investment would occur as long as interest rates were high and budget deficits remained huge.

Chart 3. Annual Mean Earnings (in thousands) of All Workers by Occupation, Sex and Race: 1979

In every occupational category, white men's mean earnings are higher than black men's; black women in some jobs earn more than white women although both earn significantly less than men

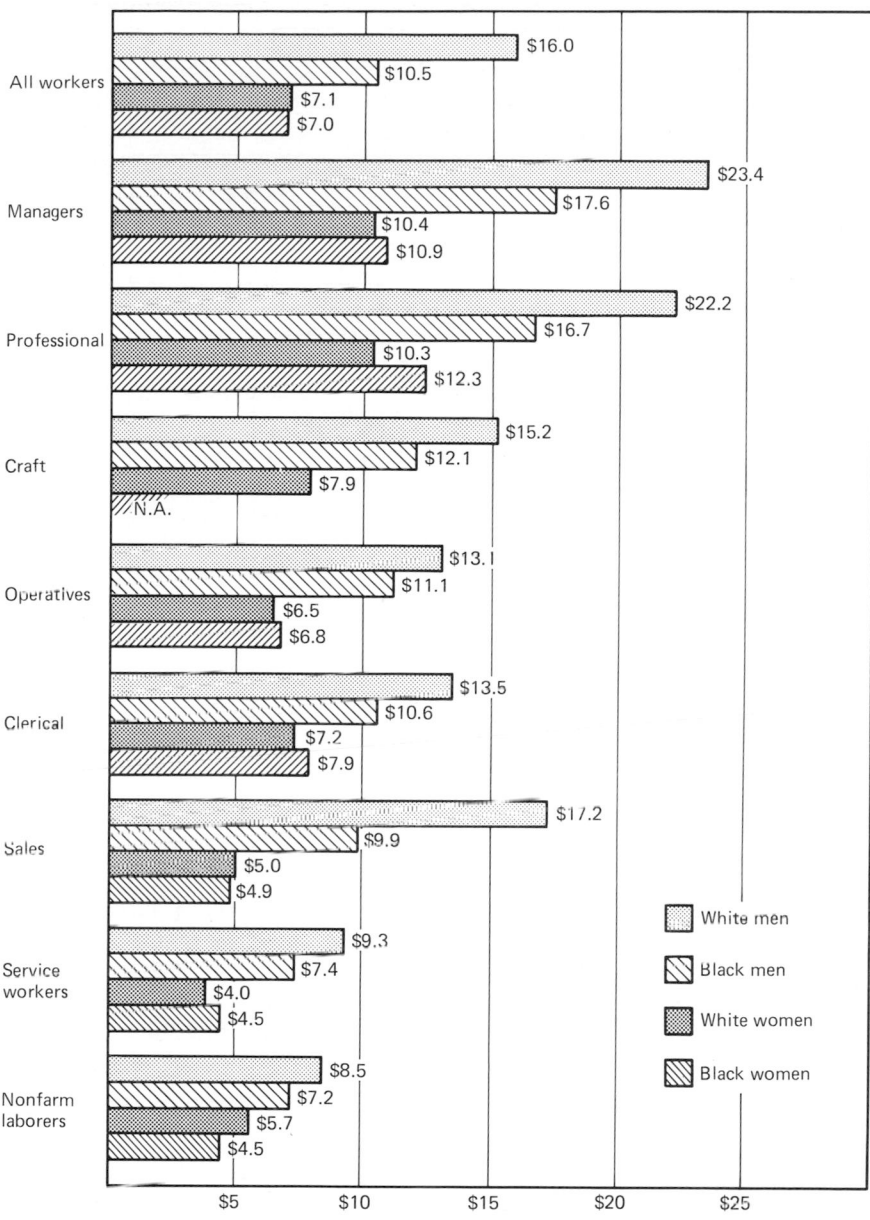

N.A. = not available.

Data: U.S. Department of Commerce, Bureau of the Census.

The net result is that total unemployment in the nation reached 9% in March 1982, its highest level since 1941, while black joblessness climbed to a record 18%. Analyzing the impact of these recent economic developments for blacks, Dr. Bernard E. Anderson, a distinguished economist writing in *The State of Black America—1982,* had this to say:

Black unemployment can be expected to rise, and black in-

come to fall significantly during the course of the current recession. Today, as often in the past, in matters of the economy, the black community is like a caboose on the train. When the train speeds up, so does the caboose; and when the train slows down, the caboose does likewise. Thus, the near term prospects for black income and employment are not good, but even beyond that, there is still a question about the potential impact of the new economic policy on black economic progress even if the policy eventually works as intended.

Chart 4. Annual Mean Earnings (in thousands) of Year-Round, Full-Time Workers by Occupation, Sex, and Race: 1979

Mean earnings of full-time black male workers are $5,700 lower than white male workers, but $3,000 to $3,500 higher than women of either race

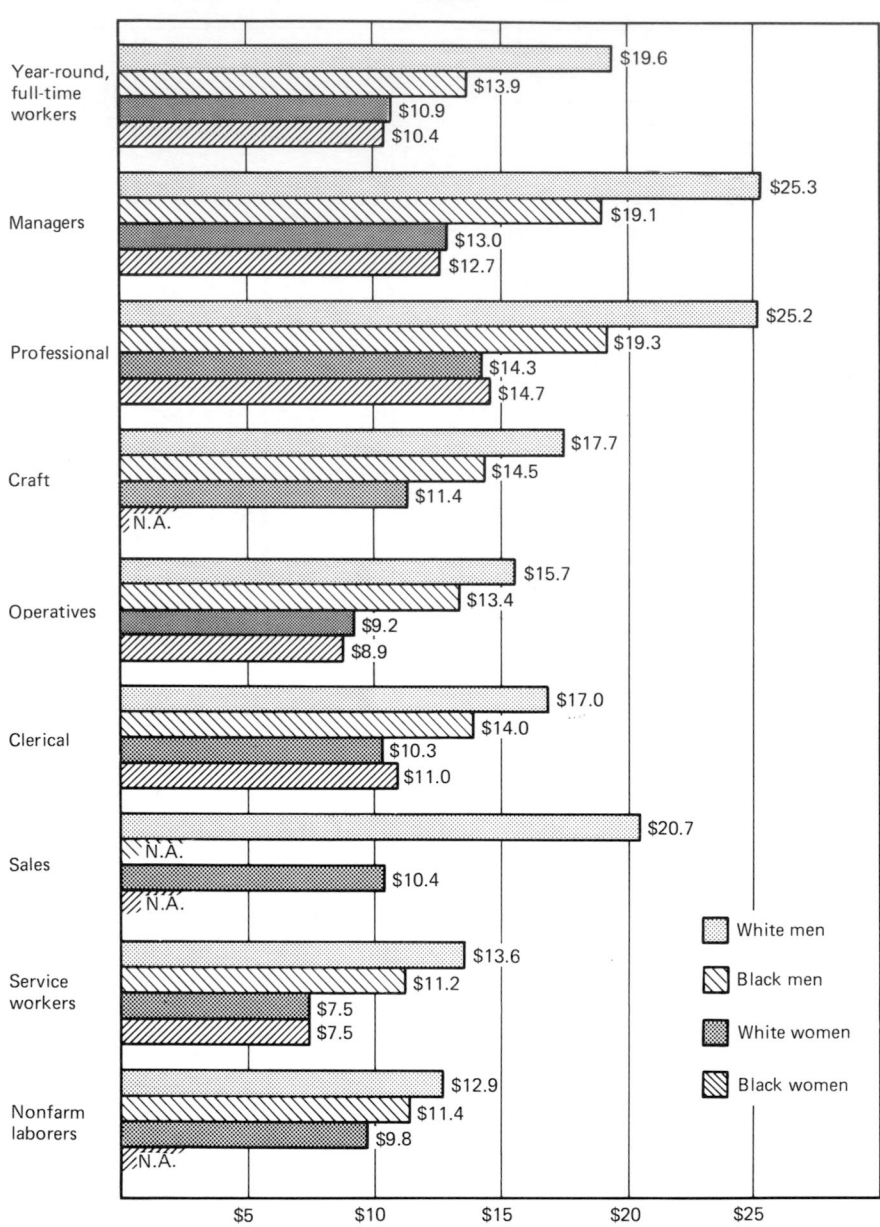

N.A. = not available.

Data: U.S. Department of Commerce, Bureau of the Census.

Declining Commitment to Minorities and the Poor During the Nixon Administration

In a perceptive and sensitive book, *Meanness Mania— The Changing Mood,* published in 1980, political scientist Gerald R. Gill looked back on the 1960s and the commitments the federal government and the larger society made to improving the lives of blacks, other minorities, and the poor. Then he looked at the seventies.

Instead of compassion, one witnesses hostility toward efforts to reduce economic inequities and to overcome the effects of past and present discrimination. Instead of appeals to achieve equal educational and economic opportunities, one hears code words like "forced busing," "white flight" and "reverse discrimination." These code words are manifestations of a spread-

Chart 5. Distribution of Total Family Income in Constant 1979 Dollars (in thousands) by Race: 1969–1979

Between 1969 and 1979, median income actually declined 2% overall. During the same period, the median income for white families rose by 6%

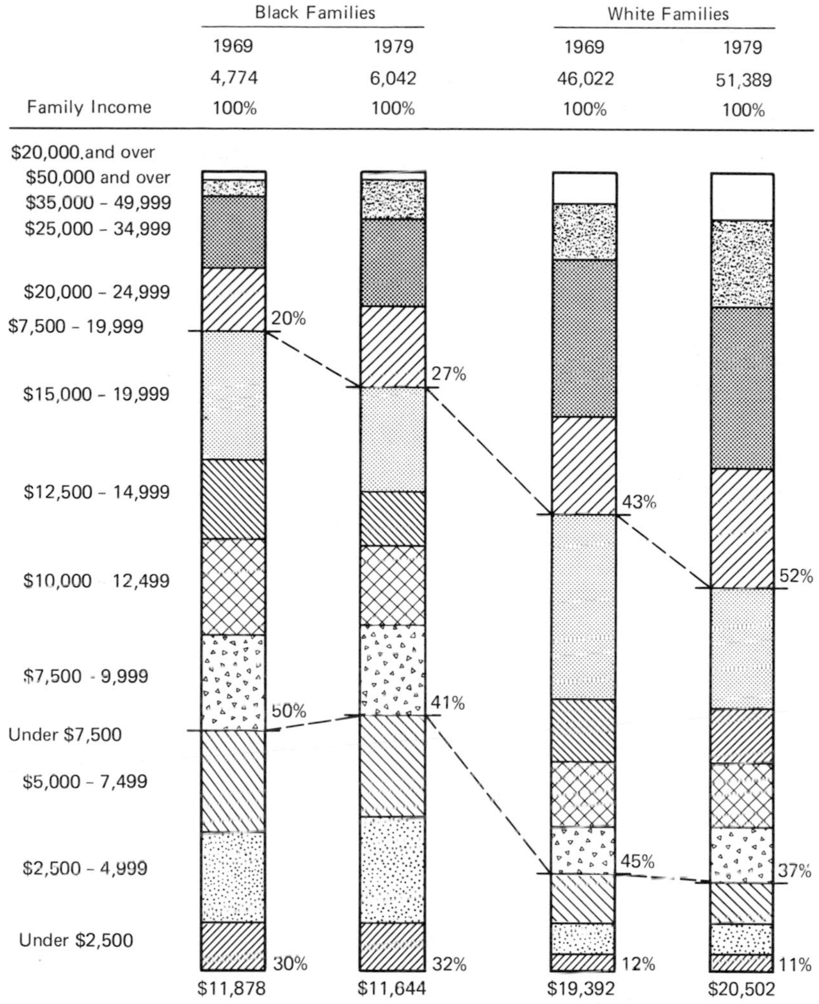

Family Income	Black Families		White Families	
	1969	1979	1969	1979
	4,774	6,042	46,022	51,389
	100%	100%	100%	100%

$20,000 and over
$50,000 and over
$35,000 – 49,999
$25,000 – 34,999

$20,000 – 24,999
$7,500 – 19,999   20%
                         27%
$15,000 – 19,999

$12,500 – 14,999
                         43%

$10,000   12,499   52%

$7,500 - 9,999

Under $7,500   50%   41%

$5,000 – 7,499

$2,500 – 4,999   45%   37%

Under $2,500
                30%   32%   12%   11%
              $11,878 $11,644 $19,392 $20,502

Data: U.S. Department of Commerce, Bureau of the Census.

ing mania within American society, a mania increasingly adamant against governmental and societal efforts to help blacks, other minorities and the poor. It is not too much to suggest that behind this mania is a growing feeling of meanness.

Gill went on to define meanness as a denoting selfishness, stinginess, and malice, and said they were "expressions of an increasing unwillingness and hostility upon the part of many citizens to share more equally the benefits of American society." The words are harsh but they reflect the rising tide of conservatism that developed over the past decade and helped create a climate in which there was a measurable declining commitment to minorities and the poor in a number of areas, including the economy.

The genesis for this lay in the Nixon Administration,

which gave currency to the term "benign neglect" to describe the preferred way of handling the problems of blacks. A major objective of Nixon during both terms of office was to dismantle the Office of Economic Opportunity, which had been created by President Johnson to conduct the so-called War on Poverty.

Nixon began by transferring some of the most popular and successful OEO programs to other agencies. For example, the Job Corps and other manpower efforts were given to the Department of Labor. Head Start, a preschool training program, was placed in the Department of Health, Education and Welfare. Despite survival of many programs, the emphasis of antipoverty activity changed. Blacks notably suffered, as sums were increasingly given to ventures supporting "middle American ethnics" and the suburbs, where few blacks live. The percentages of blacks in job training programs dropped significantly and cultural, tenant, and welfare organizing activities fell off sharply in black neighborhoods.

Following his reelection, Nixon moved more vigorously against OEO, launching concerted and prolonged attacks against its Community Action Agencies (CAAs) and legal service program. Efforts were also made to impound its funds. Under a federal court ruling that OEO could not be abolished in the face of Congressional appropriations to sustain it, Nixon retreated and allowed Congress to decide OEO's fate. It did by passing the Community Services Act, which set up the Community Services Administration, ended OEO, but continued many of its programs in other departments.

Most significantly, Nixon brought an end to the direct funding of community-based organizations to administer categorical programs for the poor. Those funds were absorbed into a broad range of "revenue-sharing" block grants that were distributed to state and local areas based more on political, rather than economic, necessity. This government decentralization was a cornerstone of Nixon's "New Federalism," which was designed to shift the primary responsibility for planning and administering a wide range of social programs to state and local governments with little federal interference. Consequently, between 1973 and 1975, Nixon created several block grants: Comprehensive Employment and Training Act (CETA) in employment and training to replace the Manpower Development and Training Act (MDTA); Community Development Block Grants (CDBG) in housing to replace Model Cities; Title XX in social services; and the Law Enforcement Assistance Administration (LEAA) in criminal justice. Although these block grants were patterned after the General Revenue Sharing (GRS) program passed in 1972, they had more restrictions on how they were to be used than GRS.

However, since funds for these block grants were distributed by politically derived formulas to localities across the nation, regardless of economic need, the proportions of minorities and other low-income groups served were much lower than those reached by the previous categorical programs. For example, a CETA evaluation conducted by the National Academy of Science found that the proportion of economically disadvantaged persons participating in CETA in its early years was markedly lower than the proportion that had participated in the MDTA employment and training programs, primarily because CETA funds were being sent to many suburban areas with low levels of unemployment, poverty, and minorities. General Accounting Office audits of the Community Development Block Grants program found that many commu-

Chart 6. Percentage of All Blacks and All Whites Below Official Poverty Level: 1969–1979

More than three of every ten blacks fall below the poverty line compared to less than one of ten whites. This pattern has changed little in ten years

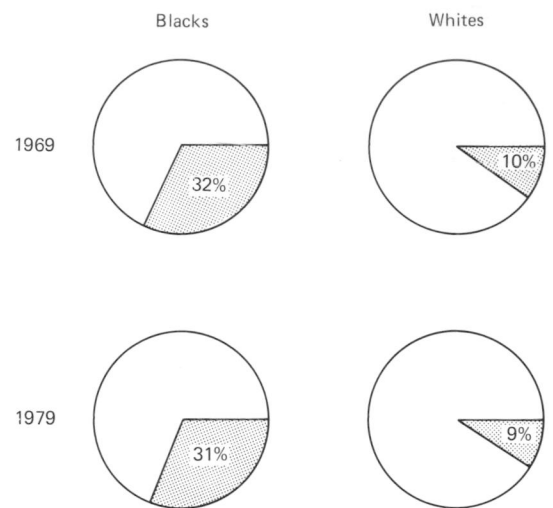

Data: U.S. Department of Commerce, Bureau of the Census.

nities were using their CDBG funds for tennis courts and other recreational facilities, rather than for low-income housing. And evaluations of other block grant programs (such as Title XX and LEAA) also revealed that sizable numbers of minorities, the poor, and other disadvantaged groups were not being reached adequately by those programs.

Although President Nixon's New Federalism was anathema to the interests of minorities and other economically disadvantaged groups, some significant efforts on behalf of the disadvantaged were made by several officials in that Administration. An Assistant Secretary of Labor, Arthur Fletcher, for example, developed the first government affirmative action guidelines for hiring minorities by private industry. Furthermore, Presidential Advisor Daniel Patrick Moynihan made a strong effort to get Congress to enact a Family Assistance Plan (FAP), which would have established the first government guaranteed income program for the poor. FAP would have provided an annual income of $1,600 for a family of four without earnings and up to $3,290 for a poor family of four with earnings. Although FAP was passed by the House of Representatives in April 1970 by a wide margin, it was unable to overcome the strong opposition in the Senate from both liberals and conservatives. But it did provide a foundation for subsequent welfare reform efforts.

It should be noted that Federal spending for the poor, which has risen from $8 billion in 1964 to $16 billion in 1969, was not, according to government fig-

Chart 7. Sources of Income for Black Families

More than half of poor black families have some earned income, even though they must rely on other sources of income as well

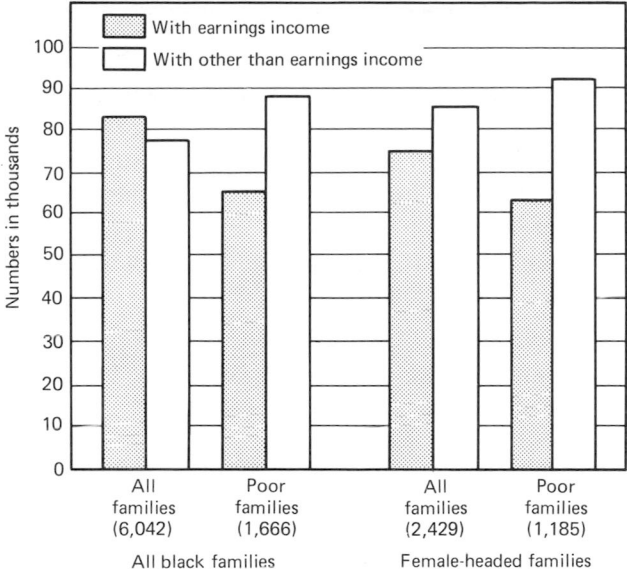

administer them was to turn them over to the states. Consequently, he announced his "New Federalism" program as part of his Economic Recovery Plan, which would consolidate more than 100 categorical programs into block grants. Furthermore, he proposed to merge into new block grants several of the existing block grant programs that Nixon had created, such as CETA, CDBG, and Title XX.

Since Reagan's economic plan called for significant increases in defense spending, it was evident that deep cuts would have to be made elsewhere if he was to reduce the cost of government. Excluded from the cuts were those programs that Reagan described as "social safety net" programs for the "truly needy." The only problem was that his "safety net" programs were primarily entitlements for the nonpoor, such as Social Security, Medicare, Railroad Retirement, Veterans Benefits, and Unemployment Compensation—which have about 80 million beneficiaries, or one third of the nation. Thus the bulk of the cuts had to come from vital programs for the poor, such as Aid to Families with Dependent Children (AFDC), food stamps, supplemental food program for women, infants, and children (WIC), school lunches, Medicaid, public housing, subsidized rent, low-income energy assistance, foster care and adoption assistance, compensatory education, and health and social services to the poor and handicapped. Block grants to states and local governments also appeared in the Reagan economic package, but disproportionately so. The major cuts in these grants included the complete elimination of the CETA Public Service Program; reducing extended jobless benefits; placing a very restrictive "cap" on Medicaid; and extensive reductions in a wide range of health, social services, community development, transportation, energy and youth employment and training programs, all of importance to the disadvantaged, a disproportionate number of whom are black.

Reagan asked Congress to approve his fiscal year 82 budget, which consisted of cuts in about 83 federal programs in order to obtain $14 billion savings in fiscal year 81 and about $49 billion in fiscal year 82.

By July 1981 Congress passed much of what President Reagan requested and approved spending cuts of about $35 billion for FY 82, which began October 1, 1981. At this time, it is still too early to assess the total impact of the cuts in social programs on the poor, but some information has been developed. For example:

Of the 350,000 CETA workers who lost their public service employment jobs, less than one fourth found employment in the private sector.

Approximately 725,000 families receiving Aid to Families with Dependent Children payments have either

ures, diminished between 1969 and 1973, although inflation took its toll and much of the money, as indicated, did not reach the poor.

During the Ford and Carter Administrations

During his two years as President, Gerald Ford continued most of Nixon's policies with respect to minorities and the poor. This was partly in response to the increasing national mood toward fiscal conservatism and partly because of the recession. The growing opposition to the use of public funds for social programs was reflected by the taxpayer revolts that emerged in the wake of the passage of Proposition 13 in California. During the Carter Administration, this translated into a Congressional obsession with "balanced budgets," while, at the same time, handing out billions of dollars in tax subsidies and loopholes to the rich and affluent. To his credit, President Carter attempted to counter this mood by targeting more programs to the disadvantaged, especially in the area of youth employment and training, but he proposed no new initiatives.

During the Reagan Administration

When Ronald Reagan took office it was with the conviction that most of the social programs created by other administrations needed to be eliminated or radically transformed, and that the most effective way to

had their grants terminated or reduced. Most of these are the working poor, usually women, whose jobs pay them so little that they had received supplemental AFDC grants to support their families. Many of them have now found that they would have more money if they quit their jobs and went on welfare full-time.

A study commissioned by the Leadership Conference on Civil Rights disclosed that the Reagan Administration budget, taxes, housing, and education policies favor whites in their effect rather than lending assistance to blacks and other minorities, who are poorer than the general population.

When Reagan submitted his budget for FY 83 early in 1982, some $20 billion additional cuts in social ser-

vice programs were proposed. This time, some reductions were proposed in Medicare and in pension benefits for federal employees, the military, veterans, and railroad workers. But the bulk of the cuts, once again, were directed at the poor. Included in the proposals were the following:

Dropping 2.6 million food stamp recipients and reducing benefits for another 15.9 million, a $2.7 billion cut.

Dropping 900,000 welfare recipients, mostly women and children, from the rolls, or reducing sharply their benefits, a $1.1 billion cut.

Dropping 500,000 families from low-rent housing assistance, a $2.4 billion cut.

Reducing employment and training assistance, which

Chart 8. Percentage of Black Families Receiving Various Types of Income Other than Earnings

More black families rely on property income than on public assistance, although poor and female-headed black families are more heavily dependent on transfer income

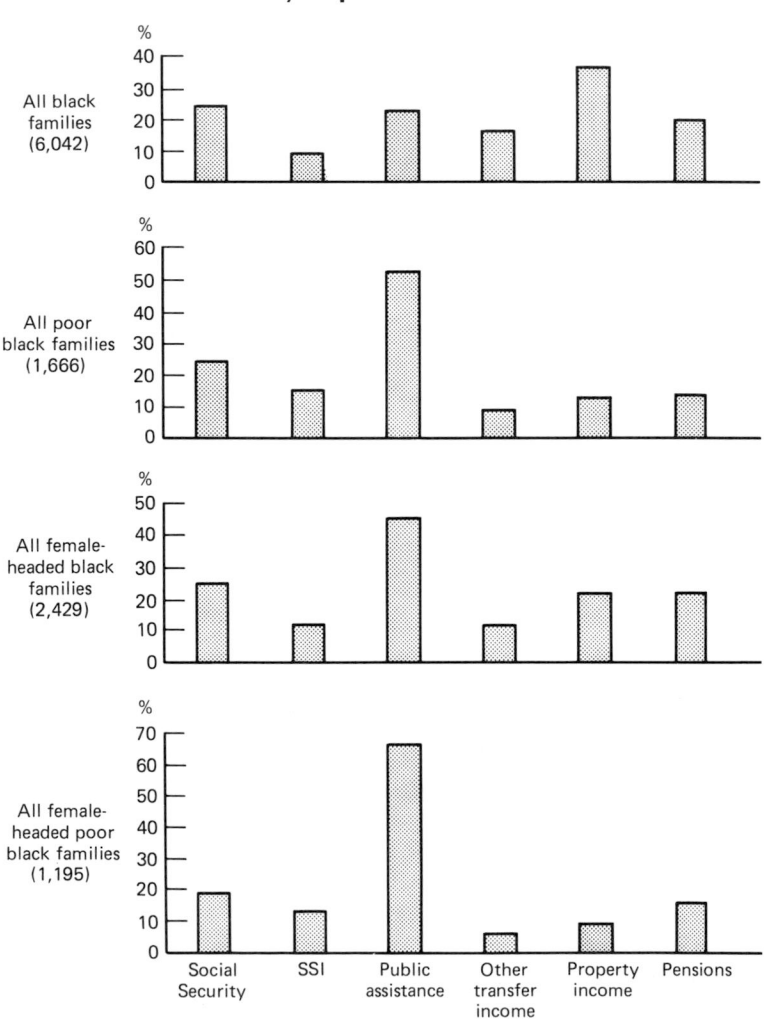

Data: U.S. Department of Commerce.

Chart 9. Percentage Distribution of Aggregate Black Family Income by Family Structure and Poverty Status: 1979

The average black family earns 83% of its income, although the 28% which are poor rely more heavily on other sources

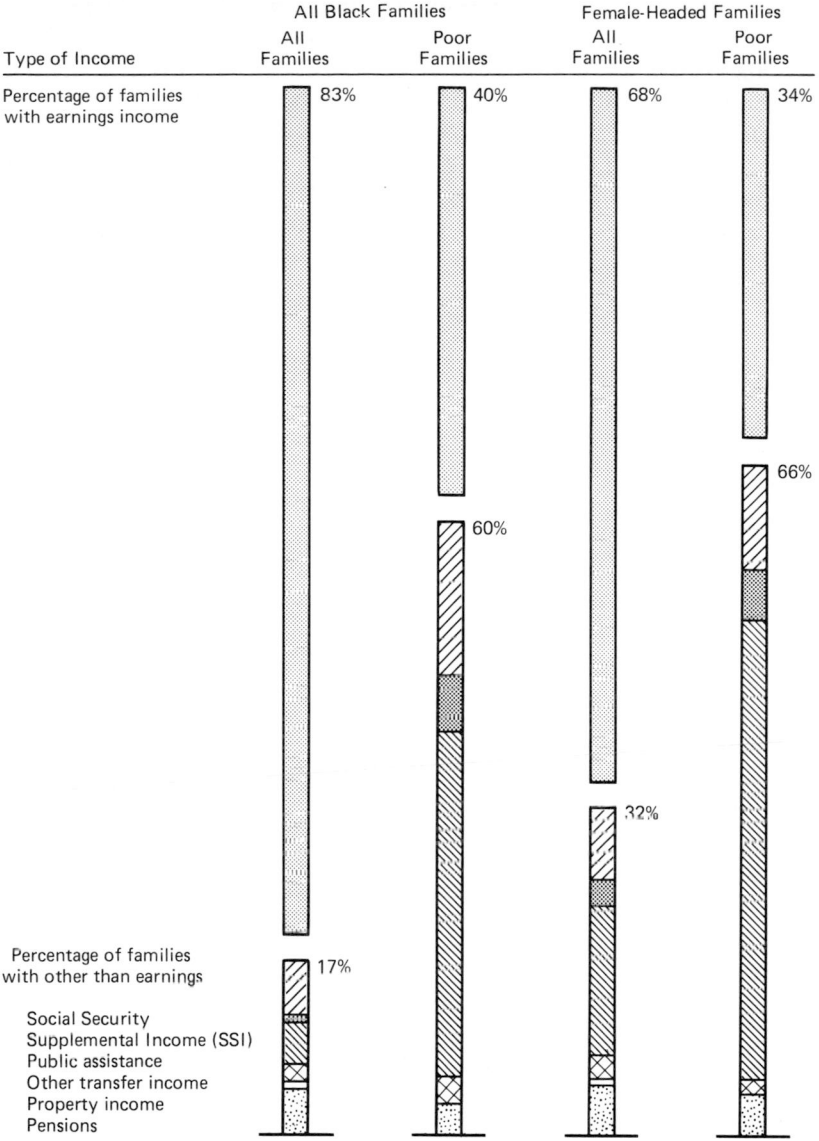

Data: U.S. Department of Commerce, Bureau of the Census.

in fiscal 1981 received $6 billion, and in fiscal 1982 received $2.2 billion, down to $1.8 billion and turning the programs into a block grant for the states.

An analysis of Reagan's FY 83 proposal by the nonpartisan Congressional Budget Office found that over half of the benefit cuts and individual tax increases would fall on the poor, those with annual incomes of under $10,000.

There were indications, however, that Congress, having cut so deeply the year before, was not in a mood to cut much deeper into social programs.

INCOME AND POVERTY PATTERNS AMONG BLACKS

Having examined the impact over the last decade on blacks of the various recessions and the eroding commitment to black economic progress, attention is now directed toward an overall appraisal of the economic status of blacks during this period. Throughout the 1970s, several new viewpoints were set forth about the nature and extent of black economic progress. The first held that blacks had made such enormous gains during the 1960s that over half of all black families were not in the middle class. This was argued most forcefully by Richard Scammon and Ben Wattenberg, two white social scientists, in *The Real Majority,* which appeared in 1971, and later in an article, "Black Progress and Liberal Rhetoric," published in the neoconservative magazine *Commentary* in 1973.

The second view held that the extraordinary progress of blacks suggested that there had been a virtual collapse of traditional patterns in the labor market and that race was no longer a factor in determining economic progress. Stated another way, class and not race was the key to progress. It was also asserted that there had been deterioration of black families due to an alleged increasing welfare-dependent "underclass," composed primarily of families headed by women and unemployed youth. Thus, it was concluded, the economic cleavage between the black middle class and underclass was wider than the gap between blacks and whites.

This view was articulated by William J. Wilson, a black sociologist at the University of Chicago, in his book *The Declining Significance of Race,* and bolstered by economists Thomas Sowell and Walter Williams, also black.

These were not arcane discussions, for if they were correct, then there was support for the position that enough had been done for blacks and there was no longer a need for such special assistance as affirmative action and minority-oriented economic programs.

Generally, however, the black intellectual community countered that the enormous economic progress of blacks was an illusion, that the economic gap within the black community had not widened significantly, and that race remains a factor in determining progress. Obviously, the views are at variance with one another. How much progress actually occurred during the 1970s among middle-income and low-income blacks? This question will now be addressed.

Middle Income Patterns

Close examination of studies heralding a surge in the black "middle class" reveal a number of deficiencies. First, most of the studies are based on data from the 1960s rather than the 1970s. Second, those that focused on the 1970s invariably omitted any systematic assessment of the impact of periodic recessions and record-level inflation on blacks. Third, many of the generalizations about income advances of black families are based on the earning gains of individuals. The danger in this is that individual income gains are not necessarily translated into family income gains. In short, if one wants to make generalizations about the progress of families, then family households and not individuals should be used as the unit of analysis. Fourth, and

Chart 10. Extent of Multiple Economic Benefits for the Poor Received by Black Households: 1979

40% of black households with under $6,000 in annual income receive *no* benefits from government programs for the poor; only 9% receive aid from five or more programs

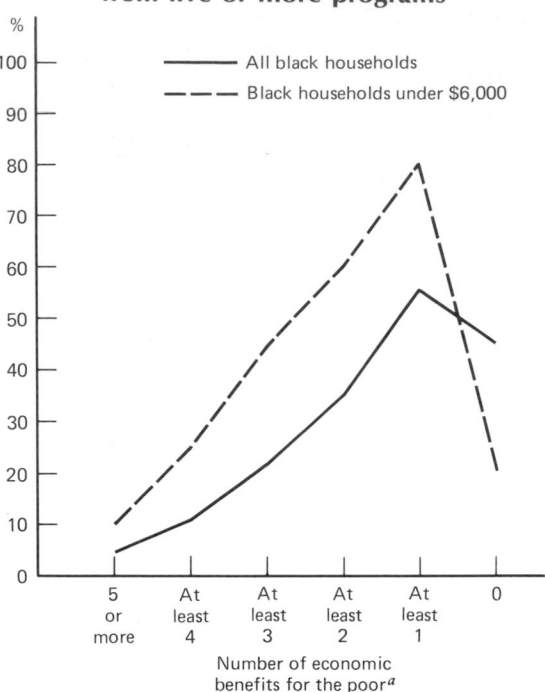

Number of economic benefits for the poor[a]

[a] Economic benefits defined as the following seven government programs for the poor: Public Assistance, Supplemental Security Income (SSI), Medicaid, food stamps, free school lunches, public housing, and subsidized rent.

Source: National Urban League Research Department, *The Myth of Income Cushions for Blacks* (1980), based on UL Black Pulse Survey data.

most important, most of these analyses fail to clearly define what they mean by "middle class." This is illustrated in the work of Wattenberg and Scammon, who arbitrarily defined all white-collar, craft, and operative (such as machinists) jobs as "middle class" or "good jobs." In fact, two fifths of the blacks holding such jobs had annual earnings below the poverty level.

What this results in is a distorted picture of the black middle class, since it places emphasis on the nature of work, rather than how much that work actually pays. In the final analysis, it is money that determines whether an individual is "middle class" or not.

Blacks, however, did make significant inroads into higher-paying positions, although the pace was slowed somewhat by periodic recessions and double-digit inflation. The proportion of all black workers in managerial, professional, and craft occupations jumped from 21 to 27% between 1970 and 1980. Interestingly, most of this occurred after 1975, when 22% of all blacks were in these higher-level jobs. Between 1975 and 1980 the number of blacks entering one of the three highest paying occupations rose by 662,000 to 2.3 million. These jobs accounted for over half (51%) of the total 1.3 million new jobs obtained by blacks during the second half of the decade. These gains helped to narrow the earnings ratio between black and white men from 61 to 65% between 1969 and 1978 and virtually closed the earnings gap between black and white women from 74 to 95%.

These occupational advances also contributed to sharp gains in the proportion of middle- and upper-income black families during the 1970s—even when income was adjusted for inflation. Using the U.S. Bureau of Labor Statistics intermediate family budget (of $20,517 in 1979) as a "middle-income" standard, the proportion of black families with real gross incomes of $20,000 or more jumped from 20 to 27% between 1969 and 1979, while increasing from 43 to 52% among white families. These income gains are largely responsible for aggregate family income among blacks rising to a record $88 billion by 1979—making the black consumer market larger than the income of many nations combined.

It is commonly believed that most of the upward advances of blacks occurred among those from "middle-class" backgrounds, while bypassing the black poor. Most studies in this area, however, have indicated that the overwhelming majority of blacks at middle-income levels or in higher-paying jobs come from working-class or poor backgrounds. A recent analysis of the origins of black men in white-collar occupations, for example, revealed that 40% of them came from working-class backgrounds, 23% from the "underclass," and only 18% from the middle class, reflecting the same general percentage that exists in the total black population.

Overall, however, blacks have made impressive advances into middle- and upper-income levels over the past decade. One out of every two new jobs obtained by blacks between 1975 and 1980 were in one of the three highest paying occupations. And more than one fourth of all black families were middle income by 1979, compared to only one fifth in 1969.

The status of the black middle class has obviously improved over the past decade or so. One note of caution, however, needs to be sounded. Because so many blacks have lately arrived at the middle-income status, their position is likely to be more precarious than that of middle-income whites. In many instances, the loss of a paycheck for even a short time could drop them out of the middle class. This precarious position is also reflected in the disproportionate number of business failures and housing defaults among blacks during the past decade.

What impact will Reagan's Economic Plan have on middle-income blacks? Certainly they will benefit from the President's tax reduction to a greater extent than low-income blacks, since the tax cuts favor the affluent. However, middle-income blacks may well be negatively affected by many of the President's cuts in social programs.

For example, the Administration proposed to cut $9.2 billion from the Basic Educational Opportunity (or Pell) Grant and the Guaranteed Student Loan Program between 1981 and 1986. If enacted, about 1.5 million college students in families with incomes under $30,000 would be disqualified from guaranteed student loans under a new "means" test, while 600,000 graduate students would be dropped from the Middle-Income Student Assistance Program.

Such wholesale cuts would significantly impede access for thousands of black youth to the primary channel that blacks have historically relied on to attain "middle-class" status—a college education. The importance of government assistance is attested to by the fact that on the campuses of many predominantly black institutions, upwards of 70% of the students receive some form of assistance, and these schools still produce the bulk of black college graduates.

Blacks in business will be affected markedly by the 33% cut in the Small Business Administration's FY 82 budget for direct loans. And the new GBA regulations that restrict maximum participation in the 8(a) set-aside program to five years will undermine the economic viability of many black businesses in their formative years. This program allows the setting aside of a certain amount of funds for contracts to minorities.

Finally, the cutbacks in social service programs will directly affect the job picture for middle-income blacks. Among professionals, 57% of black male college graduates in 1970 were employed by government, compared with 27% of comparable white college graduates; 72% of black women graduates and 56% of white women graduates were also employed by government. Professional and managerial blacks were clustered in the public sector in social work so that their numbers will be thinned considerably as the federal budget cuts for domestic social programs take their toll. For example, in Washington, D.C., the Department of Health and Human Services, a major agency for black employment, will reduce its staff by 3,000 in 1982. Also, the Community Services Administration, whose staff of more than 900 workers was 60% black, was abolished in October 1981.

Low-Income Patterns

At the same time that the percentage of middle-income blacks increased, there were changes in the ranks of

Chart 11. Number of Social Security Recipients in Current Payment Status at End of 1978, Distributed by Race (numbers in thousands)

In 1978, one in ten Social Security recipients were black; 28% of them were children, compared with 14% of white recipients

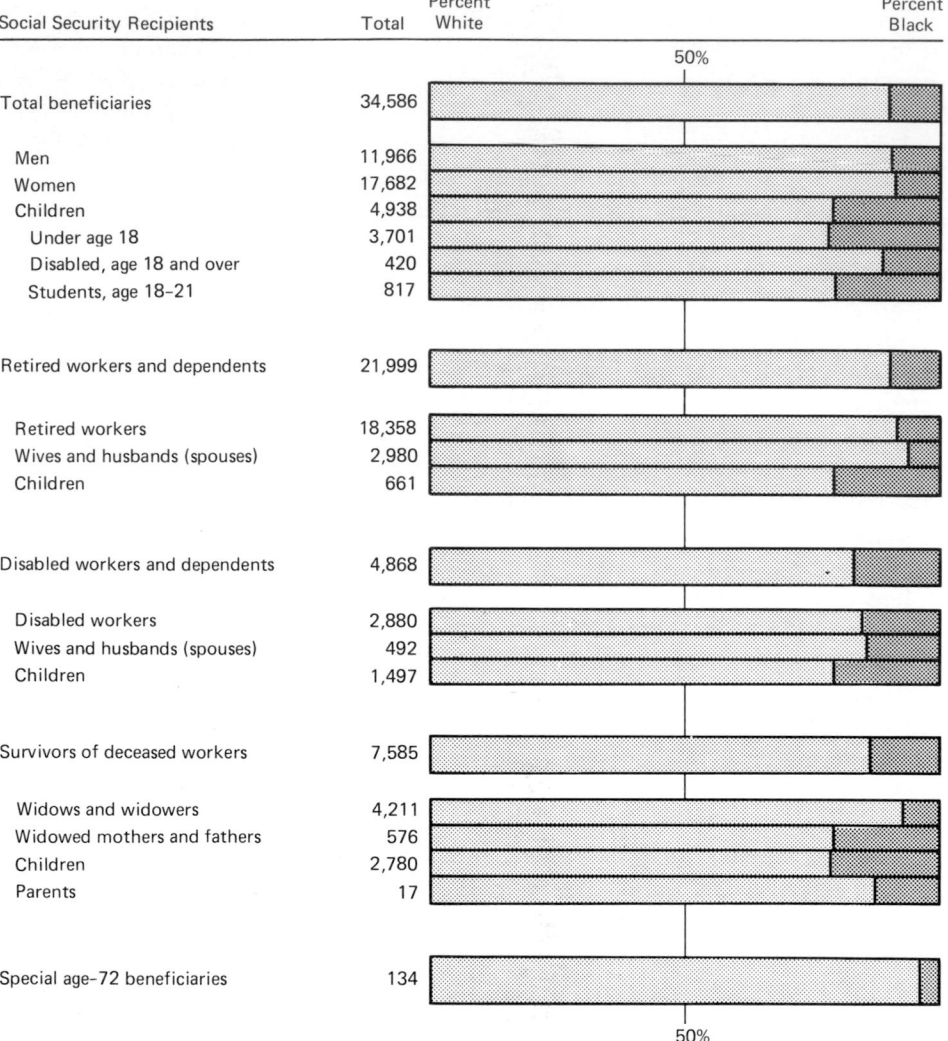

Social Security Recipients	Total	Percent White	Percent Black
Total beneficiaries	34,586		
Men	11,966		
Women	17,682		
Children	4,938		
Under age 18	3,701		
Disabled, age 18 and over	420		
Students, age 18–21	817		
Retired workers and dependents	21,999		
Retired workers	18,358		
Wives and husbands (spouses)	2,980		
Children	661		
Disabled workers and dependents	4,868		
Disabled workers	2,880		
Wives and husbands (spouses)	492		
Children	1,497		
Survivors of deceased workers	7,585		
Widows and widowers	4,211		
Widowed mothers and fathers	576		
Children	2,780		
Parents	17		
Special age-72 beneficiaries	134		

Source: U.S. Department of Health and Human Services, Social Security Administration.

low-income blacks during the 1970s. While the proportion of black families with real gross incomes under $7,500 edged up from 30 to 32%, the proportion of all blacks below the official poverty level went down from 32 to 31% between 1969 and 1979. This was in sharp contrast to the steep drop in poverty among blacks from 55 to 32% during the 1960s when the War on Poverty was operative and there was a period of economic growth. The total number of blacks in poor families, however, jumped from 6.2 to 6.6 million in the 1970s. Most of this increase in poverty occurred among female-headed families in which the number of poor persons jumped from 3.2 to 4.7 million over

the decade. Yet the percentage of female-headed black families that were poor fell from 58 to 53%. This decline indicates that the number of families headed by black women rose much faster among the nonpoor than the poor during the 1970s.

This rise in poverty among blacks is usually attributed to the increase in female-headed families. But a more complete explanation is that it is due to the rise in the number of black families headed by *unemployed* women. Employment status is a major determinant of poverty status. The chances of a black female family head being poor are only one out of four if she is working, but they are three out of four if she is unemployed. Despite their higher educational attainment and work orientation, black women heading families in 1979 were twice as likely (12.9%) to be unemployed as in 1969 (5.6%). And 54% of black female family heads were working or looking for work in 1979, compared to 51% in 1969. Among white female family heads, however, the proportion in the labor force rose more sharply than for black female family heads (from 52 to 62%). Although the jobless rate for white female family heads also doubled (from 3.6 to 7.0%) between 1969 and 1979, it was still only half the jobless rate for black female family heads by the end of the decade. The relatively larger increase of white women in the labor force during the 1970s is a major reason why, contrary to historical patterns, which found both the black husband and wife working because of economic necessity, there are more earners in white than black families today. The proportionate decline of multiple earners among black families is chiefly responsible for the widening of the gap between black and white family incomes over the past decade.

A popular justification for the deep cutbacks in social programs by the Reagan Administration is that minorities, especially blacks, have become "overdepen-dent" on welfare and other government benefits. To what extent are blacks dependent on government cash and in-kind assistance? Contrary to popular belief, the following facts should be kept in mind:

1. The overwhelming majority of the beneficiaries of government programs are white, not black. Whites make up between 58–67% of the recipients of public assistance, Supplemental Security Income (SS), food stamps, Medicaid, and housing assistance.

2. The proportion of all black families receiving public assistance rose from 18% to only 22% between 1969 and 1979.

3. Only one out of four black households receive food stamps, Medicaid, or public or subsidized housing assistance.

4. Although one fourth of all black families are on welfare, only 7% are completely dependent on it.

5. Half of all poor black households do not receive any aid from welfare, Medicaid, or food stamps.

6. Three fifths (58%) of all poor black households

Black youths who are fortunate enough to have work generally find it at low-paying, unskilled occupations.

Black-owned small businesses like this hardware store provide good services and fair prices to their local communities.

receive benefits from only two or fewer of the seven major government income support programs for the poor.

7. Public assistance accounts for only 4% of the total income of all black families, with earnings making up 83%. Similarly, among black families headed by women, earnings make up two thirds (68%) of their total income, with public assistance contributing only 15%.

What effects will the enactment of the President's economic policies have on low-income blacks? As the preceding analyses clearly indicate, economically disadvantaged individuals and families will bear the brunt of the spending cuts. But it is important to point out that the primary target of the Administration's actions was the working poor. Thus the overwhelming majority of low-income blacks will be disproportionately affected, since they are either working or looking for work.

The working poor can best be described as persons who work full time for the minimum wage or below or can only find part-time work. For example, 30%

of black female family heads who worked full-time in 1979 still remained below the official poverty level. These are hard-working breadwinners whose earnings are usually insufficient to meet the needs of their families. Consequently, they often need to supplement their poverty wages for limited periods of time with some public benefits, such as welfare, Medicaid, food stamps, school lunches, or subsidized rent. In short, it is this group, which has tried hardest to be self-reliant, that has been singled out by the Reagan Administration for undue economic hardships.

In summary, the past decade has been one of mixed blessings for black Americans in the economic sphere. There has been an increase in the percentage of black families with middle-income levels. At the same time, the overwhelming percentage of blacks remain near or below the poverty level. To compound the problem, a number of the programs that were designed to get people out of poverty have been abandoned. And further, the economic malaise of the country and the feeling that enough has been done to help blacks offers very little hope for further black economic progress in the immediate future.

SELECTED FACTS

Fact 1

Reversing historical patterns, white families now have a higher proportion of multiple earners than black families. While the proportion of black families with two or more earners fell from 54 to 47% between 1970 and 1979, the proportion among white families rose from 53 to 57%.

Fact 2

During the 1970s the earnings of black men and women gained relative to the earnings of white men and women. While the earnings ratio between black men and white men rose from 61 to 65% between 1969 and 1978, the earnings gap between black women and white women virtually closed with the ratio rising from 74 to 95%.

Fact 3

Apparently, the aftermath of the 1974–1975 recession markedly slowed the earnings gains of blacks relative to white workers. Between 1975 and 1978 the earnings ratio between black and white men remained at 65%. And, although the earnings ratio between black and white women crept up from 90 to 95% between 1975 and 1978, the gap between black women and white men held at 38%.

Fact 4

The mean earnings of all black male workers were 66% of all white male workers' earnings in 1979. Among year-round, full-time workers, black men earned 71% of what white men earned.

Fact 5

Black women and white women each earned only 44% of what white men earned in 1979. Among those working year-round, full-time, the earnings of white (56%) and black women (53%) were over half of white men's.

Fact 6

The widest gap in earnings occurs among workers in sales occupations. Black men in sales jobs earned only 57% of what all white men in such jobs earned, while white (29%) and black women (28%) earned only about one fourth of what white men earned in sales work.

Fact 7

Even when family income is adjusted for inflation, the proportion of middle- and upper-income families still rose sharply among blacks, as well as whites, during the 1970s. The proportion of families with real gross median incomes of $20,000 or more jumped from 20 to 27% among blacks and from 43 to 52% among whites between 1969 and 1979.

Fact 8

Although the percentage of low-income families fell slightly among whites between 1969 and 1979, it edged upward among blacks. The proportion of all black families with real gross incomes under $7,500 rose from 30 to 32% between 1969 and 1979, compared to a decline from 12 to 11% among white families.

Fact 9

Between 1969 and 1979, the income ratio of all black to white families fell from 61 to 57%. Among husband-wife families, however, the income gap between blacks and whites narrowed from 72 to 77%, while the gap between black and white female-headed families widened from 61 to 59%.

Fact 10

The income gap between black and white families widened significantly during the 1970s in all regions except the South. While the income ratio between black and white families fell sharply in the Northeast (from 67 to 57%), North Central (from 76 to 62%), and West (from 75 to 63%) between 1969 and 1979, the income gap held at 57% in the South.

Fact 11

Among all families, real gross income rose among whites but declined among blacks during the 1970s. Between 1969 and 1979, real gross income rose 6% among all white families but declined 2% among all black families. However, when taxes are deducted from gross income, real net income rose only 1% among whites while declining 2% among blacks.

Fact 12

Among husband-wife families, real gross income increased twice as fast among blacks (16%) than whites (8%) between 1969 and 1979. Moreover, real after-tax income among husband-wife families rose three times faster among blacks (14%) than whites (4%).

Fact 13

In families headed by women, real gross income increased just as much for blacks (5%) as for whites (4%) between 1969 and 1979. But while real spendable income in female-headed families rose 5% among whites, real net income fell 1% among blacks.

Fact 14

According to the official poverty level, 7.8 million blacks were poor in 1979. But if one uses the more accurate 150% (of the official poverty level) as the standard, the number of poor blacks rises to 11.9 million.

Fact 15

Based on the 150% poverty standard, 5.3 million black children under 18 were poor in 1979, compared to 3.7 million, according to official statistics.

Fact 16

Persons in families headed by women account for 60% of the black poor based on the official standard, but they make up 53% of the black poor using the 150% measure.

Fact 17

According to official poverty statistics, persons in male-headed families account for 24% of all black poor, but they rise to 33% based on the 150% standard.

Fact 18

Officially, 716,000 black persons 65 years and over were poor in 1979, but 1.2 million were poor based on the 150% standard.

Fact 19

Using the 150% standard, almost half (47%) of all blacks were poor in 1979, compared to 31%, officially.

Fact 20

Based on the 150% level, 59% of all black children under 18 were poor in 1979, compared to 41%, officially.

Fact 21

The proportion of all black elderly who were poor in 1979 was 59%, according to the 150% standard, but only 36% using the official poverty level.

Fact 22

Officially, 59% of all black elderly unrelated individuals were poor in 1979, but 85% were poor according to the 150% level.

Fact 23

The percentage of poor persons among all blacks and whites fell only slightly during the 1970s. While the proportion of poor black persons slipped from 32 to 31% between 1969 and 1979, the proportion of poor whites edged down from 10 to 9%.

Fact 24

The number of poor persons rose among both blacks and whites in the 1970s. The number of poor persons jumped from 7.1 to 7.8 million among blacks and from 16.7 to 16.8 million among whites between 1969 and 1979.

Fact 25

While the percentage of black children in female-headed families who were poor fell from 68 to 63% between 1969 and 1979, the number of poor black children in one-parent families jumped from 2.1 to 2.9 million.

Fact 26

Although the percentage of all black elderly who were poor fell sharply from 50 to 36% between 1969 and 1979, the number of poor black aged edged up from 689,000 to 716,000.

Fact 27

Both the number and percentage of poor white elderly declined during the 1970s. While the proportion of white elderly persons who were poor fell from 23 to 13% between 1969 and 1979, the number of poor white aged also declined from 4.1 to 2.8 million.

Fact 28

Almost three fourths (71%) of all poor blacks live in metropolitan areas, as do 59% of all poor aged blacks. Over half (56%) of all poor blacks live in central cities, as do 48% of all poor black elderly.

Fact 29

Three fourths (76%) of all poor persons in black families headed by women live in metropolitan areas, as do 56% of the poor in male-headed black families.

Fact 30

Blacks living outside metropolitan areas are more likely to be poor than those residing in metropolitan areas. Two fifths (40%) of all blacks outside metropolitan areas are poor, compared to 28% of those in metropolitan areas.

Fact 31

Half (45%) of the black aged outside metropolitan areas are poor, compared to 30% of the aged metropolitan dwellers. Similarly, 72% of the black elderly who live alone outside metropolitan areas are poor, compared to 54% of those in metropolitan areas.

Fact 32

Half (49%) of all black children under 18 who live outside metropolitan areas are poor, compared to 38% of those in metropolitan areas.

Fact 33

Over half (56%) of all poor blacks live in the South, one fifth (20%) in the North Central region, 17% in the Northeast, and only 7% in the West.

Fact 34

The highest poverty rates among blacks are found in the South (34%), while the lowest rates are in the West (24%). The rates of poverty among blacks in the Northeast (28%) and North Central regions (30%) fall between those in the South and West.

Fact 35

The proportion of black children under 18 in female-headed families who are poor is 68% in the South, 63% in the North Central region, 57% in the Northeast, and 45% in the West.

Fact 36

Black male family heads in sales occupations are just as likely (11%) to be poor as those in laborer jobs (13%). But among white male family heads, laborers are three times more likely (10%) to be poor than sales workers (3%).

Fact 37

Black female family heads in sales occupations are just as likely (39%) to be poor as those in service jobs (41%). But among white female family heads, service workers are twice as likely (27%) to be poor as sales workers (13%).

Fact 38

Among black female family heads, private sector workers are almost twice as likely (37%) to be poor as those working for the government (22%). Similarly, among black male family heads, private workers (8%) are twice as likely to be poor as government workers (4%).

Fact 39

Among female family heads, 30% of black mothers who worked full time in 1979 were poor, compared to 12% of white mothers who worked full time.

Fact 40

Among black female family heads, 60% of the mothers with children under age 3 were poor in 1979, compared to 41% of those with children between the ages of 15 and 17. Among white female family heads, half (50%) of the mothers with children under 3 were poor, compared to only 12% of those with children between 15 and 17 years old.

Fact 41

Four fifths (82%) of all black families have income from earnings, while only one fourth (22%) have income from public assistance. While half (52%) of all poor black families receive some public assistance, half (54%) of them also have earnings income.

Fact 42

Although one fourth of all black families receive public assistance, only 7% are completely dependent on it.

Fact 43

Almost three fourths (71%) of all black families headed by women have earnings income, while less than half (44%) receive public assistance. However, half (52%) of all poor black female-headed families have earnings income, while two thirds (65%) of them receive some welfare.

Fact 44

Earnings account for 83% of the total income of all black families, while public assistance makes up only 4%. Among poor black families, earnings account for 40% of their total income, while welfare makes up 34%.

Fact 45

Public assistance accounts for only 15% of the total income of all black families headed by women, with earnings making up 68%. Among poor female-headed black families, however, public assistance comprises 45% of the total income, with earnings accounting for 34%.

Fact 46

Reliance on public assistance declines sharply with increasing age. Three fourths (73%) of all black families headed by women under age 25 receive welfare, compared to only 22% of families headed by women 65 years and over.

Fact 47

Among poor one-parent black families headed by women, those with heads under 25 are 2½ times as likely (81%) to receive public assistance as those with heads 65 years and over (31%).

Fact 48

Public assistance accounts for only 41% of the total income of black families headed by women under 25, with earnings accounting for 52%. Among poor black families headed by women under 25, welfare comprises 63% of the total income, with earnings making up 29%.

Fact 49

The overwhelming majority of recipients of government benefits for the poor are white, not black. Whites account for 60% of all public assistance recipients, 64% of all SSI beneficiaries, 67% of Medicaid recipients, 63% of food stamp beneficiaries, and 58% of all recipients of public or subsidized housing.

Fact 50

About one fourth of all black households receive Medicaid (28%), food stamps (27%), and public or subsidized housing (23%), while half (50%) of the households with school-age children receive reduced-price school lunches.

Fact 51

Two out of every five black households below the official poverty level do not receive benefits from Medicaid (42%) or food stamps (41%), while two thirds (67%) do not receive either public housing or subsidized rent benefits.

Fact 52

Two thirds (65%) of all black households receive benefits from only one or none of the seven major income support programs for the poor. And 58% of all black households with income under $6,000 receive benefits from only two or less of the seven major government income transfer programs for the poor.

Fact 53

While blacks make up one tenth of all Social Security recipients, they account for one fifth of all children who receive Social Security benefits.

Fact 54

Blacks comprise only 8% of all retired workers receiving Social Security, but they are 15% of all disabled workers receiving Social Security benefits.

Fact 55

Three fifths (59%) of all black families headed by poor elderly persons rely on Social Security for over half of their total income, compared to two fifths (39%) of the families headed by non-poor aged.

Fact 56

Among black elderly living alone, 74% of those who are poor depend on Social Security for over half of their income, compared to 58% of the non-poor unrelated black elderly.

Fact 57

Ninety percent of all black elderly persons with spouses receive Social Security, compared to 80% of those without spouses. But black elderly without spouses are twice as likely to receive public assistance (39%) as those living with their spouses (22%).

Table 1. Ratio of Median Earnings of Blacks to Whites Among All Workers: 1969–1978

Occupations	1969	1975	1978
A. Earnings Ratio of Black Men to White Men			
All workers	61	66	65
Managers	60	77	81
Professional	69	73	86
Craft	71	80	84
Operatives	77	78	84
Clerical	80	92	81
Sales	58	65	67
Laborers	161	110	112
Service	84	185	110
B. Earnings Ratio of Black Women to White Women			
All workers	74	90	95
Managers	—	111	111
Professional	117	128	111
Craft	—	115	81
Operatives	87	93	101
Clerical	86	112	107
Sales	92	92	117
Laborers	—	130	161
Service	154	179	158

Data: U.S. Commerce Department, Bureau of the Census.

Table 2.   Annual Earnings by Occupation, Sex and Race: 1979

Occupation	White Men	Black Men	White Women	Black Women
A. Annual Mean Earnings of All Workers				
All workers	$16,064	$10,538	$ 7,108	$ 6,997
Managers	$23,377	$17,557	$10,432	$10,887
Professional	22,175	16,705	10,307	12,308
Craft	15,229	12,065	7,946	—
Operatives	13,138	11,154	6,526	6,763
Clerical	13,499	10,594	7,234	7,937
Sales	17,237	9,905	5,020	4,868
Service workers	9,309	7,436	3,962	4,485
Nonfarm laborers	8,507	7,248	5,734	4,509
B. Ratio of Mean Earnings of Other Workers to All White Male Workers				
All workers	100	66	44	44
Managers	100	74	44	46
Professional	100	75	46	56
Craft	100	79	52	—
Operatives	100	85	50	51
Clerical	100	78	54	59
Sales	100	57	29	28
Service workers	100	80	43	48
Nonfarm laborers	100	85	67	53

Data: U.S. Commerce Department, Bureau of the Census.

Table 3.   Annual Earnings by Occupation, Sex and Race: 1979

Occupation	White Men	Black Men	White Women	Black Women
A. Annual Mean Earnings of Year-Round, Full-Time Workers				
Year-round, full-time	$19,610	$13,908	$10,939	$10,363
Managers	25,273	19,140	12,984	12,726
Professional	25,234	19,272	14,259	14,722
Craft	17,659	14,482	11,438	—
Operatives	15,731	13,368	9,237	8,924
Clerical	17,029	13,971	10,274	10,985
Sales	20,742	—	10,363	—
Service workers	13,646	11,190	7,514	7,458
Nonfarm laborers	12,922	11,385	9,820	—
B. Ratio of Mean Earnings of Other Workers to White Male Year-Round, Full-time Workers				
Year-round, full-time	100	71	56	53
Managers	100	76	51	50
Professional	100	76	57	58
Craft	100	82	65	—
Operatives	100	85	59	57
Clerical	100	82	60	65
Sales	100	—	50	—
Service workers	100	82	55	55
Nonfarm laborers	100	88	76	—

Data: U.S. Commerce Department, Bureau of the Census.

Table 4. Total Family Income in Constant 1979 Dollars by Race: 1969–1979

Family Income	Black Families 1969	Black Families 1979	White Families 1969	White Families 1979
Total families/(thousands)	4,774	6,042	46,022	51,389
Percent	100	100	100	100
Under $7,500	30	32	12	11
Under $2,500	6	6	2	2
$2,500–4,999	11	13	4	4
$5,000–7,499	13	13	6	6
$7,500–19,999	51	41	45	37
$7,500–9,999	12	11	6	7
$10,000–12,499	12	10	8	8
$12,500–14,999	10	7	8	7
$15,000–19,999	17	12	23	15
$20,000 and over	20	27	43	52
$20,000–24,999	8	10	12	15
$25,000–34,999	9	11	20	20
$35,000–49,999	2	5	7	11
$50,000 and over	1	1	4	6
Median income	$11,878	$11,644	$19,392	$20,502

Data: U.S. Commerce Department, Bureau of the Census.

Table 5. Ratio of Gross Median Income of Black to White Families: 1969–1979

	1969	1975	1976	1979
A. By Family Structure				
All families				
Black	$ 5,999	$ 8,779	$ 9,242	$11,644
White	9,794	14,268	15,537	20,502
B/W ratio	61	62	59	57
Husband-wife families				
Black	$ 7,329	$11,526	$13,137	$16,887
White	10,241	15,125	16,501	21,824
B/W ratio	72	76	80	77
Families headed by women				
Black	$ 3,341	$ 4,898	$ 5,069	$ 6,806
White	5,500	7,651	8,226	11,452
B/W ratio	61	64	62	59
B. By Region of Residence				
Total families	61	62	59	57
Northeast	67	67	61	57
North Central	76	71	67	62
South	57	59	59	57
West	75	67	63	63

Data: U.S. Commerce Department, Bureau of the Census.

Table 6. Changes in Median Family Income in Constant 1979 Dollars Before and After Taxes [a] **by Family Structure: 1969–1979**

	Black Families			
	1969	1979	Amount	Percent
All families				
Gross income	$11,878	$11,644	−$ 234	− 2.0
Net income	10,310	10,107	− 203	− 2.0
All husband-wife families				
Gross income	$14,511	$16,887	+$2,376	+16.4
Net income	12,305	13,982	+ 1,677	+13.6
Husband and wife in labor force				
Gross income	$18.085	$20,705	+$2,620	+14.5
Net income	14,974	17,144	+ 2,170	+14.5
Wife not in labor force				
Gross income	$11,112	$11,603	+$ 491	+ 4.4
Net income	9,645	10,071	+$ 426	+ 4.5
All female-headed families				
Gross income	$ 6,615	$ 6,806	+$ 291	+ 4.4
Net income	6,205	5,939	−$ 266	− 4.3
Female-headed, year-round workers				
Gross income		$11,520		
Net income		9,999		

Data: U.S. Commerce Department, Bureau of the Census.

[a] Income after taxes (or "net" income) excludes personal income and social security payroll taxes only.

Table 7. Changes in Median Family Income in Constant 1979 Dollars Before and After Taxes [a] **by Family Structure: 1969–1979**

	1969	1979	Amount	Percent
All families				
Gross income	$19,392	$20,502	+$1,110	+5.7
Net income	16,270	16,402	+ 132	+0.8
All husband-wife families				
Gross income	$20,277	$21,824	+$1,547	+7.6
Net income	16,789	17,459	+ 670	+4.0
Husband and wife in labor force				
Gross income	$23,534	$25,313	+$1,779	+7.6
Net income	19,627	19,744	+ 117	+0.6
Wife not in labor force				
Gross income	$18,040	$18,204	+$ 164	+1.0
Net income	15,099	14,927	−$ 172	−1.1
All female-headed families				
Gross income	$10,890	$11,452	+$ 562	+5.2
Net income	9,453	9,940	+$ 487	+5.2
Female-headed, year-round workers				
Gross income		$15,417		
Net income		12,950		

Data: U.S. Commerce Department, Bureau of the Census.

[a] Income after taxes (or "net" income) excludes personal income and social security payroll taxes only.

Table 8. Number and Percent of People Below Different Poverty Levels: 1979

Family status	Below 100% of Poverty Level		Below 150% of Poverty Level		Percent	
	Number	Percent	Number	Percent	Below 100%	Below 150%
A. Blacks						
Total persons	7,838	100	11,904	100	31%	47%
65 years and over	716	9	1,198	10	36	59
In families	6,614	84	10,205	86	30	46
Children under 18	3,695	47	5,328	45	41	59
Children under 6	1,229	16	1,714	14	43	60
In male-headed	1,920	24	3,905	33	14	29
In female-headed	4,694	60	6,300	53	53	71
Children under 18	2,851	36	3,659	31	63	81
Children under 6	962	12	1,181	10	70	86
Unrelated individuals	1,143	15	1,594	13	37	51
65 years and over	390	5	561	5	59	85
B. Whites						
Total persons	16,823	100	32,545	100	9%	17%
65 years and over	2,840	17	6,504	20	13	30
In families	12,213	73	24,314	75	7	15
Children under 18	5,759	34	10,393	32	11	21
Children under 6	2,019	12	3,632	11	13	24
In male-headed	7,941	47	17,824	55	5	12
In female-headed	4,272	25	6,490	20	25	38
Children under 18	2,560	15	3,592	11	39	54
Children under 6	849	5	1,084	3	54	69
Unrelated individuals	4,351	26	7,844	24	20	36
65 years and over	1,837	11	3,834	12	27	55

Data: U.S. Commerce Department, Bureau of the Census.

Table 9. Number and Percentage of Poor, by Family Status and Race: 1969–1979

Family Status	Poor Blacks		Poor Whites	
	1969	1979	1969	1979
A. Number of Persons Below Official Poverty Level				
Total poor persons	7,095	7,838	16,659	16,823
65 years and over	689	716	4,052	2,840
In families	6,245	6,614	12,623	12,213
Children under 18	3,677	3,695	5,667	5,759
In male-headed	3,020	1,920	9,046	7,941
In female-headed	3,225	4,694	3,577	4,272
Children under 18	2,137	2,851	2,068	2,560
Unrelated individuals	850	1,143	4,036	4,351
65 years and over	336	390	2,300	1,837
B. Percent of All Persons Who Are Poor				
Total persons	32	31	10	9
65 years and over	50	36	23	13
In families	31	30	8	7
Children under 18	40	41	10	11
In male-headed	21	14	6	5
In female-headed	58	53	29	25
Children under 18	68	63	45	39
Unrelated individuals	39	37	32	20
65 years and over	75	59	45	27

Data: U.S. Commerce Department, Bureau of the Census.

Table 10. Distribution of Poor Blacks by Family Status and Residence: 1979

| Family Status | Poor Blacks | | Inside Metropolitan Areas | | | Outside Metropolitan Areas |
| | Number | Percent | Total | Central Cities | | |
				Inside	Outside	
A. Percentage Distribution of Poor Blacks Residing Inside and Outside Metropolitan Areas by Family Status						
Total poor persons	7,838	100	71	56	15	29
65 years and over	716	100	59	48	10	42
In families	6,614	100	70	56	14	30
Children under 18	3,695	100	71	56	15	29
Children under 6	1,229	100	72	57	15	28
In male-headed	1,920	100	56	39	19	44
In female-headed	4,694	100	76	62	25	24
Children under 18	2,851	100	76	62	26	24
Children under 6	962	100	75	61	25	25
Unrelated individuals	1,143	100	76	61	15	24
65 years and over	390	100	66	55	12	33
B. Percent of All Blacks Who Are Poor by Family Status and Area of Residence						
Total persons			28	31	21	40
65 years and over			30	33	23	46
In families			27	30	20	38
Children under 18			38	42	28	49
Children under 6			41	45	30	51
In male-headed			11	11	10	25
In female-headed			51	54	42	61
Children under 18			61	63	51	72
Children under 6			69	71	61	75
Unrelated individuals			34	35	30	52
65 years and over			54	54	51	72

Data: U.S. Commerce Department, Bureau of the Census.

Table 11. Distribution of Poor Blacks by Family Status and Region: 1979

Family Status	Poor Blacks Number	Poor Blacks Percent	Region of Residence North-east	Region of Residence North-Central	Region of Residence South	Region of Residence West
A. Percentage Distribution of Poor Blacks by Family Status and Region of Residence						
Total poor persons	7,838	100	17	20	56	7
65 years and over	716	100	9	15	68	8
In families	6,614	100	17	20	58	6
Children under 18	3,695	100	17	21	57	6
Children under 6	1,229	100	16	20	58	6
In male-headed	1,920	100	14	13	67	7
In female-headed	4,694	100	18	22	54	6
Children under 18	2,851	100	17	23	54	6
Children under 6	962	100	16	23	55	6
Unrelated individuals	1,143	100	18	21	51	10
65 years and over	390	100	11	18	64	7

B. Percent of All Blacks Who Are Poor by Family Status and Region of Residence

Family Status	Total	North-East	North-Central	South	West
Total persons	31	28	30	34	24
65 years and over	36	23	29	41	30
In families	30	27	29	33	22
Children under 18	41	36	40	44	30
Children under 6	43	40	43	46	33
In male-headed	14	11	9	18	12
In female-headed	53	47	55	57	38
Children under 18	63	57	63	68	45
Children under 6	70	63	73	74	55
Unrelated individuals	37	33	33	43	29
65 years and over	59	48	50	67	—

Data: U.S. Commerce Department, Bureau of the Census.

Table 12. Percentage of Family Heads Who Are Poor: 1979

Occupation of Head	Black Family Heads			White Family Heads		
	All Family Heads	Male Head	Female Head	All Family Heads	Male Head	Female Head
A. By Occupation, Sex of Head and Race						
Total employed	17%	8%	33%	4%	4%	14%
Managers, administrators	4	3	9	3	3	5
Professional, technical	8	4	16	1	1	8
Sales	21	11	39	4	3	13
Clerical	17	2	24	4	1	9
Craft	7	7	9	3	3	17
Operatives, except transport	17	8	36	5	3	15
Transport operatives	11	8	52	5	4	22
Nonfarm laborers	16	13	45	10	10	16
Service, except private household	25	7	41	10	5	27
Private household	50	8	66	39	13	45
B. Class of Worker, Sex of Head, and Race						
Total employed	17	8	33	4	4	14
Private workers	17	8	37	4	3	14
Government workers	12	4	22	3	2	11
Federal	3	1	8	1	1	7
State	18	7	26	2	1	8
Local	14	5	26	4	3	13
Self-employed	25	22	50	11	10	20

Data: U.S. Commerce Department, Bureau of the Census.

Table 13. Percentage Poor: 1979

A. Family Heads Who Are Poor, by Work Experience, Sex of Head, and Race

Work Experience	Black Family Heads			White Family Heads		
	All Family Heads	Male Head	Female Head	All Family Heads	Male Head	Female Head
Worked last year,	17	8	33	4	4	14
50–52 weeks	8	5	17	2	2	5
Worked full-time,	13	7	27	4	3	9
50–52 weeks	7	5	13	2	2	3
Did not work	55	33	71	18	12	39

B. Working Women Who Are Poor, by Work Experience, Family Status and Race

Work Experience	Black Working Mothers			White Working Mothers		
	All Working Mothers	Working Wives	Female Heads	All Working Mothers	Working Wives	Female Heads
Worked last year,	20	6	37	6	3	18
50–52 weeks	10	3	19	3	18	7
Worked full-time,	17	5	30	5	3	12
50–52 weeks	8	3	15	2	1	4
Did not work	59	29	87	16	9	74

C. Working Mothers Who Are Poor, by Age of Children, Family Status, and Race

Age of Children	Black Working Mothers			White Working Mothers		
	Working Mothers	Working Wives	Female Heads	Working Mothers	Working Wives	Female Heads
Under age 18	27	9	46	8	4	24
Under age 3	28	7	60	10	5	50
3–5 years old	28	8	50	10	5	31
6–14 years old	27	10	44	8	4	24
15–17 years old	26	10	41	4	3	12

Data: U.S. Commerce Department, Bureau of the Census.

Table 14. Black Family Income, by Family Structure and Poverty Status: 1979

Type of Income	All Black Families		Female-Headed Families	
	All Families	Poor Families	All Families	Poor Families

A. Percentage of Black Families Receiving Different Types of Income

Type of Income	All Families	Poor Families	All Families	Poor Families
Total families	6,042	1,666	2,429	1,195
With earnings income	82	54	71	52
Other than earnings	79	86	84	89
Social security	24	25	24	19
Supplemental income (SSI)	9	15	12	13
Public assistance	22	52	44	65
Other transfer income	16	9	11	7
Property income	36	12	21	9
Pensions	19	13	22	15

B. Percent Distribution of Aggregate Black Family Income

Type of Income	All Families	Poor Families	All Families	Poor Families
Total families	100	100	100	100
With earnings income	83	40	68	34
Other than earnings	17	60	32	66
Social security	6	15	8	10
Supplemental income (SSI)	1	6	3	5
Public assistance	4	34	15	45
Other transfer income	2	3	2	2
Property income	1	—	1	—
Pensions	4	3	5	4

Data: U.S. Commerce Department, Bureau of the Census.

Table 15. Income of Black Families Headed by Women, by Age of Head and Poverty Status: 1979

Type of Income	All Female-Headed Families				Poor Female-Headed Families			
	Total	Under 25 Years	25–64 Years	65+	Total	Under 25 Years	25–64 Years	65+

A. Percent of Black Families Headed by Women Receiving Different Types of Income

Type of Income	Total	Under 25 Years	25–64 Years	65+	Total	Under 25 Years	25–64 Years	65+
With earnings income	71	51	77	51	52	39	56	38
Other than earnings	84	92	81	98	89	95	87	99
Social security	24	6	19	84	19	6	17	76
Supplemental income (SSI)	12	4	9	48	13	3	11	59
Public assistance	44	73	43	22	65	81	64	31
Other transfer income	11	6	11	13	7	3	8	7
Property income	21	14	21	26	9	7	9	21
Pensions	22	15	23	21	15	12	17	6

B. Percent Distribution of Aggregate Income for Black Families Headed by Women

Type of Income	Total	Under 25 Years	25–64 Years	65+	Total	Under 25 Years	25–64 Years	65+
Total families	100	100	100	100	100	100	100	100
With earnings income	68	52	72	46	34	29	36	7
Other than earnings	32	48	28	54	66	71	64	93
Social security	8	2	6	28	10	3	9	52
Supplemental income (SSI)	3	2	2	10	5	2	5	24
Public assistance	15	41	14	5	45	63	45	14
Other transfer income	2	1	2	2	2	1	2	1
Property income	1	—	1	1	—	—	—	1
Pensions	5	3	4	8	4	3	4	1

Data: U.S. Commerce Department, Bureau of the Census.

Table 16. Number of Recipients of Cash and In-Kind Benefits by Race: 1980

Economic Benefits	Number	Percentage	White	Black
Means-tested cash aid				
Public assistance	4,398	100	60	40
Supplemental security income (SSI)	4,142	100	64	28
Other cash aid				
Social security	34,586	100	88	10
Means-tested noncash aid				
Medicaid	8,287	100	67	30
Food stamps	6,769	100	63	35
Reduced price school lunches	5,532	100	62	34
Public or subsidized housing	2,777	100	58	39
Other in-kind aid				
Medicare	19,788	100	89	10
Regular school lunches	12,049	100	89	9
Employee pension plan	38,331	100	89	9
Employee group health plan	48,824	100	89	9

Data: U.S. Commerce Department, Bureau of the Census.

Table 17. Number and Percentage of Households Receiving Noncash Benefits by Race: 1980

Type of Noncash Benefits	Black Households		White Households	
	Number	Percentage	Number	Percentage
A. All Households				
Total households	8,847	100	71,872	100
With children 5–18 years	3,785	43	22,035	31
Renter-occupied	4,618	52	21,135	29
Means-tested benefits				
Medicaid	2,495	28%	5,561	8%
Food stamps	2,376	27	4,238	6
Reduced price school lunches	1,889	50	3,429	16
Public or subsidized housing	1,075	23	1,612	8
Other in-kind benefits				
Medicare	1,964	22%	17,593	24%
Regular school lunches	1,083	29	10,704	49
Employee pension plan	3,410	39	34,204	48
Employee group health plan	4,392	50	43,397	60
B. Poor Households				
Total poor households	2,864	100	7,828	100
With children 5–18 years	1,326	46	2,439	31
Renter-occupied	1,941	68	3,934	50
Means-tested benefits				
Medicaid	1,649	58	2,656	34
Food stamps	1,701	59	2,631	34
Reduced price lunch	1,076	81	1,353	55
Public or subsidized housing	643	33	745	19
Other in-kind benefits				
Medicare	863	30	2,806	36
Regular school lunches	84	6	544	22
Employee pension plan	186	6	594	8
Employee group health plan	394	14	1,171	15

Data: U.S. Commerce Department, Bureau of the Census.

Table 18. Extent of Multiple Economic Benefits for the Poor Received by Black Households: 1979

Number of Economic Benefits for the Poor[a]	Black Households	
	Total	Under $6,000
	100	100
Less than two benefits	65	40
None of the seven benefits	45	20
One benefit	20	20
Two to three benefits	24	38
Two benefits	13	18
Three benefits	11	20
Four or more of the seven benefits	11	24
Four benefits	7	15
Five or more of the seven benefits for the poor	4	9

Source: National Urban League Research Department, *The Myth of Income Cushions for Blacks* (1980), based on NUL Black Pulse Survey data.

[a] These figures indicate the proportion of black households that receive none or some benefits from the following seven government programs for the poor: public assistance, supplemental security income (SSI), medicaid, food stamps, free school lunches, public housing, and subsidized rent.

Table 19. Number of Social Security Recipients in Current Payment Status by Race at End of 1978 (in thousands)

Social Security Recipients	Total	White	Black
Total beneficiaries	34,586	30,533	3,528
Men	11,966	10,738	1,047
Women	17,682	16,032	1,462
Children	4,938	3,763	1,019
Under age 18	3,701	2,767	806
Disabled, age 18 and over	420	365	49
Students, age 18–21	817	631	165
Retired workers and dependents	21,999	19,971	1,725
Retired workers	18,358	16,708	1,434
Wives and husbands (spouses)	2,980	2,771	164
Children	661	492	127
Disabled workers and dependents	4,868	3,971	803
Disabled workers	2,880	2,406	430
Wives and husbands (spouses)	492	412	69
Children	1,497	1,153	304
Survivors of deceased workers	7,585	6,463	995
Widows and widowers	4,211	3,888	289
Widowed mothers and fathers	576	443	117
Children	2,780	2,118	587
Parents	17	14	2
Special age-72 beneficiaries	134	129	4

Source: U.S. Department of Health and Human Services, Social Security Administration.

Table 20. Percent Distribution of Social Security Benefits Received by Elderly by Share of Total Income and Poverty Status: 1978

Social Security Share of Income	Total	Nonpoor	Poor	Percent Poor
Black Elderly Heads of Families				
Total families (millions)	0.7	0.5	0.2	—
Percent	100	100	100	25
No social security	15	12	21	37
Some social security	85	88	79	23
Under one fourth	17	22	—	6
One fourth to one half	23	26	16	17
One half to three fourths	22	21	25	29
Three fourths or more	23	19	34	38
Black Elderly Living Alone or with Nonrelatives				
Total elderly (millions)	0.7	0.3	0.4	—
Percent	100	100	100	54
No social security	16	12	20	65
Some social security	84	88	80	52
Under one fourth	3	6	1	—
One fourth to one half	14	24	5	21
One half to three fourths	25	30	21	46
Three fourths or more	42	28	53	69

Data: U.S. Department of Health and Human Services, Social Security Administration.

Table 21. Percent Distribution of Social Security Benefits Received by Elderly by Share of Total Income and Poverty Status: 1978

Social Security Share of Income	Total	Nonpoor	Poor	Percent Poor
White Elderly Heads of Families				
Total families (millions)	7.7	7.2	0.5	—
Percent	100	100	100	7
No social security	7	7	13	12
Some social security	93	93	87	6
Under one fourth	20	21	1	1
One fourth to one half	26	27	7	2
One half to three fourths	24	24	19	5
Three fourths or more	23	21	60	17
White Elderly Living Alone or with Nonrelatives				
Total elderly (millions)	6.8	5.2	1.6	—
Percent	100	100	100	24
No social security	7	6	10	35
Some social security	93	94	90	23
Under one fourth	8	11	—	—
One fourth to one half	21	27	3	4
One half to three fourths	25	27	18	19
Three fourths or more	39	29	69	43

Data: U.S. Department of Health and Human Services, Social Security Administration.

Table 22. Sources of Income of Elderly, by Race and Marital Status

Source of Income	Blacks, 65+			Whites, 65+		
	Total	With Spouse	No Spouse	Total	With Spouse	No Spouse
Number	1,552(100)	439(28)	1,113(72)	15,572	6,285(40)	9,287(60)
Percent	100	100	100	100	100	100
Earnings	25	49	16	25	40	15
Retirement benefits	87	93	84	93	94	93
Social Security	83	90	80	89	90	89
Other than social security	16	23	13	33	43	25
Public assistance	34	22	39	9	4	12
SSI	29	21	32	8	4	11
Other welfare	7	4	8	1	1	1
Income from assets	15	20	13	60	70	54
Interest	7	14	10	56	66	50
Dividends	1	1	1	18	23	14
Rent or royalty	6	9	5	11	13	9
Estates or trusts	—	—	—	2	2	2
Veterans Benefits	7	4	8	6	6	6
Unemployment insurance	2	2	1	2	3	1
Workers compensation	1	2	1	1	1	1
Personal contribution	1	2	1	1	—	1

Source: Prepared by NUL Research Department from Susan Grad and Karen Foster, "Income of the Population Aged 55 and Older, 1976," *Social Security Bulletin,* Vol. 42, No. 7, July 1979.

Data: U.S. Health and Human Services Department, Social Security Administration.

THE FEDERAL GOVERNMENT AND ASSISTANCE PROGRAMS

**The Reagan Changes ■ Federal Aid—A Brief History
■ Federal Assistance and Minorities ■ The Nixon Years
■ Ford and Carter ■ Specific Programs of Importance
to Blacks**

Drastic cuts in federal assistance programs were enacted in 1981 and more cuts were on the drawing board during the budget debates of spring 1982.

The spur to these cuts was a revolutionary change in the philosophy and policies of government. The philosophy of the Reagan Administration held that government activity on behalf of the poor was unproductive for its intended recipients, a dangerous economic burden for the nation to carry and morally questionable in and of itself. The administration also contended that cuts in assistance programs were necessary to increase military expenditures and to control a spiraling national debt that was expected to exceed $100 billion for the coming (1983) fiscal year.

As a result, funding for many programs was reduced significantly. Among affected programs were: Food Stamps, Aid to Families with Dependent Children, Medicaid, Energy Assistance, and The Job Corps.*

* See Sections on unemployment, income-earnings, and family for more specific details on reductions in federal aid during 1981 and 1982.

State and local programs were also affected adversely by cuts in federal aid. Declining tax revenues due to the recession and reductions in business, corporate and property taxes have also affected state and local programs.

Federal Aid—A Brief History

The concept of federal aid to underprivileged groups and individuals came slowly to the United States, which has traditionally valued the virtues of individual initiative and volunteerism, and has distrusted expansion of government's size and influence. The spur to such government activity was provided by the Great Depression and the magnetism of Franklin Delano Roosevelt, who became president in 1933. The cost-cutting economies of the Hoover Administration that preceded Roosevelt had failed to help the poor and unemployed or reverse the economic decline. The theories of British economist John Maynard Keynes suggested that the answer to economic depression was not for government to save money, but to stimulate its circulation and thus produce demand for goods and services. Roosevelt and his advisors felt that government spending to boost the economy was entirely compatible with America's prevailing doctrine of private enterprise and set out to press through Congress a great variety of programs that provided employment and direct monetary aid to large numbers of people who were unemployed or impoverished.

This approach was so popular it was soon embraced in fact, though not in theory, by many of Roosevelt's political opponents, and federal assistance programs expanded during the Truman and Eisenhower administrations that followed.

Federal Assistance and Minorities

Many of these programs, however, were criticized by minorities for not recognizing their underprivileged position and singling them out for special aid. Indeed, though blacks and other minorities benefited greatly from Roosevelt's "New Deal" efforts, administration of government aid often discriminated against them, especially during the 1930s in much of the aid to farmers in the South. Later in the 1950s, many blacks also charged that too much direct aid and tax relief incentives were directed to businesses and affluent citizens rather than to people with low incomes.

The concept of federal aid for disadvantaged groups reached a peak in the early 1960s, spurred in large measure by the recognition of Presidents Kennedy and Johnson that very large pockets of poverty existed in cities and rural areas, especially among minorities.

CETA has been enormously helpful to young blacks.

Kennedy encountered strong opposition from Congress, in his federal aid, as well as civil rights efforts, but many of his proposals were enacted during his administration and, following his assassination, under President Johnson.

The number of blacks participating in federally aided job programs multiplied at least fivefold between 1964 and 1969, and poverty programs started during the Kennedy and Johnson presidencies, were aiding an increasing number of people.

Decentralization involved the use of some 10,000 job training subcontractors, a step which according to the U.S. Civil Rights Commission increased the possibilities for discrimination in specific programs and decreased the possibility of adequate policing of nondiscrimination rules by federal agencies. Personnel to enforce anti-discrimination laws in federal programs was sparse and rarely spurred to action by the Administration. The basis of a "Southern Strategy" emphasized white ethnics and suburban areas where the black population is small.

Though job training of blacks was de-emphasized it remains important. In 1973 the percentage of blacks enrolled in federally assisted job training programs still constituted twice the official percentage of the nation's unemployed.

As noted in the Income and Earnings section, aid to blacks under various poverty programs has also decreased. The one area in which aid has increased since 1968 is "black capitalism," which is discussed elsewhere in this book.

The Nixon Years

The enrollment of blacks in federally assisted employment programs began to recede in 1969, during the first term of President Nixon, and did so steadily every year through 1973. Between 1971 and 1973, the only program in which the percentage of black enrollees increased was the Work Incentive Program, a program that is geared primarily to reduction of the welfare rolls. Between 1972 and 1973 the percentage of blacks enrolled in all programs dropped from 45% to 40%. The drop in black enrollees was most apparent in the JOBS program, from 43% to 26% in the two-year period.

Major reasons for the decline of black enrollment were the decentralization of training and assistance programs and the Nixon Administration's increased emphasis on aid to groups other than disadvantaged minorities.

Upon taking office in January 1975, Gerald Ford blamed much of the nation's economic ills on federal assistance programs. Said the President: "We have been self-indulgent . . . for decades we have been voting ever-increasing levels of government benefits . . . adding so many new programs . . . that their cost increases every year . . . because the number of people eligible for benefits increases." He then suggested that present programs be restrained and no new programs be added except in the field of energy.

Ford and Carter

A key area in which President Ford suggested cuts was the Food Stamp Program. In specific terms, he proposed an increase in the cost people would pay for the stamps so that the great majority of recipients of this aid would be required to pay more for food than they had previously.

The government's rationale for proposing this cut was twofold. First, the cost of the program had increased greatly, from $250 million annually in fiscal 1969 to over $4 billion in fiscal 1975, despite the fact that a great many families eligible for the benefits had not made use of them. In addition, many economists felt that food stamps contributed to large increases in food costs; that they were responsible for as much as half the rise of food prices between 1973 and 1975.

These economists suggested that a more efficient way to help poor people was via increases of direct welfare payments rather than with food stamps. This

suggestion actually appeared in the 1975 Economic Report to the President.

However, the status quo was to remain. The Administration was in no mood to grant increases in welfare payments and Congress was of no mind to saddle large blocs of voters with increases in food stamp costs. So, for the time being at least, the food stamp program survived without cuts or a substitute. But cutbacks in other federal aid were extensive—especially in areas of health and education—and in the summer of 1975 there was little prospect of restoration or increases in the near future.

With cutbacks at the federal level, many state and local governments faced severe financial strains with a result that they were often unable to produce "matching" funds which would enable them to take advantage of federal money that was available.

The election of Jimmy Carter in 1976 brought a respite to the cutbacks. Notable increases in CETA, Food Stamps, and other major programs were enacted. As his term progressed, however, Carter felt increasing pressures to cut back and in many areas did so. But, his premise that the federal government had a duty to help the impoverished and unemployed remained intact and became an issue in the 1980 presidential campaign, when Ronald Reagan opposed Carter.

Though Reagan's view carried the day, few expected

Government assistance for education has, until now, been a bipartisan must.

the massive cuts of social programs the newly elected president was to propose and pursue successfully through an acquiescent Congress. In this area, the administration's objectives and accomplishments dwarfed those of such earlier opponents of government aid as Nixon and Ford.

The administration suggested three alternatives to federal activity. One was to transfer a sizeable portion of responsibility and funds to state and local governments. Another was to ask private businesses and business groups to undertake and direct activities such as job training. Yet another was to seek to replace government aid with volunteer contributions of money and time from individuals, business, religious and social groups.

Specific Programs of Importance to Blacks

Of the hundreds of federal aid programs available, the *Negro Almanac* believes the following are of special importance to blacks. We have based our selection on each program's orientation to helping people who need economic assistance, growth and development, greater job skills, or educational direction. We have also sought to list those programs with specific orientation to blacks or minorities in general.

In some programs, support is provided directly to individuals. More often, however, funds are channeled through political subdivisions or public or private nonprofit corporations with further criteria stipulated as to the specific beneficiaries of funds.

For further information about the eligibility requirements of specific programs or on their uses or restrictions, one should contact the office of the agency listed with the "Eligibility" classification in the ensuing list.

A Caution

All individuals and groups applying for any form of assistance are urged first to inquire as to the specific information forms and documents that they must submit. This is especially important with programs aiding low income individuals such as The Food Stamp Program where extensive red tape often causes long and unproductive waiting periods. Adequate preparation can improve one's chances of qualifying and lessen the number and duration of trips to agency offices.

Also, due to the unsettled focus of Congress and the Reagan Administration toward public assistance, the continuity of programs listed in the following pages and the appropriation figures listed with them cannot be guaranteed.

FEDERAL ASSISTANCE PROGRAMS

Budget cuts may have substantially reduced the indicated budget figure for many programs though they remain in force.

Low to Moderate Income Rural Housing Loans

Agency: Department of Agriculture

Program Number: 10.410

Types of Assistance: Guaranteed/insured loans are provided to assist rural families obtain decent, safe and sanitary dwellings and related facilities.

Uses: Loans may be used to build, repair or purchase housing, sewage disposal facilities or a site on which to build them. In 1973, 116,700 loans totaling $1.7 billion were granted.

Restrictions: Dwellings for people with low or moderate income must be modest in design and cost. Applicant must be without sufficient funds to provide facilities on his own or obtain credit on reasonable terms from another source.

Related Programs of Interest (Housing)

10.411 RURAL HOUSING SITE LOANS

Aids public or private nonprofit corporations to acquire or develop land to be subdivided as building sites and sold on a nonprofit basis to low and middle income families. Limit is $100,000 unless approval for greater sum is granted by The National Farm Home Administration Office.

10.417 VERY LOW INCOME HOUSING REPAIR LOANS

Seeks through loans to give very low income rural homeowners the means to make minor repairs essential to safety and health. In 1974, the maximum loan was $2,500 plus $1,000 for water and waste disposal system or plumbing for a bathroom or kitchen. No loans for a new dwelling.

10.420 RURAL SELF-HELP HOUSING TECHNICAL ASSISTANCE

Aims to provide financial support for technical assistance to needy low income families to carry out mutual self help efforts in rural areas. Support is provided through political subdivisions or nonprofit corporations. Funds can't be used to buy land or building materials or to hire people for construction work. The idea is to pay for the technical expertise and some of the office and administrative expenses.

ELIGIBILITY FOR 10.410, 10.411, 10.417, 10.420

Contact State or local office of the Farmers Home Administration or write The Administrator, Farmers Home Administration, Washington, D.C. 20250.

Extension Service

Agency: Department of Agriculture

Program Number: 10.500

Types of Assistance: Educational programs in the areas of agricultural production and marketing, rural development, youth development and home economics.

Uses: The Extension Service program seeks to benefit farmers, producers, marketing firms, community organizations, homemakers, youth in general and 4 H Club members to benefit from technical developments and research in the areas of farming, nutrition, home management, family development, parent education, leadership development and career guidance.

The program has considerable potential for black farmers and land grant colleges, but according to 1970 reports of the Civil Rights Commission, blacks have been receiving a disproportionately small share of the funds appropriated. Total projected appropriations for fiscal 1975 were $176 million.

Restriction. By law, grants are made only to designated land grant institutions in the State and are administered by the Director of the State Extension Service.

Eligibility: Contact Extension Service, Department of Agriculture, Washington, D.C.

Food Administration

Agency: Department of Agriculture

Program Number: 10.550

Types of Assistance: The government gives away surplus food, primarily to needy families and schools, also to institutions.

Uses: To improve the diets of school children, the elderly, and needy individuals and the quality of food provided by charitable institutions.

To increase the market for food acquired via surplus food and price support programs. For fiscal 1975, assistance projected was about $500 million in food donations, only $2 million in formula grants.

Restrictions: Vary from state to state. State, federal, and local distributing agencies are designated by the government of each state. Food may not be sold, exchanged, or otherwise disposed of without permission

of the U.S. Department of Agriculture. Beneficiaries must be certified by local welfare officials as having inadequate income and resources. However, the beneficiary may be employed, unemployed, pensioned, or on strike.

Eligibility: Contact local or regional Food and Nutrition Service of the Department of Agriculture or the Food Distribution Division, Food and Nutrition Service, Department of Agriculture, Washington, D.C. 20250.

Food Stamps

Agency: Department of Agriculture

Program Number: 10.551

Type of Assistance: Government subsidies for the purchase of food, plants that produce food, and garden seeds in amounts up to 30% of income.

Uses: Mainly for low income families. Some elderly people may use stamps to pay for home delivered or institutional meals. Alcoholics and drug addicts may use stamps to pay for meals provided by programs they have enrolled in. In Alaska, recipients may use stamps to buy hunting and fishing equipment. For fiscal 1974, $3 billion was allotted, estimates for 1975 were upwards of $4 billion. Average assistance in fiscal 1974 was $18.50 per month per person.

Restrictions: Families must live in an area that has the program and be unemployed, part-time employed, working for low wages, living on small pensions, or deemed eligible by local welfare officials. As a rule, able-bodied adults must meet a work registration requirement.

Eligibility: It is estimated that only one-third of the nation's families that are eligible for stamps use them, mainly because they are not aware of the many deductions that may be taken from their income. Some of these deductions include alimony, child support, a dependent's education. For information contact the Food and Nutrition Service Regional Office or their headquarters, Department of Agriculture, Washington, D.C.

10.552 SPECIAL FOOD SERVICE PROGRAM FOR CHILDREN

Known as the "non school food program," this program seeks primarily to aid handicapped children and children from low income families that are receiving care in an institution. Aid is channeled through public and nonprofit institutions such as day care centers, settlement houses, recreation centers, and day camps. To be approved, institutions must operate a nonprofit food service for all children regardless of race, color,

There is a Special Food Service Program for needy nonschool children.

or national origin. In 1973 195,000 school children participated in the year-round program and 1,175,000 in the summer program.

10.553 SCHOOL BREAKFAST PROGRAM

Any public or private school that is exempt from income tax may receive aid which is intended to provide free or reduced price breakfasts for children who are deemed to be eligible by school officials.

10.554 NONFOOD SERVICE ASSISTANCE FOR SCHOOL SERVICE PROGRAMS (EQUIPMENT PROGRAM)

The objective is to provide funds for equipment and storage facilities to schools in low income areas so they can establish, maintain, and expand food services. Seventy-five to 100% of the cost of equipment is given. Recipients must agree to participate in the National School Lunch and/or Breakfast Program.

10.555 NATIONAL SCHOOL LUNCH PROGRAM

Seeks to provide lunch in schools for poor children of high school age and under. Is similar to the Breakfast Program, 10.553.

10.556 SPECIAL MILK PROGRAM FOR CHILDREN

The government reimburses money to schools for expenses incurred in starting and expanding distribution of fluid milk to children. Public and nonprofit schools and child care institutions are eligible, but they must agree to operate the program without regard to race, color, or national origin.

10.557 SPECIAL SUPPLEMENTAL FOOD PROGRAM FOR WOMEN, INFANTS, AND CHILDREN

This program has two principal objectives—to provide food to pregnant or lactating women identified as nutritional risks and to collect and evaluate data to identify the medical benefits of the program. Funds are provided to local public and nonprofit health service agencies which must provide health services free or at reduced cost to residents of a low income area. The program was granted no funds in 1973, but advance appropriations estimated for fiscal 1974 and 1975 were $40 million for each year.

ELIGIBILITY FOR PROGRAMS 10.552, 10.553, 10.554, 10.555, 10.556

Contact the Director, Child Nutrition Division, Food

and Nutrition Service, Department of Agriculture, Washington, D.C. 20250 or the regional office of the Food and Nutrition Service of the U.S. Department of Agriculture.

ELIGIBILITY FOR PROGRAM 10.557

Food Distribution Division, Food and Nutrition Service, Department of Agriculture, Washington, D.C. 20250, or the Regional Office of the Food and Distribution Service.

Youth Conservation Corps

Agency: Department of Agriculture

Program Number: 10.661

Type of Assistance: Employment of male and female teenagers between the ages of 15 to 18 in conservation work on public lands.

Uses: This small program employed about 4,000 young men and women in 46 states for eight weeks in fiscal 1974. All States, virtually all territories, and many local and municipal governments are eligible for grants or subgrants. The program seeks to achieve a racial mix and to bypass the personnel requirements for full-time employment of the local or state authority that carries out the program. As such it is an opportune source for brief employment of teenagers.

Restrictions: No one can be employed in this program for more than 90 days per year.

Eligibility: Contact State Foresters or Directors of Departments of Natural Resources or the Forest Service Division of Manpower and Youth Conservation Programs of the Department of Agriculture, 12th St. and Independence Avenue S.W., Washington, D.C. 20250.

Minority Business Enterprise (OMBE)

Agency: Department of Commerce

Program Number: 11.800

Type of Assistance: Grants, counseling, and research contracts, usually ranging in size from $100,000 to $350,000 are given to nonprofit organizations for channeling to an existing or potential business that is owned or controlled by one or more persons who is disadvantaged from cultural, racial, or chronic economic circumstance or background. As defined by OMBE, such persons include, but are not limited to, "Negroes, Puerto Ricans, Spanish-speaking Americans, American Indians, Aleuts, Eskimos and Orientals."

Uses: This program supports a broad range of efforts to aid minorities and develop minority businesses. The businesses can include universities and trade associations as well as financial institutions and corporations. In addition OMBE coordinates federal assistance programs for minorities, assists development of state and local programs, and conducts pilot projects designed to overcome special problems of minority businessmen.

Restrictions: Federal minority business programs have been widely criticized for supporting too many small businesses that could not succeed competitively without continuing and expensive support. As such, the government is increasingly stressing aid to larger minorities' businesses and demanding ever-increasing portents of success before committing its support.

Eligibility: Contact Regional or Local Office of the Office of Minority Business Enterprise or the Assistant Director, Administration and Field Operation Division, Office of Minority Business Enterprise, Department of Commerce, Washington, D.C. 20230.

Health Care of Children and Youth

Agency: Department of Health and Human Services

Program Number: 13.218

Type of Assistance: Grants to state health agencies for the promotion of health services for low income families.

Uses: Screening, diagnosis, treatment, correction of defects, and aftercare, both medical and dental. An estimated 550,000 children were to receive care in fiscal 1974, to be paid for by estimated allocation of $48 million. Funds for fiscal 1975 were to be supplied under program 13.232. (See below). Funds may not be used for purchase or construction of buildings.

Eligibility: Contact Regional Health Administrator, Department of Health and Human Services Regional Office or Associate Bureau Director for Maternal & Child Health, Bureau of Community Health Services, Room 12-05, Parklawn Building, 5600 Fishers Lane, Rockville, Maryland 20852.

13.217 FAMILY PLANNING PROJECTS

Grants made to state health agencies to provide persons from low income families with family planning advice, contraceptive supplies, and counseling, plus diagnostic and treatment centers for infertility. Appropriation for fiscal 1974 was $143.9 million. Estimated fiscal 1975 allocation is $97.6 million.

13.224 HEALTH SERVICES DEVELOPMENT PROJECT GRANTS

Funds to be allocated to public or non-profit private agencies, institutions, or organizations that, in accordance with plans of the state comprehensive health planning agency, propose to improve the accessibility of health care to low income families.

12.230 INTENSIVE INFANT CARE PROJECTS

Grants available to state health agencies, agencies of political subdivision of the state, and to any other public or nonprofit agency or institution to provide first-year health care to infants from low income families. In fiscal 1974, an estimated $783,000 was allocated. Fiscal 1975 allocation was to be supplied under program 13.232 (see below).

13.232 MATERNAL & CHILD HEALTH SERVICES

Grants made to state health agencies to reduce infant mortality and improve health of mothers and children in areas suffering from severe economic distress. Estimated allocation for fiscal year 1974 was $60.7 million. Estimated allocation for 1975 was to be $179 million, the increase to cover the inclusion of programs previously not under this category.

13.234 MATERNITY AND INFANT CARE PROJECTS

Grants available to health agencies of states, political subdivision, and nonprofit organizations to provide diagnostic and specialist consultation to vulnerable low-income women early in pregnancy. The aim is to reduce the incidence of mental retardation and other handicapping child-bearing conditions. Estimated allocation for fiscal 1974 $42.2 million. Funds for fiscal 1975 to be allocated under program 13.232.

ELIGIBILITY FOR 13.217

Contact Regional Health Administator, Department of Health and Human Services, or Associate Bureau Director for Family Planning Services, Health Services, Department of Health and Human Services, Rockville, Maryland.

ELIGIBILITY FOR 13.224

Contact Regional Health Administrator, Department of Health and Human Services or Associate Bureau Director for Neighborhood Health Centers, Room 12A-56, Parklawn Building, 56 Fishers Lane, Rockville, Maryland 20852.

ELIGIBILITY FOR 13.230, 13.232 AND 13.234

Regional Health Administrator, Department of Health and Human Services or Associate Bureau Director, Maternal and Child Health Services, Bureau of Community Health Service, Room 12-05, Parklawn Building, 5600 Fishers Lane, Rockville, Maryland 20852.

Several maternal and child health services are funded by the federal government.

Drug Abuse Community Service Programs

Agency: Department of Health and Human Services

Program Number: 13.235

Type of Assistance: Grants given to community mental health centers, affiliates of a community mental health center, or a public or private nonprofit agency located in an area that has no community mental health center. Provides salaries for personnel and services, inpatient, outpatient, intermediate (halfway house or partial hospitalization), 24-hour emergency service, community-wide consultation, and education services.

Uses: To reach, treat, and rehabilitate drug addicted and drug dependent persons through community based services. Estimated allocations: fiscal 1974 was $25.7 million; $12.9 million was scheduled allocation for 1975.

Eligibility: National Institute on Alcohol, Drug Abuse and Mental Health Administration, 11400 Rockville Pike, Rockville, Maryland 20852.

Migrant Health Grants

Agency: Department of Health and Human Services

Program Number: 13.246

Type of Assistance: Grants to public or private non-profit agency.

Uses: Establishment and operation of family health services clinics to raise health status of migratory seasonal farmworkers and their families. Included are: medical care to prevent or treat illness, nursing services, sanitation services, health education, training of migrants to be health aides, and coordination of services between areas and states along the same migrant stream. In fiscal 1974, 103 awards were made to grant health projects at a cost of $23.7 million. Estimated allocation for fiscal 1975 were to be $24 million.

Eligibility: Contact Regional Health Administrator or Associate Bureau Director, Migrant Health, Bureau of Community Health Services, Room 7-22, Parklawn Building, 5600 Fishers Lane, Rockville, Maryland 20852.

National Health Service Corps

Agency: Department of Health and Human Services

Program Number: 13.258

Type of Assistance: Provision of specialized health personnel to areas having critical shortages of such personnel. Applicants must be state or local health agencies, public or nonprofit private health organizations.

Uses: To provide medical, dental, nursing, psychiatric, and paramedical services to anyone within the designated area wishing it at reasonable or no cost.

Assignment and designation of personnel will be partly based upon the availability of the Service's personnel to provide the services requested.

In fiscal 1974, 183 communities, involving 4 million people, received health personnel. It is projected that in fiscal 1975, 270 communities will receive a projected 556 member staff of Health Service Corps.

Estimated allocation in fiscal 1974 was $13 million. Estimated allocation for fiscal 1975 was to be $12.3 million.

13.261 FAMILY HEALTH CENTERS

Grants available to public or private nonprofit agencies to develop health maintenance and treatment services to low income and poor people in areas with scarce health services. Funds are not to be used for services which are paid for by Medicaid, Medicare, or union health plans.

ELIGIBILITY FOR 13.258 AND 13.261

Contact Regional Health Administrator or National Health Service Corps Program Director or National

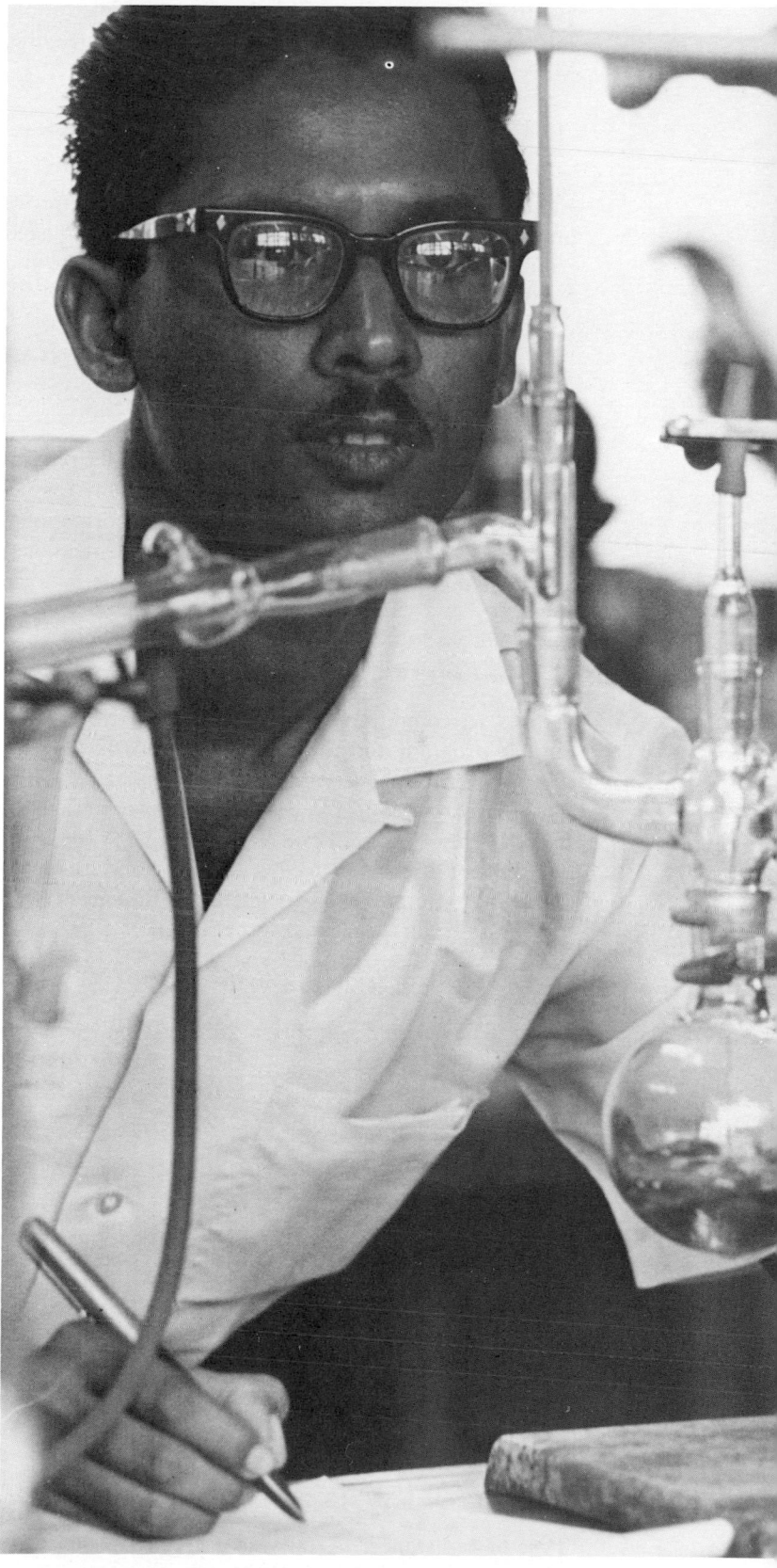

Grants are made to strengthen the biomedical research training capacity of minority schools.

Health Service Corps, Health Services Administration, Parklawn Building, 5600 Fishers Lane, Rockville, Maryland.

13.430 EDUCATIONALLY DEPRIVED CHILDREN— STATE ADMINISTRATION

Funds available to state or outlying area to improve and expand educational programs for disadvantaged children through administrative assistance to state and local educational agencies.

13.431 EDUCATIONALLY DEPRIVED CHILDREN IN STATE-ADMINISTERED INSTITUTIONS SERVING NEGLECTED OR DELINQUENT CHILDREN

Grants to state agencies directly responsible for providing free public education in state institutions for neglected or delinquent children or adult correctional institutions. Services proposed must supplement, not supplant those normally provided with State or local funds.

13.433 FOLLOW THROUGH

Grants to communities with full year Headstart or similar program and the resources to provide Follow Through's range of services. Estimated fiscal 1974 allocation $41. million. The estimated appropriation for fiscal 1975 is $35. million.

Appropriations for 13.429, 13.430, and 13.431 in fiscal 1975 are proposed for inclusion in consolidated education grants legislative program.

ELIGIBILITY FOR 13.420 AND 13.431

Contact Division of Education for the Disadvantaged, Office of Compensatory Education Programs, Bureau of School Systems, Office of Education, 7th and D Streets, S.W., Washington, D.C. 20202.

ELIGIBILITY FOR 13.433

Contact Follow Through Division, Office of Compensatory Education Programs, Bureau of School Systems, Office of Education, 7th and D Street, S.W., Washington, D.C. 20202.

Special Services for Disadvantaged Students in Institutions of Higher Education

Agency: Department of Health and Human Services

Program Number: 13.482

Type of Assistance: Grants to accredited institutions of postsecondary education.

Uses: Funds to provide assistance to low income and physically handicapped students enrolled or accepted for enrollment to initiate, continue, or resume postsecondary education.

Monies cannot be used to staff ethnic studies programs, building or outfitting tutorial or media centers, or duplicate services available through vocational rehabilitation, medicare or medicaid.

In fiscal 1974 appropriation was $23 million and it is estimated that the same sum will be allocated in fiscal 1975.

Eligibility: Director of Higher Education, Department of Health and Human Services Regional Office or Division of Student Support and Special Programs, Bureau of Postsecondary Education, Office of Education, 400 Maryland Avenue, S.W., Washington, D.C. 20202.

Health Manpower Education Initiative Awards recruit minority students.

Related Programs of Interest

13.488 TALENT SEARCH

Grants to institutions of higher education, including those with vocational and career education programs, to enable them to provide educational opportunity to young people bypassed by traditional educational procedures offering them options for continuing their education. Fiscal 1974 and fiscal 1975 allocations each $6 million.

13.492 UPWARD BOUND

Grants to institutions of higher education, including those with vocational and career education programs to carry out Upward Bound Projects which are developed to generate skill.

13.501 VOCATIONAL EDUCATION WORK STUDY

Grants to state boards for vocational education to be used for assisting economically deprived, full-time vocational education students, aged 15–20, to remain in school by providing part-time employment with public employers.

Allocation for fiscal 1974 $7.8 million. In fiscal 1975 this program proposed to be included in consolidated education grants legislative program.

13.502 VOCATIONAL EDUCATION INNOVATION

Grants and contracts to State boards for vocational education, local educational agencies, public and private agencies and organizations to develop, establish and operate occupational education programs as models for vocational education programs as models for academic, socioeconomic or other handicaps.

ELIGIBILITY FOR 13.488, 13.492

Director of Higher Education, Department of Health and Human Services Regional Office or Division of Student Support and Special Programs, Bureau of Postsecondary Education, Office of Education, 400 Maryland Avenue, S.W., Washington, D.C. 20202.

ELIGIBILITY FOR 13.501

Contact Director, Division of Vocational and Technical Education, Center for Adult, Vocational, Technical and Manpower Education, Office of Education, Washington, D.C. 20202.

ELIGIBILITY FOR 13.502

Contact Regional Office, Department of Health and Human Services or Director, Division of Research and Demonstration Bureau of Occupational and Adult Technical Education, Office of Education, Washington, D.C. 20202.

Educationally Deprived Children—Special Grants for Urban and Rural Schools

Agency: Department of Health and Human Services

Program Number: 13.511

Type of Assistance: Grants to eligible districts, based on state-conducted comprehensive survey of areas with highest concentration of children from low income areas.

Uses: Emphasis for preschool and elementary school programs to meet the special educational needs of deprived children.

Appropriation for fiscal 1974 was $47.7 million. In fiscal 1975 this program was proposed for inclusion in the disadvantaged category of consolidated education grants.

Related Programs of Interest

13.512 EDUCATIONALLY DEPRIVED CHILDREN SPECIAL INCENTIVE GRANTS

Incentive grants to state educational agencies to be used to provide an incentive for increase in state and local funding for elementary and secondary education which meets needs of educationally deprived children.

ELIGIBILITY FOR 13.511 AND 13.512

Contact Division of Education for the Disadvantaged, Office of Compensatory Educational Programs, Bureau of School Systems, Office of Education, 7th and D Streets, S.W., Washington, D.C. 20202.

Emergency School Aid Act—Basic Grants to Local Educational Agencies

Agency: Department of Health and Human Services

Program Number: 13.525

Type of Assistance: Grants to elementary and secondary local educational agencies for plans to eliminate, reduce, or prevent the isolation of minority group students in their schools.

Uses: Plans requesting funds must make available the following: remedial services, supplemental staff, teacher aids and training, guidance and counseling, curriculum development, career education, interracial activities, community activities, support services, planning, and minor remodeling.

In fiscal 1974 appropriation was $146.8 million with

authorizing legislation expiring June 30, 1974. Request for funds in fiscal 1975 was cut to $75 million.

Eligibility: Contact Emergency School Aid Director, Office of Education, Department of Health and Human Services Regional Office or Associate Commissioner, Office of Equal Educational Opportunity Programs, Bureau of School Systems, Office of Education, 400 Maryland Avenue, S.W., Washington, D.C. 20202.

Related Programs of Interest

13.526 EMERGENCY SCHOOL AID ACT—PILOT PROGRAMS

Grants to local educational agencies to assist them in eliminating, reducing, or preventing minority group isolation. Focus will be on districts having either a minimum of 15,000 minority students or a minority enrollment of at least 50%.

13.527 EMERGENCY SCHOOL AID ACT—METROPOLITAN AREA PROJECTS

Grants to local educational agencies involved in establishing and maintaining integrated schools, developing a plan to reduce minority group isolation in a Standard Metropolitan Statistical Area, or planning integrated educational parks.

13.529 EMERGENCY SCHOOL AID ACT—SPECIAL PROGRAMS AND PROJECTS

Grants to nonprofit organizations to conduct programs which support local educational agencies' efforts to meet special problems incident to desegregation, to encourage voluntary integration, or to aid schoolchildren in overcoming the educational disadvantages of minority group isolation.

13.530 EMERGENCY SCHOOL AID ACT—EDUCATIONAL TELEVISION

Grants to public or private nonprofit agencies with expertise in the development of television programming which have positive cognitive and affective value and presents multi-ethnic children's activities. Purpose is to overcome educational disadvantages of minority group isolation.

13.532 EMERGENCY SCHOOL AID ACT—SPECIAL PROGRAMS

Grants to local educational agencies and supporting public organizations which will conduct activities to help children overcome the educational disadvantages of minority group isolation.

13.533 RIGHT TO READ—ELIMINATION OF ILLITERACY

Grants to public or nonpublic school districts which will plan and implement reading and teacher training

Operation Follow Through supplements ordinary educational programs.

Head Start helps preschool children of poor families enter school on equal terms with less deprived children.

practices designed to increase functional literacy so that by 1980 99% of those 16 years of age and 90% of those over 16 will be functionally literate.

ELIGIBILITY FOR 13.526, 13.527, 13.529, 13.530 AND 13.532

Contact Associate Commissioner, Officer of Equal Educational Opportunity Programs, Bureau of School Systems, Office of Education, 400 Maryland Avenue, S.W., Washington, D.C. 20202.

ELIGIBILITY FOR 13.533

Contact Office of Education, Department of Health and Human Services Regional Office or National Right To Read Office, Office of Education, 400 Maryland Avenue, S.W., Washington, D.C. 20202.

Educational Opportunity Centers

Agency: Department of Health and Human Services

Program Number: 13.543

Type of Assistance: Grants to institutions of higher education including those with vocational and career education programs, and in exceptional cases, secondary and secondary vocational schools.

Uses: Funds to be provided for setting up services to facilitate entry into postsecondary educational programs, particularly for low income students.

Estimate allocation was $3 million for 1974 and again for fiscal 1975.

Eligibility: Contact Director of Higher Education, Department of Health and Human Services Office or Division for Student Support and Special Programs, Bureau of Postsecondary Education, Office of Education, 400 Maryland Avenue, S.W., Washington, D.C. 20202.

Child Development—Head Start

Agency: Department of Health and Human Services

Program Number: 13.600

Type of Assistance: Grants and contracts to public or private nonprofit agencies.

Uses: Funds for provision of educational, nutritional, and social services to preschool children of poor families, so that they enter school on equal terms with the less deprived children. Programs involve parents in activities of their children.

Head Start Programs are primarily for children from age 3 to age of entrance into the school system.

In fiscal 1974 allocation was $392.1 million. For fiscal 1975 estimated allocation is $430 million.

Eligibility: Contact Regional Program Director, Office of Child Development, Office of Human Development, Department of Health and Human Services or Office of Child Development, Head Start, Office of Human Development, Department of Health and Human Services, P.O. Box 1182, Washington, D.C. 20013.

Civil Rights Compliance Activities

Agency: Department of Health and Human Services

Program Number: 13.602

Type of Assistance: Investigation of complaints made by anyone who feels discriminated against in the provision of federal funds or services due to race, color, or national origin.

Uses: Enforcement of Title VI of Civil Rights Act of 1964, which prohibits Federal funds for programs that discriminate as to race, color, or national origin. This program has been extended to include anti-sex discrimination provisions.

To ensure that beneficiaries of major programs receive services without discrimination or segregation, Office of Civil Rights investigates and takes corrective steps to assure equal opportunity.

For fiscal 1974 an estimated $18.4 million allocated. For fiscal 1975 estimated allocation is $22.3 million.

Eligibility: Contact Civil Rights Directors, Department of Health and Human Services Regional Offices or Director, Office for Civil Rights, Office of the Secretary, Department of Health and Human Services, Washington, D.C. 20201.

Youth Development Delinquency Prevention

Agency: Department of Health and Human Services

Program Number: 13.610

Type of Assistance: Grants to federal, state, local public, or private nonprofit agencies. Private agencies must be in existence at least two years before applying.

Uses: To develop and implement coordinated youth service systems for the prevention of delinquency.

In fiscal 1974 estimated appropriation of $10 million supported an estimated 79 projects. For fiscal 1975 the appropriation is $15 million with no projection of number of projects to receive help.

Eligibility: Contact Office of Assistant Regional Director for Human Development or Commissioner, Office of Youth Development, Office of Human Development, Department of Health and Human Services, Washington, D.C. 20201.

Social and Rehabilitation Service

Agency: Department of Health and Human Services

Program Number: 13.707

Type of Assistance: Grants to states, District of Columbia, Puerto Rico, Virgin Islands, and Guam.

Uses: Establish, extend, and strengthen services provided by state and local public welfare programs for development of preventive and protective services which will prevent neglect, abuse, exploitation, or delinquency of children.

Monies can be used for costs of personnel, licensing of, and standard setting for child caring agencies, assisting with costs of foster care, day care, homemaker services, return of runaway children and adoptive placement of children.

Estimated appropriation in fiscal 1974 was $47.5 million with an estimated 238,000 families and 430,000 children receiving benefits. Estimated allocation for fiscal 1975 is $46 million.

Eligibility: Contact Regional Community Services, Officials of Social and Rehabilitative Service or Director, Division of Child and Family Services, Community Services Administration, Social and Rehabilitative Service, Department of Health and Human Services, 330 C Street, S.W., Washington, D.C. 20201.

Medical Assistance Program

Agency: Department of Health and Human Services

Program Number: 13.714

Type of Assistance: Grants to state and local welfare agencies.

Uses: Financial assistance to States for payments of medical assistance on behalf of cash assistance recipients.

Services include: in and out patient hospital services, laboratory and x-ray, skilled home nursing, home health for persons over 21, family planning, physicians and early periodic screening, diagnosis and treatment for individuals under 21.

State and local welfare agencies must operate under government-approved state plan.

Appropriations for fiscal 1974 estimated at $5.6 billion which supported assistance received by 27,187,000 beneficiaries. Estimated appropriation for fiscal 1975 set at $6.5 billion, with projected beneficiaries of 28,566,000.

Eligibility: Contact Regional Commissioner, Medical Services Administration, Social and Rehabilitative Service or Commissioner, Medical Services Administration, Social and Rehabilitative Services, Department of Health and Human Services, 330 C Street, S.W., Washington, D.C. 20201.

Work Incentives Program—Child Care— Employment Related Supportive Services

Agency: Department of Health and Human Services

Program Number: 13.748

Type of Assistance: Grants to state welfare agencies.

Uses: To furnish community resources to help persons receiving aid to families with dependent children become self-supporting by providing necessary child care and supportive services to registrants and participants in WIN and other man-power programs.

Estimated appropriation for fiscal 1974 was $90 million with the same amount projected as allocation for fiscal 1975.

Eligibility: Contact Regional Commissioner, Regional Coordination Committee, Social and Rehabilitation Service or Administrator, Social and Rehabilitation Service, Department of Health and Human Services, Washington, D.C. 20201.

Public Assistance—Maintenance Assistance

Agency: Department of Health and Human Services

Program Number: 13.761

Type of Assistance: Grants to state and local welfare agencies operating under approved Health and Human Services State Plan.

Uses: Financial aid to families with dependent children, emergency welfare assistance, assistance to repatriated U.S. nationals. In Guam, Virgin Islands, and Puerto Rico funds are to provide aid to the aged, blind, and permanently disabled.

Direct money payments by states covers costs for food, shelter, clothing, and other necessary items for daily living and payments for care of specified children in foster homes or institutions.

Federal funds are made available for home repairs.

Estimated allocation for fiscal 1974 was $5.4 billion with 14,300,000 beneficiaries receiving help. Estimated allocation for fiscal 1975 is $4.6 billion with projected 11,400,000 recipients.

Eligibility: Individuals should contact local welfare agency. States should contact Regional Office, or Chief, Office of Public Information, Social and Rehabilitation Service, Department of Health and Human Services, Washington, D.C. 20201.

Blood Diseases and Resources Research

Agency: Department of Health and Human Services

Program Number: 13.839

Type of Assistance: Project and research grants to any nonprofit organization engaged in biomedical research. In certain cases individuals may qualify for fellowship, award or research grant.

Uses: To further the development of blood resources and promote research on blood diseases including Sickle Cell Disease.

Funds can support salaries, equipment, supplies, travel, and patient hospitalization as required for performance of research.

Fiscal 1974 appropriation of $50.9 million supported an estimated 370 grants, 157 contracts and 48 research training fellowships. For fiscal 1975 allocation is estimated at $50.3 million, with 368 grants, 115 contracts and 80 research training fellowships projected.

Eligibility: Contact Director, Division of Blood Diseases, National Heart and Lung Institute, Bethesda, Maryland 20014.

Interest Subsidy—Acquisition and Rehabilitation of Homes for Resale to Lower Income Families

Agency: Department of Housing and Urban Development

Program Number: 14.104

Type of Assistance: Insured loans, direct payments for specified use to private nonprofit and public organizations.

Uses: Loans may be used to finance, purchase, and rehabilitate housing for resale to low income families.

Purchasers of these homes must be families, handicapped persons or single persons 62 and older whose incomes fall within specified limits.

This program was included in the overall suspension in January 1973 of subsidized housing programs.

Eligibility: Production Information: contact Director, Multifamily Underwriting Division, Housing Production and Mortgage Credit, Federal Housing Authority, Department of Housing and Urban Development, Washington, D.C. 20410. For Management Information: contact Director, Office of Loan Management, Housing Management, Department of Housing and Urban Development, Washington, D.C. 20410.

Related Programs of Interest

14.105 INTEREST SUBSIDY HOMES FOR LOWER INCOME FAMILIES

Guaranteed/insured loans and direct payments for specified use to families, handicapped persons, or single persons 62 and older whose income and assets fall within certain limits. Loans can be used to finance purchase of single-family or 2-family units or units in a multifamily dwelling which has been constructed or rehabilitated under FHA within 2 years prior to application for assistance.

14.106 INTEREST SUBSIDY PURCHASE OF REHABILITATED HOMES BY LOWER INCOME FAMILIES

Guaranteed/insured loans, direct payments for specified use to finance purchase of single-family or 2-family units or units in multifamily dwelling which has been rehabilitated by a nonprofit sponsor.

14.120 MORTGAGE INSURANCE HOMES FOR LOW AND MODERATE INCOME FAMILIES

Guaranteed/insured loans to make home-ownership more readily available to families displaced by urban

renewal as well as low and moderate income families. Loans may be used for purchase of proposed or existing low cost 1 to 4 family housing or the rehabilitation of such housing.

For fiscal 1974 an estimated $575.1 million was appropriated. The estimated allocation for fiscal 1975 is $602.4 million.

ELIGIBILITY FOR RELATED PROGRAMS OF INTEREST

Contact nearest local Housing and Urban Development Area Office or Director, Single Family Underwriting Division, Housing Production and Mortgage Credit, Federal Housing Authority, Department of Housing and Urban Development, Washington, D.C. 20410.

Public Housing—Home-Ownership for Low Income Families

Agency: Department of Housing and Urban Development

Program Number: 14.147

Type of Assistance: Project grants and direct loans to local housing authorities, authorized public agencies, or Indian tribal organizations.

Uses: To provide housing purchase opportunities for low income families by crediting amount budgeted for routine maintenance performed by tenants to family equity accounts. When family income reaches the point where permanent financing for the unit can be obtained or when equity account equals unamortized debt and closing costs, ownership passes to family.

The program was suspended in January 1973 pending comprehensive evaluation of subsidized housing. Bona fide commitments were met for fiscal 1974, but there will be no new commitments in fiscal 1975.

Eligibility: Contact Director, Publicly Financed Housing Division, Housing Production and Mortgage Credit, Department of Housing and Urban Development, Washington, D.C. 20410.

Related Program of Interest

14.148 PUBLIC HOUSING—LEASED

Project grants to local housing authorities, authorized public agency, or Indian tribal organizations providing annual contributions which permit local public agency to provide decent, safe, sanitary housing for low income families at rents they can afford to pay.

Interest subsidy programs enable lower income families to acquire and rehabilitate housing.

Eligibility: Contact Director, Publicly Financed Housing Division, Housing Production and Mortgage Credit, Department of Housing and Urban Development, Washington, D.C. 20410.

Rent Supplements—Rental Housing for Low Income Families

Agency: Department of Housing and Urban Development

Program Number: 14.149

Type of Assistance: Direct payments for specified use to nonprofit, cooperative, builder-seller, investor-sponsor, and limited distribution mortgagors.

Uses: To supplement partial payments of families within income limits prescribed for admission to public housing. Assistance covers the difference between tenants' payments and market rental, but may not exceed 70% of market rental.

Persons 62 years or older, physically handicapped, living in substandard housing and certain military personnel are also eligible to receive benefits.

Estimated allocation for fiscal 1974 was $146 million and for fiscal 1975 $192 million. This program was suspended in January 1973 pending review and evaluation of subsidized housing. Except for bona fide commitments which cannot be met under the revised public housing leasing program, additional projects will not be funded.

Eligibility: Production Information: Contact Director, Multifamily Underwriting Division, Housing Production and Mortgage Credit, Federal Housing Administration, Department of Housing and Urban Development, Washington, D.C. 20410.

Equal Opportunity in Housing

Agency: Department of Housing and Urban Development

Program Number: 14.400

Type of Assistance: Investigation and conciliation of complaints.

Uses: Any individual may file a complaint with HUD or may file suit in Federal or local court seeking injunctive relief, actual damages and not more than $1,000 in punitive damages together with court costs and reasonable attorney fees.

Individuals are assured an equal opportunity to choose housing suited to their needs and financial ability in the area in which they desire to live without discrimination because of race, color, religion, or national origin.

Estimated allocations for fiscal 1974 were $9.8 million and for fiscal 1975 $11.9 million. Anticipated number of complaints for fiscal 1974 was 2,946. Training and technical assistance has been provided to many state agencies as well as a training film for use in housing discrimination matters.

Eligibility: Contact Assistant Regional Administrator for Equal Opportunity in Department of Housing and Urban Development Regional Office or Assistant Secretary for Equal Opportunity, Department of Housing and Urban Development, Washington, D.C. 20410.

General Research and Technology Activity

Agency: Department of Housing and Urban Development

Program Number: 14.506

Type of Assistance: Project and research grants to public and/or private profit and nonprofit organizations.

Uses: Funding for research related to national housing needs, evaluation of existing housing and community development programs, and improving the environment.

The estimated allocation for fiscal 1974 was $61 million and for fiscal 1975 will be $62 million.

Some of the projects currently underway are Lead Based Paint Research, Housing Abandonment Prevention, Utilities and the Environment and Rural Housing Research.

Eligibility: Contact Assistant Secretary for Policy Development and Research, Department of Housing and Urban Development, 441 7th Street, S.W., Washington, D.C. 20410.

Public Housing—Modernization of Projects

Agency: Department of Housing and Urban Development

Program Number: 14.607

Type of Assistance: Direct loans to local housing authorities operating federally assisted public housing projects.

Uses: Loans may be used for upgrading low rent housing projects which, because of condition, location, or outmoded management policies, adversely affect the quality of living of tenants. The program must provide for the involvement of tenants in plans for rehabilitation.

HUD requested allocation of $20 million in each fiscal year 1974 and 1975 which would provide capital improvements of approximately $235 million in existing public housing projects.

Eligibility: Contact Area Director, Department of Housing and Urban Development Area Office or Office of Housing Programs, Assistant Secretary for Housing Management, Department of Housing and Urban Development, Washington, D.C. 20413.

National Historic Landmarks

Agency: U.S. Department of Interior

Program Number: 15.912

Type of Assistance: Provision of specialized services to anyone—individual, government, or corporate body—who is owner of property.

Uses: To study, identify, recognize honorifically, and encourage preservation of nationally significant historic properties.

National Historic Landmarks are selected by the National Survey of Historic Sites and Buildings. Theme studies recently completed or currently underway include sites associated with nineteenth Century Architecture, Political and Military Affairs 1865–1900 and Black History, Science and Invention and Literature, Drama and Music.

Estimated allocation for each of fiscal years 1974 and 1975 was $180,000.

Eligibility: Contact Director, National Park Service, U.S. Department of Interior, Washington, D.C. 20240.

Desegregation of Public Education

Agency: Department of Justice

Program Number: 16.100

Type of Assistance: Provision of specialized services to parent or group of parents in case of public schools, to individual or his parents in the case of public college; to applicant for employment or employee of an educational agency.

Uses: To provide equal education for children regardless of race, color, religion, sex, or national origin. To investigate, negotiate, and litigate allegations of employment discrimination by educational agencies.

Eligibility: Contact Chief, Education Section, Civil Rights Division, United States Department of Justice, Washington, D.C. 20530.

Equal Employment Opportunity

Agency: Department of Justice

Program Number: 16.101

Type of Assistance: Provision of specialized services.

Uses: To enable Attorney General to sue to enjoin discrimination in employment by state and local government agencies enforce nondiscrimination in employment provisions of Executive Order 11246, as amended, regarding government contractors and subcontractors.

Eligibility: Contact Chief, Employment Section, Civil Rights Division, U.S. Department of Justice, Washington, D.C. 20530.

Equal Enjoyment of Public Accommodations

Agency: Department of Justice

Program Number: 16.102

Type of Assistance: Provision of specialized services.

Uses: To provide equal access to all establishments offering public accommodations without regard to race, color, religion, or national origin.

The Justice Department may go to court for an injunction or other order prohibiting discrimination.

Eligibility: Contact Chief, Voting and Public Accommodations Section, Civil Rights Division, U.S. Department of Justice, Washington, D.C. 20530.

Fair Housing

Agency: Department of Justice

Program Number: 16.103

Type of Assistance: Provision of specialized services.

Uses: To provide freedom from discrimination on basis of race, color, religion, or national origin in connection with sale, rental, or financing of housing by filing suit alleging such discrimination in appropriate federal or state court.

Eligibility: Contact Chief, Housing Section, Civil Rights Division, U.S. Department of Justice, Washington, D.C. 20530.

Protection of Voting Rights

Agency: Department of Justice

Program Number: 16.104

Type of Assistance: Provision of specialized services to all U.S. citizens old enough to vote.

Uses: To provide protection of individual's right to register and vote in all local, state or federal elections without discrimination on account of race or color.

The 1970 amendments suspend the use of literacy and other tests in all states and counties not previously covered by 1965 Act, set forth uniform standards regarding durational residency requirements and absentee registration and balloting in Presidential elections and lower to 18 the minimum age for voting in federal elections.

Eligibility: Contact Chief, Voting and Public Accommodations Section, Civil Rights Division, U.S. Department of Justice, Washington, D.C. 20530.

Desegregation of Public Facilities

Agency: Department of Justice

Program Number: 16.105

Type of Assistance: Provision of specialized services to individuals.

Uses: Attorney General may bring suit for an injunction for discrimination on account of race, color, religion, or national origin in operation of public facilities

Eligibility: Contact Director, Office of Institutions and Facilities, Civil Rights Division, U.S. Department of Justice, Washington, D.C. 20530.

Community Relations Service

Agency: Department of Justice

Program Number: 16.200

Type of Assistance: Advisory services and counseling to any person, group, community, or state or local governmental unit seeking to alleviate conditions caused by discrimination based on race, color, or national origin.

To assist in developing programs and in directing available public and private resources to alleviate problems in the minority community.

In fiscal 1974 estimated allocation was $3.5 million. The estimated allocation for fiscal 1975 is $4 million.

Eligibility: Contact regional or local office or Community Relations Service, U.S. Department of Justice, Washington, D.C. 20530.

Veterans Reemployment Rights

Agency: Department of Labor

Program Number: 17.102

Type of Assistance: Advisory services and counseling, investigation of complaints, dissemination of technical information to persons (including reservists and national guardsmen) who have served on active duty or training duty for Armed Forces, or persons who have applied for enlistment or been inducted but were found not qualified.

Uses: To assist veterans of the Armed Forces, reservists, National Guardsmen, rejectees, and examinees in securing reinstatement with their employers,

the crediting of seniority, and other benefits to which the individual is entitled.

Allocation for fiscal 1974 was $2.2 million. The estimated allocation for fiscal 1975 is $2.3 million.

Eligibility: Contact nearest Department of Labor, Labor Management Services Administration Regional or Area Office or Office of Veterans Reemployment Rights, U.S. Department of Labor, Washington, D.C. 20216.

Apprenticeship Outreach

Agency: Department of Labor

Program Number: 17.200

Type of Assistance: Project grants and research contracts to local organizations.

Uses: To seek out qualified applicants from minority groups and assist them in entering apprenticeship programs.

Funds may not be used to subsidize trainees while they are in training programs.

In fiscal 1974 it is estimated that there were 9,000 indentures. Estimated allocation for fiscal 1974 was $9.3 million with an estimated allocation of $9.4 million for fiscal 1975.

Eligibility: Contact Director, Office of National Programs, Manpower Administration, U.S. Department of Labor, Washington, D.C. 20213.

Employment Service

Agency: Department of Labor

Program Number: 17.207

Type of Assistance: Project grants, advisory services, and counseling, provision of specialized services to state employment security agencies to place persons in employment.

Uses: General services including outreach, interviewing, testing, counseling, and referral.

Special services for veterans, with preferential treatment of disabled. The Employment Service emphasizes service to the poor, unemployed and underemployed, handicapped by race, age, lack of education, and assists them by supportive services, job research, and development.

Among services to youth is the Summer Employment Program designed to give priority to disadvantaged youth to enable their return to school and the recruitment, screening, and referral of young people for manpower training programs.

Special services are provided to inmates and former inmates of correctional institutions by making available placement, employment counseling and testing services.

Apprenticeship Information Centers are located in selected State employment offices to provide easily accessible sources of information.

Estimated allocation for fiscal 1974 was $443.8 million with an estimated allocation for 1975 of $444 million.

Eligibility: Contact nearest office of State Employment Security Agency or Director, Program and Management Services staff, U.S. Employment Service, Manpower Administration, U.S. Department of Labor, Washington, D.C. 20213.

Job Opportunities in the Business Sector (Jobs)

Agency: Department of Labor

Program Number: 17.212

Type of Assistance: Direct payment for specified use, training advisory services and counseling to private profit or nonprofit companies.

Uses: To enable employers to hire and train disadvantaged individuals in entry level jobs and to upgrade present employees for jobs of higher responsibility.

Estimated allocation for fiscal 1974 was $62.8 million with an estimated allocation for fiscal 1975 of $90 million.

Eligibility: Contact Regional Manpower Administration Office or Director, Office of National Programs, Manpower Administration, U.S. Department of Labor, 601 D Street, N.W., Washington, D.C. 20213.

Operation Mainstream

Agency: Department of Labor

Program Number: 17.223

Type of Assistance: Project grants to private nonprofit national organizations with emphasis on establishing projects in rural areas or towns.

Uses: To provide work training and employment activities, with necessary supportive services for chronically unemployed poor older workers.

Job opportunities may involve management, development and conservation of parks, highways, and recreational areas of federal, state, and local governments; rehabilitation of other community facilities and provision of social, health, and educational services to the poor.

Estimated allocation for fiscal 1974 was $20 million with the same figure allocated for fiscal 1975.

Eligibility: Contact Director, Office of National Programs, Manpower Administration, U.S. Department

of Labor, 607 D Street, N.W., Washington, D.C. 20213.

Work Incentives Program and Incentives (WIN)

Agency: Department of Labor

Program Number: 17.226

Type of Assistance: Project grants to state employment service agencies.

Uses: To move men and women and out-of-school youth age 16 or older from AFDC rolls into employment through training, social services, and job placement.

Services include placement or on-the-job training, work orientation, basic education, skill training, work experience to improve employability, and placement in public service employment.

Employers hiring individual under the WIN program are eligible to receive 20% tax credit on first 12 months salary paid to the individual.

Estimated allocation for fiscal 1974 was $250.4 million with an estimated allocation for fiscal 1975 of $190 million.

Eligibility: Contact local office of State employment service or Director, Office of Work Incentive Programs, Office of Manpower Development Programs, Department of Labor, Washington, D.C. 20213.

National On-The-Job Training

Agency: Department of Labor

Program Number: 17.228

Type of Assistance: Project grants to national organizations.

Uses: To provide occupational training for unemployed and underemployed persons who cannot otherwise obtain appropriate full-time employment.

Funds may be used for reimbursement of instructors, administrative costs, supplies, supplementary classroom education, trainee allowances, and supportive services.

Approximately 23,500 job placements have resulted from this program. Estimated allocation for fiscal 1974 was $14 million with the same figure allocated for fiscal 1975.

Eligibility: Contact Director, Office of National Programs, Manpower Administration, U.S. Department of Labor, 601 D Street, N.W., Washington, D.C. 20213.

Migrant Workers

Agency: Department of Labor

Program Number: 17.230

Type of Assistance: Project grants to federal, state, and local government agencies, private profit and non-profit organizations, or migrant organizations.

Uses: To help migrant and seasonal farm worker families find economically viable alternatives to agricultural labor.

Among services are relocation assistance, occupational training, education, health services, job development, and placement.

Estimated allocation for fiscal 1974 was $45 million with estimated allocation for fiscal 1975 at $52.7 million.

Eligibility: Contact Director, Office of National Programs, Manpower Administration, U.S. Department of Labor, 601 D Street, N.W., Washington, D.C. 20213.

Comprehensive Employment and Training Programs (CETA)

Agency: Department of Labor

Program Number: 17.232

Type of Assistance: Formula grants to units of state and local general government with population of more than 100,000 consortia consisting of general local government at least one of which has a population of 100,000 or more.

Uses: Funds for assistance to provide training or employment opportunities for low income, unemployed, or underemployed persons.

No monies allocated in fiscal 1974. In fiscal 1975 estimated allocation for Title I and II will be $1.6 billion.

Eligibility: Contact Regional Manpower Office or Manpower Administration, U.S. Department of Labor, 601 D Street, N.W., Washington, D.C. 20213.

Equal Employment Opportunity by Federal Contractors

Agency: Department of Labor

Program Number: 17.301

Type of Assistance: Investigation of complaints, dissemination of technical information to any individual employed by federal contractors or in federally involved construction who feels he has been the subject of discrimination.

Uses: To provide equal opportunity in the performance of Federal contracts and subcontracts. To set policy, monitoring and evaluating the compliance of Federal contractors and subcontractors.

Estimated allocation for fiscal 1974 was $29.7 million. Estimated allocation for fiscal 1975 to be $37.4 million.

Eligibility: Contact Director, Officer of Federal Contract Compliance, Employment Standards Administration, U.S. Department of Labor, Washington, D.C. 20210.

Minimum Wage and Hour Standards

Agency: Department of Labor

Program Number: 17.303

Type of Assistance: Advisory services and counseling, investigation of complaints to and by any covered employee, who unless specifically exempt, must be paid in accordance with applicable monetary standards.

Uses: To provide standards protecting wages of working persons by requiring a minimum hourly wage rate. Overtime pay and equal pay for men and women performing the same or substantially equal work is provided for.

Estimated allocation for fiscal 1974 was $23.3 million. Estimated allocation for fiscal 1975 was $28 million.

Eligibility: Contact nearest office of Employment Standards Administration or Assistant Secretary, Employment Standards Administration, U.S. Department of Labor, Washington, D.C. 20210.

Consumer Credit Protection

Agency: Department of Labor

Program Number: 17.306

Type of Assistance: Advisory services and counseling, investigation of complaints by any person whose earnings have been subjected to garnishment.

Uses: To provide restrictions on the amount of an employee's wages or salary which may be garnished, that is, beginning January 1, 1975, if an individual's weekly disposable earnings were $84 or less only the amount in excess of $63 could be garnished.

Under no circumstances may an employee be discharged from his employment by reason of garnishment for any one indebtedness.

In fiscal 1974 the estimated allocation was $459,000 with $468,000 to be allocated in fiscal 1975.

Eligibility: Contact local office of Employment Standards Administration or Assistant Secretary, Employment Standards Administration, U.S. Department of Labor, Washington, D.C. 20210.

Farm Labor Contractor Registration

Agency: Department of Labor

Program Number: 17.308

Type of Assistance: Provision of specialized services, project grants to states and state employment service agencies.

Uses: To assure more equitable treatment for migrant agricultural workers. Program provides for contractual arrangements between the contractor and the migrant worker. Requires that the contractor obtain motor vehicle liability insurance and that he insure migrant worker and his personal property against injury or damage arising from automobile accident.

Any person who, for a fee either for himself or on behalf of another person, recruits, solicits, hires, furnishes, or transports ten or more migrant workers must register under the Farm Labor Contractor Registration Act.

Estimated allocation for fiscal 1974 was $380,000. The estimated allocation for fiscal 1975 will be $418,000.

Eligibility: Contact State Employment Office, nearest Employment Standards Administration office or Assistant Secretary, Employment Standards Administration, U.S. Department of Labor, Washington, D.C. 20210.

Federal Employment for Disadvantaged Youth— Part Time

Agency: Civil Service Commission

Program Number: 27.003

Type of Assistance: Federal employment for students accepted for or enrolled in secondary school or institution of higher learning who maintain acceptable school standing and need their job earnings to stay in school.

Uses: To give disadvantaged youth, 16–21 part time employment with federal agencies which will allow them to continue their education. Work week consists of 16 hours during school year and 40 hours during extended vacation periods.

Estimated number of students participating in fiscal 1974 was 23,000. Estimated allocation for fiscal 1974 was $36 million with the same figure to be allocated for fiscal 1975.

Related Program of Interest

27.004 FEDERAL EMPLOYMENT FOR DISADVANTAGED YOUTH—SUMMER

Federal employment for disadvantaged youth, ages 16–21 with federal agencies. Economic needs criteria must be met. Minimum wage rate is paid and no special skills or experience are required. Estimated allocation for fiscal 1974 was $31 million. For fiscal 1975 the estimated allocation is $32 million.

Eligibility: Contact Civil Service Commission Regional office or Office of Youth Employment Programs, Manpower Sources Division, Bureau of Recruiting and Examining, U.S. Civil Service Commission, Washington, D.C. 20415.

Clearinghouse Services, Civil Rights and Sex Discrimination Complaints

Agency: Commission on Civil Rights

Program Number: 29.001

Type of Assistance: Dissemination of technical information, investigation of complaints.

Uses: To further opportunities for minority group members and women utilizing federal programs. Commission investigates complaints of devices to deny equal protection under the laws in voting, employment, housing, education, and administration of justice.

Estimated allocation for fiscal 1974 was $5.9 million. For fiscal 1975 estimated allocation is $6.9 million.

Eligibility: Contact nearest regional or local office or United States Commission on Civil Rights, Washington, D.C. 20425.

Job Discrimination—Investigation and Conciliation of Complaints

Agency: Equal Employment Opportunity Commission

Program Number: 30.001

Type of Assistance: Investigation of complaints by any aggrieved party or individuals knowing of discriminatory practices.

Uses: To provide for enforcement of federal prohibition against discrimination in employment based on race, color, religion, sex, or national origin.

Complaints are received, investigated, and conciliated by EEOC. Enforcement can be sought through the courts.

Estimated allocation for fiscal 1974 was $20.5 million. It is not known what the allocation will be for fiscal 1975.

Related Programs of Interest

30.002 JOB DISCRIMINATION—SPECIAL PROJECT GRANTS

Project grants and contracts with official state and

local antidiscrimination agencies to increase their capability to combat employment discrimination.

30.003 Job Discrimination—Technical Assistance

Advisory services and counseling to employees, labor unions, employment agencies, educational institutions, state and local governments to assist them in bringing their employment practices into voluntary compliance with the law and limit their liabilities to class action suits.

Fiscal 1974 allocation estimated at $1 million. No figure set for fiscal 1975.

Eligibility: Contact any EEOC field office or Director, Office of Voluntary Programs, Equal Employment Opportunity Commission, 1800 G Street, N.W., Washington, D.C. 20506.

Eligibility for 30.001

Contact any EEOC field office or Director, Office of Compliance, Equal Employment Opportunity Commission, 1800 G Street, N.W., Washington, D.C. 20506.

Eligibility for 30.002

Contact any EEOC field office or Director, Office of State and Community Affairs, Equal Employment Opportunity Commission, Room 1229-C, 1800 G Street, N.W., Washington, D.C. 20506.

Promotion of the Humanities—Fellowships in Selected Fields

Agency: National Foundation on the Arts and the Humanities

Program Number: 45.107

Type of Assistance: Project grants to citizens of the U.S. or native residents of its territorial possessions who have completed their professional training and are at an early point in their careers.

Uses: To be used for projects in historical, social, or cultural studies of American ethnic minorities and in the interrelationships between human values and science and technology.

In fiscal 1974 estimated allocation was $550,000. Estimated allocation for fiscal 1975 is $2.4 million. This figure is for a merged NEH fellowship program and will fund total independent fellowships.

Eligibility: Contact Director, Division of Fellowships, National Endowment for the Humanities, Washington, D.C. 20506.

Economic Opportunity Loans for Small Business

Agency: Small Business Administration

Program Number: 59.003

Type of Assistance: Direct loans, guaranteed/insured loans, advisory services, and counseling to people with low incomes who have been denied the opportunity to acquire adequate business financing through normal lending channels or reasonable terms.

Uses: For management assistance and loans up to $50,000 with maximum maturity of 15 years to socially or economically disadvantaged persons for small businesses.

Communications media, nonprofit enterprises, speculation in property, lending or investment enterprises, and financing of real property are excluded.

For fiscal 1974 estimated allocation was $60.8 million in direct loans and $46 million in guaranteed loans. For fiscal 1975 an estimated $60.5 in direct loans and $104.5 million in guaranteed loans are to be allocated.

Eligibility: Contact Director of Financing, Small Business Administration, 1441 L Street, N.W., Washington, D.C. 20416.

Related Programs of Interest

59.006 Minority Business Development Procurement Assistance

Specialized services are provided to black Americans, American Indians, Spanish Americans, Oriental Americans, Eskimos and Aleuts, as well as others, to insure their participation as owners of businesses in a normal competitive environment. Authority of Small Business Act to enter into procurement contracts with other federal agencies is utilized.

Estimated allocation for fiscal 1974 was $2.5 million. For fiscal 1975 estimated allocation is $3.7 million.

Eligibility: Contact Office of Business Development, Small Business Administration, 1441 L Street, N.W., Washington, D.C. 20416.

59.007 Management and Technical Assistance For Disadvantaged Businessmen

Project grants to public or private organizations having capability to provide management and technical assistance to existing or potential businessmen who are economically or socially disadvantaged or located in areas of high concentration of unemployment. In fiscal 1974 estimated allocation of funds was $5 million with the same figure allocated for fiscal 1975.

Eligibility: Contact Director of Management Assistance, Small Business Administration, 1441 L Street, N.W., Washington, D.C. 20416.

59.011 SMALL BUSINESS INVESTMENT COMPANIES

Direct loans, guaranteed insured loans, advisory services, and counseling to any chartered small business investment company with combined paid-in-capital and paid-in surplus of not less than $150,000 having qualified management and giving evidence of sound operations. MEBIC investment policy is directed toward providing assistance which will contribute to a well balanced national economy by making it easier to become the owner of small business concerns by individuals who have been disadvantaged by social or economic reasons.

Eligibility: Contact Associate Administrator, Small Business Administration, 1441 L Street, N.W., Washington, D.C. 20416.

59.019 MINORITY VENDORS PROGRAMS

Specialized services provided to minority firms which manufacture goods or perform services purchased by the nation's business community.

Small retail businesses which do not, by definition, provide product or service to major corporations are excluded from this program.

In fiscal 1974 estimated allocation was $35,000. For fiscal 1975 estimated allocation to be $40,000.

Eligibility: Contact Minority Vendors Program Field Representative in Regional Office or Assistant Administrator for Minority Enterprises, Small Business Administration, Minority Vendors Program, 1441 L Street, N.W., Washington, D.C. 20416.

COMPREHENSIVE EMPLOYMENT AND TRAINING PROGRAMS

CETA was designed to provide job training and employment opportunities for economically disadvantaged, unemployed, and underemployed persons to enable them to increase future earnings and secure self-sustaining, unsubsidized employment.

For CETA activities, prime sponsors (usually units of State or local government with a population of 100,000 or more) are responsible for developing programs responsive to local needs; these sponsors have wide discretion with regard to program design. The range of services provided includes classroom and on-the-job training, basic and remedial education, testing, job referral and development, work experience, and supportive social services. Sponsors may provide these services directly or indirectly through contracts or subgrants with such organizations as State Employment Security Agencies (SESA's), vocational agencies, schools, community groups, labor organizations, or private businesses. Prime sponsors are responsible for monitoring and evaluating programs to determine that local needs are met.

SYNOPSIS OF THE COMPREHENSIVE EMPLOYMENT AND TRAINING ACT, AS AMENDED IN 1978

Title I, Administrative Provisions

Organizational and general provisions applicable to the entire act; consolidates the procedures for planning, reporting, auditing, and other administrative requirements; authorized appropriations generally for fiscal years 1979–1982.

Title II, Comprehensive Employment and Training Services

Authorizes comprehensive work and training activities. Authorizes institutional and on-the-job training, work experience, job search assistance, and supportive services in title IIB and C. Also contains a separate counterstructural public service employment program in title IID, with new jobholders limited to economically disadvantaged persons who have been unemployed 15 of the last 20 weeks or who are receiving or are part of a family receiving welfare benefits.

Title III, Special National Programs and Activities

Authorizes special target group programs for Indians and other Native Americans, migrant and seasonal farmworkers, ex-offenders, older workers, displaced homemakers, women, and the handicapped. Continues programs of research and development, technical assistance, and labor market information.

Title IV, Youth Programs

Authorizes Job Corps residential training program, summer youth employment program, and youth programs first authorized by the Youth Employment and Demonstration Projects Act of 1977, except the Young Adult Conservation Corps, which is in title VIII.

Title V, National Commission for Employment Policy

Authorizes an advisory commission with members to be appointed by the President.

Title VI, Public Service Employment Program

Authorizes a countercyclical public service employment program. Participation is limited to unemployed persons who have been without work for 10 of the last 12 weeks and have family incomes at or below the Bureau of Labor Statistics' lower living standard level or have received public assistance 10 of the last 12 weeks.

Title VII, Private Sector Initiative Program

Authorizes a demonstration of alternative approaches to obtaining greater involvement of private sector in employment and training of the disadvantaged. Establishes Private Industry Councils with representatives from industry, business, organized labor, community-based organizations, and educational institutions to participate with prime sponsors in improving access for all CETA participants to private sector jobs.

Title VIII, Young Adult Conservation Corps

Authorizes year-round corps open both to disadvantaged and nondisadvantaged youth, 16 to 23 years old, for conservation work in national parks, forests, and other public lands.

PROGRAM PERFORMANCE IN FISCAL 1980

Selected Characteristics of CETA Participants, Fiscal 1980

Characteristic	Title IIB and C	Title III)	Title VI	Title IV	Title VII
Total	1,121,000	489,500	408,500	1,246,500	59,500
Percent	100	100	100	100	100
Male	47	50	55	51	57
Female	53	50	45	49	43
Age					
Under 22 years	48	26	24	100	36
22 to 44 years	46	62	63	—	59
45 to 54 years	4	8	8	—	4
55 years and over	2	5	6	—	1
Education					
High school student	19	3	3	73	5
High school dropout	29	30	28	14	30
High school graduate/equivalent	38	45	43	8	48
Posthigh school attendee	13	22	26	5	17
Economic status					
AFDC recipient	21	19	15	27	16
Public assistance recipient	6	8	7	6	3
OMB poverty level[a]	95	90	80	82	94
71 to 85% BLS lower living standard[b]	2	3	6	11	1
Above 85% lower living standard	3	6	19	5	3
Economically disadvantaged[c]	98	96	90	92	98
Race/ethnic group:					
White (not Hispanic)	50	51	51	38	49
Black (not Hispanic)	33	34	33	41	32
Hispanic	13	12	13	17	15
American Indian or Alaskan Native	1	2	3	2	1
Other	3	2	2	2	3
Limited English-speaking ability	6	5	5	7	6
Migrant or seasonal farm family member	1	1	1	1	1

Selected Characteristics of CETA Participants, Fiscal 1980 (*continued*)

Characteristic	Title IIB and C	Title IID	Title VI	Title IV	Title VII
Handicapped	9	6	5	6	7
Offender	9	7	6	4	9
Unemployment insurance claimant	5	9	11	1	9
Veteran status					
Veteran	8	14	15	3	12
Vietnam-era [d]	3	5	6	—	6
Special disabled	1	1	1	—	1

Source: U.S. Department of Labor, Employment and Training Administration, Office of Administration and Management.

[a] In 1980, the poverty level for a nonfarm family of four established by the Office of Management and Budget (OMB) was $7,450.

[b] The lower living standard income level established by the BLS for a nonfarm family of four in 1980 was $14,044.

[c] A person who receives, or is a member of a family that receives, cash welfare payments or has, or is a member of a family that has, a total family income (for the 6-month period prior to program application) that, in relation to family size and location, does not exceed the most recently established poverty levels determined with criteria established by OMB or 70% of the BLS lower living standard income level, whichever is higher.

[d] Served between August 5, 1964, and May 7, 1975, and under age 35.

First-time Participants and Obligations for Work and Training Programs Administered by the Department of Labor: Fiscal 1980[a] (thousands)

Program	First-Time Participants	Obligations
Total	3,699.4	$8,777,600
Comprehensive Employment and Training Act	2,609.8	8,263,700
IIB and C—Services for the disadvantaged; upgrading and retraining	795.2	2,045,300
IID—Transitional employment for the disadvantaged	231.9	1,502,500
III—Special national programs and activities	208.6	507,100
IV—Youth programs:		
Job Corps	70.6	400,900
Youth Employment and Training Programs	362.8	831,900
Summer youth programs	690.7	725,100
VI—Countercyclical public service employment	153.5	1,659,900
VII—Private Sector Initiative Program	50.2	368,000
VIII—Young Adult Conservation Corps	46.3	223,000
Work Incentive program	1,037.3[b]	247,000
Older Americans Act, title V	52.3	266,900

Source: U.S. Department of Labor, Employment and Training Administration, Office of Administration and Management.

[a] Fiscal 1980 includes the period from October 1, 1979, through September 30, 1980.

[b] Individuals receiving Work Incentive program services.

Distribution of Enrollees by Minority Status and Sex and by Selected Characteristics: CETA Participants Newly Enrolled during October 1979–September 1980[a]

Title II—Comprehensive Employment and Training Services (Total)

Selected Characteristics	All			White (excluding Hispanic)		Black (excluding Hispanic)		Hispanic		Other minorities	
	Total	Male	Female	Male	Female	Male	Female	Male	Female	Male	Female
Total	830,741	404,024	426,718	206,377	212,818	136,097	158,894	43,545	39,314	18,004	15,691
Male	404,024	404,024	—	206,377	—	136,097	—	43,545	—	18,004	—
Female	426,718	—	426,718	—	212,818	—	158,894	—	39,314	—	15,691
Minority status											
White, excluding Hispanic	419,196	206,377	212,818	206,377	212,818	—	—	—	—	—	—
Black, excluding Hispanic	294,991	136,097	158,894	—	—	136,097	158,894	—	—	—	—
Hispanic	82,860	43,545	39,314	—	—	—	—	43,545	39,314	—	—
Other minorities, total	33,695	18,004	15,691	—	—	—	—	—	—	18,004	15,691
Age at entry											
Under 16 years	36,034	22,142	13,892	10,044	5,367	9,790	7,038	2,219	1,138	88	350
16 to 19 years	199,990	93,087	106,903	47,941	47,666	32,751	44,758	9,722	11,491	2,673	2,988
20 years	109,242	53,582	55,660	26,939	25,464	17,764	23,403	6,572	4,514	2,307	2,278
Total under 21 years	345,266	168,811	176,455	84,924	78,497	60,305	75,199	18,513	17,143	5,068	5,616
21 years	485,475	235,212	250,263	121,453	134,321	75,792	83,696	25,032	22,172	12,936	10,074
Total 21 years and under	423,864	206,212	217,652	103,044	112,182	69,517	76,128	22,511	19,999	11,140	9,342
22 to 44 years	37,533	17,378	20,155	10,503	13,651	3,937	4,497	1,804	1,650	1,135	357
45 to 54 years	24,078	11,622	12,456	7,906	8,489	2,338	3,070	717	522	661	375
55 years and over	61,611	29,000	32,611	18,409	22,139	6,275	7,567	2,521	2,172	1,795	732
Total 45 years and over	345,267	168,812	176,455	84,925	78,497	60,305	75,199	18,514	17,143	5,068	5,617

Economically disadvantaged at entry	818,119	397,366	420,753	202,421	209,077	134,046	157,267	43,271	38,786	17,628	15,623
Limited ability to speak English at entry	36,403	22,190	14,213	4,940	2,726	1,824	752	7,994	6,900	7,433	3,835
Migrant or seasonal farm family at entry	6,756	3,905	2,851	378	234	451	621	2,997	1,601	79	395
Head of household at entry	317,025	198,622	118,403	108,030	73,924	63,104	31,411	18,814	7,980	8,624	5,088
Receiving unemployment insurance at application	57,394	37,476	19,918	23,516	12,259	9,455	5,452	3,113	1,628	992	579
Labor force status at entry											
Employed	8,540	3,876	4,664	2,369	3,418	985	1,032	120	149	502	64
Unemployed	678,050	329,820	348,230	170,136	177,990	108,124	126,344	36,485	31,283	15,074	12,613
Underemployed	24,390	10,170	14,219	5,308	8,684	2,567	3,256	1,082	1,814	914	465
Other	119,761	60,158	59,605	28,365	22,726	24,421	28,262	5,859	6,068	1,513	2,549
Annual family income year prior to application											
None	319,555	154,415	165,140	67,687	68,917	60,900	73,401	13,396	15,959	8,432	6,863
$1–$999	58,514	30,421	28,093	18,454	17,252	8,472	8,076	2,660	2,012	835	753
$1,000–$2,999	152,567	73,223	79,343	40,034	45,666	22,139	24,595	8,231	6,399	2,821	2,684
$3,000–$4,999	113,447	56,160	57,287	31,341	34,919	16,657	17,420	5,801	4,070	2,361	878
$5,000–$6,999	75,043	34,625	40,418	19,706	20,068	9,950	14,594	3,936	4,129	1,033	1,627
$7,000–$9,999	56,849	28,182	28,667	14,805	13,189	9,791	10,887	2,395	3,214	1,191	1,377
$10,000 or more	54,766	26,997	27,769	12,350	12,808	8,187	9,921	3,127	3,531	1,332	1,509

Source: CETA Supplemental MIS Tables by Title of Funding (Enrollees During October 1979–September 1980). Surveys conducted by the Bureau of the Census; results prepared for the Office of Program Evaluation, Employment and Training Administration, U.S. Department of Labor.

Note: Tables F-10.1 through F-10.11 fulfill the requirement in CETA, title I, section 127(d)(2), which calls for cross-tabulated participant characteristics. The data are derived from the Continuous Longitudinal Manpower Survey. Vertical and horizontal percentages are available as part of the "CETA Supplemental MIS Tables by Title of Funding." Whole numbers are provided here, so that researchers may develop percentages either vertically or horizontally to suit their own needs.
a Excludes enrollees in Puerto Rico, the Virgin Islands, the Trust Territory of the Pacific Islands, and the four rural Concentrated Employment Programs (CEPs).

THE WORK INCENTIVE PROGRAM

The Work Incentive (WIN) program, authorized by the 1968 amendments to Title IV of the Social Security Act, provides employment, training, and social services to help welfare dependents move from welfare to jobs and self-support. In fiscal 1980, WIN outlays were $395 million. In the same period, state welfare agencies reported welfare grant reductions of $632 million (on an annualized basis) as a result of job entries by WIN registrants.

WIN registration is mandated for all persons at least 16 years of age who are receiving or applying for AFDC unless they are legally exempt. Those exempt include mothers of children under 6 years of age; full-time students; persons who are ill, incapacitated, or of advanced age; persons living too far from a WIN project to make participation practicable; and mothers or other female relatives.

The WIN Population

WIN serves a diverse population, including teenagers, older workers, unemployed fathers, and women entering the labor force for the first time. About three fourths of WIN registrants are in the prime working ages of 22 to 44 years.

Although diverse, the WIN population differs significantly from the general labor force: three fourths of the WIN participants are female; more than half are minority; and fewer than half (43% in fiscal 1980) are high school graduates. In contrast, females made up only two fifths of the general U.S. labor force in 1980, minorities only one tenth, and only one fourth of the total labor force had not completed 12 or more years of school.

Females, minorities, and jobseekers who lack a high school diploma encounter greater difficulty in finding jobs and often must accept lower level, lower paying jobs. WIN registrants are often characterized by all of these disadvantages—and others.

For single parents, day-care for children is essential, but often unavailable. Transportation, health, and other problems can present major obstacles to overcoming welfare dependence. In fiscal 1980, more than 373,000 registrants were provided day-care or other social services by the WIN program, county welfare departments, or other agencies, so that participants could take jobs or prepare for employment.

Work Incentive Program, Significant Statistics: Fiscal 1979 and 1980[a]

Item	Fiscal Year		Change	
	1979	1980	Number	Percent
Intake				
New registrants	914,319	1,037,348	123,029	13.5
On board	1,487,057	1,566,848	79,791	5.4
Appraisals, total	626,147	777,531	151,384	24.2
Entered employment	296,108	283,729	−12,379	−4.2
Work and training[b]				
Total	145,487	145,632	145	0.1
WIN funded	66,085	53,625	−12,460	−18.9
Non-WIN funded	79,402	92,007	12,605	15.9

Source: U.S. Department of Labor, Employment and Training Administration, Office of Work Incentive Programs.

[a] Data do not include Puerto Rico, Guam, or the Virgin Islands.

[b] Includes on-the-job training, public service employment, institutional training, and work experience.

WIN Registrants' Hourly Entry Wages, by Sex and Race or Ethnic Group: Fiscal Year 1979 (%)

Hourly Entry Wages	Total all Groups	Sex			Race or Ethnic Group		
		UF[a]	Male, Except UF	Female	White	Black	Hispanic
Total	100.0	100.0	100.0	100.0	100.0	100.0	100.0
Less than $3	39.2	14.3	27.2	47.6	34.9	48.3	35.4
$3.00 to $3.99	35.2	31.3	33.5	36.5	35.1	34.8	38.1
$4.00 to $4.99	12.1	21.2	16.5	9.0	13.6	8.8	13.3
$5.00 to $5.99	5.6	13.6	9.5	2.9	6.8	3.3	6.0
$6.00 and over	6.1	17.3	11.7	2.2	7.5	3.3	6.0
Other[b]	1.8	2.3	1.6	1.8	2.1	1.5	1.2

[a] Unemployed fathers.

[b] Piece rates, commissions, etc.

PERSPECTIVES ON BLACK EDUCATION

Current Status ■ Education Prior to 1861 ■ Educational Efforts of the Civil War Period ■ Education Since the Civil War ■ Chronology of Educational Developments ■ Scholarships, Loans, and Awards ■ Elementary and Secondary Education Act ■ Selected Programs for Disadvantaged Children under ESEA ■ Higher Education Act ■ Vocational Education ■ Civil Rights Institutes ■ National Defense Education Act ■ Handicapped ■ Professional Education ■ Predominantly Black Colleges, Universities, and Institutes ■ Education Charts ■ Education Tables ■ Educational Films

Black efforts to attain equality in education produced notable successes in the 1970s and early 1980s. Black children accomplished significant gains relative to white children in achievement test scores. The black school dropout rate declined. Admissions of blacks to colleges, universities, and prestigious prep schools increased. And in much of the old South integration in public schools proceeded peacefully and successfully.

Yet in the early 1980s the education of America's blacks was in serious jeopardy. The Reagan Administration, in what Professor Kenneth Clark termed a "functional repeal of the *Brown* Decision," proposed and supported a series of measures that, if instituted, would eliminate effective means for integration and reward families and institutions that wished to segregate.

Victories and Defeats

Contrasts of success and failure by black students were especially evident in reports on the achievement levels of black pupils. Referring to education in inner cities, the Urban League reported in 1981 that black students "continue to lag two, even five years behind national norms." A study by the National Assessment of Educational Progress, a federally funded, state-administered program designed to measure student performance in a variety of subjects, found black high school sophomores and seniors lagging behind whites in vocabulary, math, reading, science, and civics.

However, the same tests also revealed that blacks were closing the gap when 1980 figures were compared with those of 1970. For subjects other than writing, the average difference between black and white nine-year-olds fell from about 17 percentage points in 1970 to 10–11 percentage points by 1980. For 13-year-olds, blacks closed the gap markedly in all subjects except mathematics, from 17–18 points in 1970 to 12–13 points in 1980. The analysis also indicated that improvements for nine-year-old black children were mirrored in their performance at age 13, when the same children were tested four years later.

The crucial question to blacks was whether such

progress can continue to a point where no gap exists. A provocative view on this matter was advanced by Professor Lyle Jones of North Carolina University, a director of the National Assessment study. Professor Jones contended that black children have progressed primarily because programs under the Compensatory Education Programs of the Elementary and Secondary Education Act stimulated a climate of hope. The support provided pupils and schools by these programs gave black children a sense that the country cared about their future.

The Threat

The climate of hope for black children, however, was chilled in 1981 and 1982 by proposals that threatened both blacks and the public school system itself. Among these were:

Tuition tax credits for parents earning up to $75,000 annually who send their children to private schools.

Stripping lower federal courts of the power to order busing as a remedy for segregation if children involved were to be transported more than 5 miles or longer than 15 minutes.

Elimination of efforts to desegregate entire school districts.

Cuts in funding for Public Education Programs.

According to Kenneth Clark, such policies would accelerate the white middle class's flight from public schools and result in a racial caste system in education, with whites attending private schools and public schools reserved for rejected blacks.

While these and other measures were receiving serious Administration and Congressional support, aid to public education by the federal government, and many local jurisdictions as well, was being cut.

The cuts were not as severe as President Reagan wanted, however. For fiscal 1982, the Administration sought cuts amounting to about 25% but succeeded in obtaining only 10%, from $14 billion to $12.7 billion. For fiscal 1983, the President again requested slashes of about 25%, to $9.6 billion. As of May 1982, this plan was encountering strong opposition in Congress and there was some chance that the 1983 education budget would not be reduced at all.

The Quality Issue

While most blacks regarded integration as vital, increasing concern was expressed over the quality of education their children received. Throughout the 1970s, schools in the major urban areas were beset

Kenneth Clark calls the Reagan policy a "functional repeal of the Brown decision."

by violence, vandalism, underfinancing, and the fear, hostility, and low expectations of teachers and administrators. Rigidity and overspecialization in public education also disturbed blacks.

Bernard Watson wrote in *The State of Black America, 1982,*

The need is not just a matter of lowering or raising standards but to allow enough flexibility and humanity to permeate both the schools and public policies that shape them so that students can be viewed as individuals who have the ability and motivation to use their minds constructively and create their own ways. Unfortunately, the types of policies and instructional practices that treat students as automatons or fragmented entities to be parceled out to specialists and remediators are most intensively applied to minority students and to the children of poverty.

Blacks also continued to suffer from negative perceptions of their ability to learn. The Urban League noted in *The State of Black America, 1980,* that an entire lexicon of phrases and terms such as "culturally deprived," "deficit model," "psychology of the streets," "welfare dependence," "maternal dominance," and others had been created to justify assertions that learning and excellence were beyond the reach of blacks and that they therefore should be content to accept inferior facilities and instruction as "adequate."

Though attention was focused on the poor quality of northern urban schools, inferior education apparently persisted in rural black areas of the South. In

1981 a report by the Southern Regional Council found schools in 34 predominantly black counties in Georgia and Alabama to be inferior. The Council reported that schools were better where mandatory state and federal standards were imposed or where blacks comprised a majority of the school board.

In support of this view, the Commission quoted psychologist William Ryan:

When drinking fountains were desegregated no one expected the water quality to improve; when lunch counters were desegregated the hamburgers and cokes didn't taste any better. . . . And no one expected black kids in desegregated swimming pools to start swimming faster, or preachers in desegregated churches to preach more eloquently. Segregation itself unjustly inflicts pain and suffering on black people. Desegregation is designed to stop that particular source of hurt; that's a good enough goal.

In November 1981 the U.S. Commission on Civil Rights urged that the quality issue not be used as an argument for or against integration. The Commission noted that there is strong evidence integration improves the quality of education, but added that the point of desegregation was not to improve the quality of education but to erase the caste implications of color.

The Current Status of Desegregation

In 1954 less than 1% of black students in the South attended schools with white children. By 1968, 20% of black students in the South attended schools that were more than 50% white, and by 1978, 44% did so. Nationally, in 1978, 38% of black students were in schools that contain more than 50% whites in the student body. These figures underscore two points: desegregation has progressed, and a great deal more remains to be achieved.

Integration has been delayed in many areas by lengthy litigation over various plans. In 1981 Chicago's school system remained largely segregated, despite a series of violations cited by courts since 1964. A similar pattern existed in New York City, which was also cited frequently between 1977 and 1982 for not using enough black teachers. Desegregation litigation is usually lengthy. Frequently, one case can involve 25 written opinions, 10 years, and cost the disputing parties a million dollars, before a final decision is reached and invoked.

Prolonged battles were also fought over the issue of metropolitan integration, that is, integrating a city's schools with those of its nearby suburbs. Orders and agreements for metropolitan integration of schools went into effect in St. Louis and Kansas City, Missouri, in 1981 but in early 1982 were still the subject of litigation.

Busing is rarely a logistical problem in metropolitan plans, and in fact is sometimes reduced. This was the result in Charlotte-Mecklenburg County, North Carolina, an integrated schools district of 550 square miles with 84,000 pupils. The desegregation plan there actually required less busing than had been required before desegregation. The reason: city–suburb boundaries frequently separate schools that differ racially but are not far apart.

In a survey conducted by the U.S. Commission on Civil Rights of 16 desegregated districts, only 11 showed increases in transportation costs and in no case did transportation costs rise more than 2%.

Busing as a means of desegregation is now, in the eighties, being severely tested.

Education Prior to 1861

Many Africans who came to the English colonies in 1619 as indentured servants were previous residents of West Africa, which had had a brilliant cultural and educational heritage. The West African Empire of Ghana, which became the Empire of Mali, was mentioned by Arab sources in A.D. 800. Timbuktu and Gao were prominent cultural centers of the Moslem world for 300 years. A school system was established by Emperor Askia Mohammed Toure, ruler of Songhay from 1493 to 1512. Black students and others in the Moslem world looked to the University of Sankore at Timbuktu as a major institution of higher learning. Accomplished scholars taught law, history, medicine, and literature, including the works of Plato and Aristotle.

Early supporters of the black in the United States were masters who desired to increase the economic efficiency of their labor supply, sympathetic persons who wished to help the oppressed, and zealous missionaries who taught slaves English so that they might learn the principles of the Christian religion. The Church of England, which founded the Society for the Propagation of the Gospel in Foreign Parts, was instrumental in teaching reading, prayers, and catechism to blacks and Indians of the colonies. Other religious groups such as the Quakers advocated education of blacks. Two patterns of education emerged: instruction by religious groups and emphasis on occupational training.

Early black education met great difficulties. Alexander Garden, Commissioner of North and South Carolina and the Bahamas, wrote of insuperable educational problems relating to age, race, and language, and suggested in 1740 that only those born in the colonies and under the age of 10 be educated. South Carolina, for instance, received most of her slaves directly from Africa during the eighteenth century. Over 100,000 black people were imported directly to South Carolina and Georgia prior to 1808. Charleston served as a direct point of landing by ships sailing from Africa. Many masters observed that slaves could be more useful if they acquainted themselves with the language and customs of the colonies rather than African customs and speech.

In spite of statutes which prohibited education of blacks, progress was made in urban areas. The growth of the American city made possible the contact of blacks with many people, affording an opportunity to embrace Western civilization. Many slaves became mechanics, clerks, overseers. Mulattoes, protected from the rigors of the slave codes, helped fellow blacks learn to read and write. Urban blacks had further advantage in their opportunity to attend well-regulated Sunday

The young slave Frederick Douglass being taught to read by his owner, Mrs. Auld of Baltimore.

Anthony Benezet, opponent of slavery and a teacher of black youth in colonial America.

Many states had laws prohibiting the education of blacks.

schools·which, though cloaked with the purpose of instructing blacks in the Christian religion, permitted, in many cases, the teaching of reading and writing.

Free blacks in Charleston and other metropolitan areas established societies and organizations devoted to the cause of black education. One of the earliest was the Brown Fellowship Society organized in 1790, which had as its purpose the construction and maintenance of schools for black children. Others established in Charleston were the Humane and Friendly Society (1802), the Minors Moralist (1803), and the Unity and Friendship Society. Benevolent societies of free blacks advanced the cause of education until 1830–1835 when stringent laws were passed by state legislatures limiting education of blacks—because of slave uprisings led by Denmark Vesey and Nat Turner.

The Principles of the Rights of Man, which preceded the Revolution of 1776, affected the thinking of many Americans, white and black. As early as 1787, Prince Hall, a free black and Boston property owner, petitioned the city to establish schools for black children equal in quality to those for whites. The increase in free blacks in the North and South provided pressure for more education. In 1829 Congressmen and Washington citizens founded the African Education Society with the avowed object of giving blacks academic, mechanical, and agricultural skills. Whites feared that slaves would read the literature of the French and Haitian revolutions and writings of abolitionists. Prudence Crandall met mob resistance in trying to integrate her Canterbury, Connecticut girls' school. In

spite of discouragements, black schools continued to function. In 1842 a school for Negro and Indian boys was opened in Ohio by Augustus Wattles of the American Anti-Slavery Society and Samuel Emlen, a Quaker.

Although general education for blacks had been forbidden in the South and limited in the North, many schools had been established by 1861 (see Chronology).

Educational Efforts of the Civil War Period

The Civil War successfully removed legal prohibitions against the education of the black and freed some 4,000,000 persons. As Union armies penetrated the South, blacks looked to the federal government for help, refuge, and education. In May 1863 the War Department established a Bureau of Colored Troops with schools devoted to the training of commanders of black regiments. The idea of using the army as a training school for freedmen was voiced by Representative John Hickman of Pennsylvania. Declaring that the rebellion would not have broken out if poor whites and colored people of the South had been better educated, he introduced a bill on January 27, 1863, to increase the number of "colored" regiments to 300. Although Congress defeated the proposal, the idea that the army could serve as a potential school for blacks gained many supporters. Congress later declared that proceeds from rebel property were to be used to establish a system of education in the South provided that education taught that liberty was the fundamental principle of the government of the United States, and that

The African Methodist Episcopal Zion Church school for black children in Charleston, South Carolina, in 1866.

education was available to all persons without regard to race, sex, or color.

Lincoln was well aware of his educational responsibilities to blacks. As a member of the House of Representatives, he declared on January 10, 1849, that blacks should be apprenticed and educated in the District of Columbia. Later, on August 5, 1863, he expressed his concern to General Nathaniel Banks in Louisiana that provision be made for the education of young blacks. The Proclamation of Amnesty and Reconstruction said that states must include provisions for education for freedom in order to be restored to the Union. Lincoln further showed his interest in the education of blacks by signing a bill on June 25, 1864, providing schools for black children in the District of Columbia.

Many opposed the education of blacks. In April 1860 Jefferson Davis declared that he was opposed to the use of tax money to put black and white children on the same level. Southerners feared genuine education for poorer people, black or white. Davis declared that "colored" people had already been educated by means of regular and systematic work, language, and the religion of a civilized country. On March 18, 1863, Secretary of War Stanton appointed an American Freedman's Inquiry Commission to investigate the conditions of the black population. Robert Dale Owen of Indiana, Colonel James McKay of New York, and Samuel Howe of Massachusetts traveled along the Eastern seaboard and reported that black refugees were very concerned about schools for their children and religious instruction for themselves. In Alexandria, Virginia, one of the first acts of freed blacks was to establish schools at their own expense. Many declared, however, that they still wished the presence and teaching of educated whites.

Four stages mark the attitude of the federal government toward the black during the first two years of the Civil War: (1) the black was ignored; (2) the black was declared contraband; (3) the Second Confiscation Act provided that the Army could receive blacks and take them from masters; (4) Emancipation Proclamation and Federal Guardianship.

Congress was concerned that an immense black population without education could not use freedom wisely. With Union victories, the aid of northern philanthropy was sought to provide funds for experiments in mass education of freedmen. General Frederick Augustus Mitchel, Commander of the Department of the South, epitomized the feeling of the times when he said to a black congregation:

There is a new time coming for you colored people, a better day is dawning for you oppressed and downtrodden blacks. If now you are unwilling to help yourselves, nobody will be willing to help you. I believe the good God will lift you up to a higher level than you have yet occupied, so that you and your children may become educated and industrious citizens.

Hundreds of schools were founded in "colored" regiments, contraband camps, towns, and plantations. That a public school system for blacks appeared in the South prior to the establishment of the Freedman's Bureau and with little available money is one of the wonders of American history.

An important experiment in black education took place in the Sea Islands, located between Charleston and Savannah on the Atlantic seaboard. This includes St. Helena, Port Royal, Morgan, Paris, Ladies, and Phillips islands. Lesser islands including Folly, James and others in Georgia are known collectively as "Port Royal." Possession of these islands by General Thomas W. Sherman was accomplished in November of 1861

Attorneys Charles Sumner (right) and Robert Morris began the fight against exclusion of blacks from Boston's schools in 1849. Although their test case lost, Massachusetts passed a law in 1855 which admitted blacks into the public school system.

At the end of the Civil War, public lectures by U.S. Army speakers informed black freedmen of their new status and rights.

when contraband camps were established at Hilton Head, South Carolina. Classes for pupils six to 15 years of age were organized in Beaufort, the largest town in the area, by the Reverend Peck of Massachusetts and Reverend French of New York. Black teachers supervised educational activities but were hampered by lack of funds and supplies. General Sherman divided the territory into districts and asked Congress for help in meeting administrative and educational problems of the black population. Congress failed to act, but sympathetic attention was received from relief societies in Philadelphia, New York, and Boston.

The first was known as the Educational Commission and later became the New England Freedmen's Aid Society, organized in Boston on February 7, 1862. Its object was the intellectual improvement of persons released from slavery and promotion of education among blacks. Supporters included Edward Everett Hale, Samuel Cabot, Charles Barnard, William Lloyd Garrison, and William Cullen Bryant. New York City organized the National Freedmens Relief Association on February 20, 1862. This was followed by the Port Royal Relief Committee, later known as the Pennsylvania Freedmens Relief Association, founded in Philadelphia on March 3, 1862. Many societies confederated

in 1863 to form the United States Commission for the Relief of the National Freedmen, which, in 1865, became the American Freedmans Aid Union.

General Saxton in the Department of the South declared that black children showed as much aptitude and learning as the average of children in the North and were eager to learn to read and write. Numerous and orderly schools were established in which classes were often held with teachers dispensing clothing and food from their own pocket. Cotton barns, sheds, tents, were utilized. School farms were organized and the profits used for educational purposes. Desks were often boards thrown across chairs. Yellow fever and smallpox caused hardship and even death among pupils and teachers alike. By March 1863 Port Royal had 30 schools with 40 teachers and an enrollment of over 3,000 children from eight to 12 years of age. *Hillard's Second Primary Reader* and *Wilson's Second Reader* were among the 36,000 books sent by northern agencies to the South.

The Port Royal experiment destroyed the myth of the ineducability of blacks.

Elsewhere, in North Carolina and Virginia, General Benjamin Butler laid the foundations of a labor and educational system in the area. By March 1865 school

Because of the lack of schools for blacks in the South after the Civil War, groups of children could be found studying in the streets.

attendance for 5–14 year olds was made compulsory. General Ulysses Grant and Chaplain John Eaton in the Department of Tennessee and the State of Arkansas allowed teachers from relief societies to assume a multiplicity of duties. "Schools for Negroes" were prohibited by municipal law in Memphis. By 1865, however, 51 schools with 105 teachers and 7,360 pupils were engaged in carrying out a humane educational policy. The Department of the Gulf under the direction of General Nathaniel Banks created Boards of Education with the power to levy taxes to defray educational expenses for the contrabands of Louisiana. School commenced at 8:45 and ended at 2:30, with teachers receiving a remuneration of 65 dollars per month. Black soldiers had their own schools which were supervised by black officers and chaplains.

Statistics show that by the summer of 1865, South Carolina had 10,000 pupils, 48 schools, 76 teachers, of whom 24 were black. Additional data include Georgia, with 3,603 pupils, 69 schools, 69 teachers of whom 43 were black; Florida with 1,900 pupils, 30 schools and 19 teachers; Arkansas with 10 schools, 19 teachers, 1,393 pupils; Mississippi with 31 schools, 50 teachers, and 3,396 pupils; Western Tennessee with 56 teachers, 4,095 pupils; and Alabama with 13 schools, 30 teachers, and 1,620 pupils.

Education Since the Civil War

The Congress, on July 16, 1865, passed a bill which made education an authorized function of the Bureau of Refugees, Freedmen, and Abandoned Lands (Freedmen's Bureau, which came into existence on March 3, 1865). General Oliver Otis Howard was appointed Commissioner of the Bureau and announced his intention of furthering black education by working with benevolent societies in dispensing aid. Later, Howard University was named in honor of this commissioner who, with John M. Langston, a black lawyer graduate of Oberlin College and Inspector-General of schools, worked to establish educational facilities for blacks. The influence of the Bureau declined after 1870 and ceased in 1874.

A decade after the Civil War, the character of the educational program for blacks had changed for the following reasons:

1. State education authorities began to take over administration of schools.

2. Disagreement on the question of segregation of the races.

3. Controversy as to whether schools should be purely educational or parochial.

Churches withdrew support from national organizations and established denominational societies. This proved helpful to blacks in that many permanent institutions which later became senior colleges were established. Lack of general public support led to the establishment of private funds such as the Peabody and John F. Slater funds (see Chronology). Cooperation between philanthrophic organizations and denominational societies made possible the growth of higher education for blacks, especially in the South.

Successful efforts to establish educational institutions were usually those that made no attempt at integration. The Supreme Court declared in 1883 that the Fourteenth Amendment enjoined states, not individuals, from discrimination. The decision of 1896 holding that separate and equal facilities for blacks was constitutional provoked controversy for many years. In 1899 the Court ruled that Richmond County, Georgia, could operate white schools, although there were no schools for black children. It was not until 1954 that the doctrine of "separate but equal" was declared unconstitutional, thus ending the legality of segregated facilities.

Not all black Americans had sought integration. Booker T. Washington, speaking to the Atlanta Exposition in 1895, gained white support by arguing that education would enable blacks to maintain a separate society while advancing the progress of the nation as a whole. On the other hand, William Edward Burghardt DuBois, a founder of the NAACP, demanded total equality, declaring that black schools were generally inferior to white ones.

Between 1900 and 1930 black teachers earned $100–400 per year, compared with $200–900 for their white counterparts. Segregated schools were not providing education equal to that of white schools. It was not until the Depression that federal interest in black education increased. The Civilian Conservation Corps and the National Youth Administration helped educate many blacks. Mary McLeod Bethune, who helped create Bethune-Cookman College in Florida, directed the National Youth Administration's Division of Negro Affairs. More than 600,000 black students participated in educational activities; 60,000 blacks gained occupational skills in work-study programs, 200,000 were trained by the Civilian Conservation Corps for employment in forestry and related fields. Federal projects enabled black artists to pursue their vocation. Well-known WPA intellectuals included Langston Hughes, Charles Wright, Ralph Ellison, and Richard Wright.

Mid-Twentieth Century Progress

By 1970 progress was apparent. But the ultimate aim of excellent and nonsegregated education for all the schools in the United States had not been achieved. The National Guard was continually used to control public defiance of attempts to desegregate schools. Southern states enacted 145 laws between 1954 and 1958 to protect segregation. New Rochelle, New York, was ordered to integrate its schools, which had been segregated by pattern of attendance areas. Berkeley, California, effected an integrated school plan. Dr. Harvey Scribner, a white educator and former Superintendent of Schools for Teaneck, New Jersey, sought educa-

tional change and innovation by creating a central integrated six-grade school which was successfully put into operation in an all-white suburb. Elsewhere, integration was met with sit-ins, demonstrations, and boycotts, though in a number of places it was put into effect quietly and successfully. Black mothers demonstrated in Chicago, New York, and elsewhere in the nation against poor educational conditions and *de facto* segregation. In New York, Intermediate School 201 became a center of controversy concerning integration, local responsibility, and quality education. Community control became a rallying cry and black people tried to gain control of the educational institutions which affected them.

The federal government advanced the cause of the black by initiating legislation such as Title I of the Elementary and Secondary Education Act of 1965 and Title IV of the Civil Rights Act of 1964, outlawing discrimination in the use of federal funds for educational projects. Title IV made funds available for institutions engaged in desegregation. New problems for black people arose. Between May and September 1965, over 660 black teachers were displaced for reasons relating to integration. By 1966, 5,000 black teachers had been adversely affected.

Shifts in housing patterns imposed *de facto* resegregation. *De facto* segregation results from residential housing patterns and does not violate the constitution. By contrast, *de jure* segregation arises by law or by the deliberate act of school officials and is unconstitutional. In 1955 (*Briggs* v. *Elliott*) a District Court held that the Constitution does not require integration. It merely forbids the use of governmental power to enforce segregation. In 1966 another court pointed out that this doctrine had been used to justify techniques for perpetuating school segregation. In 1969 the Fourth Circuit Court of Appeals invalidated the *Briggs* v. *Elliott* dictum. Thus in 1970 a California state court ordered the Los Angeles school board to establish a virtually uniform racial balance throughout its 711-square-mile district with 775,000 children in 561 schools.

In 1968, 55 school districts submitted acceptable plans under Title VI. Of the 35,815 black students in these districts, 31,089 (86.8%) attended schools of predominantly white enrollment. This compared with the 23.4% desegregation figure nationally, the 18.4% figure for 11 southern states, and the 10.5% figure for Alabama, Georgia, Louisiana, Mississippi, and South Carolina—the Deep South. In 1969 more than 200 Title VI "acceptable" plans called for complete desegregation in the school year 1969–1970, and over 100 called for "substantial desegregation."

Leon Panetta, former director of the Office for Civil Rights, interpreted the data as follows:

With the aid of thousands of cooperating state and local school officials who submitted raw data, we can see a stark portrayal of ethnic isolation in schools. Whether a child is isolated with his own or other minorities, he is still likely to suffer educationally as a result of this segregation according to numerous education studies.

In a regional study of black segregation, for example, it was shown that there was a great variation in the number of blacks attending 100% minority schools, from six heavily industrial northern states, where 15.4% of the blacks attended 100% minority schools, to six border states and the District of Columbia, where 25.2% of the blacks attended 100% minority schools, to five deep southern states, where 81.9% of the blacks attended 100% minority schools. (This last figure is based on 431 districts in five states out of 4,477 districts in 17 southern and border states.)

The years 1969–1970 saw the percentage of blacks in white schools double.

Nixon's Views Change

President Nixon declared in March 1970 that there was a constitutional mandate that dual school systems and other forms of *de jure* segregation be totally eliminated. School boards were requested to act in good faith and formulate plans of desegregation which best suited their needs. To obtain the benefits of integration without depriving the child of his neighborhood school, it was suggested that a portion of a child's educational activities be shared with children from other schools. Many experts considered integration a vital aid to educating the disadvantaged. James S. Coleman, author of the 1966 study on educational equality, called for massive programs to aid blacks in the 1970s.

Among new educational ideas advocated were after-school schools and "voucher systems" in which parents, black and white, can "buy" the kind of education they choose in a "market" that would generate the establishment of a variety of innovative schools. Integration and availability of educational opportunity for black and white is the ultimate goal.

In the first week of 1970, then-Secretary of Health, Education and Welfare Robert Finch announced that school districts implementing voluntary desegregation plans were making "significant and effective progress" in providing equal educational opportunity. It was difficult to reconcile this report with the 23.4% nationwide figure of black students enrolled in predominantly white public elementary and secondary schools. Some 61% of black students were shown to be isolated in 95–100% minority schools. Some 43.3 million students were represented by the ethnic data collected by the HEW Office for Civil Rights.

The Nixon administration's support of integration was waning, as the President committed himself increasingly to a "Southern Strategy," designed to appeal to Southerners and ethnics who feared the incursion of blacks and were particularly aroused by the prospect of school children being bused to achieve integration. "Busing" soon became a code word around which fretful and racist whites rallied, providing the now-discredited ex-President with the means to undercut in the 1972 election, possible third-party opposition from Governor George Wallace on the right, and support of many traditionally northern Democrat labor and middle-class voters in the center and on the left.

By the end of 1973 Congress was seriously considering strong anti-busing legislation and actual promulgation of a constitutional amendment to obviate busing for the purposes of integration.

While this was going on, however, major integration decisions were being made in the Supreme Court.

Alabama housewives marched to Washington, D.C., in 1971 to protest busing of school children.

Integration and the "Burger Court"

The Supreme Court in *Swann* v. *Charlotte-Mecklenburg Board of Education* (1971) called on lower courts to make every effort to achieve the greatest possible degree of actual desegregation taking into account the practical realities of the situation. "The Constitutional command to desegregate does not mean that every school in every community will always reflect the racial composition of the school system as a whole," declared Chief Justice Burger. In *Keyes* v. *School District No. 1 Denver, Colorado* (June 1973) the Supreme Court emphasized that the differentiating factor between *de jure* and *de facto* segregation is *purpose* or *intent* to segregate and demanded that the School Board prove that it had not intentionally effected a policy that created or maintained segregation in the core city schools. Again in *Lau* v. *Nichols* (January 1974) the Court affirmed that minority children may not be denied a meaningful opportunity to participate in the public educational program and cited Section 601 of the Civil Rights Act of 1964, which bans discrimination based "on the grounds of race, color, or national origin in any program or activity receiving federal financial assistance."

Racial violence flared in the schools after courts ordered Boston desegregation in 1974.

The Detroit Decision

On July 25, 1974, the Supreme Court of the United States declared in the *Detroit* case that integration could not be achieved by linking city schools with those of the surrounding suburbs. An integration plan involving more than one school district could be justified only if discriminatory acts in one district produced segregation in the other, or where district lines had been deliberately drawn to separate the races. The 5 to 4 *Detroit* case ruling reversed a decision of the U.S. District Court of Appeals for the Sixth Circuit (Cincinnati, December 8, 1972), which upheld a plan to link Detroit's 185,000 black pupils with the 53 suburban school districts in Oakland, Wayne, and Macomb counties surrounding the City of Detroit. The integration plan approved by Federal Judge Stephen Roth on September 27, 1971, would have affected 780,000 children.

Dr. Kenneth B. Clark, head of the Metropolitan Applied Research Corporation, and Nathaniel B. Jones, chief legal counsel for the NAACP, stated that the Detroit ruling in no way excused the larger school systems to "evade the constitutional requirement that schools be desegregated." Michigan's Governor William Milliken stated that busing was "superficial and counterproductive" and hailed the Detroit decision as a "victory for reason." Although Detroit parents, black and white, were divided on the busing issue, many stated their preference for neighborhood schools and agreed with Chief Justice Burger when he stated that "no single tradition in public education is more deeply rooted than local control over the operation of schools." Others argued that busing would have meant less crowded classrooms, greater variety of courses, and better educational facilities.

Desegregation and Violence

In spite of court decisions, desegregation efforts were hampered by violence, racial hostility, segregated housing patterns, and tradition of neighborhood schools, especially in Baltimore, Los Angeles, Boston, and Phoenix. Two hundred leaders of anti-busing groups gathered in Pontiac, Michigan (March 1972) and made plans to march to Washington to protest busing policies. Earlier, 10 school buses had been dynamited in protest against a court order to bus one third of Pontiac's 24,000 students. Virginians protested the ruling of U.S. District Judge Robert R. Merhige, Jr., later overturned in a higher court, which ordered the merger of Richmond schools with those of two surrounding counties. Thousands drove in a motorcade to protest the plan which would mix city black children with suburban white children.

Irate mothers shout disapproval of Senator Edward Kennedy for his support of desegregation.

In Atlanta (July 1973), a "compromise" plan left 83 of the city's 141 schools all black while increasing the number of desegregated schools by eight. Half of the schools' administrative posts were to be filled by blacks. NAACP's Roy Wilkins condemned the plan and suspended the Atlanta chapter after learning that the proposal had been worked out between the school board and Lonnie King, a black Atlanta businessman who was president of the Atlanta NAACP. Wilkins argued that the precedent established by the compromise was dangerous in view of the fact that Atlanta had long been considered an example of enlightened leadership in race relations.

Whites in South Boston boycotted schools and stoned buses carrying black children in September 1974, despite pleas for peace by Mayor Kevin White and Senator Edward Kennedy. However, most of Boston's whites and blacks accepted the city's busing plan with little protest.

Federal Activity

Funds to reduce racial isolation were granted under the Emergency Assistance Program begun in 1971 and the Emergency School Aid Act (Title VII of the Education Amendments of 1972). ESAA funds are used to encourage voluntary elimination, reduction, or prevention of minority group isolation. For example, students placed in educationally unjustifiable ability groupings that resulted in classroom segregation were reassigned. Black principals who had been demoted when schools desegregated were restored to their positions, and black teachers who lost jobs as schools desegregated were rehired. In one five-state region of HEW, school districts in 1974 made commitments to hire 500 black teachers to correct discriminatory attrition during the years of desegregation.

In *Adams* v. *Richardson* (U.S. Court of Appeals, District of Columbia; June 12, 1973), HEW's Office of Civil Rights was asked to move faster in enforcing Title VI of the Civil Rights Act of 1964 by taking appropriate action to end segregation in public educational institutions receiving federal funds. In Baltimore (June 1974), the city argued that withholding federal money in the absence of an acceptable desegregation plan was unfair because scattering the minority of white students (comprising less than 30% of total student population) evenly through the school system would lead to a departure from the city of white lower-middle-income families who wished to preserve their neighborhood schools.

The Carter Years

Busing and other forms of affirmative action remained the primary issues during President Carter's term (1977–1980). While most public attention focused on the *Bakke* case, a number of other important matters were fought in the courts, Congress, and regulatory agencies.

In 1979 the Supreme Court reaffirmed its previous support of busing to integrate schools. Prolonged battles were fought between the Department of Health, Education and Welfare and school boards in such cities as Chicago, Cleveland, and Pittsburgh over the validity of various integration plans and complaints against school boards for not executing integration plans that had been ordered by courts or agreed to voluntarily. By 1982 the status of Chicago's school system remained unresolved.

All in all, desegregation remained halting and tentative and of lesser significance as urban school systems became predominantly black and Hispanic. This flaw was compounded by the reluctance of courts to order and enforce interdistrict and metropolitan remedies. Consequently, to many blacks, busing became a pointless shifting of bodies rather than a positive step toward the education and integration of their children.

Conflict over busing persisted on many fronts. In California, voters approved a referendum to prohibit busing except where segregation could be shown to be intentional. A similar proposition was approved in the State of Washington, where voters outlawed busing, even when it was voluntary. Both of these laws were challenged in the courts with the outcome uncertain by the spring of 1982. A lower court found the Washington law unconstitutional. The state appealed to the Supreme Court and was supported by the U.S. Department of Justice in a switch from the government's previous opposition to the measure.

The strongest assaults on busing were undertaken in Congress. Shortly before his term expired, President Carter vetoed a bill with an anti-busing rider that would prohibit the Justice Department from bringing court cases to require busing to integrate schools. The measure was reintroduced after the inauguration of Ronald Reagan in 1981. Civil rights groups vowed to contest any such measures in the courts.

There were many pros and cons to the actions of the Carter Administration. Blacks generally applauded its initiative in establishing a separate Department of Education and Carter's refusal to accept the more extreme attacks on integration. He was criticized, however, for not taking firmer stands on monetary and moral support for public education and its integration.

CHRONOLOGY OF BLACK EDUCATION

1634 French Catholics are instrumental in providing instruction for laborers in Louisiana. The French and Spanish had liberal attitudes toward slaves. Many were respected for their worth and given privileges as freemen. Estevanico, an enlightened slave sent by Niza, the Spanish adventurer, to explore Arizona, was a favored servant of this class. French Jesuits, among them missionary Paul LeJeune, promote educational opportunities for blacks.

1685 Virginia laws prohibiting slaves from attending Quaker meetings for the purpose of instruction are denounced by the Reverend Morgan Goodwyn in a sermon preached in Westminster Abbey, London.

1695 Reverend Samuel Thomas of Goose Creek Parish, South Carolina, instructs blacks in reading and writing. Enlisting community support, he is able to educate many blacks in his parish.

1700 Monthly meeting for blacks established by William Penn. Penn advocated the emancipation of slaves that they might have opportunity for improvement. Many colonists were teaching slaves and free blacks.

1701 Chief Justice Sewall of Massachusetts publishes antislavery pamphlet, *Selling of Joseph.* The Sewall pamphlet represented the first direct attack on slavery in New England. One of the few Puritans to espouse the black cause, Sewall urged emancipation and education. Earlier, Cotton Mather and other Massachusetts Puritans made efforts to organize black people when they founded the Society of Negroes in 1693. Later, in 1717, Mather began an evening school for Indians and blacks.

1701 Organization by the Church of England of the Society for the Propagation of the Gospel in Foreign Parts for the purpose of converting and educating black slaves. Although merchants and other vested interests pressured religious groups in America to sanction slavery, the churches endorsed policies of Christianization, which proved to be the first great step in providing educational opportunity for blacks. Dr. Thomas Bray, sent to Maryland by the Bishop of London in 1669, exerted a profound influence in the conversion and education of blacks.

1704 Founding of catechizing school at Trinity Church in New York City under the direction of Elias Neau. Instruction was given regularly at this church until 1712, when blame for a local slave uprising was attributed by some masters to Neau's work. While enrollment was temporarily curtailed, instruction continued until the middle of the century, despite Neau's death in 1722.

1724 A document encouraging the Christian education of Indian, black, and mulatto children is circulated in Virginia. The document stated that slaves should be educated and that baptized children who understood the Christian religion should receive exemption from taxes until the age of 18.

1728 Nathaniel Piggott announces that he is opening a school for "instruction of Negroes in reading, catechizing, and writing."

1738 Moravians establish a mission exclusively for blacks. A mission for blacks was established by the Moravian brethren at Bethlehem, Pennsylvania. A painting of some converts prior to 1747 shows, among others, two blacks, Johannes of South Carolina and Jupiter of New York.

1743 School for black youths opens in Charlestown, South Carolina. Mr. Garden's school for training black youths opened in Charlestown, in September 1743. Supported almost entirely by the people of Charlestown, the school exerted a profound influence throughout the province. Individual missionaries saw an earnest desire among black parents to have their children instructed. Fifty-five children were taught during the day and 15 adults in the evening. Mr. Bray died in 1756.

1745 French Code Noire makes it incumbent upon masters to enlighten their slaves in order that they might grasp the principles of Christianity.

1747 Presbyterians begin religious instruction of blacks in Virginia. In 1740 Hugh Bryan, a wealthy Presbyterian, showed interest in the education of blacks and by 1755 was operating a school for slaves.

1749 Reverend Thomas Bacon preaches four sermons in Talbot County, Maryland, declaring that next to one's children, slaves enjoyed certain rights, including the right to knowledge and enlightenment.

1750 Anthony Benezet opens an evening school for Philadelphia blacks in his home. Quakers made the most conscientious efforts to fight slavery and educate blacks, permitting them to attend Quaker meetings in the face of great opposition. After teaching blacks in his home for 20 years, Benezet opened a free school for them in Philadelphia under Moses Patterson. Upon Benezet's death, money he left was used for the continuation of the school, known thereafter as Benezet House. Benezet, a French Protestant persecuted on account of his religion, had moved from France to England and later to Philadelphia. He declared that he had "found among Negroes a variety of talents as amongst a like number of whites." Besides fighting for the amelioration of the condition of blacks, he published some of America's first textbooks and urged religious equality.

1751 Society for the Propagation of the Gospel sends Joseph Ottolenghi to convert and educate blacks in Georgia. Ottolenghi, a convert from Judaism and a native of Italy, arrived in Georgia in July 1751. He "promised to spare no pains to improve the

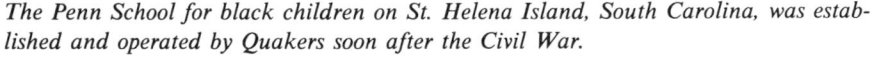

The Penn School for black children on St. Helena Island, South Carolina, was established and operated by Quakers soon after the Civil War.

Black women took the initiative in attending schools established by the Freedmen's Bureau. When these schools were burned down they were quickly rebuilt.

young children" and asked God's blessings on his educational efforts, which included reading and religious instruction to blacks. He became so successful and influential in the colonies that he was later elected a member of the Georgia Assembly and remained a member till 1765.

1773 Benjamin Rush advocates abolition of slave trade and urges education of blacks. In *An Address to the Inhabitants of the British Settlements of America upon Slavekeeping*, Benjamin Rush, a Philadelphia physician of Quaker parentage, was in contact with the most enlightened men of his time, and by persuasive argument, advanced the black cause.

1774 Benjamin Franklin opens school for blacks. While students of government were exposing the inconsistency of slaveholding among a people contending for political liberty, and men like Samuel Webster, James Swan, and Samuel Hopkins attacked slavery on economic grounds, Benjamin Franklin, Jonathan Boucher, and Dr. Rush were devising plans to educate slaves for freedom. Benjamin Franklin associated with friends of blacks and was made president of the Abolition Society of Philadelphia, which in 1774 founded a successful school for blacks.

1777 New Jersey begins educating black children. By 1801, schools are in operation in Salem, Burlington, and Trenton.

1787 New York African Free School established by the Manumission Society. Beginning with 40 students, it encountered opposition, but grew when New York required masters to teach the children of slaves to read Scripture. By 1820 more than 500 black children were enrolled.

1788 New Jersey passes an act making the teaching of slaves to read compulsory under a penalty of five pounds.

1791 Thomas Jefferson writes to Benjamin Banneker, black mathematician and astronomer. Jefferson declared that he wished to see blacks improve their condition and stated that lack of progress was due to the degraded condition of the black man in Africa and America. Writing the Declaration of Independence, he had in mind the rights of blacks as well as whites, and declared that blacks had a natural right to education and freedom. He advocated training of slaves in industrial and agricultural schools to equip them for a higher station in life.

1794 American Convention of Abolition Societies expresses hope that freedmen would participate in the

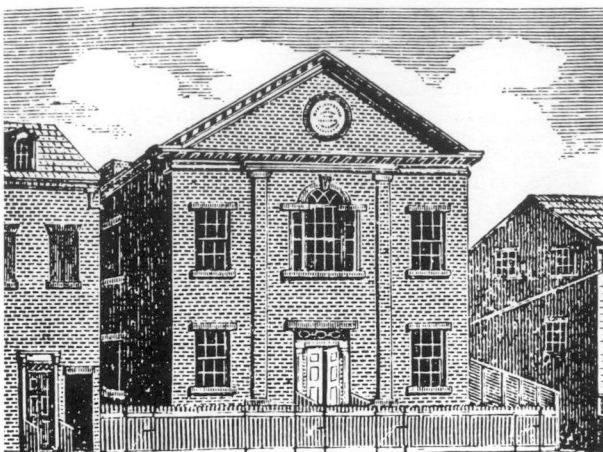

The first New York African Free School opened its doors in 1787. School No. 2 is shown here.

battle for civil rights as fast as they gained their education.

1798   School for black children established in home of Primus Hall, prominent Boston black.

1800–1830   Development of individual schools for blacks by churches, slaveholders, and free blacks. Despite legal restrictions in the South, many blacks did receive some education from their masters and in small clandestine private schools in the new nation. In 1820, for example, Boston opened an elementary school for blacks. In the District of Columbia, George Bell, Nicholas Franklin, and Moses Liverpool, former slaves, built the first schoolhouse for blacks in 1807. Unsuccessful, it opened again in 1818 under the direction of the Resolute Beneficial Society, an association of free people of color. Catholics vied with Quakers in admitting blacks to parochial schools.

During these years, a few blacks were beginning to attend colleges. (In 1826, Edward A. Jones graduated from Amherst and John Russwurm received his degree from Bowdoin. They were the first two black college graduates in the United States.)

The original building of Wilberforce University.

In Philadelphia (1804), free people of color organized a school with John Trumbull as teacher. At this time, African Episcopalians founded a school at their church. Eleven of the 16 schools in Philadelphia in 1822 were taught by teachers of African descent. In 1830 one fourth of the 1,200 black children in the schools of that city paid for their instruction, whereas in 1825 only 250 students were in attendance.

1830–1860   Curtailment of educational opportunities for blacks due to rising fear of the increasing power of slaves. This was precipitated by the fear aroused in the white population after the slave insurrection led by Nat Turner in Virginia in 1831. "Black Codes" were then enacted in several states to keep the black "in his place" by denying him access to educational facilities of any kind.

1831   Vocational education for black youth proposed by black convention. The First Annual Negro Convention was held in Philadelphia June 6–11, 1831. Delegates attended from New York, Pennsylvania, Delaware, Maryland, and Virginia. The idea was suggested by Samuel Cornish in 1827 and taken up by the Reverend S. A. Jocelyn, an antislavery white minister from New Haven. Vocational education for black youth was discussed at this and ensuing conferences held in Philadelphia, New York, and Rochester. The conference declared that colleges and high schools were needed where youth could be instructed in the manual labor system and the arts of civilized life. Money was raised for a school in New Haven, but the citizens objected and declared that "the founding of colleges for colored people was a dangerous undertaking."

1834   Prudence Crandall imprisoned and mobbed at Canterbury, Connecticut. Reaction to the education of blacks was apparent when Prudence Crandall, a young Quaker who has established a boarding school at Canterbury, tried to enroll Sarah Harris, a black girl, at her institution. When whites objected, she advertised for young women of color. Imprisonment and violence resulted.

1840   Blacks attend school with whites in Wilmington, Delaware.

1842   School for black and Indian boys opens in Ohio. Augustus Wattles, agent of American Anti-Slavery Society, and Samuel Emlen, New Jersey philanthropist, open Emlen Institute for Negro and Indian Boys, in Mercer County, Ohio. The school specialized in the teaching of agricultural and skilled crafts.

1848   Black industrial training school opens in Philadelphia at the House of Industry. By 1851 Sarah Luciana was teaching 70 youths at the training school and at the Sheppard School, another industrial institution. Other schools in operation were the Corn Street Unclassified School (1849), the Holmesburg Unclassified School (1854), and the Home for Colored Children (1859). By this date there were 1,031 pupils in the black public schools of Philadelphia; 748 in the charity schools; 211 in the benevolent schools; 331 in private schools. In all, 2,231 were in attendance, whereas 10 years earlier there were only 1,643. Besides supporting these institutions, the blacks of Philadelphia maintained many small schools and a system of lyceums and debating clubs, one of which had a library of 1,400 volumes.

1849 *Roberts* v. *City of Boston.* Robert Morris, a prominent black lawyer, and Charles Summer argued that segregation hurts white and black children alike. The suit was filed in Boston by Benjamin F. Roberts on behalf of his daughter, Sarah, who had applied under the Equal Education Act of 1845 to attend a white school closer to her home. The court ruled against Summer and a local ordinance providing for the separate education of the races was upheld. During the next six years, however, public opinion persuaded the Massachusetts legislature to repudiate the court. This was accomplished in 1855 by a law which forbade distinction of race, color, or religion for purposes of admission into the state's public schools.

1852 Students in the North become converted to the doctrine of equality in education through the efforts of President C. B. Storrs of Western Reserve College, Hudson, Ohio. By 1852 black students had attended the Institute of Easton, Pennsylvania; the Normal School of Albany, New York; Bowdoin College, Brunswick, Maine; Rutland College, Vermont; Jefferson College, Pennsylvania; Athens College, Athens, Ohio; Franklin College, New Athens, Ohio; Hanover College, near Madison, Indiana. Blacks had taken courses at the Medical School of New York, the Castleton Medical School in Vermont, the Berkshire Medical School in Pittsfield, Massachusetts, the Rush Medical School in Chicago, the Eclectic Medical School in Philadelphia, the Homeopathic College of Cleveland, and the Medical School of Harvard University. Black preachers had been educated at the Theological Seminary of Charlestown, South Carolina. Vocational schools were abundant. Statistics of 1850 and 1860 show that there was an increase in the number of black mechanics, especially in Philadelphia, Cincinnati, Columbus, the Western Reserve, and Canada. But this was probably due to the decreasing

Noon recess at the primary school for freedmen at Vicksburg, Mississippi.

A typical classroom in one of the early colleges associated with the United Negro College Fund.

prejudice of the local white mechanics toward black artisans fleeing from the South rather than to formal industrial training.

1855 Massachusetts legislature enacts law providing that no distinction be made on account of race, color, or religion, in admitting scholars to public schools.

1864 Civil War sees mass education of blacks. The Christian Commission sponsored 50 teachers who taught blacks in the Union Army. Chaplains also taught black troops. By the war's end, 20,000 had been taught to read.

1865 Founding of the Freedman's Bureau under General Oliver O. Howard. The Bureau was created by Congress on March 3, 1865, to cooperate with benevolent and religious societies in the establishment of schools for blacks. John Mercer Langston, black lawyer, and Inspector General of Schools in the Bureau, reported in August 1869 the existence of many good schools for blacks. By 1870 the Freedmen's Bureau operated over 2,600 schools in the South with 3,300 teachers educating 150,000 students. Four thousand schools were in operation prior to the abolition of the Bureau.

1865–1871 Establishment of several predominantly black institutions of higher learning. During these years, a number of important black institutions of learning were founded, including Virginia Union and Shaw University (1865); Fisk University and

Lincoln Institute (1866); Talladega College, Augusta (Georgia) Institute, Biddle University, Howard University, and Scotia Seminary (1867); Tougaloo College (1869); and Alcorn College and Benedict College (1871). Many of these colleges have changed their names since their founding.

1867 Establishment of the Peabody Fund. The two million dollar Peabody Fund was established for promotion and encouragement of intellectual, moral, and industrial education among the young of the more destitute portions of the southern and southwestern states.

1872 Alcorn College becomes the first black land grant college. This was made possible under the Morrill Act of 1862, which provided federal land grant funds for higher education. It was the Morrill Act of 1890, however, which provided that funds for black education be distributed on a "just and equitable basis." Such legislation, however, also served to strengthen the doctrine of "separate but equal," with the result that the 17 southern states maintained colleges which came to be known as "Negro land grant colleges."

1897 Founding in Washington, D.C. of the American Negro Academy. Organized on March 5, 1897, by the Reverend Alexander Crummell, black theologian and educator, the Academy has five stated objectives: (1) defense of the black against vicious assaults; (2) publication of scholarly work; (3)

fostering higher education among blacks; (4) formulation of intellectual tastes; (5) promotion of literature, science, and art.

Crummell's father was a prince and son of a West African tribal chief (Temme tribe). Crummell himself first conceived the idea of an American Negro Academy when a student at Cambridge University, England. The Academy was the first body in America to bring together black scholars from all over the world. The general purpose of the organization was to foster scholarship and culture in the black race and encourage budding black genius. In March 1897, the year of McKinley's inauguration, celebrated black scholars and writers assembled in the Lincoln Memorial Church and organized into a brotherhood of scholars. In attendance was Dunbar, the poet; DuBois, the sociologist; Scarborough, the Greek scholar; Miller, the mathematician; Grimke, the theologian; Cromwell, the historian; and many other noted educators. At Crummell's death on September 12, 1908, DuBois was elected president and stated that those with higher education must take responsibility for uplifting the black race. Many brilliant papers were published, which are still today the best discussion on Negro suffrage and southern disfranchisement.

1900 The New York legislature, under the governorship of Theodore Roosevelt, passes an act providing that no one should be denied admittance to any public school on account of race, color, or previous condition of servitude.

1902 Founding of the General Education Board, supported by John D. Rockefeller. Funds from this organization aided black education materially in such categories as endowment, scholarships, teacher training, and industrial education.

1908 Founding of the Anna T. Jeanes Fund. The Jeanes Fund sponsored the Jeanes Teacher Program to improve the quality of instruction in rural black schools.

1908 *Berea College* v. *Kentucky.* Kentucky law had made segregation mandatory. At issue was whether a private college had the right to teach blacks and whites together. The Supreme Court ruled, on technical grounds, against the college.

1913 Founding of the Julius Rosenwald Fund. The Fund provided grants for constructing schools. By 1932 more than 5,000 school buildings in 883 counties of 15 states had been built under Rosenwald sponsorship.

1932 Publication of the *Journal of Negro Education.* This organ, published at Howard University, has done much to improve educational opportunities for blacks and to democratize education in general.

1954 *Brown* v. *Board of Education.* This decision by the U.S. Supreme Court declared segregation in public schools to be unconstitutional. It was based on the theory that "the segregation of children in public schools solely on the basis of race, even though the physical facilities and other tangible factors may be equal, deprives children of the minority group of equal educational facilities." (For fuller discussion see "review" and Supreme Court section.)

1957 Little Rock crisis. After a federal court ordered desegregation in Little Rock, Arkansas, Governor Orval Faubus called out the Arkansas National Guard to prevent nine black students from entering Central High School. As a result, President Eisenhower dispatched U.S. troops to Little Rock to enforce the court order, and ultimately federalized the Arkansas National Guard as well.

1961 New Rochelle: The *Lincoln School* Case. In this case, Federal District Court Judge Irving A. Kaufman ruled that the New Rochelle Board of Education had deliberately created and maintained Lincoln as a racially segregated school. Judge Kaufman ordered the Board to present a plan to desegregate the predominantly black school at all levels. This case marked the first court decision against *de facto* segregation in the North.

1964 Passage of the Civil Rights Act. This act placed further legal restrictions on discrimination in education.

1965 Passage of the Elementary and Secondary School Education Act. This act provides funds under Title I for promoting racial integration in the public schools of the United States.

1966 Federal judge orders Lowndes County school districts to desegregate. Federal District Court Judge Frank M. Johnson, Jr. directed the Lowndes County, Alabama school board to install a sweeping desegregation order. All grades were ordered desegregated within two years. A free choice transfer system to any school was to be effected and all black teachers integrated.

1966 Teaching profession continues to appeal to black students despite emphasis on the need to diversify careers. Secretary of Labor Willard Wirtz declared that two thirds of all black college students are preparing to teach and that many of these students should be preparing for careers other than in education in order to fill positions that are finally becoming available to black applicants.

1966 The Kennedy plan for urban ghettos. Senator Robert F. Kennedy called for eradication of huge central city ghettos and criticized the deliberate location of public housing in ghettos. To help desegregate schools, he urged a program for boarding children in the suburbs.

1966 The *Chester School* case. The Court of Common Pleas of Dauphin County, Pennsylvania, decides the *Chester School* case. The court upholds the order by the Pennsylvania Human Relations Commission that the Chester school board stop assigning black teachers and clerks only to all-black schools, and that the board cease refusing to assign white teachers to a predominantly black school. The court rejects two contentions: (1) that it has authority to act against *de facto* segregation and (2) that the school board has engaged in extensive gerrymandering.

1966 The *Tometz* case against the Waukegan school board. State Circuit Court Judge Philip W. Yaeger of Illinois rejects a Waukegan school board motion to dismiss the *Tometz* case filed against it by a group of black parents.

1966 Detroit suburb agrees to integrated textbooks. The school board of Inkster, Michigan, a Detroit suburb, signs a contract with Local 1068 of the American Federation of Teachers agreeing that effective education must be integrated education. Only integrated textbooks are to be used in reading and social studies classes.

1966 Prince Edward County school board guilty of contempt. The U.S. Circuit Court of Appeals for the Fourth Circuit finds the Prince Edward County, Virginia school board guilty of contempt of court for illegally distributing state funds to be used for tuition in private schools so as to avoid desegregation.

1966 Desegregation of Plaquemine Parish, Louisiana. The public schools of Plaquemine Parish, Louisiana are ordered by a federal district court to desegregate six of 12 grades through a free choice plan.

1966 Integration in Fayette, Mississippi. In Fayette, Mississippi, 13 black children are enrolled in two formerly all-white schools as a result of an agreement between the school board and the state NAACP headed by Charles Evers.

1966 Integration question raised at I.S. 201 in Harlem. A community movement in East Harlem calls upon the school board to integrate the new intermediate school I.S. 201 or place its management under effective community control.

1967 Civil Rights Commission releases important study. The U.S. Commission on Civil Rights releases its study, *Racial Isolation in the Public Schools,* made in response to a November 1965 request by President Johnson.

1967 The *Girard College* case. Girard College in Philadelphia does not have to admit blacks under the state's Public Accommodations Act, according to a ruling by the U.S. Court of Appeals for the Third Circuit. This part of the opinion thus reverses an earlier ruling by Federal District Court Judge Joseph S. Lord III.

1967 Court of Appeals declares southern states obliged to foster integration. The U.S. Court of Appeals for the Fifth Circuit endorses an earlier ruling that six southern states have an affirmative responsibility to integrate their public schools. In April the U.S. Supreme Court declines to delay the implementation of the Court of Appeals' order. A federal court strikes down an Alabama law against the HEW desegregation guidelines as a violation of the Constitutional supremacy of Congressional legislation.

1967 Final ruling on the *Tometz* case by the Illinois Supreme Court. The Illinois Supreme Court holds unconstitutional the Armstrong law and thus reverses the earlier *Tometz* ruling. The statute, enacted in 1963, required school boards to redistrict attendance boundaries periodically to reduce segregation and prevent further segregation. The state high court finds the law to be arbitrary and unreasonable and in violation of the equal protection clause of the Fourteenth Amendment.

1967 Supreme Court upholds Court of Appeals rul-

A mathematics class in a modern black college.

ing in *Oklahoma City Dowell* case. The U.S. Supreme Court refuses to review a Tenth Circuit Court of Appeals decision in the *Oklahoma City Dowell* case, thus leaving intact a District Court order of September 5, 1965. The 1965 order called for sweeping changes in school organization; the attendance areas of various schools were to be merged to promote desegregation; a child in a racial majority would be permitted to transfer to a school in which he was in a racial minority; faculties were to be desegregated by 1970 so that the racial composition in each school approximated the systemwide composition (plus or minus a 10% tolerance).

1968 Racial imbalance in Massachusetts, the District of Columbia, and Lansing. The Massachusetts racial imbalance law withstands attack before the U.S. Supreme Court. The statute, which requires a school board to take action whenever a school's enrollment exceeds 50% nonwhite, is unsuccessfully challenged as unconstitutional by Boston school authorities. The Supreme Court rules that the suit failed to raise a substantial federal question. In the District of Columbia, the Board of Education reports on plans to effectuate the court's ruling in *Hobson* v. *Hansen*. Plans are submitted to the court regarding the reduction of racially imbalanced student bodies and faculties; measures include attendance boundary changes and busing. New teachers are assigned to achieve racial balance. Discussions are held with suburban school officials about attendance of District students in schools outside the city. The Ingham County Circuit Court rules that the Lansing school board can change attendance boundaries to bring about racial balance.

1968 Rise in population of black students recorded at predominantly white colleges in North Carolina. Between 1963 and 1967, the percentage of black students in predominantly white colleges and universities increases from 0.4 to 1.6%, according to the North Carolina Board of Higher Education.

1968 "One man, one vote" applied to school board election. The U.S. Supreme Court holds that the "one man, one vote" rule must be applied to elections of school boards and other local agencies. "Units with general governmental powers over an entire geographic area," ruled the court, "must not be apportioned among single-member districts of substantially unequal population."

1968 The Supreme Court on "open enrollment" or "freedom of choice." The Supreme Court rules unanimously that "freedom of choice" desegregation plans (called "open enrollment" in the North) must promise significant progress before being approved. Desegregation plans that result in no substantial change of segregation will be rejected. School boards are given the affirmative responsibility of finding realistic plans. The Supreme Court explicitly limits its ruling to southern and border

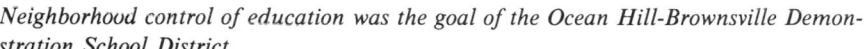

Neighborhood control of education was the goal of the Ocean Hill-Brownsville Demonstration School District.

states that had permitted legal segregation before 1954.

1968 The *Tometz* case final ruling. The State Supreme Court reverses its earlier ruling in the *Tometz* case. At issue was the 1963 Illinois Armstrong Act which required school districts to change or revise school attendance areas to prevent or end segregation. In its 1967 ruling the court invalidated the law, holding that race could not properly be a consideration in attendance area revision. Now, however, it determines that the "issue here is whether the constitution permits, rather than prohibits, voluntary state action aimed toward reducing and eventually eliminating *de facto* school segregation. The Armstrong Act was thereupon found to be constitutional."

1968 Deliberate segregation unearthed in South Holland. Legal proceedings continued in the federal complaint of deliberate segregation against School District No. 151 in South Holland, Illinois. In a deposition, Superintendent Charles B. Watts stated he was present when a school board member acknowledged that race was taken into account in locating the site of two schools. Federal attorneys introduced evidence showing that a white school board member had been allowed to enroll his children in a white school.

1968 Central issues at Ocean Hill–Brownsville in New York. The right of an experimental school district—Ocean Hill–Brownsville Demonstration School District—to transfer or dismiss teachers becomes the central issue in a continuing confrontation between the United Federation of Teachers and black parents constituting the majority of the district's governing board.

1968 The *Girard* case final ruling. In May the U.S. Supreme Court refused to review a lower court ruling that ended a 120-year-old practice of exclusion of black boys from Girard College, a free boarding school in Philadelphia. Four weeks later, numerous black mothers brought their youngsters to register for entrance in September.

1968 U.S. Circuit of Appeals declines to rule on "freedom of choice." The Fifth U.S. Circuit Court of Appeals refused to strike down 42 freedom of choice plans in four southern states. It ordered federal district courts in the states to determine by November 4 how effective the plans were. The court defined an effective plan as one that produces integration of faculties, staff, facilities, transportation, and school activities along with integration of students.

1968 U.S. Justice Department intervenes against Ku Klux Klan. The U.S. Department of Justice filed suit against a Ku Klux Klan chapter in Crenshaw County, Alabama, charging interference with a court-ordered "free choice desegregation plan." The Klan, according to federal complaint, intimidated black parents into withdrawing their children from white schools.

1968 Busing begins in South Holland, Illinois. Federal court-ordered desegregation takes effect in South Holland, Illinois without incident in September. Nine-tenths of the white enrollment as of June reentered the desegregated schools. About 800 pupils equally divided between black and white were bused daily.

1968 Federal panel in Illinois refuses to rule on per-pupil expenditure disparities between school districts. A three-man federal court panel in Illinois refused to rule unconstitutional large per-pupil expenditure disparities between school districts in the state. One suburb spent $1,283 per high school student, another $919. Plaintiffs contended state laws permitting such disparities violated the equal protection clause of the Fourteenth Amendment. Without doubt, ruled the panel, the educational potential of each child should be cultivated to the utmost and the poorer districts should have more funds, but the allocation of public revenues is a basic policy decision, more appropriately handled by a legislature than a court.

1969 Integration pressure applied to Los Angeles school district. Lawsuit filed in Los Angeles Superior Court asking that the Inglewood Unified School District be ordered to eliminate *de facto* segregation in school district number 17. The board allegedly refuses even to adopt a policy statement committing the district to integration.

1969 Move to bar erection of *de facto* segregated high school in Muncie, Indiana. Black citizens filed suit in federal court, Muncie, Indiana, to bar construction of a high school in an all-white area. The suit charged that the resulting exclusion of black children from the new facility would be in violation of their constitutional rights to equal educational opportunities.

1969 Desegregation of Mt. Vernon elementary schools. The State Supreme Court of New York upheld a state order to desegregate the Mt. Vernon elementary schools.

1969 Pennsylvania directed to achieve greater integration of schools of higher learning. Pennsylvania was directed by the Department of Health, Education and Welfare to desegregate its public colleges and universities. Pennsylvania, H.E.W. charged, "is operating a system of higher education that is segregated on a statewide basis." The state's only predominantly black school, Cheyney State, enrolls 85% black students, which amount to more than 4½ times the number of blacks in all other 13 state colleges combined.

1971 Lower courts urged to support integration. Supreme Court called upon lower courts to make every effort to achieve greatest possible degree of desegregation based on practical realities of local situations. (*Swann* v. *Charlotte-Mecklenburg Board of Education.*)

1972 New York Regents back busing. New York State Board of Regents backed use of "judicious and reasonable busing to achieve school integration."

1972 Justice Department lawyers oppose Nixon. In the Justice Department, 95 lawyers publicly expressed opposition to President Nixon's antibusing legislation.

1973 Denver challenged to disprove *de facto* segregation. Supreme Court emphasized that the differentiating factor between *de jure* and *de facto* segregation is *purpose* or *intent* to segregate and demanded that Denver School Board prove that it had not intentionally effected a policy that created or maintained segregation in the core city schools. (*Keys* v. *School District #1 Denver, Colorado.*)

1974 Affirm minority children's right in education program. Court affirmed that minority children may not be denied a meaningful opportunity to participate in public educational program and cited section 601 of Civil Rights Act of 1964 which bans discrimination based on the grounds of "race, color or national origin in any program or activity receiving federal financial assistance." (*Lau* v. *Nichols.*)

1974 HEW pressed to enforce desegregation. HEW's Office of Civil Rights urged to move faster in enforcing Title VI of Civil Rights Act of 1964 by taking action to end segregation in public education institutions receiving federal funds. (*Adams* v. *Richardson.*)

1974 Detroit Metropolitan integration plan is defeated. The *Detroit* case 5 to 4 ruling by the Supreme Court reversed a District court plan to link Detroit's 185,000 black students with the 53 suburban school districts surrounding the City of Detroit.

1974 Boston opposes integration. City of Boston resisted court order to desegregate public schools, succumbing to white demonstrations.

1974 James A. Harris becomes NEA president. The National Education Association, the nation's largest professional organization, elected James A. Harris, a black school teacher from Des Moines, Iowa, as its president.

1974 Senator Edward Kennedy prevented from speaking out on Boston desegregation issue. Senator Edward Kennedy of Massachusetts was driven from a speaker's platform by jeers and egg-throwing, while urging whites to accept the desegregation guidelines established for the Boston school system.

1975 Civil Rights Commission cites laxity in enforcement of civil rights laws in education. In a report made public on January 22, the U.S. Civil Rights Commission accused the federal government of failing to enforce the civil rights laws as they apply to education. Singled out for criticism was the Department of Health, Education and Welfare.

1975 Civil Rights Commission issues report. In a report issued March 11, the U.S. Commission on Civil Rights recommended that the federal government withhold federal aid from schools that fail to comply with desegregation directives within a 90 day period.

1975 Justice Department charges segregation in Mississippi Colleges. The U.S. Department of Justice charged that Mississippi's 25 state colleges and universities were illegally segregated. The charge was submitted to the U.S. District Court in Aberdeen.

1975 Educator issues study on integration. Dr. James S. Coleman, prominent black educator, issued a study entitled *Recent Trends in School Integration.* The core of the study concluded that integration efforts in the United States have failed and that modification of approaches was needed.

Blacks in Boston show support for the court-ordered busing program.

1975 U.S. Justice Department files suit against Detroit suburb charging segregation. The Justice Department filed suit in federal court charging Ferndale, a Detroit suburb, of operating a racially segregated school system. The suit, taken on behalf of the Office of Revenue Sharing, is the first of its kind.

1976 Black conservatives led by Thomas Sowell attack busing and affirmative action programs as ineffective and charge that government efforts in this direction benefit lawyers and government officials advocating busing more than the black children the policy is supposed to serve.

1976 Integrationists have mixed feelings about the election of Jimmy Carter to the Presidency. While they prefer him to outgoing President Gerald Ford, they feel he has been lukewarm in his support of integration.

1977 Leaders of the National Association for the Advancement of Colored People accuse several northern political leaders of abandoning support for strong measures against school districts that evade integration.

1977 Joseph Califano, Secretary of Health, Education and Welfare, blames an antidesegregation mood in Congress for a slowdown in integration efforts.

1977 A survey by the National Urban League indicates that 45% of blacks interviewed, while favoring integration, believe that an equal say in control of schools is more important.

1978 The U.S. Civil Rights Commission charges that large areas of the South have still failed to integrate their schools.

1978 By a 5 to 4 vote the Supreme Court rules that Alan Bakke, a young white man, is entitled to admission to the University of California because the university's affirmative action program for minorities discriminated against him. However, the Court also holds that college admission affirmative action programs are constitutional.

1979 Stronger federal enforcement of civil rights laws are a prerequisite. The civil rights commission charges that segregation remains most severe in the northeastern states and North Carolina. The remedy, it declares, is stronger enforcement of civil rights laws and Congressional action to enforce the Department of Health, Education and Welfare's power to order busing.

1979 A sharp decline in black high school dropouts is reported by the Census Bureau, from 35% in 1968 to 24% in 1976. The white rate remained stable at 14%.

1979 The Supreme Court sustains busing as a means to desegregate entire school systems when the policies of local officials result in racial imbalance in parts of the system.

1979 Formation of a cabinet level Department of Education is assured by a narrow 5-vote margin in the House of Representatives. The first year's budget is to be $14 million.

1979 Signs of trouble in university black studies programs surface, as Harvard's administration recommends its Afro-American Studies Department be downgraded. Russell Adams, a Howard University professor, reports that the number of college-level black studies programs has dropped from about 600 in 1961 to 250 in 1975.

1979 In Topeka, Kansas, Linda Brown joins other parents in bringing an action against the Topeka school system on the grounds that it remains segregated 25 years after her historic victory in *Brown* v. *Board of Education.*

1980 Supreme Court Justices Powell, Stewart, and Rehnquist express concern that school busing induces white flight to the suburbs.

1980 In separate decisions involving Cleveland, Ohio, and New Castle, Delaware, the Supreme Court supports busing as a means to end segregation. The Justice Department presses for speedier desegregation in Chicago. However, attempts to include suburban schools in Houston and St. Louis plans are rejected.

1980 A "Black College Day" attended by 20,000 black students is held in Washington, D.C. Its purpose is to mobilize the public to support historic black colleges, which have suffered since desegregation opened the predominantly white colleges to blacks. Tony Brown, a black writer, contends that 70% of blacks attending "white" colleges do not graduate. Meanwhile, the Justice Department contends that university systems in Texas, Louisiana, and North Carolina are segregated.

1980 Ronald Reagan is elected president. During his campaign he advocated elimination of the Department of Education, elimination of busing to achieve integration, and deep cuts in federal aid to education.

1981 A series of actions to curb busing are undertaken on several fronts. The House and Senate vote to forbid the Justice Department to use busing for integration in any but the most limited circumstances; anti-busing steps, of questionable constitutionality, are also proposed to limit the Supreme Court's power to order busing; and anti-busing constitutional amendments are proposed.

1981 Drastic cuts in federal aid to education programs are included in the Reagan budget which Congress approves and the President signs. Cuts run the gamut from the preschool Head Start program to the Pell loans for college students.

1981 The Justice Department announces it will no longer sue to desegregate entire school districts when only a part of a district discriminates. Instead, litigation is to concentrate on individual schools that discriminate. System-wide suits had become a major weapon of integrationists and had been upheld by the Supreme Court.

1982 A storm erupts as the Administration reverses its 11-year policy of denying tax exempt status to private schools and colleges that discriminate racially. Stunned by the force of broad-based opposition to its stand, the government refers the matter to Congress and the Supreme Court but defends its action as one of necessary restraint on the powers of an administrative agency.

1982 Civil rights lawyers assail the Justice Department's approval of a Chicago desegregation plan that relies extensively on voluntary student transfers.

1982 Governor Carey of New York criticizes medical schools for a 46% drop in enrollment of minorities since 1976.

1982 Efforts to eliminate the Department of Education appear to have failed as bipartisan Con-gressional support rallies around the beleaguered agency.

The importance of scholarships for blacks becomes evident when one considers the rising cost of a college education in the United States and the fact that education often provides the sole basis for the advancement of the black in our highly complex and industrialized society. The inverse relationship that exists between high college costs and low family incomes among blacks makes urgent the need for financial aid to students in predominantly black colleges.

This need is being met by an increasing number of scholarships, work-study programs, and loans. Scholarships are generally obtained from the following principal sources: colleges and universities; corporate philanthropy; religious groups; and federal, state, and local government agencies.

Below is a list of scholarship programs which are granted predominantly to black students. A guide which includes scholarships available to *all* students is published by the Scholarship Information Center of the University of North Carolina YMCA-YWCA, and can be ordered from the University of North Carolina YMCA-YWCA Human Relations Committee, Chapel Hill, North Carolina 27514. The annotated items which open this section are followed by a less detailed, but more comprehensive, listing of additional scholarship and loan sources. These have been provided courtesy of the United Negro College Fund, Research Division.

SCHOLARSHIPS

Scholarships Primarily for Black Students

National Achievement Scholarship Program for Outstanding Negro Students. *Eligibility:* High school seniors. *Where valid:* Anywhere. *Restrictions:* None. *Value:* Two hundred four-year $1,000–6,000 scholarships. *How to apply:* Through high school principal or write to: National Achievement Scholarship Program, 990 Grove Street, Evanston, IL 60201. *Basis of award:* Need and scholarship. *Deadline:* Apply very early. By December 10 of year *before* entry into college.

National Scholarship Service and Fund for Negro Students (Supplementary Scholarship Fund). *Eligibility:* High school seniors. *Where valid:* Any regionally accredited, degree-granting, INTERRACIAL institution at which campus facilities are extended equally without regard to race. *Restrictions:* Must have been counseled by organization. *Value:* Unspecified number, up to $600 per year. Renewable—**Twice Only.** *How to apply:* **Write early in Junior Year to:** NSSFNS, 6 East 82nd Street, New York, NY 10028. *Basis of awards:* **Need,** scholastic record, extracurricular activities, staff interviews, SAT tests. *Deadline:* Early in senior year for final applications.

North Carolina College at Durham $1,000 Student Scholarships. *Eligibility:* High school graduating seniors. *Where valid:* North Carolina College only. *Restrictions:* SAT score of at least 1000. *Value:* Several $1,000 grants available. Renewable. *How to apply:* Chairman of Committee on Financial Assistance to Students, North Carolina College at Durham, Box 601, Durham, NC. *Basis of awards:* SAT score of 1000 and good high school records. *Deadline:* May 1.

Herbert Lehman Education Fund. For Negroes at recently desegregated colleges in the Deep South. Apply Herbert Lehman Education Fund, 10 Columbus Circle, Suite 2040, New York, NY 10019.

Martin De Porres Foundation. For Philadelphia Catholics planning to attend nearby Catholic colleges. Apply M. H. McCloskey III, Martin De

Black graduates at commencement exercises.

Porres Foundation, 2050 Suburban Station Building, Philadelphia 3, PA.

Minority Groups Scholarship Program. (Endowed by Rockefeller Fund). *Eligibility:* High school senior. *Where valid:* Any of seven specified colleges or universities. *Restrictions:* Must be member of minority group (Negro, Mexican, Oriental in the United States). *Value:* Determined by individual college. *How to apply:* Admissions Office of particular member college. *Basis of award:* Exceptional academic drive, leadership potential, financial need. *Deadline:* Unannounced.

Polytechnic Institute of Brooklyn, New York. *Eligibility:* High school seniors. *Where valid:* Polytechnic Institute of Brooklyn, New York. *Restrictions:* None. Priority given to southern blacks. For students interested in electrical engineering. *Value:* Remedial course work in summer if needed. Full tuition and maintenance for three or more students. *How to apply:* Have principal write to Polytechnic Institute

requesting information. *Basis of award:* Need and scholarship. Interest in electrical engineering. *Deadline:* None.

Eleanor Roosevelt Scholarship Program. For students who have been actively involved in the civil rights movement. Apply CORE Scholarship, Education and Defense Fund, Inc., 150 Nassau Street, New York, NY 10038. The CORE Fund grants scholarships of up to $1,500 to cover tuition and living costs for a period of one year. Scholarships are awarded twice a year—in the spring and fall.

Alfred P. Sloan Foundation. *Eligibility:* High school seniors (½), high school juniors (½). *Where valid:* Ten major black colleges and universities. *Restrictions:* Male students only. *Value:* For juniors: Two summers remedial instruction at listed schools (Dillard University, New Orleans; Morehouse College, Atlanta). Will be granted scholarship for four years on completion of courses. For seniors: four-year grants to any of 10 schools. About 60 in

number. *How to apply:* For juniors: United Negro College Fund, 22 East 54th Street, New York, NY 10022. For seniors: Apply to listed colleges. *Basis of awards:* Need. *Deadline:* Ideally in spring.

Ralph E. Smith Freedom Scholarships. *Eligibility:* High school seniors. *Where valid:* Macalester College, St. Paul, Minnesota. *Restrictions:* Three white and three Negro awards yearly. *Value:* Four-year scholarships, maximum value $2,000 yearly. *How to apply:* Make application to Macalester and request consideration for Ralph E. Smith Freedom Scholarships. *Basis of awards:* (1) leadership, (2) scholarship, (3) desire to work toward humanitarian goals in the tradition of the American way of life. *Deadline:* March 1.

Texas Southern University School of Business, Houston, Texas Scholarships. *Eligibility:* High school senior. *Where valid:* Texas Southern University only. *Restrictions:* None, interest in business career. *Value:*

Fifteen four-year full payment grants. *How to apply:* Have guidance counselor write to Texas Southern University. *Basis of awards:* Recommendations of principal and high school counselor, results of CEB and American College Testing Program examinations. *Deadline:* March 31.

United Negro College Fund. *Eligibility:* High school seniors and college undergraduates. *Where valid:* Any of 33 listed southern Negro colleges and universities. *Restrictions:*

None. *Value:* The Fund grants money to the listed schools who then make the funds available to entering students. (In 1965, the goal was over $5,000,000.) *How to apply:* Apply to the Director of Admissions at the college or university listed. *Basis of award:* Set by each college or university. Need is certainly taken into consideration. *Deadline:* Unspecified.

John Hay Whitney Fund. The "Opportunity Fellowships" of this fund are open to citizens from a number of diverse racial and cultural

backgrounds, including Negroes. Candidates under 35 are given decided preference. Awards range to a maximum of $3,000, and are governed by the need of the candidate, as well as the nature of the program he desires to undertake. They are limited to a full year of serious graduate study. For further information (or applications), write the John Hay Whitney Foundation, 111 West 50th Street, New York, NY 10020.

Scholarships With No Racial Criteria

Cooperative College Development Program. Established with the assistance of the Alfred P. Sloan Foundation in 1965, the Cooperative Development Program extends its services to 23 southern Negro colleges and universities. The program assists member colleges in making presentations to industry, government, private foundations, and other potential sources of funds.

Lever Brothers. This organization provides 51 renewable $500 scholarships (one in each state and the District of Columbia) for study in the pharmaceutical field. Through the National Merit Program, Lever Brothers also contributes to graduate fellowships for blacks who wish to pursue a career in management.

For more information, contact state pharmaceutical associations or Public Relations Department, Lever Brothers, 390 Park Avenue, New York, NY.

National Merit Scholarship Corporation. Established by the Ford Foundation and the Carnegie Foundation of New York in 1955, the National Merit Scholarship Corporation awards about 1,600 scholarships each year to high school students who qualify both on the National Merit Scholarship Qualifying Test, given in the spring, and the Scholastic Aptitude Test, given in the autumn, and who then pass the third and final phase of competition, where the criteria are outstanding grades, extracurricular activities, and leadership qualities. Winners receive up to $1,500 per year, depending on financial need, and may enroll in the school of their choice. For information, write Mr. Edward Smith, Executive Vice President, National Merit Scholarship Corporation, 990 Grove Street, Evanston, IL.

Pulitzer Free Scholarship Committee. This committee awards 10 four-year

scholarships at $250 per year to male New York high school students. In addition, it awards graduate fellowships to a number of institutions participating in the program. For more information, contact Pulitzer Free Scholarship Committee, 105 Low Library, Columbia University, New York, NY.

Radio Corporation of America. The institutions (white and Negro) participating in the Radio Corporation of America program offer 34 undergraduate scholarships at $800 per year in various fields. In addition, RCA awards 11 fellowships for graduate study in electrical engineering, physics, electronics, dramatic arts, and journalism. The stipend is $2,100 with a supplementary $900 to a married graduate student with dependent children. An additional $500 may be made available for summer work.

General Scholarship Aid

Alcoa Foundation Scholarship Fund
Pittsburgh, Pennsylvania

Alpha Chi Rho Educational Foundation Inc.
225 Lafayette Street
New York, NY 10012

American Baptist Convention
152 Madison Avenue
New York, NY
Conditions: Student must attend Baptist college

American Machine and Foundry Company
261 Madison Avenue
New York, NY 10016

American Schools & Colleges Association
30 Rockefeller Plaza
New York, NY 10020
Conditions and Limits: 1,200 scholarships to New York and New Jersey graduates. Candidates must have worked during high school and

shown scholastic and essay-writing ability.

ASARCO Foundation
120 Broadway
New York, NY

George F. Baker Trust
2 Wall Street
New York, NY 10005

Bell Foundation, Inc.
Buffalo, NY
Conditions and Limits: 2 tuition

scholarships (Erie County Technical Institute and Niagara University).

Boy's Club of America
771 First Avenue
New York, NY 10017
Conditions and Limits: Those interested in Boy's Club career.

Campe (Ed. Lee & Jean) Foundation
U.S. Trust Company of New York
New York, NY 10005

Celanese Corp. of America
522 Fifth Avenue
New York, NY 10036

College Scholarship Service (CEEB)
Princeton, NJ
Booklet: Sponsored scholarship programs using College Board Service.

Cook (Wm. J.) Fund Scholarships
Chicago Community Trust
10 South La Salle Street
Chicago, IL 60603

Cornell Club of Buffalo
92 Pearl Street
Buffalo, NY
Conditions: For students wishing to attend Cornell.

Dedombrowski (G. Louise Robinson) Charitable Trust
Simpson, Tatcher, Baetlett
120 Broadway
New York, NY 10005

The Dillon Fund
c/o Sherman and Sterling
20 Exchange Place
New York, NY 10005

Dolan Foundation
Edward Joy Company
905 Canal Street
Syracuse 3, NY

Education Funds, Inc.
10 Dorrance Street
Providence 3, RI
Up to $2,500 per year
Renewable: Any educational expenses; no tests

Elks National Foundation Scholarship Plan
Chairman
Elks National Foundation
16 Court Street
Boston, MA
(142) High school seniors in upper five per cent of their class.
$700 to $1,500 annually

Field Foundation, Inc.
250 Park Avenue
New York, NY 10017

Fischbach Foundation, Inc.
454 Madison Avenue
New York, NY 10022

Foresight Foundation, Inc.
30 East 71st Street
New York, NY 10021

Friedman Foundation, Inc.
250 West 57th Street
New York, NY 10017

The Fund for Theological Education, Inc.
163 Nassau Street
Princeton, NJ 08540

General Motors College Scholarship Plan
General Motors Corporation
General Motors Building
Detroit 2, MI
(350) High school seniors
Up to $2,000 annually

Generoso Pope Scholarship Awards
Columbus Citizens Committee, Inc.
136 West 52nd Street
New York, NY

Grant (Ulysses S.) Scholarship Foundation
New Haven, CT

Green Foundation
167–10 Hillside Avenue
Jamaica 32, NY

Greenspan (The Henry) Foundation
469 Seventh Avenue
New York, NY 10018

Hirsch Memorial Foundation, Inc.
350 Fifth Avenue
New York, NY

Honig (Ely) Memorial Scholarship Fund
Angelo Fabrics Company, Inc.
1407 Broadway
New York, NY
Fashion Industry

Insurance Federation of New York
116 Nassau Street
New York, NY 10038
Essay Contest determines winner of scholarship.

International Supreme Council of World Masons
1775 West Forest Avenue
Detroit, MI

Interracial Scholarship Committee of Greater Hartford
Hartford Foundation for Public Giving
621 Farmington

Hartford 5, CT
Conditions: Hartford residents.

J. R. S. Foundation, Inc.
530 Fifth Avenue
New York, NY 10036

Jephson Educational Trust
c/o Chase Manhattan Plaza
New York, NY 10005

Jones (W. Alton) Foundation, Inc.
70 Pine Street
New York, NY 10005

Kiwanis Club of New York
Hotel Lexington
New York, NY 10017

Knights of Columbus Scholarships
New York State Council
486 Park Avenue
Yonkers, NY

Knights Templar Educational Foundation, Foundation Committee
Division of New York
71 West 23rd Street, Room 1527
New York, NY 10010

Levy (Adele R.) Fund, Inc.
100 Park Avenue
New York, NY 10017

Levy (Jacob) Foundation, Inc.
1440 Broadway
New York, NY

Littauer Foundation, Inc.
345 East 46th Street
New York, NY 10017

Lutheran Scholarships
National Lutheran Council
50 Madison Avenue
New York, NY 10010
Graduate Students in social work

Wheat Ridge Foundation
Scholarship Office
2590 Devon, East
Des Plaines, IL
Conditions: Lutheran students preparing careers in Lutheran Welfare Service.

Marcus Foundation, Inc.
1410 Broadway
New York, NY 10018

Mazer (The Abraham) Family Fund
477 Madison Avenue
New York, NY 10022

McCormack Foundation
5 Broadway
New York, NY 10004

McGregor Fund
2486 First National Building
Detroit 26, MI

McMillin Foundation, Inc.
435 East 52nd Street
New York, NY

Mercy College
Detroit, MI

Muehlstein Foundation, Inc.
60 East 42nd Street
New York, NY 10017

National Council of Boy Scouts of America
New Brunswick, NJ 08903
A summary of colleges and universities that offer scholarships for boy scouts.

National Honor Society Scholarships
1201 Sixteenth Street, N.W.
Washington, D.C.
Conditions: (225 high school seniors who are National Honor Society members. $500 to $5,000 for four years.

National Merit Scholarships
National Merit Scholarship Corporation
1580 Sherman Avenue
Evanston, IL
Conditions: 750 high school seniors in upper five per cent of their class. $100 to full tuition for four years.

National Methodist Scholarships
Department of Student Loans & Scholarships
P. O. Box 871
Nashville, TN 37202
Conditions: Outstanding Methodist students in Methodist colleges.

National Presbyterian College Scholarships
Office of Education Loan for Scholarships
Board of Christian Education
United Presbyterian Church in the U.S.A.
425 Witherspoon Building
Philadelphia, PA 19187
Conditions: Up to $1,000 to qualified members of Presbyterian church enrolled in Presbyterian colleges.

National Restaurant Association
Educational Director
1530 North Lakeshore Drive
Chicago, IL 60610
Conditions: 5 scholarships at $1,000

each to persons entering the field of Food Service Administration.

National Scholarship Fellowship Program of YMCA
Program of YMCA Personnel Services
National Council of MYCA
291 Broadway
New York, NY 10007
Conditions: Full time graduate professional study to prepare for YMCA work.

New York City—Board of Higher Education
Superintendent of Schools
110 Livingston Street
Brooklyn, NY

New York State Funeral Directors Association
369 Lexington Avenue
New York, NY 10017

New York State Regents College Scholarship
State Education Department
Regents Exam and Scholarship Center
Albany 1, NY
17,000 high school seniors who are residents of New York State.
$250 to $750 annually.

Jessie Smith Noyes Foundation
205 East 42nd Street
New York, NY 10017

Conditions: Undergradutes with the exception of freshmen.
Range from $500 to $1,500 with 2% interest after graduation.

Azalia P. Oberg Foundation, Inc.
Thomas & Thomas
504 Broadway, Room 1016
Gary, IN

P.E.O. Educational Fund
Executive Office
Mt. Pleasant, IO
Conditions: Women students

Proctor and Gamble Company
Scholarship Program
P. O. Box 599
Cincinnati, OH
Conditions: Full tuition plus allowance for books, fees, supplies renewable up to four years. No restrictions.

Revlon Foundation, Inc.
666 Fifth Avenue
New York, NY 10019

Henry Warren Roth Educational Fund
Henry Warren Roth
University of Pittsburgh
Pittsburgh, PA
Conditions: All undergraduates, range from $500 to $1,500 maximum 4% interest after graduation.

Federally sponsored "Double Discovery" program at Columbia University.

Rothschild Fund, Inc.
470 Park Avenue, South
New York, NY 10016

Royal A. & Mildred D. Eddy Student Loan Fund
Eddy Student Loan Fund
Thomas & Thomas
504 Broadway, Room 1016
Gary, IN
$1,500 annually
Conditions: No restrictions other than financial need; no tests; no deadline.

S & H Foundation National Scholarship Program
Educational Testing Service
Princeton, NJ
Conditions: High school seniors
Up to $1,000 renewable for four years

Sandy Hill Foundation
27 Allen Street
Hudson Falls, NY

Scholarship Foundation, Inc.
120 East End Avenue
New York, NY

Scott Fund, Inc.
Five Quaker Center
Scarsdale, NY

Schepp Leopold Foundation
551 Fifth Avenue
New York, NY 10017

Sloan (Alfred P.) Foundation
630 Fifth Avenue
New York, NY 10020
Conditions: 150 scholarships awarded to juniors and seniors in participating schools. Range from $200 to $2,400.

Society of Exploration Geophysicist
Scholarship Committee
Shell Building
Tulsa, OK 74119
Conditions: Scholarships for persons interested in a career as a geophysicist.

Social Research Foundation, Inc.
345 Park Avenue
New York, NY 10022

Henry Strong Educational Foundation
50 South LaSalle Street
Chicago, IL

Student Opportunity Scholarships
475 Riverside Drive, Room 1140
New York, NY 10027

Telluride Association
Ithaca, NY
Conditions: Students to attend Cornell

Tiffany Foundation
1083 Fifth Avenue
New York, NY 10028

Vocational Advisory Service
23 East 26th Street
New York, NY 10010

Weisberg Foundation, Inc.
29 Cooper Road
Scarsdale, NY

Western Golf Association
Golf, Illinois
Conditions: Four year scholarships to qualified caddies

Westinghouse Science Talent Search
Westinghouse Electric Corporation
East Pittsburgh, PA
Conditions: 40 high school seniors in top 10% of their class. $250 to $7,500 for four years.

White Scholarship Fund
73 Main Street
Cooperstown, NY

Woike Foundation, Inc.
1775 Broadway
New York, NY 10019

Woodrow Wilson National Fellowship Foundation
Box 642
Princeton, NJ
Conditions: 1,000 fellowships for first year graduate students interested in college teaching careers.

Business and Industry Scholarship Sources[a]

Association of American Railroads
59 East Van Buren Street
Chicago, IL

Atlantic Refining Company
260 South Broad Street
Philadelphia, PA

Boston Insurance Company
87 Kilby Street
Boston, MA

Brown and Sharpe Manufacturing Company
Providence, RI

Bryant Chucking Grinder Company
Springfield, VT

Buckeye Pipe Line Company
30 Broad Street
New York, NY

Bulova Watch Company, Inc.
Bulova Park
Flushing, NY

Chance Vought Aircraft, Inc.
P. O. Box 5907
Dallas, TX

Chicago Title & Trust Foundation
Chicago, IL

Chubb Foundation
90 John Street
New York, NY 10038

Climas Molybdenum Company
Langeloth, PA

Cummins Engine Company, Inc.
Columbus, IN

Fairchild Aircraft Division
Hagerstown, MD

Firestone Tire & Rubber Company
1200 Firestone Parkway
Akron, OH

Fisher Scientific Company
717 Forbes Street
Pittsburgh, PA

Food Fair Stores, Inc.
2223 East Allegheny Avenue
Philadelphia, PA

Ford Motor Company
Central Building
American Road
Dearborn, MI

Fruehauf Trailer Company
c/o Frank Strick Foundation
1335 Glenbrook Road
Huntingdon Valley, PA

General Dynamics Corporation
445 Park Avenue
New York, NY

General Electric Company
Schenectady, NY

General Motors Corporation
3044 West Grand Boulevard
Detroit, MI

Goodbody & Company
115 Broadway
New York, NY

Goodrich, B. F. Company
Akron, OH

Greenfield Tap & Die Corporation
Greenfield, MA

[a] Courtesy United Negro College Fund.

Gruman Engineering Company
Bethpage, NY

Greenwall, Susan Foundation
Holmdel, NJ

Gulf Oil Company
Pittsburgh, PA

Handcraft Company, Inc.
Princeton, WI

Handy & Harman
82 Fulton Street
New York, NY

Hood Dairy Foundation
500 Rutherford Avenue
Boston, MA

Hunt, C. Howard Pen Company
7th & State Streets
Camden, NJ

Imperial Coal Company
Johnstown, PA

Inland Steel Company
38 South Dearborn Street
Chicago, IL

International Business Machines Corporation
590 Madison Avenue
New York, NY

Joanna Cotton Mills
Joanna, SC

Johnstown Coal and Coke Company
Johnstown, PA

Jones & Laughlin Steel Corporation
3 Gateway Center
Pittsburgh, PA

Joy Manufacturing Company
Henry W. Oliver Building
Pittsburgh, PA

Katz Underwear Company
Honesdale, PA

Luria Engineering Company
1745 Easton Avenue
Bethlehem, PA

Mayer, Oscar & Company
Madison, WI

McCormick & Company
414 Light Street
Baltimore, MD

Mead Corporation
Dayton, OH

Merck & Company, Inc.
Rahway, NJ

National Starch Products Company
270 Madison Avenue
New York, NY

Niles-Bement-Pond Company
West Hartford, CT

Norfolk & Western Railway Company
Roanoke, VA

North American Aviation, Inc.
International Airport
Los Angeles, CA

Northern Illinois Gas Company
c/o National Merit Scholarship
Corporation
1580 Sherman Avenue
Evanston, IL

Ohio Boxboard Company
Rittman, OH

Ohio Oil Company
539 South Main Street
Findlay, OH

Ohmite Manufacturing Company
Skokie, IL

Outboard Marine Corporation
Evinrude Motors
Milwaukee, WI

Pan American Petroleum Corporation
c/o National Merit Scholarship
Corporation
1580 Sherman Avenue
Evanston, IL

Paragon Oil Company
2100 Hunters Point Avenue
Long Island City, NY

Pennsylvania Power & Light Company
901 Hamilton Street
Allentown, PA

Pennsylvania Railroad
1617 Pennsylvania Boulevard
Philadelphia, PA

Pennsylvania Salt Manufacturing Co.
Three Penn Center
Philadelphia, PA

Phelps Dodge Corporation
300 Park Avenue
New York, NY

Philip Morris, Inc.
100 Park Avenue
New York, NY

Philips Petroleum Company
Adams Boulevard
Bartlesville, OK

Pitney-Bowes, Inc.
Walnut & Pacific
Stanford, CT

Pittsburgh Plate Glass Company
632 Fort Duquesne Boulevard
Pittsburgh, PA

Pratt & Whitney Company, Inc.
Charter Oak Boulevard
West Hartford, CT

Public Service Electric & Gas Company
Newark, NJ

Pullman Company
11024 South Michigan Avenue
Chicago, IL

Purolator Products, Inc.
970 New Brunswick Avenue
Rahway, NJ

Riegel Paper Corporation
Box 170, Grand Central Station
New York, NY

Riegel Textile Corporation
Box 170, Grand Central Station
New York, NY

Riverside Memorial Chapel
180 West 76th Street
New York, NY

Rockefeller Center, Inc.
50 Rockefeller Plaza
New York, NY

Sante Fe Foundation, Inc.
Chicago, IL

Schlumberger Well Surveying Corporation
P. O. Box 2175
Houston, TX

Standard Oil Company of New Jersey
30 Rockefeller Plaza
New York, NY

Standard Oil Company of Ohio
c/o Foundation of Independent
Colleges
4554 Starret Road
Columbus, OH

Superior Tube Company
Norristown, PA

Time-Life
Time & Life Building
New York, NY

UARCO, Inc.
141 West Jackson Boulevard
Chicago, IL

United Aircraft Corporation
East Hartford, CT

United States Industries, Inc.
250 Park Avenue
New York, NY

Van Raalte Company
417 Fifth Avenue
New York, NY

Victor Adding Machine Company
3900 N. Rockwell Street
Chicago, IL

Visking Corporation
6733 West 65th Street
Chicago, IL

West Chemical Products, Inc.
(Marcuse Fund)
c/o National Merit Scholarships Corp.
1580 Sherman Avenue
Evanston, IL

Western Union Telegram Company
60 Hudson Street
New York, NY

William Manufacturing Company
Gallia & Murray Street
Portsmouth, OH

Wings Shirt Company, Inc.
4 West 33rd Street
New York, NY

Young & Rubicam, Inc.
285 Madison Avenue
New York, NY

Schmidt, Christian
3965 Germantown Avenue
Philadelphia, PA

Shatterproof Glass Corporation
c/o William B. Chase Foundation
4815 Cabot Avenue
Detroit, MI

Standard Oil Company of Indiana
910 South Michigan Avenue
Chicago, IL

Federal Financial Aid

Division of Student Financial Aid
U.S. Office of Education
Washington, D.C. 20202
(Request publication OE-55001:65)
Conditions: Loans may not exceed
$1,000 per year or $5,000 for all years
to any student.

National Defense Education Act of
1958: Students Loans for High
Education—Title II
Conditions: For the college where
student is enrolled or has been
accepted.

Architecture and Engineering

The American Institute of Architects
110 Pearl Street
Buffalo 2, NY
Conditions: 1 scholarship for student
interested in architecture as a career.

The Cooper Union (For the Advance
of Science and Art)
Director of Admissions
The Cooper Union
Cooper Square
New York, NY 10003
Conditions: Scholarships valued at

$1,500 to $2,000 per year.
Competitive—scholarships in Art,
Architecture, Engineering and
Science.

Antioch-Niagara Frontier Council
116 Hartwell Road
Buffalo 16, NY
Conditions: 2 scholarships, from $400
to $800 in engineering.

Director
Polytechnic Institute of Brooklyn
Conditions: Students wishing to

graduate in electrical engineering,
especially those from Southern Negro
high schools. All tuition and
maintenance costs.

Union Carbide Education Fund
270 Park Avenue
New York, NY 10017
Conditions: Engineering scholarships
at 35 engineering colleges and
universities.

Journalism and Drama

The Newspaper Fund
P. O. Box 300
Princeton, NJ 08540
Conditions: List of nearly $700,000 in
scholarships offered by schools and
departments of Journalism.

William Randolph Hearst Foundation
3rd and Market Streets, Suite 1018
San Francisco, CA 94103
Conditions: Grants for study to
undergraduate journalism students
range from $75 to $100 each month.

Abbott (George) Educational
Foundation, Inc.
630 Fifth Avenue
New York, NY 10020
Conditions: Students with talent in
dramatic playwriting willing to attend
the University of Rochester.

Medical and Allied Professions

American Dental Association
Council of Dental Education
222 East Superior
Chicago, IL 60611

American Association of Dental
Schools
840 North Lakeshore Drive
Chicago, IL 60611

American Medical Association
Education & Research Foundation
535 North Dearborn Street
Chicago, IL 60610
Conditions: Loans: Students admitted
to approved medical schools.

Association of American Medical Colleges
2530 Ridge Avenue
Evanston, IL
Conditions: Brochure: For sources of financial aid to medical students.

Bergen Foundation
6536 Sunset Boulevard
Hollywood 28, CA
Conditions: Loans: Nurses training.

Beta Chi Inc.
1211 Leeds Street
Utica, NY
Conditions: One scholarship of $500 for a girl to attend any accredited hospital school of nursing.

Bureau of State Services (Community Health)
U.S. Department of Health, Education, and Welfare
Washington, D.C. 20201
(Request publication 1154)
Conditions: Person enrolled or accepted for enrollment as full-time students in an accredited school of nursing having a loan fund under the Act. Students may borrow up to $1,000 an academic year.

Bureau of State Services (Community Health)

U.S. Department of Health, Education, and Welfare
Washington, D.C. 20201
(Request publication 1347)
Conditions: Persons enrolled or accepted as full-time students in a school which has a loan fund under the Act.
Establishes student loans funds, for students pursuing a degree in medicine, dentistry, optometry, or osteopathy. May obtain loans of up to $2,000 a year.

COSTEP
Surgeon General
U.S. Public Health Service
Washington, D.C.
Att: Office of Personnel
Conditions: For juniors and seniors in health related fields and students in programs of engineering and science.

The Health Profession Educational Assistance Act of 1963:
The Health Professions Student Loan Program—PTA.
Conditions: Institution where student is enrolled or has been accepted.

National Institute of Health
Division of Research Grants
U.S. Public Health Service
Bethesda, MD 20014

Conditions: Undergraduate and graduate training grants.

Navy Nurse's Corps Candidate Program
Nearest U.S. Navy Recruiting Station
Conditions: Open to students for junior and senior years in an accredited college or nursing school. Provide for tuition, salary, and/or allowance benefits.

Nurse Training Act of 1964: Nursing Student Loan Program
Conditions: Institution where student is enrolled or has been accepted.

National League for Nursing
10 Columbus Circle
New York, NY 10019
Conditions: Scholarships for persons interested in nursing.

Reyngolds Foundation, Inc.
Polikoff & Clarehen
11 West 42nd Street
New York, NY 10036
Conditions: Students of medical and social sciences.

The Surgeon General
Department of Army
Washington, D.C. 20315
Conditions: Scholarships for dietetic therapeutics fields under the Army.

Veterans

AMVETS National Foundation
P. O. Box 6038
Mid-City Station
Washington 5, D.C.
Conditions: Children whose fathers are deceased or totally disabled as a result of military service.
$2,000 total for four years.

War Orphans Education Program
Local Veterans Administration Office
Conditions: Children of servicemen who died in U.S. Armed Forces; must be between ages 18–23.
$110 monthly.

Miscellaneous Professions

The Kroger Company
1014 Vine Street
Cincinnati, OH
Areas: Freshman scholarships for students majoring in Agricultural and Home Economics at land grant colleges in the Midwest and South.

Sears, Roebuck Foundation
Appy to Dean of Land Grant College in home state.
Areas: Scholarships for male agricultural students and female home economics students.

The Ralston Purina Fellowships
Ralston Purina Company
Education Department
St. Louis, MO 63102
Areas: Scholarships for training in animal husbandry.

Allstate Foundation
10 Columbus Circle
New York, NY 10009
Areas: Scholarships for driver education to high school teachers.

National Board of Civil Air Patrol
Civil Air Patrol

Ellington Air Force Base
TX
Areas: Undergraduate and graduate scholarships awarded to Civil Air Patrol members.

Institute of Food Technology
176 West Adams Street
Chicago, IL 60603
Areas: Scholarships range from $300 to $1,000.
Scholarships for the field of Food Technology or Food Science.

A physical education class at a New York high school.

Council of Hotel, Restaurant, and Institutional Education
Statler-Hall
Ithaca, NY 14858
Areas: Summary of financial aid available to students pursuing courses of study leading to a career in hotel, restaurant, and institutional work.

Abraham & Strauss Scholarships
Areas: Executive scholarships annually for students to combine on-the-job training and studies in retailing at Adelphi College, City College, Hofstra College, Long Island University, and New York University.

National Commission for Social Work Careers
345 East 46th Street
New York, NY 10017
Areas: Handbook of graduate scholarships in the field of social work.

Public Inquiry Branch
U.S. Department of Health, Education & Welfare
Washington, D.C. 20201
Areas: Undergraduate college students and graduate students training for teaching. Provides for scholarships of up to $800 to $1,000 based on need and academic standing in high school.

Financial Aid for Spanish-Speaking Students

ASPIRA Agency Scholarships
137 West 72nd Street
New York, NY

Barnard College
New York, NY 10027
2 scholarships (Spanish speaking)

Barnard College
New York, NY 10027
1 scholarship—girl

Board of Home Missions
287 Fourth Avenue
New York, NY
4 scholarships

Mercy College
Detroit, MI
Catholic Puerto Rican students

Miami University
Oxford, OH
Conversational classes

New York Puerto Rican Scholarship Fund, Inc.
250 Church Street
New York, NY
Competitive

St. Lawrence University
Canton, NY

St. Mary of the Woods College
St. Mary of the Woods, Indiana

Southern Illinois University
Cardonale, IL

University of Arizona
Tucson, AR
10 scholarships of $360 each.

University of Chattanooga
Chattanooga, TN
Scholarships available in return for help in conversational classes.

University of New Mexico
Albuquerque, NM
Scholarship and stipend for tuition, board and room.

Student Counseling Services

College Admission Assistance Center
41 East 65th Street
New York, NY
($20.00 service fee)

College and Career Consultants
YWCA
New York, NY

National Scholarships Service and
Fund for Negro Students
6 East 82nd Street
New York, NY

New York City Board of Education
Bureau of Guidance
110 Livingston Street
Brooklyn, NY

Masons
2775 W. Forest Avenue
Detroit, MI

Alfred P. Sloan Foundation
630 Fifth Avenue
New York, NY 10020

The Dillon Fund
c/o Shearman & Sterling
20 Exchange Place
New York, NY 10005

American Baptist Convention
(in order to attend Baptist College)
152 Madison Avenue
New York, NY

George F. Baker Trust
2 Wall Street
New York, NY 10005

Jephson Educational Trust
c/o Chase Manhattan Bank
1 Chase Manhattan Plaza
New York, NY 10005

McGregor Fund
2486 First National Building
Detroit, MI

National Scholarship Service & Fund
for Negro Students
6 East 82nd Street
New York, NY 10028

Omega Psi Phi Fraternity
3104 13th Street, N.W.
Washington, D.C.

Rockefeller Foundation Scholarship
Aid
Duke University, Durham, North
Carolina
Emory University, Atlanta, Georgia
Tulane University, New Orleans,
Louisiana
Vanderbilt University, Nashville,
Tennessee
For disadvantaged graduates of
Southern high schools. Tuition varies.

Rockefeller Foundation Scholarship
Aid for Negro Students
Antioch College, Yellow Springs,
Ohio
Carleton College, Northfield,
Minnesota
Grinnell College, Grinnell, Iowa
Oberlin College, Oberlin, Ohio
Occidental College, Los Angeles,
California
Reed College, Portland, Oregon
Swarthmore College, Swarthmore,
Pennsylvania
High school juniors—Tuition for four
years.

The Eleanor Roosevelt Scholarship
Program
CORE Scholarship Education &
Defense Fund, Inc.
150 Nassau Street, Room 312
New York, NY 10038
Students who have actively been
involved in efforts to eliminate racial
prejudice and discrimination and to
secure legal rights for persons of all
races. Up to $2,000 annually.

Roosevelt University
3430 S. Michigan Avenue
Chicago, IL
Negro and Indian students wishing to
study in the college of Business
Administration, $1,500 per year.

More black adults are taking advan-
tage of college general studies courses.

General Loans

Beans Foundation
2 Broadway
New York, NY 10004
Grants and Loans: Students attending
colleges and universities.

Central Scholarship Bureau, Inc.
819 W. Monument Street
Baltimore 1, MD
Limit: $750

Insured Tuition Plan
38 Newbury Street
Boston 16, MA
Loans: No restriction on school
location.

Additional Sources of Financial Aid

Catholic Scholarships for Negroes, Inc.
Mrs. Roger L. Putnam
224 Union Street
Springfield, MA 01105

The Fund for Theological Education, Inc.
163 Nassau Street
Princeton, NJ 08540

Howard University Foreign Service Grant
Howard University
Washington, D.C.

Foreign black students learning English.

Minority Groups Scholarship Program
Write to:
Antioch College, Yellow Springs, Ohio
Carleton College, Northfield, Minnesota
Grinnell College, Grinnell, Iowa
Oberlin College, Oberlin, Ohio
Occidental College, Los Angeles, California
Reed College, Portland, Oregon
Swarthmore College, Swarthmore, Pennsylvania

Polytechnic Institute of Brooklyn, N.Y.
Electrical Engineering (priority given

to southern Negroes for remedial
courses).

Ralph L. Smith
Freedom Scholarships
Macalester College
St. Paul, Minnesota

Student Opportunity Scholarships
Room 1140
475 Riverside Drive
New York, NY 10027

Texas Southern University School of Business
Houston, TX
Home Guidance Counselor

Catholic Scholarships for Negroes
254 Union Street
Springfield, MA

Elks National Foundation
Chairman Scholarship Awards
16 Court Street
Boston, MA

Field Foundation Inc.
250 Park Avenue
New York, NY 10017

International Supreme Council of World St. Mary's College
Notre Dame, IN
1 scholarship for black girl,
competitive.

Ralph L. Smith Freedom Scholarships
Macalester College
St. Paul, MI

Texas Southern University
Houston, TX
107 high school juniors
Tuition and fees for four years.

Texas Southern University School of Business
Home Guidance Counselor
Houston, TX

John Hay Whitney Foundation
11 West 50th Street
New York, NY 10020
Graduate work in the Creative Arts
Minority groups solicit.
Range from $1,000 to $3,000/year.

ELEMENTARY AND SECONDARY EDUCATION ACT

The passage of the Elementary and Secondary Education Act of 1965 served notice of the intention of the federal government to assume direct responsibility for providing all children—particularly the disadvantaged—with quality education. The five key provisions of the act can be summarized as follows:

Title I. *Opportunity for the Disadvantaged*

This title provides funds to school districts under state plans approved by the U.S. Office of Education. During the first year of the program, Congress appropriated 775 million dollars to individual states and school districts. Each local public school is eligible to receive half the average current school expenditure per child in the state, multiplied by the number of school-age children in the district whose families earn less than $2,000 annually.

Funds may be used to benefit both public and non-public school children through such arrangements as dual enrollment, educational media centers, mobile education centers and equipment, and educational radio and television. They may also be used for broadened health programs, school breakfasts, guidance and counseling, in-service teacher training, additional teaching personnel, curriculum development, preschool training and special audio visual aids and other equipment.

Title I funds are in the form of 100% grants to state educational agencies which then allocate money to school districts according to a formula established by Congress.

Title II. *School Library and Instructional Resources*

Under Title II, Congress has authorized 100 million dollars for school library aid. Funds may be used to purchase textbooks, library books, periodicals, documents, tapes, records, physical facilities, equipment, and for administration and financing. (Under present estimates, Title II funds are expected to add about $2 per pupil annually for *each* of the nation's 47 million school children.) Funds are allocated under state plans on the basis of public and nonpublic elementary and secondary school populations.

Administrative plans under this title require the approval of the U.S. Office of Education. They must spell out criteria for fund use and provide assurance that materials will be available on an equitable basis *for all children*. Materials are loaned to private school pupils, and remain the property of the designated public agency.

Since the needs and requirements of each state vary, uniform plans are not mandatory.

Title III. *Supplementary Educational Centers*

This title is designed to help local school districts relate research to practice through the support of supplemen-

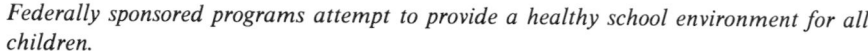

Federally sponsored programs attempt to provide a healthy school environment for all children.

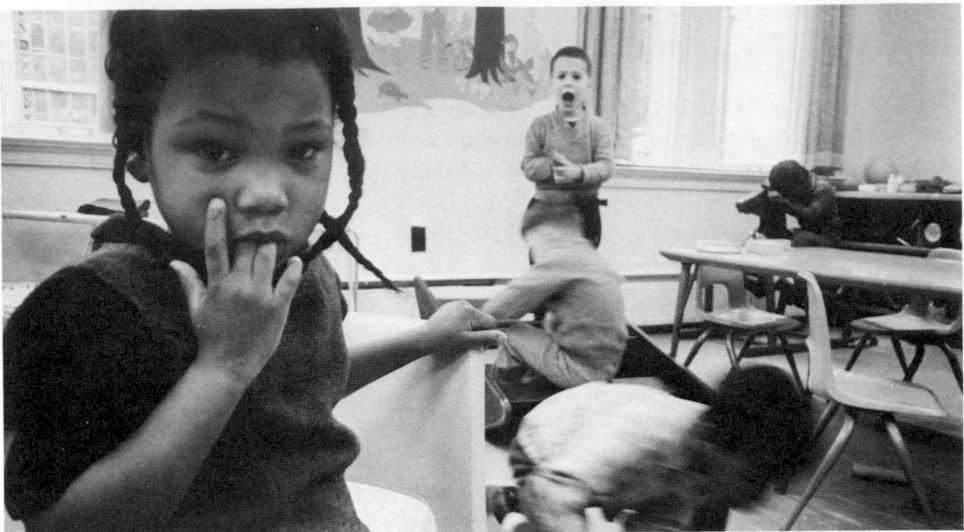

Project Head Start operates over 13,000 Child Development Centers for preschool young-sters.

tary centers and services. These must seek to improve the quality of education by providing services *not now available* to the children within a given community, such as psychological testing, audiovisual aids, radio and television, programmed materials, etc.

Congress appropriated 75 million dollars for Title III Supplementary centers for fiscal 1966. Services are available to public and nonpublic pupils on a nonsectarian basis.

Title IV. *Educational Research*

Under this title, Congress has appropriated 100 million dollars over a five-year period in an effort to improve the depth of U.S. educational research. The money is being used to construct and equip national and regional research facilities, including educational laboratories. These laboratories are regionally based, and work in such areas as basic research, curriculum development and teacher training.

Title V. *Strengthening State Education Agencies*

Under this title, Congress has appropriated 17 million dollars for the first year of a five-year program designed to strengthen state education departments. (Title V provides unmatched federal grants for the first two years, and then calls for matching state grants of from 33 to 50% of the federal total.)

Two kinds of grants—basic and experimental—are authorized under this title. Eighty-five percent of the funds must be used for basic administrative improve-

ments, with the remainder earmarked for experimental projects. Provision has also been made under Title V for the exchange of personnel between the U.S. Office of Education and state education departments in order to establish a better understanding of programs and problems.

THE HIGHER EDUCATION ACT OF 1965

The Higher Education Act of 1965 sought to "strengthen the educational resources of our colleges and universities and to provide financial assistance for students in post-secondary and higher education." In short, this act seeks to take advantage of the skills and knowledge of the university by, in effect, putting the university to work toward solving the problems of the community. The first five titles of the act may be summarized as follows.

Title I. *Community Service and Continuing Programs*

Title I authorized the appropriation of 25 million dollars in fiscal 1966 for community service and continuing education programs. The programs, set up by the states, place special emphasis on solving problems in urban and suburban areas. Each participating state has chosen an existing agency or institution to carry out this title. This agency, through a federally approved plan, has established guidelines for giving federal funds to qualifying colleges and universities.

Title II. *College Library Assistance and Library Training and Research*

Title II provided grants to colleges and universities for library materials such as books, periodicals, documents, magnetic tapes and phonograph records. These grants sometimes double and triple the funds available for library development in small and poorly supported colleges.

Title III. *Strengthening Developing Institutions*

Under this title, 55 million dollars has been provided to carry out cooperative programs and set up national teaching fellowships for developing institutions. Seventy-eight percent of the money goes to four-year colleges; the remaining 22% to two-year colleges.

To be eligible, institutions must meet the following requirements.

1. Admit as regular students only high school students, or the equivalent.
2. Award a bachelor's degree or provide a two-year program creditable toward such a degree, or a two-year technical program.
3. Be accredited, or be making reasonable progress toward reaching this status.

Title IV. *Student Assistance*

Title IV establishes educational opportunity grants and provides federally subsidized student loans. Seven million dollars has been authorized for these grants in the 1966–1967 school year. Colleges themselves administer the grants, select the eligible students, and decide on the size of individual grants.

Title V. *Teacher Programs*

Title V is aimed at improving the caliber and increasing the number of America's teachers, with a view toward thus increasing the educational opportunity offered America's elementary and secondary school children. It also establishes the National Teacher Corps (NTC), providing fellowships for graduate study. Members of the NTC are often used to visit impoverished school districts, and supplement the teaching force there.

THE HIGHER EDUCATION AMENDMENTS OF 1968

Amendments to the Higher Education Act constitute the most comprehensive aid-to-education package to take effect since the Elementary and Secondary Educa-

tion Act of 1965. These amendments not only extend through 1971 such key legislation as the National Defense Education Act, but also create six new higher education programs, including Special Services for Disadvantaged Students, Cooperative Education and Education for the Public Service. As a whole, the amendments broaden the search for talented and ambitious youths from the preschool to the Ph.D. level. The five amendments can be summarized as follows.

Title I. *Student Assistance*

Student assistance has several features which can be characterized under a number of appropriate headings. The Educational Opportunity Grant Program increases maximum student grants from $800 to $1,000 a year. The federal government is still paying interest charges on loans to borrowers in college or in their deferment period. The College Work-Study Program allows students to work more than 15 hours per week during the summer, with 80% of salary being paid by the federal government. Under Cooperative Education, grants are authorized to plan and develop programs which alternate full-time study with full-time employment. The National Defense Student Loan Pro-

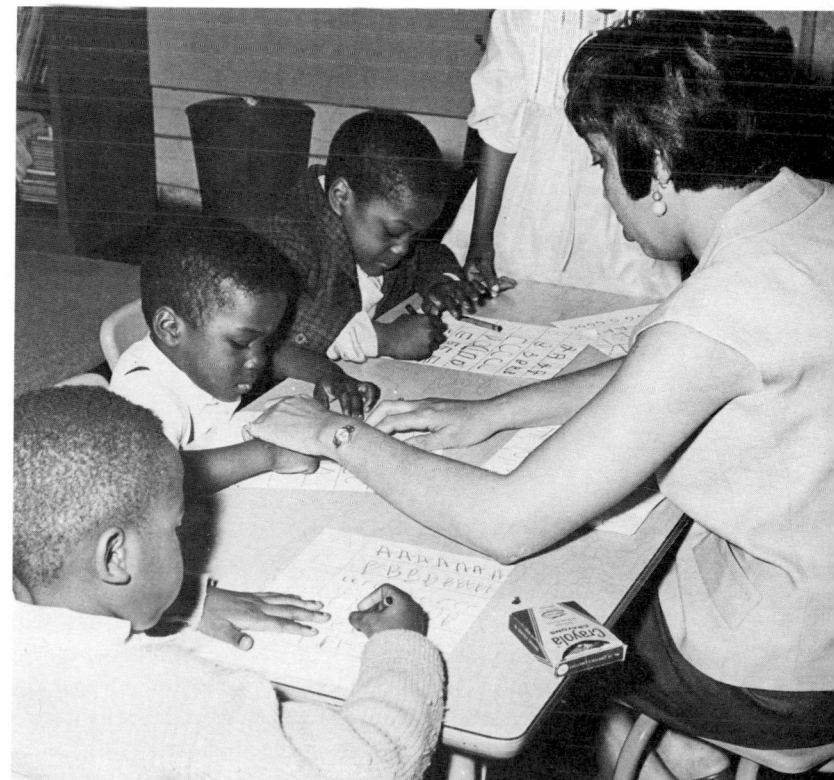

A scene from Craig Fischer's documentary The Learning Process.

gram permits teachers in low-income schools to cancel up to 100% of their loans.

Title II. *Amendments to Other Provisions of the Higher Education Act*

Other amendments to HEA offer assistance to college libraries, to junior colleges, to state educational authorities recruiting teachers and teacher aides, sharing faculty, and improving graduate programs. The Law School Clinical Experience Program (Title 9) will pay up to 90% of the cost of establishing clinical experience projects at accredited law schools.

Title III. *Amendments to Provisions of the National Defense Education Act*

The NDEA amendments include those which provide 7,500 new fellowships per year, offer short-term training sessions for guidance counselors, and extend, without change, language development.

Title IV. *Amendments to the Higher Education Facilities Act*

New legislation appended to the HEFA authorizes federal interest grants to help cover the cost of nonfederal financing of construction, and makes student health facilities eligible for building funds. These apply to both graduate and undergraduate facilities.

Title V. *Miscellaneous Amendments*

The HEA amendments extend the life of Section 12 of the National Foundation on the Arts and Humanities Act and the International Education Act of 1966. These amendments also specify instances in which Federal assistance can be cut off, to wit: when a student is convicted of a serious crime involving force or seizure of a campus facility which denies the majority access to the institution.

VOCATIONAL EDUCATION

Vocational Education Act (P.L. 88–210)

Funds are available for state vocational education programs for persons in high school, for persons who have completed or left high school, for persons who are unemployed or underemployed, and for persons who have academic, socioeconomic, or other handicaps that prevent them from succeeding in regular vocational education programs. Residential vocational schools, work-study programs, teacher-training, and research programs are included in the provisions of this Act. School systems interested in knowing more about this resource should contact their state education agency. Additional information may be obtained from the Division of Vocational and Technical Education, Bureau of Adult and Vocational Education, Office of Education, Washington, D.C. 20202.

Aid to Technical and Vocational Education (Formerly NDEA, Title VIII, P.L. 85–864, as amended by P.L. 88–210)

Grants are available to states for the development of area vocational education programs in scientific or technological fields. These programs are designed to train persons for employment as highly skilled technicians in recognized occupations requiring scientific knowledge in fields necessary for the national defense. Provision can be made for retraining and refresher courses for adults in such fields as electronics and industrial chemistry. School systems interested in knowing more about this resource should contact their state education agency. Additional information may be obtained from the Division of Vocational and Technical Education, Bureau of Adult and Vocational Education, Office of Education, Washington, D.C. 20202.

CIVIL RIGHTS INSTITUTES

Civil Rights Act of 1964, Title IV (P.L. 88–352)

Title IV provides funds to colleges and universities to conduct institutes for school personnel, grants to the school boards for in service training and the employment of advisory specialists, and technical assistance, including consultants, to enable schools to deal more effectively with educational problems caused by desegregation. Further information may be obtained from the Equal Educational Opportunities Program, Office of Education, Washington, D.C. 20202.

NATIONAL DEFENSE EDUCATION ACT

Loans to Students in Institutions of Higher Learning, Title II (P.L. 85–864, as amended by P.L. 88–665)

Undergraduate and graduate students at American colleges and universities may obtain loans under this Title to pursue their higher education. Students receiving loans who become full-time teachers in public or other nonprofit elementary or secondary schools or institutions of higher education may have up to 50% of their

Dillard University in the 1950s.

loans canceled. Additional information may be obtained from the Director, Division of Student Financial Aid, Bureau of Higher Education Programs, Office of Education, Washington, D.C. 20202.

Grants to Strengthen Subject Areas, Title III (P.L. 85–864, as amended by P.L. 88–665)

Matching grants to states are available for the purpose of strengthening education in elementary and secondary schools in the critical subjects of science, mathematics, history, civics, geography, modern foreign language, English, and reading. This is accomplished through federal grants and loans for the acquisition of laboratory and other special equipment and through federal grants for state programs of supervisory and related services in those subjects. School systems interested in knowing more about this resource should contact their state education agency. Additional information may be obtained from the Division of Program Operations, Bureau of Elementary and Secondary Education, Office of Education, Washington, D.C. 20202.

Guidance, Counseling, and Testing, Title V (P.L. 85–864, as amended by P.L. 88–865)

State education agencies may receive matching grants under this Title to establish and maintain elementary and secondary school programs of testing, guidance, and counseling. These programs are designed for the early identification of students with outstanding aptitude. School systems interested in knowing more about this resource should contact their state education agency. Additional information may be obtained from Division of Program Operations, Bureau of Elemen-

tary and Secondary Education, Office of Education, Washington, D.C. 20202.

Institutes for Advanced Study, Title XI (P.L. 88–865)

Funds are available to institutions of higher education to conduct institutes for advanced study in order to improve the qualifications of individuals engaged in the teaching of disadvantaged youth. Short-term or regular session institutes may be held; usually summer programs predominate. The law defines such youth as those who are "culturally, economically, socially, and educationally handicapped." An institute may focus on teachers whose students are rural, urban, migrant, Indian, non-English speaking, and so forth. Additional information may be obtained from the Division of Educational Personnel Training, Bureau of Elementary and Secondary Education, Office of Education, Washington, D.C. 20202.

Captioned Films for the Deaf (P.L. 85–505, as amended by P.L. 87–715)

Under this Act a service of films is available to provide cultural and educational experiences and to promote educational advancement for the deaf. The Act also supports research in the use and production of these films and for training persons in this area. Additional information may be obtained from Director, Captioned Films for the Deaf Branch, Division of Research Training and Dissemination, Bureau of Research, Office of Education, Washington, D.C. 20202.

National Technical Institute for the Deaf
(P.L. 89–36)

The National Technical Institute for the Deaf will provide a residential vocational school for postsecondary training of deaf youth for employment in high skill jobs. Additional information may be obtained from Phillip Des Marias, Office of the Secretary, Department of Health, Education, and Welfare, Washington, D.C. 20201.

BLACKS IN COLLEGES

Black enrollment in colleges increased dramatically during the 1970s, but progress was uneven and in early 1982 was threatened by proposed cutbacks in federal financial aid programs for low-income youths.

Spurred by affirmative action programs in major universities and a stunning growth in the number of two-year community, junior, and technical colleges, the number of blacks enrolled in institutions of higher learning grew from 522,000 in 1970 to over 1 million in 1980.

However, there was a shortfall of blacks in the more established and prestigious universities and in graduate schools. In 1978 blacks comprised 12.5% of the 18–24-year-old population, 9.9% of 18–24-year-olds enrolled in college, but only 5.2% of students enrolled in the 161 institutions that qualify as universities. On the other hand, blacks made up 10.3% of the students in other four-year colleges and 11% of the enrollment in two-year institutions.

Table 23 depicts the small proportion of black students admitted to the undergraduate, graduate, and first professional enrollments at 98 universities which received the most in federal funding to institutions of higher education in fiscal 1979. The significance of this table becomes clear when one considers that Congress and the government professed a commitment to the goal of equal access to higher education in the passage of the Higher Education Act of 1965 and subsequent amendments to it.

Attention must also be paid to the underrepresentation of black students in some fields of study. Because employment opportunities in other fields were scarce, black students preparing for careers have tended to major in education. In recent years more blacks have majored in such areas as the sciences and engineering, but their proportion remains abysmally low.

Blacks also remain underrepresented in faculty and administrative positions. In 1976 only 4% of the faculty and 7% of administrators in higher education were black. Of the black faculty in all of higher education over 35% were in the historically black colleges.

Blacks in Predominantly White Colleges

A concern of the 1970s was that blacks were not progressing significantly in the quality of education available to them. A spur to this concern was the large number of blacks in two-year colleges which did not offer full university or advanced degrees and offered little instruction in the sciences and advanced technology. In 1978 these two-year schools enrolled more than half of all black freshmen entering universities for the first time.

Blacks enrolled in predominantly white colleges en-

A teacher helps his students with a geometry problem.

countered a variety of difficulties, ranging from racist incidents and decline of black studies programs to a reversal of the small advances blacks had achieved in gaining admission to professional schools. Black retention rates in major universities have been low. In September 1980, at Black College Day in Washington, D.C., journalist Tony Brown asserted that seven of ten blacks attending predominantly white colleges do not graduate.

The percentage of black men and women receiving masters degrees declined during the late 1970s, as did the proportion of black men receiving bachelor's degrees. Greatest gains in these areas were recorded by Americans of Asian descent and nonresident aliens. As a group, women of all races showed the greatest increases in doctoral and first professional degrees.

In 1981 the American Bar Association reported that the proportion of blacks enrolled in accredited law schools had declined during the previous six years, from 4.7 to 4.4%. The problem stemmed as much from economic difficulties as from direct racism. In 1979 the American Medical Association reported a decline in medical school enrollment of lower-income students, largely as a result of a decline in government scholarships. The *Bakke* decision has also had an effect. Though it did not outlaw affirmative action, it did remove pressure from universities to seek black students for medical and other professional schools.

Overt discrimination remained a factor in some universities. In the late 1970s and early 1980s the government charged several states with failing to meet federal college desegregation standards. In the final days of the Carter Administration, cutoffs in federal aid to state universities in Delaware, South Carolina, Pennsylvania, West Virginia, Alabama, Florida, Missouri, and Kentucky were considered, but Reagan's Secretary of Education, Terrel Bell, decided to avoid confrontation and reopen negotiations. Texas and North Carolina were also accused of failing to desegregate their public universities properly.

Troubling incidents occurred at both the administrative and student levels in some private universities. Especially disconcerting was a 1980 draft review of admissions policies at Harvard that compared black students unfavorably with other ethnic groups and questioned whether "elite universities" such as Harvard should compete strongly for black students. Harvard was also one of many universities to curtail its black studies program. In 1979 a study released by Professor Russell Adams of Howard stated that between 1961 and the mid-1970s, the number of black studies programs offered by colleges and universities dropped from 600 to 250.

Integrationists were especially concerned to have Harvard, long regarded as the epitome of liberalism,

retreat in its programs and attitudes. The response of many blacks was that many elite white institutions were cliquish, exclusive cultures with an environment and methods of instruction that were frequently divorced from both reality and black experience.

Historic Black Colleges

For almost a century, the major resource for educating blacks at the college level was the "Historic Black Colleges" (HBCs) which are to be found in some 19 states, mostly in the South. Most HBCs were founded to teach former slaves after the Civil War, but the oldest, Cheyney State in Pennsylvania, was founded in 1837. The newest, Valley State College in Mississippi, was founded in 1950.

Sixteen of the colleges were founded in the nineteenth century as land grant colleges or later given this status to conform with federal requirements that benefits of land grant programs be available to both blacks and whites. A majority were founded as state colleges, often with significant black leadership. Elizabeth City State University, for example, was created in 1891 by a bill introduced into the North Carolina legislature by Hugh Cale, a black legislator from Pasquotank County. In 1871, when Alcorn A&M College was officially opened for Mississippi's black citizens, Hiram R. Revels, the first black elected to the U.S. Senate, resigned his seat to become the college's first president. Alcorn originated as Oakland College, a school for the education of white males.

Thirteen of the colleges were initially organized under private auspices, generally with gifts from both black and white individuals and groups. The soldiers and officers of the 62nd U.S. Colored Infantry gave $5,000 to provide funds for Lincoln University's incorporation in Missouri and are credited with the college's founding and eventual financing. Fort Valley State College was established in 1895 by leading local white and black citizens and was generously supported by gifts from Miss Anna T. Jeanes of Philadelphia. Albany State College in Georgia was begun as the Albany Bible and Manual Training Institute, receiving financial support from the Hazard family of Newport, Rhode Island, as well as from concerned local philanthropists. Financial problems led some private colleges to seek state support, and they became public institutions.

In 1964 over 51% of all blacks in college were still enrolled in the historically black colleges and universities. By 1970 the proportion was 28%, and by fall 1978, 16.5%. As recently as 1977, 38% of all blacks receiving baccalaureate degrees earned their degrees at an HBC. In the four-year college sector (other than universities), the proportion of blacks in HBCs was

32.8. Many HBCs have experienced increased enrollment of white students.

New Black Colleges

Throughout the 1970s, another group of institutions emerged, the newer predominantly black colleges (NPBCs). The number of NPBCs has increased in the last decade along with the increase in the number of black students in higher education. In 1978 there were 60 institutions whose total and full-time enrollments were more than 50% black. The large black enrollment at these institutions, 77% of which are two-year colleges, can be attributed largely to their location in major urban areas, where they provide educational opportunities to black students who may be unable to attend another type of institution and who may be forced or choose to live at home. This group of colleges enrolled nearly 13% of all blacks in higher education in the fall of 1978. A recent follow-up study of freshmen who entered two-year institutions indicates that although three out of four community college freshmen intended to get the baccalaureate degree, only one in four actually did so.

The NPBCs must constantly assure that their mission fits into the overall goal of attaining equity for blacks in higher education. In 1980 close to 20% of the freshmen in all two-year colleges came from families with annual incomes lower than $10,000. Fifty-five percent of the freshmen at HBCs came from families with incomes lower than $10,000.

Historically black colleges and universities are also facing challenges. Having been the primary providers of higher education opportunities for blacks when traditionally white institutions refused to open their doors, HBCs were constantly under pressure during the 1970s to justify their continued existence. Arguments that access now existed for blacks to attend predominantly white institutions were used to undermine the need for the continued existence of the HBCs. A landmark court decision, *Adams* v. *Richardson*, in 1969 reinforced the *Brown* decision and previous court cases which applied to desegregation of higher education institutions. That decision was intended to eradicate the "vestiges of dual systems of higher education" in states that had previously operated segregated systems of higher education. Unfortunately, it created a host of problems for the black colleges and universities by diverting public and private support and promising students from HBCs.

In 1981 President Reagan issued an Executive Order (12320) intended to show his Administration's commitment to the HBCs. This Executive Order, like one before it issued by Jimmy Carter, was intended to increase the flow of federal funds to these institutions. President Reagan's Order calls on the private sector to do their share. However, as of spring 1982, there had been no noticeable increase in funding.

In the spring of 1982, the Congress was debating the future of aid to education and student loan programs. Blacks had a great deal at stake in the outcome. Further cuts would seriously reduce the number of low-income students who could attend college and blacks would be affected disproportionately.

TRADITIONALLY AND PREDOMINANTLY BLACK COLLEGES AND UNIVERSITIES IN THE UNITED STATES [with a few indicated exceptions]

Institution	Address	President	Jr/Sr	Pub/Priv
Alabama A & M University	Normal, Alabama 35762	Dr. R. D. Morrison	Sr	Pub
Alabama State University	Montgomery, Alabama 36101	Dr. Robert L. Randolph	Sr	Pub
Albany State College	Albany, Georgia 31705	Dr. Billy C. Black	Sr	Pub
Alcorn A & M College	Lorman, Mississippi 39096	Dr. Walter Washington	Sr	Pub
Allen University	Columbia, South Carolina 29204	Dr. David W. Williams	Sr	Priv
Arkansas Baptist College	Little Rock, Arkansas 72200	Dr. J. C. Oliver	Sr	Priv
Atlanta Junior College	Atlanta, Georgia	Dr. Edwin A. Thompson	Jr	Pub
Atlanta University[a]	Atlanta, Georgia 30314	Dr. Cleveland L. Dennard	Sr	Priv
Barber-Scotia College[a]	Concord, North Carolina 28025	Dr. Mabel P. McLean	Sr	Priv
Benedict College[a]	Columbia, South Carolina 29204	Dr. Henry Ponder	Sr	Priv
Bennett College[a]	Greensboro, North Carolina 27420	Dr. Isaac H. Miller, Jr.	Sr	Priv
Bethune-Cookman College[a]	Daytona Beach, Florida 32015	Dr. Oswald P. Bronson	Sr	Priv
Bishop College[a]	Dallas, Texas 75241	Dr. Harry S. Wright	Sr	Priv
Bowie State College	Bowie, Maryland 20715	Dr. Rufus L. Barfield	Sr	Pub

TRADITIONALLY AND PREDOMINANTLY BLACK COLLEGES AND UNIVERSITIES IN THE UNITED STATES [with a few indicated exceptions]
(Continued)

Institution	Address	President	Jr/Sr	Pub/Priv
Central State University	Wilberforce, Ohio 45384	Dr. Lionel H. Newsom	Sr	Pub
Cheyney State College	Chevney, Pennsylvania 19319	Dr. Luther Burse (Interim)	Sr	Pub
Chicago State University	Chicago, Illinois 60628	Dr. Benjamin H. Alexander	Sr	Pub
Chicago Theological Seminary[b]	Chicago, Illinois	Dr. Charles S. Rooks		
Chaflin College[a]	Orangeburg, South Carolina 29115	Dr. Hubert V. Manning	Sr	Priv
Clark College[a]	Atlanta, Georgia 30314	Dr. Gloria Scott	Sr	Priv
Clinton Jr. College	Rock Hill, South Carolina 29730	Dr. S. V. Moreland	Jr	Priv
Coahoma Jr. College	Clarksdale, Mississippi 38614	Dr. McKinley C. Martin	Jr	Pub
College of the Virgin Island	St. Thomas, Virgin Island 00801	Dr. Lawrence C. Wanlass	Sr	Pub
Compton College	Los Angeles, California 90221	Dr. Abel B. Sykes, Jr.	Jr	Pub
Concordia College	Selma, Alabama 36701	Dr. Julius Jenkins	Jr	Priv
Choppin State College	Baltimore, Maryland 21216	Dr. Calvin W. Burnett	Sr	Pub
Daniel Payne College	Birmingham, Alabama 35212	Dr. Daniel T. Grant	Sr	Priv
Delaware State College	Dover, Delaware 19901	Dr. Luna I. Mishoe	Sr	Pub
Detroit Institute of Technology	Detroit, Michigan 48201	Dr. Dewey F. Barich	Sr	Pub
Dillard University[a]	New Orleans, Louisiana 70122	Dr. Samuel Du Bois Cook	Sr	Priv
District of Columbia Teachers College	Washington, D.C. 20009	Dr. Paul P. Cooke	Sr	Pub
Edward Waters College	Jacksonville, Florida 32209	Dr. Cecil W. Cone	Sr	Priv
Elizabeth City State University	Elizabeth City, North Carolina 27909	Dr. Marion D. Thorpe	Sr	Pub
Essex County College	Newark, New Jersey 07102	Dr. J. Harry Smith	Jr	Pub
Fayetteville State University	Fayetteville, North Carolina 28301	Dr. Charles Lyons, Jr.	Sr	Pub
Federal City College	Washington, D.C. 20005	Dr. Wendell P. Russell	Sr	Pub
Fisk University[a]	Nashville, Tennessee 37203	Dr. Walter J. Leonard	Sr	Priv
Florida A & M University	Tallahassee, Florida 32307	Dr. Walter L. Smith	Sr	Pub
Florida Memorial College[a]	Miami, Florida 33054	Dr. Willie C. Robinson	Sr	Priv
Fort Valley State College	Fort Valle, Georgia 31030	Dr. Cleveland Pettigrew	Sr	Pub
Friendship Jr. College	Rock Hill, South Carolina 29730	Dr. Charles W. Petress	Jr	Priv
Grambling College	Grambling, Louisiana 71245	Dr. Joseph B. Johnson	Sr	Pub
Hampton Institute	Hampton, Virginia 23368	Dr. William R. Harvey	Sr	Priv
Howard University	Washington, D.C. 20001	Dr. James E. Cheek	Sr	Priv
Huston-Tillotson College[a]	Austin, Texas 78702	Dr. John T. King	Sr	Priv
Interdenominational Theological Center[a]	Atlanta, Georgia 30314	Dr. James D. Roberts	Sr	Priv
Jackson State College	Jackson, Mississippi 39217	Dr. James A. Peoples, Jr.	Sr	Pub
Jarvis Christian College[a]	Hawkins, Texas 75765	Dr. Charles A. Berry, Jr.	Sr	Priv
Johnson C. Smith University[a]	Charlotte, North Carolina 28208	Dr. Wilbert Greenfield	Sr	Priv
Kennedy-King College	Chicago, Illinois 60621	Dr. Maceo T. Bowie	Jr	Pub
Kentucky State University	Frankfort, Kentucky 40601	Dr. W. A. Butts	Sr	Pub
Kittrell College	Kittrell, North Carolina 27544	Dr. John A. Middleton	Jr	Priv
Knoxville College[a]	Knoxville, Tennessee 36921	Dr. Clinton Marsh	Sr	Priv
Lane College[a]	Jackson, Tennessee 38301	Dr. Herman Stone, Jr.	Sr	Priv
Langston University	Langston, Oklahoma 73050	Dr. Ernest L. Holloway	Sr	Priv
LeMoyne-Owen College[a]	Memphis, Tennessee 38126	Dr. Walter L. Walker	Sr	Priv
Lincoln University	Jefferson City, Missouri 65101	Dr. Walter C. Daniel	Sr	Pub

Institution	Address	President	Jr/Sr	Pub/Priv
Lincoln University	Lincoln University, Pennsylvania 19352	Dr. James Frank	Sr	Priv
Livingstone College[a]	Salisbury, North Carolina 28144	Dr. F. George Shipman	Sr	Priv
Lomax-Hannon College	Greenville, Alabama 36037	Dr. D. M. Montgomery	Jr	Priv
Los Angeles S.W. College	Los Angeles, California 90047	Dr. W. J. Longmire	Jr	Pub
Malcolm-King: Harlem College Extension	103 East 125th Street, New York, New York 10035	Dr. Mattie Cook, Administrative Director	Jr	Priv
Malcolm X College	Chicago, Illinois 60612	Dr. E. Aikin	Jr	Pub
Manhattan Community College[b]	New York, New York	Dr. Edgar D. Draper	Jr	Pub
Manhattanville College[b]	Purchase, New York	Dr. Harold Delaney	Sr	Priv
Mary Allen Jr. College	Crockett, Texas 75835	Dr. Ira L. Clark	Jr	Priv
Mary Holmes College	West Point, Mississippi 39773	Dr. Joseph A. Gore	Jr	Priv
Martin Tech Institute[b]	Williamston, North Carolina 27892	Dr. E. M. Hunt	Jr.	Pub
Medgar Evers Community College	Brooklyn, New York	Dr. Richard D. Trent	Jr	Pub
Meharry Medical College	Nashville, Tennessee 37208	Dr. Lloyd C. Elam	Prof	Priv
Michigan State University[b]	East Lansing, Michigan	Dr. Clifton R. Wharton, Jr.	Sr	Pub
Miles College[a]	Birmingham, Alabama 35208	Dr. W. Clyde Williams	Sr	Priv
Mississippi Industrial College	Holly Springs, Mississippi 38635	Dr. Theodore R. Debro	Sr	Priv
Mississippi Valley State College	Itta Bena, Mississippi 38941	Dr. Joe L. Boyer	Sr	Pub
Mobile State (see S. D. Bishop)				
Morehouse College[a]	Atlanta, Georgia 30314	Dr. Hugh M. Gloster	Sr	Priv
Morgan State College	Baltimore, Maryland 21239	Dr. Andrew Billingsley, Jr.	Sr	Priv
Morris College	Sumter, South Carolina 29150	Dr. Luns C. Richardson	Sr	Priv
Morris Brown College[a]	Atlanta, Georgia 30314	Dr. Robert Threatt	Sr	Priv
Morristown College	Morristown, Tennessee 37814	Dr. Charles Wade	Jr	Priv
Natchez Jr. College	Natchez, Mississippi 39120	Dr. William C. Boykins	Jr	
Norfolk State College	Norfolk, Virginia 23504	Dr. Harrison B. Wilson	Sr	Pub
North Carolina A & T State University	Greensboro, North Carolina 27411	Dr. Edward Fort	Sr	Pub
North Carolina Central University	Durham, North Carolina 27707	Dr. Albert N. Whiting	Sr	Pub
Oakwood College[a]	Huntsville, Alabama 35806	Dr. Calvin B. Rock	Sr	Priv
Olive-Harvey College	Chicago, Illinois 60628	Dr. Nathaniel P. Tillman, Jr.	Jr	Pub
Paine College[a]	Augusta, Georgia 30901	Dr. Julius A. Scott	Sr	Priv
Palmer College	Columbia, South Carolina 29201	Dr. Raymond P. Carson	Jr	Priv
Paul Quinn College[a]	Waco, Texas 76704	Dr. L. H. McCloney	Sr	Priv
Philander Smith College[a]	Little Rock, Arkansas 72202	Dr. Grant S. Shockley	Sr	Priv
Prairie View A & M College	Prairie View, Texas 77445	Dr. Alvin I. Thomas	Sr	Pub
Prentiss N & I Institute	Prentiss, Mississippi 39474	Dr. Sidney James	Jr	Priv
Rust College[a]	Holly Spring, Mississippi 38565	Dr. William A. McMillan	Sr	Priv
Saint Augustine's College[a]	Raleigh, North Carolina 27602	Dr. Prezell R. Robinson	Sr	Priv
Saint Paul's College[a]	Lawrenceville, Virginia 23868	Dr. S. Dallas Simmons	Sr	Priv
Savannah State College	Savannah, Georgia 31404	Dr. Wendell G. Rayburn	Sr	Pub
S. D. Bishop State Jr. College	Mobile, Alabama 36603	Dr. Sanford D. Bishop	Jr	Pub
Selma University	Selma, Alabama 36701	Dr. M. C. Cleveland, Jr.	Sr	Priv

TRADITIONALLY AND PREDOMINANTLY BLACK COLLEGES AND UNIVERSITIES IN THE UNITED STATES [with a few indicated exceptions]
(Continued)

Institution	Address	President	Jr/Sr	Pub/Priv
Shaw College at Detroit	Detroit, Michigan 48202	Dr. Romallus O. Murphy	Sr	Priv
Shaw University[a]	Raleigh, North Carolina 27602	Dr. Stanley H. Smith	Sr	Priv
Shorter College	Little Rock, Arkansas 72114	Dr. Oley L. Griffin	Jr	Priv
Simmons University	Louisville, Kentucky 40210	Dr. William L. Holmes	Sr	Priv
South Carolina State College	Orangeburg, South Carolina 29115	Dr. M. Maceo Nance, Jr.	Sr	Priv
Southern University[a]	Baton Rouge, Louisiana	Dr. Jesse Stone	Sr	Pub
Southwestern Christian College	Terrell, Texas 75160	Dr. Jack Evans	Jr	Priv
Spelman College[a]	Atlanta, Georgia 30314	Dr. Donald M. Stewart	Sr	Priv
Stillman College[a]	Tuscaloosa, Alabama 35401	Dr. Harold N. Stinson	Sr	Priv
Theodore A. Lawson State Jr. College	Birmingham, Alabama 35228	Dr. Leon Kennedy	Jr	Pub
Talladega College[a]	Talladega, Alabama 35160	Dr. Joseph N. Gayles, Jr.	Sr	Priv
Tennessee State University	Nashville, Tennessee 37203	Dr. Frederick S. Humphries	Sr	Pub
Texas College[a]	Tyler, Texas 75701	Dr. Jimmy Ed Clark	Sr	Priv
Texas Southern University	Houston, Texas 77004	Dr. Leonard H. O. Spearman	Sr	Pub
Tougaloo College[a]	Tougaloo, Mississippi 39174	Dr. George A. Owens	Sr	Priv
Tuskegee Institute[a]	Tuskegee Institute, Alabama 36088	Dr. Benjamin Payton	Sr	Priv
University of Arkansas	Pine Bluff, Arkansas 71601	Dr. Lloyd V. Hackley	Sr	Pub
University of Maryland (Eastern Shore)	Princess Anne, Maryland 21853	Dr. William P. Hytche	Sr	Pub
Utica Jr. College	Utica, Mississippi 39175	Dr. J. Louis Stokes	Jr	Pub
Virginia College	Lynchburg, Virginia 24501	Dr. Langford Hankins	Jr	Priv
Virginia State College	Petersburg, Virginia 23803	Dr. Thomas M. Law	Sr	Pub
Virginia Union University[a]	Richmond, Virginia 23220	Dr. David Thomas Shannon	Sr	Priv
Voorhees College[a]	Denmark, South Carolina 29042	Dr. George B. Thomas	Sr	Priv
Washington Technical Institute	Washington, D.C. 20008	Dr. Cleveland L. Dennard	Jr	Pub
Wayne County Community College	Detroit, Michigan 48201	Dr. Reginald M. Wilson	Jr	Pub
Westfield State College[b]	Westfield, Massachusetts	Dr. Robert L. Randolph		
Wilberforce University[a]	Wilberforce, Ohio 45384	Dr. Charles E. Taylor	Sr	Priv
Wiley College[a]	Marshall, Texas 75670	Dr. Robert E. Hayes	Sr	Priv
Winston-Salem State University	Winston-Salem, North Carolina 27102	Dr. Harold D. Covington	Sr	Pub
Xavier University[a]	New Orleans, Louisiana 70125	Dr. Norman C. Francis	Sr	Priv

[a] United Negro College Fund member institutions

[b] Black enrollment high though not known as a traditionally black school.

For further information contact United Negro College Fund, Inc., 55 East 52nd Street, New York, N.Y. 10022, (212)PL1-0700.

COMMUNITY AND STATE COLLEGES
WITH BLACK ADMINISTRATIVE HEADS

Bronx Community College
Bronx, New York
Dr. Roscoe C. Brown, Jr., President

California State University
Fullerton, California
Dr. Jewel Plummer Cobb, President

City College of New York
New York City
Dr. Bernard Harleston, President

Essex County College
Newark, New Jersey
Dr. Zachery Yamba, President

Harris-Barber College
Raleigh, North Carolina
Charles R. Stone, President

Indian Valley Colleges
Novato, California
Constance M. Carroll, President

Manhattan Community College
New York City
Dr. Joshua L. Smith, President

Malcolm-King Harlem Extension
College
New York City
Mattie Cook, President

Maricopa Community College
District
Phoenix, Arizona
Dr. Charles A. Green, President

Medgar Evers College
Brooklyn, New York
Dr. Richard D. Trent, President

Medical College of Pennsylvania
Philadelphia, Pennsylvania
Dr. Maurice C. Clifford, President

Metropolitan State University
St. Paul, Minnesota
Reatha King, President

University of the District of Columbia
Washington, D.C.
Dr. Lisle C. Carter, Jr., President

Wayne County Community College
Detroit, Michigan
Richard Simmons, Jr., President

EDUCATIONAL FILMS WITH BLACK THEMES

The following list was compiled under the direction of Wendell Wray, Director, North Manhattan Project, Countee Cullen Branch, New York Public Library, and William Sloan, librarian of the NYPL's film division. Their kind permission makes possible its reproduction here. The films are ideal for classroom or community use.

Africa: An Introduction

Stresses the climate and geography of all parts of Africa. Shows the ruins of great civilizations, nomads in North Africa, desert oasis, life in the markets, places of worship, large cities, etc. 1972. *BFA.* (18 min)

An African Community: The Masai

Illustrates the dependence of the nomadic Masai of East Africa on the land, their adaptation to their environment, their tribal interdependence, and the roles of men, women, and different age groups. A good pictorial record; the commentary is superficial. Produced by Frank Gardonyi and Clifford Janoff, 1969. *Bailey-Film Associates.* (17 min)

African Girl—Malobi

Presents the experiences of Malobi, a 10-year-old girl of the Ibo tribe of Nigeria. There are scenes of the tribe building homes in the traditional way, her grandfather carving furniture, and Malobi attending school. Directed by Michael Hagopian. 1960. *Atlantis Productions.* (11 min)

AFRICAN VILLAGE LIFE (series title):

Annual Festival of the Dead

Follows the annual ceremony of the Dogon tribe of Mali, Africa, near the Niger River in the interesting and unusual festival they hold for those who died during the year. Produced by Julien Bryan. 1968 (14 min)

Daily Life of the Bozo

Exciting photography, without narration, but with effects and music recorded on the spot, offers an honest picture of the daily life of the Bozo tribe in Mali, near the Niger River. Photography by Hermann Schlenker. Produced by Julien Bryan. 1967. (15 min)

Fishing on the Niger River

A careful depiction of fishing on the Niger River by members of the Bozo Tribe of Mali. Natural sounds of the people at work provide the background; no narration. Photography by Hermann Schlenker. Produced by Julien Bryan. 1967. (17 min)

Herding Cattle

Records the activities of the Peul Tribe of Mali, as the men and young boys skillfully lead a herd of cattle across the Niger River. Sound background is recorded on the spot. Photography by Hermann Schlenker. Produced by Julien Bryan. 1967 (7 min) *Series by International Film Foundation*

Anansi the Spider

A folk tale from the Ashanti tribe retold in delightful abstract animation using African designs and brilliant colors to account for a troublesome spider and the origin of the moon. By Gerald McDermott. 1969. *Landmark Educational Media, Inc.* (10 min)

Ancient Games

Rafer Johnson and Bill Toomey complete in a reconstruction of the Olympic games of ancient Greece. Script by Erich Segal. 1973. *ABC Media Concepts.* (28 min)

Black African Heritage: The Congo

Aspects of the land culture of the Congo, featuring wildlife, arts and crafts, and tribal dances. Narrated by Julian Bond. Directed and filmed by Eliot Elisofon. 1972 (55 min)

Black American Dream

Black leaders reveal that today Black

Power seems to be all things to all men. Includes interviews with Stokely Carmichael and Jesse Jackson. Produced by BBC-TV. 1973. *Time-Life*. (65 min)

Black and White In South Africa

An objective appraisal of the policy of arpartheid and its background in the Union of South Africa. Produced by the National Film Board of Canada. Commonwealth of Nations series. 1958. *McGraw-Hill*. (30 min)

The Black Cop

Explores the attitudes of blacks toward black policemen, and the views of black policemen themselves. Includes interviews with police officers in New York and Los Angeles. Written and produced by Kent Garrett, for NET's Black Journal. 1969. *NET*. (15 min)

The Black G.I.

A probing exploration of the attitudes of black G.I.s serving in Vietnam. Reveals their concern about discrimination in service clubs and in promotional opportunities, about white Americans teaching racial epithets to Vietnamese, and about problems affecting blacks in the United States. Produced, written, and directed by Kent Garrett, for NET's Black Journal. 1970. *NET*. (54 min)

Black on Black: Martin Luther King

Dr. Martin Luther King explains his philosophy on nonviolence, how he favors not riots but massive civil disobedience and wants his people to organize, learn, and earn rather than "burn baby, burn." Ends with his moving speech from the night before his death. 1970. *Time-Life*. (54 min)

Black Panthers

Journalistic record of Oakland, California Black Panthers. Discussions by Huey Newton, Bill Brandt, Bobby Seale, Stokely Carmichael, and Mrs. Eldridge Cleaver. By Agnes Varda. 1969. *Grove Press*. (26 min)

Black Power

Juxtaposition of widely varying opinions and comments by Malcolm X, Eldridge Cleaver, Floyd McKissick, Martin Luther King, and others, as they view the problems and prospects of the black movement

generally and the concept of black power specifically. 1969. *Reaction Films*. (15 min)

Blue Dashiki: Jeffrey and His Neighbors

A little boy on Chicago's South Side works at odd jobs in order to earn the money to buy a beautiful blue dashiki. A film without words that should appeal to all ages. A film by Maclovia, 1969. *Encyclopedia Britannica Educational Corporation*. (14 min)

The Blues

Shows the music and some of the instruments of several country-blues singers including Sleepy John Estes, Memphis Willie B., and J. D. Short. A low-budget film in which the visuals are not synchronized with the sound. Produced by noted blues authority Samuel X. Charters. 1963. *Brandon*. (21 min)

The Blues Maker

Shows country-blues singer Fred McDowell singing and discussing his music, interspersed with scenes of rural Mississippi. Written and directed by Christian Garrison. Made by the Dept. of Educational Film Production, Univ. Extension, Univ. of Mississippi. 1969. *Univ of Miss*. (14 min)

BODY AND SOUL

Part 1: Body

History of the Negro's breakthrough in the world of sports, from Jesse Owen up to the Mexico City Olympics. Stresses the fact that few blacks have attained positions as coaches or managers; and raises the question of a black boycott of professional sports as a means of correcting this inequity. Produced by CBS News. 1968. (25 min)

Part 2: Soul

Explains how the frustration and depression of the American Negro gave rise to spirituals, revival music, jazz, the blues, and soul music. Produced by CBS News. 1968. (25 min)

Booker T. Washington

Covers the early years of Booker T. Washington and highlights the founding of Tuskegee Institute. 1972. *BFA*. (11 min)

Boy of Central Africa

Vincent Chisembwa, a teenage woodcarver from Zambia, is shown in daily life with his family: the girls fix their hair, grandfather carves, friends play instruments and make canoes, the women gather peanuts. Interesting picture of village life, but commentary is superficial. A Kevin Duffy Production, 1969. *Bailey-Film Associates*. (14 min)

Discovering American Folk Music

Singers trace the variations of folksongs from British and African origins. "The Unfortunate Rake" becomes "Streets of Laredo." "St. James Infirmary" even funny modern version on the death of a telephone lineman. Includes black treatments of traditional songs and handclapping patterns. 1969. *BFA*. (22 min)

Discovering the Music of Africa

A master drummer of Ghana demonstrates various African instruments and describes their uses. Traditional dances are also seen. A studio-made film with excessively artificial lighting. Informative, but not outstanding cinematically. Produced by Bernard Wilets. *Bailey-Film Associates*. (22 min)

Frederick Douglass

An iconographic treatment of the life of ex-slave, abolitionist, and national political figure Frederick Douglass. 1972. For children. (9 min)

DuBois Dedication

A report on the dedication of DuBois Park in Great Barrington, Mass. in October 1969, honoring the late author W. E. B. DuBois. Includes some of the speeches of Ossie Davis and Julian Bond, and interviews with other participants. Narrated by Ossie Davis. By Samuel B. Holmes. 1970. *Samuel B. Holmes*. (8 min)

East Africa

Reports on the physical geography, agriculture, handicrafts, commerce, industry, and social customs in Kenya, Uganda, and Tanganyika. Emphasizes the importance of education in the development of the diverse East African population. 1962. *Encyclopaedia Britannica Films*. (21 min)

Fabulous Harlem Globetrotters

A humorous and quickly paced demonstration of the dexterity of this famous basketball team. *Blackhawk.* (9 min)

Family of Ghana

A somewhat dated but still moving documentary of the people who live on the coast of Ghana and make their living from the sea. Conflict between the old ways and the new is represented between the father and his son. Produced by the National Film Board of Canada. Directed by Julian Biggs. National Film Board of Canada. 1958. *McGraw-Hill.* (30 min)

Felicia

Filmed in her home, school, and neighborhood in Watts, California, teenager Felicia is shown observing the area as it was in the spring of 1965, just before the Watts riots. Directed by Trevor Greenwood and produced by Stuart Roe. 1965. *University of California.* (13 min)

First World Festival of Negro Arts

Pictures scenes of the first World Festival of Negro Arts held at Dakar in 1966, showing music, dance, sculpture, painting, and the reciprocal influences of Negro art and culture in relation to the modern Western World. A pedestrian presentation of an important subject. U.S. release, 1969. *Contemporary/McGraw-Hill.* (20 min)

For All My Students

A thought-provoking and moving study of the particular problems and rewards of teaching Negro high school students. Filmed at Ravenswood High School in East Palo Alto, California. Teaching methods are examined, as are students' feelings about what is wrong with their school, their teachers, and themselves; and the doubts, convictions, frustrations, and satisfactions of the teachers are expressed. A student-made film by Bonnie Sherr under a grant from the U.S. Office of Education. Supervision by George C. Stoney. *University of California.* (36 min)

Four Women

Young women dance to Nina Simone's interpretations of the song "Four Women." Directed by Ilanga Witt.

Danced and filmed by students of the Harlem Preparatory School. 1971. (7 min)

Gabriella and Selena

A live action film based on the book by Peter Desbarats. Two middle-class girls about eight years old, one white, one black, change identities and homes for the evening and find that they've been fooled by the parents into eating things and doing jobs that both of them hate. Suitable for children (older). *BFA.* (13 min)

Game

A candid, nonsensational documentary study of a black prostitute and her pimp in New York City who openly discuss their way of life. The film includes primarily interviews and street scenes, with one brief encounter with a "client." By Jon and Abby Child. 1972. (40 min)

The Game

Negro and Puerto Rican teenagers act out their lives in a series of games which depict their situations in a New York City ghetto. A powerful and moving film. Produced by Roberta Hodes in association with Mobilization for Youth. 1967. *Grove Press.* (17 min)

Goodbye and Good Luck

A black ex-G.I. returns from Vietnam and is confronted with various black power activists. He is forced to question his reasons for having served in the military and what he wants to do in the future. Technically poor, but important subject content. Produced by William Jersey. 1967. *NET.* (30 min)

Harlem Wednesday

Paintings and sketches by American artist Gregorio Prestopino are colorfully arranged and backed with a vibrant jazz score by Benny Carter to evoke the activities and mood of a Wednesday in Harlem. Directed by John Hubley and Faith Elliot, 1959. *Brandon.* (10 min)

Al Stacey Hayes

Portrait of a black high school senior in Shelby, Mississippi and his efforts in voter registration drives. Vividly depicts the generation gap between young black southerners and their

parents and grandparents. By Joel A. Levitch, 1969. *Jason Films.* (28 min)

Heritage in Black

Panorama of the history and contributions of black people to the United States from the Revolution to present times. c.1969. *Encyclopaedia Britannica.* (27 min)

HISTORY OF THE NEGRO IN AMERICA (series title):

Part 1: 1619–1860: Out of Slavery

The development of the slave trade and the growth of slavery from the ancient world to colonial times and on through the Revolution is depicted in stills, prints, and drawing. Narrated by James Earl Jones. 1965. (17 min)

Part 2: 1861–1877: Civil War and Reconstruction

Traces the causes and effects of two critical periods in U.S. history, the Civil War and Reconstruction, and indicates how the Emancipation Proclamation, Thirteenth, Fourteenth, and Fifteenth amendments sought to protect and preserve the Negro's newly won freedom. Made from still pictures. 1965. (20 min)

Part 3: 1877–Today: Freedom Movement

Portrays the post-Reconstruction flight of the Negro, the problems of segregation, Negro heroism in World War I and II, and the advances made in the area of civil rights since 1950; uses stills, prints, drawings, and film footage. Narrated by James Earl Jones. 1965. *McGraw-Hill.* (20 min)

HISTORY OF THE NEGRO PEOPLE (series title):

Part 1. Heritage of the Negro

Explores the heritage of the Negro by examining the civilization and achievements of ancient Africa and their significance to the American Negro today. Produced by NET. 1965. (30 min)

Part 2. Negro and the South

Interviews Negroes (a teacher, a mechanic, and a minister), and whites (a mayor, a sheriff, and a judge) of Mississippi, to depict the "Southern way of life." Produced by NET. 1965. (30 min)

Part 3. Slavery

Based on actual testimony of former slaves, tells of the tragic and sometimes humorous experiences of life in the Old South and depicts the liberation of slaves by the Yankee troops. Uses Negro spirituals to help tell the story. Produced by NET. 1965. (30 min)

Part 4. Brazil: The Vanishing Negro

Depicts the interracial experiences of the Negro in Brazil and stresses that they differ markedly from the experiences of North American Negroes. Produced by NET. 1965. (30 min)

Part 5. Free at Last

Uses dramatic readings from the works of Frederick Douglass, Booker T. Washington, W. E. B. DuBois, and Marcus Garvey to trace the history of the American Negro from emancipation to the end of World War II. Produced by NET. 1965. (30 min)

Part 6. Omowale: The Child Returns Home

Pictures author John Williams, a Mississippi-born Negro, on an odyssey to Africa to explore his ancestral roots and the relationship of the American Negro to Africa and the Africans. Produced by NET. 1965. (30 min)

Part 7. New Mood

Reviews the civil rights struggle of 1955–1965 and traces the impact of the new Negro militancy on both white and Negro Americans. Produced by NET. 1965. (30 min)

Part 8. Our Country, Too

Explores the inner world of the American black: values, attitudes, and impressions of life through interviews at such places as an African rite in Harlem, a black debutante ball, the office of a black newspaper, and a black-owned radio station. Produced by NET. 1965. (30 min)

Part 9. Future and the Negro

Presents a panel discussion on the subject of the Negro's future. Discusses the economic plight of the Negro in the United States and in black nations and emphasizes the racism felt to be deeply ingrained in people throughout the world. Produced by NET. 1965. (75 min)

House on Cedar Hill

Events in the life of Frederick Douglass, the runaway slave who became an editor, orator, and statesman, are presented with skill and sensitivity, through historical documents, period drawings, photographs, and mementos found in the Douglass House in Washington, D.C. Written and directed by Carlton Moss. 1953. *Contemporary/McGraw-Hill.* (30 min)

The Hunters

A starkly beautiful documentary on the bushmen of the Kalahari Desert in Southwest Africa where continued existence depends entirely upon a man's skill and stamina as a hunter. Produced by the Film Study Center of the Peabody Museum, Harvard University. Directed by John Marshall in collaboration with Robert Gardner. 1958. *Contemporary/McGraw-Hill.* (72 min)

The Hurdler

Biographical account of Dr. Charles Drew, the research physician who discovered the value of blood plasma in transfusions and set up the first Blood Bank in the United States during World War II. The forced comparison between a hurdler and Drew's life lessens the effectiveness of the film for some audiences. Narrated by Ossie Davis. 1969. *New York Times/Arno Press.* (16 min)

I Am Somebody

A moving record of the 113-day strike by members of Local 1199B of the National Union of Hospital and Nursing Home Employees, in Charleston, S.C. during the spring of 1969. Most of the strikers were black women, and the film follows their struggle for decent wages, improved working conditions, respect and dignity. Directed by Madelyn Anderson. 1970. *Contemporary.* (28 min)

I Have A Dream

The biography of Martin Luther King made from newsreel footage of the civil rights movement during the 1950s and 1960s. Reveals his dedication to the movement and to the principles of nonviolence. *Bailey-Film Associates.* (35 min)

In Search of a Past

Three young Afro-American students visit Africa to study their racial and cultural origins and compare similarities and differences with the situation in the United States. Produced by CBS News. 1968. *Bailey-Film Associates.* (2 films; each 26 min)

In the Company of Men

Documents the role playing and sensitivity training of hardcore unemployed blacks and white foremen—techniques implemented to establish communication between these two groups in a large General Motors assembly plant in Georgia. A film by William Greaves. 1969. *William Greaves.* (52 min)

Interview with Bruce Gordon

Bruce Gordon, a 23-year-old black civil rights leader, talks of his own beliefs and hopes, the lot of the black in America, and the civil rights movement. A Harold Becker production. 1963. *Harold Becker.* (17 min)

J. T.

Just before Christmas, a lonely Harlem boy steals a radio and hides in an abandoned building. There he finds a sick cat, which he nurtures back to health and develops a sense of responsibility in the process. Presented in CBS Children's Hour; stereotyped characterizations may bother some adults. Written by Jane Wagner; directed by Robert Young; produced for CBS-TV, 1969. *Carousel Films.* (51 min)

Jackie Robinson

A graphic biography of the life of the famous ballplayer, the first black to play in the major leagues. From the television program *Biography;* produced by David Wolper, 1965. *Sterling.* (26 min)

James Weldon Johnson

An attractive biography of the famous black poet, coupled with a stunning visual treatment of the best known of his poems, "The Creation." (18 min)

Jeffries–Johnson 1910

Historical film footage and photographs retell the story of the boxing match between Jack Johnson and Jim Jeffries (the "great white hope"). Produced by Bill Kimberlin. 1972. (21 min)

The Late Show

A young black American cleans and assembles a rifle while watching the late show on television in this brief social commentary. A British Film Institute production. 1971. (12 min)

Lay My Burden Down

An important document on the economic and educational plight of black tenant farmers of the southern United States. Directed by Jack Willis for National Educational Television. 1966. *Indiana University.* (60 min)

Legend of Mark Twain

The world of author Samuel Clemens (Mark Twain) is recreated through photographs and scenes along the Mississippi near his Hannibal, Missouri home, an old Edison newsreel of Twain, and Twain's own words. Also included are dramatic scenes based on *Huckleberry Finn* and *The Jumping Frog of Calaveras County.* 1967. (32 min)

Malcolm X: Struggle for Freedom

Filmed during his trip to Europe and Africa, just three months before his assassination in the United States, Malcolm X discusses racial and other social ills of our age. Directed by Lebert Bethune. 1964. *Grove Press.* (22 min)

Martin Luther King Jr.

Still photographs and newsreel clips make up this short biography of the famed black civil rights leader. 1972. (10 min)

Martin Luther King: The Man and the March

A documentary of the late Martin Luther King, Jr.'s "Poor People's March." Shows Dr. King conferring with aides, speaking at rallies, and traveling as he solicits support for and develops the operational details of the march. Indicates the methods used by his aides to create interest and support on a local level and with other ethnic groups. Produced by Public Broadcast Laboratory of NET. 1968. *Indiana University.* (83 min)

Martin Luther King Jr.: A Man of Peace

The film centers on Dr. King receiving

the Nobel Peace Prize and his work in the Southern Christian Leadership Conference. King explains his philosophy of achieving racial equality through the use of nonviolence. Provides a look at the man, the minister, the father, and the leader of the civil rights movement. Produced by Walter Schwimmer, Inc. 1964. *Journal Films.* (30 min)

Martin Luther King Jr.: From Montgomery to Memphis

Excellent use of newsreel footage to cover the major events in Martin Luther King's civil rights struggles from the Montgomery bus boycotts through Memphis. *Bailey-Film Associates.* (27 min)

A Mask for Me, A Mask for You

A lonely little boy finds his way to the Watts Towers Art Center and finds companionship and satisfaction in creating masks and other art projects. Poor sound track, but some good visuals. 1969. *Universal Educational & Visual Arts.* (16 min)

Memory of John Earl

A black teenager refuses to submit to rude treatment by a white storekeeper and is chased and threatened with a gun by some rednecks. Powerful recreation of an actual incident in the life of the young filmmaker, John McFadden. Produced 1968. *Youth Film Distribution Center.* (6 min)

Migrant

A study of migrant workers, including many blacks and Chicanos, in Florida. Reveals problems of housing, sanitation, working conditions, schooling, and racial discrimination. 1970. Marten Car, Dir. *NBC* (52 min)

Move

Black children in third- and fourth-grade classes in Washington, D.C. learn to make animated films. Role playing is used to create the stories and sound tracks, then simple crayon pictures are drawn in sequence on paper and animated. Three short finished films are included. By Vilma Berarducci. 1971. (16 min)

My Childhood

A distinctive two-part film: part one is on Hubert Humphrey; part two, which may be used separately, is on the early years of James Baldwin.

Brilliantly directed by Arthur Barron. Produced by Metromedia Television. 1964. *Benchmark Films.* (51 min)

The Negro and the American Promise

Dr. Martin Luther King, Jr., Malcolm X, Dr. Kenneth Clark, and James Baldwin discuss their motivations, doctrines, methods, goals, and place in the American Negro's movement for social and racial equality. *Indiana University.* (60 min)

Nene de la Ruta Mora

A small boy, Nenen, from the village of Loiza Aldea, meets the "vejigante" (bogeyman) who takes him to the Fiesta de Santiago, celebrated annually by Puerto Ricans. The film shows the African and Spanish influence present in the culture. In Spanish. *Quality Film Labs.* (23 min)

Nigeria: Giant in Africa

The vastness of the country and the diverse nature of its 40 million people are stressed in this carefully documented study of the culture and geography of Nigeria. The history of the country is told through early prints and newsreel footage. Produced for the National Film Board of Canada by Ronald Dick. 1960. *McGraw-Hill.* (52 min)

No Vietnamese Ever Called Me Nigger

Three black G.I.s discuss their experiences in Vietnam, the racism that exists in the armed forces, and their dissatisfaction with life in the United States upon their return. This is intercut with scenes of a black Anti-Vietnam War protest march. By David Loeb Weiss. 1969. *Bob Maurice Paradigm.* (68 min)

Now Is The Time

Chronicles the history of the American black through emergence from the slave state over 300 years ago to 1968 where rights and equal status are demanded. Combines the sounds and rhythms of the violence of race riots with folk, rock, and hymnal music and the works of Langston Hughes, Countee Cullen, James Baldwin, Malcolm X, and Stokely Carmichael. Produced by WCAU-TV, Philadelphia. 1967. *Carousel Films.* (36 min)

The Nuer

The Nuer, a tribe of Ethiopia and the Sudan, are depicted in this beautifully photographed and detailed study. 1970. (75 min)

OF BLACK AMERICA (series title):

Black History: Lost, Stolen or Strayed

Bill Cosby reviews the achievement of Negroes which our history books have omitted and shows how Negroes have been denied recognition of their contributions to American culture. Produced by CBS News. 1968. (2 films, each 27 min)

Black World

A worldwide panel discussion in which Mike Wallace interviews prominent blacks of many countries to reveal their social and cultural problems and their reactions to current racial and political problems. Produced by CBS News. 1968. (2 films, each 26 min)

Portrait in Black and White

By means of a public opinion poll, the film explores the attitudes of blacks and whites toward each other, and the misconceptions and prejudices of each group. Produced by CBS News. 1968. (2 films, each 27 min)

The Heritage of Slavery

Traces the history of the Emancipation and explains the freed slave and his descendants; also shows the debilitating effect of slavery on the nation's social and economic life. Produced by CBS News. 1968. (2 films, each 26 min)

The Black Soldier

Surveys the black American's participation in U.S. wars, from the Revolution to the Vietnamese conflict. Produced by CBS News. 1968. (25 min)

People Who Fix Things

A black airplane mechanic, a young man who repairs musical instruments, and a tree surgeon—three workers with special repair skills talk about the satisfaction of fine craftsmanship and why they enjoy their service jobs. Directed by Paul Boorstin. 1971. (19 min)

People Who Make Things

A glimpse into the working lives of three people who are excited by and take pride in their creative skills: a young woman who designs and constructs huge wooden dolls, a young black man who is an apprentice cake decorator, and a man who works in a custom car shop.

Phyllis and Terry

Life in one of New York's ghettos as experienced by two Negro teenagers. Completely improvised, the film lets Phyllis and Terry display their wit and outspoken friendship against a background of city neighborhood. Directed by Eugene and Carol Marner. 1965. *Center for Mass Communications of Columbia University.* (35 min)

The Professionals: Basketball

Interviews famous basketball stars and team members including Wilt Chamberlain, then of the Philadelphia 76ers, and Jerry West of the Los Angeles Lakers, and shows them in action. Produced by Warner Brothers-Seven Arts. *Warner Brothers-Seven Arts.* (30 min)

Prudence Crandall

Depicts the life of nineteenth-century New England schoolteacher Prudence Crandall, who tried to open an integrated girls' school against legal and social opposition. One of the Profiles in Courage television series. For older children. Produced by Robert Saudek Associates. 1964. *Robert Saudek.* (50 min)

Rafer Johnson Story

Relates the story of Olympic decathlon champion Rafer Johnson, his early life, and his eventual triumph as one of the most honored athletes in the world. Produced by David Wolper Productions. 1964. *Sterling.* (55 min)

A. Phillip Randolph

Biography of the black labor leader who succeeded in gaining recognition for Pullman Car Porters' Union. Includes newsreel footage and an interview in which Mr. Randolph recalls his confrontations with Roosevelt and Kennedy and speaks of his continuing struggle for job equality for black Americans. Rediscovery Productions. 1971. (10 min)

Willis Reed: Center Play

Willis Reed demonstrates some of the basketball techniques that have made him famous. *Schloat Productions.* (2 parts, 10 min)

River Nile

An exploration in rich color of the course of the Nile River. Describes the civilizations that have flourished on its banks throughout history. Narrated by James Mason. Produced by Lou Hazam for NBC News. Photographed by Guy Blanchard. Directed by Ray Garner. 1962. *McGraw-Hill.* (52 min)

The Seasons Change

A report on the events surrounding the 1968 Democratic National Convention in Chicago, with emphasis on the civil rights issues involved in the interaction of police, demonstrators, and bystanders. Includes interviews with demonstrators, reporters, bystanders, convention delegates, police officials, supporters of Mayor Daley, Rennie Davis, Tom Hayden, Allen Ginsberg, Dick Gregory, Jay Miller of the American Civil Liberties Union, and others, intercut with scenes of the violence which occurred. By William Jersey. 1968. (60 min)

Sit In

A highly dramatic news analysis of the sit-in movement as it occurred in Nashville at the beginning of the sixties. The very objectivity of the film confirms the courage of the students in the face of intransigence. An NBC White Paper produced by Al Wasserman. Narrated by Chet Huntley. 1961. *McGraw-Hill.* (54 min)

Some of My Best Friends Are White

A provocative examination of America's racial problem as discussed from the point of view of the middle-class Negro involving his acceptance by society and the future of his children growing up in white suburbia. A BBC-TV production. Produced by Michael Latham. 1967. *Robeck.* (30 min)

Something to Build On

A survey of new college possibilities for black students, including a review of innovative programs, scholarship and loan information throughout the country. A Chamba Production, directed by St. Claire Bourne. 1971. (29 min)

Still a Brother: Inside the Negro Middle Class

Documents the economic, social and personal life of America's black middle-class, constituting approximately 25% of the black population. Through conversations with prominent Negroes and a study of various trends in behavior, examines the conflict between the middle-class black's personal aspirations and his commitment to the general black movement. Narrated by Ossie Davis. Produced by William Greaves and William Brance. 1967. *McGraw-Hill.* (90 min)

A Story, A Story

A beautifully executed animation of the book by Gail Haley. Anasi, a hero of African folklore, uses his wits to win a box of stories from the sky god. Narrated in the rich, West Indian accent of John Akar. (10 min)

Street of the Flower Boxes

Documents the efforts of a young boy and the people on his block to change a slum neighborhood into a more attractive and humane environment. *NBC Educational Enterprises.* (48 min)

Sunday on the River

A sensitive and poetic documentary in which members of a Harlem social club take an excursion boat trip on the Hudson River. In an atmosphere of quiet relief the Sunday tourists picnic and play, enjoying to the full their limited escape from cramped city quarters. Traditional Negro songs sung by George Tipton. Produced by Gordon Hitchens and Ken Resnick. 1961. *Hitchens.* (26 min)

Tauw

A day in the life of a young African, the eldest son of a poor family, as he tries to find employment and to deal with the tensions in his family created by hunger, the breakdown of old tribal ways, and a society in transition. Filmed in Dakar, Senegal. By Ousmane Sembene. 1970. (27 min)

The Tenement

A vivid and moving cross section of a Chicago slum dwelling and of the people who inhabit it. Their despair, their feeling, and their delicate hopes are expressed in their own words. Produced by CBS News. 1967. *Carousel.* (40 min)

A Time for Burning

Cinema verité account of a young minister's attempt and failure, to lead his congregation to taking one small step toward integration and intergroup relations in his church in Omaha. Made by William Jersey and Barbara Connell, for the Lutheran Film Associates. 1966. *Contemporary/McGraw-Hill.* (58 min)

Time of the Horn

A small black boy finds an old horn and imagines he is a great trumpeter. Has a fine jazz background. By Russell Merritt. *Journal Films.* (7 min)

Troublemakers

A moving *cinema verité* account of an unsuccessful attempt by the Students for a Democratic Society and the people of a Newark, New Jersey ghetto neighborhood to improve the living conditions of the community. Made by Robert Machover and Norman Fruchter. 1966. *Blue Van Films.* (54 min)

220 Blues

Sonny is a star high school track man, a good candidate for a college athletic scholarship, and promising future architect. His values are challenged by Larry, another young black student, who is militant and determined to make Sonny choose a side. A study

of awakening racial awareness, this is an open-ended, unresolved film intended to open discussions of issues raised. Directed by Richard Gilbert. 1970. (23 min)

Veronica

Intimate portrait of a black teenager in New Haven, Connecticut. Veronica Glover is a pretty, popular girl who finds herself torn between the demands of black classmates and her efforts to understand and be herself. Produced, directed, and edited by Pat Powell; photographed by Roger Murphy. 1969. *Jason Films.* (28 min)

The Way It Is

Documents the efforts of a New York University team of teachers and educators to redesign teaching methods and establish new ones in a ghetto Junior High School in Williamsburg, Brooklyn. Actual footage of classroom activity, which is often shocking and seemingly unbelievable, shows how it "really is." 1967. *Indiana University.* (58 min)

The Weapons of Gordon Parks

The story of the internationally known *Negro Life* magazine photographer seen at work, in his home, with his family, and on the streets of Harlem, as part of his past life is recreated. An inspiring and moving photographic essay. Directed by Warren Forma. 1967. *Contemporary/McGraw-Hill.* (28 min)

What Harvest for the Reaper?

A documentary which describes how a group of black farmworkers, recruited in Arkansas to work on farms in Long Island, get trapped in a system that keeps them perpetually in debt. Growers and processers are interviewed and the labor camps and working conditions are shown. Produced by NET. 1968. *Indiana University.* (59 min)

DISTRIBUTORS

Atlantis Productions, Inc.
894 Sheffield Place
Thousand Oaks, California 91360

Bailey-Film Associates
11559 Santa Monica Boulevard
Los Angeles, California 90025

Harold Becker
295 Fifth Avenue
New York, New York 10016
(212) 689-6160

Blue Van Films
28 West 31st Street

New York, New York 10001
(212) 524-4570

Brandon Films Inc.
221 West 57th Street
New York, New York 10019
(212) 246-4868

Carousel Films Inc.
1501 Broadway
New York, New York 10036
(212) 279–6734

Center for Mass Communications of Columbia University
440 West 110th Street
New York, New York 10025
(212) 865-2000, ext. 16

Contemporary/McGraw-Hill Films
330 West 42nd Street
New York, New York 10036
(212) 971-3333

Encyclopaedia Britannica Educational Corporation
180 East Post Road
White Plains, New York 10601
(914) 949-4142

William Greaves Production, Inc.
254 West 54th Street
New York, New York 10019
(212) 586-7710

Grove Press Cinema 16 Library
80 University Place
New York, New York 10003
(212) 677-2400

Gordon Hitchens
838 West End Avenue
New York, New York 10025
(212) 749-1652

Indiana University
Audio-Visual Center
Bloomington, Indiana 47401

International Film Foundation, Inc.
Julien Bryan, Executive Director
475 Fifth Avenue
New York, New York 10017
(212) 685-4998

Jason Films
2621 Palisade Avenue
Riverdale, New York 10463
(212) 884-7648

Journal Films
909 West Diversey Parkway
Chicago, Illinois 60614

Landmark Educational Media
1600 Broadway
New York, New York 10019
(212) 581-1090

McGraw-Hill (see Contemporary/McGraw-Hill)

NET (see Indiana University)

New York Times Library Services Dept.
229 West 43rd Street
New York, New York 10036
(212) 556-1234

Paradigm Films
2248 Broadway
New York, New York 10024
(212) 799-7543

Quality Film Laboratories, Inc.
450 West 56th Street
New York, New York 10019
(212) 586-4912

Reaction Films/Intext
Scranton, Pennsylvania 18515

Peter M. Robeck & Company, Inc.
230 Park Avenue
New York, New York 10017
(212) 689-2687

Robert Saudek Assoc.
630 Fifth Avenue
New York, New York 10020
(212) 581-1070

Sterling Educational Films
241 East 34th Street
New York, New York 10016
(212) 683-6300

Universal Education & Visual Arts
221 Park Avenue South
New York, New York 10003
(212) 777-6600

University of California Extension Media Center
Film Distribution
2223 Fulton Street
Berkeley, California 94720

Warner Brothers-Seven Arts
666 Fifth Avenue
New York, New York 10019
(212) 986-1717

Youth Film Distribution Center
4 West 16th Street
New York, New York 10011
(212) 989-7265

THE CURRENT STATUS OF BLACK EDUCATION

School Enrollment

In 1978 blacks comprised 6.6 million of the 41.6 million Americans enrolled in public elementary and secondary schools. This was 15.8% of the total enrollment. In 1974, 6.7 million blacks were enrolled, representing 14.5% of the total.

Thirty eight percent of black pupils attended schools that were more than 50% white, an increase from 1968 when only 23% of students attended schools with white majorities. However, as noted elsewhere in this section, nearly one third of the nation's schools and classrooms contained fewer than 10% whites and so could be classified as racially isolated.

When nursery schools were considered, blacks comprised a larger share of enrollment, 7.7 million out of 45 million, or 17% of the total. In 1960 blacks represented 13% of the total and in 1970, 14.8%. In 1979, 35% of public school students in central cities were black, compared with 30% in 1970 and 21% in 1960.

An increasing number of blacks attended private schools during the 1970s. In 1970 only 4% of students in private secondary schools and 6% in private elementary schools were black. In 1979 the figures had risen to 8 and 10%, respectively.

By 53 to 51%, a larger proportion of black than white children were enrolled in preprimary schools in 1979.

Educational Attainment

The proportion of the black population with fewer than five years of school has been declining rapidly, from 15% in 1970 to 10% in 1979. During the same period the percentage of blacks with four years or more of high school rose from 31 to 49%. In 1979 nearly one third of the black population 65 years of age and

Chart 1. Median School Years Completed

In 1960 the median of school years completed for blacks was 8.0 while for whites it was 10.9, a difference of three years. In 1979 the gap was only a half year.

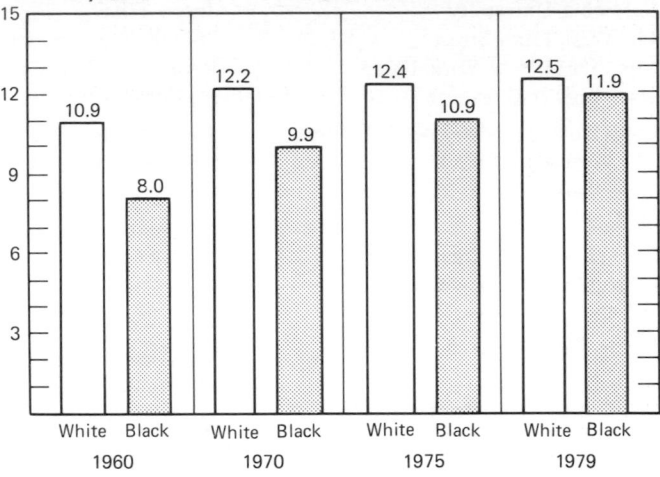

over had completed less than 5 years of school, and only 17% had four years of high school or more education.

Median years of school completed in 1979 were 11.9 for blacks and 12.5 for whites, compared to 9.9 for blacks and 12.2 for whites in 1970.

The rate of school dropouts fell for blacks and rose for whites during the 1970s. The black rate fell from 22.2 to 17.5%; the white increased from 10.8 to 11.5%.

Chart 2. Percentage of Adults Completing Four Years of High School or More: 1950 to 1979

The proportion of black adults who have completed high school nearly tripled between 1950 and 1979.

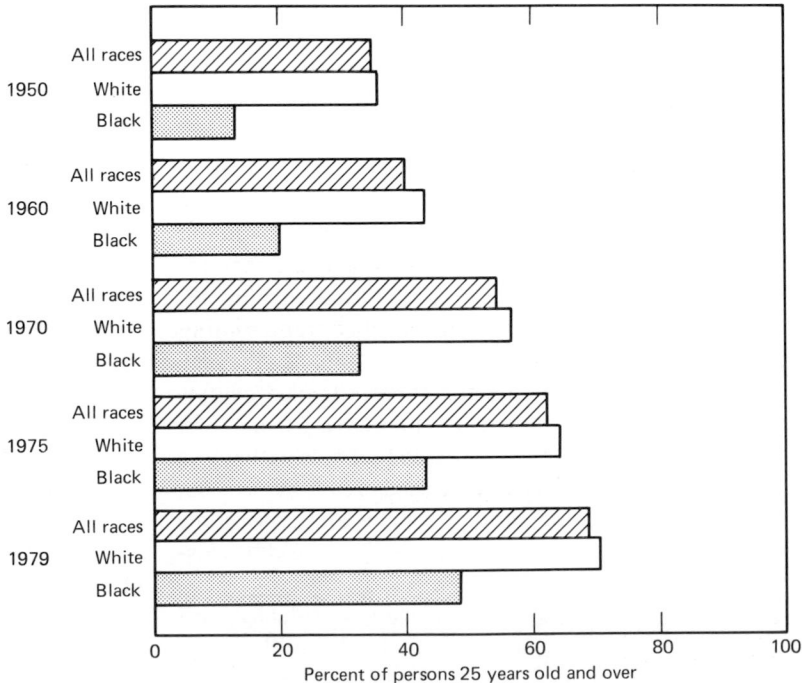

Percent of persons 25 years old and over

Source: Adapted from chart prepared by U.S. Bureau of the Census.

Chart 3. Distribution of Vocational Studies by Racial/Ethnic Group and Sex

More than one-fourth of the vocational students who attended comprehensive and vocational high schools were from minority groups. Minorities accounted for smaller proportions of vocational education enrollments in postsecondary institutions.

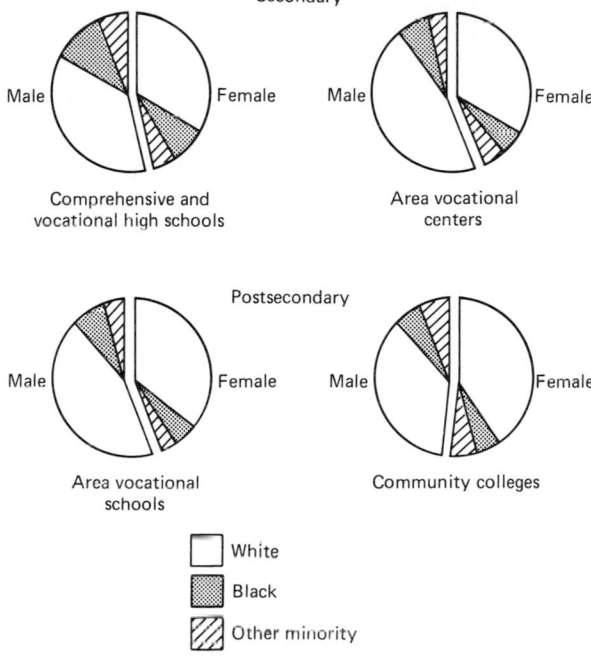

Vocational Schools

In 1979 blacks were registered in comprehensive and vocational high schools in proportions larger than their rate of the total population. Nearly 19% of students enrolled in comprehensive and vocational high schools are black, as was 11% of the instructional staff. Blacks were represented to a lesser degree in area secondary and postsecondary vocational centers and community colleges.

Black students in vocational education institutions generally specialized in traditionally female areas, such as home economics, consumer studies and homemaking, and health and office occupations.

SELECTED FACTS

Fact 1
In 1978, 44% of public schools in the Northeast and Midwest were classified as racially isolated, that is, over 90% minority. In the South less than one fourth (24%) were racially isolated, and in the West only 18%.

Fact 2
Approximately three of every five blacks over 25 years of age who live in the West, North Central, and Northeastern states have graduated from high school. In the South, however, only two in every five blacks over 25 are high school graduates.

Fact 3
In central cities over 20% of white students are enrolled in private schools, compared with only 9% of blacks. However, the proportion of blacks in public schools has more than tripled since 1970.

Fact 4
In the nation as a whole, blacks comprise 16% of the public school population but only 10% of pupils enrolled in programs for the talented and gifted. In the South 27% of the school population and only 12% of students in such programs are black. In the Northeast and Midwest, however, the proportion of blacks in such programs is about the same as their overall rate of public school enrollment.

Fact 5
A larger proportion of black than white high school seniors are enrolled in high school vocational training programs. The difference is most marked in home economics where 3½% of black seniors and less than 1% of whites are enrolled.

Fact 6
In 1978 blacks more than whites were subject to disciplinary actions in high school. Blacks constituted 16% of enrollment but 28% of explusions, suspensions, and recipients of corporal punishment.

Chart 4. Minority Distribution in Schools

In 1980 a large percentage of blacks were still enrolled in schools that had fewer than 10% white students. Areas demonstrating the highest proportion of racially isolated schools are in border states and the midwest.

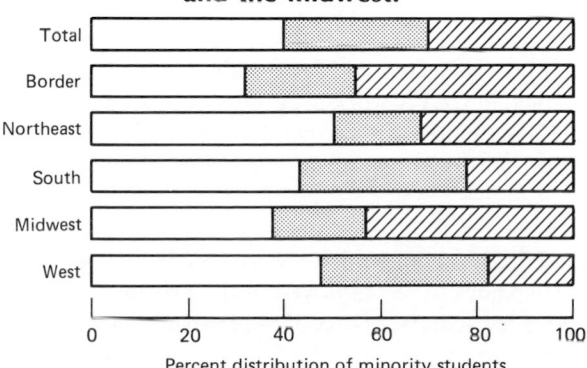

Chart 5. High School Graduates among Population 25 Years Old and Over by Region and Racial/Ethnic Group

The largest discrepancy between black and white high school graduates is in the South where some 25% fewer blacks are high school graduates.

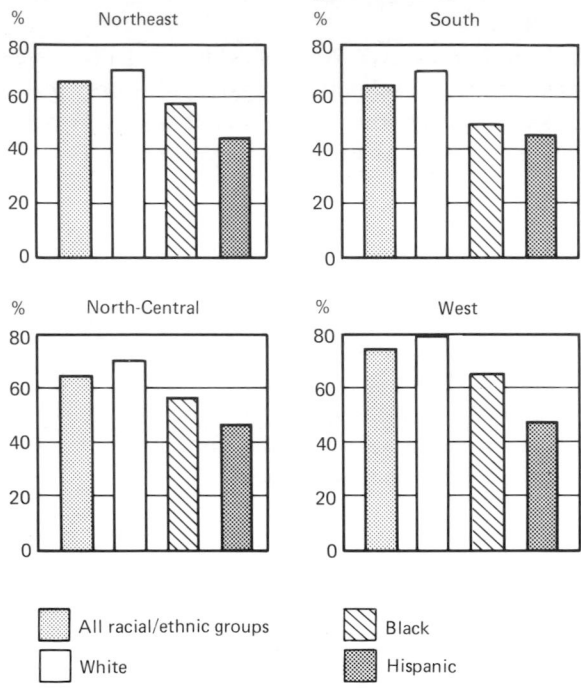

All racial/ethnic groups
White
Black
Hispanic

Fact 7

Blacks in the labor force have closed the racial gap in the number of school years completed. In 1959 only 16% of blacks and 32% of whites in the workforce had completed high school. In 1979, 40% of whites and 37% of black workers were high school graduates.

Fact 8

The proportion of whites in the work force who have college degrees remains more than twice that of black workers. In 1959 the ratio was 10% white, 4% black; in 1979 it was 18% white and 9% black.

Fact 9

In June 1980, 26% of black high school seniors were enrolled in CETA work programs, compared with only 5.4% of whites. In cooperative education, however, the proportions were closer, 12.6% black, 9.7% white.

Fact 10

Black high school students were less likely than whites or Hispanics to be employed in the private sector. The figures for seniors: blacks 35%, Hispanics 43%, whites 58%.

Fact 11

In 1976 more than three times as many doctoral degrees were conferred on nonresident aliens as on black citizens of the United States.

Fact 12

In 1976 approximately one fifth of black students pursuing professional programs were enrolled in historically black colleges.

Fact 13

Black colleges continue to be the predominant source of professional degrees in many areas of the South. Meharry Medical College conferred 96% of the dentistry and 92% of the medical degrees awarded blacks in Tennessee. Texas Southern conferred two thirds of all law degrees awarded blacks in Texas, and Howard 92% of the dentistry and 84% of the medical degrees awarded blacks residing in the District of Columbia.

Fact 14

Black college students are more likely than whites to suffer from withdrawal of financial aid. In 1974 the college dropout rate for blacks receiving financial aid was 24%, but it was 46% for blacks receiving no aid. For whites, the rates were 21% when aid was received, 29% for whites without aid.

Fact 15

A child walking to or from school is three times more likely to be injured in an accident as is a child who is being bused.

Fact 16

In 1976, 50% of the children in the United States were being bused to school. Only 3½%, however, were being bused for desegregation purposes.

Fact 17

Segregation often required more busing than integration, because blacks were frequently bused past white schools. After desegregation in Tennessee, the number of students transported declined by 20,000 and the number of miles traveled by 1,900,000 per school year. In Georgia, 14,000 more students were bused, but miles traveled dropped by 474,000 per school year.

Table 1. Median Years of School Completed (25 and over)

	1970	1975
Blacks	9.8	10.9
Whites	12.1	12.4

Source: U.S. Census, *The Social and Economic Status of the Black Population in the U.S.: An Historical View, 1790–1978,* Series P-23, No. 80, p. 93.

Table 2. School Enrollment (3–34 Years), Percent Change: 1970–1978

	White	Black
Nursery	63	75.3
Kindergarten	−9.4	5.9
Elementary	−17.9	−10.5
High school	1.4	24 1
College	26.0	95.4

Source: U.S. Census, *Population Profile of the U.S.: 1978,* No. 336, April 1979, p. 20.

Table 3. Masters Degrees Awarded to Blacks: 1964–1976

Year	Annual Increase (%)	Percentage of Total
1964		16.4
1970		19.6
1971	10.7	20.2
1972	9.2	20.7
1973	4.8	20.7
1974	5.2	21.1
1975	5.6	22.4
1976	6.6	23.4

Source: James R. Mingle, *Degree Output in the South, 1975–76: Distribution by Race* (Georgia: Southern Regional Education Board, 1978), p. 3.)

Table 4. First Year U.S. Medical School Enrollments

Year	Number		Percentage	
	Black	White	Black	White
1974–1975	1,106	12,595	7.5	85.3
1975–1976	1,036	13,156	6.8	86.0
1976–1977	1,046	13,383	6.7	85.7
1977–1978	1,085	13,732	6.7	85.1
1978–1979	1,061	14,048	6.4	85.1

Source: "U.S. Medical Student Enrollment, 1974–75 through 1978–79," Datagram.

Table 5. Total Enrollment—U.S. Law Schools

Year	Number		Percentage Black
	Black	White	
1978–1979	5,350	121,606	4.39
1977–1978	5,305	118,557	4.47
1976–1977	5,503	117,451	4.69
1975–1976	2,127	116,991	4.38
1974–1975	4,995	110,713	4.51

Source: American Bar Association, *A Review of Legal Education in the United States,* Fall 1978 (Chicago: American Bar Association, 1979), pp. 60, 63.

Table 6. Total Black Scientists: 1976 (%)

Specialization	Black	White
Computer specialists	1.6	96.3
Engineers	0.7	96.7
Mathematical specialists	3.8	93.2
Life scientists	1.4	96.2
Physical scientists	1.6	94.3
Environmental scientists	0.1	98.1
Psychologists	1.6	97.9
Social scientists	1.7	96.0

Source: Digest of Educational Statistics, 1979 ed. (Washington, D.C.: Department of Health, Education and Welfare, 1977), p. 190.

Table 7. Minority Student Enrollment by Minority Composition of Schools and Classrooms in Public Elementary/Secondary Schools, by Region: Fall 1978

Region	Minority Enrollment (thousands)	Percentage of Total Enrollment	Composition of Schools (percent distribution)				Composition of Classrooms (percent distribution)			
			Total	Predominantly White (0 to 49.9% of enrollment)	Predominantly Minority (50 to 89.9% of enrollment)	Racially Isolated (90 to 100% of enrollment)	Total	0 to 44.9% of enrollment	45 to 89.9% of enrollment	90 to 100% of enrollment
Total 50 states and D.C.	10,326	25	100	40	30	30	100	32	35	33
Northeast	1,772	21	100	30	25	45	100	24	28	48
Border states and D.C.	734	21	100	47	20	33	100	39	26	35
South	4,047	35	100	41	34	24	100	31	40	29
Midwest	1,517	15	100	38	19	43	100	34	23	43
West	2,099	28	100	46	36	18	100	38	40	22
Alaska/Hawaii	157	61	100	12	54	33	100	10	49	41

Source: U.S. Department of Education, Office for Civil Rights, *State, Regional, and National Summaries of Data from the Fall 1978 Civil Rights Survey of Elementary and Secondary Schools,* 1980.

Note: Details may not add to totals because of rounding.

Table 8. Minority Enrollment in Public Elementary and Secondary Schools, by Minority-Group School Enrollment, 1976 and 1978, and by States, 1978[a]

| State | Total Minority Enroll-ment[b] (thousands) | Minority-Group School Enrollment | | | | |
| | | Under 50% | | 90–100% | 99–100% | |
		Total (thousands)	Per-cent	(thousands)	Number (thousands)	Per-cent
Total, 1976	10,747.0	4,287.0	39.9	3,379.8	1,829.2	17.0
Total, 1978	10,336.5	4,088.4	39.6	3,115.6	1,663.9	16.1
Alabama	252.4	104.8	41.5	88.4	60.3	23.9
Alaska	25.0	12.5	50.1	8.8	3.7	14.7
Arizona	171.9	69.6	40.4	37.3	4.1	2.4
Arkansas	103.6	50.6	48.9	4.4	.8	.8
California	1,487.0	621.6	41.8	311.5	152.0	10.2
Colorado	112.6	73.1	64.9	.7	1	.1
Connecticut	93.3	47.4	50.9	25.0	7.9	8.5
Delaware	29.2	27.6	94.4	—	—	—
D.C.	109.4	.7	.6	103.0	87.4	79.9
Florida	466.1	258.3	55.4	70.5	18.1	3.9
Georgia	351.5	136.2	38.7	95.6	55.1	15.7
Hawaii	131.9	6.1	4.6	44.1	.7	.5
Idaho	11.9	11.3	94.0	—	—	—
Illinois	567.0	124.9	22.0	359.4	287.5	50.7
Indiana	119.3	57.7	48.4	36.5	22.6	19.0
Iowa	21.5	19.7	91.7	.1	.1	.2
Kansas	48.8	40.2	82.3	3.8	2.3	4.7
Kentucky	61.4	53.8	87.7	1.3	1.2	1.9
Louisiana	337.1	125.8	37.3	118.4	81.7	24.2
Maine	2.0	2.0	100.0	—	—	—
Maryland	259.9	105.7	40.7	75.2	54.2	20.8
Massachusetts	98.8	48.5	49.1	1.0	—	—
Michigan	334.1	102.0	30.5	140.1	86.6	25.9
Minnesota	38.5	35.3	91.7	.2	—	—
Mississippi	236.0	67.8	28.7	71.7	36.6	15.5
Missouri	136.9	48.6	35.5	64.7	42.9	31.3
Montana	13.0	8.5	64.9	2.7	.4	2.9
Nebraska	22.8	18.5	81.0	.8	.8	3.3
Nevada	24.9	22.6	90.7	.5	—	—
New Hampshire	1.7	1.7	100.0	—	—	—
New Jersey	345.5	113.7	32.9	140.4	54.4	15.8
New Mexico	151.1	41.3	27.3	27.9	2.5	1.7
New York	948.2	216.0	22.8	502.0	256.7	27.1
North Carolina	368.9	228.5	62.0	17.5	4.9	1.3
North Dakota	7.6	3.0	38.8	3.4	1.7	22.7
Ohio	300.9	117.2	38.9	102.6	64.6	21.5
Oklahoma	127.4	95.0	74.6	5.4	.1	.1
Oregon	33.2	30.2	91.0	.1	—	—
Pennsylvania	284.5	90.4	31.8	132.9	81.5	28.6
Rhode Island	11.8	9.9	83.4	—	—	—
South Carolina	266.4	105.5	39.6	38.8	21.2	8.0
South Dakota	9.9	7.5	76.1	.7	.1	.5
Tennessee	184.1	69.9	37.9	55.1	27.2	14.8
Texas	1,144.1	361.4	31.6	393.8	131.1	11.5
Utah	23.6	21.8	92.3	1.0	.1	.4
Vermont	.6	.6	100.0	—	—	—
Virginia	283.2	138.6	48.9	16.1	3.0	1.1
Washington	79.7	64.5	80.9	.9	.1	.1
West Virginia	21.3	19.3	91.0	.7	.7	3.4
Wisconsin	66.7	44.2	66.3	10.6	7.0	10.5
Wyoming	8.1	6.9	84.7	.3	—	—

Source: U.S. Office for Civil Rights, *State and National Summaries of Data Collected by The Elementary and Secondary Schools Civil Rights Survey, 1976* and *1978*.

[a] As of fall. "Minority group" refers to blacks, American Indians, Alaskan natives, Asian or Pacific islanders, and Hispanics. Data are based on a survey of public school districts with a substantial minority-group enrollment. Extent of undercoverage (school districts not included) will vary by state.

[b] Includes categories not shown separately.

Table 9. School Enrollment, by Race, Level, and Age: 1965–1979 [a]

Year and Age	White Total Enrolled [b]	White Elementary	White High School	White College	Black Total Enrolled [b]	Black Elementary	Black High School	Black College
1965, total	47,450	30,327	11,356	5,317	6,675	4,866	1,472	274
3 and 4 years	731	318	—	—	155	92 [c]	—	—
5–13 years	29,636	29,170	427	—	4,518	4,479	39	—
14–17 years	11,327	825	10,269	233	1,561	285	1,246	30
18–24 years	4,834	6	616	4,213	391	4	177	210
25–34 years	922	8	44	871	50	6	10	34
1970, total	51,719	31,348	12,723	6,759	7,829	5,294	1,834	522
3 and 4 years	1,181	358	—	—	250	95	—	—
5–13 years	30,460	30,066	327	—	4,997	4,915	61	—
14–17 years	12,769	898	11,639	230	1,862	279	1,558	21
18–24 years	5,979	14	661	5,304	610	5	188	416
25–34 years	1,326	5	95	1,224	109	—	23	85
1975, total	51,430	28,257	13,225	8,514	8,400	4,978	2,201	948
3 and 4 years	1,697	357	—	—	344	94	—	—
5–13 years	27,387	27,004	295	—	4,731	4,647	60	—
14–17 years	13,312	880	12,176	253	2,138	231	1,873	34
18–24 years	6,789	8	666	6,115	920	4	252	665
25–34 years	2,246	12	90	2,147	266	2	16	248
1978, total	48,843	25,973	12,893	8,514	8,416	4,809	2,278	1,020
3 and 4 years	1,622	249	—	—	385	93	—	—
5–13 years	25,353	24,968	300	—	4,566	4,501	45	—
14–17 years	12,859	737	11,892	229	2,208	207	1,964	38
18–24 years	6,738	13	644	6,077	958	8	256	694
25–34 years	2,271	6	57	2,207	300	—	13	288
1979, total	48,225	25,396	12,583	8,709	8,317	4,792	2,245	1,003
3 and 4 years	1,694	255	—	—	385	125	—	—
5–13 years	24,780	24,441	244	—	4,526	4,440	68	—
14–17 years	12,511	684	11,572	258	2,173	221	1,908	43
18–24 years	6,829	10	699	6,122	955	4	256	697
25–34 years	2,411	10	68	2,331	278	3	12	263
Percent change in total								
1965–1970	9.1	3.4	12.0	27.1	17.3	9.5	24.6	90.5
1970–1975	−.6	−9.9	3.9	26.0	7.3	−6.5	20.0	81.6
1975–1979	−6.2	−10.1	−4.9	2.3	−1.0	−3.7	2.0	5.8

[a] In thousands, except percent. As of October.

[b] Includes nursery schools, not shown separately.

[c] Data for Black and other races.

Table 10. Percentage Enrolled in School, by Age, Sex, and Race: 1970–1979

Item	3–4 Years	5–6 Years	7–9 Years	10–13 Years	14–15 Years	16–17 Years	18–19 Years	20–24 Years	25–34 Years
1970, total[a]	20.5	89.5	99.3	99.2	98.1	90.0	47.7	21.5	6.0
Male	21.2	88.9	99.3	98.8	98.2	91.3	54.4	29.3	8.4
Female	19.8	90.2	99.3	99.5	98.1	88.6	41.6	15.2	3.8
White	19.9	90.3	99.3	99.1	98.2	90.6	48.7	22.5	6.1
Black	22.7	84.9	99.3	99.3	97.6	85.7	40.1	14.2	4.2
1975, total[a]	31.5	94.7	99.4	99.3	98.2	89.0	46.9	22.4	8.5
Male	30.9	94.4	99.2	98.9	98.4	90.7	49.9	26.4	10.7
Female	32.1	95.1	99.5	99.6	98.0	87.2	44.2	18.7	6.5
White	30.8	94.8	99.4	99.3	98.3	89.3	46.5	22.7	8.5
Black	34.2	94.5	99.3	99.1	97.4	86.8	47.1	19.9	8.3
1979, total[a]	35.1	95.8	99.2	99.1	98.1	89.2	45.0	21.7	8.1
Male	34.6	96.3	99.0	98.9	98.3	90.8	46.6	23.3	8.3
Female	35.6	95.2	99.4	99.4	97.9	87.6	43.4	20.2	7.8
White	33.9	95.8	99.2	99.2	98.2	89.0	44.5	22.0	8.1
Black	40.8	96.0	99.4	98.7	97.4	90.8	46.6	18.7	7.4

Source: U.S. Bureau of the Census, *Current Population Reports,* Series P-20, No. 346 and earlier reports; and unpublished data.

[a] Includes races not shown separately.

Table 11. Black and Hispanic Enrollment in Public Elementary and Secondary Schools: 1970–1978[a]

Item	1970	1974	1976	1978
Total enrollment (thousands)	44,910	45,988	43,540	41,571
Black (thousands)	6,713	6,684	6,772	6,565
Percent black				
Of total enrollment	14.9	14.5	15.6	15.8
By minority group enrollment in				
Schools under 50%	33.1	37.1	43.2	(NA)[b]
Schools 50–100%	66.9	63.0	56.8	(NA)
Schools 95–100%	38.2	33.6	(NA)	(NA)
Schools 100%	14.0	11.4	(NA)	(NA)

Item	1970	1974	1976	1978
Total enrollment (thousands)	44,910	45,988	43,540	41,571
Hispanic (thousands)	2,275	2,577	2,797	2,884
Percent Hispanic				
Of total enrollment	5.1	5.6	6.4	6.9
By minority group enrollment in				
Schools under 50%	44.2	42.3	40.1	(NA)
Schools 50–100%	55.8	57.8	59.9	(NA)
Schools 95–100%	16.3	(NA)	(NA)	(NA)
Schools 100%	1.8	1.2	(NA)	(NA)

Source: U.S. Department of Education, Office of the Assistant Secretary for Civil Rights, *Distribution of Students by Racial/Ethnic Composition of Schools, 1970–1976* (vol. I), and *State and National Summaries of Data Collected by the Elementary and Secondary Schools Civil Rights Survey, 1976 and 1978.*

[a] As of fall. Excludes Hawaii. Data are estimated from results of a survey of public school districts with a substantial minority group enrollment. "Minority group" refers to blacks, American Indians, Alaskan natives, Asian or Pacific islanders, and Hispanics.

[b] NA = not available.

Table 12. School Enrollment of Persons 5 to 17 Years Old, by Race and Residence: 1960–1979 [a]

Race and Residence	Total Enrolled (million)						Percentage of Total Enrollment					
	1960	1965	1970	1975	1978	1979	1960	1965	1970	1975	1978	1979
White persons, total	36.8	40.9	43.2	40.7	38.2	37.3	87.0	86.1	85.2	84.1	83.2	82.9
Inside SMSAs	22.3	26.3	26.8	27.1	24.6	23.9	86.8	85.9	83.8	82.3	81.1	80.2
Inside central cities	9.6	9.8	9.2	9.4	7.9	7.5	78.7	74.2	70.2	68.7	65.7	64.7
Outside central cities	12.6	16.5	17.6	17.8	16.7	16.4	94.0	94.8	93.6	91.8	91.2	90.1
Outside SMSAs	14.5	14.6	16.4	13.6	13.6	13.4	86.8	86.9	87.7	88.0	87.1	88.2
Black and other, total	5.5	6.6	7.5	7.7	7.7	7.7	13.0	13.9	14.8	15.9	16.8	17.1
Inside SMSAs	3.4	4.3	5.2	5.9	5.7	5.9	13.2	14.1	16.3	17.7	18.9	19.8
Inside central cities	2.6	3.4	3.9	4.3	4.1	4.1	21.3	25.8	29.8	31.3	34.3	35.3
Outside central cities	.8	.9	1.2	1.6	1.6	1.8	6.0	5.2	6.4	8.2	8.8	9.9
Outside SMSAs	2.2	2.2	2.3	1.8	2.0	1.8	13.2	13.1	12.3	11.9	12.9	11.8

Source: U.S. Bureau of the Census, *Current Population Reports*, Series P-20, No. 346 and earlier reports; and unpublished data.

[a] As of October. Beginning 1970, includes nursery schools. Based on Current Population Survey.

Table 13. Preprimary School Enrollment of Children 3 to 5 Years Old, by Race and Age, and by Labor Force Status of Mother: 1967–1979[a]

Race, Age, and Labor Force Status	Number of Children (thousands)							Percentage Enrolled of Population			
	1967	1970	1975	1976	1977	1978	1979	1967	1970	1975	1979
Population, 3–5 years old	12,234	10,877	10,183	9,726	9,249	9,110	9,119				
Total enrolled[b,c]	3,864	4,075	4,954	4,790	4,577	4,584	4,664	31.6	37.5	48.6	51.1
White	3,265	3,414	4,105	3,933	3,717	3,697	3,786	31.8	37.8	48.7	50.7
Black	535	585	731	745	728	749	750	29.8	34.9	48.1	53.3
3 years old	273	454	683	603	645	759	746	6.8	13.0	21.5	24.6
4 years old	870	1,003	1,418	1,348	1,290	1,313	1,393	21.3	27.9	40.5	45.4
5 years old	2,721	2,617	2,852	2,839	2,642	2,512	2,525	65.4	69.2	81.3	83.5
All Races[c]											
With mother in labor force[d]	1,353	1,345	2,168	2,136	2,092	2,173	2,353	34.2	38.8	54.0	55.1
3 and 4 years old	466	526	973	898	992	1,017	1,139	18.1	23.5	38.0	40.5
5 years old	887	818	1,195	1,237	1,100	1,156	1,214	63.8	66.6	82.5	83.4
Married, spouse present	1,140	1,131	1,733	1,708	1,649	1,727	1,922	34.1	39.5	53.6	55.1
Other marital status	213	214	435	428	444	446	431	34.6	36.0	56.0	55.0
Employed	1,249	1,246	1,948	1,960	1,881	2,000	2,158	34.5	39.3	55.1	56.1
Full-time	817	770	1,236	1,254	1,240	1,309	1,416	33.9	38.6	55.1	55.5
Part-time	432	476	712	706	641	691	742	35.7	40.4	55.1	57.3
Mother not in labor force	2,448	2,694	2,704	2,589	2,385	2,286	2,196	30.2	37.0	45.1	47.6

White											
With mother in labor force[d]	1,053	1,031	1,723	1,668	1,592	1,666	1,833	34.7	39.1	54.0	54.6
3 and 4 years old	340	374	740	567	740	750	872	17.4	22.1	36.6	39.3
5 years old	713	657	983	1,001	852	916	961	66.2	69.2	84.1	84.4
Married, spouse present	932	913	1,449	1,399	1,334	1,408	1,583	34.7	39.1	53.3	54.8
Other marital status	120	119	273	269	258	258	250	34.6	38.9	57.8	53.0
Employed	982	959	1,566	1,561	1,458	1,567	1,706	35.2	39.3	55.0	55.7
Full-time	613	557	941	936	912	959	1,068	33.8	38.2	54.3	54.9
Part-time	369	402	625	625	546	608	638	37.7	41.0	56.2	57.0
Mother not in labor force	2,166	2,354	2,331	2,220	2,057	1,945	1,867	30.5	37.4	45.3	47.5
Black											
With mother in labor force[d]	286	281	372	414	429	427	446	32.3	36.8	52.6	57.7
3 and 4 years old	122	138	191	202	214	231	235	20.7	27.3	41.0	46.2
5 years old	163	143	181	211	215	197	212	55.3	55.6	75.2	79.1
Married, spouse present	193	192	221	255	246	243	273	31.3	39.4	53.6	57.6
Other marital status	93	89	151	158	183	184	174	34.7	32.2	51.2	58.0
Employed	252	256	313	348	362	357	387	32.3	37.9	53.5	58.6
Full-time	194	195	244	282	292	289	307	34.4	39.0	56.7	58.2
Part-time	58	61	69	66	70	68	81	26.8	34.8	44.7	60.4
Mother not in labor force	236	298	330	312	269	286	277	26.9	33.9	44.1	47.9

Source: U.S. Bureau of the Census, *Current Population Reports*, Series P-20, No. 318; and unpublished data.

[a] As of October. Civilian noninstitutional population. Includes public and nonpublic nursery school and kindergarten programs. Excludes 5 year olds enrolled in elementary school. Based on Current Population Survey.

[b] Includes children with mothers whose labor force status is unknown and children with no mother present in household, not shown separately.

[c] Includes races not shown separately.

[d] Includes children with mothers who are unemployed, not shown separately.

Table 14. School Enrollment of Persons 3 to 34 Years Old, by Level and Control of School, Race, and Spanish Origin: October 1965 to October 1980 (thousands)

Level and Control of School	1965	1970	1971	1972	1973	1974	1975	1976	1977	1978	1979	1980
All Races												
Total enrolled	54,701	60,357	61,106	60,142	59,392	60,259	60,969	60,482	60,013	58,616	57,854	57,348
Nursery school	520	1,096	1,066	1,283	1,324	1,607	1,748	1,526	1,618	1,824	1,869	1,987
Public	127	333	317	402	400	423	574	476	562	587	636	633
Private	393	763	749	881	924	1,184	1,174	1,050	1,056	1,237	1,233	1,354
Kindergarten	3,057	3,183	3,263	3,135	3,074	3,252	3,393	3,490	3,191	2,989	3,025	3,176
Public	2,439	2,647	2,689	2,636	2,582	2,726	2,851	2,962	2,665	2,493	2,593	2,690
Private	618	536	574	499	493	526	542	528	526	496	432	486
Elementary school	32,474	33,950	33,507	32,242	31,469	31,126	30,446	29,774	29,234	28,490	27,865	27,449
Public	27,596	30,001	29,829	28,693	28,201	27,956	27,166	26,698	25,983	25,252	24,756	24,398
Private	4,878	3,949	3,678	3,549	3,268	3,169	3,279	3,075	3,251	3,238	3,109	3,051
High school	12,975	14,715	15,183	15,169	15,347	15,447	15,683	15,742	15,753	15,475	15,116	14,556
Public	11,517	13,545	14,057	14,015	14,162	14,275	14,503	14,541	14,505	14,231	13,994	(NA)
Private	1,457	1,170	1,126	1,155	1,184	1,172	1,180	1,201	1,248	1,244	1,122	(NA)
College	5,675	7,413	8,087	8,313	8,179	8,827	9,697	9,950	10,217	9,838	9,978	10,180
Public	3,840	5,699	6,271	6,337	6,224	6,905	7,704	7,739	7,925	7,427	7,699	(NA)
Private	1,835	1,714	1,816	1,976	1,955	1,922	1,994	2,211	2,292	2,410	2,280	(NA)
College:												
Full time	4,414	5,763	6,204	6,314	6,089	6,351	7,105	7,176	7,196	6,979	7,010	7,147
Percent	77.8	77.7	76.7	76.0	74.4	71.9	73.3	72.1	70.4	70.9	70.3	70.2
Part time	1,261	1,650	1,883	1,999	2,090	2,476	2,592	2,773	3,021	2,859	2,968	3,033
White												
Total enrolled	47,451	51,719	52,081	51,314	50,617	50,992	51,430	50,761	50,151	48,843	48,225	47,673
Nursery school	451	893	888	1,079	1,087	1,340	1,432	1,246	1,314	1,456	1,537	1,637
Public	93	198	225	285	242	293	392	318	372	351	428	432
Private	358	695	664	794	845	1,048	1,040	929	942	1,105	1,110	1,205
Kindergarten	2,648	2,706	2,735	2,633	2,584	2,745	2,845	2,881	2,611	2,452	2,437	2,595
Public	2,086	2,233	2,207	2,185	2,139	2,268	2,363	2,423	2,153	2,009	2,069	2,172
Private	562	473	527	448	445	477	483	457	458	444	368	423
Elementary school	27,679	28,638	28,187	27,185	26,531	26,051	25,412	24,776	24,262	23,524	22,959	22,510
Public	22,976	24,923	24,720	23,869	23,506	23,063	22,351	21,947	21,312	20,551	20,174	19,743
Private	4,703	3,715	3,466	3,316	3,025	2,990	3,059	2,829	2,950	2,973	2,785	2,768
High school	11,356	12,723	12,998	12,959	13,091	13,073	13,224	13,214	13,152	12,897	12,583	12,056
Public	9,961	11,599	11,937	11,876	11,967	11,966	12,112	12,093	11,980	11,741	11,549	(NA)
Private	1,395	1,124	1,061	1,083	1,124	1,107	1,112	1,121	1,172	1,156	1,033	(NA)
College	5,317	6,759	7,273	7,458	7,324	7,781	8,516	8,644	8,812	8,514	8,709	8,875
Public	3,568	5,168	5,624	5,644	5,550	6,049	6,724	6,657	6,743	6,368	6,672	(NA)
Private	1,749	1,591	1,650	1,814	1,773	1,732	1,792	1,987	2,069	2,145	2,037	(NA)

College											
Full time	6,212	6,058	5,974	6,165	6,170	6,183	5,575	5,408	5,678	5,560	5,221	4,111
Percent	70.0	69.6	70.2	70.0	71.4	72.6	71.6	73.8	76.1	76.4	77.2	77.3
Black												
Total enrolled	8,251	8,317	8,416	8,564	8,518	8,400	8,215	7,834	7,959	8,178	7,829	7,252[b]
Nursery school	294	278	312	250	226	276	227	210	185	151	178	72
Public	180	185	210	171	146	171	121	146	113	90	129	37
Private	115	93	102	78	80	105	106	64	72	61	49	35
Kindergarten	490	497	451	496	542	468	463	423	448	464	426	407
Public	440	443	414	447	482	426	416	391	402	422	374	353
Private	50	54	38	50	60	42	47	32	46	42	53	54
Elementary school	4,259	4,296	4,356	4,337	4,430	4,509	4,585	4,473	4,573	4,877	4,868	4,796
Public	4,058	4,053	4,154	4,156	4,256	4,344	4,455	4,277	4,382	4,712	4,668	4,620
Private	202	243	202	221	175	165	131	196	191	165	200	176
High school	2,200	2,245	2,276	2,327	2,258	2,199	2,125	2,044	2,025	2,006	1,834	1,619
Public	(NA)	2,171	2,211	2,269	2,187	2,140	2,072	1,988	1,971	1,951	1,794	1,556
Private	(NA)	74	65	59	71	59	54	56	54	55	41	62
College	1,007	1,002	1,020	1,103	1,062	948	814	684	727	680	522	358
Public	(NA)	814	822	916	887	782	659	537	582	532	422	272
Private	(NA)	188	199	187	175	166	155	147	145	148	100	86
College												
Full time	723	748	753	803	817	742	589	536	525	534	427	218
Percent	71.8	74.6	73.8	72.8	76.9	78.3	72.4	78.3	72.3	78.5	81.8	79.6
***Spanish Origin*[a]**												
Total enrolled	4,263	3,608	3,455	3,516	3,623	3,741	3,620	3,171	3,257	(NA)	(NA)	(NA)
Nursery school	146	89	87	75	63	85	85	68	61	(NA)	(NA)	(NA)
Public	70	50	47	30	33	47	37	41	43	(NA)	(NA)	(NA)
Private	75	39	39	46	30	39	48	27	18	(NA)	(NA)	(NA)
Kindergarten	263	226	231	220	262	235	225	171	241	(NA)	(NA)	(NA)
Public	234	210	198	206	242	218	207	165	227	(NA)	(NA)	(NA)
Private	30	16	33	14	20	17	18	6	14	(NA)	(NA)	(NA)
Elementary school	2,363	1,934	1,893	1,874	1,934	2,062	2,040	1,884	1,879	(NA)	(NA)	(NA)
Public	2,134	1,745	1,704	1,654	1,768	1,858	1,780	1,712	1,705	(NA)	(NA)	(NA)
Private	228	189	188	220	165	204	260	172	173	(NA)	(NA)	(NA)
High school	1,048	920	868	928	932	948	916	758	834	(NA)	(NA)	(NA)
Public	(NA)	875	825	836	867	886	858	707	784	(NA)	(NA)	(NA)
Private	(NA)	45	43	92	65	61	59	51	50	(NA)	(NA)	(NA)
College	443	440	377	418	427	411	354	290	242	(NA)	(NA)	(NA)
Public	(NA)	365	315	357	354	358	297	247	213	(NA)	(NA)	(NA)
Private	(NA)	75	62	60	73	53	57	43	29	(NA)	(NA)	(NA)
College												
Full time	294	314	231	287	257	287	247	201	178	(NA)	(NA)	(NA)
Percent	66.4	71.4	61.3	68.7	69.6	69.8	69.8	69.3	73.6	(NA)	(NA)	(NA)

[a] Persons of Spanish origin may be of any race.

[b] Enrollment figures for 1965 are for black and other races.

Table 15. Percentage of Persons 3 to 34 Years Old Enrolled in School, by Age and Sex: October 1965 to October 1980

Age and Sex	1980	1979	1978	1977	1976	1975	1974	1973	1972	1971	1970	1965
Total, 3 to 34 years	49.7	50.3	51.2	52.5	53.1	53.7	53.6	53.5	54.9	56.2	56.4	55.5
3 and 4 years	36.7	35.1	34.2	32.0	31.3	31.5	28.8	24.2	24.4	21.2	20.5	10.6
5 and 6 years	95.7	95.8	95.3	95.8	95.5	94.7	94.2	92.5	91.9	91.6	89.5	84.9
7 to 13 years	99.3	99.2	99.1	99.4	99.2	99.3	99.3	99.2	99.2	99.1	99.2	99.4
14 to 17 years	93.4	93.6	93.7	93.6	93.7	93.6	92.9	92.9	93.3	94.5	94.1	93.2
18 and 19 years	46.4	45.0	45.4	46.2	46.2	46.9	43.1	42.9	46.3	49.2	47.7	46.3
20 and 21 years	31.0	30.2	29.5	31.8	32.0	31.2	30.2	30.1	31.4	32.2	31.9	27.6
22 to 24 years	16.3	15.8	16.3	16.5	17.1	16.2	15.1	14.5	14.8	15.4	14.9	13.2
25 to 29 years	9.3	9.6	9.4	10.8	10.0	10.1	9.6	8.5	8.6	8.0	7.5	6.1
30 to 34 years	6.4	6.4	6.4	6.9	6.0	6.6	5.7	4.5	4.6	4.9	4.2	3.2
Male, 3 to 34 years	50.9	51.8	52.9	54.3	55.1	56.0	56.0	56.1	57.8	59.3	59.7	58.8
3 and 4 years	37.8	34.6	34.0	32.1	30.9	30.9	28.1	24.5	24.4	20.0	21.2	10.2
5 and 6 years	95.0	96.3	95.1	94.7	95.6	94.4	94.4	92.2	91.7	90.9	88.9	84.9
7 to 13 years	99.2	99.0	99.0	99.3	99.0	99.0	99.2	99.2	99.1	98.9	99.0	99.3
14 to 17 years	93.7	94.5	93.9	94.3	94.6	94.6	93.3	93.7	94.0	95.3	94.8	93.6
18 and 19 years	47.0	46.6	47.8	48.4	48.2	49.9	45.8	47.9	51.2	55.4	54.4	55.6
20 and 21 years	32.6	31.6	31.7	34.6	33.6	35.3	34.8	34.4	37.3	38.9	42.7	37.6
22 to 24 years	17.8	17.6	19.1	19.7	20.7	20.0	19.4	19.1	21.3	23.3	21.2	21.1
25 to 29 years	9.8	10.4	10.9	12.6	13.0	13.1	12.7	11.8	12.1	11.9	11.0	9.4
30 to 34 years	5.9	6.0	6.5	7.1	6.8	7.7	6.7	5.6	5.8	6.3	5.3	4.5
Female, 3 to 34 years	48.5	49.0	49.5	50.7	51.0	51.5	51.3	50.9	52.0	53.2	53.2	52.3
3 and 4 years	35.5	35.6	34.5	32.0	31.6	32.1	29.5	23.8	24.4	22.4	19.8	10.9
5 and 6 years	96.4	95.2	95.5	96.9	95.5	95.1	93.9	92.3	92.2	92.3	90.2	84.9
7 to 13 years	99.3	99.4	99.3	99.5	99.3	99.6	99.5	99.3	99.3	99.4	99.4	99.4
14 to 17 years	93.1	92.6	93.5	93.0	92.8	92.6	92.5	92.1	92.6	93.7	93.4	92.8
18 and 19 years	45.8	43.4	43.0	44.0	44.4	44.2	40.7	38.2	41.8	43.4	41.6	37.7
20 and 21 years	29.5	28.9	27.5	29.1	30.6	27.4	26.0	26.3	26.3	26.8	23.6	19.5
22 to 24 years	14.9	14.1	13.6	13.6	13.8	12.6	11.1	10.2	8.9	8.4	9.4	6.5
25 to 29 years	8.8	8.8	7.9	9.1	7.3	7.2	6.7	5.4	5.3	4.4	4.3	3.1
30 to 34 years	7.0	6.7	6.2	6.7	5.2	5.6	4.6	3.6	3.6	3.6	3.1	2.1

Table 16. College Enrollment of Persons 14 to 34 Years Old, by Sex, Race, and Spanish Origin: October 1965 to October 1980

(thousands)

Sex, Race, and Spanish Origin	1980	1979	1978	1977	1976	1975	1974	1973	1972	1971	1970	1965
All Races												
Total, enrolled in college	10,180	9,978	9,838	10,217	9,550	9,697	8,827	8,179	8,313	8,087	7,413	5,675
Male	5,025	4,993	5,124	5,369	5,296	5,342	4,926	4,677	4,853	4,850	4,401	3,503
Female	5,155	4,986	4,714	4,848	4,654	4,355	3,901	3,502	3,460	3,236	3,013	2,172
Year of college												
First year	2,957	2,885	2,766	2,936	2,632	2,886	2,557	2,282	2,320	2,443	2,212	1,861
Second year	2,411	2,291	2,286	2,364	2,535	2,376	1,999	1,807	1,965	1,885	1,739	1,256
Third year	1,716	1,653	1,658	1,681	1,748	1,492	1,422	1,476	1,454	1,392	1,248	896
Fourth year	1,403	1,458	1,445	1,427	1,556	1,354	1,360	1,230	1,253	1,175	1,074	803
Fifth year or higher	1,692	1,691	1,681	1,810	1,680	1,589	1,490	1,385	1,322	1,192	1,140	859
White												
Total, enrolled in college	8,875	8,709	8,514	8,812	8,644	8,516	7,781	7,324	7,458	7,273	6,759	5,317
Male	4,438	4,400	4,508	4,717	4,658	4,774	4,367	4,218	4,397	4,407	4,066	3,326
Female	4,437	4,309	4,006	4,095	3,986	3,743	3,413	3,105	3,061	2,867	2,693	1,991
Black												
Total, enrolled in college	1,007	1,002	1,020	1,103	1,062	948	814	684	727	680	522	274
Male	437	434	452	490	489	442	422	358	384	363	253	126
Female	570	568	569	614	573	506	392	326	343	317	269	148
Spanish Origin[a]												
Total, enrolled in college	443	440	377	418	427	411	354	290	242	(NA)	(NA)	(NA)
Male	222	226	196	223	223	219	196	167	126	(NA)	(NA)	(NA)
Female	221	214	181	194	204	192	158	123	117	(NA)	(NA)	(NA)

[a] Persons of Spanish origin may be of any race.

Table 17. College Enrollment of Persons 3 to 34 Years Old, by Level: 1970, 1975, 1980

Race	1970	1975	1980
Black			
Total enrolled in any school	7,307,000	8,400,000	8,251,000
Enrolled in college	522,000	948,000	1,007,000
White			
Total enrolled in any school	44,960,000	51,430,000	47,673,000
Enrolled in college	6,759,000	8,516,000	8,875,000

Source: U.S. Department of Commerce, Bureau of the Census, Series P-20.

Table 18. Level of Schooling Completed by Persons 20 to 24 Years Old, by Sex: 1960, 1965, 1970, 1975, 1979

Percentage Completed One Year of College or More	Male		Female	
	Black	White	Black	White
1960	12[a]	28	13[a]	22
1965	14	36	15	26
1970	23	44	23	35
1975	25	46	28	40
1979	27	43	32	40

Source: U.S. Department of Commerce, Bureau of the Census, Series P-20.

[a] Includes person of "other races."

Table 19. College Enrollment of Persons 18 to 24 Years Old: 1965, 1970, 1975, 1980 (thousands)

Sex	Black				White			
	1965	1970	1975	1980	1965	1970	1975	1980
Both sexes								
Total persons 18 to 24 years	2,091	2,692	3,213	3,555	16,269	19,608	22,703	23,975
Number enrolled in college	210	416	665	688	4,213	5,305	6,116	6,334
Percent of total	10	15	21	19	26	27	27	26
Male								
Total persons 18 to 24 years	977	1,220	1,451	1,600	7,713	9,053	11,050	11,767
Number enrolled in college	99	192	294	278	2,593	3,096	3,326	3,224
Percent of total	10	16	20	17	34	34	30	27
Female								
Total persons 18 to 24 years	1,114	1,471	1,761	1,955	8,556	10,555	11,653	12,208
Number enrolled in college	111	225	372	410	1,620	2,209	2,790	3,110
Percent of total	10	15	21	21	19	21	24	26

Source: U.S. Department of Commerce, Bureau of the Census, Series P-20.

Table 20. **Percentage of Population 25 to 34 Years Old Who Completed 4 Years or More of College, by Sex: 1960, 1966, 1970, 1975, 1979**

Year	Black			White		
	Total	Male	Female	Total	Male	Female
1960	4.1	4.1	4.0	11.9	15.8	8.3
1966	5.7	5.2	6.1	14.6	18.9	10.4
1970	6.1	5.8	6.4	16.6	20.9	12.3
1975	10.7	12.0	9.7	22.2	26.4	18.1
1979	12.8	13.8	12.0	24.9	29.1	20.6

Source: U.S. Department of Commerce, Bureau of the Census, Series P-20.

Table 21. **Black Students Enrolled in Higher Education, by Type of Institution: Fall 1978**

	Total Black Enrollment All Institutions	Percentage in Predominantly Black Institutions	
		HBCs[a]	NPBCs[b]
All institutions	1,055,964	16.5	12.9
Public	841,113	13.7	14.4
Private	214,851	27.4	6.8
All universities	146,987	9.0	—
Public	102,162	5.0	—
Private	44,825	18.2	—
All four-year (other than universities)	466,360	32.8	5.7
Public	324,310	32.2	7.4
Private	142,050	34.0	2.1
All two-year	442,617	1.7	24.6
Public	414,641	1.3	23.5
Private	27,976	8.2	41.8

Source: National Advisory Committee on Black Higher Education and Black Colleges and Universities.

[a] HBCs = historically black colleges and universities.

[b] NPBCs = newer predominantly black colleges and universities.

Table 22.   Differences in the Black and White Population in Dropout and College Enrollment Rates: 1970, 1975, 1980 (thousands)

Age	Black			White		
	1970	1975	1980	1970	1975	1980
16 to 19 year olds						
Total population	1,855	2,167	2,237	12,642	13,898	13,613
Not a high school graduate, and						
not enrolled in school	399	378	309	1,330	1,599	1,651
Percent of total	21.5	17.4	13.8	10.5	11.5	12.1
Enrolled in college	212	293	313	2,591	2,862	2,784
Percent of total	11.4	13.5	14.0	20.5	20.6	20.5
20 to 24 years olds						
Total population	1,814	2,183	2,474	13,599	15,848	17,062
Not a high school graduate, and						
not enrolled in school	623	615	603	2,129	2,144	2,416
Percent of total	34.3	28.2	24.4	15.7	13.5	14.2
Enrolled in college	225	405	405	2,944	3,503	3,756
Percent of total	12.4	18.6	16.4	21.6	22.1	22.0
25 to 34 year olds						
Total population	2,669	3,186	3,935	21,691	26,571	30,830
Not a high school graduate, and						
not enrolled in school	1,149	1,018	905	4,773	4,268	4,017
Percent of total	43.0	32.0	23.0	22.0	16.1	13.0
Enrolled in college	85	248	289	1,224	2,147	2,328
Percent of total	3.2	7.8	7.3	5.6	8.1	7.6

Source: U.S. Department of Commerce, Bureau of the Census, Series P-20.

Table 23. Percentage of Black Enrollment at Institutions of Higher Education Which Received Largest Amounts of Federal Funding in Fiscal Year 1979 (figures based on fall 1978 enrollment)

Institution	Under-graduate	Graduate	First Professional
Johns Hopkins University, Baltimore	5.0	6.1	2.6
Howard University, Washington, DC	84.3	62.5	75.4
Massachusetts Institute of Technology, Cambridge	4.7	2.6	1.9
University of Washington, Seattle	3.5	2.0	1.4
Stanford University, Stanford, CA	5.4	2.8	4.3
University of California at Los Angeles	5.1	3.7	8.3
University of Wisconsin, Madison	2.3	2.0	3.5
University of Minnesota, Minneapolis [a]	1.6	1.2	2.0
University of California at San Diego	4.4	1.2	2.6
Harvard University, Cambridge, MA	5.2	3.8	8.5
Columbia University, New York, NY [b]	5.8	4.3	5.8
Cornell University, Ithaca, NY [a]	6.5	4.1	4.3
University of Michigan, Ann Arbor [a]	6.7	7.1	5.5 [c]
University of Pennsylvania, Philadelphia	5.7	1.7	3.6
Yale University, New Haven, CT	5.4	2.7	7.2
University of California at San Francisco	4.6	3.7	7.0
University of California at Berkeley	3.5	3.0	9.3
Pennsylvania State University, University Park [b]	2.4	2.4	3.9 [d]
University of Southern California, Los Angeles	7.2	3.8	2.5
University of Chicago, IL	3.5	4.0	3.0
University of Illinois, Urbana	3.9	2.3	2.9
University of North Carolina, Chapel Hill	6.8	6.3	8.5
Washington University, St. Louis, MO	6.7	6.5	5.8
Ohio State University, Columbus [b]	5.7	4.9	2.9
University of Colorado, Boulder [a]	2.7	1.8	2.9
Duke University, Durham, NC	4.8	2.4	6.2
New York University, New York	8.9	5.0	3.4
Gallaudet College, Washington, DC	5.5	4.0	—
University of Texas at Austin	2.6	1.6	3.5
University of Utah, Salt Lake City	0.5	0.7	1.3
Yeshiva University, New York, NY	0.1	0.2	1.3
University of Rochester, NY	3.1	1.6	1.5
Michigan State University, Lansing	5.2	4.2	8.3
University of Pittsburgh, PA [b]	10.3	7.7	3.5
University of Iowa, Iowa City	2.5	2.0	2.0
University of Miami, Coral Gables, FL	7.2	5.4	2.2
Purdue University, Lafayette, IN [b]	3.5	1.2	1.7
University of Arizona, Tucson	1.2	0.7	0.0
Texas A & M University, College Station [b]	0.7	0.4	0.2
University of California at Davis	2.9	0.6	3.3
Northwestern University, Evanston, IL	8.7	3.1	4.9
University of Alabama at Birmingham	22.0	12.4	5.2
Case Western Reserve University, Cleveland, OH	2.3	2.3	3.3
California Institute of Technology, Pasadena	1.6	0.2	—
University of Florida, Gainesville	5.2	3.3	6.0
Baylor College of Medicine, Waco, TX	—	0.0	5.1
Boston University, Boston, MA	4.6	2.3	2.1
University of New Mexico, Albuquerque [b]	1.8	1.6	1.1
University of Virginia, Charlottesville [b]	5.3	2.0	3.7
University of Tennessee at Knoxville	5.5	4.3	1.9
University of Missouri at Columbia	3.3	2.1	1.9
University of Hawaii at Manoa	0.4	0.6	0.0

[a] Main Campus not designated, used summary for all campuses.

[b] Main Campus only.

Table 23. Percentage of Black Enrollment at Institutions of Higher Education Which Received Largest Amounts of Federal Funding in Fiscal Year 1979 (figures based on fall 1978 enrollment)

Institution	Under-graduate	Graduate	First Professional
Colorado State University, Fort Collins	1.0	1.3	0.7
University of Connecticut, Storrs	3.5	1.8	3.4
University of Cincinnati, OH	12.4	6.2	6.9
University of Kentucky, Lexington	3.0	1.8	2.6
Oregon State University, Cornvallis	0.7	0.8	—
University of Kansas, Lawrence [b]	3.3	2.4	2.4
University of Maryland at College Park	7.8	5.8	—
University of Maryland, Baltimore Professional School	11.3	8.4	8.5
University of Texas Health Science Center, Dallas	4.0	0.4	2.9
North Carolina State University at Raleigh	5.7	3.7	—
Vanderbilt University, Nashville, TN	1.9	1.5	5.3
Rutgers University, New Brunswick, NJ [a]	10.0	6.4	9.8
CUNY–Mt. Sinai School of Medicine, New York, NY	—	—	5.7
Louisiana State University, Baton Rouge [b]	4.7	4.7	2.0 [e]
Georgia Institute of Technology, Atlanta [b]	6.2	3.1	—
Virginia Polytechnic Institute and State University, Blacksburg	1.8	2.5	—
University of Georgia, Athens	4.4	4.0	3.9
Temple University, Philadelphia, PA	17.9	7.0	7.7
University of Illinois Medical Center, Chicago	5.7	3.2	6.6
Princeton University, Princeton, NJ	7.3	1.9	—
George Washington University, Washington, DC	7.6	7.9	5.5
Wayne State University, Detroit, MI	25.4	15.2	9.0
University of Alaska, Fairbanks	2.3	1.2	—
Virginia Commonwealth University, Richmond	19.0	11.5	4.3
Indiana University, Bloomington	5.2	2.6	5.1
Iowa State University of Science and Technology, Ames	1.1	2.2	0.0
Emory University, Atlanta, GA	2.6	4.7	2.9
SUNY, Buffalo, NY	7.2	4.3	3.8
University of Massachusetts at Amherst	3.8	6.1	—
Georgetown University, Washington, DC	4.1	2.6	6.9
Rockefeller University, New York, NY	—	0.0	—
SUNY, Stony Brook, NY	4.8	2.1	6.4 [f]
University of California at Irvine	4.7	1.5	12.5
Carnegie-Mellon University, Pittsburgh, PA	5.0	2.9	—
University of Vermont and State Agriculture College, Burlington	0.5	0.2	0.0
Tufts University, Medford, MA	6.0	1.4	4.4
Brown University, Providence, RI	6.2	2.2	5.5
Washington State University, Pullman	1.8	1.8	0.3
College of Medicine and Dentistry of New Jersey, Newark	24.9	4.5	13.7
Kansas State University of Agriculture and Applied Science, Manhattan	2.5	2.1	1.0
University of Texas Health Science Center at Houston	7.1	5.1	2.6
New Mexico State University, Las Cruces [h]	1.7	0.7	—
Mississippi State University, Mississippi State	7.6	8.5	3.6
West Virginia University, Morgantown	1.2	1.0	0.9
Auburn University, Auburn, AL [b]	1.9	4.4	0.0
University of Nebraska, Lincoln	1.2	1.1	0.7

[c] Ann Arbor only.

[d] Hershey Medical Center.

[e] First Professional figure includes LSU Medical Center.

[f] Health Science Center at Stony Brook.

BLACKS IN COLONIAL AND REVOLUTIONARY AMERICA

The Colonial Period ■ First Settlements ■ New England ■ Slave Codes ■ Early Black Soldiers ■ Divergence of European and American Interests (1763–1770) ■ The Boston Massacre ■ Road to Revolution (1770–1775) ■ The War of Independence (1775–1783) ■ Black Military Service ■ A Chronology of Black Participation in the American Revolution ■ Biographies of Black Patriots

In 1776, delegates from 13 North American colonies declared themselves independent from the constraints and control of foreign rule and stepped dramatically onto the world stage with one of history's most articulate pronouncements of the right of all to life, liberty, and the pursuit of happiness. A nagging question then and since has been how a people moved to self-sacrifice and passion on the basis of such "self-evident"—"unalienable"—"Truths" could sanction the enslavement of fellow human beings.

For an answer to this, one might look back to ancient Greece, which like many nations since was able in its codes and conscience to reconcile the contradiction between democracy and slavery. For the America of 1776, the answer was over a century and a half in the making, starting in 1607 when a band of 107 settlers who had survived a hazardous four-month sea voyage chose a site 30 miles up the James River and settled in what was to become Jamestown, Virginia. In 1620, the Pilgrims landed in Massachusetts. Both groups, and others that followed, lacked the quantity and quality of manpower to cope with the labor and military demands of their newly founded wilderness settlements and so resorted to the use of black indentured servants.

Twenty such servants were landed and pressed into service in Jamestown in 1619 and by 1638, at the latest, a substantial number were landed in Boston.

From these early days of the seventeenth century, the ideals of liberty and equality that were to ennoble the Declaration of Independence and the peculiar institution of slavery that was to trouble many of that Declaration's framers unfolded side by side.

The Common Goal

Although the early colonies were founded for such different purposes as a refuge for religious rebels (Rhode Island) and the trading outpost of a London stock company (Virginia), the majority of colonists shared a goal. They had come seeking some variety of freedom—be it religious, political, or economic. The Pilgrims were the first of many groups who came for religious freedom. The army of poor who broached American shores were seeking freedom to work their way out of the misery into which Europe's feudal structure had consigned them. Merchants, whose self-interest was soon to mint America's dominant laissez-faire values, were to carry the flag of freedom into enterprise and trade.

Not all the passengers crossing the Atlantic, of course, traveled for idealistic purposes. Many came to impose Old World privileges on the new territory, others thought solely of accumulating wealth without regard for human values.

And the black man was brought in chains.

First Settlements

As the mother of colonies, Virginia became a model for later settlements (a role subsequently played by Massachusetts in the North) giving many local events far-reaching importance. Self-government took its first steps here. Although Jamestown began as a commercial venture equipped and financed by a company of London merchants, and was eventually taken over by the authoritarian Stuart king, the settlers acquired a large measure of control over their local affairs through an annually chosen representative assembly, the House of Burgesses, which first met in July 1619.

These early rulers of Virginia were not eager to enslave the black and when in the 1640's they finally decided to do so, they wished to restrict slavery's use and growth. There was a variety of reasons for this, fear of the bravery and military prowess of blacks

The first blacks arrived in Virginia as indentured servants in 1619, a year before the Pilgrims landed at Plymouth Rock.

among the foremost. Thus the first black born in the colonies, William Tucker, owned a birthright of freedom shared by all settlers, and by 1650 there were only some 300 blacks in all of Virginia.

Ironically, it was the very competence and strength of blacks that were to doom them, for Virginia suffered serious manpower shortages that were exacerbated by expirations of indentured servant contracts. Once free of legal bonds to work for others, these people, both white and black, sought the promises of prosperity and freedom that were developing in the colonies.

Attempts to enslave the Indians failed, largely due to their existence on the continent as unified communities able to fight for their freedom, and to avoid capture or escape. The black man, who could be brought in chains from distant lands and enslaved for life, offered an obvious, tragic, solution.

Court cases of the early 1650's show that black servants were being sold for life servitude. Reversing English common law, the House of Burgesses decreed in 1661 that children born in the colonies would be bound or free depending on the status, not of their fathers, but of their mothers.

Slavery in the New World was also to be fostered by political pressures from the Old. In the late seventeenth century, the Royal African Company emerged as a powerful influence in the English Court and Parliament. The company's most profitable commodity was slaves. Pressures were soon asserted from London on New World colonies to develop attitudes, economies, and laws conducive to the acceptance of slaves. The Company's influence was even effective in Pennsylvania where William Penn revealed willingness to accept the institution despite complaints of his fellow Quakers.

The success of the Royal African Company was also to have the effect of attracting New England shippers to the lucrative slave trade. In 1696, when the RAC's monopoly on the West African trade was broken, New England sea captains were quick to become part of massive slave incursions there.

While slavery was growing, so was the freedom of the individual settler. The filigree of navigable waterways feeding Chesapeake Bay encouraged the dispersal of tobacco plantations and other farms. In this way, the English yeoman, who returned to a central village every night, was succeeded by the American farmer, whose isolated homesteads became the steppingstones of independence.

New England

The Puritans, whose shiploads of settlers began arriving at Salem and Boston in 1629 and 1630, worked hard to build a civil government that would emblazon their spiritual beliefs. By making certain that all shares

(1632) warned his flock that it was wrong to pay taxes to which they had not consented.

The Puritans believed that the congregation of each church should be subject to no higher authority. Within a decade nearly thirty churches, each with a town around it, were scattered through the Bay Colony, New Haven, Connecticut, and Plymouth. Many of these "hivings-out" were the result of irreconcilable differences about religious matters. Minister Roger Williams, a quiet and gentle person, was one of the most rebellious thinkers of the age. He wondered aloud whether the King had any right to give the colonists land that already belonged to the Indians, argued for complete separation of church and state, and claimed that freedom of worship must be absolute. When Plymouth finally expelled him in 1635, he wintered among the Rhode Island Indians and bought land from them for his own colony.

Despite their zeal for independence, few Puritans were fond of democracy. A Calvinist categorization of people into God's blessed saints and the rest of mankind cushioned their acceptance of slavery. Massa-

A black man being sold as a slave in New Amsterdam (now New York City).

Puritan Governor William Bradford's Bible.

in their Massachusetts Bay Company were purchased by inhabitants, they became the first colony not under the control of a board of directors in England. Although church and state worked hand in glove, they were not merged. The Puritans suspected power and whoever held it. This led them to devise a well-defined system of checks and balances. "Let all the world learn to give mortal men no greater power than they are content they shall use—for use it they will," said the preacher John Cotton, words to be heeded by the United States Constitutional Convention a century and a half later. In these and similar ways the church pressed the movement for a government of law. It was the minister at Watertown, for example, who first

Religious dissenters were whipped in New England, but the Puritans' distrust of political power led to the American system of checks and balances.

chusetts Bay was the first colony to recognize this institution legally, in a document ironically entitled the *Body of Liberties* of 1641. Evidence exists that a Puritan owned black slaves in the 1620s and by 1638, when the first shipment of black slaves is believed to have reached that colony, the enslavement of Indians had already begun, with Indian villages sometimes destroyed on slender pretexts for the purpose of taking captives into bondage. Indian children under 12 were sold as late as 1706. The only New England colony to prohibit slavery was Roger Williams' Rhode Island, in its law of 1652, but that singular statute was openly violated.

Slave Codes and the Right to Bear Arms

The majority of early settlers were soldier-farmers. The growth of a plantation economy in the South, however, soon resulted in a different policy for incoming blacks. Realizing that armed slaves might try to restore their birthright by violence, Virginia relieved all blacks of their military obligations and created an all-white militia as early as 1636. The question of whether blacks should be allowed to bear arms was destined, as we shall see, to be a major problem right through the Revolution. It was here in Virginia that the first "No" was recorded.

For the next 90 years or so, white Virginians found ample persuasion to continue their exclusionist policy. Every time a slave fled into the forest, there to join and be assimilated by the Indians; every time a settlement was threatened by a slave revolt—such as the 1663 rebellion nipped in the bud in Gloucester, Virginia, or the bloody uprising at Stone, South Carolina, which resulted in the deaths of 30 whites and many more slaves—Virginia's rules reaffirmed the repressive measures they had adopted to avert racial revolution.

These stern measures were drawn up in Slave Codes that were much the same throughout the South. Slaves could not own property, carry arms, or leave their plantations without a written pass. Murder, rape, and arson were punishable by death; lesser offenses by maiming, branding, or whipping. Similar codes prevailed in the North. A large slave revolt in New York City in 1712, and public paranoia about an unproven conspiracy in 1741, were employed as justification for

Slave Codes provided for the public burning of slaves who attacked their masters.

laws and repression as severe as those found in the South. While similar laws were on the books in Pennsylvania, the blacks there had much more freedom because of the influence of the Quakers. The situation differed somewhat in New England, where the slave codes generally reflected Old Testament law, so that slaves never wholly lost their legal status as persons, and enjoyed many more rights than elsewhere in the colonies.

The Early Black Soldier

Despite their fears, settlers under siege eventually started to enlist blacks to fight beside whites. Records of King William's War (1689–1697) show that one of the first to fall in Massachusetts was "an Naygro of Colo. Tyng," slain at Falmouth. During Queen Anne's War (1702–1713), whenever levies of the white colonists failed to meet their quota, blacks were drafted and sent against the French and their Indian allies. Many armed blacks fought at Fort William Henry in New York. Those who were slaves sought freedom as their payment; those who were already free sought the wider benefits of added land and cash payments.

By 1723, Virginia saw fit to reverse its policy of excluding blacks from recruitment in the militia. In 1747, the South Carolina Company made slaves eligible for enlistment in the territorial militia according to a quota system. For every three white men in any company, one black man could be added—the 3:1 ratio abating fears of insurrection. Later, blacks were to fight for the British in the French and Indian War.

THE DIVERGENCE OF EUROPEAN AND AMERICAN INTERESTS: 1763–1770

Aftermath of the French and Indian War

The signing of the Peace of Paris on February 10, 1763, brought the French and Indian War to a close by giving Canada, Florida, and all of North America east of the Mississippi to victorious Britain. This enormous booty strained Britain's capacity to govern.

Western Indians reacted violently to Britain's replacement of France as the dominant power in their areas. Chief Pontiac, who hated the British, attacked Fort Detroit in May 1763, beginning the largest Indian uprising in American history. London's response was a Proclamation which forbade settlers from migrating into the Indian lands west of the Appalachians, and which provided for stationing a 10,000-man British army in the colonies. General Amherst handled the war badly for Britain and there were several massacres on both sides before Pontiac buried the hatchet in July 1766.

Settlers and speculators refused to honor the Proclamation Line along the Appalachian crest. Washington, one of many eminent men involved in land schemes, is known to have remarked that such a good opportunity would not be repeated. Fortunately a new treaty line was negotiated. But the British still felt it necessary to tighten their reins on the colonies and to raise money to pay for this.

To deal with these financial burdens, Prime Minister Grenville introduced the Revenue Act of 1764, which provided for a duty on molasses and contained several new trade restrictions, among them a provision that all imports from Europe and the East Indies must be routed through England. Colonists complained that the taxes would be used to support a British army in America which had failed to protect their frontiers and which contained no colonial officers. All the colonies filed protests against the Act, New York taking an irreconcilable stand against any form of Parliamentary taxation whatsoever.

Meanwhile, much of the New England clergy was registering strong negative reactions to the Archbishop of Canterbury's plan to graft the Anglican hierarchy to America. Their sermons, John Adams later remarked, did as much as anything to arouse the people's doubts about the constitutional authority of Parliament over the colonies.

Chief Pontiac led the largest Indian uprising in American history. Several massacres were committed by both sides before Pontiac buried the hatchet in 1766.

The Stamp Act

On February 6, 1765, the Prime Minister presented a proposal for duties on American stamps. The Stamp Act suggestion was especially significant because it would establish Parliament's right to levy an internal tax on the colonies. The first colonial reaction to the plan flared in the Virginia House of Burgesses where a young member, Patrick Henry, called for "no taxation without representation." Massachusetts' legislature tried to convey calm, calling for delegates from all the colonies to meet in New York City, but riots broke out and the homes of stamp distributors were ransacked.

In Boston, blacks played a significant role in protests against the Act.

When the New York meeting convened in October, the delegates acknowledged Parliament's right to legislate for the colonies, but denied it had the right to tax them in any way. This Stamp Act Congress marked the first time representatives from all the colonies as-

sembled for their own purposes. By November 1, when the stamps were slated to go on sale, there was hardly a distributor in the colonies who had not resigned his post. Business proceeded without stamps. In 1766, when it became clear the enforcement would outcost the levies to be raised, Parliament repealed the Stamp Act. But more tax proposals were to follow.

The Townshend Acts

In July 1767, Parliament passed the three Townshend Acts. The first Act imposed customs duties on a large variety of items that America had to import from Britain; the second beefed up the customs service watching American ports; the third threatened to suspend the New York assembly for its refusal to provide room and board for British soldiers according to the Quartering Act of 1765. American reaction was generally temperate. Philadelphia's John Dickinson penned 12 articles which invoked legal precedents to argue against Parliament's right to tax the colonies. In Massachu-

came running to the scene, violence and confusion escalated, and—possibly in panic, or possibly because they thought they heard an order to shoot—the British fired their weapons and killed five of the crowd. Among the dead was a leader of the protest, Crispus Attucks, a big man, said to be of terrifying looks, 47 years old, of black and Indian extraction, probably a runaway slave, perhaps a drifter, and clearly a man of courage and commanding presence. In the trial that followed, lawyer John Adams defended the soldiers with the argument that the rioters, including Attucks, were rabble. Though the soldiers were exonerated, having acted under intense provocation, the "Boston Massacre" raised popular feeling to fever heat. As Adams was to say later, in words now inscribed on the Crispus Attucks monument in Boston Common: "On that night the foundation of American independence was laid."

Patrick Henry stood in the Virginia House of Burgesses to demand "no taxation without representation."

setts, the assembly approved a circular letter to all the colonies written by Sam Adams. Although Adams was moderate in this instance, British reaction was harsh. The assembly was ordered to disband when it refused to rescind the letter. Then, on June 10, 1768, customs officers began a clean-up campaign by seizing John Hancock's ship *Liberty* for bond violations. Within a few days, the officers had been driven back to their warships by angry mobs. London responded by sending two regiments of regulars.

The Boston Massacre

Although the redcoats behaved reasonably well, and Parliament saw fit to lift all the customs duties except the tax on tea, the presence of troops gradually enflamed the citizens. Violence erupted on a cold, wet night—March 5, 1770. A crowd of angry townspeople started throwing snowballs and ice at a British soldier who had been accused of hitting a boy with his rifle butt. A nearby squadron rushed to the soldier's rescue, and someone began ringing the fire bell. Bostonians

Boston patriots tossed British tax stamps onto bonfires.

Panicky British troops opened fire on a crowd of demonstrators led by runaway slave Crispus Attucks, who became the first patriot to die for American freedom in the Boston Massacre.

Mexican artist Diego Rivera's great mural of the major events leading to the American Revolution

THE ROAD TO REVOLUTION: 1770–1775

A Festering Quiet: 1770–1773

On the day British troops were firing into the Boston mob, Parliament was moving to repeal the Townshend Acts, except the tax on tea. The concessions pacified many colonists, but Samuel Adams, Patrick Henry, and Thomas Jefferson went to work on forming the Committee of Correspondence, which soon became a revolutionary communications network. A Tory pamphleteer was eventually to acknowledge the effectiveness of the Committee by labeling it "the foulest, subtlest, and most venemous serpent ever issued from the egg of sedition."

Trouble over Tea

To save the East India Company from a bankruptcy that might have been disastrous for the Empire, the Crown gave that company's wholesalers the right to sell directly to American consumers. Immediately, American merchants of every commodity from wine

At the Boston Tea Party a band of patriots dumped 45 tons of British tea into the harbor.

to hardware demanded that the ports be closed to ships bearing the tea. In Boston, the royal governor insisted that the ships be unloaded. On the night of December 16, 1773, a band of men disguised as Indians, including John Hancock and Sam Adams, swarmed aboard the teaships and dumped 45 tons of it into the harbor.

The British were outraged. Moderates who had been sympathetic to the colonies were compromised, and in 1774 the British closed the port of Boston and demanded that Boston citizens compensate the East India Company. The Committees of Correspondence reacted with a call for unity and dispatched Paul Revere, an express rider for the Committee, southward with a message seeking solidarity from other colonies.

The Intolerable Acts

While the colonies were in agitation over the Boston blockade, Lord North (the British Prime Minister) launched a full-scale reform movement. His Intolerable Acts provided for quartering troops in Massachusetts towns, transferring military murder trials to England, and eviscerating the liberties from Massachusetts' charter. Still another act gave Quebec territorial rights

The unjust laws of British Prime Minister Lord North inflamed American resistance.

as far south as the Ohio River. When Virginia called for a general congress, all the colonies quickly agreed to meet in Philadelphia in September 1774.

The First Continental Congress

The Congress that met in Philadelphia represented every shade of American opinion, but the intense feelings prevailing in the colonies tipped the balance of power to radical elements. Britain's coercive acts had transferred the people's attention from economic to political grievances, and here the radicals were at home. Long discussions and animated addresses served to clarify American ideals and to give them a cutting edge they would not lose even in the heat of battle. The Congress resolved to disregard the Intolerable Acts and to deny Parliament's claim to tax the colonies. And the 12 separate and often jealous colonies managed to unite on a program to boycott British goods.

Perhaps even more significant, liberty was becoming a watchword. The doctrine that God created all men equal and endowed them with "natural" rights that neither laws nor men could remove swept through the towns, farms, factories, and salons of the colonies. Inevitably much of this philosophy reached blacks, the few who were free and many of the 500,000 who were not.

Reactions to Slavery

Many colonists were so preoccupied with their struggle against the British that they failed to notice the incompatibility between the philosophy that all men owned a right to freedom and the belief that some men could justly be enslaved. Others were too concerned with their personal affairs to bother with the matter. Still others grasped a doctrine which contended that blacks were "biologically inferior" and thus not entitled to considerations granted other humans. Though disproven by scientists as early as the eighteenth century, the "biological" justification for oppression was eagerly grasped by many. "Biological racism" was to re-emerge in the nineteenth century as sanction for the European conquest of Africa and in the twentieth century to serve as an excuse for Hitler's racist policies.

Other colonists, however, regarding slavery as a blight on the colonist's cause, were seriously troubled. Many of these people avoided the subject for reasons of expediency. They feared, with reason, that to make an issue of slavery could destroy the fragile unity the colonies had achieved, though in the 1770s, with the cotton gin still to be invented (1794), the dependence of the Southern economy on slave labor was in decline. Still others sought to blame the British entirely for slavery. Jefferson was to do this in his condemnation of slavery that was removed from the *Declaration of Independence.*

But there were also men and women who were ready to accept the colonists' responsibility and fight for the freedom of all people. One of them, James Otis of Massachusetts, declared in a tone reflective of the rational approach of his era: "The colonists are by law of nature free born . . . as indeed all men are, white or black. Does it follow that 'tis right to enslave a man because he is black?"

In a quieter vein, Abigail Adams wrote husband John, who wavered on the subject of slavery, that it was "iniquitous . . . to fight ourselfs for what we are daily robbing and plundering from those who have as good a right to freedom as we have."

Such words reached the ears and eyes of a great many blacks, with two significant effects. Slaves in New England began to sue for their freedom and large numbers of blacks joined the militia.

Blacks Sue for Freedom

A Massachusetts slave, Caesar Hendrick, took his master to court in 1773, arguing that he was enslaved against his will and deprived of his natural right to liberty. He was upheld by an all-white jury. It freed him and ordered his master to pay reparations, court costs, and damages.

Despite this encouraging lead, few blacks were able to follow suit. Proceedings were complicated and expensive. It was not possible to take a freedom suit to the courts in order to liberate a large number of slaves—each case had to be considered separately.

Still, for a time the climate appeared to favor elimination of slavery. In his *Summary of the Rights of British America* (1774), Thomas Jefferson stated abolition was favored by the colonies. Shortly thereafter, the Continental Congress' *Articles of Association* proposed the end of the slave trade and a boycott of all nations participating in it. And though fear of blacks was intense in the South—where four Georgia whites were killed in a slave revolt—many Southerners also favored abolition.

The Outbreak of Hostilities

On the night of April 18, 1775, 700 British troops received orders to march secretly to Concord, 18 miles away, there to destroy colonial stockpiles and to arrest John Hancock and Sam Adams. Learning of their plan, Paul Revere rode out to warn the countryside. The British hope of surprise was destroyed as church bells clanged in every village through which they passed. The troops reached Lexington as the sun rose, to find Minutemen awaiting them on the Common. Here the

Black minutemen Lemuel Haynes and Peter Salem helped drive the British back from Concord bridge, where the "shot heard round the world" sparked the American Revolution.

first skirmish took place. The British fought on to Concord bridge, where "the shot heard round the world" was fired, but by now Minutemen were pouring in from all directions. The regulars were forced to retreat under punishing rifle fire. Before they could regain the safety of Boston, 273 were killed or wounded. The colonists' casualties were 95 killed or wounded.

Black Patriots

Black men participated in the earliest battles of the Revolution. Lemuel Haynes, a gifted speaker who would become a prominent Congregationalist minister after the war, was one of many black Minutemen who defended Concord bridge. At his shoulder was Peter Salem, who had been granted his freedom to enlist. Other black men who fought in the American ranks on that first day include Pomp Blackman, Caesar and John Ferrit (father and son), Prince Estabrook (one of the wounded at Lexington), and Samuel Craft. A few weeks later, Haynes joined Primas Black and

Epheram Blackman in the celebrated capture of Fort Ticonderoga, as members of Ethan Allen's Green Mountain Boys.

The next important military engagement was the Battle of Bunker Hill (also known as Breed's Hill). The British managed to drive the Americans from their commanding position, but at a fearful cost to their regulars. When British Major John Pitcairn climbed the breastworks to shout out "The day is ours!"—a gesture not only foolhardy but premature—a black rifleman named Peter Salem shot him through, and he fell. The rifleman was honored by his companions and presented to General Washington for his feat. Salem Poor, another black combatant, was singled out for special commendation. Officers' reports to the General Court of Massachusetts praised Poor for his high standard of leadership and courage throughout the battle, making him the first acknowledged black military hero in American history. Other black freedom fighters at Bunker Hill were Barzillai Lew, a seasoned veteran who had seen combat during the French and Indian

The first great battle of the war was at Bunker Hill where two black soldiers, Salem Poor and Peter Salem, earned commendations for military leadership and valor.

War as a Massachusetts enlistee in 1760, and Cuff Whittemore, a Minuteman from Arlington. Titus Coburn, Charlestown Eads, and Sampson Taylor also fought, and Caesar Brown was one of those who gave his life that day.

Recognition that blacks could serve their country as citizens as well as soldiers was also forthcoming in 1775, when America's first abolitionist organization was formed in Philadelphia, the Pennsylvania Society for the Abolition of Slavery.

However, the courage of black fighting men and the zeal of principled whites were soon to be swept aside in the movement to exclude blacks from the armed services. Before this was to happen, the Congress was called back into session.

The Second Congress

Most of the same faces showed up when Congress convened again on May 10, 1775, but the mood was different. George Washington, now wearing the buff blue uniform of the Virginia militia, was chosen commander-in-chief of the embryonic Continental Army, then forming around Boston. Nevertheless, loyalty to the mother country did not die easily. Moderates, who wished to send an olive branch to the King, remained powerful over the next year, but they were buffeted by events, among them Washington's attack on Canada, following Ethan Allen's offensive tactics, and the British Parliament's Prohibitory Act, which made it clear that all branches of British government were united in coercing the colonies into submission. Tom Paine's *Common Sense* urged that people who would be free of tyranny must be willing to attack the tyrant. It is ridiculous, Paine said, that a continent should be ruled by an island. The hiring of German mercenaries and the burning of New England towns fueled Congressional resentment. Finally, on June 7, 1776, Rich-

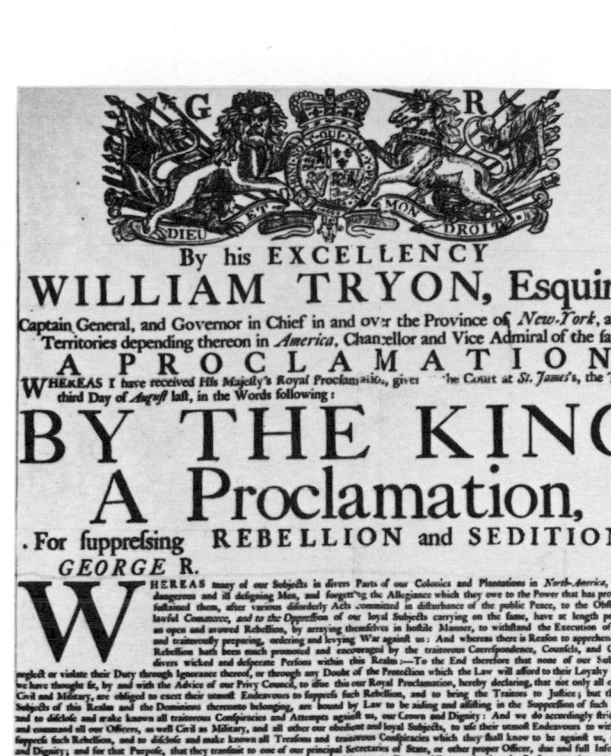

Although the British king called for all loyal subjects to put down the rebellion, the announcement of the Declaration of Independence was greeted with cheers by freedom-loving black and white Americans.

ard Henry Lee of Virginia introduced the resolution for independence.

The Declaration of Independence

While Congress pressed toward a final vote on separation from Britain, Thomas Jefferson was given the responsibility of declaring America's independence to the world. In true American fashion, he did not simply declare, he defined—for the world, for Americans, and for his own conscience. Like no nation before it, America came into being through a process in which its founders were constantly clarifying their principles.

The document Jefferson wrote enumerated the grievances which made the colonies repudiate British rule and, more profoundly, the ideals on which the colonists based their assertion of independence.

Although the ideals Jefferson cited were not new, he used them in a new way, not as a basis for philosophical speculation but to define man and to set down "natural laws" which he felt forbade human bondage.

The War of Independence: 1775–1783

The American Revolution was in many ways a revolutionary kind of war—a people's war. There was no central objective to be captured which could signal victory. America's strength did not center in any one colony or city but was scattered the length of the continent. While most eighteenth-century wars were fought by professionals, a large part of America's people would see action in this one. Washington's Continental Army never topped the 17,000 mark, but estimates

are that over 400,000 men served in it over the course of the war, mostly for short-term enlistments.

The Movement to Disarm Blacks

Conflict about whether to allow slaves, or even free black men, to bear arms was a pernicious undercurrent of the war. Despite their prowess in early battles, the blacks' welcome in the army was short-lived.

On May 29, 1775, the Massachusetts Committee of Safety, reflecting John Adams' anxiety to strengthen ties with the southern colonies, proclaimed that the enlistment of slaves "was inconsistent with the principles that are to be supported, and reflect[s] dishonor on the colony."

Men who had already risked their lives in the American cause could no longer pass muster because they were slaves.

Even Salem Poor, a hero of Bunker Hill, was nearly drummed out of the army until his masters emancipated him so that he could continue to fight. Shortly, however, all black enlistments were frozen. On July

Adjutant General Gates barred blacks from the Continental Army in 1775.

9, 1775, the adjutant general of the Continental Army, Horatio Gates, issued an order from Washington's headquarters stating that recruiting officers were no longer to accept "any stroller, Negro, or vagabond."

Southern delegates to the second Continental Congress were still unsatisfied, however, so intense was their fear of uprisings by the enormous slave populations of certain states. In South Carolina, slaves outnumbered whites, and neighboring Georgia had a population that was at least 40% slave. To minimize all risk of slaves becoming armed, South Carolina's Edward Rutledge introduced a measure in the Congress proposing that all blacks, bond or free, be discharged from the Continental Army. Although the proposal was rejected, Gen. Washington's own council of war two weeks later decided to terminate all black enlistments, a ban which Congress formalized into law on October 13, 1775. The protest of colonial generals like John Thomas, who argued that blacks made just as good soldiers as whites and that many black troops had already "proved themselves brave" in action, went unheeded. Thus, as 1775 drew to a close, it had become extremely difficult for any black to join the revolutionary forces at any level.

While the Congress' decision was clearly political, designed to keep the South from running to the British camp, its wisdom remains debatable. When the Earl of Dunmore, royal governor of Virginia, assessed the situation, he placed his colony under martial law and, on November 7, 1775, issued a proclamation offering freedom to all "indentured servants, Negroes, or others" able and willing to bear arms "for the more speedily reducing the Colony to a proper sense of their duty to His Majesty's crown and dignity." The news spread through the countryside like wildfire. Blacks, showing a great willingness to fight and die if necessary for freedom, flocked to Dunmore's "Ethiopian Regiment" at the rate of 100 fugitive slaves a week. Stepped-up

New York patriots pulled down the statue of King George in 1776.

Lord Dunmore mustered the first black regiment for Britain.

to debate the fine points of status, slaves were often armed. As a result of the longer terms for which blacks often enlisted, many of America's seasoned veterans in the latter years of the war for independence turned out to be the black troops who had been denied the right to bear arms until the situation became desperate.

The Tide Turns: 1777

Howe planned for the brunt of his forces to capture Pennsylvania, while part of his army was dispatched north, where General Burgoyne, attacking from Canada, would coordinate a three-pronged squeeze on Albany. While Howe had little difficulty, the British campaign in the north was a disaster. After a season of determined fighting and clever ruses, the colonials captured Burgoyne's force of 5,000 men at Saratoga. The victory boosted American morale and convinced France of the colonists' ability to win. French officers led by the Marquis de Lafayette were soon to be sent to help Washington, a step that was to be a turning point in the war. But the French could offer Washington little help in the brutal winter of 1777–1778.

Once again Washington had pitted his forces against the strongest part of the British Army with dire results. As Howe wintered comfortably in captured Philadelphia, Americans froze, starved, and deserted at Valley Forge. The men lacked warm clothing and shoes. While farmers sold barrels of flour and pork to the speculators in Philadelphia, the Continentals drank soup "full of burnt leaves and dirt."

It is known that the Valley Forge Army averaged about 54 blacks in each of its seven brigades. Their importance grew during this terrible winter, where their desertion rate was considerably lower than that of white Patriots.

Black Participation

Blacks made some political progress in 1777. Vermont became the first state to abolish slavery, and the Connecticut legislature passed a measure granting equal pay to white and black soldiers. Connecticut also provided for forming a fighting company of 55 slaves, as prohibitions against enlisting slaves were becoming a dead letter in Washington's mind.

Rhode Island's military situation—4,000 slaves along with unfulfilled manpower quotas—cried out for black recruitment. The state had already given the nation one black hero in Prince Whipple, a daring participant in the capture of a British general. To Washington, with the war entering a third bitter year, with manpower short, and with victory more important than the fears of slaveowners, exclusion of black men, slave or free, was becoming a wasteful indulgence.

continental patrols could not staunch the flow of manpower and, by December 1, Lord Dunmore had over 100 trained black troops. Ironically, this crisis was brought to an end only by the loyalty to America of an unidentified black man, posing as a runaway slave, who fed Lord Dunmore false reports and lured him into a disastrous attack on Norfolk, Va. Severely beaten, Dunmore's troops had to fall back to his ships and were never again able to establish a fixed camp on the mainland to which slaves could desert.

Shortly after Dunmore's defeat, Washington listened to the protests of a group of black veterans, and, reversing his policy, ordered recruiting officers to begin accepting the re-enlistments of free blacks who had already served. On January 16, 1771, Congress approved this decision, but insisted that no new black volunteers were to be accepted.

The difficulty of raising enough white troops to meet the demands of war eventually eroded America's exclusionist policy. Local militias unable to fill their muster rolls won quiet agreement from recruiting boards and reluctant slaveowners to accept free blacks as substitutes for those white men who could afford to buy their way out and wished to do so. As the war progressed, these arrangements came to involve slaves, who were declared free (compensation being awarded to the master) provided they enlist. Rhode Island passed the first slave enlistment act on February 2, 1778, raising a regiment that participated gallantly in many important battles. In 1780, Maryland became the only Southern state to enroll slave troops. Slave conscripts were at first assigned to combat-support functions, but in the heat of battle, with little time

Guerrilla commander Marion invites a captured British officer to dine with his famous volunteers.

troops occupied Savannah and threatened South Carolina. Washington chafed at the situation. Lafayette believed enlistment of only a few thousand slaves could wrest most of the South from the British.

In an attempt to obtain the cooperation of South Carolina, Washington dispatched his former aide de camp, Lieutenant Colonel John Laurens, a handsome 22-year-old native of the state and a deeply convinced abolitionist, to try to persuade the state legislature to permit enlistment of slaves. But, though South Carolina could barely raise 200 able-bodied white soldiers, and though Charleston was clearly endangered, political leaders there threatened to go over to the British if Washington insisted on arming their slaves. Frustrated and disappointed, Laurens wrote Washington that reason had been "drowned by the howlings of a triple-headed monster, in which prejudice, avarice, and pusillanimity were united."

On May 12, 1780, Charleston fell, and an army of 5,000 American troops and 300 cannon were surrendered to the British. South Carolina's fate appeared sealed, except for the daring raids of such guerrilla commanders as Francis Marion ("The Swamp Fox") and Thomas Sumter. For nearly a year, British General Cornwallis tried to force the elusive Americans to stand and fight against his larger, better-equipped army.

Blacks in the Navy

The navies of the Chesapeake Bay states, Maryland and Virginia, did not fail to capitalize on the experience and skill of the black pilots who had long been operating small craft in bay waters and river inlets. The best-known slave pilot during the war was Caesar, owned by Carter Tarrant. Caesar was at the wheel of the *Patriot* when it took possession of the *Fanny,* a British brig. In 1789, Caesar was set free. Some years later a parcel of land was awarded to his daughter in Ohio, as a reward for his services.

Another black naval hero was James Forten, who joined the navy at 14. He was taken prisoner by the British while serving as powderboy on the *Royal Lewis.* Forten became friends with the ship captain's son and was invited to accompany him back to England, where a life of wealth and aristocratic privilege awaited. Forten's answer to this suggestion was, "I am a prisoner here for the liberties of my country. I never, NEVER shall prove a traitor to her interests."

Black prisoners rarely were considered eligible for exchange. Usually they were sent to the West Indies and sold in the slave market. Transferred to a British prison ship, Forten made plans to escape by hiding himself in a chest. At the last moment, however, he relinquished his hiding place to Daniel Brewton, who he thought would be more valuable to the American

Tacitly bypassing his own standing order, Washington endorsed a Rhode Island plan which called for slaves serving in its forces to be freed and their owners to be reimbursed by the state (which would be ultimately paid by Congress). As in Connecticut, the same pay scale was to apply equally to white and black troops.

The plan paid off handsomely. In the Battle of Rhode Island (August 1778) a regiment of 125 blacks, 95 of them slaves, held its ground against three concerted British-Hessian attacks, thus enabling six brigades of American troops to make a successful retreat with all their equipment. The resistance of the black regiment earned the admiration of friend and foe alike. Barely past the recruit stage, they had inflicted casualties of 6:1 on the professionals who fought for the British. Many of the same blacks were to fight later at Ponts Bridge, in New York.

The War in the South

After 1778, British efforts in the North were limited to blockade and local raiding operations. The significant fighting was now in the South where, with Tory and Indian support, Britain hoped to reestablish control. In a brief winter campaign, 1778–1779, British

The American Navy grew into a respected fighting force during the Revolution, relying often on the skill of black pilots and crewmen.

cause. Brewton publicly praised Forten's heroism when he got to Philadelphia. Forten himself was eventually to become a renowned abolitionist and civic leader.

Blacks and the British Forces

American loyalists lobbied against the use of black troops by His Majesty's armies. The recruitment of blacks was further undercut by a dandyish atmosphere that prevaded the royal forces. It was fine for rebellious colonials to use blacks, redmen, and the like, but the British Army was too gentlemanly and disciplined to employ such rabble in any but menial capacities. As it turned out, the British refusal to arm slaves in the South sealed the Crown's fate in the war, for victories were badly needed below the Potomac to counter American successes in the North, and the only source of manpower was slaves.

The Fortification of Virginia

In 1781, England's General Cornwallis, feeling secure after victories in North Carolina, decided he could move the war to Virginia. Traveling overland from Charleston, Cornwallis' forces lived off the countryside, supplied by blacks who foraged successfully despite Cornwallis' stripping them of arms. Reaching Virginia in May, the British dug in around Yorktown and Portsmouth with the help of 1,000 black laborers. As they had throughout their Southern campaigns, the British made superior use of the blacks in supportive capacities.

The brutality of the British to their black men showed up clearly in a outbreak of smallpox. Underclothed and underfed, an "immense number of Negroes," in the words of a British commander on the scene, "died in the most miserable manner" to be, as another British officer suggested, "strewn about rebel plantations" for the purposes of spreading the plague.

In the Continental Army, on the other hand, blacks were serving in military capacities.

Spies, Couriers, and Guides

Black men assumed many key intelligence roles during the war, but especially in the Virginia campaign. The most famous slave spy was named James, the property of William Armistead, and so sometimes referred to as James Armistead. He saw service with Lafayette in 1781. James' reports from the enemy base at Portsmouth won such high praise from the French general that the Virginia legislature gave James his freedom. Thirty-three years later, in 1819, it occurred to someone that James might be deserving of a pension for services rendered, whereupon the legislature voted the former spy a $40.00 annual pension for the rest of his life. When Lafayette returned to America, in 1824, he remembered to look up James—who was by then calling himself James Lafayette.

Saul Mathews, another slave spy who operated in Virginia during the Cornwallis operation, completed many missions behind British lines, returning with detailed information of enemy movements that enabled Continental strategists to form effective battle plans.

Many blacks volunteered for hazardous spying missions behind enemy lines.

Some ten years after the close of the war, Mathews petitioned for, and was awarded, his freedom.

Yorktown

The climax of the war for independence came at Yorktown. Cornwallis was trapped in his fortifications by the sudden appearance of a French fleet of 20 warships under Admiral de Grasse. Learning the news in New York, Washington speedily slipped past the main British army in Philadelphia and turned up outside Yorktown. Cornwallis had no choice but to surrender, which he did on October 19, 1781.

Though fighting was to continue for months, and the British were to linger on beyond that, the defeat at Yorktown marked the end of British power south of Canada. After Yorktown, all Britain's efforts were bent toward getting her troops home safely and negotiating peace. The Americans had won their independence and would soon draft the Constitution.

Blacks after Yorktown

The fortunes of blacks following Yorktown varied enormously. Hundreds of slaves, freed to fight and labor on both sides, were re-enslaved by conquering American and French officers. The French returned some slaves but many were kept to meet a diversity of fates. Some found freedom in the North, a few in France, and many were sold into slavery in the West Indies.

The British kept many slaves behind their lines. When the royal ships departed, the evacuees included slaves of owners who had remained loyal to the Crown, black captives, and ex-slaves who had been promised freedom for their wartime help. A few slaves who had fought with the British waged guerrilla warfare from the Georgia and South Carolina swamps until their defeat in 1786.

In the States, most of the slaves who had served in the armed forces were freed, though deceitful and

French General Lafayette, shown with his orderly, pressed General Washington to create black regiments.

This romanticized painting of Cornwallis' surrender pays tribute to the major contributors to the American victory.

occasionally successful attempts were made to re-enslave them. The country was already beginning to polarize. Slaves belonging to loyalist owners were generally freed in the North but not in the South. Economic factors were probably conclusive. The North, with new trading opportunities developing, had little reason to keep slaves, but the South felt a need for slaves to replace wartime losses and to harvest the cotton that was becoming its dominant crop.

The force of ideology, however, should not be dismissed. Abolitionist convictions grew stronger in the North. The Philadelphia Society, whose anti-slavery activities had been suspended during the war, resumed operations. Pennsylvania's program of gradual abolition went into effect. Finally, in 1783, Massachusetts ended slavery and granted the vote to black taxpayers. The road to the future was now charted.

The American Victory

America's victory was formally sealed by the Treaty of Paris in 1783. America had won a victory in a war of revolution unlike any other. The American Revolution, as writer Hannah Arendt was to put it some 200 years later, "succeeded where all others were to fail, namely, in founding a new body politic stable enough to survive the onslaught of centuries to come."

By the end of the revolutionary struggle, America's feet were planted firmly on the world stage. By word and arms, a new nation had carved itself out of the wilderness.

A CHRONOLOGY OF BLACK PARTICIPATION IN THE AMERICAN REVOLUTION

1770, March 5   Panicky British troops open fire on a crowd of protestors apparently led by runaway slave Crispus Attucks; Attucks is the first of five patriots to die for freedom in what history remembers as the Boston Massacre.

1770, March 12   The Massachusetts *Gazette* publishes Paul Revere's celebrated engraving of the Boston Massacre, which inflames American resentment of Britain.

1770, June 28   Quaker Anthony Benezet opens the first nonsegregated school for black and white children in Philadelphia.

1770, October 24   Lawyer John Adams bases the defense of Capt. Preston, whose troop committed the Boston Massacre, on the responsibility of Crispus Attucks for the bloodshed; Preston is found innocent, but colonial public opinion now leans strongly toward revolution.

1772, June 9   A black man named Aaron participates in the burning of the British revenue cutter *Gaspee* off the coast of Rhode Island.

1772, June 22   Slavery is abolished in England by the Mansfield decision, which further states that any slave brought to the British Isles must be freed.

1773, January 6   Blacks petition the governor of Massachusetts for equal rights and for an end to slavery; two weeks later a follow-up petition with more signatures is sent to the Massachusetts assembly.

1773, February 17   The slave trade is stifled in Pennsylvania by imposing a 20 pounds sterling tax on every imported slave.

1773, March 13   Jean Baptiste Point du Sable, a black trader, founds the first permanent settlement on the present site of Chicago, Illinois.

1773, April 5   White ministers Samuel Hopkins and Ezra Stiles enroll free black John Quaumino and slave Bristol Yamma in a radical program to train blacks for missionary work in Africa.

1773, April 20   Slaves petition the Massachusetts legislature to be allowed to earn money to buy their freedom.

1773, July 5   The Lord Mayor of London presents a copy of *Paradise Lost* to Phillis Wheatley, the black American poet.

1773, November   Massachusetts slave Caesar Hendricks takes his master to court "for detaining him in slavery"; the all-white jury frees Hendricks and awards him damages.

1773, November 6   Quaker merchant Moses Brown of Rhode Island voluntarily frees his slaves.

1774, March 8   The Massachusetts General Assembly passes a measure prohibiting the importation of slaves, but is unexpectedly suspended by the royal governor on the following day.

1774, May 27   Massachusetts blacks send a petition to royal Governor General Thomas Gage, denouncing slavery as evil and destructive of natural rights.

1774, September 7   Abigail Adams, in a letter to her husband, John, writes: "It always appeared a most iniquitous scheme to me to fight ourselfs for what we are daily robbing and plundering from those who have as good a right to freedom as we have."

1774, October 2   The Continental Congress votes for discontinuance of the slave trade after December 1, 1774.

1774, October 26   Massachusetts blacks enlist in the Minuteman companies being organized by the Committee of Safety.

1774, November 2   Slaves revolt in St. Andrew's Parish, Georgia.

The capture of Fort Ticonderoga, in which Lemuel Haynes and two other black fighting men took part.

Pompy _____, Prince _____, Prince Estabrook (wounded), Pomp Blackman (at both battles), Cato Stedman, Cato Boardman, Cuff Whitmore, and Cato Wood.

1775, April 24 Minuteman Salem Poor hurries to enlist in Captain Simon Edgel's Framingham company, which will see action at Bunker Hill.

1775, May 1 Lemuel Haynes and two other black volunteers in Ethan Allen's Green Mountain Boys take part in America's first aggressive military action, the capture of Fort Ticonderoga.

1775, May 3 Seasot _____ and Pharaoh _____ enlist in Colonel Scamman's "Regiment on Foot"; they too, will fight on Bunker Hill.

1775, May 29 The Massachusetts Committee of Safety suddenly prohibits the enlistment of slaves as "inconsistent with the principles that are to be supported, and reflecting dishonor on this colony."

1775, June 16 Colonel William Prescott of the Massachusetts militia leads his regiment, which contains many black veterans of Lexington and Concord, to the top of Bunker Hill, where they prepare for a British attack.

1775, June 17 Black soldiers distinguish themselves at the Battle of Bunker Hill; among the day's heroes are Salem Poor, Barzlllai Lew, Cuff Whitmore, and Peter Salem, who is credited with shooting Brit-

1775, March 8 Thomas Paine publishes his first essay, "African Slavery in America," which denounces slavery, calls for abolition, and demands that blacks be given land in payment for long years of slavery.

1775, March 10 Daniel Boone's expedition sets out for Kentucky guided by an aged black slave.

1775, April As war becomes imminent, Maryland slavcowners petition Governor Robert Eden for arms and ammunition to put down possible slave uprisings.

1775, April 14 America's first Abolition Society elects as officers Benjamin Franklin and Benjamin Rush.

1775, April 18 The midnight rides of Paul Revere and William Dawes alert the Minutemen, many of whom are black volunteers, that the British are coming.

1775, April 19 Black American Minutemen fighting in the first battles of the Revolution at Lexington and Concord include Peter Salem, Lemuel Haynes,

Black rifleman Peter Salem stopped a British charge at Bunker Hill by picking off an enemy major.

ish major John Pitcairn; two of America's 100 dead are free black men.

1775, July Virginia opens the militia to all free male persons; an unforeseen consequence is that many slaves manage to pass themselves off as free, and sign up.

1775, July 3 Prince Hall founds the first lodge of black freemasons in Boston.

1775, July 9 Horatio Gates, the adjutant general of the new American army (distinct from state militias), orders recruiting officers not to enroll any "stroller, negro, or vagabond."

1775, August 3 Connecticut brigantine *Minerva* signs on two black marines, Peter _____ and Gist _____.

1775, August 18 White pilot and well-to-do slave-owner Jerry _____, of South Carolina, is hanged for supplying weapons to slaves and advising them to join the British.

1775, September 26 The Continental Congress hears, but rejects, South Carolinian Edward Rutledge's proposal to discharge all blacks, free or slave, from the army.

1775, October 8 Bowing to Southern pressures, General Washington's council of war decides to exclude blacks from the Continental Army.

1775, October 13 Congress legalizes the General's resolution barring blacks from the army.

1775, October 14 Congress authorizes the Continental navy, in which black sailors, both free and slave, serve from the very beginning.

1775, October 24 General John Thomas protests to John Adams that it is a mistake for the army to reject black soldiers, many of whom "have proved themselves brave" in action.

1775, November 7 The Earl of Dunmore, Virginia's royal governor, issues his famous proclamation offering freedom to slaves who will desert their rebel masters and join the British army.

1775, November 10 South Carolina authorizes the hiring of slaves to build fortifications, with payment to be made to their masters.

1775, November 23 Southern newspapers mount a bitter attack on Lord Dunmore's call for blacks to enlist as British troops.

1775, November 25 Slaves are reported to be flocking to join Lord Dunmore, where they are not only welcomed to serve but promised freedom after the war.

1775, December 1 Nearly 300 runaway slaves in Virginia have reached Lord Dunmore's positions; they are officially dubbed the "Ethiopian Regiment."

Newspaper woodcuts for runaway slave notices

1775, December 5 Salem Poor's extraordinary bravery at the battle of Bunker Hill is praised by 14 officers who send a petition on his behalf to the General Court of Massachusetts.

1775, December 8 A patriotic black American posing as a runaway slave dupes Dunmore into believing that Norfolk's Great Bridge is inadequately guarded.

1775, December 9 Dunmore attacks the Great Bridge with 600 troops and is badly defeated; he is forced to flee to his ships, where the "Ethiopian Brigade," gradually devastated by disease, never takes part in another major encounter.

1775, December 13 The Virginia Convention publishes a broadside offering to pardon runaway slaves if they will promptly return from Lord Dunmore's brigade; slaves captured in battle will be sold to the West Indies.

1775, December 30 After listening to the protests of free black veterans, General Washington reverses his policy and orders recruiting officers to accept their enlistments; he also promises to ask Congress to reconsider the question of allowing blacks to serve.

1776, January 1 General Washington writes to John Hancock, president of the Continental Congress, to press for a decision allowing the enlistment of free black soldiers.

1776, January 16 Granting General Washington's re-

Captured slaves being sent to the West Indies

Black casualties were heavy when the outnumbered Americans were driven from Long Island in 1776.

quest, the Congress approves the re-enlistment of free black veterans but insists that no new black volunteers are to be accepted.

1776, January 18   South Carolina's Council of Safety sends out a militia captain with 34 Catawba Indians on a scouting patrol to catch runaway slaves.

1776, January 22   Negro Jack is one of 15 privates from West Hartford who join the army invading Canada.

1776, January 23   Adopting the exclusionist policies of the central government, Massachusetts bans blacks, Indians, and mulattos from serving in its militia.

1776, February 28   General Washington invites poet Phillis Wheatley to Cambridge headquarters to thank her for a poem in his honor.

1776, March   Free black Scipio Fayerweather refuses to join the British in their evacuation of Boston despite reprisals in which they tear down his house.

1776, March 17   In New York City, Captain Benjamin Egbert's 59-man company contains 11 black soldiers.

1776, March 26   Congress resolves to draft Indians.

1776, April   South Carolina authorizes the death penalty for slaves who defect to join the British.

1776, April 6   Congress bans the importation of slaves into the 13 colonies.

1776, April 13   Two fugitive slaves attempting to join a British man-of-war are captured by the Virginia navy and hung "as an example to others."

1776, April 23   To prevent black defections to the British force in the area of Charleston, S.C., General R. H. Lee orders all blacks who can fight to be "secured immediately and sent up to Norfolk."

1776, May   Surriname Wanton and Loushir _____ are two black sailors aboard the U.S. brig *Cabot* when it captures a British merchantman; because they are slaves, their 120 pounds share of the booty is given to their owner.

1776, June   Spain joins France as an ally of America bringing black troops from Louisiana into the combat; these troops include militia companies of free blacks and slaves commanded by black officers of the line.

1776, June   Virginia navy pilot Minny _____, a slave volunteer, is killed attempting to board an enemy vessel in the Rappahannock River.

1776, June 17   Thomas Hubey is hanged for conspiracy against General Washington, after his plot was exposed by black serving girl Phoebe Francis.

The hangman at Nathan Hale's execution was Bill Richmond, a fifteen-year-old black American who fought with the British. Richmond later became heavyweight champion of England.

1776, July 4 The *Declaration of Independence* is adopted in Philadelphia, but only after voting out Thomas Jefferson's sharp condemnation of the slave trade as "cruel war against human nature itself, violating its most sacred rights of life and liberty."

1776, July 23 Major Thomas Price tells the Maryland Council of Safety that he has seen the bodies of dead blacks washed ashore from Lord Dunmore's ships, where an epidemic is ravaging the troops.

1776, August 6 Lord Dunmore finally gives up and sails for the West Indies; the best black troops remaining from the "Ethiopian Regiment" sail for Sandy Hook where they will fight in the principal British army.

1776, August 12 Georgia assigns black pilots to patrol state waterways and seacoast.

1776, August 27 Black casualties are heavy in Washington's defeat at the Battle of Long Island.

1776, September 16 At the Battle of Harlem Heights, a major skirmish in Washington's withdrawal to Valley Forge, many black militiamen see action.

1776, September 22 The British hang Nathan Hale as an American spy; the hangman is 15-year old loyalist slave, Bill Richmond, who in later years becomes Europe's heavyweight boxing champion.

1776, October 10 The U.S. Cavalry is formed, but few blacks see service in this elite branch; an exception is free black John Banks of Goochland, Va., who rides for two years in Theodorick Bland's regiment.

1776, December 3 Silas Deane urges Americans to stir up slave rebellions in Jamaica, but his plan is not implemented.

1776, December 17 Congress gives General Washington specific authority to raise troops; the quotas he levies on the various states finally lead to the general acceptance of black enlistments, eventually including slaves.

1776, December 25 Washington makes his famous midnight crossing of the icy Delaware; many black soldiers are in the boats, including Prince Whipple and Oliver Cromwell.

1776, December 26 American troops, including many black militiamen, earn an important victory in the Battle of Trenton.

1777 Cato Carlile and Scipio Africanus, freeborn blacks from New England coastal towns, enlist for service under Captain John Paul Jones; the navy welcomes black men who know the sea, whether they be free or slave.

1777, January 13 A black petition to end slavery is sent to the Massachusetts House of Representatives, arguing that every principle which impelled America to break with England pleads for abolition; signers include Prince Hall.

1777, April Black pilot Dick _____ is hired by the Maryland state navy.

1777, April 9 John Jay urges that New York's Constitution abolish slavery.

1777, May 2 The Connecticut legislature officially considers recruiting slaves, votes against it, but finally permits drafted men to supply black substitutes for their army service.

1777, May 6 Virginia moves to prevent slaves enlisting as though they were free by making it mandatory for a black man to have a certificate of freedom from the county judge before he can sign up.

1777, May 12 Several blacks sail on the frigate *Boston,* including Cato Austin, number one gunner on the starboard watch.

1777, June Moved by a black petition, Massachusetts drafts a bill abolishing slavery, but the measure is tabled by John Adams' deft behind-the-scenes politicking for fear that it would imperil friendly relations with Southern states.

1777, June 7 Ty, the best-known black American fighting for the British, leads a raiding party of 20 black and white troops in the capture of two American captains and some stock.

1777, July 2 Vermont, not one of the original 13 states, becomes the first U.S. territory to abolish slavery.

1777, July 9 Black commando Tack Sisson spearheads a daring raid to capture British Major General Richard Prescott from his own headquarters.

1777, August 4 Reflecting the bigotry of some Ameri-

Two black soldiers with General Washington when he crossed the Delaware River were Oliver Cromwell and Prince Whipple.

can commanders, General Philip Schuyler complains of the high number of black soldiers in his reinforcements as a disgrace to American arms, but this army shortly wins the great victory over Burgoyne at Saratoga.

1777, September Ty, the feared black commando working for the British, is mortally wounded in his squad's attack on the house of Captain Joshua Hardy.

1777, September 5 Virginia legislators are alarmed by the continued flight of slaves to join British forces, yet they will not allow slaves to enlist on the American side.

1777, September 10 Many black veterans see action in the Battle of Brandywine, including Samuel Charlton, Oliver Cromwell, John Frances (wounded), and artilleryman Edward Hector, who risks his life to keep the enemy from capturing an ammunition wagon.

1777, October 4 Samuel Charlton, a 17-year-old slave enlisted as his master's substitute, is one of the black soldiers fighting in the daring attack on the British at Germantown.

1777, October 22 Black and white troops stand firm to repel a British attack on Delaware River's Fort Mercer.

1777, October 23 A Hessian officer's diary reads: "The Negro can take the field instead of his master, and therefore no regiment is to be seen in which there are not Negroes in abundance, and among them are able-bodied and strong fellows."

1777, November Connecticut's largest vessel, the *Oliver Cromwell,* carries five black marines in its patrol of the Lesser Antilles and the Azores.

1777, November 15 The Articles of Confederation, which govern the states during the Revolution, are adopted; the document makes no reference to black people.

1777, December 11 Washington begins his retreat to Valley Forge; many soldiers will desert during this terrible winter, but black troops less than whites.

1778, January 1 Rhode Island's two battalions are severely depleted at Valley Forge; General James Varnum proposes to Washington that the state be allowed to meet its quota by raising a slave-soldier regiment, and Washington agrees.

1778, January 19 With the Southern colonies reluctant to use blacks as soldiers, General Washington suggests to Maryland, Virginia, and the Carolinas that blacks be employed in combat-support functions.

1778, February 2 Rhode Island passes the first slave enlistment act, which provides that slaves who serve for the duration of the war will be declared free and grants them the same pay and bounties as whites.

1778, February 23 The organization of Rhode Island's black 1st Regiment officially begins.

1778, April Massachusetts passes an act legalizing the enlistment of blacks, but turns down artillery

American soldiers proved their will during the starving winter at Valley Forge.

captain Thomas Kench's proposal to raise a black regiment.

1778, April   Black civil rights leader Prince Hall enlists at Medford, Mass., receiving a bounty of $100.

1778, June 8   Georgia's Council of Safety empowers Colonel Andrew Williamson to hire or impress black laborers to repair state roads.

1778, June 28   At Monmouth courthouse, the last great battle in the North, 700 black troops fight under General Washington in an attack that rattles the main core of the British army.

1778, July 28   The newly recruited, black 1st Rhode Island Regiment is sent out on a planned combat-support mission as one of its first assignments.

1778, July 29   Admiral D'Estaing's French fleet arrives at Newport, R.I., to coordinate a land-sea attack against the British.

1778, August   Names on Northern muster roles show that black soldiers are bearing arms in exchange for their freedom; one Connecticut regiment includes Jeffery Liberty, Pomp Liberty, Sharp Liberty, Cuff Liberty, Dick Freedom, Ned Freedom, Cuff Freedom, Peter Freeman, Jube Freeman, and Prinnis Freeman.

1778, August 10   A hurricane forces Admiral D'Estaing to seek Boston harbor, leaving New Hampshire General Sullivan facing a much stronger British force on Rhode Island; part of Sullivan's command is the new black regiment.

1778, August 11   In the Battle of Rhode Island, Colonel Greene's raw First Regiment of 125 black soldiers holds the lines against four hours of British-

Hessian assaults, enabling the entire American army to escape a trap.

1778, August 24   Muster rolls show 775 black troops in the Continental army; 148 are serving in General Samuel Parson's brigade.

1778, November 4   French Admiral D'Estaing sails from Boston for the West Indies to recruit blacks.

1778, December 10   John Jay, an advocate of black rights, is elected president of the Continental Congress.

1778, December 29   The British capture Savannah, Ga., thanks to aged slave guide Quamino Dolly, who volunteers to lead them through a heavy swamp to the undefended rear of the American position.

1779, February   After taking Savannah and Augusta, General Henry Clinton's army is joined by large numbers of runaway slaves who, barred from joining Georgia's militia, have defected to the British in order to fight for their freedom.

1779, February 16   Freed to enlist as his master's substitute, artilleryman Abner Dabney of Georgia shows "bravery and fortitude" in the Battle of Kettle Creek, while sustaining a broken thigh.

1779, March   At the head of a "half-white and half-black army," Bernardo Galvez, Spanish governor of Louisiana, drives the British from the Mississippi Valley.

1779, March 14   Alexander Hamilton urges Congress to allow slaves to enlist, reminding them that "the contempt we have been taught to entertain for the blacks, makes us fancy many things that are founded neither in reason nor experience."

1779, March 16   Henry Laurens writes Washington that the British could be driven from Georgia if the American forces were strengthened by 3,000 blacks from South Carolina.

The Battle of Rhode Island, where the first black American regiment took the field

1779, March 29 Congress urges South Carolina and Georgia to immediately enlist 3,000 black soldiers; this so incenses the privy council of South Carolina that it recommends withdrawing from the Revolution.

1779, May 11 A black petition to end slavery is sent to the general assembly of Connecticut.

1779, May 12 An unidentified black civilian provides American general William Moultrie with detailed information about surprise British troop deployments.

1779, May 18 Massachusetts frees six black sailors captured from the British, provided they enlist in the state navy.

1779, May 26 South Carolina stubbornly rejects a Congressional proposal to form a black militia, even though Charleston is threatened and the state can barely raise 750 white men for active duty—partly because so many citizens have to remain at home preventing their slaves from revolting or deserting to the British.

1779, June Admiral D'Estaing enlists both white and black slaves in the West Indies.

1779, June 30 To recruit blacks for the British army, General Clinton proclaims that rebel "Negroes who reach the British lines are free."

1779, July 2 General Horatio Gates, now impressed by black fighting men, writes a letter on behalf of runaway slaves who "assist us in securing our freedom at the risk of their own lives."

1779, July 15 Black spy Pompey _____ brings the information which General Anthony Wayne uses to storm Stony Point, N.Y.

1779, August Black trader Jean Baptiste Point du Sable is arrested by royal troops in Wisconsin for his anti-British sentiments.

1779, September 14 South Carolina's naval commissioners issue orders for the recruiting of black seamen.

1779, September 23 The Father of the American Navy, John Paul Jones in the *Bonhomme Richard,* whose crew includes free black seaman, defeats the *Serapis* in the Atlantic.

1779, October 9 Admiral D'Estaing's 3,600-strong army, including 545 black troops from Santo Domingo, is beaten back from an ill-advised attack on Savannah, but the black unit holds off a British counterattack, preventing a rout.

1779, November The army from Louisiana, containing a majority of black troops and several black officers, captures Mobile and Pensacola; six black officers are decorated for bravery.

Revolutionary flagship The Bonhomme Richard, *whose crew numbered several blacks, won America's first great naval victory over the British man-of-war* Serapis.

Long before leading the black revolution in Haiti, King Henri Christophe was a teenage soldier at the Battle of Savannah. Relying heavily on black labor, the British encircled Charleston in a steel ring.

1779, November 12 Blacks petition the New Hampshire legislature to outlaw slavery.

1779, December 7 Papers for the Virginia navy's *Tempest* show four blacks aboard; it is probable that at least 140 black seamen served on the state fleet during the war.

1779, December 9 Eighteen-year-old Jabez Jolly enlists in Captain Rufus Lincoln's company of the 7th Massachusetts Regiment as a drummer, a typical assignment of black soldiers.

1780, February 9 Paul Cuffe and six other free black residents of Massachusetts petition the legislature demanding the right to vote since they pay taxes; the case is eventually decided in their favor.

1780, February 26 Concerted British forces attack Charleston, S.C., which the state legislature would rather leave inadequately defended than protect by arming blacks.

1780, March Writing from Charleston, General Benjamin Lincoln alerts Washington that the enlistment of slaves is necessary for the safety of the town, but the South Carolina assembly will not consent.

1780, March 1 Pennsylvania becomes the first state to pass a measure abolishing slavery; emancipation is to be gradual.

1780, April 1 The British encircle Charleston in a steel ring made possible by using blacks in combat-support functions more extensively than anywhere else in the war.

Many black veterans fought in the strategic victory at Cowpens, South Carolina, which is often considered the best executed American battle of the war.

1780, May 12 Charleston surrenders to the British, who dispatch patrols of blacks and noncommissioned officers to dismount and remove the captured guns.

1780, May 17 The British army that has conquered Charleston, South Carolina's largest city, is swelled by runaway slaves.

1780, June 1 Connecticut organizes a 52-man black company, which fights as a separate unit until November 1782.

1780, June 3 British commander-in-chief Clinton proclaims freedom to fugitive slaves of rebel masters, provided they serve the British faithfully till the end of the war.

1780, July The Hospital Department in Virginia signs on a black woman slave, promising to pay her master a fixed rate as long as she is employed; this practice of hiring slaves for combat-support functions is common.

1780, July 9 After twice debating freedom petitions pressed by slaves, the New Hampshire legislature postpones further deliberations "to a more convenient opportunity."

1780, August 16 Black wagonners and laborers participate on both sides as the British crush the Americans at Camden, S.C.

1780, September 3 Henry Laurens, who has strongly advocated creation of black regiments in the South, falls captive to the British.

1780, October Maryland authorizes slave enlistments, the only Southern state to do so during the Revolutionary War.

1780, October 19 Pennsylvania prohibits the importation of slaves.

1780, November 22 In an effort to secure more white volunteers, the Virginia legislature considers a bill to give a slave to every new recruit, but the measure is rejected.

1780, November 28 James Madison tries to convince the Virginia assembly to liberate certain slaves for enlistment, but slaveowner opposition is inflexible.

1781 Slave Cuffee _____, pilot of Virginia Commodore Richard Barron's ship, dies of wounds received at the wheel.

1781 James Forten, not yet 15 years old, enlists as a powderboy on the Pennsylvania privateer *Royal Lewis*.

1781 Military dispatches praise black Jupiter _____, who "saved four guns during the time the enemy were in Richmond."

1781 In one of the best-executed operations of the

war, the largely black army of Louisiana takes control of Florida.

1781, January 18 Many black veterans fight in the strategic victory at Cowpens, S.C., which is often considered the best-executed American battle of the war.

1781, February 5 General Cornwallis gives the order that blacks are not to be armed under any circumstances.

1781, March 20 New York passes a law freeing slaves whose masters allow them to enlist; the masters are to receive a compensation of 500 acres per emancipation.

1781, March 25 Richard Barnes in Maryland writes to Governor Lee of Virginia describing, with great concern, the favorable reaction of blacks to the sight of British ships in the area.

1781, March 27 Lafayette takes James Armistead into his service as a spy.

1781, April Quok Walker brings a freedom suit against his master on the basis of Massachusetts' constitution, which states that "all men are born free and equal"; Walker will win his freedom.

1781, May 4 Rhode Island's black regiment suffers heavy casualties at Point Bridge, N.Y., in a futile attempt to save the life of its commanding officer, Colonel Greene.

1781, May 9 Jefferson appeals to the Virginia legislature to draft slaves into the army as laborers, if nothing else, but the legislature will go no further than petitioning masters to lease out their bondsmen.

1781, May 10 The Maryland legislature decrees that all free black men are eligible for the draft.

1781, June Smallpox, aggravated by unsanitary conditions, kills great numbers of blacks laboring for the British.

1781, June Virginia slave Saul Matthews, an American spy, returns with crucial information about British defenses and, that very night, leads the successful raid which forces Cornwallis to abandon his strong position at Portsmouth, Va.

1781, July 4 Black troops make up one-fourth of the army assembled at White Plains headquarters.

1781, July 13 British General Leslie conceives a plan to use the corpses of 700 black smallpox victims to spread the disease around rebel plantations.

1781, July 20 Petitioning for a force of 400 black troops, Lafayette writes to Washington: "Nothing but a treaty of alliance with the Negroes can find us dragoon horses, and it is by this means the enemy have so formidable a cavalry."

1781, August 13 Black patriot Nicholas _____, of Kent County, Del., rides to Dover to give the alarm that the British are coming.

1781, September 6 At the Battle of Groton Heights the fierce tenacity of hugely outnumbered Americans infuriates the ultimately victorious British into killing their captives, including black orderly Jordan Freeman, who had speared the British major in hand-to-hand fighting, and black volunteer Lambo Latham.

1781, September 8 Fort Griswold surrenders to the British following heavy casualties to its garrison, which included many black soldiers.

1781, October 1 The Virginia schooner *Patriot* is taken by the British; among the many black crewmen made prisoner is veteran James Ranger.

1781, October 6 The American army begins the climactic siege of Cornwallis at Yorktown; blacks serve on both sides but are generally restricted to laboring roles for the British.

1781, October 19 Slave James Robinson wins a gold medal at the Battle of Yorktown, where Cornwallis' defeat marks the end of Britain's major war effort.

1781, October 22 Visiting Lafayette's camp, defeated General Cornwallis is surprised to find that his chief black spy is really an American double agent; although unidentified, the black man is probably James Armistead.

1781, December 9 Rhode Island's skillful General Nathanael Green is dispatched to the Southern theater, where he bluntly tells South Carolina's gover-

American militia uniforms in 1782: Massachusetts (left) *and New Jersey*

nor that slave enlistments are necessary to protect the state's territory.

1782, February 25 Instead of arming blacks, South Carolina offers a slave bounty to each new white recruit.

1782, May 19 Describing South Carolina's refusal to allow blacks to bear arms, Laurens writes Washington that the voice of reason was "drowned by the howlings of a triple-headed monster, in which prejudice, avarice and pusillanimity were united."

1782, July 21 5,000 fugitive slaves chose to leave with the British as they evacuate Savannah, Ga.

1782, August Caesar Perry ranks first in a Massachusetts list of noncommissioned officers and privates entitled to length of service honors; many black soldiers in the 1st Rhode Island Regiment served for five consecutive years.

1782, November 10 Furnished with troop information by a black who has lived with the Shawnee tribe, General G. R. Clark routs Indian-loyalist forces at Piqua.

1782, November 16 Many of 3,500 Virginians conscripted to level the works at Yorktown are blacks.

1782, November 20 Preliminary peace agreement is signed in Paris; the British fail to comply with the provision to return fugitive slaves to their rebel masters despite British promises of freedom for service.

1782, December 16 The British evacuation of Charleston, S.C., is completed; 5,327 escaped slaves leave with them to be resettled in Jamaica, St. Lucia, Halifax, East Florida, and England.

1783, April 19 War is over, Congress declares; more than 5,000 blacks have served in the American forces, and another 1,000 have borne arms for the British.

1783, June 13 Rhode Island's black regiment is disbanded at Saratoga, N.Y.

1783, October Virginia puts up for sale most of the state-owned slaves in its navy when it disbands that force; the few retained to man the state's two remaining vessels, such as Joseph Ranger, William Bush, and Jack Knight, are given their freedom in 1789.

1783, October 20 The Virginia legislature forbids the re-enslavement of black veterans who had been promised freedom for their military service.

1783, November 29 For the final evacuation of British subjects from New York City, the British commissioners compile a detailed list of evacuees, which includes 2,722 blacks.

John Hancock presented this flag to Boston's black regiment, which called itself the "Bucks of America."

1783, December 4 For his retirement banquet and farewell to his officers, General Washington chooses New York City's Fraunces Tavern, a famous black-owned restaurant.

1784, February 13 Rhode Island's assembly legislates that all children of slaves born after March 1, 1784 shall be born free.

1784, April 4 Despite efforts by his former master to re-enslave him, honorably discharged Ned Griffin is guaranteed his freedom by the South Carolina legislature.

1784, April 22 Jefferson draws up an ordinance for the government of the Northwest Territory, which recommends the exclusion of slavery.

1784, September 1 Peter Williams, who later becomes one of the founders of the AME Zion Church in New York, is freed from his loyalist master.

1784, November 20 General Lafayette writes a letter commending James Armistead's services to the Continental army; Virginia's state legislature eventually buys Armistead his freedom.

BLACK PATRIOTS IN THE ERA OF THE AMERICAN REVOLUTION

CRISPUS ATTUCKS
Patriot
c. 1723–1770

Crispus Attucks, a runaway slave, holds the place of honor in the American Revolution as "the first to defy,

the first to die." He earned this honor on March 5, 1770, the night of the infamous Boston Massacre, when British troops fired into an unruly crowd of Bostonians, killing five of them. Many historians cite this incident as the beginning of the war for independence.

The most widely accepted account of what Attucks did that night was given by John Adams during the subsequent trial of the British soldiers. According to what Adams told the jury, Attucks undertook "to be the hero of the night; and to lead this army with banners, to form them in the first place in Dock Square, and march them up to King Street with their clubs." When the crowd reached the soldiers, it was Attucks who "had hardiness enough to fall in upon them, and with one hand tooke hold of a bayonet, and with the other knocked the man down." At this point the panicked soldiers fired, and in the echoes of their volley, as five men fell dying to the wintry street, the seeds of the American Revolution were sown.

As a runaway slave, Crispus Attucks seems to have taken the first step for independence in more than one way. Certainly, no account of the American struggle for freedom would be complete without remembering his heroic dedication to liberty.

Protestor Crispus Attucks was killed in the Boston Massacre.

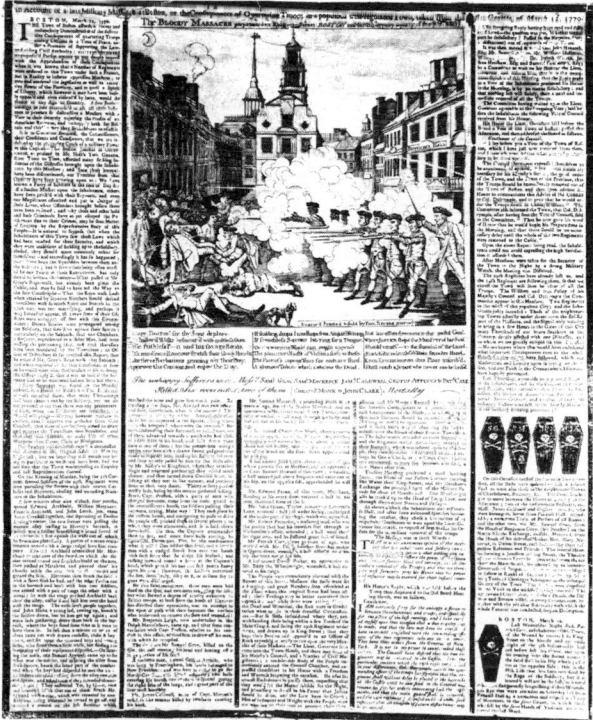

Contemporary newspapers headlined the incident with Paul Revere's famous engraving.

SAMUEL CHARLTON
Soldier
1760–1843

Samuel Charlton was enlisted in the American forces by his master when he was only 16 or 17 years old. Like many other black men, he was ordered to take his master's place in the fighting. Despite this wartime service, he went back to slavery when the war was over and was not liberated until his master's will freed all his slaves and provided Charlton with a special pension.

Charlton saw action at the battles of Brandywine, Germantown, and Monmouth. Historians estimate that of the 15,000 troops at Monmouth—Washington's historic attack on the British evacuating Philadelphia—700 were black. Many of these men were veterans of the terrible winter at Valley Forge, when cold, hunger, and inadequate clothing thinned the ranks of the patriots. Records from this desperation point in American history show that black men deserted at a lower rate than whites.

When Charlton was freed, he and his wife moved to New York City, where he lived for the rest of his life.

OLIVER CROMWELL
Soldier
1753–1853

Oliver Cromwell served in the American revolutionary forces for 6 years and 9 months, much longer than most of the patriots, and saw action in many important battles. Besides being present at the surrender of Cornwallis at Yorktown, he was one of the valiant soldiers who crossed the Delaware River with Washington on Christmas night in 1776.

Born in Columbus, N.J., Cromwell enlisted in the Second New Jersey Regiment, under the command of Colonel Israel Shreve. He participated in the battles of Trenton and Princeton in 1776–1777, Brandywine in 1777, Monmouth in 1778, and Yorktown in 1781. When he was discharged he was awarded an Army pension of $96 a year in recognition of his honorable service. He settled on a farm in his native state and, after raising a large family, lived to be 100 years old.

WILLIAM FLORA
Soldier, business leader
1755–1820

Long after his comrades had retreated into the fort at Norfolk, Va., William Flora stood his ground on the Great Bridge, defending it against the British attack of December 9, 1776. His bravery is credited with sparking an American victory that eventually forced the British to withdraw from Norfolk. Born in Ports-

Black infantryman Jordan Freeman killed the British commander at the Battle of Groton Heights.

mouth, Va., he was one of the 1,000 free blacks in that colony at the outbreak of the Revolution. Although the British governor tried to win the support of the black population, Flora was among the leaders of the majority who joined the American side. After the war, he received the standard 100-acre land bounty and became a successful livery stable operator. When the War of 1812 broke out, he quickly leaped to his country's defense once more, enlisting as a marine on a gunboat.

JORDAN FREEMAN
Soldier
?–1781

Like the majority of black infantrymen, orderly Jordan Freeman was assigned to noncombative battle-support functions. When the chance to fight came at the Battle of Groton Heights, however, he fought valiantly and gave his life in one of the fiercest combats of the Revolution.

The Battle of Groton Heights took place on September 6, 1781, when a British force under traitor Benedict Arnold was sent to capture the port of New London. Although victory was impossible, the hugely outnumbered Americans put up a terrible resistance. Jordan Freeman was in the thick of the action. When the British stormed the fortifications, it was Freeman who met the British major in vicious hand-to-hand fighting and speared him fatally. British casualties were so high in this battle that when they finally triumphed, they madly bayonetted their captives. Dying alongside Freeman was Lambo Latham, another black orderly who had insisted on volunteering for that day's fighting. The courage of these men stands as an undying example of the mettle of the majority of unknown black infantrymen.

LEMUEL HAYNES
Minuteman, Clergyman
1753–1833

Lemuel Haynes was the son of a black father and a white mother. Deserted by his mother, he was brought up by Deacon David Rose of Granville, Mass. Extraordinarily precocious, he began writing adult sermons while still a youngster, but his preparation for the ministry was interrupted by the advent of the Revolution. Answering Paul Revere's midnight call to arms, he fought in the war's first battle, at Lexington on April 19, 1775. He joined the regular forces and served with

Lemuel Haynes interrupted his preparations for the ministry to bear arms for America.

Ethan Allen's Green Mountain Boys at the capture of Fort Ticonderoga.

After the war he became pastor of the Congregational Church of Middle Granville and, in 1786, he transferred to Torrington, Conn., becoming the first black minister of a church with a white congregation. Famous as a sermon writer, he served as a pastor in Vermont and New York until his death in 1833.

EDWARD HECTOR
Soldier
c. 1744–1834

One of the few black men who served in the artillery regiments, Edward Hector was a private in Captain Hercules Courtney's company of the Third Pennsylvania Artillery. After enlisting in March 1777, he served valorously in the Battle of Brandywine, where he had charge of an ammunition wagon. The Americans were forced to retreat, and the order was given to abandon the wagons to the enemy. Hector courageously disobeyed the order, and not only brought his team, wagon, and cargo to safety, but stopped a few times on the field of battle to gather up weapons that had been cast away by fleeing soldiers. However, Hector became one of the forgotten veterans of the Revolution. The Pennsylvania legislature refused to award him a pension for his service and did not see fit to grant him any recompense until 1833, when he was sent a $40 donation.

AGRIPPA HULL
Soldier
c. 1759–?

Agrippa Hull, a free-born black man from Massachusetts, enlisted at the age of 18. He served for six years, four of them under General Tadeusz Kosciuszko. Assigned to a unit of military surgeons, he assisted at many field operations and amputations. After his discharge, he returned to the Massachusetts town of Stockbridge, where he was a respected citizen.

PRINCE HALL
Fraternal Leader, Civil Rights Activist
1735–1807

Prince Hall, the founder of black freemasonry, was one of America's first civil rights leaders. Born in the British West Indies, he migrated to Boston as a young man and rose to become an influential member of the black community there. In January 1777 he was the prime force behind a black petition to end slavery which was sent to the Massachusetts House of Representatives, arguing that every principle which impelled America to break with England pleaded for immediate abolition. Although small in stature, Hall enlisted in the Medford militia and served in the armed forces during the Revolution. After the war, he obtained a charter from Masons in England for African Lodge Number 459, which is the oldest black fraternal organization in America. True to the ideals of freemasonry, Hall was dedicated to helping his fellowmen. He was self-educated and had a high regard for schooling. As early as 1787, he lobbied for the organization of schools for black children in Boston. Another important petition drawn up under his leadership was the 1788 document which raised a public outcry against the kidnapping and sale into slavery of free blacks. Until his death, Hall remained a notable citizen of Massachusetts, where he was a property owner with full voting rights. Many masonic lodges celebrate September 7 as Prince Hall Day.

JAMES ARMISTEAD LAFAYETTE
American spy

Although born a slave, James Armistead was willing to risk his life behind enemy lines collecting information for the American cause. The many valuable reports he furnished the Marquis de Lafayette enabled the French commander to check the troop advances of British General Cornwallis, setting the stage for Washington's 1781 victory at Yorktown, which crushed the Crown's North American empire south of Canada. In recognition of these services, Armistead was granted his freedom by the Virginia legislature

James Armistead Lafayette, one of America's intelligence agents

in 1786. It was not until 1819, however, that Virginia finally thought to award him a pension of $40 a year along with a grant of $100. He adopted the surname "Lafayette" in honor of his former commander who, on an 1824 trip to the United States, did not fail to pay him a visit.

BARZILLAI LEW
Soldier
1743–1793

Adventurous Barzillai Lew was the son of a free father who had immigrated to Massachusetts from Haiti. A cooper by trade, he joined Captain Thomas Farrington's volunteers for nine months of combat during the French and Indian wars of the 1760s. When the Revolution broke out, he enlisted in May 1775, and saw action at the Battle of Bunker Hill and the siege of Boston. He continued to serve for the full six years of hostilities as a soldier and a fifer. Because of his courage and seasoned skills, this veteran was chosen for many daring guerrilla assignments in New England.

SAUL MATTHEWS
Soldier, Spy

Born a slave in Virginia, Saul Matthews won his freedom for "many essential services rendered to the Commonwealth during the . . . war." Although he had joined the American forces as a rifleman, his most memorable exploit was as a spy. To dislodge British General Cornwallis from his control of Portsmouth, the Americans desperately needed information about his fortifications. Matthews penetrated enemy lines, carefully collected the necessary data, and led a successful raiding party against the British on the very night of his return. So many British prisoners were taken that Cornwallis was forced to abandon his strong position.

SALEM POOR
Soldier

Salem Poor was a member of a predominantly white Massachusetts regiment, who distinguished himself so gallantly in the Battle of Charleston in 1775 that 14 officers sent a petition on his behalf to the General Court of Massachusetts. The petition says, in part: "Salem Poor of Col. Frye's Regiment . . . behaved like an Experienced officer, as well as an Excellent Soldier. . . . We would only begg leave to Say in the Person of this Negro Centers a Brave and gallant Soldier. The reward due to so great and Distinguished a caracter, We Submit to the Congress." Poor went on to serve at Valley Forge and White Plains.

JOSEPH RANGER
Seaman

Joseph Ranger, a free black man, enlisted in Virginia's navy in 1776 and served on four of her ships of war during the Revolution. He was crewman of the *Jefferson* when the British exploded it during a James River combat. Undaunted, he joined the *Patriot,* on which he served until a defeat shortly before Yorktown ended with the whole crew being taken prisoner. After the end of hostilities, Ranger continued to serve on Virginia ships until the last of them was retired in 1787. His 11-year term of enlisted service is apparently one of the longest on record for the American revolutionary forces. Following his discharge, he received a land grant of 100 acres and a pension of $96 per year for life.

JAMES ROBINSON
Soldier
1753–1868

The story of James Robinson exemplifies the bad treatment received by many black veterans of the Revolution. Although he was promised his freedom for serving in the American army, and despite the fact that he won a gold medal for military valor at Yorktown, James Robinson's reward was to be sold down the river into the harsh slavery of the deep South. This came about because his master died, and the heirs refused to honor the promise of freedom. It would have been predictable for Robinson to become bitter and resentful. However, when war broke out again in 1812, he gallantly answered Andrew Jackson's call for riflemen at the Battle of New Orleans. When the fighting was over, Robinson once more returned to a life of slavery on a cotton plantation. He never gave in, however. Although condemned to servitude, he lived to be 115 years old and, when the Emancipation Proclamation was finally written, he was there to hear it. This extraordinary man, who had twice fought for American freedom, was able to live the last years of his life as a free citizen.

PETER SALEM
Soldier
?–1816

Peter Salem was one of the patriots who manned the breastworks at Bunker Hill on June 17, 1775. According to contemporary accounts, he was the marksman who shot British Major Pitcairn dead when he leapt on the wall and claimed victory. Because he was a slave, Salem was almost drilled out of the army shortly after that feat when the Congress decided to use only free men in the Continental Army. However, his owners, the Belknaps of Framingham, gave him his freedom so that he could continue to fight. He was one of the many black soldiers who served valiantly in the cause of freedom for all Americans.

TACK SISSON
Soldier

Commando Tack Sisson participated in many raids behind enemy lines in New England. His most famous

Heeding the command not to "fire until you see the whites of their eyes," Peter Salem shot British Major Pitcairn at the Battle of Bunker Hill.

This famous picture of Washington crossing the Delaware shows Prince Whipple manning the first starboard oar.

exploit was the daring capture of British Major General Prescott in his own headquarters, and the subsequent escape with his prize through enemy lines. This high-ranking abduction was necessary to bait a prisoner exchange for captured American Major General Charles Lee. The colonel in charge of the Rhode Island militia hand-picked a squadron of 44 men, and he and Sisson were among the three commandos who finally crept to the British general's quarters, subdued a sentry, broke down the door, and captured their quarry. They returned through the sentries without any problems and the operation was a complete success, although, as the *London Chronicle* reported, the British general had been carried off "without his breeches."

CAESAR TARRANT
Ship Pilot
1755–1796

Caesar Tarrant was one of a number of knowledgeable black pilots spawned by the Chesapeake Bay waterways whose skills were put at the service of the American Revolution. A Virginia slave, Tarrant served in that state's navy for over four years, until his bark, the *Patriot,* was captured just before the battle of York-

town. He is known to have been at the helm during a famous sea encounter with a British privateer. When the war was over, the Virginia legislature emancipated Tarrant for his services. He became a wealthy landowner.

PRINCE WHIPPLE
Soldier

One of George Washington's most loyal comrades-in-arms was Prince Whipple, a black man born in Amabon, Africa. History has it that Whipple was sent to America as a child to get an education but that he was sold into slavery on his arrival at Baltimore. In any event he succeeded in joining the Continental forces as a bodyguard to General Whipple of New Hampshire, whose name he took, and served in many of General Washington's campaigns. After enduring the hardships of the retreat from Long Island, he was one of the soldiers to have the privilege of being in the boat with Washington during the famous Christmas night crossing of the Delaware. This event is commemorated in Emanuel Gottlieb Leutze's inspiring painting of the event. Prince Whipple is buried in North Cemetery, Portsmouth, N.H.

BLACK SERVICEMEN AND THE MILITARY ESTABLISHMENT

The Nation's Wars ■ A Chronology of Military Events ■ Black Congressional Medal of Honor Winners ■ Black Graduates of the U.S. Military Academy ■ Black Graduates of the U.S. Naval Academy ■ Black Graduates of the U.S. Air Force Academy ■ Black Cadets Enrolled at the Service Academies ■ Black Armed Forces Brass ■ Black War Heroes

The experience of settling America, and the burden of defending it, have been shared by people of many continents. Black men, too, have built the nation, forged its destiny in peace, and defended it in war. They began serving America long before the nation had come into being and they have fought long and honorably in every major American conflict.

As in other areas of American life, the black man in the military establishment has been subject to discriminatory treatment and second-class status. In the Revolutionary War, he achieved parity with the white patriot only because conditions were too desperate to impose artificial barriers between men in the field; in the War of 1812, he excelled on land and sea when emergency conditions required his involvement; during the Civil War, he was a pawn until his importance was recognized by both sides and he was thrust into the heat of battle, often without adequate preparation and with the added risk of being slaughtered by a vengeful enemy.

The black soldier fought on America's frontier at the close of the nineteenth century, developing great camaraderie with white counterparts of the same hardy and robust breed. Even in Cuba, during the Spanish-American War, much of this mutual respect for each other's combat prowess was in evidence between the four black regiments and Teddy Roosevelt's "Rough Riders." In both world wars, however, a cumbersome and often insensitive military bureaucracy imposed conditions which created class divisions between the men and so contributed to the systematic demoralization of most black forces. Blacks sought to fight alongside white men, but were summarily rejected—often on the uninformed grounds thay they possessed no military tradition worthy of recognition. With the coming of integration in 1948, black men widened their role in combat and support functions, often exhibiting a sense of pride in personal excellence and sometimes cultivating a framework of exclusivity. Today, both trends are in evidence: the constant policing by the military itself of placement and promotion opportunities, and the dynamic drive by young black men to express their manhood even before considering questions of involvement with whites. Whatever the merits of these policies and attitudes, one thing remains indisputable: black men have served with valor and distinction in all of America's wars, and have come away with a substantial share of its major citations and decorations.

THE FIRST BLACK SOLDIERS

The American Revolution (1775–1781)

American blacks fought in most major battles of the Revolutionary War including Lexington and Concord, Bunker Hill, Trenton, Long Island, Savannah, Valley Forge, and Yorktown. In the most serious prewar clash between the Americans and the British, the Boston Massacre of 1770, one of the five colonists who fell was runaway slave Crispus Attucks. Attucks was in the vanguard of marchers protesting the general presence of British "occupation" forces in Boston and a specific incident involving the alleged beating of an unruly youth by a British "lobster-back."

After war broke out in 1775, General George Washington at first moved to bar all black enlistments in the Continental Army but was forced to modify his stand as soon as the British governor of Virginia, Lord Dunmore, promised to free all blacks who would desert their masters and fight for the British Crown. Washington then recommended that free blacks be allowed to enlist in the Continental Army, although many of the 5,000 who eventually saw combat were in reality slaves who passed muster because of the difficulty recruiters encountered in meeting their monthly quotas.

Blacks served in a variety of capacities—as spies, as pilots, as infantrymen, and as laborers, cooks, and teamsters. Some were with the Minutemen at Lexington and Concord; others wintered with Washington at Valley Forge, crossing the Delaware with him enroute to surprising the Hessians quartered at Trenton. Two blacks—Peter Salem and Salem Poor—were singled out for gallantry at the Battle of Bunker Hill in 1775. Lemuel Haynes, a minister, served at Lexington and with the Ticonderoga expedition. All told, between 8,000 and 10,000 blacks served in the colonial armies of the Revolution. Statistics are available for some states including Massachusetts (572 blacks); Virginia (250 blacks); Rhode Island (one all-black battalion and hundreds of other blacks scattered through "white" regiments); Connecticut (49 blacks in the 2nd Company, Third Regiment); New Hampshire (almost every black of military age); Maryland (780 blacks in one regiment, others in mixed ranks); New York (two battalions of blacks as of 1780); New Jersey and Pennsylvania (mixed battalions).

Blacks serving in the Revolutionary Navy were, generally ordinary seamen or orderlies, but not a few were pilots, especially in the coastal patrol boats of the individual states.

Black sailors were impressed from U.S. ships by the British Navy.

(For a more detailed account see the section on Blacks in Colonial and Revolutionary America.)

The War of 1812

On a June morning in 1807, the British man-of-war *Leopard* attacked the U.S. Navy's *Chesapeake*, killing three men and wounding 18 others in a skirmish outside Norfolk harbor. British officers then boarded the *Chesapeake* and threw irons on four alleged Royal Navy deserters, among them three black seamen, Daniel Martin, William Ware, and John Strachan. Impressment of U.S. seamen was one of the issues which culminated in the War of 1812, a conflict waged primarily at sea. Its most celebrated battle—the Battle of New Orleans—was fought after a peace treaty had been signed in Ghent, Belgium.

The most famous naval figure associated with the war is Oliver Hazard Perry, who requested reinforcements for a projected battle at Lake Erie in 1813, and was appalled when his immediate superior, Commodore Isaac Chauncey, sent him a parcel of "blacks, soldiers, and boys." The word used to describe the reinforcements: "motley."

Chauncey, in his turn, was irritated at his subordinate's sharp criticism, though his reply is subdued and philosophical:

I have yet to learn that the color of the skin or the cut and trimmings of the coat can affect a man's qualificatons or usefulness. I have fifty blacks on board this ship and many of them are my best men; and these people you call soldiers have been to sea from two to seventeen years; and I presume you will find them as good and useful as any men on board your vessel.

Perry changed his appraisal once the "motley" brigade proved itself under fire. They seemed, in his words, "absolutely insensible to danger," despite the far-from-ideal circumstances under which they had served. The lack of fresh water, for example, had been particularly critical on board ship, impairing the health of many and causing widespread discomfort.

Nathaniel Shaler of the schooner *Governor Tompkins* registered similar approval of the combat prowess of one of his crew members during a subsequent sea engagement. One man, according to Shaler,

ought to be registered in the book of fame, and remembered with reverence as long as bravery is considered a virtue. He was a black man, by the name of John Johnson. A twenty-four-pound shot struck him in the hip, and took away all the lower part of his body. In this state, the poor brave fellow lay on the deck, and several times exclaimed to his shipmates: "Fire away, my boys; no haul a color down." The other was also a black man, by the name of John Davis, and was struck in much the same way. He fell near me, and several times requested to be thrown overboard, saying he was only in the way of others.

"When America has such tars, she has little to fear from the tyrants of the ocean."

The most famous land battle of the war found Old Hickory, Andrew Jackson, so hard pressed for troops that he was forced to issue a call for black recruits in a letter to Louisiana's Governor Claiborne. Jackson declared:

They must be either for us, or against us. Distrust them and you make them your enemies, place confidence in them, and you engage them by every dear and honorable tie to the interest of the country, who extends to them equal rights and privileges with white men.

His address to the "Free Colored Inhabitants" of Louisiana is far more exalted in tone.

As sons of freedom, you are now called upon to defend our most inestimable blessing. As Americans, your country looks with confidence to her adopted children for a valorous support, as a faithful return for the advantages enjoyed under her mild and equitable government. As fathers, husbands and brothers, you are summoned to rally around the standard of the eagle, to defend all which is dear in existence . . .

To every noble-hearted, generous freeman of color, volunteering to serve during the present contest with Great Britain, and no longer, there will be paid the same bounty in money and lands, now received by the white soldiers of the United States, viz. one hundred and twenty-four dollars in money, and one hundred and sixty acres of land . . .

Due regard will be paid to the feelings of freemen and soldiers.

Black sailors fought in every sea engagement of the War of 1812. Shown here is the Battle of Lake Erie.

General Andrew Jackson issued an urgent call for black recruits for the Battle of New Orleans, a victory in which black riflemen played an important role.

You will not, by being associated with white men in the same corps, be exposed to improper comparisons or unjust sarcasm. As a distinct, independent battalion or regiment, pursuing the path of glory, you will, undivided, receive the applause and gratitude of your countrymen.

Given the era, "feelings" could hardly be expected to hold much weight among brusque frontiersmen of the Jackson breed. Still, they had been brought up by the general himself, apparently out of regard for a code of chivalry which had some relevance among southern gentlemen. Such chivalry, however, was not the primary concern when it came to the matter of the men's pay which was held up by some subordinate. Outraged, Jackson quickly ordered that the men be paid whether they were "white, black, or tea."

Applause and gratitude held little appeal for the average southerner who had participated in the glorious victory over the British. After all, what value could there be in according to the black man a share of the triumph? Surely, it might cause him to feel a dangerous sense of importance even as it dramatized his undeniable competency with combat weapons in a critical situation. Thus the annual New Orleans parade commemorating the event afforded blacks little opportunity to feel that they had played a part in this significant chapter of American military history. Ironically, the next time black drummer boy Jordan B. Noble marched through the streets of town was in 1862—the year Union troops took possession of New Orleans.

Noble had wanted to stay in service. But he was declared ineligible in the aftermath of an 1820 General Order which stated: "No Negro or Mulatto will be received as a recruit of the Army."

THE CIVIL WAR (1861–1865)

The Crispus Attucks incident (the Boston Massacre), the *Chesapeake-Leopard* debacle, the John Brown Raid—all have a common denominator as skirmishes which portended the arrival of full-scale war in these United States.

By 1859 slavery had so aroused the indignation of black and white activists (compromises had kept the agitation in check, but the Dred Scott decision of 1857 had added fuel to the flames of the cause) that there seemed little chance to avoid an armed showdown over the issue. White abolitionist John Brown was never one to wait for a battle, however. Crucial to his strategy was the element of surprise and the prospect of guerrilla warfare. On October 16, 1859, Brown and a band of 21 men—five of them black—seized the arsenal at Harpers Ferry and held it for a few precious hours until federal troops commanded by Robert E. Lee forced him to fight. Brown's capture did not appease the outraged South, which interpreted the very gesture as symptomatic of the North's alleged willingness to attempt the forcible overthrow of slavery. Relatively few abolitionists would ever publicly advocate such a posture, however, since they realized that the more explicit they became, the more they increased the risk of publicizing the struggle as racial rather than sectional.

Those hanged alongside Brown at Charleston in December 1859 included Dangerfield Newby, a runaway slave; John A. Copeland, a North Carolinian; Sheridan Leary, a harness maker and a freedman; and Shields Green, a sailor from South Carolina. (Black Green died alongside white Brown.) One of the five,

Osborne Perry Anderson, escaped death, only to write his memoirs and eventually to serve in the Union Army.

Once the South determined to bring the issue to the battlefield, it was not, as is often implied, an appreciably weaker foe than the North. In arms and material, yes, but not in the coherence of its aims and the passion of its defenders. The South knew at once what the stakes were; the North was, conversely, ambiguous and equivocal.

None realized the indecisiveness of the North better than Lincoln, a man whose demonstrated moral aversion to slavery should suffice to prove the efficacy of his intentions. It is well to remember, however, that Lincoln came to abolition by guarded states, not in one grand, uninterrupted movement. Originally he argued containment of slavery, that is, prevention of its spread to the Western Territories. For those touched by its blight, he proposed resettlement in Africa, mainly out of a genuine realization that little hope existed for a reconciliation of the races in the South. Compensation of the slaveowner was an unsavory part of this proposed course of action, a gesture embraced by Lincoln mainly in keeping with his stated objective of "preserving the Union."

Political considerations aside, however, there was clearly little resolve cementing the fighting men of the North in their approach to the war. Lincoln issued an initial order calling for 75,000 volunteers—whites only. Black frontiersman Jacob Dodson came forward with an offer to raise 300 black volunteers to defend Washington, D.C. Over 100 Wilberforce students followed suit by attempting to join Union forces. These and all other gestures of black support were rejected for political reasons.

As in the Revolutionary War, however, military concerns soon became the overriding issue. The South could put the black man to use tilling the soil and performing other functionary labors which freed the white gentry to fight the war. The North had no such ready-made class to provide a similarly needed service.

Blacks themselves held the answer. Would they remain loyal to their immediate oppressors, those who, however benevolent, owned them outright, or would they seek refuge in another territory which might potentially alter their condition? For obvious reasons, the risk was worth taking. The black tide of humanity soon flowing into Union lines volunteered to do teamster work, to build roads and fortifications, to forage for units in the field, to load weapons, to serve as personal valets—whatever was needed to guarantee *de facto* freedom. By the summer of 1861, Lincoln had gone so far as to instruct Union commanders not to return such fugitive slaves to their place of origin. Pressure was already mounting to plug up all the military loopholes that were making victory dubious.

In 1862 one of the "contraband" (this was the name applied to black refugees entering Union lines, a name usually applied to materiel) brought in a Confederate gunboat he had sailed out of Charleston harbor at

Battle of Lake Champlain.

An escaped slave in the Union Army, from an 1860s Harpers' *drawing*

the First South Carolina Volunteers but was unable to requisition the necessary equipment and uniforms to incorporate the group properly. Jim Lane of Kansas, an abolitionist and Free Soiler who later became a U.S. senator, cut through the mass of red tape by organizing the First and Second Regiments of Kansas Colored Volunteers. Being frontier soldiers, they were perhaps less preoccupied with the formal regalia of their station. They had two brief and successful skirmishes with the enemy—one at Clay County, Mississippi, the other at the Osage River in Bates County, Missouri. "They fought like tigers," said one Confederate observer. Still another Union commander was comparatively quick to realize the virtues of "Africa." The word "Africa" is extracted from General Ben Butler's own quote in which he professed willingness to "call on Africa to intervene," and confidence that he would not "call in vain." The First Regiment Louisiana Native Guards were mustered into the U.S. Army on September 27, 1862. They fought under the impressive name *Chasseurs D'Afrique*.

By January 1, 1863, it was clear that the nation was at a historic crossroads. The Union was torn asunder, its armies unable to bring the rebellious South to heel. It would be presumptuous to claim that the Emancipation Proclamation changed all of this; but it would be equally foolish to see no connection between the Union victory and the freedom promised slaves by the document. Lincoln's edict not only pronounced the dread word "freedom" but also paved the way for black participation in the conflict—not as support units, but as fighting men.

Three years, the recruiting order stated, not three months as Lincoln's first summons had dictated. By the summer of 1863, Mayor George Stearns of Medford, Massachusetts, reported, somewhat obtusely, that "colored men" were beginning "to understand they gain nothing by standing off but if they would gain their rights and secure protection at the hands of government they must rally at its call." The implication that blacks were hanging back, waiting for whites to get the job done, is not only insulting, it is woefully inaccurate. Dodson and the Wilberforce students were among those who knew otherwise.

Word from Massachusetts read as follows:

Massachusetts now welcomes you to arms as her soldiers. She has but a small colored population from which to recruit. She has full leave of the General Government to send one regiment to the war, and she has undertaken to do it. Go quickly and help fill up this first colored regiment from the North. I am authorized to assure you that you will receive the same wages, the same rations, the same equipment, the same protection, the same treatment, and the same bounty secured to white soldiers. . . .

dawn's early light. Robert Smalls was declared a hero, and declared himself and his family free men. There was compensation, too, for the singular deed of valor in the form of prize booty from the U.S. Senate.

Elsewhere, some white generals sought to obtain a clear directive from Washington, D.C. on the possible use of black fighting men. "Black Dave" Hunter raised

A black infantry regiment counterattacks after stopping a Confederate cavalry charge.

Thus the 54th and the 55th took the banner of the U.S. Army and marched into South Carolina to face the entrenched legions of Fort Wagner in July 1863. Even after the Union batteries had pummeled the fort in an effort to soften it up for an infantry attack, it was virtually unscathed and ready for the onslaught. "Forward Fifty-Fourth! For God and Governor Andrew," regimental commander Robert Gould Shaw bellowed to his men. The men charged into withering barrages of small-arms fire, held ranks, and reached the outer parapet before Shaw fell. A few feet away lay black standard bearer William H. Carney, Company C, shot several times. Carney managed to drag himself to safety, the colors always held aloft. Miraculously, he got back, but over 1,500 of his comrades didn't. His regiment alone lost more men than all the Confederate forces combined.

Battles in which black casualties were high were numerous throughout the war. At Port Hudson, Louisiana, in May 1863, 600 men were left dead on the battlefield after what amounted to near suicidal charges against the enemy. The First and Third Louisiana Negro Regiments, raised in New Orleans, were the primary units involved in the engagement. Of them, General Nathanael Banks said:

The highest commendation is bestowed upon them by all officers in command. . . . [The] history of this day proves conclu-
sively . . . that the Government will find in this class of troops effective supporters and defenders.

Elsewhere up the Mississippi, at Miliken's Bend, the 9th Louisiana, the 11th Louisiana, and the 1st Mississippi were attacked by Confederate troops further spurred by the knowledge that their adversaries were black troops. Untrained troops who relied on instinct to survive, they prevented the Confederates from realizing their objective, and once again proved what one eyewitness put into words.

Tauntingly it has been said that Negroes won't fight. Who says it . . . when the Battle of Milliken's Bend finds its place among the heroic deeds of this war? . . . [The] freed slaves will fight.

They fought, too, at the Battle of Olustee in Florida where, according to one press report,

the First North Carolina and the Fifty-fourth Massachusetts . . . did admirably. The First North Carolina held the positions it was placed in with great tenacity, and inflicted heavy losses on the enemy. . . . The Fifty-fourth sustained the reputation they had gained at Fort Wagner, and bore themselves like soldiers throughout the battle.

Perhaps it was combat fatigue that triggered the upsurge of a new issue: equal pay for equal risks. The

This black battalion was ambushed by "rebels and bloodhounds" in South Carolina.

black units which had been recruited on the basis of Union slogans promising "the same wages" as all other campaigners had begun to protest shortly after the Fort Wagner struggle. Their pleas had been reasonable and subdued; their arguments logical and persuasive. "[Are] we soldiers," they asked, "or are we laborers? We have done a soldiers duty. Why can't we have a soldiers pay?"

Among their supporters were such prominent Bostonians as Oliver Wendell Holmes and Charles Eliot Norton and such capable field commanders as General Ben Butler, who was appalled at the logic of paying white soldiers an extra $3.50 a month as a clothing allowance when "the colored man fills an equal space in the ranks while he lives, and an equal grave when he falls." It was not until 1864 that the Army Appropriation Act finally succeeded in obliterating the invidious racial distinction which institutionalized separate pay ledgers.

This was the year of one of the most infamous and demoralizing combat episodes of the war, the brutal Fort Pillow Massacre. The few black survivors of the bloody affair were unanimous in their condemnation of the fighting practices of Confederate forces. Their butchery not only increased Union casualties at the close of the day but bore ugly testimony to the hysteria and hatred gripping certain elements of the Confederacy. Only desperate men could have clubbed wounded soldiers, burned them alive, or impaled them on buildings and trees. Hospital patients were sabered to death in their beds; women and children were slain without quarter by men either gone berserk or so furious with rage that hardly a shred of reason or compassion prevailed. Though the massacre was condemned after an official inquiry, no concrete measures were taken to impose a severe penalty on the offices who had somehow permitted, or even justified, the bloodshed.

Another key battle of the war in which black soldiers were subjected to undue pressure and risk occurred at the crater near Petersburg, Virginia, in the

summer of 1864. The military objective of the battle was to destroy a small fort protecting Confederate lines. Union General Ambrose Burnside ordered his men to dig a tunnel under the fort, lay explosive mines in the excavation, and blow up the obstruction. The strategy then called for an assault wave to engage the enemy. Black troops, originally singled out to lead the attack, were withdrawn in an eleventh-hour gesture by General Grant himself. After mines were detonated, leaving a gigantic crater in the middle of the battlefield, three white divisions made a rush at the enemy, but they were unable to reach the lines and forced to seek refuge in the crater itself. Exposed and immobilized, they were virtual sitting ducks for Confederate sharpshooters.

Black reserve troops were immediately summoned to the rescue, but were soon slowed down in their spirited advance by demoralized white troops. Still, they formed a tiny beachhead at the crest of the crater, hanging on tenaciously until they too were forced to retreat. By this time, however, they found themselves lodged between white Union and white Confederate forces. The results of this impasse were disastrous. Panic-stricken Union troops fired wildly into the ranks of their black comrades, even as well-disciplined Confederate forces took full advantage of the desperate plight of the black troops. A Union colonel reported:

The bravest [white troops] lost heart and men who distrusted Negroes vented their feelings freely. Some colored men . . . found a worse fate than death in the charge. . . . [Some] white men bayoneted blacks who fell into the crater.

The Battle of Nashville, fought in December 1864, was one of the few engagements in which the coordinated efforts of both black and white troops resulted in the effective repulsion of Confederate forces. Union General James B. Steedman explained:

All, white and black, nobly did their duty as soldiers and evinced cheerfulness and resolutions, such as I have never seen excelled in any campaign of the war in which I have borne a part.

Overall, the extent of black participation in the war can be tabulated with reasonable accuracy, both in terms of the kinds of units in which they were enrolled and the geographical distribution of such troops. Besides the 186,000 combat troops, there were more than 200,000 members of so-called service units. Of the combat troops, nearly 100,000 were mustered into service through the federal government, with the remainder being raised through state levy. Regionally, there were some 34,000 soldiers from the New York-New England area, including Pennsylvania and New Jersey. An additional 12,000 came from the West, including its territories. Over 45,000 came from border states, which Lincoln had feared he would lose and whose loyalty and manpower proved to be valuable adjuncts to the Union victory. Over 93,000 were raised in the rebellious states of the South, which might have done well to utilize black manpower, had it been possible.

Organizationally, black units were subdivided into 120 combat infantry regiments (close to 100,000 men), seven cavalry regiments (over 7,000 men), 12 heavy artillery regiments (over 12,000 men), and 10 companies of light artillery with over 1,300 men. These men saw combat in more than 200 battles classified either as full-scale engagements or minor skirmishes.

Not all black participants in the war served with Union forces. Indeed, as hostilities ground to a close, the South searched desperately for some last-ditch measure to stave off defeat. In agonizing frustration, some southern authorities entertained the notion of arming slaves, rationalizing this proposed policy by claiming that many blacks would still regard the South as their homeland, and so fight to save it from "foreign" encroachment, while others would follow their masters out of fear or personal loyalty.

On at least one occasion, the South gave at least momentary consideration to a formal proposal to recruit slaves. The proposal was made by General Pat Cleburne, an Irish supporter of the Confederacy, who broached the subject at a meeting of senior officers in 1864. Since every slave, in Cleburne's view, was a potential free man, he constituted an ever-present source of rebellion within the Confederacy itself, as well as an instant collaborator with Union troops. What had been a source of southern strength at the outset of the war was now "one of our chief sources of weakness." Cleburne proposed that the South turn slavery from weakness to strength again, by boldly and resolutely promising freedom to all slaves who would enlist.

His proposal was signed by three other generals and a handful of lower-echelon officers from his own command, but the high command listened in stunned silence. "I will not attempt to describe my feelings," one Confederate officer later wrote, "on being confronted with a proposal so startling in its character, so revolting to Southern sentiment, Southern pride and Southern honor. . . . If this thing is once openly proposed to the Army, the total disintegration of that Army will follow in a fortnight."

Dejectedly, General Cleburne put away his proposal. The war ground on as before. On the very day of Lee's surrender to Grant at Appomattox, black Union troops were still under fire on other battlegrounds, serving under such commanders as General Birney and General Sherman. Black soldiers were complemented by some 200,000 black civilians employed by the Union Army as laborers, cooks, teamsters, and in other support functions.

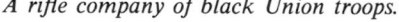
A rifle company of black Union troops.

All told, one out of every four Union navy men—29,511 in all—was black. They fulfilled a variety of roles on vessels engaged in coastal blockades and in pursuit craft activity, hunting down enemy privateers and gun runners. Black river and harbor pilots were among the best operating in the states. Others served as gunners, loaders, coal heavers, stewards, and firemen. On the docks, black men were equally active as laborers unloading supplies and other equipment. Blacks served aboard the *Kearsage* when she destroyed the *Alabama,* aboard the *Monitor* on its famed engagement with the *Merrimac,* and aboard Farragut's flagship in the Battle of Mobile Bay.

Four black sailors won Congressional Medals of Honor for valor in combat conditions. (For full details, see the list of winners elsewhere in this section.)

The Confederate "Experiment"

No definitive record exists to determine just how many black soldiers fought on the side of the Confederacy during the Civil War. Most who were readied for combat, however, were freedmen rather than slaves. The latter were generally engaged in construction work on roads, fortifications, and canals. They were also regarded as the "Army of the Soil," workers whose primary function was to tend and harvest the crops which helped feed an army in the field.

The largest of the black units was the First Louisiana Volunteer Regiment, also known as the Native Guards and consisting of nearly 1,000 men. The volunteers had answered Governor Moore's call to arms, issued on March 21, 1862:

The Governor and Commander-in-Chief, relying implicitly upon the loyalty of the free colored people of this city and state . . . calls upon them to maintain their organization and be prepared for such orders as may be transmitted to them.

There were at the time in New Orleans some 13,000 or so free blacks, many of them direct descendants of men who had fought with Andrew Jackson during the War of 1812. Many were educated men of property, even slaveowners themselves, who felt that emancipation and a Union victory would only bring an end to their privileged status.

There may have been no more than 150 soldiers in the 15 other black militia units serving throughout the country. This figure remains dubious, however. It is based on the muster roll of a Mississippi militia unit with 12 black infantrymen. Many more are known to have served in the defense of Richmond toward the close of the war, and presumably were also present in numbers greater than 12 in the First South Carolina Volunteer Regiment. One black officer, a Colonel

Gregg (regiment unknown), surrendered his life on the battlefield of Fredericksburg.

The fate of the First Louisiana Militia remains shrouded in mystery, however. There is no report of their having followed regular Confederate troops out of the city when it was evacuated following the triumphant entry of the Union Forces in the spring of 1862. Four months later, in August to be exact, General Ben Butler reorganized the Native Guards and recruited them for the Federal side.

An 1862 issue of *Harpers' Magazine* provides full insight into the scope of black activity during the war:

The works before Charleston, commenced late in 1860, were mainly thrown up by large gangs of negroes [sic] from the plantations, and by free negroes [sic] of Charleston, of whom 150 in a single day offered their services to the Governor of South Carolina. In April the Lynchburg Republican *proposed "three cheers for the patriotic free Negroes of Lynchburg," of whom seventy had "tendered their services to the governor to act in whatever capacity may be assigned them in defense of the state." It was triumphantly announced that all the fortifications required for the harbor of Norfolk could be erected by the voluntary labor of negroes [sic]. In June the Legislature of Tennessee passed an act authorizing the governor to receive into the military service of the state all male free persons of color between the ages of fifteen and fifty; and if a sufficient number did not volunteer they were to be impressed. The Southern newspapers of 1861 were full of accounts of colored volunteers. One told of a grand display, held November 23 at New Orleans, where 28,000 troops were reviewed, among whom was a "regiment composed of 1400 free colored men." The works of Manassas Junction were mainly thrown up by the slaves of the neighboring planters. In February, 1862, the Virginia House of Delegates passed a bill ordering the enlistment of free colored persons for six months. On the 10th of March, Mr. Foote declared in the Confederate Congress that, when Nashville was surrendered, 1000 or 1500 slaves had been called out and employed on the fortifications. In November, Governor Brown of Georgia, called for slaves to complete the fortifications of Savannah; if these were not voluntarily tendered a levy would be made upon every planter in the state of one slave out of five, which would give a working force of 15,000. Subsequent to this time still more stringent measures were taken to bring negroes [sic] into the Confederate service.*

It was not until July 17, 1862 that Congress authorized President Lincoln to employ "persons of African descent" in the naval and military service of the United States. On August 15, 1862, President Davis bitterly denounced "two at least of the generals of the United States" for exciting servile insurrection, and "arming and training slaves for warfare against their masters, citizens of the Confederacy." Clearly, however, from the evidence at least, it was a case of military charges and propaganda.

By the spring of 1865, the Confederates, poised upon

Private John Henry at Headquarters, 3rd Army, in October 1863. From the Matthew Brady Collection.

the abyss of defeat, again broached the subject of arming slaves. Again *Harpers' Magazine* reported the particulars with unfailing accuracy:

In September, 1864, the Governor of Louisiana urged upon the Secretary of War that the time had come to put into the army every able-bodied negro [sic] as a soldier "I would," he said, "free all able to bear arms, and put them into the field at once." In his message in November Mr. Davis discussed the question. It was to be viewed, he said, "solely in the light of policy and our domestic economy." Late in February, 1865, Lee strongly urged the employment of negroes [sic] as soldiers. "I think," he said, "the measure not only important, but necessary. I do not think our white population can supply the necessities of a long war. I think those who are employed should be freed. It would not be just or wise to require them to remain as slaves." An impressment or draft he thought would not bring out the best class; he would rather call upon those who are willing to come, with the consent of their owners.

An Act of Congress was ultimately passed (the margin of victory was a lone vote) which empowered the Confederacy to experiment with the idea of using slaves on a limited scale and granting them freedom for their efforts. Critics regarded the motion as an admission of despair to foreign observers, an abandonment of the very principles for which the Confederacy was ostensibly fighting, a gesture which would further demoralize their own white forces, and a decision which would remove too much needed black manpower from the fields. Though the matter remained academic, the stipulations of the enactment are intriguing and revealing:

1. Pay and rations the same for both white and black troops.

2. A quota from each state "not exceeding 300,000 troops . . . to be raised . . . irrespective of color."

3. Eligibility for no more than 25% of the male slaves of any state.

4. "Nothing in this act shall be construed to authorize a change in the relation [between master and slave]."

The last condition was, of course, logically impossible, the desperately incongruous act of a faltering enemy seeking vainly to preserve its ebbing life by arming its natural enemy.

CIVIL WAR BATTLES ENGAGED IN BY THE UNITED STATES COLORED TROOPS (USCT)

Black soldiers played a major role in the Civil War. Nearly 200,000 black combat troops fought in the Union Army, and one of every four men in the Union Navy was black. Blacks saw action in all sections of the country and in all types of warfare; some of the more significant battles in which they participated are listed below.

Amite River	Ash Bayou
Appomattox Court House	Ashepoo River
Arkansas River	Ashwood Landing

Athens	Clinton	Fort Taylor	Laurence
Barrancas	Coleman's Plantation	Fort Wagner	Little Rock
Bayou Bidell	Columbia	Franklin	Liverpool Heights
Bayou Boeuf	Concordia Bayou	Ghent	Madison Station
Bayou Macon	Cow Creek	Glasgow	Magnolia
Bayou St. Lewis	Cox's Bridge	Goodrich's Landing	Marengo
Bayou Tensas	Dallas	Grand Gulf	Mariana
Bayou Tunica	Dalton	Gregory's Farm	Marion
Bermuda Hundreds	Darbytown Road	Haines' Bluff	Marion County
Berwick	David's Bend	Hall Island	McKay's Point
Big Creek	Decatur	Harrodsburg	Meffleton Lodge
Big River	Deep Bottom	Hatcher's Run	Memphis
Big Springs	Deveraux Neck	Helena	Milliken's Bend
Black Creek	Drewry's Bluff	Henderson	Milltown Bluff
Black River	Dutch Gap	Holly Springs	Mitchell's Creek
Boggs' Mill	East Pascagoula	Honey Hill	Morganzia
Boyd's Station	Eastport	Hopkinsville	Moscow Station
Boykin's Mills	Fair Oaks	Horse Head Creek	Mound Plantation
Bradford Spring	Federal Point	Indian Bay	Mount Pleasant Landing
Brawley Fork	Fillmore	Indian Town	Mud Creek
Brice's Cross Roads	Floyd	Indian Village	Murfreesboro
Brigsen Creek	Fort Adams	Island Mound	Nashville
Brush Creek	Fort Anderson	Island No. 76	Natchez
Bryant's Plantation	Fort Blakely	Issequena County	Natural Bridge
Cabin Creek	Fort Brady	Jackson	New Kent Court House
Cabin Point	Fort Burnham	Jacksonville	New Market Heights
Camden	Fort Donelson	James Island	Olustee
Cedar Keys	Fort Gaines	Jenkin's Ferry	Owensboro
Chapin's Farm	Fort Gibson	John's Island	Pass Manchal
Charleston	Fort Jones	Johnsonville	Palmetto Ranch
Chattanooga	Fort Pillow	Jones' Bridge	Petersburg
City Point	Fort Pocahontas	Joy's Ford	Pierson's Farm
Clarkesville	Fort Smith	Lake Providence	Pine Barren Creek

The effect of the Emancipation Proclamation was the start of an exodus north and west.

Black rebel pickets seen through a federal officer's field glass.

Pine Barren Ford
Pine Bluff
Plymouth
Point Lookout
Point of Rocks
Point Pleasant
Poison Springs
Port Hudson
Powhatan
Prairie d'Anne
Pulaski
Raleigh
Rector's Farm
Richland
Richmond
Ripley
Roache's Plantation
Rolling Fork
Rooseville Creek
Ross Landing
Sabine River
Salkehatchie
Saltville
Sand Mountain
Sandy Swamp
Scottsboro
Sherwood
Shipwith's Landing
Simpsonville
Smithfield
South Tunnel

Spanish Fort
St. John's River
St. Stephens
Steamer *Alliance*
Steamer *Chippewa*
Steamer *City Belle*
Steamer *Lotus*
Suffolk
Sugar Loaf Hill
Sulphur Branch
Swift Creek
Taylorsville
Timber Hill
Town Creek
Township
Trestle
Tupelo
Vicksburg
Vidalia
Wallace Ferry
Warsaw
Waterford
Waterloo
Waterproof
White Oak Road
White River
Williamsburg
Wilmington
Wilson's Landing, Wharf
Yazoo City
Yazoo Expedition

LATER WARS

Indian Wars on the Frontier

At the close of the Civil War, several USCT regiments remained on active duty for a time, but Congress later authorized the creation of only two regular regiments of cavalry (the 9th and the 10th) and two of infantry (the 24th and the 25th). Known to the Indians as "Buffalo Soldiers," they served on isolated posts located in Texas and the Southwest—building roads, stringing telegraph wire, escorting groups crossing Indian territory, and scouting hostile tribes as well. During this period, 12 blacks won Congressional Medals of Honor for bravery in combat. (See Black Congressional Medal of Honor section for names and units.)

The first action between black troopers and Indians came 40 miles east of Fort Hays, Kansas in September 1867 when 40 troopers on duty protecting workers of the Kansas Pacific Railroad engaged 300 Cheyenne; the last action of black troopers and Indians was likewise the last armed fight between the U.S. Army and the Indian on this continent and took place on January 9, 1918 between Troop E of the 10th Cavalry and a well-armed band of Yaqui Indians 25 miles west of Nogales, Mexico, in Bear Valley, Arizona. Between these years the black soldiers on the American frontier played important roles in General Phillip Sheridan's

Mustered out black volunteers rejoin their loved ones in Little Rock, Arkansas.

campaign against the Cheyennes and Arapahoes and in subduing the Apache uprisings of the Southwest led by Victorio, Mangus Colorado, and Geronimo.

The most famous Indian uprising punctuating those years occurred at the Little Big Horn in the Dakota Territory between June 25 and 26, 1876. This is one of history's most frightfully memorable battles, largely because it resulted in the extermination of three whole U.S. battalions, led by Colonel George Armstrong Custer, at the hands of Sioux and Cheyenne Indians. It is not generally known that a black cavalryman by the name of Isaiah Dorman fought and fell at the Little Big Horn.

Originally an interpreter and scout, Dorman was an escaped slave who made his way into Indian territory and lived there for some years before taking an Indian wife. The "black white man," as the Indians called him, was trusted by them even though he worked for the white man. It would seem that he enjoyed the role of intermediary between the U.S. government (represented by the cavalry) and the Sioux nation (represented by an explosive mixture of volatile young chiefs and their more reluctant elders).

While reconnoitering the area through which Custer had decided to ride, Dorman detected various signs of a hostile Indian presence. His warnings were com-

A "Buffalo Soldier," the name given to black troopers by the Indians.

The black 10th Cavalry patrolled the high plains of the Old West for over fifty years.

municated to Custer, who paid as little heed to them as he paid to his War Department orders to avoid an armed confrontation. He led his men—Dorman among them—right into the trap the Indians had laid.

Dorman was one of those who fell. He was found on the battlefield by a bevy of Sioux women whose custom it was to circulate among the wounded, stripping them of arms and valuables. He was not scalped, according to one version of the story, because Sitting Bull himself intervened once he had learned his old friend was among the day's victims. Seeing that it was too late to save him, the chief then requested that he be spared from the customary ritual of mutilation designed, in Indian eyes, to prevent the victim from passing into the spirit world as a "whole man."

Although battles such as these tend to etch themselves into the public consciousness, it is well to remember that the glamorous or adventurous aspects of frontier life were generally far outweighed by the prosaic and uneventful routine of garrison or escort duty.

No chronicler of the West has captured the authentic flavor of life in these regiments more dramatically than author/illustrator Frederic Remington. In much of his writing, Remington recreates the up-front aura of the 10th Cavalry—not a stately, majestic, spruced-up lot of men suited for parades and other ceremonial gestures, but a rough-and-ready detail of "old soldiers who know what it is all about, this soldiering." The all-black 10th, Remington tells us, "never had a soft detail since it was organized," and was composed exclusively of "good horses and hardy men, divested of

military fuss." Remington respected men such as these, for he knew that it was they who were best equipped to grapple with the rigors of the frontier and to subdue "the great strange stretches of the high plains." The soldiers "in the colored regiments" were all veterans with several years of frontier life behind them, men who could never be replaced, men whose like would "never come again." The artist admired the obvious physical equipment of the black cavalrymen—fellows who were "great chested, broad shouldered (and) bull-necked," ideally built to contend with the rigors of the strenuous life.

The sociological significance of the passing of the frontier may have been lost on the men themselves but was of primary concern to the artist observer. Remington not only correctly identified the signs of encroaching civilization but captured its essential flavor with noteworthy sensitivity and unmistakable sympathy for the meritorious service of the Army regular.

The country through which we were then operating was howling wilderness; it is now traversed by railroads and covered with villages and farms. Children at play unwittingly trample the grass over the graves of soldiers who gave their lives that they might live and thrive, and communities throughout the West generally send representatives to Congress some of whom, in the peace and plenty of their comfortable homes, fail to recognize, in Washington, the hardships, privations, and sacrifice of life suffered by the army, before their prosperity could be possible or the lives of their constituents assured.

In this the simple duty of soldiers was performed, and no

Artist Frederic Remington recorded the everyday life of the 10th Cavalry. Above, an outposted sentry; below, a trooper takes a drink on the trail.

credit is claimed, but should not the record of past deeds such as these accompanied by the prosperity that has followed, at least guarantee a more generous feeling for the army by all citizens, more especially by those who are called upon to support it?

The Spanish-American War (1898)

It was the jingoistic Spanish-American War which roused the nation to reconsider the status of its black frontier regiments. The diary of a black sergeant of the 25th Infantry, Frank Pullen, suggests the hardships which the unit had undergone at its duty stations in Minnesota and, later, the Dakotas and Montana:

This gallant regiment of colored soldiers served eighteen years

in that climate, where, in winter, which lasts five months or more, the temperature falls as low as 55 degrees below zero, and in summer rises to over 100 degrees in the shade and where mosquitoes rival the Jersey breed.

Considering the isolation, drudgery, and discomfort the troops had undergone, it is not surprising that they reacted with unvarnished enthusiasm when news reached them that they were to embark for Cuba to avenge the sinking of the *Maine*.

Despite the ostensible importance of their patriotic mission, the men were at times subjected to considerable harassment and to humiliating affronts. They were jeered at whistle stops in southern towns; they were not only given separate quarters on government transport ships, but officially forbidden to socialize in any manner with white troops while enroute to their destinations; they ate in separate sections of the mess hall, which they entered only after white troops were all seated; they took their morning coffee alone after their white counterparts were finished.

Despite these indignities, black soldiers fought spiritedly and with great determination during the brief encounter. One white Southerner who saw them in action commented: "Of all the men I saw fighting, there were none to beat the 10th Cavalry and the colored infantry, and I don't mind saying so." Rough Rider Frank Knox, a cohort of Theodore Roosevelt's, promised that many of the black cavalrymen who had rushed up San Juan Hill would "live in my memory forever."

Roosevelt, on the other hand, recalled incidents in which black troopers had allegedly shown a tendency to "drift to the rear." In a magazine article, he described his stalwart intercession at crucial points to prevent mass desertions but neglected to take into account the possibility that orders from actual battle zones may have governed the men's behavior. As it turned out, Sergeant Preston Holliday of the 10th Cavalry later explained that black soldiers were often ordered to the rear to remove casualties or to stock up on rations, water, and other supplies. Other white Rough Riders backed the sergeant, although they did not command the same audience Roosevelt addressed.

As in other wars, conflicting white opinions concerning the calibre of black troops determined, to a large degree, their overall deployment and combat effectiveness. Individual heroes like Private T. C. Butler of the 25th Infantry and Sergeant Major Edward L. Baker of the 10th Cavalry (as well as six other Medal of Honor winners) distinguished themselves in combat at El Cavey, Santiago, and San Juan Hill, but the mass of black men who tried desperately to participate in the conflict were discouraged, delayed, or rejected.

In the South, National Guard units did not accept

Heroic charge of black regulars near Santiago, Cuba, during the Spanish-American War. The regiments participating were the 9th and 10th Cavalry and the 24th and 25th Infantry.

black volunteers; elsewhere volunteer regiments found the War Department in Washington, D.C. sluggish in responding to their pleas for active involvement. Among the state militias which were eventually raised pursuant to Congressional authorization were the 9th Ohio (a unit commanded by former West Pointer Charles Young), the 3rd Alabama Infantry, the 3rd North Carolina Infantry, the 6th Virginia, the 23rd Kansas, the 8th Illinois, two infantry companies from Indiana, and Company L of the 6th Massachusetts (otherwise an all-white regiment).

Officer promotions during the war were scanty, al-

Troop H, 10th Cavalry.

Action at Las Gusimas.

though some black men were advanced on the basis of combat heroism. In most cases, however, few command positions were meted out to black officers at the head of regimental-sized units. There was also a distinct reluctance on the part of American authorities to utilize black troops as part of the overall occupying force on the island after hostilities ended.

Significantly, some black critics of the war pointed to it as little more than an exerise in American imperialism, and saw black involvement in it as a double tragedy. In the view of historian Kelly Miller, blacks were in the awkward position of being subject to a form of domination at home which they themselves imposed on people fighting for liberation in Cuba and the Philippines.

World War I (1917–1918)

When the United States declared war on Germany on April 6, 1917, the call went out for thousands of black volunteers to help supply the war zones in France and Germany. Segregated in the draft and in a lone officer's training camp, and allowed at first to volunteer only as laborers in the Army and as servants in the Navy, blacks were assigned to the American Expeditionary Force, serving as stevedores, road builders, wood choppers, railroad hands, mechanics, gravediggers—in short, as cogs in the war machinery.

Black combat troops were organized into two divisions (the 92nd and the 93rd), each composed of four regiments. The 92nd consisted of the 365th to 368th regiments, and the 93rd was made up of the 369th to 372nd regiments. The most famous of the regiments was unquestionably the "Fighting 369th," an outgrowth of the old 8th Illinois, and a contingent well-stocked with New Yorkers. This unit landed at Brest, France in the spring of 1918, went into action in the Champagne sector, and remained on the front lines for 191 consecutive days without losing a trench, retreating an inch, or surrendering a prisoner. The unit

A famous regiment in World War I was the black "Fighting 369th," which remained on the front lines for 191 consecutive days without losing a trench or surrendering one prisoner.

Black infantrymen in France.

that the troops were badly motivated, cowardly, and a detriment to overall morale. As a result, the unit saw little action at the front.

The behind-the-scenes racial arrangements of U.S. military officials were not disclosed until *Crisis* correspondent W. E. B. DuBois uncovered a blatantly discriminatory document which explored the "official" U.S. position on the use and status of black troops.

Young black officer candidates were not aware of these disturbing policies when they pleaded so earnestly with Washington congressmen for the creation of a training camp. The Des Moines, Iowa camp which finally came into existence, graduated hundreds of junior officers, among them Charles Houston, later dean of Howard University's Law School. Houston's experiences in France led him to exclaim: "There [is] no sense of dying in a world ruled by them. German pris-

was awarded the Croix de Guerre by the appreciative French.

Two members of the 369th showed particular valor in combat and became the most celebrated black heroes of the war. Privates Henry Johnson, an Albany, New York, redcap, and Trenton, New Jersey resident Needham Roberts, while on forward observer duty, were suddenly overrun by a sizable band of German infiltrators. Though wounded, Roberts held the enemy at bay for a time by lobbing hand grenades into their midst. Low on supplies and losing strength, Roberts was soon overwhelmed by the Germans and in the process of being dragged off to German lines. Johnson then rushed the enemy with a bolo knife, creating such a diversion and inflicting so many casualties that he managed singlehandedly to disperse the invaders. The next morning, four German bodies were found, and Unit Commander William Hayward praised the "two brave Colored boys" who had fought "like tigers at bay." The French added their approval by nominating the men for the nation's highest military honor, the Croix de Guerre.

The other three black regiments were also brigaded with the French. The 370th saw action north of the Oise-Aisne canal; the 371st and the 372nd regiments helped defend the Meuse-Argonne front and earned the Croix de Guerre (with Palm) for their efforts.

The 92nd Division, left under American command, fared badly in comparison to its sister unit—largely because of familiar taunts by southern commanders

A trainload of recruits starts moving.

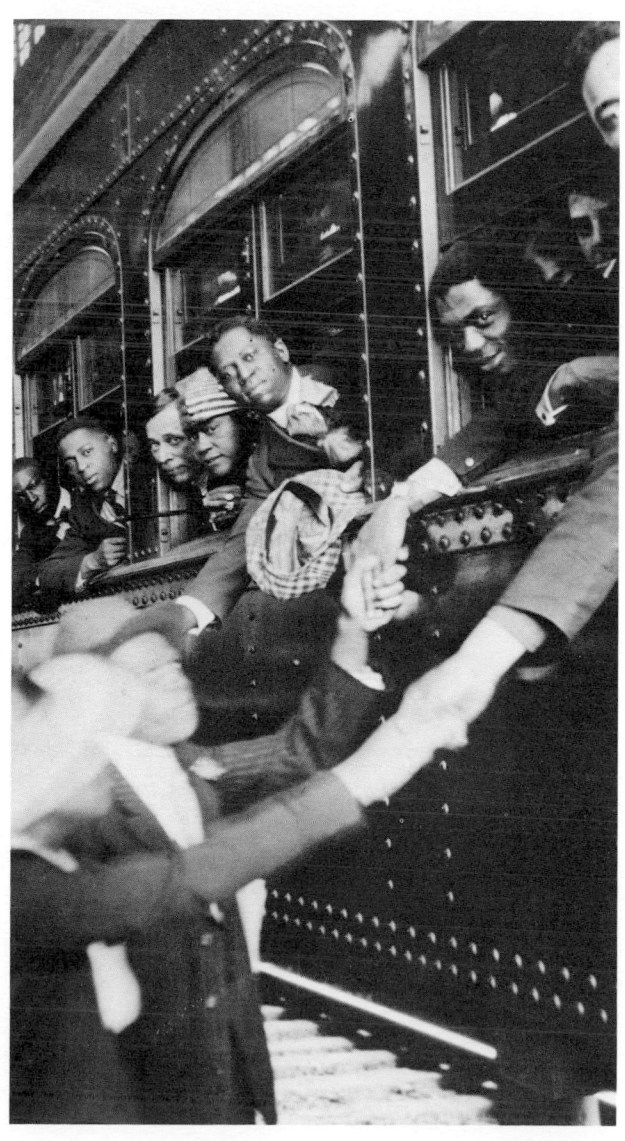

oners were kinder than our white American comrades."

After the famous parade up Fifth Avenue which marked the triumphant return of the 369th to Harlem, Dr. DuBois served notice on America that returning black servicemen meant to realize full equality under the law as first-class citizens:

We stand again to look America squarely in the face. It lynches . . . it disfranchises. . . it insults us. . . . We return fighting. Make way for Democracy! We saved it in France, and by the great Jehovah, we will save it in the U.S.A.

World War II black infantrymen in Italy (top) *and an Air Force sergeant in the Pacific.*

World War II (1941–1945)

World War II blasted its way onto the American scene on the infamous morning of December 7, 1941, when Japanese fighters flew over Pearl Harbor and rained a hail of bombs and bullets on the slumbering U.S. naval base there. Among the battle vessels sunk or reduced to helpless hulks was the U.S.S. *Arizona,* the ship on which black messman Dorie Miller was routinely going about his duties collecting laundry when the ear-splitting sounds of battle sirens and exploding shells rent the air. Miller rushed up on deck, and instantly hauled his wounded captain to safety. Moments later, he sprung into action behind an anti-aircraft gun he had never been trained to operate. Firing calmly and accurately, he brought down four Zero fighter planes before the cry to abandon ship was heeded by all survivors.

On May 7, 1942, messman Dorie Miller was cited for bravery by Fleet Admiral Chester Nimitz, who decorated him with a Silver Star and so acknowledged the nation's debt to a black man of "extraordinary courage." The medal did not bring with it an instant promotion, or a transfer to a line of duty which might have been more in keeping with Miller's demonstrated aptitudes or preferences. After returning from a trip back to Harlem, where he drummed up support for U.S. war bonds, Miller was assigned to the *Liscome Bay,* which went down in the Pacific on November 25, 1944, with no survivors.

There seems little doubt that the treatment accorded black servicemen was a contributing factor to the severe disillusionment gripping elements of the black community with the announcement of war. Dr. DuBois, for example, sensed instantly that blacks would continue to face the double burden of defending a nation abroad even as that nation, by virtue of its domestic policies, had not yet assured all of its citizens equal protection under the Constitution. Both Bayard Rustin and Elijah Muhammad were conscientious objectors during the war; Rustin on pacifist grounds and Muhammad in consequence of his religious separatism. (Muhammad was indicted for pro-Japanese sympathies in 1942.)

Still, most black civilians rallied to the side of the nation, endorsed the war effort, and sought to make a vital contribution to it. In the case of air cadet Yancy Williams, that endorsement involved a fearless insistence on the right of prospective black airmen to join the Air Force as fighter pilots, not merely ground jockeys or maintenance personnel. Williams, a Howard graduate, threatened a lawsuit, whereupon the Air Force quickly succumbed to the pressure of adverse publicity and opened its Jim Crow training facility at Tuskegee Institute.

The Navy, however, was equally lax in withdrawing the restrictions under which black sailors were forced to serve until pressure from the White House overturned existing policies of apathy and neglect. By the summer of 1942, some trainees in segregated camps and schools were receiving instructions as gunner's mates, petty officers, quartermasters, and coxswains. Despite these gestures, by 1945 the Navy was still operating under a *de facto* quota system which kept some one out of every 20 black seamen in the messman's branch.

The most important branch of the military complex remained the Army, however. Here, by the end of 1942, it was apparent that there was widespread reluctance to utilize black combat forces abroad. One unit of black engineers had been sent to Liberia to prepare landing strips for anticipated combat missions over North Africa, but War Plans Chief Dwight D. Eisenhower was frankly doubtful that large blocks of black troops could be indiscriminately assigned to overseas duty in Europe. In the Pacific theater, Generals Douglas MacArthur and Millard F. Harmon responded more to manpower needs than to an anticipated maze of social roadblocks and circumspect pressures. "Please disabuse yourself," wrote MacArthur to Washington, "of any idea that I might return these troops after your decision to dispatch them."

Black troops of the 93rd Division later fought at Bougainville and the Treasury Islands, and joined MacArthur in a historic moment of triumph and national glory when the Philippines were retaken in October 1944. By then, black marines had helped win the Battle of Saipan, and black engineers had pitched in to build the Burma Road on the Asian mainland. Black aviation engineers had built runways and landing strips in New Caledonia, the point of origin for the Air Force escort bombers that struck the Japanese in the crucial Battle of the Coral Sea, fought in 1942.

The 92nd also saw combat overseas, although its record was by far the most controversial of all black fighting units. General Benjamin O. Davis, the Army's first black general, joined the unit overseas in Italy, where he shot a propaganda film entitled *Teamwork* in an effort to prepare the American public for the advent of black combat troops on the European firing line. Great Britain's crusty and indomitable leader Winston Churchill, on hand to offer words of encouragement, was followed by dozens of white correspondents sent to improve public relations. Perhaps the most transparent public relations episode was the "battlefield promotion" invented by General Mark Clark to demonstrate the vital combat role already being played by the 92nd when it had not in fact taken its positions on the Gothic Line. General Clark rashly promoted First Lieutenant Charles F. Gandy of Wash-

ington, D.C., as a gesture to allay black criticism of the promotion policies in effect for back officers. Clark simply plucked the captain's bars off one of his white staff members and placed them on the shoulders of a man he had designated, clairvoyantly it seemed, as one who ought to be made visible.

Other problems of morale, level of training, and competence were simply overlooked by the high command of the 92nd. There were some initial combat successes, largely against light resistance along Highway 12 enroute to the foothills of the Apennines. Once

Colonel Benjamin O. Davis, Jr., commanding officer of the 99th Pursuit Squadron

General Patton pins a silver star on a member of the all-black 761st tank battalion.

in the mountains, however, the 92nd faltered badly. Some ran; some hesitated; some advanced sluggishly and without any combat crispness and determination. Still, there were contingents which engaged the enemy aggressively and fought earnestly to capture key objectives. Mass frustration, mismanagement, and confusion keynoted the experience as a whole, however. Lieutenant Colonel Marcus Ray, a black officer, conceded he was "heartsick," but was emphatic in denying the 92nd was "a complete failure as a combat unit."

Other black units performed many missions without any stigma of controversy. General Eisenhower, watching a black battalion charge the beach at Normandy, commended the troops for carrying out their mission "with courage and determination." General George S. Patton found the all-black 761st Tank Battalion worthy of fighting in his select company. "I would never have asked for you," he told them bluntly, "if you weren't good." The men were good enough to be on hand for the German capitulation in Austria.

At the Battle of the Bulge, Germany's last-ditch attempt to drive a wedge into Allied lines, black troops were called into action on an emergency basis to help withstand a ferocious Nazi assault. General Lanham

commented that he had "never seen soldiers who have performed better in combat." Again, neither proficiency nor praise was sufficient to override rigid patterns of segregation. The "heroes" were returned to their all-black units as soon as the crisis passed.

The 99th Pursuit Squadron remains the most glamorous black unit associated with World War II. Commanded by Colonel Benjamin O. Davis, this unit had flown over 500 combat missions and more than 3,000 sorties against the Germans by the summer of 1944. After being attached to the 332nd Fighter Group, the record of the unit grew even more impressive. By the spring of 1945, it boasted of nearly 1,600 combat missions and over 15,000 sorties; it destroyed Messerschmitts in the air and on the ground, and terrorized enemy shipping as well in the role of the roving marauder.

Neither the Navy nor the Marines could boast of such an accomplished unit. The Merchant Marine, on the other hand, had recruited some 24,000 black members, most of whom had had ample opportunity to win their spurs in a relatively unencumbered and desegregated environment. Eighteen Liberty ships were actually named for black men, including the S.S. *Frederick Douglass* and the S.S. *Robert L. Vann*.

Pressure mounted in the wake of World War II to continue to break down the most onerous patterns of racial segregation and to assure blacks—both in and out of service—the opportunity to make professional progress commensurate with their ability.

Blacks could point to impressive statistics as a testimonial to their unflagging commitment to the war effort. Three million had registered for service; 700,000 had served in the Army, 165,000 in the Navy, 5,000 in the Coast Guard, 17,000 in the Marines, and 4,000 in the WAVES and WACS.

Despite the record, recognition was not forthcoming until pressure was applied. In June 1948 A. Philip Randolph made extensive preparations to urge blacks to resist induction into a segregated Armed Forces. His League for Nonviolent Civil Disobedience against Military Segregation threatened to cause heavy embarrassment to the Truman Administration. After studying the situation carefully, President Truman decided not only to issue Executive Order 9981 barring segregation in the Armed Forces, but also to appoint a blue-ribbon panel to study equality of treatment and opportunity throughout the Armed Forces. The resulting group, the Fahy Committee, still found considerable evidence of unconscionable manipulation in the training patterns of black enlisted men, but reported that segregation was largely a thing of the past in the Army, Navy, Marines, and Air Force. Remnants of all-black units were to surface one last time before being officially doomed to oblivion: in the Korean War.

Three Mustang fighter pilots in Korea.

Korea

On June 25, 1950, North Korean forces, armed with Soviet weapons, ripped across the 38th parallel, driving hard for the Republic of Korea (ROK) capital at Seoul. Seventeen days after the Korean bombshell burst, the men of the 24th Infantry Regiment, a unit which, for all of its 81 years, had been composed entirely of black combatants, landed in Korea from Japan. The 24th entered the grim fighting against an enemy which had all but routed the ROK army, and forced them into one strategic retreat after another. It was a somber beginning. Then, on July 22, 1950, the *New York Times* reported that the important railhead city of Yech'on had been recaptured by attacking black American soldiers of the 24th Infantry. And the New York *Daily News* headlined: "Negroes Gain 1st Korea Victory." Thus remnants of an all-black unit were credited with the first victory for U.N. forces in Korea.

Despite this initial success, terrible controversy surrounded the performance of many black fighting units during the war. As in other wars, criticism of black units was sometimes unduly harsh. In January 1951 NAACP counsel Thurgood Marshall was dispatched to Japan to investigate the conditions surrounding court-martial proceedings involving 32 blacks convicted of violating the 75th Article of War. Of the 32, half had been sentenced to death or life imprisonment, and the remainder anywhere from 10 to 50 years.

After examining the trial records, Marshall found that several of the deliberations which had resulted in the conferral of life sentences had lasted less than an hour. Four life sentences had been issued in a space ranging from 42 to 50 minutes, hardly time for the observance of court formalities and the presentation of adequate arguments.

Later interviews with the prisoners uncovered other germane facts. One soldier had actually been in an Army hospital at the time he was accused of being absent without leave; another had falsified his age in order to enlist, and was not yet 18 at the time of his conviction; four others were found guilty of cowardice even though they were doing mess duty behind the battle lines at the time of their alleged disappearance. Five other men had been placed on trial in the aftermath of a confused withdrawal during which they had become separated from their unit. An examination of the trial testimony showed that the captain who testified against them had given three different versions of what happened on the night in question. Despite these discrepancies, the captain was promoted to major, and the five men were convicted of being AWOL. In all, 32 black GIs had been sentenced to imprisonment for criminal behavior as opposed to only two whites. Moreover, many of the convicted blacks, though accused of the same offense as the convicted whites, had been given far stiffer penalties.

From Japan, Marshall went on to Korea, where

he conducted many interviews with infantrymen who claimed that their officers frequently berated them and made no effort whatsoever to disguise their contempt for "nigger troops." Marshall concluded his investigation by maintaining that the frequency of such episodes not only contributed to the high rate of casualties but also encouraged the practice of scapegoating—the habit of blaming black troops for every conceivable combat snafu.

Marshall's findings offered convincing proof that many blacks were being accused by, and tried before, officers who held them in the kind of prejudicial contempt which made legal justice a virtual impossibility. The NAACP gathered enough evidence to reverse many of the court-martials entirely and to lighten sentences in the majority of other cases. It also succeeded in drawing renewed attention to the numerous instances of combat heroism by blacks.

Two black infantrymen received Congressional Medals of Honor, both of them awarded posthumously. Private William H. Thompson, one of the designees, had manned a machine-gun nest singlehandedly and remained at his post until his buddies withdrew to safety. Sergeant Cornelius H. Charlton, the other medal winner, had led three valiant attacks up an enemy-held hill and, though wounded, somehow continued to fire until the enemy emplacement under attack was destroyed.

Private Edward O. Cleaborn was honored by an official ceremony in his home town of Memphis, Tennessee, for covering the withdrawal of his comrades, including wounded buddies, while under fire on a ridge near the town of Kuri. Cleaborn's parents, presented with the Distinguished Service Cross, were told how their son had wiped out the Communist machine-gun crews threatening Company A of the 24th. He had mowed down enemy infiltrators which had outflanked the platoon, staying at his post and pumping his weapon until it grew hot enough to burn his hand. Everyone had made it back . . . except Private Cleaborn.

Lieutenant Harry Sutton was so conspicuous in fighting off a Communist breakthrough at Hungnam beachhead in December 1950 that the ridge he and his black infantry platoon had defended came to be known as "Sutton's Ridge." Sutton was later killed by Communist machine-gun fire while fighting in the Suwon sector, and thus never got to wear his Silver Star back home.

Among the black heroes who survived the rigors of combat were Lieutenant Ellison Wynn, acting commander of Company B, 9th Infantry Regiment. When dawn broke after a night attack, Lieutenant Wynn, out of ammunition, threw rocks and C-ration cans at scores of charging Chinese troops attempting to

Lieutenant General Benjamin O. Davis, Jr. takes command of U.N./U.S. Forces in Korea.

overrun his position near the Yalu River. Wynn was thus able to cover the retreat of 34 men, losing only four.

Sergeant Arthur Dudley, holder of a Distinguished Service Cross, was known to his war-weary senior officers on the line as "the best damn squad leader in Korea." The head of an international and interracial squad consisting of three KATUSAs (Koreans attached to the U.S. Army), and four Americans (one of them black), Dudley personally accounted for 53 enemy dead while under fire with the 19th Regiment. He had received his DSC for heroism displayed at the Battle of Ch'angyong, near the Naktong River, early in August 1950.

By the end of the Korean War, deactivation and reorganization had proceeded throughout the various military echelons. All black infantry units were discontinued, their men redistributed elsewhere. The 9th and 10th Cavalries were reconstituted as the all-black 509th and 510th Tank Battalions, and white replacements soon filtered into them. Statistics showed that only 88 all-black concentrations were still identifiable within the Army's structure, and 95% of black personnel were serving in integrated units. These included units stationed in Alaska and Australia, along with the Orient. Only in Europe and the United States did a few pockets of segregation remain.

Vietnam

During the brief period of cease-fire which intervened between the end of the Korean War and the intensification of the conflict in Vietnam, the Kennedy Administration proceeded energetically with a program designed to ferret out the remaining vestiges of discrimination in the Armed Forces. President Kennedy, speaking through his Secretary of Defense Robert McNamara, impressed upon the military establishment the need for fostering friendship and equal opportunity for black servicemen, both on and off base. By 1965, however, it was apparent that the nation was no longer on a peacetime footing; statistics released by the Department of Defense showed that almost 15% of the infantrymen serving in Vietnam were black. Added to these were 5.1% of the Navy, 8.9% of the Marine Corps, and 8.3% of the Air Force. The grand total: 9.3% of the Armed Forces.

The figures, and the war itself, generated tremendous controversy in the black community. In 1965 Malcolm X claimed that the U.S. government was "causing American soldiers to be murdered every day, for no reason at all." Two years later, Martin Luther King, Jr., reminded the American public that "the Negro" had always managed to become a "100% citizen in warfare," but was always reduced to a "50% citizen on American soil." The most famous defector from the ranks was heavyweight champion Muhammad Ali, who declared himself a conscientious objector on religious grounds as a Black Muslim. Ali was convicted of violating the Selective Service Act, and stripped of his championship as well.

Still, most young blacks were willing to answer the draft board's call when it came. Private First Class Milton Olive, 19, of Chicago, was typical of the young black men who risked, and sometimes lost, their lives in arduous battle far from the familiar sounds of home. Olive was blown to bits by an exploding grenade on which he had fallen to save the lives of his comrades, and posthumously awarded the Congressional Medal of Honor. By mid-1969, nine other blacks had joined Olive as recipients of the medal: Captain Riley L. Pitts, First Lieutenant Ruppert L. Sargent, Sergeant Rodney M. Davis, Sergeant Matthew Leonard, Sergeant Donald R. Long, SP5 Lawrence Joel, SP5 Clarence E. Sasser, SP5 Dwight H. Johnson, and PFC James Anderson, Jr.

Like Olive, many perished in combat. For Sergeant Davis, the end came in Quahg Nam on September 6, 1968 when, like Olive, he threw himself on a live grenade to protect his comrades.

Black servicemen stationed in Vietnam saw duty in hazardous combat zones and in the full spectrum of support functions. They could be found patrolling the Mekong Delta, advising the South Vietnamese Army at Pleiku, repairing jet planes on aircraft carriers in the Gulf of Tonkin (or flying them over Hanoi), joining the gruelling sieges (as at the Citadel of Hue after the Tet Lunar New Year offensive) or the bloody fights (as at Hill 875, Dakto), wading across the treacherous rice paddies, and slashing through the barely penetrable bamboo thickets. Black men in the ranks were unloading ships, digging latrines, driving trucks, servicing warplanes, and walking mountain ranges, even as black desk men and strategists were planning battles, practicing international law, and running press centers, to name but a few of their diversified assignments.

According to *New York Times* reporter Thomas Johnson, officers in the Military Assistance Command

A search and destroy mission in Vietnam, where the U.S. infantry was 13 percent black.

A black paratrooper crosses a native-built bridge in Kontum Province.

said that the 173rd Airborne Brigade, a crack outfit with heavy black representation, was "the best performing unit in Vietnam." In elite combat units like these, one out of every four combat troops was a black man; elsewhere in Vietnam's battle zones, the ratio fell to one out of every five men apt to see action. This same ratio prevailed among the Army's front-line supervisors (ranging in rank from PFC to Master Sergeant).

Until General Davis retired (to become Cleveland's Public Safety Director) two of the 1,342 admirals and generals in the U.S. military establishment were black. General Davis was last assigned to deputy command of MacDill Air Force Base in Florida after serving as full commander of the 13th Air Force in the Philippines and, prior to that, in a Korean headquarters assignment. The other was Lieutenant General Frederic E. Davison, appointed Brigadier General in July 1968, and named deputy commanding officer of the 199th Infantry Brigade in Vietnam. He was the highest ranked of 35 black senior officers in the U.S. Army at the time of his promotion.

By 1969 it had become apparent that many young black combat troops were beginning to exhibit the same trends toward racial separatism that had characterized the behavior of white troops. Experience quickly showed that such efforts at racial elitism, spawned no doubt by the constancy of rejection on the part of white troops, constituted a dangerous menace to the peace and well-being of all concerned. The primary cause of the difficulty was the unwillingness of the biased white GI to accept black troops; the more obvious manifestation of the problem was reflected in the black GI's contempt for his intransigent white counterpart.

At Fort Bragg, North Carolina, in the summer of 1969, for instance, racial unrest flared into a full-fledged brawl when 35 black troops at an enlisted men's club squared off with a squad of about 25 white MPs. The club was described as a voluntarily segregated meeting place for black soldiers who, like their white counterparts, had opted for exclusivity in their after-hours leisure and recreation. Such a withdrawal, thought to be harmless enough on the surface, allowed young men to lock up their assorted complaints, nourish their private rages, and magnify their gnawing grievances and suspicions. Though the Bragg incident had no tragic outcome, it afforded unmistakable evidence that a base camp could be transformed into gangland turf as soon as two militantly uncompromising factions found an explosive issue around which to rally.

The violence which erupted at the Marine base in Kaneohe, Hawaii, bore some similarities to the Bragg fisticuffs, although the rumble on the island centered on more readily discernible discriminatory trends, such as inequities in military discipline and punishment, as well as unjust favoritism involving promotions. The black-power salute rendered by a group of black leathernecks brought the series of provocations to a flash point, resulting in a donnybrook which left 16 injured and three hospitalized.

At Camp Lejeune, North Carolina, one white Marine died in the aftermath of an interracial brawl whose origins were not immediately apparent. Even before the incident, however, an Ad Hoc Committee on Equal Treatment and Opportunity had outlined some of the more deliberate practices which could lead to racial confrontations, including *de facto* segregation in housing, bars, and barber shops. Still, the Committee had not proceeded beyond the warning-and-advice stage by the time the tragedy struck.

The Marine Corps responded, several weeks later, with a directive which restated the integration policies of the Corps, ordered all officers and men to observe them, and added a pair of human touches which might have been amusing if the situation had not become so serious:

1. Natural haircuts, with certain minimal modifications, would henceforth be allowed.
2. Black-power salutes would be permitted so long as they were intended as greetings between "brothers" and not in defiance of the Corps.

The Army quickly realized that orders regarding haircuts and ghetto salutes were not substantive enough measures to prevent further outbreaks. This was communicated to Washington officials, who began to formulate a preliminary blueprint for easing the conflicts and preventing their escalation. Structural reform was clearly required, and the Department of Defense offered concrete proposals to clear the air and improve the racial climate within the military establishment. Implicit in its formula was the assumption that the Armed Services could not merely quarantine the problems of the civilian community with a stern and inflexible mandate. Instead, the Armed Services would have to face up to every vestige of bias which both raw recruits and seasoned commanders had inherited from civilian life. Such defects would have to be dissected in special indoctrination courses and mandatory biracial councils on such problems as housing, recreation,

officer-soldier relationships and promotion opportunities.

With such vigorous and affirmative action, the Armed Services sought to overcome the failures which rank-and-file violence underscored and recover its acknowledged position as a stalwart leader in the fight to achieve integration in American life.

BLACK SERVICEMEN IN THE 1970s

Between 1970 and 1975, major issues facing blacks in the armed forces were:

1. Continuing interracial tensions between black and white personnel, often resulting in disproportionate punishment of black servicemen.
2. Widespread application to blacks of administrative "other-than-honorable" discharges.
3. The use of coded discharges, in which numbers printed on separation papers alluded to pre-

An infantryman (below) *rests after returning from combat. At right, a black student undergoing Recondo Training descends from a UH-ID helicopter.*

Viet Cong flags taken by Marines of the 1st Division after brief firefight.

sumed behavior and personality problems of individual servicemen.

4. Unequal application of military justice.

In 1972 the Defense Department issued "The Search for Military Justice," the formal report of a special task force set up by Defense Secretary Melvin Laird. The report "affirmed that vestiges of discrimination remain in the military system," and went on to prove that blacks and Hispanics are involved in more disciplinary incidents than Caucasians and are punished more severely. Cited as major causes of inequities in military justice were:

1. Societal racism and preservice factors such as education and language disadvantages.

2. Mistrust and suspicion of and by people in command.

3. Coerced induction in lieu of civilian jail terms.

4. Heavy assignment of blacks into combat and service units and deficient training and use of blacks in technically skilled assignments.

Discharges and Punishment

In 1972 blacks comprised about 13% of discharged servicemen but received 33% of the dishonorable discharges, 21% of bad conduct discharges, 16% of undesirable discharges, and 20% of general discharges.

According to the National Association for the Advancement of Colored People, over one third of the discharges of minorities for Vietnam era veterans have been dishonorable, bad conduct, or less than honorable.

A count of military prisoners in Germany in 1971 showed that the proportion of black prisoners ranged from 40 to 50%, or more than three times the percentage of black servicemen stationed there. More than three fifths of prisoners convicted for willful disobedience or assault were black.

Blacks also received a higher proportion than Caucasians of Article 15, or "Company Punishment." Article 15 of the Uniform Code of Military Justice allows company commanders to impose nonjudicial punishment for various infractions. Article 15s have traditionally served two somewhat contrasting purposes. They are a compromise mechanism to reduce the severity of a punishment and mark on a serviceman's record, roughly similar to plea bargaining in civilian courts. And they are a means for junior officers to act against enlisted men with relatively little chance that unfair actions exercised under the Article will come to the attention of higher authorities.

In many units, Article 15 punishment was often used by company level officers to discourage blacks from military career ambitions or reenlistments, in contradiction to the policies of the Defense Department and many higher officers. The problem was compounded by the traditional service policy of leaving maximum discretion in disciplinary action to commanders at the company or battalion level.

Administrative Discharges

Although not widely known, a whole gamut of discharges exists between the "honorable" and "dishonorable" extremes. These are known as administrative discharges and are given for a variety of official reasons ranging from "the good of the service" to "unsuitability" and "unfitness." Although some of these discharges are classified as honorable, the majority have fallen into "general" and "undesirable" categories. According to the NAACP, in Europe in the early 1970s blacks received about 45% of all discharges issued below the "honorable" category. Though servicemen could appeal these and were entitled to counsel, fear and a paucity of legal knowledge prevented all but a few from doing so. And, often, less than honorable discharges were accepted by individual servicemen as an alternative to unexpired stockade terms or to a court martial and the likelihood of incarceration.

Less than honorable discharges can have the effect of branding a person for life, affecting career, earning ability, relations with civilian law enforcement agencies, and receipt of veterans' benefits. Though such discharges can be appealed, the appeal mechanism has been cumbersome and very few appeals have succeeded—only 5% by estimate of the NAACP.

Upper echelons of the Armed Forces have moved to reduce abuses. All-volunteer military service is in great part dependent on the enlistments, hopes, and positive attitudes to military service among minorities of all education levels. The Marine Corps has an-

nounced its intention to recruit at least 100 black officers annually. The Air Force wishes to raise its proportion of black officers. To do this and obtain enough enlisted personnel the services must improve their reputation among blacks, a reputation tarnished by inequities in military justice and assignments, and the Vietnam War, where a disproportionate number of blacks were killed in a venture unpopular with great segments of black, and white, Americans.

Improvements

The findings of "The Search for Military Justice" were underscored in 1972 by serious interracial battles aboard two Navy ships, the *Kitty Hawk* and *Constellation*, incidents in which the overwhelming number of servicemen blamed and detained were minorities. Blacks fought the case, with the NAACP undertaking legal proceedings. In December 1973, all convictions were reversed.

In January 1974, the Secretary of Defense eliminated coded discharges, which had labeled many ex-servicemen, often on the basis of supposition or rancor rather than fact, as homosexuals, drug users, or generally unstable.

The Defense Department ruling also entitled blacks

Navy Petty Officer Karl Graham checks a radar sensor control panel.

who had been discharged to scratch out or otherwise conceal the code numbers on their separation papers. The NAACP declared this to be unsatisfactory and demanded that administrative discharges be eliminated. They also sought to have veterans with coded discharges guaranteed the right to full veteran's benefits.

However, for all the very serious problems, the position of blacks in the services seems to be improving. And in many ways, military life is less discriminatory than civilian life.

Vast changes have begun to occur in the military—especially in the status of the black officer. Current attention to affirmative action has led the military to develop programs for the black serviceman. And in the 1980s increasing numbers of women are joining the military, working side by side with men in all aspects of military life. Women are being trained as pilots and navigators on noncombat aircraft. But even in the 1980s there is evidence of discrimination and racism in all branches of the military. Despite glowing reports of plans of affirmative action by the branches of service, such organizations as the NAACP and the American Civil Liberties Union have criticized the military's steps in meeting that plan.

In the late sixties and the early seventies there was a rash of incidents within the military in which black servicemen experienced the type of harassment they considered racial. The NAACP contacted the Defense Department and pressed for a general investigation, which resulted in affirmative action policies by all branches of the military. Those racial incidents seemed to have abated by the mid 1970s and the early part of 1980—when a black, Clifford Alexander, was Secretary of the Army. However, with the change of administration, there was a downgrading of affirmative action and the mechanisms that had been put into place in an attempt to curb the racist policies within the armed services.

The NAACP points up one incident that occurred on February 19, 1982 in the Phillips Building, Headquarters U.S. Army Engineer Division, Europe, in Frankfurt, Germany. The NAACP said that it had received reports that an Equal Employment Opportunity Officer, identified as Mrs. Patsy Moore, had been observed in full regalia of the Ku Klux Klan, visiting several division offices of the U.S. Army Engineers in Europe.

In a letter to Percy A. Pierre, Acting Secretary of the Army, Samuel Wright, the NAACP's Armed Forces Director, said, "An EEOC officer represents a unique position in our military services as elsewhere, seeking to redress inequality because of race that crops up in our American society and cultural structure. In view of her obvious adherence to the basic tenets

of the KKK philosophy by her outrageous conduct, we respectfully demand an inquiry into this entire matter for appropriate action by the Army. Such action would, of course, include removal of Mrs. Moore from her EEOC position, if this incident is verified."

In 1979 the American Civil Liberties Union charged the Navy with what it termed "widespread discrimination" against blacks and other minority members seeking to enter the service. John Shattuck, director of the A.C.L.U.'s Washington office, said that the recruitment policies of the Navy excluded qualified black youth instead giving preference to whites who were not as qualified. Statistically, the Navy has had the lowest percentage of blacks and other minorities in its enlisted and officer ranks. In 1978 the Navy had 8.6% of blacks in comparison to 26.3% in the Army, 17.6% in the Marines, and the Air Force with 13%. However, in a statement following Shattuck's charge, the Navy denied the allegation, stating that its "policy was to ensure that all racial groups have an equal opportunity for advancement. Equal opportunity in the Navy has improved through various management initiatives."

A report by the A.C.L.U. called "The White Man's Navy: Keeping the Blacks Out," compiled by the organization's director, William Olds, said, "Getting minorities into the Navy has been mind-boggling for Navy recruiters. A member of the Navy, based in Maryland, said only about 10 percent of blacks in his particular recruitment zone was able to enter the Navy in 1978 despite the fact that all were qualified and had passing grades on the qualification test. He observed that he had never seen a 'White Charlie' or a 'White Bravo' rejected." ("Alphas," "Charlies," and "Bravos" represent military jargon for A, B, and C scores.)

In 1962 President John Kennedy reestablished the Committee on Equal Opportunity in the Armed Forces, and the body was asked to look into the general problem of equal opportunity for Armed Forces members and their families. The major findings of the report were:

1. Black advancements in the military since 1949 were meager, and much remained to be done to achieve equality of opportunity.

2. Blacks in the military and their families were suffering daily humiliation and degradation in communities near bases at which they were compelled to serve.

3. No one in the military was charged with the responsibility to listen to equal opportunity complaints.

4. Installation commanders lacked specific direc-

Anti-aircraft shoulder-launched "Smart" missile, part of the modern "technical" army.

tives to guide them in dealing with off-base discrimination and, in fact, did not view this as a military command responsibility.

The major outcome of the report was a directive, "Equal Opportunity in the Armed Forces," which:

1. Created within the Office of the Secretary of Defense a Civil Rights Office.
2. Established, as policy, the responsibility of military commanders to oppose discriminatory practices affecting military personnel and their families and to foster equal opportunity for them, both in the military and in surrounding communities.
3. Authorized procedures for use of the off-limits sanctions in matters involving discrimination.
4. Directed the military services to issue the necessary regulations and orders to implement equal opportunity.

In assessing its affirmative action plan for fiscal year 1980, all branches of the military said that they were continuing their commitment to full equality for all members.

The United States Air Force said that commanders are responsible for managing its equal opportunity and treatment programs. The USAF said that during 1980 commanders continued to implement sound career development programs which provide Air Force people the opportunity to progress regardless of their race, creed, sex, national origin, or age. The Air Force said that it made excellent progress in increasing its numbers of minorities and women. The number of minority officers rose 9.6% over fiscal year 1979. Officer end strength increases included 435 blacks, 157 Hispanics, and 85 minorities. Minority enlisted force representation increased by 3%. Enlisted end strength increases included 2,294 blacks, 359 Hispanics, and 505 other minorities.

The Air Force said that its ROTC scholarships are used to procure the best qualified applicants to meet pilot, navigator, missile, technical, doctor, and nurse requirements. The Air Force said that it awarded scholarships to as many qualified minority and women officer candidates as possible through central scholarship selection boards.

The U.S. Army, in its affirmative action report, said that minority officer recruitment is being expanded to include appointments in specialty and professional areas, and the U.S. Military Academy has instituted long-range innovative programs to assist in meeting and sustaining goals in the years ahead. The Army's report also pointed out that although minority chaplains continue to be underrepresented, the accessions for all minorities are increasing. To recruit more minority chaplains, the Office of the Chief of Chaplains is planning to take measures to ensure chaplain visits to church conferences and seminars in the proximity of their installations to actively solicit qualified candidates.

The report of the U.S. Navy noted that its 1980 demography continued to show an increase in minority representation. The Navy said that its officer programs to increase minority representation are centered on the Naval Academy Preparatory School (NAPS) and the Broadened Opportunity for Officer Selection and Training (BOOST) efforts to prepare potential candidates for the rigors of college-level academic work. The Navy said that it met its 60% goal of minority students at BOOST and continues to strive toward a 50% goal at NAPS. On discrimination complaints, the Navy said that the number of complaints reviewed within various Navy headquarters had increased during 1979. The report noted that initial monitoring of cases concerning sexual harassment indicated the existence of this form of discriminatory practice in the force. The Navy said that initiatives to address these issues started through the use of training materials and aides to inform personnel of their rights to seek redress. During fiscal year 1980, the Navy chartered a Minority Officer Accession Study to recommend initiatives necessary to achieve the fiscal year 1985 end strength goal. The study concluded that the potential pool of eligible minorities is limited in terms of low Scholastic Aptitude Test scores and the preponderance of backgrounds in nontechnical fields. Sixteen initiatives were recommended to increase minority officer accessions. The initiatives included increasing minority affairs advisor billets at the U.S. Naval Academy from two to six, establishing a fifth NROTC unit on a predominantly black college campus, and expanding contact with minority colleges or universities, counselors, students, and organizations.

In assessing its affirmative action plan for 1980, the U.S. Marine Corps said that minorities increased by approximately 1% of the total enlisted population for a total of 30.7%, and minority officer strength remained the same at 5.8% with an increase among black officers and a slight decrease among Hispanic officers. The Marine Corps said that the readily apparent area of concern is the disproportionately low number of minority officers, both male and female, when compared to the minority population within the enlisted force. The report pointed out that its program to provide equitable distribution of minorities within occupational fields continues to show success. Mental group test classification scores used to determine school eligibility were reduced by 10 points for high school graduates. The Marine Corps noted that its goal is to attain a representation of minorities and women in each occupational field comparable to its composition of minorities and women in the total grade structure.

A CHRONOLOGY OF MILITARY EVENTS
(1770–1982)

1770, March 5 Crispus Attucks, "a mulatto fellow about 27 years of age . . . 6 feet 2 inches high, short, curled hair, his knees nearer together than common," is the first to fall in the "Boston Massacre."

1775, May 20 The Hancock and Warren Committee decides to use free blacks in the conflict but rejects slaves.

1775, June 17 Peter Salem, a former slave in Framington, Massachusetts, becomes a hero of the day at Bunker Hill by shooting British Major Pitcairn, the officer who had ordered the British to fire on the Minutemen at Lexington.

1775, July 9 George Washington directs colonial recruiters not to enlist "any deserter from the ministerial army, nor any stroller, black or vagabond or person suspected of being an enemy to the liberty of America."

1775, November 7 The British Colonial Governor of Virginia, John Murray, Earl of Dunmore, seeks to recruit blacks for the loyalist cause. His recruits become known as "Dunmore's Ethiopian Regiment."

1776, January 16 The Continental Congress accepts a December 30, 1775 proposal from Washington for the enlistment of free blacks. During the war approximately 5,000 blacks serve in the Colonial Army.

1776, April 15 John Martin, the first black Marine, enlisted for service in the Continental brig *Reprisal*.

1776, December 25 Blacks Prince Whipple and Oliver Cromwell cross the Delaware with Washington. By this time more blacks are serving among white units than fighting in separate units. Many are "substitutes" for whites. One separate unit distinguishes itself: men from Massachusetts who proudly call themselves "The Bucks of America."

1778, August 29 At the Battle of Rhode Island, an all-black regiment from Connecticut "distinguishes itself by deeds of desperate valor" against German mercenaries fighting for the British.

1779, July 15 Pompey Lamb, posing as a vegetable vendor, aids materially in the capture of Stony Point by General Anthony Wayne. Spies and saboteurs like Lamb were active in many roles and on many fronts during the war.

1807, June 22 The American man-of-war *Chesapeake* is capured by the British frigate *Leopard* in one of the key skirmishes that led to the War of

1812. Three black sailors are among those impressed aboard the British vessel.

1813, September 12 Captain (later Commodore) Oliver Hazard Perry wins a decisive victory against the British in the Battle of Lake Erie. The Commander reverses earlier criticisms regarding the possible effectiveness of black sailors.

1814, September 21 General Andrew Jackson calls on all black citizens to enlist in the defense of New Orleans.

1814, December 23–24 The Battle of Chalmette Plains or the Battle of New Orleans: Black troops hold a strategic position in Jackson's defense force and contribute materially to the crushing defeat of the British. After the black troops and others have some trouble collecting their pay, Jackson angrily writes: "Receive my orders for the payment of the necessary muster roll without inquiring whether the troops are white, black or tea."

1846, May 13 Few blacks see combat during the Mexican War. It is largely a war supported by the South and West and thus chiefly a white man's affair. Blacks who do participate go mostly as personal servants.

1856, October 18 First black listed on Navy muster rolls as sailmaker.

1861, June 28 The Tennessee Legislature authorizes the enlistment of free blacks between 15 and 50 years of age. Many southern blacks work on fortifications and, through their labor on plantations, help feed the bulk of the Confederate force. There are occasional all-black units in the early years of the war, but almost every Confederate regiment has its share of blacks who accompany white masters into battle and occasionally see action.

1861, August 6 The Confiscation Act declares that property used in direct or indirect acts against the Union are lawful prizes of war. Slaves who fit this category are considered free.

1862, May 9 General David "Black Dave" Hunter, holding captured South Carolina territory, begins to enlist blacks. This is the first organized attempt to use black manpower for combat duty in the War. By August, however, military pressures force Hunter to disband his "First South Carolina Volunteers."

1862, May 12 Robert Smalls, a black pilot, takes the Confederate Transport CSS *Planter* out of Charleston harbor and delivers her to the Union Squadron. Smalls is later named Captain of the *Planter.*

1862, July 16 Congress authorizes the enlistment of blacks "for the purpose of constructing entrench-

ments, of performing camp service, or any war service for which they may be found competent." The Enlistment Act, signed the next day, provides that whites with the rank of private should receive $13 a month and $3.50 for clothing, but blacks of the same rank are to receive $7 and $3, respectively. Pay is not equalized until 1864.

1862, October 28 The First Kansas Colored Volunteers, the first official all-black unit in the Civil War, fights a victorious skirmish at Island Mound, Missouri.

1863, January 1 President Abraham Lincoln formally issues the Emancipation Proclamation.

1863, January 13 The first Kansas Colored Volunteers are formally mustered.

1863, May 22 The Bureau of Colored Troops is established by the War Department. Union black troops are organized into 165 regiments of light and heavy artillery, cavalry, infantry and engineers. They are called "United States Colored Troops."

1863, May 27 During the attack on Port Hudson, the First Louisiana Native Guards fight valiantly, despite heavy losses. Captain Andre Cailloux distinguishes himself with a heroic death at the head of his men.

1863, October 2 Dr. A. T. Angusta is appointed surgeon of the 17th Regiment, U.S. Colored Volunteers. He is said to be the first commissioned black medical officer.

1863, December 25 Robert Blake wins Navy Medal of Honor for distinguished service aboard the USS *Marblehead.*

1864, June 19 Joachim Pease wins Navy Medal of Honor for gallant conduct aboard the USS *Kearsage* near Cherbourg, France.

1864, August 4 William Brown, James Mifflin, and John Lawson win the Navy Medal of Honor for heroic acts aboard a Union gunboat during the battle of Mobile Bay.

1865, March 13 A black enlistment bill is passed in the South. The action, originally initiated in 1864, comes too late to affect outcome of the war.

1865, March 17 Aaron Anderson wins Navy Medal of Honor for heroic action aboard the USS *Wyandank* at Mattox Creek, Virginia.

1865, April 9 Surrender at Appomattox.

1866, July 28 The 9th and 10th all-black Cavalry Regiments are formed under provisions of an Act of Congress. The 38th, 39th, 40th and 41st Infantry Regiments are also formed.

1869, March 3 A consolidation of the 38th and 41st makes the 24th all-black Infantry Regiment. A con-

The charge of the 22nd Negro Regiment, Petersburg, Virginia, June 16, 1864, painted by Andre Castaigne.

solidation of the 39th and 40th makes the 25th All-black Infantry Regiment. The four regiments, mostly staffed by white officers, patrol the plains and participate in the opening of the western frontier in the late nineteenth century.

1872, September 21 First black, John H. Conyers, admitted to U.S. Naval Academy.

1872, December 26 Joseph Noil wins Navy Medal of Honor for a daring rescue at sea aboard the USS *Powhatan* off Norfolk.

1877, June 15 Henry O. Flipper is the first black to graduate from West Point. Other black graduates follow in 1887 (John H. Alexander) and 1889 (Charles Young). A fourth, B. O. Davis, Jr., completed his training at the Point in 1936.

1898, February 11 Daniel Atkins wins Navy Medal of Honor for gallant conduct aboard the USS *Cushing*.

1898, July 20 Robert Penn wins Navy Medal of Honor for heroic action aboard the USS *Iowa* off Santiago de Cuba.

1906, August 13 One man is killed and several are wounded in Brownsville, Texas after racial disturbances involving black infantrymen of the 25th. When the men of the 25th refuse to identify those who participated in the violence, President Theodore Roosevelt takes extreme action and dishonorably discharges three whole companies. The Senate, in 1908, upholds his action in the "Brownsville Affair."

1917, March 25 The District of Columbia National Guard is called up to help protect the nation's capital; black units are included, reluctantly.

1917, May 1 The Central Committee of Negro College Men is set up at Howard University to prove the willingness of blacks to fight.

1917, May 12 Black leaders succeed in getting a black officer's training base at Des Moines, Iowa. The camp opens on June 15.

1917, May 18 Passage of a Selective Service Act greatly increases black participation in the Expeditionary Force.

1917, July 5 Registration Day. Some 700,000 blacks register for the draft.

1917, October 5 Secretary of War Newton D. Baker announces the appointment of Emmett J. Scott, secretary to Booker T. Washington, as Special Assistant to the Secretary of War serving as "confidential adviser in matters affecting the interests of the 10 million blacks of the United States and the part they play in connection with the present war." Scott remains in the position until June 1919.

1917, October 24 Formation of the 92nd Division, an all-black unit.

1917, December 27 The 369th Infantry Regiment of the 93rd arrives in Brest, the first black unit overseas. After training, they move up to the fighting front in April of 1918. Fighting with the French, they create an enviable record. In 191 days of front line action, the regiment never loses a man, a trench or a foot of ground, Soon the 369th is known to the Germans as the "Hell Fighters."

1917, March 28   "The Bulletin #35 Incident." General C. L. Ballou, commander of the 92nd Division, in response to discrimination against a black NCO at a theater in Kansas, orders "all colored members . . . [to] refrain from going where their presence will be resented . . . The sergeant is guilty of the greater wrong in doing anything, no matter how legally correct."

1918, May 15   "The Battle of Henry Johnson." When rifle fire fails to stop advancing Germans and his fellow sentry, Needham Roberts, has been captured, Henry Johnson attacks the enemy with his bolo knife, freeing his friend and forcing the Germans into retreat. Both he and Roberts receive the highest French military award, the Croix de Guerre—the first Americans of the war to do so.

1918, August 7   A document is circulated among the French entitled "Secret Information Concerning Black-American Troops." It describes the necessity for separating blacks and whites. The 92nd division, at the front, finds itself confronted with German propaganda aimed at undermining black loyalty to a country which enjoins them to fight for rights abroad they still do not have at home.

1918, September 26   The 368th Infantry Regiment of the 92nd begins a mission against the enemy which ends in confusion and disorder. Despite honorable records of the majority of black units, this incident is offered by many in the military and the white press as proving black inability to survive combat pressure. Secretary of War Baker later makes the following statement: "The circumstances disclosed by a detailed study of the situation do not justify the highly colored accounts which have been given of the troops in the action, and they afford no basis at all for any of the general assumptions with regard to the action of colored troops in this battle and elsewhere in France."

1919, February 17   The famed 369th marches up Fifth Avenue to Harlem through cheering crowds. The celebration over, most black units are quickly disbanded except for the four permanent regiments. Finally, as blacks and whites fresh from the service compete for jobs, increased racial friction occurs. By year's end, some 25 race riots have breached the peace.

1923, July 12   A War Department directive provides for use of blacks in emergencies—and then only on a limited scale. The letter adds: "No Negro troops are to be mobilized in the state of Texas." Military policy becomes even more specific in 1938 with the recommendation that blacks be accepted in proportion to the general population—at that time about 9% of the total.

1939, September 11   West Virginia State College is granted the right to establish the first black Civilian Pilot Training Program approved in peacetime.

1940, September 16   Congress passes a Selective

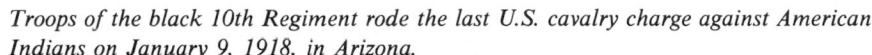

Troops of the black 10th Regiment rode the last U.S. cavalry charge against American Indians on January 9, 1918, in Arizona.

Training and Service Act containing the following antidiscrimination clause: "In the selection and training of men under this Act, and in the interpretation and execution of the provisions of this Act, there shall be no discrimination against any person on account of race or color." The 10% quota system is not regarded as discriminatory.

1940, September 27 With U.S. entry into the war more and more probable, President Franklin D. Roosevelt receives a delegation of three blacks, Walter White, A. Philip Randolph, and T. Arnold Hill, concerning utilization of black manpower in the war effort.

1940, October 9 With Roosevelt's initials, Assistant Secretary of War Robert Patterson issues a memo declaring the initial policy on the use of black troops: segregation as usual. "It has been proven satisfactory over a long period of years and to make changes would produce situations destructive to the morale and detrimental to the preparations for national defense."

1940, October 25 Colonel B. O. Davis, Sr., veteran of the Spanish-American War, becomes the first black general officer.

1940, November 1 The Office of the Civilian Aide to the Secretary of War in matters of black rights is established for William H. Hastie, dean of Howard University Law School. This is a position similar to the one occupied by Emmett Scott during World War I. Hastie holds the office until February 1943. Colonel Campbell Johnson, black head of Reserve Officer Training at Howard University, is made special aide to draft director Lewis B. Hershey.

1941, February 10 The first all-black officered regular Army Infantry Regiment (366th) is activated.

1941, March 21 A 99th Fighter squadron of black aviators is activated.

1941, May 1 The first black Signal Unit (275th Cons. Co.) is activated.

1941, June 1 The first black Tank Battalion (758th) is activated.

1941, July 1 Integrated Officers' Candidate Schools open, the first major step toward an integrated Army.

1941, July 19 Inaugural ceremonies are held at Tuskegee Institute, beginning black air training, which culminates in the 99th squadron.

1941, July 25 President Roosevelt issues Executive Order 8802 forming the FEPC.

1941, December 7 The Japanese attack Pearl Harbor. Black mess steward Dorie Miller mans a machine gun during the attack and downs four Japanese fighters, winning a Navy Cross.

1942, February 6 The first black military police battalion (730th) is activated.

1942, March 7 First black pilots complete training and are commissioned into the Air Corps. Included among them is West Point graduate B. O. Davis, Jr., son of the Army's first black general.

1942, March 24 The first black numbered Station Hospital (25th) is activated.

1942, April 7 Secretary of Navy Frank Knox initiates a policy calling for acceptance of blacks in the general service in the Navy and Reserves of the Marine and Coast Guard.

Major Charity Adams reviews her WAC troops during World War II.

1942, April 14 The first black officer is commissioned into the Coast Guard: Ensign Joseph C. Jenkins, a graduate of the Coast Guard Academy.

1942, May 15 The 93rd Infantry Division is activated.

1942, June 1 The Marine Corps begins the enlistment of blacks at the Marine Training Center, Camp Lejeune, North Carolina. The Navy, too, begins to accept blacks in positions other than the stewards branch.

1942, July 20 With the formation of the Women's Army Auxiliary Corps (WAC), black women are accepted with whites.

1942, August 24 Colonel B. O. Davis, Jr., takes command of the newly formed 99th Squadron.

1942, October 13 The 332nd all-black Fighter Group is activated, joining the 99th.

1942, October 15 The 92nd Division is activated.

1942, November 13 Leonard Roy Harmon wins Navy cross for extraordinary action aboard the USS *San Francisco* in the Solomon Islands.

1942, December 5 Executive Order 9279 requires all services to accept recruits through the Selective Service System. The order portends a greater percentage of blacks in service.

1943, February 19 Truman K. Gibson, Jr., succeeds William H. Hastie as Civilian Aide. Gibson, Assistant since November 1940, officially becomes Civilian Aide in September 1943, and stays in the position until November of 1945.

1943, February 28 The Navy makes a decision to induct blacks into all branches of the service according to their percentage of the total population, 10%. The announcement is made next month.

1943, April 16 The 1st Marine Depot company was the first black unit to be sent overseas in World War II.

1943, April 24 The 99th arrives in North Africa at Oued N'ja, is moved to Fardjourna and attached to the 33rd Fighter Group.

1943, June 1 The third black air unit, the 477th Bomb Group, is activated.

1943, June 12 William Pinckney awarded Navy Cross for heroism while serving aboard the USS *Enterprise* during the Battle of Santa Cruz Islands.

1943, June 20 Race tension explodes in the most serious race riot of the war in Detroit. The cause is largely black exclusion from the huge military efforts which are lucrative to civilian defense workers.

1943, July 2 Black pilots see action over Italy, and down their first aircraft.

1943, August 31 USS *Leonard Roy Harmon* commissioned as first naval vessel named for a Negro.

1943, November 12 Dorie Miller lost at sea, presumed dead. Awarded the Navy Cross for heroic actions during attack on Pearl Harbor.

1944, January 3 The 332nd enters the European theater.

1944, January 27 The 99th distinguishes itself over the Anzio-Nettuno beachhead. Eight confirmed hits are scored. The black air units, especially the 99th, go on to establish an outstanding combat record. Numerous black pilots will win the Distinguished Flying Cross by the end of the war.

1944, February 23 The Navy Department announces that two anti-submarine vessels being commissioned will be manned by all-black crews. The two all-black vessels, the USS *Mason* and the *PC-1253*, will only have one black officer aboard between them.

1944, March 17 Thirteen blacks become first group to be commissioned as Naval officers.

1944, March 20 The first Naval vessel with a predominantly black crew was commissioned as the USS *Mason* at the Boston Naval Shipyard.

1944, April 14 *PC-1264* commissioned at the Navy Yard, New York City, as the second naval vessel with predominantly black crew of officers and men.

1944, May 1 Charles F. Anderson becomes the first black in the Marine Corps to be promoted to Sergeant Major, highest noncommissioned rank among enlisted men.

1944, May 20 Secretary of the Navy Forrestal orders all naval vessels to be integrated. A group of 25 preselected ships are thoroughly briefed before the blacks arrive in August.

1944, June 6 D-Day. The 320th Negro Anti-aircraft Barrage Balloon battalion helps with the landing.

1944, July 3 The 99th is attached to the 332nd.

1944, July 8 In an attempt to partially remedy the cause of most racial incidents still breaking out in service, the War Department forbids racial discrimination in recreation and transportation facilities on all Army stations. Serious riots occur at Fort Bragg, Camp Robinson, Camp Davis, Camp Lee, and Fort Dix.

1944, August 9 The "Port Chicago Mutiny": after an ammunition explosion at the docks near San Francisco on July 17, black stevedores, some of them with advanced technical training, refuse to return to work. They are then brought to trial and sentenced to 8–15 years hard labor. Thurgood Marshall appeals the case and wins an acquittal in January of 1946.

Black marines on the beach at Iwo Jima

1944, October 19 Black women are notified they will be admitted into the WAVES. The first are sworn in on November 13 and the first WAVE officers graduate from training at Smith College on December 21.

1944, December 26 The Germans strike back at the Allies, creating a bulge in the broad advancing force. A directive is issued by Lieutenant General John C. H. Lee for black volunteers to be integrated by platoons into the white units fighting in the area. The move succeeds but does not usher in a new policy.

1945, January 31 The "Bulge" is neutralized. Most officials still refuse to recognize the Bulge Experiment as any kind of precedent, but rather simply as a successful special case.

1945, February 7 During a planned attack on the German Gothic Line on the Cinquale Canal, elements of the all-black 92nd Division reportedly fall back in a disordered retreat and are accused of "melting away" in the face of enemy resistance. "Failure" is again trotted out as proof of the black's inability to endure combat pressure. Segregation continues to evade exposure as the real culprit.

1945, March 8 The first black nurse is sworn in the Navy Nurse Corps in New York City. She is Phyllis Mae Dailey.

1945, March 24 The 332nd stages a raid over Berlin and later receives a Distinguished Unit Citation for its bravery.

1945, April 13 The Navy lifts all restrictions on the number and type of auxiliary vessels to which black personnel can be assigned.

1945, July 23 An urgent appeal goes out "to qualified women to join with the two Negro commissioned officers and the 54 enlisted WAVES in playing an active part in a speedy victory."

1945, August 25 Reviewing the Bulge Experiment, General George C. Marshall agrees that the results of the integrated force should be regarded as a special case and not lead to premature judgments.

1945, October 4 Secretary of War Robert P. Patterson sets up the Gillem Board to study the use of black manpower in the armed forces.

1945, October 17 The 332nd returns triumphantly to the U.S.

1945, November 10 The first black Marine officer, Frederick C. Branch, was commissioned a second lieutenant in the Marine Corps Reserve.

1946, January 2 Lieutenant Colonel Marcus H. Ray, fresh from the Italian campaign, becomes Civilian Aide, a post he holds until July 1947.

1946, February 27 Secretary of the Navy James V. Forrestal announces: "Effective immediately, all restrictions governing the types of assignments for which Negro Navy personnel are eligible are hereby lifted. Henceforth, they shall be eligible for all types of assignments in all ratings in all activities and all ships of the Naval Services."

1946, March 4 The Gillem report calls for the continuation of the 10% quotas and is released as "War Department Circular 124" on April 27, 1946.

1946, June 23 The first group of 31 black officers are integrated into the Regular Army.

1946, December 5 Executive Order 9808 establishing the President's Commission on Civil Rights.

1947, March 15 Ensign John W. Lee is the first black officer to be transferred into the Regular Navy.

1947, October 29 The Office of Civilian Aide is transferred to the Office of the Secretary of Defense. James C. Evans officially begins his duties in this post in January, 1948.

1948, February 2 President Truman issues a Civil Rights message to Congress which states: "During the recent war and in the years since its close we have made much progress toward equality of opportunity in our armed services without regard to race, color, religion or national origin. I have instructed the Secretary of Defense to take steps to have remaining instances in the armed services eliminated as rapidly as possible. The personnel policies and practices of all the services in this regard will be made consistent."

1948, February 12 The first black nurse is integrated into the Regular Army Nurse Corps.

1948, April 1 The *New York Times* announces that

A. Philip Randolph has formed a Committee against Jim Crow in the Military Service and Training. The group threatens mass civil disobedience and black boycott of the draft.

1948, June 9 The first black doctor is integrated into the Regular Army Medical Corps.

1948, June 23 The Republican Party platform states "We are opposed to the idea of racial segregation in the armed forces of the United States."

1948, July 1 ROTC units are established at Morgan State University, Florida A & M, and Southern University, predominantly black schools.

1948, July 1 First blacks augmented into Regular Marine Corps.

1948, July 15 The Democratic Party platform states: "We call upon the Congress to support our President [to guarantee] the right of equal treatment in the service and defense of our nation."

1948, July 17 A. Philip Randolph impresses on President Truman the "bipartisan mandate to end military segregation."

1948, July 25 Training centers for blacks and whites are established at Fort Riley, Kansas and Fort Ord, California.

1948, July 26 President Truman issues Executive Order 9981, setting up a Committee to study Equality of Treatment and Opportunity in the Armed Services (the Fahy Committee).

1948, October 23 The Navy commissions and assigns to duty its first black aviator, Ensign Jessie Brown.

1949, April 6 Secretary of Defense Louis Johnson directs the Secretaries of the Army, Navy, and Air Force to examine their personnel practices in line with Executive Order 9981.

1949, April 28 Now under the Defense Department the title Civilian Aide is changed to Civilian Assistant to the Secretary of Defense. James C. Evans still occupies the position.

June 1 The 332nd Fighter Wing is deactivated at Lockbourne Air Force Base and integrated into the Regular Air Force throughout the world. Integration seems to proceed more smoothly within the military than with the civilian community.

1949, June 3 Wesley A. Brown of Washington, D.C. graduates from the U.S. Naval Academy, the first black in its history.

1949, June 7 The Secretary of Defense approves of the Department of Navy's policies under Executive Order 9981.

1949, June 23 Secretary of the Navy Francis Matthews declares: "It is the policy of the Navy Department that there shall be equality of treatment and opportunity for all persons in the Navy and Marine Corps without regard to race, color, religion or national origin."

1949, September 30 A nondiscriminatory job policy adopted by Army. All school courses opened to blacks.

1949, October 1 New Army Secretary Gordon Gray issues orders abolishing black quotas.

1950, January 16 The Department of the Army promulgates Special Regulations 600–629–1, "Utilization of Negro Manpower," and declares its new policy: Blacks with special skills will be "assigned to any . . . unit without regard for race or color."

1950, March 27 Quotas in Army enlistments are officially abolished.

1950, May 22 The Report of the President's Committee on Equality of Treatment and Opportunity in the Armed Services (Fahy Committee), "Freedom to Serve," is issued.

1950, July 20 The first United States victory in Korea is won by the all-black 24th Infantry Regiment.

1950, October 20 The 9th and 10th Cavalry are converted into the 509th and 510th black Tank Battalions and integrated with white units on March 7, 1952 and December 31, 1953 respectively. The 25th Infantry is broken into smaller units and integrated with white units during early 1951 and 1952.

1950, December 4 Ensign Jesse L. Brown becomes first black to win the Navy's Distinguished Flying Cross for heroic action over Korea.

1951, June 21 In Korea, the first black since the Spanish American War is posthumously awarded the Medal of Honor.

1951, July 21 The Army makes its first cautious press release concerning its integration plans. They announce that the 24th Infantry Regiment will be broken up and that plans are underway to integrate the Far Eastern Command.

1951, July 26 The Department of the Army announces plans for the complete racial integration of the Far Eastern Command. Integration has, however, already existed to a greater or lesser extent for some time in Korea.

1951, October 1 The 24th Infantry Regiment is deactivated and its personnel are integrated into white units. Much of the 24th is already spread out among white units in Korea.

1951, November 1 The Draft Form of Project Clear (three volumes), "Utilization of Negro Manpower in the Army," is issued. It clearly shows that an integrated force is effective, even much more effective than a segregated service.

1952, April 1 Plans for racial integration throughout

A naval reservist photographer's mate first class answers recruiting station phone.

the Army's European Command are announced. Meanwhile, the Air Force has been at work and now announces complete integration of its personnel.

1952, October 1 The first black Marine pilot, Frank E. Petersen, Jr., was commissioned a second lieutenant and received his wings.

1953, August 20 Secretary of the Navy Robert Anderson directs the elimination of segregation in all facilities at Naval shore installations.

1954, January 12 The Secretary of Defense Charles Wilson announces that "the operation of all school facilities located on military installations shall be conducted without segregation on the basis of race or color."

1954, May 17 The Supreme Court hands down its historic decision on the unconstitutionality of school segregation. The armed forces already had moved to break down segregationist practices.

1954, June 11 The Secretary of Defense provides a program "to familiarize contracting officers" with the Department's policies on discrimination. On paper, at least, integration is finally a general policy within the military establishment.

1966, February 1 Thomas D. Parham, Jr., becomes first black chaplain to attain rank of Captain.

1967, September 1 Minority Officer Recruiting Effort (MORE) established at Navy Bureau of Personnel, Washington, D.C.

1968, August 21 The Medal of Honor was posthumously awarded to the first black Marine recipient, PFC James Anderson, Jr.

1968, May 19 First Naval Reserve Officer Training Corps established at Prairie View A&M.

1969, January 24 A report released in Saigon by the Army contends that "all indications point to an increase in racial tensions" in the Army. Insufficient numbers of black junior officers and disproportionately heavy punishment for black soldiers are cited as major causes.

1970, May 17 Prairie View A&M (Texas) University NROTC commissions first group of 11 Naval Reserve Ensigns and two Marine Corps second lieutenants.

1970, December Seven black soldiers petition the Secretary of Army to investigate bias against black soldiers stationed in Germany.

1970, December 17 Chief of Naval Operations Admiral E. R. Zumwalt issued Z-66, a directive outlining specific actions to be taken by all U.S. Naval Personnel to ensure equal opportunity.

1971, February 8 Secretary of the Navy John Chafee announced that a destroyer escort would be named in honor of Ensign Jesse L. Brown, the first black naval aviator.

1971, March 15 Defense Secretary Laird announces program to end discrimination in Armed Forces. Included are mandatory race relations classes in basic training and a Defense Department Race Relations Institute to train teachers of race relations.

1971, April 28 Captain Samuel L. Gravely selected to become the U.S. Navy's first black admiral.

1971, May 13 Three blacks are among 80 colonels promoted to Brigadier General. This raises number of black generals to four. The Air Force has one black general and on June 2 Navy Captain Samuel L. Gravely is named the first black admiral.

1971, June 3 Representative Shirley Chisholm charges that racial tension between Germans and black soldiers stationed in Germany is critical.

1971, June 13 Twenty airmen are injured in a racial clash at Sheppard Air Force Base, Texas. On June 24, similar conflicts erupt at Travis Air Force Base, California.

1971, July 24 Twelve high-ranking military officers are reprimanded and transferred for failure to comply with Defense Department race relations policies.

1971, September 1 The Defense Department announces that blacks now comprise 10% of the nation's forces in Vietnam and that this percentage is greater than the percentage of black soldiers being killed in action. In 1969 blacks accounted for 8.5% of the soldiers and over 13% of deaths.

1972, September 28 The first black to complete 30 years of service as a Marine, Sergeant Major Edgar R. Huff, retired.

1972, October and November Interracial skirmishes involving over 100 crewmen break out on the ships *Kitty Hawk* and *Constellation.*

1973, May 21 Daniel James, Jr., named Lieutenant General, becomes the highest ranking black in the Armed Forces.

1973, June Secretary of Army Robert F. Froehlke orders reversal of all the discharges without honor imposed on 167 black soldiers of the 25th Infantry Regiment in 1907, following the riots in Brownsville, Texas. Records of all the men were cleared.

1974, April 19 The first permanent Marine Corps facility to be named for a black Marine, Camp Johnson, at Camp Lejeune, North Carolina, was dedicated to the memory of Sergeant Major Gilbert H. "Hashmark" Johnson, USMC (Ret.)

1974, February Captain Gerald Thomas becomes the second black Rear Admiral in U.S. Navy history and is assigned to Pacific Destroyer Squadron 9.

1974, June and July Forty-three black sailors refuse to report to the U.S. *Midway,* charging racial bias, long hours, and mistreatment aboard their aircraft carrier. This is the second ship-jumping incident aboard the *Midway* in two years.

1974 July The Reverend Alice Henderson, a black woman, is commissioned a chaplain in the U.S. Army, becoming the only female chaplain, black or white, in the country's armed forces.

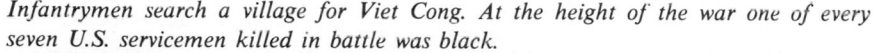

Infantrymen search a village for Viet Cong. At the height of the war one of every seven U.S. servicemen killed in battle was black.

1974, July Five black women are among the group of 15 women who become the first female cadets at the U.S. Merchant Marine Academy at Kings Point, New York.

1974, July Brigadiers Julius W. Becton, 47, and Harry W. Brooks, Jr., 45, are promoted to the rank of Major General in the U.S. Army.

1974, November Jill Brown becomes the first black woman to qualify as a pilot in the U.S. armed forces. Brown is in the Navy.

1975, May Lieutenant Donna P. Davis becomes the first black woman physician in the Naval Medical Corps.

1975, August General Daniel "Chappie" James, Jr., becomes Commander-in-Chief of the North American Air Defense Command (NORAD) on the same day that he is promoted to the first black four-star general in U.S. military history.

1976, May 6 Midshipman First Class Mason C. Reddix, Jr., of San Antonio becomes the first black in the history of the U.S. Naval Academy to earn the highest midshipman's rank. Midshipman First Class Derwood C. Curtis of Chicago is named Regimental Commander.

1976, June 7 Edward Scarborough, a member of the Defense Manpower Commission, says that a report about the military written for the Commission by Kenneth J. Coffey and Frederick J. Reeg suppressed evidence of racial discrimination in all four major services. Scarborough says that the report showed that Armed Service recruiting policies were "racially motivated" but he says those findings did not appear in the final report.

1976, June 19 A hearing by the military manpower subcommittee of the House Armed Services Committee into the Marine Corps recruitment and training practices. Harry Hiscock, a former Marine private, one of the witnesses, tells of harsh treatment at the hands of drill instructors.

1976, July 1 Two former Marine recruiters testify before a House Armed Services Subcommittee that they were ordered to limit the number of blacks they took into the corps.

1976, August 1 Veteran Columbia, South Carolina NAACP lawyer Matthew J. Perry, Jr. confirmed by the Senate as a judge in the U.S. Court of Military Appeals in Washington. He is the first civil rights lawyer in the South to gain a judicial position during the Ford Administration.

1976, September 2 The Army reorganizes part of its college scholarship program in an attempt to double the number of black officers in the ROTC within 10 years.

1976, December 6 The Marine Corps begins pretrial hearings for three black Marines who face charges stemming from a November 13, 1976 incident. The alleged assailants had attacked a group of white marines holding a party because they thought the party was a meeting of Marine Ku Klux Klan members.

1977 Togo West becomes the first black sworn in as Navy General Counsel.

1977 Clifford Alexander, Jr. becomes the first black Secretary of the Army. He has a budget of $28.8 billion and supervises over 1.3 million Army regulars and others. He also supervises 370,000 civilian employees.

1977, September 25 A report by the Rand Corporation terms the volunteer military a success while conceding that the percentage of black enlisted men had risen from about 8 in 1960 to approximately 16 at the present. The report contends that the proportion of enlisted blacks would have increased by about the same amount under the draft.

1977, November 15 Dr. John White, an assistant secretary of defense, says that more than 40% of the recruits for the volunteer armed forces were being discharged before completion of their first term. He said the discharge rate was more than twice what it had been during the draft era and among the factors he cited were lack of literacy, medical problems, financial hardships, and poor performance. White said that blacks accounted for 20% of new enlistees in fiscal 1977, up from 2% from fiscal 1976.

1978 Majors Frederick D. Gregory and Gulon S. Bluford, along with Dr. Ronald McNair, begin training as astronauts.

1978, February 2 Federal contracts totaling $240 million earmarked for the nation's minority business sector for defense purposes in fiscal year 1979.

1978, March 16 General Daniel "Chappie" James, the first black four-star general is buried. General James had earned more than 24 awards and commissions. Representative Louis Stokes (D. Ohio) urges legislation to construct a memorial to James at Alabama's Tuskegee Institute where the general received his wings.

1978, June 1 The Black Panthers of World War II receives the Distinguished Presidential Unit citation award for "courageous and professional actions." The honor was presented to retired Army Lieutenant Colonel Charles Gates, president of the 761st Tank Battalion Association, by Army Secretary Clifford Alexander, Jr. during a ceremony at Fort Meyer, Virginia.

1978, June 29 Brigadier General Harvey Williams

denied entry to a disco in Bonn, Germany until someone mentions his rank. Williams said after the incident that American GIs "of all races, but primarily black" are turned away at doors of 10 nightspots in the German capital.

1978, August 3 W. Graham Claytor, Jr., Secretary of the Navy, says the Supreme Court's controversial *Bakke* decision "leaves the legality of Navy affirmative action programs, both military and civilian, unchallenged."

1978, August 15 Army Chief of Staff General Bernard W. Rogers writes that "black soldiers receive disproportionate numbers of punitive discharges, are overrepresented in confinement facilities and are charged with more serious offenses per 1,000 soldiers than white soldiers." At the same time an internal Army study of equal opportunity claims that there had been "significant progress" in race relations in the Army.

1978, August 24 U.S. Navy Captain Richard E. Williams is the first black to assume duties as Commander of Air Wing Four at the Naval Air Station in Corpus Christi, Texas.

1978, November The Army drafts a plan aimed at young college-bound men that would reduce some enlistments to two years from three and offer a better GI bill. Army officials deny that the plan is aimed at changing the racial composition of the Army by attracting whites. Blacks compose about 30% of the Army, which numbers 770,000

1978, December 6 Pentagon reports that the percentage of black soldiers in the Army's enlisted ranks doubled over the past eight years.

1979 Second Lieutenant Marcella A. Hayes becomes the first black woman pilot in the U.S. armed forces in November. She is only the fifty-fifth woman out of 48,000 officers to graduate from the Army Aviation School in Fort Rucker, Alabama.

1979, January 4 Lieutenant General Julius W. Becton sworn in as commanding general of headquarters, VLL Corps, in Frankfort, Germany. The command includes two infantry divisions and one German Panzer division.

1979, February 8 Army Secretary Clifford Alexander promotes five blacks to the rank of general. Those promoted by Alexander are Arthur Holmes, an ordnance officer; John Michael Brown, a West Point graduate attached to the infantry; Colon Powell, an infantry officer; John Forte, an air defense artillery officer; and Edward Honor of the transportation corps.

1979, April 1 Lieutenant Colonel Reginald Jones becomes the first black munitions staff officer in the Munitions and Missile Division in the U.S. Air Force in Washington, D.C.

1979, April 12 Former POW Air Force Colonel Fred Cherry claims the Air Force failed to safeguard against the misspending of his wages while he was a prisoner of war. The U.S. Court of claims rules that the Air Force had allowed the colonel's wife, whom he divorced, to squander his military pay.

1979, April 27 Frank E. Petersen of the U.S. Marine Corps becomes the first black Brigadier General in the Marine Corps. General Petersen is the Director, Facilities and Senior Division, Installations and Logistics Department Headquarters, Marine Corps, Washington, D.C.

1979, June 15 The U.S. Navy is charged with widespread discrimination against blacks and other minorities. John Shattuck, Washington Director of the American Civil Liberties Union, states that the Navy uses a quota system restricting minority access to the Navy by giving preference to whites having the same or fewer qualifications than blacks.

1979, July 5 Army Assistant Secretary Percy Pierre praised on Capitol Hill "for presenting to Congress the most readable and honest presentation on the needs of the Army." The report, which involves military needs against a background of Soviet build-up, is also credited with "pulling no punches because the Army admits its failures, refuses to portray the Russians as 10 feet tall, and provides examples which clearly explain military needs."

1979, July 23 Deputy Assistant Secretary of Defense for Equal Opportunity M. Kathleen Carpenter says she believes there is "a new racism" appearing in the military. Carpenter says it is a form of backlash from affirmative action programs.

1979, August 17 Master Chief Boatswain's Mate Jesse J. Holloway becomes the first chief petty officer of the Pacific Fleet.

1979, August 2 Representative Ronald V. Dellums (D. Calif.), vice chairperson of the Congressional Black Caucus and a member of the House Armed Services Committee, says the 17-member CBC strongly opposes the reinstitution of the military draft during peacetime.

1979, August 29 The Navy announces that all ship and shore commanders have been ordered to use their full powers to "deal effectively with racist activity."

1979, September 20 Bill Daniels, an Oakland, California civilian Army employee who is an amputee, among a trio of people receiving the title of Handicapped Employees of the Year.

1980, March General Hazel W. Johnson becomes the

Nineteen-year-old Lance Corporal Felicia A. Lynch, part of the new Marine Corps.

first black woman promoted to the rank and position of Brigadier General, Chief of the U.S. Army Nurse Corps. Brigadier General Johnson received her Ph.D. from Catholic University in Washington, D.C.

1980, May 28 Lieutenant Vincent K. Brooks becomes the first black West Point cadet to hold the post of "Captain of the Cadets."

1980, December Ensign Brenda Robinson becomes the first black female aviator in the U.S. Navy assigned to the Fleet Logistics Support Squadron Forty in Norfolk, Virginia.

1981, March 23 A New York-based research team for the Veterans Administration releases a study stating that Vietnam veterans suffer from "significantly more" emotional, social, educational, and job-related problems than do military veterans who did not serve in Vietnam. The study shows that unemployment among black Vietnam veterans was more than three times as high as for white Vietnam veterans.

1982, February 19 The NAACP calls on Acting Secretary of the Army Percy A. Pierre to investigate the complaint against an Equal Employment Officer, Mrs. Patsy Moore, who was said to have been wearing the full regalia of the Ku Klux Klan while visiting several division offices of the U.S. Army Engineers in Europe.

BLACK MILITARY HEROES

In view of the absence of racial identification of many military records dating from the Civil War, it is difficult to determine how many black servicemen have been awarded the Medal of Honor. By pinpointing a number of segregated units in which blacks served until World War II, however, the editors of this volume have been able to verify the names of 46 blacks who have won this coveted award since it was instituted during the Civil War. The Department of Defense is at present compiling a definitive list of all black CMH recipients. According to the preliminary information gathered by this agency, 46 black soldiers have won the medal: 16 in the Civil War; 14 in the Indian wars; 5 in the Spanish-American War; 2 during the Korean Conflict; and 11 in the Vietnamese War. Of the 8 winners in the Navy, 5 were honored for their exploits during the Civil War, 1 for a feat of peacetime bravery (1872), and 2 in the Spanish-American War.

Pending further research, the following list is offered to our readers, along with biographical data where available.

ARMY

Civil War (1861–1865)

1863

Sergeant William H. Carney, *Company C. 54th Massachusetts Colored Infantry.* Born in New Bedford, Massachusetts, Carney was the first black to win the Congressional Medal of Honor. He was cited for valor on June 18, 1863 during the Battle of Fort Wagner, South Carolina, in which he carried the colors and led a charge to the parapet after the standard bearer had been felled by rifle fire. During this battle, Carney was twice severely wounded. His medal was issued on May 23, 1900.

1864

Private William H. Barnes, * *Company C, 38th U.S. Colored Troops.* Born in St. Mary's County, Maryland.

Sergeant William H. Carney, first black Congressional Medal of Honor winner

First Sergeant Powhatan Beaty,* *Company G, 5th U.S. Colored Troops.* Born Richmond, Virginia.

First Sergeant James H. Bronson,* *Company D, 5th U.S. Colored Troops.* Born in Indiana County, Pennsylvania.

Sergeant-Major Christian A. Fleetwood,* *4th U.S. Colored Troops.* Born in Baltimore, Maryland.

Private James Gardiner,* *Company I, U.S. Colored Troops.* Born Gloucester, Virginia.

Sergeant James H. Harris,* *Company B, 38th U.S. Colored Troops.* Born in St. Mary's County, Maryland.

Sergeant Alfred B. Hilton,* *Company H, 4th U.S. Colored Troops.* Born in Harford County, Maryland.

Sergeant-Major Milton M. Holland,* *5th U.S. Colored Troops.* Born in Austin, Texas.

Corporal Miles James,* *Company B, 36th U.S. Colored Troops.* Born in Princess Anne County, Virginia.

First Sergeant Alexander Kelly,* *Company F, 6th U.S. Colored Troops.* Born in Pennsylvania.

First Sergeant Robert Pinn,* *Company I, 5th U.S. Colored Troops.* Born in Stark County, Ohio.

First Sergeant Edward Radcliff,* *Company C, 38th U.S. Colored Troops.* Born in James County, Virginia.

Private Charles Veal,* *Company D, 4th U.S. Colored Troops.* Born in Portsmouth, Virginia.

Sergeant-Major Thomas Hawkins,* *6th U.S. Colored Troops.* Born in Cincinnati, Ohio, Hawkins was cited for valor in the Battle of Deep Bottom, Virginia on July 21, 1864. He was credited with the rescue of his regimental colors from the enemy. His medal was issued on February 8, 1870.

Sergeant Decatur Dorsey, *Company B, 39th U.S. Colored Troops.* Born in Howard County, Maryland, Dorsey was cited for valor in the Battle of Petersburg, Virginia, on July 30, 1864. When his regiment was driven back to Union lines, he carried the colors and rallied the men in his unit. His medal was issued on November 8, 1865.

Indian Wars (1870–1890)

Sergeant Emanuel Stance, *Troop F, 9th U.S. Cavalry.* Born in Carroll County, Louisiana, Stance was cited for valor in the Battle of Kickapoo Springs, Texas. An outstanding Indian scout, he was awarded his medal on June 28, 1870.

Corporal Clinton Greaves, *Troop C, 9th U.S. Cavalry.* Born in Madison County, Virginia, Greaves was cited for valor in the Battle of Florida Mountain, New Mexico, on June 24, 1877. His medal was issued on June 26, 1879.

Sergeant Thomas Boyne, *Troop C, 9th U.S. Cavalry.* Born in Prince George's County, Maryland. Boyne was cited for bravery in action during two New Mexico battles in 1879. His medal was issued on January 6, 1882.

Sergeant John Denny, *Troop B, 9th U.S. Cavalry.* Born in Big Flats, New York, Denny was cited for removing a wounded comrade to a place of safety while under heavy fire in Las Animas Canyon, Mexico, on September 18, 1879. His medal was issued on November 27, 1894.

Sergeant Henry Johnson, *Troop D, 9th U.S. Cavalry.* Born in Boynton, Virginia, Johnson was cited for valor in the Battle of Milk River, Colorado, on October 25, 1879. While under heavy fire, he fought his way to a creek to bring water to the wounded. His medal was issued on September 22, 1890.

Sergeant George Jordan, *Troop K, 9th U.S. Cavalry.* Born in Williamson County, Tennessee, Jordan was cited for bravery in two battles; one at Fort Tulersu,

---

* These 13 men won their awards for valor during the Battle of New Market Heights on September 29, 1864. With the exception of Sergeant James H. Harris, all were awarded their citations on April 6, 1865.

New Mexico, on May 14, 1880, the other at Carrizo Canyon, New Mexico, on August 12, 1881.

Sergeant Thomas Shaw, *Troop K, 9th U.S. Cavalry.* Born in Covington, Kentucky, Shaw was cited for valor in Carrizo Canyon, New Mexico, on August 12, 1881. He forced the enemy back after holding his ground in a dangerous position. His medal was issued in December, 1890.

First Sergeant Moses Williams, *Troop I, 9th U.S. Cavalry.* Born in Carroll County, Pennsylvania, Williams was cited for valor in the Battle of Cuchillo Negro Mountains, New Mexico, on August 16, 1881. His medal was issued on November 12, 1896.

Private Augustus Walley, *Troop I, 9th U.S. Cavalry.* Born in Reisterstown, Maryland, Walley was cited for bravery in action in the Battle of Cuchillo Negro Mountains, New Mexico, on August 16, 1881. His medal was issued on October 1, 1890.

Sergeant Brent Woods, *Troop B, 9th U.S. Cavalry.* Born in Pulaski, Kentucky, Woods was cited for valor in New Mexico on August 19, 1881. His medal was issued on July 12, 1894.

Sergeant Benjamin Brown, *Company C, 24th Infantry Regiment.* Born in Virginia, Brown won his award nipping an attempted robbery in Arizona on May 11, 1889. His medal was issued on February 19, 1890.

Corporal Isaiah Mays, *Company B, 24th Infantry Regiment.* Born in Carter's Bridge, Virginia, Mays was cited for gallantly stopping an attempted robbery in Arizona on May 11, 1889. Like Brown, he was awarded his medal on February 19, 1890.

Corporal William O. Wilson, *Troop I, 9th U.S. Cavalry.* Born in Hagerstown, Maryland, Wilson was cited for bravery in the Sioux campaign of 1890. His medal was issued on September 17, 1891.

Sergeant William McBryar, *Troop K, 10th U.S. Cavalry.* Born in Elizabeth, North Carolina, McBryar was cited for bravery in an engagement against Apache Indians in Arizona on March 7, 1890. His medal was issued on May 15, 1890.

Spanish-American War (1898)

Private Dennis Bell,* *Troop H, 10th U.S. Cavalry.* Born in Washington, D.C.

Private Fitz Lee,* *Troop M, 10th U.S. Cavalry.* Born in Dinwiddie County, Virginia.

Private William H. Thompkins,* *Troop G, 10th U.S. Cavalry.* Born in Paterson, New Jersey.

Private George Wanton,* *Troop M, 10th U.S. Cavalry.* Born in Paterson, New Jersey.

* Cited for bravery at Tayabacoa, Cuba. They received their medals on June 23, 1899.

Sergeant-Major Edward L. Baker, *10th U.S. Cavalry.* Born in Laramie County, Wyoming, Baker was cited for bravery in the underfire rescue operation of a wounded comrade in Santiago, Cuba, on July 1, 1898. His medal was issued on July 3, 1902.

Korean War (1950–1953)

Pfc. William Thompson, *Company M, 24th Infantry.* Born in Brooklyn, New York, Thompson was the first black to win the CMH since the Spanish-American War. He lost his life on August 6, 1950 after fighting off the enemy singlehandedly during a withdrawal operation. The medal was awarded in June 1951.

Sergeant Cornelius Charlton, *Company C, 24th Infantry.* Born in the Bronx, New York, Charlton was the second black to win the Congressional Medal of Honor in Korea. On June 2, 1951, he was killed while leading a platoon attack on a Communist-held ridge. The medal was awarded on February 12, 1952.

Vietnam (1965–1973)

PFC Milton L. Olive III, *Company B, 503rd Infantry, 173rd Airborne Brigade.* While participating in a search-and-destroy operation in the vicinity of Phu Coung on October 22, 1965, PFC Milton Olive saved the lives of his fellow soldiers by falling on a live grenade and absorbing the shock of its blast with his body. Olive was cited for conspicuous gallantry by the President of the United States at the White House on Thursday, April 21, 1966, at which time the Medal was awarded posthumously to his parents. Born in Chicago on November 7, 1946, Olive attended parochial school in his native city and later went to Saints Junior College High School for three years. He took basic combat training at Fort Knox, Kentucky, and also attended a number of service schools. During his service tour, he won the Combat Infantryman Badge, the Armed Forces Expeditionary Medal, and the Purple Heart with an Oak Leaf Cluster. Olive died a few weeks before his twentieth birthday.

PFC James Anderson, Jr., *Company F, 2nd Battalion, 3rd Marine Division.* Like PFC Olive before him, James Anderson, Jr. reacted instantaneously to danger "with complete disregard for his own personal safety," grabbing a live grenade thrown into the midst of his platoon, pulling it to his chest and curling around it as it exploded. The shock was so great that other Marines received shrapnel wounds from the fragmentation. Anderson was killed instantly. The highly decorated soldier (he

The parents of PFC Milton Olive accept his posthumous Medal of Honor from President Lyndon Johnson.

had won the Purple Heart and several service medals) was a native of Los Angeles, California, where he was born January 22, 1947.

Sergeant First Class Webster Anderson, *Battery A, 2nd Battalion, 320th Artillery, 101st Airborne Division.* Complete disregard for his personal safety and the ability to function in an exemplary fashion while under fire earmarked Sergeant Anderson for the Medal of Honor, presented him by President Nixon at the White House on November 24, 1969. Anderson, a native of Winnsboro, South Carolina, entered the U.S. Army on September 11, 1953.

Sergeant First Class Eugene Ashley, Jr., *Company C, 5th Special Forces Group [Airborne], 1st Special Forces.* Born in Wilmington, North Carolina, on October 12, 1931, Ashley was killed in action during an attempted rescue operation at Camp Lang Vei in Vietnam. Ashley lost his life while being carried from the summit of the hill from which he and his men had dislodged the enemy. He was killed by an artillery shell.

PFC Oscar P. Austin, *Company E, 2nd Battalion, 1st Marine Division.* On February 23, 1969, PFC Oscar P. Austin threw himself on an enemy grenade to protect an injured Marine, and later was mortally wounded when he lunged in front of a fallen comrade who was exposed to enemy rifle fire. Austin was cited for "inspiring initiative and selfless devotion to duty." A native of Nacogdoches, Texas, Austin was born January 15, 1948. He completed high school in Phoenix, Arizona, and joined the Marine Corps in April 1968. Austin had won other medals, including the Purple Heart, before being designated a Medal of Honor winner.

Sergeant Rodney M. Davis, *Company B, 1st Battalion,*

1st Marine Division. During a heavy battle in Quang Nam Province (Republic of Vietnam), Sergeant Rodney M. Davis and his platoon were pinned down by mortars, heavy automatic and small arms fire. Unable to withstand the enemy assault, the Marines were lodged in a trench and in danger of being overrun by the enemy. A grenade lobbed in from close range landed in the trench, threatening the lives of the entire unit. Sergeant Davis "instantly" threw himself upon it in what was described as "a final valiant act of complete self-sacrifice." Davis died September 6, 1967. Born in Macon, Georgia, in 1942, he had enlisted in the Corps on August 31, 1961.

PFC Robert H. Jenkins, *Company C, 3rd Reconnaissance Battalion, 3rd Marine Division.* PFC Robert H. Jenkins was killed in action on the morning of March 5, 1969 while occupying a defense position south of the DMZ. Jenkins and his comrade constituted a two-man fighting emplacement manning a machine gun. When a North Vietnamese grenade was thrown into their midst, Jenkins seized his comrade, shielding him from the full impact of the explosion. He died later of injuries sustained on the scene. Born June 1, 1948, Jenkins was a graduate of Central Academy High School in Palatka, Florida. He enlisted in the Marines in 1968.

Specialist Six Lawrence Joel, *HQ & HQ Company, 1st Battalion [Airborne], 503rd Infantry, 173rd Airborne Brigade.* One of the earlier winners of the Medal of Honor, Specialist Joel was cited for "gallantry and intrepidity at the risk of his life above and beyond the call of duty" while serving as a medical aidman in a combat operation on November 8, 1965. Despite his own wounds, Joel left his cover to minister to several fallen comrades, giving them plasma, pain killers, and other necessary medication while under a continuous barrage. Joel, a native of Winston-Salem, North Carolina, was born February 22, 1928.

PFC Ralph H. Johnson, *Company A, 1st Reconnaissance Battalion, 1st Marine Division.* As part of a 15-man reconnaissance patrol deep in enemy territory, PFC Ralph H. Johnson was manning an observation post on Hill 146 when a heavily armed, platoon-sized Vietnamese force attacked his position. A grenade tossed into the three-man fighting hole occupied by Johnson and two comrades threatened the lives of all until Johnson flung himself on the device, absorbing its shattering fragments. Johnson was killed in action on March 5, 1968, less than a year after he had enlisted in the Regular Marine Corps. Johnson was born in Charleston, South Carolina, January 11, 1949.

Specialist Five Dwight Hal Johnson, *Company B, 1st Battalion, 69th Armor, 4th Infantry Division.* Climbing fearlessly out of his disabled tank, Johnson, armed only with a .45 caliber pistol, engaged the heavily armed enemy and killed several North Vietnamese. After running out of ammunition, he returned to his tank, where he grabbed a submachine gun before braving yet another enemy barrage. Johnson also rescued comrades and killed several North Vietnamese at close range. A native of Detroit, Michigan, Johnson is a graduate of Northwestern High School. He was born May 7, 1947.

Private First Class Garfield M. Langhorn, *Troop C, 7th Squadron [Airmobile], 17th Cavalry, 1st Aviation Brigade.* A radio operator, Langhorn lost his life after falling on a grenade thrown into the midst of a group of wounded men he was helping rescue during a helicopter mission. Born in 1948 in Cumberland, Virginia, Langhorn attended Riverdale High School before being inducted into service in 1968.

Platoon Sergeant Matthew Leonard, *Company B, 1st Battalion, 16th Infantry, 1st Infantry Division.* Sergeant Leonard was awarded the Medal of Honor in 1967 for "conspicuous gallantry and intrepidity in action" during combat operations near Suoi Da in Vietnam. Surviving numerous assaults and several gunshot wounds, Leonard showed remarkable "fighting spirit" and qualities of "heroic leadership." Leonard is a native of Eutaw, Alabama, and was born on November 26, 1929.

Sergeant Donald Russell Long, *Troop C, 1st Squadron, 4th Cavalry, 1st Infantry Division.* Sergeant Long was killed in action during an attack on his troop by a Viet Cong regiment on June 30, 1966. Long abandoned the relative safety of his armored personnel carrier and exposed himself to withering enemy fire while carrying the wounded to evacuation helicopters. He was killed by an exploding grenade whose shock he absorbed with his body. Born August 27, 1939, Long was a native of Blackfork, Ohio.

Captain Riley Leroy Pitts, *Company C, 2nd Battalion, 27th Infantry, 25th Infantry Division.* Captain Pitts died in Vietnam on October 31, 1967 after leading an airmobile assault in the vicinity of Ap Dong. The captain risked his life when a grenade which he had lobbed against the entrenched enemy rebounded off the dense jungle foliage and threatened to explode in the midst of his men. Pitts fell on the grenade but, miraculously, it failed to explode. He was later mortally wounded during an exchange of gunfire with the enemy. Captain Pitts, a native of Fallis, Oklahoma, was born October 15, 1937.

Lieutenant Colonel Charles Calvin Rogers, *1st Battalion, 5th Artillery, 1st Infantry Division.* Rogers is the highest ranking black officer to have received the Medal of Honor while on active duty in Vietnam. Rogers served in the embattled country from November 1967 to November 1968, and was cited for exceptional gallantry while on duty with the 1st Infantry Division. Despite several wounds, Colonel Rogers rallied the beleaguered men of a fire support base which was in danger of being overrun by a numerically superior enemy, and prevented it from being captured. Rogers' citation singled out his "relentless spirit of aggressiveness, conspicuous gallantry and intrepidity in action."

First Lieutenant Ruppert L. Sargent, *HQ & HQ Company, 3rd Battalion, 60th Infantry, 9th Infantry Division.* Lieutenant Sargent died in action on March 15, 1967.

Specialist Five Clarence Eugene Sasser, *HQ & HQ Company, 3rd Battalion, 60th Infantry, 9th Infantry Division.* Medical aidman Clarence E. Sasser was awarded the Medal of Honor in recognition of his heroic efforts, under fire, on behalf of wounded comrades stranded in an exposed rice paddy. Sasser himself was wounded, but stayed at his post for several hours tending others. Born September 12, 1947 in Chenango, Texas, Sasser is a graduate of Marshal High School in Angleton, Texas.

Staff Sergeant Chester Sims, *Company D, 2nd Battalion [Airborne], 501st Infantry, 101st Airborn Division.* Squad leader Sims distinguished himself in action on February 21, 1968 while his company was engaged in a furious assault of a heavily fortified enemy position. While advancing his unit, Sims heard the unmistakable noise of a concealed booby trap and unhesitatingly hurled himself on the device, absorbing its shock with his body. Vice President Agnew presented the medal posthumously at the White House on December 21, 1969. Sims, a native of Port Saint Joe, Florida, was born June 18, 1942.

First Lieutenant John E. Warren, Jr., *Company C, 2nd Battalion* [*Mechanized*], *22nd Infantry, 25th Infantry Division.* The bravery of Lieutenant Warren cost him his life in Vietnam on January 14, 1969. Warren and his men were moving through a rubber plantation to join a friendly unit when they were set upon by a well-fortified enemy. The lieutenant maneuvered his men to within six feet of the enemy bunker, at which point a grenade was thrown into their midst. Warren fell on the grenade and saved three others. A native of Brooklyn, New York, Lieutenant Warren was born November 16, 1946.

NAVY

Civil War

Aaron Anderson, *Landsman.* Served on board the USS *Wyandank* during a boat expedition up Mattox Creek, 17 March 1865. Participating with a boat crew in the clearing of Mattox Creek, Anderson carried out his duties courageously in the face of a devastating fire which cut away half the oars, pierced the launch in many places, and cut the barrel of a musket being fired at the enemy. (General Order 59, June 22, 1865.)

Robert Blake, *Contraband.* On board the U.S. Steam Gunboat *Marblehead* off Legareville, Stono River, December 25, 1863, in an engagement with the enemy on John's Island. Serving the rifle gun, Blake, an escaped slave, carried out his duties bravely throughout the engagement which resulted in the enemy's abandonment of positions, leaving a caisson and one gun behind. (General Order 32, April 16, 1864.)

William Brown, *Landsman.* Born 1836, Baltimore. Accredited to Maryland. On board the USS *Brooklyn* during its successful attacks against Fort Morgan rebel gunboats and the ram *Tennessee* in Mobile Bay on August 5, 1864. Stationed in the immediate vicinity of the shell whips which were twice cleared of men by bursting shells, Brown remained steadfast at his post and performed his duties in the powder division throughout the furious action which resulted in the surrender of the prize Southern ram *Tennessee* and in the damaging and destruction of batteries at Fort Morgan. (General Order 45, December 31, 1864.)

John Lawson received the U.S. Naval Medal of Honor for heroism in the Battle of Mobile Bay, 1864.

John Lawson, *Landsman.* Born 1837. Accredited to Pennsylvania. On board the flagship USS *Hartford* during its successful attacks against Fort Morgan, rebel gunboats and the rebel ram *Tennessee* in Mobile Bay on August 5, 1864. Wounded in the leg and thrown violently against the side of the ship when an enemy shell killed or wounded the six-man crew at the shell whip on the berth deck, Lawson, upon regaining his composure, promptly returned to his station and, although urged to go below for treatment, steadfastly continued his duties throughout the remainder of the action. (General Order 45, December 31, 1864.)

James Mifflin, *Engineer's Cook.* Born 1839, Richmond. Accredited to Virginia. On board the USS *Brooklyn* during its successful attacks against Fort Morgan, rebel gunboats and the Southern ram *Tennessee* in Mobile Bay on August 5, 1864. Stationed in the immediate vicinity of the shell whips which were twice cleared of men by bursting shells, Mifflin remained steadfast at his post and performed his duties in the powder division throughout the furious action which resulted in the surrender of the prize rebel ram *Tennessee* and in the damaging and destruction of batteries at Fort Morgan. (General Order 45, December 31, 1864.)

Joachim Pease, *Seaman.* Born Long Island, New York. Accredited to New York. Served as a seaman on board the USS *Kearsarge* when that vessel destroyed the *Alabama* off Cherbourg, France, June 19, 1864. Acting as loader on the No. 2 gun during his bitter engagement, Pease exhibited marked coolness and good conduct and was highly recommended by his divisional officer for gallantry under fire. (General Order 45, December 31, 1864.)

Interim (1871 to 1898)

Daniel Atkins, *Ship's Cook, First Class.* Born 1867, Brunswick. Accredited to Virginia. On board the USS *Cushing* on February 11, 1898. Showing gallant conduct, Atkins attempted to save the life of Ensign Joseph C. Breckenridge, U.S. Navy, who fell overboard at sea from that vessel on that date. (General Order 489, May 20, 1898.)

Joseph B. Noil, *Seaman.* Born 1841, Nova Scotia. Accredited to New York. Serving on board the USS *Powhatan* near Norfolk, December 26, 1872. Noil saved Boatswain J. C. Walton from drowning.

Spanish-American War

Robert Penn, *Fireman First Class.* Born October 10, 1872, City Point. Accredited to Virginia. On board the USS *Iowa* off Santiago de Cuba, July 20, 1898. Performing his duty at the risk of serious scalding at the time of the blowing out of the manhole gasket on board the vessel, Penn hauled the fire while standing on a board thrown across a coal bucket one foot above the boiling water which was still flowing from the boiler. (General Order 501, December 14, 1898.)

BLACK GRADUATES OF U.S. MILITARY ACADEMY (1877–1982)

Class of 1877

Flipper, Henry O.

Class of 1887

Alexander, John H.

Class of 1889

Young, Charles W.

Class of 1936

Davis, Benjamin O., Jr.

Class of 1941

Fowler, James, D.

Class of 1943

Davenport, Clarence M.
Tresville, Robert B., Jr.

Class of 1944

Francis, Henry M.

Class of 1945

Davis, Ernest J., Jr.
Rivers, Mark E., Jr.

Class of 1946

McCoy, Andrew A., Jr.

Class of 1949

Howard, Edward B.
Smith, Charles L.

Class of 1950

Carlisle, David K.
Green, Robert W.

Class of 1951

Brown, Norman J.
Robinson, Roscoe, Jr.
Wainer, Douglas F.
Woodson, William B.
Young, James R., Jr.

Class of 1953

Corprew, Gerald
Hughes, Bernard C.
Worthy, Clifford

Class of 1954

Lee, Ronald B.
Robinson, Hugh G.
Turner, LeRoy C.

Class of 1955

Batchman, Gilbert R.
Brown, John M.
Cassells, Cyrus C., Jr.
Hamilton, John M., Jr.
Olive, Lewis C., Jr.

Class of 1956

Blunt, Robert R.

Class of 1957

Bradley, Martin G.
McCullom, Cornell, Jr.

Class of 1958

Brunner, Ronald S.

Class of 1959

Baugh, Raymond C.
Kelley, Wilbourne A., III

Class of 1960

Dorsey, Ira

Class of 1961

Brown, Reginald J.
Quinn, Kenneth L.

Class of 1962

Gorden, Fred A.

Class of 1963

Banks, Edgar, Jr.
Handcox, Robert C.
Ivy, William L.
Jackson, David S.

Class of 1964

Miller, Warren F., Jr.
Ramsay, David L.

Class of 1965

Anderson, Joseph B.
Conley, James S.
Hester, Arthur C.
Jenkins, Harold A., Jr.

Class of 1966

Cox, Ronald E.
Davis, Thomas B., III
Ramsay, Robert B.

Class of 1967

Fowler, James D., Jr.
Whaley, Bobby G.

Henry O. Flipper (left) *was the first black graduate of West Point* (Class of 1877). *Ten years later, John H. Alexander became the second.*

Class of 1968

Copeland, Rene G.
Flowers, Ernest, Jr.
Garcia, Victor
Howard, James T.
Jordan, Larry R.
Martin, John T., III
Outlaw, LeRoy B.
Robinson, Benny L.
Rotie, Wilson L., Jr.
Tildon, Ralph B.

Class of 1969

Cooper, Cornelius M., Jr.
Cousar, Robert J., Jr.
Groves, Sheridon H.
Hackett, Jerome R.
Minor, James A., Jr.
Steele, Michael F.
Tabela, Francis E.
Williams, Michael M.

Class of 1970

Mason, Robert E.
Morgan, Roderick H.
Price, Willie J.
Reid, Trevor A.
Robinson, Bruce E.
Steel, Gary R.
Thomas, Kenneth L.

Class of 1971

Anderson, Edgar
Brice, David L.
Dedmond, Tony L.
Edwards, Joe F.
Freeman, Robert E.
James, Kevin T.
Plummer, William W.

Class of 1972

Burns, Cornelius
Mension, Danny L.
Squires, Percy

Class of 1973

Adams, Jesse B.
Bell, Richard, Jr.
Bivens, Courtland C., II
Bonner, Garland C.
Christopher, Clyde J.
Coats, Charles S., Jr.
Coleman, Frederick D.
Crisp, William Ira
Edwards, Lawrence D.
Ferguson, Mercer E.
Fountain, Foster F., III
Gains, Michael B.
Jenkins, Gil S.
Johnson, Edward C., Jr.
Lewis, Brett H.

Martin, Edwin L.
Moore, William I.
Perry, William H.
Robinson, Lenwood, Jr.
Rowe, Dennis W.
Sayles, Andre H.
Sutton, Lloyd I.
Topping, Gary E.
Twitty, Theophlise K.

Class of 1974

Anderson, Gary J.
Banks, Allan A.
Best, Marshall
Braxton, Maceo
Bryant, Albert
Chachere, Ernest G.
Elmore, Terry E.
Fowler, David L.
Helton, Dwight A.
Holmes, Keith B.
Hughes, Samuel J., III
Hunter, Joseph
Jones, Harvey D., Jr.
King, Jimmie D.
Lewis, Kevin M.
Lynch, Myron C.
Mallory, Phillip L.
Reid, Ronny E.
Sample, Allen L.
Spaulding, Milton C.
Taylor, Theodore R.

Topping, Gerald W.
Wallace, Michael D.
Wheeler, Clayton R.

Class of 1975

Anderson, D. T.
Armstong, B. M.
Austin, L. J., III
Benn, J. F., Jr.
Boddie, O. B., Jr.
Bradley, R.
Briggs-Hall, M. A.
Brown, A. B. Jr.
Byrd, J. E.
Cheese, R. A.
Dupree, D. W.
Dyer, A. G.
Hanford, C. B.
Harris, D. L.
Harris, J. W., III
Hicks, J. E.
Johnson, E. A., Jr.
Johnson, R. E.
Jones, J. D., III
Jordan, N. C.
Lewis, S. J.
Maney, E. K.
Mooney, D. L.
Peters, V. M.
Pinkney, R. M.
Shaw, E. E., Jr.
Smith, M. L.

South, C. H., Jr.
Taylor, P. L., III
Thigpen, W. L.
Williams, D. L.
Williams, J. P.

Class of 1976

Alexander, M. A.
Austin, C. W.
Bivins, D. K.
Brown, J. L.
Chase, R. P.
Collins, L. C.
Crecy, W. G.
Crocker, V. B.
Crofton, W. T.
Dixon, M. L.
Elam, A.
Fields, G.
Floyd, J. N.
Grammer, J. K.
Hayes, A. B.
Hicks, P. L.
Jett, S. A.
Johnson, R. L.
Little, L. L.
Louis, V. D.
Lullen, J. J.
McKenzie, C.
Miles, H. A.
Morgan, E. R.
Owens, J. F.
Perry, M. J.
Pruitt, W. H.
Ricks, S. J.
Shelton, L. E.
Simpson, P. R.
Sims, K. E.
Slate, L. K.
Smith, M. A.
White, M. A.
Whitlock, W. P.
Williams, H. M.

Class of 1977

Belcher, Gerald J.
Beverly, Raymond N.
Butler, Cranson A.
Carson, Ivory D.
Chapman, Reginal K.
Clark, Edward D.
Clay, James
Collins, Vincent R.
Daily, Anthony B.
Eugene, Bernhard G.
Howell, Mitchell A.
Jackson, Arthur D.
Jones, Curtis L.

Lewis, Brett A.
Lunsford, Joseph M.
Lynem, Joseph P.
McFadden, Reginald
Miott, Rory Q.
Mitchell, Robert L.
Mosby, William E.
Pace, Gerald D.
Peebles, Darrell
Ross, James L.
Sanders, Carl E.
Scott, Kenneth L.
Scriber, Phillip H.
Taliaferro, Jerry
Terry, William R.
Thompson, Terrance
Vaughn, James A.
Washington, Donald
Williams, Calvin
Wilson, Alfred A.
Wilson, Michael B.

Class of 1978

Adams, D. C.
Allen, C. D.
Alston, L. M.
Bassa, R. L.
Beatty, W. D.
Bastick, T. P.
Bowman, Q. V.
Bulls, H. E.
Cade, B. D.

Carter, R. L.
Clark, M. C.
Collins, T. W.
English, M. A.
Ford, S. H.
Fore, H. R.
Fry, D. L.
Grant, R. A.
Hall, M. H.
Hamilton, W.
Hargrove, P. H.
Harris, C. A.
Herndon, H. E.
Hollingsworth, J.
Holman, S. E.
Johns, O. H.
Johnson, H. E.
Jourdan, L. T.
King, G.
Landry, P. G.
Lewis, D. G.
Mallory, R. P.
Martin, Q. R.
Miles, F. M.
Mingilton, M. D.
Mitchell, C.
Mobley, D. L.
Moseley, D. L.
Moseley, M. M.
Moye, M. D.
Nixon, W. J.
Owens, C. D.
Ouslley, G. M.
Pilgrim, C. F.

Price, W. W.
Scribner, C. F.
Seaton, M. J.
Smith, C.
Taylor, T. T.
White, W. L.
Wilson, K. H.
Winton, G. J.
Young, V. J.

Class of 1979

Adams, William D.
Ash, Toney L.
Austin, Michael D.
Balom, Curtis, II
Beasley, Michael D.
Bonds, Marcus B.
Brannon, Gregory K.
Brooks, Leo A.
Brundidge, Clennie
Bullard, Edward J.
Clark, David C.
Clemons, Edward F.
Darlington, Loyd
Deramus, Lawrence D.
Fowlkes, Essex
Fuller, Duane E.
Gordon, Robert L.
Griffin, Wesley B.
Hall, Kevin L.
Hardrick, Harold S.
Hooper, Charles W.
Howard, Maroc L.

Lieutenant Vincent K. Brooks, the first black cadet to hold the post of Captain of Cadets. Class of 1980

Hughes, Bernard C.
Jackson, Stanley M.
Jennings, Tony O.
Macklin, Philip D.
McCall, James T.
McKissick, Isaac V.
Miller, Kevin L.
Mitchell, Chris T.
Oliver, Joseph P.
Petit, Jules G.
Pettus, Carlous T.
Sears, Walter A.
Sledge, Nathanial H.
Sobers, Arthur A.
Staten, Michael U.
Stewart, John
Tabler, Anthony D.
Taylor, Clarence E.
Traylor, Jimmie L.
Veney, David W.
Walter, Clifford S.
Wilkerson, Joseph W.
Williams, C., Jr.
Williams, James I.
Williams, Thomas
Willis, Michael B.
Yancey, David T.
Yeldell, Anthony L.

Class of 1980

Beans, Michael K.
Bland, Andrew R.
Brooks, Vincent K.
Dallas, Joy S.
Dennis, Daryl C.
Ellerbe, Michael D.
Gayle, Michael D.
Gillis, Reginald R.
Grace, Karl F.
Grayer, Curtis A.
Harrington, W. D.
Hervey, George A.
Hilliard, John F.
Jones, Ernest W.
Jones, Jeffery
Laney, Mark N.
Mattingly, John A.
Mays, George S.
Miles, Lloyd
Perdue, Rodney
Rivers, Eddie L.
Robinson, Hugh G.
Scott, James C.
Shepherd, Gilbert
Sledge, William T.
Stephens, Gregory B.
Strode, Tollie
Turner, Henry C.
Walter, Priscilla

Class of 1981

Bland, Melvin H.
Britton, Randy A.
Cook, Jeffrey S.
Cooper, Kieth L.
David, James E.
Davis, Archie L.
Delahoussaye, P. J.
Evans, Leroy M.
Freeman, Thomas
Gates, James A.
Gibson, Byron J.
Grady, Norman M.
Graham, David G.
Green, Emmett F.
Hall, Kimetha G.
Harris, Daryl E.
Hembrey, James E.
Hill, James B.
Hines, Curtis T.
Jackson, Christopher H.
Johnson, Hiram N.
Lambright, Michael
Luster, Robert A.
Lyons, Dereck E.
Mazyck, Alphonse F.
Miner, Michael D.
Peterson, Darryl W.
Petty, James E.
Pittard, Dana J.
Polite, Anita M.
Porter, Ronald A.
Pullen, Harvey L.
Reid, Carlton B.
Shields, Robert L.
Somersall, Paul O.
Streets, Kevin A.
Stroud, Andrew B.
Taylor, John J.
Thompson, Kevin S.
Topping, Kenneth L.
Turrentine, Larry C.
Webb, Anthony V.
Wilkins, Stephen M.
Williams, Eddie E.
Williams, Michael G.
Wilson, Duane K.

Class of 1982

Almore, Arthur
Austin, Stanley
Bell, Oliver
Bennett, Jerryl
Bland, Christopher
Boston, Stephen
Boutte, Brian M.
Buchanan, Mickey
Callahan, Dennis

Cofield, William
Coleman, Joseph
Dabney, Harold
Dodson, Walter
Dunn, James F.
Goodwin, Michael
Grammer, Nadja
Hackney, John K.
Hargraves, William
Harris, David D.
Heard, Lance
Hervey, Cardell, Jr.
Hollifield, Rodney
Johnson, Chris
Jones, Emmett
Jones, Kermit
Knotts, Lester

Lowry, William I.
Malloy, Brian
Miller, Cliff
Miller, Marlon
Mosby, Stewart
Perry, Benjamin, II
Powell, Webster
Pullen, Harvey L.
Skinner, Eugene
Spencer, Michael
Terry, Gary L.
Thomas, David L.
Wilkins, David
Williams, Gary
Wilmer, Archie, III
Wynder, Allen

BLACK GRADUATES OF U.S. NAVAL ACADEMY
(1949–1982)

Class of 1949

Brown, W. A.

Class of 1952

Chambers, L. C.

Class of 1953

Taylor, R. R.

Class of 1954

Raiford, J. D.

Class of 1955

Gregg, L. P.

Class of 1956

Baudit, H. S.
Sechrest, E. A.

Class of 1957

Jamison, V. L.
Slaughter, K. W.

Class of 1958

Fennell, G. M., Jr.

Class of 1959

Bruce, M. D.
Bush, W. S., III

Clark, M. E.
Powell, W. E.

Class of 1961

Byrd, W. Z.
Johnson, M., Jr.
Shelton, J. A.

Class of 1962

Jackson, J. T.
McCray, D.

Class of 1963

Newton, R. C.

Class of 1964

Jones, W. C.
McDonald, J. F., Jr.
Prout, P. M.
Thomas, B. F.

Class of 1965

Carter, S. J., Jr.
Grayson, F. F., Jr.
Reason, J. P.

Class of 1967

Huey, C. W.
Tzomes, C. A.

Class of 1968

Bolden, C. F., Jr.

Clark, W. S., Jr.
Lucas, R. G.
Simmons, D. F.

Class of 1969

Carr, E. F.
Jones, F. E.

Class of 1970

Freeman, J. B.
Greene, E. L.
Henry, B. A.
Roberts, M. C.
Watson, A. J.
Williams, L. V.

Class of 1971

Collier, C. M.
Porter, J. F.
Shaw, H. M., Jr.

Class of 1972

Burnette, E. A.
Coleman, A. B.
Crump, W. L., Jr.
Jones, N. M.
Keaser, L. W.
Lovely, E.
Mason, M. T.
McMillian, J. A.
Rucks, C. H.
Smith, E. M.
Staton, E. M.
Tindall, J. S.

Class of 1973

Calhoun, L. W.
Caliman, K. H.
Campbell, J. H.
Evans, W. G.
Faust, H. L.
Jackson, J. E.
Jones, L. W.
Kennard, W. M.
Samuels, R. G.
Shockley, R. L.
Watts, R. D.
Young, E. C.

Class of 1974

Corpin, O. D.
Dunn, K. D.
Jolly, E. L.
Kirk, F. L.

Minor, T. E.
Montgomery, D.
Rasin, S. E.
Robinson, C.
Tate, J. D.

Class of 1975

Ardine, J. E.
Baily, C. E.
Everet, W. M.
Graves, B. E.
Grover, R. O.
Hampton, M. L.
Hargrove, C.
Harris, W. M.
Jackson, D. E.
Jackson, J. T.
Lawson, H.
Merrell, W.
Miller, K. E.
Montgomery, W. J.
Nollie, T. C.
Robinson, J. W.
Russell, D.
Washington, M. B.
Watson, L. J.
Williams, R. B.
Willis, C. J.

Class of 1976

Bass, R. G.
Boyd, C. C., Jr.
Brown, C. A.
Clark, A. W., Jr.
Cole, C.
Curtis, D. C.
Davis, N., Jr.
Dennis, J. I.
Ellis, R. L.
Epps, J. B.
Ford, E., Jr.
Franklin, D. W.
Giron, B. A.
Halton, E. S.
Harris, W. J.
Hicks, G. R.
Holmes, E. I.
Howard, R.
Jenkins, G.
Lassiter, I. W.
Leonard, K. E.
Liscomb, J. C.
Littlejohn, G. A.
Miles, D. A.
Mitchell, R. I.
Moore, G.
Owens, I. H.
Paulding, O.

Payton, L., Jr.
Pritchett, R. R.
Queen, G. A.
Reddix, M. C.
Sears, W. T.
Sharperson, C. H.
Smith, J. B., Jr.
Sparks, J. E., Jr.
Stevens, M. K.
Walton, D. F.
Woumnm, E. D.

Class of 1977

Adair, S. A.
Almeida, J. M.
Anderson, K.
Bonner, D. R.
Booker, C. B.
Booker, R. L.
Brinkly, R. W.
Bruce, P. J.
Burns, M. W.
Byrd, G. L.
Caeser, J. S.
Caldwell, R. L.
Campbell, A. L.
Clay, J. L.
Cook, D.
Davis, P. L. E.
Deane, L. E.
Dory, C. E.
Ellison, W. L., Jr.
Faulkner, R. M.
Floyd, M. L.
Foster, A. P.
Franklin, D. E.
Garcia, B. A.
Gilmore, E. J.
Goodrum, R. A.
Graham, D. F.
Gray, S. G.
Hallman, C.
Handy, C. D.
Hardy, J. T., Jr.
Harrington, J.
Hill, M. L.
Hithon, C. J.
Ivey, C. G.
Jackson, L., Jr.
Lee, S., Jr.
Lockett, K. V.
Lockley, J.
Long, A., IV
McNair, E. R.
McNeil, R. A.
Mitchell, R. V.
Nacoste, P. J.
Ray, D. D.

Rogers, M. L.
Roxe, M. V.
Sapp, J. K.
Sawyer, G. R.
Schoolfield, D. J.
Seldon, R. W.
Smith, J. W.
Station, G. V.
Trass, K. R.
Tucker, M.
Turner, E. A.
Valentine, J.
Washington, V. L.
Wright, E. J.

Class of 1978

Abernethy, T. S.
Anderson, D. E.
Andre, C. A.
Bramlett, L.
Carter, B. W.
Cato, A. M.
Cook, D.
Crawford, T.
Dyer, M. A.
Fields, M. H.
Flanagan, G.
Goodman, R. O., Jr.
Guillory, V. G.
Haney, C. E. D.
Harris, B. F.
Johnson, M. R.
Johnston, M. R.
Jones, S. E.
Jubert, G. A.
King, M. E.
Knight, R. L.
Marchant, B. F.
Meadows, F. J.
Miller, L. E.
Moore, C. E.
Mosley, E. K.
Newby, L. D.
Perry, C. A.
Peterson, J. C., Jr.
Prince, L. O., Jr.
Reddick, M. P., Jr.
Redvict, P. C.
Robinson, W. I.
Saddler, M. R.
Scott, R. W.
Sears, M. E.
Stallings, J. B.
Taylor, R. R.
Thompson, L. B.
Williams, A.
Williams, M. G., Jr.
Winns, A. L.
Wood, D. L.

Woods, H. M.
Wray, K. L.
Young, O. W.

Class of 1979

Adams, J., Jr.
Allen, M. T.
Ballard, W. W.
Beam, D. A.
Berry, E. C.
Brooks, S. E.
Burrell, A. K.
Cousin, D. G.
Darring, P. I.
Gibson, M. A.
Green, N. B.
Jackson, K. L.
Johnson, A. J., Jr.
Johnson, M. D.
Jones, H.
Jones, L. H., Jr.
Jones, S. A.
Lewis, W. D.

Martin, W. B.
Massie, W. R.
McCoy, L. J.
McKenzie, S. S.
Miller, A. B.
Monroe, G. A.
Norgrove, K. E.
Smith, A. R.
Wilder, C. R.
Wise, J. E.
Womack, K.
Woodward, C. C., Jr.

Class of 1980

Atkins, M.
Barnhill, L.
Bradley, E.
Brown, G. V.
Burks, L. J.
Carmichael, B.
Character, D.
Clark, C. B.
Clark, I. R., Jr.

Coker, M., Jr.
Colvin, J. T.
Cooper, S. L.
Cornish, B. F.
Dancy, J. G.
Daniel, F.
Dennis, D. C.
Figgins, R. L.
Gay, E. L.
Grooms, B. E.
Hodge, R. R.
Jackson, B. K.
Jiles, A. W.
Johnson, R.
Johnson, R.
Josia, A. H.
Mack, T. A.
Manns, E.
McCauley, L. H.
Meyers, C. L.
Mines, J. L.
Minor, I. L.
Mosley, A. S.
Nemecek, R. A.
Paul, W.
Raymond, D. K.
Shorts, V.
Smith, B. E.
Smith, V. C.
Sneed, M.
Thompson, C.
Thornton, C.
Trass, R. E.
Vonlipsey, R. K.
Walker, J. L.
White, T.
Williams, N.
Wilson, C. A.

Class of 1981

Abernathy, R.
Bailey, P. E.
Barnes, A. P.
Brownlee, E.
Butler, R. A.
Coker, T.
Curry, B.
Denkler, G.
Evans, W. T.
Gainer, C.
Green, L. R.
Gross, K. J.
Harness, K. N.
Herrod, A. L.
Howard, A. M.
Jackson, B. D.
Jackson, R. C., III

Knock, J. A.
Lee, F. A.
McCree, V.
McElroy, D. M.
Mines, G.
Nixon, M.
Oliver, B. C.
Pace, G. H.
Perez, M. C.
Reaves, J. C.
Redden, S. D.
Ricks, D. L.
Roberts, W.
Swoope, A. M.
Taylor, R. L.
Thomas, A. A.
Tolbert, K. C.
Ware, R. E.
Weems, R. A.

Class of 1982

Banks, M. E.
Baptiste, B.
Batchlor, C. D.
Bates, A. Y.
Baugh, K. A.
Bennett, D. C., Jr.
Butts, W. S.
Carodine, C. K.
Cole, P.
Davis, N. M.
Dixon, D. S.
Ferrell, T. J.
Gay, W. H., Jr.
Goodson, E. H.
Gray, A. M.
Hayes, S. K., Jr.
Hazzard, D. M.
Howard, M. J.
Leisch, J. K.
Malcolm, M. W.
McLain, J. S.
Meyers, E. A.
Morris, M. J.
Nobles, W. E., Jr.
Odom, A. A.
Palmer, D. K.
Parker, C. T.
Reagans, E., Jr.
Rogers, W. F., III
Simons, J. M.
Terrell, W. A.
Tondu, J. L.
Watson, R. K.
Wiggins, C. A.
Williams, A.
Winbush, N. W. C., II

Midshipman Donna Hazzard, graduate of Annapolis, 1982.

BLACK GRADUATES OF THE U.S. AIR FORCE ACADEMY (1963–1982)

Class of 1963

Bush, Charles V.
Payne, Isaac
Sims, Roger B.

Class of 1964

Gregory, Frederick D.

Class of 1965

Beaman, Arthur L.
Plummer, Bentley V.
Thomas, Charles A.
Wiley, Fletcher H.

Class of 1967

Cunningham, Thomas L.

Class of 1968

Ecung, Maurice
Gibson, Samuel B.
Groves, Weldon K.
Moore, Francis M.
Thompson, James E.

Class of 1969

Hopper, John D.
Howland, Walter T.
Little, Kenneth H.
Love, James E.
Spooner, Richard E.
Stevenson, Kenneth E.

Class of 1970

Arnold, Harry
Battles, Dorsey
Bowie, Harold V.
Bryant, Robert S.
Elliot, Norman L.
Jones, Reuben D., Jr.
Key, George
Mohr, Dean B., Jr.

Class of 1972

Bassa, Paul, Jr.
Harrison, Booker
Henderson, Clyde R.
Jones, Raymond J.
McDonald, Michael
Meredith, Keith S.
Nelson, Michael V.
Parks, Reginald D.
Rhaney, Mahlon C., Jr.
Ross, Joseph D., Jr.
Rucker, Raymond I., Jr.
Slade, John B., Jr.

Class of 1973

Abraham, Robert E.
Baker, Richard A.
Bolton, Robert M.
Butler, Ernest E., Jr.
Childress, Charlie Jr.
Dunn, Arther L.
Gilbert, Robert L.
Harrison, Herbert A.
Hodges, Rudnaldo
Lewis, Gerald E.
Mitchell, David L.
Mitchell, Joseph R., Jr.
Mitchell, Orderia F.
Stallworth, Charles E.
Thompson, William L.
Way, Spencer, Jr.

Class of 1974

Berry, William M., III
Bryant, Frederic B., Jr.
Caldwell, Richmond H., Jr.
Collins, Dennis F.
Crenshaw, Ronald L.
Hairston, Carlton P.
Lockette, Emory W., Jr.
McAlpin, Sherman E.
Murphy, Franklin
Robinson, Neal T.
Scott, Darryl A.
Smith, Clarence D., Jr.
Tarleton, Gadson J., III
Timberlake, Marion A.
Walker, Philip E.
Watson, Ronald W.
Webb, Lance C.

Class of 1975

Benjamin, Philip G., II
Bready, Alvin
Cason, Wilbert, Jr.
Cosby, Willie J., III
Crenshaw, Larry D.
Franklin, George E., Jr.
Graves, Jeffrey C.
Hargrove, Julius L.
Kendall, Phillip L.

Osborne, William B.
Roberts, Randy W.
Smith-Harrison, Leon I.
Whitley, Kenneth L.
Williams, Douglas L., II

Class of 1976

Allen, Calvin L.
Benton, Jimmie L.
Butler, Michael W.
Campbell, Stephen C.
Correia, Stanley C.
Crosley, Hilton C.
Dantzler, Willie C.
Dorman, Glenn A.
Felder, Lloyd R.
Franklin, William H.
Gandy, Edward R., Jr.
Garner, Larry E.
Gray, Robert M.
Hoyes, Michael B.
Johnson, Anthony R.
Kyle, Gary A.
Levell, Edward A.
Macklin, Winfred H., Jr.
Manson, Harold C.
Miller, Michael P.
Norris, Johnnie E., Jr.
Palms, Wilfred G. R.
Pannell, Garland J.
Powers, Ahart W.
Reed, Raymond, Jr.
Ross, Dave M.
Williams, Gregory
Williams, John F.
Williams, Mark R.
Williams, Roderick M.

Class of 1977

Adams, Craig F.
Bailey, Zachery E.
Balancierre, Milton G., III
Clegg, Robert S.
Cosby, Ricky Joe
Crafton, Wilson D., Jr.
Cromer, DeJuan
Cross, Michael A.
Gipson, Anthony
Grady, Walter A.
Johnson, Sterling
Jones, Clarence D.
Jones, Daryl L.
Lee, Williams C.
Lyle, Harron V.
McReynolds, James C., Jr.
Parker, Thomas G.
Peters, Burnett W., III
Ratchford, Monroe J.

Robinson, Vernon L., III
Scott, Lynn M.
Shropshire, Theodore V.
Singletery, James
Smith, Gregory F.
Wallace, Frank L.
Wells, Kennard R.
White, Kenneth R.

Class of 1978

Allen, Martin W.
Clemons, Russell
Clethen, Eric L.
Cooper, Gary Lee
Cox, Andrew H.
Crowe, Lelvin, Jr.
Dean, Garry C.
Drake, Ricky J.
Ghiden, Reginald
Gilmore, Samuel L.
Gravatt, Wayne K.
Harrison, Oliver
Hawkins, Michael
Henderson, Herbert
Hicks, John E.
Holder, Livingston L.
Lankford, Morgan
Lawrence, Michael
Lee, Lyman Anthony
Mason, Linwood Jr.
Mills, Raymond G.
Moye, Arthur L.
Rice, Edward A.
Richardson, Anthony
Shaw, William J.
Simons, James T.
Stewart, Moses Jr.
Temple, David J.
Woodfork, Isaac K.
Wrenn, Mark L.

Class of 1979

Allen, Travis Leverne, Jr.
Alston, Stephen Maurice
Austin, Christopher Lynn
Belt, James Michael
Blake, Gregory Nathaniel
Bordenave, Paul Basil, Jr.
Brown, Al Christopher
Brundidge, Gregory Lynn
Colvin, James Thomas, Jr.
Donald, Edward Gregory
Dubose, Ted
Duvalle, Reginald Alfred
Faulkner, Paul Edward
Francois, Frank, Jr.
Gilchrist, Lenue, Jr.
Hall, Richard Patrick

Harris, Junious Leo, III
Holmes, Reginald Carwin
Jones, Vernon Dale
Leonard, Steven Douglas
Maxwell, Richard P.
Mitchell, Verner Devone
Murry, Curtis R.
Osler, Benjamin Franklin
Pate, Walter Randolph, Jr.
Pearson, Ricardo
Petterson, Hernes Juan, Jr.
Pointer, Ronald Lynn
Ramirez, Juanito Esteban
Rayfield, William L., II
Robinson, Eddie
Sawyer, Willis Elmer, Jr.
Smith, Gregory Lee
Sowards, Mark Anthony
Thomas, Michael Allan
Warner, Curt Elliot
Watkins, Steven David
Williams, Asa Romero

Class of 1980

Adams, Daniel Sinclair, Jr.
Alexander, David Lavone, III
Ball, Shelby Gregory
Batts, Stephen Michael
Benjamin, Gail Frances
Benjamin, Vaughn Philip, Jr.
Benn, Mack, III
Best, James Henry
Burrell, Hugh Francis
Campbell, Jeffrey Oikawa
Campbell, Patrick Edward
Desbordes, David Anthony
Floyd, Kevin Steven
Fortson, Michael Loren
Glenn, Michael Leslie
Gray, Ronald Patrick
Gunn, Willie Arthur
Harris, Andre William
Hill, Walter Bryan
Jones, William, Jr.
Knuckles, Gwendolyn
Lester, Thomas, Jr.
Mack, Oscar, Jr.
Mallory, Patrick Anthony
Marshall, Brian
Payton, Timothy James
Robinson, Thomas Elwood, Jr.
Ross, Michael Donnell
Saxon, Frank, IV
Sears, Alvin Darrel
Strickland, Robert Henry, Jr.
Turman, Beverly Carol
Upshur, Robert Adrian, Jr.
Walters, Donald Eric
Warr, Dartanian

White, Michael Philip
Woodland, Paul Stanley

Class of 1981

Anderson, Alan Keith
Andrews, Dale
Blount, Robert, Jr.
Brooks, Frank Kelly, Jr.
Burks, Eric Stanley
Butler, Craig Alan
Campbell, Andre Kazuo
Carroll, Marvin Dee
Clark, David Anthony
Cloud, Albert Thomas, Jr.
Coleman, Clarence J. C., Jr.
Cox, Michael Andre
Dennis, Sheldon
Derry, Heyward, Jr.
Dismuke, Theophus Danier
Dortch, Joseph
English, Nelson William
Evans, Adolphus, Jr.
Garvin, Eric Darryl
Griffin, Drees Catera
Guess, James Allen, Jr.
Gunter, Gurnie Cornelius, Jr.
Handy, Dexter Raphael
Harris, Timothy Alan
Hasty, Thomas Jefferson, III
Ingram, Mark Everett
Jenkins, Craig Michael
Johnson, Ernest Jerome, Jr.
Jones, Reginald Lewis
Knight, Gregory Guy
Manning, Kelvin Monroe
Perry, Phillip Leon
Phillips Charles Edward, Jr.
Richardson, Ernest Ikuo
Rosier, Isaac, Jr.
Silas, Michael Owen
Smith, Kenric
Stevens, Cecil Doyle, Jr.
Stewart, Alfred James
Stewart, Freddie, Jr.
Streeter, Xavier Lewis
Wallace, Everton Ricardo
Wright, Robert Franklin

Class of 1982

Bankole, Cullen R.
Barnes, Marion E., II
Berry, Carson C.
Bizzell, William A.
Buchanan, Julia M.
Christian, Nathaniel D.
Craft, Raymond, Jr.
Davis, Earl Q.
Davis, Elton D.

Davis, Michael N.
Duncan, Marc B.
Francisco, Raymond A.
Graham, Nancy F.
Hamilton, Gregory J.
Hill, Larry D.
Hithe, Troy A.
Howard, Richard N., II
Hunigan, Kirk A.
Jackson, Antoine
Jackson, Johnny L.
Jackson, Walter L., Jr.
James, George F., III
Jarrell, Allen K.
Johnson, Jonnie
Johnson, Thomas L.
Jones, Daryl P.
Jones, Jerome S.
Lewis, Gregory L.
Lofton, Victor E.
Mack, Lin A.
Maize, Robert D.
Maragh, Vivet V.

Mason, John R., Jr.
Moragne, Jeffrey A.
Payne, Glenn R.
Richards, Thomas L.
Riles, Jeffrey M.
Roath, Anthony S.
Robinson, Kenneth L.
Shelton, Cynthia
Singletery, Rodney
Smith, Elva D.
Smith, James E.
Smith, Kathryn L.
Stevenson, Martha
Stevenson, Mary
Temple, Alan J.
West, Steven A.
White, Alex, Jr.
Williams, Billy W.
Williams, Darryl A. C.
Williams, Edward L.
Willis, Cynthia
Wolters, Tod D.

BLACK CADETS AT THE U.S. MILITARY ACADEMY

Class of 1983

Alexander, William
Allen, Clinton O.
Allen, William T.
Babers, Charles R.
Bell, Jonathon A.
Blow, Jerry
Brinkley, Marc A.
Cary, Richard J.
Copeland, Anthony
Crumlin, Michael A.
Crutcher, Charlie
Daniel, Jeffrey A.
Davis, Alfrazier J.
Fitzgerald, Gregory
Foster, Steven P.
Gates, Willie E.
George, Marc C.
Hamilton, Marcus K.
Hayes, Morris G.
Hooper, Marc
Hopson, Mark J.
Jackson, Julius H.
Jackson, Libby Ann
Johnson, Christine
Johnson, Regina
Lighthall, Donnell
McCall, Vincent D.
McFadden, Willie J.
Morgan, Thomas, Jr.
Neason, Clarence, Jr.

Newkirk, Bryan T.
Oakes, Patrick B.
Poinsette, Kenneth
Porter, John
Pruitt, Larry II.
Ridgeley, Raymond
Rodriguez, Anthony
Stubblefield, Lavern
Thompson, James A.
Thomas, Johnny F.
Vaughn, John K.
Walker, Gerald J.
Williams, Cardell
Williams, Darryl A.
Williams, Michael

Class of 1984

Alsberry, Dennis M.
Armstrong, Bryan J.
Baldwin, Cleophas
Banks, Robert C., Jr.
Bradley, Sherry J.
Boyd, Daniel O.
Brooks, Alfred L.
Brown, Kenneth
Brown, Marvin C., Jr.
Celestan, Gregory J.
Cobb, Alma J.
Cuerington, Andre M.
Delphin, Julie A.
Dow, Thurman E.

Dunham, Andrea M.
Gales, Byron E.
Gamble, Eddie L.
Gardner, Kelvin G.
Gaston, Angela M.
Gordon, Paul G.
Grayer, Gerren S.
Green, Kent M.
Harris, William C., III
Hinton, Robert C.
Howard, Rory J.
Jefferson, William H.
Johnson, Derek
Johnson, Derek V.
Johnson, Faith A.
Jones, Kevin
Lambert, Alexander L.
McCloud, William P.
McNair, Kerry V.
Mickens, Stanley, V.
Morgan, Gregory L.
Myers, Cynthia L.
Myhand, Rickey C.
Newsome, Earl
Oatis, Demetrius C.
Oliver, Ernest M.
Peterson, Paul M.
Reever, Darryl K.
Rhodes, Robert E.
Richardson, Ricky W.
Robinson, Bruce E.
Rogers, Beverly Y.
Shaw, Everett M.
Sistrunk, Thomas M., III
Smith, Daryl G.
Smith, Troy L.
Sparkman, Gary N.
Steele, Marcus E.
Tai, Neville P.
Thomas, Fern J.
Tunnell, Harry D.
Waters, Anthony J.
Watford, Roslyn A.
White, Ronald O.
Wilson, Henry L.
Wilson, Tee Gee

Class of 1985

Adams, Reginald O.
Abins, Elton D.
Allen, Michael C.
Allen, Reginald M.
Asberry, Herman, III
Augustine, Harvey, III
Banks, Daniel T.
Babers, Alex L., III
Baisden, Michael K.
Baptiste, Martin W.
Barring, Troy A.

Bishop, Gary P.
Black, Aurelia L.
Blount, Anthony, L.
Bowling, Anthony
Brown, James B.
Bryant, Vincent D.
Carr, Angela D.
Carroll, Catherine L.
Clark, Geoffrey R.
Clark, Michelle
Collins, Michael L.
Corbett, Carl D.
Corbett, Jeffrey C.
Curry, Clarence W.
Dallas, Jeffrey B.
Davis, Amah A.
Devore, Matthew A.
Eberhart, Jimmie L.
Edmond, Pamela
Gary, Michael W.
Gaston, Patrick B.
Gilbreat, Byron J.
Giles, Edward E.
Goodly, Timothy W.
Greenhouse, Paul S.
Griffin, Eric S.
Griffin, Oliver C., II
Hamilton, Marvin C.
Harris, Charles H.
Harris, Mark C.
Harrison, Ora E.
Holiday, Herschel S.
Hollingsworth, Jarvis
Hood, Brian M.
Hope, Charles J.
Horton, Michael P.
Jacobs, Ronald
Jackson, Samuel D. J.
Johnson, Calvin V.
Johnson, Mark D.
Johnson, Mark S.
Jones, Leon, Jr.
Jones, Melvin, Jr.
Jones, Luis D.
Jordan, Jansen J.
King, Rhonda H.
Labee, Kevin A.
Ladson, Gary L.
Lane, Charles B.
Lawson, John
Lipscomb, Racheaud
Lockett, Philip W.
Lowery, Veronica A.
Madden, Vernard C.
Manzy, Tyrone J.
Marshall, Jacqueline Y.
McCloud, Jamie L.
McDow, William E.
McKeloy, William K.
McLoyer, Bryford G., Jr.

Milburn, Dwayne S.
Moore, Kevin D.
Morris, John S.
Myers, Robert T.

Newsome, Mike
Otey, Francoise Y.
Owens, Ronald Jr.
Patrick, Bruce A.

BLACK CADETS AT THE U.S. NAVAL ACADEMY

Class of 1983

Alexander, Catherine D.
Barclift, Michael R.
Battle, John Clayborne
Bedell, Kevin Fredric
Blackwell, Jacqueline
Blake, James A.
Butler, Christopher L.
Carter, George R.
Clark, Jerome A.
Coles, James R., III
Crockett, Jerry M.
Crozier, Wilbur V.
Deberry, Dennis
Edmondson, Michael J.
Fears, George Michael
Finley, Julian G.
Gatson, Darryl Keith
Hale, Kevin T.
Hester, Gina Loraine
Hicks, Warren T.
Hundley, Herbert
Jackson, Eric Keith
Jackson, Stephen Mark
James, Kenneth Angelo
Jones, Eugene Weston
Key, Kevin Donell
Lakins, Darryl David
Mackay, Leo Sidney, Jr.
Martin, Robert Cason
McClusky, Kenneth W.
McCoy, Angelo A.
McNeil, Franklin N., Jr.
Miller, Kevin Lavord
Mitchell, Troy Michael
Moore, Richard A.
Outing, Donald Anthony
Posey, Brian Wenford
Raines, Clinton, Jr.
Roane, Elmer W., Jr.
Robinson, Russell L.
Rupp, John
Scissum, Adolph C.
Smith, Henry C.
Smith, Leonard, Jr.
Thames, Tyrone M.
Tyree, William D., III
Wallington, Joseph T.
Waye, Reginald B.
Williams, Joseph E., Jr.
Williams, Leo W., II

Williams, Yolanda Y.
Wilson, Joe David, Jr.
Wilson, Kenneth
Wrice, Jesse Edward, Jr.

Class of 1984

Abbott, Denise Michelle
Andrews, Jeffrey Alan
Andrews, Tae Wan
Baker, Beverly Muriel
Brown, Conrad Nelson, Jr.
Brown, Jeffrey Darryl
Chambers, Cliffton Durell
Clayton, Eric Von
Curbeam, Robert Lee, Jr.
Darden, Ronald Karl
Davis, Christopher Darnell
Davis, Jacqueline Renee
Fegan, Frederick Morris
Flaggs, Moreatha Yvette
Fortune, Idean Josephine, II
Gaines, Leonard Salmon
Hosch, Willie H.
Howard, James Heyward
Howard, Kevin Thomas
Hudson, Derek Dewitt
Jones, Michael Lawrence
Kizzee, Carlos Perry
Law, Leitia Lynne
Manning, Cameron Alan
Marshall, Lawrence Eugene
McDonald, Ronald Keith
McKinney, Billy Lynn
Neal, Sherman Evon
Newhouse, Darryl Brian
Nixon, Randall Lamar
Parrish, Demetrius John, Jr.
Peoples, Gerald Keith
Price, Lenny Francis
Rasbury, Stanley Okoye
Shepherd, Michael Andrew
Skinner, Steven Gregory
Smith, David Hanson
Smith, Jonathan Jerome
Stephens, Carla Renee
Stevens, Monica
Taylor, James, Jr.
Tillman, Willard, Jr.
Turner, Jean-Francois
Walton, Terrance Bernard
Wilson, Joslyn Grant, Jr.

Wilson, Woodrow, III
Wright, Darin Claude

Class of 1985

Adams, Thomas Lee, III
Adkins, Lemonte Andre
Alexander, Lewis B., Jr.
Atkinson, David
Betton, Christopher R.
Biggs, Jeffrey S.
Bryan, Curtis E., Jr.
Burke, Christopher K.
Bugg, Lois
Bush, Rani Dale
Coleman, Austin Hughes
Daniel, Jeffrey Allen
Davis, Bruce Gary
Dejoie, Bertel Jacques
Dillard Mark Vincent
Figgins, Gerald Dale
Flowers, Michael L.
Gex, Geoffrey David
Graham, Michael Ray
Greenwood, Michael D.
Hacker, Bruce Laurence
Harris, Paul, Jr.

Henry, Frederick D.
Hines, Joseph Emanuel
Johnson, Dreste M.
Jones, Warren R., Jr.
Keyes, Warren F.
Maddox, Mario Renara
Marsh, Laurence A.
McCallum, Napoleon
McKinney, Roberta V.
Melvin, Barry S.
Mills, Charlie H., III
Mimms, Bernard F.
Moore, David Joseph
Moore, Michael Thomas
Morant, Kevin
Nolan, Charles H., Jr.
Parham, Thomas D., III
Phelps, Peter M.
Phillip, Lester U.
Pierce, Carlton
Pleasant, Mervin A., III
Rhoe, Reginald M.
Richmond, Phillip Paul
Studevan, Colin C.
Wallace, Eric K.
Williams, Byron A.
Williams, Steven Craig

BLACK CADETS AT THE U.S. AIR FORCE ACADEMY

Class of 1983

Aikens, Johnny, III
Anderson, Nicole P.
Babers, Alonzo C.
Bland, Othello, Jr.
Brisbon, Harris L.
Brown, Virginia G.
Bullock, Jay P.
Cannon, Kevin A.
Carter, Norris E.
Cephas, Earl F.
Childress, Iris R.
Collins, Brian D.
Corbett, Dorian I.
Davis, Howard D., Jr.
Dooley, Bryan P.
Evans, Quintin A.
Ford, Apryl A.
Gibbs, Gregory C.
Glover, Kendall R.
Gobern, Alexis M., Jr.
Gore, Kevin A.
Gould, Patrick A.
Grant, Cecil A., Jr.
Graves, Ronald E.
Hall, Nathaniel C.

Harris, Charles H., Jr.
Harris, Johnnie C., Jr.
Head, Robert L., Jr.
Hockaday, Cleophas S., Jr.
Holloway, Theodore P.
Holmes, Stewart E., Jr.
Hudson, Tony D.
Hunter, Raymond A.
Johnson, Roger E.
Johnson, Steven B.
Jones, Charles D.
Jones, Herbert H., Jr.
Lewis, Errol I.
Lofton, Ricky O.
McCray, Cleveland R.
McDaniel, Donald A.
Moore, Kyle R.
Moreland, Carol L.
Peart, Michael A.
Peterson, Eugene G., Jr.
Pratt, Bryan P.
Richardson, Derrick M.
Robinson, Donovan O.
Rogers, John F., III
Samuda, Eric F.
Sears, Emanuel O.
Simmons, Richard I.

Simpson, Dorothy E.
Singleton, Harold L., Jr.
Smith, Donald R.
Sullivan, Konda H.
Tingman, Kenneth R.
Valentine, Lee A.
Veal, Kenny
Washington, Erwin V.
Williams, Bernard S., Jr.
Williams, Troy M.
Wilson, Jahn D.
Winston, Moses B.
Yancy, Daniel M.

Class of 1984

Aiken, Charles H., Jr.
Allen, Cheryl A.
Aubert, Steven F.
Aycock, Kent D.
Baker, Herman L., Jr.
Banks, Melody C.
Barrant, Winston I.
Best, Leonard Jr.
Bethea, Mark I.
Billups, Aundra E.
Boyd, Robin D.
Bradley, Dave W.
Burke, John C.
Calderon, Joseph P.
Callahan, Mark A.
Chatman, Cleophus D.
Clark, Andrea D.
Clark, Warren H.
Collins, Colleen A.
Conway, Norphesia G.
Crews, Alfred, Jr.
Cross, Clarice
Dawson, Jay W.
Dieudonne, Carl H.
Dixon, Charles I.
Drew, Benjamin A., Jr.
Dugue, Brett A.
Dulaney, Keith L.
Elliott, Grady N.
Eubanks, James C., Jr.
Fisher, Christopher S.
Foster, Derek C.
Freeman, Myron
Glass, George C.
Glass, Robert C., Jr.
Gomes, Marie E.
Goodman, Anthony L.
Greer, Byron L.
Griffis, Craig E.
Hamilton, Caleb L.
Hargrove, Reginald P.
Harris, William J., Jr.
Haynes, Victor C.
Healy, Steven J.

Hill, Douglas E.
Hill, Prince A.
Hood, Charles M., III
Hurst, Thurston L.
Jackson, Ingrid M.
Johnson, David C.
Johnson, Stephen T.
Jones, Marvin E.
Joseph, Garland R.
King, Konrad
Leblanc, Stewart M.
Lewis, Randy
Major, Derrick S.
Malone, Michael L.
Marshall, Gregory
Martin, Mark A.
McClary, Wayne H.
McGlotten, Douglas L.
Milteer, Michael N.
Milton, Elbert, Jr.
Moore, Lee
Myers, Chris A.
Owens, John E.
Paige, Clive A.
Petteway, Malcolm
Phanord, Bettina A.
Phifer, Julia C.
Prince, John H.
Randall, Ivan T.
Reaves, Irving W.
Revels, Allen R.
Ross, Hubert A.
Rozier, David E.
Rucker, Sharon L.
Sanders, Samuel T.
Scott, Lamont G.
Scott, Leon C., Jr.
Seals, Regan W.
Sheppard, Gwendolyn M.
Smith, Eugenio R.
Smith, Susan E.
Smith, Marcel R.
Strong, Crystal L.
Suber, Craig J.
Tann, Martin C.
Taylor, John D.
Thom, Maxie C.
Thomas, Andre L.
Thomas, Michael J.
Tucker, Wade L.
Valentine, Fred L., Jr.
Westbrook, James B., II
Wickliffe, Carlton P.
Wigfall, James E.
Williams, Anthony W.
Williams, Daniel E.
Williams, David H.
Williams, Douglas
Williams, Horace L.
Willis, Cedric C.

Class of 1985

Abram, Dorera J.
Adkins, Thomas A.
Allen, Marc L.
Anderson, Jerry D.
Baker, Robert K.
Banks, Kenneth
Barnes, Glenn D.
Barnum, Usher L.
Baylor, William L., III
Bessellieu, Susan P.
Black, Michael B.
Blackmon, Elihu R.
Boswell, Anthony O.
Boyd, Randy D.
Bridgers, Matthew X.
Brown, Gerald Q.
Brown, Regina J.
Brown, William C.
Broussard, Kerri L.
Burns, Bennie L.
Butler, Derrick D.
Byrd, Edward L.
Cameron, Von M.
Carter, Miguel A.
Cleaves, Chevalier P.
Corns, Toi V.
Dawkins, Keith A.
Devane, Mark W.
Dixon, Kevin W.
Dobbs, Deric K.
Dorsey, Alfred M.
Douglas, Robert H.
Durante, Paris A.
Eady, Monica J.
Evans, Kenneth C.
Evans, Robert A.
Ferrell, Melodi L.
Fields, Mark K.
Foster, Nagaila
Garrett, Gerald B.
Gest, Robert IV
Gibbs, Gregory L.
Gilmore, Robert E.
Gilyard, Reginald H.
Gordon, Eric L.
Gould, Evelyn J.
Graham, Anterro A.
Grant, Karl A.
Griffith, Rodney N.
Griggs, Gordon J.
Harris, Philecia L.
Harris, Wanda D.
Harvey, Dwight E.
Hatchett, Danielle L.
Hayes, Jesse D.
Hines, Hugh L.
Hodge, Nicole C.

Holsey, Reginald C.
Hussain, Kobir
Ivory, James C.
Jackson, Larry D.
Jackson, Reginald W.
James, Thomas M.
Johnson, Ellis
Jones, Charles E., Jr.
Jones, William A.
Jordan, Jonathon D.
Kelley, Russell V.
Larkins, Charles G.
Lesane, Jonathan
Luster, Maurice
Mason, Gerald M.
Mayes, Bobby L.
McClary, Carl W.
McElhannon, Neal B.
McKnight, Ivan S.
Mills, Johnny R.
Modesty, Ronald K.
Moore, Vernon L.
Mooreland, Christopher J.
Morton, Clarence R., II
Nixon, Kevin M.
Paige, Clive A.
Patterson, Edward A., II
Perry, David F. D.
Philpotts, Gregory M.
Pickett, Marquis D.
Randolf, Mark J.
Richardson, Darrell K.
Ross, Anthony D., Jr.
Ross, Arthur, Jr.
Russell, Frank E., II
Sampson, Rodney N.
Scott, Alton J.
Simmons, Cedric D.
Sisson, Michael A.
Smith, Ronald G.
Sowell, Michael T.
Stewart, Dennis J.
Street, Christopher L.
Streeter, Charles A.
Thomas, Douglas
Timberlake, Douglas E.
Ussery, Harold A.
Walker, Gary L.
Walton, James D.
Washington, Joyce D.
Washington, Robert A.
Weathersby, George
Wiggins, Joseph, Jr.
Williams, Albert H.
Williams, Frank Q.
Williams, Jeffrey D.
Woods, Robert A., Jr.
Wright, Wanda A.

BLACK ARMED FORCES BRASS

BRIGADIER GENERAL ROBERT BRADSHAW ADAMS
Director of Resources and Management, Office of the Deputy Chief of Staff for Logistics, United States Army, Washington, D.C.

General Adams was born in Buffalo, New York. He received a BBA degree in accounting/auditing from Canisius College and BBA and MBA degrees in automated data processing from George Washington University. During his 25-year career in the U.S. Army, General Adams has been Finance Officer of the 23rd Infantry Division and was later Finance Officer of the 196th Infantry Brigade in Vietnam; Commandant, U.S. Army Institute of Administration, Fort Benjamin Harrison, Indiana; Deputy Commander for Integration, U.S. Army Administration Center, Fort Benjamin Harrison, Indiana; and Assistant Comptroller for Resource Policy and Financial Planning, Office of the Comptroller of the Army, Washington, D.C. He has received the Bronze Star Medal, the Legion of Merit with two oak leaf clusters, the Meritorious Service Medal with an Oak Leaf Cluster, and the Army Commendation Medal with an oak leaf cluster.

BRIGADIER GENERAL JULIUS WESTLEY BECTON, JR.
Deputy Commanding General U.S. Army Training Center, Infantry, Fort Dix, N.J.

General Becton began his service career when he was called to active duty in July 1944, from the Air Corps

Lieutenant General Julius W. Becton, Jr.

Enlisted Reserve, which he joined in 1943. He attended the Infantry Officer Candidate School at Fort Benning, Georgia, and graduated in 1945.

His assignments include Commanding Officer, Second Squadron, Seventh Cavalry, 101st Airborne Division, United States Army, Vietnam. His medals and awards are the Silver Star with Oak Leaf Cluster, Legion of Merit with Oak Leaf Cluster, Distinguished Flying Cross, Bronze Star Medal with Oak Leaf Cluster, five awards of the Air Medal with V Device, Army Commendation Medal with Oak Leaf Cluster, Purple Heart with Oak Leaf Cluster, Combat Infantry Badge (2d Award), and the Parachutist Badge.

BRIGADIER GENERAL JAMES T. BODDIE, JR.
Deputy Director for Operations, National Military Command Center, Organization of the Joint Chiefs of Staff, Washington, D.C.

General Boddie was born in 1931 in Baltimore and received his bachelors degree from Howard University. He is a graduate of the Academic Instructors School and Squadron Officer School, both located at Maxwell Air Force Base, Alabama. He received his commission through the Air Force Reserve Officers Training Corps program and was awarded the Convair Aviation Association Award for his outstanding accomplishments as a cadet. In June 1965 General Boddie joined the 4453rd Combat Crew Training Wing, Davis-Monthan Air Force Base, Arizona, where he flew and instructed in F-4s. The following year he volunteered for combat duty in Southeast Asia and was assigned to the 559th Tactical Fighter Squadron, Cam Ranh Bay Air Base, Republic of Vietnam, in October 1966. General Boddie is a command pilot with more than 4,000 hours in jet fighter aircraft. His military decorations and awards include the Legion of Merit, Distinguished Flying Cross, Meritorious Service Medal with two oak leaf clusters, Air Medal with 13 oak leaf clusters, Air Force Commendation Medal, Air Force Outstanding Unit Award ribbon with three oak leaf clusters and "V" device, Combat Readiness Medal and the National Defense Service Medal.

BRIGADIER GENERAL ELMER T. BROOKS
Commander of the 381st Strategic Missile Wing, McConnell Air Force Base, Kansas

A native of Washington, D.C., General Brooks received a bachelor of arts degree in zoology from Miami of Ohio University and was commissioned through the Air Force Reserve Officers Training Corps. He received a master of science degree from George Washington University. General Brooks has served in Houston as a flight control technologist for Gemini and Apollo space missions at the National Aeronautics and space Administration's Manned Spacecraft Center. He was also vice commander of the 381st Missile Wing, a Titan II intercontinental ballistic missile unit at McConnell Air Force Base. He assumed command of that wing in January 1979. His awards include the Defense Superior Service Medal with one oak leaf cluster, Meritorious Service Medal with one oak leaf cluster, and the Joint Service Commendation Medal.

BRIGADIER GENERAL HARRY WILLIAMS BROOKS, JR.
Assistant Division Commander, U.S. Army 2nd Infantry Division, 8th Army

General Brooks was commissioned a Second Lieutenant in 1949 through Officer Candidate School. He earned a B.S. from University of Omaha in business administration.

During his career he was assigned Commanding Officer, Second Battalion, 40th Artillery, 199th Infantry Brigade, Vietnam; Special Assistant to Deputy Commanding Officer, 199th Infantry Brigade, Vietnam; Commanding Officer, 72d Field Artillery Group, Europe; and Army Director of Equal Opportunity Programs, Office of the Deputy Chief of Staff for Personnel, Washington, D.C.

He has been awarded the Legion of Merit with Oak Leaf Cluster, Bronze Star Medal with Oak Leaf Cluster, Meritorious Service Medal, seven awards of the Air Medal and the Army Commendation Medal.

BRIGADIER GENERAL LEO AUSTIN BROOKS
Commanding General, United States Army Troop Support Agency, Fort Lee, Virginia

General Brooks was born in Washington, D.C. and received his B.S. degree in music education from Virginia State College and his M.S. in financial management from George Washington University. During his 26 years in the U.S. Army, General Brooks' assignments have been Assistant for Budget and Congressional Coordinators, Office, Deputy Chief of Staff for Logistics, Washington, D.C.; Deputy Secretary of the General Staff, U.S. Army Materiel Command, Washington, D.C.; Commander, 13th Corps Support Command, Fort Hood, Texas, and Director of Industrial Operations, Fort Hood, Texas. He has received the Legion of Merit with two oak leaf clusters, the Army Commendation Medal with an oak leaf cluster, the Bronze Star Medal, the Meritorious Service Medal, and the Joint Service Commendation Medal.

BRIGADIER GENERAL COVERDALE BROWN, JR.
Deputy Commandant, U.S. Army War College, Carlisle Barracks, Pennsylvania

General Brown was born in New Orleans and received

his bachelor of arts degree in history from West Virginia State College and his master of arts degree in government from Indiana University. He has been Commander of the 519th Military Intelligence Battalion, 525th Military Intelligence Group in Vietnam; Deputy Chief, Soviet/East European Division; Directorate for Estimates and later Chief, Ground Forces/Mutual Balanced Forced Reduction Branch, Soviet-Warsaw Pact Division; Directorate for Intelligence Research, Defense Intelligence Agency, Washington, D.C.; Deputy Chief of Staff for Intelligence, U.S. Army Forces Command, Fort McPherson, Georgia; and Assistant Vice Director for Estimates and Deputy Vice Director for Foreign Intelligence, Defense Intelligence Agency, Washington, D.C. General Brown has received the Meritorious Service Medal with an oak leaf cluster, the Joint Service Commendation Medal, the Army Commendation Medal, and the Master Parachutist Badge.

BRIGADIER GENERAL JOHN MITCHELL BROWN
Deputy Director of Materiel Plans and Programs, Office of the Deputy Chief of Staff for Research, Development, and Acquisition, U.S. Army, Washington, D.C.

General Brown was born in Vicksburg, Mississippi and received his bachelor of science degree in engineering from the U.S. Military Academy. He received his MBA degree in comptrollership from Syracuse University and attended the advanced management program at the University of Houston. General Brown has been Commander, 1st Battalion, 87th Infantry, 8th Infantry Division, U.S. Army in Europe; Executive to the Comptroller of the Army in Washington, D.C.; Assistant Chief of Staff Comptroller, U.N. Command, U.S. Forces Korea, and the Eighth U.S. Army; and Assistant Division Commander, 2nd Infantry Division, Korea. He has received the Legion of Merit, the Bronze Star Medal, the Meritorious Service Medal, the Army Commendation Medal with two oak leaf clusters, the Combat Infantryman Badge, the Parachutist Badge, and the Ranger Tab.

MAJOR GENERAL WILLIAM E. BROWN, JR.
Commander of the 17th Air Force

General Brown was born in the Bronx, New York. He received a bachelor of science degree from Pennsylvania State University and has acquired graduate credits toward a masters degree in systems management from the University of Southern California. He also attended the Harvard Business School's advanced management program. General Brown was stationed at McGuire Air Force Base in New Jersey for seven years. During his stay, he flew the F-84 Thunderjet,

Major General William E. Brown, Jr.

the F-86D, and the F-102 Delta Dagger with the 2nd and 332nd Fighter-Interceptor Squadrons and the New York Air Defense Sector. He is a command pilot with more than 4,900 flying hours. General Brown's decorations and awards include the Legion of Merit with two oak leaf clusters, the Distinguished Flying Cross with one oak leaf cluster, the Air Medal with four oak leaf clusters, the Air Force Commendation Medal with two oak leaf clusters, the Purple Heart, the Air Force Outstanding Unit Award, the Combat Readiness Medal, and the Republic of Korea Presidential Unit Citation.

BRIGADIER GENERAL CUNNINGHAM CAMPBELL BRYANT
The Adjutant General, District of Columbia National Guard, Washington, D.C.

General Bryant entered the enlisted reserve at Howard University in 1942 as an Army ROTC cadet. He was called to active duty in 1943 and was commissioned as a Second Lieutenant after completing Infantry Officer Candidate School at Fort Benning in 1944.

He served as Company Commander with the 317th Combat Engineer Battalion and the 92d General Service Regiment. After he was released from active duty in 1949, he remained in the U.S. Army Reserve until 1954.

He has been awarded the Bronze Star Medal, Army Commendation Medal, Purple Heart, Army of Occupation Medal (Germany), World War II Victory Medal, National Defense Service Medal, European-African Middle Eastern Campaign Medal with two stars, American Campaign Medal, and the Combat Infantry Badge.

BRIGADIER GENERAL ROSCOE CONKLIN CARTWRIGHT
Assistant Division Commander, U.S. Army 3rd Infantry Division, Europe

In 1942 General Cartwright was commissioned a Second Lieutenant through Officer Candidate School. He has served as Commanding Officer, 108th Artillery Group, Pacific-Vietnam; Deputy Commanding Officer, U.S. Army Support Command, Cam Ranh Bay; Chief, Budget and Five Year Defense Program, Coordination Division, Manpower and Forces Directorate, Office of the Assistant Chief of Staff for Force Development, Washington, D.C.; and Director of Management Review and Analysis, Office of Comptroller of the Army, Washington, D.C. He has been awarded the Legion of Merit with oak leaf cluster, Bronze Star Medal with two oak leaf clusters, Meritorious Service Medal, three awards of the Air Medal and the Army Commendation Medal with two oak leaf clusters.

General Cartwright died December 1974 in an air crash in Virginia.

MAJOR GENERAL ANDREW PHILLIP CHAMBERS
Commanding General, U.S. Army Readiness and Mobilization Region VII, Fort Sam Houston, Texas

Major Chambers was born in Bedford, Virginia and received his B.S. from Howard University and his M.S. from Shippensburg State College. During his 26 years in the military, General Chambers' assignments have included Deputy Commander, 1st Brigade, 8th Infantry, 8th Infantry Division, Europe; Deputy Director and later Director, Equal Opportunity Programs, Office, Deputy Chief of Staff for Personnel, Washington, D.C.; Director, Personnel, Inspector General, Pacific Command, Camp H. M. Smith, Hawaii; and Assistant Division Commander, 1st Cavalry Division, Fort Hood, Texas. He has received the Defense Superior Service Medal, the Legion of Merit, the Soldier's Medal, the Bronze Star Medal with V device, the Meritorious Service Medal with an oak leaf cluster, the Air Medal, the Army Commendation Medal with two oak leaf clusters, the Combat Infantryman Badge, and the Senior Parachutist Badge.

BRIGADIER GENERAL THOMAS E. CLIFFORD
Deputy Commanding General, 17th AF, Ramstein, Germany

General Clifford was commissioned as a member of the ROTC at Howard University in March 1949. Later

he was an all-weather jet pilot with the 5th Fighter Interceptor Squadron, McGuire AFB a fighter pilot attached to the 449th Interceptor Squadron in Alaska, and then with the 437th at Oxnard Air Force Base.

He was weapons training officer and flight commander, 329th Fighter Interceptor Squadron, George Air Force Base, California; management analyst, U.S. Air Forces.

He has been awarded the Legion of Merit with oak leaf cluster and Air Force Commendation Medal with one oak leaf cluster.

COLONEL EUGENE RUFUS CROMARTIE
Deputy Provost Marshal, U.S. Army, Europe, and Seventh Army

Colonel Cromartie was born in Wabasso, Florida. He received his bachelor of science degree in social science from Florida A&M University and his master of science in education/guidance and counseling from the University of Dayton. Colonel Cromartie, during his military career, has been Commander, 503rd Military Police Battalion, Fort Bragg, North Carolina; Provost Marshal, 82nd Airborne Division, Fort Bragg; Special Assistant to the Commanding General, U.S. Army Criminal Investigation Command, Falls Church, Virginia; and Commander, First Region, U.S. Army Criminal Investigation Command, Fort Meade, Maryland. Colonel Cromartie has received the Bronze Star Medal with an oak leaf cluster, the Meritorious Service Medal with two oak leaf clusters, the Army Commendation Medal with an oak leaf cluster, and the Parachutist Badge.

MAJOR GENERAL JERRY RALPH CURRY
Deputy Assistant Secretary of Defense (public affairs), Washington, D.C.

A native of McKeesport, Pennsylvania, General Curry received his BE degree in general education from the University of Nebraska-Omaha and his master of arts degree in international relations from Boston University. He obtained his Ph.D. in religious theology from Luther Rice Seminary. General Curry has been Commander of the 2nd Battalion, 30th Infantry, 3rd Infantry Division (mechanized), U.S. Army in Europe; Commander, 3rd Brigade, 8th Infantry Division (mechanized), U.S. Army, Europe; Deputy Commanding General, U.S. Army Military District of Washington, Washington, D.C.; Assistant Division Commander, 4th Infantry Division (Mechanized), Fort Carson, Colorado; and Commanding General, U.S. Army Test and Evaluation Command, Aberdeen Proving Ground, Maryland. General Curry has received the Legion of Merit with an oak leaf cluster, the Bronze Star Medal, the Meritorious Service Medal with an oak leaf cluster, Air Medals, the Army Commendation Medal with two oak leaf clusters, the Navy Commendation Medal, the Combat Infantryman Badge, the Parachutist Badge, and the Master Army Aviator Badge.

MAJOR GENERAL FREDERICK ELLIS DAVISON
Commanding General, 8th Infantry Division, U.S. Army, Europe

General Davison entered Howard University in Washington, D.C., in 1934 and earned B.S. and M.S. degrees in zoology and chemistry. While earning his baccalaureate degree, he completed Army ROTC and was commissioned a Second Lieutenant in the Infantry Reserve in 1939.

During his career he was assigned as Chief, Reserve Forces Division, Office Deputy Under Secretary of the Army, Washington, D.C.; Commanding Officer, Third Training Brigade, U.S. Army Training Center, Air Defense.

His awards include the Distinguished Service Medal, Legion of Merit with oak leaf cluster, Bronze Star Medal, forty-nine awards of the Air Medal, Army Commendation Medal with two oak leaf clusters, Bronze Star Medal (infantryman's) Badge, Second Award.

BRIGADIER GENERAL DONALD JOSEPH DELANDRO
Deputy, The Adjutant General for Administrative Systems and Executive Director, Military Postal Service, the Adjutant General Center, U.S. Army, Washington, D.C.

General Delandro is a native of New Orleans. He received his bachelor of science degree in business administration from Southern University A&M College and his MBA degree from the University of Chicago. His assignments during his 24-year career in the U.S. Army have included Adjutant General, 23rd Infantry Division (America), Vietnam; Executive Officer, Weapons Systems Analysis Directorate, Office, Assistant Vice Chief of Staff, Washington, D.C.; Chief of Staff, U.S. Army Military Personnel Center, Alexandria, Virginia; and Chief of Staff, U.S. Army Recruiting Command, Fort Sheridan, Illinois. Among the decorations and badges General Delandro has received are the Legion of Merit with an oak leaf cluster, the Bronze Star Medal, the Meritorious Service Medal, the Air Medal, the Joint Service Commendation Medal, and the Army Commendation Medal with an oak leaf cluster as well as the Parachutist Badge.

BRIGADIER GENERAL OLIVER WILLIAMS DILLARD
Deputy Chief of Staff for Intelligence, Headquarters, U.S. Army Forces Command, Fort McPherson, Georgia

General Dillard began his service career in 1945 when he was inducted into the U.S. Army. He was accepted into the Infantry Officer Candidate School at Fort Benning, Georgia, and was commissioned a Second Lieutenant in 1947.

His first three years of duty as a commissioned officer consisted of various assignments within the 365th Infantry Regiment, which was involved in basic training of recruits. His assignments also include Assistant Professor of Military Science at A & T College, Greensboro, North Carolina, Commanding Officer, 5th Combat Support Training Brigade, Fort Dix, New Jersey; Director of Intelligence Support.

He has been awarded the Silver Star, Legion of Merit with two oak leaf clusters, Bronze Star Medal with oak leaf cluster, Army Commendation Medal with oak leaf cluster, Purple Heart, Combat Infantryman's Badge, and the Vietnamese Army Distinguished Service Order (2d class).

MAJOR GENERAL HENRY DOCTOR, JR.
Director, Personnel, Training and Force Development, U.S. Army Materiel Development and Readiness Command, Alexandria, Virginia

General Doctor, born in Oakley, South Carolina, was commissioned a Second Lieutenant through the Army ROTC following graduation in 1954 with a bachelor of science degree in general agriculture from South Carolina State College. He also received his master of arts degree in counseling and psychological services from Georgia State University. General Doctor's assignments have included Commander, 1st Battalion, 29th Infantry, 197th Infantry Brigade, Fort Benning, Georgia; Chief, Modern Volunteer Army Control Group, U.S. Army Infantry Center, Fort Benning, Georgia; Director of Enlisted Personnel Management, U.S. Army Military Personnel Center, Alexandria, Virginia; and Assistant Division Commander, 24th Infantry Division, Fort Stewart, Georgia. He has been awarded the Legion of Merit, the Bronze Star Medal, the Meritorious Service Medal, the Air Medal, the Army Commendation Medal with three oak leaf clusters, and the Combat Infantryman Badge.

BRIGADIER GENERAL ARCHER L. DURHAM
Commander of the 76th Airlift Division, Military Airlift Command, Andrews Air Force Base, Maryland

General Durham was born in 1932 in Pasadena, California. He received a bachelor of science degree in political science from Utah State University in 1960 and a master of science degree in international affairs from the George Washington University in Washington, D.C. in 1975. General Durham began his military career in 1953 as an aviation cadet and in April 1954 received his commission and pilot wings at Laredo Air Force Base, Texas. In July 1977 he took command of the 1606th Air Base Wing, Kirtland Air Force Base, New Mexico, a position he held until February 1979. He next served as commander of the 436th Military Airlift Wing at Dover Air Force Base, Delaware, until February 1980. He is a command pilot with more than 6,000 flying hours. His military decorations and awards include the Legion of Merit with one oak leaf cluster, Meritorious Service Medal with one oak leaf cluster, and the Air Force Commendation Medal with one oak leaf cluster.

BRIGADIER GENERAL ALONZO L. FERGUSON
Commander, 21st North American Air Defense Command Region at Hancock Field, New York; Commander, 21st Aerospace Defense Command Region, and Commander, 21st Air Division, Air Defense Component of the Tactical Air Command

General Ferguson began active duty in 1952 after completion of flight and jet training. Born in Washington, D.C., General Ferguson graduated from Howard University with a bachelor of science degree in psychology. General Ferguson served at Headquarters Tactical Air Command, Langley Air Force Base, Virginia as chief of the weapons systems branch under the deputy for operations from January 1968 to July 1971. General Ferguson returned to South Korea in 1974 and in March 1975 was named Vice Commander of the 355th Tactical Fighter Wing at Davis-Monthan Air Force Base, Arizona. His military decorations and awards include the Silver Star with one oak leaf cluster, the Legion of Merit, the Defense Meritorious Service Medal, Meritorious Service Medal with one oak leaf cluster, the Air Medal with 13 oak leaf clusters, and the Air Force Commendation Medal with one oak leaf cluster.

BRIGADIER GENERAL JOHNNIE FORTE, JR.
Director of Personnel, J-1 Inspector General, U.S. European Command

General Forte was born in New Boston, Texas and received his bachelor of science degree in political science from Prairie View University and his master of science in public administration from Auburn University. General Forte has been commander, 41st Civil Affairs Company, Civil Operations and Rural Development Support, U.S. Military Assistance Command in Vietnam; Commander, 4th Battalion, 61st Air Defense Artillery, 4th Infantry Division (Mechanized), Fort

Carson, Colorado; and Liaison Officer to the U.S. Air Force, Europe, U.S. Army Europe Liaison Group, Ramstein Air Force Base, Germany. General Forte has received the Legion of Merit with the oak leaf cluster, the Meritorious Service Medal, the Army Commendation Medal with two oak leaf clusters, the Air Force Commendation Medal, and the Aircraft Crewman Badge.

MAJOR GENERAL ROBERT CLARENCE GASKILL
Deputy Director, Defense Logistics Agency, Cameron Station, Alexandria, Virginia

General Gaskill is a native of Yonkers, New York. He received his bachelor of arts degree in business administration from Howard University and his MBA degree also in business administration from George Washington University. He was commissioned a Second Lieutenant through the Army ROTC program. His assignments during his 28-year career have been Commanding General, 1st Support Brigade, U.S. Army, Europe; Commanding General, Letterkenny Army Depot, Chambersburg, Pennsylvania; Deputy Commanding General, 21st Support Command, U.S. Army, Europe; Deputy Commandant, U.S. Army War College, Carlisle Barracks, Pennsylvania. He has received the Legion of Merit, the Meritorious Service Medal, and the Army Commendation Medal each with an oak leaf cluster.

REAR ADMIRAL SAMUEL L. GRAVELY, JR.
Commander, Cruiser Destroyer Flotilla Two

Admiral Gravely enlisted in the U.S. Naval Reserve in 1942. He transferred from the Reserve to the U.S. Navy in 1955.

He has been Assistant Battalion Commander, Naval Training Center, Great Lakes; Communications Officer, Electronics Officer, and later Executive Officer and Personnel Officer of the USS PC 1264 submarine chaser; Communications Watch Officer, Fleet Training Group, Norfolk, Virginia; Assistant to the Officer in Charge for Recruiting, Naval Recruiting Station; and Officer Procurement, Washington, D.C.

He has been awarded the Meritorious Service Medal, Navy Commendation Medal (with Gold Star and Combat V), Korean Presidential Unit Citation Ribbon, Naval Reserve Medal, American Campaign Medal, World War II Victory Medal, National Defense Service Medal (with Bronze Star), China Service Medal, Korean Service Medal (with two Bronze Stars), U.N. Service Medal, Armed Forces Expeditionary Medal, Vietnam Service Medal (with four Bronze Stars), and Republic of Vietnam Campaign Medal (with device).

Admiral Gravely.

BRIGADIER GENERAL EDWARD GREER
Deputy Commanding General, U.S. Army Training Center, Engineer, Fort Leonard Wood, Missouri

General Greer was commissioned through the Army ROTC in 1948 from West Virginia State College. He was born in Gary, West Virginia.

His assignments include Commanding Officer, First Battalion, Seventh Artillery, U.S. Army, Pacific-Korea; Author-Instructor, Department of Command, U.S. Army Command and General Staff College, Fort Leavenworth, Kansas; Deputy Commander, XXIV Corps Artillery, U.S. Army, Pacific-Vietnam; Commanding Officer, 108th Artillery Group, U.S. Army, Pacific-Vietnam; and Assistant Director, Directorate for Reserve Forces; Plans, Programs and Budgets, Office, Assistant Secretary of Defense, Washington, D.C.

His medals and awards are the Silver Star, Legion of Merit with oak leaf cluster, Bronze Star Medal with oak leaf cluster, Air Medal, Joint Service Commendation Medal, and Army Commendation Medal with oak leaf cluster.

BRIGADIER GENERAL ARTHUR JAMES GREGG
Deputy Director of Supply and Maintenance, for Logistics, U.S. Army, Washington, D.C.

General Gregg was born in Florence, South Carolina. He attended St. Benedict's College, Atchison, Kansas, and earned a B.S. degree in business administration. He was commissioned a Second Lieutenant through Officer Candidate School in 1950.

His assignments include Commanding Officer 96th Quartermaster Battalion, Fort Riley, Kansas; Commanding Officer, Nahbollenbach Army Depot, U.S. Army, Europe; Director of Troop Support, Office, Deputy Chief of Staff for Logistics, U.S. Army. He has been awarded the Legion of Merit with oak leaf cluster, Meritorious Service Medal, Joint Service Commendation Medal, and Army Commendation Medal with two oak leaf clusters.

BRIGADIER GENERAL DAVID M. HALL
Deputy Chief of Staff, Comptroller, Air Force Logistics Command, Wright-Patterson Air Force Base, Ohio

General Hall was born in 1928 in Gary, Indiana where he graduated from Roosevelt High School. He earned a bachelors degree in business administration from Howard University, Washington, D.C. and a masters degree in educational sociology from the Agricultural and Technical State University of North Carolina, Greensboro. General Hall was assigned to the Air Force Accounting and Finance Center, Denver, in September 1967. He was chief of the Computer Operations Division in the Directorate of Data Automation until 1969 when he joined a software development division as an analyst-programmer. In March 1971 he was assigned to Scott Air Force Base, Illinois, where he became chief of the Computer Operations Division for Military Airlift Command headquarters, and in March 1972 he became the assistant for social actions in the office of the Deputy Chief of Staff for Personnel at Scott. General Hall became the deputy base commander for Scott Air Force Base in May 1974 and base commander in February 1975. His military deco-

Lieutenant General Arthur S. Gregg.

rations and awards include the Legion of Merit, Meritorious Service Medal with one oak leaf cluster, and the Air Force Commendation Medal with one oak leaf cluster.

BRIGADIER GENERAL JAMES REGINALD HALL, JR.
Assistant Deputy Chief of Staff for Personnel, U.S. Army Forces Command, Fort McPherson, Georgia

General Hall was born in Anniston, Alabama and received a B.A. degree in political science from Morehouse College in Atlanta and an M.S. degree in public administration from Shippensburg State College in Pennsylvania. His assignments have included Personnel Management Officer, Infantry Branch, Officer Personnel Directorate, Office of Personnel Operations in Washington, D.C.; Commander 1st Battalion, 9th Infantry, 2nd Infantry Division, Korea; Chief, Army Wide Test Branch, Skill Progression Directorate; and later Executive Officer, Office, Deputy Chief of Staff for Training and Schools, U.S. Army Training and Doctrine Command, Fort Monroe, Virginia; Commander, 4th Regiment, U.S. Corps of Cadets, U.S. Military Academy, West Point; Commander, 197th Infantry Brigade, Fort Benning, Georgia; and Secretary, U.S. Army Infantry School, Fort Benning, Georgia. His awards and decorations include the Legion of Merit, the Bronze Star Medal, Meritorious Service Medal with the oak leaf cluster, Army Commendation Medal with oak leaf cluster, the Combat Infantryman Badge, and the Parachutist Badge.

MAJOR GENERAL TITUS C. HALL
Commander of the Lowry Technical Training Center, Lowry Air Force Base, Colorado

General Hall entered active duty with the U.S. Air Force in 1942 after he received his bachelor of science degree in electrical engineering from Tuskegee Institute, Alabama. A native of Pflugerville, Texas, General Hall also earned a masters degree in systems engineering from the University of Southern California in 1971. The General attended basic navigator flying school at Ellington Air Force Base, Texas, and advanced bombing and navigation school at Mather Air Force Base, California, from March 1956 to January 1958. General Hall became chief avionics engineer for the B-1 strategic manned bomber at Headquarters Aeronautical Systems Division, Wright-Patterson Air Force Base, Ohio, in March 1972. General Hall became deputy for systems, now reconnaissance and electronic warfare systems, Headquarters Aeronautical Systems Division, Wright-Patterson Air Force Base, in July 1978. He is a master navigator with 4,000 flying hours in the FB-111s, EF-111s, F-4G Wild Weasels, and the U.S. Navy A-7Ds. His military decorations and awards

Major General Titus C. Hall.

include the Distinguished Service Medal, Legion of Merit, Distinguished Flying Cross, Bronze Star Medal, Meritorious Service Medal with one oak leaf cluster, and the Air Medal with two oak leaf clusters.

MAJOR GENERAL JAMES FRANK HAMLET
Commanding General, U.S. Army 4th Infantry Division (Mechanized), Fort Carson, Colorado

General Hamlet was born in Alliance, Ohio. A student at Tuskegee Institute in Alabama when he enlisted in the U.S. Army in 1942, he was commissioned a Second Lieutenant in 1944 through Officer Candidate School.

His career has been marked by command and staff officer assignments at all levels of command. A senior aviator and qualified parachutist, he has extensive combat experience, including three years of combat command time in Vietnam.

General Hamlet's assignments include Chief, Doctrine and Systems Division, U.S. Army Combat Development Command Combat Arms Group, Fort Leavenworth, Kansas; Commanding Officer, Eleventh Aviation Group, First Cavalry Division, U.S. Army Vietnam.

He has been awarded the Distinguished Service Medal, Legion of Merit with two oak leaf clusters, Distinguished Flying Cross, Soldier's Medal, Bronze Star Medal with oak leaf clusters, 49 awards of the Air Medal, Army Commendation Medal with three oak leaf clusters, and the Combat Infantryman Badge.

Major General James F. Hamlet.

BRIGADIER GENERAL ARTHUR HOLMES, JR.
Director of Readiness, U.S. Army Material Development and Readiness Command, Alexandria, Virginia

General Holmes was born in Decatur, Alabama and received a B.S. degree in chemistry from Hampton Institute in Hampton, Virginia. He received an MBA degree from Kent State University. General Holmes also attended the Field Artillery School's basic course, The Ordnance School's advanced course, the U.S. Army Command and General Staff College, and the U.S. Naval War College. His assignments have included Commander, 724th Maintenance Battalion, 24th Infantry Division, Fort Riley, Kansas; Chief, Materiel Program Coordination Section, later Chief, Weapons and Combat Vehicles Section, Materiel Analysis Branch, Materiel Acquisition Directorate, Office, Deputy Chief of Staff for Logistics, U.S. Army, Washington, D.C.; Commander, 62nd Maintenance Battalion, U.S. Army, Qui Nhon Support Command, Vietnam; Commander, Division Support Command, 1st Infantry Division (mechanized) Fort Riley, Kansas; and Executive to the Secretary of the Army, Washington, D.C. He has received the Legion of Merit, the Bronze Star Medal, the Meritorious Service Medal with oak leaf cluster, the Joint Service Commendation Medal, and the Army Commendation Medal with two oak leaf clusters.

BRIGADIER GENERAL EDWARD HONOR
Deputy Director for Planning and Resources, Logistics Directorate, Organization of the Joint Chiefs of Staff, Washington, D.C.

General Honor was commissioned a Second Lieutenant through the Army ROTC in 1954 from Southern University A&M College where he received a B.A. degree in education. He was born in Melville, Louisiana. General Honor has been Commander, 36th Transportation Battalion, U.S. Army Cam Ranh Bay Support Command, Vietnam; Assistant Chief of Staff, Security, Plans and Operations, U.S. Army Cam Ranh Bay Support Command, Vietnam; Chief, Transportation Service Branch, Transportation Division, Office Deputy Chief of Staff for Logistics, U.S. Continental Army Command, Fort Monroe, Virginia; Commander, Military Traffic Management Command, Transportation Terminal Group-Europe, Rotterdam, Netherlands; and Director for Plans, Doctrine, and Systems, U.S. Army Materiel Development and Readiness Command, Alexandria, Virginia. He has received the Legion of Merit with three oak leaf clusters, the Bronze Star Medal, the Meritorious Service Medal, and the Army Commendation Medal all with an oak leaf cluster, and the Joint Service Commendation Medal.

BRIGADIER GENERAL BENJAMIN LACY HUNTON
Commander, U.S. 97th Army Reserve Command, Fort Meade, Maryland

General Hunton was commissioned a Second Lieutenant, Infantry, through Army ROTC upon graduation from Howard University in 1940, and entered active duty in 1942. He was assigned to the 368th Infantry Regiment, the Infantry School and Assistant Professor of Military Science at Howard University. He was released from active duty in August 1949.

During his Army Reserve status he served as Battalion Commander, 428th Infantry Regiment; Battalion Commander, Executive Officer, and Commander, 317th Infantry Regiment, 80th Infantry division; and upon redesignation of the unit to 80th Division (training), he became Commander, First Brigade.

General Hunton's present civilian occupation is Assistant Director, Education and Training, U.S. Bureau of Mines, Department of Interior, Washington, D.C.

BRIGADIER GENERAL AVON C. JAMES
Director of Computer Resources, Office of the Comptroller of the Air Force, Headquarters U.S. Air Force, Washington, D.C.

General James was born in Hampton, Virginia and earned his bachelors degree from Morgan State University in 1951. General James was assigned in July 1972 as a computer systems staff officer with the Automatic Data Processing Equipment Selection directorate at Hanscom Air Force Base, Massachusetts; in July 1973 he was assigned as Chief of Staff, Electronic Systems Division, Air Force Systems Command at Hanscom Air Force Base. In June 1978 General James was assigned as the First Deputy Commander for Data Automation, Headquarters Air Force Communications Command, Scott Air Force Base, Illinois. His military decorations and awards include the Legion of Merit with one oak leaf cluster, Meritorious Service Medal, the Air Force Commendation Medal with one oak leaf cluster, and the Air Force Organizational Excellence Award.

BRIGADIER GENERAL CHARLES B. JIGGETTS
Director, Communications and Data Processing, J-6, Pacific Command, Camp H. M. Smith, Hawaii

General Jiggetts was born in Henderson, North Carolina and received a bachelor of arts degree in political science from Howard University, Washington, D.C. In the fall of 1971, General Jiggetts was assigned as the Military Assistant to the Director of the Office of Telecommunications Policy, Executive Office of the President of the United States. In July 1974 he became Vice Commander of the Northern Communications Area of the Air Force Communications Service. He became Commander of that unit in July 1976. His military decorations and awards include the Distinguished Service Medal, Legion of Merit with one oak leaf cluster, Bronze Star Medal, Meritorious Service Medal, Joint Service Commendation Medal, and the Air Force Commendation Medal.

BRIGADIER GENERAL HAZEL WINIFRED JOHNSON
Chief, Army Nurse Corps, Office of the Surgeon General, U.S. Army, Washington D.C.

General Johnson was born in West Chester, Pennsylvania and received her bachelor of science degree in nursing from Villanova University, her master of arts degree in nursing education from Columbia University, and her Ph.D. in educational administration from Catholic University. General Johnson's assignments during her 22 years in the military have included Project Officer, Development Branch, Materiel Development Division, Surgical Directorate, U.S. Army Medical Research and Development Command, Washington, D.C.; Dean, Walter Reed Army Institute of Nursing, Walter Reed Army Medical Center, Washington, D.C.; Chief Nurse, U.S. Army Medical Command, Korea; and Special Assistant to the Chief, Army Nurse Corps, Washington, D.C. General Johnson has been awarded the Legion of Merit, the Meritorious

Brigadier General Hazel W. Johnson.

Service Medal, and the Army Commendation Medal with an oak leaf cluster.

BRIGADIER GENERAL JAMES FRANKLIN McCALL
Comptroller, U.S. Army Materiel Development and Readiness Command, Alexandria, Virginia

General McCall received his B.S. degree in economics from the University of Pennsylvania and was commissioned a Second Lieutenant through the OCS at the university in 1958. He was born in Philadelphia and received an MBA degree in comptrollership from Syracuse University. General McCall has served as a Military Assistant, Office of the Assistant Secretary of the Army (Financial Management) in Washington, D.C.; Commander, 1st Battalion 31st Infantry, 2nd Infantry Division, Eighth Army, Korea; Commander, 4th Training Brigade, U.S. Army Armor School, Fort Knox, Kentucky; and Chief, Procurement Programs and Budget Division, Materiel Plans and Programs Directorate, Office of the Deputy Chief of Staff for Research, Development, and Acquisition, U.S. Army, Washington, D.C. His decorations and badges include the Parachutist Badge, the Combat Infantry Badge, Meritorious Medal, the Legion of Merit with an oak leaf cluster, and Air Medals. He also received the Army Commendation Medal with an oak leaf cluster.

MAJOR GENERAL EMMETT PAIGE, JR.
Commanding General, U.S. Army Electronics Research and Development Command, Adelphi, Maryland

General Paige received his B.A. degree in business administration from the University of Maryland and an MBA in public administration from Pennsylvania State University. General Paige was born in Jacksonville, Florida and during his career has been awarded the Legion of Merit with two oak leaf clusters, the Bronze Star Medal, the Joint Service Commendation Medal, the Meritorious Medal, and the Army Commendation Medal. He has been Commander, 361st Signal Battalion, 1st Signal Brigade, U.S. Army Strategic Communications Command-Vietnam; Staff Officer, Voice Networks Branch, Operations Directorate, Defense Communications Agency, Washington, D.C.; Commander, 11th Signal Group, U.S. Army Communications Command, Fort Huachuca, Arizona; and Commanding General, U.S. Army Communications Research and Development Command, Fort Monmouth, New Jersey.

BRIGADIER GENERAL JULIUS PARKER, JR.
Deputy Chief of Staff for Intelligence, United States Army Forces Command, Fort McPherson, Georgia

General Parker was born in New Braunfels, Texas and received a B.S. degree in biology and chemistry from Prairie View A&M University and an M.S. degree in public administration from Shippensburg State College. He was commissioned a Second Lieutenant in 1955 from Prairie View through the school's ROTC

Major General Winston D. Powers.

program. General Parker has served as a Combat Intelligence Staff Officer, later Chief, Ground and Special Systems Branch, Doctrine and Systems Division, later Ground Surveillance Officer, Tactical Surveillance and Reconnaissance Branch, Doctrine and Surveillance Division, Office, Assistant Chief of Staff for Intelligence, U.S. Army, Washington, D.C.; Strategic Research Analyst, Strategic Studies Institute, U.S. Army War College, Carlisle Barracks, Pennsylvania; Commander, 501st Military Intelligence Group, U.S. Army Intelligence and Security Command, Korea, and Executive to the Assistant Chief of Staff for Intelligence, Washington, D.C. He has received the Parachutist Badge, the Combat Infantry Badge, the Purple Heart, the Army Commendation Medal with an oak leaf cluster, the Meritorious Service Medal with three oak leaf clusters, the Air Medal, and the Bronze Star Medal with V device and with an oak leaf cluster.

BRIGADIER GENERAL FRANK E. PETERSEN
Director, Facilities and Services Division, Installation and Logistics Department, Headquarters Marine Corps, Washington, D.C.

Brigadier General Frank E. Petersen was born March 2, 1932 in Topeka, Kansas, and graduated from Topeka High School in 1949. He attended Washburn University in Topeka and received his B.A. degree from George Washington University in 1967. He completed his masters degree in 1973 at that university. He began flight training through the Naval Aviation Cadet Program at the Naval Air Station in Pensacola, Florida, and at Corpus Christi, Texas. In October 1952 he was designated a Naval Aviator and commissioned a Second Lieutenant in the Marine Corps Reserve. During the Korean conflict, in 1953, he flew 60 combat missions and was awarded the Distinguished Flying Cross and the Air Medal with one silver star denoting five subsequent awards. His decorations and medals include the Legion of Merit with Combat V, the Distinguished Flying Cross, Meritorious Service Medal, Air Medal with Numeral 14, Purple Heart, Combat Action Ribbon, Presidential Unit Citation, Korean Service Medal with two bronze stars, Vietnam Service Medal with two bronze stars, and United Nations Service Medal.

BRIGADIER GENERAL COLIN LUTHER POWELL
Senior Military Assistant to the Deputy Secretary of Defense, Office of the Secretary of Defense, Washington, D.C.

General Powell was born in New York City and received his B.S. degree in geology from City University. He received his MBA degree from George Washington University. General Powell was commissioned a Second Lieutenant through the ROTC in 1958. He has received the Defense Superior Service Medal, the Legion of Merit with an oak leaf cluster, the Bronze Star Medal, the Soldiers Medal, the Purple Heart, the Parachutist Badge, the Ranger Tap, and the Joint Service Commendation Medal. General Powell has served as Assistant Chief of Staff in Vietnam; Commander, 2nd Brigade, 101st Airborne Division (Air Assault) Fort Campbell, Kentucky, and Commander, 1st Battalion, 32nd Infantry, 2nd Infantry Division, Eighth Army.

MAJOR GENERAL WINSTON D. POWERS
Deputy Chief of Staff for Communications, Electronics and Computer Resources for the North American Air Defense Command and U.S. Aerospace Defense Command at Peterson Air Force Base, Colorado; Chief, Systems Integration Office, Aerospace Defense Center

General Powers was born in New York City and earned his bachelor of arts degree from McKendree College, Illinois. General Powers attended graduate school at the George Washington University and completed the Industrial College of the Armed Forces. In 1974 General Powers returned to Korea as commander of the 2146th Communications Group and director of communications-electronics for the 314th Air Division at Osan Air Base. General Powers became deputy director of telecommunications and command and control resources, Office of the Assistant Chief of Staff, Communications and Computer Resources, Headquarters U.S. Air Force in September 1975. He became the director in 1978. He is a master navigator with more than 4,000 flying hours. His military decorations and awards include the Meritorious Service Medal with two oak leaf clusters, the Air Medal with one oak leaf cluster, the Air Force Commendation Medal, the Presidential Unit Citation emblem, and the Outstanding Unit Award ribbon.

BRIGADIER GENERAL BERNARD P. RANDOLPH
Director of Space Systems, and Command, Control and Communications, Office of the Deputy Chief of Staff, Research, Development and Acquisition, Headquarters U.S. Air Force, Washington, D.C.

A native of New Orleans, General Randolph received his bachelor of science degree in chemistry from Xavier University of Louisiana in New Orleans. He also earned the bachelor (*magna cum laude*) and master of science degrees in electrical engineering from the University of North Dakota, Grand Forks, through the Air Force Institute of Technology program in 1964 and 1965, respectively. In July 1980 General Randolph became Vice Commander of the Warner Robins Air Logistics Center, Robins Air Force Base, Georgia. His

military decorations and awards include the Legion of Merit with one oak leaf cluster, Bronze Star Medal, the Meritorious Service Medal, the Air Force Commendation Medal, and the Presidential Unit Citation emblem.

BRIGADIER GENERAL HUGH GRANVILLE ROBINSON
Division Engineer, U.S. Army Engineer Division Southwestern, Dallas, Texas

General Robinson was born in Washington and received a B.S. degree in military science from the U.S. Military Academy and an M.S. degree in civil engineering from the Massachusetts Institute of Technology. General Robinson has been Executive Officer, 45th Engineer Group, U.S. Army, Pacific-Vietnam; Staff Officer, Regional Capabilities Branch, War Plans Division, Plans Directorate, Office, Deputy Chief of Staff for Military Operations, U.S. Army, Washington, D.C.; Commander, 3rd Regiment, U.S. Corps of Cadets, U.S. Military Academy, West Point; and District Engineer, U.S. Army Engineer District, Los Angeles, California. His decorations and badges include the Joint Service Commendation Medal, the Parachutist Badge, the Presidential Service Badge, the Army Commendation Medal with an oak leaf cluster, along with the Legion of Merit and the Bronze Star Medal both with oak leaf clusters.

BRIGADIER GENERAL JACKSON EVANDER ROZIER, JR.
Commanding General, U.S. Army Ordnance Center and School, Aberdeen Proving Ground, Maryland

General Rozier was born in Richmond, Virginia and earned his B.S. degree in educational administration from Morgan State University in Baltimore. He received his M.A. degree also in educational administration from Howard University in Washington, D.C. His assignments have included Personnel Management Officer and Executive Officer, U.S. Army Military Personnel Center, Alexandria, Virginia; Commander, 801st Maintenance Battalion, 101st Airborne Division (Air Assault), Fort Campbell, Kentucky; and Commander, Division Support Command, 8th Infantry Division (mechanized), U.S. Army, Europe. He has received the Meritorious Service Medal and the Army Commendation Medal both with the oak leaf cluster and the Parachutist Badge.

BRIGADIER GENERAL FRED CLIFTON SHEFFEY
Operations and Maintenance Resources, Office of Deputy General Staff for Logistics, Department of the Army Headquarters

During the past 10 years, General Sheffey has been Chief, Clothing and Textile Material Section, Supply

Branch, Quartermaster Division, 3rd Logistical Command, U.S. Communications Zone, Europe; Assistant Division Supply Officer, 4th Infantry Division, Fort Lewis, Washington; Executive Officer, 4th Supply and Transport Battalion, 4th Infantry Quartermaster Battalion, Fort Lewis, Washington; Commanding Officer, 266th Quartermaster Battalion, later 266th Supply and Service Battalion, Fort Lewis, Washington, and later U.S. Pacific-Vietnam; Logistical Plans Officer, later Chief, Plans and Policy Branch, G-4 Section, U.S. Vietnam, U.S. Pacific-Vietnam; Chief, Facilities Branch.

He has been awarded the Legion of Merit with two oak leaf clusters, Bronze Star Medal, Army Commendation Medal, Purple Heart, and Combat Infantry Badge.

BRIGADIER GENERAL GEORGE MACON SHUFFER, JR.
Assistant Deputy Chief of Staff for Personnel, U.S. Army Europe and 7th Army

General Shuffer was commissioned a Second Lieutenant in 1943 through Officer Candidate School. During his tour of duty he was assigned as Commanding Officer Second Battalion, Second Infantry, Fort Devens, Massachusetts; Assistant for Continuity of Operations Plans, Office, Assistant Secretary of Defense, Washington, D.C.; Commanding Officer, 193d Infantry Brigade, U.S. Army Forces Southern Command, Fort Kobbe, Canal Zone.

He has been awarded the Silver Star with two oak leaf clusters, Legion of Merit with two oak leaf clusters, Bronze Star Medal with V device and two oak leaf clusters, five awards of Air Medal, Army Commendation Medal, Purple Heart, Combat Infantryman's Badge with the third award, and the Parachutist Badge.

BRIGADIER GENERAL ISAAC DIXON SMITH
Commanding General, U.S. Army Second Reserve Officer Training Corps Region, Fort Knox, Kentucky

General Smith was born in Wakefield, Louisiana and received his B.S. degree in agriculture from Southern University. He earned his M.A. degree in public administration from Shippensburg State College. General Smith has been Commander, 8th Battalion, 4th Artillery, XXIV Corps Artillery, U.S. Army in Vietnam; Commander, 2nd Battalion, 75th Field Artillery, 36th Field Artillery Group, V Corps Artillery, U.S. Army, Europe; Special Assistant to the Commander, Third Reserve Officer Training Corps Region, Fort Riley, Kansas; and Chief, Reserve Forces Division, Office of the Assistant Secretary of the Army, Washington, D.C. He has received the Silver Star, the Legion of Merit with an oak leaf cluster, the Bronze Star Medal,

and the Army Commendation Medal with two oak leaf clusters.

BRIGADIER GENERAL LUCIUS THEUS
Special Assistant for Social Actions, Directorate of Personnel Plans, Deputy Chief of Staff, Personnel, Headquarters U.S. Air Force, Washington, D.C.

General Theus entered the Army Air Corps in December 1942, as a private. In January 1946 he was commissioned as a Second Lieutenant. He has served as squadron adjutant, Tuskegee Army Air Field, Alabama; Base Statistical Control Officer, Lockbourne Air Force Base, Ohio; Commander of the Statistical Control Flight and Depot Statistical Control Officer, Erding Air Depot, Germany; Chief of the Material Logistics Statistics Branch, Office of the Deputy Chief of Staff, Comptroller, Headquarters U.S. Air Force, Washington, D.C.

His military decorations and awards include the Legion of Merit, Bronze Star Medal, Air Force Commendation Medal with oak leaf cluster, Air Force Outstanding Unit Award Ribbon, Good Conduct Medal, and the Republic of Vietnam Commendation Medal.

REAR ADMIRAL GERALD E. THOMAS
Commander Cruiser-Destroyer Group FIVE

Born in Natick, Massachusetts, Gerald Thomas became a member of the Naval Reserve Officers Training Corps Unit during his student days at Harvard, and upon graduation in 1951 was commissioned Ensign. While attached to the cruiser *Worcester,* as a lieutenant as of November 1955, he studied Russian at the Defense Language Institute and qualified as a Russian interpreter, after which he served at the National Security Agency, Fort Meade, Maryland. His first command was in 1962 aboard the USS *Impervious,* an ocean minesweeper then operating in the western Pacific.

His major permanent duty assignments have been Assistant Head, College Training Programs Section, Bureau of Naval Personnel; student, Naval War College; commanding officer, USS *Bausell;* executive officer, NROTC, Prairie View College; commanding officer, NROTC, Prairie View College; student, Yale University; and commander, Destroyer Squadron NINE.

Admiral Thomas' medals and awards include the Meritorious Service Medal, the Navy Commendation Medal with Combat 'V', the Navy Occupation Service Medal with Europe Clasp, the National Defense Service Medal with Bronze Star, the Armed Forces Expeditionary Medal (Vietnam), and the Vietnam Service Medal with two Bronze Stars.

BRIGADIER GENERAL GUTHRIE LEWIS TURNER, JR.
Commanding General, Madigan Army Medical Center, Tacoma, Washington

General Turner was born in Chicago and received a direct appointment to the U.S. Army as a Second Lieutenant in 1953. He received his B.S. degree in biology from Shaw University in Raleigh, North Carolina and his M.D. degree from Howard University. General Turner also received a masters degree in public health from Harvard University. He has been Assistant Chief, Department of Aviation Medicine, U.S. Army Hospital, Fort Rucker, Alabama; Commander, Beach Army Hospital; and surgeon, U.S. Army Primary Helicopter Center and School, Fort Wolters, Texas; Surgeon, VII Corps, U.S. Army, Europe; Commander, 130th General Hospital, U.S. Army, Europe; and consultant for Aviation Medicine, Office of the Surgeon General, U.S. Army, Washington, D.C. General Turner has received the Senior Flight Surgeon badge, the Master Parachutist Badge, the Legion of Merit, air medals, and the Army Commendation Medal.

MAJOR GENERAL HARVEY DEAN WILLIAMS
Commanding General, U.S. Army Readiness and Mobilization Region III and Deputy Commanding General, First U.S. Army, Fort Meade, Maryland

General Williams was born in Whiteville, North Carolina and received his B.A. degree in political science from West Virginia State College and his M.S. degree

in international relations from George Washington University. His assignments have included Commander, 1st Battalion, 92nd Artillery, I Field Force, U.S. Army Pacific-Vietnam; Military Advisor, U.S. Arms Control and Disarmament Agency, Washington, D.C.; Commander, U.S. Army Garrison, Fort Myer, Virginia; and Commanding General, VII Corps Artillery, U.S. Army, Europe. His commendations and awards include the Legion of Merit, the Bronze Star Medal with an oak leaf cluster, the Army Commendation Medal with three oak leaf clusters, along with Air Medals.

OUTSTANDING MILITARY FIGURES

ENSIGN JESSE L. BROWN
1926–1950

Jesse L. Brown was the first black American to become a naval aviator and the first black naval officer to be killed in action during the Korean War.

Born in Hattiesburg, Mississippi, he attended Ohio State University. In October 1948 he qualified as an aviator and became the first black man to wear the Navy wings. When the Korean War broke out he entered the combat as a pilot with the 32nd Fighter Squad and quickly rose to section leader. For his daring attacks on enemy transportation facilities and military installations at Wonsun, Songjin, and Sinanju, he

Ensign Jesse L. Brown, a hero of the Korean War.

earned the Air Medal. On December 4, 1950, he was dispatched to fly close air support for the marines fighting near Chosin Reservoir. As he repeatedly returned to strafe enemy positions, his low-flying craft was hit by hostile fire and almost immediately crashed. He died in the wreckage. Ensign Brown was posthumously awarded the Distinguished Flying Cross for his exceptional courage, airmanship, and devotion to duty.

In 1973 he became the first black man to have a naval vessel named in his honor. The USS *Jesse L. Brown,* Commissioned at the Boston Naval Yard, is a new type of destroyer escort.

LIEUTENANT GENERAL BENJAMIN O. DAVIS, JR.
1912–

Described by a former instructor as "the closest thing to a model cadet I ever saw," General Benjamin O. Davis rose to become the highest ranking black military man in the United States.

Born in Washington in 1912, Davis was educated in Alabama (his father taught military science at Tuskegee) and, later, in Cleveland, where he graduated as president of his class with one of the highest scholastic averages in the city.

Davis attended Western Reserve University and the University of Chicago before accepting an appointment to the U.S. Military Academy in 1932. Davis survived the silent treatment as a cadet, and graduated 35th in his class of 276.

After serving in the infantry for five years, he transferred to the Army Air Corps in 1941 and was among the first six black air cadets to graduate from the Advanced Army Flying School in 1942.

As Commander of the 99th Fighter Squadron (and later commander of the all-black 332nd Fighter Group) Davis flew 60 missions in 224 combat hours during World War II, winning several medals, including the Silver Star.

Davis became a Lieutenant General in 1965 and closed out his career as deputy commander of the U.S. Strike Command at McDill Air Force Base in Tampa, Florida. In civilian life, Davis worked briefly in the administration of Cleveland's black mayor Carl Stokes, resigning after a policy dispute.

BRIGADIER GENERAL BENJAMIN OLIVER DAVIS, SR.
1877–1970

Benjamin Oliver Davis, Sr., was the first black American to become a general in the U.S. Army. He deserves exceptional recognition for his distinguished 50-year military career, which began with the Spanish-American War. Promoted to Brigadier General in 1940, he supervised the World War II progress of integration policy in the European military theater.

Benjamin O. Davis, Sr., became the first black general in the U.S. Army in 1940.

Born in the nation's capital, General Davis graduated from Howard University and joined the army during the emergency of 1898. At the end of that war with Spain, he reenlisted in the 9th Cavalry and was made Second Lieutenant in 1901. Black promotions were rare in those years, but Davis rose through the officer's ranks until he was made a full Colonel in 1930. During that time, in addition to his military commands, he was a professor of military science and tactics at Wilberforce and Tuskegee universities, military attache to Liberia, and instructor of the 372nd Infantry of the Ohio National Guard. After his promotion to Brigadier General and his service in World War II, he became an assistant to the inspector general in Washington, D.C. until his retirement in 1948.

Among General Davis' many awards and decorations are the Distinguished Service Medal, the Bronze Star Medal, the Grade of Commander of the Order of the Star of Africa, from the Liberian government, and the French Croix de Guerre with Palm. General Davis died on November 26, 1970.

LIEUTENANT HENRY O. FLIPPER
1877–1940

The first black officer to graduate from West Point and the first to be assigned to a command position in a black unit after the Civil War, Henry O. Flipper was the victim of a controversial court-martial proceeding which cut short the career of one of the most promising black military men to wear the uniform of an American soldier.

Flipper was not defeated by the debacle, however. He went on, as a civilian, to become a notable figure on the American frontier—as a mining engineer and consultant and later, as a translator of Spanish land grants.

Flipper tried on many occasions to vindicate himself, befriending such prominent Washington officials as Senator A. B. Fall of New Mexico. When Fall became Secretary of the Interior, Flipper became his assistant until the infamous Teapot Dome affair severed their relationship.

Flipper returned to Atlanta at the close of his mining career, living with his brother, an AME bishop, until his death in 1940. His quest to remove the stain of "conduct unbecoming an officer and a gentleman" remained unfulfilled to his dying day, partly because certain records which might shed light on the situation are not yet open for public scrutiny.

GENERAL DANIEL JAMES, JR.
1920–1978

Appointed Commander of NORAD on August 29, 1975, Daniel "Chappie" James was the first black four-star general in U.S. military history. Before coming to this post, he had been a flying ace in the Korean War, had served as Deputy Secretary of Defense, and was Vice Commander of Military Airlift Command.

Born on February 11, 1920 in Pensacola, Florida, he attended Tuskegee Institute, where he took the Army Air Corps program and was commissioned a Second Lieutenant in 1943. During the Korean War, James flew 101 combat missions in F-51 and F-80 aircraft. After the war, he performed various staff assignments until 1957, when he graduated from the Air Command and Staff College at Maxwell Air Force Base, Alabama. In 1966 he became Deputy Commander for Operations of the 8th Tactical Fighter Wing stationed in Thailand, before promotion to Commander of the 7272nd Flying Training Wing at Wheelus Air Force Base in Libya.

James became a Brigadier General in 1970, a Lieutenant General in 1973, and a Four-Star General in 1975. He has received numerous civilian awards. His military awards include Legion of Merit with one oak leaf cluster, Distinguished Flying Cross, Air Medal with 10 clusters, Distinguished Unit Citation, Presidential Unit Citation, and Air Force Outstanding Unit Award. General James was widely known for his speeches on Americanism and patriotism. One citation

General Daniel James, Jr., receives his fourth star in August 1975.

he received reads in part: "fighter pilot with a magnificent record . . . and eloquent spokesman for the American Dream we so rarely achieve."

He died of a heart attack at the age of 58 in Colorado Springs, February 25, 1978. General James had suffered from a heart condition and had retired from the Air Force for medical reasons earlier that month.

HENRY JOHNSON
1897–1929

A member of the 15th National Guard of New York, which became the 369th Infantry, Henry Johnson was probably the most famous black soldier to have fought in World War I.

The 369th itself was the first group of black combat troops to arrive in Europe. After a summer of training, the group saw action at Champagne and fought its way to the Rhine River in Germany, receiving the Croix de Guerre from the French government. Johnson and another soldier (Needham Roberts) were the first Americans to receive this French medal for individual heroism in combat.

During a night skirmish, Johnson fought off an entire German patrol single-handedly, rescuing his wounded comrade from almost certain capture in the process. He personally accounted for four dead, a host of wounded, and a virtual stockpile of abandoned equipment. Wounded himself, he lost a shin bone and had several broken bones in one of his feet.

Johnson was cited by the French as a "magnificent example of courage and energy." He was later promoted to sergeant.

DORIE MILLER
1919–1943

A messman aboard the USS *Arizona,* Dorie Miller had his first taste of combat at Pearl Harbor on December 7, 1941, when he manned a machine gun and brought down four Japanese planes.

Born on a farm near Waco, Texas in 1919, Miller was the son of a sharecropper and grew up to become star fullback on the Moore High School football team in his native city. At 19 he enlisted in the U.S. Navy,

and was nearing the end of his first hitch at the time of the Pearl Harbor attack.

For his heroism, Miller was awarded the Navy Cross, which was conferred by Admiral Chester W. Nimitz, the Commander in Chief of the Pacific Fleet.

He remained a messman during the hostilities, serving aboard the aircraft carrier *Liscome Bay* and being promoted to Mess Attendant Third Class. He was killed in action in the South Pacific in December of 1943. Miller was commended for "distinguished devotion to duty, extreme courage, and disregard of his personal safety during attack."

Miller was one of several "noncombatant" blacks who distinguished themselves for heroism during combat. Others included Leonard Roy Harmon of the USS *San Francisco;* William Pinckney of the USS *Enterprise,* and Elbert H. Oliver of the USS *Intrepid.* Harmon and Pinckney were awarded the Navy Cross; Oliver, the Silver Star.

Admiral Nimitz awards the Navy Cross to Dorie Miller for heroism at Pearl Harbor.

COLONEL CHARLES YOUNG
1864–1922

Charles Young saw his first major combat during the Spanish-American War, less than 10 years after he had become the third black to have graduated from the U.S. Military Academy at West Point.

Born on March 12, 1864 in Mayslick, Kentucky, Young moved to Ripley, Ohio with his parents at an early age. Having finished high school, he taught for a time until winning an appointment to West Point in 1884. Upon graduation, Young was commissioned a Second Lieutenant in the 10th Cavalry, an all-black unit, In 1894 he became a military instructor at Wilberforce University in Ohio and, with the outbreak of the Spanish American War, was reassigned to the 9th Ohio Regiment, which was transferred to Cuba.

After the war Young served in the Philippines and in Haiti, and also in the Mexican campaign of 1915, where he commanded a squadron of the 10th Cavalry which rescued a group of ambushed white soldiers near Parral, Mexico. Declared physically unfit for service overseas in World War I. Young rode on horseback from his home in Xenia, Ohio to Washington, D.C. where, to no avail, he protested the decision of the War Department to retire him from active duty.

Five days before the Armistice, however, Young was ordered to Camp Grant in Illinois to take charge of trainees. Sent to Liberia after completing this assignment. Young helped organize the army there.

He died in 1922 of a fever contracted while he was on furlough in Nigeria, and was buried with full military honors at Arlington National Cemetery in Virginia.

Table 1. Black Servicemen and Women on Active Duty around the World (December 31, 1974)

Service	Officers (%)[a]	Enlisted (%)	Total (%)
Army	6,924 (8.1)	220,631 (32.8)	227,555
Navy	1,703 (2.58)	55,577 (16.81)	57,280 (10.67)
Marine Corps	735	37,654	38,389 (20.3)
Air Force	4,836 (4.9)	78,229 (16.8)	83,065 (14.7)
Total	14,198	392,091	406,289

[a] Includes Commissioned and Warrant Officers.

Table 2. Distribution of Blacks by Percentage within Each Service (December 31, 1974)

Service	Officers	Enlisted	As Of
Army			81
Navy	2.58	11.81	81
Marine Corps	4.0	22.1	81
Air Force	4.9	16.8	81

Table 3. Statistics on Black Commissioned and Warrant Officers (December 31, 1974)

Grade (Army, Air Force, Marine)	Grade (Navy)	Number (Percentage)			
		Army	Navy	Air Force	Marine Corps
General	Admiral	24 (5.6)	3 (1.12)	11 (32)	1 (1.5)
Colonel	Captain	222 (4.8)	32 (0.85)	97 (1.8)	0 (0)
Lieutenant Colonel	Commander	522 (4.7)	43 (0.56)	290 (2.3)	8 (.5)
Major	Lieutenant Commander	752 (4.6)	176 (1.36)	422 (2.3)	52 (1.8)
Captain	Lieutenant	2,346 (8.3)	628 (3.35)	1,837 (5.2)	206 (4.3)
First Lieutenant	Lieutenant (JG)	17.57 (12.0)	335 (3.58)	1,181 (8.6)	259 (5.6)
Second Lieutenant	Ensign	11.22 (11.9)	329 (3.24)	998 (7.1)	112 (4.2)
Warrant Officer	Warrant Officer		257 (4.45)		108 (7.2)
Total Officers and Percentages			1,703 (2.58)	4,836 (4.9)	735 (4.0)

Table 4. Statistics on Black Enlisted Personnel (number and percent of black personnel in each grade)

Grade	Army	Navy	Air Force	Marine Corps
E-9	812 (21.8)	203 (6.07)	478 (10.2)	784 (15.1)
E-8	34,70 (26.2)	473 (5.57)	1,197 (12.9)	459 (15)
E-7	11,052 (24.4)	1,617 (5.36)	4,830 (14.4)	1,304 (15.9)
E-6	19,499 (25.2)	4,471 (6.61)	8,148 (15.6)	2,565 (19.5)
E-5	42,328 (34.2)	8,110 (9.63)	19,763 (19.6)	5,706 (20.9)
E-4	67,909 (39.4)	11,630 (13.19)	18,711 (17.6)	5,805 (20.7)
E-3	36,130 (34.9)	11,195 (14.86)	16,920 (16.6)	11,447 (26.1)
E-2	22,781 (32.2)	11,972 (15.91)	3,810 (14.2)	6,993 (2.4)
E-1	16,650 (27.1)	5,905 (14.27)	4,372 (14.0)	3,791 (19.7)
Total Enlisted	220,631 (32.8)	55,577 (10.67)	78,229 (16.8)	37,654 (22.1)

THE BLACK AMATEUR AND PROFESSIONAL ATHLETE

Baseball ■ Basketball ■ Football ■ Boxing ■ Track and Field ■ Golf ■ Horse Racing ■ Tennis ■ Wrestling ■ Outstanding Black Athletes

There were still heroes, and the excitement of winning and losing remained a powerful attraction. Yet as the decade of the 1980s began, the pure enjoyment of major league sports had been tainted. Outside of the exclusive domain of the arena of competition, side issues were growing as important as the games themselves. And disenchanted fans were directing their pique at individual players as well as front office powers.

During this period where the sports world endured more bitter with the sweet, black athletes figured prominently. In the areas of high scoring and individual achievement, there was more than ample representation. When all-star teams were selected, when championships were won, when most valuable player selections were made, blacks maintained a high profile.

In some cases, black athletes were able to gain impressive salaries while participating in team sports. There were times when a few talented fighters were able to command astronomical fees for single title boxing matches.

By the mid-1970s, talented blacks were graduating from All-American college careers to rookie acclaim within a year and then eventual superstardom status as veteran professionals. And these superstars opened the doors for scores of additional athletes with exceptional ability, who contributed greatly to team success.

In certain sports, boxing and basketball in particular, blacks were predominant. And as young college-trained players continued to join the ranks, black pioneers were belatedly honored by being inducted into the Halls of Fame representing the sports in which they participated.

As the 1970s passed, notable firsts were achieved as blacks gained managerships in baseball, head coaching positions in basketball, and support coaching positions in professional football. These breakthroughs were significant for symbolizing the fact that men of unquestioned athletic ability could apply their organizational skills and formulate strategy just as important to winning.

Another indication of progress was the increase in referees and umpires, who broadened the impact of black participation on the playing field. And behind the scenes, administrative positions reflecting a variety of levels of support activity were increasingly filled by blacks.

As the 1980s arrived, it became increasingly difficult to imagine what most professional sports would be like without the participation of black athletes.

Yet those nagging problems were a more pressing concern. Fans were distracted by contract negotiations leading to highly publicized multimillion dollar player contracts and labor disputes—which in one unsettling case climaxed in an extended strike that halted major league baseball at midseason.

In addition, tacitly condoned incidents of aggression on the field resulted in injuries that tragically left some players crippled for life. And an often ugly mood spilled into a new element of hostility between players and fans, reflected in more and more violent confrontations—especially at hockey and basketball games, but elsewhere as well.

When President Jimmy Carter withdrew the U.S. Olympic Team from the 1980 summer games in Moscow, the boycott added a new frustration of political influence. And while a total of 61 nations joined together in the boycott, the action was a heartbreaking conclusion to literally years of training for scores of young hopefuls. Unofficially, the United States had been the winner of 13 of the previous games.

All the while, television had intruded into a close relationship with major league sports, expanding schedules to the benefit of all. While some had predicted the extensive coverage would reach a saturation point, a new cable network soon developed—which provided round-the-clock sports programming. Within a short time, it had won over a loyal audience.

In an atmosphere occasionally tinged with uncertainty and controversy, black athletes continued to excel while sharing in the world of professional and amateur sports. Even in losing efforts on losing teams, they were still winners for just having made it into the circle of one of America's remaining corps of heroes.

The Early Days

The first black major league baseball player was not Jackie Robinson but probably Bud Fowler, who played for a Newcastle, Pennsylvania, team in 1872. In 1884 Moses Fleetwood Walker, a barehanded catcher and graduate of Oberlin College, played for Toledo in the old major league American Association. However, in the 1880s, as segregation was becoming established as a way of life, these and other blacks were increasingly excluded from major league play, continued to the minor leagues, and gradually eased out.

In the early 1900s John McGraw, the great manager of the New York Giants, tried three times with short-lived success to bring black ball players on to his team. They were represented as American "Indians" but soon were exposed and McGraw was forced to release them. The men were Charles Grant and Jose Mendez, pitchers, and Andrew Foster, a pitching coach who had taught Christy Mathewson. In 1925 a black Latin, Ramon Herrera, played for the Boston Red Sox. Perhaps unknown, other blacks "passed" successfully during the 1888–1946 period.

Blacks and whites did, however, play openly against one another. Starting in 1884, blacks organized their own teams and then their own leagues. To these teams came some of the great, unheralded baseball players of all time: George Stovey, Josh Gibson, Oscar Charleston, and of course Satchel Paige, and in the 1940s, to the Kansas City Monarchs, Jackie Robinson.

In the 1920s pitcher Smokey Jo Williams and his team, the Lincoln Giants, shut out the National League champion Philadelphia Phillies 1 to 0 in an exhibition game in New York after the World Series. Henceforth, no more exhibition games between whole major league teams and black teams were permitted. But individuals of both races did play beside and against one another, especially in Winter Baseball in the Caribbean, where blacks excelled. Black professional baseball teams blossomed at the turn of the century. In the 1920s a black professional baseball league was formed primarily through the efforts of Andrew "Rube" Foster, a black baseball pitcher who in 1905 had won 51 of 55 games. The "Negro National League" had franchises in Indianapolis, Kansas City, Chicago, Detroit and St. Louis. Several years later, a "Negro American League" was established and an all-black world series was annually held.

Basketball

The basketball color line was broken in 1951 with the signing of Chuck Cooper by the Boston Celtics. Cooper was the son of Charles Cooper, who was a superstar on the all-black Harlem Renaissance pro basketball team. The Harlem Renaissance, or the Rens, as it was called, was founded in 1923 and was widely considered the best basketball team of its time. They usually had to hold the score down to maintain spectator interest. The Rens record: 1,588 won, 239 lost. Another great all-black basketball team still going strong is the Harlem Globetrotters. The Globetrotters started to play in the early 1920s as The Savoy Big Five.

Football

The breaking of the modern day color line in pro football occurred shortly after World War II when a goodly number of black players were recruited by the pro teams. In its early days, around the turn of the century, pro football utilized black ball players, and many colleges had black players on their rosters from the time of the sport's inception. William H. Lewis from Harvard University was in 1892 the first black All American. One of the early great black pro football players was Henry McDonald, who played for the Rochester Jeffersons and later the Akron Giants. Fritz Pollard, another all-time great in pro football, was playing at

Josh Gibson, greatest hitter in Negro Leagues history, was voted to Cooperstown in 1972.

about the same time as McDonald. Around 1930 the recruiting of blacks for pro football ceased and in major league pro football there were no black athletes until after World War II.

Black Coaches

In professional sports, coaching assignments by blacks began in the 1950s and increased several-fold in the following two decades.

In baseball, John Buck O'Neil became a coach of the Cubs in 1962. Thirteen years later, Frank Robinson—the only player to win the MVP (most valuable player) award in the National and American leagues—became the first black manager when he joined the Cleveland Indians.

In 1978 Larry Doby, who followed Jackie Robinson as an early pioneer in baseball, managed the Chicago White Sox for a portion of the season. During the 1981 season, Frank Robinson returned as an active manager in the same year that Maury Wills—who had set the base-stealing record—made his debut as a manager with the Seattle Mariners.

In 1966 Bill Russell was named coach of basketball's Boston Celtics. After guiding the team to national championship status, the talented former center retired to sports broadcasting. In 1974, however, a lucrative contract beckoned and he returned to coaching at the helm of the Seattle Supersonics.

In 1975 blacks were coaching at five franchises of the National Basketball Association. Russell was at Seattle, Ray Scott at Detroit, Al Attles at San Francisco, K. C. Jones in Washington, and Lenny Wilkins in Portland. Soon Willis Reed would join the ranks as coach of the New York Knicks.

In 1981 Elston Howard was on the coaching staff of the New York Yankees. There were 14 assistant coaches working in the National Football League, following in the footsteps of Lowell Perry, who was a pioneer for that sport in 1957.

Willie Wood, who played for the Green Bay Packers and was named an assistant coach for the San Diego Chargers, became a head coach of the Toronto Argonauts of the Canadian Football League.

The Black in Professional Baseball

On April 10, 1947, Jackie Robinson broke the color barrier in major league baseball. He immediately excelled and was named rookie of the year. And as the Brooklyn Dodgers went on to win six league pennants, Robinson continued as a mainstay of the team, soon being cited as the league MVP.

Since that first historic season, a host of black baseball players in major league baseball have followed as stars in the Robinson tradition. Don Newcombe, Roy Campanella, Elston Howard, Monty Irvin, and Larry Doby are among the score of pioneers whose achievements were later complemented by a new breed of superstar who made an impact on professional baseball with precedent-setting entries on the record books.

While Jackie Robinson complained of his treatment by some fans, the crowds who cheered the great American summer pastime 30 years later paid little attention to the racial background of the player. For, more often than not, black players were giving those fans more than enough to cheer about. By the 1970s blacks were on the roster of every team in the league and were joined in increasing numbers by talented players from Puerto Rico, the Dominican Republic, Venezuela, and other parts of Latin America. Among the stars who excelled was Hank Aaron, who became the all-time home run leader; Lou Brock, who set an all-time single season mark for stealing bases with 118; Willie Mays, acclaimed as baseball's greatest center fielder; and Frank Robinson, the only player to win the MVP award in both the National and American leagues.

For their efforts in winning scoring, batting, base stealing, and RBI titles, blacks became regular participants in the most valuable player selections as well as being designated to play in the annual all-star games. Soon several, including Robinson, Mays, and even the

Great second baseman Jackie Robinson steals home. He was the first black player to break the color barrier in the majors.

Negro League's standout Satchel Paige, were voted into the Baseball Hall of Fame.

As the 1980s began, there were new talents such as Reggie Jackson, who batted his 400th home run during that season, and his teammate Dave Winfield, who in 1981 became baseball's highest paid player when the Yankees signed him to a 10-year, $22 million contract.

The 1981 Season

The two big stories of 1981 involved a chubby, 20-year-old rookie from Mexico who provided such inspiration for the Los Angeles Dodgers that they won their first World Series in years, and a 50-day strike that resulted in 714 canceled games, a split season, and the greatest feeling of disaffection baseball fans had ever experienced.

For Fernando Valenzuela, his major league debut would result in being honored with the Cy Young Award. For the New York Yankees, who won their fourth division title, there was disappointment when their fortunes against the Dodgers proved to be just the reverse of the 1978 season.

And while Dave Winfield was not a hero of the World Series, both he and Reggie Jackson performed admirably during the season as just two among several black players who exhibited formidable batting power. Veterans like Rod Carew, Ken Singleton, and George Foster managed to maintain their hitting stride of previous seasons, as did Amos Otis, Ben Oglivie, and Andrew Dawson.

A rookie on the Montreal Expos, Tim Raines, made an early impression as he built up an impressive record for stealing bases. (Montreal was a contender during the close of the season playoffs.)

And while blacks distinguished themselves with their batting prowess throughout the major leagues, pitchers like Jim Bibby and Rudy May were to influence the outcome of individual games during the course of the season.

During the summer, on a nostalgic note, 50 former players of the Negro Baseball League met for a reunion in Ashland, Kentucky and provided fascinating commentary on the role of blacks in one of America's great pastimes. From the groundwork they laid and the contributions blacks made in 1981, there was a general consensus that the future bode well for blacks in major league baseball.

1982 NATIONAL LEAGUE ROSTER OF MINORITY PLAYERS

Atlanta Braves

Chris Chambliss—IF
Luis Gomez—IF
Gary Matthews—OF
Claudell Washington—OF

Chicago Cubs

Leon Durham—OF
Steve Henderson—OF
Ferguson Jenkins—P
Lynn McGlothen—P
Jerry Morales—OF
Lee Smith—P
Tye Waller—IF
Bump Willis—IF

Cincinnati Reds

German Barranca—IF
Cesar Cedeno—OF
Dave Concepcion—IF
Dan Driessen—IF
Rafael Landestoy—IF
Eddie Milner—OF
Mario Soto—P
Alex Trevino—C
Duane Walker—OF

Houston Astros

Jose Cruz—OF
Kiko Garcia—IF
Luis Pujols—C
Tony Scott—OF

Los Angeles Dodgers

Dusty Baker—OF
Pedro Guerrero—OF
Ken Landreaux—OF
Alejandro Pena—P
Ted Power—P

Jorge Orta—OF
Dave Stewart—P
Derrel Thomas—OF
Fernando Valenzuela—P

Montreal Expos

Ray Burris—P
Warren Cromartie—OF
Andre Dawson—OF
Wallace Johnson—IF
John Milner—IF
Rowland Office—OF
Al Oliver—IF
Tim Raines—OF
Rodney Scott—IF
Frank Traveras—IF
Jerry White—OF

New York Mets

Hubie Brooks—IF
George Foster—OF
Jesse Orosco—P
Ellis Valentine—OF
Mookie Wilson—OF

Philadelphia Phillies

Luis Aguayo—IF
Dick Davis—OF
Ivan DeJesus—IF
Bo Diaz—C
Julio Frenko—IF
Garry Maddox—OF
Gary Matthews—OF
Sid Monge—P
Manny Trillo—IF
Ozzie Virgil—C

Pittsburgh Pirates

Jim Bibby—P
John Candelaria—P
Mike Easler—OF

Lee Lacy—OF
Bill Madlock—IF
Willie Montanez—IF
Omar Moreno—OF
Dave Parker—OF
Tony Pena—C
Johnny Ray—IF
Bill Robinson—IF
Enrique Roma—P
Eddie Solomon—P
Willie Stargell—IF, OF

St. Louis Cardinals

Joaquin Andujar—P
Julio Gonzalez—IF
David Green—OF
George Hendrick—OF
Tito Landrum—OF
Orlando Sanchez—C
Lonnie Smith—OF
Ozzie Smith—IF

San Diego Padres

Randy Bass—IF
Juan Bonilla—IF
Luis DeLeon—P
Juan Eichelberger—P
Ruppert Jones—OF
Sixto Lexcano—OF
Broderick Perkins—IF
Mario Ramirez—IF
Gene Richards—OF
Garry Templeton—IF
Luis Salazar—IF

San Francisco Giants

Chili Davis—OF
Al Holland—P
Jeff Leonard—OF
Joe Morgan—IF
Reggie Smith—IF
Max Venable—OF

1982 AMERICAN LEAGUE ROSTER OF MINORITY PLAYERS

Baltimore Orioles

Benny Ayala—OF
Al Bumbry—OF
Dan Ford—OF
Dennis Martinez—P
Tippy Martinez—P
Jose Morales—C
Eddie Murray—IF

Boston Red Sox

Luis Aponte—P
Tony Perez—IF
Jim Rice—OF
Julio Valdez—IF

California Angels

Don Baylor—OF
Juan Beniquez—OF
Rod Carew—IF
Reggie Jackson—OF
Angel Moreno—P
Jose Moreno—IF
Luis Sanchez—P

Chicago White Sox

Juan Agosto—P
Solomon Barojas—P
Ron LeFlore—OF
Aurelio Rodriguez—IF

Cleveland Indians

Miguel Dilone—OF
Bake McBride—OF
Andre Thornton—IF

Detroit Tigers

Enos Cabell—IF
Larry Herndon—OF
Lynn Jones—OF
Chet Lemar—OF
Elias Sosa—P

Kansas City Royals

Vida Blue—P
Cesar Geronimo—OF
Grant Jackson—P
Lee May—IF
Hal McRae—OF
Amos Otis—OF
U. L. Washington—IF
Frank White—IF
Willie Wilson—OF

Milwaukee Brewers

Cecil Cooper—IF
Larry Hisle—OF
Ben Oglivie—OF

Minnesota Twins

Fernando Arroyo—P
Bobby Castillo—P
Jesus Vega—IF
Ron Washington—IF

New York Yankees

Oscar Gamble—OF
Ken Griffey—OF
Rudy May—P
John Mayberry—OF
Jerry Mumphrey—OF
Willie Randolph—IF
Dave Winfield—OF

Oakland Athletics

Tony Armas—OF
Rickey Henderson—OF
Cliff Johnson—C
Davey Lopes—IF
Dwayne Murphy—OF
Mike Norris—P

Seattle Mariners

Thad Bosley—OF
Estaban Castillo—IF
Al Cowens—OF
Julio Cruz—IF
Todd Cruz—IF
Lamar Johnson—IF
Ed Nunez—P

Texas Rangers

Lamar Johnson—IF
Mario Mendoza—IF
Leon Roberts—OF
Bill Sample—OF

Toronto Blue Jays

Damaso Garcia—IF
Roy Lee Jackson—P
Luis Leal—P
Lloyd Moseby—OF
Willie Upshaw—IF
Otto Velez—OF
Al Woods—OF

RECORD SETTERS

Black Batting Champions (National League)

Player	Year	Avg.	Player	Year	Avg.
Jackie Robinson, *Bklyn.*	1949	.342			
Willie Mays, *N.Y. Giants*	1954	.345	Roberto Clemente, *Pitt.*	1967	.357
Hank Aaron, *Mil.*	1956	.328	Rico Carty, *Atl.*	1970	.366
Hank Aaron, *Mil.*	1959	.355	Billy Williams, *Chi.*	1972	.333
Roberto Clemente, *Pitt.*	1961	.351	Ralph Garr, *Atl.*	1974	.353
Tommy Davis, *L.A.*	1962	.346	Bill Madlock, *Chi.*	1975	.354
Tommy Davis, *L.A.*	1963	.326	Bill Madlock, *Chi.*	1976	.339
Roberto Clemente, *Pitt.*	1964	.339	Dave Parker, *Pitt.*	1977	.338
Roberto Clemente, *Pitt.*	1965	.329	Dave Parker, *Pitt.*	1978	.334
Matty Alou, *Pitt.*	1966	.342	Bill Madlock, *Pitt.*	1982	.341

Black Batting Champions (American League)

Player	Year	Avg.
Tony Oliva, *Minn.*	1964	.323
Tony Oliva, *Minn.*	1965	.321
Frank Robinson, *Balt.*	1966	.316
Rod Carew, *Minn.*	1969	.332
Alex Johnson, *Cal.*	1970	.329
Tony Oliva, *Minn.*	1971	.337
Rod Carew, *Minn.*	1972	.318
Rod Carew, *Minn.*	1973	.350
Rod Carew, *Minn.*	1974	.364
Rod Carew, *Minn.*	1975	.359
Rod Carew, *Minn.*	1977	.388
Rod Carew, *Minn.*	1978	.333

Black Home Run Champions (American League)

Player	Year	Total
Larry Doby, *Cleve.*	1952	32
Larry Doby, *Cleve.*	1954	32
Frank Robinson, *Balt.*	1966	49
Dick Allen, *Chi.*	1972	37
Reggie Jackson, *Oak.*	1973	32
Dick Allen, *Chi.*	1974	32
Reggie Jackson, *Oak.*	1975	36
George Scott, *Mil.*	(*tie*)	36
Jim Rice, *Bos.*	1977	39
Jim Rice, *Bos.*	1978	46
Reggie Jackson, *N.Y.*	1980	41
Eddie Murray, *Balt.*	1981	22

Black Home Run Champions (National League)

Player	Year	Total
Willie Mays, *N.Y. Giants*	1955	51
Hank Aaron, *Mil.*	1957	44
Ernie Banks, *Chi.*	1958	47
Ernie Banks, *Chi.*	1960	41
Orlando Cepeda, *S.F.*	1961	46
Willie Mays, *S.F.*	1962	49
Willie McCovey, *S.F.*	1963	44
Willie Mays, *S.F.*	1964	47
Willie Mays, *S.F.*	1965	52
Hank Aaron, *Atl.*	1966	44
Hank Aaron, *Atl.*	1967	39
Willie McCovey, *S.F.*	1968	36
Willie McCovey, *S.F.*	1969	45
Willie Stargell, *Pitt.*	1971	48
Willie Stargell, *Pitt.*	1973	44
George Foster, *Cinn.*	1977	52
George Foster, *Cinn.*	1978	40

Black Most Valuable Player Awards (National League)

Player	Year
Jackie Robinson, *Bklyn.*	1949
Roy Campanella, *Bklyn.*	1951
Roy Campanella, *Bklyn.*	1953
Willie Mays, *N.Y. Giants*	1954
Roy Campanella, *Bklyn.*	1955
Don Newcombe, *Bklyn.*	1956
Hank Aaron, *Mil.*	1957
Ernie Banks, *Chi.*	1958
Ernie Banks, *Chi.*	1959
Maury Wills, *L.A.*	1962
Willie Mays, *S.F.*	1965
Roberto Clemente, *Pitt.*	1966
Orlando Cepeda, *St.L.*	1967
Bob Gibson, *St.L.*	1968
Willie McCovey, *S.F.*	1969
Joe Morgan, *Cinn.*	1975
Joe Morgan, *Cinn.*	1976
George Foster, *Cinn.*	1977
Dave Parker, *Pitt.*	1978
Willie Stargell, *Pitt.*	1979

Maury Wills was the National League's MVP of 1962.

Black Most Valuable Player Awards
(American League)

Player	Year
Elston Howard, *N.Y.*	1963
Zoilo Versalles, *Minn.*	1965
Frank Robinson, *Balt.*	1966
Vida Blue, *Oak.*	1971
Dick Allen, *Chi.*	1972
Reggie Jackson, *Oak.*	1973
Rod Carew, *Minn.*	1977
Jim Rice, *Bos.*	1978
Don Baylor, *Cal.*	1979

Black Runs-Batted-In Leaders (National League)

Player	Year	Total
Monte Irvin, *N.Y. Giants*	1951	121
Hank Aaron, *Mil.*	1957	126
Ernie Banks, *Chi.*	1958	129
Ernie Banks, *Chi.*	1959	143
Hank Aaron, *Mil.*	1960	126
Orlando Cepeda, *S.F.*	1961	142
Tommy Davis, *L.A.*	1962	153
Hank Aaron, *Mil.*	1963	130
Hank Aaron, *Atl.*	1966	127
Orlando Cepeda, *St.L.*	1967	111
Willie McCovey, *S.F.*	1968	105
Willie McCovey, *S.F.*	1969	126
Willie Stargell, *Pitt.*	1973	119
George Foster, *Cinn.*	1976	121
George Foster, *Cinn.*	1977	149
George Foster, *Cinn.*	1978	120
Dave Winfield, *S.D.*	1979	121

Black Runs-Batted-In Leaders (American League)

Player	Year	Total
Larry Doby, *Cleve.*	1954	126
Frank Robinson, *Balt.*	1966	122
Dick Allen, *Chi.*	1972	113
Reggie Jackson, *Oak.*	1973	117
Lee May, *Balt.*	1976	109
Larry Hisle, *Minn.*	1977	119
Jim Rice, *Bos.*	1978	139
Don Baylor, *Cal.*	1979	139
Cecil Cooper, *Minn.*	1980	122
Eddie Murray, *Balt.*	1981	81

THE BLACK IN PROFESSIONAL BASKETBALL

The first black man to play as a professional in the National Basketball Association (NBA) was Chuck Cooper, a forward who signed a contract with the Boston Celtics in 1951. He remained with the team for six years. Former Harlem Globetrotters star Nat "Sweetwater" Clifton joined the pro ranks later in 1951, playing with the New York Knicks.

Within the decade, many of the top players in both leagues were black. Bill Russell, K. C. Jones, and Sam Jones were at Boston; Ray Felix and Willie Naulls were at New York, and Elgin Baylor starred at Minneapolis.

The 1960s

By 1964 most NBA teams had five or six black players, all accomplished athletes contributing to their respective squads as they were called upon.

The incomparable Wilt Chamberlain, for instance, soon held virtually every scoring record. In fact, he scored an incredible 100 points in a game against the Knicks on March 2, 1962 and repeated the feat again before he retired.

As the decade progressed, new players joined the ranks. Kareem Abdul-Jabbar, the New York City teen who, as a standout at UCLA, led his team to three NCAA championships, signed with the Milwaukee Bucks. During the 1969–1970 season, the Bucks ranked second in a division known for its tough standards.

Other outstanding players included Elvin Hayes, who won the NBA scoring title in his rookie year. Willis Reed, with the Knicks, would win the MVP Award twice within a 10-year period.

San Francisco Giant slugger Willie McCovey won the 1969 MVP award.

Bill Russell, first black basketball coach.

The Early 1980s

As the decade began, another powerful center had come to dominate the league. Kareem Abdul-Jabbar had steadily grown to become a phenomenal star with the Los Angeles Lakers. His contributions through the year led the team to victory as the NBA champs on May 16, 1980 as they defeated the Philadelphia 76ers. When the final game was played, Abdul-Jabbar was injured and rookie guard Earvin (Magic) Johnson incredibly substituted at center, contributing 42 points and being named MVP for the tournament.

In defeating the 76ers, the Lakers faced off against Julius Erving, fast becoming a perennial basketball superstar. With solid, exciting play, he continued to be one of the major attractions in pro sports.

In the following year, the Boston Celtics took the NBA crown with Cedric Maxwell walking away with MVP honors as the east coast team defeated the Denver Rockets. And in 1982 Kareem Abdul-Jabbar led the Lakers in regaining the crown.

Despite intense defensive pressure, Chamberlain led NBA scoring for seven straight seasons.

The 1970s

In the 1970s black representation grew even more substantial. During the 1973–1974 season, Bob McAdoo of the Buffalo Braves was a standout. In only his second season, he scored 2,261 points and rolled up a 30.6-point scoring average, both tops in the league. The towering center also established himself as an excellent rebounder with a 15.1 average, third highest in the NBA.

Other outstanding players were Jabbar of the Bucks (later the Los Angeles Lakers), who would become a dominant force as center and the central force of his teams. Two other ranking centers in the league were Hayes with the Washington Bullets and Nate Thurmond with the Chicago Bulls.

Julius Erving was the top player of the New York Nets of the American Basketball Association (ABA) during the 1973–1974 season (before it merged into the NBA later in the decade). Nicknamed "Dr. J." and "The Doctor," he was the league's top scorer with 2,299 points, averaging 27.4 points per game. George McGinnis of the Indiana Pacers was another top scorer of the ABA during the decade.

During the 1974–1975 season, the dominance of black players continued as four of the top five players in the three categories of scoring, rebounding, and assists were black. The top NBA scorer was again McAdoo, the top rebounder was Wes Unseld, and the top playmaker, Kevin Porter. Both Unseld and Porter played at Washington.

During the decade, Moses Malone became the first player to be drafted into the NBA directly from high school and Wayne Embry became the first black general manager of an NBA team.

1981 NBA ROSTER OF BLACK PLAYERS

Atlanta Braves

John Drew
Eddie Johnson
Tree Rollins
Dan Roundfield
Rory Sparrow
Freeman Williams

Boston Celtics

Nate Archibald
Charles Bradley
M. L. Carr
Gerald Henderson
Cedric Maxwell
Robert Parish

Chicago Bulls

Artis Gilmore
David Greenwood
Tracy Jackson
Larry Kenon
Ronnie Lester
Rickey Sobers
Reggie Theus
James Wilkes
Orlando Woolridge

Cleveland Cavaliers

Ron Brewer
Kenny Carr
James Edwards
Jeff Huston
James Silas
Bobby Wilkerson

Dallas Mavericks

Mark Aguirre
Rolando Blackman
Brad Davis
Jay Vincent

Denver Nuggets

T. R. Dunn
Alex English
Billy McKinney
Dave Thompson

Detroit Pistons

Phil Hubbard
Ron Lee
John Long
Isiah Thomas
Terry Tyler

Golden State Warriors

Ricky Brown
Joe Barry Carroll
World Free
Bernard King
Larry Smith

Houston Rockets

Elvin Hayes
Tom Henderson
Major Jones
Moses Malone
Calvin Murphy
Robert Reid
Bill Willoughby

Indiana Pacers

Johnny Davis
George Johnson
George McGinniss
Lewis Orr
Herb Williams

Kansas City Kings

Leon Douglas
Larry Drew
Phil Ford
Eddie Johnson
Reggie King
Cliff Robinson
Mike Woodson

Los Angeles Lakers

Jim Brewer
Kareem Abdul-Jabbar
Michael Cooper
Earvin "Magic" Johnson
Eddie Jordan
Bob McAdoo
Mike McGee
Norm Nixon
Jamaal Wilkes

Milwaukee Bucks

Junior Bridgeman
Quinn Buckner
Harvey Catchings
Bob Lanier
Marques Johnson
Scott May
Sidney Moncrief

New Jersey Nets

James Bailey
Otis Birdsong
Darwin Cook
Len Elmore
Albert King
Sam Lacey
Ray Tolbert
Foots Walker
Buck Williams
Ray Williams

New York Knicks

Alex Bradley
Reggie Carter
Bill Cartwright
Maurice Lucas
Michael Ray Richardson
Campy Russell
Randy Smith
Marvin Webster
Sly Williams

Philadelphia 76ers

Mike Bantom
Maurice Cheeks
Earl Cureton
Darryl Dawkins
Julius Erving
Lionel Hollins
Caldwell Jones
Andrew Toney

Phoenix Suns

Dudley Bradley
Walter Davis
Dennis Johnson
Larry Nance
Len Truck Robinson
Charlie Scott

Portland Trailblazers

Billy Ray Bates
Calvin Natt
Kelvin Ransey
Michael Thompson
Darnell Valentine
Kermit Washington

San Antonio Spurs

Gene Banks
George Gervin
George Johnson

Mike Mitchell
Johnny Moore

San Diego Clippers

Michael Brooks
Joe Bryant
Charlie Criss
Phil Smith
Brian Taylor
Jerome Whitehead

Seattle Supersonics

Freddie Brown
John Johnson
Greg Kelser
Lonnie Shelton
Ray Tolbert
Gus Williams

Washington Bullets

Greg Ballard
Jim Chones
Spencer Haywood
John Lucas
Rick Mahorn

Utah Jazz

Adrian Dantley
Rickey Green
Darrell Griffith

The colleges are the farm teams for the pros; many a spectacular college star failed in the pros.

RECORD SETTERS

Black NBA Scoring Leaders

Player	Year	Pts.	Avg.
Wilt Chamberlain, *Phil.*	1959–1960	2707	37.9
Wilt Chamberlain, *Phil.*	1960–1961	3303	38.4
Wilt Chamberlain, *Phil.*	1961–1962	4029	50.4
Wilt Chamberlain, *S.F.*	1962–1963	3586	44.8
Wilt Chamberlain, *S.F.*	1963–1964	2948	36.5
Wilt Chamberlain, *Phil.*	1964–1965	2534	34.7
Wilt Chamberlain, *Phil.*	1965–1966	2649	33.5
Dave Bing, *Det.*	1967–1968	2142	27.1
Elvin Hayes, *S.D.*	1968–1969	2327	28.4
Lew Alcindor, *Mil.*	1970–1971	2596	31.7
Kareem Abdul-Jabbar, *Mil.*	1971–1972	2822	34.8
Nate Archibald, *K.C.-O*	1972–1973	2719	34.0
Bob McAdoo, *Buff.*	1973–1974	2261	30.6
Bob McAdoo, *Buff.*	1974–1975	2831	34.5
Bob McAdoo, *Buff.*	1975–1976	2427	31.1
George Gervin, *San Ant.*	1977–1978	2232	29.2
George Gervin, *San Ant.*	1978–1979	2365	29.6
George Gervin, *San Ant.*	1979–1980	2585	33.1
Adrian Dantley, *Utah*	1980–1981	2452	30.7

Black NBA Rebounding Leaders

Player	Year	Rebounds
Maurice Stokes, *Roch.*	1956–1957	1256
Bill Russell, *Bost.*	1957–1958	1564
Bill Russell, *Bost.*	1958–1959	1612
Wilt Chamberlain, *Phil.*	1959–1960	1941
Wilt Chamberlain, *Phil.*	1960–1961	2149
Wilt Chamberlain, *Phil.*	1961–1962	2052
Wilt Chamberlain, *S.F.*	1962–1963	1946
Bill Russell, *Bost.*	1963–1964	1930
Bill Russell, *Bost.*	1964–1965	1878
Wilt Chamberlain, *Phil.*	1965–1966	1943
Wilt Chamberlain, *Phil.*	1966–1967	1957
Wilt Chamberlain, *Phil.*	1967–1968	1952
Wilt Chamberlain, *L.A.*	1968–1969	1712
Elvin Hayes, *S.D.*	1969–1970	1386
Wilt Chamberlain, *L.A.*	1970–1971	1493
Wilt Chamberlain, *L.A.*	1971–1972	1572
Wilt Chamberlain, *L.A.*	1972–1973	1526
Elvin Hayes, *Wash.*	1973–1974	1463
Bob McAdoo, *Buff.*	1974–1975	1155

Player	Year	Rebounds
Kareem Abdul-Jabbar, *L.A.*	1975–1976	1383
Kareem Abdul-Jabbar, *L.A.*	1976–1977	1090
Truck Robinson, *N.O.*	1977–1978	1288
Moses Malone, *Hous.*	1978–1979	1444
Moses Malone, *Hous.*	1980–1981	1180

Black NBA Assist Leaders

Player	Year	Assists
Oscar Robertson, *Cinn.*	1960–1961	690
Oscar Robertson, *Cinn.*	1961–1962	899
Guy Rodgers, *S.F.*	1962–1963	825
Oscar Robertson, *Cinn.*	1963–1964	868
Oscar Robertson, *Cinn.*	1964–1965	861
Oscar Robertson, *Cinn.*	1965–1966	847
Guy Rodgers, *Chi.*	1966–1967	908
Wilt Chamberlain, *Phil.*	1967–1968	702
Oscar Robertson, *Cinn.*	1968–1969	772
Lenny Wilkens, *Sea.*	1969–1970	683
Norm Van Lier, *Cinn.*	1970–1971	832
Nate Archibald, *K.C.-O*	1972–1973	910
Kevin Porter, *Wash.*	1974–1975	650
Don Watts, *Sea.*	1975–1976	661
Don Buse, *Ind.*	1976–1977	685
Kevin Porter, *N.J.*	1977–1978	837
Kevin Porter, *Det.*	1978–1979	1099
Michael Ray Richardson, *N.Y.*	1979–1980	832
Kevin Porter, *Wash.*	1980–1981	734

THE BLACK IN PROFESSIONAL FOOTBALL

The 1970s

In the 1970s outstanding black players excelled at virtually every offensive and defensive position. For the first time, quarterback James Harris of the Los Angeles Rams was consistently successful as a week-to-week starter and helped to overcome the stereotype of black signal callers performing erratically and failing under pressure.

During the 1974 season, Harris—who graduated from fabled Grambling College—was the NFC's second leading passer. Two years later he would capture the crown in that category.

Quarterbacking was an important concern among observers who watched numerous blacks excel at college and then fail or not be allowed to try out in that position. With responsibility for leading the offense, gaining acceptability and respectability in that position was a crucial goal for those outstanding college players and their supporters.

In time, Joe Gilliam joined the Pittsburgh Steelers and performed admirably as a backup quarterback for a team that would claim the Super Bowl title in unprecedented fashion. In 1978 Doug Williams became an offensive standout as he quarterbacked an expansion team, the Tampa Bay Buccaneers, to contender status within three years. By that time, Vince Evans had become a successful backup signal caller with the Chicago Bears.

During the decade, blacks virtually dominated the year-end statistics in pass receiving, rushing, and for a time, scoring. While these records on offense continued to fall, there were notable achievements by blacks on the defensive teams as well.

Linemen anchored defensive lines and made vital contributions to team efforts in the secondary areas as well. Each year new players were joining the NFL and making their reputations in short order. Within time, half of all the active players in the league were black.

Soon the Football Hall of Fame gave recognition to a number of blacks, including all-pro Willie Davis of the Green Bay Packers, Herb Adderly of the Packers and Dallas Cowboys, Jim Brown of the Cleveland Browns, Roosevelt Brown of the New York Giants, David (Deacon) Jones of the Rams, San Diego Chargers, and Washington Redskins, Lenny Moore of the Baltimore Colts, and Gale Sayers of the Chicago Bears.

And each year, new collegiate wonders would join the ranks. George Rogers, a star at the University of South Carolina, became the seventh black in a row to win the coveted Heisman Trophy in 1980. And while Rogers was excelling as a rookie with the New Orleans Saints, Marcus Allen of USC became the 1981 winner, the eighth black honored with college football's most coveted individual award.

The 1980 Season

In January the Pittsburgh Steelers had won an unprecedented fourth Super Bowl victory by defeating the Los Angeles Rams in the fifteenth championship contest.

When the season started that fall, the Steelers were plagued by injuries and got off with a series of four losses before changing to winning ways. At Buffalo, a young runner named Joe Cribbs was providing the kind of excitement not seen since the retirement of O. J. Simpson. The Philadelphia Eagles also appeared strong, with receiver Harold Carmichael contributing substantially each week. At Atlanta, a back named William Andrews and a receiver named Wallace Francis combined for a tremendous offensive threat.

As the season drew to a close, the Eagles beat the Minnesota Vikings 42–7 as the playoff series began.

One of the greatest, Gale Sayers.

Oakland overcame the Cleveland Browns 14–12 and the Dallas Cowboys defeated Atlanta, 30–27. In the final game, the Buffalo Bills were vanquished by the San Diego Chargers. In the next competition Oakland and Philadelphia moved up as contenders in Super Bowl XV.

As the final score indicated, Oakland overwhelmed the Eagles, with quarterback Jim Plunkett throwing for three touchdowns. While the offensive line was credited with giving Plunkett the time he needed, Cliff Branch, who caught two of the TD passes, and Kenny King, who caught the third—a record 80-yard pass—were certainly heroes that day. Rod Martin, a defensive standout, was also singled out for praise after catching three interceptions—another Super Bowl record to aid the Raiders in their second world championship.

Other standouts during the 1980–1981 season were Earl Campbell, the Houston Oiler who led the league in rushing; John Jefferson, who was the leading receiver with 1,340 yards and 13 touchdowns, and Tony Dorsett of the Cowboys, who rushed for 160 yards in a single game. Veterans Chuck Muncie, Wilbert Montgomery, Billy Sims, and Mike Pruitt all provided excitement and solid offensive statistics throughout the season.

The 1981 Season

The San Francisco 49ers defeated the Cincinnati Bengals in Super Bowl XVI, as two teams who had never reached the championships played to a 26–21 decision. The game marked the culmination of a season in which the two ultimate contenders were praised most for the talent of their respective quarterbacks and the strategy of their coaches.

A number of black players were instrumental in bringing the West Coast team its first victory, however. Earl Cooper caught a crucial touchdown pass, and Dwight Hicks was on the receiving end of an intercepted pass that helped to bring about the Bengal's downfall.

During the playoffs preceding the championship game, Doug Williams quarterbacked his team into contention while several heroes produced playoff opportunities for the New York Giants and Jets, in a rare outburst of spirited play for the second major story of the season.

Among the perennial offensive standouts during the season were Walter Payton at Chicago, Earl Campbell at Houston, Tony Dorsett at Dallas, and Chuck Muncie at San Diego.

REPRESENTATIVE ROSTER OF BLACK PLAYERS IN THE NATIONAL FOOTBALL LEAGUE

Atlanta Falcons

William Andrews—RB
Bobby Butler—DB
Lynn Cain—RB
Wally Francis—WR
Alfred Jackson—WR
Al Jenkins—WR
Earl Jones—DB
James Mayberry—RB
Junior Miller—TE
Reggie Smith—WR
Matthew Teague—DE

Baltimore Colts

Cleveland Franklin—RB
Bubba Green—DT
Steve Henry—DB
Ricky Jones—LB
Jimmy Moore—G
Reggie Pinkney—DB
Sanders Shiver—LB
Marvin Sims—RB
Eddie Smith—LB
Hosea Taylor—DT
Donnell Thompson—DT

Buffalo Bills

Buster Barnett—TE
Rufus Bess—DB
Curtis Brown—RB
Jerry Butler—WR
Joe Cribbs—RB
Byron Franklin—WR
Roland Hooks—RB
Ron Jessie—WR
Roosevelt Leaks—RB
Frank Lewis—WR
Isaiah Robertson—LB
Lucius Sanford—LB
Sherman Write—De

Chicago Bears

Marcus Anderson—WR
Todd Bell—DB
Vince Evans—QB
Leslie Frazier—DB
Roland Harper—RB
Reuben Henderson—DB
Noah Jackson—G
Willie McClendon—RB
Emery Moorehead—WR
Alan Page—DT
Walter Payton—RB
Mike Singletary—LB

Rickey Watts—WR
Otis Wilson—LB
Emanuel Zanders—G

Cincinnati Bengals

Charles Alexander—RB
Don Bass—WR
Louis Breeden—CB
Gary Burfey—DE
Oliver Davis—S
Eddie Edwards—DE
Archie Griffin—RB
Ray Griffin—DB
M. L. Harris—TE
Pete Johnson—RB
Bobby Kemp—S
Ken Riley—DB
John Simmons—DB
Dave Verser—WR
Wilson Whitley—NT
Reggie Williams—LB

Cleveland Browns

Autrey Beamon—DB
Ron Bolton—DB
Henry Bradley—DT
Gary Davis—RB
Hanford Dixon—DB
Ricky Feacher—WR
Elvis Franks—DE
Calvin Hill—RB
Eddie Johnson—LB
Cleo Miller—RB
Ozzie Newsome—TE
Greg Pruitt—RB
Mike Pruitt—RB
Reggie Rucker—WR
Clarence Scott—DB
Charles White—RB

Dallas Cowboys

Benny Barnes—DB
Larry Bethea—DT
Dennis Thurman—DB
Tony Dorsett—RB
Bill Joe DuPree—TE
John Dutton—DT
Tony Hill—WR
Butch Johnson—WR
Ed Jones—DE
James Jones—RB
Harvey Martin—DE
Robert Newhouse—RB
Timmy Newsome—FB
Herbert Scott—G

Ron Springs—RB
Everson Walls—DB
Steve Wilson—DB

Denver Broncos

Rubin Carter—DT
Aaron Kyle—DB
Brison Manor—DE
Claudie Minor—T
Haven Moses—WR
Riley Odoms—TE
Tony Reed—RB
Dennis Smith—DB
Roland Solomon—DB
Rick Upchurch—WR

Detroit Lions

Jimmy Allen—DB
Luther Bradley—DB
Dexter Bussey—RB
William Gay—DE
Curtis Green—DE
Alvin Hall—DB
James Hunter—DB
Horace King—RB
Ulysses Norris—TE
Tracy Porter—WR
Billy Sims—RB
Vince Thompson—RB

Green Bay Packers

Leotis Harris—G
Maurice Harvey—DB
Estus Hood—DB
John Jefferson—WR
Ezra Johnson—DE
James Lofton—WR
Terdell Middleton—RB
Guy Prather—LB

Houston Oilers

Adger Armstrong—RB
Harold Bailey—WR
Jesse Baker—DE
Elvin Bethea—DE
Robert Brazile—LB
Ken Burrough—WR
Earl Campbell—RB
Ronnie Coleman—RB
Leon Gray—T
Michael Holston—WR
Vernon Perry—DB
Avon Riley—LB
Carl Roaches—WR

Morris Towns—T
Willie Tullis—WR
J. C. Wilson—DB

Kansas City Chiefs

Curtis Bledsoe—RB
Carlos Carson—WR
M. L. Carter—DB
Deron Cherry—DB
Herb Christopher—DB
Joe Delaney—RB
Al Dixon—TE
Clark Gaines—RB
James Hadnot—RB
Eric Harris—DB
Billy Jackson—RB
Willie Scott—TE
J. T. Smith—WR

Los Angeles Rams

Cullen Bryant—RB
Preston Dennard—WR
Reggie Doss—DT
Lewis Gilbert—TE
LeRoy Irvin—DB
Johnnie Johnson—DB
Willie Miller—WR
Jeff Moore—WR

Rod Perry—DB
Jackie Slater—T
Lucius Smith—DB
Ivory Sully—DB
Jewerl Thomas—RB
Wendell Tyler—RB
Billy Waddy—WR

Miami Dolphins

Elmer Bailey—WR
Andra Franklin—RB
Cleveland Green—T
Duriel Harris—WR
Eddie Hill—RB
Nat Moore—WR
Tony Nathan—RB
Ricky Ray—DB
Gerald Small—DB
Fulton Walker—DB

Minnesota Vikings

Ted Brown—RB
Tony Galbreath—RB
Leo Lewis—WR
Eddie Payton—KR
Ahmad Rashad—WR
Jarvis Redwine—RB
Willie Teal—DB

John Turner—DB
Sammy White—WR
Rickey Young—RB

New England Patriots

Julius Adams—DE
Ray Clayborn—DB
Anthony Collins—RB
Sam Cunningham—RB
Vagas Ferguson—RB
Harold Jackson—WR
Roland James—DB
Keith Lee—DB
Stanley Morgan—WR
Dwight Wheeler—T

New Orleans Saints

Sam Adams—G
Larry Hardy—TE
Rickey Jackson—LB
Derland Moore—DT
Johnnie Poe—DB
George Rogers—RB
Jimmy Rogers—RB
Aundra Thompson—WR
Toussaint Tyler—RB
Wayne Wilson—RB

Billy Taylor of the New York Giants.

New York Giants

Leon Bright—RB
Harry Carson—LB
Larry Flowers—DB
Ike Forte—RB
Earnest Gray—WR
Mark Haynes—DB
Louis Jackson—RB
Terry Jackson—DB
Gary Jeter—DE
Frank Marion—LB
George Martin—DE
Johnny Perkins—WR
Leon Perry—RB
Danny Pittman—WR
Beasley Reece—DB
Lawrence Taylor—LB
J. T. Turner—G

New York Jets

Jerome Barkum—TE
Derrick Gaffney—WR
Bruce Harper—RB
Jesse Johnson—DB
Bobby Jones—WR
Johnny Lam Jones—WR
Freeman McNeil—RB
Tom Newton—RB
Marvin Powell—T
Darrol Ray—DB
Abdul Salaam—DT
Wesley Walker—WR
Chris Ward—T

Oakland Raiders

Malcolm Barnwell—WR
Morris Bradshaw—WR
Cliff Branch—WR
Raymond Chester—TE
Mike Davis—DB
Cedric Hardman—DE
Frank Hawkins—RB
Lester Hayes—DB
Ken Hill—DB
Monte Jackson—DB
Henry Lawrence—T
Rod Martin—LB
Odis McKinney—DB
Cleotha Montgomery—RB
Burgess Owens—DB
Johnny Robinson—DT
Art Shell—T
Gene Upshaw—G
Arthur Whittington—RB

Philadelphia Eagles

Billy Campfield—RB
Harold Carmichael—WR
Herman Edwards—DB
Carl Hairston—DE
Jo Jo Heath—DB
Wally Henry—WR
Wilbert Montgomery—RB
Calvin Murray—RB
Hubert Oliver—RB
Booker Russell—RB
Charles Smith—WR

Reggie Wilkes—LB
Brenard Wilson—DB
Roynell Young—DB

Pittsburgh Steelers

Mel Blount—DB
Bennie Cunningham—TE
Russell Davis—RB
Joe Greene—DT
L. C. Greenwood—DE
Franco Harris—RB
Ron Johnson—DB
Donnie Shell—DB
Lynn Swann—WR
Calvin Sweeney—WR
J. T. Thomas—DB
Sidney Thornton—RB
Anthony Washington—DB
Dwayne Woodruff—DB

St. Louis Cardinals

Ottis Anderson—RB
Mel Gray—WR
Roy Green—DB
Jeff Griffin—DB
Willard Harrell—RB
Charles Johnson—DB
Randy Love—RB
Wayne Morris—RB
Bruce Radford—DE
Herb Williams—DB

San Diego Chargers

Carlos Bradley—LB
James Brooks—RB
Willie Buchanson—DB
Wes Chandler—WR
James Harris—QB
Wyatt Henderson—DB
Charlie Joiner—WR
Gary Johnson—DT
Leroy Jones—DE
Woodrow Lowe—LB
Chuck Muncie—RB
Dwight Scales—WR
Clarence Williams—RB
Kellen Winslow—TE
Wilbur Young—DE

San Francisco 49ers

Dwight Clark—TE
Earl Cooper—FB

Timmy Brown holds the game record for most touchdowns scored from kickoff returns.

Johnny Davis—RB
Walt Easley—RB
Willie Harper—LB
Dwight Hicks—S
Amos Lawrence—RB
Ronnie Lott—DB
Saladin Martin—DB
Ricky Patton—RB
Lawrence Pillars—DE
Eason Ramson—TE
Archie Reese—DT
Fred Solomon—WR
Keena Turner—LB
Eric Wright—DB
Carlton Williamson—DB
Charles Young—TE

Seattle Seahawks

Fred Anderson—DE
Theotis Brown—RB

Ken Easley—DB
Robert Hardy—DT
John Harris—DB
David Hughes—RB
Horace Ivory—RB
Sam McCullum—WR
Vic Minor—DB
Keith Simpson—DB
Rodell Thomas—LB

Tampa Bay Buccaneers

Ricky Bell—RB
Theo Bell—WR
Cedric Brown—DB
Gerald Carter—WR
Tony Davis—RB
Jimmie Giles—TE
Kevin House—WR
Hugh Green—LB
Cecil Johnson—LB

Gordon Jones—WR
James Owens—RB
Lee Roy Selmon—DE
Norris Thomas—DB
Doug Williams—QB

Washington Redskins

Perry Brooks—DT
Rickey Claitt—RB
Calvin Clark—DE
Melvin Jones—G
Curtis Jordan—DB
Joe Lavender—DB
Dexter Manley—DE
Terry Metcalf—RB
Art Monk—WR
Lemar Parrish—DB
Ricky Thompson—WR
Joe Washington—RB

RECORD SETTERS

Black NFL Rushing Leaders

Player	Year	Yards
Jim Brown, *Cleve.*	1957	942
Jim Brown, *Cleve.*	1958	1527
Jim Brown, *Cleve.*	1959	1329
Jim Brown, *Cleve.*	1960	1257
Jim Brown, *Cleve.*	1961	1408
Jim Brown, *Cleve.*	1963	1863
Jim Brown, *Cleve.*	1964	1446
Jim Brown, *Cleve.*	1965	1544
Gale Sayers, *Chi.*	1966	1331
Leroy Kelly, *Cleve.*	1967	1205
Leroy Kelly, *Cleve.*	1968	1239
Gale Sayers, *Chi.*	1969	1032
Larry Brown, *Wash.*	1970	1125
John Brockington, *G.B.*	1971	1105
Larry Brown, *Wash.*	1972	1216
John Brockington, *G.B.*	1973	1144
Lawrence McCutcheon, *L.A.*	1974	1109
Walter Payton, *Chi.*	1976	1390
Walter Payton, *Chi.*	1977	1852
Walter Payton, *Chi.*	1978	1395
Walter Payton, *Chi.*	1979	1610
Walter Payton, *Chi.*	1980	1460

Black AFL Rushing Leaders

Player	Year	Yards
Cookie Gilchrist, *Buff.*	1962	1096
Clem Daniels, *Oak.*	1963	1098
Cookie Gilchrist, *Buff.*	1964	981
Paul Lowe, *S.D.*	1965	1121

Player	Year	Yards
Jim Nance, *Bost.*	1966	1458
Jim Nance, *Bost.*	1967	1216
Paul Robinson, *Cinn.*	1968	1023
Floyd Little, *Den.*	1970	901
Floyd Little, *Den.*	1971	1133
O. J. Simpson, *Buff.*	1972	1251
O. J. Simpson, *Buff.*	1973	2003
All-time NFL record		
Otis Armstrong, *Den.*	1974	1407
O. J. Simpson, *Buff.*	1975	1817
O. J. Simpson, *Buff.*	1976	1503
Earl Campbell, *Hous.*	1978	1450
Earl Campbell, *Hous.*	1979	1697
Earl Campbell, *Hous.*	1980	1434

Black NFL Scoring Leaders

Player	Year	Points
Jim Brown, *Cleve.*	1958	108
Lenny Moore, *Balt.*	1964	120
Gale Sayers, *Chi.*	1965	132
Leroy Kelly, *Cleve.*	1968	120
Chuck Forman, *Minn.*	1975	132
Billy Sims, *Det.*	1980	96

Black AFL Scoring Leaders

Player	Year	Points
Gene Mingo, *Den.*	1962	137
O. J. Simpson, *Buff.*	1975	138
Earl Campbell, *Hous.*	1980	78

Black NFL Receiving Leaders				Black AFL Receiving Leaders		
Player	Year	Catches		Player	Year	Catches
Bobby Mitchell, *Wash.*	1962	72		Lionel Taylor, *Den.*	1962	77
Charley Taylor, *Wash.*	1966	72		Lionel Taylor, *Den.*	1963	78
Charley Taylor, *Wash.*	1967	70		Lionel Taylor, *Den.*	1965	85
Clifton McNeil, *S.F.*	1968	71		Marlin Briscoe, *Buff.*	1970	57
Dick Gordon, *Chi.*	1970	71		Lydell Mitchell, *Balt.*	1974	
Harold Jackson, *Phil.*	1972	62		Lydell Mitchell, *Balt.*	1975	60
Harold Carmichael, *Phil.*	1973	67		Reggie Rucker	1976	
Claude Young, *Phil.*	1974	63		MacArthur Lane, *K.C.*	1977	
Chuck Forman, *Minn.*	1975	73		Lydell Mitchell, *Balt.*	1978	
Drew Pearson, *Dall.*	1976	50		Joe Washington	1979	82
Ahmad Rashad, *Minn.*	1977	51		Kellen Wenslow, *S.D.*	1980	89
Rickey Young, *Minn.*	1978	88				
Ahmad Rashad, *Minn.*	1979	80				
Earl Cooper, *S.F.*	1980	83				

THE BLACK IN PROFESSIONAL BOXING

The black prize fighter has been active in America for well over two centuries. In fact, the first American heavyweight contender was a black, Tom Molineaux, a Virginia slave. Molineaux lost two championship fights against the English titleholder, Tom Crib, in 1810 and again 1811.

With the advent of the twentieth century, the black boxer came to occupy a place of ever-growing importance in American ring annals—in particular after Jack Johnson, regarded by many as the greatest fighter of all time, won the heavyweight championship of the world in 1908.

By the 1930s blacks were challenging for supremacy in other divisions as well. Henry Armstrong had be-

The first American heavyweight contender was Tom Molineaux, a Virginia slave, who fought two championship bouts against English titleholder Tom Crib, in 1810 and 1811.

come featherweight, lightweight, and welterweight champion of the world—the first and only fighter to hold three titles at once. Joe Louis had already been world heavyweight champion for almost 10 years when Ray Robinson took the welterweight crown at the end of 1946. Robinson moved up to the middleweight championship in the 1950s and came close to taking the light-heavyweight title from Joe Maxim, losing only after wilting in the heat at Yankee Stadium in 1952.

Throughout most of this era (in fact, for all but five years since 1937), blacks have retained the heavyweight championship of the world. Although there have been many champions in all divisions, we are listing the records of only the heavyweight titleholders, along with those of Henry Armstrong and Ray Robinson, two of the greatest black champions in other divisions.

Certainly the most prominent figure in the past two decades was Muhammad Ali (who boxed first under the name Cassius Clay). Winner of the heavyweight boxing title three times, Ali continued to challenge contenders even after his third loss, succumbing to a younger Trevor Berbick in a bout in the Bahamas in December 1981. He was then on the verge of his fortieth birthday.

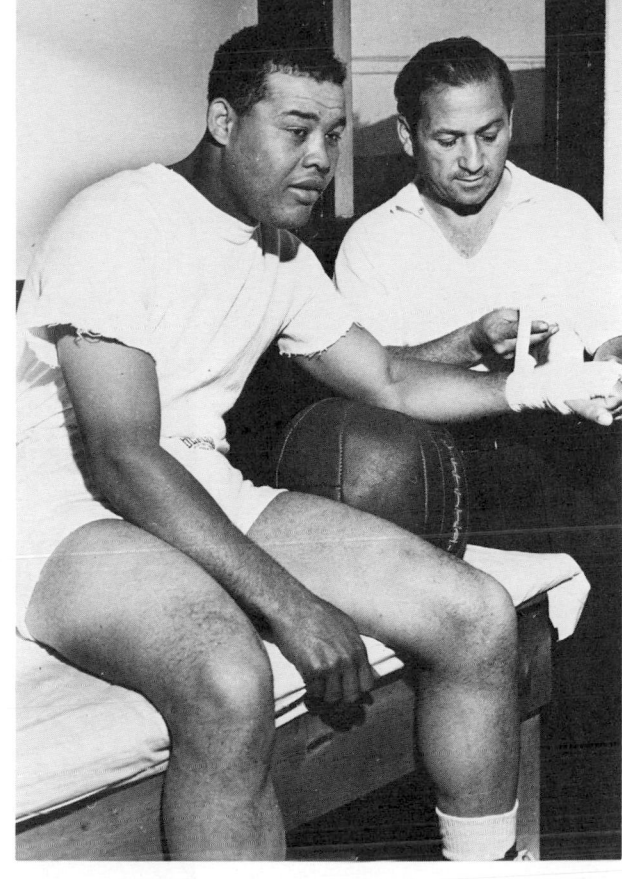

"The Brown Bomber," Joe Louis.

Sugar Ray Robinson won this classic battle with Gene Fullmer by KO in round 5.

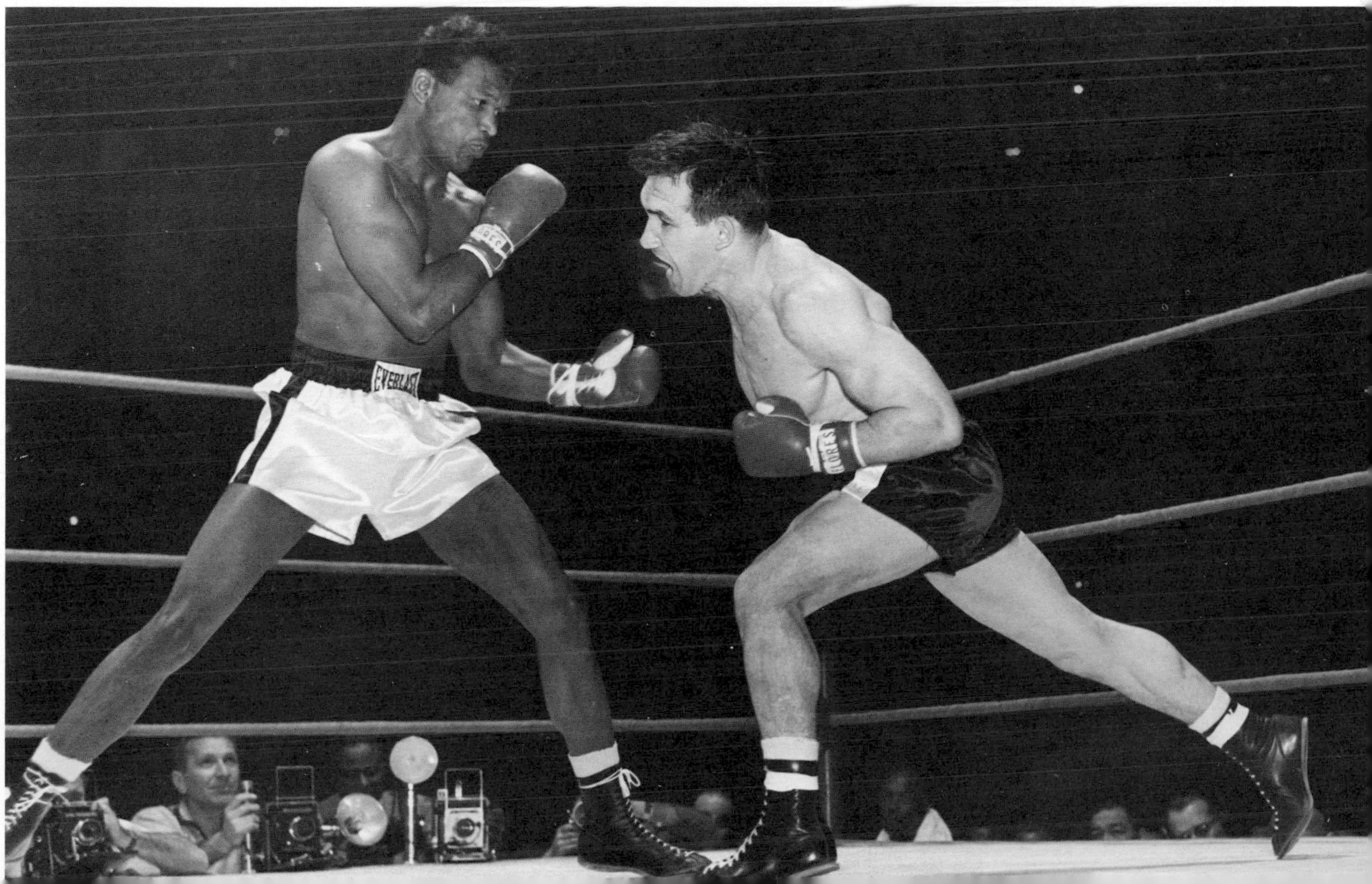

Muhammad Ali, possibly the best heavyweight ever, shown here with the title belt.

After winning the Olympic gold medal in 1960, Ali turned pro and defeated reigning champ Sonny Liston. Over the next 20 years, he was at the center of attention as he lost the title after refusing to register for the draft. Of course, he then went on to win it twice more.

Even while Ali remained in the picture, a host of strong competitors came into focus. George Foreman and Joe Frazier were among those who faced Ali in the ring. Larry Holmes, 1968 Olympic gold medalist, and Leon Spinks, 1976 gold medal winner, both fought Ali during the decade. In 1981 Foreman preceded Ali in an unsuccessful comeback bid.

In another interesting turnabout, Ed "Too Tall" Jones left a successful pro football career as a defensive end with the Dallas Cowboys to try a career in boxing. Within a year he returned to the Cowboys.

Sugar Ray Leonard, a 1976 Olympic gold medal winner as a light welterweight, then turned pro, ultimately winning the title after facing Roberto Duran. Later, boxing against Thomas Hearns, the WBA champ, he was victorious in a highly publicized match which made him the undisputed champ in that weight class. (The following records are reprinted here through the courtesy of Nat Fleischer and *Ring* magazine.)

BLACK BOXING CHAMPIONS (ALL DIVISIONS)

Heavyweight

Name	Years Held
Jack Johnson	1908–1915
Joe Louis	1937–1949
Ezzard Charles	1949–1951
Jersey Joe Walcott	1951–1952
Floyd Patterson	1956–1959; 1960–1962
Sonny Liston	1962–1964
Muhammad Ali (Cassius Clay)	1964–1967; 1974
Joe Frazier	1970–1973
George Foreman	1973–1974
Muhammad Ali	1974–1978
Ken Norton (WBC)	1978
Larry Holmes (WBC)	1978
John Tate (WBA)	1979
Mike Weaver (WBA)	1980

Light Heavyweight

Name	Years Held
Battling Siki	1922–1923
John Henry Lewis	1935–1939
Archie Moore	1952–1961
Harold Johnson	1961–1963
Jose Torres	1965–1966
Dick Tiger	1966–1968
Bob Foster	1968–1975
Marvin Johnson (WBC)	1978
Matthew Saad Muhammad (WBC)	1979
Eddie Mustava Muhammad (WBA)	1980
Michael Spinks (WBA)	1981

Middleweight

Name	Years Held
Tiger Flowers	1926–1931
Gorilla Jones	1931–1932
Sugar Ray Robinson	1951; 1951–1952; 1955–1957; 1957; 1958–1960

Randy Turpin	1951
Dick Tiger	1962–1963; 1965–1966
Emile Griffith	1966–1967
Marvin Hagler	1980

Welterweight

Name	Years Held
Joe Walcott	1901–1904; 1904–1906
Young Jack Thompson	1931
Henry Armstrong	1938–1940
Sugar Ray Robinson	1946–1951
Johnny Bratton	1951
Kid Gavilan	1951–1954
Johnny Saxton	1954–1955; 1956
Virgil Akins	1958–1960
Benny Kid Paret	1960–1961
Emile Griffith	1963–1966
Curtis Cokes	1966–1969
Jose Napoles	1969–1970; 1971
Sugar Ray Leonard (WBC)	1979
Thomas Hearns (WBA)	1980
Sugar Ray Leonard (WBA)	1981

Muhammad Ali hits the canvas in the fifteenth round of Superfight I, on the way ⟨
a losing decision to Joe Frazier.

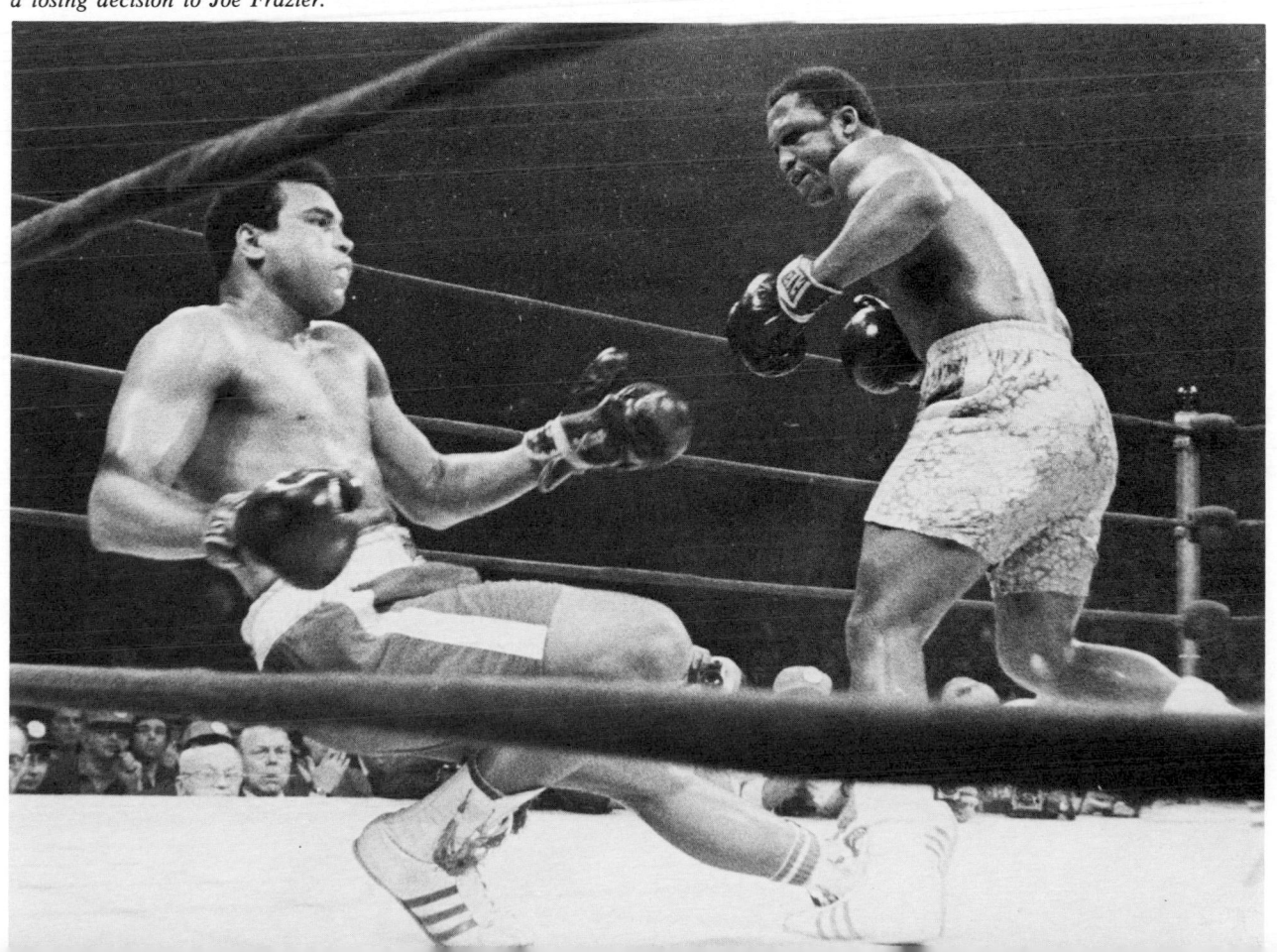

Lightweight

Name	Years Held
Joe Gans	1901–1908
Henry Armstrong	1938–1939
Beau Jack	1942–1944 (New York)
Bob Montgomery	1944–1947 (New York)
Ike Williams	1945–1947 (NBA); 1947–1951
Jimmy Carter	1951–1952; 1952–1954; 1954–1955
Wallace Bud Smith	1955–1956
Joe Brown	1956–1962

Featherweight

Name	Years Held
George Dixon	1890–1899
Kid Chocolate	1932–1934 (New York)
Henry Armstrong	1937–1938
Chalky Wright	1941–1942
Sandy Saddler	1948–1949; 1950–1957
Hogan Kid Bassey	1957–1959
Davey Moore	1959–1963

Bantamweight

Name	Years Held
George Dixon	1890–1892
Panama Al Brown	1929–1935
George Pace	1940
Harold Dade	1947
Jimmy Carruthers	1953–1954

TITLE BOUTS OF BLACK CHAMPIONS

Muhammad Ali

February 25, 1964
    Sonny Liston, Miami Beach   KO 7
May 25, 1965
    Sonny Liston, Lewiston, Maine   KO 1
November 22, 1965
    Floyd Patterson, Las Vegas   KO 12
March 29, 1966
    George Chuvalo, Toronto   W 15
May 21, 1966
    Henry Cooper, London   KO 6
August 6, 1966
    Brian London, London   KO 3
September 10, 1966
    Karl Mildenberger, Frankfurt   KO 12

November 14, 1966
    Cleveland Williams, Houston   KO 3
February 6, 1967
    Ernie Terrell, Houston   W 15
March 22, 1967
    Zora Folley, New York   KO 7
March 8, 1971
    Joe Frazier, New York   L 15
October 29, 1974
    George Foreman, Kinshasa, Zaire   KO 8
March 24, 1975
    Chuck Wepner, Cleveland   KO 15
May 16, 1975
    Ron Lyle, Las Vegas   KO 11
June 30, 1975
    Joe Bugner, Malaysia   W 15
October 1, 1975
    Joe Frazier, Manila   KO 14
February 20, 1976
    Jean-Pierre Coopman, San Juan   KO 5
April 30, 1976
    Jimmy Young, Landover, Maryland   W 15
May 25, 1976
    Richard Dunn, Munich   KO 5
September 28, 1976
    Ken Norton, New York   W 15
May 16, 1977
    Alfredo Evangelista, Landover, Maryland   W 15
September 29, 1977
    Ernie Shavers, New York   W 15
February 15, 1978
    Leon Spinks, Las Vegas   L 15
September 15, 1978
    Leon Spinks, New Orleans   W 15
October 2, 1980
    Larry Holmes, Las Vegas

Henry Armstrong

(*Fought early in career as Melody Jackson. Won 58 out of 62 amateur bouts.*)

October 29, 1937
    Petey Sarron, New York   KO 6
May 31, 1938
    Barney Ross, Long Island City, New York   W 15
August 17, 1938
    Lou Ambers, New York   W 15
November 25, 1938
    Ceferino Garcia, New York   W 15
December 5, 1938
    Al Manfredo, Cleveland   KO 3
    (*Won welterweight title. Relinquished featherweight title.*)
August 22, 1939
    Lou Ambers, New York   L 15
December 11, 1939
    Jimmy Garrison, Cleveland   KO 7

October 4, 1940
Fritzie Zivic, New York — L 15
January 17, 1941
Fritzie Zivic, New York — KO by 12

Joe Brown

August 24, 1956
Wallace (Bud) Smith, New Orleans — W 15
February 13, 1957
Wallace (Bud) Smith, Miami Beach — KO 11
June 19, 1957
Orlando Zulueta, Denver — KO 15
December 4, 1957
Joe Lopes, Chicago — KO 11
May 7, 1958
Ralph Dupas, Houston — KO 8
July 23, 1958
Kenny Lane, Houston — W 15
February 11, 1959
Johnny Busso, Houston — W 15
June 3, 1959
Paolo Rosi, Washington, D.C. — KO 8
December 2, 1959
Dave Charnley, Houston — KO 5
October 28, 1960
Cisco Andrade, Los Angeles — W 15
April 18, 1961
Dave Charnley, London — W 15
October 28, 1961
Bert Somodio, Quezon City — W 15
April 21, 1962
Carlos Ortiz, Las Vegas — L 15

(*Brown retired in the mid-1960s.*)

Ezzard Charles

June 22, 1949
Joe Walcott, Chicago — W 15
August 10, 1949
Gus Lesnevich, New York — KO 7
October 14, 1949
Pat Valentino, San Francisco — KO 8
August 15, 1950
Freddy Beshore, Buffalo — KO 14
September 27, 1950
Joe Louis, New York — W 15
December 5, 1950
Nick Barone, Cincinnati — KO 11
January 12, 1951
Lee Oma, New York — KO 10
March 7, 1951
Joe Walcott, Detroit — W 15
May 30, 1951
Joey Maxim, Chicago — W 15
July 18, 1951
Joe Walcott, Pittsburgh — KO by 7
June 5, 1952
Joe Walcott, Philadelphia — L 15
June 17, 1954

Rocky Marciano, New York — L 15
September 17, 1954
Rocky Marciano, New York — KO by 8

(*Charles announced his retirement from the ring on 12/1/56.*)

George Foreman

January 22, 1973
Joe Frazier, Kingston, Jamaica — KO 2
September 1, 1973
Joe (King) Roman, Tokyo, Japan — KO 1
March 26, 1974
Ken Norton, Caracas, Venezuela — KO 2
October 29, 1974
Muhammad Ali, Kinshasa, Zaire — KO by 8

Bob Foster

March 24, 1968
Dick Tiger, New York — KO 4
January 22, 1969
Frankie DePaula, New York — KO 1
May 24, 1969
Andy Kendall, West Springfield, Massachusetts — KO 4
April 4, 1970
Roger Rouse, Missoula, Montana — KO 4
June 27, 1970
Mark Tessman, Baltimore — KO 10
November 18, 1970
Joe Frazier, Detroit — KO by 2
(*Heavyweight title fight*)
March 2, 1971
Hal (T.N.T.) Carroll, Scranton, Pennsylvania — KO 4
April 24, 1971
Ray Anderson — W 15
October 29, 1971
Tommy Hicks, Scranton, Pennsylvania — KO 8
December 16, 1971
Brian Kelly, Oklahoma City — KO 3
April 7, 1972
Vincente Rondon, Miami Beach — KO 2
June 27, 1972
Mike Quarry, Las Vegas — KO 4
September 26, 1972
Chris Finnegan, London — KO 14
August 21, 1973
Pierre Fourie, Albuquerque, New Mexico — W 15
December 1, 1973
Pierre Fourie, Johannesburg — W 15
June 17, 1974
Jorge Ahumada, Albuquerque, New Mexico — D 15

(*Foster retired as champion on 9/16/74. He had a final record of 51–6–1 and never lost to a light heavyweight, all his losses coming at the hands of heavyweights.*)

Joe Frazier

March 4, 1968
    Manuel Ramos, New York   TKO 2
December 1, 1968
    Oscar Bonavena, Philadelphia   W 15
June 23, 1969
    Jerry Quarry, New York   TKO 7
February 16, 1970
    Jimmy Ellis, New York   TKO 5
    (*Wins Undisputed Official Title*)
November 18, 1970
    Bob Foster, Detroit   KO 2
March 8, 1971
    Muhammad Ali, New York   W 15
January 15, 1972
    Terry Daniels, New Orleans   KO 4
May 25, 1972
    Ron Stander, Omaha   KO 5
January 22, 1973
    George Foreman, Kingston, Jamaica   KO by 2

Emile Griffith

April 1, 1961
    Benny Paret, Miami Beach   KO 13
    (*Won welterweight title*)
June 3, 1961
    Gaspar Ortega, Los Angeles   KO 12
September 30, 1961
    Benny Paret, New York City   L 15
March 24, 1962
    Benny Paret, New York City   KO 12
    (*Paret died ten days later from injuries suffered in this fight*)
July 13, 1962
    Ralph Dupas, Las Vegas   W 15
December 8, 1962
    Jorge Fernandez, Las Vegas   KO 9
March 21, 1963
    Luis Rodriguez, Los Angeles   L 15
June 8, 1963
    Luis Rodriguez, New York City   W 15
September 22, 1964
    Brian Curvis, London   W 15
March 30, 1965
    Jose Stable, New York   W 15
December 10, 1965
    Manuel Gonzalez, New York   W 15
April 25, 1966
    Dick Tiger, New York City   W 15
    (*Won middleweight title and had to relinquish welterweight title*)
July 13, 1966
    Joey Archer, New York   W 15
January 23, 1967
    Joey Archer, New York   W 15
April 17, 1967
    Nino Benvenuti, New York   L 15

September 29, 1967
    Nino Benvenuti, New York   W 15
March 4, 1968
    Nino Benvenuti, New York   L 15
October 18, 1969
    Jose Napoles, Los Angeles   L 15
    (*Welterweight title fight*)
September 25, 1971
    Carlos Monzon, Buenos Aires   KO by 14
    (*Middleweight title fight*)
June 2, 1973
    Carlos Monzon, Monte Carlo   L 15
    (*Middleweight title fight*)

Larry Holmes

June 9, 1978
    Ken Norton, Los Vegas   W 15
    (*Won WBC Heavyweight Title*)
November 10, 1978
    Alfredo Evangelista, Las Vegas   KO 7
    (*Retained WBC Heavyweight Title*)
March 23, 1979
    Osvaldo Ocasio, Las Vegas   KO 7
    (*Retained WBC Heavyweight Title*)
June 22, 1979
    Mike Weaver, New York   KO 12
    (*Retained WBC Heavyweight Title*)
September 28, 1979
    Earnie Shavers, Las Vegas   KO 11
    (*Retained WBC Heavyweight Title*)
February 3, 1980
    Lorenzo Zanon, Las Vegas   KO 6
    (*Retained WBC Heavyweight Title*)
March 31, 1980
    Leroy Jones, Las Vegas   KO 8
    (*Won Vacant World Heavyweight Title*)
July 7, 1980
    Scott LeDoux, Bloomington   KO 7
    (*Retained World Heavyweight Title*)
October 2, 1980
    Muhammad Ali, Las Vegas   KO 11
    (*Retained World Heavyweight Title*)
April 11, 1981
    Trevor Berbick, Las Vegas   W 15
    (*Retained World Heavyweight Title*)
June 12, 1981
    Leon Spinks, Detroit   KO 3
    (*Retained World Heavyweight Title*)
November 6, 1981
    Renaldo Snipes, Pittsburgh   KO 11
    (*Retained World Heavyweight Title*)

Jack Johnson

December 26, 1908
    Tommy Burns, Sydney   W 14
May 19, 1909
    P. Jack O'Brien, Philadelphia   ND 6
June 30, 1909
    Tony Ross, Pittsburgh   ND 6

Larry Holmes, another all-time great.

September 9, 1909

    Al Kaufman, San Francisco   ND 10

October 16, 1909

    Stanley Ketchel, Colma, California   KO 12

July 4, 1910

    James J. Jeffries, Reno, Nevada   KO 15

July 4, 1912

    Jim Flynn, Las Vegas   W 9

November 28, 1913

    Andre Spoul, Paris   KO 2

June 27, 1914

    Frank Moran, Paris   W 20

April 5, 1915

    Jess Willard, Havana, Cuba   KO by 26

    (*Died June 10, 1946, Raleigh, North Carolina*)

Sonny Liston

September 25, 1962

    Floyd Patterson, Chicago   KO 1

    (*Won World Heavyweight Championship*)

July 22, 1963

    Floyd Patterson, Las Vegas   KO 1

    (*World Heavyweight Title*)

February 25, 1964

    Cassius Clay, Miami Beach   KO by 7

May, 25, 1965

    Cassius Clay, Lewiston, Maine   KO by 1

    (*Liston was found dead in his home in 1971*)

Joe Louis

June 22, 1937
    James J. Braddock, Chicago   KO 8
August 30, 1937
    Tommy Farr, New York   W 15
February 23, 1938
    Nathan Mann, New York   KO 3
April 1, 1938
    Harry Thomas, Chicago   KO 5
June 22, 1938
    Max Schmeling, New York   KO 1
January 25, 1939
    John Henry Lewis, New York   KO 1
April 17, 1939
    Jack Roper, Los Angeles   KO 1
June 28, 1939
    Tony Galento, New York   KO 4
September 20, 1939
    Bob Pastor, Detroit   KO 11
February 9, 1940
    Arturo Godoy, New York   W 15
March 29, 1940
    Johnny Paychek, New York   KO 2
June 20, 1940
    Arturo Godoy, New York   KO 8
December 16, 1940
    Al McCoy, Boston   KO 6
January 31, 1941
    Red Burman, New York   KO 5
February 17, 1941
    Gus Dorazio, Philadelphia   KO 2
March 21, 1941
    Abe Simon, Detroit   KO 13
April 8, 1941
    Tony Musto, St. Louis   KO 9
May 23, 1941
    Buddy Baer, Washington, D.C.   W disq. 7
June 18, 1941
    Billy Conn, New York   KO 13
September 29, 1941
    Lou Nova, New York   KO 6
January 9, 1942
    Buddy Baer, New York   KO 1
    (*Donated purse to Naval Relief Fund*)
March 27, 1942
    Abe Simon, New York   KO 6
    (*Donated purse to Naval Relief Fund*)
June 19, 1946
    Billy Conn, New York   KO 8
September 18, 1946
    Tami Mauriello, New York   KO 1
December 5, 1946
    Jersey Joe Walcott, New York   W 15
June 25, 1948
    Jersey Joe Walcott, New York   KO 11
    (*Louis announced his retirement as undefeated world heavyweight champion on March 1, 1949*)
September 27, 1950
    Ezzard Charles, New York   L 15

(*Final record: 68–3 with 54 by KO. Elected to Boxing Hall of Fame in 1954*)

Jose Napoles

April 18, 1969
    Curtis Cokes, Los Angeles   KO 13
June 29, 1969
    Curtis Cokes, Mexico City   KO 10
October 18, 1969
    Emile Griffith, Los Angeles   W 15
February 15, 1970
    Ernie Lopez, Los Angeles   KO 15
December 3, 1970
    Billy Backus, Syracuse   KO by 4
June 4, 1971
    Billy Backus, Los Angeles   KO 8
December 14, 1971
    Hedgemon Lewis, Los Angeles   W 15
March 28, 1972
    Ralph Charles, London   KO 7
June 10, 1972
    Adolph Pruitt, Monterrey, Mexico   KO 2
February 28, 1973
    Ernie Lopez, Los Angeles   KO 7
June 23, 1973
    Rober Menetrey, Grenoble   W 15
September 22, 1973
    Clyde Gray, Toronto   W 15

Floyd Patterson

November 30, 1956
    Archie Moore, Chicago   KO 5
July 29, 1957
    Tommy Jackson, New York   KO 10
August 22, 1957
    Pete Rademacher, Seattle   KO 6
August 18, 1958
    Roy Harris, Los Angeles   KO 12
May 1, 1959
    Brian London, Indianapolis   KO 11
June 26, 1959
    Ingemar Johansson, New York   KO by 3
June 20, 1960
    Ingemar Johansson, New York   KO 5
March 13, 1961
    Ingemar Johansson, Miami Beach   KO 6
December 4, 1961
    Tom McNeeley, Toronto   KO 4
September 25, 1962
    Sonny Liston, Chicago   KO by 1
    (*Lost World Heavyweight Title*)
July 22, 1963
    Sonny Liston, Las Vegas   KO by 1
November 22, 1965
    Muhammad Ali, Las Vegas   KO by 12
September 14, 1968
    Jimmy Ellis, Stockholm   L 15
    (*WBA heavyweight title fight*)

Ray Robinson

(*Won Golden Gloves featherweight title in 1939 and lightweight title in 1940 in New York and in intercity competition. Engaged in 85 amateur bouts. Had 69 KOs [40 in first round]. Boxed as Walker Smith.*)

December 20, 1946		
Tommy Bell, New York	W	15
(*Won Vacant World Welterweight Title*)		
June 24, 1947		
Jimmy Doyle, Cleveland	KO	8
December 19, 1947		
Chuck Taylor, Detroit	KO	6
June 28, 1948		
Bernard Docusen, Chicago	W	15
July 11, 1949		
Kid Gavilan, Philadelphia	W	15
June 5, 1950		
Robert Villemain, Philadelphia	W	15
August 9, 1950		
Charley Fusari, Jersey City	W	15
August 25, 1950		
Jose Basora, Scranton	KO	1
October 26, 1950		
Carl Olson, Philadelphia	KO	12
February 14, 1951		
Jake La Motta, Chicago	KO	13
July 10, 1951		
Randy Turpin, London	L	15
September 12, 1951		
Randy Turpin, New York	KO	10
March 13, 1952		
Carl (Bobo) Olson, San Francisco	W	15
April 16, 1952		
Rocky Graziano, Chicago	KO	3
June 25, 1952		
Joey Maxim, New York	KO by	14

December 9, 1955		
Carl (Bobo) Olson, Chicago	KO	2
May 18, 1956		
Carl (Bobo) Olson, Los Angeles	KO	4
January 2, 1957		
Gene Fullmer, New York	L	15
May 1, 1957		
Gene Fullmer, Chicago	KO	5
September 23, 1957		
Carmen Basilio, New York	L	15
March 25, 1958		
Carmen Basilio, Chicago	W	15
January 22, 1960		
Paul Pender, Boston	L	15
June 10, 1960		
Paul Pender, Boston	L	15
December 3, 1960		
Gene Fullmer, Los Angeles	D	15
March 4, 1961		
Gene Fullmer, Las Vegas	L	15

Jersey Joe Walcott

December 5, 1947		
Joe Louis, New York	L	15
June 25, 1948		
Joe Louis, New York	KO by	11
June 22, 1949		
Ezzard Charles, Chicago	L	15
March 7, 1951		
Ezzard Charles, Detroit	L	15
July 18, 1951		
Ezzard Charles, Pittsburgh	KO	7
June 5, 1952		
Ezzard Charles, Philadelphia	W	15
September 23, 1952		
Rocky Marciano, Philadelphia	KO by	13
May 15, 1953		
Rocky Marciano, Chicago	KO by	1

(*Walcott retired to become a parole officer and a referee*)

Floyd Patterson, the first fighter to win back the world heavyweight championship.

Mike Weaver

March 31, 1980
    John Tate, Knoxville   KO 15
    (*Won WBA Heavyweight Title*)
October 25, 1980
    Gerrie Coetzee, Bophuthatswana   KO 13
    (*Retained WBA Heavyweight Title*)
October 3, 1981
    James (Quick) Tillis, Rosemont, Ill.   W 15
    (*Retained WBA Heavyweight Title*)

THE BLACK IN TRACK AND FIELD

The number of black stars produced in track and field is such that the compilation of a roster of stars quickly becomes something approaching a herculean task. In view of this fact, we have decided instead to provide a number of lists containing the names of black World, Olympic, and American record holders. Biographies of outstanding black performers in track and field will be found in the last subsection of this sports section.

World Track and Field Records Held by American Blacks

Holder/Distance or Event	Time, Height, or Distance	Year
Bob Hayes/100 yd	9.1	1963
Jim Hines/100 yd	9.1	1967
Charlie Greene/100 yd	9.1	1967
John Carlos/100 yd	9.1	1969
Tommie Smith/220 yd (turn)	20.0	1966
Tommie Smith/220 yd (str. way)	19.5	1966
Curtis Mills/440 yd	44.7	1969
Charlie Greene/100 m	9.9	1968
Jim Hines/100 m	9.9	1968
Ronnie Ray Smith/100 m	9.9	1968
Tommie Smith/200 m (turn)	19.8	1968
Tommie Smith/200 m (str. way)	19.5	1966
Lee Evans/400 m	43.8	1968
Charlie Greene/400 m relay	38.2	1968
Mel Pender		
Ronnie Ray Smith		
Jim Hines		
Earl McCullough/440 yd relay	38.6	1967

Holder/Distance or Event	Time, Height, or Distance	Year
O. J. Simpson		
Lennox Miller		
Lee Evans		
Tommie Smith/800 m relay	1:22.1	1967
Lee Evans		
Tommie Smith/880 yd relay	1:22.1	1967
Vince Matthews		
Ron Freeman/1,600 m relay	2:56.1	1968
Larry James		
Lee Evans		
Lennox Yearwood		
Kent Bernard/1 mi relay	3:02.8	1966
Edwin Roberts		
Wendell Mottley		
Lee Calhoun/120 yd high hurdles	13.2	1960
Earl McCullough/120 yd high hurdles	13.2	1967
Erv Hall/120 yd high hurdles	13.2	1969
Willie Davenport/120 yd high hurdles	13.2	1969
Lee Calhoun/110 m high hurdles	13.2	1960
Earl McCullough/110 m high hurdles	13.2	1967
Willie Davenport/110 m high hurdles	13.2	1969
Bob Beamon/long jump	29'2¼"	1968
Otis Davis (team)/1,600 m relay	3:02.2	1960
Eddie Hart/100 m	9.9	1972
John Smith/440 yd	44.5	1971
Rod Milburn/120 yd, 3'6" hurdles	13.0	1971
Larry Black/4 × 100 m relay (2 turns)	38.2	1972
Gerald Tinker		
Eddie Hart		
Randy Williams/long jump	27'7⁄₁₆"	1972
Vince Matthews/400 m	44.7	1972
Rod Milburn/110 m hurdle	13.2	1972
Wilma Rudolph/100 m	11.2	1961
Wilma Rudolph/200 m	22.9	1960
Willye White/400 m relay	44.3	1961
Ernestine Pollards		
Vivian Brown		
Wilma Rudolph		
Mattline Render/4 × 110 yd run	44.7	1971
Iris Davis		
Gale Fitzgerald/4 × 440 yd run	3:38.8	1971
Cheryl Toussaint		
Renaldo Nehemiah/110 m hurdles	12.93	1981
Edwin Moses/400 m hurdles	47.13	1980

American Track and Field Records Held by Black Women

Holder/Distance or Event	Time, Height or Distance	Year
Wilma Rudolph/100 m dash	11.2	1961
Wilma Rudolph/200 m dash	22.9	1960
Mildred McDaniel/running high jump	5′9½″	1956
Rosie Bonds/80 m low hurdles	10.8	1964
Willye White/Running broad jump	24′6″	1964
Earlene Brown/4 Km shot put	54′9″	1960
Earlene Brown/distance throw	176′10½″	1960
Evelyn Ashford/100 m dash	10.90	1981
Evelyn Ashford/200 m dash	21.83	1979

Track and Field Achievements of Black U.S. Olympic Team Members

Place, Year, Athlete	Distance or Event	Position
St. Louis, 1904		
George C. Poag	200 m hurdles	3rd
George C. Poag	400 m hurdles	3rd
London, 1908		
J. B. Taylor (team)	1,600 m relay	1st—3.29.4
Paris, 1924		
Dehart Hubbard	Running broad jump	1st—24′5⅛″
Edward Gourdin	Running broad jump	2nd—23′10⅞″
Los Angeles, 1932		
Eddie Tolan	100 m dash	1st—10.3 [a]
Ralph Metcalfe	100 m dash	2nd—10.3
Eddie Tolan	200 m dash	1st—21.2
Ralph Metcalfe	200 m dash	3rd—21.5
Edward Gordon	Running broad jump	1st—25′¾″
Berlin, 1936		
Jesse Owens	100 m dash	1st—10.3 [b]
Ralph Metcalfe	100 m dash	2nd—10.4
Jesse Owens	200 m dash	1st—20.7 [c]
Matthew Robinson	200 m dash	2nd—21.1
Archie Williams	400 m run	1st—46.5
James DuValle	400 m run	2nd—46.8
John Woodruff	800 m run	1st—1.52.9
Fritz Pollard, Jr.	110 m hurdles	3rd—14.4
Cornelius Johnson	High jump	1st—6′8″ [c]
Jesse Owens	Running broad jump	1st—26′5 5/16″ [a]
Jesse Owens (team)	400 m relay	1st—39.8 [d]
Ralph Metcalfe (team)	400 m relay	1st—39.8 [d]
London, 1948		
Harrison Dillard	100 m dash	1st—10.3
Norwood Ewell	100 m dash	2nd—10.4
Norwood Ewell	200 m dash	1st—21.1
Mal Whitfield	400 m run	3rd—46.9
Willie Steele	Running broad jump	1st—25′8″
Herbert Douglass	Running broad jump	3rd—24′9″
Lorenzo Wright	Running broad jump	4th—24′9″
Harrison Dillard		
Norwood Ewell		

Place, Year, Athlete	Distance or Event	Position
Lorenzo Wright (team)	400 m relay	1st—40.6
Mal Whitfield (team)	1,600 m relay	1st—3.10.4
Audrey Patterson	200 m dash	3rd—25.2
Alice Coachman	High jump	1st—5'6¼"
Helsinki, 1952		
Andrew Stanfield	200 m dash	1st—20.7
James Gathers	200 m dash	3rd—20.8
Ollie Matson	400 m run	3rd—46.8
Mal Whitfield	400 m run	6th—47.8
Mal Whitfield	800 m run	1st—1.49.2 [c]
Reginald Pearman	800 m run	6th
Harrison Dillard	110 m hurdles	1st—13.7 [c]
Jerome Biffle	Running broad jump	1st—24'10"
Meredith Gourdine	Running broad jump	2nd—24'8⁷⁄₁₆"
Harrison Dillard		
Andrew Stanfield (team)	400 m relay	1st—40.1
Ollie Matson		
Mal Whitfield (team)	1,600 m relay	2nd—3.04.1
Bill Miller	Javelin	2nd—237'8¾"
Milton Campbell	Decathlon	2nd—6,975 pts.
Mae Faggs	100 m dash	6th
Catherine Hardy		
Mae Faggs		
Barbara Jones (team)	400 m relay	1st—45.9 [a]
Melbourne, 1956		
Andrew Stanfield	200 m dash	2nd—20.7
Charles Jenkins	400 m run	1st—46.7
Lou Jones	400 m run	5th—48.1
Arnold Sowell	800 m run	4th—1.48.3
Lee Calhoun	110 m hurdles	1st—13.5
Josh Culbreath	400 m hurdles	3rd
Charles Dumas	High jump	1st—6'11¼" [c]
Gregory Bell	Running broad jump	1st—25'8¼"
Ira Murchison (team)	400 m relay	1st—39.5 [c]
Lou Jones		
Charles Jenkins (team)	1,600 m relay	1st—3.04.8
Milton Campbell	Decathlon	1st—7,937 pts.
Rafer Johnson	Decathlon	2nd—7,587 pts.
Mildred McDaniel	High jump	1st—5'9¼" [a]
Willye White	Running broad jump	2nd—19'11¾"
Mae Faggs		
Margaret Matthews		
Isabelle Daniels		
Wilma Rudolph (team)	400 m relay	3rd—45.5
Rome, 1960		
Les Carney	200 m dash	2nd—20.6
Lee Calhoun	110 m hurdles	1st—13.8
Willie May	110 m hurdles	2nd—13.8
Hayes Jones	110 m hurdles	3rd—14.0
John Thomas	High jump	1st—7'¼"
Ralph Boston	Running broad jump	1st—26'7¾" [c]
Irv. Roberson	Running broad jump	2nd—26'7⅜"
Ira Davis	H., S., & J.	4th—53'11"
Otis Davis (team)	1,600 m relay	1st—3.02.2
Rafer Johnson	Decathlon	1st—8,392 pts. [c]
Wilma Rudolph	200 m dash	1st—24.0
Earlene Brown	Shot put	3rd—53'10⅜"

Place, Year, Athlete	Distance or Event	Position
Martha Judson		
Lucinda Williams		
Barbara Jones		
Wilma Rudolph (team)	400 m relay	1st—44.5 [b]
Tokyo, 1964		
Robert Hayes	100 m dash	1st—9.9 [a]
Mel Pender	100 m dash	7th—10.4
Henry Carr	200 m dash	1st—20.3
Paul Drayton	200 m dash	2nd—20.5
Ulis Williams	400 m run	5th—46.0
Hayes Jones	110 m hurdles	1st—13.6
Paul Drayton		
Robert Hayes (team)	400 m relay	1st—39.0 [b]
John Thomas	High jump	2nd—7'1¼"
John Rambo	High jump	3rd—7'1"
Ralph Boston	Running broad jump	2nd—26'4"
Ira Davis	H., S., & J.	5th—52'1¼"
Wyomia Tyus	100 m dash	1st—11.4
Edith McGuire	100 m dash	2nd—11.4
Marilyn White	100 m dash	3rd—11.6
Rosie Bonds	80 m hurdles	8th—10.8
Willye White		
Wyomia Tyus		
Marilyn White		
Edith McGuire (team)	400 m relay	2nd—43.9
Eleanor Montgomery	High jump	8th—5'7¼"
Willye White	Running broad jump	12th—19'8¼"
Earlene Brown	Shot put	12th—48'6¼"

[a] Olympic and world record.

[b] Ties Olympic and world record.

[c] Olympic record.

[d] World record.

[e] World record, disallowed, wind.

Jesse Owens, who infuriated Adolf Hitler in the 1936 Olympics.

Black Gold Medal Winners at the 1968 Mexico City Olympics

Athlete/Distance or Event	Time or Distance
Jim Hines/100 m dash	9.9
Tommie Smith/200 m dash	19.8
Lee Evans/400 m dash	43.8
Willie Davenport/110 m hurdles	13.3
Charlie Greene	
Mel Pender	
Ronnie Ray Smith	
Jim Hines (team)/400 m relay	38.2
Vince Matthews	
Ron Freeman	
Larry James	
Lee Evans (team)/1,600 m relay	2:56.1
Bob Beamon/Long jump	29'2¼"
Wyomia Tyus/100 m	11.0
Madeline Manning/800 m	2:00.9

Black Medal Winners at the 1972 Munich Olympics

Athlete/Distance or Event	Position
Larry Black/200 m	2nd—20.2
Vince Matthews/400 m	1st—44.7
Wayne Collett/400 m	2nd—44.8
Rod Milburn/100 m hurdles	1st—13.2[a]
Eddie Hart/4 × 100 m relay	1st—38.2[a]
Randy Williams/Long jump	1st—27'½"
Jeff Bennett/Decathlon	3rd—7,974 pts.
Mable Fergerson	
Madeline Manning	
Cheryl Toussaint (team)/ 4 × 400 m relay	2nd—3:25.2

[a] Ties world record.

Black Medal Winners at the 1976 Montreal Olympics

Athlete	Time or Distance
Edwin Moses/400 m hurdles	47.64

Gold medal winner Tommie Smith (center) *and silver medal winner John Carlos* (right) *give the black power salute at the 1968 Olympics in Mexico City.*

Rod Milburn (left) *sets a blistering pace over 120 yard high hurdles on his way to a time of 13.0 seconds.*

THE BLACK GOLFER

In the late 1960s golfers Lee Elder and Pete Brown began to challenge Charlie Sifford as the most successful black pro playing on the PGA circuit. Sifford was the first black golfer to win admission to the Professional Golfers Association. His most successful money-winning year was 1967, when he earned $57,000, largely on the heels of a spectacular triumph in the Hartford Open. This occurred a full 10 years after he had become the first black man to capture a nationwide tournament, the Long Beach Open in which he defeated Eric Monti in a sudden-death playoff. Sifford slipped to $33,000 in 1968, the year Lee Elder made a rush at top prize money in the American Classic at Akron, Ohio. Playing against one of the all-time greats, Jack Nicklaus, Elder finished the course at 8 under par, for 280. A sudden death playoff, carried on nationwide television, pitted him against Nicklaus, whom he played stroke for stroke until the fifth hole, at which point Elder missed a putt and had to settle for a little over $12,000, rather than first-prize money of $25,000. Still, by year's end, Elder finished the tour with earnings of more than $31,000.

Another up-and-coming black golfer, Pete Brown, was the third leading black money winner in 1968 with some $8,300. Brown came from nowhere three years later to capture the San Diego Open, winning $30,000 in a sudden-death playoff against Britain's Tony Jacklin.

The top woman golfer, at least judging from her numerous national titles over the past decade, is Ethel Funches, who won the 1968 championship at Lanston Golf Course in Washington, D.C. Althea Gibson, the former tennis great, tried golfing for a while, but performed indifferently, winning only $2,700 in 1968.

On April 22, 1974 Lee Elder won a sudden-death playoff against Peter Oosterhuis at the Monsanto Open in Pensacola, Florida. Elder's victory thus made him the first black to qualify for the 1975 Masters Tournament. In April 1975 Elder did play in the Masters but failed to make the second-round cut.

Sand flies as Lee Elder blasts out of a trap on his way to winning the Monsanto Open.

THE BLACK IN HORSE RACING

From the time of the first running of the Kentucky Derby in 1875 until 1911, the last year a black jockey (Jess Conley) rode in the event, black riders were featured performers in the gala pageantry which surrounded the annual Churchill Downs classic. No less than 11 black jockeys have won a total of 15 Kentucky Derbies in the history of the event. The race was every bit as glamorous and thrilling in its early days as it is now; audiences were as tense and as animated; the clubhouse, the grandstand, the lawns, the flower beds, the track itself were all meticulously and irreproachably prepared for the rush of excitement that was to grip thousands of onlookers for the race's few, but unforgettable, moments. The stable scene was dominated not only by black jockeys, but by black trainers, exercise riders, grooms, and stable boys—a whole cadre of skilled black racetrack people without whom the glorious and magical atmosphere of uproarious and suspenseful competition would never have developed.

These were men more preoccupied with the attraction of sport than with the blandishments of money. They cherished the moment; they loved the horses; victory inspired them, even as defeat crushed them. Two great black jockeys towered over their contemporaries: Isaac Murphy (the Colored Archer) and Jimmy Winkfield.

Except for Murphy (three-time winner of the Derby) and Winkfield (twice winner of the same racing classic), few of the early black jockeys who once dominated the riding end of the sport are known to the public. One of the reasons is that jockeys were not generally identified in the programs of the early days. Another is that, as the sport was transformed into a big business with staggeringly lucrative purses for owners and high annual income for jockeys, black aspirants were gradually phased into the more menial aspects of turf life, shunted aside by a base professionalism which completely undercut their long and distinguished association with the sport.

Winkfield might possibly have competed with Murphy for top honors as the leading black jockey of all time, but the wiry little Kentuckian left the United States to ride in Europe, where he won such prominent races as the Polish Derby, the Grand Prix de Baden, the Emperor's Purse, the Moscow Derby, and the Russian Derby. At the time of the Russian Revolution, he was reportedly making $100,000 a year, but was forced to flee to France in the wake of the upheaval. Winkfield continued to race on the Continent, winning several important races in France, Italy, and Spain. In 1930, after amassing a total of 2,600 winners on tracks all over the globe, Winkfield retired, built a stable near Paris, and bred a string of successful racehorses until he was driven out by the Nazis in World War II. In 1953 Winkfield returned to Maisons-Lafitte, and was able to remodel his stable and remain in business.

Winkfield was not the first black man to win the derby. That feat was accomplished by Oliver Lewis, who rode his mount (Aristides) to victory in the first running of the event in 1875, during which 14 of the 15 starters in the race were ridden by black mounts.

In recent years, the best-known black jockey has been Bob McCurdy, a native of Atlantic City. McCurdy posted over 100 victories in 1963, and earned over $60,000 at his profession. He also won the jockey championship at the Garden State park meet with 27 wins. He is the first black man to ride at Tropical Park, Florida. Interviewed regarding the potential for black jockeys in the business today, McCurdy claims "the sport is wide open for Negroes now." McCurdy will succeed, says George Howell, "because he has had a good upbringing."

Still, as late as 1967, the *New York Times* wrote: "In recent years, Negro jockeys could be counted on the fingers of one hand."

Black Winners of the Kentucky Derby (1875–1895)

Jockey	Mount	Year
Oliver Lewis	Aristides	1875
Billy Walker	Baden Baden	1877
Barrett Lewis	Fonso	1880
Babe Hurd	Apollo	1882
Isaac Murphy	Buchanan	1884
Erskine Henderson	Joe Cotton	1885
Isaac Lewis	Montrose	1887
Isaac Murphy	Riley	1887
Isaac Murphy	Kingman	1891
Alonzo Clayton	Azra	1892
James Perkins	Halma	1895

James Long is one of the few black jockeys in modern racing. Black riders dominated the sport in the last century.

THE BLACK TENNIS PLAYER

The most outstanding black tennis stars have been Arthur Ashe and Althea Gibson. Miss Gibson, winner of both the Wimbledon and U.S. championships in 1957 and 1958 while in her early thirties, was the first black athlete to win a major tennis title. At that time, Arthur Ashe was a teenager who was playing in the semifinals of the under-15 division of the National Junior Championships, which he won in 1960 and 1961. Ashe's most successful year on the court was in 1968 when, as a member of the U.S. Davis Cup Team, he guided the United States to its first championship in five years. Ashe won every match in the Cup preliminaries, showing particularly impressive form against Premjit Lall and Ramanathan Krishnan of India. The United States thus qualified to play Australia, and Ashe, despite an ailing elbow, won the opening match against Ray Ruffels in four sets. He did not play again until the final match, by which time the U.S. had already clinched the crown. (Ashe lost the final to Bill Bowery, 2–6, 6–3, 11–9, 8–6.)

Even more impressive was Ashe's sensational showing in the U.S. Open Tournament, a competition featuring the world's best players, regardless of professional or amateur standing. Ashe, an amateur, defeated Tom Okker of Holland in a grueling five-set match, thus earning his rightful plaudits as the world's top amateur player. Ashe won other tournaments that year, including the U.S. amateur title. Ashe became a pro tennis player in the early 1970s, and became one of the top money winners on the tour. After cardiac surgery ended Ashe's playing career, he became the captain of the U.S. Davis Cup team.

There has been a long tradition of "black" tennis much the same as has existed in baseball. One black player, Jimmie McDaniel, once played U.S. Singles champion Don Budge, and was easily defeated by him, although inexperience and lack of opportunity to play in championship competition were clearly factors influencing the outcome. The first black to play in the U.S. Lawn Tennis Singles Championships, Dr. Reginald S. Weir, did not appear until 1948.

Arthur Ashe lofts the Wimbledon Cup after decisively winning the men's singles final in the English classic. Ashe's brilliant play, coming shortly after his World Championship Tennis (WCT) triumph, established him as one of the dominant figures in pro tennis.

THE BLACK IN WRESTLING

Relatively few blacks have claimed world championships in professional wrestling, but this sport is not without its black participants. Jack Claybourne, one of the earlier successful black pro wrestlers, did lay claim to the black world's heavyweight title by pinning Rufus Jones in 1943. Seven years later, Don Blackman was reported to be the only black to hold a world's wrestling title, that of light-heavyweight champion. Woody Strode, the football star turned Hollywood actor, was also active for a time as a wrestler, as were Bobo Brazil, Shag Thomas, Frank James, and "Black Panther" Mitchell. Black women also perform in this sport from time to time.

MISCELLANEOUS SPORTS

Other competitive sports which deserve some mention include swimming and bowling, although blacks have not achieved prominence in either of these.

A National Negro Bowling Association was established in Detroit in 1939, two years before the first black bowling alley was opened in Cleveland. By the early 1960s J. Wilbert Sims had won for himself a solid reputation as a topflight black bowler, but his performance could not be matched by too many other black bowlers. Clearly "separate competition" has contributed in part to the black's "separate development" in this sport.

Swimming exhibits a similar pattern, inasmuch as it had been difficult for blacks to find suitable recreational facilities in which to develop their skills. Lack of good coaching, the difficulty in finding standard-sized pools nearby, and the consequent inability to develop a systematic method of training are all related factors which must be taken into account in any attempted evaluation of the black's performance in swimming.

Hockey is another sport in which blacks have not yet come to the fore. At the present time, there is only one black in pro-hockey, despite the fact that some blacks have managed to play minor league hockey. Again, access to the facilities, as well as cost of the equipment, must be cited as contributory factors for the lack of participation.

Only one black, Cicero Murphy, has ever competed for the world's billiards championship. Murphy defeated his first rival in the 1965 playoffs by a 150–32 count, and lost to his second opponent, 150–105. Murphy seems destined to win permanent rating among the world's best in this sport.

Blacks are notably absent in any large numbers from a host of other sports which are conventionally associated with higher-income groups, including boating, big-game hunting, fishing, and even camping.

Cicero Murphy, ranking competitor for the world billiard championship.

OUTSTANDING BLACK ATHLETES

HANK AARON
Baseball

Hank Aaron hit more home runs than anyone else in the history of major league baseball. He attained this plateau with his second home run of the 1974 season, a shot which marked his 715th career round-tripper and thus broke the previous record of 714 which had been held by the immortal Babe Ruth. At the advanced age of 40, Aaron finished that season with 20 homers and brought his career mark to a total of 733, a record to which he added 22 more to complete his career with a total of 755.

Born in Mobile, Alabama on February 5, 1934, Aaron played sandlot ball as a teenager. He then played for a team called the Black Bears, but soon thereafter,

signed a $200-per-month contract with the Indianapolis Clowns of the Negro American League. He began as a shortstop and went 10-for-11 in a doubleheader on his first day.

He was purchased by the Boston Braves in June of 1952 and proceeded to hit .336 at Eau Claire of the Northern League. The following season, playing for Jacksonville, his .362 average led the South Atlantic League. This led to a promotion to the Braves, then based in Milwaukee, and the beginning of his brilliant major league career in 1954.

In his second big league season, he hit .314, socked 27 homers, and drove in 106 runs, numbers which were to become routine for Aaron in the years ahead.

He enjoyed perhaps his finest season in 1957, when he was named Most Valuable Player and led his team to a world championship. His stats that year included a .322 average, 44 homers, 132 runs batted in, and 118 runs scored.

Over his career, Aaron has won a pair of batting titles and hit over .300 in 12 seasons. He won the home run and RBI crowns 4 times apiece, hit 40 or more homers 8 times, and hit at least 20 for 20 consecutive years, a National League record. In addition, he was named to 20 consecutive all-star teams.

In November 1974, after playing for Atlanta since 1966, Aaron was traded to the present Milwaukee franchise (now the Brewers), enabling him to finish his career in the city where he began and which became a home town to him.

In January 1982 Aaron received 406 of 415 votes from the Baseball Writers Association as he was elected into the baseball Hall of Fame. While some observers complained that his election should have been unanimous, it was still an overwhelming tribute to a man who held some 13 major league records in an outstanding career.

KAREEM ABDUL-JABBAR
Basketball

A dominant force in professional basketball, Kareem Abdul-Jabbar was named the Most Valuable Player of the NBA for six seasons. A standout with the Los Angeles Lakers during many of their most memorable seasons, Jabbar, born Ferdinand Lewis Alcindor, Jr., at 7' 1½" tall, was easily the most sought after high school basketball player during the 1960s, particularly after he established a New York City record of 2,067 points and 2,002 rebounds in leading Power Memorial High School to three straight schoolboy championships. Power won 95 and lost only six during Lew Alcindor's years with the team; 71 of these victories were consecutive.

Hank Aaron—he broke Babe Ruth's lifetime home run record.

Taller than Wilt Chamberlain at the time of his entrance to UCLA, Jabbar combined great height with catlike moves and a deft shooting touch to lead UCLA to three consecutive NCAA Championships. Twice, as a sophomore and a senior, he was chosen the top collegiate player in the country. He finished his career at UCLA as the ninth all-time collegiate scorer, accumulating 2,325 points in 88 games for an average of 26.4 points per game. After leading UCLA to its third consecutive NCAA title, Jabbar signed a contract with the Milwaukee Bucks of the NBA calling for $1.4 million.

In his rookie season, 1969–1970, he wasted little time showing any doubters that he was worth every penny of it by leading the Bucks, a recently established expansion club, to a second place finish in the Eastern Division, only a few games behind the division winners—the New York Knickerbockers. Jabbar won personal acclaim for his outstanding play in the 1970 NBA All-Star game, combining with the Knicks' Willis Reed to lead the East to victory. After being voted Rookie of the Year, he went on to win the scoring championships in 1971 and 1972. He was one of the keys to the Bucks' world championship in 1971. In 1973 he finished second in scoring with a 30.2 point average, but he had become dissatisfied with life in Milwaukee. At the end of the 1974–1975 season he was traded to the L.A. Lakers.

A serious person both on and off the court, Abdul-Jabbar is a convert to the Hanafi Muslims. Greatly influenced by the life and struggles of Malcolm X, he believes that the Islamic religion (as distinct from the nationalistic Black Muslims) and determined effort have much to offer for a good life.

MUHAMMAD ALI
Boxer

Heavyweight champ for the second time, Muhammad Ali (born Cassius Clay) is recognized as one of the great figures in ring history.

Born in Louisville, Kentucky, he started boxing because he thought it was "the quickest way for black people to make it." After winning the 1960 Olympic gold medal as light-heavyweight, he turned pro. He also turned Black Muslim, although the sect strongly disapproves of boxing, and changed his name in 1963.

In February 1964 Ali won the world heavyweight championship by KO'ing Sonny Liston. Nine successful title defenses followed before Ali's famous war with the Army began. Refusing to serve in the Armed Forces (1967), Ali maintained that it was contrary to Muslim tenets. He also remarked: "I ain't got nothing against them Viet Congs." Stripped of his title and banned from boxing in the United States, Ali faced prison, but he refused to back down and was finally

Agility and intelligence combined with his height make Jabbar an awesome ballplayer.

vindicated by the Supreme Court in 1970. Coming back to the ring after a 3½ year layoff, he worked his way up for another title shot. Biggest matches along the way were Superfights I and II against Joe Frazier in which Ali suffered his first loss and then evened the score.

Few fans gave Ali a chance against Champ George Foreman when they met in Zaire on October 30, 1974. A 4–1 underdog at ring time, Ali amazed the boxing world by using his brains and speed to exhaust and then KO his stronger, six-years-younger opponent. After regaining the crown, Ali KO'd Chuck Wepner and Ron Lyle, and decisioned Joe Bugner. His earnings for 1975, as of July, were over $6,000,000.

In December of 1981, Muhammad Ali entered the ring in a bout against Canadian heavyweight Trevor Berbick. It was a rare occasion where not many besides those at the Bahamas site paid much attention as Ali lost in a decision—his second defeat (the previous being at the hands of Larry Holmes) in two years. It was an inauspicious end to a career for a fighter who had won the heavyweight title three times.

Ali fast approaching his 40th birthday, had resisted suggestions that he not venture into the ring against younger and stronger fighters. Still, after 20 years, it was obviously difficult for the man who had been called champ and so dominated the sport that he had become one of the great figures in ring history. A popular talk show guest and even star of a movie about his life, *The Greatest,* Ali was named Athlete of the Decade for the 1970s by the Associated Press.

As he gets older Ali's personal dedication to helping black people everywhere becomes increasingly more generous, and he now places special emphasis on setting a good example for black youth.

HENRY ARMSTRONG
Boxer

The only fighter ever to hold three titles at the same time is Henry Armstrong, who accomplished this feat on August 17, 1938, when he added the lightweight championship to the featherweight and welterweight titles which he had won earlier.

Armstrong was born on December 12, 1912 in St. Louis, and orphaned five years later. One of 13 children, he managed not only to get through eight grades, but to graduate from Vashon High School as well.

In 1929, while fighting under the name of Melody Jackson, he was knocked out in his professional debut in Pittsburgh. Within two weeks, however, he had won his first fight and, for the next eight years, he learned his trade from coast to coast, fighting all comers until he was finally given a shot at the featherweight title on October 20, 1937. Armstrong defeated Petey Sarron, knocking out a champion who had never before been off his feet.

Less than a year later, on May 31, 1938, Armstrong picked up his second title with a decision over welter-weight champion Barney Ross. Within three months he copyrighted his own triple crown, winning a decision over lightweight champion Lou Ambers.

Inducted into the Black Athletes Hall of Fame in 1975, Armstrong is now a minister living in Norwood, Missouri.

ARTHUR ASHE
Tennis

Arthur Ashe was named captain of the U.S. Davis Cup team in 1981. Inactive as a competition player after suffering a heart attack in 1979, Ashe had been the world's leading black professional tennis star for nearly a decade. In a sport traditionally closed to blacks because of its private-club setting and the financial cost involved, Ashe rose to be the No. 1 amateur tennis player in America in the late 1960s before turning pro. Twice ranked as the number one player in the world, Ashe was winner at various times of Wimbledon, the Australian Open, the U.S. Open, the U.S. Clay Court Championships, and the World Championship Tennis Tournament.

Ashe was a former president and active member of the board of directors of the Association of Tennis Professionals and a co-founder of the National Junior Tennis League. Late in his career, he also served as a television sports commentator.

Born in 1943 in Richmond, Virginia, Ashe learned the game at the Richmond Racket Club, which had been formed by local black enthusiasts. Dr. R. W. Johnson, who had also served as an advisor and benefactor to Althea Gibson, sponsored Ashe's tennis career, spending thousands of dollars and a great deal of time with him.

By 1958 Ashe reached the semifinals in the under-15 division of the National Junior Championships. In 1960 and 1961, he won the Junior Indoors Singles title. Even before he finished high school, he was ranked 28th in the country.

In 1961 Ashe entered UCLA on a tennis scholarship. Since then, on the way to winning the U.S. Amateur Tennis Championship and the U.S. Open Tennis Championship, in addition to becoming the first black man ever named to a Davis Cup Team, Ashe beat most of the world's top players. Tennis great Pancho Gonzales said: "He has the fastest service since mine."

In 1975 Ashe had to be recognized as one of the world's great tennis players having defeated Jimmy Connors at Wimbledon as well as taking the World Championship Tennis (WCT) singles title over Bjorn Borg. At Wimbledon he defeated Connors 6–1, 6–1, 5–7, 6–4.

Ashe is also the author of the books *Advantage Ashe* and *Portrait in Motion.*

ELGIN BAYLOR
Basketball

The owner of a National Basketball Association team once made a serious offer to trade his entire team for Elgin Baylor of the Lakers—and was quickly turned down! The Laker star is rated among the top three or four players who ever played basketball, his proneness to injury notwithstanding.

Born in 1936 in Washington, D.C., Baylor first became an All-American while attending Spingarn High School. He and R. C. Owens (later a professional football star) then joined forces to lead the College of Idaho to a 23–4 record. When Baylor transferred to Seattle University, he became an All-American as the team won 45 out of 54 games over the next two years, losing to Kentucky in the 1958 NCAA finals.

In 1959 Baylor made a sensational professional debut. He was the first rookie to be named Most Valuable Player in the All Star Game. That same year, he was named to the All-League team, and set a scoring record of 64 points in a single game. After five years as a superstar, Baylor ripped off part of his kneecap during a 1965 playoff game against the Bullets. Constant work brought him back to competitive form, but he never reached his former greatness. His career point total of 23,149 is fourth highest in NBA history, and his field goal average of 27.4 is second. His best year was 1961–1962, when he averaged 38.2 points a game. When he retired in 1968, Baylor had made the All-Pro first team nine times and had played eight consecutive All-Star games.

Inducted into the Black Athletes Hall of Fame in 1975, Baylor is now assistant coach of the Utah Jazz.

Elgin Baylor, one of basketball's all-time top five.

JIM BROWN
Football

A Football Hall of Fame honoree, Jim Brown is still acknowledged by some observers to be the greatest offensive back in the history of football. In many circles, he is viewed as the best all-around athlete since the legendary Jim Thorpe.

The greatest offensive back in football history—Jimmy Brown.

Brown was born February 17, 1936 on St. Simon Island, Georgia, and moved to Manhasset, Long Island at the age of seven. At Manhasset High School he became an outstanding competitor in baseball, football, track and field, basketball, and lacrosse. At graduation, he had a choice of 42 college scholarships, as well as professional offers from both the New York Yankees and the Boston Braves.

Brown chose Syracuse University, where his athletic prowess gained him national recognition. An All-American performer in both football and lacrosse, he turned down the opportunity to compete in the decathlon at the 1956 Olympics because it would have conflicted with his football schedule. When he graduated from Syracuse in 1957, he spurned a three-year $150,000 offer to become a professional fighter.

Brown's 1957 entry into professional football with the Cleveland Browns was emblematic of the manner in which he would dominate the game in the decade to come. He led the league in rushing; paced Cleveland to a division championship; and was unanimously named Rookie of the Year.

Thereafter, Brown broke rushing and scoring records in both single season and lifetime totals, and he was All-League fullback virtually every season. His records include most yards gained, lifetime—12,312, and most touchdowns, lifetime—106. He was voted Football Back of the Decade for 1950–1960.

Brown announced his retirement in the summer of 1966, deciding to devote his time to a budding movie career, and to the improvement of black business. He has made several films, including *Rio Conchos, The Dirty Dozen, Ice Station Zebra, Year of the Cricket, The Split, The Riot,* and *100 Rifles.* In addition to his movie-making activities, he is president and founder of the Negro Industrial and Economic Union, an organization that arranges financing for black businessmen and provides business expertise.

ROY CAMPANELLA
Baseball

The only black baseball star to be named Most Valuable Player for three separate years is Roy Campanella, who won this coveted title in 1951, 1953, and 1955. He is also a member of the Baseball Hall of Fame.

Campanella, the fourth black to establish himself in the modern major leagues, was born in Philadelphia in 1921 and began playing semi-pro baseball 15 years later with the Bacharach Giants. In time, he became part of the hectic life of black professional baseball—touring the states in buses with the Baltimore Elites during the summer, and playing Latin American ball in winter.

In 1945 Campanella turned down the opportunity to become the first black in the major leagues when he mistakenly understood Branch Rickey's offer to be a contract with a rumored black team in Brooklyn. A few days later, he learned from Jackie Robinson that the offer had involved the possibility of playing with the Brooklyn Dodgers of the National League.

In 1946 Campanella was signed by the Dodgers and, along with pitcher Don Newcombe, assigned to their Nashua, New Hampshire team. Two years later, Branch Rickey delayed Campanella's debut with the Dodgers by deciding instead to break the color barrier of the American Association, specifically at St. Paul.

Before the year was out, however, Campanella was brought up to Brooklyn. Over the next eight years, the Dodger star played with five National League pennant winners, and one world championship team. He played on seven consecutive National League All-Star teams (1949–1955).

In January of 1958, Campanella's career as a player was ended by an automobile accident which left him paralyzed, and confined to a wheel chair. Today, he remains active in the game as a sports commentator.

In March 1975 he was inducted into the Black Athletes Hall of Fame in Las Vegas, Nevada.

WILT CHAMBERLAIN
Basketball

Elected to the Basketball Hall of Fame in 1979, Wilt Chamberlain is ranked as the greatest offensive player in the history of the sport. He led the NBA in scoring from 1959 to 1967, and held the single game record of 100 points—a feat he achieved twice.

Chamberlain was born in Philadelphia on August 21, 1936. By the time he entered high school, he was already 6'11", two inches short of his present height.

Unlike most men this tall, Chamberlain is strong, agile, and fast. He has run a 47-second quarter-mile, put a 16-pound shot 55 feet, and high-jumped 6 feet 10 inches. When he graduated from high school, he had his choice of 77 major colleges, and 125 smaller ones. He chose Kansas University, but left after his junior year with two years of All-American honors behind him. He then played with the Harlem Globetrotters before joining the Philadelphia Warriors of the NBA in 1959.

Although dominating the sport with the Philadelphia 76ers (1959–1967) and with the Los Angeles Lakers (1968–1972), Chamberlain was a member of only two championship teams, Philadelphia (1961) and Los Angeles (1972). For his gargantuan effort in defeating the Knicks in the latter series, including playing the final game with both hands painfully injured, he was voted MVP. At the start of the 1974 season, he jumped the Lakers to become player-coach of the San Diego Conquistadors (ABA) for a reported $500,000 contract.

Wilt Chamberlain holds most major basketball records, such as: for single games, most points (100); most field goals made (36); most free throws (28); most rebounds (55). His career records are: most rebounds (23,924); highest scoring average (30.1); most points (31,419); most field goals made (12,681); most free throws attempted (11,862).

ROBERTO CLEMENTE
Baseball

Roberto Clemente was one of the greatest major league baseball players of all time. A devout student of physical condition, he excelled in every facet of the game, and, following 18 big league seasons, seemed capable of playing forever. On December 31, 1972, however, while heading a relief mission for earthquake victims in Nicaragua, his plane crashed shortly after takeoff from San Juan, Puerto Rico, ending his life and career at the age of 38. A fund to continue the relief effort was established in his name.

Born in Carolina, Puerto Rico on August 18, 1934, Clemente was signed by the Brooklyn Dodgers and shipped to their Montreal farm club in 1954. He was drafted by the Pittsburgh Pirates in the off-season and quickly established himself as a major leaguer the following year.

He hit .311 in 1956 but didn't come into his own until the 1960s. His batting averages speak for themselves: .351 in '61, .339 in '64, .329 in '65, .317 in '66, .357 in '67, .345 in '69, .352 in '70, .341 in '71, and .312 in '72.

Clemente also proved himself as an outstanding World Series performer, hitting a combined .362 for the 1960 and 1971 fall classics. His .414 against the Baltimore Orioles in '71 deserves more than honorable mention, especially remembering that he was 37 at the time.

Overall, he won 4 batting titles and was named to 12 All-Star teams. In addition, he earned the league's Most Valuable Player Award in 1966. He achieved his 3,000th base hit, coincidentally, with the final hit of his career.

In the spring of 1973, Clemente was voted into the Hall of Fame in a special election by the Baseball Writers Association of America. His lifetime batting average was .317. In 1975 he was posthumously inducted into the Black Athletes Hall of Fame.

LEE ELDER
Golf

Lee Elder became the first black to play in the coveted Masters Golf Tournament in Augusta, Georgia in 1975. Although he missed the cut that time, he knew he'd be back.

Born in Washington, D.C. in 1935, Elder picked up golf as a 15-year-old caddie in Dallas. After his father's death during World War II, Elder moved his mother to Los Angeles, where he met and traveled with the famed black golfer Ted Rhodes. While learning from Rhodes he was drafted by the Army where he was allowed to sharpen his skills as captain of the golf team at Fort Lewis, Washington. In 1960, after his discharge, he taught at the Langston Golf Course. In 1962 he debuted as a pro winning the United Golf Association (a black organization) National Title. He debuted in the PGA in November 1967 in the Cajun Classic of New Orleans, finishing one stroke out of the money. Prior to his participation on the PGA tour Elder had done 17 years on the Negro tour (participating in close to 50 tournaments). In 30 tournaments as a PGA rookie (1968), Elder earned $38,000 (40th on PGA list of money-winners). Elder was the first black pro to reach $1 million in earnings.

JULIUS ("DR. J") ERVING
Basketball

One of the most exciting players in professional basketball, Julius Erving invariably brings crowds to their feet with such moves as leaping from the foul line to slam dunk the ball. A standout with the Philadelphia 76ers, after several seasons with the New York Nets, Erving was scoring champ and Most Valuable Player of the ABA three times. Between his combined seasons with the two teams, he became the thirteenth player to score 20,000 points.

Born in Hempstead, Long Island, on February 22, 1950, Erving was raised by his mother, who worked as a domestic after his father deserted the family. Throughout a childhood in low-income housing he was always confident he could do something with his life if he stuck to his goals. "I saw that basketball could be my way out and I worked hard to make sure that it was."

As a player at Roosevelt High School, Erving made the All-County and All-Long Island teams while keeping a scholastic average in the 80s. At graduation he chose the University of Massachusetts from many athletic scholarships. Dropping out after junior year, he hired the services of a management firm and signed a $500,000 contract for four years with the Virginia Squires of the ABA. Voted Rookie of the Year in 1972, he renegotiated his contract and eventually landed with the Nets for $2.8 million for four years.

In his first season with the Nets (1973), he led the league in scoring for the second consecutive year and paced his team to the ABA championship. Although bothered by tendonitis in 1974, he had another great year, but the Nets were eliminated in the early rounds of the playoffs. After being traded to the 76ers, Erving became a favorite with Philadelphia fans. He led the 76ers to the NBA championship finals in 1982.

ALTHEA GIBSON
Tennis

Black participation in the world of tennis is so rare that Althea Gibson's rise to the top is truly one of America's more remarkable success stories. In a sport which is traditionally developed on the more affluent private club circuit, she became the most accomplished female player in the world after learning to play paddle tennis on a play street in Harlem.

Born in Silver, South Carolina on August 25, 1927, Miss Gibson was raised in Harlem. After her paddle tennis days, she entered and won the Department of Parks Manhattan Girls' Tennis Championship. In 1942, she began to receive professional coaching at the interracial Cosmopolitan Tennis Club and, a year later, won the New York State Negro Girls Singles Title. In 1945 and 1946, she won the National Negro Girls Singles championship and, in 1948, began a decade of domination of the same title in the Women's Division.

A year later Miss Gibson entered Florida A & M, where she played tennis and basketball for the next four years. In 1950 she was runner-up for the National Indoor Championship and, that same year, became the first black to play at Forest Hills.

The following year she became the first black to play at Wimbledon. In 1957 she won the Wimbledon singles crown, and teamed with Darlene Hard to win the doubles championship as well. When she returned to New York, she was greeted by a ticker-tape parade in recognition of her position as the best woman tennis player in the world.

Since then, Miss Gibson has engaged in public relations work with a bakery firm.

BOB GIBSON
Baseball

Bob Gibson has won more games than anyone else in the history of the St. Louis Cardinals. Despite numerous injuries and ailments throughout his career, he has proven himself as one of the game's top performers.

Born in Omaha, Nebraska on November 9, 1935, Gibson began as a basketball player with the Harlem Globetrotters. He soon turned to baseball, however, and after attending Creighton, signed with the Cardinals in 1957. Following an apprenticeship in the minor leagues, he spent his first full season with the big club in 1961.

Pitching ace Bob Gibson chalked up seven consecutive World Series victories.

He went on to lead his team to pennants in 1964 and 1967, and was instrumental in both World Series victories.

His best year, however, was 1968. He was named Most Valuable Player, led the Cardinals to another pennant, and earned the Cy Young Award, posting a 22-9 record and an incredible 1.12 earned run average, a mark which stands as the lowest for a performance of no less than 200 innings. He also struck out a record 17 batters in a World Series game.

Gibson's other career achievements include a 21-win season and a pair of 19-win performances, a major league record of 8 years with 200 or more strikeouts, a record 7 consecutive World Series victories, a no-hitter (8/14/71), a second Cy Young Award, over 2,900 strikeouts, 55 shutouts, a 4-strikeout inning, and 8 all-star appearances. At the end of 1973 he had boosted his won-lost record to 237-151, for a lifetime percentage of .611.

He also boasts a hitting prowess which includes 22 career home runs, an impressive statistic for a pitcher, and is the only hurler with two World Series homers to his credit.

HARLEM GLOBETROTTERS
Basketball

The most widely known black team in the world is

the Harlem Globetrotters, whose comic brand of basketball has captivated audiences around the globe.

The original Globetrotters, formed in the 1927–1928 basketball season by Abe Saperstein, traveled to local engagements by automobile. The present-day Globetrotters are really three separate troupes playing simultaneously in different parts of the world under the name "Harlem Globetrotters."

The Globetrotters have become more an entertainment package than an athletic team, playing against familiar opponents who travel with them and follow the script. But the athletic ability of the group has always been there when needed. Such stars as Sweetwater Clifton and Wilt Chamberlain went from the Globetrotters to stardom in the National Basketball Association. Other stars have included Reece "Goose" Tatum, and dribbling sensation Marcus Haynes. The current lead clown is Meadowlark Lemon.

The Globetrotters played before the largest audience to see a basketball game when 75,000 fans jammed into Berlin's Olympic Stadium.

BOB HAYES
Track, Football

Known as the "world's fastest human," Olympic sprint champion Bob Hayes became one of professional football's most dazzling performers as a split end and flanker back for the Dallas Cowboys of the National Football League. However, it is his track achievements that remain most impressive.

Hayes still holds the world record for the 100 yard dash, 9.1 seconds, a mark he set on June 21, 1963. At the 1964 Olympics in Tokyo, Hayes came away with two gold medals for victories in the 100 meter dash and the 400 meter relay.

Born on December 20, 1942, in Jacksonville, Florida, Hayes played football in high school, and later attended all-black Florida A & M. He first captured the national track spotlight in 1961 by equalling the then world record of 9.3 seconds for the 100. Two years later, he set his own long-standing record at the National AAU championships in St. Louis, Missouri.

The Harlem Globetrotters have astounded fans the world over with their amazing feats of basketball wizardry.

After finishing college, Hayes signed to play football with the Dallas Cowboys. In 14 games he caught 46 passes for 1,003 yards and 12 touch-downs. In 1965 he led the league in TD pass receptions (12) and average yardage per reception (21.8). He was leading TD pass receiver again in 1966, and punt yardage return leader (276) in 1967. Continuing to be one of the reasons for the Cowboy's dominance of the NFL's Eastern Division, he played in the 1971 and 1972 Superbowls.

Now retired from sports, Hayes is associated with the Consolidated Wig Corp. of Dallas, Texas.

REGGIE JACKSON
Baseball

Because of his outstanding performance in the early fall Reggie Jackson became known as "Mr. October." During his years with the Oakland Athletics and New York Yankees, Jackson captured or tied 13 World Series records to become baseball's greatest record holder for the fall classic.

Reggie Jackson ranks among baseball's crop of players with proven superstar ability. His temperament, long reported to be as explosive and dynamic as his skill with the bat, gave him the drive to reach the top.

Born in Wynecote, Pennsylvania, he followed his father's encouragement to become an all-around athlete in Cheltenham High School, where he ran the 100 in 9.7, starred at halfback, and batted .550. An outstanding football and baseball collegian at Arizona State U, he left after sophomore year to join the Athletics (then located in Kansas City), having been passed over by the New York Mets' draft because, it is rumored, he was considered too hot to handle.

In 1968, his first full season, he hit 29 homers and batted in 74 runs, but made 18 errors and struck out 171 times, the second worst seasonal total in baseball history. He hit 49 homers in 1969, but feuding over money with owner Charlie Finley led to a bad year in 1970. Playing winter ball that year under Frank Robinson's managership seemed to get Jackson back on the track. His performance continued to improve and in 1973 he batted .293, led the league in home runs (32), RBIs (117), and slugging average (.531), and won the MVP.

While with the Oakland Athletics, Jackson appeared as the team participated in three straight World Series—1972, 1973, and 1974. Oakland won each of the championships and Jackson was named series MVP in 1973. Later, with the New York Yankees, Jackson was again prominent as the Yankees participated in the series of 1977, 1978, and 1981. In 1977 he was named series MVP after hitting five home runs, three in the crucial sixth and deciding game.

The first of the big money free agents, Jackson hit 144 homers, drove in 461 runs, and boosted his total career home runs to 425 while with the Yankees for five seasons. In January 1982, after an often stormy tenure, he signed with the California Angels.

JACK JOHNSON
Boxer

Jack Johnson, the first black heavyweight champion, won the crown from Tommy Burns in Sydney, Australia on December 26, 1908. Nat Fleischer, the editor of *Ring* magazine and a foremost boxing authority, has said: "After years devoted to the study of heavyweight fighters, I have no hesitation in naming Jack Johnson as the greatest of them all. He possessed every asset."

Johnson was born in Galveston, Texas in 1878, the son of a school janitor. He was so tiny as a boy that he was nicknamed "Li'l Arthur," a name that stuck with him throughout his career. As a young man, he hoboed around the country, making his way to Chicago, Boston, and New York, and learning the fighting trade by working out with veteran professionals whenever he could. When he finally got his chance at the title, he had already been fighting for nine years and had lost only three of some 100 bouts.

With his victory over Burns, Johnson became the center of a bitter racial controversy, as the American public clamored for the former white champion, Jim Jeffries, to come out of retirement and recapture the crown. When the two fought on July 4, 1910 in Reno, Nevada, Johnson knocked out Jeffries in the fourteenth round.

In 1913 Johnson left the United States because of legal entanglements. Two years later he defended his title against Jess Willard in Havana, Cuba and was knocked out in the twenty-sixth round. His career record was 107 wins, 6 losses.

In 1946 Johnson died in an automobile crash in North Carolina. He was inducted into the Boxing Hall of Fame in 1954.

RAFER JOHNSON
Track and Field

Rafer Johnson holds the Olympic record (set in 1960) for points scored in the decathlon, considered to be the toughest test of all-around athletic ability in the world of sports.

The decathlon consists of 10 events (Greek: deka means 10, athlos means contest) designed to test strength, speed, and agility under the most grueling of conditions. The events are the 100-meter dash, the broad jump, the shot put, the high jump, the 400-meter run, the 100-meter hurdles, the discus throw, the pole vault, the javelin toss, and the 1,500-meter

Jack Johnson, the first black heavyweight champion (1906).

run. Only an athlete with a considerable combination of athletic skills and endurance can compete in such a formidable event.

Johnson was born in Hillsboro, Texas on August 18, 1935, and competed in his first decathlon in 1954 while attending UCLA, where he was president of the student body.

In spite of a knee injury in the 1956 Olympics at Melbourne, Australia, Johnson competed in the event, and finished second to Milt Campbell, another American black who was the first of his race to win an Olympic decathlon.

Competing in Moscow in 1958, Johnson shattered the world record with a total of 8,302 points. Two years later, at the Olympics in Rome, Johnson won the decathlon gold medal with another record-breaking performance, amassing 8,392 points to gain recognition as "the greatest all-around athlete in the world." He is now a director of the Kennedy Foundation.

LEROY KELLY
Football

Leroy Kelly was a dominant force throughout his playing days in the National Football League. Never considered a finesse player, his ability to eat up opposing defenders along with yardage earned him acclaim as one of the league's most powerful running backs.

Born in Philadelphia on May 20, 1942, Kelly attended Morgan State University before joining the Cleveland Browns in 1964. Following two years as apprentice to the great Jim Brown, he became a regular and, soon thereafter, began to prove his star ability.

After leading the league in average yardage on punt returns (15.6) in 1965, he achieved back to back rushing titles in 1967 and 1968, amassing over 1,200 yards each season. His 1968 season made him the third three-time 1,000-yard gainer in NFL history, and he also led in scoring with 20 TDs, a feat seldom accomplished.

Rafer Johnson set the Olympic decathlon record in 1960.

Kelly was an All-Pro selection from 1966 through 1969 and, at the end of his 10-year career, ranked fourth on the National Football League's all-time rushing list with a career mark of 7,274 yards.

He is now a member of Base Enterprises in Los Angeles, a TV producing company.

SUGAR RAY LEONARD
Boxer

In 1981 Sugar Ray Leonard was named Athlete of the Year by ABC-TV's Wide World of Sports and Sportsman of the Year by *Sports Illustrated* magazine.

Just 25 years old, the 1976 Olympic gold medal winner was the undisputed professional welterweight champion. After his Olympic victory, Leonard had embarked on a professional boxing career in 1977 and proceeded to win 25 fights, 16 of them by knockouts, while losing none.

Before a Las Vegas crowd on November 30, 1979,

Leonard KO'd Wilfredo Benitez to win the welterweight crown for the first time. In June 1980 he fought Roberto Duran in Montreal. The purse for that fight was $9.5 million—the largest in boxing history—and Leonard lost by decision. In a climatic November rematch—this time with a purse of $7 million—Leonard won the title back in a New Orleans bout as Duran quit in the eighth round, claiming stomach cramps.

Then, as a two-time World Boxing Council champ, he faced off against Thomas Hearns, the tough World Boxing Association and became the undisputed welterweight champ with a fourteenth-round TKO.

Besides being a talented athlete, Leonard was praised for his sportsmanlike demeanor and his wise business sense, which some observers felt would set a pattern for the boxer of the 1980s. This young multimillionaire and close companion to his wife and son is both a colorful personality and outstanding image for his profession.

JOE LOUIS
Boxer

Joe Louis held the heavyweight championship longer than anyone else (11 years, eight months, and seven days), and defended it more often than any other heavyweight champion. His 25 title fights were more than the combined total of the eight champions who preceded him.

Born in a sharecropper's shack in Chambers County, Alabama in 1914, Louis moved to Detroit as a small boy. Taking up boxing later as an amateur, he won 50 out of 59 bouts (43 by knockout) before turning professional in 1934. He quickly gained a reputation in the Midwest and in 1935 came East to meet Primo Carnera, the former champion who was then staging a comeback. Louis knocked out Carnera in six rounds, and earned his nickname, "The Brown Bomber."

After knocking out ex-champion Max Baer, Louis suffered his lone pre-championship defeat at the hands of Max Schmeling, the German titleholder who knocked him out in the twelfth round. Less than a month later, Louis knocked out another former champion, Jack Sharkey, in three rounds. After defeating a number of other challengers, he was given a title fight with Jim Braddock on June 22, 1937. He stopped Braddock in the eighth round, and began the long championship reign that was to see him defending his crown as often as six times in six months (1941), and

Sugar Ray Leonard

battering Schmeling to the canvas in one round in their 1938 return bout.

One of Louis' greatest fights was his 1941 come-from-behind thirteenth-round-knockout of Billy Conn. After winning a disputed decision over Joe Walcott in 1947, Louis knocked out the Jersey challenger six months later, and then went into retirement.

His later comeback attempts against the likes of Ezzard Charles and Rocky Marciano were unsuccessful.

Joe Louis died April 12, 1981 at the age of 67.

WILLIE MAYS
Baseball

In his 21 seasons with the Giants, Willie Mays hit more than 600 home runs. Besides being a solid hitter, Mays also has been called the game's finest defensive outfielder and perhaps its best baserunner as well.

Born in Fairfield, Alabama on May 6, 1931, Mays made his professional debut on July 4, 1948 with the Birmingham Black Barons. He was signed by the Giants in 1950 and reached the major leagues in 1951—in time to become the National League's Rookie of the Year with 20 home runs, 68 RBIs, and the sensational fielding which contributed to his team's pennant victory.

After two years in the Army, Mays returned to lead the Giants to the World Championship in 1954, gaining recognition as the league's Most Valuable Player for his 41 homers, 110 RBIs and .345 batting average.

After the Giants moved to San Francisco, Mays continued his phenomenal home run hitting, and led his team to a 1962 pennant. A year later, *Sport* magazine named him "the greatest player of the decade." He won the MVP award again in 1965, after hitting 52 home runs and batting .317.

Traded back to the New York National League team (the Mets) before the 1972 season, he continued to play outfield and first base. At the end of the 1973 season, his records included 2,992 games (3rd on the all-time list), 3,283 hits (7th), and 660 home runs (3rd).

Willie Mays is one of the only seven ballplayers to have hit four home runs in one game. In addition to that he was the only black member of the living all-time baseball team selected in 1969 by the Baseball Writer's Association of America. After acting as a coach for the Mets, Mays left baseball to pursue a business career. He was elected to the Baseball Hall of Fame in 1979.

Baseball immortal Willie Mays collected over 3,250 hits in 22 seasons.

JESSE OWENS
Track and Field

The track and field records Jesse Owens once set have all been eclipsed, but his reputation as one of the first great athletes with the combined talents of a sprinter, low hurdler, and a broad jumper has hardly diminished with the passing of time.

Born on September 12, 1913 in Danville, Alabama, Owens moved to Ohio at an early age. The name "Jesse" derived from the way a teacher pronounced his initials, "J. C." In 1932, while attending East Technical High School in Cleveland, Owens gained national fame with a 10.3 clocking in the 100-meter dash.

Two years later Owens entered Ohio State University and for the next four years made track history, becoming universally known as "The Ebony Antelope." While competing in the Big Ten Championships at Ann Arbor, Michigan on May 25, 1935, Owens had what has been called "the greatest single day in the history of man's athletic achievements." In the space of about 70 minutes, he tied the world record for the 100-yard dash and surpassed the world record for five other events, including the broad jump, the 220-yard low hurdles, and the 220-yard dash.

In 1936, at the Berlin Olympics, Owens won four gold medals, at that time the most universally acclaimed feat in the history of the games. When Adolf Hitler refused to present him medals he had won in the various competitions, Owens' fame became even more widespread as a result of the publicity.

SATCHEL PAIGE
Baseball

Long before Jackie Robinson broke the color barrier of "organized baseball," Satchel Paige was a name well-known to the general sports public. As the outstanding performer in "Negro baseball," Paige had become a legendary figure whose infrequent encounters with major league players (he defeated Dizzy Dean in a 1–0 game in 1933 and, four years later, was called "the best pitcher I ever faced" by Joe DiMaggio) added considerable laurels to his athletic reputation.

Paige was born in Mobile, Alabama in September 1904, and began playing semi-pro ball while working as an iceman and porter. In the mid-1920s he became a professional with the Birmingham Black Barons and later, while playing at Chattanooga, acquired the nickname "Satchel" because of his "Satchel-sized feet."

For the next two decades, Paige compiled a phenomenal record. In 1933 he won 31 games and lost four. The following year, he pitched for a Brunswick, North Dakota team which reportedly took 104 out of 105 games, with Paige himself starting a total of 29 games over a one-month span. Along with Josh Gibson and

other black stars, Paige, also dominated winter ball in Latin America during the 1930s.

In 1942 Paige led the Kansas City Monarchs to victory in the Negro World Series, and four years later he helped them to the pennant by allowing only two runs in 93 innings, a performance which included a skein of 64 straight scoreless innings.

In 1948, when he was brought up to the major leagues, Paige was well past his prime, but he still was able to contribute six victories in Cleveland's pennant drive. Four years' later, while pitching for the St. Louis Browns, he was named to the American League All-Star squad.

Up until the 1969 baseball season Paige was primarily active on the barnstorming circuit with the Harlem Globetrotters and a host of other exhibition teams. It was in 1969 that the Atlanta Braves, in an attempt to make Paige eligible for baseball's pension plan, signed him to a one-year contract as coach.

Satchel Paige died in June 1982.

PELE
Soccer

The undisputed all-time king of world soccer is Edson Arantes do Nascimento, known to his fans as Pele. He has led his Santos (Brazil) Football Club to five South American championships and two world championships (1962, 1963) and has sparked the Brazilian National Team's first World Cup victory (1958) and its defense of the title (1962). In international competition, he has maintained an awesome average of nearly a goal a game.

Born in Tres Coracocs, Brazil, on October 23, 1940, Pele began playing soccer as a youngster. His father had been a minor league soccer player besides working as a civil servant. At 15 Pele left the provinces, and his $2 a month job as a shoemaker's apprentice, and within a year he had won a starting berth on the major league Santos team.

Famous for his speed and ball control, Pele has performed many remarkable feats. In the 1962 defense of the World Cup in Lisbon, Portugal, he scored three goals and passed for two others in Brazil's 5–2 triumph.

Pele's private life is quiet and serious. Concerned with setting a good example for youth, he refuses to do cigarette or alcohol commercials. In response to U.S. interviewers he said that, despite being married to a white woman, he's "never been faced with any kind of race problems. . . . In Brazil no one thinks that way."

Pele, soccer's all-time goal leader with a total of 1,281 points in 22 years, was the highest paid player in any professional sport, receiving $4.75 million for two years—about 100 games—with the New York Cosmos. He retired and became a good will ambassador for the sport, appearing in the feature film *Victory* with Sylvester Stallone.

WILLIS REED
Basketball

After seven seasons with the New York Knicks—which included two world championships and several playoff berths—Willis Reed returned to the team as head coach during the 1977–1978 season. His debut proved to be quite a challenge and he stayed with the team only until the beginning of the following season. By the 1981–1982 season he decided to return to coaching—this time on the college level at Creighton University.

A native of Louisiana, Reed spent his boyhood picking cotton around his hometown of Bernice, where he was born in 1943. He attended Grambling College, where he was discovered by Red Holzman, then the Knicks' chief scout.

Reed led the Knicks in scoring and rebounding on his way to becoming Rookie of the Year in 1965. As he matured, he captured rave notices from opposing centers who admired his shooting prowess and jarring "picks." In 1970, when the Knicks won their first title, Reed was voted three separate MVP awards: one for the regular season, one for the All-Star game, and one for the playoffs. Particularly memorable was his astonishing comeback after being injured in the fifth game of the playoffs against the Los Angeles Lakers. With Reed sidelined, Chamberlain dominated the sixth game and the Lakers romped to a 135–113 victory. In the seventh and deciding game, Reed took the floor, his mobility seriously impaired by his injured leg and hip, and scored the first two baskets of the night. The Knicks won the game handily and took the title back to New York.

At 6'9" and 240 pounds, Reed is not at all big for a center. However, he was named to the All Star team his first seven seasons. He missed the 1972 season because of knee trouble. Able to return in 1973 after operations, he captained the Knicks to their second title and won the playoff MVP. Unfortunately, continued knee problems ended his career.

Reed is active in a number of business ventures, including a basketball camp and a farm in Louisiana.

OSCAR ROBERTSON
Basketball

Standing 6'5", Oscar Robertson is remembered as the best "small man" in professional basketball—particularly in view of his outstanding scoring and playmaking ability. Averaging 25.7 points a game, he ended up as the second leading scorer in NBA history, with a point total of 26,710.

Born on November 29, 1938 in Charlotte, Tennes-

Oscar Robertson drives for the hoop and second highest point total in NBA history.

see, Robertson is the great-grandson of Marshall Collier, an ex-slave who died in 1954 at the age of 116, allegedly the oldest person in the United States at that time. The Robertsons moved to Indianapolis when Oscar was three. As soon as he and his brothers were old enough, they began playing basketball at the local YMCA. Oscar's oldest brother, Baily, later played briefly for the Harlem Globetrotters.

At Crispus Attucks High School, Robertson led his team to the first unbeaten season in Indiana history, a 45-game winning streak, and two consecutive state championships. He was All-State for three years, broke numerous individual scoring records, and was named a high school All-American. In addition to starring on the baseball and track teams, Robertson also was a member of the National Honor Society.

At the University of Cincinnati, Robertson became the nation's leading scorer as a sophomore, then went on to set 14 major collegiate records while leading his team to 89 wins in 98 games.

As a professional with the Cincinnati Royals, he became the game's leading backcourt scorer. He holds the records for highest assist average in the season (11.5 in 1964–1965) and for most assists in a career: 9,887. While second to Chamberlain in free throws attempted, he ranks first in free throws made. Three times MVP (1961, 1964, and 1969), Robertson was traded to the Milwaukee Bucks, becoming a key part of the 1970–1971 championship team.

He is now a TV sports announcer.

FRANK ROBINSON
Baseball

Frank Robinson is major league baseball's first black manager. Named to the head post of the Cleveland Indians in October of 1974, he lost none of the calm control that carried him through 18 consistently good seasons as a player. On the first day of the 1975 season he put himself into the lineup as designated hitter and boomed career home run 575.

Robinson left the Indians, but was hired for a new manager's position with the San Francisco Giants during the 1981 season. At season's end, his contract was extended an additional two years. In January 1982 he was voted into the Baseball Hall of Fame.

Born in Beaumont, Texas in 1936, Robinson moved with his family to Oakland, California at the age of five. During his teens, he was a football and baseball star at McClyronds High School (which also produced Bill Russell, Vada Pinson, and Curt Flood). After graduation in 1953, he signed with the Cincinnati Reds.

In his first year of professional ball, Robinson batted .348 and led Ogden, Utah to the Pioneer League pennant. The following year, he batted .336 in the Sally League.

In 1956 he made a smash debut in the major leagues, hitting 38 homers and winning Rookie of the Year honors. Over the next eight years, he hit 259 homers and had 800 RBIs, an outstanding record, but one which was often underpublicized playing in the shadow of such greats as Willie Mays and Hank Aaron.

In 1961, Robinson was named Most Valuable Player for leading Cincinnati to the National League pennant. Five years later, Robinson won the American League's Triple Crown and became the first player to win the MVP in both leagues. By the end of the 1973 season he had hit .297 in 2,432 games with 2,614 hits, 1,639 runs, and 1,613 RBIs.

JACKIE ROBINSON
Baseball

Jackie Robinson's pioneer efforts in breaking the color barrier in organized baseball not only opened the door for other black players but for black athletes in all major American sports.

Robinson's importance, however, can never be limited to the sociological feat which he performed. It was solely on the basis of his playing baseball that he was named, on July 3, 1962, to the Hall of Fame in Cooperstown, New York.

Born in Cairo, Georgia on January 31, 1919, Robinson was raised in Pasadena, California. At UCLA he gained All-American honorable mention as a halfback, but he left college in his junior year to play professional football for the Los Angeles Bulldogs. After serving as an Army lieutenant during World War II, Robinson returned to civilian life with the hope of becoming a physical education coach. To achieve this, he felt he had to make a name for himself and, for this reason, decided to spend a few seasons in black baseball.

In 1945, while he was playing with the Kansas City Monarchs, Branch Rickey of the Brooklyn Dodgers assigned him to the Montreal Royals, the team's top farm club, where he was to be groomed for a career in the majors.

On April 10, 1947, the Dodgers announced that they had purchased Robinson's contract and the following day he began his major league career. When he retired in 1956, he had compiled an outstanding record as a hitter, fielder, and base-stealer.

During a 10-year career, he hit .311 in 1,382 games with 1,518 hits, 947 runs, 273 doubles, and 734 RBIs. He stole home 19 times, once in World Series play. He won the National League's Most Valuable Player award in 1949, and played on six National League pennant winners, as well as one world championship team.

After retirement, Robinson became a bank official, president of a land development firm, and a director of programs to combat drug addiction. He died on October 24, 1972 in Stamford, Connecticut.

Baseball's first black manager, Frank Robinson, won MVP awards in both leagues.

"SUGAR RAY" ROBINSON
Boxer

Sugar Ray Robinson is often labeled the greatest fighter pound-for-pound in the history of boxing.

Born Walker Smith in Detroit on May 3, 1920, he took the name Robinson from the certificate of an amateur boxer whose identity enabled him to meet the age requirements for getting a match in Michigan. The "Sugar" came from his having been dubbed "the sweetest fighter."

As a 10-year-old boy, Robinson had watched a Detroit neighbor, Joe Louis, train for an amateur boxing career. When Robinson moved to New York two years later, he began to spend most of his time at local gyms in preparation for his own amateur career.

After winning all 89 of his amateur bouts and the 1939 Golden Gloves featherweight championship as well, he turned professional in 1940 at Madison Square Garden, fighting for the first time on a card headlined by the Fritzie Zivic-Henry Armstrong fight. (Armstrong, Robinson's idol, lost the fight.) A year later, Robinson himself decisioned Zivic, and, three months after that, knocked him out.

After several years of being "the uncrowned king of the welterweights," Robinson beat Tommy Bell in an elimination title bout in December 1946. He successfully defended the title for five years and, on February 14, 1951, took the middleweight crown from Jake La-Motta.

In July 1951 he lost the title to Randy Turpin, only to win it back two months later. Retiring for a time, Robinson subsequently fought a series of exciting battles with Carl "Bobo" Olsen, Carmen Basilio, and Gene Fullmer before retiring permanently, on December 10, 1965, with six victories in title bouts to his credit—more than any other fighter in history.

Bad investments have whittled away his fortune. He is the founder of the Sugar Ray Robinson Youth Foundation in Los Angeles.

WILMA RUDOLPH
Track and Field

Wilma Rudolph is the only American woman runner ever to win three gold medals in the Olympic Games. Her performance is all the more remarkable in light of the fact that she had double pneumonia and scarlet fever as a young child and could not walk without braces until age 11.

Born on June 23, 1940, in St. Bethlehem, Tennessee, she soon moved with her family to Clarksville, the town in which she grew up. At an early age, she survived an attack of double pneumonia and scarlet fever, but was left with the use of her right leg only. Through daily leg massages administered in turn by different members of her family, she progressed to the point where, at the age of eight, she was able to walk only with the aid of a special left shoe. Three years later, however, she discarded the shoe, and began joining her brother in backyard basketball games.

At Burt High School in Clarksville, Miss Rudolph broke the state basketball record for girls while a sophomore. As a sprinter, she was undefeated in all her high school track meets.

In 1957 she enrolled at Tennessee State University and began to set her sights for the Olympics in Rome three years later. In the interim she gained national recognition in collegiate meets, setting the world record for 200 meters in July 1960.

In the Olympics she earned the title of the "World's Fastest Woman" by winning gold medals for the 100-meter dash; the 200-meter dash (Olympic record); and for anchoring the 400-meter relay (world record). She was named by the Associated Press as the U.S. Female Athlete of the Year for 1960, and also won United Press Athlete of the Year honors.

She is assistant director of athletics for the Mayor's Youth Foundation in Chicago.

BILL RUSSELL
Basketball

Bill Russell, who led the Boston Celtics to 11 titles, 8 in a row, is regarded as the finest defensive basketball player in the game's history. The 6'10" star is also the first black to coach and play for a National Basketball Association team. His style of play is credited with revolutionizing basketball.

Russell was born on February 12, 1934 in Monroe, Louisiana. The family moved to Detroit when he was nine. Two years later, after his mother died, they continued on to Oakland. There, at McClyronds High School (the starting point for numerous black professional athletes), Russell proved to be an awkward but determined basketball player who eventually received a scholarship to the nearby University of San Francisco.

In college, Russell came into his own, in his sophomore year becoming the most publicized athlete on the West Coast. Over the next two years, his fame spread across the nation as he led his team to 60 consecutive victories (a collegiate record) and two straight NCAA titles.

The Celtics had never won the title before Russell's arrival, but since his specialties (blocking shots, rebounding outstandingly) were added to their attack, they became the most successful team in the history of professional sports, winning the world championship eight years in a row. Russell himself was named Most Valuable Player on five separate occasions (1958, 1961–1963, 1965).

Wilma Rudolph won the 1960 Olympic gold medals for the 100 meter run, 200 meter run, and 400 meter relay.

After the 1968–1969 season, having led the Celtics to their eleventh NBA crown, Russell retired as both coach and player. The move had its impact on the team, for the next season (1969–1970) the Celtics failed to make the playoffs for the first time in a good many years. The NBA's Most Valuable Player five times, Russell is the NBA leader in career minutes (40,726) and second in career rebounds (21,721).

After retirement, Russell was a color commentator on NBC-TV's NBA Game of the Week. In 1974 he returned to active basketball, accepting a lucrative contract to be head coach and general manager of the Seattle Supersonics. That year, he was inducted into the Basketball Hall of Fame.

GALE SAYERS
Football

Gale Sayers was an All-Pro running back with the Chicago Bears from 1965 to 1971, during which time he was considered football's greatest offensive weapon. In 1965 the 200-pound 22-year-old Sayers combined great speed and agility with explosive power to capture Rookie of the Year Honors in the National Football League in what was surely the most remarkable debut in professional football. Not only did Sayers win the scoring title but, in the process, he also broke the league scoring record with 22 touchdowns (including six in one game).

Sayers was born in Wichita, Kansas and moved to Omaha, Nebraska in 1952. At the University of Kansas, he earned All-American honors and received $50,000 for signing with the Bears.

A dazzling runner from scrimmage, he was also adept at punt and kickoff returns and showed pass-catching and pass-throwing ability. In 1966, having set the scoring standard the previous year, Sayers led the league in rushing with 1,231 yards. In 1968, en route to one of his best years ever, Sayers suffered a crippling knee injury. During the off season, there was much speculation as to whether Sayers would ever be able to play again. In the 1969 season Sayers not only played but led the league in rushing as well, with 1,032 yards.

In March 1975, accepting his nomination to the Black Athletes Hall of Fame from O. J. Simpson, he asked today's black stars to "drop back down and give young black athletes wise counsel about the pitfalls of professional sports."

CHARLES SIFFORD
Golf

Charlie Sifford started caddying at the age of nine in his hometown of Charlotte, North Carolina. As a 13-year-old Sifford won a Charlotte tournament for caddies. In the late 1930s he moved to Philadelphia, where it was somewhat easier for a black golfer to gain access to a golf course.

From 1947 to 1953 Sifford worked between matches as private golf instructor and sometime chauffeur and valet to singer Billy Eckstine, who later offered Sifford the financial support he needed to keep playing golf. From 1953 on he won the Negro National title six times. In the late fifties Charlie got to play in a few tournaments on the PGA tour. In 1967 on the tour Sifford earned $57,000. In 1968 he added $33,000 more from competing on the tour. In 1968 he won the first PGA tournament of the year, the Los Angeles Open, copping the $20,000 first prize. The victory was his second major one (he had earned $20,000 in 1967 while winning the Hartford Open).

O. J. SIMPSON
Football

Orenthal J. Simpson may have been the finest running back in pro football. Nicknamed "The Juice," he holds rushing records for most yards in a single game and most yards in a single season.

Born in San Francisco on July 9, 1947, Simpson began his football days at the University of Southern California, culminating with a Heisman Trophy in 1968. A year prior to that, he was a member of the relay team which set a world record of 38.6 seconds in the 440-yard run. A year after graduation, ABC Sports voted him College Player of the Decade.

He signed with the Buffalo Bills in 1969 and, three years later, achieved his first rushing title, gaining over 1,200 yards.

Then came his record-breaking 1973 season. On opening day, he rushed for 250 yards against the New England Patriots, breaking the record of 247 yards held by Willie Ellison. He gained an astonishing 2,003 yards for the entire season, surpassing the previous mark of 1,863 yards held by Jim Brown. In addition, he scored 12 touchdowns, averaged 6 yards per carry, and had more rushing yardage than 15 of the other NFL clubs. He was named Player of the Year and won the Jim Thorpe Trophy.

Recently retired from football, O. J. has begun a movie career with feature parts in *The Towering Inferno* and *The Klansman,* and he also works for ABC-TV sports.

PAUL WARFIELD
Football

Paul Warfield combined speed with great hands to baffle defenses from his first year in the league, leading to All-Pro recognition in four of his first seven seasons.

Born in Warren, Ohio on November 28, 1942, Warfield attended Ohio State University.

In 1964, his first year with the Cleveland Browns, he caught 52 passes, good for 920 yards and 9 touchdowns. Similar seasons followed. In 1968, he made 50 receptions, gained 1,067 yards, and scored 12 touchdowns. A year later he posted 42 catches, gained 886 yards, and recorded 10 scores.

Warfield was traded to the Miami Dolphins in 1970 and, the following year, had another outstanding season (43/996/11). In addition, he went on to help the Dolphins to three consecutive Super Bowl appearances. At the end of the 1974 season Warfield jumped from Miami to sign a seven-figure contract with the Memphis Southmen of the World Football League.

OTHER NOTABLE BLACK BASEBALL PLAYERS

Name	Position	Born
Tommie Agee	of	1942
Dick Allen	1b	1942
Felipe Alou	of	1935
Jesus Alou	of	1943
Matty Alou	of	1938
Dusty Baker	of	1949
Gene Baker	if	1918
Dan Bankhead	p	1924
Sammy Bankhead	if	1905
Ernie Banks	ss	1931

Name	Position	Born	Name	Position	Born
Earl Battey	c	1935	Tony Oliva	of	1940
Johnny Beckwith	of	1902	Al Oliver	of	1946
James "Cool Papa" Bell	of	1905	Amos Otis	of	1947
Paul Blair	of	1944	Tony Perez	1b	1942
Vida Blue	p	1949	Vada Pinson	of	1938
Bobby Bonds	of	1946	Juan Pizarro	p	1937
Chet Brewer	p	1902	Floyd Robinson	of	1936
Johnny Briggs	of	1944	Manny Sanguillen	c	1944
Lou Brock	of	1939	George Scott	1b	1944
Gates Brown	of	1939	Ken Singleton	of	1947
Ollie Brown	of	1944	Reggie Smith	of	1945
Ray Brown	p	1903	Charlie Spikes	of	1951
Willard Brown	of	1921	Willie Stargell	of	1941
Billy Bruton	of	1929	Luis Tiant	p	1940
Bert Campaneris	ss	1942	Bobby Tolan	of	1945
Jose Cardenal	of	1943	Quincy Troupe	c	1922
Leo Cardenas	ss	1938	Bob Veale	p	1935
Rod Carew	2b	1945	Zoilo Versalles	ss	1940
Rico Carty	of	1939	Leon Wagner	of	1934
Dave Cash	2b	1948	Bob Watson	of	1946
Cesar Cedeno	of	1951	Bill White	1b	1934
Orlando Cepeda	1b	1937	Roy White	of	1943
Donn Clendenon	1b	1935	Billy Williams	of	1938
Nate Colbert	1b	1946	Earl Williams	1b	1948
Wes Covington	of	1932	Maury Wills	ss	1932
Willie Crawford	of	1946	Don Wilson	p	1945
Mike Cuellar	p	1937	Earl Wilson	p	1935
Tommy Davis	of	1939	Jimmy Wynn	of	1942
Willie Davis	of	1940			
Larry Doby	of	1924			
Al Downing	p	1941			
Dock Ellis	p	1945			
Curt Flood	of	1938			
Andy "Rube" Foster	p	1879			
Ralph Garr	of	1945			
Josh Gibson	c	1911			
Tony Gonzalez	of	1936			

OTHER NOTABLE BLACK FOOTBALL PLAYERS

Name	Position	Born
Herb Adderly	DB	1939
Lem Barney	CB	1946
Bill Bell	T	1909
Bobby Bell	LB	1942
Elvin Bethea	DE	1946
Verlon Biggs	DE	1942
Emerson Boozer	RB	1943
John Brockington	RB	1949
Bob Brown	DT	1940
Larry Brown	RB	1947
Timmy Brown	RB	
Willie Brown	CB	1941
Fred Carr	LB	1946
Charlie Cowan	T	1938
Curley Culp	DT	1946
Clem Daniels	RB	
Earl Edwards	DE	1946
Carl Eller	DE	1942
Chuck Foreman	RB	1949
John Gilliam	WR	1945
Cornell Green	DB	1940
Joe Greene	DT	1947

Additional names from the left column (baseball):

Name	Position	Born
Tommy Harper	of	1940
Jim Ray Hart	3b	1941
George Hendrick	of	1949
Willie Horton	of	1942
Elston Howard	c	1929
Monte Irvin	of	1919
Ferguson Jenkins	of	1943
Alex Johnson	of	1942
Cleon Jones	of	1942
Buck Leonard	1b	1907
Dave Lopes	2b	1946
Juan Marichal	p	1937
Carlos May	of	1948
Lee May	1b	1943
John Mayberry	1b	1950
Al McBean	p	1938
Willie McCovey	1b	1938
Hal McRae	of	1946
Willie Montanez	1b	1948
Joe Morgan	2b	1943
Manny Mota	of	1938

OTHER NOTABLE BLACK FOOTBALL PLAYERS
(*continued*)

Name	Position	Born
L. C. Greenwood	DE	1947
Roosevelt Grier	DB	
Cedrick Hardman	DE	1949
Franco Harris	RB	1950
Calvin Hill	RB	1947
Winston Hill	T	1942
Claude Humphrey	DE	1944
Harold Jackson	WR	1946
Roy Jefferson	WR	1944
Jimmy Johnson	CB	1938
Ron Johnson	RB	1948
Walter Johnson	DT	1943
Deacon Jones	DB	
Dick "Night Train" Lane	RB	
Willie Lanier	LB	1945
Floyd Little	RB	1942
Larry Little	G	1945
Carl "Spider" Lockhart	DB	1943
John Mackey	TE	
Jim Marshall	DE	1938
Reggie McKenzie	G	1950
Lenny Moore	RB	
Mercury Morris	RB	1947
Alan Page	DT	1945
Jim Parker	T	1934
Woody Peoples	G	1943
Don Perkins	RB	1938
Joe "The Jet" Perry	RB	1927
Fritz Pollard	RB	1895
Jethro Pugh	DT	1944
Mel Renfro	CB	1942
Paul Robeson	RB	1898
Dave Robinson		
Paul Robinson	RB	1947
Charlie Sanders	TE	1946
Art Shell	T	1947
Paul Smith	DT	1945
Ron Smith	DB	1943
Matt Snell	RB	
Bruce Taylor	CB	1948
Charley Taylor	WR	1942
Lionel Taylor	WR	
Otis Taylor	WR	1942
Duane Thomas	RB	1947
Gene Upshaw	G	1945
Gene Washington	WR	1947
Warren Wells	WR	1944
Charley West	RB	1899
Ernie Wheelwright	RB	1939
Freeman White	WR	1943
Travis Williams	RB	1946
Willie Williams	DB	1942
Bill Willis	G	1928
Rayfield Wright	T	1945
Tank Younger	RB	1921

OTHER NOTABLE BLACK BASKETBALL PLAYERS

Name	Position	Born
Nate Archibald	G	1948
Dick Barnett	G	1936
Dave Bing	G	1943
Austin Carr	G	1948
Phil Chenier	G	1950
Wayne Embry	C	1937
Walt Frazier	G	1945
Artis Gilmore	C	1948
Hal Greer	G	1936
Elvin Hayes	C	1945
Spencer Haywood	F	1949
Lou Hudson	G	1944
Lucious Jackson	F	1941
Sam Jones	F	1933
Bob Lanier	C	1948
Bob Love	F	1942
Bob McAdoo	C	1951
George McGinnis	F	1950
Earl Monroe	G	1944
Nate Thurmond	C	1941
Wes Unseld	F	1946
Chet Walker	F	1940
Jo Jo White	G	1946
Sidney Wicks	F	1949
Lenny Wilkens	G	1937

OTHER NOTABLE BLACK TRACK AND FIELD STARS

Name	Born
Dave Albritton	1918
Johnny Borican	1918
Ralph Boston	1940
Earlene Brown	1935
Frank Budd	1925
John Carlos	1946
Alice Coachman	1921
Josh Culbreath	1935
Willie Davenport	1943
Harrison Dillard	1923
Howard P. Drew	1890
Eddie Hart	1948
Jimmy Hines	1946
DeHart Hubbard	1899
Cornelius Johnson	1918
Ralph Metcalfe	1910
Rod Milburn	1950
Ira Murchison	1933
Mel Pender	1937
Tommie Smith	1944
John Thomas	1941
Edward Tolan	1911
Mal Whitfield	1921
Johnny "Longjohn" Woodruff	1917

OTHER NOTABLE BLACK BOXERS

Name	Division	Born
Henry Aldridge	middleweight	1946
Paul Armstead	lightweight	1937
Hogan "Kid" Bassey[a]	bantamweight	1932
Joe Brown[a]	lightweight	
Panama Al Brown[a]	bantamweight	1904
Ezzard Charles[a]	heavyweight	
Curtis Cokes[a]	welterweight	1939
Jimmy Ellis[a] (WBA)	heavyweight	1944
Zora Folley	heavyweight	
George Foreman[a]	heavyweight	1949
Bob Foster[a]	light heavyweight	
Joe Frazier[a]	heavyweight	1944
Joe Gans[a]	lightweight	1874
George Godfrey	heavyweight	1853
Emile Griffith[a]	middleweight	1938
Beau Jack[a]	lightweight	1921
Peter Jackson	heavyweight	1861
Harold Johnson[a]	light heavyweight	
Doug Jones	heavyweight	
Sam Langford	heavyweight	1886
John Henry Lewis[a]	light heavyweight	1914
Sonny Liston[a]	heavyweight	
Eddie Machen	heavyweight	
Tom Molineaux	heavyweight	1784
Bob Montgomery[a]	lightweight	1919
Archie Moore[a]	light heavyweight	
Davey Moore[a]	featherweight	
Jose Napoles[a]	welterweight	
Ken Norton	heavyweight	
Benny "Kid" Paret[a]	welterweight	
Floyd Patterson[a]	heavyweight	
Luis Rodriguez[a]	welterweight	1937
Joe "Sandy" Saddler[a]	featherweight	1926
Johnny Saxton[a]	welterweight	
Battling Siki[a]	light heavyweight	1897
Bob Smith	heavyweight	1840
Ernie Terrell[a] (WBA)	heavyweight	1935
Mervine Thompson	heavyweight	1869
Dick Tiger[a]	light heavyweight	1929
Bob Travers	heavyweight	1836
Gil Turner	middleweight	1928
Jersey Joe Walcott[a]	heavyweight	1914
Cleveland Williams	heavyweight	
Ike Williams[a]	lightweight	1923
Harry Wills	heavyweight	1889
Jackie Wilson[a]	featherweight	1909
Chalky Wright[a]	featherweight	1917

[a] Denotes champion.

BLACK WRITERS, SCHOLARS, AND POETS

Present Issues ■ The Harlem Renaissance ■ Activism ■ Outstanding Literary Figures

In the wake of the civil rights "revolution" of the 1960s, the voices of black Americans were being raised and heard as never before, and major publishing houses became eager to put into print the expressions of black writers. For a time, the reading public expressed active interest in the many previously ignored black themes and perspectives, but such interest was relatively short-lived. Toward the end of the 1970s black writers were discovering that white-owned publishing houses were becoming increasingly inaccessible.

Many black writers began to write books for children and for young people using African or Afro-American settings. Black writers found that the market for young people was far better than that for black adult books. Black poets and novelists, however, continue to publish books of poetry and novels dealing with the black problem in today's society. Black playwrights also wrote and had many of their contemporary plays produced on stage, and a few blacks wrote in the area of science fiction.

Books by such authors as Richard Wright and Zora Neale Hurston were revived and there were bio-bibliographies, autobiographies, and biographies written about many of the black writers.

One of the more important development in black writing was the emergence of the black woman. Black women received further recognition through the white feminist movement and publishing houses that were kind to women. Perhaps the biggest trend in black writing has been the Alex Haley *Roots* syndrome. The resounding success of *Roots* stimulated great interest in Africa and black geneology and history. Many books of family geneology have been written and published. Such historical novels and plays as *The Chaneysville Incident* and *The Brownsville Raid* were written, all of which perhaps had been greatly stimulated by the *Roots* phenomenon. Many books on the history of blacks in the various sections of the Middle West, the Far West, the South, and the North were published— mainly by noncommercial or university presses. The authors of these books were black as well as white writers.

The Issue

The issue that permeates the writings of all members of acknowledged minorities, be they Eskimoes, Jews, Rosicrucians, or blacks, is whether to try in their writings to further the particular cause of their group or, through observation and self-expression, to help illuminate the universal human condition. Though the two goals are not always mutually exclusive, few writers can avoid a commitment to one position or the other at some point during their career.

The great problem faced by the black writer to this day, and especially before the Renaissance of the 1920s, was that he was not allowed a choice. Literary dominion in the United States—the establishment of publishers, editors, critics, and professors—has been lodged in the hands of whites, whose tastes determined the authors who were to be published, promoted, and praised. Until the 1920s these people, often innocently, left no room for those blacks who chose to write in the black idiom.

Much of the early literature produced by American blacks (as with Phillis Wheatley) was merely imitative of the general literature of the time, its racial facet being the attempt to exhibit the writer's intrinsic effort as sufficient refutation of the belief that the black was an inherently inferior creature. Other early works were little more than pious tracts written to assure the masters that the servants wanted nothing more than to serve in religious humility, as in the case of Jupiter Hammon. In contrast to these, however, there was also a long succession of autobiographical narratives by former slaves who chose to attack the existing system in an attempt to force "White America" to look into the human face of "Negro America."

From the post-Reconstruction period to the decade of the 1920s, much of American black literature was an attempt to show the general public that blacks could be as respectably middle class in outlook and ideals as whites. If much of "Negro America" was unable to afford the creature comforts of such an environment, it could still produce literary commentaries which would at least show a people happily laughing at their assigned lot.

It was in the 1920s that black literature made a sharp change of direction, removing itself once and for all from polite and straitlaced conventions and its grinning, dancing, ingratiating manner. With the emergence of the "Harlem School" came a sense of racial pride which expressed itself in earthy, realistic terms—the protests of both the black and white establishments notwithstanding.

Self-Expression and the Renaissance

Oddly, despite acclaim for many authors and poets of the Harlem Renaissance, black writers were never considered part of American literature, or at best were viewed as a distant phase of it. Blacks could, as Willard Motley and Frank Yerby were to do, write as individual observers without reference to their racial interests or background. But despite the integrationist political stance of leading American publishers and critics, black writers were never regarded as part of the nation's overall intellectual fabric and, absurdly, anthologies of black writing were frequently selected, edited, and prefaced by whites.

The cause of this—rather than blatant prejudice—was a kind of parochial racism, particularly found in

Alain Locke defined the aims of the black artists of the Harlem Renaissance.

the English departments of universities, which found it hard to accept writers who did not follow in the hallowed Dryden to T. S. Eliot tradition which tended to emphasize exquisiteness of language and to derogate the unabashed self-expression which was the hallmark of the Harlem School.

Renaissance self-expression had emerged in large measure because the moralizing writings of blacks prior to this era had failed to reach white consciences and abate racism. Much of this writing by Douglass, duBois, and James Weldon Johnson was of excellent caliber and truly reflected the experience of blacks. But it remained for Alain Locke to stress to blacks of post-World War I America that whites were not really paying much attention and that the time had come for blacks to cease propagandizing and reach into themselves to express their suffering through art rather than pamphleteering. Thus, though they did not abrogate interest in the black cause, the political objectives of Renaissance writers were largely beneath the surface. Grievances and objectives were not spelled out. Readers were encouraged to draw their own conclusions.

The ideology of self-expression was underscored by Ralph Ellison, when he noted: "If *Invisible Man* is free from ideological penalties suffered by Negroes in

Poet and diplomat James Weldon Johnson wrote "Lift Every Voice and Sing."

this country, it is because I tried to the best of my ability to transform these elements into art."

Wright and Activism

This view was not seriously challenged until 1940 when, with economic depression still present and world war brewing, Richard Wright appeared as an important writer and declared that with racism still rampant in the United States, "art for art's sake" was an indulgence that blacks could not afford. And Claude McKay, who had been a harbinger of the Renaissance, expressed fierce and direct protest in his poem "If We Must Die."

Wright, however, was no separatist. A strong theme in his writing was that the black was part of an American culture which in turn rejected him. As such, though politically radical, Wright's literary efforts coincided with much of the ideology of the civil rights movement of the 1950s and 1960s.

The militancy and violence of the 1960s shaped not only new leaders of the black cause but a new breed of activist writers who, far from belonging to an established black intellectual elite, wrote of the passions and experiences that emerge from people in direct conflict with society. Much leading black literature of the

late 1960s came from men bred in the conflicts of streets and prisons. Foremost among these writers were Eldridge Cleaver, George Jackson, Ron Karenga, and Malcolm X. Imamu Baraka had also been involved in bouts with the law.

By the 1970s black writers had achieved a position of respect in the American intellectual scene even if they, and black critics, still remained outsiders. Black studies faculties at universities added to this stature, though many were being eliminated by 1975.

The writers reviewed in this section have been included for their historical and/or aesthetic importance. In this limited space, the list can only be representative, although it can serve as a vital springboard for developing a greater understanding of the contributions made by the American black writer—both to the mainstream and to the tributaries of the American literary experience.

MAJOR BLACK LITERARY FIGURES

RAYMOND ANDREWS
Novelist
1934

Born in Madison, Georgia, Raymond Andrews left his sharecropper farm home at 15 to live, work, and attend high school at night in Atlanta. After graduation, he served in the U.S. Air Force (1952–1956) and

Raymond Andrews, first recipient of the annual James Baldwin Award, shown here in a sketch by his brother, well-known artist Benny Andrews.

attended Michigan State University before moving to New York City where he worked in a variety of jobs: airline reservations clerk, hamburger cook, photo librarian, proofreader, inventory taker, mailroom clerk, messenger, air courier dispatcher, and bookkeeper. And all the while he was writing.

His first novel, *Appalachee Red* (1978), set in the black neighborhood of a northern Georgia town called Appalachee, was widely acclaimed. In the view of the reviewer for the *St. Louis Globe Democrat,* it marked the literary debut of a significant modern American novelist of the stature of a Richard Wright or James Baldwin. The following year Raymond Andrews was the first recipient of the annual James Baldwin Prize presented by The Dial Press at a ceremony attended by Baldwin.

Andrews' second work, *Rosiebelle Lee Wildcat Tennessee: A Novel* (1980), chronicled the 40-year reign in Appalachee, beginning in 1906, of the spiritual and temporal leader of the black community there. And like his previous novel, it was illustrated by his brother Benny.

Now working on his third novel, Raymond Andrews lives in New York City with his wife, Heidi, a classical singer from Switzerland, and their two cats.

MAYA ANGELOU
Writer, Poet, Actress
1928

Born in St. Louis, Maya Angelou spent her formative years shuttling between that city, a tiny, totally segregated town in Arkansas, and San Francisco where she realized her ambition of becoming that city's first Negro streetcar conductor.

In the 1950s she studied dancing with Pearl Primus in New York, later appearing as a nightclub singer in New York and San Francisco. She has worked as an editor for *The Arab Observer,* an English-language weekly published in Cairo; lived in Accra, Ghana, where under the black nationalist regime of Kwame Nkrumah she taught music and drama; and studied cinematography in Sweden. She became a national celebrity in 1970 with the publication of *I Know Why the Caged Bird Sings,* the first volume of her autobiography, which detailed her encounters with southern racism and a prepubescent rape by her mother's lover.

In 1971 she produced *Just Give Me a Cool Drink of Water 'fore I Die: The Poetry of Maya Angelou;* in 1975 *Oh Pray My Wings Are Gonna Fit Me Well* (poetry); and in 1979 *And Still I Rise* (poetry). In 1977 she was nominated for an Emmy award for her

By 1982 Maya Angelou had become the most visible black writer in the country.

portrayal of Nyo Boto in the television adaptation of the best-selling novel *Roots.*

Three more volumes of her autobiography have been published: *Gather Together in My Name* (1974); *Singin' and Swingin' and Gettin' Merry Like Christmas* (1976); and *The Heart of a Woman* (1981).

The extravagantly tall, multitalented Angelou lives in Winston-Salem, North Carolina with her husband, Paul De Feu.

JAMES BALDWIN
Novelist, Essayist
1924

James Baldwin is one of the most widely quoted black writers of the past two decades.

Born in New York City, Baldwin turned to writing after an early career as a boy preacher in Harlem's storefront churches. He attended Frederick Douglass Junior High School in Harlem and later graduated from De Witt Clinton High School, where he was editor of the school magazine. Three years later, he won a Eugene Saxton Fellowship, which enabled him to write full-time. Now a resident of France, since leaving the United States, Baldwin has also been a resident of Turkey.

Baldwin's first novel, *Go Tell It on the Mountain,* was published in 1953, receiving good critical notices.

Two years later his first collection of essays, *Notes of a Native Son,* again won favorable critical acclaim. This was followed in 1956 by the publication of his second novel, *Giovanni's Room,* set in Paris. His second collection of essays, *Nobody Knows My Name,* brought him into the literary spotlight and established him as a major voice in American literature.

In 1962, *Another Country,* Baldwin's third novel, was a critical and commercial success. A year later, he wrote *The Fire Next Time,* an immediate best-seller and already regarded as one of the most brilliant essays written in the history of the black protest.

Since then, two of Baldwin's plays—*Blues for Mister Charlie* and *The Amen Corner*—have been produced on the New York stage, where they achieved modest success.

His novel *Tell Me How Long The Train's Been Gone* was published in 1968. Baldwin himself regards it as his first "grown-up novel," but it has generated little enthusiasm among critics.

Much to the distress of his public, Baldwin then entered an extended fallow period, and the question of whether he had stopped writing was widely debated. After a silence of several years, he published the 1974 novel *If Beale Street Could Talk.* In this work, the problems besetting a ghetto family in which the younger generation is striving to build a life for itself are portrayed with great sensitivity and humor. Baldwin's skill as a novelist is evident as he sets and solves the difficult problem of conveying his own sophisticated analyses through the mind of his protagonist, a young woman. To many critics, however, the novel lacks the undeniable relevance and fiery power of Baldwin's early polemical essays.

Baldwin's other works include *Going to Meet the Man* (short stories), *No Name in the Street, One Day When I Was Lost,* a scenario based on Alex Haley's *The Autobiography of Malcolm X, A Rap on Race* with Margaret Mead, and *A Dialogue* with Nikki Giovanni. He is one of the rare authors who works well alone or in collaboration. Other books by Baldwin are *Nothing Personal* (1964) with photographs by Richard Avedon; *The Devil Finds Work* (1976), about the movies; his big sixth novel *Just Above My Head* (1979); and *Little Man, Little Man: A Story of Childhood* (1977). He has written 16 books including the book for children, and has co-authored three others. There are six books about Baldwin's life and writings including a reference guide and bibliography.

Just Above My Head, published in 1979, dealt with

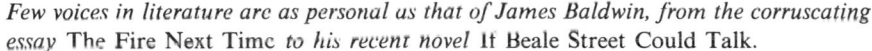

Few voices in literature are as personal as that of James Baldwin, from the corruscating essay The Fire Next Time *to his recent novel* If Beale Street Could Talk.

the intertwined lives from childhood to adulthood of a gospel singer, his brother, and a young girl who is a child preacher. The next year Baldwin's publisher announced *Remember This House,* described as his "memoirs, history and biography of the civil rights movement" interwoven with the biographies of three assassinated leaders: Martin Luther King, Jr., Malcolm X, and Medgar Evers. This literary tour de force is expected to take several years to produce.

Meanwhile, in his lectures Baldwin appears to remain pessimistic about the future of race relations.

IMAMU AMIRI BARAKA (Leroi Jones)
Poet, Playwright, Essayist
1934

(For biography see Civil Rights section.)

LERONE BENNETT, JR.
Historian
1928

Lerone Bennett, Jr. is often referred to as the "resident historian" of the Johnson Publishing Company, publisher of *Ebony, Jet,* and *Ebony Jr.*

Bennett was born in Clarksdale, Mississippi, and was educated in the public school system of Jackson, where he worked on his high school paper and edited the local Negro Weekly, *The Mississippi Enterprise.* At Morehouse College in Atlanta he was editor of the student newspaper and, after graduation, became a reporter and later city editor of the *Atlanta Daily World.*

Bennett joined Johnson in 1953 and worked as associate editor of *Jet* and *Ebony* before being named the latter's first senior editor in 1960.

His books include *Before the Mayflower* (1962), *The Negro Mood And Other Essays* (1964), *What Manner of Man* (a biography of Martin Luther King published in 1964), *Confrontation, Black and White* (1965), *Black Power, U.S.A., The Human Side of Reconstruction 1867–1877* (1967), and *Pioneers in Protest* (1968), *The Challenge of Blackness* (1972), *The Shaping of Black America* (1974), and *Wade in the Water: Great Moments in Black History* (1979). Bennett received the Literature Award from the American Academy of Arts and Science in 1978.

In 1969 he published a revised and enlarged edition of *Before the Mayflower.* He is also a lecturer and teacher of black history.

JOHN W. BLASSINGAME
Historian

A professor of history for many years at Yale University, he is the editor of *New Perspectives on Black Studies* (1973), the author of *Black New Orleans: 1860–1880* (1973), the co-editor with Mae G. Henderson and Jessica M. Dunn of *Antislavery Newspapers and Periodicals* (3 vols., 1980–1981), author of *The Slave Community: Plantation Life in the Antebellum South* (1972), editor of *Slave Testimony: Two Centuries of Letters, Speeches, Interviews and Autobiographies* (1976), and author with Mary F. Berry of *Long Memory: The Black Experience in America* (1981). Blassin-

Searing dramatist Imamu Amiri Baraka has emerged as a political leader.

game is also editing the 14 volumes of the Frederick Douglass papers—15,000 documents of speeches, debates, interviews, editorials, essays, poems, and correspondence. The first book of the series *The Frederick Douglass Papers: Series One (Speeches, Debates and Interviews)*, Volume I, *1841–46* was published in 1979 by Yale University Press.

ARNA BONTEMPS
Poet, Novelist, Anthologist
1902–1973

Arna Bontemps was one of the most productive black writers of the twentieth century. Born in Alexandria, Louisiana and raised in California, Arna Bontemps received his B.A. degree from Pacific Union College in Angwin in 1923. The next year, his poetry first appeared in *Crisis* magazine, the NAACP periodical edited by Dr. W. E. B. DuBois. Two years later, *Golgotha Is a Mountain* won the Alexander Pushkin Award, and in 1927 *Nocturne at Bethesda* achieved first honors in the *Crisis* poetry contest. *Personals,* Bontemps collected poems, was published in 1963.

In the late 1920s, Bontemps decided to try his hand at prose and over the next decade produced such novels as *God Sends Sunday* (1931), *Black Thunder* (1936), and *Drums at Dusk* (1939).

His books for young people include *We Have To-*

The prolific Arna Bontemps.

morrow (1945) and *Story of the Negro* (1948). Likewise of literary merit are such children's books as *Sad-Faced Boy* (1937) and *Slappy Hooper* (1946). He edited *American Negro Poetry* and two anthologies, with Langston Hughes among others.

Bontemps also served for many years as the chief librarian at Fisk University in Nashville, Tennessee.

In 1968 he completed the editing of a volume of children's poetry. Other publications have been *Anyplace But Here* (published in 1966 in collaboration with Jack Convoy), *Black Thunder* (1968 reprint), *Great Slave Narratives* (1969), *The Harlem Renaissance Remembered: Essays,* and *The Old South.* He also edited several anthologies. In 1978 Charles H. Nichols edited the *Arna Bontemps/Langston Hughes Letters, 1925–1967,* selected correspondence of two of the most important black U.S. writers from the Harlem Renaissance to the 1960s—an event in black belles-lettres. Robert E. Fleming's *James Weldon Johnson and Arna Wendell Bontemps: A Reference Guide* was published in 1979.

DAVID BRADLEY
Novelist
1950

Born in Bedford, Pennsylvania, Bradley grew up in a rural area. His father, a minister who had attended the University of Pittsburgh and New York University and wrote several books on the history of the Methodist church, was most responsible for Bradley's interest in writing. When he was nine years old, he wrote a play, *Martian Thanksgiving,* which was performed by his Cub Scout troop. Bradley entered the University of Pennsylvania in 1968 and majored in English and creative writing, preparing for a writing career. While an undergraduate he wrote the novel *South Street,* published in 1975, about the black underclass on South Street in Philadelphia. He rejected the civil rights struggle for power of the 1960s by his black fellow students at the university. Believing that blacks were powerless with no way of getting any power, he gravitated to the powerless underclass on South Street. After graduating from college, Bradley's postgraduate research in American history at the University of London sent him back to the story he had heard in Bedford about the 13 escaped slaves who asked to be killed rather than recaptured, and the 13 unmarked graves discovered by his mother. His fourth version of this big novel about those runaway slaves was finally published in the spring of 1981 as *The Chaneysville Incident.* The book received many glowing reviews and in 1982 was selected as one of the six novels or books of short stories nominated for the second annual P.E.N./Faulkner Award for fiction. Bradley is a professor of English at Temple University in Philadelphia.

WILLIAM STANLEY BRAITHWAITE
Poet, Critic
1878–1962

In the early part of his career, it was not generally known that William Stanley Braithwaite was black although his name was familiar to many readers through his book reviews for the *Boston Transcript* and such books of poetry as *Lyrics of Life and Love* (1904) and *The House of Falling Leaves* (1908).

From 1913 to 1929 Braithwaite published an annual *Anthology of Magazine Verse* which brought before the public many of the works of such noted American poets as Edgar Lee Masters, Vachel Lindsay, and Carl Sandburg long before they were ever published in book form.

Braithwaite's other books include *The Book of Elizabethan Verse* (1906), *The Book of Georgian Verse* (1908), *The Book of Restoration Verse* (1909), his *Selected Poems* (1948), and a biography of the Bonti Family. *The William Stanley Braithwaite Reader,* edited by Philip Butcher, was published in 1972.

The recipient of the NAACP's Spingarn Medal in 1918, Braithwaite spent most of his later years in education, serving notably as professor of creative literature at Atlanta University.

BENJAMIN BRAWLEY
Literary Historian
1882–1939

Although he wrote a number of poems and short stories, the major portion of Benjamin Brawley's work was in the field of literary and social history.

Brawley was born in Columbia, South Carolina and educated at Morehouse College, the University of Chicago, and Harvard. He later taught at Morehouse, Shaw, and Howard.

His books include *A Short History of English Drama* (1921); *A New Survey of English Literature* (1925); *The Negro Genius* (1937), a biography of Paul L. Dunbar; *A Short History of the American Negro;* and *Negro Builders and Heroes* (1937). The latter was written two years before his death.

GWENDOLYN BROOKS
Poet
1912

Gwendolyn Brooks is one of seven blacks to win Pulitzer Prizes in various fields. (Duke Ellington was nominated for the Pulitzer Prize in music in 1965 but was turned down amid controversy and resignation of judges.) Miss Brooks received this prestigious award in 1950 for *Annie Allen,* a volume of her poetry which had been published a year earlier.

Miss Brooks was born in Topeka, Kansas, moved

In 1950 Gwendolyn Brooks became the first black writer to win a Pulitzer Prize.

to Chicago at an early age, and was educated there, graduating from Wilson Junior College in 1936.

She had her first taste of ghetto life during her first job as secretary to a "spiritual advisor" who sold "love drops." Although unfamiliar with these conditions from her native environment, she was nonetheless alert enough to realize that they could offer her much in the way of unique material for her writing.

In 1945 she completed a book of poems, *A Street in Bronzeville,* and was selected by *Mademoiselle* as one of the year's 10 most outstanding American women. She was made a fellow of the American Academy of Arts and Letters in 1946, and received Guggenheim Fellowships for 1946 and 1947.

In 1949 she won the Eunice Tietjen Prize for Poetry in the annual competition sponsored by *Poetry* magazine. She was poet laureate of the state of Illinois.

Her other books include a collection of children's poems, *Bronzeville Boys and Girls* (1956); a novel, *Maud Martha* (1953); and two books of poetry, *The Bean Eaters* (1960) and *Selected Poems* (1963). She has also written *In the Mecca, Riot, The World of Gwendolyn Brooks, Report from Part One: The Autobiography of Gwendolyn Brooks, Family Pictures, Beckonings, Aloneness, Primer for Blacks,* and *To Disembark.*

Her poems and stories have also been published in magazines and the anthologies *Soon, One Morning,* and *Beyond the Angry Black.* She has edited *A Broadside Treasury* and *Jump Bad, A New Chicago Anthol-*

Claude Brown's life story forms the basis for Manchild in the Promised Land.

ogy. George Kent, a black professor of English at the University of Chicago, is writing a biography of Gwendolyn Brooks with access to her notebooks.

CLAUDE BROWN
Author
1927

Claude Brown's claim to literary fame rests largely on his best-selling autobiography *Manchild in the Promised Land,* which was published in 1965 when its author was 28.

The book is the story of Brown's life in Harlem and, in the process, becomes a highly realistic documentary of life in the ghetto. It tells of Brown's escapades with the Harlem Buccaneers, a "bopping gang," and of his later involvement with the Forty Thieves, an elite stealing division of this same gang.

After attending the Wiltwyck School for emotionally disturbed and deprived boys, Brown returned to New York, was later sent to Warwick Reform School three times, and eventually made his way downtown to a small loft apartment near Greenwich Village. Changing his style of life, Brown finished high school and went on to graduate from Howard University in 1965.

Brown began work on his book in 1963, submitting a manuscript of some 1,500 pages which was eventually cut and reworked into the finished product over a two-year period. Brown completed law school in the late

1960s and is now practicing in California. In 1976, he published *The Children of Ham* about a group of young blacks living as a family in a condemned Harlem tenement, begging, stealing, and doing whatever is necessary to survive.

STERLING BROWN
Poet, Critic
1901

In the period immediately following the Harlem Renaissance, Sterling Brown received favorable attention for *Southern Road,* a volume of poetry published in 1932 (reprinted in 1974). In contrast to the urban environment of the Harlem school, Brown drew his material from the rural South.

Born in Washington, D.C., Brown was educated at Williams College and Harvard. Except for brief periods during which he has served as visiting lecturer at the New School for Social Research, Vassar, and at the University of Minnesota, he has spent his entire teaching career at Howard University. He has now retired.

In the 1930s, Brown received a Guggenheim Fellowship and the following year published two works: *The Negro in American Fiction,* and *Negro Poetry and Drama* in 1937 (both reprinted in 1969). He was one of the three editors of *The Negro Caravan* (1941, 1969), authored many magazine articles, and in 1974 published *The Last Ride of Wild Bill,* a book of poetry. In 1980 *The Collected Poems of Sterling Brown,* edited by Michael S. Harper, was published and was co-winner of the Anisfield-Wolf Award for 1980.

WILLIAM WELLS BROWN
Novelist, Dramatist
1815–1884

Williams Wells Brown was the first American black to publish a novel, the first to publish a drama, and the first to publish a travel book.

Born a slave in Lexington, Kentucky and taken to St. Louis as a young boy, Brown worked for a time in the offices of the *St. Louis Times,* and then took a job on a riverboat in service on the Mississippi. In 1834 Brown fled to Canada, taking his name from a friendly Quaker whom he met there. While working as a steward on Lake Erie ships, he educated himself and became well known as a public speaker. In 1849 he went to England and Paris to attend the Peace Congress, remaining abroad for five years.

His first published work, the *Narrative of William H. Brown,* went into three editions within eight months. A year later, a collection of his poems was published, *The Anti-Slavery Harp,* and in 1852 his travel book *Three Years in Europe* appeared in London.

Brown's *Clotel, or the President's Daughter,* a melodramatic novel about miscegenation, was first published in London in 1853. As the first novel by an American black (it subsequently went through two revisions), its historical importance transcends its aesthetic shortcomings.

Brown's other books include the first Negro drama, *The Escape, or a Leap for Freedom* (1858); *The Black Man: His Antecedents, His Genius, and His Achievements* (1863); *The Negro in the American Rebellion: His Heroism and Fidelity* (1867); and *The Rising Son* (1874).

ED BULLINS
Dramatist, Essayist, Poet
1935

Ed Bullins was born in Philadelphia and grew up in Los Angeles. Bullins is a writer of drama, and one of the founders of the Black Arts/West in the Fillmore District of San Francisco. He patterned this experiment after the Black Arts Repertory Theater School in Harlem, which was founded and directed by Imamu Baraka and is active in analyzing the black experience in America. In 1977, when *Daddy,* the sixth play in his "20th-Century Cycle" opened at the New Federal Theatre in New York's Henry Street Settlement, Bullins in an interview with the *New York Times* foresaw black theatrical producers taking plays to cities with large black populations and spreading out unless something happens to kill the economy. A leader of the black theater movement and creator of more than 50 plays, he has yet to have a play produced on Broadway.

Bullins' main themes are the violence and tragedy of drug abuse and the oppressive life style of the ghetto. He presents his material in a realistic and naturalistic style. From 1965 to 1968 he wrote *The Rally, How Do You Do; Goin'a Buffalo; Clara's Old Man; The Electronic Nigger;* and *In The Wine Time.* He has also produced *The Fabulous Miss Maine.*

He has been a creative member of Black Arts Alliance, working with Baraka in producing films on the West Coast.

Bullins has been connected with the New Lafayette Theater in Harlem where he was a resident playwright. His books are *Five Plays, New Plays from the Black Theatre* (editor), *The Reluctant Rapist, The New Lafayette Theatre Presents, The Theme Is Blackness, Four Dynamite Plays, The Duplex, The Hungered One: Early Writings,* and *How Do You Do: A Nonsense Drama.*

PHILIP BUTCHER
Essayist, Scholar
1918

Philip Butcher was born in Washington, D.C., and attended Howard University where he received an A.B. in 1942 and an M.A. in 1947. He pursued his education at Columbia University where he was awarded a Ph.D. in 1956.

After serving in the U.S. Army during World War II, he received fellowships from the General Education Board (1948) and from the John Hay Whitney Foundation (1951).

The works of Philip Butcher can be found in *Opportunity, Phylon, Journal of Negro History, CLA Journal, Shakespeare Quarterly,* and *The American Literary Realism.* His essays present vital analyses of, and key insight into, the works of major American writers.

His two books on George W. Cable were published by Columbia University Press and Twayne Publishers. He edited *The William Stanley Braithwaite Reader,* which was published in 1972. He also wrote *The Minority Presence in American Literature* (1977).

Ed Bullins has captured wide audiences with The Taking of Miss Janie.

CHARLES WADDELL CHESNUTT
Novelist
1858–1932

Charles Waddell Chesnutt was the first black writer to deal with the race question from the Negro's point of view.

Born in Cleveland, Ohio, in 1858, Chesnutt moved to North Carolina with his family at the age of eight. Largely self-educated, he was admitted to the Ohio bar in 1887, the same year in which his first story, "The Gophered Grapevine," was published in the *Atlantic Monthly*. This was followed in 1899 by two collections of his stories—*The Conjure Woman* and *The Wife of His Youth*.

His first novel, *The House Behind the Cedars* (1900), dealt with a young girl's attempt to "pass" for white. A year later, *The Marrow of Tradition* examined the violence of the post-Reconstruction period. His final novel, *The Colonel's Dream,* was published in 1905 and typified Chesnutt's basically ingratiating approach to his art, one which the writers of the Harlem School were later to reject. Chesnutt also wrote a biography, *Frederick Douglass.* There has been a great revival of interest in Chesnutt in recent years with the publication of six or more books about him.

ALICE CHILDRESS
Playwright, Novelist, Actress
1920

Born in Charleston, South Carolina, she studied acting at the American Negro Theatre and attended Radcliffe Institute from 1966 to 1968 through a Harvard University appointment as a scholar-writer. Her plays are *Florence* (one-act play), *Gold Through the Trees, Just a Little Simple* (based on Langston Hughes' *Simple Speaks His Mind*), *Trouble in Mind, Wedding Band, Wine in the Wilderness, When the Rattlesnake Sounds: A Play about Harriet Tubman.* Childress also edited *Black Scenes* (1971), excerpts from plays in the Zenith series for children. Her other books are *Like One of the Family: Conversations from a Domestic's Life* (1956), *A Hero Ain't Nothing but a Sandwich* (1973) (novel), and *A Short Walk* (1979), a novel. Childress' play *Trouble in Mind* won the Obie Award in 1956 as the best original off-Broadway production.

JOHN HENRIK CLARKE
Essayist, Editor, Anthologist
1915

Born in Union Springs, Alabama in 1915, Clarke spent most of his early youth in Columbus, Georgia. Since 1933 Clarke has been a resident of New York City, for the most part in Harlem. He has written for a number of magazines and newspapers, among them *Black World, Negro History Bulletin, New York Amsterdam News,* and *The Pittsburgh Courier.* Clarke was a co-founder of *Harlem Quarterly* in 1950 and since 1962 has been an associate editor of *Freedomways.* Since 1974 he has been a professor in Black Studies at Hunter College, New York City. His specialty is African history, but he also teaches Afro-American history.

Some of the books edited by Clarke include *Harlem: A Communication in Transition* (1964, 1970); *Harlem U.S.A.* (1965, 1971); *American Negro Short Stories* (1966); *William Styron's Nat Turner, Ten Black Writers Respond* (1968); *Malcolm X: The Man and His Times* (1969); and *Marcus Garvey and the Vision of Africa* (1973). Other books edited by Clarke are *Harlem* (short stories, 1970); *Slave Trade and Slavery* (1970) with Vincent Harding; *Pan-Africanism and the Liberation of Southern Africa: A Tribute to W. E. B. DuBois* (1978); and *Dimensions of the Struggle Against Apartheid, A Tribute to Paul Robeson* (1979).

JOSEPH SEAMON COTTER, SR.
Poet
1861–1949

Though he did not, in his youth, attend school past the third grade, Joseph Seamon Cotter, Sr. achieved distinction during his lifetime as a poet—primarily in the dialect idiom. Cotter's earliest work, *A Rhyming* (1895), was followed in later years by the prize-winning "Tragedy of Pete," which was awarded an *Opportunity* Prize during the Harlem Renaissance. His *Collected Poems* appeared in 1938. Cotter published seven other books.

Born at Bardstown, Kentucky, Cotter worked in various odd jobs during his youth and became a schoolteacher in Louisville after he returned to his schooling at the age of 22. His poetry reflects more than 50 years' experience as a teacher, and is a dynamic mixture of the storytelling art, the young man's thirst for racial leadership, and the tutor at work. His dialect poetry is mindful of Paul Laurence Dunbar at his best, although Cotter tends to be more racially critical than his more famous peer.

JOSEPH SEAMON COTTER, JR.
Poet
1895–1919

Young Joseph Seamon Cotter, Jr. followed in his father's footsteps as a poet, although he enjoyed the benefit of collegiate training at Fisk University in Nashville. Sickly, Cotter was forced to abandon the school in his second year after contracting tuberculosis. His only distinguished work, *The Bank of Gideon,* a thin volume of only 30 pages, was published in 1918, shortly before his death.

Countee Cullen was a leading figure in the Harlem Renaissance.

COUNTEE CULLEN
Poet
1903–1946

Countee Cullen was one of the leading figures in the Harlem Renaissance.

Born Countee Porter on May 30, 1903 in Baltimore, he was orphaned at an early age and adopted by Reverend Frederick Cullen, pastor of New York's Salem Methodist Church. At New York University, Cullen won Phi Beta Kappa honors and was awarded the Witter Bynner Poetry Prize. In 1925, while still a student at New York University, Cullen completed *Color*, a volume of poetry which received the Harmon Foundation's first gold medal for literature two years later.

In 1926 he earned his M.A. at Harvard and a year later finished both *The Ballad of the Brown Girl* and *Copper Sun*. This was followed in 1929 by *The Black Christ*, written during a two-year sojourn in France on a Guggenheim Fellowship. In 1927 he edited *Caroling Dusk: An Anthology of Verse by Negro Poets*. The book was reprinted in 1972.

Upon his return to New York City, Cullen began a teaching career in the public school system. During this period, he also produced a novel, *One Way to Heaven* (1932); *The Medea and Other Poems* (1935); *The Lost Zoo* (1940); and *My Lives and How I Lost Them* (1942).

In 1947, a year after his death, Cullen's own selections of his best work were collected in a volume published under the title *On These I Stand*.

ELDRIDGE CLEAVER
Author, Civil Rights Leader
1935

(For biography see Civil Rights section)

ARTHUR P. DAVIS
Essayist, Scholar
1904

Arthur P. Davis was born in Hampton, Virginia. He received his Ph.D. from Columbia University in 1942. He has served as a college professor at North Carolina College (1927–1928) and at Virginia Union (1929–1944).

Davis is most noted for co-editing *The Negro Caravan* (1941) with Sterling A. Brown and Ulysses Lee. He published a book based on his doctoral dissertation, called *Issac Watts: His Life and Works* (1943).

A leading critic of Negro literature, many of Davis' essays can be found in *Phylon, Common Ground*, and *Opportunity*. His most famous essays have been analyses of works by Phillis Wheatley, Langston Hughes, Countee Cullen, and writers of the Harlem Renaissance. He recently retired as an English teacher from Howard University where he had been a professor since 1944.

Davis is the editor, with Saunders Redding, of *Cavalcade, Negro American Writing from 1760 to the Present* published in 1971. His book *From the Dark Tower: Afro-American Writers 1900 to 1960* was published in 1974.

MARTIN R. DELANEY
Essayist, Author
1812–1885

Most of Martin R. Delaney's writing was concerned with the search for identity and self-realization. Delaney, a native of Charlestown, Virginia, was widely read and traveled, and developed in his lifetime a dynamic and expressive black power ethic.

One of Delaney's first serious ventures was to trace his lineage to the African chieftains whom he believed were his actual forefathers. Delaney pursued formal education with resolve and vigor once his parents had escaped from Virginia to western Pennsylvania. He eventually studied medicine at Harvard University Medical School and while a practicing physician in Pittsburgh, was instrumental in putting down a cholera epidemic there.

Prior to the outbreak of the Civil War, Delaney led an investigation into the Niger Valley in West Africa, later publishing an official report of his explorations in a study which contained specific recommendations for black repatriation. During the war itself, Delaney served as a medical officer, rising to the rank

Major Martin R. Delaney penned an early political analysis of race.

(1966), *Empire Star* (1966), *The Einstein Intersection Out of the Dead City* (1968), and *Nova* (1968). *Babel-17* and *The Einstein Intersection* both won Nebula Awards from the Science Fiction Writers of America, as have his short stories "Aye, and Gomorrah" and "Time Considered as a Helix of Semi-Precious Stones," which also won a Hugo Award at the World Science Fiction Convention at Heidelberg. Delany co-edited the speculative fiction quarterly *Owark*, Nos. 1, 2, 3, 4 with his wife, National Book Award winning poet Marilyn Hacker. It was published by Popular Library in New York. The Delanys have a daughter. He wrote, directed, and edited the half-hour film *The Orchid*. In 1975 Delany was Visiting Butler Chair Professor of English at the State University of New York at Buffalo. His novels and short stories of the 1970s are *Diftglass: Tales of Speculative Fiction* (1971) and The Fall of the Towers trilogy (1971), *Captives of the Flame, The Tower of Toron,* and *City of a Thousand Suns.* He has also published *The Tides Lust* (1973) and *Tales of Neveryon. Dhalgren* (1975) is the big major novel of this brilliant young writer, published when he was 32 years old. His last three books are the novel *Triton* (1976), *Empire: A Visual Novel* with Howard V. Chaykin, and *Heavenly Breakfast: An Essay on the Winter of Love* (1979), an autobiographical look back by Delany of his youthful adventures of the winter and spring of 1967–1968. *Galaxy* magazine has called Delany "the best science fiction writer in the world." Michael W. Peplow and Robert S. Bravard's *Samuel R. Delany: A Primary and Secondary Bibliography* was published in 1980.

OWEN DODSON
Dramatist, Poet
1914

Poet/dramatist Owen Dodson's most ambitious work revolves about the Father Divine legend and is, with punnish intent, entitled *The Divine Comedy*. The play was produced at the Yale University Theatre in 1938.

A native of Brooklyn, Dodson attended Bates College and went on to earn a Master of Fine Arts degree from Yale. His alma mater also presented Dodson's *The Garden of Time*. Success in university theater led to the play's later appearances at predominantly black universities throughout the South.

Dodson later went into teaching at the Atlanta University complex, although he was commissioned to write a play about the Amistad Mutiny, a shipboard slave uprising in the 1840s. His traditional and experimental verse and short stories were published in several quarterlies and anthologies. He has now retired after many years at Howard University. His books are *Powerful Long Ladder, Boy at the Window* (novel) and *The Confession Stone.*

of major. Reconstruction found him active in politics, albeit unsuccessfully.

Retirement enabled him to prepare his most ambitious work, *Principles of Ethnology* (1879). His best-known work, however, remains a political tract entitled *The Condition, Elevation, Emigration and Destiny of the Colored People of the United States, Politically Considered* (1852). He also wrote the novel *Blake,* published in 1870. *Search for a Place* by Delaney and Robert Campbell was published in 1869.

Delaney died in Xenia, Ohio, home of Wilberforce University.

SAMUEL R. DELANY
Science Fiction Writer
1942

Born in Harlem and a published writer at the age of 19, Delany has been a prolific writer of science fiction, novelettes, and novels. His first book was *The Jewels of Aptor* (1962), followed by *Captives of the Flame* (1963), *The Towers of Toron* (1964), *City of a Thousand Suns* (1965), *The Ballad of Beta-2* (1965), *Babel-17*

PAUL LAURENCE DUNBAR
Poet
1872–1906

The first black poet to gain a national reputation in the United States, Paul Laurence Dunbar was also the first to use Negro dialect within the formal structure of his work.

Born of former slaves in Dayton, Ohio, Dunbar went to work as an elevator operator after graduating from high school. His first book of poetry, *Oak and Ivy,* was privately printed in 1893 and was followed by *Majors and Minors,* which appeared two years later. Neither book was an immediate sensation, but there were enough favorable reviews in such magazines as *Harper's* to encourage Dunbar in the pursuit of a full-fledged literary career. In 1896, Dunbar completed *Lyrics of a Lowly Life,* the single work upon which his subsequent reputation was irrevocably established.

Before his untimely death in 1906, Dunbar had become the dominant presence in the world of American Negro poetry. His later works included *Lyrics of Love and Laughter* (1903), *Lyrics of Sunshine and Shadow* (1905), and *Complete Poems,* published posthumously in 1913.

Paul Lawrence Dunbar introduced the nation to black dialect in formal poetry.

This last work contains not only the dialect poems which were his trademark but many poems in conventional English as well. The book has enjoyed such enormous popularity that it has, to this day, never gone out of print. He also published four novels including *The Sport of Gods* and *The Uncalled,* and four volumes of short stories. There are several biographies of Dunbar.

RALPH ELLISON
Novelist, Essayist
1914

Ralph Ellison's critical and artistic reputation rests largely on a single masterpiece, his first and only novel, *Invisible Man.* Acclaimed by virtually all who have read it, the novel was given the National Book Award for fiction in 1952. It had been years in the making, and its success heralded the emergence of a major writing talent.

Ellison was born in Oklahoma City, Oklahoma and came to New York City in the late 1930s, after having studied music at Tuskegee Institute for three years. At first interested in sculpture, he turned to writing after coming under the influence of T. S. Eliot's poetry,

son was the subject of a *New Yorker* magazine profile in 1976.

MARI EVANS
Poet

A poet first noticed in the early 1960s, Mari Evans is noted for her ability to jolt her readers with the beauty of blackness.

Born in Toledo, Ohio, she studied at the University of Toledo. In 1963 her poetry was published in *Phylon, Negro Digest,* and *Dialog.* Two years later she was awarded a John Hay Whitney Fellowship.

One of her better known works is probably *The Alarm Clock,* which deals with the rude awakening of the black American to the white "Establishment." It captures and summarizes the scene of the sixties in the United States.

Miss Evans has been employed as a television producer-director. She also teaches at Purdue University in Indiana. Her books are *I Am A Black Woman* and *Where Is All the Music?* (for adults); *J. D., I Look at Me, Singing Black, The Day They Made Benuni,* and *Jim Flying High,* which are for children. Her poems appear in over 40 textbooks and anthologies.

RONALD L. FAIR
Novelist
1932

Ronald L. Fair was born in Chicago in 1932. He spent two years at a local business college and was a court reporter from 1955 to 1966. He published his first novel, *Many Thousand Gone,* in 1965 and his second novel, *Hog Butcher,* in 1966. Since then, he has taught at Columbia College in Chicago, at Northwestern University, and at Wesleyan University in Connecticut. Fair's third book, *World of Nothing,* consisting of two novellas, was published in several anthologies and magazines. His third novel, *We Can't Breathe,* published in 1971, is an autobiographical work about Fair's growing up in a black ghetto. He has lived in Europe since 1971. Winner of a Guggenheim Fellowship, he published *Rufus,* a book of poems, in Germany in 1976.

JESSIE REDMON FAUSET
Novelist
1886–1961

Jessie Redmon Fauset was one of the last mainstays of the so-called traditional school of Negro literature. Written in a genteel style, her novels deal primarily with middle-class blacks and are in sharp contrast to the work produced by the young writers of the Harlem School who sought to capture the stark realism of life in the Negro ghetto.

An an editor of *Crisis,* Miss Fauset often champi-

Invisible Man *was written by Ralph Ellison.*

and as a direct consequence of his friendship with Richard Wright.

In 1955 the American Academy of Arts and Letters awarded Ellison the *Prix de Rome,* which enabled him to live and write in Italy for a time. Since then, he has lectured at New York University and at Bennington College, and has been writer-in-residence at Rutgers University.

His second published work was *Shadow and Act,* a book of essays which appeared in 1964. Excerpts from his second novel have been published in several literary journals. There are three books of essays on him and his novel.

He has retired as distinguished professor at New York University in New York City and was awarded an honorary Doctor of Letters degree in 1974 by Harvard University.

The thirtieth anniversary edition of *Invisible Man* with a new introduction by Ellison was published in 1982.

Elected to the National Institute of Arts and Letters and the American Academy of Arts and Letters, Elli-

oned the works of the young writers, even though their direction ran counter to her own. She herself was a prolific Renaissance novelist, publishing four books over a ten-year span: *There is Confusion* (1924), *Plum Bun* (1928), *The Chinaberry Tree* (1931), and *Comedy American Style* (1933).

ELTON FAX
(For biography see Art section.)

RUDOLPH FISHER
Novelist, Short Story Writer
1897–1934

Rudolph Fisher was born in Washington, D.C. and raised in Providence, Rhode Island. He attended Brown University and Howard Medical School. He came to New York to study biology at Columbia University's College of Physicians and Surgeons and then went on to specialize in roentgenology.

"The City of Refuge," Fisher's first short story, was written while he was still in medical school and depicted Harlem life during the 1920s. It was subsequently reprinted in the anthology *The Best Short Stories of 1925*.

Fisher's two novels, *The Walls of Jericho* (1928) and *The Conjure Man Dies* (1932), never became as popular as his short stories. Other short stories by Fisher are "Ringtail," "High Yaller," "The Promised Land," and "Miss Cynthie."

CHARLOTTE L. FORTEN
Author, Poet
1837–1914

A member of the distinguished Forten family (her grandfather James served in the Revolutionary War), Charlotte Forten attended school in Salem, Massachusetts, winning early honors for her poetry while at Higginson Grammar School. (She was unable to obtain an education in her native city of Philadelphia because of race.)

Her education prepared her for a career in teaching, which she pursued until the Civil War when she served as an agent with the Freedmen's Aid Society at Port Royal, St. Helena Island, off South Carolina.

Her best-known writing was a series of articles entitled *Glimpses of New England,* which was published in the *National Anti-Slavery Standard.* Other articles on life in the Sea Islands were printed in *Atlantic Monthly,* a publication which gave her widespread circulation. *The Journal of Charlotte Forten,* edited by Roy Allen Billington, was published in 1961.

Though her work is by no means lasting literature, it is important for the exposure Miss Forten gave to racial prejudice in antebellum New England in a mid-dle-class atmosphere, and for her equally relevant characterization of the Sea Islands.

JOHN HOPE FRANKLIN
Historian
1915

Black history has had no more scholarly spokesman in the last two decades than John Hope Franklin, whose classic analysis of American history and the blacks place in it, *From Slavery to Freedom* (1947), is ranked in the company of the most authoritative studies of the period. It has gone through many editions and is still in print.

A native of Rentiesville, Oklahoma, Franklin graduated from Fisk University in 1935, and later received his M.A. and Ph.D. degrees from Harvard. Since then, he has taught at Howard, Fisk University, Alabama State Teachers College, and Brooklyn College and has received Rosenwald and Guggenheim Fellowships for research.

In addition to numerous articles in professional journals, Franklin has an impressive list of full-length book credits, including *The Free Negro in North Carolina, 1790–1860* (1943); *The Civil War, Diary of James Ayers* (1947); *Reconstruction After the Civil War* (1961); *The Emancipation Proclamation* (1963); *The Negro in Twentieth Century America* (1967); *Color and Race* (1968); *An Illustrated History of Black Ameri-*

John Hope Franklin analyzes the black role in American history.

cans; *Americans; Racial Equality in America;* and *A Southern Odyssey: Travelers in the Antebellum North.*

Franklin, who has retired as a professor of History at the University of Chicago, co-edited with August Meier *Black Leaders of the Twentieth Century* (1982), a volume in the Blacks in the New World series (general editor is August Meier).

E. FRANKLIN FRAZIER
Historian, Sociologist
1894–1962

Once chairman of Howard University's sociology department, E. Franklin Frazier is best remembered for his controversial book *Black Bourgeoisie,* in which he expounded the theory that the black middle class was isolating itself from the problems of marginal or poverty-stricken blacks. He was an authority on the black family among other subjects.

Born in Baltimore in 1894, Frazier graduated from Howard in 1916 and received his Ph.D. from the University of Chicago in 1931. Three years later, he began a 25-year period in the sociology department of Howard, interrupting his tenure there on occasion to teach at Columbia, New York University, and other universities.

In 1940 and again the following year, Frazier was a Guggenheim fellow in Brazil and the West Indies. He became president of the American Sociological Society in 1948 and a year later was named Chairman of UNESCO's committee of experts on race. Later he served as chief of UNESCO's Applied Science Division in Paris.

Frazier died at George Washington University Hospital after a long illness. He had retired from Howard in 1959. His books include *The Negro Family in the United States, The Negro in the United States, The Negro Church in America,* and *The Free Negro Family and Race and Culture Contacts in the Modern World.*

CHARLES FULLER
Playwright
1939

He became "stagestruck" in his high-school days, when he went to the Old Walnut Street Theater in his native Philadelphia and saw a Yiddish play starring Molly Picon and Menasha Skulnik. Fuller didn't understand a word of it, "but it was live theater, and I felt myself responding to it."

In 1959, Fuller entered the Army and served in Japan and South Korea, after which he attended Villanova University and La Salle College. While Fuller was working as a housing inspector in Philadelphia, the McCarter Theater in Princeton, New Jersey produced his first play. The theme was intermarriage, and

Pulitzer Prize winner Charles Fuller.

its creator is quick now to tag it "one of the world's worst interracial plays." However, during this time he met members of The Negro Ensemble Company and in 1974 he wrote his first play for them, *In the Deepest Part of Sleep.* "I decided then that I wanted to do something bigger and beyond myself, something historical, that would stand *outside* normal black theater. I wanted to open up black theater so that it couldn't be labeled that easily." For NEC's tenth anniversary Fuller wrote *The Brownsville Raid* about the black soldiers who were dishonorably discharged on President Teddy Roosevelt's orders in 1906 after a shoot-out in Brownsville, Texas. The play was a hit and Fuller followed it a few seasons later with *Zooman and the Sign,* a melodrama that won two Obie awards.

A Soldiers Play, which won a Pulitzer Prize in 1982, is his fourth play for The Negro Ensemble Company. This drama dealing with a murder set in a backwater New Orleans Army camp in 1944 opened NEC's fifteenth anniversary season in 1981 with a long run and was hailed by the *New York Times* as "tough, taut and fully realized."

The recipient of the Guggenheim Foundation Fellowship, the Rockefeller Foundation, and the National Endowment for the Arts and CAPS Fellowships in playwrighting, Fuller describes himself as a playwright who happens to be black, rather than a black playwright.

Ernest J. Gaines, novelist and short story writer.

Nikki Giovanni is a successful young author who often reads her poetry on TV.

ERNEST J. GAINES
Novelist, Short Story Writer
1933

Although Ernest J. Gaines had written three novels and many short stories, it was not until the publication of *Bloodline,* a book of short stories, in 1968 that he began to receive considerable attention.

Gaines was born on a plantation in Louisiana. He moved to California in 1949 where he did his undergraduate study at San Francisco State College. In 1959 he received the Wallace Stegner Fellowship in creative writing. The following year he was awarded the Joseph Henry Jackson Literary Award.

His first novel to be published was *Catherine Carmier* (1964). Other novels by Gaines are *Of Love and Dust* (1967), *Barren Summer* (completed in 1963 but never published), *The Autobiography of Miss Jane Pittman* (1971), *A Warm Day in November* (for young people), and *In My Father's House* (1978). The 1974 television production of *The Autobiography of Miss Jane Pittman* with Cicely Tyson boosted his reputation quite a bit.

NIKKI GIOVANNI
Poet
1943

Nikki Giovanni was born in Knoxville, Tennessee. She studied at Fisk University and at the University of Pennsylvania. Her first book of poetry, *Black Feeling, Black Talk,* published in the mid-1960s was followed by *Black Judgment* in 1968. These two were combined as *Black Feeling, Black Talk, Black Judgment* in 1970.

In 1974 her poems were to be found in many black literature anthologies and she had also become a media personality through her TV appearances where she read her poetry. Many of her poems were put to soul or gospel music accompaniment. One such recording is *Truth Is on Its Way.*

Giovanni is a prolific author. Her other books are *Re-creation, Spin a Soft Black Song; Night Comes Softly: Anthology of Black Female Voices; My House; Gemini: An Extended Autobiographical Statement; Ego Tripping and Other Poems for Young People; A Dialogue* (with James Baldwin); and *A Poetic Equation: Conversations Between Nikki Giovanni and Margaret Walker.* Wilberforce University in Xenia, Ohio, gave her an honorary Doctor of Humanities degree in 1972 when she was 28 years old. Later books by Giovanni are *The Women and the Men: Poems* (1975), *Cotton Candy on a Rainy Day* (1978), and *Vacation Time: Poems for Children* (1980). Her most recent work, *Vacation Time,* a collection of poems for children, was dedicated to her son, Tommy. In 1981, a newspaper reporter noted that Giovanni, one of the premiere black revolutionary poets of the 1960s, appeared to have shed all trace of the angry, bitter radical. Explaining her transformation, Giovanni said, "One winds down. We've touched on every sore that anybody in the world ever had and I think we ought to do some healing. I'm not downgrading anger, but how long can you stay angry?"

Besides writing and lecturing, today Giovanni is also a volunteer in the Cincinnati public schools system, where she teaches poetry.

SHIRLEY GRAHAM
Biographer
1907–1977

Born in Indianapolis, Indiana, Miss Graham received her B.A. degree in 1934 at Oberlin College and her M.A. from the same institution a year later. While at Oberlin, she wrote and composed her first musical play, *Tom-Tom,* which was produced in 1932. She then studied music in Paris for years, and later taught at Morgan State and Tennessee State universities.

During a short stint with the Chicago Federal Theatre, she directed, designed, and composed for *Little Black Sambo* (1937) and created *The Swing Mikado* (1938). In 1941, while she was a Rosenwald Fellow at the Yale University Drama School (1938–1941), her play *Dust to Earth* was produced there. A later work, *Elijah's Raven,* was produced in Cleveland.

In 1944, in collaboration with George Lipscomb, she published her first biography for young people, *Dr. George Washington Carver, Scientist.* A year later she wrote *Paul Robeson, Citizen of the World,* and in 1949 completed *The Story of Phillis Wheatley.*

Miss Graham received a Guggenheim grant in 1947 and a year later won the Julian Messner Award for *There Was Once A Slave.* In 1950, *Your Most Humble Servant,* a biography of Benjamin Banneker, won the Anisfield-Wolf prize.

She married W. E. B. DuBois in the 1950s and went to Ghana with him in 1961. She lived in Cairo, Egypt, until her death. Her other books are *Booker T. Washington; His Day Is Marching On: A Memoir of W. E. B. DuBois; Gamal Abdel Nasser: Son of the Nile; Zulu Heart,* a novel; *Jean Baptiste Point Le Sable, Founder of Chicago; The Story of Pocahontas; Julius K. Nyerere: Teacher of Africa;* and *DuBois: A Pictorial Biography* (1978).

ALEX HALEY
Journalist, Novelist
1921

The author of the widely acclaimed novel *Roots* was born in Ithaca, New York and reared in Henning, Tennessee. The oldest of three sons of a college professor father and a mother who taught grade school, Haley graduated from high school at 15 and attended college for two years before enlisting in the U.S. Coast Guard as a messboy in 1939.

A voracious reader, he began writing short stories while working at sea, but it took eight years before small magazines began accepting some of his stories.

By 1952, the Coast Guard had created a new rating for Haley, Chief Journalist, and he began handling U.S. Coast Guard public relations. In 1959, after 20 years' military service, he retired from the Coast Guard and launched a new career as a freelance writer. He eventually became an assignments writer for *Reader's Digest* and moved on to *Playboy* where he initiated the "Playboy Interviews" feature.

One of the personalities Haley interviewed was Malcolm X—an interview that inspired Haley's first book, *The Autobiography of Malcolm X* (1965). Translated into eight languages, the book has sold over 6 million copies.

Pursuing the few slender clues of oral family history told him by his maternal grandmother in Tennessee, Haley spent the next 12 years traveling three continents tracking his maternal family back to a Mandingo youth, named Kunta Kinte, who was kidnaped into slavery from the small village of Juffure, in The Gambia, West Africa. During this period, he lectured extensively in the United States and in Great Britain on his discoveries about his family in Africa and wrote many magazine articles on his research in the 1960s and the 1970s. He received several honorary doctor of letters degrees for his work.

The book *Roots,* excerpted in *Reader's Digest* in 1974 and heralded for several years, was finally published in the fall of 1976 with very wide publicity and reviews. In January 1977, ABC-TV produced a 12-hour series based on the book, which set records for the number of viewers. With cover stories, book reviews, and interviews with Haley in scores of magazines and many newspaper articles, the book became the number one national best-seller, sold in the millions, and was published as a paperback in 1977. *Roots* became a phenomenon. It was serialized in the *New York Post* and the *Long Island Press.* Instructional packages, lesson plans based on *Roots* and other books about *Roots* for schools were published along with phonograph records and tapes of Haley and *Roots.* He quickly became a multimillionaire.

All of this stimulated interest in Africa and in black

genealogy. The U.S. Senate passed a resolution paying tribute to Haley and comparing *Roots* to *Uncle Tom's Cabin* by Harriet Beecher Stowe in the 1850s. The book got all sorts of awards, including the National Book Award for 1976 special citation of merit in history and a special Pulitzer Prize in 1976 for making an important contribution to the literature of slavery. Haley received more honorary doctorates from colleges and universities. There was criticism of the errors in *Roots,* and then there was a 1977 lawsuit brought by Margaret Walker Alexander charging that *Roots* plagiarized her novel *Jubilee;* Harold Courlander also filed a suit charging that *Roots* plagiarized his novel *The African.* Courlander received a settlement said to be hundreds of thousands of dollars after several passages in *Roots* were found to be almost verbatim from *The African.* Haley claimed that researchers helping him had given him this material without citing the source.

Haley received the NAACP's Spingarn Medal for 1977 for *Roots.* Four thousand deans and department heads of colleges and universities throughout the country in a survey conducted by *Scholastic Magazine* selected Haley as America's foremost achiever in the literature category. (Dr. Martin Luther King, Jr. was selected in the religious category.) The ABC-TV network presented another series, *Roots: The Next Generation,* in February 1979 (also written by Haley). *Roots* had sold almost 5 million copies by December 1978 and had been reprinted in 23 languages. Haley later with Norman Lear produced a TV series about his childhood in Henning. His next book is supposed to be *My Search for Roots,* or *How I Wrote Roots,* but from newspaper reports his plans may have changed. *Presence Africaine* magazine had a special issue (Fall 1978) on *Roots.* There are also two related books, David L. Wolper and Quincy Troupe's *The Inside Story of TV's Roots* (1978) and Leslie A. Fiedler's *The Inadvertent Epic: From Uncle Tom's Cabin to Roots* (1979).

JUPITER HAMMON
Poet
1720?–1800?

Hammon was the first black to be published in America. *An Evening Thought, Salvation by Christ, with Penitential Cries* appeared in 1761, when Hammon was a slave belonging to a Mr. Lloyd of Long Island, New York.

Due to his fondness for preaching, the major portion of Hammon's poetry is religious in tone, and is usually dismissed by critics as being of little aesthetic value because of its pious platitudes, faulty syntax, and forced rhymes. Hammon's best-known work is a prose piece, *An Address to the Negroes of the State of New York,* delivered before the African Society of New York City on September 24, 1786. This speech was published the following year and went into three editions.

LORRAINE HANSBERRY
Dramatist
1930–1965

The artistic reputation of Lorraine Hansberry rests largely on the success of her first play, *A Raisin in the Sun,* which was awarded the New York Drama Critics Circle Award for the year 1959. (Miss Hansberry is the first black to win this award.)

In Lorraine Hansberry's plays entertainment blends with mental stimulation.

Born in Chicago, Miss Hansberry studied art at Chicago's Art Institute, the University of Wisconsin, and, finally, in Guadalajara, Mexico.

She wrote *Raisin* while living in New York's Greenwich Village, having conceived it after reacting distastefully to what she called "a whole body of material about Negroes. Cardboard characters. Cute dialect bits. Or hip-swinging musicals from exotic scores." It opened on Broadway on March 11, 1959, at a time when it was generally held that all plays dealing with Negroes were "death" at the box-office. Produced, directed, and acted by blacks, it was later made into a successful movie starring Sidney Poitier. It was then converted to *Raisin,* a musical which won a Tony Award in 1974.

Her second Broadway play, *The Sign in Sidney Brustein's Window,* dealt with "the western intellectual poised in hesitation before the flames of involvement." Shortly after its Broadway opening, Miss Hansberry succumbed to cancer on January 12, 1965 in New York City.

Her books, in addition to the two published plays, are *To Be Young, Gifted and Black; The Movement: Documentary of a Struggle for Equality* (text); and *Les Blancs: The Collected Last Plays of Lorraine Hansberry.*

FRANCES E. W. HARPER
Poet, Abolitionist
1825–1911

Frances Ellen Watkins Harper was born in Baltimore of free parents, and orphaned a few years later. She attended a school for free Negroes conducted by her uncle, William Watkins, interrupting her formal education at the age of 13 to find employment as a nursemaid.

While she was still in her teens, Miss Harper's poetry and prose were published in a volume called *Autumn Leaves.* Her biggest commercial success came in Philadelphia in 1854, when she published *Poems on Miscellaneous Subjects,* which sold 10,000 copies in its first five years.

Her next work, *Moses, A Story of the Nile,* appeared in 1869. Three years later, she completed *Sketches of Southern Life,* which is notable for its attempt to recreate the speech of American Negroes while avoiding dialect. Her other books of poetry are *Poems* (1871, 1895, 1900), *Atlanta Offering, Effie Alton, Eventide, Forest Leaves, Idylls of the Bible, The Sparrow's Fall. Iola Leroy: On Shadows Uplifted* is a novel.

MICHAEL S. HARPER
Poet
1938

Michael S. Harper was born in Brooklyn, New York, but lived for many years in California. He studied creative writing at the Iowa University Writers' Workshop and has published poems in the magazines *Poetry, Southern Review, Quarterly Review of Literature, Negro Digest, December,* and others. He has been writer-in-residence, visiting lecturer, and associate professor of English at several colleges. Since 1974, Harper has been an associate professor of English at Brown University, Providence, Rhode Island. His books of poetry are *Dear John, Dear Coltrane: Poems* (1970); *History Is Your Own Heartbeat; Photographs: Negatives: History as Apple Tree; Song: I Want a Witness; Debridement; Poems; Nightmare Begins Responsibility* (1974); and *Images of Kin: New and Selected Poems* (1977).

MIDDLETON A. "SPIKE" HARRIS
Historian
1910–1977

Born and schooled in New York City, Middleton A. Harris' early formal education began at P.S. 9 in

Middleton Harris ferrets out the secrets of black history.

Brooklyn and continued through Brooklyn's Manual Training High School and the Manhattan Textile High School. He later attended Howard University, graduating with a degree in sociology.

After college, Harris became a social worker, directing numerous youth groups before joining the City of New York as a parole officer. During World War II, "Spike" served as social director for the American Red Cross in the South Pacific.

Curiosity about his family beginnings started Harris on his lifelong quest for his own origins and for the largely buried elements of black history. Like Joel Rogers, Harris realized that the history of his people was dispersed and would require intensive research. Thus he wrote letters to government officials, conducted investigations of records in local courthouses, and relentlessly followed every lead. Over the years, Harris was able to accumulate a vast personal collection of memorabilia, mementos, tokens, souvenirs, and diversified keepsakes germane to the history of blacks.

Harris' personal library of rare books, graphics, audiovisual materials, and duplicates of government records relative to the history of the black provides a treasure trove for scholars. Some of this material is now in the Schomburg Collection in New York City. As President of Negro History Associates, Harris had successfully assumed responsibility for generating interest in what he calls the "lost pages of our national history." He dedicated four historical plaques in Manhattan which pertain to episodes involving black contributions or achievements.

Harris is also the author of a unique guidebook of Manhattan Island as seen from the vantage point of a black observer. The book, *A Negro History Tour of Manhattan,* contains several startling, revealing, and intriguing facts and incidents. *The Black Book,* edited by Middleton Harris, Morris Levitt, Roger Furman, and Ernest Smith was published in 1974. At the time of his death Harris was working on a book, yet unpublished, titled *The Black Man and the Sea.*

JAMES HASKINS
Writer
1941

James Haskins was a public school teacher in New York City in the late 1960s. His first book, *Diary of a Harlem School Teacher* (1970), was the result of this experience. He then began to write and edit books for children and adults. They were *Profiles of Black Power; A Piece of the Power: Four Black Mayors; Black Manifesto for Education; Jokes from Black Folks; Religious;* and *From Lew Alcindor to Kareem Abdul Jabbar* (1972). In 1974 Haskins was teaching at the Experimental College at Staten Island Community and Manhattanville Colleges. His other works are *Pinckney*

Benton Stewart Pinchback; The Psychology of Black Language (with High F. Butts); *Adam Clayton Powell: Portrait of a Marching Black; Jobs in Business and Office; Witchcraft, Mysticism and Magic in the Black World; Ralph Bunche: A Most Reluctant Hero; Babe Ruth and Hank Aaron: The Home Run Kings; The War and the Protest: Viet Nam and Resistance; Profiles in Nonviolence.*

From 1975 to the present Haskins has devoted full time to writing mostly for young people and children, sometimes in collaboration. He has written *The Creoles of Color of New Orleans; Fighting Shirley Chisholm; The Picture Life of Malcolm X; Dr. J: A Biography of Julius Erving; The Story of Stevie Wonder; Children Have Rights Too; The Consumer Movement; Your Rights, Past and Present; Pele: A Biography; Teen-Age Alcoholism; Aging in America: The Great Denial; A Time To Win: The Story of the Kennedy Foundation's Special Olympics for the Mentally Retarded; Always Movin On: The Life of Langston Hughes; The Cotton Club* (now being made into a film); *Scott Joplin; James Van Der Zee: The Picture Takin' Man; The Life and Death of Martin Luther King, Jr.;* and *I'm Gonna Make You Love Me: The Story of Diana Ross.* A few other earlier titles by Haskins not listed here make him the author of 36 to 40 books.

ROBERT E. HAYDEN
Poet
1913–1980

Poet Robert E. Hayden, a graduate of Wayne University, who was chief researcher on Negro history and folklore for the Federal Writers Project in 1936, later went on to do advanced work in English, play production, and creative writing at the University of Michigan. While there, he won the Jule and Avery Hopwood Prize for poetry twice. Hayden also completed radio scripts and a finished version of a play about the Underground Railroad, *Go Down Moses.*

His first book of poems, *Heart-Shape in the Dust,* was published in 1940 shortly before he assumed the music and drama critic function for the *Michigan Chronicle.* He taught at Fisk University from 1946 to the early 1970s and later at the University of Michigan. His works include *The Lion and the Archer* (with Myron O'Higgins), *A Ballad of Remembrance; Selected Poems; Words in the Mourning Time;* and *The Night-Blooming Cereus.* He edited *Kaleidoscope: Poems by American Negro Poets* and *Afro American Literature: An Introduction* (with David J. Burrows and Frederick R. Lapsides). His other books are *Figure of Time, Angle of Ascent: New and Selected Poems,* and *American Journal* (poems). In 1975 the Academy of American Poets elected him its Fellow of the Year, and in 1976 he was awarded the Grand Prize for Poetry at the

A scene from the screen version of Chester Himes' novel Cotton Comes to Harlem.

First World Festival of Negro Arts in Dakar, Senegal. From 1976 to 1978, he served as Consultant in Poetry at the Library of Congress. He was a professor of English at the University of Michigan at the time of his death in 1980.

CHESTER HIMES
Novelist
1909

Chester Himes began his career as a writer of popular material and later moved to biting satiric fiction.

Born in Jefferson City, Missouri, Himes was educated at Ohio State University, has lived in France, and now lives in Spain.

In 1945 he completed his first novel, *If He Hollers Let Him Go,* the story of a black working in a defense plant. His second book, *The Lonely Crusade* (1947), was set in similar surroundings.

Since then, Himes has written many other books: *The Third Generation* (1954); *Cotton Comes to Harlem* (1965); and *Pinktoes* (1965). Recently he published *The Quality of Hurt: The Autobiography of Chester Himes* and *Black on Black: Baby Sister and Selected Writings.*

Himes suffered a stroke that has confined him to a wheelchair. He now lives with his wife in Alicante, Spain and in 1977, they came to New York for the publication of the concluding volume of his autobiography *My Life of Absurdity.* At that time in answer to a question about his work habits, he told a reporter: "I do a little writing after breakfast and I think about what I would write if I had the strength."

GEORGE MOSES HORTON
Poet
1797–1883?

George Moses Horton was born in slavery in North Carolina. While working as a janitor at the University of North Carolina, Horton wrote light verse for some students in exchange for spending money.

Some of his early poems were printed in the newspapers of Raleigh and Boston. When Horton published his first book of poems in 1829, he entitled it *The Hope of Liberty* in the belief that profits from its sales would be sufficient to pay for his freedom. His hopes did not materialize, however, with the result that he remained a slave until the coming of Emancipation.

This book was reprinted in 1837 under the title *Poems by a Slave.*

In 1865, he published *Naked Genius,* a poem containing many bitter lines about his former condition which are in sharp contrast to the conformist verse of earlier black poets. Richard Walser's *The Black Poet* about Horton was published in 1967.

LANGSTON HUGHES
Poet
1902–1967

Langston Hughes belongs in the ranks of the major American writers of the twentieth century.

Born in Joplin, Missouri, Hughes moved to Cleveland at the age of 14, graduated from Central High School, and spent a year in Mexico before studying at Columbia University. After roaming the world as a seaman and writing some poetry as well, Hughes returned to the United States, winning the Witter Bynner Prize for undergraduate poetry while attending Lincoln University, later his alma mater (1928). Two years later, he received the Harmon Award and, in 1935, with the help of a Guggenheim Fellowship, traveled to Russia and Spain.

The long and distinguished list of Hughes' prose works includes *Not Without Laughter* (1930), a novel,

Black poet laureate Langston Hughes.

and *The Big Sea* (1940) and *I Wonder as I Wander* (1956), his autobiography. To this must be added such collections of poetry as *The Weary Blues* (1926); *The Dream Keeper* (1932); *Shakespeare in Harlem* (1942); *Fields of Wonder* (1947); *One Way Ticket* (1947); and *Selected Poems* (1959).

Hughes was also an accomplished song lyricist, librettist, and newspaper columnist. Through his newspaper columns, he created Jesse B. Simple, a Harlem character who saw life on the musical stage in *Simply Heavenly.* There are also several volumes of the *Simple Columns.*

Throughout the 1960s, Hughes edited several anthologies in an attempt to popularize black authors and their works. Some of these are *An African Treasury* (1960); *Poems from Black Africa* (1963); *New Negro Poets: U.S.A.* (1964); and *The Best Short Stories by Negro Writers* (1967). Published after his death were *The Panther and the Lash: Poems of Our Times* (1969) and *Good Morning Revolution: Uncollected Writings of Social Protest.* Hughes wrote many plays, including *Emperor of Haiti* and *Five Plays by Langston Hughes.* *Mulatto* was produced on Broadway in the 1930s. He also wrote gospel song plays such as *Tambourines to Glory, Black Nativity,* and *Jericho—Jim Crow.*

In tone and spirit, Hughes remained a poet with a twist of gray humor. Sadness, rather than anger, seemed his primary emotion. There are seven books about Hughes written for adults and children since his death in 1967.

ZORA NEALE HURSTON
Novelist
1903–1960

Once placed in "the front rank of American writers" for her mastery of folklore, Zora Neale Hurston was born and raised in an all-black town in Florida (Eatonville), an experience that left a deep imprint on her later literary efforts.

After traveling north as a maid with a Gilbert and Sullivan company, she acquired her education at Morgan State, Howard, and Columbia. While at Howard, under Alain Locke's influence, she became a figure in the Negro Renaissance, publishing short stories in *Opportunity* and serving with Langston Hughes and Wallace Thurman on the editorial board of the magazine *Fire.*

In 1934 *Jonah's Gourd Vine* was published after her return to Florida. Her more important novel, *Their Eyes Were Watching God,* appeared three years later and then *Moses, Man of the Mountain* (1939), was followed in 1948 by *Seraph on the Suwanee.* Her other three works are books of folklore and her autobiography.

Toward the end of her life, Miss Hurston was a

drama instructor at the North Carolina College for Negroes in Durham. She died in obscurity and poverty on January 28, 1960. Since then, six of her works have been reprinted with new introductions and Alice Walker edited *A Zora Neale Hurston Reader.* These books plus two books about Hurston and her works constitute a Hurston revival.

FENTON JOHNSON
Poet
1888–1958

Fenton Johnson was born in Chicago in 1888, and received his formal education there, in the public school system and at the University of Chicago. In 1914 Johnson completed his first volume of poetry, *A Little Dreaming,* followed in 1916 by *Visions of the Dusk and Songs of the Soil.* Johnson's prose works include *Tales of Darkest America* (1920) and a book of short stories.

His last work, *The Daily Grind: 42 W.P.A. Poems,* was listed in 1963 in the *Paul Breman Heritage Series* but was never published.

GEORGIA DOUGLAS JOHNSON
Poet
1886–1966

Georgia Douglas Johnson was born in Atlanta and educated at Atlanta University and at the Oberlin Conservatory in Ohio.

Her initial interest was in musical composition, but gradually she turned toward lyric poetry. After teaching school in Alabama, she moved to Washington, D.C. with her husband, who had been appointed as Recorder of Deeds by President William Howard Taft. While in the nation's capital, she too engaged in government work while completing such books as *The Heart of Woman* (1918), *Bronze* (1922), and *An Autumn Love Cycle* (1928). Her last book, *Share My World,* was published in 1962.

JAMES WELDON JOHNSON
Poet, Lyricist, Civil Rights Leader
1871–1938

(For biography see Civil Rights section, p. 000.)

JUNE JORDAN
Poet, Novelist
1936

Born in Harlem of parents from Jamaica, West Indies, June Jordan attended Barnard College and the University of Chicago. She has been married and has a son. She has taught Afro-American literature, English, and writing at several colleges and universities and was co-founder and co-director of The Voice of the Children, Inc., a creative workshop. Her poems have been published in many magazines, newspapers, and anthologies. She received a Rockefeller Grant in creative writing for 1969. Her books for children and young people are *Fannie Lou Hamer* (1972); *His Own Where* (1971), her first novel nominated for the National Book Award; *Who Look at Me* (1969); *Dry Victories* (1972); *New Room, New Life* (1974); and *The Voice of the Children: Writings by Black and Puerto Rican Young People* (1970, 1974), edited by Jordan and Terri Bush. Her books for adults are *Soulscript* (1970), edited by Jordan; *Some Changes* (1971); *New Day Poems of Exile and Return* (1973); *Things That I Do in the Dark: Selected Poems* (1976); and *Passion: New Poems 1977–1980* (1980).

WILLIAM MELVIN KELLEY
Novelist
1937

William Melvin Kelley's first novel, *A Different Drummer* (1962), was widely acclaimed for its provocative theme and imaginative development. The story concerns the mass exodus of the black inhabitants of an imaginary Southern state.

Born in New York City, Kelley is a graduate of the Fieldston School and of Harvard, where he studied under Archibald MacLeish and John Hawkes. He has won the Dana Reed Literary Prize and the Rosenthal Foundation Award of the National Institute of Arts and Letters. He was author-in-residence at New York State University College at Geneseo.

In 1964, a collection of his stories appeared under the title *Dancers on the Shore.* The following year his second novel was published, *A Drop of Patience. Dem,* a surrealistic fantasy, was published in 1967. His fourth novel, *Dunsford Travels Everywhere,* was published in 1970. He now lives with his family in Paris, France.

JOHN OLIVER KILLENS
Novelist
1916

John Oliver Killen's first novel, *Youngblood* (1954), dealt with life in a southern black family, a theme which Killens knew well, having been born into just such an environment in Macon, Georgia.

Killens studied at three black colleges then the Terrell Law School, at Columbia, and at New York University. From 1936 to 1942—and again in 1946 after completing his military service—Killens worked with the National Labor Relations Board in Washington, D.C.

After serving as head of the Harlem Writers' Workshop, Killens second novel, *And Then We Heard the*

John Killens expresses his ideas in novels, essays, and film scripts.

Thunder, was published in 1963. Prior to that, he had written the script for *Odds Against Tomorrow,* a film which starred Harry Belafonte in 1959. He has taught creative writing at Fisk, Columbia, and Howard universities.

Killens' book of essays, *Black Man's Burden,* appeared in 1965. His later works are *Sippi* (1967), a novel; the film script for the *Silim Slaves* (1969); *The Cotillion* (1971), a novel; and *The Trial Record of Denmark Vesey* (1970); *Great Gittin' Up Morning* (1972), a biography of Denmark Vesey; and *A Man Ain't Nothin' But A Man: The Adventures of John Henry* (1975). He lives with his family in Brooklyn, New York and teaches writing at Medgar Evers College in Brooklyn.

JULIUS LESTER
Essayist, Critic

Julius Lester, a forceful advocate of the black militant movement, is the author of *Look Out, Whitey! Black Power's Gon' Get Your Mama; To Be A Slave; Revolutionary Notes; Black Folktales; Search for the New Land; The Seventh Son; The Thought and Writings of W. E. B. DuBois; Long Journey Home: Stories from Black History; Two Love Stories; The Knee High Man and Other Tales;* and *Who I Am.*

To Be A Slave (1968) was the 1968 Newbery Medal runner-up. His writings have appeared in *The Village Voice, The Guardian, The Movement, Broadsides, Lib-*

erator, and *Sing Out.* In addition, Lester has made records for Vanguard Records. His reviews appear frequently in the pages of the *New York Times.* His autobiography, *All Is Well,* was published in 1976. *This Strange New Feeling* (1982) is a compilation of love stories of newly freed slaves.

ALAIN LEROY LOCKE
Critic
1886–1954

Alain Leroy Locke shares the spotlight—along with Benjamin Brawley and Sterling Brown—as a critic and chronicler of the Harlem Renaissance.

Locke was born in Philadelphia and educated at Harvard and, as a Rhodes scholar, at Oxford. He served for many years as chairman of the philosophy department at Howard University, but his main contribution to American culture lies in his efforts to make

Julius Lester, the essayist as provocateur.

the public aware of the Negro's aesthetic achievements—from the art and artifacts of Africa to the poetry and novels of the American writer.

In 1925 Locke edited *The New Negro,* a volume which sought to define the aims of the black artists then in the full flush of the Harlem Renaissance. Consisting of the representative work of a number of young black writers, this anthology served notice of the existence of a new literary self-image for the Negro, founded partly on an uncompromising demand for equal rights.

Locke's championing of the new writers who had outgrown what he called "the pathetic overcompensation of a group inferiority complex" helped promote a number of outstanding literary works written by blacks during the postwar period.

Locke died in 1954 while in the midst of collecting material for what he hoped would be his greatest contribution to American letters. This work, later completed by Margaret Just Butcher, is entitled *The Negro in American Culture* (1956). His other works are *The Negro and His Music, Negro Art: Past and Present,* and *The Negro in Art.* Eugene C. Holmes, retired professor of philosophy at Howard University, died before he completed the biography of Locke that he was writing.

RAYFORD W. LOGAN
Historian
1897

Rayford W. Logan is a native of Washington, D.C., where he received a public school education prior to attending Harvard and Williams College.

During World War I, Logan served abroad with the 372nd Infantry of the segregated 93rd Division, a unit which was brigaded with French troops overseas. After the war, Logan went into teaching, first at Virginia Union University, then at Atlanta University, and last at Howard. While there, he became an assistant to Carter Woodson in the Washington-based Association for the Study of Negro Life and History. In this capacity, he contributed numerous articles to a variety of scholarly and popular periodicals, edited *The Attitude of the Southern White Press Toward Negro Suffrage, 1932–1940* (1940), and wrote a study entitled *The Diplomatic Relations of the United States with Haiti, 1776–1891* (1941).

Logan has written numerous other books since then, including *The Negro in the United States* (1957); *The Betrayal of the Negro from Rutherford B. Hayes to Woodrow Wilson* (1965); *The American Negro* (with Irving S. Cohen); and *Howard University: The First Hundred Years 1867–1967.* He is now editing with Michael R. Winston the *Dictionary of American Negro Biography.*

CLARENCE MAJOR
Poet, Novelist
1936

Clarence Major, although born in Atlanta, Georgia, was essentially a product of the elementary and high school system of Chicago where his family had moved shortly after his birth. He attended the Art Institute of Chicago and later studied English and journalism. His poems, short stories, and essays have been published in many magazines and anthologies. He was an associate editor of *Umbra* magazine and is a contributing editor of *The Journal of Black Poetry.* In 1974 he was living in New York City and taught literature and creative writing at Sarah Lawrence College. Major has been a visiting writer at many colleges and universities. He has written or edited many books: three novels and a novelette: *All-Night Visitors* (1969), *No* (1973), *Reflex and Bone Structure* (1975), and *Emergency Exit* (1980); *The New Black Poetry* (anthology); *Dictionary of Afro-American Slang;* and five books of poetry: *Swallow the Lake, Symptoms and Madness, Private Line, The Cotton Club* and *The Syncopated Cakewalk.* Logan has also written *The Dark and Feeling: Black American Writers and Their Work* (1974).

PAULE MARSHALL
Novelist, Short Story Writer
1929

Paule Marshall was born in Brooklyn, New York, and graduated from Brooklyn College as a Phi Beta Kappa. In Barbados (the birthplace of her parents) she wrote her first novel, *Brown Girl, Brownstones* (1959, reprinted twice in 1970 and also in 1981), which deals with the dislocation one experiences in moving from the tropics to the cruel reality of a home in Brooklyn.

Marshall is also the author of *Soul Clap Hands and Sing* (1961) which is a collection of four short stories or novellas set in Brazil, Barbados, British Guiana, and Brooklyn. Her big novel, entitled *The Chosen Place, The Timeless People,* was published in 1969. She is now working on her fourth book.

JULIAN MAYFIELD
Novelist, Essayist, Editor
1928

Julian Mayfield was born in Greer, South Carolina, and at the age of 10 moved with his family to Washington, D.C. Upon completing high school, he served in the Army in the Pacific. At the conclusion of World War II he attended Lincoln University in Pennsylvania. As with many other artists, he was employed in a myriad of unrewarding jobs. He acted in the Broadway play *Lost in the Stars* and in the film *Up Tight!* Mayfield spent many years in Africa, Europe, and the Caribbean. Much of his work can be found in the *Puerto Rico World Journal, The African Review* in Accra, *Commentary, The New Republic, The Nation, Negro Digest,* and *Freedomways.*

His novels include *The Hit* (1957), *The Long Night* (1958), and *The Grand Parade* (1961). His works have been translated into French, Japanese, Czech, and German. He was a teaching fellow at Cornell University and by 1974 was living in Guyana. He edited *Ten Times Black* (short stories) in 1972. He has been a writer in residence at several colleges.

CLAUDE McKAY
Poet
1890–1948

Claude McKay is generally regarded as the herald of the Harlem Renaissance.

Born the son of a farmer in Jamaica (then British West Indies), McKay began writing early in life. Two books of his poems—*Songs of Jamaica* and *Constab Ballads*—were published just after he turned 20. In both, he made extensive use of the Jamaican dialect known as *patois.*

In 1913 McKay came to America to study agriculture at Tuskegee Institute and at Kansas State University, but his interest in poetry induced him to move to New York City, where he published his work in small literary magazines.

McKay then made a trip abroad, visiting England. While there, he completed a collection of lyrics entitled *Spring in New Hampshire.* When he returned to the United States, he became associated editor of *The Liberator* under Max Eastman. In 1922 he completed *Harlem Shadows,* a landmark work during the Harlem Renaissance period.

McKay then turned to the writing of such novels as *Home to Harlem* (1928), *Banjo* (1929), and four other books including an autobiography and a study of Harlem. *The Passion of Claude McKay: Selected Prose and Poetry 1912–1948* edited by Wayne Cooper, was published in 1973. McKay traveled extensively abroad before returning to the United States, where he died. His final work, *Selected Poems,* was published posthumously in 1953.

During World War II, when Winston Churchill addressed a joint session of the U.S. Congress in an effort to enlist American aid in the battle against Nazism, the climax of his oration was his reading of the famous poem *If We Must Die,* which is taken from a stirring poem originally written by McKay to assail lynchings and mob violence in the South. McKay's *Trial by Lynching* (1967), edited and translated stories, and his *The Negroes in America* (1979 or 1980), edited and translated from the Russian language, have also been published.

Short Story specialist James A. McPherson.

JAMES A. McPHERSON
Short Story Writer
1943

James McPherson, born in Savannah, Georgia, received his B.A. degree in 1965 from Morris Brown College in Atlanta, a law degree from Harvard University in 1968, and an M.F.A. degree from the University of Iowa in 1969. He has taught writing at several universities and is a contributing editor of *Atlantic Monthly.* His short stories have appeared in several magazines. *Hue and Cry,* a collection of short stories published in 1969, was highly praised by Ralph Ellison. A Guggenheim Fellow in 1972–1973, McPherson's second book of short stories, *Elbow Room,* was published in 1977 and was given the Pulitzer Prize for fiction in 1978. He has been teaching fiction writing for several years at the University of Virginia in Charlottesville. McPherson was one of the three black writers who, with Elma Lewis, were awarded five-year grants by the McArthur Foundation of Chicago in

1981 for exceptional talent. His grant was $192,000. After this happened, he left the University of Virginia with his wife and son to keep to his privacy and is now teaching writing at another university.

KELLY MILLER
Historian
1863–1939

(For biography see Civil Rights section)

LOFTEN MITCHELL
Dramatist
1919

Raised in the Harlem of 1920s, Loften Mitchell first began to write as a child, creating scripts for backyard shows he and his brother put on. After completing junior high school, he decided to enroll at New York Textile High because he had been promised a job on the school newspaper there. But Mitchell soon realized that he needed the training of an academic high school and, with the help of one of his teachers, transferred to DeWitt Clinton.

Graduating with honors, Mitchell found a job as

Playwright Loften Mitchell.

an elevator operator and a delivery boy to support himself while he studied playwriting at night at the City College of New York. However, he met a professor from Talladega College in Alabama who helped him win a scholarship to study there. He graduated with honors in 1943, having won an award for the best play written by a student.

After two years of service in the Navy, Mitchell enrolled as a graduate student at Columbia University in New York. A year later, he accepted a job with the Department of Welfare as a social investigator and continued to go to school at night. During this time he wrote one of his first successful plays, *Blood in the Night,* and in 1957 he wrote *A Land Beyond the River,* which had a long run at an off-Broadway theater and was published as a book.

The following year Mitchell won a Guggenheim award, which enabled him to return to Columbia and write for a year. Since then, he has written a new play, *Star of the Morning,* the story of Bert Williams, famous black entertainer.

In 1967 Mitchell published a study entitled *Black Drama,* the story of the American Negro in the theater. His other books are *Tell Pharaoh,* a play, and *The Stubborn Old Lady Who Resisted Change* (1973), a novel, and *Voices of the Black Theatre* (1976). Mitchell also wrote the books for the Broadway musicals *Ballads for Bimshire* (1963) and *Bubbling Brown Sugar* in the 1970s, as well as a 1979 musical, *Cartoons for a Lunch Hour.*

TONI MORRISON
Novelist, Editor
1931

Born in Lorain, Ohio, she received a B.A. degree from Howard University in 1953 and an M.A. from Cornell in 1955. After working as an instructor in English and the humanities at Texas Southern University and Howard University Morrison eventually became a senior editor at Random House in New York City, a job she still holds. Morrison has been responsible for the publication of many books by blacks at Random House: Middleton Harris' *The Black Book,* which she edited, and books by Toni Cade Bambara and others. In 1971–1972 she was also an associate professor at the State University of New York at Purchase. Formerly married, she has two sons. Her first novel, *The Bluest Eye,* was published in 1970. Her second novel, *Sula,* was published in 1974 and won a 1975 Ohioana Book Award. Morrison's third novel, *Song of Solomon* (1977), was very widely reviewed and received the 1978 award in literature of $3,000 from the American Academy and Institute of Arts and Letters. Her fourth novel, *Tar Baby* (1981) was even more widely reviewed. *Newsweek* magazine's front cover story on

Morrison's life and writings called her the best of the black writers today. She was elected to the American Institute of Arts and Letters in 1981 and gave the keynote address at the American Writers' Congress in New York City in the fall of that year. Barbara Christian's *Black Women Novelists* (1980) has a section on her first three novels; and there is an interview with Morrison in Michael S. Harper and Robert B. Stepto's *Chant of Saints: A Gathering of Afro-American Literature, Art and Scholarship* (1979). She has written the story for the musical *Storyville*, which is about jazz music originating in the brothels of New Orleans.

WILLARD MOTLEY
Novelist
1912–1965

Because most of his work dealt with poor whites on Chicago's West Side, it was not generally known that Willard Motley was black.

Born in a middle-class Chicago neighborhood, Motley wrote his first book, *Knock on Any Door,* in 1947. One of the first naturalistic novels to deal with the problem of juvenile delinquency, it enjoyed enormous commercial success before being made into a Hollywood film starring Humphrey Bogart.

In 1951, Motley completed *We Fished All Night,* an attempt to describe the impact of World War II on three young Chicagoans. Seven years later, a sequel to his first novel was published under the title *Let No Man Write My Epitaph,* also made into a movie.

Motley died of gangrene in Mexico City on March 4, 1965, a year before his last novel, *Let Noon Be Fair,* was published. Jerome Klinkowitz edited *The Diaries of Willard Motley,* published in 1978.

ALBERT MURRAY
Essayist, Novelist
1916

Born in Nokonis, Alabama, Albert Murray received a B.A. from Tuskegee Institute and an M.A. from New York University and has completed additional study at several other universities. He has been a visiting professor and a lecturer at many universities since he retired from the U.S. Air Force as a major some years ago. Murray's short stories and essays are found in numerous anthologies of black writing. His first book was *The Omni-Americans: New Perspectives on Black Experience and American Culture* (1970). This was followed by *South to a Very Old Place* (1972); then *The Hero and the Blues* (1973), a collection of the Paul Anthony Buck lectures (ninth series) at the University of Missouri, Columbia. His fourth book was a novel, *Trainwhistle Guitar* (1974), the first part of a trilogy of novels to be published. Murray's biggest

book was *Stomping the Blues* (1976), a profusely illustrated discussion of the aesthetic values of blues music and how these values originated and the blues developed as an art in the black communities. His writings on Duke Ellington's music have also been published elsewhere. *Stomping the Blues* will be reprinted in the Vintage Book series. Murray has lived with his wife and daughter in New York City for many years. He has influenced many young black writers such as Stanley Crouch of the *Village Voice* newspaper, Jerrvis Anderson of *The New Yorker* magazine, and many others.

WILLIAM C. NELL
Historian, Journalist
1816–1874

The most important contribution of William C. Nell to American military history is his *The Colored Patriots of the American Revolution* (1855), a factual, vividly descriptive account of the role played by blacks in the wars in 1776 and 1812.

Though he had little formal education, Nell struggled impressively to improve his condition, and eventually came to be a close friend of William Lloyd Garrison, with whom he was closely associated in the publication of *The Liberator.* Other abolitionists associated with Garrison encouraged Nell in his writing, and two of them—Wendell Phillips and Harriet Beecher Stowe—contributed introductions.

Nell not only documented rare and underpublicized events of the Revolutionary War and the War of 1812, but also painstakingly sifted his sources to separate fact from hearsay. His account of the Boston Massacre is particularly helpful in understanding the full implication of the event—both when it happened and generations later.

DANIEL A. PAYNE
Historian, Educator
1811–1893

Education and expansion of the Negro church were the two activities which occupied most of Daniel Payne's professional career, although he found time late in life to record his experiences in a number of valuable publications.

Born in Charleston, South Carolina, Payne was educated at the school of the Miner's Moralist Society in his native city and later at the Gettysburg Lutheran Seminary. Payne ran a private school for blacks in antebellum Charleston until 1835—the year a state law against schools for Negro children was passed. Forced to close down, he moved to Philadelphia where he established a similar operation.

During the Civil War, after urging President Lin-

The Reverend Daniel A. Payne, author of The History of the A.M.E. Church.

coln to sign a bill emancipating slaves in the District of Columbia, Payne urged the African Methodist Episcopal Church to purchase Wilberforce. Payne served as president of the school for some 16 years.

In retirement, Payne turned to writing. His most important full-length work is *The History of the A.M.E. Church* (1891). He also wrote *Recollections of Seventy Years* (1888).

ANN PETRY
Novelist, Short Story Writer, Critic
1911

Ann Petry was born in Old Saybrook, Connecticut, where her father was a druggist. After graduating from the College of Pharmacy at the University of Connecticut, she went to New York where she found employment as a social worker and newspaper reporter, studying creative writing at night.

Her early short stories appeared in *Crisis* and *Pylon*. In 1946, after having received a Houghton Mifflin Fellowship, she completed and published her first novel, *The Street*. This was followed by *Country Place* (1947) and *The Narrows* (1953). She then wrote *The Drugstore Cat; Harriet Tubman; Tituba of Salem Village; Legends of Saints;* and a fourth book for children and young people. *Miss Muriel and Other Stories* (1971) is for adults.

BENJAMIN QUARLES
Historian
1904

A specialist in military history, Benjamin Quarles has done extensive research on the Revolutionary and Civil wars and has produced two full-length books dealing with the blacks' role in these conflicts.

Born in Boston and educated in the public schools there, Quarles has also studied at Shaw University in North Carolina and at the University of Wisconsin. He has taught for many years at Dillard University in New Orleans and at Morgan State University in Baltimore, and served as an associate editor of the *Journal of Negro History*.

The recipient of Rosenwald Fellowships and the University of Wisconsin President Adams Fellowship in Modern History, Quarles has completed a number of books on Negro history and life, including full-length studies of Frederick Douglass and Abraham Lincoln.

His books are *Frederick Douglass* (1948); *Lincoln and the Negro* (1962); *The Negro in the Civil War* (1953); *The Negro in the American Revolution* (1961); *The Negro in the Making of America* (1964); *Black Abolitionists;* and *Allies for Freedom: Blacks and John Brown*. He has edited *Blacks on John Brown; Frederick Douglass* (Great Lives Observed Series); *The Black American: A Documentary History,* with Leslie H. Fishel, Jr.; and *Narrative of the Life of Frederick Douglass*.

J. SAUNDERS REDDING
Critic
1906

J. Saunders Redding has written a number of perceptive appraisals of black literature, completed a novel, an autobiography, and several volumes of history.

Born in Wilmington, Delaware, Redding received his undergraduate and graduate degrees from Brown University where he won Phi Beta Kappa honors. In 1944, he received the Mayflower Award for the best book by a resident of North Carolina. A 1945–1946 Guggenheim Fellowship enabled him to take a leave from his teaching position at Hampton Institute in Virginia.

Redding's books are *To Make a Poet Black* (1939); *No Day of Triumph* (1942); *Stranger and Alone* (1950); *They Came in Chains* (1950); *On Being Negro in America* (1951); *An American in India* (1955); *The Lonesome Road* (1958); and *The Negro*.

In recent years, Redding has assumed several prominent and important educational and consulting assignments. His reviews on black historical, cultural, and scholarly themes have often appeared in the *New York Times*. He is the editor with Arthur P. Davis of *Caval-*

cade: *Negro American Writing from 1760 to the Present* (1971) and earlier *Reading for Writing* (1952) with Ivan E. Taylor. He is still a professor at Cornell University, Ithaca, New York.

ISHMAEL REED
Novelist, Poet
1938

Powerfully imaginative Ishmael Reed is one of America's most promising young novelists, with a great ability to create characters with ideas.

Born in Chattanooga, Tennessee, he grew up in Buffalo, New York, learned to write in New York City, and wised up in Berkeley, California, where he now lives and teaches at the university. His first volume of poetry published in the United States, *Conjure* (1972), was nominated for the National Book Award, as was his third novel, *Mumbo Jumbo* (1972). He has also published *Chattanooga,* a second volume of poetry, and four other novels: *The Free-lance Pallbearers, Yellow Back Radio Broke Down, The Last Days of Louisiana Red,* which appeared in 1974, and *Flight to Canada* (1976).

Reed edited the breakthrough anthology *19 Necromancers from Now* and *The Yardbird Reader,* Volume I. His poetry has appeared in numerous anthologies and magazines, including *The Poetry of the Negro, The New Black Poetry, The Norton Anthology, Cricket,* and *Scholastic* magazine. His *Shrovetide in Old New Orleans* (1978) is a collection of essays.

JOEL A. ROGERS
Historian
1880–1966

For more than 50 years, Joel A. Rogers was one of the foremost black historians and journalists in the United States.

Born in Jamaica, West Indies, Rogers came to the United States in 1906. Originally a journalist, he covered Haile Selassie's coronation as Emperor of Ethiopia in 1930 and, five years later, became the first black war correspondent in U.S. history by reporting the Italo-Ethiopian War for the *Pittsburgh Courier.*

Rogers was a member of the American Geographical Society and the Academy of Political Science. He was the author of numerous newspaper and magazine articles and wrote an illustrated feature ("Your History") for the *Pittsburgh Courier.* His books are *From Superman to Man* (1917); *As Nature Leads* (1919); *World's Greatest Men of African Descent* (1931); *Real Facts About Ethiopia* (1935); *Sex and Race* (3 vols., 1940–1944); *World's Great Men of Color* (2 vols., 1947, 1972); *Nature Knows No Color Line;* and *Africa's Gift to America.*

Although the work of Joel Rogers has at times been challenged for the accuracy of its documentation and interpretation, it is nonetheless impressive when one considers that Rogers was conducting much of his research at a time when black historians were very rare in the United States.

Rogers continued to work on a number of manuscripts until his death in New York City in January 1966.

DAVID RUGGLES
Author
1810–1849

David Ruggles probably gained his most lasting fame because he aided Frederick Douglass' escape from slavery but he is worthy of recognition in his own right.

Described as a jack-of-all-trades, Ruggles seems to have been a self-educated activist who was involved with the ministry, opened a reading room in New York *exclusively* for Negroes, served as Secretary of the Committee of Vigilance of New York, ran a magazine, deluged the press with antislavery letters, and somehow found time to be proprietor of a spa.

His books are both polemical in tone and somewhat effusive, but they give considerable evidence of the man's unbounded enthusiasm and debating excellence. They are *The "Extinguisher" Extinguished, or David M. Reese, M.D.; Used Up* (1834); and *An Antidote for a Poisonous Combination Recently Prepared by a "Citizen of New York," alias Dr. Reese.*

SONIA SANCHEZ
Poet, Playwright
1934

Sonia Sanchez was born in Birmingham, Alabama. She studied at New York University and Hunter College in New York City. She is married to Etheridge Knight, a black writer of poetry and fiction. She has taught at San Francisco State College and is now teaching in the Black Studies Department of Temple University in Philadelphia. Her plays are published in the special black drama number of *The Drama Review* (Summer 1968) and in *New Plays from the Black Theatre* (1969) edited by Ed Bullins. Her poems have been published in many magazines and anthologies. Books written or edited by her are six volumes of poetry: *Homecoming* (1969); *We a Badd DDD People* (1970); *It's a New Day; A Blues Book for Blue Black Magical Women; Love Poems* (1975); and *I've Been a Woman;* two anthologies edited by her: *Three Hundred and Sixty Degrees of Blackness Comin at You, An Anthology of the Sonia Sanchez Writers Workshop at Countee Cullen Library in Harlem* (1971); and *We Be Word Sorcerers: 25 Stories by Black Americans* (1974). In

1975 she was working on another book, *Behind the Bamboo Curtain,* an account of her recent visit to the Peoples' Republic of China. She has also written *A Sound Investment* (1978), a collection of short stories.

GEORGE S. SCHUYLER
Journalist, Author
1895–1977

George S. Schuyler was born in Providence, Rhode Island in 1895. Educated in the Syracuse public schools, Schuyler served as a first lieutenant in World War I and returned to civilian life as a newspaperman for such publications as the *Pittsburgh Courier, Crisis, Opportunity,* and *The Nation.*

Schuyler graduated into fiction as his style matured, publishing a novel, *Black No More* (1931), and a slave account entitled *Slaves, Today: A Story of Liberia* (1931). Other sketches and short stories appeared in Harlem publications which highlighted the work of black writers before the onset of the Depression. Schuyler drew heavily from his military experience (he was in the U.S. Army from 1912 to 1920), and from various odd jobs to create the setting and mood for his various vignettes. His autobiography, *Black and Conservative,* was published in 1966; Michael W. Peplow's *George S. Schuyler* appeared in 1980.

NATHAN ALEXANDER SCOTT, JR.
Critic, Essayist
1925

Nathan A. Scott, Jr. is a critic of modern literature who has written extensively on the relationships between the literary and religious imagination.

Born in Cleveland, Scott attended the University of Michigan and the Union Theological Seminary in New York. He received his Ph.D. from Columbia University at the age of 24. He later became Chairman of the Theology and Literature Field of the Divinity School at the University of Chicago.

Scott's essays are noted for their diversity and quality. His works have appeared frequently in journals such as *Review of Metaphysics* and *Christian Century,* as well as *Saturday Review* and *The Kenyon Review.*

In addition to his teaching, lecturing, and essays, Scott has written or edited many books: *Rehearsals of Discomposure: Alienation and Reconciliation in Modern Literature* (1952); *Modern Literature and the Religious Frontier* (1958); *Samuel Beckett* (1965); *The Broken Center: Studies in the Theological Horizon of Modern Literature* (1966); *Craters of the Spirit: Studies in the Modern Novel* (1968); *Forms of Extremity in the Modern Novel; Adversity and Ernest Hemingway; Grace; Negative Capability; The Poetry of Civic Virtue: Eliot, Malraux, Auden;* the essay on Black Writing in the *Harvard Guide to Contemporary American Writing* (1980) edited by Daniel Hoffman; and *Three American Moralists: Mailer, Bellow, Trilling.*

NTOZAKE SHANGE
Playwright, Poet
1948

Born in Trenton, New Jersey, Ntozake Shange graduated from Barnard College and received her masters degree from the University of Southern California. She studied Afro-American dance and gave many poetry readings in California. Shange taught at Sonoma College in California. Her play *For Colored Girls Who Have Considered Suicide When the Rainbow is Enuf,* a choreopoem, was first produced in California after her dance-drama *Sassafrass* was presented in 1975. *For Colored Girls* showed real talent and was later produced in New York City where it had a long run before going on the road. Other works by Shange that have been produced on the stage are *Spell #7; A Photograph: Lovers in Motion;* and *Boogie Woogie Landscapes. For Colored Girls* has been published twice as a book and Shange's book *Three Pieces* (1981) contains *Spell #7, A Photograph: Lovers in Motion,* and *Boogie Woogie Landscapes.*

WILLIAM STILL
Journalist, Editor
1821–1902

William Grant Still was the nineteenth century's foremost chronicler of the Underground Railroad, having compiled numerous case histories involving fugitive slaves. Perhaps the most harrowing and revealing escapade involved an encounter with a man who turned out to be his brother—an escapee from Alabama. That episode strengthened Still's resolve to keep records on as many slaves as possible. Still kept these records from 1850 to 1860 and in 1872 compiled a thick volume entitled *Underground Railroad Records.*

Still himself was born free, only because his parents had escaped separately from Maryland's eastern shore to New Jersey. The young man was frequently involved in forwarding passengers to safety in Canada, and also aided survivors of the Harpers Ferry debacle to escape from Virginia. In 1861, Still organized a social, civil, and statistical clearinghouse to collect and preserve historical materials relating to blacks. Some 20 years later, he founded the first YMCA branch for Negroes. He engaged in civil rights and welfare work until his death.

ELLEN TARRY
Author
1906

Ellen Tarry's service as the "Story Lady" of Friendship House, a Catholic community center in Harlem, brought her into close contact with the actual person who served as the model for "Hezekiah Horton," the character she created in the book of the same name. This same character appears in *The Runaway Elephant*, which was enthusiastically received by critics and public alike at its publication in 1950.

The Runaway Elephant was illustrated by cartoonist Oliver Harrington, whose "Bootsie" is one of the best-known cartoon characters in the black press.

Born in Birmingham, Alabama, Miss Tarry was educated in a Southern convent school and converted to Catholicism. Later a journalist in the South and in New York, she began her work in Harlem in 1929, becoming associated with Catherine De Hueck, founder of Friendship House; she went on to establish a similar institution in Chicago. During World War II she served as a staff member of the National Catholic Community Service.

Her books include *Katherine Drexel* (1958); *Martin de Porres* (1963); and *Young Jim: The Early Years of James Weldon Johnson* (1967). Her autobiography *The Third Door* was published in 1955. Tarry's most recent book, *The Other Toussaint* (1981), a biography of Pierre Toussaint, traces this postrevolutionary black's life from Haiti to New York where he became hairdresser to most of the great society ladies of that era.

LUCY TERRY
Poet
1730–1821

Lucy Terry is generally considered to be the first black poet in America. In a ballad which she called "Bars Fight," she recreated an Indian massacre which occurred in Deerfield, Massachusetts in 1746 during King George's War. (Although of little poetic value, "Bars Fight" has been hailed by some historians as the most authentic account of the massacre.)

A semiliterate slave in the household of Ensign Ebenezer Wells, she won her freedom and was married to a freedman named Prince. The Prince house served as a center for young people who gathered to listen to their hostess's storytelling. Lucy Terry was a strong woman who argued eloquently for her family's rights in several cases. See *Black Woman: A Fictionalized Biography of Lucy Terry Prince* (1973) by Bernard and Jonathan Katz.

HOWARD THURMAN
Author
1900–1981

Almost all of Howard Thurman's considerable writing has centered on religious themes and been printed in such publications as *Christian Century, The World To-* morrow, *The Southern Workman, Christendom, The Journal of Religion,* and *Religion and Life. With Head and Heart: The Autobiography of Howard Thurman* (1979) along with other achievements Thurman won the religious award in the Ebony American Achievement Award for 1979.

He was co-founder of the Interracial Interdenominational Fellowship Church of San Francisco. In 1978, *Ebony* magazine published an article titled "Howard Thurman: 20th Century Holy Man." He died in his home in San Francisco in 1981.

Born in Florida and educated at the Florida Baptist Academy (later Florida Normal Institute), Thurman later received collegiate training at Morehouse and Rochester Theological Seminary, the Oberlin Divinity School, and Haverford. In 1935 Thurman led a "pilgrimage of friendship" of students of religion to colleges in Burma, India, and Ceylon. Later, he was pastor and religious advisor at Oberlin, Morehouse, and Howard. He was also professor of Christian theology at Howard. His many books include *The Negro Spiritualist Speaks of Life and Death; Deep River; The Luminous Darkness; The Inward Journey; Disciplines of the Spirit;* and an essay called *Why I Believe There Is a God.*

WALLACE THURMAN
Novelist, Playwright
1902–1934

Death claimed Wallace Thurman not long after he had produced two of his major works, a play, *Harlem* (1929), and a novel, *The Blacker the Berry,* published the same year. His other major literary effort was *Infants of the Spring,* published in 1932.

Born in Salt Lake City, Utah and educated at the University of Southern California, Thurman served on the editorial staffs of *The Messenger* and of Macaulay Publishing Company. He was also involved in a pair of short-lived magazine ventures, *Fire* and *Harlem. The Blacker the Berry* and *Fire* have been reprinted.

MELVIN B. TOLSON
Poet
1900–1966

Born in Moberly, Missouri, educated at Fisk, Lincoln, and Columbia universities, Tolson had been a contributor to many newspapers and to publications such as *Arts Quarterly* and *American Poets.* The recipient of several prizes from state and local organizations, he has also won the National Poetry Contest for his poem "Dark Symphony." *Rendezvous with America,* published in 1944, was his first volume of poetry. In 1951 *Poetry* magazine presented him with the Bess Hokin Award for a poem called "Foe."

To date, his best-known work is probably *Libretto*

for the Republic of Liberia (1953). Another of his narrative poems, *Harlem Gallery,* was published in 1965 as a book. He taught for many years at Langston University in Oklahoma. Joy Flasch's *Melvin B. Tolston* (1972) is in *Twayne U.S. Authors Series.* Tolson's *A Gallery of Harlem Portraits* was published posthumously.

JEAN TOOMER
Novelist, Poet
1894–1967

Jean Toomer's *Cane,* published in 1923, has been called one of the three best novels ever written by an American black, the others being Richard Wright's *Native Son* and Ralph Ellison's *Invisible Man.* According to Columbia University critic Robert Bone, "*Cane* is by far the most impressive product of the Negro Renaissance."

A mixture of poems and sketches, *Cane* was written during that period in which most black writers were reacting against earlier "polite" forms by creating works marked by literary realism. Toomer even went beyond this realm to the threshold of symbol and myth, using a "mystical" approach which is much more akin to the contemporary mood than it was to the prevailing spirit of his own day.

Born in Washington, D.C. in 1894, Toomer was educated for law at the University of Wisconsin and

Jean Toomer led the novel beyond literary realism.

Kidnapped into slavery, Gustavus Vassa lived to become a spokesman for abolition.

City College of New York before he turned to writing. His transcendental bent is said to have stemmed in part from his early study under Gurdjieff, the Russian mystic.

Cane sold only 500 copies on publication, and was still little known until it was reprinted recently with new introductions. A lot has been written about Toomer and *Cane* in recent years including a *Cane* casebook. Toomer also published quite a bit of poetry. Darwin T. Turner edited *The Wayward and The Seeking: A Collection of Writings by Jean Toomer,* a book of his poetry, short stories, dramas, and autobiography.

GUSTAVUS VASSA
Author
1745?–1801?

Gustavus Vassa was born in 1745 in Benin in Southern Nigeria. At the age of 11 he was kidnaped and shipped to the New World as a slave. His masters included a Virginia plantation owner, a British officer, and a Philadelphia merchant from whom he eventually purchased his freedom.

Vassa then settled in England where he worked diligently for the elimination of slavery. He even went so far as to present a petition to Parliament calling for its abolition.

His autobiography, *The Interesting Narrative of the Life of Oloudah Equiano, or Gustavus Vassa,* was published in London in 1789 and went through five editions in the next five years. It is regarded as a highly informative account of the evils of slavery as it affected both master and slave.

Vassa died around 1801. *Equian's Travels* has also been published recently.

ALICE WALKER
Poet, Novelist
1944

Alice Walker was born in Eatonton, Georgia, has lived in Mississippi, and in 1974 moved to New York City. She was educated at Spelman College, Atlanta, Georgia and at Sarah Lawrence College, Bronxville, New York.

Her short stories and poems have been published in *Freedomways, Essence,* and other magazines and anthologies. She has been writer-in-residence and teacher at Jackson State College and Tougaloo College in Mississippi and is a prolific writer. Her first book was poetry titled *Once* published in 1968. Her second book, published in 1970, was a novel, *The Third Life of Grange Copeland.* A second book of poetry, *Revolutionary Petunia & Other Poems,* was published in 1972. She also wrote *In Love and Trouble: Stories of Black Women* (1973) and *Langston Hughes, American Poet* (1974), for children; *Meridian* (1976), a novel; *Good Night, Willie Lee, I'll See You in the Morning* (1979), poetry; and *You Can't Keep A Good Woman Down* (1981), short stories.

DAVID WALKER
Pamphleteer
1785–1830

(For biography see Civil Rights section, p. 000.)

MARGARET WALKER
Poet, Novelist
1915

Margaret Walker was born on July 7, 1915 in Birmingham, Alabama, and received her early education in Alabama, Louisiana, and Mississippi. She earned her B.A. from Northwestern University and her M.A. from the University of Iowa (1940).

In 1942, Miss Walker published *For My People* and two years later was awarded a Rosenwald Fellowship for creative writing. She has taught English and literature at Livingston College in North Carolina, at West Virginia State College, and at Jackson State College in Mississippi. Her novel appeared in 1966 and is entitled *Jubilee. For My People* was reprinted in 1969. Her other works are *Prophets for a New Day, How I Wrote Jubilee, October Journey,* and *A Poetic Equation:*

Conversations Between Nikki Giovanni and Margaret Walker. She has contracted for and is completing a book about Richard Wright, who she knew in Chicago. June 17, 1976, was proclaimed Margaret Walker Alexander Day by the mayor of her native Birmingham.

ERIC WALROND
Essayist, Short Story Writer
1898–1966

Eric Walrond was born in Georgetown, Guyana, came to Harlem in 1918, and studied at Columbia University and The City College of New York while he held several odd jobs. He became associate editor of *The Negro World* in 1923.

Two years later he wrote an essay entitled "On Being Black" which was published in *The New Republic* and brought him a measure of attention from the literary world.

Tropic Death, his first and only book, was published in 1926. It is a collection of stories depicting the contrast between the natural beauty of the American tropics and the poverty, disease, and death of its inhabitants. Walrond lived for many years in London, where he died in 1966.

SAMUEL RINGGOLD WARD
Author
1817–1864

Primarily a serious orator, although his writing was laced with much humor and satire, Samuel Ringgold Ward published only one full-length book in his lifetime, *The Autobiography of a Fugitive Negro* (1855).

An escapee from slavery, Ward was raised in New York, where he was sufficiently educated to teach school and become a preacher. He soon extended his involvements to include the antislavery cause and was eventually forced to flee to Canada because of his fiery speechmaking on behalf of fugitive slave Jerry McHenry. Ward remained an active lecturer in Canada and England. He died in Jamaica during the Civil War. His book was reprinted in 1968 by Arno Press.

CHARLES WESLEY
Historian
1895

Charles H. Wesley, president from 1942 until the mid-1960s of Central State University, is one of America's major black historians.

Born in Louisville, Kentucky, Wesley studied at Fisk, Howard, Harvard, Yale, Columbia, and the Guilde International in Paris. Among his many awards were scholarships from Yale (1913) and Harvard (1920–1921), and a Guggenheim Fellowship (1930–1931).

Escaped slave Samuel R. Ward had to flee the United States because of his fiery speechmaking.

Wesley served as professor and dean of Howard. He is the author of such works as *Negro Labor in the United States, 1850–1925; A Study in American Economic History* (1927); *Richard Allen, Apostle of Freedom* (1935); *The Collapse of the Confederacy* (1937); and *The Negro in the Americas* (1940).

His most recent works include *Neglected History* (1965); *In Freedom's Footsteps* (1968); *The Quest For Equality* (1968); and *Henry Arthur Callis: Life and Legacy* (1978). Wesley was for several years director of the Association for the Study of Afro-American Life and History.

PHILLIS WHEATLEY
Poet
1753?–1784

Born in Senegal, Phillis Wheatley was brought to the United States as a slave and received her name from Mrs. Susannah Wheatley, the wife of the Boston tailor who had bought Phillis.

Miss Wheatley received her early education in the household of her master. Her interest in writing stemmed from her reading of the Bible and the classics under the guidance of the Wheatleys' daughter, Mary.

In 1770 her first poem was printed under the title

A Poem by Phillis, A Negro Girl on the Death of Reverend George Whitefield. Her book *Poems on Various Subjects: Religious and Moral* was published in London in 1773. After a trip to England for health reasons she returned to the United States and was married. She published the poem *Liberty and Peace* in 1784, shortly before her death. Most of the old books of her poems, letters, and memoirs and about her life were reprinted in the late 1960s and early 1970s. Two books about her are Julian D. Mason, Jr.'s *The Poems of Phillis Wheatley* (1966) and William H. Robinson's *Phillis Wheatley, A Biography* (1981).

Although George Washington was among her admirers (she had once sent him a tributary poem, which he graciously acknowledged), her poetry is considered important today largely because of its historical role in the growth of American Negro literature. In its style and thematic preoccupations, Miss Wheatley's poetry reflects Anglo-Saxon models, rather than her African heritage. It is nevertheless, a typical example of the verse manufactured in a territory—the British colonies—not yet divorced from its maternal origins.

WALTER WHITE
Journalist, Novelist
1893–1955

(For biography see Civil Rights section, p. 000.)

JOHN EDGAR WIDEMAN
Novelist
1941

John Wideman was born in Washington, D.C. and educated at the University of Pennsylvania and at Oxford University where he was a Rhodes Scholar. Rhodes Scholars are selected because of their excellence in more than one field. Wideman was an outstanding basketball player and scholar at the University of Pennsylvania. He attended the University of Iowa Writers' Workshop and was associate professor of English at the University of Pennsylvania. Wideman has been professor of English at the University of Wyoming for some years. His first novel, *A Glance Away,* was published in 1967 when he was 26 years old. His second novel, *Hurry Home,* was published in 1970. Wideman's third novel is *The Lynchers* (1973). His novels have always received enthusiastic reviews by the literary critics. Wideman is also a reviewer of black novels and books about black literature and music for the *New York Times Book Review.* In 1981 he published two paperback books: *Hiding Place,* a novel based on his family history; and *Damballah,* related short stories about his family history.

GEORGE WASHINGTON WILLIAMS
Historian
1849–1891

George Washington Williams was the writer of a pair of definite works on the black experience in the Civil War and the period stretching from the Jamestown landing to the end of Reconstruction. Williams' major works are *The History of the Negro Race in America from 1619–1880* and *A History of the Negro Troops in the War of the Rebellion* (1888).

A native of Bedford Spring, Pennsylvania, Williams enlisted in the Union Army at the age of 14, served through the war, and went on to become a lieutenant-colonel in the Mexican army. After the fall of Maximilian, he moved west, serving in several Indian campaigns on the frontier. Later he attended Howard University and Newton Theological Seminary, the latter after he had decided on a career in the ministry. His career eventually reached into journalism (he conducted two newspapers), into law (he practiced in Ohio), and into politics (he served in the Ohio state legislature and as Minister to Haiti). Williams subsequently became interested in the Congo and entered the service of the Belgian government. He died in England while still in the service of Leopold II, the Belgian King. *A History of the Negro Race* was recently reprinted.

JOHN A. WILLIAMS
Novelist
1925

John A. Williams was born in Jackson, Mississippi but grew up in Syracuse, New York. Educated locally, he also took both his undergraduate and graduate degrees at Syracuse University.

His first novel, *The Angry Ones,* was published in 1960, and was followed within a year by a second offering, *Night Song.* In 1962 Williams wrote the text for *Africa: Her History, Lands and People.* That same year, he won the Roman Fellowship of the American Academy in Rome, the unanimous choice of the jury here. The award, however, was rescinded by officials in Rome in an unprecedented action, which caused considerable controversy.

Williams wrote *Sissie* (1936) and *This Is My Country Too* (1965) and has written or edited many other books: *Beyond the Angry Black* (1966); *The Man Who Cried I Am* (1967); *The Most Native of Sons; Captain Blackman; Sons of Darkness; Sons of Light; Flashbacks: A Twenty-Year Diary of Article Writing;* and *Mothersill and the Foxes.*

In 1970 Williams published a controversial work in which he lamented the alleged "failure" of Dr. Martin Luther King, Jr. The book, *The King God Didn't Save,* professed to be an objective appraisal of the life

Controversial independent thinker John Williams.

and work of the slain civil rights leader. His eighth novel is *Click Song* (1982), about racism in the publishing industry. Williams' other works include *West Virginia and The Captains of Industry* (1976) and *Y'bird* (1978).

CARTER WOODSON
Historian
1875–1950

Carter Woodson was for many years, along with W. E. B. DuBois, the main voice in American Negro historiography.

Born in New Canton, Virginia, Woodson attended Berea College, the University of Chicago, Harvard, and the Sorbonne in Paris. He and others organized the Association for the Study of Negro Life and History in 1915.

In 1921 Woodson organized Associated Publishers in order to produce textbooks and other supplementary material on blacks, which, at the time, was not readily accepted by most publishers. A year later he retired from academic life to become Director of the Association for the Study of Negro Life and History and continued as editor of the *Journal of Negro History,* started

A pioneer in the intellectual history of the black American, Carter Woodson.

Richard Wright drew on his personal experience to dramatize racial injustice

in 1916. (Woodson had taught at the elementary and high school level, and served as Dean of the School of Liberal Arts of Howard University.)

Many of Woodson's books have become the foundations upon which contemporary historians have based their own research. These include *The Education of the Negro Prior to 1861* (1915); *A Century of Negro Migration* (1918); *The Negro in Our History* (1922); *The Rural Negro* (1930); *The Miseducation of the Negro, The Mind of the Negro, History of the Negro Church, The African Background Outlined,* and *The Negro and the History of the Negro Church.*

Woodson died in Washington, D.C. on April 3, 1950.

RICHARD WRIGHT
Novelist
1908–1960

The work of Richard Wright is still used as the yardstick by which black novelists in America are measured. It was Wright who, in the 1940s, set the standard for a whole generation of prose writers, including Ralph Ellison and James Baldwin.

Born on a plantation near Natchez, Mississippi, Wright drew on his personal experience to dramatize racial injustice and its brutalizing effects. In 1938, under the auspices of the WPA Illinois Writers Project, Wright published *Uncle Tom's Children,* a collection of four novellas based on his Mississippi boyhood memories. The book won an award for the best work of fiction by a WPA writer, and Wright received a Guggenheim Fellowship.

Two years later, *Native Son,* a novel of Chicago's Negro ghetto, further enhanced Wright's reputation. A Book-of-the-Month Club choice, it was later a successful Broadway production under Orson Welles' direction and was filmed in South America with Wright himself in the role of Bigger Thomas. He published *12 Million Black Voices* in 1941.

In 1945 Wright's largely autobiographical *Black Boy* was selected by the Book-of-the-Month Club and went on to become a second best-seller.

Wright later moved to Paris where he continued to write fiction and nonfiction including *The Outsider* (1953); *Black Power* (1954); *Savage Holiday* (1954–1955); *The Color Curtain* (1956); *The Long Dream*

(1958); *Lawd Today* (1963); *Fight Men* (1961); and *White Man Listen* (1957).

Wright died on November 28, 1960. There are over a dozen adult books about Wright, two casebooks on *Native Son,* a children's book, and a critical pamphlet in a writers series. These include a *Richard Wright Reader* (1978) and Addison Gayle, Jr.'s *Richard Wright: Ordeal of a Native Son* (1980).

FRANK YERBY
Novelist

Frank Yerby, a commercially successful writer, has published over 30 novels which have sold more than 20 million copies and earned for their author a gross amount in excess of 10 million dollars.

Born in Augusta, Georgia in 1916, Yerby studied at Fisk University and the University of Chicago, and taught briefly at Florida A&M and Southern University before moving to Detroit in 1942 to work in a wartime assembly plant.

His early work often dealt with significant social issues such as race. In 1944, for example, *Harper's* published his short story "Health Card," which won a special O. Henry award. Later, after studiously researching the ingredients of popular fiction, Yerby turned his talent to the creation of swashbuckling costume novels which were an immediate success.

In 1949 he published *The Foxes of Harrow,* soon to become a best-seller and a successful movie as well. His commercial successes then became an annual occurrence: *The Vixens* (1947); *The Golden Hawk* (1948); *Pride's Castle* (1949); *Floodtide* (1950); *A Woman Called Fancy* (1951); *The Saracen Blade* (1952); and many others.

Yerby has lived in Europe since 1952. His other books—*The Old Gods Laugh, An Odor of Sanctity, Goat Song,* and *The Dahomean*—are departures from the "costume motif," and he has himself expressed a desire to create literature of greater substance. Yerby's recent books are *The Girl from Storyville: A Victorian Novel* (1972); *The Voyage Planned* (1974); *Tobias and the Angel* (1975); *A Rose for Ana Maria* (1976); *Fair Oaks* (1977); *Hail the Conquering Hero* (1978); *The Darkness at Ingraham's Crest: A Tale of the Slaveholding South* (1979); and *Floodtide* (1980).

AL YOUNG
Poet, Novelist
1939

Born in Ocean Springs, Mississippi, Al Young is the son of a professional musician and auto worker. Young attended the University of Michigan, studied creative writing at Stamford University, and received a B.A. degree from the University of California at Berkeley

in 1969. A musician and a teacher of writing, his works are *Dancing Poems* (1969); *Snakes* (1970), a novel; *The Song Turning Back into Itself* (1971), poetry; *Earth, Air, Fire and Water* (1971), poetry; *Who Is Angelina?* (1974), a novel; *Geography of the Near East* (1976), poetry; *Sitting Pretty* (1976), a novel; *Ask Me Now* (1981), a novel; *The Blues Don't Change; New and Selected Poems* (1981); and *Bodies and Soul: Musical Memoirs* (1982).

NOTABLE BLACK PLAYWRIGHTS

Name	Dates
Garland Anderson	1886–1939
Marita Bonner	1905
Theodore Browne	1910
Hazel Bryant	
Ben Caldwell	
Steve Carter	
Bob Cole	
N. R. Davidson	1940
Philip Hayes Dean	
Tom Dent	
Val Ferdinand	1947
J. E. Franklin	
Ruth Gaines-Shelton	1873
Neil Harris	
Abraham Hill	
Errol Hill	
J. Leubrie Hill	1873–1916
Adrienne Kennedy	1931
Lew Leslie	1890–1963
William MacKey	1861–1918
William Marshall	1924
John Matheus	1887–1935
May Miller	
Ron Milner	1938
Barbara Molette	
Alice D. Nelson	1875–1958
Thomas D. Pawley	1917
Louis Peterson	1922
Lennox Raphael	1940
Alex Rogers	
John M. Ross	
Ruth Gaines Shelton	1849–1891
Jesse Shipp	1859–1934
Wole Soyinka	
Eulalie Spence	1894
Evan Walker	
Joseph Walker	1935
Richard Wesley	1935
Edgar White	1947
Vantile Whitfield	
Frank Wilson	1886–1956
Marvin X	

OTHER NOTABLE BLACK WRITERS

Name	Craft	Dates
George Leonard Allen	Poet	1905–1935
Samuel Allen	Poet, essayist	1917
Jervis Anderson	Novelist	
Russell Atkins	Poet	1926
William Attaway	Novelist	1912
Kofi Awoonor	Poet	
Toni Cade Bambara	Poet, educator	
Gwendolyn B. Bennett	Poet	1902
Hal Bennett	Novelist	1930
James Boggs	Essayist	1919
Donald Bogle	Poet	
John H. Bracey, Jr.	Writer	1941
Jonathan Brooks	Poet	1904–1945
James E. Campbell	Poet	1860–1905
Catherine Cater	Novelist	1918
Ocania Chalk	Writer	
William Calvin Chase	Journalist, editor	1854–?
Marcus Christian	Poet	1900
Leslie M. Collins	Poet	1914
Cyrus Coltee	Writer	1910
Orde Coombs	Poet	
Waring Cuney	Poet, musician	1906
Margaret Danner	Poet	1915
Frank Marshall Davis	Poet	1905
Clarissa Delaney	Poet	1901–1927
William Demby	Novelist	1922
Alfred A. Duckett	Journalist	1918
James A. Emanuel	Poet	1921
Julia Fields	Poet	1938
Nick Aaron Ford	Editor, critic	1904
Timothy Thomas Fortune	Editor, pamphleteer	1855–1928
Hoyt W. Fuller	Journalist	1927
Addison Gayle, Jr.	Critic, essayist	1932
Dick Gregory	Satirist, social activist	1932
Yvonne Gregory	Writer	1919
Angelina W. Grimké	Poet, teacher	1880–1958
Rosa Guy	Novelist	1925

Name	Craft	Dates
Warren Halliburton	Author, educator	1924
Charles V. Hamilton	Author, educator	1929
Donald Jeffrey Hayes	Poet	1904
Calvin Hernton	Essayist	1932
Frank Hercules	Novelist	1917
Leslie Pinckney Hill	Author	1880–1960
Carl W. Hines, Jr.	Poet	1940
M. Carl Holman	Poet, journalist	1919
Frank Horne	Poet	1899
Alton Hornsby, Jr.	Editor	
Kristin Hunter	Novelist	1931
Lance Jeffers	Writer	1919
Ted Joans	Poet, artist	1928
Charles Johnson	Novelist	
Charles Spurgeon Johnson	Editor	1895–1956
Gayle Jones	Author, playwright	1949
George E. Kent	Critic	1920
Etheridge Knight	Poet	1931
Don L. Lee	Editor, poet	1942
John Lovell, Jr.	Author, educator	1907
Naomi Long Madgett	Poet	1923
Sharon Bell Mathis	Novelist	1937
Louise Meriwether	Author	
Pauli Murray	Poet, lawyer	1910
Walter Dean Myers	Author	1937
Larry Neal	Poet	1937
Effie Lee Newsome	Author, poet	1885
Gloria C. Oden	Poet	1923
Earl Ofari	Writer	1945
Myron O'Higgins	Poet	1918
Roi Ottley	Journalist	1906–1960
Lindsay Patterson	Editor	
Raymond Patterson	Poet	1929
Oliver Pitcher	Poet, actor	1923
Dudley Randall	Poet	1914
T. J. Reddy	Novelist	
Eugene B. Redmond	Poet	
Clayton Riley	Writer	1935
Conrad Kent Rivers	Poet	1933
Carolyn M. Rodgers	Poet	
Charlemae H. Rollins	Author, bibliographer	1897
Gil Scott-Heron	Poet, musician	1949

Name	Craft	Dates	Name	Craft	Dates
Ann Allen Shockley	Editor		James M. Whitfield	Writer	1830–
Rev. William J. Simmons	Biographer	1849– 1890			1870
William Gardner Smith	Novelist, journalist	1926– 1974	George W. Williams	Historian, legislator	1849– 1891
Thomas Sewell	Writer	1930	Lucy Ariel Williams	Writer	1905
Anne Spencer	Poet, librarian	1882	Charles V. Willie	Writer	1927
			Charles Wright	Novelist	1932
Robert Staples	Writer	1942	Bruce McM. Wright	Writer	1918
Darwin T. Turner	Critic, editor	1931	Jay Wright	Author, poet	1935
Charles Enoch Wheeler	Writer	1909			

THE BLACK ARTIST

A Brief History of the Black Artist in America ■ Black Museums and Galleries ■ Black Exhibitions ■ Black Artists' Organizations ■ Outstanding Black Artists

The constructive lessons of African art are among the soundest and most needed of art creeds today. They offset with equal force the banalities of sterile, imitative classicism and the superficialities of literal realism. They emphasize intellectually significant form, abstractly balanced design, formal simplicity, restrained and unsentimental emotional appeal. Moreover, Africa's art creed is beauty in use, vitally rooted in the crafts, and uncontaminated with the blight of the machine. Surely the liberating example of such art will be as marked an influence in the contemporary work of Negro artists as it has been in that of the leading modernists: Picasso, Modigliani, Matisse, Epstein, Lipchitz, Brancusi and others too numerous to mention. (Aluin Locke, Professor of Philosophy, Howard University, 1931)

This comment, by one of America's foremost art critics over 40 years ago during the height of the Harlem Renaissance, underscores the problems and promise of what blacks, interested in expanding their artistic skills, have encountered throughout their history in the United States. The substantial contributions of black artists have been achieved against numerous obstacles. Foremost among these obstacles are:

Blacks in the western world and also Europe were long cut off from the artistic heritage of Africa, a heritage now known for enormous achievements as far back as the fifteenth century. As Locke points out, "the liberating example" of African art was used by white Europeans long before American blacks.

From colonial days to the present, black talent has been encouraged and recognized on a very limited basis by reigning art establishments and connoisseurs of the United States, though some white insti-

tutions, such as the Rosenwald Fund in the early twentieth century, did subsidize promising blacks.

Themes and expressions of black life, whether they relate to slave, sharecropper, or ghetto life, have rarely been regarded as prime moneymakers by leading merchants and curators of the art world.

Few blacks attained the economic security of leisure essential to creativity and patronage of artists.

Early European Art

That blacks could excel in Euro-American art forms was firmly established in seventeenth-century Spain by the success of Juan de Pareja, a slave, apprentice, and pupil of the great master Velasquez. Many of Pareja's works were of such quality they were mistakenly accepted as Velasquez' own and hung in the great museums and mansions of western Europe. Today, Pareja's paintings, properly credited to him, hang in the Dulwich Gallery in London, the Prado in Madrid, the Munich Gallery, and the Hermitage in Leningrad. Pareja's talent was recognized in his lifetime and in 1652 he was manumitted by King Philip IV.

Another well-known seventeenth-century black artist, Sebastian Gomez, a servant of Murillo, was discovered painting secretly at night in his master's studio after Murillo's pupils had departed. Gomez was made a pupil of the master and eventually, known as The Mulatto of Murillo, became famous for paintings and murals in Seville.

Although Pareja and Gomez were black artists, their genius was nurtured in a European setting and tradition. Cut off from their African heritage, they naturally worked in the same style and format as their white contemporaries. Their paintings were devoted

From the folk art collection of Abbe Aldrich Rockefeller, a watercolor entitled The Old Plantation *by an unknown eighteenth-century artist.*

to the religious themes and aristocratic portraits desired by the art world of that historical era.

BLACK ARTISTS IN AMERICA—A BRIEF REVIEW

Blacks in Early America

The only eighteenth-century black artist in colonial America to have been recorded, Scipio Morehead, of whom no known work survives, also painted in the style of the dominant white culture, in this case classical allegories resembling work of Romney and Reynolds, British masters of the era. Morehead's artistic endeavors were aided by two prominent women who lived in Boston where he was a slave. The wife of his clergyman master, who was a patron of the arts, encouraged him, and poet Phillis Wheatley praised his work publicly.

Whatever other work of excellence lay unrecognized, or wrongly attributed to whites, whatever black talent lay dormant because essential materials were unavailable, will never be known. Nor will we ever know how many black drawings, sketches, sculptures might now be accepted for their excellence by the art world but were discarded because the themes did not conform to the preconceptions of their time.

That there were other unrecorded black artists in the eighteenth century, as well as a great many craftsmen, is certain. According to historian James Porter, skilled blacks interested in buying their freedom worked as sign painters, silversmiths, cabinet and coach makers, ornamentalists, and shipwrights. Eugene Warbourg, a black sculptor from New Orleans, became well known for his ornamental gravestones and eventually went to study in Europe. Much colonial iron and metal work on eighteenth-century mansions, churches, and public buildings was created and executed by blacks and occasionally reached heights that can be classified as fine art. However, the names of the black artists and artisans involved are rarely known.

Nineteenth Century

The black presence in nineteenth-century art is better documented. Blacks able to overcome the immense obstacles to their performance and recognition in-

Among examples of fine craftsmanship produced by slave labor are these brass locks and hinges.

cluded Duncanson, Simpson, Bannister, Johnston, Douglass Bowser, Edmonia Lewis, Tanner, Harper, and Meta Warwick Fuller.

These talents generally performed in the prevailing fashion of American art at the time, which was to copy the styles and techniques then popular in Europe. And many went to Europe to study, attained recognition, and eventually settled there, among them two women sculptors, Lewis and Fuller.

Many black artists attempted to escape the classical tradition into which they were confined and painted themes closer to their heritage and existence. Some fine portraits of black freedmen were performed by talented but obscure black artists in the rural South during the period from 1870 into the early part of this century. Henry Tanner's paintings of the 1880s and Meta Fuller's sculptures of peasant blacks stemmed from this unheralded school of black art.

Twentieth Century

From 1900 to the 1920s, black artists continued to work in the stilted, imitative styles of the late nineteenth century. In 1913 the now famous New York Armory Show of European cubist and modernist painters swept the art world in a totally different direction, which in retrospect bears traces of important African influences. But it was not until after World War I that twentieth-century trends in art and respect for the African idiom and negritude began to manifest itself in the paintings of black America. Out of this period came Archibald Motley, Palmer Hayden, Mal-

This frontispiece from Phillis Wheatley's Poems *is thought to be the work of Scipio Morehead.*

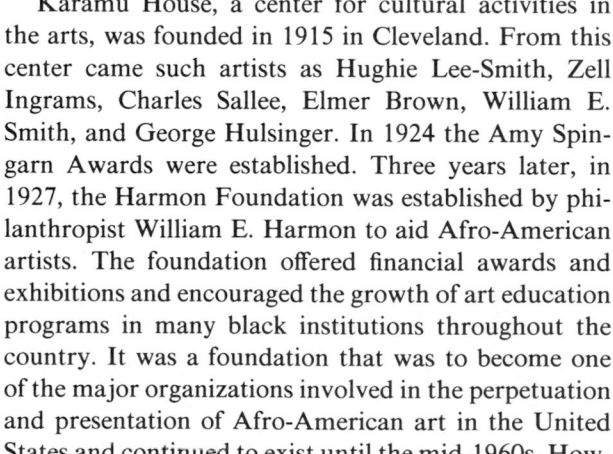

The very gifted Edmonia Lewis.

Meta Vaux Warrick Fuller's bronze Water Boy, *in the National Archives, Washington, D.C.*

vin Gray Johnson, Laura Wheeler Waring, and W. E. Scott.

Karamu House, a center for cultural activities in the arts, was founded in 1915 in Cleveland. From this center came such artists as Hughie Lee-Smith, Zell Ingrams, Charles Sallee, Elmer Brown, William E. Smith, and George Hulsinger. In 1924 the Amy Spingarn Awards were established. Three years later, in 1927, the Harmon Foundation was established by philanthropist William E. Harmon to aid Afro-American artists. The foundation offered financial awards and exhibitions and encouraged the growth of art education programs in many black institutions throughout the country. It was a foundation that was to become one of the major organizations involved in the perpetuation and presentation of Afro-American art in the United States and continued to exist until the mid-1960s. Howard University established its first art gallery, under the directorship of James V. Herrings, in 1930.

The 1930s brought the depression and the Works Progress Administration. Black artists abandoned by the white philanthropists of the 1920s were rescued by the W.P.A. Aaron Douglas, Augusta Savage, Charles Alston, Hale Woodruff, and Charles White created murals and other works for public buildings under this program. In 1939, the Baltimore Museum Show, the first exhibition of black artists to be held in a southern region, presented the works of Richmond Barthe, Malvin Gray Johnson, Henry Bannarn, Florence Purviance, Hale Woodruff, Dox Thrash, Robert Blackburn, and Archibald Motley.

The Harlem Art Center and The Chicago South Side Community Art Center also began with the W.P.A.

The search for a black identity and the expression of black militancy were the most pervasive themes of black art in the 1950s and 1960s. Emotions could not always be contained on canvas, channeled into familiar forms, or exhibited in traditional settings. Art literally took to the streets of the ghetto to meet with, appeal to, and celebrate the people, as was richly illustrated in the Chicago and Detroit murals. Artists also demonstrated an abiding preoccupation with social themes. Black art had become their vehicle to champion the cause of the "people." Others felt that art should be separated from politics and remain an expression of the individual not necessarily with reference to race. The two views occasionally clashed, producing dissension among black artists, but also contributing to the vitality and diversity of black art.

Modern Science in Medicine, *Charles Alston's heroic mural, was executed in the 1930s for Harlem Hospital.*

BLACK MUSEUMS AND GALLERIES

The 1960s was an era which saw a great many radical changes in both the social and the cultural aspects of the United States. Afro-Americans throughout the country were demanding political and social recognition. Afro-Americans added cultural recognition to those demands. No longer satisfied with the limited support of such philanthropic organizations as the Harmon Foundation, these artists looked for alternative forms of exposure. The result of their demands was an outpouring of galleries, community art centers, and community art galleries and programs established within the major art museums around the country.

In New York City, the *Acts of Art Gallery,* established by Nigel Jackson, a former artist turned adminis-

The National Conference of Artists held its second annual meeting in 1954, convening (from left) Jimmy Mosley, Samella Lewis, F. Spellman, Phillip Hampton, Venola Jennings, Juanita Moulon, James Porter, Eugene Brown, and Hayward Oubre.

trator, provided exhibition space for contemporary artists. A not-for-profit organization, the gallery was dedicated to promoting these artists and providing them with the opportunity to attract collectors interested in their work. The gallery exhibitions included the works of such artists as James Denmark, Dinga McCannon, Frank Wimberly, Ann Tanksley, Don Robertson, Llod Toones, Lois Mailou Jones, Jo Butler, Robert Threadgill, and Faith Ringgold. The Acts of Art Gallery in 1971 was to become the center for the controversial Whitney Rebuttal Show.

The *Cinque Gallery,* another New York gallery, was the concept of three distinguished artists—Romare Bearden, Norman Lewis, and Ernest Crichlow. The gallery was named after the famous African prince Cinque, who in 1839 led a successful revolt aboard the slave ship *Amistad,* won his freedom, and returned to Africa. It was the wish of Bearden, Crichlow, and Lewis to establish an exhibition space specifically for young Afro-American artists who needed to learn the process of being a professional artist. This was 1969. Several years later, when it was discovered that there were many artists over the age of 30 who also needed this kind of opportunity, the age limit was taken away. By the end of the 1970s, the Cinque Gallery opened its doors to all new and emerging artists.

The *Weusi Ya Nambe Yasana Gallery,* also in New York, was one of the few cooperative community galleries to come out of the late 1960s. Housed in a brown-

stone in Harlem, the gallery was established to present the art work of its members. Headed by Ademola Olagebefola, the other members included Otto Neals, Kay Brown, and Jean Taylor.

Genesis II was one of the alternative profit-making galleries that emerged out of the 1960s. Like many of its kind, the gallery functioned out of the dealer's apartment to cover the cost of overhead expenses. The dealer would invite his or her clients to come view the works in a living environment so that they might better appreciate the art work. Also, at these gatherings, they had the opportunity to meet other collectors as well as meet the artist and talk in detail about the work. The concept was a good one because it afforded the Afro-American a greater opportunity to develop supporting collectors and to have a real market for their art work.

Just Above Midtown, Inc. was the first organization to move into the gallery district in New York City. Established in 1976, it set up its operation base in a modest space on 57th Street in midtown Manhattan. Under the directorship of Linda Bryant, the organization presented many of the leading contemporary artists of the 1970s—David Hammons, Senga Nengudi, Randy Williams, and Howardena Pindell, to name just a few. It was a costly venture but it did place the Afro-American artist in direct competition with other American artists. The selection was purely a black aesthetic one and it proved once and for all that the black aesthetic could stand up to the mainstream American vision. No longer could art critics fall back on the excuse that they could not go up to Harlem or out to Queens or Brooklyn to see the art; it was right there in midtown. Eventually, the cost of living took its toll and Just Above Midtown, Inc. found that in order for it to continue to function it had to move to a not-for-profit structure. When that happened, the organization expanded its programing to include workshops for artists—how to develop a portfolio, etc.—performance pieces, musical concerts, and film programs. By the end of 1979, Just Above Midtown, Inc. moved from 57th Street to a larger space on Franklin Street in the Tribeca section of New York, changed its name to the *Just Above Midtown/Downtown Alternative Art Center,* and opened its doors to all vanguard, new-wave artists.

The *Studio Museum of Harlem* began in 1969 under the direction of Edward Spriggs. Set up as a place for artists who needed working space, it eventually branched out into a cultural center where the artists could display their work, meet other artists and art supporters, and hold concerts, panel discussions, and other art-related activities. The Studio Museum of Harlem had become, by 1972, the cultural center of New York for the Afro-American community. Important

Artists Mel Edwards (left) *and Vincent Smith at the opening exhibition of The Studio Museum in Harlem.*

retrospectives were presented such as the works of Palmer Hayden, Hale Woodruff, Beauford Delaney, and James Van Der Zee. There was the Lewis H. Michaux Book Fair, which took place for three years (1976–1979) under the direction of Special Program Coordinator David Jackson. Lewis Michaux was a legend in the world of bookselling, and he established a bookstore on 125th Street and Lenox Avenue which became a landmark center for people from around the world who were interested in literature of or about Afro-Americans, Africans, Caribbeans, and South Americans. The store opened in 1930 and continued to exist for the next 44 years. It was called The National Memorial African Book Store.

While under the directorship of Edward Spriggs, the museum began a special holiday celebration, Kwansa, inviting the whole neighborhood—fathers, mothers, and children—to come into the museum and dance, sing, and eat with the artists. Dancer Chuch Davis would come to lead off the dancing, ending with the entire room filled with guests in the center of the floor dancing. By 1980, the museum had grown out of its two-floor loft space and moved into an old office building on 125th Street and 7th Avenue. The new space provided the museum with additional exhibition galleries, larger office areas, and space for its growing collection and the artist-in-residence program.

The *New Muse* in Brooklyn also began in the late 1960s, offering the Afro-American Brooklyn community the same kinds of art programs presented at the Studio Museum. In addition to the art programs, the

James Gittens of the Bed-Stuy Sculpture Workshop shows children how to work with clay.

New Muse also offered lessons in jazz music with bassist Reggie Workman, who headed the program.

The *Store Front Museum* in Queens was established to satisfy the artistic needs of its community. Offering art classes in painting and drawing, its focus was more in the direction of the performing arts—dancing and drama.

The *Hatch-Billops Collection* in New Jersey, while not a museum or gallery, was an important organization which grew out of the demonstrations of the 1960s. Based on the understanding that no one will protect your history or present your history the way you do, the collection began in 1969 with the taping of the history of some black theater artists. It is a collection of more than 604 taped interviews and panel and media events of, about, or by artists. There are over 10,000 slides and 3,000 books, clippings, files, letters, memorabilia, programs, photographs, drawings, scrapbooks, and videotapes. This collection is one of the most complete reference centers focusing on Afro-American art—visual, literary, and theatrical. It is a collection available to artists, scholars, and students.

Galleries and museums for Afro-American artists were developing throughout the country. In Los Angeles, Dr. Samella Lewis, a painter, art historian, and professor at Claremont College, founded the *Contemporary Crafts Center.* In 1967 Alonzo and Dale Davis established and directed the *Brockman Gallery Produc-*

tions, a nonprofit gallery showing contemporary Afro-American art and the work of other minority groups. This gallery has been involved with the promotion and collection of this work.

In Chicago, the *DuSable Museum* was established in 1961 under the directorship of Margaret Burroughs to provide the South Side community with an art center. The museum grew out of an art center that was established under the Works Progress Administration during the depression period. Some of the artists presented here include Charles White, Elizabeth Catlett, Gordon Parks, Rex Gorleigh, William McBride, Jr. and Eldzier Cortor.

On the East Coast, in Boston, the museum of the *National Center of Afro-American Artists,* under the curatorship of Edmond Gaither, is a multimedia art center, featuring dance, theater, visual arts, film, and educational programs.

In Washington, D.C., the *Museum of African Art,* also known as the *Frederick Douglass Institute,* exists in a Victorian row house on Capitol Hill, nestled in the shadow of the Supreme Court. Formerly the home of Frederick Douglass, a former slave who became an advisor to President Lincoln, this museum was established in 1964 to help promote and render familiar to Americans the artistic heritage of Africa. The walls and gallery space are devoted exclusively to African art and culture. The collection, one of the largest and

Local artist Joan Maynard works with children at New York's Bedford-Lincoln Neighborhood Museum.

most diverse of its kind in the United States, consists of some 6,500 works—traditional carvings, musical instruments, and textiles with particular emphasis on works from Nigeria, Ghana, Liberia, the Ivory Coast, and Zaire. The museum's educational programs range from elementary school to college-level accredited courses. There is also the Eliot Elisofon Photographic Archives, which contains some 150,000 slides and motion pictures available to the public for a fee.

The *Smith-Mason Gallery-Museum,* also located in Washington, D.C., is a four-story Victorian house established in 1968 to present its permanent collection, which features paintings, sculptures, and graphics of Afro-American and Caribbean artists. The works remain on permanent display.

Black Exhibitions and Mainstream Art Institutions

Leading mainstream museums during the late 1960s and early 1970s responded to the demands being made by Afro-American artists to open their doors and hire Afro-American scholars as curators and administrators. At the time of the intensive demonstrations, Kynastan McShine, a young West Indian who had already established his reputation as a strong curator at the Jewish Museum, moved on to become the Assistant Curator of Painting and Sculpture at The Museum of Modern Art. Howardena Pindell had just begun her career at the Museum of Modern Art as the Assistant Curator of Drawings and Prints, would later move on to become the Associate Curator of Drawings and Prints, and would in 1980 resign from that position to pursue her career as an artist. But this was not satisfactory to the artists, who demonstrated and wrote letters demanding that jobs be made available to black art historians. In 1968 Gylbert Coker was the first Afro-American to be hired at the Guggenheim Museum in an administrative trainee position. She later went on to work at the Museum of Modern Art as a cataloguer in the museum's registration department. Cheryl McClenny became the second Afro-American to work at the Guggenheim in an administrative position. She went on to direct the Museum Collaborative Programs for the City of New York, and in 1978 she became an administrator with the National Endowment for the Arts in Washington, D.C.

From the Whitney Museum's Museum Studies Program came Faith Weaver and Horace Brockington. Faith Weaver went on to teach American Art History at the School of Visual Arts, and Horace Brockington has established himself as one of the finest curators producing imaginative exhibitions in New York. His presentations include "Another Generation" for The Studio Museum of Harlem (1978), which set the stage for Afro-American Abstraction, which was presented two years later at P.S. 1, an alternative art center. The Brooklyn Museum opened its Community Gallery and hired Henri Ghent, who began to produce some very important exhibitions, including several Afro-American exhibitions, which were sent to Europe.

The largest community program existed in the Metropolitan Museum of Art in New York City. There, people like Randy Williams, Florence Hardney, Dolores Wright, Cathy Chance, and Lowery Sims were actively presenting the artworks of Afro-American and other minority artists to the Metropolitan Museum's audience. By 1977 Lowery Sims was made the museum's first Afro-American assistant curator within the museum's Twentieth-Century Department, under the curatorial guidance of Henry Geldzahler.

The mainstream museums have, over the years, chosen to handle the Afro-American artist in a variety of ways. Always willing to collect the work, seldom were they willing to show it in total before the 1960s. The Museum of Modern Art, for example, presented the work of Horace Pippin back in 1936 in an "American Primitives" exhibition, and in 1955 Roy DeCarava's photography of a young black mother and her children walking across a Harlem lot was included in the "Family of Man" exhibition. Yet it wasn't until 1968 that the museum sponsored a large exhibition of Afro-American artists dedicated to the Reverend Martin Luther King, Jr. In 1971, as the result of a great deal of pressure from Afro-American artists' groups, the museum offered a two-man retrospective for Romare Bearden and Richard Hunt. Between 1968 and 1971 the Museum of Modern Art presented works by Afro-American artists in its collections, as part of collection exhibitions, or through the Lending Services selection.

The Whitney Museum of American Art occasionally presented the works of Afro-American artists within some of its exhibitions, but it wasn't until the pressures of the 1960s that it presented its "Contemporary Black Artists" show in 1971. The exhibition proved to be controversial, with artists complaining

that the selection had been elitist and demanding that the museum open its doors to Afro-American scholars. It did not, and the Whitney Counterexhibition was held at the Acts of Art Gallery.

The artists included in the Whitney exhibition were Roland Ayers, Frank Bowling, Marvin Brown, Walter Cade, Catti James, Barbara Chase-Riboud, Manuel Hughes, Bankley Hendricks, Alvin Loving, Rom Lloyd, Hughie Lee-Smith, Lloyd McNeill, Alernon Miller, Norma Morgan, Howardena Pindell, Mavis Pusey, Betye Saar, Raymond Saunders, Thomas Sills, Alma Thomas, John Torress, Charles White, and Todd Williams. There have been a few one-person exhibitions held for Afro-American artists—Mel Edwards, Mahler Ryder, Alma Thomas, Minnie Evans, and Jacob Lawrence in 1974.

In 1973 the New York Cultural Center, in association with Fairleigh Dickinson University, put together the largest all-black exhibition in the country. Guest curator was artist Benny Andrews. The exhibition also included a lecture series which dealt with all areas of the arts—dance, theater, film, and painting and drawing. Invited to speak on these subjects were black and white curators, administrators, and artists.

The Jacob Lawrence Exhibition at the Whitney Museum in 1974 opened with a gala, drawing Raymond Saunders, Dorothy White, Haywood Rivers, Ed Clark, Camille Billops, Joe Overstreet, Benny Andrews, Louise Parks, Bob Blackburn, Romare Bearden, Norman Lewis, Herbert Gentry, and Vincent Smith, among others.

Dr. Regina Perry was invited by the Metropolitan Museum of Art in 1976 to produce an exhibition called "Selections of Nineteenth-Century Afro-American Art." It was an exhibition which highlighted, for the first time, many early Afro-American portrait painters and landscape artists, and it even made attempts to document some important slave artifacts and put them into an aesthetic rather than sociological perspective. Also at that time, Lowery Sims was putting together an exhibition of selected works by twentieth-century Afro-American artists from the museum's collection for the Bedford-Stuyvesant Restoration Corporation. It was an attempt, on the museum's part, to share its collection with a community of people who might not otherwise visit the museum and certainly would not see these particular works from the collection. Three years later, Ms. Sims mounted another exhibition of Afro-American paintings from the twentieth-century collection. This time the exhibition was inside the Metropolitan Museum.

The Newark Museum of Art in New Jersey held its first black exhibition back in 1944. The exhibition included the works of Richmond Barthe, Romare Bearden, and William Edmonson. Thirty years later, in 1974, the museum presented its second Afro-American art exhibit, "Black Artists: Two Generations." The curator was Paul Waters.

BLACK ARTIST ORGANIZATIONS AND MOVEMENTS

Black artist organizations have been portals through which many black artists entered the art world, whether their personal forums were to be in storefronts or established galleries.

In 1953 a group of artists and art educators primarily from Florida and Georgia met at Florida A & M College. This meeting, whose guest speaker was Hale Woodruff, sparked the beginning of the *National Conference of Artists.* This auspicious beginning was sponsored by Florida A & M's Art Department, which was at that time headed by Dr. Samella Lewis. The purpose of the gathering was to establish a national organization which would address itself to the needs of black artists. In 1954 a second meeting was held at Lincoln University in Jefferson City, Missouri. Those present were Samella Lewis, James Parks, James Porter, Hayward Oubre, Margaret Burroughs, Jimmy Mosley, Venola Seals Jennings, F. L. Spellman, Phillip Hampton, Marion Perkins, Juanita Moulon, Eugene Jesse Brown, and Bernard Goss. By 1959, at a meeting at Atlanta University, the N.C.A. had been established as a viable organization of art educators, historians,

and artists themselves. It is one of the largest and most unusual organizations of its time.

Spiral, a New York-based organization, was active between 1963 and 1966. Its gallery-meeting place was housed on Christopher Street on the lower west side of Manhattan. The first exhibition was held in 1965. A membership of 15 included Romare Bearden, Reginald Gammon, Emma Ammos, Charles Alston, Hale Woodruff, Richard Mayhew, Al Hollingsworth, Calvin Douglass, Merton Simpson, Earl Miller, Felrath Hines, Norman Lewis, Perry Ferguson, William Majors, and James Yeargans. In 1966 it officially closed its doors when it was dispossessed.

Art West Associated, founded in Los Angeles in the early 1960s, is a conference of southern California artists. Its founder and director, Ruth Waddy, has co-edited two volumes on black art published by Contemporary Crafts of Los Angeles.

Art West Associated North, a sister organization to A.W.A., was organized by Evangeline Montgomery in Berkeley, California. Ms. Montgomery has been the black art consultant to the Oakland Museum of Art and Rainbow Sign of Berkeley.

In 1968 a group of black artists joined efforts to form an organization called *AFRI-COBRA,* an acronym for African Commune of Bad Relevant Artists. As stated in its tenets, art is to serve the people. In an attempt to fulfill this aim, art must have specific colors, style, form, and intent. The original members were Jeff Donaldson, a painter and now chairman of the art department at Howard University, Wadsworth Jarrell, and Gerald Williams. Carolyn Mims Lawrence, Barbara Jones Hogu, Frank Smith, Howard Mallory, Napoleon Henderson, and Nelson Stevens joined later.

In New York in 1968, the *Black Emergency Cultural Coalition* gained prominence when it formed to protest the Whitney Museum's exclusionary show "American Artist of the 1930's." BECC charged that the Whitney exhibition excluded notable black artists who had painted during the thirties. Led by Henri Ghent, Vivian Browne, and Faith Ringgold, a counter-exhibition entitled "Invisible Artists: 1930" was mounted at the Studio Museum of Harlem.

In 1969 BECC picketed the Metropolitan Museum, which was staging the "Harlem On My Mind" exhibition, a large multimedia show, which many believe misrepresented the Harlem community.

Following the Metropolitan Museum protest, the critical attention of the BECC turned again to the Whitney. Deciding that it had not responded to its original protest, the Coalition formed a picket line on the sidewalk surrounding the museum and demanded full participation for black artists in the museum's exhibitions. As a result, several blacks were included in subsequent annuals and in 1971 the first black art exhibition at the Whitney, "Contemporary Black Art in America," was held. However, a rebuttal show was held again, this time at Acts of Art Gallery, for the Whitney had failed to include blacks on the curatorial level, a necessary step in the selection of works slated for exhibition.

During the early 1970s, the BECC developed art programs in correctional institutions throughout New York State, an innovation soon adopted elsewhere in the nation.

In 1971, a New York-based organization, the *Where We At Together Black Women,* was developed as an art collective. Co-founded by Dinga McCannon, Key Brown, and Faith Ringgold, this group of female artists joined together in a team effort to curate their own exhibitions and promote their art work. This group is perhaps one of the oldest of the women's art groups.

Workshops

In 1949, the Printmaking Workshop of New York, under the direction of its founder, Bob Blackburn, opened its doors to provide working space for printmakers. The workshop, besides providing space for artists, has also printed the work of such artists as Norman Lewis, Eldzier Cortor, Vivian Browne, Camille Billops, Benny Andrews, Romare Bearden, Charles Alston, Ernest Crichlow, and many, many, more.

The original Children's Art Carnival was initiated in the garden of the Museum of Modern Art under a tent during the summer of 1942. It was a means of introducing parents to the fact that the Museum of Modern Art had an art school for children which operated during the school year. During President John F. Kennedy's term of office, his wife, Jacqueline, requested that a replica of the Children's Art Carnival be sent to the World's Fair in Brussels, Belgium to serve as an example of quality art education provided for the programs and better schools. The concept was so well received that it was decided by the Museum of Modern Art that a site should be found for this new Carnival project. In 1969 a space was provided by the Harlem School of the Arts. It was a large open garage on St. Nicholas Avenue.

The Carnival's activities focus on the needs of individual youngsters. Providing students with vehicles for expressing themselves, the Carnival staff has developed tools to help the teachers better understand their students. The Carnival is designed to provide service for preschool-age children, up to high school youngsters, as well as the handicapped. The Carnival offers free classes, which include painting, puppetry, clay and 3-D construction, printmaking, and photography.

A sculpting workshop in Brooklyn.

Spray Can Graffiti

In 1972, in New York City, black and Hispanic teenagers combined the paint spray can and street pride into a colorful art form, "wall graffiti," which at the time of writing is embroiled in heated artistic and political controversy.

The content of wall graffiti is usually no more than the name of a street gang or the nickname of the individual painter and the name or number of the street on which he lives or to which gives his loyalty. The lettering, however, is frequently, and lavishly flamboyant. Very often the lettering covers the entire length of a 60-foot train or a block-long construction wall.

The New York City government and the Metropolitan Transit Authority have been outraged by the graffiti and prevailed upon courts to order painters caught in the act to clean up their handiwork, a very difficult task given the chemical content of the paint. The officials argue that in addition to violating public property, graffiti represents hooliganism and resentment and has to cease, regardless of artistic merit.

Art and black militancy in the 1960s—a mood, an explosion of emotion, a philosophical exposition, a celebration of the people.

However, defenders of graffitists soon came forward, many of them from the art world. A New York gallery located some outstanding graffitists, put them to work on canvas, and had a show. Choreographer Twyla Tharp choreographed a ballet for the Joffrey Company, "Deuce Coupe," showing dancers moving against a background provided by boys painting with spray cans on ceiling-hung sheets of paper.

The defense of graffiti was that it continues the historic tradition of wall paintings and murals, which, in an organized form, the city was encouraging and, furthermore, that it was far superior in artistic expression to the commercial advertisements that are put up on walls and in public transportation facilities.

Whatever it represents, graffiti serves an important purpose to blacks and others who live and work in America's increasingly dank and grimy cities. It both permits artistic expression and brightens the environment without vulgarity or banality. This, argue graffiti defenders, has been the purpose of all wall art from cave paintings through the great Mexican muralists of early twentieth century to the present day. And, as defenders of graffiti point out, the street art of blacks is almost never obscene and is rarely affixed to attractive buildings.

BLACK ARTISTS OF THE EIGHTEENTH, NINETEENTH, AND EARLY TWENTIETH CENTURIES

JOHN JAMES AUDUBON (Also known as JEAN RABINE, JEAN-JACQUES FORGERE)
Painter
1785–1851

Some Notable Works: *Portrait of Henri De Gallon; Portrait of John Cleives Simms*

John James Audubon was the son of a French merchant sea captain and planter and his Afro-Caribbean mistress. Born on April 26, 1785, in Les Cayes (now Aux Cayes) in the French colony of Saint-Dominique (now Haiti), Audubon was taken to his father's home in France, Coueron, near Nantes, along with his half-sister following the death of his mother. He was six years old. After a suitably discreet period of time, both he and his sister were formally adopted by the captain's legal wife, Anne Moynet.

As a youngster in France, Audubon began to collect his specimens and draw, receiving a basic education during the French Revolution. In the summer of 1803, to escape conscription into Napoleon's army, to acquire business training, and to avoid the increasing social problems caused by the circumstances of his birth, Audubon was sent to Mill Grove, his father's farm near Philadelphia. Living the life of a young dandy, he met Lucy Bakewell, the daughter of a nearby plantation owner. They married five years later in 1808 and moved to Kentucky to establish a general store at the falls of the Ohio River. For a brief period Audubon painted portraits of frontier gentry, gave art lessons, and worked as a taxidermist. Later he began to travel down the Mississippi River in search of specimens to draw. He and his family lived in New Orleans for a time, and then Audubon took his bird drawings and sailed for England, where his work was appreciated, and then he published *The Birds of America.*

EDWARD MITCHELL BANNISTER
Painter
1828–1901

Some Notable Works: *After the Storm; Sabin Point; Driving Home the Cows; Pleasant Pastures; Narragansett Bay; Swale Land; Sad Memories*

Born in Nova Scotia, Bannister was the son of a West Indian father and Afro-American mother. Both parents died when he was very young. Bannister moved to Boston in the early 1850s, where he learned to make solar plates and worked as a photographer.

Influenced by the Barbizon style popular at this time, Bannister's paintings convey his own love of the quiet beauty of nature and his pleasure in picturesque scenes with cottages, cattle, dawns, sunsets, and small bodies of water.

In 1871 Bannister moved from Boston to Providence, Rhode Island, where he lived until his death. He was the only nineteenth-century Afro-American artist who did not travel to Europe to study art, believing that he was an American and that he wished to paint as an American. Bannister became one of the most outstanding artists in Providence in the 1870s and 1880s, and in 1880 was to become one of seven founders of the Providence Art Club, which later became known as the Rhode Island School of Design.

ROBERT DUNCANSON
Painter
1817–1872

Some Notable Works: *Portraits: William and Freeman Cary; Nicholas Longworth; The Berthelets of Detroit; Bishop Payne; Murals at Taft Museum; Romantic Landscape*

Robert Duncanson was the son of an Afro-American mother and a Scottish-Canadian father. Born in upstate New York, he was to spend much of his childhood in Canada. At some point in his youth, he and his

Robert S. Duncanson, America's first black studio artist, painted the Hudson River scene Mural *in 1848.*

mother moved to Mt. Healthy, Ohio, where in 1840 the Western Freedman's Aid Society, an antislavery group, raised funds to send him to Glasgow, Scotland, where he could study art. Returning to Cincinnati three years later, Duncanson turned to the local newspaper where he advertised as the proprietor of a daguerreotype studio, and although he seemed to have been gaining a reputation as a painter, he continued to work at his daguerreotype until 1855, when he began to devote all of his time to his painting. Like many landscape artists of this time, Duncanson traveled around the United States drawing his compositions from the images of nature before him. In 1853 he made his second trip to Europe—this time to visit Italy, France, and England.

It is interesting to note that Duncanson was active during and after the Civil War, yet with the exception of his painting of Uncle Tom and Eva, Duncanson made no attempts to present the turmoil that was taking place within America or the social pressures that he experienced. In September 1872 Duncanson, while at the height of his success, suffered a severe mental breakdown and ended his life on December 21 in the Michigan State Retreat in Detroit.

MINNIE EVANS
Painter
1892

Minnie Eva Jones was born on December 1, 1892 in a log cabin in Long Creek, Pender County, North Carolina. In 1893 she moved with her mother, grandmother, and great-grandmother to Wilmington, North Carolina, where she spent her childhood. In 1908 she married Julis Evans, the body servant of Mr. Pembroke Jones.

Minnie Evans began to draw in 1935, working with crayon, pencil, and ink, on the backs of discarded stationery. In 1961 Evans was given her first exhibition at the Little Gallery in Wilmington, which was followed by her first New York exhibition "The Lost World of Minnie Evans" in 1966 at the Church of the Epiphany and at St. Clement's Episcopal Church. Also in 1966, Evans began to make collages, covering her earlier drawings with oil paint and ink and pencil. Her work was exhibited in 1969 at the Davison Art Center, Wesleyan University, in Middletown, Connecticut. Her first European exhibition was held in 1970 in the Portal Gallery in London, and in 1975 Evans was given a one-person exhibition at the Whitney Museum of American Art.

META VAUX WARRICK FULLER
Sculptor
1877–1968

Some Notable Works: *The Awakening of Ethiopia; Richard B. Harrison; The Talking Skull; John*

Meta Vaux Warrick Fuller was born in 1877 in Philadelphia and educated at the School of Industrial Art and the Pennsylvania Academy. Her interest in sculpture led her to study with Charles Grafly and then with Rodin at the Academie Colarossi in Paris.

In 1903 and again in 1904, her group entitled *The Wretched* (considered by most experts to be her masterpiece) was exhibited at the Paris Salon. In 1910 most of her works were destroyed by fire, but her subsequent efforts were exhibited by the Harmon Foundation and the Boston Art Club, among others.

Today her work can be found in the Cleveland Museum. She died in 1968 at the age of 90.

WILLIAM HARPER
Painter
1873–1910

Some Notable Works: *Autumn Landscape; Afternoon at Montigny; Landscape; An Autumn Day in France*

William Harper was born in 1873 in Canada, and died 37 years later in Mexico City, at a time when many critics already considered his work superior to Henry Ossawa Tanner's.

Harper was a protege of Tanner and, along with him, came to be regarded as one of the truly significant American black painters of the nineteenth century.

ISAAC HATHAWAY
Sculptor, Ceramicist
1871–?

Some Notable Works: *Busts of Frederick Douglass, Booker T. Washington and Paul Dunbar; Memorial coins of Booker T. Washington and George Washington Carver*

Isaac Hathaway's major works are portrait busts, the most famous of which are those of Frederick Douglass, Paul Laurence Dunbar, and Booker T. Washington. He was also commissioned by the U.S. Mint to design the memorial coins issued in honor of Booker T. Washington and George Washington Carver.

Born in Lexington, Kentucky in 1871, Hathaway studied in the Art Department of the New England Conservatory of Music and the Ceramics Department of Pittsburgh Normal College. One of America's outstanding ceramicists, he was for many years head of the Ceramics Department at Alabama State Teachers College in Montgomery.

JULIEN HUDSON
Painter
Active 1831–1844

Some Notable Works: *Self-Portrait; Colonel Jean Michel Fortier, Jr.*

Julien Hudson was a native of New Orleans. He studied in Paris and upon his return to New Orleans taught art and portrait painting. On December 3, 1831 Hudson published a notice in the New Orleans *Courier* announcing his return from Paris and advertising his services as a portrait painter to the ladies and gentlemen of New Orleans. Although there are only two known works by Hudson, both are dated and signed.

MAY HOWARD JACKSON
Sculptor
1877–1931

Some Notable Works: *Busts of Paul Laurence Dunbar; Dean Kelly Miller of Howard University, Francis J. Grimke; Head of a Negro Child*

Born in 1877 in Philadelphia (the same year and place as fellow sculptor Meta Vaux Warrick Fuller), Mrs. Jackson was educated at J. Liberty Tadd's Art School in her native city, and at the Pennsylvania Academy. She had her own art studio in Washington, D.C. from 1902 until her death in 1931.

Executing busts of famous people remained her

A work by the best-known black portrait painter of the nineteenth century, Joshua Johnston.

Julien Hudson's Self-Portrait.

forte, although after 1914 she became preoccupied with the production of black thematic sculpture.

Mrs. Jackson's work has been exhibited at the National Academy of Design, the New York Emancipation Exposition, and the National Academy of Art in New York City.

In addition to lecturing and exhibiting, Mrs. Jackson taught sculpture at Howard University for several years.

JOSHUA JOHNSTON
Painter
c. 1765–1830

Some Notable Works: *Portrait of a Cleric; In the Garden; Benjamin Franklin and Son*

The best known black portrait artist of the eighteenth and early nineteenth centuries was Joshua Johnston, from Baltimore. Over the years, researchers have uncovered some two dozen of his paintings. It is believed that Johnston, who was active in Baltimore, was probably manumitted because he is listed in the Baltimore Directories between 1769 and 1824 as a "free householder of colour, portrait painter," with a studio in various central locations.

It is believed that Johnston may have been a former slave of Charles Willson Peale, the artist who is also known for having started a drawing school in Maryland in 1795, a school which was to encourage the development of the Pennsylvania Academy in Philadelphia, or he may have seen examples of Peale's work and begun to copy his style. It is also possible that Johnston had seen the work of Peale's son Rembrandt Peale and studied his style as well.

One could call Johnston a primitive painter, probably for the most part self-taught. His work had a quaint simplicity, honesty, and charm. He depicted subjects with enormous warmth and sensitivity. The gentle qualities of Johnston demonstrate themselves most readily in *Portrait of a Cleric,* his only known black subject.

EDMONIA LEWIS
Sculptor
1845–1890

Some Notable Works: *Hiawatha; The Marriage; Hagar in the Wilderness; Madonna and Child; Forever Free; The Death of Cleopatra*

Edmonia Lewis was America's first black woman artist and also the first of her race and sex to be recognized as a sculptor.

Born in 1845 in upstate New York, she was the daughter of a Chippewa Indian mother and a free black father. From 1859 to 1863, under the patronage of a number of abolitionists, she was educated at Oberlin

Edmonia Lewis created Hagar in the Wilderness.

College, the first American college to admit women on a nonsegregated basis.

After completing her schooling, Miss Lewis moved to Boston where she studied with Edmund Brackett and did a bust of Colonel Robert Gould Shaw, the commander of the first black regiment raised in the state of Massachusetts during the Civil War.

In 1865 she moved to Rome, where she soon became prominent. Returning to the United States, she fulfilled many commissions, including a bust of Henry Wadsworth Longfellow which was executed for the Harvard College Library.

Her works are fine examples of the neoclassical sculpture that was fashionable in her lifetime.

Miss Lewis is believed to have died in Rome in 1890.

SCIPIO MOORHEAD
Artist
c. 1773–?

Recognition is given Scipio Moorhead as a symbolic gesture to all the unknown blacks who contributed to the American art scene. There are today no known works by Moorhead in existence and of course no way of evaluating his place among artists. Memory of him is preserved primarily by the slave poet Phillis Wheatley, who dedicated a poem "To S.M., a Young African Painter, on Seeing His Works." In a penciled note of the 1773 edition of Miss Wheatley's *Poems on Various Subjects, Religious and Moral,* she identifies S.M. as "Scipio Moorhead, Negro servant to the Rev. John Moorhead of Boston whose genius inclined him that way."

The talent of Scipio Moorhead was initially recognized and cultivated by Sarah Moorhead, wife of the Reverend, a teacher of art and an expert in drawing techniques, japanning, and painting on glass. It is possible Scipio painted the unsigned portrait of Phillis Wheatley that was used as a frontispiece for several of her works.

PATRICK REASON
Artist-Engraver
1817–1852

Some Notable Works: *De Witt Clinton (engraving); Granville Sharp (engraving); Am I Not a Man and a Brother? (engraving copy); Treadmill in Jamaica (illustrations)*

At the age of 13 in the year 1830, Patrick Reason designed the frontispiece for Charles Andrew's *History of the African Free Schools.* Through the patronage of abolitionist organizations, Reason was apprenticed to a white engraver and subsequently became an independent engraver and draftsman himself.

For many years, Reason was actively involved in the abolitionist movement and much of his work was designed as propaganda for abolitionist organizations.

WILLIAM SIMPSON
Painter
1818–1872

Some Notable Works: *Portrait of Bishop J. W. Loguen, Portrait of Carolina E. S. Loguen*

William Simpson was a prolific painter in Boston around the 1860s, but only two works that he produced are available to us today, both at the Howard University Art Gallery in Washington, D.C. The paintings

reveal enormous competence and general artistic sensibility.

Born in Buffalo, New York in 1818, Simpson became the apprentice of Matthew Wilson around 1854 and worked with him some six years before moving on to Boston, where he lived until his death.

HENRY OSSAWA TANNER
Painter
1859–1937

Some Notable Works: *Daniel in the Lions' Den; He Healed the Sick; Christ Walking on the Water; Flight into Egypt; Lions in the Desert; The Disciples on the Road to Bethany; The Sabot Makers; Banjo Lesson*

Alain Locke has called Henry Ossawa Tanner the leading talent of the "journeyman period" of black American art.

Born in Pittsburgh in 1859, Tanner chose painting rather than the ministry as a career, overcoming the strong objections of his father, an African Methodist Episcopal bishop. After attending the Pennsylvania Academy of Fine Arts, he taught at Clark University in Atlanta, supplementing his salary by working as a photographer. Some of Tanner's most compelling work—such as *The Banjo Lesson* (1890)—was produced during this period, with Tanner himself emerging as the most promising black artist of his day.

In 1891, however, Tanner abandoned black subject matter and left the United States for Paris, where he concentrated on religious themes. In 1896, his *Daniel in the Lion's Den,* a mixture of realism and mystical

Engravings by Patrick Reason are the copperplate of Henry Bibb (top) *and* DeWitt Clinton (bottom).

Henry Tanner, the most respected black artist of his time.

Tanner's The Thankful Poor.

symbolism, won honorable mention at the Paris Salon. The following year, the French government purchased his *Resurrection of Lazarus.*

In 1900, Tanner received the Medal of Honor at the Paris Exposition and the Lippincott Prize.

Tanner died in 1937.

EUGENE WARBOURG
Sculptor
1825–1867

Some Notable Works: *Bust of John Bason Brown; Le Pecheur; Le Premier Baiser*

Born a freeman in New Orleans, Eugene Warbourg, a stonemason by trade, shared a workshop with his brother Daniel, also a stonemason. Eugene demonstrated a strong talent for sculpturing and received his formal training from a French artist of the vicinity called Gabriel. He was so successful that in 1852 jealousy and economic rivalry caused him to leave the

United States for Europe where he stayed until his death. His best known American work is that of John Young Mason, a marble bust now at the Virginia Historical Society in Richmond.

A. B. WILSON
Painter
(active 1840–1848)

Notable Work: *Portrait of Bishop Payne*

Not much is known about A. B. Wilson except that he was the son of a member of the Bethel A. M. E. Church in Philadelphia. His one known painting is the group portrait of Bishop Payne and his family, which is an unusual narrative with an angel floating above. A portrait of John Cornish, a lithographic copy, is more conventional, still the sensitivity of the religious and social philosophies of both images reveal the intensity of the individual.

BLACK ARTISTS OF THE HARLEM RENAISSANCE

RICHMOND BARTHE
Sculptor
1901

Some Notable Works: *Singing Slave; Maurice Evans; Lot's Wife; Henry O. Tanner*

Born in 1901 in Bay St. Louis, Mississippi, Barthe was educated at the Art Institute in Chicago from 1924 to 1928. He studied under Charles Schroeder and Albin Polasek.

Barthe's first love was painting, but it was through his experiments with sculpture that he began initially to gain critical attention in 1927. His first commissions were busts of Henry Ossawa Tanner and Toussaint L'Ouverture. The acclaim resulting from them led to a one-man show in Chicago and a Rosenwald Fellowship for study in New York City.

Barthe's work has been exhibited at several major American museums, including the Metropolitan Museum of Art in New York City. In 1946 he received the first commission given to a black for a bust slated in New York University's Hall of Fame. A year later he was one of a committee of 15 artists chosen to help modernize the sculpture in the Catholic churches of the United States.

Barthe holds membership in the National Academy of Arts and Letters.

WILLIAM E. BRAXTON
Painter
1878–1932

Some Notable Works: *Figural Study; Seascape; Portraits of Ira Aldridge; Alexander Pushkin; D'Artagnan*

Born in Washington, D.C. where he received his early education, Braxton came to New York where he studied art at Adelphi College. He never attained financial success and so worked at many jobs. Early in his life he was an office boy, later he became a valet, and still later a pullman porter. Braxton is considered the first American black to work as an expressionist

The poignant, powerful touch of Richmond Barthe is exemplified in these two sculptures.

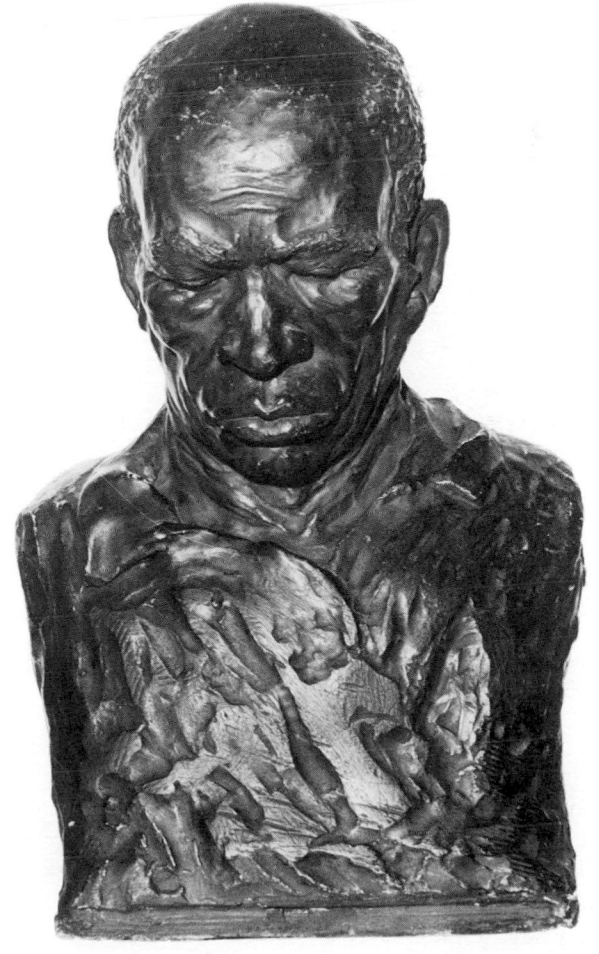

painter. His major work was probably *Figural Study,* which is now in the Schomburg collection.

ALLAN ROHAN CRITE
Painter, Illustrator
1910

Some Notable Works: *Beneath the Cross of St. Augustine; City of God; Tyre Jumping; Book Illustrations; Were You There; These Spirituals*

Born in Plainfield, New Jersey in 1910 where he attended public school, he attended the Boston Museum of Fine Arts School and later the Massachusetts School of Art at Boston University. He completed works for the M. I. T. chapel, for Grace Church in Martha's Vineyard, and Holy Cross Church in Morrisville, Vermont among many others.

AARON DOUGLAS
Painter
1899

Some Notable Works: *Murals in the Countee Cullen Branch of the New York City Public Library; Illustrations*

in books by Cullen, James Weldon Johnson, Alain Locke, Langston Hughes; Alexander Dumas; Marion Anderson

Born in Topeka, Kansas in 1899, Aaron Douglas has achieved considerable eminence as a muralist, illustrator, and academician.

As a young man, Douglas studied at the University of Nebraska, Columbia University Teachers College, and l'Academie Scandinave in Paris. He has had one-man exhibits at the universities of Kansas and Nebraska and has also exhibited in New York at the Gallery of Modern Art. In 1939 Douglas was named to the faculty of Fisk and later became head of its Department of Art Education.

ALICE GAFFORD
Painter
1886

Some Notable Works: *Tea Party* (1968); *Flowers* (1956)

Mrs. Alice Gafford is among the pioneer black artists who have worked in the Los Angeles area for several generations.

Born in Kansas in 1886, Mrs. Gafford studied at the Otis Art Institute, at UCLA, and with private tutors. Mrs. Gafford is a member of several local art associations and has exhibited her work all over the United States. It is today represented in several private collections.

PALMER C. HAYDEN
Painter
1893–1973

Some Notable Works: *Southern Scenes and City Streets Series; John Henry Series*

Palmer Hayden painted sophisticated landscapes and street scenes, gentle and humorous portraits, satirical caricatures, and canvases protesting the plight of blacks in the United States.

Hayden was born in Widewater, Virginia and served in the Army during World War I, after which he studied at Boothbay Colony, Maine, under Asa G. Randall and in 1925 at Cooper Union in New York City, where he earned his bread and canvas by housecleaning and washing windows. At the first Harmon Exhibit of African American Art in 1926, he was awarded the Gold Medal. He then studied in Paris and Boston, returning to the United States in 1933, the year in which he received the Rockefeller award in art.

Detail from Alice Gafford still life.

Died Wid His Hammer in His Hand *from Palmer Hayden's* John Henry Series.

MALVIN GRAY JOHNSON
Painter
1896–1934

Some Notable Works: *Self Portrait; Turkeys at Roost; Portrait of a Soldier; Meditation*

Johnson was born in Greensboro, North Carolina in 1896. He is noted especially for the pictures made in Brightwood, Virginia in the late summer of 1934. Along with Hale Woodruff, he was one of the first black artists to incorporate modern concepts of cubism in his paintings.

SARGENT JOHNSON
Sculptor
1888–1967

Some Notable Works: *Sammy; Esther; Golden Gate Exposition Aquatic Park murals; Forever Free*

Sargent Johnson, who three times won the Harmon Foundation's medal as the outstanding artist of his race in the nation, worked in stylized idioms, heavily influenced by the art forms of Africa, in sculpture, mural bas-reliefs, metal sculpture, and ceramics.

Born in Boston, he studied at the Worcester Art School and moved west to the San Francisco Bay area in 1915, where his teachers were Beniamino Bufano and Ralph Stackpole. He exhibited at the San Francisco Artists Annual, 1925–1931; Harmon Foundation, 1928–1931, 1933; Art Institute of Chicago, 1930; Baltimore Museum, 1939; American Negro Exposition, Chicago, 1940. He was the recipient of numerous awards and prizes.

From the beginning of his career he spoke of his sculpture as an attempt to show the "natural beauty and dignity of the pure American Negro" and wished to present "that beauty not so much to the white man as to the Negro himself. Unless I can interest my race, I am sunk."

WILLIAM H. JOHNSON
Painter
1901

Some Notable Works: *Booker T. Washington; Young Man in Vest; Descent from the Cross; On a John Brown Flight*

William H. Johnson has been a pioneer black modernist whose ever-developing work has gone from abstract expressionist landscape and flower studies, influenced by Van Gogh, to studies of black life in America, and finally to abstract figure studies in the manner of Rouault.

Born in Florence, South Carolina, he studied at the National Academy of Design; Cape Cod School of Art, under Charles Hawthorne; southern France, 1926–1929; Denmark and Norway, 1930–1938. Exhibits include Harmon Foundation (Gold Medal in 1929); Aarlins, Denmark, 1935; Baltimore Museum, 1939; American Negro Exposition, Chicago, 1940. One-man shows Copenhagen, 1935; Artists Gallery, New York, 1938.

LOIS MAILOU JONES
Painter
1905

Some Notable Works: *Old Street in Montmartre; Jennie; Speracedes; Series; Paris, Haiti, Africa*

Lois Mailou Jones, a multifaceted artist who first gained recognition in the world of fashion with her textile designs and fashion illustrations, later turned to working in oils and watercolors, presenting a variety of figurative images that covered her interpretation of the Caribbean, Africa, Europe, and the United States.

Born in Boston, Lois Mailou Jones studied at the High School of Practical Arts and then went on to the Boston Museum School of Fine Arts and the Designers School. In 1930 Jones became a professor at Howard University, where she taught courses in design and watercolor painting.

ARCHIBALD MOTLEY
Painter
1891

Some Notable Works: *The Jockey Club; The Plotters; Parisian Scene; Black Belt*

Archibald Motley touched on many topics and themes in his work but none was more gratifying to him than his candid depictions of black Americans.

Born in New Orleans, Motley's artistic talent was apparent by the time he attended high school. His father wanted him to become a doctor, but Archibald insisted on art and began formal education at the Art

Archibald Motley's Chicken Shack.

Institute of Chicago, earning his subsistence by working as a day laborer. During this time Motley came in contact with the driftwood, scavengers, and hustlers of society, who are now immortalized in his street scenes.

In 1928 Motley had a one-man show at the New Galleries in downtown New York and became the first artist, black or white, to make the front page of the *New York Times.*

JAMES A. PORTER
Art Historian, Painter
1905–1970

Some Notable Works: *On a Cuban Bus; Portrait of F. A. as Harlequin; Dorothy Porter; Nude*

James A. Porter is a painter of considerable scholarship, famous both for his original works and for his studies.

Born in Baltimore, he studied at Howard University (B.S.); Art Students League, New York; Sorbonne; and New York University (M.A.). He has enjoyed numerous travel grants enabling him to study African and European art at first hand.

Among his ten one-man shows are Port-au-Prince, Haiti, 1946; Dupont Gallery, Washington, D.C., 1949; and, Howard University, 1965. His works are in the collections of Howard University; Lincoln University, Missouri; Harmon Foundation; IBM; and others. He is the author of the classic *Modern Negro Art* (1943), and numerous articles.

He was a delegate to the UNESCO Conference on Africa, Boston, 1961 and to the International Congress of African Art and Culture, Salisbury, Southern Rhodesia, 1962. Since 1953 he has been chairman of the Department of Art, and director of the Gallery of Art at Howard University.

In 1965, at the twenty-fifth anniversary of the founding of the National Gallery of Art, he was named "one of America's Most Outstanding Men of the Arts."

AUGUSTA SAVAGE
Sculptor
1900–1962

Some Notable Works: *Lift Every Voice and Sing; The Chase; Black Women; Lenore, Gamin*

A leading sculptor who emerged during the Negro Renaissance, Augusta Savage was one of the artists represented in the first all-black exhibition in America, sponsored by the Harmon Foundation at International House in New York City. In 1939 her symbolic group piece *Lift Every Voice and Sing* was shown at the New York World's Fair Community Arts Building.

Miss Savage was born in Florida, studied at Talla-

Sensitive portrayals of the human condition were found in W. E. Scott's paintings.

hassee State Normal School, at Cooper Union in New York City, and in France as the recipient of Carnegie and Rosenwald fellowships. She was the first black to win acceptance in the National Association of Women Painters and Sculptors.

WILLIAM EDOUARD SCOTT
Painter
1884

Some Notable Works: *Haitian Man; Blind Sister Mary; Mexican Scene*

William Edouard Scott was born in Indianapolis in 1884 and studied at the Art Institute in Chicago between 1904 and 1908. He later went on to Paris, where he studied at the Julien and Colossi academies and privately under Henry O. Tanner.

In 1907, at the age of 23, Scott won first prize for a mural at the Chicago Shakespeare Festival and went on to a series of successful exhibitions in the United States and a Harmon Gold Medal in 1927. In 1931 he visited Haiti on a Rosenwald Fellowship to paint "Negro types" of the island. It was there that whatever inhibitions Scott had faded and he reached the peak of his originality and brilliance of expression. Upon his return to the United States he painted numerous murals in public buildings throughout the country.

JAMES VAN DER ZEE
Photographer
1886

James Van Der Zee was born on June 29, 1886, in Lenox, Massachusetts. His parents had moved there from New York in the early 1880s after serving as maid and butler to Ulysses S. Grant, who then resided at 34th Street in New York City. The second of six children, James grew up in a family filled with creative people. Everybody painted, drew, or played an instrument, so it was not considered out of the ordinary when, upon receiving a camera outfit for premiums in 1900, Van Der Zee became interested in photography.

By 1906 Van Der Zee moved to New York, married, and took on odd jobs to support his new and growing family. In 1907 they moved to Phoetus, Virginia, where he worked in the dining room of the Hotel Chamberlin in Old Point Comfort, Virginia. During this time he worked as a photographer on a part-time basis. In 1909 he returned to New York.

By 1915 Van Der Zee had his first photography job as assistant in a small concession in the Gertz Department Store in Newark, New Jersey. With the money he saved from this job he was able to open his own studio in 1916 on 135th Street. World War I had begun and many young soldiers came to the studio to have their pictures taken. Over the course of a half century, James Van Der Zee would record the visual history of Harlem. His subjects include Marcus Garvey, Daddy Grace, Father Divine, Joe Louis, Madame Walker, and many more.

In 1969 the exhibition "Harlem On My Mind," produced by Thomas Hoving, then director of the Metropolitan Museum of Art, brought James Van Der Zee international recognition.

LAURA WHEELER WARING
Artist, Educator
1887–1948

Some Notable Works: *Alonzo Aden; W. E. Burghardt DuBois; James Weldon Johnson; Mother and Daughter*

Born in 1887 in Hartford, Connecticut, this portrait painter and illustrator received her first training at the Pennsylvania Academy of Fine Arts, where she studied for six years. In 1914 she won the Cresson Memorial Scholarship, which enabled her to continue her studies at the Academie de la Grande Chaumiere in Paris.

Mrs. Waring returned to the United States as an art instructor at Cheyney State Teachers College in Pennsylvania, eventually becoming head of the art department there. Her work, particularly portraits, has been exhibited at several leading American art galleries. In 1927 she received the Harmon Award for achievement in fine art. Mrs. Waring with Betsy Graves Reyneau completed a set of 24 repaintings of other of their works titled *Portraits of Outstanding*

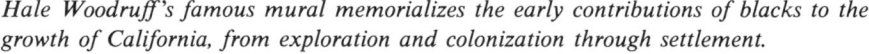

Hale Woodruff's famous mural memorializes the early contributions of blacks to the growth of California, from exploration and colonization through settlement.

Americans of Negro Origin for the Harmon Foundation in the 1940s.

Mrs. Waring was also the director in charge of the black art exhibits at the Philadelphia Exposition in 1926 and was a member of the national advisory board of Art Movements, Inc.

She died in 1948.

HALE WOODRUFF
Painter, Muralist
1900–1979

Some Notable Works: *Ancestral Remedies; The Little Boy; The Amistad Murals*

Hale Woodruff's paintings have been largely modernist landscapes and formal abstractions, but he has also done rural Georgia scenes evocative of the "red clay" country.

Born in 1900 in Cairo, Illinois, Woodruff is a graduate of the John Herron Art Institute in Indianapolis. Encouraged by a bronze award in the 1926 Harmon Foundation competition, Woodruff went to Paris to study at both the Academie Scandinave and the Academie Moderne, as well as with Henry Ossawa Tanner.

In 1931 he became art instructor at Atlanta University and five years later accepted a similar post at New York University. In 1939 he was commissioned by Talladega College to do *The Amistad Murals,* an episodic depiction of a slave revolt.

In 1948, Woodruff teamed up with Charles Alston to work on the Golden State Mutual Life Insurance Company Murals in California, which presented the contribution of Afro-Americans to the history of the development of California. Woodruff's last mural assignment came in 1950 when he developed the series of mural panels for Atlanta University entitled "The Art of the Negro."

Hale Woodruff died in 1979 after creating a body of works with styles that moved from the figurative, to the Impressionistic period of his Paris experience, to a brief exploration of the cubist visual concepts, to moving comfortably into the abstract style. With all of these stylistic developments, Hale Woodruff also became one of America's strongest mural painters.

BLACK ARTISTS FROM THE DEPRESSION THROUGH WORLD WAR II

CHARLES ALSTON
Painter, Sculptor, Muralist
1907–1972

Some Notable Works: *Frederick Douglass* (1968); *Nobody Knows* (1966); *Blues Song* (1958); *Blues with Guitar and Bass* (1957); *Sons and Daughters* (1966); *School Girl* (1958)

It is the mural of painter Charles Alston that has established his reputation and insured his fame as a black American artist of importance.

Alston's California mural focuses on the post-Civil War period. Blacks participated in all the state-building activities, as well as in their own struggle against racist discrimination.

Born in Charlotte, North Carolina in 1907, Alston studied at Columbia University in New York, receiving B.A. and M.A. degrees. He was later awarded several fellowships and grants to launch his painting career.

Alston's paintings and sculpture are in such collections as those of IBM and the Detroit Museum. His murals depicting the history of medicine adorn the facade of Harlem Hospital in New York. Alston is a member of the National Society of Mural Painters.

WILLIAM ARTIS
Sculptor
1914

Notable Work: *Head of a Girl* (1933)

William Artis, one of the first black Americans to achieve recognition for his work in ceramics, is now a professor of art at Mankato State College.

Born in Washington, North Carolina, he studied at Alfred University and later at Syracuse University under Ivan Nestrovic. Among the major national shows in which his works have been exhibited are the Harmon Foundation exhibitions, the surveys of Afro-American art at the Albany Institute of History and Art in 1945, and the City College of New York in 1967. The largest collection of his works is at Atlanta University; he is also represented at Howard University, Fisk University, Chadron State College, the National Portrait Gallery of the Smithsonian Institution, the Joslyn Art Museum, Omaha; and the IBM collection, Chicago.

ROMARE BEARDEN
Painter, Collagist
1914

Some Notable Works: *Street Corner; He Is Arisen; The Burial*

Romare Bearden was born in Charlotte, North Carolina. His family moved to Pittsburgh and later to Harlem. Bearden studied with George Grosz at the Art Students League and later, on the G.I. Bill, went to Paris where he met Matisse, Joan Miro, and Carl Holty. A product of the new generation of Afro-Americans who had migrated from the rural areas of the South to the urban cities of the North, Bearden's work reflected the era of industrialization. His would become the visual images that would reflect the city life, the music—jazz—the city people. Bearden's earlier works belonged to the school of Social Realism, but after his return from Europe his images became more abstract.

In the 1960s Bearden changed his approach to his picture-making and began to make collages, soon becoming one of the best known collagists in the world.

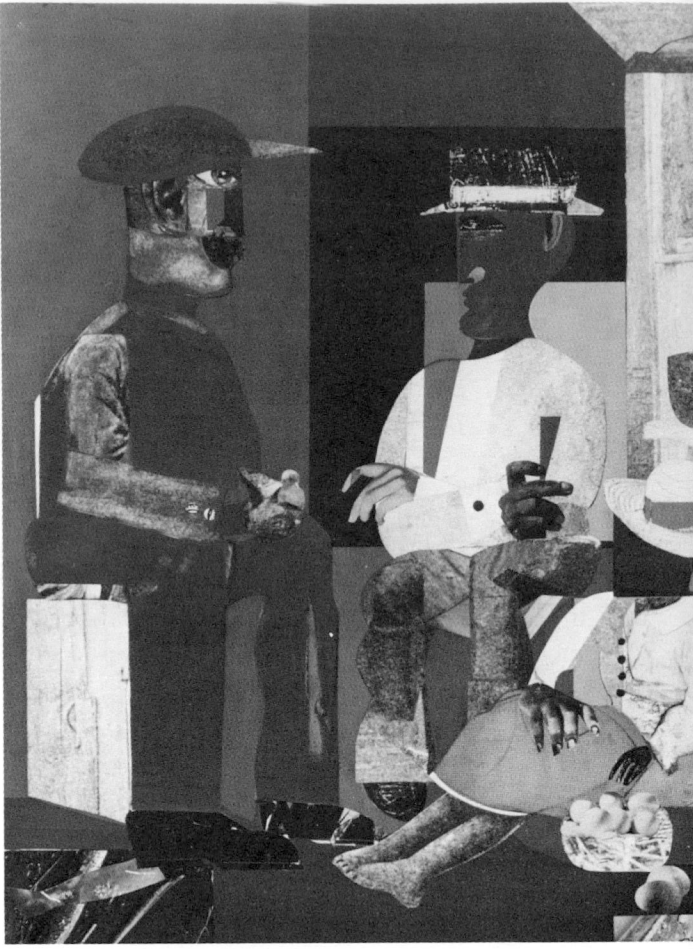

Romare Bearden's collage Eastern Barn.

His images are haunting montages of his memories of past experiences, of stories told to him by other people. They are for Bearden "an attempt to redefine the image of man in terms of the black experience."

JOHN BIGGERS
Painter
1924

Some Notable Works: *Cradle; Mother and Child; The Contributions of Negro Women to American Life and Education*

John Biggers has been a leading figure in Social Realism as a painter, sculptor, printmaker, and teacher, and an outstanding surrealistic muralist as well.

Born in Gastonia, North Carolina in 1924, Biggers has derived much of his subject matter from the contributions made by blacks to the development of the United States.

While teaching at Texas Southern University, Biggers has become a significant influence on several young black painters.

Bob Blackburn's massive figures convey towering strength.

ROBERT BLACKBURN
Printmaker
1921

Some Notable Works: *Boy with Green Head; Negro Mother*

Robert Blackburn was born in New York City. He studied at the Harlem Workshop, the Art Students League, and the Wallace Harrison School of Art. His exhibits include Art of the American Negro, 1940; Downtown Gallery, New York; Albany Museum; Contemporary Art of the American Negro, 1966; and numerous print shows in the United States and Europe. His work is represented in the Library of Congress, the Brooklyn and Baltimore museums, and the Atlanta University Collections. He is a member of the art faculty of Cooper Union and has established a graphic workshop in New York City.

MARGARET BURROUGHS
Painter, Sculptor
1917

Some Notable Works: *Mexican Landscape; Head; Black Queen; Two Girls*

Margaret Burroughs brings her formidable talents as painter, sculptor, educator, writer, illustrator, and graphic artist to bear upon the situations of the black and of the artist in America.

Born in St. Rose Parish, Louisiana, she studied at Chicago Normal School; Art Institute of Chicago (B.A.., M.A.E.); Teachers' College, Columbia University; Northwestern University; and in Mexico City. She is a founder of the Museum of Negro History, Chicago; The South Side Community Art Center, Chicago; and the National Conference of Artists.

Her numerous exhibitions include American Exposition, Chicago, 1940; San Francisco Civic Museum, 1949; Market Place Gallery, New York, 1950; House of Friendship, Moscow, 1967; Elmhurst College, 1970. Her work can be found in the collections of Howard University; Alabama State Normal; Atlanta University; DuSable Museum of African-American History, Chicago; Johnson Publishing Company; and the Oakland Museum.

WILLIAM CARTER
Painter, Muralist
1909

Some Notable Works: *Missouri Snow; Clouds Over Kuilock; Small Town Dandy; Hermits; Demi-Monde; Portrait of Rev. Joseph Branham*

Muralist William Carter was one of the leading black painters active during the early 1940s, a comparatively productive period for blacks in American art.

Born in Missouri in 1909, Carter received his education at the Art Institute of Chicago and the University of Illinois. Though he is primarily known as a muralist, Carter is equally adept on canvas.

ELDZIER CORTOR
Painter, Educator
1915

Some Notable Works: *Day Clean; Vision of Sunset; Oak Table; The Woman; Environment; The Merchants*

Born in Chicago in 1915, Cortor received his art education at Chicago Art Institute, Institute of Design, Columbia University, and Pratt Graphic Art Center.

ERNEST CRICHLOW
Painter, Illustrator
1914

Some Notable Works: *Young Boy; The White Fence; The Domestic; Lend Me Your Hand; Young Hand;* Illustrations for *Two is a Team* (1945); *Corrie and the Yankee* (1959)

The black child has never been more effectively employed as subject matter than in the work of Ernest Crichlow. Although adolescence and motherhood are often recurring themes in Crichlow, it is through his portrayal of the touching simplicity of children that he has made his most memorable contribution.

Crichlow was born in 1914 in New York City, and received art instruction at New York University and the Art Students League.

Ernest Crichlow is a master at rendering sensitive portrayals of youth.

In the 1930s he worked on Federal art projects in North Carolina and New York and exhibited in many galleries, among them the Harlem Community Art Center and Federal Gallery in New York. Crichlow has taught art at Shaw and other universities and is a founder of the Cinque Gallery in New York City.

BEAUFORD DELANEY
Painter
1910–1979

Some Notable Works: *Greene Street; Yaddo; Head of a Poet; Snow Scene*

Born in Knoxville, Tennessee, Beauford Delaney was described by his elder brother Samuel as a "remarkably dutiful child." His father, the Reverend Samuel Delaney, and his mother, Delia Johnson Delaney, understood and recognized Beauford Delaney's artistic talent, as well as that of his brother Joseph, and when the time came they encouraged them in the development of their skills. For Beauford Delaney, recognition came by way of an elderly white artist of Knoxville, Lloyd Branson. Branson gave him lessons and after a time urged him to go to a city where he might study and come into contact with the art world.

In 1924 Beauford Delaney went to Boston to study at the Massachusetts Normal School, later studying at the Copley Society, where he took evening courses while working full-time at the South Boston School of Art. From Boston, Delaney moved on to New York, swept up, like many artists during this period, by the Harlem Renaissance.

It was in New York that Delaney took on the life of a bohemian, living in the village in cold water flats. Much of his time was spent painting the portraits of the personalities of the day, such as Louis Armstrong, Ethel Waters, and Duke Ellington. In 1938 Beauford Delaney gained national attention when *Life Magazine,* in an article on "negroes," featured a photograph of him surrounded by a group of his paintings at the annual outdoor exhibition in Washington Square in New York. In 1945 Henry Miller wrote the essay "The Amazing and Invariable Beauford Delaney," which was later reprinted in *Remember to Remember.* The essay describes Delaney's bohemian lifestyle in New York during the 1940s and 1950s.

The fifties was the era of Rome. Every artist in New York saw Rome as the "New Paris" and rushed off to study and absorb its culture. Delaney, receiving money from a young benefactor, also rushed off to Rome. Taking the *Ile de France,* he sailed to Paris, next visiting Greece, Turkey, Northern Italy—but somehow he never got to Rome. Returning to Paris for one more visit, Delaney began to paint, make new friends, and create a new social life filled with the famous and the soon-to-be-famous, like James Baldwin, who at that time had not yet become a famous novelist. Paris was to become Beauford Delaney's home, and he would live out his life in that city.

By 1961 Delaney was producing paintings at such an intense rate that the pressure began to wear upon his strength, and he suffered his first mental collapse. Confined to a clinic in Vincennes, his dealer and close friends began to organize Delaney's life, hoping to help relieve some of the pressure, but it was of little use. For the rest of his life, Delaney was to continue to suffer repeated breakdowns, and by 1971 was back in a sanitarium, where he was to remain until his death in 1979.

Beauford Delaney's numerous exhibitions included Artists Gallery, New York in 1948; Roko Gallery, New York, 1950–1953; Musée d'Art Moderne, Paris, 1963; American Negro Exposition, Chicago, 1940; and Newark Museum, 1971. His work can be found in the collections of the Whitney Museum of American Art, New York, the Newark Museum, New Jersey, and the Morgan State College in Baltimore, Maryland.

JOSEPH DELANEY
Painter
1904

Some Notable Works: *Portraits: Eartha Kitt; Chester A. Arthur III; Eleanor Roosevelt; Tallulah Bankhead*

Joseph Delaney's art celebrates the personal. His portraits, many of which have been executed on sidewalks, record the expressions of momentary contact with other human beings.

Born in Knoxville, Tennessee, he did considerable drawing on his own before enrolling in the Art Students League in 1930 and eventually studying with Thomas Hart Benton, George Bridgeman, and Alexander Brooke. From 1932 to 1971 he exhibited work and did portraits on the sidewalks of New York, in Washington Square Park, Prospect Park, two World's Fairs, museums, and galleries. In 1968 he taught at Vermont Academy under a grant from the Ford Foundation. He has had one-man shows at McClung Museum Gallery, University of Tennessee, 1970; and The Studio Museum, Harlem, 1971.

Delaney says that his doing portraits was a natural result of talking with interested people and sitting out on the street during the Washington Square Outdoor Art Shows.

WILLIAM EDMONSON
Sculptor
1882–?

Some Notable Works: *Choir Girls; Lion; Sculpture of Animal*

William Edmonson was a stonecutter, self-taught in sculpture.

Born in Davidson County, Kentucky, he supported himself as a stonemason until the late 1930s. His work was discovered by Mrs. Meyer Dahl-Wolfe, who has an extensive private collection, and who brought it to the attention of the Museum of Modern Art. In an exhibition of self-taught artists, his work was received extremely well. In May 1938 he had a one-man exhibit at the museum. Private collectors and museums have purchased his few sculptures, which are vigorously executed original primitives.

ELTON FAX
Illustrator, Writer
1909

Some Notable Works: *Steelworker; Ethiopia Old & New; Contemporary Black Leaders; Through Black Eyes*

Elton Fax stands among America's leading fine artists and illustrators. He is also a noted essayist. Both his drawings and his writings reflect a proud interest in the African legacy of the American black.

Born in Baltimore, he graduated from Syracuse University (B.F.A., 1931). He taught at Claflin University from 1935 to 1936, and was an instructor at the Harlem Community Art Center from 1938 to 1939. His work has been exhibited at the Baltimore Art Museum, 1939; American Negro Exposition, 1940; the Metropolitan Museum of Art; and Visual Arts Gallery,

Author-illustrator Elton Fax at work in his studio.

New York, 1970. Examples of his work hang in some of the nation's best university collections, including Texas Southern, the University of Minnesota, and Virginia State University.

Publications by Fax are *Africa Vignettes, Garvey, Seventeen Black Artists, Black Artists of the New Generation. The Portfolio Black and Beautiful* features his art work, and he has written *Hashar,* about the life of the peoples of Soviet Central Asia and Kazakhstan.

FRED FLEMISTER
Painter
1916

Some Notable Works: *Man with a Brush* (1950); *The Mourners* (1942); *Self-Portrait* (1945)

Fred Flemister was born in Atlanta. He studied at Morehouse College and under Hale Woodruff at Atlanta University, 1935–1939; and he was a scholarship student at John Herron Art Institute, Indianapolis, 1940–1941. Before his Army service, he was for a time an instructor in art at Atlanta University.

His exhibits have been seen at the Albany Institute of History and Art, 1945; Xavier University, 1963; City College of New York, 1967; and Smith College Museum of Art. His work is represented in the Atlanta University Collections.

RONALD JOSEPH
Painter
1910

Some Notable Works: *Card Players; Park Avenue Market; Mood; Family Group*

Ronald Joseph is considered by many to be America's foremost black abstractionist painter.

Born in St. Kitts, British West Indies, he came to study at the Art Students League and has since studied and taught at the Harlem Art Center.

His exhibitions include Harlem Art Center, 1938, 1939; Baltimore Museum, 1939; American Negro Exposition, 1940; Library of Congress, 1940; and City College of New York, 1967.

Joseph's work receives a great deal of attention from his contemporaries. It is particularly important in terms of the development of black consciousness, and has recently been studied against the backdrop of militancy in the arts.

JACOB LAWRENCE
Painter
1917

Some Notable Works: *The Life of Toussaint L'Ouverture* (41 panels—1937); *The Life of Harriet Tubman* (40 panels—

1939); *The Negro Migration Northward in World War* (60 panels—1942).

Born in 1917 in Atlantic City, New Jersey, Jacob Lawrence received his early training at the Harlem Art School and the American Artist School. His rise to prominence was ushered in by his painting of several series of biographical panels commemorating important episodes in Afro-American history. A narrative painter, Lawrence creates the "philosophy of Impressionism" within his work. Capturing the essential meaning behind the natural appearance of a historical moment or personality, Lawrence creates a formal series of several dozen small paintings which relate the course of a particular historic event in American history, such as *The Migration Series* (". . . and the Migrants kept coming"), which traces the migration of the Afro-American from the South to the North, or the discussion on the course of a man's life (e.g., Toussant L'Ouverture and John Brown).

Jacob Lawrence is a visual American historian. His paintings record the Afro-American in trade, theater, mental hospitals, and neighborhoods, or running in the Olympic races. Lawrence's works are found in such

Jacob Lawrence's Tombstones.

collections as the Metropolitan Museum of Art, Museum of Modern Art, and Whitney Museum of American Art.

HUGHIE LEE-SMITH
Painter
1915

Some Notable Works: *Portrait of a Sailor; Old Man and Youth; Waste Land; Little Diana; Aftermath*

Hughie Lee-Smith has received more than a dozen important prizes, including the Founders Prize of the Detroit Institute of Arts (1953) and the Emily Lowe Award (1957).

Born in Florida in 1915, Smith was awarded the Gilpin Players Scholarship at the Cleveland School of Art and later studied under Sarkis Sarkisian. He received his B.S. from Wayne University.

Smith is a member of Allied Artists of America, the Michigan Academy of Arts, Sciences & Letters, and the Artists Equity Association.

MARION PERKINS
Sculptor
1908–1961

Notable Work: *Mother and Child* (1956)

Mood study of Jacob Lawrence, considered one of America's finest artists.

Marion Perkins' sculpture was the art at which he excelled, but it was just one of his creative talents, which included painting, the writing of poetry and plays, and teaching.

Born in Marche, Arkansas, he received his secondary education in Chicago, but in art he was largely self-taught. His early sculptures were worked on while he tended a newspaper stand on Chicago's South Side. He later studied privately with Simon Gordon, and the two men became close friends.

Perkins exhibited at the Art Institute of Chicago; American Negro Exposition, 1940; Xavier University, 1963; and Rockland College, Illinois 1965.

As artist in residence at Jackson State College in Mississippi, Perkins founded a scholarship fund for art students at that college, which is where much of his sculpture can be seen today.

HORACE PIPPIN
Painter
1888–1946

Some Notable Works: *John Brown Goes to a Hanging; Flowers with Red Chair; The Den; The Milk Man of Goshen; Dog Fight Over the Trenches*

Horace Pippin is known as a major primitive painter and has been ranked in the company of Henri Rousseau as a self-taught artist.

Pippin was born in 1888 in West Chester, Pennsylvania, and painted steadily from 1920 until his death in 1946. Among his most vivid portrayals on canvas are the battle scenes which he remembered from his own experience in World War 1, during which he was wounded and partially paralyzed.

Pippin's work was discovered in the late 1930s. From that time on, he was championed by many critics as the finest black painter in America.

CHARLES SEBREE
Painter, Illustrator, Theater Designer
1914

Some Notable Works: *The Clown; Illustrations for Countee Cullen's book The Lost Zoo; Harlem Saltimbanques*

Charles Sebree was born in Madisonville, Kentucky. He studied at the Art Institute of Chicago and worked for the Easel Division of the Illinois Federal Art Project (1936–1938).

He has exhibited at the International Watercolor Society, 1935; American Negro Exposition, Chicago, 1940; Institute of Modern Art, Boston, 1943; City College of New York, 1967; James A. Porter Gallery, 1970; and others. Among the collections in which his work is represented are those of the Renaissance Society; University of Chicago; Thornton Wilder; National

Primordial themes and forms, Horace Pippin's Buffalo Hunt.

Archives; and the New York Public Library Schomburg Art Collection.

DOX THRASH
Painter, Printmaker
1893

Some Notable Works: *Mary Lou; Harmonica Blues; Surface Mining*

Dox Thrash is co-inventor of the graphic technique of the carborundum print, which facilitates combination plates.

Born in Griffin, Georgia, he studied art through correspondence course till 1908; at the Art Institute of Chicago under Seyffert, Naughton, and Poole, 1919–1922; and under Earl Horton of Graphic Sketch Club, Philadelphia.

His exhibitions include Graphic Sketch Club, 1933, 1934, 1935; New York World's Fair, 1939, 1940; American Negro Exposition, 1940; Newark Museum, 1970; and James A. Porter Gallery, 1970. His work is represented in the National Archives.

BILL TRAYLOR
Painter
1854–1947

Some Notable Works: *Turkeys; Horse-Man; He Smells a Cow*

Bill Traylor was born a slave in 1854 on the George Traylor plantation near Benton, Alabama. Freed in

Bill Traylor was born a slave in 1854. He began drawing when he was approximately 82. His first New York Exhibit took place when he was 88 years old.

1864, Traylor chose to remain a farmer on the plantation, where he was to spend most of his life. By the late 1930s, Traylor was alone and without work. Living in the back room of the Ross-Clayton Funeral Home, a "Negro" funeral parlor, Traylor, in order to earn a living, began to draw on bits of scrap paper he found in the streets. His works were soon discovered by a white dealer in Montgomery, Alabama. He was given his first one-person exhibition at New South, an art center in Montgomery, in 1940, and in a brief time he gained national attention.

In 1942 Traylor's works were exhibited at Fieldston School in New York. Traylor's surreal world belongs to that of Mark Twain, Walt Whitman, and Zora Neal Hurston. His images, abstract ideas of life and reality, never imitate natural forms but create new ones. His mules, cats, dogs, and men and women meeting under the street lights were created in a folk idiom that was as un-self-conscious and spontaneous as an old spiritual. It spoke of the simple country life—the custom and the daily activities.

During World War II Traylor lived with his children in Detroit, Washington, and possibly elsewhere as well. It was during this time that he had a leg amputated because of gangrene. Traylor returned to Montgomery and Monroe Street in 1946, where he once again slept from place to place, ending up sleeping regularly in a shoe repair shop. In 1947 he moved into his daughter's home in Montgomery, where he died.

CHARLES WHITE
Painter
1918

Some Notable Works: *Let's Walk Together; Frederick Douglass Lives Again; Women; Gospel Singer*

Charles White is an eminent exponent of social art. His paintings have used as their subject matter the notable achievements of famous American blacks as well as the suffering of the lowly and the anonymous.

White was born in 1918 in Chicago, and was influenced as a young boy by Alain Locke's critical review of the Harlem Renaissance: *The New Negro.*

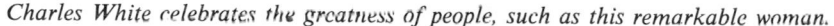

Charles White celebrates the greatness of people, such as this remarkable woman.

At the age of 23, White won a Rosenwald Fellowship which enabled him to work in the South for two years, during which time he painted a celebrated mural depicting the black's contribution to American democracy. It is now the property of Hampton Institute in Virginia.

The bulk of White's work is done in black-and-white, a symbolic motif which he feels gives him the widest possible purview.

ELLIS WILSON
Painter
1899

Some Notable Works: *Lunch Hour; Field Workers; Four Sisters; Marchande*

Ellis Wilson is a chronicler of Afro-American history.

Born in Mayfield, Kentucky, he studied at the Art Institute of Chicago. He was awarded the Charles S. Peterson Prize in Fine Arts for his African poster, and won a Guggenheim Fellowship in 1944.

His exhibitions include Harmon Foundation; Atlanta University; Detroit Museum; New York World's Fair, 1939; Contemporary Arts, New York, 1948, 1951; and James A. Porter Gallery, 1970. His work is represented in various museums and private collections, including the Schomburg Collection of the New York Public Library.

JOHN WILSON
Painter, Printmaker, Educator
1922

Some Notable Works: *Roxbury Landscape* (oil, 1944); *Trabajador* (print, 1951); *Child with Father* (graphic, 1969)

John Wilson is both an extremely versatile and fecund artist as well as possessor of considerable erudition.

Born in Boston, he studied at Boston Museum of Fine Arts; Fernand Leger School, Paris; The Institute Politecnico, Mexico City; and others. He has been a teacher at Boston Museum, Pratt Institute, and is currently at Boston University.

His very numerous exhibits include Albany Institute, 1945; Library of Congress National (and International) Print Exhibit(s); Smith College; Carnegie Institute; and American International College, Springfield, Massachusetts, 1971, one-man. Wilson's work is represented in the collections of the Museum of Modern Art; Schomburg, New York; Department of Fine Arts, French Government; Atlanta University; and Bezalel Museum, Jerusalem.

BLACK ARTISTS: WORLD WAR II TO THE PRESENT

JULES ALLEN
Photographer
1947

In 1978 Jules Allen established himself in the New York art world with a two-man exhibition shared with Frank Stewart at The Studio Museum of Harlem. In 1979 his work appeared in a group photography exhibition at Gallery 22. For Allen, photography provides the means to document the unique esthetics of African Americans. Light and form are his poetry, and Allen captures the different ways in which black people take pictures.

Jules Allen also worked as a production photographer for the play *For Colored Girls Who Have Considered Suicide When the Rainbow Is Enuf* in Rio de Janeiro, Brazil, and was the co-producer and assistant cameraman for the film *Americans in Havana, Cuba.*

CAMILLE BILLOPS
Ceramic Sculptor

Some Notable Works: *Tenure, Black American, Portrait of an American Indian* (ceramic sculptures); *Year after Year* (painting)

A sculptor of note in the art and retailing world, Camille Billops was born in California, graduated from California State College in 1960, and then studied sculpture on the West Coast under a grant from the Huntington Hartford Foundation. In 1960 she had her first exhibition at the African Art Exhibition in Los Angeles, followed in 1963 by an exhibit at the Valley Cities Jewish Community Center in Los Angeles. In 1966 she participated in a group exhibition in Moscow. Since then, her multifaceted artistic talents, which include poetry, book illustration, and jewelry-making, have earned the praise of critics throughout the world, particularly in Ceylon and Egypt, where she has lived and worked.

Billops has also taught extensively. In 1975 she was active on the faculties of the City University of New York and Rutgers State University, New Jersey. In addition, she has conducted special art courses in the New York City jail (the Tombs) and in 1972 lectured in India for the United States Information Service on black American artists. She participated in an exhibit at the New York Cultural Center in 1973.

STAR BULLOCK
Painter

Notable Work: *Landscape One*

Star Bullock was born in Washington, D.C. She studied at Howard University (B. F. A., M. F. A.); the Brooklyn Museum School; with Reuben Tam; and at the University of Massachusetts (M. Ed.). Her works have been exhibited in the Smithsonian Institute, the Boston Museum, Howard University, the Studio Museum, and the Museum of the Philadelphia Civil Center. She joined the faculty of Howard University in 1969 where she now teaches design and painting.

ELIZABETH CATLETT
Painter
1919

Some Notable Works: *Black Unity* (1968); *Target Practice* (1970); *Mother and Child* (1972)

The granddaughter of North Carolina slaves, Elizabeth Catlett was raised in the Northwest Washington, D.C. district. As a young woman she attempted to gain admission into a then all-white art school, Carnegie Institute of Technology in Pittsburgh, Pennsylvania. She was refused entry and instead went to Howard University. It was 1936 and she was an honor student. In 1940 she went on to study at the University of Iowa, where she became the first of their students to receive an M. F. A.

Catlett accepted teaching positions at various black colleges in order to earn a living, but by 1946 she had moved to Mexico, where she eventually settled. Always a promoter of human struggle—visually concerned with the recording of economic, social, and political themes, Catlett became involved with the Civil Rights Movement so deeply that it contributed greatly to her philosophy of life and art. Between 1941 and 1969, Catlett won eight prizes and honors, four in Mexico and four in America.

DANA CHANDLER
Painter
1941

Some Notable Works: *Fred Hampton's Door; Martin Luther King Jr. Assassinated; Death of Uncle Tom; Rebellion '68; Dynamite; Death of a Bigot; The Golden Prison*

Dana Chandler is one of the most visible, outspoken, and provocative black painters on the American scene. Chandler's huge, colorful black power murals are spotted throughout the ghetto area of Boston, a constant reminder of the resolve and determination manifested by the new breed of young black urban dwellers—proud and even scornful.

"All this stuff whites are buying," Chandler says, "tells the black man a lot about where the white community is at, namely, nowhere."

Talented and outspoken Dana Chandler exhibits his provocative Fred Hampton's Door.

Chandler's easel works are bold and simple. One, *The Golden Prison,* shows a black man with a yellow and red striped flag "because America has been yellow and cowardly in dealing with the black man." Another, *Freddie Hampton's Door,* shows a bullet-splintered door replete with a stamp of U.S. government approval.

Born in Lynn, Massachusetts, Chandler received his B.S. from the Massachusetts College of Art in 1967.

RAVEN CHANTICLEER
Fashion Designer

Progressive fashion designer Raven Chanticleer designs clothes for New York City's most famous stores as well as for leading personalities in the society and entertainment worlds.

Born in New York of Haitian parents, he attended Fashion Institute of Technology, the University of Texas (B.A.), and the University of Paris (M.A.). His clients have included Louis Armstrong, Billie Holiday, Eartha Kitt, Dorothy Dandridge, Mr. and Mrs. Percy Sutton, The Jackson Five, and Muhammad Ali. In addition to designing, Chanticleer devotes time to helping institutions such as Willowbrook School for the Retarded, Harlem Prep, penal institutions, and senior citizens' and children's centers.

EDWARD CLARK
Painter

Some Notable Works: *The Big Egg; Vetheuil, Summer 1968; Vetheuil, Fall 1968; Paris Rose; Calm Force*

Edward Clark is an adherent of the 1950s "action school" of painting whose philosophical and psychological view of painting holds that it is a purely visual experience whose primary constituent elements are nothing but color and movement.

Born in New Orleans, he studied at the Art Institute of Chicago and L'Academie de la Grand Chaumière. His one-man shows include Gallery Creuze, Paris, 1966; Brata Gallery, New York, 1958; United States Embassy, Paris, 1969; Prince Street Gallery, New York, 1971; and South Houston Gallery, New York, 1974. His work has also been shown at the Modern Museum, Tokyo and Kyoto; Boston Museum of Fine Arts, 1970; and University of Texas, 1970.

Clark has resided alternately in Paris and New York. His search for the best method to express movement extending beyond the limits of the canvas has led him to a prolonged exploration of the dynamics of the ellipse.

Sam Gilliam's works are bold and brilliant blazes of color on unusual canvases.

ROY DECARAVA
Painter, Photographer
1919

Some Notable Works: *Woman Resting, Subway Stairs, 1952; Billy Holliday Singing, 1955; Stairwell 127th Street, 1955*

Roy DeCarava is an urban man. His existence in New York City prepared him for his destined work as a photographer. He began as a commercial artist in 1938 by studying painting at Cooper Union. This was followed by classes at the Harlem Art Center from 1940–1942, where he concentrated on painting and printmaking. By the mid-1940s, he began to use photography as a convenient method of recording ideas for his paintings. In 1958 DeCarava gave up his commercial work and became a full-time freelance photographer. Edward Steichen, a very important photographer at this time, began to study his work and suggested that he apply for a Guggenheim Fellowship. Winning the award allowed DeCarava the financial freedom to take his pictures and tell his story. One of DeCarava's photographs from this body of work appeared in Steichen's exhibition "Family of Man" at the Museum of Modern Art. Later, Langston Hughes worked with DeCarava to create the book *Sweet Flypaper of Life.*

JOHN DOWELL
Painter
1941

Some Notable Works: *Tomorrow's Solo; Tune Break Away; To Open Time*

Born in Philadelphia and educated in Seattle, Dowell moved back to Philadelphia to teach and work. As full professor of printmaking and chairman of the department at Tyler School of Art, Dowell divides his time between the running of his classroom and his own artwork. In 1976 Dowell formed the Visual Arts Ensemble, which consists of a saxophone, cello, percussion, and Dowell at the piano. The group has traveled throughout Europe and the United States performing many of Dowell's paintings and watercolors. Influenced by East Asian art forms, from which the musical sounds are improvised, the group dissects, plucks, and hammers out the visual forms.

SAM GILLIAM
Painter

Some Notable Works: *Watercolor 4* (1969); *Herald,* (1965); *Carousel Change* (1970); *Mazda* (1970)

Mississippi-born Sam Gilliam produces hanging canvases which are laced with pure color pigments rather than shades or tones. The artist bunches these pigments in weird configurations on drooping, drapelike canvases, giving the effect, in the words of *Time Magazine,* of "clothes drying on a line." His canvases are said to be "like nobody else's, black or white."

Gilliam took his M.A. from the University of Louisville, and was awarded a National Endowment of Humanities and Arts Grant in 1966. Since then, he has had one-man shows at the Washington Gallery of Modern Art, Jefferson Place Gallery, and Adams-Morgan Gallery in Washington, D.C.

Gilliam has also been represented in several group exhibitions, including the First World Festival of Negro Arts in Dakar, Senegal (1966), "The Negro in American Art" at UCLA (1967), the Whitney Museum's American Art Annual (1969).

In 1968, 1969, and 1970 his work was displayed in one-man shows at Washington, D.C.'s Jefferson Place, and in 1971 he was featured in a one-man show at New York City's Museum of Modern Art.

In 1980 Sam Gilliam was commissioned, with 13 other artists, to design an art piece for installation in the Atlanta, Georgia Airport Terminal, one of the largest terminals in the world and the first to install contemporary artwork on its walls for public viewing.

DAVID HAMMONS
Painter
1939

Some Notable Works. *America the Beautiful* (1969); *American Hung-Up* (1970); *Injustice Case* (1970); *Pray for America* (1969)

Born in Springfield, Illinois, the youngest of 10 children in a family on welfare, David Hammons passed the home of Abraham Lincoln every day on his way to school, and somehow derived from this experience an abiding preoccupation with the American flag, a recurring theme in his early work. From the flag, Hammons went on to incorporate the Spade into his visual constructions. Hair, wire, eggs, found objects, recycled objects—Hammons finds no need to purchase art supplies, believing that art is the product of the mind and not of the store.

Art critic John Perreault identified Hammons as "a very active new energy source." As an artist, he works to use and communicate his background and his life within his work. In 1980 Hammons was identified as one of the artists to watch in the 1980s. His installation work in such exhibitions as Afro-American Abstraction, presented at P.S. 1 in New York, and a window installation for the New Museum in New York, both done in 1980, and a group installation done at the Studio Museum of Harlem brought David Hammons into the art world as one of America's top young artists.

The paintings of David Hammon are a militant outcry against oppression.

RICHARD HUNT
Painter
1935

Some Notable Works: *Man on a Vehicular Construct* (1956); *Arachve* (1956); *Linear Spatial Theme* (1962); *The Chase* (1965)

Richard Hunt was born in Chicago and began his formal career after studying at the School of the Art Institute of Chicago, where he received a number of awards.

After graduating in 1957, Hunt was given the James Nelson Raymond Traveling Fellowship. He later taught at the School of the Art Institute of Chicago and at the University of Illinois. From 1962 to 1963, he pursued his craft while under a Guggenheim Fellowship.

Hunt has had several one-man shows and been included in major exhibits throughout the United States. His work can also be seen in, among others, the permanent collections of the Museum of Modern Art and the Cleveland Museum of Art.

His work hangs in museums in Cleveland, Chicago, Houston, and Buffalo and was featured in "The Ameri-

Extending Horizontal Form *typifies Richard Hunt's interest in spatial concepts.*

can Negro Artists Show" held in Dakar, Senegal in 1966.

DANIEL JOHNSON
Painter
1938

Some Notable Works: *Homage to Rene D'Harnoncourt; Yesterday; Death of Tarzan; Eve; Study for a Church Altar; Big Red; Wendell*

Though a native of the Los Angeles Watts ghetto, Daniel Johnson does not attribute his creative instincts to his color. Instead, he believes that questions of race "are frivolous" and "have nothing to do with the consciousness of people who attempt to make art."

His own works, seen in prominent display at Manhattan's French & Co. in 1970, are painted sculptures which have already sold for upwards of $3,500. Critic Margit Rowell says of his work: "The sensation of a temporal, even acoustical experience—for which one was unprepared and which is intangible—is perhaps the most unsettling aspect of one's first encounter" with Johnson's work. Otherwise, the visual impact is one of strict sobriety—the total absence of extraneous forms and preoccupation.

Johnson holds a B.F.A. from Chouinard Art Institute (1960). He has befriended, or studied with, such giants as Larry Rivers, Willem de Kooning, and Alberto Giacometti. In 1961 he was awarded the Stanton Fellowship; within two years, he was touring the South collecting common objects for constructions. By 1966, he was fully involved in developing the technique of using high polishes for surface-painted wood.

RICHARD MAYHEW
Painter
1924

Some Notable Works: *West* (1965); *Field* (1950); *Thorn Bush*

Richard Mayhew's oils have earned wide critical respect. His awards include John Hay Whitney Fellowship, 1958; MacDowell Colony Foundation, 1958; Ingram Merrill Foundation Grant, 1960; National Institute of Arts and Letters Grant, 1965; and Benjamin Altman Award, National Academy of Design, 1970.

Born in Amityville, New York, he studied at the Brooklyn Museum School. Among his very numerous exhibitions have been the American Academy of Arts and Letters; Boston Museum; Brooklyn Museum; Museum of Modern Art; Whitney Museum; and in 1974, a one-man show at the Midtown Gallery, New York. Some of the collections which include his works are Albion College, Michigan; Brooklyn Museum; Whitney Museum; Olsen Foundation, Connecticut; Evansville Museum; and New York University.

GERALDINE MCCULLOUGH
Sculptor
1928

Some Notable Works: *Bessie Smith; View from the Moon; Toad Hall Front; Atomic Rose; Phoenix*

Geraldine McCullough's steel and copper abstraction "Phoenix" won the George D. Widener Gold Medal at the 1964 exhibition of the Pennsylvania Academy of Fine Arts. In capturing this award, her name was added to a roster of distinguished artists who have already won the same honor, including Jacques Lipchitz and Theodore Roszak. Of further note was the fact that this had been her first showing in a major national exhibition.

A native of Arkansas, McCullough has lived in Chicago since she was three and is a 1948 graduate of the Art Institute there.

EARL MILLER
Painter
1930

Some Notable Works: *Tone Poems with Two Blue Squares; Accordion Flyer; American Flyer; Steller*

Among the most talented new Afro-American artists exhibiting in America since 1950 is Earl Miller, born in Seattle in 1930.

Miller studied in the United States until 1957, first at Pratt Institute in Brooklyn (1954–1956), later at the Art School of the Brooklyn Museum (1956), and finally at the Art Students League. He also attended the Akademie der Bildenden Kunste in Munich in 1963.

Miller has had several one-man exhibits, notably at New York's Phoenix Gallery (1961) and the Town Hall in Marbella, Spain (1962). In 1968 and 1969 he was among those featured at the American Greetings Gallery, the Lever House, the Museum of Modern Art, and Brooklyn College, all in New York.

CLARENCE MORGAN
Painter
1950

Some Notable Works: *Upper Volta; Linear Notation; Neon Juke*

Clarence Morgan grew up in Philadelphia, where he received his B.A. at the University of Pennsylvania. In 1978 Morgan took on the role of art instructor at East Carolina University. There he stresses the importance of color, form, composition, and their position in space, principles that he adheres to in the development of his own work.

Morgan's visual style is a layering process which produces paintings heavy with noisy rhythms rising and falling across the surface. Personal and intimate, both in scale and content, these works, like those of artists Howardena Pindell and Betye Saar, involve a selective and intuitive eye that searches, gathers, and accumulates the materials which ultimately provide the energy of the works. His exhibitions include "Small Works" at New York University and "Paper in Particular" at Columbia College in Columbia, Missouri, both in 1980.

NORMA MORGAN
Painter, Engraver

Some Notable Works: *Storm over Hawort Moor* (painting); *Glen in Badenoch* (engraving)

Norma Morgan is a well-known younger New York artist, at home with both traditional and abstract

Stellar, *acrylic on canvas by Earl Miller.*

themes. Much of her work has been inspired by travels through remote areas in England and Scotland, and she is especially drawn to subjects, whether natural objects or people, which show their struggle with the forces of erosion.

Born in New Haven, Connecticut, she attended the Hans Hoffman School of Fine Art and the Art Students League. She has taken part in many invitational and touring exhibitions.

Her engravings are represented in the collections of the Philadelphia Museum, the Library of Congress, the American Federation of Arts, Washington's National Gallery of Art, the Victoria and Albert Museum in London, the Glasgow Museum, and such private collections as those of Nelson Rockefeller and Ruth Ford.

Norma Morgan's engraving David in the Wilderness.

SENGA NENGUDI
Painter-Sculptor
1943

Some Notable Works: *R.S.V.P. XIII; Ritual Chant; Inside Out*

Born in Chicago, Illinois, Senga Nengudi has always been interested in the process of art. During her early development stages—school at the California State University, the Weseda University in Tokyo, Japan and then back to California State University for her masters degree—Nengudi was more concerned with the process than the final result. First she created images made by filling vinyl bags with water, thereby developing a loose, flowing rhythm. Later she switched to filling the bags with mud, creating an art form that was more earthy in texture but was too difficult to install and move. One of the pieces from this series was exhibited in "8 Black Artists" in Geneva, Switzerland.

From this point, Nengudi moved on to working with nylon body stockings, which allowed her to draw upon her knowledge of weight, stretch, and balance. Filling the stockings with sand, Senga Nengudi had found a substance that allowed her to control and distribute the weight of her pieces without destroying the images' naturalness. Her more recent works have concerned themselves less with the final piece itself and more with the performance of the piece. Working with artists Frank Marane and Maren Hassinger, Nengudi has developed a series of performance pieces that have been presented in California.

HAYWOOD OUBRE
Painter

Notable Work: *Colorwheel* (1962)

Hayward Oubre explores the properties of color within the framework of scientific research.

He attended Dillard University, New Orleans (M.F.A.), and went on to teach art at Tuskegee Institute, Alabama; Florida A&M University, Tallahassee; Alabama State College, Montgomery. He is currently chairman of the Art Department at Winston-Salem University, North Carolina.

His works have been exhibited at Atlanta University, Georgia; Walker Art Center, Minneapolis; Isaac Delgado Museum, New Orleans; Art Directions Gallery, New York; and Southern Illinois University, Carbondale.

JOSEPH OVERSTREET
Painter
1934

Some Notable Works: *The New Jemima* (1964); *Justice, Faith, Hope, and Peace* (1968); *Indian Sun* (1969)

Joe Overstreet's fine paintings are proud statements of deep feelings.

Born in Conehatta, Mississippi in 1934, Joe Overstreet studied at the California School of Arts and Crafts and participated in "New Black Artists," seen at the Brooklyn Museum in 1969.

Overstreet's canvases have of late eschewed racial themes to concentrate instead on vivid color and original configuration. Thus many of his abstractions are based on a medley of African and Indian colors. When they are exhibited, the canvases are often held in place by guy wires.

Overstreet's work is equally memorable when it deals with racial subject matter. Noteworthy are *Jazz in 4/4 Time* (oil on canvas) and *Keep on Keeping On* (oil on canvas).

HOWARDENA PINDELL
Painter
1943

Some Notable Works: *Memory Test; Inflation; You Have a Friend at Chase; Lake Lilies for Kim*

Born in Philadelphia, Howardena Pindell received her education at Boston University and Yale University. She first gained national recognition for her artistic skills in 1969 with the exhibition "American Drawing Biennial XXIII" at the Norfolk Museum of Arts and Sciences in Virginia. By the mid-1970s, Pindell's work began appearing in such exhibitions as "Eleven Americans in Paris," Gerald Piltzer Gallery, Paris, 1975; "Recent Acquisitions; Drawings," Museum of Modern Art, New York, 1976; and "Pindell: Video Drawings," Sonja Henie Onstad Foundation, Oslo, Norway, also in 1976.

Around this same time, Howardena Pindell began to travel around the world as a guest speaker. Some of her lectures included "Current American and Black American Art: A Historical Survey" at Madras College of Arts and Crafts, Madras, India, 1975; "Black Artists, U.S.A.," Academy of Art, Oslo, Norway, 1976.

FAITH RINGGOLD
Painter

Some Notable Works: *The Flag Is Bleeding; Flag for the Moon; Die Nigger; Mommy & Daddy; Soul Sister*

Committed to a revolutionary perspective both in politics and in aesthetics, Faith Ringgold is a symbolic expressionist whose stark paintings are acts of social reform directed toward educating the consciousness of her audience. Her most intense focus has been upon the problematic of being black in America. Her works highlight the violent tensions which tear at American society, including the discrimination suffered by women.

Born in Harlem in 1934, she was raised by parents who took care to make sure that she would enjoy the benefits of a good education. She attended the City College of New York, receiving her B.S. in 1955 and her masters in Fine Arts in 1959.

Her boldly political work has been well-received and widely shown. She has had several one-person shows, the first in 1968, and her paintings are included in the collections of the Chase Manhattan Bank, New York City; the Museum of Modern Art; the Bank Street College of Education, New York City; and Melvin Van Peebles.

In 1972 Ringgold became one of the founders of the Women Students and Artists for Black Liberation, an organization whose principal goal is to make sure that all exhibitions of black artists give equal space to paintings by men and women. In line with her interest in sexual parity, she has donated a large mural depicting the roles of women in American society to the Women's House of Detention in Manhattan.

Aesthetically, she believes that "black art must use its own color black to create its light, since that color is the most immediate black truth." Her most recent paintings have been an attempt to give pictorial realization to this vision.

BETYE SAAR
Painter-Sculptor
1926

Betye Saar was born in California in 1926. She went to college, got married, and raised her children—all the while creating artwork, images built upon discarded pieces of old dreams, postcards, photographs, flowers, buttons, fans, and ticket stubs. Her motifs range from the fetish to the everyday object. In 1978 Saar was one of a select group of American female artists to be discussed in a documentary film entitled *Spirit Catcher: The Art of Betye Saar.* It appeared on WNET/13 in New York as part of "The Originals: Women in Art" series. Her exhibitions include an installation piece especially designed for the Studio Museum of Harlem in 1980, and several one-person exhibitions at the Monique Knowlton Gallery in New York in 1981.

SKUNDER (ALEXANDER BOGHOSSIAN)
Painter
1937

Skunder is the first Ethiopian whose paintings have been purchased by the Museum of Modern Art in New York, and the first African to have a work hanging in the Musée d'Art Moderne in Paris.

Born in Addis Ababa, he took second prize at the National Art Exhibition, 1955, and received a scholarship to study abroad. After two years in London he went on to study at the Ecole des Beaux Arts and La Grande Chaumière in Paris, as well as with leading artists.

His exhibitions include London Contemporary Arts Society, 1956; Merton Simpson Gallery, New York, 1961; Biennale de Sao Paolo, Brazil, 1967; and Contemporary Art of Africa, Montgomery, Alabama, 1969. Skunder is presently Artist-in-Residence at Howard University.

VINCENT SMITH
Painter
1929

Some Notable Works: *Repairing a Bombed Church; Peace and Freedom Party; Molotov Cocktail; The People Cry Out; Sharecropper's Shack; Black Family*

Vincent Smith, born in 1929, belongs to the social commentary school of artists—those who explore themes relating to the rise of black militancy and the aspirations of black youth.

A native of Brooklyn, Smith studied at the Art Students League (1953) and continued his training at the

Brooklyn Museum School of Art. In 1957 he received a John Hay Whitney Fellowship.

Smith has exhibited widely in the East and has even had several one-man shows.

BOB THOMPSON
Painter
1937–1966

Some Notable Works: *Ascension to the Heavens; Untitled Diptych; The Dentist* (1963); *Expulsion and Nativity* (1964)

The death of Bob Thompson took from the black art world one of its outstanding painters, a man who had studied extensively here in the United States and also traveled widely in Europe and North Africa, living in Paris (1961–1962), Ibiza (1962–1963), and Rome (1965–1966).

Born in Louisville, Kentucky, Thompson studied at the Boston Museum School in 1955 and later spent

Caledonia Flight, by Bob Thompson.

three years at the University of Louisville. In 1960 Thompson participated in a two-person show at Zabriskie Gallery and two years later received a John Hay Whitney Fellowship.

For the next several years, Thompson had several one-man exhibitions in such leading U.S. cities as New York and Chicago. His work was also seen in Spain. He died in Rome at the age of 29.

Thompson's work is in several permanent collections around the country, including the Chrysler Museum in Provincetown, Massachusetts. In 1970 Thompson's work was featured in the Afro-American Artist exhibition at the Boston Museum of Fine Arts.

CLIFTON WEBB
Painter-Sculptor
1950

Some Notable Works: *Landscape; The Raft; A Closer Connection*

Born in New Orleans on August 7, 1950, Webb was raised in Baton Rouge, Louisiana. Involved with the inner relationship of African people and Afro-American people, Webb approaches his interest in African art forms through a shared sense of musical order. His objects are often arranged in a polyrhythmic structure emphasizing the individuality of the various items used within the total work. Webb's synthesizing of African and Meso-American sensations through the use of raw materials provides an element of fetishistic, eccentric, and kinetic energies that makes his works both funky and magically endowed.

JACK WHITTEN
Painter
1939

Some Notable Works: *Psychic Square 1; First Frame* (1971)

Painter Jack Whitten was born in Bessemer, Alabama in 1939 and studied at Tuskegee Institute and Southern University in Baton Rouge, Louisiana before coming North to receive his BFA degree from Cooper Union in New York.

Whitten, who teaches at Pratt Institute, received a Whitney Fellowship in 1964. His second one-man show was given at the Allan Stone Gallery in February 1970. He was also represented in the 1969 Whitney Museum of American Art Annual.

OTHER NOTABLE ARTISTS

Name	Craft	Dates
Ron Adams	Painter	1934
Emma Amos	Painter	1938
Benny Andrews	Painter	1930
Dorothy Atkins	Painter, sculptor	1936
Casper Banjo	Sculptor	
Malcolm Bailey	Painter, illustrator	1947
Jene Ballentine	Painter, architect	1942
Henry W. Bannard	Painter	1910
Cleveland Bellow	Painter	1946
Arthur Berry	Sculptor	1923
Eloise Bishop	Painter	1921
Betty Blayton	Painter, sculptor	1937
Gloria Bohanon	Painter (abstract)	1941
Shirley Bolton	Painter	1942
Frank Bowling	Painter	1936
David P. Bradford	Painter	1937
Peter Bradley	Painter	1940
Arthur L. Britt	Painter (abstract)	1934
Grafton Tyler Brown	Painter	1841–1918
Fred Brown	Painter (abstract)	1941
Vivian E. Browne	Painter	1929

Jack Whitten at a gallery opening.

Name	Craft	Dates	Name	Craft	Dates
Henry Brownlee	Painter	1940	Wes Hall	Painter	1934
Margaret Burroughs	Painter, sculptor, illustrator	1917	Phillip J. Hampton	Painter	1922
			Edward A. Harleston	Painter	1882
Nathaniel Bustion	Painter (surrealist)	1942	John T. Harris	Painter	1908
Sheryle Butler	Designer	1947	Bob Heliton	Photographer	1934
Arthur Carraway	Painter	1927	Dion Henderson	Painter	1941
William Carter	Painter		William Henderson	Painter	1943
Bernie Casey	Painter	1939	Ernest Herbert	Painter (abstract)	1932
Yvonne Catchings	Painter		Felrath Hines	Painter	1918
Mitchell Caton	Muralist	1930	Alvin Hollengsworth	Painter	1931
Barbara Chase-Riboud	Sculptor	1939	Humbert Howard	Painter	1915
George Clach	Sculptor		Julien Hudson	Painter	c. 1830
Claude Clark	Painter	1914	Howard Humbert	Painter	1915
Edward Clark	Painter	1926	Richard Hunt	Painter, sculptor	1925
Floyd Coleman	Painter	1937	Bill Hutson	Painter	1936
Donald F. Coles	Painter	1947	Suzanne Jackson	Painter	1944
Dan Concholar	Painter	1939	Walter Jackson	Sculptor	1940
Eldzier Cortor	Painter	1915	Rosalind Jeffries	Painter	1938
Marva Cremer	Painter	1942	Daniel Lorne Johnson	Sculptor	1938
Doris Crudup	Painter	1933	David Johnson	Painter	1938
Iris Crump	Sculptor	1933	Benjamin Jones	Painter	1941
William Curtis	Painter	1939	Henry B. Jones	Painter	1889
Emilio Cruz	Painter	1938	Tonnie Jones	Sculptor	
Alonzo Davis	Painter	1942	Jack Jordan	Sculptor	1925
Bing Davis	Painter	1937	Cliff Joseph	Painter	1922
Dale Davis	Painter	1945	Ronald Joseph	Painter	1910
Charles C. Dawson	Painter	1889	Paul Keene	Painter (abstract)	1920
Avel de Knight	Painter	1933	Gwendolyn Knight	Painter, sculptor	
Murray De Pillars	Painter		Compton L. Kolowole	Painter	1931
Robert R. d'hue	Painter (abstract)	1917	Doyle Lane	Ceramicist	1953
Kenneth Dickerson	Painter (abstract)	1935	Raymond Lark	Painter	1939
David Diskill	Painter	1931	James Lewis	Painter	1923
Jeff Donaldsen	Painter		Larry Lewis	Painter	1927
David Driskell	Painter	1931	Norman Lewis	Painter	1916
Eugenia V. Dunn	Painter	1918	Samella S. Lewis	Painter	
Eugene Eda	Painter, muralist	1939	Tom Lloyd	Sculptor	1929
William Edmonson	Sculptor	1882	Juan Logan	Painter	1940
Marion A. Epting	Painter (modern)	1940	Juan Logan	Sculptor	1946
Frederick J. Eversley	Sculptor	1941	Willie F. Longshore	Painter	1933
Cyril Fabio	Sculptor	1921	Edward Loper	Painter	1916
Kenneth Falana	Painter	1940	Edward Love	Sculptor	1936
William M. Farrow	Painter	1885	Alvin Loving	Painter	1935
John Farrar	Painter	1927	David Mann	Painter	1927
Tom Feelings	Painter, draftsman	1933	Lloyd McNeill	Painter	1936
Allan R. Freelon	Painter	1895	Leon Meeks	Painter	1940
Ibibio Fundi	Sculptor	1929	Earl Miller	Painter	1930
Reginald Gammon	Painter	1921	Ron Moore	Painter	1944
Herbert Gentry	Painter	1921	Isaac Nommo	Painter	1940
William Giles	Painter	1930	William Pajaud	Painter	1925
Robert Glover	Collage artist, painter	1941	Denise Palm	Painter (abstract)	1951
			James Dallas Parks	Painter, printmaker, sculptor	1907
Rex Gordeigh	Painter	1902			
Robert H. Green	Painter (abstract)		Robert S. Pious	Painter, illustrator	1908
Donald O. Greene	Painter (abstract)	1940	Larry Potter	Painter	
Stephen Greene	Painter	1918	Leslie Price	Painter (abstract)	1945
Eugene Grigsby	Painter (abstract)	1918	Nancy E. Prophet	Sculptor	1890
Henry Gridgell	Craftsman	1826–1895	William Pryor	Painter	1949
Ron Griffin	Sculptor	1938	Noah Purifoy	Sculptor	1917

Name	Craft	Dates	Name	Craft	Dates
Roscoe Reddix	Painter	1933	Charlene Tull	Painter	1945
Jerry Reed	Painter	1949	Les Twiggs	Painter	1934
Robert Reid	Painter	1924	Alfred Tyler	Painter, drawing	1933
John Rhoden	Sculptor	1918	Anna Tyler	Painter (abstract)	1933
Gary A. Rickson	Painter, muralist	1942	Bernard Upshur	Painter, woodcuts	1936
Haywood Rivers	Painter	1922	Florestee Vance	Painter	1940
Joseph Ronald	Painter		Ruth G. Waddy	Painter	1909
Raymond Saunders	Painter	1934	William Walker	Painter, muralist	
Christopher Shelton	Sculptor	1933	Carole Ward	Sculptor	1943
Thomas Sills	Painter	1914	James Watkins	Painter	1925
Jewel Simon	Painter, sculptor	1911	Richard Waytt	Painter	1955
Walter Simon	Painter	1916	James L. Wells	Painter	1902
Merton D. Simpson	Painter	1928	Jack White	Sculptor	1940
Alvin Smith	Painter	1933	Walter Williams	Painter	1920
Arthur Smith	Jeweler	1923	William T. Williams	Painter	1942
Thelma J. Streat	Painter	1912	Ed Wilson	Sculptor	1925
Rod Taylor	Sculptor	1932	Fred Wilson	Sculptor	1932
Alma W. Thomas	Painter	1896	Stanley Wilson	Sculptor	1947
Lovett Thompson	Sculptor		Estella Wright	Sculptor	
Roberta Thompson	Painter	1928	Charles Young	Painter	1930
Russ Thompson	Painter	1922	Milton Young	Painter (abstract)	1935
Dox Thrash	Painter	1893			

INVENTORS AND SCIENTISTS

Anonymity and Achievement ■ Biographies of Outstanding Scientific Pioneers ■ Black Scientific Organizations ■ List of Inventions by Blacks in the Nineteenth Century

America's earliest black scientists and inventors are buried in the anonymity that concealed their contributions to prerevolutionary America. While Bannaker's eighteenth-century successes in timepieces and urban planning are known and applauded, numerous achievements of seventeenth- and eighteenth-century blacks in architecture, agriculture, and masonry cannot be identified. Thus, while it is increasingly recognized that blacks had a significant impact on the design and construction of plantations and public buildings in the South and that rice farming in the Carolinas might not have been possible without blacks, the individuals who spearheaded these accomplishments remain unknown.

Prior to the Civil War, in one of history's most absurd bureaucratic fiats, slaves could neither be granted patents nor assign patents to their masters. The theory behind this was that since slaves were not citizens they could not enter into contracts with their owners or the government. As a result, the efforts of slaves were dismissed or, if accepted, credited entirely to their masters, and one can only speculate on the part blacks played in significant inventions they are known to have worked on. One such area of speculation concerns the grain harvester of Cyrus McCormick. Jo Anderson, one of McCormick's slaves, is believed to have played a major role in the creation of the McCormick harvester, but available records are insufficient to determine the degree of Anderson's importance in the invention.

The inventions of free blacks were, however, recorded. The first patent granted a black was probably Henry Blair's 1834 seed planter patent. But again, records fail the historian, for the race of patent-seekers was rarely noted. Blair may well have had numerous predecessors. Other black inventions were not patented for various reasons, as was the case with ice cream, invented by Augustus Jackson of Philadelphia in 1832.

The Reconstruction era unleashed the creativity that had been suppressed in blacks. Between 1870 and 1900, though some 80% of black adults in the United States were illiterate, blacks were awarded several hundred patents. Notable among these were the shoe last (Jan Matzeliger, 1883), a machine for making paper bags (William Purvis, 1884), assorted machinery-lubricating equipment (Elijah McCoy, from 1872), an automatic railroad car coupler (Andrew Beard, 1897), and the synchronous multiplex railroad telegraph (Granville Woods, 1888).

The contributions of black scientists are better known than those of black inventors, partly because of the recognition awarded George Washington Carver, an agricultural scientist who, incidentally, refused to patent his inventions. However, it is not widely known, as this section reports, that black scientists contributed enormously to the development of blood plasma, open heart surgery, and cortisone, all vital ingredients of modern health care.

The achievements of black inventors and scientists of the mid-twentieth century have been increasingly obscured by reasons more complex than blatant racial prejudice. An important element is the replacement of the individual inventor by government and corporate research and development teams. Individuals, whatever their race, receive less recognition. Thus it is that creators of such devices as the computer, television, heart pacers, and lasers are relatively obscure while such names as Bell, Edison, and Marconi are imparted to every school child.

Although blacks have not laid claim to inventions and patents in great numbers, black colleges in the 1980s have been advancing their curriculums in science and technology. Black students have chosen majors that will get them jobs both before and behind the scene with the national space program. Since that day when the late Major Robert H. Lawrence was the first black astronaut, more and more blacks have begun training for future orbital flights. And at black colleges, students are preparing experiments to be used in manned space missions.

ARCHIE ALEXANDER
Engineer
1887–1958

Born in Ottumwa, Iowa, Archie Alexander graduated from the University of Iowa with a Bachelor of Science in 1912. Although advised to avoid a career in engineering because of racial prejudice by the head of the University, Alexander persisted and gained recognition. After working for a bridge construction firm for a time, he founded his own business, and in the next 11 years completed contracts amounting to $4,500,000. One of his most satisfying jobs was the construction of a million-dollar heating plant using tunnels running under the Iowa River for his alma mater. In 1945 this institution awarded him an honorary degree.

BENJAMIN BANNEKER
Inventory, Mathematician, Almanac-Maker
1731–1806

Benjamin Banneker's mechanical inventiveness led him, in 1761, to construct what was probably the first clock made in America—a wooden "striking" clock so accurate that it kept perfect time and struck each hour unfailingly for more than 20 years.

Born in Ellicott, Maryland of a free mother and slave father, who ultimately purchased his own freedom, Banneker himself was considered free and thus able to attend an integrated private school, where he secured the equivalent of an eighth-grade education.

His aptitude in mathematics and knowledge of astronomy enabled him to predict the solar eclipse of 1789. Within a few years, he began publishing an almanac which contained tide tables, data on future eclipses, and a listing of useful medicinal products and formulas. This almanac was the first scientific book written by

a black American, and it appeared annually for more than a decade.

Banneker's major reputation, however, stems from his service as a surveyor on the six-man team which helped lay out the blueprint for Washington, D.C. When the chairman of the committee, Major L'Enfant, abruptly resigned and returned to France with his plans, Banneker's precise memory enabled him to reproduce the plans in their entirety.

ANDREW J. BEARD
Inventor
c. 1850–1910

In 1897, Andrew J. Beard received $50,000 for an invention which has since prevented the death or maiming of countless railroad men.

Benjamin Banneker, America's first black scientist, helped plan Washington, D.C.

While working in an Alabama railroad yard, Beard had seen men lose hands, even arms, in accidents occurring during the manual coupling of railroad cars. The system in use involved the dropping of a metal pin into place when two cars crashed together. Men were often caught between cars and crushed to death during this split-second operation.

Beard's invention, called the "Jenny Coupler," was an automatic device which secured two cars by merely bumping them together.

HENRY BLAIR
Inventor
c. 1804–1860

On October 14, 1834, Henry Blair of Maryland was granted a patent for a corn-planting machine and, two years later, a second patent for a similar device used in planting cotton.

In the registry of the Patent Office, Blair was designated "a colored man"—the only instance of identification by race in these early records. Since slaves could not legally obtain patents, Blair was evidently a free man and is probably the first black inventor to receive a U.S. patent.

CHARLES F. BOLDEN, JR.
NASA Astronaut
1946

Major Charles F. Bolden of the U.S. Marine Corps was born August 19, 1946 in Columbia, South Carolina. He received a bachelor of science degree in electrical science from the U.S. Naval Academy in 1968 and a master of science in systems management from the University of Southern California in 1978. Major Bolden was commissioned a second lieutenant in the U.S. Marine Corps after his graduation from Annapolis in 1968. He underwent flight training at Pensacola, Florida, Meridian, Mississippi, and Kingsville, Texas before being designated a naval aviator in May 1970. In June 1979 he was graduated from the U.S. Naval Test Pilot School at Patuxent River, Maryland and was assigned to the Naval Air Test Center's Systems Engineering and Strike Aircraft Test Directorates. Major Bolden was selected as an astronaut by NASA in May 1980. In August 1981 he completed a one-year training and evaluation period making him eligible for assignment as a pilot on future space shuttle flight crews.

OTIS BOYKIN
Inventor
1920

Otis Boykin's career began as a laboratory assistant testing automatic controls for airplanes. Boykin in-

Charles F. Bolden, selected as an astronaut by NASA in 1980.

vented a wide range of electronic devices, one of them a type of resistor now used in many computers, radios, television sets, and other electronically controlled devices. He also developed a control unit for artificial heart stimulators, a variable resistor used in guided missiles, small components such as thick-film resistors for computers, a burglar-proof cash register, and a chemical air filter. His innovations have been used both in the military and commercially.

GEORGE E. CARRUTHERS
Physicist
1940

Dr. George Carruthers is one of the two naval research laboratory people responsible for the Apollo 16 lunar surface ultraviolet camera/spectrograph, which was placed on the lunar surface in April 1972. It was Carruthers who designed the instrument while William Conway adapted the camera for the lunar mission. The spectrographs, obtained from 11 targets, include the first photographs of the ultraviolet equatorial bands of atomic oxygen that girdle the earth.

Carruthers, born and raised on Chicago's south side, built his first telescope at the age of 10. He received his Ph.D. in physics from the University of Illinois in 1964, the same year that he started employment with the Navy. Carruthers is the recipient of the National Aeronautical Space Agency (NASA) Excep-

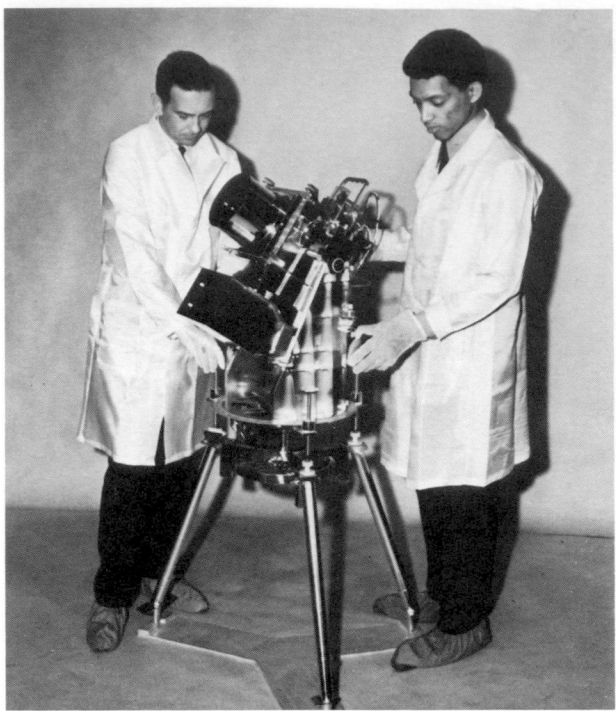

Dr. George Carruthers (right) *designed this lunar surface ultraviolet camera/spectrograph for Apollo 16.*

CHARLES DREW
Blood Plasma Researcher
1904–1950

The techniques developed by Charles Richard Drew for separating and preserving blood, and his advanced research in the vital field of blood plasma, helped save countless lives during World War II.

Born in Washington, D.C., Drew graduated from Amherst College in Massachusetts, where he received the Messman Trophy for having brought the most honor to the school during his four years there. He was not only an outstanding scholar but the captain of the track team and a star halfback on the football team.

After receiving his medical degree from McGill University in 1933, Drew returned to Washington, D.C., to teach pathology at Howard. In 1940, while taking his D.Sc. degree at Columbia University, he wrote a dissertation on "banked blood" and soon became such an expert in this field that the British government called upon him to set up the first blood bank in England.

During World War II, Drew was appointed director of the American Red Cross blood donor project and later served as chief surgeon of Freedmen's Hospital in Washington, D.C.

He was killed in an automobile crash.

tional Scientific Achievement medal for his work on the ultraviolet camera/spectrograph.

ULYSSES GRANT DAILEY
Surgeon
1885–1961

Ulysses Grant Dailey served for four years (1908–1912) as surgical assistant to Dr. Daniel Hale Williams, founder of Provident Hospital and noted heart surgeon.

Born in Donaldsonville, Louisiana, Dailey graduated in 1906 from Northwestern University Medical School, where he was appointed a demonstrator in anatomy. He later studied in London, Paris, and Vienna and in 1926 set up his own hospital and sanitarium in Chicago. His name was soon associated with some of the outstanding achievements being made in anatomy and surgery.

For many years an associate editor of the *Journal of the National Medical Association,* Dr. Dailey traveled around the world in 1933 under the sponsorship of the International College of Surgeons, of which he was a Founder Fellow.

In 1951 and again in 1953 the U.S. State Department sent him to Pakistan, India, Ceylon, and Africa. A year later he was named honorary consul to Haiti.

Dr. Charles R. Drew developed the preserving technique for blood transfusions.

GEORGE WASHINGTON CARVER
Agricultural Scientist
1864–1943

George Washington Carver devoted his life to research projects connected primarily with southern agriculture. The products he derived from the peanut and the soybean revolutionized the economy of the South by liberating it from an excessive dependence on cotton.

Born a slave in Diamond Grove, Missouri, Carver was only an infant when he and his mother were abducted from his owner's plantation by a band of slave raiders. His mother was sold and shipped away but her son was ransomed by his master in exchange for a race horse.

At the age of 13, Carver was already on his own. By working as a farm hand, he managed to obtain a high school education. He was admitted as the first black student of Simpson College, Indianola, Iowa. He then attended Iowa Agricultural College (now Iowa State University) where, while working as the school janitor, he received a degree in agricultural science in 1894. Two years later he received a master's degree from the same school and became the first black to serve on its faculty. Within a short time his fame spread, and Booker T. Washington offered him a post at Tuskegee.

Dr. Carver never patented any of the many discoveries he made while at Tuskegee, saying "God gave them to me, how can I sell them to someone else?" In fact, in 1938 he donated over $30,000 of his life's savings to the George Washington Carver Foundation and willed the rest of his estate to the organization so his work might be carried on after his death.

Carver is buried alongside Booker T. Washington. His epitaph reads: "He could have added fortune to fame, but caring for neither, he found happiness and honor in being helpful to the world."

DAVID N. CROSTHWAIT, JR.
Engineer
1898

Some of David Crosthwait's inventions and patents are the automatic water feeder, 1920; automobile indicator, 1921; thermostat-setting apparatus, 1928; vacuum heating system, 1929; and the vacuum pump, 1930.

Born in Nashville, Tennessee, Crosthwait attended high school in Kansas City and went on to receive a B.S. and M.S. in engineering from Purdue University.

As a supervisor with the firm C. A. Durham of Michigan City, Indiana, Crosthwait designed and diagnosed heating systems and installations.

In his capacity as consultant and technical advisor to utility companies of metropolitan areas, Crosthwait helped develop the method and apparatus for heating the 70-story Radio City Music Hall in New York City.

MEREDITH GOURDINE
Physicist
1929

Dr. Meredith Gourdine was born in New Jersey and grew up in the streets of Harlem and Brooklyn. From his ideas in the field of electrogasdynamics (EGD), Dr. Gourdine built a million-dollar corporation, and through his manufacturing firm he found a successful method to use the principles of EGD to convert gas to electricity for everyday use. Dr. Gourdine attended Cornell University and received his Ph.D. in engineering science from California Institute of Technology. While a student at Cornell, Dr. Gourdine was in Olympic competition in Helsinki, Finland as a broad jumper, missing first place by 4 centimeters.

LLOYD AUGUSTUS HALL
Chemist
1894

As the chief chemist and director of research for Griffith Laboratories of Chicago, Lloyd Hall discovered curing salts for the preserving and processing of meats, thus revolutionizing the meat-packing industry. He has more than 25 patents registered for processes used in the manufacturing and packing of food products, especially meat and bakery products.

An honor graduate in science from East High School of Aurora, Illinois, Hall received a B.S. in pharmaceutical chemistry from Northwestern University. He continued his training with graduate work at the University of Chicago and University of Illinois and then embarked on his unique and fruitful career.

WILLIAM A. HINTON
Medical Scientist
1883–1959

Long one of the world's authorities on venereal disease, Dr. William A. Hinton is responsible for the development of the Hinton test, a reliable method for detecting syphilis. He also collaborated with Dr. J. A. V. Davies on what is now called the Davies-Hinton test for the detection of this same disease.

Born in Chicago, Hinton graduated from Harvard in 1905 and, seven years later, finished his studies at Harvard Medical School.

For three years after graduation, he was a voluntary assistant in the pathological laboratory at Massachusetts General Hospital. This was followed by eight years of laboratory practice at the Boston Dispensary and at the Massachusetts Department of Public Health.

Hinton then became an assistant lecturer in preventive medicine and hygiene at the Harvard Medical School. In 1949 he became the first black to be granted a professorship there.

Though he lost a leg in an automobile accident, Dr. Hinton remained active in teaching and at the Boston Dispensary Laboratory, which he directed from 1916 to 1952.

He died in Canton, Massachusetts.

KATHERINE JOHNSON
Aerospace Technologist
1918

Katherine Johnson was born in West Virginia and is an aerospace technologist at the National Aeronautics and Space Administration's Langley Research Center in Hampton, Virginia. Ms. Johnson was a pioneer in the studies of new navigation procedures to determine more practical ways to track manned and unmanned space missions. Because of her work she was the recipient of the Group Achievement Award presented to NASA's Lunar Spacecraft and Operations Team. Ms. Johnson has also analyzed data gathered by tracking stations around the world during the lunar orbital missions—the moon shots.

FREDERICK McKINLEY JONES
Technician
1892–1961

In 1935 Frederick McKinley Jones inaugurated the first successful application of mechanical refrigeration techniques to railroad cars and trucks, enabling them to ship perishable food products over long distances. Previously, foods were packed in ice so slight delays led to spoilage. Jones's new method instigated a change in eating habits and patterns of the entire nation and allowed the development of food production facilities in almost any geographic location.

Jones was born in Cincinnati. His mother died when he was a boy and he moved to Covington, Kentucky, where he was raised by a priest until he was 16. When he left the rectory, Jones worked as a pinboy, mechanic's helper, and, finally, as chief mechanic on a Minnesota farm. He served in World War I and in the late 1920s his mechanical fame spread when he developed a series of devices to adapt silent movie projectors to talkies.

Jones also developed an air conditioning unit for military field hospitals, a portable x-ray machine, and a refrigerator for military field kitchens.

During his life, a total of 61 patents were issued in Jones's name.

PERCY JULIAN
Chemist
1898

The research of Dr. Percy Julian has helped create derivative drugs which are in widespread use by sufferers from arthritis.

Born in Montgomery, Alabama, Julian attended DePauw University in Greencastle, Indiana. He graduated Phi Beta Kappa and was valedictorian of his class after having lived during his college days in the attic of a fraternity house where he worked as a waiter.

For several years Julian taught at Fisk and Howard universities, as well as at West Virginia State College, before attending Harvard and the University of Vienna.

He later headed the soybean research department

Frederick Jones stands in front of a refrigerated food truck based on his patents.

of the Glidden Company and then formed Julian Laboratories in order to specialize in the production of sterols, which he extracted from the oil of the soybean. The method perfected by Dr. Julian eventually lowered the cost of sterols to less than 20 cents a gram, and ultimately enabled millions of people suffering from arthritis to obtain relief through the use of cortisone, a sterol derivative, at a price within their means.

In 1935 Julian synthesized the drug physostigmine, which is used today in the treatment of glaucoma.

ERNEST E. JUST
Biologist
1883–1941

Ernest Just formulated new concepts of cell life and metabolism and initiated pioneer investigations of egg fertilization, artificial parthenogenesis, and cell division.

Born in Charleston, South Carolina, Just received his B.A. with high honors from Dartmouth and his Ph.D. from the University of Chicago. He began teaching at Howard University and by 1912 had become professor of zoology.

A member of Phi Beta Kappa, Just received the Spingarn Medal in 1914 and served as associate editor of *Physiological Zoology, The Biological Bulletin,* and *The Journal of Morphology.* He wrote two books and more than 60 papers on his field and served as vice-president of the American Society of Zoologists.

SAMUEL L. KOUNTZ
Surgeon
1930–1981

Dr. Samuel L. Kountz was an international leader in transplant surgery who performed 500 kidney transplants, believed to be the most to be performed by any physician to date. Dr. Kountz was head of surgery at the Downstate Medical Center and chief of general surgery at Kings County Hospital Center, both in Brooklyn, New York. Born in Lexa, Arkansas, he graduated third in his class at the Agricultural, Mechanical and Normal College of Arkansas in 1952. He pursued graduate studies at the University of Arkansas, earning a degree in chemistry. Senator J. W. Fulbright, who he met while a graduate student, advised him to apply for a scholarship to medical school. Kountz won the scholarship on a competitive basis and was the first black to enroll at the University of Arkansas Medical School in Little Rock. Dr. Kountz was responsible for finding out that large doses of the drug methylprednisolone could help reverse the acute rejection of a transplanted kidney. The drug was used for a number of years in the standard management of kidney transplant patients.

Dr. Samuel L. Kountz, an international leader in transplant surgery.

In 1964, working with Dr. Roy Cohn, one of the pioneers in the field of transplantation, Dr. Kountz made medical history by transplanting a kidney from a mother to a daughter—the first transplant between humans who were not identical twins. At the University of California in 1967, Dr. Kountz worked with other researchers to develop the prototype of a machine which is now able to preserve kidneys up to 50 hours from the time they are taken from the body of a donor. The machine, called the Belzer Kidney Perfusion Machine, was named for Dr. Folkert O. Belzer, who was Dr. Kountz's partner. Dr. Kountz died in 1981 after a long illness contracted on a trip to South Africa in 1977. The illness was never diagnosed and Dr. Kountz remained brain-damaged until the time of his death.

LEWIS HOWARD LATIMER
Inventor, Draftsman, Engineer
1848–1928

Lewis Howard Latimer was employed by Alexander Graham Bell to make the patent drawings for the first telephone, and later went on to become chief draftsman for both the General Electric and Westinghouse companies.

Born in Chelsea, Massachusetts, on September 4, 1848, Latimer enlisted in the Union Navy at the age of 15 and began the study of drafting upon completion of military service. In 1881 he invented a method of making carbon filaments for the Maxim electric incandescent lamp which he patented. In 1881 Latimer supervised installation of electric light in New York, Philadelphia, Montreal, and London for the Maxim-Weston Electric Company. In 1884 he joined the Edison Company.

THEODORE K. LAWLESS
Dermatologist
1892

Theodore K. Lawless, one of the leading skin specialists in the United States, was born in Thibodeaux, Louisiana. He was educated at Talladega College in Alabama and at Kansas, Columbia, and Harvard universities before receiving his M.D. from Northwestern.

From 1924 until 1941 Lawless taught at the Northwestern School of Medicine and did special research in Vienna, Freiburg, and Paris, where he made valuable contributions to the scientific treatment of syphilis and leprosy.

The dermatology clinic at the Beilinson Hospital Center for Israel was erected largely through his efforts, and bears his name, as does a chapel at Dillard University in New Orleans.

In 1929 Lawless won the Harmon Award in medicine, and he was later awarded the Spingarn Medal (1954).

ROBERT H. LAWRENCE, JR.
Pilot-Scientist
1935–1967

Air Force Major Robert H. Lawrence, Jr. was the first black astronaut to be appointed to the Manned Orbiting Laboratory. Lawrence was a native of Chicago, and while still in elementary school he became a model airplane hobbyist and a chess enthusiast. Lawrence became interested in biology during his high school days at Englewood High School in Chicago. As a student at Englewood, Lawrence excelled in chemistry and track, placing top in the 440 and 880. When he graduated, he placed in the upper 10% of the class. Lawrence entered Bradley University, joining the Air Force Reserve Officer's Training Corps and attaining the rank of lieutenant colonel, the second highest ranking cadet at Bradley. Lawrence was commissioned a second lieutenant in the U.S. Air Force in 1956 soon after he received his bachelor's degree in chemistry. Following a stint at an air base in Ger-

many, Lawrence entered Ohio State University through the Air Force Institute of Technology as a doctoral candidate. At Ohio State Lawrence earned a number of A's in courses such as nuclear chemistry, photochemistry, chemical kinetics, advanced inorganic chemistry, and thermodynamics. Major Lawrence's career came to an end in 1967 when his F-104D Starfighter jet crashed on a runway in a California desert.

MILES VANDAHURST LYNK
Physician and Attorney
1871–1956

Dr. Miles Vandahurst Lynk, M.D., Esq., born June 3, 1871 near Brownsville, Tennessee was founder, editor, and publisher of the first black medical journal. The journal, called *Medical and Surgical Observer,* was first published in December 1892 and ran for 18 months. At the age of 19, Dr. Lynk first received his M.D. degree from Meharry Medical College. Dr. Lynk was one of the organizers of the first black national medical association. The organization later became the National Medical Association. He also founded and was president of the School of Medicine at the University of West Tennessee.

JAN MATZELIGER
Inventor
1852–1889

The shoe-lasting machine invented by Jan Matzeliger not only revolutionized the shoe industry but also made Lynn, Massachusetts, the "shoe capital of the world."

Born in Paramaribo, Dutch Guiana, Matzeliger found employment in the government machine works at the age of 10. Eight years later he immigrated to the United States, settling in Philadelphia, where he worked in a shoe factory. He later moved to New England, settling permanently in Lynn.

The Industrial Revolution had by this time resulted in the invention of machines to cut, sew, and tack shoes, but none had been perfected to last a shoe. Seeing this, Matzeliger lost little time in designing and patenting just such a device, one which he refined over the years to a point where it could adjust a shoe, arrange the leather over the sole, drive in the nails, and deliver the finished product—all in one minute's time.

Matzeliger's patent was subsequently bought by Sydney W. Winslow, who established the United Shoe Machine Company. The continued success of this business brought about a 50% reduction in the price of shoes across the nation, doubled wages, and improved working conditions for millions of people dependent on the shoe industry for their livelihood.

Matzeliger died when only 37, long before he had the chance to realize a share of the enormous profit derived from his invention.

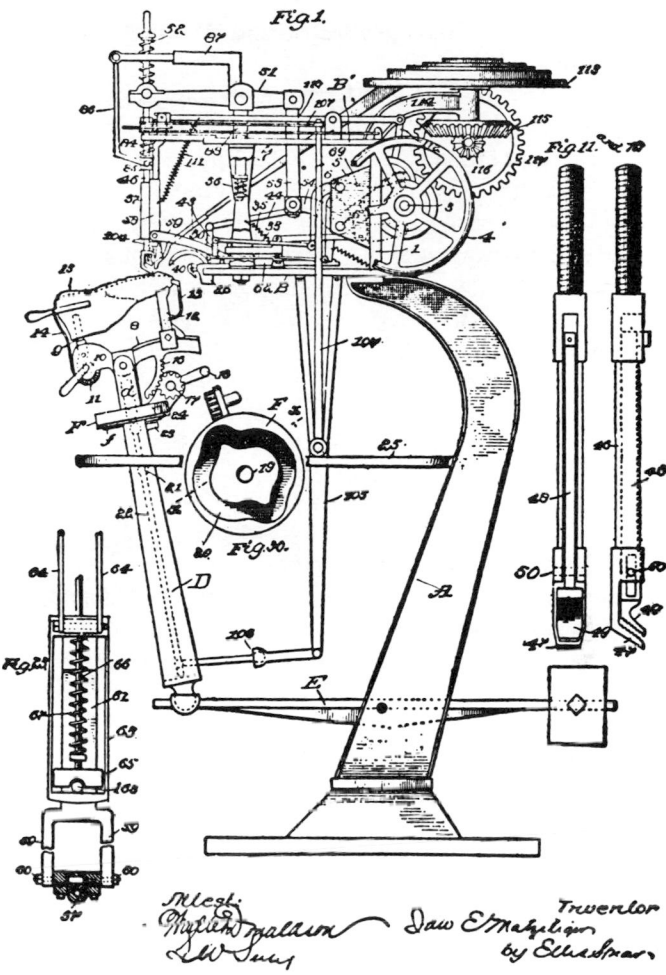

The shoe-lasting machine invented by Jan Matzeliger cut American shoe prices in half and doubled wages.

ELIJAH McCOY
Inventor
1844–1928?

Elijah McCoy's inventions were primarily connected with the automatic lubrication of moving machinery. Perhaps his most valuable design was the "drip cup," a tiny container filled with oil whose flow to the essential moving parts of heavy-duty machinery was regulated by means of a "stopcock." The drip cup was a key device in perfecting the overall lubrication system used in large industry today.

Born in Canada, McCoy moved to Ypsilanti, Michigan, after the Civil War and, over the next 40 years, acquired some 57 patents for devices designed to streamline his automatic lubrication process.

W. DELANO MERIWETHER
Research Hematologist
1943

Dr. W. Delano Meriwether is a clinical and research hematologist who has studied leukemia and sickle cell anemia. Dr. Meriwether is also known for his athletic prowess and is an award-winning sprinter. Born in Nashville, Tennessee, Meriwether attended Michigan State University on an academic scholarship. He left Michigan State after three years and became the first black to enroll at Duke University School of Medicine in Durham, North Carolina. At Duke, Dr. Meriwether studied on a National Medical Fellowship from the Sloan Foundation.

Dr. Meriwether joined the Baltimore Cancer Research Center in 1969 as a clinical associate, and for a year he worked with young leukemia patients and researched the effects of experimental drugs on leukemic mice. Dr. Meriwether took up running evenings on a high school track to keep his mind off the tragedy of leukemia. In 1973, Dr. Meriwether received a White House Fellowship and was assigned to the Department of Health, Education and Welfare as a special assistant. He went on fact-finding missions to the Sahel drought area of the sub-Sahara, to South Africa, and to the Soviet Union. At the end of his year's assignment he became special assistant to Assistant Secretary for Health Dr. Theodore Cooper. He spent most of his time working on federal nutrition programs until he was appointed in 1976 director of the national swine flu immunization program.

JAMES W. MITCHELL
Chemist

James W. Mitchell, an outstanding chemist, is best known for his contributions and achievements in ad-

vancing the accuracy of trace element analyses. For his research, Mitchell received the 1981 Percy L. Julian Outstanding Research Award.

A native of Durham, North Carolina, Mitchell is head of the Analytical Chemistry Department at Bell Laboratories in Murray Hill, New Jersey. In his research, Mitchell found techniques for identifying extremely small quantities of trace elements and contaminants in high-purity materials. He also worked on processes for producing ultra-high-purity chemicals.

Mitchell received his B.S. degree in chemistry from North Carolina Agriculture and Technical State University in Greensboro, North Carolina and a Ph.D. in analytical chemistry from Iowa State University. He has published a number of articles and is co-author of *Contamination Control in Trace Element Analysis.*

GARRETT A. MORGAN
Inventor
1877–1963

The value of Garrett Morgan's "gas inhalator" was first acknowledged during a successful rescue operation of several men trapped by a tunnel explosion in the Cleveland Waterworks some 200 feet below the surface of Lake Erie. During the emergency, Morgan, his brother, and two other volunteers—all wearing inhalators—were the only men able to descend into the smoky, gas-filled tunnel, and save several workers from asphyxiation.

Orders for the Morgan inhalator soon began to pour into Cleveland from fire companies all over the nation but, as soon as Morgan's racial identity became known, many of them were canceled. In the South, it was necessary for Morgan to utilize the services of a white man to demonstrate his invention. During World War I the Morgan inhalator was transformed into a gas mask used by combat troops.

Born in Paris, Kentucky, Morgan moved to Cleveland at an early age. His first invention was an improvement on the sewing machine which he sold for $150. In 1923, having established his reputation with the gas inhalator, he was able to command a price of $40,000 from the General Electric Company for his automatic traffic sign.

Morgan died in Cleveland, the city which had awarded him a gold medal for his devotion to public safety.

Both the gas mask and the traffic light were invented by Garrett Morgan. An early version of his gas safety helmet is shown.

NORBERT RILLIEUX
Inventor
1806–1894

Norbert Rillieux's inventions were of great value to the sugar-refining industry. The method formerly used called for gangs of slaves to ladle boiling sugarcane juice from one kettle to another—a primitive process known as "The Jamaica Train."

In 1845, Rillieux invented a vacuum evaporating pan (a series of condensing coils in vacuum chambers) which reduced the industry's dependence on gang labor and helped manufacture a superior product at a greatly reduced cost. The first Rillieux evaporator was installed at Myrtle Grove Plantation, Louisiana, in 1845.

In the following years, factories in Louisiana, Cuba, and Mexico converted to the Rillieux system.

A native of New Orleans, Rillieux was the son of Vincent Rillieux, a wealthy engineer, and Constance Vivant, a slave on his plantation. Young Rillieux's higher education was obtained in Paris, where his extraordinary aptitude for engineering led to his appointment at the age of 24 as an instructor of applied mechanics at L'Ecole Centrale. Rillieux returned to Paris permanently in 1854, securing a scholarship and working on the deciphering of hieroglyphics.

When his evaporator process was finally adopted in Europe, he returned to inventing with renewed interest—applying his process to the sugar beet. In so doing, he cut production and refining costs in half.

Rillieux died in Paris on October 8, 1894, leaving behind a system which is in universal use throughout the sugar industry, as well as in the manufacture of soap, gelatin, glue, and many other products.

HILYARD R. ROBINSON
Architect

Robinson was trained in architecture at the University of Pennsylvania, the Columbia University School of Architecture, and the University of Berlin.

In 1926 his design was chosen for the historic restaurant in the Henry Hudson Hotel in Troy, New York.

Mechanical genius Norbert Rillieux invented the evaporating pan which revolutionized many industries, starting with sugar-refining.

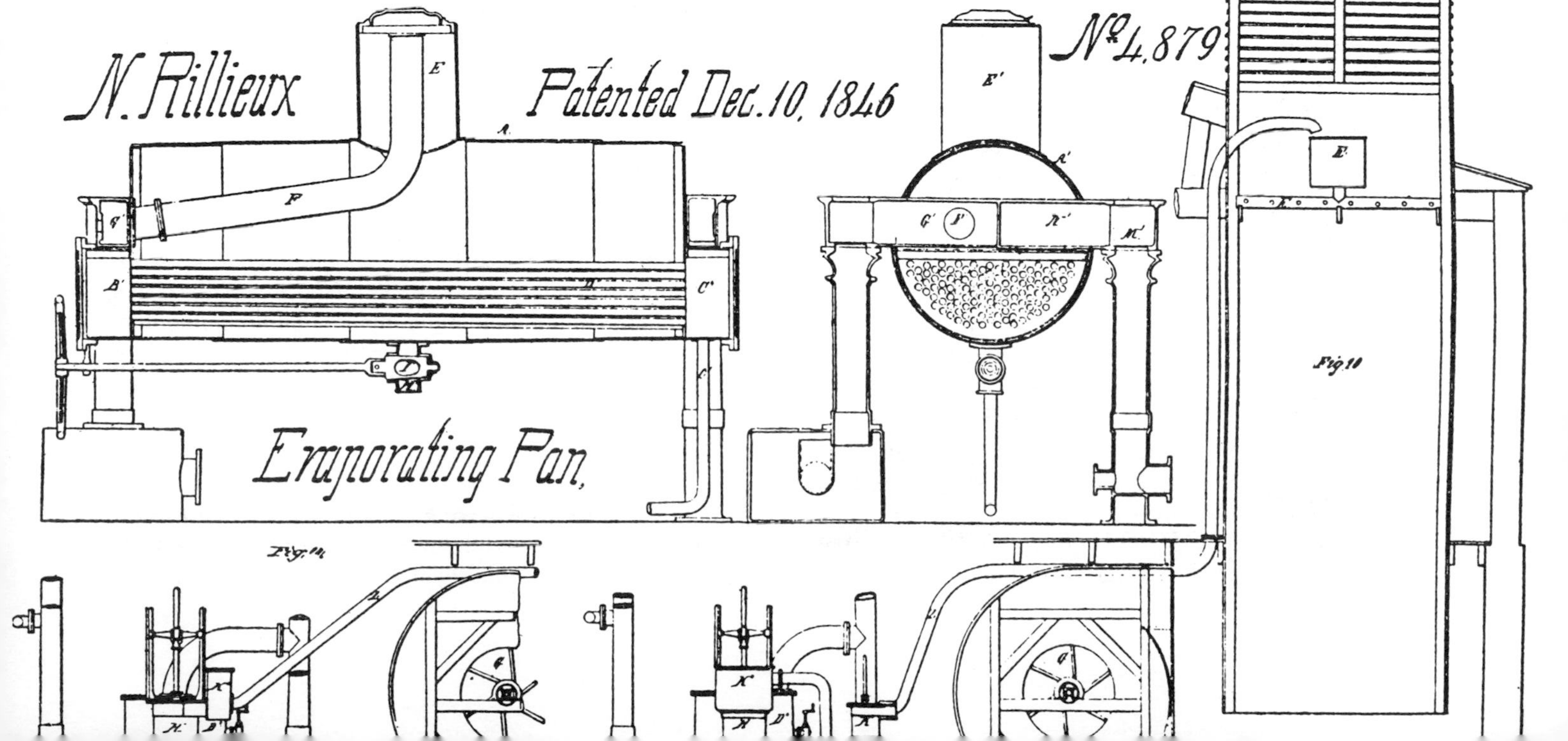

N. Rillieux   Patented Dec. 10, 1846   Nº 4,879

Evaporating Pan.

The toggle harpoon invented by Lewis Temple doubled the whaling catch of nineteenth-century New England.

In 1927 he received the first, second, and fourth prizes offered by the professional journal *Architecture*.

Robinson was responsible for organizing and conducting the slum housing survey in the District of Columbia in 1933. He was professor of architecture and chairman of the department at Howard University for 13 years. In 1934 he was appointed consulting architect to the National Capitol Advisory Committee and senior architect for the United States Suburban Resettlement Administration.

The $1.8 million Langston Public Works Administration Housing Project for Negroes was his most outstanding project. In 1940, he completed the Alabama Avenue S.E. government housing project and collaborated with Paul R. Williams in the design of the men's dormitory at Howard University.

LEWIS TEMPLE
Inventor
1800–1854

The toggle harpoon invented by Lewis Temple so improved the whaling methods of the nineteenth century that it more than doubled the catch for this leading New England industry.

Little is known of Temple's early background, except that he was born in Richmond, Virginia, in 1800,

and had no formal education. As a young man he moved to New Bedford, Massachusetts, then a major whaling port.

Finding work as a metalsmith, Temple modified the design of the whaler's harpoon and, in the 1840s, manufactured a new version of the harpoon which allowed lines to be securely fastened to the whale. Using the "toggle harpoon," the whaling industry soon entered a period of unprecedented prosperity.

Temple, who never patented his harpoon, died destitute.

DANIEL HALE WILLIAMS
Surgeon
1856–1931

A pioneer in open heart surgery, Daniel Hale Williams was born in Holidaysburg, Pennsylvania. His father died when he was 11, and his mother deserted him after apprenticing him to a cobbler. He later worked as a roustabout on a lake steamer and as a barber before finishing his education at the Chicago Medical College in 1883.

Williams opened his office on Chicago's South Side at a time when Chicago hospitals did not allow black doctors to use their facilities. In those days, operations were often performed on kitchen tables in tenements

Dr. Daniel Williams was a pioneer in heart surgery.

For the next four days, the patient, James Cornish, lay near death, his temperature far above normal and his pulse dangerously uneven. An encouraging rally then brought him out of immediate danger, terminating the crisis period. Three weeks later, minor surgery was performed by Dr. Williams to remove fluid from Cornish's pleural cavity. After recuperating for still another month, Cornish was fully recovered and able to leave the hospital, scarred but cured.

An uproar of publicity greeted Dr. Williams' later announcement that his heart surgery had been successful. Much of it was negative, in the sense that skeptics doubted that a black doctor could engineer such a significant breakthrough. Unaffected by the notoriety, Williams continued a full-time association with Freedmen's Hospital.

Dr. Williams died in 1931 after a lifetime devoted to his two main interests—the NAACP and the construction of hospitals and training schools for black doctors and nurses.

O. S. (OZZIE) WILLIAMS
Aeronautical Engineer
1921

O. S. (Ozzie) Williams was the first black person to be hired by Republic Aviation, Inc., as an aeronautical engineer. Later he joined Greer Hydraulics, Inc., where he became a group project engineer and helped develop the first airborne radar beacon for locating crashed aircraft. Williams, a specialist in small rocket engine design, was also associated with the Reaction Motors Division of Thiokol Chemical Corporation. Williams joined Grumman International in 1961 and was in charge of developing and producing the control rocket systems that guided lunar modules during moon landings.

PAUL R. WILLIAMS
Architect
1894

Paul R. Williams is a renowned architect of the environmentalist school who seeks to fuse homes to a closer feeling and relationship with their surroundings.

Born in Los Angeles, Williams graduated from Polytechnic High School and studied at the University of Southern California. He was certified as an architect in 1915 and worked in the office of a landscape architect.

Early in his career Williams conceived many fine civic and institutional buildings in the young, booming city of Los Angeles, including the Shriner Auditorium and the First Methodist Church. Movie stars and moguls observing Williams's talent then engaged his services to build many of their elaborate dwellings.

scattered through the Black Belt. Dr. Williams helped put an end to this practice by founding Provident Hospital, which was open to patients of all races.

At Provident Hospital in 1893, Dr. Williams performed the operation upon which his later fame rests. On July 10 of that year, a patient was admitted to the emergency ward with a knife wound in an artery lying a fraction of an inch from the heart. With the aid of six staff surgeons, Williams made an incision in the patient's chest and operated successfully on the artery.

The operation performed by Williams was an astonishing feat. The doctor began by making a six-inch incision and detaching the fifth rib from the breastbone, so he could settle down to work through a 2×1½-inch opening. After securing the left internal mammary artery, he inspected the heart, noting instantly that the pericardium had been punctured by the knife. The heart muscle, too, had been nicked, but the wound here was not serious enough to require suturing or stitching. Dr. Williams then repaired the pericardium, sutured the chest opening, and completed the momentous operation.

GRANVILLE T. WOODS
Inventor
1856–1910

During his lifetime, Granville Woods obtained some 50 patents, including one for an incubator which was the forerunner of present machines capable of hatching 50,000 eggs at a time.

Born in Columbus, Ohio, Woods attended school until he was 10. He was first employed in a machine shop, and continued to improve his mechanical aptitude by working on a railroad in 1872, in a rolling mill in 1874, and later by studying mechanical engineering at college. In 1878 Woods became an engineer aboard the *Ironsides,* a British steamer, and within two years was handling a steam locomotive on the D&S Railroad.

In 1887 Woods patented the most advanced of his many inventions—the Synchronous Multiplex Railway Telegraph. This device was designed to avert accidents by keeping each train informed of the whereabouts of the train immediately ahead or following it by enabling communication between stations from moving trains.

Woods marketed this product, and others which followed, through his own company. A perusal of the patent files in Washington, D.C., shows Woods to have been an extremely prolific inventor. In the 20-year span between 1879 and 1899, no less than 23 separate inventions bear his name. In 1887 alone, he registered seven separate inventions with the Patent Office, all of them connected with the ingenious railway communications system he devised.

Woods died in New York City.

LOUIS TOMPKINS WRIGHT
Medical Researcher
1891–1952

Dr. Louis Tompkins Wright, one of the country's outstanding surgeons and medical researchers, is known for the first extensive study of the intradermal method of smallpox vaccination, the design of a special brace for patients with head and neck injuries, the first use of chlortetracycline, a new antibiotic, on humans, and the use of drugs to treat cancer patients. Dr. Wright was born in LaGrange, Georgia, and was a graduate of Harvard Medical School. He was the first black person to be appointed to the staff of New York Hospital and in 1939 was also the first black to be elected to a fellowship in the American College of Surgeons.

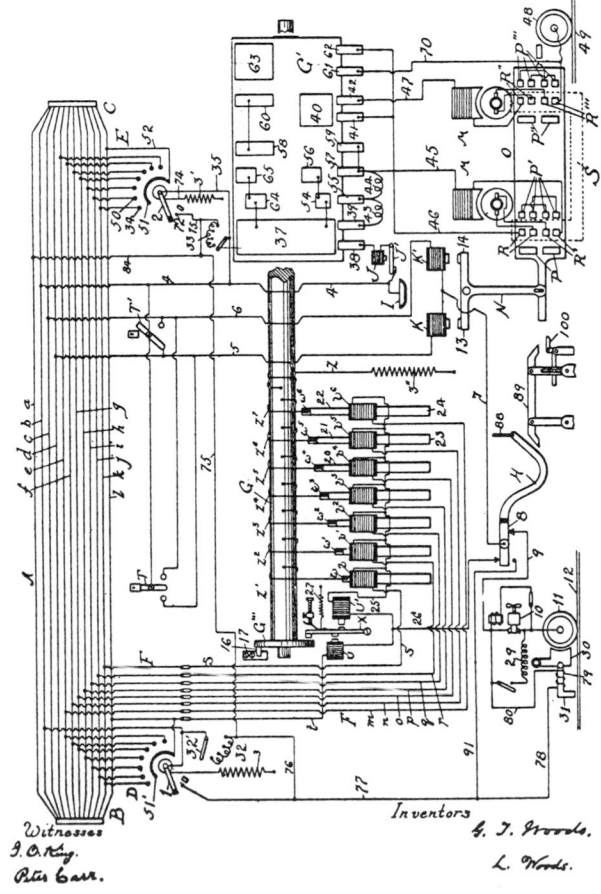

Inventor Granville Woods obtained some 50 patents.

OTHER NOTABLE BLACK INVENTORS AND SCIENTISTS

Name	Occupation	Dates
Dr. William Harry Barnes	Medical specialist	1887–1945
Charles F. Baxter	Scientist	1927–
Jesse F. Berry	Engineer	1932–
Max J. Bond, Jr.	Architect	1935–
Edward Alexander Bouchet	Physicist-educator	1852–1918
Herman Russell Branson	Scientist-educator	1914–
Ernest Coleman	Physics researcher	1942–
Annie Easley	Energy researcher	1932–
Lloyd Noel Ferguson	Chemist	1918–
Solomon C. Fuller	Neurologist	1872–1953
James Harris Green	Scientist	
James Harris	Nuclear chemist	1932–
James Henderson	Scientist	1917–
Henry Aaron Hill	Scientist	1915–

Name	Occupation	Dates
Dr. William Augustus Hinton	Medical specialist	1883–1959
Defield T. Holmes	Scientist	
Dr. Rebecca Lee	Physician	1833–
Robert P. Madison	Architect	1923–
Huey Perry Malone	Engineer	1935–
Julia M. Martin	Chemist	1924–
Samuel Proctor Massie, Jr.	Scientist	1919–
Caldwell McCoy	Energy researcher	1933–
Louis W. Roberts	Physicist	1913–
Dr. John Sweat Rock	Physician	1825–1866
David W. Robinson	Scientist	1933–
Elijah Saunders	Cardiologist	1934–
Dr. Roland Scott	Pediatrician	
Dr. James McCune Smith	Physician	1813–1865
Vertner W. Tandy	Architect	1885
Julius H. Taylor	Physicist	1914–
Lawnie Taylor	Physicist	
Moddie Daniel Taylor	Scientist	1942–1976
James Tyson Tildon	Scientist	1931–
Virgil G. Trice, Jr.	Nuclear researcher	1926–
Dr. Jane Cooke Wright	Surgeon	1919–
Ronald E. Zanders	Engineer	1933–

BLACK SCIENTIFIC ORGANIZATIONS

American Association of Blacks in Energy

James Caldwell (Secretary)
1429 Larimer Square
Denver, CO 80802

Chairman: Rufus McKinney, Washington, DC

Founded: 1977

Purpose: To insure that Black Americans and other minorities gain their adequate share of representation and participation in the development and implementation of this nation's activities involving energy.

Membership: 300; open to managerial and professional employees of energy-related businesses, trade associations and government agencies; consultants, educators, and students in related disciplines who support the purposes of the association.

Dues: $25; $50 Gold Star Sustaining

Association of Third World Anthropologists (ATWA)

Department of Sociology-Anthropology

Morgan State University
Baltimore, MD 21239

Presidents (joint): Dr. Mario Zamora, Williamsburg, VA; Dr. Stefan Goodwin, Baltimore, MD

Founded: 1977

Purpose: To make anthropology more sensitive and responsive to the views and needs of Third World peoples; to make anthropology less prejudiced against Third World peoples by making it less ethnocentric in its use of language, paradigms, and conceptual grids; to genuinely incorporate Third World professionals into its organizations and their perspectives into the mainstream of its literature.

Membership: 110 (on every continent except Australia); open to all anthropologists and specialists in cognate disciplines interested in achieving the purposes or objectives.

Dues: $26 institutional; $15 fellows and associates; $10 students; Gratis by special request to limited numbers of overseas persons unable to pay.

Publications: The *ATWA Research Bulletin*—quarterly

Atlanta Council of Black Professional Engineers

148 International Boulevard, Suite 448
Atlanta, GA 30303

President: Calvin Espy, Atlanta, GA

Founded: 1976

Purpose: To develop an awareness in the Black community of the opportunities available in engineering.

Membership: 75; open to practicing engineers and technicians.

Publications: *Atlanta Council of Black Professional Engineers*—quarterly

Los Angeles Council of Black Professional Engineers

Federal Building
P.O. Box 945
Los Angeles, CA 90053

President: Sylvia Weatherford, Torrence, CA

Founded: 1969

Purpose: To promote an interest in, recruit, and retain minorities in academic and professional careers in engineering. This objective is accomplished through the Council's committees on youth motivation, college relations, summer work exposure, newsletter, special projects, planning and operations, pan-African committee, and its Mathematics-Engineering Science Achievement (MESA) center.

Membership: 200; open to engineering, mathematics, and computer science professionals

Dues: none

Publications: newsletter—monthly

National Conference of Black Political Scientists

Department of Political Science
Morgan State University
Baltimore, MD 21239

President: Dr. Elsie Scott, Washington, DC

Founded: 1971

Purpose: To bring black political scientists together to maximize their role in the liberation of black people; to promote the study of political science with particular reference to the black experience; to reflect on the proper means by which political scientists can approach the study of politics with a view toward enriching the black experience; to facilitate the solving of professional problems that are unique to black political scientists.

Membership: 300; open to any political or social scientists and others interested in the political life and liberation of black people and who pay the requisite dues for a given year.

Dues: $20 per year

Publications: *Journal of Political Repression*—quarterly

National Dental Association

Mrs. Rubye C. Porter, Administrator
5506 Connecticut Avenue, NW, Suite 24
Washington, DC 20015
President: Dr. Elisha Richardson, Nashville, TN

Founded: 1913

Purpose: To promote the interests of dentistry in general and of minority dentists in particular; to represent the interests of the minority population with respect to health care, especially dental care.

Membership: 2,000+; open to dentists and four affiliated groups: The Auxiliary of NDA, The National

Dental Hygienists Association (NDHA). The National Dental Assistants Association (NDAA), and The Student National Dental Association (SNDA).

Dues: $125 per year

Publications: *NDA Quarterly*; and a bimonthly newsletter

National Organization for the Professional Advancement of Black Chemists and Chemical Engineers

Dr. Clarence Tucker
Polaroid Corporation
1265 Main Street
Waltham, MA 02154

President: Dr. James H. Porter, Cambridge, MA

Founded: 1972

Purpose: To develop programs to assist blacks in realizing their full potential in the fields of chemistry and chemical engineering.

Membership: 700; open to persons who support and are willing to attain the objectives of the organization; full membership—a bachelors or advanced degree in chemistry or the equivalent; associate membership—all others.

Dues: $35 full membership; $15 associate membership; no dues student membership

Publications: Newsletter—quarterly; proceedings of national meetings—annually

National Society of Black Engineers

317 Clermont Avenue
Brooklyn, NY 11205

Chairperson: Carolynn Cooper, Brooklyn, NY

Founded: 1971

Purpose: To promote black scholastic achievement; to insure the completion of a science or engineering program with a degree once a student has entered the university; to promote the social standing of the black student in the sciences and engineering; to establish and maintain tutorial programs for college, high school, and junior high school students; to provide college, high school, and junior high school students with proper engineering counseling; to assist in job placement; and to strive toward a better understanding among all engineers regardless of race, creed or color.

Membership: 4,000 (approximately); open to undergraduate and graduate students in engineering or applied science; junior membership open to junior high and high school students; auxiliary memberships are available to professional engineers and corporations.

Dues: Exempt, honorary and junior members; $1,500 corporate membership; $25 senior associate; $12 associate; $3 affiliate and member

Publications: Newsletter—three times a year; national conference proceedings—yearly; technical conference proceedings—yearly

National Society of Black Physicists

Dr. Shirley Jackson
Bell Laboratories
600 Mountain Avenue
Murray Hill, NJ 07974

President: Dr. Shirley Jackson

Founded: 1978

Purpose: To promote the professional well-being of black physicists within the scientific community and within society at large, and to develop and support efforts to increase opportunities for and the number of blacks in physics.

Membership: About 50; open to persons who have a Ph.D. in physics and/or are employed as professional physicists, or are currently matriculating toward a doctoral degree in physics.

Dues: $20

Publications: Newsletter published periodically; proceedings of annual meeting.

Organization of Black Scientists, Inc.

P.O. Box 8715
Washington, DC 20011

President: Dr. Franklin Hamilton, Atlanta, GA

Founded: 1971

Purpose: To identify, provide, and administer research and educational goals of black scientists.

Membership: 600 (with local chapters in several cities); open to anyone active in natural sciences or mathematics and who will further the objectives of the organization.

Dues: $10

Publication: Newsletter

INVENTIONS BY BLACKS
1871–1900[a]

Inventor	Invention	Date	Patent
Abrams, W. B.	Hame attachment	Apr. 14, 1891	450,550
Allen, C. W.	Self-leveling table	Nov. 1, 1898	613,436
Allen, J. B.	Clothes line support	Dec. 10, 1895	551,105
Ashbourne, A. P.	Process for preparing coconut for domestic use	June 1, 1875	163,962
Ashbourne, A. P.	Biscuit cutter	Nov. 30, 1875	170,460
Ashbourne, A. P.	Refining coconut oil	July 27, 1880	230,518
Ashbourne, A. P.	Process of treating coconut	Aug. 21, 1877	194,287
Bailes, William	Ladder scaffold-support	Aug. 5, 1879	218,154
Bailey, L. C.	Combined truss and bandage	Sept. 25, 1883	285,545
Bailey, L. C.	Folding bed	July 18, 1899	629,286
Bailiff, C. O.	Shampoo headrest	Oct. 11, 1898	612,008
Ballow, W. J.	Combined hatrack and table	Mar. 29, 1898	601,422
Barnes, G. A. E.	Design for sign	Aug. 19, 1889	29,193
Beard, A. J.	Rotary engine	July 5, 1892	478,271
Beard, A. J.	Car-coupler	Nov. 23, 1897	594,059
Becket, G. E.	Letter box	Oct. 4, 1892	483,525
Bell, L.	Locomotive smoke stack	May 23, 1871	115,153
Bell, L.	Dough kneader	Dec. 10, 1872	133,823
Benjamin, L. W.	Broom moisteners and bridles	May 16, 1893	497,747
Benjamin, M. E.	Gong and signal chairs for hotels	July 17, 1888	386,286
Binga, M. W.	Street sprinkling apparatus	July 22, 1879	217,843
Blackburn, A. B.	Railway signal	Jan. 10, 1888	376,362
Blackburn, A. B.	Spring seat for chairs	Apr. 3, 1888	380,420
Blackburn, A. B.	Cash carrier	Oct. 23, 1888	391,577
Blair, Henry	Corn planter	Oct. 14, 1834	
Blair, Henry	Cotton planter	Aug. 31, 1836	
Blue, L.	Hand corn shelling device	May 20, 1884	298,937
Booker, L. F.	Design rubber scraping knife	Mar. 28, 1899	30,404
Boone, Sarah	Ironing board	Apr. 26, 1892	473,653
Bowman, H. A.	Making flags	Feb. 23, 1892	469,395
Brooks, C. B.	Punch	Oct. 31, 1893	507,672
Brooks, C. B.	Street-sweepers	Mar. 17, 1896	556,711
Brooks, C. B.	Street-sweepers	May 12, 1896	560,154
Brooks, Hallstead and Page	Street-sweepers	Apr. 21, 1896	558,719
Brown, Henry	Receptacle for storing and preserving papers	Nov. 2, 1886	352,036
Brown, L. F.	Bridle bit	Oct. 25, 1892	484,994
Brown, O. E.	Horseshoe	Aug. 23, 1892	481,271
Brown & Latimer	Water closets for railway cars	Feb. 10, 1874	147,363
Burr, J. A.	Lawn mower	May 9, 1899	624,749
Burr, W. F.	Switching device for railways	Oct. 31, 1899	636,197
Burwell, W.	Boot or shoe	Nov. 28, 1899	638,143
Butler, R. A.	Train alarm	June 15, 1897	584,540
Butts, J. W.	Luggage carrier	Oct. 10, 1899	634, 611
Byrd, T. J.	Improvement in holders for reins for horses	Feb. 6, 1872	123,328
Byrd, T. J.	Apparatus for detaching horses from carriages	Feb. 6, 1872	123,328
Byrd, T. J.	Apparatus for detaching horses from carriages	Mar. 19, 1872	124,790
Byrd, T. J.	Improvement in neck yokes for wagons	Mar. 19, 1872	124,790
Byrd, T. J.	Improvement in car couplings	Dec. 1, 1874	157,370
Campbell, W. S.	Self-setting animal trap	Aug. 30, 1881	246,369
Cargill, B. F.	Invalid cot	July 25, 1899	629,658
Carrington, T. A.	Range	July 25, 1876	180,323
Carter, W. C.	Umbrella stand	Aug. 4, 1885	323,397

[a] In cases where an inventor has patented several variations on the same basic invention, a composite entry has been devised.

Inventor	Invention	Date	Patent
Certain, J. M.	Parcel carrier for bicycles	Dec. 26, 1899	639,708
Cherry, M. A.	Velocipede	May 8, 1888	382,351
Cherry, M. A.	Street car fender	Jan. 1, 1895	531,908
Church, T. S.	Carpet beating machine	July 29, 1884	302,237
Clare, O. B.	Trestle	Oct. 9, 1888	390,752
Coates, R.	Overboot for horses	Apr. 19, 1892	473,295
Cook, G.	Automatic fishing device	May 30, 1899	625,829
Coolidge, J. S.	Harness attachment	Nov. 13, 1888	392,908
Cooper, A. R.	Shoemaker's jack	Aug. 22, 1899	631,519
Cooper, J.	Shutter and fastening	May 1, 1883	276,563
Cooper, J.	Elevator device	Apr. 2, 1895	536,605
Cooper, J.	Elevator device	Sept. 21, 1897	590,257
Cornwell, P. W.	Draft regulator	Oct. 2, 1888	390,284
Cornwell, P. W.	Draft regulator	Feb. 7, 1893	491,082
Cralle, A. L.	Ice-cream mold	Feb. 2, 1897	576,395
Creamer, H.	Steam feed water trap	Mar. 17, 1895	313,854
Creamer, H.[a]	Steam trap feeder	Dec. 11, 1888	394,463
Cosgrove, W. F.	Automatic stop plug for gas oil pipes	Mar. 17, 1885	313,993
Darkins, J. T.	Ventilation aid (variation)	Feb. 19, 1895	534,322
Davis, I. D.	Tonic	Nov. 2, 1886	351,829
Davis, W. D.	Riding saddles	Oct. 6, 1896	568,939
Davis, W. R., Jr.	Library table	Sept. 24, 1878	208,378
Deitz, W. A.	Shoe	Apr. 30, 1867	64,205
Dickinson, J. H.	Pianola	Mich., 1899	
Dorsey, O.	Door-holding device	Dec. 10, 1878	210,764
Dorticus, C. J.	Device for applying coloring liquids to sides of soles or heels of shoes	Mar. 19, 1895	535,820
Dorticus, C. J.	Machine for embossing photo	Apr. 16, 1895	537,442
Dorticus, C. J.	Photographic print wash	Apr. 23, 1875	537,968
Dorticus, C. J.	Hose leak stop	July 18, 1899	629,315
Downing, P. B.	Electric switch for railroad	June 17, 1890	430,118
Downing, P. B.	Letter box	Oct 27, 1891	462,093
Downing, P. B.	Street letter box	Oct 27, 1891	462,096

[a] Creamer also patented five steam traps between 1887 and 1893.

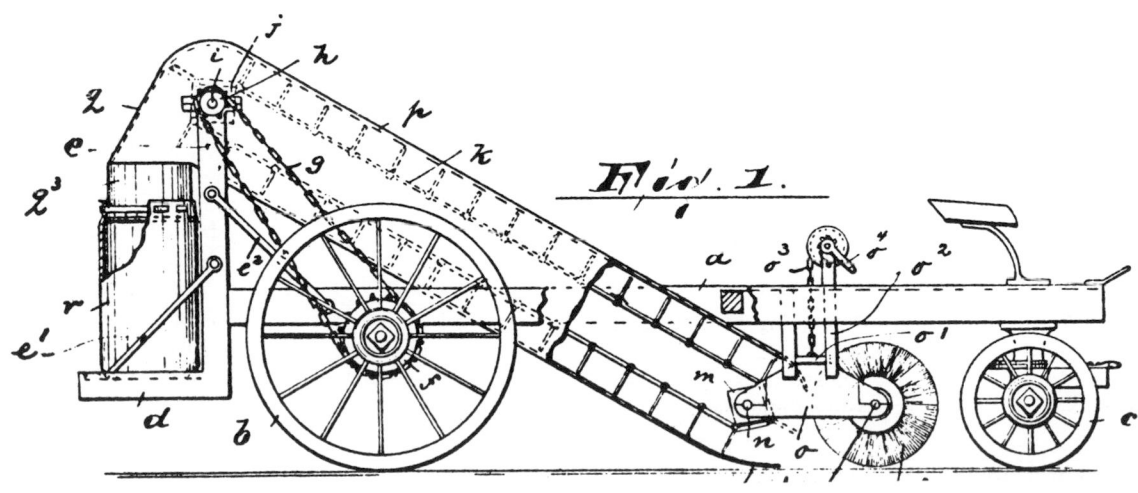

Inventor	Invention	Date	Patent
Dunnington, J. H.	Horse detachers	Mar. 16, 1897	578,979
Edmonds, T. H.	Separating screens	July 20, 1897	586,724
Elkins, T.	Dining, ironing table, and quilting frame combined	Feb. 22, 1870	100,020
Elkins, T.	Chamber commode	Jan. 9, 1872	122,518
Elkins, T.	Refrigerating apparatus	Nov. 4, 1879	221,222
Evans, J. H.	Convertible settees	Oct. 5, 1897	591,095
Faulkner, H.	Ventilated shoe	Apr. 29, 1890	426,495
Ferrell, F. J.	Steam trap	Feb. 11, 1890	420,993
Ferrell, F. J. [b]	Apparatus for melting snow	May 27, 1890	428,670
Fisher, D.	Joiners' clamp	Apr. 20, 1875	162,281
Fisher, D. C.	Furniture castor	Mar. 14, 1876	174,794
Flemming, F., Jr.	Guitar (variation)	Mar. 3, 1886	338,727
Forten, J.	Sail control	Mass. Newspaper 1850	
Goode, Sarah E.	Folding cabinet bed	July 14, 1885	322,177
Grant, G. F.	Golf tee	Dec. 12, 1899	638,920
Grant, W.	Curtain rod support	Aug. 4, 1896	565,075
Gray, R. H.	Bailing press	Aug. 28, 1894	525,203
Gray, R. H.	Cistern cleaners	Apr. 9, 1895	537,151
Gregory, J.	Motor	Apr. 26, 1887	361,937
Grenon, H.	Razor stropping device	Feb. 18, 1896	554,867
Griffin, F. W.	Pool table attachment	June 13, 1899	626,902
Gunn, S. W.	Boot or shoe (variation)	Jan. 16, 1900	641,642
Haines, J. H.	Portable basin	Sept. 28, 1897	590,833
Hammonds, J. F.	Apparatus for holding yarn skeins	Dec. 15, 1896	572,985
Harding, F. H.	Extension banquet table	Nov. 22, 1898	614,468
Hawkins, J.	Gridiron	Mar. 26, 1845	3,973
Hawkins, R.	Harness attachment	Oct. 4, 1887	370,943
Headen, M.	Foot power hammer	Oct. 5, 1886	350,363
Hearness, R.	Detachable car fender	July 4, 1899	628,003
Hilyer, A. F.	Water evaporator attachment for hot air registers	Aug. 26, 1890	435,095
Hilyer, A. F.	Registers	Oct. 14, 1890	438,159
Holmes, E. H.	Gage	Nov. 12, 1895	549,513
Hunter, J. H.	Portable weighing scales	Nov. 3, 1896	570,553
Hyde, R. N.	Composition for cleaning and preserving carpets	Nov. 6, 1888	392,205
Jackson, B. F.	Heating apparatus	Mar. 1, 1898	599,985
Jackson, B. F.	Matrix drying apparatus	May 10, 1898	603,879
Jackson, B. F.	Gas burner	Apr. 4, 1899	622,482
Jackson, H. A.	Kitchen table (variation)	Oct. 6, 1896	569,135
Jackson, W. H.	Railway switch	Mar. 9, 1897	578,641
Jackson, W. H.	Railway switch	Mar. 16, 1897	593,665
Jackson, W. H.	Automatic locking switch	Aug. 23, 1898	609,436
Johnson, D.	Rotary dining table	Jan. 15, 1888	396,089
Johnson, D.	Lawn mower attachment	Sept. 10, 1889	410,836
Johnson, D.	Grass receivers for lawn mowers	June 10, 1890	429,629
Johnson, I. R.	Bicycle frame	Oct. 10, 1899	634,823
Johnson, P.	Swinging chairs	Nov. 15, 1881	249,530
Johnson, P.	Eye protector	Nov. 2, 1880	234,039
Johnson, W.	Egg beater	Feb. 5, 1884	292,821
Johnson, W.	Velocipede	June 20, 1899	627,335
Johnson, W. A.	Paint vehicle	Dec. 4, 1888	393,763
Johnson, W. H.	Overcoming dead centers	Feb. 4, 1896	554,223
Johnson, W. H.	Overcoming dead centers	Oct. 11, 1898	612,345
Jones, F. M.	Ticket dispensing machine	June 27, 1939	2,163,754
Jones, F. M.	Air conditioning unit	July 12, 1949	2,475,841

[b] Ferrell also patented eight valves between 1890 and 1893.

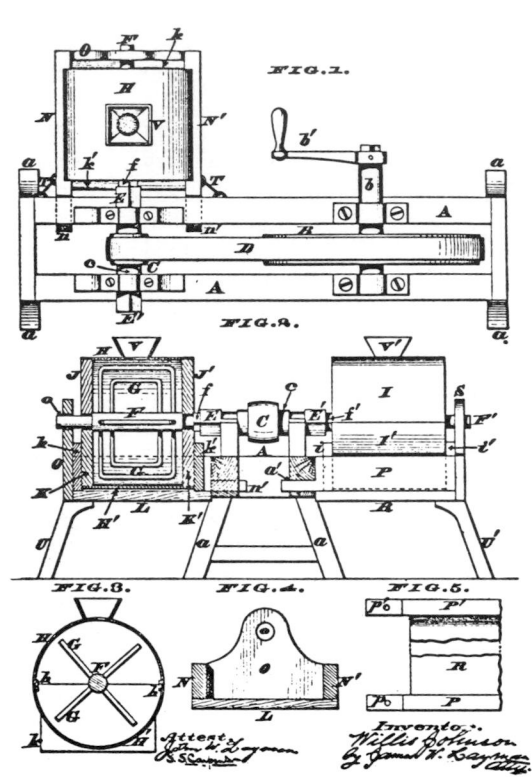

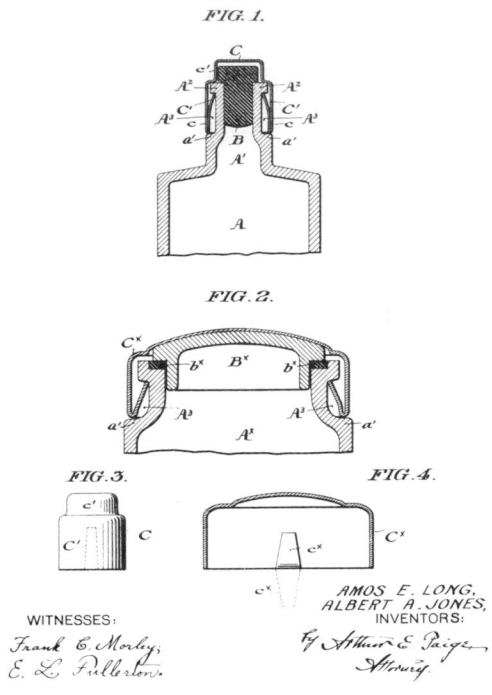

Inventor	Invention	Date	Patent
Jones, F. M.	Two-cycle gasoline engine	Nov. 28, 1950	2,523,273
Jones, F. M.	Starter generator	July 12, 1949	2,475,842
Jones, F. M.[a]	Thermostat and temperature control system	Feb. 23, 1960	2,926,005
Jones & Long	Caps for bottles	Sept. 13, 1898	610,715
Joyce, J. A.	Ore bucket	Apr. 26, 1898	603,143
Latimer, L. H.	Manufacturing carbons	June 17, 1882	252,386
Latimer, L. H.	Apparatus for cooling and disinfecting	Jan. 12, 1886	334,078
Latimer, L. H.	Locking racks for hats, coats, and umbrellas	Mar. 24, 1896	557,076
Latimer & Nichols	Electric lamp	Sept. 13, 1881	247,097
Latimer & Tregoning	Globe support for electric lamps	Mar. 21, 1882	255,212
Lavalette, W.	Printing press (variation)	Sept. 17, 1878	208,208
Lee, H.	Animal trap	Feb. 12, 1867	61,941
Lee, J.	Kneading machine	Aug. 7, 1894	524,042
Lee, J.	Bread crumbing machine	June 4, 1895	540,553
Leslie, F. W.	Envelope seal	Sept. 21, 1897	590,325
Lewis, A. L.	Window cleaner	Sept. 27, 1892	483,359
Lewis, E. R.	Spring gun	May 3, 1887	362,096
Linden, H.	Piano truck	Sept. 8, 1891	459,365
Little, E.	Bridle-bit	Mar. 7, 1882	254,666
Loudin, F. J.	Sash fastener	Dec. 12, 1892	510,432
Loudin, F. J.	Key fastener	Jan. 9, 1894	512,308
Love, J. L.	Plasterers' hawk	July 9, 1895	542,419
Love, J. L.	Pencil sharpener	Nov. 23, 1897	594,114
Marshall, T. J.	Fire extinguisher (variation)	May 26, 1872	125,063

[a] Jones also patented multiple devices related to gas engines and temperature control between 1939 and 1960.

Inventor	Invention	Date	Patent
Marshall, W.	Grain binder	May 11, 1886	341,599
Martin, W. A.	Lock	July 23, 1889	407,738
Martin, W. A.	Lock	Dec. 30, 1890	443,945
Matzeliger, J. E.	Mechanism for distributing tacks	Nov. 26, 1899	415,726
Matzeliger, J. E.	Nailing machine	Feb. 25, 1896	421,954
Matzeliger, J. E.	Tack separating mechanism	Mar. 25, 1890	423,937
Matzeliger, J. E.	Lasting machine	Sept. 22, 1891	459,899
McCoy, E.	Lubricator for steam engines	July 2, 1872	129,843
McCoy, E.	Lubricator for steam engines	Aug. 6, 1872	130,305
McCoy, E.	Steam lubricator	Jan. 20, 1874	146,697
McCoy, E.	Ironing table	May 12, 1874	150,876
McCoy, E.	Steam cylinder lubricator	Feb. 1, 1876	173,032
McCoy, E.	Steam cylinder lubricator	July 4, 1876	179,585
McCoy, E.	Law sprinkler design	Sept. 26, 1899	631,549
McCoy, E.	Steam dome	June 16, 1885	320,354
McCoy, E.	Lubricator attachment	Apr. 19, 1887	361,435
McCoy, E.	Lubricator for safety valves	May 24, 1887	363,529
McCoy, E. [a]	Drip cup	Sept. 29, 1891	460,215
McCoy & Hodges	Lubricator	Dec. 24, 1889	418,139
McCree, D.	Portable fire escape	Nov. 11, 1890	440,322
Mendenhall, A.	Holder for driving reins	Nov. 28, 1899	637,811
Miles, A.	Elevator	Oct. 11, 1887	371,207
Mitchell, C. L.	Phoneterism	Jan 1, 1884	291,071
Mitchell, J. M.	Cheek row corn planter	Jan 16, 1900	641,462
Moody, W. U.	Game board design	May 11, 1897	27,046
Morehead, K.	Reel carrier	Oct. 6, 1896	568,916
Murray, G. W.	Combined furrow opener and stalk-knocker	Apr. 10, 1894	517,960
Murray, G. W.	Cultivator and marker	Apr 10, 1894	517,961
Murray, G. W.	Planter	June 5, 1894	520,887
Murray, G. W.	Cotton chopper	June 5, 1894	520,888
Murray, G. W.	Fertilizer distributor	June 5, 1894	520,889
Murray, G. W.	Planter	June 5, 1894	520,891
Murray, G. W.	Planter and fertilizer distributor reaper	June 5, 1894	520,892
Murray, W.	Attachment for bicycles	Jan 27, 1891	445,452
Nance, L.	Game apparatus	Dec. 1, 1891	464,035
Nash, H. H.	Life-preserving stool	Oct. 5, 1875	168,519
Newson, S.	Oil heater or cooker	May 22, 1894	520,188
Nichols & Latimer	Electric lamp (variation)	Sept. 13, 1881	247,097
Nickerson, W. J.	Mandolin and guitar attachment for pianos	June 27, 1899	627,739
O'Conner & Turner	Alarm for boilers	Aug. 25, 1896	566,612
O'Conner & Turner	Steam gage	Aug. 25, 1896	566,613
O'Conner & Turner	Alarm for coasts containing vessels	Feb. 8, 1898	598,572
Outlaw, J. W.	Alarm for coasts containing vessels	Feb. 8, 1898	598,572
Outlaw, J. W.	Horseshoes	Nov. 15, 1898	614,273
Perryman, F. R.	Caterers' tray table	Feb. 2, 1892	468,038
Peterson, H.	Attachment for lawn mowers	Apr. 30, 1889	402,189
Phelps, W. H.	Apparatus for washing vehicles	Mar. 23, 1897	579,242
Pickering, J. F.	Air ship	Feb. 20, 1900	643,975
Pickett, H.	Scaffold	June 30, 1874	152,511
Pinn, T. B.	File holder	Aug. 17, 1880	231,355
Polk, A. J.	Bicycle support	Apr. 14, 1896	558,103
Pugsley, A.	Blind stop	July 29, 1890	433,306
Purdy, W.	Device for sharpening edged tools	Oct. 27, 1896	570,337
Purdy, W.	Design for sharpening edged tools	Aug. 16, 1898	609,367
Purdy, W.	Device for sharpening edged tools	Aug. 1, 1899	630,106
Purdy & Peters	Design for spoons	Apr. 23, 1895	24,228

[a] In addition, McCoy held 16 different patents for lubricators designed between 1873 and 1899.

Inventor	Invention	Date	Patent
Purdy & Sadgwar	Folding chair	June 11, 1889	405,117
Purvis, W. B.	Bag fastener	Apr. 25, 1882	256,856
Purvis, W. B.	Hand stamp	Feb. 27, 1883	273,149
Purvis, W. B.	Fountain pen	Jan. 7, 1890	419,065
Purvis, W. B.	Electric railway (variation)	May 1, 1894	519,291
Purvis, W. B.	Magnetic car balancing device	May 21, 1895	539,542
Purvis, W. B. [a]	Electric railway switch	Aug. 17, 1897	588,176
Queen, W.	Guard for companion ways and hatches	Aug. 18, 1891	458,131
Ray, E. P.	Chair supporting device	Feb. 21, 1899	620,078
Ray, L. P.	Dust pan	Aug. 3, 1897	587,607
Reed, J. W.	Dough kneader and roller	Sept. 23, 1884	305,474
Reynolds, H. H.	Window ventilator for railroad cars	Apr. 3, 1883	275,271
Reynolds, H. H.	Safety gate for bridges	Oct. 7, 1890	437,937
Reynolds, R. R.	Nonrefillable bottle	May 2, 1899	624,092
Rhodes, J. B.	Water closets	Dec. 19, 1899	639,290
Richardson, A. C.	Hame fastener	Mar. 14, 1882	255,022
Richardson, A. C.	Churn	Feb. 17, 1891	466,470
Richardson, A. C.	Casket-lowering device	Nov. 13, 1894	529,311
Richardson, A. C.	Insect destroyer	Feb. 28, 1899	620,363
Richardson, A. C.	Bottle	Dec. 12, 1899	638,811
Richardson, W. H.	Cotton chopper	June 1, 1886	343,140
Richardson, W. H.	Child's carriage	June 18, 1889	405,599
Richardson, W. H.	Child's carriage	June 18, 1889	405,600
Richey, C. V.	Car coupling	June 15, 1897	584,650
Richey, C. V.	Railroad switch	Aug. 3, 1897	587,657
Richey, C. V.	Railroad switch	Oct. 26, 1897	592,448
Richey, C. V.	Fire escape bracket	Dec. 28, 1897	596,427
Richey, C. V.	Combined hammock and stretcher	Dec. 13, 1898	615,907
Rickman, A. L.	Overshoe	Feb. 8, 1898	598,816
Ricks, J.	Horseshoe	Mar. 30, 1886	338,781
Ricks. J.	Overshoes for horses	June 6, 1899	626,245
Rillieux, N.	Sugar refiner (evaporating pan)	Dec. 10, 1846	4,879
Robinson, E. R.	Electric railway trolley	Sept. 19, 1893	505,370
Robinson, E. R.	Casting composite	Nov. 23, 1897	594,386
Robinson, J. H.	Lifesaving guards for locomotives	Mar. 14, 1899	621,143
Robinson, J. H.	Lifesaving guards for street cars	Apr. 25, 1899	623,929
Robinson, J.	Dinner pail	Feb. 1, 1887	356,852
Romain, A.	Passenger register	Apr. 23, 1889	402,035
Ross, A. L.	Runner for stops	Aug. 4, 1896	565,301
Ross, A. L.	Bag closure	June 7, 1898	605,343
Ross, A. L.	Trousers support	Nov. 28, 1899	638,068
Ross, J.	Bailing press	Sept. 5, 1899	632,539
Roster, D. N.	Feather curler	Mar. 10, 1896	556,166
Ruffin, S.	Vessels for liquids and manner of sealing	Nov. 20, 1899	737,603
Russell, L. A.	Guard attachment for beds	Aug. 13, 1895	544,381
Sampson, G. T.	Sled propeller	Feb. 17, 1885	312,388
Sampson, G. T.	Clothes drier	June 7, 1892	476,416
Scottron, S. R.	Adjustable window cornice	Feb. 17, 1880	224,732
Scottron, S. R.	Cornice	Jan. 16, 1883	270,851
Scottron, S. R.	Pole tip	Sept. 21, 1886	349,525
Scottron, S. R.	Curtain rod	Aug. 30, 1892	481,720
Scottron, S. R.	Supporting bracket	Sept. 12, 1893	505,008
Shanks, S. C.	Sleeping car berth register	July 21, 1897	587,165
Shewcraft, Frank	Letter box		Detroit, Mich.
Shorter, D. W.	Feed rack	May 17, 1887	363,089

[a] Purvis also patented 10 paper bag machines between 1884 and 1894.

Inventor	Invention	Date	Patent
Smith, J. W.	Improvement in games	Apr. 17, 1900	647,887
Smith, J. W.	Lawn sprinkler	May 4, 1897	581,785
Smith, J. W.	Lawn sprinkler	Mar. 22, 1898	601,065
Smith, P. D.	Potato digger	Jan. 21, 1891	445,206
Smith, P.D.	Grain binder	Feb. 23, 1892	469,279
Snow & Johns	Liniment	Oct. 7, 1890	437,728
Spears, H.	Portable shield for infantry	Dec. 27, 1870	110,599
Spikes, R. B.	Combination milk bottle opener and bottle cover	June 29, 1926	1,590,557
Spikes, R. B.	Method and apparatus for obtaining average samples and temperature of tank liquids	Oct. 27, 1931	1,828,753
Spikes, R. B.	Automatic gear shift	Dec. 6, 1932	1,889,814
Spikes, R. B.	Transmission and shifting thereof	Nov. 28, 1933	1,936,996
Spikes, R. B.	Self-locking rack for billiard cues	around 1910	not found
Spikes, R. B.	Automatic shoeshine chair	around 1939	not found
Spikes, R. B.	Multiple barrel machine gun	around 1940	not found
Standard, J.	Oil stove	Oct. 29, 1889	413,689
Standard, J.	Refrigerator	July 14, 1891	455,891
Stewart, E. W.	Punching machine	May 3, 1887	362,190
Stewart, E. W.	Machine for forming vehicle seat bars	Mar. 22, 1887	373,698
Stewart, T. W.	Mop	June 13, 1893	499,402
Stewart, T. W.	Station indicator	June 20, 1893	499,895
Stewart & Johnson	Metal bending machine	Dec. 27, 1887	375,512
Sutton, E. H.	Cotton cultivator	Apr. 7, 1878	149,543
Sweeting, J. A.	Device for rolling cigarettes	Nov. 30, 1897	594,501
Sweeting, J. A.	Combined knife and scoop	June 7, 1898	605,209
Taylor, B. H.	Rotary engine	Apr. 23, 1878	202,888
Taylor, B. H.	Slide valve	July 6, 1897	585,798
Temple, L.	Toggle harpoon	1848	
Thomas, S. E.	Waste trap	Oct. 16, 1883	286,746
Thomas, S. E.	Waste trap for basins, closets, etc.	Oct. 4, 1887	371,107
Thomas, S. E.	Casting	July 31, 1888	386,941
Thomas, S. E.	Pipe connection	Oct. 9, 1888	390,821
Toliver, George	Propeller for vessels	Apr. 28, 1891	451,086
Tregoning & Latimer	Globe supporter for electric lamps	Mar. 21, 1882	255,212
Walker, Peter	Machine for cleaning seed cotton	Feb. 16, 1897	577,153
Walker, Peter	Bait holder	Mar. 8, 1898	600,241
Waller, J. N.	Shoemaker's cabinet or bench	Feb. 3, 1880	224,253
Washington, Wade	Corn husking machine	Aug. 14, 1883	283,173
Watkins, Isaac	Scrubbing frame	Oct. 7, 1890	437,849
Watts, J. R.	Bracket for miners' lamp	Mar. 7, 1893	493,137
West, E. H.	Weather shield	Sept. 5, 1899	632,385
West, J. W.	Wagon	Oct. 18, 1870	108,419
White, D. L.	Extension steps for cars	Jan. 12, 1897	574,969
White, J. T.	Lemon squeezer	Dec. 8, 1896	572,849
Williams, Carter	Canopy frame	Feb. 2, 1892	468,280
Williams, J. P.	Pillow sham holder	Oct. 10, 1899	634,784
Winn, Frank	Direct acting steam engine	Dec. 4, 1888	394,047
Winters, J. R.	Fire escape ladder	May 7, 1878	203,517
Winters, J. R.	Fire escape ladder	Apr. 8, 1879	214,224
Woods, G. T.	Steam boiler furnace	June 3, 1884	299,894
Woods, G. T.	Telephone transmitter (variation)	Dec. 2, 1884	3,088,176
Woods, G. T.	Apparatus for transmission of messages by electricity	Apr. 7, 1885	315,368
Woods, G. T.	Relay instrument	June 7, 1887	364,619
Woods, G. T.	Polarized relay	July 5, 1887	366,192
Woods, G. T.	Electromechanical brake	Aug. 16, 1887	368,265
Woods, G. T.	Telephone system and apparatus	Oct. 11, 1887	371,241
Woods, G. T.	Electromagnetic brake apparatus	Oct. 18, 1887	371,655

Inventor	Invention	Date	Patent
Woods, G. T.	Railway telegraphy	Nov. 15, 1887	373,383
Woods, G. T.	Induction telegraph system	Nov. 29, 1887	373,915
	Overhead conducting system for electric railway	May 29, 1888	383,844
Woods, G. T.	Electromotive railway system	June 26, 1888	385,034
Woods, G. T.	Tunnel construction for electric railway	July 17, 1888	386,282
Woods, G. T.	Galvanic battery	Aug. 14, 1888	387,839
Woods, G. T.	Railway telegraphy	Aug. 28, 1888	388,803
Woods, G. T.	Automatic safety cut-out for electric circuits	Jan. 1, 1889	395,533
Woods, G. T.	Automatic safety cut-out for electric circuits	Oct. 14, 1889	438,590
Woods, G. T.	Electric railway system	Nov. 10, 1891	463,020
Woods, G. T.	Electric railway supply system	Oct. 31, 1893	507,606
Woods, G. T.	Electric railway conduit	Nov. 21, 1893	509,065
Woods, G. T.	System of electrical distribution	Oct. 13, 1896	569,443
Woods, G. T.	Amusement apparatus	Dec. 19, 1899	639,692
Wormley, James	Lifesaving apparatus	May 24, 1881	242,091

THE BLACK ENTERTAINER IN THE PERFORMING ARTS

Early American Theater ■ Blackface and Minstrelsy ■ Post-Civil War Theater Groups ■ Serious Drama ■ The Renaissance ■ The 1930s to the Present ■ Black Theater Companies ■ Famous Entertainers

The black contribution to the world of American entertainment has been powerful, personal, and profound. The black presence has been felt to a degree far greater than could normally be expected, given the clear population minority blacks represent and the barely peripheral place which American society often provides them. Nonetheless, much of what the world at large considers uniquely American in the performing arts can be traced directly to black performers and their heritage.

For more than a century, the most formidable obstacle faced by black entertainers was that they were often excluded—both as spectator and participant—from those public places of entertainment which are the logical training ground for any performer. Nevertheless, from the earliest days of slavery, entertainment was one of the few avenues of expression open to blacks.

In the book *Black Magic*, Langston Hughes and Milton Meltzer document that the "first stage for the captive Africans was the open deck of a slave ship. There, on the way to the Americas, blacks in chains, when herded up on deck for exercise, were forced to sing and dance in the open air for the amusement of the crew." After reaching the southern plantations, the African traditions, rhythms, and dances that had survived the cultural transplantation combined with a developing folk tradition to form the basis for black American entertainment. Drawings, paintings, and patches of oral history depict the rich folklore which provided virtually the only entertainment and means of self-expression for black slaves.

As singers, dancers, or bones players, slaves were often called upon to perform for their masters and, if talented enough, were even hired out by them to entertain others. Numerous newspaper advertisements for slave entertainers of the antebellum period can be found in *Readings in Black American Music* by Eileen Southern. Best remembered of the slave entertainers is Blind Tom, a talented pianist, whose many concerts in the United States and Europe won fame for himself and profit for Colonel Bethune, his owner. Blind Tom's story has been dramatized by Theodore Ward in the musical *Charity*.

Slaves also used the medium of religious songs (considered "safe" by the masters) to express their dissatisfaction with their lot. In this fashion, "Go Down Moses," "Oh Freedom," "God's Gonna Cut You Down," and many other spirituals have become part of the vast oral tradition created by the black musical artist. After the Civil War, the Fisk Jubilee Singers extended the realm of the Negro spiritual to the international arena by going on a tour of Europe with "Negro" music as the basis of their repertoire.

Tribal music and dances kept alive on colonial plantations gradually blended into Afro-American culture.

European Traditions

While blacks were beginning to build up Afro-American culture in the fields and slave shacks of plantations, the American theater was still growing from European roots. This cultural lag showed itself in a peculiar, unnatural conception of blacks on the stage.

From the role of the black magus in the medieval plays to Othello on the Elizabethan stage, the black was most often presented as the "noble Moor." Shakespeare himself believed that Moors were Negroes, even without scientific verification. His investiture of Othello with the alleged personal attributes and moral characteristics of "the Negroes" of Elizabethan England was by no means accidental, nor was it even an unusual dramatic license for Shakespeare.

Othello was followed, in 1696, by *Oroonoko,* a tragedy in five acts written by Thomas Southerne. The hero was an African prince stolen from Angola during the reign of Charles II and sold as a slave in the West Indies. The "noble Moor" image was dying, fading into another stereotype. On stage, Oroonoko had black skin and woolly hair, spoke in the stilted blank verse of the period, and showed more traits assignable to the buffoon than to an African prince.

Another stage black of dubious authenticity was Mungo, slave hero of the comic opera *The Padlock.* The stage role was at least played by an Englishman who had studied the manners and dialect of the black man he was trying to impersonate. However, the writing reflected little real contact with any black cultural

context. The result was that Mungo was a further step in the development of the low stereotype. This stereotype was given a powerful expression in the character Friday, in *Robinson Crusoe,* who is portrayed as having no options other than remaining a low-born savage or becoming a contented, ignorant servant.

This poor fellow was the chief black image imported to the American theater. Apparently the first black character in an American play appeared in *The Disappointment: or, The Force of Credulity* in 1767. The character, a comic stereotype, was named "Raccoon." From these beginnings the history of blacks in the American theater can be seen as two centuries of progress in replacing stereotypes with the real thing.

Early American Theater

In the United States, references to the black actor are rare in any setting prior to 1821. A unique handbill of "The African Company," at "The Theatre in Mercer Street, in the rear of the 1 Mile Stone, Broadway," refers to two dramatic offerings: *Tom and Jerry* and *Obi, or Three Fingered Jack.* These are believed to be the only traces of a company of black amateurs who played in New York about 1820 or 1821.

At the same epoch New York City was host to the foundation of the African Grove Theatre. Little is known about the origins of this important theater. One Henry Brown wrote *King Shotaway,* generally recognized as the first drama by a black man in the United States. Brown is also credited with founding

FAMOUS CANADIAN JUBILEE SINGERS

MALE QUARTETTE, PLANTATION LULLABIES.

Talented black performers like the Canadian Jubilee Singers were internationally famous in the last century

the African Grove. This black-operated theater was one of only four theaters (the other three were white operated) that existed in New York City before 1830. During the early 1820s, this house presented regular performances by the famous tragedians James Hewlitt, from the West Indies, and Ira Aldridge. Unfortunately, hostile white audiences, segregated into the back of the auditorium, caused disturbances that eventually forced the theater to close. By 1824 Ira Aldridge, one of the great Shakespearean actors of the nineteenth century, had gauged there was no future for his talents in the Americas and left for Europe, where he enjoyed a highly successful career, his most memorable role being Othello, for which he received numerous royal awards.

Blackface and Minstrelsy

Comic roles were the forte of the white-turned-black actor. In 1823, at the Globe Theatre in Cincinnati, Edwin Forrest played a black in a farce called *The Tailor in Distress,* singing and dancing, and winning the praise from a black onlooker that he was indeed

"nigger all over." Other eminent American actors who donned blackface include "Sol" Smith and Bernard Flaherty. In 1850, when Edwin Booth was 17, and a year after his debut at the Boston Museum, he gave an entertainment with a friend at the courthouse in Belair, Maryland. Along with selections from *Richelieu* and *Julius Caesar,* they also sang, with blackened faces, a number of Negro melodies, "using appropriate dialogue," as Mrs. Asia Booth Clarke records in the memoirs of her brother. Ralph Keeler is among the most prominent of the stage Negroes of later years. His *Three Years a Negro Minstrel,* first published in the *Atlantic Monthly* for July 1869, is instructive reading, and gives an excellent idea of the wandering minstrel of that period.

Thomas D. Rice, though not the originator, was the man who made so-called Ethiopian minstrelsy popular on both sides of the Atlantic. The history of "Jim Crow Rice," as he was affectionately called for many years, was recounted with particular vividness in the columns of the *New York Times,* June 5, 1881. Back of the Louisville theater was a livery stable kept by a man named Crow. The actors could look into the stable yard from the windows of their dressing rooms and were fond of watching the movements of an old and decrepit slave who was employed by the proprietor to do odd jobs. The slave, who called himself Jim Crow, was physically deformed—the right shoulder was drawn up high, and the left leg was stiff and crooked at the knee. As he walked with his painful, but at the same time ludicrous, limp, he was in the habit of crooning an old tune, to which he had applied words of his own. At the end of each verse he gave a peculiar step, "rocking de heel" in the manner that has since become so general among the long generations of his delineators. The words of his refrain were as follows:

> Wheel about, turn about
> Do jis so,
> An' ebery time I wheel about
> I jump Jim Crow.

Rice closely watched this unconscious performer, and recognized in him a character entirely new to the stage. He wrote a number of verses, quickened and slightly changed the air (made up exactly like the original), and appeared before a Louisville audience, which reportedly went mad with delight, recalling him on the first night at least 20 times. And so Jim Crow, reinforcing the image of the black buffoon, jumped into the dramatic pantheon.

Rice aside, the first band of black minstrels was organized in the boardinghouse of Mrs. Brooks, in Catherine Street, New York, late in the winter of 1842,

White minstrels caricatured blacks and black music in the period from 1830 to 1860. From left are George Christy, Charley White, and T. D. Rice (the original "Jim Crow").

and it consisted of "Dan" Emmet, "Frank" Brower, "Billy" Whitlock, and "Dick" Pelham. They opened at the Chatham Theatre, New York, on February 17, 1843, and later toured other American cities before going on to Europe. Not until after the Civil War did black performers begin appearing regularly in minstrel shows, and then usually under the supervision of white managers.

What the review of minstrelsy indicates is that, although much credit was due to the minstrel, the basic popularity was dependent on the black melody he introduced and on the characteristic bones, banjo, and tambourine upon which he accompanied himself. It was certainly the song, not the singer, which once moved Thackeray to write:

I heard a humorous balladist not long since, a minstrel with wool on his head and an ultra-Ethiopian complexion, who performed a Negro ballad that I confess moistened these spectacles in a most unexpected manner. I have gazed at thousands of tragedy queens dying on the stage and expiring in appropriate blank-verse, and I never wanted to wipe them. They have looked up, be it said, at many scores of clergymen without being dimmed; and behold, a vagabond with a corked face and a banjo sings a little song, strikes a wild note, which sets the heart thrilling with happy pity.

Despite Joel Chandler Harris' contention that he'd never seen a banjo in the hands of a black on any of the plantations of middle Georgia, there is much evidence of the instrument's popularity. George Washington Cable, in a pre-Civil War work, quotes a popular Creole ditty in which "Musieu Bainjo" is mentioned

in every line; Maurice Thompson says the banjo is a common instrument among the field hands in North Georgia, Alabama, and Tennessee, and describes a rude banjo manufactured by its "dusky" performer out of a flat gourd, strung with horsehair. In Jefferson's *Notes on Virginia,* printed in 1784, the following statement is worthy of note: "In music they [the blacks] are more generally gifted than the whites with accurate ears for tune and time, and they have been found capable of imagining a small catch." In a footnote, Jefferson adds: "The instrument proper to them is the banjar, which they brought hither from Africa."

After the Civil War—Black Theater Groups

After the war, blacks formed their own groups, among them the Charles Hicks Georgia Minstrels and Lew Johnson's Plantation Minstrel Company. These groups copied their white counterparts' style of blackened face with red and white lines around the mouth. Audiences were usually segregated—whites on one side, blacks on the other. The important thing, however, was that black people had finally achieved a tenuous access to the American stage. Among the best known of these black minstrels was William C. Handy, who joined the W. A. Mahara Minstrels in 1896.

Female choruses were added to the previously all-male shows before the turn of the century. An example was *The Creole Show* (1891). When Bob Cole's *A Trip to Coontown* combined music with plotline in 1898, the black American musical was born. Cole worked with Sissieretta Jones in conceiving *Black Patti's Trou-*

Blackface minstrel troupes gave their audiences music and dances "borrowed" from blacks mixed with racist comedy routines.

badours, which toured widely to great acclaim. *Clorindy—The Origin of the Cakewalk,* with book by Paul Laurence Dunbar and music by Will Marion Cook, was a smash hit at New York's Casino Roof Garden.

These black minstrel shows flourishing in the mid- and late 1800s usually carried bands consisting of only four instruments, tambourine, bones, fiddle, and banjo. These were the first black theater orchestras. At the beginning of this century black bands frequently traveled with carnivals, tent shows, and vaudeville companies. At the turn of the century and into the 1920s and 1930s black pit orchestras were popular as was black theater. This situation changed in the 1940s and 1950s when black musicians were employed in the theater only occasionally, and then only under pressure.

Ragtime

The ragtime musical took a long stride closer to Broadway. In the shows of the Williams and Walker Com-

pany, this novel style of music flashed across the New York stage. Of all the Williams and Walker shows, from *Sons of Ham* through *Abyssinia* and *Bandanna Land,* the most successful was *In Dahomey,* which featured the work of Will Marion Cook, Paul Laurence Dunbar, and Jesse Shipp. This show toured both the United States and Europe following its first production in 1903.

The first decade of this century saw the heyday of black musicals and vaudeville. Minstrelsy disappeared from the professional circuit. Unfortunately, George Walker's ill health led to the dissolving of the company. Bert Williams left to join the Follies in 1911. When Walker died a year later, another epoch in black theater history ended.

The cakewalk, the dance that had become an American craze by the turn of the century, was derived from the blacks' "chalk-line" walk, which they had presented at the 1876 celebration of the Centennial of American Independence in Philadelphia.

First Serious Themes

Besides the wealth of light musicals, the early 1900s witnessed the beginnings of serious black theater. The first attempts met with little public support. Scott Joplin wrote an opera, *Treemonisha,* in 1915, but could not find a producer, although friends backed it for a one-night run. In the 1970s when the musical score for *The Sting* was adapted from his compositions and *Treemonisha* became a hit on Broadway, Joplin finally received his due. The themes of lynching and racial injustice were addressed by Angela Grimké's *Rachel* in a 1916 NAACP production. Although the play received attention and sparked controversy, the production was not a success.

THEATRE,

IN MERCER STREET,
In the rear of the 1 Mile Stone.
Broadway.
African Company.
Saturday Evening, June 7th,

Will be presented with new Scenery prepared expressly for this Piece
the Musical Extravaganza of

Tom & Jerry,
Or, Life in London.

Got up under the Direction of Mr, Brown.
Scene I.

Life in the Country.

Corinthian Tom,	Mr, Williams
Jerry Hawthorn	Jackson

Life on Foot

Logic,	Mr, Bates
Tommy Green	Mr, Jackson

Life on Horse Back.

Honorable Dick Trifle	Mr. Matthews
Gallton ,	Mr, Bates

Life in Fancy.

Cap	Mr, Dusenberry
Primrose	Mr, Jackson
Miss Tartan	Miss Peterson
Jane	Miss Johnson

Life in the Dark.

Watchman	Mrs. Smith
Dusty Bob	Mr, Johnson

Life in Rags,

Crib	Mr, Wilson
African Sal	Mr, Jackson

Life in Bond Street,

Cats	Miss Davis
Sue	Miss Foot

Life in Wapping

Mr, Davis	Miss Johnson

In The course of the Evening an additional Scene

Life in Limbo—Life in Love.

VANGO RANGE in Charleston

On the Slave Market.

Slaves	By the Company
Auctioneer	Mr, Smith

In the Course of the Evening a variety of

Songs & Dances.

The whole to conclude with the Pantomime of

OBI:
Or, Three Finger'd Jack.

Obi,	Mr. Bates	Planter,	Mr. Johnson.
	Planter's Wife,	-	Miss Hicks.

Box Tickets 75 Cents, Pit. 50, Cents, Gallery 37 1-2.

On MONDAY Evening next,
Tom & Jerry, or. *Life in New-York,*
With an Additional Scene,
Life in Fulton-market!!!
And FORTUNE'S FROLIC.

On April 5, 1917 the production of three one-act plays by poet Ridgely Torrance, with music conducted and performed by blacks, marked "the first time anywhere in the United States for black actors in the dramatic theater to command the serious attention of the critics, the general press, and public."

The Renaissance

During World War I, small houses kept alive the spirit of black theater, preparing the way for the great Renaissance of the 1920s when hundreds of theaters sprang up all around the country. Some were simple movie houses which offered live entertainment at intermission; others were tent shows nostalgically clinging to the minstrel tradition. Many of them were eventually organized into the T.O.B.A. (Theatre Owners Booking Association), which operated into the beginning of the Great Depression. With member theaters across the country, including the Howard in Washington, D.C. and the Booker T. in St. Louis, T.O.B.A. provided work for many black actors and performers.

Harlem's Lafayette Theatre first received wide notice for its 1915 production of Miller and Lyles' *Darkydom.* In 1919 Anita Bush joined with Charles Gilpin to form the Lafayette Players, a touring company which enjoyed many successes. A year later Gilpin became famous for his creation of the role of Brutus Jones in Eugene O'Neill's *Emperor Jones,* and Bush went on to form her own stock company.

Russell and Rowena Jelliffe, white social workers devoted to integrated theater, founded Cleveland's Karamu Theatre in 1916.

The Twenties

The "Negro" or "Harlem" Renaissance, which reached its peak in the 1920s, was an era of general harvest in black arts. This was the time of Howard philosopher Alain Locke's "New Negro" movement, Carter Woodson founded the Association for the Study of Negro Life and History, and, throughout the nation, artists' groups, theater groups, and writers' workshops came together, gelled, and produced. Every aspect of theater was touched by the energies of the Renaissance.

The early 1920s saw the growth and success of the Ethiopian Art Players, founded in Chicago. In 1923 this company brought the production of Willis Richardson's *Chip Woman's Fortune* to New York City. Two years later, Garland Anderson's *Appearances* be-

A company of black amateurs performed in New York City around 1820.

came the first full-length drama by a black playwright to reach Broadway.

From the ragtime rhythms of the Williams and Walker era came musicals which imaginatively combined jazz and ragtime themes. The team of Miller and Lyles, starting at the Lafayette Theatre, joined with Noble Sissle and Eubie Blake. Together, they created *Shuffle Along,* one of the most popular shows in American theater since 1900. In 1921 *Shuffle Along* came to the Howard Theatre in Washington, D.C., for two weeks, then opened at the 63rd Street Theatre in New York City, and went on to become an international success. Josephine Baker was catapulted to stardom in a cast full of notables, including Florence Mills and Caterina Jarboro on stage and William Grant Still and Hall Johnson in the orchestra. All became famous in their own right.

With the success of this production, a new genre was adopted, and other shows followed the style and format of *Shuffle Along.* Sissle and Blake went on to produce *Chocolate Dandies;* Miller and Lyles came out with *Runnin' Wild, Keep Shufflin',* and *Rang Tang.*

In 1924 Paul Robeson opened in O'Neill's *All God's Chillun Got Wings.* A controversy ensued, but the play had its clear effect: Rose McClendon, Abbie Mitchell, Jules Bledsoe, and Frank Wilson were cast in white playwright Paul Green's *In Abraham's Bosom,* which won the Pulitzer Prize.

The twenties was a great period for black musicals. Lew Leslie's *Blackbirds of 1928* starred the famous singer and dancer Bill Robinson. *Blackbirds of 1929* had music by Eubie Blake. Across the country the Renaissance spirit was manifest in many community-oriented productions.

Harlem was an oasis of black theater. The Crescent Theatre, the Lincoln Theatre, as well as the Lafayette and the Harlem Experimental Theatre in 1928, preceded and encouraged the Negro Art Theatre, Harlem Community Players, and the Dunbar Garden Players.

Elsewhere in America, W.E.B. DuBois had founded the Krigwa Players, sponsored by *Crisis* magazine, with member groups in various cities. The Krigwas mostly performed one-act plays. Among great playwrights they produced were Georgia Douglass Johnson, Willis Richardson, and Eulalie Spence.

Richardson and May Miller were invited by Carter Woodson to write plays for Negro History Week, which was organized in part by playwright and educational theater proponent Randolph Edmonds. Richardson eventually published *Plays and Pageants from the Life of the Negro* and, with May Miller (Sullivan), *Negro History in Thirteen Plays.*

In sum, the creative energy of the Renaissance fed three very positive developments: the creation of the

Sensational Florence Mills, acclaimed as the leading black entertainer of her time.

new musicals, the growth of black drama, and the expansion of the historical-educational theater movement.

The Thirties

In the early 1930s, there was a brief reversion. Black professional theater work was limited to stereotyped roles in plays and films by white writers, such as *Green Pastures* by Marc Connelly. By the middle of the decade, however, black theater was reasserting itself. Langston Hughes' *Mulatto* went to Broadway with Rose McClendon in the lead. Hall Johnson's musical *Run Little Chillun* was well received. In 1935 Dick Campbell joined forces with Rose McClendon to form the Negro People's Theatre, which enjoyed some early successes but came unstuck after the death of McClendon. Many of the members moved on to the Negro Unit of the Federal Theatre Project.

Founded under the sponsorship of the Works Progress Administration (WPA), the Negro Unit became the primary source of employment for black theater workers. The Lafayette Theatre was the core of the East Coast movement, with shows such as Orson Welles' *Macbeth,* cast in a Haitian setting. Other productions included William Dubois' *Haiti,* Frank Wilson's *Walk Together, Children,* and *Meek Moses,* and Rudolph Fisher's *The Conjure Man Dies.* In California, Clarence Muse directed Hall Johnson's *Run Little Chillun,* and in Seattle, the Federal Theatre performed Theodore Browne's *Natural Man.* When Congress cut off federal funds in 1939, the work stopped.

Independent community theaters fought for their lives during the Depression. The Harlem Suitcase Theatre was one. Founded by Langston Hughes and Louise Patterson in 1937, it opened with Hughes' *Don't You Want To Be Free?* This theater lasted just two years. Hughes then sought to spread his idea of a Negro People's Theatre by founding the New Negro Theatre (1939) in Los Angeles.

Dick Campbell and Muriel Rahn formed the Rose McClendon Players in the late 1930s. The group variously featured Canada Lee, Dooley Wilson, Frederick O'Neal, Ossie Davis, Ruby Dee, and Maxwell Glanville. Early productions included *Goodbye Again* by Arthur Kobers and *Having a Wonderful Time.* Moving to the 124th Street Library basement, the Rose McClendon Workshop Theatre opened officially in 1939 with Abram Hill's *On Strivers' Row.* The show was a big hit and has been revived frequently.

The Forties

The American Negro Theatre (ANT) was formed in Harlem in 1940 by Abram Hill, Frederick O'Neal, and former members of the McClendon Players. ANT produced Hill's *On Strivers' Row* and *Walk Hard,* Theodore Brown's *Natural Man,* and Owen Dodson's *The Garden of Time.* Subsequently, Hill adapted *Anna Lucasta* for ANT presentation. The cast included Hilda Simms, Fred O'Neal, Alice Childress, Alvin Childress, and Earle Hyman. By the time *Anna Lucasta* reached Broadway in 1944, where it was destined to remain nearly three years, the cast variously included the talents of Canada Lee, Ossie Davis, Ruby Dee, and Frank Silvera. Despite its apparent success and support, ANT survived only a few years, the stresses of World War II playing a large part in its downfall.

Paul Robeson's portrayal of Othello, in the longest run a Shakespearean play has ever received in America, is often considered the peak of his prodigious career. Theodore Ward, one of America's leading playwrights, came out with two dramas in the late forties. His *Big White Fog* was produced as part of the Negro Playwrights' Company, and featured Canada Lee. In 1947 his *Our Lan'* reached the Broadway stage, but the script had been fatally watered down by director Eddie Dowling, and the play never received the acclaim it deserved.

Canada Lee electrified Broadway in Native Son.

By the end of the decade, many black actors and writers were among the casualties of the "Red Scare." The blacklisting of Paul Robeson and Canada Lee epitomized the outrage.

The Fifties

These years are noted for the formation of small production companies and for little black activity on Broadway. But between the Committee for the Negro in the Arts, founded in 1951, and Lorraine Hansberry's award-winning *Raisin in the Sun* in 1959, many worthy productions were staged.

William Branch's *Medal for Willie* had its first production (1951) by the Committee. The play had a successful run, but elicited controversial reactions from both whites and blacks. Branch himself was inducted into the Army the day after the show opened. An earlier production of the Committee, Alice Childress' *Just a Little Simple,* adapted from Langston Hughes' *Simple Speaks His Mind* columns, opened at the Club Baron in the fall of 1950, but had only a short run.

Two companies successful in this period were Roger Furman's Negro Art Players and the Group formed by Maxville Glanville and Julian Mayfield. Both came to the stage in 1952. The Negro Art Players did such productions as Furman's *The Quiet Laughter,* T. Williams' *Mooney's Kids Don't Cry,* and Charles Griffin's *Oklahoma Bearcat.* Mayfield and Glanville opened with one-acts: *A World Full of Men* and *The Other Foot* by Mayfield, and Ossie Davis' *Alice in Wonder.* In 1953 Davis rewrote this one-act into *The Big Deal,* presented at the New Playwrights Theatre.

Louis Peterson's *Take a Giant Step* reached Broadway in 1953 with Frederick O'Neal, Pauline Meyers, Frank Wilson, and Louis Gossett's debut. Though favorably reviewed, the production suffered from empty seats and shortly died. It was revived three years later, off-Broadway, with Bill Gunn, Beah Richards, and Godfrey Cambridge.

In downtown Manhattan, the Greenwich Mews Theatre helped black theater survive the fifties. William Branch's *In Splendid Error* had a 1954 showing. The same year saw a production of Alice Childress' *Trouble in Mind*, starring Clarice Taylor and Hilda Simms. In 1957 Loften Mitchell's *Land Beyond the River* ran nearly a year, featuring, at various times, Diana Sands, Charles Griffin, Ivan Dixon, Douglas Turner Ward, and Roscoe Lee Brown.

Lorraine Hansberry's tragically short career flowered in 1959 when *Raisin in the Sun* reached New York after several small northeastern productions. The cast eventually included Ossie Davis, Diana Sands, Ruby Dee, and Sidney Poitier. Hansberry was awarded the Drama Critics' Circle Award.

The Sixties

These years were a complex, uneven, and fertile period for black drama. A curious and tragic ambivalence affected both the artist and the actor, for the success of being courted in public by the foundations was played out against the backdrop of aborted lives and insufficient social change.

At the onset of the 1960s, black playwright Loften Mitchell reflected on the situation of his peers with some optimism, noting that such fellow playwrights as William Branch, Alice Childress, Louis Peterson, Theodore Ward, Langston Hughes, Gertrude Jeanette, Harold Holifield, Charles Sebree, and Lorraine Hansberry were either in production or the beneficiaries of critical acclaim. Within six years, the burst of promise had shriveled into despair. Lorraine Hansberry was dead after her second play, *The Sign in Sidney Brustein's Window*, had opened to mixed reviews; William Branch's *Wreath for Udomo* was performed successfully in Cleveland, but found little sympathy on the English stage; Alice Childress withdrew her *Trouble in Mind* when she grew disillusioned over hot-then-cold producers; Julian Mayfield's *417* found few dedicated backers; Louis Peterson suffered a heart attack and needed six months to recuperate. Loften Mitchell, though he produced (*Tell Pharaoh* and *Ballad of the Winter Soldiers*), had become mistrustful. The difficulties were not strictly racial, but they were not totally divorced from racial alienation either.

The early sixties, swelling to the climax of the Civil Rights movement, had been a time of idealism and activism. *Fly Blackbird*, with book by James V. Hatch and music by C. Bernard Jackson, gives a lively musical portrayal of this era. The cast opening at the Metro Theatre in Los Angeles in 1961 included Micki Grant, Josie Dotson, Thelma Oliver, Camille Billops, George Takei, and Russ Ellis. The New York run, adding Avon Long to the cast, opened in 1962 to critical acclaim and won the Obie Award for best musical off-Broadway. Though it was not financially rewarding, Ossie Davis' 1961 *Purlie Victorious* was another of the era's optimistic hits.

By the time Adrienne Kennedy's *Funnyhouse of a Negro* opened at the Circle-in-the-Square (1963), integrationist ideals had begun to surrender to more nationalist politics, such as those eloquently dramatized by Imamu Amiri Baraka (then LeRoi Jones) and his Black Arts Theatre. Based in Harlem, because of a felt need to reside in the black community in order to speak truthfully about blacks, the theater went public with *Experimental Death #1* and quickly made a name for itself. Baraka's classic *Dutchman* went on to win an Obie and has had several revivals; *The Toilet* and *The Slave* also earned widespread recognition and acclaim, though white reviewers were stunned by the playwright's vehemence. In the late sixties Baraka founded radical Spirit House in Newark's ghetto and continued to carry out his cultural ideals within the framework of that city's political struggles. By 1975, however, Baraka had abandoned his black nationalism for a political perspective oriented along class rather than color lines. In 1982 he was teaching history at the State University of New York's Stony Brook campus.

Another black big name to gather impact during the sixties was James Baldwin, whose angry plays appalled some white theatergoers. His *Amen Corner*, first produced at Howard University in 1954, was picked up by Frank Silvera's Theatre for Being on the West Coast in the early sixties. The play struggled to Broadway in 1965, with a brilliant lead played by Beah Richards, but ran for less than three months. *Blues for Mister Charlie*, opening in New York under the direction of Burgess Meredith and starring Diana Sands, Al Freeman, Jr., and Rip Torn, also had an acclaimed but limited Broadway run.

Langston Hughes was another big name prominent during this period, but his was an idiom reflecting wit and widsom rather than rage and rebuttal. He had a number of successes on and off Broadway.

There were more disappointments than surprises in the late sixties. Childress' *Wedding Band* went unproduced, as did much of the work of Mitchell. Along came Howard Sackler with a play called *The Great White Hope*, an ideal vehicle for James Earl Jones in the role of the first black heavyweight champion,

Jack Johnson. The play was a success though, in the words of Mitchell, it did not have "one well-constructed scene." It was followed by the lusitanic *Big Time Buck White* which not even Muhammad Ali could save.

Other controversial plays which spanked the white public exposed racism both historically and in contemporary terms. They took their raps, though this did not in any way alter their efficacy. Among those included in this category are *Slave Ship* (Imamu Amiri Baraka), *Ceremonies in Dark Old Men* (Lonnie Elder), and *No Place to be Somebody* (Charles Gordone).

The abrasive spirit of the 1960s focused on the tensions building in American society. If it did not resolve them, it at least exposed them.

Black Theater Companies

Aided by grants from the Ford Foundation, playwright Ed Bullins and artistic director Robert Macbeth founded the New Lafayette Theatre in 1966. Toward the goal of developing a successful theater for black people in their own community, the New Lafayette produced the works of Baraka, Milner, Neil Harris, Marvin X, Richard Welsley, Martie Charles, Milburn Davis, and Bullins, to name but a few. Workshops in all aspects of the theater provided rich training for young people. *Black Theatre Magazine,* which published a total of six issues over the course of the theater's existence, was the first national periodical to devote itself exclusively to black theater. Unfortunately, the group ran out of funding in the early seventies, and the doors of the New Lafayette closed.

Douglas Turner Ward, actor-turned-playwright, had two one-acts, *Days of Absence* and *Happy Ending,* produced at the St. Marks Playhouse in 1966. Winning two Obies for them (writing and acting), Ward gave impetus to an entire movement which culminated in the formation of the foundation-sponsored Negro Ensemble Company (NEC).

Black Theater Across the Nation

The success of black companies has not been limited to New York. The Free Southern Theatre was founded in 1963 by Gilbert Moses, John O'Neal, and Doris Derby. Making its base in Jackson, Mississippi, the group produced the plays of Tom Dent, Val Ferdinand, and Gilbert Moses. In New Orleans, the group's affiliate, Blkartsouth, adhered to the traditions of the Krigwa, New Lafayette, and Spirit House Movements. *Nkombo* was the quarterly published by the group. California's Inner City Cultural Center was founded in the late sixties and involved such diverse activities as touring dance groups and a local travel service.

Inner City sponsored a repertory company which produced many plays of note. Other theaters formed around the country included Marvin X and Ed Bullins' Black Arts/West in San Francisco and Woodie Kings' Concept-East Theater in Detroit.

The late sixties also saw the resurgence of the black educational theater movement, which was begun in the early 1900s by Dr. Carter Woodson and Dr. Randolph Edmonds, then chairman of the drama department at Florida A&M University.

The Seventies and Early Eighties

By the early 1970s there were more than 60 black community theaters functioning throughout the United States. In 1970 the Negro Ensemble Company's production of *River Niger* moved to Broadway, attracting large audiences. In 1971 Melvin Van Peebles had two musicals running simultaneously on Broadway, *Ain't Supposed to Die a Natural Death* and *Don't Play Us Cheap*. In 1972 critic Howard Thompson, writing in the *New York Times,* described *A Revival; Change! Love Together! Organize!* as "impressive, vivid and often gripping"; it was the initial regularly scheduled offering of a major production by the National Black Theater located in Harlem and partly supported by the National Endowment for the Arts. Reviewing *Black Visions,* four playlets by Sonia Sanchez, Neil Harris, and Richard Wesley, presented by Joseph Papp at the storefront annex to the Public Theater in New York, both *Time* and *Newsweek* magazines commented on the "new" black theater. T. E. Kalem in the May 1, 1972 issue of *Time* wrote:

Current plays written by blacks about blacks display strange and interesting aspects of the prickly pride of the outcast. They almost brazenly embrace some of the least admirable notions about blacks held by many whites—that they can be lazy, foulmouthed, deadbeats addicted to alcohol, gambling, and promiscuity. Another aspect of black drama is that it bears a surprising relationship to the class-conscious plays of the '30s. The manner is naturalistic. The tone is hortatory. The focus is not on individuals but on a downtrodden group undergoing a consciousness-raising exercise.

Jack Kroll in the April 17, 1972 issue of *Newsweek* wrote:

The American black man, from slavery on, has always been trapped in reality, and his art, especially his music, has always been the most brilliant example in Western culture of redeeming the time. . . . The new black theater continues this tradition, but it goes beyond redeeming the time, and begins to shape a new time, a time that has always been hinted and heralded in the rhythms of American black art. In Black Visions *one can see in microcosm the answer to the perennial black question, "What's happening?"*

What's happening is that the growing number of remarkable people—writers, actors, directors, designers and a remarkable number of people who combine these roles—are engaged in an extraordinary attempt to hold the mirror up to the unnature of the American black man's life. . . . The new black theater is preparing for transformation by insisting on reality. From this strong base, hopefully it will, as the brilliant black director Robert Macbeth says, "be moved on by the swell of reality" into a theater that has a chance to be unique for its mixture of esthetic form and social power.

Throughout the 1970s, there were notable black successes on Broadway as well as many Off-Broadway productions. In 1974 *Sizwe Banzi Is Dead* by Athol Fugard, a white South African, opened to critical acclaim on Broadway. Its stars, black actors John Kani and Winston Ntshona, both won Tony Awards. In 1975 *The Wiz,* the black musical version of the children's classic *The Wizard of Oz,* opened on Broadway, with a book by William F. Brown and music and lyrics by Charles Smalls. In 1976 poet Ntozake Shange's verse play *For Colored Girls Who Have Considered Suicide When the Rainbow Is Enuf* moved from Joseph Papp's Public Theatre to Broadway where it had the greatest success of any serious black play since Lorraine Hansberry's *A Raisin in the Sun* in 1959. In

the same year, 1976, there was the musical *Bubbling Brown Sugar* by Loften Mitchell (with Rosetta LeNoire) with music by Duke Ellington, Eubie Blake, Cab Calloway, and others and *Your Arms Too Short to Box with God* conceived and directed by Vinnette Caroll with music and lyrics by Alex Bradford and Micki Grant.

In 1978 *Ain't Misbehavin,* conceived and directed by Richard Maltby, Jr., with most of the music and lyrics by Fats Waller (who died in 1943), opened on Broadway, winning the New York Drama Critics Circle Award and the Tony Award as best musical. *Timbuktu,* based on the musical *Kismet,* opened the same year starring Eartha Kitt. Also in 1978, *Eubie,* a tribute to the great Eubie Blake, opened on Broadway.

In the mid-1970s a television production about the Black experience became an American phenomenon. The American Broadcasting Company's dramatization of Alex Haley's book *Roots* on eight consecutive evenings was viewed by an estimated 130 million people and on seven evenings ranked among the Top Ten in all-time TV ratings. Other television productions followed, including Cicely Tyson's award-winning performance in "The Autobiography of Miss Jane Pittman," Leslie Uggams and Olivia Cole in "Backstairs

Fats Waller's music and very talented cast received the coveted Tony Award for Ain't Misbehavin', *a smash Broadway success.* (left to right:) *Ken Page, Charline Woodard, Armelia McQueen, Andre De Shields, and Luther Henderson* (at the piano).

at the White House," Tyson in "A Woman Called Moses," and, of course, "Roots: The Next Generation."

As the new decade began Samm-Art Williams' play *Home,* produced by the Negro Ensemble Company during the 1979–80 season, won a Drama Desk Award and moved to Broadway where it was nominated for two Tony Awards.

In 1980 Athol Fugard's *A Lesson from Aloes* moved

from the Yale Repertory Theater to Broadway where it was nominated for a Tony Award as best play and won the New York Drama Critics Circle Award as best play of 1980.

In the spring of 1982 Broadway had four long-running black musicals, one black drama, and a famous black actor doing Shakespeare. *Dreamgirls,* a smash hit loosely based on the singing group The Supremes, won 13 1982 Tony Award nominations; *Lena Horne, The Lady and Her Music* was a highly acclaimed one-woman performance which had won a special Tony Award in 1981; Duke Ellington's *Sophisticated Ladies* was described by the *New York Times* as "a stroke of genius"; *Waltz of the Stork* was Melvin Van Peebles' new comedy musical which he wrote, directed, and acted in; *Master Harold . . . and the Boys,* by Athol Fugard, had moved from the Yale Repertory Theater in New Haven were it had been highly praised to the Lyceum Theatre on Broadway where it was nominated for three Tony Awards; and James Earl Jones was appearing in *Othello.*

At the same time Off-Broadway, the Negro Ensemble Company was presenting *A Soldier's Play* by Charles Fuller, which won a 1982 Pulitzer Prize, and *One Mo' Time,* written and directed by Vernel Bagneris, was still at the Village Gate. And there were other black productions Off-Off-Broadway.

OUTSTANDING BLACK ENTERTAINERS

ALVIN AILEY
Dancer, Choreographer

Alvin Ailey, founder of the Alvin Ailey American Dance Theatre, has won international fame as both dancer and choreographer.

Ailey studied dancing after graduating from high school where he was a star athlete. With a short stint in college behind him, he formed his own dance group in 1961 and began giving four concerts annually. A year later, the Ailey troupe made an official State Department tour of Australia, receiving accolades throughout the country. One critic called it "the most stark and devastating theatre ever presented in Australia."

After numerous appearances as a featured dancer with Harry Belafonte and others, Ailey performed in a straight dramatic role with Claudia McNeil in Broadway's *Tiger, Tiger Burning Bright.*

In 1965 Ailey took his group on one of the most

The versatile Gregory Hines and sultry Judith Jamison in a scene from the Broadway hit Duke Ellington's Sophisticated Ladies.

successful European tours ever made by an American dance company. In London it was held over six weeks to accommodate the demand for tickets, and in Hamburg it received an unprecedented 61 curtain calls.

A German critic called this performance "a triumph of sweeping, violent beauty, a furious spectacle. The stage vibrates. One has never seen anything like it."

During the mid-seventies Ailey, among his other professional commitments, devoted much time to creating special jazz dance sequences for America's Bicentennial celebration.

IRA ALDRIDGE
Actor
1807–1867

Ira Aldridge was one of the leading Shakespearean actors of the nineteenth century. Although he was denied the opportunity to exhibit his talent to the American public, the fame which he won abroad is more than enough to establish him as one of the landmark figures in the annals of international theater.

Aldridge's origins are obscure. Some accounts give his birthplace as Africa; others name Bel-Air, Maryland; still others list New York City. His birthdate

Ira Aldridge stands among the great nineteenth-century Shakespeareans.

ranges from 1804 to 1807. It seems clear that he attended the African Free School in New York until he was around 16, at which time he left home.

His early dramatic training centered around the African Grove Theatre in New York in 1821. His first role was in *Pizarro,* and he subsequently played a variety of small roles in classical productions before accepting employment as a steward on a ship bound for England.

After studying briefly at the University of Glasgow in Scotland, Aldridge went to London in 1825, appearing in the melodrama *Surinam, or a Slave's Revenge.* For the next eight years, he toured the provinces learning his craft. When he finally appeared in London's Theatre Royal in 1833, his Othello was acclaimed as brilliant by the critics. For the next three decades he toured the continent with great successes, appearing before several members of European royalty.

Aldridge died in Lodz, Poland, on August 7, 1867. He is honored by a tablet housed in the New Memorial Theatre in Stratford-upon-Avon, England.

EDDIE (ROCHESTER) ANDERSON
Comedian
1906–1977

For many years Eddie Anderson was the only black performing regularly on a network radio show. As the character Rochester on the Jack Benny program, he became one of the most widely known black American entertainers.

Anderson was born in Oakland, California in 1906, the son of Big Ed Anderson, a minstrel performer, and Ella Mae, a tightwire walker. During the 1920s and early 1930s Anderson traveled throughout the Middle and Far West singing, dancing, and clowning in small clubs. On Easter Sunday, 1937, he was featured on Benny's radio show in what was supposed to be a "one-shot" appearance, but Anderson was such a hit that he quickly became a regular on the program.

Anderson is best known for his work with Benny (in television, as well as on radio), but he also appeared in a number of movies, including *Star Spangled Rhythm* and *Cabin in the Sky.*

Anderson made a point of staying out of public view. He made a rare public appearance when he attended the funeral of his longtime friend Jack Benny in 1974. Anderson died on February 28, 1977 at the age of 71.

PEARL BAILEY
Singer

With her easy style and impromptu wit, Pearl Bailey has starred as singer, actress, author, and United Nations representative during her long career.

Pearl Bailey and Cab Calloway in Hello Dolly.

Born March 29, 1918 in Newport News, Virginia, she moved to Philadelphia with her family in 1933. She began to sing at small clubs in Scranton, Pennsylvania and in Washington, D.C. before becoming the vocalist for Cootie Williams and later for Count Basie. In 1941 she had her first successful New York engagements at the Village Vanguard and the Blue Angel, and during World War II she toured with the U.S.O. Bailey made her New York stage debut in 1946 in *St. Louis Woman,* for which she won a Donaldson Award as the year's most promising new performer.

In 1952 in London she married drummer Louis Bellson, who is white. He now acts as her musical conductor and they continue to tour in many parts of the world. They have two adopted children, Tony and Dee Dee.

During the 1950s Bailey appeared in the movies *Carmen Jones* and *Porgy and Bess* and on Broadway in *House of Flowers.* In the 1950s and 1960s she was a recording artist, nightclub headliner, and television performer. In 1967 she received a special Tony Award for her starring role on Broadway in *Hello, Dolly* and in 1968 she published her autobiography, *The Raw Pearl.*

In the 1970s she was named a special adviser to the United States Mission to the United Nations. In 1976 she had another book published, *Hurry Up, America, And Spit,* a collection of prose, poetry, and letters. That same year she did the movie *Norman, Is That You?* with Redd Foxx, appeared in Washington, D.C. in *Something To Do,* a musical saluting the American worker, and received an award from the Screen Actors Guild for Outstanding Achievement in Fostering the Finest Ideals of the Acting Profession. Georgetown University made her an honorary doctor of Human Letters in 1977, and in 1978 she enrolled as a student at Georgetown stating that she wanted to prepare for a career in teaching.

In January 1980 she did a one-night concert at Radio City Music Hall in New York. In 1981 she was the voice of the cartoon character "owl" in the Disney movie *The Fox and the Hound.* The movie was described as "a story of two friends who didn't know they were supposed to be enemies" and it also aptly describes Bailey's long involvement in furthering human understanding and international relations.

JOSEPHINE BAKER
Chanteuse, Stage Star
1906–1975

A legend in her own time, and one of America's foremost entertainment expatriates, Josephine Baker first became an internationally famous variety show dancer and a celebrated music hall star in Paris during the 1920s. From then on she continued to win applause for her polished performances, her supple, lithe dance movements, and her sultry and engaging voice. By today's standards, her material would be considered only mildly risque; in the context of her time, however, it was considerably more bold and shocking.

Born in St. Louis on June 3, 1906, Baker received little formal education, first leaving school at the age of eight to supplement the family income by working as a kitchen helper and baby-sitter. While still in elementary school, she took a part-time job as a chorus girl, a job she repeated at age 17 in Noble Sissle's musical comedy *Shuffle Along,* which played Radio City Music Hall in 1923. Her next show was *Chocolate Dandies,* followed by a major dancing part in *La Revue Nègre,* an American production that introduced *le jazz hot* to Paris in 1925.

Baker later left the show to create her most sensational role, that of the "Dark Star" of the Folies Bergère. At the height of her act, she appeared topless on a mirror, clad only in a protective waist shield of rubber bananas. The spectacular dance made her an overnight star and a public figure with a rabid following. In true "star" tradition, she catered to her fans and to her success by adopting such flamboyant eccen-

Josephine Baker at the Casino de Paris in 1931

tricities as walking pet leopards down the Champs Elysees.

In 1930, after completing an around-the-world tour, she made her debut as a singing and dancing comedienne at the Casino de Paris. Critics called her a "complete artist, the perfect master of her tools." In time, she ventured into films, starring alongside French idol Jean Gabin, and into light opera, performing in *La Creole,* an operetta about a Jamaican girl.

During World War II, she served first as a Red Cross volunteer, and later did underground intelligence work through an Italian Embassy attache. After the war, the French government decorated her with the Legion of Honor. She returned to the entertainment world, regularly starring at the Folies Bergère, appearing on French television, and going on still another lengthy international tour.

In the early 1950s, Josephine Baker earned another reputation—not as a lavish and provocative entertainer but as a warm-hearted and devoted friend of humanity. She used her fortune to adopt and tutor a group of orphaned babies of all races, retiring from the stage in 1956 to devote all her time to her "rainbow family." Within three years, however, her "experiment in brotherhood" had taken such a toll on her finances that she was forced to return to the footlights, starring in *Paris, Mes Amours,* a musical based in part on her own fabled career.

Baker survived numerous financial crises without a public hint of despair, or audible groans of discouragement. Illness hardly managed to slow down or otherwise deter her indomitable spirit. Through her long life, she retained her most noteworthy stage attributes—an intimate, subdued voice, coupled with an infectiously energetic and vivacious manner.

Baker died in Paris on April 12, 1975, after opening a gala show to celebrate her fiftieth year in show business.

HARRY BELAFONTE
Singer

Although he has not made a film, appeared on television, or had a hit record in years, Harry Belafonte's performances are still standing room only around the world.

Born March 1, 1927 in New York City, he moved to the West Indies at the age of eight and returned at 13 to New York where he attended high school. In 1944 he joined the Navy. After his discharge, while working as a janitor, he became interested in drama. He studied acting at Stanley Kubrick's Dramatic Workshop and also with Erwin Piscator at the New School for Social Research in New York City where his classmates included Marlon Brando and Walther Matthau. A successful singing engagement at The Royal Roost, a New York jazz club, led to other engagements around the country. But Belafonte, dissatisfied with the music he was performing, returned to New York, opened a restaurant in Greenwich Village, and studied folk singing. He first appeared as a folk singer in the 1950s and "helped give folk music a period of mass appeal" according to John S. Wilson in a 1981 *New York Times* article. During his performances at the Palace Theater in New York, Belafonte had audiences calypsoing in the aisles.

Belafonte produced the first integrated musical shows on television, which won two Emmy Awards and resulted in his being fired by the sponsor. The famous incident in which white British singer Petula Clark touched his arm while singing a song caused a national furor in pre-civil rights America. When Dr. Martin Luther King marched in Montgomery, Alabama and Washington, D.C., Harry Belafonte joined him and brought along a large contingent of performers. Touring in the stage musical *Three for Tonight* in which he also had appeared on Broadway, Belafonte was forced to flee in the middle of a performance in Spartanburg, South Carolina and be rushed to the airport in the mayor's car when word came that the Klu Klux Klan was marching on the theater.

Belafonte also appeared on Broadway in John Murray Anderson's *Almanac,* and his movies include *Carmen Jones, The Angel Levine, Odds against Tomorrow, Buck and the Preacher, Uptown Saturday Night, Island in the Sun,* and *The World, the Flesh, and the Devil.*

In the 1960s and early 1970s he appeared on television and in nightclubs. In 1968 he substituted for Johnny Carson as host of "The Tonight Show." In 1970 he did an ABC-TV special, "Harry and Lena,"

Playing a Jewish angel in The Angel Levine, *Harry Belafonte glares past Milo O'Shea at a skeptical Zero Mostel.*

with Lena Horne, and also appeared with her at Caesar's Palace in Las Vegas.

In the 1980s, coming out of what *Ebony* magazine in a 1981 article described as a self-imposed semiseclusion, he appeared in his first dramatic role on television in the NBC-TV presentation of "Grambling's White Tiger." In 1981 Columbia Records released his first album in seven years, "Loving You Is Where I Belong," mostly ballads. In April 1981 he began a 7½-month tour of the United States, Europe, and Australia which he described as cleaning up unfulfilled commitments so that he could devote himself daily to developing outlets in the third world for black and minority group artists who, after finding acceptance in the 1970s in this country in the wake of the civil-rights movement, are now being bypassed by motion pictures, the recording industry, and the theater. He also is planning to turn his full attention to other projects such as getting black plays and black actors into American regional theaters.

Belafonte and his wife, Julia, who is white, live in a cooperative apartment in a Manhattan building which he purchased many years ago when he was denied another apartment because of his race. They were married in 1957 and have two children, David, a sound engineer, and Gina, a college student. Belafonte has two other daughters from a previous marriage, Shari, an actress, and Adrienne, a weaver in West Virginia.

JAMES HUBERT "EUBIE" BLAKE
Musician-Composer

Eubie Blake was born in Baltimore, the son of former slaves, on February 7, 1883, the last of 10 children and the only one to survive beyond two months. His mother worked as a laundress, his father as a stevedore. One day in 1888, as a child of five, he strayed from his mother's side while she was shopping in downtown Baltimore and disappeared into a musical instrument store that had an organ displayed just inside the entrance, climbed on the organ stool, and fingered the keys.

The store manager insisted on placing a $75.00 organ in the Blake home for 25¢ a week. Young James played so well, he started taking piano lessons with the renowned teacher Margaret Marshall. The following year he was taught musical composition by Llewelyn Wilson, who at one time conducted an all-black symphony orchestra sponsored by the city of Baltimore.

At 17 Blake started playing piano professionally. In 1915 Sissle and Blake, together with Miller and Lyles, created one of the pioneers of black shows, *Shuffle Along,* which was produced on Broadway. "I'm Just Wild About Harry" was one of the hits of this show. The show was produced again on Broadway in 1952. Eubie Blake and Noble Sissle sold their first song, "It's All Your Fault," to Sophie Tucker in 1915 and her introduction of the song started them on their way.

In the early 1930s Blake collaborated with Andy Razaf and wrote the musical score for Lew Leslie's *Blackbirds*. Out of this association came the hit "Memories of You."

During World War II Blake was appointed musical conductor for the United Services Organizations (USO) Hospital Unit. In 1946 he announced his "retirement" and proceeded to enroll in New York University, completing a course, "The Schillinger System of Composition," a method of composing based on higher mathematics, although he had never finished grade school.

In 1966, Blake attended a concert given by a young black girl at Baltimore's Peabody Conservatory of Music. In 1890 the conservatory color bar was so rigid they objected to his carrying his mother's laundry bundles past their building. Three years later, Blake recorded a two-record album entitled "The Eight-Six Years of Eubie Blake."

In 1973 Biograph issued a two-record set of all his known available piano rolls, "Eubie Blake: Blues and Rags" and "Eubie Blake, 1921, Vol. 2." Later he put out two disks on his own label, "Eubie Blake, Rags to Classics" and "Eubie Blake and His Friends." From 1973 through 1981 he performed in concerts in this country and abroad. In 1976 New World Records issued a new album of songs from *Shuffle Along*. In 1978 the Broadway show *Eubie* opened, a tribute to him featuring 24 of his songs. In the spring of 1981 he made his first appearance on cable TV, taped during his February 1981 concert at Carnegie Hall in New York, where he headlined an evening of jazz greats. That concert also produced a record album and a video disk cassette.

Eubie Blake has received honorary doctorates from numerous colleges and universities. For many years his most frequently requested song was "Charleston Rag," which he composed in 1899 and which had to be written down by someone else because he could not then read music. Among his most famous songs were "How Ya' Gonna Keep 'Em Down on the Farm," "Love Will Find a Way," and "You're Lucky to Me."

Blake's first wife, Avis, died in 1939 after 31 years of marriage. In 1945 he married Marion Taylor, who now acts as his agent and manager.

Though known as the master of ragtime, Blake has always most loved the music of the masters. In the intimacy of his Brooklyn studio, Blake rarely plays music of the type with which the world reveres him.

JAMES BLAND
Composer
1854–1911

James Bland was an accomplished minstrel comedian, but his fame rests largely on his work as a composer of more than 600 popular songs.

Born in Flushing, New York on October 22, 1854, Bland moved to Washington, D.C. at an early age. His father, Allan M. Bland, one of the country's earliest Negro college graduates, had been appointed an examiner in the U.S. Patent Office there.

Bland himself attended Howard University, studying music and beginning to create his own tunes. His more famous songs include "Carry Me Back to Old Virginny," "Oh, Them Golden Slippers," and "In the Evening by the Moonlight."

Bland died of pneumonia on May 5, 1911.

More than a quarter of a century after his death, when "Carry Me Back to Old Virginny" was recommended by the Virginia Conservation Committee to become the official state anthem, many people were surprised to learn that the song had actually been written by Bland, and not by Stephen Foster, as was popularly believed. In January 1940 it became the official state anthem.

JAMES BROWN
Singer

James Brown is America's leading exponent of big-beat "soul" music, a highly personal blending of blues and gospel forms with a driving beat.

Master of ragtime Eubie Blake still performs at 98.

Soul on tour with James Brown

Brown was born in 1934 and raised in Augusta, Georgia. He formed his own group, which was discovered during a recording session in a Macon, Georgia radio station in 1956.

He first appeared at the Apollo Theater in New York's Harlem in 1959 and has since appeared there more than 25 times.

With a style made up of frenzied wails and intricate, speedy dance steps, Brown rose to the top of the rock field. Annoyed by the fact that the American public was neglecting its native "down home" music while embracing its synthetic British imitations, Brown organized his own troupe to tour the country with the "genuine article."

With a 40-man ensemble known as "The James Brown Show," he played on the road for 340 days in 1965 and grossed over a million dollars. He drew crowds of 11,000 in Los Angeles; 15,000 in Annapolis, Maryland, and 27,000 in Atlanta. Estimates of future earnings ran as high as $3,000,000 annually.

His hit songs include "Please, Please, Please," "It's a Man's World," and "I Feel Good."

In 1968 Brown toured military bases in the Pacific for the USO. He also came under attack for his endorsement of President Nixon. Brown, who has been called "The Godfather of Soul," records for Polydor Records. At one time he owned five radio stations. In 1980 he appeared in the movie *Blues Brothers*. In 1981 and 1982 he was touring his show across the country. He lives in California.

JOHN BUBBLES
Singer, Dancer

Song-and-dance man John Bubbles was born in 1902 in Louisville and, at the age of seven, teamed with a fellow bowling alley pinboy, Ford (Buck) Washington, in what was soon to become one of the top vaudeville acts in show business. Throughout the 1920s and 1930s, Buck and Bubbles played the top theaters in the country at salaries of up to $1,750 a week.

The two appeared in several films, including *Cabin in the Sky*. Bubbles captured additional fame as Sportin' Life in the 1935 version of *Porgy and Bess*.

After Buck's death in 1955, Bubbles virtually disappeared from show business until 1964 when he teamed up with Anna Maria Alberghetti in a successful nightclub act. Since then, he has made numerous appearances with Johnny Carson, toured Vietnam with Bob Hope, and released several successful records.

In 1979, at the age of 77 and partially crippled from a 1967 stroke, he recreated his characterization of "Sportin' Life" for a one-night show entitled *Black Broadway* at Avery Fisher Hall of New York's Lincoln Center. The show was repeated in 1980 for a limited engagement at Town Hall in New York. In the fall of 1980 Bubbles received the Lifetime Achievement Award from the American Guild of Variety Artists and a Certificate of Appreciation from New York presented by Mayor Koch at City Hall. At that time he was living in Los Angeles.

HARRY T. BURLEIGH
Composer
1866–1949

Of Harry T. Burleigh, Alain Locke has said: "More than any other single person, Mr. Burleigh as arranger, composer, and baritone soloist played the role of a pathbreaking ambassador of Negro music to the musically elect." Burleigh's pioneer work in introducing Negro spirituals on the concert stage and his transcription of songs which had been previously transmitted only orally constitutes a major contribution to the field of American music.

Burleigh was born in Erie, Pennsylvania on December 2, 1866, the grandson of a blind slave who had been dismissed by his Maryland owners when he was unable to work. Burleigh's mother, a college graduate, supported the family after her husband's death by working as the janitor of a local school.

Singing in several choirs in Erie, Burleigh was urged to seek a scholarship to the National Conservatory of Music, one which he ultimately received with the aid of composer Edward MacDowell's mother. In 1900 he joined the choir of Temple Emanu-El in New York, the first Negro to have sung in that synagogue, one of the nation's largest. He was, for some 53 years, soloist at St. George's Episcopal Church in New York City, and received the NAACP Spingarn Medal in 1917 for "excellence in creative music."

Burleigh's concert tours included appearances before numerous presidents and members of royalty. In addition to his arrangements of such spirituals as "Deep River" and "Were You There," he composed 250 original songs.

ANITA BUSH
Singer, Actress
1883–1974

Anita Bush was busily involved in the theater during her early childhood. Her father was the tailor for the Bijou, a large neighborhood theater in Brooklyn, and Anita would carry the costumes to the theater for him, thus giving her a backstage view of performers and productions. Her singing/acting career took off full swing while she was in the chorus of the Williams and Walker Company from 1903 to 1909. With Williams and Walker, she performed in such hits as *Abyssinia* and *In Dahomey,* which had a successful European tour. When the group split up in 1909, she went on to form the Anita Bush Stock Company, which included her own show of chorus girls, plus such greats as Charles Gilpin and Dooley Wilson, with whom she also worked as part of the founding group of the Lafayette Players. Bush died February 16, 1974.

CAB CALLOWAY
Bandleader, Singer

During the 1930s Cab Calloway was one of the best known black entertainers in the United States.

Calloway was born on Christmas Day in 1907 in Rochester, New York. At the age of 22, he was already being booked in New York's famous Cotton Club, a unique musical feat considering the number of well-known musicians active during this era. Calloway's band alternated with the Duke Ellington Orchestra at the Cotton Club throughout the 1930s. It was during this period that Calloway wrote and recorded the song which became an enormous international success and his personal theme song—"Minnie the Moocher."

Calloway has been featured along with his band in such movies as *Big Broadcast, International House,* and *Stormy Weather.*

Since 1948 he has worked with small groups and has also been seen in such shows as the Broadway revival of *Porgy and Bess* in 1950, in which he played the part of Sportin' Life. In the 1960s Calloway appeared with Pearl Bailey on Broadway in *Hello Dolly.*

Also a talented composer, his compositions include "St. James Infirmary," "Lady With a Fan," and "That Man's Here Again."

In the mid-seventies Calloway appeared in a nostalgic review called *Cotton Club* and in 1980 at Town Hall in a Tribute to the Big Bands.

Calloway also appeared at Belmont Park, the Brooklyn Academy of Music, various night spots, and in a one-night performance when his daughter, Chris Calloway, opened an engagement in New York in 1981. In 1976 the book *Of Minnie the Moocher and Me* by Cab Calloway and Bryant Robbins was published. It is an autobiography and documentary collage of remembrances of former employees, friends, and children. Calloway also published a pamphlet, *Hipster's Dictionary.* Calloway will probably always be remembered as "the Hi-De-Ho Man," and he calls himself the ultimate practitioner of "jive."

GODFREY CAMBRIDGE
Comedian, Actor
1933–1976

Godfrey Cambridge gained considerable distinction both as a comedian and as an actor. Born in New York, Cambridge was raised in Harlem and attended grammar school in Nova Scotia while living there with his grandparents. His parents had emigrated from British Guiana. After finishing his schooling in New York at Flushing High School and Hofstra College, he began to study acting.

Cambridge made his Broadway debut in *Nature's Way,* and was featured in *Purlie Victorious,* both on stage and, later, on screen. He has also appeared off-Broadway in *Lost in the Stars, Take a Giant Step,* and *The Detective Story.* He won the Obie award for the 1960–1961 season's most distinguished off-Broadway performance in *The Blacks.*

As a comedian, he appeared on the Jack Paar show, the Johnny Carson show, and many other variety hours. His material, drawn from the contemporary racial situation, was often presented in the style associated with the new wave of black comedians.

Cambridge has also performed dramatically on many television series. In 1965 he starred in the stock version of *A Funny Thing Happened on the Way to the Forum.*

One of Cambridge's most memorable roles was as the star of a seriocomic Hollywood film offering, *The Watermelon Man.* In it the comedian played a man who turns color overnight, a transformation which not only shocks his friends, but leaves his movie wife (Estelle Parsons) somewhat baffled. The action turned on Cambridge's zesty and unhesitating approach to the role.

During the mid-seventies Cambridge appeared to be in semiretirement, making few public appearances.

Cambridge was a compulsive eater who once

Godfrey Cambridge shows his comic flair.

dramatic role on live stage came in 1962 when she played opposite Richard Kiley in *No Strings,* as a love-sick fashion model sharing a writer's digs in Paris.

Carroll was born in the Bronx, the daughter of a subway conductor and a nurse. She joined the Abyssinian Baptist Church choir as a Tiny Tot and, at the age of 10, won a Metropolitan Opera scholarship. Singing lessons held little appeal to her, however, so she continued her schooling at the High School of Music and Art, a "wonderful, beautiful oasis in my life." As a concession to her parents, she enrolled at New York University, where she was to be a sociology student, but stage fever led her to an appearance on a television talent show netting her $1,000. A subsequent appearance at the Latin Quarter launched her professional career.

In 1954 Carroll appeared in *House of Flowers,* winning favorable press notices as a refreshing personality "with a rich, lovely, easy voice." In that year, she also appeared in a film version of *Carmen Jones,* as Myrt.

Movie and television appearances kept her busy until 1958, the year she was slated to appear as an Oriental in Richard Rodgers' *Flower Drum Song.* The part did not materialize, however, largely due to Carroll's height and makeup problems.

Three years later, Rodgers cast her as a high-fashion model playing opposite a hesitant and troubled Pulitzer Prize author. The show was not a smashing success, but Carroll's performance received good notices. The show was titled *No Strings.*

In the late 1960s, Miss Carroll was cast as lead in the television series *Julia* in which she played a nurse

weighed 300 pounds. In 1974 he moved with his wife, Audrey, to Ridgefield, Connecticut, where they were the first blacks and targets for racial harassment. Godfrey Cambridge died at the age of 43 in California on November 29, 1976. He was stricken on a Warner Brothers set where he was playing the role of Ugandan dictator Idi Amin in the television film "Victory at Entebbe."

DIAHANN CARROLL
Singer, Actress

The stunning Diahann Carroll, the first black ingenue to star in a long-running network television series, has had a diversified career in films, on stage, in nightclubs, and in the recording industry. Her most important

Charm radiates from Diahann Carroll.

and war widow. Carroll won a Tony for her performance in the Broadway production *No Strings.* Some of her films include *Porgy and Bess, Goodbye Again, Paris Blues,* and in 1974, *Claudine* with James Earl Jones, a serious comedy in which she played a mother struggling to raise children in Harlem, a role for which she was nominated for an Academy Award.

Following the death of her husband in 1981, she was making only occasional appearances. She lives in California.

VINETTE CARROLL
Actress

Unlike many of her contemporaries who started young, Vinette Carroll didn't decide upon a career in the theater until the age of 25. Coming from a science-oriented family, Carroll had first intended to enter the field of psychology. As her life progressed, she went from part-time acting classes at the New School to two years of stock work, during which time she worked hard at developing the theatrical tools for expressing "the things I was feeling in my gut."

Born in New York City, Vinette Carroll lived in Jamaica, West Indies from the age of three until she was 11. She earned a B.A. in psychology from Long Island University, an M.A. in psychology from New York University, and had completed all of the course work a Ph.D. at Columbia University.

As an actress she won an Obie for her performance in the play *Moon on the Rainbow Shawl* and an Emmy for the TV special "Beyond the Blues." She played Sojourner Truth in the CBS television special "We the Women" and appeared in the movies in *One Potato, Two Potato, Up the Down Staircase,* and *Alice's Restaurant.*

Moving beyond acting to become artistic director of the Urban Arts Corps, she conceived and directed the award-winning musical *Don't Bother Me, I Can't Cope,* which reached Broadway in 1972. Her next Broadway musical was *Your Arm's Too Short to Box with God,* which opened December 1976, and the same year, with Micki Grant, *I'm Laughin' but I Ain't Tickled.*

NAT "KING" COLE
Singer, Pianist
1919–1965

The style and smooth delivery of Nat "King" Cole made him one of the most imitated singers ever produced in American popular music. His death from cancer in 1965 came after he had already enjoyed many successful years at the top of his profession.

Cole was born on March 17, 1919, in Montgomery, Alabama (the family name was Coles, but Cole

Nat "King" Cole ruled the airwaves with his silken voice.

dropped the "s" when he formed the *King Cole Trio* years later) When he was five, the family moved to Chicago, and he was soon playing piano and organ in the church where his father served as minister. While attending Phillips High School, Cole formed his own band, and also played with small combos, including one headed by his brother Edward, a bassist.

In 1936 Cole joined the touring company of *Shuffle Along.* When it folded in Los Angeles, he found work in small clubs there. In 1937 *The King Cole Trio* was formed quite by accident when the drummer in his quartet failed to appear for a scheduled performance. That same year, Cole made his singing debut when a customer insisted he sing "Sweet Lorraine" (a number he later recorded with great success).

Cole's first record was made in 1943. It was his own composition ("Straighten Up and Fly Right"), and sold more than 500,000 copies. Over the years, one hit followed another in rapid succession—"Paper Moon," "Route 66," "I Love You for Sentimental Reasons," "Chestnuts Roasting on an Open Fire," "Nature Boy," "Mona Lisa," "Too Young," "Pretend," "Somewhere Along the Way," "Smile," and many others.

Cole died in 1965, from cancer, at the height of his career and shortly after he finished the celebrated movie *Cat Ballou.*

BILL COSBY
Comedian

Bill Cosby was the first black actor to star in a network television series (*I Spy*), and also the first to win an

The ubiquitous Bill Cosby, stand-up comic, actor, TV personage, and supersalesman.

Emmy, collecting three in a row and eventually three more. He also was the first black entertainer in a network television role that was not racially motivated.

A native of Philadelphia, Cosby dropped out of high school to become a medic in the Navy, obtaining his diploma while in service. On becoming a civilian, he entered Temple University, where he played football and worked evenings as a bartender.

While doing this work, he began to entertain the customers with his comedy routines and, encouraged by their reception, left Temple in 1962 to pursue a career in show business. He began by playing small clubs around Philadelphia and New York's Greenwich Village. Within two years he was playing the top nightclubs around the country and making television appearances on the Johnny Carson (he acted as guest host during Carson's absence), Jack Paar, and Andy Williams shows.

In the 1970s he appeared regularly in nightclubs in Las Vegas, Tahoe, and Reno and did commercials for such sponsors as Jell-O, Del Monte and Ford. In 1980 he did a comedy concert at Carnegie Hall in New York. From 1969 until 1972 he had his own TV series, *The Bill Cosby Show.* He has recorded more than 27 albums and has received five Grammy Awards. He appeared in such films as *Uptown Saturday Night, Let's Do It Again, A Piece of the Action,* and the award-winning television movie "To All My Friends On Shore."

In 1975 Random House published his book, *Bill Cosby's Personal Guide to Tennis or Don't Lower the Lob, Raise the Net.* For several years he was involved in educational television with the Children's Television Workshop. He returned to college, spending five years at the University of Massachusetts earning a masters degree and then a doctorate in education in 1977 when he was 39 years old. He had received his bachelors degree from Temple University.

Cosby and his wife, Camille, live in rural New England with their five children.

RUPERT CROSSE
Actor
1928–1973

Actor Rupert Crosse's most important film role was as Ned McCaslin, the black companion of Steve McQueen in the uproarious screen adaptation of William Faulkner's Pulitzer Prize-winning novel, *The Reivers.* Crosse was nominated for an Academy Award as best supporting actor for his outstanding performance.

Born in Nevis, British West Indies, Crosse moved to Harlem at an early age, but returned to Nevis at the age of seven, after the death of his father. Reared by his grandparents and strongly influenced by his grandfather, a schoolmaster, Crosse received a solid education before returning to the United States, where he attended Benjamin Franklin High School. He later worked at odd jobs before spending two years in service in Germany and Japan.

Once out of service, Crosse renewed his educational pursuits, finishing high school and entering Bloomfield College and Seminary in New Jersey. Though he intended to become a minister, it was obvious from the jobs he held—machinist, construction worker, and recreation counselor—that his career plans were not yet definite.

Crosse subsequently enrolled at the Daykarhanora School for the stage, studying the acting craft and appearing in the Equity Library Theatre off-Broadway production *Climate of Eden.* He then transferred to John Cassavetes' workshop, where he helped create *Shadows,* winner of a Venice Film Festival Award. Crosse's first Hollywood role was in a Cassavetes movie, *Too Late Blues.* Other film credits are *The Wild Seed* and *Ride in the Whirlwind.*

Stage credits are also numerous, including appearances in *Sweet Bird of Youth, The Blood Knot,* and *Hatful of Rain.* Television viewers have seen Crosse in "Dr. Kildare," "I Spy," and "The Man from U.N.C.L.E.," as well as several other series. Crosse's big film break came in 1968 during an appearance at an Actors Studio production of *Echoes* at UCLA.

The actor had the ability to play American black roles and to interpret various African and West Indian characters. An ardent Yoga enthusiast and a practitioner of karate, Crosse believed his hobbies and experience broadened his ability to feel comfortable with a wide variety of roles.

Rupert Crosse died of cancer on March 5, 1973 at the age of 45 at his sister's home in Nevis, West Indies.

OSSIE DAVIS, RUBY DEE
Acting Team

The Ossie Davis-Ruby Dee husband and wife team has won notable accolades in the American theater. Acting together or separately, the Davises have also performed successfully on television, in movies, and in cabarets.

Davis grew up in Waycross, Georgia, and attended Howard University in Washington, D.C., where Dr. Alain Locke suggested he try for an acting career in New York. After completing service in the Army, he landed his first role in 1946 in *Jeb*, the play in which he met Dee. (Two years later, they were married.)

After appearing in the movie *No Way Out*, Davis won Broadway roles in *No Time for Sergeants, Raisin in the Sun,* and *Jamaica*. In 1961 he and Dee starred in *Purlie Victorious*, which Davis himself had written. Two years later, they repeated their roles in the movie version, *Gone Are the Days.*

Davis' other movie credits include *The Cardinal* and *Shock Treatment*. He has also written a number of TV scripts, and has acted on such television series as "The Defenders," "The Nurses," and "East Side, West Side."

He also directed such films as *Cotton Comes to Harlem* and *Black Girl*. His play *Escape to Freedom: A Play about Young Frederick Douglass* had its debut at Town Hall in New York and later was published by Viking Junior Books.

Ruby Dee was born in Cleveland but grew up in Harlem, taking her undergraduate training at Hunter College in New York. In 1942 she appeared in *South Pacific* with Canada Lee and, five years later, met Ossie Davis while they were both playing in *Jeb*.

Her movies include *No Way Out, Edge of the City, Raisin in the Sun,* and *The Balcony*. She has appeared often on network television.

In 1965 she was the first black actress to appear in major roles at the American Shakespeare Festival in Stratford, Connecticut. She wrote a musical satire *Take It from the Top*, in which she appeared with her husband in a showcase run at the Henry Street Settlement Theatre in New York in 1979.

Ossie Davis and Ruby Dee were involved in the civil rights struggle long before it became a "fashionable" cause. In 1970 they received the Frederick Douglass Award from the Urban League and in 1975 Actors Equity presented them with the Paul Robeson Citation "for outstanding creative contributions both in the performing arts and in society at large."

As a team they recorded several talking story albums for Caedmon. In 1974 they produced "The Ruby Dee/Ossie Davis Story Hour," which was sponsored by Kraft Foods on more than 60 stations of the National Black Network. Together they founded the Institute of New Cinema Artists to train selected youths for jobs in films and television, and then founded The Recording Industry Training Program to develop jobs in the music industry for disadvantaged youths.

In 1981 Alcoa funded a television series on the Public Broadcasting System titled "With Ossie and Ruby" using guests to provide an anthology of the arts. The show began its second season in the spring of 1982.

Ossie Davis and Ruby Dee live in a large house in New Rochelle, in New York's Westchester County. They have two daughters, a son, and a grandson born in May 1982.

SAMMY DAVIS, JR.
Singer, Dancer, Comedian, Actor

Sammy Davis, Jr. is often called "the world's greatest entertainer" (a title which attests to his remarkable versatility as singer, dancer, actor, mimic, and musician).

Davis was born in New York City on December 8, 1925 and, four years later, was appearing in vaudeville with his father and "uncle" in the Will Mastin Trio. In 1931 Davis made his movie debut with Ethel Waters in *Rufus Jones for President*, and followed this with an appearance in *Season's Greetings*.

Throughout the 1930s, the Will Mastin Trio continued to play vaudeville, burlesque, and cabarets. In 1943 Davis entered the Army and served for two years writing, directing, and producing camp shows. After his discharge, he rejoined the trio, which in 1946 cracked the "big-time" club circuit with a successful Hollywood engagement.

Davis recorded a string of hits ("Hey There," "Mr. Wonderful," "Too Close for Comfort") during his continued climb to the top of show business. In November 1954 he lost an eye in an automobile accident, but this did not in any way interfere with his career. He scored a hit in his first Broadway show *Mr. Wonderful* (1956), and later repeated this success in *Golden Boy*.

In 1959 he played Sportin' Life in the movie version of *Porgy and Bess*. Other Davis movies include *Oceans 11* and *Robin and the Seven Hoods*. In 1966 his autobiography *Yes, I Can* was a best seller, and he starred in his own network television series.

The complete entertainer, Sammy Davis, Jr., sings a sermon in Sweet Charity.

In 1968 the National Association for the Advancement of Colored People awarded him its Spingarn Medal. In the 1970s Davis appeared in films, television, and nightclubs. In 1972 he was involved in a controversy over his support of Richard Nixon attested by a famous photograph of Nixon hugging Davis at the 1972 Republican Convention. In 1974 Davis renounced his support of Nixon and Nixon's programs. In the same year his TV commercials for Japan's Suntory Whiskey won the grand prize at the Cannes Film Festival, and the National Academy of TV Arts and Sciences honored him for his unique contributions to TV.

In 1975 he became host of an evening talk and entertainment show. In 1980 he marked his fiftieth anniversary as an entertainer and the Friars Club honored him with its Annual Life Achievement Award.

Davis has been married three times. His first marriage was in 1959 to singer Loray White. He married his second wife, actress Mai Britt, in 1961 and she is the mother of his three children. In 1970 he married dancer Altovise Gore.

KATHERINE DUNHAM
Dancer, Choreographer

Katherine Dunham has for many years been one of the leading exponents of primitive dance in the world of modern choreography. She has used her training in anthropology and her study of primitive rituals from tropical cultures to create unique dance forms which blend native qualities with sophisticated Broadway stage settings.

Born in Chicago on June 22, 1910, Dunham attended the University of Chicago, where she majored in anthropology. With the aid of a Rosenwald Fellowship, she was able to visit the Caribbean and Brazil to further her research in her chosen field.

In the 1930s she founded the Dunham Company using Dunham techniques. She has been called the mother of Afro-American dance.

In 1940 she appeared in *Cabin in the Sky,* a musical for which she had done the choreography. She later toured the United States with her own dance group and, after the war, also played to enthusiastic audiences in Europe.

Among her best-known choreographic pieces are *Bhahiana* and *Burrell House.* Under the pseudonym Kaye Dunn, Dunham has writen several articles and books on primitive dance.

On January 15, 1979 (Martin Luther King's Birthday) at Carnegie Hall in New York she received the 1979 Albert Schweitzer Music Award, and selections from her dance repertory from 1938 to 1975 were staged. In recent years she founded a free school to teach her dance techniques in East St. Louis. Dunham is married to stage designer John Pratt.

GAIL FISHER
Actress

Gail Fisher won the Emmy Award from the Academy of Television Arts and Sciences and garnered four additional Emmy nominations for her co-starring role as Peggy Fair, secretary to Mike Connors, in the CBS-TV series "Mannix."

Fisher was born in Potters Crossing, New Jersey—often referred to as "the worst rural slum on the eastern seaboard." Gail's father, a carpenter, died when she was two, leaving her mother $8.45.

In 1960 Fisher appeared in the first Ford Grant production performed by the San Francisco Actors' Workshop and drew rave reviews for her role in *The Rocks Cried Out,* which lasted for three months. In 1961 she became the first black to do a national TV commercial with lines.

In 1967 the producers of the TV show "Mannix" chose Gail to play the Peggy Fair role. "I read for the part five times and got it," she said before adding, "Peggy replaced a bank of computers and a man to make room for me in the show." It appears as though the move was beneficial to all parties. Gail has received the producer's nod for Emmy consideration every season, and the series, after Fisher joined it, grew in the ratings.

Gail's penchant is for creative expression, be it painting, decorating or lyric writing. She is also known to be one of Hollywood's finest pool players.

In 1982 she was appearing on the television series "General Hospital," a daytime "soap."

Fisher has been married several times and has two daughters.

REDD FOXX
Comedian

Redd Foxx's most famous role was Fred Sanford, the junkman on the popular NBC-TV series "Sanford and Son," which began in 1972. It was considered to be the second most popular role on television (the first being Archie Bunker). As a result Foxx became one of the highest paid actors in show business. In 1976 it was reported that he was earning $25,000 per half-hour episode plus 25% of the producer's net profit.

Coincidentally, Sanford is actually Foxx's family name. He was born John Elroy Sanford in St. Louis and both his father and his brother are named Fred. As a boy he concocted a washtub band with two friends and played for tips on street corners, earning as much as $60 a night. At 14, Foxx and the band moved to Chicago. The group broke up in World War II. Foxx moved to New York, worked as a rack pusher in the garment district, but, persevering, began to find entertainment spots in night clubs and on the black vaudeville circuit. While in New York he played pool with

Redd Foxx portrays one of TV's favorite characters.

a hustler named Malcolm Little, who was to change his name to Malcolm X.

In the early 1950s Foxx tried Hollywood. He had a brief stint with the Dinah Washington Show, but mostly survived by combining vaudeville and sign painting.

His comedy act was X-rated adult entertainment, which limited his bookings. His first real success came in 1955 when he began to record party records. He has done more than 50 of them which sold over 20 million copies. His television career was launched in the 1960s with guest appearances on The Today Show, The Tonight Show, and others. He also began to appear in the Las Vegas nightclubs. Throughout the long run of "Sanford and Son," Foxx was in disputes with his producer over money. Originally he was not receiving a percentage of the show's profits, so he sat out several episodes resulting in a breach of contract suit filed by the producers. There were also racial undertones with Foxx referring to himself as a "tuxedo slave" and pointing to white stars who owned a percentage of their shows. Eventually he broke with the show and with NBC. He then signed a multimillion dollar, multiyear contract with ABC, which resulted in a disastrous comedy variety hour which he quit on the air in October 1977.

He has also done a TV situation comedy "My Buddy" for ABC-TV which he wrote and starred in, and served as executive producer. In 1978 ABC filed a breach of contract suit. In 1979 Foxx was back at NBC planning a sequel to "Sanford and Son."

Foxx had done a movie for MGM in 1976, *Norman, Is That You?* He continued his appearances in nightclubs in Las Vegas and New York. He also had a deal with CBS Inc., which in 1981 was suing him for a second time, allegedly to recover advances not paid back. In 1979 a book, *Redd Foxx, B.S.,* was published. It was collection of chapters written by his friends.

In 1973 Foxx received the Entertainer of the Year Award from the National Association for the Advancement of Colored People. In 1974 he was named police chief of Taft, Oklahoma, an all-black village of 600 people. He also was running a Los Angeles nightclub to showcase aspiring young comedians, both black and white. Foxx also did numerous prison shows, probably more than any other famous entertainer, and he paid for the shows out of his own pocket.

ARETHA FRANKLIN
Singer

The uncontested modern queen of "Soul," Aretha Franklin is a vigorous and talented performer who reigns over the pop music field. She has already reached the magic figure of one million sales on several singles and long-playing albums, all of which are characterized by a lively and pulsating rhythm and a compelling, infectious beat. Some of her music stems straight from the openly emotional jubilant gospel choir tradition in which her father, Reverend C. L. Franklin, was immersed during his evangelical years in Memphis and Detroit; she is, however, equally capable of delivering a warm blues number or a rhythmically explosive solo reminiscent of her mentor, Ray Charles. Whatever the music calls for, her style radiates a relaxed natural honesty that critics regard as an admirable trademark.

Born in 1942, Franklin moved to Detroit at the age of two, and grew up teaching herself the gospel songs and piano accompaniment which were to form the basis of her early career. Her success on the gospel circuit inspired her to test the pop music field, but she was only modestly successful until 1966, when she signed a contract with Atlantic Records, a company specializing in rhythm and blues performers.

Franklin has had 21 gold records and has won 10 Grammy Awards. One of the secrets of her astonishing success was the breakthrough which black music itself was finally achieving. Much of it had been copied and adulterated by white artists familiar with its driving rhythms and throbbing vitality. When Franklin came along, black artists were finally beginning to be appreciated nationally as the originators and prime interpreters of such music. In the words of one observer, it no longer needed to be "manicured" or "sanitized."

In 1976 Aretha Franklin made her first European tour. That same year, cheering and foot-stomping crowds greeted her at a performance at Lincoln Center in New York City. In 1981 she did a concert series at the City Center in New York.

In 1980 she signed with a new record label, Arista;

Aretha Franklin is a warm and natural performer.

her highly successful album "Aretha" came out in 1981, launching the popular single release "United Together" followed by "What a Fool Believes" and "Can't Turn You Loose."

Franklin appeared in the Universal film *The Blues Brothers* in 1980. Franklin had been married to her manager, Ted White in the 1960s. In 1978 she married actor Glynn Turman.

AL FREEMAN, JR.
Actor

Al Freeman, Jr. has won recognition for his many roles in the theater and motion pictures. His title role, portrayal in the television film "My Sweet Charlie" earned him an Emmy Award nomination.

Freeman was born in San Antonio, Texas, the son of late pianist Al Freeman, Sr., and Lottie Coleman Freeman. After attending primary schools there, Freeman continued his education in Ohio, then moved to the West Coast to study law at Los Angeles City College. Encouraged by fellow students to audition for a campus production, he decided to change his major to theater arts when he returned to college following a tour of duty with the Army in Germany.

He did radio shows and appeared in little theater productions in the Los Angeles area before performing in his first Broadway play, *The Long Dream*. Other Broadway credits include *Golden Boy, Blues for Mr. Charley, Look to the Lilies, The Dozens, Medea, Tiger, Tiger Burning Bright, Conversations at Midnight, The Long Dream*, and *Kicks and Company*.

Off-Broadway Freeman worked in *The Premise, Trumpets of the Lord, The Slave, Great McDaddy*, and *Measure for Measure* and *Troilus and Cressida* for the New York Shakespeare Festival. He has also done more than a dozen feature films including *Dutchman, Finian's Rainbow, The Lost Man, The Detective*, and *Castle Keep*.

Freeman has appeared in such TV series as "The Defenders," "The FBI," "Naked City," and is featured as Lt. Ed Hall in ABC's daytime drama "One Life to Live," estimated to have 25% black audience. He also appeared on TV in Norman Lear's "Hot l Baltimore."

CHARLES GILPIN
Actor
1878–1930

Charles Gilpin has been described by Margaret Just Butcher as "the first modern American Negro to establish himself as a serious actor of first quality."

Gilpin was born in Virginia in 1878 and, after a brief period in school, began work as a printer's devil. In 1890 he began to travel with vaudeville troupes, a

Charles S. Gilpin, the dean of serious black American actors

practice he continued for two decades, working as a printer, elevator operator, prizefight trainer, and porter during long interludes of theatrical unemployment.

From 1911 to 1914 he toured with a group called the Pan-American Octette, and in 1914 he had a bit part in *Old Ann's Boy.* Two years later he organized and managed the Lafayette Theatre Company, one of the earliest black stock companies in New York.

After Eugene O'Neill saw Gilpin in *Abraham Lincoln,* he was chosen to play the lead in *Emperor Jones,* the role in which he starred from 1920 to 1924. (In 1921, he was named winner of the NAACP Spingarn Award for his theatrical accomplishment.)

Gilpin lost his voice in 1926 and was forced to earn his living once again as an elevator operator. He died in 1930.

RICHARD B. HARRISON
Actor
1864–1935

Richard B. Harrison is one of the few actors to gain national prominence on the basis of one role, a feat which he accomplished with his characterization of "De Lawd" in *Green Pastures.*

Harrison was born in Canada in 1864 and moved to Detroit as a young boy. There he worked as a waiter, porter, and handyman, using whatever money he could save to attend the theatrical offerings playing in town. After studying drama in Detroit, he made his professional debut in Canada in a program of readings and recitations.

For three decades he entertained black audiences with one-man performances of *Macbeth, Julius Caesar,* and *Damon and Pythias,* as well as with poems by Shakespeare, Poe, Kipling, and Paul Laurence Dunbar. In 1929, while serving on the faculty of North Carolina A&T as a drama instructor, he was chosen for the part in *Green Pastures.*

When he died in 1935, Harrison had performed as "De Lawd" 1,656 times. His work had won him the 1930 Spingarn Medal and several honorary degrees as well.

GEOFFREY HOLDER
Actor, Dancer, Choreographer, Director, Costume Designer, Writer, Painter

Geoffrey Holder is an artistic man for all seasons. He also is an imposing presence, 6 feet, 6 inches tall, handsome, with a shaved head.

Born in Trinidad, he left school to become the costume designer for his brother's dance troupe, which he took over in 1948 leading the dancers, singers, and steel band musicians through a series of successful small revues to the Carribean Festival in Puerto Rico where they represented Trinidad. His appearances with his troupe in the mid-1950s were so popular that he is credited with launching the calypso vogue.

Early in his career he appeared in New York as a featured dancer in *House of Flowers,* later dancing with the Metropolitan Opera and as a guest star on many television shows. He also appeared in many TV dramas and in the films *Live and Let Die,* a James Bond adventure, and *Dr. Doolittle,* the children's classic starring Rex Harrison.

He received two Tony Awards in 1976 as director and as costume designer for the Broadway show *The Wiz,* the all-black adaptation of *The Wizard of Oz.* In 1978 he directed and choreographed the successful Broadway musical *Timbuktu.*

He is the recipient of a Guggenheim Fellowship for painting and his impressionist paintings have been shown in galleries such as the Corcoran in Washington, D.C. Holder also has written two books. *Black Gods, Green Islands* is a retelling of West Indian legends and *Geoffrey Holder's Carribean Cookbook* is a collection of recipes which he also illustrated.

He appeared in the film *Annie,* based on the hit Broadway musical, playing Punjab, a character from the original comic strip. In early 1982 he was planning a new project, *A Voodoo Tragedy,* the story of Elektra, which he proposed to direct, costume, choreograph, and film in Haiti.

Holder is married to the ballet dancer Carmen deLavallade. They have one son, Leo.

The lovely Lena Horne, song stylist extraordinaire

LENA HORNE
Singer, Actress

Lena Horne has been called the most beautiful woman in the world, an opinion which has been no small factor in the continued success of her stage, screen, and nightclub career.

Born on June 30, 1917, in Brooklyn, she joined the chorus line at the Cotton Club in 1933, and then left to tour as a dancer with Noble Sissle's orchestra. She was given a leading role in *Blackbirds of 1939,* but the show folded quickly, whereupon she left to join Charlie Barnett's band as a singer. She made her first records (including the popular "Haunted Town") with Barnett.

In the early 1940s she worked at New York's Cafe Society Downtown and, from there, went to Hollywood where she was the first black woman ever to sign a term contract in films.

Her films include *Panama Hattie* (1942), *Cabin in the Sky* (1943), *Stormy Weather* (1943), and *Meet Me in Las Vegas* (1956). In 1957 she took a break from her nightclub schedule to star in her first Broadway musical, *Jamaica.*

Her most popular recordings include "Stormy Weather," "Blues in the Night," "The Lady Is a Tramp," and "Mad about the Boy."

In the 1970s Lena Horne was appearing in night-clubs and concerts, but her greatest recent success was on Broadway. On May 12, 1981 Lena Horne opened a one-woman show called *Lena Horne: The Lady and Her Music.* It was a critical and box-office success. Although it opened too late to qualify for the Tony Award nominations, the show was awarded a special Tony at the June ceremonies. In December of that year she received New York City's highest cultural award, The Handel Medallion.

Horne was married for 23 years to Lennie Hayton, a white composer, arranger, and conductor, who died April 24, 1971. She had been married previously at a young age to Louis Jones, with whom she had two children. Her son, Edwin, died at the age of 29 in 1970 of a kidney ailment. She also has a daughter, Gail Lumet, and grandchildren.

An extremely generous and gracious woman, Horne has devoted much time quietly and unobtrusively in the interest of many humane causes.

EDDIE HUNTER
Vaudevillian
1888–1974

Eddie Hunter, star of vaudeville, got his start as an elevator operator in a building frequented by the great tenor Enrico Caruso. Hunter had been writing comedy parts on the side and Caruso encouraged and helped him. By 1923 Hunter's show *How Come,* a musical revue, reached Broadway.

Hunter performed himself in the majority of the shows he wrote. *Going to the Races,* produced at the Lafayette Theatre in Harlem, had Hunter and his partner live onstage, interacting with a movie of themselves flashed on the screen. Hunter considered this show one of his best. As one of the principal performers in *Blackbirds,* he toured Europe in the late twenties; his show *Good Gracious* also toured Europe.

Depicting himself as "the fighting comedian," Hunter developed a reputation for his struggle against racial discrimination in the performing arts. He frequently told the story about Phoenix, Arizona, where the male members of the show were forced to sleep in the theater where they were performing; accommodations for blacks simply did not exist at the time. In contrast, Hunter characterized his European receptions as being generally free of prejudice. There, he felt he received the respect and recognition due him.

By 1923 Hunter had a full recording contract with Victor Records. His recordings have included "It's Human Nature to Complain," "I Got," and "My Wife Mamie." Shortly thereafter, he suspended his singing career to begin traveling with a new show he had developed. But when talking movies came into being, time and the public ran out on people like Eddie Hunter and the types of shows he produced. Vaudeville was dying, if not already dead. Eddie Hunter retired from show business and entered the real estate business in the 1930s.

Hunter lived in Harlem, where he managed over 20 buildings. He died there in 1974 at the age of 86.

EARLE HYMAN
Actor

When Earle Hyman made his debut in Eugene O'Neill's *Emperor Jones* in Oslo, Norway, he became the first American to perform a title role in a Scandinavian language. Hyman had originally become acquainted with Norway during a European trip made in 1957. He had planned to spend only two weeks in the Scandinavian country, but found himself so enchanted with it that he all but forgot the rest of Europe.

When he returned to New York, he resolved at once to learn Norwegian and, for practice, began to study the role of Othello (which he was doing for the Great Lakes Shakespeare Festival of 1962) in that language. By sheer coincidence, the director of *Den Nationale Scene* Theatre of Bergen, Norway, invited him to play Othello there in the spring of the following year, a performance which marked Hyman's first success in the Norwegian theater.

Two years later Hyman returned to Norway to play *Emperor Jones* for a different theater company, and was greeted with high critical acclaim for his portrayal; he stayed for six years. Due to the interest of the Norwegian people in his life, Hyman has been the subject of several radio broadcasts and numerous television interviews. He still spends six months each year in Scandinavia playing "Othello" and other classical roles. A bronze bust of the actor as Othello has been erected in the Norwegian theater where Hyman performed, and he has also been presented with an honorary membership in the Norwegian Society of Artists, the third foreigner and first American to be so honored.

Born in North Carolina in 1926, Hyman began his acting career with the American Negro Theatre in New York, after which he appeared in eight Broadway productions and over 100 television programs. He is also a five-year veteran of the American Shakespeare Festival at Stratford, Connecticut.

His many on and off-Broadway credits include *Mister Johnson, Waiting for Godot, No Time for Sergeants, St. Joan* (with Diana Sands at Lincoln Center), Lorraine Hansberry's *Les Blancs,* Edward Albee's *Lady from Dubuque,* and the black version of Eugene O'Neill's *Long Day's Journey into Night* (at the Public Theatre in 1981). In the mid-1970s he also appeared on a daytime "soap" "Love of Life."

REX INGRAM
Actor
1895–1969

A major movie and radio personality of the 1930s and 1940s, Rex Ingram was born in 1895 aboard the *Robert E. Lee,* a Mississippi riverboat on which his father was a stoker. He attended military schools where he displayed an interest in acting.

After working briefly as a cook for the Union Pacific Railroad and as head of his own small window-washing business, Ingram gravitated to Hollywood where in 1919 he appeared in the original Tarzan film. Roles in such classics as *Lord Jim, Beau Geste, King Kong,*

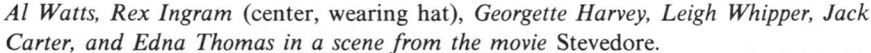

Al Watts, Rex Ingram (center, wearing hat), *Georgette Harvey, Leigh Whipper, Jack Carter, and Edna Thomas in a scene from the movie* Stevedore.

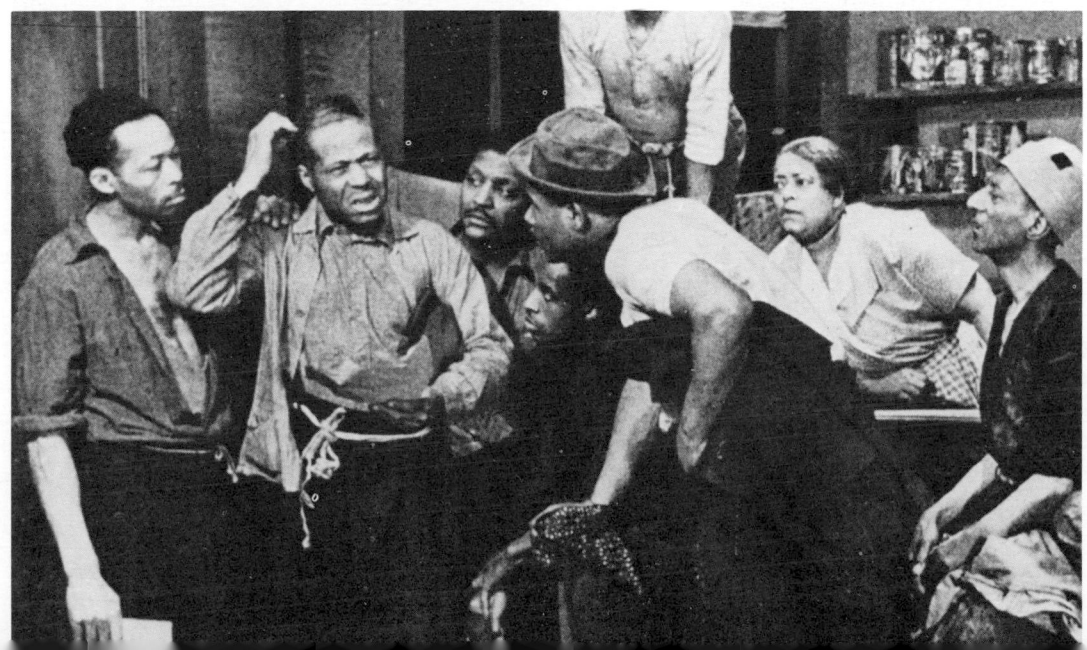

Green Pastures and *Huckleberry Finn* followed. During the late twenties and early thirties, Ingram also appeared prominently in legitimate theater in San Francisco. In the late thirties he was to star in daytime radio soap operas and in WPA theater. This launched a distinguished career in New York on the legitimate stage and in television, which was to last into the 1960s. In 1957 he played Pozzo in *Waiting for Godot*. During this period, he appeared periodically in motion pictures, his last role being in *Your Cheating Heart* in 1964.

MAHALIA JACKSON
Gospel Singer
1911–1972

The rich contralto of Mahalia Jackson—with its great range and singular control—has no equal in performing the original compositions of "gospel," a unique musical form produced by the style of worship prevalent in many black churches.

Mahalia Jackson was born in New Orleans on October 26, 1911. She was acquainted with the records of Bessie Smith and other blues singers but, at home, her preacher father confined the family's listening habits to strictly religious music.

She moved to Chicago at 16 and joined the Salem Baptist choir, saving enough from her work as a hotel maid to open her own beauty shop. In 1934 she made her first record, "God Gonna Separate the Wheat from the Tares," but she did not achieve national fame until 1945 with "Move On Up a Little Higher," which ultimately sold over a million copies.

Over the next few years, her fame was even greater in Europe than at home. In 1950, however, she gave a highly successful concert at Carnegie Hall in New York City. After that, she had several hit records and has made guest appearances on major television shows.

Her best-known record albums include "Bless This House," "Sweet Little Jesus Boy," and "The World's Greatest Gospel Singer."

Jackson died on January 27, 1972 ending a career that brought traditional gospel music to huge audiences through her truly remarkable voice and presentation. At the time of her death Jackson had been devoting much time to civil rights causes.

JUDITH JAMISON
Dancer

Judith Jamison, the leading dancer of the interracial Alvin Ailey Dance Theater, emerged in the 1970s as the first black superstar of American dance.

Tall, fluid, and spirited, Jamison portrays a wide gamut of black roles, many of which have been especially choreographed for her by Ailey, including two roles in "Cry," a 20-minute solo depicting the nobility and suffering of black women in which Jamison plays both a slave and black queen. Her talent for comedy is portrayed in her famous "parasol" role in "Revelations."

Born in Philadelphia, Jamison started to study dance at the age of six and was discovered in her early twenties by choreographer Agnes De Mille, who felt her spontaneity should be encouraged. Notes the great dancer: "Being on stage is the second most uninhibited thing I do. I turn myself totally inside out. I am preoccupied with the audience. I'm trying to turn them on, not the critics or the other dancers."

In the 1980s Jamison scored a great success on Broadway in *Sophisticated Ladies,* a musical featuring the music of Duke Ellington.

JAMES EARL JONES
Actor

James Earl Jones is one of the most prominent black actors in the United States today, having starred in a variety of Shakespearean roles as well as a number of contemporary avant-garde theatrical productions.

Jones (whose actor father Robert Earl Jones was featured in the movie *One Potato, Two Potato*) was born in Tate County, Mississippi, and raised by his grandparents on a farm near Jackson, Michigan. He turned to acting after a brief period as a premedical student at the University of Michigan (from which he graduated cum laude in 1953) and upon completion

James Earl Jones as King Lear

of military service with the Army's Cold Weather Mountain Training Command in Colorado.

After drifting to New York, Jones studied at the American Theatre Wing, making his off-Broadway debut in 1957 in *Wedding in Japan*. Since then, he has appeared in more than 30 plays on and off Broadway, including *Sunrise at Campobello, The Cool World, The Blacks, The Blood Knot,* and *Anyone, Anyone.* Jones holds a number of awards, including the 1961 Obie and the 1961–1962 Daniel Blum Theatre World Award.

Jones' progress as an actor was, in a sense, slow and deliberate, rather than meteoric, until he portrayed Jack Jefferson in the Broadway smash hit *The Great White Hope.* The play, based on the life of Jack Johnson, the first black heavyweight champion, invariably reminded audiences of the career of Muhammad Ali. In 1969 Jones received the Tony Award for the best dramatic actor in a Broadway play, and the Drama Desk award for one of the best performances of the 1968–1969 New York season.

In the 1970s Jones was appearing in roles traditionally performed by white actors. Among the performances was King Lear and an award-winning performance as Lenny in Steinbeck's *Of Mice and Men.*

In 1978 Jones appeared in the highly controversial *Paul Robeson,* a one-man show on Broadway. Many leading blacks advocated a boycott of the show because they said it did not measure up to the man himself. But critics gave the show high praise.

In 1980 Jones starred in Athol Fugard's *A Lesson from Aloes,* which was a top contender for a Tony Award that year. He also appeared in the Yale Repertory Theater Production of *Hedda Gabler.* In the spring of 1982 he co-starred with Christopher Plummer on Broadway in *Othello* in a production acclaimed as one of the best ever done of the Shakespearean tragedy.

Among his films have been *Dr. Strangelove* and *River Niger.* He was the screen voice of Darth Vader in *Star Wars* and its sequel *The Empire Strikes Back,* and he made the horror movie, *Red Tide* and the adventure *Conan the Barbarian.* On television he portrayed author Alex Haley in "Roots: The Next Generation," and narrated documentaries for the Public Broadcasting System. In 1977 he was reported to command $200,000 for his performance in a movie.

In 1976 Jones was elected to the Board of Governors of the Academy of Motion Picture Arts and Sciences. In 1979 New York City presented him with the "Mayor's Award of Honor for Arts and Culture." He received an honorary Doctorate of Humane Letters from the University of Michigan in 1971 and the Michigan Club of New York Man of the Year Award in 1976.

Jones has a home in Pawling, New York. In March

Leadbelly's songs mixed sweet music and raw wit.

1982, he married his *Othello* co-star, white actress Cecilia Hart.

HUDDIE (LEADBELLY) LEDBETTER
Folk Singer
1888–1949

A legendary figure in the history of American entertainment is Huddie Ledbetter, known widely as "Leadbelly." The violence of Ledbetter's personal life sometimes tends to obscure the major contribution he made to the folk music revival in the United States.

Ledbetter was born in Mooringsport, Louisiana in 1888, and raised in Texas where he learned to play accordion and guitar. From 1903 until 1917 he worked in the Louisiana-Texas area. In 1918 he was jailed for murder under the name Walter Boyd. Seven years later he was pardoned, but in 1930 he was jailed again for attempted homicide and this time served four years in prison. (There seems to be no basis for the legend that Ledbetter was freed by the Governor of Louisiana because "he played the sweetest 12-string guitar in the whole wide world.")

Discovered by folklorist Alan Lomax, Ledbetter recorded for the Library of Congress and played numerous nightclub engagements during the 1940s. In 1949 he toured France successfully and, during this period, began to spark a general interest both at home and abroad in American folk music. Some of his songs, such as "On Top of Old Smoky" and "Irene Good

Night," became commercial successes when recorded by others.

He died in New York City on December 6, 1949.

CANADA LEE
Actor
1907–1951

Canada Lee is best known for his work in the 1941 Broadway version of *Native Son,* in which he played Bigger Thomas, and for his performance in the 1952 film *Cry the Beloved Country.*

Lee was born in Manhattan on May 3, 1907. After studying violin as a young boy, he ran off to Saratoga with the intention of becoming a jockey. Failing in this, he returned to New York and began a boxing career. By 1926 he had turned professional after winning 90 out of 100 fights, including the national amateur lightweight title.

Over the next few years he won 175 out of some 200 fights against such top opponents as Jack Britton and Vince Dundee. In 1933 a detached retina brought an end to his ring career. (He had acquired his name when a ring announcer could not pronounce his real name—Lee Canetaga.)

In 1934 Lee was a struggling musician when he successfully auditioned at the Harlem YMCA for his first acting role in a WPA production of *Brother Mose.*

In 1941 Orson Welles, who had met him in the production of the Federal Theatre's Negro *Macbeth,* chose him to play Bigger Thomas in the stage version of Richard Wright's famed novel *Native Son. New York Times* critic Brooks Atkinson called him "a superbly imaginative player."

In 1944 Lee served as narrator of a radio series called "New World Comin'," the first such series devoted to the race question. That same yer, he also appeared in Alfred Hitchcock's film *Lifeboat,* and in the Broadway play *Anna Lucasta.*

Lee died in 1951.

JACKIE (MOMS) MABLEY
Comedienne
1897–1975

Although she was virtually unknown to the general public, Jackie (Moms) Mabley was a favorite of black audiences for almost half a century. Late in her life her comedy record albums made her "an overnight success almost 50 years in show business."

Mabley was born Loretta Mary Aiken in North Carolina, and entered show business as a teenager when the team of Buck and Bubbles gave her a bit part in a vaudeville skit called *Rich Aunt from Utah.*

With the help of comedienne Bonnie Bell Drew, Mabley developed a monologue, and was soon being booked on the black vaudeville circuit. Influenced by such teams as Butterbeans and Susie, she developed her own comic character, that of a world-weary old woman in a funny hat and droopy stockings, delivering her gags with a mixture of sassy folk wisdom and sly insights. Her first big success came in 1923 at Connie's Inn in New York.

Her first record album "Moms Mabley at the U.N." was a commercial success, and was followed by "Moms Mabley at the Geneva Conference." In 1962 she made her Carnegie Hall debut on a program with Cannonball Adderley and Nancy Wilson. Her subsequent record successes made her the favorite of a new generation.

Moms Mabley died May 23, 1975 at the age of 78 in White Plains (New York) Hospital. She had lived in Greenburgh, New York and was survived by five children.

JOHNNY MATHIS
Singer

Records and nightclub engagements have combined to establish Johnny Mathis as one of the most successful pop singers. Mathis was born in San Francisco on September 30, 1935, and won an athletic scholarship to San Francisco State College, where he set a high-jump record. In 1935, while watching a friend perform in a San Francisco nightclub, he answered a request to sing, and was discovered by the club's owner. He was soon signed to a recording contract and begin to tour the nightclub circuit.

In 1958 he sang the title song and was featured in the movie *A Certain Smile.* Since then, he has made countless television appearances and is one of the few

Johnny Mathis cutting a record.

singers on the current scene whose appeal is not limited to members of a single age group.

His biggest hits include "Chances Are," "It's Not For Me to Say," and "Twelfth of Never."

Mathis has more than 50 gold and platinum albums and singles. His "Greatest Hits" album stayed on the *Billboard* bestseller charts for a record 490 weeks. In 1978, almost 23 years after his first record was released, he had the number one pop single for the first time, "Too Much, Too Little, Too Late" (with singer Deniece Williams).

Mathis continues to tour the world doing concerts and nightclubs. He also has done television specials. He lives in the Hollywood Hills in California.

HATTIE McDANIEL
Actress
1898–1952

The first black to win an Oscar was Hattie McDaniel, who received the Motion Picture Academy's highest award in 1940 as the year's best supporting actress in *Gone with the Wind.*

McDaniel was born on June 10, 1898 in Wichita, Kansas and moved to Denver, Colorado as a child. After singing on Denver radio as an amateur for some time, she entered vaudeville professionally and, by 1924, was a headliner on the Pantages circuit.

By 1931 she had made her way to Hollywood where, after a slow start (during which she supported herself as a maid and washer woman), she gradually began to get more movie roles. *Judge Priest, The Little Colonel,* and *Showboat* were some of the movies in which she appeared, along with *Saratoga* and *Nothing Sacred.* Her portrayal of a "mammy" figure in *Gone with*

the Wind is still regarded as a kind of definitive interpretation of this role.

In addition to her movie roles, she also had ample success on radio during the 1930s, particularly as Hi-Hat Hattie. She followed this in the 1940s in the title role of the very successful "Beulah" series.

McDaniel died on October 26, 1952.

FLORENCE MILLS
Stage Performer
1895–1927

When Florence Mills died in New York City in November of 1927, she had been acclaimed as the leading black entertainer of her time. As a singing and dancing comedienne, she had become a star not only on Broadway but in London and Paris as well.

Mills was born in Washington, D.C. on January 25, 1895, and made her debut there at the age of five in *Sons of Ham.* In 1903 the family moved to Harlem, and in 1910 she joined her sisters in an act known as The Mills Trio. She later appeared with a group called The Panama Four. (One of its members was Ada "Bricktop" Smith.)

In 1920 she appeared in *Shuffle Along,* a prototype among Negro musicals, and her success led to a long engagement at The Plantation, a New York night spot. After a successful appearance in London, she returned to the United States in 1924 to star in *From Dixie to Broadway,* the show in which she sang the song that became her trademark, "I'm Just a Little Blackbird Lookin' for a Bluebird." Later, her own *Blackbirds* revue was a great success in London and Paris.

Mills returned to the United States in 1927. Exhausted by her work abroad, she entered the hospital

Arthur Mitchell gives the illusion of effortless grace.

Sherman Helmsley, Melba Moore, Novella Nelson, and Cleavon Little in Purlie, *which won star acclaim for Moore's big voice.*

on October 25 for a routine appendectomy, and died suddenly a few days later.

ABBIE MITCHELL
Singer, Actress
1884–1960

Most celebrated as a concert artist, Abbie Mitchell also displayed her versatility in the areas of serious acting and light musical comedy. At the age of 13, she came to New York City from Baltimore, joining Will Marion Cook's Clorindy Company and, later, achieving her first real success with the Williams and Walker Company. (Mitchell married Cook while still in her teens and bore him a son, Mercer, now a diplomat in Africa.)

By 1923 Mitchell had performed in nearly every European country, and returned home to give the first of her many voice concerts in the United States at the Mother A.M.E. Zion Church in New York.

Mitchell also performed with many opera companies and acted in several plays, including *Stevedore* in 1934 and *Coquette* with Helen Hayes. She also headed the voice department at Tuskegee Institute for three years.

She died in 1960 after a long illness.

MELBA MOORE
Singer, actress

With her powerful voice, polychrome personality, and wide range of singing styles, Melba Moore has become one of the brightest new stars in the international entertainment world.

Born in New York City, daughter of singer Melba "Bonnie" Smith and jazz saxophonist Teddy Hill, she spent her early years in Harlem and the rest of her childhood in a middle-class part of Newark, New Jersey. This mixture of backgrounds has contributed much to the unique range of her personality. After graduating from Montclair State Teachers College, she taught elementary school music for a year and began working her way into show business doing lounge work and some background voice sessions for recording companies. She successfully auditioned for the Broadway opening of *Hair* in 1968 and, in her 18-month stint with the show, went up the rungs from ordinary tribe member to female lead. In 1970 she created the musical role of Lutiebelle in *Purlie,* where she received rave reviews and rousing ovations for her rendition of "I Got Love." She also won the Antoninette Perry Award for best supporting actress in a musical, the

New York Critics Award, and the Drama Desk Award for best actress in a musical.

In 1978 she appeared on Broadway in the musical *Timbuktu.* In 1981 she did *Inacent Black,* a comedy with music, on Broadway. She has had straight acting roles in two movies, *Pigeons* and *Lost in the Stars.* On television she guest starred on talk and variety shows, played Harriet Tubman in the 1976 ABC-TV series "The American Woman: Portraits in Courage," and won both the Emmy and the Peabody Award for the PBS Children's series "Big Blue Marble." She was the first black artist to be featured in a one-woman concert at the Metropolitan Opera House in New York, has appeared in concert around the world, and has done many nightclub engagements.

She recently has been involved in producing her own record albums. In 1980 Moore introduced her new sportswear line "500 Francs for Melba Moore," designed, she said, for "a better fit for black women who tend to be smaller waisted and wider hipped."

CLARENCE MUSE
Actor
1889–1979

Perhaps best known for his film acting, Clarence Muse was also successful as a director, playwright, and actor on the legitimate stage.

Born in Baltimore, Muse's parents came from Virginia and North Carolina, a grandfather from Martinique. After studying law at Dickinson University in Pennsylvania, Muse sang as part of a hotel quartet in Palm Beach, Florida. A subsequent job with a stock company took him on tour through the South with his wife and son. Coming to New York, he barely scraped a living together, mostly performing as a vaudevillian.

After several plays with the now-famous groups of The Lincoln Theatre and The Lafayette Players in Harlem, and then a Broadway stint in *Dr. Jekyll and Mr. Hyde,* where white roles were played by blacks in white-face creating quite a controversy, Muse had established himself as an able actor and singer.

His first movie role was in *Hearts in Dixie,* produced at the William Fox Studio, in which Muse played the role of a 90-year-old man. Later he returned to the stage for the role of a butler in the show called *Under the Virgin Moon.* After Muse wrote the theme song, the title was changed to his *When It's Sleepy Time Down South.* Both the song and the show were hits. Muse recalls six encores on opening night.

When the Federal Theatre Project in Los Angeles presented Hall Johnson's *Run Little Chillun,* Clarence Muse directed the show. After a successful run for two years, Muse adapted *Way Down South* for the screen.

During his career he appeared in 219 films and was at one time one of the highest paid black actors, often portraying faithful servant "Uncle Tom" characters. His last film was *Black Stallion* in 1979. He also appeared over the years in concerts and on radio.

Muse died October 13, 1979, the day before his ninetieth birthday. He lived in Perris, California on his Muse-a-While Ranch. He was survived by his third wife, Irene, a son and a daughter.

In October 1980 he was the subject of a segment of the PBS series "Western Exposure"—"Clarence Muse: Black Star of the Silver Screen."

FREDERICK O'NEAL
Actor

Frederick O'Neal is the first black to hold the position of President of Actor's Equity. The honor of leading his profession's union is a fitting tribute to his long years of service to the American theater as both actor and teacher.

O'Neal was born August 27, 1908 in Brookville, Mississippi. After his father's death in 1919, he moved with his family to St. Louis, finishing high school there, and then appearing in Urban League dramatic productions.

In 1927, with the help of some friends in St. Louis, O'Neal founded the Ira Aldridge Players, the second Negro acting group in America. For the next 10 years, he played in 30 of its productions. In 1937 he came to New York and, three years later, helped found the American Negro Theatre. Today, its alumni include such established stars as Sidney Poitier, Earle Hyman, Harry Belafonte, Ruby Dee, Ossie Davis, and Hilda Simms.

O'Neal himself starred in *Anna Lucasta,* and was later featured in *Take a Giant Step, The Winner,* and several other stage productions. In the 1944–1945 season, he won the Derwent Award and the Drama Critics Award for the best supporting performance by an actor on Broadway.

His films include *Pinky* and *The Man with the Golden Arm.* He has also appeared on several TV dramatic and comedy shows.

Devoting full time to Actor's Equity, O'Neal was in 1970 elected International President of the Associated Actors and Artists of America, the parent union which included all of the show business performers' unions. He became president and chairman of the board of the Schomburg Corporation to raise money to conserve and preserve materials in the center, to solicit material, and to work toward construction of a new building. He was a member of the New York State Council on the Arts, President of the Catholic Interracial Council, chairman of the AFL-CIO Civil

Rights Committee, and vice president of the A. Philip Randolph Institute. In 1980 he received the National Urban Coalition's Distinguished Trade Unionist Award.

GORDON PARKS
Photographer, Composer, Author, Director

Gordon Parks, long acclaimed internationally as a photographer, has recently become a leading producer of black films. He is also a composer (*First Concerto for Piana and Orchestra*) and novelist (*The Learning Tree*).

Born in Fort Scott, Kansas, Parks moved to St. Paul, Minnesota, and attended high school there for a time while engaging in a variety of odd jobs. Having chosen photography as a career in 1937, Parks went to Chicago, where he became closely associated with the South Side Community Art Center.

A one-man exhibit of his work eventually led to a Rosenwald Fellowship, after which he accepted a gov-

ernment assignment in the Overseas Division of the Office of War Information.

After World War II, Parks made a number of documentaries for a large New Jersey oil firm, and was later taken on as a staff photographer for *Life*. Since then, he traveled widely, lived abroad, and captured a number of impressive awards, including Magazine Photographer of the Year (1961), the Newhouse Award from Syracuse University, and NAACP's Spingarn Award in 1972.

Parks also has won awards for his writing. His subject matter has included such diverse topics as Black Muslims, Paris of the 1920s, and the plight of all oppressed peoples in U.S. ghettos. His music has been performed in New York, Venice, and Philadelphia.

In addition to *The Learning Tree,* Parks has written an autobiography entitled *A Choice of Weapons* (1965). For National Educational Television, he has produced three documentaries which focus on ghetto life. In 1968 he was the director of the motion picture version of *The Learning Tree.*

His other movies have included *Shaft* and its sequel *Shaft's Big Score, Super Cops,* and *Leadbelly.*

In 1968 his book *A Poet and His Camera* was published. In 1978 he published *Flavio,* the story of a Rio de Janeiro slum child who had become famous because of an earlier picture essay which Parks had done for *Life* magazine. In 1977, with three partners, he gained control of *Essence,* the largest magazine for black women, to prevent the magazine from falling into the hands of whites.

SIDNEY POITIER
Actor

In 1965 Sidney Poitier became the first black to win an Oscar for a starring role, receiving this award for his performance in *Lilies of the Field.* Seven years earlier, Poitier had been the first black actor nominated for the award for his portrayal of an escaped convict in *The Defiant Ones.*

Poitier was born on February 20, 1927 in Miami, but moved to the Bahamas with his family at a very early age. At 15 he returned to Miami, later riding freight trains to New York City, where he found employment as a dishwasher. With the coming of Pearl Harbor, he enlisted in the Army and served on active duty for four years.

Back in New York, he auditioned for the American Negro Theatre, but was turned down by director Frederick O'Neal. After working diligently to improve his diction, Poitier was accepted in the theater group and received acting lessons in exchange for performing backstage chores.

In 1950 he made his Hollywood debut in *No Way*

The first black actor to win an Academy Award was Sidney Poitier.

Out, and followed this with successful appearances in *Cry the Beloved Country* (1952), *Red Ball Express* (1952), *Go, Man, Go* (1954), *Blackboard Jungle* (1956), *Goodbye, My Lady* (1956), *Edge of the City* (1957), *Band of Angels* (1957), *Something of Value* (1957), and *Porgy and Bess* (1959), among others.

Poitier starred on Broadway in 1959 in Lorraine Hansberry's award-winning *Raisin in the Sun,* and repeated this success in the movie version of the play in 1961.

His notable recent films include *To Sir with Love* and *Heat of the Night* in 1967, *Guess Who's Coming to Dinner* with Spencer Tracy and Katherine Hepburn in 1968, *Buck and the Preacher* in 1972 and *A Warm December* in 1973 in both of which he acted and directed, *Uptown Saturday Night* in 1974 for the now defunct First Artists Company (which he had formed with Barbra Streisand, Paul Newman and Steve McQueen), and *A Piece of the Action* in 1977. In 1978 he directed Richard Pryor and Gene Wilder in *Stir Crazy.*

Poitier spent two years writing his memoirs. *This Life* was published by Knopf in 1980. In 1981, Citadel Press published *The Films of Sidney Poitier* by Alvin H. Marill.

Poitier has six daughters, four from his first marriage to Juanita Hardy and two from his second marriage to Joanna Shimkus, in 1976.

RICHARD PRYOR
Comedian, Actor, Writer

"Pryor: Hollywood's Hottest Star" was the headline in a New York newspaper in the spring of 1982. Pryor was starring in two movies simultaneously running in New York, *Live on the Sunset Strip* and *Some Kind of Hero,* both of them taking in millions of dollars at the box office. His movie fee was said to be $3,000,000 plus more than a third of the gross profit.

This was the same Richard Pryor who in June 1980 lay near death for six weeks in the Sherman Oaks (California) Burn Center after an accident in which he had turned himself into a flaming torch.

In June 1981 he was on the cover of *People* magazine and the movie he had been making at the time of the accident, *Bustin' Loose,* was a hit.

Before his accident his life had been filled with violence, fights, lawsuits, drugs, alcohol. After his recovery he was said to be a changed man.

In an interview with Ernie Johnston, Jr., former managing editor of the *New York Amsterdam News* soon after his release from the hospital, Pryor told Johnston, "What is good is getting high on energy. I get high on myself now and I really like Richard. Dope is for dopes," he said in the interview.

An amazingly talented actor as well as a comic, sensational Richard Pryor.

Richard Franklin Lennox Thomas Pryor III was born in Peoria, Illinois in 1940. His grandmother owned a bar and brothel and both his parents worked there. But he was strictly brought up, going to church and to parochial school until his family's profession was discovered. He transferred to public school where his long history of being in trouble began.

His interest in show business began when he was seven while sitting in on drums at Peoria's famous Door Club and watching impromptu performances by Louis Armstrong, Count Basie, and Duke Ellington. His first professional job was at a small club in Canada followed by his first New York job at The Wha? coffee house (when he was hired, he had only 33 cents in his pocket). An appearance on the Ed Sullivan Show led to his first movie, *The Busy Body,* in 1966 followed by *Wild in the Streets.* His movie *Stir Crazy* was one of the top ten grossers in Hollywood history.

Pryor also is a writer and creator of comedy. His work as a writer on the Lily Tomlin specials resulted in two Emmy Awards. He collaborated with Mel Brooks in putting together *Blazing Saddles,* for which he received the American Writers Guild Award and The American Academy of Humor Award.

It was Pryor who created the role of Piano Man in *Lady Sings the Blues,* starring Diana Ross as Billie

Holliday. His first Grammy was for "Craps after Dark" in 1971. In 1974 he won a Grammy for his album "That Nigger's Crazy" and in 1976 another Grammy for the album "Bicentennial Nigger." He also had a nightclub act in the late 1970s. By 1980, four of his comedy albums were gold.

He now lives on the island of Maui in Hawaii where he says he is seeking privacy. He continues to make movies and had several new projects scheduled for 1982.

Pryor has been married several times and has four children.

WILLIS RICHARDSON
Playwright

The great playwright Angelina Grimké taught at the Washington, D.C. high school attended by Willis Richardson. Upon seeing a school production of one of her plays, Richardson commented to a friend that he could write a better play than that, and within a year he had set about the task. Alain Locke and Montgomery Gregory liked Richardson's work and suggested he send it to W. E. B. DuBois at *Crisis,* which was sponsoring plays and productions. *Crisis* promptly accepted and produced Richardson's *Chip Woman's Fortune* along with Oscar Wilde's *Salome.* In 1923 *Chip Woman's Fortune* became the first drama by a black writer to reach Broadway.

In 1930 Dr. Carter Woodson, who had founded the Association for the Study of Negro Life and History, and was sponsoring a national Negro History Week, asked Richardson to edit a book of plays about black history. The result was *Plays and Pageants for the Life of the Negro,* 12 plays, including Richardson's own *The King's Dilemma* and *The House of Sham,* both one-acts for children. In 1935 Richardson collaborated with May Miller (Sullivan), poet and sometimes playwright, to write *Negro History in Thirteen Plays,* using some materials provided by Dr. Woodson.

Willis Richardson, who was 84 years old in 1974, has written nearly 30 one-act plays and almost a dozen three-acts. Besides *Chip Woman's Fortune,* perhaps his most famous, there are *The Broken Banjo, The Amateur Prostitute, Flight of the Natives, The Visiting Lady,* and *Joy Rider.* Throughout his career, Richardson has devoted himself to portrayals of the lives and history of blacks in America, as well as actively participating in the black theater movement in and around Washington, D.C. Of the many groups he worked with, his mutual endeavors with Carter Woodson and the Howard Theatre are the most noteworthy.

Active in a theatrical career which in itself would mean full-time commitment to more average talent,

Richardson spent over 40 years of his life as a full-time employee of the Government Engraving Office.

PAUL ROBESON
Actor, Singer
1898–1976

Paul Robeson earned worldwide fame in a variety of roles—as athlete, actor, singer, and scholar. Born in Princeton, New Jersey on April 9, 1898, Robeson is the son of a runaway slave who put himself through Lincoln University and later became a Presbyterian minister.

Robeson entered Rutgers on a scholarship, and won a total of 12 letters in track, football, baseball, and basketball. In 1917 and again in 1918 he was named All-American by Walter Camp, who later called him "the greatest defensive end that ever trod the gridiron." In addition to his athletic exploits, his academic ability gained him Phi Beta Kappa honors in his junior year.

In 1923 Robeson won a law degree from Columbia, financing his schooling by playing professional foot-

The great Paul Robeson as the Emperor Jones

ball. While at Columbia, Robeson was seen by Eugene O'Neill in an amateur play. After making his professional debut in *Taboo* (1922), Robeson appeared in O'Neill's *All God's Chillun Got Wings* and *Emperor Jones.*

Called upon to whistle in the latter play, Robeson sang instead, and his voice met with instant acclaim. In 1925 he made his concert debut with a highly successful program of all-Negro music. He went on to such stage successes as *Show Boat, Porgy,* and *Othello.* (When he did *Othello* in 1943 in New York, his ovation was called "one of the most prolonged and wildest . . . in the history of the New York theatre.")

A world traveler in the Soviet Union, Asia, and Europe, Robeson spoke several languages, including Chinese, Russian, Gaelic, and Spanish.

Robeson's political affiliations at times tended to attract even more publicity than his artistic career. In 1950, for instance, he was denied a passport after refusing to sign an affidavit as to whether or not he had ever belonged to the Communist Party. Eight years later, the U.S. Supreme Court ruled that the refusal to sign such an affidavit was not valid grounds for denial of a passport. Robeson subsequently settled in London, making a number of trips to the continent (and to the U.S.S.R. as well) before returning to the United States in 1963.

Robeson died January 23, 1976 in Philadelphia, Pennsylvania.

BILL (BOJANGLES) ROBINSON
Dancer
1878–1949

Throughout his long career on stage and in movies, Bill Robinson was known as the "King of Tap Dancers."

Robinson was born on May 25, 1878 in Richmond, Virginia and, being orphaned early, was raised by his grandmother, a former slave. By the time he was eight, he was earning his own way dancing in the street for pennies and working as a stable boy.

In 1887 he toured the South in a show called *The South Before the War* and, the following year, moved to Washington, D.C. where he began working as a stable boy. By 1896 he had teamed up with George Cooper in vaudeville. This act had success on the Keith circuit until the slump of 1907 caused it to fold. Robinson returned to Richmond to work as a waiter, and, a year later, was discovered by a theatrical manager who soon had him working as a cabaret and vaudeville headliner.

In 1927 he starred on Broadway in *Blackbirds,* and in 1932 he had top billing in *Harlems Heaven,* the first all-Negro talking movie. Later, he scored a Hollywood success teaching his famous stair dance to Shirley

Temple in *The Little Colonel.* Robinson made 14 movies, including *The Littlest Rebel, In Old Kentucky, Rebecca of Sunnybrook Farm, Stormy Weather,* and *One Mile from Heaven.*

Robinson died on November 25, 1949.

DIANA ROSS
Actress, Singer

As lead singer with the Supremes, Diana Ross was part of one of the most popular singing groups in musical history. More recently, she's been on her own, garnering raves from critics, college students, and nightclub goers.

Born in Detroit, Diana Ross grew up in a low-rent housing project where she played baseball, sewed her own clothes, and sang with girl friends after school. When she was 14 and had failed to win a singing role in a school musical, she and two friends, Mary Wilson and Florence Ballard, decided to form a musical group of their own. In 1960, in their senior year in high school, the three were hired by Motown Records to sing background and play record hops with Marvin Gaye and Mary Wells.

After finishing high school, the trio was named the Supremes and went on tour with the Motor Town Revue. Their first record to make the charts was "Let Me Go the Right Way." Then "Where Did Our Love Go?" reached number one on the national charts. Over a period of 10 years, the Supremes had 15 consecutive smash hit singles, and at one point they had five consecutive records in the number one position on the charts.

In 1969 Diana Ross decided she was ready to go out on her own. She appeared on the television special "Like Hep" and stole the show from such veteran performers as Dinah Shore, Lucille Ball, and Rowan and Martin. She then went on a nightclub tour and also starred on her own television special "Diana." In 1972 she played Billie Holiday in the film *Lady Sings the Blues.*

Other films followed including *Mahogany* and *The Wiz.* She received a Tony Award for her Broadway show *An Evening with Diana Ross.* Her concert career continues and in 1979 she appeared at Radio City Music Hall and that same year signed a 2.52 million dollar contract for 72 performances at Resorts International in Atlantic City. She has had more number one records than any other artist in the history of the charts, and she recently signed a 20 million dollar contract with RCA Records. In 1981 she had a television special on CBS.

She lives with her three daughters in a 35-room house in Connecticut.

Diana Ross (right), *Cindy Birdsong* (left), *and Mary Wilson—the Supremes—one of the top recording groups of the sixties.*

NIPSEY RUSSELL
Comedian

One of the first "stand-up" comedians to gain success with jokes drawn from the contemporary racial situation is Nipsey Russell. Long before similar material had found its way to the general public via television appearances by various black comedians, Russell was delighting Harlem audiences with his routines at Smalls Paradise and the Baby Grand.

Born in Atlanta, Georgia, Russell at the age of six began to tour the South as a child performer. During his final years in high school, he lived in Cincinnati, and later attended college there earning his B.A. in English in 1946 (with four years out for duty as an Army captain).

Russell has had a running part in television's "Car 54, Where Are You?" and was a frequent guest on Arthur Godfrey's show. He first came to national attention on The Tonight Show when he was a guest of Orson Bean who was substituting for host Jack Paar. Paar subsequently had Russell on the show many times. He has also worked as a panelist on such shows as "Missing Links."

In the 1970s he co-hosted the television shows "The Wide World of Comedy" and the "Les Crane Show." In the 1980s he was appearing in nightclubs and on cruises and doing television variety and quiz shows. Russell lives in Manhattan.

HILDA SIMMS
Actress

Hilda Simms was born Hilda Moses in Minneapolis in 1920, the oldest of 13 children. Her family was very poor, and she worked at many odd jobs to help out before she won a scholarship to the University of Minnesota. After she had been in school for a year and a half, she left to marry William Simms and, shortly afterward, accepted a teaching fellowship at Hampton Institute in Virginia where she also worked for her B.S. degree.

Having completed her course of study at Hampton, Simms left for New York City, working as a singer for several different radio stations before playing the lead in the 1944 production of *Anna Lucasta,* a role which was to make her famous.

The play was a production of the American Negro Theater of Harlem, and was first performed in a tiny theater in the basement of the 135th Street public library in New York. It was subsequently brought to Broadway, where opening night reviewers had high praise for the "beauty and intelligence" of Miss Simms' characterization.

The actress has an interest in writing (she has begun one novel) and has been an active worker in political campaigns. She became a featured columnist in *Tuesday* magazine. Recently she was director of Theater Therapy Addiction Research and Treatment Center.

NINA SIMONE
Singer, Pianist

Nurtured in the tradition of Billie Holiday and fortified as well by years of classical training, Nina Simone is one of the most original and versatile black concert performers to have come along in the past decade. Implicit in her work is a deep-seated racial pride which burns through her music and suffuses her audiences with its liberating intensity and driving force. Her singing style is too individual to classify simply as jazz, popular, folk, gospel, or any other style. Like her piano playing, it is fraught with elements from many recognizable idioms, all of which are blended and contrasted in a highly evocative and spellbinding manner.

Born Eunice Kathleen Waymon on February 21, 1935 in Tryon, North Carolina, Simone exhibited extraordinary virtuosity on the piano early in life but found herself hampered by lack of money to pursue proper training. A dedicated and unselfish teacher soon moved to overcome the difficulty, establishing a fund which enabled her outstanding pupil to attend high school in North Carolina, where young Eunice excelled academically, in extracurricular activities, and in her musical development. She continued her education later at Juilliard and at the Curtis Institute of Music, but was finally forced to support herself by teaching piano privately.

The turning point in her career came in 1954 when she found a job in an Atlantic City nightclub, ostensibly as a performer on the piano, not as a vocalist. Her smashing success in both capacities convinced her that show business was a worthy career for her unique talents. Her first hit record thereafter was a haunting version "I Loves You, Porgy," from the score of Gershwin's celebrated *Porgy and Bess.* At later recording sessions, she discovered a further gift for composition, and thus has come to write more than 50 of her own songs, including the bitter and controversial lament, "Wild is the Wind."

Since 1960, the year she was named Most Promising Singer of the Year, Simone has grown in stature as a concert and nightclub entertainer. She prefers the concert hall, where she feels she can "get more out of myself . . . call on every resource . . . give on a huge scale."

These widely acclaimed performances have placed her time and again among the top 10 performers in national and international jazz polls. In 1966 she was designated Woman of the Year by the Jazz at Home Club in New York City. The following year the National Association of Television and Radio Announcers named her Female Jazz Singer of the Year.

The gifted actress Cicely Tyson in The Autobiography of Miss Jane Pittman, *from young woman to centenarian.*

NOBLE SISSLE
Songwriter
1889–1975

Noble Sissle reaped his early successes teamed up with the great Eubie Blake. Sissle wrote the lyrics and sang them in performance; Blake wrote and played the music. Together they wrote the famous "I'm Just Wild about Harry," which was picked up by the Truman campaign of 1948.

Shuffle Along, the first black musical with a love theme, made Sissle and Blake famous. Joining forces with the writing and comedy team of Miller and Lyles, Sissle and Blake wrote the words and music to over a dozen songs for the show. *Shuffle Along* became a huge success in the United States and Europe, where it had a prolonged tour.

As with most black performers in the early 1900s, Sissle and his troupe would have to travel as far as 20 or 30 miles out of their way from where they were performing in order to find a place to eat and sleep, since blacks were not welcome in the white hotels of the towns they played.

Other Sissle and Blake shows included *Keep Shufflin'* and *Chocolate Dandies*. Sissle attributed his business and popular decline to the increased acceptance of rock and roll music, but said his long popularity was due to "beautiful music."

Noble Sissle died December 17, 1975 at his home in Tampa, Florida.

CICELY TYSON
Actress

During the early 1970s Cicely Tyson emerged as America's leading black dramatic star. This she achieved with two sterling performances—as Rebecca, the wife of a southern sharecropper in the film *Sounder;* and as the lead in a television special, *The Autobiography of Miss Jane Pittman*, the story of an ex-slave who past her hundredth year challenges racist authority by deliberately drinking from a "white only" water fountain as a paunchy white deputy sheriff looks on ominously.

Though both roles were of southern women, Cicely Tyson was born in New York City. She was raised strictly by a very religious, proper mother, who associated movies with sin and forbade Cicely to attend them. When 18, Cicely became a secretary, but one day she stood up before an office of fellow workers, announced that God did not put her on Earth to pound a typewriter and walked out.

Blessed with poise and natural grace, Cicely became a model, appearing on the cover of America's two foremost fashion magazines, *Vogue* and *Harper's Bazaar* in 1956. Interested in acting, she started to study

drama and in 1959 appeared on a CBS culture series, *Camera Three,* with what is believed to be the first African natural hair style on television.

Her star rising, Cicely Tyson won a role in an off-Broadway production of Jean Genet's *The Blacks,* for which she received the 1962 Vernon Rice Award. She then played a lead part in the CBS-TV series *East Side, West Side.*

From this, Cicely Tyson moved into film parts in *The Comedians, The Heart Is a Lonely Hunter,* and others. Critical acclaim led to the role of Rebecca in *Sounder,* for which she was nominated for an Academy Award and named Best Actress by the National Society of Film Critics. She won an Emmy TV acting trophy for *Jane Pittman.*

More than most stars, Cicely Tyson demands to be judged solely on her professional ability, making little effort to garnish her image. She will not say whether or not she was married, remarks frankly that she is not sure pregnancy in an unmarried relationship is grounds for marriage, and refuses to confirm or deny that she herself has had a son and daughter out of wedlock. In 1974 she was the first actor, of any race or sex, to be honored with a day by the Harvard University Faculty Club, and in 1975 firmly declared that she would not participate in any film she regarded as black exploitation.

Her recent films have included *The Blue Bird, River Niger,* and *Wilma.* On television she did "Roots" and "King," and portrayed Harriet Tubman in "A Woman Called Moses" and Chicago schoolteacher Marva Collins in a television movie.

In 1979 Marymount College presented her with an honorary Doctor of Fine Arts. Tyson owns a house on Malibu Beach in California. In November 1981 she married jazz trumpeter Miles Davis in Amherst, Massachusetts.

LESLIE UGGAMS
Singer, actress

Once dubbed a black Shirley Temple, scintillating Leslie Uggams has been a popular performer since her childhood. Nevertheless, abiding undisputed fame did not come to the versatile entertainer until she opened on Broadway in the much-heralded musical *Hallelujah Baby.* The show was given the lift and verve it needed to survive by Uggams' dynamic and impressive performance.

Born in the Washington Heights section of New York City in May 1943, Uggams enjoyed a comfortable childhood. She made her singing debut at the age of six, performing with the choir of St. James Presbyterian Church in New York, and followed shortly thereafter with her acting debut in the television series "Beulah."

Singer Leslie Uggams has been a popular performer since childhood.

Uggams developed her poise and stage presence early in life, attending the Professional Children's School, where she was chosen student body president in her senior year.

Later she won $25,000 on the popular TV quiz show "Name That Tune," gaining the opportunity, as well, to renew her interest in a singing career. In 1961 Uggams became a regular on the Mitch Miller show, a variety offering featuring old favorites. She was at the time the only black performer appearing regularly on network television.

Throughout the 1960s, Uggams appeared in numerous nightclubs and filled several supperclub and television engagements. Her big break came when she was signed as a replacement for Lena Horne in *Hallelujah Baby,* a show which represented a kind of musical chronicle of the civil rights movement. Billed as "pure sunshine" and worth the price of admission by herself, Uggams was elevated to instant stardom and received a Tony Award for her performance. On television she appeared as Kizzy in "Roots" and in "Backstairs at the White House," a miniseries.

In 1965 Uggams married a white man, Grahame Pratt, and she has two children.

Uggams has written a beauty book (*The Leslie Uggams Beauty Book*) dedicated to her two early mentors,

Harry Salter and Mitch Miller, both of the "Name That Tune" era. The pair had "nothing to do with her beauty," one New York reporter once pointed out, "but a great deal to do with its intelligent exploitation."

In May 1982 Leslie Uggams was appearing in a new Broadway show, *Blues in the Night,* at the Rialto Theater in New York City.

BEN VEREEN
Dancer, Actor

Ben Vereen was born in the Bedford-Stuyvesant section of Brooklyn, New York and attended the High School of Performing Arts in Manhattan. Vereen was also an active member of the Pentecostal Church. His dancing ability was uncovered almost accidentally after he had been sent to dance school by his mother. Vereen would have preferred playing stickball with neighborhood kids. Vereen has been called America's premier song and dance man and his talents were discovered by Sammy Davis, Jr. while performing in the chorus of *Sweet Charity.*

Many have said that Vereen is the most gifted, energetic, and multifaceted entertainer since Davis. Vereen starred in the ABC comedy series "Tenspeed and Brown Shoe" and is known for his television specials. The most notable special was "Ben Vereen—His Roots," which won seven Emmy Awards. He also portrayed Louis "Satchmo" Armstrong and received wide acclaim for his role of Chicken George in the original "Roots" and also for his performance in "Jubilee."

Vereen is best known for his Broadway role in *Pippin,* which won him a Tony Award. He was also nominated for a Tony for his co-starring role in *Jesus Christ Superstar.*

He has appeared at the White House on several occasions, and during the 1980 inauguration of President Ronald Reagan Vereen came under fire from blacks after he appeared in blackface on national television.

ADAM WADE
Singer, Actor

Multitalented Adam Wade came to the performing arts via the basketball court and the laboratory of polio-vaccine discoverer Dr. Jonas Salk, for whom he worked as a research assistant.

Born in Pittsburgh, he won a basketball scholarship to Virginia State College and later studied biochemistry at the University of Pennsylvania. Although he had been singing since childhood, his professional start did not come until he did a songwriting friend the favor of singing some of his lyrics to a New York recording agent. Liking the voice more than the words, the agent

The legendary vaudeville team of Bert Williams and George Walker

signed Wade in 1960 to sing "Tell Her for Me," which became a hit and launched his career, followed by "Ruby" in 1961. After considerable early success as a vocalist, he turned to drama and has appeared in many stage, television, and movie roles. As host on the CBS show "Musical Chairs" he became the first black entertainer to host a daily game show. In the mid-1970s he also was preparing a nightclub act with two female vocalists.

THEODORE WARD
Playwright

One of the America's greatest living playwrights, Theodore Ward, has been virtually ignored by the theater establishment. Long an active advocate of racial equality and social justice, Ward's plays have consistently served as artistic witness of the history of black people in the United States.

When his play *Big White Fog* reached the "legitimate" stage in 1940, Ralph Ellison noted, "Seldom in literature or on stage has the inner dignity of an oppressed people struggling to affirm its nationhood risen so indestructibly, so magnificently, as in the Negro family portrayed in *Big White Fog*." The same words would ring true for most of Ward's more than 15 full-length dramas. Yet his work has appeared on Broadway just once: *Our Lan'* in 1947. Since that production, Ward has not had a nationally noticed production, in spite of numerous grants and awards, including the Theatre Guild Award, a John Simon Guggenheim Fellowship, and the National Theatre Conference.

Born on September 15, 1902, in Thibodeaux, Louisiana, Ward was the son of a schoolteacher. Running away from home after the death of his mother, he spent much of his teens wandering from city to city, from coast to coast, working in menial employment.

Ward was most prolific during the years between 1930 and 1950. Besides his two best known works, *Big White Fog* and *Our Lan'*, Ward's other plays include *The Daubers*, a play about the social and political implications of drug abuse in a black middle-class family, *Charity*, a musical portrayal of the life of the famed slave performer Blind Tom, *John Brown, Even the Dead Arise, Whole Hog or Nothing*, and *The Creole*, based on a story by Frederick Douglass concerning a black revolt aboard a slave ship.

In 1980 Ward could be reached through Free So Theater, 1328 Dryades, New Orleans, Louisiana 70113.

ETHEL WATERS
Singer, Actress
1900–1977

The distinguished career of Ethel Waters spanned half a century, and made its mark in virtually every entertainment medium—stage, screen, television, and recordings.

Ethel Waters was born on October 31, 1900, and spent most of her childhood in Chester, Pennsylvania. At the age of 17, she was singing professionally at the Lincoln Theatre in Baltimore. During this early phase of her career, she became the first woman to perform W. C. Handy's "St. Louis Blues" on stage.

After several years in nightclubs and vaudeville, she made her Broadway debut in the 1927 review *Africana*. In 1930 she appeared in *Blackbirds,* and in 1931 and 1932 she starred in *Rhapsody in Black.* The following year she was featured with Clifton Webb and Marilyn Miller in Irving Berlin's *As Thousands Cheer.* In 1935 she co-starred with Bea Lillie in *At Home Abroad* and, three years later, she played the lead in *Mamba's Daughters.*

In 1940 she created her greatest role in *Cabin in the Sky,* a triumph which she repeated in the 1943 movie version. Her other films include *Rufus Jones for President* (1931), *Tales of Manhattan* (1941), *Cairo* (1942), *Stage Door Canteen* (1943), and *Pinky* (1949).

Her autobiography, *His Eye Is on the Sparrow,* was a 1951 Book-of-the-Month Club selection. The title is taken from a song which she sang during her memorable performance in the 1950 stage success *Member of the Wedding.*

Ethel Waters sang at a worship service at the White House in 1971, and was invited again to attend the wedding of Tricia Nixon. In her obituary *The New York Times* noted, "In the last two decades of her life, her religious spirit came to the fore more and more and more. She was brought up as a Roman Catholic but said she was a Baptist, a Methodist, 'everything that's help to people.' Through the Billy Graham crusades she rededicated herself to Jesus." Waters died September 1, 1977 in Chatsworth, California, at the home of friends with whom she lived.

BERT WILLIAMS
Vaudevillian
1876–1922

The legendary Bert Williams is considered by many to be the greatest black vaudeville performer in the history of the American stage. His considerable success extended into the realm of musical comedy as well.

Born in 1876 in the Bahamas, Williams moved to New York with his family, and then on to California, where he graduated from high school. After studying civil engineering for a time, he decided instead to try his hand at show business.

In 1895 he teamed with George Walker to form a successful vaudeville team. Five years later, they opened in New York in *The Sons of Ham* and were acclaimed for the characterizations that became their stock-in-trade . . . Walker as a dandy, and Williams in blackface, complete with outlandish costumes and "Negro" comic dialect. The show ran for two years.

In 1902 their show *In Dahomey* was so popular that they took it to England, and met with equal success there. The partners continued to produce shows such as *The Policy Players, Bandanna Land,* and *Abyssinia* until Walker's death in 1909.

Thereafter, Williams worked as a featured single in the Ziegfeld Follies, touring America for 10 years in several versions of the show. His most famous songs were *Woodman, Spare That Tree; O, Death, Where is Thy Sting;* and *Nobody,* his own composition and trademark.

Williams died of pneumonia on March 4, 1922.

DEMOND WILSON
Actor

Demond Wilson's mother admired Bill Robinson and wanted her son to become a famous dancer too. But the family flat in Harlem where he was born in 1947 had linoleum floors—and tap dancing destroyed the linoleum. So Demond was put in the bathroom, where the floor was covered with a harder, mosaic-type tile, and told to dance.

When he was 4, Demond's mother took him to try out for a part in the Broadway play *Green Pastures* starring William Marshall. He got the part—a cherub in heaven.

After Wilson outgrew his mother's prodding he enrolled in Hunter College in New York where he studied drama and the arts. Two years later he dropped out to make some money, then he was drafted and sent to Vietnam.

After being discharged, Wilson went on tour with *Boys in the Band,* a play with a homosexual theme. "That was the one thing my folks weren't too happy about," said Wilson, "They were relieved when I got in my old car and drove to Hollywood."

Then things happened fast. Wilson won a part in *The Organization* starring Sidney Poitier, and then a role in a segment of "All in the Family" as a burglar. It was that role which led to his audition for the part of Lamont Sanford in the popular TV show *Sanford and Son* in which he co-starred with Redd Foxx. He also appeared in the TV situation comedy "Baby, I'm Back." In the mid-1970s he also was appearing in Las Vegas with a new nightclub act.

Flip Wilson, one of the big names and truly original talents in comedy

FLIP WILSON
Comedian

Flip Wilson has reached the pinnacle of stardom in the entertainment world with a series of original routines and ethnic characters rivaled only by Bill Cosby. Wilson's hilarious monologues, seen on a number of network television shows, made him perhaps the most visible black comedian of the early 1970s.

Born on December 8, 1933 and named Clerow, he was the tenth in a family of 24 children, 18 of whom survived. The family was destitute with his father being a painter, and Wilson was a troublesome child during his youth in Jersey City. He ran away from reform school several times, and was ultimately raised in foster homes.

Wilson's comic talents first surfaced during a hitch in the Air Force. While in service, he was sent overseas to the Pacific theater, where he entertained his buddies with such preposterous routines as "The Sex Habits of the Coconut Crab."

Back in civilian life, he became a bellhop and part-time showman, but constant economic pressure left him without adequate time to refine his spontaneous material. Opportunity struck in 1959 when a Miami businessman gave him $50 a week for a year, thus enabling him to concentrate on the evolution of a successful style.

For the next five years or so, Wilson was a regular at the Apollo in Harlem. In 1965 he began a series

of nationwide appearances on the "Tonight Show." Long-term contracts and several hit records have followed in quick sequence since then, and Wilson has become firmly established as one of the big names and truly innovative talents in the comedy profession.

With "The Flip Wilson Show" in the early seventies, he became the first black to have a weekly prime time TV show with his own name. He became famous for his original character creations such as "Geraldine." On January 31, 1972 he was on the cover of *Time* magazine. In 1976 he made his dramatic debut on TV in the ABC series *Six Million Dollar Man*.

Wilson has been national president of the American Cancer Society. In 1975 his common-law wife of 17 years and the mother of his four children filed for divorce in Florida.

In the early 1980s he was doing nightclubs and television specials. Wilson lives in California.

STEVIE WONDER
Singer, pianist, composer

Stevie Wonder was born in 1950 in Saginaw, Michigan. Blind since birth, Wonder began his professional career recording with Motown in Detroit. At the height of his career in the mid-1970s, Wonder had recorded

Stevie Wonder's records have been at the top of the charts since the mid-seventies. He has over a dozen gold records.

more than 12 gold records. During the time frame of 1975 and 1976, Wonder received more singing awards than any other pop singer. He has recorded such hits as "I Call It Pretty Music," "Fingertips," and "Uptight." He has also appeared in the movies *Bikini Beach* and *Muscle Beach Party*.

In the 1980s Wonder began to speak out and lead demonstrations in Washington, D.C. to press for the birthdate of Dr. Martin Luther King, Jr. to be made a national holiday. His recording "Happy Birthday to You" became a part of the January 15th birthdate of Dr. King and the record is played by disk jockeys across the country as part of the King memorial.

PLAYS BY AND ABOUT BLACKS

Title	Author	Date of Production
The Black Doctor	Ira Aldridge	1847
The Brown Overcoat	Victor Sejour	1858
The Escape: or, A Leap for Freedom	William Wells Brown	1858
Caleb, the Degenerate	Joseph Cotter, Sr.	1901
Rachel	Angelina Grimké	1916
Mine Eyes Have Seen	Alice Dunber Nelson	1918
They that Sit in Darkness	Mary Burrill	1919
Balo	Jean Toomer	1924
Appearances	Garland Anderson	1925
The Church Fight	Ruth Gaines Shelton	1925
A Sunday Morning in the South	Georgia Douglass Johnson	1925
For Unborn Children	Myrtle Smith Livingston	1926
'Cruiter	John Matheus	1926
Flight of the Natives	Willis Richardson	1927
The Purple Flower	Marita Bonner	1928
Meek Mose	Frank Wilson	1928
Undertow	Eulalie Spence	1929
Graven Images	May Miller	1929
Harlem	Wallace Thurman with William Jordan Rapp	1929
Job Hunters	H. F. V. Edward	1931
Run Little Children	Hall Johnson with Lew Cooper	1933
Louisiana	Augustus Smith	1933
Bad Man	Randolph Edmonds	1934
Legal Murder	Dennis Donoghue	1934
Little Ham	Langston Hughes	1935
Mulatto	Langston Hughes	1935
Don't You Want to Be Free?	Langston Hughes	1937
Natural Man	Theodore Browne	1937
Big White Fog	Theodore Ward	1938

Title	Author	Date of Production
Divine Comedy	Owen Dodson	1938
Limitations of Life	Langston Hughes	1938
Dry August	Charles Sebree	1938
Joy Exceeding Glory	George Norford	1938
Native Son	Richard Wright and Paul Green	1941
Walk Hard	Abram Hill	1944
District of Columbia	Stanley Richards	1945
On Strivers' Row	Abram Hill	1945
Our Lan'	Theodore Ward	1947
A Medal for Willie	William Branch	1951
Gold through the Trees	Alice Childress	1952
Take a Giant Step	Louis Peterson	1953
The Amen Corner	James Baldwin	1954
In Splendid Error	William Branch	1954
Mrs. Patterson	Charles Sebree with Greer Johnson	1954
Trouble in Mind	Alice Childress	1955
A Land Beyond the River	Loften Mitchell	1956
Simply Heavenly	Langston Hughes	1957
A Raisin in the Sun	Lorraine Hansberry	1959
Fly Backward	C. Bernard Jackson and James V. Hatch	1960
The Drinking Gourd	Lorraine Hansberry	1960
Marcus in the High Grass	Bill Gunn	1960
Purlie Victorious	Ossie Davis	1961
Moon on a Rainbow Shawl	Errol John	1962
Tambourines to Glory	Langston Hughes	1963
Walk in Darkness	William Hairston	1963
The Slave	Imamu Amiri Baraka	1964
Blues for Mister Charlie	James Baldwin	1964
The Sign in Sidney Brustein's Window	Lorraine Hansberry	1964
Funnyhouse of a Negro	Adrienne Kennedy	1964
Dutchman	Imamu Amiri Baraka	1964
Star of the Morning	Loften Mitchell	1964
Day of Absence	Douglas Turner Ward	1965
The Owl Answers	Adrienne Kennedy	1965
The Zulu and the Zayda	Ossie Davis	1965
Goin' a Buffalo	Ed Bullins	1966
Who's Got His Own	Ronald Milner	1966
The Tumult and the Shouting	Thomas Pawley	1969
Daddy Goodness	Richard Wright (produced posthumously)	1968

Title	Author	Date of Production	Title	Author	Date of Production
Wine in the Wilderness	Alice Childress	1969		music and lyrics by Charles Smalls	
Black Love Song #1	Val Ferdinand	1969	*Black Picture Show*	Bill Gunn	1975
No Place to Be Somebody	Charles Gordone	1969	*The Taking of Miss Janie*	Ed Bullins	1975
The Duplex	Ed Bullins	1969	*The First Breeze of Summer*	Leslie Lee	1975
Job Security	Martie Charles	1970			
Ain Supposed to Die a Natural Death	Melvin Van Peebles	1971	*Dr. Jazz*	Paul Carter Harrison	1975
Don' Play Us Cheap	Melvin Van Peebles	1972	*For Colored Girls Who Have Considered Suicide When the Rainbow Is Enuf*	Ntozake Shange	1976
Don't Bother Me, I Can't Cope	Micki Grant	1972			
The River Niger	Joseph Walker	1973			
Black Girl	J. E. Franklin	1973	*Bubbling Brown Sugar*	Loften Mitchell with Rosetta Le Noire; music by Duke Ellington	1976
My Sister, My Sister	Ray Aranha	1973			
Short Eyes	Miguel Pinero	1974			
The Sirens	Richard Wesley	1974			
The Prodigal Sister	J. (Jenny) E. Franklin; music by Micki Grant, lyrics by Micki Grant and J. E. Franklin	1974	*Your Arm's Too Short to Box With God*	Conceived by Vinnette Carroll; music and lyrics by Alex Bradford and Micki Grant	1976
Sizwe Banzi Is Dead	Athol Fugard, John Kani, Winston Ntshona	1975	*The Brownsville Raid*	Charles H. Fuller, Jr.	1976
The Wiz	William F. Brown,	1975	*Eden*	Steve Carter	1976

Bruce Strickland, Frozine Jo Thomas, Peggy Alston, and Carol Woods in the smash New Orleans musical One Mo' Time, *now in its third year.*

Title	Author	Date of Production
I'm Laughin' but I Ain't Tickled	Vinnette Carroll and Micki Grant	1976
Soldiers of Freedom	Louis Rivers	1977
Eubie	Conceived by Julianne Boyd; music by Eubie Blake; lyrics by Noble Sissle, Anzy Razas, Johnny Brandon, F. E. Miller, Jim Europe	1978
Timbuktu	Luther Davis; music and lyrics by Robert Wright and George Forrest	1978
Ain't Misbehavin'	Richard Maltby, Jr.; music and lyrics by Fats Waller (posthumously)	1978
Home	Samm-Art Williams	1979
One Mo' Time	Conceived by Vernel Bagneris	1979
Comin' Uptown	Philip Rose and Peter Udell; music by Gary Sherman; lyrics by Peter Udell	1979
A Lesson from Aloes	Athol Fugard	1980
Sophisticated Ladies	Duke Ellington (music); Donald McKayle (concept)	1981
Lena Horne, The Lady and Her Music	Musical direction by Harold Wheeler	1981
Dreamgirls	Tom Eyen; music by Henry Krieger; lyrics by Tom Eyen	1981
A Soldier's Play	Charles Fuller	1982
Master Harold . . . And The Boys	Athol Fugard	1982
Waltz of the Stork	Melvin Van Peebles	1982

OTHER BLACK ENTERTAINERS

Name	Category	Birthdate
Mary Alice	Actress	1941
Jonelle Allen	Actress	1944
William Duncan Allen	Pianist	1908
Osceola Archer	Actress	1920
Peggy Alston	Singer/actress	n.a.
Joseph Attles	Actor	1903
Priscilla Baskerville	Singer/actress	n.a.
Hinton Battle	Dancer/actor	n.a.

Melvin Van Peebles produced, directed, and stars in Waltz of the Stork *with Bob Carten, C. J. Critt, and Mario Van Peebles.*

Name	Category	Birthdate
Cynthia Belgrave	Actress	1900
Fran Bennett	Actress	1935
Charles Blackwell	Actor	1935
Sherri Brewer	Actress	1922
Charles Brown	Actor	n.a.
Chelsea Brown	Actress	1946
George Stanford Brown	Actor	1924
Graham Brown	Actor	1924
Jim Brown	Actor	1936
Roscoe Lee Brown	Actor	1925
Betty E. Burghardt	Actress	1922
Vinie Burrows	Actor	1925
Gregg Burge	Dancer/actor	n.a.
Leon Bibb	Singer	1926
Jules Bledsoe	Singer	1900
Johnny Brown	Comic	1945
Dick Campbell	Actor	1946
Thelma Carpenter	Actor	1922
Ben Carter	Actor	1912
Alvin Childress	Actor	1952
Rolf Coleman	Actor	1946
Nell Carter	Singer/actress	n.a. [a]
Adolph Caesar	Actor	n.a.
Brian Evaret Chandler	Actor	n.a.
Scatman Crothers	Comic	1905
Dorothy Dandridge	Actress	1924
Clifton Davis	Actor	1945
Peter DeAnda	Actor	1941

[a] Not available.

Name	Category	Birthdate	Name	Category	Birthdate
Carmen de Lavallade	Dancer	1930	Julian Mayfield	Actor	1928
Loretta Devine	Singer/actress	n.a.	Whitman Mayo	Actor	1904
Ivan Dixon	Actor	1934	Barbara McNair	Singer	1939
Josie Dotson	Actor	1936	Claudia McNeil	Actress	1917
O. L. Duke	Actor	n.a.	Butterfly McQueen	Actress	1911
Nat Dickerson	Singer	n.a.	Theresa Merritt	Actress	1903
Arthur Duncan	Dancer	1945	Flournoy Miller	Actor	1887
Roy Felix Eaton	Pianist	n.a.	Zakas Mohoe	Actor	n.a.
Mercedes Ellington	Dancer/actress	n.a.	Lynne Moody	Actress	1902
Mercer Ellington	Musician	n.a.	Manton Moreland	Comic	1901
Lola Falana	Singer	c1944	Pauline Myers	Actress	1900
Step 'N Fletchit	Comic	1900	Denise Nicholas	Actress	1946
Roger Furman	Actor	1936	Maidie Norman	Actress	1936
Charles Gordone	Actor	1925	Odetta	Singer	1930
Louis Gossett	Actor	1936	Ron O'Neal	Actor	1937
Shirley Graham	Actress	1904	Judy Pace	Actress	1950
Micki Grant	Singer/composer	1946	Cecil Perrin	Actor	1945
Theresa Graves	Actress	1945	Lincoln T. Perry	Actor	1902
Roosevelt Grier	Actor	1933	Walter Raines	Actor	1940
Timmy Grimes	Comic	1925	Sheryl Lee Randolph	Singer/actress	n.a.
Danny Glover	Actor	n.a.	Tracy Reed	Actor	1900
Robert Guillaume	Actor/singer	1927	Beah Richards	Actress	1900
Dick Gregory	Comedian	1932	Larry Riley	Actor	n.a.
Charles Griffin	Actor	1937	Roger Robinson	Actor	1941
Moses Gunn	Actor	1929	Percy Rodriguez	Actor	1925
Ed Hall	Actor	1931	Sugar Chile Robinson	Pianist	1939
Juanita Hall	Actress	1914	Diana Sands	Actress	1934
Ina Hartman	Actress	1926	Harold Scott		1935
Hilda Haynes	Actress	1935	Bobby Short	Pianist/singer	1924
Lloyd Haynes	Actor	1926	Frank Silvera	Actor	1914
Sherman Hemsley	Actor	1938	Nat Simmons		1901
George Hillman	Actor	1934	Muriel Smith		1923
Gregory Hines	Dancer/actor	n.a.	Bruce Strickland	Singer/actor	n.a.
Maurice Hines	Dancer/actor	n.a.	Clarice Taylor		1902
Ernest Hogan	Comic	1924	Barbara Ann Teer	Actress	1936
Jennifer Holliday	Singer/actress	n.a.	Frozine Jo Thomas	Singer/actress	n.a.
Robert Hooks	Actor	1937	Lois Towles	Pianist	n.a.
Ida Hubbard	Actress	1900	George Walker	Comic	1873
Phyllis Hyman	Singer/actress	n.a.	J. J. Walker	Actor/comedian	1952
Samuel L. Jackson	Actor	n.a.	Douglas Turner Ward	Actor	1930
Judith Jamison	Dancer/actress	n.a.	Richard Ward	Actor	1935
Blind Lemon Jefferson	Singer	1897	Vernon Washington	Actor	1927
Brent Jennings	Actor	n.a.	Charles Weldon	Actor	n.a.
Dots Johnson	Actor	1903	Leigh Whipper	Actor	1876
Robert Earl Jones	Actor	1900	Jane White	Actress	1921
Woodie King	Actor	1937	Josh White	Singer	1908
George Kirby	Comic	1939	Slappy White	Comic	1930
Eartha Kitt	Singer/actress	1928	Napoleon Whiting	Actor	1901
Ted Lange	Actor	n.a.	Red Wilcher	Singer/actor	n.a.
Roger Lawson	Actor	1942	Clarence Williams III	Actor	1939
Rosetta Le Noire	Actress	1911	Dooley Wilson	Actor	1884
Eugene Lee	Actor	n.a.	Theodore Wilson	Actor	1903
Philip Lindsay	Actor	1924	Andre Womble	Actor	1940
Cleavon Little	Actor	1939	Stevie Wonder	Pianist/singer/composer	1950
Avon Long	Dancer	1910			
Aubrey Lyles	Actor	1884	Allie Woods		1940
Pigmeat Markham	Comic	1900	Carol Woods	Singer/Actress	n.a.

BLACK CLASSICAL MUSICIANS: OUTSTANDING ARTISTS OF THE BLACK CLASSICAL TRADITION

Composers ■ Conductors ■ Musicians ■ Singers ■

The role of the black in the history of music is finally being given serious attention. Recent discoveries of excellent black symphonic music, both contemporary and two centuries old, have begun to ventilate the stereotype of black music as a limited program of spirituals, jazz, and the blues. Even more important, studies of comprehensive musicology (the study of music in relation to the culture and society in which it exists) are beginning to focus on the unique, non-European nature of black music.

Black music looks back to Africa, not Europe, as the Old World. Whereas the European tradition often considers music in the realm of "art for art's sake," African music is first and foremost a social function. It is such an important part of daily life that ritual and social events cannot even happen without exactly proper music. As a result, despite the lack of formal theory, both African music and the traditional African audience have always been among the world's most sophisticated.

Social functionalism, following Dr. Rene-Dominique de Lerma's analysis, has continued to be one of the chief characteristics of Afro-American music.

Never sinking to the level of acoustical decoration, the music remains a key force of events: the Civil Rights movement could not have evolved as it did without the songs of the freedom marchers. Other characteristic elements of black American music, according to Dr. de Lerma, are participant "confusion" (such as the interplay of audience, performer, composer, and arranger), the scale and barform phrasing of the blues, a sense of lively unity with the environment, "speaking" instruments (like Louis Armstrong's trumpet), and inspiration's intense need to find a voice. These are the non-European elements that give traditional Afro-American music its distinctive quality. This degree of complexity might seem exaggerated to students of the European tradition, but black composers have begun to display the sophistication of their musical heritage and of their individual creative talents in classical Western forms also.

Black symphonic music falls into two categories: blackstream music, synonymous with Gunther Schuller's *Third Stream,* which is serious music influenced by the ethnic background described above; and traditional European music created by black composers.

Until a few years ago, composers of either style were largely unknown, but the public relations efforts and researches of Paul Freeman, Dr. de Lerma, C. Edward Thomas and the Afro-American Music Opportunities Association have brought to light a great many first-rate symphonic compositions both old and new. Among the best blackstream pieces are William Grant Still's *Afro-American Symphony* (1931) and Ornette Coleman's *Skies of America.* Examples of black symphonic music in which there is no obvious contribution from the black heritage are the Chevalier de Saint Georges' *Symphonic Concertante* (1782) and Ulysses Kay's *Markings* (1966).

Organizations such as the Afro-American Music Opportunities Association and the Dance Theater of Harlem have been an integral part of clasical music. The Afro-American Music Opportunities Association, in existence since 1969, was formed out of the need for more acknowledgment of black music and musicians. Since its formation, C. Edward Thomas has developed his concepts into viable and dynamic programs which have already substantially changed American musical sociology.

AAMOA has put out its own record label for non-symphonic repertoires with the release of David Baker's *Sonata for Piano and String Quartet* in a performance which features Brazilian virtuoso Helena Freire.

The Dance Theater of Harlem was founded by Arthur Mitchell not only to teach black children but to teach children of all races dance and especially the classical ballet. The company, formed following the assassination of Dr. Martin Luther King, Jr., has won international acclaim and is probably the youngest company appearing throughout the world. Mitchell, the founder and artistic director, attended New York City's High School of Performing Arts and was the first male graduate to receive the annual Dance Award from the school. Mitchell made his debut with the New York City ballet in 1955 in George Balanchine's "Western Symphony." Since its founding, Mitchell has built the company into a strong group with a repertoire that has the distinction of being unique and at the same time appealing to an audience both young and old, black and white.

Over the past few years, there has been an awareness and a renewed interest in black classical music. Still, however, there are more female singers dominating the concert stage than male singers. Simon Estes, in a January 3, 1982 *New York Times* interview, said, "When I tell people about this problem, they say, 'Look, we have Leontyne Price, Shirley Verrett, Grace Bumbry, Martina Arroyo,' and I say, 'Yes, but how many black men?' 'Well . . . , I never thought of that.'" They can't think of another black man singing major roles in opera. Yet there are probably eight black men who are qualified to do it right now."

Persons close to the opera scene as well as opera singers, both male and female, agree that black men haven't made it as big in the field because of the sex image they portray. Most agree that at one time the black male was seen as virile and threatening to whites; such stereotypic attitudes have changed over the years, giving black males more opportunity in many areas of endeavor.

The Metropolitan Opera has 15 black artists on its roster plus two in the chorus. The New York City Opera has 11 black singers in principal roles with two conductors and one stage director. Prior to World War II, there were no black singers in any opera house in the United States, but now they are accepted almost anywhere.

The formation of Opera Ebony provided an avenue for blacks to accept classical music. In the 1980s the black composer and the classical musician can be appreciated more because of a long and varied heritage within the mainstream of American music.

In Harlem, the Harlem School of the Arts has been a vehicle through which black youngsters have been exposed to the classical arts. Many classical performers as well as jazz and pop musicians have participated in workshops at the school.

OUTSTANDING ARTISTS: COMPOSERS, CONDUCTORS, MUSICIANS, SINGERS

ADELE ADDISON
Soprano
1925

Adele Addison received her musical training at Westminster Choir College (Mus. B., 1946) and the University of Massachusetts (1963). After making her recital debut at Town Hall, New York City, in 1952, she went on many annual recital tours of the United States and Canada. In 1963 she made a tour of the Soviet Union under the cultural exchange program. She has appeared with the New England, New York City, and Washington opera companies. Her premiere performances include John La Montaine's *Fragments from the Song of Songs* with the New Haven Symphony (1959) and Poulenc's *Gloria* with the Boston Symphony (1961). She performed the soloist opening concert at Philharmonic Hall of Lincoln Center in 1962, and she is a trustee of Westminster Choir College.

Messo-soprano Betty Lou Allen recently appeared with the Santa Fe and Washington opera companies.

BETTY LOU ALLEN
Mezzo-Soprano
1930

Born in Campbell, Ohio, Betty Lou Allen studied at Wilberforce University and toured with Leontyne Price as the Wilberforce Sisters. She continued her musical studies at the Hartford School of Music (1950) and the Berkshire Music Center (1951), and studied voice with Sarah Peck Moore, Paul Ulanowsky, and Zinka Milanov. Her New York debut was in Virgil Thompson's *Four Saints in Three Acts* with the New York City Opera Company (1953) and her formal opera debut was at the Teatro Colon, Buenos Aires (1964). She has been a soloist with major symphonies on many tours as well as in Bernstein's *Jeremiah* Symphony. She opened the Lyndon Baines Johnson Library Concert Hall (1971) and has appeared with the Santa Fe and Washington opera companies.

MARIAN ANDERSON
Contralto
1902

At the peak of her career, Marian Anderson was regarded as the world's greatest contralto. When she made her Town Hall debut in New York on December 31, 1935, Howard Taubman, the *New York Times* reviewer, described it as "music-making that probed too deep for words."

Marian Anderson was born on February 27, 1902 in Philadelphia and, as a young choir girl, demonstrated her vocal talents by singing parts from soprano, alto, tenor and bass. At the age of 19, she began studying with Giuseppe Boghetti and, four years later, appeared as soloist with the New York Philharmonic. After a short engagement with the Philadelphia Symphony Orchestra, she traveled to Europe on a scholarship granted by the National Association of Negro Musicians.

It was on Easter Sunday in 1939 that Miss Anderson gave what is perhaps her most memorable concert—singing on the steps of the Lincoln Memorial after having been barred from making an appearance at Constitution Hall by the Daughters of the American Revolution (DAR).

In 1955, after years of successful concert work, she made her Metropolitan Opera debut in Verdi's *A Masked Ball.* Two years later, a State Department tour took her around the world. In September of 1958, Miss Anderson was named to the U.S. delegation to the United Nations.

Now retired, she lives with her husband, Orpheus Fisher, in Danbury, Connecticut.

In 1982 when Marian Anderson celebrated her eightieth birthday, Grace Bumbry and Shirley Verrett sang at New York City's Carnegie Hall in tribute to Mrs. Anderson. Ms. Verrett hailed Mrs. Anderson as "a dream maker." Ms. Verrett and Ms. Bumbry are

both former recipients of Marian Anderson scholarships.

THOMAS J. ANDERSON
Composer, Educator
1928

Thomas Jefferson Anderson was born in Coatesville, Pennsylvania. His mother was a musician, and as a teenager he toured with a jazz orchestra. His music shows influences from jazz, the post-Webern composers, and traditional African music.

Anderson studied at West Virginia State College (B.M., 1950), Pennsylvania State University (M.E., 1951), Aspen School of Music, and University of Iowa (Ph.D., 1958). He was composer-in-residence with the Atlanta Symphony Orchestra on a grant from the Rockefeller Foundation during the 1969–1971 seasons. His present post is chairman of the music department of Tufts University.

The composer's most widely performed works have been *Chamber Symphony* (1968); *Squares* (1965), an essay for orchestra, and *Personals* (1966), a cantata for narrator, chorus, and brass ensemble. He has also written music for band (*In Memoriam Zach Walker*), works for piano (*Watermelon*), and various compositions for solo voice and for chorus.

MARTINA ARROYO
Soprano
1939

Martina Arroyo, a New York native, made her debut at the Metropolitan Opera in February 1965 in the title role of *Aida* and has since sung engagements with opera houses in Vienna, Berlin, Buenos Aires, London, and Hamburg. In addition to operatic appearances, she has also been a frequent guest soloist with many of the world's major orchestras.

In addition to Aida, Miss Arroyo's Metropolitan repertoire includes Donna Anna in *Don Giovanni,* Liu in *Turandot,* Leonora in *Il Trovatore,* Elsa in *Lohengrin,* and the title role of *Madame Butterfly.* These have been developed since 1958, the year she made her debut in Carnegie Hall in the American premiere of Pizzetti's *Murder in the Cathedral:* that same year she made her Metropolitan debut as the celestial voice in *Don Carlo.*

On opening night of the 1970–1971 Met opera season Miss Arroyo sang Elvira in *Ernani,* and she opened the 1971–1972 season as Elizabeth in *Don Carlo.*

Ms. Arroyo sang at the White House in 1977 sharing the bill with Andre Previn and Isaac Stern at a dinner

Martina Arroyo as Leonora in Verdi's La Forza del Destino.

for 26 heads of state marking the signing of the Panama Canal treaty.

DAVID BAKER
Composer
1931

David N. Baker, a composer of great promise, directs the jazz studies program at Indiana University. Born in Indianapolis, he obtained his B.A. and M.A. in music education from the university there. He taught music in the public schools of Indianapolis and at Indiana Central College and Lincoln University (Missouri) before returning to his alma mater as a faculty member. Baker has logged considerable experience with both jazz bands and college and municipal symphony orchestras. He was a member of Quincy Jones' All-Star Jazz Orchestra which toured Europe in 1961. Among his better known works is a cello sonata that Janos Starker plays. Paul Freeman has praised Baker's talent as that of a "black Bartok."

KATHLEEN BATTLE
Soprano

An active orchestral soloist, Kathleen Battle made her Met debut in 1977 as the Shepherd in *Tannhäuser*, and has also been heard there as Sophie in *Werther* and Blondchen in *The Abduction from the Seraglio*. She has sung with the symphonies of Chicago, Boston, and Cincinnati, as well as with the New York and Berlin Philharmonics. She is a graduate of the University of Cincinnati's Conservatory of Music. The 1980–1981 season included her first Metropolitan Opera performances of Elvira in *The Italian Girl in Algiers* as well as debuts with the Zurich Opera and the Lyric Opera of Chicago. In 1982 she received critical kudos for her Rosina in the Met's *Barber of Seville*. Ms. Battle was born in Portsmouth, Ohio.

MARGARET BONDS
Composer, Pianist
1913

Margaret Bonds has written several scores for the stage as well as concert works. Born in Chicago, she was encouraged by her mother, a talented organist, to develop her musical gifts. After receiving an M.A. in music from Northwestern, she continued her studies at Juilliard. Her awards include a Rosenwald Fellowship, a Roy Harris Scholarship, and a Wanamaker Award. Her best known works are *Migration*, a ballet; *Spiritual Suite for Piano; Mass in D Minor; Three Dream Portraits;* and, of the many songs, "The Ballad of the Brown King" and "The Negro Speaks of Rivers."

GWENDOLYN BRADLEY
Soprano

Gwendolyn Bradley was born in New York City but grew up in Bishopville, South Carolina. Ms. Bradley was a finalist in the 1977 Metropolitan Opera National Council auditions. She is a graduate of the North Carolina School of the Arts and attended both the Curtis Institute of Music and the Academy of Vocal Arts in Philadelphia and has studied with Margaret Harshaw and Seth McCoy. Ms. Bradley made her Metropolitan Opera debut as the Nightingale in the Met premiere of Raval's "L'Enfant et les Sortileges" in February 1981. Since making her professional operatic debut in 1976 with the Lake George Opera Festival as Nanetta in *Falstaff*, she has been heard as Titania in *A Midsummer Night's Dream* with the Central City Opera, Lakme with Opera/South, and Aurelia in *Rumpelstiltskin* with the Opera Company of Philadelphia. Ms. Bradley has sung with the Philadelphia Orchestra, the Kansas City Philharmonic, and the Charleston Symphony. During 1980–1981 she appeared with the Los Angeles Philharmonic at the Hollywood Bowl and with the Seattle Symphony.

HAROLD J. BROWN
Composer
1909

Harold J. Brown is a composer and choral conductor. He was born in Shellman, Georgia and received a B.A. degree from Fisk University in Nashville, Tennessee in 1923. He received his M.A. degree in 1931 from Indiana University. He has taught at Florida A & M College and at Southern University. Brown was music director at Karamu House and the Huntington Play-

Margaret Bonds plays her Spiritual Suite for Piano.

house in Cleveland. He wrote the oratorio *The Saga of Rip Van Winkle* and *The African Chief,* a cantata.

GRACE BUMBRY
Mezzo-Soprano
1937

Grace Bumbry is the first black performer to have sung at the Wagner Festival in Bayreuth, Germany, and one of the few young singers who can boast of having been called to play a command performance at the White House. Miss Bumbry sang at a formal state dinner opening Washington's official social season in 1962 as a guest of the Kennedys and the nation.

A native of St. Louis, Missouri, Miss Bumbry, like many black singers, had her first exposure to music in a church choir, singing with her brothers and her

The brilliant singing of Grace Bumbry wins worldwide acclaim.

parents at the Union Memorial Methodist Church in St. Louis. After studying voice locally, she won a nationwide talent contest in 1954, and went on, with scholarship aid, to study successively at Boston and Northwestern universities. At the latter school, she attended master classes in opera and lieder given by the famed singer and teacher Lotte Lehmann. Later competitions led to several important cash awards, as well as contacts with such important personages as Marian Anderson.

Beginning in 1959, Miss Bumbry traveled to various European countries, performing in the operatic capitals of the world. On July 23, 1961, Wieland Wagner, grandson of Richard Wagner, shocked many traditionalists by selecting Miss Bumbry to sing the role of Venus in *Tannhäuser,* a role which conventionally calls for a figure of so-called Nordic beauty, usually a tall and voluptuous blond. Miss Bumbry proceeded to give a performance which won acclamation from both the harshest and the kindest of critics, all of whom praised her both for her physical radiance and her brilliant singing.

After her Bayreuth engagement, Miss Bumbry returned to the United States for a concert debut at Carnegie Hall. Her recital was only moderately successful, however. Over the years, critics seemed to question her ability to evolve as a full-fledged interpreter of German lieder, many preferring instead to view her as the possessor of a big voice whose calibre and quality are more suited for opera. To some extent, it would seem that she concurs in this analysis, being on record as having once said: "My style is really Verdi. This is my heart and soul."

In 1974 Miss Bumbry returned to the Met to sing Santuzza in *Cavalleria Rusticana.* She has since appeared successfully with various opera companies as Dalilah, Lady Macbeth, Medea, and other great dramatic roles, which have become her speciality.

On January 31, 1982, Ms. Bumbry joined Shirley Verrett on the stage of Carnegie Hall in New York City to pay tribute to Marian Anderson on her eightieth birthday. Ms. Bumbry sang Adriana's entrance aria from Cilea's *Adriana Lecouvreur* entirely in mezza voice. On December 6, 1981, Ms. Bumbry had also appeared in a benefit concert at Carnegie Hall for Artists to End Hunger.

SAMUEL COLERIDGE-TAYLOR
Composer
1875–1912

Coleridge-Taylor was one of England's most celebrated composers at the turn of the century.

Born to a doctor from Sierra Leone and a British mother, he showed musical gifts at age five and, ten years later, entered the Royal College of Music in Lon-

Samuel Coleridge-Taylor was a celebrated turn-of-the-century composer.

don. There he studied with Sir Charles Wood and Sir Charles Villiers Stanford. Fame was his with the premiere of *Hiawatha's Wedding Feast*.

The beautiful aria "Onaway! Awake, Beloved," became one of the most popular and frequently recorded songs of the period.

In 1901 the Coleridge-Taylor Society was founded in Washington, D.C. specifically to study and perform his music. Harry Burleigh was one of the soloists to perform under the composer's baton soon after, along with a 200-voice choir, 52 musicians from the U.S. Marine Band, and the supplementary strings required by the *Hiawatha* music. The composer was very warmly received in this country. James Weldon Johnson and Booker T. Washington were among his friends, and he was President Theodore Roosevelt's guest at the White House.

ROQUE CORDERO
Composer, Educator
1917

Roque Cordero is respected as one of Latin America's most creative talents because of his abilities as a violinist, a conductor, and a composer who incorporates popular Panamanian forms into concert music.

Born in Panama, his interests developed from popular songwriting to classical music at the age of 17. Four years later, he was appointed director of the Orquesta Sinfonica de la Union Musical in Panama, and he later joined the Orquesta Sinfonica de Panama as violist. In 1943 he began studying abroad. He was engaged by the University of Minnesota as Artistic

Director of the Institute of Latin-American Studies and, after completing his course of study, was awarded a Guggenheim Fellowship. Dr. Cordero is presently music editor for the publishing company of Peer International Corporation and is professor of music at Illinois State University.

PHILIP CREECH
Tenor

Philip Creech is a native of Hempstead, New York and a graduate of Northwestern University. Creech performed with Margaret Hillis' Chicago Symphony Chorus from 1973 to 1975 and frequently appeared as tenor soloist. Since 1976 he has sung with the Chicago Symphony, the Boston Symphony, the New York Philharmonic, and the Cincinnati Symphony. Creech made his debut at the Salzburg Festival in 1979 singing in the Berlioz *Requiem*. He made his Metropolitan Opera debut in September 1979 as Beppe in the season's premiere of Leoncavallo's *Pagliacci,* and was heard later that season as Edmondo in the premiere and subsequent live overseas telecast of the new production of Puccini's *Manon Lescaut.* Creech has also appeared at the Met as Tonio in *Pagliacci.*

OSCEOLA DAVIS
Soprano

Osceola Davis is a native of New Jersey and a graduate of the Philadelphia Musical Academy. She received further vocal training at the Curtis Institute of Music, where she sang Gilda in *Rigoletto* and Despina in *Così fan Tutte.* Ms. Davis went to Germany to sing with the Staatstheater am Gaertnerplatz in Munich, where her roles included Rosina in *The Barber of Seville,* Blondchen in *The Abduction from the Seraglio,* Olympia in *The Tales of Hoffman,* Esmeralda in *The Bartered Bride,* and Papagena in *The Magic Flute.* She returned to the United States in 1979.

WILLIAM LEVI DAWSON
Composer, Conductor
1898

Born in Anniston, Alabama, Dawson attended Tuskegee Institute and later enrolled at the Hornes Institute for fine arts in Kansas City, Kansas. In 1927 he received an M.A. in music from the American Conservatory. One of Dawson's famous orchestral compositions, the *Negro Folk Symphony,* was premiered in 1934 by the Philadelphia Orchestra under the direction of Leopold Stokowski. Critics were moved by the music's "dramatic feeling," "directness of melodic speech," and "sumptuous orchestration." Inspired by Dvorak, Dawson's goal, in his own words, was "to write a symphony in the Negro folk idiom, based on authentic folk, but in the same symphonic form used by the composers of the (European) romantic-nationalist school."

JAMES DEPREIST
Conductor
1936

A gifted and versatile musician, James DePreist has been active in several areas of music as a performer, composer, arranger, and conductor. It is in the last-named field that he has been most often acclaimed by musicians and critics alike as a young man of rare ability. This estimate was confirmed in 1965 when he was appointed assistant conductor of the New York Philharmonic.

Born in Philadelphia on November 21, 1936, De-Preist studied piano and percussion from the age of 10, but did not decide on a musical career until he reached his early twenties. After graduating from high school, he entered the Wharton School of the University of Pennsylvania as a prelaw student, receiving a B.S. in 1958 and an M.A. in 1961.

DePreist also studied music history, the theory of harmony, and orchestration at the Philadelphia Conservatory of Music, and composition with the distinguished American composer Vincent Persichetti.

In 1962 the State Department sponsored a cultural exchange tour of the Near and the Far East, engaging DePreist as an American specialist in music. During this tour, DePreist was stricken with polio, paralyzed in both legs, and flown home for intensive therapy.

James De Preist is assistant conductor of the New York Philharmonic.

Within six months he had fought his way back to the point where he could walk with the aid of crutches and braces. Courage, determination, and talent carried him to the semifinals of the 1963 Dmitri Mitropoulos International Music Competition for Conductors.

After another overseas tour as conductor in residence in Thailand, DePreist returned to the United States, appearing with the Minneapolis International Symphony Orchestra, the New York Philharmonic, and the Philadelphia Orchestra.

In 1964, he recorded what is perhaps his most satisfying triumph, capturing first prize in the Mitropoulos International Competition. Another highlight of his career occurred on June 28, 1965 when he conducted Marian Anderson's farewell concert at Philadelphia's Robin Hood Dell.

CHEVALIER DE SAINT-GEORGES
Composer
1739–1799

The Chevalier de Saint-Georges is considered to be the first man of African ancestry to have made a major impression on European music.

Born on the Caribbean island of Guadeloupe to an African-slave mother and a French father, he displayed early talent on the violin. He studied with François Gossec, whom he succeeded as concertmaster of the celebrated Concert des Amateurs in 1769. His musical output was enormous, including several operas, 11 symphonies concertantes, a dozen string quartets, 10 violin concertos, and other instrumental and vocal works. His hours away from the composing table were as full of life as his music. He was one of Europe's outstanding swordsmen, an expert swimmer and boxer, and colonel of an all-black regiment that included the father of Alexandre Dumas.

Saint-Georges is stylistically and chronologically pre-Classic. Within the frequently pastel-hued hedonism of his music can be found the French progenitors of the string quartet and the basic architecture of the sonata form for violin and piano.

DEAN DIXON
Conductor
1915

In 1941 Dean Dixon became the first black and, at 26, the youngest musician ever to conduct the New York Philharmonic Orchestra.

Dixon was born in Manhattan on January 10, 1915, and graduated from DeWitt Clinton High School in 1932. Exposed to classical music by his parents (as a small boy he was regularly taken to Carnegie Hall), Dixon formed his own amateur orchestra at the Harlem YMCA while he was still in high school.

Dean Dixon conducts the Frankfurt Orchestra.

On the basis of a successful violin audition, he was admitted to the Juilliard School, where he received his B.S. in 1936. Three years later he acquired his master's from Columbia.

The Dean Dixon Symphony Society, which he had formed in 1932, began to receive financial support from the Harlem community in 1937, and in 1941, at the request of Eleanor Roosevelt, Dixon gave a concert at the Heckscher Theater. He was later signed by the musical director of NBC radio to conduct the network's summer symphony in two concerts. Two months after the NBC concerts he made his debut with the New York Philharmonic.

Dixon is currently (1975) director of the Frankfurt Orchestra in Frankfurt, Germany. He makes his home there although he makes occasional visits to the United States to conduct.

MATTIWILDA DOBBS
Coloratura Soprano
1925

One of the world's most gifted coloratura sopranos is Mattiwilda Dobbs. Now residing in Sweden, where she is a national favorite, Miss Dobbs has gained international fame with a voice that has been described as one "of often miraculous beauty . . . fascinating ease and uncanny accuracy."

Born in Atlanta, Georgia on July 11, 1925, Miss Dobbs graduated from Spelman College in 1946 as class valedictorian, having majored in voice training. After studying Spanish at Columbia, where she re-ceived her master's degree, she went on to Paris for two years on a Whitney Fellowship.

In October 1950, competing against hundreds of singers from four continents, she won the International Music Competition held at Geneva. She made her professional debut in Paris, and then became the first black to sing a principal role at La Scala in Milan.

On March 8, 1954, she made her Town Hall debut in New York in the one-act opera *Ariadne auf Naxos,* and received a rousing ovation. A year later she repeated the success with her first concert recital on the same stage.

Since then, she has made numerous recordings, including *The Pearl Fishers* and *Zaïde,* and has toured the world with great success. She is currently a mainstay in the world of Swedish opera.

RUDOLPH DUNBAR
Composer
1917

A native of British Guiana, Rudolph Dunbar received his musical education at the Institute of Musical Art in New York as well as in Paris and Leipzig. In addition to being a musical conductor, Dunbar is also a clarinetist. He made his debut with the NBC Symphony Orchestra in New York City and has conducted in Great Britain and throughout the United States. He is the author of *A Treatise on Clarinet Playing* and is known widely for the composition *Dance of the 20th Century.*

TODD DUNCAN
Actor, singer
1903

Although thinking of himself primarily as a teacher, Todd Duncan has made notable contributions to the world of theater and concert.

Duncan was born into a well-to-do family in Danville, Kentucky on February 12, 1903. He graduated from Butler University in Indianapolis in 1925 and began a teaching career—first at a junior high school and then in Louisville at the Municipal College for Negroes.

In 1934 he appeared in New York in a single performance of an all-black version of the opera *Cavalleria Rusticana.* On the strength of this alone, he was auditioned less than a year later by George Gershwin, and received the role of Porgy in *Porgy and Bess.* He was such a success that he repeated his performance in the role in the 1938 and 1942 revivals of the play.

In 1940 he was a featured performer on Broadway in *Cabin in the Sky.* When the play closed, he headed for Hollywood to appear in the movie *Syncopation.* His concert repertoire includes German lieder and

Simon Estes, the new Metropolitan Opera star.

French and Italian songs. Duncan retired in 1965 after singing at President Lyndon B. Johnson's inaugural. Only once has he broken his retirement and that was in 1972 to sing the title role of *Job* at Washington's Kennedy Center. In 1978 Duncan was honored by the Washington Performing Arts Society with a dinner dance at the Sheraton Park Hotel. He still teaches voice in his home in Washington.

SIMON ESTES
Bass-Baritone

Simon Estes was the first black man to sing at the Bayreuth Festival, appearing in the title role of a new production of *Der Fliegende Holländer,* a portrayal

Simon Estes as the Landgrave in Wagner's Tannhäuser.

he repeated there in three subsequent seasons. A native of Centerville, Iowa, Estes attended the University of Iowa and received a full scholarship to Juilliard studying under Sergius Kagan and Christopher West. He won the Munich International Vocal Competition in 1965 and subsequently was the silver medalist in the Tchaikovsky Competition in 1966. Estes made his operatic debut as Ramfis in *Aida* at the Deutsche Oper Berlin and since then has appeared in most of the world's major opera houses, including La Scala, the Hamburg State Opera, the Bavarian State Opera of Munich, the Vienna State Opera, the Lyric Opera of Chicago, the San Francisco Opera, and the Zurich Opera. He made his debut at the Metropolitan Opera in 1982, foregoing the honor of singing the national anthem on baseball's opening day—the day of his Met debut. He has appeared as soloist with most of the world's leading symphony orchestras. Estes was heard with the National Symphony of Washington at the opening of the Kennedy Center's Concert Hall in 1971. Estes spent the early part of his career making a name for himself in Europe. The grandson of a slave, Estes has been called the world's foremost bass-baritone.

LOUIS MOREAU GOTTSCHALK
Composer, Pianist
1829

Louis Moreau Gottschalk was, perhaps, the first black composer born in the United States to achieve international renown. Chopin praised his debut at the Salle Pleyel in April 1844, and Berlioz, with whom he studied, applauded his "sovereign power."

Born in New Orleans, Gottschalk was a violin prodigy at six years of age and later became a brilliant concert pianist. He was already something of a European matinee idol when he first appeared in New York, on February 10, 1853, and his romantic compositions enjoyed a wide vogue.

Although Gottschalk went to Paris when he was 13 to study with Halle, Stamaty, and Maleden, much of his music reflected the Creole environment of his early childhood. One of his best-known compositions, *La Bamboula,* is based on the sights and sounds of New Orleans' Congo Square. His autobiographical book, *Notes of a Pianist,* provides an interesting description of his background and method of composition.

RERI GRIST
Coloratura Soprano

Reri Grist, one of America's best coloratura sopranos, has sung at most of the world's great opera houses,

Louis Moreau Gottschalk enjoyed international fame for his music.

including La Scala, Vienna State, Britain's Royal Opera, and the Met.

Miss Grist first came to national attention in the role of Consuela in Leonard Bernstein's *West Side Story,* and compounded this success in a performance of Mahler's *Fourth Symphony* with the New York Philharmonic.

When Dr. Herbert Graf, the former stage director of the Met, left in 1960 to become Director of the Zurich Opera, he persuaded many operatic talents, including Miss Grist, to accompany him there. While in Europe, Miss Grist was asked by Stravinsky to sing under his baton in *Le Rossignol.* In July 1964 she made a successful debut at the renowned Salzburg Festival in Austria. She now resides in Austria, where she is a national favorite.

HELEN EUGENIA HAGAN
Pianist
1893–1964

Born in Portsmouth, New Hampshire, Ms. Hagan is a graduate of the Yale University School of Music.

Reri Grist as Sophie in Richard Strauss' Der Rosenkavalier.

She received a Samuel Simmons Sanford Fellowship to study two years abroad and made her New York City debut in Aeolian Hall. Ms. Hagan was later on the faculty at Bishop College in Dallas, Texas.

HILDA HARRIS
Mezzo-Soprano

Hilda Harris is a native of Warrenton, North Carolina and has been heard frequently with the New York City Opera where her roles include Cherubino in *The Marriage of Figaro,* Orsini in *Lucrezia Borgia,* Smeton in *Anna Bolena,* and Nicklausse in *Tales of Hoffman.*

Ms. Harris has also sung with the San Diego Opera, the Pittsburgh Opera, and the companies of Miami, St. Paul, and Fort Worth. She made her Metropolitan debut as the Wardrobe Mistress/The Schoolboy in the 1976–1977 premiere of Alban Berg's *Lulu.* Ms. Harris is an active orchestral soloist, having been heard with the New York Philharmonic, the Pittsburg Symphony, the Buffalo Philharmonic, and the Houston Symphony, as well as with orchestras in England, Holland, Luxembourg, and Switzerland.

ROLAND HAYES
Tenor
1887–1977

The success of Roland Hayes in the concert field played a great part in broadening the opportunities later afforded such singers as Paul Robeson and Marian Anderson.

Hayes was born of former slave parents in Curryville, Georgia on June 3, 1887. His tenant-farmer father was crippled by an accident and died when Hayes was 12. Determined that her seven children would not share her illiteracy, Hayes' mother sent them to Chattanooga, Tennessee, where they set up a rotating system whereby one brother worked while the others attended school. Hayes was employed in a machine shop but, when his turn came to go to school, he passed it up, continuing to supply the family income while he studied at night.

In 1917 he became the first black to give a recital in Boston's Symphony Hall. Three years later he traveled to London and gave a royal command performance, following this up with other successes on the continent. Over the years, his rich, delicate tenor voice was used to good advantage in programs blended from Negro spirituals, folk songs, operatic arias, and German lieder.

Hayes gave a well-received farewell concert at Carnegie Hall in New York on the occasion of his seventy-fifth birthday in 1962.

During his career, Hayes received many awards and citations including eight honorary degrees and the NAACP's Spingarn Medal for the most outstanding achievement among blacks in 1925.

Hayes died in Boston on January 1, 1977 at the age of 89.

ISOLA JONES
Mezzo-Soprano

Since making her Met debut in 1977 as Olga in *Eugene Onegin,* Isola Jones has been heard there in more than a dozen roles, including Maddalena in *Rigoletto,* which was telecast "Live from the Met," Lola in *Cavalleria Rusticana,* Mercedes in *Carmen,* and a Musician in

Ulysses Kay composes elegant symphonic music.

Manon Lescaut, which was also televised in the "Live from the Met" series. Ms. Jones is a native of Chicago and a graduate of Northwestern University. She has sung Carmen with the Stamford State Opera and has been heard at Santa Fe, with the symphonies of Chicago, Los Angeles, Cleveland, Boston, and at the Ravinia Festival.

ULYSSES KAY
Composer, Educator
1917

Ulysses Simpson Kay is a traditionally trained classical composer and the creator of eloquent symphonic music.

Born in Tucson, he won a scholarship to the Eastman School of Music and went on to study with Paul Hindemith at Yale and Otto Luening at Columbia. He spent the years 1942–1945 in the Navy, where he played with the bands, and 1949–1952 in Rome studying music as a Fulbright fellow. He has visited the Soviet Union on a cultural exchange program and is currently Distinguished Professor of Music at Herbert H. Lehman College in New York.

Kay is a prolific composer. His works for voice, chamber groups, and orchestra include *Choral Triptych, Six Dances* (for string orchestra), *Fantasy Variations* (for orchestra), *Sinfonia in F,* and *The Boor* (an opera). He is regularly performed and recorded throughout the United States and Europe.

Although his uncle was King Oliver, the legendary cornet player, Kay believes that jazz is a much more limited medium than symphonic music, where "you can express everything."

HENRY LEWIS
Conductor
1933

Henry Lewis attracted worldwide attention in the 1970s because of his conductorial abilities. He was the first black conductor of a leading American symphony orchestra when he was named to head the New Jersey Symphony Orchestra. Lewis was also the first black person to conduct *La Bohème* at the Metropolitan Opera in New York. He has served as assistant conductor of the Los Angeles Philharmonic and also formed and conducted his own orchestra, the Los Angeles Chamber Orchestra.

DOROTHY MAYNOR
Soprano
1910

Within a short time after her debut at New York's Town Hall in 1939, soprano Dorothy Maynor was being acclaimed by critics as a leading American singer. Since then, she has appeared as a soloist with almost every major symphony orchestra in the United States, and has made concert tours in Europe, Canada, and Latin America.

Born Dorothy Leigh Mayner (she changed the spelling of her last name when she became a singer) on September 3, 1910 in Norfolk, Virginia, she was raised in an atmosphere of music and singing. Nevertheless, she was originally intent on becoming a home economics teacher and, with this in mind, entered Hampton Institute at the age of 14. She received her B.S. degree in 1933 and, shortly afterwards, was heard by the director of the Westminster Choir, who made it possible for her to receive a scholarship at Westminster Choir College in Princeton, New Jersey.

In 1935 she graduated with a B.M. degree and left for New York to study voice. After four years of directing a choir and teaching, she felt that she was ready for her New York debut, which took place in November of 1939. She had previously received support from Serge Koussevitzky, the conductor of the Boston Symphony Orchestra, who had once heard her sing and exclaimed: "The whole world must hear her!"

Miss Maynor has made several recordings for RCA Victor, and has been a guest artist on both radio and television. When not on tour, she lives in New York City with her husband, the Reverend Shelby A. Rooks of St. James Church.

In 1975 Miss Maynor was elected to the Metropolitan Opera's board of directors, becoming the first black to sit on the Met board. She is founder of the Harlem School of the Arts in St. James Presbyterian Church, which is pastored by her husband. The school is now a huge complex on St. Nicholas Avenue in New York's Harlem.

Robert McFerrin singing the role of Valentin in Faust.

ROBERT MCFERRIN
Baritone
1921

Born in Marianna, Arkansas, Robert McFerrin studied at Fisk University (1940–1941), Chicago Municipal College (1941–1942; 1946–1948), and Kathryn Turney Long School (1953). He sang the title role in *Rigoletto* with the New England Opera Company (1950), was a baritone soloist in the Lewisohn Stadium Summer Concert Series (1954), and made his Metropolitan Opera debut with the role of Amonasro in *Aida* (1955). He has been a guest professor of voice at Sibelius Academy, Finland (1959) and served as a member of the voice faculty at Nelson School of Fine Arts in Nelson, B.C., Canada.

MYRA MERRITT
Soprano

Myra Merritt, a native of Washington, D.C., is a member of the Metropolitan Opera company's Young Artist Program. Ms. Merritt is a graduate of the Peabody Conservatory of Music where she studied with Flora Wend. She has been heard with the Washington Opera as Fleurette in Offenbach's *Christopher Columbus* and in the title role of Lehar's *The Merry Widow*. In 1981

Ms. Merritt sang Musetta in *La Bohème* with the Houston Grand Opera and has been heard with them as both Clara and Lily in their New York performances of *Porgy and Bess.* She made her Metropolitan Opera debut in January 1982 as the Shepherd in *Tannhäuser.*

LEONA MITCHELL
Soprano

Leona Mitchell is a native of Enid, Oklahoma and a graduate of Oklahoma University and subsequently a winner of the San Francisco Kurt Herbert Adler Award. Ms. Mitchell has been heard with the San Francisco Opera, the Washington Opera Society, the Houston Opera, and at the Gran Teatro del Liceo in Barcelona as Mathilde in Rossini's *William Tell.* Her orchestral appearances include concerts with the Cleveland Orchestra, the London Symphony, and the New Jersey Symphony. During the summer of 1980 she sang Bess in the Cleveland Orchestra Blossom Festival production of *Porgy and Bess* and performed the same role in their subsequent recording of the work. Ms. Mitchell made her Metropolitan Opera debut as Micaela in *Carmen* in December 1975 and since then has been heard there as Lauretta in *Gianni Schicci,* Pamina in *The Magic Flute,* and Madame Lidoine in *Dialogues of the Carmelites.*

Leona Mitchell as Mme. Ledoine in a scene from Poulenc's Dialogues of the Carmelites.

JESSYE NORMAN
Soprano

Jessye Norman grew up in Augusta, Georgia and attended Howard University in Washington, D.C. on a full scholarship. Ms. Norman graduated from Howard in 1967 with a music degree. Following her graduation from Howard, Ms. Norman spent what she calls "an unhappy summer" at the Peabody Conservatory in Baltimore but according to the soprano she couldn't put up with the "rat race" there so she enrolled at the University of Michigan to study with Pierre Bernac, one of the world's top teachers of art song. Ms. Norman has spent a great deal of her time in Germany and in 1969 she was signed to a three-year contract by the Deutsche Oper in West Berlin where she was immediately put into major parts. She made her debut as Elisabeth in *Tannhäuser.* Soon after, she sang the Countess Almaviva opposite Dietrich Fisher-Dieskau in *The Marriage of Figaro.* Before her debut in Berlin, she had sung in the Howard University chorus and appeared in small recitals, contests, and auditions.

COLERIDGE-TAYLOR PERKINSON
Composer
1932

Coleridge-Taylor Perkinson has been a figure in explorative musical movements in both Hollywood and New York.

Born in New York, Perkinson took graduate and postgraduate degrees from the Manhattan School of Music (1953, 1954), before going on to study at the Berkshire Music Center, the Mozarteum, and the Netherland Radio Union Hilversum. Becoming first composer-in-residence for the Negro Ensemble Company, he wrote the music for many plays, including Peter Weiss' *Song of the Lusitanian Bogey,* Ray McIver's *God Is a (Guess What?),* and Errol Hill's *Man Better Man.* In 1965, when the Symphony of the New World was organized in New York, Perkinson was named associate conductor. His concert pieces include *Concerto for Violin and Orchestra* (1954) and *Attitudes* (1964), written for black opera star George Shirley. Perkinson has also composed music for television and radio programs, documentary films (*Crossroads Africa*), and ballet ensembles.

JULIA PERRY
Composer
1927

Julia Perry, born in Akron, Ohio, studied composition, piano, and voice at the Westminster Choir School in Princeton, New Jersey. After taking her M.A. there, she continued her musical studies at Juilliard, at the Berkshire Music Center, and in Europe with Luigi

Dallapiccola and Nadia Boulanger. Her best-known works are *Stabat Mater* (1951), for solo voice and string orchestra; *A Short Piece for Orchestra* (1952); *Pastoral* (1969), for flute and strings; and *Homunculus, C. F.* (1969), for soprano and percussion. She has also written two operas, *The Bottle* and *The Cask of Amontillado.*

LEONTYNE PRICE
Lyric Soprano
1927

Leontyne Price is one of the world's leading lyric sopranos. Her career in concerts and opera has brought her the praise of public and critics alike.

Miss Price was born in Laurel, Mississippi on February 10, 1927, and received her B.A. in 1948 from the College of Education and Industrial Arts (now Central State College) in Wilberforce, Ohio. She later accepted a scholarship to Juilliard where she studied with Florence Page Kimball.

After seeing her in the student production of Verdi's *Falstaff,* Virgil Thompson, the noted composer and critic, selected her to sing in the revival of his *Four Saints in Three Acts,* which was performed on Broadway for two weeks in 1952. She then played the role of Bess in the 1952 revival of *Porgy and Bess,* and continued in the part on a tour sponsored by the U.S. State Department.

During the run of *Porgy and Bess,* she introduced works by Stravinsky, Henri Saguet, John La Montaine and others at such places as the Metropolitan Museum in New York and Constitution Hall in Washington, D.C.

Miss Price made her Metropolitan debut in *Il Trovatore* on January 27, 1961. Since then, she has made numerous recordings of operas and operatic arias. She was married to the noted black bass baritone William Warfield.

Just one season after she had made her Met debut as Leonora in Verdi's *Il Trovatore,* Miss Price had her first Met opening in 1961 in the title role of Puccini's *The Girl of the Golden West.* Since then, she has made numerous recordings of operas and operatic arias. She opened the new Metropolitan Opera House at Lincoln Center in Barber's *Antony and Cleopatra.*

In the world of opera, Miss Price ranks alongside Birgit Nilsson, Joan Sutherland, and Renata Tebaldi as one of the most esteemed and celebrated sopranos of the contemporary era. Her voice is said to be the perfect Verdi voice; her *Aida* is often regarded as the paragon against which all others should be measured.

On April 20, 1982 Miss Price opened the convention of the Daughters of the American Revolution in Constitution Hall with a concert honoring Marian Anderson. It was in 1939 that Miss Anderson was barred from appearing in Constitution Hall by the DAR, prompting Eleanor Roosevelt to resign in anger from the organization. In September 1981 Miss Price opened the 1981–1982 concert series at Rutgers University in New Brunswick, New Jersey, which marked her first New Jersey appearance after 15 years. In 1977 she was awarded the San Francisco Opera medal in honor of the twentieth anniversary of her debut with the company.

FLORENCE QUIVAR
Mezzo-Soprano

A native of Philadelphia, Florence Quivar is a graduate of the Academy of Music and was a member of the Juilliard Opera Theater. She has been a soloist with practically all of the major symphony orchestras in the United States, including the New York Philhar-

Leontyne Price is said to have the perfect Verdi voice.

monic, the Cleveland Orchestra, the Cincinnati Symphony, and the Boston Symphony. Ms. Quivar made her debut in New York in 1973 as soloist for the Verdi *Requiem* with the National Orchestral Association at Carnegie Hall, and has also sung that work with Giulini and the Los Angeles Philharmonic and with Muti and the Philadelphia Orchestra. Since Ms. Quivar's Metropolitan Opera debut as Marina during the 1977–1978 opening night performance of *Boris Godunov,* she has been heard there as Suzuki in *Madama Butterfly,* Fides in *Le Prophète,* and Isabella in *L'Italiana in Algeri.*

PHILIPPA SCHUYLER
Pianist
1932–1969

Philippa Schuyler was at one time considered to be one of America's most outstanding musical prodigies. Remembered as a mature concert pianist who died tragically at the height of her powers, she first gained recognition for her piano artistry and original compositions as a child.

Born on August 21, 1932 in New York City, Miss Schuyler was already playing the piano at the age of two and began composing a year later. By the time she was eight, she had some 50 compositions to her credit. (Her published works include *Six Little Pieces* and *Eight Little Pieces.*)

At 12, her first symphonic composition (*Manhattan Nocturne*) was performed at Carnegie Hall, and the following year her scherzo (*Rumplestiltskin*) was written and subsequently performed by the Dean Dixon Youth Orchestra, the Boston Pops, the New Haven Symphony Orchestra, and the New York Philharmonic. Miss Schuyler herself was a soloist with the last-named orchestra.

In 1953 she made her debut at Town Hall in New York. She then traveled in some 50 countries on goodwill concert tours sponsored by the U.S. State Department.

Gifted also as a writer, Miss Schuyler was the author of such books as *Adventures in Black and White* (1960), and *Who Killed the Congo?* (1962).

GEORGE SHIRLEY
Tenor
1934

Tenor George Shirley has sung more than 20 leading roles at the Metropolitan since his debut there as Fernando in *Così Fan Tutte* on October 24, 1961.

Shirley, winner of the 1960–1961 Metropolitan Opera auditions, was born April 18, 1934 in Indianapolis, and moved to Detroit in 1940. There he began giving vocal recitals in churches, deciding on a musical career

Tenor George Shirley sings over twenty roles with the Metropolitan Opera company.

after playing baritone horn in the community band. In 1955 he graduated from Wayne State University in Detroit with a B.S. in musical education.

After his discharge from the Army in 1959 he began serious vocal studies with Themy S. Georgi. In June of that year he made his operatic debut as Eisenstein in Strauss's *Die Fledermaus,* performing with the Turnau Players in Woodstock. A year later he won the American Opera Auditions, whereupon he journeyed to Milan, Italy, making his opera debut there in Puccini's *La Bohème.*

In 1961 his career was given tremendous impetus by his victory in the Metropolitan Opera auditions. Recording, opera, and television engagements were numerous that year. In 1963 he made his debut at Carnegie Hall with the Friends of French Opera, singing opposite Rita Gorr in Massenet's *La Navarraise.*

Since then, he has sung with several of the Met's

leading divas, including Renata Tebaldi in *Simon Boccanegra* and Birgit Nilsson in *Salome*. By now, Shirley has so broadened and refined his repertory that he is at home in virtually every major opera culture in Europe. He has made several European tours, performing with the leading orchestras on the continent and at the most prestigious opera houses there.

In 1973 Shirley initiated a radio program on WQXR (N.Y.) entitled *Afro-American Artists in the Classical Field.*

In 1974 he sang the title role in Mozart's *Idomeneo* at the Glyndeburne Festival, and he has remained a favorite at the Met over the years.

ANDREW SMITH
Baritone

A native of Lexington, Kentucky, Andrew Smith received his bachelors degree from Kentucky State University and his masters from Roosevelt University. Smith also pursued doctoral studies at Northwestern University. He made his operatic debut in 1969 with Beverly Sills at Chicago's Grant Park Summer Festival in *La Traviata*. He has been heard with the Chicago Symphony, the Cleveland Orchestra, the Buffalo Philharmonic, and he toured with the Houston Grand Opera's production of *Porgy and Bess*. Smith is a member of the New York City Opera and made his Metropolitan Opera debut in the premiere of *Billy Budd*, singing the role of the First Mate.

HALE SMITH
Composer, Teacher

Hale Smith composes symphonic music whose elements stretch from avant garde concepts of tone rows to erotic Brazilian dances.

Born in Cleveland, Ohio, Smith's musicianship was nurtured at the Jeliffe's Karamu House in Cleveland, Ohio, where he had the opportunity to write scores for such stage productions as Lorca's *Yerma* and *Blood Wedding*. *Contours for Orchestra*, perhaps his best known work, builds its virile power by balancing abrasive, protesting brass against cool strings. Other works include *In Memoriam: Beryl Rubinstein* (chorus and chamber orchestra); *Epicedial Variations* (violin and piano); and *Music for Harp and Orchestra*.

WILLIAM GRANT STILL
Composer
1895–1978

William Grant Still was acclaimed as the "dean of black composers." He has numerous firsts to his credit, and his musical inspiration and skills united both classical and folk traditions.

Born in Woodville, Mississippi, Still received his early musical training at home. He attended Wilberforce University and then studied at the Oberlin Conservatory of Music and the New England Conservatory. Work with George W. Chadwick and Edgar Varese completed his formal studies.

Still's early work was as an arranger for jazz orchestras, but he soon turned to composition, making use of his jazz background in a more classical framework. It was the performance of his *Afro-American Symphony* in 1931 by the Rochester Philharmonic under Howard Hanson that brought him real recognition. This was the first time a major orchestra had performed a full-length piece by a black American composer. In 1936 Still became the first black to conduct a major American orchestra when he gave a program of his own compositions at the Hollywood Bowl.

He won two Guggenheim Fellowships during his lifetime. One was in 1944 and the other in 1961. In 1939 he was invited to compose the theme song for New York's world's fair.

Still wrote seven operas as well as composing music for films (*Pennies from Heaven*), radio, and television (*Perry Mason* and *Gunsmoke*). His numerous serious works reflect many sides of black life. Stokowski called him "one of our greatest American composers."

Still died in December 1978 in a nursing home in Los Angeles at the age of 83.

HOWARD SWANSON
Composer
1909–1978

Howard Swanson was born in Atlanta and raised in Cleveland, where he studied at the Institute of Music. He was taught composition by Herbert Elwell. In 1938 he won a Rosenwald Fellowship to study with Nadia Boulanger in Paris. Returning to the United States, he devoted himself to composition, and in 1950 he won wide acclaim as well as serious attention as an American composer when his *Short Symphony*, written in 1948, was performed by the New York Philharmonic with Dmitri Mitropoulos conducting. In 1952 this symphony won the New York Critics' Award. One of Swanson's well-known works is the song "The Negro Speaks of Rivers," based on a poem by Langston Hughes, which Marian Anderson has sung in recital.

Swanson died in 1978 at New York Hospital. In 1979 at the St. James Presbyterian Church in New York City a concert was given by the Triad Chorale as a memorial to him and William Grant Still.

ARTHUR THOMPSON
Baritone

Baritone Arthur Thompson is a graduate of the Hartt College of Music and the Juilliard School. He is a

Shirley Verrett as Cassandra in Berlioz' Les Troyens.

former member of the Metropolitan Opera Studio and has been heard with the Juilliard Opera Theater, the Chautauqua Opera, the Aspen Summer Opera, and the Yale Summer Opera Theater. Thompson has also been heard as a soloist with the St. Louis Symphony, the Miami Symphony, the Hartford Symphony, the Milwaukee Symphony, and the Pro Arte Chorale. He was also heard as St. Ignatius Loyola in Thomson's *Four Saints in Three Acts* during the first season of the Mini-Met in 1973. Thompson made his Metropolitan Opera debut in 1974 in *Madama Butterfly,* and has also been heard there in *Boris Godunov, Fidelio, Tosca, Lohengrin,* and *Otello.*

SHIRLEY VERRETT
Mezzo-Soprano

Mezzo-soprano Shirley Verrett is a striking and talented recitalist and opera performer whose most elec-

trifying role has been in the title role of Bizet's *Carmen,* which she has performed to rave notices in the great opera houses of the world.

Born of a musical family in New Orleans, Miss Verrett moved to California at the age of five, but had no formal voice training during her childhood, largely because her father felt singing would involve his daughter in too precarious a career. Still, he offered his daughter the opportunity to sing in church choirs under his direction, and provided her with an ample education at Ventura College, where she majored in business administration. By 1954 she was a prosperous real estate agent, but her longing for an artistic career had become so acute that she decided to take voice lessons in Los Angeles and train her sights on the concert stage after all.

After winning a television talent show in 1955, she enrolled at the Juilliard School on a scholarship, taking her diploma in voice some six years later. Her debut at Town Hall in 1958 was not a sensational one, earning plaudits for her "sensitive, imaginative . . . comprehension," even as it inspired the conclusion that she was perhaps only an "earnest, conscientious" singer who was well coached and adequately prepared.

At Spoleto, Italy in 1962, she delivered an excellent *Carmen* and was praised for a "warm vibrant voice and earthy womanliness." A year later, she performed at Lincoln Center in New York, where her recital was said to be "simply without flaws, simply a great event in the annals of American music-making."

By 1964 her *Carmen* had improved so dramatically that the New York *Herald Tribune* critic was able to claim it was "the finest" performance "seen or heard in New York" for the past generation. Other performances in such roles as Orfeo in Gluck's *Orfeo ed Euridice*, Ulrica in Verdi's *Un Ballo de Maschera* and recently Leonora in Beethoven's *Fidelio* have been met with comparable acclaim.

In 1982, Miss Verrett appeared with Grace Bumbry in a concert honoring Marian Anderson on her eightieth birthday. Miss Verrett sang the "Salce" and "Ave Maria" from Verdi's *Otello*. In September 1977 she appeared with conductor Zubin Mehta on WNET-TV's "Live From Lincoln Center." The *New York Times* has hailed Miss Verrett as "a singer of intelligence, beauty and good vocal endowment." Her yearly recital tours take her to the major music centers throughout the country.

GEORGE WALKER
Concert Pianist, Educator
1922

George Walker's music has a strong foundation in his distinguished career as a concert recitalist.

Born in Washington, D.C., he studied at Oberlin, the Curtis Institute of Music, and at the Eastman School, where he completed his doctorate. His teachers included Rudolf Serkin, Giancarlo Menotti, and Robert Casadesus. Following his well-received Town Hall debut in 1945, Walker gained 20 seasons of experience touring the United States, Canada, and Europe. He is currently a professor at Rutgers University in Newark.

Recently, Dr. Walker's compositions have inclined toward pointillistic and serial styles; however, the neoclassical disciplines which shaped his earlier works are still in evidence. His major works include the *Address for Orchestra, Gloria in Memoriam* for women's voices and organ, and *Variations for Orchestra,* which exemplifies his stylistic development.

William Warfield, a distinguished concert baritone.

WILLIAM WARFIELD
Baritone

One of the most distinguished concert baritones in the world today is William Warfield, who made his debut at New York's Town Hall in March 1950.

Warfield was born in West Helena, Arkansas, and later moved with his family to Rochester, New York, where he attended school. The son of a Baptist minister, he received early training in voice, organ, and piano and, in 1938, while a student at Washington Junior High School, won the vocal competition at the Music Educators National Convention in St. Louis.

He then studied at the Eastman School of Music and the University of Rochester, receiving his A.B. while in the Army, where he worked in intelligence because of his fluency in Italian, French, and German. At the close of World War II he returned to Eastman before spending a year traveling with the national company of *Call Me Mister.*

After his resounding New York debut in 1950, he made an unprecedented tour of Australia under the auspices of the Australian Broadcasting Commission. A year later he made his movie debut in *Show Boat.*

Warfield then appeared on several major television shows and starred in the NBC television version of *Green Pastures.* Between 1952 and 1959 he made five international tours under the auspices of the U.S. State Department.

His performances as Porgy in the various revivals of *Porgy and Bess* have made him the best-known

Andre Watts, one of America's most gifted young pianists, performs with the New York Philharmonic.

singer in this role. He was married to Leontyne Price, the brilliant opera star whom he met during a *Porgy and Bess* production.

In 1966 he appeared in a revival of the Jerome Kern-Edna Ferber classic, *Showboat.* In 1971 he performed the role in Austria.

ANDRE WATTS
Pianist

One of America's most gifted young pianists, Andre Watts achieved a substantial degree of fame while playing under the baton of Leonard Bernstein of the New York Philharmonic.

Born in Nuremberg, Germany of a Hungarian mother and an American G.I. father, Watts spent the first eight years of his life on Army posts in Europe before moving to Philadelphia, his current place of residence. By the time he was nine, he was already good enough to perform as a soloist with the Philadelphia Orchestra.

At the age of 17, Watts appeared on television in one of Leonard Bernstein's Young People's Concerts and was a huge success. After graduating from Lincoln Prep in Philadelphia, he enrolled at Baltimore's Peabody Conservatory of Music.

On one occasion, when Glenn Gould became ill just prior to a performance with the New York Philharmonic, Bernstein chose Watts as a last-minute replacement. At the conclusion of the concerto, Watts received a standing ovation not only from the audience but from the orchestra as well.

In June 1966 Watts made his debut in London, and a month later was the soloist for the two-day Philharmonic Stravinsky Festival at Lincoln Center.

In the 1970s Watts gave a concert in Teheran as part of the coronation festivities for the Shah of Iran and later at a state dinner for Congo's President Mobutu he was presented with the African republic's highest honor, the Order of the Zaire. Watts also performed at President Richard M. Nixon's inaugural concert.

OLLY WILSON
Composer
1937

Olly Wilson, one of the nation's leading young composers, won the first International Electronic Music Competition (Dartmouth, N.H., 1968) with his *Cetus*.

Born in St. Louis, Wilson's high school clarinet playing led to a scholarship at hometown Washington University. After taking a Ph.D. in composition at the State University of Iowa, he began focusing on electronic music at Illinois' Studio for Experimental Music. His practical experience has included playing double bass with symphony orchestras in St. Louis and Cedar Rapids, Iowa, and also with jazz groups.

He has since spent a year of research in Africa, particularly Ghana, and is currently a faculty member at Berkeley.

Wilson's best-known works are the *Sextet* (1963), *Three Movements for Orchestra* (1964), and *Cetus* (1967). Even prior to turning to electronic sounds, Dr. Wilson's employment of traditional media stressed innovative sonorities, with such works as *Wry Fragments* (1961) for tenor and percussion; *And Death Shall Have No Dominion* (1963), tenor and percussion; and *Chanson Innocent* (1965), for contralto and two bassoons. Wilson's style springs from his belief that a black composer's "reality" is different. He draws upon a wide spectrum of music not normally regarded as part of the Euro-American tradition.

OTHER NOTABLE CLASSICAL MUSICIANS

Composers

Name	Born
Alton Augustus Adams	1889–?
Walter Anderson	1915
Thomas Green Bethune	1849–1908
Edward Boatner	1898
J. Harold Brown	1902
Harry Thacker Burleigh	1866–1949
Melville Charlton	1880
Edgar Rogie Clark	1917
Charles L. Cooke	1891–1958
Noel G. DeCosta	1929
Claude Brindis DeSala	?–d. 1912
R. Nathaniel Dett	1882–1943
Carl Diton	1886
Shirley Lola Graham DuBois	1906–1977
Azalia Hackley	1867–1922
Margaret Harris	
Noral Holt	
Hall Johnson	1888
J. Rosamund Johnson	1873–1954
Penman Livingood	1895
Carman Leroy Moore	1936
Undine Smith Moore	1905
Karl H. Porter	
Clarence Cameron White	1880–1960
John Wesley Work	1901–1967

Concert Artists

Name	Talent	Born
William Duncan Allen	Pianist	1908
Flora Batson Bergen	Singer	1865 ?
Carol Brice	Singer	1918
Annie Wiggins Brown	Singer	1915
Lillian Fuanti	Singer	
Elizabeth Taylor Greenfield	Singer	1809–1876
Hazel Harrison	Pianist	1881–?
Sissieretta Jones	Singer	1868–1933
Abbie Mitchell	Singer-actress	1845–1924
Nellie Brown Mitchell	Singer	
Etta Moten	Singer	
Othello Pumphrey	Singer	1921
Muriel Rahn	Singer	
Helen Thigpen	Singer	
Camilla E. Williams	Singer	
Maria Selika Williams	Singer	

THE JAZZ SCENE

The Medium and Its Background ■ New Orleans Beginnings ■ Milestones ■ Outstanding Jazz Artists

Composed of West African rhythms and European harmonic elements, jazz music came together as an identifiable sound in America's black ghettos in the early years of this century. The sound was not simply different, it was one of the rare new beginnings in the history of music—a blend of African and European legacies in an improvisational style. Perhaps the style had to be improvisational to give voice to the novel interplay of cultures in the American setting, especially to express the feelings and experience of black people as they came into contact with the dominant white culture. It is from that kind of cultural shock that the simultaneous withdrawal and embrace of improvisational jazz music seemed to develop. While it is not racial music, most of the great figures in jazz history have been black, and it is to their genius that the world pays homage when it embraces this music, calling it America's only original artistic contribution to the culture of the world.

Jazz stands out from other Afro-American musical idioms because of its improvisational basis. By nature, jazz is a player's music, and the players are always free to improvise. Usually this improvisation appears as a spontaneous melodic ornamentation of a theme, but the player is free to invent a new melody if he wishes, provided he keeps to the chord changes (harmonic progression) of the original theme. This improvisational style not only guarantees the aliveness of jazz songs but was in fact responsible for forging jazz's fundamental characteristics: syncopated rhythm; the simultaneous playing of individual melody lines by members of a group; the use of vocal techniques in instrumental music; and the interpreter's free introduction of special melodic features, like glissandi or blue ("flatted") notes. These characteristics can be seen nascent in the musical roots of jazz.

West African rhythms were hammered into work songs and spirituals in the plantation fields of the South. From these chants sprang the high, melancholic note of the blues, which is by far the most important and influential background idiom of jazz. Beginning in pre-Emancipation times, the blues developed from primitive laments, some consisting of only incessant moans, into songs of sorrow and yearning cooled with satire. Both the irony and the intense feelings were conveyed by the singer through spontaneously inflected pitches and tones, blues techniques that led to the bent notes of jazz improvisations and to the intimate interplay of voice and instrument that fecundates jazz songs. Among the earliest and finest duets of this kind are the collaborations of Louis Armstrong and the great blues singer Bessie Smith, such as their version of *St. Louis Blues* (1925). Bessie's *Lost Your Head Blues* (1926), with its great emotional impact, is often mentioned as one of the best introductions to the blues. Other great blues, showing this tradition's range and evolution, are Robert Johnson's *Hellhound on My Trail* (1937), Jelly Roll Morton's *Dead Man Blues* (1926), Sidney Bechet's *Blue Horizon* (1944), Duke Ellington's *Ko-ko* (1940), Charlie Parker's *Parker's Mood* (1948), Thelonious Monk's *Misterioso* (1948), Sonny Rollins' *Blue 7* (1956), and Charles Mingus' *Hora Decubitus* (1963).

If the blues breathed soul into jazz, then ragtime was the clay of its body. This keyboard version of the polka put together the multithemed structure of early jazz. Ragtime's character (and nationwide popularity) came from its introduction, in right-hand melodies, of gay syncopations over the heavy oom-pah rhythm of its cakewalk bass line. The first great rag was Scott Joplin's *The Maple Leaf Rag* (1897). Tom Turpin of St. Louis (*The Harlem Rag, The Bowery*

In New Orleans bamboo drums and many-vowelled African chants made the music for exuberant and sensuous dance marathons.

Buck, and *The Buffalo*) and Louis Chauvin, a great natural piano player, are other founding fathers of ragtime. Their delightful music brought a wide public to the outskirts of jazz, which is more rhythmically varied than ragtime.

Although jazz was being created simultaneously in various parts of the Southwest during the late 1800s, it is the Storyville red-light district of New Orleans that is generally accepted as its prime breeding ground. With a dozen bands, many trios, and other musicians employed every night, it is little wonder that jazz sprang up here. Even last century New Orleans was known for its music, particularly the black population's enjoyment of true African material. As late as two decades after the Civil War, every weekend saw the famous Congo Dances performed, in which crude instruments (bamboo or hollow-log drums, African banjos, and bone castanets) and many-voweled Congolese chants made the music for exuberant and sensuous dance marathons. Buddy Bolden, the leader of the first great jazz orchestra, was able to attend these fetes into his teens.

Typical of New Orleans musicians, Bolden considered improvisation (but not note reading) an essential part of musical skill, was accustomed by the chants to the endless repetition of short motifs, and had had no formal training or teachers to show him the supposed limitations of his instrument, the cornet. While classical music had subordinated the brasses to the strings, self-taught musicians like Bolden were able to hit on undreamed of technical possibilities for the brass and to create an appropriate and unique jazz style.

Bolden's band played dance jobs primarily, and used the seven pieces standard in New Orleans groups: the cornet, playing the melody most of the time, was considered the leader; the clarinet played a faster moving part and filled in at the end of phrases with characteristic "breaks"; the trombone sometimes supported the others with a sort of rhythmic bass and also took its own countermelody in the best style of New Orleans music; a violin was used; and the rhythm section consisted of drums, guitar, and string bass. Pianos were not included originally, but they eventually found a home in Storyville. Among the first to play there was Jelly Roll Morton, whose compositions include the *King Porter Stomp* and the *Milneburg Joys* (originally the *Pee Hole Blues*). Among the other great and influential figures produced by New Orleans jazz were cornetists Freddy Keppard and Joseph "King" Oliver, clarinetist and soprano saxophonist Sidney Bechet, clarinetists Johnny Dodds and Jimmy Noone, and, of course, Louis Armstrong.

The route followed by Armstrong's horn—from New Orleans to Chicago to New York— was the path by which jazz reached the rest of America. Louis' greatest talent was his ability to ennoble the most banal themes by syncopatic paraphrase. He inspired musicians of all kinds all over the world and was part of the collaborations (along with King Oliver, Fletcher

Henderson, and Don Redman) from which emerged the "big band" jazz that found wide popularity in the mid-1930s and began the "swing" era.

The big band style was perfected by Duke Ellington, who used the dance band as a vehicle of personal artistic expression. His works from the great period (1938–1942) include *Rumpus in Richmond, Harlem Air Shaft,* and *Concerto for Cootie.* Like Morton before him, Ellington was a synthesizer who cared more for the total piece than for individual performances. His chief sidemen and soloists were trumpeter Charles "Cootie" Williams, cornetist Rex Stewart, trombonists Lawrence Brown and Joe Norton, clarinetist Barney Bigard, tenor saxophonist Ben Webster, alto saxophonist Johnny Hodges, and baritone saxophonist Harry Carney. Ellington's blend of sophistication and funk repays the most careful listening.

Count Basie's innovative orchestra, which came out of Kansas City in 1936, led jazz beyond the "swing" momentum. Playing with new lightness, the rhythm section's lead was taken, not by Jo Jones' drums, but by Walter Page's strong string bass. The leader's piano simplified earlier styles (he had been originally influenced by Thomas "Fats" Waller and Earl "Fatha" Hines), but with an inimitably airy touch. Basie's most famous performance is the instrumental blues *One O'Clock Jump.*

In the middle 1940s, the light legato style fashioned by tenor saxophonist Lester Young, the greatest of the Basie soloists, was elaborated into a major innovation: bebop. Chiefly, this new music centered on the work of trumpeter John "Dizzy" Gillespie, alto saxophonist Charlie Parker, and pianist Thelonious Monk. Other participants included drummers Kenny Clarke and Max Roach, pianist Earl "Bud" Powell, and bassist Oscar Pettiford. The big band was superseded by small groups, usually quintets; Parker's contrast of brief, rhythmically terse phrases alternating with long, flowing bursts of lyric melody dominated the scene; and the harmonic language of jazz became increasingly chromatic.

After Parker's death in 1955, Monk's synthesis of the saxophonist's innovations set the pace for jazz. Two of Monk's associates on his classic recordings (many of which were made between 1948 and 1954) were vibraphonist Milt Jackson and tenor saxophonist Theodore "Sonny" Rollins. Meanwhile, a composer and bassist of importance appeared in Charles Mingus, who laid down a bass line of such variety that it virtually ceased to be a mere accompaniment and became a contrapuntal part of the spontaneous musical texture.

Throughout the 1960s, black jazz musicians continued to explore, expand, and extend the language of jazz. Consonant with their origins and experience, the new breed of performers, playing a style they called

Jazz burst onto the New York City scene in the 1920s. Band leader Jelly Roll Morton was one of the first to appear in New York.

The New Thing, drew heavily on African sources, even as they recreated—at times furiously, at other times effortlessly—the turmoil of their private lives. Tenor saxophonist John Coltrane won the admiration of his peers not only for his revolutionary "sheets of sound" technique, but for his quiet and convincing evangelical fervor—the manner of a priest, as one colleague described it. Now dead, Coltrane leaves behind Ornette Coleman, an alto sax virtuoso whose music is more consciously and deliberately angry than spiritual.

In the 1970s and into the 1980s, there appears to be more of an awareness of jazz. There are some who say that jazz has been dead for a period of time and that today there is a resurgence of the music. However, many who are close to the music form will know that jazz never died and that more and more people are becoming aware of the music.

During the summer months some cities put together "Jazzmobiles" featuring jazz artists in outdoor concerts. In New York City during the summer of 1981, drummer Art Blakey appeared in an outdoor jazzmobile festival to a jam-packed audience. The Blakey concert, like so many other outdoor concerts by jazz artists, prompted many people to bring chairs and blankets and sit under the stars to listen to jazz sounds on a summer night.

When radio station WRVR-FM in New York City switched its format from an all-jazz station to country and western, the changeover brought a public outcry from the jazz community. The station management stated that the reason for the switchover was because of a dying jazz audience. However, the numbers of people who protested against the switch plus the numbers of jazz enthusiasts who frequent jazz clubs is testimony to the popularity of jazz. And so radio stations, including public radio, continue scheduling jazz formats as part of their programming.

More and more bars and night clubs are featuring a "jazz only" entertainment policy as well. Not only does this policy give jazz buffs an opportunity to listen to their favorite sounds played by jazz artists, but it affords an opportunity for many of the older jazz musicians to work. These musicians wouldn't have had the chance to work otherwise because of the stiff competition in the larger clubs.

Many young people are also swinging over to jazz and college-age students as well as young adults make up a sizable portion of the audience at jazz concerts. Quite a few colleges and universities are scheduling workshops and lectures by jazz artists. Through this program, which has been established by such institutions, young people are being exposed to jazz at an early age and they are learning about the "greats" of the jazz world.

Jazz artists who heretofore have been a forgotten people are now coming into their own. Their names

Joe "King" Oliver and the Creole Band introduced New Orleans Jazz to San Francisco in 1921.

are plastered across the fronts of night clubs as featured attractions, and newspapers are giving recognition to them by having columns devoted to jazz.

Jazz has also attracted the attention of public relations people so much that there are those who gear their public relations only to the jazz trade.

Today's players incorporate the origins of jazz into their own personal larger framework. Movement and mood do not simply overpower the creative performer who, along with pianist Cecil Taylor, seeks "a higher plane than he could ordinarily achieve," and an acceptance of the "energy of God." There is too much variety in today's jazz for a short summary or even an umbrella definition. Perhaps Monk had the last word when he said, "Jazz is freedom. Think about that. You think about that."

OUTSTANDING JAZZ MUSICIANS

LILIAN (LIL) HARDIN ARMSTRONG
Piano, singer, composer
1902–1971

Lil Armstrong, born in Memphis, was married to Louis Armstrong. She played and wrote music for many of Armstrong's Hot Five and Hot Seven concerts and recordings. She also played in King Oliver's band and led various bands and combos of her own in New York and Chicago. Characteristically, it was while playing at a Tribute to Louis Armstrong Concert at Chicago's Civic Center Plaza that Lilian Armstrong collapsed and died of a heart attack on July 7, 1971.

LOUIS ARMSTRONG
Trumpet
1900–1971

Born on the Fourth of July at the turn of the twentieth century, Louis Armstrong was one of the most influential and durable of all jazz artists. He is, quite simply, one of the most famous people in the entire world.

On New Year's Eve in 1914, Armstrong was arrested in New Orleans for firing a pistol and sent to the Colored Waifs Home. There he first learned to play the cornet. His skill increased with the experience he gained from playing in the Home's band. When he was finally released from the institution, he was already proficient enough with the instrument to begin playing for money.

Befriended by his idol, King Oliver, Armstrong quickly began to develop the jazz skills which he had, until then, been able to admire only from a distance. When Oliver left for Chicago in 1919, a place was opened up for Armstrong as a member of the Kid Ory band in New Orleans.

In 1922 Oliver asked Armstrong to join him in Chicago as second cornet with his Creole Jazz Band. The duets between "Dippermouth" (as Armstrong was called) and "Papa Joe" (Oliver's nickname) soon became the talk of the Chicago music world.

Two years later Armstrong joined the Fletcher Henderson band at the Roseland Ballroom in New York City where, at Henderson's suggestion, he switched from cornet to trumpet, the instrument he played from then on. In 1925 he returned to Chicago to play with Erskine Tate. During the next four years he made a

Singer, pianist, composer Lil Harden was one of the greatest.

Louis Armstrong, mentor and model for generations of jazz musicians

series of recordings which brought him worldwide fame in musical circles.

In 1929 Armstrong returned to New York and there, in the revue "Hot Chocolates," scored his first triumph with a popular song (Fats Waller's "Ain't Misbehavin' "). This success was a turning point in his career inasmuch as he then began to front big bands, playing and singing popular songs rather than blues or original instrumentals.

In 1932 Armstrong headlined the show at the London Palladium, where he acquired the nickname "Satchelmouth" (since then abbreviated to "Satchmo"). From 1932 to 1935 he toured Europe, returning to the United States to film *Pennies from Heaven* with Bing Crosby. He continued to evolve from the status of musician to that of entertainer, and his singing soon became even more important than his playing. In 1947 he formed a small group which was an immediate success. He continued to work in this context.

The influence of Louis Armstrong on the history of jazz is so pervasive that it has on occasion been blithely dismissed by those who have found fault with him for not "keeping up with the changes." It is clear, however, that Armstrong's continued success as a soloist and entertainer helped make jazz a vital force in the general culture of the United States and, to some degree, of the entire world.

In March 1971 Armstrong suffered a heart attack in New York, after a particularly heavy stint there.

On the critical list for two months, he finally succumbed in July, dying in his sleep.

The great musician apparently had little fear of death, in fact often anticipated his funeral with wit. "They're going to blow over me" Armstrong had forecast of his final rites. "Cats will be coming from everywhere to play. I had a beautiful life. When I get to the Pearly Gates I'll play a duet with Gabriel. We'll play 'Sleepy Time Down South.' He wants to be remembered for his music just like I do."

WILLIAM (COUNT) BASIE
Piano, Bandleader
1904

Count Basie is generally regarded as leader of the best jazz band in the United States and, consequently, one of the major influences on jazz as a whole.

His musical career ranges from a boyhood spent watching the pit band at the local movie theater (he

Count Basie's light keyboard touch gave new style to the big bands.

later learned the organ techniques of Fats Waller by crouching beside him in the Lincoln Theater in Harlem) to his dual triumphs in 1957 when his became the first American band to play a royal command performance for the Queen of England, and the first black jazz band ever to play at the Waldorf Astoria Hotel in New York City.

During the early 1920s, Basie toured in vaudeville. Stranded in Kansas City, he joined Walter Page's Blue Devils. (Jimmy Rushing was the singer.) After this band broke up, Basie joined Benny Moten and, in 1935, formed his own band at the Reno Club in Kansas City, where a local radio announcer soon dubbed him "Count."

At the urging of critic John Hammond, Basie brought his group to New York City in 1936. Within a year he had cut his first record and was well on his way to becoming an established presence in the jazz world.

The Basie trademark was a rhythm section, which featured Basie's own clean, spare piano style and outstanding soloists like Lester Young and Sweets Edison in the early years, and Lucky Thompson, J. J. Johnson, Clark Terry, and Benny Powell in the later period.

Except for the years 1950 and 1951 when he had a small group, Basie has led a big band for more than 30 years. In some way immune to changing fashion, the Basie band has completed numerous global tours and successful recording engagements without ever suffering an appreciable decline in its popularity. In 1974, on his seventieth birthday, the Count was honored at a "Royal Salute" party by virtually every big name in jazz.

Count Basie was honored at Radio City Music Hall in New York City in 1982. Among those honoring The Count were Dionne Warwick and Lena Horne.

SHIRLEY BASSEY
Singer
1937

Shirley Bassey's melodious voice and dynamic style make her one of the best female vocalists ever to come out of England. While her recordings are excellent, her most exciting work is done in live performances before nightclub and concert audiences.

Born in Cardiff, Wales, she was raised in the rundown Tiger Bay section and taught herself to sing by listening to the radio. She had to leave school in her early teens to help support her family. Her first singing job was in the chorus of a touring show, *Memories of Al Jolson*. She continued picking up spots in small clubs and minor shows until the success of her 1956 single "Banana Boat Song" turned the spotlight on her. The next few years brought such hits as the English version of "Climb Ev'ry Mountain" and "As Long

The dynamic and versatile Shirley Bassey.

as He Needs Me." Coming to the United States in 1961, she opened with a sensational performance in New York's Persian Room and went on to a successful tour.

Her versatility as a singer has enabled her to broaden out from ballads to include folk-rock and soul songs in her repertoire. In 1965 she sang the title theme from the movie *Goldfinger*. Her U.S. concerts have been very well received by both audiences and critics. Among her more recent hits are "Shirley Bassey Is Really Something," "Something Else," "I Capricorn," "Diamonds Are Forever," and "Never, Never, Never."

SIDNEY BECHET
Soprano Saxophone
1897–1959

Sidney Bechet was the first jazzman to achieve recognition on the soprano saxophone, and also one of the first to win acceptance in classical circles as a serious musician.

In 1919 Bechet played in England and on the Continent with Will Marion Cook's Southern Syncopated Orchestra. Even before this, his clarinet and soprano sax had been heard in the bands of King Oliver and Freddie Keppard.

During the early 1920s Bechet made a series of records with Clarence Williams' Blue Five, worked briefly with Duke Ellington (one of his great admirers),

Early jazz forms were pioneered by Sidney Bechet on the soprano saxophone and clarinet.

and then returned to Europe and the United States with Noble Sissle before forming his own trio. He took up residence in France toward the end of his career, and he died there in 1959.

JIMMY BLANTON
Bass
1921–1942

During his brief life, Jimmy Blanton changed the course of jazz history by originating a new way of playing the string bass. Playing the instrument as if it were a horn, he lifted it from a rhythmic back up to a melodic focal point.

Born in St. Louis, Missouri, he played with Jeter Pillars and Fate Marable before joining Duke Ellington in 1939. Until this time the string bass rarely played anything but quarter notes in ensemble or solos, but Blanton began sliding into eighth- and sixteenth-note runs, introducing melodic and harmonic ideas that were totally new to the instrument. His skill put him in a different class from his predecessors. Tonal clarity and melodic imagination made him the first true master of the bass and demonstrated the instrument's unsuspected range in improvisational dynamics.

BUDDY BOLDEN
Cornet
1868–1931

Buddy Bolden, a barber by trade, formed the first jazz band in the 1890s. By the turn of the century, his cornet was so popular that he was often called upon to sit in with a number of bands on a single evening.

His cornet style was the starting point for a chain of musicians from King Oliver to Louis Armstrong or, put another way, from New Orleans to Chicago. Since his career predated the recording of jazz, the only lasting memorial to his talent lies in the oral tradition which carries on his legend, and in the recorded successes of his proteges.

Bolden was committed to East Louisiana State Hospital in 1907, and remained there until his death in 1931.

EARL BOSTIC
Alto Saxophone, Composer
1913–1965

Earl Bostic was born in Tulsa, Oklahoma and early developed a florid, outgoing style and sound that had enormous appeal for a cross section of audiences, making him one of the best-selling jazz recording artists of the early 1950s. Bostic played with a wide range of jazz artists, among them Joe Pass, Shelly Manne, Richard Holmes, and Al McKibbon.

OSCAR BROWN, JR.
Composer, Singer
1926

The many talents of Oscar Brown, Jr. make it necessary to view him as both a creative artist working behind the scenes and a dynamic interpreter delivering original and highly innovative "up-front" material to beguiled, and often enraptured, audiences.

Brown's talents first achieved nationwide recognition in the early 1960s. *Time Magazine* characterized him as "the best new entertainer" in show business "since Belafonte" in 1962, quoting *Ebony Magazine*,

Jean Pace and Oscar Brown, Jr. performed together in Joy.

which viewed him as a "hip Negro folk poet," and Lorraine Hansberry, who called him "a startling genius."

Brown subsequently demonstrated the full measure of his jazz, folk music, and blues talents in the off-Broadway musical *Joy. New York Times* critic Clive Barnes called composer/singer Brown "an artist of great merit" and "a major talent."

Brown, a native of Chicago, was born in 1926. He first gained a reputation as a jazzman playing Mister Kelly's there in the 1950s.

RAY BROWN (RAYMOND MATTHEWS)
Bass
1926

Ray Brown is perhaps the most versatile bass player living today and is in demand around the world. He was born in Pittsburgh. Early in 1951, he joined Oscar Peterson's Trio in an association that lasted 15 years. During this time, he and Peterson produced award-winning records and were in constant demand for concerts. Since leaving Peterson in 1966, Brown joined forces with Laurindo Almeida, Shelly Manne, and Bud Shank. This group toured in Australia, New Zealand, Mexico, and Canada. Brown's work includes regular appearances on the Merv Griffin television show.

RAY CHARLES
Singer, Piano
1932

Ray Charles is the vital link between contemporary jazz and the long-forgotten wellspring of early jazz.

Charles uses what might be called a "down home" style to transmit contemporary musical ideas. He has succeeded to the point where he is one of the few musicians in our time to be acclaimed by jazz professionals and the general public alike.

Blinded at the age of six, Charles received his first musical training at a school for the blind in St. Augustine, Florida. Originally from Georgia, he left school there at the age of 15 to play local engagements. Two years later, he formed a trio which had some success in the Northwest. In 1954 he organized an even larger rhythm and blues group.

Ray Charles breathes soul into jazz.

In 1957 his first LP was released, consisting of a potpourri of instrumentals drawn from pop, gospel, and modern jazz sources. His singing and pianoplaying found particular favor with a number of jazz artists who were reacting against what they felt was a growing tendency for jazz to become overscored and underfelt. In Charles, they saw an artist who had restored both a sense of "soul" and instrumental "funkiness" to the jazz idiom.

CHARLIE CHRISTIAN
Electric Guitar
1917–1942

Jimmy Blanton was playing with the Fate Mirable orchestra in St. Louis when he was discovered by Duke Ellington in 1939. Before that time, the bass was an instrument whose use was confined to the production of a steady, monotonous beat, one which was always subordinate to the more "glamorous" instruments.

Blanton, however, refused to be limited by quarternote traditions. He improvised on his bass as freely as if it were a horn, using unique runs of eighth and sixteenth notes, and experimenting with ideas in melody and harmony that had never before been seriously considered for the bass. His technical skill was so great that no one seriously questions his designation as the first true bass master.

In 1941 Blanton contracted tuberculosis, and he died the following year.

Charlie Christian did for the electric guitar what Jimmy Blanton had done for the bass.

Christian joined Benny Goodman in 1939 and, after only two years with the Goodman sextet, achieved considerable fame as the first electric guitarist to use single-string solos. In his after-hour activities at such Harlem clubs as Minton's, he was an early contributor to the jazz revolution which would one day come to be called Bop. (Christian is even credited by some with having coined the word.)

In 1941, like Blanton, he contracted tuberculosis and, the following year, he too died.

KENNY CLARKE
(Liaqat Ali Salaam)
Drums
1914

Kenny Clarke was one of the "founding fathers" of the Bop movement. Along with Charlie Parker, Dizzy Gillespie, and Thelonious Monk, Clarke made Minton's in Harlem *the* late-hour haunt for jazz buffs and musicians alike in the 1940s.

A pioneer figure in the use of drums as a solo instrument and not just as a background presence, he was the first musician to move away from the blatant use of cymbals to a more subtle style in which he maintained a steady rhythm with the top cymbal while "dropping bombs" with surprise bass-drum sounds.

Clarke hails from a musically inclined Pittsburgh family. While still in school, he began the study of vibes, piano, and trombone, as well as musical theory. His early professional experience was gained with Roy Eldridge and Edgar Hayes. (He traveled to Finland and Sweden with Hayes in 1937.)

In the early 1940s he played with Teddy Hill and then moved into Minton's, where his presence was strongly felt on the Bop scene. Throughout this decade, he continued to work with Dizzy Gillespie, Coleman Hawkins, Tadd Dameron, and others. In 1951 he toured with Billy Eckstine, and the following year he helped organize the Modern Jazz Quartet, remaining with this group for the next three years. After freelancing around New York for a year, he moved to France where he continued to work with a long list of visiting American talents.

Clarke's integrated use of the drums with other soloists has become a staple of contemporary jazz.

ORNETTE COLEMAN
Alto Saxophone
1930

It has often been said that the Bop revolution in jazz marked the beginning of a new musical era, but the music of Ornette Coleman has called that generalization into question. For all its intricacies, its radical harmonic departures which shocked those who first heard them, and its extremely free adherence to melodic lines, Bop may well have been the end of an old era rather than the beginning of a new one, since the core of its uniqueness was built around the concept of improvisation based on chord patterns.

Ornette Coleman's style, however, represents a sharp break with this latter tradition. As a result of this, he has often been dismissed by many musicians (as well as by much of the general jazz public) as little more than "a noisemaker."

Coleman is largely self-taught on his alto. His early professional experience consisted of a series of irregular spots with rhythm and blues bands in New Orleans, Texas, and California. While working as an elevator operator in Los Angeles in the mid-1950s, Coleman undertook a textbook study of harmony and theory before evolving a new style phase.

Arguments have raged since he completed his first major recording session in New York City in 1957. Some feel that the squeaks, bleats, and other sounds which are produced with his plastic horn, not to mention the sounds he has recently begun to experiment with on violin, are meaningless. Others, however (including John Lewis), are convinced that he is easily

The music which Coltrane was creating—like that of Ornette Coleman, Archie Shepp, and others—was the subject of great controversy in its heyday. Coltrane used his tenor to produce harsh, strange sounds which defied easy categorization. The overall effect of his music was regarded as unpleasant and unnerving by many of his listeners, including those who have always felt they were truly open to jazz experimentation.

Some always maintained that Coltrane's music was "meaningless," a charge which at least one fellow musician, J. J. Johnson, took great pains to refute, professing to see in the Coltrane-Monk relationship a parallel with that of Parker and Gillespie.

For all of the difficulty which his music presents to fellow musicians and critics, and likewise to the general listening public, Coltrane remained the most influential presence for young tenor men seeking to make their mark. The dissonance with which he was

Alto sax virtuoso Ornette Coleman

the most original and gifted jazz artist since Parker, Gillespie, and Monk.

At this juncture, only time can provide the necessary perspective with which to pass judgment on the emerging school of harsh, atonal jazz, of which Coleman is undoubtedly a major exponent.

JOHN COLTRANE
Tenor Saxophone
1926–1967

John Coltrane played tenor in a variety of settings during his musical career. In the 1940s he was with a small combo featured in Philadelphia, then a U.S. Navy band playing in Hawaii, and, lastly, a rhythm and blues group. Throughout the 1950s, he saw service with some of the greats of contemporary jazz: Dizzy Gillespie, Miles Davis, and Thelonious Monk.

Saxophonist John Coltrane won kudos with his revolutionary "sheets of sound" technique.

experimenting was a distinct keynote of jazz through-out the 1960s.

EDDIE (LOCKJAW) DAVIS
Tenor Saxophone
1921

Eddie Lockjaw Davis was born in New York City and taught himself to play the tenor saxophone only eight months after purchasing the instrument. He worked with Cootie Williams band from 1942 to 1943, then with Lucky Millinder, Andy Kirk, and Louis Armstrong. From 1945 to 1952 he had his own combo and played mainly at Minton's in Harlem. In 1955 he and organist Shirley Scott joined forces to form a trio which lasted until 1957 at which time he visited Britain and France with Count Basie's big band. Davis still plays in New York jazz clubs.

MILES DAVIS
Trumpet
1926

Miles Davis has played a major role in effecting the transition from the hard, aggressive stance of Bop to the softer, more subtle shadings of the "cool school."

As a teen-age musician in St. Louis in the early 1940s, Davis sat in with his idols Charlie Parker and Dizzy Gillespie when they passed through town with the Billy Eckstine Band.

In 1945 his well-to-do father sent him to the Juilliard School of Music in New York. Within a short time, Davis was working the 52nd Street clubs with Parker and Coleman Hawkins, and touring with the bands of Billy Eckstine and Benny Carter.

In the late 1940s Davis formed a nine-piece band of his own, including Lee Konitz, Gerry Mulligan, John Lewis, and Max Roach. The group was highly

Miles Davis of the "cool school."

praised by other musicians but was a commercial failure.

Except for brief hiatuses due to illness, Davis has been an important jazz presence since 1950, regarded as the leading trumpet in the field.

In the late sixties and early seventies, Davis attracted an enthusiastic following from urban rock audiences, adding percussionist, flutist, and electric organ to his usual accompaniment of electric piano, saxophone, bass, and drums.

Davis enjoys the response, but remains above all keen to please himself. "In Europe they like everything you do; the mistakes and everything. That's a little bit too much. I wouldn't like to sit up there and play without anybody liking it, but you don't have to applaud me."

ERIC DOLPHY
Alto Sax, Bass Clarinet, Composer
1928–1964

Eric Dolphy is greatly admired by musicians. Although his linear derivations were from Charlie Parker, his attack on alto sax and bass clarinet had a fierce bite that sprang from earlier jazz. His mastery of the bass clarinet has never been equaled.

Born in Los Angeles, his first recognition came with the Chico Hamilton quintet of 1958–1959. In 1960 he joined Charles Mingus in New York, and in 1961 he played many club dates with trumpeter Booker Little before joining John Coltrane for some historic tours, concerts, and recordings. Dolphy also played in a group with trumpeter Freddie Hubbard and recorded with Ornette Coleman, then experimenting with a plastic saxophone. In 1964, while on tour again with Mingus in Europe, he decided to stay abroad, where he recorded with Dutch, Scandinavian, and German rhythm sections. He died in Berlin of a heart attack possibly brought on by diabetes.

Dolphy was the winner of *Down Beat* magazine's New Star award for alto, flute, and miscellaneous instruments in 1961, and was elected to that magazine's Hall of Fame in 1965. His legacy includes many recordings for Prestige, Blue Note, Impulse, and smaller companies, both as leader and sideman.

Charles Mingus said of Dolphy that he had the "great capacity to talk in his music . . . He knew the level of language which very few musicians get down to."

ROY (LITTLE JAZZ) ELDRIDGE
Trumpet, Singer
1919

Roy Eldridge was born in Pittsburgh, Pennsylvania and began playing in the late 1920s with Speed Webb and Zach Whyte. Eldridge then began performing with McKinney's Cotton Pickers, Teddy Hall, and Fletcher Henderson. Eldridge has been hailed as one of the most influential trumpeters in the history of jazz. In 1950 he put together his own quintet and has also played with several smaller bands. In the 1940s Eldridge played with Artie Shaw and Sammy Kaye.

Eric Dolphy, a musician's musician.

DUKE ELLINGTON
Piano, Bandleader, Composer
1899–1974

Duke Ellington is believed by many critics to have made the most pervasive contribution to the development of jazz in the United States. Though the lion's share of Ellington's fame hinges on the numerous "standards" he composed, it is his work as the leader of a jazz orchestra that has won him the respect and admiration of fellow musicians

Ellington was born into a moderately well-to-do family in Washington, D.C. The name "Duke" was easily fitted to the dapper young man with the courtly manner. A gifted painter, Ellington was offered a scholarship to the Pratt Institute of Fine Arts in New York City, but he decided instead to play local music dates and paint commercial signs. By 1918 he was doing well enough with his dance bands, featuring such talents as Sonny Greer on drums and Elmer Snowden on piano.

In 1923, at the urging of Fats Waller, Ellington made a trip to New York City, working in Harlem for Bricktop (Ada Smith). He then became leader of his own group and moved down to the Kentucky Club, where the band began to record under the name of Ellington's Kentucky Club Orchestra.

In 1924 Ellington wrote his first revue score for *Chocolate Kiddies,* a show which ran for two years in Germany but never reached Broadway. From 1927 to 1932, Ellington and his orchestra held forth at the Cotton Club on Lenox Avenue (except for a brief hiatus in 1930 when he appeared in his first movie, Amos and Andy's *Check and Double Check*).

During the Cotton Club period, Ellington's orchestral genius gained him a national reputation, particularly through his records and his network broadcasts. Brilliant solo performances by such artists as Barney Bigard, Johnny Hodges, and Cootie Williams set the pace for many later jazz orchestrations—not his single-line melodies—which earned him the plaudits of his fellow musicians.

In 1927 Ellington introduced the wordless use of the voice as a jazz instrument, and in 1931 he broke through the traditional three-minute time limit set for commercial records. His later use of a miniature concerto context as a framework for compositions played by specific jazz soloists, and his creation of original works for new concerts are among the other significant contributions he made to the realm of jazz.

The big bands found their apotheosis in Duke Ellington, who used the huge jazz ensembles for personal artistic expression. Standing behind Ellington is the great jazz vocalist Ella Fitzgerald.

Through European tours first begun in the 1930s, the Ellington sound was brought live to an international public which had, even then, long acclaimed his preeminence in the jazz domain. In 1943 his "Black, Brown and Beige" was regarded as the most important attempt of its time to fuse jazz elements with the formal concert idiom.

The roster of Ellington personnel through the years is among the most impressive in the history of jazz . . . Ben Webster, Juan Tizol, Ray Nance, Oscar Pettiford, Louis Bellson, Harry Carney, Johnny Hodges, and many others.

The whole world of music was saddened by Ellington's death on May 24, 1974. Even today the Duke continues to exert a unique and powerful influence on jazz around the world, both through the music he left behind and through the galaxy of musicians who served in his great band.

ELLA FITZGERALD
Singer
1918

Ella Fitzgerald has emerged as the top female vocalist in virtually every poll conducted among jazz musicians during the last decade. No other jazz vocalist has been as unanimously acclaimed as she.

Discovered in 1934 by Chick Webb during an amateur contest at Harlem's Apollo Theatre in New York City, she cut her first side with Webb a year later. In 1938 she recorded "A Tisket, A Tasket," a novelty number which brought her commercial success and made her name widely known among the general public. Among musicians, however, her reputation stemmed from her singular ability to use her voice like an instrument, improvising effortlessly in a clear style filled with rhythmic subtleties.

For more than 40 years Ella Fitzgerald has been the leading jazz interpreter of a popular song.

ROBERTA FLACK
Singer
1940–

During the early 1970s Roberta Flack rose from a musical cult figure in Washington to become one of the most popular female singers in the world. Her two smash singles—"First Time Ever I Saw Your Face" and Norman Gimbel's beautiful "Killing Me Softly With His Song"—established her as a major force in contemporary music.

Roberta Flack was born in Asheville, North Carolina, and as a child moved with her family to Richmond and then to Arlington, Virginia. Her family was musical, her mother playing church organ and her father

Roberta Flack in performance

the piano in what Roberta calls "A primitive Art Tatum style."

Roberta entered Howard University on a scholarship at 15, graduating three years later with a B.A. in music education. She accepted teaching jobs in Farmville, North Carolina, then later in Washington, D.C. and then took a part-time job accompanying opera singers at a restaurant in the Georgetown section of Washington. She also directed an amateur production of *Aida*. In 1967, after three years with the D.C. school system, she decided to try a music career.

In 1967 Roberta started a regular singing gig at Mr. Henry's Pub in Washington. Word of her talent soon spread and many entertainers who were in Washington would make it a point to see her. Les McCann was so impressed that he brought Roberta to Atlantic Records where she recorded her first album called *First Take*. Roberta's first smash single "The First Time Ever I Saw Your Face" was taken from this album. She quickly followed up with another success, "Killing Me Softly With His Song" and a hit album *Quiet Fire*.

Roberta Flack handles a wide variety of contemporary material with a soulful and mellow-smooth personal style that transcends categorization. The flexibility and purity of her delivery has produced a star who promises more in years to come.

Erroll Garner, piano stylist.

ERROLL GARNER
Jazz Piano, Composer
1921–1977

A keyboard artist who played and composed by ear in the tradition of the founding fathers of jazz, Erroll Garner won the international acclaim of jazz lovers, serious music critics, and the general public. Strong and bouncy left-hand rhythms and beautiful melodies are the trademarks of his extremely enjoyable music. He is the best selling jazz pianist in the world.

Born in Pittsburgh, Garner grew up in a musical family and began picking out piano melodies before he was three years old. He started taking piano lessons at six, but his first and only piano teacher gave up on him when she realized he was playing all her assignments by ear instead of learning to read notes. At seven he began playing regularly on Pittsburgh radio station KDKA. He dropped out of high school to play with a dance band and came to New York in 1939 as an accompanist for nightclub singer Ann Lewis. With guitarist "Tiny" Grimes and bassist "Slam" Stewart, he formed a trio which toured the East Coast. In 1946 he recorded "Laura," which sold a half million copies, and his fame began to grow. On March 27, 1950 he gave a solo recital at Cleveland's Music Hall, and in December a concert at New York's Town Hall.

Gradually recitals and recording sessions took the place of nightclub performances.

Although much of his early music was lost because it was not written down, his later works were taken down by arrangers as he composed them. When Garner played his own compositions with an orchestra, the orchestra played from the arranger's score, while he played from memory.

Garner won musical awards in many countries. As he grew older he devoted most of his time to composing scores for ballet, movies, and Broadway shows, and to concerts and recording sessions, from which he earned over a quarter of a million dollars yearly.

DIZZY GILLESPIE
Trumpet
1917

Dizzy Gillespie and Charlie Parker were co-founders of the most revolutionary movement in jazz during the 1940s—the phenomenon known simply as Bop. The role which each played in this revolution has long been a subject of considerable controversy. Billy Eckstine, whose band at one time included both Gillespie and Parker, has defined Parker's role more as instrumentalist, and Gillespie's more as writer and arranger. Whatever their particular contributions were, however, it cannot be disputed that the sum total of their ideas has brought about a directional change in jazz which continues to the present time.

Gillespie studied harmony and theory at the Lauringburg Institute in North Carolina and, after moving to Philadelphia and gaining more professional experience there, he joined the Teddy Hill band where he replaced his early idol "Little Jazz" Roy Eldridge, who had moved to the Fletcher Henderson Orchestra.

He toured Europe with Teddy Hill during 1939 and, when he returned to New York to play with Mercer Ellington and Cab Calloway, his bop experimentation was already beginning to develop and he had also begun his career as an arranger. After working with Ella Fitzgerald, Benny Carter, Charlie Barnet, Earl Hines, and others, he joined Eckstine's band in 1944.

Since Bop has become nationally known, Gillespie has toured Europe, the Middle East, and Latin America with big bands and quintets, some of which have been subsidized by the U.S. State Department.

EVANS TYREE GLENN
Trombone
1912–1974

Evans Tyree Glenn was one of the most accomplished jazz trombonists in the music world. He was born in Corsicana, Texas and played with many great bands during his career. Among the bands Glenn played with are those of Duke Ellington, Cab Calloway, Benny

Carter, and Don Redman. The trombonist also formed his own groups and played many jazz engagements in the New York City area.

WARDELL GRAY
Tenor Saxophone
1921–1955

Wardell Gray was born in Oklahoma City. Gray, perhaps more than any early modern saxophone player, influenced a whole generation of horn players with his rapid, accurate, and harmonic tones. He started on clarinet in Detroit and worked with Earl Hines in 1943, later joining Benny Carter, Billy Eckstine, and the Gene Norman jazz troupe. In 1948 he came to New York to join the Benny Goodman sextet and later Goodman's big band. With Count Basie and Tadd Dameron, Gray was a direct descendant of the Lester Young school and later he came under the influence of Charlie Parker, showing a large tone and aggressive swing making him perhaps the Sonny Stitt of that period. Cut off by an untimely death, Wardell, in a slim period of time, made his mark on the development of jazz.

BENNIE GREEN
Trombone, Composer
1923–1977

Bennie Green was born in Chicago of a musical family. In 1942 he joined Earl Hines but entered the Army in 1943 where he played with the Army band in Illinois. In 1946 he rejoined Hines, staying until 1948 after which he worked with Gene Ammons and Charlie Ventura. Green has been described as one of the most facile and inspired trombonist of his time.

JOHN A. GRIFFIN
Tenor Saxophone
1928

Johnny Griffin was born in Chicago and has played with most of the prominent jazz personalities over the years. Among them have been Art Blakey, Thelonious Monk, and Eddie Lockjaw Davis. Griffin, like many Chicago musicians, preferred to stay and play in the Windy City, and much of his early development took place there. In December 1962 he moved to Europe and played all over the continent. He lived in Paris in the late 1960s and later moved to Holland, where he owned a farm. In the late 1970s Griffin moved back to the United States, celebrating the occasion with outstanding concerts and recordings with his friend Dexter Gordon.

Dizzy Gillespie with his horn

LIONEL HAMPTON
Vibraphone
1909

Lionel Hampton was the first jazz musician to feature the vibes, an instrument which has since come to play a vital role in small-combo jazz. His first recorded solo on the instrument was in 1930 on "Memories of You," which featured Louis Armstrong, then fronting the Les Hite band in California.

Hampton later left Hite's band to form his own Los Angeles group. When Benny Goodman heard him in 1936, he used him on a record date with Teddy Wilson and Gene Krupa, and then persuaded him to sign on with the Goodman tour on a permanent basis.

Hampton played with the Goodman Quartet until 1940, the year he formed his own permanent orchestra. The following year, it scored its first big hit: "Flyin' Home."

Hampton enjoyed great commercial success in the 1940s and 1950s in such places as Israel, Europe, Australia, and North Africa.

Lionel Hampton most recently has been active in the development of housing in the Harlem community of New York City. A complex of houses has been named for his late wife, The Gladys Hampton Houses between Frederick Douglass Boulevard and St. Nicholas Avenue. Hampton was also honored in 1979 at the White House by President Ronald Reagan.

HERBERT JEFFREY (HERBIE) HANCOCK
Keyboards, Composer
1940

Herbie Hancock was born in Chicago and has notably been associated with the piano, although in recent years he has turned to electronics as a vehicle of communication in his music: electric guitar, electric bass, electric piano, echo-plex, phase shifter, and synthesizer. In 1963 he traveled and played with Miles Davis, establishing himself as a composer and instrumentalist of the first rank. While with Davis, Hancock recorded with numerous groups and became firmly established as a major jazz figure. He has won many awards,

Lionel Hampton at the drums

Herbie Hancock, a composer and instrumentalist of the first rank

including *Down Beat* Jazzman of the Year in 1974 and *Cash Box* and *Playboy* Awards of the Year in 1974. Hancock has also written screenplays and television specials. In 1972 Hancock moved to Los Angeles, where he continues to play and compose as he enjoys success and fame.

W. C. HANDY
Composer
1873–1958

Although he began as a cornetist and bandleader in the 1890s, W. C. Handy's fame as the "Father of the Blues" rests almost entirely on his work as a composer.

After studying at Kentucky Musical College, Handy toured with an assortment of musical groups, becoming the bandmaster of the Mahara Minstrels in 1896.

In 1909, during a political campaign in Memphis, Handy wrote *Mr. Crump,* a campaign song for E. H. "Boss" Crump. Three years later, the song was published as the *Memphis Blues.*

In 1914 Handy published his most famous song, *St. Louis Blues,* and, that same year, also wrote *Yellow Dog Blues.* Some others that have become perennial favorites are *Joe Turner Blues* (1915); *Beale Street Blues* (1916); *Careless Love* (1921); and *Aunt Hagar's Blues* (1922).

In the 1920s Handy became a music publisher in New York. Despite his failing sight, he remained active until his death in 1958. His songs extended beyond the world of jazz to find their way into the general field of popular music in innumerable forms. Their popularity continues unabated even today.

COLEMAN HAWKINS
Tenor Saxophone
1904–1969

With the position occupied by the tenor saxophone in jazz today, it is difficult to imagine that, until Coleman Hawkins came along, this instrument was not seriously considered as a suitable jazz vehicle. The full, rich tone which Hawkins brought to the tenor has helped make it one of the most vital instruments in the contemporary jazz ensemble.

When Hawkins took up the tenor at the age of nine, he had already had four years of training on piano and cello. He continued his studies at Washburn College in Topeka, Kansas and in 1922 toured with Mamie Smith's Jazz Hounds. The following year, he began a 10-year stint with Fletcher Henderson's band.

Hawkins left Henderson in 1934 to tour England and the Continent, recording with Django Reinhardt, Benny Carter, and others. When he returned to the United States in 1939, he recorded his first commercial hit, "Body and Soul," with his own band.

Unlike many of his contemporaries, Hawkins was open to the experimentation of the young musicians of the 1940s. In 1944, for example, he formed an all-star band for the first Bop record session, and he gave help and encouragement to Dizzy Gillespie, Charlie Parker, and others he admired.

With the advent of the "cool school," Hawkins lapsed into temporary decline, but the warmth of his style has been recognized anew by scores of young musicians attempting to duplicate his "soul" sound.

ALBERT (AL) HIBBLER
Singer
1915

Al Hibbler was born in Little Rock, Arkansas, and has been blind since birth. His early influence was Pha Terrell of the Andy Kirk band. Hibbler formed and led his own band in Texas and later joined Jay McShann's band in 1942. After leaving McShann, he freelanced in New York City, gaining national fame while touring with Duke Ellington from 1943 to 1951. Hibbler has a tonal quality once described by Ellington as "tonal pantomime." Hibbler still lives in New York and makes rare appearances.

EARL (FATHA) HINES
Piano
1903

Except for increased technical proficiency, the piano style of Earl "Fatha" Hines has barely changed from what it was in the late 1920s.

Hailing from a Pittsburgh background musically rounded out by his trumpeter father and organist mother, Hines originally planned to launch a concert career, but he was soon caught up in the world of jazz. Forming his own trio while still in high school, he began to play in local clubs before moving on to Chicago as a "single" (a solo act).

While there, he made a series of records with Louis Armstrong's Hot Five, and soon became known as "the trumpet-style pianist." Because of the exciting single-note use of his right hand, the intricacy of his style was well beyond that of any of his contemporaries, and served as a touchstone for a succeeding generation of pianists.

In 1928 Hines formed his own band at the Grand Terrace in Chicago. For the next 20 years, this band served as a proving ground for the best instrumentalists and innovators of the period (from Bud Johnson and Walter Fuller in the early era to Dizzy Gillespie and Charlie Parker in the later years).

From 1948 to 1951, Hines worked again with Armstrong. Since then, he has been active with his own small groups on the West Coast and has, on occasion, toured both the United States and the Continent.

MILTON J. (MILT) HINTON
Bass
1909

Milt Hinton was born in Vicksburg, Mississippi and is considered one of the greatest of bass players. He has played with many of the top jazz artists, including Cab Calloway, Count Basie, Louis Armstrong, Teddy Wilson, and Benny Goodman. Hinton has appeared in concerts throughout the United States and on numerous television shows.

The one and only Earl (Fatha) Hines

"Lady Day"—Billie Holiday

BILLIE HOLIDAY
Singer
1915–1959

Billie Holiday, dubbed "Lady Day" by Lester Young, belongs to the great blues tradition dominated by such figures as Ma Rainey and Bessie Smith.

While still a young girl, she moved from her hometown of Baltimore to New York City and, in 1929, began her singing career in an assortment of Harlem night spots. Four years later, she cut her first sides with Benny Goodman and, from 1935 to 1939, established her reputation with a series of records made while she was vocalist with Teddy Wilson, Count Basie, Artie Shaw, and several other all-star bands.

Although Billie Holiday is often compared with Bessie Smith, her style and material were really far removed from those of the older singer. In fact, there is no earlier jazz artist who is known to have had a direct influence on Billie Holiday. What she shared with Bessie Smith and other blues singers was an ability to project a universal sense of loneliness—that feature which is thought to be at the core of true blues artistry.

In such classic records as "Strange Fruit" and "God Bless the Child," she departed from popular material to score her greatest artistic triumphs, depicting the harsh reality of Southern lynchings and the personal alienation she had experienced because of it.

Miss Holiday died of lung congestion and other ailments in Metropolitan Hospital, New York City.

Once addicted to drugs and alcohol, she had written in her 1956 autobiography: "All dope can do for you is kill you—and kill you the long, slow, hard way."

J. J. JOHNSON
Trombone
1924

J. J. Johnson stands alone as the unchallenged master of the jazz trombone. He is the first musician to have adapted this instrument to the demanding techniques called for by the advent of Bop.

Early in his career, Johnson displayed such skill in performing high-speed and intricate solos that those who knew him only from records found it hard to believe that he was actually using a slide—and not a valve—trombone.

Johnson spent the 1940s touring with Benny Carter, Count Basie, Woody Herman, and Dizzy Gillespie. During these years, his trombone was as widely imitated as the trumpet and alto of Gillespie and Parker, respectively.

In the 1950s Johnson retired for a time, only to return as part of Kai Winding's *Jay and Kai Quintet.* This group soon began to tour Europe and the United States with great commercial success.

For the last generation, Johnson's ability as a composer has also been widely praised. In 1959 he performed several of his works with the Monterey Festival Workshop Orchestra

JAMES P. JOHNSON
Piano
1891–1955

The name of James P. Johnson is less known than that of his most famous protege, Fats Waller, but Johnson nonetheless made a substantial contribution in the field of jazz piano and popular show music.

Johnson was the master of the "stride piano," an instrumental style which derives its name from the strong, striding, left-hand style of the player. "Stride piano" came into its own during the 1920s, particularly in conjunction with the phenomenon known as the "rent party." Such a party was held for the purpose of raising rent money, and involved the payment of an admission fee which entitled a "patron" to food, drink, conviviality, and a stride piano session.

Duke Ellington and Count Basie were among the many who sharpened their skills in the rent party training ground. In fact, the influence of the stride piano was heard in popular music for the next two decades.

Johnson was also an early bridge between the worlds of jazz and Broadway. Numbered among his song hits are "If I Could Be With You," "Charleston," and "Runnin' Wild."

*Scott Joplin, now recognized as one of
America's greatest composers*

SCOTT JOPLIN
Composer
1868–1917

At the start of 1970, the name Scott Joplin was known
only to connoisseurs of ragtime. His remains lay buried
in an unmarked pauper's grave in New York City's
Borough of Queens and his music had been consigned
to oblivion.

Then, in 1970, Nonesuch Records released a recording of Joplin's rags on a classical label. The record
pulled raves from critics of classical music, among
them Harold Schonberg of the *New York Times.* In
1971 the New York City Public Library sponsored a
concert of Joplin's work at Lincoln Center by pianists
Mary Lou Williams, William Bolcom and Joshua Rif-
kin, and singers Barbara Christopher, Clamma Dale,
and Michael Gordon. In 1972 a full-scale performance
of Joplin's opera *Treemonisha* was staged by the Afro
American Music Workshop in Atlanta. In 1973 Joplin
rags were adapted for *The Sting,* a successful movie.
By 1975 Scott Joplin's music was the rage of both
the popular and classical music worlds, the former

buying records and tapes of his rags by the million,
the latter seriously debating whether he should be rated
with Ives and Gershwin in the top rank of American
composers.

The popular success of Joplin's themes in *The Sting*
obscures the key fact about his music and life: he was
a serious composer of talent and versatility whose most
earnest efforts were ignored and rejected because it
was inconceivable to the American musical establishment that the black idiom, or indeed any black individual, could be associated with "serious" music. Thus,
during his lifetime, Joplin was acclaimed as the King
of Ragtime, but when he presumed to venture into
the forms of grand opera, he was ignored and destroyed.

Joplin felt that rag would become the "classical"
music of the United States, and that this would reflect
an assimilation of African and American black folk
themes with classical compositional devices into music
with mixed urban and minstrel roots. Much of this
view was accepted, tacitly at least, by established classical composers of his period, such as Igor Stravinsky,

who wrote rag music, and Debussy, who wrote cakewalk music clearly modeled on rag.

Incredibly, rag, an interracial product of the American Midwest, was acceptable in concert halls only when composed by European whites.

Scott Joplin, whose father had been a slave, was born in Texas in 1868. He early displayed musical talent and was given piano lessons, free, by a local German music teacher. In his teens, he left home and became an itinerant pianist, playing in saloons and bordellos of Mississippi River towns, then in St. Louis and Chicago, and then in Sedalia, Missouri, where he settled in 1894. In Sedalia, he worked in a honky tonk, studied harmony and composition at a local black college, and in 1897 composed "Maple Leaf Rag," which was published in 1899.

"Rag" was an instant success, rewarding Joplin sufficiently to allow him to leave the honky tonks, marry, and move to St. Louis where he taught and composed. In 1899 he wrote a long, choreographed song, "The Ragtime Dance," and in 1903 copyrighted his first opera, *A Guest of Honor,* which was in ragtime. Unusual for their time, neither was successful, but Joplin's short ragtime works continued to be in great demand.

In 1907, Joplin moved to New York where he started work on *Treemonisha,* a folk grand opera. Publishers would not consider such a thing, let alone one by a black pianist from the honky tonks of the Midwest, and Joplin had to publish *Treemonisha,* at his own expense, in 1911. However, he could not find a producer and his orchestration of it was lost. In 1916, in desperation, he unsuccessfully staged a piano version of *Treemonisha* in Harlem. Finally broken, and a victim of syphilis, Joplin was committed to a State Hospital and died the next year.

For the next 55 years, Joplin's name and music were kept alive by a small band of disciples such as James Scott and Joseph Lamb, but much of his music, including *A Guest of Honor,* has been lost.

Treemonisha—An Opera by Scott Joplin

Scott Joplin's major work—for 11 voices—consists of 27 set pieces, and overture, instrumental preludes to the second and third acts, arias, ensembles, recitative choruses—in short, it is a grand opera. It was originally composed for piano accompaniment only, then orchestrated by Joplin, probably in an attempt to improve its chances for acceptance (production). The music is evocative of standard opera of its period, Joplin's black heritage, and his genius for ragtime composition.

The story reflects Joplin's views, and that of many blacks and civil rights advocates of that time, that education of blacks was the most effective weapon against racism and prejudice.

In the story, Treemonisha is an 18-year-old orphan girl with an education who becomes leader of recently freed slaves on a Southern plantation and refuses to allow her followers to punish their oppressors, because this would be unjust and a confirmation of ignorance. It clearly calls for blacks to acquire education and assert themselves.

B. B. KING
Singer-Musician
1925

B. B. King has become one of the most successful artists in the history of the blues. Each of his albums and singles have outsold each previous release and topped those of Bessie Smith, Billie Holiday, Robert Johnson, Big Bill Broonzy, and others.

B. B.'s career really started when as a boy of 14 in Indianola, Mississippi, he met a preacher who played the guitar. B. B. soon owned his own guitar, which he bought for eight dollars, paid out of meager wages he earned working in the cotton fields. From that time on, B. B. spent his spare time singing and playing the guitar with other budding musicians in the town, and listening to itinerant blues guitarists who came to Indianola clubs. Although he loved to sing the blues, he had to do it away from home since such "lowdown" music was not sung in his religious household. In the early 1940s he would travel to a nearby town where he would stand on street corners and play. Sometimes he'd come home with as much as 25 dollars.

After the war, B. B. hitchhiked to Memphis where a fellow musician, remembering him from Indianola,

Versatile guitarist B. B. King in concert

got B. B. a performing job at the 16th Street Grill. He was paid 12 dollars a night, five nights a week, and room and board. B. B. then found a spot on a newly opened radio station in Memphis called WDIA. He played 10 minutes each afternoon, then became a disc jockey. The station named him "The Boy from Beale Street" and thereafter Riley B. King was known as "B. B."

B. B.'s first record was made in 1949 on RPM. He had a number one disc on the rhythm and blues charts in 1950 and has been known nationally ever since. A change of managers then led to a new direction, away from the "chitlin' circuit" and into prestigious "pop"-oriented clubs, colleges, and the fast-growing field of pop festivals.

A series of personal appearances on major television shows sparked his popularity. In 1969 B. B. toured Europe, starting with the Royal Albert Hall in London and continuing throughout England, France, Germany, Switzerland, Denmark, and Sweden. Returning to the United States he joined a 14-city tour with the Rolling Stones.

He later performed at Carnegie Hall in New York

Rahsaan Kirk, a serious and creative innovator

City. Shortly thereafter *Down Beat* magazine voted B. B. the number one blues artist in its annual international critic's poll.

RAHSAAN ROLAND KIRK
Composer; Flute, Tenor Sax, Manzello, etc.
1936–1977

At first called "gimmicky" by the critics, Roland Kirk proved to be one of the most exciting jazz instrumentalists on the circuit. His variety of instruments was matched only by the range of his improvisational styles, often switching in the middle of a number from a dissonant, Hawkins-like exploration to a tonal solo based on a conventional melody.

Born in Columbus, Ohio, Kirk was technically blind, having been able to see nothing but light from infancy. Educated at the Ohio State School for the Blind, he began picking up horns at the age of nine. At 19, while touring with Boyd Moore, he started experimenting with playing more than one instrument at one time. Finding obscure horns like the stritch and the manzello, he worked out a technique for playing three-part harmony through the use of trick fingering.

In 1960 Ramsey Lewis helped Kirk get his first recording date (with Argo Records). In 1961 he played with Charles Mingus' group, and later that year he went on the international circuit.

Among his many compositions are *Three for Dizzy; Hip Chops; The Business Ain't Nothin' but the Blues; From Bechet, Byas, & Fats;* and *Mystical Dreams.*

JOHN LEWIS
Pianist, Composer
1920

John Lewis has become an international force in the world of jazz as an arranger, conductor, composer, and instrumentalist.

Raised in a middle-class environment in Albuquerque, New Mexico, Lewis studied music and anthropology at the University of New Mexico until 1942. After three years in the Army, he went to New York City to become pianist and arranger with Dizzy Gillespie's band. Two years later at Carnegie Hall, Gillespie's band performed Lewis' first major work, "Toccata for Trumpet and Orchestra."

After a European tour with Gillespie, Lewis returned to the United States to play with Lester Young and Charlie Parker, and to arrange for Miles Davis. In 1952, after having finished his studies at the Manhattan School of Music, Lewis founded the group upon which a major part of his reputation rests: The Modern Jazz Quartet (MJQ). Throughout the 1950s, this group developed an international reputation in spite of some carping that its material was too charted to be truly called jazz.

Lewis has never confined his creativity to the MJQ but has constantly assumed a variety of roles, ranging from conducting in Germany to serving as music director of the highly acclaimed Monterey Jazz Festival.

ABBEY LINCOLN
Singer
1930

"This is a WOMAN singing, and more specifically it is a Negro woman, because part of this striking liberation of Abbey's singing has come from a renewed and urgent pride in herself as a Black Woman." This assessment of Abbey Lincoln's talent, style, and direction, made by critic Nat Hentoff, places her among the great jazz singers of our time.

Born Anna Marie Wooldridge in Chicago, Miss Lincoln graduated from Kalamazoo Central High School in Kalamazoo, Michigan and later studied music for a number of years in Hollywood under several prominent vocal and dramatic coaches.

She began her professional career in Jackson, Michigan in 1950. Since then she has performed in movies (*Nothing but a Man*), made records (*Abbey Is Blue, Straight Ahead*), played several prominent clubs, and appeared on nationwide television. More important, she has been hailed by many of the outstanding black jazz performers of our era, including Coleman Hawkins, Benny Carter, and Charles Mingus, as a singer to be classed with the likes of Billie Holiday.

JIMMY LUNCEFORD
Bandleader
1902–1947

"The Lunceford style"—although its originator himself never played an instrument while recording with his band (except on the record of *Liza*)—was one which influenced many bandleaders and arrangers up to the 1950s, including Sonny Dunham, Sonny Burke, and Tommy Dorsey. The Lunceford band reigned with those of Duke Ellington, Count Basie, and Benny Goodman as the leading and most influential of the big jazz orchestras in the 1930s.

A native of Fulton, Missouri, Lunceford received his B.A. at Fisk University and later studied at City College in New York. After having become proficient on all reed instruments, Lunceford began his own career as a "leader" in Memphis in 1927. By 1934 he was already an established presence in the field of jazz. During the next decade, the Lunceford band was known as the best-disciplined and most showmanly black jazz ensemble in the nation.

The Lunceford vogue faded after 1942, by which time the band was already experiencing several changes of personnel. Lunceford died of a heart attack in 1947 while the band was on tour.

JIMMY MCGRIFF
Organist
1936

Jazz organist James Harrell McGriff was born in Philadelphia and comes from a musical family. His father, Harrell, and his mother, Beatrice, both played the piano. By the time McGriff finished Roosevelt and Germantown high schools, he was playing bass, drums, sax, and vibes. Although he possessed excellent musical ability, McGriff thought that he was big enough to become a policeman and enrolled at the Penn Institute of Criminology in Philadelphia. However, while he was enrolled at the institute, he began to hang out in a club three miles from Philadelphia where Lynn Hope, Jimmy Smith, Donald Bailey, Lee Morgan, Don Gardner, Al Cass, and Eddie McFadden were playing. He was tempted to drop out of school and pursue a musical career—until he caught Smith, Cass, and Thornel Schwartz at a club in Trenton, New Jersey. He was hooked the first night he went in to listen. His records have been best sellers since the McGriff version of the Ray Charles tune "I Got a Woman" hit the international spotlight in 1962. His album *City Lights* in 1981 brought the total of McGriff's compositions on record to an impressive number of 79. In the fall of 1981 McGriff was a participant in Norfolk State University's (Norfolk, Virginia) Eminent Scholars Program. McGriff has played clubs and concert dates all over the world.

CHARLES MINGUS
Bass, Composer
1922–1981

Charles Mingus was to the young jazz musician of the 1960s what Charlie Parker and Dizzy Gillespie were to the same group in the two previous decades.

Mingus emerged from classical training in Los Angeles in solfeggio and trombone to become one of jazz's most original bassists. His musical background ranges from five years of study with H. Rheinschagen of the New York Philharmonic to professional stints with Louis Armstrong, Kid Ory, Lionel Hampton, Red Norvo, Charlie Parker, Stan Getz, Duke Ellington, Bud Powell, and Art Tatum (a roster which literally spans the entire history of jazz).

Mingus came into his own as a composer in the mid-1950s. His experiments were directed at expanding the arbitrary limitations he felt had been imposed on jazz. Some of the effects he created (including atonali-

Pioneering bass player Charles Mingus, whose background includes classical training, took the bass from simple accompaniment and gave it a sophisticated contrapuntal role.

ties and dissonances) generated the sort of furor which greeted the advent of Bop a decade earlier.

In 1964 Mingus made his first appearance at the Monterey Jazz Festival with a specially assembled large band to play "Meditations." The powerful performance ranks as one of the high points in Mingus' career.

Mingus played little during the latter half of the 1960s, writing an autobiography called *Beneath the Underdog,* which was published in 1971. It catalyzed new interest in Mingus' music and he began to play again.

In February 1972 he made a comeback concert at Philharmonic Hall, appearing with a 20-piece band and several surprise guests and playing to a sell-out house. In 1974 he appeared at Carnegie Hall with Rahsaan Roland Kirk.

THE MODERN JAZZ QUARTET
Instrumentalists

The Modern Jazz Quartet, formed in 1952, established the right of jazz to be performed on the world's great concert stages.

In 1957 the Quartet broke European barriers to jazz with a series of successful appearances in its staidest concert halls. This triumph was capped in 1970 when the MJQ was asked to perform in Venice's La Fenice opera house.

Another MJQ pioneering success: the first solo jazz performance at the Berkshire Music Barn, in Massachusetts.

With one exception, in 1954, the Quartet has operated with the same personnel since its inception. In that year, Connie Kay replaced Kenny Clarke. John Lewis is the pianist and musical director, Milt Jackson plays the vibraharp and is principal soloist, and Percy Heath rounds out the group.

In 1972 the MJQ presented a twentieth anniversary concert in Carnegie Hall to the applause of public and critics alike.

THELONIOUS SPHERE MONK
Piano
1917–1982

Thelonious Monk's popularity with the general public dates largely from the middle 1950s. However, within the world of professional jazz musicians, his role as an important pioneer in the development of Bop had been acknowledged long before then.

Along with Charlie Parker and Dizzy Gillespie, Monk had been a vital member of the jazz revolution which took place in the early 1940s. Some musicians

Formed in 1952, the Modern Jazz Quartet brought jazz to the world's great concert stages. MJQ's personnel were (left to right) John Lewis, Connie Kay, Percy Heath, and Milt Jackson.

Thelonius Monk, "the most important jazz composer since Ellington."

(among them Art Blakey) have felt that Monk actually predated his more renowned contemporaries. This view notwithstanding, Monk's piano technique and his talent as a composer in the new idiom made him a leader in the development of modern jazz.

Aside from some brief work with the Lucky Millander band and with Coleman Hawkins, Monk generally was the only leader of his own small groups. He has been called the most important jazz composer since Ellington. Many of his compositions (*Round About Midnight, Ruby My Dear*) have been established jazz standards for some time.

Monk's spare and serious piano style spawned scores of imitators. He managed, nonetheless, to remain unique as both an instrumentalist and composer, maintaining his own musical integity and his melodic originality.

Thelonious Monk died in Englewood, New Jersey in 1982.

FERDINAND (JELLY ROLL) MORTON
Piano
1885–1941

Among the many controversial aspects of Jelly Roll Morton's life was his claim that he had "invented jazz in 1901." Although Morton's boast was often scored by many, his talents as a soloist, composer, and arranger place him in the forefront of the early jazz innovators.

A pianist in New Orleans from 1902 until the close of the Storeyville era, Morton lived in California from 1917 to 1922. Using the name "Morton's Red Hot Peppers" from 1926 to 1930, he cut a series of records which were to bring him a nationwide reputation. During this period of prosperity, Morton also became widely known for the diamond filling he wore in one of his teeth as a success symbol.

When jazz fashions changed in the 1930s, Morton fell into eclipse. By 1937 he was running an obscure nightclub in Washington, D.C.

In 1938 Morton made a number of recordings for the Library of Congress—playing, singing, and narrating the major incidents of his life and career. These recordings brought him some renewed attention but within two years he had lapsed back into obscurity—this time in Los Angeles, where he died in 1941.

THEODORE (FATS) NAVARRO
Trumpet
1923–1950

Fats Navarro was born in Key West, Florida. Navarro started playing trumpet at age 13. He played tenor sax with the Walter Johnson band in Miami. Navarro was first heard in the Northeast as a member of Andy

Kirk's band from 1943 to 1944 after Dizzy Gillespie heard him and recommended him to Billy Eckstine, with whom he played for 18 months. In 1947–1948 Fats played with Illinois Jacquet, Lionel Hampton, and Coleman Hawkins. He also worked briefly with Tadd Dameron in 1948–1949. Navarro came up in the Bop era of the 1940s and was ranked with Dizzy Gillespie and Miles Davis as one of the great trumpet players during that period.

JOSEPH (KING) OLIVER
Cornet
1885–1938

Joe Oliver first earned the sobriquet "King" in 1917 after winning a kind of "open combat" solo contest against the likes of Freddie Keppard, Manuel Perez, and a host of other cornetists who filled the Storeyville nights with the first sounds of New Orleans jazz.

Strongly influenced by Buddy Bolden in the early part of his career, Oliver soon teamed up with Kid Ory and organized what was to become the leading jazz band in New Orleans.

During the Storeyville era, Oliver met and befriended Louis Armstrong. Lacking a son of his own, he became Armstrong's "unofficial father," giving the boy his old horn, and sharing with him the musical

Cornetist Joe Oliver, one of the "founding fathers of jazz."

knowledge which he had acquired over the years. In return for these favors, Armstrong treated him with great respect, referring to him always as "Papa Joe."

With the closing of Storeyville, Oliver left for Chicago, whereupon Armstrong replaced him in Ory's band. By 1922, however, Oliver was in a position to summon Armstrong to play in his Creole Jazz Band as second cornetist.

In 1923 the Creole Jazz Band made the first series of recordings by a black jazz group. (Except for a few numbers by Kid Ory, almost no pure black jazz had ever been recorded.)

The duets of Oliver and Armstrong put Chicago on the jazz map of the United States. Some years later, however, changing tastes caused Oliver's music to decline in popularity so that, by the time he moved to New York in 1928, his best years were already behind him.

In the early 1930s Oliver made an unsuccessful tour of the South before finally settling in Savannah, Georgia, where he worked in a poolroom until his death in 1938.

EDWARD (KID) ORY
Trombone
1886–1973

Kid Ory's musical career is in many ways emblematic of the story of jazz itself. Both reached a high point in New Orleans during the first two decades of this century; both moved north during the 1920s, only to lapse into obscurity in the 1930s before being revived in the next two decades.

Ory was the best known of the so-called tailgate trombonists. He led his own band in Los Angeles until 1924 when he moved to Chicago to play with King Oliver and others. In 1926, together with Armstrong, he recorded his own composition "Muskrat Ramble."

He returned to the West Coast in 1929 and, after playing for a time with local bands, retired to run a successful chicken ranch from 1930 to 1939. In the 1940s, he returned gradually to music with Barney Bigard, Bunk Johnson, and other New Orleans notables. When "Muskrat Ramble" was commercially revived in 1956, Ory's name became known to a whole new generation.

He toured Europe successfully in 1956, and again in 1959, and has to this day continued to be a favorite in San Francisco nightclubs.

CHARLIE (BIRD) PARKER
Alto Saxophone
1920–1955

The influence of Charlie Parker on the development of jazz has been felt not only in the realm of the alto

saxophone, which he dominated, but on the whole spectrum of jazz ideas. The astounding innovations which he introduced melodically, harmonically, tonally, and rhythmically made it impossible for any jazz musician from the mid-1940s to the present time to develop his own style without reflecting some of Parker's tonal patterns, with or without acknowledgment.

Parker left school at 15 to become a professional, spending his early years with a group of fun-loving musicians in Kansas City, his hometown. After wandering about the Midwest for a time, Parker arrived in New York in 1939. Working sporadically in Harlem, he recorded his first sides with Jay McShann two years later. It was at this time that Parker met Dizzy Gillespie, who was developing parallel ideas and who would become known as co-founder with Parker of the Bop movement some four years later.

In the early 1940s, Parker played with the bands of Noble Sissle, Earl Hines, Cootie Williams, Andy Kirk, as well as the original Billy Eckstine band — the first big band formed expressly to feature the new jazz style in both solos and arrangements.

In 1945 Parker formally launched the Bop movement by cutting a series of sides with Gillespie's rhythm section. Although Parker was soon revered by a whole host of younger musicians, his innovations met with a great deal of opposition from traditional jazz musicians and critics.

In 1946 Parker suffered a complete breakdown and was confined to a state hospital in California. Six months later he was back recording with Erroll Garner. From this point on until his death from a heart attack in 1955, he confined most of his activity to working with a quintet in the New York area, making his final appearance in 1955 at Birdland, the club which had been named in his honor.

OSCAR PETERSON
Piano
1925

Oscar Peterson began classical study of the piano at the age of six in his native Canada and, in less than a decade, was playing regularly on a local radio show.

In 1944 he became a featured soloist with Johnny Holmes, one of the top bands in Canada, and his reputation soon spread throughout the United States jazz world. He continued to resist offers from Jimmie Lunceford and others to tour the States but in 1949 was persuaded by Norman Granz to come to New York City for a Carnegie Hall appearance. The following year he began to record and to tour the United States for Granz.

Peterson's international reputation stems from his annual European tours. His original group used bass (Ray Brown) and guitar (Barney Kessel, Herb Ellis)

Oscar Peterson bridges Swing and Bop.

Restless innovator Dewey Redman.

but, when Ellis left in 1958, Peterson hired drummer Ed Thigpen to fill out the trio.

The initial reaction to Peterson in the United States was often one of curt dismissal. He was first thought of as nothing but a composite of other pianists, but gradually it came to be recognized that he was forming a creative bridge between two jazz generations—Swing and Bop—using the very best elements of both to make his own highly personal statement.

OSCAR PETTIFORD
Bass
1922–1960

Oscar Pettiford was the leading bassist in the Bop era of jazz. Building his own style on the foundation which had been established by the late Jimmy Blanton, Pettiford achieved renown as the most technically capable and melodically inventive bassist in the jazz world of the late 1940s.

Pettiford was born on an Indian reservation and raised in Minneapolis. Until he was 19, he toured with the family band (father and 11 children), and was well known in the Midwest. In 1943 Charlie Barnet heard him in Minneapolis and hired him to team up with bassist Chubby Jackson.

Pettiford left Barnet later that year and became a regular at Minton's in the era during which Bop was being born. Later, he led his own group on 52nd Street and also played with Coleman Hawkins, Duke Ellington, and Woody Herman.

Pettiford's fame grew during the 1950s through his recordings and his tours of Europe and the Orient. In 1958 he settled permanently in Europe, where he

continued to work with a number of groups until his death in Copenhagen in 1960.

DEWEY REDMAN
Tenor Saxophone
1931

Dewey Redman has spent most of his life in search of a greater knowledge of his instrument, the tenor saxophone, constantly reevaluating his relationship to his music.

Dewey was born in Ft. Worth, Texas, started playing the clarinet when he was 12, taking private lessons briefly for six months before he turned to self-instruction. At 15 he got a job with an eight-piece band that performed in church as the minister passed the collection plate.

At Prairie View A&M College, Dewey teamed up with a piano and bass player to work in local clubs, found a spot in the Prairie View "swing" band, and graduated in 1953 with a degree in industrial arts and a grasp on a new instrument he had worked on in college, the saxophone.

After a stint in the Army, Dewey obtained a masters degree in Education at North Texas State and taught school and directed school bands in West and South Texas.

In 1959 he moved to Los Angeles, where he found the music scene to be very cliquish, and then to San Francisco, where he remained for seven years, studying music, working out his own theories on chord progressions, improvisation and technique. In 1967 Dewey went to New York City, fell in with Ornette Coleman, who brought him into his quartet with Dave Izenson on bass and Ornette Coleman, Jr. on the drums.

In 1973 Dewey was dividing his playing time between solo efforts and gigs with Ornette Coleman and Keith Jarrett and composition of *Peace Suite,* dedicated to the late Ralph Bunche.

DON REDMAN
Saxophone, Composer
1900–1964

The first composer-arranger of any consequence in the history of jazz, Don Redman was known in the 1920s as a brilliant instrumentalist on several kinds of saxophones. He also made a number of records with Bessie Smith, Louis Armstrong, and other top-ranking jazz artists.

Born in Piedmont, West Virginia in 1900, Redman was a child prodigy who played trumpet at the age of three, joined a band at six, and later studied harmony, theory, and composition at the Boston and Detroit conservatories.

During most of the 1930s, Redman led his own band, regarded as one of the leading black orchestras of the day, and the first to play a sponsored radio series. In 1940 Redman went into the composing phase of his career with such bands as Paul Whiteman and Jimmy Dorsey.

After 1951 Redman became musical director for Pearl Bailey. From 1954 to 1955, he appeared in a small acting role in *House of Flowers* on Broadway. Thereafter, he returned to recording, cutting several albums for a number of companies. Redman died in 1964.

MAXWELL (MAX) ROACH
Percussion, Composer
1925

Max Roach, born in Brooklyn, New York, is considered to be one of the key figures in the development

Percussionist Max Roach is considered to be the elder statesman of the modern jazz era.

of jazz in the 1940s. He was the original drummer in Charlie Parker's quintet. It has been stated that Max Roach plays the drums as if he invented the first set. Roach has played with so many musicians living and deceased he is considered to be the elder statesman of the modern jazz period. He is currently professor of music at the University of Massachusetts in Amherst.

JIMMY RUSHING
Singer
1903–1972

The song "Mister Five by Five," written in tribute to him, is an apt description of Jimmy Rushing, who was often called the greatest male vocalist in jazz history.

Rushing played piano and violin as a boy, but he entered music professionally as a singer in the after-

Jimmy Rushing, the original "Mr. Five-by-Five," is often called the greatest male jazz vocalist.

hours world of California in 1925. Over the years since then, Rushing has been linked with leading bands and musicians: with Walter Page from 1927 to 1928, Benny Moten in 1929 and, from 1935 to 1940, as a mainstay with the famed Count Basie band.

Rushing formed his own small group when he left Basie and, in the ensuing years, worked most often as a "single." Following the rediscovery of the blues in the mid-1950s, Rushing regained the widespread popularity he had achieved with earlier generations.

His nightclub and theater engagements were usually highly successful, and his world tours on his own and also with Benny Goodman earned him critical acclaim and commercial success. His style endured across four decades of jazz largely because it is noted for its great warmth, a sure, firm melodic line, and a swinging use of rhythm.

Jazz lost its premier male singer when Jimmy Rushing died on June 8, 1972.

BESSIE SMITH
Singer
1894–1937

Bessie Smith rose from the most abject poverty to become the most popular black entertainer of her day.

Bessie was "discovered" at the age of 13 by Ma Rainey, the first of the great blues singers. Years later, while singing in Selma, Alabama, Bessie was heard by Frank Walker, the recording director of Columbia, a company which was then experiencing serious financial difficulties. In those days, most of the popular recordings of the blues were the so-called urban blues, rendered by such singers as Mamie Smith (no relation). Walker's decision to record a less polished country blues singer created a furor of protest at Columbia, but it also established a personality who has since left a great imprint on the history of vocal jazz. In 1923 Bessie Smith recorded "Down Hearted Blues"—a number which sold over 2 million records in a single year.

From 1924 to 1927 Bessie Smith earned better than $2,000 a week, and was accompanied on her records by the top jazz musicians of her day, including Louis Armstrong and James P. Johnson. Within a short time, however, changing fashions, mismanagement of her funds, and other personal problems all combined to reduce her popularity and bring her career to the brink of ruin.

In 1933 John Hammond arranged a recording session in tribute to her past greatness. Four years later, just before Hammond was to leave for Mississippi to bring her North, she met with a fatal automobile accident, bleeding to death after being refused admission to a segregated hospital in the South.

Bessie Smith influenced most blues singers who followed her.

MAXINE SULLIVAN
Singer
1911

Maxine Sullivan was born Marietta Williams in Homestead, Pennsylvania. Ms. Sullivan was doing radio work and performing with the Red Hot Peppers in Pittsburgh when she was discovered. Her first recording session resulted in the best seller, "Loch Lomond." Ms. Sullivan appeared with the John Kirby band in the 1930s. Following a tour with Benny Carter in 1941, she went into retirement for a short period. She began singing in nightclubs in the New York area during the mid-forties, and in 1948 and 1954 she toured Europe. Ms. Sullivan, who also worked as a nurse, occasionally appears around the New York City jazz circuit.

ART TATUM
Piano
1910–1956

In 1932 a young, almost totally blind pianist from Ohio—Art Tatum by name—arrived in New York City as an accompanist for Adelaide Hall. The first records he cut with her that year gave rise to questions of style which are still being debated today.

Within a year, Tatum's work at the Onyx Club on 52nd Street had made him the talk of the jazz world in New York. After a few years in Chicago, he went abroad in 1938, experiencing his greatest success in London. In his early years, Tatum worked almost exclusively as a soloist, but in 1943 he formed a trio (Slam Stewart on bass, Tiny Gaines on guitar), continuing to perform in this context until his death.

Tatum's emergence was extremely disconcerting to many musicians who felt that his style was far too classical to be truly placed in the category of jazz. Most musicians, however, recognized that Tatum's astounding technical skills and harmonic experimentations were simply years ahead of their time.

No one has yet qualified Tatum's technical virtuosity, though young pianists by the score have tried to do so. More important, however, Tatum seldom let his dexterity overshadow his basic jazz orientation. When he died of uremia in 1956, he had won the respect and acclaim reserved for those who totally dominate their art.

SARAH VAUGHAN
Singer
1924

When a high school junior from Newark, New Jersey, whose only previous singing experience had been with a church choir, stepped onto the stage of Harlem's Apollo Theater on Amateur Night in 1942 and sang "Body and Soul," the audience lost no time whistling and applauding her into first place.

Sarah Vaughan had agreed to enter the amateur contest purely by chance—on a dare from a friend—and it was chance too that brought both Earl (Fatha) Hines and Ella Fitzgerald to the audience that night. Shortly afterward Miss Vaughan signed as vocalist with Hines' band, and stayed with him for two years until she was booked into Manhattan's Cafe Society Downtown, where she remained for a six-month engagement.

The next year, she met and married trumpeter George Treadwell, who left his job to become her agent. Since then, Miss Vaughan has become one of the most sought after of jazz and popular artists, earning a six-figure income annually. Her first record, "It's Magic," sold over 2 million copies, and two others—"Don't Blame Me" and "I Cover the Waterfront"—have since become jazz standards.

THOMAS (FATS) WALLER
Piano
1904–1943

The son of a former pastor of Harlem's Abyssinian Baptist Church, Fats Waller received his early training in the classical idiom.

Already an accompanist for Bessie Smith and other blues greats at the age of 15, Waller was also a piano and organ soloist in cabarets and theaters. He was the first to successfully use the organ as a jazz instrument. During the 1920s, Waller joined his idol James

Sarah Vaughan has been a popular singer for forty years.

P. Johnson in touring the "rent parties" of Harlem, and in developing the "stride piano" which soon set the pace for a number of up-and-coming younger pianists. In 1932, while touring Europe, Waller and the eminent French organist Marcel Dupre gave a private recital in the Notre Dame Cathedral in Paris.

Waller's skill as a popular composer led to such hits as "Ain't Misbehavin' " and "Honeysuckle Rose."

LESTER (PREZ) YOUNG
Tenor Saxophone
1909–1959

It was Lester Young who gave Billie Holiday the name "Lady Day" when both were with Count Basie, and it was Lady Day in turn who christened Lester Young "President" (later shortened to "Prez").

Young spent his youth on the carnival circuit in the Midwest with his musical family, choosing to concentrate on the tenor saxophone, only one of the many instruments he was able to play.

When Young took over Coleman Hawkin's chair in Fletcher Henderson's orchestra, he was criticized for not having the same style as his predecessor. As a result of this, he returned to Kansas City to play with Andy Kirk, and then with Count Basie from 1936 to 1940. During the Basie years, Young and Hawkins were the two most vital influences on the tenor as a jazz instrument. Hardly a tenor man from the middle 1940s through the 1950s achieved prominence without building on the foundations laid by Lester Young. Young is considered to be a major figure involved in the transition between the big, rich tenor style and the quiet, moody "cool school."

Young suffered a complete breakdown in 1956, and died three years later after having made a brief European comeback.

OTHER NOTABLE JAZZMEN

Name	Forte	Dates
Cannonball Adderley	Sax, leader	1928–1975
Nat Adderley	Trumpet	1931
Red Allen	Trumpet	1908–1969
Albert Ammons	Piano	1907–1949
Albert Ayler	Tenor sax	1936
Benny Bailey	Trumpet	1925–1967
Buster Bailey	Saxophone	1902
Dave Bailey	Drums	1926
Danny Barker	Guitar	1909
Denzil Best	Drums	1917
Barney Bigard	Clarinet	1906
George Braith	Soprano sax	1939
Lawrence Brown	Trombone	1905
Pete Brown	Alto sax	1906

Name	Forte	Dates
Donald Byrd	Trumpet	1932
Cab Calloway	Bandleader	1907
Mutt Carey	Trumpet	1892–1948
Harry Carney	Baritone sax	1910
Bruno Carr	Drums	1928
Scoop Carry	Alto sax	1915
Benny Carter	Alto sax	1907
Ron Carter	Bass	1937
Al Casey	Guitar	1915
Buddy Catlett	Bass	1933
Sidney Catlett	Drums	1910–1951
Don Cherry	Trumpet	1936
Buck Clayton	Trumpet	1911
Jimmy Cobb	Drums	1929
Cozy Cole	Drums	1909
Bill Coleman	Trumpet	1904
Hank Crawford	Alto sax	1934
James Crawford	Drums	1910
Ted Curson	Trumpet	1935
Richard Davis	Bass	1930
Sidney DeParis	Trumpet	1903–1967
Johnny Dodds	Clarinet	1892–1940
Baby Dodds	Drums	1898–1959
Natty Dominique	Trumpet	1896
Ed Durham	Trombone	1906
Billy Eckstine	Vocalist	1914
Harry Edison	Trumpet	1915
Teddy Edwards	Tenor sax	1924
Ethel Ennis	Vocalist	1934
Booker Ervin	Tenor sax	1930
Herschel Evans	Tenor sax	1909–1939
Pops Foster	Bass	1892–1969
Gil Fuller	Composer, bandleader	1920
Victor Gaskin	Bass	1934
Dexter Gordon	Tenor sax	1923
Grant Green	Guitar	1911
Edmond Hall	Clarinet	1901–1967
Tubby Hall	Drums	1895–1946
Jimmy Hamilton	Clarinet	1917
Lil Hardin	Piano	1903
Otto Hardwicke	Alto sax	1904
Eddie Harns	Tenor sax	1934
Jimmy Harrison	Trombone	1900–1931
Louis Hayes	Drums	1937
J. C. Heard	Drums	1917
Percy Heath	Bass	1923
Fletcher Henderson	Piano, bandleader	1898–1952
Joe Henderson	Tenor sax	1937
Jay C. Higginbotham	Trombone	1906–1973
Andrew Hill	Drums	1937
Johnny Hodges	Alto sax	1906–1970
Red Holt	Drums	1932
Darnell Howard	Clarinet	1892–1966
Freddie Hubbard	Trumpet	1938
Paul Humphrey	Drums	1935
Bobby Hutcherson	Vibes	1941
Bessie Jackson	Singer	n.a.
Cliff Jackson	Piano	1902–1970

Name	Forte	Dates	Name	Forte	Dates
Quentin Jackson	Saxophone	1909	John Patton	Organ	1936
Hilton Jefferson	Alto Sax	1903–1968	Esther Phillips	Vocalist	1935
Bill Johnson	Bass	1872–?	Charles Tommy Potter	Bass	1918
Bud Johnson	Trombone	1910	Bud Powell	Piano	1924–1966
Keg Johnson	Trombone	1908–1967	Russell Procope	Saxophone	1908
Lonnie Johnson	Guitar	1889–1970	Lou Rawls	Singer	1935
Manzie Johnson	Drums	1915	Jerome Richardson	Saxophone	1920
Pete Johnson	Piano	1904–1967	Sam Rivers	Tenor sax	1930
Elvin Jones	Drums	1918	Luis Russell	Piano	1902–1963
"Philly Jo" Jones	Drums	1923	Johnny St. Cyr	Banjo, guitar	1890–1966
Quincy Jones	Arranger, composer	1933	Bud Scott	Banjo, guitar	1890–1949
Connie Kay	Drums	1927	Hazel Scott	Piano, singer	1920
Wynton Kelly	Piano	1931	Shirley Scott	Organ	1934
Al Killion	Trumpet	1916–1950	Bola Sete	Guitar, lute	1928
John Kirby	Bass, leader	1908–1952	Charlie Shavers	Trumpet	1917
Billy Kyle	Piano	1914	Orvell Shaw	Bass	1923
Tommy Ladnier	Trumpet	1900–1939	Archie Shepp	Tenor sax	1937
Jusef Lateef	Saxophone	1921	Wayne Shorter	Tenor sax	1933
Harland Leonard	Saxophone	1904	Ormer Simeon	Clarinet	1902–1959
John Levy	Bass	1912	Tab Smith	Saxophone	1909
Ed Lewis	Trumpet	1909	Les Spann	Guitar, flute	1932
Meade Lux Lewis	Piano	1905–1964	O'Neil Spencer	Drums, singer	1909–1944
Ramscy Lewis	Piano	1935	Billy Strayhorn	Arranger	1915–1970
John Lindsay	Bass	1894–1950	Buddy Tate	Saxophone	1915
Melba Liston	Arranger	1926	Art Taylor	Drums	1929
Johnny Lytle	Piano	1935	Cecil Taylor	Piano, arranger	1933
Joseph K. Marshall	Drums	1902–1948	John Tchicai	Saxophone	1936
Les McCann	Piano	1935	Clark Terry	Trumpet	1920
Carmen McRae	Singer	1922	Walter Thomas	Tenor sax	1907
Donald Mills*	Singer	1915	"Lucky" Thompson	Tenor sax	1924
Harry Mills*	Singer	1913	Stanley Torrentine	Tenor sax	1934
Herbert Mills*	Singer	1912	McCoy Tyner	Piano	1938
John Mills*	Singer	1889	Mal Waldron	Piano	1926
George Mitchell	Trumpet	1899–?	Clara Ward	Vocalist	1924
Hank Mobley	Tenor sax	1930	Jack Washington	Saxophone	1912–1964
Lee Morgan	Trumpet	1938	Julius Watkins	French horn	1921
Benny Morton	Trombone	1907	Anthony Williams	Drums	1945
Bennie Moten	Piano, leader	1894–1935	John Williams	Saxophone	1903
Tricky Sam Nanton	Trombone	1904–1948	Marion Williams	Vocalist	1927
Oliver Nelson	Piano, arranger	1932	Nancy Wilson	Vocalist	1937
David Newman	Saxophone	1933	Shadow Wilson	Drums	1919
William Frank Newton	Trumpet	1906–1954	Phil Woods	Alto sax	1931
Albert Nicholas	Clarinet	1900	Reggie Workman	Bass	1937
Jimmy Noone	Clarinet	1895–1944	Gene Wright	Bass	1923
Joe Orange	Trombone	1941	Lamar Wright	Trumpet	1912
Jimmy Owens	Fluegelhorn	1943	Larry Young	Organ	1940
Walter Page	Bass	1900–1957			

* Entries refer to the group which performed together as "The Mills Brothers"

THE BLACK IN FILMS

A Historical Survey of the Black in Film (1902–1982)
■ Annotated List of Films with Black Themes or Actors

In the early 1980s, black exploitation films were on the decline and fewer and fewer black stars were being featured in movies. This drew the concern of the NAACP, which mounted a protest against the film industry to get more blacks before the cameras. The NAACP's protest included urging blacks to boycott movie houses across the country. This was a sharp reaction that followed a long period of attempts to make films echo reality.

A SURVEY OF BLACKS IN FILMS

Films of the pre-World War I period which featured black characters invariably fell into one or the other of two categories: the slapstick variety portraying the black as a clown or fool; or the sentimental melodrama full of laughing, hymn-singing slaves toiling contentedly for their benevolent masters. With very few exceptions, these roles were played not by black actors but by whites in blackface. Perhaps the most noteworthy film of this era was D. W. Griffith's 1915 production *The Birth of a Nation,* in which the portrayal of the Reconstruction period black as a corrupt, lawless villain invoked a storm of controversy and protest.

The 1920s

After World War I the casting of blacks to depict blacks increased. But, far from portending any change in philosophy, the black servant, bellhop, maid, straight man—the black lackey—became an established vehicle for winning a few cheap laughs from the audience.

The motion picture industry was growing rapidly during the twenties, becoming America's prime mode of entertainment. During this era, there was little recognition that the movies were not only entertainment but an enormous propaganda machine that inordinately influenced the thinking and the behavior of its audience. Nothing in the movies during those early years did justice to the black American.

In 1922, with D. W. Griffith's *One Exciting Night,* a type had been born: the black as a blubbering, superstitious coward whose hair turned white at the approach of even the mildest form of danger. The other genre of black roles popular in the 1920s was the cannibalistic savage in jungle pictures about "darkest Africa." Probably the most true-to-life depiction of blacks in this period was in Hal Roach's "Our Gang" comedies in which black and white children played together naturally and generally as equals.

However, there was little serious attempt to tap the acting potential black actors possessed. In 1928 hope was kindled by Paul Sloane of Fox who was given the assignment of directing an all black motion picture for the studio entitled *Hearts in Dixie.* But with its premiere in 1929 there was new disappointment, as the same routine movie cliches regarding blacks were executed on a grand production scale. Lacking plot, story line, or sophistication, the movie was merely a succession of "darkies" picking cotton, praying, and getting together to sing spirituals. Later that year, King Vidor of MGM released *Hallelujah,* a more adept film that used several black actors. However, real thoughtfulness about life among black Americans was still lacking. The characters did not ring true. What was portrayed was more a white fantasy of the separated black society.

The Thirties

Bad as it was, *Hallelujah* was nonetheless a milestone. The comment and criticism concerning the movie, both

Paul Robeson plays a porter who becomes a potentate in the classic The Emperor Jones.

pro and con, had much to do with work that followed, such as *Arrowsmith* in 1932, directed by the Hollywood great, John Ford. Clarence Brookes, a black actor, played a black physician who had a stature, sincerity, and ability the moviegoing public had been taught to associate with white heroes.

In 1933 Paul Robeson starred in *The Emperor Jones,* a major motion picture effort that failed financially but received excellent critical reviews.

For blacks, the advent of sound in motion pictures meant an endless parade of routines akin to those produced at the well known Cotton Club in Harlem. The 1930s for the most part was an era of commercial exploitation, as singers, dancers, and jazz musicians from the New York stage and night club circuit appeared in countless Hollywood musicals, usually in all-Negro productions, or in segregated sequences in otherwise all-white films. Integrated jazz groups were never shown. Performers such as Cab Calloway, Louis Armstrong, Lena Horne, and Hazel Scott became box-office names, with the musical serving as a vehicle for the discovery and popularization of much significant black talent. At the same time, the myth of the Negro as irrepressible "rhythm man" was reinforced— a myth which found its most demeaning expression in the grinning, shuffling, eye-rolling antics of Stepin Fetchit, Mantan Moreland, and Sleep 'n' Eat, among others. Even black films made independently of the major studios by black or, on occasion, white producers followed Hollywood stereotypes of character and situation, although they at least utilized accurate local color motifs. Shoddily produced and acted, they made little effort to alter the already-distorted Negro film image.

The contributions of two directors, Mervyn Le Roy and Fritz Lang, offset these trends to some extent.

In producing films which showed blacks to possess the qualities and emotions of ordinary human beings, or which dealt with the theme of intolerance, they prepared the way for more understanding treatment and more realistic themes in the years to come. Documentary films of the early 1940s also helped correct many Hollywood stereotypes by showing blacks at work, pursuing education, or in the armed services.

The Forties and the War

The new liberalism of the World War II years, with a concern for morale at home and support of the country's fighting men of all colors, had a corrective influence on the black's film image. In such pictures as *Of Mice and Men* and *Strange Incident* blacks appeared as dignified citizens, often as heroic or semiheroic figures. Fewer films were made glorifying the Old South. The 1940s also saw increasingly vocal protest by the black and the liberal press, and by such groups as the NAACP and the International Film and Radio Guild. Pressure from these sources did much to eliminate offensive dialogue and stereotypical roles and brought such major victories as the abandonment, in 1946, of plans for a new production of *Uncle Tom's Cabin.*

After World War II

Gradually, following the war, the worst racial offenses began to disappear from the scene. The scatterbrained maid, shuffle-foot janitor, and crazed savage have virtually disappeared. Black actors and actresses had begun to find roles worthy of their talent. In 1939, for example, Hattie McDaniel won an Academy award for her supporting role as a stereotyped "Mammy" in *Gone With the Wind.* By contrast, Sidney Poitier's 1965 best actor award was for a role (*Lilies of the Field*) which showed a black assuming his responsibilities with strength and skill in a natural, amicable relationship with a group of whites dependent on him.

Themes that were taboo well into the 1930s and beyond are now dealt with more frankly: where once it was daring to examine the color bar with a story about blacks "passing" for white, nowadays a number of films show interracial love affairs and marriages. Moreover, the contemporary urban, educated, black sophisticated in speech, dress, and tastes is more and more "visible" in both minor and major roles.

When blacks began to assert themselves with a more strident form of protest during the 1960s, the film industry took note. *Uptight* was based on the events in a major ghetto following the assassination of Martin Luther King. And as blacks forged ahead in the film industry, Gordon Parks led a quiet revolution, as he became the first black to direct a film (*The Learning Tree*) for a major studio. Then Melvin Van Peebles made an independent film, *The Night The Sun Came Out,* which grossed over $10 million. Soon more than 15 blacks had directed feature films for major studios or independent distributors and the industry had to acknowledge the impact of black performers and their following among moviegoing America.

The Seventies

In the early 1970s, the film industry started to produce movies in great quantity with the huge black moviegoing audience in mind. Almost all were action films with superheroes of the stud type. These films made huge sums of money and helped to rejuvenate a financially ailing Hollywood.

While Hollywood was gaining in benefits from what was to be called "The Black Film Boom," identity problems were emerging from the new films for black audience. By the summer of 1972, there had been na-

tional media attention to the phenomenon which had acquired the label "blaxploitation."

Leaders of every major black organization—Jesse Jackson of PUSH, Roy Innis of CORE, Roy Wilkins of the NAACP, and Ralph Abernathy of SCLC and Vernon Jordan of the Urban League—were condemning most of the films which dealt with the themes of violence and extolled unsavory characters such as pimps and drug dealers. Concern was also expressed by black intellectuals. Psychologist Alvin F. Poussaint, a Harvard professor, wrote of the films: "The same insidious message is there: blacks are violent, criminal, sexy savages who imitate the white man's ways as best they can."

Blaxploitation Ends and New Era Begins

In Hollywood, some 400 concerned black artists working in the industry met to discuss the black image in contemporary films. The result: an organization was formed called The Coalition Against Blaxploitation.

Hollywood's romanticized version of the Old South spawned many black characters like those in Carolina *(top left); in* I Am a Fugitive from a Chain Gang *(lower left) blacks are portrayed with more human complexity and nobility;* Birth of the Blues *(below) was a major 1941 musical.*

Its purpose: to meet with studio and industry union heads to improve the image of blacks on screen and their working lot in Hollywood as well.

In that time, new stars emerged, particularly popular athletes and pretty singers. They were followed by new producers and other personnel behind the cameras in production capacities.

In 1973 10 films created primarily for black audiences were nominated for Academy Awards. In 1972 Isaac Hayes, a composer, won an Oscar for his theme song for *Shaft.*

The commercial success of these films was unexpected and very quickly—and expectedly—the industry responded with a profusion of similar films. In what could be described as a sudden explosion, there were scores of films boasting more blacks working before the cameras and as a part of the crews than Hollywood had ever witnessed at any time in its history. Virtually all of the superficial action-adventure films generated concern among critics and activists angry about the emphasis on black anti-heroes.

The phenomenon known as the black exploitation film boom virtually disappeared as quickly as it had arrived. Some observers had accurately predicted its demise, and soon it was obvious that audiences had begun to tire of the action, violence, and titillation. Some producers continued to release such low-budget projects over the next five years, but they were all rejected by theatergoers looking for something new and different.

During this period of transition, musicals and biographical dramas were released. If there was a new trend of movies with wide acceptance, it was reflected in a revival of the comedy genre—which had a history of negative acceptance among many blacks objecting to what they felt were stereotypic performances.

The films during the decade of the 1970s, however, proved to be successful entertainment, which appealed to a broad cross section of the moviegoing public, becoming unqualified commercial successes.

Specifically, the talents of a Hollywood veteran and an unpredictable neophyte meshed to established a trend that would continue successfully for years. The veteran—Sidney Poitier—had thrived through a precedent-setting career as an actor and was venturing into the world behind the camera as a director. The neophyte—Richard Pryor—had become a cult hero among the young as a tough-talking and hilarious street comic. When the two collaborated (with a gallery of other major black actors) in *Uptown Saturday Night,* a new era of black involvement in films was inaugurated. The film was a modest box office success, but it lead to separate career paths for the two principals reflective of increasing impact and power within the industry.

By 1980 Poitier and Pryor had reunited as director and actor in *Stir Crazy,* and the results were predictably successful. Poitier had grown over the previous decades to become the most prominent black presence in the movie industry. As he concentrated on a series of films, refining his expertise as a director, Pryor soon became one of Hollywood's top media stars of the 1970s. In film after film, each presenting a role unique within itself, he emerged as a consistent box office draw and an increasingly popular performer.

The previously mentioned decline in the purely exploitational action films during this time resulted in a loss of work for such performers as the actor-athletes who had thrived on those movies. Blacks who had worked behind the cameras in positions ranging from producer and director to stuntman and cameraman were also hard-pressed to find regular employment.

In the constantly changing world of movies, however, new faces were being recruited and they were often experienced, stage-trained actors and actresses like James Earl Jones, Lou Gossett, Billy Dee Williams, Cicely Tyson, and Diahann Carroll.

As predominantly black projects became increasingly rare, these skilled performers were cast in films designed to appeal to audiences in general. Producers

Blackula, *a movie some called a "blaxploitation" film.*

A scene from the 1859 play The Octoroon, *which was made into a movie in 1913.*

had realized that to gear a film solely for the black audience was self-defeating in terms of commercial success. Now the emphasis was on "crossover" films with mass appeal. So, in the space of some 10 years, the role of blacks on the screen had changed dramatically. The Hollywood-Beverly Hills chapter of the NAACP and the Black Film-Makers Hall of Fame sought to honor achievement and encourage a higher quality of performance in separate awards ceremonies.

And even in the absence of exploitation films, it was not necessarily a time of optimism. Hollywood's unsettling economic problems sharply reduced the number of films made. A lot of projects were left waiting and numerous talented people were forced to vie for painfully few roles. Yet it has been challenges such as this that have been accepted by each hopeful that ever came to Hollywood. And there was no indication that those among the generation of the 1980s would be any less determined to achieve their definition of success than the blacks who had preceded them.

The following is a list of representative films in which blacks have either starred, played feature roles, or otherwise made significant contributions.

FILMS FEATURING BLACK ACTORS OR WITH BLACK THEMES: 1902–1982

Off to Bloomingdale Asylum. 1902 (French). Produced by George Méliès. First appearance of Negroes in film. Slapstick comedy.

The Wooing and Wedding of a Coon. 1905. All-Negro. Undisguised mockery of Negro couple.

Fights of a Nation. 1905. Negro depicted as cake-walker, buck-dancer, and razor-thrower.

The Slave. Biograph, 1909. Directed by D. W. Griffith.

The Sambo Series. 1909–1911. Produced by Sigmund Lubin. All-Negro comedies similar to Rastus series.

The Rastus Series. About 1910. Produced by Sigmund Lubin. Series of all-Negro short comedies. Central character a Negro buffoon of small intelligence.

The Judge's Story. Thanhauser, 1911. A Southern judge moves a jury to leniency for an accused Negro.

Probably first film to give a measure of sympathy to Negro character.

The Battle. Biograph, 1911. Directed by D. W. Griffith. The first of Griffith's glorifications of the Old South.

The Dark Romance of a Tobacco Can. Essanay, 1911. Man horrified to find girl he proposes to is Negro.

For Massa's Sake. Pathe, 1911. With Crane Wilbur. Devoted slave tries to sell himself to pay master's gambling debts.

The Debt. 1912. Tragedy of interracial love.

In Slavery Days. Rex, 1913. Directed by Otis Turner. With Robert Z. Leonard, Margarita Fischer, Edna Maison. Wicked octoroon foiled.

The Octoroon. 1913. From the play by Dion Boucicault. With Guy Coombes, Marguerite Courtot. The tragedy of whites with Negro blood.

Coon Town Suffragettes. 1914. Produced by Sigmund Lubin. All-Negro. Southern "Mammys" try to keep their no-good husbands out of saloons.

Dark Town Jubilee. 1914. The first attempt to star a Negro, in this case Bert Williams, the well-known New York vaudevillian. Badly received by white audiences.

The Wages of Sin, The Broken Violin, etc. About 1914. Oscar Micheaux, independent producer. Series of all-Negro films.

Uncle Tom's Cabin. World, 1914. Directed by William R. Daly. From the novel by Harriet Beecher Stowe. With Sam Lucas, Irving Cummings, Marie Eline, and a cast of Negro players. The featuring of Negro actor Sam Lucas, rather than a white actor in blackface, created a precedent. This was the third film version of the novel; the first, in 1909, directed by Edwin S. Porter, seriously distorted the abolitionist intent of the book into a sentimental tale about slaves who "know their place." In 1927 Negro actor Charles Gilpin left the filming of a new production over a dispute about the characterization of Uncle Tom.

The Birth of a Nation. Epoch, 1915. Directed by D. W. Griffith. From the novel *The Clansman* by Thomas Dixon. With Mae Marsh, Lillian Gish, Henry B. Walthall, Robert Harron, Wallace Reid, George Seigmann, Walter Long, George Reed, Ralph Lewis, Elmo Lincoln, Elmer Clifton, Donald Crisp, Raoul Walsh, Joseph Henaberry, Eugene Pallette, Bessie Love, Jennie Lee, Howard Gaye, Tom Wilson, Erich von Stroheim, and others. Negroes as corrupt and brutal villains in Reconstruction-period South, with the Ku Klux Klan having a "just" triumph. Film caused storm of indignation in the North, was banned in some cities.

The Nigger. Fox, 1915. From the novel by Edward Sheldon. With William Farnum.

The "Our Gang" Comedies. Produced by Hal Roach. Negro children, including Farina, Stymie Beard, and Buckwheat, playing together with whites.

The Greatest Thing in Life. 1918. Directed by D. W. Griffith. Includes episode of a white soldier in World War I kissing his Negro comrade-in-arms as he died. Griffith was accused of planting the scene to appease critics of his racially biased *Birth of a Nation*.

Ten Nights in a Bar-Room. Coloured Players Film Corporation, about 1920. All-Negro with Charles Gilpin.

One Exciting Night. 1922. Directed by D. W. Griffith. First example of Negro as contemptible comic relief.

Broken Chains. 1924. Shows Negro as a murderous agitator.

The Florian Slappey Series. About 1925–1926. Written and produced by Octavus Roy Cohen, a Negro. All-Negro, "blackface" humor.

Melancholy Dame. 1929. Written and directed by Octavus Roy Cohen. All-Negro with Evelyn Preer, Eddie Thompson, Spencer Williams.

Hearts in Dixie. 1929. Directed by Paul Sloane. The first of Hollywood's All-Negro films, with Clarence Muse, Stepin Fetchit, Mildred Washington in stereotyped roles.

Hallelujah. MGM, 1929. Directed by King Vidor. From the novel by Wanda Tuchock. All-Negro, with Daniel Haynes, Nina Mae McKinney, Victoria Spivey, William Fountain, Harry Gray, Fannie Belle de Knight, Everett McGarritty. Usual

In the Our Gang *comedies the pint-sized heroes inhabit a world of mischief and pranks where race doesn't matter.*

Although Halleluja *was filled with stereotypes, it did attempt to be serious, dramatic, and passionate.*

stereotypes, though not as extreme as in *Hearts in Dixie.* Had very favorable press.

East of Borneo. Universal, 1932. Directed by George Melford. With Charles Bickford, Rose Hobart, Lupita Tovar, Noble Johnson. Typical Hollywood jungle film, in which Negro players were featured mostly as cannibals, head-hunters, and repulsive savages.

The Black King. Southland, 1932. Directed by Bud Pollard. From the story by Donald Heywood. With Vivian Baber, Harry Gray, Knolly Mitchell, Mary Jane Watkins. One of the first big independent all-Negro film productions.

Arrowsmith. 1932. Directed by John Ford. With Ronald Coleman, Clarence Brooks. Negro doctor given same stature as white doctor.

I Am a Fugitive from a Chain Gang. Warners, 1932. Directed by Mervyn LeRoy. With Paul Muni, Everett Brown. Sympathetic, realistic portrayal of Negro prisoner.

The Emperor Jones. Krimsky-Cochran, 1933. Directed by Dudley Murphy, under supervision of William C. DeMille. From the play by Eugene O'Neill. With Paul Robeson, Dudley Diggs, Frank Wilson, Rex Ingram, George Stamper, Fredi Washington, Ruby Elzy, Brandon Evans, Taylor Gordon. Significant in that it gave a Negro actor a leading part in a film also featuring whites. Dealt seriously with a Negro theme.

Hypnotized. World Wide, 1933. Directed by Mack Sennett. With George Moran, Charlie Mack, Ernest Torrence, Wallace Ford, Maria Alba. Typical of comedies featuring well-known "blackface" minstrels.

The Cabin in the Cotton. Warners, 1933. Directed by Michael Curtiz. From the novel by Henry Kroll. With Richard Barthelmess, Bette Davis, Dorothy Jordan, Henry B. Walthall, Clarence Muse, "Snowflake."

Judge Priest. Fox, 1935. Directed by John Ford. With Will Rogers, Tom Brown, Anita Louise, Henry B. Walthall, Rochelle Hudson, Hattie McDaniel, Stepin Fetchit. A comedy drama about a judge who is not in conformance with a Southern town regarding blacks.

Helldorado. 1935. Directed by James Cruze. With Richard Arlen, Madge Evans, Ralph Bellamy, James Gleason, Henry B. Walthall, Stepin Fetchit. Negro frightened by a "ghost," the butt of the humor.

Imitation of Life. Universal, 1935. Directed by John M. Stahl. From the novel by Fannie Hurst. With Claudette Colbert, Warren William, Ned Sparks, Louise Beavers, Fredi Washington, Rochelle Hudson, Sebie Hendricks, Dorothy Black, Alan Hale, Hazel Washington. A light-skinned Negro girl makes a desperate bid to pass as white. The film dealt seriously

with this problem, but also had a "Mammy" role more in the foreground.

So Red the Rose. Paramount, 1935. Directed by King Vidor. With Margaret Sullivan, Walter Connolly, Randolph Scott, Daniel Haynes, Clarence Muse. Depicts the revolt against slavery as the work of a few Negro opportunists misleading the contented masses.

Show Boat. Universal, 1936. Directed by James Whale. From the operetta by Edna Ferber and Jerome Kern. With Irene Dunne, Paul Robeson, Allan Jones, Charles Winninger, Helen Morgan, Queenie Smith, Helen Westly, Donald Cook, Hattie McDaniel, Clarence Muse. A musical review and love story set on the Mississippi River in the 1880's.

The Littlest Rebel. Twentieth-Century Fox, 1936. Directed by David Butler. With Shirley Temple, John Boles, Jack Holt, Bill Robinson, Karen Morley, Quinn Williams, Willie Best, Frank McGlynn Sr., Hannah Washington. Typical Hollywood Civil War picture, totally sympathetic to the South and Southerners.

The Singing Kid. Warners, 1936. Directed by William Keighley With Al Jolson, Sybil Jason, Allen Jenkins, Lyle Talbot, Wini Shaw, Edward Everett Horton, Cab

The first movie with an all-black cast was Hearts in Dixie, *an exuberant musical spectacle about the stereotypical happy plantation workers.*

Carolina *was an extremely romanticized depiction of the Old South.*

Calloway. Negro shown in natural, friendly relationship with white.

Spirit of Youth. Independent, 1937. With Joe Louis, Clarence Muse. Poor Negro fights his way to the top as a boxer.

The Black Legion. Warners, 1937. Directed by Archie Mays. With Humphrey Bogart, Dick Foran, Erin O'Brien Moore, Ann Sheridan, Robert Barrat, Joseph Sawyer, Paul Harvey, Henry Brandon, John Litel. An attack on the Ku Klux Klan.

The Green Pastures. Warners, 1937. Directed by William Keighley and Marc Connelly. All-Negro with Rex Ingram, Oscar Polk, Eddie Anderson, Frank Wilson, Ernest Whitman, William Cumby, Edna Mae Harris, Al Stokes, David Bethea, George Reed, Clinton Rosemond. Interprets the Negro idea of heaven. Did little to correct stereotypes, but gave many

Negro actors chances for important roles.

Pennies from Heaven. Columbia, 1937. Directed by Norman McLeod. With Bing Crosby, Madge Evans, Edith Fellowes, Donald Meek, John Gallaudet, Louis Armstrong, Charles Wilson. Musical.

They Won't Forget. Warners, 1937. Directed by Mervyn LeRoy. Adapted from the Graham Greene novel *Deep in the Deep South.* With Claude Rains, Allyn Joslyn, Gloria Dickson, Edward Norris, Clinton Rosemond. Indictment of Southern values, including treatment of Negro.

Mystery in Swing. Goldberg, independent, 1938. Produced and directed by Arthur Dreifuss. All-Negro with Monte Howley, Marguerite Whitten, Bob Webb, Sybil Lewis, Josephine Edwards, F. E. Miller, Haley Harding, Jess Lee

Brooks. Murder of a famous jazz bandleader.

One Mile from Heaven. Twentieth-Century Fox, 1938. Directed by Allan Dwan. With Claire Trevor, Sally Blane, Douglas Fowley, Fredi Washington, Bill Robinson, Eddie Anderson. Fredi Washington as Negro foster mother of a white child.

Mr. Creeps. Toddy Pictures, 1938. All-Negro, with Mantan Moreland, F. E. Miller. Comedy.

The Adventures of Huckleberry Finn. MGM, 1939 (earlier production, 1932). Directed by Richard Thorpe. From the novel by Mark Twain. With Mickey Rooney, Walter Connolly, William Frawley, Rex Ingram, Lynne Carver, Elizabeth Risdon, Victor Kilian, Minor Watson, Clara Blandick.

Harlem on the Prairie. Buell, 1939.

Claimed as "the first independent all-Negro Western film."

Gone with the Wind. Selznick, 1939. Directed by Victor Fleming. From the novel by Margaret Mitchell. With Vivien Leigh, Clark Gable, Leslie Howard, Olivia de Haviland, Thomas Mitchell, Evelyn Keyes, Barbara O'Neill, Hattie McDaniel, Butterfly McQueen, Oscar Polk, Adrian Morris, Ben Carter, Eddie "Rochester" Anderson. Negro depicted in "Mammy" and "Uncle Tom" tradition. Hattie McDaniel won an Academy Award for best supporting actress.

Man About Town. Paramount, 1939. Directed by Mark Sandrich. With Jack Benny, Dorothy Lamour, Eddie "Rochester" Anderson, Binnie Barnes, Edward Arnold, Monty Woolley. Typical Benny-"Rochester" comedy of 1939-1944 period.

Bronze Venus. Toddy Pictures, 1940. All-Negro, with Lena Horne, Ralph Cooper. The life of a great musical star.

Chasing Trouble. Monogram, 1940. Directed by Howard Bretherton. From a screenplay by Mary McCarthy. With Frankie Darro, Mantan Moreland, Marjorie Reynolds, Milburn Stone, Cheryl Walker. White boy and Negro friend chase crooks together.

One Tenth of Our Nation. American Film Centre, 1940. Directed by Henwar Rodakiewiecz. Documentary showing inadequate conditions of education among Negroes in the South.

Of Mice and Men. Hal Roach, 1940. Directed by Lewis Milestone. From the book by John Steinbeck. With Burgess Meredith, Lon Chaney, Betty Field, Charles Bickford, Leigh Whipper. Dignified portrayal of Negro ranch worker.

Maryland. Twentieth-Century Fox, 1940. Directed by Henry King. With Walter Brennan, Fay Bainter, Brenda Joyce, John Payne, Charlie Ruggles, Hattie McDaniel, Marjorie Weaver, Sydney Blackmer, Clarence Muse, George Reed, Ben Carter, Ernest Whitman, Zack Williams, Thaddeus Jones, Clinton Rosemond, Jesse Graves. Romance of the South with several Negro players featured prominently as comic relief.

Murder on Lenox Avenue. Goldberg, independent, 1941. Directed by Arthur Dreifuss. All-Negro, with Mamie Smith, Alex Lovejoy, Dene Larry, Norman Astwood, Gus Smith, Edna Mae Harris, Alberta Perkins, George Williams. A murder mystery set in Harlem.

A Place to Live. Philadelphia Housing Association, 1941. Directed by Irvin Lerner. Documentary on housing conditions among Negroes and whites in Philadelphia.

Birth of the Blues. Paramount, 1941. Directed by Victor Scheitzinger. With Bing Crosby, Mary Martin, Brian Donlevy, Eddie "Rochester" Anderson, J. Carrol Naish, Warren Hymer, Horace MacMahon, Ruby Elzy. A musical review which features whites learning about blues and popularizing.

Affectionately Yours. Warners, 1941. Directed by Lloyd Bacon. With Merle Oberon, Dennis Morgan, Rita Hayworth, Ralph Bellamy, George Tobias, James Gleason, Hattie McDaniel, Butterfly McQueen. Goodnatured "Mammy" types.

In This Our Life. Warners, 1942. Directed by John Huston. From the novel by Ellen Glasgow. With Bette Davis, Olivia de Haviland, George Brent, Dennis Morgan, Charles Coburn, Frank Craven, Billie Burke, Lee Patrick, Hattie McDaniel, Ernest Anderson. Dignified portrayal of young Negro studying to be lawyer, victimized by Southern prejudice and injustice. Placed on Honor Roll of Race Relations for 1942.

Henry Brown, Farmer. U.S. Department of Agriculture, 1942. Directed by Roger Barlow. Narration by Canada Lee. Documentary on the life of a Negro farmer in Alabama.

Syncopation. RKO Radio, 1942. Directed by William Dieterle. With Adolphe Menjou, Jackie Cooper, Bonita Granville, George Bancroft, Ted North, Todd Duncan. Negro trumpet player teaches jazz to white girl. Sympathetic handling of race relations.

Panama Hattie. MGM, 1943. Directed by Norman Z. McLeod. Based on the play by Herbert Fields and B. G. de Sylva. With Ann Sothern, Red Skelton, Rags Ragland, Ben Blue, Marsha Hunt, Virginia O'Brien, Carl Esmond, the Berry Brothers, Nyas, James and Warren, Lena Horne. Lena Horne's first major screen role.

Stormy Weather. Twentieth-Century Fox, 1943. Directed by Andrew Stone. With Lena Horne, Bill Robinson, Cab Calloway, Katherine Dunham, Harold and Fayard Nicholas, Ada Brown, Dooley Wilson, Babe Wallace, Ernest Whitman, Zuttie Singleton, F. E. Miller, Nicodemus Stewart. All-Negro musical.

Dixie. Paramount, 1943. Directed by Edward Sutherland. With Bing Crosby, Dorothy Lamour, Billy de Wolfe, Marjorie Reynolds, Lynne Overman, Raymond Walburn, Eddie Foy, Jr. Biography of Daniel Emmett, the first blackface minstrel and composer of "Dixie."

Tales of Manhattan. Twentieth-Century Fox, 1943. Directed by Julian Duvivier. With Charles Boyer, Rita Hayworth, Ginger Rogers, Henry Fonda, Charles Laughton, Edward G. Robinson, Paul Robeson, Eddie "Rochester" Anderson, Ethel Waters, Clarence Muse. Paul Robeson, enticed back from his self-imposed exile in Britain to make this film, was so disturbed by his "darky" role he declared he would never again accept such a part in a Hollywood film.

Cabin in the Sky. MGM, 1943. Directed by Vincente Minnelli. All-Negro, with Lena Horne, Eddie "Rochester" Anderson, Ethel Waters, Rex Ingram, Kenneth Spencer, Ernest Whitman, Mantan Moreland, Louis Armstrong, Oscar Polk, Buck and Bubbles, Duke Ellington, John Sublett, Willie Best. Musical fantasy. Brought prominence to Lena Horne and to Katherine Dunham ballet.

Strange Incident. Twentieth-Century Fox, 1943. Directed by William Wellman. From the novel *The Oxbow Incident* by Walter V. T. Clark. With Henry Fonda, Dana Andrews, Anthony Quinn, and Leigh Whipper as Negro preacher who makes dignified, eloquent plea against lynching of white rustlers.

Bataan. MGM, 1943. Directed by Tay Garnett. With Robert Taylor, George

Murphy, Thomas Mitchell, Lee Bowman and Kenneth Spencer as a black G.I. Won special award from NAACP.

Sahara. Columbia, 1944. Directed by Zoltan Korda. With Humphrey Bogart, Rex Ingram. Negro soldier in heroic role.

Carnival in Rhythm. Warners, 1944. A short film devoted to Katherine Dunham and her Negro ballet.

Lifeboat. Twentieth-Century Fox, 1944. Directed by Alfred Hitchcock. With Tallulah Bankhead, John Hodiak, Henry Hull, Walter Slezak, Canada Lee, Hume Cronyn, Mary Anderson, Heather Angel. Survivors in the lifeboat include an intelligent, heroic Negro.

Dr. George Washington Carver. MGM, 1945. With Clinton

Rosemond. Documentary based on the life and work of the Negro scientist.

The House I Live In. MGM, 1945. With Frank Sinatra. A plea for racial tolerance; won special Academy Award.

Jammin' the Blues. Warners, 1945. Directed and photographed by Gjon Mili. Semidocumentary of a "jam session" in a Negro club.

We've Come a Long, Long Way. "Negro Marches On." 1945. Produced and directed by Jack Goldberg. Narration by Elder Michaux. A documentary cavalcade of the Negro race.

Brewster's Millions. Edward Small, 1946. Directed by Alan Dwan. From the novel by George B. McCutcheon. With Dennis O'Keefe, Helen Walker,

Eddie "Rochester" Anderson, June Havoc, Gail Patrick, Mischa Auer, Joseph Sawyer, John Litel, Herbert Dudley, Neil Hamilton. Film was banned in Memphis because Negro "acted too snappy and socialized too much with whites."

Ziegfeld Follies. MGM, 1946. Directed by Vincente Minnelli. With William Powell, Virginia O'Brien, Lucille Ball, Esther Williams, James Melton, Marion Bell, Victor Moore, Fred Astaire, Lucille Bremer, Keenan Wynn, Lena Horne, Red Skelton, Judy Garland, Gene Kelly, Kathryn Grayson, Edward Arnold, Cyd Charisse, Robert Lewis, Avon Long. A musical review using as background the life of Florence Ziegfeld. Cute stereotype cameos performed by blacks.

Saratoga Trunk. Warners, 1946. Directed by Sam Wood. From the novel by Edna Ferber. With Ingrid Bergman, Gary Cooper, Flora Robson. In a psychological throwback to earlier days, Flora Robson played an important role in "blackface."

Mildred Pierce. Warners, 1946. Directed by Michael Curtiz. Based on the novel by James M. Cain. With Joan Crawford, Jack Carson, Zachary Scott, Eve Arden, Bruce Bennett, Ann Blyth, Lee Patrick, Butterfly McQueen, Moroni Olsen, Charles Trowbridge, Chester Clute. Butterfly McQueen in one of the "stupid maid" parts she subsequently announced she would no longer accept.

The Brotherhood of Man. Brandon, 1946. A color cartoon based on *The Races of Mankind by* Ruth Benedict and Gene Weltfish. Antiprejudice message.

Till the End of Time. R.K.O. Radio, 1946. Directed by Edward Dmytryk. With Dorothy McGuire, Robert Mitchum, Guy Madison, Bill Williams, Tom Tully, Jean Porter, William Gargan. Subplot in which whites defend Negro against Fascist talk.

Song of the South. R.K.O. Radio-Disney, 1947. Produced by Walt

Ethel Waters (left) *and Jeanne Crain* (right) *in* Pinky *(1949).*

Disney. Based on the "Uncle Remus" stories. With Ruth Warrick, James Baskett, Lucille Watson, Hattie McDaniel, Luana Patten, Bobby Driscoll. NAACP and IFRG tried to stop the filming because of stereotyped character of Uncle Remus.

Uncle Tom's Cabana. MGM, 1947. Produced by Fred Quimby. Typical comedy short film emphasizing the stereotype.

What a Guy. Toddy Pictures, 1947. All-Negro, with Ruby Dee.

The Burning Cross. Somerset-Screen Guild, 1947. Directed by Walter Colmes. With Hank Daniels, Virginia Patton, Joel Fluellyn, Dick Rich, Raymond Bond, Mat Willis. Ku Klux Klan expose.

The Jackie Robinson Story. 1948. With Jackie Robinson, Ruby Dee, Joel Fluellyn, Louise Beavers. The story of Robinson's breakthrough to the major leagues and his early playing career.

Gangsters on the Loose. Toddy Pictures, 1948. All-Negro with Ralph Cooper. Teresa Thompson. Gangster picture about a double-crosser.

The Betrayal. Released by Astor Pictures, 1948. Produced by Oscar Micheaux. All-Negro cast in this story about a young Negro farmer in South Dakota who refuses the love of a woman he believes is white—only to marry her after discovering she is Negro.

Lost Boundaries. 1949. With Bill Greaves, Canada Lee, Beatrice Pearson. Concerns a New Hampshire physician "passing" for white, and his children who are unaware of their Negro blood.

Home of the Brave. 1949. With James Edwards as a Negro soldier torn by discrimination and hatred.

Pinky. 1949. With Ethel Waters, Jeanne Crain, Fred O'Neal, Kenny Washington, Nina Mae McKinney. A fair-skinned Negro girl refuses marriage with a white doctor.

The Quiet One. 1949. With Estelle Evans, Sadie Stockton, Donald Thompson. The juvenile delinquency problem.

Ethel Waters and Eddie Anderson headlined the all-star cast of Cabin in the Sky.

Intruder in the Dust. 1949. From the story by William Faulkner. With Juano Hernandez. A Negro is accused of murdering a white man.

Miracle in Harlem. 1949. Directed by Jack Kemp. Original screenplay and story by Vincent Valentini. All-Negro cast in this story about "murder and mayhem" in Harlem.

Stars in My Crown. 1950. Produced by William H. Wright for MGM. Juano Hernandez as an aged Negro in this film about a parson in a Southern town after the Civil War.

No Way Out. Twentieth-Century Fox, 1950. With Sidney Poitier, Bobby Darin, Linda Darnell, Mildred Joanne Smith, Fred O'Neal, Dots Johnson, Maude Simmons, Ruby Dee, Ossie Davis. The first Negro intern at a white hospital finds he must battle prejudice.

Show Boat. 1951. "Ole Man River" is sung by William Warfield in this revival of the 1927 stage production and the 1929 movie.

Bright Victory. 1951. With James Edwards. Concerns prejudice in a hospital for the blind once the white patients discover a blind Negro soldier is among them.

Native Son. 1951. With Richard Wright, Gloria Madison, Willa Pearl Curtiss. The movie version of Richard Wright's novel.

The Breaking Point. 1951. With Juano Hernandez. A white-Negro friendship.

The Well. 1951. With Maidie Norman, Ernest Anderson, Christine Larson, Bill Walker, Alfred Grant, Benjamin Hamilton. Rescue operations for a Negro child trapped in a mine shaft.

Tarzan's Perils. 1952. A Tarzan adventure film, with Dorothy

Juano Hernandez (center) *gives an extraordinary performance in the powerful, realistic drama* Intruder in the Dust.

Canada Lee portrays a South African village priest in Cry the Beloved Country.

Dandridge in the lead as African princess.

Lydia Bailey. 1951. With Ken Renard, Juanita Moore, William Marshall. Story of Toussaint L'Ouverture, liberator of Haiti.

To Live Together. 1951. A documentary produced by B'nai Brith. Depicts an interracial camp for Chicago children.

The Harlem Globetrotters. Columbia, 1951. With Thomas Gomez, Dorothy Dandridge, Bill Walker, Harlem Globetrotters team. Fiction plot, interspersed with Globetrotter games.

Member of the Wedding. Paramount, 1951. Stars Ethel Waters opposite Julie Harris in the screen version of Carson McCullers' play. Miss Waters gives a powerful portrayal of a cook who befriends a troubled young girl.

The Medium. 1951. Produced by Walter Lowenthal. Directed by Gian-Carlo Menotti, and based upon his play of the same name about a "phony" spiritualist. Leo Coleman, a Negro, plays the part of Toby, a mute gypsy boy.

The Steel Helmet. Lippert Pictures, 1951. Produced by Samuel Fuller. Features James Edwards in a low-budget picture about the adventures of an American infantry patrol detailed to occupy a Korean temple and set up an observation post. Edwards plays the part of a Negro medic.

Cry the Beloved Country. United Artists, 1952. Sidney Poitier along with Canada Lee in this screen version of Alan Paton's novel about South Africa.

Red Ball Express. Universal, 1952. Sidney Poitier as a member of Korea's famed trucking outfit.

Bright Road. MGM, 1953. Harry Belafonte, Dorothy Dandridge, Philip Hepburn in this story about a small, troubled boy and his schoolmaster.

The Joe Louis Story. United Artists, 1953. Stars Hilda Simms, Coley Wallace, and others in a film based on the famous boxer's life.

Go Man, Go. United Artists, 1954. Sidney Poitier as a member of the Harlem Globetrotters, along with Dane Clark and actual players on the team.

New Faces. Twentieth-Century Fox, 1954. Eartha Kitt along with June Carroll, Ronny Graham, and others in this screen version of the Broadway musical.

The Glenn Miller Story. Universal, 1955. Produced by Aaron Rosenberg. Louis Armstrong in this film biography of the famous bandleader.

Trial. MGM, 1955. Produced by Charles Schnee; directed by Mark Robson. Based on the novel by Don Mankiewicz, the screen version concerns the defense of a Mexican who is tried on a murder charge in a California town. Juano Hernandez is the judge.

Blackboard Jungle. MGM, 1956. Produced by Pandro S. Berman. Featuring Sidney Poitier in a film dealing with slum schools and juvenile delinquency.

Goodbye, My Lady. Warner Brothers, 1956. Sidney Poitier in a supporting role as a young farmer who is involved in the problems confronting sharecroppers in the Louisiana swamp country. Brandon De Wilde and Phil Harris are also featured.

Safari. Columbia, 1956. Produced by Adrian D. Worker. Features Earl Cameron, Orlando Martins, and Cy Grant in a story about hunting down the Mau Mau and life in Africa.

That Certain Feeling. Paramount, 1956. Produced and directed by Norman Panama, Melvin Frank, I. A. L. Diamond, and William Altman. Based on the play *The King of Hearts* by Jean Kerr. Features Pearl Bailey as a lyrical maid (she sings two numbers) in a comedy farce.

Edge of the City. United Artists. 1957. Sidney Poitier along with John Cassavetes and Jack Warden in a story about racial bigotry along the waterfront.

Island in the Sun. 1957. Produced by Darryl F. Zanuck. Harry Belafonte stars opposite Joan Fontaine in this story of interracial romance written by Alec Waugh.

Meet Me in Las Vegas. MGM, 1957. Produced by Joe Pasternak. Lena Horne is featured in this musical along with a host of other stars.

Something of Value. MGM, 1957.

Anna Lucasta was a successful 1958 film with Eartha Kitt, Sammy Davis, Jr., and Frederick O'Neal. Shown here is a scene from the play with Hilda Simms and Canada Lee, originally produced by the American Negro Theatre in Harlem.

Stars Sidney Poitier in the screen adaptation of the Robert Ruark novel about the Mau Mau revolt in Kenya.

The Benny Goodman Story. Universal, 1957. Produced by Aaron Rosenberg. Stars Sammy Davis, Jr., Lionel Hampton, and Teddy Wilson in the life story of the famous jazzman.

The Defiant Ones. United Artists, 1957. Produced by Stanley Kramer. Involves the trials of two escaped convicts—one white, the other Negro. Sidney Poitier opposite Tony Curtis.

Anna Lucasta. United Artists, 1958. Produced by Sidney Harmon. Eartha Kitt, Sammy Davis, Jr., Frederick O'Neal, Rex Ingram, Henry Morgan star in this film about the problems of a young woman who has left home to become a streetwalker.

St. Louis Blues. Paramount, 1958. Produced by Robert Smith. All-Negro cast with Nat Cole, Eartha Kitt, Pearl Bailey, Cab Calloway, Ella Fitzgerald, Mahalia Jackson, Juano Hernandez, and Billy Preston in the life and times of W. C. Handy.

The Decks Ran Red. 1958. Dorothy Dandridge opposite Curt Jurgens in a film which deals with life aboard a slave ship.

The March of the Hawk. Universal-International, 1958. Sidney Poitier opposite Eartha Kitt in a story about the struggle for equality in Africa. Poitier plays a peaceful man at odds with his brother, the "hawk" who is dedicated to violence and war.

Black Orpheus. A Lopert Films release, 1959. Produced by Sacha Gordine. All-Negro cast in this story of a young couple who fall suddenly and rapturously in love, only to be separated by death as in the ancient Greek legend.

Night of the Quarter Moon. MGM, 1959. Produced by Albert Zugsmith. Stars Nat Cole, James Edwards, Marguerite Belafonte, and Billy Daniels in a story of interracial love.

Odds Against Tomorrow. United Artists, 1959. Produced by Robert Wise. Stars Harry Belafonte, Carmen de Lavallade, along with Robert Ryan, Shelley Winters, and Ed Begley. Story of the planning and execution of a crime, with three men (one a Negro). Musical score written by John Lewis. Screenplay by John Oliver Killens.

Porgy and Bess. Columbia, 1959. Produced by Samuel Goldwyn; directed by Otto Preminger. Based on the play by Dubose and Dorothy Heyward. Stars Sidney Poitier, Dorothy Dandridge, Sammy Davis, Jr., Pearl Bailey, and others.

Sapphire. J. Arthur Rank, 1959. Produced by Michael Ralph; directed by Basil Dearden. Featuring Earl Cameron, Gordon Heath, Harry Baird, Nigel Patrick, Yvonne Mitchell, Michael Craig, and Paul Massie in a mystery with racial overtones. (The murdered girl turns out to be a Negro.)

Tamango. Hal Roach Release, 1959. Produced by Rene G. Vauttoux, Roland Gerard, Sig Shore, and Joe Harris. Based on the novel by Prosper Merimee, with Dorothy Dandridge, Curt Jurgens, Jean Servais, and Alex Cressah. Concerns the slave trade, and what happens on a slaver bound from Africa to Cuba.

The Sound and the Fury. 1959. Produced by Jerry Wald. Features Ethel Waters along with Margaret Leighton, Joanne Woodward, Yul Brynner, and Jack Warden in the film version of the Faulkner novel. Miss Waters is Dilsey, the family cook.

The World, the Flesh and the Devil. 1959. Stars Harry Belafonte, along with Inger Stevens and Mel Ferrer. An interracial theme in a story which takes place at the end of the world.

All the Young Men. Columbia, 1960. Sidney Poitier, along with Alan Ladd and Mort Sahl, in this story about what happens to a small detachment of marines in Korea whose command is taken over by a Negro.

Let No Man Write My Epitaph. Columbia, 1960. Produced by Boris D. Kaplan. Bernie Hamilton appears in this film version of Willard Motley's novel.

Sergeant Rutledge. Warner Brothers, 1960. Produced and directed by John Ford. Stars Woody Strode in a tale of the Old West set in Arizona after the Civil War. The sergeant (Strode) is accused of violating and strangling a white girl, and of murdering her father, his commanding officer. Also features, Jeffrey Hunter, Constance Towers, and Billie Burke.

Shadows. 1960. Directed by John Cassavetes. Focuses on the rootlessness of the urban Negro in Greenwich Village.

Take a Giant Step. United Artists, 1960. Produced by Julius J. Epstein. Stars Johnny Nash, Ruby Dee, Frederick O'Neal, Beah Richards in the screen version of Louis Peterson's play about a young man growing up.

The Adventures of Huckleberry Finn. MGM, 1960. Produced by Samuel Goldwyn, Jr. Archie Moore plays Jim in this modern version of the Mark Twain novel.

The Crowning Experience. Directed, produced, and presented by Moral Rearmament, 1960. All-Negro cast in the screen version of the life of Mary McLeod Bethune.

A Raisin in the Sun. Columbia, 1961. Sidney Poitier, Claudia McNeil, Diana Sands in this film based on Lorraine Hansberry's award-winning play about an urban Negro family.

Biography of a Rookie. Wolper-Sterling Prod., 1961. Narrator, Mike Wallace. Story of the rise of Dodger baseball player Willie Davis to the major leagues.

Guns of the Trees. 1961. Produced by Jonas Mekas. This film juxtaposes the lives of two married couples, one white, the other Negro.

Paris Blues. United Artists, 1961. Sidney Poitier, Paul Newman, Joanne Woodward, Diahann Carroll in this film about two expatriate jazzmen living in Paris, and their romantic adventures with two American girls on the loose.

The Intruder. 1961. Produced by Roger Gorman. Based on a novel by Charles Beaumont, this film concerns an anti-integrationist who goes to a small Southern town to arouse the townspeople against integration in the local schools.

The Young One. 1961. Produced by George P. Werber. Stars Bernie Hamilton and Zachary Scott. A Negro (Hamilton) escapes to an isolated island over which Scott serves as a kind of warden.

A Taste of Honey. Continental Pictures, 1962. Produced by Tony Richardson. Features Paul Danquah as the Negro sailor who gets involved with a young white girl. Also seen are Dora Bryan and Rita Tushingham.

Carmen Jones. Twentieth-Century Fox, 1962. Produced and directed by Otto Preminger. Dorothy Dandridge, Harry Belafonte, Olga James, Pearl Bailey, and Diahann Carroll in this revised version of Bizet's opera.

Oceans 11. 1962. Produced by Frank Sinatra. The famous "clan" with Sammy Davis, Jr. in a prominent role as a member of a daring gang that plans to hold up Las Vegas nightspots.

Pressure Point. United Artists, 1962. Sidney Poitier cast as a social worker who attempts to rehabilitate wrongdoer Bobby Darin.

The Connection. 1962. Vivid screen portrayal of Negroes in the narcotics underworld. Based on Jack Gelber's play.

An Affair of the Skin. 1963. Produced by Ben Maddow. Diana Sands as a Negro heroine in Greenwich Village. Featuring Viveca Lindfors, Kevin McCarthy.

Convicts 4. Allied Artists, 1963. Produced by A. Ronald Lubin. Sammy Davis, Jr. along with Richard Conte in a prominent role as a convict who contemplates escape.

Gone Are the Days. 1963. Directed by Nicholas Webster. Based on the play *Purlie Victorious* by Ossie Davis.

Sergeants 3. United Artists, 1963. Produced by Frank Sinatra. Stars Sammy Davis, Jr., along with Sinatra and Peter Lawford, as members of a U.S. Cavalry unit which fights a number of frontier battles.

The Cool World. 1963. Produced by Shirley Clarke. Based on Warren Miller's novel. An important film document about Negro life in Harlem.

The Greenwich Village Story. 1963. Produced by Jack O'Connell. Features Negroes as background presences in party sequences, street and restaurant scenes and, in general, as part of the Village milieu.

To Kill a Mockingbird. Universal, 1963. Produced by Alan J. Pakula; directed by Robert Mulligan. Based on Harper Lee's best selling novel of 1960, this film has Brock Peters and Estelle Evans in prominent roles. The story concerns the defense of a Negro on trial for allegedly raping a white girl.

Black Like Me. 1964. Directed by Carl Lerner. Based on the novel of the same title by John Howard Griffin. A white man (James Whitmore) passes for Negro.

Free, White and 21. American International, 1964. Directed by Larry Buchanan; stars Frederick O'Neal. Carefree, wild, abandoned whites and their world of tinsel and gold.

Johnny Cool. United Artists, 1964. Producer-director William Asher. Based on the novel *The Kingdom of Johnny Cool* by John McPartland. Sammy Davis, Jr. in the role of "Educated," a sophisticated "hanger-on" in the underworld's gambling casinos. Plot turns on underworld life and intragang rivalry.

Lilies of the Field. United Artists, 1964. Sidney Poitier as a traveling vagabond who befriends a group of nuns and wins their friendship and understanding.

Living Between Two Worlds. 1964. Directed by Robert Johnson. Deals with a mother-son conflict within a Negro family in Los Angeles.

Nothing but a Man. 1964. Produced by Michael Roemer. The award-winning story of a Negro laborer and his romance. Stars Ivan Dixon and Abbey Lincoln.

One Potato, Two Potato. 1964. Directed by Larry Peerce. A love affair involving a Negro man and a white divorcee. The Negro is played by Bernie Hamilton.

The Long Ships. Columbia, 1964. Sidney Poitier as a powerful sultan in a costume drama. Also features Richard Widmark.

The Streets of Greenwood or Ivanhoe Donaldson. 1964. Directed by Harold Becher. A feature-length documentary illustrating the civil rights struggle in the United States.

Cat Ballou. Columbia, 1965. Produced by Harold Hecht. Nat Cole is featured as a traveling minstrel.

Major Dundee. Columbia, 1965. Produced by Jerry Bresher. Brock Peters is featured as a member of the U.S. Cavalry.

None but the Brave. Warner Brothers, 1965. Produced and directed by Frank Sinatra. Rafer Johnson plays an Army officer on patrol in the South Pacific.

Synanon. Columbia, 1965. Produced and directed by Richard Quine. Features Eartha Kitt, Bernie Hamilton, Chuck Connors, Stella Stevens, and Edmund O'Brien. The rehabilitation of drug addicts through the now-famous "Synanon" method.

The Carpetbaggers. Paramount, 1965. Produced by Joseph E. Levine; based on the novel by Harold Robbins. Featuring Archie Moore in the role of Jedediah.

The Greatest Story Ever Told. 1965. The story of the ministry of Christ. Sidney Poitier as the Ethiopian who is converted to Christianity.

The Hill. 1965. Produced by Sidney Lumet. Features Ossie Davis as a West Indian soldier-prisoner known as Jacko King. Based on the play by Ray Rigby about a British detention camp in North Africa during World War II.

The New Interns. Columbia, 1965. Ena Hartman in an important role as a nurse.

The Pawnbroker. Landau, 1965. Produced by Worthington Miner. This film with Brock Peters, Juano Hernandez, and Rod Steiger depicts life in Harlem. One of the earliest films

for which a Negro, Quincy Jones, wrote the musical score.

A Man Called Adam. 1966. Produced by Sammy Davis, Jr. Stars Sammy Davis, Jr., along with Cicely Tyson, Ossie Davis, and Louis Armstrong in the story of a problem-ridden musician.

Blues for Lovers. Twentieth-Century Fox, 1966. Produced by Alexander Salkind. Features Ray Charles along with his orchestra and singers in a story about a small boy's need for understanding.

Booker T. Washington. Encyclopedia Britannica Films, 1966. Collaborator: John Hope Franklin. Tells the dramatic story of Washington's life and career.

Duel at Diablo. 1966. Sidney Poitier plays a feared gunslinger in this Western.

Hurry Sundown. 1966. Produced by Otto Preminger. Stars Diahann Carroll, Robert Hooks, Rex Ingram in a movie based on the best-selling novel.

Our Man Flint. Twentieth-Century Fox, 1966. Ena Hartman has a featured role as bigwig's (Lee J. Cobb) secretary.

Patch of Blue. MGM, 1966. Produced by Pandro S. Berman. A moving story about a blind girl befriended by a young Negro. Stars Sidney Poitier, Elizabeth Hartman, Shelley Winters, Ivan Dixon, Wallace Ford.

Rio Conchos. Twentieth-Century Fox, 1966. Produced by David Weisbart. Ex-football star Jim Brown, now an actor, as U.S. Cavalry Sergeant Ben Franklin, one of four men out to recover stolen rifles.

The Appaloosa. Universal, 1966. Frank Silvera in this modern Western starring Marlon Brando.

The Cincinnati Kid. MGM, 1966. Produced by Martin Ransohoff, Cab Calloway in a prominent role as a traveling card shark in a film about top-flight poker players.

The Girl Nobody Knew. Universal, 1966. Ena Hartman is cast as a sophisticated New Yorker who moves in top social circles.

The Slender Thread. Paramount, 1966. Sidney Poitier opposite Anne

Bancroft as the psychiatrist who saves her life.

The Bedford Incident. 1966. Sidney Poitier along with Richard Widmark in a story about life on a U.S. warship.

Dutchman. 1967. Produced by Gene Persson. Based on the off-Broadway play by Leroi Jones. Starring Shirley Knight and Al Freeman, Jr.

In the Heat of the Night. Mirisch Corporation, 1967. Director Norman Jewison presents a drama of racial hate and prejudice fictionally set in an ugly little Mississippi town. The stars Rod Steiger and Sidney Poitier (Virgil Tibbs) are well-realized characters. Quincy Jones composed the music and Ray Charles sang the title song.

Now Is the Time. 1967. Carousel Films. 36 minutes. WCAU-TV, Philadelphia. Chronicles the history of the American Negro and his emergence from a 300-year old "pagan" slave state. Shows him as of 1968, a crucial year in which he demands his rights and equal status. Combines the sounds and rhythms of the violence of race riots with folk, rock, and hymnal music. Features the works of Langston Hughes, Countee Cullen, James Baldwin, Malcolm X, and Stokely Carmichael.

Some of My Best Friends Are White. Robeck, 1967. Producer Michael Lathem. A provocative examination of America's racial problem as discussed from the point of view of the middle-class Negro involving his acceptance by society and the future of his children growing up in white suburbia. A BBC-TV Production.

The Weapons of Gordon Parks. Color. 28 minutes. 1967. Contemporary–McGraw-Hill. The story of the internationally known black photographer seen at work, in his home, with his family, and on the streets of Harlem, as part of his past life is recreated. An inspiring and moving photographic essay. Directed by Warren Forma.

The President's Analyst. Paramount, 1967. Screenwriter/director Theodore J. Flicker came up with this smartly filmed Hollywood comedy with a distinctly intellectual turn. Godfrey Cambridge featured alongside James Coburn. The story is a take-off on governmental security, automation, and international intrigue involving U.S. and foreign agents.

A Time for Burning. 1967. Conceived, directed, and edited by William C. Jersey and Barbara Connell, this film deals with a crisis that actually occurred in Omaha, Nebraska, when a Lutheran minister tried to inspire church members to destroy the barriers existing between themselves and the Negro ghetto.

Up the Down Staircase. Warner Brothers-Seven Arts, 1967. Director Robert Mulligan casts Jose Rodriguez in an adaptation of the best-selling novel about a big-city school system.

To Sir, With Love. Columbia, 1967. Director James Clavell here paints a picture of a Negro teacher who takes a post in a tough London school and battles to reach rebellious youngsters. Starring Sidney Poitier.

Doctor Doolittle. Twentieth-Century Fox, 1967. Director Richard Fleisher has multitalented Geoffrey Holder in this musical based on a series of stories bearing the same title. The film is one big, colorful, imaginative burst of animal-people fun.

Portrait of Jason. Filmmakers,. 1967. Director Shirely Clarke's intimate marathon interview with a self-described male prostitute, himself a Negro. The star bares his soul in an all-night camera session for director Clarke. The film comes off as a first-rate sociopsychological documentary.

The Dirty Dozen. MGM, 1967. Director Robert Aldrich hs ex-football star Jim Brown in this tough, he-man, ribald film about war prisoners who are given a chance to redeem themselves by embarking on a perilous World War II mission.

The Night of the Living Dead. Walter Reade, 1968. Director, George A. Romero. The story involves corpses reawakened by radiation who roam the countryside killing and devouring cities. Stars Duane Jones.

The Scalphunters. United Artists, 1968. Directed by Sidney Pollack. Black power Western involving a furtrapper with a captured runaway slave stalking a scalphunting gang to

Ossie Davis and Burt Lancaster in a scene from The Scalphunters.

retrieve stolen furs. A Negro, trying to gain his freedom by outwitting whites, proves that white supremacy isn't omnipotent. Ossie Davis is in this one along with Burt Lancaster.

Guess Who's Coming to Dinner. Columbia Pictures, 1968. Director Stanley Kramer draws on a top-level cast which includes Sidney Poitier, Spencer Tracy, and Katherine Hepburn. The story deals with the question of interracial love and the problems of mixed marriage. The cast also includes Beah Richards.

For Love of Ivy. Cinerama, 1968. Director Daniel Mann. This film stars Sidney Poitier, Abbey Lincoln, and Leon Bibb. A love affair between the luscious Ivy (Abbey Lincoln) and a suave businessman (Sidney Poitier). Quincy Jones composed the music.

Negro Kingdoms. Color. 16 minutes. 1968. Atlantis. Reveals the high level of culture and society of slavery existing in West Africa prior to the era of slavery through treatment of the

changing climate of Africa, trans-Saharan trade, the growth of Islam, and the story of medieval Mali and Ghana.

If He Hollers, Let Him Go! (Cinerama Releasing, 1968.) Theme of this film is injustice to a black man hunted down following his escape from prison for a crime he did not commit. Stars Raymond St. Jacques, Barbara McNair, Dana Wynter, and Kevin McCarthy.

P. J. Universal, 1968. Rough, tough, violent private-eye story dircted by John Gulleria with Brock Peters in a top-level role.

Mingus. Filmmakers, 1968. Close-up of bassplayer and composer Charlie Mingus as he and his five-year-old daughter await eviction by the City of New York. The film is laced with intercuts of Mingus as a musician.

Dark of the Sun. MGM, 1968. Director Jack Cardiff off to the Congo on a story involving killing, gore, and

double-dealing. Jim Brown prominent in this one.

Split Decision. Filmmakers, 1968. Fighter Jose Torres is followed in this film during preparations for his bout with Dick Tiger. The film manages to give some insight into the boxing profession.

The Story of a Three Day Pass. Sigma III, 1968. Black director Melvin Van Peebles tells a story of a young Negro on a three-day pass in Paris, of his weekend encounter with a white girl, as well as some white buddies from camp. This film gives tremendous insight in the gap between what people feel and what they encounter.

Robby. Bluewood, 1968. Writer/ director Ralph C. Bluemke produces a sincere film about a white lad marooned on an island along with a Negro youngster. Both develop a friendship, only to be cruelly separated by racism after their rescue.

The Biggest Bundle of Them All. MGM, 1968. Director Ken Annakin produced this big caper spoof featuring an aging, exiled gangster in Italy who leads gang of amateurs in carefully planned heist. Starring Godfrey Cambridge.

Finian's Rainbow. Warner Brothers-Seven Arts, 1968. This long-time hit and favorite of Broadway's yesteryear is directed by Francis Ford Coppola and has a fresh movie look. Al Freeman, Jr. with Fred Astaire, Petula Clark, Tommy Steele and a completely integrated cast.

The Heart Is a Lonely Hunter. Warner Brothers-Seven Arts, 1968. Robert Ellis Miller directd this poignant film based on Carson McCullers' novel about loneliness in a Southern town. Cicely Tyson featured with Percy Rodrigues.

Ice Station Zebra. MGM, 1968. Director John Sturges put Jim Brown in this suspenseful cold-war thriller about a U.S. nuclear war submarine on a secret mission to a polar region with an unknown saboteur aboard.

The Split. MGM, 1968. Director Gordon Fleming stars Jim Brown as a tough criminal who decides on one last caper before retiring—robbing the Los Angeles Coliseum.

Salt and Pepper. United Artists, 1968. Director Richard Donner put together this frantic comedy about London club owners caught in a plot to overthrow the British government. Peter Lawford is Pepper, and Sammy Davis, Jr. is Salt.

The Learning Tree. Warner Brothers-Seven Arts, 1969. Photojournalist-musician Gordon Parks with a reflective film based upon his novel about a Negro youngster growing up in Kansas in the 1920s. Parks also composed the music. Stars include Kyle Johnson, Alex Clarke, Estelle Evans, and Dana Elcar.

The Lost Man. Universal, 1969. Director Robert Alan Aurthur cast Sidney Poitier as a hunted Negro militant in flight after a robbery to get funds for his movement fails. Also featuring Al Freeman, Jr. and Leon Bibb.

Float Like a Butterfly, Sting Like a Bee. Grove Films, 1969. Directed and filmed by William Klein, this film is a visually excellent, fascinating study of Cassius Clay, now Muhammad Ali. A factual biography with great moments from his ring career.

Putney Swope. Cinema V, 1969. Director Robert Downey tells what happens when a group of Negroes takes over an ad agency. Arnold Johnson, Laura Greene, along with a huge amusing cast.

Terry Whitmore for Example. Grove Films, 1969. Director Bill Brodie presents a young Negro who, after having won a medal for heroism as a marine in Vietnam, defects to Sweden.

Ace High. Paramount, 1969. The world-famed Colizzi presents a western featuring intellectually attuned hombres, including Brock Peters.

Death of a Gunfighter. Universal, 1969. A marvelous western with an interracial marriage theme. Involves a town marshal who kills too easily

Sidney Poitier marries the daughter of Spencer Tracy and Katherine Hepburn in Guess Who's Coming to Dinner.

The Last Man dramatized black militancy in Philadelphia.

and alienates his town. Lena Horne as the wife, Richard Widmark as her husband.

100 Rifles. Twentieth-Century Fox, 1969. Director Tom Gries presents a drama about the Mexican persecution of Yaqui Indians. The hero is Jim Brown and the heroine is Raquel Welch.

Topaz. Alfred Hitchcock Universal Production Release, 1969. This is the film version of the Leon Uris bestselling novel of the same title dealing with international espionage. Roscoe Lee Browne plays the role of an espionage agent.

Bye, Bye Braverman. Warner Brothers-Seven Arts, 1969. Director Sidney Lumet has Godfrey Cambridge in this film dealing with a slice of ethnic life in Brooklyn, New York.

Slaves. Walter Reade, 1969. This controversial drama takes a bold look at the system of slavery as it occurred in the United States and stars Ossie Davis along with Dionne Warwick.

Castle Keep. Columbia Pictures, 1969. Director Sydney Pollack casts Al

Freeman, Jr. in this unusual war film about a small unit of U.S. servicemen who try to hold a castle against advancing Germans during World War II.

Change of Mind. Cinerama Release, 1969. Director Robert Stephens casts Raymond St. Jacques in this film about the brain of a white district attorney transplanted into the brain of a Negro man.

Two Gentlemen Sharing. American International Pictures, 1969. Director Ted Kotcheff put this film together about a young white man who shares a flat with an equally young Negro in London. An assortment of problems follows—equally shared by Robin Phillips and Hal Frederick.

Sweet Charity. Universal, 1969. Director Bob Fosse made the transition from stage to screen with singular intelligence, imagination, and cinematic flair in this successful Broadway stage hit. Sammy Davis, Jr. is an appealing part of the action.

Up Tight. Paramount, 1969. Director/producer Jules Dassin set his locale in Cleveland, Ohio, to tell an honest powerful drama of a poor, sincere Negro man caught in a changing world.

The Informer. Screen version of the Liam O'Flaherty story, 1969. The very able cast includes Raymond St. Jacques, Julian Mayfield, Ruby Dee, Frank Silvera, and Roscoe Lee Browne. Booker T. Jones composed the music.

Wild in the Streets. American International Pictures, 1969. Director Barry Shear put together this film about the explosive movement of the young to win the vote at age 15 and take over the U.S. government, with the "older generation" forcibly retired after age 35. Richard Pryor, comedian-turned-actor, plays a prominent role.

Joanna. Twentieth-Century Fox, 1969. This well told British drama describes a world where life is free and easy. Its theme also covers an interracial love affair. Starring Glenna Forster Jones, Genevieve Waite, and Calvin Lockhart.

The Comedians. MGM, 1969. Directed and produced by Peter Glenville. This film presents the

sinister image of a rigid reign of terror in a Carribbean country under a black dictatorship. Negroes in top-level roles include Roscoe Lee Browne, George S. Brown, James Earl Jones, Raymond St. Jacques, and Cicely Tyson.

Flame in the Streets. Atlantic, 1969 release (original 1962). Released again in 1969, this absorbing drama set in England deals with Negro and white civil, social, and labor relationships, and the double-edged problem of mixed marriage. Stars Earl Cameron, Sylvia Sims, John Wills, and Johnny Sekka.

The Riot. Paramount, 1969. Director Buzz Kulik made this film on location at the Arizona State Prison. Starring Jim Brown in a story about a prison break.

The Rievers. A Cinema Center Film Presentation, 1969. Director Mark Rydell based this film version on the Faulkner novel of the same title. The amusing story about the turn-of-the-century South co-starred Steve McQueen and Rupert Crosse, a Negro actor nominated for an Academy Award in a supporting role.

Hello Dolly. Twentieth-Century Fox, 1969. Director Gene Kelly did the screen adaptation of this well-known Broadway play with finesse and great skill. The story hasn't changed. Dolly, a female jack-of-all-trades, is at it again. Barbra Streisand along with Walter Matthau, and Louis Armstrong.

First World Festival of Negro Arts. Color, 20 minutes. Contemporary–McGraw-Hill, 1969. Scenes of the first

Burt Lancaster and Al Freeman, Jr., team up in Castle Keep.

Sweet Charity's *chorus line works out a song.*

World Festival of Negro Arts held at Dakar in 1966, showing music, dance, sculpture, painting and the reciprocal influence of Negro art and culture in relation to the Western world.

I Have a Dream. 35 minutes. 1969. The biography of Martin Luther King made from newsreel footage of the civil rights movement during the 1950s and 1960s. Reveals his dedication to the movement and to the principles of nonviolence.

Martin Luther King: The Man and the March. 83 minutes. 1969. Produced by Public Broadcast Laboratory of NET. A documentary on the late Doctor Martin Luther King, Jr.'s "Poor People's March." Shows Dr. King conferring with aides, speaking at rallies and traveling as he solicits support for, and develops the operational details of, the March. Indicates the methods used by his aides to create interest and support on a local level and with other ethnic groups.

Three in the Attic. American International Pictures, 1969. Director Richard Wilson. This film tells the story of a campus Don Juan kidnaped and held in the attic by three of his girl friends. Judy Pace along with Christopher Jones.

No Vietnamese Ever Called Me Nigger. Bob Maurice Paradigm, 1969. 68 minutes. Three black G.I.'s discuss their experiences in Vietnam, the racism that exists in the armed forces,

and their dissatisfaction with life in the U.S. upon their return.

The Watermelon Man. Columbia Pictures, 1970. Director Melvin Van Peebles (see also *The Story of a Three Day Pass,* 1969), in his American film debut, casts Godfrey Cambridge and Estelle Parsons in a film about a man

who turns color overnight. What happens when that transformation becomes known to his associates and friends makes for a story perched on the fine edge between comedy and tragedy.

The Angel Levine. United Artists, 1970. Jan Kadar directed this film which casts Harry Bellafonte as the angel opposite Zero Mostel whom he seeks to convince that he is for real.

Last of the Mobile Hot-Shots. Warner Brothers, 1970. A Sidney Lumet Production. The film version of *The Seven Descents of Myrtle,* a play by Tennessee Williams adapted for the screen by Gore Vidal, tells the story of two brothers; one white, one black and the women they both love. Filmed largely on location in and around Baton Rouge, Louisiana. Stars Robert Hooks, Lynn Redgrave, and James Coburn.

My Sweet Charlie. Universal, 1970. Directed by Lamont Johnson, this boy-meets-girl story initially premiered on NBC. Stars Patty Duke and Al Freeman, Jr.

End of the Road. Allied Artists Film,

The Watermelon Man *is a tragicomedy about a white man suddenly turning black.*

1970. Directed by Aram Avakian. This film stars James Earl Jones as Doctor D. in a story involving one man's attempt to straighten out his life, only to find more difficulty lies at the end of the road.

Tick . . . Tick . . . Tick . . . MGM, 1970. Directed by Ralph Nelson. This drama stars Jim Brown, George Kennedy, and Frederic March and centers around the aftermath of a bitter election campaign for sheriff in a small rural county in the Deep South.

Patton. Fox, 1970. A monumental performance by George C. Scott as World War II General George S. Patton. Karl Malden as General Bradley, along with the late James Edwards in his last film.

Super Fly. Warner Brothers, 1971. Actor Ron O'Neal became a folk hero and a target of outrage simultaneously after playing a role as Priest in this sympathetic portrait of a drug pusher.

Sweet Sweetback's Badasssss Song. Cinemation, 1971. Filmmaking Melvin Van Peebles involved himself in virtually every aspect of this X-rated film about the radicalization and subsequent revolt of a black stud. Controversial but independent and a precedent-setter.

Shaft. MGM, 1971. Photogenic Richard Roundtree made his film debut with director Gordon Parks in this adventure tale about a black New York City private eye.

Skin Game. Warner Brothers, 1971. Lou Gossett co-stars with James Garner in this film about two con men who take on town after town in the old West. Gossett plays a slave in this comedy, although he is actually a well-educated, but crooked man.

Right On. Independent, 1971. Filmmakers Woody King and Herbert Danska filmed the Last Poets, an activist group of performers as they rapped about the black condition and intercut representative scenes of Harlem life in this documentary.

The Organization. United Artists, 1971. Sidney Poitier portrays detective Tibbs again in this drama set in modern San Francisco. Barbara McNair co-stars as his wife.

Man and Boy. Levitt-Pickman, 1971. Bill Cosby invested huge sums of his own money to produce this film about a black family on the Western frontier. A pioneer effort and warm story.

Honkey. Jack Harris Ent., 1971. Brenda Sykes starred in this tepid drama about an interracial teenage love affair that was more soap opera than anything else.

The Bus Is Coming. Independent, 1971. K-Calb was the black production company that made this drama about a black Vietnam veteran who returns home to a racially tense town after his activist brother has been killed by police.

Brother John. Columbia, 1971. Sidney Poitier plays the key role in this drama about a man who returns to a small Southern town for a funeral and confronts the establishment on a number of issues.

Black Jesus. Cannon, 1971. Woody Strode stars in this Italian-made allegorical drama about a man who becomes a sacrificial lamb in an African struggle. The central figure is reminiscent of the Christ person.

Across 110th Street. United Artists, 1972. The emphasis is on crime in this heavy handed drama about a territory war between the uptown and downtown mobs for control of the Harlem rackets. Yaphet Kotto in a key role as a police lieutenant.

Black Gunn. Columbia, 1972. Jim Brown stars in this takeoff as a superpowerful operator who takes on established crime and wins handily.

Trouble Man. Twentieth-Century Fox, 1972. Ivan Dixon made his film debut as a director working with actor Robert Hooks in this action film about a ghetto trouble shooter who free-lances and attempts to protect the community from outside gangsters.

Farewell Uncle Tom. Cannon, 1972. An Italian-made film about slavery in the United States.

Black Girl. Cinerama, 1972. Ossie Davis directed this film version of a successful off-Broadway play about the life in a black family. Emphasis was on the inter-relationship between three generations of women under one roof.

Lady Sings the Blues. Paramount, 1972. Motown Records entered the movie business with this film and won five Academy Award nominations. Diana Ross made her film debut as singer Billie Holiday in one of the most important film biographies about a black character.

Hickey and Boggs. United Artists, 1972. Bill Cosby teams with his old

Jewish angel Harry Belafonte drinks Passover wine with a troubled Zero Mostel.

Diana Ross plays singer Billie Holiday in The Lady Sings the Blues.

television co-star Robert Culp in this film about two aging private detectives and their careers. A rare screen role for Cosby.

Hammer. United Artists, 1972. Fred Williamson stars in this film about a boxer who attempts to fight off corruption in boxing as well as keep his title in the ring.

Sounder. Twentieth-Century Fox, 1972. Nominated for four Academy Awards, this film was based on a best-selling story and adapted for the screen by Lonne Elder III. Paul Winfield and Cicely Tyson starred as the parents of a depression era black family in the South. Both were nominated for their realistic portrayals.

Melinda. MGM, 1972. Calvin Lockhart stars in this story about a black disc jockey who becomes involved in all kinds of intrigues and successfully solves the murder of his pretty girlfriend.

Blacula. American International,

Red Foxx as a junkman in the hilarious Cotton Comes to Harlem.

1972. A black version of the story about Count Dracula with William Marshall as the Count Mamuwalde (Blacula) who turns up in contemporary society and ventures

forth in a journey of death but is ultimately exposed and killed.

The Man. Paramount, 1972. James Earl Jones stars as the title character in this film version of the best-selling novel about the first black man to be elected president of the United States.

Super Fly. Warner Brothers, 1972. A film probing deep inside a successful drug pusher and his relationship with his women. A controversial effort that was roundly criticized by those who felt the filmmakers themselves were short on drugs.

The Limit. Cannon, 1972. A Yaphet Kotto production written to shed light on the difficult task to handle: that of a black motorcycle policemen. The film awkwardly proposes several problems with no real resolution.

The Final Comedown. New World, 1972. Billy Dee Williams stars in this drama about black revolution in the ghetto. Oscar Williams directed this film which was sponsored in part by grants from the American Film Institute.

Black Rodeo. Cinerama, 1972. Basically a documentary on contemporary black cowboys in the rodeo circuit today. Also comments from various celebrities who have seen the cowboys at work.

Come Back Charleston Blue. Warner Brothers, 1972. Television director

Fred Williamson is the hero of the western The Legend of Nigger Charlie.

Mark Warren makes his film debut with Raymond St. Jacques and Godfrey Cambridge recast as two Harlem detectives in this film based on novelist Chester Himes' books.

Shaft's Big Score. MGM, 1972. The follow-up adventure of the handsome black private eye in New York City. A bag of money and a chase that involves virtually every mode of transporation in existence. Richard Roundtree stars.

Malcolm X. Warner Brothers, 1972. An excellent documentary about the slain rights leader that was later nominated for an Academy Award.

Top of the Heap. Fanfare, 1972. Actor Christopher St. John quickly becomes a writer and director in this film about the life of a big city black cop.

The Legend of Nigger Charley. Paramount, 1972. A house slave on a Virginia plantation gets fed up and runs away to the West where he quickly adapts and becomes a hero. Fred Williamson stars.

Buck and the Preacher. Columbia, 1972. Sidney Poitier made his directorial debut working on this Western in which he co-starred with Harry Belafonte and Ruby Dee.

Cool Breeze. MGM, 1972. An unlikely team of bank thieves are the key players in this film which was fashioned after a 1950 drama. Thalmus Rasulala starred.

Man and Boy. Levitt-Pickman, 1972. Bill Cosby produced and starred in this Western drama about a black family. Despite careful attention to make an important film, technical problems robbed the production of much of its potential.

Georgia, Georgia. Cinerama, 1972.

Diana Sands stars in this film about a black singer on tour in Europe. Made on location in Sweden by producer Jack Jordan, it was a milestone for efforts of blacks to work in Europe.

Soul Soldier. Fanfare, 1972. Former Olympic winner Rafer Johnson among the cast in this poor film about life of the all-black cavalry on the Western frontier after the Civil War.

Five on the Black Hand Side. United Artists, 1973. An off-Broadway play was the inspiration for this comedy about a black middle class family. Brock Peters made his co-producing debut and many of the original cast members became part of the film.

Jimi Plays Berkeley. Independent, 1973. A documentary on rock singer Jimi Hendricks with specific emphasis on a concert he played at Berkeley.

The Slams. MGM, 1973. Prison life is the background for this film about life in a penitentiary and an attempt is made to reveal some insight into how this unique society operates. Jim Brown stars.

The Hit. Paramount, 1973. Billy Dee Williams is the key character in this story of a government agent who uses his expertise to track down the source of drug traffic in Europe and then wipe all the kingpins out of operation.

Maurie. National General, 1973. Bernie Casey stars in the title role of this semifictional account of the life of basketball great Maurice Stokes, who was permanently incapacitated by a tragic accident at the height of his pro career. Well acted and well produced.

Save the Children. Paramount, 1973. Filmed entirely on location at the 1972 PUSH Expo in Chicago, this music documentary featuring the finest black talent working at the time was a major effort that also featured as many talented blacks in the crucial positions behind the cameras, including director Stan Lathan.

The Spook Who Sat by the Door. United Artists, 1973. Based on Sam Greenlee's powerful novel about black revolution, this action drama proved to be as potent onscreen. Directed by Ivan Dixon with Lawrence Cook and J. A. Preston starring.

Slaughter's Big Ripoff. American International, 1973. Jim Brown versus the Mafia is the theme in this action drama that pits Brown against a West Coast syndicate. A sequel to *Slaughter.*

Scream Blacula Scream. American International, 1973. Modeled after the Dracula character, Blacula is played by William Marshall. He comes to life and terrorizes a contemporary town for several weeks before being discovered by a nosy investigator. A sequel to *Blacula.*

Gordon's War. Twentieth-Century Fox, 1973. Ossie Davis and Paul Winfield team as director and star of this adventure film about a Vietnam veteran who returns home and seeks about to destroy drug dealers responsible for his wife's death by overdose.

Cleopatra Jones. Warner Brothers, 1973. Former model Tamara Dobson is the leading lady in this film about an attractive drug fighter who becomes a community hero as much as an activist.

The Soul of Nigger Charley. Paramount, 1973. A runaway slave becomes a folk hero in the West as he fights his way away from bounty hunters and helps out some Mexican allies. Fred Williamson stars.

Ganja and Hess. Kelly-Jordan, 1973. Writer-director Bill Gunn is the key figure in this independently made and distributed production about a doctor's obsession with blood. Much more in heavily symbolic terms about the black experience. An extremely successful film at the Cannes festival.

The Mack. Cinerama, 1973. Max Julien and Richard Pryor are the key figures in this portrait of a highly successful pimp and the lifestyle that he pursues. A significant collection of negative images and plenty of violence.

Book of Numbers. Avco Embassy, 1973. Actor Raymond St. Jacques makes his directing and producing debut in this film based on the life of Southern society with an emphasis on numbers running. Good natured fun a major asset in this film based on a novel by Robert Dean Pharr.

The Harder They Fall. New World, 1973. Reggae star Jimmy Cliff stars in this Jamaican-produced film about a singer and his encounters with the

Max Julien explains his success as a Mack to Richard Pryor in The Mack.

system. A first from the islands and a revealing portrait of Caribbean life.

Wattstax. Columbia, 1973. A marathon concert covering a wide range of black music provides the basis for this concert and commentary film about the black experience in America. Comedian Richard Pryor and man on the street interviews are two unique features in this film, which was co-produced by Stax Records.

Black Caesar. American International, 1973. The story of a ghetto youth who grows up to take over operation of Harlem mob activity once controlled by the Mafia. Fred Williamson's title character modeled after former Edward G. Robinson role.

Black Mama, White Mama. American International, 1973. Filmed on location in the Philippines, this drama of a black and a white female convict who escape from jail handcuffed together reveals little more than a predictable chase and outcome.

Trick Baby. Universal, 1973. A novel by Iceberg Slim was the inspiration for this film about two con men working the ghetto. Mel Stewart stars as the key team member who loses at the ultimate game of life.

The Super Cops. United Artists, 1974.

Based on the exploits of two real life renegade New York City cops who made some 400 drug arrests, this Gordon Parks, Sr. directed adventure about drug warring in the ghetto marked the fourth film for the dean of black filmmaking.

Thomasine and Bushrod. Columbia, 1974. Max Julian and Vonetta McGee are the key figures in this turn-of-the-century Western about a bank robbing team. Colorful characters and a sense of humor make this black-written and produced effort informative and entertaining.

Conrack. Twentieth-Century Fox, 1974. Based on the true story of a white teacher who spends a school year on an isolated isle off the South Carolina coast, this warm drama featured local talent and many of the behind the camera artists who brought the black family film *Sounder* to the screen.

Foxy Brown. American International, 1974. Pam Grier plays a nurse in this film of violence and sex. She avenges the death of her boyfriend by singlehandedly taking on an entire crime syndicate and winning.

Catch My Soul. Cinerama, 1974. Folk singer Richie Havens plays the key role of Othello in this filmed rock version of the famous Shakespearean play. An interesting idea that was an audience flop.

The Black Six. Cinemation, 1974. Six mean looking professional football players make a formidable crime-fighting team in this poorly made drama and action film. Rosalind Miles co-stars.

Three Tough Guys. Paramount, 1974. Film scorer Isaac Hayes stars as a fired police lieutenant who teams with a priest to solve a major ghetto murder. One of the first Italian-produced black films made in America.

Blazing Saddles. Warner Brothers, 1974. A film of Mel Brooks which satirizes virtually everything possible in Hollywood Westerns. Cleavon Little stars as a black sheriff sent to work in racist town in a plot that ultimately backfires in the face of a corrupt state officer.

Black Belt Jones. Warner Brothers, 1974. Jim Kelly, an actual Black Belt karate champ, plays the title role in this take-off on oriental martial arts films. Ex-Playboy Bunny Gloria Hendry co-stars in this action drama laced with humor.

Hell Up In Harlem. American International, 1974. Fred Williamson stars as gangster Tommy Gibbs who uses all his ingenuity to regain control of the Harlem mob operations after they've been taken over by the white forces of evil. A sequel to *Black Caesar.*

Sugar Hill. American International, 1974. Marki Bey stars as a young nightclub owner on a Caribbean isle whose boyfriend is slain. She seeks out the forces of voodoo to avenge his death. A rare black horror film.

That Man Bolt. Universal, 1974. Ex-footballer Fred Williamson stars as a high priced courier carrying a valuable prize from Hong Kong to Mexico. Pure James Bond story with exotic locales, pretty women, and lots of action.

Willie Dynamite. Universal, 1974. The last film role for Diana Sands and the first directorial job for stage mentor Gil Moses. Roscoe Orman stars in the title role of an arrogant but doomed pimp and Miss Sands as a reformed prostitute converted to a social worker.

Bone. Cannon, 1974. Yaphet Kotto stars as a frustrated rapist who invades and terrorizes the home as a wealthy but dishonest television personality and his insecure wife. Commercially unsuccessful satire on a very sensitive topic.

Abby. American International, 1974. William Marshall and Carol Speed head the cast of this horror-oriented drama.

Amazing Grace. United Artists, 1974. Slappy White and Moms Mabley make rare film appearances in this good-natured comedy.

Claudine. Twentieth-Century Fox, 1974. Diahann Carroll and James Earl Jones head a stellar cast in this well-received romantic comedy.

Black Belt Jones. Warner Bros., 1974. Jim Kelly and Gloria Hendry are featured in this action drama about a martial arts hero.

The Education of Sonny Carson. Paramount, 1974. Rony Clanton stars in this sensitive drama about a ghetto youth whose life is a product of his surroundings.

Lost in the Stars. American Film Theater, 1974. Brock Peters, Melba Moore, and Raymond St. Jacques appear in this film adaptation of a noted opera.

The Take. Columbia, 1974. Billy Dee Williams stars in the central role of this drama about police activity.

The Klansmen. Paramount, 1974. O. J. Simpson appears in this angry drama about hatred and violence in the South.

Three The Hard Way. Allied Artists, 1974. Jim Brown, Fred Williamson, and Jim Kelly star in this action drama about three superheroes who take on corrupt forces. Gordon Parks, Jr. directed.

Together Brothers. Twentieth-Century Fox, 1974. Lincoln Kilpatrick stars in the suspense drama about a group of youngsters who take on a deadly villain in their community.

Truck Turner. American International, 1974. Isaac Hayes takes a turn at acting, portraying a tough private investigator.

Uptown Saturday Night. Warner Bros., 1974. Sidney Poitier stars and directs this light-hearted comedy with the able participation of such talents as Bill Cosby and Harry Belafonte.

Boss Nigger. Dimension, 1975. Fred Williamson stars and serves as producer of this action drama typical of his tough-guy hero roles.

Cornbread, Earl and Me. American International, 1975. Moses Gunn and Bernie Casey are among the stars of this sincere drama about the interaction between close friends.

Cleopatra and the Casino of Gold. Warner Bros., 1975. Tamara Dobson appears as a tough lady who can hold her own as she uses charm and her wits to take on a challenging assignment.

Aaron Loves Angela. Columbia. Gordon Parks, Jr. directs this romantic drama which stars Kevin Hooks and Irene Cara as two urban young people.

Cooley High. American International, 1975. Glynn Turman stars in this feature about life in a high school community of fascinating characters.

Friday Foster. American International, 1975. Pam Grier and Yaphet Kotto star in this action drama about a femme private eye.

Let's Do It Again. Warner Bros., 1975. Another Poitier-directed effort with Jimmy Walker among the newcomers to the cast that again included Bill Cosby in a comedy romp.

Mahogany. Paramount, 1975. Diana Ross and Billy Dee Williams star in this romantic drama about a woman who fulfills her dream to become a celebrity fashion model.

Mandingo. Paramount, 1975. Heavyweight boxer Ken Norton is among the cast of this racy drama about the goings-on at a plantation during slavery days.

Sheba Baby. American International, 1975. Pam Grier headlines another action vehicle obviously conceived with her in mind.

TNT Jackson. New World, 1975. Jeanne Bell stars in this drama whose title tells it all.

Report to the Commissioner. United Artists, 1975. Yaphet Kotto stars as a police officer in this hard-hitting drama about a major case in New York City.

Bingo Long and the Traveling All-Stars

and Motor Kings. Universal, 1976. James Earl Jones, Billy Dee Williams, and Richard Pryor star in this humorous and often poignant drama about the early Negro baseball teams that barnstormed around the country.

Car Wash. Universal, 1976. Richard Pryor had a cameo role in this rollicking comedy directed by Mark Warren depicting a day of activity in an establishment where a diverse group carries on the business.

Countdown at Kusini. Columbia, 1976. Ossie Davis directed this drama about the politics of an African country.

Drum. United Artists, 1976. Ken Norton and Yaphet Kotto star in this film which reverts to depicting an earlier generation of slave-era stereotypes.

Mother, Jugs and Speed. Twentieth-Century Fox, 1976. Bill Cosby is one of the principals in this comedy about the operation of an ambulance service.

Norman, Is That You? United Artists. Redd Foxx and Pearl Bailey star in this tepid comedy about a married couple whose son presents them with an unusual problem.

Rocky. United Artists, 1976. Carl Weathers is featured as a ring antagonist in Sylvester Stallone's drama about a struggling boxer.

Silver Streak. Twentieth-Century Fox, 1976. Richard Pryor teams with Gene Wilder in a comedy set aboard a cross-country train.

Brothers. Warner Bros., 1977. Bernie Casey, Vonetta McGee, and Ron O'Neal are among the principals in this drama about black militancy.

The Cassandra Crossing. ITC, 1977. O. J. Simpson worked with an international cast in this suspense drama about a train plagued with a potential disaster.

The Deep. Columbia, 1977. Lou Gossetts stars as a menacing presence on a Caribbean island who becomes a principal foe as a group of treasure hunters attempt to recover a fortune.

The Greatest. Columbia, 1977. Paul Winfield starred among an all-star cast of actors including Muhammad Ali in a dramatization of the flamboyant boxing champ's life.

Greased Lightning. Warner Bros.,

1977. Richard Pryor and Pam Grier star in this drama based on the life of Wendell Scott, one of the nation's most prominent black racing car drivers.

A Hero Ain't Nothing but a Sandwich. New World, 1977. The Alice Childress novel became the basis for this drama starring Paul Winfield and Cicely Tyson.

A Piece of the Action. Warner Bros., 1977. Sidney Poitier directed this comedy after again assembling a team of prominent black actors including Bill Cosby, who again portrayed his sidekick.

Short Eyes. Paramount, 1977. Nathan George was among the talented cast in this film adaptation of Miguel Pinero's acclaimed stage drama.

Which Way Is Up? Universal, 1977. Richard Pryor starred in three different roles in this comedy-drama about compromise and sticking with convictions.

Blue Collar. Universal, 1978. The plight of the working man is dramatized in this film which marked a departure from the roles Richard Pryor generally played.

California Suite. Columbia, 1978. Bill Cosby and Richard Pryor star in this Neil Simon comedy about guests at a California hotel.

The Boys in Company C. Columbia, 1978. Stan Shaw is among the principals in this gritty drama about

a group of Marine recruits sent to fight in the Vietnam War.

FM. Universal, 1978. Cleavon Little stars as a disc jockey at a small station battling to keep its successful format.

Scott Joplin. Universal, 1978. Billy Dee Williams stars in the title role of this biographical drama about the noted ragtime composer.

Apocolypse Now. United Artists, 1979. Albert Hall stars in a central role of this Francis Ford Coppola drama about the Vietnam War.

The Fish That Saved Pittsburgh. United Artists, 1979. Julius Erving and Meadowlark Lemon star in this Gilbert Moses film about a sports phenomenon with humorous overtones.

Richard Pryor in Concert. Independent, 1979. Filmed as Pryor performed, this straightforward film proved to be an unexpected hit.

Rocky II. United Artists, 1979. Carl Weathers as a fighter going up against Sylvester Stallone as the great white hope.

Airplane. Paramount, 1980. Kareem Abdul Jabbar found his way to the cockpit of a fictional airliner in this spoof on disaster films.

All That Jazz. Twentieth-Century Fox, 1980. Ben Vereen stars as a Broadway performer in this acclaimed drama inspired by the career of a famous director.

The Blues Brothers. Universal, 1980.

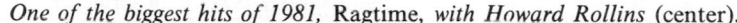

One of the biggest hits of 1981, Ragtime, *with Howard Rollins* (center).

Some Kind of Hero *once again demonstrated the enormous talent of Richard Pryor.*

Aretha Franklin, James Brown, and Cab Calloway are among the performers who make rare cameo appearances in this comedy about two men on the lam.

Brubaker. Twentieth-Century Fox, 1980. Yaphet Kotto stars in this Robert Redford drama about a man attempting to expose corruption in a prison system.

The Empire Strikes Back. Twentieth-Century Fox. Billy Dee Williams stars as one of the principal heroes in this tremendously successful sequel to the science fiction adventure *Star Wars.*

Fame. United Artists, 1980. Irene Cara stands out among the talented young performers in this musical drama about youngsters attempting to excel at a performing arts high school.

The Hunter. Paramount, 1980. LeVar Burton stars as a young fugitive who becomes a friend of the bounty hunter who picked him up in this drama that was Steve McQueen's last film.

Stir Crazy. Columbia, 1980. Richard Pryor stars again with Gene Wilder about a mismatched pair of con men in this comedy directed by Sidney Poitier.

Wholly Moses. Columbia, 1980. Richard Pryor stars with Dudley Moore in this comedy which unsuccessfully attempted to parody the noted biblical character.

Bustin' Loose. Universal, 1981. Richard Pryor stars with Cicely Tyson in this heart-warming comedy about a man who transports a lively group of youngsters across the country by bus.

Carbon Copy. Avco Embassy, 1981. Denzell Washington stars as the black son of a white man who is totally unprepared for this revelation years after his son's birth.

Fort Apache The Bronx. Twentieth-Century Fox, 1981. Pam Grier stars as a deadly prostitute in this grim drama starring Paul Newman as a police officer working in a notorious Bronx ghetto.

Nighthawks. Universal, 1981. Billy Dee Williams stars with Sylvester Stallone in a suspense drama about New York City police attempting to locate and apprehend a European terrorist.

Body and Soul. Cannon, 1981. Leon Isaac Kennedy wrote this drama about a young boxer obviously inspired by a John Garfield film of a previous era. He stars in the central role with his wife Jayne Kennedy and Muhammad Ali also appearing.

Ragtime. Paramount, 1981. Moses Gunn, Howard E. Rollins, and Debbie Allen appeared with James Cagney in an acclaimed adaptation of E. L. Doctorow's novel about life in New York when ragtime music would become a reflection of the turn-of-the-century epoch. Howard E. Rollins was nominated for an Academy Award for his performance.

Penitentiary I and II. Gerry Gross Org., 1981, 1982. Leon Isaac Kennedy in these moving films about prison life and the struggles of a boxer.

Some Kind of a Hero. United Artists, 1982. Richard Pryor stars with Olivia Cole and Lynn Moody about a returning Vietnam veteran adjusting to society.

Live on Sunset Strip. Paramount Pictures Corp., 1982. Stars Richard Pryor in a solo stand-up routine.

Amin, The Rise and Fall. Twin Continental, 1982. Joseph Olita stars as Idi Amin, former Ugandan president, showing how he ruled the country.

THE BLACK PRESS AND BROADCAST MEDIA

A Survey of the Mass Media ■ Black Reporters on White Newspapers ■ Prominent Black Publishers and Journalists ■ Guide to Black Newspapers and Periodicals ■ Broadcast Media ■ Broadcast Personalities ■ Guide to Radio Stations with Black Programming

The past two decades saw a rise in black influence and representation in America's print and broadcast media. There was a big increase in the number of black-operated and oriented radio stations, a rise in television programs featuring black themes and performers, and also in the number of black journalists and commentators employed by general interest newspapers and broadcasters. There was an explosion of special-interest magazines catering to blacks. Blacks successfully challenged cases of discriminatory programming and employment by television and radio stations.

However, blacks also suffered reverses, especially black newspapers. Since the 1970s, over 200 black newspapers ceased publication. Until 1975, there was only one major black daily, *The Chicago Defender,* when another black publication, *The Daily Challenge* began publishing on a daily basis in Brooklyn, New York. There are now three with the addition of the *Atlanta Daily World* based in Atlanta, Georgia. As the 1980s began, 194 black weekly newspapers were being published in 36 states and the District of Columbia.

The Afro-American and the *Courier* were publishing national editions, and a new national newspaper, *The National Leader,* was launched in 1982. From 120 blacks on white publications in the 1970s, the number rose to 3,000 by 1982. Despite these gains by blacks

in newsrooms across the country, there is still a per capita underrepresentation among the nation's reporters and broadcasters and particularly in editorial policy-making positions. Blacks account for fewer than 1% of the editorial jobs on daily publications. In 1979 Robert Maynard became the first black editor-publisher of a daily newspaper, *The Oakland Tribune-East Bay Today* in Oakland, California.

In 1981 Pam Johnson was named publisher of the *Ithaca Journal* in Ithaca, New York, becoming the first black female publisher in the country.

BLACK NEWSPAPERS AND JOURNALISTS

The black press in the United States is heir to a great, largely unheralded tradition. It began with the first black newspaper, *Freedom's Journal* (edited and published by Samuel Cornish and John B. Russwurm), which appeared in New York City on March 16, 1827. *Freedom's Journal* sought to plead the black case before the American public. *The North Star,* the newspaper of the celebrated abolitionist Frederick Douglass, dedicated itself to much the same cause when its first edition appeared in Rochester, New York on December 3, 1847.

Black journalism experienced a rapid growth in the era immediately following the Civil War. Several peri-

The black press in America goes back to 1827 when Freedom's Journal *was published by Samuel Cornish and John B. Russwurm. In 1975 there were over 100 black newspapers, and some 35 of them had a circulation exceeding 20,000 per issue.*

odicals began publication but, more important, the "political" press came into its own, reflecting the black's newfound awarenes of himself.

By the 1880s, the black's ability to establish a substantial cultural environment in many cities of the North, led to the creation of a new wave of publications, including the Washington *Bee,* the Indianapolis *World,* the Philadelphia *Tribune,* the Cleveland *Gazette,* and the New York *Age.* By 1900 there were no less than three dailies, one each in Norfolk, Kansas City, and Washington, D.C.

Among famous black editors of this era were W. M. Trotter, editor of the Boston *Guardian,* a self-styled "radical" paper that showed no sympathy for the so-called conciliatory stance of Booker T. Washington, Robert S. Abbott whose Chicago *Defender* pioneered in the use of headlines and other techniques of mass circulation, and T. T. Fortune of the New York *Age,* who championed free public schools in an age when many opposed the idea.

The black press set the goal of keeping the black public informed of vital issues and creating an appropriate forum for voicing black sentiment on such issues, exposing political injustice and corruption, exhorting the black to become more aware of his achievements and the opportunities open to him. While on the one hand it demanded that society as a whole provide better schools, improved sanitation, and more comprehensive police protection, it likewise threw its support behind black self-help groups like the NAACP and the National Negro Business League.

Believing that urbanization, for all its drawbacks, still offered blacks more promise than a rural environment, the black press backed migration to the North as a means of escaping southern oppression. Most black papers were behind American involvement in World War I and sought actively to encourage blacks to fight for their country.

Between the World Wars

Between the two World Wars, black journalists were major leaders and advocates in the civil rights cause. Roy Wilkins, for example, achieved prominence, and

The Afro-American Building in Baltimore, Maryland, serves as headquarters for one of the nation's largest black newspaper chains.

recognition by the NAACP, as a vigorous journalist in Minnesota and Missouri during the 1920s and early 1930s. In 1940 there were over 200 black newspapers, mostly weeklies with local readership, and about 120 black magazines in the country. The Pittsburgh *Courier,* a weekly, had the largest circulation, about 140,000 per issue.

Many of these papers did not regard America's entry into World War II as sufficient reason to relax their vigilance, especially when the armed forces' determination to maintain segregation became apparent. Some papers headlined news that commanders were refusing to accept black troops except in menial roles and that blacks were victims of injustices on military bases and in nearby communities in many parts of the South. In 1942 the Justice Department threatened about 20 editors with sedition charges, and many black papers found it difficult to obtain newsprint. The NAACP negotiated an unofficial settlement in which black papers tamed their criticism and were able to obtain essential supplies.

The 1950s and 1960s

After World War II black papers suffered from troubles similar to those that afflicted most of America's newspapers—competition for readers and advertisers from radio and television and increasing costs of operation. These problems were compounded by an increasing demand for black journalists from large metropolitan dailies, a demand that was spurred by government pressure and a realization among white publishers that it was absurd to have white reporters continually assigned to cover black communities.

Black papers simply could not compete with the salaries, prestige, and benefits offered by large metropolitan dailies. For example, in 1975, black papers commonly started reporters at salaries of $110 a week,

while some major white papers paid salaries of $400 a week to reporters with a few months experience.

The presence of black journalists on major papers was a benefit to blacks as a whole, but black papers lost many of their most experienced and competent people.

In response to declining circulation, many papers sought almost entirely to entertain readers, concentrating on local social and crime news and omitting news of developments and issues important to blacks. Often, when they reported such matters, accounts were based largely on rewrites of accounts in general newspapers or culled from radio and TV newscasts.

Criticism of papers with this orientation peaked in the later 1960s and early 1970s, when the political consciousness of blacks was ascending and black citizens began to recall the great contributions of black journalists from the days of Abolition through World War II. In response, the National Newspapers Publishers Association, a group representing some 30 black papers, scheduled workshops and trips abroad to acquaint editors and reporters with important news centers and news sources. A result was a trend to more progressive and interpretive reporting.

The 1970s

Black papers were also enlivened in the 1960s and 1970s by a new breed of owners. Typical of the trend was the purchase in 1971 of the New York *Amsterdam News.*

A group of investors headed by lawyer–Wall Street broker Clarence B. Jones, organized under the name of Inner City Broadcasting, purchased the Harlem-based newspaper from its original owners. Jones served two years as editor and publisher. Immediately after Jones departed and was succeeded by general manager John L. Procope, the group exercised an option and gained full ownership of WBLS, one of the nation's rare FM stations with a "soul" format.

Sengstacke Enterprises, the largest black newspaper chain in the nation, also grew strongly in the last decade. Its Chairman, John H. Sengstacke, entered the newspaper business in the 1930s after studying both printing and business administration in college. As head of a chain of 11 newspapers, Sengstacke's group turned in $5 million in overall sales in 1973. Sengstacke's papers include The Chicago *Daily Defender,* the Memphis *Tri-State Defender,* and eight papers in the Pittsburgh Courier chain.

Chester L. Washington, the first black reporter on the *Los Angeles Times,* became head of the Los Angeles Central News-Wave Publications in 1974. With a total audience of 233,000, *News Wave* is the largest black newspaper operation in any single metropolitan area. Washington's papers stress black news and rarely feature crime news.

In the 1970s the Houston *Forward Times* and the Milwaukee *Courier* made a mark after only a few years of publishing. In 1973 the *Courier* earned a profit of $114,000 with a circulation of 13,000. Under publisher and owner Jerrel W. Jones, it won six editorial awards.

An older black paper, the *Baltimore Afro-American,* expanded from Baltimore to include editions catering to Newark, Philadelphia, Washington, D.C., and Richmond. The paper is run by John H. Murphy, III, grandson of John Murphy, Sr. who founded the paper in 1892.

However, in 1975, black newspapers presented a picture of mixed success. Despite the increases in ethnic and political consciousness that marked the decade, black newspapers, like other ethnic papers in the United States, remained largely marginal operations with small staffs and little advertising.

Only about 100 black newspapers were in existence in 1975 and only some 35 of these had a circulation exceeding 20,000 per issue. The largest of these, the weekly *Amsterdam News* of New York had a circulation of about 85,000 per issue in 1974, but still had to struggle along with an editorial staff of six.

Black newspapers remained largely dependent on black readers, many of whom were more responsive to the general press, with its daily coverage and variety of features, than to papers oriented to blacks. In 1975 no major black newspaper in the country reached more than 20% of the black community it catered to and the coverage of most was appreciably less. The *Amsterdam News,* for example, reached only about 10% of New York City's blacks.

The 1980s

A number of newspapers that began publishing in the late 1960s and in the 1970s were out of business by the beginning of the 1980s mainly due to their inability to attract advertising, both locally and nationally, and because of general economic decline during that period.

Most of the newspapers found that they couldn't survive solely on small business advertisements and they didn't have the capital to continue publishing and building circulation figures in order to attract the major advertisers. The local advertiser for the most part were unable to pay rates requested of large businesses and much of the national and big store chain advertising went to the white-run newspapers.

Major advertisers also began to watch their budget

President Eisenhower addresses black leaders at a 1958 meeting sponsored by the National Newspaper Publishers' Association.

in that period of economic decline and placed their dollars where they felt they could get the most mileage—in major commercial newspapers.

Because much of the advertising went to major publications, newspapers such as the New York *Amsterdam News* and the *Afro-American* in Baltimore felt the impact. However, those newspapers as well as more of the older publishing publications were able to hold their regular lineage, but in many cases failed to attract new advertising.

Coupled with the fact that advertising was the focal point of survival, those publishers venturing into the newspaper field also found that they didn't have the necessary capital to survive. They needed money in order to promote their product in order to develop a readership which meant advertising dollars.

Many publishers starting newspapers didn't have that type of capital. Whereas at one time black newspapers had a built-in readership in the black community, publishers in the 1970s and the 1980s were learning that a new upscale readership of young and educated blacks existed. They realized that readers of black newspapers had a need for more national and international coverage, especially news from the African continent. Many black newspapers failed to provide this coverage.

Therefore, black newspaper publishers began to take a hard look at how to make their publications survive and some went the route of developing "metros" or controlled circulation newspapers, commonly called "giveaways."

Through this method, publishers were able to increase their circulation and therefore compete for national advertisers. Dr. Carlton B. Goodlet, publisher of the San Francisco *Metro Reporter,* a string of newspapers on the West Coast, has been successful in such a venture.

Along with reassessing their circulation methods, many black newspapers began to take a look at their products editorially. Many publishers and editors began to deemphasize murders, sensationalist headlines, and blood and gut pictures found on the pages of many black publications. Instead, there were more community-oriented stories and pictures coverage of African affairs.

In 1982 a national publication was born, *The National Leader,* with Claude Lewis as editor. Lewis had been an associate editor at the Philadelphia *Bulletin* before its demise earlier in 1982. The newspaper began publishing during the spring of 1982 and presented stories around the United States, Africa, and features and information about the black communities across the country.

The closing of *The Bulletin, The Chicago Daily News, The Washington Star,* and *The Cleveland Press*

all had an impact upon the black community and placed additional demands on the black press to produce new newspapers. Black communities were learning that their outlet for news had been closed and black publications began to cover the communities more and present more news relevent to blacks. However, because of the closing of the major newspapers, it did not make a significant change in the advertising picture for black newspapers because much of the advertising went to other white run newspapers or to radio and television.

A Scarborough Report on black newspaper audience readership put out by the Amalgamated Publishers Inc. (API) stated that 82.2% of readers of API newspapers found that the publications dealt with subjects of special interest to them while 58.9% found subjects of special interest in daily publications. Of API newspapers readers, 69.9% stated that they found an understanding of their life in the publications; 40.4% found it in daily newspapers. API represents 88 leading, black community newspapers in 68 markets and the study represented only those markets within the top 50 metropolitan areas where there is an API newspaper.

Black Reporters

In the mid-1960s, during the urban unrest, black reporters were hired by major daily newspapers across the country. Until the mid-1970s, the number of blacks on white publications numbered about 120. In the 1980s, the number had risen to more than 3,000 blacks. Although the number is far more than in the 1960s, blacks are still not adequately represented in the policy-making positions on daily newspapers. The *New York Post,* which boasts of being the largest circulating newspaper in the country, has only one black on its staff, a black woman photographer. The *Washington Post* is perhaps the largest employer of blacks of any newspaper in the country with a total of close to 50 in all categories.

In 1981 Janet Cooke, a reporter for *The Washington Post,* won the Pulitzer Prize for her story on an 8-year-old drug addict, which later turned out to be a phony story. Her actions created a furor in newsrooms across the country and thus made the work of other black reporters suspect.

In 1982 William Hilliard, who had been managing editor of the *Portland Oregonian,* was named editor to head editorial direction of the newspaper. Hilliard has also served on the Pulitzer Prize board along with other black journalists such as Bob Maynard, publisher of the *Oakland Tribune-East Bay Today,* and Joel Dreyfuss of *Black Enterprise Magazine.*

Magazines

A significant development of the 1970s was the advent of a new class of special interest magazines. Johnson Publications was very much in the vanguard, with *Ebony Jr.,* a youthful version of its popular general interest magazine, *Ebony.* The company also converted *Tan,* a woman's magazine, into a successful show business and personality monthly called *Black Stars.*

Essence editor Ida Lewis departed from her position at that woman's digest and created *Encore,* a journal that appealed to a multiracial audience with a format similar to three major news weeklies, *Time, Newsweek,* and *U.S. News and World Report. Encore* was one of the first of the new magazines to base itself in the black community, but to develop its editorial appeal to a wide base in order to attract increased readership and advertising.

Earl G. Graves, a young businessman, embarked on a concept to publish a monthly digest of news,

commentary, and informative articles for blacks interested in business enterprise. Heavily subsidized initially, *Black Enterprise* soon achieved prominence as one of the more sophisticated magazines in the country.

Another young man, Allan Barron, established *Black Sports,* a magazine geared to highlight the tremendous impact blacks have at all levels of competitive athletics. A spin-off of the publication was the Black Hall of Fame, which has become a prominent institution in the community.

Players magazine, a nationally distributed version of *Playboy,* started on the West Coast, flourished immediately, and built a substantial readership in both the black and general markets. *Soul Journey,* a monthly travel magazine began publishing and capitalized on the huge leisure market among blacks.

In 1981 a new national competitor to women-oriented *Essence,* called *Elam,* published for several months but ceased publication in 1982.

In Chicago, a magazine called *Black Family* began publishing in 1981 with Mary Ellen Strong as publisher.

Meanwhile, magazines such as *Black Enterprise* and *Essence* continued to show strong growth. *Black Enterprise* has become known for its top 100 black companies and has become widely quoted in national publications.

Essence is considered the top in a field of women's magazines geared to black women and has steadily gained in its circulation since its inception. The magazine has added more departments relevant to the black woman of the 1980s.

Popular black magazines include general-interest Ebony; Essence, *oriented toward the black woman; and* Encore, *a multiracial news digest.*

BLACK REPORTERS, EDITORS, PHOTOGRAPHERS, AND COLUMNISTS ON MAJOR NEWSPAPERS

Atlanta Constitution

Tony Cooper
Linda Horton
Burnis Morris (assistant city editor)
Ernest Reese (sports)

Atlanta Journal

Chet Fuller
John Head (assistant city editor)
Clem Richardson
Prentiss Rogers (sports)
Angela Terrell

Boston Globe

Ken Cooper
Jackie Green
Ron Hutson
Judy Jackson
Robert Jordan
Diane Lewis

Victor Lewis
Norman Lockman
Don Lowery
Jim McBride
Valerie Montague
Viola Osgood
Gayle Pollard
Fletcher Roberts
John Robinson
Miriam Tarver
Larry Whiteside

Chicago Tribune

Monroe Anderson
Joyce Brown
Vernon Jarrett
Leanita McClain
John White

Charlotte News

Ramona Clark
Ted DeAdyler
Deborah Gates
Cassandra Lawton
David Porter (assistant city editor)
Osker Spicer
Gail Westry (copy editor)

Detroit Free Press

Bruce Britt
Donna Britt-Gibson
Betty DeRamus
Andrea Ford
Brenda Gilchrist
Moses Harris
Kim Heron
Greg Huskisson
Luther Jackson III
Ben Johnson
Jackie Jones
Larry Olmstead
Ruth Seymour
Cassandra Spratling
Monte Trammer
Joyce Walker-Tyson
Susan Watson

Detroit News

June Brown
Denice Crittenden
Larry Davis
David Grant
Jim McFarlan
Carl Payne
Arlena Sawyer
Michael Tucker
Monroe Walker

Louisville Courier-Journal

Mervin Aubespin
Marie Bradby
Leon Carter
Michael Days

Cheryl Devall
Angela Dotson
Keith Harriston
Donna Whitaker

Louisville Times

Bruce Branch
Michelle Chandler
Delma Francis
Clarence Matthews
Milford Reid

Newsday

Mike Alexander
Dennis Bell
Sid Cassesse
Merle English
Sheryl Fitzgerald
Betty Logan
Bill Mason
Charles Moses
Les Payne (national editor)
Morris Thompson

New York Daily News

Willie Anderson (photographer)
Earl Caldwell (columnist)
Ron Claiborne
Clarence Davis (photographer)
Steve Duncan (copy editor)
David Hardy
James Harncy
Bob Herbert (City Hall bureau chief)
Ron Howell (Harlem bureau chief)
Keith Moore
Cynthia Raymond
Rufus Rivers (copy editor)
Joan Shepard
Dave Sims (sports)
Causewell Vaughan (Bronx editor)
Joyce White
Hugh Wyatt (health affairs editor)

New York Post

Lenore Davis (photographer)

New York Times

Lee Daniels
Paul Delaney (national editor)
C. Gerald Frazier (arts and entertainment writer)
Dorothy Gaiter
George Goodman
Judith Gummings
Al Harvin (sports)
Don Hogan-Charles (photographer)
Ernest Holsendolph
Les Ledbetter
Sheila Rule
Nathaniel Sheppard
E. R. Shipp
Ron Smothers
Reginald Stuart

Ron Smothers, Paul Delany, and Judith Cummings are journalists with the New York Times.

Oakland Tribune-East Bay Today

Marilyn Bailey (assistant city editor)
Sharon Bibb (copy editor)
Mary Ellen Butler (features editor)
Gerald Davis
Skye Dent (editorial writer)
Kenneth Green (photographer)
Juadine Henderson (assistant city editor)
Denise Holt (education writer)
Lonnie Isabel
Annette John (sports writer)
Sidney Jones (columnist)
Will Jones (assistant city editor)
Brenda Lane-Worthington (columnist)
Robert Maynard (editor, publisher, president)
Tina Pania (copy editor)
Brenda Payton
Doris Worsham (columnist)

Philadelphia Daily News

Lorenzo Biggs
Joseph Blake
Prentice Cole
Wayne Faircloth
Juan Gonzalez
Frederick Lowe
Valerie Russ
Gene Seymour
Elmer Smith
Chuck Stone (columnist)
Leon Taylor
Linn Washington
Barnett Wright
Earni Young

The Star-Ledger, Newark, New Jersey

Edna M. Bailey
Kathy Barrett-Carter
Frederick V. Boyd
Bill Bright
Frederick W. Byrd
Kevin Dilworth
Larry Hall (editor, This Week-Newark)
Jason Jett
Lisa Peterson
Ernest Roberson
Stanley E. Terrell
Joan Whitlow (medical editor)
Kenneth Woody

The Washington Post

Vivian Aplin-Brownlee (assistant national editor)
Vanessa Barnes-Hillian
Alice C. Bonner
LaBarbara Bowman
Warren Brown
Dorothy Butler-Gilliam (metro-columnist)
Earl K. Chism (Treasurer, Washington Post Company)
Milton Coleman (city editor)
Leon D. Dash
Ellsworth Davis (night photo editor)
Herbert H. Denton
David DuPree
Cheryl Eaves (assistant news editor)
Sandra R. Gregg
Carla Hall
Neil Henry

Graig Herndon (photographer)
Michael Hill (assistant editor-style section)
Donald Huff
Athelia Knight
Leah Y. Latimer
Matthew Lewis (assistant managing editor-photography)
Wanda Lloyd (assistant editor)
Harold J. Logan (assistant-to-the-publisher)
Michel Marriott
Michel McQueen
Courtland Milloy, Jr.
Tom Morgan (editor, District Weekly)
Carol Porter (graphics)
Jacquelyn Powell (copy editor-style section)
Rudolf Pyatt
William Raspberry (columnist)
Vincent E. Reed (vice president-communications)
Keith B. Richburg
Joe Ritchie (foreign desk editor)
Eugene Robinson (assistant city editor)
Edward D. Sargent
Jane Seaberry
Jube Shiver, Jr.
Fred Sweets
Jacqueline Trescott
Joseph D. Whitaker
Ronald D. White
Michael Wilbon
Juan Williams
Leon Wynter

PROMINENT BLACK PUBLISHERS AND BROADCAST EXECUTIVES

EARL G. GRAVES
Publisher and Broadcast Executive
1935

In the 1970s Earl Graves emerged as one of America's leading publishers and exponents of black entrepreneurship. Within a few short years his magazine, *Black Enterprise,* was accepted as the authority on the progress of minorities in business and as an important advocate for an active, socially responsive, black middle class.

Born in Brooklyn, Graves graduated from Morgan State College. In 1966 he was hired to a position on the staff of Robert Kennedy, then Senator from New York. In 1968 he organized Earl Graves Associates, a firm which serves as a consultant on urban affairs,

black economic development and publishes *Black Enterprise.*

Graves represented a new wave of blacks in publishing. His magazine is polished, topical, thorough, and distinctive in its own right.

He also has interests in radio as President of EGG Dallas Broadcasting, Inc., which operates KNOK-AM and KNOK-FM in Fort Worth, Texas.

RAGAN A. HENRY
Broadcast and Newspaper Executive, Attorney
1934

Ragan A. Henry has been President of Broadcast Enterprises National, Inc. since 1973 and is President of *The National Leader,* a new black national newspaper launched in May 1982, both headquartered in Philadelphia. He serves as President of radio stations in several states (see Guide in this chapter). He also

Earl Graves, rapidly becoming one of the most important publishers in the country.

is a partner in the Philadelphia law firm of Wolf, Black, Schorr, and Solis-Cohen.

Henry was born in Sadiesville, Kentucky on February 2, 1934. He received his A.B. from Harvard College in 1956 and his L.L.B. from Harvard Law School in 1961. He also attended Temple University Graduate School in 1963. Prior to joining his current law firm, he had been a partner in the Philadelphia firm of Goodis, Greenfield, Henry and Edelstein from 1964 to 1977.

Henry has been a Visiting Professor at Syracuse University's S. I. Newhouse School of Communications since 1979 and was a lecturer at LaSalle College from 1971–1973. He serves on the boards of directors of Continental Bank, Abt Associates, Inc., National Association of Black Owned Broadcasters (President of the Board), LaSalle College, and the Hospital of the University of Pennsylvania. He had been chairman of the John McKee Scholarship Committee Fellowships, Noyes and Whitney Foundations.

JOHN H. JOHNSON
Publisher
1918

One of the America's foremost businessmen, John H. Johnson sits at the head of the most prosperous and powerful black publishing company in the United States. Beginning with *Negro Digest* in 1942, and following with *Ebony* in 1945, Johnson built a chain of journalistic successes that now includes *Jet, Ebony, Jr.,* and book publishing.

Born in Arkansas City, Arkansas, Johnson, at age six, lost his father, a mill worker, and was raised by his mother and stepfather. His segregated schooling was obtained locally until the family moved to Chicago. Johnson attended DuSable High School in Chicago, excelling academically and in extracurricular activities, writing for the yearbook and school paper.

After graduation, an insurance executive heard a speech delivered by Johnson, and was so impressed he offered him a partial scholarship at the University of Chicago. After two years, however, Johnson quit classes, although he entered the Northwestern School of Commerce in 1938, studying for an additional two years before joining the Supreme Liberty Life Insurance Company.

While running the company's house organ, it occurred to Johnson that a digest of weekly or monthly gathered news items of special interest and importance to the black community might achieve a wide black readership. The idea resulted in the creation of *Negro Digest*, a periodical containing both news reprints and feature articles. Of the latter, perhaps the most beneficial to circulation was Eleanor Roosevelt's contribution, "If I Were a Negro."

Buoyed by success, Johnson decided to approach the market with yet another offering, a pictorial magazine patterned after *Life*. The first issue of *Ebony* sold

John H. Johnson directs the most prosperous and powerful black publishing company in the United States.

out its press run of 25,000 copies and soon became a permanent staple in the world of journalism, as big companies began to advertise regularly in it. Johnson ran ads for both consumer merchandise and ethnic products, mainly hair- and skin-conditioning items. The world of "special markets" was born.

In style, tone, and format, *Ebony* glamorized American life and appealed both to middle-class citizens who felt they were already participating in the milieu he described, and to poor blacks who modeled their aspirations on the world of fulfillment he so effectively created.

From its preoccupation with frothy glamor and eye-catching photographs, *Ebony* evolved over the years into a family-style magazine devoting much of its coverage to black success stories, show business personalities, and other unusual facets of black life. For a time, much of its material was so superficial and innocuous that it succeeded in alienating many black activists, but as its circulation grew and its outlook changed, it took a more aggressive editorial stance.

In addition to serving as President and Publisher of Johnson Publishing Company, Inc., Johnson is Chairman and Chief Executive Officer of Supreme Life Insurance Company, Chairman of WJPC-AM in Chicago, and President of Fashion Fair Cosmetics. He serves on the boards of directors of The Greyhound Corporation, Verex Corporation, Marina Bank, Supreme Life Insurance Company, and Zenith Radio

Publisher John H. Murphy III in his office at the Baltimore Afro-American.

Corporation. Johnson also serves as a Trustee for The Art Institute of Chicago and United Negro College Fund; on the Advisory Council, Harvard Graduate School of Business; as a Director, Chamber of Commerce of the United States, The Advertising Council, Junior Achievement, and Chicago USO. In 1972 Johnson was appointed to the Urban Transportation District of Chicago. He has received honorary doctoral degrees from 16 colleges and universities, and many honors and awards from civil and professional organizations.

CLARENCE B. JONES
Publisher and Lawyer
1931

With a background in civil rights litigation, investment financing, publishing, and broadcasting, Clarence Jones is one of New York City's more influential and knowledgeable citizens.

Born in Philadelphia, Jones graduated from Columbia University and Boston University Law School and then practiced as an attorney, specializing in civil rights and copyright cases for a New York City law firm. During this period, he was counsel for Dr. Martin Luther King, Jr. and the Southern Christian Leadership Conference. In 1968 and again in 1972, he served as a delegate from New York State to the Democratic Convention.

Jones was also an observer at Attica prison during the uprising there in 1971.

In 1971 Jones, as head of Inner City Broadcasting, led a group of investors in the purchase of the New York *Amsterdam News,* the nation's largest black newspaper. Inner City Broadcasting also owned radio station WLIB and has full ownership of WBLS-FM.

JOHN H. MURPHY III
Publisher
1916

John Murphy III is the great-nephew of John Murphy Sr., founder of the Baltimore *Afro-American,* which John III now heads. Murphy was born in Baltimore and raised in Philadelphia where at the age of nine he started his newspaper career by covering an *Afro-American* delivery route.

In 1937 Murphy graduated from Temple University in Philadelphia with a degree in Business Administration. He immediately joined the *Afro-American* staff, working in both editorial and publishing capacities, under Dr. Carl Murphy, his uncle.

From 1961 to 1974 he was President of the Afro-American Newspapers, and since 1974 has been Chairman of the Board of Directors.

Murphy serves on the boards of Amalgamated Publishers, Inc., National Newspaper Publishers Association, Council on Equal Business Opportunities, National Aquarium at Baltimore, Provident Hospital, Baltimore School for the Arts, and Baltimore City Literacy Commission. He is a former member of the U.S. Civil Rights Commission.

Murphy has received numerous honors and awards from civic, educational, charitable, and journalistic organizations.

JOHN HERMAN HENRY SENGSTACKE
Publisher
1912

A nephew of the great publisher Robert Abbott, John H. Sengstacke has achieved fame in his own right, and today heads several publishing companies.

Born in Savannah, Sengstacke received a B.A. from Hampton Institute in 1933. Upon graduation, he went to work with Robert Abbott, attended school to learn printing, and wrote editorials and articles for three Abbott papers. In 1934 he became Vice President and General Manager of the company.

During World War II, Sengstacke was an advisor to the U.S. Office of War Information, during a period of severe tension between the government and black press. He also presided over the Chicago rationing board.

In 1940, after the death of his uncle, Sengstacke became President of the Robert S. Abbott Publishing Company. In 1905 his uncle had founded the weekly *Defender.* In 1956, Sengstacke founded the *Daily Defender,* one of only three black dailies in the country. In 1940 he founded the Negro Newspaper Publishers Association, now known as the National Newspaper Publishers Association, and served six terms as president. Today he is president of Tri-State Defender, Inc., Florida Courier Publishing Company, New Pittsburgh Courier Publishing Company, and Amalgamated Publishers, Inc., and chairman of Michigan Chronicle Publishing Company and Sengstacke Enterprises, Inc., and treasurer of Chicago Defender Charities, Inc.

Sengstacke has served in leadership positions with many professional, educational, and civic organizations, received a number of presidential appointments, and is the recipient of several academic awards. He is currently a trustee of Bethune-Cookman College, Chairman of the Board of Provident Hospital and Training School Association, member of the board of directors of the American Society of Newspaper Editors, on the Advisory Board of the Boy Scouts of America, and a principal in Chicago United.

John Sengstacke heads the mighty Chicago Defender.

CHESTER LLOYD WASHINGTON
Publisher

Chester L. Washington is a rare breed—a reporter who became a publishing executive. He is now publisher of The Wave newspapers, 12 newspapers, and 4 weekly news magazines, in Los Angeles.

Washington was born in Pittsburgh, where he completed his primary education, and was graduated from Pittsburgh's Business High School. For several years he was employed by the Pittsburgh *Courier* as legal secretary for Robert L. Vann, then publisher of the *Courier.*

He earned his B.A. degree at Virginia Union University where he taught typewriting in Richmond's Evening High School, after winning the area's typewriting championship.

Following graduation from Virginia Union, Washington returned to the *Courier* where he eventually became secretary of The Courier Corporation.

In 1949 Washington became the first black full-time reporter for the *Mirror-News,* owned by the *Los Angeles Times.* While there he specialized in coverage of superior court cases.

In 1960 he went to the *Los Angeles Sentinel* as a reporter, covering the Civic Center. In 1961 he was

promoted to editor and in 1965 was named editor-in-chief.

In September 1966 he purchased the *Central News* and *Southwest News*. Then, in 1971, the *Central News* and *Southwest News* were merged with the five newspapers of The Wave Publications, which became the Central News-Wave Publications. He created three additional weeklies for a total of 10. Central News-Wave Publications is now the largest black-owned newspaper chain in the United States. In 1979 it made its first appearance on the *Black Enterprise* magazine's list of the top 100 black owned businesses. The newspapers also have won several journalism awards.

Washington is chairman of the Los Angeles County Parks and Recreation Commission, was a member of the California State Bicentennial Commission, and serves on the Coliseum Commission. He is active in many educational, youth, and civic organizations. He participated in a speaking tour at colleges in Sweden under the auspices of the State Department, and was a member of the American Delegation to Israel. At dedication ceremonies in March 1982, the Western Avenue Golf Course in Los Angeles was renamed the Chester L. Washington Golf Course. The course hosts many well-known tournaments.

FAMOUS PUBLISHERS OF THE PAST

ROBERT S. ABBOTT
Founder of the Chicago *Defender*
1870–1940

A founding father of black journalism in the United States, Robert S. Abbott realized a lifelong dream when the first issue of his Chicago *Defender* rolled off the presses on May 5, 1905.

A native of St. Simon Island, Georgia, Abbott studied at Beach Institute in Savannah, and later did his undergraduate work at Claflin College in Orangeburg, South Carolina. Some 12 years later, he took the advice of his stepfather, John J. Sengstacke, and learned the printing trade. Migrating to Chicago, he attended Kent Law School and took a job in a printing house until he completed his law studies in 1899.

After wandering around the country for a time, Abbott returned to Chicago and decided to devote all his energies to founding the *Defender*, which he initially sold on a door-to-door basis. Over the next 15 years, the paper's circulation climbed into the hundreds of thousands.

Abbott died in 1940, whereupon the *Defender* was inherited by his nephew, John H. Sengstacke, who introduced a daily edition of the paper in 1956.

John Henry Murphy launched the Afro-American *in 1890.*

JOHN HENRY MURPHY
Founder, Baltimore *Afro-American*
1840–1922

John Henry Murphy was born a slave in Maryland. After his emancipation at the age of 23, he worked another 27 years in menial jobs. Then at age 50, inspired by a desire to represent the black cause with honor and integrity, Murphy launched the Baltimore *Afro-American,* which to this day remains a prominent force in the black community.

At first, Murphy set the paper's type himself, having acquired this skill during his forties. Throughout, he insisted that his paper maintain political and editorial independence. The paper grew and is now under the helm of Murphy's grandson, John H. Murphy III.

JOHN B. RUSSWURM
Co-Publisher, *Freedom's Journal*
1799–1851

John B. Russwurm is conventionally identified as the second black to have graduated from a U.S. college. Edward A. Jones graduated from Amherst some 11 days before he did in 1826.

Russwurm took his degree at Bowdoin in 1826, and by 1827 he was engaged in editing the first Negro newspaper, *Freedom's Journal*. His colleague in this effort was the Reverend Samuel E. Cornish, pastor of the African Presbyterian Church in New York. (The paper changed its name to *Rights of All* in 1830.)

In 1828 Russwurm migrated to Liberia, finding in the new colony a "promised land." He remained there until his death some 23 years later, eventually becoming superintendent of schools.

A GUIDE TO BLACK NEWSPAPERS

National Weekly Newspapers

National Afro-American
628 N. Eutaw Street
Baltimore, MD 21201
Circulation: 6,092

Bilalian News **(American Muslim
Mission)**

7801 S. Cottage Grove
Chicago, IL 60619
Circulation: 150,000

New National Courier
315 E. Carson Street, P.O. Box 2939
Pittsburgh, PA 15230

Circulation: 7,956

The National Leader
1422 Chestnut Street
Philadelphia, PA 11902
Circulation:

National Newspaper Supplements

Black Monitor
Black Media, Inc.
507 Fifth Avenue
New York, NY 10017
Circulation: 1,000,000
(cooperatively published supplement
to 110 black newspapers)

Dawn Magazine
628 N. Eutaw Street
Baltimore, MD 21203
Circulation: 900,000 (distributed
once a month in local and national
black newspapers)

National Scene
L. H. Stanton Publications, Inc.
507 Fifth Avenue
New York, NY 10017
Circulation: 792,773 (monthly
supplement to 23 weekly newspapers)

Daily Newspapers

The Daily Challenge
1368 Fulton Street
Brooklyn, NY 11216
Circulation: 72,500 (publishes every
day except Saturday)

Chicago Daily Defender
Robert S. Abbott Publishing Co.
2400 S. Michigan
Chicago, IL 60616
Circulation: 17,349 (Monday–
Friday), 18,250 (Saturday)

Atlanta Daily World
145 Auburn Avenue
Atlanta, GA 30335
Circulation: 18,500 (Monday,
Tuesday, Thursday, Friday), 22,500
(Saturday)

Weekly Newspapers

Alabama

Birmingham: *Times*–P.O. Box 10503,
Birmingham (35204); 36,000

Birmingham: *World*–312 N. 17th St.,
Birmingham (35203); 9,200

Florence: *Shoals News-Leader*–P.O.
Box 427, Florence (35630); 10,000

Huntsville: *Huntsville Weekly*–2227
Bell Avenue, N.W., Huntsville
(35805); 2,000

Mobile: *Beacon*–P.O. Box 1407, 2311
Coastarides St., Mobile (36601); W;
5,200

Mobile: *Inner City News*–P.O. Box
1545, Mobile (36633); 16,000

Montgomery: *Montgomery/Tuskegee
Times*–P.O. Box 9133, Montgomery
(36108); 10,000

Tuscaloosa: *Courier*–P.O. Box 2055,
Tuscaloosa (35401); 14,000

Arizona

Phoenix: *Informant*–222 North 9th
St., Phoenix (85034); W; 5,300

Phoenix: *The Phoenix Press Weekly*–
P.O. Box 8753, Phoenix (85066);
25,000

Arkansas

Little Rock: *Arkansas Weekly
Sentinel*–P.O. Box 4520, Little Rock
(72214); 2,500

Little Rock: *Statewide Mediator*–500
E. Markham, Suite 300, Little Rock
(72201); 51,749

California

Bakersfield: *Bakersfield News
Observer*–1219 20th St., Bakersfield
(93301); 20,000

Carson: *Carson Courier*–402 E.
Sepulveda, Carson (90745); 12,000

Fresno: *California Advocate*–P.O. Box
11826, 450 Fresno St., Fresno (93775);
46,000

Los Angeles: *Sentinel*–1112 E. 43rd
St., Los Angeles (90011); 32,258

Los Angeles: *Central News-Wave
Publications*–2621 W. 54th St., Los
Angeles (90043); 210,000

Los Angeles: *Herald Dispatch*–3741
W. Stocker, Los Angeles (90008);
20,000

Los Angeles: *Watts Times*–2112 Park
Grove Ave., Los Angeles (90007);
10,000

Oakland: *Post*ᶜ–630 20th St., Oakland
(94612); 94,000

Pasadena: *L.A./Pasadena Metro
Gazette*–83 E. Orange Grove Blvd.,
Suite 4, Pasadena (91103); 40,000

Quartz Hill: *Metro Star Group:
Bakersfield, Antelope Valley, Los
Angeles*–42 353 47th St. West, Quartz
Hill (93534); 19,000

Sacramento: *Los Angeles Happenings*–
P.O. Box 209, Sacramento (95801);
124,000

Sacramento: *Observer*–P.O. Box 209,
3540 4th Ave., Sacramento (95801);
92,800

San Bernardino: *Precinct Reporter*–
1673 W. Baseline St., San Bernardino
(92411); 30,000

San Diego: *Voice and Viewpoint News*–P.O. Box 95, 4684 Federal Blvd., San Diego (92112); 10,000

San Francisco: *San Francisco Metro Reporter*–1366 Turk St., San Francisco (94115); 121,772

Colorado

Denver: *Denver Weekly News*–2547 Welton St., Denver (80205); 15,000

Connecticut

Hartford: *Inquirer*–P.O. Box 1260, Hartford (06101); 66,000

Delaware

Wilmington: *Delaware Valley Star*–1050 A.S. Market St., Wilmington (19801); 10,000

District of Columbia

Washington: *Afro-American And Tribune*[b]–2002 11th St. N.W., Washington (20001); 10,101

Washington: *Informer*–1343 H St. N.W., Washington (20005); 45,000

Washington: *The New Observer*–811 Florida Ave. N.W., Washington (20001); 24,000

Florida

Daytona Beach: *Times*–P.O. Box 1110, Daytona Beach (32015); 10,000

Fort Lauderdale: *Gazette*–P.O. Box 5304, Fort Lauderdale (33310); 21,000

Fort Pierce: *Chronicle*–1527 Ave D, Fort Pierce (33450); 7,000

Jacksonville: *Florida Star-News*–P.O. Box 40629, Jacksonville (32203); 26,050

Jacksonville: *Jacksonville Advocate*–860 Sorrento Road, Jacksonville (32207); 5,000

Miami: *Florida Courier*–1466 N.W. 62 St., Miami (33147); 4,496

Miami: *The Liberty News*–Northside Shopping Center, 188 North Plaza, Miami (33147);

Miami: *Miami Times*–900 N.W. 54th St., Miami (33127); 24,160

Orlando: *Florida Sun & Mirror*–P.O. Box 2488, Orlando (32802); 5,000

Orlando: *Sun Review*–4020 W. Columbia St., Orlando (32805); 4,000

Orlando: *Times*–2393 W. Church St., Orlando (32805); 10,000

Pensacola: *Pensacola Voice*–213 E. Young St., Pensacola (32503); 32,700

Riveria Beach: *Gold Coast Star News*–P.O. Box 6002, 206 No. Flagler Ave., Riveria Beach (33060); 7,500*

Sarasota: *Weekly Bulletin*–P.O. Box 2560, Sarasota (33578); 17,500

St. Petersburg: *Weekly Challenger*–Suite C, 2500 9th St. S., St. Petersburg (33705); 15,300

Tallahassee: *Capitol Outlook*–P.O. Box 31, Tallahassee (32302); 5,000

Tampa: *News Reporter*–1610 N. Howard Ave., Tampa (33607); 5,759

Tampa: *Sentinel-Bulletin*[b]–2207-21 Ave., Tampa (33601); 39,806

West Palm Beach: *Florida Photo News*–P.O. Box 1583–46, 601 Clematis St., West Palm Beach (33402); 2,288

Georgia

Albany: *Albany/Macon Times*–141 West Broad, Albany (31705); 46,000

Albany: *Southwest Georgian*–P.O. Box 1943, Albany (33701); 10,000

Atlanta: *The Atlanta Inquirer*–787 Parsons St. S.W., Atlanta (30314); 40,000

Atlanta: *Atlanta People's Crusader*–551 Houston St. N.E., Atlanta (30312); 20,000

Atlanta: *Atlanta Voice*–P.O. Box 92405, Atlanta (30315); 37,500

Augusta: *News Review*–P.O. Box 953, Augusta (30903); 3,025

Columbus: *Times*–2230 Buena Vista Rd., Columbus (31906); 20,000

Cordele: *Southeastern News*–P.O. Box 461, Cordele (31015); 20,000

Macon: *Courier*–P.O. Box 52D, Macon (31208); 7,500

Macon: *Macon Times*–813 Forsyth, Macon (31201); 32,000

Savannah: *Savannah Herald*–P.O. Box 41, 1803 Barnard St., Savannah (31402); 6,000

Savannah: *Tribune*–P.O. Box 2066, Savannah (31402); 6,000

Illinois

Champaign: *Spectrum*–Station A.P.O. Box 2285, Champaign (61820)

Chicago: *Chicago Metro News*–Suite 101, 2600 S. Michigan Ave., Chicago (60616); 70,205

Chicago: *Citizen Newspapers*–412 E. 87 St., Chicago (60619); 65,000

Chicago: *Independent Bulletin Newspapers*–2042 W. 95th St., Chicago (60643); 47,000

Chicago: *New Crusader*–6429 Martin Luther King Dr., Chicago (60637); 39,411

Chicago: *Observer*–6040 S. Harper, Chicago (60637); 30,000

Chicago: *Shoreland*–11740 S. Elizabeth St., Chicago (60643); 20,000

Chicago Hts.: *Tri-City Journal*–1406 Park Ave., Chicago Hts.; 30,000

Decatur: *Decatur Voice*–3180 N. Woolford Rd., Rm. 31, Decatur (62526); 5,000

East St. Louis: *Monitor*–1501 State St., East St. Louis (62205); 17,000

Evanston: *North Shore Examiner*–909 Pitner Ave., Evanston (60202)

Rockford: *The Rockford Chronicle*–605 West State Street, Rockford (61102)

Indiana

Ft. Wayne: *Ft. Wayne Frost Illustrated*–124 West Wayne St., Ft. Wayne (46802); 2,000

Gary: *Gary Crusader*–1549 Broadway, Gary (46407); 14,856

Gary: *Info*–P.O. Box 587, Gary (46407); 9,000

Indianapolis: *Herald*–723 N.W. St., Indianapolis (46205); 27,200

Indianapolis: *Indianapolis Recorder*–2901 N. Tacoma Ave., Indianapolis (46218); 9,880

Iowa

W. Des Moines: *New Iowa Bystander*–P.O. Box 65640, W. Des Moines (50265); 3,000

Kansas

Kansas City: *Kansas City Globe*–1125 Grand Suite 1102, Kansas City (64106); 19,000

Kansas City: *Kansas City Voice*–2727 N. 13th St., Kansas City (66104); 34,000

Kentucky

Louisville: *The Defender Newspaper*–1720 Dixie Highway, Louisville (40210); 2,654

Louisiana

Alexandria: *Alexandria News Weekly*–P.O. Box 608, Alexandria (71301); 13,700

Baton Rouge: *Community Leader* (Group)–1210 North Blvd., Baton Rouge (70802); 46,013

New Orleans: *Black Data Weekly*–P.O. Box 51933, New Orleans (70151); 15,000

New Orleans: *Louisiana Weekly*–640 S. Rampart St., New Orleans (70150); 9,197

Shreveport: *Shreveport Ebony Tribune*–P.O. Box 3857, Shreveport (71103)

Shreveport: *Shreveport Sun*–P.O. Box 9328, Shreveport (71109); 8,500

Maryland

Baltimore: *Afro-American*[b]–628 N. Eutaw St., Baltimore (21201); Tues., 19,762–Sat., 21,343

Baltimore: *African-American News & World Report*–325 E. 2nd Street, Baltimore (21218); 10,000

Massachusetts

Roxbury: *Bay State Banner*–25 Ruggles St., Roxbury (02119); 10,500

Michigan

Benton Harbor: *Citizen*–P.O. Box 216, Benton Harbor (49022); 17,000

Detroit: *Detroit/Ecorse Telegram*–4122-10th St., Detroit (48229); 11,000

Detroit: *Michigan Chronicle*–479 Ledyard St., Detroit (48201); 30,856

Flint: *Spokesman*–3604 W. Saginaw St., Flint (48405); 9,000

Grand Rapids: *Grand Rapids Times*–P.O. Box 2521, 346 Wealthy St. S.E., Grand Rapids (49501); 9,000

Jackson: *Jackson Blazer*–1305 Francis St., Jackson (49204); 3,500

Minnesota

Minneapolis: *Minneapolis Spokesman & Recorder*–3744-4th Ave. S., Minneapolis (55409); 13,810

Minneapolis: *St. Paul Recorder*–3744 4th Ave. S., Minneapolis (55409); 11,340

Minneapolis: *Twin Cities Courier*–Suite 501, 84 S. 6th St., Minneapolis (55402); 16,202

Mississippi

Jackson: *Jackson Advocate*–115 E. Hamilton, Jackson (39202); 8,000

Meredian: *Memo Digest*–2511 Fifth St., Meredian (39301); 5,000

Missouri

Kansas City: *Call*–P.O. Box 477, 1715 E. 18th St., Kansas City (64141); 10,085

St. Louis: *St. Louis American*–3910 Lindell Blvd., St. Louis (63108); 9,000

St. Louis: *St. Louis Argus*–4595 Martin Luther King Drive, St. Louis (63113); 24,117

St. Louis: *St. Louis Crusader*–4371 Finney Ave., St. Louis (63113); 24,000

St. Louis: *St. Louis Evening Whirl*–8544 Riverview Blvd., St. Louis (63147); 40,000

St. Louis: *St. Louis Sentinel*–Suite 206, 3338 Olive St., St. Louis (63103); 9,665

Nebraska

Omaha: *Omaha Star*–2216 N. 24 St., Omaha (68111); 30,000

Nevada

Las Vegas: *Las Vegas Voice*–616 North "II" St., Las Vegas; 10,000

Reno: *The Reno Observer*–328 E. Taylor, Reno (89505); 5,000

New Jersey

East Orange: *Grafrica News*–28 Emerson St., East Orange (07018); 24,000

Newark: *New Jersey Afro-American*–Suites 200–201, 11 Hill St., Newark (07102); 4,405

Newark: *Newark/Essex Greater News*–585 Broad St., Newark (07102); 50,000

Willingboro: *Willingboro Tri-County News*–P.O. Box 248, Willingboro (08046); 10,000

New York

Brooklyn: *"Big Red-Newspaper"*–40 Empire Blvd., Brooklyn (11225); 34,000

Buffalo: *Buffalo Challenger*–1303 Fillmore, Buffalo (14211); 16,000

Buffalo: *Buffalo Criterion*–625 William St., Buffalo (14211); 4,000

Buffalo: *Buffalo Fine Print News*–Box 57, Buffalo (14205); 16,000

Hastings-On-Hudson: *Westchester County Press*–61 Pinecrest Drive, Hastings-On-Hudson (10706); 7,143

Hempstead: *N.Y.-L.I. Courier*–507 Fulton Ave., Hempstead; 4,900

New York: *The Black American*–41 Union Square, New York (10003); 126,000

New York: *New York Amsterdam News*–2340 Frederick Douglass Blvd., New York (10027); 51,161

New York—Brooklyn: *New York Recorder*–P.O. Box D, N.Y. Station, New York—Brooklyn (11207); 29,000

New York—Queens: *New York Voice*–78-36 Parsons Blvd., New York—Queens (11366); 92,000

Poughkeepsie: *Mid Hudson Herald*–15 Smith St., Poughkeepsie (12602); 4,500

Rochester: *Communicade*–P.O. Box 7933 Rochester (14606); 3,000

Syracuse: *The Impartial Citizen*–P.O. Box 98, 1313 S. Saline St., Syracuse (13205); 3,000

North Carolina

Charlotte: *Charlotte Post*–1524 West Blvd., Charlotte (28208); 4,000

Durham: *Carolina Times*–923 Old Fayetteville St., Durham (27701); 12,086

Greensboro: *Peacemaker*–P.O. Box 20853, Greensboro (27420); 10,200

Raleigh: *The Carolinian*–518 E. Martin St., Raleigh (27601); 9,500

Wilmington: *Wilmington Journal*–P.O. Box 1618, 412 S. 7th St., Wilmington (28402); 8,766

Winston-Salem: *Chronicle*–516 N. Trade St., Winston-Salem (27102); 4,026

Ohio

Akron: *Reporter*–P.O. Box 2042, Akron (44309); 35,000

Bedford: *Cleveland Metro*–22801 Aurora Rd., Bedford (44116); 55,000

Cincinnati: *Cincinnati Herald*–863 Lincoln Ave., Cincinnati (45206); 4,852

Cleveland: *Call and Post*–1949 E. 105 St., Cleveland (44101); 26,670

Columbus: *Columbus Onyx*–1312 East Broad St., Columbus (43205); 35,000

Dayton: *Jetstone News*–627 Salem Ave., Dayton (45406); 24,000

Toledo: *The Toledo Journal*–1816 Bancroft, Toledo (43607)

Youngstown: *Buckeye Review*–P.O. Box 1436, 632 Belmont Ave., Youngstown (44502); 4,000

Oklahoma

Oklahoma City: *Black Chronicle*–P.O. Box 17498, Oklahoma City (73136); 3,000

Oklahoma City: *Black Dispatch*–1301 North Eastern Ave., Oklahoma City (73117); 6,500

Tulsa: *Oklahoma Eagle*–122 N. Greenwood Ave., Tulsa (74120); 32,000

Oregon

Portland: *Observer*–P.O. Box 3137, Portland (97208); 11,525

Portland: *Skanner*–P.O. Box 5455, Portland (97228); 10,000

Pennsylvania

Philadelphia: *Afro American*–427 S. Broad St., Philadelphia (19107); 842

Philadelphia: *New Observer*–1218 Chestnut St., Suite 503, Philadelphia (19107); 30,000

Philadelphia: *Philadelphia Spirit*–211 So. 53rd St., Philadelphia (19130); 10,000

Philadelphia: *Tribune*ᵇ–524–26 S. 16th St., Philadelphia (19146); 19,091

Pittsburgh: *Homewood Bruston News*–121 S. Highland Mall, Pittsburgh (15206); 11,750

Pittsburgh: *New Pittsburgh Courier*–315 E. Carson St., Pittsburgh (15230); 8,582

South Carolina

Charleston: *Charleston Chronicle*–534 King St., Charleston (29403); 6,000

Columbia: *Black News*–1310 Harden St., Columbia (29211); 24,900

Columbia: *Orangeburg Black Voice*–P.O. Box 11128, Columbia (29211); 6,000

Florence: *The Key*–P.O. Box 491, Florence (29503); 7,000

Orangeburg: *Afro Weekly*–460 Sullen N.E., Orangeburg (29115); 3,000

Tennessee

Memphis: *Mid-South Express*–1425 Elvis Presley Blvd., Memphis (38106); 35,000

Memphis: *Tri-State Defender*–124 E. Calhoun Ave., Memphis (38101); 8,707

Texas

Austin: *Capitol City Argus*–P.O. Box 2171, 1704 E. 12 St., Austin (78767); 7,500

Dallas: *Dallas Weekly*–P.O. Box 15832, Dallas (75212); 40,000

Dallas: *Freedoms' Journal*–2814 S. Beckley, Dallas (75224)

Dallas: *Great Circle News*–3101 Forest Ave., Dallas (75215)

Dallas: *Post Tribune*–2726 S. Beckley Ave., Dallas (75224); 18,587

Fort Worth: *Fort Worth Como Monitor*ᶜ–P.O. Box 885, 5529 Wellesley Ave., Fort Worth (76101); 1,000

Fort Worth: *Fort Worth Mind*–1632 D. E. Berry St., Fort Worth (76119); 12,955

Fort Worth: *Metro Cities News*–3204 E. Rosedale Ave., Fort Worth (76105); 2,050

Ft. Worth: *Times*–P.O. Box 1341, Ft. Worth (76101); 50,000

Houston: *Defender*–4406 Chartes St., Houston (77004); 8,000

Houston: *Forward Times*–4411 Alemeda Rd., Houston (77004); 116,701

Houston: *Globe-Advocate*–P.O. Box 8147, 3221 Southmore Blvd., Houston (77004); 10,000

Lubbock: *Lubbock Digest*–Lubbock (79404); 4,000

San Antonio: *San Antonio Register*–1501 E. Commerce St., San Antonio (78296); 5,640

Texarkana: *Texarkana Courier*–504 W. 3rd St., P.O. Box 6066, Texarkana

Virginia

Charlottesville: *Charlottesville-Albemarle Tribune*–1055 Grady Ave., Charlottesville (22903); 3,300

Danville: *Danville News & Observer*–P.O. Box 163, Danville (24541); 5,000

Norfolk: *Journal and Guide* (Group)–1516 Princess Ann Rd., Norfolk (23504); 84,249

Richmond: *Richmond Afro-American and Planet*–301 East Clay St., Richmond (23219); 8,223

Roanoke: *Roanoke Tribune*–P.O. Box 6021, Roanoke (24017); 1,885

Washington

Seattle: *Facts News*–2803 E. Cherry St., Seattle (98122); 20,000

Seattle: *Medium*–P.O. Box 22047, Seattle (98122); 15,000

Wisconsin

Milwaukee: *Community Journal*–3612 N. Greenbay Ave., Milwaukee (53212); 23,269

Milwaukee: *Milwaukee Courier*–2431 W. Hopkins, Milwaukee (53206); 8,900

Milwaukee: *Star*–2431 W. Hopkins St., Milwaukee (53206); 25,000

ᵃ Three times weekly.
ᵇ Twice weekly.
ᶜ Twice monthly.

A GUIDE TO BLACK PERIODICALS

Magazines

About Time

30 Genessee Street
Rochester, NY 14611
Circulation: 16,280 (monthly)

Beauty Trade

15 Columbus Circle
New York, NY 10022

Circulation: 2,680,000 (monthly)

Black Affairs

Suite 1121
National Press Building
Washington, DC 20045
(bi-weekly)

The Black Collegian

1240 Broad Street
New Orleans, LA 70125
Circulation: 254,818 (bi-monthly)

Black Enterprise

Earl G. Graves Publishing Co.
295 Madison Avenue

New York, NY 10027
Circulation: 230,000 (monthly)

Black Family

332 North Michigan Avenue
Chicago, IL 60601
Circulation:

Black News

10 Claver Place
Brooklyn, NY 11238
(monthly)

Black Odyssey

J.F.F. Communications
114 E. 28 Street
New York, NY 11434
(monthly, travel and leisure magazine)

Black Stars

Johnson Publishing Co.
820 S. Michigan Avenue
Chicago, IL 60605
Circulation: 200,000 (monthly;
lifestyles of Blacks who have achieved
success, especially in the
entertainment industry)

Blac-Tress

Harris Publications
79 Madison Avenue
New York, NY 10016
Circulation: 150,000 (six times a
year; beauty and hair fashions)

Disco That

250 West 57th Street, Suite 224
New York, NY 10019

Dollar and Sense

840 E. 87 Street, Suite 202
Chicago, IL 60619
Circulation: 91,476 (six times a year;
Business magazine)

Eagle & Swan

Port Royal Communications Network
155 E. 55 Street
New York, NY 10022
Circulation: 110,000 (six times a
year; special interest for military
service personnel)

Ebony

Johnson Publishing Co.
820 S. Michigan Avenue
Chicago, IL 60605
Circulation: 1,250,000 (monthly;
general interest picture article format)

Encore

Tanner Publications
155 E. 55 Street
New York, NY 10022
Circulation: 170,000 (monthly)

Equal Opportunity

Equal Opportunity Publications, Inc.
Box 202
Centerport, NY 11721
Circulation: 15,000 (three times a
year; minority student magazine)

Essence

1550 Broadway
New York, NY 10036
Circulation: 650,000 (monthly;
women's magazine)

First World

1580 Avon Avenue, S.W.
Atlanta, GA 30311
Circulation: 20,000 (quarterly)

Freedomways

799 Broadway
New York, NY 10003
Circulation: 10,000 (quarterly;
review of the Freedom Movement)

Great Black Group
   Bronze Thrills
   Jive
   Help
   Soul
   Soul Confessions

Sepia Publishing Corporation
1220 Harding Street
Fort Worth, TX 76102
Circulation: 150,000 (monthly; true
romance and confessional magazines)

Jet

Johnson Publishing Company
820 S. Michigan Avenue

Chicago, IL 60605
Circulation: 700,000 (weekly; digest
size national news magazine)

Journal of Black Studies

Sage Publications
275 S. Beverly Drive
Beverly Hills, CA 90212
Circulation: (quarterly)

Negro Traveler and Conventioneer

11717 S. Vincennes
Chicago, IL 60643
Circulation: 72,000 (bi-monthly;
guide to travel)

Players

8060 Melrose Avenue
Los Angeles, CA 90046
Circulation: 200,000 (monthly;
black men's magazine)

Sepia

1220 Harding Boulevard
Fort Worth, TX 76102
Circulation: 50,000 (monthly;
topical and contemporary, oriented to
young black families)

Soul

6331 Hollywood Boulevard
Los Angeles, CA 90028
Circulation: 225,000 (bi-weekly;
entertainment coverage for young
blacks)

Soul Teen

Sepia Publishing Corporation
1220 Harding Street
Fort Worth, TX 76102
Circulation: 50,000 (monthly;
features and photos on black
entertainment personalities)

Uptown (*The Voice of Central Harlem*)

Minisink Town House
646 Lenox Avenue
New York, NY 10037
(monthly)

Association, Professional, and Collegiate Publications

Afro-American Journal

Martin Center
3561 N. College Avenue
Indianapolis, IN 46205
(quarterly)

Afro-Americans in New York Life and History

Afro-American Historical Association
of the Niagara Frontier
Box 1663
Hertel Station

Buffalo, NY 14216
(semiannually)

Atlanta University Bulletin

Office of Public Relations
Atlanta University
Atlanta, GA 30314
Circulation: 8,500 (semi-annually)

Black American Literature Forum

Indiana State University School of Education
Terre Haute, IN 47809
Circulation: (quarterly)

Black Law Journal

University of California at Los Angeles School of Law
Los Angeles, CA 90024
Circulation: 5,000 (three times a year)

Black Male/Female Relationships

Black Think Tank
1801 Bush Street
San Francisco, CA 94109
Circulation: 10,000 (quarterly)

Black News Digest

Department of Labor
Office of Information
200 Constitution Avenue, N.W.
Washington, DC 20210
Circulation: 2,000 (weekly)

Black Perspective in Music

Foundation for Research in the Afro-American Creative Arts, Inc.
Drawer I
Cambria Heights, NY 11411
Circulation: 1,000 (semi-annually)

Black Scholar (Journal of Black Studies and Research)

Black World Foundation
Box 908
Sausalito, CA 94965
Circulation: 25,000 (six times a year)

Black Writers News

4019 S. Vincennes Avenue
Chicago, IL 60653
Circulation: 5,000 (quarterly)

Campus Digest

Tuskegee Institute
Bulletin Publishing Co.
Auburn, AL 36830
Circulation: 4,000 (weekly)

Core

Congress of Racial Equality Magazine
1916–38 Park Avenue
New York, NY 10037

Crisis

National Association for the Advancement of Colored People
1790 Broadway
New York, NY 10019
Circulation: 119,000 (monthly)

Culture—A Journal of Black Consciousness

Institute of Positive Education
7524 S. Cottage Grove Avenue
Chicago, IL 60619
Circulation: 12,500 (quarterly; formerly *Black Books Bulletin*)

Everybody

Ruffin Publications
2514 N. 24 Street
Omaha, NE 68111
Circulation: 94,198 (monthly)

Gold Torch

Central State University
Wilberforce, OH 45384
Circulation: 2,400 (weekly)

Hampton Script

Hampton Institute
Hampton, VA 23368
Circulation: 2,800–3,000 (semiannually)

Ivy Leaf

Alpha Kappa Alpha Sorority
5211 S. Greenwood Avenue
Chicago, IL 60615
(quarterly)

Journal of the National Medical Association

292 Madison Avenue
New York, NY 10017
Circulation: 24,000 (monthly)

Journal of National Black Associations

Charles Williams-Kerr Enterprises, Inc.
Box 2063
Hyattsville, MD 20784
(quarterly)

Journal of Negro Education

Howard University, Bureau of Educational Research
2400 Sixth Avenue N.W.
Washington, DC 20059
Circulation: 3,000 (quarterly)

Journal of Negro History

Association for the Study of Afro-American Life and History
1407 14th Street N.W.
Washington, DC 20005
Circulation: 6,500 (quarterly)

Maroon Tiger

Morehouse College
Atlanta, GA 30314
Circulation: 2,000 (every three weeks)

Morehouse College Bulletin; The Alumnus

Morehouse College
Public Relations and Alumni Affairs
Atlanta, GA 30314
Circulation: 6,500 (quarterly)

Negro History Bulletin

Association for the Study of Afro-American Life and History
1407 14th Street N.W.
Washington, DC 20005
Circulation: 22,000 (bi-monthly)

Southern Digest

Southern University
Baton Rouge, LA 70813
Circulation: 10,000 (weekly)

Urban League Review

(National Urban League Research Department)
Transaction Periodicals Consortium
Rutgers University
New Brunswick, NJ 08903
(semiannually)

Religious Publications

AME Church Review

African Methodist Episcopal Church
468 Lincoln Drive N.W.
Atlanta, GA 30318
Circulation: 4,500 (quarterly)

American Baptist

American Baptist Churches in the U.S.A.
Valley Forge, PA 19481
Circulation: 122,000 (monthly)

Baptist Leader

Baptist Churches in the U.S.A.
Baptist Board of Educational Ministries
Valley Forge, PA 19481
Circulation: 17,000 (monthly)

Journal of Religious Thought

Howard University Divinity School
2900 Van Ness Street N.W.
Washington, DC 20008
Circulation: 400 (semiannually)

Message

Southern Publishing Association
1900 Elm Hill Pike

Nashville, TN 37202
Circulation: 75,000–125,000 (bimonthly)

Star of Zion

African Methodist Episcopal Zion
Church
P.O. Box 31005
Charlotte, NC 20202
Circulation: 6,200 (weekly)

Voice of Mission

African Methodist Episcopal Church
(New York)
475 Riverside Drive
New York, NY 10027
Circulation: 3,500 (monthly)

TELEVISION

The 1970s

The mid-1970s saw a mixed picture of black progress in television. Black performers and programs of interest to blacks were slowly increasing, but there were no black-owned conventional television stations in the United States. A black-led group in Detroit did hold a license and expected to start a station soon (WGPR), and Howard University was expected to launch a station in 1976. One cable-operating station in Gary, Indiana was black-owned.

Outside the continental United States, WSVI-TV in Christiansted, Virgin Islands, was owned by blacks.

The importance of black ownership was underscored by the paucity of black programming by the major networks. No network had, in 1975, a program concerned with the needs or history of the black community; such undertakings were restricted to special one-time efforts, like *The Autobiography of Miss Jane Pittman* (1974), a CBS venture which was nominated for nine Emmy Awards and won two.

Major network news programs also omitted blacks, especially programs of the question and answer type where reporters interview political leaders. Black journalists rarely appeared on CBS's *Face the Nation* or ABC's *Issues and Answers.*

Blacks were, however, given greater exposure as performers, in such light entertainment programs as *Good Times* and the *Flip Wilson Show,* and they did appear more frequently in local news programming. The 1974 season brought about a new comedy series, *That's My Mama,* starring Clifton Davis and Theresa Merritt, while *Sanford and Son* continued. In the adventure realm, former *Laugh-In* star Theresa Graves became the title character in a woman detective series entitled *Get Christie Love.*

Following the success of *Jane Pittman,* plays by Alice Childress and Lonnie Elder III—namely *Wedding Band* and *Ceremonies in Dark Old Men*—were brought to the home screen.

In New York, WABC had been successful with the cultural affairs program *Like It Is* since 1967. A loss to blacks in the New York area was the decision by CBS, Channel 2, to drop *Black Arts,* a weekly 30-minute program devoted to the cultural and intellectual contributions of black Americans.

A strong record for black broadcasters and performers had been turned in by station WAGA, Atlanta.

The 1980s

By the 1980s, television had become a dominant force in the lifestyle of most Americans, including blacks. No longer a luxury but a fixture in most households, it played for an average of nearly seven hours a day and generated a profound effect on those viewers who sought it for entertainment and information. As years passed, new records were being set as estimated audiences exceeded 100 million on popular entertainment and sports broadcasts.

For all of its inherent influence, there was perhaps no single industry more sensitive to the concerns of its huge, multifaceted constituency.

Though some groups and individuals had voiced anger over portrayals by black actors and actresses in such series as *Amos 'n' Andy, Beulah,* and *The Jack Benny Show,* it wasn't until the 1970s that a concerted effort evolved from several quarters. With the realization that the resolve of advocacy from the outside was not always sufficient to make an impression, blacks working within the industry began to work toward the goal of building a more representative minority presence in what went out over the airwaves as well as in the creative, technical, and management work force.

In addition, Benjamin Hooks and Tyrone Brown were able to add their voices to the minority cause as members of the Federal Communications Commission, the government body assigned to regulate the broadcast industry and insure that each broadcasting organization only receives a license as long as it continues to meet the needs of its viewing audience.

Commercial television touched the sensibilities of viewers through a combination of news presentations, entertainment programming, and the incessant commercials that keep the industry alive. With hour after hour spent by adults and impressionable children day after day, many observers began to develop an increased awareness of the impact the medium was having on its viewers.

The first object of attention, of course, was the programming on the air. Of all the shows on the air starring or featuring blacks in prominent roles, situation comedies consistently proved to be the most popular with viewing audiences. Not every program proved successful, but series like *Sanford and Son,* often ranked as the top show of the week, and *The Jeffersons,* also a regular among the top 10 shows, were excellent examples.

As these series came and went, however, there was one major miniseries that captivated 130 million viewers for a solid week and certainly became the media story involving black television for the decade. The program was called *Roots* and for eight consecutive nights, in early 1977, it captured the interest of American viewers like few programs ever aired prior to that time. The dramatization of Alex Haley's best-selling book tracing his ancestry back to Africa, the program was praised for more than its entertainment value. Following its presentation, National Urban League director Vernon Jordan described *Roots* as "the single most spectacular educational experience in race relations in America."

The *Roots* experience certainly had a profound impact on the television industry as well as the American public. It was not only a symbol of pride but of hope that the drama's success might signal a shift in programming depicting the many aspects of the black experience in America. It was not long before most observers were disappointed.

When NBC-TV broadcast a powerful dramatization of the life of Dr. Martin Luther King, Jr. a few months later (with the full cooperation of Coretta King), the program was roundly criticized by black leaders and failed to attract a substantial audience. Following a new trend of presenting programs about factual individuals, the networks presented television films about people like Harriet Tubman (*A Woman Called Moses*), Olympic gold medalist Wilma Rudolph (*Wilma*), and baseball great Satchel Paige (*Don't Look Back*). During this period there was also a dramatization of a sensational Deep South rape trial (*Judge Horton and the Scottsboro Boys*), and Cicely Tyson starred in *The Marva Collins Story.*

Alex Haley wrote a sequel to *Roots,* which picked up the story and traced his family tree into the twentieth century. While not as spectacularly successful as the initial presentation, it did attract a large audience. During this time, some of America's most prominent black stage-trained actors moved to Hollywood. When series like *Paris* with James Earl Jones and *The Lazarus Syndrome* starring Lou Gossett failed, however, there

A scene from NBC's powerful dramatization of the life of Martin Luther King, Jr., with Paul Winfield and Cicely Tyson.

Diff'rent Strokes, *with Gary Coleman* (right) *& Todd Bridges, has been a fairly popular NBC sitcom.*

appeared to be a general rejection of blacks in serious roles.

From time to time, there were dramas written by blacks that garnered critical acclaim, if not substantial ratings success. Melvin Van Peebles wrote *The Sophisticated Gents* while Maya Angelou adapted her book, *I Know Why a Caged Bird Sings* and wrote *Sister, Sister.*

All the while, the new comedy series blossomed. *Sanford* was brought back for a brief unsuccessful run while new shows proliferated. Among the titles were *Good Times, One in a Million, What's Happening, That's My Mama, Baby, I'm Back, Benson, Diff'rent Strokes,* and *Gimme a Break.*

While there was concern about many of the previously mentioned programs, nothing rallied the black community to action like *Beulah Land,* an NBC miniseries about the Deep South during the antebellum period. Basically the story of a strong-willed woman who persevered through hardships before, during, and after the Civil War, the program ran into protests about its characterization of black slaves even as it was being filmed. As the highly publicized outcry grew, the network held meetings with concerned blacks and the program was postponed from the initial telecast time. It eventually did air (with moderate ratings success),

but the episode marked an important time for blacks who had banded together and strongly expressed their discontent, bringing about some changes in the roles portrayed by black actors and actresses.

One of the issues raised during the *Beulah Land* controversy was that attacking television programming would have the ultimate effect of forcing black talent out of work when the protests succeeded. This was a sensitive issue since most black actors and actresses were out of work at any given time. Among many of television's most successful series, blacks were able to work in roles that did not emphasize their race. Ron Glass portrayed a detective in *Barney Miller,* Ted Lange an amiable bartender in *Love Boat,* and Madge Sinclair a nurse in *Trapper John, M.D.*

Yet there was a prevailing feeling that blacks were underrepresented in prime-time television. Daytime dramas, also known as soap operas, grew in audience interest—expanding from its traditional base of women at home to college students, professionals, and others. Here again, there were times when some of the 14 or so programs had no blacks in the casts at all.

Even though there were popular series like *Fat Albert* (inspired by the Bill Cosby characters) and *The Jackson Five* (based on the teen rock group) on Saturday morning children's television schedules, these ani-

Bryant Gumble, anchorman of NBC's Today Show.

mated series were the symbol of hope for more programming in this part of the weekly network schedules.

While the battle for more input continued in the entertainment realm, news grew to become more and more important on the networks as well. As surveys continued to indicate that more and more Americans were getting most of their awareness of world events from television, there were increased efforts to seek more black participation in news gathering and reporting.

On the network level, Max Robinson became the first black to become a regular co-anchor for an evening news program when he joined ABC-TV's *World News Tonight.* Bryant Gumble, a versatile sportscaster, also made news in early 1982 when he became the first black co-host for NBC's *Today* show. Irv Crosse, a former athlete, became a regular CBS sportscaster, providing expert commentary during the professional football season.

There are over 1,000 television stations in the United States—some affiliated with the networks, others independent, and still others part of the educational television operation. At the beginning of the 1980s, only eight of those stations were owned by blacks. With the concerns addressed by black owners, it is felt that impact will be made in the local market and felt even at a national level.

Public Television

The hopes of many blacks for programming rested in programs like those produced on the local level. Tony Brown, former Dean of the Howard University School of Communications, continued to produce *The*

Tony Brown Journal. The oldest and only black public affairs program in the country, it remained a victim

The charming Xernona Clayton hosts a weekly talk show on Ted Turner's Atlanta Station.

KNXT-TV, Los Angeles' Insider Outsider *discusses vital civic issues each Sunday.*

to erratic scheduling in many cities. *For You Black Woman,* another syndicated program aimed at black women, suffered a similar fate. With all that the networks might do, the hope of many was that a valuable alternative would be more of those black-produced programs to add a balance to the images that had become a way of life for so many black Americans.

Cable Television

The most significant development in broadcasting and the one deemed to have the most impact on television in the future was the advent of cable or pay television. Conceived as an alternative to network television, the systems seemed initially geared to viewers with specialized tastes. Most prominent among the programming were movies, shown without commercials and material edited out by the networks when deemed objectionable.

Soon there was a network broadcasting sports 24 hours a day and another bringing news around the clock. As more systems began and diversified their programming, cable began to grow at an increasing pace. Soon, there was a discernible decline in network viewing.

Without question, cable would be a major, if not predominant, medium of the 1980s and beyond. There had been hope that blacks would be able to capitalize on the growing medium and become owners of cable systems since many of the early franchises were in large cities with significant black populations. When it became obvious that this was a lucrative market to be tapped, many large corporations seeking to diversify joined in competing for the chance to operate a system.

Still, some black-owned companies like Inner City Broadcasting in New York City have successfully bid for systems. It is hoped that Black Entertainment Television, a network that will distribute black programming to systems around the country, will be able to survive in this increasingly competitive marketplace. For all involved, the biggest obstacle will be funding,

Charlayne Hunter-Gault makes frequent appearances on the McNeil-Lehrer report for PBS-TV.

The
Ossie
Davis
& Ruby Dee
Story Hour

Black-oriented radio programming gains impetus on the new National Black Network.

not only to buy the systems but to construct them and then operate them.

RADIO

With a faithful and loyal audience, radio stations with programming geared for blacks appeared to be a prominent part of a thriving industry. In the mid-1970s, some 30 of those 100 stations were owned by blacks. By 1981, the total of black-owned radio stations had increased fourfold to 130. At that time, there were more than 9,000 stations (AM, FM, and FM educational) in the United States.

Proportionally, blacks were found to be a more frequent and responsive audience than whites. As a result, astute advertisers were able to tap into a lucrative marketplace, often at the expense of traditional avenues including black newspapers and magazines. Many major corporations were among those sought to reach the ever expanding black buying power traced back to the black community. By buying time on stations with proven popularity among blacks, they received just those returns they were seeking.

With soul and jazz music broadening its appeal into the white market, a new success in building audiences was noted. One of the more spectacular examples of the phenomenon occurred with WBLS-FM in New

York. Owned by Inner City Broadcasting, it became the top station in New York for an extended period of time.

With proper management, radio stations proved to be a worthy investment. Owners of individual stations were able to buy into new markets and use their expertise to build viable broadcast corporations. As black publishers diversified, John Johnson (*Ebony* and *Jet*), Inner City Broadcasting (associated with New York's *Amsterdam News*), and Earl Graves (*Black Enterprise*) became successful station owners.

As many of the stations grew from their limited local status, there was a parallel movement to cooperate in broadcasting efforts. The National Black Network was an important example of an effort to broaden the scope of local newscasts with national reporting with a black perspective.

Clearly, the most successful enterprise involving blacks in all of the media, radio—despite obstacles that remain until today—will establish a pattern proving that responsible black ownership and programming can meet the needs of a diversified audience and lead to a medium that entertains and informs just the way it was conceived to do.

RADIO AND TELEVISION PERSONAGES

DENISE BAKER
NBC News Correspondent

NBC News Correspondent Denise Baker joined the Northeast Bureau of NBC News in January 1981. Based in New York, Baker covers stories throughout the Northeast.

She joined NBC News in July 1979 as a correspondent in Pittsburgh and, until her move to New York, covered stories in the Pittsburgh area, western Pennsylvania, southwestern New York, West Virginia, Ohio, and Kentucky.

Before joining NBC News she was a correspondent for WETA-TV, the PBS station in Washington, D.C. (from April 1978) and covered local and national affairs. Among her assignments was anchoring the WETA special program *Who Killed King?*, telecast nationally on the PBS Network. For her work in public affairs she was nominated for two Emmy Awards.

She began her broadcasting career in September 1974, at WGN Radio in Chicago, where she produced the station's late-night talk program, "Extension 720," during which listeners phoned in their opinions on a variety of topics.

Baker was born in Chicago. She was graduated from Yale University with a B.A. degree in English and received her masters degree from the Medill School of Journalism at Northwestern University.

J. Tabor Bolden, Jr. is an executive with NBC-TV.

J. TABER BOLDEN, JR.
Vice President, Station Affairs
NBC-TV

After serving three years as Station Manager of WRC-TV, the NBC television station in Washington, D.C., J. Taber Bolden, Jr. was named to the newly created position of Vice President, Station Affairs, NBC Televi-

sion Stations. The appointment was effective in December 1976.

Before joining WRC-TV, Bolden had been Director, Personnel of NBC Washington. He came to the network after working for RCA for 12 years. He began his career at NBC as an administrator of training in January 1968 and was later promoted to Director, Management Development, a position he held until his move to Washington.

Bolden started with RCA as a Training Specialist in the Engineering Personnel area in Camden, New Jersey, in 1955. In 1961 he moved to the RCA Aerospace Systems Division and held other positions until his move to NBC.

A native of Cleveland, Bolden received a B.A. degree in psychology from Boston University and a masters degree in education. He also did postgraduate study in behavioral science at Temple University.

ANNA MONIQUE BOND
NBC News

Anna Monique Bond began her WABC-TV New York career in November 1970 as an administrative assistant to the Director of Local News and Public Affairs.

Prior to her appointment as a reporter in August 1973, Bond was a WABC-TV newswriter for the station's news program telecast during the early morning *A.M. New York* series. She also served as a part-time producer of weekend news programs, as a remote and field producer for various local news stories and fea-

Television news reporter Anna Bond covers an outdoor concert at Lincoln Center in New York City.

tures, and prepared news copy and edited film for presentation on the 6 and 11 o'clock editions of *Eyewitness News.*

Bond has also been a news researcher and assistant to the station's Vice President and General Manager and administrative assistant to the News and Public Affairs Director.

Bond joined NBC-TV in New York in 1982 and now co-anchors the local weekend news programs.

ED BRADLEY
Co-Editor, *60 Minutes*
CBS-TV

Ed Bradley replaced Dan Rather as a co-editor of *60 Minutes,* the weekly news magazine at the beginning of the 1981–1982 season. Prior to that, he had been a principal correspondent for *CBS Reports* since September 1978. From November 1976 until that time, he had served as CBS News White House Correspondent. In addition to *CBS Reports,* Bradley had been anchor of the CBS *Sunday Night News* from November 1976 to May 1981. Bradley's new duties included being co-anchor of CBS News daytime broadcast, *Up to the Minute.*

After working as a reporter for WDAS Radio in

Ed Bradley, TV news journalist and co-editor of 60 Minutes.

Philadelphia, Bradley was a reporter for WCBS Radio in New York. He joined CBS News as a stringer in the Paris Bureau in 1971. In a few months, he was transferred to the Saigon Bureau, where he remained until he was assigned to the CBS News Washington Bureau in June 1974. He had been named a correspondent in April 1973.

His documentary assignments include *What's Happened to Cambodia?*, *CBS Reports: The Boat People, The Boston Goes to China,* and *Blacks in America: With All Deliberate Speed?* His other assignments include reports broadcast on "CBS Evening News with Walter Cronkite," "CBS News Sunday Morning," and "CBS News Magazine."

A native of Pennsylvania, Bradley received a B.S. degree in education from Cheyney State College in Cheyney, Pennsylvania.

JAROBIN GILBERT, JR.
Vice President, NBC-TV

Jarobin Gilbert, Jr. was named to the newly created position of Vice President, NBC Television Network in February 1981. Previously, he was Vice President, Olympic Administration, and Director, Olympic Administration, NBC Sports. He had joined the company in November 1977 and was responsible for the coordination of planning for the network's 1980 Olympic coverage (ultimately canceled when President Carter called a boycott of the Moscow games).

Prior to joining NBC, Gilbert was associated with the US–USSR Trade and Economic Council in Moscow as a Director of Projects. He worked with the State Department/U.S. Information Agency before joining the US–USSR Council. An internationalist by training, he reads, writes, and speaks several languages including Russian, French, and German.

Gilbert is a graduate of Harvard University, where he emphasized linguistics and Slavic languages. He also studied international law and Soviet law at Columbia University.

MAL GOODE
ABC News Correspondent

Mal Goode had been with the *Pittsburgh Courier* 14 years when in 1962 he joined ABC to cover the United Nations. His first test was the Cuban missile crisis, just two months later, during which Goode distinguished himself with incisive TV and radio reports during the long hours of U.N. debate.

Goode was born in White Plains, Virginia; educated in the public schools of Homestead, Pennsylvania, and graduated from the University of Pittsburgh. He was employed for 12 years as a laborer in the steel mills while in high school and college and for five years

Mal Goode reports from the United Nations.

after graduation. In 1936 he was appointed to a post in Juvenile Court and became Boys Work Director of the Centre Avenue Y.M.C.A., where he led the fight to eliminate discrimination in Pittsburgh branches of the Y.

Goode served with the Pittsburgh Housing Authority for six years and in 1948 joined the *Pittsburgh Courier.* The following year he started a career in radio with station KQV, doing a 15-minute news show two nights each week. In 1950 he started a five minute daily news program on WHOD.

Goode was named News Director of WHOD in 1952. He and his sister, the late Mary Dee, had the only brother-sister team in radio for six years. He was the first black to hold membership in the National Association of Radio and TV News Directors.

For two months in 1963 he joined with three colleagues to conduct courses in journalism for 104 African students in seminars at Lagos, Nigeria; Addis Adaba, Ethiopia; and Dar es Salaam, Tanzania.

GORDON GRAHAM
NBC News Correspondent

Gordon Graham has been an NBC News correspondent in Washington, D.C., since January 1971, covering the House of Representatives and general assignments.

Between 1968 and 1971 he was a news reporter

for two years for KNBC Television, Los Angeles. Prior to joining KNBC he was a reporter and writer for KRON, San Francisco.

Graham was born in Coshocton, Ohio, in 1936. He majored in broadcasting at Ohio University and was graduated with a B.F.A. degree in 1958. His first news job from 1962 to 1965 was with KGFJ, a Los Angeles radio station, first as a reporter, subsequently as a News Director.

BRYANT GUMBLE
Co-Anchor, *Today*
NBC-TV

Bryant Gumble was named co-anchor (with Jane Pauley) of *Today* in January 1981—the first black in such a regular position on the long-running NBC News morning program.

Prior to that time, Gumble had made regular sports reports on *Today,* although his primary responsibilities were with NBC Sports as host of pregame programming during coverage of the National Football League, Major League Baseball, and other sports broadcasts.

He began his broadcasting career in October 1972 when he was named a weekend sportscaster for KNBC, the NBC station in Los Angeles. Within a year, he

Today anchorman Bryant Gumble.

became weekday sportscaster and was appointed the station's Sports Director in 1976. He remained in that post until July 1980.

Prior to embarking on his career in television, Gumble was a sports writer. After submitting his first piece to *Black Sports* magazine in 1971, he was given additional free-lance assignments and was soon hired as a staff writer. Within eight months he was elevated to Editor-in-Chief.

A native of New Orleans, Gumble grew up in Chicago. He received a liberal arts degree from Bates College in Lewiston, Maine in 1970.

EUGENE D. JACKSON
Broadcast Executive

Eugene D. Jackson is president of Unity Broadcasting Network in New York City, parent company of the National Black Network, and of four radio stations of which Jackson is also president—WDAS-AM and FM in Philadelphia and KATZ-AM and WZEN-FM in St. Louis.

Jackson was born in Wauhomis, Oklahoma on September 5, 1943. He received a B.S. degree from the University of Missouri at Rolla in 1967 and an M.S. from Columbia University in 1971.

Jackson serves on the boards of directors of the National Association of Broadcasters, the Council of Concerned Black Executives Freedom National Bank, and Trans Africa (1977). He was a member of the Council on Foreign Relations in 1978 and on the board of governors of the International Radio and TV Society from 1974 to 1976.

From 1969 to 1971 he directed major industry programs for the Interracial Council for Business Opportunity in New York City. He was a production and project engineer for the Black Economic Union in New York City from 1968 to 1969 and an industrial engineer for Colgate-Palmolive from 1967 to 1968.

CAROL JENKINS
NBC News

Carol Jenkins has learned the value of a broad knowledge during her experience as a network correspondent for ABC News, as a reporter and anchorwoman for WOR-TV, and since February, 1973, with WNBC-TV, where she was a general assignment reporter, and anchored the 1 A.M. news.

With WNBC-TV, Jenkins has also covered returning POWs and interviewed New York City Mayors Lindsay and Beame, Governors Rockefeller and Wilson, and Senators Javits and Buckley.

Jenkins was born in Montgomery Alabama, in 1944 and moved with her family to Jamaica, New York,

Carol Jenkins reports the news on NBC.

when she was three. She attended Boston University where she received a B.A. She also has a M.A. from New York University.

Honors as a broadcaster include the Harlem Preparatory School Service Award (1971), Ophelia DeVore School, Outstanding Achievement Award (1972), and Alabama State University Alumni Association Outstanding Achievement Award (1972).

JOHN JOHNSON
ABC News

WABC-TV *Eyewitness News* reporter John Johnson was born in Harlem and grew up in the Bedford-Stuyvesant section of Brooklyn, New York. Johnson received his masters degree with honors from the City University of New York. After six years with the New York Board of Education as a teacher, dean of students, and assistant principal, he became Associate Professor of Fine Arts at Lincoln University. From Lincoln, Johnson won a fellowship to Indiana University to complete his Ph.D. in the Arts.

From 1968 to 1971 Johnson was with ABC network documentaries, during which time he rose from an associate producer to producer/director/writer. Included among his documentaries was the widely acclaimed *To All the World's Children,* narrated by Rod Steiger, for which Johnson won a Christopher Award for his directing.

TV newsman John Johnson has won acclaim as a producer, writer, and director of network documentaries.

Johnson has also won acclaim as writer/narrator for the Emmy Award-winning *People, Places and Things* program dealing with natural childbirth.

ROYAL KENNEDY
ABC News Chicago Correspondent

Royal Kennedy was named an ABC News Chicago Correspondent in April 1978. Kennedy had been a reporter for WMAQ-TV since June 1975. She was a general assignment reporter, anchored a consumer segment of the station's *Beat the System* series, and anchored local newscasts during the *Today* show telecasts on WMAQ.

She began her news career as a copy editor and researcher for *Playboy* magazine in Chicago in June 1969, and then joined WDSU-TV, New Orleans, in September 1971. She was a general assignment reporter and anchored local newscasts during the *Today* show.

Kennedy moved on to WKYC-TV, the NBC-owned station in Cleveland, in April 1973, to become a general assignment reporter, host of a weekly public affairs program, and anchorperson for *Today* show local newscasts.

The recipient of numerous awards and honors, Kennedy won a Cleveland Emmy for "outstanding individual achievement" as a producer-reporter of a five-part series on rape. The rape series also earned her a citation for "excellence in reporting a legal issue" from the American Association of Trial Lawyers. She has also received a San Francisco State Journalism Award for

a five-part series on abortion, which she produced and reported.

Kennedy majored in history at Ohio University. She attended Dartmouth College and studied journalism at Columbia University.

EMERY KING
NBC News Correspondent

As of April 1980, Emery King became an NBC News correspondent, based in Washington, D.C., on general assignment. Prior to joining NBC News, King had been a reporter covering politics and the Illinois State House for WBBM-TV, Chicago, since 1977. From 1973 until 1977, he was a reporter/anchor with WBBM NewsRadio in that city.

Between 1972 and 1973 King was with radio station WWCA in Gary, Indiana, as a reporter, and during the period from 1970 to 1972 he held the same post with radio station WJOB in Hammond, Indiana. From 1967 until 1971, he attended Purdue University studying speech and drama.

LEON LEWIS
Radio Commentator

The Peabody Award citation received by Harlem radio station WLIB in 1966 was a milestone in the career of dialogue jockey Leon Lewis, now Ombudsman for WMCA's *Call for Action*. The WLIB show hosted by Lewis consisted of any early evening talk marathon

Leon Lewis opened the radio microphones to the Harlem community.

(*Community Opinion*) in which ghetto residents could voice their grievances, air their feelings, and, perhaps more importantly, take advantage of underpublicized community services available to deal with specific problems.

Lewis frequently cultivated relationships with local legal, educational, and political experts who volunteered free advisory and consulting services. To their surprise and dismay, they often found themselves squirming nervously under a constant barrage of pointed questions. Lewis generally stayed out of the fray, except for an occasional quiet and philosophical

remark that brought the confrontations to a satisfying close.

Still, by abating many tensions, WLIB, in the words of the Peabody citation, "gave Harlem a safety valve. It developed *Community Opinion*, a radio program permitting citizens of Harlem to voice their feelings, frankly and openly, via a hot line telephone interview, heard not only by the Negro community, but by the entire city.

"In addition, the station provided details of how listeners could avail themselves of existing vital community service. At WLIB community involvement is more than just a station phrase." In recognition, WLIB received a Peabody Award for outstanding local radio education during 1966.

Veteran newsman Lewis, born in Troy, New York in 1917, has worked in a variety of radio and journalism jobs, including that of sales manager for an Albany station and circulation manager for the *Amsterdam News.* Glib and resourceful, he was not able to break into New York radio at first, but he found a ready career on the ethnic air waves.

After his success at WLIB, however, opportunity beckoned, and Lewis joined WMCA as Assistant Public Affairs Director in 1967. Over the years, several of his documentaries won prestigious journalism awards and even led to a teaching career at Fordham University.

Nothing seems to satisfy Lewis better than his early morning rendezvous with the unpredictable and fascinating potpourri of characters who vie for attention on his show, constantly seeking to either put him on the defensive or joke about his own idiosyncrasies.

For Lewis, though, there has always been a discernible mission to be accomplished at his secluded outpost. While at WLIB, he once found succinct words to sum it up: "The walls of the ghetto are so high," he said, "that people can't see in and they can't see out. I'd like to see those walls come tumbling down."

ROBERT W. MATTHEWS
NBC Radio News Manager

Robert W. Matthews, Manager, NBC Radio News, in Washington, D.C. supervises and coordinates the gathering of news stories for local and national presentation.

Prior to joining NBC News as Duty Manager in January 1969, Matthews was a reporter/assignment editor for CBS-TV News in New York. He began his career in television in 1964 as a reporter and weekend anchorman for WBAL-TV News, Baltimore. He later became News Manager, the first black newsman in the country to assume that post at a major TV station.

Matthews got his start in journalism in 1948 with

the Afro-American Newspaper chain in Baltimore. His 15 years in various news posts with that organization culminated in his assignment as editor of the magazine section.

Before joining WEBB Radio in Baltimore in 1963 as news director, he worked for the Annapolis *Evening Capitol* and Baltimore *News-American* newspapers.

A native of Detroit, Matthews attended Lane College in Jackson, Tennessee, and Wayne State University in Detroit.

GIL NOBLE
ABC News

Channel 7's *Eyewitness News* late-night weekend anchorman Gil Noble has been honored with several professional awards, including an Emmy for hosting *Like It Is.*

In addition, Noble has been honored with the Golden Mike Award of the National Association of Television and Radio Artists, and the John B. Russwurm Award of the New York Urban League.

In 1975 Noble was artist in residence at Seton Hall University, Orange, New Jersey, where he teaches two courses, the first time a black journalist has appeared

and become involved in the Communications Department at Seton Hall.

In October 1971 Noble hosted the first televised program ever devoted to sickle cell anemia. The *Like It Is* special, *Attica: The Unanswered Questions,* cohosted by Noble and Geraldo Rivera, won a Tonge Shaeffer Award.

Jazz: The American Art Form, a documentary produced by Noble in October 1972, was another unprecedented step for black representation in the media.

Born and raised in Harlem, Noble taught himself to play the piano and became one of the leading pianists in New York City. He is a graduate of DeWitt Clinton High School in the Bronx and attended City College at night.

Noble spent two years in the Army Medical Corps. When back in New York, he worked as a clerk and occasionally as a male model. In 1962 he became a part-time announcer for WLIB-Radio. At this time, he also had a professional music combo, *The Gil Noble Trio,* which was playing at night clubs in New York. He auditioned for WABC-TV in 1967 and his first assignment was coverage of the Newark riots. His work there landed him the job and Noble has been reporting for Channel 7 ever since.

NORMA QUARLES
NBC News Correspondent

Norma Quarles became an NBC News correspondent based in Chicago in October 1978. She had been producing and reporting the *Urban Journal* series for *Newscenter 5* at WMAQ-TV for a year at that time.

Before joining WMAQ, Quarles was an award-winning reporter for *Newscenter 4* on WNBC-TV in New York, where she also anchored the early local news broadcasts during the *Today* show.

A native New Yorker and an alumna of Hunter College and City College of New York, Quarles worked as a buyer for a New York specialty shop before moving to Chicago where she became a licensed real estate broker. In 1965 she began her broadcast career in Chicago at WSDM Radio, working as a news reporter and disk jockey. She later returned to New York where she joined NBC in 1966 for a one-year training program. After three years with WKYC-TV in Cleveland, she was transferred to WNBC-TV where in 1973 she won a Front Page Award and a Sigma Delta Chi Deadline Club Award for her film story *The Stripper.*

STANLEY ROBERTSON
NBC Vice President

Stanley Robertson, Vice President, Motion Pictures for Television, NBC-TV joined NBC-TV in 1957 as

Gil Noble of ABC-TV has a weekly news feature, Like It Is, *as well as reporting duties.*

Norma Quarles, NBC news correspondent based in Chicago.

a page and served in the Music Library and Music Rights Department. In 1965 he was named Manager, Film Program Operations, West Coast. He was promoted to Director, Motion Pictures for Television, in March 1970, and elevated to Vice President in April 1971.

A native of Los Angeles, Robertson graduated from Los Angeles City College and then majored in telecommunications for three years at the University of Southern California. While at college he was a reporter for the Los Angeles *Sentinal* and as associate editor of *Ebony* magazine.

In 1975 Robertson was a member of the Board of Directors of the Hollywood Radio and Television Society and served on the Board of Governors, Hollywood Chapter, National Academy of Television Arts and Sciences.

MAX ROBINSON
ABC News Correspondent

Max Robinson joined ABC News in June 1978 as head of the National Desk in Chicago on *ABC News World*

News Tonight. The new program premiered in July 1978. Robinson covers major news events that occur in the heartland of the nation and anchors the evening news from the Midwest. He is the first network anchorman to broadcast regularly from a city other than New York or Washington.

Robinson came to ABC News for WTOP-TV in Washington, D.C., where he had been anchoring the station's *Eyewitness News* since 1969. He also anchored news specials and public affairs programs for that station. He received widespread praise last year for his coverage of the Hanafi Muslim siege in the nation's capital.

Robinson had been a correspondent for WRC-TV in Washington from 1966 until 1969. There he anchored the *Today in Washington Early Morning News* and covered Capitol Hill, the White House, and the District Building.

He began his career as a studio floor director at WTOP-TV in 1965, becoming a news reporter shortly thereafter. He is the recipient of three Emmy Awards, the Capital Press Club Journalist of the Year Award, and the Ohio State Award, as well as an award from the National Education Association.

An accomplished painter, he has taught communicative arts and television production at Federal City College. He attended Oberlin College and learned Russian as a language specialist in the Air Force Language Institute at Indiana University.

Robinson helped found the Association of Black Journalists, a group whose efforts are aimed at encouraging blacks in journalism.

BARBARA ROWAN
NBC News Correspondent

Barbara Rowan has been a correspondent based in the Houston bureau since she joined NBC News in January 1981. Before that, she had been a reporter/anchor for WDIV-TV, the NBC affiliate in Detroit, from August 1978. She covered the Republican National Convention in that city in 1980.

Rowan was a reporter and weekend anchor for WDTN-TV, the NBC affiliate in Dayton, Ohio in 1977–1978, and covered the school desegregation hearings and the United Mineworkers' strike, among other stories. From September 1975, to August 1977, she was a reporter, anchor, and program host for WKBW-TV, the ABC affiliate in Buffalo, New York.

She has won numerous honors for her work in broadcasting, including the Michigan Education Association's School Bell Award in 1980 for "outstanding and objective reporting" of the lengthy Armada (Michigan) teachers' strike. In 1978 she won a Distinguished Service Award in Newscasting and Communication from St. Agnes Parish in Dayton. She received a Special Services Award in 1977 from the Western New York Chapter of the National Society for Autistic Children. In 1976 she won the Black Achievement in Industry Award from the Community Action Foundation in Buffalo, and was named Outstanding Woman of the Year by the Niagara Falls Professional and Businesswoman's Association.

BERNARD SHAW
CNN News Correspondent

Bernard Shaw is currently the Washington correspondent for the Cable News Network (CNN). Previously Shaw was with ABC News as Miami Bureau Chief in 1977. He later became a correspondent for the CBS News Washington Bureau. While at CBS he broke the story that Representative Wayne Hays would resign. He also did an exclusive interview with Attorney General John Mitchell at the height of the Watergate scandal. Shaw filed a major report on marijuana for the *CBS Evening News,* following travel and research in the South and Midwest.

Shaw wrote and anchored radio newscasts and did the same on the *Washington Week* program. He was a special correspondent on the children's specials

Bernard Shaw is CNN's major Washington correspondent.

What's an Election About and *What the Oil Crisis Is About.*

Prior to joining CBS News, Shaw was a reporter for Group W, Westinghouse Broadcasting Company, based first in Chicago and then in Washington (1966–1971). Shaw served as Group W's White House Correspondent during the last year of the Johnson Administration (1968). His other assignments included local and national urban affairs, the struggles of the Mexican Americans and Puerto Ricans, and the plight of the American Indians in Billings, Montana. In 1966 he reported on the aftermath of the assassination of Dr. Martin Luther King, Jr. in Memphis and his funeral in Atlanta.

Born in Chicago, Shaw attended the University of Illinois, Chicago Circle Campus, where he majored in history.

PIERRE MONTÉ (PEPE) SUTTON
Broadcast Executive

Pierre Sutton is President of Inner City Broadcasting Corporation in New York City and President of its radio stations in New York and California. He is the son of Percy E. Sutton, chairman of the board of Inner City Broadcasting and former Borough President of Manhattan.

Pierre Sutton was born in New York City on February 1, 1947. He received a B.A. degree from the University of Toledo in 1968 and attended New York University in 1972.

He began his career in 1971 as Vice President of Inner City Research and Analysis Corporation, was Executive Editor of the *New York Courier* newspaper in 1971–1972, served as Public Affairs Director for WLIB radio from 1972 to 1975, was Vice President of Inner City Broadcasting from 1975 to 1977, and became President in 1977.

During the past decade he has served as a board member of the Minority Investment Fund, First Vice President of the National Association of Black Owned Broadcasters, Chairman of the Harlem Boy Scouts, member of the board and executive committee of the New York City Marathon, a trustee of the Alvin Ailey Dance Foundation, a board member of the Better Business Bureau of Harlem, and a member of the board of the Hayden Planetarium.

BOB TEAGUE
NBC News

Bob Teague has been an anchorman for late night news, a moderator and panelist for interview programs, and a sportscaster.

Teague was born in Milwaukee in 1929. In 1950

Bob Teague, NBC-TV special assignments reporter.

Veteran executive producer Lem Tucker.

he received a B.S. degree in journalism from the University of Wisconsin, where he starred in football.

Following his graduation, the *Milwaukee Journal* provided a wide scope for his talents: he covered sports, wrote book reviews, and served as a reporter. At the *New York Times,* starting in 1956, Teague covered a variety of sports events.

He has been honored with the Amistad Award from the American Missionary Association "for his dignity and journalistic skill."

He has written three books, *Climate of Opinion* published in 1962, *Letters To A Black Boy* in 1968, and his autobiography was published in 1982.

LEM TUCKER
CBS News Correspondent

Lem Tucker joined ABC News in January 1972, from WOR-TV in New York where he was News Director and an executive producer for special news presentation. He was assigned to ABC News' Chicago Bureau, and was later transferred to ABC News headquarters in New York.

From 1965 through July 1970, Tucker was with NBC News where he was awarded an Emmy for his reporting on hunger in the United States, a series of seven reports broadcast during 1968 and 1969.

A native of Saginaw, Michigan, Tucker is a graduate of Central Michigan University. He served briefly as an administrative assistant to the Auditor General of Michigan before entering the Army in 1960. He was discharged in 1962 with the rank of first lieutenant and worked in the public relations department of Buick Motors in Flint, Michigan, before joining NBC News.

A GUIDE TO BLACK BROADCAST MEDIA

Television

California

N. John Douglass, President
National Group Television
KSTS-TV 48
2349 Bering Drive
San Jose, CA 95131

Washington, D.C.

Ted Ledbetter, President
Channel 50
6507 Chillum Place, N.W.
Washington, DC 20012

Arnold Wallace, General Manager
WHMM-TV (PBS)
(Noncommercial)
Howard University

2600 4th Street, N.W.
Washington, DC 20059

Maine

Dr. Jasper Williams, Sr., Chairman
Seaway Comm.
WVII-TV
41 Farm Road
Bangor, ME 04401

Michigan

Dr. William V. Banks, Pres.
WGPR, Inc.
WGPR-TV
3146 East Jefferson Street
Detroit, MI 48207

Mississippi

Aaron Henry, Chairman
TV-3, Inc.

WLBT-TV
P.O. Box 1712
Jackson, MS 38205

New Jersey

Donald McMeans, President
Renaissance Broadcasting Co.
WRBV-TV
145 Tyler Drive
Willingboro, NJ 08046

New York

Ragan Henry, President
BENI
WHEC-TV
191 East Avenue
Rochester, NY 14604

Texas

Dr. Robert Lee, President
PRIMA, Inc.
KLBK-TV
7400 S. University Avenue
Lubbock, TX 79408

Dr. Robert Lee, President
PRIMA, Inc.
KTXS-TV
P.O. Box 2997
Abeline, TX 79604

Wisconsin

Dr. Jasper Williams, Sr., Chairman
Seaway Comm.
WAEO-TV
Box 858
S. Oneida Avenue
Rhinelander, WI 54501

Radio

Alabama

Bob Carl Bailey, President
Muscle Shoals Broadcasting
WZZA-AM
P.O. Box 2562
Muscle Shoals, 35560

Bob Carl Bailey, President
Muscle Shoals Broadcasting
WTQX-AM
P.O. Box 1307
Selma, 36701

George H. Clay, President
All Channel TV Service
WBIL-AM
P.O. Box 666
Tuskegee, 36083

George H. Clay, President
New World Communications
WBIL-FM
P.O. Box 666
Tuskegee, 36083

A. G. Gaston, President
Booker T. Washington Broadcasting
Co.
WENN-AM
1523 5th Avenue
Birmingham, 35203

A. G. Gaston, President
Booker T. Washington Broadcasting
Co.
WENN-FM
1523 5th Avenue
Birmingham, 35203

Viola M. Garrett, President
Garrett Broadcasting Inc.
WEUP-AM

2606 Jordan Lane
Huntsville, 35806

Arkansas

John Green, President
Quadras, Inc.
KDEW-AM
P.O. Box 326
Dewitt, 72042

John Green, President
Quadras, Inc.
KDEW-FM
P.O. Box 326
Dewitt, 72042

George Ivory, President
Southwest Communications Inc.
KYDE-AM
P.O. Box 5086
Pine Bluff, 71611

California

Willie Davis, President
All Pro Broadcasting Co.
KACE-FM
1710 East 111th Street
Los Angeles, 90059

Lloyd Edwards, President
Golden Gate Broadcasting
KMPX-FM
655 Sutter Street
San Francisco, 94102

Dr. Carlton Goodlett, President
Frontier Communications, Inc.
KLIP-AM
P.O. Box 129
Fowler, 93625

Steveland Morris, President
TAXI Productions
KJLH-FM
3847 S. Crenshaw, Boulevard
Los Angeles, 90008

John Pembroke, President
Goodwill Broadcasting Co.
KJOP-AM
15279 Hanford Armona Road
Lemoore, 93245

Ed Roper, President
KFOX Radio, Inc.
KFOX-FM
123 West Torrance Boulevard
Redondo Beach, 90277

Pierre Sutton, President
Inner City Broadcasting Corp.
KRE-AM
601 Ashby Avenue
Berkeley, 94710

Pierre Sutton, President
Inner City Broadcasting Corp.
KBLX-FM
601 Ashby Avenue
Berkeley, 94710

Pierre Sutton, President
Inner City Broadcasting Corp.
KGFJ-AM
5900 Wilshire Boulevard
Suite 33
Los Angeles, 90036

Pierre Sutton, President
Inner City Broadcasting Corp.
KUTE-FM
5900 Wilshire Boulevard
Suite 33
Los Angeles, 90036

Ed Wright, President
Wright Communications Corp.
KNAC-FM
320 Pine Avenue, Suite 1100
Long Beach, 90802

Connecticut

John Catlett, General Manager
Hartcom, Inc.
WKND-AM
P.O. Box 1480
Windsor, 06095

Frank Jacobs, President
Delta Communications Corp.
WNOU-FM
P.O. Box 98
Willimatic, 06226

Harold Lawson, President
Lawson Broadcasting Co.
WNAB-AM
Broadcast Center
Bridgeport, 06608

District of Columbia

James Queen
District Group Communications
WUST-AM
815 V Street, N.W.
Washington, 20001

Dewey Hughes, President
Almic Broadcasting Co.
WOL-AM
680 Wisconsin Avenue, N.W.
Washington, 20007

Robert Taylor, General Manager
WHUR-FM
Howard University
2600 4th Street, N.W.
Washington, 20059

Howard Sanders, Vice President and
General Manager
WYCB-AM
National Press Building
Washington, 20036

Florida

Ragan Henry, President
Broadcast Enterprises
National Inc.
WPDQ-AM
9090 Hogan Road
Jacksonville, 32216

Ragan Henry, President
BENI
WFYV-FM
9090 Hogan Road
Jacksonville, 32216

Art Gilliam, President
Gilliam Communications
WERD-AM

P.O. Box 2467
Jacksonville, 32203

Rudolph McCleod, President
Gulf South Communications Ltd.
WTMP-AM
P.O. Box 1101
Tampa, 33601

Georgia

Dorothy Brunson, President
Brunson Broadcasting
WIGO-AM
1922 W. Peachtree Street
Atlanta, 30309

Ragan Henry, President
BENI
WAOK-AM
401 Peachtree Street, N.E.
Room 1947
Atlanta, 30365

Benjamin M. Tucker, Chairman/
General Manager
Black Communications Corp. of
Georgia, Inc.
WSOK-AM
P.O. Box 1288
Savannah, 31402

Illinois

John H. Johnson, President
Johnson Publishing Co.
WJPC-AM
820 South Michigan Avenue
Chicago, 60605

Wesley South, President
WXOL-AM
3350 South Kedzie Avenue
Chicago, 60623

Indiana

Anderson Schweich
Chicago Metro Assurance Co.
WLTH-AM
3669 Broadway Street
Gary, 46409

Ragan Henry, President
BENI
WTLC-FM
P.O. Box 697
Indianapolis, 46206

Kansas

Dr. Marvin Wilson, President
Shawnee Broadcasting Inc.
KTPK-FM
910 First National Bank Tower
Topeka, 66603

Charlie Pride, President
Long-Pride Broadcasting
KEYN-AM

2829 Salina Avenue
Wichita, 67204

Charlie Pride, President
Long-Pride, Broadcasting
KEYN-FM
2829 Salina Avenue
Wichita, 67204

Louisiana

Henry Cotton, President
North Delta Broadcasting, Inc.
KTRY-AM
P.O. Box 1075
Bastrop, 71220

Henry Cotton, President
North Delta Broadcasting, Inc.
KTRY-FM
P.O. Box 1075
Bastrop, 71220

Thomas Lewis, President
Inter Urban Broadcasting
WYLD-AM
2906 Tulane Avenue
New Orleans, 70019

Thomas Lewis, President
Inter-Urban Broadcasting
WYLD-FM
2906 Tulane Avenue
New Orleans, 70119

Ben Johnson, President
Winnfield Life Broadcasting
P.O. Box 60475
WXOK-AM
Baton Rouge, 70896

Maryland

Dorothy Brunson, President
Brunson Broadcasting Corp.
WEBB-AM
Clifton and Dennison Streets
Baltimore, 21216

Ragan Henry, President
BENI
WITH-AM
5 Light Street
Baltimore, 21202

Massachusetts

Ken Nash, President
Ken Nash Communications
WILD-AM
390 Commonwealth Avenue
Boston, 02215

Michigan

Dr. William V. Banks, President
WGPR, Inc.
WGPR-FM
3146 East Jefferson Street
Detroit, 48207

Mrs. Mary Bell, President
Bell Broadcasting Corp.
WCHB-FM
32790 Henry Ruff Road
Inkster, 48141

Mrs. Mary Bell, President
Bell Broadcasting Corp.
WJZZ-FM
2994 East Grand Boulevard
Detroit, 48202

Richard Culpepper, President
WKWM-AM
P.O. Box 828
Kentwood, 49508

Vernon Merritt, President
Flint Metro Mass Media
WDZZ-FM
1980 East Genesee Towers
1 East Flint Street
Flint, 48501

Pierre Sutton, President
Inner City Broadcasting Corp.
WLBS-FM
15565 Northland Drive
Room 200 E
Southfield, 48075

Mississippi

Vernon C. Floyd, President
Circuit Broadcasting Co.
WORV-AM
604 Gussie Avenue
Hattiesburg, 39401

William Jackson, President
Interchange Communications
WESY-AM
P.O. Box 340
Greenville, 38701

William Jackson, President
Interchange Communications
WBAD-FM
P.O. Box 4426
Greenville, 38701

Missouri

Andrew Carter, President
KPRS Broadcasting Corp.
KPRS-FM
3 Crown Center, Suite 118
Kansas City, 64108

Andrew Carter, President
KPRS Broadcasting Corp.
KPRT-AM
3 Crown Center, Suite 118
Kansas City, 64108

Johnny Roland, President
Bronco Media, Inc.
KIRL-AM

P.O. Box 1374
St. Charles, 63301

Eugene Jackson, President
Unity Broadcasting Corp.
KATZ-AM
1139 Olive St.
St. Louis, 63101

Eugene Jackson, President
Unity Broadcasting Corp.
WZEN-FM
1139 Olive Street
St. Louis, 63101

New Jersey

James N. Wade, President
Wade Broadcasting, Inc.
WSSJ-AM
Radio CATV
1315 Walnut Street
Suite 716–20
Philadelphia, 19107

Larry Hayes, President
Atlantic Business
Community Development Corp.
WUSS-AM
1500 Absecon Avenue
Atlantic City, 88401

Daniel Robinson, Chairman
1430 Associates
WNJR-AM
1700 Union Avenue
Union, 07083

New York

Andrew Langston, President
Monroe County Broadcasting Co.
WDKX-FM
1337 East Main Street
Rochester, 14607

Ron Davenport, President
Sheridan Broadcasting Corp.
WUFO-AM
89 LaSalle Avenue
Buffalo, 14214

Pierre Sutton, President
Inner City Broadcasting Corp.
WBLS-FM
801 2nd Avenue
New York, 10017

Pierre Sutton, President
Inner City Broadcasting Corp.
WLIB-AM
801 2nd Avenue
New York, 10017

Norman T. Pinkard, Chairman
P&L Broadcasting of Johnstown,
NY, Inc.
WMYL-AM

P.O. Box 307
Johnstown, 12095

Norman T. Pinkard, Chairman
P&L Broadcasting of Johnstown,
NY, Inc.
WIZR-FM
Johnstown, 12095

North Carolina

Ralph Coleman, President
WARR, Inc.
WARR-AM
P.O. Box 577
Warrentown, 27589

Ms. Mutter Evans, President
Evans Broadcasting Corp.
WAAA-AM
P.O. Box 11197
Winston-Salem, 27106

Garfield Harris, President
Harris Communications
WGIV-AM
2520 Toomey Avenue
Charlotte, 28203

S. N. Lennon, President
Ebony Enterprises, Inc.
WVOE-AM
P.O. Box 328
Chadburn, 28431

Charles O. Johnson, President
Radio Station Weed, Inc.
WRSU-FM
P.O. Box 2666
Rocky Mount, 27801

Ohio

Ragan Henry, President
BENI
WCIN-AM
106 Glenwood Avenue
Cincinnati, 45217

Ragan Henry, President
BENI
WBLZ-FM
804 First National Bank Building
3rd and High Streets
Hamilton, 45011

LaRue Turner, President
WELX-AM
P.O. Box 219
Xenia, 45385

Oklahoma

Jimmy Miller, President
All American Broadcasting, Inc.
KAEZ-FM
P.O. Box 11333
Oklahoma City, 73136

Pennsylvania

Eugene Jackson, President
Unity Broadcasting Corp.
WDAS-AM
Belmont Avenue and Edgley Road
Philadelphia, 19131

Eugene Jackson, President
Unity Broadcasting Corp.
WDAS-FM
Belmont Avenue and Edgely Road
Philadelphia, 19131

Ron Davenport, President
Sheridan Broadcasting Corp.
WYJZ-AM
1811 Boulevard of the Allies
Pittsburgh, 15219

Ron Davenport, President
Sheridan Broadcasting Corp.
WAMO-FM
1811 Boulevard of the Allies
Pittsburgh, 15219

James Drayton, President
Phyldel Communications Corp.
WVAM-AM
2727 Albert Drive
Altoona, 16602

James Drayton, President
Phyldel Communications Corp.
WVAM-FM
2727 Albert Drive
Altoona, 16602

Dr. Samuel Hart, President
Hart Broadcasting Co., Inc.
WYIS-AM
400 Main Street
Phoenixville, 19460

Noble Blackwell, President
Lifestyle Productions
WCDL-AM
Salem Road
Carbondale, 18407

Noble Blackwell, President
Lifestyle Productions
WCDL-FM
Salem Road
Carbondale, 18407

Ragan Henry, President
BENI
WJAS-AM
Broadcast Plaza
Crane Avenue
Pittsburgh, 15220

Rhode Island

Henry Hampton, President
East Providence Broadcasting
WHIM-AM

125 Eastern Avenue
East Providence, 02914

South Carolina

I. S. Leevy Johnson, President
Nuance Corporation
WOIC-AM
P.O. Box 565
Columbia, 29202

I. S. Leevy Johnson, President
Nuance Corporation
WTWF-FM
P.O. Box 758
Moncks Corner, 29202

Mary Forbes, Chairman
Trident Communications
WQIZ-AM
P.O. Box 903–904
St. George, 29202

Mary Forbes, Chairman
Trident Communications
WDWQ-FM
P.O. Box 903–904
St. George, 29202

William & Vivian Galloway
WSIB-AM
1210 Boundary Street
Bufort, 29902

Tennessee

Samuel Howard, President
Phoenix of Nashville
WVOL-AM
P.O. Box 8085
1320 Brick Church Pike
Nashville, 37207

Art Gilliam, President
Gilliam Communications
WLOK-AM
363 S. 2nd Street
Memphis, 38103

Dr. Thomas Crawford, President
Broadcast Media of Knoxville
WBMX-AM
P.O. Box 6920
Knoxville, 37914

Texas

Dr. John B. Coleman, President
KCOH, Inc.
KCOH-AM
5011 Almeda Street
Houston, 77001

Earl G. Graves, President
EGG Dallas Broadcasting, Inc.
KNOK-AM
3601 Kimbo Street
Fort Worth, 76111

Earl G. Graves, President
EGG Dallas Broadcasting, Inc.

KNOK-FM
3601 Kimbo Street
Fort Worth, 76111

Virginia

Shirley Everette, President
Everette Broadcasting
WPAK-AM
P.O. Box 4949
800 Old Plank Road
Farmville, 23901

Tyrone Dickerson, President
Drum Communications
WENZ-AM
4719 Nine Mile Road
Richmond, 23901

Dr. Charles Cummings, President
WKIE-AM
6001 Wilkinson Road
Richmond, 23227

Levi Willis, Sr., President
Willis Broadcasting
WPCE-AM
1010 Park Avenue
Norfolk, 23227

Levi Willis, Sr., President
Willis Broadcasting
WOWI-FM
1010 Park Avenue
Norfolk, 23227

Cicero M. Green, Jr., President
North Carolina Mutual
Communications
WBMG-AM
P.O. Box 180
Williamsburg, 23185

Cicero M. Green, Jr., President
North Carolina Mutual
Communications
WBCI-FM
P.O. Box 180
Williamsburg, 23185

Washington

Patrick Prout, President
KUJ-AM
P.O. Box 513
Walla Walla, 99362

Willie Davis, President
All Pro Broadcasting Co.
KQIN-AM
P.O. Box 66160
Burien, 98166

Lloyd Edwards, President
Golden Gate Broadcasting
KYAC-AM
Seattle, 98101

Wisconsin

Willie Davis, President
All Pro Broadcasting Co.
WLUM-FM
12800 W. Bluemond Road
Elmgrove, 53122

Willie Davis, President
All Pro Broadcasting Co.
WAWA-AM
12800 Bluemond Road
Elmgrove, 53122

Jerrel W. Jones, President
Courier Communications
WNOU-AM
3815 North Teutonia Avenue
Milwaukee, 53206

Professional Media Organizations

Amalgamated Publishers, Inc.
45 West 45th Street
New York, NY 10036
President, John H. Sengstacke
(212) 489-1220

Black Anti-Defamation Coalition
1765 N. Highland–Box 426
Los Angeles, CA 90028
Executive Director, Robert E. Price

Black Awareness in Television
13217 Livernois Avenue
Detroit, MI 48238
Executive Director, David Rambeau
(313) 931-3427

The Black Filmmaker Foundation
1 Centre Street
WNYC-TV 26th Floor
New York, NY 10007
Executive Director, Denise Oliver
(212) 619-2480

Black Media, Inc.
507 5th Avenue, Suite 1101
New York, NY 10017
President, Benjamin H. Wright
(212) 867-0983

Black Owned Communication Alliance
P.O. Box 2757 Grand Central Station
New York, NY 10017
Executive Director, Terrie Williams
(212) 586-0370

The BMI Cooperative
PHC, 410 Central Park West
New York, NY 10025
Chairman, Calvin Rolark
(212) 222-3555

Broadcast Enterprises Nationwide Inc.
1422 Chestnut Street, 8th Floor
Philadelphia, PA 19102
President, Ragan A. Henry
(215) 563-2910

Capital Press Club
P.O. Box 19403
Washington, DC 20036
President, Janet Dewert
(202) 797-3746

Delta Sigma Theta Telecommunications, Inc.
1951 Pembridge Place
Detroit, MI 48207
President, Mrs. Lillian Benbow
(313) 483-5460

Minority Telecommunications Corp.
166 Madison Avenue
New York, NY 10016
President, Roy Thompson
(212) 686-6850

National Association of Black Journalists
P.O. Box 2089
Washington, DC 20013
President, Bob Reid
(202) 737-0277

National Association of Black Owned Broadcasters
1629 K Street, N.W., Suite 302
Washington, DC 20006
Executive Director, Nate Boyer
(202) 293-1137

National Association of Media Women
157 W. 126th Street
New York, NY 10027

President, Ella Kay Mays
(212) 666-1320

National Black Media Coalition
1802 T Street, N.W., Suite B
Washington, DC 20009
Chairman, Pluria Marshall
(202) 387-8155

National Black Network
1350 Avenue of the Americas, 24th Floor
New York, NY 10019
President, Eugene Jackson
(212) 586-0610

National Black Programming Consortium, Inc.
700 Bryden Road, Suite 135
Columbus, OH 43215
Executive Director, Mable Haddock
(614) 461-1536

National Newspaper Publishers Association
770 National Press Building
Washington, DC 20045
Executive Director, Steve Davis
(202) 638-4473

School of Communications—Howard University
Washinton, DC 20059
Dean, Lionel C. Barrow
(202) 636-7491

Sheridan Broadcasting Network
1745 S. Jefferson Davis Highway
Suite 404
Arlington, VA 22202
President, Skip Finley
(703) 685-2146

THE BLACK RELIGIOUS TRADITION

A History of Black Religion in the United States ■ Black Denominations: The Baptists and the Methodists ■ Other Predominantly Black Churches ■ Black Participation in Predominantly White Churches ■ Roman Catholicism ■ Black Jews ■ Mormon Policy Toward Blacks ■ Black Churchmen ■ Gospel Music

Since the 1960s the history and precepts of black religion in the United States have undergone exhaustive reexamination by religious leaders and scholars. The long dominant view of black Christianity in the United States is that religion was brought to blacks by white missionaries and served mainly as an ally of oppressors by promising the ultimate reward of salvation in heaven while withholding hope of release from earthly bondage. Conservative historians tended to laud this function of the black church as a source of comfort for blacks while liberals deplored it as a tool of oppression.

These views were honestly held and there was much evidence to support them. African traditions were ruptured along with the family structure by the manner in which slaves were transported and sold here. And as Charles S. Johnson noted in 1934, black churches like others did "hold out a world of escape from the hard experiences of life common to all" and "provide a large measure of the recreation and relaxation from the physical stress of life."

Under such circumstances, it was logical to deduce that the black religious tradition in the United States started when white missionaries, in the eighteenth century, were first permitted to spread the gospel among slaves. But in reviewing this period here, one must bear in mind a caution offered by W. E. B. DuBois in 1924:

Religion in the United States was not simply brought to blacks by missionaries. To treat it that way is to miss the essence of the black action and reaction upon American religion. We must think of the black as transplanting to the United States a certain spiritual entity, and an unbreakable set of old-world beliefs, manners, superstitions, and religious observances . . . a philosophy of life.

A more recent view suggested by theologian Henry H. Mitchell and others holds that black Christianity in the United States represents

a deeply spiritual world view that has not been contaminated by white rationalism and materialistic manipulation. What was mistaken by whites for childlike, simple faith was in fact a product of sophisticated African spiritual heritage which had already achieved profound transcendence over material things. . . . Because the culture of racism has denied the black man the possibility of realizing his own dignity, all black religion has, of necessity, been concerned with the affirmation and support of black selfhood.

The black church has been the primary identification for blacks both spiritually and politically as well as an important force in the survival and growth of black culture. The American black church is the pillar of the black community and is the religious, political, social, and economic base of the community.

Much of the political fervor manifested in the black

Bishop Christopher Rush (left), *eloquent orator and ardent abolitionist, laid the groundwork for expansion of the AME Zion church; Quakers like John Woolman* (above left) *treated slaves like brothers; Dr. Benjamin Rush* (right) *championed the black's right to education.*

community has its roots in the religious organization.

A very large section of the social life of the black community stems from the church: traveling tours, dinners, songfests, dances, teas, and fashion shows all play an important part in the fundraising efforts of the church, thereby causing the black church to be the greatest economic investment for black people.

During the turbulent civil rights era of the sixties, the black church often served as the meeting ground for protests and strategy parleys—a place to mobilize black people in their fight against racism.

The late Dr. Martin Luther King, Jr. was especially effective in using the church to carry out his voter registration projects in the south and to hold civil rights rallies.

Because the church was the only meeting place where blacks could congregate in the South because of segregation policies at other public facilities, it became the focal point during that era, which resulted in ministers becoming involved in speaking out on issues affecting black people. Churches all over the country then began to get involved in the civil rights struggle.

The church has produced many political leaders from the ranks of ministers as well as from its lay membership. Dr. Martin Luther King, Jr. was perhaps the most noted minister to come out of the black church and emerge as a national leader.

Other ministers who became involved in politics or who spoke out on the quality of life for black people include Reverend Ralph Abernathy, Reverend Joseph

Lowery, former U.N. Ambassador, and current Mayor of Atlanta Andrew Young, Congressman Walter E. Fauntroy, Reverend Jesse Jackson, Reverend Wyatt Tee Walker, NAACP executive director Benjamen Hooks, and former New York State Senator H. Carl McCall.

Black churches, especially in the south, were being used to promote voter registration and to advance the civil rights cause, and they became the target of the bombings that took many lives during the 1960s. Even today political candidates go directly to the church to solicit support in their campaigns for elective office. Candidates feel that through the church, they can reach a major percentage of the black community because it is the church where a large number of blacks are found on Sunday mornings.

The black church recently became involved with nonreligious programs such as operating daycare centers, setting up programs for the elderly, after-school programs for youth, Boy and Girl Scout programs, and many other events that benefit the community at large.

Dr. Kelly Miller Smith, a specialist in black religion, wrote that the black church is "the moral authority of the black community, and its buildings are where that community gathers. The line of demarcation between the black secular community and the black religious community, or the church, is at times invisible."

Efforts are being made increasingly to pull all church denominations together and to mobilize the institutional leadership and power of the black church. One such organization is the 17 million-member coalition called the Congress of National Black Churches, which is chaired by Bishop John Hurst Adams of the African Methodist Church.

BLACK CHRISTIANITY IN THE EIGHTEENTH CENTURY

In the mid-eighteenth century, just before the signing of the Declaration of Independence, there were no black churches or church organizations in the colonies. A few sparsely organized congregations of free blacks met, often secretly, in diverse places, but there were few black Christians, the British largely having confined conversion efforts to Indians. One exception was the Quakers, as William Penn had established a monthly Friends meeting for blacks as far back as 1700.

Though Christian dissenters such as the Germantown Mennonites were important in the founding of the American colonies, and nonconformists such as George Fox and John Wesley were among the first articulate English-speaking foes of slavery, the tardy start of Christianity among blacks was to be expected. Two forces—religious indifference among white settlers and fear that Christian conversion of blacks would undermine white supremacy—were much more powerful than the ideals of a few Quakers and Mennonites.

Early colonizers were generally lethargic about organized religion; fewer than half belonged to churches. Many who did attend services eschewed evangelizing and tended to interpret their faith in terms of proper personal ethics rather than adherence to a formal doctrine or spreading of the gospel.

In such a setting, missionary work among heathen blacks, who were widely presumed by British settlers to have no soul, was scarcely a priority.*

The colonists' religious indifference was compounded by several fears, one of which was that if blacks were allowed to congregate for church purposes, they would also want to congregate to plot rebellions. Moreover, if blacks were taught Christian doctrines of brotherhood and equality of all mankind before God, they would protest the precept that whites had a moral authority over blacks—something that was staunchly believed by white colonists in general and slaveholders in particular.

By the start of the eighteenth century, all southern states plus New York and New Jersey had enacted statutes which decreed that conversion to Christianity did not entitle slaves to freedom; Virginia was the first state to do so in 1669. Nevertheless, fears remained strong and the few missionaries who were interested in reaching black souls were opposed by slaveholders and usually denied access to slave quarters.

The White Evangelists

In the 1740s the religious environment of the colonies started to change drastically. Spurred by such formidable men as George Whitefield, an Anglican, and Gilbert Tennent, a Presbyterian, religious revivals were mounted from New England to Georgia.

The first of the colorful oratorical preachers in the tradition that later was to include Billy Sunday and Billy Graham, George Whitefield traveled the length of the Eastern seaboard preaching that a decent orderly life of itself could not lead to salvation, that man must accept Christ or suffer an eternal, burning Hell. With his mastery of English and a booming voice that Benjamin Franklin estimated could reach 30,000 people in the open air, Whitefield shook the casual attitudes of colonial Protestants and, followed by the nearly equally eloquent Tennent, shattered the prevailing conservatism among the New World's religious leaders.*

Religious consciousness was revitalized with a new sense of reform and a new independence among laymen within the church structure itself. This spiritual climate bode well for the direction of the colonial seekers of independence and provided the groundwork for future abolitionist movements.

Thus black religion in the United States is now being reexamined as an important force in the survival and growth of black culture in this country rather than merely as a means of "escapism" for people who suffered.

In addition, an increasing number of churchmen, white and black, also contend that features of worship found in many black churches, notably shouting-back participation by the congregation, musical improvisation, melodic license in hymn singing, and lack of inhibition with which these aspects of worship are carried out contain ingredients of spiritual freedom that dominant white churches have mistakenly rejected in their emphasis on formalistic worship and social respectability. Rock services and group participation by worshippers are now increasingly found among white congregations.

Christianity and Slavery

During the mid-eighteenth century the "radical left" of the time, the anticrown revolutionaries, were also making an impact against slavery by advancing the egalitarian precepts that were to provide the ideals of the war for independence. Such sentiments as "all

---

* This was in contrast to Latin America where slaves were routinely converted to Catholicism. Indeed, the French *Code Noir* of 1685 required that slaves be baptized and provided religious instruction.

* At first Whitefield opposed slavery, but he tempered his stance when he decided that an orphanage of his in Georgia could not survive without slave labor. He later owned slaves himself and was influential in the removal of proscriptions against slavery that had existed in Georgia.

Black camp meeting in the rural South during Reconstruction.

men are by nature free and independent" and "have the right to life, liberty and the pursuit of happiness" did not persuade the framers of the Constitution to abolish slavery but did contribute greatly to the growth of abolitionist sentiment.

Egalitarian notions increasingly permeated church groups. By 1769 Dr. Samuel Hopkins, minister of the First Congregationalist Church at Newport, Rhode Island, declared the incompatibility of Christianity and slavery. Hopkins, who had been a slaveholder himself, made a house-to-house campaign to arouse abolitionist sentiment. In 1773 Hopkins and Ezra Stiles, who was later to become president of Yale University, conceived a project to train blacks as missionaries for work in Africa. Two slaves, Bristol Yamma and John Quaniero, were selected for this experiment, given freedom, and schooled in the divinities. Money for their manumission was raised through the congregation. In 1774 Yamma and Quaniero entered Princeton to further their studies, but the outbreak of the American Revolution caused the project to be canceled.

As the black and white populations of the mid-eighteenth-century colonies increased, there were only moderate increases in church membership. Greatest gains were made by the Baptists, Presbyterians, and Quakers.

Most important, a religious plurality and liberty to worship or not to worship had developed in the colonies. This crystallized into the constitutional concept that church and state be separate.

THE FIRST BLACK CHURCHES

As the religious revival swept the country, white missionaries and ministers in the mid-eighteenth-century colonies moved through the South from plantation to plantation conducting services and providing religious training to blacks. Slaves were often used to assist white ministers, and on rare occasions a particularly able slave was purchased and freed to travel with a minister. However, although these black assistants grew to excel in their ministry, they could not hold the title of minister. Slaveholders insisted that black slaves not meet under their own leadership and successfully thwarted black religious workers from being elevated to the position of minister.

Because of segregation, blacks tended to gather in small groups and worship in their own style. For formal services, black freemen and members of the slave church congregations would request permission to use the white churches and were allowed to worship between the services for whites. Only a white preacher or minister was allowed to officiate, however.

The first effort for blacks to organize a church independently took place between 1773 and 1775 at Silver

Rural clergymen, post-Civil War.

Bluff, South Carolina, 12 miles from Augusta, Georgia, with the creation of a black Baptist church. Leadership of this church was attributed to a Mr. Parmer, first name unknown. David George, another black, also served at Silver Bluff during its early days.

The slaveowner who allowed this group to organize was George Galphin, who became a patron of the congregation. Galphin, an anticrown colonist, fled in 1778 when the British overran Georgia, and the church was temporarily disbanded. In 1781, after the Revolutionaries' victory, it was revived by the Reverend Jesse Peters.

A second black church was founded in Savannah, Georgia by George Liele, a former servant of a British officer who was previously a leader in the Silver Bluff Baptist church. Liele left with the British forces and successfully organized a church in Jamaica.

In 1780 the Freewill Baptists, formed in New Durham, New Hampshire, took an antislavery stance that was later to exempt them from William Lloyd Garrison's attacks on Protestants for indulging slavery. Garrison wrote:

It gives me great pleasure to mention one Christian denomination that deserves to be excepted from the censures I have been compelled to bestow upon the rest. I allude to the Freewill Baptists who from the beginning refused to receive slaveholders into communion, and most of whom were prompt to espouse the doctrine of emancipation.

By the late eighteenth century Presbyterians were also beginning a renunciation of slavery. In 1787 resolutions in New York and Philadelphia were approved stating general principles in favor of the idea of "universal liberty, that prevail in America" and of the interest which many of the states had in promoting abolition of slavery. These Presbyterians also resolved that slaveholders would give slaves a "suitable education as may prepare them for better enjoyment of freedom."

Also in the 1780s Bishop Coke of the Methodist (Baptist) Church was preaching that slavery was "the vilest [institution] that ever saw the sun." He urged General Washington to sign an antislavery petition and lend his influence to the cause of abolition. Washington declined to sign the petition but stated he was member of the Assembly and that he would support such a resolution if it came to a hearing. It did not.

The changing attitudes of New England churchmen were significant. It is often forgotten that the Puritans were the first settlers to justify slavery theologically, with their view that slaves were the progeny of Ham and condemned to servitude forever.

ADDITIONAL BLACK CHURCHES

Black Catholics

Before the Civil War, black Catholics in the United States were largely confined to Baltimore, New Orleans, St. Augustine, and Key West, the Catholic Church in the United States having made little effort to convert blacks. However, Catholics increased conversion efforts after the Civil War and by the end of

Zealous abolitionist William Lloyd Garrison was known as "The Great Liberator."

the nineteenth century there were some 200,000 black Catholics in the United States, two papers devoted to their interests, the *St. Joseph's Advocate* of Baltimore and the *American Catholic Tribune* of Cincinnati. The first black priest, ordained in 1886, was Augustus Tolton.

He was followed in Savannah by Andrew Bryan, a courageous and articulate man who was feared by whites. Bryan was often waylaid, assaulted, and beaten viciously. However, he continued his influential work, was ordained a minister, and died a natural death in 1812.

Black Protestants

Blacks also organized churches in other parts of the South—in Petersburg, Virginia in 1776 and Richmond in 1780. These and other churches were formed by bold enterprising men such as Henry Evans, who established the first Methodist Church with an all-black congregation in Fayetteville, North Carolina in 1790. Evans, originally from Virginia, was a shoemaker by trade and born free. A devoted religious man, he settled in Fayetteville where he set out to help blacks of the area by bringing them closer to God. He was denied the right to preach by the town council and so was forced to hold his services secretly. However, Evans' honesty, integrity and earnest pleadings to the town council eventually convinced authorities to allow him to preach in the town. His church was incorporated into the black AME Zion Church in 1866.

One very prominent, respected black preacher of the time was Black Harry Housier who traveled with Bishop Asbury of the Methodist Church. The Methodist Bishop Coke wrote in 1784: "I have had the pleasure

Many black preachers have been blessed with great oratorical gifts.

of hearing Harry Housier preach several times. I sometimes give notice immediately after preaching that in a little while he will preach to the blacks, but the whites always stay to hear him."

A very prominent black minister of the late eighteenth century was John Chavis. Born free in Oxford, North Carolina in 1763, Chavis was a soldier in the Revolutionary Army, attended Princeton University, and was appointed a minister by the Presbyterian Church to serve among blacks. He eventually set up a school where he taught both white and black students classics in preparation for college. Many of his students, such as Senator Charles Manly, in later years achieved status and recognition in government.

Beginning of AME Church

The growing number of blacks within the Methodist denomination and a rigid set of segregationist standards moved blacks in the direction of formally organizing their own church. The first was to emerge in Philadelphia under the leadership of Richard Allen and Absalom Jones and to be known as the Bethel African Methodist Episcopal Church.

The Philadelphia Church was to start as a direct result of violence by whites. Absalom Jones, a thrifty black from Delaware who had bought his and his wife's freedom, worshipped with whites in St. George's Methodist Church, as did other Philadelphia blacks. One day in 1787 Jones was jerked from his knees while praying and ordered to move to the balcony. The upshot was that Jones, together with Richard Allen, started to organize independently. The immediate result, in 1787, was the Free African Society. Then in

The Reverend Andrew Bryan spread the Gospel in Georgia.

The Reverend Absalom Jones, a Philadelphia pastor and church organizer

1793 Allen formed the Bethel African Methodist Episcopal Church (AME) while Jones, ordained in the Episcopal Church in 1794, became pastor at St. Thomas' Episcopal Church.

The separate courses followed by Allen and Jones was the forerunner of a split in black Protestantism that prevails to this day. Jones followed a course close to the style and procedures of established white churches, while Allen set out to appeal almost solely to blacks by displaying empathy with their experience and views. Inevitably, the approach of the two groups was to part further, the churches affiliated with white denominations following a more staid, ceremonial course and forcefully preaching education and social benefits for blacks, while the latter tended to concentrate on the distinctiveness and emotions of blacks while often eschewing social protest.

However, it would be grossly misleading to assume that the latter group played no part in black political progress. Such great leaders as Martin Luther King, Jr., Leon Sullivan, and Jesse Jackson were to emerge from such religious organizations.

Though Allen resisted help from whites, it was Methodist Bishop Asbury who obtained a church for him in 1793 and in 1799 ordained him a Deacon. The AME grew, sprouting branches in Pennsylvania, Maryland, Delaware, and New Jersey and by 1822 had moved south to Charleston.

Beginning of AME Zion Church

In New York City, James Varick was to follow a course similar to Allen's. In 1796 members of the Methodist Episcopal Church in New York hired a house and started to hold separate meetings. In 1799 they formally organized their own church. In 1820 they officially seceded from the Methodist Church when that group refused to ordain Varick. In 1822 Varick was elected Bishop of the AME Zion Church.

Similar patterns developed in other churches; for example, in Philadelphia in 1809 where blacks, denied worship in a local Baptist church, formed an African Baptist Church under the leadership of a Reverend Burrows. Also in 1809 blacks established the Abyssinian Baptist Church, in Boston, under Thomas Paul.

Recolonization

Black ministers in the early nineteenth century were to become involved in African recolonization efforts, some as missionaries. One of these, the Baptist Lott Cary went to Liberia in 1821 where he worked until his death seven years later.

Blacks such as Cary were ambivalent to recolonization. On the one hand, they saw it as a way of spreading the word of God, but on the other they felt it contrary to the best interests of blacks. One leading black who later supported recolonization was Bishop Daniel Payne of the AME Church, another was Alexander Crummell, an Episcopalian minister from New York City.

Other black churchmen favored recolonization and missionary work in the West Indies.

Powerful A.M.E. leader Daniel Coker later emigrated to Liberia.

Wendell Phillips speaking against slavery on Boston Common.

The Effect of Slave Revolts

The march of Christianity among blacks—always suspect to many whites—was soon to meet strong opposition in 1822, following suppression of Denmark Vesey's plot to revolt. White fears of the consequences of allowing blacks to organize for religious worship were stirred by the ingenuity of Vesey's planning and by the fact that Vesey himself was a member of the African Methodist Church. Numerous black churches in the South were forced to go underground, a step that was to further the "blackness" of black religions in the United States.

The Nat Turner revolt of 1830 resulted in further restrictions on the freedom of blacks to move about and organize. However, during the period from 1822 to the outbreak of the civil war in 1861, there was a substantial increase in the number of black Christian congregations and church organizations. Noteworthy increases occurred in the West where itinerant preachers spread the gospel. One of these, William Paul Quinn, a missionary of the AME, had set up nearly 50 churches with over 2,000 members by the early 1830's in Western Pennsylvania, Ohio, and Illinois. By 1836 the AME had 86 churches and nearly 8,000 members throughout the country, and during that year the first organization of black Baptist churches, the Providence Baptist Association, was formed in Ohio. By 1850 there were 150,000 black members of the Baptist Church.

Christians and Abolition

Of great urgency during this time was the involvement of black and white churchmen in the abolitionist struggle, on both sides. Abolitionist leaders were, ironically,

slow to accept black churchmen. In 1836 abolitionists vetoed a move to have a black minister address them. Many churches, pressured from both sides, adopted carefully developed fence-sitting positions. The Methodist Episcopal Church, which had condemned slavery in 1780, announced in 1836 that it had no wish to interfere in the relationship between master and slave as it then existed. In 1842 an Episcopal Convention in Pennsylvania adopted a resolution excluding representatives from black churches. In 1844 Methodists in the South seceded from their church when northern church leaders declared that a bishop could not own slaves.

Firmest opposition to slavery continued to come from Quakers, who sought to buy slaves in order to free them and who encouraged blacks to attend Friends meetings. Their stance was supported by individual ministers of conscience in all major churches who sought, often successfully, to encourage blacks to worship in their congregations and to send representatives to their conventions.

During the Civil War, Lincoln acknowledged the importance of religion to blacks when he appointed Henry McNeal Turner, an elder in the Methodist Episcopal Church, as Chaplain for the black 1st Regiment.

Religion and Reconstruction

Black church membership expanded greatly after the Civil War. Greatest growth was achieved by the Baptists, who had 500,000 members by 1870. The Methodist Episcopal Church, while split into northern and southern divisions, also grew, with separate black church conferences emerging in the South. The African Methodist Episcopal Church, which had gone underground in the South in the Civil War, also grew. Membership in the African Methodist Episcopal Zion Church boomed from 25,000 in 1860 to 200,000 in 1870.

Meanwhile in the Catholic Church, Father Patrick Healy and James Augustine Healy, who were brothers, were to assume important posts, the former becoming president of Georgetown University in 1873, the latter a Bishop in 1875, and then an assistant to the papal throne.

The Churches and Segregation

The history of black Christianity after the Civil War is also being subjected to reexamination. There is no doubt that churchmen, both white and black, adjusted to segregation efforts following Reconstruction and frequently encouraged it. Until recently, this has been almost universally regarded as a negative, retrogressive step, which furthered the humiliation and degredation of blacks that was to be given legitimacy in the 1896 "separate but equal" decision of the U.S. Supreme Court.

In general, southern churches completely excluded blacks from both churches and church organizations. Northern churches often forced blacks to worship in separate and most unequal structures, and subordinated them within individual churches and church or-

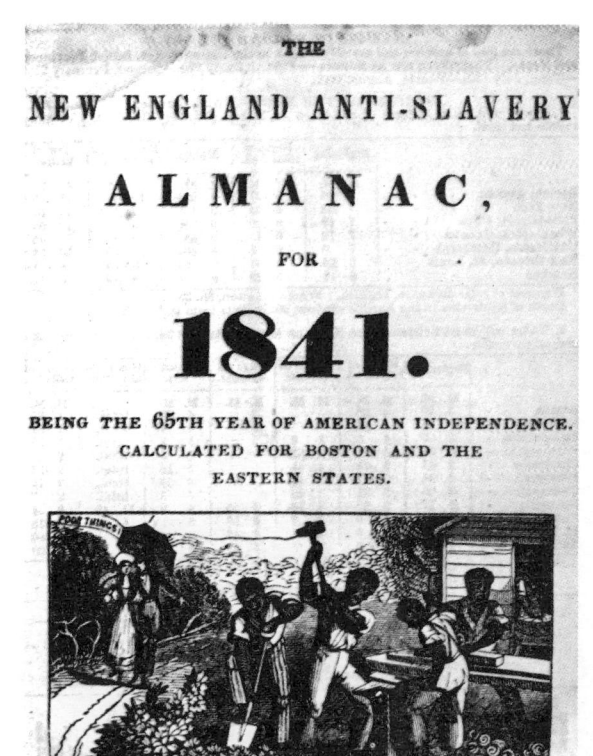

Abolitionist periodicals raised public consciousness.

ganizations, but not sharing the racial fanaticism then prevalent in the South, did not wish to suffer the diminution of church membership that would result from complete exclusion of blacks from church membership.

The reunification of the Methodist Church reflected the different concerns of northern and southern Protestants, the latter insisting on considerable independence as a condition of reunion.

However, in the latter part of the nineteenth century as in the 1970s, there were those who felt strongly that separation of the races was essential to the survival and self-respect of blacks. In many cases, black clergymen were a vital source of racial pride.

A comment by a black student at Tugaloo University, Mississippi in 1894, as reported by the Reverend A. F. Beard, D.D., secretary of the American Missionary Association, underscores the fact that charges against black churches for encouraging obsequiousness and acceptance of their low status were not altogether correct.

I find the Negro lacks race pride. He despises his own makeup. Who of you ever heard any Negro say that he thought the general characteristics of his race were as becoming as those of other races? Nor are they. The Anglo-Saxon is proud of his race characteristics. The Indian is, also, but the Negro despises himself, and would be anything else than what God has made him. But how can we escape hell if we hate ourselves because we are Negroes, when this is the divine wisdom of a just God? We may talk about improving our homes by getting an education as much as we please, but we will never be anything until we have race pride, and try to carry out the great plan of God who made us and knew what is best for us. Let us be genuine Negroes, pure and good, and not desire a drop of other blood in our veins.

THE TWENTIETH-CENTURY BLACK CHURCH

The influence of religious institutions among blacks probably peaked in the first decade of the twentieth century. With the start of the massive migration from the rural South to northern cities, the small community structures on which the church's authority rested were ruptured. Churches remained very important to blacks and to their adjustment to urban life, but their authority diminished. By 1926 the Congregationalist Church was to report that less than half of America's black population and less than one third of blacks who lived in large northern cities had a religious affiliation.

Many black church leaders ascribed the decline in religious interest primarily to a national trend produced by rising acceptance of evolutionary and scientific interpretations of the meaning of existence and to the growing strength of Socialism and other anticlerical political viewpoints. However, many black civil rights leaders and some church leaders themselves charged that churches, with what in the 1960s was to become labeled as "irrelevance," lacked interest in the day-to-day housing, employment, and education problems that plagued blacks.

Christianity and Political Activism in the Sixties

Churches spawned some of the great leaders of the twentieth century, men such as Powell, King, Abernathy, and most recently Jesse Jackson. These ministers were to use their churches as a base for uniting blacks politically. In so doing, they did not eschew traditional Christian doctrines or organized religion but sought to ally Christian faith with social militancy. Religion to these men and other activist ministers was not a pacifier, but a spur to action. For, they maintained, if God was in man, then man was worthy of respect from others and by the law. To exploit human beings, be they black or white, was to deny God.

Dr. King took special pains to point out the compatibility between his activism and religious worship. His reconciliation of passive resistance with Christianity contributed substantially to his reputation as one of the great Americans of the twentieth century and his receipt of the Nobel Peace Prize. There was also in King's theology, as well as that of other postwar Christians, an affinity for Ghandian doctrines of nonviolence. King held staunchly to his pacifist views, in the face of black critics who considered nonviolence a failure, and in the mid 1960s became one of the first Americans to oppose military involvement in Vietnam, when he equated war and racism.

In addition to the rising activism of the black clergy, there were three other major postwar developments in black religion, each of which emerged strongly in the 1960s:

The growth of the Nation of Islam, frequently known as the Black Muslims.

The prominence received by the concept of the "Black Messiah," as advanced by the Reverend Albert Cleague of Detroit.

Communities look to their pastors for both spiritual and temporal leadership.

The demands of blacks for monetary reparation from white-dominated religious groups.

The Nation of Islam

From its outset during the 1920s and 1930s, the Nation of Islam stressed the superiority of blacks as a race. According to the founder of the religion, who was known variously as W. D. Fard, Farad Muhammad, Wally Farad, and F. Muhammad Ali, mankind was originally black, but people had a weak and evil side which was white. The two halves became separated and whites were given some 6,000 years to reign, until 1984, when blacks would again rule.

In the 1930s, Fard disappeared and was succeeded as head of the movement by Elijah Poole, who became known as Elijah Muhammad. Muhammad declared that Fard was Allah and that he, Muhammad, was Allah's messenger, selected by Allah to inform blacks of their heritage, rights, and responsibilities.

The Nation of Islam also differed from more conventional religions in the directness of its appeal to what some sociologists have come to call the "black underclass"—people who are unemployed, prison inmates, or living by their wits in the street.

Along with their doctrines of black integrity, the Nation preaches discipline, abstinence, honor, cleanliness, and self-sufficiency. By 1975, when Elijah Muhammad died, it had an estimated 160,000 members, operated several schools, a university, and thriving businesses in such fields as publishing, agriculture, and food processing and retailing, and had earned the respect of whites and more theologically conservative blacks.

It was under the leadership of the now-retired Dr. Mohammed Abdul-Rauf that a reconciliation was made between the conventional Muslims and the Nation of Islam (Black Muslims). Dr. Abdul-Rauf, in private consultations, gained concessions from the Black Muslims to change practices that were not in conformity with the best traditions of Islam.

There are close to 3 million Muslims in the United States with a large concentration in the Washington, D.C. area. *The Muslim News* is the national publication.

The Black Messiah

Another religious concept associated with black pride and the impoverished was the Black Messiah movement led by the Reverend Albert Cleague in Detroit. Established in Detroit in the 1960s, Cleague's militant group asserted that there was no reason the Messiah could not be black and proceeded to challenge such groups as The United Church of Christ to allocate

James Forman delivering the 1969 Black Manifesto demanding $500,000 from white churches in reparation for the injustices of slavery and racism.

positions of responsibility in church hierarchies for black churchmen and to give substantial sums of church money for improvements of conditions in ghettos.

Reparations

The move for reparations reflected a growing tendency for blacks to demand economic aid from white-dominated institutions. The most widely publicized demand for reparations was made by James Forman, head of the now-defunct Student Non-Violent Coordinating Committee, in 1968 when, in the midst of Sunday services at New York City's Riverside Church, he strode to the pulpit and demanded $500 million as repayment to blacks for past abuses by white Americans.

The Council of Churches and other white-led churches responded by setting up organizations to advance funds to disadvantaged groups, but little money changed hands; the net effect of Forman's demand was to raise the consciousness of whites. Moreover, not all blacks supported Forman's view. The Reverend Joseph Jackson, head of the Black National Baptist

Convention, for example, attacked the National Council of Churches for establishing a black development corporation in reaction to Forman's demands.

Blacks within major national and international church groups also challenged their leadership. In Chicago, black priests protested the appointment policy of the Archbishop. Blacks petitioned the Vatican for a separate rite for black Catholics in the United States. Dissension between white and black Catholics in the United States peaked in 1971 when the U.S. Conference of Catholic Bishops omitted funding for the National Office of Black Catholics.

In 1973, a black, The Most Reverend Joseph Lawson Howze, was named Auxiliary Bishop of Mississippi. Harold Perry, a Roman Catholic Bishop in Louisiana, is also black.

Enrollment of minorities in seminaries has slowly risen from 808 in 1970 to 1,061 in 1972. Hispanic enrollment in 1972 was 264, less than 1% of seminary population.

By contrast with established religions, racial conflict has long been rare and racial integration extensive among Pentecostal groups.

Black Churches Remain Dominant

In 1980 the majority of America's black Christians continued to worship within churches that appealed primarily to blacks and generally had all-black congregations. A thread uniting these congregations and distinguishing them from white-dominated groups is the verbal feedback of congregations during sermons, the music of black hymns, the melodic license of congregants to improvise in church singing, and a greater tendency of black than white preachers in their fiery utterances to be positive, to offer hope more than to warn of damnation, and to avoid dwelling on the sins and dangers of religious or lay threats, such as "Socialists" or "intellectuals."

Once despised by theologians and intellectuals as crude and naive, the black church has increasingly become an object of respect and admiration. In part this is attributable to rising race consciousness among blacks and increasing respect among the general public for people willing, without embarrassment, "to do their thing." Also, awareness slowly dawned that there is probably no more truly black institution in the United States than the black church.

As Henry H. Mitchell observes:

It is important to remember that there is a distinct black religious experience today because there was and is a distinct black experience in America and because that experience was given religious interpretation by men, most of whom were ignorant of the white tradition. Their interpretations were made on the basis of their African background and peculiar experience in America, as this experience could be articulated with their knowledge of the Bible. The theological world has therefore, a fresh datum of experience, far more free . . .

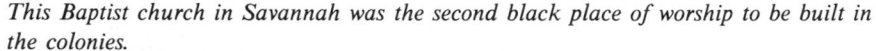

This Baptist church in Savannah was the second black place of worship to be built in the colonies.

[*of European influences*] *than can be found elsewhere in America.*

Black churches have grown stronger because they served the needs of their congregations, both spiritually and socially. While the black church frequently has been accused of "otherworldly escapism," it is also true that the civil rights movement of the sixties would not have been possible without the leadership and facilities of the churches. The proof of this participation is seen in the multitude of churches that were burned and bombed and the religious leaders who were jailed and otherwise persecuted.

The Black Church and Current Religious Conservatism

The rise of the "Moral Majority" movement in the 1980s was greeted with general ambivalence by black churches. In two major cities, black ministers headed up citywide chapters of the Moral Majority and one black minister formed a national conservative organization of his own.

But while most black churches, specifically the Baptists, agreed with the Moral Majority on such doctrinal matters as belief in God, The Holy Spirit, deity of Jesus Christ, the Fall of Man, doctrine of sin, salvation, and redemption, they diverged on issues such as racism and politics.

The Reverend Frank Madison Reid, Bishop in the African Methodist Church, summed up the major problem that blacks had with the Moral Majority: "There is a lot about the movement's inflexibility, intolerance and passion for annihilation that makes me think of the Great Inquisition and the Dark Ages. Church people must pray and think together."

The Reverend William Jones, Jr., President of the National Black Minister's Conference, was even more succinct, in an open letter to Moral Majority leader Reverend Jerry Falwell: "You, Dr. Falwell, are a champion of the American system. I, sir, refuse to champion any system that historically and presently engages in the systematic demeaning, degrading and dehumanizing of millions of lives and is in conflict with the ethic espoused by Jesus of Nazareth." He noted that the John Birch Society and Ku Klux Klan were supporting the movement.

Thus it seemed as if there would be little outpouring of support for the Moral Majority by black churches; indeed, many black religious organizations, such as the Progressive National Convention, took official stands against the religious right as early as 1980.

The Baptist church has been a major force in black religious life since the Civil War.

BLACK DENOMINATIONS

Baptists: History and Worship

The Baptist church became a major force in black religious life in the years immediately following the Civil War. By 1870 (four years after North Carolina had launched the movement), Baptist state conventions had been organized throughout the South.

The Consolidated American Baptist Convention, organized in 1867 and lasting until 1880, represented the black's first attempt to create a national body independent of, and separate from, white-dominated groups. With the dissolution of this convention, three smaller ones sprang up: the Foreign Mission Baptist Convention of the U.S.A. (1880), the American Na-

tional Baptist Convention (1880), and the American National Educational Baptist Convention (1893). These organizations were then united as the National Baptist Convention of the U.S.A.

The National Baptist Convention, U.S.A., Inc. is the parent convention of black Baptists. It's membership in 1981 was 6.3 million, up from 515 million in 1958. Dr. Joseph H. Jackson has been president of the Convention since 1953.

The National Baptist Convention of America was organized in 1880 and is usually referred to as the "unincorporated body." In 1981 it had a membership of 6,300,000. The Convention is based in Jacksonville, Florida. (Correspondence should be addressed to Albert E. Chew, 2823 North Houston, Fort Worth, TX 76106.)

Officers of the National Baptist Convention, U.S.A., Inc.

Officers

Pres., Rev. J. H. Jackson
405 E. 31st Street
Chicago, IL 60616

Vice-Pres.-at-Large, Rev. E. D.
Billoups
904 N. 33rd Street
Baton Rouge, LA 70802

Vice-Pres.: Rev. C. H. Hampton
605 S. 32nd Street
San Diego, CA 92113

Rev. David Matthews
P.O. Box 627
Indianola, MS

Rev. A. E. Campbell
2500 Carnes Avenue
Memphis, TN 38114

Rev. Sandy F. Ray
574 Madison Street
Brooklyn, NY 11221

Sec., Rev. T. J. Jemison
915 Spain Street
Baton Rouge, LA 70802

Stat., Dr. B. Joseph Johnson, Sr.
1211 Hunter Street, NW
Atlanta, GA 30314

Hist., Rev. E. T. Caviness
10515 Tacoma Avenue
Cleveland, OH 44108

Officers of Boards

Foreign Mission Board
701 S. 19th Street
Philadelphia, PA 19146
Sec., Rev. William J. Harvey, III

Sunday School Publishing Board
330 Charlotte Avenue
Nashville, TN 37201
Exec. Dir., Mrs. C. N. Adkins

B.T.U. Board
412 4th Avenue
Nashville, TN 37219

Education Board
903 Looney Street
Memphis, TN 38107
Chpsn., Rev. W. H. Brewster

Evangelism Board
7201 Claremont Street
Albuquerque, NM 87110
Sec., Rev. W. C. Trotter

Laymen's Movement
Pres., Walter Cade
537 N. 82nd Street
Kansas City, KS 66112

Woman's Auxiliary Convention
584 Arden Park
Detroit, MI 48202
Pres., Mrs. Mary O. Ross

Congress of Christian Education
3620 Oak Street
Kansas City, KS 66104
Pres., Dr. E. A. Freeman

Periodical

National Baptist Voice   (s-m)
902 N. Good Street
Dallas, TX 75204
Rev. C. A. Clark, Ed.

Officers of the National Baptist Convention of America

Officers

Pres., Dr. James C. Sams
954 Kings Road
Jacksonville, FL 32204

Corr. Sec., Albert E. Chew
2823 N. Houston
Fort Worth, TX 76106

Treas., Dr. John Francis
3715 Dryades
New Orleans, LA 70115

Hist., Rev. Marvin C. Griffin
1010 E. Tenth Street
Austin, TX 79102

Other Organizations

Baptist Training Union
Chpsn., Rev. Alexander Bernard
3069 Orchard Street
Indianapolis, IN 46218

Benevolent Board
Chpsn., Rev. W. M. Bowie

3401 Southmore Boulevard
Houston, TX 77004

Educational Board
Chpsn., Rev. J. B. Adams
609 S.W. 9th Street
Belle Glade, FL 33430

Evangelical Board
Chpsn., Dr. E. H. Branch
4919 Rosedale Circle
Houston, TX 77004

Foreign Mission Board
Exec. Sec., Rev. Robert H. Wilson
National Baptist Convention of
America
P.O. Box 223665
Dallas, TX 75222

Home Mission Board
Chpsn., Dr. Luke K. Mingo
3993 S. King Drive
Chicago, IL 60653

Junior Mission Auxiliary
Pres., Ms. Susan Turner

Mission Number Two Auxiliary
Pres., Ms. Hattie L. E. Williams
1166 Rapides Street
Alexandria, LA 71301

National Baptist Brotherhood
Pres., Dr. Ira L. Clark
3615 Rosedale Street
Houston, TX 77004

National Baptist Youth Convention
Pres., Quaford Coleman

4269 S. Figueroa Street
Los Angeles, CA 90037

National Ushers Auxiliary
Pres., Sr. Katie Allen
1806 Chestnut Avenue
Austin, TX 78702

Nurses Corps
Exec. Sec., Sr. Ernestine Sims
5007 N. Roman
New Orleans, LA 70117

Senior Woman's Auxiliary
Pres., Mrs. Fannie C. Thompson
516 E. Waverly Street
Tuscon, AZ 85705

Officers of the Progressive National Baptist Convention, Inc.

Officers

Pres., Dr. Ralph W. Canty
Savannah Grove Baptist Church
c/o 312 S. Main Street
Sumter, SC 29150

Gen. Sec., Rev. C. J. Malloy, Jr.
601 50th Street, N.E.
Washington, DC 20019
Tel. (202) 396-0558

Dir., Publicity, Dr. George Lawrence
Antioch Baptist Church of Christ
828 Greene Avenue
Brooklyn, NY 11221

Other Organizations

Dept. of Christian Education
Sec., Rev. C. B. Lucas
3815 W. Broadway
Louisville, KY 40211

Women's Auxiliary
Pres., Ms. Peggy A. Garnett
313 Oak Street
Elmwood Pl.
Cincinnati, OH 45216

Home Mission Bd.
Exec. Dir., Dr. Joseph O. Bass
601 50th Street, N.E.
Washington, DC 20019

Congress of Christian Education
Pres., Rev. Howard W. Creecy
Mt. Moriah Baptist Church
200 Ashby Street, S.W.
Atlanta, GA 30314

Baptist F. M. Bureau
Rev. George F. Bell, Sr.
Tasker Street Baptist Church
2010 Tasker Street
Philadelphia, PA 19145

Periodical

Baptist Progress   (q)
Mt. Carmel Baptist Church
712–14 Quincy Street
Brooklyn, NY 11221
Rev. V. Simpson Turner, Ed.

Methodists: History and Worship

Large numbers of blacks joined the Methodist Church in prerevolutionary times. In some areas they were organized into separate congregations presided over by white preachers, while in others they participated in services on a segregated basis (occupying special seats, and taking communion only after their white counterparts had done so). Dissatisfaction with the latter system grew so pronounced that, by 1785, several influential members of Methodist churches in the North had voted to establish their own places of worship. The leader in this movement, Richard Allen, was himself a freedman and a convert to Methodism.

The black Methodist movement experienced its first flowering after the Civil War, at which time many rural churches in the South showed an inclination to accept its leadership. In part this phenomenon was due to the greater mobility enjoyed by the black—

both preacher and convert—as a result of emancipation. Despite its growth, however, the Methodists never succeeded in matching the appeal generated by the Baptist movement. Nevertheless, the Methodists of today lay claim to more than 2 million members.

As in the case of the Baptists, Methodist worship has tended to reflect the religious mentality and spiritual expectations of the black masses. As such, it is usually evangelistic in tone and relies heavily on the dynamism and personality of the preacher, rather than on any strict adherence to articles of faith.

The AME Church

In 1816 Richard Allen, then a deacon of Bethel Church, called together representatives of separate black churches which had been established in Delaware, Maryland, and New Jersey. The meeting resulted in the formation of the African Methodist Episcopal (AME) Church.

Right Reverend Richard Allen, first bishop of the A.M.E. Church.

across the United States, has a membership of 1.9 million. The number of churches has declined sharply, from 6,000 in the 1970s to slightly more than 3,000 in the 1980s. Membership expanded by 800,000, however.

The AME's chief governing bodies are the General Conference, the Council of Bishops, and the General Board. The main work of the church is carried out through a number of lesser boards and departments in charge of such fields as missionary endeavor, education, and evangelism.

AME Official Directory Through 1981

This church began in 1787 in Philadelphia when persons in St. George Methodist Episcopal Church withdrew as a protest against color segregation. In 1816 the denomination was started, led by Rev. Richard Allen, who had been ordained deacon by Bishop Asbury, and who was ordained elder and elected and consecrated bishop.

The AME Church, which has parishes in Africa, Canada, and the islands of the Caribbean as well as

Officers

Senior Bishop, Bishop William F. Ball, Sr.
1002 Kirkwood Avenue
Nashville, TN 37203

Gen. Sec., A.M.E. Church, Dr. Richard Allen Chappelle, Sr.
P.O. Box 183
St. Louis, MO 63166

Pres., Council of Bishops, Bishop H. Hartford Bookins
4908 Crenshaw Boulevard
Los Angeles, CA 90008

Sec. Council of Bishops, Bishop Vinton R. Anderson
2685 Halleck Drive
Columbus, OH 43209

Pres. General Board, Bishop Frank C. Cummings
2138 St. Bernard Avenue
New Orleans, LA 70119

Sec. General Board, Dr. Richard Allen Chappelle, Sr.
P.O. Box 183
St. Louis, MO 63166

Treas., A.M.E. Church, Dr. Joseph C. McKinney
2311 M Street N.W.
Washington, DC 20037

Historiographer, Dr. Henderson Davis
P.O. Box 88143
Indianapolis, IN 46208

Pres. Judicial Council, Dr. Luna I. Mishoe
Delaware State College
Dover, DE 19901

Departments

Missions
Dr. John W. P. Collier, Jr.
475 Riverside Drive, Room 1926
New York, NY 10027

Church Extension
Dr. Hercules Miles, Sec.-Treas.
3526 Dodier
St. Louis, MO 63107

Christian Education
Dr. Edgar Mack, Sec.
500 8th Avenue S
Nashville, TN 37203

Evangelism
Dr. G. H. J. Thibodeaux, Dir.
1150 Portland Avenue
Shreveport, LA 71103

Publications
Dr. Henry A. Belin, Jr., Sec.-Treas.
500 8th Avenue S.
Nashville, TN 37203

Pension
Dr. J. M. Granberry, Sec.-Treas.
500 8th Avenue S.
Nashville, TN 37203

Minimum Salary
Dr. Ezra M. Johnson
280 Hernando Street
Memphis, TN 38126

Lay Organization
Mr. J. D. Williams, Connectional Pres.
3232 E. 30th Street
Kansas City, MO 64124

Women's Missionary Society
Mrs. Wilhelmina Lawrence, Pres.
2311 M Street N.W.
Washington, DC 20037

Religious Literature Department
Dr. Therion E. Cobbs, Editor-in-Chief
500 8th Avenue S.
Nashville, TN 37203

Periodicals

A.M.E. Christian Recorder
Dr. Robert H. Reid, Ed.
500 8th Avenue S.
Nashville, TN 37203

A.M.E. Review
Dr. William D. Johnson, Ed.
468 Lincoln Drive N.W.
Atlanta, GA 30318

Voice of Missions
Dr. John W. P. Collier, Jr., Ed.
475 Riverside Drive, Room 1920
New York, NY 10027

Women's Missionary Magazine
Mrs. Delores Williams
3912 Washington Boulevard
Indianapolis, IN 46205

Secret Chamber
Dr. G. H. J. Thibodeaux, Ed.
1150 Portland Avenue
Shreveport, LA 71103

This old painting shows Deacon Peter Williams, one of the founders of the A.M.E. Zion Church, standing in the doorway of New York's John Street Methodist Episcopal Church.

Bishops in the United States

First District
Richard Allen Hildebrand
29 Bala Avenue, Suite 222
Bala Cynwyd, PA 19004

Second District
John Hurst Adams
1221 Massachusetts Avenue N.W.,
Suite C
Washington, DC 20005

Third District
Vinton R. Anderson
2685 Halleck Drive
Columbus, OH 43209

Fourth District
Hubert N. Robinson
7220 N. Illinois Street
Indianapolis, IN 46260

Fifth District
H. Hartford Brookins
4908 Creshaw Boulevard
Los Angeles, CA 90008

Sixth District
Frederick Hilborn Talbot
208 Auburn Avenue N.E.
Atlanta, GA 30303

Seventh District
Frank M. Reid, Jr.
2522 Barhamville Road
Columbia, SC 29204

Eighth District
Frank C. Cummings
2138 St. Bernard Avenue
New Orleans, LA 70119

Ninth District
Phillip R. Cousin
1403 Miami Circle
Birmingham, AL 35214

Tenth District
Henry W. Murph
2812 Kendall Lane
Waco, TX 76705

Eleventh District
Samuel S. Morris
915 Old Grove Manor
Jacksonville, FL 32207

Twelfth District
Fred C. James
6514 Sherry Drive
Little Rock, AR 72204

Thirteenth District
William F. Ball, Sr.
1002 Kirkwood Avenue
Nashville, TN 37203

Special Assignment
Harold I. Bearden
644 Skipper Drive NW
Atlanta, GA 30318

Retired Bishops

O. L. Sherman
2525 Chester
Little Rock, AR 72206

D. Ward Nichols
2295 Seventh Avenue
New York, NY 10030

Ernest L. Hickman
120 Oakcrest Drive S.W.
Atlanta, GA 30311

Harrison J. Bryant
4000 Bedford Road
Baltimore, MD 21207

H. Thomas Primm
2820 Monaco Parkway
Denver, CO 80207

The African Methodist Episcopal Zion Church

In 1796 Bishop Francis Asbury acceded to the request of black members of the Methodist Episcopal Church in New York for permission to hold meetings under their own auspices. Among those who participated in this movement were James Varick, Francis Jacobs, William Brown, Peter Williams, June Scott, Samuel Pontier, Thomas Miller, William Hamilton, Abraham Thompson, William Miller. They fitted out an old building on Cross Street, between Mulberry and Orange streets, which had previously been used as a stable, as a place of worship. Thus was born the prototype of the African Methodist Episcopal Zion Church. The founders, however, did not declare their underlying purpose at once and withheld their new name from the public until 1799.

Prominent among those who attended the meeting in 1799, when it was decided to make public their purpose and declare the name of the first African Methodist Church in America, were George E. Moore,

Thomas Sipkins, David Bias, George White, Thomas Cook, John Teesman, and George Collins with those named above. The first Board of Trustees consisted of Francis Jacobs, William Brown, Thomas Miller, Peter Williams, Thomas Sipkins, William Hamilton, George Collins.

The first church frame was built in 1800 on the corner of Church and Leonard streets. A year later, on February 16, 1801, the church was officially incorporated. The General Conference of the Methodist Episcopal Church, through Reverend John McClaskey, recognized the new body on April 6, 1801.

The first elders elected in the AMEZ Church were Abraham Thompson and James Varick. These, with Leven Smith, were ordained elders June 17, 1821, by Reverend James Covel, D.D., Reverend Sylvester Hutchinson, and Reverend William Stilwell, elders of the Methodist Episcopal Church. Local deacons, ordained by the Methodist Episcopal Conference, officiated in the African Methodist Episcopal Zion Church prior to 1800.

The first Conference was held in Zion Church, New York, June 21, 1821. Reverend William Phoebus, of the Methodist Church, presided. At this Conference a form of "Limited Episcopacy" was established, and James Varick was elected the first Bishop—then called "Superintendent." The first Discipline for the African Methodist Episcopal Zion Church was adopted October 25, 1820.

The first attempt to effect the "Organic Union" of the African Methodist Episcopal and African Methodist Episcopal Zion churches was made August 17, 1820, at the residence of Mr. William Brown, Leonard Street, New York, by the officials of the African Methodist Episcopal Zion Church and Bishop Richard Allen. The merger was not accomplished, however.

The original title of the African Methodist Episcopal Zion Church was The African Methodist Episcopal Church, the word "Zion" being used only accommodatively. Since the sister church had adopted the same title, however, the General Conference of 1848 made the Zion a part of the corporate title to avoid confusion.

The policy of the church has been Episcopal Meth-

Bishop J. Clinton Hoggard, president of the Board of Bishops, A.M.E. Zion Church.

odism in its entirely from its beginning. Changes have been minimal, except that in 1868 the limit of Episcopal tenure was extended during life on good behavior. The form of consecration also varied, and the imposition of hands was introduced.

This is the first Methodist church to admit women to all functions save ordination. It was also the only black Methodist church that declared against slavery, the measure being incorporated in its first Copy of Discipline, 1820. This action proved a means of keeping it out of the South until 1862–1863.

Latest figures (1979) place the membership at 1,125,176, up from 900,000 in 1970.

Officers of the African Methodist Episcopal Zion Church Through 1981

Officers

Pres., Board of Bishops, Bishop J. Clinton Hoggard
6401 Sunset Lane
Indianapolis, IN 46260

Sec., Board of Bishops, Bishop Charles H. Foggie
1200 Windermere Drive
Pittsburgh, PA 15218

Asst. Sec., Bishop John H. Miller
6211 Red Bird Court
Dallas, TX 75232

Other Agencies

Gen. Sec.-Aud., Earle E. Johnson
P.O. Box 32843
Charlotte, NC 28232

Fin. Sec., Ms. Madie L. Simpson
P.O. Box 31005
Charlotte, NC 28230

A.M.E. Zion Publishing House: Mr. Lem Long, Jr., General Mgr.
P.O. Box 30714
Charlotte, NC 28230

Dept. of Overseas Missions: Rev. Kermit J. DeGraffenreidt, Sec.-Treas.

475 Riverside Drive, Suite 1910
New York, NY 10015

Dept. of Home Missions, Pensions,
and Relief: Rev. Jewett Walker,
Sec.-Treas.
P.O. Box 30846
Charlotte, NC 28231

Dept. of Christian Education: Rev.
G. L. Blackwell, Sec.
128 E. 58th Street
Chicago, IL 60637

Dept. of Church School Literature:
Ms. Mary A. Love, Ed.
P.O. Box 31005
Charlotte, NC 28230

Dept. of Church Extension: Mr. Lem
Long, Jr., Sec.-Treas.
P.O. Box 31005
Charlotte, NC 28231

Dept. of Evangelism: Rev. J. Dallas
Jenkins, Sr., Dir.
4550 Laurel Drive
Dayton, OH 45417

Dept. of Public Relations: Gregory R.
Smith, Dir.
344 Hawthrone Terrace
Mt. Vernon, NY 10550

Dept. of Public Health: Samuel C.
Coleman, M.D., Dir.
128 Grove Street
Hot Springs National Park, AR 71901

Woman's Home and Overseas
Missionary Society: Gen. Pres., Mrs.
Alcestis Coleman
120–19 Nashville Boulevard
St. Albans, NY 11412
Exec. Sec., Mrs. Lonia Gill
2864 Whistler Street
Whistler, AL 36612
Treas., Mrs. Farris Williams
3507 8th Street
Tuscaloosa, AL 35401

Periodicals

Star of Zion (w)
Rev. M. B. Robinson, Ed.
P.O. Box 31005
Charlotte, NC 28230

Quarterly Review (q)
Missionary Seer
Rev. Kermit J. DeGraffenreidt, Ed.
475 Riverside Drive, Suite 1910
New York, NY 10115

Church School Herald (q)
Ms. Mary A. Love, Ed.
P.O. Box 31005
Charlotte, NC 28230

Bishops

First Episcopal Area
Bishop William Melton Smith
3753 Springhill Avenue
Mobile, AL 36608

Second Episcopal Area
Bishop Alfred G. Dunston, Jr.
P.O. Box 19788
Philadelphia, PA 19143

Third Episcopal Area
Bishop Charles H. Foggie
1200 Weidemere Drive
Pittsburgh, PA 15218

Fourth Episcopal Area
Bishop Clinton J. Hoggard
6401 Sunset Lane
Indianapolis, IN 47260

Fifth Episcopal Area
Bishop James W. Wactor
709 Edgehill Road
Fayetteville, NC 28302

Sixth Episcopal Area
Bishop Clinton R. Coleman
3513 Ellamont Road
Baltimore, MD 21215

AMEZ Bishop Stephen Spottswood is the chairman of the National Board of Directors of the NAACP.

Seventh Episcopal Area
Bishop Arthur Marshall, Jr.
P.O. Box 41138
Benn Hill Station
Atlanta, GA 30331

Eighth Episcopal Area
Bishop John H. Miller
6211 Red Bird Court
Dallas, TX 75232

Ninth Episcopal Area
Bishop George J. Leake
220 W. 10th Street
Charlotte, NC 28202

Tenth Episcopal Area
Bishop Ruben L. Speaks
P.O. Box G
Roosevelt, NY 11575

The CME Church

The Christian Methodist Episcopal (CME) Church, known until 1956 as the Colored Methodist Episcopal Church, is the third largest black Methodist body in the United States.

Like many black churches, it came into being after the Civil War when some 250,000 segregated or otherwise restricted blacks belonging to the Methodist Episcopal (ME) Church South appealed to the General Conference for the right to form their own church.

In December 1870 the first General Conference of the CME Church was held in Jackson, Tennessee, where two black bishops—Henry Miles and Richard H. Vanderhorst—were elected. Since then, the two churches have cooperated in many ways, primarily in the field of education. (The CME Church operates three colleges, several secondary schools, and a seminary.)

Latest membership figures (1965) show a total of over 466,000 communicants. (The secretary of the Conference is Reverend Nichales Thomas, 664 Vance Avenue, Memphis, TN 38126.)

CME Official Directory Through 1982

Officer

Sec., Rev. N. Charles Thomas
P.O. Box 74
Memphis, TN 38101

Other Organizations

General Board of Missions
Chpsn. Bishop Joseph C. Coles, Jr.
2780 Collier Drive NW
Atlanta, GA 30018
Gen. Sec., Rev. Lymell Carter
4210 Belgrade
Houston, TX 77045

General Board of Christian Education
Chpsn., Bishop James L. Cummings
5517 W. 63rd Street
Los Angeles, CA 90056
Gen. Sec., Dr. W. R. Johnson, Jr.
Board of Christian Education
1474 Humber Street
Memphis, TN 38101

General Board of Publication Services
Chpsn., Bishop J. Madison Exum
654 E. Frank Avenue
Memphis, TN 38101
Gen. Sec., Rev. E. Lynn Brown
P.O. Box 2018
Memphis, TN 38106

General Board of Fiscal Services
Chpsn., Bishop C. A. Kirkendoll
308 10th Avenue W.
Birmingham, AL 35204
Gen. Sec., Dr. O. T. Peeples
P. O. Box 1704
Memphis, TN 38101

General Board of Personnel
Chpsn., Bishop C. D. Colemen
2330 Sutter Street
Dallas, TX 75216
Gen. Sec., Rev. N. Charles Thomas
P.O. Box 74
Memphis, TN 38101

General Board of Evangelism
Chpsn., Bishop P. R. Shy
6322 Elwynne Drive
Cincinnati, OH 45236

Gen. Sec., Rev. Anzo Montgomery
17626 Scottsdale Boulevard
Shaker Heights, OH 44120

General Board of Lay Activities
Chpsn., Bishop Nathaniel L. Linsey
6524 16th Street N.W.
Washington, DC 20012
Gen. Sec., I. Carlton Faulk
1222 Rose Street
Berkeley, CA 94702

Woman's Missionary Council
Pres., Mrs. Thelma Dudley
P.O. Box 5245
Orlando, FL 32855
Patron Bishop, Bishop Elisha P.
Murchison
11470 Northway
St. Louis, MO 63136

Periodicals

Christian Index (w)
P.O. Box 665
Memphis, TN 38101
Rev. Othal H. Lakley, Ed.

Eastern Index (bi m)
501 N Street N.W.
Washington, DC 20001
Rev. Gene Williams, Ed.

Missionary Messenger
1634 Garden Street
Shreveport, LA 71101
Cora B. Williams, Ed.

Western Index
971 E. 43rd Street
Los Angeles, CA 90011
Rev. W. H. Graves, Ed.

Bishops

First District
Bishop J. Madison Exum
564 Frank Avenue
Memphis, TN 38101
Tel. (901) 942-9336

Second District
Bishop P. Randolph Shy
6322 Elwynne Drive
Cincinnati, OH 45236
Tel. (513) 984-6825

Third District
Bishop E. P. Murchison
11470 Northway
St. Louis, MO 63136
Tel. (314) 741-5837

Fourth District
Bishop Henry C. Bunton, Jr.
109 Holcomb Drive
Shreveport, LA 71103
Tel. (318) 222-6284

Fifth District
Bishop C. A. Kirkendoll
308 10th Avenue W.
Birmingham, AL
Tel. (205) 252-3541

Sixth District
Bishop Joseph C. Coles, Jr.
2780 Collier Drive
Atlanta, GA 30018
Tel. (404) 752-7800

Seventh District
Bishop Nathaniel L. Linsey
6524 16th Street N.W.
Washington, DC 20012
Tel. (202) 828-8070

Eighth District
Bishop C. D. Coleman
2330 Sutter Street
Dallas, TX 75216
Tel. (214) 942-5781

Ninth District
Bishop James L. Cummings
5517 W. 63rd Street
Los Angeles, CA 90056
Tel. (213) 649-1704

THE LOST-FOUND NATION OF ISLAM IN THE WEST: THE BLACK MUSLIMS

Pigeonholed in the 1960s as a fanatical antiwhite separatist movement, the Black Muslims became, in the 1970s, a major economic and educational force in America's black community.

The Muslims are a religious organization in the sense that they worship a supreme being. (There is no God but Allah. Muhammad is His Apostle.) In addition, many of their admonitions and disciplines can be likened to the puritanism of some religious groups. Followers are expected to abstain from alcohol, tobacco, and cosmetics. Children are educated in sect-oriented schools.

After the assassination of Malcolm X, the Muslim

organization was saddled with the reputation of being a fierce and fanatic hate group, fearlessly self-righteous and ready to seek vengeance and retribution for alleged wrongdoing. Since then, however, the fiery rhetoric of Elijah Muhammad has cooled, and the Messenger has displayed a keen interest in developing the Nation's economic self-sufficiency. Muslim's economic holdings extend throughout the United States and beyond, to the Caribbean and Central America.

In Chicago, where the Muslims are headquartered, The Nation manages publishing, trucking, egg, meat, baking, retailing, restaurant, and apparel manufacturing operations. Muslims also own modern cattle, dairy, poultry, and produce farms in Alabama, Georgia, and Michigan, having survived, in 1970, the poisoning of much of its Alabama herd. Value of the Nation's holdings is estimated at about $60 million.

Starting in the early 1970s, the Nation started to alter its membership base, expanding its appeal from prisons and ghetto streets to the black middle class. Much of the reason for this was the need for professional specialists to man its growing economic ventures. However, the Muslims still reject membership and offers of help from whites, even white governments. The Nation has refused help from the United States government but has borrowed $3 million from Libya to finance purchase of a temple in Chicago.

The Muslims also operate some 50 schools and colleges, from which whites are also excluded. The Muslim schools have an excellent reputation and frequently surpass public school systems in academic achievement.

RASTAFARIANS

Rastafarians, who wear their hair in matted "dreadlocks" and smoke marijuana as part of their faith, have grown in popularity in the United States and Britain since the sect was born in Jamaica in the 1930s. Members of the religion regard Ethiopian Emperor Haile Selassie, who died in 1975, as God.

Marcus Garvey, a Jamaican-born nationalist who advocated a back-to-Africa movement in the United States in the early 1920s, is also a central figure in the faith. Garvey founded the Universal Negro Improvement Association in Harlem in the 1920s with the message that "Africa was for the Africans" and urged blacks to look back to the motherland, where a black King would be crowned soon.

He was deported to Jamaica in 1927.

In 1930 Lij Ras Tafari Makonnen ascended to the throne of Ethiopia and took the titles of His Imperial Majesty, Haile Selassie I, Power of the Holy Trinity, 225th Emperor of the 3,000 year-old Ethiopian Empire, Elect of God, Lord of Lords, King of Kings, Heir to the Throne of Solomon, and Conquesting Lion of the Tribe of Judah. Rastafarians hailed him as Jah, the living God on earth.

Today, Rastas differ on specific dogma, but they basically believe they are descended from black Hebrews exiled in Babylon and therefore are true Israelites. They also believe that Haile Selassie is the direct descendent of Solomon and Sheba, and that God is black.

Most white men, they believe, have been worshipping a dead god and have attempted to teach the blacks to do likewise. They believe the Bible was distorted by King James I and that the black race sinned and was punished by God with slavery. They view Ethiopia as Zion, the Western world as Babylon, and believe that one day they will return to Zion. They preach love, peace, and reconciliation between races but warn that Armageddon is now.

Rastas don't vote, tend to be vegetarians, abhor alcohol, and wear their hair in long, uncombed plaits called dreadlocks. The hair is never cut, since it is part of the spirit, nor is it ever combed.

They never use the word "last" because it expresses retrogression and a Rastaman can only go forward. Marijuana is the holy herb, regarded as a sacramental gift, and the Bible is quoted as proof of this: "And thous shalt eat the herb of the field" (Gen. 3:18).

The movement in America grew rapidly in the fifties and sixties, and accelerated with the emergence of reggae musician Bob Marley, the first Rastafarian to become a pop superstar, and the 1966 visit of Selassie to Jamaica. Selassie died in 1975 and Marley died in 1981.

There are an estimated 50,000 Rastas in Britain and almost a million in the United States, approximately 80,000 of whom live in New York City, mainly in Brooklyn where there is a high concentration of West Indians and Haitians.

OTHER PREDOMINANTLY BLACK CHURCHES

The following is a list of black churches and religious organizations now active in the United States. Inevitably, such a list can only offer a brief glimpse into the prevailing religious mood of the black churchgoer in the United States today.

The *African Orthodox Church* was founded in 1921 by Archbishop George Alexander McGuire, once a priest in the Protestant Episcopal Church. At first associated with the Marcus Garvey movement, this church is today an autonomous and independent body adhering to an "orthodox" confession of faith. Its nearly 6,000 members worship in some 25 to 30 churches.

"We Shall Overcome" is sung as a hymn during black congregational services.

The organization's headquarters are at 122 West 129th Street, New York City.

The *African Union First Colored Methodist Protestant Church, Inc.* grew out of the Methodist Episcopal Church in 1805, although it did not become a distinct denomination until fully eight years later. Today, it has more than 30 churches and a membership of some 5,000. Headquarters for the organization are at 602 Spruce Street, Wilmington, Delaware.

The *Apostolic Overcoming Holy Church of God* was incorporated in Alabama in 1919. Evangelistic in purpose, it emphasizes sanctification, holiness, and the power of divine healing. As of 1956, it had a membership of 75,000 people in some 300 congregations. The headquarters of the organization are at 1807 S. Mott Drive, Mobile, Alabama.

Christ's Sanctified Holy Church was organized in 1903 from among the members of a Negro Methodist church. The last available figures put church membership at 600. This church, which holds its annual conference in September, has its headquarters at South Cutting Avenue and East Spencer Street in Jennings, Louisiana.

The *Church of Christ, Holiness, U.S.A.* was organized by Bishop C. P. Jones in 1896. The avowed mission of this body is to proclaim the gospel, seek the conversion of sinners, and perfect them in their Christian belief. Some 150 churches belong to this group, which has a membership of about 7,500. The organiza-

tion, with headquarters at 329 East Monument Street, Jackson, Mississippi, has an annual national convention in August.

The *Church of God and Saints of Christ* was organized in 1896 in Lawrence, Kansas by William S. Crowdy, who held the belief that blacks were descended from the 10 lost tribes of Israel. Crowdy's followers today observe the Old Testament calendar, using Hebrew terminology for the months, and are sometimes referred to as "Black Jews." National headquarters for the organization were established in Philadelphia in 1900. In 1917 international headquarters were set up at Belleville, R.F.D. 1, Portsmouth, Virginia, site of the quadrennial general conference. The organization's more than 200 churches have a membership of some 38,000.

The *Church of God in Christ* was organized in Arkansas in 1895 by Elders C. P. Jones and C. H. Mason. Today, the organization has over 4,000 churches and a membership of better than 400,000. Annual conferences are held in the 5,000-seat Mason's Temple in Memphis, Tennessee. Headquarters are at 958 Mason Street, Memphis.

The *Church of the Living God* was founded in 1889 in Wrightsville, Arkansas by William Christian. Believers practice baptism by immersion, foot-washing, and the use of water in the dispensation of the sacrament. The churches—or temples as they are called— are organized along fraternal order lines. A national assembly is held by the group on the seond Tuesday in October on a biennial basis. The close-to-300 churches in the movement claim a membership of over 43,000.

The *Churches of God, Holiness* were organized by K. H. Burruss in Georgia in 1914. Headquarters are at 170 Ashby Street, N.W., Atlanta, Georgia. Membership in the group's 40-odd churches totals some 25,000.

The black churches of the *Cumberland Presbyterian Church* were established with their own ecclesiastical organization in 1869. Nowadays, the general assembly of the Second Cumberland Presbyterian Church in U.S. (formerly Colored Cumberland Presbyterian Church) meets annually in June. Total membership in the church's more than 854 places of worship in the United States stands at some 94,574.

The *Fire Baptized Holiness Church* was organized in Atlanta, Georgia in 1898. Its headquarters today are at 556 Houston Street, Atlanta, Georgia. The general council for its 50-odd churches (membership, c. 1,000) meets annually.

The *Free Christian Zion Church of Christ* was organized in 1905 at Redemption, Arkansas by a company of black ministers who were associated with a variety of Methodist-inclined denominations. Church membership today stands at approximately 20,000. Headquarters for the organization, which has an annual general assembly in November, are in Nashville, Arkansas.

The *House of God, Which Is the Church of the Living God, the Pillar and Ground of the Truth, Inc.* was organized by R. A. R. Johnson in 1918. A small body which meets annually in October, it has about 100 churches and a membership approaching 2,500.

The *Independent AME Denomination* was founded in Jacksonville, Florida in 1907 by 12 elders who had withdrawn from the AME Church. Information on this body is scant, although it is known that, as of 1940, it had 12 churches and an inclusive membership of 1,000.

The *Kodesh Church of Immanuel* was founded in 1929 by the Reverend Frank R. Killingsworth, leader of a group which had withdrawn from the African Methodist Episcopal Zion Church. According to its last report, it had five churches, and a membership of 326.

The *National Baptist Evangelical Life and Soul Saving Assembly of U.S.A.* was founded in 1921 by A. A. Banks, who envisioned that it would become a charitable, educational, and evangelical body. The church, with headquarters at 441 Monroe Avenue, Detroit, Michigan, has a general assembly for its close to 60,000 members who worship in some 260 churches across the United States.

The *National David Spiritual Temple of Christ Church Union (Inc.), U.S.A.* was organized in 1921 by the Most Reverend David William Short, originally a Baptist minister. The organization's headquarters are at 545 W. 92nd Street, Los Angeles, California. A national assembly is held annually in August. Membership has already passed 40,000.

The *National Primitive Baptist Convention of the U.S.A.,* founded in 1907, differs from similar bodies in its general opposition to the notion of extensive organization. Headquarters of this body are at 2116 Clinton Avenue, West, Huntsville, Alabama.

The *Reformed Methodist Union Episcopal Church* was founded in Charleston, South Carolina by a group which had withdrawn from the African Methodist Episcopal Church there. Doctrinally, this church closely resembles the Methodist Episcopal Church. Headquarters for the more than 30 churches are in Charleston, South Carolina; membership is estimated at over 11,000. The church also has an annual general conference.

The *Reformed Zion Union Apostolic Church,* organized in 1869 at Boydton, Virginia by a minister of the AME Zion Church (Elder James R. Howell of New York), espouses doctrines which are generally in accord with those of the Methodist Episcopal Church. Its annual conference, held in August, is superseded by a quadrennial general conference, the last of which was held in 1966. It has over 50 churches, and a membership of about 16,000.

Triumph the Church and Kingdom of God in Christ was organized in 1902 in Georgia by the Elder E. D. Smith, who taught sanctification and the second coming of Christ. The church has quarterly and annual conferences, as well as a quadrennial international religious congress. Headquarters are at 213 Furrington Avenue, S.E., Atlanta, Georgia. Membership has grown rapidly in recent years, and is now approaching 60,000.

The *Union American Methodist Episcopal Church,* founded by Rev. Peter Spencer in Delaware in 1813, is reputed to be the first all-black Methodist denomination in the United States. Until 1850 the organization went by the name of the "Union Church of Africans." That year, however, a split occurred, whereupon the main body adopted the name by which it is currently known. The latest figures made available by the organization show it to have 256 churches and 27,560 members.

The *United Free Will Baptist Church* set up its organization in 1870, and has since maintained close ties with the Free Will Baptists. It has a general conference every three years and is headquartered at Kinston College, 1000 University Street, Kinston, North Carolina. Membership stands at about 100,000; churches number close to 900.

The *United Holy Church of America, Inc.* was founded in 1886 at Method, North Carolina. This body recognizes baptism by immersion and the Lord's Supper, and meets quadrennially. Its headquarters are at both 500 Gulley Street, Goldsboro, North Carolina and 31 Miami Avenue, Columbus, Ohio. Its membership is approaching 30,000, while its churches are nearing the 500 mark in number.

"WHITE CHURCHES"

The term "white churches" is used to identify those churches which, while having predominantly white congregations, have large numbers of black worshippers on a generally nonsegregated basis. Among others, these include: the Methodist Church (c. 370,000); the Protestant Episcopal Church (c. 78,000); Seventh Day Adventists (c. 50,000), and the Congregational Church (c. 38,000). Since not all churches base their tabulations of membership on a racial breakdown, it is hazardous to estimate the number of blacks in such churches, although a figure of 800,000 has been advanced.

Black members of "white churches" generally enjoy the rights of full participation. In the Methodist Church, for example, black bishops serve side by side and on an equal footing, with their white counterparts.

Catholicism

Missionary activities have intensified, particularly since the early 1960s, resulting in a tripling of black membership; in 1982 the Catholic Office of Black Ministry reported a black membership of 1.3 million, up from 700,000 in 1963. The Catholic church thus became the fourth largest religious organization among American blacks, following the two Baptist conventions and the AME denomination.

Black participation in the church has not been without dissension. In the early 1970s, for example, blacks petitioned the Vatican for a separate rite for black Catholics in the United States. Later, black and white Catholics spoke out against each other when the U.S. Conference of Catholic Bishops omitted funding for the National Office of Black Catholics in 1971.

However, the church has sought to elevate black leaders: in 1966 Harold Robert Perry of Lake Charles, Louisiana, became the first black bishop; Joseph Lawson Howze followed in his footsteps in 1973. On February 10, 1982, New York City's Terence Cardinal Cooke created the posts of Episcopal Vicar for black community development and Vicar of Harlem, and named Emerson Moore, pastor of St. Charles Borromeo Church in Harlem, to handle the dual role. Moore thus became the nation's first black monsignor.

Black enrollment in seminaries has increased substantially: in 1970, 808 black students were reported in seminary studies; by 1980, the enrollment had reached 2,205. However, blacks still constitute only about 4.4% of the entire student population. Also, more than 600 of the students attend one of five predominantly black institutions.

The Black Jews

There are believed to be approximately 44,000 so-called black Jews (they are actually more appropriately classified as members of Ethiopian Hebrew congregations) in the United States. These Jews, located in such cities as Philadelphia, Boston, Chicago, Los Angeles, and New York, are mainly natives of the West Indies or the American South, although they consistently trace their ancestry and heritage back to Africa. Clannish, and fully involved, the black Jews continue to live successfully in poor or lower middle-class neighborhoods, despite the high crime rates prevalent in settings such as these. Both their religious optimism and the strong parental authority exercised on offspring contribute to the inherent stability of the group. New York's Wentworth A. Matthew, leader of Harlem's Ethiopian Hebrew Congregation, credits the strength and solidarity of his group to the presence of a "tower-

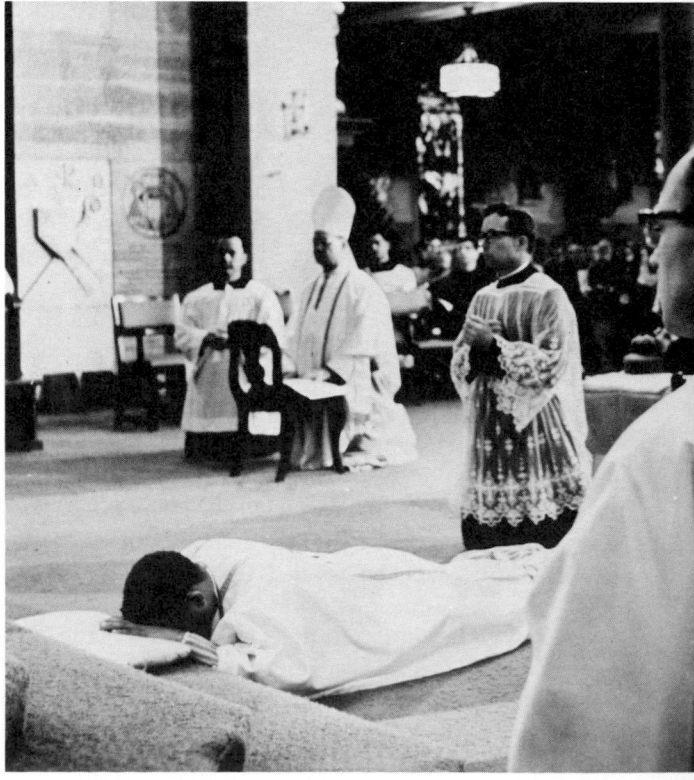

The consecration of Bishop Harold R. Perry in New Orleans

A black rabbi stands in front of his Bronx synagogue.

ing" father figure and a tenacious mother who "sets the tone and the mood" of family life.

Like Jews everywhere, the Ethiopian Hebrew congregations observe the rituals and holidays stemming from ancient Jewish traditions. Thus they celebrate such joyous occasions as the liberation of the Jews from bondage in Egypt by reading the Passover stories and participating in the family *seder.*

Their form of worship, the *Sephardic,* originated with the Jews in Spain and Portugal and was carried by them to the lands of Latin America and the islands of the West Indies. Thus the Spanish influence is evident in the ethnic composition of the congregations, which often includes Spanish and Portuguese members.

Like many American Jews, the Ethiopians identify strongly with Israel. Despite the Jewish values which suffuse their lives, young blacks in the congregation are sensitive to pressures to identify with the black movement. In most cases, however, cultural and philosophical preoccupations continue to eclipse racial matters as concerns which unify and connect the community.

Race, however, is still an issue which tends to fragment the black Jews and becloud their status. Thus some black Jews seek to identify with the universal Jewish world, whose nationhood is centered in the state of Israel, while others, sensing the suspicion and uneasiness that might be generated by their presence in many areas of the white (including the Jewish) world, prefer to remain in small, unrelated clusters or decentralized factions.

Though many have worshipped as Jews for years, they often cannot produce the necessary documents required to prove to a rabinnical court their eligibility to call themselves Orthodox Jews. Some do not qualify as Jews in the strict religious sense of the term, being persons neither born of a Jewish mother nor brought into the faith by a properly ordained rabbi.

The isolaton of the black Jews contributes to the difficulty of finding absolute verification of their Jewish origins. Most trace their forbears to West or East Africa and are linked in some way to the Ethiopian Jews known as Falashas.

Mormonism

On January 9, 1970, Mormon leaders around the world were informed of church policy toward the black. The text of the official Mormon position follows:

In view of confusion that has arisen, it was decided at a meeting of the first presidency and the quorum of the twelve to restate the position of the church with regard to the Negro both in society and in the church.

First, may we say that we know something of the suffering of those who are discriminated against in a denial of their civil rights and constitutional privileges. Our early history as a church is a tragic story of persecution and oppression.

Our people repeatedly were denied the protection of the law. They were driven and plundered, robbed and murdered by mobs who in many instances were aided and abetted by those sworn to uphold the law. We as a people have experienced the bitter fruits of civil discrimination and mob violence.

We believe that the Constitution of the United States was divinely inspired, that it was produced by "wise men" whom God raised up for this "very purpose," and that the principles embodied in the Constitution are so fundamental and important that, if possible, they should be extended "for the rights and protection" of all mankind.

In revelations received by the first prophet of the church in this dispensation, Joseph Smith (1804-1844), the Lord made it clear that it is "not right that any man should be in bondage one to another." These words were spoken prior to the Civil War. From these and other revelations have sprung the church's deep and historic concern with man's free agency and our commitment to the sacred principles of the Constitution.

It follows, therefore, that we believe the Negro, as well as those of other races, should have his full constitutional privileges as a member of society, and we hope that members of the church everywhere will do their part as citizens to see that these rights are held inviolate. Each citizen must have equal opportunities and protection under the law with reference to civil rights.

However, matters of faith, conscience, and theology are not within the purview of the civil law. The first amendment to the Constitution specifically provides that "Congress shall make no law respecting an establishment of religion, or prohibiting the free exercise thereof."

The position of the Church of Jesus Christ of Latter-Day Saints affecting those of the Negro race who choose to join the church falls wholly within the category of religion. It has no bearing upon matters of civil rights. In no case or degree does it deny to the Negro his full privileges as a citizen of the nation.

This position has no relevancy whatever to those who do not wish to join the church. Those individuals, we suppose, do not believe in the divine origin and nature of the church, nor that we have the priesthood of God. Therefore, if they feel we have no priesthood, they should have no concern with any aspect of our theology on priesthood so long as that theology does not deny any man his constitutional privileges.

A word of explanation concerning the position of the church: The Church of Jesus Christ of Latter-Day Saints owes its origin, its existence, and its hope for the future to the principle of continuous revelation. "We believe all that God has revealed, all that He does now reveal, and we believe that He will yet reveal many great and important things pertaining to the Kingdom of God."

From the beginning of this dispensation, Joseph Smith and all succeeding presidents of the church have taught that Negroes, while spirit children of a common father, and the progeny of our earthly parents Adam and Eve, were not yet to receive the priesthood, for reasons which we believe are known to God, but which He has not made fully known to man.

Our living prophet, President David O. McKay, has said, "The seeming discrimination by the church toward the Negro is something which originated with man; but goes back into the beginning with God. Revelation assures us that this plan antedates man's mortal existence, extending back to man's pre-existent state."

President McKay has also said, "Sometime in God's eternal plan, the Negro will be given the right to hold the priesthood."

Until God reveals His will in this matter, to Him whom we sustain as a prophet, we are bound by that same will. Priesthood, when it is conferred on any man comes as a blessing from God, not of men.

We feel nothing but love, compassion, and the deepest appreciation for the rich talents, endowments, and the earnest strivings of our Negro brothers and sisters. We are eager to share them with men of all races the blessings of the gospel. We have no racially segregated congregations.

Were we the leaders of an enterprise created by ourselves and operated only according to our own earthly wisdom, it would be a simple thing to act according to popular will. But we believe that this work is directed by God and that the conferring of the priesthood must await His revelation. To do otherwise would be to deny the very premise on which the church is established.

We recognize that those who do not accept the principle of modern revelation may oppose our point of view. We repeat that such would not wish for membership in the church, and therefore the question of priesthood should hold no interest for them.

Without prejudice they should grant us the privilege afforded under the Constitution to exercise our chosen form of religion just as we must grant all others a similar privilege. They must recognize that the question of bestowing or withholding priesthood in the church is a matter of religion and not a matter of constitutional right.

We extend the hand of friendship to men everywhere and the hand of fellowship to all who wish to join the church and partake of the many rewarding opportunities to be found therein.

This position stood until a landmark decision in 1978, when Church leader Spencer W. Kimball, after "hours of supplicating the Lord for divine guidance," had a revelation to allow "all males 12 years and older to be admitted to the priesthood."

On June 8, 1978, a letter went out to all general and local priesthood officers of the Church of Jesus Christ of Latter-Day Saints throughout the world:

As we have witnessed the expansion of the work of the Lord over the earth, we have been grateful that people of many nations have responded to the message of the restored gospel, and have joined the Church in ever-increasing numbers. This, in turn, has inspired us with a desire to extend to every worthy member of the Church all of the privileges and blessings which the gospel affords.

Aware of the promises made by the prophets and presidents of the Church who have preceded us that at some time, in God's eternal plan, all of our brethren who are worthy may receive the priesthood, and witnessing the faithfulness of those from whom the priesthood has been withheld, we have pleaded long and earnestly in behalf of these, our faithful brethren, spending many hours in the Upper Room of the Temple supplicating the Lord for divine guidance.

He has heard our prayers, and by revelation has confirmed that the long-promised day has come when every faithful, worthy man in the Church may receive the holy priesthood, with power to exercise its divine authority, and enjoy with his loved ones every blessing that flows therefrom, including the blessings of the temple.

Accordingly, all worthy male member of the Church may be ordained to be priesthood without regard for race or color. Priesthood leaders are instructed to follow the policy of carefully interviewing all candidates for ordination to either the Aaronic or the Melchizedec Priesthood to insure that they meet the established standards for worthiness.

We declare with soberness that the Lord has now made known His will for the blessing of all His children throughout the earth who will hearken to the voice of His authorized servants, and prepare themselves to receive every blessing of the gospel.

Two days after this announcement, Joseph Freeman, Jr., 26, a Salt Lake City telephone repairman and father of three, became the first black man ordained to the priesthood.

Although there are more than four million Mormons worldwide, membership is not broken down by race or nationality; thus it is not known how many black men have been ordained since.

NONAFFILIATED CHURCHES: THE EVANGELICAL MOVEMENT

One of the by-products of black migration from rural to urban areas has been the development of the so-called store front church, that is, one which serves those poor who are forced to live within the confines of what is known as "the inner city," or in other ghetto quarters. Such churches are usually set up in vacant stores which lend themselves readily to adaptation as appropriate meeting places. In some cases, such groups are affiliated with larger bodies; in others, they are individual units maintained by a single, self-appointed evangelist.

BLACK CHURCHMEN

The pioneer minister of the early churches was not only responsible for the material needs of his congregation but was also a primary force in promoting its material welfare. By working with abolitionist societies, by helping to sponsor the Underground Railroad, and by directing a number of forums for the voicing of black protest sentiment, the black minister managed to establish his church as the focal point of every significant movement designed to improve the political and social status of his congregation.

Although the importance of black churchmen is said to be declining in importance today, several major contemporary figures—the Reverend Jesse Jackson and the Reverend Ralph Abernathy to name just two—continue to exert a good part of their influence on the national scene through the pulpit. Biographies of some of these people are contained in the Civil Rights section.

This section takes into account both the historical importance of the individual and the position he occupied within the framework of the religious belief he espoused.

RICHARD ALLEN
Founder, African Methodist Episcopal (AME) Church
1760–1831

For biography see Civil Rights section.

JOHN M. BURGESS
Former Bishop, Episcopal Diocese of Massachusetts
1909

The Right Reverend Burgess, who earned the distinction of becoming the first black Episcopal bishop in the United States, was born in Grand Rapids, Michigan. He received both an A.B. and M.A. from Michigan University by 1931 and went on to graduate from the Episcopal Theological School in Cambridge, Massachusetts in 1934.

After serving in various posts, Reverend Burgess was named chaplain of Howard University in 1946 and canon of the Episcopal Cathedral in Washington, D.C. in 1951. Five years later he moved to Boston where he served as superintendent of the Episcopal City Mission until 1962, when he was appointed Suffra-

New York Minister W. Sterling Cary, president of the National Council of Churches

gan Bishop. His historical moment came in 1970, with his election as Bishop of the Diocese, and he served in that post until 1976, when he retired and moved to Connecticut.

W. STERLING CARY
Former President, National Council of Churches
1927

Once a prominent political activist and New York-based minister in the United Church of Christ, Reverend W. Sterling Cary became the first black president of the National Council of Churches in 1972. He served a three-year term, through 1974, and later moved to Illinois to become the Conference Minister for the Illinois Conference of the Church of Christ. He also served on the Church of Christ's governing board for many years until 1981.

Born in 1927 in Plainfield, New Jersey, Reverend Cary holds a B.A. from Morehouse College and a B.D. from the Union Theological Seminary. During his career, he earned a reputation for his antiwar positions and advocated extensive welfare reform, low-income housing, and strict enforcement of fair employment statutes. He also adhered to moderate theological positions and urged reconciliation between Christians who interpret the Bible conservatively and those who choose a more liberal path.

GEORGE WYLIE CLINTON
Bishop, AMEZ Church
1859–1921

An activist who was buffeted about by the ebb and flow of black fortunes after the Civil War, George

Wiley Clinton was born in Lancaster County, South Carolina and raised in the home of his grandparents with whom he and his mother lived, his father having died when Wiley was very young. In 1874 he entered South Carolina University, but he had to leave in 1877 when Governor Wade Hampton closed the school to blacks. He returned home to help his family harvest the season's crops and then became a teacher in a public school for blacks while studying law in the office of two lawyers in Lancaster. While doing so, he heeded advice in the writings of Blackstone, the great legal scholar, to study the Bible and in 1879 became a licensed preacher.

In 1891 Clinton returned to Brainard Institute in Chester, South Carolina to complete his formal education, teaching there to help pay his fees. In the 1890s he became pastor of the John Wesley Church in Pittsburgh, and in 1896 he was consecrated a bishop in the AMEZ.

During his career, Bishop Clinton was a prominent writer on church and political matters. He participated in the Southern Sociological Congress and in work of the Federal Council of the Churches of Christ in America.

FATHER DIVINE
The Peace Mission Cult
1877–1965

Father Divine was the founder of the Peace Mission Cult, a nonritualistic religious movement whose followers worshipped their leader as God incarnate on earth.

Mystery shrouds the early identity and real name of Father Divine. There is reason to believe he was born George Baker in 1877 on Hutchinson's Island in Georgia. Before the turn of the century, he lived in East Baltimore, where he preached in local Sunday schools. In 1907 he became a disciple of Sam Morris, a Pennsylvania black who called himself Father Jehovia. Two years later he switched over to John Hickerson's "Lift Ever, Die Never" group before returning to Georgia where he began his own campaign to promote himself as a "divine messenger."

Threatened by local authorities (he was once booked as "John Doe, alias God"), Father Divine left Georgia in 1914 and later settled in New York City, where he worked as a kind of employment agent for the few followers still loyal to him. Calling his meeting place "Heaven," he soon attracted a larger following and moved to Sayville, Long Island, where he was once sentenced to six months in jail as a public nuisance.

Four days after his trial, the judge in his case died of a heart attack, whereupon Father Divine was quoted as having said: "I hated to do it." The ensuing publicity enhanced his popularity.

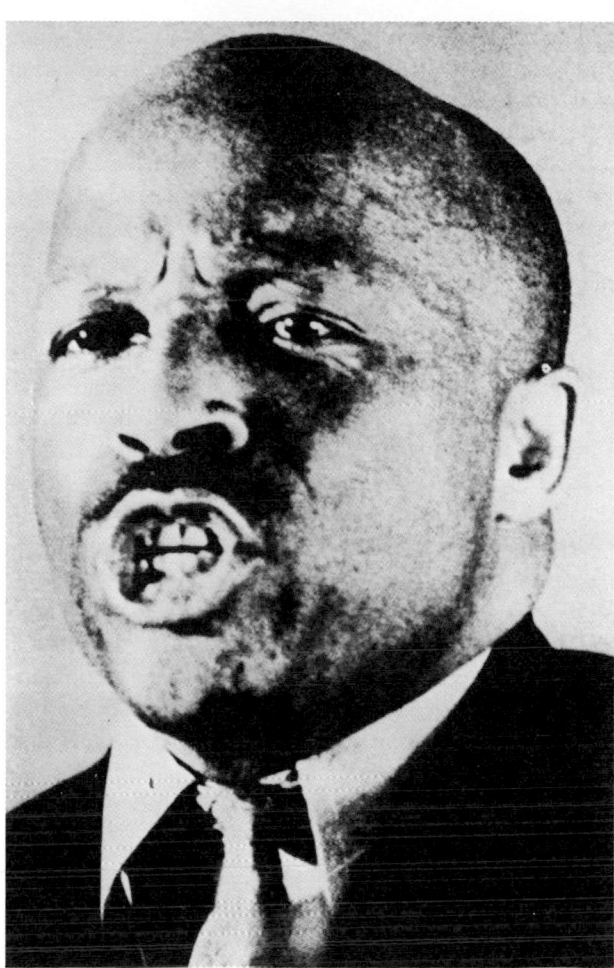

Father Divine believed he could "produce God and shake the earth with it."

The Divine movement grew by leaps and bounds in the 1930s and 1940s, with "Father" speaking across the country and publicizing his views in the *New Day*, a weekly magazine published by his organization. In 1946 he married his "Sweet Angel," a 21-year-old Canadian stenographer known thereafter as Mother Divine.

In 1953 Father Divine acquired Woodmont, a 73-acre estate in lower Merion township on Philadelphia's Main Line. In later years he came to refer to it as the showcase of the "Kingdom of Peace."

Many believers in the Father Divine cult pointed with pride to the way their leader had provided them with food and lodging over the years, at prices well within the range of their pocketbooks. The low-cost service originated in the Depression years, and has continued to be a hallmark of the missions every since then.

Spiritually, Father Divine fostered what amounted to a massive cooperative agency, based on the communal spirit of the Last Supper. Services included songs and impromptu sermons and were conducted without Scripture readings and the use of a clergy.

Father Divine himself died peacefully at Woodmont on September 10, 1965. His wife pledged to continue the work of the movement, whose property holdings were then estimated at $10 million.

GARDNER C. TAYLOR
Concord Baptist Church of Chirst
1918

Reverend Taylor is widely regarded as the dean of the nation's black preachers. He received a B.A. degree from Leland College in 1937 and B.D. degree from Oberlin Graduate School of Theology in Baton Rouge in 1940.

Reverend Taylor has long been a community activist. He demonstrated for civil rights with Martin Luther King in Brooklyn in the 1960s and was one of 700 clergymen arrested during such demonstrations. He is the past president of the Council of Churches and past vice president of the Urban League in New York City.

Reverend Taylor has been the pastor at the Concord Baptist Church of Christ in Brooklyn for more than 30 years.

ELIJAH JOHN FISHER
1858–1915

Elijah Fisher exemplifies the great charismatic black preachers of the nineteenth and early twentieth centuries who, with very little formal education, built large religious institutions, counseled racial pride, and expounded the cause of blacks as a people.

Born in La Grange, Georgia, the youngest of eight boys in a family of 17 children, Fisher's father was an unordained preacher of a Baptist congregation that met in a white church. Fisher worked in a Baptist parsonage as a boy slave, and was taught to read by a former house slave and a white missionary. In his teens, he worked in mines in Alabama and then as a butler, all the while studying theology in his own time. Though losing a leg in an accident, Fisher in his early twenties became pastor of several small country churches, then in 1889 of the Mount Olive Baptist Church in Atlanta. In that year, when past the age of 30, he enrolled in the Atlanta Baptist Seminary, later to become Morehouse College, passed his examinations, went on to preach in Nashville and then to Chicago where he led the Olivet Baptist Church from 1902 until his death.

Throughout his life, Dr. Fisher continued his studies, preached from coast to coast, and involved the Church in youth work, food programs for poor people, and black-run businesses. An active member of the Republican party, Fisher strongly criticized blacks who advised their breathren to rely solely on the good will of whites and publicly criticized Booker T. Washington for not speaking out against lynching.

JAMES AUGUSTINE HEALY
First Black Catholic Bishop
1830–1900

James Augustine Healy was the first black Catholic bishop in the United States. For 25 years he presided over a diocese covering the states of Maine and New Hampshire.

A native of Macon, Georgia, Healy received his education in the North, first at Franklin Park Quaker School in Burlington, New York and later at Holy Cross in Worcester, Massachusetts. After graduating from the latter with first honors. Healy continued his studies abroad, and was ordained in Paris at Notre Dame Cathedral in 1854. He then returned to the United States.

Pastor of a predominantly Irish congregation which was at first reluctant to accept him, Bishop Healy performed his priestly duties with devotion and eventually won the respect and admiration of his parishioners—particularly after performing his office during a typhoid epidemic.

Thereafter, he was made an assistant to Bishop John

James A. Healy was the first black American to become a Roman Catholic bishop.

Fitzpatrick of Boston, who appointed him chancellor and entrusted him with a wide variety of additional responsibilities. In 1875 he was named Bishop of Portland, Maine.

Bishop Healy died in 1900. (His brother, Patrick Francis Healy, was a Jesuit priest who served as president of Georgetown University from 1873 to 1882.)

JOSEPH LAWSON HOWZE
Auxiliary Bishop of Mississippi
1925

Born in Daphne, Alabama, Reverend Howze attended Junior College in Alabama, graduated with a B.S. in Education from Alabama State University, and taught sciences in the public schools of Mobile. During the 1940s, Howze increasingly questioned the desirability of a public school teaching career for himself and in 1950 entered Epiphany Apostolic College in Newburgh, New York. In 1959 he graduated from St. Bonaventure University, New York and entered the priesthood. In 1973 he was named to his current post, becoming the second black bishop presently in the Catholic Church, the other being Bishop Perry of Louisiana.

JOSEPH H. JACKSON
President, National Baptist Convention, U.S.A., Inc.

Dr. Joseph H. Jackson has been the leader of some 5 million U.S. black Baptists since 1953, the year he was elected to the presidency of the National Baptist Convention, U.S.A., Inc. Dr. Jackson has steered the organization into new spheres of influence, notably into a more activist role in the civil rights struggle.

One of the most ambitious ventures initiated under Dr. Jackson has been the Liberian land investment program whereby Baptists hope to develop extensive farms on some 100,000 acres of Liberian land, and thus raise additional funds to help sponsor their missionary labors in Africa. The Convention has also purchased 400 acres in Fayette County, Tennessee, and owns a Nashville publishing house with sales of close to $1 million annually.

Dr. Jackson holds a B.A. from Jackson College, an M.A. from Creighton University, and a B.D. from Rochester Colgate School of Divinity. He is a member of the Central Committee of the World Council of Churches and a vice president of the World Baptist Alliance. He has visited Asia, Africa, Europe, and the Middle East, taped messages for the Voice of America, preached in Russia, written campaign literature for John F. Kennedy, and attended the 1962 Second Vatican Council in Rome. He is pastor of Olivet Baptist Church in Chicago.

ISAAC LANE
Bishop, Colored Methodist Church
1834–1937

A great religious leader and educator, whose life spanned more than a century, Isaac Lane was born a slave in Jackson, Tennessee. Self-educated, in 1856 he was granted a license to exhort, a category assigned blacks who were forbidden to preach, in the Methodist Episcopal Church, South.

Lane was ordained a minister in 1865 and in 1873 was made a bishop, at a salary so low he had to raise cotton to supplement his income and support his family, which contained 11 children. In the 1890s, he established Lane College in Jackson with $9,000 he himself raised.

ELIJAH MUHAMMAD
Spiritual Leader of the Nation of Islam
1897–1975

Perhaps the United States' most significant and controversial religious leader of the twentieth century, Elijah Muhammad was born Elijah Poole in Sandersville, Georgia in 1897. His father, a Baptist preacher, had been a slave.

As a boy, Elijah worked as a sawmill helper and field boy, later as a laborer for the Southern Railroad and as a foreman for a brick company. At the age of 26, he moved with his wife and two children (he was to have eight children in all) to Detroit where he worked at several jobs, including one for Chevrolet.

In Detroit in 1930 Poole met Fard Muhammad, also known as W. D. Fard, who had founded the Black Nation of Islam. Poole soon became Fard's chief assistant and in 1932 went to Chicago where he established the Nation of Islam's Temple, Number Two, which soon became the largest. In 1934 he returned to Detroit. When Fard disappeared in that year, political and theological rivals accused Poole of foul play. He returned to Chicago where he organized his own movement, in which Fard was deified as Allah and Elijah (Poole) Muhammad became known as Allah's Messenger. This movement soon became known as the Black Muslims.

During World War II Elijah Muhammad expressed support for Japan, on the basis of its being a nonwhite country, and was jailed for sedition. The time Muhammad served in prison was probably significant in his later, successful attempts to convert large numbers of black prison inmates, including Malcolm X, to the Nation of Islam. During the 1950s, and especially during the 1960s, the Nation grew under Muhammad's leadership, surviving internal differences between Muhammad and Malcolm X. In the late 1960s and early 1970s Elijah Muhammad moderated the Nation's criticism of whites without compromising its message of black integrity. When Muhammad died in 1975 the Nation was an important religious, political, and economic force among America's blacks and in this country's major cities.

Elijah Muhammad was a leader whose significance was too great to assess shortly after his death. But some factors stand out. In many respects, Muhammad resembled the great black religious leaders of the late nineteenth and early twentieth centuries. He appealed to the racial consciousness and pride of blacks and he advocated discipline and abstinence in personal living. But he was clearly unique in three ways.

His message on the virtues of being black was explicit and uncompromising.

In addition to preaching the importance of self-sufficiency for blacks, he sought successfully through the Nation's schools and business enterprises to provide vehicles for attaining this self-sufficiency.

He built the first strong, national religious group in the United States that appealed primarily to the unemployed and underemployed city dweller. In his later years, Muhammad made some attempts to broaden the Nation's appeal to the growing black middle class, but a preponderance of the Nation's membership continued to come from the ranks of poor people who sought to live with pride and decency in America's black ghettos.

THOMAS PAUL
Baptist Leader
1773–1831

Thomas Paul is credited with having begun the movement to establish independent black Baptist churches in the United States.

Organizing a congregation of free blacks in a church on Jay Street in Boston (1805), Paul soon became so famous that he was invited to speak before white con-

Reverend Thomas Paul organized the first black Baptist church in Boston.

gregations in New York City where blacks were maintained as "segregated brethren." The First Baptist Church soon granted 16 of its members the right to organize a separate congregation under Paul's leadership. (It later became known as Abyssinian Baptist Church.)

Paul also carried his message to the Caribbean, spending six months in Haiti under the auspices of the Massachusetts Baptist Society. He later returned to the United States, continuing his work in the North until his death in 1831.

HAROLD ROBERT PERRY
Auxiliary Bishop of New Orleans

Harold Robert Perry was consecrated a Bishop of New Orleans on January 6, 1966—and thus became the first black Catholic bishop in the United States in the twentieth century.

One of six children, Perry was born the son of a rice-mill worker and a domestic cook in Lake Charles, Louisiana. He entered the Divine Word Seminary in Mississippi at the age of 13, was ordained a priest in 1944, and spent the next 14 years in parish work. In 1958 he was appointed rector of the seminary.

Louisiana has the largest concentration of black Catholics in the South, some 200,000 in all.

Perry is one of five black bishops now serving in Catholic parishes around the nation. Others include Joseph Howze in Biloxi, Mississippi; James Lyke in Cleveland, Ohio; Joseph Francis in Newark, New Jersey; and Eugene Marino in Washington, D. C.

ADAM CLAYTON POWELL, SR.
Pastor, Abyssinian Baptist Church
1865–1953

Adam Clayton Powell, Sr.—father of the late Harlem congressman— was largely responsible for building the Abyssinian Baptist Church into one of the most celebrated black congregations in the world.

Born in the backwoods of Virginia in 1865, Powell attended school locally and, between sessions, worked in the mines of West Virginia. After deciding to enter the ministry, he began his studies at Wayland Academy (now Virginia Union University), working his way through as a janitor and waiter. He later attended the Yale University School of Divinity and served as pastor of the Immanuel Baptist Church in New Haven.

Powell became pastor of Abyssinian in 1908—when it had a membership of only 1,600 and indebtedness of over $100,000. By 1921 the church had not been made solvent but was able to move into a $350,000 Gothic structure at its present location on 138th Street in Harlem.

During the depression Powell opened soup kitchens for Harlem residents and served thousands of meals. Later he and his son campaigned vigorously to expand job opportunities and city services in Harlem.

Powell retired from Abyssinian in 1937. He died in 1953, at which time the church was being pastored by his son.

STEPHEN GILL SPOTTSWOOD
1897–1974

Bishop of the African Episcopal Zion Church from 1952 to 1972 and board chairman of the National Association for the Advancement of Colored People from 1961 until his death in 1974, Bishop Spottswood embodied the religious faith and intellectual incisiveness that has produced so many effective black religious activists.

Reverend Spottswood was born in Boston, attended Albright College, Gordon Divinity School, and then received a Doctor of Divinity from Yale University.

As a religious leader, Bishop Spottswood was president of the Ohio Council of Churches and served on the boards of numerous interfaith conferences as well as heading the AMEZ church. His activity with NAACP started in 1919, when he joined the organization. He was appointed to the national board in 1955. In 1971 he became the center of a political storm when he chastised the Nixon administration for its policies toward blacks and refused, under strong pressure from the administration, to retract his comments.

GOSPEL MUSIC IN THE UNITED STATES

Gospel music, a function of the camp-meeting spiritual, blues, and jazz, has as its theme uninhibited praise and joyous worship of God. Major rhythms of gospel pieces are up-tempo and syncopated, but their melodies remain simple enough to enable large numbers of untrained musicians to master the playing and singing. Their harmonies are generally uncomplicated, although they have of late begun to show the influence of other musical forms.

The main performer in gospel is an outstanding soloist who is usually backed by a combination of singers able to provide him or her with a moving foundation on which to base improvisations. (This is, then, not unlike jazz where the group often forms a fabric around and through which the soloist may move.) Another major aspect of gospel is the highly repetitious "drive" which seeks to raise the fervor of the audience by building a hypnotic effect over it. The repeated phrases of the "drive" are intended to sway the listener and create a mood which mounts to an apex of power.

The Utterbach Concert Ensemble blends the fervor of gospel with classical and contemporary harmony.

Historical Roots

The rich, vibrant gospel music of the American black— an integral part of most traditional black religious services—can be grouped into two main styles or divisions: spirituals themselves, with their poignant and soulful quality ("Deep River," "Were You There," "Nobody Knows the Trouble I've Seen"), and camp-meeting songs, sung in part by a "leader" and then taken up by a "congregation," or chorus.

Along with traditional hymns, spirituals were sung during worship services in black Baptist or Methodist churches and were also heard in conjunction with the work songs which the black devised to help him through his wearisome field labors. The "field holler," a combination of yell and yodel developed by black slaves in the South, eventually became a component of solo blues, a musical diary through which blacks expressed despair and hopelessness.

Spirituals, hymns, and blues—these were the three ingredients which contributed most significantly to the development of gospel music in the post-Emancipation era. The black was free but remained a creature apart from the rest of humanity, still clinging to the single institution around which much of his social life revolved: the church.

Choral or communal singing in the black church

soon came to be a highly organized practice. Certain arrangements of traditional spirituals then began to incorporate ideas from the blues idiom, together with a more syncopated, up-tempo style. In the early 1900s, a blues pianist, Thomas A. Dorsey, was sufficiently impressed by some of this music to write original tunes using this form. Dorsey was later responsible for popularizing it across the country by going on tour with Sallie Martin, a religious singer.

The leader–congregation style eventually gave way to the soloist–background method of performing. In this way, several soloists began to gain widespread fame for their artistic achievement. In the late 1930s, for example, Miss Roberta Martin of Chicago brought together several young soloists of varying styles and outstanding ability and formed a small, mixed group known as the Roberta Martin Singers. (This group is still in existence today.) Elsewhere in Chicago, Miss Mahalia Jackson was also on her way to becoming an international celebrity through her singular renditions of black gospel music. In the East, it was Clara Ward and the Ward Singers, given their original impetus by Mrs. Gertrude Ward. The Ward Singers introduced new techniques into their performances, employing all-female voices singing together in unusually high-pitched harmony and using synchronized theatrical motions and movements in their presentations.

Postwar Trends

During World War II "jubilee" singing had a run of popularity, involving as it did male quartets who sang a type of arranged spiritual. Perhaps the most representative of these groups in this era was the Golden Gate Quartet. Radio appearances by such choral ensembles as The Wings Over Jordan group helped popularize the gospel style even further, making thousands of people more acutely aware of a coming musical trend. Soon, the recording industry (Apollo and Gotham records) took a more active interest in cultivating this brand of music. One of the first big recording successes for gospel was "Old Ship of Zion" by the Roberta Martin Singers, featuring the voice of Norsalus McKissick.

The music itself quickly became separated into two camps: gospel and quartet. Gospel included all-male, all-female, or mixed groups using piano or organ as accompanying instruments, whereas quartet involved all-male groups whose accompaniment was always provided by a guitarist. Gospel singers generally used colorful choir robes, whereas quartet groups were identified by conventional coat and trousers.

The first gospel recording which sold over a million copies—"Surely God Is Able" (Savoy Records)—was made during the late 1940s by Clara Ward and her group. Soon thereafter the Alex Bradford Singers recorded "Too Close to Heaven" (Specialty Records), a tune which approximated the success of "Surely." Gospel arrangers then began to pore through the pages of hymnals in search of appropriate material for the growing number of revivals, festivals, and other programs.

In the 1950s, the Davis Sisters came to dominate the gospel field, ushering in the era of "song battles" between competing groups which would try to outdo each other in the intensity and fervor of their performances. Some of the most popular tunes recorded by the Davis Sisters were "Jesus," "Reign in Jerusalem," "He'll Understand," "Plant My Feet on Higher Ground," and "Twelve Gates to the City." (Perhaps the archrivals of the Davis Sisters during these years were the Gospel Harmonettes of Birmingham, led by Dorothy Love. Among the leading tunes recorded by the Harmonettes were "I'm Sealed," "You Must Be Born Again," "That'sa Enough," and "Lord, You've Been Good to Me.")

The leading quartet groups of this period included The Dixie Hummingbirds, The Nightingales, The Harmonizing Four, and The Soul Stirrers. (Sam Cooke, later to gain great fame in the popular music field, was once a regular performer with the last-named group, and had such hits as "Nearer to Thee" and "Touch the Hem of His Garment.")

The Impact of Gospel

Gospel had profound effects on rock 'n' roll performers like Ray Charles and James Brown, both of whom retained the same inflections used by the gospel singer. In fact, many churches in which gospel music is sung have served as a kind of unintentional training ground for rock 'n' roll, popular, and jazz musicians whose trademark came to be called "soul."

Over the years, gospel forms have often been incorporated into more programmed arrangements in an effort to blend the fervor and excitement of the music itself with the form and texture of classical music.

Inevitably, gospel music achieved the international spotlight. Instrumental in this was Langston Hughes, whose singsong plays *Black Nativity, Jericho, Jim Crow,* and *Trumpets for the Lord* were successful abroad. In many respects, gospel's European success paralleled that of the Fisk Jubilee Singers, who toured Europe in 1870.

In the 1960s, gospel started to move from the churches into auditoriums across the country where jazz and folk music enthusiasts lined up to hear performances. Along with jazz and spirituals, gospel was recognized as a significant black contribution to American culture and the world of music.

Table 1. Summary of Current and Noncurrent Statistics on Black Churches

Faith	Churches	Membership	Clergy	Date of Last Report
African Methodist Episcopal Church	3,050	1,970,000	3,938	1979
African Methodist Episcopal Zion Church	6,020	1,125,176	6,716	1979
African Orthodox Church	25	6,000	50	1957
Apostolic Overcoming Holy Church of God	300	75,000	350	1956
Christian Methodist Episcopal Church	2,598	466,718	2,214	1965
Christian Unity Baptist Association	5	345	9	1970
Christ's Sanctified Holy Church	30	600	30	1957
Church of Christ Holiness in U.S.A.	159	9,829	76	1965

Table 1. Summary of Current and Noncurrent Statistics on Black Churches (*continued*)

Faith	Churches	Membership	Clergy	Date of Last Report
Church of God and Saints of Christ	217	38,217		1959
The Church of God in Christ	4,500	425,000	6,000	1965
Church of the Living God	276	45,320	376	1964
Fire Baptized Holiness Church	53	998		1958
Free Christian Zion Church of Christ	742	22,260	340	1956
House of God, Which is the Church of the Living God, the Pillar and Ground of the Truth, Inc.	107	2,350	170	1956
Kodesh Church of Immanuel	5	326	28	1980
National Baptist Convention of America	11,398	2,668,799	28,574	1956
National Baptist Convention in the U.S.A., Inc.	26,000	5,500,000	27,500	1958
National Primitive Baptist Convention Inc.	606	250,000	636	1975
Progressive National Baptist Convention Inc.	655	521,692	863	1967
Reformed Methodist Union Episcopal Church	17	3,800	26	1976
Reformed Zion Union Apostolic Church	50	16,000		1965
Second Cumberland Presbyterian Church in the U.S.A.	121	30,000	125	1959
Triumph the Church and Kingdom of God in Christ Inc.	475	54,307	1,375	1972
United Free Will Baptist Church	836	100,000	915	1952
United Holy Church of America, Inc.	470	28,980	400	1960

Table 2. Catholic Percentage of the Black Population: Major Dioceses of the United States

City	Catholic Percentage of Black Population	Black Percentage of Total Population	Change in Black Population 1960–1970	Number of Black Catholics	Black Percentage of Catholic Population
Albany	1.7	2.3	7,916	500	0.1
Alexandria	2.3	36.2	23,599	9,000	10.6
Amarillo	0.8	4.9	−2,296	288	0.3
Atlanta	0.4	20.6	76,976	2,600	3.8
Austin	1.1	14.0	4,567	1,500	1.0
Baltimore	4.1	21.1	105,458	20,814	4.4
Baton Rouge	6.8	32.9	8,101	12,960	7.8
Belleville	4.0	9.9	11,707	3,312	2.8
Birmingham	0.7	20.0	−76,469	3,342	7.8
Boston	3.6	3.6	50,422	5,000	0.2
Brooklyn	3.2	19.9	396,940	30,000	1.9
Buffalo	2.6	6.5	27,280	3,000	0.4
Camden	4.2	12.2	26,210	5,425	1.6
Charleston	0.6	30.4	−40,250	4,978	10.6
Chicago	6.6	20.4	330,491	80,000	3.1
Cincinnati	1.8	10.0	46,937	5,000	0.9
Cleveland	2.3	13.3	88,614	9,000	0.9
Columbus	2.0	5.2	−5,261	1,957	1.1
Corpus Christi	6.1	3.2	1,175	1,000	0.5
Covington	1.5	3.9	−4,510	800	0.8
Dallas	0.3	17.4	67,796	1,500	1.3
Detroit	5.2	16.9	198,493	40,000	2.7
Erie	6.3	1.8	2,086	1,015	0.4
Evansville	4.1	2.8	786	500	0.5
Ft. Worth	0.8	8.5	23,363	910	1.2
Fresno	7.5	4.5	5,359	4,000	1.5
Galveston	7.0	20.2	105,709	33,210	10.3
Gary	4.1	15.7	27,168	5,000	2.6

Table 2. Catholic Percentage of the Black Population: Major Dioceses of the United States (*continued*)

City	Catholic Percentage of Black Population	Black Percentage of Total Population	Change in Black Population 1960–1970	Number of Black Catholics	Black Percentage of Catholic Population
Indianapolis	4.8	7.7	38,494	7,650	3.6
Kansas City, KS	4.2	6.5	6,944	2,500	1.8
Kansas City, MO	7.4	9.8	29,425	9,050	6.6
Lafayette, LA	47.2	25.1	15,961	80,237	20.2
Lansing	0.7	7.1	38,517	800	0.3
Little Rock	0.3	18.3	−36,342	1,100	1.9
Los Angeles	5.7	8.6	317,081	45,000	2.5
Louisville	4.8	10.3	19,717	6,000	3.0
Miami	1.6	14.4	85,710	5,828	1.0
Milwaukee	12.4	5.9	50,159	15,000	2.1
Mobile—Birmingham	1.7	36.9	−335	8,000	18.3
Monterey—Fresno	0.3	3.0	5,359	49	>0.1
Nashville	0.5	9.1	8,396	1,500	2.8
Natchez	0.9	36.7	−99,973	7,542	9.0
Newark	1.8	14.2	149,564	8,000	0.6
Oklahoma City	6.3	6.5	15,804	6,000	10.4
Omaha	2.7	5.1	10,430	1,000	0.5
New Orleans	21.8	25.7	−36	75,000	11.2
New York	5.6	17.3	225,970	50,000	2.7
Oakland	7.4	12.4	65,833	15,060	4.5
Owensboro	1.3	7.7	−363	700	1.5
Pittsburgh	1.4	7.2	9,238	2,500	0.2
Portland	3.1	1.3	8,067	800	0.4
Raleigh	0.2	30.4	71,490	2,156	6.3
Reno	7.2	5.6	14,278	2,000	2.1
Richmond	0.9	22.8	59,222	7,446	6.9
Sacramento	9.7	5.6	33,270	8,000	3.5
St. Augustine	0.7	22.0	14,282	1,500	3.2
St. Louis	9.5	15.6	66,664	29,000	5.6
St. Paul	9.2	1.5	11,548	3,000	0.5
San Diego	9.1	4.4	55,756	10,550	2.6
San Francisco	3.1	13.6	254,894	11,000	1.8
Savannah	0.5	33.2	−12,423	3,500	9.9
Seattle	3.9	2.4	22,106	2,500	0.9
Toledo	2.4	5.6	15,937	2,000	0.6
Trenton	0.9	7.1	52,984	1,500	0.1
Tucson	1.6	2.9	2,261	300	0.1
Tulsa	1.5	6.9	3,004	1,200	2.7
Washington	10.4	33.0	201,322	71,304	17.8
Wichita	11.3	4.4	6,683	4,200	5.0
Wilmington	1.4	16.7	17,852	2,000	1.7

NATIONAL BLACK ORGANIZATIONS

Fraternities ■ Sororities ■ Professional Societies ■ Religious and Cooperative Associations ■ Lodges ■ Brotherhoods ■ Benevolent Orders ■ Various Incorporated Groups

During the 1970s and early 1980s, the tenor and orientation of black organizations increasingly reflected the desire of blacks to work on their own behalf, independent of control by whites, and to explore black history and heritage. Many organizations were also formed to develop and explore business opportunities for blacks, this in response to government programs encouraging minority enterpreneurship. However, traditional black groups of a professional and fraternal nature remained prominent as did racially integrated organizations with social and political objectives. Groups stressing economic progress by poor tenants, welfare recipients, etc., of all races increased in importance in the mid-1970s. Also notable in the 1970s was the increasing prominence of black women in positions of leadership. For example, Margaret Bush Wilson became board chairman of the National Association for the Advancement of Colored People. Another trend was the emergence of black caucuses within white groups. The most notable of these was formation of the Congressional Black Caucus in the House of Representatives. Others appeared within such professional societies as the American Bar Association, to complement the efforts of groups consisting entirely of blacks.

A Brief History

Throughout their history on these shores, blacks have displayed a remarkable capacity to organize in pursuit of their political and personal objectives. The nature of these organizations of course has varied in terms of what was permitted, by whites, as well as what was sought by blacks.

Until the late eighteenth century, blacks were frequently forbidden by white laws and policies to organize in more than the most informal and limited sense. Thus black organizations that did exist were clandestine and unrecorded, and the first black organization in what is now the United States cannot be identified. Probably it was some camp of runaway slaves in Virginia in the seventeenth century. Some of these camps survived as independent communities for many years with their own government, rules, and procedures, and so certainly qualify as "organizations."

In the 1770s, following zealous efforts by white evangelists, a small number of blacks in South Carolina and Georgia were permitted to form their own churches (as discussed elsewhere in this volume). At about the same time, black slaves in New England were organizing, with sympathetic whites, to sue for their freedom in Massachusetts courts.

The Free African Society formed by Richard Allen in Philadelphia in 1787 is generally viewed as the United States' first black organization of note. In many respects, its orientation was a model for groups to follow. It was founded by a clergyman, in great part so blacks could worship without interference from harassing whites, but it soon became a factor in the education and political status of blacks. The influence of clergymen in lay black groups remains important to this day, with Reverends Jesse Jackson of Operation

The A. Philip Randolph Institute has been effective both in labor conference rooms and in the streets, getting people to take an active role in their communities.

PUSH, Cecil Williams of the Glide Memorial Church, and John Lewis of the Voters Education Project but three of many current examples.

In the nineteenth century, organizations concerned with issues important to blacks were invariably dominated by whites. Blacks had little influence in abolitionist and "back to Africa" efforts, though black leaders and heroes such as Paul Cuffe and Frederick Douglass did emerge.

During Reconstruction and into the early twentieth century a great many black groups were formed. The thrust of most was toward education, betterment, and religious training, and in many cases also a reassurance of whites that blacks posed no threat to the nation's segregationist order. Other organizations, however, such as the National Colored Farmers Alliance, sought, with unfortunately little success, to strengthen the economic and political position of blacks.

In the early twentieth century, led by W. E. B.

DuBois, a black intelligentsia increasingly came to the fore, to struggle for the rights of blacks, first in the Niagara Movement founded in 1905, then in the National Association for the Advancement of Colored People, which succeeded it in 1910, and the Urban League shortly thereafter.

Less noted by historians, but of great significance during the early decades of this century was the formation and growth of professional, business, and labor groups such as the National Medical Association, the National Negro Business League, the National Newspaper Publishers Association, the Brotherhood of Sleeping Car Porters, and scores of others.

Though less publicized than civil rights and black power groups, they have also contributed enormously to the progress of blacks and it is such organizations as well as those with political objectives which are listed and briefly described in the ensuing pages.

PROMINENT BLACK ORGANIZATIONS*

A. Philip Randolph Institute

260 Park Avenue South
New York, NY 10010
(212) 533-8000

To promote institutional changes in this country's social and economic structure through political action programs and a broad-based national coalition of minorities, the poor, and working people. The Institute believes the labor movement occupies a pivotal role within this alliance.

Afram Associates, Inc.

68–72 East 131 Street
New York, NY 10037
(212) 690-7010

To develop a depository of information and research for use by the community's action groups; to reprint and circulate articles on critical social issues; to formulate and implement research about the problems of minority groups; to provide staff services to groups involved with consumers and the community and, ultimately, to promote self-understanding, self-determination, and true liberation.

African American Institute

833 United Nations Plaza
New York, NY 10017
(212) 661-0800

To strengthen African-American understanding, to inform America about Africa, and to help further African development.

African American Scholars Council, Inc.

1001 Connecticut Avenue NW, Suite 1119
Washington, DC 20036
(202) 785-4743

An educational organization to promote social, economic, and human resources of the African continent.

African Bibliographic Center, Inc.

1346 Connecticut Avenue NW, #901
Washington, DC 20036
(202) 233-1392

To disseminate information on African affairs in the United States and abroad. The information is selected primarily on a "need to know" basis by print and electronic media forms.

African Methodist Episcopal Church

2311 M Street
Washington, DC 20037
(202) 337-3930

Operates a Home and Foreign Mission Board as well as maintaining churches; supports schools, hospitals, and other public facilities in eight overseas missions in South and Central America, the West Indies, and Africa.

Africare

1601 Connecticut Avenue NW
Washington, DC 20009
(202) 462-3614

To offer people an opportunity to relate to Africa; especially reawakened blacks. To make a tangible contribution to the development of Africa and facilitate opportunities for Africa to set its own direction.

Afro American Cultural Foundation

394 Tarrytown Road
White Plains, NY 10607
(914) 761-4778

To improve the self-esteem of blacks, change the attitude of whites toward black people and their talents, to raise awareness of the potentials and problems of black people and help eliminate latent and induced prejudices.

Afro-American Cultural and Historical Society

1839 East 81 Street
Cleveland, OH 44104
(216) 795-3121

To build an International African and Afro-American Historical Society Museum and Library; erect monuments in Cleveland honoring Colonel Charles Young and Reverend John Malvin, Cleveland's first ordained black minister. To integrate textbooks in the school system and promote the study of Afro-American history. To obtain official national holidays honoring Harriet Tubman, Crispus Attucks, Colonel Young, Mary McLeod Bethune, and Dr. Martin Luther King, Jr.

Afro-American Music Hall of Fame and Musicians, Inc.

P.O. Box 3901
Youngstown, OH 44505
(216) 746-7189

To ensure that the works of the Afro-Americans in the world of rhythm and blues, jazz, and gospel music will live

* This section also lists some organizations which, while nonblack, focus on minority issues. These groups are set off by an asterisk.

The Afram staff operates one of the Harlem community's chief information agencies.

on, to enlighten, to educate, and to entertain all those who visit the Hall of Fame so they will feel fulfillment and they will pass on the works of their ancestors and the Hall of Fame.

Afro-American Music Opportunities Association, Inc.

2909 Wayzata Boulevard
Minneapolis, MN 55405
(612) 377-3730

To help place black performers in professional ensembles; black music specialists on college campuses; assist these individuals in educational opportunities, materials, and repertoire; assemble information on black music history and make it readily available to the public; serve as a repository and clearinghouse on all aspects of black music.

The Afro-American Patrolmen's League

7126 South Jeffery Boulevard
Chicago, IL 60649
(312) 667-7384

Elevate the image of black policemen, especially in the black community; seek fair hiring and promotion practices of black police; represent needs of minority people to police departments; elevate police performance and act as a check on unethical police practices; lessen danger and increase understanding between police and citizens, improve relations between black and white police.

American Association for Affirmative Action

State University College at Buffalo
GC 405
1300 Elmwood Avenue
Buffalo, NY 14222
(716) 878-6210

To implement affirmative action and equal opportunity nationwide and serve as a liaison to private and governmental agencies involved with compliance in employment and education.

American Association of Mesbics

915 15th Street, N.W., Suite 700
Washington, DC 20005
(202) 347-8600

To foster capital formation and promote development of venture capital for small businesses. The organization is also a research and information resource.

American Bridge Association

555 Kappock Street
Riverdale, NY 10463
(212) 543-2910

Provides a competitive arena to develop the skills of bridge players and, through its tournaments, fosters vocational excellence and good citizenship.

Ancient Egyptian Arabic Order Nobles Mystic Shrine, Inc.

Imperial Recorder's Office
65 Cadillac Square, Suite 3111
Detroit, MI 48226
(313) 961-9148

A worldwide charitable and benevolent organization sponsoring action programs to curb delinquency and drug abuse among black youngsters. Also lends support to education through its scholarship efforts.

Alliance Enterprise Corporation

1616 Walnut Street, Suite 802
Philadelphia, PA 19103
(215) 732-2812

To make the maximum contribution within capital resource limitations to the economic growth of the minority business community.

Alpha Kappa Alpha Sorority, Inc.

5211 South Greenwood Avenue
Chicago, IL 60615
(312) 684-1282

To cultivate and encourage high scholastic and ethical standards, to promote unity and friendship among college women, to study and help alleviate problems concerning girls and women in order to improve the social stature, to maintain a progressive interest in college life, and to be of service to all mankind.

Alpha Phi Alpha Fraternity, Inc.

4432 Martin Luther King, Jr. Drive
Chicago, IL 60653
(312) 373-1819

To promote a more perfect union among college men, aid in and insist upon personal progress of membership; further brotherly love and a fraternal spirit; discountenance evil; destroy all prejudices, preserve the sanctity of the home, the personification of virtue and chastity of woman; aid downtrodden humanity in its efforts to achieve higher social, economic, and intellectual status.

American Committee on Africa

164 Madison Avenue
New York, NY 10016
(212) 532-3700

To establish an organization in the United States fully sympathetic with and actively supporting the struggle for freedom of the people of Africa.

American Economic Association

1313 Twenty-First Avenue South
Nashville, TN 37212
(615) 322-2595

To encourage economic research, especially historical and statistical study; issue publications on economic subjects; promote perfect freedom of economic discussion.

American Library Association Black Caucus

Bureau of Academic and Research Libraries
99 Washington Avenue
Albany, NY 12230

Serve as a clearinghouse for black librarians; review, analyze, evaluate and recommend to the American Library Association actions on the needs of black librarians in the areas of recruitment, development, advancement, and general working conditions.

The American Society for Training and Development

P.O. Box 5307
Madison, WI 53705
(608) 274-3440

A professional society devoted exclusively to the education, development, and expansion of the skills and standards of members in the training and development profession.

The American Committee on Africa focuses on Third World problems.

American Society of Planning Officials

1313 East 60 Street
Chicago, IL 60637
(312) 947-2560

To evolve the best techniques for guiding development in cities, regions, states, and the nation. Facilitates communication among all groups in the planning field. Seeks to provide professional aid to the planner.

The Amistad Research Center

Dillard University
New Orleans, LA 70122
(504) 944-0239

The center is a historical research library which collects primary source material on the histories and cultures of America's ethnic minorities. Its 8,000,000 manuscript pieces comprise the world's largest collection of original material on the Afro-American and on race relations in the United States. Although privately funded, the center is a public archive open to all students of American Ethnic history.

Arizona Contractors' Service Center, Inc.

1800 North Central, Suite 201
Phoenix, AZ 85004
(602) 267-7541

Management assistance for minority contractors in the state of Arizona.

The Association for Black Management in Health Care, Inc.

120 Liberty Street
New York, NY 10006
(212) 682-5595

Health systems economic development to advance the participation and involvement in service provision in health care delivery.

Association of Black Psychologists

P.O. Box 2929
Washington, DC 20013
(202) 462-7553

To unite black professionals and students of psychology in order to enhance the psychological well-being of black people. It also seeks to influence the mental health of the black community through research and developing policies on the local, state, and national levels.

Association for the Integration of Management, Inc.

280 Park Avenue
West Building, 33F
New York, NY 10017
(212) 687-7075

To achieve full particpation in the management by minority group men and women; to accelerate the movement of minority group men and women into key positions in management.

The Association for the Study of Afro-American Life and History, Inc.

1401 Fourteenth Street, N.W.
Washington, DC 20005
(202) 667-2822

To promote an appreciation of the life and history of the black man,

Architect's model of the Amistad Research Center, world's largest collection of Afro-American source material.

encourage an understanding of his present status, and enrich the promise of the future.

Association of Social and Behavioral Scientists

Box 5522
Durham, NC 27707
(919) 684-3175

To study the weakness in social science offerings with the view of recommending improvements. To think through some of the most difficult and perplexing problems confronting blacks from the black point of view, with the intent of working out satisfactory methods and plans for acquainting the student with and developing within him a philosophy and an attitude that will enable him to confront the baffling problems that he will face throughout life.

Association for the Study of Afro-American Life and History

1401 14th Street, N.W.
Washington, DC 20005
(202) 667-2822

Promotes the appreciation of the life and the history of the black American. The association also encourages a better understanding of present black life while at the same time working to enrich the promise of the future.

Association of United Contractors of America, Inc.

360 West 125 Street
New York, NY 10027
(212) 663-0900

To help eliminate discrimination against minority groups in all phases of building construction and general business, thereby contributing to the general growth of the country through economic well-being and stability.

Atlanta Associated Contractors and Trade Council, Inc.

825½ Cascade Avenue, S.W.
Atlanta, GA 30311

To assist minority contractors in developing and creating new businesses; to improve those already in existence, to assist and/or encourage successful minority contractors in expanding existing business.

Members of the Black Economic Research Center. Robert S. Brown (center) *is staff leader.*

Audience Development Committee, Inc.

969 Third Avenue
New York, NY 10022
(212) PL 9-2424

To generate more recognition, understanding, and awareness of the arts in the black community.

Bedford-Stuyvesant Restoration Corporation

1368 Fulton Street
Brooklyn, NY 11216
(212) 636-1100

The social, physical, and economic redevelopment of the Bedford-Stuyvesant community.

Bancap Corporation

420 Lexington Avenue
New York, NY 10017
(212) 684-6460

Economic development of minority group members.

Black Affairs Center, Inc.

1200 Fifteenth Street, N.W., Suite 608
Washington, DC 20005
(202) 872-1787

Provides training, consultation, and applied survey research and evaluation for individuals, educational institutions, organizations—public/private, communities, and religious groups. Adapts the use of behavioral science technology to meet the often neglected and overlooked needs of the black community.

Black Child Development Institute, Inc.

1028 Connecticut Avenue, N.W.,
Suite 514
Washington, DC 20036
(202) 659-4010

To ensure that every black child receives comprehensive developmental services; assist black parents and communities in making policies and decisions that affect black children; ensure that programs dealing with a black child are consistent with the reality of his experience and recognize the strengths of his family and community.

Black Development Foundation, Inc.

442 Pratt Street
Buffalo, NY 14204
(716) 855-1703

To promote economic development in the city of Buffalo, specifically in the disadvantaged community; to mobilize local municipal governments and coordinate state and federal grants to further the economic aid.

Black Economic Research Center

112 West 120 Street
New York, NY 10027
(212) 666-0310

To focus attention and skills on the economic aspects of the black condition with a view toward discovering more effective ways of winning the full measure of dignity, security, power, and economic well-being for blacks.

Black Economic Union of Greater Kansas City

2502 Prospect Avenue
Kansas City, MO 64127
(816) 924-6789

To assist minorities to join the "mainstream" of the American economy.

The Black Emergency Cultural Coalition

463 West Street
New York, NY 10014
(212) 924-6666

Action-oriented watchdog organization to implement rights and aspirations of artists. To encourage participation and employment of blacks in educational, curatorial, and policymaking areas of art institutions; to uphold the validity of art as an agent for social and cultural growth and change; to stimulate, develop, and sustain interest of black youth in the exploration of art.

Black Law Students Union

Yale Law School
127 Wall Street
New Haven, CT 06520
(203) 486-2029

To promote the interests of Afro-American and African students; to focus and articulate the viewpoints of black students; to improve the quality of life for black students in law schools.

Black Methodists for Church Renewal, Inc.

890 Beckwith Street, S.W.
Atlanta, GA 30314
(404) 758-8118

To assist in strengthening the black church within the predominantly white structure; to eradicate racism within the total society; and ensure that the church serves the total community and administers to the needs of the total person.

Black Music Association

Inner Visions
1500 Locust Street, Suite 1905
Philadelphia, PA 19102
(215) 545-8600

To protect the interests of

professionals in the music field. The BMA also funds scholarships for young musicians and provides education and career guidance.

Black Psychiatrists of America

25 West 11th Street
New York, NY 10011
(212) 242-4500

To serve as a resource for information and training on the special mental health needs of the black community and to provide a network for its members.

Black Resources, Inc.

507 Fifth Avenue, Suite 803
New York, NY 10017
(212) 972-1260

A resource on race-related matters for corporations, government agencies and institutions.

The Black Theatre Alliance, Inc.

1564 Broadway, #701
New York, NY
(212) 245-3125

To solve common problems, share central resources, and work for the development of community resident and community-oriented theater.

The Black Scholar

P.O. Box 908
Sausalito, CA 94965
(415) 332-3130

Publication of serious essays on topics of concern to the black community.

Black Women's Community Development Foundation

1028 Connecticut Avenue, N.W.,
Suite 1010
Washington, DC 20036
(202) 296-7565

To foster communication among black women in the United States; identification of issues and problems of particular relevance to black women and program development relevant to these issues; and the operation of a Juvenile Justice Project, a community-based program for the personal development and counseling of young women referred to the Project by the courts.

Brotherhood of Sleeping Car Porters

AFL, CIO, CLC
103 East 125 Street
New York, NY 10035
(212) 348-2245

Railroad service union.

Burger Wing Mesbic, Inc.

P.O. Box 520783
Biscayne Annex
Miami, FL 33152
(305) 274-7011

Finance minority-owned Burger Wing franchised restaurants throughout the United States

Center for Community Economic Development

1878 Massachusetts Avenue
Cambridge, MA 02140
(617) 547-9695

To promote community-based economic development; work on research which will have an impact on state and national policies for community-based economic development, and strengthen active projects in the field through publications and newsletter.

The Center for Venture Management

811 East Wisconsin Avenue
Milwaukee, WI 53202
(414) 272-5421

Research into nature of new venture formation; into nature of the entrepreneur and into the ecology of new and small business.

Chi Eta Phi Sorority

3029 13th Street, N.W.
Washington, DC 20009
(202) 526-7866

To provide health-care service and recruit new professionals in the nursing field. The sorority also encourages continuing education for nurses.

Children's Defense Fund of the Washington Research Project

1763 R Street, N.W.
Washington, DC 20009
(202) 483-1470

To guarantee the right to an education for children who have been excluded or misclassified; protect children's right to privacy of records kept by various social agencies, with particular attention to guidelines for data banking and information retrieval systems; protect children from medical experimentation or other harmful research procedures and guarantee fair and humane services under the juvenile justice system.

The Church of What's Happening Now

832 Seventh Street, N.E.
Washington, DC 20002
(202) 547-8549

To apply freeing power of the gospel to those that are oppressed; to work with other ministers to get the church back into the forefront of the liberation struggle.

Coalition of Black Trade Unionists

P.O. Box 13055
Washington, DC 20009
(202) 452-4837

To get more blacks into labor while at the same time strengthening the trade union movement in order to improve the socioeconomic level of minorities.

Coalition of 100 Black Women

60 East 86th Street
New York, NY 10028
(212) 560-2840

To look into the root causes of institutionalized racism to determine ways and means by which change can be brought about; assess and analyze issues which affect black women specifically; seek effective solutions to major problems confronting blacks; attempt to equalize life results for blacks generally and black women specifically and bring about a commitment for change in the black communities in order to improve our society.

College Service Bureau, Inc.

1625 Eye Street, N.W., Suite 725
Washington, DC 20006
(202) 293-6366

Educational services to colleges and universities. Assists organization with identification of black professionals, without regard to race.

Combined Opportunities, Inc.

5050 North Broadway
Chicago, IL 60640
(312) 275-3871

Seeks to increase the participation of individuals from minority groups in the free enterprise system by providing investment loan funds to, and arranging or providing management assistance for, small businesses that are at least 51% owned and operated by minority individuals and organizations, presently restricted to the state of Illinois.

Commission for Racial Justice United Church of Christ

297 Park Avenue South
New York, NY 10010
(212) 475-2121

To increase the involvement of the United Church of Christ in the continuing struggle for racial justice and to assist in making this involvement relevant; assist the national black community and other minority groups to become self-determinative, self-directed, and self-controlled whereby meaningful social change can be effected; assist the black constituency of the UCC to become effectively organized, thereby contributing to the empowerment of Black United Churches of Christ.

Committee for a Free Mozambique

616 West 116 Street
New York, NY 10027
(212) 662-2323

To educate groups and people about the southern African struggle, especially as it relates to Mozambique and to American involvement in African colonialism.

Community Law Offices

176 East 106 Street
New York, NY 10029
(212) 369-2007

The provision of civil and criminal representation to poor persons who reside in the communities of Harlem and East Harlem.

Community Tax Aid, Inc.

Box 1040, Cathedral Station
New York, NY 10025

To give free income tax service to low-income people (for example, less than $7,500 for a family of four) by volunteer professionals.

Congress for Racial Equality

1916 Park Avenue
New York, NY 10027
(212) 690-3678

The national liberation of black (African) people in the United States. To give black people control of the political, economical, and social instruments that control their lives.

Congressional Black Caucus

H 2344 House Annex N2
Washington, DC 20515
(202) 225-1691

The CBC serves as a catalyst for the economic, educational, and social concerns of black people and other underrepresented Americans. A yearly legislative agenda is drawn up outlining the major policies supported by the caucus. Among the policies supported by the CBC are full employment, national health care, education, minority business assistance, urban redevelopment, welfare reform, and international relations.

Continental Societies, Inc.

4225 Bellamy Street
Columbus, GA 31903
(404) 568-2255

A service organization improving the welfare of disadvantaged children through its sponsorship of shoe funds, clothing, and toy banks as well as tutorial programs, concert scholarships, art exhibits, and cultural tours.

Delta Sigma Theta, Inc.

1707 New Hampshire Avenue, N.W.
Washington, DC 20009
(202) 483-5460

A national public service organization of women committed to educational and economic development; community and international involvement; improvement of mental health, housing, and urban development.

Dignity Institute of Technology

P.O. Box 1670
San Francisco, CA 94101
(415) 524-7762

To learn how many and what type of black scientists we have among us; allow a familiarization among black scientists; direct black minds in scientific areas; keep abreast of black students developing in scientific areas regardless of educational institution they may attend.

The Diuguid Fellowship Program

795 Peachtree Street, N.W., Suite 484
Atlanta, GA 30308
(404) 874-4891

To help women whose career and professional goals have been deferred because of marriage or other reasons. Fellowships make funds available for one year of intensive retraining or concentrated study on a full-time or part-time basis. No racial or religious restrictions.

The Drifters, Inc.

8825 South Luella Street
Chicago, IL 60617
(312) 721-2831

To provide an opportunity for friendships and good fellowship between women of member cities with similar background, interests, and desires. To participate within and among chapters in social, civic, educational, and charitable activities.

East Central Committee for Opportunity, Inc.

Central Administration Building
Mayfield, GA 31059
(404) 465-3201

To create new opportunities for employment; provide for capital accumulation; establish minority-owned businesses; develop new community services and mobilize indigenous persons within the community to effectively utilize all the resources available to them for the purpose of achieving a sound socioeconomic community.

East Harlem Food Buying Federation

237 East 104th Street
New York, NY 10024
(212) LE 4-7900

This union of 11 food cooperatives, involving some 600 families, was organized in 1973 to provide top-quality fresh fruits and vegetables at prices 40% cheaper than retail supermarkets. Merchandise is purchased twice weekly at the city's largest wholesale market by volunteer

workers, and the entire savings is passed on to the families involved.

Economic Development Corporation of Greater Detroit

1501 Fisher Building
Detroit, MI 48202
(313) 873-9300

Promote and assist minority economic development.

Enterprises Now, Inc.

898 Beckwith Street, S.W.
Atlanta, GA 30314
(404) 753-1163

To make loans and investments in small minority businesses.

Equal Opportunity Finance, Inc.

224 East Broadway
Louisville, KY 40202
(502) 583-0601

To help disadvantaged individuals begin, expand, or improve business operations. Loans, investments, and technical assistance are considered for minority or socially disadvantaged persons in the states of Kentucky, Ohio, Indiana, and West Virginia.

The Equitable Life Community Enterprises Corp.*

1285 Avenue of the Americas,
Location 15-M
New York, NY 10019
(212) 554-4978

To invest in minority-owned companies that have been in existence three to five years and are located in New York State.

Eric Clearinghouse on Urban Education*

Box 40
Teachers College, Columbia University
New York, NY 10027
(212) 678-3437

A national information storage and retrieval system supported by the National Institute of Education of the U.S. Department of Education and Welfare. Its purposes are to provide ready access to educational literature for subsequent information analysis activities. ERIC Clearinghouse on Urban Education collects, evaluates, and disseminates published and unpublished materials concerning the

education of urban children and youth.

Executive Secretariat of the Organization of African Unity

211 East 43 Street
New York, NY 10017
(212) 697-8334

To promote the unity and solidarity of the African states; coordinate and intensify cooperation and efforts to achieve a better life for people of Africa; eradicate all forms of colonialism from Africa; and promote international cooperation with regard to the United Nations Charter and the Universal Declaration of Human Rights.

Federation of Masons of the World and Federation of Eastern Stars

1017 East 11th Street
Austin, TX 78702
(512) 477-5380

Supports projects for the good of the public and also donates financially to disadvantaged students desiring to go to college.

Free Southern Theater

1328 Dryades Street
New Orleans, LA 70113
(504) 581-5091

To use theater, a viable cultural form, to advance the struggles of black and oppressed people from the burden of exploitation and oppressive conditions. To educate and motivate social change.

Florida Crown Minority Enterprise Small Business Investment Company

604 Hogan Street
Jacksonville, FL 32202
(904) 353-6161

Invests seed capital in businesses which are at least 51% owned by minorities—blacks, Indians, disadvantaged whites, Mexicans, Puerto Ricans, etc.

Forsyth County Investment Company

305 Pepper Building
Winston-Salem, NC 27101
(919) 724-3676

To provide venture capital financing and management consulting services to small concerns.

The Foundation for Research and Education in Sickle Cell Disease

423 West 120 Street
New York, NY 10027
(212) 222-8500

To coordinate local activities with a national education program and to allocate funds for research on all levels.

Frontiers International

5915 West Gerard Avenue
Philadelphia, PA 19151
(215) 476-4089

With a membership of 2,500, this club supports a broad cross section of community projects. Each chapter operates autonomously, and the organization as a whole develops major projects, such as funding the medical battle against vitiligo.

Frontiers International, Inc.

1901 West Girard Avenue
Philadelphia, PA 19151
(215) CE 5-5959

To direct community activities when no other group or organization is functioning adequately in a given area.

Gamma Phi Delta Sorority

2927A Harper
Berkeley, CA 94703
(415) 845-1630

The aims of the sorority are to encourage and finance the education and training of women and to support health projects for deprived and retarded children. Educational aid is also provided to needy students who do not benefit from the scholarship program.

Girl Friends, Inc.

16255 West Nine Mile Road
North Park Square, Apt. 101
Southfield, MI 48075
(313) 956-0133

Friendship.

Glide Memorial United Methodist Church

Glide Urban Center
330 Ellis Street
San Francisco, CA 94102
(415) 771-6300

Creating change; making positive change possible; coalition building; celebrations; provide a free health clinic, food, housing, and transportation clinic; drug abuse and alcoholic referral and a program for prisoners presently confined or encountering reentry difficulties on release.

Grand United Order of Odd Fellows

12th and Spruce Streets
Philadelphia, PA
(215) PE 5-8774

Charity and education.

Greater Philadelphia Venture Capital Corporation, Inc.

Lewis Tower Building, Suite 920
22 South 15 Street
Philadelphia, PA 19102
(215) 734-3415

To provide long-term equity or seed capital and managerial assistance to minority-owned corporations in the Delaware Valley area.

Gulf South Venture Corporation

Commerce Building, Suite 1202
821 Gravier Street
New Orleans, LA 70112
(504) 523-7386

To provide venture capital to existing and emerging business enterprises in which American minorities own at least 51%. To promote industrial economic development in the Gulf South region.

The Haitian & Co-Arts Association, Inc.

165 Park Row, Suite 8-D
New York, NY 10038
(212) 732-9735

Created by Andre Letellier, Haitian-born U.S. citizen to help eliminate hunger, eradicate disease, combat illiteracy, and promote multitrade development and vocational schools plus improve farming in the rural areas of Haiti.

Harlem River Consumers Cooperative, Inc.

270 Lenox Avenue
New York, NY 10027
(212) 472-7252

Organized in 1969 to help blacks gain control of business in Harlem in order to provide food and housing at reasonable prices to the Harlem community.

Imperial Court, Daughters of Isis

Prichard Building, Room 404
Ninth Street and Sixth Avenue
Huntington, WV 25701
(304) 523-5241

To unite in one common bond of friendship the mother, wife, sister,

Cora Walker heads the Harlem River Consumers Coop, a neighborhood approach to marketing.

daughter, and widow of all Nobles of the Mystic Shrine; give true expression fraternally to the Ancient Tradition of the Order; practice charity and benevolence; promote general welfare and inculcate honor and integrity as symbolized in the Legend of the Egyptian Queen—"The Goddess of Isis."

Improved Benevolent Protective Order of Elks of the World

P.O. Box 159
Winton, NC 27986
(919) 358-7661

Through a variety of civic, educational, and religious programs, the organization has raised more than $100,000 yearly in scholarship assistance. Instruction in preventive medicine is also provided to its 450,000 members.

Independence Capital Formation, Inc.

3049 East Grand Boulevard
Detroit, MI 48202
(313) 875-7669

To provide venture capital financing and assistance, particularly to the minority community.

Inner City Business Improvement Forum

3049 East Grand Boulevard
Detroit, MI 48202
(313) 875-4700

To promote minority entrepreneurship by providing advisory, technical, managerial, loan packaging, financing assistance to help Detroit's black inner city become a strong economic entity.

The Institute of the Black World, Inc.

87 Chestnut Street, S.W.
Atlanta, GA 30314
(404) 523-7805

A community of black scholar-activists convinced that blacks must move to control the definition of our past and present if we are to become masters of our future. Committed to doing tasks of research, analysis, and advocacy which will forward the struggles of the black community toward self-understanding, self-determination, and ultimate liberation.

Interracial Council for Business Opportunity

800 Second Avenue
New York, NY 10017
(212) 599-0677

To assist minority businessmen in the development and management of their own enterprises.

Iota Phi Lambda Sorority, Inc.

2561 4th Avenue
Los Angeles, CA 91803
(213) 732-7607

The sorority develops programs and scholarships to promote interest in business education among high school and college girls. Other goals are the cultivation of leadership personalities and the intellectual enrichment of members through higher education.

Jack and Jill of America, Inc.

1029 LaPleins Drive
East St. Louis, IL 62203
(618) 397-6314; (618) 398-4823

The 30,000 members financially aid education and community projects; since 1968 the Jack and Jill Foundation has awarded more than $250,000 in grants.

The Joint Center for Political Studies

1301 Pennsylvania Avenue, N.W., Suite 400
Washington, DC 20004
(202) 626-3500

To provide research, education, technical assistance, and information for the nation's black and other minority elected officials, to respond to minority-group aspirations to participate in the political process, and to enhance the effectiveness of minorities at every level of government.

Kappa Alpha Psi Fraternity, Inc.

2320 North Broad Street
Philadelphia, PA 19132
(215) 228-7184

To provide housing, scholarships, loans, and job placement for its collegiate members. The fraternity also provides social interaction for members. On the community level, the fraternity sponsors Little League sports, a tutorial program, and a leadership training group.

Knights of Peter Claver

1821 Orleans Avenue
New Orleans, LA 70116
(504) 821-4225

Promote civic improvements; encourage Lady Apostolic and Catholic action; provide financial assistance to sick members; award scholarships; foster recreational assemblies and facilities and develop youth.

Leadership Conference on Civil Rights

2027 Massachusetts Avenue, N.W.
Washington, DC 20036
(202) 667-1780

Seeks an integrated, democratic, plural society, in which every individual is accorded equal rights, opportunities, and justice without regard to race, religion, ethnic origin, or sex; and in which every group is accorded an equal opportunity to enter fully into the general life of the society with mutual acceptance and regard for differences.

Liberty House Cooperative

P.O. Box 3468
Jackson, MS 39207
(601) 969-7522

To provide work for poor rural Mississippians through craft cooperatives; publicize co-ops and market items nationally by means of mail-order catalog, advertising in national magazines, etc.

The Links, Inc.

1522 K Street, N.W., Suite 404
Washington, DC 20005
(202) 783-3888

To enrich the lives of its members and the community by promoting educational, civic, and cultural activities. Financial assistance is provided by The Links to the NAACP, the United Negro College Fund, and the National Urban League.

Lokahi Pacific

P.O. Box 767
Kihei, Maui, HI 96753
(808) 879-1517

Lokahi seeks to develop new skills, to broaden the county's economic base, and to increase the income level of the disadvantaged.

Mesbic Financial Corporation of Dallas

P.O. Box 6228
Dallas, TX 75222
(214) 632-0445

Provide debt and equity capital and management assistance to selected businesses in the Dallas-Fort Worth area which are owned by disadvantaged small businessmen.

Metropolitan Applied Research Center

60 East 86 Street
New York, NY 10028
(212) 628-7400

To serve as a catalyst for change and advocate for the poor and powerless in American cities.

Metropolitan Contractors Association

4450 Oakman Boulevard
Detroit, MI 48204
(313) 933-6470

Develop and administer educational programs for minority contractors.

Minority Contractors Assistance Project, Inc.

1211 Connecticut Avenue, N.W., Suite 312
Washington, DC 20036
(202) 833-1840

Increase participation of minority groups in building industry; provide technical and financial assistance to local associations of minority contractors; multiply and upgrade at all skill levels the minority workforce in the construction industry; assist core city residents to participate in rebuilding of their own communities; expand minority opportunities in mortgage, surety brokerage, engineering, and other construction-related fields.

Minority Equity Capital Company, Inc.

470 Park Avenue South
New York, NY 10016
(212) 889-0880

Venture capital, equity-oriented investments in larger, ongoing minority-owned businesses where such an investment will aid businesses in undertaking major growth or expansion.

Most Worshipful National Grand Lodge Free and Accepted Ancient York Masons Prince Hall Origin, National Compact, U.S.A. Inc.

26070 Tryon Road
Oakwood Village, OH 44146
(216) 232-9495

The organization's main thrust is giving generously each year to the United Negro College Fund. Scholarships are also granted to nonmembers of the organization and it also supports sickle cell anemia research.

Mother Waddles' Perpetual Mission

3700 Gratiot
Detroit, MI 48207
(313) 925-0901

The mission was founded in 1957 to provide food, shelter, clothing, and medical care to the needy. Staffed by volunteers, and open 24 hours a day, it also offers religious services, day and evening classes, and counseling.

Motor Enterprises, Inc.*

General Motors Corporation
13–152 General Motors Building
3044 West Grand Boulevard
Detroit, MI 48202
(313) 556-4273

To provide financing to minority businessmen in communities where General Motors has plant operations. Along with financing, Motor Enterprises offers managerial and technical assistance to those businessmen granted loans.

National Alliance of Black School Educators

1430 K. Street, N.W., Suite 702
Washington, DC 20005
(202) 638-7970

To make a strong commitment to the education of all children and black children in particular; to provide a coalition of black educators; create a forum for the exchange of ideas and techniques; identify and develop black professionals who will assume leadership positions in the education of black children.

National Association for the Advancement of Colored People

1790 Broadway
New York, NY 10019
(212) 245-2100

To end all barriers to racial justice and guarantee full equality of opportunity and achievement in the United States.

NAACP Legal Defense and Educational Fund, Inc.

Ten Columbus Circle
New York, NY 10019
(212) 586-8397

To provide free legal assistance to people and organizations involved in racial discrimination suits. The fund also handles suits related to voting rights, housing, and education as well as the administration of criminal justice.

National Association for Equal Opportunity in Higher Education

2243 Wisconsin Avenue, N.W.
Washington, DC 20007
(202) 333-3855

To promote the widest possible sensitivity to the complex factors involved and the institutional commitment required to create successful higher education programs for students from groups buffeted by the racism, exploitation, and neglect of the economic, educational, and social institutions of America.

National Association of Black Accountants

1642 R Street, N.W.
Washington, DC 20009
(202) 387-7066

To encourage members of minority groups to enter the profession of accounting; stimulate acquaintance and fellowship among members of minority groups; provide opportunities for members to increase their knowledge of accounting practices and individual capabilities.

National Association of Black Journalists

P.O. Box 2089
Washington, DC 20013
(202) 737-0277

To provide an ongoing educational program for black journalists and to assist them in upgrading their professional skills so that they may get into management positions.

The prestigious and very effective NAACP dates back to 1909. In this 1945 photo, the old National Offices show their wartime austerity.

National Association of Black Manufacturers

1910 K Street, N.W., Suite 600
Washington, DC 20006
(202) 785-5133

To promote interest of all minority-owned manufacturing firms; seek domestic and foreign markets for products of minority manufacturers; bring large industrial firms together with small business corporations; develop communication between NABM and other industrial associations, labor unions, and various governmental agencies; and encourage minority young people to enter industry.

National Association of Black Women Attorneys, Inc.

1625 Eye Street, N.W., Suite 626
Washington, DC 20006
(202) 822-9124

To increase opportunities for minorities in the legal profession by expanding options of professionals and through scholarship assistance for students.

National Association of Black Social Workers

1969 Madison Avenue
New York, NY 10035
(212) 369-0639

To develop social programs in the black community and make contributions to the enhancement of social work.

National Association of Colored Women's Clubs, Inc.

5808 Sixteenth Street, N.W.
Washington, DC 20011
(202) 726-2044

To promote the education of women and girls; raise the standard of the home; work for moral, economic, social, and religious welfare of women and children; protect the rights of women and children who work; and obtain for all women the opportunity of reaching the highest standards in all fields of human endeavor.

The National Association of Health Services Executives

551 Fifth Avenue
New York, NY 10017
(212) 867-0027

Dissemination of information, educational material, job position clearing house, research in health care.

National Association of Market Developers, Inc.

201 Ashby Street, N.W., Suite 306
Atlanta, GA 30314
(404) 688-9075

To encourage young people to enter the marketing profession while at the same time promoting professionalism among its members through seminars and regional workshops.

National Baptist Convention of America

Second Missionary Baptist Church
954 Kings Road
Jacksonville, FL 32204
(904) 354-8268

The organization does missionary work in Africa, the Caribbean, and

South America. Its primary effort is to support its evangelical work through education and fundraising.

National Baptist Convention, U.S.A., Inc.

405 East 31st Street
Chicago, IL 60616
(312) 842-1081

To support black Baptist colleges, universities, and seminaries. Scholarship assistance is also provided for its members and missionary work is conducted by the Convention in the United States, Africa, the Caribbean, the Bahamas, and South America.

National Beauty Culturists League, Inc.

25 Logan Circle, N.W.
Washington, DC 20005
(202) 332-2695

Formed to upgrade professional standards in the cosmetology field and at the same time assuring equal opportunity through fair licensing and state regulation practices. Training courses in beauty and business techniques are also offered through the League.

National Black Caucus of Local Elected Officials

1301 Pennsylvania Avenue, N.W., Suite 400
Washington, DC 20004
(202) 626-3500

To have an impact upon the National League of Cities and The United States Conference of Mayors as well as other policymaking bodies that influence issues of concern to black people. Membership in the caucus represents 44 states and the District of Columbia.

National Black Caucus of State Legislators

1012 14th Street, Suite 706
Washington, DC 20005
(202) 347-6020; (301) 578-0400

Designed to promote a more effective leadership among its members; also functions as an information resource and network for blacks in state legislatures.

National Black Child Development Institute

1463 Rhode Island Avenue, N.W.
Washington, DC 20005
(202) 387-1281

Dedicated to the enactment of public policies to better the welfare and development of black children.

National Black Nurses Association

P.O. Box 18358
Boston, MA 02118
(617) 266-9703

Serves as a job bank and recruits for the nursing field. The association also functions as an information resource for federal agencies concerned with health care. In addition, it monitors federal legislation.

The National Association of Planners

Cablecommunications Resource Center
1900 L Street, N.W., Suite 205
Washington, DC 20036

Increase numbers of minority persons participating in planning; make technical planning information and sources available to planners in minority communities; improve quality and number of planning departments in black schools; make planning profession and education more relevant to needs of minority communities; develop a national

National Association of Black Social Workers officers (from left:) *President Jay Chunn, Treasurer Lenora Delaney, Secretary Andreye Johnson, and Vice President Howard Brabson.*

communication system between minority planners.

National Association of Media Women, Inc.

157 West 126 Street
New York, NY 10027
(212) 850-1886

Enrich lives of its members through exchange of ideas and experiences; create opportunities for women in mass communications; institute programming to hasten recognition and advancement in the field; and influence young women to seek careers in the media.

National Association of Minority Contractors

1518 K Street, N.W., Room 401
Washington, DC 20005
(202) 347-8259

Represent economic development and organizational interests of minority construction workers throughout United States. Committed to gaining economic parity for minority contractor and minority craftsman. Attempts to organize minority contractors at local level so that they may better compete.

National Association of Negro Business and Professional Women's Clubs

1806 New Hampshire Avenue, N.W.
Washington, DC 20009
(202) 483-4880

To protect interest of business and professional women; create good fellowship and spirit of cooperation among business and professional women; direct interest of members toward united action for improved social, educational, and civic conditions; encourage youth through education and job opportunities, recognize achievements of women in business and professions and make a record of these achievements so all people may be informed of their heritage.

National Association of Negro Musicians

4330 Fullerton Street
Detroit, MI 48238
(313) 934-7448

Created as a communications network for black musicians, this organization

disseminates music and job information and seeks to promote the appreciation of black music.

National Alliance of Postal and Federal Employees*

1644 11 Street, N.W.
Washington, DC 20001
(202) 332-4313

Promulgate better working conditions for blacks, minorities, and women in the Postal Service and federal government.

National Association of Real Estate Brokers

3520 Connecticut Avenue, N.W., Suite 21
Washington, DC 20008
(202) 966-5100

Housing reform for minorities; seminars for real estate brokers in management, appraisal, development, and conversions.

National Bankers Association

499 South Capitol Street, S.W.
Washington, DC 20003
(202) 488-5550

To strengthen existing member banks, increase their numbers, and ultimately increase the economic impact of minority-owned banks in their communities.

National Bar Association

1900 L Street, Suite 203
Washington, DC 20036
(202) 463-4200

Established in the 1920s to encourage young blacks to enter the legal profession, this organization now represents some 4,000 black lawyers across the country. Legal scholarships and personal counseling are offered.

The National Black Christian Education Resources Center

Education for Christian Life and Mission
Division of Education and Ministry
National Council of Churches, in cooperation with JED* Black Church Education Team
475 Riverside Drive
New York, NY 10027
(212) 870-2772

To identify, collect, evaluate, and disseminate information about

resources available for programs based on the black experience.

National Black Police Association

P.O. Box 138
Jamaica, NY 11412
(516) 379-9549

Chartered in 1972, the association has three goals: (1) to improve the relationship between police departments, institutions, and black communities; (2) to recruit minority police officers across the country; and (3) to eliminate police corruption, brutality, and racial discrimination.

National Black Sisters' Conference

3508 Fifth Avenue
Pittsburgh, PA 15213
(412) 621-9677

To develop personal resources of individual sisters for the deepening of spirituality and promotion of unity and solidarity among black religious women. To importune our society to respond with Christian enthusiasm to the need for eradicating powerlessness and poverty by responsibly encouraging white people to address themselves to the roots of racism in their own social, professional, and spiritual milieu.

National Business League

4324 Georgia Avenue, N.W.
Washington, DC 20011
(202) 726-6200

To promote commercial and financial developments of blacks and other minorities in the United States; expose problems of its members and provide technical assistance.

National Center for Voluntary Action

1785 Massachusetts Avenue, N.W.
Washington, DC 20036
(202) 797-7800

Strengthens volunteer services and organizations in their efforts to prevent and alleviate social problems; serves as a source of information on volunteer programs; assists in development of central community volunteer services; provides leadership in education and training of volunteer leaders; encourages public awareness of voluntary action.

National Committee Against Discrimination in Housing, Inc.

1425 H Street, N.W., Suite 410
Washington, DC 20005
(202) 783-8150

To test equality of treatment of black and white housing applicants by real estate brokers and rental offices; gather evidence of racial discrimination by lending institutions; testify at hearings on behalf of state and municipal fair housing measures; combat misuses of local zoning to exclude low-income families; to create a local awareness of fair housing laws and to stabilize interracial neighborhoods by counteracting block-busting techniques through person-to-person contact.

National Committee for the Defense of Political Prisoners

P.O. Box 1184
New York, NY 10027

Defense and support of blacks arrested or imprisoned for alleged political offenses or viewpoints.

National Committee for Self-Development of People

475 Riverside Drive, Room 1260
New York, NY 10027
(212) 870-2563

Funds programs of community groups to increase self-determination, build relationships between subcommunities and surrounding economic, political, and social institutions; attract other resources. Seeks to avoid the dangers of paternalism and discourage individual alienation from social origins.

National Conference of Black and Nonwhite Laymen and Staff of the YMCA

100 North Arlington Avenue
East Orange, NJ 07017
(201) 673-5588

To overcome the practices, procedures, and policies of the YMCA that subordinate nonwhites because of their race and provide the leadership for survival and future of the YMCA in nonwhite communities.

National Conference of Black Churchmen

Atlanta, GA
(404) 524-8010

To unite black churches and black church people in efforts to unify, develop, and strengthen the black community; promulgate the vitality and life style of black families; enhance the contribution of black churches and black people in the larger religious fellowship across racial, national, denominational, and sectarian lines.

National Conference of Black Lawyers

126 West 119 Street
New York, NY 10026
(212) 866-3501

Carries on a program of litigation, including defense of the politically unpopular and affirmative action suits on community issues; monitors governmental activity affecting the black community; serves the black bar through lawyer referral, job placement, legal education programs, watchdog activity on law school admission and curriculum; defends advocates facing judicial and bar sanctions.

National Conference of Black Mayors

1430 Peachtree Street, N.E., Suite 318
Atlanta, GA 30309
(404) 892-0127

Formed in 1974, the NCBM works to channel greater financial aid and managerial resources into the communities served by black mayors. The organization places a great emphasis on sewage and water projects. It is a charter member of the National Demonstration Water Project. Some of the other issues of NCBM are the improvement of public utilities and the development of low-income housing.

The indefatigable Mother Waddles, whose Perpetual Mission cares for the needy without fanfare.

National Council for Equal Business Opportunity, Inc.

1211 Connecticut Avenue, N.W.,
Suite 310
Washington, DC 20036
(202) 293-3960

Assist individuals, groups, and organizations in economic development projects; technical assistance and professional counseling of all types, including business planning for individuals, organizations and their members for the economic development of low-income or low-employment areas.

National Council of Negro Women

815 Second Avenue
New York, NY 10017

A 45-year-old organization focusing the resources and energies of its constituents on the social, economic, and political aspects of American life. Its program efforts for youth include career development and juvenile justice. Other important concerns of the organization are leadership development, women's history, and public health.

National Dental Association

5506 Connecticut Avenue, N.W.,
Suite 24
Washington, DC 20015
(202) 244-7555

To promote the art and science of dentistry; raise the standards of the dental profession and of dental education; sponsor and work for enactment of just dental laws; promote betterment of public health; work persistently for elimination of religious and racial discrimination and segregation from American dental institutions, clinics, and organizations.

The National Fellowship Fund

795 Peachtree Street, N.E.
Atlanta, GA 30308
(404) 874-4891

Provide qualified black personnel for careers in higher education in the United States through the stimulation of doctoral study in the basic biological and physical sciences, humanities, and social sciences. Awards are available to black Americans who plan to continue on to the doctoral degree in preparation for a career in higher education.

National Funeral Directors and Morticians Association

734 West 79th Street
Chicago, IL 60620
(312) 487-3603

Founded in 1924, the NFDMA seeks to maintain high standards for the benefit of the public and their own business community. The organization conducts workshops and seminars, sponsors research, and represents the interests of its constituency before the various federal, state, and local governing bodies.

National Insurance Association

2400 S. Michigan Avenue
Chicago, IL 60616
(312) 842-5125

To improve professional standards within the insurance industry and bring about a better public understanding of its services. The group also provides technical assistance for its members and facilitates management and operating manpower development.

National Medical Association

1720 Massachusetts Avenue, N.W.
Washington, DC 20036
(202) 659-9623

To raise the standards of the medical profession and medical education; stimulate favorable relationships among all physicians; nurture growth and diffusion of medical knowledge; sponsor education of the public concerning all matters affecting public health; sponsor enactment of just medical laws and eliminate religious and racial discrimination and segregation from American medical institutions.

National Medical Association Foundation, Inc.

2109 E Street, N.W.
Washington, DC 20037
(202) 338-8266

To promote programs providing comprehensive health care and residential accommodations, together with related facilities, for inhabitants of the core cities of metropolitan areas and other medically deprived areas in the United States; improve the quality of medical care; enhance the image of the physician and demonstrate his or her concern for the health of the poor.

National Medical Fellowships, Inc.

250 West 57 Street
New York, NY 10019
(212) 246-4293

To create more physicians from groups currently underrepresented in medicine—blacks, American Indians, Puerto Ricans, and Mexican-Americans—by giving financial aid to medical students from those groups needing it.

National Minority Business Campaign

1016 Plymouth Avenue
Minneapolis, MN 55406
(612) 522-3323

To publish a national directory of minority-owned firms.

National Newspaper Publishers Association

770 National Press Building
Washington, DC 20045
(202) 638-4473

To unify, strengthen, and improve the black press.

The National Office for Black Catholics

734 Fifteenth Street, N.W.
Washington, DC 20005
(202) 347-4260

To enable black Catholics assume greater responsibility for and participation in the Catholic Church; assist black Catholics and the Church in general; make an effective contribution to the needs of the total black community; and bring the Catholic Church to recognition and elimination of racism within its own structure and assume a more forceful stand against racism in America.

National Optometric Association

55 Marietta Street, N.W., Suite 1935
Atlanta, GA 30303
(404) 523-7028

Minority recruitment for optometric profession; education of public to profession of optometry, better primary optometric and health care delivery.

National Organization of Black Law Enforcement Executives

Metro-Plex
8401 Corporate Drive, Suite 360
Landover, MD 20785
(301) 459-8344

The National Sharecroppers Fund helps co-op farms compete with the large industrialized farm operation. Aerial photo shows the fund's experimental farm and training center in Anson County, North Carolina.

NOBLE works for a greater community involvement in the criminal justice system and increases the sensitivity by law enforcement agencies to the problems of the black police officer and the black community.

National Pharmaceutical Association

Howard University College of Pharmacy and Pharmacal Sciences
2300 Fourth Street, N.W.
Washington, DC 20059
(202) 636-6530

To provide an atmosphere to exchange ideas among minority pharmacists; continue education; stimulate positive community relationships for the minority pharmacist; contribute financially to charitable causes and promote enforcement and enactment of just health-care legislation.

National Scholarship Service and Fund for Negro Students

1776 Broadway
New York, NY 10019
(212) 757-8100

To provide to black and other high school juniors and seniors increased access to postsecondary institutions through a computerized college

advisory and counseling service. Limited supplementary scholarship assistance available to students who complete the application process and demonstrate need.

National Sharecroppers Fund

2128 Commonwealth Avenue
Charlotte, NC 28205
(704) 334-3051

To help low-income farm and other rural people develop programs and services they need to live a good life and remain on the land. NSF maintains an experimental farm and training center in Wadesboro, NC and legislative and research office in Washington, DC, provides services and technical help to cooperatives and other self-help groups in rural areas, and publishes reports and newsletters on developments of concern to rural people.

National Small Business Association*

1225 Nineteenth Street, N.W.
Washington, DC 20036
(202) 296-7400

Demands revision of tax laws, adoption of a sound fiscal and economic policy, establishment of a fair management-labor policy; opposes

growth of unnecessary government authority, regulations, and reports which burden the limited resources of independent business; promotes government policies that permit independent business to obtain its fair share of government contracts.

National Smart Set

140 West End Avenue, Apt. 12H
New York, NY 10023

Formed in 1937, the organization's programs benefit young people. The group also contributes to the United Negro College Fund annually.

National Supreme Council, Ancient and Accepted Scottish Rite Masons, Inc.

5040 Joy Road
Detroit, MI 48204
(313) 834-5597

To fraternize with the brothers; aid the widows and orphans of the brother masons, dispensing charity where needed; assist in any programs, projects, etc., that will benefit mankind as a whole; help make our society better by providing the necessities of life for all people regardless of race, creed, color, or national origin.

National Technical Association, Inc.

1425 H Street, N.W., Suite 701
Washington, DC 20005
(202) 638-6370

To increase participation by minorities in the technical fields by disseminating information on educational and career opportunities. The group also makes the public aware of minority contributions to modern technological advancement.

National Tenants Organization, Inc.*

425 Thirteenth Street, N.W., Suite 1010
Washington, DC 20004
(202) 347-4458

Continuing the development of local tenant organizations to become effective in obtaining decent housing for themselves; expansion of legal rights for tenants as part of a broad-based consumer movement in this country.

National United Licencees Beverage Associations, Inc.

1938 Ninth Street, N.W.
Washington, DC 20001
(202) 232-6888

To promote the fellowship with others engaged in the same business, seek uniformity in commercial usages, and distribute statistics and information of value.

National Urban Coalition

1201 Connecticut Avenue N.W., Suite 400
Washington, DC 20036
(202) 331-2400

To link the needs of the private job sector to more effective occupational education and training. Its aim is to build economically stronger and physically sounder urban neighborhoods around the country and to stabilize communities through the reduction of violence and delinquency.

National Urban League

500 East 62nd Street
New York, NY 10021
(212) 310-9000

To achieve equal opportunity for all Americans, especially members of minority groups.

National Welfare Rights Organization

1420 N Street, N.W.
Washington, DC 20005
(202) 483-1531

To secure those legal, economic, and human rights to which poor people are now entitled by federal law; to advocate for true welfare reform which will bring dignity, justice, and the right to self-determination to the poor.

Negro Actors Guild, Inc.

1674 Broadway
New York, NY 10019
(212) 245-4343

To elevate, foster, and promote good fellowship and the spiritual welfare of actors and those connected with the theatrical profession; render service to members of the profession in time of illness and distress; champion and uphold the highest standards of the stage and elsewhere; and attend and support performances adhering to such standards.

Negro Labor Committee

312 West 125 Street
New York, NY 10027
(212) UN 4-3295

To organize and guide black workers into bona fide trade unions and establish the solidarity of black and white labor.

New York City Task Force on Youth Motivation*

c/o St. Regis Paper Company
633 Third Avenue
New York, NY 10017
(212) 697-4400, ext. 225

To inspire and encourage minority youth to stay in school and obtain their high school diploma.

New York State Urban Development Corp.*

1345 Avenue of the Americas
New York, NY 10019
(212) 974-7000

To help build low- and moderate-income housing.

North Street Capital Corporation

250 North Street
White Plains, NY 10625
(914) 631-3000

Help businesses owned or controlled by socially and economically

disadvantaged persons, and members of minority groups in particular. Especially interested in those businesses (or business ideas) that show potential for bank financing.

Office for the Advancement of Public Negro Colleges

One Dupont Circle, Suite 710
Washington, DC 20036
(202) 293-7120

This group, which is affiliated with the National Association of State University and Land Grant Colleges and the American Association of State Universities and Colleges, works to enhance public awareness of the contributions of those institutions to American society.

Office of Human Rights

American Personnel and Guidance Association
1607 New Hampshire Avenue, N.W.
Washington, DC 20009
(202) 483-4633

To develop a roster of resource people who are representative of and responsible to minority group communities.

Omega Psi Phi Fraternity

2714 Georgia Avenue, N.W.
Washington, DC 20001
(202) 667-7158; (800) 424-2442

The 26,000-member organization formed at Howard University in 1911 undertakes civic and community service projects and also lends financial support to the NAACP as well as the United Negro College Fund.

Operation PUSH

(People United to Save Humanity)
930 East 50 Street
Chicago, IL 60615
(312) 373-3366

Basic contention is that it does very little good to have the *right* to do certain things without the *ability*. We have the right to attend any school, to eat in any restaurant, stay in any motel, and live in any neighborhood, but we do not have the money to pay the tuition, the bill, or the house note. Operation PUSH addresses the economic question through research, education, and direct action.

Opportunities Industrialization Centers of America, Inc.

100 West Coulter Street
Philadelphia, PA
(215) VI 9-3010

Training, counseling, and employment program for developing vocational skills of community people regardless of race, creed, sex, or color within the broad field of industry.

Opportunity Capital Corp.

235 Montgomery Street, Suite 1226
San Francisco, CA 94104
(415) 392-5696

Provide long-term equity financing for minority-owned businesses.

Pan American Contractors Service Center

2211 East Missouri Avenue, Suite E-243
El Paso, TX 79903
(915) 545-2758

Investments in minority-owned businesses.

Phi Beta Sigma Fraternity, Inc.

145 Kennedy Street, N.W.
Washington, DC 20011
(202) 726-5434

The 65,000-member fraternity established in 1914 promotes brotherhood and community service. The fraternity instills in its membership the desire to pursue scholastic excellence, and program support is given to education through scholarships and tutorial services.

Phi Delta Kappa Sorority

Mrs. Arthur Mae Norris, Supreme Basileus
1337 South Hall Street
Montgomery, AL 36106
(205) 262-0875

The sorority, founded in 1923 for the purpose of promoting sisterhood, encourages higher education among its membership and the community at large.

Pioneer Capital Corporation

1440 Broadway
New York, NY 10018
(212) 594-4860

Investments in minority-owned companies.

Progress Venture Capital Corp.

1501 North Broad Street
Philadelphia, PA 19122
(215) PO 9-3484

Provide capital and technical assistance to minority entrepreneurs.

Resource Placement and Development, Inc.

77 Maple Street
Springfield, MA 01105
(413) 733-3121

Recruit minorities to match companies' employment opportunities.

Rutgers Minority Investment Company

92 New Street
Newark, NJ 07102
(201) 648-5287

Active in assisting and encouraging minority-owned small businesses.

Sedfre, Inc.

315 Seventh Avenue, 7th Floor
New York, NY 10001
(212) 741-0800

To provide training and technical assistance to those organizations and institutions that are involved in all of the dimensions of community development.

Seminole Employment Economic Development Corp.

1011 South Sanford Avenue
P.O. Box 2076
Sanford, FL 32771
(305) 323-4360

Provide opportunities for employment at the highest skill levels possible; develop new salable skills; reduce unemployment; curb emigration; and develop managerial talent among the disadvantaged in the economic life of Seminole County.

Seven Hills Neighborhood Houses

701 Lincoln Park Drive
Cincinnati, OH 45203
(513) 721-2512

Work with neighborhood residents who, in the search for a useful and satisfying life, have the least number of alternatives open to them by reason of color, discrimination, lack of educational training, minimal access to full employment, inadequate health

facilities, few opportunities for home ownership, and too few resources to solve basic problems of survival in the city.

Sigma Gamma Rho Sorority, Inc.

7311 South Yates Boulevard
Chicago, IL 60649
(313) 731-4661

To encourage academic achievement while at the same time nurturing special talents and leadership ability. The sorority has as one of its goals promotion of community involvement among its membership.

Sigma Pi Phi Fraternity ("The Boule")

69 Fifth Avenue, Apt. 9G
New York, NY 10001
(212) 247-5850

The oldest black Greek letter fraternal society, Sigma Pi Phi fraternity has commitments to philanthropic and charitable causes. These funds are channeled through its tax-exempt foundation.

The Solomon Fuller Institute

127 Mt. Auburn Street
Cambridge, MA 02138
(617) 661-9446

Dedicated to research and study; devising methods of disseminating information which will have a positive effect on the mental health of all people, particularly black and other minority groups. Projects reflect a desire to improve and increase the conditions which will enable people to function and relate to each other so each person can realize his fullest, healthy potential.

Southern Africa Committee

244 East 27 Street
New York, NY 10011
(212) 741-3480

Inform and activate people concerning the issues of Southern Africa through the monthly magazine AFRICA containing articles and information about military, political, economic, and social developments in South Africa, Zimbabwe (Rhodesia), Namibia, Angola, and the former Portuguese colonies of Mozambique and the new Republic of Guinea-Bissau.

Southern Association of Black Administration Personnel

District Administrative Officers
Florida Junior College at Jacksonville
Jacksonville, FL 32205
(904) 387-8346

To articulate needs of black students in higher education; research, develop, and coordinate recruiting techniques for black students in the South; investigate and develop economic resources for black students, and minimize attrition rates of black students in higher education.

Southern Christian Leadership Conference

334 Auburn Avenue, N.E.
Atlanta, GA 30303
(404) 522-1420

To function as an eleemosynary organization, more particularly to organize and maintain Christian guidance to help improve civic, religious, economic, and cultural conditions in the nation. This organization hopes to achieve its purposes through nonviolent direct action, lectures, dissemination of literature, and other means of public instruction.

Southern California Minority Capital Corp.

2651 South Western Avenue, Suite 303
Los Angeles, CA 90018
(213) 731-8211

To financially assist small businesses on a venture capital basis.

The Southern Fellowship Fund

795 Peachtree Street, N.E., Suite 484
Atlanta, GA 30308
(404) 874-4891

To provide a cadre of qualified persons for faculty and staff of colleges in the United States. Primary emphasis is placed on providing black talent, but others who are on the staff of black colleges and who have commitments to continuing careers in these institutions are eligible.

Southern Poverty Law Center

1001 South Hull Street
Montgomery, AL 36101
(205) 264-0286

To provide free legal aid for the financially handicapped. The group works with legal aid groups and with the local branches of the American Civil Liberties Union.

Southern Regional Council, Inc.

52 Fairlie Street, N.W.
Atlanta, GA 30303
(404) 522-8764

To alert, sensitize, educate, and mobilize Southerners on issues which will broaden opportunity and enhance quality of life for its people, primarily in areas of education, economic development, health, and housing.

Southwest Virginia Community Development Fund

401 First Street, N.W.
Roanoke, VA 24016
(703) 344-6624

To reduce unemployment and underemployment in depressed areas through the creation of economically sound, community-owned industries that will hire and train unemployed and underemployed persons.

Tactics (Technical Assistance Consortium To Improve College Services)

2001 S Street, N.W., Suite 503
Washington, DC 20009
(202) 232-7738

To create and maintain a pool of deployable manpower capable of dealing with institutional problems identified by the colleges; assist colleges in efforts to strengthen academic programs; establish and maintain a closer interface between federal programs and institutions for their mutual benefit and ensure that colleges become knowledgeable about government and nongovernment funding programs.

Tau Gamma Delta Sorority, Inc.

2207 Baker Street
Baltimore, MD 21216
(301) 669-2421

The 38-year-old sorority of college-educated women encourages educational opportunities for young people through its National Service Project and scholarship program. The organization also assists charitable institutions.

Third World Press

7524–26 South Cottage Grove
Chicago, IL 60619
(321) 651-1095

Makes available low-priced, quality books that can be purchased in most bookstores; publishes works of social and political analysis, as well as creative and critical writing aimed at raising the consciousness of third-world people, wherever they may be.

Transafrica, Inc.

1325 18th Street, N.W., Suite 202
Washington, DC 20036
(202) 223-9666

The organization is designed to promote an active U.S. policy on African and Caribbean issues. Transafrica also monitors federal legislation.

United Golfers Association

James Morrow, President
(Direct communications via local Professional Golf Association offices.)

Founded in Stone, MA, in 1926, the association represents some 20,000 golfers in 89 golf clubs across the United States. A scholarship fund and junior golfer interest programs are emphasized.

United Church of Christ, Commission for Racial Justice

105 Madison Avenue, Rooms 1102–1120
New York, NY 10016
(212) 683-5656

Criminal justice, penal reform, consumer advocacy, higher education, black family life, community organization, and retarded offender advocacy are supported by the commission's interdenominational and ecumenical programs.

United Mortgage Bankers of America, Inc.

840 East 87 Street
Chicago, IL 60619
(312) 994-7200

To unite black persons interested in mortgage banking; exchange information and establish educational programs for recruiting blacks into banking.

United Negro College Fund

500 East 62nd Street
New York, NY 10021
(212) 644-9600

UNCF is the fundraising arm of 41 private, accredited, four-year institutions of higher learning, located in the southern region of the United States with the exception of one in Ohio.

United States Commission on Civil Rights*

1121 Vermont Avenue, N.W.
Washington, DC 20425
(202) 254-6600

Investigates denials of voting rights; collects information about denials of equal protection of the laws under the Constitution; appraises federal laws and policies regarding equal protection of laws; serves as a national clearing house for information about denial of equal protection and submits reports, findings, and recommendations to the President and Congress.

Urban Bankers Coalition

c/o Robert Samuels
Manufacturers Hanover Trust
350 Park Avenue
New York, NY 10022
(212) 350-3109

To inform young people about opportunities in the banking industry; assist fellow employees to take advantage of opportunities for advancement in banking; promote economic improvement of the community and individuals through financial education and counseling.

The Urban Fund, Inc.

1525 East 53 Street
Chicago, IL 60615
(312) 455-0080

Equity financing of minority businesses in manufacturing and distribution.

Urban Ventures, Inc.

Tower Three, 18th Floor
825 South Bayshore Drive
Miami, FL 23131
(305) 371-4691

Help minority industry with business investments.

Venture Capital, Inc.

P.O. Box 1434
Little Rock, AR 72203
(501) 374-9977

Provide financing and management services for economically and socially oriented businesses.

Veterans' Association, Inc.

369th Regiment Armory
2366 Fifth Avenue
New York, NY 10037
(212) WA 6-5800

To assist the men and women veterans in any problems that might arise; acquaint them with the veterans benefits available; participate in community activities, especially as they pertain to youth, and to sponsor the Annual Dr. Martin Luther King, Jr. Memorial Parade on Fifth Avenue in New York in May of each year.

Voter Education Project, Inc.

52 Fairlie Street, N.W.
Atlanta, GA 30303
(404) 522-7495

To assist minority political participation in the 11 southern states—Alabama, Arkansas, Florida, Georgia, Louisiana, Mississippi, North Carolina, South Carolina, Tennessee, Texas, and Virginia; to provide assistance to black public officials in those states.

Washington Task Force on African Affairs

P.O. Box 13033
Washington, DC 20009
(202) 223-1392

To collect data and furnish analyses relevant to United States-Africa relations; assure consideration of black America in U.S. policies and activities with respect to Africa; to methodically build a constituency for African issues in the United States.

The Whitney M. Young, Jr. Academic and Intern Fellowship Program

795 Peachtree Street, N.W., Suite 484
Atlanta, GA 30308
(404) 874-4891

To fittingly memorialize Whitney M. Young, Jr. by providing training and

developmental opportunities for people in the areas of interracial cooperation; human resources; social services and corporate social responsibility in relationships with minorities.

Women's Auxiliary to the National Medical Association

1627 Mill "B" Lane Avenue
Savannah, GA 31405
(601) 534-8686

To increase interest in the National Medical Association; to aid and encourage the medical profession in its effort to educate the public in matters of sanitation and health; to promote acquaintances among doctors' families.

Youth Pride, Inc.

1536 You Street, N.W.
Washington, DC 20009
(202) 483-1900

To reclaim the lives of young inner-city black men who come from hard-core problem-ridden levels of society. Pride does this by recruiting them from the streets, enrolling them in a work-study program for which they are salaried, and placing them with both public and private employers. YPI's basic philosophy is self-respect, self-help, and self-sufficiency.

Zeta Phi Beta Sorority, Inc.

1734 New Hampshire Avenue, N.W.
Washington, DC 20009
(202) 387-3103

Scholarship, service, and community action.

The Zion Non-Profit Charitable Trust

Progress Plaza Shopping Center
1501 North Broad Street
Philadelphia, PA 19122
(215) 769-3484

To develop residential and commercial real estate; to build and manage residential, industrial, and commercial property; provide technical and financial assistance to minority business and education, and training to minority entrepreneurs. Motivational guidance, tutorial help, and financial assistance to selected students are also provided.

THE BLACK WOMAN

Blacks and Women's Liberation ■ Historical Perspectives ■ Current Trends ■ Outstanding Black Women

Because women must work harder than men to achieve the same recognition and earn the same money, black women have, throughout their history on these shores, labored under a double burden. They have had to struggle for the emancipation of their race, while contending with prejudices and policies in American life that discriminate against women. Thus the rise of the women's movement in the early 1970s presented black women with a hard question: Is it productive to fight for the rights of minorities and women at the same time, or will involvement in one inevitably detract from success in the other? As debate on this continued into the 1980s, Representative Shirley Chisholm observed that in many respects it was more difficult to be a woman than a black. Aileen Fernandez became leader of what has probably been the women's movement's most potent force, the National Organization for Women (NOW).

Feminists, both black and white, pointed out that many of the nation's sexist laws and procedures exerted their most adverse effect on black women. Examples cited included anti-abortion laws, which have the effect of increasing the cost of abortions to astronomical prices that few black women can afford, state labor laws that deny certain "strenuous" well-paying jobs to women, and welfare laws that rupture homes by denying aid to families that contain an able-bodied male.

However, while granting validity to these points, many blacks, both men and women, were deeply disturbed by the women's movement. In part their concern stemmed from the focus of much of the movement. Many blacks felt that feminists were unduly preoccupied with the problems and careerist aspirations of professional whites to the neglect of pressing job, housing, health, and education problems suffered more by black than white women.

In addition, many blacks, among them psychiatrist Alvin Poussaint, charged that the women's liberation movement was being used to perpetuate discriminatory practices in employment; that white women were being hired for positions that could be filled by blacks, male or female.

Carrying this assertion further, many blacks contended that the women's liberation movement (and the environmentalist movement as well) was a national copout, a retreat from the fight for racial justice to a less violent and controversial arena of justice for women. People supporting this view asserted that during the late 1960s and early 1970s the decline of the movement for racial justice and the rise of women's liberation coincided, until the latter gained preeminence in the consciences and priorities of the American government and public.

However, partisans of racial and sexual equality found much in common. In the summer of 1975, representatives of the two causes joined in the defense of Joanne Little, a North Carolina woman indicted for first degree murder after she killed a male prison guard whom she alleged had raped her while she was in jail pending an appeal of her conviction on a burglary charge.

Historical Perspectives

Inevitably, the women's movement is of interest to black women. Since the early days of slavery, black women have been deprived of rights society has traditionally granted women, namely to marry and raise a family. As slaves, women consistently found their mates, their children, or themselves sold abruptly to distant owners. And if by chance families were not ruptured in such a manner, long, rigorous hours of labor obliterated opportunities to fulfill the responsibilities and enjoy the pleasures that have been regarded as concomitants of motherhood. Even black women fortunate enough to live in physical comfort as the mistresses of slaveowners were denied the perquisites of wives and mothers. Unlike many female slaves in Latin American nations, their status was seldom recognized socially or legally.

It is ironic that black women were—and indeed still are—given special status as nurse and confidante to the children of white mothers they serve, while being deprived of the opportunity to shower the same appropriate attentions on their own children.

On many occasions, even before the Civil War, the two streams—black rights and women's rights—have merged. The battles for the black vote and the vote for women, for education of blacks and women, were often fought on the same ground. In the mid-nineteenth century, for instance, Frederick Douglass and the Forten sisters, all blacks, were fighting for black emancipation and the rights of women, and were aided in their work by a number of white abolitionists (e.g., Sarah and Angelina Grimké). In Philadelphia and Boston especially, many black and white families united to form antislavery societies dedicated to the causes of emancipation and education.

After Emancipation, one of the first discernible trends among black women was the development of a strong club movement, designed to improve their overall welfare and increase opportunities open to them. At that time, such leading black educators as Fannie Jackson Coppin, Charlotte Hawkins Brown, and Nannie Helen Burroughs came into prominence, to be joined later by Mary McLeod Bethune and Mary Church Terrell, among others.

Matriarchy and Current Trends

Much has been written of the matriarchal structure of black society, from the postwar era down to the present day. Whatever conclusions are drawn, there can be little doubt that the black woman has often been called upon to compensate for the failure (through no fault of his own) of the black man to find suitable, dependable employment in an intensely competitive and racist society. Cases in which women become the marginal family breadwinner—the sole financial support of the group—inevitably involve a reversal of traditional roles for both partners, and contribute in some measure to the hazards faced by the blacks.

Black women have strengthened their positions considerably in the twentieth century by their entry into more skilled and better-paying jobs made possible through higher educational achievement. As opportunities have opened up, the black woman has been quick to make the transition from low-paid, unskilled domes-

tic, farm, and operative jobs to employment in clerical, professional, technical, sales, and service jobs. But in comparison to whites, black women still lag far behind. In an effort to increase upward mobility, many black women have opted for national women's movements. This has caused dissention among blacks who feel that the feminists have put the various black movements on the back burner of social priorities.

The social trends and economic troubles of the 1970s and early 1980s have strained the fragile alliance between the women's and black movements. On one hand, such organizations as NOW participated importantly with blacks in equal opportunity litigation that improved the lot of both women and blacks. And blacks and women shared a concern about preachments from the radical right which sought to portray the aspirations of both groups as immoral. But to many blacks, the priorities of feminists, such as the right to abortion and the Equal Rights Amendment, were subordinate to the issues of economic survival manifested by inflation, recessions, and the competition to blacks of both sexes presented by the rapid increase of white women in the nation's labor force.

OUTSTANDING BLACK WOMEN

Whatever the pros and cons of the feminist cause for blacks as a whole, the number of prominent black women in American life has grown substantially. Many of these outstanding women have their biographies given below. Biographies of other prominent black women may be found in the sections of the *Almanac* devoted to their major fields or the section on Prominent Black Americans.

MARGARET W. ALEXANDER
College Administrator, Author

Director of black studies at Jackson State College in Mississippi, Margaret W. Alexander is also the author of many books, including the bestselling *Jubilee*, a novel about the Civil War. Born in Birmingham, she attended Northwestern University (B.A., English) and the University of Iowa (M.A. and Ph.D., English). Her writing has won many prizes, including the Yale Award for Younger Poets. She has taught college English since 1949.

SADIE T. M. ALEXANDER
Lawyer

Sadie Alexander set a series of precedents in pursuing her distinguished career as a lawyer. She was the first black woman to earn a Ph.D. degree in the United States and the first woman to earn a law degree from the University of Pennsylvania. In 1927, she became the first black woman to be admitted to the bar in the state of Pennsylvania.

Before graduating with honors from the University of Pennsylvania in 1918, Mrs. Alexander had acted as the associate editor of the university's law review. She then received a scholarship for a year's graduate study, and was also awarded the Frances S. Pepper Fellowship in Economics for the year 1920–1921.

Besides belonging to several church and law associations, Mrs. Alexander has served on the Board of Directors of the New York City branch of the National Urban League. The author of several articles, she was the editor of *Who's Who Among Negro Lawyers* in 1949.

Mrs. Alexander now lives in semiretirement in Philadelphia.

AUGUSTA BAKER
Librarian, Children's Specialist

During her distinguished 37-year career with the New York Public Library, Augusta Baker rose to the position of Coordinator of Children's Services. Under her knowledgeable and sensitive leadership, library materials for juveniles were greatly expanded in both kind and degree. Although she retired from the library in 1974, she continues to teach the art of storytelling at Columbia University and to lecture at colleges around the country.

Augusta Baker founded the New York Public Library's collection of children's books about black life.

After taking her bachelors degree in library science from the State University of New York, Albany, in 1934, she founded the New York Public Library's James Weldon Johnson Memorial collection of children's books about black life. In addition to contributing to numerous professional journals, she is the author of *The Black Experience in Books for Children* and two collections of folk tales, *The Talking Tree* and *The Golden Lynx.* Her extensive knowledge of juvenile literature has made her an active consultant for NBC-TV's children's programming, as well as for the successful *Sesame Street* series.

The recipient of many professional honors, Mrs. Baker is associated with the New York Library Association and the American Library Association, where she has served on the Executive Board (1968–1972). In 1975 Mrs. Baker was elected to an honorary life membership in the American Library Association, one of only 55 such memberships awarded in the 100 years of the association's existence.

IDA B. WELLS BARNETT
Antilynching Crusader
1864–1931

Born in Mississippi and educated at Rusk University, Ida Wells Barnett was one of the few women in the South who engaged in a vigorous campaign against the lynching practices common at that time. She was affiliated with several newspapers, most prominently as the editor of *Free Speech* in Memphis.

In 1895 her first pamphlet against lynching, *The Red Record,* was compiled. Mrs. Barnett also wrote several other pamphlets and articles during the years when her speaking engagements took her across the United States and to Europe as well.

After having become chairman of the Anti-Lynching Bureau of the National African Council, she organized and became the first president of the Negro Fellowship League in 1908. Five years later, her social work began to center in Chicago, where she was appointed probation officer. She left this post in 1915, having been elected Vice-President of the Chicago Equal Rights League. From then on, Mrs. Barnett devoted most of her time to civil rights activities.

She died in 1931.

BRENETTA H. BARRETT
State Official

Brenetta H. Barrett is currently director of Illinois' human resources administration. Prior to her appointment, she was national vice chairman for the 1972 First National Conference on Business Opportunities for Women. A native of Chicago, she attended Chicago Loop College and DePaul University. She is a board member of the Illinois ACLU, and has served on the advisory board of the Illinois Citizens for Medical Control of Abortions.

MARY TREADWELL BARRY
Executive

Mary T. Barry is an executive and co-founder of the Pride corporations, which provide work-training, job placement, and business ownership opportunities for black youths and inner city black males. Born in Lexington, Ky., she studied at Fisk University, Ohio State University, and Antioch Law School in Columbia, Md. She is a member of the Washington, D.C. chapter of the National Association of Market Developers, Inc., the Washington, D.C. Citizens for Better Public Education, Inc., and the American Management Association.

CHARLOTTA A. BASS
Vice-Presidential Candidate
1890–1961

Chosen unanimously by the Progressive Party convention in 1952, Mrs. Charlotta A. Bass became the first black woman to run for the nation's second-highest political office—Vice President of the United States.

Born in Little Compton, R.I. in 1890, Mrs. Bass studied at Brown University, Columbia University, and U.C.L.A. While a resident of Los Angeles, Mrs. Bass was the editor and publisher of the *California Eagle*, the oldest black newspaper on the West Coast.

Until 1948, Mrs. Bass was a member of the Republican party, and had even served as Western Regional Director for Wendell Willkie in his 1940 presidential campaign. In 1950, however, Mrs. Bass ran for Congress in the 14th District of Los Angeles on the ticket of the Progressive party, which she herself had helped found two years earlier.

During her newspaper career, she was known as a vigorous opponent of the Ku Klux Klan and an outspoken foe of discrimination in employment.

Mrs. Bass died in 1961.

DAISY BATES
Little Rock Integrationist

Mrs. Daisy Bates first captured the national spotlight in 1957 during the Little Rock crisis in which President Eisenhower was forced to use federal troops to effect the admission of nine black children to Central High School. As Arkansas president of the NAACP, Mrs. Bates submitted to arrest and other attempts at intimidation while standing firm in the struggle to integrate the school.

Born in Huttig, Ark., Mrs. Bates attended school in Memphis and later went to Philander Smith and Shorter colleges in Little Rock. She married L. Christopher Bates in 1941, the same year they organized a weekly newspaper, The Arkansas *State Press,* which has since become one of the most influential of its kind in the South. In 1946 Mrs. Bates and her husband were convicted on contempt charges for criticizing a Circuit Court trial, but the Arkansas Supreme Court later reversed the decision.

Mrs. Bates has recounted her integration experiences in her book *The Long Shadow of Little Rock,* published in 1962. Ever critical of discriminatory policies, she led a 1972 attack on Nixon's cut of OEO funds for Mitchellville, Ark., calling the budgetary measure a form of economic genocide. In March 1974 Mrs. Bates and the nine children who integrated Little Rock's white Central High School in 1957 were honored for their courage by the National Black Political Convention.

MARY McLEOD BETHUNE
Administrator, Division of Negro Affairs, National Youth Administration (NYA)
1875–1955

Mary McLeod Bethune is such a major figure in black American history that no comprehensive discussion of it is possible without recalling her contributions.

Born on July 10, 1875, she gained her special insight into the everyday problems of the average black youth while growing up on a farm in Mayesville, S.C. As a young woman, she spent some seven years at Scotia Seminary in North Carolina and later did further study at the Moody Bible Institute in Chicago—all this with the intention of eventually becoming a missionary. But when this proved impossible (her application for a post in Africa was turned down by the Presbyterian Board of Missions in New York), she turned instead to teaching.

Herbert Hoover was the first American president to utilize her abilities when, in 1930, he invited her to a White House Conference on Child Health and Protection. Franklin D. Roosevelt was quick to follow his predecessor's lead by asking her to serve on the Advisory Committee of one of the organizations he helped establish—the National Youth Administration (NYA). In 1935, after a year spent laying the foundations for the NYA, her work had so impressed the President that he was persuaded to set up an Office of Minority Affairs, with Mrs. Bethune as administrator. This established a precedent, for it was the first post of its kind ever to be held by an American black woman.

Congressional appropriations for the NYA continued from 1936 through 1944, and Mary Bethune's title was soon changed to the more specific one of Director of the Division of Negro Affairs. Her duties consisted

Mary McLeod Bethune dedicated her career to teaching and government service.

largely in granting funds to deserving students (particularly blacks) who could not otherwise have continued graduate study.

During the 1930s she was one of the leading figures (and the only woman) in the unofficial "Black Cabinet" which had begun the fight for advanced integration in the U.S. government.

In later years Mrs. Bethune was instrumental in establishing what is now known as Bethune-Cookman College, a merger of her own school (The Daytona Educational and Industrial School for Negro Girls) with the Cookman Institute.

Mrs. Bethune died in 1955 at the age of 80. Though she had been the holder of many important awards—among them the 1935 Spingarn Medal—her greatest achievement was the legacy of a lifelong career dedicated to young people, one which won her worldwide recognition and acclaim.

DOROTHY BOLDEN
Labor Leader

Fighting for good job conditions and fair employment opportunities for domestic workers, Dorothy Bolden founded and serves as president of the National Domestic Workers Union. Her interest in improving home situations has also led her to become director of the Homemaking Skills Training Program in Atlanta. Born in Fulton County, Ga., she attended high school there before going on to study at the Chicago School

of Dress Designers. She is on the board of directors of the Welfare Rights Organization, a member of the Atlanta Legal Aid Society, and a member of the League of Women Voters. Her homemaking skills project teaches consumer rights, nutrition, child care, budgeting, cooking, and housekeeping.

RUTH J. BOWEN
Booking Agent

Ruth J. Bowen is founder and president of Queen Booking Corp., New York City. Born in Danville, Va., and raised in Brooklyn, N.Y., she studied business administration at New York University and UCLA.

After marrying Billy Bowen, one of the original Inkspots, she began to gain show business experience by handling her husband's business affairs. A friendship with Dinah Washington, who urged Mrs. Bowen to assume all her management responsibilities, led to the founding of Queen Booking, which has grown to be the largest black-owned entertainment agency in the country, grossing over $800,000 annually.

The only woman to head her own booking agency, Mrs. Bowen handles such talent as Stevie Wonder, Sammy Davis, Jr., Aretha Franklin, Redd Foxx, Ray

Ruth Bowen is president and founder of the nation's largest black-owned entertainment agency.

Charles, and Gladys Knight and the Pips. She is a member, and former president, of the Rinkydinks Club, and is a member of Operation Push.

CHARLOTTE HAWKINS BROWN
Educator
1882–1961

Although she was raised and educated in Cambridge, Mass., Charlotte Hawkins made yearly visits with her parents to her birthplace in Henderson, N.C., and as she grew older, became interested in improving educational facilities for black people in the South.

With the aid of her benefactor, Alice Freeman Palmer, she received training as a teacher at Salem (Mass.) Normal School and at Wellesley College, later accepting a position from the American Missionary Association as a teacher in a small school near Sedalia, N.C.

Lack of funds, however, forced the Association to close the school in 1902. Conscious of the community's urgent need for educational facilities, Miss Hawkins decided to work in Sedalia without a salary, and to establish her own school there. By 1904 she had raised enough money to construct the first building of what was to become Palmer Memorial Institute. A midwinter conflagration burned the school's wooden structure to the ground in 1917, but Mrs. Brown turned the disaster into an opportunity for further growth and improvement. With the assistance of loyal friends in both New England and North Carolina, she raised enough money to construct the sturdy brick buildings which are still in use.

In addition to her distinguished work as an educator, Mrs. Brown (she married Edward S. Brown in 1911) served as president of the Federation of Women's Clubs of North Carolina, and as vice-president of the National Association of Colored Women. She was also well-known as a lecturer on interracial subjects.

Mrs. Brown resigned as president of Palmer in 1952 but remained as director of finance until 1955. Mrs. Brown died in 1961 in Greensboro, N.C.

DOROTHY LAVINIA BROWN
Physician

Dorothy L. Brown holds the positions of clinical professor of surgery at Meharry Medical College in Nashville, director of Student Health Service at Meharry and Fisk universities, and chief of surgery at Riverside Hospital. Born in Philadelphia, she spent the first 12 years of her life in a foster home. She is a graduate of Bennett College (B.A., 1941) and Meharry Medical College (M.D., 1948). As a member of Tennessee's legislature, Dr. Brown wrote and sponsored the state's only attempt at abortion reform, which was rejected,

and she was then defeated in her own attempts for reelection. Dr. Brown enjoys the distinction of being the first black woman general surgeon in the South, and she was also the first single woman in Tennessee permitted to adopt a child. She is a fellow of the American College of Surgeons.

HALLIE Q. BROWN
Teacher, Elocutionist, Writer
1845?–1949

A distinguished lecturer and elocutionist who traveled throughout the United States and several European countries, Hallie Q. Brown was born in Pittsburgh, but moved with her family at an early age to Ontario, Canada. Having completed her early education, she returned to the United States and attended Wilberforce College in Ohio, graduating with a B.S. degree in 1873.

Before she began her lecture tours with the Wilberforce Grand Concert Company, Miss Brown taught for several years at plantation schools in the South and later at Allen University (South Carolina) and Tuskegee Institute (Alabama). She also returned to her alma mater to teach and serve as a trustee.

Between 1905 and 1912, Miss Brown served as president of both the Ohio State Federation of Women and National Association of Colored Women, establishing the latter organization's scholarship fund.

Miss Brown was the author of several books, among them *First Lessons in Public Speaking* and *Homespun Heroines and Other Women of Distinction.*

NANNIE HELEN BURROUGHS
Educator
1883–1961

Nannie Helen Burroughs began her career as a bookkeeper and associate editor of the Philadelphia *Christian Banner* but, because of her longstanding interest in the church, decided after a year to leave her position with the paper in order to devote all her energies to social service.

Working for the Association of Colored Women, she organized the Women's Industrial Club in Louisville, which specialized in teaching domestic skills to black girls. In 1907 she began her work with the National Baptist Convention, playing an important role in founding the National Training School for Women and Girls, which opened in 1909 with her as president. Though most of her time was devoted to the school, Miss Burroughs was also particularly active as a member of both the National Association of Colored Women and the National Association for the Advancement of Colored People.

Vinie Burrows, a performing actress, is extremely active in civil affairs.

VINIE BURROWS
Performing Artist

Vinie Burrows is a founding member of Women for Racial and Economic Equality. A native of New York City, Vinie Burrows began her theatrical career as a child actress with Helen Hayes on the New York stage. She has appeared both on and off Broadway with such stars as Ossie Davis, James Earl Jones, Mary Martin, Ben Gazzara, and Cicely Tyson. Ms. Burrows created a one-woman show, called *Walk Together Children*, which is an exploration of the black presence in America, using poetry, prose and song. The show has received rave reviews from the more than 900 colleges in the United States and in Holland, Sweden, Nigeria, Algeria, and Viet Nam.

Vinie Burrows has had feature articles published in national magazines and produces a weekly live radio show focusing on concerns of women. Her concern for political, economic, and social democracy is evidenced in her role as an NGO (Nongovernmental Organization) Permanent Representative to the United Nations where she is closely involved with women's issues, disarmament, and the struggle against apartheid.

MADELYN CHENNAULT
Educator, Psychologist

One of the handful of black women in the United States qualifying for a license to practice clinical psychology, Madelyn Chennault is both Calloway Professor of Educational Psychology at Fort Valley (Ga.) State College and director of the school's forward-looking "crisis clinic." The clinic offers its services to members of the college and to the local community. Born in Atlanta, she took degrees from Morris Brown College, the University of Michigan, and Indiana University before completing her doctoral internship in clinical psychology at the University of Georgia. She belongs to the Association of Black Psychologists and the American Association of University Professors.

MAY EDWARD CHINN
Physician
1896–1980

Dr. May Edward Chinn was born in 1876 in Great Barrington, Massachusetts. Her father was William Lafayette Chinn, a slave who escaped from the Chinn Plantation in Lancasta, Virginia in 1864. The Chinn family moved from Great Barrington in 1899.

In 1921 May passed tests at New York's Teachers College which qualified her for the music course there. She was a pianist and was an accompanist for Paul Robeson for a four-year period. While at Teachers College, she came to the attention of a professor through a paper she had written on sewage disposal, which ultimately led to medical studies.

In 1926 she was graduated from the Bellevue Hospital Medical College and was admitted to an internship at Harlem Hospital. Her early work in cancer detection earned her high professional praise and in 1944 she was invited to join the staff of the Strang Clinic, where she remained for 29 years. By 1978 Dr. Chinn had become a consultant to the Phelps-Stokes Fund where she remained until her death on December 1, 1980. Dr. Chinn was the recipient of numerous awards. Among them were the doctor of science degree from New York University and an honorary doctorate from Columbia University.

She was the first black female intern at Harlem Hospital and for many years the lone female doctor in Harlem.

XERONA CLAYTON
Television Producer and Hostess

Xerona Clayton produces and hosts *The Xerona Clayton Show,* which focuses on current events from an activist viewpoint, on WAGA-TV in Atlanta. A native of Muskogee, Okla., she graduated from Tennessee

State University (B.A., 1952) and taught in the public school systems of Chicago and Los Angeles before joining the Southern Christian Leadership Conference. Mrs. Clayton is a consultant for the Atlanta Model Cities Program and a member of American Women in Radio and Television and of the Atlanta Press Club.

LENORA COLE-ALEXANDER
Administrator

Dr. Lenora Cole-Alexander is the ninth woman to head the Labor Department's Women's Bureau since it was created in 1920. As director, she is responsible for carrying out the agency's mandate to formulate standards and policies promoting the welfare of working women and to advance their employment opportunities. A native of Buffalo, New York, Dr. Cole-Alexander has been involved in a number of professional and community service activities. She has served on the boards or commissions of the Washington, D.C. Chamber of Commerce, the D.C. Rental Accommodations Commission, National Association of Student Personnel Administrators, National Council of Negro Women, American Council on Education, and Washington Opportunities for Women.

Dr. Cole-Alexander was educated at the State University of New York at Buffalo, where she received her bachelors degree in 1957 and her masters in 1969 and Ph.D. in 1974. Prior to being named to her Labor Department post, Dr. Cole-Alexander was vice president for student affairs at the University of the District of Columbia. She has also served as vice president for student life at American University in Washington, D.C. and was assistant to the vice president for student affairs and interim director, Cooperative College Center at the State University of New York in Buffalo from 1969 to 1973.

MARVA N. COLLINS
Educator

Marva N. Collins is well known for her educational work in Chicago, where she established her own school to teach slow learners. Mrs. Collins was the subject of a special television program in which Cicely Tyson played the role of the noted educator. Mrs. Collins, an Alabama native, taught in the Chicago school system for 14 years but became concerned with the type of education black youngsters were receiving. In 1975 she opened the Westside Preparatory School in her home and since then she has been teaching basic education to youngsters on Chicago's West Side. Mrs. Collins graduated from Chicago Teacher's College and is a recipient of the Watson Washburn Award for Excellence in Education.

ANNA JULIA COOPER
Educator
1858–1964

This noted educator was, as early as the age of 11, acting as a student-teacher at St. Augustine Normal School, the institution which she attended in her native city of Raleigh, N.C. She was later to return there to teach for two years after she had become a full professor.

Dr. Cooper married the Reverend G. A. C. Cooper in 1877 and, four years later, left for Oberlin College in Ohio, where she taught and continued to pursue her own studies at the same time. Upon graduation in 1885, she became a professor of modern languages and science at Wilberforce University. However, her primary work in the field of educational administration came during her 50-year association with the old M Street High School in Washington, D.C. (later to become Dunbar). She served there as both instructor and principal.

In addition to her career as a teacher, Dr. Cooper wrote *A Voice from the South,* a well-received book on the racial problem which appeared in 1892. In 1925, at the age of 66, she received a Ph.D. from the Sorbonne in Paris, and later became president of Frelinghuysen University, a school for unemployed blacks which she ran in her own home in Washington, D.C.

Dr. Cooper died on February 27, 1961, at the age of 105.

LOUISE M. DARGANS
Administrator

Louise M. Dargans became known as the "good right hand" of New York Congressman Adam Clayton Powell after joining his staff in 1946. Today, as Chief Clerk of the House Committee on Education and Labor, she is one of the two blacks who heads a committee staff, and the only woman employed as chief clerk of a House committee.

The youngest of nine children, Miss Dargans was born in Daytona Beach, Fla., and moved to New York with her parents at the age of seven. In 1938 she graduated from Hunter College and went on to work for the New York State Department of Labor, the Office of Price Administration, and the Internal Revenue Service.

ANGELA DAVIS
Political Activist

Born in Birmingham, Ala., Angela Davis grew up in a segregated middle-class neighborhood, which became known as "Dynamite Hill" because of the terrorist attacks of white nightriders. After taking part in the mid-1950s civil rights demonstrations, she won a scholarship to a progressive high school in New York City, which prepared her for Brandeis University, where her intellectual leftism was sharpened by philosopher Herbert Marcuse. After two years of advanced study in Germany, she returned to the United States because she felt she had to take an active political role here.

Earning her masters degree at the University of California, San Diego, she worked with SNCC, the Black Panthers, and the Communist Party, eventually joining the last in 1968. Shortly thereafter, she was hired by UCLA to teach philosophy and fired twice by the Board of Regents over the strong protests of faculty and students after FBI leaks had identified her as a Party member. Counted against her were the speeches she gave in the cause of the Soledad Brothers. Then, in 1970, guns she had legally bought were used in a courtroom shootout and she became a fugitive on the FBI's "Most Wanted" list. Captured two months later, she spent 16 months in jail before coming to trial for murder and conspiracy. Needing only 13 hours of deliberations, the jurors acquitted her of all charges in June 1972.

Since then she has focused on the long-range revolutionary goals that affect not only blacks but all working people of the United States. To this end she has helped organize the National Alliance Against Racist and Political Repression, which now has 20 chapters. Despite university pleas, the California Regents refuses to rehire her. Her autobiography, *Angela Davis,* was published in 1974.

CHRISTINE R. DAVIS
Publishing Executive

Christine Ray Davis was born in Nashville and began her education as a music major at Fisk University. However, she left Fisk in 1935 and completed her higher education at Tennessee State College, majoring in business administration.

Her first job was as secretary and research assistant in a Boston law firm. Later, she left for Washington, D.C., to become administrative assistant to Arthur W. Mitchell, the Democratic Congressman from Illinois. She held this position until 1942 when Mitchell retired, after which she began to work for his successor, William L. Dawson.

In 1949 Dawson became chairman of the Committee on Expenditures (now the Committee on Government Operations), and appointed Mrs. Davis chief clerk. When the Democrats won control of the House in 1954, Dawson appointed her Staff Director of the Committee.

Mrs. Davis has been the recipient of several awards for her work in government, among them the citation of "Outstanding Woman of the Year," given her by the National Council of Negro Women in 1949. She also holds the award for "distinguished achievement in government affairs" from the National Association of Colored Women's Clubs.

Mrs. Davis is now a member of the staff of *Tuesday* magazine.

JULIETTE DERRICOTTE
Educator
1897–1931

Raised in Athens, Ga., Juliette Derricotte was educated in the public schools there and at Talladega College, then a small school in Alabama operated by the American Missionary Association. Some 11 years after graduating from Talladega in 1918, Miss Derricotte became the first woman trustee of the college.

In the intervening years, she traveled across the United States, speaking at many colleges and educational conferences. In both 1924 and 1928 she was chosen to be a delegate representing American college students at the convention of the General Committee of the World's Student Christian Federation.

She later became the National Student Secretary for the Y.W.C.A. but resigned from this position in 1929 in order to become Dean of Women at Fisk University.

She died two years later in an automobile accident.

DOROTHY B. FEREBEE
Physician

A physician who received her medical degree with honors from Tufts Medical School in Massachusetts, Dr. Dorothy Ferebee has been active all her life in civic and social affairs. She began her medical career in Washington, D.C., where she served for several years on the Board of Directors of the Southeast Settlement House.

For seven summers, she worked among black sharecroppers in Mississippi on a health project which was sponsored by the Alpha Kappa Alpha Sorority. Dr. Ferebee later became president of this society, and also succeeded Mary McLeod Bethune as president of the National Council of Negro Women.

In 1951 Dr. Ferebee was sent by the U.S. Labor Department to study the problems of women in Germany, and she later visited Africa as a delegate to an international conference of women of African descent.

Besides maintaining her own medical practice, Dr. Ferebee acts as the head of the Student Health Service at Howard University and is a full professor of preventive medicine at the Howard School of Medicine.

PHYLLIS T. GARLAND
Journalist

Phyllis ("Phyl") Garland is a journalism professor at Columbia University in New York City. The former *Ebony* editor is an expert on black music and musicians and her book, *The Sound of Soul: The Story of Black Music,* is used as a text in many high school and college music courses. Born in McKeesport, Pa., she studied journalism at Northwestern University. While writing for the Pittsburgh *Courier* newspaper, she received the 1962 Golden Quail award as "outstanding feature writer."

GLORIA GASTON
Diplomat

A career diplomat, Gloria Gaston is a member of the Foreign Services Office of the Department of State. She became the first black woman to occupy a post of major importance in the Agency for International Development (AID) when she was appointed Human Resources Development Officer for the Bureau of Latin America in 1970.

A graduate of the University of Washington (B.A., 1948), Miss Gaston has done graduate work at the New School for Social Research in New York City. Her first government assignment was as a Peace Corps liaison officer (1962–1964). Later she served in the Sudan with a Columbia research team gathering data on possible investment programs there.

Miss Gaston has also held a number of important posts with private organizations—among them the Bank Street College of Education, the National Conference of Christians and Jews, and the American Society of African Culture.

REGINA GOFF
Professor, Retired Public Official

A specialist in child development and welfare, Dr. Regina Goff has worked in the field of education for many years. From 1965 to 1971 she was Assistant Commissioner responsible for programs for the disadvantaged in the U.S. Office of Education, Washington, D.C.

Born in St. Louis in 1917, she received a B.A. in Education from Northwestern University in 1936 and, later, both an M.A. and a Ph.D. in child development from Columbia University. She has taught both nursery school and kindergarten, and has served as chairman of the department of child development at Florida A & M, state supervisor of Negro elementary schools for the Florida Department of Education, and professor of education at Morgan State College in Baltimore.

In 1955 Dr. Goff was appointed consultant to the Ministry of Education in Iran by the International Cooperation Administration (now the Agency for International Development). In 1971 she accepted a professorship at the University of Maryland.

She is a member of the American Psychological Association and president of the Maryland Association of Teachers of Education.

JESSIE P. GUZMAN
Educator

The distinguished teaching career of Jessie P. Guzman, which began in 1918 in the schools of Greensboro, N.C., came to an end in 1965 when she retired as professor of history and director of the Department of Records and Research at Tuskegee Institute in Alabama.

A native of Savannah, Mrs. Guzman was educated at Clark College in Atlanta, Columbia University, and the University of Chicago. Before her appointment to the Tuskegee faculty in 1924, Mrs. Guzman had taught at Dillard University in New Orleans and had served as a secretary to the New York City Bible Society. She left Tuskegee after one year to join the faculty of Alabama State Teachers College in Montgomery, but returned to the former school in 1930 to begin an uninterrupted 34-year tenure there. She served as teacher, research assistant, and dean of women at Tuskegee prior to accepting the positions she held at the time of her retirement.

A leader in the civic affairs of her community, Mrs. Guzman has also written some 15 books, pamphlets, and articles. In 1947 and again in 1952 she was the editor of the *Negro Year Book,* and she later served as secretary to the Southern Conference Educational Fund and as director of the Tuskegee branch of the NAACP. She now lives in retirement in Tuskegee.

ANNA ARNOLD HEDGEMAN
Educator

After serving as an administrator in several political and social welfare organizations, Dr. Anna Arnold Hedgeman joined with her husband, Merritt A. Hedgeman, to establish the Hedgeman Consultant Service in 1967. Clients include educational institutions, civic, business, and community organizations.

Born in Marshalltown, Ia., Dr. Hedgeman was educated at Hamline University, the University of Minnesota, and the New York School of Social Work. After teaching for two years in Mississippi, she worked in various executive capacities for the YMCAs of Ohio, Jersey City, New York, and Philadelphia for 12 years.

In 1944 she was named executive director of the National Council for the Fair Employment Practices Commission, a position which she held for four years. From 1949 to 1953 she served as assistant to the admin-

Former public administrator Anna Arnold Hedgeman is now an organizational consultant.

istrator of the Federal Security Agency (now the Department of Health, Education, and Welfare). In 1954 she became a member of New York Mayor Robert F. Wagner's cabinet with liaison responsibility for eight city departments. From 1963 to 1968 she served as associate director of the Department of Social Justice and director of ecumenical action for the National Council of Churches in 1967.

The recipient of many awards, Dr. Hedgeman is on the boards of the National Conference of Christians and Jews and the United Seamen's Service, and is a member of the National Urban League and the Community Council of New York.

DOROTHY I. HEIGHT
Administrator

Before becoming the fourth president of the National Council of Negro Women, Dorothy Height had for many years served as a member of the organization's Board of Directors, later becoming its executive director. Miss Height is also the Associate Director for Leadership Training Services for the Young Women's Christian Association of the United States. From 1952 to 1955 she served as a member of the Defense Advisory Committee on Women in the Services, having been appointed by General George C. Marshall.

A native of Richmond, Va., Miss Height holds a masters degree from New York University and has also studied at the New York School of Social Work. In the fall of 1952 she served as a visiting professor at the Delhi School of Social Work in New Delhi, India. Six years later, Miss Height was appointed to the Social Welfare Board of New York by Governor Averell Harriman, and was reappointed by Governor Nelson Rockefeller in 1961 for another five years.

In 1960 Miss Height was sent to five African countries by the Committee on Correspondence to make a study of women's organizations there. In addition to the presidency of the National Council of Negro Women, Miss Height also holds the office of vice-president of the National Council of Women of the United States.

In May 1973 she was elected president of Women in Community Services, Inc. Her recent accomplishments include designing a vast program sponsored by the Agency for International Development and serving as a chief architect for the 1974–1975 International Women's Year program.

Dorothy Height is president of the National Council of Negro Women.

AILEEN C. HERNANDEZ
Public Affairs Consultant

Aileen C. Hernandez is a consultant and lecturer on urban affairs and public relations. From 1965 to 1966 she was a commissioner on the U.S. Equal Employment Opportunity Commission.

Born in New York City, Mrs. Hernandez attended Howard University in Washington, D.C., where she was active in student civil rights work. In 1959 she received an M.A. from Los Angeles State College, and she has since studied at New York University, UCLA, and the University of Oslo in Norway.

She has had several years' experience with the educational program of the International Ladies Garment Workers Union on the West Coast and, in the summer of 1960, toured six Latin American countries under the auspices of the State Department, giving lectures on labor education and reporting on the position of minority groups in the United States.

Mrs. Hernandez is a member of several national organizations, including the NAACP, the Urban League, and Americans for Democratic Action. In 1961 she was selected "Woman of the Year" by the Community Relations Conference of Southern California. In 1971 she was elected president of NOW (the National Organization for Women).

CHARLOTTE MOTON HUBBARD
Public Official

Charlotte Hubbard has had a long and distinguished career in communications and politics. Appointed in May of 1964 as Deputy Assistant Secretary of State for Public Affairs, she served in the highest permanent federal position ever held by a black woman until her retirement in 1970.

Born in Hampton, Va., Mrs. Hubbard received a junior college certificate in home economics from Tuskegee Institute, a B.S. in education at Boston University, and did graduate work both at the latter school and at Bennington College. Before joining the government, she was an instructor and later an associate professor of physical education at Hampton Institute.

In 1942 Mrs. Hubbard—largely on the recommendation of Eleanor Roosevelt—was named recreation representative in what became the Department of Health, Education and Welfare, her main job being that of organizing communities where a particular need for welfare and recreational facilities existed.

Some 10 years later, Mrs. Hubbard became the first black person to be appointed to an important position with a television station (WTOP-TV) in Washington, D.C. From 1958 to 1963 she was public relations assistant of the United Givers Fund, an organization linking local and national welfare agencies.

She is a trustee of Southeastern College, on the board of governors of the Women's National Democratic Club, and on the board of directors of the Educational Community Association. In 1970 she was named one of the Foremost Women in Communications.

JANE EDNA HUNTER
Social Worker
1882–1971

Jane Hunter spent the early years of her life in her home state of South Carolina, before taking nurses training in Virginia and then migrating north in search of a better job. However, she had great difficulty finding suitable employment in Cleveland, and it was not until she met the secretary to the physician of John D. Rockefeller that she received any real help in securing a satisfactory position.

By this time, she was acutely aware of the need for an institution to aid other black women coming to Cleveland in search of employment. With this in mind, she called the first meeting of the Working Girls' Home Association (later renamed the Phyllis Wheatley Association) in 1911. Although the early years of the Association were ones of hardship, it was able to expand both its boarding facilities and other services after

Jean Blackwell Hutson is curator of New York's prestigious Schomburg library.

receiving a substantial grant from Rockefeller in 1917.

Although much of her time was occupied by her obligations to the Association, Miss Hunter was able to study law for four years at Baldwin Wallace College. She was admitted to the bar in 1925, after which she continued her work with the Association. Under her guidance, several similar organizations have been established in leading cities across the country.

Miss Hunter died in Cleveland in January 1971, at the age of 89. In her will she bequeathed $427,107 to aid young women in South Carolina.

CHARLAYNE HUNTER-GAULT
Journalist

Charlayne Hunter-Gault is an anchorwoman for WNET television news and was formerly a reporter for *The New York Times* and chief of that newspaper's Harlem bureau, which she founded in the late 1960s to make certain that reportage about black persons would begin to "provide stories about human beings rather than sociological stereotypes."

Born in Due West, S.C., she pioneered the admission of black women to the University of Georgia (B.A., journalism, 1963). By graduation time her writing style was fine enough to win her a berth on the staff of the prestigious *New Yorker* magazine as a "Talk of the Town" contributor and a short story writer. Leaving the magazine in 1967, she accepted a Russell Sage Fellowship at Washington University to pursue her studies in the social sciences and simultaneously began her career in media news, working with WRL/NBC News, Washington, D.C.

JEAN BLACKWELL HUTSON
Library Administrator

Jean Blackwell Hutson served as curator of the prestigious Schomburg Collection of Negro Life and History for more than 25 years. The Schomburg Collection is a special noncirculating library and autonomous research division within the New York Public Library system. The collection grew immensely under Mrs. Hutson's guidance, which reflects her expert acquisitions, alert reading of the expanding relevance of black studies materials, and internationalist outlook. The Schomburg now has vertical files, microfilm, tapes and records, and photographs in addition to books and periodicals from all over the world. It is the single most important repository on black culture and achievement in the United States.

A native of Summerfield, Fla., Mrs. Hutson earned her B.A. in 1935. A year later she received a B.S. from the Columbia School of Library Service. Her first assignment in the New York Public Library system was as branch librarian of Woodstock in the Bronx.

She has been with Schomburg since 1948, although she took a leave of absence in 1964–1965 to serve as assistant librarian at the University of Ghana. After her return to New York, she served as chairman of the Harlem Cultural Council.

Mrs. Hutson has been a lecturer at City College and belongs to numerous organizations which cultivate interest in, and promote the study of, the heritage of Africa. These include the American Society of African Culture and the African Studies Association. Mrs. Hutson is a Delta, and a member of the NAACP, the National Urban League, and the American Library Association.

BEVERLY JOHNSON
Fashion Model

One of the world's top high fashion models, Beverly Johnson is an outspoken and career-minded young woman from Buffalo, N.Y. Smart enough to win a full academic scholarship to Boston's Northeastern University, she left for New York City after her freshman year to see if she'd find the instant modeling success her friends predicted. She did. Within two years she was a star in the high fashion world, and in August 1974 she landmarked the first black cover for *Vogue* magazine. Her professional dedication coupled with beautifully photogenic features and figure make her

Beverly Johnson is the first black model to appear on the cover of Vogue.

one of today's most sought after mannequins. When a radio host recently commented that she was the "biggest black model in the business," she replied: "No, I'm not. I'm the biggest model—period."

MAIDA SPRINGER KEMP
Labor Leader

Maida Springer Kemp is a general organizer and member of the international staff of the International Ladies Garment Workers Union, and is a consultant for the African Labor History Center. Born in Panama City, Panama, she studied at Wellesley College, Rand School of Social Sciences in New York, and with the education department of the ILGWU. She joined the Dressmakers Union (AFL-CIO) in 1933, became a member of its executive board (1938–1942), and was a captain in the Women's Health Brigade (1942–1944). She served in East and West Africa as a representative in the Department of International Affairs, AFL-CIO, (1959–1965), was an ILGWU organizer in the Southwestern United States (1965–1968), and organized the Midwestern Regional Office of the A. Philip Randolph Institute (1969–1972). She is vice president of the National Council of Negro Women, a member of the board of the DuSable History Museum, and a life member of the NAACP.

ELIZABETH DUNCAN KOONTZ
Educator, Government Official

Mrs. Elizabeth Duncan Koontz has devoted most of her professional life to the field of classroom education, having served as a teacher in the public schools of Salisbury, N.C., from 1938 to 1965, the year she became president of the 1.1-million-member National Education Association (NEA). A year later she was appointed Director of the Women's Bureau in the Department of Labor and, in a related assignment, named U.S. Delegate to the U.S. Commission on the Status of Women. Mrs. Koontz resigned her directorship in late 1972.

Early in her teaching career, she developed what became a lifelong interest in "supposedly mentally retarded" children, whom she herself generally classifies as slow learners needing only patience and understanding before they will develop the same rate of perception and level of skill as other less-neglected pupils.

Mrs. Koontz was once head of North Carolina's all-black NEA affiliate, as well as the Association's largest division, the 820,000-member Association of Classroom Teachers. Once in office as NEA head, she made it clear that she anticipated trouble as soon as teachers began to organize, agitate, and strike for higher pay and improved conditions. When the NEA did in fact stage strikes, she advised communities to

Elizabeth Duncan Koontz has served as Director of the U.S. Dept. of Labor Women's Bureau.

adjust to teachers' demands and support bona fide attempts to upgrade the caliber of teaching candidates by making the profession more lucrative.

LUCY LANEY
Educator
1854–1933

Lucy Craft Laney, born a slave in Macon, Ga., rose to become the founder and principal of Haines Normal Institute in Georgia. Her work was made possible largely through the early efforts of her master's sister, who taught her to read at the age of four and later enabled her to enter Atlanta University.

After graduating from the first class there, Miss Laney taught for several years in the public schools of Savannah before accepting an invitation from the Presbyterian Board of Missions for Freedmen to start a private school in Atlanta. When the funds from the Board were not forthcoming, Miss Laney decided to raise the money for the school herself. In 1886, the school was first opened in the remodeled basement of a church, and, though beset by financial difficulties, was able to accommodate over 200 pupils by its second year.

Such generous financial aid was received from Mrs. F. E. H. Haines of Milwaukee that it was soon decided to name the school after its benefactor. Further allocations from the Presbyterian Mission Board, together with donations of land from other sources, made it possible for Haines to expand from a one-room school to the prospering educational community of over 1,000 students which it is today.

MARJORIE LAWSON
Lawyer

In August of 1962, Marjorie M. Lawson became the first black woman to be appointed to a judgeship by a president of the United States, and the first black woman ever to be approved by the Senate for a statutory appointment. She resigned from the bench in 1965 and is now back in private practice.

Born in Pittsburgh in 1912, Mrs. Lawson graduated from the University of Michigan in 1933 and received a Certificate in Social Work there the next year. In 1939 she earned the Bachelor of Law degree from the Terrell Law School in Washington, D.C., and in 1950 from the Columbia University School of Law.

Admitted to the District of Columbia Bar in 1939, Mrs. Lawson engaged in private practice with her husband, Belford V. Lawson, Jr., until the time of her appointment to the bench. She wrote a weekly public affairs column for 15 years for the Pittsburgh *Courier*.

She has held a variety of social work positions, often employing her capacity as a lawyer to act as counsel for families in the Juvenile Court of the District of Columbia. She has also been active in several organizations dealing with housing and employment problems, among them the National Urban League, and has held the post of Vice-President of the National Council of Women.

In 1958, Mrs. Lawson became race relations advisor to Senator John F. Kennedy and, upon his nomination for the presidency, was named director of civil rights for his campaign. In 1962 Kennedy named her to his Committee on Equal Employment Opportunity.

JEWELL JACKSON McCABE
Community Affairs Specialist

Jewell Jackson McCabe is president of the National Coalition of 100 Black Women and is Director of WNET-TV/Thirteen's Government and Community Affairs Department in New York City. As director of that department, Ms. McCabe plays an important role in Thirteen's relations with federal, state, and city governments, and with major community relations organizations in the tristate metropolitan area.

The daughter of broadcast pioneer Hal Jackson, Ms. McCabe, who attended Bard College, has been an active leader in civic and community affairs for a number of years. In her short career, Ms. McCabe has distinguished herself as an important spokesperson and role model for today's contemporary black woman. She has been recognized by several national organiza-

Jewel Jackson McCabe, extensively involved in many vital social issues.

tions, including the Women's Equity Action League (WEAL), which is the leading national women's advocacy group, and the national YWCA, which saluted her for outstanding service on behalf of women in business. Ms. McCabe has become an advisor to leaders in the public and private sector related to minority issues and concerns. She serves on the boards of the National Urban Coalition, the Overseas Education Fund, Community Council of Greater New York, Lenox Hill Hospital, and the New York Urban League. She is also a member of the Board of Directors of Planned Parenthood of New York, the Women's Forum, and the Executive Committee of the Association for a Better New York, the Policy Committee of the New York Partnership chaired by David Rockefeller, and a Commissioner for the New York City Commission on the Status of Women.

ERNESTINE McCLENDON
Theatrical Agent

Ernestine McClendon Enterprises, named for its owner and founder, is a theatrical agency which represents several hundred well-known television, movie, stage, and radio actors, as well as writers, directors, and variety acts. Born in Norfolk, Va., Ms. McClendon began her career as a stage actress. Moving on to teaching, she organized the Harlem Workshop. She was the first theatrical agent to be recognized by all unions and was one of the major people responsible for getting blacks into television commercials. She won the Woman's Award (1969) and was named one of Two Thousand Women of Achievement (1970).

ROSALIE J. McGUIRE
Educator

Rosalie J. McGuire is president of the National Association of Negro Business and Professional Women's Clubs, Inc. Born in Baltimore, she studied at Morgan State College (B.A.), New York University (M.A.), and Johns Hopkins and Columbia universities. Entering the profession of education, she became principal of Bentalou Elementary School in Baltimore. She has been first vice president of the Maryland League of Women's Clubs, co-chairman of Baltimore's Provident Hospital Development Program, and national education chairperson and national first vice president of the NBPWC. Mrs. McGuire is on the board of directors of Provident Hospital and is a member of the National Council of Women of the United States and the President's Committee on the Employment of the Handicapped.

MILDRED MITCHELL-BATEMAN
Psychiatrist, Administrator

When Mildred Mitchell-Bateman became director of West Virginia's Department of Mental Health in 1962, she advanced the causes of both black and women's rights, becoming the country's first female mental health chief and the state's first black department head. She has shown her fitness for the post by increasing the number of West Virginia communities offering mental health services from four to 54 and by her success in obtaining much more Federal money for her state. Born in Cordele, Ga., she was a student at Johnson C. Smith University (B.S., 1941), Women's Medical College of Pennsylvania (M.D., 1946), and the Menninger School of Psychiatry (three-year residency, 1957). After internship in New York and private practice in Philadelphia, she transferred to Lakin State Hospital, where she worked as physician, clinic director, and superintendent, until assuming her present position.

JEANNE NOBLE
Educator, Guidance Expert

Dr. Jeanne Noble is a full professor at Brooklyn College School of Education in New York City, where she works with graduate students in the guidance and counseling programs. In July 1975 she was appointed by President Ford to the National Advisory Council on Professional Development.

Professor Jeanne Noble was named to the National Advisory Council on Professional Development.

Eleanor Holmes Norton was New York City Commissioner of Human Rights and Chairwoman of the Equal Employment Opportunities Commission.

A product of a poverty-stricken environment in Albany, Ga., she graduated from Howard University before going on to take two postgraduate degrees at the Teachers College of New York's Columbia University. Having specialized in guidance and developmental psychology, Dr. Noble returned to her hometown to teach social science at Albany State College. She later was a visiting professor at Tuskegee Institute and the University of Vermont, and has taught human relations at New York University.

With her extensive background in the fields of education and social service, Dr. Noble was well-equipped to accept Sargent Shriver's 1964 offer to head a committee in drawing up plans for the Girls' Job Corps. Her other activities in the field of social service include work with the Girl Scouts, HARYOU-ACT in Harlem, the National Social Welfare Assembly, and the President's Commission on the Status of Women. In 1975 she was chairperson for the Arts and Letters Committee of Delta Sigma Theta. In addition to publishing articles in several professional journals, she is author of *The Negro Woman's College Education*.

In 1963 Dr. Noble was named by *Ebony* magazine as "one of the 100 most influential Negroes of the Emancipation Centennial Year." She received the 1965 Bethune-Roosevelt Award for service in the field of education.

ELEANOR HOLMES NORTON
Attorney

Born in Washington, D.C., Eleanor Holmes Norton is a graduate of Antioch College and holds masters and law degrees from Yale University. In 1977 Mrs. Norton was appointed chairperson of the Equal Employment Opportunity Commission (EEOC). Mrs. Norton also has headed the New York City Human Rights Commission, a post she was appointed to in 1970. She has long included sex among the irrational factors which sometimes cause discrimination and has worked diligently to remove this consideration from the list of acceptable job criteria. She is a former black history teacher and participated in the freedom marches as a SNCC worker. While chairman of the New York City Human Rights Commission, Mrs. Norton co-hosted a Sunday morning television program along with Art Rust, Jr.

In 1968, while serving as a Civil Liberties Attorney, Mrs. Norton demonstrated her dedication to principle by pressing for the right of George Wallace to hold an outdoor rally at Shea Stadium. She followed through on her stand despite stiff opposition from the mayor and noisy protests from other liberal quarters.

ESTELLE MASSEY OSBORNE
Nurse

With her appointment in February of 1945 to the faculty of New York University, Estelle Osborne became the first black woman instructor at that school. She began her duties with the Department of Nursing Education in the spring of that year.

Prior to her appointment, Mrs. Osborne had already had a long career in nursing and allied fields. An instructor of nursing at Harlem and Lincoln hospitals from 1929 to 1931, she later served as director of the Freedmen's Nursing School and of the Homer Phillips School in St. Louis. She was also a consultant on the staff of the National Nursing Council for War Service.

Active throughout her life in public health organizations, Mrs. Osborne has also served as vice-president of the National Council of Negro Women. In 1943, the "Estelle Massey Scholarship" was established in her honor at Fisk University, and in 1946 she was the recipient of the Mary Mahoney Award in recognition of her contributions to nursing.

Mrs. Osborne is now retired and living in Queens, N.Y.

ROSA PARKS
Civil Rights Activist

There is about her name no discernible ring nor aura of distinction. There is about her dress and manner no singular, commanding, or memorable uniqueness. Her story, however, is one of the most inspirational to come out of the civil rights movement, a simple message to all that human dignity cannot interminably be undermined by brute force.

On the evening of December 1, 1955, Rosa Parks boarded a public bus in Montgomery, Ala., took a seat with the other passengers, and prepared to relax for 15 minutes or so before arriving home. As the bus began to fill up, however, the number of seats dwindled until, within a few minutes, there were none left. As soon as the white bus driver noticed that a black woman was occupying a seat in the "white" section of the bus while a white passenger was standing, he ordered the "offender" to the rear.

The "offender" did not make a scene when she refused. She did not scream; she did not whine; she did not threaten; she did not exhort. She simply did not move, thus forcing those who would force her to move to make the next move.

Rosa Parks was arrested, jailed, and brought to trial while the rest of the once quiescent black community refused to ride public buses. Mrs. Parks was the catalyst in the Montgomery boycott, the first public confrontation which brought the name of Martin Luther King, Jr., into the ears of America.

Bernice Fletcher Powell, president of the Coalition of 100 Black Women of New York.

Mrs. Parks paid dearly for her courage. Her husband, a barber, became ill from the pressure; the family ultimately moved to Detroit, where Parks resumed his profession. Mrs. Parks did sewing and alterations at home until she found a job as a dressmaker.

In Detroit, she has since become active in youth work, job guidance, cultural and recreational planning—the daily grind of a community activist. Dr. King, while he lived, once called her "the great fuse that led to the modern stride toward freedom." She made the stride while sitting still.

Mrs. Parks is presently a receptionist-secretary to Representative John Conyers. A religious person, she serves as deaconess of St. Matthews A.M.E. church in Detroit. She accepts many speaking engagements because she wants to help "young people grow, develop, and reach their potential."

DOROTHY PORTER
Library Administrator, Author

Dorothy Porter is former librarian of Howard University's Moorland-Spingarn Collection in Washington, D.C., which she shepherded to its enormous collection of more than 165,000 books and reference tools dealing with black history and culture. Born in Warrenton, Va., she studied at Howard University (A.B., 1928) and Columbia University (B.S., library science, 1931; M.S., 1932). She is the author of several articles on black history for various books and scholarly journals, a member of Phi Beta Kappa, and the winner of many awards, including a 1971 Distinguished Service Award from the student body of Howard's College of Liberal Arts. Since her retirement, she lives in Washington, D.C.

ERSA H. POSTON
Government Official

Ersa H. Poston, a top official with the Federal Civil Service Commission, was born in Paducah, Ky. and is a 1942 graduate of Kentucky State College. She received her M.A. degree in 1946 in social work from Atlanta University. Mrs. Poston was formerly director of the New York State Office of Economic Opportunity and in 1967 was appointed president of the New York Civil Service Commission. She began her career working in various youth programs and in 1964 was named confidential assistant to Governor Nelson Rockefeller. Mrs. Poston is a member of a number of organizations and has received many awards and citations for her community involvement.

BERNICE FLETCHER POWELL
Public Information Specialist

Bernice Fletcher Powell is president of the Coalition of 100 Black Women of New York, an organization of women from a cross section of the business, corporate, and private sector of the city. Born in Washington, D.C., Mrs. Powell is special assistant for public information, Women's Division of the Governor's Office of New York. She is a board member of the New York Urban League and is chairperson of the Riverside Church Video Project. Mrs. Powell received her B.A. from Wilson College and her M.S. from Columbia University Graduate School of Journalism.

VIRGINIA ESTELLE RANDOLPH
Social Worker
1876–1958

Concerned with the problems of youth, Virginia E. Randolph was both a teacher and a social worker in the area of juvenile affairs. Born of slave parents in Richmond, Va., she was able to receive an education at the Bacon School and the City Normal School, both in her native city. At the age of 16, she took her first teaching job in Goochland County, Va., holding it for three years before moving to a small schoolhouse in Henrico County.

In 1908 she accepted an important appointment as the first supervisor of the Jeanes Fund, a philanthropic organization established by Anna Jeanes, a Philadelphia Quaker, to finance black rural schools in the South. Having for many years emphasized the importance of vocational training for youth, Miss Randolph often worked in conjunction with the Richmond Juvenile and Domestic Relations Court and in 1926 received the Harmon Award in recognition of her outstanding social service.

She retired in 1948 as supervisor of education in Henrico County, and was honored the next year at an appreciation service given her by many educators of both races.

LILLIAN ROBERTS
Labor Leader

Lillian Roberts is the Commissioner of Labor for the New York State Labor Department. Mrs. Roberts was formerly the Associate Director of District Council 37 of the American Federation of State, County and Municipal Employees (AFSCME), AFL-CIO. As associate director of AFSCME, Mrs. Roberts headed the largest union in New York City. She was sworn in as Commissioner of Labor by New York Governor Hugh Carey on July 2, 1981. Mrs. Roberts began her career in 1945 in Chicago as a nurse's aide and operating room technician. During the years of 1958 and 1965 she was employed by AFSCME District Councils 19 and 34 to organize state mental health employees and volunteer hospital workers in Illinois.

In 1965, Mrs. Roberts came to New York City as Hospital Division Director for DC 37. Governor Carey named Mrs. Roberts a trustee of the State University of New York in 1979 and she has served as an International Vice President of the national AFSCME organization and at the Governor's request, she has served on the State Advisory Council on Substance Abuse.

She has been cited by a number of groups for her dedication to human rights and for her work in furthering minority-labor relations.

LUCILLE MASON ROSE
Civil Servant

As New York City's Commissioner of Employment, Lucille Mason Rose oversees an agency which attempts to find skilled job openings and then train unskilled and uneducated workers to qualify for the jobs. Born in Richmond, Va., she came to Brooklyn's Bedford-Stuyvesant section as a young child when her family moved North. While attending Girls' High, she joined the local branch of the NAACP. She has always been a firm believer in diligent work and personal responsibility. When her husband enlisted in World War II,

she enrolled as a welding trainee at the Brooklyn Navy Yard to earn money for their house mortgage.

In 1949 Mrs. Rose joined the Department of Social Services. She graduated from Brooklyn College at night in 1963 (B.A., economics), and was shortly thereafter appointed director of the Bedford-Stuyvesant field office of the city's Department of Labor. When the poverty programs centralized neighborhood employment services in 1966, Mrs. Rose became the first director of the Bedford-Stuyvesant Manpower Center. Mayor Lindsay appointed her first deputy commissioner of the Manpower and Development Agency in 1970, where she remained until November 1972, when she was named to be the city's employment chief.

Under Mrs. Rose's direction, the city's employment agency locates employment openings and then trains people on the job, a program which avoids the old pitfall of training workers for nonexistent jobs. "Our main concern," she says, "is to get poor people into jobs."

BETTY SHABAZZ
Community Activist

The widow of Malcolm X, Betty Shabazz is currently dedicating the major part of her energies to raising their children according to his principles and ideas. Born in Detroit, she studied at Tuskegee Institute, Brooklyn State Hospital School of Nursing (R.N.), and Jersey City State College (B.A., public health education; certified school nurse). She is a director of the African-American Foundation, the Day Care Council of Westchester County, and the Women's Service League; a trustee of the National Housewives League; and a co-chairman of the advisory board of the *Amsterdam News* newspaper. She lives in Mt. Vernon, N.Y.

NAOMI SIMS
Fashion Model

Naomi Sims manages to be both one of America's leading fashion models and a dedicated community worker. This diversity of talents can be traced back to her school days when she was a scholarship student at both the Fashion Institute of Technology and New York University (psychology). Born in Oxford, Mississippi, she was the first black model to appear in a television commercial, to grace the cover of a major women's magazine (*Ladies Home Journal*), and to be featured in *Vogue*. She has been on the cover of *Life*, and in 1969/70 was voted Model of the Year by International Famous Mannequins.

Naomi Sims is one of America's leading high fashion models.

JUANITA STOUT
Municipal Court Judge

The first woman ever to reach the bench in Pennsylvania is Juanita Kidd Stout, who was appointed Judge of the Philadelphia Municipal Court by Governor David L. Lawrence in September of 1959. In November of that year, Judge Stout ran in a city-wide election and won a 10-year term, thus becoming the nation's first elected black woman judge.

Judge Stout earned her Master of Laws and Doctor of Jurisprudence degrees at the University of Indiana, and was admitted to the bar in the District of Columbia in 1950 and in Philadelphia in 1954.

Since 1959 she has served as a judge of Philadelphia's Juvenile Court, a position which at times has proven to be a dangerous one. Her safety has often been threatened by those who feel that her methods of dealing with delinquent youth are too severe, but she also has many supporters who feel that her stringent measures have done much to reduce Philadelphia's delinquency rate.

LYNNETTE DOBBINS TAYLOR
Executive

Lynnette Dobbins Taylor is executive director of the international sorority Delta Sigma Theta, and is a member of the boards of directors of the National Friends of Public Broadcasting Corporation and the National Center for Voluntary Action. Born in Birmingham, she attended Alabama State Teachers College (B.S., 1939) and Wayne State University (M.S., 1948). In her career she has been New York editor of the *Chicago Defender* and the *Detroit Tribune,* principal of Roosevelt Elementary School, and a program analyst for the Office of Economic Opportunity. She is a director of college and youth activities for the American Red Cross and a member of the Public Committee on Truth in Lending Legislation.

MARY CHURCH TERRELL
Women's Rights Advocate
1863-1954

An active leader all her life in the campaign for equal rights, Mary Church Terrell was born the year the Emancipation Proclamation was issued and died only a few months after segregation had been declared unconstitutional by the *Brown* v. *Board of Education* decision of 1954.

A graduate of Oberlin College in 1884, Mrs. Terrell was appointed to the District of Columbia school board in 1895 and, in the following year, became one of the charter members of the National Association of Colored Women. She was consistently active in politics, campaigning against the practice of segregation in the United States, and on several occasions acting as a delegate from her country to international conferences.

Born of ex-slave parents in Memphis, Mary Church Terrell chose to make her home in Washington, D.C., a city which remained segregated until 1953. In that year, she headed a committee of Washington citizens who demanded enforcement of a 75-year-old law prohibiting discrimination against "respectable persons" in restaurants. In the resulting test case, the U.S. Supreme Court ruled that the old law was still valid, thus paving the way for the beginning of integration in the public accommodations of the nation's capital.

A year later, having seen the initiation of a new policy which she herself had done much to bring about, Mary Church Terrell died in Annapolis, Md., at the age of 90.

GLORIA E. A. TOOTE
Attorney

Dr. Gloria E. A. Toote, regarded as a high-ranking black in the Republican Party, is a New York City attorney. Dr. Toote is a former teacher and was Assistant Secretary for Equal Opportunity of the Housing and Urban Development agency. She was also a HUD contract compliance officer. Dr. Toote is also founder, owner, and builder of Town Sound Studios and is a self-taught recording expert. She has been featured in the *Chicago Tribune*, *Ebony*, *Jet*, and the *Washington Post*.

CHARLESZETTA WADDLES
Clergywoman

Dedicated to religious and social action, Mother Charleszetta Waddles founded her Perpetual Mission in Detroit in 1957 to help the poor. The mission, which never closes its doors, offers food, shelter, clothing, medical care, and instruction to the needy.

Born in St. Louis, she moved to Detroit and married Payton Waddles, then a Ford Motor Company employee, and raised a family of 10 children. She founded her mission as a nonprofit, nondenominational, religious, charitable organization serving metropolitan Detroit. Staffed mainly by volunteers, the mission operates on funds from private contributions. Mother Waddles leads the worship and directs the social services. Perhaps she is known best for the kitchens she maintains on "Skid Row," where she serves approximately 7,500 meals each month at 35¢ per meal or free to those with no money. Her work has merited numerous humanitarian and outstanding community service awards, including letters of commendation from Vice Presidents Hubert Humphrey and Lyndon Johnson, and from President Richard Nixon. She has had her own radio and television programs and is advisory consultant to Detroit's Shelby Hotel.

Mother Waddles operates with the philosophy that the church should make itself relevant to the needs of the people, and that if a person needs assistance then it is up to the church, above all, to give it to him or her.

MADAME C. J. WALKER
Cosmetics Manufacturer
1869–1919

Madame C. J. Walker who, because of her innovations in the cosmetics business, was to become one of the wealthiest and most famous women of her race, experienced an early life of poverty and hardship. Born to ex-slave parents in Delta, La., Sarah McWilliams was orphaned at the age of seven, married at 14, and was left a widow with a small child at the age of 20.

Deciding to begin a new life, she traveled to St. Louis and worked as a laundress in order to send her daughter to school. In the 1890s she married Charles J. Walker and, under the name of Madame C. J. Walker, subsequently made famous her new hair-styling formula.

In 1910 she went to Indianapolis to begin the manufacture of her hair preparations, later adding a complete line of toiletries and cosmetics to her products. As her business expanded, she established many Walker schools of beauty culture across the country. In the process, she became the first black woman millionaire.

Before her death in 1919, Madame Walker was well-known for her philanthropic activities: she made large bequests to the NAACP, the YMCA of St. Louis, Tuskegee Institute, and Bethune-Cookman College, and also stipulated in her will that two-thirds of the profits of her company should be given to charitable organizations.

Today, students from several foreign countries come to the United States to receive training at the Walker beauty schools, and over 2,000 agents represent the Walker system in the country and abroad.

CORA WALKER
Attorney, Businesswoman

Cora Walker is best known for bringing to Harlem a cooperative supermarket. Although some have tried to undermine the venture, it has drawn community support. Mrs. Walker was born in Charlotte, N.C., but grew up in the Bronx. She attended St. John's University in Brooklyn and went on to study law. Her public career has involved her in numerous legal and civic projects. Often quoted as a severe critic of the Harlem community, Mrs. Walker has come under fire

Cora Walker, coordinator and legal counselor of the Harlem Co-op Supermarket.

from many political regulars who feel her views are distorted.

MAGGIE LENA WALKER
Banker
1867–1934

Born in Richmond, Va., Maggie L. Walker had no specific training for the banking career in which she was later to achieve such notable success. After graduating from high school, she taught for several years before starting as secretary to the Independent Order of St. Luke, a black organization in Virginia.

During this time, she helped establish branches of the Order throughout Virginia and West Virginia. In 1899 she became secretary-treasurer of the organization. Under her guidance, the Order was restored to financial solvency and grew to include an insurance concern and a banking establishment. The latter, which became known as the Consolidated Bank and Trust Company, functioned with Mrs. Walker serving as chairman of the board. She also established and supervised the *St. Luke Herald,* the newspaper which was the official organ of the Order of St. Luke.

A contributor to several charitable organizations, Mrs. Walker was also an organizer and president of the Council of Colored Women, a director of the

NAACP, and a board member of the National Urban League.

She died in 1934.

MARY DAWSON WALTERS
Librarian

Associate professor of library administration at Ohio State University in Columbus, Mary Dawson Walters doubles as head of the library's acquisition department. The responsibilities of this position include keeping the library abreast of the latest advances in scholarship and allocating a budget of over $1 million a year. A native of Mitchell County, Ga., she is a graduate of Savannah State College (B.S., home economics, 1949) and Atlanta University (M.S., library science, 1957). When she accepted her present appointment in 1961, Mrs. Walters became the first black person to head one of Ohio State's library departments. She has received the Who's Who in Library Service Award (1965) and the Two Thousand Women of Achievement Award (1972).

BENNETTA B. WASHINGTON
Administrator

Dr. Bennetta B. Washington is special assistant to William H. Kolberg, assistant secretary of labor for manpower, U.S. Department of Commerce.

Born in Winston-Salem, N.C., she moved as a child to Washington, D.C., with her parents. She received both B.A. and M.A. degrees from Howard University, and later a Ph.D. in sociology from the Catholic University of America.

In 1941 she began working as a counselor in the public school system of Baltimore, leaving in 1944 to act as program director for young adults at the Phillis Wheatley Y.W.C.A. in Washington, D.C. From 1946 to 1965, Dr. Washington worked first as counselor in the Washington schools, then as principal of several different high schools.

In 1965 she was appointed Director of the Women's Job Corps, a branch of the Office of Economic Opportunity, where she remained until accepting her present post.

FRANCES CRESS WELSING
Psychiatrist

Following in the Hippocratic footsteps of both her father and her grandfather, Frances Cress Welsing became a doctor. She is currently assistant professor of pediatrics at Freedmen's Hospital and Howard University School of Medicine in Washington, D.C. Born in Chicago, she received her training at Antioch College and Howard University School of Medicine. She is the author of *The Cress Theory of Color-Confrontation and Racism,* and is a member of the National Medical Association, the American Medical Association, and the American Psychiatric Association.

GERALDINE WHITTINGTON
Civil Servant

During her secretarial career in government service, Geraldine Whittington was one of President Lyndon Johnson's traveling secretaries and later served in the Office of the Chief of Protocol.

Born in West River, Md., she began her career in 1950 as a secretary for the Veterans Administration. By 1961 she had become executive assistant to the Administrator of the Agency for International Development, and was called upon to work as a secretary to Ralph Durgan, special assistant to President John F. Kennedy. In 1963 she joined the staff of Bill Moyers, press secretary to Lyndon Johnson. In December of that year, President Johnson invited her to work with him during his subsequent campaign.

Retired after an illness, Miss Whittington now lives in Washington, D.C.

MARGARET BUSH WILSON
Civil Rights Activist

Mrs. Margaret Bush Wilson is a St. Louis lawyer who has been in the civil rights and public service arena for a number of years. As chairman of the national board of the NAACP, Mrs. Wilson sits at the helm of the 450,000-member organization, the oldest and the largest civil rights body and often regarded as the most feared but yet most respected and the most consulted group in the world.

Mrs. Wilson has served as an assistant attorney general of Missouri, acting legal services specialist in the federal government's war against poverty, and other government positions. She has been associated with the NAACP virtually all her life and is a former president of the St. Louis branch. A member of the national board of directors since 1963, Mrs. Wilson is the first black woman to serve in the NAACP's top policymaking position.

Mrs. Wilson's determination to become a lawyer overshadowed her father's desires for her to merely enter one of the female professions such as nursing, teaching, or social work. Her father was a long-time NAACP member and the first successful black real estate broker in St. Louis.

Following Mrs. Wilson's graduation from Talladega College, where she majored in economics and mathematics, she returned to St. Louis where she entered the Lincoln University School of Law. Her first assignment following her admission to the Missouri bar

Margret Bush Wilson is Chairman, National Board, NAACP.

in 1943 was to act as counsel for the Real Estate Brokers Association of St. Louis, of which her father was president. She obtained the association's corporate charter. She is a founder of the Model Housing Corporation in St. Louis, which was established to get federal funds in order to improve housing for poor people. Mrs. Wilson took part in a national board hearing in 1972 that resulted in overturning the Atlanta NAACP chapter's compromise policy of allowing that city's school system to remain partially segregated.

JANE C. WRIGHT
Surgeon, Educator

Jane C. Wright is a noted surgeon and educator who was born in New York City. Dr. Wright was director of cancer chemotherapy research and instructor in research surgery at the State University of New York Downstate Medical Center and later became associate dean and professor of surgery at the hospital.

Dr. Wright succeeded her father, Dr. Louis Wright, at Harlem Hospital Cancer Research Foundation as director. As head of the foundation, Dr. Wright pioneered tests in the use of chemotherapy on tumors and other abnormal growths.

She received a B.A. degree from Smith College in

Northhampton, Mass. in 1942 and her M.D. degree in 1945 from New York Medical College.

Dr. Wright has also been an assistant resident in internal medicine at Bellevue Hospital in New York City and was also chief medical resident at Harlem Hospital.

NOTABLE BLACK WOMEN OF THE PAST

Name	Career	Dates
Sarah Allen	Missionary pioneer	1764–1849
Caroline Still Anderson, M.D.	Physician	1849–1919
Maria Louise Baldwin	Educator	1856–1919
Janie Porter Barrett	Educator	1870–1949
Delilah L. Beasley	Historian, journalist	1871–1934
Mother Matilda Beasley	Educator, social worker	1834–1903
Ann Marie Becraft	Educator	1805–1833
Rosa Dixon Bowser	Educator	1885–1931
Sue M. Brown	Club leader, organizer	1877–1941
Mary Ann Shadd Cary	Abolitionist, educator	1823–1893
Myrtle Foster Cook	Teacher, civic leader	1870–1951
Fannie Jackson Coppin	Teacher, missionary	1835–1912
Anna Murray Douglass	Underground railroad conductor	n.a.–1882
Sarah Mapps Douglass	Abolitionist, educator	1806–1882
Elleanor Eldridge	Writer	1785–1845
Sarah Harris Fayerweather	Underground railroad conductor	1820–1870
Susan E. Frazier	Woman's Guild founder	1866–1901
Nora A. Gordon	Teacher, missionary	1866–1901
Ida Gray, M.D.	Dentist	1867–n.a.
Charlotte Forten Grimké	Teacher, writer, poet	1838–1914
Emma Azalia Hackley	Teacher, creative artist	1867–1922
Maude Cuney Hare	Music teacher	1874–1936
Annie Wealthy Holland	Educator	1871–1934
Anna Elizabeth Hudlun	Social worker	1840–1911
Adella Hunt Logan	Educator	1863–1915
Victoria Earle Matthews	Social worker	1861–1898
Emma Grayson Merrit	Educator	1860–1933
Gertrude Bustill Mossell	Newspaper editor	1855–?
Mary Ella Mossell	Teacher, missionary	1853–1866
Alice Dunbar Nelson	Author, editor	1875–1935

Name	Career	Dates
Mary Jane Patterson	Educator	1840–1894
Mary Smith Kelsey Peake	Teacher	1823–1862
Frances E. L. Preston	Lecturer	1844–1929
Georgianna Frances Putnam	Educator	1839–1914
Charlotta G. Pyles	Abolitionist	1806–1880
Sarah Remond, M.D.	Abolitionist, physician	1815–n.a.
Josephine St. Pierre Ruffin	Woman's club organizer	1842–1924
Susie Shorter	Teacher, writer	1859–1912
Georgianna R. Simpson	Professor, linguistics	1866–1944
Amanda Berry Smith	African missionary	1836–1915
Sallie W. Stewart	Teacher, clubwoman	1881–1951
Mary B. Talbert	Educator, social reformer	1866–1923
Susan Paul Vashon	Teacher, nurse	1838–1912
Josephine Turpin Washington	Journalist, teacher	1861–1949
Margaret Murray Washington	Woman's club organizer	1865–1925
Olivia Davidson Washington	Fund-raiser	1859–1889
Lulu Williams	Teacher, social reformer	1874–1945
Josephine Silone Yates	Educator, writer	1852–1912

PROMINENT BLACK AMERICANS: BIOGRAPHIES OF NOTABLE MEN AND WOMEN

Increasingly important on the American scene are black men and women who are making day-to-day contributions to the social, cultural, and economic progress of the nation. The brief biographies given here offer a cross-sectional view of this burgeoning group. Although many of the people named here are distinguished, they are not so much celebrities as part of the fiber of the country. If they share one distinguishing characteristic, it is decision-making responsibility. The following selection does not intend to be inclusive, but to sketch a representative sample of the growing number of blacks enjoying the challenge of significant careers and assuming increasing responsibility for our national future.

WILLIAM AIKEN
Certified Public Accountant

President of the National Association of Black Accountants, William Aiken is a partner in his own New York-based CPA firm of Aiken, Wilson & Brown. Born in New York City in 1934, he is a member of the board of the Ethical-Fieldston Fund and the Business Advisory Board of the Borough of Manhattan Community College.

MILTON BURK ALLEN
Attorney

As Maryland State Attorney for Baltimore, Milton Allen is the only black person elected chief prosecutor of a large American city. Born in Baltimore in 1917, he graduated from Coppin State Teachers College in 1938, served as a naval officer in World War II, and obtained a law degree from Maryland University in 1948. After becoming one of Baltimore's most successful civil rights defense and criminal attorneys, he was selected in 1966 to chair the Baltimore Criminal Courts Committee and was elected chief prosecutor in 1970.

JIM ANDERSON
Community Development Activist, Actor

Working to unite neighbors into functioning communities, Jim Anderson has developed several projects, including the East Harlem Food Buying Federation, which provides fresh produce to over 600 families in 11 separate neighborhood clubs at less than 60% of retail costs. Born in Harlem in 1929, he has been a Golden Gloves boxer, a dock worker, and a principal actor with the Living Theatre.

Hannah Diggs Atkins is an Oklahoma state representative.

SARAH A. ANDERSON
Legislator

Sarah A. Anderson was a member of the Pennsylvania House of Representatives for 18 years prior to her retirement in 1972. Her work led to the establishment of the state's Commission on the Status of Women in 1964. She sponsored the Pennsylvania Equal Rights Amendment guaranteeing equal treatment to women.

HANNAH DIGGS ATKINS
Legislator

Oklahoma state representative Hannah Diggs Atkins plays an important role on the governor's Commission on Women. Born in Winston-Salem, N.C. in 1923, she was a law librarian at Oklahoma State Library before her electoral victory. She is the first black woman in Oklahoma history to chair a committee in the legislature.

J. EDWARD ATKINSON
Executive

J. Edward Atkinson directs public relations for the Carnation Co. in Los Angeles, where his functions include liaison work with black community groups. Born in Denver in 1914, he is the author of *Black Dimensions in Contemporary American Art* (1971) and a member of the L.A. Mayor's Area Advisory Board.

JAMES S. AVERY
Executive

James S. Avery manages the giant Exxon Corporation's public relations programs in New York, New Jersey, and the six New England states. His responsibilities include developing liaison with the political governments in his region. Born in Cranford, N.J., in 1923, he takes an active role in several civic and educative organizations and is grand basileus of Omega Psi Phi.

JOHN A. AXAM
Librarian

John A. Axam directs the mobile division of Philadelphia's Free Library. Through the Reader Development Program he founded, he supervises library service to institutions and to undereducated and young adults. Born in Cincinnati in 1930, he is a member of the Pennsylvania Library Association and the board of the Crime Prevention Association.

WARREN H. BACON
Administrator

Warren H. Bacon is a personnel executive for Chicago's Inland Steel Co. Born in Chicago in 1923, he is a member of the American Iron and Steel Institute,

James S. Avery, an Exxon executive Ebony *terms one of the 100 most important blacks in America.*

a director of Hyde Park Federal Savings & Loan Association of Chicago, and president of Urban Ventures, Inc., which aids minority entrepreneurs.

DONALD J. BEAN
Dentist

Dr. Donald J. Bean is the first black to be appointed by the New York State Board of Dental Examiners. The Board of Dental Examiners is composed of eleven dentists, three public representatives, and two dental hygienists. Dr. Bean is a product of the New York City Public School System and a graduate of Howard University College of Dentistry. He is a past president of the Greater Metropolitan New York Dental Society and presently a member of the Board of Trustees of the National Dental Association. He also serves as a clinical instructor on the staff of New York Medical College and is responsible for the training of residents at Metropolitan Hospital and Bird S. Coler Hospital in New York City. His dental practice is in Jamaica, New York.

AL BELL
Executive

Al Bell worked his way from an AM disc jockey to board chairman of Stax Records, Inc., in Memphis,

Dr. Donald Bean, member of the New York State Board of Dental Examiners.

Former baseball great Joe Black, now a vice president of Greyhound.

Tenn. Born in Little Rock, Ark., in 1940, he is now one of the most powerful men in the American record industry. He also serves as executive vice president of Stax, which produces Isaac Hayes, the Staple Singers, and Rufus Thomas.

EDWARD B. BELL
Executive

Former professional football player Edward B. Bell is now an executive with Atlantic Richfield, where he coordinates urban marketing programs and activities for the merchandising department. Born in Philadelphia in 1931, he has been a guided missile instructor at Fort Monmouth, N.J., and a national treasurer of the National Association of Market Developers.

ANDREW BILLINGSLEY
Educator

Author of *Black Families in White America*, Andrew Billingsley is the president of Morgan State College. Born in Marion, Ala., in 1926, he received degrees from Grinnel College, Boston University, the University of Michigan, and Brandeis. His concern for social welfare is shown by his work on the board of directors of the Council on Social Work Education, the Publications Advisory Commission, and the Child Welfare League of America.

JOE BLACK
Executive

In his corporate position as vice president of special markets for the Greyhound Corporation, Joe Black has the responsibility of the development and recommendation of policies, practices, programs, and procedures of marketing for the black consumer market. Born in Plainfield, N.J., in 1924, he became the first black pitcher in the big leagues in 1952 when he joined the Brooklyn Dodgers and was named the National League's Rookie of the Year. After a career in which he came to be considered one of the top relievers in the sport, he joined Greyhound in 1962, rapidly rising to important administrative posts. He is a member of the Task Force on Youth Motivation under the National Alliance of Businessmen (NAB) and of the National Association of Market Developers (NAMD).

JAMES BOGGS
Author

Born in Marion Junction, Ala., in 1919, self-educated James Boggs worked in a Detroit automobile plant until he was 48 years old before deciding to quit his job and start writing "to project a vision of what we must do in this country to develop another way for man to live." His books *The American Revolution: Pages from a Negro Worker's Notebook* and *Racism and the Class Struggle* have become a fundamental part of the ideology of the black revolution.

JAMES E. BOOKER
Public Relations Consultant

After 18 years as an award-winning columnist and political editor on the *Amsterdam News,* James Booker formed his own firm to deal with the public relations aspects of civil rights, urban affairs, minority economic development, and government relations. Born in Riverhead, N.Y., in 1926, he is also a university lecturer and TV commentator.

HILDAGARDEIS BOSWELL
Legislator

Hildagardeis Boswell serves Maryland as a state representative and a specialist with the State Commission on Human Relations. Born in Daisytown, Pa., in 1934, she was nearly cheated of her election by fraud, but took her case to the courts and won an upset. She co-sponsored the controversial bill which proposes three-year renewable marriage contracts.

MILLER W. BOYD
Psychologist

Research psychologist Miller W. Boyd co-directs the Academy of Urban Service, Inc., in his home town of St. Louis. Born in 1934, he is a prolific psychological journal contributor, former director of Experiment in Higher Education, and a member of the National Association of Education for Young Children and the National Council for Black Child Development.

RAYMOND A. BROWN
Attorney

Raymond A. Brown has been described by many as the "black F. Lee Bailey" and an associate in his law firm called him "the greatest lawyer in America." Raymond Brown tackles the tough ones, including some of the more socially and politically controversial figures of the time. He has represented Rubin (Hurricane) Carter, Imamu Amiri Baraka, Linden, N.J. Mayor and State Senator John T. Gregorio, former Camden, N.J. Mayor Angelo Errichetti, Sam (The Plumber) DeCavalcante, Angelo (Gyp) DeCarlo, and the Black Panther Party of New Jersey. The Montclair, N.J. resident, who has his law practice in Jersey City, also represents major corporations from time to time, although his specialty is criminal law.

Brown was born in Jacksonville, Florida but grew up in Jersey City. He graduated from Florida A&M University where he played football, and finished Fordham Law School at night by working during the day. Brown has been a civil rights activist and was jailed in the 1960s along with Percy Sutton, lawyer and former Manhattan Borough President. He is a former president of the Jersey City branch of the NAACP, a board member of the Boy Scouts of America, and was a delegate to the White House Conference on Children in 1960 and to the White House Conference on the Aged in 1961. In 1967 Brown was appointed to the Commission on Civil Disorders to investigate the underlying causes of Newark and Plainfield race riots.

ROSCOE C. BROWN, JR.
Educator

Roscoe C. Brown is president of Bronx Community College and was formerly director of the Institute of Afro-American Affairs at New York University. Born in Washington, D.C., in 1922, he was a squadron commander in the USAF, hosted the Emmy award winning TV series *Black Arts,* has more than 50 publications to his credit (including co-editing the first edition of *The Negro Almanac*), and is an active consultant for the city, state, and federal government.

ROBERT S. BROWNE
Economist

Robert S. Browne created and heads New York's Black Economic Research Center, which provides technical assistance to black economic development programs. A man of principle, he renounced a promising career with the U.S. aid program in Cambodia (1955–1957) and Vietnam (1958–1961) and went on to give speeches

Dr. Roscoe C. Brown, Jr. is president of Bronx Community College.

against U.S. policies in Southeast Asia. Born in Chicago in 1924, he is vice president of the National Sharecroppers Fund and a member of the board of the American Commission on Africa.

MANFORD BYRD, JR.
Administrator

Manford Byrd, Jr., is deputy superintendent of the Chicago Public School System, which is the second largest in the country. Born in Brewton, Ala., in 1928, he began teaching in the Chicago schools in 1949. He is a trustee of Central College and a board member of Chicago State University and of the Joint Negro Appeal.

LEROY CALLENDER
Engineer

One of the nation's foremost consulting engineers, LeRoy Callender got his start at renowned Brooklyn

Technical High School, graduating first in its architectural design class in 1950. After designing buildings for the U.S. Army in Korea, he graduated from the City College of New York, then worked on a nuclear power plant for the Consolidated Edison Company before forming his own firm in 1969. In 1975, Callender completed the first phase design of York College, a projected university in New York City, and formed a second company, Callender & Smith, which specializes in waterworks development.

THEOPHILUS CAVINESS
Clergyman

The Reverend Caviness is pastor of Cleveland's Greater Abyssinia Baptist Church and president of that church's Federal Credit Union. Born in Marshall, Tex., in 1928, he serves as the historian and a member of the board of the National Baptist Convention, U.S.A., and is a member of the Zoning Board of Appeals of the City of Cleveland.

JAMES E. CHEEK
Educator

James Cheek was named president of Howard University in 1969, becoming one of the youngest major American university heads. Born in Roanoke Rapids, N.C., in 1932, he obtained three theological degrees—from Shaw, Colgate, and Drew universities—but was interested in an academic rather than clerical career. In 1963 he became president of Shaw, rescued that institution from financial collapse, and acquired a reputation as one of academia's most gifted administrators and diplomats.

CHARLES DARRETT CHURCHWELL
Administrator

Charles Darrett Churchwell is associate provost of Miami University in Oxford, Ohio. Born in Dunnellon, Fla., he is an alumnus of Morehouse College, Atlanta University, and the University of Illinois. He is the author of *A History of Education for Librarianship, 1919–1939*.

KENNETH BANCROFT CLARK
Psychologist, Social Critic

Gifted scholar Kenneth B. Clark heads Clark, Phipps, Clark & Harris, Inc., an executive consulting firm specializing in affirmative action in race relations matters. Born in the Panama Canal Zone in 1914, he performed important psychological research cited by the Supreme Court in its 1954 ruling outlawing segregation in the schools. A regular contributor to professional journals, he is the author of *Dark Ghetto: Dilemmas of Social*

Kenneth Clark spearheaded psychological research leading to civil rights reforms.

Power and is one of the chief organizers behind Harlem Youth Opportunities Unlimited (HARYOU).

RICHARD V. CLARKE
Entrepreneur

The founder and president of Richard Clarke Associates, Inc., a pioneer firm in the recruitment of black executives, has a wide range of business successes to his credit. He publishes the magazines *Opportunities for the College Graduate* and *Contact,* operates Hallmark Holidays travel agency, and is a consultant to several federal, state, and private agencies.

MAURICE LIONEL COLVIN
Administrator

Maurice Colvin serves Corpus Christi, Tex., as administrative assistant to the city manager, the highest municipal post ever held there by a black, and is administrator of the Human Relations Committee. Born in Prairie View, Tex., in 1932, he became one of the original members (and chairman) of the Human Relations Committee, which coordinates programs against racial and ethnic discrimination.

JAMES R. COWAN
State Official

James Cowan, M.D., is commissioner of health for the State of New Jersey. Born in Washington, D.C., in 1916, he became chief of surgery at the U.S. Army's 26th Station Hospital in Regensburg, Germany. He went on to a post as senior attending physician at East Orange General Hospital before becoming the first black state commissioner of health in the United States.

ARNOLD (JERSEY JOE WOLCOTT) CREAM
State Official

Former world heavyweight champion Arnold Cream, who boxed under the name of Jersey Joe Wolcott, is Commissioner of Athletics for the State of New Jersey. Prior to that position, Jersey Joe was New Jersey's State Director of Special Olympics, a program involv-

Former boxing champion Arnold "Jersey Joe Wolcott" Cream now heads New Jersey's Special Olympics Program.

ing sports projects for handicapped children. He had also been sheriff in his hometown of Camden, N.J. Born in 1914, he began his professional boxing career at 15, and finally, in 1951, he knocked out Ezzard Charles with a left hook to become, at 37, the oldest man ever to win the crown. A family man of strong religious beliefs, he uses his present post to help people.

GEORGE W. CROCKETT, JR.
Jurist

Now in his second term as Recorder's Court judge in Detroit, George W. Crockett continues his distinguished career as an unswerving opponent of racism. Born in Jacksonville, Fla., he has been a senior attorney for the U.S. Department of Labor and a general counsel for the United Auto Workers-CIO. He was the lawyer in the case which opened the Atlanta union to black auto workers and has set several judicial precedents in cases involving black rights.

WILLIE L. DANIELS
Stockbroker

Willie L. Daniels formed and directs Daniels & Bell, Inc., the first black member firm on the New York Stock Exchange. Born in Valdosta, Ga., he began working on Wall Street in 1960 and was ready in 1971 to open his own brokerage, which now holds two seats on the exchange and does business throughout the United States and Europe. He is a member of the Lawyers Club and a director of the Young Adult Institute & Workshop.

GEORGIA M. DAVIS
Legislator

Georgia M. Davis enjoys the double distinction of being the first black and the first woman elected to the Kentucky State Senate, where she is chairwoman of the Subcommittee on Wages and Hours. Born in Springfield, Ky., in 1923, she owns a restaurant, a laundry, and a dry cleaning establishment. Always active in civil rights causes, she was a charter member of Allied Organizations for Civil Rights and an organizer of the Kentucky Christian Leadership Conference.

C. C. DEJOIE, JR.
Executive

C. C. Dejoie, Jr., publishes the *Louisiana Weekly,* the only black newspaper in New Orleans, his hometown. Born in 1914, he entered the newspaper business in 1938 and has on-the-staff experience of all its aspects. He has been president and treasurer of the National Newspaper Publishers Association and is a member

Former New York City Welfare Commissioner James Dumpson is now a dean at Fordham University.

of the group that owns the New Orleans Saints football team.

JAMES R. DUMPSON
Administrator

Professor James R. Dumpson is dean of Fordham University's Graduate School of Social Service. Born in 1909, his 25-year career in the New York Department of Welfare was capped by his appointment as city welfare commissioner in 1959. A member of many organizations and societies, he has been named to several presidential commissions on welfare, drug abuse, and child welfare.

ROY EATON
Music Production Executive

Performer and music writer Roy Eaton is president of Roy Eaton Music in Roosevelt Island, New York. The versatile musician has made a number of radio and television appearances as a performer and writer, and has had articles published in several magazines. Roy Eaton is best known as a concert pianist and made his debut with the Chicago Symphony Orchestra in 1951, appearing the next year at New York City's Town Hall. Prior to forming his own company, Roy Eaton was vice president and music director of Benton and Bowles, Inc. At B&B, he was responsible for supervising the creation and production of all music for the agency's radio and television commercials. Among the well-known jingles he has composed are "Start the day a little bit better" for General Foods' Post Cereals and a jingle for Kent Cigarettes which is believed to be the first use of modern jazz in commercial jingles.

Roy Eaton holds baccalaureate degrees from both the Manhattan School of Music and CCNY, and a masters degree from The Manhattan School of Music. He has also taught music history at the U.S. Armed Forces Institute.

CHRISTOPHER FAIRFIELD EDLEY
Administrator

Christopher Fairfield Edley serves as executive director of the United Negro College Fund. Born in Charleston, W.Va., in 1928, he has held a wide range of private and governmental legal posts and was program officer of the Ford Foundation from 1963–1973. Mr. Edley graduated magna cum laude from Howard University in 1949 and received his law degree from Harvard Law School in 1953. He is a board member of The Great Atlantic and Pacific Tea Company, The Bowery Savings Bank, American Airlines, C.I.T. Financial Corporation, and the National Bank of North America. In 1950 Mr. Edley was the recipient of the John Hay Whitney Fellowship and received the Distinguished Alumni Award from Howard University in 1979. He has also received a number of other honors and awards from colleges and fraternal organizations.

A. WILSON EDWARDS
City Official

A. Wilson Edwards supervises the police and fire departments of Louisville, Ky. Born in Frankfort, Ky., in 1908, he began his career as a patrolman in 1935. He served as a security officer at the inaugurations of presidents Eisenhower and Johnson, and as a security advisor to President William V. S. Tubman of Liberia and Colonel Tran Minh Cong, police chief of Da Nang.

NELSON JACK EDWARDS
Union Official

As international vice president of the United Auto Workers, and a member of that union's International Executive Board, Nelson Jack Edwards represents some 400,000 black and white workers in the automobile and aerospace industries. Born in Lowndes County, Ala., in 1917, he began his career at 17 with the Southern Oil Co., working 12 hours a day at 15¢ an hour. In 1936 he made the move to the UAW, was soon elected chairman of the overwhelmingly

Roy Eaton, versatile musician and president of Roy Eaton Music Corporation.

Jean R. Esquerre is an executive with Grumman Aerospace Corporation.

of the Huntington Station Youth Development Association, former Labor and Industry Chairman of the Huntington Township branch of the NAACP, and president of the Urban League of Long Island. Mr. Esquerre was born in Yonkers, N.Y. and during World War II he served as a radio operator-gunner in the United States Army Air Force 477th B-25 Medium Bomber Group. He received a B.S. in Engineering Technology from Empire State College, State University of New York, and has studied mechanical engineering and industrial management at the City College of New York and New York University.

W. LEONARD EVANS, JR.
Publisher

W. Leonard Evans, Jr., is president of Chicago-based Tuesday Publications, Inc., which creates monthly magazine inserts for 22 major newspapers. Born in Louisville, Ky., in 1914, he was awarded Lincoln University's Citation of Merit for Outstanding Contributions to Journalism in 1968 and the National Newspaper Award from the Poor Richard Club in 1970. He

white Ford Motor local, and became the first black member of the UAW board in 1962.

LLOYD CHARLES ELAM
Educator

As president of Meharry Medical College in Nashville, Lloyd Charles Elam has devoted much of his energies to expanding the faculty, the physical plant, and student enrollment. Born in Little Rock, Ark., 1928, he arrived at Meharry in 1961 to found and chair the department of psychiatry. He serves on the Advisory Committee to the National Academy of Sciences, the National Board of Medical Examiners, and the National Association for Equal Opportunity in Higher Education.

JEAN R. ESQUERRE
Corporate Executive

Jean R. Esquerre is assistant to the president of the Grumman Aerospace Corporation and Director of the corporation's Opportunity Development Department. Mr. Esquerre is responsible for Grumman's equal employment and Affirmative Action programs. Very active in civic affairs, Mr. Esquerre is a member of the Society of Automotive Engineers and the Alpha Phi Alpha Fraternity. He is past president of the Board

W. Leonard Evans is president of Tuesday Publications.

is a member of the boards of the National Conference of Christians and Jews, the Advertising Council, Inc., Fisk University, and the University of Chicago.

CLARENCE C. FINLEY
Executive

As executive vice president of Burlington House Products Group in New York, Clarence C. Finley is probably the most important black executive in the United States. Starting as a $12-a-week file clerk in 1942, he has risen to the second spot in a corporation that does over $250 million yearly business and employs nearly 7,000 people. He was born in Chicago.

LUTHER H. FOSTER
Educator

Luther H. Foster is the president of renowned Tuskegee Institute. Born in Lawrenceville, Va., in 1913, he pursued his education at Virginia State College, Harvard School of Business Administration, and the University of Chicago. Since becoming Tuskegee's president in 1953, he has augmented the college's buildings, strengthened its financial underpinning, and greatly increased service programs for the disadvantaged. He is a trustee of the United Negro College Fund.

ERWIN A. FRANCE
City Official

Erwin A. France serves Chicago as administrative assistant to the mayor and as director of Model Cities—the Chicago Committee on Urban Opportunity Program. Born in St. Louis in 1938, he has divided his career between public service and higher education. Besides teaching at several universities, he has been director of the Chicago Youth Opportunity Centers and deputy director of the Illinois State Employment Service for the Chicago central city.

FRANKIE M. FREEMAN
Attorney

Frankie M. Freeman serves on the U.S. Commission on Civil Rights and is associate general counsel of the St. Louis Housing and Land Clearance Authorities. Born in Danville, Va., her career has included instructing business law at College Center of the Fingerlakes as well as being a practicing lawyer. Often honored for her civil rights work, she is a member of several bar associations, the National Association of Housing and Redevelopment Officials, and the League of Women Voters.

MARY E. FRIZZELL
Fraternal Leader

Mary E. Frizzell is president of the Women's Missionary Society of the A.M.E. Church and has been involved in missionary work for nearly 25 years. Under her guidance, the missionary education department of the society has developed leadership courses in adult work, published inspirational literature, maintained a reference book service, and established a correspondence school. She was born in Mayfield, Ky.

D. PARKE GIBSON
Marketing Specialist

Author of *The $30 Billion Negro*, D. Parke Gibson heads his own national marketing and public relations consulting firm, which publishes monthly newsletters on black consumers and on race-related developments in corporation policies and communication. Born in Seattle, he is a member of the American Marketing Association, the National Association of Market Developers, and the Public Relations Society of America.

SIMEON GOLAR
Judge

Following an outstanding career as an administrator in New York City government, Simeon Golar was named a municipal judge in Queens. His position prior to judicial appointment was chairman of the NYC Housing Authority, where he regulated construction and management of low- and middle-income housing in the metropolis. Born in Chester, S.C., in 1928, he attended City College of New York and New York University Law School. He is an officer of the National Association of Housing and Redevelopment Officials.

BERRY GORDY, JR.
Entrepreneur

One of the great business successes, Berry Gordy, Jr., parlayed an $800 loan into gigantic Motown Industries, which grosses over $50 million a year. Born in Detroit, Mich., he had 15 fights as a Golden Gloves featherweight before joining the U.S. Army in Korea. As president and board chairman of Motown, he has introduced many new artists to the public and to fame, including Smokey Robinson and the Miracles, the Temptations, the Four Tops, the Supremes, and Martha and the Vandellas.

BOOKER GRIFFIN
Broadcast Journalist

Media personality Booker Griffin is director of news and community relations at radio station KGFJ in Los Angeles and is a featured columnist for the *Los*

Simeon Golar is a municipal judge in Queens, New York.

Angeles Sentinel newspaper. His radio responsibilities include reviewing the news to be broadcast, designing community relations programs, and coordinating public service announcements and the station's services to listeners. He was born in Gary, Ind., in 1938.

GILROYE A. GRIFFIN, JR.
Executive

Gilroye A. Griffin, Jr., is a member of the board of directors of Kenyon & Eckhardt, a New York advertising agency. He also serves the firm as vice president of corporate administration and associate counsel. Born in Columbia, S.C., in 1938, he attended Dartmouth College and Columbia University. On the job he supervises all of the company's corporate and advertising legal matters and is director of personnel.

JUNIUS GRIFFIN
Executive

Junius Griffin formed his own public relations firm in Hollywood, Calif., in 1972. Born in Stonega, Va., in 1929, he abandoned a promising career in journalism to become a public relations aide to Martin Luther King, Jr., served as director of public relations for

the SCLC, and was an executive of Motown Records. He is a member of the boards of trustees and of governors of the Martin Luther King Center for Social Change and a member of the board of the U.S. Commission on Civil Rights.

CHARLES V. HAMILTON
Educator

Charles V. Hamilton heads New York's Metropolitan Applied Research Center (MARC), which was formed to research social problems related to community development. Born in Muskogee, Okla., in 1927, he taught at several universities and has published widely. His magazine credits include *The New York Times* magazine, *Harvard Educational Review,* and *Black World,* and he is the author of *The Black Preacher in America* (1972) and *The Black Experience in American Politics* (1973). He is vice president of the American Political Science Association.

NATHAN HARE
Publisher

Author of *The Black Anglo-Saxon,* Nathan Hare is president and founder of The Black World Foundation and publisher of *The Black Scholar.* Born in Slick, Okla., in 1933, he has taught at Howard University and San Francisco College, where he was the country's first coordinator of a black studies program, and has published several articles in *Saturday Review, Ramparts, Black World, Newsweek,* and the *Times* of London. Mr. Hare was a professional fighter under the name Nat Harris. He is a member of the National Steering Committee of the African Liberation Day.

BERNARD W. HARLESTON
Educator

Dr. Bernard W. Harleston is the ninth president of the City College of New York. At CCNY, he has emphasized the importance of maintaining the college's 135-year-old tradition of academic excellence and service to the young people of New York City, particularly those who might not otherwise have attended college. A summa cum laude graduate of Howard University, Dr. Harleston received his doctorate in experimental psychology in 1955 from the University of Rochester, where he began his teaching career. He joined Tufts University as an assistant professor of psychology in 1956 and was away from the institution from 1968 to 1970, when he was provost and later acting president of Lincoln University in Pennsylvania. A member of Phi Beta Kappa, Dr. Harleston holds an honorary Doctor of Science degree from the University of Rochester and he received the John H. Franklin Award

Dr. Bernard W. Harleston is president of the City College of New York.

OLLEN B. HINNANT
Attorney

Ollen B. Hinnant is Assistant General Counsel of the Prudential Insurance Company in Newark, N.J. and is a member of the U.S. National Commission for the United Nations Educational, Scientific and Cultural Organization (UNESCO). Former President Gerald Ford also appointed Mr. Hinnant a member of the State Appeal Board of the Selective Service System of New Jersey. The Newark attorney is active in a number of organizations which include the Planned Parenthood Association of America, the American Bar Association, and the National Bar Association where he is chairperson of the Institutional Law Section. He has been named in editions of *Who's Who in the East, Who's Who in Black America,* and *Who's Who in New Jersey* and the *International Register of Profiles.* Mr. Hinnant was born in Lexington, Ky. and received his B.A. degree from Kentucky State University in Frankfort, Kentucky and his J.D. degree from the University of Kentucky Law School in 1955 prior to undertaking postgraduate studies at New York University.

from the Tufts University African American Cultural Center in 1980. His articles on psychology and education have appeared in scholarly journals and his papers and lectures have been presented to many professional associations. Dr. Harleston was born in New York City.

EDWARD W. HAWTHORNE
Physician

A pioneer in the study of cardiac functioning and hypertension, Dr. Hawthorne has contributed importantly to the research of high blood pressure, an affliction which strikes a far greater proportion of black than white Americans. Born in 1924, he is a graduate of Howard Medical School and took his Ph.D. in physiology from the University of Illinois. Named chairman of Howard's Physiology Department, he pioneered methods of recording heart functioning in conscious animals. In 1974 he was appointed chairman of the Hypertension Research Center's Advisory Committee of the National Heart and Lung Institute.

Ollen B. Hinnant is an executive with the Prudential Insurance Company in Newark, New Jersey.

J. CLINTON HOGGARD
Clergyman

As bishop of the 6th Episcopal District of the African Methodist Episcopal Zion Church, J. Clinton Hoggard oversees the Indiana, Kentucky, North Alabama, and the East Tennessee-Virginia conferences. Born in Jersey City, N.J., he graduated from Rutgers University in 1939 and took a graduate B.D. degree at New York's Union Theological Seminary in 1942. From 1952 to 1972 he served as secretary-treasurer of the AMEZ's Department of Foreign Missions, during which time he earned an international reputation as a diligent and altruistic churchman, with a deep dedication to religious ideals. Consecrated a bishop in 1970, he is a member of the World Council of Churches, the National Council of Churches of Christ in the U.S.A., the NAACP, and the ACLU.

DONALD LEE HOLLOWELL
Federal Executive

As a regional director of the Equal Employment Opportunity Commission, Donald Lee Hollowell works to eliminate discriminatory hiring practices in the southeastern United States. Born in Wichita, Kan., in 1917, he began the private practice of law in Atlanta, Ga., in 1952, has handled several school desegration and public accommodation cases, and was legal representative for Martin Luther King, Jr., and Ralph D. Abernathy.

M. CARL HOLMAN
Administrator

Former deputy director of the U.S. Commission on Civil Rights, M. Carl Holman is now president of the National Urban Coalition, taking up the responsibilities formerly exercised by A. Philip Randolph and the late Whitney M. Young, Jr. During his presidency he has initiated a spectrum of programs designed to focus the united strength of urban minorities against their common problems. Born in Minter City, Miss., in 1919, he is also a prize-winning poet and playwright.

RAYMOND W. HOOD
Legislator

Raymond W. Hood is Democratic party leader in the Michigan House of Representatives. Elected from the 14th District of Detroit, his hometown, he is chairman of the Public Health Committee, vice-chairman of the Labor Committee, and a member of the Elections Committee and the Conservation and Recreation committees. Born in 1936, he was first elected in 1964, becoming the youngest black legislator in Michigan history.

ROY DAVAGE HUDSON
Educator

President of Virginia's Hampton Institute since 1970, Roy Davage Hudson was formerly a pharmacology faculty member at the University of Michigan Medical School and had served as an associate dean of Brown's Graduate School. Born in Chattanooga, Tenn., in 1930, he is a board member of the Virginia Peninsula Industrial Committee and the National Association for Equal Opportunity in Higher Education.

NATHANIEL R. JONES
Attorney

General counsel of the National Association for the Advancement of Colored People, Nathaniel Jones was born in Youngstown, Ohio, in 1926. He obtained a Bachelor of Law Degree from Youngstown University in 1956, served as executive director of that city's Fair Employment Practices Commission, and then became an assistant United States Attorney for the Northern District of Ohio. In 1967, Jones was general counsel for President Lyndon Johnson's Commission on Civil

NAACP General Counsel Nathaniel R. Jones.

Disorders (also known as the Kerner Commission). Named NAACP general counsel in 1969, Jones has earned distinction as a champion of black servicemen and has sparked major revisions in the United States military justice system.

VIRGINIA L. JONES
Librarian

Virginia L. Jones, whose career as a librarian began at Louisville Municipal College in 1934, is director of Atlanta University's School of Library Sciences. Born in Cincinnati, Ohio, in 1912, she has been an instructor in library science and a university dean. A former president of the Association of American Library Schools, she sits on the executive board of the American Library Association and is a member of the President's Advisory Committee on Library Training and Research.

FREDERICK DOUGLASS JORDAN
Clergyman

Bishop Frederick Douglass Jordan is ecumenical prelate of the A.M.E. Church. Born in Atlanta in 1901, he is chairman of the Commission on Union of Black Methodist Churches and of the Commission on the Consultation on Church Union, and a member of the executive committee of the World Methodist Council and of the governing board of the National Council of the Churches of Christ in the U.S. He has been a leader in building up the A.M.E. Church in Africa.

E. J. JOSEY
Librarian

E. J. Josey heads the New York State Education Department's Bureau of Academic and Research Libraries, where he charts the development of specialized research library services. Born in Norfolk, Va., in 1924, he organized the first NAACP college chapter in the South in 1963 and was the first chairman of the Black Caucus of the American Library Association. He is the author of *What Black Librarians Are Saying* and *The Black Librarian in America*.

MARTIN LUTHER KING, SR.
Clergyman

The Reverend Martin Luther King, Sr., retired as pastor of the Ebenezer Baptist Church, Atlanta, in 1975. Born in Stockbridge, Ga., in 1899, he was named 1972 Clergyman of the Year by the Georgia Region of the National Conference of Christians and Jews. Father of the martyred civil rights leader, he is a member of the boards of SCLC, the Citizens Trust Co., and the Carrie-Steele-Pitts Children's Home.

BARBARA LAMONT
Television Newscaster

Barbara Lamont is co-host of New York City's WNEW-TV *Black News* and a key member of the channel's *10 O'Clock News*. Born in 1925, she received the Newswoman's Guild Award for excellence in reporting in 1973 for her two documentaries, *Guyana* and *Brownstone Fever*. She is the author of *City People* and a Democratic district leader in Manhattan.

HARRISON EDWARD LEE
Educator

Professor Harrison Edward Lee is director of public relations at Prentiss Institute Jr. College in Mississippi. Born in Talladega, Ala., in 1922, he has taught at several colleges and is an accomplished poet as well as a journalist and news broadcaster. He is a member of the Voter's League and the NAACP.

ROBERT O. LOWERY
City Official

Robert O. Lowery became the first black fire commissioner of a major city when he was appointed to that post in New York City on January 1, 1966. Born in Buffalo, N.Y., in 1916, he joined the New York Fire Department in 1942 and worked his way up the ranks. His administration is noteworthy for its honesty, public education programs, and attempts to recruit minority personnel.

ERNEST DUKE McNEIL
Attorney

Ernest Duke McNeil is founder and senior partner of his own law firm and president of Chicago's Woodlawn Organization. Born in Memphis in 1936, he is co-founder of UHURU, a legal foundation, and of the Organization of Black American Culture, chairman of the Black Businessmen's Association, and president of Hustlers Discount Records. A recent candidate for mayor of Chicago, he was cited by Power, Inc., for Outstanding Contributions to Black Liberation in 1972.

JAMES P. McQUAY
Furrier

James McQuay is known as "The Black Furrier" because he is the only black in the wholesale-retail fur manufacturing business. McQuay opened his first store in Harlem with $460. It took him seven years to get to the point where he was making a living for himself. At the beginning Mr. McQuay did most of the manual labor himself, but as time went on and business picked up, he did less and less. Since 1963 Mr. McQuay has

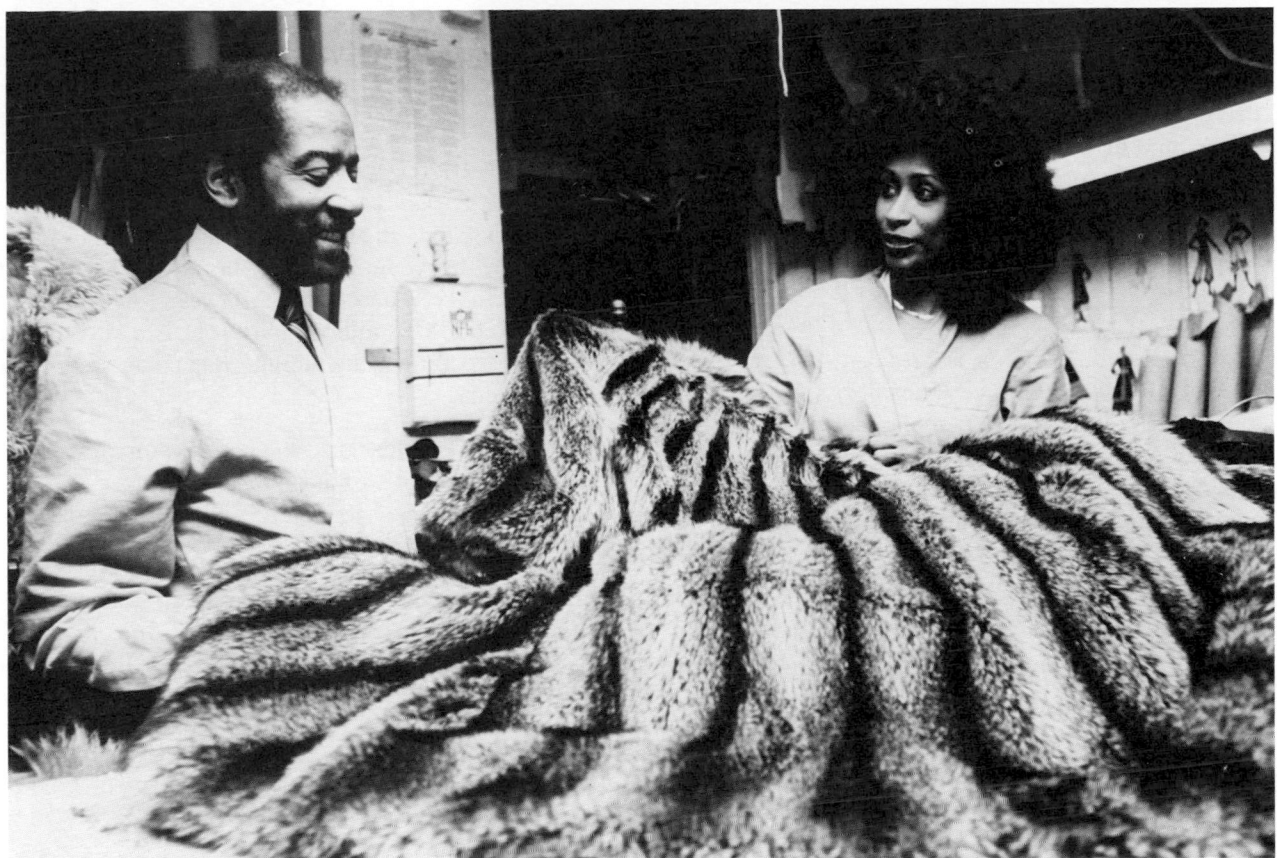

James McQuay is the only black in wholesale-retail fur manufacturing to own his own business.

operated in the heart of the wholesale fur district in New York City, making custom-made coats, producing specialty items for several prestigious stores, and remodeling, repairing, and altering old furs. His clientele includes entertainers, politicians, community and business leaders from all over the nation. Mr. McQuay's designs are also in demand all across the nation for various fashion galas.

CLARENCE M. MITCHELL, JR.
Attorney

Clarence M. Mitchell is chief of the NAACP's Washington, D.C., Bureau and is legislative chairman of the Leadership Conference on Civil Rights. Born in Baltimore in 1911, he has played an important role in much civil rights legislation and helped direct the successful legal battle against ex-President Nixon's nominations of judges Clement Haynesworth and G. Harrold Carswell to the U.S. Supreme Court. He was awarded the 1969 Spingarn Medal.

L. PEARL MITCHELL
Humanitarian

L. Pearl Mitchell is a former director of the NAACP and functionary of Alpha Kappa Alpha sorority. Born

Chief of the NAACP's Washington, D.C., Bureau, Clarence M. Mitchell, Jr.

in Wilberforce, Ohio, she began teaching music in 1915, worked as a juvenile probation officer in Cleveland for 20 years, and served as director of membership drives for the NAACP. In 1965 she coordinated several AKA fund drives which raised nearly $500,000 in life memberships for the NAACP. Langston Hughes' poem "I dream" is dedicated to her.

RICHARD DAVID MORRISON
Educator

Richard David Morrison is president of Alabama A & M University. Born in Utica, Miss., in 1910, he joined the college in 1937, rising to chairman of the Agriculture Division before being appointed college president in 1962. Since then he has directed a fundamental reorganization of the school, gaining it full academic accreditation as a university, increasing student enrollment 60%, and constructing several new buildings.

JOHN A. MORSELL
Administrator

John A. Morsell serves both as assistant executive director of the NAACP and as a member of the New York City Board of Higher Education. Born in Pittsburgh in 1912, he became an eminent sociological researcher, focusing on racial integration and civil rights questions, before joining the NAACP in 1956. He is a Fellow of the American Sociological Association and a member of the American Association for Public Opinion Research.

WINSTON E. MOORE
State Official

Director of the Cook County (Chicago) Department of Corrections Winston Moore was born in New Orleans in 1929. He obtained a B.S. from West Virginia State College and an M.S. in psychology from the University of Louisville. In 1961 he joined the Illinois Youth Commission as a psychologist and soon became a clinic director. In 1968 he was named warden of the Cook County Jail and was appointed Director of the county's penal system in 1969.

HUGO A. OWENS
City Official, Dentist

A member of the Dental Staff of the Portsmouth, Va. General Hospital and president of the Portsmouth branch of the NAACP, Hugo A. Owens became the first black city councilman in Chesapeake County history in 1970, and has since been reelected to that post. Born in 1917, he served in the U.S. Army during World War II and graduated from Howard University Dental

College in 1947. He is a formidable organizer of community action and public opinion.

HENRY G. PARKS, JR.
Executive

Henry G. Parks, Jr., is founder and president of H. G. Parks, Inc., the famous sausage makers in Baltimore. Born in Atlanta in 1916, he started his present company in 1951 and, within 20 years, had brought sales past the $10 million mark. He is a director of several corporations including Magnavox and First Pennsylvania.

JOHN A. PEOPLES
Educator

John A. Peoples was appointed president of Mississippi's Jackson State College in 1967. Born in Starkville, Miss., in 1926, he began his career in education as an instructor of mathematics in Gary, Ind., in 1951. His memberships include the Institute for Educational Management, the American Association for Higher Education, and HEW's Advisory Committee on Accreditation and Institutional Eligibility.

CHANNING E. PHILLIPS
Administrator

As president of the Housing Development Corp. in Washington, D.C., the Reverend Channing E. Phillips supervises the firm's real estate transactions and property management. Born in Brooklyn, N.Y., in 1928, he has taught at several colleges and, at the 1968 Democratic National Convention in Chicago, he became the first black American ever nominated for the office of President of the United States.

ERSA HINES POSTON
State Official

Ersa Hines Poston became president of the New York State Civil Service Commission in 1967, taking on a department with 900 employees and a yearly budget of $10 million. Born in Paducah, Ky., in 1921, she began her career with the Hartford Tuberculosis and Health Association in 1946 and has been a confidential assistant to Governor Nelson Rockefeller and director of the New York State Office of Economic Opportunity.

ALVIN POUSSAINT
Psychiatrist

Alvin Poussaint is associate dean of students at the Harvard University Medical School, where he also teaches psychiatry. Born in New York City in 1934, he has taught at Tufts University Medical School, has

Reverend Samuel Proctor is pastor of New York's famous Abyssinian Baptist Church.

Mahlon T. Puryear directs the Economic Development Department of the National Urban League.

written several articles as well as the book *Why Blacks Kill Blacks* (1972), and is one of the founding fellows of The Black Academy of Arts and Letters.

JOHN L. PROCOPE
Editor, Publisher

In 1974 John L. Procope took the reins as editor and publisher of the New York *Amsterdam News,* one of the nation's more important and prestigious black newspapers, with a circulation of 91,000. In an era marked by black newspaper failures, he has successfully redirected his paper's focus toward significant national events rather than concentrating on community events of limited appeal. A native of New York City, he attended Morgan State College and did graduate work in marketing at New York University.

SAMUEL DeWITT PROCTOR
Clergyman

Reverend Samuel DeWitt Proctor is pastor of New York's famous Abyssinian Baptist Church and is a professor of education at Rutgers University. Born in Norfolk, Va., in 1921, he was ordained in 1943 and has held several important posts in government, education, and the church. He is a trustee of Meharry Medical College, the National Urban League, and Ottawa University, and is the author of *The Young Negro in America, 1960-1980.*

MAHLON T. PURYEAR
Administrator

Mahlon T. Puryear is director of the Economic Development Department of the National Urban League. Born in Winston-Salem, N.C., in 1915, he has been a college teacher, a personnel counselor for Wright Aeronautical Corp., and has served in various capacities with the Urban League since 1951. In 1968 he became president of Manpower Consultants to direct their projected coordination of employer needs and school programs.

ROYAL W. PURYEAR
Educator

Royal W. Puryear is president of Miami's Florida Memorial College, an accredited Southern Association senior college that he built up from a two-year institution. Born in Winston-Salem, N.C., in 1912, he began his teaching career in the public schools of his hometown and has been associate pastor of St. John the Baptist Church in Dallas and president of Butler College in Tyler, Tex.

JAMES A. RUSSELL, JR.
Educator

James A. Russell, Jr., is president of Saint Paul's College in his hometown of Lawrenceville, Va. Born in 1917, he taught for many years at Hampton Institute, where he developed outstanding engineering and technology programs to train young black men and women for positions in industry. He has received several awards, including the 1971 Outstanding Educator of America.

FRED L. SHUTTLESWORTH
Clergyman

The Reverend Fred L. Shuttlesworth serves as pastor of the Greater New Light Baptist Church in Cincinnati, Ohio, and is the national secretary of the Southern Christian Leadership Conference (SCLC). Born in Montgomery, Ala., in 1922, he organized the Alabama Christian Movement for Human Rights in 1952 and was an important aide to Martin Luther King, Jr.

WILLIAM E. SIMS
Educator

William E. Sims has been president of Oklahoma's Langston University since 1970. Born in Chickasha, Okla., in 1921, he served in the U.S. Navy as a musician from 1942 to 1946 and taught public school in Tulsa, before joining the Langston faculty as a professor of music and band director in 1953. He is a member of the Adult Education Association and has worked with the Oklahoma Humanities Task Force.

ASA T. SPAULDING, SR.
Executive

Asa T. Spaulding is president of his own consulting firm in Durham, N.C., which he formed in 1968 after retiring from the presidency of North Carolina Mutual Life Insurance Co., the largest black-controlled insurance company in the world. Born in Columbus County, N.C., in 1902, he worked at North Carolina Mutual for 36 years, was named the first black director of W. T. Grant in 1964, and is an advisor to many governmental commissions and philanthropic organizations.

EDWARD S. SPRIGGS
Executive

Artist and author Edward S. Spriggs is the executive director of The Studio Museum of Contemporary Black Art in Harlem, New York City. Born in Cleveland in 1934, he has worked as a freelance graphic artist, a sound technician, and a film editor. A consultant to the New York State Council on the Arts, he edits *Black Dialogue* magazine, and he is a member of the American Association of Museums and the International Council of Museums.

WILLIAM H. STAFFORD
Executive

As executive director of the New York Community Training Institute, Inc., William H. Stafford is a recognized leader in the development of programs to solve the problems of training men and women in the nation's poverty areas. Born in Valdosta, Ga., in 1929, he graduated from Kentucky State College and holds a masters degree from Adelphi University School of Social Work. Prior to his present position, he worked for several years with the New York City Youth Board and gave counseling in special manpower programs for the Board of Education and for Mobilization for Youth. He has been instrumental in developing many programs which operate in New York City's 26 poverty areas, providing training in management, comprehensive health, nontraditional degree programs, economic development, housing, management and maintenance, and board operations and institutional development.

REMBERT EDWARDS STOKES
Educator

A.M.E. minister Rembert Edwards Stokes has been president of Wilberforce University since 1956. Born in Dayton, Ohio, in 1917, he was formerly dean of the school's Payne Theological Seminary. He is a trustee of the Cleveland Chapter of the National Conference of Christians and Jews and a member of the Ohio Mental Health Association, the National Council of Churches, and the American Association for the Advancement of Science.

LEON HOWARD SULLIVAN
Clergyman, Executive

Founder and board chairman of the Opportunities Industrialization Centers of America, the Reverend Leon Sullivan was born in Charleston, W.Va., in 1922 and ordained a Baptist minister in 1941. In 1944 he was prominent in A. Philip Randolph's successful threat to march on Washington to obtain jobs for blacks. During this period, Sullivan served as an aide to the Rev. Adam Clayton Powell, Jr., while the latter was running for Congress. In 1951 Sullivan was named pastor of the Zion Baptist Church, Philadelphia, and in 1964 formed OIC, which soon became one of the largest and most prestigious job training organizations in the world. In 1971 Rev. Sullivan was named a director of General Motors.

ALVIN I. THOMAS
Educator

President of Prairie View A & M College since 1966, Alvin I. Thomas had formerly served the school as industrial arts instructor, woodwork instructor, director of industrial education, and dean of the school of Industrial Education and Technology. Born in New Orleans in 1925, he has been a consultant for the public schools of Texas, Kansas, California, and Ohio, and for Dow Chemical, Litton Industries, and the U.S. Office of Education. He is a member of the National Education Association and the Texas Rural Development Commission.

FRANKLIN THOMAS
Attorney, Administrator

Franklin Thomas, president of the Ford Foundation, is the first black person to head a major philanthropic organization. An attorney, Thomas served as president and chief executive officer of the Bedford-Stuyvesant Restoration Corporation in Brooklyn from 1967 to 1977, where he helped establish neighborhood businesses, renovate local residences, and create thousands of new jobs. Thomas was born in the Bedford-Stuyvesant section of Brooklyn in a stable working-class environment and was the only member of his family to go to college. As a youngster growing up in Bed-Stuy, Thomas avoided street gangs and became active in the Boy Scouts. He developed his skill in basketball on black-top courts and went on to Franklin K. Lane High School where he was captain and star of the basketball team. He also excelled academically. At Columbia University, Thomas starred on the basketball team and was voted the Ivy League's most valuable player in 1955 and 1956. He became the first black student to serve as captain of the team. In 1963 and 1964 Thomas worked as an adviser and attorney in the regional New York office of the Federal Housing and Home Finance Agency and in 1964 he was appointed assistant United States attorney for the Southern District of New York. Thomas was appointed deputy police commissioner of New York City in 1965, the fourth black man to serve in that position. He has served as a director or trustee of several organizations, including the John Hay Whitney Foundation, the Foreign Policy Study Foundation, and the Columbia Law School Alumni Association. Thomas has been on the boards of directors of such corporations as the Columbia Broadcasting System, the Aluminum Corporation of America, the Cummins Engine Company, Allied Stores Corporation, and the New York Life Insurance Corporation.

Eugene Toomer is Vice President for Employee Relations at Alexander's Department Stores.

JAMES S. THOMAS
Clergyman

Bishop James S. Thomas watches over the nearly 1,000 congregations of the United Methodist Church in Iowa and directs the Church's assistance programs. Born in Orangeburg, S.C., in 1919, he has been instrumental in securing Church support for black private colleges, launching the program by which 11 black colleges of the Methodist Church gained accreditation from the Southern Association of Schools and Colleges.

EUGENE A. TOOMER
Executive

In his post as vice president for Employee Relations and Urban Affairs at Alexander's Department Stores, Eugene Toomer has been instrumental in implementing Equal Opportunity efforts and programs for 13 stores and more than 13,000 employees. Born in Macon, Georgia, in 1921, he earned his B.A. at Kentucky State University, where he was an All-American football player, and his M.A. at Wayne State University. He is on the executive board of Edges, on the board of directors of the Bronx-Manhattan Mental Health Association, and is the president of the Consumer Distribution Committee for Retail Industries.

WILLIAM H. TOWNSEND
Legislator

A member of the Arkansas House of Representatives, William H. Townsend is also a practicing optometrist in Little Rock. Born near West Point, Miss., in 1914, he became the first black optometrist licensed in Arkansas in 1950 and is now president of the Arkansas Council on Human Relations, vice president of the Arkansas Optometric Association, and treasurer of Professional Services, Inc. He is a trustee of Mt. Zion Baptist Church in Little Rock.

JACKIE VAUGHN III
Legislator

Michigan state representative Jackie Vaughn III wrote his state's ground-breaking voting rights bill for 18-year-olds. Born in Birmingham, Ala., in 1939, he studied social science at Oxford University as a Fulbright Scholar and Fellow, and was the first black to be elected president of the Young Democrats of Michigan.

JOHN THOMAS WALKER
Clergyman

The Rt. Reverend John Thomas Walker, bishop of the Episcopal Diocese of Washington, D.C., was born in Barnesville, Ga., in 1925. Placing great emphasis on social and educational reform, he provides an active chairmanship to the Negro Student Fund. He is a member of the boards of trustees of Absalom Jones Theological Institute in Atlanta, St. Paul's School in New Hampshire, and the National Cathedral School for Girls in Washington, D.C.

LUCIUS WALKER, JR.
Clergyman

The Reverend Lucius Walker, Jr., is executive director of the Inter-religious Foundation for Community Organization in New York City, which provides economic assistance for black community development. Born in Roselle, N.J., in 1930, he is a member of the Black Foundation Executives and sits on the board of trustees of Shaw University and Andover Newton Theological School.

WYATT TEE WALKER
Clergyman

Former chief of staff to Martin Luther King, Jr., the Reverend Wyatt Tee Walker is minister of the Canaan Baptist Church of Christ in New York City, and was

Reverend Wyatt Tee Walker advised New York Governor Nelson Rockefeller on urban affairs.

urban affairs assistant to the governor of New York. Born in Brockton, Mass., in 1929, he has conducted sensitivity seminars on racial polarization for IBM, New York Bell Telephone Co., and Consolidated Edison. Under his direction the Canaan Baptist Church has grown physically and financially and has added several new social programs.

WILLIAM J. L. WALLACE
Educator

William J. L. Wallace is president of West Virginia State College in Institute, W.Va. Born in Salisbury, N.C. in 1908, he is a member of the West Virginia Advisory Committee, the U.S. Commission on Civil Rights, and the Farmers Home Administration. He was awarded the Outstanding Civilian Service Medal of the Army in 1972.

HAROLD WASHINGTON
Legislator

Harold Washington serves his native Chicago as state representative from the 26th District. Born in 1922, he is an attorney in the firm of Washington and Washington, founded by his father, and has been an assistant corporation counsel for the city of Chicago and an arbitrator with the Illinois Industrial Commission.

WALTER WASHINGTON
Educator

Walter Washington is president of Alcorn A & M College in Lorman, Miss., the oldest land-grant college in the nation, where he has initiated a dynamic program of renovation and improvements. Born in Hazlehurst, Miss., in 1923, he is a member of the Mississippi Advisory Commission on Vocational Education, vice chairman of the secondary commission of the Southern Association of Colleges and Schools, and a member of the state board of directors of the Boy Scouts of America.

LEVI WATKINS
Educator

Founder and former president of Owen College in Memphis, Levi Watkins is now president of Alabama State University in Montgomery. Born in Montgomery, Ky., he is a vice president of the Alabama Commission on Higher Education and a member of the Advisory Board on Health and Environmental Quality.

BARBARA M. WATSON
Federal Official

Barbara M. Watson is former administrator of the Bureau of Security and Consular Affairs of the U.S. State Department in Washington, D.C. Born in New York City in 1918, she has operated a successful modeling school, worked as an attorney with the New York City Board of Statutory Review, and was executive director of the New York City Commission to the United Nations (1964–1966). She is a member of the board of directors of the United Mutual Life Insurance Co.

KENNETH L. WEBSTER
Legislator

Kenneth L. Webster is a member of the Maryland House of Delegates from Baltimore's 5th District and is also a community relations assistant for the Model Cities Housing Development. Born in Baltimore in 1935, he served in the Strategic Air Command and is a member of the Black United Front, the Baltimore Advisory Council of Vocational Education, and the New Democratic Coalition of Maryland.

LEONARD 12X WEIR
Policeman

New York City patrolman Leonard 12X Weir is founder and president of the National Society of Afro-American Policemen. Born in New York in 1931, he has been a patrolman since 1959, and his current assignment is in the Internal Affairs Division, which investigates police corruption. He is a member of the Nation of Islam and the owner of a book and natural foods store.

VERDA F. WELCOME
Legislator

Verda F. Welcome is a state senator from Baltimore's 4th District. Born in Lake Lure, N.C., she became the first woman and the first black to be elected to Baltimore's senate in 1963. She sponsored the 1967 "Miscegenation Bill" repealing the ban on interracial marriage and the 1968 bill to prohibit racial discrimination in the sale of new housing.

LAWRENCE DOUGLAS WILDER
Legislator

Virginia state senator Lawrence Douglas Wilder was born in Richmond in 1931. The only black in the state senate, he has worked for laws on open housing and sickle cell anemia, and has served as chairman of the Virginia Legislative Council Sub-Committee. He maintains a private law practice.

WILLIAM R. WILKES
Clergyman

A.M.E. bishop William R. Wilkes is now responsible for the episcopal district of Kentucky and Tennessee. Born in Eatonton, Ga., in 1902, he has served the Church in many capacities. During his tenure as bishop of Ohio he was instrumental in adding many new buildings to the campus of Wilberforce University.

A. CECIL WILLIAMS
Clergyman

The Reverend A. Cecil Williams is minister of Celebrations and Involvement at the Glide Memorial United Methodist Church in San Francisco. Born in San Angelo, Tex., in 1929, he takes an initiatory role in multi-racial social reform. He has served as co-chairman for the Congress of Racial Equality, is a trustee of the Martin Luther King Center for Social Change, and hosts a weekly TV public affairs program.

Social activist A. Cecil Williams is Minister of Celebrations and Involvement at San Francisco's Glide Memorial United Methodist Church.

CHANCELLOR WILLIAMS
Educator

Dr. Chancellor Williams is a retired Howard University history professor who grew up in Bennettsville, S.C. As a child, Williams wanted to know more about the social positions of blacks during that time period. Dr. Williams has written eight books, among them *The Destruction of Black Civilization: Great Issues of a Race from 4500 B.C. to 2000 A.D.* He has a B.A. in education and an M.A. degree in history, both from Howard University. His Ph.D. in history and sociology is from American University. Williams has spent his lifetime rediscovering the truth of the African past.

EDDIE N. WILLIAMS
Executive

As president of the Joint Center for Political Studies in Washington, D.C., Eddie N. Williams tries to meet the information and technical needs of minority elected officials affiliated with the National Black Caucus. Born in Memphis in 1932, he has served at the University of Chicago as vice president for public affairs and as director of the Center for Public Study. He is chairman of the Fellowship Committee of the National Drug Abuse Council and is vice chairman of the board of trustees of the National Children's Television Workshop.

HARDY WILLIAMS
Legislator

Democrat Hardy Williams was elected to the Pennsylvania legislature from his hometown of Philadelphia in 1970. An attorney with a private practice, he is a member of the Lawyers Committee for Civil Rights, the Philadelphia Council for Community Advancement, and Community Legal Services. He was born in 1931.

NATHAN WRIGHT, JR.
Educator

Professor Nathan Wright, Jr., teaches urban affairs at the State University of New York in Albany. Born in Shreveport, La., in 1923, he is a prolific author, with more than 300 published articles to his credit, and his award-winning books include *Black Power and Urban Unrest, What Black Educators Are Saying,* and *Ready to Riot.* He has been a columnist for the *Newark Star-Ledger,* chairman of the 1967 and 1968 National and International Conferences on Black Power in Newark and Philadelphia, and was one of the participants in the "Journey of Reconciliation" in CORE's 1967 freedom ride.

OTHER PROMINENT BLACK AMERICANS

Name	Occupation	Birthdate
Adams, Albert W., Jr.	Administrator	Nov. 22, 1948
Adams, John D.	PR executive	Mar. 16, 1943
Alexander, Louis G.	Bank executive	Feb. 14, 1910
Alexander, William H.	Legislator, lawyer	Dec. 10, 1930
Allen, Aris T.	Legislator, physician	Dec. 27, 1910
Allen, George Louis	Businessman, legislator	Nov. 26, 1910
Allen, George M.	Legislator	Nov. 14, 1933
Allen, Willie	Clergyman	July 12, 1921
Alphran, R. Marchand	Corporate manager	
Amos, Larry C.	Corporate attorney	July 28, 1935
Anderson, Marcellus J., Sr.	Businessman	June 21, 1900
Arlene, Herbert	Legislator	Sep. 15, 1917
Atkins, Thomas I.	Legislator	Mar. 2, 1939
Barbee, Lloyd A.	Legislator	Aug. 17, 1925
Barnes, Eugene M.	Legislator	July 24, 1931
Barnett, Brenetta Howell	State official	June 28, 1932
Bates, Nathaniel	Mayor	Sep. 9, 1931
Bearden, Harold I.	Clergyman	Mar. 8, 1910
Bell, Thomas M.	Legislator, businessman	Jan. 23, 1948
Bennett, Marion D.	Clergyman, legislator	May 31, 1936
Billington, Clyde	Legislator, realtor	Aug. 29, 1934
Bishop, Cecil	Clergyman	May 12, 1930
Black, Leona R.	County official	Jan. 5, 1924
Blackwell, Lucien E.	Legislator	Aug. 1, 1931
Blackwell, Robert B.	Public official	Nov. 4, 1921
Blakeley, Ulysses Buckley, Sr.	Clergyman	Nov. 29, 1911
Bodden, Wendell N.	Administrator	Mar 8, 1930

Name	Occupation	Birthdate
Bolden, Darwin W.	Executive	Aug. 8, 1932
Bolden, Dorothy	Administrator	
Bonner, Isaiah H.	Clergyman	July 27, 1890
Boone, Charles H.	Marketing specialist	Mar. 13, 1932
Booth, L. Venchael	Clergyman	Jan. 17, 1919
Borders, William H.	Clergyman	Feb. 29, 1905
Bowen, William F.	Legislator	Jan. 30, 1929
Brailey, Troy	Legislator	Aug. 26, 1916
Branch, Dorothy S.	Clergywoman	Feb. 4, 1922
Caldwell, James F.	Tax counsel	May 22, 1930
Carr, Charles V.	Legislator, businessman	Nov. 9, 1903
Carter, James Y.	Legislator	Apr. 20, 1915
Carter, Matthew G.	Business executive	Oct. 16, 1915
Cashin, John L., Jr.	Dentist, politician	Apr. 16, 1928
Charbonnet, Louis, III	Legislator, businessman	Mar. 12, 1939
Cherry, Gwen S.	Legislator	Aug. 27, 1923
Chess, Sammie, Jr.	Judge	Mar. 28, 1934
Chester, Joseph A., Sr.	Legislator	Mar. 4, 1914
Clark, Caesar A. W.	Clergyman	Dec. 13, 1914
Clark, Robert G.	Legislator	Oct. 3, 1929
Cleveland, Jones	Clergyman	Dec. 5, 1931
Clyburn, James E.	Gubernatorial aide	July 21, 1940
Coleman, Charles A.	Administrator	Feb. 23, 1921
Colter, Cyrus J.	Public official	Jan. 8, 1910
Compton, James W.	Administrator	Apr. 7, 1939
Connor, George C., Jr.	Legislator	May 28, 1921
Cooper, Peggy	Attorney	Apr. 7, 1947
Copes, Glenda L.	Business executive	Oct. 18, 1943
Coston, Bessie	Administrator	Nov. 29, 1916
Cousins, William, Jr.	Legislator, attorney	Oct. 6, 1927
Cullers, Vincent T.	Executive	
Curls, Phillip B.	Legislator	Apr. 2, 1942
Daniel, David	Administrator	Jan. 2, 1906
Daniels, Hayzel B.	Jurist	Feb. 7, 1907
Dargon, Charles A.	Executive	
Darnell, Emma I.	City official	Mar. 1, 1937
Davis, Charles A.	Administrator	Sep. 29, 1922
Davis, Corneal A.	Legislator	Aug. 28, 1900
Davis, Edward D.	Businessman	Feb. 1, 1904
Dawkins, Maurice A.	Administrator	Jan. 29, 1921
Dean, James E.	Legislator	1945
Dean, Walter R.	Legislator	Dec. 12, 1934
Dilday, William H., Jr.	Executive	Sep. 14, 1937
Ditto, Frank	Community leader	
Dixon, Isaiah, Jr.	Legislator	Dec. 23, 1922
Dixon, Julian C.	Legislator	
Doss, Lawrence P.	Administrator	June 16, 1927
Douglas, Herbert P., Jr.	Executive	Mar. 9, 1922
Douglass, Calvin A.	Legislator	Sep. 1, 1909

Name	Occupation	Birthdate	Name	Occupation	Birthdate
Douglass, John W.	Legislator	Mar. 19, 1942	Jones, Paul R.	Federal executive	1930
Dunham, Robert	Restaurateur	1932			
Dunmore, Albert J.	Administrator	June 4, 1915	Jones, Sidney A., Jr.	Judge	July 2, 1909
Edgill, John W.	Executive	Sep. 13, 1921	Jordon, Orchid I.	Legislator	Aug. 15, 1910
Edwards, Alfred L.	Federal official	Aug. 6, 1920	Kidd, Mae Street	Legislator	
Edwards, George H.	Legislator	Feb. 13, 1911	King, Edward B., Jr.	Executive	Aug. 17, 1939
Elliott, Daisy	Legislator	Nov. 26, 1919	King, Lawrence C.	Executive	
Evans, Samuel L.	Administrator	Nov. 11, 1902	Kornegay, Francis A.	Executive	Sep. 14, 1913
Ewell, Raymond W.	Legislator	Dec. 29, 1928	Lewis, Aubrey C.	Executive	1937
Fielding, Herbert V.	Legislator	July 6, 1923	Lewis, Byron	Executive	Dec. 25, 1931
Fields, Charles L.	Executive	Oct. 28, 1932	Lewis, Edward	Executive	May 15, 1940
Fierce, Hughlyn F.	Executive		Lewis, Elma I.	Administrator	Sep. 15, 1929
Fitzpatrick, William T.	Administrator	Jan. 20, 1889	Lewis, Elsie Makel	Educator	May 2, 1914
Foggie, Samuel L.	Executive	Apr. 16, 1927	Lyles, Leonard E.	Executive	Jan. 26, 1936
Frazier, Leonard G.	Legislator		McClendon, Ernestine	Businesswoman	Aug. 17, 1921
Frost, Wilson	City official	Dec. 27, 1925	McGee, Henry W.	Postal official	Feb. 7, 1910
Gardner, Betram E.	Banker	1915	McGuire, Rosalie J.	Educator	Jan. 27, 1910
Gaston, Arthur G., Sr.	Businessman	July 4, 1892	Melton, Mitchell W.	Legislator	Apr. 6, 1943
Goode, Malvin R.	Media consultant	Feb. 13, 1908	Moore, Daniel A.	Executive	Nov. 20, 1935
			Moore, George A.	TV producer	Feb. 8, 1914
Goward, Russell	Legislator	Aug. 25, 1935	Moore, Hilliard T., Sr.	City official	Aug. 18, 1925
Granger, Shelton B.	Civic official	Feb. 21, 1921	Norford, George E.	Administrator	Jan. 18, 1918
Graves, Curtis M.	Administrator	Aug. 26, 1938	Owens, Jesse	Marketing executive	Sep. 12, 1913
Graves, Earl Gilbert	Executive	1935			
Greene, Bill	Legislator	Nov. 15, 1931	Payton, Sallyanne	White House aide	May 18, 1943
Hamer, Fannie Lou	Community leader	Oct. 6, 1917	Reid, Maude K.	Administrator	
Hamilton, Paul L.	Curriculum specialist	Apr. 1, 1941	Reynolds, Hobson R.	Administrator	Sep. 13, 1898
			Rhodes, Joseph, Sr.	Legislator	Aug. 14, 1947
Hampton, Leroy	Executive	Apr. 20, 1927	Richardson, George C.	Legislator	Feb. 19, 1929
Hancock, Wayman E., Jr.	Marketing representative	Jan. 2, 1937	Robertson, William B.	Legislator	Jan. 31, 1933
Harris, Charles F.	Executive	Jan. 3, 1934	Robinson, William P., Sr.	Legislator	Mar. 15, 1911
Harris, J. Robert	Marketing analyst	Apr. 1, 1944	Rollins, Joseph W., Jr.	Manpower expert	Mar. 10, 1920
Hayes, Reginald C.	Executive	Apr. 1, 1928	Sanders, Charles L.	Consultant	Aug. 10, 1938
Hayes, Robert L.	Executive		Sears, Arthur, Jr.	Consultant	July 1, 1928
Hicks, William H.	Legislator	Aug. 27, 1925	Seymour, Frank M.	Businessman	Dec. 16, 1916
Hobson, Charles	Broadcast journalist	June 23, 1926	Sheffield, Horace L.	Librarian, union official	
Holloway, Ruth L.	Administrator	Apr. 22, 1932	Sherwood, Kenneth N.	Businessman	Aug. 10, 1930
Holmes, David S., Jr.	Legislator	Aug. 11, 1914	Simmons, Leonard	Public official	May 2, 1920
Holomon, Frank	Legislator	Jan. 10, 1934	Singleton, Mary L.	Legislator	Sep. 20, 1926
Hoover, Odie W., Jr.	Clergyman	Sep. 21, 1921	Smith, Herman B., Jr.	Administrator	Feb. 12, 1927
Hunter, Clarence H.	Administrator	Nov. 1, 1925	Smith, Kelly M., Sr.	Clergyman	Oct. 28, 1920
Hunter, James	Executive	May 27, 1936	Smith, Nate	Library specialist	Feb. 23, 1929
Irby, Roy	Executive	June 7, 1918			
Jackson, George E.	Executive	Jan. 29, 1931	Thomas, Franklin A.	Administrator	May 27, 1934
Jackson, Johnny, Jr.	Legislator	Sep. 19, 1943	Wedgeworth, Robert, Jr.	Administrator	July 31, 1937
Jackson, Samuel C.	Administrator	May 8, 1929			
Jarrett, Vernon D.	Journalist	June 19, 1921	Wright, Stephen J.	Educator	Sep. 8, 1910
Jeffries, Leroy N.	Market consultant	Aug. 14, 1911			
Johnson, E. Marie	Businesswoman				
Johnson, George E.,	Businessman	June 16, 1927			
Jones, Benjamin E.	Administrator	Sep. 8, 1935			
Jones, Johnnie A.	Legislator	Nov. 30, 1919			

BLACK FIRSTS: A COMPILATION OF INTERESTING DEBUT EVENTS

The following list of firsts describes a wide spectrum of pioneering events in black American history. Many of the moments described possess considerable intrinsic significance—such as the first publication of a novel by a black author in 1853, or the selection of the first interracial jury in 1865 for the trial of ex-Confederate president Jefferson Davis—while other events listed are merely interesting. To all of these breakthroughs, great and small, an undeniable human interest attaches, for they tell of people who refused to accept old limitations. Seen as a whole, the list has an even greater importance, for it takes on a historical shape. From this perspective, the individual stories of courage and daring combine to reveal a very personal and nontheoretical chart of the progress of equal opportunity and black achievement in America.*

1621 **William Tucker** becomes the first black child born in the American colonies. A native of Jamestown, Virginia, his birthright entails the same privileges of freedom and liberty enjoyed by the white children of the colony.

1623 The first black in the colonies to be baptized a Christian is a child named **Anthony,** son of Isabel

---

* This section does not repeat many of the most important firsts in civil rights, science, the arts, and entertainment, which are dealt with at length in their respective sections of the *Almanac,* especially in the biographies of the individuals involved.

---

and William, who becomes a member of the Anglican Church in Jamestown.

1783 **James Derham,** born a slave in Philadelphia in 1762, becomes the first black physician in the United States. After learning medicine, while serving as an assistant to his master (a doctor by profession), Derham purchased his freedom in 1783, and went on to develop a thriving practice with both black and white clientele. By 1788 he was considered to be one of the leading physicians in New Orleans. Dr. Benjamin Rush, a famous contemporary of Derham, once said of him: "I have conversed with him upon most of the acute and epidemic diseases of the country where he lives. I expected to have suggested some new medicines to him, but he suggested many more to me."

1786 **Lemuel Haynes,** who served in the Revolution as a minuteman, becomes the first black minister with a white congregation.

1795 First black missionary minister to work with Indians is **John Morront** of New York. He is ordained as a Methodist minister on May 15 in London, England. Among his converts to the Christian faith were a Cherokee chieftain and his daughter.

1826 The first black college graduate, **John Russwurm,** receives his degree from Bowdoin College in Maine in 1826. (This claim is disputed in some sources, which maintain that Edward A. Jones graduated from Amherst a few days earlier than Russ-

CLOTEL;

OR,

THE PRESIDENT'S DAUGHTER:

A Narrative of Slave Life

IN

THE UNITED STATES.

BY

WILLIAM WELLS BROWN,

A FUGITIVE SLAVE, AUTHOR OF "THREE YEARS IN EUROPE.

With a Sketch of the Author's Life.

"We hold these truths to be self-evident: that all men are created equal; that they are endowed by their Creator with certain inalienable rights, and that among these are LIFE, LIBERTY, and the PURSUIT OF HAPPINESS." — *Declaration of American Independence.*

Title page of the first novel published by a black American author.

wurm.) Russwurm was one of the editors of *Freedom's Journal,* the first black newspaper printed in the United States.

1834 First black to obtain a patent from the U.S. Patent Office is **Henry Blair** of Greenosa, Maryland. Blair's invention is a corn planter. He later invents a cotton seed planter.

1845 First black lawyer to be formally admitted to the bar is **Macon B. Allen** after he passes the state bar examination in Worcester, Massachusetts. He had practiced law previously for two years in Maine, a state in which no license was required at the time.

1853 First novel written by a black American and published is a work of **W. W. Brown,** entitled *Clotelle A Tale of the Southern States.* The American edition is published by James Redfaith of Boston. The novel is 104 pages and sells for 10 cents.

1860 First professional baseball team to tour various parts of the country is called the **Brooklyn Excelsiors.** They play in cities of New York State (such as Troy, Buffalo, and New York) on a regular basis. On an irregular basis they play in various cities of the South and West.

1861 The first black is wounded in the Civil War—65-year-old **Nicholas Biddle** of Pottsville, Pennsylvania. An escaped slave who has attached himself

to a troop unit heading for the defense of Washington, D.C., he is stoned by an angry mob in Baltimore. His scalp cut to the bone, Biddle manages to escape further injury only with the aid of his white comrades-in-arms.

1862 **Mary Patterson** becomes the first black woman in the United States to earn an M.A. degree, awarded her by Oberlin College.

1863 The first black to be appointed a chaplain in the U.S. Army is **Henry McNeal Turner.**

1865 **Martin R. Delany** becomes the first black to reach the rank of Major in the U.S. Army. A graduate of Howard University Medical School, Delany served in the Medical Corps. He was also a writer.

1865 The first black school below the Mason Dixon Line is established in Lexington, Kentucky—in the same building over which the first Confederate flag was raised in Kentucky.

1865 The selection of the first interracial jury indicts **Jefferson Davis,** former President of the Confederate States of America. On December 3, 1868 the case comes to trial but is dismissed by President Johnson's amnesty proclamation on December 25, 1868.

Bishop Henry Turner was the first black chaplain in the U.S. Army.

The 54th Massachusetts, the only black regiment in the line, led the attack on Fort Wagner on July 18, 1863. Inset shows Nicholas Biddle, the first black wounded in the Civil War.

1865 The first black newspaper in the South—*The Colored American*—is published in Augusta, Georgia, edited by J. T. Shutten.

1865 **John Rock** becomes the first black lawyer to be admitted to practice before the U.S. Supreme Court. His admittance is moved by Senator Charles Sumner of Massachusetts. Chief Justice Salmon P. Chase presides.

1866 First black state representatives to sit in any state legislature are **Charles Lewis Mitchell** and **Edward Garrison Walker** of Boston. Both are elected at the same time to the Massachusetts State Legislature.

1872 The first black delegates to the presidential nominating convention of a major party appear at the Republican Convention in Philadelphia.

1872 The first black midshipman to attend the U.S. Naval Academy is **Henry Conyers** of South Carolina. Conyers did not graduate, however, and left the academy on November 11, 1873.

1872 The first black woman lawyer, **Charlotte E. Roy,** receives her degree from Howard University School of Law in Washington, D.C.

1873 The first black municipal judge, **M. W. Gibbs,** is elected in Little Rock, Arkansas.

1873 **Susan McKinney,** believed to be the first black woman to enter the medical profession formally, is certified as a physician. (Records at the medical college of the New York Infirmary indicate that **Dr. Rebecca Cole** was the first black woman physician in the United States, having practiced from 1872 to 1881.)

1873 **William Monroe Trotter,** becomes Harvard University's first black Phi Beta Kappa and the founder of the Boston Guardian newspaper.

1875 **Oscar Lewis,** is the first black jockey to win the Kentucky Derby. He rode Aristides at Churchill Downs in Louisville.

1879 In Boston, **Mary E. Mattoney** is the first black woman to receive a diploma in nursing from New England Hospital for Women and Children.

1882 The first daily newspaper to be owned by a black, *The Cairo Illinois Gazette,* is published by W. S. Scott.

1884 **Moses Fleetwood Walker** becomes the first black major league baseball player, for Toledo in the American Association.

1884 **John Roy Lynch** becomes the first black to preside over a national political convention, becoming temporary chairman of the Republican Party's national convention after being nominated by Henry Cabot Lodge of Massachusetts. The nomination was seconded by Theodore Roosevelt, Lynch received 424 votes; his opposition, George William Curtis, received 384.

1884 The first black baseball team, the **Cuban Giants,** is formed in New York City by Frank Thompson from a group of black waiters at a Long Island hotel.

1885 First black state legislator to represent a constituency in which the majority are white is **Bishop Benjamin William Arnett** of the AME Church. He represented Green County, Ohio from 1885 to 1887.

1885 The first black Protestant Episcopal Bishop in the United States, the **Reverend Samuel David Ferguson,** is elected to the House of Bishops in 1884 and consecrated at Grace Church in New York City in 1885.

1885 **Jonathan Jasper Wright** is the first black to be elected to the State Supreme Court of South Carolina. He had also been the first black to be admitted to the bar in Pennsylvania.

1890 **Thomy Gafon,** a real estate speculator and moneylender in Louisiana, is probably the first black millionaire in the United States. The *Afro-American Almanac* of 1896 complains that "in politics [Gafon was] rather more conservative than an old-fashioned planter and not at all desirous of seeing the colored people rule the state."

1890 First medical journal written for and by blacks is published in Jackson, Mississippi. The first editor of the publication is **Bandaburst Lynk, M.D.** The journal lasted 18 months.

1892 The first black college football game is played between **Biddle College** and **Livingstone College.** Biddle wins 4 to 0.

1890 **George Dixon** of Halifax, Nova Scotia, becomes the first black to win a world boxing title, when he beats Nunc Wallace in 18 rounds in London. Dixon was a bantamweight.

1903 **Lena Walker** becomes the first black woman bank president. Miss Walker was the founder and chief executive of the Saint Luke Penny Savings Bank in Richmond, Virginia.

1910 First black to be awarded a coveted Rhodes Scholarship is **Alain Leroy Locke** of Philadelphia. Locke received his B.A. degree from Howard University in 1908 and under his Rhodes Scholarship he studied at Oxford University in England. Locke was a certified teacher in the Philadelphia school system.

1918 First black Bishop of the Episcopal Church was **Edward Thomas Demley.**

Fritz Pollard was the first black to play pro football for a major team.

1919 **Fritz Pollard** becomes the first black to play professional football for a major team, the Akron Indians. In 1916 Pollard had been the first black to play in the Rose Bowl, for Brown University.

1926 First black woman lawyer to practice before the U.S. Supreme Court is **Violette M. Anderson** of Chicago.

1929 In the first black post season "bowl" football game in history, the **Prairie View Bowl,** Atlanta University defeats Prairie View 6 to 0.

1931 **Estele Massey Osborne** became the first black recipient in the United States of a masters degree in nursing education. She is a 1931 graduate of Columbia's Teachers College.

1933 The first transcontinental flight by black civilian pilots is made by **Charles Alfred Anderson** of Bryn Mawr, Pennsylvania and **Albert Ernest Forsythe** of Atlantic City.

1935 **Mrs. Gertrude Elise Ayer,** the first black woman to serve as a school principal in the New York City public school system, is appointed to her post at P.S. 24 (Madison Avenue and 128th Street).

1938 **Crystal Bird Fauset** becomes the first black woman elected to a state legislature in the United States, acquiring this distinction when she was named to the Pennsylvania House of Representatives on November 8, 1938. Miss Fauset died in 1965.

In 1940, Hattie McDaniel became the first black to win an Oscar.

1939 First black woman to become a judge, **Jane Matilda Bolin,** is appointed to the bench of the Court of Domestic Relations by Mayor Fiorello La Guardia of New York City.

1940 First black to win an Oscar from the Academy of Motion Pictures Arts and Sciences is **Hattie McDaniel** as best supporting actress for her performance in *Gone with the Wind.* Star billing in the movie went to Clark Gable and Vivian Leigh.

1940 **Benjamin O. Davis, Sr.** is promoted to the rank of brigadier general in 1940, thus becoming the first black to hold this post in the U.S. Army. Born in 1877, career officer Davis made second lieutenant in 1901 and rose through the ranks until he was promoted to full colonel in 1930. He retired in 1948. (His son, Lieutenant General Benjamin O. Davis, Jr. was formerly a general in the Air Force. His last assignment was as chief of staff of U.S. Forces in Korea, and Chief of Staff of the U.N. Commission there. After World War II, Davis was the first black to command an air base—Godman Field in Kentucky. He became the first black general in the history of the Air Force on October 27, 1954.)

1940 The first postage stamp honoring a black, the **Booker T. Washington stamp,** goes on sale at Tuskegee Institute. Valued at 10 cents, the stamp belongs to the Famous American Series and bears a picture

of Washington's head. Its issuance comes at the culmination of a seven-year campaign which had originally been sponsored by Major R. R. Wright, president of the Citizens and Southern Bank and Trust Company of Philadelphia. (Seven years later, a stamp honoring George Washington Carver was issued on the fourth anniversary of the renowned scientist's death. The stamp is of three-cent denomination, and bears a picture of Carver's head.)

1942 **Bernard W. Robinson,** a medical student at Harvard, becomes the first black to be commissioned an officer in the U.S. Navy. Robinson was the first black ensign in the U.S. Naval Reserve.

1943 **Dr. W. E. B. DuBois** becomes the first black admitted to the National Institute of Arts and Letters. At the time of his admittance, Dr. DuBois headed the Department of Sociology at Atlanta University.

1943 The first Liberty Ship named for a black, the **George Washington Carver,** is launched from a New Jersey shipyard to begin its career of carrying war cargo to Europe during WW II.

1944 The USS *Harmon* becomes the first fighting ship of the U.S. named for a black man. Leonard Roy Harmon won the Navy Cross for his heroism aboard the U.S.S. *San Francisco* in a battle with the Japanese near the Solomon Islands. Harmon died of wounds suffered during the engagement.

1944 First black accredited White House news correspondent is **Harry McAlpin,** who represented the *Daily World* of Atlanta, Georgia. He was, as well, the representative for the press service of the Negro Newspaper Publishers Association.

The first U.S. coin and stamps honoring black citizens were issued in the 1940s.

1945 First black nurse to be commissioned in the Navy Reserve Corps is **Phyllis Mae Dolly.** Miss Dolly, a registered nurse from New York City was sworn in as an Ensign.

1945 First black appointed as a Judge of the Custom's Court is **Irving Charles Mollison** of Chicago, Illinois.

1946 **Roy Campanella,** a catcher for Nashua, New Hampshire, in the New England League, becomes the first black to manage an organized baseball team on the field, when the regular manager Walt Alston is evicted from the field by the umpire. Nashua wins the game when a black pitcher, Don Newcombe, hits a pinch hit home run.

1946 The first coin honoring a black was a 50¢ piece which bears a relief bust of **Booker T. Washington,** the founder of Tuskegee Institute. The coin was issued in May, 1946.

1947 **Dan Bankhead** of the Brooklyn Dodgers becomes the first black pitcher in the major leagues. The first black pitcher in the American League follows in 1948. He is **Leroy Satchell Paige** whose age at the time is variously estimated between 41 and 54. Paige wins six, loses one, has an earned run average of 2.47. Though of advanced years, Paige was to have many successful years in the major leagues and then in the minors before his final season with Portland in the Pacific Coast League in 1961.

1947 **Louis Lautier,** Washington Bureau Chief of the Negro Newspaper Publishers Association, becomes the first black issued credentials for both the Senate and the House press galleries. Lautier is admitted to the galleries after a Senate Rules Committee overrode the refusal of the Standing Committee of Newspaper Correspondents to grant him the necessary credentials.

1947 **John Lee** of Indianapolis, Indiana, becomes the first black commissioned officer in the Regular Navy. His first assignment upon being commissioned was on the U.S.S. *Kearsage.*

1948 First appointed black clerk of the Supreme Court of the United States is **William Thaddeus Coleman, Jr.** of Philadelphia. His appointment was made by Supreme Court Justice Felix Frankfurter.

1948 First black commissioned officer in the Regular U.S. Marine Corps is **John Earl Rudder.**

1949 **Wesley A. Brown** becomes the first black to graduate from the Naval Academy at Annapolis. **Henry O. Flipper** became the first black to graduate from West Point on June 15, 1877.

1949 First black pilot in U.S. Naval Reserve is **Jesse Leroy Brown** from Hattiesburg, Virginia. On De-

Jesse L. Brown plays backgammon after becoming the first black U.S. Naval pilot.

cember 4, 1950 at Changjin Reservoir in Korea, Jesse Brown became the first black naval pilot to be killed in action.

1949 **Dr. Peter Marshall Murray** of New York is the first black to be appointed to the American Medical Association's policy-making body.

1949 **Jackie Robinson** becomes the first black baseball player to win his league's "Most Valuable Player" award while with the National League Brooklyn Dodgers. The first black to win the award three times was **Roy Campanella** of the Brooklyn Dodgers, in 1951, 1953, and 1955.

1950 **Gwendolyn Brooks** won the Pulitzer Prize for her volume of poetry. She was the first black woman to win the award and also the first black woman elected to the National Institute of Arts and Letters.

1950 First black judge of a Circuit Court of Appeals is **William Henry Hastie,** who was also the first black to be appointed governor of the American Virgin Islands.

1950 The first black to play in organized hockey is **Arthur Dovington** with the Atlantic City Seagulls of the Eastern Amateur League. He played for only one season, 1950–1951.

1951 The first black Deputy Police Commissioner, **William L. Rowe,** is appointed to this position in New York by Mayor Vincent Impellitieri. He com-

Mayor Impellitieri swears in William Rowe as New York City's first black deputy police commissioner.

pleted his term of service in 1954. Rowe was employed by the *Pittsburgh Courier* newspaper chain for some 16 years before entering government service. As an overseas correspondent he covered World War II from Guadalcanal to Tokyo and was cited for bravery in the Solomon Islands.

1951 **Janet Collins** is the first black to dance for the Metropolitan Opera in New York. Miss Collins, signed by an agent of the company in 1951, made her debut in *Aïda*.

1954 **Dr. James Joshua Thomas** becomes the first black pastor of the Reformed Dutch Church. He is installed as minister of the Mott Haven Reformed Church in the Bronx, New York City.

1954 The first black radio network, called the **National Negro Network,** begins programming. The New York outlet was station WOV. The first program of the network, a soap opera titled *The Story of Ruby Valentine,* starred Juanita Hall and was carried on 40 stations. The program, sponsored by Philip Morris and Pet Milk, ran five days a week.

1955 The first black Methodist minister of an all white congregation is **Reverend Simon Peter Montgomery** of Pineville, South Carolina. At that time he was appointed minister of the Mystic Methodist Church in Old Mystic, Connecticut.

1956 The first athlete to high jump over seven feet

is a black, **Charles Dumas.** The feat is performed at the Coliseum in Los Angeles. At the time Dumas was 19 and a freshman at Compton College.

1958 First black minister with two all-white congregations is the **Reverend Joseph Reed Washington,** who serves as minister of the Methodist Church in Newfield, Maine and in the Congregational Church of West Newfield. The distance between the two churches is three miles.

1958 **Ruth Carol Taylor** becomes the first black airline stewardess. A graduate nurse from Ithaca, New York, Miss Taylor worked for Mohawk Airlines.

1959 **John McLendon** becomes the first black to coach an integrated professional basketball team, the Cleveland Pipers of the National Industrial Basketball League.

1961 First black appointed as a District Court judge is **James Benton Parsons.** Judge Parsons had been a Justice on the State Supreme Council of Illinois.

1962 The first black warship commander, **Lieutenant Commander Samuel L. Gravely,** assumes command of the U.S.S. *Falgout,* a destroyer escort.

1966 **Emmett Ashford,** the first black umpire in the major leagues, makes his debut in the American League inaugural between the Cleveland Indians and the Washington Senators.

Born in Los Angeles, Ashford attended Jefferson High School and Los Angeles City College. Before receiving his major league assignment at the age

Emmett Ashford, the first black umpire in the major leagues.

of 51 (four years before compulsory retirement age), Ashford had umpired in the Dominican Republic for three winter seasons (1958, 1959, 1964), and in several minor leagues as well, including the Pacific Coast League where he was Umpire-in-Chief as of September 1965.

1967 **Bill Russell,** star center of the world-champion Boston Celtics, becomes the first black to direct a major league sports team when he is named to succeed Red Auerbach as coach of that team.

1968 Chairman of the District of Columbia Democratic delegation, **Reverend Channing Phillips,** a favorite son, is placed in nomination for President at the Democratic convention in Chicago. Phillips receives 67½ votes. At the same time, the Peace and Freedom Party of New York State announces that Dick Gregory would run for this office on its ballot.

1968 Archbishop Terence J. Cooke names **Reverend Harold A. Salmon** the first black pastor in the N.Y. Archdiocese and Vicariate Delegate for Harlem in

The first black "Mr. America," Chris Dickerson.

Judge A. Leon Higgenbotham was first black elected as a trustee of Yale University.

1968. Reverend Salmon is put in charge of Harlem's largest parish, St. Charles Borromeo.

1968 **Henry Lewis** is the first black named director of an American orchestra (the Newark-based New Jersey Symphony). Other black conductors—Dean Dixon and Everett Lee—had found regular podiums in Europe; Lewis, however, was the first to be appointed in the United States.

1969 **Joseph L. Searles, III** becomes the first black man proposed for a seat on the New York Stock Exchange. Searles, formerly an aide in the administration of New York City Mayor John Lindsay, had resigned to become one of the three floor traders, as well as a general partner, for Newburger, Loeb & Co.

1969 **Federal Judge A. Leon Higginbotham, Jr.,** is elected a trustee of Yale University, the first black to be so honored. The judge, who succeeded New York's Mayor John Lindsay, defeated five other candidates in nationwide balloting in April and May 1969. Some 25,000 of Yale's 75,000 eligible alumni took part.

1970 **Chris Dickerson** becomes the first black man to win the title "Mr. America," one of 15 bodybuilding titles which Dickerson has earned. Among the others are Mr. California, Mr. Eastern America, Mr. Junior U.S.A. Born one of triplets in Montgomery, Alabama on August 25, 1939, Dickerson was an outstanding athlete throughout his school years, and showed an early interest in a singing career. The desire to improve his voice quality and breath control led him into bodybuilding in the mid-1960s.

1970 **Renard Edwards** becomes the first black musician to play for the Philadelphia Orchestra when he is hired as a violist for the 1970–1971 season. Edwards was formerly with the Symphony of the New World, an integrated orchestra one-third to one-half of whose members are blacks.

1971 **Dr. James Allen Colston** becomes the first black to head a college in New York State (and possibly the first to head a "predominantly white" college in the United States) when he is appointed president of the two-year Bronx Community College in New York City.

1973 **Thomas Bradley** of Los Angeles and **Coleman Young** of Detroit become the first blacks to be elected mayors of cities with populations exceeding one million.

1975 The U.S. Navy commissions **Dr. Donna P. Davis** as a lieutenant in the Navy's medical corps, making Lt. Davis the first black woman physician in the corps history.

1975 **Frank Robinson** becomes the first black man to manage a major league baseball team, and leads his Cleveland Indians to an opening-day victory over the New York Yankees, hitting a home run himself.

1976 **Attorney Ernest A. Finney, Jr.** of Sumpter, South Carolina becomes the state's first black Circuit Court Judge. Finney was selected by fellow lawyers for the judgeship.

1976 **Dr. W. J. Yelder** becomes the first black principal at Selma, Alabama High School. The school board passed over Dr. Yelder in 1975 and appointed Roy Wilson, a white, to the position. However, Federal Judge Bernard Hand ordered the appointment of Yelder after a lengthy legal battle.

1977 **William Bryant** becomes the first black chief U.S. District Court Judge in Washington, D.C. Bryant, a former U.S. District Court judge, appointed by President Lyndon Johnson, had won early fame as a criminal lawyer. He argued the *Mallory* case before the Supreme Court, which led to the decision that arrested criminal suspects must be presented before a magistrate as rapidly as possible.

1978 **Karen Farmer** becomes the first black member of the Daughters of the American Revolution. It was the DAR that refused to allow Marian Ander-

Frank Robinson, the first black to coach a major league baseball team.

son to perform in concert in Washington, D.C. in 1939.

1978 **Right Reverend Emerson Moore, Jr.** named first black monsignor of the Catholic Church in the United States. Monsignor Moore is pastor of St. Charles Borromeo Church in New York City. He was ordained a priest in the historic St. Patrick's Cathedral in 1964.

1979 **John Glover** named first black FBI field office chief in charge of the Milwaukee, Wisconsin FBI office. Glover was the first black agent to be named an inspector at FBI headquarters in Washington, D.C.

1979 U.S. Army **Second Lieutenant Marcella A. Hayes,** a graduate of the University of Wisconsin and the Army ROTC program, earns her aviator wings and becomes the first black woman pilot in U.S. armed services history.

1979 **Loren Monroe** becomes first black named as Michigan's state treasurer. Monroe was born in Thomasville, Georgia and holds degrees in law and accounting.

1979 **Audrey Neal** the first black woman or woman of any ethnic group to become a longshoreman on the eastern seaboard. Neal works at the Bayonne Military Ocean Terminal in New Jersey.

1980 **Dr. Levi Watkins, Jr.** performs the first surgical implantation of the automatic implantable defibrillator in the human heart. The device corrects an ailment known as ventricular fibrillator, or arrhythmia, which prevents the heart from pumping blood.

1981 **Dr. Lenora Cole-Alexander** becomes the first black to head the U.S. Labor Department's Women's Bureau.

1981 **Pamela Johnson** is named publisher of the *Ithaca Journal* and becomes the first black woman to hold such a position with a major newspaper in the United States.

1981 **Dr. Ruth Love** became the first black to serve as superintendent of the Chicago school system. Before her appointment to this top post, Dr. Love held the same position in Oakland, California.

1981 **Lillian Roberts** named the first black woman to head the New York State Labor Department. She was appointed commissioner of the department July 2, 1981.

SLAVERY IN THE AMERICAS

The Transatlantic Slave Trade ■ Slavery in Colonial America ■ The Nation Divided by Slavery (1776–1865) ■ The Great Debate: A Summary of Arguments for and against Slavery ■ Comparisons with Latin America and the Caribbean ■ Slave Conspiracies in the United States with Chronology ■ Leaders of Slave Revolts in the United States ■ Abolition of Slavery by Country and Date

The transatlantic slave trade hoisted its first anchor in 1517 when Spain resolved to encourage immigration to its American possessions by granting each loyal settler the right to own 12 black slaves. Time had already shown that the American Indian was unable to adjust to the rigors of European-administered slavery. Indians died in large numbers, either from disease or from the constant pressure of forced labor, but the African's will to live made him valuable. Most of these early slaves were sent to work on the plantations or in the mines of the Caribbean islands, or in Spanish and Portuguese holdings in South and Central America. Slavery gained its first foothold in the British colonies of North America in 1619, when the settlement of Jamestown, Va., bartered with a Dutch warship for 20 blacks captured from a Latin American slave ship.

While historical headcounts vary, the number of black persons who reached lives of slavery in the New World is now put at around 10 million. Nearly 600,000 were brought in the sixteenth century, 2 million in the seventeenth century, 5 million in the eighteenth century, and 3 million in the nineteenth century. Added to these must be an enormous number who died between capture and their intended arrival in America. It is estimated that 15% died of disease on the noxiously overcrowded "Middle Passage" from Africa to the Caribbean, and another 30% during the brutal three-month training period in the West Indies before they were shipped on to the American mainland.

Although Spain and Portugal were the first powers to import slaves to their colonies, much of the traffic was conducted by the Dutch, French, and British. The majority of the slaves they transported came from the territories of the modern states of Senegal, Gambia, Guinea, Sierra Leone, Liberia, Upper Volta, Ivory Coast, Ghana, Togo, Benin, Nigeria, Cameroon, Gabon, the Congo Republic, and the Republic of the Congo. It is to these lands that most black people now living in the Americas can trace their ancestry.

The African Roots of Slavery

West Africa was the birthplace of three powerful tribal empires: Ghana, Mali, and Songhay. Despite their complexity and advancements, these societies retained the custom of slavery and commonly sold captives taken in war. As early as the ninth century, the Ghanaian king was trading slaves to Arab merchants for goods from the Mediterranean and the East. Although this early slave trade is now believed to have been a two-way affair, the balance gradually shifted. As the

Captives from an enemy tribe being marched to the slave coast of Africa for sale.

centuries passed, the mud-walled city of Timbuktu became both a university and the famous southern hub of trade across the Sahara. Horses, steel, and woven goods came south and were paid for by gold, ivory, cotton, and slaves.

When fifteenth-century Portuguese explorers became the first modern Europeans to reach West Africa by sea, they found slave trading was part of the social fabric, as it was back in Portugal. However, the opening of a direct sea route immediately changed things for the worse. Once the Portuguese began turning over guns for captives, the slave trade became a vicious trap. An African king could not refuse to raid for slaves or the traders would cut off his gun supply, making his own people defenseless before the raids of others. It was in this way that the great Mani-Congo kingdom was brought to ruins. Furthermore, there was an immense difference between the slavery which the Europeans exported and that which had existed in black Africa.

African slavery was not a stigma of human inferiority. As in the ancient world, many slaves were men of accomplishment and learning. Most important, African slavery was not based on race. The gulf between master and slave could be bridged, and often was crossed within a few generations. Dahomean kings were known to choose the sons of slaves to succeed to the throne. West African slavery was more like medieval serfdom than the slavery that developed in the Americas. In these lands, where race became the badge of slavery, the slave's heaviest chain was the color of his skin, his condition became irrevocable for his life and the lives of his descendants, and enslavement began to be taken as a mark of racial inferiority. When, as happened in North America, a race was enslaved by another race, the gulf between master and slave became filled with terrors. Not the least terrible is the schizophrenic barbarization of the whites who grafted a primitive social relationship onto an industrial and civilized society.

THE COLONIAL UNITED STATES: 1619–1787

Europeans who colonized the North American mainland generally intended to settle there for good. They brought their wives and children, and went about building a society for themselves. They were reluctant to import slaves directly from Africa, fearing them too savage and violent. The Caribbean islands, huge plantations where brutal work conditions were the norm, became a midstation at which those blacks were "seasoned" for several months before completing the journey from Africa to the New World.

From Indentured Servant to Slave

Many Europeans (chiefly of English, German, and Scotch-Irish ancestry) who immigrated to the colonies as laborers came as "indentured servants." They had voluntarily bound themselves over to the service of a master for a number of years in payment for passage and board. Most who came involuntarily were debtors and paupers who had been deported and were obliged to work seven years before achieving their freedom. Among them were some children who had been kidnapped, shipped to the colonies, and then sold into service.

The 20 blacks who landed at Jamestown in 1619 were accepted into the community as indentured servants. On the completion of their contracts, they automatically enjoyed the liberties and privileges of the "free laboring class," including the right to own property. Other blacks arrived, and some prospered. Anthony Johnson, who seems to have graduated from servant to freeman by 1622, was rich enough to import five servants of his own by 1651, for which he obtained 250 acres from the colony's government. A black carpenter, Richard Johnson, imported two white servants in 1654 and was given 100 acres. But these men were the exceptions, and the rule they proved was that a fissure was cracking open between black and white servitude.

Beginning in the 1640s, the black ceased to be regarded as a servant and came to be assigned the status of a "chattel slave"—one who remained a fixed item of personal property for the duration of his life. Of three runaways in 1640, two whites were sentenced to four extra years as servants, but a black was given a life term. By the 1650s black chattels were commonly being sold for life, and in 1661 the House of Burgesses formally recognized the institution of black slavery.

The erosion of black indentured servitude followed a similar course in the sister colony of Maryland, where the slave law passed in 1663 was even more specific. "All negroes," the law proclaimed, "or other slaves within the province, [and] all negroes (sic) to be hereafter imported, shall serve *durante vita*."

With the passage of time, white indentured servants gradually disappeared from the colonial labor market, particularly after liberalized legislation enabled them to acquire freedom and land. This accelerated the flow of black workers into the colonies and encouraged planters to institutionalize the notion of perpetual black servitude. Practical considerations for such a move included the fact that black runaways could be detected more easily than fugitive whites. Moreover, since the incoming black was not a Christian, he was regarded as product of a primitive, savage culture, and hence fit for nothing better than an animal's life of unbroken labor. Of course, even when the black later accepted Christianity, his status was in no way altered. As early as 1667 Virginia wrote into statute that "bap-

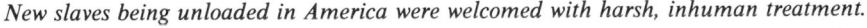

New slaves being unloaded in America were welcomed with harsh, inhuman treatment.

James Otis argued that blacks had just as much right to freedom as whites, an unpopular view since much of the work in the colonies was done by slave labor. Black slaves are shown boiling out sugar cane on a colonial plantation.

tism doth not alter the condition of the person as to his bondage or freedom." Color remained the real cutting edge, and ultimately, in the mind of white colonists, color razored the black man from the ranks of humanity and cast him, once and for all, into the immutable role of slave.

The Spread of Slavery

Of the 13 original colonies, only Pennsylvania put up any sustained opposition to the use of slavery. Rhode Island had an antislavery ordinance on the books, but it was openly violated. And Massachusetts, the cradle of liberty, was actually the first colony to make perpetual bondage legal. Nevertheless, the conditions of slavery differed significantly from North to South.

The New England colonies played a principal role in the slave trade, but they had little reason to buy slaves themselves. By 1700 blacks amounted to only about 1,000 in a population of 90,000. As the economy of the area was diversified, so too were the occupations of the blacks. Many were skilled craftsmen, and there are records of black physicians. Furthermore, the Puritan heritage asserted itself in an Old Testament kind of slavery, which did not deny the slave's existence as a human being. Blacks could own property, they could testify in court against whites, and the law regulated the way a master could treat slaves.

The Mid-Atlantic states were familiar with small slaveholdings; slaves comprised 12% of the population of eighteenth-century New York. In addition to laboring on farms, they worked as domestics and craftsmen. Although the Quakers in Pennsylvania passed laws against the slave trade in 1688, 1693, and 1696—protesting that it violated the principles of Christianity and the rights of man—their statutes were overruled by Parliament in 1712. The behavior of slaves in these colonies was controlled, as in the South, by strict slave codes, under which the slaves were stripped of most rights. Slavery may have been mild in Pennsylvania, but the codes were enforced with frightening severity in New York.

The colonial South was divided into the tobacco-raising provinces of Virginia, Maryland, and North Carolina, and the huge rice and indigo plantations now comprising South Carolina and Georgia. Since tobacco was often raised on family farms, the slave population of the Chesapeake Bay area never reached the intense concentrations created in the deeper South. Terrified of uprisings, slaveholders devised ever harsher slave codes. A slave could not own anything, carry a weapon, or even leave his plantation without a written pass. There were many capital crimes, and small offenses were commonly punished by whipping, maiming, and branding. In the area where 90% of colonial blacks lived, a slave had no rights even to defend himself against a white man, and, as far north as Virginia, it was impossible for a white man to be convicted of the murder of a slave.

The Revolutionary Era and the Constitution

The spirit of revolution that gripped the American continent in the 1770s shook acceptance of slavery. Even the economic structure seemed open to change,

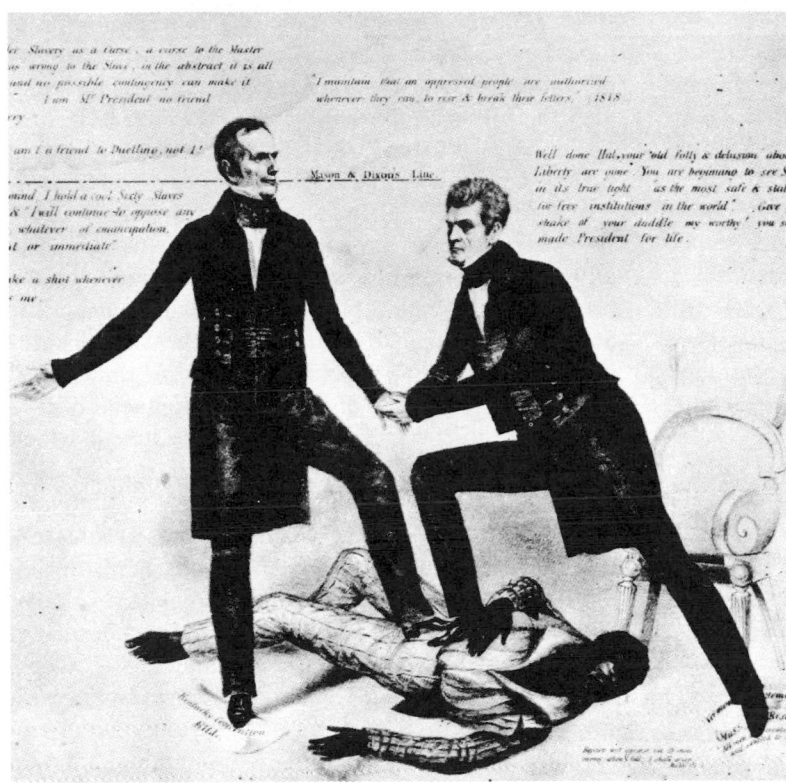

An 1839 cartoon showing southerners Henry Clay (left) and John Calhoun stepping on a slave.

which surrounded him. A slave had no free moments, every gesture was watched, but this means that whites had no free moments either. Inside its glittering plantation houses, the Old South was a nerve-wracked, armed camp, or as Frederick Law Olmstead called it, "a police state."

Abolition

The abortive Nat Turner rebellion of 1831 was a turning point in the history of the black slave. From this point until the outbreak of the Civil War, the slave was relentlessly harassed. Manumission was almost completely suspended.

This period also marked a decline in the "repatriation" movement which had been sponsored largely by the American Colonization Society. The idea of returning free blacks to their "ancestral homeland" had been in part motivated by sincere humanitarian impulses, but it had also had its sinister side. By 1830, the more than 300,000 free blacks in the United States constituted an important element in the population, particularly in the South where their presence struck fear into the planter aristocracy. While Northerners contributed support and donations, Southern patrols were out threatening blacks who were unenthusiastic about emigrating to Liberia.

With the downplaying of repatriation, however, came the creation of the New England Antislavery

Society and publication of the first issue of the crusading abolitionist journal, *The Liberator.* As colonization and manumission lost their momentum, abolition quickly sprang to the fore as a compelling moral alternative, drawing much of its strength from the dedication of an impressive array of leaders, including William Lloyd Garrison, Theodore Dwight Weld, James Forten, Robert Purvis, and David Ruggles. By 1833, the new American Anti-Slavery Society was demanding immediate abolition and stressing the rhetoric of racial equality.

In the South abolition only hardened the already congealed opinion of the slaveholding class. Slavery, said such champions as Thomas Roderick Dew, was necessary for economic survival; it had enabled the white man to create a unique and progressive culture; it was even countenanced by Christianity as a means of converting the black pagan from heathenism. Above and beyond these rationalizations lay the ultimate racist ideology which has characterized the thinking of many whites. The black was, in their view, biologically inferior—a fact which they would at times assert without any seeming malice.

Toward War and Emancipation

As positions polarized and battle lines were drawn, the politics of the slavery question vaulted into the foreground of American life. The Fugitive Slave Act

(1850), the Compromise of 1850, the publication of *Uncle Tom's Cabin* (1852), the Kansas-Nebraska Act (1854), the Dred Scott decision (1857), the Harpers Ferry raid (1859)—these and countless other events were connected with the attempt to resolve the slavery issue.

"Slavery" and "Preservation of the Union" were the paramount issues of the Civil War. It can be said that both questions had to be resolved simultaneously, or not at all. However, Abraham Lincoln, elected to the presidency as a racial moderate in 1860, argued that the federal government had no right to prohibit slavery in the South, and that preserving the Union was the sole issue.

If I could save the Union without freeing any slave, I would do it; if I could save it by freeing all the slaves, I would do it; and if I could save it by freeing some and leaving others alone, I would also do that. What I do about slavery and the colored race, I do because I believe it helps save the Union. . . .

As tension with the South mounted, Lincoln sponsored the Confiscation Act of 1861, which provided for the emancipation of slaves who had been used for insurrectionary purposes in the South. Within two years, free black regiments were responding to the Union slogan that they could at last fight for their own freedom.

By May 1862 Lincoln was prepared to move even closer to the position advocated by the Radical Republicans: complete abolition. In September of that year, the President issued a preliminary Emancipation Proclamation—holding out to slaveowners the possibility of compensation, and continuing to suggest to freedmen the prospect of voluntary colonization in Africa.

On January 1, 1863, a further proclamation declared that all slaves living in the *seceded states* of the Confederacy were to be "thenceforward, and forever free." It conferred legal, though not actual, emancipation on three-fourths of the slave population, yet made no provisions for some 800,000 blacks living outside the South who remained technically enslaved. Constitutional emancipation did not come *for all slaves* until 1865 with the passage of the thirteenth amendment—the single, all-embracing legislative enactment which brought the United States steps closer to its motto: "Land of the Free."

The story of the black freedman during Reconstruction, and of the black population in general during the twentieth century, belongs to another province of American history. For our purposes, slavery as a *legal* concept ended in the year 1865, although its repercussions continue to plague our society down to our own time.

THE GREAT DEBATE: ARGUMENTS FOR AND AGAINST SLAVERY

Civilized man has produced several arguments in favor of, or violently opposed to, the institution of slavery. We attempt here to indicate them in summary form.

As Northern armies advanced near their plantations, scores of slaves slipped away to seek the Union lines and freedom.

Slaves being herded to a Deep South auction house.

In Defense of Slavery

The established classes within most ancient and medieval societies assumed that certain groups of people were inherently inferior. In modern times, this theory is embodied in the term "white supremacy."

Agricultural and industrial surpluses could not be produced, nor could public works projects or cultural monuments be undertaken, without use of slave labor. Slavery was needed to create wealth and grandeur.

The advancement of culture, thought to be the natural province of the "leisure class," could not exist unless menial and commonplace services were provided by a laboring class.

Slave ownership was a primary attribute of power and distinction within certain societies.

Slavery afforded Christianity a means of converting the slave from paganism.

Slavery was profitable to those engaged in the trade. Their well-being was not isolated but contributed instead to the good fortune of others.

In Opposition to Slavery

The inherent inferiority of any group of people cannot be scientifically demonstrated.

Slavery was morally indefensible, since it involved the denial of two inalienable rights: personal freedom and equality of birth.

Slavery was inhumane, awakening the most brutal instincts within the slaveowner.

Slavery caused the physical, mental, and moral degradation of the slave.

Slavery was contrary to such Christian principles as brotherly love and the sanctity of the individual in the sight of God.

Slavery deprived the slave of a sense of identity and pride, causing him to lose confidence in his own capacities—intellectual and otherwise.

COMPARISONS WITH LATIN AMERICA

Slavery in Spanish and Portuguese colonies was regulated by a code of laws that stretched back to Roman

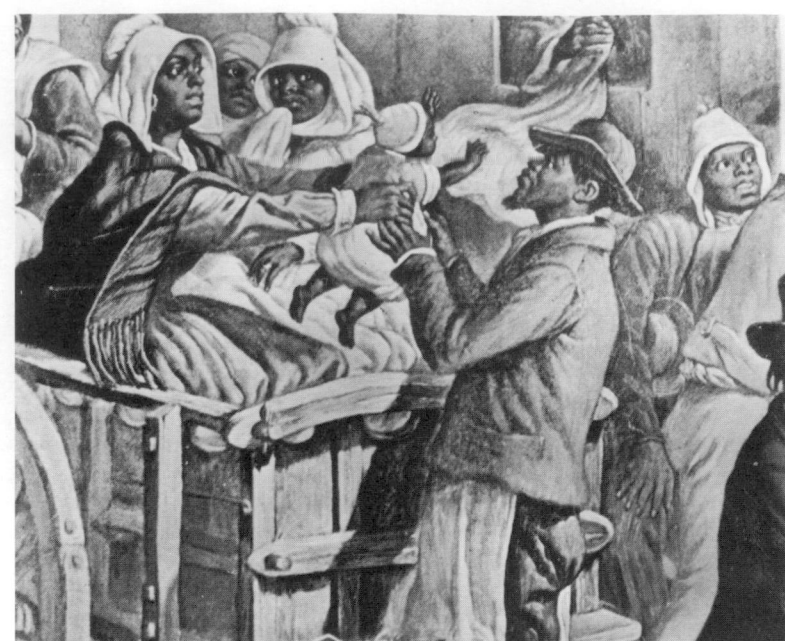

A slave family being separated by sale at the railroad station. A chief difference between North and South American slavery was that slave families had no legal rights in the United States.

traditions and had been influenced by Church jurists. Instead of allowing considerable local autonomy, as the British did, the Iberian crowns regulated overseas affairs with a paternal hand. Slaves were numbered among the monarch's subjects, not simply considered property to be disposed of as the owner wished. The Church, accepting slavery as a labor system, zealously exercised her role as guardian of public morals to insure that slaves were treated as human beings. Not only was missionary activity intense, but human rights were upheld.

Many historians argue that the Latin American system was far more humane than that of the British colonies. While North American slaves were rarely given their freedom, manumission was a common practice in Latin countries, favored by both law and social approval. While North American jurists ruled that preventing the separate sale of family members would tamper with owners property rights—putting property higher than slave marriage—the South American church insisted that slave unions be sacramentalized, and Latin law forbade the separate sale of husband, wife, and children under the age of 10. While North American courts refrained from interfering in the master's nearly absolute power over his slaves, South American justice took an active role. Slave crimes were prosecuted in court, and if a slave was murdered the case was often tried as if the victim had been a free citizen. Mistreatment could not only cost the master fines but win freedom for the slave. Finally, South American slaves could own property and were guaranteed times in which they could work for themselves.

In retrospect, North American slaves were consis-

tently regarded as objects, with both laws and customs pushing them deeper and deeper into the role of "thing," whereas South American societies made some effort to protect the slave's humanity.

The conclusion that Latin American slavery was more humane has been disputed, however. Certain historians point to the fact that in Brazil, the largest importer of slaves to the south, the death rate was much higher than in the United States, as were suicides, and that there was also intense dehumanization, many slaves being forced by owners to wear masks, a practice rare in the United States. These historians also cite the frequency of Latin American slave resistance, which sometimes took the form of wholesale insurrections. In the 1550s, for example, there were frequent outbreaks of violence in Cartagena (Colombia). During the seventeenth century, similar upheavals occurred in Bahia and Rio de Janeiro, despite the fact that blacks in these areas enjoyed a relative measure of well-being at that time. It may be suggested in reply that greater well-being, and the sharper sense of human rights it gave to the slaves, would encourage rebellion, whereas slaves who were absolutely crushed would be unlikely to revolt.

One factor enhancing Brazil's reputation for humane slavery was the emergence of a mulatto class which, after emancipation, rose to a respectable and fairly secure place in Brazilian society, while in the United States mulattoes were defined out of the white world as bearers of black blood. A major cause of this exclusion was that blacks were always a minority in the English mainland colonies—never more than 20% of the overall population of what was to become the United States—while in Brazil, Europeans (especially European women) were always in the minority. As a result, white women on the northern continent were more influential within the social structure, and thus in a position to prevent widespread miscegenation. In Brazil, more European men had children by female slaves, and were more ready to acknowledge their offspring. Ultimately, it is hard to gauge how frequently the mixture of races occurred in the United States because of the social sanctions against it.

Another difference between the American continents was that in the United States, despite notable exceptions, slaves were largely confined to agricultural labor, while in Latin America they were needed in skilled trades. In the north, these trades were mostly filled by whites and often rigidly segregated to preclude competition, a practice that worsened as abolition gained ground and after the collapse of Reconstruction.

The Caribbean

Scholars are tantalized by the great disparity between slavery on the English islands of the Carribean and slavery in the English provinces of the North American mainland. Caribbean slavery, after the discovery of the value of sugar around 1650, became one of the most brutal systems of servitude known to history. The death rate of blacks was enormous, as the grossest and most avaricious of Englishmen were attracted to the quick wealth and wild living style the islands then offered. By 1680, almost all the 40,000 slaves in Barbados worked for some 175 planters, and by 1700, in the West Indies, six major islands held some 270,000 black slaves under the control of a few hundred whites.

Wherever possible these overcrowded warrens spurred revolt. In Jamaica alone, there were six major uprisings between 1650 and 1700.

Of the English mainland colonies, South Carolina appears to have been closest in economy and style to Barbados and Jamaica. By 1700, as rice became an important crop and adventurers moved from the West Indies to develop it, blacks comprised a majority of the population.

Slavery, of course, developed differently over time and space, a fact often overlooked in the passions with which the "peculiar institution" has been attacked and defended. In Virginia, in the seventeenth century, slavery developed slowly, whites consistently outnumbering blacks by 6 and 7 to 1. White slaveholders often worked beside blacks and encouraged their mastery of trades to better contribute to the self-sufficient life style then prized in Virginia. However, skilled slaves were the most rebellious, the most able to plot, forage, and escape successfully, a factor that contributed to restrictions on the trades blacks could pursue and to

limitations on manumission and the liberties of free blacks. It was these "mobile" blacks who stunned Virginia with the skill and intensity of the planned Prosser uprising of 1800.

SLAVE CONSPIRACIES IN THE UNITED STATES

Slave rebellions in the West Indies were larger and more successful than those on the North American mainland. In the U.S. South, whites outnumbered blacks and maintained the solid front of a unified ruling class, unconcerned until the Civil War about invasion from the outside. The Indies were far less stable politically and militarily, and in many areas the population was overwhelmingly black. Thus large effective societies consisting of escaped slaves existed throughout the Caribbean. In some cases rebellious slaves had been trained to fight for their captors as soldiers, a factor that was rare in the United States.

However, the growing list of rebellions and communities of escaped blacks in the United States refutes for all time the picture of the American slave as docile and content.

Little is known specifically of slave revolts between the seventeenth and nineteenth centuries, and only three major uprisings have been documented. These were led by Prosser, Vesey, and Turner, whose brief biographies are listed below. A fourth famous revolt, Cinque's capture of the *Amistad*, occurred off the coast of Cuba.

Other slave leaders are known only remotely, by a name or poster, posted briefly on a pole or courthouse. From the skimpy records of available history, *The Negro Almanac* has compiled the following list of slave uprisings prior to the Civil War.

CHRONOLOGY OF U.S. SLAVE REBELLIONS AND CONSPIRACIES, 1663–1863

1663 Servant betrays first serious plot of black slaves and white servants in Gloucester, Va.

1687 A planned uprising by a group of slaves to take place during a funeral was quelled in northern Virginia.

1691 Mingoe, an escaped slave from Middlesex County, and his followers attack white settlement in Rappahannock County, Va., for food and ammunition.

1711 Sebastian, an escaped slave, leads maroon attacks on a white South Carolina community. In 1729, an Indian hunter tracks and kills him.

1712 Slave revolt in New York results in the death of nine whites and the execution of 21 slaves.

1730 In Williamsburg, Va., a black rebellion was precipitated when a rumor circulated to the effect that all baptized persons would be set free.

1739 Other revolts in South Carolina are squashed, 44 of a band on the way to St. Augustine, Fla. perished in an ambush, more than 30 of the slaves led by Cato at Stono River are killed. A third insurrection with no record of casualties took place in Berkeley County, S.C.

1741 Reports of slave conspiracy in New York City lead to execution of 31 slaves and five whites.

1771 Bands of fugitive slaves commit robberies in Savannah and Ebenezer, leading to a joint effort by militiamen and Indians against them.

1786 Band of slaves promised freedom for service by British formed a group called soldiers of the King of England and carry on guerrilla warfare on banks of Savannah River. Their settlement is attacked by militia from Georgia and South Carolina, with heavy casualties suffered.

1792 In Chesterfield and Charles City counties, Va., maroons are tracked down after flurries of marauding. Ten runaways are captured with the help of dogs.

1795 General of the Swamps, maroon leader and five of his group are killed by hunting party.

1800 Conspiracy of Gabriel Prosser and some 1,000 followers betrayed by two slaves. Gabriel and 15 others hanged.

1802 Tom Copper, leader of maroon camp in Elizabeth City, North Carolina, instigates insubordination among slave population.

1811 Slave revolt in Louisiana suppressed by U.S. troops.

1811 A community of runaways settled in Cabarras County, N.C. resolved to hold out against any force was wiped out.

1812 During July 80 slaves escape from Georgia to go east to Florida, arousing them. In September, Captain Williams and 20 men, on their way to assist Colonel Smith, were routed, attacked, and killed by maroons and Indians. In February 1813, after numerous battles a black fort is destroyed.

1816 Black fort on Appalachicola Bay destroyed by cannon after 10-day siege; 270 men, women, and children are killed.

1816 In Ashepoo, S.C. a large maroon community which carried on continuing plundering missions is defeated by Major-General Youngblood. Large numbers of blacks are killed and captured.

1818 Andrey, alias Billy James, a.k.a. Abaellino, leader of some 30 runaway slaves, has a $100 reward

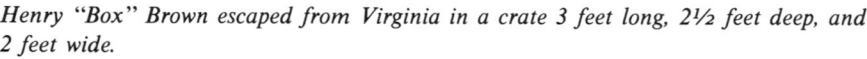

Henry "Box" Brown escaped from Virginia in a crate 3 feet long, 2½ feet deep, and 2 feet wide.

Many runaway slaves fled to the depths of the Dismal Swamp in North Carolina.

posted on him for carrying on attacks in Princess Anne County, Va.

1819 The slave outlaw Harry, leader of a runaway slave company, is killed by whites on an expedition against maroons. Harry had a reward of $200 on his head.

1819 Slaves in Augusta, Ga., planned to burn the city. Their leader, Coco, also known as Coot, was caught and executed.

1821 Rebellion led by Isam, alias General Jackson, took place through concerted activities of maroon groups in Onslow, Carteret, and Bladen counties in North Carolina. Joint action planned by outlaws, field hands, and some free blacks against slaveholders. It took 300 militiamen 23 days to subdue the insurrection.

1822 Betrayal by a house slave of Denmark Vesey conspiracy involving thousands of blacks in Charleston, S.C. and environs. Four whites, 131 blacks arrested; 37 hanged (including Vesey and five of his aides).

1823 Bob Ferebee, outlaw slave leader, captured and executed.

1827 In Mobile County, Ala., maroon community built a stockade fort which fell after a three-day attack by armed slaveholders.

1829 Race riot in Cincinnati, Ohio. More than 1,000 blacks migrate to Canada.

1830 Maroon communities cause insubordination in Sampson, Bladen, Onslow, New Hanover, and Dublin counties, N.C. According to one leader, Moses, an uprising was planned with considerable arms, ammunition, runners, and food supply.

1831 Nat Turner Revolt in Southampton County, Va. results in the death of 60 whites. Turner is captured and hanged.

1836 Squire, leader of a three-year-old group of maroons near New Orleans, is killed by a guard of soldiers.

1841 Slave revolt on *Creole,* a ship en route from Hampton, Va. to New Orleans. The slaves sail the vessel to the Bahamas, where they are granted asylum and emancipated.

1859 John Brown and his followers (13 whites and five blacks) attack Harpers Ferry. Of the five blacks, two are killed, two are captured, and one escapes.

LEADERS OF SLAVE REVOLTS IN THE UNITED STATES

GABRIEL PROSSER
Slave Insurrectionist
1775?–1800

Little is known of the early life of Gabriel Prosser. Born around 1775, he was a coachman belonging to Thomas Prosser of Henrico County, Va.

The revolt which Prosser planned was remarkable not only for the skill of its organization but also for the large numbers of people who were to take part in it. The environs of Richmond, Va.—chosen as the site of the rebellion—had some 32,000 slaves, but only 8,000 whites, including a number of French and Quakers, groups which Prosser felt would be sympathetic to his cause.

Prosser planned the revolt for the end of August, reasoning that there would be plenty to eat at the harvest, and that his followers would thus be spared any shortage of important supplies. He intended to kill all slaveowners but to spare the French, Quakers, elderly women, and children. Eventually, he hoped that the remaining 300,000 slaves in Virginia would follow his lead and take over the entire state.

The plans laid, it was decided to meet at the Old Brook Swamp outside of Richmond on the last night of August, and to martial forces there for the attack on the city. A severe rainstorm, however, made it impossible for many of the slaves to assemble, and the plot was betrayed by a pair of house slaves who did not wish their master killed.

Panic quickly swept Richmond, and martial law was declared. Most slaves implicated in the conspiracy were rounded up and hanged, at least until it became apparent that this procedure would soon decimate the area's slave population. Less severe sentences were then meted out by the courts.

Prosser himself was captured in the hold of the schooner *Mary* when it docked at Norfolk after a trip from Richmond. Brought back in chains, he was interrogated by the governor but refused to divulge any information on the nature of his plans or on the identities of his compatriots. Prosser was hanged on October 7, 1800.

DENMARK VESEY
Slave Insurrectionist
1767–1822

Another serious uprising of the nineteenth century was led by Denmark Vesey, a slave who for 20 years had sailed with his master, Captain Vesey, to the Virgin Islands and Haiti, the latter an independent island ruled by blacks.

Born in 1767, Vesey was sold by his master at an early age but later repurchased because he was an epileptic. Vesey enjoyed a considerable degree of mobility in his native Charleston, S.C., eventually securing his own freedom by paying his master $600 of a $1,500 sum won in a lottery. He later became a Methodist minister, using his church as a base from which to recruit supporters for his plan to take over Charleston—a plan set to go into operation on the second Sunday in July of 1822.

Nat Turner plotting his insurrection.

As in the case of Prosser, the Vesey plan was betrayed by a slave who alerted the white authorities of the city. Hundreds of blacks were quickly rounded up, and Vesey himself was taken prisoner after a two-day search.

Vesey, who was literate, was extremely adept at cross-examining witnesses at his trial but was unable to deny that his intended purpose was the overthrow of the city. Sentenced to death, he was hanged with some of his co-conspirators on July 2, 1822.

Some of Vesey's collaborators probably escaped to fight as maroons in the Carolinas.

NAT TURNER
Slave Insurrectionist
1800–1831

Nat Turner, the best-known of the three major slave revolutionaries, was strongly drawn by a kind of visionary mysticism through which he heard "voices" and believed in a special destiny. An avid reader of the Bible, he also prayed, fasted, and ultimately felt that God wanted him to conquer Southampton County in Virginia.

Recruiting a handful of conspirators, Turner struck isolated white homes within his immediate area and, within 48 hours, had built up his band to 60 armed men. Terrorizing the county, they killed 55 whites before deciding to attack the county seat of Jerusalem.

While en route, Turner's men were overtaken by a posse and dispersed, with Turner himself taking refuge in the forbidding confines of what was known as the Dismal Swamp. Remaining there for six weeks, he was finally captured, brought to trial, and, along with 16 other blacks, sentenced to death by hanging.

JOSEPH CINQUE
Amistad Mutineer
1811–1852

In Havana, Cuba, in 1839, Joseph Cinque, an African who had been sold into slavery there, was purchased by some Spaniards and put aboard a ship, the *Amistad,* for transportation to Puerto Principe. The *Amistad* was caught in a storm, and the crew exhausted itself keeping the ship afloat. Noting the opportunity, Cinque led the other slaves in seizing the ship. They killed the entire crew except for two men left alive to navigate. Cinque ordered a course set for Africa but had no knowledge of navigation and did not realize that his captives headed north rather than east. The ship was sighted off Long Island and taken to port in Connecticut, where the blacks were put in prison.

However, abolitionists took up their cause. Cinque was released and went on a lecture tour to raise funds for judicial appeals. Cinque spoke in the Mendi lan-

Joseph Cinque, painted from life by Nathaniel Jocelyn.

guage, which was translated, and became known as an excellent speaker. In 1841, with John Quincy Adams presenting their case, the Supreme Court ruled that the slaves be released.

Together with five white missionaries, Cinque returned to Africa.

ABOLITION OF SLAVERY BY DATE AND COUNTY

The first European nation to abolish slavery in the New World was France (1794), which provided for the theoretical, if not actual, emancipation of all slaves in the French West Indies. The distinction of being the first nation in the Western Hemisphere actually to do away with slavery belongs to Haiti (1804). Slavery was abolished in England in 1772, and the British slave trade halted in 1807. It was not until 1833, however, that Parliament passed an act eliminating slavery, after payment of compensation to slaveowners, in all British overseas possessions including Canada, the mainland colonies in Central and South America, and the island colonies in the Caribbean. The measure was not fully enforced until 1838.

On the Spanish and Portuguese mainland colonies the abolition of slavery was linked with the independence struggles of various subject territories. Slaves were freed in the United Provinces of Central America (1824); in Mexico (1829); in Latin America, to all intent and purpose, by 1855; in Cuba (1886); and in Brazil (1888). In Spain and Portugal themselves, slavery was declared illegal in 1872 and 1856, respectively.

England—1771 Legal decision; 1833 Act of Parliament
France—1794 (ineffectively enforced in colonies)
British Colonies—1807 (measure enforced in 1838)
Haiti—1804
Jamaica—1804
British Guiana—1827
Mexico—1829

Bolivia—1831
Uruguay—1842
West Indies—1842
Colombia—1851
Venezuela—1854
Paraguay—1862
United States—1865
Puerto Rico—1873
Cuba—1898
Brazil—1888
Spain—1872
Portugal—1856
Russia—1851
Peru—1860

SUB-SAHARAN AFRICA: THE EMERGING NATIONS

A Brief History ■ Africa and Oil ■ Chronology (3000 B.C.–A.D. 1982) ■ Sub-Saharan Nations ■ North African Nations ■ European Dependencies

With the independence of Angola, Mozambique, and The Cape Verde Republic in the mid-1970s, all but one of Africa's 47 Sub-Saharan nations had achieved independence from colonial rulers.

In many of these new nations, events following independence were more tumultuous than the struggle for freedom itself. Nearly two-thirds of the new nations experienced nonconstitutional changes in their governments and more than half came under the control of military leaders.

However, such brutal dictators as Amin of Uganda and Bokassa of the Central African Republic were eventually deposed by more moderate leaders. Other nations, such as Tanzania, Gambia, Botswana, Kenya, and Ivory Coast have experienced relatively stable leadership from the first days of independence.

Some areas suffered from wars. Chad was invaded by Libya and Eritrea continues its long war of secession from Ethiopia which had annexed it in 1962. A long dispute rages between Morocco, Mauritania, and indigenous forces over control of the Western Sahara. In Namibia, South Africa and forces seeking unconditional self-determination continue the guerrilla war which dates back to the 1960s.

In several areas conflict between the United States and the USSR has intensified. Both powers seek to establish military facilities at various strategic points along Africa's 19,000-mile coastline, particularly in East Africa. In 1980 the U.S. State Department reported that 37,000 Cuban military personnel were acting as Soviet proxies in 14 African nations, most heavily in Angola and Ethiopia. However, some nations previously identified with anti-western policies, among them Guinea, Mozambique, Somalia, and Zimbabwe are seeking to expand trade and technical relations with the West.

Because of its prolonged, extreme, and rigid policies of racial segregation, the Union of South Africa remains a nation of profound interest to blacks in the United States. In the spring of 1982 the Union's Prime Minister P. W. Botha suggested that the country establish a new constitution to moderate some of his country's more stringent racial policies. Though Botha was attacked from the right for merely suggesting modifications of apartheid, blacks were skeptical that concessions would be no more than window dressing.

AFRICA—AN OVERVIEW

Sub-Saharan Africa encompasses some 9.3 million of Africa's 11.6 million square miles and 340 million of its 400 million inhabitants. It includes all but six most

northern and most Arabic of the continent's nations: Egypt, Libya, Algeria, Tunisia, Morocco, and Western Sahara. Most of the area is situated in tropical latitudes and a great deal of it is desert.

In recent years archeologists have come to believe modern man originated in Africa some 2½ million years ago and eventually expanded to other continents. Three racial groups, Bushmanoid, Pygmoid, and Negroid developed, with the latter becoming dominant through its skills in hunting, farming, and domesticating animals. A group classified linguistically as *Niger Congo* came to control much of Southern Africa. Other subgroups speaking Bantu extended to the East, dominating and almost eliminating the Pygmoid and Bushmanoid people.

During much of this period, Caucasoids moved from Europe and the Near East into North and Northeast Africa. Bedouins came in the seventh to tenth century, and between the tenth and eighteenth centuries large numbers of Moslems emigrated to East Africa.

Sophisticated societies developed, among them the Kush, between 700 B.C. and A.D. 200 and the ancient Ghana, Kanen, Mali Songhai, and the Haissa states. In the Congo, the Kingdoms of Lunda, Lula, Bushong, and Kongo were founded, probably between the sixteenth and eighteenth centuries. On the Guinea Coast, the city states of Benin, Ite, Oyo, Ashanti, and Yoruba date back to the fifteenth century. These states traded extensively in gold, ivory, salt, and livestock.

Significant trade with Europe started in the fifteenth century, with the slave trade an important part. An estimated 10 to 30 million people were sold into slavery by the mid-nineteenth century.

The interior of Africa was first exposed to Europeans in the eighteenth century by missionaries, traders, and adventurers. Their reports of Africa's resources eventually spurred European conquest and direct control of virtually all of Sub-Saharan Africa. Between 1879 and 1900 most of the continent was conquered. By 1900 only Ethiopia and Liberia, of the current 47 Sub-Saharan nations, were free of European control. The Union of South Africa achieved a large measure of independence in 1910 when the British granted it dominion status.

Freedom for black-dominated regions, however, was withheld until a decade after World War II. In 1957, independence movements started with a rush in Kenya, Ghana, and Guinea. (By 1980, only one country remained under foreign control.)

Population

Sub-Saharan population is most heavily concentrated in Nigeria, Southern Ghana, along the Gulf of Guinea, Benin and Togo, the Nile Valley, in Northern Sudan, the East Africa highlands of Ethiopia, Rwanda, Burundi and Tanzania, eastern Zaire, the eastern and southern coasts, and the inland High Veld of South Africa.

The desert and mountain regions are largely uninhabited. Population growth is rapid, estimated as 2 to 3% annually; the urbanization rate is 11%. Until recently, 90% of Africa's people lived in rural areas. In 1978 African cities with populations exceeding 1 million included Accra, Ghana; Addis Ababa, Ethiopia; Cape Town and Johannesburg, South Africa; Ibadan and Lagos, Nigeria; and Kinshasa, Zaire.

About 5 million people of predominantly European descent and one million Asians live in Africa. Life expectancy in Africa in 1980 was 43 years. In the rest of the developing world it was 53 and in the United States, 71. Illiteracy is estimated at 80%.

The diversity of Africa's people is underscored by the existence of over 800 languages and dialects, only less than 10 of which are used by over 1 million persons.

Economy

Africa produces 95% of the world's diamonds, 87% of its cobalt, 65% of its gold, and 54% of its chrome. Agricultural development has been notably successful in Kenya and Ivory Coast. Nigeria and Angola are major producers of oil.

However, poverty has been extreme, especially in arid, landlocked areas such as Chad, Mali, and Upper Volta. Africa's overall per capita food production declined by 1.4% annually in the 1970s and serious grain shortages are in prospect for 1990 if this trend is not reversed. In 1978 the average daily food intake for Africans was very low—1950 calories with 55 grams of protein, and these figures were declining.

Agricultural development has been hindered by deforestation by colonial rulers, poor transportation, and political policies designed to hold down food prices.

Another problem is that many African nations suffer from economic dependence on a single export product and are thus very sensitive to fluctuations in world markets. Nigeria, for example, is heavily dependent on oil and suffered severely during the oil glut of 1981.

United Nations; Supranational Organizations

In 1980 all independent Sub-Saharan nations belonged to the United Nations, collectively comprising nearly 30% of the General Assembly's membership of 152.

The most notable African organization is the Organization of African Unity, formed in 1963. Based in Addis Ababa, the OAU seeks to form an African concensus on major world issues and to further the economic development of African nations. OAU has four important organizational components: an Assembly of Heads of State and Government; a Council of (Foreign) Ministers; the General Secretariat; and a Commission of Mediation, Conciliation and Arbitration.

As with other major international groups, the OAU has had little success in resolving major disputes, but remains important as a forum for dialogue and negotiation on major issues.

CHRONOLOGY OF IMPORTANT EVENTS IN AFRICAN HISTORY: 3000 B.C.–A.D. 1975

3000 B.C. Tasili Frescoes, rock murals located in southeast Algeria, give evidence of an early black pastoral civilization (believed to date back to 6000 B.C.).

1200 B.C. Beginnings of Nok culture (in Nigeria): an advanced black civilization with a great tradition of terra cotta sculpture (lasting until 200 B.C.).

1100 B.C. The Phoenicians found the city of Utica in Tunisia.

813 B.C. The Phoenicians found the city of Carthage, a center of trade in North Africa and later a bitter rival of the Roman Empire.

650 B.C. Beginnings of the Kingdom of Axum in Ethiopia (lasting until A.D. 650.).

631 B.C. The Greeks found the city of Cyrene in North Africa.

470 B.C. Hanno of Carthage explores the coast of West Africa as far south as Sierra Leone.

350 B.C. Meroe, the capital of ancient Nubia, falls to Ethiopia.

332 B.C. Conquest of Egypt by Alexander the Great, who later builds the city of Alexandria.

168 B.C. Colonization of Egypt by Rome.

A.D. 100 Introduction of Christianity into North Africa.

300 Beginnings of the kingdom of Ghana in the Western Sudan.

320 Introduction of Christianity in the Kingdom of Axum (present-day Ethiopia).

800 Founding of Arab colonies in Madagascar and Zanzibar; organization of Arab expeditions into East Africa in search of slaves.

800 Zenith of the black kingdom of Ghana—extending from the Atlantic coast to Timbuktu, "the land of gold" (lasting until 1240).

1000 Zenith of the Great Zimbabwe civilization of Rhodesia, site of a highly developed black culture marked by architectural wonders.

1054 Beginnings of the conquest of West Africa by Moslem Berber tribes.

1100 Zenith of the Songhai kingdom of West Africa, with its capital at Timbuktu.

1147 Conquest of portions of North Africa by the Almohades, fierce Berber Moslems who establish hegemony over the region.

1269 Fall of the Berber's North African Empire.

1300–1500 Zenith of Ife, a holy city in Nigeria noted for its fine sculpture.

1307 West Africa ruled by Mandingo Empire, successor to the Ghana and Songhai kingdoms.

1350 Beginnings of Benin, seat of a royal court and Nigerian city famed for bronze sculpture (lasting until 1897).

1400 Emergence of a Baluba Kingdom in the Congo.

1415 Arrival of Portuguese in West Africa; beginnings (under Prince Henry the Navigator) of trade with, and exploration of, West Africa.

1471 Portuguese begin mining of precious metal on "Gold Coast."

1482 Portuguese colonize Angola.

1488 Portuguese explorer, Bartholomew Diaz, reaches Cape of Good Hope at the southern tip of Africa.

1491 Portuguese explorer, Vasco da Gama, rounds the Cape, and sails up the East African coast en route to Asia.

1493–1529 Defeat of Mandingos by the Songhai Empire, headed by Askia Mohammed.

1503–1507 Loe Africanus of Morocco explores the Sudan.

1508–1515 Portuguese colonize Mozambique.

1513–1517 Conquest of Hausa states by Songhai Empire; blacks succeed Arabs, and form Hausa Confederation to carry on prosperous trade (West Africa).

1571–1603 Zenith of Kanem (Bornu) Empire in Lake Chad region, West Africa.

1590–1618 Defeat of Songhai by Moroccans who gain control over much of West Africa.

1592 England's Sir John Hawkins plays active role in slave trade between Africa and the Americas.

1618 Pedro Paez of Spain discovers the source of the Blue Nile in Ethiopia.

1652 Founding by the Dutch of Cape Town, South Africa.

1660 Rise of the Bambara Kingdom in Niger (West Africa).

1672 Founding in England of the Royal Africa Company for the cultivation of trade in West Africa.

1697–1893 Rise of Ashanti Kingdom (noted for its high-quality gold work) in what is now Ghana.

1713 Asiento Treaty enables British to monopolize slave trade to Latin America.

1787 Great Britain acquires Sierra Leone (West Africa) through treaties with local chieftains.

1795 England's Mungo Park explores Gambia, the Niger River regions, and the interior of West Africa.

1807 Great Britain abolishes the slave trade.

1808 Sierra Leone becomes a British Crown Colony, with Gambia falling under its administration.

1814 Great Britain secures possession of the Cape of Good Hope through the Peace of Paris.

1815 France, Spain, and Portugal abolish the slave trade.

1821 Sierra Leone, Gold Coast, and Gambia are united to form British West Africa.

1822–1827 Hugh Clapperton and Dixon Denham explore the Sudan, Nigeria, and other territories in West Africa.

1827 Rene Caillie of France reaches Timbuktu.

1835–1837 The Great Boer Trek from the Cape Colony to the Transvaal (South Africa).

1840–1870 Dr. David Livingstone explores Central Africa, discovering Lakes Ngami and Nyasa, and reaching the Upper Zambezi River.

1845–1855 Heinrich Barth of Germany leads scientific expeditions into the Sahara and the Sudan.

1847 Liberia becomes the first independent republic in Africa.

1858 Richard Burton and John Speke of England discover Lake Tanganyika.

1861–1864 Samuel Baker of England discovers Lake Albert and Murchison Falls and explores the Nile's tributaries in Ethiopia.

1867–1871 The discovery of diamonds in South Africa; Kimberly becomes the center of the diamond industry and the mecca for fortune hunters.

1869 Gustav Nachtigal of Germany explores the central Sahara.

1871 Great Britain annexes the Orange Free State (South Africa).

1873–1874 Great Britain conquers the Ashanti Kingdom of the Gold Coast region.

1874–1889 Henry Morton Stanley explores the Congo River from its source to its mouth.

1875–1883 Pierre de Brazza of France explores southern and western Africa; founds Brazzaville.

1876 Exploitation of the Congo begins under King Leopold II of Belgium.

1877 Annexation of the Transvaal (South Africa) by Great Britain.

1878–1890 Emin Pasha (Eduard Schnitzer) of Germany explores Central Africa.

1879 Outbreak of the British–Zulu war, with British winning decisive victory at Ulundi.

1880 Founding of Brazzaville in the Congo by France.

1881 Tunisia accepts status as French protectorate (Treaty of Bardo).

1884 Germany annexes Southwest Africa; establishes control over Cameroons and Togoland.

1885 Germany proclaims a protectorate over Tanganyika.

1886 Gold rush to Witwatersrand in southern Transvaal (South Africa).

The storming of Taba-Basio by Boers and British in 1865.

A Portuguese sentry and a Lorenzo Marquez tribesman in the 1890s.

1888 Formation of the British East Africa Company.

1889 Germany relinquishes its claim on Uganda to Great Britain.

1890–1897 Cecil Rhodes, British diamond tycoon, becomes leading empire-builder in Africa.

1893 Great Britain establishes protectorate over Ashanti Kingdom (West Africa) and Nyasaland (Central Africa).

1896 Ethiopian forces, victorious in the Battle of Adua, force Italy to withdraw from Ethiopia.

1896–1925 Carl E. Ackley of the United States explores various parts of Africa.

1898–1899 France assigns the name "French West Africa" to its West African possessions.

1899 Nigeria becomes a British protectorate.

1899–1902 Great Britain defeats the Boers in South Africa; annexes the Orange Free State and the Transvaal.

1902 Louis Gentil of France explores portions of Morocco and the Atlas Mountains of North Africa.

1904–1935 Leo Frobenius of Germany makes 12 expeditions into Africa.

1905 Italy assumes control of Somaliland.

1908 Belgium annexes the Congo Free State.

1910 Formation of the Union of South Africa (composed of Cape of Good Hope and Natal provinces, Transvaal and Orange Free State), with Luis Botha as first premier.

1911 Annexation of Libya by Italy.

1912 Partition of Africa completed (only Ethiopia and Liberia independent).

1914 France and Great Britain conquer German colonies of Togo and Cameroons.

1923 Rhodesia (named after Cecil B. Rhodes) is divided into Northern and Southern Rhodesia.

1926 Firestone Rubber Company purchases one million acres of land in Liberia to be used in the development of rubber plantations.

1930 Haile Selassie I is crowned as Emperor of Ethiopia.

1935–1942 Invasion and conquest of Ethiopia by Italy.

1945 Mandated League of Nations territories are transferred to the control of the Trusteeship Council of the United Nations.

1945–1966 Independence comes to Africa; European domination ends, except in Southern Africa.

1946 India breaks diplomatic relations with the Union of South Africa because of alleged mistreatment of its Indian minority.

In the streets of Luanda, Angolans celebrate their newly gained independence from Portugal.

A political rally in Sangmelima, Cameroon.

1948 D. F. Malan and the National Party elected in South Africa on apartheid platform.

1950 Seretse Khama sent into exile from Bechuanaland.

1952 Independence for Libya (North Africa).

1952–1960 Mau-Mau violence in Kenya (East Africa).

1953 Egypt proclaims itself a republic.

1954 Revolt begins in Algeria.

1956 Tunisia and Morocco gain independence from France.

1956 Sudan proclaims itself a republic.

1957 Ghana becomes first independent "black dominion" in the British Commonwealth.

1958 First conference of independent African states convenes in Accra, Ghana.

1958 Arch supporter of apartheid, Henrik Verwoerd, is elected Prime Minister of South Africa.

1958 Guinea votes for independence from France; rest of French West Africa joins French Community.

1960 Independence for Cameroun, Togo, Malagasy Republic, Congo (Leopoldville), Somali Republic, Dahomey, Niger, Upper Volta, Ivory Coast, Chad, Central African Republic, Congo (Brazzaville), Gabon, Senegal, Mali, Nigeria, and Mauritania.

1960–1963 Tribal war and anarchy prevail in the Congo until United Nations forces restore order; Premier Patrice Lumumba assassinated.

1961 Independence for Tanganyika.

1961 Death of Dag Hammarskjold, Secretary General of the UN, in a plane crash in Northern Rhodesia.

1961 Sierra Leone becomes independent within the British Commonwealth.

1962 Independence for Algeria, Burundi, Rwanda, and Uganda.

1963 Independence for Kenya (with Jomo Kenyatta as prime minister) and Zanzibar.

1964 Independence for Malawi and Zambia.

1964 Tanzania (composed of Tanganyika and Zanzibar) united under Julius Nyerere.

1964 Moise Tshombe named premier of Congo.

1965 Independence for Gambia.

1965 Ahmed Ben Bella overthrown in Algeria by Colonel Houari Boumedienne.

1965 General Joseph Mobutu seizes power in Congo (Leopoldville); General Christophe Soglo ousts Sourou Migan-Apithy in Dahomey.

1965 Rhodesia declares unilateral independence from Great Britain.

1966 Colonel Jean-Bedel Bokassa overthrows President David Dacko of the Central African Republic; Lieutenant Colonel Sangoule Lamizane seizes power in Upper Volta.

1966 Assassination of Abubakar Tafawa Balewa, chief of state in Nigeria; General Aguiyi Ironsi heads caretaker military government.

1966 Kwame Nkrumah overthrown in Ghana by Sandhurst-trained officers under the leadership of General Joseph A. Ankrah.

1966 Assassination of South African premier, Henrik Verwoerd.

1966 Independence for Basutoland (Lesotho) and for Bechuanaland (Botswana). Lesotho is ruled by Premier Leabua Jonathan, whereas Botswana has as its prime minister Seretse Khama.

1967 Congolese President Joseph Mobutu nationalizes the Union Minere du Haut-Katanga, the Belgian mining concern which produces three-fourths of the nation's mineral exports, and accounts for nearly one-half of his government's revenues. The company, on the other hand, withholds more than 10 million dollars in royalties, and suspends its tax payments which normally run some two million dollars per month.

1969 A new Rhodesian constitution severs all ties with Great Britain and institutionalizes white minority rule and racial supremacy for an indefinite period.

1969 Kenya's Economic Planning Commissioner Tom Mboya is assassinated in Nairobi, sparking sporadic clashes between Luo tribesmen and members of the Kikuyu.

1970 Two and a half years of civil war in Nigeria end with the capitulation of the Biafran secessionists to federal authorities in Lagos. At the time of the surrender, Biafra has shrunk to a 3,000-square-mile area with a population of three million. On May 30, 1967, at the time it declared its independence, Biafra consisted of a 30,000-square-mile area peopled by 14 million tribesmen, most of them Ibos. Announcement of the surrender is made by Maj. Gen. Philip Effiong, successor to Odumegwu Ojukwu who had fled the country. In an attempt

Victorious General Yakubu Gowon became Nigerian chief of state.

to quell rumors of an impending bloodbath, Nigerian commander Major General Yakubu Gowon declares a general amnesty "for all those misled into attempting to disintegrate the country." Gowon calls the surrender "one of the greatest moments in the history of our nation, a great moment of victory for unity and national reconciliation." As he talks, a million Biafran refugees search the scorched and barren countryside for food and shelter; victims of the political struggle which has caused widespread famine and mass starvation. Relief offers from nations deemed hostile are rejected by General Gowon, but the General expresses "warm appreciation" for U.S. and British gestures. Withal, Biafra remains etched in the memory of Western man as a grim chapter of human horror and barbarism; a reminder that not even the cries of innocent children for food will prevent men from clashing doggedly over divergent points of view.

1971 Strained relations between Rhodesia and Great Britain are relieved when the two countries restore normal relations in November. Rhodesian Prime Minister Ian Smith, had broken ties with the United Kingdom in 1965, when Britain objected that the nation's new constitution did not allow blacks sufficient rights.

1972 Ghana's Prime Minister, Kafi A. Busia, is overthrown in a bloodless coup by Army officers during a visit by Busia to London for medical treatment. Leaders of the uprising, which was headed by Colonel Ignatius Kutu Achaempong, dissolve Parliament.

1972 Black opposition to the Rhodesian government rises as it becomes apparent that Prime Minister Smith will do little to increase their representation in the nation's public and economic life.

1972 President Amin of Uganda expels all Indians and Pakistanis who have British passports. Some 25,000 leave the country.

1972 After 17 years, the civil war in Sudan between Moslem and Christian forces is unofficially ended. Arab Moslem factions had controlled the north of the country, Christian and Pagan forces the south.

1972 Sheik Abeid Amani Karume of Zanzibar is assassinated by a commando team and succeeded in power by Aboud Jumbe. Though Zanzibar is part of Tanzania, Karume had been extremely powerful in his own domain. Jumbe had the support of Tanzanian President Nyerere.

1972 Border disputes between Morocco and Algeria are officially resolved when King Hassan of Morocco and Algerian President Boumedienne sign a

Members of the women's detachment of Mozambique's guerrilla fighters have a short rest.

treaty in Rabat. Leaders of 23 African nations attended the event.

1972 The government of the Union of South Africa bans student marches and meetings after students at Witwatersrand and Capetown Universities protest the nation's apartheid policies.

1973 Egypt and the United States renew diplomatic relations after a break of six years. The "October War" between Egypt and Israel is stopped by cease fire and prisoner exchange in November. Also in November, Arab diplomats meeting in Algeria announce an oil embargo on countries supporting Israel and their intent to reduce oil production and exports. Embargo affects virtually all of Western Europe, Japan, and the United States. In December the price of oil is doubled. Embargo is lifted on all countries except the United States, Netherlands, and Denmark.

1973 Large numbers of African nations break diplomatic ties with Israel, in efforts to firm relations with Arab countries.

1974 The Ethiopian Army, in a coup, seizes Addis Ababa. Emperor Haile Selassie agrees to free political prisoners and accedes to a new constitution. Though the new leaders agree to let Selassie remain as Emperor, he is slowly stripped of his powers and then deposed. The Emperor had ruled Ethiopia for 58 years.

1974 In August, at a conference in Algiers, Portugal agrees with African representatives to grant freedom to Portuguese Guinea and the Cape Verde Islands. Portuguese Guinea is to become Guinea Bissau. Cape Verde inhabitants are to vote on whether they wish to be independent or join Guinea Bissau. In September, at a meeting in Zambia, Portugal signs agreement with Frelimo (Front for the Liberation of Mozambique) that institutes a provisional government there, with freedom set for June 25, 1975. White settlers resist briefly, capturing the radio station, but give up when they are rebuffed by the Portuguese Army. Freedom is also promised to Angola, with a date set for November 1975.

1975 Signs of change appear in the foreign policy of South Africa as Prime Minister Vorster visits many black African nations and seems to reduce support for the white government in Rhodesia. However, though blacks start to appear in South African athletic events, the policy of apartheid remains firm.

1975 Numerous efforts at agreement between the Rhodesian government and black forces collapse, as Smith avoids transfer of power and black groups fight among themselves. By the summer of 1975 the days of absolute white rule in Rhodesia seem to be numbered.

1975 An assassination attempt in June against President Mobutu of Zaire fails. Mobutu implies that the United States was behind the attempt.

1975 After 470 years of colonial rule, on June 25, the Portuguese flag is lowered throughout Mozambique and what seems to be Africa's most Marxist government takes over. Samora Machel, 41-year-old Frelimo leader, is sworn in as President. Portugal affirms intent to leave Angola, despite possibility of civil war there and rising emigration of white settlers.

1976 Lieutenant Colonel Jean-Baptiste Bagaza, a Tutsi, leads a bloodless coup in Burundi and ousts President Michel Micombero, who was in his second term. Bagaza assumes the presidency two days after the coup, suspends the Constitution, and heads a 30-member Supreme Revolutionary Council.

1976 The U.N. Security Council unanimously condemns South Africa's "illegal occupation" of Namibia and calls for free elections under U.N. supervision.

1976 Murtala Ramat Muhammad, who assumed leadership in Nigeria following a coup in 1975, is assassinated during another coup attempt. Lieutenant General Olusegun Obasanjo succeeds the slain leader and captures and executes Muhammad's assassins.

1976 The Republic of Seychelles is granted independence from Britain as republic within the Commonwealth. A year later, the first president, James

A woman's detachment of the FRELIMO army that fought for Mozambique independence.

President William L. Tolbert of Liberia, shown here with U.N. Secretary General Kurt Waldheim in 1974, was deposed in a coup led by Master Sergeant Samuel Doe on April 12, 1980. Tolbert's execution, with a number of family members, ended years of rule by the Tubman family.

Mancham is ousted for what is termed "lavish spending."

1976 Somalia leader, Mohamed Siad Barre, dissolves the Supreme Revolutionary Council and forms the Somali Revolutionary Socialist Party, as the nation's only legal party.

1976 A third attempted coup against Sudan President Gafaar Muhammed al-Nimeiry leaves 1,000 rebels and loyal troops dead following a fierce battle in Khartoum. President Nimeiry blames Libyan President Muammar Qaddafy for instigating the attempt; Sudan breaks relations with Libya.

1976 Morocco formally assumes control of the northern two thirds of Western Sahara; Mauritania assumes the southern third while Polisario proclaims the establishment of an independent Saharan Arab Democratic Republic as government-in-exile. Mohammed Ould Ahmed is named Prime Minister.

1977 Zairean refugees in Angola invade Zaire's Shaba Province, prompting President Mobutu Sese Seko to charge Angola and the Soviet Union with the invasion. The regime of Agostinho Neto, the Soviet Union, and Cuba denied this, but in May 1978 another invasion takes place.

1977 A small, but fierce, battle is fought at Cotonou in which Beninese exiles are repulsed by the forces of Major Mathieu Kerekou. A U.N. mission of inquiry later reports that the invaders had been flown in from Gabon which leads Kerekou to sharply criticize Gabonese President Bongo.

1977 The Supreme Revolutionary Council in Burundi gives Lieutenant Colonel Jean-Baptiste Bagaza a mandate for a renewable five-year term and proposes its own dissolution and a return to civilian rule once the Tutsi-dominated political party, Unity and National Progress (UPRONA), has been restored.

1977 President Marien N'Gouabi of the Congo is assassinated by a four-man hit squad and the power of the country shifts to an 11-member committee headed by Colonel Joachim Yhombi-Opango, who suspends the Constitution and reportedly seeks Western aid for the nation.

1977 The Republic of Djibouti is born after more than 98% of the population votes for independence. Three days following the election, Issa leader Hassan Gouled is unanimously elected President. Two months later Afar leader Ahmed Dini is named head of a 15-member Council of Ministers.

1977 Somali rebels in Ethiopia's Ogaden Province cut the railway to Djibouti. There is fear that Somali will annex the tiny nation. Somali still considers Djibouti a "land to be redeemed" which makes relations between the nations strained.

1977 King Hassan of Morocco sends 1,500 Moroccan troops to Zaire to help President Mobuto defeat an invasion force from Angola.

1977 South Africa experiences the worst outbreak of racial violence since the Sharpeville riots in 1960. The bloodshed begins in the black township of Soweto outside Johannesburg, growing out of black student protests against the compulsory use of Afrikaans. As a result, many theaters and opera houses are desegregated.

1977 Rioting intensifies in South Africa following the death of anti-apartheid activist Steven Biko from a head injury while in prison. The government invokes some of its strictest apartheid policies in two decades by closing down the leading black newspaper, arresting its editor, and banning a number of protest groups.

1978 Algerian President Colonel Houari Boumedienne dies after a long illness. Chadli Bendjedid, secretary-general of the National Liberation Front, assumes the presidency. When Boumedienne took over the presidency in 1965, he sought to restore financial stability and maintain good economic and financial relations with France and the United States until 1967.

1978 A 10-day "summit" meeting convenes at Camp David with U.S. President Jimmy Carter, Israeli Prime Minister Menachem Begin, and Egyptian President Anwar Sadat. The summit results in two documents—A Framework for Peace in the Middle

These brass figurines from Cameroon were made by the lost-wax process, which has been practiced for many centuries in West Africa. Called Suah Dua ("juju men" in English) the figures wear the fibered costumes used for religious ceremonies.

The haff-bearer of the King of Togoland, from a nineteenth-century engraving.

East and A Framework for a Peace Treaty Between Israel and Egypt.

1978 Kenya's President Jomo Kenyatta, known as "The Old Man," dies and is succeeded by Daniel Arap Moi, who had been vice president. Moi is declared president for the remainder of Kenyatta's five-year term and in 1979, he is reelected for another five-year term.

1978 Libya breaks its relations with Egypt following the Camp David accord and fortifies their mutual border.

1978 Nigeria's 12-year state of emergency ends and a ban on political party activity is lifted. In mid-1979 elections are held which place a number of federal representatives, state legislators, and state governors in power with Alhaji Shehu Shagari as president.

1978 United States President Jimmy Carter's visit to Nigeria is the first to Africa by an American president since President Franklin Roosevelt stopped in Liberia during World War II.

1978 Sierra Leone becomes a one-party state with a new Constitution adopted by referendum and Siaka Stevens is reelected president for a seven-year term.

1979 Angola's President Agostinho Neto dies in Moscow, where he had been undergoing medical treatment. MPLA/Party of Labor Chairman Jose Eduardo dos Santos becomes president.

1979 While Central African Republic's President Jean-Bedel Bokassa is in Libya, he is deposed by former President Dacko, aided by French military forces.

1979 Colonel Joachim Yhombi-Opango of the Congo resigns under pressure from the Central Committee of the Congolese Labor Party. Late in 1979 he is arrested and demoted to a private soldier.

1979 The President of Equatorial Guinea, Macie Nguema Biyogo, is deposed in a coup led by his nephew, Lieutenant Colonel Teodoro Obiang Nguema Mbazogo, who formed a Supreme Military Council. Macie was executed a month after being deposed for the crimes of genocide, treason, and embezzlement.

1979 Protests over a price increase of rice lead to riots in Monrovia, Liberia, which result in more than 40 deaths, 500 injuries, and property damage estimated at $35 million. The government reversed itself and lowered the price of rice—a brief period of calm followed.

1979 Colonel Mohamed Mahmoud Ould Ahmed Louly, President of Mauritania, concludes a peace treaty with Polisario, a Saharan independence group backed by Algeria by withdrawing Mauritanian troops. Moroccan troops immediately occupy the land.

1979 A 171-member People's Assembly is elected in Somalia under a new constitution and Mohamed Siad Barre is confirmed as President for a six-year term.

1979 Major General Maphevu Dlamini, who had been Prime Minister of Swaziland since 1976, dies. Prince Mandabala Fred Dlamini is designated as his successor.

1979 The Amin regime is overthrown in Kampala following an invasian by Tanzanian and exiled Ugandan forces. Amin's eight-year reign had been a horror reminiscent of Hitler's purges in Germany.

1979 Zambia endures several Rhodesian commando attacks, including an attack on Lusaka. However, later in the year, Zambia, Rhodesia (to be known as Zimbabwe), and Angola sign a pact to end support for each other's exiled opposition forces, as well as to cooperate with transportation needs.

Afrikaaner guns and horses conquered ancestral lands from primitive tribes.

1979 In Rhodesia, white voters choose to ratify a new constitution which enfranchises all blacks, establishes a black majority Senate and Assembly, and changes the country's name to Zimbabwe.

1979 Algerian President Chadli Bendjedid frees deposed President Ben Bella from a 14-year "house arrest."

1980 President Ahmadou Ahidjo of Cameroon is elected to a fifth term, having faced no organized opposition in his reelection efforts. In 1979 the Ahidjo administration had tried to mediate regional factions but in 1980, sought instead to protest Libya's participation in the disputes.

1980 Algerian Minister of Executive Affairs Behzad Nabair persuades the Iranian government to retain the $3 billion in Iranian assets against which the banks had legal claims.

1980 Fifty-two American hostages are released to Algerian custody and flown to Algiers en route to the United States. The release of the hostages coincided with the inauguration of President Ronald Reagan. President Reagan delegated former President Jimmy Carter to serve as the official U.S. representative to greet the released hostages.

1980 The National People's Assembly adopted Cape Verde Island's first constitution, expected to emulate in Guinea-Bissau's. Four days after Guinea-Bissau adopts a similar constitution, the mainland government under President Luis Cabral is overthrown in a military coup.

1980 President Jean-Bedel Bokassa of the Central African Republic is sentenced to death for crimes that include murder, cannibalism, and embezzlement. President Dacko, however, undermines his own popularity on his second attempt at leadership by keeping several high ranking officials from the hated Bokassa regime in office and creating one-party rule again.

1980 Civil war breaks out in Chad when Hissein Habre, who had been the Defense Minister, challenges President Goukhouni Queddei. During this period, some 80,000 civilians flee the capital of Ndjamena, the site of much of the fighting.

1980 During a trip to France, Hassan Gouled of Djibouti asks that a truce in the Horn of Africa be made. Djibouti, as a neutral state, is willing to facilitate peace discussions between Somali and Ethiopia. He suggests regional agreements in nomadic migration, freedom of travel in the Ogaden, and joint economic development plans.

1980 Guinea's President Sekou Toure barely escapes an assassination attempt which claims several lives and injures 30 bystanders. Following the assassination, he immediately calls Guineans to "remobilize" and "unite against intruders." In 1981 Toure is reelected president.

1980 The Ivory Coast enters a slight recession, but anticipates renewed economic progress under the continued guidance of its president, Felix Houphouet-Boigny. The Ivory Coast has the reputation of being one of the most prosperous, highly developed and politically stable African countries. In the past two decades, the Ivory Coast has tripled its agricultural exports.

1980 While Gabriel Baccus Matthews is awaiting trial after he had called for a general strike to overthrow the government in Liberia, a coup is held and President William R. Tolbert, Jr. and more than two dozen government leaders are killed. Master Sergeant Samuel Doe, leader of the coup, frees Matthews and appoints him as foreign minister.

1980 Libya gives military support in the Chadian civil war, thereby helping the Goukhouni Woddei government defeat insurgent forces.

1980 King Hassan of Morocco, under pressure from other African leaders at the Organization of African Unity summit in Nairobi, Kenya, agrees to a cease fire with the Polisarios. It is decided that a referendum under international supervision be used to determine the future of the territory.

1980 Niger attends the OAU emergency summit on Chad and joins the Central African Republic, Cameroon, Guinea, Senegal, Sudan, and Togo in calling for Libya's immediate withdrawal from Chad.

1980 President Leopold Sedar Senghor of Senegal retires as leader of the Senegalese Progressive Union. He was considered one of the most highly respected intellectuals in Africa. He had been president since 1960.

1980 Robert Mugabe's Zimbabwe African National Union-Patriotic Front party wins 57 of the 80 Assembly seats reserved for blacks and Joshua Nkomo's ZAPU-Patriotic Front wins another 20 seats, leaving three seats for Bishop Abel Muzorewa's council. Mugabe is sworn in as Prime Minister of Zimbabwe.

1981 President Ronald Reagan asks Congress to repeal a 1976 ban on military aid to the tattered National Union for the Total Independence of Angola (UNITA) rebels, but Congress refuses partly because of lobbying pressures from American oil businesses which have interests in Angola's oil-rich Cabinda section.

1981 The National People's Assembly of Cape Verde Islands reelects Aristides Pereira as President and revokes all constitutional provisions relating to a union with Guinea-Bissau. Earlier, the Cape Verde wing of the African Party for the Independence of Guinea and Cape Verde (PAIGC) cut its association with the Guinea-Bissau wing of the party and formed its own party, the African Party for the Independence of Cape Verde (PAICV).

1981 President Dacko of the Central African Republic is elected to a six-year term by a slim margin. His opponents protest that the election was rigged and begin demonstrations against him.

1981 General Andre Kolingba, commander of the Central African Republic Army, deposes President Dacko and places all political parties in suspension, declaring rule under the Military Committee of National Redress.

1981 Egyptian President Anwar Sadat is assassinated in full view of thousands of Egyptians by a small force of terrorists. Sadat's assassins are captured, put on trial, and executed within five months.

1981 The Reagan Administration closes the Libyan embassy in Washington, citing Libya's connection to international terrorism as the reason. Relations between the countries have not improved though U.S. oil companies remain active in Libya and some 2,000 U.S. citizens continue to work there.

1981 Tanzania faces bankruptcy and the 18 million population is faced with daily shortages of staples such as bread, soap, and cooking oil.

1981 Robert Mugabe of Zimbabwe dismisses Joshua Nkomo as Home Minister; Nkomo leaves in protest. Mugabe also discharges Edgar Tekere, the Planning Minister.

1981 Jerry Rawlings, who had lost in a presidential balloting against Dr. Hilla Limann during a 1979

General Odumegwu Ojukwu led the 30-month war for Biafran secession, but was defeated.

election in Ghana, leads a coup against Limann. Following the coup, Rawlings dismisses Ghana's parliament, bans political parties, and suspends the Constitution. Rawlings is an admirer of Libya's Muammar Qaddafi.

1982 Negotiations are completed between Senegal and Gambia whereby the nations will unite in a confederation known as Senegambia. Public opinion in both countries is divided about the merger.

1982 Kenya's President Daniel Arap Moi accuses the 100,000 Asians of "ruining the country's economy" and pledges to deport any Asians found hoarding or smuggling currency regardless of their citizenship in Kenya.

1982 A previous U.S. policy is reversed by the Reagan Administration and support is stepped up for Morocco's King Hassan's government, in order to help stabilize that country and to reestablish American military bases there.

1982 President Mobuto Sese Seko, who brought a degree of stability to impoverished Zaire renews diplomatic relations with Israel, saying that his representative would live in Jerusalem thereby giving tacit recognition of Israel's annexation of the controversial Holy City.

1982 Nigerian President Shenhu Shagari reportedly pardons ex-Biafran leader C. Odumegwu Ojukwu, paving the way for his return home from exile in the Ivory Coast where he has been a successful businessman due to the help of President Houghphet Boigny. Nigeria's Ambassador to the United Nation's and a close friend of Shagari, Alhaji Maitama Sule is said to have been instrumental in the pardon.

1982 A wave of strikes across South Africa by some 10,000 African workers in the automobile and commercial sectors occurs the first of May. The key issues are mounting lay-offs due to recession and a demand for a minimum wage of $2 an hour.

1982 President Arap Moi of Kenya, chairman of the Organization of African Unity (OAU), joins the president of Chad, Goukoni Oueddi, in asking the U.N. Security Council to help pay for the African peace-keeping force in troubled Chad. The force is made up of troops from Senegal, Nigeria, and Zaire and has been patrolling since 1981.

1982 Zimbabwean officials announce that the country's capital city, Salisbury, will be renamed Harare, in honor of the second anniversary of the nation.

The successful fight for independence in Angola ended Portugal's 500 years of African colonization.

SUB-SAHARAN AFRICA

Angola

Date of independence: **November 11, 1975**
Area: **481,351 sq. miles (1% cultivated, 44% forested, 22% meadow, 33% fallow)**
Population: **7,250,000 (est. 1981)**
Capital: **Luanda**
Monetary unit: **Kwanza**
Nationality: **Angolan**
Religion: **84% animist, 12% Roman Catholic, 4% Protestant**
Language: **Portuguese (official), native dialects**
Literacy: **10–15%**
Type of government: **Republic**
Political parties/leaders: **Popular Movement for Liberation of Angola–Labor Party (MPLA) (only legal party), also National Front for Liberation of Angola (FNLA)**
Monetary conversion rate: **40.643 escudos = $1 (Nov. 1977)**
Principal economic resources: **Coffee, sisal, corn, cotton, sugar, oil, diamonds, tobacco, timber**

History at a Glance

The Congo River (the northern border of Angola) was discovered in 1482 by the Portuguese navigator Diogo Cao, who was followed by a number of other Portuguese explorers. Settlements were soon established and, by 1575, the town of Luanda had been founded. Except for a brief period between 1641 and 1648 during which it was under Dutch control, Angola has been one of Portugal's major overseas dominions and a primary source of tropical products and raw materials.

Until the abolition of the slave trade in 1836, Angola

served as the chief supplier of slaves bound for Brazil and other parts of South America. The territory's boundaries were first fixed by an international treaty signed by the major European powers at the Berlin Conference of 1884–1885.

The tribes of the Angolan interior were gradually pacified during the first two decades of the 20th century and, by 1951, Portugal had imposed the status of an overseas province upon the territory. However, African representation in government and equal citizenship rights were slow in coming to Angola.

Guerrilla opposition to colonial rule erupted in 1961 and continued for 13 years despite fierce reprisals from Portuguese forces. In 1974 with Portugal itself in the midst of a revolt, Lisbon announced plans to relinquish control of the last of its African colonies.

At the time of the government turnover, three principal independence forces were operating in Angola: the Popular Movement for the Liberation of Angola (MPLA), led by Dr. Agostinho Neto, which controlled much of the central region plus oil-rich Cabinda; the National Front for the Liberation of Angola (FNLA), which had established a government-in-exile in Zaire in 1963 under the leadership of Holden Toberto and controlled most of the northeast section; and the National Union for the Total Independence of Angola (UNITA), which controlled the eastern part of Angola under the leadership of Dr. Jonas Savimbi.

The three groups initially signed a pact with Portuguese officials declaring Angola's independence on November 11, 1975. However, four months later, the MPLA forces, backed by Soviet weapons and advisors, established a new government under MPLA auspices and ousted the rival factions.

Two weeks later, FNLA–UNITA announced the formation of a rival Democratic People's Republic of Angola and claimed the central highlands city of Huambo as its capital.

Conflict grew between the factions, with the Soviets aiding the MPLA with some 18,000 Cuban troops and the United States sending aid to the FNLA group through Zaire.

In early February 1976, the MPLA captured Huambo and other key cities, forcing FNLA and UNITA to resort to guerrilla warfare. Meanwhile, the Organization of African Unity announced that the MPLA was formally admitted to its membership and on December 1, 1976, Angola, under MPLA rule, was also admitted to the United Nations.

On September 10, 1979 President Neto died in Moscow, where he had been undergoing medical treatment, and on September 21, MPLA–Party of Labor Chairman Jose Eduardo dos Santos became President.

FNLA forces dwindled to practically nothing in

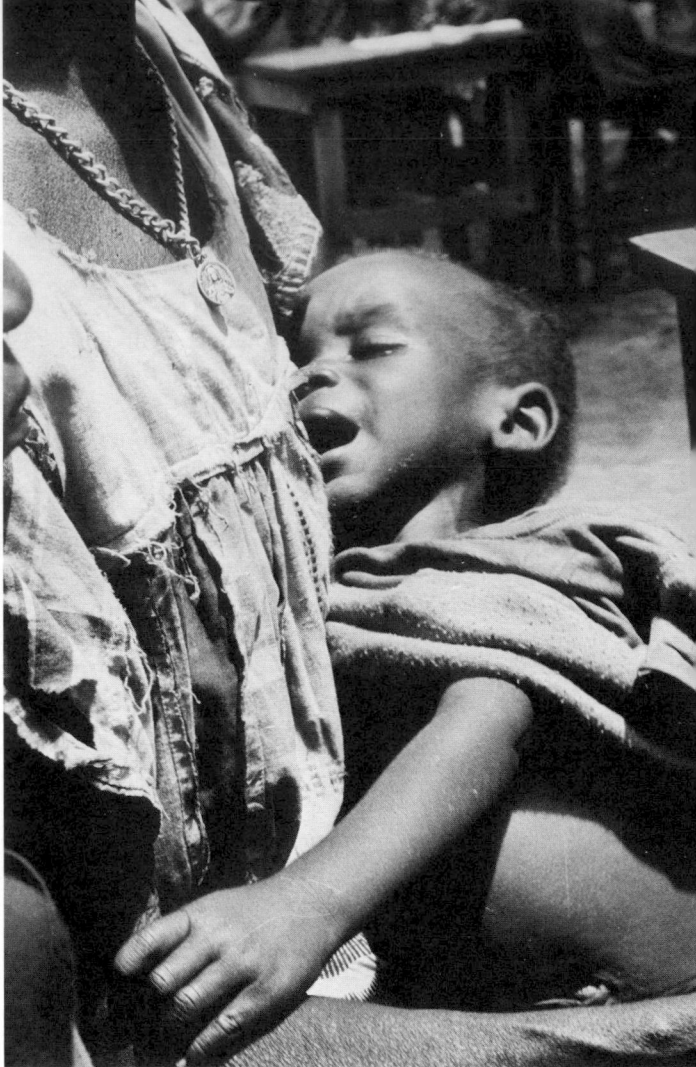

This starving infant is one of the casualties of the Biafran War.

later years, but the UNITA forces under Dr. Savimbi continued to offer resistance.

Angola has been embroiled in numerous fights between groups in neighboring Namibia, South Africa, and Zaire. In March 1977, Zairean refugees in Angola invaded Zaire's Shaba Province, prompting Zairean President Mobutu to charge Angola with collaborating with the Soviet Union to invade Zaire. The Neto regime, the Soviet Union, and Cuba denied this, but in May 1978 another invasion took place. This time, the United States and France joined Mobutu in protesting the invasion. Denials were again heard, but negotiations began, resulting in a nonaggression pact between the countries on October 12, 1979.

In the south, Luanda supported the South West African People's Organisation (SWAPO) in regular cross-border raids through Namibia. Angola later sustained a three-week raid by South African troops in June 1980.

In March 1981 President Reagan asked Congress

to repeal a 1976 ban on military aid to the tattered UNITA rebels, but Congress refused to repeal the ban.

Benin (formerly Dahomey)

Date of independence: **August 1, 1980**
Area: **43,483 square miles**
Population: **3,665,000 (1981 est.)**
Capital: **Porto-Novo (official); Coronou (*de facto*)**
Monetary unit: **Franc CFA**
Nationality: **Beninese**
Religion: **12% Muslim, 8% Christian, 80% animist**
Language: **French (official), tribal dialects**
Literacy: **20%**
Type of government: **Marxist one party state**
Political parties/leaders: **People's Revolutionary Party of Benin (established 1975)**
Monetary conversion rate: **212.72 Communaute Financiere Africaine (CFA) francs = U.S. $1 (1979)**
Principal economic resources: **Oil, palms, peanuts, cotton, coffee, tobacco, corn, rice, iron ore**

History at a Glance

Long before the Portuguese arrived in the sixteenth century, the modern nation of Benin (formerly Dahomey) was already heir to a long and proud tradition replete with mighty armies, glittering cities, and lavish palaces. At the height of its power, Benin (then much larger than it is today) exchanged ambassadors with the French court of King Louis XIV.

The Portuguese (who discovered Benin's ancient capital of Abomey) were soon followed by the Dutch, English, French, and Spanish, all of whom shared a common interest: the slave trade.

During the nineteenth century, the French imposed protectorate status on the territory. In 1904 Benin was made part of the Federation of French West Africa. The territory's first real stride toward independence occurred under the Constitution of 1947 when, as an overseas member of the French Union, it won the right to send representatives to the Chamber of Deputies in Paris. By 1952 a territorial assembly had been established. Four years later, under the *loi-cadre* (the Enabling Act which gave most of French West African territories a greater share in self-government), universal suffrage was instituted.

Benin accepted French President Charles de Gaulle's Constitution of 1958 and proclaimed itself an autonomous republic, with full membership in the French Community. Two years later, Dahomey opted for full independence, with Hubert Maga as President.

In the first of five coups in 10 years, the Maga government was deposed in 1963 by a military group led by General Christophe Soglo. Soglo stepped aside when a general election in January 1964 elected President Sourou-Migan Apithy, but took back the reins of power in 1965 after numerous political crises in the civilian government.

Soglo was himself deposed in December 1967 by a military coup led by Major Maurice Kouandete and an interim regime was established under Lieutenant Colonel Alphone Alley.

When a general election attempted in May 1968 failed, former Foreign Minister Dr. Emile-Derlin Zinsou was appointed President of the civilian regime. However in December 1969, the Zinsou government was overthrown, again by Kouandete, and military rule remained until another election was attempted in May 1970.

This time the military forces established a Presidential Council made up of the country's three leading politicians: Justin Ahomadegbe and former Presidents Apithy and Maga.

Kouandete, in his third coup, tried to overthrow the triumvirate, but failed. Eight months later, however, another coup led by Major Mathieu Kerekou succeeded in abolishing the presidential council.

Kerekou announced that the country was to become a Marxist-Leninist state and significantly altered national economic and industrial operations. On November 30, 1975, Kerekou changed the name of the country from Dahomey to Benin after an African kingdom that flourished in the seventeenth century.

The Benin People's Revolutionary Party was established as the new one-party system and remains in power, although an illegal party, the Front for the Liberation and Rehabilitation of Dahomey, was also formed at the time of Kerekou's takeover.

A small, but fierce battle was fought at Cotonou in January 1977 in which Beninese exiles were repulsed by Kerekou's forces. A U.N. mission of inquiry later reported that the invaders had been flown in from Gabon, which led Kerekou to sharply criticize Gabonese President Bongo. Bongo immediately ordered some 6,000 Benin nationals expelled from that country.

Kerekou accepted conversion to the Islamic faith and continued to maintain close ties with Libya's Colonel Muammar Qaddafi.

Benin is one of the smallest and most densely populated states in Africa. It is primarily an agricultural state, with palm products, cotton, and groundnuts as principal exports.

Botswana

Date of independence: **September 30, 1966**
Area: **222,000 square miles**
Population: **819,000 (est. 1981)**
Capital: **Gaborone**

Monetary unit: **Pula**
Nationality: **Botswana**
Religion: **85% Animist, 15% Christian**
Language: **English (official), Tswana**
Literacy: **22% English, 32% Tswana**
Type of government: **Parliamentary republic**
Political parties/leaders: **Botswana Democratic Party, Botswana National Front, Botswana People's Party, Botswana Independence Party**
Monetary conversion rate: **1 pula = $1.22 (1979)**
Principal economic resources: **Diamonds, copper, nickel, salt, coal, beef**

History at a Glance

Landlocked Botswana has been reliant on outside assistance to shore up its economy. Although its traditional principal industry has been cattle-raising, discovery of copper, nickel, and diamond deposits in the late 1960s opened a highly profitable source of revenue. In fact, diamonds and copper-nickel matte accounted for about 70% of Botswana's export earnings in 1979. Tourism, consisting mainly of safaris to hunt lions and swamp antelope, continues to flourish.

Until his death on July 13, 1980, President Khama sought to preserve Botswana's independent position in African and world affairs, as well as an uncompromisingly anti-apartheid policy on the home front. He was succeeded by Dr. Quett Ketumile Masire, who had served as Vice President and Minister of Finance and Development Planning since Botswana's independence.

In 1979 a highway connection with Zambia, financed with U.S. aid, gave Botswana an "opening to the north" and provided the country with its first communications link with a nation under African majority rule. Since then, Botswana has added 15,000 kilometers of roads, a railway to South Africa, and three airports.

Besides building a major roadway north, Botswana has taken other steps to establish its independence from South Africa. In 1979 it withdrew from the South African monetary union to create its own central bank. However, Botswana maintains a customs union agreement with South Africa and 45,000 of its residents continue to work in South Africa, a majority of them in diamond mines.

In 1975 the majority of Botswana's population remained impoverished. Per capita income was about $70 and less than 10% of its residents held paid employment.

Burundi

Date of independence: **July 1, 1962**
Area: **10,747 square miles**
Population: **4,650,000 (est. 1981)**

Capital: **Bujumbura**
Monetary unit: **Burundi franc**
Nationality: **Burundi**
Religion: **60% Christian (mostly Catholic), 2% Muslim, 38% Animist**
Language: **Kirundi and French (official), Swahili**
Literacy: **15% in Kirundi, 3% in French**
Type of government: **Republic, military government, one-party socialist**
Political parties/leaders: **National Party of Unity and Progress (only legitimate party)**
Monetary conversion rate: **90 Burundi francs = $1 (1980)**
Principal economic resources: **Coffee, tea, cotton, food crops**

History at a Glance

The early history of Burundi strongly parallels that of its northern neighbor, Rwanda. The first-known inhabitants of both regions were the Twa, a tribe of pygmy hunters who were gradually pushed back into the jungle by the agriculturally inclined Hutu, a Bantu-people.

In the fifteenth century, the Tutsi (of Hamitic stock) entered the area from the northeast, establishing a caste-oriented, feudal society. Headed by an omnipotent chieftain, or mwami, the Tutsi became the ruling class and obliged the Hutu to tend the fields and produce food for everyone.

In 1858 the English explorers John Speke and Richard Burton became the first white men in the area when they crossed Burundi in search of the headwaters of the Nile River. Thirteen years later, Stanley and Livingstone landed at Usumbura and explored the Ruzizi River region. Ultimately, however, it was the Germans who succeeded in consolidating control over the territory as a result of agreements reached with other major European powers at the Berlin Conference (1884–1885).

During World War I, Belgium replaced Germany as the power administering the territory. In 1923 the League of Nations formalized this arrangement by granting the Belgian king a special mandate over the combined territory of Ruanda-Urundi. This mandate remained operative until 1946, at which time the United Nations substituted a system of trusteeship.

By this time, it was clear that Ruanda and Urundi were developing along separate paths which would, without proper supervision, lead to a possible collision course. To the north, Ruanda seemed bent on a republic form of government; to the south, Urundi continued to favor a monarchical structure. In the 1961 elections, Urundi expressed its preference for a constitutional monarchy, headed by Prince Rwagasore, a son of the mwami. Later that same year, the prince was assassinated by rival nationalists.

The UN stepped into the ensuing power vacuum, recommending that a united Ruanda-Urundi declare itself independent by July 1, 1962. With one significant exception, the deadline and the conditions were met by both territories. Ruanda became the Republic of Rwanda; Urundi, the Kingdom of Burundi. Since then, however, outbreaks of violence between the Tutsi and Hutu tribes have disrupted Burundi and undermined the welfare of her people.

In 1972 the antagonism between the Hutu and Tutsi tribes erupted into tribal warfare which claimed at least 100,000 lives and drove an additional 80,000 into exile. The 1972 crisis started not in the rivalry between the Tutsi and the Hutu, but in a political division within the dominant Tutsi minority.

The Tutsi consolidated their leadership position under the strict regime of President Michel Micombero, the former Commander-in-Chief who deposed the last Tutsi King (Mwame), Ntare V, in 1966.

Micombero's government blamed the conflict on the Hutu, who then became victims of tribal violence that followed. The violence continued for some time after the crisis was officially over with the induction of a new "reconciliation" cabinet in July 1972. International relief efforts returned economic conditions to normal by the end of 1972, but tensions remained high and prevented Micombero from carrying out his previously stated intention of reviving the constitutional form of government he suspended in 1966.

On November 1, 1976, Lieutenant Colonel Jean-Baptiste Bagaza, a Tutsi, led a bloodless coup and ousted Micombero, who was in his second term. Bagaza assumed the presidency two days later, suspended the Constitution, and headed a 30-member Supreme Revolutionary Council.

Miniature of a swinging suspension bridge typical of the southern Cameroons.

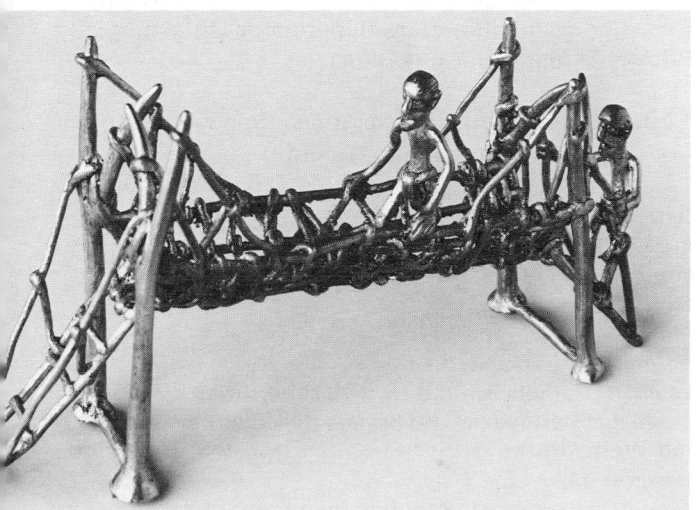

In 1977 the Council gave Bagaza a mandate for a renewable five-year term and proposed its own dissolution and a return to civilian rule once the Tutsi-dominated political party, Unity and National Progress (UPRONA), had been restored.

One of the 12 poorest countries in the world, with a per capita GNP of barely $150 in 1979, Burundi continues to depend mostly on its coffee exports for revenue. Cotton and tea production has been recently established. Deposits of cobalt, copper, nickel, platinum, and uranium have been discovered in recent years, but remain largely undeveloped because of inadequate transportation.

Cameroon

Date of independence: **January 1, 1960**
Area: **183,569 square miles**
Population: **8,650,000 (est. 1981)**
Capital: **Yaounde**
Monetary unit: **Communaute Financiere Africaine (CFA) franc**
Nationality: **Cameroonian**
Religion: **50% Animist, 25% Christian, 10% Muslim**
Language: **English/French (official), tribal dialects**
Literacy: **South 40%, North 10%**
Type of government: **One-party presidential regime**
Political parties/leaders: **Cameroonian National Union (established 1966)**
Monetary conversion rate: **212.7 CFA francs = $1 (1979)**
Principal economic resources: **Cocoa, coffee, timber, aluminum, cotton**

History at a Glance

The first European to explore any part of present-day Cameroon was Fernando Po, a Portuguese who arrived in the territory in 1472. (Po was followed by a number of Portuguese navigators who found the territory's main waterways overloaded with prawn, a crustacean known in their language as "camaraos.") Portuguese interests soon gave way to those of the English and the Germans.

Germany had already established trading posts and factories at various points along the West African coast before becoming interested in basing her African colonial empire in the Cameroons. In 1884 with the approval of England, she placed the territory under protectorate status. Prior to World War I, the Germans concentrated on developing the resources of the interior, cultivating banana and coffee plantations, building roads and railroads, and establishing a communications network.

During World War I, the German Cameroons were seized by French, British and Belgian troops. In 1915 the territory known as "New Cameroons" (an addi-

A marketplace in Mankon.

tional portion which had been ceded to Germany by France in 1911) was returned to France and incorporated into French Equatorial Africa. Later that year, the French and the British agreed to rule the rest of the territory jointly. New Cameroons remained part of French Equatorial Africa; the eastern sector became East Cameroon, while the western area adjoining Nigeria was dubbed British Cameroons.

Between the two world wars, the French contributed significantly to the development of the territory's resources, although they did little to encourage self-sustaining political institutions. In 1946 the territory was placed under international trusteeship and in 1957, France granted Cameroon full internal autonomy. A year later, the Cameroonian Legislative Assembly voted to declare the territory independent by 1960, with Ahmadou Ahidjo as chief of state. During this same period, John Foncha emerged as the key figure behind the independence movement in the British Cameroons. After a short period of unrest culminating with the appearance of French troops in East Cameroon, a national assembly was elected and Ahidjo was returned to office as president of the newly created Republic of Cameroon.

In 1961 the Northern British Cameroons were incorporated into the Republic of Nigeria as the Sarduana Province, while the Southern British Cameroons joined the Cameroon Republic. After a constitution had finally been drafted and approved, the Cameroon Republic came into being as the combined states of East and West Cameroon. Ahidjo serves as President of the republic; Foncha, as Vice-President.

Throughout the 1960s, Cameroon maintained close ties with France, its chief economic benefactor. Internationally, the country generally supported the Western bloc, although it signed economic and cultural agreements with the Soviet Union and its satellites.

In 1972 Cameroon's federal structure gave way to a unitary republic under a new constitution. Legislative power was placed in the hands of a 120 member National Assembly, elected directly.

As part of President Ahidjo's plan to encourage a regime of national unity and social justice, a five-year economic plan (1972–1976) was initiated. He faced no organized opposition and on April 5, 1980 was reelected to a fifth term as President.

A prominent problem of late has been the civil war in Chad, Cameroon's northern neighbor, which has driven some 100,000 refugees into Cameroon. The Ahidjo Administration tried in 1979 to mediate regional factions, but in 1980 sought instead to protest Libya's participation in the disputes.

Cameroon's economy is primarily agricultural. Cocoa, coffee, palm products, tea, bananas, and cotton are major exports. The most important manufacturing industry is aluminum processing.

Cape Verde Islands (Santa Antas, Boa Vista, Sao Nicolau, Sao Vicente)

Date of independence: July 5, 1975
Area: 1,557 square miles
Population: 330,000 (est. 1981)
Capital: Praia
Monetary unit: Cape Verde escudo
Nationality: Cape Verdian
Religion: Catholicism mixed with superstition
Language: Portuguese and crioula (blend of Portuguese and West African)
Literacy: 14%
Type of government: Republic (one-party socialist)

Residents of the Cameroons examine garments at a used clothes market.

Political parties/leaders: **African Party for the Independence of Cape Verde (PAICV)**
Monetary conversion rate: **53.6 escudos = $1**
Principal economic resources: **Fish, bananas, salt, flour, corn**

History at a Glance

The Cape Verde Islands, uninhabited when they were discovered by the Portuguese in 1456, were first settled toward the end of the sixteenth century, when African slaves were brought in from Portuguese Guinea to work the land. In 1587 the islands were placed under the administration of a colonial governor.

For the next two centuries, the population of the islands grew steadily, particularly with the influx of Genoese and Spanish immigrants. Great Britain established a coaling station on the island of Sao Vicente in the eighteenth century, a move which also involved the founding of a settlement. On occasion, famine has caused some of the island's inhabitants to emigrate to the African mainland or to the United States.

Although Portuguese rule of the Cape Verde Islands was more benign than that of its other African possessions, rebellious uprisings started as early as 1956. Neighboring mainland country Guinea-Bissau rebels fought Portuguese troops and often the two countries found themselves allied against the common ruler.

When Portuguese rule of the islands finally ended in July 1975, it seemed appropriate to many that the islands would merge with Guinea-Bissau.

During the 1970s, two major independence movements developed: the mainland-based African Party for the Independence of Guinea and Cape Verde (PAIGC), which advocated the union of the islands and the mainland; and the Democratic Union of Cape Verde (UDCV), headed by Joao Baptista Monterio, which opposed a union.

When Cape Verde was liberated from Portuguese rule, a transitional government was set up via the election of a 56-member National People's Assembly. However, only members of the PAIGC participated in the election and it appeared that the majority of people wanted unification.

In July 1975 the Assembly elected Aristides Pereira, the secretary general of PAIGC as President of Cape Verde, and Major Pedro Pires, who had engineered independence agreements for both Guinea-Bissau and Cape Verde, was made Prime Minister. Later, the countries were governed through President Pereira as Secretary General and Guinea-Bissau's President Luis Cabral as Deputy Secretary.

Although a union between the two countries appeared inevitable, signs of trouble appeared in January 1977 when a Unity Council, formed to examine the means of unification, announced that it must move cautiously in order to establish "a common strategy of development."

On September 7, 1980, the National People's Assembly adopted Cape Verde's first constitution, which was expected to emulate Guinea-Bissau's. However, on November 14, 1980, four days after Guinea-Bissau adopted a similar constitution, the mainland government under Cabral was overthrown in a military coup. The reasons for this were partly because the black Guinea-Bissau people did not want to be dominated by the mostly mestizo population of Cape Verde.

Three weeks after the coup, Cape Verde's President Pereira pledged that his country would not interfere with the internal affairs of Guinea-Bissau, and on February 12, 1981, the National People's Assembly both reelected Pereira as President and revoked all constitutional provisions relating to a union with Guinea-Bissau. Earlier, the Cape Verde wing of the PAIGC cut its association with the Guinea-Bissau wing of the party and formed its own party, the African Party for the Independence of Cape Verde (PAICV).

Cape Verde is strategically located along sea routes taken by tankers carrying oil from the Mid-East to Europe. However, the country remains unaligned and has diplomatic and trade relations with both the Soviet bloc and the Europen Economic Community.

The islands suffer from a scarcity of fresh water and experienced a decade-long drought from 1968 to 1978. Fish, bananas, corn, and salt are principal exports.

This traditional ironworker makes arrows and farm tools.

Central African Republic

Date of independence: **August 13, 1960**
Area: **241,343 square miles**
Population: **2,000,000 (est. 1981)**
Capital: **Bangui**
Monetary unit: **CFA franc**
Nationality: **Central African**
Religion: **40% Protestant, 28% Catholic, 24% Animist, 8% Muslim**
Language: **French (official)**
Literacy: **5–10%**
Type of government: **Democratic republic with a single party—presently under military rule**
Monetary conversion rate: **225.50 Communaute Financiere Africaine (CFA) = $1 (1980)**
Principal economic resources: **Cotton, coffee, peanuts, livestock, diamonds, titanium**

History at a Glance

The territory of what is now the landlocked Central African Republic was first settled by France in 1887 pursuant to the Berlin Conference (1884–1885), which had established French rights to all land lying beyond the right bank of the Congo River. Early French explorers of this region were particularly concerned with solidifying France's control over all territory between Brazzaville and Lake Chad. With this in mind they set up the first French outpost of any major consequence at Bangui (the site of the present capital) in 1889. Within five years, the territory had become the French colony of Ubangi-Shari, a name derived from its two main rivers. In 1905 Ubangi-Shari was united with Chad and, five years later, became one of the four territories constituting French Equatorial Africa.

During both world wars, the territory was effectively utilized as a base for French military operations—in the first case, against the Germans in the Cameroons and then in conjunction with the Free French forces active in Africa from 1940 to 1944.

Following World War II, Ubangi-Shari was granted a greater degree of autonomy, sending elected representatives to the French Senate and Chamber of Deputies in Paris. Under the 1946 constitution, all inhabitants of the region were officially designated as citizens of France. In 1958 Ubangi-Shari changed its name to the Central African Republic, and voted to join the French Community as an autonomous republic. Two years later, it voted for full independence with David Dacko as President.

Dacko introduced one-party rule and steered his regime toward a closer alignment with the government of Communist China. In 1964 this policy led to official recognition of the Chinese regime which, by then, had launched an ambitious program of economic aid in the Central African Republic.

On January 1, 1966, the Dacko regime was overthrown in a military coup led by colonel Jean-Bedel Bokassa, who proved to be one of Africa's most unpredictable and cruel leaders. In the 13 years he ruled this impoverished nation, Bokassa appointed himself President for Life, created—and later abolished—a Council of the Central African Revolution, changed the country's government from a republic to a parliamentary monarchy, crowned himself Emperor Bokassa I in a lavish ceremony, and survived numerous coup attempts, one of which involved his son-in-law. He brutally enforced martial law and was reported to have tortured and murdered school children who refused to wear official school uniforms in 1979.

Bokassa cut relations with China, but began a courtship with the Soviet bloc and Libya's Colonel Muammar Qaddafi. On September 21, 1979, while Bokassa was in Libya, he was deposed by former president Dacko, who was aided by French military forces.

The new government put Bokassa on trial in absentia, as the Emperor had fled to Ivory Coast, and in December 1980, sentenced him to death for crimes that included murder, cannibalism, and embezzlement.

President Dacko, however, undermined his own popularity on his second attempt at leadership; he kept several high-ranking officials from the hated Bokassa regime in office and set up a one-party rule again.

In March 1981 Dacko was elected to a 6-year term as President by a slim margin, but opponents protested that the election was rigged and began demonstrations against him.

On September 1, 1981, General Andre Kolingba, Commander of the Central African Republic Army, deposed Dacko, placed all political parties in suspension, and declared rule under the Military Committee of National Redress.

Farming, animal husbandry, and food processing are main sources of employment in Central African Republic. Diamond exports were the leading source of revenue in 1978–1979 and uranium resources are still being tapped. However, economic diversification has been hampered by lack of transportation facilities and the fact that Emperor Bokassa squandered virtually all of the national treasury during his reign.

Chad

Date of independence: **August 11, 1960**
Area: **495,752 square miles**
Population: **4,602,000 (est. 1981)**
Capital: **N'Djamena**
Monetary unit: **CFA franc**
Religion: **50% Muslim, 5% Christian, 45% Animist**
Language: **French (official), Arabic, Sara**
Literacy: **5–10%**

Chad's President Tombalbaye conferring with former U.N. Secretary General U Thant.

Type of government: **Republic**
Political parties/leaders: **Chad National Liberation Front, several other parties, one opposition group**
Monetary conversion rate: **225.80 francs = $1 (1980)**
Principal economic resources: **Cotton, cattle, fish, livestock, oil, uranium.**

History at a Glance
Ancient history records the existence of several African empires which flourished between the Niger River and the Upper Nile; the Baguirmi and Wadai Empires are known to have held sway within the boundaries of the present Chadian republic. In the fourteenth century Islamic invaders from North and West Africa penetrated as far south as Wadai, and used this land as a fertile hunting ground for the flourishing slave trade.

(One of the long-range results of this human exploitation has been the development of a deep-seated hostility between Chadian blacks and their former Arab masters.)

Initial European contact with the territory dates back to 1822, although exploration did not begin in earnest until 1853. During the 1890s, the French pushed their way northwards from the Middle Congo region and, by 1897, had reached the shores of Lake Chad itself. Before the turn of the century, boundaries had been fixed between adjacent French, British and German territories in the area.

In 1910 Chad became one of the territories constituting French Equatorial Africa, but its economy developed slowly due to the lack of markets for its produce. By 1930 it was already being affected adversely by the onset of the world depression.

During World War II, the colony rallied to the side of the Free French and became an important staging area for Allied troops earmarked for battle on the North African front. As a reward for its loyalty, Chad was granted a greater degree of autonomy in 1946, and began sending elected representatives to the French National Assembly. In 1958 Chad became a member state of the French Community.

An independence movement, led by the first Premier and President Francois Tombalbaye, gained complete freedom for Chad on August 11, 1960. A struggle for political control began. A coup in 1963 was rebuffed and a new constitution and government under President Tombalbaye was established. Dissatisfaction with his policies grew, however, and in 1966, the Chad National Liberation Front (Frolinat) was formed.

President Tombalbaye tried hard to keep his country together until his assassination on April 13, 1975 during a coup by army and police units. He was succeeded by General Felix Malloum, who received endorsement from a number of former opposition groups, except Frolinat.

Frolinat, under the military leadership of Hissein Habre, fought Libyan forces in northern Chad in June 1976, and later sought help from the Malloum regime. When Malloum refused assistance, Habre lost control of the main wing of the Frolinat to Goukhouni Oueddei, who in turn decided to cooperate with the Libyans. Frolinat launched several offensives against Chadian cities and by June 1978, was in control of the northern two-thirds of the country. This time, President Malloum treated the force with more seriousness and on August 29, announced the appointment of Habre as prime minister under a "basic charter of national reconciliation."

The honeymoon between Malloum and Habre was short-lived, and following an abortive coup against Malloum in February 1979, fighting broke out between the factions.

Nine rival groups met in Lagos, Nigeria in March 1979 and agreed to form a provisional government and named former Frolinat leader Oueddei as President. However, fighting broke out again in March 1980 when Habre, now the Defense Minister, challenged President Oueddei, and a bloody civil war began.

During this period, some 80,000 civilians fled the capital of N'Djamena, the site of much of the fighting.

Habre's forces, the Armed Forces of the North (FAN), secured the capital, but Libyan troops, in support of President Oueddei, attacked and captured the city in June 1980. Libyan troops, under instruction of Muammar Qaddafi, stormed into Chad throughout the rest of the year and beat back Habre's army—virtually annexing the entire country much to the consternation of the rest of the world, aware of Qaddafi's expansionist dreams.

French President Francois Mitterand first tried to woo President Oueddei from Qaddafi, offering him unconditional French aid to rebuild Chad's army and economy. Nigeria and Senegal also pledged to supply troops to Chad, as did, on a lesser scale, Zaire, Benin, and Gabon.

Finally, at the North-South Cancun Summit in Mexico in October 1981, President Mitterand publicly appealed for the Organization of African Unity to create a peace-keeping force to replace the Libyans in Chad.

This time, President Oueddei complied and served Qaddafi an eviction notice, calling for complete Libyan withdrawal from N'Djamena and evacuation of Chad within a year. Qaddafi had promised to withdraw if asked and, with the world watching, withdrew his 10,000 troops from all Chadian land except a narrow, uranium-rich region in Northern Chad which Libya has long claimed as its own.

Qaddafi is up for the chairmanship of the OAU and observers have speculated that he might be interested in improving his image. Others thought his congenial withdrawal was geared to allow Chad to plunge deeper into economic and political chaos, thus making a merger with Libya more palatable to the Chadians. Libya has kept Chad afloat with oil shipments and food supplies and President Oueddei would not be able to survive a complete severance in trade. The year-long Libyan occupation also has served to keep Habre and numerous other factions in line.

Chad's economy is almost exclusively agricultural, with farming, livestock, and fish. Attempts at locating significant mineral deposits have been unsuccessful; the only known uranium and other mineral deposits are located in the northern-most region, which is occupied by Libya.

Comoros

Date of independence: **July 6, 1975**
Area: **718 square miles**
Population: **306,000 (est. 1981)**
Capital: **Moroni**
Monetary unit: **CFA franc**
Nationality: **Comoran**
Religion: **Islamic**
Language: **French, Arabic, Swahili**
Literacy: **15%**

Type of government: 3 islands form independent republic; 4th island remains French territorial community
Political parties/leaders: Federal Assembly, other parties
Monetary conversion rate: 225.80 francs = $1 (1980)
Principal economic resources: Perfume essences, copra, coconuts, cloves, spices

History at a Glance

The Comoros Islands—Grand Comoro, Anjouan, Moheli, and Mayotte—are volcanic islands in the Indian Ocean between Mozambique and Madagascar.

Through the centuries, the Comoros have been invaded by a succession of groups from the coast of Africa, Persian Gulf, Indonesia, and Madagascar and ruled by many Arab sultans. In 1505 Portuguese explorers came, and Arab migrants brought the Muslim faith. Between 1843 and 1912 France set up colonial rule over the Comoros, placing them under the administration of the Governor-General of Madagascar. Later, wealthy, French and Arab merchants established plantations on the islands.

Following a 1968 student strike, France decided to permit formation of legal political parties in the islands and within four years, pro-independence forces were strong. Under French approval, three of the Comoros Islands declared themselves independent on July 6, 1975 with Mayotte voting to remain under French administration. The main reason for this separation is that Mayotte's population is mostly Christian while the other islands are Muslim.

A month after independence, Justice Minister Ali Soilih staged a coup with the help of mercenaries and overthrew the nation's first president, Ahmed Abdallah. Soilih implemented drastic reforms, lowering the voting age to 14, destroying all records, and killing many Comorans. His socialist leanings did not please the population, however, and after two unsuccessful coup attempts, Soilih was desposed on May 13, 1978 by a revolt aided by some of the same mercenaries he had employed three years earlier.

Soilih was killed shortly thereafter, allegedly during an escape attempt.

After the coup, Ahmed Abdallah and Mohammed Ahmed formed a "military and political directorate" until a constitution and republic were formed on October 1. Ahmed stepped down two days later and Abdallah regained the presidency.

Tensions following the coup continue to cause problems, but the major effort of the government is to revive a stagnant economy and persuade Mayotte to join an economic federation. (Mayotte has 14% of Comoros' population.)

Comoros is one of the world's poorest and least developed nations. Besides its economic and political upheavals, a volcano on Grande Comore erupted in April 1976, causing havoc and dispossessing some 500 families.

Comoros is the leading producer of ylang-yland, a critical element in perfume production, and the second largest producer of the world's vanilla supply. However, the country must still import 40% of its food.

Congo

Date of independence: August 15, 1960
Area: 132,046 square miles
Population: 1,580,000 (est. 1980)
Capital: Brazzaville
Monetary unit: CFA franc
Nationality: Congolese
Religion: 50% Animist, 49% nominal Christian, 1% Muslim
Language: French (official), Lingala, Kikongo
Literacy: 20%
Type of government: Republic (military regime established September 1978)
Political parties/leaders: Congolese Labor Party, Colonel Denis Sassou-Nguessou
Monetary conversion rate: CFA francs 225.80 = $1 (1980)
Principal economic resources: Sugar cane, wood, coffee, cocoa, crude oil, tobacco

Delcommune dam supplies hydropower to the Congo's largest mining operation.

Louvanium University campus in Leopoldville.

History at a Glance

During the sixteenth century, the territory of today's Congo (Brazzaville) Republic was part of the so-called Congo Empire, which is believed to have extended as far south as Angola. Prior to this time, the sole Europeans in the area had been the Portuguese who discovered the mouth of the Congo River in 1484.

France established numerous trading companies during the seventeenth century, showing particular interest in slaves and ivory as items of commerce. Following the abolition of the slave trade, France undertook the exploration of the interior, a task hampered by its dense forests and barely navigable rivers. In 1880 a local chieftain signed a treaty with French explorer Pierre Savorgnan de Brazza, placing his domain under the protection of France. Five years later, the major European powers recognized French claims to the entire region lying beyond the right bank of the Congo River. In 1908 France installed a governor-general in Brazzaville, the present-day capital of the republic. Two years later, Middle Congo (as it was then called) was made a separate colony within the framework of French Equatorial Africa.

In 1940 Middle Congo joined Chad in declaring its support of the Free French forces under the leadership of Charles de Gaulle. During the war, it played a valuable strategic role in accommodating troops ultimately bound for combat in various parts of the Sahara Desert.

By 1956 Middle Congo had achieved full local autonomy. Two years later, it became an independent state within the French Community, changing its name to the Congo Republic. Fulbert Youlou, the mayor of Brazzaville, was elected president in 1960, the same year the Congo opted for full independence. Youlou was deposed three years later in the wake of popular unrest following passage of a bill designed to institute one-party rule in the country.

Under Youlou's successor, Alphonse Massamba-Debat, the Congo cultivated close ties with China, and sought to implement a national policy which Debat characterized as "scientific socialism." When Debat introduced Cuban advisers, however, utilizing them as a kind of private militia, the regular army staged a coup d'etat in 1968, installing President Marien N'Gouabi as head of state.

During his eight years as president, N'Gouabi proclaimed a "people's republic" and formed the official party, the Congolese Labor Party, complete with constitution, in January 1970. Later, student unrest and alleged plots against the regime caused a shake-up and in 1973, the Constitution was rewritten and the post of prime minister reestablished.

President N'Gouabi was assassinated by a four-man hit squad on March 18, 1977, and the power of the country went to an 11-member committee headed by Colonel Joachim Yhombi-Opango, who suspended the Constitution and reportedly sought Western aid for the nation. Opango also had former president Massamba-Debat, who was accused of masterminding the N'Gouabi assassination, executed on March 25. Shortly thereafter, Opango named Major Denis Sassou-Nguesso as First Vice President of the Military Committee.

Opango's sympathy toward the West, however, earned him enmity from his fellow party member and he resigned under pressure from the Central Committee of the Congolese Labor Party on February 5, 1979. He was later arrested and in late 1979 demoted to a private soldier. Meanwhile, Sassou-Nguesso was named President, a decision which was later confirmed by an election.

President Sassou-Nguesso has renewed relations with the Soviet Union, Cuba, and China, as well as the United States. He is on good terms with most of the Congo's neighbors, with the exception of Zaire, which has accused the Congo of both launching surreptitious guerrilla attacks against it as well as stockpiling weapons with Benin and Guinea.

Oil, timber, and potash are among the Congo's most important resources, along with copper, lead, and zinc.

Djibouti

Date of independence: June 27, 1977
Area: 8,800 square miles
Population: 286,000 (est. 1981)
Capital: Djibouti
Monetary unit: Djibouti franc
Nationality: Afar or Issa
Religion: 94% Muslim, 6% Christian
Language: French (official), Somali, Afar, Arabic
Literacy: 5%
Type of government: Republic
Political parties/leaders: Four major political parties
Monetary conversion rate: 173.38 Djibouti francs = $1 (1980)
Principal economic resources: Goats, sheep, camels

History at a Glance

French control over this portion of Somaliland dates back to an omnibus treaty signed by France and a number of Danakil tribal chieftains in 1862. Seven years later, concurrent with the opening of the Suez Canal, a number of French development companies were established in the region. In 1896 France annexed the territory as a colony after having signed additional treaties with Danakil and Issa chieftains. The all-important railroad which links Addis Ababa (Ethiopia) to the sea was completed in 1917.

After World War II, French Somaliland became an overseas territory, and gained complete internal autonomy in 1956. Two years later, the local assembly voted to retain its territorial status.

In 1964 a conference of nonaligned nations placed the issue of French Somaliland on its agenda, and called upon France to grant the territory immediate independence. The Somalian delegate to the United Nations later asked that body to take up the same question, but political leaders within the territory itself rejected this proposal on the grounds that it involved "annexationist designs." Consequently, French Somaliland reaffirmed its loyalty to France.

In 1967 when the area voted to remain part of France, rioting erupted among Somalis who wished to join Somalia. In 1972 President Pompidou of France affirmed that the country had direct ties with France. It is run by a French appointed high commissioner, and an elected Chamber of Deputies. It is represented in the French Parliament by a Senator and Deputy.

Both Ethiopia and Somalia claim this territory and French departure could lead to a war for it.

Djibouti is an important terminus and a vital port for Ethiopia. The Addis Ababa-Djibouti one track railroad carries about one third of Ethiopia's exports over its 486 miles.

Equatorial Guinea

Date of independence: October 12, 1968
Area: 10,830 square miles
Population: 346,000 (est. 1981)
Capital: Malabo
Monetary unit: Ekvele
Nationality: Equatorial Guinean
Religion: 99% population nominally Christian
Language: Spanish (official), Fang
Literacy: 20% (1975)
Type of government: Republic
Political parties/leaders: La Transition (formerly National Unity Party of Workers)
Monetary conversion rate: 159.50 bipkwele = (1980)
Principal economic resources: Cocoa, wood, coffee

History at a Glance

Fernando Poo was discovered by Fernao de Po of Portugal in 1471, at which time it was given the name Formosa. (Annobon, an island lying some 400 miles to the southwest, was discovered a year later.) Portugal ceded both islands to Spain in 1778. From 1827 to 1843, Great Britain received permission from Spain to use Fernando Poo as a base for hunting down slave-runners. During this period, a number of Sierra Leonean Creoles and West Indian Maroons were liberated on the island. In 1904 Fernando Poo and Rio Muni became known as the West African Territories and, later, as Spanish Guinea. This territory acquired the status of a province in 1960. Rio Muni was ceded to Spain by Portugal in 1778 and reconfirmed as a Spanish possession at the Berlin Conference (1884–1885). Spain, however, did not take over its administration until about 1900.

When the colonies sought independence in the late 1960s, progress was hampered by differences between mainland Fang, which wanted to sever all ties with Spain, and the island Bubi, which preferred a semi-autonomous government with connections to Spain. A compromise constitution was reached and passed by a people's election on August 11, 1968 by a 63% majority. During a presidential election a month later, a mainland Fang, Macias Nguema Biyogo, was elected president and on October 12, 1968, the nation, Equatorial Guinea was born.

In 1969 President Macia (who later changed his

name to Macie) seized emergency power when a series of tribal rivalries engendered unrest. As Macie's cruel politics emerged, opposition arose and soon he was forced to squelch a major coup against him. During this time of turmoil, Macie executed more than 200 political enemies and hundreds of skilled workers, and forced most of the Spaniards still living in the country to flee. Macie quickly established a one-party state, and declared himself President for Life in July 1972.

During Macie's 11-year rule, which was supported by the Soviet bloc nations, Equatorial Guinea was dubbed the "Auschwitz of Africa." Macie was deposed on August 3, 1979 in a coup led by his nephew, Lieutenant Colonel Teodoro Obiang Nguema Mbasogo, who formed a Supreme Military Council. Macie was executed a month later for the crimes of genocide, treason, and embezzlement.

Obiang has since reopened churches, released all political prisoners, returned confiscated property, and is working to reconstruct the country with the help of Spain.

The economy of the nation is based on cocoa, timber, bananas, palm products, and coffee. However, economic progress was stunted by the mass murder of so many of the nation's workers under the Macie regime.

Equatorial Guinea is Africa's only Spanish-speaking nation.

Ethiopia

Date of independence: September 12, 1974
Area: 471,799 square miles
Population: 33,388,000 (est. 1981)
Capital: Addis Ababa
Monetary unit: Birr
Nationality: Ethiopian
Religion: 35–40% Ethiopian Orthodox, 40–45% Muslim, 15–20% Animist

An agriculturist examines a coffee tree at an experimental farm in Ethiopia.

Language: Amharic (official), English
Literacy: 5%
Type of government: Military rule since 1974
Political parties/leaders: Commission for Organizing the Party of the Working People of Ethiopia, 3 clandestine parties, 3 separatist groups, lesser opposition groups
Monetary conversion rate: 2.07 birr = $1 (1980)
Principal economic resources: Coffee, barley, wheat, corn, potash, salt, gold, copper, platinum

History at a Glance

Ethiopia is one of the oldest nations in the world, and the oldest in Africa south of the Sahara Desert. Its original settlers, the Cushites, were descendants of the Galla and Sidama tribes which occupied the territory prior to 1000 B.C. From the tenth to the seventh centuries B.C., Semitic peoples from southern Arabia entered Ethiopia, and it is their offspring which became the lineal descendants of the Amhara and Tigrai tribes found there today. In the writings of the fifth century B.C. Greek historian Herodotus, one encounters a reference to the Ethiopians as "the most just men" and, even in Homer, they are spoken of as the "blameless race."

Haile Selassie, late Emperor of Ethiopia, paid an official visit to the United Nations in 1967. He is shown being greeted by Secretary General U Thant.

Donkeys and cars share a street in Addis Ababa.

Traditionally, Menelik, the first son on King Solomon and the Queen of Sheba, is regarded as the founder of the Ethiopian Empire, which is said to date back to 1000 B.C. The earliest authenticated history of the area describes Ethiopia as a pagan empire with its capital at Axum.

Christianity was introduced in the fourth century A.D., and survived the onslaughts of Moslem hordes which in the seventh century imposed the religion of Islam on northeastern Africa. For a time, the Axum dynasty fell into decline and was threatened with extinction by the Zagwe dynasty which was founded by Takla Haimanot. In 1260 with the accession of Yekuma Amlak, the Axum line was restored and the reputed link with Solomon reestablished. Emperor Amda Seyon I later imposed Ethiopian rule over the Moslem principalities which had sprung up to the east and south.

In the sixteenth century, Moslem power reasserted itself when the Somalis (with the aid of the Ottoman Turks) began a holy war that threatened to engulf the entire kingdom. Though the Ethiopians received help from Portugal, they were saved largely due to the heroic exploits of their legendary emperor, Prester John.

The next three centuries, characterized by anarchy, cultural decadence, religious controversy, and other divisive influences, resulted in the partitioning of Ethiopia by a number of rival pretenders to the throne. Allegiance to a central government was not rekindled until 1855 when the Emperor Theodore II, himself a one-time petty chieftain, succeeded in subjugating a number of other dissident chieftains. However, when Theodore committed suicide in 1869, the country was once again plunged into strife.

In 1885 Italy capitalized on the discordant situation by capturing the seaport of Massawa, thus gaining a secure foothold in Eritrea. Menelik II, one of Ethiopia's great reform emperors, thereupon signed a face-saving treaty with Italy, maintaining that it was with his approval that a protectorate was being established over the country. Italy attempted to force the issue to total conquest by launching an invasion in 1895, but was forced to withdraw after a humiliating defeat.

Menelik II turned his energies to the development of the interior of his country—building a rail line, establishing more schools, improving communications and introducing postal service. After the death of Menelik in 1913, his successor Lij Yassu embraced the Moslem faith—a gesture which led to his being deposed by Ras Tafari Menkonnen, a grand-nephew of Menelik. Later Ras (prince) Tafari made Judith (Lij Yassu's aunt) empress, and assumed the role of regent until her death in 1930. He was then crowned as emperor in his own right, and ascended the throne as Haile Selassie I, the Lion of Judah.

Five years later, with the invasion of Ethiopia by Italy, he was forced to flee his country. His plea for international intervention, aired before the League of Nations, went largely unheeded, and he then took up his exile in Great Britain. On May 5, 1941, however, he triumphantly re-entered Addis Ababa at the head of a liberating army and was restored to his throne.

In 1952 with the approval of the United Nations, Eritrea was linked to Ethiopia as a federated state. Ten years later, its status was changed to that of an Ethiopian province.

During the postwar period, Ethiopia modernized its institutions somewhat. A liberalized constitution was put into effect, and Haile Selassie attempted to

Ethiopia's poverty is manifest in the central market at Harrar.

function as a kind of moderating influence between African nationalists on the one hand, and the last heirs to the European colonial tradition on the other.

In Ethiopia itself, a coup d'etat was attempted in 1960 by members of the Imperial Guard under the leadership of Crown Prince Asfa Wassan. The revolt was quickly crushed, and its chief leaders (with the exception of the Crown Prince, the emperor's son) were executed.

Throughout the 1960s, Ethiopia attempted to establish itself as a political headquarters and cultural center for the rest of emergent Africa. This is symbolized in the pride of Addis Ababa, the imposing edifice known as Africa Hall, headquarters of the Organization of African Unity and the United Nations Economic Commission for Africa.

Though a symbol of black culture and progress, Ethiopia remained in the grip of a feudal system in which over half the nation's rural population was required to turn over some three-fourths of their crops to landlords.

In 1974 Haile Selassie was overthrown by a military coup, which announced sweeping land reform measures. However, opposition from both large and small landlords threatened implementation.

Emperor Haile Selassie died at the age of 83 on August 27, 1975 while still in detention. Earlier, on March 21, Lieutenant Colonel Mengistu Haile-Mariam, leader of the Provisional Military Administrative Council (PMAC), decreed formal abolition of the monarchy with the intention of reorganizing Ethiopia by socialism.

A number of officials were executed for "counter-revolutionary crimes" and the Mengistu regime enacted an indiscriminate "red terror" from December 1977 to February 1978 in order to establish their control.

Following the 1974 coup, revolt in Eritrea escalated into full-scale war with Ethiopia and the Eritrean Independence Front, armed by Libya and other Arab states, demanded full independence. Some 22,000 government troops were sent into combat in February 1975, and thousands of deaths were reported in the ensuing months.

Somalian rebels supported Eritrea's fight, but when the Soviets diverted their support from Somalia to Ethiopia, the tide of war turned and by March 1978, badly beaten Somalis retreated to their homeland, leaving Eritrea still under Ethiopian control. Guerrilla activity in that region remained strong in 1980.

Ethiopia is one of the world's poorest countries in terms of per capita GNP. It has an agricultural economy with a principal export of coffee. Gold is mined commercially and deposits of copper, potash, and natural gas recently have been discovered. Most technical and economic assistance is supplied by communist nations.

Gabon

Date of independence: **August 17, 1960**
Area: **103,089 square miles**
Population: **1,508,000 (1981 est.)**
Capital: **Libreville**
Monetary unit: **CFA franc**
Nationality: **Gabonese**
Religion: **55%–75% Christian, 1% Muslim, Animist**
Language: **French (official), Fang**
Literacy: **Reportedly 80% of children in school, but total is lower**
Type of government: **Republic (since 1964 one-party regime)**
Political parties/leaders: **Gabonese Democratic Party**
Monetary conversion rate: **CFA francs 225.80 = $1 (1980)**
Principal economic resources: **Cocoa, coffee, timber, iron ore, oil, manganese**

History at a Glance

The first Europeans to visit and explore the territory of Gabon were the Portuguese, who arrived toward the end of the fifteenth century and established trading posts at the mouth of the Ogowe River. French missionaries followed soon after, only to be succeeded by groups of European slave traders.

By 1815 the slave trade had been abolished, thus obliging the French to concentrate on exploitation of the territory's other resources, notably her forests. This policy brought about the development of several coastal ports, and the signing of a number of treaties with local rulers. The French agreed to protect the interests of these chieftains in return for access to the regions they controlled.

At the Congress of Berlin (1884–1885), the major European powers agreed to recognize French control over the land lying beyond the right bank of the Congo River (subsequently known as the French Congo). Five years later, Gabon became a part of this region, although it did not come to exist as a distinct administrative entity until 1893. In 1910 it achieved colonial status within what was then called French Equatorial Africa.

After World War II, Gabon was made an Overseas Territory of the French Union, and given the right to be represented in the French Parliament by a senator and a deputy of its own choice. In 1958 the colony voted to become fully autonomous within the framework of the French Community and, two years later, declared itself a fully independent republic, with Leon M'Ba as premier.

M'Ba was returned to office a year later, this time with the title of president of Gabon. In 1964 the Gabonese army temporarily overthrew the government, but the deposed M'Ba was reinstated by French President Charles de Gaulle who ordered French troops airlifted into Libreville to quell the rebellion.

In 1967 M'Ba died, and was replaced by Albert-Bernard Bongo, who had been elected vice president in the spring of that year.

President Bongo gave priority to his nation's economic development, and national unity. Gabon's unusual wealth of mineral resources helped this country to attain first place among black African nations in per capita output, estimated at $3,300 in 1979.

Bongo declared Gabon a one-party state in March 1968 and announced a "renovation" policy that included formation of the Gabonese Democratic Party (PDG). The party accorded unanimous support in parliamentary elections in 1969, 1973, and 1980.

Gabon remains a member of the French Community and has received French military support in deterring Libyan (via Chad) overtures of expansionism.

Natural resources include abundant supplies of oil, manganese, uranium, and timber. Gabon also has iron ore reserves estimated at 1 billion tons.

Gambia

Date of independence: **February 18, 1965**
Area: **4,361 square miles**
Population: **615,000 (est. 1981)**
Capital: **Banjul**
Monetary: **Dalasi**
Nationality: **Gambian**
Religion: **85% Muslim, 15% Animist, Christian**
Language: **English (official), Mandinka, Wolof**
Literacy: **10%**
Type of government: **Republic**
Political parties/leaders: **People's Progressive Party, four opposition parties**
Monetary conversion rate: **1.68 dalasi = $1 (1980)**
Principal economic resources: **Peanuts, fish**

History at a Glance

Gambia is the smallest nation in Africa. The first reference to Gambia in the historical records of antiquity occurs in the reports of voyages made by Carthaginian explorers. Hanno's writings lend support to the theory that an entrance was made into the Gambian estuary as far back as 450 B.C.

The first Europeans to set foot in Gambia were led by Alvise de Cadamosto and Antoniotto Usodimare, both of whom were in the service of Portugal's Prince Henry the Navigator (1455).

Later, Gambia became part of England's ambitious colonization schemes for West Africa, with a settlement being founded at Fort James, a small island some 20 miles from the mouth of the Gambia River. English merchants in increasing numbers were granted royal charters to trade in West Africa, often competing with their French counterparts. Not until the Treaty of Versailles (1783) did the English establish a clearcut priority in the area.

In 1821 Gambia was placed under the control of a British colonial administration based in Sierra Leone. It became a colony in its own right until 1888 when it was provided with its own governor and legislative and executive councils.

Gambia's path to independence in the 20th century was peaceful and gradual. The nation's present Constitution, introduced in 1960, established a representative assembly headed by a chief minister. Modeling its governmental institutions on those of Great Britain, Gambia achieved final independence on February 18, 1965 with Dawda K. Jawara as Prime Minister. On the first anniversary of its independence, Gambia opted for a republican form of government.

Gambia has avoided the extravagant and, at times, grandiose economic projects which have brought some of her more famous neighbors to the brink of financial ruin. Careful and deliberate, the tiny country has met its budget and staked out realistic, rather than improbable goals.

Prime Minister Dawda Kairaba Jawara was elected President in 1970 and was reelected in 1972. Sir Dawda has maintained a cordial relationship with his bordering neighbor, Senegal.

Like many African nations, Gambia has been troubled by drought and inflation. While Gambia may lose a preferred market for its peanut crop due to Britain's joining the Common Market, direct involvement with the Common Market may well offset this potential loss.

In February 1982 negotiations were completed between Senegal and Gambia whereby the nations will unite in a confederation known as Senegambia.

Public opinion in both countries is divided as to the desirability of the merger—Gambians are concerned that their river-hugging nation will become just another province in Senegal, especially since the latter is 17 times larger in size and has a population 10 times larger than Gambia's.

Under the agreement, Senegal and Gambia will remain sovereign nations, but will integrate their security forces and communications networks and undertake an economic and monetary union. President Abdou Biouf of Senegal will be President of Senegambia and President Jawara will be Vice-President.

Integration has already been achieved by virtue of Gambia's small reserves; Senegal's 5,000 troops have already provided protection. Both nations are pro-West and have severed diplomatic ties with Libya.

There are sure to be problems reconciling the Gambialan dalasi with the Senegalese franc as the rates of exchange are incompatible.

Ghana

Date of independence: **March 6, 1957**
Area: **92,099 square miles**

Sir Dauda Jawara, Prime Minister of Gambia, addressing people of the village of Queenala during an electoral campaign.

Population: 11,529,000 (est. 1981)
Capital: Accra
Monetary unit: New Cedi
Religion: 45% Animist, 43% Christian, 12% Muslim
Language: English (official), Akan, Mole-Dagbani, Ewe languages
Literacy: 25%
Type of government: Republic
Political parties/leaders: People's National Party, five opposition parties
Monetary conversion rate: 2.75 new cedi = $1 (1980)
Principal economic resources: Cocoa, timber, coconuts, coffee, rubber, gold, diamonds, bauxite, manganese, fish

History at a Glance

Modern Ghana takes its name from an ancient African empire which flourished in the Western Sudan from the fourth through the twelfth centuries.

Ghana's first contact with the nations of Europe dates back to the 15th century when a band of Portuguese seafarers landed on the "Gold Coast," as it was then called, and began to trade in the area's plentiful gold dust. The Portuguese were followed by the Dutch, the Danes, the Swedes, the Prussians and, finally, by the English who in 1807 prohibited the lucrative slave trade which had begun to replace gold as the most profitable commodity in the territory.

The English remained the dominant European power in Ghana during the nineteenth century, although their hegemony was often threatened by frequent tribal uprisings of the powerful and well-organized Ashanti Confederation. Ashanti territory, however, was annexed by the English in 1900, and incorporated with the Northern Protectorates into the already-existing Gold Coast Colony. In 1922 Togoland, formerly under German control, was given to Great Britain, which administered this territory, too, as part of the Gold Coast.

After World War II, Ghana gradually came to have more say about its political destiny, first by participating actively in the rewriting of a constitution, then by electing its own representatives to a duly constituted parliament. On March 6, 1957, Ashanti, the Northern Protectorates, the Gold Coast and British Togoland declared their independence, adopted the name of Ghana, and immediately joined the British Commonwealth. Officially, Ghana became a republic on July 1, 1960, continuing under the leadership of President Kwame Nkrumah, who held absolute power until he himself was overthrown on February 24, 1966 while on a visit to Red China.

The National Liberation Council then established a military government, installing J. A. Ankrah as head of state.

In July 1972, Colonel Ignatius K. Acheampong headed a group of military leaders who seized govern-

A tribal chief in Ghana.

ing power from the civilian Prime Minister, Kofi A. Busia, while he was in London undergoing medical treatment.

However, Colonel Acheampong was forced to resign on July 5, 1978, and was immediately succeeded by his deputy, Lieutenant General Frederick Akuffo. Less than a year later, Akuffo was deposed in a coup led by junior military officers and an Armed Forces Revolutionary Council (AFRC) was established under Flight Lieutenant Jerry Rawlings, who had been undergoing a court martial for staging an unsuccessful coup a few months earlier.

Rawlings had former presidents Acheampong, Akuffo, and Brigadier Akwasi Afrifa executed in addition to a number of other high-ranking military and civilian officials, causing international protests.

Rawlings stepped aside when Dr. Hilla Limann of the People's National Party won a presidential balloting in July 1979, but led a coup against Limann on New Year's Eve 1981. He has since dismissed Ghana's

A woman in traditional dress walks past the new state library in Accra, Ghana.

parliament, banned political parties, and suspended the Constitution. Rawlings is a devout admirer of Libya's Muammar Qaddafi and sees Libya as a "revolutionary dream." He appears to be leading Ghana down a similar path, having established a "people's government" in early 1982.

Like several other African countries, Ghana has failed to diversify its export crops and has depleted its natural resources causing grave economic difficulties. The cocoa crop, which was a massive 420,000 tons in the early 1960s, dropped to 270,000 tons in 1979. The country's mines, which once produced 35% of the world's gold, supplied only 1% in 1979. Inflation has reached 120%.

Guinea

Date of independence: **October 2, 1958**
Area: **94,926 square miles**
Population: **5,574,000 (est. 1981)**
Capital: **Conakry**
Monetary unit: **Syli**
Nationality: **Guinean**
Religion: **75% Muslim, 25% Animist, 1% Christian**
Language: **French (official), several tribal dialects**
Literacy: **5–10%**
Type of government: **Republic (one-party presidential regime)**
Political parties/leaders: **Democratic Party of Guinea, National Liberation Front of Guinea (illegal)**

Monetary conversion rate: **19.46 Sylis = $1 (1980)**
Principal economic resources: **Palm oil, bananas, rice, coconuts, peanuts, bauxite, gold, diamonds**

History at a Glance

Modern-day Guinea is linked historically with the ancient Ghanian kingdom of West Africa. The territory is believed to have been ruled by a succession of dynasties, the most celebrated of which was headed by the Malinke chieftain, Sundiata, founder of the Mali Empire. The last Malinke emperor was deposed in the seventeenth century, some two centuries after the first Europeans (the Portuguese) had begun to explore the area.

Portuguese, French, and British traders were engaged in competitive trade along Guinea's coast long before the Peace of Paris (1814) secured for France the most advantageous position in the region. By 1849 the French had proclaimed a protectorate over the Guinea coast.

Opposition to French rule from the inhabitants of the interior was widespread during the last decades of the nineteenth century. In 1879 the famous Malinke chieftain, Almany Samoury Toure (a direct ancestor of Guinea's Sekou Toure), seized Kankan in the Upper Guinea region, and began terrorizing French settlers.

By that time, Guinea was being administered as a separate colony, its name having been changed from Rivieres du Sud to French Guinea. Up until World War I, a number of chieftains from the hinterlands continued to harass the colonial authorities, but this did not prevent the French from holding together the federation they had imposed on their West African territories.

The inhabitants of Guinea became French citizens in 1946, and won the right to vote in 1957. A year later, the electorate rejected an offer of independence within the French Community, preferring instead complete independence with Sekou Toure as President. The French immediately withdrew all economic and financial aid, and recalled the trained technical and administrative personnel needed to operate an efficient bureaucracy. For a time, Guinea received aid from the Soviet Union and China, although it has since been assisted by the United States and other Western nations as well. Since their independence, Guinea, Ghana, and Mali have been closely allied as members of the Union of African States.

Although an avowed Marxist, Toure has followed a foreign policy of nonalignment, and cultivated particularly close ties with Kwame Nkrumah (deposed as President of Ghana in 1966).

Toure offered Nkrumah a huge welcome after the latter entered Guinea in exile, naming him co-president.

Members of a U.N. commission cross over a makeshift bridge during Guinea Bissau's struggle for independence from Portugal.

After a serious internal crisis (a Portuguese–Guinean exile attack on its capital city—1970–1972) that decimated a large percentage of its governing class, Guinean President Toure turned to improving his nation's social and economic conditions. Ample supplies of natural resources such as bauxite and iron ore helped make his job easier. In 1975 Toure formed a company with Saudi Arabia, Kuwait, Egypt, and Libya to mine bauxite in the country's north.

Toure calls Guinea a "people's state" and has stressed the use of "national" languages as a replacement for French, has replaced the franc with the syli,

has removed beggars from public view, and has included women in the governmental process.

He also has improved relations with Liberia, Sierra Leone, Nigeria, Cameroon, Algeria, and since 1978, Senegal and the Ivory Coast.

Despite peaceful overtures to other nations, on May 14, 1980, Toure barely escaped an assassination attempt which claimed the lives of others and injured 30 additional bystanders. Toure immediately called Guineans to "remobilize" and "unite against intruders." He was reelected President in 1981.

Committee on the decolonization of Africa meets in Conakry.

Guinea-Bissau

Date of independence: **September 10, 1974**
Area: **13,948 square miles**
Population: **580,000 (est. 1981)**
Capital: **Bissau**
Monetary unit: **escudo**
Nationality: **Guinean**
Religion: **66% Animist, 30% Muslim, 4% Christian**
Language: **Portuguese, several tribal dialects**
Literacy: **3–5%**
Type of government:
Political parties/leaders: **Revolutionary Council, Major Joao Bernardo Vieira**
Monetary conversion rate: **35.2 escudos $1 (1978)**
Principal economic resources: **Palm oil, rice, coconuts, peanuts, bauxite**

History at a Glance

Portuguese sailors first visited this portion of Guinea in 1446, some 100 years before it was to become a source of slaves. Cape Verdeans set up trading posts here and, by the nineteenth century, had imposed their administration over the entire territory. The tribes of the interior, however, were not fully subjugated until after World War I and only then with difficulty. Nationalism quickly grew during the Angola uprising of the 1960s.

Guinea-Bissau achieved *de facto* independence in 1974 with Portugal's other African colonies and was expected to unite with Cape Verde Islands under a common government.

For five years, measures toward unification were taken under the guidance of a mutually representative National People's Assembly. But, in November 1980, when a Cape Verde-based constitution was adopted in Guinea-Bissau under President Luis Cabral's leadership, Vice President Major Joao Bernardo Vieira led a military coup against Cabral, deposed him, and revoked the Constitution. Vieira immediately set up a Revolutionary Council with himself as Premier.

Cabral was denounced as having helped "corrupt the meaning of unity" between the two countries and was expected to be put on trial. Vieira, however, continued to entertain hopes that a unification between the two countries could be arranged. However, Cape Verde leaders have since taken steps to disassociate themselves politically from the new council.

Guinea-Bissau has received Soviet assistance since 1978. Recently, the country has experienced trouble with neighboring Guinea over an offshore oil exploration site.

Major exports are peanuts, palm products, fish, and shrimp. Economic development has been hindered by insufficient capital, skilled labor, and transportation.

Ivory Coast

Date of independence: **August 7, 1960**
Area: **124,503 square miles**
Population: **8,313,000 (est. 1981)**
Capital: **Abidjan**
Monetary unit: **CFA franc**
Nationality: **Ivorian**
Religion: **66% Animist, 22% Muslim, 12% Christian**
Language: **French (official), 60 native dialects (primarily Dioula)**
Literacy: **65%**
Type of government: **Republic (one-party presidential regime)**
Political parties/leaders: **Democratic Party of the Ivory Coast, President Felix Houphouet-Boigny**
Monetary conversion rate: **225.80 CFA francs = $1 (1980)**
Principal economic resources: **Coffee, cocoa, timber, palm oil, petroleum, iron ore**

History at a Glance

The first Europeans to establish themselves in what is today the Ivory Coast were the Portuguese, whose commercial activities date back to the fifteenth century. Other European nations (principally Holland and England) soon began to compete for their share of the thriving slave market, and for gold, ivory, and spices as well. With different aims in view, French missionaries established a foothold in this region by settling at Assinie in 1687.

It was not until the nineteenth century, however, that the economic exploitation of the Ivory Coast was begun in earnest. In 1842 France established a protectorate over the coastal region and built up a number of trading posts, primarily at Assinie and Grand Bassam. French control was gradually extended into the interior through a number of treaties signed with various local chieftains. In 1893 the territory was placed under the control of a French governor. The administrative organization and military pacification of the area engaged the energies of the French until 1912.

After World War I, the colony flourished as a producer of hardwoods, cocoa, coffee, and bananas. Both European planters and African cultivators shared in the wealth produced by these exports.

In 1933 France linked Upper Volta with the Ivory Coast in the hope of inducing the former territory to provide a source of cheap labor for the latter. The plan failed, however, and the Ivory Coast was soon returned to its original status.

At the close of World War II, the Ivory Coast officially became an overseas territory of the French Union. By 1956 it had gained self-autonomy; by 1958, it had become an independent republic and a member of the French Community and, by 1960, it had attained

Armed with a spear, a watchman stands guard at the Ivory Coast Bouake Dam.

complete independence, as a republic, headed by a popularly elected president, Felix Houphouet-Boigny.

Since then, the Ivory Coast has retained close economic ties with France, disavowing all help from countries with alleged communist affiliations. Foreign companies operate relatively free of intervention.

The Ivory Coast has relied heavily on foreign investment to modernize the capital, improve public health, and eliminate primitive housing.

Relying heavily on foreign investment and expertise, Boigny, in 1974, set as a goal a 7.7% increase in gross domestic product based on a $1 billion 5 year plan. Already the Bandama River dam at Kossou (which will provide irrigation for nearby farm communities and substantial fish catch) has been opened as a result of this program. A port at San Pedro in the undeveloped southwestern area was completed in 1971.

The Ivory Coast has earned the distinction of being one of the most prosperous, highly developed, and politically stable countries in Africa, having tripled its agricultural exports in the past two decades. Although it entered a slight recession in 1980, Ivorians anticipate only renewed economic progress under the continued guidance of Boigny.

American and Spanish-owned oil companies have been drilling for off-shore oil since 1975 and it is expected that by the mid-1980s, the Ivory Coast will be self-sufficient in oil production, though agriculture will remain the staple of the country's economy.

Kenya

Date of independence: **December 12, 1963**
Area: **224,960 square miles**

Members of fishermen's families await return of the fishermen.

Population: **16,424,000 (est. 1981)**
Capital: **Nairobi**
Monetary unit: **Kenya shilling**
Religion: **56% Christian, 36% Animist, 7% Muslim, 1% Hindu**
Language: **Swahili (official), English**
Literacy: **27%**
Type of government: **Republic within Commonwealth**
Political parties/leaders: **Kenya African National Union**
Monetary conversion rate: **7.57 shillings = (1980)**
Principal economic resources: **Coffee, sisal, tea, cotton, livestock, wildlife**

History at a Glance
Archeological excavations in Kenya have unearthed

In the right foreground stands Kenya's Prime Minister Jomo Kenyatta, wearing a beaded cap. Other African leaders include (left to right:) Milton Obote (Uganda); Cyrille Adoula (former premier of the Congo), and, at far right in traditional African dress, Kenneth Kaunda of Zambia. The occasion is the opening meeting of the Pan-African Movement for East and Central Africa (PAFMECA).

bones, instruments, and several other artifacts (some of which may be 30,000 years old) in the Great Rift Valley. It has been determined that the earliest known inhabitants of the region buried their dead ceremoniously—a practice generally associated with relatively advanced cultures. Archeologists have also linked Kenya with an Iron Age civilization.

Long before the Portuguese arrived in Africa in the fifteenth century, the region was visited by Greek merchants and Arab slave traders. With the arrival of Vasco da Gama in 1498, the Portuguese established new trading posts and succeeded in suppressing Arab influence for the next two centuries. In 1729 however, the Arabs regained their influence, exercising sway for more than 150 years, during which time an Arab empire was established throughout East Africa.

European explorers again became active in the area in the nineteenth century, particularly the Englishmen Rebman and Kraft, and John Speke, who discovered Lake Victoria in 1858. During the next few decades, Great Britain and France put into effect what has been called the "spheres of influence policy" of partitioning

East and Central Africa. In 1887 Great Britain obtained a lease on the main coastal dominion of the Sultan of Zanzibar, the island from which the Arabs exercised considerable control over Kenya. Eight years later, Kenya (including the Sultan's coastal strip) was declared a British protectorate.

Beginning in the twentieth century, settlement of the territory was undertaken on a large scale by the British, the South Africans, and Asians most of whom were from the Indian subcontinent. As a rule, white Europeans acquired exclusive rights over the most desirable land in Kenya: the so-called "White Highlands." After World War I, the protectorate became a British Crown Colony and the coastal strip was given the status of a protectorate.

During the next three decades, sharp divisions between the Crown, the settlers (both white and Indian), and the natives resulted in an explosive situation—culminating in 1952 with the outbreak of the "Mau Mau" rebellion. This uprising was characterized by savage butchery on all sides and eventually claimed some 12,000 lives. When the state of emergency was finally declared at an end in 1960, some 80,000 suspected "Mau Mau" members were in prison, including Jomo Kenyatta, convicted leader of the rebellion.

Majority rule by the Africans was in the process of being introduced even as the "Mau Mau" revolt raged. In 1954 however, Tom Mboya, leader of the elected Africans, expressed his dissatisfaction with the existing political arrangement and rejected a newly proposed constitution. In 1960 an African delegation finally accepted the British blueprint for a transitional government. A year later, Kenyatta was released from prison and quickly returned to the leadership of the Kenya African National Union (KANU). In 1963 KANU won control of the legislature and, with British approval, introduced a program of internal self-government. In October of the same year, the Sultan of Zanzibar relinquished all rights to his mainland dominion. A month later, Kenya became an independent republic within the British Commonwealth with Kenyatta as President.

In 1969 Tom Mboya, the expected successor to Kenyatta, was assassinated, triggering a period of civil strife and abolition of the opposition party, Kenya People's Union. Opposition to the Kenyatta reign continued into the 1970s, with a few attempts to overthrow the government. Kenyatta and his Vice President, Daniel Arap Moi, were reelected in 1974, but not without political crises and the assassination of an opposition leader.

Kenyatta, who was known as "The Old Man," died in his bed at a rest home on August 22, 1978 and was immediately succeeded by Moi, who was later declared President for the remainder of Kenyatta's five-year term. He was reelected in 1979 for another five-year term.

A domestic problem for years has been the substantial Asian Indian population in Kenya. In 1982 President Moi accused the 100,000 Asians of "ruining the country's economy" and pledged to deport any Asian found hoarding or smuggling currency—regardless of their citizenship in Kenya.

The per capita annual income of the Kenyan Asians is estimated to be $15,000 while the overall per capita income of Kenya's 17 million blacks is less than $400.

In recent years, there have been shortages of rice and flour. Falling world prices for Kenya's main exports of coffee and tea have severely hurt the economy.

Lesotho

Date of independence: **October 4, 1966**
Area: **11,720 square miles**
Population: **1,437,000 (est. 1981)**
Capital: **Maseru**
Monetary unit: **South African Rand/Loti**
Nationality: **Basotho**

Religion: **70% Christian, Animist**
Language: **Sesotho (all population), English**
Literacy: **40%**
Type of government: **Constitutional monarchy**
Political parties/leaders: **Basotho National Party, four opposition parties**
Monetary conversion rate: **1 loti = $1.34 (1980)**
Principal economic resources: **Corn, wheat, sorghum, barley, diamonds**

History at a Glance

An enclave within the Republic of South Africa, Lesotho, then known as Basutoland, first became a battleground in 1831, when Basuto tribes engaged in open warfare against the Boers who were advancing northward from South Africa. In 1867 having been defeated by the Boers, the Basuto asked for and received British protection in return for granting England full sovereignty rights. In 1964 Basutoland won internal autonomy and made known its intention of becoming independent as the Kingdom of Lesotho in October of 1966. Motlotlehi Moshoeshoe II is King and its Prime Minister is Chief Leabua Jonathan.

Until then, the territory was governed by a paramount chief and by a British high commissioner in charge of defense, foreign affairs, and internal security.

Upon assuming independence, Prime Minister Jonathan pursued policies of peaceful coexistence with his larger, richer, and more potent neighbor, South Africa. The relationship was not without some uneasiness, however. In the words of Jonathan, the country has been desirous of "choosing our friends," while at the same time "living with our neighbors."

Lesotho has been enjoying a 5-year "holiday from politics" declared by its Prime Minister, Leabua Jonathan in 1970 when elections were suspended. As part of this holiday, leaders of the opposition party have been released from detention. Prime Minister Jonathan has also tried to establish some type of independent relationship vis-a-vis South Africa by declaring his disapproval of South African apartheid. However, Lesotho's geographic and economic dependence on South Africa (where some 40% of the male population are employed) lessens chances of upheaval in the relations of the two countries. In the meantime, Lesotho has replaced some British and South African government personnel with U.N. people.

In recent years, Chief Jonathan's popularity has decreased due to charges of corruption and nepotism. His principal rival, Ntsu Mokhekle, reportedly is amassing a guerrilla force in the Lesotho mountains with some 500 men and 65 Libyan-trained insurgents.

Understandably, Chief Jonathan has become sensitive to South African loyalties; although that government has supported him in the past, South African-made weapons have been discovered among the rival camps. In August 1980, Chief Jonathan met with South African Prime Minister Pieter Botha and held "candid and highly constructive" talks.

Although Lesotho has one of the highest literacy rates among African nations, it remains one of the largest aid recipients in the Third World. Lesotho residents continue to work as migrant laborers in South African mines, constituting almost a quarter of that work force.

Liberia

Date of independence: **July 26, 1847**
Area: **43,000 square miles**
Population: **1,830,000 (est. 1981)**
Capital: **Monrovia**
Monetary unit: **Liberian dollar**
Nationality: **Liberian**
Religion: **80% Animist, Muslim, Christian**
Language: **English (official)**
Literacy: **24%**
Type of government: **Highly centralized military rule**
Political parties/leaders: **All suspended, but three parties remain in existence**
Monetary conversion rate: **$1 Liberian = $1 (1980)**
Principal economic resources: **Rubber, rice, palm oil, iron ore, diamonds**

History at a Glance
Portuguese adventurers of the fifteenth century were most likely the first white men to see and explore the Liberian coast from Cape Mount to Cape Palmas.

The first permanent settlement of this territory at Cape Mesurado in 1822 was sponsored by the American Colonization Society, a private corporation which financed the return of free blacks to Africa. By 1839 the group of settlements which had sprung up in the interim found it mutually advantageous to join forces

and to establish a commonwealth. Liberia's first governor was Thomas Buchanan, a cousin of James Buchanan, the fifteenth president of the United States. Eight years later, on July 26, the commonwealth proclaimed itself an independent republic.

For the remainder of the nineteenth century, Liberia was ruthlessly carved up by a host of European nations, which were interested not only in exploiting its natural resources, but also in preventing it, as a nation of free blacks, from becoming a base for the dissemination of ideas politically dangerous to colonial territories in adjacent areas.

Soon after the turn of the century, the United States directly intervened to save Liberia from financial ruin, made imminent as a result of disastrous foreign loans negotiated largely through British concessionaires. Particularly hard-hit by the Depression of the 1930s, Liberia found itself further humiliated by an international scandal involving corrupt government officials who were condoning a thriving forced-labor trade.

Due to its strategic value, Liberia became an important base for Allied military operations in Africa during World War II. The country did not become financially solvent, however, until its defaulted loans were paid off by the Firestone Corporation, which then invested heavily in the development of many new rubber plantations. The wealth flowing from this booming industry has helped to improve public health and educational facilities in the country, which is now ruled, for the most part, by some 15,000 Americo-Liberian descendants.

Liberia's constitution is modeled on that of the United States. However, only African descendants may become citizens. Real estate ownership is permitted only to citizens.

According to some reliable historians, the "natives" of the interior have been exploited by the Americo-

William U.S. Tubman, President of Liberia, being welcomed in Monrovia in 1963. In 1980 the Tubman family grip on Liberia was destroyed in a successful revolution.

Liberians in much the same way as their forebearers had once been at the hands of southern slaveholders.

William V. S. Tubman, the President between 1943 and 1971, was a leading supporter of the concept of a West African common market.

In July 1971 President Tubman died following surgery and was succeeded by his long-time associate, Vice President William R. Tolbert, Jr.

In the years under Tolbert, allegations of corruption and misadministration grew. On April 14, 1979, protests over a price increase of rice led to riots in Monrovia resulting in more than 40 deaths, 500 injuries, and property damage estimated at $35 million. The government reversed itself and lowered the price of rice, and a brief period of calm followed.

Although Liberia had been a *de facto* one-party state since 1869, Tolbert decided to allow the People's Progressive Wing (PPP) to operate legally, under the leadership of Gabriel Baccus Matthews. When Matthews called for a general strike in February 1980 to overthrow the government, he was arrested and the PPP banned.

On April 12, 1980, before Matthews could come to trial, a coup was held by insurgents from the army, and Tolbert and more than two dozen government leaders were killed. Master Sergeant Samuel Doe, who had led the coup, established a People's Redemption Council (PRC), freed Matthews, and appointed him Foreign Minister.

Doe's rule has been marred by numerous executions, the most notable example being when he lined up all the Tolbert officials and executed them on a Monrovian beach. Initially, control was to pass from his hands, but Doe has promoted himself from Master Sergeant to General to Commander-in-Chief of Liberia's 5,000-man army, apparently intending to maintain his position. He also had his staunchest critic in the PRC, Weh Syen, and four others arrested in mid-August 1980 and tried by a secret military court. Found guilty, the five men were led past a howling mob to military barracks, where they were beaten to death that night.

Liberian finances have slipped disastrously low under Doe. He appointed Colonel Harrison Pennue, a Doe loyalist, to collect some $36 million owed by private debtors to the defunct Bank of Liberia. But so far, although millions of dollars in cash have been collected by Pennue, nothing has been turned over to the bank.

Despite PRC excesses, American aid still flows to this long-time ally. Foreign aid was slashed by the Reagan Administration, but U.S. annual assistance leaped from $8 million during Tolbert's presidency to $68.3 million in 1981.

Doe is expected to remain in power for some time, but has faced assassination attempts in recent months.

Madagascar

Date of independence: **June 30, 1960**
Area: **226,657 square miles**
Population: **8,754,000 (est. 1981)**
Capital: **Antananarivo**
Monetary unit: **Malagasy franc**
Nationality: **Malagasy**
Religion: **50% Animist, 41% Christian, 7% Muslim**
Language: **Malagasy (official), French**
Literacy: **45%**
Type of government: **Republic**
Political parties/leaders: **National Front for the Defense of the Malagasy Socialist Revolution**
Monetary conversion rate: **225.80 Malagasy francs = $1 (1980)**
Principal economic resources: **Rice, livestock, coffee, vanilla, sugar, cloves, graphite, chromium, coal**

History at a Glance

The language, customs, and culture of the Malagasy Republic (formerly known as Madagascar) are closely associated with those of other Indonesian peoples who are believed to have migrated in great numbers to the island even before the Christian era. Arab traders and African slaves began arriving in the seventh century A.D.

Portuguese explorers became aware of the island's existence in the fifteenth century. They were followed by French, Dutch, and English traders. In the seventeenth century, France attempted for a time to establish her own colonies in the southern portion of the island, but abandoned the area. This left open the way for Malagasy to become a popular pirate haunt. The famous Captain Kidd laid over on occasion.

By this time, the three main kingdoms on the island—the Merina, the Sakalava, and the Betsimisaraka—were establishing themselves in the central, western, and eastern reaches of the island. Near the end of the eighteenth century, the Merina kingdom, headed by its greatest ruler, Andrianampoinimerina, made a first attempt to extend its dominion over the entire island. Radama I not only continued in his father's footsteps, but went further—imposing a ban on the slave trade. Opposition to French influence hardened after the death of Radama I; Christian persecution intensified and European settlers were eventually obliged to leave the island altogether.

By 1885 France had reasserted itself in the territory with the establishment of a protectorate that was recognized in 1890 by Great Britain in return for French recognition of British control in Zanzibar. French forces occupied the capital in 1895, but did not stamp out opposition in the south until 10 years later.

The move toward independence showed signs of gaining momentum in Madagascar as far back as the post-World War I decade. In 1940 British troops occupied the territory, maintaining themselves there until French administration could be restored under General de Gaulle's Free French government.

In 1946 Madagascar became an overseas territory of France, a move denounced by various nationalist elements. A bloody rebellion broke out against French rule in 1947. Before peace was restored a year later, some 60,000–90,000 Malagasy had lost their lives. Conservative business and political interests on the island gained support and, in 1958, succeeded in leading the territory to independence within the framework of the French Community. Two years later, the Malagasy Republic became a sovereign independent nation, retaining close ties with France.

The republic's first president, Philibert Tsiranana, leader of the pro-French Social Democratic Party, spent much of his time assuaging ethnic rivalries between the Merina people (Protestants) and the *cotiers* (Roman Catholics).

Tsiranana was ousted in a coup in May 1972. A referendum in October of the same year approved General Gabriel Ramanantsoa as head of a new government.

With unemployment and inflation high, General Ramanantsoa resigned on February 5, 1975. His leftist successor, Colonel Richard Ratsimandrava, was assassinated six days later by a machine gun ambush in Antananarivo.

On June 15, 1975, Commander Didier Ratsiraka was named President. He announced that the country would follow a socialist course and nationalized all banks, insurance companies, and mineral sources.

The Ratsiraka regime has been plagued by at least two coup attempts, civil unrest, and scarcities of food and other essential commodities.

The name of the country was changed to Madagascar on December 21, 1975.

Malawi

Date of independence: **July 6, 1974**
Area: **45,747 square miles**
Population: **6,243,000 (est. 1981)**
Capital: **Lilongwe**
Monetary unit: **Kwacha**
Nationality: **Malawian**
Religion: **Predominantly Animist, some Christian, Muslim**
Language: **Chichewa (official), English, Tombucka**
Literacy: **40%**
Type of government: **One-party state**
Political parties/leaders: **Malawi Congress Party, exile opposition groups**
Monetary conversion rate: **Kwacha = $1.21 (1980)**
Principal economic resources: **Tobacco, tea, peanuts, sugar, cotton**

History at a Glance

Malawi, known as Nyasaland prior to its independence, was first settled by an agricultural people of Bantu origin who appeared in the Lake Nyasa area some 2,000 years ago and then moved southward to the Shire River Valley. Later migrations by the Yao and Nyanja peoples from the neighborhood of the southern Congo eventually led to population pressures and tribal conflicts in the lake Nyasa region.

The first European to sight the lake was probably a Portuguese, Casper Boccaro, in 1616, but discovery of it is credited to David Livingstone, the Scottish explorer who arrived there in 1859. By this time, Nyasaland was an important base for Arab slave traders, whose operations were not checked until a number of Christian missionaries appeared in the area.

British influence in Nyasaland reached its zenith during the last four decades of the nineteenth century. The African Lakes Company, having followed the missionaries into the territory in 1878, quickly became embroiled in sharp competition with the Arab ivory traders on the northern end of Lake Nyasa. By 1891 the British had fully consolidated their political position in the region and given it protectorate status.

Hostility to British colonial policies first manifested itself in Nyasaland in 1915 when John Chilembwe, an American-trained African religious leader, led an armed revolt which, though unsuccessful, helped crystallize the political aspirations of the African inhabitants. After World War II, Great Britain tried to establish a federation made up of its three important Central African territories—Northern Rhodesia, Southern Rhodesia, and Nyasaland. Despite its opposition to the idea, Nyasaland was forced in 1953 to join a move which fanned the growing flames of nationalist fervor in the territory. Nyasaland lost no time in protesting to the Queen herself that the federation was dominated by a white minority intent on institutionalizing the notion of perpetual European political superiority. Fearing likewise that the federation might achieve complete independence from Great Britain, Nyasaland became ripe for revolt—particularly with the return of Dr. H. Kamuzu Banda in 1958. Within a year, an uprising did occur, and several Africans were killed. As a consequence, the Nyasaland African Congress (NAC), the main nationalist party, was outlawed, and its leaders, including Dr. Banda, imprisoned.

In 1960 the British government accepted the fact-finding report of an investigating commission which maintained that the original uprising had been caused by popular dissatisfaction with the idea of federation.

Upon his release from prison, Dr. Banda formed the Malawi Congress Party (MCP) which won widespread support at the polls. This encouraged England to institute constitutional reforms leading to internal autonomy for Nyasaland, which seceded from the federation in 1963 and became an independent state, adopting the name "Malawi" a year later.

In 1967 Malawi took the initiative among black African republics in establishing trade relations with the white-dominated nations of southern Africa. Despite the criticism he incurred, Banda remained steadfast in his conviction that Malawi should trade "with the devil" if it becomes necessary to improve the economic status of the nation.

Under the leadership of Dr. Banda, Malawi has maintained a rather peaceful coexistence with South Africa, Zimbabwe, and Mozambique. His party continues to exercise complete control of the government, but opposition movements operate out of neighboring Tanzania and Mozambique.

Though Malawi has considerable bauxite resources, it still is primarily an agricultural nation, with tea, tobacco, peanuts, and cotton accounting for 90% of its exports. Economic growth has resulted from Commonwealth, the European Economic Community, and World Bank aid. Per capita income in 1980 was $200.

Mali

Date of independence: **September 22, 1960**
Area: **478,764 square miles**
Population: **6,817,000 (est. 1981)**
Capital: **Bamako**
Monetary unit: **Mali Franc**
Nationality: **Malian**
Religion: **90% Muslim, 9% Animist, 1% Christian**
Language: **French (official), Mande, other dialects**

Literacy: **less than 5%**
Type of government: **Republic (civilian rule)**
Political parties/leaders: **Mali People's Democratic Union**
Monetary conversion rate: **451.60 francs = $1 (1980)**
Principal economic resources: **Millet, sorghum, corn, rice, sugar, cotton, bauxite, iron ore**

History at a Glance

What is now known as Mali was, in the fourth century A.D., only a portion of the larger and far more influential empire of Ghana. By the eighth century, Ghana was known to the Moslem Arab world as the land of gold. It later became a source of wealth for Spain and North Africa before entering into a period of decline which culminated in its overthrow in the mid-thirteenth century by a Moslem empire named Mali.

Perhaps the most famous of Mali's many emperors was the fabled Mansa Musa, who conquered Timbuktu and the vast regions of the Middle Niger. On one of his pilgrimages to Mecca, he is reported to have taken along some 500 slaves and to have distributed 50,000 ounces of gold. On his return from Mecca, he brought with him a number of Moslem tutors and men of learning, and thus fostered the growth of Timbuktu as a center of medieval African scholarship.

Due to persistent pressure on its frontiers, Mali declined in power in the fourteenth and fifteenth centuries, eventually giving way to the Songhai kingdom of Gao which, in its turn, was overcome by armed hosts from Morocco. During the nineteenth century, the territory finally achieved a degree of unity under the banner of Islam, but this was short-lived due to

The port of Mopti in Mali, a place of continuous activity.

Fishermen casting their net on the Niger River in Mali.

French military intervention and the extension of French administrative control.

Mali was known at this time as the French Soudan, a vast and underdeveloped country which was to have little importance until World War II when it became a rallying point for the Free French. Even in 1958 the Soudan was still only one of the numerous French West African territories which accepted the de Gaulle Constitution and voted for membership in the French Community.

A year later, Soudan, Senegal, Dahomey, and Upper Volta drafted their own constitution calling for the creation of a Federation of Mali. Only Senegal and Soudan, however, ratified the document. Shortly thereafter, the Mali Federation appealed to France for recognition by, and complete sovereignty within, the French Community. Although this request was granted, the federation collapsed almost immediately, largely because of the sharp differences existing between key politicians in each territory.

Under the leadership of Modibo Keita, Mali declared itself an independent state and embarked on its own program of development.

In 1965 Bamako was the site of an epoch-making conference between the heads of state of Ghana, Algeria, and Mali, all nations desirous of creating a closely knit Pan African group to rival the French-oriented Afro-Malagasy Common Organization.

Keita subsequently set the nation on a course of alignment with the Chinese brand of "socialism." The economy fell completely into the hands of state enterprises, operated with the help of more than 1,000 technicians. This policy produced a counter-revolutionary fervor among a group of young Army officers who, in 1968, overthrew Keita and installed a National Liberation Committee, headed by Lieutenant Moussa Traore.

Mining and petroleum codes were revised in 1969 to encourage more systematic prospecting in extant resources of bauxite, uranium, iron ore, gold, manganese, and petroleum among others.

In the early 1970s Chinese and Soviet influence waned in the country, French aid doubled, and France joined Mali's three-year economic plan.

Mali, a landlocked country, is mainly agricultural and pastoral. The Sahelian drought which struck sub-Saharan nations in 1973–1974 led to severe famine and mass starvation in Mali.

The drought was later followed by an equally devastating rainfall; 1.8 million Malians were affected, thousands were killed.

The country is run effectively by the army. General Traore was elected to a five-year term as President and Prime Minister on June 19, 1979 and the Constitution was approved in 1974.

In 1974 traditional border disputes between Mali and Upper Volta, her southern neighbor, flared and scores of Malians were killed.

Mali remains one of the dozen poorest countries in the world with a per capita GNP of $140 in 1979.

Mauritania

Date of independence: **November 28, 1960**
Area: **397,953 square miles**
Population: **1,713,000 (est. 1981)**
Capital: **Nouakchott**
Monetary unit: **Ouguiya**
Nationality: **Mauritanian**
Religion: **100% Muslim**
Language: **French (official), Arabic**
Literacy: **10%**
Type of government: **Republic (military control)**
Political parties/leaders: **Suspended, but a number of small parties do exist**
Monetary conversion rate: **45.85 ouguiyas = $1 (1980)**
Principal economic resources: **Sugar cane, rice, iron ore, gypsum, fish**

History at a Glance

In its early history, Mauritania was the scene of successive waves of southward migration by Arabs and Berbers, both of whom conquered the indigenous black inhabitants. Perhaps the most important invaders were the nomadic Tuareg Berbers who often carried out raids on the Morocco–Ghana caravan route, and thus disrupted the commerce between the great black empires of the Western Sudan in the eleventh century. Islam became a potent force during the fourteenth and fifteenth centuries when Arab invaders from Egypt drove out the Berbers. Attracted by the gum trade, the Portuguese arrived in the fifteenth century, setting up trading posts along Mauritania's southern boundary—the Senegal River. For the next four centuries, the French slowly pushed their way northward from Senegal and, by signing appropriate treaties with several Moorish chieftains, came to exercise hegemony over most of the desert zone of Mauritania.

The French retaliated against the frequent raids of Moorish tribes early in the twentieth century by extending their authority over more and more of the territory. By 1909, they had added to the Adrar region, bordering on the Spanish Sahara, to their dominion. The territory of Mauritania was established as an administrative unit in 1920, at which time the city of Saint-Louis in Senegal was made its capital. At the same time, Mauritania became a part of French West Africa, a loosely knit federation set up in the French colonial holdings.

After World War II, Mauritania received the same colonial concessions from France as did the other territories in the region. In 1946 it assumed partial control of its own affairs through the election of its own assembly and sent representatives to the French National Assembly in Paris, as well as to the Assembly of the French Union. Work was begun on the new capital of Nouakchott in 1957. A year later, Mauritania approved the Constitution of the Fifth French Republic and decided in favor of membership within the French Community. Complete independence was not achieved until 1960.

Mauritania and Morocco planned to divide the territory of the former Spanish Sahara after the departure of Spain in November 1975. Although Mauritanian troops moved into the region, they were rebuffed by the Polisario, a Saharan independence group backed by Algeria. Mauritania broke diplomatic relations with Algeria in 1976 after Algeria recognized the area as an independent state.

Increased military spending and high casualties were incurred when Mauritania tried to maintain control of its southern third of Western Sahara and unrest grew on the home front. On July 10, 1978, President Moktar Ould Daddah was deposed in a bloodless coup and Lieutenant Colonel Mustapha Ould Salek installed as Head of State.

Western Sahara continued to occupy national interest and President Salek spent the next few months trying to get a "global settlement" concerning that desert territory, but was unsuccessful. In March 1979 he dismissed several leaders who were sympathetic to the Polisario and relinquished the office of Prime Minister to Lieutenant Colonel Ahmed Ould Bouceif, who was highly esteemed. Barely a month later, Bouceif was killed in an airplane crash and was succeeded on May 31 by Lieutenant Colonel Mohamed Khouna Ould Haidalla.

President Salek was forced to resign three days later and the ruling body, the Military Committee for National Salvation (CMNS), named Lieutenant Colonel Mahomed Mahmoud Ould Ahmed Louly as President.

Colonel Louly concluded a peace treaty with Polisario in August 1979 and ended hostilities by withdrawing Mauritanian troops. Moroccan troops immediately occupied the land.

Colonel Louly only held power for six months and then was removed by a junta on January 4, 1980 with Prime Minister Haidalla named President.

Under President Haidalla, economic reconstruction has become a priority. The Sahelian drought of 1968–1974 devastated the land, wiping out 80% of the country's cattle, one-third of its camels and more than half the sheep and goats. Still, 85% of the population works in agriculture, fishing, or livestock. Modern Mauritanians participate in the mining of iron ore, which accounts for 75% of the nation's export earnings.

With military withdrawal from Western Sahara complete and an economic program underway, the major domestic issue confronting the leadership is growing unrest among blacks and Haratines, who protest the adoption of Arabic ways. Though the CMNS has outlawed slavery, many blacks and Haratines continue to be employed in menial or laborious jobs.

Mauritius

Date of independence: March 12, 1968
Area: 790 square miles
Population: 967,000 (est. 1981)
Capital: Port Louis
Monetary unit: Mauritian rupee
Nationality: Mauritian
Religion: 51% Hindu, 33% Christian, 6% Muslim
Language: English (official), Hindi, Creole, Chinese
Literacy: 60% over 21, 90% school age
Type of government: Independent state, recognizes Elizabeth II as Chief of State
Political parties/leaders: Independence Party, Mauritian Social Democratic Party, 5 opposition parties
Monetary conversion rate: 7.83 Mauritian rupees = $1 (1980)
Principal economic resources: Sugar cane, rice, cut diamonds, tobacco, iron ore

History at a Glance

Mauritius is located in the Indian Ocean some 500 miles east of Madagascar. It was discovered by Portuguese sailors in the early sixteenth century and first settled by the Dutch who gave it its name in 1598. After the Dutch withdrew in 1710, the French claimed the island (renaming it Ile de France), but lost it to British forces in 1810. Four years later, British sovereignty was recognized by the Peace of Paris. With the abolition of slavery in the British Empire in 1834, Mauritius absorbed large numbers of migrant laborers from the Asian subcontinent. Some 200,000 Mauritians are of mixed French and African origin; the remainder are mostly Indo-Mauritians.

In 1967 Mauritius became self-governing, with Labour party leader Seewoosagur Ramgoolam appointed as Prime Minister. Racial and labor unrest involving the island's Creole and Moslem population followed, but the island maintained sufficient equilibrium to declare its independence in 1968.

This racially mixed country is faced with the three-headed problem of a limited economy, racial and social tension, and population increase of 1.4% per year.

More than 90% of the island's arable land is devoted to sugar cane production, the bulk of the country's exports. However, falling sugar prices after 1975 have caused severe economic difficulties. In October 1979, Mauritius was faced with double-digit inflation and balance-of-payment problems. The government, under Ramgoolam, now in his eighties, took a 23% currency devaluation in return for aid from the International Monetary Fund. Economic problems have caused labor unrest and a leftist coalition may be forming against the present government.

Mozambique

Date of independence: June 25, 1975
Area: 302,328 square miles
Population: 10,517,000 (est. 1981)
Capital: Maputo
Monetary unit: Metical
Nationality: Mozambican
Religion: 65% Animist, 21% Christian, 10% Muslim
Language: Portuguese (official), many tribal dialects
Literacy: 15% (1974)
Type of government: One-party socialist
Political parties/leaders: Mozambique Liberation Front; three illegal parties
Monetary conversion rate: 28.57 meticals = $1 (1980)
Principal economic resources: Cotton, cashew nuts, sugar, tea, copra, coal, iron ore

History at a Glance

Mozambique was first visited by the Portuguese explorer Vasco da Gama in the course of his voyage to India and the Far East in 1498. Settlements along the coastal areas were established in the sixteenth century, during which time the slave trade also prospered. By 1878 this trade had been abolished and boundary settlements reached between adjacent British and German territories.

In 1951 the territory's status was changed to that of an overseas Portuguese province. African nationalism in Mozambique was slow to develop, with no definite trend in evidence until 1962 when the Mozambique Liberation Front was formed. Fighting broke out in 1964.

At first, the Portuguese fragmented the rebels and forced them underground, but the guerrillas held on and led by the Frelimo movement, slowly gained the upper hand. In 1974 with guerrillas in control of much of the country, the Portuguese announced that they would depart in 1975. In June 1975 the Social Frelimo leader, Samora Machel, became President.

While not racked with the degree of internal dissensions that plagued transition in Angola, and though Machel promised to heal internal differences, Mozambique's young government faced many difficulties. Hopes for substantial economic aid from Portugal were dissipated by that country's internal problems. Economic troubles were further aggravated by flooding of the Limpopo River and emigration of some 160,000 of the nation's 200,000 Portuguese. However, aid was forthcoming from China which in 1974 and 1975 retained half of Frelimo's 12,000-man army.

After a brief period of cooperation with its landlocked neighbor, Rhodesia, Mozambique closed its border in 1976 when fighting broke out, cutting Rhodesia off from its 1,700-mile coastline on the Indian Ocean. Mozambique suffered mightily during the Rhodesian war, in effect serving as a rear base for Robert

Mugabe's guerrilla army. President Machel later estimated that Rhodesian forces attacked his nation 350 times, killing more than 1,000 Mozambicans and costing the country $550 million in revenue.

After Zimbabwe achieved its independence in 1980, rail and highway communications with Mozambique were resumed.

Mozambique is a Marxist state, although by early 1980 the economic state had deteriorated so that limited private ownership and foreign investment were encouraged. Although it still depends heavily on the Soviet bloc countries, Mozambique has also accepted millions in aid from Western nations. Domestically, Mozambique also maintains economic trade with South Africa, although it is committed to black majority rule there.

Illiteracy in this nation is 98% and the government is trying to educate about 200,000 persons a year. Cashew nuts are a major export, but a number of mineral deposits have been discovered recently.

Namibia

Area: 318,259 square miles
Population: 1,137,000 (est. 1981)
Capital: Windhoek
Monetary unit: South African Rand
Nationality: Namibian
Religion: Christian, Animist
Language: Africaans (principal), German, English
Literacy: High for whites, low for nonwhites
Type of government: U.N. Mandate
Political parties: South West African People's Organization (SWAPO), UNITA, FNLA, Democratic Turnhalle Alliance (DIA)
Monetary conversion rate: 1 rand = $1.34 (1980)
Principal economic resources: Corn, millet, diamonds, copper, lead, zinc, fish

History at a Glance
Great Britain was the first European nation to set foot in what is now the territory of Namibia, having gained control of a number of offshore islands, as well as the Walvis Bay region, by 1878. Germany established a protectorate over the mainland in 1884, acquired a number of trading concessions there, and established full administrative control in 1908.

Captured by South African troops in 1915, South West Africa became a South African mandated territory in 1920, retaining this status until the close of World War II, when South Africa sought unsuccessfully to annex the territory outright, rather than place it under the trusteeship of the United Nations as other colonial powers had done.

Soon thereafter, representatives of the African population in the territory were sent as petitioners to air their grievances before the United Nations. In 1962 Ethiopia and Liberia brought suit against South Africa before the International Court of Justice at The Hague, Netherlands, maintaining that the rights of the South-West African population had consistently been violated by the administering power.

On July 18, 1966, the Court dismissed the suit on the grounds that Ethiopia and Liberia did not have sufficient legal interest to obtain a judgment on the case's merits. This setback was regarded as a severe blow to the foes of apartheid.

The territory, governed by a South African administrator, is divided into the police zone (white settlement areas) and the reserve area (for native inhabitants only).

In 1966 the U.N. General Assembly declared that the South African mandate was terminated and, within a year, appointed a council to administer the territory until independence. In 1968 the territory was renamed Namibia.

South Africa, however, refused to relinquish administration.

In 1970 the U.N. Security Council condemned South Africa for its illegal control of the area and, in 1971, the International Court of Justice concurred. In 1973 a part of the north, Ovamboland, received limited self-government.

In 1975 pressures for independence for Namibia persisted in the United Nations and in Africa itself. Spearheading the movement is the Southwest Africa People's Organization (SWAPO), whose leaders live in exile. Vorster has declared that he would like to grant freedom to Namibia, but will not deal with SWAPO. In reply SWAPO, which is recognized by both the United Nations and the Organization for African Unity as Namibia's legal representative, charges that South Africa wishes to maintain control of Namibia's richer areas through puppet homelands.

On January 31, 1976, a U.N. Security Council resolution unanimously condemned South Africa's "illegal occupation" of Namibia and called for free elections under U.N. supervision.

A draft constitution, calling for representation of the 11 major racial and ethnic groups, was approved by Turnhalle delegates on March 9, 1977, but SWAPO refused to cooperate. The five Western members of the U.N. Security Council, including the United States, also opposed the move. Further talks with South African Prime Minister Vorster and the Western powers resulted in a declaration of the Turnhalle formula as still "predominantly ethnic, [which] lacked neutrality and appeared to prejudice the outcome of free election."

Preparation for a 1978 balloting continued, despite the opposition. Administrator General Matthinus

Steyn worked to dismantle the apartheid system, including the Mixed Marriages Act, and pass laws.

SWAPO boycotted the December balloting and the Turnhalle Alliance was declared the victor with 82% of the vote.

In May 1979 the South African government agreed to the Constituent Assembly's request that the body be reconstituted as a National Assembly, although the Assembly would not have the power to alter the status of the territory. Meanwhile, SWAPO guerrilla forces and South African troops continued to fight.

In 1979 Angolan President Neto proposed the creation of a 60-mile-wide demilitarized zone along the Angolan-Namibian border to prevent incursions from either side.

The Reagan Administration has supported Namibia's independence, but has stipulated that when Namibia wins its freedom, it must send the 20,000 Cuban troops stationed there home.

Niger

Date of independence: August 3, 1960
Area: 489,189 square miles
Population: 5,660,000 (est. 1981)
Capital: Niamey
Monetary unit: CFA franc
Nationality: Nigerien
Religion: 80% Muslim, Animist, Christian
Language: French (official), many dialects

Portrait of a modern construction worker in Nigeria with the traditional markings of tribal initiation on his face.

Literacy: 6%
Type of government: Republic (military regime since 1974)
Political parties/leaders: Banned
Monetary conversion rate: 225.80 CFA francs = $1 (1980)
Principal economic resources: Peanuts, cotton, livestock, sorghum, uranium, coal, iron

History at a Glance

The territory known today as Niger was, for most of its early history, a crossroads of migration between white peoples of North Africa and black peoples of the Lake Chad region. The Kanem Bornu Empire was only one of several powerful states which emerged in this area during the eighth and ninth centuries. This empire was overthrown in the tenth century by the Hausa states which lay in the southern reaches of Niger, and by the Songhai Kingdom which held sway in the western half of the country until the sixteenth century, when it was itself destroyed by an invading Moroccan army.

The first European explorer in the area was the fabled Scot, Mungo Park (1805). Later Major Dixon Denham and Lieutenant Hugh Clapperton were sent by Great Britain to explore the Niger River and they reached Lake Chad after crossing the Sahara Desert from Tripoli.

By 1900 the French had pushed their way eastward despite fierce opposition from the Tuareg tribe. In 1901 Niger was declared a military district and became part of a larger territorial unit known as Haut-Senegal et Niger. Sporadic revolts continued right up until the eve of World War I, at which time they were quelled with the aid of British forces from Nigeria. In 1922 Niger was officially declared a French colony.

Due to its lack of strategic importance, the territory remained virtually unaffected by World War II. Nationalism and, with it, the growth of political parties became inevitable once France allowed her West African territories a greater share in self-government. In 1958 Niger approved the new French Constitution and, within two years, had become a fully independent state.

The President of Niger, Hamani Diori, embarked upon an ambitious economic program which called for long-term cooperation with France. He survived one assassination attempt in April 1965. In 1970 he was reelected to a five year term.

A massive drought from 1968 to 1974 had devastating consequences for this landlocked nation; half of the 4 million population experienced starvation. The United States and other nations sent some 200,000 tons of food to Niger; however, when President Diori was accused of mishandling the relief supplies, discontent grew.

On April 15, 1974, President Diori was ousted by

a military coup led by Lieutenant Colonel Seyni Kountche, who suspended both the Constitution and the only political party, the Niger Progressive Party. Kountche installed a 12-man military government and adopted diplomatic relations with a number of communist states while maintaining a conservative posture in regional affairs.

In 1980 Niger's attention was focused on the civil war in neighboring Chad, with concern about Libya's involvement. In December 1980 Niger attended the OAU emergency summit on Chad and joined the Central African Republic, Cameroon, Guinea, Senegal, the Sudan, and Togo in calling for Libya's immediate withdrawal from Chad.

Agriculture and livestock are the primary livelihood of 90 percent of the Nigeriens while uranium mining accounts for the majority of the country's foreign earnings.

Nigeria

Date of independence: **October 1, 1960**
Area: **356,667 square miles**
Population: **79,445,000 (est. 1981)**
Capital: **Lagos**
Monetary unit: **Naira**
Religion: **47% Muslim, 34% Christian, 18% Animist**
Language: **English (official), Hausa, Yoruba, Ibo**
Literacy: **25%**
Type of government: **Federal republic (since 1979)**
Political parties/leaders: **National Party of Nigeria, Nigerian People's Party, 3 minority parties**
Monetary conversion rate: **1 Naira = $1.84 (1980)**
Principal economic resources: **Peanuts, cotton, cocoa, rubber, yams, cassava, livestock, oil, natural gas, coal, tin, processed rubber**

History at a Glance

Little is known of the early peoples who inhabited Nigeria. During the Middle Ages, Northern Nigeria was in contact with the kingdoms of the western Sudan and the nations lying to the north of the Sahara Desert as well. Islam was established as the major religion in Nigeria during the fifteenth century, by which time the Ife and Benin kingdoms were flourishing.

Contact between the coastal peoples of Nigeria and the nations of Europe was based upon the exploitation of slaves who were removed from the territory in astounding numbers. The British abolished the slave trade in 1807 and, with the discovery of the mouth of the Niger River in 1830, extended their economic influence into the interior. In 1861 they annexed the island of Lagos, an important center in the palm oil trade. Toward the end of the century, they swept into the eastern regions of Nigeria, establishing the Oil Riv-

Teenagers draw water in a rural village in the Western Region of Nigeria, an oil-rich country battling widespread poverty.

ers Protectorate (1885) and the Niger Coast Protectorate (1893).

British influence in Nigeria was formally recognized by the Berlin Conference of 1884–1885. Over the next 15 years, Great Britain gained control of an even more substantial piece of territory in Northern Nigeria, where a third protectorate was established.

In 1914 these separate administrative areas were combined into the Colony and Protectorate of Nigeria, introducing a system of indirect rule which enabled local chieftains to exercise a significant degree of control over their own affairs.

Nationalism became a potent force in Nigeria after World War II, primarily under the leadership of Nnamdi Azikiwe, Obafemi Awolowo, and Alhaji Sir Abubakar Tafawa Balewa. In 1960 Nigeria became a fully independent federation within the framework of the British Commonwealth and, three years later, opted for a republican government.

Early in 1966, Nigeria was the scene of the bloodiest military coup any black African nation has suffered to date. Prime Minister Tafawa Balewa was assassinated and a military government headed by General J. Aguiyi-Ironsi seized power. This government abolished the existing constitution, eliminated the offices of president and prime minister, and dismissed the premiers of Nigeria's semi-autonomous regions (the Northern, the Western, the Eastern and the Midwestern).

Later that year, Aguiyi-Ironsi was deposed by Lieutenant Colonel Yakubu Gowon, head of a new military junta. When anti-Ibo rioting began anew late in 1966, Ibos from all over the nation began flocking back to their homeland in the Eastern Region. Soon the new state of Biafra was created, and civil war engulfed the country.

In January 1970, after 31 months of civil war, the Republic of Biafra surrendered to the federal government, leaving an estimated 1 million persons, mostly inhabitants of the defeated state, homeless and starving. A massive international relief operation kept the death toll lower than might have been anticipated;

overall cost of the war was estimated at $840 million.

Gowon's nine-year rule ended on July 1975 when he was deposed in a bloodless coup while at an OAU summit in Uganda. By the beginning of August, a Supreme Military Council was reorganized as well as a 25-member Federal Executive Council, with coup leader Brigadier General Murtala Ramat Muhammad in position of leadership. Muhammad's rule was only temporary—he was assassinated on February 13, 1976, during a coup attempt. Lieutenant General Olusegun Obasanjo succeeded the slain leader as Chairman of the Supreme Military Council and captured and executed Muhammad's assassins.

On September 12, 1978, Nigeria's 12-year state of emergency ended and a ban on political party activity was lifted.

Elections were held in mid-1979 which placed a number of federal representatives, state legislators, and state governors in power and Alhaji Shehu Shagari as President.

Typical dress identifies these women as Western Yorubas, one of Nigeria's three major tribes. Africa's most populous nation also amalgamates the seminomadic Northern Hausas and the Eastern Ibos.

Nigeria's National Training Scheme for Vocational Instructors and Foremen holds classes at the Yaba Trade Center in Lagos. Qualified instructors take an 8-month course in teacher training, while trainees take a 15-month City and Guilds Advanced Craft course.

In October after the elections, power transferred peacefully from military to multiparty civilian rule and was hailed as a good example for other African states.

The only significant outbreak of domestic violence since then was in December of 1980 when a fundamentalist Islamic Yan Izala sect began preaching. Rioting broke out for 10 days at Kano, leaving 200 dead.

Nigeria is one of the most richly endowed African nations in natural resources. It ranked seventh in world oil production in 1977 with revenues of $10 billion. Unfortunately, a deficit in balance payments of $960 million forced the country to severely restrict importation of consumer goods.

On March 31, 1978, President Carter came to visit—the first visit by an American President since President Franklin Roosevelt stopped in Liberia during World War II.

Rwanda

Date of independence: **July 1, 1962**
Area: **10,169 square miles**
Population: **5,258,000 (est. 1981)**
Capital: **Kigali**
Monetary unit: **Rwanda franc**
Nationality: **Rwandan**
Religion: **45% Catholic, 9% Protestant, 1% Muslim, Animist**
Language: **Kinyarwanda (official), French, Kiswahili**
Literacy: **25%**
Type of government: **Republic**
Political parties/leaders: **All banned following 1973 coup**
Monetary conversion rate: **92.84 Rwanda francs = $1 (1980)**
Principal economic resources: **Coffee, tea, beans, potatoes, cassiterite, wolfram**

History at a Glance

The history of Rwanda, a tiny country adjacent to Zaire, has been largely one involving the strained relationship between the Tutsi and the Hutu tribes.

The Hutu comprise some 90% of the population, but have long been subjugated by the tall, disciplined Tutsi, sometimes referred to as Watusis.

A nomadic pastoral people, the Tutsi first entered Rwanda in the fifteenth century, subjugating its inhabitants, the Hutu and Twa. The Tutsi instituted a caste system and came to function as the feudal overlords of the Hutu tribe, which was composed mainly of farmers. The Twa slowly retired into the surrounding jungle in search of wild game.

The first white men to pass through Rwanda were the English explorers John Speke and Richard Burton, who crossed the territory in 1858 during their search for the southernmost source of the river Nile. In 1871 Stanley and Livingstone landed at Usumbura (now in Burundi) after having first explored the Ruzizi River region. They were soon to be followed by German explorers and by Roman Catholic missionaries.

The status of both Rwanda (originally spelled Ruanda) and Burundi (then known as Urundi) was first determined by the Berlin Conference of 1884–1885. Ultimately, Rwanda was made a distinct colony by Germany and given its own administrative headquarters at Kigali.

Following World War I, Germany was forced to surrender this territory to Belgium, which was awarded a mandate over once-again-united Ruanda-Urundi by the League of Nations. In 1946 although it continued to be administered from the Belgian Congo, it was made a trust territory by the United Nations.

During the next decade, fierce tribal clashes became more frequent in Ruanda-Urundi. The politically awakened Hutu tribe, in particular, grew more militant

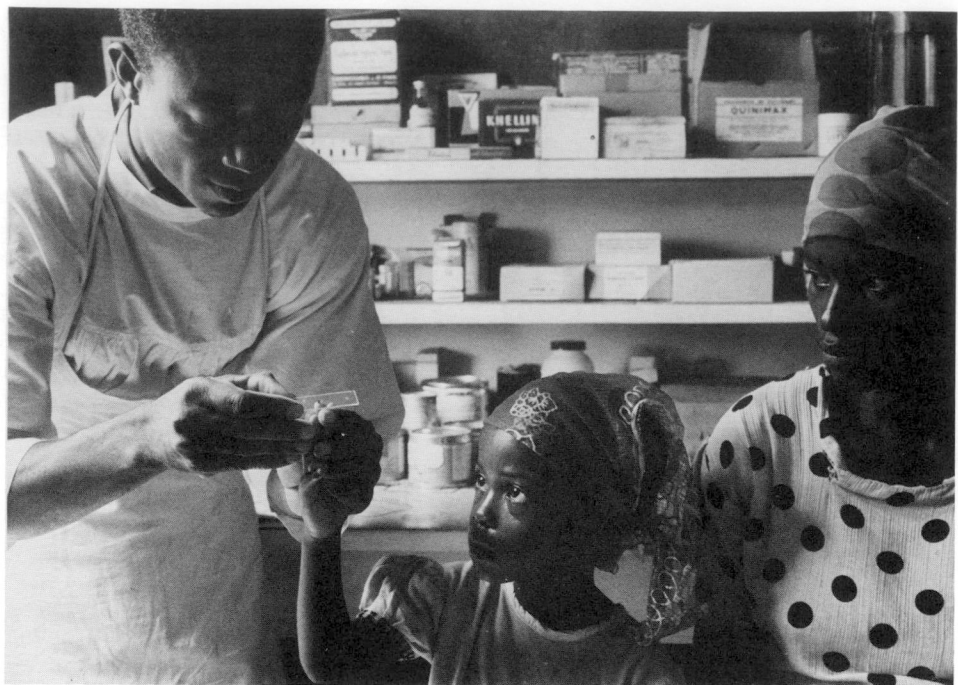

Throughout Africa a developing network of rural public health services combats endemic diseases.

and self-assertive toward its aristocratic Tutsi overlords. Finally, in 1960, an outbreak of violence caused large numbers of Tutsi to flee to neighboring countries. That same year, Belgium withdrew from the Congo, and thus served notice of her intention to sever formal political ties with her African colonies. A year later, a U.N. commission called for legislative elections and a referendum to decide on the fate of the mwami (a tribal king with absolute power). The people voted to abolish the mwami's major governing powers and to set up instead a republican form of government.

On July 1, 1962, with Gregoire Kayibanda as its President, Rwanda declared its independence and formally separated itself from Burundi which, by contrast, retained a monarchist form of government. Some 200,000 Tutsi were driven into exile.

Due largely to its limited size, its landlocked position, and its meager resources, Rwanda continues to depend on agriculture and tourism to better its economy.

President Kayibanda was legally barred from seeking another term in 1973, but when he tried to alter the Constitution to provide for another term, hostile elements arose and a bloodless coup on July 5, 1973 overthrew his regime.

The new government, under the leadership of Major General Juvenal Habyarimana, suspended parts of the constitution and banned all political parties. In 1976 however, a new legal party, the National Revolutionary Movement for Development, was organized.

Under Habyarimana, Rwanda has taken a distinctly "anti-imperialist" turn and became the first African nation to break relations with Israel as a result of the October 1973 war. It has also supported liberation movements in Southern Africa, and opened closer relations with Burundi, Zaire, and Tanzania.

Rwanda is the most densely populated state in Africa due mainly to the population's strict Catholic beliefs about family planning. It is still one of Africa's poorest nations with a per capita income of $106. Coffee and tea are the leading cash exports and many Rwandan farmers grow a species of flower (chrysanthemum) which is processed into an insecticide.

Sao Tome and Principe

Date of independence: July 10, 1975
Area: 372 square miles
Population: 86,000 (est. 1981)
Capital: Sao Tome
Monetary unit: Dobra
Nationality: Sao Tornean
Religion: Roman Catholic, Evangelical, Seventh Day Adventist
Language: Portuguese (official)
Literacy: 5%–10%
Type of government: Republic
Political parties/leaders: Unicameral Popular Assembly is the supreme organ of the state and designates the President
Monetary conversion rate: 40.64 escudos = $1 (1977)
Principal economic resources: Cocoa, coconut, palm oil, coffee, bananas, copra

History at a Glance

Most of the people inhabiting Sao Tome and Principe are descendants of the original Portuguese colonists and African slaves from Gabon and other parts of the Guinea coast as far south as Angola. The Angolares, descendants of Angolan slaves shipwrecked in the sixteenth century, live along the south and west coast of Sao Tome. They have been joined there by a large number of migrant laborers who have come from other Portuguese territories on the mainland for the purpose of working on the numerous plantations scattered through the islands.

The islands are located about 125 miles west of the African coast in the Gulf of Guinea.

Independence was granted on July 12, 1975 as part of Portugal's dissolution of its African possessions; most of the Europeans on the islands left at this time.

Dr. Manuel Pinto da Coasta assumed the presidency with the support of the Movement for the Liberation of Sao Tome and Principe (MLSTP). A constitution was approved on December 12, 1975 which named a Popular Assembly as the supreme organ of the state, but neither Assembly members nor da Coasta have undergone reelection. In recent years, the government has survived a number of plots and attempted coups.

The islands were once the world's leading producer of cocoa, but production has diminished somewhat. Cocoa still supplies three quarters of the country's export revenue.

Senegal

Date of independence: **August 20, 1960**
Area: **75,750 square miles**
Population: **5,823,000 (est. 1981)**
Capital: **Dakar**
Monetary unit: **CFA franc**
Nationality: **Senegalese**
Religion: **80% Muslim, 15% Animist, 5% Catholic**
Language: **French (official), Wolof vernacular**
Literacy: **10%**
Type of government: **Republic**
Political parties/leaders: **Socialist Party, Senegalese Democratic Party, African Independence Party**
Monetary conversion rate: **225.80 CFA francs = $1 (1980)**
Principal economic resources: **Peanuts, millet, cotton, rice, sorghum**

History at a Glance

Parts of what is today Senegal were at different times ruled by the empires of Tekrur, Ghana, and Mali, the last of which reached the zenith of its power in the fourteenth century.

The first Europeans to arrive in this general area— along the Cape Verde peninsula and in the estuary of the Gambia River—were the Portuguese, who were soon followed by the English and the French. French activity was concentrated around the trading post of Saint Louis and the island of Goree, just outside the city of Dakar.

A fisherman approaches the Senegal River to cast his net.

In the nineteenth century, the French began cultivating peanuts in the valleys of Senegal, and this crop came to be the staple of a predominantly agricultural economy.

On the political front, four large municipalities (Saint Louis, Goree, Dakar, and Rufisque) won the right to choose a single deputy to be seated in the French parliament. However, the first African deputy was not elected until 1914. At the end of World War II, Senegal, as part of the French Union, was permitted to send two representatives to the Chamber of Deputies in Paris.

In 1946 a constitution was drawn up, and a territorial assembly established. By 1957, universal suffrage had been introduced. A year later, Senegal ratified the new Constitution of French president de Gaulle, thus becoming an autonomous republic within the French Community.

Senegal joined the short-lived Mali Federation in 1959, only to withdraw a year later when the Legislative Assembly declared the country independent.

Leopold Sedar Senghor, who was leader of the Senegalese Progressive Union and considered to be one of the most highly respected intellectuals in Africa, served as President from 1960 until his retirement in 1980. Senghor's tenure was not wholly peaceful—he survived at least one coup attempt—but he supervised three revisions of the constitution, reinstituted the post of prime minister and in 1976, passed an amendment sanctioning three political parties, each with a prescribed ideology. Although he was reelected for a fourth five-year term in 1978, Senghor announced his resignation in November 1980. Abdou Diouf, who had served as Prime Minister for 11 years, succeeded him on January 2, 1981.

Senegal is formally unaligned but pro-Western and retains close ties with France. It has participated in several African development groups and strengthened relations with Gambia, Liberia, Guinea, and Ivory Coast.

Severe droughts in recent years forced the government to apply stringent economic policies which in turn have sparked student unrest and demonstrations. Peanuts remain the principal export, accounting for one-third of the country's exports, but successive poor harvests have necessitated foreign assistance.

Seychelles

Date of independence: **June 29, 1976**
Area: **107 square miles**
Population: **64,000 (est. 1981)**
Capital: **Victoria**
Monetary unit: **Seychelles rupee**
Religion: **90% Roman Catholic**
Language: **English (official), Creole**

Literacy: **60% (adult), 75% (school age children)**
Type of government: **Republic**
Political parties/leaders: **Seychelles People's United Party**
Monetary conversion rate: **6.51 rupee = $1.00 U.S. (1980)**
Principal economic resources: **Cinnamon, coconut, fish**

History at a Glance

Discovered by Portugal in 1505, the Seychelles became a pirates' base until they were settled by France in the mid-eighteenth century. In 1794 Great Britain took control of the islands and, by 1810, had made them a dependency of the British colony of Mauritius. Four years later, at the signing of the Peace of Paris, the French officially ceded them to Great Britain. In 1903 the Seychelles became a separate colony, with a governor as well as executive and legislative councils.

Though blessed with a pleasant climate, the Seychelles are very poor. Unemployment has risen as plantations have increasingly mechanized. The annual birthrate, 38 per 1,000, is very high.

The Republic of Seychelles consists of 92 islands in the Indian Ocean northeast of Madagascar.

They were seized from France by the British in 1810 and remained a colony until independence was granted on June 29, 1976. The state is an independent republic within the Commonwealth.

The first president, James Mancham, was ousted on June 5, 1977 after a year-long rule of "lavish spending" and Prime Minister France Albert Rene was installed as the new head of state. In balloting conducted under a single-party socialist system, Rene was confirmed in office for a five-year term.

The main objective of Seychelles foreign policy is the "return" of a number of small islands still under British control. Meanwhile, the Seychelles People's Progressive Front (SPPF) has called for the dismantling of all foreign military bases in the region.

There have been demonstrations against the socialist tendency of the Rene government and a contingent of Tanzanian troops were asked for, and received, in 1979.

Copra accounts for about two-thirds of the export earnings followed by fish and cinnamon. Tourism has increased due to the opening of an international airport on the main island of Mahe.

Sierra Leone

Date of independence: **April 27, 1961**
Area: **27,699 square miles**
Population: **3,131,000 (est. 1981)**
Capital: **Freetown**
Monetary unit: **Leone**
Nationality: **Sierra Leonean**

Religion: 70% Animist, 25% Muslim, 5% Christian
Language: **English (official), Mende, Temne, Krio dialects**
Literacy: **10%**
Type of government: **Republic (presidential regime)**
Political parties/leaders: **All People's Congress**
Monetary conversion rate: **1.06 leones = $1 (1980)**
Principal economic resources: **Diamonds, bauxite, chromite, iron ore, coffee, cocoa, ginger, rice**

History at a Glance

Founded in 1787 by Granville Sharp, an English abolitionist, Sierra Leone was first settled by black slaves who had been brought to England and freed there.

Granted a royal charter in 1799, Sierra Leone ("The Province of Freedom") was first governed by a town council, complete with a mayor and aldermen. However, after several attacks on the settlement by hostile tribes, Great Britain decided to bring the colony under the direct administration of the Crown. When the English parliament ruled the slave trade illegal in 1807, Sierra Leone came to be utilized as a base from which slave runners could be hunted down.

The frontiers of Sierra Leone were not settled until late in the nineteenth century. At this time, the hinterlands of the territory were declared a British protectorate, a move which caused considerable tribal unrest. The Mende and Temne peoples in particular were opposed to a hut tax imposed by the officials of the Crown.

In 1924 the Constitution under which the colony had been governed was revised to provide for the election of three Sierra Leoneans to posts on the Legislative Council. Again, in 1951, a new Constitution was promulgated, ushering in a system of party rule through a duly elected African majority, whose decisions, however, were still subject to the veto of an English resident. Five years later, the Legislative Council gave way to a House of Representatives, consisting of 39 members and 12 chiefs.

In 1958 Dr. Milton Margai formed the first Cabinet and, three years later, the country achieved full independence within the British Commonwealth. Prime Minister Margai died in 1964 and was succeeded by his brother, Albert, who was overthrown in 1967 by Siaka Stevens, head of the All People's Congress. Stevens was temporarily overthrown by an army coup, but was reinstated in 1968.

While Sierra Leone clings to a British-like two-party system, there is an increasing concentration of power in the hands of Stevens and his All People's Congress. The authority of the Sierra Leone People's Party, which had ruled the country until 1967, has lessened. While a Republican regime was proclamed in 1971, the APC actually controls the country as of 1975.

Under a new constitution adopted by referendum in early June 1978, Sierra Leone became a one-party state and Stevens was reelected president for a seven-year term on June 14.

Basically an unaligned nation, Sierra Leone had maintained cordial relations with neighboring Guinea and Liberia until the latter's civilian government was overthrown in 1980.

High unemployment, escalating oil prices, and shortages of consumer goods have led to student unrest and demonstrations in recent years. Diamonds, bauxite, and rutile are major export minerals, but resources are rapidly being depleted. The International Monetary Fund, World Bank group, and European Economic Community are among the foreign interests trying to help Sierra Leone's government reverse inflation.

Somalia

Date of independence: **July 1, 1960**
Area: **246,199 square miles**
Population: **3,753,000 (est. 1981)**
Capital: **Mogadishu**
Monetary unit: **Somali shilling**
Nationality: **Somali**
Religion: **Muslim**
Language: **Somali, Arabic, Italian, English**
Literacy: **5–10%**
Type of government: **Republic**
Political parties/leaders: **Somali Revolutionary Socialist Party (since 1976)**
Monetary conversion rate: **6,295 Somali shillings = $1 (1980)**
Principal economic resources: **Livestock, bananas, sorghum, peanuts, sugar cane, cotton, maize**

History at a Glance

The ancient Egyptians visited Somalia (Land of Aromatics) during the pre-Christian era in search of incense and aromatic herbs.

From A.D. 900 to 1400 the eastern coast of the territory was part of the Zenj Empire, which fell in the fifteenth century to Portugal. Later, Arabs from Muscat and Oman asserted their control over Somalia's major coastal centers, to be replaced in the nineteenth century by the Sultan of Zanzibar.

European contact with this region dates back to 1839, the year that Aden came under the domination of Great Britain. Effective control was not established, however, until the English signed between 1884 and 1886, a number of "protectorate" treaties with various Somali chieftains in the north. The Italians, meanwhile, began to expand into Southern Somalia in 1885, establishing administrative control and consolidating their territory by extensive military operations. Great Britain first began to administer her protectorate through the Colonial Office in 1905, and was embroiled in conflict with a rebellious local chief until 1920.

From 1934 to 1936, Italy used Somalia as a staging area for the invasion of Ethiopia, establishing at the same time a colonial government to administer most of Somalia, as well as Ogaden (the eastern portion of Ethiopia and the home of many Somalis).

During World War II, Italian troops occupied British Somaliland, but they lost control of this region with their defeat in 1941 at the hands of the British. Italian Somaliland was itself occupied by British troops until 1950, at which time it was returned to Italy under a 10-year trusteeship arrangement. By then, the United Nations had already decided that Italian Somaliland should receive its independence by 1960. (In 1954, matters had been complicated somewhat by the transference of a portion of British controlled Ogaden to Ethiopia.) Unification of the two territories and their subsequent independence was achieved in 1960.

Since then, Somali-inhabited sections of both Kenya and Ethiopia have repeatedly expressed a desire to be reunited with Somalia. In 1953 diplomatic relations were severed with Kenya over this issue, and, two years later, fighting broke out with Ethiopia over much the same question. As might be expected, Somalia has also advocated self-determination for the inhabitants of French Somaliland, including the port of Djibouti, terminus of the Ethiopian railroad.

In 1967 a popular election put President Abdirashid Ali Shermarke in office and Mohammed Haji Ibrahim Egal as Prime Minister. These two men guided Somalia into Western-oriented relationships and conciliation with neighboring states.

However, a 1969 coup led by Major General Mohammed Siad Barre ended in Shermarke's assassination and a reorganization of the country along socialist lines. Soon foreign banks and other foreign-controlled establishments were nationalized and local governments were introduced in eight regions and 48 districts.

On July 1, 1976, Barre dissolved the Supreme Revolutionary Council, which had been instituted at the time of the coup, and formed the Somali Revolutionary Socialist Party, the nation's only legal party. In late 1979 a 171-member People's Assembly was elected under a new Constitution and Barre was confirmed as President for a six-year term.

Initially, Barre maintained close ties with the Soviet Union, allowing the Soviets to build a naval base at Berbera in return for assistance in building up Somalia's 9,000-man army. This relationship came to a close in 1977.

Seasonal migrations by Somali herdsmen have historically strained relations with neighboring countries and in 1977, Somalia openly backed rebels in the Ogaden desert, which had been occupied by Ethiopia since the turn of the century. The Soviet Union disapproved of Somalia's action, which was heavily involved in the new Marxist government being formed in Ethiopia after Emperor Haile Selassie's ouster in 1974, and stopped military aid to Somalia. Somalia in turn expelled some 1,500 Soviet personnel and broke diplomatic relations with Soviet bloc countries.

Eventually, after full-scale fighting, Somalia conceded defeat in the Ethiopian desert and in March 1978 accepted some $13 million in U.S. food. Military aid was refused, however, unless Somalia gave up claims to northern Kenya, the Ogaden, and the Republic of Djibouti, all of which were contained in "Greater Somalia." Barre refused to do this and relationships between these countries have remained uneasy.

However, U.S.–Somalian military arrangements have been amended. In January 1980, $2 billion worth of arms and economic aid was given to this coastal country in exchange for bases for U.S. planes and ships. Eight months later, $25 million more in military aid was given for additional military bases.

South Africa

Date of independence: **1934**
Area: **471,445 square miles**
Population: **23,771,970 (est. 1980)**
Capital: **Pretoria**
Monetary unit: **Rand**
Nationality: **South African**
Religion: **Christian, Hindu, Muslim**
Language: **English (official), Afrikaans**
Literacy: **Whites 100%, blacks 50%**
Type of government: **Republic**
Political parties/leaders: **National Party, four white opposition parties, 11 non-white parties**
Monetary conversion rate: **1 rand = $1.34 (1980)**
Principal economic resources: **Corn, wool, wheat, sugar cane, gold, diamonds, platinum, uranium**

History at a Glance

Fossils discovered in South Africa lend evidence to speculation that the country is one of the earliest homes of mankind. Before Bartholomew Diaz of Portugal discovered the Cape of Good Hope in 1488, this huge area was inhabited by Bushmen, nomadic hunters confined to the western uplands, and by Hottentots, a pastoral people settled largely in its southern and eastern coastal sectors. At the same time, however, there was increased migration from the north by Bantu-speaking peoples who today live primarily in "reserves" set aside for them by the government.

On Christmas Day in 1497, Vasco da Gama discovered Natal, bordering on the Mozambique Channel, but South Africa itself did not come to be settled by Europeans until 1652. In that year, Jan van Riebeeck brought the first colonists into the Cape of Good Hope region under the sponsorship of the Dutch East India

Barbed wire fences mark the boundaries of black living areas in South Africa, which is ruled by a racist white minority government.

Company. The settlers began to import slaves from West Africa almost immediately and, with the scarcity of European women, eventually entered into mixed marriages which produced the so-called Cape Colored people. The Dutch, who were known as Boers, or "farmers," were soon joined by French, Scandinavian, and German immigrants who adopted the name "Afrikaaners" to distinguish themselves from the rest of the population.

The first contacts with Bantu-speaking Africans were made along the Great Fish River in the 1730s. By 1778 boundaries had been set up to separate the settlers from the Africans. Within the year, the first Kaffir War had broken out between the Xhosa tribesmen and the colonists.

In 1795 Great Britain took charge of the Cape region and, by 1815, pursuant to the Treaty of Vienna, had extended official control over the territory. English settlers began arriving in 1820. From the outset, England granted the free "Cape Colored" people the same legal and political privileges as white people and, in fact, abolished slavery in 1834. Two years later, the Dutch (Boers), alienated by these policies, undertook their great northward trek, defeating Bantu tribesmen

in the interior, to found the Natal, Transvaal, and Orange Free State territories.

The British, however, followed close on the heels of the Boers annexing Natal in 1843, Kaffraria in 1847, Griqualand West in 1874, Bechuanaland in 1885, and Zululand and Tongaland in 1887. In 1848 the Orange Free State was taken over by the British, only to regain its independence six years later. The Transvaal was made independent in 1852, annexed in 1877, and returned to independence in 1881, the same year in which Swaziland achieved this status.

Despite the preponderance of British political influence, economic factors in the territory accounted for much of its social development during the nineteenth century. The growth of the sugar cane plantations in Natal led to the importation of thousands of east Indians who worked off their period of indenture and then remained in the territory as tradesmen and fishermen. The discovery of diamonds along the Orange and Vaal Rivers (1868) and of gold on the Witwatersrand (1886) hastened the fanatically systematic creation of separate white and black communities. Within the white communities, however, friction between the Dutch farmers and the "outsiders" (English and others) soon led to armed conflict, culminating in the Boer War, which was won by the British in 1902.

The Union of South Africa was formed in 1910 and consisted of the two Boer republics, which by then had been granted self-government by the British, and the Cape and Natal provinces. In 1926 South Africa was given equal legal status with Great Britain, and the right to associate freely with the sovereign members of the British Commonwealth.

Despite the restoration of peace, Boer–English relations continued to be marked by wholesale bitterness and recrimination. Two political parties emerged—the Unionists on the one hand advocating cooperation with Great Britain and the Boer supremacists (the group in power today) who ultimately conceived and executed the policy of "apartheid," or separate racial development.

During both world wars, Boer nationalists attempted to prevent South Africa from participating on the Allied side. They first managed to consolidate effective control over the country in 1948, the year in which Prime Minister Daniel Malan came to power. Since then, white-supremacist policies have become even more firmly entrenched, particularly now that industrial development has brought a tremendous improvement in the living standards of white South Africans.

In 1959 the Nationalists passed the Promotion of Bantu Self-Government Act which provided for the creation of eight separate autonomous states for blacks only. Two years later, concurrent with its withdrawal from the British Commonwealth, South Africa opted for a republican form of government, although its constitution barely changed.

South Africa continued to refine its program of apartheid, turning a deaf ear to the protests of the United Nations, the rest of Africa, and most of the civilized world. The state, then headed by Prime Minister Hendrik F. Verwoerd, had taken stern measures to suppress all forms of political opposition, censoring the press and other media, imprisoning citizens for up to six months with no formal charges and without a trial—in short, declaring all forms of objectionable activity as communist-inspired.

Late in 1966 Prime Minister Verwoerd was assassinated by Dimitrio Tsafendas, a white, who, ironically, thought that Verwoerd was doing too much for the black population.

Since then, under Prime Minister Balthazar J. Vorster, South Africa has strengthened its defense establishment in anticipation of stepped-up guerrilla activity and possible sea and air attacks emanating from its black neighbors to the North. At the same time, the United Nations has sought desperately to take control of South West Africa due to South Africa's imposition of apartheid there, but has been unable to dislodge the republic from the mandated territory.

The late 1960s and early 1970s were an economic boom time for South Africa, though two thirds of the national income went to the white fifth of the population.

One critical issue of the early 1970s was the renewal of interest in the future of South-West Africa, a former German territory, that has been ruled by South Africa since World War I. Local leaders appealed for help from the United Nations to gain independence under the name Namibia, and the country was under U.N. jurisdiction by a 1966 General Assembly resolution. South Africa has repeatedly refused to acknowledge Namibia and has been ousted from the United Nations and remains barred from the General Assembly to date.

A series of crises arose in the mid-1970s. When the Angola civil war began in 1975–1976 Prime Minister Vorster sent 4,000 troops to help the doomed National Union for the Total Independence of Angola, which eventually was defeated by the Soviet-backed Popular Movement for the Liberation of Angola. On the other side of the continent, unrest in Zimbabwe (formerly Rhodesia) was growing and military aid was sent there as well.

In 1977 South Africa experienced the worst outbreak of racial violence since the Sharpeville riots in 1960. The bloodshed, which began in the black township of Soweto, a suburb of Johannesburg, grew out of black student protests against the compulsory use of Afrikaans as the language of instruction. As a result, many theaters and opera houses were desegregated, though the Vorster government has given no indication of wanting to end apartheid restrictions altogether. Instead, it has insisted that the blacks in South Africa are not segregated because of their race but rather because they represent distinct "nations" to which special political and constitutional arrangements should be made. It was in accordance with this philosophy that independence was granted to the "homelands" of Transkei in October 1976, Bophuthatswana in December 1977, and Venda in September 1979.

Rioting intensified greatly after September 12, 1977, after the controversial death of anti-apartheid activist Steven Biko, when it was discovered that he died from a head injury while in prison. As a result, the government invoked some of its strictest policies in two decades, closing down the leading black newspaper, arresting its editor, and banning a number of protest groups.

Prime Minister Vorster was forced to resign on June 4, 1979, following a scandal involving $11 million which was supposed to have been used to buy *The Washington Star* for propaganda purposes.

Prime Minister Peter Botha has eased job restrictions and extended black union rights. He also has appointed a multiracial advisory council which includes whites, Asians, and coloreds, but pointedly excludes blacks.

Numerous nations have cut trade with South Africa because of its apartheid practices and occupation of Namibia. However, the Reagan Administration recently offered "strategic cooperation" if Prime Minister Botha allows Namibia true independence and moves away from apartheid.

South Africa is the first African country to experience the full force of the industrial revolution. Its gold mines supply about two thirds of the gold produced by non-Communist countries. Other important mineral products include coal, diamonds, copper, asbestos, chrome, and platinum. Agriculturally, South Africa is self-sufficient in most foods.

South African Dependency of Bophulthatswana

Date of independence: **December 6, 1977**
Area: **15,571 square miles**
Population: **1,350,000 (est. 1981)**
Capital: **Mmabatho**
Monetary unit: **South African rand**
Religion: **Methodist, Lutheran, Anglican**
Language: **Setswana, also English, Africaan**
Political party: **Bophuthatswana Democratic Party**
Monetary conversion rate: **1 rand = $1.30 (1980)**
Principal economic resource: **Platinum**

South African Dependency of Transkei

Date of independence: **October 26, 1976**
Area: **16,675 square miles**
Population: **2,300,000 (est. 1981)**
Capital: **Umtata**
Monetary unit: **South African rand**
Religion: **66% Christian, 24% Animist**
Language: **Xhosa, English, Africaan**
Political parties: **Transkei Congress Party, two opposition parties**
Monetary conversion rate: **1 rand = $1.30 (1980)**
Principal economic resources: **Tea, beans, corn, sorghum, timber**

South African Dependency of Venda

Date of independence: **September 13, 1979**
Area: **2,861 square miles**
Population: **528,000 (est. 1981)**
Capital: **Thohyandou**
Monetary unit: **South African rand**
Religion: **Christian, tribal**
Language: **English, Africaans**
Political parties: **Venda National Party, Venda Independence Party (opposition)**

Monetary conversion rate: **1 rand = $1.30 (1980)**
Principal economic resources: **Meat, tea, fruit, timber, graphite**

Sudan

Date of independence: **January 1, 1956**
Area: **967,494 square miles**
Population: **19,385,000 (est. 1981)**
Capital: **Khartoum**
Monetary unit: **Sudanese pound**
Religion: **73% Sunni Muslim, 23% Pagan, 4% Christian**
Language: **Arabic (official), Nubian, English**
Literacy: **5–10%**
Type of government: **Republic (under military control since May 1969)**
Political parties/leaders: **Sudanese Socialist Union, President Ja'far Muhammad Numayri**
Monetary conversion rate: **Sudanese pound = $2 (1980)**
Principal economic resources: **Cotton, peanuts, sesame seeds, gum Arabic, sorghum, wheat, sugar cane**

History at a Glance

Sudanese history reflects the country's natural division between the predominantly Arab North (which for centuries has lived in close contact with the civilizations of Egypt, Rome, Byzantium, and Turkey) and the black-dominated South (which has been virtually isolated from significant contact with North African and Near Eastern culture).

In antiquity, the center of Sudan lay in what is today the eastern portion of the territory that is, in the vicinity of the kingdom of Meroe (750 B.C.–A.D. 300) which even ruled Egypt for a time.

Beginning in the ninth century A.D., nomadic tribes from neighboring Egypt penetrated other areas of the Sudan, intermarrying with the indigenous peoples of the Upper Nile region. From 1500 to 1820, control over most of central and northern Sudan rested with a confederation of tribes ruled and administered by the "Black Sultans" of the Funj dynasty.

In 1820 Sudan was conquered by the Ottoman viceroy of Egypt, Mohammed Ali. Some 50 years passed before the Khedive Ismail led a campaign against the slave trade and, as a result, moved down the Nile into the Southern Sudan.

Soon after, several Sudanese tribes rallied to the side of Muhammad Ahmad, who proclaimed himself the Mahdi, a religious leader believed to be acting under the inspiration of Allah, and led a number of Sudanese tribes in a successful revolt against Anglo-Egyptian rule. The Mahdi took possession of Khartoum and put to death the British governor, General Charles Gordon. In 1898 Anglo-Egyptian forces under General Kitchener defeated the Mahdi's successor in the battle of Obdurman. British rule was then established through a nominal Anglo-Egyptian condominium (a

A girl winnows hand-threshed rice at a U.N. agricultural station designed to promote modern methods of farming among primitive tribesmen. The Sudanese government has set up a number of such experimental farms to raise the living standard of the population.

jointly ruled territory) which remained in effect until 1955.

Sudanese nationalism became a force after World War I, when differences were growing more pronounced between Moslem Northerners and the black tribes of the South who were falling under the influence of Christian missionaries and the British educational system. The split gradually widened between those seeking union with Egypt and those advocating the establishment of a separate state.

During World War II, British-led Sudanese troops complied an outstanding combat record, particularly against superior and better equipped Italian forces. Later, several schemes for a unified state encompassing the entire Nile Valley were advanced, but agreement was not reached by the negotiating parties, Great Britain, Egypt, and the Sudan, until 1953, the year Egypt's King Farouk was deposed.

The new republic of Sudan came into being three years later. Within a short time, the government had launched its Arabization-of-the-South program which had widespread repercussions, leading to the eventual overthrow of the existing parliamentary regime by a military junta headed by Lieutenant General Ibrahim Abbud. In 1964 a popular revolution swept the army aside but, by this time, the question of Sudanese unity threatened to plunge the nation into civil war.

Though secessionist activity subsided in the late 1960s, the Sudan was still troubled by internal turmoil and a growing financial deficit. The nation relinquished

American aid in 1967 after breaking ties with the United States over the Arab–Israeli war. Two years later, a military coup headed by Gafaar Muhammed al-Nimeiry took over and set a socialist course.

A constitutional calm crept into the Sudan with al-Nimeiry's inauguration as President in 1971. Though beset by both communist and pro-Egyptian elements, Nimeiry has managed to pursue a moderate course. Three southern provinces of the country were given their own regional government, thus ending long-standing guerrilla warfare in this area.

In 1972 the Sudan resumed diplomatic relations with the United States, and stressed friendly relations with Ethiopia, Uganda, and its other neighbors. This shift in focus led to a decline in its friendship with Egypt.

In 1973 the United States Ambassador and charge d'affaires and a Belgian diplomat were killed by "Black September" Palestinian terrorists. The terrorists were convicted by a Sudanese court, but later freed by the Sudanese government and turned over to a Palestinian group in Egypt.

Numerous internal problems, including persistent charges of corruption, led to six cabinet reorganizations between 1970 and 1975.

In 1976 a third attempted coup against President Nimeiry left 1,000 rebels and loyal troops dead after

Members of the Dinka tribe stack sisal fiber, an indigenous substitute for jute.

a fierce battle in Khartoum. President Nimeiry blamed Libyan President Muammar Qaddafy for instigating the attempt and Sudan broke relations with Libya. Firing squads later executed 81 convicted rebels. President Nimeiry also charged the Soviets with complicity in the attempt and expelled 90 Soviet advisors.

Tensions between Egypt and Sudan had been strong, but in February 1974 an agreement coordinating political and economic strategies between the countries was signed. In 1979 Sudan distinguished itself by not breaking relations with Egypt, although, like all other Arab countries, it rejected the Egyptian–Israeli peace treaty.

Sudan also has been ostracized for publicly backing the Eritrean rebel movement in its fight against the pro-Soviet Ethiopian central government.

Cotton is the only major cash crop, followed by gum arabic, of which Sudan produces four fifths of the world's supply. Domestic petroleum production has recently begun.

Swaziland

Date of independence: **September 6, 1968**
Area: **6,703 square miles**
Population: **566,000 (est. 1981)**
Capital: **Mbabane**
Monetary unit: **Lilangeni**
Nationality: **Swazi**
Religion: **57% Christian, 43% Animist**
Language: **English, Siswati (both official)**
Literacy: **25%**
Type of government: **Monarchy**
Political parties/leaders: **King Sobhuza II**
Monetary conversion rate: **1 Lilangeni = $1.34 (1980)**
Principal economic resources: **Corn, livestock, sugar cane, citrus fruits, cotton, rice, pineapple**

A Swazi woman walks toward Mbabane, capital of the small, landlocked country.

History at a Glance

Swaziland was settled in the early nineteenth century by the Swazi, a people of Bantu stock who had been driven from their homelands in northern Zululand by the Zulus. Swazi independence was guaranteed by Great Britain in 1881 and, three years later, by the Republic of South Africa. In 1890 a British-South African-Swazi government was established, with South Africa declaring a protectorate over the territory four years later. After the Boer War, Swaziland was administered by the governor of Transvaal. In 1907 it was placed under the control of the British High Commissioner for South Africa.

In 1967 Swaziland won a measure of self-government under a new constitution and, a year later, achieved full independence under King Sobhuza II. In 1972 Swaziland held its first general election since independence in 1968. A hint of opposition crept into the political pattern of the country, though it was not strong enough to keep the ruling Imbokodvo National Movement from forming another one-party government. The INM favors heightened cooperation with its neighbor, South Africa.

Major General Maphevu Dlamini, who had served as Prime Minister since 1976, died on October 25, 1979. Prince Mandabala Fred Dlamini was designated his successor a month later.

King Sobhuza, now in his eighties, is the world's longest reigning monarch. He has maintained good relations with South Africa and established diplomatic relations with Mozambique during 1976.

The economy is quite diversified, considering the country's small size and population. Production of iron ore, which once accounted for a quarter of the export earnings, virtually ceased by the end of the 1970s. Coal mining, on the other hand, is increasing and additional minerals such as tin, barites, and silica have been found in some abundance.

Tanzania

Date of independence: December 9, 1961
Area: 364,898 square miles
Population: 18,420,000 (est. 1981)
Capital: Dar es Salaam
Monetary unit: Shilling
Religion: 40% Animist, 30% Christian, 30% Muslim
Language: English (official), Swahili, local languages
Literacy: 61%
Type of government: Republic (single party)
Political parties/leaders: Revolutionary Party of Tanzania
Monetary conversion rate: 8.18 shillings = $1 (1980)
Principal economic resources: Sugar, maize, rice, wheat, cotton, coffee, iron, coal, natural gas

History at a Glance

Since 1959 Tanzania has been able to claim the distinction of being the aboriginal home of mankind. It was in this year that Dr. L. S. B. Leakey discovered *homo zinjanthropus* in the Olduvai Gorge near Serengeti National Park. Knowledge of the early history of the region is scant, although it is certain that East Africa as a whole was involved in trade with Greece, Arabia, Persia, India, and even China.

The coastal region of Tanzania, then known as Tanganyika, first attracted Arab colonists from Oman in the eighth century A.D. and Persian settlers a century later. For the next 500 years, a number of coastal towns enjoyed considerable commercial prosperity. During this period, Islam gained a secure foothold along the coast and the Swahili language and culture developed among the Bantu tribes of the region.

Portugal came on the scene in the sixteenth century, wresting the Indian Ocean trade from the Arabs and conquering the coastal towns under the latter's control. The Portuguese themselves were driven from their coastal holdings during the next two centuries by Arab slave traders based in Zanzibar and loyal to the Omani sultans. The height of Arab influence on the mainland occurred in the nineteenth century under the Imam Seyyid Said. The plantation system introduced by Zanzibar around 1840 led to an extension of the slave trade which brought about considerable tribal unrest and warfare.

The first Europeans to explore the interior of Tanzania were the Englishmen Burton and Speke, who crossed the territory in 1857 in search of the headwaters of the Nile River. After the Berlin Conference of 1884–1885, Germany established a protectorate extending over the areas of Rwanda and Burundi (German East Africa). In 1890 Germany purchased a portion of the coast from the Sultan of Zanzibar, and gradually began to extend its influence farther into the interior, encountering stiff resistance from the Afri-

can population. The Germans established plantations, built railways, improved communications, and substituted a system of forced labor for the slave trade.

After Germany's defeat in World War I, Tanzania was mandated to Great Britain by the League of Nations and retained this status until it was taken over by the United Nations after World War II.

By 1954 African nationalism had reached such a fever pitch in the territory that the Tanganyika African National Union (TANU) petitioned the United Nations to persuade Great Britain to establish a timetable for the specific steps leading to independence. In September 1960 Julius Nyerere became Tanganyika's chief minister. By the end of 1961 the territory had become fully independent.

Meanwhile, Zanzibar had likewise begun to press Great Britain for autonomy. In 1964 shortly after Zanzibar had won its independence under an Arab-controlled government, a popular revolt was staged by the African-supported Afro-Shirazi party. Both the sultan and the prime minister were deposed, and a republican government headed by Abeid Karume was installed. Three months later, Zanzibar merged with Tanganyika, creating what was at first called the United Republic of Tanganyika and Zanzibar and has since come to be known as Tanzania.

In 1967 President Julius K. Nyerere undertook an extensive program of nationalization that covered banks, trading companies, insurance firms, and the food-processing industry. Despite the program, the President emphasized that private investment would still be welcome in his country, operating in partnership with the National Development Corporation.

During the 1970s, Tanzania was torn by both domestic and foreign conflict. Zanzibar suffered political unrest in 1972 when assassins killed a political leader, Abeid Amani Karume. His replacement, Aboud Jumbe, is more of a moderate. In 1972 Tanzania was once again fighting with its neighbor, Uganda. A peace settlement was worked out through the various leaders of African countries that make up the East African community to which both Uganda and Tanzania belong. However, as the government of General Amin in Uganda became entrenched, tensions between the countries increased, threatening the unity of the East African Community (Kenya, Tanzania, and Uganda), which had long been viewed as an outstanding example of African regional cooperation. Tanzanian youths applying for work in Uganda disappeared, Ugandan rebels tried to use Tanzania as a base of operations, and prospects for an East African Federation, long a dream of Julius Nyerere, seemed to have collapsed.

An invasion by Ugandan troops in November 1978 was followed by a fierce counterattack in January 1979, in which 5,000 Tanzanian troops were joined by 3,000

Ugandan exiles. Within the month, full-scale war had developed with the Tanzanian force pushing north to capture Kampala on April 11.

Despite pressure from opposition groups, Nyerere kept his troops in Uganda in open support of Ugandan President Milton Obote until the national elections in December 1980. In 1981, however, Nyerere withdrew his troops, citing a $1 million-a-month drain on the Tanzanian economy as the principal reason.

By 1981 Tanzania was all but bankrupt. The country's 18 million people faced daily shortages of such staples as bread, soap, and cooking oil.

In 1974–1975 Nyerere began implementing a socialist economic plan, called "ujamaa", by moving 11 million peasants into some 8,000 collective villages. Today, 40% of the villagers have clean tap water and 35% are serviced by medical clinics. School enrollment is improved and average life expectancy has increased to 51 years.

However, the clinics and schools are only shells of progress—books and drugs alike are hard to come by. Other problems have resulted from ideological rigidity. In the farm collectives, workers must walk to and from the farms instead of working their own land. It is not uncommon for a worker to walk 10 miles 40 times in order to deliver a harvest to a village home.

Oil production cost increases and the $500 million spent on the Ugandan war have somewhat destroyed Tanzania's economic stability. However, modernization plans have been enhanced by the completion of the Tanzam Railway, which links Dar es Salaam and the Zambian copper belt, begun in 1976 with support from China.

Togo

Date of independence: **April 27, 1960**
Area: **21,622 square miles**
Population: **2,601,000 (est. 1981)**
Capital: **Lome**
Monetary unit: **CFA franc**
Nationality: **Togolese**
Religion: **75% Animist, 20% Christian, 5% Muslim**
Language: **French (official), four major African languages**
Literacy: **54.9% of school age children**
Type of government: **Republic (under military rule since 1967)**
Political parties/leaders: **Rally of the Togolese People**
Monetary conversion rate: **CFA 225.80 francs = $1 (1980)**
Principal economic resources: **Yams, manioc, millet, sorghum, cocoa, coffee, rice**

History at a Glance
Togo was first settled by the Ewe people, who migrated

A woman potter in Togoland.

there from the Niger Valley between the twelfth and the fourteenth centuries.

During the next two centuries, the territory was frequently visited by the Portuguese, who instituted a thriving slave trade in Grand Popo and Petit Popo, two of Togo's coastal villages. The Portuguese were then displaced, first by the French, who established trading posts in the area, and then by the Germans, who ultimately won control over the territory by signing a treaty with the chief of Togo, then only a village on the coast. The Germans later applied the name Togo to the entire territory.

The Togolese capital of Lome was established in 1897 and, within a few years, boundary settlements had been arranged with England and France. These agreements paid scant attention to existing tribal unities, with the result that a number of groups found themselves simultaneously incorporated into three distinct colonial areas—Ghana, Togo, and Dahomey.

During World War I, England took over control of the coastal areas (British Togoland), whereas France administered Togo's interior (French Togoland). In

1922 the League of Nations sanctioned this wartime arrangement.

In 1945 England and France relinquished their holds on Togo to the United Nations. Two years later, the Ewe people sent the first of a number of petitions to the United Nations requesting assistance in the achievement of tribal and national unification. After nine years of debate (differences had to be resolved not only between England and France, but also between a number of conflicting tribes), a plebiscite was held in British Togoland, which was incorporated into the Republic of Ghana when that nation became independent in 1957.

French Togoland voted for full autonomy within the French Community, a decision opposed at first by the United Nations. In 1960 the Republic of Togo became a sovereign nation, with Sylvanus Olympio as Prime Minister. When Olympio was assassinated in 1963, Nicholas Grunitzky, living in exile in Dahomey at the time, became Prime Minister.

President Etienne Eyadema, who seized power in 1967 through a military coup, has since legitimized his office by "popular referendum." His election in 1972 so pleased him that he released all political prisoners.

In 1969 Eyadema established a national political party, the Rally of the Togolese People (RTP), through which he organized the labor unions and women. He has not enjoyed a serene presidency; his life has been threatened on numerous occasions including one serious attempt in October 1977 by a group of professional mercenaries. Eyadema was reelected unanimously for a seven-year term in December 1979 (there were no opponents) and the next month he released 34 out of 45 reported political prisoners. However, opponents claim that those released were not "real political prisoners" and that hundreds of others remain incarcerated.

Togo is one of the smallest and poorest African countries. Coffee, cocoa, and most recently, cotton are its primary exports. Phosphates are the most important mining activity, and a substantial amount of smuggling between Togo and Ghana enhances the country's meager economy. (Authorities have estimated that as much as a third of Togo's cocoa exports begin in Ghana, but are smuggled into Togo in exchange for luxury items.)

Tunisia

Date of independence: **March 20, 1956**
Area: **63,170 square miles**
Population: **6,644,000 (est. 1981)**
Capital: **Tunis**
Monetary unit: **Dinar**

Nationality: **Tunisian**
Religion: **98% Muslim, 1% Christian, 1% Jewish**
Language: **Arabic (official), French**
Literacy: **50%**
Type of government: **Republic**
Political parties/leaders: **Destourian Socialist Party, four major illegal parties**
Monetary conversion rate: **1 dinar = $2.39 (1980)**
Principal economic resources: **Wheat, olives, citrus fruits, grapes, dates, oil, phosphates**

History at a Glance

Tunisia is the site of the ancient empire of Carthage, which once vied with Rome for power in the Mediterranean and in North Africa, but was finally defeated in 146 B.C. in the last of the three Punic Wars. Tunisia was occupied by the Vandals in the fifth century A.D.; by the Byzantines a century later, and by the Arabs for many centuries thereafter. The Arabs used Tunisia as a base from which to extend their power and the religion of Islam south and west into sub-Sahara Africa, and northward to Sicily.

The Turks seized Tunisia in 1574, holding it for three centuries, during which the territory was ruled by governors from Istanbul or by descendants of the Husayn dynasty.

In the late nineteenth century, France imposed a protectorate over the territory by armed force. By 1880 Great Britain, Italy, and France had established a control commission to supervise Tunisia's tottering finances. Once France had a clear field, though, she proceeded with a program of heavy investments which helped Tunisia modernize itself. In return, she benefitted from Tunisia's unstinting loyalty during World War I.

Tunisian nationalism was an outgrowth of a moderate reform movement begun by the Destour Party in the 1920s. Led by Habib Bourguiba, the Neo-Destour Party of the next decade was activist in character, and able to negotiate with France from a position of strength after World War II.

In 1951 the French rejected a Tunisian demand for internal autonomy, a decision which touched off a wave of unrest punctuated by terrorism. In 1955 a Franco-Tunisian treaty was signed in Paris and, a year later, Tunisia was granted full independence. A new constitution went into effect in 1959, and Bourguiba became first president.

Two years later, Tunisia attempted a blockade of the French naval base at Bizerte, a move which provoked the armed intervention of France and led to the massacre of several Tunisian civilians. Tension eased gradually and, in 1963, the base was evacuated by France.

Since then, Tunisia has nationalized all foreign-owned land in an effort to initiate a program of internal reform. In response, the French withdrew their technical experts, suspended financial aid, and eliminated export subsidies. The United States took up part of the slack by donating surplus grain, and by supporting a large public works program.

Tunisia ended its traditionally neutral role in the Arab world when it joined with the majority of Arab League members in condemning Egypt for signing a peace treaty with Israel. After Egypt was expelled from the League in 1979, Tunis became the headquarters for the League. Difficult relations with neighboring Algeria were smoothed over in 1979, but Tunisia broke all ties with Libya after its mining town of Gafsa was seized in 1980 by insurgents who were allegedly trained in Libya. To date, Tunisia has tried to move toward more conservative policies and seek foreign investment and tourism revenues.

Bourguiba, now in his eighties, has long been the head of Tunisia's only legal party, the Socialist Destourian Party, but has been forced by internal pressures to recognize other parties. In recent years, the country has been faced with a staggering birth rate, 20% unemployment, student unrest, and increasingly radical Islamic movements. Moreover, Bourguiba's failing health has made him vulnerable, although he was elected President for Life in 1974.

In 1981 he announced that free elections for National Assembly would be held and allowed campaigning, rallies, and free airtime for opposing political party candidates. However, only 6% of the population voted for opposing parties, and incidents of intimidation, ballot stuffing, and other outrageous voting discrepancies were reported.

Agriculture accounts for 45% of the labor force and industry is expanding slowly. Tunisia claims the first steel mill in northwest Africa.

Uganda

Date of independence: **October 9, 1962**
Area: **91,133 square miles**
Population: **14,139,000 (est. 1981)**
Capital: **Kampala**
Monetary unit: **Uganda shilling**
Nationality: **Ugandan**
Religion: **60% nominally Christian, 15% Muslim**
Language: **English (official), Luganda, Swahili**
Literacy: **20–40%**
Type of government: **Republic**
Political parties/leaders: **Uganda People's Congress, three opposition parties**
Monetary conversion rate: **7.57 Uganda shillings = $1 (1980)**
Principal economic resources: **Coffee, tea, cotton, tobacco, sugar, copper**

History at a Glance

According to the testimony of contemporary archeologists, tiny landlocked Uganda was the site of a highly developed African civilization long before European explorers opened up this portion of the African continent. Africans of Bantu stock built up a relatively advanced Iron Age civilization there. It remained intact until Hamitic peoples from the northeast overcame the Bantu.

The two mightiest kingdoms in the area were the Buganda to the north and the Bunyoro to the south. Arab slave traders took advantage of the clash between these two groups, which reached a climactic stage in the mid-nineteenth century.

In 1862 John Hanning Speke and Captain J. A. Grant explored the territory for Great Britain, as did Samuel Baker who discovered Lake Albert. Baker later returned to Uganda as a foreign agent for Egypt which had its own expansionist interests in the regions of the lower Nile. In 1875 Henry Stanley arrived in Uganda, and was followed by Christian missionaries seeking to win favor with the Kabaka (the king of Buganda).

In 1894 consistent with the role it had assigned itself in the carving up of Africa into different "spheres of influence," Great Britain established a formal protectorate over Buganda. In 1900 Sir Harry Johnstone negotiated the Uganda Agreement, giving the Buganda Kingdom a privileged position within the British-controlled territory. A year later, similar agreements were concluded with the kingdoms of Toro and Ankole.

In the first decade of the twentieth century, Sir Hesketh Bell, the British commissioner, drafted a program designed to assist development of cotton as a staple crop. Thus Uganda was spared the upheaval which later afflicted neighboring Kenya, where the predominant system of free speculation in land allowed white Europeans to win control of the choicest land and to establish a plantation-based economy.

After World War II, Buganda established a federation which would allow each territory to maintain its autonomy. But in 1962 a coalition government headed by A. Milton Obote was voted into power. Agreement with the petty kingdoms of the territory as to their status and representation was reached before the end of the year when independence came.

In 1966 President Obote moved to unify Uganda by removing Mutesa, suspending the Constitution, abolishing the federal system, and assuming all ruling power. A year later, the traditional kingdoms were abolished, and Obote was named President under a new republican constitution.

In 1971 Idi Amin, a 43-year-old general, seized power and became President. The following year Amin ejected two thirds of his country's 75,000 Asian residents. This ejection caused great hardship to those who were forced to leave and dealt a grievous blow to Uganda's economy.

Increasingly, Amin became known as one of the world's more ruthless and eccentric leaders. After praising Hitler for his racial policies, Amin fired his female foreign minister for putatively having sexual realtions with a Frenchman in a lavatory in the Paris airport, and in 1975 he nearly executed a British lecturer for referring to him as a "village tyrant."

Meanwhile, numerous Tanzanians, Kenyans, Europeans, and Americans working in Uganda had been jailed or disappeared, and Amin developed a policy of Ugandanization which, to many, seems aimed at removing Ugandans sympathetic with former president Obote, or with the apparent, periodic attempts of Tanzanian President Nyerere to overthrow Amin.

Perhaps even more serious to Ugandans were monetary inflation, declining agricultural production, and corruption in the government. In 1975 such basics as soap, eggs, flour, and tobacco were scarce, despite the fact that Uganda is a large tobacco producer.

Amin had his defenders, among them Roy Innes, head of America's Congress of Racial Equality, to whom Amin granted Ugandan citizenship. Defenders of Amin maintained that his policies were necessitated by the manner in which Uganda's resources had been exploited by foreign companies. For example, it is charged that a Canadian company that mines Ugandan copper had never given Uganda any income from its copper exports, as a result of an agreement signed in the 1940s.

Following an invasion by Tanzanian and exile Ugandan forces, the Amin regime was overthrown in Kampala on April 10–11, 1979. Amin's eight-year reign had been a horror reminiscent of Hitler's purges in Germany. His paranoia resulted in countless deaths of innocent men and women, and in 1977 Amnesty International reported that 300,000 had died under his rule.

No African leaders denounced Amin, however, until Tanzania's Nyerere took up the fight. The only one to come to Amin's defense was Libya's Muammar Qaddafi, who sent in troops until the battle was lost and later allowed Amin safe refuge in Libya.

A brief interim government was established and former President Obote returned from exile in Tanzania, where he was reelected through a newly established National Assembly.

Peace is slow in coming to this nation. Scores of people have been murdered by Obote's army and secret police organizations still roam the countryside. Inflation is extremely high—an average worker's monthly wages will buy food for only three days. Tanzanian troops remained for a year to ensure Obote's position, but there are numerous small opposition parties which force Obote to maintain sharp control.

The Ugandan economy is in disastrous shape as the Amin regime controlled virtually all industrial and manufacturing concerns and bled them dry. Today, agriculture and fishing account for about half of gross domestic product while coffee accounts for more than 90% of exports.

Upper Volta

Date of independence: **August 5, 1960**
Area: **105,869 square miles**
Population: **6,970,000 (est. 1981)**
Capital: **Ouagandougou**
Monetary unit: **CFA franc**
Nationality: **Upper Voltan**
Religion: **75% Animist, 20% Muslim, 5% Christian**
Language: **French (official); tribal languages**

Masai facial incisions traditionally protected the bearer from being sold into slavery.

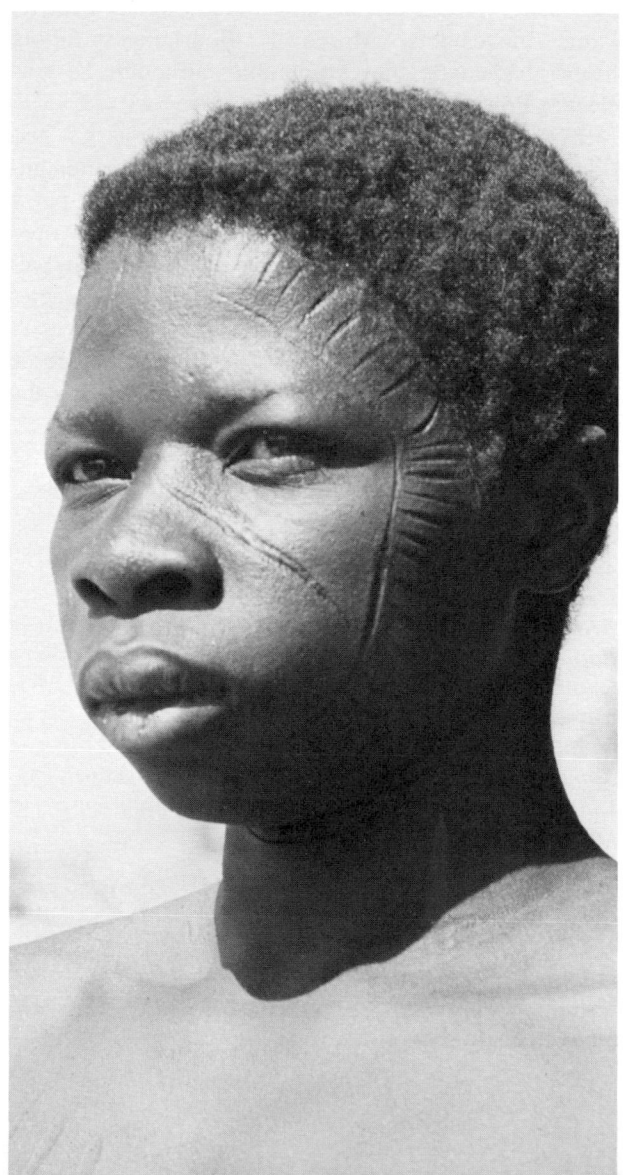

Girls of Yargo pounding newly harvested millet.

Literacy: 5%–10%
Type of government: Military
Political parties/leaders: Voltan Democratic Union, Voltan Progressive Union
Monetary conversion rate: CFA 225.80 = $1 (1980)
Principal economic resources: Millet, sorghum, corn, rice, livestock, peanuts, sugar cane, cotton

History at a Glance

The early history of Upper Volta is largely concerned with the exploits of the Mossi people who migrated from the east between the eleventh and thirteenth centuries. During the following two centuries, there is evidence indicating that the Mossi conducted highly successful raids on the wealthy trading cities along the Niger River. Checked eventually by the armed might of the Songhai Empire, the Mossi organized the territorial spoils they had acquired into the states of Tenkodogo, Yatenga, and Ouagadougou, each of which was ruled by a moro naba (king). Of the three reigning kingdoms, Ouagandougou was unquestionably the most powerful.

The Mossi finally settled down to a life of commerce, engaging profitably in the export of gold, kola nuts, and slaves. In the eighteenth century, the Ashanti, from Ghana, made significant military inroads into Mossi territory. The rest of it was conquered in 1896 by a French lieutenant in command of a single infantry battalion.

Governed at first as part of the Ivory Coast, Upper Volta was separated from this territory in 1969 and made a single administrative unit. In 1933 it was parceled up among Niger, French Sudan, and the Ivory Coast.

After World War II, however, Upper Volta was reconstituted as a separate territory in response to the wishes of the Mossi, and to curb the growth of the African Democratic Rally, an interterritorial political party which was gaining widespread support throughout West Africa. Upper Volta accepted the French Constitution of 1958, thereby becoming an autonomous unit within the French Community. Two years later, the territory became completely independent, although retaining close ties with metropolitan France.

In 1966 Maurice Yameogo, President of Upper Volta, was deposed by Lieutenant Colonel Sangoule Lamizane after several days of rioting in Ouagadougou concerning the issue of pay cuts for government employees.

Throughout the late 1960s, Chief of Staff Lamizana effectively headed the country and prevented any further erosion of its precarious financial position.

In 1970 Upper Volta returned to a constitutional government under Lamizana, but soon suffered two natural disasters: a severe drought in 1973 and famine in 1974. Political fighting between Lamizana and ex-President Tameogo resulted in Lamizana, with the Army, taking control of the government and dissolving the National Assembly and suspending the 1970 constitution. A new cabinet was formed in February 1974 with Lamizana continuing as both President and Prime Minister.

In yet another governmental reorganization in 1977,

Lamizana announced that a constitutional referendum would take place soon with both presidential and legislative elections, though he would not stand as a candidate. On November 27, 1977, the majority of the population voted for democratic rule in the referendum. However, Lamizana reneged on his promise not to run for the presidency and won in the 1978 election.

Upper Volta had been one of two multiparty democracies (Senegal was the other) in French Africa, until November 25, 1980, when the regime was overthrown in a military coup led by former Foreign Minister Colonel Saye Zerbo.

Under Zerbo's rule, all political activity was banned, former leaders were arrested, and the constitution was suspended. The Military Committee of Reform for National Progress was formed and an 11-member "directing committee," headed by Zerbo, installed.

There has been civil unrest in the country and two unsuccessful countercoups against the Zerbo regime, but the country remains firmly under his control.

Upper Volta remains one of the poorest countries in Africa, with $113 (1977) per capita income and more than 80% of the population engaged in subsistence agriculture.

Zaire

Date of independence: **June 30, 1960**
Area: **905,562 square miles**
Population: **29,742,000 (est. 1981)**
Capital: **Kinshasa**
Monetary unit: **Zaire**
Nationality: **Zairian**
Religion: **60% Christian, 35% Animist**
Language: **French, English, Lingala, Swahili, Kikongo, Chiluba (all official)**
Literacy: **5% (fluency in French)**
Type of government: **Republic**
Political parties/leaders: **Popular Movement of the Revolution, four exile groups**
Monetary conversion rate: **2.99 zaire = $1 (1980)**
Principal economic resources: **Coffee, palm oil, rubber, tea, cotton, copper, cobalt, zinc, industrial diamonds, manganese, tin, gold**

History at a Glance

The first known inhabitants of the Congro are believed to have been pygmy tribes who eventually came to be dominated by Bantu and Nilotic groups engaged in sedentary agriculture.

In 1482 the Portuguese explorer Diago Cao visited the mouth of the Congo River, but the world became aware of the potential wealth of the territory only after Henry Stanley made his fabled trip down the Congo River in 1877. Rumors of great riches induced King Leopold II of Belgium to commission Stanley to conduct further explorations and sign commercial treaties with local chieftains for access to the region. Within a year Leopold had formed the International Association of the Congo, a development company in which he himself was the chief stockholder. At the Berlin Conference of 1884–1885, the major European powers recognized the Independent State of the Congo, with Leopold as its absolute monarch. However, a subsequent scandal concerning the treatment accorded Congolese mine and plantation workers forced the king to transfer his territory to Belgium in 1908. Rechristened the Belgian Congo, the territory was sufficiently stable to campaign against the Germans during World War I.

African nationalism did not emerge as a potent factor in the Congo for more than a decade after World War II had ended. In 1959 rioting broke out in Leopoldville and soon spread. Belgium quickly indicated willingness to establish a gradual timetable for self-rule, but pressure from the Congolese eventually persuaded the Belgians to accept June 30, 1960 as the date for complete independence. At the time of the original agreement between both negotiating parties, it had been clearly established that Belgium would continue to provide technical and economic aid to the Congo after independence and assist in the training of Congolese administrators and politicians. The Congolese had no national political organization apart from a conglomeration of over 200 minor groups split along religious, personal, tribal and regional lines.

Independence on June 30, 1960 was followed by a collapse of national authority. Intertribal fighting broke out; secessionist movements gained momentum; the army dismissed its European officers and stood in open rebellion against the central government. Less than two weeks after independence, Moise Tshombe complicated matters further by announcing the secession of the mineral-rich Katanga province. Belgian civil servants and professionals left the country *en masse,* creating an enormous vacuum in the government. Faced with chaos, the new republic appealed to the United Nations, which responded with massive aid funneled through the hastily organized Fund for the Congo. The United Nations backed these measures with a multinational armed force whose instructions were to avoid becoming embroiled in political and military controversies.

Politically, the initial struggle shaped up between the adherents of Patrice Lumumba, the Belgian-appointed first prime minister who advocated creation of a strong centralized government, and the supporters of chief of state Joseph Kasavubu, who favored a looser type federal system which allowed for a greater degree of provincial autonomy.

At one point, Lumumba and Kasavuba took turns

dismissing each other, but parliament quickly re-scinded both dismissals, only to see itself dismissed by Kasavuba, whose military backers took Lumumba prisoner. Lumumba was then delivered into the hands of Katanga authorities who subsequently reported that he had been killed while trying to escape. A U.N. investigating commission later disclosed that Lu-mumba had probably been executed.

In July of 1961, Cyrille Adoula, a moderate, was named premier. Adoula attempted to negotiate with Tshombe for the termination of Katanga's secession, an issue which involved the direct intervention of U.N. Secretary-General Dag Hammarskjold. Hammar-skjold was killed in an air crash in September 1961 while en route to a meeting with Tshombe in Elisabeth-ville.

During the summer of 1962, the United Nations once again submitted reconciliation proposals to the disputing parties. It was not until the latter part of the year, however, that negotiators succeeded in con-vincing the reluctant Tshombe to end the secession of Katanga, and thus restore a measure of unity and stability to the country.

The followers of Lumumba, however, remained far from being pacified. Across the Congo River, in the Brazzaville Republic, they set up a self-styled "govern-ment in exile," headed by Christophe Gbenye. Guer-rilla action and other subversive tactics soon spread to the eastern part of the Congo. Through its embassy in the tiny Kingdom of Burundi, Communist China gave the rebels substantial backing, whereas the Soviet Union began to funnel arms and other provisions to the rebels through Algeria and Egypt. Incidents of butchery and pillaging grew in number and severity; missionaries were slain; innocent civilians indiscrimi-nately slaughtered.

In the summer of 1964, Tshombe returned to the Congo and was quickly sworn in as the nation's new premier. Within a short time, however, Stanleyville had fallen to the rebels, who consolidated their control over much of the eastern territory. Congo forces, aided by Belgian mercenaries and possibly also by the United States Central Intelligence Agency, succeeded in stem-ming the tide toward the end of the year, at which time Belgian paratroopers liberated Stanleyville and rescued most of the white hostages being held there. Communist-block nations, as well as several other Afri-can and non-aligned countries, were quick to denounce this joint U.S.-Belgian action.

Within the year, Tshombe had once again been ousted from office—this time by President Joseph Ka-savubu who installed Evariste Kimba (slain since then) as premier.

The Kasavubu-Tshombe rivalry had been closely watched by Colonel Joseph Mobutu, head of the army.

In December of 1965, Mobutu deposed Kasavubu, can-celed the scheduled presidential elections and installed himself as head of a "regime of exception."

The new president nationalized the Union Minière, the Belgian copper mining operation that had been a lucrative economic force since colonial days. The plane carrying exiled Tshombe was hijacked in 1967 and he was held prisoner in Algeria until his death from a heart attack on June 29, 1969.

In 1969 when trouble erupted at the University of Lobanium, Mobutu curtailed his involvement with re-gional associations concerned with the rest of Africa, choosing instead to consolidate his power at home and keep in touch with internal political developments. As a result, he dismissed his popular Foreign Minister Justin Bomboke, replacing him with former Premier Cyrille Adoula, considered a less ambitious and ener-getic politician.

In 1972 President Mobutu decided to end Zaire's membership in the French-oriented African Malagasy and Mauritius Common Organization (OCAM). The ruling People's Revolutionary Movement (MPR) of-fered Mobutu the title of President for Life, but he rejected it. However, he eliminated political opposition in order to win a seven-year term as President in 1970 and again in 1977.

Among his first actions was to invite the United States, South Africa, and Japan to invest in Zaire, in order to replace Belgian interests. He also nationalized much of the economy, barred religious instruction in the schools, and decreed the adoption of African names.

Mobutu is known for his corrupt policies. While most of Zaire's 40 million people are suffering from lack of food, Mobutu and some "300 familes" live in luxury.

Mobutu backed the National Front for the Libera-tion of Angola during the Angolan civil war of 1975–1976, and only reluctantly acknowledged the victory of the Soviet-backed Popular Movement for the Libera-tion of Angola.

On March 8, 1977, thousands of invaders calling themselves the Congolese National Liberation Front pushed into the mineral-rich Shaba region, threatening the mining center of Kilwezu. This attack was repulsed with the help of 1,500 Moroccan troops, airlifted by French military forces. Mobutu denounced the invad-ers as Soviet-inspired and Cuban-led, but other sources declared the invaders as residents of Katanga (now known as Shaba) who had fled to Angola in 1963 at Tshombe's defeat.

A second invasion, on May 15, 1978, saw the cap-ture of Kilwezi and slaughter of 100 Europeans and 300 blacks. This time France and Belgium intervened directly while 1,000 Foreign Legion paratroopers quelled the Angolan rebels and evacuated some 2,000 Europeans.

President Carter sent some military aid and backed Mobutu's renewed accusations of Soviet and Cuban influence in the invasion.

A seven-nation African security force was formed following the bloodshed to protect the Shaba region until August 1979, allowing Kolwezi to rebuilt itself.

The lengthy war between Zaire and Angola was ended when Angolan President Agostinho Neto visited Zaire in August 1979; President Mobutu reciprocated in October. The countries share a 1,250-mile border.

Mobutu ended speculation about renewed political activity in February 1980 when he declared "as long as I live, there will never be a biparty or a multiparty system in Zaire." Activities of all political parties had been banned since 1965 and the MPR remains the only functioning party. However, the Mobutu regime has been accused of harboring as many as 1,000 political prisioners and killing or torturing hundreds each year.

As many as a dozen exile groups, many located in Belgium, are also known to exist.

The Shaba region holds the world's richest diamond, copper, and zinc deposits and is the largest known cobalt reserve, supplying 90% of the world's cobalt. Also, in 1975, offshore oil was discovered.

However, despite these assets, Zaire's economy continued to hover on the brink of disaster because of corruption, mismanagement of state enterprises, an inflation rate that reached 100% in 1979 (and later fell 37% in 1980), and a massive foreign debt of $5 billion.

Zambia

Date of independence: **October 24, 1964**
Area: **290,585 square miles**
Population: **6,015,000 (est. 1981)**
Capital: **Lusaka**
Monetary unit: **Kwacha**
Nationality: **Zambian**
Religion: **82% Animist, 17% Christian, 1% Hindu, Muslim**
Language: **English (official), tribal languages**
Literacy: **28%**
Type of government: **One-party state**
Political parties/leaders: **United National Independence Party**
Monetary conversion rate: **1 Kwacha = $1.24 (1980)**
Principal economic resources: **Maize, tobacco, cotton, sugar cane, copper, zinc, lead, cobalt, coal**

History at a Glance

Archeological discoveries in the Gwembe Valley near Lusaka in 1964 uncovered such artifacts as copper wire, pottery specimens, and iron gongs dating to the nineth century. It is also believed that the people of this period, 850–1000, were skilled in the art of weaving cloth.

The first European to explore the territory was the Scotsman David Livingstone. He was followed by representatives of the British South Africa Company which gradually edged its way across the Zambezi River until, by 1924, it had extended its influence as far north as the Belgian Congo.

Since the mineral wealth of Northern Rhodesia, as it was then called, was not immediately apparent, the British did not feel it necessary to give the territory colonial status, particularly since it was under the direct jurisdiction of the Colonial Office. In 1925 however, the rich ore deposits in what is today known as the Copper Belt were discovered, and Europeans flocked northward.

The political tactics of the European settler had a twofold objective: to minimize the authority of the British Crown in the territory and, at the same time, to prevent Africans from uniting.

The political strength of Africans crystallized slowly in Northern Rhodesia. It was not until 1948 that they won the right to be represented by non-Europeans. Five years later, the British government decided to include the territory in a newly created federation, consisting of Northern and Southern Rhodesia and Nyasaland.

In 1959 an investigating commission of the Crown reported that the majority of the population in both Northern Rhodesia and Nyasaland were violently opposed to union with Southern Rhodesia on the grounds that racial discrimination was institutionalized there. The European-dominated United Federal Party (UFP) contested the findings of the commission, and took issue with the pro-African United National Independence Party (UNIP) over the question of dissolving the federation.

With the eventual withdrawal of Nyasaland, relations between the two Rhodesias became even more strained, and the federation was officially dissolved in 1963.

A year later, Northern Rhodesia became independent, as Zambia, with Kenneth Kaunda as its premier. Late in 1965, following Rhodesia's unilateral declaration of independence from Great Britain, Zambia, as a member of the British Commonwealth, requested and received the protection of British troops.

Reelected in 1968, Zambian Kaunda has diminished his country's dependence on imports obtained from Rhodesia, but purchased heavily in South Africa, where racial segregation is probably more thorough and repugnant than anywhere else in the world.

In December 1974 Zambia became a one-party country. President Kaunda attributed this to declining

Decolonization demonstration at the airport of Lusaka, awaiting members of the decolonization committee.

copper revenues, tribal warfare, guerrilla activities in outlying regions and an influx of approximately 40,000 refugees from other African lands. Zambia, he said, could no longer tolerate political opposition if it was to get on with the "humanist society" he wished to encourage.

Development in Zambia has been hindered by the fact that its economy is based on the world copper market. Copper accounts for 90% of Zambia's export earnings.

By 1975 Zambia had evolved from a British-type democracy stressing private enterprise into a one party nation in which the government controlled most important industries and the disposition of much of the country's labor force. In June 1975, Kaunda decreed that all unemployed workers in towns would have to return to their villages and aid in the production of food.

However, Zambia has remained a respected force in Africa. It has long opposed racial discrimination and provided asylum for exile groups. During 1979 Zambia endured several Rhodesian (now known as Zimbabwe) commando attacks including an attack on Lusaka on April 13, 1979. Later in the year, Zambia, Rhodesia, and Angola signed a pact to end support for each other's exiled opposition forces, as well as to cooperate with transportation. A critical railway, built with funds from China, runs through the Zambian interior to the Tanzanian port of Dar es Salaam.

Besides copper, Zambia is a major exporter of cobalt, lead, manganese, sulfur, and zinc.

Zimbabwe

Date of independence: **November 11, 1965**
Area: **150,803 square miles**
Population: **7,621,000 (est. 1981)**
Capital: **Horare (April 1982)**
Monetary unit: **Zimbabwe dollar**
Religion: **51% syncretic (Christian-Animist), 24% Christian**
Language: **English (official), Shona and Ndebele**
Literacy: **25–30% black, nearly 100% white**
Type of government: **Independent (British style democracy)**
Political parties/leaders: **Zimbabwe African National Union, Patriotic Front, Rhodesian Front, eight other parties**
Monetary conversion rate: **$1 Zimbabwe = $1.59 (1980)**
Principal economic resources: **Tobacco, corn, sugar, cotton, livestock, gold, copper, cobalt, nickel, tin**

History at a Glance

The Rhodesian plateau is believed to have been settled some 2,000 years ago by a group of farmers who had mastered the use of iron. After the eighth century A.D., descendants of this group began trading gold and ivory with the Arabs on the east coast of Africa. The great stone structures of Zimbabwe, near Fort Victoria, were probably built between the eleventh and fifteenth centuries, shortly before the Vakaranga tribe moved northward to establish a state which extended over the northern and eastern Rhodesian plateau and the Mozambique lowlands.

The Portuguese were the first Europeans in the region, arriving between 1514 and 1569. At the end of the seventeenth century, the Monomatapa tribe and their Portuguese overlords were defeated by the Changamires who then held sway until the nineteenth century, the time of the great Zulu emigration from Natal. This emigration ushered in the era of Matabele rule at much the same time that David Livingstone, the Scottish missionary and explorer, was opening up the entire region to European exploitation. Livingstone's reports in 1875–1876 were chiefly responsible for the establishment of two Scottish missions in the territory of Nyasaland.

British entry into this region precipitated a series of conflicts with the Portuguese who had laid claim to the whole of Central Africa in the hope of linking Angola on the west with Mozambique on the east. Cecil B. Rhodes, holder of the controlling interest in the diamond mines of South Africa, sent his agents into the territory to obtain mining concessions from a number of the local chieftains. In 1888 Lobengula, the powerful and legendary chief of the Matabele, signed such a treaty with the British, thus preventing Portuguese or Boer (South African) penetration. Within a year, the discovery of extensive gold deposits enabled Rhodes to acquire a charter giving him the right to form the British South Africa Company and to exploit the area.

In 1890 the company sent a group of European settlers into Mashonaland, where they founded the town of Salisbury, site of the present capital. Meanwhile, Lobengula had granted Edward A. Lippert, a German concessionaire, the sole right to dispose of land in territory he controlled. This did not stop Rhodes from buying the concession and from continuing to send in settlers until 1893, the year of the unsuccessful Matabele rebellion. In 1897 a Mashona uprising was crushed by the British, and Rhodes was able to promote the development of the territory without interference.

For the next 20 years, conflicts arose between the settlers who sought an increasing degree of self-government and the British South Africa Company, which was subject only to the supervisory control of the high commissioner in South Africa. In 1922 the settlers finally won the right to establish a government separate from that of South Africa. A year later, the territory was annexed to the Crown, a move which made British subjects of all African inhabitants.

Southern Rhodesia (as it was then called) then divided its total land mass into two basic areas: mining and industrial regions (for European settlement), and native reserves and forest lands (for Africans only). Through this system, the Europeans received some 52 million acres of the choicest land.

After World War II, European settlers in neighboring Northern Rhodesia and Nyasaland merged into a federation embracing the three territories. The Federation of Rhodesia and Nyasaland came into being in 1953, and had a stormy life for the 10 years it survived. African resentment in Nyasaland flared into violence in 1959, during which time a state of emergency was declared in Nyasaland and Northern Rhodesia, African-controlled governments came into being and succeeded in getting Great Britain to agree to independence talks.

In 1962 the UN General Assembly censured Southern Rhodesia in an official resolution calling for the passage of a new constitution there. This pressure only led to the creation of a right-wing, white-supremacist government headed by Prime Minister Ian Smith, who was to defy Great Britain late in 1965 by declaring unilateral independence and withdrawing from the British Commonwealth. Economic sanctions imposed in 1966 by Great Britain and other members of the United Nations did not succeed in breaking the determination of Rhodesia's minority to maintain its hold on the country.

Three years later, the predominantly white electorate of Rhodesia voted overwhelmingly in a referendum to abandon all pretext at professing loyalty to the Queen and to support a constitution guaranteeing white supremacy indefinitely.

Rhodesian black nationalists, based in neighboring Zambia, intensified guerrilla actions in the early 1970s. The Smith government held out effectively, but in 1974 the success of the Frelimo Movement in Mozambique changed the picture drastically. Some 80% of Rhodesia's exports had traditionally passed through Mozambique to such ports as Beira and Lourenco Marques on the Indian Ocean. Also, with the Portuguese preparing to leave Mozambique, the government of South Africa began slowly to withdraw police and military forces it had dispatched to the aid of the Smith government and seemed to pressure Smith to reach an accord with black leaders. Smith made overtures to black groups in early 1975 and discussions of a new constitution, granting blacks greater power started.

Divisions between Rhodesian blacks—Bishop Abel Muzorewa of the African National Congress and Ndabangi Sithole of the Zimbabwe African National Union as moderates versus Robert Mugabe and Joshua Nkomo of the Patriotic Front as advocates of guerrilla force—intensified in 1977. By July, white Rhodesian residents were fleeing by the hundreds and the economy began to falter.

On March 3, 1978, Smith, Muzorewa, Sithole, and Chief Jeremiah Chirau signed an agreement to transfer power to the black majority by December 31, and constituted themselves as an Executive Council with

Smith as Prime Minister. However, the Patriotic Front Leaders denounced this action and no recognition was granted.

On January 30, 1979, white voters chose to ratify the new Constitution which enfranchised all blacks, established a black majority Senate and Assembly, and changed the country's name to Zimbabwe. Muzorewa's party received more than 67% of the vote although the Patriotic Front members lobbied for a boycott.

A turnabout in power came in February 29, 1980 when Mugabe's ZANU-Patriotic Front party won 57 of the 80 Assembly seats reserved for blacks and Nkomo's ZAPU-Patriotic Front won another 20 seats—leaving only three seats for Muzorewa's council. Mugabe was sworn in as Prime Minister on April 18, 1980. Reverend Canaan Sodindo Banana, the only nominated candidate, was sworn in for a six-year term on April 18.

Mugabe, a Marxist, has worked to unite the many factions still in Zimbabwe and pledged his support for continuation of a free-market economy. Help comes from Western nations, with Britain offering a two-year $165 million aid program and the United States giving $15 million for rural rehabilitation and $2 million to rebuild rural clinics.

In January 1981 Mugabe dismissed Nkomo as Home Minister and discharged Planning Minister Edgar Tekere, after he had been tried (and acquitted) of the murder of a white farmer.

Later that year Mugabe received $1.8 billion in Western aid for the next three years.

However, whites still continue to move out of the country, threatening Zimbabwe's farm and industrial production.

Zimbabwe is well endowed with natural resources and exports tobacco, sugar, asbestos, chrome, and copper.

On April 18, 1982, Zimbabwe officials announced that the country's capital city, Salisbury, would be renamed Harare in honor of the second anniversary of the nation.

FRENCH AFRICAN DEPENDENCIES

Comoro Islands (Grand Comore, Anjouan, Moheli, Mayotte)

Area: **838 square miles**
Population: **271,000**
Capital: **Moroni**
Monetary unit: **CFA franc**
Language: **French, Malagasy**
Principal economic resources: **Coconuts, cloves, vanilla, copra, sisal, rice**

History at a Glance

It is believed that the Comoro Islands, which are located some 300 miles northwest of Malagasy, were first visited in the pre-Christian era by Phoenician traders from North Africa. They were later invaded by Arabs from the Persian Gulf region.

Much later (in 1503), the Portuguese discovered the islands again, but it was not until 1517 that an actual landing by the French took place. Malagasy invaders were also active in the area during this period. In 1843 the Malagasy ruler of Mayotte ceded that island to France, and in 1865 the local rulers of Moheli signed a treaty of friendship with this European nation. A French protectorate was eventually established over Anjouan, Grande Comore and Moheli, islands which were administered jointly with Madagascar.

In 1946 the Comoros acquired overseas territorial status and, by 1961, had achieved full internal autonomy.

A high commissioner appointed in Paris administers the islands, together with an elected territorial assembly. In turn, the Comoros are represented in Paris by two Deputies and a Senator in the French Parliament.

Reunion

Area: **969 square miles**
Population: **460,000**
Capital: **Saint Denis**
Monetary unit: **CFA franc**
Language: **French, Malay, Hindi**
Principal economic resources: **Sugar cane, geranium, vetiver**

History at a Glance

Located 450 miles east of Malagasy, Reunion was an uninhabited volcanic island at the time of its discovery in 1528 by Pedro de Mascarenhas, a Portuguese explorer. By 1649, it had fallen under the control of France and was called "Bourbon Island." Having served originally as a French penal colony, it was later settled by blacks, Malays, Indo-Chinese, Chinese, and Malabar Indians.

In 1665 the French East India Company established an outpost there. Coffee, which by 1715 had become the major agricultural staple of the island, was replaced in importance after 1800 by sugar cane.

Reunion, which received its present name in 1793, was made an overseas department of France in 1947.

A prefect appointed in Paris administers Reunion together with an elected general council. Reunion sends three Deputies and two Senators to the French Parliament in Paris.

Reunion's per capita income in 1972 exceeded

$1,000, making it, after Libya, Africa's wealthiest country.

SPANISH AFRICAN DEPENDENCIES

Spanish North Africa (consisting of Ceuta and Melilla)

Area: 12 square miles
Population: 165,000
Language: Spanish
Principal economic resources: Fish, tourism

History at a Glance

Built on the site of an ancient Phoenician colony, Ceuta is believed to have been the locale of one of the fabled Pillars of Hercules. It was taken over from the Arabs by Portugal in 1415, only to fall under Spanish control in 1580. Melilla, the site of the initial uprising which launched the Spanish Civil War in 1936, has belonged to Spain since 1496. Both Ceuta and Melilla are part of Metropolitan Spain, and the population is predominantly Spanish.

UNITED KINGDOM AFRICAN DEPENDENCIES

St. Helena (Tristan da Cunha, Ascension Island, and Gough, Nightingale, and Inaccessible Islands)

Area: 47 square miles
Population: 6,000
Capital: Jamestown
Monetary unit: British pound
Language: English
Principal economic resources: Hemp, timber, vegetables, flax

History at a Glance

St. Helena, located in the Atlantic 1,200 miles west of the African continent, was sighted by the Portuguese explorer Juan de Nova Castelle in 1502, but was first claimed by the Dutch in 1633. By 1659, it was garrisoned by the British East India Company which withstood an armed attack by the Dutch in 1673.

Perhaps St. Helena's major claim to fame is the fact that Napoleon was exiled there in 1815, the year of his disastrous defeat at Waterloo. He remained there until his death in 1821.

In 1834 St. Helena became a British Crown Colony. It is now administered by a governor, who is assisted by executive and advisory councils.

COUNTRIES OF NORTH AFRICA

Algeria

Date of independence: July 3, 1962
Area: 919,591 square miles
Population: 20,500,000 (est. 1981)
Capital: Algiers
Monetary unit: Dinar
Nationality: Algerian
Religion: 99% Muslim, 1% Christian and Hebrew
Language: Arabic (official), French, Berber dialects
Literacy: 25% (5% Arabic, 9% French, 11% both)
Type of government: Republic
Political parties/leaders: National Liberation Front, Secretary-General Chadli Bendjedid
Monetary conversion rate: 1DA = U.S. $.024
Principal economic resources: Oil, natural gas, wheat, barley, grapes, citrus fruits

History at a Glance

Algeria (ancient Numidia) did not exist as a unified territory until 1848, at which time the French finally

These Algerian shepherds follow a traditional lifestyle, but their country is modernizing rapidly.

subdued the Berber inhabitants from whom they had originally taken much of the fertile land along the coastal area. (Before this, Algeria had been ruled by Carthage, Rome, and a succession of Arab invaders, the most powerful of whom had established a Moorish empire uniting Algeria with Morocco and Spain.)

Effective control of Berber outposts in the Sahara region was not achieved by the French until the first decade of the twentieth century. During World War II, many Algerian nationalists cooperated with the Allies in the hope of gaining a greater degree of autonomy. Having failed in this, a group of discontented factions united in 1954 under the banner of two revolutionary associations: the *Front de Liberation Nationale* (FLN) and the *Mouvement Nationale Algerien* (MNA). Both groups, though at odds with each other, began to undermine French interests in the territory—first by terrorism and subversion and, ultimately, by open revolt.

Politically, this revolt was instrumental in bringing about the fall of the Fourth French Republic in 1958 and the rise to power of Charles de Gaulle, hero of the French resistance during World War II and the man to whom the army and the *colons* (European colonists in Algeria) looked to as their savior. This group, which centralized its opposition to the Algerian nationalists in the Secret Army Organization (OAS), eventually (though unsuccessfully) sought to overthrow de Gaulle when he advocated negotiations with the FLN and self-determination for Algeria. Ultimately, the following choices were open to the rebels: absolute independence (with no ties to the mother country); incorporation into France as an overseas province; or federal autonomy involving closer ties with France. Algeria chose self-determination in a 1961 referendum and, a year later, voted for the third of the above alternatives.

A cease fire was achieved in 1962, followed by the formation of a sovereign state headed by Premier Youssef Ben Khedda. He in turn was overthrown by a military coup d'etat which supported Ahmed Ben Bella, then Vice-Premier. Elected on a single-party slate in 1962, Ben Bella announced that Algeria would follow a socialist course of development, with a non-aligned foreign policy.

In 1965 Ben Bella was deposed in a bloodless, army-backed coup by Colonel Houari Boumedienne, President and Defense Minister.

Boumedienne sought to restore financial stability and maintain good economic and financial relations with France and the United States until 1967, when Algeria joined the war against Israel and entered the Arab bloc. Thereafter, Algeria received most of its developmental support from the Soviet Union.

Algeria expanded petroleum and natural gas exports, with the United States as its chief trading part-ner, until 1976. However, in 1977 and 1978, like other oil-exporting countries, Algeria slowed its general industrial expansion and turned to increasing its oil and gas output and reviving agricultural livelihoods.

Boumedienne died in December 1978 after a long illness, and Chadli Bendjedid, Secretary-General of the National Liberation Front, assumed the presidency. On July 4, 1979, Bendjedid freed former President Ben Bella, who had been imprisoned for the past 14 years.

Algeria played a key role in the release of the 52 American hostages in Iran. Algerian Minister of Executive Affairs Behzad Nabavi was a chief negotiator between the United States and Iran, and helped achieve a critical breakthrough on January 17, 1980 when he persuaded the Iranians to allow U.S. banks to retain the $3.7 billion in Iranian assets against which the banks had legal claims.

The hostages were released three days later to Algerian custody and flown to Algiers, where they were greeted for the first time in 444 days by U.S. officials.

Egypt

Date of independence: June 18, 1953
Area: 386,659 square miles
Population: 43,236,000 (est. 1981)
Capital: Cairo
Monetary unit: Egyptian pound
Religion: 94% Muslim
Language: Arabic (official)
Literacy: 44%
Type of government: Republic (under presidential rule)
Political parties/leaders: National Democratic Party, three opposition parties, several illegal groups
Monetary conversion rate: 1 pound = $1.43 (1980)
Principal economic resources: Cotton, wheat, rice, corn, manganese, oil, gold, nickel, tungsten

History at a Glance

The site of one of the world's oldest civilizations, Egypt was a name in recorded history long before its upper and lower kingdoms were united (c. 3200 B.C.). The "golden age" of Egypt was reached during the eighteenth dynasty, about 1570 B.C., at which time the New Empire superceded it. As this kingdom weakened, invasion by foreign conquerors, particularly the Assyrians, the Persians (525 B.C.), and the Macedonians under Alexander the Great (332 B.C.), became more and more devastating.

For the next three centuries, Egypt was effectively ruled by the Ptolemaic dynasty which fell to Rome in 31 B.C. when Caius Octavius, later to become the Emperor Augustus, defeated the combined forces of Cleopatra and Marc Antony at the Battle of Actium.

In A.D. 340 Egypt was made part of the Eastern

Until recently most of the agriculture in the United Arab Republic was done by ancient methods.

Roman Empire (Byzantium). Three centuries later, it fell under Arab control and became a center of the Islamic world. Arab domination was not ended until 1250 when the Mamelukes, slaves of non-Arabic stock, gained supremacy, only to be engulfed in their own turn by the Ottoman Empire, centered in Constantinople (1517). In 1798 the armies of Napoleon Bonaparte occupied Egypt, but within three years, were ousted by British and Turkish forces. In 1805 the Ottoman Turks appointed Mohammed Ali pasha, or governor, of the territory. Backed by the power of the Turks, he was able, by 1811, to eliminate the last vestiges of Mameluke influence in Egypt. The dynasty which Mohammed Ali founded eventually proved to be Egypt's last royal line.

The nineteenth century was a time of ambitious planning in Egypt. Land reform and improved methods for cotton cultivation were introduced, and construction was begun on the Suez Canal, linking the Mediterranean with the Red Sea. With the opening of the canal in 1869, Egypt became a transportation center of international significance—so much so that, in 1882, Great Britain sent in troops to quell a threatened rebellion. In the process, Britain also took over the government, solidifying her rule over all territory as far south as the Sudan.

With the outbreak of World War I, Great Britain established a protectorate over this area as well. By 1922 Egypt had won back a degree of sovereignty. Britain continued, however, to exercise control over foreign affairs, defense, communications, and the Anglo-Egyptian Sudan to the South.

Between the wars, Egyptian nationalism was centered in the Ward Party, first led by Sa'ad Zaghul Pasha and later by Dahas Pasha. In 1936 the year

Farouk I ascended the throne, an Anglo-Egyptian treaty was signed under which Britain restricted its occupation forces to specified areas, mainly along the Suez Canal route.

During World War II, Cairo became the Middle Eastern headquarters for British forces and a key military staging ground for the Allies. In 1948 fighting broke out between Egypt and Israel which had only just acquired its independence. After nine months, in which the Egyptians were severely beaten, a truce was declared, but army dissatisfaction continued to smolder. In 1952 a group called the Society of Free Officers revolted against the monarchy. Led by General Mohammed Naguib, though the guiding genius was Colonel Gamal Abdel Nasser, the coup forced Farouk to abdicate and led to the establishment of a republic on June 18, 1953. Within a year, Nasser had gained absolute control of the country, and entered into a series of agreements with the Unted States, Great Britain, and other U.N. members to help build a new dam at Aswan. Nasser also negotiated with the Soviet Union for economic aid and arms shipments, a move which finally caused the United States to withhold promised financial assistance. Nasser, however, countered this move by seizing and nationalizing the Suez Canal on July 26, 1956. This action was followed by an Israeli invasion of the Sinai Peninsula, and by British and French military intervention in the Port Sa'id area. However, a Soviet ultimatum, backed in part by the United States, led to the forced withdrawal of these troops and to the subsequent restoration of peace and order by UN forces.

In 1958 Egypt and Syria combined their states into a single entity—the United Arab Republic (UAR), a federation under one chief of state, governed by a common legislature and defended by a unified army. That same year, Yemen joined the federation which came to be known as the United Arab States (UAS). The union lasted until 1961, when the Syrian army revolted, causing the withdrawal of Syria from the federation. By the end of the year, Egypt had broken off relations with Yemen as well.

In May 1967, at the insistence of Nasser, the U.N. peacekeeping force was withdrawn. Shortly thereafter, on June 5, Israeli forces struck and by June 10 had occupied the entire Sinai Peninsula and reached the Suez Canal, when a cease fire instituted by the United Nations halted hostilities. In August 1970, Egypt and Israel agreed to a cease fire, though clashes along the Canal were to continue. In September, Nasser died and was succeeded by Anwar el Sadat.

Despite increased hopes for peace, tensions persisted as Egypt and her Arab allies, notably Syria, Iraq, Algeria, and Libya sought unsuccessfully to obtain an Israeli withdrawal to her 1967 boundaries. In October 1973 Egyptian forces attacked again, along with the Syrians on Israel's northern frontier. After initial successes by Egypt, the Israelis again prevailed, occupying the town of Suez. A disengagement agreement was reached in January 1974, under which Israel withdrew from the Suez Canal's west bank.

In February 1974 Egypt and the United States reestablished diplomatic relations, which had been broken in 1967. In July 1975, extremely intense and sensitive negotiations regarding the degree and speed of Israeli withdrawal from the Sinai had been underway for over a year, with Egypt demanding complete withdrawal from all its occupied land and Israel seeking to maintain a measure of occupation in some of Sinai's strategic areas.

U.S. Secretary of State Henry Kissinger pursued "shuttle diplomacy" between Cairo and Jerusalem to expand areas of agreement. Israel yielded on the possession of the Mitla and Giddi passes in the Sinai and the Abu Rudeis oil field in the peninsula. Both sides agreed to annual renewal of the U.N. peacekeeping force in the Sinai and allowed the United States to assume a mediating position.

Sadat received blistering accusations from Arab countries who perceived his actions with Israel as betrayal, but in 1977 Saudi Arabia and other Arabian Gulf states agreed to lend Egypt $1.5 billion. Sadat also gained U.S. aid to combat a 30% inflation rate and serious unemployment.

A 1976 referendum gave Sadat the right to run for a second six-year term and he achieved a 99.9% vote of approval.

Sadat garnered both praise and anger when he flew to Jerusalem at the invitation of Prime Minister Menachem Begin to plead for peace before Israel's Knesset on November 20, 1977. Among the members of the Arab world, only Morocco, Tunisia, Sudan, and Oman voiced support.

Egypt's own Foreign Minister Ismail Fahmy resigned in disgust. Negotiations lagged in Jerusalem after several weeks, and the Egyptian contingent returned home. The major problem had been Israel's refusal to discuss the ultimate status of the West Bank and Gaza Strip, which Sadat had proposed to be placed under Jordanian and Egyptian administration, respectively.

Progress for peace remained bogged down until 1978 when a historic 10-day "summit" at Camp David was convened by U.S. President Carter. The meeting of Begin, Sadat, and Carter resulted in two documents—A Framework for Peace in the Middle East and Framework for a Peace Treaty Between Israel and Egypt—signed by the leaders at the White House on September 17, 1978. Negotiations continued in order to work out details and a timetable for the treaty, and on March 26, 1979, the completed treaty was signed; a month later the 31-year state of war between Egypt and Israel was officially ended.

In reaction, the Arab League convened in Baghdad to approve resolutions to isolate Egypt. By midyear, all League members except Oman, Somalia, and Sudan had severed relations with the Sadat regime and Cairo was suspended from numerous Arab groups.

Egypt weathered the tactics, thanks to the nominal participation of Saudi Arabia and increased economic aid from Western countries including France, West Germany, and Japan.

Undercurrent tensions in Egypt remained, exploding in July 1981 when Sadat was assassinated in full view of thousands of Egyptians by a small force of terrorists. Anwar el-Sadat died during the ambush and the assassins were captured, put on trial, and executed within five months.

Under the leadership of Mohamed Hossny Mubarak, Egypt is expected to continue on the course pioneered by Sadat.

Libya

Date of independence: **December 24, 1951**
Area: **679,358 square miles**
Population: **3,341,000 (est. 1981)**
Capital: **Tripoli**
Monetary unit: **Dinar**
Nationality: **Libyan**
Religion: **97% Muslim**
Language: **Arabic, Italian, English**
Literacy: **35%**
Type of government: **Republic (Constitutional overhaul in 1977)**
Political parties/leaders: **Banned**

Monetary conversion rate: **1 dinar = $3.38 (1980)**
Principal economic resources: **Wheat, barley, olives, dates, oil, natural gas**

History at a Glance

Both Carthage and Rome left their imprint on Libya in the pre-Christian era—Carthage along the Tripolitania coast, then Greece in the portion known as Cyrenaica. By the third century B.C., Rome had replaced Greece as the dominant power in the region and, with the destruction of Carthage, went on to become the sole empire builder throughout most of North Africa.

In the third century A.D., with Rome already in a state of decline, Emperor Diocletian assigned Tripolitania to the western part of the Roman Empire and Cyrenaica to the eastern portion of it. By 431, however, Rome could no longer protect these outlying territories, and they were overrun by hordes of Vandal invaders. In the sixth century, Emperor Justinian's military commander, Belisarius, conquered the territory and placed it under the suzerainty of the Byzantine Empire. The first of what were to become frequent Arab invasions occurred in 643, the year which ushered in three centuries of almost continuous religious and dynastic conflicts. During this period, Tripolitania manifested a tendency to identify itself with the Western world, whereas Cyrenaica became more closely associated with Egypt to the east.

In 1510 Tripoli was seized by the Spanish who were

in turn overcome by Ottoman Turks. From 1711 to 1835, Libyan territory was controlled by the Karamanli family, which wrested virtual autonomy from the Turks whose capital was in Constantinople. Ultimately, the Turks regained their power, only to lose it again to Italy in 1911. Over the next two decades, the Italians worked their way inland with marked effectiveness.

During World War II, Libya was occupied by Italian, German, and finally British and Free French forces. When the war ended, the United Nations voted to create an independent state—a decision which was put into effect two years later with the establishment of a federated kingdom embracing Tripolitania and Cyrenaica (now known as Fezzan and Barquah).

Libya was once considered a country largely devoid of natural resources, but in the late 1950s with the discovery of oil, this desert nation became a rapidly growing world power. In 1979 Libya had the highest per capita gross national product ($8,000) of any African nation.

After the discovery of oil, Libya's foreign policy was formed: anti-Western sentiments were voiced, especially regarding foreign-dominated petroleum companies and the presence of foreign military bases on Libyan soil.

The period following the June 1967 Arab–Israeli conflict saw a succession of prime ministers. In September 1968, while King Idris I was abroad, Colonel Muammar Qaddafi seized control of the government and established a revolutionary regime under the military-controlled Revolutionary Command Council (RCC).

The new regime employed a combination of puritanical Islamic codes and radical Arab nationalism. By 1970 Western military bases were evacuated and the Italian and Jewish communities forced to leave. The regime also began to acquire shares in the nation's oil industry and by 1976, controlled about two thirds of production.

Under Qaddafi, Libya has made a strong commitment to Arab unity, total war against Israel, and shown a willingness to use oil as a political weapon. It has given support to many radical Islamic, terrorist, and dissident groups around the world, including Uganda's Idi Amin, Polisario of Western Sahara, and the Palestinian Liberation Organization. Libya broke relations with Egypt following the Camp David accords in 1978 and fortified their mutual border.

The most blatant military action, however, came in December 1980, when Libya gave military support in the Chadian civil war, helping the Goukhouni Wod-

This typical Libyan farmer still uses a camel to plough his fields.

dei government defeat insurgent forces. Equally ignominious was the 2,000-man Libyan army sent in 1979 to Uganda to assist Amin against Ugandan rebels and Tanzanian forces. Qaddafi later offered asylum to the ousted Amin and his family.

The U.S. Embassy in Tripoli has been closed since February 7, 1979, and four Libyan embassy members were expelled from Washington in May after they were accused of threatening Libyan students in America. On July 14, a scandal erupted when it was revealed that Billy Carter, brother of President Carter, had registered as a Libyan agent. A Senate investigation was launched when it was further revealed that Carter had taken $220,000 from Libyan officials.

Qaddafi has a goal of building a continent-wide Islamic Saharan state, and in January 1981, announced that Chad and Libya would be merging. This appears unlikely however since a similar merger with Syria, proposed in September 1980, has proved unsuccessful.

The Reagan Administration closed the Libyan embassy in Washington on May 6, 1981, citing Libya's connection to international terrorism as the reason. Relations between the two countries have not improved although U.S. oil companies remain active in Libya and some 2,000 U.S. citizens continue to work there.

Libya, which was renamed in 1977 as the Socialist People's Libyan Arab Hamahiriya, is governed by the General People's Congress, with a general secretariat.

Carpet weavers at the School of Popular Arts in Tetuan; Morocco.

Morocco

Date of independence: **March 2, 1956**
Area: **275,115 square miles (following a 1976 annexation of a section of Western Sahara)**
Population: **21,524,000 (est. 1981)**
Capital: **Rabat**
Monetary unit: **Dirham**
Nationality: **Moroccan**
Religion: **98.7% Muslim, 1.1% Christian, 0.2% Jewish**
Language: **Arabic (official), French, Berber dialects**
Literacy: **20%**
Type of government: **Constitutional monarchy**
Political parties/leaders: **National Assembly of Independents, nine other parties**
Monetary conversion rate: **4.33 dirhams = $1 (1980)**
Principal economic resources: **Phosphates, iron, manganese, barley, wheat, citrus fruits, fish, silver, lead, coal**

History at a Glance

Morocco shares with the rest of North Africa a long history of domination by foreign powers, but differs from its neighbors in that it was never completely overrun by either Rome or the Ottoman Empire.

In ancient times, the Berbers, the earliest known inhabitants of Morocco, were invaded by Phoenicians and Carthaginians. In the early centuries of the Christian era, they suffered the same fate at the hands of the Vandals, Byzantines, and Arabs. In 683 Morocco fell under the influence of Islam, but, for all its unifying effect, religion did not succeed, in the next four centuries, in eliminating conflict between numerous petty chieftains.

From the eleventh to the thirteenth centuries, Morocco was ruled by the Almoravid, Almohade, and Marinid dynasties and enjoyed a period of relative political stability and intellectual development. Under the Sa'adi kings, Morocco experienced its period of greatest prosperity. Its strong army protected it from Turkish invasions while its own spoils of victory enabled it to build a magnificent capital at Marrakesh.

By the middle of the sixteenth century, however, Spain and England controlled most of the country's major seaports. Were it not for the tenacity of the Filali dynasty, these nations would certainly have attempted to gain control of the interior as well. The Filali king Mawlay Isma'il (1672–1727) managed for a time to preserve Moroccan independence by driving the Spanish from Lavache and the English from Tangier.

The establishment of diplomatic relations with France in 1682 led to an expansion of Moroccan trade

Moroccan folklore produces many master musicians and dancers.

during the following two centuries and, ultimately, to French military occupation (1844). In 1860 Spain invaded and occupied northern Morocco, necessitating the signing in 1880 of an international agreement to guarantee Morocco's territorial integrity. By 1904, however, France and Spain had secretly agreed to divide up all of Morocco between themselves. Two years later, the Act of Algeciras established the principle of commercial equality for European nations trading in the region, although policing of the act's provisions was left to France and Spain. In 1912 Morocco was divided into French Morocco (a protectorate with Rabat as its capital), Spanish Morocco (a protectorate with Tetuan as its capital), Southern Morocco (administered as part of Spanish Sahara), and the international zone of Tangier.

In 1921 Berber nationalism reached fever pitch, culminating in the Rif War during which Abd el-Krim inflicted several crucial defeats on both the French and Spanish before himself being captured and exiled in 1926. Guerrilla fighting continued until 1934.

During World War II, Allied forces landed in Morocco, where they were soon joined by large detachments of Moroccan troops who fought on the side of the Free French. At the war's end, Sultan Sidi Mohammed demanded independence for his country, but was exiled instead in 1952—a gesture which triggered massive anti-French demonstrations lasting for nearly two years. With her already humiliating defeat in Indo-China, France was now forced to loosen her grip on Morocco, to allow Sidi Mohammed to return in 1955 and to grant the territory (including Tangier and the French and Spanish zones) complete independence a

year later. Muhammad V then ascended the throne as the first modern-day king of Morocco.

After his death in 1961, the King was succeeded by his son, Hassan II, who faced an uphill battle to win popular support and maintain a stable government. In the early 1970s, he survived two separate assassination attempts.

A new constitution was accepted by a popular referendum in 1972, but change in the political process has been slow.

Early in 1969 Morocco persuaded Spain to surrender the tiny enclave of Ifni on the Mediterranean, signed an accord minimizing political and military frictions with its leftist neighbor Algeria, and worked out terms with the European Common Market to achieve associate status. Morocco has further asked Spain to give up offshore oil prospecting rights to Couta and Melilla, two Spanish enclaves on Morocco's north coast.

The country's major concern in recent years has been the Moroccan takeover of Western Sahara. In 1975 tens of thousands of Moroccans crossed into Spanish Sahara to give evidence that the northern party of that territory was historically part of Morocco. At the same time, Mauritania occupied the southern half of the land in defiance of Spanish threats to resist such a takeover. In November 1975, Spain relinquished claims to Spanish Sahara and struck a deal with Morocco and Mauritania: Morocco would administer the northern two-thirds and Mauritania would take over the southern third.

However, when the two countries moved to establish their dominion in February 1976, Polisario, an independence group, declared a government-in-exile in Algeria. Within two years, Polisario undermined Mauritania's rule in western Sahara and Mauritania renounced its claims on the territory. Moroccan troops immediately invaded the southern third of the country and to date continue to fight Polisario forces.

King Hassan maintains firm day-to-day military control while his popularity has soared. The 21 million Moroccans believe so strongly in Morocco's historic claims to Western Sahara that they are firmly united behind King Hassan as never before during his reign.

Morocco is not without its economic problems, however. Forty percent of the 1981 budget went to military concerns and the country suffers from unemployment and drought. Increasing import costs triggered rioting in Casablanca in June 1980.

In 1980 under pressure from other African leaders at the Organization of African Unity summit in Nairobi, King Hassan agreed to a ceasefire with the Polisarios, and it was decided that a referendum under international supervision be used to determine the future of the territory.

A Saharan refugee camp near Zag, southern Morocco, during the dispute to oust Spanish colonial rule.

Meanwhile in March 1982, the Reagan Administration reversed previous U.S. policy and stepped up support for King Hassan's government, in order to help stabilize the country and to reestablish American military bases there.

On another front, King Hassan sent 1,500 Moroccan troops to Zaire to help President Mobuto Sese Seko defeat an invasion from Angola in 1977.

Western Sahara

Date of independence: **Spanish dominion ended February 28, 1976; Morocco and Mauritania assumed responsibility**
Area: **102,000 square miles**
Population: **101,000**
Capital: **El Aioun**
Monetary unit: **Moroccan and Mauritanian currencies**
Nationality: **Saharan**
Religion: **Muslim**
Language: **Hassaniya Arabic**
Literacy: **Saharans 5%, Moroccans 20%**
Type of government: **Undetermined (Under Moroccan administrative control)**
Political party: **Polisario**
Monetary conversion rate: **4.33 dirhams = $1 (1980)**
Principal economic resources: **Phosphates**

History at a Glance

For centuries, the territory now known as Western Sahara has been the home of desert nomads. Its coastline was first annexed by Spain in 1884, with penetration further inland by the 1930s.

Morocco, with longstanding historical rights to Western Sahara, sent thousands of soldiers to attack the territory in 1957 immediately after achieving its own independence. That invasion was quelled by Spanish and French forces and assistance from Western Sahara territorial divisions of Saguia el Hamra and Rio de Oro.

Interest in the land again heightened in 1963 with the discovery of one of the world's richest phosphate deposits in Bu Craa. During the next 12 years, Morocco pressured Spain to relinquish claims to Western Sahara, using a United Nations referendum, guerrilla activity, and a legal challenge in the International Court of Justice. Meanwhile, newly independent Mauritania lobbied from the south with claims to parts of Western Sahara.

Bowing to pressure, Spain formally announced its intention to give up claims to the land in May 1975 and in a Madrid conference in November of that year, administrative control of the territory was divided between Morocco and Mauritania—excising Western Sahara's eastern neighbor, Algeria.

As might have been expected, some inhabitants of Western Sahara felt the country should be self-governing, and in the fall of 1975 they formed the Popular Front for the Liberation of Saguia el Hamra and Rio de Oro (Polisario).

On February 28, 1976, Morocco formally assumed control of the northern two thirds of Western Sahara; Mauritania assumed control of the southern third. Meanwhile, Polisario proclaimed the establishment of an independent Saharan Arab Democratic Republic, as government-in-exile and named Mohammed Ould Ahmed as Prime Minister.

Several months later, a World Court ruling said

that Moroccan and Mauritania claims to the region were limited and had little bearing on the question of self-determination. Nevertheless, in November 1976 Morocco's King Hassan ordered 300,000 unarmed Moroccans to enter the territory in what was called "The Green March."

Polisario moved its headquarters from Mauritania to a more sympathetic Algeria, where it flourished in safety and received supplies from Libya. In July 1978, Polisario showed its strength by contributing to the overthrow of Mauritania's President Moktar Ould Dadda. A year later, Mauritania, beset by domestic troubles, renounced claims to Western Sahara at a conference held in Algeria, with Polisario officials in attendance.

Morocco seized the opportunity and sent troops into the southern third of the country, in effect annexing the entire country. Polisario in turn launched raids into Morocco itself, starting the first of many hit-and-run skirmishes.

Much of Western Sahara's nomadic population has been forced to either join Polisario refugee camps in Algeria or flee the region. The rest live in a few coastal towns, but little now remains of the nomadic lifestyle.

There are an estimated 15,000 Polisario fighters, who claim a "liberated zone" 30 miles from the Algerian town of Tindouf. Meanwhile, some 85,000 Moroccan troops stand watch behind a 400-mile long, 20-foot-high sand wall, fortified by land mines, which protects the Western Saharan capital of El Aioun and the northern regions, richest in phosphates.

The Polisario has been using Soviet-made weapons and missiles to drive out the Moroccans while King Hassan has sought military aid from the West. Since 1980 an uneasy truce has been called. However, military observers say negotiations for peace are remote and the situation is in a stalemate.

The Polisario has worked to gain recognition from other African countries, and by 1980 received a diplomatic nod from 45 nations.

BLACKS IN THE WESTERN HEMISPHERE

**North America ■ Central America ■ South America ■
The Caribbean ■ Independent Nations ■ European
Dependencies ■ North American Dependencies**

The status of blacks in Western Hemisphere nations can be divided broadly into three categories. In the English-speaking countries of the United States and Canada, blacks comprise an identifiable minority. On many islands of the Caribbean, blacks are a majority of the population, sometimes, as on Barbados and Jamaica, an overwhelming majority. And in other areas, notably on the continental mainland, from Mexico south to Argentina, blacks have largely been absorbed into the mainstream of their country's population. South Americans who are predominantly a mixture of black and Indian are known as Zambos. Those who are primarily a mixture of Caucasian and American Indian are known as mestizos, and those who are a mixture of Caucasian and black are, as in the United States, referred to as mulattoes.

In tens of millions of cases, the Latin American is a mixture of all three strains. Because intermarriage has been accepted in so much of Latin America, black consciousness and racial, political, and cultural activity as such is minimal. Our description of these countries is brief. We give somewhat more space to Mexico and Canada because of their proximity to the United States and to other nations where the black presence is apparent and significant. However, it should not be thought that blacks have played a minor role in the history of other countries. Blacks, both slave and free, were prominent in the armies of Bolivar and San Martin in the liberation of South America from Spain. Bolivar was an avid opponent of slavery and, as slavery was culminated in Latin America—in contrast to feelings in the United States of America—there was little bitterness or resistance to the incorporation of blacks into the social fabric of the countries in which they lived.

NORTH AMERICA

Canada

Blacks comprise a minuscule portion of Canada's population, less than 25,000, or 0.1% of the total. Though the income and living conditions of Canada's blacks are much lower than those of its whites, Canada's major race problem reflects its treatment of the Indians and Eskimos, who total about 200,000 and whose life expectancy is little more than half that of whites.

Blacks were prominent in the early seventeenth-century explorations and development of Canada by French explorers and Jesuit missionaries. The first slaves were Indians. The first black slave is believed to have been a native of Madagascar (Malagasy) and to have been sold to a French resident of Quebec in 1628. As French Canada expanded, slaves were purchased in the United States.

In 1749 the British brought slaves to Halifax, and slavery was legalized in British Canada in 1762. Slavery increased shortly thereafter, when the British took all of Canada in the French and Indian Wars. Many British fleeing from the revolutionary colonies to the south after 1775 brought slaves with them.

British slave codes were more severe than the French, under whom slaves could marry, own property, and maintain parental rights.

However, the British were not to sustain slavery for long. London had divided Canada into two governments, Upper Canada and Lower Canada. The governor of Upper Canada, Colonel James Simcoe, an ardent abolitionist, induced the areas's legislature to pass laws forbidding importation of slaves and freeing every slave born in the area by the age of 25. As a result, slavery in Upper Canada soon collapsed.

Similar legislation was not enacted in Lower Canada, but by 1800 the Courts, through complex legal decisions, established the principle that a slave could leave his master whenever he wished. In the Maritime Provinces, courts also acted so as to eliminate slavery in fact if not in theory. Slavery was formally abolished in Canada in 1833.

Meanwhile, starting slowly in the eighteenth century, Canada was becoming a haven for slaves fleeing across her southern borders. Slaves who had served with the British in the American War for Independence came to Halifax from New York in large numbers in 1782 and 1783. Though many were to migrate to Freetown on the West Coast of Africa, others stayed. In 1826 Canada defied the United States and formally refused to return fugitive slaves. In 1829, the legislature of Lower Canada announced that every slave that entered the Province was immediately free, a declaration that gave impetus to the underground railroad and stimulated moves for resettlement by blacks in Canada.

The passage of the Fugitive Slave Act in 1850 meant that any escaped slave who remained in the U.S.A. was to be returned to his owner. Within a year after passage of the Law, some 10,000 slaves arrived in Canada, welcomed by a majority of Canadians who provided communities and services for them. In 1858, Canada served as a refuge for John Brown to plan his attack on Harpers Ferry.

Blacks were accepted into the mainstream of Canadian life, were allowed to choose separate or integrated schools, were elected to local office and served as officers in the Canadian Army. Black laborers contributed substantially to the expansion of the Canadian Pacific Railroad, as immigrants from Eastern and Southern Europe were to contribute to the development of railroads in the United States. Black skilled laborers were much in demand. By 1861 at the outbreak of the U.S. Civil War, there were 50,000 blacks in Canada, some pioneering above the Arctic Circle.

However, after the Civil War, feelings of fear and jealousy that had been festering among white Canadians led to discrimination in employment and schools. Blacks started to re-emigrate to the U.S.A. in large numbers, feeling that, with slavery outlawed there, a bright future awaited them. By 1871, the black population of Canada dipped to about 20,000. It has remained at about that level since.

NORTH AMERICA

There are no laws in Canada barring blacks from full opportunities in housing, education and the professions. But blacks are largely excluded from better jobs and housing and without the hope of legal recourse that does exist, whatever its shortcomings, in the United States.

A number of Canada's blacks continue to live in rural areas settled by escaped slaves, but the majority live in or near major cities in the East. Earlier slaves and migrants from the U.S.A. have been joined by blacks from the West Indies.

Mexico

Blacks accompanied the Spanish as conquerors to Mexico in the sixteenth century, and later were brought in large numbers as slaves. It is estimated that there were 150,000 black slaves in Mexico in the sixteenth century. One of the earlier slaves, Estevanico, is credited with opening up the northern interior lands of what is now New Mexico and Arizona, to Spanish conquest.

The use of slavery dropped sharply in the eighteenth and early nineteenth centuries. In 1829 Mexico abolished slavery in all its states except Texas, allowing it to remain there to pacify the United States. As slavery in the United States moved westward into Texas, Mexico became a haven for escaped slaves who slipped into the heart of the country and blended with the population.

Since the sixteenth century, Mexico's blacks have intermarried with Indians and whites so that their African heritage is no longer clearly identifiable. Some 100,000 blacks, about 0.5% of the population, do live in Mexico, mostly in the port cities of Vera Cruz and Acapulco. Blacks in lesser density live in Mexico City and in border cities across the Rio Grande River from Texas.

SOUTH AMERICA

Argentina

Blacks comprise a very small portion of the population of Argentina, which is one of South America's most Europeanized countries. Black population is estimated at about 30,000. In part, this low figure represents absorption of blacks into the general population.

Bolivia

About 2% of the population of Bolivia is classified as black. Cultural factors, primarily those involving the Spanish and Indian populations, are of greater import in this country than the race question. Two thirds of the population is Indian.

Brazil

Brazil is the "melting pot" of South America. The Brazilian heritage is a compound of several diverse elements, blacks from Africa, Asians from Japan, Caucasians from Europe, mostly Portugal, and the country's aboriginal population. Official figures indicate that about 11% of Brazil's population of 105 million is black, another 26% is of mixed origins, 62% is European. However, the numbers of Brazilians with some African descent may be considerably greater, since children of mixed black and European parentage were commonplace during the days of slavery.

Slavery was introduced into Brazil in the 1530s, expanded greatly after 1540, when sugar became important, and grew most rapidly between 1580 and 1640, when Spain controlled the country. Estimates of the total number of slaves brought to Brazil varies from 6 to 20 million. Slavery did not finally end in Brazil until 1888.

Blacks in Brazil occasionally succeeded in establishing their own states within the country, the most famous being Palmares, which survived from 1630 to 1697, and at its peak had a population of 20,000. Palmares was a Kingdom with a capital, a well-developed economy and a remarkably efficient and courageous army. In the 19th century, Moslem blacks frequently came near to controlling the post city of Bahia.

Though slavery in Brazil was often extremely brutal, and the death rate of blacks on sugar, coffee and cotton plantations was enormous, large numbers of Africans achieved freedom. About 25% of Brazil's blacks were free during slavery.

During the nineteenth century, free blacks intermarried so rapidly their numbers fell from about 400,000

SOUTH AMERICA

in 1800 to 20,000 by 1888 when slavery was finally abolished. Free blacks enjoyed full legal equality both during the period of slavery and after it was abolished.

In Brazil slaves who served masters in cities were often allowed to seek part-time and temporary employment elsewhere. They were able to read and write and develop employable skills. Blacks became important to the development and economy of the country and some became prominent in public life. Nilo Pecanha served as vice president and briefly as president of Brazil in the first decade of this century. Blacks also achieved fame in Brazil's intellectual and artistic life.

Brazil is the only large South American country that has a sizable number of churches, periodicals and cultural groups oriented to blacks.

Chile

Blacks have been less important to the development of Chile than to other South American nations, though blacks soldiers did fight in San Martin's Army in the nineteenth century when he liberated Chile from Spain. About two thirds of Chile's population is of mixed European and Spanish ancestry, about one third is European. The black population is less than 5,000.

Colombia

Colombia's population typifies the Spanish, African and Indian mixture found in South America with perhaps a larger proportion of African stock than is evidenced in most other countries on the South American mainland—a factor that is largely due to the country's location on the Caribbean Sea. Some 600,000 of Colombia's 15 million people are regarded as black. The territory that now comprises Colombia was one of the first locations in South America to which black slaves were brought in the sixteenth century. Blacks reside mostly along the coastal areas and in Colombia's tropical valleys. Blacks are noted in Colombia for their conspicuous contribution to its armed forces.

Ecuador

About 500,000 of Ecuador's 5 million people are classified as black. Some 2 million are Indian. Blacks and

A banana plantation in Colombia.

people of black, European and Indian mixture mostly reside along the Atlantic coast.

Paraguay

Paraguay's 3 million inhabitants are largely a mixture of European and Guarani Indian. Blacks make up about 0.5% of 15,000 of the population.

Peru

Black slave-soldiers accompanied Pizarro in his sixteenth-century conquest of Peru and saved subsequent conquistadores from defeat by the Indians. In the eighteenth century, blacks made up over one fifth of the population of Lima. Peru was the last nation in Spanish South America to abolish slavery, not doing so until 1855. Today some 550,000 of Peru's 16 million inhabitants are regarded as black.

Uruguay

Uruguay is widely regarded as South America's most Europeanized country. About 15,000 of its 3 million inhabitants are black and Uruguay's proportion of mulattoes and mestizos is perhaps the lowest in South America.

Venezuela

About 900,000 of Venezuela's 12 million people are black and another 500,000 are Zambos. In the sixteenth and seventeenth centuries, Caracas was a major center for the import of slaves. In the early nineteenth century, blacks and mulattoes comprised more than half of the population of The Captaincy General of Caracas, as Venezuela was known then. Blacks remain a significant part of the country because of its proximity to the Caribbean and employment opportunities that have been available in this oil-rich nation.

CENTRAL AMERICA

Belize—formerly British Honduras

About 60% of the inhabitants of Belize are of mixed black-white parentage. Most blacks are of West Indian origin.

Costa Rica

Only 2% of the population of Costa Rica is black. Most blacks are of Jamaican origin and, together with a small number of mulattoes, are settled in the Limon Province.

El Salvador

Less than 5,000 of El Salvador's 4 million inhabitants are classified as black.

Guatemala

The relatively few blacks and mulattoes in Guatemala inhabit the Caribbean and Pacific lowland areas.

Honduras

Some 2% of the Honduras population is black. The dominant strain is a mixture of Spanish and Indian blood.

Nicaragua

Blacks comprise some 9% of the population in sparsely inhabited Nicaragua. They are settled mainly along the Miskito Coast.

Panama

Roughly 65% of the inhabitants of Panama are classified as mestizo or mulatto—i.e., mixed white and Indian, or mixed white and black. In part this reflects large numbers of blacks brought to Panama to build the Panama Canal. (See United States Dependencies: Panama Canal Zone.)

THE CARIBBEAN

The end of slavery in the Caribbean in the 1830s did little to help the area's blacks. Still dependent for a living on the plantation-type economy dominant in the area, blacks tended in large numbers to enter into debt-ridden, subordinate relations with landowners, much like the tenant farming system many American blacks were forced into after the Civil War. Some blacks, however, taking advantage of the short labor supply in West Indian towns and cities, moved to urban areas where they acquired skills and higher living standards. On many islands, they filled lower civil service posts and became sources of manpower to the police and military. In some cases, a few blacks eventually worked their way into their island's upper social strata, themselves becoming landowners and public officials. But the vast majority remained impoverished. This was also true in Haiti, despite the fact that blacks owned the land and ran the government. Most holdings there were, and are, very small. Since its freedom, Haiti has largely been ruled by a mulatto elite.

In the 1860s, denial of suffrage to all but a few

CARIBBEAN ISLANDS

blacks and, on some islands, large scale importation of cheap contract labor from India, led to unsuccessful rebellions by blacks. One rebellion in Jamaica was ruthlessly suppressed at a cost of thousands of lives and burning of black neighborhoods.

Economic conditions, education and political rights slowly improved until the end of World War II, when Britain, facing the need of dissolving most of its Empire, and prodded by black West Indians, started to grant independence to most of its Caribbean territory. A Federation of the West Indies, containing Jamaica, Trinidad and Tobago and Barbados, was formed in 1958, but could not function well over the great distances between the islands, and was dissolved in 1962.

Despite freedom, most Caribbean nations continue to suffer from an inequitable distribution of wealth, a matter which in turn induces large scale emigration of educated blacks. Many of these contributed substantially to the development of the United States. John Russwurm, Marcus Garvey, and Claude McKay were immigrants from the British West Indies.

Poor living standards have also created large amounts of emigration to Britain and the United States. In the eastern part of the United States, Jamaicans are frequently imported to perform short term agricultural jobs, such as apple picking in Vermont. In 1975 unemployment in Jamaica was about 20% of its workforce. In Puerto Rico, despite massive infusion of American investment, unemployment was at 17%.

The following territories are discussed in this section.

Bahama Islands
Barbados
Cuba
Dominican Republic
Guyana (in South America)
Haiti
Jamaica
Trinidad and Tobago
French American Dependencies
    French Guiana (in South America)
    Guadeloupe
    Martinique
Netherlands American Dependencies
    Netherlands Antilles
    Surinam (in South America)
United Kingdom American Dependencies
    Bermuda
    British Virgin Islands
    Cayman Islands
    Leeward Islands
    Turks and Caicos Islands
    Windward Islands
United States Dependencies
    Corn Islands
    Panama Canal Zone
    Puerto Rico
    Swan Islands
    Virgin Islands of the U.S.

Barbados

Date of independence: November 30, 1966
Area: 166 square miles
Population: 256,000 (January 1981)
Capital: Bridgetown
Monetary unit: Barbados dollar
Ethnic divisions: 80% African, 17% mixed, 4% European

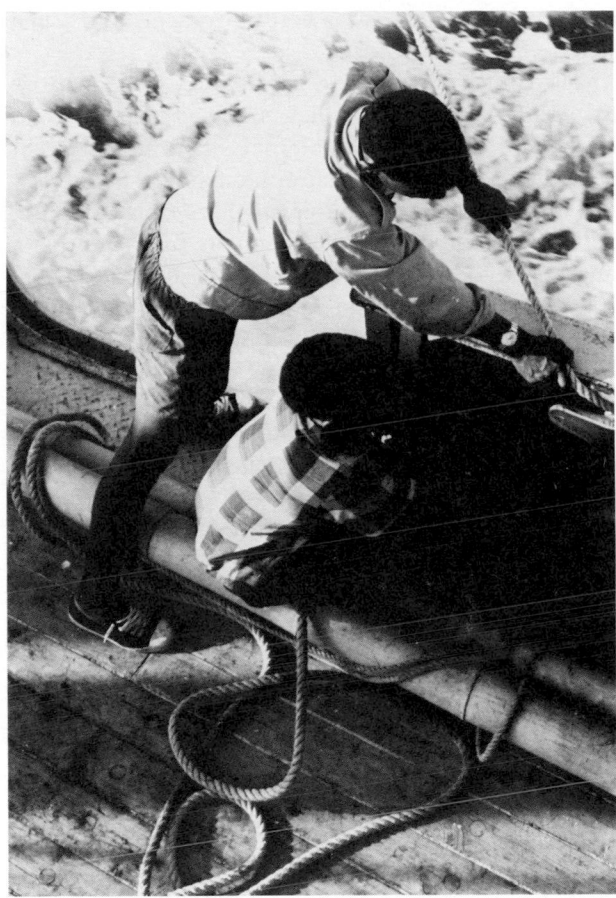

Fishing trainees aboard the Alcyon, *a ship of the Caribbean Fishery Development Project.*

Religion: 70% Anglican, Roman Catholic, Methodist, Moravian
Language: English
Literacy: Over 90%
Type of government: Independent sovereign state within the Commonwealth since November 1966 recognizing Elizabeth II as Chief of State
Political parties leaders: Barbados Labor Party (BLP), J. M. G. "Tom" Adams; Democratic Labor Party (DLP), Errol Barrow
Monetary conversion rate: 2 Barbados dollars = U.S. $1 (December 1980)
Principal economic resources: Tourism, sugar milling, light manufacturing

History at a Glance

The most easterly of the Caribbean Islands, Barbados was originally the home of the Arawak Indians, although it was probably uninhabited when the first British settlers arrived in 1627. Barbados is an island in the Atlantic located some 300 miles north of Venezuela. It is only 21 miles long and at its widest point is 14 miles across. Land patents were granted to members of the English nobility but returned to the Crown

in 1652. Slavery was legally abolished in 1834, the last of the slaves liberated four years later.

The constitution of Barbados, among the oldest in the Commonwealth, is based largely on convention. Universal adult suffrage was introduced in 1951, elected ministers in 1954, a cabinet system in 1958, and full internal autonomy in 1961. The bicameral legislature was headed by a Crown-appointed governor, who in turn appointed a premier empowered to name a five-member cabinet.

Despite the coming of independence in November 1966, the "bajans" retained strong political and cultural ties with England. Though an independent parliamentary democracy, they have remained within the British Commonwealth and preserved their allegiance to Queen Elizabeth II who in 1974 was represented in the country by Sir Winston Scott. J. M. G. Adams became Prime Minister in 1976. Barbados has been called the "Little England" of the Caribbean. The country played a leading role in the West Indies Federation (1958–1962) and supplied the organization's only prime minister, Sir Grantley Adams. J. M. G. ("Tom") Adams is Sir Grantley's son.

Cuba

Date of independence: May 20, 1902
Area: 44,218 square miles
Population: 9,796,000 (January 1981)
Capital: Havana
Monetary unit: Peso (noncommercial rate December 1980)
Ethnic divisions: 51% Mulatto, 37% white, 11% Negro, 1% Chinese
Religion: At least 85% nominally Roman Catholic before Castro assumed power
Language: Spanish
Literacy: About 96%
Type of government: Communist state
Political parties/leaders: Cuban Communist Party (PCC), First Secretary Fidel Castro Ruz, Second Secretary Raul Castro Ruz
Monetary conversion rate: 1 Peso = U.S. $1.38 (nominal)
Principal economic resources: Sugar milling, petroleum refining, food and tobacco processing, textiles, chemicals, paper and wood products, metals

History at a Glance

Cuba was discovered by Christopher Columbus during his first voyage to America. In 1511 the Spanish appointed a governor, Diego Velasquez, who established Santiago as the capital and founded Havana just south of where it lies today. By 1523, the African slave had become a familiar sight on the island. Yet, during this period, Cuba was of even greater importance as an embarkation point for Spanish explorers bound for the Central and South American mainlands. The treasures of Mexico obtained by the conquistadores invariably passed through Havana on their way back to Europe, with the result that the northern coast of Cuba was often despoiled by French and English pirates preying on Spanish shipping. In 1762 the English occupied Havana and held Cuba for nearly a year before returning it to Spain in exchange for Florida. The English occupation encouraged a greater spirit of national unity and stimulated free trade.

Most of Spanish America managed to win independence in the early decades of the nineteenth century, but not Cuba. In 1868, Carlos Manuel de Cespedes, a wealthy planter, granted his slaves their freedom and agitated for revolution against Spain. For the next decade or so, guerrillas were holed up in the hills of eastern Cuba, but their efforts against the combined strength of the colonial government and the Spanish army proved fruitless. In 1892, while in exile in the United States, Jose Marti founded the Cuban Revolutionary Party and three years later, issued the famous *grito de Baire* (call to arms). The insurrection lasted for three years, though Marti was killed in the initial engagement against Spanish forces.

The cause of the revolutionaries aroused considerable sympathy in the United States, both in private and official circles. Consequently, it hardly came as a surprise when the United States declared war on Spain after the U.S. battleship *Maine* was blown up in Havana harbor on February 15, 1898. Spanish resistance on both land and sea was easily overcome and Cuba was declared independent.

The United States, however, did force Cuba to ratify the Platt Amendment which specified that it could intervene in the island's internal affairs in the event it became necessary to insure the maintenance of law and order. In addition to this, much of Cuba's wealth, natural and otherwise, was soon in the hands of a number of American absentee owners. Revolts against Yankee imperialism brought about the periodic intervention of U.S. Marines—in 1906, 1912, and again in 1920. Finally, in 1934, during the first administration of Franklin D. Roosevelt, the Platt Amendment was abrogated. (The United States, however, retained possession of a naval base at Guantanamo Bay.)

During World War I, Cuba enjoyed a brief period of prosperity due to the growth of its gold reserves, but sugar prices soon declined, giving rise to widespread unemployment and national hardship. In 1925 Gerardo Machado began an eight-year reign as dictator. His successor was overthrown in 1934 by an army sergeant, Fulgencio Batista y Zaldivar. More clever than his predecessor, Batista held power by installing puppet presidents whom he then deposed at will. In 1940 he had himself elected president and allowed a new constitution to be passed. After his four-year term was over, he continued, nonetheless, to be a potent force in Cuban politics—a fact borne out by his seizure of power in 1952.

Road construction in Barbados.

On July 26, 1953, a group of young firebrands staged an abortive raid on the army barracks at Fort Moncada. Led by Fidel Castro, the uprising was quickly suppressed and Castro himself thrown into prison. He was released under a 1954 presidential amnesty, only to begin the immediate organization of what he came to term the sequel to the "26th of July" movement. Two years later, he and a small group of revolutionary forces (including his trusted aide Ernesto "Che" Guevara of Argentina) landed in Oriente province, where they holed up in the Sierra Maestra Mountains. The rebellion spread across the island and, within three years, Batista has been forced into exile. The "26th of July" movement swept Castro into power as premier in 1959.

Members of the revolutionary cabinet then undertook to rule the country by decree, ostensibly until those reforms to which the movement had been dedicated could be put into effect. Castro himself disavowed ties with Communism.

By 1960, however, the government plunged ahead with a comprehensive scheme of land expropriation, one which affected U.S. property holdings with disturbing frequency. Anti-Communist cabinet members were soon purged and Cuba became a base for other Latin American revolutionary movements.

In 1961 the United States, at this time still Cuba's chief hemispheric customer, decided to sever diplomatic relations with the Castro regime. The Cuban government countered this move by nationalizing U.S. oil refineries for having refused to process Soviet crude oil, whereupon the United States decided in its turn to eliminate Cuba's sugar quota. Trade and general relations with Soviet-bloc nations and Communist China offset some of the deficit incurred by the loss of U.S. markets. Late in 1960, Castro labeled Cuba a socialist country and, within a year, declared himself to be a follower of Marxist-Leninist doctrine.

In 1961 a group of Cuban exiles—financed, trained, and organized by the Central Intelligence Agency—undertook an amphibious invasion of the island at the Bay of Pigs. Within three days, however, Cuban military forces defeated the invaders, taking some 1,200 men prisoner. (The captives were later used by Castro as human barter for U.S. supplies.)

By 1962 all major means of production and distribution, as well as communication and other public services, were in the hands of the state.

That same year, evidence gathered from U.S. aerial reconnaissance photographs of Cuba established that the Soviet Union had begun to install ballistic missiles capable of reaching American soil. Moving decisively, President Kennedy quickly initiated a blockade of the island and issued an ultimatum calling for the immediate withdrawal of all such offensive weapons. This action brought the world to the brink of war, averted only after the Soviets backed down in the face of Kennedy's demand.

Castro remained in control, however, and continued to spread revolutionary propaganda throughout the rest of Latin America. In 1965 he instituted a program whereby all Cubans wishing to go to the United States (excepting those males eligible for military service) would be permitted to do so.

Castro has since reported that 1970 was a turning point in Cuban affairs. Viewing a decade of revolution, he assured the people that agricultural programs would continue to put plenty of food on their tables and on the shelves of their stores. He also maintained that Cuban industry was making remarkable strides and would bring the country out of its underdeveloped status before 1975.

In 1973 Cuba and the U.S. signed an agreement providing for extradition of hijackers of planes or vessels brought by Americans to Cuba or by Cubans to the U.S.

In 1975 there were hints that the United States and Cuba might soon resume diplomatic and trade relations. Cuba's efforts to direct other Latin American nations toward a Communist path had largely failed and her foreign policy appeared more moderate. Many Latin American nations that had broken relations with Cuba indicated a wish to restore them and Senators Pell and Javits of the United States had made a visit to Cuba and then introduced a resolution in the Senate asking President Ford to try to improve relations with Cuba. Secretary of State Kissinger also hinted at interest in friendlier relations.

However, prospects for normalization were clouded by reports that in the early 1960s, the United States Central Intelligence Agency had sought to have Fidel Castro assassinated and that perhaps the Cuban government had been involved in the 1963 assassination of President Kennedy.

In 1980 both foreign and domestic issues were dominated by the massive emigration of Cuban citizens mainly orchestrated by the Castro regime. Touching off the exodus was the influx of 10,000 Cubans into the Peruvian embassy at Havana after the government had withdrawn its police guard following a dispute over the right of political asylum.

Dominican Republic

Date of independence: February 27, 1809
Area: 18,816 sq. miles
Population: 5,762,000
Capital: Santo Domingo
Monetary unit: Peso
Ethnic divisions: 73% Mulatto, 16% white, 11% black

Religion: 95% Roman Catholic
Language: Spanish
Literacy: 68%
Type of government: Republic
Political parties/leaders: Reformist Party, Dominican Revolutionary Party, Dominican Liberation Party, others
Monetary conversion rate: 1 peso = U.S. $1.00
Principal economic resources: Tourism, sugar, sugar processing, nickel mining, bauxite mining, gold mining, textiles, cement

History at a Glance

The eastern portion of the island of Hispaniola, the portion which forms today's Dominican Republic, was originally known as Quisqueya—"mother of all lands." It was first settled by the warlike Carib Indians, who were succeeded by the peace-loving and agriculturally inclined Arawaks.

In 1492 Christopher Columbus became the first European to land on the island, claiming it for Spain. Within the next two decades, Hispaniola became a base from which Spain initiated her conquest of the New World. By 1517 cattle and horses were being raised on the island and sugar cane had become the staple of its agricultural economy. At that time, the population was estimated to be about 60,000, a substantial portion of which were black slaves. The discovery of Mexico and Peru, the ravages of a smallpox epidemic, and the excesses of Dutch, English, and French buccaneers, led to a sharp population decline and Hispaniola soon outlived its usefulness as a staging ground for the Spanish conquests.

In 1697 Spain was forced by the Treaty of Ryswick to acknowledge French dominion over the western third of the island (Haiti). A century later it also lost control of the eastern two-thirds of Hispaniola (Santo Domingo) in the aftermath of a slave uprising. Toussaint L'Ouverture, the liberator of Haiti, conquered Santo Domingo in 1801, but the Dominicans, fearing the Haitian's rule, backed a French force which soon succeeded in overcoming them. Haiti achieved independence in 1804, but Saint Domingue (as it was rechristened by the French) remained under French control until 1809 when Juan Sanchez Ramirez defeated the French at Palo Hincado and proclaimed the founding of the first Dominican Republic.

Spain regained control of this territory under the Treaty of Paris (1814), but in 1821 another republic was founded, this time by Jose Munez de Caceres. Within a year, however, Santo Domingo was once again overrun by Haiti, which occupied the territory for some 22 years, a period marked by the departure of most land-owning whites, fierce racial and cultural animosities, and an atmosphere heavy with oppression and violence. In 1884 a secret group known as La Trinitaria organized a successful revolt which once more restored the independent republic of Santo Domingo.

During the next 20 years Dominican history ran an unpredictable course, punctuated by petty internecine rivalries, further threatened invasions by Haiti, and several changes of government. In 1861 President General Santana invited Spain to annex the country and, during the next four years, it was administered as a Spanish colony. Spanish troops withdrew in 1865, ushering in still another period of almost continuous revolution and widespread governmental corruption.

In 1870 Santo Domingo was on the verge of being annexed by the United States, but the U.S. Senate refused to ratify the necessary treaty. By 1905 the country teetered on the brink of bankruptcy and political chaos and the United States assumed control of Dominican customs. In 1915, following a presidential assassination and the overthrow of several chief executives, the United States set up an economic council to stabilize the island's economy. A year later, a military government under Captain H. S. Knapp was established. This government remained in power until 1924 when Dominican sovereignty was restored and U.S. forces withdrew. (The customs control mission remained until 1941.)

In 1930 Rafael Leonidas Trujillo Molina was elected president and ushered in a 30-year period of rule during which Santo Domingo became his personal property. Aided by his family, Trujillo became an absolute dictator who quashed all attempts at resistance by murder, imprisonment, and other grisly forms of intimidation. Reelected in 1934, 1940, and 1947, Trujillo did manage to improve economic conditions in his country, achieve administrative stability, balance the budget and free the nation from domestic and foreign debt. In the process, however, he accumulated an enormous private fortune, estimated at from 900 million to 1.5 billion dollars.

In 1961 Trujillo was assassinated and a wave of terror swept the island as his son, Air Force General Rafael Trujillo Martinez, seized power. Special investigators from the Organization of American States (OAS) reported that the new repressions were even more ruthless than the old.

Over the next four years, the influence of the Trujillo family was eradicated. The country was ruled by two presidents, two councils of state, and two juntas. Coup and counter-coup verged on the order of the day. The situation was further complicated by near-war with Haiti and by guerrilla activity sponsored by pro-Castro Dominicans.

In 1965 the ruling civilian junta was overthrown in a military uprising which triggered a civil war involving rebel forces laced with Castroite supporters and hard-core Communists. Almost at once the United

States intervened militarily, ostensibly on the grounds that it was protecting American nationals. In May of that year an inter-American contingent was created by the Organization of American States and dispatched to the scene to serve as an occupational force. The major factions agreed on the installation of Hector Garcia-Godoy as provisional president in the summer of 1965. A year later Joaquin Balaguer was elected president, whereupon U.S. combat troops were withdrawn.

Balaguer, who was reelected in 1970, kept the nominal allegiance of the military, but at a high price. The national budget allocated more than 17% of its expenditures to military upkeep. The expansion of the U.S. sugar quota helped the country, but political unrest, labor problems, and dwindling tourism offset much of the gain from this source. About two thirds of the Republic's population is mulatto and mestizo, about 12% is black.

Silvestre Antonio Guzman Fernandez of the Dominican Revolutionary Party succeeded Dr. Joaquin Balaguer following an election on May 16, 1978. Fernandez has been applauded for many sweeping reforms while in office. He has also met resistance especially from his own Dominican Revolutionary Party (PRD), concerning maneuvering for the 1982 election. Although he stated that he would not seek another term, Fernandez has made no effort to implement a 1978 PRD campaign pledge to seek a constitutional amendment that would bar reelection. In 1979 Fernandez ousted his principal rival, Salvador Jorge Blanco, as president of the party.

Guyana (formerly British Guiana)

Date of independence: May 26, 1966
Area: 83,000 square miles
Population: 850,000 (January 1981)
Capital: Georgetown
Monetary unit: Guyana dollar
Ethnic divisions: 51% East Indians, 43% Negro and Negro mixed, 4% Amerindian, 2% white/Chinese
Religion: 57% Christian, 33% Hindu, 9% Muslim, 1% other
Language: English
Literacy: 86%
Type of government: Republic within Commonwealth
Political parties/leaders: People's National Congress (PNC), L. F. S. Burnham, People's Progressive Party (PPP), Cheddi Jagan, Working People's Alliance (WPA), Rupert Roopnarine, Walter Omawale, Eusi Kwayana, United Force (UF) Feilden Singh
Monetary conversion rate: Floating with U.S. dollar, 1 U.S. $ = G $2.55 (1980)
Principal economic resources: Bauxite mining, alumina production, sugar and rice milling, timber

History at a Glance

Spanish sailors first charted the coastline of what is now Guyana in 1499, but the territory was not settled until 1620, by the Dutch West Indies Company. By 1746 the Dutch had founded settlements in Essequibo, Demerara, and Berbice. But they lost control of these areas to the English—first in 1796, then in 1803, and, finally, in 1814. The colony of British Guiana was formed in 1831.

With the abolition of slavery in 1837, most blacks settled down on the land they had worked or migrated to the towns. The aristocratic planter class exerted pressure on the government for the importation of indentured servants from India to work on the plantations. Today most of the sugar workers are East Indians, whereas the urban population is predominantly of African origin—a factor of great importance in current political trends in the country.

In 1928 British Guiana was granted a limited representative government along with a new constitution. In 1953 another constitution was put into effect, calling for the establishment of a bicameral legislature and an increase in the elected majority of the lower house. Because of charges of Communist subversion, however, England suspended the elections, instituting instead an interim government which ruled until 1957 when new elections were held. Victory went to the People's Progressive Party (PPP), headed by Dr. Cheddi Jagan, who was named minister of trade and industry.

In 1961 British Guiana was granted full autonomy. That same year, elections held under still another constitution resulted again in a majority victory for the PPP which controlled the Legislative Assembly. A year later, Dr. Jagan, by then the premier, submitted an austerity program calling for compulsory savings and for a property tax. Announcement of this program triggered a violent general strike, which could not be put down until British troops arrived on the scene.

In 1963 there was further unrest with the passage of a labor relations bill which appeared to make it possible for Dr. Jagan to favor the interests of certain unions. Racial friction heightened between the East Indian followers of Dr. Jagan and the black-dominated urban population, many of whom occupied civil service posts. Strikes and even more violent upheavals seriously affected Guiana's economy and large losses were suffered by the sugar and bauxite industries.

Late in 1964 the People's National Congress (PNC), headed by Forbes Burnham, wrested control from the PPP by winning the national elections. The PNC, however, was only able to form a government with the aid of the United Force Party, a right-wing, business-oriented group, encouraging close ties with the West. British Guiana became independent under its new name of Guyana on May 26, 1966, with Burnham

Ceramics has become an important small industry in Haiti.

remaining in power as the duly elected prime minister. Guyana was declared a republic in 1970.

Guyana then became involved in a feud with its western neighbor, Venezuela, which laid claim to more than half the entire territory of the new republic. The dispute was officially resolved for a period of 12 years, by an agreement in 1970. In 1974 Forbes Burnham was still Prime Minister.

Today Ptolemy A. Reid is Prime Minister, and former Prime Minister Forbes Burnham is president. Guyana gained widespread attention in 1978 when 911 persons died in a mass murder–suicide at a remote settlement in Guyana founded by a sect from the United States known as the People's Temple led by Reverend Jim Jones. Jones, on November 19, 1978 had ordered his followers to die (the victims were either shot or forced to drink poisoned Kool-Aid) after his aides had killed U.S. Representative Leo J. Ryan of California. Three journalists who were with Ryan were also killed.

Haiti

Date of independence: January 1, 1804
Area: 10,714 square miles
Population: 5,945,000 (1981)
Capital: Port-au-Prince
Monetary unit: Gourde

Ethnic divisions: Over 90% Negro, nearly 10% Mulatto, few whites
Religion: 10% Protestant, 75% to 80% Roman Catholic (of which an overwhelming majority also practice voodoo)
Language: French (official) spoken by only 10% of the population; all speak Creole
Literacy: 10 to 12%
Type of government: Republic
Political parties/leaders: National Unity Party, Haitian Christian Democratic Party, Haitian Christian Democratic Party of June 27, Haitian National Christian Party, United Haitian Communist Party (PUCH), illegal (communist)
Monetary conversion rate: 5 Gourdes = U.S. $1 (December 1980)
Principal economic resources: Sugar refining, textiles, flour milling, cement manufacturing, bauxite mining, tourism, light assembly industries

History at a Glance

Christopher Columbus discovered the island of Hispaniola (the western half of which is today called Haiti) in 1492 and established a settlement on the north coast near the present city of Cap Haitien. The Spanish colonists lost little time in wiping out the island's Indian inhabitants, a policy which eventually made it necessary for the Spanish crown to import slaves from Africa for plantation labor.

By 1625 French privateers, operating from the island of Tortuga, were successful in expelling the Spanish along the northern coast and paving the way for French colonies to spring up. With sugar as the basis of the plantation economy, the French brought more and more slaves from West Africa. In 1697 under the Treaty of Ryswick, Spain ceded the western portion of Hispaniola to France. Under French rule, St. Domingue (as this area was then called) became one of the most prosperous territories in the Caribbean.

By the eighteenth century, four distinct social groupings had emerged on the island: the white French planter; the Creole; the freed black and the black slave. The Creoles—sandwiched, as it were, between the white and black—found themselves striving desperately for the privileges accorded the white minority while living in fear of being overrun by the blacks.

It was not until the French Revolution in 1789 that the explosive potential inherent in such a social situation began to reveal itself. Haiti's half a million black slaves became increasingly imbued with a desire for freedom. In 1791 an uprising was suppressed by the French, but the movement never lost its momentum due largely to the fervor and genius of a self-educated

A tinsmith at work in his shop.

slave and former soldier, Toussaint L'Ouverture. Within two years, Toussaint had conquered the entire island, promulgated a new constitution, and abolished slavery. In 1802, however, a huge force sent by Napoleon recaptured the island. Toussaint himself was betrayed and, after being taken prisoner, was shipped to France where he died.

However, his successor, Jean Jacques Dessalines, another black general who had risen in the ranks, continued this struggle and overcame the French forces in 1803. A year later, Dessalines proclaimed the independence of St. Domingue and restored to it the original Indian name of Haiti ("land of mountains"), in the process taking for himself the title of emperor.

When Dessalines was assassinated in 1806, the nation soon became divided into a northern kingdom ruled by Henri Christophe and a southern republic administered by Alexandre Sabes Petion, a mulatto. France lost control of Santo Domingo, the eastern portion of the island, in 1808.

The next decade was marked by widespread agricultural reform and by internal political manipulation which accomplished little for the principals involved in it.

Claude Duvalier married Michelle Bennett on May 17, 1980 in a ceremony attended by 4,000 guests, estimated to have cost from $3 million to $5 million. During 1980 a steady exodus of refugees migrated toward the United States, reaching a high of 15,000. They have been denied refugee status, but the Haitian "boat people" finally have been accorded the same temporary entrance rights as Cubans who arrived by boat earlier.

Jamaica

Date of independence: August 6, 1962
Area: 4,411 square miles
Population: 2,255,000
Capital: Kingston
Monetary unit: Jamaican dollar
Ethnic divisions: African 75.3%, Afro-European 15.1%, Chinese and Afro-Chinese 1.2%, East Indian and Afro-East Indian, 3.4%, White 3.2%, others 0.9%
Religion: Predominantly protestant, some Roman Catholic and spiritualist cults
Language: English
Literacy: Although government claims 82%, only about half are functionally illiterate
Type of government: Independent state within the Commonwealth
Political parties/leaders: Jamaica Labor Party (JLP), People's National Party (PNP), Michael Manley
Monetary conversion rate: 1 Jamaican dollar = U.S. 0.5613 (December 1980)
Principal economic resources: Bauxite mining, textiles, food processing, light manufacturing, tourism, bananas, rum

History at a Glance

Jamaica was discovered by Christopher Columbus on May 2, 1494, on his second voyage to the New World. Some 15 years later, it was settled by the Spanish who systematically exterminated its original inhabitants, the Arawak Indians, replacing them with slaves brought from Africa to work the plantations. The name Jamaica was derived from an Arawak Indian word, Xaymaca. Jamaica is the third largest island in the Caribbean and the largest and most populous of the independent Commonwealth nations in the area.

The English conquered the island in 1655, at which time a group of slaves (the Maroons) fled into the interior, where they established a number of strongholds from which they made sporadic raids on the English settlers. This situation lasted until 1740, the year the Maroons were granted virtual autonomy over their own lands.

Jamaica soon became a base of operations for buccaneers raiding the Spanish Main. On the whole, however, the English continued to maintain a slave-operated plantation economy based on such crops as sugar, cocoa, and coffee. With the abolition of slavery in 1834, the settlers were forced to recruit other sources of cheap labor, resorting to the importation of East Indian and Chinese farm hands. In 1846 the removal of the tariff protection for colonial produce entering the British market set off a violent dispute between the planter-dominated Jamaican legislature and the Crown on the one hand, and the planter-dominated administration and the Jamaican freedmen on the other. This conflict culminated in the Morant Bay uprising of 1865, which led to the imposition of Crown-colony status one year later. The growth of banana cultivation, improvement of internal transportation and communication, and reform in the political administration improved the status of the islanders somewhat, but insurmountable barriers continued to separate most groups within Jamaican society, which was largely class-centered

The Depression of the 1930s aggravated already-existing problems to such an extent that England felt it necessary to dispatch a royal investigating commission to the island. The commission's report led to the drafting of the 1944 constitution which permitted Jamaicans a wider degree of self-government.

Cabinet government was introduced in 1953, five years before the island became a member of the West Indies Federation. Jamaica withdrew from this organization in 1961. Full self-government came in 1959; independence within the British Commonwealth was achieved three years later. Thereafter, the Prime Minister was Sir Alexander Bustamante, leader of the Jamaican Labour Party (JLP). Bustamante was succeeded in office in 1967 by Hugh Shearer.

In 1972 Michael Manley of the People's National Party defeated the People's Labor Party to become Prime Minister. In 1975 Manley was host to a meeting of British Commonwealth Prime Ministers in Kings-

An open air market in Kingston, Jamaica.

ton, at which time he affirmed Jamaica's intent to remain in the Commonwealth. He has been trying to forge closer ties with Africa through such means as inviting leaders like Julius Nyerere of Tanzania to visit Jamaica and encouraging the appointment of a research fellow in linguistics to trace surviving African influences in Jamaican English.

In international affairs, Manley described Jamaica as a "third world" nation suffering from the ever-present problem of receiving low prices for exports of raw materials and having to pay steeply rising prices for imports of manufactured goods from industrially advanced countries.

Prime Minister Edward Philip George Seaga of the Jamaica Labour Party succeeded Manley following an election on October 30, 1980. The magnitude of the JLP victory was a function of the poor economic situation that had developed in the last couple of years while Manley ruled. There had been a decline in bauxite earnings along with an escalating oil import cost which generated an inflation rate exceeding 25%. There also had been a 33% unemployment rate plus a cumulative decline of 16% in the Gross National Product since 1974. Soon after the election, Seaga issued a call for a "Marshall Plan" to aid Jamaica and other Caribbean countries.

Trinidad and Tobago

Date of independence: August 31, 1962
Area: 1,980 square miles
Population: 1,176,000 (January 1981)
Capital: Port-of-Spain
Monetary unit: Trinidad and Tobago dollar
Ethnic divisions: 43% black, 40% East Indian, 14% mixed, 1% white, 2% other
Religion: 26.8% Protestant, 31.2% Roman Catholic, 23.0% Hindu, 6.0% Muslim, 13.0% unknown
Language: English
Literacy: 95%
Type of government: Independent state
Political parties/leaders: People's National Movement, United Labor Front (ULF), Democratic Labor Party (DLP), Democratic Action Congress (DAC), West Indian National Party (WINP)
Monetary conversion rate: TT $2.40 = U.S. $1 (Tied to U.S. dollar in 1976)
Principal economic resources: Oil, asphalt, cocoa, sugar, molasses, rum, tourism

History at a Glance

Christopher Columbus discovered Trinidad and Tobago on July 31, 1498, bestowing the name "La Trinidad" (Spanish for "The Trinity") on the larger of the

A Trinidad constable pauses on the principal street of Port-of-Spain.

The offices of Tobago's premier occupy a nineteenth-century mansion.

two islands. A Spanish governor was placed in charge of Trinidad in 1522, at which time the island became a supply station for ships en route to South America. Settlers attempting to colonize Trinidad during these years met with opposition from the Carib Indians and from British buccaneers then active in the Caribbean. Sir Walter Raleigh, for example, burned St. Joseph in 1595.

In time, however, the Spanish did manage to establish settlements and introduce a plantation-based economy heavily dependent on slave labor from West Africa. In 1725 a severe blight all but wiped out the cocoa crop, and agriculture was at a virtual standstill for the next 50 years. In 1783 the Spanish government began inviting immigrants of other nationalities to help colonize the islands, an offer which attracted many Frenchmen who acquired free land grants. (The distinctive French-Creole flavor in today's Trinidad is directly traceable to this influx of French settlers.)

Trinidad was captured by the British in 1797 and formally ceded to Great Britain by Spain five years later (The Treaty of Amiens). Trinidad became a Crown Colony and was linked to Tobago.

In the nineteenth century sugar proved to be the island's agricultural staple. Cultivation of this crop was made possible by the utilization of slave labor.

When slavery was abolished in 1834, the landowners resorted to the importation of more than 150,000 Hindu and Moslem "contract workers" from India. A good number of them remained in Trinidad once their contracts had expired, finding work in the cocoa industry which experienced a revival in the late nineteenth century. Since then, sugar and petroleum have grown in importance.

Independence was granted Trinidad and Tobago jointly in 1962, with Dr. Eric Williams serving the new nation both as prime minister and head of the majority party, the People's National Movement. In 1970 Trinidad was rocked by Black Power demonstrations and a mutiny in its armed forces, both of which were overcome by the government.

Williams died unexpectedly on March 29, 1981. George Chambers was immediately invested as Williams' interim successor. On May 9, 1981, Chambers was formally elected leader of the People's National Movement. Williams had led the country for a quarter of a century and prior to his death there had been no obvious successor to him. Williams had insisted that anyone designated as a successor should be selected for party, not personal, responsibility.

After its discovery by Columbus, Tobago too went virtually ignored until 1616, when colonists from Great Britain first appeared among the island's Carib Indian inhabitants. England gained permanent possession of Tobago in 1814 and ruled it for much of the nineteenth century from the Windward Island of Grenada. Tobago became a Crown Colony in 1877 and was linked to Trinidad in 1888. Since then, it has remained associated with the latter in all phases of its political, economic, and social development.

FRENCH AMERICAN DEPENDENCIES

French Guiana

Area: 35,135 square miles
Population: 66,000 (January 1981)
Capital: Cayenne
Monetary unit: Franc
Ethnic divisions: 95% black or mulatto, 5% caucasian, 10,000 East Indian, Chinese
Religion: Roman Catholic
Language: French
Literacy: 73%
Type of government: Overseas department and region of France
Political parties/leaders: Parti Socialiste Guyanais (PSG), Leopold Heder Senator; Union du Peuple Guyanaise (UAG)
Monetary conversion rate: 4.21 French francs = U.S. $1 (1980)
Principal economic resources: Timber, rum, gold mining, production of rosewood essence, space center

History at a Glance

French Guiana first was colonized in 1604 and was formally awarded to France in 1667 by the Peace of Breda. During the French Revolution, it served both as a penal colony and a place of exile. The territory's permanent borders were not settled until 1854.

Since 1947 French Guiana has been an overseas department of France, represented in the French parliament by one senator and one deputy. The territory of Inini, included within it, has a status equivalent to that of a Parisian *arrondissement* (an administrative district).

Most of the inhabitants are mulattoes. There are several tribes of aboriginal Indians in the interior. Most descendants of free or fugitive black slaves have settled along the rivers and coastal lowlands.

French Guiana is north of Brazil and east of Suriname on the northeast coast of South America. In 1958 French Guiana accepted the new Constitution of the French Fifth Republic, while remaining an Overseas Department of the French Republic.

Guadeloupe (Basse-Terre, Grand Terre)

Area: 687 square miles
Population: 317,000 (January 1981)
Capital: Basse-Terre
Monetary unit: French Franc
Ethnic divisions: 90% black or mulatto, less than 5% East Indian, 5% caucasian, Lebanese, Chinese
Religion: Roman Catholic
Language: French, creole, patois
Literacy: Over 70%
Type of government: Overseas department and region of France
Political parties/leaders: Rassemblement Pour la Republique (RPR), Gabriel Lisette; Communist Party of Guadeloupe (PCG); Progressive Party of Guadeloupe (PPG), Henri Rodes; Independent Republicans; Federation of the Left
Monetary conversion rate: 4.21 French francs = U.S. $1 (1980)
Principal economic resources: Bananas, rum, sugar cane, fishing, tourism, agricultural processing

History at a Glance

Guadeloupe was discovered by Christopher Columbus in 1493 during his second voyage to the New World. A permanent colony was established there by France in 1635. Since then, with the exception of two brief periods during which the island was occupied by Great Britain, Guadeloupe has been in the hands of the French. An overseas department of France since 1946, it is represented in Paris by three deputies and two senators.

The inhabitants of Guadeloupe are either black or a mixture of black and the French settlers who first arrived in the seventeenth century.

Fervent demonstrations for independence erupted in 1967. In response, France increased its economic and educational subsidies to Guadeloupe.

Guadeloupe is located 300 miles southeast of Puerto Rico and consists of the twin islands of Basse-Terre and Grande-Terre and five dependencies—Marie-Galante, Les Saintes, LaDesirade, St. Barthelemy, and the northern half of St. Martin.

Martinique

Area: 425 square miles
Population: 312,000 (Jan. 1981)
Capital: Fort-de-France
Monetary unit: Franc
Ethnic divisions: 90% African and African-Caucasian-Indian mixture, less than 5% East Indian, Lebanese, Chinese, 5% caucasian
Religion: 95% Roman Catholic, 5% Hindu and Pagan African
Language: French, creole, patois
Literacy: Over 70%
Type of government: Overseas department of France
Political parties/leaders: Rassemblement Pour la Republique, (RPR), Emile Maurice; Progressive Party of Martinique (PPM), Aime Cesaire; Communist Party of Martinique (PCM); Democratic Union of Martinique, and Federation of the Left
Monetary conversion rate: 4.21 French francs = U.S. $1 (1980)
Principal economic resources: Tourism, bananas, sugar, rum, fishing

History at a Glance

Christopher Columbus discovered Martinique in 1502. It was first colonized by the French in 1635 and has remained under the control of France for all but two short periods of its history: from 1762 to 1763, during the Seven Years War and from 1794 to 1815, during the Napoleonic Wars. In both instances, Great Britain temporarily occupied the island.

In 1902 Mount Pelee erupted and completely destroyed the city of St. Pierre, together with its 30,000 inhabitants.

Martinique is represented in the French parliament by three deputies and two senators. An appointed prefect is chief administrator and is assisted by a 36-member general council. The island has been an overseas department of France since 1946.

Martinique is in the Lesser Antilles and about 300 miles northeast of Venezuela. A new Constitution of the French Fifth Republic was approved in 1958 and Martinique has since remained an Overseas Department of the French Republic. The people of Martinique are mostly black, or of Carib Indian or European descent.

NETHERLANDS AMERICAN DEPENDENCIES

Netherlands Antilles

Area: 817 square miles
Population: 243,000 (Jan. 1981)
Capital: Willemstad, Curacao
Monetary unit: Florin
Ethnic divisions: Racial mixture with African, Caribbean Indian, European, Latin and Oriental influences, negroid characteristics dominant on Curacao, Indian on Aruba
Religion: Roman Catholic, sizable Protestant and smaller Jewish minorities
Language: Officially Dutch; Papiamento, a Spanish Portuguese-Dutch-English dialect with English widely spoken
Literacy: 95%
Type of government: A territory within the Kingdom of the Netherlands
Political parties/leaders: Indigenous to each island
Monetary conversion rate: 1.8 Netherlands Antillean florins (NAF) = U.S. $1 official
Principal economic resources: Oil (Aruba and Curacao), boatbuilding (Saba), cotton, sugar, cane (Saint Maarten), agriculture (St. Eustatius), tourism

History at a Glance

Curacao, the largest of the Netherlands Antilles, was discovered in 1499 by Aloso de Ojeda and Amerigo Vespucci, but Spain did not begin colonizing the island until 1527. In 1634 the Dutch, under Johannes van Walkeeck, seized the islands, including Aruba and Bonaire and installed Peter Stuyvesant as governor. During the Napoleonic Wars, the English occupied them, but they were restored to the Netherlands in 1816.

Saba was first occupied by the Dutch in the seventeenth century, while St. Eustatius, in the hands of the Dutch since 1632, served as a supply depot for England's American colonies before and during the Revolutionary War. (It is traditionally credited with having been the first foreign post to render a salute to the American flag in 1776.) The island changed hands several times before being permanently restored to the Netherlands in 1841. Saint Maarten, occupied by the Dutch and French in 1648, was later divided between them.

The Netherlands Antilles, a part of the kingdom of the Netherlands, has had complete internal autonomy since 1954. Executive power is wielded by a governor who represents the Dutch sovereign.

The people are mostly a mixture of black, Indian, Spanish, and Dutch strains.

Suriname (Dutch Guiana)

Area: 63,251 square miles
Population: 400,000
Capital: Paramaribo
Monetary unit: Suriname guilder
Ethnic divisions: 40% Creole (black and mixed), 37% Hindustani, 15% Javanese, 2.6% American Indian, 1.7% Chinese, 1.7% European
Religion:
Language: Dutch (official), English (widely spoken)
Literacy: 80%
Type of government: Parliamentary democracy with military participation
Political parties/leaders: Bruma (principal leftist party), Progressive Party, Javanese Farmers Party, Reformed Progressive Party
Monetary conversion rate: 1 Surinam guilder = U.S. $0.560
Principal economic resources: Bauxite, lumbering, rice, sugar cane, citrus fruits, coconuts, bananas

History at a Glance

In the sixteenth century Spaniards in search of gold were the first Europeans to set foot on Suriname, but they left when no treasure was found. In 1625 the British, French, and Dutch began to vie for control of the territory. Under the Treaty of Breda (1667), Great Britain agreed to cede it to the Netherlands in return for the colony of New Amsterdam (later New York). Dutch control, however, was not recognized by other European powers until the Treaty of Paris at the end of the Napoleonic Wars.

In 1954 Suriname was granted full internal autonomy in accordance with the provisions of a new statute put into effect by the king of the Netherlands. (This charter united the Netherlands, Suriname, and the Netherlands Antilles on a basis of equality and as constituents by a governor who is assisted by a cabinet and by an elected legislative council.)

The black inhabitants of Suriname, representing about 40% of the population, are descendants of fugitive slaves who were imported from Africa before 1865. Other major groups include: Indians (from the Asian subcontinent), Indonesians; Creoles (persons of mixed descent), and aboriginal Indians.

Dr. Henk Chin A Sen was designated Prime Minister by the National Military Council and sworn into office on March 15, 1980. Sen assumed office following the ouster of Henck Alfonsius Eugene Arron with few recriminations taken against members of the previous government. During the year a number of changes occurred within the National Military Council with a generally conservative outlook gradually turning toward a more leftist idealogy.

Suriname, formerly called Dutch Guiana, lies on the north-central coast of South America. It is bordered by Guyana on the west, French Guiana on the east, and Brazil to the south.

UNITED KINGDOM AMERICAN DEPENDENCIES

Bermuda

Area: 21 square miles
Population: 64,000 (January 1981)
Capital: Hamilton
Monetary unit: Bermuda dollar
Ethnic divisions: 59% black, 41% white
Religion: 47.5% Church of England, 38.2% other Protestant, 10.2% Catholic, 4.1% other
Language: English
Literacy: Virtually 100%
Type of government: British colony
Political parties/leaders: United Bermuda Party (UBP), J. David Gibbons; Progressive Labor Party (PLP), Lois Browne Evans
Monetary conversion rate: 1 Bermuda dollar = U.S. $1
Principal economic resources: Tourism, finance

History at a Glance

Discovered in 1515 by the Spaniard Juan de Bermudez, Bermuda was first settled by a group of British colonists who had been shipwrecked in 1609 while en route to Virginia. The islands were officially acquired by the British Crown in 1684.

In modern times, the British have established a naval base on Ireland Island, while the United States has leased sites for military bases on two other islands.

A Crown Colony, Bermuda has the oldest British colonial legislature. It is administered by a governor who represents the sovereign and is assisted by a nine-member executive council. The British maintain control over foreign affairs and the Bermudan police.

The current population breakdown lists 60% as black or mixed and 40% as white.

In 1973 the governor Sir Richard Sharples and an aide were assassinated and a state of emergency was declared. Motives for the crime remain obscure. However, there was much rioting in December 1977 after two blacks had been hanged for a series of murders, including the assassination of the Governor. British troops were called in to restore order.

British Virgin Islands

Area: 59 square miles
Population: 12,000
Capital: Road Town
Monetary unit: U.S. dollar
Language: English
Principal economic resources: Fish, livestock, tourism

History at a Glance

Great Britain obtained title to these 40-odd islands and islets in 1666 and, until 1960, administered them as part of the Leeward Islands. At present, the government is headed by a Crown-appointed administrator who is assisted by both executive and legislative councils.

The administration of the British Virgin Islands is headed by a governor, James Alfred Davidson, and its representative institutions include a mainly elected Legislative Council and an appointed Executive Council. The governor chooses the chief minister from the legislature. H. Lavity Stoutt is currently chief minister.

Almost the entire population is of African descent.

Cayman Islands (Grand Cayman, Little Cayman, Cayman Brac)

Area: 100 square miles
Population: 14,000
Capital: Georgetown
Monetary unit: Cayman Islands dollar
Language: English
Principal economic resources: Farming, fishing

History at a Glance

Christopher Columbus discovered the Cayman Islands in 1503, naming them "Tortugas" due to the profusion of turtles in the surrounding waters.

Once it became clear that the Spanish did not intend to colonize them, the British sent in settlers from nearby Jamaica. The islands remained a dependency of Jamaica until its independence in 1959, when they became subject to a new constitution providing for a Crown-appointed administrator, a legislative assembly, and an executive council.

One out of every five Cayman Islanders is classified as black; approximately half of the population is of mixed blood; the rest is European.

Leeward Islands (Antigua, Barbuda, Redonda, St. Kitts-Nevis-Anguilla, Montserrat)

Area: 356 square miles
Population: 161,000
Language: English
Principal economic resources: Agriculture, tourism, sugar

History at a Glance

When the Leeward Islands were discovered by Christopher Columbus in 1493, they were inhabited by Carib Indians. St. Kitts was the first English settlement in the Caribbean (1623); Nevis was colonized five years later and Montserrat in 1632. The French captured some of the islands in 1666 and again in 1782, but they were returned to the British under the Treaty of Versailles (1783).

Significant contitutional changes were first introduced in the nineteenth century, particularly after the abolition of the slave trade (1808). Although suffrage was extended, the small farmer and the laboring class still found themselves not truly represented.

In 1956 the separate colonies were united to form the territory of the Leeward Islands and, two years later, were incorporated into the Federation of the West Indies which lasted until 1962.

Today each territorial unit has a Crown-appointed administrator, as well as executive and legislative councils.

Most of the population is an intermixture of European settlers and the descendants of West African slaves.

In 1967 Antigua and a St. Christopher Nevis-Anguilla Federation were granted full control of their domestic affairs.

Bahama Islands

Date of independence: July 10, 1973
Area: 5,380 square miles
Population: 249,000
Capital: Nassau (New Providence Island)
Monetary unit: Bahamian dollar
Ethnic divisions: 80% black, 10% white, 10% mixed
Religion: 29% Baptist, 23% Church of England, 23% Roman Catholic, 7% Methodist
Language: English
Type of government: Independent Commonwealth since July 1973 which recognizes Elizabeth II as chief of state
Political parties/leaders: Progressive Liberal Party, Lynden O. Pindling; Bahamian Democratic Party (BDP) Henry Bostwick; Free National Movement (FNM), Cecil Wallace-Whitfield
Monetary conversion rate: 1 Bahamian dollar (B$1) = U.S. $1
Principal economic resources: Tourism, cement, oil refining, lumber, salt production, rum, aragonite, pharmaceuticals, spiral weld, steel pipe

History at a Glance
Christopher Columbus first set foot in the New World on the island of San Salvador (now called Watling's Island) in the Bahamas on October 12, 1492. The first settlers of the Bahamas, however, were British who came from Bermuda in the seventeenth century. British companies subsequently brought in large numbers of African slaves to work the plantations. The first royal governor, appointed in 1717, made the islands safe for colonization by permanently driving off the many pirates, among them the notorious Bluebeard, who had utilized the Bahamas as a base of operation. The islands were claimed by the French in the eighteenth century, then captured by the Spanish, in 1781. The English, however, quickly regained control of them via the Treaty of Paris (1783).

During the U.S. Civil War, confederate blockade runners operated out of the Bahamas, as did rum runners during the American prohibition era. In 1940 the United States established naval bases in the area.

The Bahamas are administered by a governor, who is assisted by legislative and executive councils. The constitution has existed virtually unchanged since 1729.

On July 10, 1973, the Bahamas obtained their independence and assumed the status of an independent member of the British Commonwealth. Lynden O. Pauling of the Progressive Liberal Party is Prime Minister. Following an overwhelming election by the Progressive Liberal Party in 1968, the Bahamas gained greater autonomy. The party, led by Pauling, won 30 of 38 seats in Parliament in a 1977 election.

The Bahamas, since World War II, has become established as an important center of banking and finance. Its banking laws promise anonymity as does Switzerland. It is also a major center for gambling.

The Bahamas make up an archipelago of some 700 islands plus uninhabited inlets (2,400), as well as cays 50 miles off Florida's coast. Twenty-two of the islands are inhabited, the most important being New Providence where Nassau is located.

Turks (Grand Turk; Salt Cay) and Caicos (South Caicos, North Caicos) Islands

Area: 166 square miles
Population: 6,000
Capital: Grand Turk
Language: English
Principal economic resources: Salt, crayfish, sisal, conch products

History at a Glance
Though discovered by Ponce de Leon in 1512, the Turks and Caicos Islands remained uninhabited until 1678, when the Bermudians settled there to mine salt. They were expelled by the Spanish in 1710, but soon returned, only to survive several Spanish and French attacks.

In 1848 the islands became a separate colony under the administration of Jamaica before being annexed by the latter in 1873. They were again separated from Jamaica when it became independent in 1962. Since then they have been administered by a British resident who is assisted by an executive council and a legislative assembly.

Most of the inhabitants are either of African or mixed descent.

Windward Islands (Dominica, Grenada, Saint Lucia, Saint Vincent)

Area: 825 square miles
Population: 335,000

Principal economic resources: Livestock, fish
Language: English

History at a Glance

The Windward Islands were inhabited by Indians when they were discovered by Columbus in 1493. Later settled by the English, they soon became a battleground between the indigenous Caribs, the English, and the French. Carib opposition was, to all intent and purpose, eliminated toward the beginning of the eighteenth century, when the remaining Indians were deported to areas near Honduras. During much the same period, Great Britain won important territorial concessions under the Treaty of Versailles (1783) and at the Congress of Vienna (1815).

Africans worked the fields until slavery was abolished, at which time they were replaced by East Indians and Portuguese. Despite the introduction of limited voting rights, the descendants of the land-working class remained essentially unrepresented until the twentieth century.

In 1956 the four territories—Dominica, Grenada, Saint Lucia, and Saint Vincent—were combined to form the Windward Islands and, two years later, incorporated into the Federation of the West Indies (dissolved in 1962).

The islands are governed by a Crown-appointed administrator, aided by executive and legislative councils.

The population is an intermixture of European settlers, the descendants of West African slaves, and Carib Indians.

In 1967 Dominica, Grenada, and St. Lucia were granted self-government with Britain retaining control of foreign affairs. St. Vincent received similar status in 1969.

UNITED STATES DEPENDENCIES

Corn Islands

Area: 4 square miles
Language: English
Principal economic resources: Coconuts

History at a Glance

The Corn Islands (Great Corn and Little Corn) were leased to the United States by Nicaragua in 1916 as a means of protecting a contemplated canal across the latter country. The lease was signed for a 99-year period.

Panama Canal Zone

Area: 560 square miles (372 are land)
Population: 45,000

A flower vendor carries her wares in a basket on her head.

Language: English, Spanish
Principal economic resources: Canal operations

History at a Glance

The Canal Zone is a 50-mile-long, five-mile-wide strip lying between the Atlantic and Pacific Oceans, on both sides of the Panama Canal. It was granted in perpetuity to the United States by virtue of a United States–Panamanian treaty signed in 1903.

Since 1959 the residents of the zone (half of whom were born in the continental United States, the rest from Panama or the zone itself) had grown vehement in their demands for its restoration to Panama. On occasion, student demonstrations flared to the point of violence before being suppressed.

The canal was operated by the U.S.-owned Panama Canal Company under the terms of the Panama Canal Act of 1950. The governor of the zone was also the president of the company. Canal Zone legislation remained in the hands of the U.S. Congress.

By 1967 U.S. and Panamanian negotiators produced

draft treaties that would provide for Panamanian participation in canal management, profit-sharing between Panama and the United States, and a measure of dual sovereignty. The treaties were obstructed by the forceful overthrow of Panamanian President Arnulfo Arias in 1968, and in 1970 Panama repudiated the treaty. In 1973 the United States vetoed a United Nations Security Council resolution that would have called for negotiation of a new treaty that recognized Panamanian sovereignty. However, in 1974 the two countries entered negotiations which would eventually hand over control to Panama and in the meantime increase Panamanian influence and revenues.

Two treaties were signed in Washington on September 7, 1977 and though Panama endorsed it in a plebiscite on October 23, the treaties were barely approved by the U.S. Senate on March 16 and April 18, 1978. During a visit to Panama by President Carter on June 16, 1978, documents of the ratification were exchanged. There was a delay in the implementation of the treaties due to a U.S. Senate stipulation that ratification would not be deemed complete until passage of enabling legislation by the Congress or until March 31, 1979, or whichever was first. On October 1, 1979, the American flag was lowered within the Canal Zone and the administrative authority for the canal was then formally transferred to a binational Panama Canal Commission.

Puerto Rico (Culebra, Mona, Vieques)

Area: 3,435 square miles
Population: 2,920,000
Capital: San Juan
Religion: Roman Catholic
Language: Spanish, English
Type of government: Democracy
Political parties/leaders: Popular Democratic Parrty, New Progressive Parrty, Puerto Rican Socialist Party, Puerto Rican Independence Party
Principal economic resources: Coffee, tobacco, sugar cane, tourism, dairy farming, manufacturing industries

History at a Glance
Discovered by Columbus in 1493 on his second voyage to the New World, Puerto Rico was soon conquered by the Spaniard Ponce de Leon, who was appointed governor of the island in 1509. The indigenous Carib Indians, almost all of whom were utilized by the Spaniards as plantation laborers, were eventually wiped out—to be replaced in 1513 by African slaves. Puerto Rico was held by the English in 1598 and San Juan was beseiged by the Dutch in 1625. Otherwise, Spanish control remained unchallenged until the Spanish-American War.

The island was captured by U.S. forces during this conflict and ceded outright to the United States under

Puerto Rico's beautiful beaches and luxury hotels cater to an economically important tourist industry.

the Treaty of Paris (1898). In 1900 Congress established a local administration—with a governor appointed by the American president, an executive council, and an elected house of delegates. Puerto Ricans were granted U.S. citizenship in 1917.

After World War II, Congress provided that the governor of the island be an elected official, whereupon, in 1948, Luis Munoz Marin was chosen for this office. In 1950 a further act of Congress enabled Puerto Rico to draft its own constitution and, in three years, it became a U.S. Commonwealth.

Since then, Puerto Rican politics have been dominated by the Popular Democratic Party. Marin's hand-picked successor, Roberto Sanchez Villela, was elected in January 1965. This party is committed to the retention of Commonwealth status. Emigration to the mainland, a major factor in the 1950s, has declined in recent years. Despite the preponderance of popular support for the Democrats, two other parties have managed to gain some foothold: the Statehood Republican Party, which advocates statehood for the island, and the Independence Party, which seeks complete independence for Puerto Rico. In a 1967 referendum, Puerto Rico voted to remain a Commonwealth.

Many Puerto Ricans today are of mixed black and Spanish ancestry. For the most part, the original Indian inhabitants of the island were exterminated in the sixteenth century.

In 1968 Luis A. Ferre, long an advocate of statehood, was elected governor of the island as a candidate of the New Progressive Party. Ferre made it clear, however, that statehood would depend on a separate plebiscite which would be run apart from the general election.

In the late 1960s and early 1970s, Puerto Rico came increasingly to resemble the United States, especially in the area of San Juan which was being disrupted more and more often by road and office building construction and some of the Western Hemisphere's most spectacular traffic jams. Labor disputes intensified in 1974, leading to sabotage of large sections of the island's water supply. However, the relatively unexplored portion of the island's center, the Cordillera Central, remained relatively undeveloped and an example of tropical lushness where the brilliant flamboya blooms in cone-shaped symmetry from tall trees and oranges and grapefruit grow waiting to be picked on trees alongside the roads.

In 1975 the Governor of Puerto Rico was Rafael Hernandez Colon.

In 1979 former governor Hernandez Colon was designated as the gubernatorial candidate by the Popular Democratic Party for the 1980 election. The PPD called for administration by the Commonwealth of most of the transferred federal funds, the right to nego-

tiate international trade agreements and to create a 200-mile economic zone in order to ensure local control of marine resources and potential offshore petroleum deposits. The New Progressive Party won the governorship by 0.3% of the votes cast with Carlos Romero Barcelo assuming office. Barcelo had been expected to call for a 1981 plebiscite on statehood, but after his election he decided to defer plans on the issue.

Swan Islands

Area: 4 square miles
Population: Less than 100 (on Big Swan)
Language: English
Principal economic resources: Guano

History at a Glance

The Swan Islands (Big Swan and Little Swan) were discovered in the early sixteenth century, and have been in the possession of the United States since 1863, although the Central American republic of Honduras has laid claim to them. The islands, now the site of a lighthouse and a radio station, are believed to be a base of operations for the Central Intelligence Agency.

Following years of dispute, in 1971 the United States signed a treaty which recognized Honduran sovereignty over the islands. On September 1, 1972, the treaty ratifications were exchanged.

Virgin Islands (St. Croix, St. Thomas, St. John)

Date of independence:
Area: 133 square miles
Population: 64,500
Capital: Charlotte Amalie
Ethnic divisions: 80% black or mulatto
Language: English
Principal economic resources: Fish, tourism, rum

History at a Glance

Discovered by Christopher Columbus in 1493, the Virgin Islands (an archipelago of 74 islands) is now divided into two distinct clusters; the U.S. Virgin Islands (three main islands, 65 islets) and the British Virgin Islands (six main islands).

The American group was originally settled by the Danish West India Company, which first colonized St. Thomas in 1672. In 1683 St. John was likewise claimed by this company and, by 1733, St. Croix had been acquired from France. Some 20 years later, the holdings of this company were taken over by the Danish crown, which then reconstituted them as a royal colony, The Danish West Indies.

The United States bought the territory from Denmark in 1917 for some 25 million dollars and granted citizenship to its inhabitants 10 years later. In 1931 its administration was transferred from the U.S. Navy Department to the Department of the Interior.

Limited self-government for the territory dates back to 1936, although the internal administration of the islands continues to be in the hands of a governor appointed by the President of the United States. (The first black governor, William H. Hastie, was appointed in 1946.) Under the terms of the 1954 Revised Organic Act of the Virgin Islands, local legislative power rests in the hands of a unicameral chamber composed of 11 popularly elected senators.

Under the terms of the constitution now in effect, the United States retains the authority to introduce and enact legislation to govern the territory. The courts are also controlled by the United States, with an American district judge serving as the territory's highest judicial officer.

Pursuant to a bill passed by Congress in 1968, the governor of the island is an elected, rather than an appointed, official. Dr. Melvin Evans, the first native black governor, came to office in mid-1969. In 1970 Dr. Evans was elected governor in the Virgin Islands' first popular election.

In 1972 the Virgin Islands were granted the right to send one nonvoting delegate to the House of Representatives. Island residents enjoy the same rights as mainlanders with the exception that they may not vote in a presidential election.

In 1973 and 1974 simmering economic and racial problems erupted, with fervent Black Power agitation and a series of murders disturbing the area's tranquility and tourism.

A SELECTED BIBLIOGRAPHY

Biography ■ Culture and Society ■ Economics ■ Education ■ General Works ■ History ■ Juvenile Books ■ Literature ■ Politics ■ Slavery ■ Africa

Recent years have seen a great increase in the publication of material dealing with blacks and civil rights. Because so many new books and articles have been published in these areas since 1971, the following bibliography does not repeat the listings already printed in the 1967 and 1971 editions of *The Negro Almanac,* and the reader interested in basic source material should not neglect those volumes. Furthermore, to make the torrent of new information easier to handle and to help the student encounter a sufficiently large selection of current material on any given subject, this bibliography has been subdivided into 11 areas: biography, culture and society, economics, education, general, history, juvenile, literature, political, slavery, and Africa. The materials included were compiled by Ernest Kaiser of the Schomburg Collection of the New York Public Library. Subject breakdown of the books was completed by the *Almanac* staff.

Other important bibliographies are *A Bibliography of Black Literature,* available from the Office of Adult Services of the New York Public Library; *The Black Experience in Children's Books,* selected by Barbara Rolluck, available from the Office of Branch Libraries, New York Public Library; *The Negro in the United States: A Selected Bibliography,* compiled by Dorothy Porter, available from the Superintendent of Documents / U.S. Government Printing Office / Washington, D.C.; and *A Bibliography of Negro History and Culture for Young Readers,* compiled by Miles M. Jackson, available from the University of Pennsylvania Press.

General

This section encompasses a potpourri of subjects, including religion, sports, music, cooking, and art.

A

Ahye, Molly. *Golden Heritage: The Dance in Trinidad and Tobago.* Petit Valley, Republic of Trinidad and Tobago: Heritage Cultures, Ltd., 1979.

Allen, Walter C. *Hendersonia: The Music of Fletcher Henderson and His Musicians. A Bio-Discography.* (Jazz Monographs No. 4.) The Author, P.O. Box 1382, Highland Park, N.J. 08904, 1973.

Andrews, Benny. *Between the Lines: 70 Drawings and 7 Essays.* New York: Pella Publishing Co., 1979.

Andrews, Malachi. *Psychoglackology.* Berkeley, Cal.: Achebe Enterprises, 1975.

Anselment, Carol and Donald B. Gibson (eds.). *Black and White: Stories of American Life.* New York: Washington Square Press, 1971.

Avery, Charles E. *Black Traces: A Photographic Essay.* New York: Carlton Press, 1973.

B

Bailey, Pearl. *Pearl's Kitchen: An Extraordinary Cookbook.* New York: Harcourt Brace Jovanovich, 1973.

———. *Duey's Tale.* New York: Harcourt Brace Jovanovich, 1975.

The Barnett-Aden Collection. Washington, D.C.: The Anacostia Neighborhood Museum, Smithsonian Institution, 1981.

Black American Music: Past and Present. Boston: Crescendo Publishing Co., 1974.

Black List: The Concise Reference Guide to Publications and Broadcasting Media of Black America, Africa and the Caribbean. New York: Panther House Ltd., 1971.

Black Music in Our Culture: Curricular Ideas on the Subjects, Materials and Problems. Kent, Ohio: Kent State University Press.

The Black Photographers Annual. Black Photographers Annual, Inc., 55 Hicks St., Brooklyn, N.Y. 11201, 1973, 1974.

Blawis, Patricia Bell. *Tijerina and the Land Grants: Mexican Americans in the Struggle for their Heritage.* New York: International Publishers.

Blockson, Charles L. with Ron Fry. *Black Genealogy.* Englewood Cliffs, N.J.: Prentice-Hall, 1977.

Bogle, Donald. *Brown Sugar: Eighty Years of America's Black Female Superstars.* New York: Crown Publishers, 1980.

Bowser, Pearl and Joan Eckstein. *Princess Pamela's Soul Food Cookbook.* New York: New American Library, 1971.

Boyd, Herb (ed.). *Roots: Some Student Perspectives Readings in Black History and Culture.* Detroit: College of Lifelong Learning, Division of Community Services, Wayne State University, 1977.

Brashler, William. *The Bingo Long Traveling All-Stars and Motor Kings.* New York: Harper & Row, 1973.

C

Clark, Chris and Sheila Rush. *How to Get Along with Black People: A Handbook for White Folks—and Some Black Folks Too.* New York: Third Press.

Cleage, Jr., Albert B. *Black Christian Nationalism: New Directions for the Black Church.* New York: William Morrow.

Coles, Robert. *The Buses Roll.* New York: W. W. Norton, 1975.

Cone, James H. *The Spirituals and the Blues: An Interpretation.* New York: Seabury Press, 1972.

D

Dance, Martin E. (ed.). *The Black Press, 1827–1890: The Quest for National Identity.* New York: Putnam, 1971.

Dance, Stanley. *The World of Count Basie.* New York: Scribner, 1980.

———. *The World of Earl Hines.* New York: Scribner, 1978.

Darden, Norma Jean and Carole Darden. *Spoonbread and Strawberry Wine: Recipes and Reminiscences of a Family.* New York: Anchor Press/Doubleday, 1979.

Davis, Lenwood G. and Janet L. Sims. *Black Artists in the United States: An Annotated Bibliography of Books, Articles, and Dissertations on Black Artists, 1779–1979.* Westport, Conn.: Greenwood Press, 1980.

DeCock, Liliane and Reginald McGhee (eds.). *James Van Der Zee.* Dobbs Ferry, N.Y.: Morgan and Morgan, 1974.

de Lerma, Dominique-Rene (ed.). *Reflections on Afro-American Music.* Kent, Ohio: Kent State University Press, 1974.

D'Emilio, John. *The Civil Rights Struggle: Leaders in Profile.* New York: Facts on File, 1980.

Dett, R. Nathaniel. *The Collected Piano Works of R. Nathaniel Dett.* Evanston, Ill.: Summy-Birhcard Co., 1973.

Dixon, Robert and John Godnich. *Recording the Blues.* New York: Stein and Day, 1973.

Doty, Robert. *Contemporary Black Artists in America.* New York: Dodd, Mead, 1971.

Drake, St. Clair. *The Redemption of Africa and Black Religion.* Chicago: Third World Press, 1973.

Dunham, Katherine. *Kasamance: A Fantasy.* New York: Third Press, 1975.

E

Ellison, Curtis W. and E. W. Metcalf, Jr. *William Wells Brown and Martin R. Delaney: A Reference Guide.* Boston: G. K. Hall, 1978.

F

Fax, Elton C. *Through Black Eyes: Journeys of a Black Artist to East Africa and Russia.* New York: Dodd, Mead, 1974.

Feather, Leonard. *From Satchmo to Miles.* New York: Stein and Day, 1973.

Fiedler, Leslie A. *The Inadvertent Epic: From Uncle Tom's Cabin to Roots.* New York: Simon and Schuster, 1980.

Flynn, James J. *Negroes of Achievement in Modern America.* New York: Dodd, Mead, 1971.

Foxx, Redd and Norma Miller. *The Redd Foxx Encyclopedia of Black Humor.* Los Angeles: Ward Ritchie Press, 1978.

Frazier, Walt and Ira Berkow. *Rockin' Steady: A Guide to Basketball and Cool.* Englewood Cliffs: N.J.: Prentice-Hall, 1974.

G

Galton, Lawrence. *The Silent Disease: Hypertension.* New York: Crown Publishers, 1973.

Garvin, Richard M. and Edmond G. Addeo. *The Midnight Special: The Legend of Leadbelly.* New York: Bernard Geis Associates.

Gary, Lawrence E. (ed.). *Mental Health: A Challenge to the Black Community.* Ardmore, Pa.: Dorrance & Co., 1979.

Gaver, Jessyca Russell. *Sickle Cell Disease: Its Tragedy and Its Treatment.* New York: Lancer Books, 1973.

Gerber, Israel J. *The Heritage Seekers.* Middle Village, N.Y.: Jonathan David Publishers, 1978.

Giovanni, Nikki. *Vacation Time: Poems for Children.* New York: William Morrow, 1981.

Goddard, Chris. *Jazz Away From Home.* New York: Paddington Press, 1980.

Goldman, Alan H. *Justice and Reverse Discrimination.* Princeton, N.J.: Princeton University Press, 1980.

Gonzales, Babs. *Movin on Down the Line.* Newark, N.J.: Ezpudience Publishing, 1979.

Gould, William B. *Black Workers in White Unions: Job Discrimination in the United States.* Ithaca, N.Y.: Cornell University Press, 1977.

Gregory, Dick. *Dick Gregory's Nature Diet for Folks Who Eat: Cookin' With Mother Nature.* New York: Harper & Row, 1973.

Grier, Roosevelt. *Rosey Grier's Needlepoint for Men.* New York: Walker and Co., 1974.

Grier, William H. and Price M. Cobbs. *The Jesus Bag.* New York: McGraw-Hill, 1971.

Groia, Philip. *They All Sang on the Corner.* Setauket, N.Y.: Edmond Publishing Co., 1975.

Grosvernor, Verta Mae. *Thursdays and Every Other Sunday Off: A Domestic Rap.* New York: Doubleday, 1973.

Gutman, Bill. *Morris, Johnson, Hill, Little* (Great Running Backs #2), New York: Grosset & Dunlap/Tempo Books, 1975.

Gwaltney, John L. *The Thrice Shy.* New York: Columbia University Press, 1971.

H

Hamilton, Virginia. *Paul Robeson: The Life and Times of a Free Man.* New York: Harper & Row, 1975.

Handy, D. Antoinette. *Black Music Opinions & Reviews.* Ettrick: Virginia State College, B.M. & M., 1979.

Hano, Arnold. *Muhammad Ali: The Champion.* New York: Putnam, 1978.

Harnan, Terry. *African Rhythm—American Dance: A Biography of Katherine Dunham.* New York: Knopf, 1974.

Harris, Middleton, Morris Levitt, Roger Furman, and Ernest Smith (eds.). *The Black Book.* New York: Random House, 1974.

Haskins, Jim. *The Cotton Club.* New York: Random House, 1978.

———— with Kathleen Benson. *Scott Joplin.* New York: Doubleday, 1978.

Haskins, James. *Witchcraft, Mysticism and Magic in the Black World.* New York: Doubleday, 1974.

Hayes, Elvin and Bill Gilbert. *They Call Me "The Big E."* Englewood Cliffs, N.J.: Prentice-Hall, 1979.

Hayes, Bob. *The Black American Travel Guide.* New York: Straight Arrow/World, 1971.

Haynes, Robert V. *A Night of Violence: The Houston Riot of 1917.* Baton Rouge: Louisiana State University Press, 1977.

Heilbut, Tony. *The Gospel Sound.* New York: Simon and Schuster.

Holder, Geoffrey. *Geoffrey Holder's Caribbean Cookbook.* New York: Viking Press.

Holmes, Jr., Oakley N. (comp.). *The Complete Annotated Resource Guide to Black American Art.* Jacksonville: Black Artists in America, 1980.

Hough, Jr., John T. *A Peck of Salt: A Year in the Ghetto.* Boston: Little, Brown.

Houston, Robert. *Legacy to an Unborn Son.* Boston: Beacon Press, 1971.

Huggins, Nathan Irvin. *Harlem Renaissance.* New York: Oxford University Press, 1971.

J

Jackson, Bruce (ed.). *Wake Up Dead Man: Afro-American Worksongs from Texas Prison.* Cambridge, Mass.: Harvard University Press, 1972.

Jackson, Irene V. *Afro-American Religious Music: A Bibliography and a Catalogue of Gospel Music.* Westport, Conn.: Greenwood Press, 1980.

Jackson, Reggie. *Reggie Jackson's Scrapbook.* New York: Dutton, 1978.

Jay, James M. *Negroes in Science: Natural Science Doctorates, 1876–1969.* Detroit: Balamp Publishing Co.

Vlach, M. *The Afro-American Tradition in Decorative Arts.* Cleveland: Cleveland Museum of Art, 1979.

Jazz People. Photographs by Ole Brask. Text by Dan Morgenstern. Foreword by Dizzy Gillespie. Introduction by James Jones. New York: Harry N. Abrams, 1977.

Johnson, Bobby. *Monroe . . . (an avenue).* The Author, 30 Prince St. #6 Rochester, N.Y., 1981.

Johnson, Samuel M. *Often Back: The Tales of Harlem.* New York: Vantage Press.

Jones, W. and Jim Washington. *Black Champions Challenge American Sports.* New York: David McKay Co.

Joplin, Scott. *The Best of Scott Joplin: A Collection of Original Ragtime Piano Compositions.* Long Island City, N.Y.: Publishers Central Bureau, 1974.

————. *The Collected Works of Scott Joplin* (2 vols.). Edited by Vera Brodsky Lawrence. New York: New York Public Library, Lincoln Center, 1971.

K

Kennebeck, Edwin. *Juror Number Four: The Trial of Thirteen Black Panthers as Seen from the Jury Box.* New York: W. W. Norton, 1973.

Kennington, Donald. *The Literature of Jazz: A Critical Guide.* Chicago: American Library Association.

Kickingbird, Kirke and Karen Ducheneaux. *One Hundred Million Acres.* New York: Macmillan, 1973.

L

Landay, Eileen. *Black Film Stars.* New York: Drake Publishers, 1974.

Leonard, Walter J. *Black Lawyers: Training and Results, Then and Now.* P.O. Box 1091, Boston: Senna & Shih, 1978.

Lewis, Edna and Evangeline Peterson. *Edna Lewis Cookbook.* Indianapolis: Bobbs-Merrill, 1974.

Lewis, Samella. *Art: African American.* New York: Harcourt Brace Jovanovich, 1978.

———— and Ruth G. Waddy (eds.). *Black Artists on Art.* Vol. II. Los Angeles: Contemporary Crafts Publishers.

Linde, Shirley Motter. *Sickle Cell: A Complete Guide to Prevention and Treatment.* New York: Pavilion Publishing Co., 1972.

Lipsky, Richard. *How We Play the Game: Why Sports Dominate American Life.* Boston: Beacon Press, 1981.

Lovell, Jr., John. *Black Song: The Forge and the Flame.* New York: Macmillan.

M

Major, Clarence. *The Cotton Club.* Detroit: Broadside Press, 1973.

Manning, Steve. *The Jackson Five.* Indianapolis: Bobbs-Merrill, 1977.

Mapp, Edward. *Blacks in American Films: Today and Yesterday.* Metuchen, N.J.: Scarecrow Press.

————. *Directory of Blacks in the Performing Arts.* Metuchen, N.J.: Scarecrow Press, 1979.

Masterpieces of Primitive Art. The Nelson A. Rockefeller Collection. Photographs by Lee Boltin. Text by Douglas Newton. New York: Knopf, 1979.

McCutcheon, Lynn. *Rhythm and Blues.* Arlington, Va.: R. W. Beatty Ltd.

Mensh, Elaine and Harry Mensh. *Behind the Scenes in Two Worlds.* New York: International Publishers, 1978.

Mitchell, Henry H. *Black Preaching.* New York: Lippincott, 1971.

Moore, Archie. *Any Boy Can.* Englewood Cliffs, N.J.: Prentice-Hall.

Mossell, Gertrude E. H. (Bustill). *The Work of Afro-American Woman.* Freeport, N.Y.: Books for Libraries.

Murray, James P. *To Find an Image: Black Films from Uncle Tom to Super Fly.* Indianapolis: Bobbs-Merrill, 1974.

N

Nelson, Hart M., Raytha L. Yokley, and Anne K. Nelson (eds.). *The Black Church in America.* New York: Basic Books, 1971.

Nicholas, Denise. *Denise Nicholas/Beauty Book. A Complete Guide to Good Grooming and Feminine Beauty from Head to Toe.* New York: Cornerstone Library, 1971.

Noble, Peter. *The Negro in Films.* New York: Arno Press, 1971.

O

Odegaard, Charles E. *Minorities in Medicine: From Receptive Passivity to Positive Action—1966–76. Report of a Study.* New York: Josiah Macy, Jr. Foundation, 1979.

Oliver, Paul. *Savannah Syncopaters: African Retentions in the Blues.* New York: Stein and Day.

Osei, G. K. *Caribbean Women: Their History and Habits.* New York: University Place Book Shop, 1979.

Owens, J. Garfield. *All God's Chillun: Meditations on Negro Spirituals.* Nashville: Abingdon Press, 1971.

P

Pallister, Jan. *The Bruised Reed: Black Songs from the Latin Tongues.* New York: Librairie de France, 1978.

Parris, Guichard and Lester Brooks. *Blacks in the City: A History of the National Urban League.* Boston: Little, Brown.

Patterson, Willis C. (comp.). *Anthology of Art Songs by Black American Composers.* Melville, N.Y.: Edward B. Marks Music Corp., 1979.

Peters, Margaret. *The Ebony Book of Black Achievement.* Chicago: Johnson Publishing Co.

Piro, Richard. *Black Fiddler.* New York: William Morrow.

Porter, Kenneth W. *The Negro on the American Frontier.* New York: Arno Press, 1971.

Pyramid Films Catalog. Santa Monica, Cal., 1978.

R

Rivelli, Pauline and Robert Levin. *The Black Giants.* New York: World Publishing Co., 1971.

Roach, Hildred. *Black American Music, Past and Present.* Boston: Crescendo Publishing Co., 1975.

Roberts, Hermese E. *The Third Ear: A Black Glossary.* New York: English Language Institute, 1971.

Romare, Bearden: 1970–1980. Mint Museum, Department of Art. Charlotte, N.C., 1981.

Rowan, Carl T. *Just Between Us Blacks.* New York: Random House, 1975.

Rublowsky, John. *Black Music in America.* New York: Basic Books, 1971.

S

Sale, R. T. *The Blackstone Rangers: A Reporter's Account of Time Spent on Chicago's South Side.* New York: Random House.

Sample, Johnny (with Fred J. Hamilton and Sonny Schwartz). *Confessions of a Dirty Ballplayer.* Introduction by Joe Namath. New York: Dial Press, 1971.

Schafer, William J. and Johannes Riedel. *The Art of Ragtime: Form and Meaning of an Original Black American Art.* Baton Rouge: Louisiana State University Press, 1974.

Schiffman, Jack. *Uptown: The Story of Harlem's Apollo Theatre.* Foreword by Flip Wilson. New York: Cowles Book Co., 1971.

Schoener, Allon (ed.). *Harlem on My Mind: Cultural Capital of Black America 1900–1978.* New York: Dell, 1980.

Sidran, Ben. *Black Talk: How the Music of Black America Created a Radical Alternative to the Values of Western Literary Tradition.* New York: Holt, Rinehart and Winston, 1971.

Sims, Naomi. *How to be a Top Model.* New York: Doubleday, 1981.

Sirkis, Nancy. *One Family.* Introduction by Julian Bond. Boston: Little, Brown, 1971.

Smith, Anthony. *The Geopolitics of Information: How Western Culture Dominates the World.* New York: Oxford University Press, 1981.

Speed, Carol. *Inside Black Hollywood.* Los Angeles: Holloway House, 1981.

Squires, Gregory D. *Affirmative Action: A Guide for the Perplexed.* East Lansing: Institute for Community Development and Services, Michigan State University, 1978.

Starke, Catherine Juanita. *Black Portraiture in American Fiction: Stock Characters, Archetypes and Individuals.* New York: Basic Books, 1971.

Still, William Grant, Robert B. Haas, Paul H. Slattery, et. al. *William Grant Still and the Fusion of Cultures in American Music.* Los Angeles: Black Sparrow Press, 1972.

The Story of Civil Rights as Seen by the Black Church in America. Elgin, Ill.: David C. Cook Publishing Co., 1972.

T

Thomas, Valerie M. *Accent African: Traditional and Contemporary Hair Styles for the Black Woman.* New York: COL-BOB Associates, 1975.

Thompson, Robert Farris. *African Art in Motion: Icon and Art in the Collection of Katherine Coryton White.* Berkeley: University of California Press, 1980.

Thurman, Howard. *The Search for Common Ground.* New York: Harper & Row, 1971.

Tirro, Frank. *Jazz: A History.* New York: W. W. Norton, 1982.

Tomorrow's Woman. Washington, D.C.: National Council of Negro Women, Inc., 1972.

Turner, Patricia. *Afro-American Singers: An Index and Preliminary Discography of Long-Playing Recordings of Opera, Choral Music and Song.* Autumn 1978 Supplement. Minneapolis.

V

Vaughan, Ruby Carmichael. *The New Breed: Getting to Know You.* Smithtown, N.Y.: Exposition Press, 1981.

Viorst, Milton. *Fire in the Streets: America in the 1960s.* New York: Simon and Schuster, 1981.

W

Walden, Barbara with Vicki Lindner. *Easy Glamour: The Black Woman's Definitive Guide to Beauty and Style.* New York: William Morrow, 1981.

Wallenstein, Steve and George Fisher with Jacob Brackman. *Backfire: Ordeal at Cornell.* New York: Chelsea House Publishers, 1971.

Walton, Ortiz M. *Music: Black, White & Blue.* New York: William Morrow, 1973.

Washington, M. Bunch. *The Art of Romare Bearden: The Prevalence of Ritual.* New York: Harry N. Abrams, 1974.

Weinberg, Kenneth G. *A Man's Home, A Man's Castle.* New York: McCall Publishing Co., 1971.

Weisberg, Harold. *Frame-Up: The Martin Luther King/James Earl Ray Case.* New York: Outerbridge & Dienstfrey.

Who's Who Among Black Americans 1980–1981. Edited by William C. Matney, 3202 Doolittle Dr., Northbrook, Ill. 60062, 1981.

Williams, Ethel L. and Clifton L. Brown (comps.). *Afro-American Religious Studies: A Comprehensive Bibliography with Location in American Libraries.* Metuchen, N.J.: Scarecrow Press, 1972.

Williams, Loretta J. *Black Freemasonry and Middle-Class Realities.* Columbia: University of Missouri Press, 1981.

Williams, Roger W. *The Bond: An American Family.* New York: Atheneum, 1971.

Wilmer, Valerie. *As Serious as Your Life: The Story of the New Jazz.* Westport, Conn.: Lawrence Hill, 1981.

The Wiz Book. Introduction by Sidney Lumet. New York: Berkley Publishing Corp., 1979.

Wolseley, Roland E. *The Black Press, U.S.A.* Ames: Iowa State University Press, 1971.

Z

Ziegenhals, Walter E. *Urban Churches in Transition.* New York: Pilgrim Press, 1979.

History

Books listed here are either specifically about history or have a general historical perspective.

A

Afro-American Encyclopedia. Miami: Educational Book Publishers, 10 vols., 1974.

Allen, James Egert. *Black History—Past and Present.* New York: Exposition Press, 1972.

Alvarez, Joseph A. *From Reconstruction to Revolution: The Blacks' Struggle for Equality.* New York: Atheneum, 1971.

Anderson, Osborne P. *A Voice from Harper's Ferry.* New York: World View Publishers, 1975.

Aptheker, Herbert. *Afro-American History: The Modern Era.* New York: Citadel Press, 1971.

———. (ed.). *A Documentary History of the Negro People in the United States 1910–1932.* Secaucus, N.J.: Citadel Press, 1973.

——— (ed.). *A Documentary History of the Negro People in the United States 1932–1945.* Secaucus, N.J.: Citadel Press, 1975.

Athearn, Robert G. *In Search of Canaan: Black Migration to Kansas 1879–80.* Lawrence: The Regents Press of Kansas, 1980.

Avery, Burniece. *Walk Quietly Through the Night and Cry Softly.* Detroit: Balamp Publishing, 1977.

B

Banner, Warren M. *Research to Answer What Blacks Ought to Have.* Ardmore, Pa.: Dorrance, 1978.

Baraka, Imamu Amiri (ed.). *African Congress: A Documentary of the First Modern Pan-African Congress.* New York: William Morrow, 1972.

Bigsby, C. W. E. *The Second Black Renaissance: Essays in Black Literature.* Westport, Conn.: Greenwood Press, 1980.

Black Contributions to Science and Energy Technology. Washington, D.C.: U.S. Department of Energy, 1979.

Blackwood, Paul E. *How and Why Wonder Book of—The Civil War.* New York: U.S. Office of Education/Grosset and Dunlap, 1980.

Boggs, James and Grace Lee. *Revolution and Evolution in the Twentieth Century.* New York: Monthly Review Press, 1974.

Bracey, Jr., John H., August Meier, and Elliott Rudwick (eds.). *The Afro-Americans: Selected Documents.* Boston: Allyn and Bacon, 1972.

Brawley, James P. *Two Centuries of Methodist Concern: Bondage, Freedom and Education of Black People.* Atlanta: Clark College, 1974.

Breen, T. H. and Stephen Innes. *Myne Owne Ground: Race and Freedom on Virginia's Eastern Shore, 1640–1676.* New York: Oxford University Press, 1980.

Brown, Letitia Woods. *Free Negroes in the District of Columbia 1790–1846.* New York: Oxford University Press, 1972.

Buah, F. K. *A New History for Schools and Colleges.* New York: Macmillan.

C

Carlisle, Rodney P. *Prologue to Liberation: A History of Black People in America.* New York: Appleton-Century-Crofts, 1972.

Carroll, John M. (ed.). *The Black Military Experience in the American West.* New York: Liveright Publishing Corp.

Cohn, Michael and Michael K. H. Platzer. *Black Men of the Sea.* New York: Dodd, Mead, 1979.

Countries of the World and Their Leaders Yearbook 1980. Detroit: Gale Research, 1980.

Craig, E. Quita. *Black Drama of the Federal Theatre Era: Beyond the Formal Horizons.* Amherst: University of Massachusetts Press, 1980.

Curley, Edmund F. *Crispus Attucks: The First to Die.* Philadelphia: Dorrance, 1975.

D

David, Jay and Elaine Crane (eds.). *The Black Soldier from the American Revolution to Vietnam.* New York: William Morrow.

Dillard, J. L. *Black Names.* The Hague, Netherlands: Mouton, 1980.

Directory of African Studies in the United States, 1973. Waltham, Mass.: African Studies Association, Brandeis University, 1973.

Dorn, Edwin. *Rules and Racial Equality.* New Haven, Conn.: Yale University Press, 1980.

DuBois, W. E. B. *The Correspondence of W. E. B. DuBois.* Edited by Herbert Aptheker. Amherst: University of Massachusetts Press, 1973.

E

Ebony Pictorial History of Black America: Vol. I—African Past to the Civil War; Vol. II—Reconstruction to Supreme Court Decision 1954; Vol. III—Civil Rights Movement to Black Revolution; Vol. IV— The 1973 Year Book. Chicago: Johnson Publishing Co., 1971 and 1975.

Ehrlich, Walter. *They Have No Rights: Dred Scott's Struggle for Freedom.* Westport, Conn.: Greenwood Press, 1980.

Emery, Lynne Fauley. *Black Dance in the United States from 1619 to 1970.* Palo Alto, Cal.: National Press Books, 1972.

Encyclopedia of the Negro in Africa and America. St. Clair Shores, Mich.: Negro History Press, 1973.

Encyclopedia of the Third World, George Thomas Kurian (ed.). New York: Facts on File, 1979.

Engs, Robert Francis. *Freedom's First Generation: Black Hampton, Virginia, 1861–1890.* Philadelphia: University of Pennsylvania Press, 1980.

Epstein, Dena J. *Sinful Tunes and Spirituals: Black Folk Music to the Civil War.* Urbana: University of Illinois Press, 1980.

F

Faggett, Harry Lee. *Black and Other Minorities in Shakespeare's England.* Prairie View, Tex.: Prairie View A&M, 1973.

Farley, Reynolds. *Growth of the Black Population.* Chicago: Markham Publishing Co., 1972.

Fredo, Michael W. *They Was Just Niggers.* Ontario, Cal.: Brasch and Brasch Publishers, 1980.

Fehrenbacher, Don E. *The Dred Scott Case: Its Significance in American Law and Politics.* New York: Oxford University Press, 1979.

Fife, Christopher (ed.). *African Studies Since 1945: A Tribute to Basil Davidson.* New York: Holmes & Meier, 1980.

Fleming, Thomas. *Give Me Liberty: Black Valor in the Revolutionary War.* New York: Scholastic Book Services, 1973.

Foner, Jack. *Blacks and the Military in American History: A New Perspective.* New York: Praeger, 1974.

Foner, Philip S. *American Socialism and Black Americans: From the Age of Jackson to World War II.* Westport, Conn.: Greenwood Press, 1978.

———. *Blacks in the American Revolution.* Westport, Conn.: Greenwood Press, 1980.

———. *Essays in Afro-American History.* Philadelphia: Temple, 1979.

——— (ed.). *W. E. B. DuBois Speaks: Speeches and Addresses, 1890–1919* (2 vols.). New York: Pathfinder Press, 1971.

——— and R. Lewis (eds.). *The Black Worker. Vol. I: From Colonial Times to 1869; Vol. II: During the Era of the National Labor Union.* Philadelphia: Temple University Press, 1978.

Foster, William Z. *The Negro People in American History.* New York: International Publishers, 1973.

Fowler, Arlen L. *The Black Infantry in the West 1869–1891.* Westport, Conn.: Greenwood Publishing Corp.

Frank, Gerold. *An American Death: The True Story of the Assassination of Dr. Martin Luther King, Jr., and the Greatest Manhunt of Our Time.* New York: Doubleday, 1972.

Fredrickson, George M. *The Black Image in the White Mind: The Debate on Afro-American Character and Destiny, 1817–1914.* New York: Harper & Row, 1971.

G

Garrett, Romeo B. *Famous First Facts About Negroes.* New York: Arno Press, 1972.

Garrison, William Lloyd. *The Letters of William Lloyd Garrison,* Vol. II. *A House Dividing Against Itself, 1836–1840.* Edited by Louis Ruchames. Cambridge, Mass.: Harvard University Press.

George, Carol V. R. *Segregated Sabbaths: Richard Allen and the Emergence of Independent Black Churches, 1760–1840.* New York: Oxford University Press, 1973.

Gerber, David A. *Black Ohio and the Color Line, 1860–1915.* Urbana: University of Illinois Press, 1977.

Gerteis, Louis S. *From Contraband to Freedman: Federal Policy toward Southern Blacks, 1861–1865.* Westport, Conn.: Greenwood Press, 1974.

Golden, James L. and Richard D. Rieke (comps.). *The Rhetoric of Black Americans.* Columbus, Ohio: Charles E. Merrill, 1975.

Goldman, Peter. *The Death and Life of Malcolm X.* New York: Harper & Row, 1980.

Greene, Robert Ewell. *Black Defenders of America, 1775–1973: A Reference and Pictorial History.* Chicago: Johnson Publishing Co., 1974.

Groh, George W. *The Black Migration: The Journey to Urban America.* New York: Weybright and Talley, 1972.

Grosso, Sonny and John Devaney. *Murder at the Harlem Mosque.* New York: Crown Publishers, 1978.

H

Hamilton, Charles V. *The Black Preacher in America.* New York: William Morrow, 1973.

Harding, Vincent. *The Other American Revolution: A Brief History of the Struggle for Black Freedom.* Atlanta: Published by the Center for Afro-American Studies, Atlanta University and the Institute of the Black World, 1980.

Harlan, Louis R. (ed.). *The Booker T. Washington Papers.* Urbana: University of Illinois Press, 1974.

Harley, Sharon and Rosalyn Terborg-Penn (eds.). *The Afro-American Woman: Struggles and Images.* Port Washington, N.Y.: Kennikat Press, 1979.

Hayden, Robert C. *Eight Black American Inventors.* Reading, Mass.: Addison-Wesley, 1973.

Hedgeman, Anna Arnold. *The Gift of Chaos.* New York: Oxford University Press, 1977.

Higginbotham, Jr., A. Leon. *In the Matter of Color: Race & the American Legal Process, the Colonial Period.* New York: Oxford University Press, 1978.

Higgins, Jr., Chester (photos) and Orde Coombs (text). *Some Time Ago: A Historical Portrait of Black Americans, 1850–1950.* New York: Anchor/Doubleday, 1981.

Higham, John (ed.). *Ethnic Leadership in America.* Baltimore: Johns Hopkins University Press, 1980.

Hine, Darlene Clark. *Black Victory: The Rise and Fall of the White Primary in Texas.* Millwood, N.Y.: KTO Press, 1980.

Hodges, Norman E. W. *Breaking the Chains of Bondage: Black History from Its Origin in Africa to the Present.* New York: Simon and Schuster, 1973.

Holt, Delores L. and Langley Newman. *Black History Playing Card Deck.* New York: U.S. Games Systems, 1980.

Hornsby, Jr., Alton. *The Black Almanac: From Involuntary Servitude (1619–1860) to the Age of Disillusionment (1964–1971).* Woodbury, N.Y.: Barron's Educational Series, 1972.

———, (ed.). *In the Cage: Eyewitness Accounts of the Freed Negro in Southern Society 1877–1929.* Chicago: Quadrangle Books, 1971.

Huggins, Nathan I., Martin Kilson, and Daniel M. Fox (eds.). *Key Issues in the Afro-American Experience.* New York: Harcourt Brace Jovanovich.

Hughes, Langston, Milton Meltzer, and C. Eric Lincoln. *A Pictorial History of Blackamericans.* New York: Crown Publishers, 1974.

Hyman, Harold M. *A More Perfect Union: The Impact of the Civil War and Reconstruction on the Constitution.* New York: Knopf, 1973.

I

Irvine, Keith. *The Rise of the Colored Races.* New York: W. W. Norton.

J

Jackson, Florence. *The Black Man in America 1905–1932.* New York: Franklin Watts, 1974.

———. *The Black Man in America 1791–1861.* New York: Franklin Watts, 1971.

Jacobs, Paul and Saul Landau with Eve Pell. *To Serve the Devil.* Vol. I: *Natives and Slaves;* Vol. II: *Colonials and Sojourners.* New York: Random House, 1971.

Jacobs, Wilbur R. *Dispossessing the American Indian: Indians and Whites on the Colonial Frontier.* New York: Scribner, 1972.

Johnson, Abby Arthur and Ronald Maberry Johnson. *Propaganda and Aesthetics: The Literary Politics of Afro-American Magazines in the Twentieth Century.* Amherst: University of Massachusetts Press, 1980.

Johnson, Jesse J. *A Pictorial History of Black Servicemen [Air Force, Army, Navy, Marines] 1619–1970—Missing Pages in United States History.* The Author, Hampton, Va., 1972.

Jones, Bessie and Bess Lomax Hawes. *Step It Down: Games, Plays, Songs, and Stories from the Afro-American Heritage.* New York: Harper & Row, 1972.

K

Kailin, Clarence S. *Black Chronicle: An American History Textbook Supplement.* Madison: Wisconsin Dept. of Public Instruction, 1974.

Kaplan, Sidney. *The Black Presence in the Era of the American Revolution, 1770–1800.* Washington, D.C.: National Portrait Gallery, Smithsonian Institution, 1973.

Katz, William Loren. *The Black West: A Documentary and Pictorial History.* New York: Doubleday, 1971.

Katzman, David M. *Before the Ghetto: Black Detroit in the Nineteenth Century.* Urbana: University of Illinois Press, 1972.

Katznelson, Ira. *Black Men, White Cities: Race, Politics, and Migration in the United States, 1900–1930, and Britain, 1948–1968.* New York: Oxford University Press, 1973.

Keegan, Frank L. *Blacktown, U.S.A.* Boston: Little, Brown, 1971.

Kilian, Crawford. *Go Do Some Great Thing: The Black Pioneers of British Columbia.* Seattle: University of Washington Press, 1979.

Kirby, John B. *Black Americans in the Roosevelt Era: Liberalism and Race.* Knoxville: University of Tennessee Press, 1981.

Klinkowitz, Jerome (ed.). *The Diaries of Willard Motley.* Ames: Iowa State University Press, 1979.

Kohn, Bernice. *The Amistad Mutiny.* New York: McCall Publishing Co., 1971.

Kolchin, Peter. *First Freedom: The Responses of Alabama's Blacks to Emancipation and Reconstruction.* Westport, Conn.: Greenwood Press, 1973.

L

La Brie III, Henry G. *A Survey of Black Newspapers in America.* Kennebunkport, Ma.: Mercer House Press, 1980.

Lacy, Dan. *The White Use of Blacks in America.* New York: Atheneum.

Ladner, Joyce A. *Tomorrow's Tomorrow: The Black Woman.* New York: Doubleday, 1971.

Lerner, Gerda. *The Majority Finds Its Past: Placing Women in History.* New York: Oxford University Press, 1980.

——— (ed.). *Black Women in White America: A Documentary History.* New York: Pantheon Books, 1972.

Levilain, Guy Viet. *Cultural Identity, Negritude and Decolonization: The Haitian Situation in the Light of the Socialist Humanism of Jacques Roumain and Rene Depestre.* New York: American Institute for Marxist Studies, 1978.

Lightfoot, Claude M. *Human Rights U.S. Style: From Colonial Times Through the New Deal.* New York: International Publishers, 1978.

Littlefield, Jr., Daniel F. *The Cherokee Freedmen: From Emancipation to American Citizenship.* Westport, Conn.: Greenwood Press, 1979.

Locating Information by and about Afro-Americans, Compiled by Rita Sparks and DeWitt S. Dykes. Rochester, Mich.: Oakland University Libraries, 1977.

Lowenberg, Bert James and Ruth Bogin (eds.). *Black Women in Nineteenth-Century American Life: Their Words, Their Thoughts, Their Feelings.* University Park: Pennsylvania State University Press, 1977.

Lynch, Hollis R. *The Black Urban Condition: A Documentary History, 1866–1971.* New York: Thomas Y. Crowell, 1973.

M

Maynard, Aubre de L. *Surgeons to the Poor: The Harlem Hospital Story.* New York: Appleton-Century-Crofts/Medical/Nursing Publishers, 1978.

McBride, David. *The Afro-American in Pennsylvania: A Critical Guide to Sources in the Pennsylvania State Archives.* Harrisburg: Pennsylvania Historical and Museum Commission, 1980.

McFarlin, Annjennette Sophie. *Black Congressional Reconstruction Orators and Their Orations 1869–1879.* Metuchen, N.J.: Scarecrow Press, 1977.

McKay, Claude. *The Negroes in America.* Edited by Alan L. McLeod. Translated by Robert J. Winter. Port Washington, N.Y.: Kennikat Press, 1980.

McManus, Edgar J. *Black Bondage in the North.* Syracuse, N.Y.: Syracuse University Press, 1973.

Meier, August and Elliott Rudwick. *Black Detroit and the Rise of the UAW.* New York: Oxford University Press, 1980.

Meier, Matt S. and Rivera Meier. *The Chicanos: A History of Mexican Americans.* New York: Hill and Wang, 1972.

Meyer, Howard N. *The Amendment that Refused to Die.* Radnor, Pa.: Chilton Book Co., 1973.

Mezu, S. O. and Ram Desai (eds.). *Black Leaders of the Centuries.* Buffalo, N.Y.: Black Academy Press, 1972.

Miller, Donald L. *An Album of Black Americans in the Armed Forces.* New York: Franklin Watts, 1971.

Miller, Marc S. (ed.). *Working Lives: The "Southern Exposure" History of Labor in the South.* New York: Pantheon Books, 1981.

Moquin, Wayne. *Great Documents in American Indian History.* New York: Praeger, 1971.

——— and Charles Van Doren (eds.). *A Documentary History of the Mexican Americans.* New York: Praeger, 1971.

Morris, James. *The Preachers.* New York: St. Martin's Press, 1973.

Moses, Wilson Jeremiah. *The Golden Age of Black Nationalism, 1850–1925.* Hamden, Conn.: Shoe String Press, 1978.

Moss, Jr., Alfred A. *The American Negro Academy: Voice of the Talented Tenth.* Baton Rouge: Louisiana State University Press, 1981.

Mullen, Robert W. *Blacks in America's Wars: The Shift in Attitudes from the Revolutionary War to Vietnam.* New York: Pathfinder Press, 1974.

Muray, Nickolas. *Muray's Celebrity Portraits of the Twenties and Thirties: 135 Photographs by Nickolas Muray.* New York: Dover Publications, 1978.

N

Newby, I. A. *Black Carolinians: A History of Blacks in South Carolina from 1895 to 1968.* Columbia: University of South Carolina Press, 1973.

Newman, Richard. *Black Index: Afro-Americans in Selected Periodicals 1907–1949.* New York: Garland, 1981.

Nkrumah, Kwame. *Revolutionary Path.* New York: International Publishers, 1973.

Noble, Jeanne. *Beautiful, Also, Are the Souls of My Black Sisters: A History of the Black Woman in America.* Englewood Cliffs, N.J.: Prentice-Hall, 1979.

Nunez, Benjamin. *Dictionary of Afro-Latin American Civilization.* Westport, Conn.: Greenwood Press and the African Bibliographic Center, 1981.

O

Oakley, Giles. *The Devil's Music: A History of the Blues.* New York: Taplinger Publishing Co., 1977.

Ortiz, Roxanne Dunbar. *Roots of Resistance: Land Tenure in New Mexico, 1680–1980.* Los Angeles: Chicano Studies Research Center, University of California, 1981.

Osei, G. K. *20 Interesting Facts About the Caribbean Peoples.* New York: Alkebu-Lan Books, 1977.

P

Painter, Nell Irvin. *The Narrative of Hosea Hudson: His Life as a Negro Communist in the South.* Cambridge, Mass.: Harvard University Press, 1980.

Peavy, Charles D. *Afro-American Literature and Culture since World War II: A Guide to Information Sources.* Detroit: Gale Research Co., 1981.

Pennsylvania Heritage, Vol. 4, No. 1, Dec. 1977. Harrisburg, Pa.: Pennsylvania Historical and Museum Commission, 1978.

Perdue, Robert E. *The Negro in Savannah, 1865–1900.* Jericho, N.Y.: Exposition Press, 1973.

Perry, Lewis. *Radical Abolitionism: Anarchy and the Government of God in Antislavery Thought.* Ithaca, N.Y.: Cornell University Press, 1973.

Pre-Civil War Black History Series #1. Cleveland: New Day Press, Case Western Reserve University, 1973.

Preiswerk, Roy and Dominique Perrot. *Ethnocentrism and History: Africa, Asia and Indian America in Western Textbooks.* New York: Nok Publishers, 1981.

Q

Quarles, Benjamin. *Black History's Diversified Clientele.* The Second Annual Rayford W. Logan Lecture of the Department of History. Washington, D.C.: Howard University, 1971.

———. *The Negro in the American Revolution.* New York: W. W. Norton, 1973.

R

Rice, Lawrence D. *The Negro in Texas, 1894–1900.* Baton Rouge: Louisiana State University Press, 1972.

Richards, Leonard L. *"Gentlemen of Property and Standing": Anti-Abolition Mobs in Jacksonian America.* New York: Oxford University Press, 1971.

Richardson, Jr., Fredrick Douglas. *The Genesis and Exodus of NOW.* New York: Vantage Press, 1979.

Roach, Hildred. *Black American Music: Past and Present.* Boston: Crescendo Publishers, 1974.

Roucek, Joseph S. and Thomas Kiernan (eds.). *The Negro Impact on Western Civilization.* New York: Philosophical Library, 1972.

Ross, B. Joyce. *J. E. Spingarn and the Rise of the NAACP.* New York: Atheneum, 1972.

Ross, Jack C. and Raymond H. Wheeler. *Black Belonging: A Study of the Social Correlates of Work Relations among Negroes.* Westport, Conn.: Greenwood Publishing Corp., 1971.

Rossi, Peter H. (ed.). *Ghetto Revolts.* Chicago: Aldine, 1971.

S

Salter, Jr., John R. *Jackson, Mississippi: An American Chronicle of Struggle and Schism.* Hicksville, N.Y.: Exposition Press, 1979.

Salvador, George. *The Black Yankee.* Chicago: William S. Sullwold Publishers, 1973.

Shick, Tom W. *Behold the Promised Land: A History of Afro-American Settler Society in Nineteenth-Century Liberia.* Baltimore: Johns Hopkins Press, 1981.

Simmons, Charles W. and Harry W. Morris (eds.). *Afro-American History.* Columbus, Ohio: Charles E. Merrill Publishing Co., 1974.

Simon, George T., et al. *The Best of the Music Makers.* New York: Doubleday, 1981.

Sitkoff, Harvard. *A New Deal for Blacks: The Emergence of Civil Rights as a National Issue. Vol. I: The Depression Decade.* New York: Oxford University Press, 1979.

———. *The Struggle for Black Equality, 1954–1980.* New York: Farrar, Straus & Giroux, 1981.

Sloan, Irving. *The Negro in Modern American History Textbooks.* Washington, D.C.: American Federation of Teachers, 1972.

——— (ed.). *The Blacks in America, 1492–1977: A Chronology & Fact Book.* Dobbs Ferry, N.Y.: 1979.

Smallwood, James M. *Time of Hope, Time of Despair: Black Texans During Reconstruction.* Port Washington, N.Y.: Kennikat Press, 1981.

Smith, Dwight L. (ed.). *Afro-American History: A Bibliography.* Santa Barbara, Cal.: American Bibliographical Center, 1975.

Smith, Jessie Carney. *Black Academic Libraries and Research Collections: An Historical Survey.* Westport, Conn.: Greenwood Press, 1978.

Smith, Page. *The Shaping of America—A People's History of the Young Republic.* New York: McGraw-Hill, 1981.

Sochen, June (ed.). *The Black Man and the American Dream: Negro Aspirations in America 1900–1930.* Chicago: Quadrangle, 1971.

The Social and Economic Status of the Black Population in the United States, 1971. Current Population Reports, Series P-23, No. 42; iv. Washington, D.C.: U.S. Dept. of Commerce, Social and Economic Statistics Administration, Bureau of the Census, 1971.

The Social and Economic Status of the Black Population in the United States, 1972. Current Population Reports; iv. Washington, D.C.: U.S. Dept. of Commerce, Bureau of the Census, 1973.

Sollors, Werner (ed.). *A Bibliographic Guide to Afro-American Studies.* Berlin: John F. Kennedy-Institute for North American Studies, Free University, 1973.

Southall, Geneva H. *Blind Tom: The Post-Civil War Enslavement of a Black Musical Genius.* Minneapolis: Challenge Productions, 1981.

Southern, Eileen. *The Music of Black Americans: A History.* New York: W. W. Norton, 1971.

Sowell, Thomas. *Ethnic America: A History.* New York: Basic Books, 1981.

Sterling, Dorothy. *The Making of an Afro-American: Martin Robinson Delany, 1812–1885.* New York: Doubleday, 1971.

———. (ed.). *Speak Out in Thunder Tones: Letters and Other Writings by Black Northerners, 1787–1865.* New York: Doubleday.

Stevenson, Janet. *The School Segregation Cases.* New York: Franklin Watts.

Stuckey, Sterling (ed.). *The Ideological Origins of Black Nationalism.* Boston: Beacon Press, 1972.

Synnestvedt, Sig. *The White Response to Black Emancipation.* New York: Macmillan, 1973.

T

Terrill, Tom E. and Jerrold Hirsch (eds.). *Such as Us: Southern Voices of the Thirties.* Chapel Hill: University of North Carolina Press, 1978.

Thompson, Mindy. *The National Negro Labor Council: A History.* New York: American Institute for Marxist Studies, 1978.

Thorpe, Earl E. *Black Historians: A Critique.* New York: William Morrow, 1971.

Toll, Robert C. *Blacking Up: The Minstrel Show in Nineteenth-Century America.* New York: Oxford University Press, 1975.

Townsend, Linda and Dupree Davenport. *The History of Blacks in the Coast Guard from 1790.* Washington, D.C.: Department of Transportation, 1977.

Trelease, Allen W. *White Terror: The Ku Klux Klan Conspiracy and Southern Reconstruction.* New York: Harper & Row, 1971.

Tuttle, Jr., William M. *Race Riot: Chicago in the Red Summer of 1919.* New York: Atheneum, 1971.

V

Van Der Slik, Jack R. (ed.). *Black Conflict with White America: A Reader in Social and Political Analysis.* Columbus, Ohio: Charles E. Merrill Publishing Co., 1973.

Van Sertima, Ivan. *They Came Before Columbus (The African Presence in Ancient America).* New York: Random House, 1977.

W

Waldron, Edward E. *Walter White and the Harlem Renaissance.* Port Washington, N.Y.: Kennikat Press, 1979.

Walker, Clarence E. *A Rock in a Weary Land: The African Methodist Episcopal Church During the Civil War and Reconstruction.* Baton Rouge: Louisiana State University Press, 1981.

Walker, Peter. *Moral Choices: Memory, Desire, and Imagination in Nineteenth-Century American Abolition.* Baton Rouge: Louisiana State University Press, 1979.

Wallace, Phyllis A., with the assistance of Linda Datcher and Julianne Malveaux. *Black Women in the Labor Force.* Cambridge: Massachusetts Institute of Technology Press, 1981.

Weaver, John D. *The Brownsville Raid.* New York: W. W. Norton, 1971.

Weston, Rubin F. *Racism in U.S. Imperialism: The Influence of Racial Assumptions on American Foreign Policy, 1893–1946.* Columbia: University of South Carolina Press.

Whitlow, Roger. *Black American Literature: A Critical History.* Chicago: Nelson-Hall Publishers, 1978.

Williams, Chancellor. *The Destruction of Black Civilization: Great Issues of a Race from 4500 B.C. to 2000 A.D.* Dubuque, Iowa: Kendall/Hunt Publishing Co.

Willliams, David J. *Eleanor Roosevelt's Niggers.* Coral Reef, Fla.: Neptune, 1978.

Williams, Jamye and Mcdonald. *The Negro Speaks: The Rhetoric of Contemporary Black Leaders.* New York: Noble and Noble.

Winks, Robin. *The Blacks in Canada: A History.* New Haven, Conn.: Yale University Press, 1971.

Winston, Henry. *Africa's Struggle for Freedom, the USA and the USSR: A Selection of Political Analyses, Assembled and with an Introduction.* New York: New Outlook Publishers, 1973.

Wood, Peter H. *Black Majority: Negroes in Colonial South Carolina from 1670 through the Stono Rebellion.* New York: Knopf, 1975.

Y

Young, Henry J. *Major Black Religious Leaders 1755–1940.* Nashville: Abingdon Press, 1981.

———. *Major Black Religious Leaders Since 1940.* Nashville: Abingdon Press, 1981.

Z

Zangrando, Robert L. *The NAACP Crusade Against Lynching 1909–1950.* Philadelphia: Temple University Press, 1981.

Africa

A

Adelcye, R. A. *Power and Diplomacy in Northern Nigeria 1804–1906.* New York: Humanities Press, 1972.

Africa Research Group. *Race to Power: The Struggle for Southern Africa.* New York: Anchor Press/Doubleday, 1974.

Africa Seen by American Negro Scholars. Edited by the staff of The American Society of African Culture, New York.

Africa '71: A Reference Volume on the African Continent. By the editorial staff of *Jeune Afrique* magazine. New York: Africana Publishing Corp., 1972.

Against Racism, Apartheid and Colonialism: Documents Published by the GDR, 1949–1977. Berlin: Staatsverlag of GDR, 1979.

Ajayi, J. F. A. and Michael Crowder (eds.). *History of West Africa.* Vol. I. New York: Columbia University Press, 1974.

———, and Ian Espie (eds.). *A Thousand Years of West African History.* New York: Humanities Press, 1972.

Akintoye, S. A. *Revolution and Power Politics in Yorubaland 1840–1893: Ibadan Expansion and the Rise of Ekitiparapo.* New York: Humanities Press, 1972.

Alagoa, E. J. *Jaja of Opobo: The Slave Who Became a King.* London: Longman Group, Ltd.

Allen, Samuel W. (ed.). *Poems from Africa.* New York: Thomas Y. Crowell, 1973.

Anderson, Kaj B. *African Traditional Architecture: A Study of the Housing and Settlement Patterns of Rural Kenya.* New York: Oxford University Press, 1979.

Apple, Arnold. *Son of Guyana.* New York: Oxford University Press, 1973.

Armah, Ayi Kwei. *Two Thousand Seasons.* Chicago: Third World Press, 1980.

Arnold, Millard (ed.). *Steve Biko: Black Consciousness in South Africa.* New York: Random House, 1979.

Awoonor, Kofi and G. Adali-Mortty, (eds.). *Messages: Poems from Ghana.* New York: Humanities Press, 1972.

Ayandele, E. A., A. E. Afigbo, R. J. Gaxin, and J. D. Omer-Cooper. *The Growth of African Civilization, The Making of Modern Africa,* Vol. 2: *The Late 19th Century to the Present Day.* New York: Humanities Press, 1972.

B

Bain, Mildred and Ervin Lewis (eds.). Foreword by Alex Haley. *From Freedom to Freedom: African Roots in American Soil. Selected Readings Based on Roots: The Saga of an American Family.* Milwaukee: Purnell Reference Books, 1977.

Balandier, George, Jacques Maquet, et al. *Dictionary of Black African Civilization.* New York: Leon Amiel, Publisher, 1975.

Balima, Mildred G. (comp.). *Botswana, Lesotho and Swaziland: A Guide to Official Publications, 1868–1968.* Washington, D.C.: Library of Congress, 1972.

Banfield, Beryle. *Africa in the Curriculum: A Teacher's Guide.* New York: Edward W. Blyden Press, 1972.

Barrett, Leonard E. *Soul-Force: African Heritage in Afro-American Religion.* New York: Anchor/Doubleday, 1974.

———. *The Sun and the Drum: African Roots in Jamaican Folk Tradition.* Atlantic Highlands, N.J.: Humanities Press, 1977.

Bates, Robert H. *Unions, Parties and Political Development: A Study of Mineworkers in Zambia.* New Haven, Conn.: Yale University Press, 1972.

Beier, Ulli (ed.). *Political Spider: Stories from* Black Orpheus. New York: Africana Publishing Corp., 1972.

ben-Jochannan, Yosef. *Africa: Mother of Western Civilization.* New York: Alkebu-Lan Books.

———. *African Origins of the Major Western Religions.* New York: Alkebu-Lan Books.

Bennett, Norman R. *Africa and Europe.* New York: Africana Publishing Co., 1975.

Black Africa. New York: New York Times and Arno Press, 1973.

Blyden, Edward Wilmot. *Black Spokesman: Selected Published Writings of Edward Wilmot Blyden.* New York: Humanities Press, 1972.

Boahen, A. Adu. *Topics in West African History.* London: Longmans, Green, 1972.

Boone, Sylvia Ardyn. *West African Travels: A Guide to People & Places.* New York: Random House.

Bowser, Frederick P. *The African Slave in Colonial Peru, 1525–1650.* Stanford, Cal.: Stanford University Press, 1974.

Brooks, Lester. *Great Civilizations of Ancient Africa.* New York: Four Winds Press, 1972.

C

Cabral, Amilcar. *Cabrat on Nkrumah.* Newark, N.J.: Jihad Productions, 1973.

———. *Return to the Source: Selected Speeches by* Amilcar Cabral. New York: Monthly Review Press, 1975.

Carroll, David. *Chinua Achebe.* New York: Twayne Publishers, 1972.

Cartey, Wilfred (ed.). *Palaver: Modern African Writings.* New York: Thomas Nelson, 1972.

Chernoff, John Miller. *African Rhythm and African Sensibility.* Chicago: University of Chicago Press, 1980.

Chuks-orji, Ogonna. *Names from Africa: Their Origin, Meaning and Pronunciation.* Chicago: Johnson Publishing Co., 1972.

Clammer, David. *The Zulu War.* New York: St. Martin's Press, 1973.

Clarke, John Henrik (ed.). *Pan-Africanism and the Liberation of Southern Africa: A Tribute to W. E. B. DuBois.* New York: African Heritage Studies Association in cooperation with the United Nations Center Against Apartheid, 1974.

Clark, John Pepper. *Casualties: Poems 1966/68.* New York: Africana Publishing Corp., 1972.

Clark, Leon E. (ed.). *Through African Eyes: Cultures in Change.* New York: Praeger Publishers, 1972.

Clifford, Mary Louise. *The Land and People of Sierra Leone.* Philadelphia: Lippincott, 1974.

Collins, Harold R. *Amos Tutuola.* New York: Twayne Publishers, 1972.

Collins, Paul and Tom Lee. *Black Portrait of an African Journey.* Grand Rapids, Mich.: Wm. B. Eerdmans Publishing Co., 1972.

Collins, Robert O. (ed.). *Problems in African History.* Englewood Cliffs, N.J.: Prentice-Hall, 1972.

Contemporary African Art. New York: Africana Publishing Corp., 1972.

Cook, Mercer and Stephen E. Henderson. *The Militant Black Writer in Africa and the United States.* Madison: University of Wisconsin Press, 1972.

Cornwall, Barbara. *The Bush Rebels: A Personal Account of Black Revolt in Africa.* New York: Holt, Rinehart and Winston, 1972.

Courlander, Harold. *A Treasury of African Folklore: The Oral Literature, Traditions, Myths, Legends, Epics, Tales, Recollections, Wisdom, Sayings, and Humor of Africa.* New York: Crown Publishers, 1975.

———. *Tales of Yoruba Gods and Heroes.* New York: Crown Publishers, 1973.

Crane, Louise. *Ms. Africa: Profiles of Modern African Women.* Philadelphia: Lippincott, 1973.

Crowley, Daniel J. (ed.). *African Folklore in the New World.* Austin: University of Texas Press, 1979.

Curtin, Philip D. and others (eds.). *Africa Remembered: Narratives by West Africans from the Era of the Slave Trade.* Madison: University of Wisconsin Press, 1972.

D

Dadie, Bernard Bertin. *Climbie.* New York: Africana Publishing Corp., 1972.

Daggs, Elisa. *All Africa.* New York: Hastings House Publishers, 1972.

Damachi, Ukandi Godwin. *Nigerian Modernization: The Colonial Legacy.* New York: Third Press, 1972.

Daniels, George M. (ed.). *Drums of War: The Continuing Crisis in Rhodesia.* New York: Third Press, 1975.

Dathorne, O. R. *The Black Mind: A History of African Literature.* Minneapolis: University of Minnesota Press, 1975.

——— and Willfried Feuser (eds.). *Africa in Prose.* Baltimore: Penguin Books, 1972.

Davidson, Basil. *The African Genius: An Introduction to African Social and Cultural History.* Boston: Atlantic-Little Brown, 1972.

———. *Discovering Our African Heritage.* Boston: Ginn and Co., 1972.

———. *Let Freedom Come: Africa in Modern History.* Boston: Atlantic-Little Brown, 1979.

Davis, Lenwood G. *Construction Building and Planning in Selected African Cities.* P.O. Box 229, Monticello, Ill.: Council of Planning Librarians, 1977.

d'Azevedo, Warren L. (ed.). *The Traditional Artist in African Societies.* Bloomington: Indiana University Press, 1974.

Desai, R. and L. Szabo. *African Society and Culture.* New York: Africana Publishing Corp., 1972.

Desmond, Cosmas. *The Discarded People: An Account of African Resettlement in South Africa.* Baltimore: Penguin African Library, 1972.

Dietz, Betty Warner and Michael B. Olatunji. *Musical Instruments of Africa: Their Nature, Use and Place in the Life of a Deeply Musical People.* New York: John Day Co., 1972.

Diop, Cheikh Anta. *Black Africa: The Economic and Cultural Basis for a Federated State.* Westport, Conn.: Lawrence Hill, 1979.

———. *The Cultural Unity of Black Africa.* Chicago: Third World Press, 1978.

Diop, Cheikh Anta. *The African Origin of Civilization: Myth and Reality.* New York: Lawrence Hill, 1973.

———. *The Cultural Unity of Negro Africa.* Paris: Presence Africaine.

Du Bois, W. E. B. *The Negro.* New York: Oxford University Press, 1972.

Duerden, Dennis and Cosmo Pieterse. *African Writers Talking: A Collection of Interviews.* London: Heinemann Educational Books, 1972.

Dickie, John and Alan Rake. *Who's Who in Africa.* London: Wheatsheaf House.

Directory of African Studies in the United States, 1974–1975 (4th edition). Syracuse, N.Y.: African Studies Association, Syracuse University.

Drachler, Jacob (ed.). *Black Homeland/Black Diaspora: Cross Currents of the African Relationship.* Port Washington, N.Y.: Kennikat Press, 1975.

Dugan, James and Lawrence Lafore. *Days of Emperor and Clown: The Italo-Ethiopian War, 1935–36.* New York: Doubleday, 1973.

E

Ephson, Dr. I. S. *Gallery of Gold Coast Celebrities.* Accra, Ghana: Ilen Publications, Ltd.

F

Fage, J. D. (ed.). *Africa Discovers Her Past.* New York: Oxford University Press, 1972.

———, and Roland A. Oliver (eds.). *Papers in African Pre-History.* London: Cambridge University Press, 1972.

Fagg, William (intro.). *The Art of Central Africa: Sculpture and Tribal Masks.* New York: New American Library, 1972.

Feelings, Muriel. *Moja Means One: Swahili Counting Book.* New York: Dial Press, 1972.

Feinstein, Alan. *African Revolutionary: The Life and Times of Nigeria's Aminu Kano.* New York: Quadrangle/The New York Times Book Co., 1973.

Fife, Christopher (ed.). *African Studies Since 1945: A Tribute to Basil Davidson.* London: Longman, 1978.

First, Ruth. *The Barrel of a Gun.* London: Allen Lane, The Penguin Press, 1972.

Fraser, Douglas (ed.). *African Art as Philosophy.* New York: Interbook Inc., 1975.

Frobenius, Leo (ed.). *African Nights: Black Erotic Folk Tales.* New York: Herder and Herder, 1972.

Fuja, Abayomi. *Fourteen Hundred Cowries and Other African Tales.* New York: Washington Square Press, 1974.

Fuller, Hoyt W. *Journey to Africa.* Chicago: Third World Press, 1972.

———. *The Turning of the Wheel/or Are Black Men Serious.* Chicago: Institute of Positive Education, 1973.

Fyfe, Christopher. *Africanus Horton, 1835–1883: West African Scientist and Patriot.* New York: Oxford University Press, 1972.

G

Gardner, Cliff. *Black Caesar, Pirate.* Atlanta: Peachtree Publishers, 1981.

Geiss, Immanuel. *The Pan-African Movement, A History of Pan-Africanism in America, Europe and Africa.* New York: Africana Publishing Co., 1975.

Gerard, Albert S. *Four African Literatures: Xhosa, Sotho, Zulu, Amharic.* Berkeley: University of California Press, 1972.

Gerhart, Gail M. *Black Power in South Africa: The Evolution of an Ideology.* Berkeley: University of California Press, 1980.

Gibson, Richard. *African Liberation Movements: Contemporary Struggles against White Minority Rule.* New York: Oxford University Press, 1972.

Griffiths, Gareth. *A Double Exile: African and West Indian Writing Between Two Cultures.* Atlantic Highlands, N.J.: Humanities Press, 1979.

H

Handyside, Richard (ed. and trans.). *Revolution in Guinea: Selected Texts by Amilcar Cabral.* New York: Monthly Review Press, 1972.

Harris, Elizabeth. *Ghana: A Travel Guide.* Flushing, N.Y.: Aburi Press, 1977.

Harris, Joseph E. *Africans and their History.* New York: New American Library, 1973.

——— (ed.). *Africa and Africans as Seen by Classical Writers: The William Leo Hansberry African History Notebook,* Vol. II. Washington, D.C.: Howard University Press, 1979.

Harrison, Paul Carter. *The Drama of Nommo.* New York: Grove Press, 1973.

Hatch, John. *Tanzania: A Profile.* New York: Praeger, 1972.

Head, Bessie. *Maru.* New York: McCall Books, 1972.

Heinz, Hans-Joachim and Marshall Lee. *Namkwa: Life Among the Bushmen.* Boston: Houghton Mifflin, 1980.

Herdeck, Donald E. *African Authors: A Companion to Black African Writing 1300–1973.* Volume I. Detroit: Gale Research Co., 1974.

Hill, Adelaide C. and Martin Kilson. *Apropos of Africa: Afro-American Leaders and the Romance of Africa.* New York: Anchor/Doubleday and Humanities Press.

Hiskett, Mervyn. *The Sword of Truth: The Life and Times of the Shehu Usuman Dan Fodio.* New York: Oxford University Press, 1975.

Huet, Michel (photographer). *The Dance, Art and Ritual of Africa.* Translated by Jean-Louis Paudrat. New York: Pantheon Books, 1979.

Hull, Richard. *African Cities and Towns Before the European Conquest.* New York: W. W. Norton, 1977.

Hutchinson, Louise Daniel. *Out of Africa: From West African Kingdoms to Civilizations.* Washington, D. C.: Smithsonian Institution Press, 1981.

I

Ikime, Obaro and S. O. Osoba (eds.). *Tarikh,* Vol. 3, No. 4: *Independence Movements in Africa* (Part 1). New York: Humanities Press, 1972.

International Tribute to Frantz Fanon. Record of the Special Meeting of the United Nations Special Committee against Apartheid, 3 November 1978. New York: United Nations Centre Against Apartheid, 1981.

Irwin, Graham W. (ed.). *Africans Abroad: A Documentary History of the Black Diaspora in Asia, Latin America and the Caribbean During the Age of Slavery.* Irvington, N.Y.: Columbia University Press, 1977.

J

Jackson, John G. *Introduction to African Civilizations.* New York: University Books, 1972.

———. *Man, God and Civilization.* Secaucus, N.J.: University Books.

Jahn, Jaheinz. *Neo-African Literature: A History of Black Writing.* New York: Grove Press, 1972.

——— and Claus Peter Dressler. *Bibliography of Creative African Writing.* New York: Krasu Reprint, 1972.

Jefferson, Louise. *African Life and Culture.* New York: Zenith/Doubleday, 1975.

———. *The Decorative Arts of Africa.* New York: Viking Press, 1974.

Johnson, Christine C. *ABC's of African History.* New York: Vantage Press, 1972.

Jones, Edward L. *Profiles in African Heritage.* Seattle: University of Washington Press, 1975.

Joseph, Joan. *Black African Empires.* New York: Franklin Watts, 1974.

July, Robert W. *A History of the African People.* New York: Scribner, 1974.

K

Kahn, Jr., E. J. *The First Decade: A Report on Independent Black Africa.* New York: W. W. Norton, 1972.

Kalanzi, Benny. *The Mysteries of African Music.* Dayton, Ohio: McAfree Music Corp., 1975.

Karimakwenda, F. Tongotarisa. *The Feelings and Thoughts of a Zimbabwean.* New York: United Brothers Communications Systems, 1977.

Katz, Naomi and Nancy Milton (eds.). *Fragment from a Lost Diary and Other Stories: Women of Asia, Africa and Latin America.* New York: Pantheon Books, 1974.

Kaunda, Kenneth. *The Riddle of Violence.* New York: Harper & Row, 1981.

Keesing's Research Report 6. *Africa Independent: A Study of Political Developments.* New York: Scribner, 1972.

Kennedy, Scott. *In Search of African Theatre.* New York: Scribner, 1974.

Killian, G. D. *African Writers on African Writing.* Evanston, Ill.: Northwestern University Press, 1974.

Klein, Martin and G. Wesley Johnson (eds.). *Perspectives on the African Past.* Boston: Little, Brown, 1972.

Knappert, Jan. *Myths and Legends of the Congo.* New York: Humanities Press, 1972.

L

LaGuma, Alex (ed.). *Apartheid: A Collection of Writings on South African Racism by South Africans.* New York: International Publishers, 1972.

Langley, J. Ayodele. *Pan-Africanism and Nationalism in West Africa 1900–1945.* New York: Oxford University Press, 1974.

Laurence, Margaret. *Long Drums and Cannons: Nigerian Dramatists and Novelists.* New York: Praeger Publishers, 1972.

Leakey, Richard E. and Roger Lewin. *People of the Lake: Mankind and its Beginnings.* New York: Anchor Press/Doubleday, 1979.

Lee, Don L. *From Plan to Planet: Life Studies: The Need for Afrikan Minds and Institutions.* Detroit: Broadside Press, 1973.

Legum, Colin, I. William Zartman, Steven Langdon and Lynn K. Mytelka. *Africa in the 1980s: A Continent in Crisis.* New York: McGraw-Hill, 1979.

Leiris, Michel and Jacqueline Delange. *African Art.* New York: Golden Press Publishers, 1972.

Lindfors, Bernth (ed.). *Forms of Folklore in Africa: Narrative, Poetic, Gnomic, Dramatic.* Austin: University of Texas Press, 1978.

Littlefield, Jr., Daniel F. *Africans and Seminoles: From Removal to Emancipation.* Westport, Conn.: Greenwood Press, 1977.

Liyong, Taban Lo. *Eating Chiefs: Lwo Culture from Lolwe to Malkal.* New York: Humanities Press, 1972.

Lynch, Hollis R. *Black American Radicals and the Liberation of Africa: The Council on African Affairs 1937–1955.* Ithaca, N.Y.: Africana Studies and Research Center, Cornell University, 1979.

M

Mackonnen, Ras. *Pan-Africanism from Within* as recorded and edited by Kenneth King. New York: Oxford University Press, 1975.

Makeba, Miriam. *The World of African Song.* Chicago: Quadrangle Books, 1972.

Makward, Edris and Leslie Lacy (eds.). *Contemporary African Literature.* New York: Random House, 1972.

Maquet, Jacques. *Africanity: The Cultural Unity of Black Africa.* New York: Oxford University Press.

———. *Civilizations of Black Africa.* New York: Oxford University Press, 1972.

Marsh, Clifton E. *Journey to Shanara: A Love Story and a Proposal to Freedom.* Syracuse, N.Y.: Shanara Publications, 1975.

Marx, Karl and Frederick Engels. *On Colonialism.* New York: International Publishers, 1972.

Mazrui, Ali A. *Ancient Greece in African Political Thought.* Evanston, Ill.: Northwestern University Press, 1972.

———, and Hasu H. Patel (eds.). *Africa in World Affairs: The Next Thirty Years.* New York: Third Press.

Mbiti, J. S. *African Religions and Philosophy.* New York: Praeger, 1972.

McCall, Daniel F. and Edna G. Bay (eds.). *African Images: Essays in African Iconology.* New York: Africana Publishing Co., 1977.

McKenzie-Rennie, Rhoda. *Nkrumah: Greatest of Modern Philosophers.* New York: Vantage Press, 1977.

Mitchison, Naomi. *African Heroes.* New York: Farrar, Straus & Giroux, 1972.

Moore, Basil (ed.). *The Challenge of Black Theology in South Africa.* Richmond, Va.: John Knox Press, 1975.

Moore, Gerald (ed.). *Wole Soyinka.* New York: Africana Publishing Corp., 1972.

Morrison, Donald G., et al. *Black Africa: A Comparative Handbook.* Riverside, N.J.: The Free Press, 1973.

Motley, Mary Penick. *Africa: Its Empires, Nations, and People.* Detroit: Wayne State University Press, 1972.

Mphahlele, Ezekiel. *The Wanderers.* New York: Macmillan, 1972.

Munford, Clarence J. *Production Relations, Class and Black Liberation: A Marxist Perspective in Afro-American Studies.* Amsterdam, The Netherlands: B. R. Gruner, 1979.

Murphy, E. Jefferson. *History of African Civilization.* New York: Thomas Y. Crowell, 1973.

Mutiso, Gideon-Cyrus M. *Messages: An Annotated Bibliography of African Literature for Schools.* Upper Montclair, N.J.: Montclair State College Press, 1972.

N

Naylor, Penelope. *Black Images, The Art of West Africa.* New York: Doubleday, 1975.

Nketia, J. H. Kwabena. *The Music of Africa.* New York: W. W. Norton, 1975.

Nkrumah, Kwame. *Class Struggle in Africa.* New York: International Publishers, 1972.

Nolen, Barbara (ed.). *Africa Is Thunder and Wonder.* New York: Scribner, 1972.

Nyerere, Julius K. *Man and Development: Binadamu Na Maendeleo.* New York: Oxford University Press, 1975.

———. *Ujamaa: Essays on Socialism.* New York: Oxford University Press, 1972.

O

Obbo, Christine. *African Women: Their Struggle for Economic Independence.* Westport, Conn.: Lawrence Hill, 1981.

Odarty, Bill. *A Safari of African Cooking.* Detroit: Broadside Press, 1972.

Ogot, B. A. and J. A. Kiernan (eds.). *Zamani: A Survey of East African History.* New York: Humanities Press, 1972.

Okigbo, Christopher. *Labyrinths with "Path of Thunder."* New York: Africana Publishing Corp., 1972.

Okoye, Felix N. *The American Image of Africa: Myth and Reality.* Buffalo, N.Y.: Black Academy Press.

Okpaku, Joseph (ed.). *New African Literature and the Arts.* Vols. 1 and 2. New York: Thomas Y. Crowell/Third Press, 1972.

———. *New African Literature and the Arts.* Vol. 3. New York: Third Press, 1972.

———. *Nigeria, Dilemma of Nationhood: An African Analysis of the Biafran Conflict.* Westport, Conn.: Greenwood Publishing Co., 1972.

Olney, James. *Tell Me Africa: An Approach to African Literature.* Princeton, N.Y.: Princeton University Press, 1972.

Osei, G. K. *The African: His Antecedents, His Genius, and His Destiny.* Secaucus, N.J.: University Books.

Ottoway, Marina and D. Ottoway. *Ethiopia: Empire in Revolution.* New York: Holmes and Meier, 1979.

Oxford Library of African Literature. 15 vols. New York: Oxford University Press, 1972.

P

Pan-African Seminar on the Juche Idea of Comrade Kim Il Sung. Beirut, Lebanon: Preparatory Committee, Dar Al-Talia, 1974.

Pellow, Deborah. *Women in Accra: Options for Autonomy.* Algonac, Mich.: Reference Publications, 1978.

Pieterse, Cosmo and George Hallett. *Present Lives Future Becoming: A South African Landscape in Words and Pictures.* The Green, Richmond, Surrey, England: Hickey Press Ltd., 1975.

———, and Donald Munro (eds.). *Protest and Conflict in African Literature.* New York: Africana Publishing Corp., 1972.

Pittman, John. *Africa Calling: "Isolate the Racists!" The Liberation Struggle in Southern Africa.* New York: New Outlook Publishers, 1974.

Polakoff, Claire. *Into Indigo: African Textiles and Dyeing Techniques.* New York: Anchor/Doubleday, 1981.

Polatnick, Florence T. *Zambia's President, Kenneth Kaunda.* New York: Julian Messner, 1972.

——— and Alberta L. Saletan. *Shapers of Africa.* New York: Julian Messner, 1972.

R

Radin, Paul (ed.). *African Folktales.* Princeton, N.J.: Princeton University Press, 1972.

Raeburn, Michael. *We Are Everywhere: Narratives from Rhodesian*

Guerrillas. Introduction by James Baldwin. New York: Random House, 1979.

Rich, Evelyn Jones and Immanuel Wallerstein. *Africa: Tradition and Change*. New York: Random House, 1973.

Roberts, John Storm. *Black Music of Two Worlds*. New York: Praeger, 1972.

Robinson, William H. (ed.). *Nommo: An Anthology of Modern Black African and Black American Literature*. New York: Macmillan, 1972.

Roland, Joan G. (ed.). *Africa: The Heritage and the Challenge. An Anthology of African History*. Greenwich, Conn.: Fawcett Publications, 1974.

Rotberg, Robert I. (ed.). *Rebellion in Black Africa*. New York: Oxford University Press, 1972.

———, and Ali A. Mazrui (eds.). *Protest and Power in Black Africa*. New York: Oxford University Press, 1972.

Rubin, Neville. *Cameroun: An African Federation*. New York: Praeger, 1972.

S

Samkange, Stanlake. *African Saga: A Brief Introduction to African History*. Nashville: Abingdon Press.

Sampson, Magnus. *Makers of Modern Ghana: From Philip Quarcoo to Aggrey*, Vol. I. Accra, Ghana: Anowuo Educational Publications.

Schwab, Peter (ed.). *Biafra*. New York: Facts on File, 1972.

———. *Ethiopia & Haile Selassie*. New York: Facts on File, 1972.

Sergeant, Howard (ed.). *African Voices*. New York: Lawrence Hill and Co.

Shaw, Thurstan. *Nigeria: Its Archaeology and Early History*. London: Thames and Hudson, 1979.

Shelton, Austin J. (ed.). *The African Assertion: A Critical Anthology of African Literature*. New York: Odyssey Press, 1972.

Shostak, Marjorie. *Nisa: The Life and Words of a !Kung Woman*. Cambridge, Mass.: Harvard University Press, 1981.

Simo, Rene. *The Little Gringo: Love and Martyrdom in Cameroon*. Jericho, N.Y.: Exposition Press, 1974.

Sithole, Ndabaningi. *Obed Mutezo: The Mudzimu Christian Nationalist*. New York: Oxford University Press, 1972.

Smirnov, S. R. (ed.) *A History of Africa, 1918–1967*. Moscow: Nauka Publishing House (Institute of African Studies, Academy of Sciences).

Smith, Robert S. *Kingdoms of the Yoruba*. New York: Barnes and Noble.

Smith, Stewart. *U.S. Neo-Colonialism in Africa*. New York: International Publishers, 1974.

Smith, William Edgett. *We Must Run While They Walk: A Portrait of Africa's Julius Nyerere*. New York: Random House, 1972.

Snowden, Jr., Frank M. *Blacks in Antiquity: Ethiopians in the Greco-Roman Experience*. Cambridge: Belknap Press, 1972.

South Africa: Time Running Out. The Report of the Study Commission on U.S. Policy Toward Southern Africa. Berkeley: University of California Press, 1981.

Southern Africa: A Time for Change. New York: Friendship Press, 1972.

Soyinka, Wole. *Collected Plays*. New York: Oxford University Press, 1973.

———. *The Man Died: Prison Notes of Wole Soyinka*. New York: Harper & Row, 1973.

———. *Opera Wonyosi*. Bloomington: Indiana University Press, 1981.

Stokke, Olav (ed.). *Reporting Africa: In African and International Mass Media*. New York: Africana Publishing Corp., 1972.

Strage, Mark. *Cape to Cairo: Rape of a Continent*. New York: Harcourt Brace Jovanovich, 1974.

Sub-Saharan Africa. New York: Anchor Press/Doubleday, 1975.

Sub-Saharan Africa: A Guide to Serials. Washington, D.C.: The Library of Congress, 1972.

T

Tarikh. Atlantic Highlands, N.J.: Humanities Press, 1979.

Thompson, Vincent Bakpetu. *Africa and Unity: The Evolution of Africanism*. New York: Humanities Press, 1972.

Tindall, P. E. N. *A History of Central Africa*. New York: Praeger, 1972.

To Be Born a Nation: The Liberation Struggle for Namibia. SWAPO Department of Information. Westport, Conn.: Lawrence Hill, 1981.

Trask, Willard R. (ed.). *Classic Black African Poems*. New York: Eakins Press, 1972.

U

UNESCO. *Africa: Survey on the Scientific and Technical Potential of the Countries of Africa*. Paris: UNESCO, 1972.

U.S. Military Involvement in Southern Africa. Edited by Western Massachusetts Association of Concerned African Scholars. Boston: South End Press, 1979.

Uya, Okon Edet. *African History: Some Problems in Methodology and Perspectives*. Ithaca, N.Y.: African Studies and Research Center, Cornell University, 1981.

V

Vambe, Lawrence. *From Rhodesia to Zimbabwe*. Pittsburgh: University of Pittsburgh Press, 1977.

W

Wassing, Rene S. *African Art: Its Background and Tradition*. New York: Harry N. Abrams, 1972.

Wastberg, Per (ed.). *The Writer in Modern Africa: African-Scandinavian Writers' Conference*. New York: Africana Publishing Corp., 1972.

Wauthier, Claude. *The Literature and Thought of Modern Africa: A Survey*. New York: Praeger, 1972.

Weinstein, Brian. *Eboue*. New York: Oxford University Press, 1972.

Weisbord, Robert G. *Ebony Kinship: Africa, Africans, and the Afro-American*. Westport, Conn.: Greenwood Publishing Co., 1974.

Welsh, David. *The Roots of Segregation: Native Policy in Natal*. New York: Oxford University Press, 1972.

Were, Gideon S. and Derek A. Wilson. *East Africa through a Thousand Years: A History of the Years A.D. 1000 to the Present Day*. New York: Africana Publishing Co., 1972.

Wilhoit, Francis M. *The Politics of Massive Resistance*. New York: George Braziller, 1974.

Willett, Frank. *African Art*. New York: Praeger, 1972.

Williams, Chancellor. *The Destruction of Black Civilization: Great Issues of a Race from 4500 B.C. to 2000 A.D.* Chicago: Third World Press, 1975.

Williams, Lorraine A. (ed.). *Africa and the Afro-American Experience: Eight Essays*. Washington, D.C.: Howard University Press, 1978.

Witherell, Julian W. (comp.). *French-Speaking Central Africa: A Guide to Official Publications in American Libraries*. Washington, D.C.: Library of Congress, Supt. of Documents, Government Printing Office, 1974.

Woodson, Carter G. *The African Background Outlined: Or, Hand-*

book for the Study of the Negro. Westport, Conn.: Negro Universities Press/New American Library, 1972.

Woronoff, Jon. *Organizing African Unity.* Metuchen, N.J.: Scarecrow Press, 1972.

Y

Yerby, Frank. *The Dahomean.* New York: Dial Press, 1972.

Z

Zaslavsky, Claudia. *Africa Counts.* Boston, Mass.: Prindle, Weber & Schmidt, 1972.

Zell, Hans M. and Helene Silver (eds.). *A Reader's Guide to African Literature.* New York: Africana Publishing Co., 1972.

Slavery

Much recent scholarship has investigated the facts of slave life and the fight for abolition in U.S. history.

A

Aptheker, Herbert. *Heavenly Days in Dixie or, The Time of their Lives: A Critical Review of* Time on the Cross: The Economics of American Negro Slavery by Robert W. Fogel and Stanley L. Engerman. New York: *Political Affairs,* 1975.

B

Berlin, Ira. *Slaves without Masters: The Free Negro in the Antebellum South.* New York: Pantheon Books, 1975.

Blassingame, John W. *Black New Orleans: 1860–1880.* Chicago: University of Chicago Press, 1973.

———. *The Slave Community: Plantation Life in the Antebellum South.* New York: Oxford University Press, 1972.

Boateng, Yaw M. *The Return.* New York: Pantheon Books, 1978.

Bormann, Ernest G. (ed.). *Forerunners of Black Power: The Rhetoric of Abolition.* Englewood Cliffs, N.J.: Prentice-Hall, 1971.

Bracey, Jr., John H., August Meier and Elliott Rudwick (eds.). *American Slavery: The Question of Resistance.* Belmont, Cal.: Wadsworth, 1971.

C

Cable, Mary. *Black Odyssey: The Case of the Slave Ship Amistad.* New York: Viking Press, 1971.

Chapman, Abraham (ed.). *Steal Away: Stories of Runaway Slaves.* New York: Praeger, 1971.

Craton, Michael. *Sinews of Empire: A Short History of British Slavery.* New York: Anchor/Doubleday, 1975.

Crow, John W. *Star of Africa.* Hicksville, N.Y.: Exposition Press, 1977.

D

Daedalus, Spring 1974 on *Slavery, Colonialism and Racism.* 1974.

Daniel, Pete. *The Shadow of Slavery: Peonage in the South, 1901–1969.* Urbana: University of Illinois Press, 1973.

Davis, David Brion. *The Problem of Slavery in the Age of Revolution, 1770–1823.* Ithaca, N.Y.: Cornell University Press, 1975.

Degler, Carl N. *Neither Black nor White: Slavery and Race Relations in Brazil and the United States.* New York: Macmillan.

Dillard, J. L. *Black English: Its History and Usage in the United States.* New York: Random House, 1972.

Duff, J. and P. Mitchell (eds.). *The Nat Turner Rebellion: The Historical Event and the Modern Controversy.* New York: Harper & Row, 1971.

E

Escott, Paul D. *Slavery Remembered: A Record of Twentieth-Century Slave Narratives.* Chapel Hill: University of North Carolina Press, 1980.

Everett, Susanne. *The Slaves: An Illustrated History of the Monstrous Evil.* New York: Putnam, 1979.

F

Feldstein, Stanley. *Once a Slave: The Slaves' View of Slavery.* New York: William Morrow, 1971.

Franklin, H. Bruce. *The Victim as Criminal and Artist in America: Literature from the American Prison.* New York: Oxford University Press, 1979.

G

Genovese, Eugene. *From Rebellion to Revolution: Afro-American Slave Revolts in the Making of the Modern World.* Baton Rouge: Louisiana State University Press, 1980.

H

Hill, Herbert. *Black Labor and the American Legal System.* Washington, D.C.: Bureau of National Affairs, 1978.

Horsmanden, Daniel. *The New York Conspiracy.* Boston: Beacon Press, 1971.

Howard, Thomas (ed.). *Black Voyage: Eyewitness Accounts of the Atlantic Slave Trade.* Boston: Little, Brown.

Huggins, Nathan Irvin. *Black Odyssey: The Afro-American Ordeal in Slavery.* New York: Pantheon Books, 1978.

K

Kromer, Helen. *The Amistad Revolt, 1839: The Slave Uprising Aboard the Spanish Schooner.* New York: Franklin Watts, 1973.

L

Lane, Ann J. (ed.). *The Debate Over Slavery: Stanley Elkins and His Critics.* Urbana: University of Illinois Press, 1971.

Litwack, Leon F. *Been in the Storm So Long: The Aftermath of Slavery.* New York: Knopf, 1979.

M

McColley, Robert. *Slavery and Jeffersonian Virginia.* Urbana: University of Illinois Press, 1974.

Mintz, Sidney W. (ed.). *Slavery, Colonialism, and Racism.* New York: W. W. Norton, 1975.

Moore, Wilbert E. *American Negro Slavery and Abolition: A Sociological Study.* New York: Third Press.

Mullin, Gerald W. *Flight and Rebellion: Slave Resistance in 18th Century Virginia.* New York: Oxford University Press.

N

Nichols, Charles H. (ed.). *Black Men in Chains: Narratives by Escaped Slaves.* New York: Lawrence Hill & Co., 1974.

Novak, Daniel A. *The Wheel of Servitude: Black Forced Labor After Slavery.* Lexington: University Press of Kentucky, 1978.

P

Pease, Jane H. *They Who Would Be Free: Blacks' Search for Freedom, 1830–1861.* New York: Antheneum, 1975.

—— and William H. Pease. *Bound with Them in Chains: A Biographical History of the Antislavery Movement.* Westport, Conn.: Greenwood Publishing Co., 1973.

A Pictorial History of the Slave Trade. Translated by Bonnie Christen. Geneva: Editions Minerva, S.A., 1971.

Perdue, Theda. *Slavery and the Evolution of Cherokee Society, 1540–1866.* Knoxville: University of Tennessee Press, 1980.

Price, Richard (ed.). *Maroon Societies: Rebel Slave Communities in the Americas.* New York: Anchor/Doubleday, 1974.

R

Raboteau, Albert J. *Slave Religion: The "Invisible Institution" in the Antebellum South.* New York. Oxford University Press, 1979.

Rawick, George P. *The American Slave: A Composite Autobiography.* Vol. 1: *From Sundown to Sunup: The Making of the Black Community.* Westport, Conn.: Greenwood Publishing Co., 1972.

Redding, Saunders. *They Came in Chains: Americans from Africa.* Philadelphia: Lippincott, 1973.

Roark, James L. *Masters Without Slaves: Southern Planters in the Civil War and Reconstruction.* New York: W. W. Norton, 1977.

Robinson, Donald. *Slavery in the Structure of American Politics, 1765–1820.* New York: Harcourt Brace Jovanovich.

S

Schwarz-Bart, Andre. *A Woman Named Solitude.* New York: Atheneum, 1973.

Scott, John Anthony. *Hard Trials on My Way: Slavery and the Struggle Against It 1800–1860.* New York: Knopf, 1975.

Sobel, Mechal. *Trabelin' on: The Slave Journey to an Afro-Baptist Faith.* Westport, Conn.: Greenwood Press, 1979.

Sorin, Gerald. *Abolitionism: A New Perspective.* New York: Praeger, 1972.

Stanley, A. Knighton. *The Children Is Crying: Congregationalism among Black People.* New York: Pilgrim Press, 1979.

Starobin, Robert S. (ed.). *Blacks in Bondage: Letters of American Slaves.* New York: New Viewpoints: Franklin Watts.

——. *Denmark Vesey: The Slave Conspiracy of 1822.* Englewood Cliffs, N.J.: Prentice-Hall, 1971.

T

Tragle, Henry Irving. *The Southampton Slave Revolt of 1831: A Compilation of Source Material.* Amherst: University of Massachusetts Press, 1971.

U

Uya, Okon E. *From Slavery to Public Service: Robert Smalls, 1839–1915.* New York: Oxford University Press, 1971.

W

Woodward, C. Vann. *American Counterpoint: Slavery and Race in the North-South Dialogue.* Boston: Little, Brown, 1971.

Y

Yetman, Norman R. (ed.). *Life Under the Peculiar Institution: Selections from the Slave Narrative.* New York: Holt, Rinehart and Winston, 1971.

Education

Books in this category are related directly to the education process and schooling.

A

Access of Black Americans to Higher Education: How Open Is the Door? Washington, D.C.: National Advisory Committee on Black Higher Education and Black Colleges and Universities, 1980.

Almost as Fairly: The First Year of Title IX Implementation in Six Southern States. Atlanta: American Friends Service Committee, Southeastern Public Education Program, 1977.

Andrews, Malachi and Paul T. Owens. *Black Language.* New York: Seymour Smith Publisher, 1974.

Arnez, Nancy L. *Partners in Urban Education: Training the Inner-City Child.* Morristown, N.J.: Silver Burdett, 1975.

B

Ballard, Allen B. *The Education of Black Folk: The Afro-American Struggle for Knowledge in White America.* New York: Harper & Row, 1973.

Banks, James A. and Jean D. Grambs (eds.). *Black Self-Concept: Implications for Education and Social Science.* New York: McGraw-Hill.

Bell, Jr., Derrick A. *Race, Racism and American Law.* Boston: Little, Brown, 1980.

—— (ed.). *Shades of Brown: New Perspectives on School Desegregation.* New York: Teachers College Press, Columbia University, 1980.

Bibliographic Guide to Black Studies: 1979. Boston: G. K. Hall, 1980.

Blassingame, John W. (ed.). *New Perspectives on Black Studies.* Urbana: University of Illinois Press, 1971.

Bowles, Frank and Frank A. DeCosta. *Between Two Worlds: A Profile of Negro Higher Education.* New York: McGraw-Hill, 1971.

Bramwell, Jonathan. *Courage in Crisis: The Black Professional Today.* Indianapolis: Bobbs-Merrill, 1973.

Brigham, John C. and Theodore A. Weissbach (eds.). *Racial Attitudes in America: Analyses and Findings of Social Psychology.* New York: Harper & Row, 1973.

Bullock, Paul. *Aspiration vs. Opportunity: "Careers" in the Inner City.* Ann Arbor, Mich.: The Institute of Labor and Industrial Relations, 1974.

Butler, Addie Louise Joyner. *The Distinctive Black College: Talladega, Tuskegee and Morehouse.* Metuchen, N.J.: Scarecrow Press, 1978.

C

Chrisman, Robert and Nathan Hare (eds.). *Contemporary Black Thought: The Best from the Black Scholar.* Indianapolis: Bobbs-Merrill, 1974.

D

Drum: Black Literary Experience at the University of Massachusetts. Amherst: MA. 1980.

Du Bois, W. E. B. *The Education of Black People: Ten Critiques 1906–1960.* Edited by Herbert Aptheker. Amherst: University of Massachusetts Press, 1973.

E

Education and Black Struggle: Notes from the Colonized World. Cambridge, Mass.: Harvard University, *Harvard Educational Review.*

Equal Education Opportunity: More Promise Than Progress. Washington, D.C.: Institute for the Study of Educational Policy, Howard University Press, 1979.

Eysenck, H. J. *The I.Q. Argument.* Freeport, N.Y.: The Library Press, 1971.

F

Ford, Nick Aaron. *Black Studies: Threat or Challenge?* Port Washington, N.Y.: Kennikat Press, 1973.

Foster, Marcus A. *Making Schools Work: Strategies for Changing Education.* Philadelphia: The Westminster Press, 1971.

Franklin, Vincent P. *The Education of Black Philadelphia: The Social and Educational History of a Minority Community, 1900–1950.* Philadelphia: University of Pennsylvania Press, 1980.

Freimarck, Vincent and Bernard Rosenthal (ed.). *Race and the American Romantics.* New York: Schocken Books, 1972.

From Isolation to Mainstream: Problems of Colleges Founded for Negroes. New York: McGraw-Hill.

G

Garrett, James and the Center for Black Education staff (eds.). *The Struggle for Black Education: 1968–1971.* Washington, D.C.: Drum and Spear Press, 1973.

Greer, Colin. *Cobweb Attitudes: Essays on Educational and Cultural Mythology.* New York: Teachers College Press, Columbia University.

H

Haskins, Jim (ed.). *Black Manifesto for Education.* New York: William Morrow.

Hauser, Stuart T. *Black and White Identity Formation: Studies in the Psychosocial Development of Lower Socioeconomic Class Adolescent Boys.* New York: Wiley, 1972.

Heath, G. Louis. *Red, Brown & Black Demands for Better Education.* Philadelphia: Westminster Press, 1972.

Hillson, Jon. *The Battle of Boston, Busing and the Struggle for School Desegregation.* New York: Pathfinder Press, 1978.

I

Irvin, Leonard B. (comp.). *Black Studies: A Bibliography.* Brooklawn, N.J.: McKinley Publishing Co., 1974.

J

Jefferson, Keith. *The Hyena Reader.* Sacramento, Cal.: Black River Writers West, 1977.

Jencks, Christopher, et al. *Inequality: A Reassessment of the Effect of Family and Schooling in America.* New York: Basic Books, 1972.

Jensen, Arthur R. *Educability and Group Differences.* New York: Harper & Row, 1973.

———. *Genetics and Education.* New York: Harper & Row, 1973.

Johnson, Harry A. *Multimedia Materials for Afro-American Studies.* New York: R. R. Bowker, 1972.

Jones, Reginald L. (ed.). *Black Psychology.* New York: Harper & Row, 1973.

Josey, E. J. (ed.). *What Black Librarians Are Saying.* Metuchen, N.J.: Scarecrow Press, 1973.

———. *The Black Librarian in America.* Metuchen, N.J.: Scarecrow Press, 1971.

K

Kochman, Thomas (ed.). *Rappin' and Stylin' Out: Communication in Urban Black America.* Urbana: University of Illinois Press, 1972.

L

Levin, Henry M. (ed.). *Community Control of Schools.* New York: Simon and Schuster, 1971.

Lightfoot, Claude M. *The Effect of Education on Racism: The Two German States and the USA.* New York: New Outlook Publishers, 1974.

Lightfoot, Sara Lawrence. *Worlds Apart: Relationships Between Families and Schools.* New York: Basic Books, 1978.

Locke, Louis G., W. M. Gibson, G. Arms and G. Petty (eds.). *TLE Six: Options for the 1970s.* New York: Holt, Rinehart and Winston.

M

Mabee, Carleton. *Black Education in New York State: From Colonial to Modern Times.* N.Y.: Syracuse University Press, 1980.

Marcus, Sheldon and Philip D. Vairo (eds.). *Urban Education: Crisis or Opportunity?* Metuchen, N.J.: Scarecrow Press, 1973.

Media and the Disadvantaged: Instructional Technology as the Equalizer for Disadvantaged Students. Stanford, Cal.: ERIC Clearinghouse on Media and Technology, Stanford Center for Research and Development in Teaching, Stanford University, 1973.

Mercer, Walter A. *Teaching in the Desegregated School.* New York: Vantage Press, 1973.

Minorities in Two-Year Colleges: A Report and Recommendations for Change. Washington, D.C.: Institute for the Study of Educational Policy, Howard University, 1981.

Moore, Eleanor I. *And the Truth Shall Set You Free.* Smithtown, N.Y.: Exposition Press, 1981.

Moore, Jr., William and Lonnie H. Wagstaff. *Black Education in White Colleges: Progress and Prospects.* San Francisco, Cal.: Jossey-Bass, 1974.

Morange, Lenora and Rudolph. *Our Baby's Early Years.* Washington, D.C.: Len Champs Publishers.

Morris, Lorenzo. *Elusive Equality: The Status of Black Americans in Higher Education.* Washington, D.C.: Howard University Press, 1980.

Mosteller, Frederick and Daniel P. Moynihan (eds.). *On Quality of Educational Opportunity: Papers Deriving from the Harvard University Faculty Seminar on the Coleman Report.* New York: Random House.

Murphy, E. Jefferson and Harry Stein. *Teaching Africa Today: A*

Handbook for Teachers and Curriculum Planners. New York: Citation Press, 1975.

N

Newman, Katherine D. (ed.). *The American Equation: Literature in a Multi-Ethnic Culture.* Boston: Allyn and Bacon, 1971.

O

Ogbu, John U. *Minority Education and Caste: The American System in Crosscultural Perspective.* New York: Academic Press, 1979.

P

Peterson, Marvin W., R. T. Blackburn et al. *Black Students on White Campus: The Impacts of Increased Black Enrollments.* Ann Arbor, Mich.: Institute for Social Research, 1979.

R

Reeves, Donald. *Notes of a Processed Brother.* New York: Pantheon Books.

Richardson, Ken, David Spears and Martin Richards (eds.). *Race and Intelligence: The Fallacies behind the Race-IQ Controversy.* Baltimore: Penguin Books, 1972.

S

Schatz, Walter (ed.). *Directory of Afro-American Resources.* New York: R. R. Bowker Co., 1971.

Schultz, Jr., Michael J. *The National Educational Association and the Black Teacher.* Coral Gables, Fla.: University of Miami Press, 1971.

Scott, J. Irving E. *The Education of Black People in Florida.* Philadelphia: Dorrance, 1975.

Senna, Carl (ed.). *The Fallacy of I.Q.* New York: Third Press, 1973.

Sinclair, Robert L. (ed.). *A Two-Way Street: Home-School Cooperation in Curriculum Decisionmaking.* Boston: Institute for Responsive Education, 1981.

Smith, Arthur L. (ed.). *Language, Communication and Rhetoric in Black America.* New York: Harper & Row, 1973.

Smith, Sr., Charles H. E. *An Historical Look at the Roots of Black Education in Portsmouth.* The Author, 106 Pecan Dr., Princess Anne, Md., 1978.

Smith, Ed. *Black Students in Interracial Schools: A Guide for Students, Teachers and Parents.* Garrett Park, Md.: Garrett Park Press, 1981.

Sowell, Thomas. *Black Education: Myths and Tragedies.* New York: David McKay.

Spivey, Donald. *Schooling for the New Slavery: Black Industrial Education 1868–1915.* Westport, Conn.: Greenwood Press, 1979.

Spradling, Mary Mace (ed.). *In Black and White: A Guide to Magazine Articles, Newspaper Articles and Books Concerning More Than 15,000 Black Individuals and Groups.* Detroit: Gale Research Co., 1981.

Stanford, Barbara Dodds and Karima Amin. *Black Literature for High School Students.* Urbana, Ill.: National Council of Teachers of English, 1979.

Starting Out Right: Choosing Books about Black People for Young Children: Pre-School through Third Grade. Madison: Wisconsin Department of Public Instruction, Division for Administrative Services, 1972.

T

Teaching Black: An Evaluation of Methods and Resources. Redwood City, Cal.: San Mateo County Office of Education, 1972.

The What and How of Teaching Afro-American Culture and History in the Elementary Schools. Albany, University of the State of New York, State Education Dept., 1973.

Thomas, Gail E. (ed.). *Black Students in Higher Education: Conditions and Experiences in the 1970s.* Westport, Conn.: Greenwood Press, 1981.

Thompson, Daniel C. *Private Black Colleges at the Crossroads.* Westport, Conn.: Greenwood Press, 1974.

U

United Federation of Teachers. *History of Black Americans: A Study Guide and Curriculum Outline.* New York, 1973.

V

Vaughn, William Preston. *Schools for All: The Blacks and Public Education in the South, 1865–1877.* Lexington: University Press of Kentucky, 1977.

W

Webster, Staten W. *The Education of Black Americans.* New York: John Day, 1975.

West, Earle H. (ed.). *The Black American and Education.* Columbus, Ohio: Charles E. Merrill Publishing Co., 1975.

Wilkinson, III, J. Harvie. *From Brown to Bakke: The Supreme Court and School Integration 1954–1978.* New York: Oxford University Press, 1978.

Williams, Lorraine A. and Madlyn Calbert. *A Curriculum in Black History for Secondary Schools.* Washington, D.C.: Howard University, Department of History.

Willie, Charles V. *Race Mixing in the Public Schools.* New York: Praeger Publishers, 1974.

—— and Arline McCord. *Black Students at White Colleges.* New York: Praeger, 1973.

—— and Ronald R. Edmonds (eds.). *Black Colleges in America: Challenge, Development, Survival.* New York: Teachers' College Press, 1979.

Wolpin, R. *The New Negro on Campus: Black College Rebellions in the 1920s.* Princeton, N.J.: Princeton University Press, 1975.

Y

Yarmolinsky, Adam, Lance Liebman and Corinne S. Schelling (eds.). *Race and Schooling in the City.* Cambridge, Mass.: Harvard University Press, 1981.

Juvenile

This section lists works written specifically for elementary, junior high, and high school students.

A

Abdul, Raoul. *Famous Black Entertainers of Today.* New York: Dodd, Mead, 1973.

Adoff, Arnold. *Black Is Brown Is Tan.* New York: Harper & Row, 1973.

B

Baker, Augusta. *The Black Experience in Children's Books.* Office of Children's Services. New York Public Library, 1971.

Banks, Ernie and Jim Enright. *"Mr. Cub."* Chicago: Follett.

Benig, Irving (ed.). *The Children: Poems and Prose from Bedford-Stuyvesant.* New York: Evergreen Press, 1971.

Billingsley, Andrew and Jeanne M. Giovannoni. *Children of the Storm: Black Children and American Child Welfare.* New York: Harcourt Brace Jovanovich, 1972.

Black History/Museum Committee (eds.). *Sunaru: A Multimedia Guide for the Black Child.* Philadelphia: Black History Museum, 1980.

Brandon, Jr., Brumsic. *Outta Sight, Luther!* New York: Paul S. Eriksson, 1972.

Brimberg, Stanlee. *Black Stars.* New York: Dodd, Mead, 1974.

Broderick, Dorothy M. *Image of the Black in Children's Fiction.* Ann Arbor, Mich.: R. R. Bowker, 1974.

Brodie, Fawn M. *Thomas Jefferson: An Intimate History.* New York: W. W. Norton, 1974.

Brown, Josephine Stephens. *The Way of the Shadows.* Jericho: N.Y.: Exposition Press, 1973.

Bruner, Richard. *Black Politicians.* New York: David McKay, 1971.

Burroughs, Margaret T. G. *What Shall I Tell My Children Who Are Black?* The Author, 3806 S. Michigan Ave., Chicago, Ill. 60653, 1971.

C

Childress, Alice. *A Hero Ain't Nothin' But a Sandwich.* New York: Coward, McCann & Geoghegan, 1973.

Clifton, Lucille. *The Boy Who Didn't Believe in Spring.* New York: Dutton, 1973.

————. *Everett Anderson's Christmas Coming.* New York: Holt, Rinehart and Winston.

Cohen, Barbara. *Thank You, Jackie Robinson.* New York: Lothrop, Lee and Shepard, 1974.

Coombs, Orde. *Do You See My Love for You Growing?* New York: Dodd, Mead, 1972.

———— (ed.). *What We Must See: Young Black Storytellers.* New York: Dodd, Mead, 1971.

Cottle, Thomas J. *Black Children, White Dreams.* Boston: Houghton Mifflin, 1974.

Crowell Biographies for Children Just Beginning to Read: Gordon Parks, Malcolm X, Charles Drew, Jackie Robinson, Wilt Chamberlain, Cesar Chavez, Jim Thorpe, Marian Anderson and others. New York: Thomas Y. Crowell, 1971.

D

Delany, Samuel R., et al. *The Shores Beneath, Novellas.* New York: Avon Books, 1971.

Deveaux, Alexis. *Spritis in the Street.* New York: Anchor/Doubleday, 1974.

Dobrin, Arnold. *Voices of Joy, Voices of Freedom.* New York: Coward, McCann & Geoghegan, 1972.

Du Bois, W. E. B. *Selections from the Brownies' Book.* Millwood, N.Y.: Kraus-Thomson Organization, 1980.

E

Edwards, Sally. *When the World's On Fire.* New York: Coward, McCann & Geoghegan, 1972.

Evans, Mari. *JD.* New York: Doubleday, 1974.

F

Feelings, Muriel. *Jambo Means Hello: Swahili Alphabet Book.* New York: Dial Press, 1974.

Feelings, Tom. *Black Pilgrimage.* New York: Lothrop, Lee & Shepard, 1972.

The Firebird Library. Englewood Cliffs, N.J.: Scholastic Book Services, 1974.

Froman, Robert. *Racism.* New York: Delacorte Press, 1972.

Funke, Lewis. *The Curtain: The Story of Ossie Davis.* New York: Grosset and Dunlap.

G

Gaines, Ernest J. *A Long Day In November.* New York: Dial Press, 1971.

Gee, Maurine H. *Chicano, Amigo.* New York: William Morrow, 1972.

Giovanni, Nikki. *Ego Tripping and Other Poems for Young People.* New York: Lawrence Hill and Co., 1974.

————. *Spin a Soft Black Song: Poems for Children.* New York: Hill and Wang, 1971.

Gouldner, Helen P. *Teacher's Pets, Troublemakers and Nobodies: Black Children in Elementary School.* Westport, Conn.: Greenwood Press, 1979.

Graham, Lorenz. *Hongry Catch the Foolish Boy.* New York: Thomas Y. Crowell, 1973.

Greenfield, Eloise. *Rosa Parks.* New York: Thomas Y. Crowell, 1974.

Gross, Martha. *The Possible Dream: 10 Who Dared.* Philadelphia: Chilton Books, 1971.

Gross, Mary Anne (ed.). *Ah Man, You Found Me Again.* Boston: Beacon Press.

Guy, Rosa. *The Disappearance.* New York: Delacorte Press, 1980.

————. *The Friends.* New York: Holt, Rinehart & Winston, 1974.

———— (ed.). *Children of Longing.* New York: Bantam Books, 1971.

H

Hamilton, Virginia. *Justice and Her Brothers.* New York: Greenwillow Books, 1979.

————. *The Planet of Junior Brown.* New York: Macmillan, 1971.

Harper, Michael S. *History Is Your Own Heartbeat.* Urbana: University of Illinois Press, 1971.

Harris, Sheldon H. *Paul Cuffee: Black America and the African Return.* New York: Simon and Schuster, 1972.

Harrison, Deloris. *Journey All Alone.* New York: Dial Press, 1971.

Haskins, James. *A Piece of the Power: Four Black Mayors.* New York: Dial Press, 1972.

————. *Pinckney Benton Stewart Pinchback.* New York: Macmillan, 1973.

I

Irwin, Hadley and Annabelle Irwin. *We Are Mesquakie: We Are One.* Old Westbury, N.Y.: Feminist Press, 1981.

J

Jackson, Jesse. *The Sickest Don't Always Die the Quickest.* New York: Doubleday, 1971.

Jacobs, William J. *Hannibal: An African Hero.* New York: McGraw-Hill, 1973.

Johnston, Johanna. *Paul Cuffee: America's First Black Captain.* New York: Dodd, Mead, 1971.

Jordan, June. *Dry Victories.* New York: Holt, Rinehart and Winston, 1973.

———. *His Own Where.* New York: Thomas Y. Crowell, 1971.

——— and Terri Bush (comp.). *The Voice of the Children.* New York: Holt, Rinehart and Winston, 1971.

K

Klein, Aaron E. *The Hidden Contributors: Black Scientists and Inventors in America.* New York: Doubleday, 1971.

L

Larrick, Nancy (ed.). *Somebody Turned on a Tap in These Kids.* New York: Delacorte Press, 1971.

Lester, Julius. *Long Journey Home: Stories from Black History.* New York: Dial Press, 1972.

M

MacCann, Donnarae and Gloria Woodard (eds.). *The Black American in Books for Children: Readings in Racism.* Metuchen, N.J.: Scarecrow Press, 1973.

Mathis, Sharon Bell. *Teacup Full of Roses.* New York: Viking Press, 1972.

Matturri, Joanna and Hy Dales (eds.). *Inner City Reflections in Black and White: A Collection of Visuals by Young Photographers.* New York: Washington Square Press, 1973.

Meriwether, Louise. *The Freedom Ship of Robert Smalls.* Englewood Cliffs, N.J.: Prentice-Hall, 1972.

Mitchell, George. *I'm Somebody Important: Young Black Voices from Rural Georgia.* Urbana: University of Illinois Press, 1972.

Mohr, Nicholasa. *Nilda.* New York: Harper & Row, 1974.

Myers, Hector F., Phyllis G. Rana and Marcia Harris (comps.). *Black Child Development in America 1927–1977: An Annotated Bibliography.* Westport, Conn.: Greenwood Press, 1981.

O

O'Gorman, Ned. *The Children Are Dying.* New York: New American Library/Signet, 1979.

P

Parish, Helen Rand. *Estebanico.* New York: Viking Press, 1975.

S

Schiesel, Jane. *The Otis Redding Story.* New York: Doubleday, 1974.

Segal, Edith. *The Greatest Wonder. Just Poems, Answer Poems, Guessing Poems, Dance Poems for Young People.* Drawings by Samuel Kamen. New York: Philmark Press, 1979.

Shoberg, Lore. *Willy!* New York: McGraw-Hill, 1975.

Steptoe, John. *Birthday.* New York: Holt, Rinehart and Winston, 1972.

———. *Train Ride.* New York: Harper & Row, 1971.

T

Thomas, George B. *Young Black Adults: Liberation and Family Attitudes.* New York: Friendship Press, 1975.

Thomas, Ianthe. *Walk Home Tired, Billy Jenkins.* New York: Harper & Row, 1975.

W

Wagenvoord, James. *Hangin' Out: City Kids, City Games.* Philadelphia: Lippincott, 1974.

Walkin, Edward. *Black Fighting Men in U.S. History.* New York: Lothrop, Lee & Shepard, 1973.

Werstein, Irving. *The Storming of Fort Wagner: Black Valor in the Civil War.* New York: Scholastic Book Services, 1971.

Williams, Walter E. *Youth and Minority Unemployment.* Stanford, Cal.: Hoover Institution, Stanford University, 1979.

Literature

This list contains both literary criticism and works of fiction, including novels, poetry, and drama.

A

Abcarian, Richard (ed.). *Richard Wright's* Native Son: *A Critical Handbook.* Belmont, Cal.: Wadsworth, 1971.

Abdul, Raoul (ed.). *The Magic of Black Poetry.* New York: Dodd, Mead, 1972.

Abish, Walter. *Alphabetical Africa.* New York: New Directions, 1975.

Abubadika, Mwlimu Imiri (Sonny Carson). *The Education of Sonny Carson.* New York: W. W. Norton.

Achebe, Chinua. *Girls at War and Other Stories.* New York: Doubleday, 1973.

———. *Morning Yet on Creation Day.* Garden City, N.Y.: Anchor/Doubleday, 1981.

Adoff, Arnold (ed.). *Brothers and Sisters: Modern Stories by Black Americans.* New York: Macmillan.

———. *The Poetry of Black America: Anthology of the 20th Century.* New York: Harper & Row, 1973.

Afro-American Literature: Fiction, Drama, Poetry, Nonfiction (4 vols.). Boston: Houghton Mifflin.

Alhamisi, Ahmed Akinwole. *Holy Ghosts: Poems.* Broadside Press, 1972.

Anderson, Elijah. *A Place on the Corner.* Chicago: University of Chicago Press, 1979.

Angelou, Maya. *Gather Together in My Name.* New York: Random House, 1974.

———. *Just Give Me A Cool Drink of Water 'Fore I Diiie: The Poetry of Maya Angelou.* New York: Random House, 1971.

———. *And Still I Rise: A Book of Poems.* New York: Random House, 1979.

———. *Oh Pray My Wings Are Gonna Fit Me Well.* New York: Random House, 1981.

Arata, Esther Spring, et al. *More Black American Playwrights: A Bibliography.* Metuchen, N.J.: Scarecrow Press, 1979.

Archer, Leonard C. *Black Images in the American Theatre.* Brooklyn, N.Y.: Pageant-Poseidon Ltd., 1973.

Atkinson, J. Edward (ed.). *Black Dimensions in Contemporary American Art.* New York: New American Library, 1971.

Awoonor, Kofi. *The House by the Sea.* Greenfield Center, N.Y.: Greenfield Review, 1979.

B

Bailey, Gertrude Blackwell. *If Words Could Set Us Free.* Jericho, N.Y.: Exposition Press, 1974.

Bailey, Leonead Pack (ed.). *Broadside Authors and Artists: An Illustrated Biographical Directory.* Detroit: Broadside Press, 1974.

Baker, Jr., Houston A. *A Many-Colored Coat of Dreams: The Poetry of Countee Cullen.* Detroit: Broadside Press, 1975.

———. *Long Black Song: Essays in Black American Literature and Culture.* Charlottesville: University Press of Virginia, 1972.

———, (ed.). *Black Literature in America.* New York: McGraw-Hill, 1971.

Baker, Ross K. (ed.). *The Afro-American: Readings.* New York: Van Nostrand-Reinhold, 1971.

Baker, Jr., Houston A. (ed.). *Reading Black: Essays in the Criticism of African, Caribbean and Black American Literature.* Ithaca, N.Y.: Cornell University Press, 1978.

Bakish, David. *Richard Wright.* New York: Frederick Ungar Publishing Co., 1973.

Baldwin, James and Nikki Giovanni. *A Dialogue.* Philadelphia: J. B. Lippincott, 1973.

Baldwin, James. *If Beale Street Could Talk.* New York: Dial Press, 1974.

———. *No Name in the Street.* New York: Dial Press, 1972.

———. *One Day, When I Was Lost: A Scenario Based on Alex Haley's "The Autobiography of Malcolm X."* New York: Dial Press, 1973.

———, and Jerry Jenkins in collaboration with Hank Aaron. *Bad Henry.* Radnor, Pa.: Chilton Book Co., 1974.

Bambara, Toni Cade (ed.). *Tales and Stories for Black Folks.* New York: Doubleday.

———. *Gorilla, My Love.* New York: Random House, 1972.

Banks, Phyllis M. and Virginia M. Burke (eds.). *Black Americans: Images in Conflict.* Indianapolis: Bobbs-Merrill.

Baraka, Amiri. *The Motion of History & Other Plays.* N.Y.: William Morrow, 1979.

———. *Selected Plays and Prose of Amiri Baraka/Le Roi Jones.* New York: William Morrow, 1980.

Barker, Ben. *The Time of the Terrorists.* Los Angeles: Crescent Publications, 1978.

Barksdale, Richard K. and Kenneth Kinnamon (eds.). *Black Writers of America: A Comprehensive Anthology.* New York: Macmillan, 1972.

Barrax, Gerald. *An Audience of One.* Athens: University of Georgia Press, 1980.

Barrett, C. Lindsay (Eseoghene). *The Conflicting Eye.* Detroit: Broadside Press, 1973.

Bascom, William. *African Art in Cultural Perspective: An Introduction.* New York: Norton, 1973.

Bates, Arthenia J. *Seeds Beneath the Snow: Vignettes from the South.* Washington, D.C.: Howard University Press, 1978.

Bearden, Romare and Harry Henderson. *6 Black Masters of American Art.* New York: Doubleday/Zenith, 1972.

Bebey, Francis, *Agatha Moudio's Son.* New York: Lawrence Hill, 1974.

Beckham, Barry. *Runner Mack.* New York: William Morrow.

Bell, Bernard W. *The Folk Roots of Contemporary Afro-American Poetry.* Detroit: Broadside Press.

Berman, Paul (ed.). *Yo Better Believe It: Black Verse in English.* New York: Penguin Books, 1973.

Black Artists in America. New York: Black Artists in America. Horace Mann Lincoln Institute, Columbia University, 1973.

The Black Review No. 1: Essays, Poetry and Short Stories. New York: William Morrow, 1971.

Blakely, Henry. *Windy Place.* Detroit: Mich.: Broadside Press, 1975.

Bogus, Diane. *I'm Off to See the Goddamn Wizard, Alright!* The Author, 7902 South Perry, Chicago, Ill., 1972.

Bogus, S. Diane. *Woman in the Moon.* Inglewood, Cal.: WIM Publications, 1980.

Bone, Robert. *Down Home: A Study of the Afro-American Short Story from its Beginnings through the Harlem Renaissance.* New York: Putnam, 1977.

Bontemps, Arna (ed.). *American Negro Poetry.* New York: Hill and Wang, 1974.

———. *The Harlem Renaissance Remembered: Essays.* New York: Dodd, Mead, 1972.

Booker, Merrel Daniel, Sr., et. al. (eds.). *Cry at Birth.* New York: McGraw-Hill, 1971.

Bradlee Jr., Ben. *The Ambush Murders: The True Account of the Killing of Two California Policemen.* New York: Dodd, Mead, 1980.

Braithwaite, Edward. *The Arrivants: A New World Trilogy: Rights of Passage, Islands, Masks.* New York: Oxford University Press, 1973.

Brashler, William. *Josh Gibson: A Life in the Negro Leagues.* New York: Harper & Row, 1978.

Brooks, Gwendolyn. *The World of Gwendolyn Brooks.* New York: Harper & Row, 1971.

Brown, Lloyd W. (ed.). *The Black Writer in Africa and the Americas.* Los Angeles: Hennessey & Ingalls, 1973.

Brown, Patricia, Don L. Lee and Francis Ward (eds.). *To Gwen with Love: An Anthology Dedicated to Gwendolyn Brooks.* Chicago: Johnson Publishing Co.

Brown, Sterling. *The Last Ride of Wild Bill.* Detroit: Broadside Press, 1974.

———. *Southern Road.* Boston: Beacon Press, 1975.

Brutus, Dennis. *A Simple Lust.* New York: Hill & Wang, 1973.

Buerkle, Jack V. and Danny Barker. *Bourbon Street Black: The New Orleans Black Jazzman.* New York: Oxford University Press, 1973.

Bullins, Ed. *The Duplex: A Black Love Fable in Four Movements.* New York: William Morrow, 1971.

———. *Four Dynamite Plays.* New York: William Morrow.

———, (ed.). *The New Lafayette Theatre Presents: Plays with Aesthetic Comments by 6 Black Playwrights.* New York: Doubleday, 1974.

———. *The Theme is Blackness: The Corner and Other Plays.* New York: William Morrow, 1973.

Burnett, Whit (ed.). *Black Hands on a White Face: A Timepiece of Experience in a Black and White America.* New York: Dodd, Mead, 1971.

Butcher, Margaret Just. *The Negro in American Culture.* New York: Knopf, 1972.

Butcher, Philip (ed.). *The William Stanley Braithwaite Reader.* Ann Arbor: University of Michigan Press, 1973.

C

Cabral, Amilcar. *Unity and Struggle: Speeches and Writings.* New York: Monthly Review Press, 1980.

Caldwell, Ben, Ronald Milner, Ed Bullins and Leroi Jones. *A Black Quartet: Four New Black Plays.* New York: New American Library, 1971.

Canada, James L. *Reality Is My Awareness Sense.* East Weymouth, Mass.: Gemini Book Village, African and Third World Books, 1975.

Cannady, Joan (ed.). *Black Images in American Literature.* Rochelle Park, N.J.: Hayden, 1978.

Carter, Vincent O. *The Bern Book: A Record of a Voyage of the Mind.* New York: John Day, 1973.

Chapman, Abraham (ed.). *New Black Voices.* New York: New American Library, 1972.

Chase, Judith Wragg. *Afro-American Art and Craft.* New York: Van Nostrand Reinhold, 1973.

Cheyney-Coker, Syl. *Concerto for an Exile.* New York: Humanities Press, 1973.

Childress, Alice (ed.). *Black Scenes.* New York: Doubleday (Zenith Books), 1971.

————. *A Short Walk.* New York: Coward, McCann & Geoghegan, 1980.

Christian, Barbara T. *Black Women Novelists: The Development of a Tradition, 1892–1976.* Westport, Conn.: Greenwood Press, 1980.

Clarenmon, Neil. *West of the American Dream: Visions of an Alien Landscape.* New York: William Morrow, 1973.

Clarke, Austin. *When He Was Free and Young and He Used to Wear Silks.* Boston: Little, Brown, 1973.

Clarke, John Henrik (ed.). *Dimensions of the Struggle against Apartheid: A Tribute to Paul Robeson.* New York: U.N. Center Against Apartheid, and African Heritage Studies Association, 1980.

Cleaver, Eldridge. *Soul on Fire.* Waco, Tex.: Word Books, 1979.

Clifton, Lucille. *An Ordinary Woman.* New York: Random House, 1975.

Cobb, Charlie. *Everywhere Is Yours.* Chicago: Third World Press, 1971.

Collier Paperback Reprint Series (of Afro-American, African and West Indian novels), 1974.

Collins, Marie (ed.). *Black Poets in French.* New York: Scribner, 1972.

Connor-Bey, Brenda (ed.). *Afro-Realism: A New Era in Third World Literature.* Men Wem Writers' Workshop, New York City, 1980.

Conrad, Earl. *Club.* San Francisco: West-Lewis Publishing Co., 1974.

Colter, Cyrus. *The Hippodrome.* Chicago: Swallow Press, 1973.

————. *The Rivers of Eros.* Chicago: Swallow Press, 1972.

Cook, Bruce. *Listen to the Blues.* New York: Scribner, 1973.

Cooke, M. G. (ed.). *Modern Black Novelists: A Collection of Critical Essays.* Englewood Cliffs, N.J.: Prentice-Hall.

Cornish, Sam. *Generations.* Boston: Beacon Press, 1971.

Cortez, Jayne. *Festivals and Funerals.* The Author, P.O. Box 249, NY 10014.

Cox, Joseph Mason Andrew. *Land Dimly Seen.* New York: Cox and Hopewell Publishers, 1975.

Cruz, Victor Hernandez. *Mainland.* New York: Random House, 1973.

Cullen, Countee (ed.). *Caroling Dusk: An Anthology of Verse by Negro Poets.* New York: Harper & Row, 1974.

Cuney, William Waring. *Storefront Church.* London: Paul Bremen Ltd.

D

Dace, Letitia. *Le Roi Jones [Imamu Amirti Baraka]: A Checklist of Works by and About Him.* London: Nether Press, Ltd., England, 1971.

Dance, Daryl Cumber. *Shuckin' and Jivin': Folklore from Contemporary Black Americans.* Bloomington: Indiana University Press, 1979.

Davis, Arthur P. and Saunders Redding (eds.). *Cavalcade: Negro American Writing from 1760 to the Present.* Boston: Houghton Mifflin, 1971.

Davis, George. *Coming Home.* New York: Random House.

————. *Love, Black Love.* New York: Anchor Press/Doubleday, 1978.

Davis, Nolan. *Six Black Horses.* New York: Putnam.

DeCosta, Miriam (ed.). *Blacks in Hispanic Literature: Critical Essays.* Port Washington, N.Y.: Kennikat Press, 1977.

DeJongh, James and Carles Cleveland. *City Cool.* New York: Random House, 1978.

Delany, Samuel R. *Dhalgren.* New York: Bantam Books, 1975.

————, and Marilyn Hacker (eds.). *Quark #2: 20 Pieces of Speculative Fiction.* New York: Paperback Library, 1971.

de Lone, Richard H. *Small Futures: Children, Inequality and the Limits of Liberal Reform.* New York: Harcourt Brace Jovanovich, 1980.

Denby, Charles. *Indignant Heart: A Black Worker's Journal.* Boston: South End Press, 1980.

Deodene, Frank and William P. French. *Black American Fiction Since 1952: A Preliminary Checklist.* Chatham, N.J.: The Chatham Bookseller, 1972.

Dodge, Robert K. and Joseph B. McCullough. *Voices from Wah-Kno-Tah: Contemporary Poetry of Native Americans.* New York: International Publishers, 1974.

Du Bois, W.E.B. *The Correspondence of W.E.B. Du Bois: Volume III: Selections 1944–1963.* Edited by Herbert Aptheker. Amherst: University of Massachusetts Press, 1978.

————. *W.E.B. Du Bois: A Bibliography of His Published Writings* Edited by Paul G. Partington. The Editor, 7320 S. Gretna Ave., Whittier, Cal., 1978.

————. *Prayers for Dark People.* Edited by Herbert Aptheker. Amherst: University of Massachusetts Press, 1980.

Duckett, Alfred. *Raps.* Chicago: Nelson-Hall, 1974.

Dumas, Henry. *Ark of Bones and Other Stories.* Carbondale: Southern Illinois University Press, 1971.

————. *Rope of Wind and Other Stories.* New York: Random House, 1980.

Dundes, Alan (ed.). *Mother Wit from the Laughing Barrel: Readings in the Interpretation of Afro-American Folklore.* Englewood Cliffs, N.J.: Prentice-Hall, 1973.

Durem, Ray. *Take No Prisoners.* (Vol. 17 Heritage Series) London: Paul Bremen Ltd., 1972.

E

Eastland, Terry and William J. Bennett. *Counting by Race: Equality from the Founding Fathers to Bakke and Weber.* New York: Basic Books, 1980.

Elder, Arlene A. *The "Hindered Hand": Cultural Implications of Early African-American Fiction.* Westport, Conn.: Greenwood Press, 1980.

Ellington, Edward Kennedy. *Music Is My Mistress.* New York: Doubleday.

Emecheta, Buchi. *The Joys of Motherhood.* New York: George Braziller, 1980.

Evans, Mari. *Jim Flying High.* New York: Doubleday, 1980.

Exum, Pat Crutchfield (ed.). *Keeping the Faith: Writings by Contemporary Black American Women.* Greenwich, Conn.: Fawcett Publications, 1975.

F

Fairbanks, Carol and Eugene A. Engeldinger. *Black American Fiction: A Bibliography.* Metuchen, N.J.: Scarecrow Press, 1979.

Felton, Harold W. *James Weldon Johnson.* New York: Dodd, Mead, 1971.

Figueroa, John (ed.). *Caribbean Voices: Combined Edition.* New York: Robert B. Luce, 1974.

Figueroa, Jose-Angel. *East 110th Street.* Broadside Press, 1973.

Fisher, Dexter and Robert B. Stepto (eds.). *Afro-American Literature: The Reconstruction of Instruction.* New York: Modern Language Association of America, 1980.

Fisher, William H. *Free at Last: A Bibliography of Martin Luther King, Jr.* Metuchen, N.J.: Scarecrow Press, 1978.

Ford, Nick Aaron (ed.). *Black Insights.* Waltham, Mass.: Ginn and Co., 1971.

Forrest, Leon. *There Is a Tree More Ancient than Eden.* New York: Random House, 1973.

A Freedomways Reader: Afro-America in the Seventies. Edited by

Ernest Kaiser. Foreword by James Baldwin. New York: International Publishers, 1979.

French, William P., Michel J. Fabre, Amritjit Singh and Genevieve E. Fabre. *Afro-American Poetry and Drama, 1760–1975: A Guide to Information Sources.* Detroit: Gale Research, 1980.

G

Gayle, Jr., Addison. *Claude McKay: The Black Poet.* Detroit: Broadside Press, 1972.

———. *The Way of the New World: The Black Novel in America.* New York: Anchor/Doubleday, 1975.

Gibson, Donald B. (ed.). *Five Black Writers: Essays on Wright, Ellison, Baldwin, Hughes and LeRoi Jones.* New York: New York University Press, 1971.

———. *Modern Black Poets: A Collection of Critical Essays.* Englewood Cliffs, N.J.: Prentice-Hall, 1973.

Gilder, George. *Visible Man: A True Story of Post-Racist America.* New York: Basic Books, 1979.

Gill, Gerald R. *Meanness Mania: The Changed Mood.* Washington, D.C.: Howard, 1981.

Giovanni, Nikki. *Cotton Candy on a Rainy Day.* New York: William Morrow, 1979.

———. *My House.* New York: William Morrow, 1972.

———. *A Poetic Equation: Conversations between Nikki Giovanni and Margaret Walker.* Washington, D.C.: Howard University Press, 1974.

Glasgow, Douglas. *The Black Underclass.* San Francisco: Jossey-Bass, 1978.

Glass, Frankcina. *Marvin & Tige.* New York: St. Martin's Press, 1978.

Gonzales, Babs. *I Paid My Dues: Good Times . . . No Bread.* New York: Lancer Books, 1971.

Green, Gerald. *Blockbuster.* New York: Doubleday, 1972.

Greene, J. Lee. *Time's Unfading Garden: Ann Spencer's Life and Poetry.* Baton Rouge: Louisiana State University Press, 1978.

Greenlee, Sam. *Blues for an African Princess.* Chicago: Third World Press, 1971.

Gregg, Ernest. *And the Sun God Said: That's Hip.* New York: Harper & Row, 1972.

Guillen, Nicolas. *Man-Making Words: Selected Poems of Nicolas Guillen.* Translated from the Spanish and edited by Robert Marquez and David Arthur McMurray. Amherst: University of Massachusetts Press, 1979.

———. *Tengo.* Detroit: Broadside Press, 1975.

H

Hampden-Turner, Charles. *From Poverty to Dignity: A Strategy for Poor Americans.* New York: Anchor/Doubleday, 1974.

Hansberry, Lorraine. *Les Blancs: The Collected Last Plays of Lorraine Hansberry.* New York: Random House, 1972.

Hardeman, Jr., B. A. *A Book of Poems.* The Author, P.O. Box 40158, San Francisco, Cal. 94140

Hardeman, Jr., Beauregard (B. Rap). *Metamorphosis of Supernigger: The Poems by B. Rap.* The Author, P.O. Box 40158, San Francisco, Cal. 94140, 1973.

Harper, Michael S. and Robert B. Stepto (eds.). *Chant of Saints: A Gathering of Afro-American Literature, Art and Scholarship.* Urbana: University of Illinois Press, 1980.

Harper, Michael S. *Images of Kin: New and Selected Poems.* Urbana: University of Illinois Press, 1978.

Harper, Michael S. *Song: I Want a Witness.* Pittsburgh: University of Pittsburgh Press, 1973.

Harris, William J. *Hey Fella Would You Mind Holding This Piano a Moment: A Book of Poems.* Serendipity Books, 1974.

Haskins, James. *I'm Gonna Make You Love Me: The Story of Diana Ross.* New York: Dial Press.

Haskins, Jim. *Jokes from Black Folks.* Garden City, N.Y.: Doubleday, 1973.

Hatch, James V. and Omanii Abdullah (compilers & editors). *Black Playwrights, 1823–1977; An Annotated Bibliography of Plays.* New York: R. R. Bowker, 1978.

Hatch, James V. and Ted Shine. *Black Theater, U.S.A.: Forty-Five Plays by Black Americans, 1847–1972.* New York: Macmillan, 1974.

Hayden, Robert. *American Journal.* Taunton, Massachusetts: Essendi Press, 1980.

Hayden, Robert. *The Night-Blooming Cereus.* London: Paul Breman Ltd., 1972.

Hayden, Robert. *Words in the Mourning Time.* New York: October House, 1971.

Heard, Nathan C. *To Reach a Dream.* New York: Dial Press, 1972.

Hemenway, Robert (ed.). *The Black Novelist.* Columbus, Ohio: Charles E. Merrill Publishing Co., 1971.

Henderson, Stephen. *Understanding the New Black Poetry: Black Speech and Black Music as Poetic References.* New York: William Morrow, 1973.

Henry, Lauchland. *Tough Me Inside.* Scarsdale, N.Y.: High Q Publications, 1977.

Hernton, Calvin. *Scarecrow.* New York: Doubleday, 1974.

Hersey, John (ed.). *Ralph Ellison: A Collection of Critical Essays.* Englewood Cliffs, N.J.: Prentice-Hall, 1974.

Hicks, Nora Louis. *Slave Girl Reba and Her Descendants in America.* Jericho, N.Y.: Exposition Press, 1974.

Higgins, Jr., Chester (photographs); Orde Coombs (text). *Drums of Life: A Photographic Essay on the Black Man in America.* New York: Anchor Press/Doubleday, 1974.

Himes, Chester. *Black on Black: Baby Sister and Selected Writings.* New York: Doubleday, 1973.

Hoffman, Nancy and Florence Howe. *Women Working: An Anthology of Stories and Poems.* Old Westbury, N.Y.: Feminist Press, 1980.

Hopkins, Lee Bennett (ed.). *On Our Way: Poems of Pride and Love.* New York: Knopf, 1974.

Hopkins, Pauline. *Contending Forces: A Romance Illustrative of Negro Life North and South.* Carbondale: Southern Illinois University Press, 1979.

Houston, Helen Ruth. *The Afro-American Novel 1965–1975: A Descriptive Bibliography of Primary and Secondary Material.* Troy, N.Y.: Whitson, 1979.

Horizon Six. *The Best of 40 Acres of Poetry.* P.O. Box 21, New York, 10027.

Hudson, Theodore R. *A LeRoi Jones [Amiri Baraka] Bibliography.* The Author, 1816 Varnum St., N.E., Washington, D.C. 20018, 1972.

———. *From Le Roi Jones to Imamu Baraka: The Literary Works.* Durham, N.C.: Duke University Press, 1974.

Hunter, Kristin. *Guest in the Promised Land.* New York: Scribner, 1974.

Hunter, Kristin. *The Lakestown Rebellion.* New York: Scribner, 1980.

Hurston, Zora Neale. *I Love Myself When I Am Laughing . . . and Then Again When I Am Looking Mean and Impressive. A Zora Neale Hurston Reader.* Edited by Alice Walker. Old Westbury, N.Y.: Feminist Press, 1980.

I

Images: An Anthology of Black Literature. New York: Curriculum Bulletin, 1971–72 Series, No. 3. Bureau of Curriculum Development, Board of Education of the City of New York, 1972.

Images, US. A magazine of student poetry and illustrations from Frederick Douglass High School, 225 Hightower Road, N.W., Atlanta, Ga., 30318, 1974.

Inge, M. Thomas, Maurice Duke, and Jackson R. Bryer (eds.). *Black American Writers: Bibliographical Essays.* New York: St. Martin's Press, 1979.

Index to Periodical Articles by and About Blacks, 1973. Boston: G. K. Hall, 1979.

J

Jackson, Blyden. *Operation: Burning Candle.* New York: Third Press, 1974.

———. *Totem.* New York: Third Press, 1975.

———. *The Waiting Years: Essays on American Negro Literature.* Baton Rouge: Louisiana State University Press, 1977.

Jackson, Bruce (comp.). *"Get Your Ass in the Water and Swim Like Me."* Cambridge, Mass.: Harvard University Press, 1975.

Jackson, Bruce. *Killing Time: Life in the Arkansas Penitentiary.* Ithaca, N.Y.: Cornell University Press, 1978.

Jackson, John R. *Soulful Sounds.* Jericho, N.Y.: Exposition Press, 1974.

Jackson, George A. *A Case Study of Mr. Cage: Toleration Over Assertion or Assertion Over Toleration.* Hicksville, N.Y.: Exposition Press, 1979.

Jackson, Richard L. *The Black Image in Latin American Literature.* Albuquerque: University of New Mexico Press, 1977.

Jackson, Jesse. *A Discussion with the Reverend Jesse Jackson.* Edited transcript. American Enterprise Institute, 1979.

Jacobs, W. Richard and Ian Jacobs. *Grenada: The Route to Revolution.* Havana, Cuba: Casa de las Americas, 1981.

James, C. L. R. *The Future in the Present: Selected Writings.* Westport, Conn.: Lawrence Hill, 1978.

Jeffers, Lance. *Grandsire.* Detroit: Lotus Press, 1979.

Jemie, Onwuchekwa. *Langston Hughes: An Introduction to the Poetry.* New York: Columbia University Press, 1977.

Joans, Ted. *Afrodisia: New Poems.* New York: Hill and Wang, 1971.

Johanson, Donald C. and Maitland A. Edey. *Lucy: The Beginnings of Humankind.* New York: Simon and Schuster, 1981.

Johnson, B. B. *Death of a Blue-Eyed Soul Brother.* New York: Paperback Library.

Johnson, Lemuel. *The Devil, the Gargoyle and the Buffoon: The Negro as Metaphor in Western Literature.* Port Washington, N.Y.: Kennikat Press, 1974.

Jones, Faustine Childress. *The Changing Mood in America: Eroding Commitment?* Washington, D.C.: Howard University Press, 1978.

Jones, Jymi. *The Fruit Theory.* Philadelphia: Dorrance, 1973.

Jordan, June. *Passion: New Poems 1977–1980.* Boston: Beacon Press, 1981.

———. *Things That I Do in the Dark: Selected Poems.* New York: Random House, 1977.

Jordan, June. *Some Changes.* New York: Richard W. Baron Book/ Dutton, 1971.

Jordan, Norman. *Above Maya.* Cleveland: Jordan Press, 1971.

K

Kearns, Francis E. (ed.). *Black Identity: A Thematic Reader.* New York: Holt, Rinehart and Winston, 1972.

Kellner, Bruce (ed.). *"Keep A-Inchin' Along": Selected Writings of Carl Van Vechten About Black Art and Letters.* Westport, Conn.: Greenwood Press, 1981.

Kemp, Arnold. *Eat of Me: I Am the Savior.* New York: William Morrow, 1972.

King, Woodie, (ed.). *Black Short Story Anthology.* New York: Columbia University Press, 1973.

———, (ed.). *Black Spirits: A Festival of New Black Poets in America.* New York: Random House, 1972.

———, and Earl Anthony (eds.). *Black Poets and Prophets. The Theory, Practice, and Esthetics of the Pan-Africanist Revolution.* New York: New American Library, 1972.

———, and Ron Milner (eds.). *Black Drama Anthology.* New York: Columbia University Press.

Klineman, George, Sherman Butler, and David Conn. *The Cult That Died.* New York: Putnam, 1981.

Klotman, Phyllis Rauch. *Humanities through the Black Experience.* Dubuque, Iowa: Kendall/Hunt Publishing Co., 1981.

Kinnamon, Kenneth. *The Emergence of Richard Wright: A Study in Literature and Society.* Urbana: University of Illinois Press, 1972.

Kramer, Aaron (ed.). *On Freedom's Side: An Anthology of American Poems of Protest.* New York: Macmillan, 1973.

L

La Guma, Alex. *In the Fog of the Season's End.* New York: Third Press, 1973.

——— and Dick Gregory. *Code Name "Zorro": The Murder of Martin Luther King, Jr.* Englewood Cliffs, N.J.: Prentice-Hall, 1977.

Lane, Mark. *The Strongest Poison.* New York: Hawthorn Books, 1980.

Lane, Ronnie M. (ed.). *Face the Whirlwind.* Grand Rapids, Mich.: Pilot Press, 1974.

Langione, Jon F. *A Cruel Way to Live.* Jericho, N.Y.: Exposition Press, 1974.

Lawrence, Bill. *Nigger, Go Home!* Hicksville, N.Y.: Exposition Press, 1979.

Lee, Don L. (Mwalimu Haki R. Madhubuti). *Book of Life.* Detroit: Broadside Press, 1974.

———. *Dynamite Voices I: Black Poets of the 1960's.* Detroit: Broadside Press, 1973.

Lee, Helen Jackson. *Nigger in the Window.* New York: Doubleday, 1978.

Les Cenelles: A Collection of Poems by Creole Writers of the Early Nineteenth Century. Translated by Regine Latortue and Gleason R. Adams. Boston: G. K. Hall, 1980.

Lester, Julius. *Two Love Stories.* New York: Dial Press, 1972.

Lindfors, Bernth (ed.). *Black African Literature in English: A Guide to Information Sources.* Detroit: Gale Research Co., 1980.

Littleton, Arthur C. and Mary W. Burger (eds.). *Black Viewpoints.* New York: New American Library, 1971.

Loftis, N. J. *Exiles and Voyages.* New York: Black Market Press, 1971.

Long, Doughty. *Black Love Black Hope.* Detroit: Broadside Press, 1971.

———. *Song for Nia: A Poetic Essay in Three Parts.* Detroit: Broadside Press.

Long, Richard A. *Ascending and Other Poems.* Chicago: Du Sable Museum of African American History, 1977.

——— and Eugenia Collier (eds.). *Afro-American Writing: An Anthology of Prose and Poetry.* New York: New York University Press, 1973.

Lorde, Audre. *Between Our Selves.* Berkeley, Cal.: Eidolon Editions, 1977.

———. *The Black Unicorn.* New York: W. W. Norton, 1978.

———. *The New York Head Shop and Museum.* Detroit: Broadside Press, 1975.

Lowenfels, Walter (ed.). *From the Belly of the Shark: A New Anthology of Native Americans.* New York: Random House, 1974.

M

Macebuh, Stanley. *James Baldwin: A Critical Study.* New York: Third Press, 1973.

Madgett, Naomi Long. *Pink Ladies in the Afternoon.* Detroit: Lotus Press.

Major, Clarence. *Emergency Exit.* New York: Fiction Collective, 1981.

———. *No.* New York: Emerson Hall Publishers.

———. *Symptoms & Madness.* New York: Corinth Books, 1971.

———. *The Syncopated Cakewalk.* New York: Barlenmir House, 1974.

Maguire, Daniel C. *A New American Justice: Ending the White Male Monopolies.* New York: Doubleday, 1981.

Malamud, Bernard. *The Tenants.* New York: Farrar, Straus and Giroux, 1971.

Maldonado-Denis, Manuel. *The Emigration Dialectic: Puerto Rico and the USA.* New York: International Publishers.

Mandela, Nelson. *The Struggle Is My Life.* London: International Defence & Aid Fund for Southern Africa, 1979.

Margolies, Edward and David Bakish. *Afro-American Fiction, 1853–1976: A Guide to Information Sources.* Detroit: Gale Research Co., 1980.

Mason, Clifford. *When Love Was Not Enough.* New York: Playboy Paperbacks.

The Massachusetts Review, Vol. 18, Nos. 3 and 4, Autumn and Winter 1977. Amherst: Memorial Hall, University of Massachusetts, 1978.

Mayfield, Julian (ed.). *Ten Times Black.* New York: Bantam Books, 1972.

Mays, James A., *M.D. Chameleon.* Los Angeles: Crescent Publications, 1978.

Mays, James A. *Mercy is King.* Los Angeles: Crescent Publications, 1975.

Mberi, Antar S. K. *A Song Out of Harlem: Poems.* Clifton, N.J.: The Humana Press, 1981.

Mberi, Antar Sudan Katara. *Bandages and Bullets: In Praise of the African Revolution.* Cambridge, Mass.: West End Press, 1977.

Meaddough, R. J. *The Retarded Genius.* New York: Troisieme-Canadian Publishers, 1979.

Mezu, S. Okechukwu (ed.). *Modern Black Literature.* Buffalo, N.Y.: Black Academy Press, 1972.

Miller, Jake C. *The Black Presence in American Foreign Affairs.* Washington, D.C.: University Press of America, 1979.

Miller, R. Baxter. *Langston Hughes and Gwendolyn Brooks: A Reference Guide.* Boston: G. K. Hall, 1979.

Miller, Ruth, (ed.). *Backgrounds to Black-american Literature.* Scranton, Pa.: Chandler Publishing Co., 1971.

——— (ed.). *Black American Literature: 1760 to Present.* Beverly Hills, Cal.: Glencoe Press, 1971.

Miller, Wayne Charles (ed.). *A Gathering of Ghetto Writers—Irish, Italian, Jewish, Black, Puerto Rican.* New York: New York University Press, 1972.

Mirer, Martin (ed.). *Modern Black Stories.* Woodbury, N.Y.: Barron's Educational Series, 1973.

Mitchell, Loften. *The Stubborn Old Lady Who Resisted Change.* New York: Emerson Hall, 1974.

Morrison, Joan and Charlotte Fox Zabusky. *American Mosaic. The Immigrant Experience in the Words of Those Who Lived It.* New York: E. P. Dutton, 1981.

Morrison, Toni. *Sula.* N.Y.: Knopf, 1972.

Morrow, E. Frederic. *Forty Years a Guinea Pig: A Black Man's View from the Top.* Philadelphia: Pilgrim Press, 1981.

Mtshali, Oswald Mbuyiseni. *Sounds of a Cowhide Drum.* New York: The Third Press Viking, 1972.

Murray, Albert. *The Hero and the Blues.* Columbia: University of Missouri Press, 1975.

———. *South to a Very Old Place.* New York: McGraw-Hill, 1971.

Murray, Alma and Robert Thomas (eds.). *The Black Hero.* Englewood Cliffs, N.J.: The Scholastic Black Literature Series, 1971.

Myers, Lena Wright. *Black Women: Do They Cope Better?* Englewood Cliffs, N.J.: Prentice-Hall, 1981.

McKay, Claude. *The Passion of Claude McKay: Selected Prose and Poetry 1912–1948.* New York: Schocken Books, 1974.

McKluskey, John. *Look What They Done to My Song.* New York: Random House, 1975.

N

New City Voices: Anthology of Black Literature. South Ozone Park, N.Y.: Metamorphoses, Inc., 1981.

Newman, Dorothy K., Nancy J. Amidei, Barbara L. Carter, Dawn Day, William J. Kruvant, and Jack S. Russell. *Protest, Politics, and Prosperity: Black Americans and White Institutions. 1940–75.* New York: Pantheon Books, 1978.

Newton, Huey P. *To Die for the People: The Writings of Huey P. Newton.* New York: Random House, 1972.

Nichols, Charles H. (ed.). *Arna Bontemps/Langston Hughes Letters, 1925–1967.* New York: Dodd, Mead, 1980.

Ngugi, James. *Petals of Blood.* New York: Dutton, 1978.

Nielson, David Gordon. *Black Ethos: Northern Urban Negro Life and Thought, 1890–1930.* Westport, Conn.: Greenwood Publishing Corp., 1977.

No Crystal Stair: A Bibliography of Black Literature. New York: Office of Adult Services, New York Public Library, 1971.

Norfolk Prison Brothers. *Who Took the Weight? Black Voices from Prison.* Boston: Little, Brown.

O

O'Brien, John (ed.). *Interviews with Black Writers.* New York: Liveright, 1974.

O'Daniel, Therman B. (ed.). *Langston Hughes—Black Genius: A Critical Evaluation.* New York: William Morrow, 1971.

Okpewho, Isadore. *The Victims.* New York: Doubleday, 1972.

Oliver, Clinton F. and Stephanie Sills (eds.). *Contemporary Black Drama from* A Raisin in the Sun *to* No Place to Be Somebody. New York: Scribner, 1971.

Oliver, Paul. *The Story of the Blues.* Philadelphia: Chilton Book Co., 1971.

Olumo (Jim Cunningham). *The Blue Narrator.* Chicago: Third World Press, 1975.

Ortego, Philip D. *We Are Chicanos: An Anthology of Mexican-American Literature.* New York: Washington Square Press, 1973.

The Oxford Library of African Literature. Oxford: London: Clarendon Press, 1973.

P

Panorama GDR. IMPRESSIONS: OF THE BIRTH AND GROWTH OF THE GDR—VOICES FROM ALL OVER THE WORLD. Panorama, Wilhelm Pieck Str. 49, 1054 Berlin, GDR.

Parker, Percy Spurlark. *Good Girls Don't Get Murdered.* New York: Scribner, 1975.

Parks, Gordon. *Flavio.* New York: W. W. Norton, 1978.

Parks, Gordon. *In Love.* New York: Lippincott, 1971.

Patterson, Lindsay. *A Rock Against the Wind: Black Love Poems.* New York: Dodd, Mead, 1974.

—— (ed.). *Black Theatre: A 20th Century Collection of the Work of Its Best Playwrights.* New York: Dodd, Mead, 1971.

P'Bitek, Okot. *Song of a Prisoner.* New York: Third Press, 1972.

Perry, Margaret. *A Bio-Bibliography of Countee P. Cullen, 1903–1946.* Westport, Conn.: Greenwood Publishing Corp., 1971.

Petry, Ann. *Miss Muriel and Other Stories.* Boston: Houghton Mifflin, 1972.

Pharr, Robert Deane. *Giveadamn Brown.* New York: Doubleday, 1978.

——. *S.R.O.* New York: Doubleday, 1971.

Philpot, William M. (ed.). *Best Black Sermons.* Valley Forge, Pa.: Judson Press, 1973.

Plumpp, Sterling. *Black Rituals.* Chicago: Third World Press, 1973.

Popkin, Michael (compiler and editor). *Modern Black Writers.* New York: Frederick Ungar Publishing Co., 1978.

Porter, Dorothy (ed.). *Early Negro Writing 1760–1837.* Boston: Beacon Press.

Porter, Dorothy B. (ed.). *Afro-Braziliana: A Working Bibliography.* Boston: G. K. Hall, 1979.

Porter, John R. *Dating Habits of Young Black Americans: And Almost Everybody Else's Too.* Dubuque, Iowa: Kendall/Hunt Publishing Co., 1981.

Powell, Virgil S. *Adeline, A Child of Yani.* Hicksville, N.Y.: Exposition Press, 1980.

Powlis, Laverne. *The Black Woman's Beauty Book.* New York: Doubleday, 1980.

Prestwidge, K. J. *Wisdom Teeth.* The Author, 76–11 160th St., Flushing, N.Y. 11366, 1973.

Price, Robert E. *Blood Lines.* Los Angeles: Poets Pay Rent, Too, Togetherness Productions, 1979.

Pugh, Charles. *The Hospital Plot.* Port Washington, N.Y.: Ashley Books, 1980.

Q

Quarles, Benjamin (ed.). *Blacks on John Brown.* Urbana: University of Illinois Press, 1972.

R

Randall, Dudley (ed.). *The Black Poets.* New York: Bantam Books.

——. *More to Remember: Poems of Four Decades.* Chicago: Third World Press, 1973.

Four Decades. Chicago: Third World Press, 1973.

Ray, David and Robert M. Farnsworth (eds.). *Richard Wright: Impressions and Perspectives.* Ann Arbor: University of Michigan Press, 1974.

Redmond, Eugene B. *Songs from an Afro/Phone.* Black River Writers, P.O. Box 1591, East St. Louis, Ill. 62205, 1973.

Reed, Ishmael. *Chattanooga: Poems.* New York: Random House, 1974.

——. *Conjure: Selected Poems, 1963–1970.* Amherst: University of Massachusetts Press, 1973.

——. *Mumbo Jumbo.* New York: Doubleday, 1972.

——. *Shrovetide in Old New Orleans.* New York: Doubleday, 1978.

Reid, Inez Smith. *"Together" Black Women.* New York: Emerson Hall Publishers, 1972.

Reilly, J. Terrance. *Black!* Myra House, Box 148, Poughkeepsie, N.Y., 1973.

Riboud, Barbara Chase. *From Memphis & Peking.* New York: Random House, 1975.

——. *Sally Hemings.* New York: Viking Press, 1979.

Robinson, Jackie and Alfred Duckett. *I Never Had It Made.* New York: Putnam, 1972.

Robinson, Jr., William H. (ed.). *Early Black American Prose.* Dubuque, Iowa: Wm. C. Brown Co., 1971.

Roc, John. *Winter Blood.* New York: Pocket Books, 1973.

Rodgers, Carolyn M. *The Heart as Ever Green.* New York: Anchor Press/Doubleday, 1979.

Rosenblatt, Roger. *Black Fiction.* Cambridge, Mass.: Harvard University Press, 1975.

Russell, Ross. *Bird Lives! The High Life and Hard Times of Charlie [Yardbird] Parker.* New York: Charterhouse Books Inc., 1973.

S

Salkey, Andrew. *In the Hills Where Her Dreams Live.* Sausalito, Cal.: Black Scholar Press, 1981.

Sanchez, Sonia. *I've Been a Woman: New and Selected Poems.* Sausalito, Cal.: Black Scholar Press, 1979.

——. *A Sound Investment.* Chicago: Third World Press, 1980.

—— (ed.). *We Be Word Sorcerers: 25 Stories by Black Americans.* New York: Bantam Books, 1974.

Schraufnagel, Noel. *From Apology to Protest: The Black American Novel.* Deland, Fla.: Everett-Edwards, Inc., 1975.

Schuman, R. Baird (ed.). *A Galaxy of Black Writing.* Durham, N.C.: Moore Publishing Co.

Scott, Jr., Nathan A. *Three American Moralists: Mailer, Bellow, Trilling.* Notre Dame, Ind.: University of Notre Dame Press, 1974.

Scott-Heron, Gil. *The Vulture.* New York: World Publishing Co., 1971.

Schockley, Ann Allen. *Loving Her.* Indianapolis: Bobbs-Merrill, 1975.

—— and Sue P. Chandler (eds.). *Living Black American Authors: A Biographical Directory.* Ann Arbor, Mich.: R. R. Bowker Co., 1974.

Shange, Ntozake. *Nappy Edges.* New York: St. Martin's Press, 1979.

——. *Three Pieces.* New York: St. Martin's Press, 1981.

Shipps, Charles Kadia. *Black Nemesis.* Detroit: Harlo Press, 1974.

Shuman R. Baird (ed.). *A Galaxy of Black Writing.* Durham, N.C.: Moore Publishing Co., 1979.

Simmons, Gloria M. and Helene D. Hutchinson (eds.). *Black Culture: Reading and Writing Black.* New York: Holt, Rinehart and Winston, 1973.

Sims, Janet L. (comp.). *Marian Anderson: An Annotated Bibliography and Discography.* Westport, Conn.: Greenwood Press, 1981.

—— (comp.). *The Progress of Afro-American Women: A Selected Bibliography and Resource Guide.* Westport, Conn.: Greenwood Press, 1981.

Smith, Patrick. *Angel City.* St. Petersburg, Fla.: Valkyrie Press, 1979.

Somerville, Rose M. (ed.). *Intimate Relationships: Marriages, Family and Lifestyles through Literature.* New York: Prentice-Hall, 1975.

Southerland, Ellease. *Let the Lion Eat Straw.* New York: Scribner, 1979.

Soyinka, Wole. *The Interpreters.* New York: Africana Publishing Corp., 1972.

Spalding, Henry D. (ed.). *Encyclopedia of Black Folklore and Humor.* Middle Village, N.Y.: Jonathan David Publishers.

Staples, Robert. *The World of Black Singles: Changing Patterns of Male/Female Relations.* Westport, Conn.: Greenwood Press, 1981.

Stetson, Erlene (ed.). *Black Sister: Poetry by Black American Women, 1746–1980.* Bloomington: Indiana University Press, 1981.

T

Thelwell, Michael. *The Harder They Come: The Story of Rhygin.* New York: Grove Press, 1980.

Three Hundred and Sixty Degrees of Blackness Comin at You. An Anthology of the Sonia Sanchez Writers Workshop at Countee Cullen Library in Harlem. New York: 5X Publishing Co., 1971.

Tolson, Melvin B. *A Gallery of Harlem Portraits.* Edited by Robert M. Farnsworth. University of Missouri Press, 1980.

Trommer, Joseph F. (ed.). *A Casebook on Ralph Ellison's Invisible Man.* New York: Thomas Y. Crowell, 1974.

Turner, Darwin T. (ed.). *The Wayward and the Seeking: A Collection of Writings by Jean Toomer.* Washington, D.C.: Howard University Press, 1981.

———, Jean Bright and Richard Wright (eds.). *Voices from the Black Experience: African and Afro-American Literature.* Waltham, Mass.: Ginn and Co., 1971.

Turner, David T. *In a Minor Chord: Three Afro-American Writers and Their Search for Identity.* Carbondale: Southern Illinois University Press, 1971.

——— (ed.). *Black Drama in America: An Anthology.* New York Fawcett Publishing Co.

Toure, Askia Muhammad. *Songhai!* New York: Songhai Press, 1972.

U Tam'si Tchicaya. *Selected Poems.* New York: Humanities Press, 1972.

V

Van Der Zee, James (photographs). *The Harlem Book of the Dead.* Poetry by Owen Dodson. Text by Camille Billops. Dobbs Ferry, N.Y.: Morgan & Morgan, 1979.

Van Dyke, Henry. *Dead Piano.* New York: Farrar, Straus and Giroux, 1971.

Van Peebles, Melvin. *Ain't Supposed to Die a Natural Death.* New York: Bantam Books, 1973.

W

Wagner, Jean. *Black Poems of the United States: From Laurence Dunbar to Langston Hughes.* Urbana: University of Illinois Press, 1973.

Walcott, Derek. *Another Life.* New York: Farrar, Straus & Giroux, 1973.

———. *The Star-Apple Kingdom.* New York: Farrar, Straus and Giroux, 1979.

Walker, Alice. *In Love and Trouble: Stories of Black Women.* New York: Harcourt Brace Jovanovich, 1974.

———. *Revolutionary Petunias & Other Poems.* New York: Harcourt Brace Jovanovich, 1973.

Walker, Joseph A. *The River Niger: A Play.* New York: Mermaid Dramabook/Hill & Wang, 1974.

———. *October Journey.* Detroit: Broadside Press, 1974.

Walker, Margaret. *How I Wrote Jubilee.* Chicago: Third World Press, 1972.

Washington, Mary Helen (ed.). *Midnight Birds: Stories of Contemporary Black Women Writers.* New York: Anchor/Doubleday, 1981.

Washington, William D. and Samuel Beckoff (eds.). *Black Literature: An Anthology of Outstanding Black Writers.* New York: Simon & Schuster, 1973.

Watkins, Mel and Jay David (eds.). *To Be a Black Woman: Portraits in Fact and Fiction.* New York: William Morrow, 1971.

Weisman, Leon and Elfreda S. Wright (eds.). *Black Poetry for All Americans.* New York: Globe Book Co., 1973.

Westlake, Neda M. and Otto Albrecht (eds.). *Marian Anderson: A Catalog of the Collection at the University of Pennsylvania Library.* Philadelphia: University of Pennsylvania Press, 1981.

Whitlow, Roger. *Black American Literature: A Critical History.* Totowa, N.J.: Littlefield, Adams & Co., 1975.

Wideman, John Edgar. *The Lynchers.* New York: Harcourt Brace Jovanovich, 1973.

Wilder, Charles. *Another Side of the Blues: Seven Stories.* Smithtown, N.Y.: Exposition Press, 1981.

Wilentz, Ted and Tom Weatherly (eds.). *Natural Process: An Anthology of New Black Poetry.* New York: Hill and Wang, 1971.

Wilkes, Alfred W. *Little Boy Black.* New York: Scribner, 1971.

Williams, John A. *Flashbacks: A Twenty-Year Diary of Article Writing.* New York: Doubleday, 1975.

———. *Mothersill and the Foxes.* New York: Doubleday, 1975.

Williams, Kenny J. *They Also Spoke: An Essay on Negro Literature in America, 1787–1930.* Nashville: Townsend Press.

Williams, Ora. *American Black Women in the Arts and Social Sciences: A Bibliographic Survey.* Metuchen, N.J.: Scarecrow Press, 1974.

Williams, Sherley Anne. *Give Birth to Brightness: A Thematic Study in Neo-Black Literature.* New York: Dial Press.

Wilmer, Valerie. *Jazz People.* Indianapolis: Bobbs-Merrill, 1971.

Wilson, Merzie. *Nealites: Doc Genius and Henry the Stud.* New York: Vantage Press, 1981.

Wright, Charles. *Absolutely Nothing to Get Alarmed About.* New York: Farrar, Straus and Giroux, 1973.

Wright, Jay. *The Homecoming Singer.* New York: Corinth Books.

Y

Yellin, Jean Fagan. *The Intricate Knot: Black Figures in American Literature, 1776–1863.* New York: New York University Press, 1973.

Yerby, Frank. *A Darkness at Ingraham's Crest.* New York: Dial Press, 1980.

———. *The Voyage Unplanned.* New York: Dial Press, 1975.

Biography

The following works include biographies and autobiographies for both the general audience and for juveniles.

A

Afro-American Artists—A Bio-Bibliographical Directory. Boston: Boston Public Library, 1973.

Albertson, Chris. *Bessie.* New York: Stein and Day, 1973.

Ali, Muhammad with Richard Durham. *The Greatest: My Own Story.* New York: Random House, 1981.

Allyn, Paul. *The Picture Life of Herman Badillo.* New York: Franklin Watts. 1972.

Anderson, Jervis. *A Philip Randolph: A Biographical Portrait,* New York: Harcourt Brace Jovanovich, 1973.

B

Bailey, Pearl. *Talking to Myself.* New York: Harcourt Brace Jovanovich, 1971.

Baker, Jim. *O. J. Simpson.* New York: Grosset and Dunlap, 1975.

Baker, Josephine and Jo Bouillon. *Josephine.* Translated from the French by Mariana Fitzpatrick. New York: Harper & Row, 1978.

Barksdale, Richard K. *Langston Hughes: The Poet and His Critics.* Chicago: American Library Association, 1978.

Bearden, Jim and Linda Jean Butler. *Shadd: The Life and Times of Mary Shadd Cary.* Toronto: NC Press, 1978.

Bedini, Silvio. *The Life of Benjamin Banneker: The Definitive Biography of the First Black Man of Science.* New York: Scribner.

Berkow, Ira. *Oscar Robertson: The Golden Year 1964.* Englewood Cliffs, N.J.: Prentice-Hall, 1971.

— I —

— O —

— P —

— Q —

— R —

— T —

– U –

— Y —

— Z —